175 YEARS OF DICTIONARY PUBLISHING

Collins

175 YEARS OF DICTIONARY PUBLISHING

Writer's Thesaurus of the English Language

HarperCollins Publishers
Westerhill Road
Bishopbriggs
Glasgow
G64 2QT
Great Britain

First Edition 2010

Reprint 10 9 8 7 6 5 4 3 2 1 0

HOME EDITION
ISBN 978-0-00-737127-3

EXPORT EDITION
ISBN 978-0-00-741251-8

www.collinslanguage.com

A catalogue record for this book is available from the British Library

Typeset by Davidson Publishing Solutions, Glasgow

Printed in India by Gopsons Papers Ltd

Acknowledgements
We would like to thank those authors and publishers who kindly gave permission for copyright material to be used in the Collins Word Web. We would also like to thank Times Newspapers Ltd for providing valuable data.

Contents

Editorial Staff

Editors
Ian Brookes
Robert Groves
Michael Munro
Anne Robertson
Kate Wild

Essays written by
Daphne Day
Lorna Gilmour
Gavin Gray
Robert Groves
Orin Hargraves
Lesley Haughton
Andrew Holmes
Cordelia Lilly
John Miller
Michael Munro
Claire Newton
Anne Robertson
Liam Rodger
Kate Wild

Computing Support
Thomas Callan

For the publisher
Gerry Breslin
Lucy Cooper
Kerry Ferguson
Elaine Higgleton

Foreword

A thesaurus is an invaluable tool for a writer. It allows you to look up a common word and find other words with the same meaning or nearly the same meaning. Thus it can provide you with a range of alternatives for a word you do not wish to overuse, and it can also suggest a more exact or effective word when the word that immediately comes to mind is not quite suitable.

Collins Writer's Thesaurus has a number of features that help you to find the best word for any occasion. The entries are arranged in a single 'A to Z' listing so that you do not need to consult an index before finding the list of alternative words (synonyms). Once you look up a word, its synonyms are listed in order of salience, so that the first ones are the closest matches to the main word, whereas words that occur later in the list may have a slightly different meaning or connotation (while still being valid alternatives in certain contexts).

Some words can be used with several different meanings, and to help you identify the precise meaning you want, the synonyms of these words are split up into different numbered groups. A 'key synonym' in bold type comes as the first item in each group of synonyms, and the specific sense under discussion is further demonstrated by a phrase or sentence in italics, so it should always be quite clear to which meaning the different groups of synonyms apply.

Two further features may provide inspiration for writers. The presence of an opposite word (antonym) after many senses may suggest alternative ways of formulating an idea. Moreover, many words in the thesaurus are illustrated or exemplified by apt quotations. Some of these quotations are familiar (although the original sources are not always well known), while others may provide new ways of thinking about a particular word or concept.

However, what makes *Collins Writer's Thesaurus* really stand out from other thesauruses is the inclusion of over one hundred specially commissioned essays about the use of English, interspersed at regular intervals throughout the text. These essays aim to shed light on the ways that some acclaimed writers of the past have used the English language. There are over eighty essays analysing the style of classic prose-writers including novelists such as Jane Austen and DH Lawrence, short-story writers such as Edgar Allan Poe and Katherine Mansfield, and children's authors such as Lewis Carroll and Kenneth Grahame. Some eminent non-fiction writers are also covered, such as Abraham Lincoln (whose language is recorded in his speeches and letters).

As well as essays on individuals, there are several essays discussing the way that certain linguistic features are treated in classic literature in general. These include analyses of some aspects of style which are considered problematic or controversial today, such as the split infinitive and the use of *who* and *whom*. In addition, there are six essays comparing the language used in *The Times* and *The Sun*, showing how the use of English in a newspaper with a perceived highbrow readership differs from one at the opposite end of the spectrum.

What all of the essays have in common is that they look at how writers use English by analysing a *corpus*, a searchable collection of electronic texts. Corpus analysis makes it possible, for example, to make statistical comparisons between an eighteenth-century writer's use of a word and the use of that word in modern English, thus highlighting which words a writer privileges over other words. The preferences of a writer may sometimes reflect the state of the English language at the time when the writer was working, but they may also say something about the subjects that preoccupied the writer and the effects that the writer was seeking to achieve.

The process of writing often involves a choice between one word and another. A thesaurus presents a writer with a full palette of words and offers the possibility of making a choice between them. This thesaurus shows how writers of the past have chosen words wisely; it is hoped it will help writers of today compose wise words as well.

Using this Thesaurus

Main Entry Words

Main entry words are printed in large blue bold type:

altogether

Variant Spellings

Common acceptable variant spellings are shown in full:

dramatize *or* **dramatise** VERB

Fixed Phrases

Fixed phrases are printed in small blue bold type:

acquainted ADJECTIVE
acquainted with **1 = familiar with**, aware of, in on, experienced in, conscious of, informed of, alive to, privy to, knowledgeable about, versed in, conversant with, apprised of, cognizant of, up to speed with, *au fait* with

Parts of Speech

Parts of speech are shown in small capitals. Where a word has several senses for one part of speech, the senses are numbered:

edition NOUN **1 = printing**, publication: *a rare first edition of a Dickens novel* **2 = copy**, impression, number: *The Christmas edition of the catalogue is out now.* **3 = version**, volume, issue

A change of part of speech is signalled by an empty arrow:

antique NOUN **= period piece**, relic, bygone, heirloom, collector's item, museum piece, object of virtu: *a genuine antique*
▷ ADJECTIVE **1 = vintage**, classic, antiquarian, olden: *antique silver jewellery*

Alternatives

The key synonym for each sense is given in black bold type, with other alternatives given in roman:

altogether ADVERB **1 = absolutely**, quite, completely, totally, perfectly, fully, thoroughly, wholly, utterly, downright, one hundred per cent *(informal)*, undisputedly, lock, stock and barrel

Examples Example sentences are given in italics:

annual ADJECTIVE **1 = once a year**, yearly: *the annual conference of the trade union movement* **2 = yearlong**, yearly: *annual costs, £1,600*

Opposites Opposites are given after the list of alternatives:

enemy NOUN **= foe**, rival, opponent, the opposition, competitor, the other side, adversary, antagonist
OPPOSITE: friend

Related Words Related words are introduced by a black arrow:

garden NOUN **= grounds**, park, plot, patch, lawn, allotment, yard (*U.S. & Canad.*), forest park (*N.Z.*) ▸ *related adjective:* horticultural

Labels Labels show the restricted region or register of a word or phrase:

babble VERB **1 = gabble**, chatter, gush, spout, waffle (*informal, chiefly Brit.*), splutter, gaggle, burble, prattle, gibber, rabbit on (*Brit. informal*), jabber, prate, earbash (*Austral. & N.Z. slang*): *They all babbled simultaneously.*

Usage Notes Usage notes are introduced by the heading **USAGE**:

USAGE
The use of *actress* is now very much on the decline, and women who work in the profession invariably prefer to be referred to as *actors*.

Quotations Quotations are introduced by the heading **QUOTATIONS**:

QUOTATIONS
An actor's a guy who, if you ain't talking about him, ain't listening
[Marlon Brando]

Proverbs

Proverbs are introduced by the heading **PROVERBS**:

> **PROVERBS**
> *Every eel hopes to become a whale*

Cross References

Cross references, given in black bold, refer the user to another entry where full information is given:

enquire *see* **inquire**

Cross references to themed panels are introduced by an empty arrow:

star NOUN **1 = heavenly body**, sun, celestial body: *The nights were pure with cold air and lit with stars.* **2 = celebrity**, big name, celeb (*informal*), megastar (*informal*), name, draw, idol, luminary, leading man *or* lady, lead, hero *or* heroine, principal, main attraction: *Not all football stars are ill-behaved louts.*
▷ PLURAL NOUN **= horoscope**, forecast, astrological chart: *There was nothing in my stars to say I'd have problems.*
▷ VERB **= play the lead**, appear, feature, perform: *He's starred in dozens of films.* ▷ *See themed panel* **Stars and Constellations** *on facing page*

Themed Panels

Themed panels are in blue boxes:

apocalypse NOUN **= destruction**, holocaust, havoc, devastation, carnage, conflagration, cataclysm

FOUR HORSEMEN OF THE APOCALYPSE

white – Christ	black – Famine
red – War	pale – Death

List of Essays by Page Order

List of Essays by Theme

The Language of…

Newspaper Language

Authorial Style

A Close-up on Classic Literature

Writing Tips

Subject Word Lists

List of Themed Panels

Abbreviations

AD	anno Domini
Austral.	Australia/Australian
BC	before Christ
Brit.	British
Canad.	Canada/Canadian
e.g.	for example
esp.	especially
etc.	et cetera
N.Z.	New Zealand
®	trademark
RC	Roman Catholic
S.	South
Scot.	Scottish
S.M.S.	Short Message Service
US	United States

Aa

aback ADVERB
taken aback = **surprised**, thrown, shocked, stunned, confused, astonished, staggered, startled, bewildered, astounded, disconcerted, bowled over *(informal)*, stupefied, floored *(informal)*, knocked for six, dumbfounded, left open-mouthed, nonplussed, flabbergasted *(informal)*

abandon VERB **1** = **leave**, strand, ditch, leave behind, walk out on, forsake, jilt, run out on, throw over, turn your back on, desert, dump, leave high and dry, leave in the lurch: *He claimed that his parents had abandoned him.* **2** = **stop**, drop, give up, halt, cease, cut out, pack in *(Brit. informal)*, discontinue, leave off, desist from: *The authorities have abandoned any attempt to distribute food.* **OPPOSITE:** continue **3** = **give up**, resign from, yield, surrender, relinquish, renounce, waive, cede, forgo, abdicate: *efforts to persuade him to abandon his claim to the presidency* **OPPOSITE:** keep
▷ NOUN = **recklessness**, dash, wildness, wantonness, unrestraint, careless freedom: *He has splashed money around with gay abandon.* **OPPOSITE:** restraint
abandon ship = **evacuate**, quit, withdraw from, vacate, depart from: *The crew prepared to abandon ship.* **OPPOSITE:** maintain

abandoned ADJECTIVE **1** = **unoccupied**, empty, deserted, vacant, derelict, uninhabited: *abandoned buildings that become a breeding ground for crime* **OPPOSITE:** occupied **2** = **deserted**, dropped, rejected, neglected, stranded, ditched, discarded, relinquished, left, forsaken, cast off, jilted, cast aside, cast out, cast away: *a newsreel of abandoned children suffering from cold and hunger* **3** = **uninhibited**, wild, uncontrolled, unbridled, unrestrained, unconstrained: *people who enjoy wild, abandoned lovemaking* **OPPOSITE:** inhibited

abandonment NOUN **1** = **desertion**, leaving, forsaking, jilting: *memories of her father's complete abandonment of her* **2** = **evacuation**, leaving, quitting, departure, withdrawal: *the abandonment of two North Sea oilfields* **3** = **stopping**, cessation, discontinuation: *Rain forced the abandonment of the next day's competitions.* **4** = **renunciation**, giving up, surrender, waiver, abdication, cession, relinquishment: *their abandonment of the policy*

abate VERB **1** = **decrease**, decline, relax, ease, sink, fade, weaken, diminish, dwindle, lessen, slow, wane, subside, ebb, let up, slacken, attenuate, taper off: *The storms soon abated.* **OPPOSITE:** increase **2** = **reduce**, slow, relax, ease, relieve, moderate, weaken, dull, diminish, decrease, lessen, alleviate, quell, mitigate, attenuate: *a government programme to abate greenhouse gas emissions* **OPPOSITE:** increase

abatement NOUN **1** = **decrease**, slowing, decline, easing, sinking, fading, weakening, relaxation, dwindling, lessening, waning, subsiding, ebbing, cessation, let-up, slackening, diminution, tapering off, attenuation: *Demand for the product shows no sign of abatement.* **2** = **reduction**, slowing, relief, easing, weakening, dulling, decrease, lessening, cutback, quelling, moderation, remission, slackening, mitigation, diminution, curtailment, alleviation, attenuation, extenuation: *noise abatement*

abattoir NOUN = **slaughterhouse**, shambles, butchery

abbey NOUN = **monastery**, convent, priory, cloister, nunnery, friary

abbreviate VERB = **shorten**, reduce, contract, trim, cut, prune, summarize, compress, condense, abridge **OPPOSITE:** expand

abbreviated ADJECTIVE = **shortened**, shorter, reduced, brief, potted, trimmed, pruned, cut, summarized, compressed, concise, condensed, abridged **OPPOSITE:** expanded

abbreviation NOUN = **shortening**, reduction, résumé, trimming, summary, contraction, compression, synopsis, précis, abridgment

abdicate VERB **1** = **resign**, retire, quit, step down *(informal)*: *The last French king abdicated in 1848.* **2** = **give up**, yield, hand over, surrender, relinquish, renounce, waive, vacate, cede, abjure: *Edward chose to abdicate the throne, rather than give Mrs Simpson up.* **3** = **renounce**, give up, abandon, surrender, relinquish, waive, forgo, abnegate: *Many parents simply abdicate all responsibility for their children.*

abdication NOUN **1** = **resignation**, quitting, retirement, retiral *(chiefly Scot.)*: *the abdication of Edward VIII* **2** = **giving up**, yielding, surrender, waiving, renunciation, cession, relinquishment, abjuration: *Edward was titled Duke of Windsor after his abdication of the throne.*

abdomen NOUN = **stomach**, guts *(slang)*, belly, tummy *(informal)*, midriff, midsection, makutu *(N.Z.)*, puku *(N.Z.)*
▸ *related adjective:* abdominal

abdominal ADJECTIVE = **gastric**, intestinal, visceral

abduct VERB = **kidnap**, seize, carry off, run off with, run away with, make off with, snatch *(slang)*

abduction NOUN = **kidnapping**, seizure, carrying off

aberrant ADJECTIVE **1** = **abnormal**, odd, strange, extraordinary, curious, weird, peculiar, eccentric, queer, irregular, erratic, deviant, off-the-wall *(slang)*, oddball *(informal)*, anomalous, untypical, wacko *(slang)*, outré, daggy *(Austral. & N.Z. informal)*: *His rages and aberrant behaviour worsened.* **2** = **depraved**, corrupt, perverted, perverse, degenerate, deviant, debased, debauched: *aberrant sexual crimes*

aberration NOUN = **anomaly**, exception, defect, abnormality, inconsistency, deviation, quirk, peculiarity, divergence, departure, irregularity, incongruity

abet VERB **1** = **help**, aid, encourage, sustain, assist, uphold, back, second, incite, egg on, succour: *We shall strike hard at terrorists and those who abet them.* **2** = **encourage**, further, forward, promote, urge, boost, prompt, spur, foster, incite, connive at: *The media have abetted the feeling of unreality.*

abetting NOUN = **help**, backing, support, aid, assistance, encouragement, abetment, abettal

abeyance NOUN
in abeyance = **shelved**, pending, on ice *(informal)*, in cold storage *(informal)*, hanging fire, suspended

abhor VERB = **hate**, loathe, despise, detest, shrink from, shudder at, recoil from, be repelled by, have an aversion to, abominate, execrate, regard with repugnance *or* horror **OPPOSITE:** love

abhorrent ADJECTIVE = **hateful**, hated, offensive, disgusting, horrible, revolting, obscene, distasteful, horrid, repellent, obnoxious, despicable, repulsive, heinous, odious, repugnant, loathsome, abominable, execrable, detestable

abide VERB **1** = **tolerate**, suffer, accept, bear, endure, brook, hack *(slang)*, put up with, take, stand, stomach, thole *(Scot.)*: *I can't abide people who can't make up their minds.* **2** = **last**, continue, remain, survive, carry on, endure, persist, keep on: *to make moral judgements on the basis of what is eternal and abides*
abide by something = **obey**, follow, agree to, carry out, observe, fulfil,

stand by, act on, comply with, hold to, heed, submit to, conform to, keep to, adhere to, mind: *They have got to abide by the rules.*

abiding ADJECTIVE = **enduring**, lasting, continuing, remaining, surviving, permanent, constant, prevailing, persisting, persistent, eternal, tenacious, firm, fast, everlasting, unending, unchanging **OPPOSITE:** brief

ability NOUN **1 = capability**, power, potential, facility, capacity, qualification, competence, proficiency, competency, potentiality: *No one had faith in his ability to do the job.* **OPPOSITE:** inability **2 = skill**, talent, know-how *(informal)*, gift, expertise, faculty, flair, competence, energy, accomplishment, knack, aptitude, proficiency, dexterity, cleverness, potentiality, adroitness, adeptness: *Her drama teacher spotted her ability.*

> **QUOTATIONS**
> From each according to his abilities, to each according to his needs
> [Karl Marx *Critique of the Gotha Programme*]

abject ADJECTIVE **1 = wretched**, miserable, hopeless, dismal, outcast, pitiful, forlorn, deplorable, pitiable: *Both of them died in abject poverty.* **2 = servile**, humble, craven, cringing, fawning, submissive, grovelling, subservient, slavish, mean, low, obsequious: *He sounded abject and eager to please.* **OPPOSITE:** dignified **3 = despicable**, base, degraded, worthless, vile, sordid, debased, reprehensible, contemptible, dishonourable, ignoble, detestable, scungy *(Austral. & N.Z.)*: *the kind of abject low-life that preys on children*

ablaze ADJECTIVE **1 = on fire**, burning, flaming, blazing, fiery, alight, aflame, afire: *Shops, houses and vehicles were ablaze.* **2 = bright**, brilliant, flashing, glowing, sparkling, illuminated, gleaming, radiant, luminous, incandescent, aglow: *The chamber was ablaze with light.* **3 = passionate**, excited, stimulated, fierce, enthusiastic, aroused, animated, frenzied, fervent, impassioned, fervid: *He was ablaze with enthusiasm.*

able ADJECTIVE = **capable**, experienced, fit, skilled, expert, powerful, masterly, effective, qualified, talented, gifted, efficient, clever, practised, accomplished, competent, skilful, adept, masterful, strong, proficient, adroit, highly endowed **OPPOSITE:** incapable

able-bodied ADJECTIVE = **strong**, firm, sound, fit, powerful, healthy, strapping, hardy, robust, vigorous, sturdy, hale, stout, staunch, hearty, lusty, right as rain *(Brit. informal)*, tough, capable, sturdy, Herculean, fighting fit, sinewy, fit as a fiddle **OPPOSITE:** weak

abnormal ADJECTIVE = **unusual**, different, odd, strange, surprising, extraordinary, remarkable, bizarre, unexpected, curious, weird, exceptional, peculiar, eccentric, unfamiliar, queer, irregular, phenomenal, uncommon, erratic, monstrous, singular, unnatural, deviant, unconventional, off-the-wall *(slang)*, oddball *(informal)*, out of the ordinary, left-field *(informal)*, anomalous, atypical, aberrant, untypical, wacko *(slang)*, outré, daggy *(Austral. & N.Z. informal)* **OPPOSITE:** normal

abnormality NOUN **1 = strangeness**, deviation, eccentricity, aberration, peculiarity, idiosyncrasy, irregularity, weirdness, singularity, oddness, waywardness, unorthodoxy, unexpectedness, queerness, unnaturalness, bizarreness, unusualness, extraordinariness, aberrance, atypicalness, uncommonness, untypicalness, curiousness: *Further scans are required to confirm any abnormality.* **2 = anomaly**, flaw, rarity, deviation, oddity, aberration, exception, peculiarity, deformity, monstrosity, irregularity, malformation: *Genetic abnormalities are usually associated with paternal DNA.*

abnormally ADVERB = **unusually**, oddly, strangely, extremely, exceptionally, extraordinarily, overly, excessively, peculiarly, particularly, bizarrely, disproportionately, singularly, fantastically, unnaturally, uncannily, inordinately, uncommonly, prodigiously, freakishly, atypically, subnormally, supernormally

abode NOUN = **home**, house, quarters, lodging, pad *(slang)*, residence, habitat, dwelling, habitation, domicile, dwelling place

abolish VERB = **do away with**, end, destroy, eliminate, shed, cancel, axe *(informal)*, get rid of, ditch *(slang)*, dissolve, junk *(informal)*, suppress, overturn, throw out, discard, wipe out, overthrow, void, terminate, drop, trash *(slang)*, repeal, eradicate, put an end to, quash, extinguish, dispense with, revoke, stamp out, obliterate, subvert, jettison, repudiate, annihilate, rescind, exterminate, invalidate, bring to an end, annul, nullify, blot out, expunge, abrogate, vitiate, extirpate, kennet *(Austral. slang)*, jeff *(Austral. slang)* **OPPOSITE:** establish

abolition NOUN = **eradication**, ending, end, withdrawal, destruction, removal, overturning, wiping out, overthrow, voiding, extinction, repeal, elimination, cancellation, suppression, quashing, termination, stamping out, subversion, extermination, annihilation, blotting out, repudiation, erasure, annulment, obliteration, revocation, effacement, nullification, abrogation, rescission, extirpation, invalidation, vitiation, expunction

abominable ADJECTIVE = **detestable**, shocking, terrible, offensive, foul, disgusting, horrible, revolting, obscene, vile, horrid, repellent, atrocious, obnoxious, despicable, repulsive, base, heinous, hellish, odious, hateful, repugnant, reprehensible, loathsome, abhorrent, contemptible, villainous, nauseous, wretched, accursed, execrable, godawful *(slang)* **OPPOSITE:** pleasant

abomination NOUN **1 = outrage**, bête noire, horror, evil, shame, plague, curse, disgrace, crime, atrocity, torment, anathema, barbarism, bugbear: *What is happening is an abomination.* **2 = hatred**, hate, horror, disgust, dislike, loathing, distaste, animosity, aversion, revulsion, antagonism, antipathy, enmity, ill will, animus, abhorrence, repugnance, odium, detestation, execration: *He had become an object of abomination.*

aboriginal ADJECTIVE = **indigenous**, first, earliest, original, primary, ancient, native, primitive, pristine, primordial, primeval, autochthonous

aborigine NOUN = **original inhabitant**, native, aboriginal, indigene

abort VERB **1 = terminate** *(a pregnancy)*, miscarry: *the latest date at which a foetus can be aborted* **2 = stop**, end, finish, check, arrest, halt, cease, bring *or* come to a halt *or* standstill, axe *(informal)*, pull up, terminate, call off, break off, cut short, pack in *(Brit. informal)*, discontinue, desist: *The take-off was aborted.*

abortion NOUN **1 = termination**, feticide, aborticide, miscarriage, deliberate miscarriage: *They had been going out a year when she had an abortion.* **2 = failure**, disappointment, fiasco, misadventure, vain effort: *the abortion of the original nuclear project* **3 = monstrosity**

abortive ADJECTIVE = **failed**, failing, useless, vain, unsuccessful, idle, ineffective, futile, fruitless, unproductive, ineffectual, miscarried, unavailing, bootless

abound VERB = **be plentiful**, thrive, flourish, be numerous, proliferate, be abundant, be thick on the ground, superabound: *Stories abound about when he was in charge.*
abound with *or* **in something = overflow with**, be packed with, teem with, be crowded with, swell with, crawl with, swarm with, be jammed with, be infested with, be thronged with, luxuriate with: *Venice abounds in famous hotels; In troubled times, the roads abounded with highwaymen and brigands.*

about PREPOSITION **1 = regarding**, on, re, concerning, touching, dealing with, respecting, referring to, relating to, concerned with, connected with, relative to, with respect to, as regards, anent *(Scot.)*: *She knew a lot about food.* **2 = around**, over, through, round, throughout, all over: *For 18 years, he wandered about Germany, Switzerland and Italy.* **3 = near**, around, close to, bordering, nearby, beside, close by, adjacent to, just round the corner from, in the neighbourhood of, alongside of, contiguous to, within sniffing distance of *(informal)*, at close quarters to, a hop, skip and a jump away from *(informal)*: *The restaurant is somewhere about here.*

▷ ADVERB **1 = approximately**, around, almost, nearing, nearly, approaching, close to, roughly, just about, more or less, in the region of, in the vicinity of, not far off: *The rate of inflation is running at about 2.7 per cent.* **2 = everywhere**, around, all over, here and there, on all sides, in all directions, to and fro, from place to place, hither and thither: *The house isn't big enough with three children running about.*

about to = on the point of, ready to, intending to, on the verge *or* brink of: *I think he's about to leave.*

about-turn NOUN **= change of direction**, reverse, reversal, turnaround, U-turn, right about (turn), about-face, volte-face, turnabout, paradigm shift: *The decision was seen as an about-turn for the government.*

▷ VERB **= change direction**, reverse, about-face, volte-face, face the opposite direction, turn about *or* around, turn through 180 degrees, do *or* perform a U-turn *or* volte-face: *She about-turned abruptly and left.*

above PREPOSITION **1 = over**, upon, beyond, on top of, exceeding, higher than, atop: *He lifted his arms above his head.* **OPPOSITE:** under **2 = senior to**, over, ahead of, in charge of, higher than, surpassing, superior to, more powerful than: *the people above you in the organization* **OPPOSITE:** subordinate to **3 = before**, more than, rather than, beyond, instead of, sooner than, in preference to: *I want to be honest, above everything else.*

▷ ADVERB **= overhead**, upward, in the sky, on high, in heaven, atop, aloft, up above, skyward: *A long scream sounded from somewhere above.*

▷ ADJECTIVE **= preceding**, earlier, previous, prior, foregoing, aforementioned, aforesaid: *Write to the above address.*

▸ *related prefixes:* super-, supra-, sur-

abrasion NOUN **1 = graze**, scratch, trauma *(Pathology)*, scrape, scuff, chafe, surface injury: *He had severe abrasions to his right cheek.* **2 = rubbing**, wear, scratching, scraping, grating, friction, scouring, attrition, corrosion, wearing down, erosion, scuffing, chafing, grinding down, wearing away, abrading: *The sole of the shoe should be designed to take constant abrasion.*

abrasive ADJECTIVE **1 = harsh**, cutting, biting, tough, sharp, severe, bitter, rough, hard, nasty, cruel, annoying, brutal, stern, irritating, unpleasant, grating, abusive, galling, unkind, hurtful, caustic, vitriolic, pitiless, unfeeling, comfortless: *She was unrepentant about her abrasive remarks.* **2 = rough**, scratching, scraping, grating, scuffing, chafing, scratchy, frictional, erosive: *an all-purpose non-abrasive cleaner*

▷ NOUN **= scourer**, grinder, burnisher, scarifier, abradant: *Avoid abrasives, which can damage the tiles.*

abreast ADVERB **= alongside**, level, beside, in a row, side by side, neck and neck, shoulder to shoulder: *a group of youths riding four abreast*

abreast of *or* **with = informed about**, in touch with, familiar with, acquainted with, up to date with, knowledgeable about, conversant with, up to speed with *(informal)*, in the picture about, *au courant* with, *au fait* with, keeping your finger on the pulse of: *We'll keep you abreast of developments.*

abridge VERB **= shorten**, reduce, contract, trim, clip, diminish, decrease, abstract, digest, cut down, cut back, cut, prune, concentrate, lessen, summarize, compress, curtail, condense, abbreviate, truncate, epitomize, downsize, précis, synopsize *(U.S.)* **OPPOSITE:** expand

abridged ADJECTIVE **= shortened**, shorter, reduced, brief, potted *(informal)*, trimmed, diminished, pruned, summarized, cut, compressed, curtailed, concise, condensed, abbreviated **OPPOSITE:** expanded

abroad ADVERB **1 = overseas**, out of the country, beyond the sea, in foreign lands: *About 65 per cent of our sales come from abroad.* **2 = about**, everywhere, circulating, at large, here and there, current, all over, in circulation: *There is still a feeling abroad that this change must be recognised.*

abrupt ADJECTIVE **1 = sudden**, unexpected, hurried, rapid, surprising, quick, swift, rash, precipitate, hasty, impulsive, headlong, unforeseen, unanticipated: *His abrupt departure is bound to raise questions.* **OPPOSITE:** slow **2 = curt**, direct, brief, sharp, rough, short, clipped, blunt, rude, tart, impatient, brisk, concise, snappy, terse, gruff, succinct, pithy, brusque, offhand, impolite, monosyllabic, ungracious, discourteous, uncivil, unceremonious, snappish: *He was abrupt to the point of rudeness.* **OPPOSITE:** polite **3 = steep**, sharp, sheer, sudden, precipitous: *narrow valleys and abrupt hillsides* **OPPOSITE:** gradual

abruptly ADVERB **1 = suddenly**, short, unexpectedly, all of a sudden, hastily, precipitately, all at once, hurriedly: *He stopped abruptly and looked my way.* **OPPOSITE:** gradually **2 = curtly**, bluntly, rudely, briskly, tersely, shortly, sharply, brusquely, gruffly, snappily: *'Good night then,' she said abruptly.* **OPPOSITE:** politely

abscess NOUN **= boil**, infection, swelling, blister, ulcer, inflammation, gathering, whitlow, blain, carbuncle, pustule, bubo, furuncle *(Pathology)*, gumboil, parulis *(Pathology)*

abscond VERB **= escape**, flee, get away, bolt, fly, disappear, skip, run off, slip away, clear out, flit *(informal)*, make off, break free *or* out, decamp, hook it *(slang)*, do a runner *(slang)*, steal away, sneak away, do a bunk *(Brit. slang)*, fly the coop *(U.S. & Canad. informal)*, skedaddle *(informal)*, take a powder *(U.S. & Canad. slang)*, go on the lam *(U.S. & Canad. slang)*, make your getaway, do a Skase *(Austral. informal)*, make *or* effect your escape

> **QUOTATIONS**
> abscond: to 'move in a mysterious way', commonly with the property of another
> [Ambrose Bierce *The Devil's Dictionary*]

absence NOUN **1 = time off**, leave, break, vacation, recess, truancy, absenteeism, nonappearance, nonattendance: *A bundle of letters had arrived for me in my absence.* **2 = lack**, deficiency, deprivation, omission, scarcity, want, need, shortage, dearth, privation, unavailability, nonexistence: *In the absence of a will, the courts decide who the guardian is.*

> **QUOTATIONS**
> Absence makes the heart grow fonder,
> Isle of Beauty, Fare thee well!
> [Thomas Haynes Bayly *Isle of Beauty*]
>
> Absence is to love what wind is to fire; it extinguishes the small, it inflames the great
> [Comte de Bussy-Rabutin *Histoire amoureuse des Gaules*]
>
> That out of sight is out of mind
> Is true of most we leave behind
> [Arthur Hugh Clough *That Out of Sight*]
>
> Among the defects of the Bill, which were numerous, one provision was conspicuous by its presence and another by its absence
> [Lord John Russell *Speech to his constituents, 1859*]

absent ADJECTIVE **1 = away**, missing, gone, lacking, elsewhere, unavailable, not present, truant, nonexistent, nonattendant: *He has been absent from his desk for two weeks.* **OPPOSITE:** present **2 = absent-minded**, blank, unconscious, abstracted, vague, distracted, unaware, musing, vacant,

preoccupied, empty, absorbed, bemused, oblivious, dreamy, daydreaming, faraway, unthinking, heedless, inattentive, unheeding: *'Nothing,' she said in an absent way.*
OPPOSITE: alert
absent yourself = stay away, withdraw, depart, keep away, truant, abscond, play truant, slope off *(informal)*, bunk off *(slang)*, remove yourself: *He pleaded guilty to absenting himself without leave.*

QUOTATIONS
> Greater things are believed of those who are absent
> [Tacitus *Histories*]

absentee NOUN **= nonattender**, stay-at-home, truant, no-show, stayaway

absent-minded ADJECTIVE **= forgetful**, absorbed, abstracted, vague, absent, distracted, unaware, musing, preoccupied, careless, bemused, oblivious, dreamy, faraway, engrossed, unthinking, neglectful, heedless, inattentive, unmindful, unheeding, apt to forget, in a brown study, ditzy *or* ditsy *(slang)*
OPPOSITE: alert

absolute ADJECTIVE **1 = complete**, total, perfect, entire, pure, sheer, utter, outright, thorough, downright, consummate, unqualified, full-on *(informal)*, out-and-out, unadulterated, unmitigated, dyed-in-the-wool, thoroughgoing, unalloyed, unmixed, arrant, deep-dyed *(usually derogatory)*: *A sick person needs to have absolute trust in a doctor.* **2 = supreme**, sovereign, unlimited, ultimate, full, utmost, unconditional, unqualified, predominant, superlative, unrestricted, pre-eminent, unrestrained, tyrannical, peerless, unsurpassed, unquestionable, matchless, peremptory, unbounded: *He ruled with absolute power.*
3 = autocratic, supreme, unlimited, autonomous, arbitrary, dictatorial, all-powerful, imperious, domineering, tyrannical, despotic, absolutist, tyrannous, autarchical: *the doctrine of absolute monarchy*
4 = definite, sure, certain, positive, guaranteed, actual, assured, genuine, exact, precise, decisive, conclusive, unequivocal, unambiguous, infallible, categorical, unquestionable, dinkum *(Austral. & N.Z. informal)*, nailed-on *(slang)*: *He brought the absolute proof that we needed.*

absolutely ADVERB **1 = completely**, totally, perfectly, quite, fully, entirely, purely, altogether, thoroughly, wholly, utterly, consummately, every inch, to the hilt, a hundred per cent, one hundred per cent, unmitigatedly, lock, stock and barrel: *She is absolutely right.* **OPPOSITE:** somewhat
2 = definitely, surely, certainly, clearly, obviously, plainly, truly, precisely, exactly, genuinely, positively, decidedly, decisively, without doubt, unquestionably, undeniably, categorically, without question, unequivocally, conclusively, unambiguously, beyond any doubt, infallibly: *'It's worrying, isn't it?' 'Absolutely.'*

absolution NOUN **= forgiveness**, release, freedom, liberation, discharge, amnesty, mercy, pardon, indulgence, exemption, acquittal, remission, vindication, deliverance, dispensation, exoneration, exculpation, shriving, condonation

absolve VERB **= excuse**, free, clear, release, deliver, loose, forgive, discharge, liberate, pardon, exempt, acquit, vindicate, remit, let off, set free, exonerate, exculpate
OPPOSITE: condemn

absorb VERB **1 = soak up**, drink in, devour, suck up, receive, digest, imbibe, ingest, osmose: *Refined sugars are absorbed into the bloodstream very quickly.* **2 = engross**, hold, involve, fill, arrest, fix, occupy, engage, fascinate, preoccupy, engulf, fill up, immerse, rivet, captivate, monopolize, enwrap: *a second career which absorbed her more completely than acting ever had*

absorbed ADJECTIVE **= engrossed**, lost, involved, fixed, concentrating, occupied, engaged, gripped, fascinated, caught up, intrigued, wrapped up, preoccupied, immersed, dialled in, locked in, riveted, captivated, enthralled, rapt, up to your ears

absorbent ADJECTIVE **= porous**, receptive, imbibing, spongy, permeable, absorptive, blotting, penetrable, pervious, assimilative

absorbing ADJECTIVE **= fascinating**, interesting, engaging, gripping, arresting, compelling, intriguing, enticing, preoccupying, enchanting, seductive, riveting, captivating, alluring, bewitching, engrossing, spellbinding **OPPOSITE:** boring

absorption NOUN **1 = soaking up**, consumption, digestion, sucking up, osmosis: *Vitamin C increases absorption of iron.* **2 = immersion**, holding, involvement, concentration, occupation, engagement, fascination, preoccupation, intentness, captivation, raptness: *He was struck by the artists' total absorption in their work.*

abstain from VERB **= refrain from**, avoid, decline, give up, stop, refuse, cease, do without, shun, renounce, eschew, leave off, keep from, forgo, withhold from, forbear, desist from, deny yourself, kick *(informal)*
OPPOSITE: abandon yourself

QUOTATIONS
> abstainer: a weak person who yields to the temptation of denying himself a pleasure
> [Ambrose Bierce *The Devil's Dictionary*]

abstention NOUN **1 = abstaining**, non-voting, refusal to vote: *Abstention is traditionally high in Columbia.*
2 = abstinence, refraining, avoidance, forbearance, eschewal, desistance, nonindulgence: *The goal is complete abstention from all mind-altering substances.*

abstinence NOUN **= abstention**, continence, temperance, self-denial, self-restraint, forbearance, refraining, avoidance, moderation, sobriety, asceticism, teetotalism, abstemiousness, soberness
OPPOSITE: self-indulgence

QUOTATIONS
> If God forbade drinking, would he have made wine so good?
> [Cardinal Richelieu]
>
> I am a beer teetotaller, not a champagne teetotaller
> [George Bernard Shaw]
>
> Refrain to-night, And that shall lend a kind of easiness
> To the next abstinence: the next more easy;
> For use almost can change the stamp of nature
> [William Shakespeare *Hamlet*]
>
> Abstinence is as easy to me, as temperance would be difficult
> [Samuel Johnson *Correspondence with Mrs. Hannah More*]
>
> To many, total abstinence is easier than perfect moderation
> [St. Augustine of Hippo *On the Good of Marriage*]

abstract ADJECTIVE **= theoretical**, general, complex, academic, intellectual, subtle, profound, philosophical, speculative, unrealistic, conceptual, indefinite, deep, separate, occult, hypothetical, generalized, impractical, arcane, notional, abstruse, recondite, theoretic, conjectural, unpractical, nonconcrete: *starting with a few abstract principles* **OPPOSITE:** actual
▷ NOUN **= summary**, résumé, outline, extract, essence, summing-up, digest, epitome, rundown, condensation, compendium, synopsis, précis, recapitulation, review, abridgment: *If you want to submit a paper, you must supply an abstract.*
OPPOSITE: expansion
▷ VERB **= extract**, draw, pull, remove, separate, withdraw, isolate, pull out, take out, take away, detach, dissociate, pluck out: *The author has abstracted poems from earlier books.*
OPPOSITE: add

abstracted ADJECTIVE **= preoccupied**, withdrawn, remote, absorbed, intent, absent, distracted, unaware, wrapped up, bemused, immersed, oblivious, dreamy, daydreaming, faraway, engrossed, rapt, absent-minded, heedless, inattentive, distrait, woolgathering

abstraction NOUN **1 = concept**, thought, idea, view, theory, impression, formula, notion, hypothesis, generalization, theorem, generality: *Is it worth fighting in the name of an abstraction?* **2 = absent-mindedness**, musing, preoccupation, daydreaming, vagueness, remoteness, absence, inattention, dreaminess, obliviousness, absence of mind, pensiveness, woolgathering, distractedness, bemusedness: *He noticed her abstraction and asked, 'What's bothering you?'*

absurd ADJECTIVE **= ridiculous**, crazy *(informal)*, silly, incredible, outrageous, foolish, unbelievable, daft *(informal)*, hilarious, ludicrous, meaningless, unreasonable, irrational, senseless, preposterous, laughable, funny, stupid, farcical, illogical, incongruous, comical, zany, idiotic, nonsensical, inane, dumb-ass *(slang)* **OPPOSITE:** sensible

absurdity NOUN **= ridiculousness**, nonsense, malarkey, folly, stupidity, foolishness, silliness, idiocy, irrationality, incongruity, meaninglessness, daftness *(informal)*, senselessness, illogicality, ludicrousness, unreasonableness, preposterousness, farcicality, craziness *(informal)*, bêtise *(rare)*, farcicalness, illogicalness

> **QUOTATIONS**
> absurdity: a statement of belief manifestly inconsistent with one's own opinion
> [Ambrose Bierce *The Devil's Dictionary*]

absurdly ADVERB **= ridiculously**, incredibly, unbelievably, foolishly, ludicrously, unreasonably, incongruously, laughably, irrationally, implausibly, preposterously, illogically, inanely, senselessly, idiotically, inconceivably, farcically

abundance NOUN **1 = plenty**, heap *(informal)*, bounty, exuberance, profusion, plethora, affluence, fullness, opulence, plenitude, fruitfulness, copiousness, ampleness, cornucopia, plenteousness, plentifulness: *a staggering abundance of food* **OPPOSITE:** shortage **2 = wealth**, money, funds, capital, cash, riches, resources, assets, fortune, possessions, prosperity, big money, wad *(U.S. & Canad. slang)*, affluence, big bucks *(informal, chiefly U.S.)*, opulence, megabucks *(U.S. & Canad. slang)*, tidy sum *(informal)*, lucre, pretty penny *(informal)*, pelf, top whack *(informal)*: *What customers want is a display of lushness and abundance.*

> **QUOTATIONS**
> ... a good land and a large ... a land flowing with milk and honey
> [*Bible: Exodus*]

abundant ADJECTIVE **= plentiful**, full, rich, liberal, generous, lavish, ample, infinite, overflowing, exuberant, teeming, copious, inexhaustible, bountiful, luxuriant, profuse, rank, well-provided, well-supplied, bounteous, plenteous **OPPOSITE:** scarce

abundantly ADVERB **= plentifully**, greatly, freely, amply, richly, liberally, fully, thoroughly, substantially, lavishly, extensively, generously, profusely, copiously, exuberantly, in plentiful supply, luxuriantly, unstintingly, bountifully, bounteously, plenteously, in great *or* large numbers **OPPOSITE:** sparsely

abuse NOUN **1 = maltreatment**, wrong, damage, injury, hurt, harm, spoiling, bullying, exploitation, oppression, imposition, mistreatment, manhandling, ill-treatment, rough handling: *an investigation into alleged child abuse* **2 = insults**, blame, slights, curses, put-downs, libel, censure, reproach, scolding, defamation, indignities, offence, tirade, derision, slander, rudeness, vilification, invective, swear words, opprobrium, insolence, upbraiding, aspersions, character assassination, disparagement, vituperation, castigation, contumely, revilement, traducement, calumniation: *I was left shouting abuse as the car sped off.* **3 = misuse**, corruption, perversion, misapplication, misemployment, misusage: *an abuse of power*
▷ VERB **1 = ill-treat**, wrong, damage, hurt, injure, harm, mar, oppress, maul, molest, impose upon, manhandle, rough up, brutalize, maltreat, handle roughly, knock about *or* around: *She had been abused by her father.* **OPPOSITE:** care for **2 = insult**, injure, offend, curse, put down, smear, libel, slate *(informal, chiefly Brit.)*, slag (off) *(slang)*, malign, scold, swear at, disparage, castigate, revile, vilify, slander, defame, upbraid, slight, inveigh against, call names, traduce, calumniate, vituperate: *He alleged that he was verbally abused by other soldiers.* **OPPOSITE:** praise

abusive ADJECTIVE **1 = violent**, wild, rough, cruel, savage, brutal, vicious, destructive, harmful, maddened, hurtful, unrestrained, impetuous, homicidal, intemperate, raging, furious, injurious, maniacal: *her cruel and abusive husband* **OPPOSITE:** kind **2 = insulting**, offensive, rude, degrading, scathing, maligning, scolding, affronting, contemptuous, disparaging, castigating, reviling, vilifying, invective, scurrilous, defamatory, insolent, derisive, censorious, slighting, libellous, upbraiding, vituperative, reproachful, slanderous, traducing, opprobrious, calumniating, contumelious: *He was alleged to have used abusive language.* **OPPOSITE:** complimentary

abut VERB **= adjoin**, join, touch, border, neighbour, link to, attach to, combine with, connect with, couple with, communicate with, annex, meet, unite with, verge on, impinge, append, affix to

abysmal ADJECTIVE **= dreadful**, bad, terrible, awful, appalling, dismal, dire, ghastly, hideous, atrocious, godawful *(informal)*

abyss NOUN **= chasm**, gulf, split, crack, gap, pit, opening, breach, hollow, void, gorge, crater, cavity, ravine, cleft, fissure, crevasse, bottomless depth, abysm

academic ADJECTIVE **1 = scholastic**, school, university, college, educational, campus, collegiate: *the country's richest and most famous academic institutions* **2 = scholarly**, learned, intellectual, literary, erudite, highbrow, studious, lettered: *The author has settled for a more academic approach.* **3 = theoretical**, ideal, abstract, speculative, hypothetical, impractical, notional, conjectural: *These arguments are purely academic.*
▷ NOUN **= scholar**, intellectual, don, student, master, professor, fellow, pupil, lecturer, tutor, scholastic, bookworm, man of letters, egghead *(informal)*, savant, academician, acca *(Austral. slang)*, bluestocking *(usually derogatory)*, schoolman *(U.S. rare)*: *He is an academic who believes in winning through argument.*

academy NOUN **= college**, school, university, institution, institute, establishment, seminary, centre of learning, whare wananga *(N.Z.)*

accede to VERB **1 = agree to**, accept, grant, endorse, consent to, give in to, surrender to, yield to, concede to, acquiesce in, assent to, comply with, concur to: *Why didn't he accede to our demands at the outset?* **2 = inherit**, come to, assume, succeed, come into, attain, succeed to *(of an heir)*, enter upon, fall heir to: *when Henry VIII acceded to the throne*

accelerate VERB **1 = increase**, grow, advance, extend, expand, build up, strengthen, raise, swell, intensify, enlarge, escalate, multiply, inflate, magnify, proliferate, snowball: *Growth will accelerate to 2.9 per cent next year.* **OPPOSITE:** fall **2 = expedite**, press, forward, promote, spur, further, stimulate, hurry, step up *(informal)*, speed up, facilitate, hasten, precipitate, quicken: *The government is to accelerate its privatisation programme.* **OPPOSITE:** delay **3 = speed up**, speed, advance, quicken, get under way, gather momentum, get moving, pick up speed, put your foot down *(informal)*, open up the throttle, put on speed: *Suddenly the car accelerated.* **OPPOSITE:** slow down

acceleration NOUN **= hastening**, hurrying, stepping up *(informal)*, expedition, speeding up, stimulation, advancement, promotion, spurring, quickening

accent NOUN **= pronunciation**, tone, articulation, inflection, brogue, intonation, diction, modulation, elocution, enunciation, accentuation:

a

He has developed a slight American accent. ▷ VERB **= emphasize**, stress, highlight, underline, bring home, underscore, accentuate, give emphasis to, call *or* draw attention to: *She had a round face accented by a little white cap.*

QUOTATIONS

The accent of one's birthplace lingers in the mind and in the heart as it does in one's speech
[Duc de la Rochefoucauld *Maximes*]

I don't have an English accent because this is what English sounds like when spoken properly
[Jimmy Carr *The Tonight Show with Jay Leno (US TV chat show)*]

accentuate VERB **= emphasize**, stress, highlight, accent, underline, bring home, underscore, foreground, give emphasis to, call *or* draw attention to **OPPOSITE:** minimize

accept VERB **1 = receive**, take, gain, pick up, secure, collect, have, get, obtain, acquire: *All old clothes will be gratefully accepted by the organizers.* **2 = take on**, try, begin, attempt, bear, assume, tackle, acknowledge, undertake, embark on, set about, commence, avow, enter upon: *Everyone told me I should accept the job.* **OPPOSITE:** reject **3 = acknowledge**, believe, allow, admit, adopt, approve, recognize, yield, concede, swallow *(informal)*, buy *(slang)*, affirm, profess, consent to, buy into *(slang)*, cooperate with, take on board, accede, acquiesce, concur with: *I do not accept that there is any kind of crisis in the industry.* **4 = stand**, take, experience, suffer, bear, allow, weather, cope with, tolerate, sustain, put up with, wear *(Brit. slang)*, stomach, endure, undergo, brook, hack *(slang)*, abide, withstand, bow to, yield to, countenance, like it or lump it *(informal)*: *Urban dwellers have to accept noise as part of city life.*

acceptability NOUN **= adequacy**, fitness, suitability, propriety, appropriateness, admissibility, permissibility, acceptableness, satisfactoriness **OPPOSITE:** unacceptability

acceptable ADJECTIVE **1 = satisfactory**, fair, all right, suitable, sufficient, good enough, standard, adequate, so-so *(informal)*, tolerable, up to scratch *(informal)*, passable, up to the mark: *There was one restaurant that looked acceptable.* **OPPOSITE:** unsatisfactory **2 = pleasant**, pleasing, welcome, satisfying, grateful, refreshing, delightful, gratifying, agreeable, pleasurable: *a most acceptable present*

acceptance NOUN **1 = accepting**, taking, receiving, obtaining, acquiring, reception, receipt: *The party is being downgraded by its acceptance of secret donations.* **2 = acknowledgement**, agreement, belief, approval, recognition, admission, consent, consensus, adoption, affirmation, assent, credence, accession, approbation, concurrence, accedence, stamp *or* seal of approval: *a theory that is steadily gaining acceptance* **3 = taking on**, admission, assumption, acknowledgement, undertaking, avowal: *a letter of acceptance* **4 = submission**, yielding, resignation, concession, compliance, deference, passivity, acquiescence: *He thought about it for a moment, then nodded his reluctant acceptance.*

accepted ADJECTIVE **= agreed**, received, common, standard, established, traditional, confirmed, regular, usual, approved, acknowledged, recognized, sanctioned, acceptable, universal, authorized, customary, agreed upon, time-honoured **OPPOSITE:** unconventional

access NOUN **1 = admission**, entry, passage, entrée, admittance, ingress: *The facilities have been adapted to give access to wheelchair users.* **2 = entrance**, road, door, approach, entry, path, gate, opening, way in, passage, avenue, doorway, gateway, portal, passageway: *a courtyard with a side access to the rear gardens*

accessibility NOUN **1 = approachability**, availability, readiness, nearness, handiness: *the town's accessibility to the city* **2 = availability**, possibility, attainability, obtainability: *growing fears about the cost and accessibility of health care*

accessible ADJECTIVE **= handy**, near, nearby, at hand, within reach, at your fingertips, reachable, achievable, get-at-able *(informal)*, a hop, skip and a jump away **OPPOSITE:** inaccessible

accession
accession to = succession to, attainment of, inheritance of, elevation to, taking up of, assumption of, taking over of, taking on of

accessory NOUN **1 = extra**, addition, supplement, convenience, attachment, add-on, component, extension, adjunct, appendage, appurtenance: *an exclusive range of bathroom accessories* **2 = accomplice**, partner, ally, associate, assistant, helper, colleague, collaborator, confederate, henchman, abettor: *She was charged with being an accessory to the embezzlement of funds.* ▷ ADJECTIVE **= supplementary**, extra, additional, accompanying, secondary, subordinate, complementary, auxiliary, abetting, supplemental, contributory, ancillary: *Minerals are accessory food factors required in maintaining health.*

accident NOUN **1 = crash**, smash, wreck, collision, pile-up *(informal)*, smash-up *(informal)*: *She was involved in a serious car accident last week.* **2 = misfortune**, blow, disaster, tragedy, setback, calamity, mishap, misadventure, mischance, stroke of bad luck: *5,000 people die every year because of accidents in the home.* **3 = chance**, fortune, luck, fate, hazard, coincidence, fluke, fortuity: *She discovered the problem by accident.*

QUOTATIONS

Accidents will occur in the best-regulated families
[Charles Dickens *David Copperfield*]

now and then there is a person born who is so unlucky that he runs into accidents
which started out to happen to somebody else
[Don Marquis *archys life of mehitabel*]

accidental ADJECTIVE **1 = unintentional**, unexpected, incidental, unforeseen, unintended, unplanned, unpremeditated: *The jury returned a verdict of accidental death.* **OPPOSITE:** deliberate **2 = chance**, random, casual, unintentional, unintended, unplanned, fortuitous, inadvertent, serendipitous, unlooked-for, uncalculated, contingent: *His hand brushed against hers; it could have been accidental.*

accidentally ADVERB **= unintentionally**, casually, unexpectedly, incidentally, by accident, by chance, inadvertently, unwittingly, randomly, unconsciously, by mistake, haphazardly, fortuitously, adventitiously **OPPOSITE:** deliberately

acclaim VERB **= praise**, celebrate, honour, cheer, admire, hail, applaud, compliment, salute, approve, congratulate, clap, pay tribute to, commend, exalt, laud, extol, crack up *(informal)*, eulogize: *He was acclaimed as the country's greatest modern painter.* ▷ NOUN **= praise**, honour, celebration, approval, tribute, applause, cheering, clapping, ovation, accolades, plaudits, kudos, commendation, exaltation, approbation, acclamation, eulogizing, panegyric, encomium: *She won critical acclaim for her performance.* **OPPOSITE:** criticism

acclaimed ADJECTIVE **= celebrated**, famous, acknowledged, praised, outstanding, distinguished, admired, renowned, noted, highly rated, eminent, revered, famed, illustrious, well received, much vaunted, highly esteemed, much touted, well thought of, lionized, highly thought of **OPPOSITE:** criticized

accolade NOUN **1 = honour**, award, recognition, tribute: *the ultimate accolade in the sciences* **2 = praise**, approval, acclaim, applause, compliment, homage, laud *(literary)*, eulogy, congratulation, commendation, acclamation *(formal)*, recognition, tribute, ovation, plaudit: *We're always pleased to receive accolades from our guests.*

accommodate VERB **1 = house**, put up, take in, lodge, board, quarter, shelter, entertain, harbour, cater for, billet: *Students are accommodated in homes nearby.* **2 = help**, support, aid, encourage, assist, befriend, cooperate with, abet, lend a hand to, lend a helping hand to, give a leg up to (*informal*): *He has never made an effort to accommodate photographers.* **3 = adapt**, match, fit, fashion, settle, alter, adjust, modify, compose, comply, accustom, reconcile, harmonize: *She walked slowly to accommodate herself to his pace.*

accommodating ADJECTIVE **= obliging**, willing, kind, friendly, helpful, polite, cooperative, agreeable, amiable, courteous, considerate, hospitable, unselfish, eager to please, complaisant **OPPOSITE:** unhelpful

accommodation NOUN **1 = housing**, homes, houses, board, quartering, quarters, digs (*Brit. informal*), shelter, sheltering, lodging(s), dwellings: *The government is to provide accommodation for 3,000 homeless people.* **2 = adaptation**, change, settlement, compromise, composition, adjustment, transformation, reconciliation, compliance, modification, alteration, conformity: *Religions have to make accommodations with larger political structures.*

accompaniment NOUN **1 = backing music**, backing, support, obbligato: *He sang to the musical director's piano accompaniment.* **2 = supplement**, extra, addition, extension, companion, accessory, complement, decoration, frill, adjunct, appendage, adornment: *The recipe makes a good accompaniment to ice-cream.*

accompany VERB **1 = go with**, lead, partner, protect, guide, attend, conduct, escort, shepherd, convoy, usher, chaperon: *Ken agreed to accompany me on a trip to Africa.* **2 = occur with**, belong to, come with, supplement, coincide with, join with, coexist with, go together with, follow, go cheek by jowl with: *This volume of essays was designed to accompany an exhibition.*

accompanying ADJECTIVE **= additional**, added, extra, related, associate, associated, joint, fellow, connected, attached, accessory, attendant, complementary, supplementary, supplemental, concurrent, concomitant, appended

accomplice NOUN **= partner in crime**, ally, associate, assistant, companion, accessory, comrade, helper, colleague, collaborator, confederate, henchman, coadjutor, abettor

accomplish VERB **= realize**, produce, effect, finish, complete, manage, achieve, perform, carry out, conclude, fulfil, execute, bring about, attain, consummate, bring off (*informal*), do, effectuate **OPPOSITE:** fail

accomplished ADJECTIVE **= skilled**, able, professional, expert, masterly, talented, gifted, polished, practised, cultivated, skilful, adept, consummate, proficient **OPPOSITE:** unskilled

accomplishment NOUN **1 = achievement**, feat, attainment, act, stroke, triumph, coup, exploit, deed: *The accomplishments of the past year are quite extraordinary.* **2** (*often plural*) **= talent**, ability, skill, gift, achievement, craft, faculty, capability, forte, attainment, proficiency: *She can now add basketball to her list of accomplishments.* **3 = accomplishing**, effecting, finishing, carrying out, achievement, conclusion, bringing about, execution, completion, realization, fulfilment, attainment, consummation: *His function is vital to the accomplishment of the mission.*

accord NOUN **1 = treaty**, contract, agreement, arrangement, settlement, pact, deal (*informal*): *The party was made legal under the 1991 peace accords.* **2 = sympathy**, agreement, concert, harmony, accordance, unison, rapport, conformity, assent, unanimity, concurrence: *I found myself in total accord.* **OPPOSITE:** conflict
▷ VERB **= grant**, give, award, render, assign, present with, endow with, bestow on, confer on, vouchsafe, impart with: *On his return home, the government accorded him the rank of Colonel.* **OPPOSITE:** refuse
accord with something = agree with, match, coincide with, fit with, square with, correspond with, conform with, concur with, tally with, be in tune with (*informal*), harmonize with, assent with: *Such an approach accords with the principles of Socialist ideology.*

accordance NOUN
in accordance with = in agreement with, consistent with, in harmony with, in concert with, in sympathy with, in conformity with, in assent with, in congruence with

accordingly ADVERB **1 = consequently**, so, thus, therefore, hence, subsequently, in consequence, ergo, as a result: *We have different backgrounds. Accordingly we will have different futures.* **2 = appropriately**, correspondingly, properly, suitably, fitly: *It is a difficult job and they should be paid accordingly.*

accost VERB **= confront**, challenge, address, stop, approach, oppose, halt, greet, hail, solicit (*of a prostitute*), buttonhole

account NOUN **1 = description**, report, record, story, history, detail, statement, relation, version, tale, explanation, narrative, chronicle, portrayal, recital, depiction, narration: *He gave a detailed account of what had happened that night.* **2 = importance**, standing, concern, value, note, benefit, use, profit, worth, weight, advantage, rank, import, honour, consequence, substance, merit, significance, distinction, esteem, usefulness, repute, momentousness: *These obscure little groups were of no account in national politics.* **3 = ledger**, charge, bill, statement, balance, tally, invoice, computation: *He kept a detailed account of all expenditures.*
▷ VERB **= consider**, rate, value, judge, estimate, think, hold, believe, count, reckon, assess, weigh, calculate, esteem, deem, compute, gauge, appraise, regard as: *The first day of the event was accounted a success.*
account for something 1 = constitute, make, make up, compose, comprise: *Computers account for 5% of the country's electricity consumption.* **2 = explain**, excuse, justify, clarify, give a reason for, give an explanation for, illuminate, clear up, answer for, rationalize, elucidate: *How do you account for the company's high staff turnover?* **3 = put out of action**, kill, destroy, put paid to, incapacitate: *The squadron accounted for seven enemy aircraft in the first week.*
on account of = by reason of, because of, owing to, on the basis of, for the sake of, on the grounds of: *He declined to give the speech on account of a sore throat.*

accountability NOUN **= responsibility**, liability, culpability, answerability, chargeability

accountable ADJECTIVE **= answerable**, subject, responsible, obliged, liable, amenable, obligated, chargeable

accountant NOUN **= auditor**, book-keeper, bean counter (*informal*)

accounting NOUN **= accountancy**, auditing, book-keeping

accoutrements PLURAL NOUN **= paraphernalia**, fittings, dress, material, clothing, stuff, equipment, tackle, gear, things, kit, outfit, trimmings, fixtures, array, decorations, baggage, apparatus, furnishings, trappings, garb, adornments, ornamentation, bells and whistles, impedimenta, appurtenances, equipage

accredit VERB **1 = approve**, support, back, commission, champion, favour, guarantee, promote, recommend, appoint, recognize, sanction, advocate, license, endorse, warrant, authorize, ratify, empower, certify, entrust, vouch for, depute: *The degree programme is fully accredited by the Institute of Engineers.* **2 = attribute**, credit, assign, ascribe, trace to, put down to, lay at the door of: *The discovery of runes is, in Norse mythology, accredited to Odin.*

accredited ADJECTIVE **= authorized**, official, commissioned, guaranteed, appointed, recognized, sanctioned, licensed, endorsed, empowered, certified, vouched for, deputed, deputized

a

accrue VERB **= accumulate**, issue, increase, grow, collect, gather, flow, build up, enlarge, follow, ensue, pile up, amass, spring up, stockpile

accumulate VERB **= build up**, increase, grow, be stored, collect, gather, pile up, amass, stockpile, hoard, accrue, cumulate **OPPOSITE:** disperse

accumulation NOUN **1 = collection**, increase, stock, store, mass, build-up, pile, stack, heap, rick, stockpile, hoard: *accumulations of dirt* **2 = growth**, collection, gathering, build-up, aggregation, conglomeration, augmentation: *The rate of accumulation decreases with time.*

accuracy NOUN **= exactness**, precision, fidelity, authenticity, correctness, closeness, truth, verity, nicety, veracity, faithfulness, truthfulness, niceness, exactitude, strictness, meticulousness, carefulness, scrupulousness, preciseness, faultlessness, accurateness **OPPOSITE:** inaccuracy

accurate ADJECTIVE **1 = precise**, right, close, regular, correct, careful, strict, exact, faithful, explicit, authentic, spot-on, just, clear-cut, meticulous, truthful, faultless, scrupulous, unerring, veracious: *This is the most accurate description of the killer to date.* **OPPOSITE:** inaccurate **2 = correct**, right, true, exact, faithful, spot-on (*Brit. informal*), faultless, on the money (*U.S.*): *Their prediction was accurate.*

accurately ADVERB **1 = precisely**, rightly, correctly, closely, carefully, truly, properly, strictly, literally, exactly, faithfully, meticulously, to the letter, justly, scrupulously, truthfully, authentically, unerringly, faultlessly, veraciously: *The test can accurately predict what a bigger explosion would do.* **2 = exactly**, rightly, closely, correctly, definitely, truly, properly, precisely, nicely, strictly, faithfully, explicitly, unequivocally, scrupulously, truthfully: *His concept of 'power' could be more accurately described as 'control'.*

accusation NOUN **= charge**, complaint, allegation, indictment, impeachment, recrimination, citation, denunciation, attribution, imputation, arraignment, incrimination

accuse VERB **1 = point a** *or* **the finger at**, blame for, denounce, attribute to, hold responsible for, impute blame to: *He accused her of having an affair with another man.* **OPPOSITE:** exonerate **2 = charge with**, indict for, impeach for, arraign for, cite, tax with, censure with, incriminate for, recriminate for: *Her assistant was accused of theft and fraud by the police.* **OPPOSITE:** absolve

accustom VERB **= familiarize**, train, coach, discipline, adapt, instruct, make used, school, season, acquaint, inure, habituate, acclimatize, make conversant

accustomed ADJECTIVE **1 = used**, trained, familiar, disciplined, given to, adapted, acquainted, in the habit of, familiarized, seasoned, inured, habituated, exercised, acclimatized: *I was accustomed to being the only child amongst adults.* **OPPOSITE:** unaccustomed **2 = usual**, established, expected, general, common, standard, set, traditional, normal, fixed, regular, ordinary, familiar, conventional, routine, everyday, customary, habitual, wonted: *He took up his accustomed position at the fire.* **OPPOSITE:** unusual

ace NOUN **1 = one**, single point: *the ace of hearts* **2 = expert**, star, champion, authority, winner, professional, master, pro (*informal*), specialist, genius, guru, buff (*informal*), wizard (*informal*), whizz (*informal*), virtuoso, connoisseur, hotshot (*informal*), past master, dab hand (*Brit. informal*), maven (*U.S.*): *former motor-racing ace Stirling Moss*
▷ ADJECTIVE **= great**, good, brilliant, mean (*slang*), fine, champion, expert, masterly, wonderful, excellent, cracking (*Brit. informal*), outstanding, superb, fantastic (*informal*), tremendous (*informal*), marvellous (*informal*), terrific (*informal*), mega (*slang*), awesome (*slang*), dope (*slang*), admirable, virtuoso, first-rate, brill (*informal*), bitchin' (*U.S. slang*), chillin' (*U.S. slang*), booshit (*Austral. slang*), exo (*Austral. slang*), sik (*Austral. slang*), ka pai (*N.Z.*), rad (*informal*), phat (*slang*), schmick (*Austral. informal*), beaut (*informal*), barrie (*Scot. slang*), belting (*Brit. slang*), pearler (*Austral. slang*): *It's been a while since I've seen a really ace film.*

acerbic ADJECTIVE **= sharp**, cutting, biting, severe, acid, bitter, nasty, harsh, stern, rude, scathing, acrimonious, barbed, unkind, unfriendly, sarcastic, sardonic, caustic, churlish, vitriolic, trenchant, acrid, brusque, rancorous, mordant

ache VERB **1 = hurt**, suffer, burn, pain, smart, sting, pound, throb, be tender, twinge, be sore: *Her head was hurting and she ached all over.* **2 = suffer**, hurt, grieve, sorrow, agonize, be in pain, go through the mill (*informal*), mourn, feel wretched: *It must have been hard to keep smiling when his heart was aching.*
▷ NOUN **1 = pain**, discomfort, suffering, hurt, smart, smarting, cramp, throb, throbbing, irritation, tenderness, pounding, spasm, pang, twinge, soreness, throe (*rare*): *You feel nausea and aches in your muscles.* **2 = anguish**, suffering, pain, torture, distress, grief, misery, mourning, torment, sorrow, woe, heartache, heartbreak: *Nothing could relieve the terrible ache of fear.*

achievable ADJECTIVE **= attainable**, obtainable, winnable, reachable, realizable, within your grasp, graspable, gettable, acquirable, possible, accessible, probable, feasible, practicable, accomplishable

achieve VERB **= accomplish**, reach, fulfil, finish, complete, gain, perform, earn, do, get, win, carry out, realize, obtain, conclude, acquire, execute, bring about, attain, consummate, procure, bring off (*informal*), effectuate, put the tin lid on

achievement NOUN **1 = accomplishment**, effort, feat, deed, stroke, triumph, coup, exploit, act, attainment, feather in your cap: *a conference celebrating women's achievements* **2 = fulfilment**, effecting, performance, production, execution, implementation, completion, accomplishment, realization, attainment, acquirement, carrying out *or* through: *It is the achievement of these goals that will bring lasting peace.*

> **QUOTATIONS**
> When I look at the works of the masters, I see what they have done. When I consider my own trifles, I see what I ought to have done
> [Johann Wolfgang von Goethe]
>
> If there were an instrument by which to measure desire, one could foretell achievement
> [Willa Cather *The Professor's House*]

achiever NOUN **= success**, winner, dynamo, high-flyer, doer, go-getter (*informal*), organizer, active person, overachiever, man *or* woman of action, wheeler-dealer (*informal*)

aching ADJECTIVE **1 = painful**, suffering, hurting, tired, smarting, pounding, raw, tender, sore, throbbing, harrowing, inflamed, excruciating, agonizing: *The aching joints and fever should last no longer than a few days.* **2 = longing**, anxious, eager, pining, hungering, craving, yearning, languishing, thirsting, ardent, avid, wishful, wistful, hankering, desirous: *He has an aching need for love.*

acid ADJECTIVE **1 = sour**, sharp, tart, pungent, biting, acidic, acerbic, acrid, acetic, vinegary, acidulous, acidulated, vinegarish, acerb: *These wines are rather hard, and somewhat acid.* **OPPOSITE:** sweet **2 = sharp**, cutting, biting, severe, bitter, harsh, stinging, scathing, acrimonious, barbed, pungent, hurtful, sarcastic, sardonic, caustic, vitriolic, acerbic, trenchant, mordant, mordacious: *a comedy told with compassion and acid humour* **OPPOSITE:** kindly

acidity NOUN **= sourness**, bitterness, sharpness, pungency, tartness, acerbity, acridness, acidulousness, acridity, vinegariness, vinegarishness

acknowledge VERB **1 = admit**, own up, allow, accept, reveal, grant, declare, recognize, yield, concede, confess, disclose, affirm, profess, divulge, accede, acquiesce, 'fess up (*U.S. slang*): *He acknowledged that he was a drug addict.* **OPPOSITE:** deny **2 = greet**, address, notice, recognize, salute,

The Language of Robert Louis Stevenson

The novelist, short story writer, poet, and essayist Robert Louis Stevenson (1850-1894) was born in Edinburgh, into a family of engineers and lighthouse builders, but he was a sickly child and his leanings were always towards writing. He loved travel and his first book was *Travels with a Donkey in the Cevennes* (1878), but he is best remembered as the author of such novels as *Treasure Island* (1883), *Kidnapped* (1886), and *The Strange Case of Dr Jekyll and Mr Hyde* (1886).

Stevenson's love of travel is perhaps nowhere better expressed than in a well-known quotation from his *Virginibus Puerisque* (1881): 'To travel hopefully is a better thing than to arrive.' This attitude is shown in his language in his typical use of verbs. For example, the verb *leave* is much more common in his writing than *return*.

> There are few things more renovating than to **leave** Paris, and the long alignment of the glittering streets, and to bathe the senses in this fragrant darkness of the wood.

Similarly, the verb *move* is found in Stevenson far more frequently than its opposite, to *stop*. And while Stevenson does feature female characters (not only in the eponymous *Catriona*, 1893), it cannot be surprising that the noun *ship*, so evocative of the romance of voyaging, is more ubiquitous anywhere in his works than, say, *woman:*

> The sea has a rude, pistolling sort of odour, that takes you in the nostrils like snuff, and carries with it a fine sentiment of open water and tall **ships**.

Stevenson's novels are mostly historical in context, whether he is dealing with the Scottish Highlands in the aftermath of the Jacobite rebellion (as in *Kidnapped*, 1886, or *The Master of Ballantrae*, 1888) or the Spanish Main in the age of the great pirates (as in *Treasure Island*, 1883), but he is also deeply interested in the supernatural, especially in its interplay with evil in the human spirit. We can see an indication of this vein in Stevenson's work when we realize that one of his favourite adjectives is *strange*, which is to be found in his writing much more often than such more homely descriptive terms as, for example, *pretty*. Not only in his stories of the supernatural (such as *Thrawn Janet* and *Markheim*), there are plenty of *strange doings* to be met with, *strange sights* to see and wonder at, and *strange sensations* to be experienced. Even more prominently, the word appears in the very title of one of his most famous novels, *The Strange Case of Dr Jekyll and Mr Hyde* (1886).

It was in the latter book, of course, that Stevenson contributed a new phrase to the English language. This tale of a dual personality, half good and half devilishly evil, so resonated with its readers that to this day everyone immediately understands what is meant when reference is made to a 'Jekyll-and-Hyde personality.'

A dominant part of Stevenson's make-up was his Scottishness. While he spent much of his adult life abroad, not least because his poor health necessitated a less demanding climate, he never forgot his native land and continually evoked it in his fiction until his last days. Indeed, when he died suddenly in Samoa he was working on yet another Scottish-set novel, the uncompleted *Weir of Hermiston*. This Scottishness is shown in his choice of language, especially in the dialogues of his Scots characters in novels such as *Kidnapped*, where terms like *ay*, *thrawn*, and *ye* are liberally used, lending an immediate authenticity to his record of their speech:

> 'Well,' said I, 'I am tired indeed, but I could walk as far again, if that was all.' '**Ay**, but it **isnae**,' said Alan, 'nor yet the half.'

nod to, accost, tip your hat to: *He saw her but refused to even acknowledge her.* **OPPOSITE:** snub **3 = reply to**, answer, notice, recognize, respond to, come back to, react to, write back to, retort to: *They sent me a postcard acknowledging my request.* **OPPOSITE:** ignore

a

acknowledged ADJECTIVE **= accepted**, admitted, established, confirmed, declared, approved, recognized, well-known, sanctioned, confessed, authorized, professed, accredited, agreed upon

acknowledgment *or* **acknowledgement** NOUN **1 = recognition**, allowing, understanding, yielding, profession, admission, awareness, acceptance, confession, realization, accession, acquiescence: *He appreciated her acknowledgement of his maturity.* **2 = greeting**, welcome, notice, recognition, reception, hail, hailing, salute, salutation: *He smiled in acknowledgement and gave her a bow.* **3 = appreciation**, answer, thanks, credit, response, reply, reaction, recognition, gratitude, indebtedness, thankfulness, gratefulness: *Grateful acknowledgement is made for permission to reprint.*

acme NOUN **= height**, top, crown, summit, peak, climax, crest, optimum, high point, pinnacle, culmination, zenith, apex, apogee, vertex **OPPOSITE:** depths

acolyte NOUN **1 = follower**, fan, supporter, pupil, convert, believer, admirer, backer, partisan, disciple, devotee, worshipper, apostle, cohort *(chiefly U.S.)*, adherent, henchman, habitué, votary: *To his acolytes, he is known simply as 'The Boss'.* **2 = attendant**, assistant, follower, helper, altar boy: *When they reached the shrine, acolytes removed the pall.*

acquaint VERB **= tell**, reveal, advise, inform, communicate, disclose, notify, enlighten, divulge, familiarize, apprise, let (someone) know

acquaintance NOUN **1 = associate**, contact, ally, colleague, comrade, confrère: *He exchanged a few words with the man, an old acquaintance of his.* **OPPOSITE:** intimate **2 = relationship**, association, exchange, connection, intimacy, fellowship, familiarity, companionship, social contact, cognizance, conversance, conversancy: *He becomes involved in a real murder mystery through his acquaintance with a police officer.* **OPPOSITE:** unfamiliarity

> **QUOTATIONS**
> Should auld acquaintance be forgot,
> And never brought to mind?
> [Robert Burns *Auld Lang Syne*]
>
> I look upon every day to be lost, in which I do not make a new acquaintance
> [Samuel Johnson]
>
> acquaintance: a person whom we know well enough to borrow from, but not well enough to lend to
> [Ambrose Bierce *The Devil's Dictionary*]

acquainted ADJECTIVE **acquainted with = familiar with**, aware of, in on, experienced in, conscious of, informed of, alive to, privy to, knowledgeable about, versed in, conversant with, apprised of, cognizant of, up to speed with, *au fait* with

acquiesce VERB **= submit**, agree, accept, approve, yield, bend, surrender, consent, tolerate, comply, give in, conform, succumb, go along with, bow to, cave in *(informal)*, concur, assent, capitulate, accede, play ball *(informal)*, toe the line, hoist the white flag **OPPOSITE:** resist

acquiescence NOUN **= agreement**, yielding, approval, acceptance, consent, harmony, giving in, submission, compliance, obedience, conformity, assent, accession, concord, concurrence

acquire VERB **= get**, win, buy, receive, land, score *(slang)*, gain, achieve, earn, pick up, bag, secure, collect, gather, realize, obtain, attain, amass, procure, come into possession of **OPPOSITE:** lose

acquisition NOUN **1 = acquiring**, gaining, achievement, procurement, attainment, acquirement, obtainment: *the President's recent acquisition of a helicopter* **2 = purchase**, buy, investment, property, gain, prize, asset, possession: *her latest acquisition, a bright red dress*

acquisitive ADJECTIVE **= greedy**, grabbing, grasping, hungry, selfish, avid, predatory, rapacious, avaricious, desirous, covetous **OPPOSITE:** generous

acquit VERB **= clear**, free, release, deliver, excuse, relieve, discharge, liberate, vindicate, exonerate, absolve, exculpate: *He was acquitted of disorderly behaviour by magistrates.* **OPPOSITE:** find guilty **acquit yourself = behave**, bear yourself, conduct yourself, comport yourself: *Most men acquitted themselves well throughout the action.*

acquittal NOUN **= clearance**, freeing, release, relief, liberation, discharge, pardon, setting free, vindication, deliverance, absolution, exoneration, exculpation

acrid ADJECTIVE **1 = pungent**, biting, strong, burning, sharp, acid, bitter, harsh, stinging, irritating, caustic, astringent, vitriolic, highly flavoured, acerb: *The room filled with the acrid smell of tobacco.* **2 = harsh**, cutting, biting, sharp, bitter, nasty, acrimonious, caustic, vitriolic, trenchant, mordant, mordacious: *He is soured by acrid memories he has dredged up.*

acrimonious ADJECTIVE **= bitter**, cutting, biting, sharp, severe, hostile, crabbed, sarcastic, embittered, caustic, petulant, spiteful, churlish, astringent, vitriolic, acerbic, trenchant, irascible, testy, censorious, rancorous, mordant, peevish, splenetic, mordacious **OPPOSITE:** good-tempered

acrimony NOUN **= bitterness**, harshness, rancour, ill will, virulence, sarcasm, pungency, asperity, tartness, astringency, irascibility, peevishness, acerbity, churlishness, trenchancy, mordancy **OPPOSITE:** goodwill

acrobat NOUN **= gymnast**, balancer, tumbler, tightrope walker, rope walker, funambulist

across PREPOSITION **1 = over**, on the other *or* far side of, past, beyond: *Anyone from the houses across the road could see him.* **2 = throughout**, over, all over, right through, all through, covering, straddling, everywhere in, through the whole of, from end to end of, over the length and breadth of: *The film opens across America in December.* ▷ ADVERB **= from side to side**, athwart, transversely, crossways *or* crosswise: *Trim toenails straight across using nail clippers.*

across-the-board ADJECTIVE **= general**, full, complete, total, sweeping, broad, widespread, comprehensive, universal, blanket, thorough, wholesale, panoramic, indiscriminate, all-inclusive, wall-to-wall, all-embracing, overarching, all-encompassing, thoroughgoing, without exception *or* omission, one-size-fits-all **OPPOSITE:** limited

act VERB **1 = do something**, perform, move, function, go about, conduct yourself, undertake something: *I have no reason to doubt that the bank acted properly.* **2 = play**, seem to be, pose as, pretend to be, posture as, imitate, sham, feign, characterize, enact, personify, impersonate, play the part of: *They were just acting tough.* **3 = perform**, mimic, mime: *She told her parents of her desire to act.* ▷ NOUN **1 = deed**, action, step, performance, operation, doing, move, blow, achievement, stroke, undertaking, exploit, execution, feat, accomplishment, exertion: *My insurance covers acts of sabotage.* **2 = pretence**, show, front, performance, display, attitude, pose, stance, fake, posture, façade, sham, veneer, counterfeit, feigning, affectation, dissimulation: *His anger was real. It wasn't just an act.* **3 = law**, bill, measure, resolution, decree, statute, ordinance, enactment, edict: *an Act of Parliament* **4 = performance**, show, turn, production, routine, presentation, gig *(informal)*, sketch: *Numerous bands are playing, as well as comedy acts.* **act for someone = stand in for**, serve, represent, replace, substitute for, cover for, take the place of, fill in for, deputize for, function in place of: *Because we travel so much, we asked a broker to act for us.*

act on *or* **upon something** **1 = obey**, follow, carry out, observe, embrace, execute, comply with, heed, conform to, adhere to, abide by, yield to, act upon, be ruled by, act in accordance with, do what is expected: *A patient will usually listen to the doctor's advice and act on it.* **2 = affect**, change, influence, impact, transform, alter, modify: *The drug acts very fast on the central nervous system.*

act up = misbehave, carry on, cause trouble, mess about, be naughty, horse around *(informal)*, give trouble, give someone grief *(Brit. & S. African)*, give bother: *I could hear him acting up downstairs.*

acting NOUN **= performance**, playing, performing, theatre, dramatics, portraying, enacting, portrayal, impersonation, characterization, stagecraft: *She has returned home to pursue her career in acting.*
▷ ADJECTIVE **= temporary**, substitute, intervening, interim, provisional, surrogate, stopgap, pro tem: *The new acting President has a reputation for being independent.*

QUOTATIONS

The art of acting consists in keeping people from coughing
[Ralph Richardson]

She ran the whole gamut of emotions from A to B
[Dorothy Parker (of Katherine Hepburn)]

Acting deals with very delicate emotions. It is not putting up a mask. Each time an actor acts he does not hide; he exposes himself
[Jeanne Moreau *The New York Times*]

action NOUN **1 = deed**, move, act, performance, blow, exercise, achievement, stroke, undertaking, exploit, feat, accomplishment, exertion: *He was the sort of man who didn't like his actions questioned.* **2 = measure**, act, step, operation, manoeuvre: *The government is taking emergency action to deal with the crisis.* **3 = lawsuit**, case, cause, trial, suit, argument, proceeding, dispute, contest, prosecution, litigation: *a libel action brought by one of the country's top bureaucrats* **4 = energy**, activity, spirit, force, vitality, vigour, liveliness, vim: *Hollywood is where the action is now.* **5 = effect**, working, work, force, power, process, effort, operation, activity, movement, influence, functioning, motion, exertion: *Her description of the action of poisons is very accurate.* **6 = battle**, war, fight, fighting, conflict, clash, contest, encounter, combat, engagement, hostilities, warfare, fray, skirmish, sortie, affray: *Ten soldiers were wounded in action.*

activate VERB **= start**, move, trigger (off), stimulate, turn on, set off, initiate, switch on, propel, rouse, prod, get going, mobilize, kick-start *(informal)*, set in motion, impel, galvanize, set going, actuate
OPPOSITE: stop

activation NOUN **= start**, triggering, turning on, switching on, animation, arousal, initiation, mobilization, setting in motion, actuation

active ADJECTIVE **1 = busy**, involved, occupied, engaged, tiring, lively, energetic, bustling, restless, on the move, strenuous, tireless, on the go *(informal)*: *Having an active youngster about the house can be quite wearing.*
OPPOSITE: sluggish **2 = energetic**, strong, spirited, quick, vital, alert, dynamic, lively, vigorous, potent, animated, vibrant, forceful, nimble, diligent, industrious, sprightly, vivacious, on the go *(informal)*, alive and kicking, spry, full of beans *(informal)*, bright-eyed and bushy-tailed *(informal)*: *the tragedy of an active mind trapped by failing physical health*
OPPOSITE: inactive **3 = in operation**, working, live, running, moving, acting, functioning, stirring, at work, in business, in action, operative, in force, effectual, astir: *Guerrilla groups are active in the province.*

activist NOUN **= militant**, partisan, organizer, warrior

activity NOUN **1 = action**, work, life, labour, movement, energy, exercise, spirit, enterprise, motion, bustle, animation, vigour, hustle, exertion, hurly-burly, liveliness, activeness: *There is an extraordinary level of activity in the market.* OPPOSITE: inaction
2 = pursuit, act, project, scheme, task, pleasure, interest, enterprise, undertaking, occupation, hobby, deed, endeavour, pastime, avocation: *Activities range from canoeing to birdwatching.*

actor *or* **actress** NOUN **= performer**, player, artiste, leading man *or* lady, Thespian, luvvie *(informal)*, trouper, thesp *(informal)*, play-actor, dramatic artist, tragedian *or* tragedienne: *You have to be a very good actor to play that part.*

USAGE

The use of *actress* is now very much on the decline, and women who work in the profession invariably prefer to be referred to as *actors*.

QUOTATIONS

An actor's a guy who, if you ain't talking about him, ain't listening
[Marlon Brando]

Actors should be treated like cattle
[Alfred Hitchcock]

I'm an actor. An actress is someone who wears boa feathers
[Sigourney Weaver]

actual ADJECTIVE **1 = genuine**, real, true, confirmed, authentic, verified, truthful, bona fide, dinkum *(Austral. & N.Z. informal)*: *They are using local actors or the actual people involved.*
OPPOSITE: unreal **2 = real**, substantial, concrete, definite, tangible: *She had written some notes, but she hadn't started the actual work.* OPPOSITE: theoretical

USAGE

The words *actual* and *actually* are often used when speaking, but should only be used in writing where they add something to the meaning of a sentence. For example, in the sentence *he actually rather enjoyed the film*, the word *actually* is only needed if there was originally some doubt as to whether he would enjoy it.

actuality NOUN **1 = reality**, truth, substance, verity, materiality, realness, substantiality, factuality, corporeality: *It exists in dreams rather than actuality.* **2 = fact**, truth, reality, verity: *You may theorise, but we are concerned with actualities.*

actually ADVERB **= really**, in fact, indeed, essentially, truly, literally, genuinely, in reality, in truth, in actuality, in point of fact, veritably, as a matter of fact

acumen NOUN **= judgment**, intelligence, perception, wisdom, insight, wit, ingenuity, sharpness, cleverness, keenness, shrewdness, discernment, perspicacity, sagacity, smartness, smarts *(slang, chiefly U.S.)*, astuteness, acuteness, perspicuity

acute ADJECTIVE **1 = serious**, important, dangerous, critical, crucial, alarming, severe, grave, sudden, urgent, decisive: *The war aggravated an acute economic crisis.*
2 = sharp, shooting, powerful, violent, severe, intense, overwhelming, distressing, stabbing, cutting, fierce, piercing, racking, exquisite, poignant, harrowing, overpowering, shrill, excruciating: *His back is arched as if in acute pain.*
3 = perceptive, sharp, keen, smart, sensitive, clever, subtle, piercing, penetrating, discriminating, discerning, ingenious, astute, intuitive, canny, incisive, insightful, observant, perspicacious: *His relaxed exterior hides an extremely acute mind.*
OPPOSITE: slow

adage NOUN **= saying**, motto, maxim, proverb, dictum, precept, by-word, saw, axiom, aphorism, apophthegm

adamant ADJECTIVE **= determined**, firm, fixed, stiff, rigid, set, relentless, stubborn, uncompromising, insistent, resolute, inflexible, unrelenting, inexorable, unyielding, intransigent, immovable, unbending, obdurate, unshakable
OPPOSITE: flexible

adapt VERB **1 = adjust**, change, match, alter, modify, accommodate, comply, conform, reconcile, harmonize, familiarize, habituate, acclimatize: *Things will be different and we will have to* *adapt.* **2 = convert**, change, prepare, fit, fashion, make, shape, suit, qualify, transform, alter, modify, tailor, remodel, tweak *(informal)*, metamorphose, customize: *Shelves were built to adapt the library for use as an office.*

adaptability NOUN **= flexibility**, versatility, resilience, variability, convertibility, plasticity, malleability, pliability, changeability, pliancy, adjustability, compliancy, modifiability, adaptableness, alterability

adaptable ADJECTIVE **1 = flexible**, variable, versatile, resilient, easy-going, changeable, modifiable, conformable: *They are adaptable foragers that can survive on a wide range of foods.* **2 = adjustable**, flexible, compliant, malleable, pliant, plastic, modifiable, alterable: *He hopes to make the workforce more adaptable and skilled.*

adaptation NOUN **1 = acclimatization**, naturalization, habituation, familiarization, accustomedness: *Most creatures are capable of adaptation when necessary.* **2 = conversion**, change, shift, variation, adjustment, transformation, modification, alteration, remodelling, reworking, refitting: *He won two awards for his screen adaptation of the play.*

add VERB **1 = count up**, total, reckon, sum up, compute, add up, tot up: *Banks add all the interest and other charges together.* **OPPOSITE:** take away **2 = include**, attach, supplement, increase by, adjoin, annex, amplify, augment, affix, append, enlarge by: *He wants to add a huge sports complex to the hotel.*
add to something = increase, boost, expand, strengthen, enhance, step up *(informal)*, intensify, raise, advance, spread, extend, heighten, enlarge, escalate, multiply, inflate, magnify, amplify, augment, proliferate: *Smiles and cheerful faces added to the general gaiety.*
add up 1 = count up, add, total, count, reckon, calculate, sum up, compute, tally, tot up, add together: *More than a quarter of seven-year-olds cannot add up properly.* **2 = make sense**, hold up, be reasonable, ring true, be plausible, stand to reason, hold water, bear examination, bear investigation: *They arrested her because her statements did not add up.*
add up to something = mean, reveal, indicate, imply, amount to, signify: *All this adds up to very bad news for the car industry.*

addict NOUN **1 = junkie** *(informal)*, abuser, user *(informal)*, druggie *(informal)*, freak *(informal)*, fiend *(informal)*, mainliner *(slang)*, smackhead *(slang)*, space cadet *(slang)*, pill-popper *(informal)*, head *(slang)*, pothead *(slang)*, dope-fiend *(slang)*, cokehead *(slang)*, acidhead *(slang)*, hashhead *(slang)*: *He's only 24 years old and a drug addict.* **2 = fan**, lover, nut *(slang)*, follower, enthusiast, freak *(informal)*, admirer, buff *(informal)*, junkie *(informal)*, devotee, fiend *(informal)*, adherent, rooter *(U.S.)*, zealot, groupie *(slang)*, aficionado: *She's a TV addict and watches as much as she can.*
▸ *related suffix:* -holic

addicted ADJECTIVE **= hooked**, dependent

addiction NOUN **1 = dependence**, need, habit, weakness, obsession, attachment, craving, vulnerability, subordination, enslavement, subservience, overreliance: *She helped him fight his drug addiction.* **2** *(with* **to***)* **= love of**, passion for, attachment to, fondness for, zeal for, fervour for, ardour for: *I've developed an addiction to rollercoasters.*

> **QUOTATIONS**
> Every form of addiction is bad, no matter whether the narcotic be alcohol or morphine or idealism [Carl Gustav Jung *Memories, Dreams, Reflections*]

addictive ADJECTIVE **= habit-forming**, compelling, compulsive, causing addiction *or* dependency, moreish *or* morish *(informal)*

addition NOUN **1 = extra**, supplement, complement, adjunct, increase, gain, bonus, extension, accessory, additive, appendix, increment, appendage, addendum: *This book is a worthy addition to the series.* **2 = inclusion**, adding, increasing, extension, attachment, adjoining, insertion, incorporation, annexation, accession, affixing, augmentation: *It was completely refurbished with the addition of a picnic site.* **OPPOSITE:** removal **3 = counting up**, totalling, reckoning, summing up, adding up, computation, totting up, summation: *simple addition and subtraction problems* **OPPOSITE:** subtraction
in addition to = as well as, along with, on top of, besides, to boot, additionally, over and above, to say nothing of, into the bargain: *There's a postage and packing fee in addition to the repair charge.*

additional ADJECTIVE **= extra**, more, new, other, added, increased, further, fresh, spare, supplementary, auxiliary, ancillary, appended

additive NOUN **= added ingredient**, artificial *or* synthetic ingredient, E number, extra, supplement

addled ADJECTIVE **= confused**, silly, foolish, at sea, bewildered, mixed-up, muddled, perplexed, flustered, befuddled

address NOUN **1 = direction**, label, inscription, superscription: *The address on the envelope was illegible.* **2 = location**, home, place, house, point, position, situation, site, spot, venue, lodging, pad *(slang)*, residence, dwelling, whereabouts, abode, locus, locale, domicile: *The workmen had gone to the wrong address at the wrong time.* **3 = speech**, talk, lecture, discourse, sermon, dissertation, harangue, homily, oration, spiel *(informal)*, disquisition: *He had scheduled an address to the people for that evening.*
▹ VERB **1 = give a speech to**, talk to, speak to, lecture, discourse, harangue, give a talk to, spout to, hold forth to, expound to, orate to, sermonize to: *He will address a conference on human rights next week.* **2 = speak to**, talk to, greet, hail, salute, invoke, communicate with, accost, approach, converse with, apostrophize, korero *(N.Z.)*: *The two ministers did not address each other directly.*
address yourself to something = concentrate on, turn to, focus on, take up, look to, undertake, engage in, take care of, attend to, knuckle down to, devote yourself to, apply yourself to: *We have addressed ourselves to the problem of ethics throughout.*

adept ADJECTIVE **= skilful**, able, skilled, expert, masterly, practised, accomplished, versed, masterful, proficient, adroit, dexterous: *He is an adept guitar player.* **OPPOSITE:** unskilled
▹ NOUN **= expert**, master, genius, buff *(informal)*, whizz *(informal)*, hotshot *(informal)*, rocket scientist *(informal, chiefly U.S.)*, dab hand *(Brit. informal)*, maven *(U.S.)*: *He was an adept at getting people to talk confidentially to him.*

adequacy NOUN **= sufficiency**, capability, competence, suitability, tolerability, fairness, commensurateness, requisiteness, satisfactoriness

adequate ADJECTIVE **1 = passable**, acceptable, middling, average, fair, ordinary, moderate, satisfactory, competent, mediocre, so-so *(informal)*, tolerable, up to scratch *(informal)*, presentable, unexceptional: *One in four people are without adequate homes.* **OPPOSITE:** inadequate **2 = sufficient**, enough, capable, suitable, requisite: *an amount adequate to purchase another house* **OPPOSITE:** insufficient

adherent NOUN **= supporter**, fan, advocate, follower, admirer, partisan, disciple, protagonist, devotee, henchman, hanger-on, upholder, sectary: *Communism was gaining adherents in Latin America.* **OPPOSITE:** opponent
▹ ADJECTIVE **= adhering**, holding, sticking, clinging, sticky, tacky, adhesive, tenacious, glutinous, gummy, gluey, mucilaginous: *an adherent bandage*

adhere to VERB **1 = follow**, keep, maintain, respect, observe, be true, fulfil, obey, heed, keep to, abide by, be loyal, mind, be constant, be faithful: *All members adhere to a strict code of practice.* **2 = be faithful**, follow, support, respect, observe, be true, obey, be devoted, be attached, keep to, be loyal: *He urged them to adhere to the values of Islam.* **3 = stick to**, attach to, cling to, unite to, glue to, fix to, fasten to, hold fast to, paste to, cement to, cleave to, glue on to, stick fast to, cohere to: *Small particles adhere to the seed.*

adhesion NOUN **= sticking**, grip, attachment, cohesion, coherence, adherence, adhesiveness

adhesive NOUN **= glue**, cement, gum, paste, mucilage: *Glue the mirror in with a strong adhesive.*
▷ ADJECTIVE **= sticky**, holding, sticking, attaching, clinging, adhering, tacky, cohesive, tenacious, glutinous, gummy, gluey, mucilaginous: *adhesive tape*

ad hoc ADJECTIVE **= makeshift**, emergency, improvised, impromptu, expedient, stopgap, jury-rigged (*chiefly Nautical*): *An ad hoc committee was set up to examine the problem.*
OPPOSITE: permanent

adjacent ADJECTIVE **= adjoining**, neighbouring, nearby, abutting: *The fire quickly spread to adjacent shops.*
OPPOSITE: far away

adjoin VERB **= connect with** *or* **to**, join, neighbour (on), link with, attach to, combine with, couple with, communicate with, touch on, border on, annex, approximate, unite with, verge on, impinge on, append, affix to, interconnect with

adjoining ADJECTIVE **= connecting**, nearby, joined, joining, touching, bordering, neighbouring, next door, adjacent, interconnecting, abutting, contiguous

adjourn VERB **= postpone**, delay, suspend, interrupt, put off, stay, defer, recess, discontinue, put on the back burner (*informal*), prorogue, take a rain check on (*U.S. & Canad. informal*)
OPPOSITE: continue

adjournment NOUN **= postponement**, delay, suspension, putting off, stay, recess, interruption, deferment, deferral, discontinuation, prorogation

adjudge VERB **= judge**, determine, declare, decide, assign, pronounce, decree, apportion, adjudicate

adjudicate VERB **1 = decide**, judge, determine, settle, mediate, adjudge, arbitrate **2 = judge**, referee, umpire

adjudication NOUN **= judgment**, finding, ruling, decision, settlement, conclusion, verdict, determination, arbitration, pronouncement, adjudgment

adjudicator NOUN **= judge**, referee, umpire, umpie (*Austral. slang*), arbiter, arbitrator, moderator

adjunct NOUN **= addition**, supplement, accessory, complement, auxiliary, add-on, appendage, addendum, appurtenance

adjust VERB **1 = adapt**, change, settle, convert, alter, accommodate, dispose, get used, accustom, conform, reconcile, harmonize, acclimatize, familiarize yourself, attune: *I felt I had adjusted to the idea of being a mother very well.* **2 = change**, order, reform, fix, arrange, alter, adapt, revise, modify, set, regulate, amend, reconcile, remodel, redress, rectify, recast, customize, make conform: *To attract investors the country has adjusted its tax laws.* **3 = modify**, arrange, fix, tune (up), alter, adapt, remodel, tweak (*informal*), customize: *Liz adjusted her mirror and edged the car out.*

adjustable ADJECTIVE **= alterable**, flexible, adaptable, malleable, movable, tractable, modifiable, mouldable

adjustment NOUN **1 = alteration**, setting, change, ordering, fixing, arrangement, tuning, repair, conversion, modifying, adaptation, modification, remodelling, redress, refinement, rectification: *A technician made an adjustment to a smoke machine at the back.* **2 = acclimatization**, settling in, orientation, familiarization, change, regulation, settlement, amendment, reconciliation, adaptation, accustoming, revision, modification, naturalization, acculturation, harmonization, habituation, acclimation, inurement: *He will need a period of adjustment.*

administer VERB **1 = manage**, run, control, rule, direct, handle, conduct, command, govern, oversee, supervise, preside over, be in charge of, superintend: *Next summer's exams will be straightforward to administer.*
2 = dispense, give, share, provide, apply, distribute, assign, allocate, allot, dole out, apportion, deal out: *Sister came to watch the nurses administer the drugs.* **3 = execute**, do, give, provide, apply, perform, carry out, impose, realize, implement, enforce, render, discharge, enact, dispense, mete out, bring off: *He is shown administering most of the blows.*

administration NOUN
1 = management, government, running, control, performance, handling, direction, conduct, application, command, provision, distribution, governing, administering, execution, overseeing, supervision, manipulation, governance, dispensation, superintendence: *Standards in the administration of justice have degenerated.* **2 = directors**, board, executive(s), bosses (*informal*), management, employers, directorate: *They would like the college administration to exert more control.* **3 = government**, authority, executive, leadership, ministry, regime, governing body: *He served in posts in both the Ford and Carter administrations.*

administrative ADJECTIVE **= managerial**, executive, management, directing, regulatory, governmental, organizational, supervisory, directorial, gubernatorial (*chiefly U.S.*)

administrator NOUN **= manager**, head, official, director, officer, executive, minister, boss (*informal*), agent, governor, controller, supervisor, bureaucrat, superintendent, gaffer (*informal, chiefly Brit.*), organizer, mandarin, functionary, overseer, baas (*S. African*)

admirable ADJECTIVE **= praiseworthy**, good, great, fine, capital, noted, choice, champion, prime, select, wonderful, excellent, brilliant, rare, cracking (*Brit. informal*), outstanding, valuable, superb, distinguished, superior, sterling, worthy, first-class, notable, sovereign, dope (*slang*), world-class, exquisite, exemplary, first-rate, superlative, commendable, top-notch (*informal*), brill (*informal*), laudable, meritorious, estimable, tiptop, A1 *or* A-one (*informal*), bitchin' (*U.S. slang*), chillin' (*U.S. slang*), booshit (*Austral. slang*), exo (*Austral. slang*), sik (*Austral. slang*), ka pai (*N.Z.*), rad (*informal*), phat (*slang*), schmick (*Austral. informal*), beaut (*informal*), barrie (*Scot. slang*), belting (*Brit. slang*), pearler (*Austral. slang*) **OPPOSITE:** deplorable

admiration NOUN **= regard**, surprise, wonder, respect, delight, pleasure, praise, approval, recognition, affection, esteem, appreciation, amazement, astonishment, reverence, deference, adoration, veneration, wonderment, approbation

admire VERB **1 = respect**, value, prize, honour, praise, appreciate, esteem, approve of, revere, venerate, take your hat off to, have a good *or* high opinion of, think highly of: *He admired the way she had coped with life.* **OPPOSITE:** despise
2 = adore, like, love, desire, take to, go for, fancy (*Brit. informal*), treasure, worship, cherish, glorify, look up to, dote on, hold dear, be captivated by, have an eye for, find attractive, idolize, take a liking to, be infatuated with, be enamoured of, lavish affection on: *I admired her when I first met her and I still think she's marvellous.*
3 = marvel at, look at, appreciate, delight in, gaze at, wonder at, be amazed by, take pleasure in, gape at, be awed by, goggle at, be filled with surprise by: *We took time to stop and admire the view.*

admirer NOUN **1 = fan**, supporter, follower, enthusiast, partisan, disciple, buff (*informal*), protagonist, devotee, worshipper, adherent, votary: *He was an admirer of her grandmother's paintings.* **2 = suitor**, lover, boyfriend, sweetheart, beau, wooer: *He was the most persistent of her admirers.*

admissible ADJECTIVE **= permissible**, allowed, permitted, acceptable, tolerated, tolerable, passable, allowable **OPPOSITE:** inadmissible

admission NOUN **1 = admittance**, access, entry, introduction, entrance, acceptance, initiation, entrée, ingress: *There have been increases in hospital admissions of children.*
2 = confession, admitting, profession,

a

a

declaration, revelation, concession, allowance, disclosure, acknowledgement, affirmation, unburdening, avowal, divulgence, unbosoming: *She wanted an admission of guilt from her father.*

admit VERB **1 = confess**, own up, confide, profess, own up, come clean (*informal*), avow, come out of the closet, sing (*slang, chiefly U.S.*), cough (*slang*), spill your guts (*slang*), 'fess up (*U.S. slang*): *Two-thirds of them admit to buying drink illegally.* **2 = allow**, agree, accept, reveal, grant, declare, acknowledge, recognize, concede, disclose, affirm, divulge: *I am willing to admit that I do make mistakes.* **OPPOSITE:** deny **3 = let in**, allow, receive, accept, introduce, take in, initiate, give access to, allow to enter: *Security personnel refused to admit him or his wife.* **OPPOSITE:** keep out

admittance NOUN **= access**, entry, way in, passage, entrance, reception, acceptance

admittedly ADVERB **= it must be admitted**, certainly, undeniably, it must be said, to be fair *or* honest, avowedly, it cannot be denied, it must be allowed, confessedly, it must be confessed, allowedly

admonish VERB **1 = reprimand**, caution, censure, rebuke, scold, berate, check, chide, tear into (*informal*), tell off (*informal*), reprove, upbraid, read the riot act to someone, carpet (*informal*), chew out (*U.S. & Canad. informal*), tear someone off a strip (*Brit. informal*), give someone a rocket (*Brit. & N.Z. informal*), slap someone on the wrist, rap someone over the knuckles: *They admonished me for taking risks with my health.* **OPPOSITE:** praise **2 = advise**, suggest, warn, urge, recommend, counsel, caution, prescribe, exhort, enjoin, forewarn: *Your doctor may one day admonish you to improve your posture.*

admonition NOUN **= reprimand**, warning, advice, counsel, caution, rebuke, reproach, scolding, berating, chiding, telling off (*informal*), upbraiding, reproof, remonstrance

ado NOUN **= fuss**, to-do, trouble, delay, bother, stir, confusion, excitement, disturbance, bustle, flurry, agitation, commotion, pother

adolescence NOUN **= teens**, youth, minority, boyhood, girlhood, juvenescence

adolescent ADJECTIVE **1 = young**, growing, junior, teenage, juvenile, youthful, childish, immature, boyish, undeveloped, girlish, puerile, in the springtime of life: *adolescent rebellion* **2 = teenage**, young, teen (*informal*), juvenile, youthful, immature: *An adolescent boy should have an adult in whom he can confide.*
▷ NOUN **= teenager**, girl, boy, kid (*informal*), youth, lad, minor, young man, youngster, young woman, juvenile, young person, lass, young adult: *Adolescents are happiest with small groups of close friends.*

adopt VERB **1 = take on**, follow, support, choose, accept, maintain, assume, select, take over, approve, appropriate, take up, embrace, engage in, endorse, ratify, become involved in, espouse: *Pupils should be helped to adopt a positive approach.* **2 = take in**, raise, nurse, mother, rear, foster, bring up, take care of: *There are hundreds of people desperate to adopt a child.* **OPPOSITE:** abandon

adoption NOUN **1 = fostering**, adopting, taking in, fosterage: *They gave their babies up for adoption.* **2 = embracing**, choice, taking on, taking up, support, taking over, selection, approval, following, assumption, maintenance, acceptance, endorsement, appropriation, ratification, approbation, espousal: *the adoption of Japanese management practices*

adorable ADJECTIVE **= lovable**, pleasing, appealing, dear, sweet, attractive, charming, precious, darling, fetching, delightful, cute, captivating, cutesy (*informal, chiefly U.S.*) **OPPOSITE:** hateful

adoration NOUN **= love**, honour, worship, worshipping, esteem, admiration, reverence, estimation, exaltation, veneration, glorification, idolatry, idolization

adore VERB **= love**, honour, admire, worship, esteem, cherish, bow to, revere, dote on, idolize **OPPOSITE:** hate

adoring ADJECTIVE **= admiring**, loving, devoted, worshipping, fond, affectionate, ardent, doting, venerating, enamoured, reverential, reverent, idolizing, adulatory **OPPOSITE:** hating

adorn VERB **= decorate**, enhance, deck, trim, grace, array, enrich, garnish, ornament, embellish, emblazon, festoon, bedeck, beautify, engarland

adornment NOUN **1 = decoration**, trimming, supplement, accessory, ornament, frill, festoon, embellishment, frippery: *A building without any adornment or decoration.* **2 = beautification**, decorating, decoration, embellishment, ornamentation: *Cosmetics are used for adornment.*

adrift ADJECTIVE **1 = drifting**, afloat, cast off, unmoored, aweigh, unanchored: *They were spotted adrift in a dinghy.* **2 = aimless**, goalless, directionless, purposeless: *She had the growing sense that she was adrift and isolated.*
▷ ADVERB **= wrong**, astray, off course, amiss, off target, wide of the mark: *They are trying to place the blame for a policy that has gone adrift.*

adroit ADJECTIVE **= skilful**, able, skilled, expert, bright (*informal*), clever, apt, cunning, ingenious, adept, deft, nimble, masterful, proficient, artful, quick-witted, dexterous **OPPOSITE:** unskilful

adulation NOUN **= extravagant flattery**, worship, fawning, sycophancy, fulsome praise, blandishment, bootlicking (*informal*), servile flattery **OPPOSITE:** ridicule

adult NOUN **= grown-up**, mature person, person of mature age, grown *or* grown-up person, man *or* woman: *Children under 14 must be accompanied by an adult.*
▷ ADJECTIVE **1 = fully grown**, mature, grown-up, of age, ripe, fully fledged, fully developed, full grown: *a pair of adult birds* **2 = pornographic**, blue, dirty, offensive, sexy, erotic, porn (*informal*), obscene, taboo, filthy, indecent, sensual, hard-core, lewd, carnal, porno (*informal*), X-rated (*informal*), salacious, prurient, smutty: *She was the adult film industry's hottest property.*

adulterer *or* **adulteress** NOUN **= cheat** (*informal*), love rat (*slang*), love cheat (*slang*), fornicator

adulterous ADJECTIVE **= unfaithful**, cheating (*informal*), extramarital, fornicating, unchaste

adultery NOUN **= unfaithfulness**, infidelity, cheating (*informal*), fornication, playing the field (*slang*), extramarital sex, playing away from home (*slang*), illicit sex, unchastity, extramarital relations, extracurricular sex (*informal*), extramarital congress, having an affair *or* a fling
OPPOSITE: faithfulness

QUOTATIONS

What men call gallantry, and gods adultery,
Is much more common where the climate's sultry
[Lord Byron *Don Juan*]

Do not adultery commit
Advantage rarely comes of it
[Arthur Hugh Clough *The Latest Decalogue*]

It is not marriage but a mockery of it, a merging that mixes love and dread together like jackstraws
[Alexander Theroux *An Adultery*]

Adultery is the application of democracy to love
[H.L. Mencken]

The first breath of adultery is the freest; after it, constraints aping marriage develop
[John Updike *Couples*]

advance VERB **1 = progress**, proceed, go ahead, move up, come forward, go forward, press on, gain ground, make inroads, make headway, make your way, cover ground, make strides, move onward: *Rebel forces are advancing on the capital.* **OPPOSITE:** retreat **2 = accelerate**, speed, promote, hurry (up), step up (*informal*), hasten, precipitate, quicken, bring forward, push forward, expedite, send forward, crack on *(informal)*: *Too much protein in the diet may advance the ageing process.* **3 = improve**, rise, grow, develop, reform, pick up, progress, thrive, upgrade, multiply, prosper, make strides: *The country has advanced from a rural society to an industrial power.* **4 = suggest**, offer, present, propose, allege, cite, advocate, submit, prescribe, put forward, proffer, adduce, offer as a suggestion: *Many theories have been advanced as to why this is.* **OPPOSITE:** withhold **5 = lend**, loan, accommodate someone with, supply on credit: *I advanced him some money, which he promised to repay.* **OPPOSITE:** withhold payment

▷ NOUN **1 = down payment**, credit, fee, deposit, retainer, prepayment, loan: *She was paid a £100,000 advance for her next two novels.* **2 = attack**, charge, strike, rush, assault, raid, invasion, offensive, onslaught, advancement, foray, incursion, forward movement, onward movement: *They simulated an advance on enemy positions.* **3 = improvement**, development, gain, growth, breakthrough, advancement, step, headway, inroads, betterment, furtherance, forward movement, amelioration, onward movement: *Air safety has not improved since the advances of the 1970s.*

▷ MODIFIER **= prior**, early, previous, beforehand: *The event received little advance publicity.*

in advance = beforehand, earlier, ahead, previously, pre-need, in the lead, in the forefront: *The subject of the talk is announced a week in advance.*

advanced ADJECTIVE **= sophisticated**, foremost, modern, revolutionary, up-to-date, higher, leading, recent, prime, forward, ahead, supreme, extreme, principal, progressive, paramount, state-of-the-art, avant-garde, precocious, pre-eminent, up-to-the-minute, ahead of the times **OPPOSITE:** backward

advancement NOUN **1 = promotion**, rise, gain, growth, advance, progress, improvement, betterment, preferment, amelioration: *He cared little for social advancement.* **2 = progress**, advance, headway, forward movement, onward movement: *her work for the advancement of the status of women*

advantage NOUN **1 = benefit**, use, start, help, service, aid, profit, favour, asset, assistance, blessing, utility, boon, ace in the hole, ace up your sleeve: *A good crowd will be a definite advantage to the team.* **OPPOSITE:** disadvantage **2 = lead**, control, edge, sway, dominance, superiority, upper hand, precedence, primacy, pre-eminence: *Men have created an economic position of advantage over women.* **3 = superiority**, good, worth, gain, comfort, welfare, enjoyment, mileage *(informal)*: *The great advantage of home-grown fruit is its magnificent flavour.*

advantageous ADJECTIVE **1 = beneficial**, useful, valuable, helpful, profitable, of service, convenient, worthwhile, expedient: *Free exchange of goods was advantageous to all.* **OPPOSITE:** unfavourable **2 = superior**, dominating, commanding, dominant, important, powerful, favourable, fortuitous: *She was determined to prise what she could from an advantageous situation.*

advent NOUN **= coming**, approach, appearance, arrival, entrance, onset, occurrence, visitation

adventure NOUN **= venture**, experience, chance, risk, incident, enterprise, speculation, undertaking, exploit, fling, hazard, occurrence, contingency, caper, escapade: *I set off for a new adventure in the US on the first day of the year.*

▷ VERB **= venture**, risk, brave, dare: *The group has adventured as far as the Alps.*

> **QUOTATIONS**
> An adventure is only an inconvenience rightly considered. An inconvenience is only an adventure wrongly considered
> [G.K. Chesterton *All Things Considered*]

adventurer NOUN **1 = mercenary**, rogue, gambler, speculator, opportunist, charlatan, fortune-hunter: *ambitious political adventurers* **2 = venturer**, hero, traveller, heroine, wanderer, voyager, daredevil, soldier of fortune, swashbuckler, knight-errant: *A round-the-world adventurer was killed when her plane crashed.*

adventurous ADJECTIVE **= daring**, dangerous, enterprising, bold, risky, rash, have-a-go *(informal)*, hazardous, reckless, audacious, intrepid, foolhardy, daredevil, headstrong, venturesome, adventuresome, temerarious *(rare)* **OPPOSITE:** cautious

adversary NOUN **= opponent**, rival, opposer, enemy, competitor, foe, contestant, antagonist **OPPOSITE:** ally

adverse ADJECTIVE **1 = harmful**, damaging, conflicting, dangerous, opposite, negative, destructive, detrimental, hurtful, antagonistic, injurious, inimical, inopportune, disadvantageous, unpropitious, inexpedient: *The decision would have no adverse effect on the investigation.* **OPPOSITE:** beneficial **2 = unfavourable**, bad, threatening, hostile, unfortunate, unlucky, ominous, unfriendly, untimely, unsuited, ill-suited, inopportune, disadvantageous, unseasonable: *Despite the adverse conditions, the road was finished in just eight months.* **3 = negative**, opposing, reluctant, hostile, contrary, dissenting, unwilling, unfriendly, unsympathetic, ill-disposed: *Wine lakes and butter mountains have drawn considerable adverse publicity.*

adversity NOUN **= hardship**, trouble, distress, suffering, trial, disaster, reverse, misery, hard times, catastrophe, sorrow, woe, misfortune, bad luck, deep water, calamity, mishap, affliction, wretchedness, ill-fortune, ill-luck

advert NOUN **= advertisement**, bill, notice, display, commercial, ad *(informal)*, announcement, promotion, publicity, poster, plug *(informal)*, puff, circular, placard, blurb

advertise VERB **= publicize**, promote, plug *(informal)*, announce, publish, push *(informal)*, display, declare, broadcast, advise, inform, praise, proclaim, puff, hype, notify, tout, flaunt, crack up *(informal)*, promulgate, make known, apprise, beat the drum *(informal)*, blazon, bring to public notice

advertisement NOUN **= advert** *(Brit. informal)*, bill, notice, display, commercial, ad *(informal)*, announcement, promotion, publicity, poster, plug *(informal)*, puff, circular, placard, blurb

advice NOUN **1 = guidance**, help, opinion, direction, suggestion, instruction, counsel, counselling, recommendation, injunction, admonition: *Don't be afraid to ask for advice when ordering a meal.* **2 = instruction**, notification, view, information, warning, teaching, notice, word, intelligence: *Most have now left the country on the advice of their governments.*

> **QUOTATIONS**
> There is nothing we receive with so much reluctance as advice
> [Joseph Addison *The Spectator*]
>
> It was, perhaps, one of those cases in which advice is good or bad only as the event decides
> [Jane Austen *Persuasion*]
>
> The best way to give advice to your children is to find out what they want and advise them to do it
> [Harry S. Truman]

advisable ADJECTIVE **= wise**, seemly, sound, suggested, fitting, fit, politic, recommended, appropriate, suitable, sensible, proper, profitable, desirable, apt, prudent, expedient, judicious **OPPOSITE:** unwise

advise VERB **1 = recommend**, suggest, urge, counsel, advocate, caution, prescribe, commend, admonish, enjoin: *I would strongly advise against it.* **2 = notify**, tell, report, announce, warn, declare, inform, acquaint, make known, apprise, let (someone) know: *I must advise you of my decision to retire.*

> **QUOTATIONS**
> Advise none to marry or go to war
> [George Herbert *Outlandish Proverbs*]
>
> Thou dost advise me, Even so as
> I mine own course have set down
> [William Shakespeare *The Winter's Tale*]

a

adviser NOUN = **counsellor**, authority, teacher, coach, guide, lawyer, consultant, solicitor, counsel, aide, tutor, guru, mentor, helper, confidant, right-hand man, consigliere

advisory ADJECTIVE = **advising**, helping, recommending, counselling, consultative

advocacy NOUN = **recommendation**, support, defence, championing, backing, proposal, urging, promotion, campaigning for, upholding, encouragement, justification, argument for, advancement, pleading for, propagation, espousal, promulgation, boosterism, spokesmanship

advocate VERB = **recommend**, support, champion, encourage, propose, favour, defend, promote, urge, advise, justify, endorse, campaign for, prescribe, speak for, uphold, press for, argue for, commend, plead for, espouse, countenance, hold a brief for *(informal)*: *He advocates fewer government controls on business.* **OPPOSITE:** oppose
▷ NOUN **1** = **supporter**, spokesman, champion, defender, speaker, pleader, campaigner, promoter, counsellor, backer, proponent, apostle, apologist, upholder, proposer: *He was a strong advocate of free market policies.* **2** = **lawyer**, attorney, solicitor, counsel, barrister: *When she became an advocate there were only a few women practising.*

aegis NOUN = **support**, backing, wing, favour, protection, shelter, sponsorship, patronage, advocacy, auspices, guardianship

aesthetic ADJECTIVE = **ornamental**, artistic, pleasing, pretty, fancy, enhancing, decorative, tasteful, beautifying, nonfunctional

affable ADJECTIVE = **friendly**, kindly, civil, warm, pleasant, mild, obliging, benign, gracious, benevolent, good-humoured, amiable, courteous, amicable, cordial, sociable, genial, congenial, urbane, approachable, good-natured **OPPOSITE:** unfriendly

affair NOUN **1** = **matter**, thing, business, question, issue, happening, concern, event, subject, project, activity, incident, proceeding, circumstance, episode, topic, undertaking, transaction, occurrence: *The government has mishandled the whole affair.*
2 = **relationship**, romance, intrigue, fling, liaison, flirtation, amour, dalliance: *A married male supervisor was carrying on an affair with a colleague.*

affect[1] VERB **1** = **influence**, involve, concern, impact, transform, alter, modify, change, manipulate, act on, sway, prevail over, bear upon, impinge upon: *Millions of people have been affected by the drought.*
2 = **emotionally move**, touch, upset, overcome, stir, disturb, perturb, impress on, tug at your heartstrings *(often facetious)*: *He loved his sister, and her loss clearly still affects him.*

affect[2] VERB = **put on**, assume, adopt, pretend, imitate, simulate, contrive, aspire to, sham, counterfeit, feign: *He listened to them, affecting an amused interest.*

affectation NOUN = **pretence**, show, posing, posturing, act, display, appearance, pose, façade, simulation, sham, pretension, veneer, artifice, mannerism, insincerity, pretentiousness, hokum *(slang, chiefly U.S. & Canad.)*, artificiality, fakery, affectedness, assumed manners, false display, unnatural imitation

affected[1] ADJECTIVE = **pretended**, artificial, contrived, put-on, assumed, mannered, studied, precious, stiff, simulated, mincing, sham, unnatural, pompous, pretentious, counterfeit, feigned, spurious, conceited, insincere, camp *(informal)*, la-di-da *(informal)*, arty-farty *(informal)*, phoney *or* phony *(informal)*: *She passed by with an affected air and a disdainful look.* **OPPOSITE:** genuine

affected[2] ADJECTIVE = **touched**, influenced, concerned, troubled, damaged, hurt, injured, upset, impressed, stirred, altered, changed, distressed, stimulated, melted, impaired, afflicted, deeply moved: *Staff at the hospital were deeply affected by the tragedy.* **OPPOSITE:** untouched

affecting ADJECTIVE = **emotionally moving**, touching, sad, pathetic, poignant, saddening, pitiful, pitiable, piteous

affection NOUN = **fondness**, liking, feeling, love, care, desire, passion, warmth, attachment, goodwill, devotion, kindness, inclination, tenderness, propensity, friendliness, amity, aroha *(N.Z.)*

affectionate ADJECTIVE = **fond**, loving, kind, caring, warm, friendly, attached, devoted, tender, doting, warm-hearted **OPPOSITE:** cool

affiliate VERB = **associate**, unite, join, link, ally, combine, connect, incorporate, annex, confederate, amalgamate, band together

affiliated ADJECTIVE = **associated**, united, joined, linked, allied, connected, incorporated, confederated, amalgamated, federated, conjoined

affiliation NOUN = **association**, union, joining, league, relationship, connection, alliance, combination, coalition, merging, confederation, incorporation, amalgamation, banding together

affinity NOUN **1** = **attraction**, liking, leaning, sympathy, inclination, rapport, fondness, partiality, aroha *(N.Z.)*: *There is a natural affinity between the two.* **OPPOSITE:** hostility
2 = **similarity**, relationship, relation, connection, alliance, correspondence, analogy, resemblance, closeness, likeness, compatibility, kinship: *The two plots share certain obvious affinities.* **OPPOSITE:** difference

affirm VERB **1** = **declare**, state, maintain, swear, assert, testify, pronounce, certify, attest, avow, aver, asseverate, avouch: *'The place is a dump,' she affirmed.* **OPPOSITE:** deny
2 = **confirm**, prove, sanction, endorse, ratify, verify, validate, bear out, substantiate, corroborate, authenticate: *Everything I had accomplished seemed to affirm that opinion.* **OPPOSITE:** refute

affirmation NOUN **1** = **declaration**, statement, assertion, oath, certification, pronouncement, avowal, asseveration, averment: *The ministers issued a robust affirmation of their faith in the system.*
2 = **confirmation**, testimony, ratification, attestation, avouchment: *The high turnout was an affirmation of the importance of the election.*

affirmative ADJECTIVE = **agreeing**, confirming, positive, approving, consenting, favourable, concurring, assenting, corroborative **OPPOSITE:** negative

affix VERB = **attach**, add, join, stick on, bind, put on, tag, glue, paste, tack, fasten, annex, append, subjoin **OPPOSITE:** remove

afflict VERB = **torment**, trouble, pain, hurt, wound, burden, distress, rack, try, plague, grieve, harass, ail, oppress, beset, smite

TERMS OF AFFECTION

angel	dearheart	cat	petal	sweetie pie
babe *or* babes	dear one	lamb	pet lamb	sweets
baby	doll	little one *or* little 'un	poppet	tiger
bean	duck	love	precious	toots
beloved	flower	loved one	princess	treacle
bunnykins	fluffy bunny	lover	pumpkin	treasure
chicken	goose	munchkin	puppy	truelove
chicken bunny	honey	muppet	pussycat	weasel
darling	honey bunny	pepperpot	star	
dear	kitten	pet	sugar	
dearest	kitty *or* kitty		sweetheart	

Adjectives in 'The Times' and 'The Sun'

It is to be expected that linguistic analysis should pinpoint differences between two newspapers at opposite ends of the spectrum, such as the highbrow *Times* and the populist *Sun*.

Some interesting differences can be found in the distribution of everyday adjectives in the two newspapers. *Big* is used with about equal frequency, while *massive* is over three times as frequent in *The Sun* and *large* is nearly three times as frequent in *The Times*. Both use *large* to refer to amounts (*large amount, large proportion, large number*), but *The Times* also refers to *large firms* and *large houses*, which *The Sun* is more likely to express with *big*. *The Sun* uses the more hyperbolic *massive* more frequently, especially in the phrases *massive selection, massive boost,* and *a massive game*, as in:

That's why Sunday is such a **massive game** for both teams. (*The Sun*)

The adjective *total* is slightly more frequent in *The Times*; more interesting is its sense distribution in the two newspapers. *The Times* tends to use it in the sense 'relating to a sum', for example in *total sale, total cost,* and *total revenue. The Sun*, on the other hand, more frequently uses it as an intensifier meaning 'complete' or 'absolute', as in:

It is an absolute disgrace and a **total waste** of taxpayers' money. (*The Sun*)

However, *The Times* has its own favourite intensifying adjective. *Vast* occurs three times more often in *The Times*, usually in relation to amount (*vast majority, vast sum*) or size (*vast crowd, vast expanse*), but also in cases where it no longer has connotations of size and space and has become a simple intensifier, as in:

He was supported by the vast **sophistication** of the American political system. (*The Times*)

Difficult occurs with equal frequency in the two newspapers, as does *hard. Challenging* is more frequent in *The Times*, occurring in phrases such as *challenging times, a challenging year,* and *challenging work. Tough* is more frequent in *The Sun*, and it also differs in sense distribution in the two newspapers. Both refer to *tough decisions* and to people being *tough*, but in addition to these *The Times* more frequently uses *tough* in the sense 'strict' (as in *tough stance, tough regulations*), while *The Sun* more frequently uses it in the sense 'difficult' (as in *tough game, tough challenge*).There are also variations in words meaning 'unbelievable' and 'very good' (meanings which often overlap). Both *fantastic* and *amazing* are nearly three times as frequent in *The Sun* as in *The Times*. One of *The Sun's* favourite adjectives is *bizarre*, which occurs sixteen times more often than it does in *The Times*, frequently collocating with *twist* and *outburst. Incredible* occurs two and a half times more often and *unbelievable* three times more often in *The Sun*, frequently modifying *achievement, experience,* and *effort*, and often modified by an adverb for emphasis, as in:

It took an **absolutely incredible effort** to get a bronze. (*The Sun*)

Stunned occurs six times more often and *shocked* three times more often in *The Sun*. Furthermore, almost all the uses in *The Times* are either the past tense of the verb ('Ms. Horlick **stunned** the stock market last week') or a passive form bordering on a predicative adjective ('the entire family **are shocked** and devastated'). In *The Sun*, on the other hand, *shocked* and *stunned* are often used attributively, as in:

Witnesses said **shocked** Nadine sobbed,
'My poor babies, my poor babies'. (*The Sun*)

The few cases of this structure in *The Times* refer not to shocked or stunned people, but to atmospheres or emotions such as *shocked silence, shocked amusement,* and *stunned disbelief.*

affliction NOUN **= misfortune**, suffering, trouble, trial, disease, pain, distress, grief, misery, plague, curse, ordeal, sickness, torment, hardship, sorrow, woe, adversity, calamity, scourge, tribulation, wretchedness

affluence NOUN **= wealth**, riches, plenty, fortune, prosperity, abundance, big money, exuberance, profusion, big bucks *(informal, chiefly U.S.)*, opulence, megabucks *(U.S. & Canad. slang)*, pretty penny *(informal)*, wad *(U.S. & Canad. slang)*

affluent ADJECTIVE **= wealthy**, rich, prosperous, loaded *(slang)*, well-off, opulent, well-heeled *(informal)*, well-to-do, moneyed, minted *(Brit. slang)* **OPPOSITE:** poor

afford VERB **1 = have the money for**, manage, bear, pay for, spare, stand, stretch to: *The arts should be available at prices people can afford.* **2 = bear**, stand, sustain, allow yourself: *We cannot afford to wait.* **3 = give**, offer, provide, produce, supply, grant, yield, render, furnish, bestow, impart: *The room afforded fine views of the city.*

affordable ADJECTIVE **= inexpensive**, fair, cheap, reasonable, moderate, modest, low-price, low-cost, economical **OPPOSITE:** expensive

affront VERB **= offend**, anger, provoke, outrage, insult, annoy, vex, displease, pique, put *or* get your back up, slight: *One example that particularly affronted him was at the world championships.*
▷ NOUN **= insult**, wrong, injury, abuse, offence, slight, outrage, provocation, slur, indignity, slap in the face *(informal)*, vexation: *She has taken my enquiry as a personal affront.*

affronted ADJECTIVE **= offended**, cross, angry, upset, slighted, outraged, insulted, annoyed, stung, incensed, indignant, irate, miffed *(informal)*, displeased, peeved *(informal)*, piqued, tooshie *(Austral. slang)*

afloat ADJECTIVE **1 = floating**, on the surface, buoyant, keeping your head above water, unsubmerged: *Three hours is a long time to try and stay afloat.* **OPPOSITE:** sunken **2 = solvent**, in business, above water: *Efforts were being made to keep the company afloat.* **OPPOSITE:** bankrupt

afoot ADJECTIVE **= going on**, happening, current, operating, abroad, brewing, hatching, circulating, up *(informal)*, about, in preparation, in progress, afloat, in the wind, on the go *(informal)*, astir

afraid ADJECTIVE **1 = scared**, frightened, nervous, anxious, terrified, shaken, alarmed, startled, suspicious, intimidated, fearful, cowardly, timid, apprehensive, petrified, panicky, panic-stricken, timorous, faint-hearted: *She did not seem at all afraid; He's afraid to sleep in his own bedroom.* **OPPOSITE:** unafraid **2 = reluctant**, slow, frightened, scared, unwilling, backward, hesitant, recalcitrant, loath, disinclined, unenthusiastic, indisposed: *He seems to live in an ivory tower, afraid to enter the real world.* **3 = sorry**, apologetic, regretful, sad, distressed, unhappy: *I'm afraid I can't help you.* **OPPOSITE:** pleased

afresh ADVERB **= again**, newly, once again, once more, over again, anew

after PREPOSITION **1 = at the end of**, following, subsequent to: *After breakfast she phoned for a taxi.* **OPPOSITE:** before **2 = following**, chasing, pursuing, on the hunt for, on the tail of *(informal)*, on the track of: *People were after him for large amounts of money.*
▷ ADVERB **= following**, later, next, succeeding, afterwards, subsequently, thereafter: *tomorrow, or the day after*

aftereffect NOUN *(usually plural)* **= consequence**, wake, trail, aftermath, hangover *(informal)*, spin-off, repercussion, afterglow, aftershock, delayed response

aftermath NOUN **= effects**, end, results, wake, consequences, outcome, sequel, end result, upshot, aftereffects

afterwards *or* **afterward** ADVERB **= later**, after, then, after that, subsequently, thereafter, following that, at a later date *or* time

again ADVERB **1 = once more**, another time, anew, afresh: *He kissed her again.* **2 = also**, in addition, moreover, besides, furthermore: *And again, that's probably part of the progress of technology.* **there again** *or* **then again = on the other hand**, in contrast, on the contrary, conversely: *They may agree, but there again, they may not.*

against PREPOSITION **1 = beside**, on, up against, in contact with, abutting, close up to: *She leaned against him.* **2 = opposed to**, anti *(informal)*, opposing, counter, contra *(informal)*, hostile to, in opposition to, averse to, opposite to, not in accord with: *She was very much against commencing the treatment.* **3 = in opposition to**, resisting, versus, counter to, in the opposite direction of: *swimming upstream against the current* **4 = in preparation for**, in case of, in anticipation of, in expectation of, in provision for: *You'll need insurance against fire, flood and breakage.*

age NOUN **1 = years**, days, generation, lifetime, stage of life, length of life, length of existence: *He's very confident for his age.* **2 = old age**, experience, maturity, completion, seniority, fullness, majority, maturation, senility, decline, advancing years, declining years, senescence, full growth, matureness: *Perhaps he has grown wiser with age.* **OPPOSITE:** youth **3 = time**, day(s), period, generation, era, epoch: *the age of steam and steel*
▷ PLURAL NOUN **= a long time** *or* **while**, years, centuries, for ever *(informal)*, aeons, donkey's years *(informal)*, yonks *(informal)*, a month of Sundays *(informal)*, an age *or* eternity: *The bus took ages to arrive.*
▷ VERB **1 = grow old**, decline, weather, fade, deteriorate, wither: *He seemed to have aged in the last few months.* **2 = mature**, season, condition, soften, mellow, ripen: *Whisky loses strength as it ages.*

aged ADJECTIVE **= old**, getting on, grey, ancient, antique, elderly, past it *(informal)*, age-old, antiquated, hoary, superannuated, senescent, cobwebby **OPPOSITE:** young

ageing *or* **aging** ADJECTIVE **= growing old** *or* **older**, declining, maturing, deteriorating, mellowing, in decline, senile, long in the tooth, senescent, getting on *or* past it *(informal)*: *He lives with his ageing mother.*
▷ NOUN **= growing old**, decline, decay, deterioration, degeneration, maturation, senility, senescence: *degenerative diseases and premature ageing*

QUOTATIONS

But at my back I always hear
Time's wingèd chariot hurrying near
[Andrew Marvell *To his Coy Mistress*]

Grow old along with me!
The best is yet to be
[Robert Browning *Rabbi Ben Ezra*]

ageless ADJECTIVE **= eternal**, enduring, abiding, perennial, timeless, immortal, unchanging, deathless, unfading **OPPOSITE:** momentary

agency NOUN **1 = business**, company, office, firm, department, organization, enterprise, establishment, bureau: *a successful advertising agency* **2 = medium**, work, means, force, power, action, operation, activity, influence, vehicle, instrument, intervention, mechanism, efficiency, mediation, auspices, intercession, instrumentality: *a negotiated settlement through the agency of the UN*

agenda NOUN **= programme**, list, plan, schedule, diary, calendar, timetable

agent NOUN **1 = representative**, deputy, substitute, advocate, rep *(informal)*, broker, delegate, factor, negotiator, envoy, trustee, proxy, surrogate, go-between, emissary: *You are buying direct, rather than through an agent.* **2 = author**, officer, worker, actor, vehicle, instrument, operator, performer, operative, catalyst, executor, doer, perpetuator: *They regard themselves as the agents of change in society.* **3 = force**, means, power, cause, instrument: *the bleaching agent in white flour*

aggravate VERB **1 = make worse**, exaggerate, intensify, worsen, heighten, exacerbate, magnify, inflame, increase, add insult to injury, fan the flames of: *Stress and lack of sleep can aggravate the situation.* **OPPOSITE:** improve **2 = annoy**, bother, provoke, needle *(informal)*, irritate, tease, hassle *(informal)*, gall, exasperate, nettle, pester, vex, irk, get under your skin *(informal)*, get on your nerves *(informal)*, nark *(Brit., Austral. & N.Z. slang)*, get up your nose *(informal)*, be on your back *(slang)*, rub (someone) up the wrong way *(informal)*, get in your hair *(informal)*, get on your wick *(Brit. slang)*, hack you off *(informal)*: *What aggravates you most about this country?* **OPPOSITE:** please

aggravating ADJECTIVE **1 = annoying**, provoking, irritating, teasing, galling, exasperating, vexing, irksome: *You don't realise how aggravating you can be.* **2 = worsening**, exaggerating, intensifying, heightening, exacerbating, magnifying, inflaming: *Stress is a frequent aggravating factor.*

aggravation NOUN **1 = annoyance**, grief *(informal)*, teasing, irritation, hassle *(informal)*, provocation, gall, exasperation, vexation, irksomeness: *I just couldn't take the aggravation.* **2 = worsening**, heightening, inflaming, exaggeration, intensification, magnification, exacerbation: *Any aggravations of the injury would keep him out of the match.*

aggregate NOUN **= total**, body, whole, amount, collection, mass, sum, combination, pile, mixture, bulk, lump, heap, accumulation, assemblage, agglomeration: *society viewed as an aggregate of individuals*
▷ ADJECTIVE **= collective**, added, mixed, combined, collected, corporate, assembled, accumulated, composite, cumulative: *the rate of growth of aggregate demand*
▷ VERB **= combine**, mix, collect, assemble, heap, accumulate, pile, amass: *We should never aggregate votes to predict results under another system.*

aggregation NOUN **= collection**, body, mass, combination, pile, mixture, bulk, lump, heap, accumulation, assemblage, agglomeration

aggression NOUN **1 = hostility**, malice, antagonism, antipathy, aggressiveness, ill will, belligerence, destructiveness, malevolence, pugnacity: *Aggression is by no means a male-only trait.* **2 = attack**, campaign, injury, assault, offence, raid, invasion, offensive, onslaught, foray, encroachment: *the threat of massive military aggression*

aggressive ADJECTIVE **1 = hostile**, offensive, destructive, belligerent, unkind, unfriendly, malevolent, contrary, antagonistic, pugnacious, bellicose, quarrelsome, aggers *(Austral. slang)*, biffo *(Austral. slang)*, inimical, rancorous, ill-disposed: *Some children are much more aggressive than others.* **OPPOSITE:** friendly **2 = forceful**, powerful, convincing, effective, enterprising, dynamic, bold, militant, pushing, vigorous, energetic, persuasive, assertive, zealous, pushy *(informal)*, in-your-face *(slang)*: *He is respected as a very competitive and aggressive executive.* **OPPOSITE:** submissive

aggressor NOUN **= attacker**, assaulter, invader, assailant

aggrieved ADJECTIVE **= hurt**, wronged, injured, harmed, disturbed, distressed, unhappy, afflicted, saddened, woeful, peeved *(informal)*, ill-used

aghast ADJECTIVE **= horrified**, shocked, amazed, stunned, appalled, astonished, startled, astounded, confounded, awestruck, horror-struck, thunder-struck

agile ADJECTIVE **1 = nimble**, active, quick, lively, swift, brisk, supple, sprightly, lithe, limber, spry, lissom(e): *He is not as strong and agile as he was at 20.* **OPPOSITE:** slow **2 = acute**, sharp, quick, bright *(informal)*, prompt, alert, clever, lively, nimble, quick-witted: *She was quick-witted, and had an extraordinarily agile mind.*

agility NOUN **1 = nimbleness**, activity, suppleness, quickness, swiftness, liveliness, briskness, litheness, sprightliness, spryness: *She blinked in surprise at his agility.* **2 = acuteness**, sharpness, alertness, cleverness, quickness, liveliness, promptness, quick-wittedness, promptitude: *His intellect and mental agility have never been in doubt.*

agitate VERB **1 = stir**, beat, mix, shake, disturb, toss, rouse, churn: *Gently agitate the water with a paintbrush.* **2 = upset**, worry, trouble, disturb, excite, alarm, stimulate, distract, rouse, ruffle, inflame, incite, unnerve, disconcert, disquiet, fluster, perturb, faze, work someone up, give someone grief *(Brit. & S. African)*: *The thought of them inheriting all these things agitated her.* **OPPOSITE:** calm

agitated ADJECTIVE **= upset**, worried, troubled, disturbed, shaken, excited, alarmed, nervous, anxious, distressed, rattled *(informal)*, distracted, uneasy, unsettled, worked up, ruffled, unnerved, disconcerted, disquieted, edgy, flustered, perturbed, on edge, fazed, ill at ease, hot under the collar *(informal)*, in a flap *(informal)*, hot and bothered *(informal)*, antsy *(informal)*, angsty, all of a flutter *(informal)*, discomposed, aerated **OPPOSITE:** calm

agitation NOUN **1 = turbulence**, rocking, shaking, stirring, stir, tossing, disturbance, upheaval, churning, convulsion: *Temperature is a measure of agitation of molecules.* **2 = turmoil**, worry, trouble, upset, alarm, confusion, excitement, disturbance, distraction, upheaval, stimulation, flurry, outcry, clamour, arousal, ferment, disquiet, commotion, fluster, lather *(informal)*, incitement, tumult, discomposure, tizzy, tizz or tiz-woz *(informal)*: *She was in a state of emotional agitation.*

agitator NOUN **= troublemaker**, revolutionary, inciter, firebrand, instigator, demagogue, rabble-rouser, agent provocateur, stirrer *(informal)*

ago ADVERB **= previously**, back, before, since, earlier, formerly

> **USAGE**
> Although *since* can be used as a synonym of *ago* in certain contexts, the use of *ago* and *since* together, as in *it's ten years ago since he wrote that novel*, is redundant. Instead, it would be correct to use *it is ten years since he wrote that novel*, or *it is ten years ago that he wrote that novel*.

agonize VERB **= suffer**, labour, worry, struggle, strain, strive, writhe, be distressed, be in agony, go through the mill, be in anguish

agonized ADJECTIVE **= tortured**, suffering, wounded, distressed, racked, tormented, anguished, broken-hearted, grief-stricken, wretched

agonizing ADJECTIVE **= painful**, bitter, distressing, harrowing, heartbreaking, grievous, excruciating, hellish, heart-rending, gut-wrenching, torturous

agony NOUN **= suffering**, pain, distress, misery, torture, discomfort, torment, hardship, woe, anguish, pangs, affliction, throes

agrarian ADJECTIVE **= agricultural**, country, land, farming, rural, rustic, agrestic **OPPOSITE:** urban

agree VERB **1 = concur**, engage, be as one, sympathize, assent, see eye to eye, be of the same opinion, be of the same mind, be down with *(informal)*: *I'm not sure I agree with you.* **OPPOSITE:** disagree **2 = correspond**, match, accord, answer, fit, suit, square, coincide, tally, conform, chime, harmonize: *His second statement agrees with the facts.*
agree on something = shake hands on, reach agreement on, settle on, negotiate, work out, arrive at, yield to, thrash out, accede to, concede to: *The warring sides have agreed on a ceasefire.*
agree to something = consent to, grant, approve, permit, accede to, assent to, acquiesce to, comply to, concur to: *All 100 senators agreed to postponement.*
agree with someone = suit, get on, be good for, befit: *I don't think the food here agrees with me.*

agreeable ADJECTIVE **1 = pleasant**, pleasing, satisfying, acceptable, delightful, enjoyable, gratifying, pleasurable, congenial, to your liking, to your taste, likable or likeable: *more agreeable and better paid occupations* **OPPOSITE:** unpleasant

a

2 = **friendly**, pleasant, nice, sociable, affable, congenial, good-natured, likable *or* likeable: *I've gone out of my way to be agreeable to his friends.* 3 = **consenting**, willing, agreeing, approving, sympathetic, complying, responsive, concurring, amenable, in accord, well-disposed, acquiescent: *She was agreeable to the project.*

QUOTATIONS
I do not want people to be very agreeable, as it saves me the trouble of liking them a great deal
[Jane Austen]
My idea of an agreeable person is a person who agrees with me
[Benjamin Disraeli *Lothair*]

agreed ADJECTIVE = **settled**, given, established, guaranteed, fixed, arranged, definite, stipulated, predetermined: *There is a discount if goods do not arrive by the agreed time.*
OPPOSITE: indefinite
▷ INTERJECTION = **all right**, done, settled, it's a bargain *or* deal, O.K. *or* okay *(informal)*, you're on *(informal)*, ka pai *(N.Z.)*: *That means we move out today. Agreed?*

agreement NOUN 1 = **treaty**, contract, bond, arrangement, alliance, deal *(informal)*, understanding, settlement, bargain, pact, compact, covenant, entente: *a new defence agreement* 2 = **concurrence**, harmony, compliance, union, agreeing, concession, consent, unison, assent, concord, acquiescence: *The talks ended in acrimony rather than agreement.*
OPPOSITE: disagreement
3 = **correspondence**, agreeing, accord, similarity, consistency, analogy, accordance, correlation, affinity, conformity, compatibility, congruity, suitableness: *The results are generally in agreement with these figures.*
OPPOSITE: difference

agricultural ADJECTIVE = **farming**, country, rural, rustic, agrarian, agronomic, agronomical, agrestic

agriculture NOUN = **farming**, culture, cultivation, husbandry, tillage, agronomy, agronomics

aground ADVERB = **beached**, grounded, stuck, shipwrecked, foundered, stranded, ashore, marooned, on the rocks, high and dry

ahead ADVERB 1 = **in front**, on, forwards, in advance, onwards, towards the front, frontwards: *He looked straight ahead.* 2 = **at an advantage**, in advance, in the lead: *Children in smaller classes were 1.5 months ahead in reading.* 3 = **in the lead**, winning, leading, at the head, to the fore, at an advantage: *Australia were ahead throughout the game.* 4 = **in advance**, in front, before, onwards, in the lead, in the vanguard: *You go on ahead. I'll catch you up later.*

aid NOUN 1 = **help**, backing, support, benefit, favour, relief, promotion, assistance, encouragement, helping hand, succour: *He was forced to turn to his former enemy for aid.*
OPPOSITE: hindrance 2 = **helper**, supporter, assistant, aide, adjutant, aide-de-camp, second, abettor: *A young woman employed as an aid spoke hesitantly.*
▷ VERB 1 = **help**, second, support, serve, sustain, assist, relieve, avail, subsidize, abet, succour, be of service to, lend a hand to, give a leg up to *(informal)*: *a software system to aid managers in decision-making*
OPPOSITE: hinder 2 = **promote**, help, further, forward, encourage, favour, facilitate, pave the way for, expedite, smooth the path of, assist the progress of: *Calcium may aid the prevention of colon cancer.*

aide NOUN = **assistant**, supporter, deputy, attendant, helper, henchman, right-hand man, adjutant, second, helpmate, coadjutor *(rare)*

ail VERB 1 = **trouble**, worry, bother, distress, pain, upset, annoy, irritate, sicken, afflict, be the matter with: *a debate on what ails the industry* 2 = **be ill**, be sick, be unwell, feel unwell, be indisposed, be *or* feel off colour: *He is said to be ailing at his home in the country.*

ailing ADJECTIVE 1 = **weak**, failing, poor, flawed, unstable, feeble, unsatisfactory, deficient, unsound: *A rise in overseas sales is good news for the ailing economy.* 2 = **ill**, suffering, poorly, diseased, sick, weak, crook *(Austral. & N.Z. informal)*, feeble, invalid, debilitated, sickly, unwell, infirm, off colour, under the weather *(informal)*, indisposed: *She stopped working to care for her ailing mother.*

ailment NOUN = **illness**, disease, complaint, disorder, sickness, affliction, malady, infirmity, lurgy *(informal)*

aim VERB 1 = **try for**, want, seek, work for, plan for, strive, aspire to, wish for, have designs on, set your sights on: *He was aiming for the 100 metres world record.* 2 = **point**, level, train, direct, sight, take aim (at): *He was aiming the rifle at me.*
▷ NOUN = **intention**, end, point, plan, course, mark, goal, design, target, wish, scheme, purpose, direction, desire, object, objective, ambition, intent, aspiration, Holy Grail *(informal)*: *a research programme that has failed to achieve its aim*

aimless ADJECTIVE = **purposeless**, random, stray, pointless, erratic, wayward, frivolous, chance, goalless, haphazard, vagrant, directionless, unguided, undirected
OPPOSITE: purposeful

air NOUN 1 = **wind**, blast, breath, breeze, puff, whiff, draught, gust, waft, zephyr, air-current, current of air: *Draughts help to circulate air.* 2 = **atmosphere**, sky, heavens, aerosphere: *They fired their guns in the air.* 3 = **tune**, song, theme, melody, strain, lay, aria: *an old Irish air* 4 = **manner**, feeling, effect, style, quality, character, bearing, appearance, look, aspect, atmosphere, tone, mood, impression, flavour, aura, ambience, demeanour, vibe *(slang)*: *The meal gave the occasion an almost festive air.*
▷ VERB 1 = **publicize**, tell, reveal, exhibit, communicate, voice, express, display, declare, expose, disclose, proclaim, utter, circulate, make public, divulge, disseminate, ventilate, make known, give vent to, take the wraps off: *The whole issue was thoroughly aired at the meeting.* 2 = **ventilate**, expose, freshen, aerate: *Once a week she cleaned and aired each room.*
▶ *related adjective:* aerial

QUOTATIONS
air: a nutritious substance supplied by a bountiful Providence for the fattening of the poor
[Ambrose Bierce *The Devil's Dictionary*]

PROVERBS
Fresh air keeps the doctor poor

airborne ADJECTIVE = **flying**, floating, soaring, in the air, hovering, gliding, in flight, on the wing, wind-borne, volitant

aircraft NOUN = **plane**, jet, aeroplane, airplane *(U.S. & Canad.)*, airliner, kite *(Brit. slang)*, flying machine

airfield NOUN = **airport**, airstrip, aerodrome, landing strip, air station, airdrome *(U.S.)*

airily ADVERB = **light-heartedly**, happily, blithely, gaily, animatedly, breezily, jauntily, buoyantly, high-spiritedly

airing NOUN 1 = **ventilation**, drying, freshening, aeration: *Open the windows and give the bedroom a good airing.* 2 = **exposure**, display, expression, publicity, vent, utterance, dissemination: *We feel able to talk about sex, but money rarely gets an airing.*

airless ADJECTIVE = **stuffy**, close, heavy, stifling, oppressive, stale, breathless, suffocating, sultry, muggy, unventilated OPPOSITE: airy

airplane NOUN = **plane**, aircraft, jet, aeroplane, airliner, kite *(Brit. slang)*, flying machine

airport NOUN = **airfield**, aerodrome, airdrome *(U.S.)*

airs PLURAL NOUN = **affectation**, arrogance, pretensions, pomposity, swank *(informal)*, hauteur, haughtiness, superciliousness, affectedness: *We're poor and we never put on airs.*

airy ADJECTIVE 1 = **well-ventilated**, open, light, fresh, spacious, windy, lofty, breezy, uncluttered, draughty, gusty, blowy: *The bathroom is light and airy.* OPPOSITE: stuffy 2 = **light-hearted**, light, happy, gay, lively, cheerful, animated, merry, upbeat *(informal)*, buoyant, graceful, cheery, genial, high-spirited, jaunty, chirpy *(informal)*, sprightly, debonair,

nonchalant, blithe, frolicsome: *He sailed past, giving them an airy wave of the hand.* **OPPOSITE:** gloomy
3 = insubstantial, imaginary, visionary, flimsy, fanciful, ethereal, immaterial, illusory, wispy, weightless, incorporeal, vaporous: *'launch aid', an airy euphemism for more state handouts* **OPPOSITE:** real

aisle NOUN **= passageway**, path, lane, passage, corridor, alley, gangway

ajar ADJECTIVE **= open**, gaping, agape, partly open, unclosed

akin ADJECTIVE
akin to = similar to, like, related to, corresponding to, parallel to, comparable to, allied with, analogous to, affiliated with, of a piece with, kin to, cognate with, congenial with, connected with *or* to

alacrity NOUN **= eagerness**, enthusiasm, willingness, readiness, speed, zeal, gaiety, alertness, hilarity, cheerfulness, quickness, liveliness, briskness, promptness, avidity, joyousness, sprightliness
OPPOSITE: reluctance

alarm NOUN **1 = fear**, horror, panic, anxiety, distress, terror, dread, dismay, fright, unease, apprehension, nervousness, consternation, trepidation, uneasiness: *The news was greeted with alarm by MPs.*
OPPOSITE: calmness **2 = danger signal**, warning, bell, alert, siren, alarm bell, hooter, distress signal, tocsin: *As soon as the door opened he heard the alarm go off.*
▷ VERB **= frighten**, shock, scare, panic, distress, terrify, startle, rattle, dismay, daunt, unnerve, terrorize, put the wind up *(informal)*, give (someone) a turn *(informal)*, make (someone's) hair stand on end: *We could not see what had alarmed him.*
OPPOSITE: calm

alarmed ADJECTIVE **= frightened**, troubled, shocked, scared, nervous, disturbed, anxious, distressed, terrified, startled, dismayed, uneasy, fearful, daunted, unnerved, apprehensive, in a panic
OPPOSITE: calm

alarming ADJECTIVE **= frightening**, shocking, scaring, disturbing, distressing, terrifying, appalling, startling, dreadful, horrifying, menacing, intimidating, dismaying, scary *(informal)*, fearful, daunting, fearsome, unnerving, hair-raising, bloodcurdling

albeit CONJUNCTION **= even though**, though, although, even if, notwithstanding, tho' *(U.S. poetic)*

album NOUN **1 = record**, recording, CD, single, release, disc, waxing *(informal)*, LP, vinyl, EP, forty-five, platter *(U.S. slang)*, seventy-eight, gramophone record, black disc: *He has a large collection of albums and cassettes.*
2 = book, collection, scrapbook: *She showed me her photo album.*

alchemy NOUN **= magic**, witchcraft, wizardry, sorcery, makutu *(N.Z.)*

alcohol NOUN **1 = drink**, spirits, liquor, intoxicant, juice *(informal)*, booze *(informal)*, the bottle *(informal)*, grog *(informal, chiefly Austral. & N.Z.)*, the hard stuff *(informal)*, strong drink, Dutch courage *(informal)*, firewater, John Barleycorn, hooch *or* hootch *(informal, chiefly U.S. & Canad.)*: *No alcohol is allowed on the premises.* **2 = ethanol**, ethyl alcohol: *Products for dry skin have little or no alcohol.*
▸ *related mania:* dipsomania

alcoholic NOUN **= drunkard**, drinker, drunk, boozer *(informal)*, toper, soak *(slang)*, lush *(slang)*, sponge *(informal)*, carouser, sot, tippler, wino *(informal)*, inebriate, dipsomaniac, hard drinker, tosspot *(informal)*, alky *(slang)*, alko *or* alco *(Austral. slang)*: *He admitted publicly that he was an alcoholic.*
▷ ADJECTIVE **= intoxicating**, hard, strong, stiff, brewed, fermented, distilled, vinous, inebriating, spirituous, inebriant: *tea, coffee, and alcoholic beverages*

alcove NOUN **= recess**, corner, bay, niche, bower, compartment, cubicle, nook, cubbyhole

alert ADJECTIVE **1 = attentive**, careful, awake, wary, vigilant, perceptive, watchful, ready, on the lookout, circumspect, observant, on guard, wide-awake, on your toes, on the watch, keeping a weather eye on, heedful: *He had been spotted by an alert neighbour.* **OPPOSITE:** careless
2 = quick-witted, spirited, quick, bright, sharp, active, lively, brisk, on the ball *(informal)*, nimble, agile, sprightly, bright-eyed and bushy-tailed *(informal)*: *His grandfather is still alert at 93.*
▷ NOUN **= warning**, signal, alarm, siren: *Due to a security alert, the train did not stop at our station.* **OPPOSITE:** all clear
▷ VERB **= warn**, signal, inform, alarm, notify, tip off, forewarn: *I was hoping he'd alert the police.* **OPPOSITE:** lull

alertness NOUN **= watchfulness**, vigilance, agility, wariness, quickness, liveliness, readiness, circumspection, attentiveness, spiritedness, briskness, nimbleness, perceptiveness, carefulness, sprightliness, promptitude, activeness, heedfulness

alias NOUN **= pseudonym**, pen name, assumed name, stage name, nom de guerre, nom de plume, sock puppet *(Computing)*: *He had rented a house using an alias.*
▷ ADVERB **= also known as**, otherwise, also called, otherwise known as, a.k.a. *(informal)*: *Richard Thorp, alias Alan Turner*

alibi NOUN **= excuse**, reason, defence, explanation, plea, justification, pretext

alien NOUN **= foreigner**, incomer, immigrant, stranger, outsider, newcomer, asylum seeker, outlander: *The woman had hired an illegal alien for child care.* **OPPOSITE:** citizen
▷ ADJECTIVE **1 = foreign**, outside, strange, imported, overseas, unknown, exotic, unfamiliar, not native, not naturalized: *They were afraid of the presence of alien troops in the region.*
2 = strange, new, foreign, novel, remote, unknown, exotic, unfamiliar, estranged, outlandish, untried, unexplored: *His work offers an insight into an alien culture.* **OPPOSITE:** similar
alien to = unfamiliar to, opposed to, contrary to, separated from, conflicting with, incompatible with, inappropriate to, repugnant to, adverse to: *Such an attitude is alien to most businessmen.*

alienate VERB **= antagonize**, anger, annoy, offend, irritate, hassle *(informal)*, gall, repel, estrange, lose the affection of, disaffect, hack off *(informal)*: *The government cannot afford to alienate either group.*

alienation NOUN **= estrangement**, setting against, divorce, withdrawal, separation, turning away, indifference, breaking off, diversion, rupture, disaffection, remoteness

alight[1] VERB **1 = get off**, descend, get down, disembark, dismount: *Two men alighted from the vehicle.* **2 = land**, light, settle, come down, descend, perch, touch down, come to rest: *A thrush alighted on a branch of the pine tree.*
OPPOSITE: take off

alight[2] ADJECTIVE **1 = lit up**, bright, brilliant, shining, illuminated, fiery: *Her face was alight with happiness.* **2 = on fire**, ignited, set ablaze, lit, burning, aflame, blazing, flaming, flaring: *The rioters set several buildings alight.*

align VERB **1 = ally**, side, join, associate, affiliate, cooperate, sympathize: *The prime minister is aligning himself with the liberals.* **2 = line up**, even, order, range, sequence, regulate, straighten, coordinate, even up, make parallel, arrange in line: *A tripod would be useful to align and steady the camera.*

alignment NOUN **1 = alliance**, union, association, agreement, sympathy, cooperation, affiliation: *His alignment with the old administration cost him the election.* **2 = lining up**, line, order, ranging, arrangement, evening, sequence, regulating, adjustment, coordination, straightening up, evening up: *a link between the alignment of the planets and events on earth*

alike ADJECTIVE **= similar**, close, the same, equal, equivalent, uniform, parallel, resembling, identical, corresponding, akin, duplicate, analogous, homogeneous, of a piece, cut from the same cloth, like two peas in a pod: *We are very alike.*
OPPOSITE: different
▷ ADVERB **= similarly**, identically, equally, uniformly, correspondingly, analogously: *They even dressed alike.*
OPPOSITE: differently

alive ADJECTIVE **1 = living**, breathing, animate, having life, subsisting, existing, functioning, alive and kicking, in the land of the living (*informal*): *She does not know if he is alive or dead.* **OPPOSITE:** dead **2 = in existence**, existing, functioning, active, operative, in force, on-going, prevalent, existent, extant: *Factories are trying to stay alive by cutting costs.* **OPPOSITE:** inoperative **3 = lively**, spirited, active, vital, alert, eager, quick, awake, vigorous, cheerful, energetic, animated, brisk, agile, perky, chirpy (*informal*), sprightly, vivacious, full of life, spry, full of beans (*informal*), zestful: *I never expected to feel so alive in my life again.* **OPPOSITE:** dull
alive to = aware of, sensitive to, susceptible to, alert to, eager for, awake to, cognizant of, sensible of: *You must be alive to opportunity!*

all DETERMINER **1 = the whole amount**, everything, the whole, the total, the sum, the total amount, the aggregate, the totality, the sum total, the entirety, the entire amount, the complete amount: *I'd spent all I had, every last penny.* **2 = every**, each, every single, every one of, each and every: *There is built-in storage space in all bedrooms.*
▷ ADJECTIVE **= complete**, greatest, full, total, perfect, entire, utter: *In all fairness, she isn't dishonest.*
▷ ADVERB **= completely**, totally, fully, entirely, absolutely, altogether, wholly, utterly
▸ *related prefixes:* pan-, panto-

allay VERB **= reduce**, quiet, relax, ease, calm, smooth, relieve, check, moderate, dull, diminish, compose, soften, blunt, soothe, subdue, lessen, alleviate, appease, quell, mitigate, assuage, pacify, mollify

allegation NOUN **= claim**, charge, statement, profession, declaration, plea, accusation, assertion, affirmation, deposition, avowal, asseveration, averment

allege VERB **= claim**, hold, charge, challenge, state, maintain, advance, declare, assert, uphold, put forward, affirm, profess, depose, avow, aver, asseverate **OPPOSITE:** deny

alleged ADJECTIVE **= claimed**, supposed, declared, assumed, so-called, apparent, rumoured, stated, described, asserted, designated, presumed, affirmed, professed, reputed, hypothetical, putative, presupposed, averred, unproved

allegedly ADVERB **= supposedly**, apparently, reportedly, by all accounts, reputedly, purportedly

allegiance NOUN **= loyalty**, duty, obligation, devotion, fidelity, homage, obedience, adherence, constancy, faithfulness, troth (*archaic*), fealty **OPPOSITE:** disloyalty

PROVERBS
You cannot run with the hare and hunt with the hounds

allegorical ADJECTIVE **= symbolic**, figurative, symbolizing, emblematic, parabolic

allegory NOUN **= symbol**, story, tale, myth, symbolism, emblem, fable, parable, apologue

allergic ADJECTIVE **= sensitive**, affected, susceptible, sensitized, hypersensitive: *I'm allergic to cats.*
allergic to = averse to, opposed to, hostile to, loath to, disinclined to, antipathetic to: *He was allergic to risk.*

allergy NOUN **1 = sensitivity**, reaction, susceptibility, antipathy, hypersensitivity, sensitiveness: *Food allergies result in many and varied symptoms.* **2 = dislike**, hatred, hostility, aversion, loathing, disgust, antipathy, animosity, displeasure, antagonism, distaste, enmity, opposition, repugnance, disinclination: *I developed an allergy to the company of couples.*

alleviate VERB **= ease**, reduce, relieve, moderate, smooth, dull, diminish, soften, check, blunt, soothe, subdue, lessen, lighten, quell, allay, mitigate, abate, slacken, assuage, quench, mollify, slake, palliate

alley NOUN **= passage**, walk, lane, pathway, alleyway, passageway, backstreet

alliance NOUN **= union**, league, association, agreement, marriage, connection, combination, coalition, treaty, partnership, federation, pact, compact, confederation, affinity, affiliation, confederacy, concordat **OPPOSITE:** division

allied ADJECTIVE **1 = united**, joined, linked, related, married, joint, combined, bound, integrated, unified, affiliated, leagued, confederate, amalgamated, cooperating, in league, hand in glove (*informal*), in cahoots (*U.S. informal*): *forces from three allied nations* **2 = connected**, joined, linked, tied, related, associated, syndicated, affiliated, kindred: *doctors and other allied medical professionals*

all-important ADJECTIVE **= essential**, central, significant, key, necessary, vital, critical, crucial, pivotal, momentous, consequential

allocate VERB **= assign**, grant, distribute, designate, set aside, earmark, give out, consign, allow, budget, allot, mete, share out, apportion, appropriate

allocation NOUN **1 = allowance**, share, measure, grant, portion, quota, lot, ration, stint, stipend: *During rationing we had a sugar allocation.* **2 = assignment**, allowance, rationing, allotment, apportionment, appropriation: *Town planning and land allocation had to be co-ordinated.*

allot VERB **= assign**, allocate, designate, set aside, earmark, mete, share out, apportion, budget, appropriate

allotment NOUN **1 = plot**, patch, tract, kitchen garden: *He was just back from a hard morning's toil on his allotment.* **2 = assignment**, share, measure, grant, allowance, portion, quota, lot, ration, allocation, stint, appropriation, stipend, apportionment: *His meagre allotment of gas had to be saved for emergencies.*

allotted VERB **= assigned**, given, allocated, designated, set aside, earmarked, apportioned

all-out or **all out** ADJECTIVE **= total**, full, complete, determined, supreme, maximum, outright, thorough, unlimited, full-scale, optimum, exhaustive, resolute, full-on (*informal*), unrestrained, unremitting, thoroughgoing, unstinted: *He launched an all-out attack on his critics.* **OPPOSITE:** half-hearted
▷ ADVERB **= energetically**, hard, strongly, sharply, heavily, severely, fiercely, vigorously, intensely, violently, powerfully, forcibly, forcefully, with all your might, with might and main: *We will be going all out to make sure it doesn't happen again.*

allow VERB **1 = permit**, approve, enable, sanction, endure, license, brook, endorse, warrant, tolerate, put up with (*informal*), authorize, stand, suffer, bear: *Smoking will not be allowed.* **OPPOSITE:** prohibit **2 = let**, permit, sanction, authorize, license, tolerate, consent to, countenance, concede to, assent to, give leave to, give the green light for, give a blank cheque to: *He allows her to drive his Mercedes 300SE.* **OPPOSITE:** forbid **3 = give**, provide, grant, spare, devote, assign, allocate, set aside, deduct, earmark, remit, allot: *Please allow 28 days for delivery.* **4 = acknowledge**, accept, admit, grant, recognize, yield, concede, confess, acquiesce: *He allows that the development may result in social inequality.*
allow for something = take into account, consider, plan for, accommodate, provide for, arrange for, foresee, make provision for, make allowances for, make concessions for, keep in mind, set something aside for, take into consideration: *You have to allow for a certain amount of error.*

allowable ADJECTIVE **= permissible**, all right, approved, appropriate, suitable, acceptable, tolerable, admissible, sufferable, sanctionable

allowance NOUN **1 = portion**, lot, share, amount, measure, grant, pension, subsidy, quota, allocation, stint, annuity, allotment, remittance, stipend, apportionment: *He lives on an allowance of £70 a week.* **2 = pocket money**, grant, fee, payment, consideration, ration, handout, remittance: *The boy was given an allowance for his own needs.* **3 = concession**, discount, reduction, repayment, deduction, rebate: *those earning less than the basic tax allowance*

alloy NOUN = **mixture**, combination, compound, blend, hybrid, composite, amalgam, meld, admixture: *Bronze is an alloy of copper and tin.*

all right ADJECTIVE **1 = satisfactory**, O.K. *or* okay *(informal)*, average, fair, sufficient, standard, acceptable, good enough, adequate, so-so *(informal)*, up to scratch *(informal)*, passable, up to standard, up to the mark, unobjectionable: *'How was the school you attended?' 'It was all right.'*
OPPOSITE: unsatisfactory
2 = well, O.K. *or* okay *(informal)*, strong, whole, sound, fit, safe, healthy, hale, unharmed, out of the woods, uninjured, unimpaired, up to par: *Are you all right now?* **OPPOSITE:** ill
▷ ADVERB = **satisfactorily**, O.K. *or* okay *(informal)*, reasonably, well enough, adequately, suitably, acceptably, passably, unobjectionably: *Things have thankfully worked out all right.*

allude to VERB = **refer to**, suggest, mention, speak of, imply, intimate, hint at, remark on, insinuate, touch upon

allure NOUN = **attractiveness**, appeal, charm, attraction, lure, temptation, glamour, persuasion, enchantment, enticement, seductiveness: *It's a game that has really lost its allure.*
▷ VERB = **attract**, persuade, charm, win over, tempt, lure, seduce, entice, enchant, lead on, coax, captivate, beguile, cajole, decoy, inveigle: *The dog was allured by the smell of roasting meat.*

alluring ADJECTIVE = **attractive**, fascinating, enchanting, seductive, tempting, sexy, intriguing, fetching, glamorous, captivating, beguiling, bewitching, come-hither, hot *(informal)* **OPPOSITE:** unattractive

allusion NOUN = **reference**, mention, suggestion, hint, implication, innuendo, intimation, insinuation, casual remark, indirect reference

ally NOUN = **partner**, friend, colleague, associate, mate, accessory, comrade, helper, collaborator, accomplice, confederate, co-worker, bedfellow, cobber *(Austral. & N.Z. old-fashioned, informal)*, coadjutor, abettor, E hoa *(N.Z.)*: *He is a close ally of the Prime Minister.* **OPPOSITE:** opponent
ally yourself with something *or* **someone = unite with**, join, associate with, connect with, unify, league with, affiliate with, collaborate with, join forces with, confederate, band together with: *He will have to ally himself with the new movement.*

almighty ADJECTIVE **1 = all-powerful**, supreme, absolute, unlimited, invincible, omnipotent: *Let us now confess our sins to Almighty God.*
OPPOSITE: powerless **2 = great**, terrible, enormous, desperate, severe, intense, awful, loud, excessive: *I had the most almighty row with the waitress.*
OPPOSITE: slight

almost ADVERB = **nearly**, about, approaching, close to, virtually, practically, roughly, all but, just about, not quite, on the brink of, not far from, approximately, well-nigh, as good as

alms PLURAL NOUN = **donation**, relief, gift, charity, bounty, benefaction, koha *(N.Z.)*

aloft ADVERB **1 = in the air**, up, higher, above, overhead, in the sky, on high, high up, up above: *Four of the nine balloons were still aloft the next day.*
2 = upward, skyward, heavenward: *He lifted the cup aloft.*

alone ADJECTIVE **1 = solitary**, isolated, sole, separate, apart, abandoned, detached, by yourself, unattended, unaccompanied, out on a limb, unescorted, on your tod *(slang)*: *He was all alone in the middle of the hall.*
OPPOSITE: accompanied **2 = lonely**, abandoned, deserted, isolated, solitary, estranged, desolate, forsaken, forlorn, destitute, lonesome *(chiefly U.S. & Canad.)*, friendless: *Never in her life had she felt so alone.*
▷ ADVERB **1 = solely**, only, individually, singly, exclusively, uniquely: *You alone should determine what is right for you.*
2 = by yourself, independently, unaided, unaccompanied, without help, on your own, unassisted, without assistance, under your own steam: *He was working alone, and did not have an accomplice.* **OPPOSITE:** with help

> **QUOTATIONS**
> I want to be alone
> [Greta Garbo *Grand Hotel (film)*]

aloof ADJECTIVE = **distant**, cold, reserved, cool, formal, remote, forbidding, detached, indifferent, chilly, unfriendly, unsympathetic, uninterested, haughty, unresponsive, supercilious, unapproachable, unsociable, standoffish
OPPOSITE: friendly

aloud ADVERB = **out loud**, clearly, plainly, distinctly, audibly, intelligibly

alphabet NOUN = **letters**, script, writing system, syllabary

already ADVERB = **before now**, before, previously, at present, by now, by then, even now, by this time, just now, by that time, heretofore, as of now

also ADVERB = **and**, too, further, plus, along with, in addition, as well, moreover, besides, furthermore, what's more, on top of that, to boot, additionally, into the bargain, as well as

alter VERB **1 = modify**, change, reform, shift, vary, transform, adjust, adapt, revise, amend, diversify, remodel, tweak *(informal)*, recast, reshape, metamorphose, transmute: *They have never altered their programmes.*
2 = change, turn, vary, transform, adjust, adapt, metamorphose: *Little had altered in the village.*

alteration NOUN **1 = change**, adjustment, shift, amendment, conversion, modification: *Making some simple alterations to your diet will make you feel fitter.* **2 = adjustment**, change, amendment, variation, conversion, transformation, adaptation, difference, revision, modification, remodelling, reformation, diversification, metamorphosis, variance, reshaping, transmutation: *Her jacket and skirt were still awaiting alteration.*

altercation NOUN = **argument**, row, clash, disagreement, dispute, controversy, contention, quarrel, squabble, wrangle, bickering, discord, dissension

alternate VERB **1 = interchange**, change, alter, fluctuate, intersperse, take turns, oscillate, chop and change, follow one another, follow in turn: *Her gentle moods alternated with calmer states.* **2 = intersperse**, interchange, exchange, swap, stagger, rotate: *Now you just alternate layers of that mixture and eggplant.*
▷ ADJECTIVE **1 = alternating**, interchanging, every other, rotating, every second, sequential: *They were streaked with alternate bands of colour.*
2 = substitute, alternative, other, different, replacement, complementary: *alternate forms of medical treatment*
▷ NOUN = **substitute**, reserve, deputy, relief, replacement, stand-by, makeshift: *In most jurisdictions, twelve jurors and two alternates are chosen.*

alternating ADJECTIVE = **interchanging**, changing, shifting, swinging, rotating, fluctuating, occurring by turns, oscillating, vacillating, seesawing

alternative NOUN = **substitute**, choice, other, option, preference, recourse: *New treatments may provide an alternative to painkillers.*
▷ ADJECTIVE = **different**, other, substitute, alternate: *There were alternative methods of transport available.*

alternatively ADVERB = **or**, instead, otherwise, on the other hand, if not, then again, as an alternative, by way of alternative, as another option

although CONJUNCTION = **though**, while, even if, even though, whilst, albeit, despite the fact that, notwithstanding, even supposing, tho' *(U.S. poetic)*

altitude NOUN = **height**, summit, peak, elevation, loftiness

altogether ADVERB **1 = absolutely**, quite, completely, totally, perfectly, fully, thoroughly, wholly, utterly, downright, one hundred per cent *(informal)*, undisputedly, lock, stock and barrel: *She wasn't altogether sorry to be leaving.* **2 = completely**, all, fully, entirely, comprehensively, thoroughly, wholly, every inch, one hundred per cent *(informal)*, in every respect: *The choice of language is altogether different.* **OPPOSITE:** partially **3 = on the whole**, generally, mostly, in general, collectively, all things considered, on average, for the most part, all in all, on balance, in toto *(Latin)*, as a whole: *Altogether, it was a delightful town garden.* **4 = in total**, in all, all told, taken together, in sum, everything included, in toto *(Latin)*: *Altogether seven inmates escaped.*

USAGE
The single-word form *altogether* should not be used as an alternative to *all together* because the meanings are very distinct. *Altogether* is an adverb meaning 'absolutely' or, in a different sense, 'in total'. *All together*, however, means 'all at the same time' or 'all in the same place'. The distinction can be seen in the following example: *altogether there were six or seven families sharing the flat's facilities* means 'in total', while *there were six or seven families all together in one flat*, means 'all crowded in together'.

altruism NOUN **= selflessness**, charity, consideration, goodwill, generosity, self-sacrifice, philanthropy, benevolence, magnanimity, humanitarianism, unselfishness, beneficence, charitableness, greatheartedness, bigheartedness **OPPOSITE:** self-interest

altruistic ADJECTIVE **= selfless**, generous, humanitarian, charitable, benevolent, considerate, self-sacrificing, philanthropic, unselfish, public-spirited **OPPOSITE:** self-interested

always ADVERB **1 = habitually**, regularly, every time, inevitably, consistently, invariably, aye *(Scot.)*, perpetually, without exception, customarily, unfailingly, on every occasion, day in, day out: *Always lock your garage.* **OPPOSITE:** seldom
2 = forever, for keeps, eternally, for all time, evermore, till the cows come home *(informal)*, till Doomsday
3 = continually, constantly, all the time, forever, repeatedly, aye *(Scot.)*, endlessly, persistently, eternally, perpetually, incessantly, interminably, unceasingly, everlastingly, in perpetuum *(Latin)*: *She was always moving things around.*

amalgam NOUN **= combination**, mixture, compound, blend, union, composite, fusion, alloy, amalgamation, meld, admixture

amalgamate VERB **= combine**, unite, ally, compound, blend, incorporate, integrate, merge, fuse, mingle, alloy, coalesce, meld, commingle, intermix **OPPOSITE:** divide

amalgamation NOUN **= combination**, union, joining, mixing, alliance, coalition, merger, mixture, compound, blend, integration, composite, fusion, mingling, alloy, amalgamating, incorporation, amalgam, meld, admixture, commingling

amass VERB **= collect**, gather, assemble, compile, accumulate, aggregate, pile up, garner, hoard, scrape together, rake up, heap up

amateur NOUN **= nonprofessional**, outsider, layman, dilettante, layperson, non-specialist, dabbler

amateurish ADJECTIVE **= unprofessional**, amateur, crude, bungling, clumsy, inexpert, unaccomplished, unskilful **OPPOSITE:** professional

amaze VERB **= astonish**, surprise, shock, stun, alarm, stagger, startle, bewilder, astound, daze, confound, stupefy, flabbergast, bowl someone over *(informal)*, boggle someone's mind, dumbfound

amazement NOUN **= astonishment**, surprise, wonder, shock, confusion, admiration, awe, marvel, bewilderment, wonderment, perplexity, stupefaction

amazing ADJECTIVE **= astonishing**, striking, surprising, brilliant, stunning, impressive, overwhelming, staggering, sensational *(informal)*, bewildering, breathtaking, astounding, eye-opening, wondrous *(archaic, literary)*, mind-boggling, jaw-dropping, stupefying

ambassador NOUN **= representative**, minister, agent, deputy, diplomat, envoy, consul, attaché, emissary, legate, plenipotentiary

QUOTATIONS
An ambassador is an honest man sent to lie abroad for the commonwealth
[Henry Wotton]

ambience NOUN **= atmosphere**, feel, setting, air, quality, character, spirit, surroundings, tone, mood, impression, flavour, temper, tenor, aura, complexion, vibes *(slang)*, vibrations *(slang)*, milieu

ambiguity NOUN **= vagueness**, doubt, puzzle, uncertainty, obscurity, enigma, equivocation, inconclusiveness, indefiniteness, dubiety, dubiousness, tergiversation, indeterminateness, equivocality, doubtfulness, equivocacy

ambiguous ADJECTIVE **= unclear**, puzzling, uncertain, obscure, vague, doubtful, dubious, enigmatic, indefinite, inconclusive, cryptic, indeterminate, equivocal, Delphic, oracular, enigmatical, clear as mud *(informal)* **OPPOSITE:** clear

ambition NOUN **1 = goal**, end, hope, design, dream, target, aim, wish, purpose, desire, intention, objective, intent, aspiration, Holy Grail *(informal)*: *His ambition is to sail round the world.* **2 = enterprise**, longing, drive, fire, spirit, desire, passion, enthusiasm, warmth, striving, initiative, aspiration, yearning, devotion, zeal, verve, zest, fervour, eagerness, gusto, hankering, get-up-and-go *(informal)*, ardour, keenness, avidity, fervency: *a mixture of ambition and ruthlessness*

QUOTATIONS
Ambition is the growth of every clime
[William Blake *King Edward the Third*]

Well is it known that ambition can creep as well as soar
[Edmund Burke *Letters on a Regicide Peace*]

Ambition, in a private man a vice,
Is in a prince the virtue
[Philip Massinger *The Bashful Lover*]

Ambition must be made to counteract ambition
[James Madison *The Federalist Papers*]

Ah, but a man's reach should exceed his grasp,
Or what's a Heaven for?
[Robert Browning *Andrea del Sarto*]

The glorious fault of angels and gods
[Alexander Pope *Elegy to the Memory of an Unfortunate Lady*]

PROVERBS
Every eel hopes to become a whale

ambitious ADJECTIVE
1 = enterprising, spirited, keen, active, daring, eager, intent, enthusiastic, hopeful, striving, vigorous, aspiring, energetic, adventurous, avid, zealous, intrepid, resourceful, purposeful, desirous: *He's a very ambitious lad.*
OPPOSITE: unambitious
2 = demanding, trying, hard, taxing, difficult, challenging, tough, severe, impressive, exhausting, exacting, bold, elaborate, formidable, energetic, strenuous, pretentious, arduous, grandiose, industrious: *Their goal was extraordinarily ambitious.*
OPPOSITE: modest

ambivalence NOUN **= indecision**, doubt, opposition, conflict, uncertainty, contradiction, wavering, fluctuation, hesitancy, equivocation, vacillation, irresolution

ambivalent ADJECTIVE **= undecided**, mixed, conflicting, opposed, uncertain, doubtful, unsure, contradictory, wavering, unresolved, fluctuating, hesitant, inconclusive, debatable, equivocal, vacillating, warring, irresolute
OPPOSITE: definite

amble VERB **= stroll**, walk, wander, ramble, meander, saunter, dawdle, mosey *(informal)*

ambush VERB **= trap**, attack, surprise, deceive, dupe, ensnare, waylay, ambuscade, bushwhack *(U.S.)*: *Rebels ambushed and killed 10 patrolmen.*
▷ NOUN **= trap**, snare, attack, lure, waylaying, ambuscade: *A policeman has been shot dead in an ambush.*

The Language of Wilkie Collins

A prolific writer of so-called sensation novels, William Wilkie Collins (1824–89), is regarded by many as the father of detective fiction. Among his best-known works are *The Woman in White*, *The Moonstone*, *Armadale* and *No Name*, all of which were first serialized in periodicals before appearing in book form.

Even though it is about a century and a half since they were written, Collins' popular novels still read easily and excitingly, and draw in the modern reader with their suspense, mystery, flowing lines and relatively short sentences. He believed there to be 'two main elements in the attraction of all stories – the interest of curiosity, and the excitement of surprise' and, because many of his novels were originally serialized, Collins had to ensure that his readers would want to read on after each instalment. Unusually, in both *The Moonstone* and *The Woman in White* the stories are told through a series of first-person accounts by different narrators, something which brings a sense of immediacy.

For a present-day reader, while the texts read very easily and fluidly, there are little linguistic details that remind us that the language, not to mention the world, has moved on since Collins' time: for example, characters *borrow* money *of* people rather than *from* them; and they would *fain have* done certain things; there are many references to *scoundrels*, a word that seems rather dated now; and a *fly* may refer to a hirable carriage. Certain spellings too are no longer current (*to-day, to-morrow, in the mean while*). Very often, the formal register of certain Latinate words seems unwarranted to us today when a more neutral or common alternative would seem more natural:

> We could only find time to pursue this occupation by sitting up late at night.

> His next proceeding was stranger still.

> On returning from Mrs. Vesey's, I instructed Marian to write (observing the same caution which I practised myself) to Mrs. Michelson.

In *The Haunted Hotel* there is a reference to middle age which suggests that in Collins' day, the middle years may have been thought to start much earlier than in our times:

> She was dressed in dark colours, with perfect taste; she was of middle height, and (apparently) of middle age – say a year or two over thirty.

In Collins' time, *sex* never referred to anything so vulgar as sexual intercourse; as today, it often indicated the category of being male or female, especially female (*the female sex, her sex*) and the expression *the sex* was sometimes used to refer to women:

> The doctor laughed softly. 'So like a woman!' he remarked, with the most exasperating good humour. 'The moment she sees her object, she dashes at it headlong the nearest way. Oh, **the sex**! **the sex**!'

> 'Never mind **the sex**!' I broke out, impatiently. 'I want a serious answer – Yes or No?'

> The opinion which declares that vanity is a failing peculiar to **the sex** is a slander on women.

In Collins' writings, characters make many references to *the gentle sex, the fair sex, the weaker sex, the enchanting sex, the soft sex*, and so on, expressions that in the past would not have jarred as much as now, as these days they tend to be avoided except in ironic, humorous, or misogynistic language by all but the most old-fashioned. As Collins was an advocate of female rights (and also of the rights of other groups whose treatment he considered unfair), and as he increasingly used his novels to point out social injustice, one may detect a certain irony in some of the more disparaging remarks about women, especially when uttered by strong, reliable female characters such as Marian Halcombe in *The Woman in White*:

> We are such fools, we can't entertain each other at table. You see I don't think much of my own sex, Mr. Hartright – which will you have, tea or coffee? – no woman does think much of her own sex, although few of them confess it as freely as I do.

> Women can't draw – their minds are too flighty, and their eyes are too inattentive.

a

ameliorate VERB = **improve**, better, benefit, reform, advance, promote, amend, elevate, raise, mend, mitigate, make better, assuage, meliorate

> USAGE
> *Ameliorate* is sometimes confused with *alleviate* but the words are not synonymous. *Ameliorate* comes ultimately from the Latin for 'better', and means 'to improve'. The nouns it typically goes with are *condition* and *situation*. *Alleviate* means 'to lessen', and frequently occurs with *poverty*, *suffering*, *pain*, *symptoms*, and *effects*. Occasionally *ameliorate* is used with *effects* and *poverty* where the other verb may be more appropriate.

amenable ADJECTIVE = **receptive**, open, susceptible, responsive, agreeable, compliant, tractable, acquiescent, persuadable, able to be influenced **OPPOSITE:** stubborn

amend VERB = **change**, improve, reform, fix, correct, repair, edit, alter, enhance, update, revise, modify, remedy, rewrite, mend, rectify, tweak *(informal)*, ameliorate, redraw: *The committee put forward proposals to amend the penal system.*

amendment NOUN **1 = addition**, change, adjustment, attachment, adaptation, revision, modification, alteration, remodelling, reformation, clarification, adjunct, addendum: *an amendment to the defence bill* **2 = change**, improvement, repair, edit, remedy, correction, revision, modification, alteration, mending, enhancement, reform, betterment, rectification, amelioration, emendation: *We are making a few amendments to the document.*

amends PLURAL NOUN = **compensation**, apology, restoration, redress, reparation, indemnity, restitution, atonement, recompense, expiation, requital: *He wanted to make amends for causing their marriage to fail.*

amenity NOUN **1 = facility**, service, advantage, comfort, convenience: *The hotel amenities include a health club and banqueting rooms.* **2 = refinement**, politeness, affability, amiability, courtesy, mildness, pleasantness, suavity, agreeableness, complaisance: *a man of little amenity* **OPPOSITE:** rudeness

American ADJECTIVE = **Yankee** *or* **Yank**, U.S.: *the American ambassador at the UN* ▷ NOUN = **Yankee** *or* **Yank**, Yankee Doodle: *The 1990 Nobel Prize for medicine was won by two Americans.* ▷ *See themed panel* **English and American Equivalences** *on facing page*

> QUOTATIONS
> I am willing to love all mankind, except an American
> [Dr. Johnson]
>
> Good Americans, when they die, go to Paris
> [Thomas Gold Appleton]

amiable ADJECTIVE = **pleasant**, kind, kindly, pleasing, friendly, attractive, engaging, charming, obliging, delightful, cheerful, benign, winning, agreeable, good-humoured, lovable, sociable, genial, affable, congenial, winsome, good-natured, sweet-tempered, likable *or* likeable **OPPOSITE:** unfriendly

amicable ADJECTIVE = **friendly**, kindly, brotherly, civil, neighbourly, peaceful, polite, harmonious, good-humoured, amiable, courteous, cordial, sociable, fraternal, peaceable **OPPOSITE:** unfriendly

amid *or* **amidst** PREPOSITION **1 = during**, among, at a time of, in an atmosphere of: *He cancelled a foreign trip amid growing concerns of a domestic crisis.* **2 = in the middle of**, among, surrounded by, amongst, in the midst of, in the thick of: *a tiny bungalow amid clusters of trees*

amiss ADJECTIVE = **wrong**, mistaken, confused, false, inappropriate, rotten, incorrect, faulty, inaccurate, unsuitable, improper, defective, out of order, awry, erroneous, untoward, fallacious: *Their instincts warned them something was amiss.* **OPPOSITE:** right

take something amiss = take as an insult, take wrongly, take as offensive, take out of turn: *He took it amiss when I asked to speak to someone else.*

ammunition NOUN = **munitions**, rounds, shot, shells, powder, explosives, cartridges, armaments, materiel, shot and shell

amnesty NOUN = **general pardon**, mercy, pardoning, immunity, forgiveness, reprieve, oblivion, remission, clemency, dispensation, absolution, condonation

amok *or* **amuck** ADVERB
run amok = go mad, go wild, turn violent, go berserk, lose control, go insane, go into a frenzy

among *or* **amongst** PREPOSITION **1 = in the midst of**, with, together with, in the middle of, amid, surrounded by, amidst, in the thick of: *They walked among the crowds in the large town square.* **2 = in the group of**, one of, part of, included in, in the company of, in the class of, in the number of: *Among the speakers was the new American ambassador.* **3 = between**, to: *Most of the furniture was distributed among friends.* **4 = with one another**, mutually, by all of, by the whole of, by the joint action of: *The directors have been arguing amongst themselves.*

amoral ADJECTIVE = **unethical**, nonmoral, unvirtuous

> USAGE
> *Amoral* is sometimes confused with *immoral*. The *a-* at the beginning of the word means 'without' or 'lacking', so the word is properly used of people who have no moral code, or about places or situations where moral considerations do not apply: *the film was violent and amoral*. In contrast *immoral* should be used to talk about the breaking of moral rules, as in: *drug dealing is the most immoral and evil of all human activities.*

amorous ADJECTIVE = **loving**, in love, tender, passionate, fond, erotic, affectionate, ardent, impassioned, doting, enamoured, lustful, attached, lovesick, amatory **OPPOSITE:** cold

amorphous ADJECTIVE = **shapeless**, vague, irregular, nondescript, indeterminate, unstructured, nebulous, formless, inchoate, characterless, unformed, unshaped, unshapen **OPPOSITE:** definite

amount NOUN **1 = quantity**, lot, measure, size, supply, mass, volume, capacity, extent, bulk, number, magnitude, expanse: *I still do a certain amount of work for them.* **2 = total**, whole, mass, addition, sum, lot, extent, aggregate, entirety, totality, sum total: *If you always pay the full amount, this won't affect you.*

amount to something 1 = add up to, mean, total, equal, constitute, comprise, aggregate, purport, be equivalent to: *The banks have what amounts to a monopoly.* **2 = come to**, become, grow to, develop into, advance to, progress to, mature into: *My music teacher said I'd never amount to anything.*

> PROVERBS
> *Many a mickle makes a muckle*

> USAGE
> Although it is common to use a plural noun after *amount of*, for example in *the amount of people* and *the amount of goods*, this should be avoided. Preferred alternatives would be to use *quantity*, as in *the quantity of people*, or *number*, as in *the number of goods*.

amour NOUN = **love affair**, relationship, affair, romance, intrigue, liaison, affaire de coeur *(French)*

ample ADJECTIVE **1 = plenty of**, great, rich, liberal, broad, generous, lavish, spacious, abounding, abundant, plentiful, expansive, copious, roomy, unrestricted, voluminous, capacious, profuse, commodious, plenteous: *The design gave ample space for a good-sized kitchen.* **OPPOSITE:** insufficient **2 = large**, great, big, full, wide, broad, extensive, generous, abundant, voluminous, bountiful: *a young mother with a baby resting against her ample bosom*

amplification NOUN **1 = increase**, boosting, stretching, strengthening, expansion, extension, widening, raising, heightening, deepening, lengthening, enlargement, intensification, magnification, dilation, augmentation: *a voice that needed no amplification* **2 = explanation**, development, expansion, supplementing, fleshing out, elaboration, rounding out,

ENGLISH AND AMERICAN EQUIVALENCES

English	American	English	American	English	American
aeroplane	airplane	estate agent	realtor	pub *or* public house	bar
American football	football	estate car	station wagon	public school	private school
antenatal	prenatal	fire lighter	fire starter	purse	pocketbook
aubergine	eggplant	first floor	second floor	pushchair	stroller
autumn	fall	flat	apartment	quaver	eighth note
bad-tempered	mean	flick knife	switch blade	quilt *or* eiderdown	comforter
banknote	bill	football	soccer	railway	railroad
bat	paddle	foyer	lobby	receptionist	desk clerk
benefit	welfare	fringe	bangs	reverse charge	collect
bin *or* dustbin	trashcan	garden	yard	ring road	beltway
biscuit	cookie	gear lever	stick shift	roll *or* bap	bun
black pudding	blood sausage	goose pimples	goose bumps	rubber	eraser
blinds	shades	ground floor	first floor	rubbish	trash *or* garbage
bonnet (car)	hood	hair grip	bobby pin	semibreve	whole note
boot (car)	trunk	hairpin bend	switchback	semi-detached	duplex
braces (teeth)	retainer	handbag	purse	semiquaver	sixteenth note
braces (lingerie)	suspenders	hessian	burlap	shop	store
breve	double whole note	high street	main street	silencer	muffler
broad bean	fava bean	holiday	vacation	skip	dumpster
building society	savings and loan	indicator	blinker	skirting board	baseboard
burgle	burglarize	invigilator	proctor	sleeper (railway)	tie
candy floss	cotton candy	ironmonger	hardware store	slowcoach	slowpoke
car	automobile	jam	jelly	soft drink	soda
car park	parking lot	janitor	caretaker	spanner	wrench
chemist	drug store	lawyer	attorney	spring onion *or* salad onion	scallion
chips	French fries	lift	elevator	state school	public school
clothes peg	clothes pin	mangetout	snowpea	stream	creek
coffin	casket	mate	friend	surgical spirit	rubbing alcohol
condom	rubber	merry-go-round	carousel	sweet	candy
cornflour	corn starch	methylated spirits	denatured alcohol	tap	faucet
courgette	zucchini	mince	ground beef	tarmac	asphalt
crisps	chips *or* potato chips	minim	half note	telegram	wire
crossroads	intersection	nappy	diaper	thread	cotton
crotchet	quarter note	neat (of drinks)	straight	tights	pantihose
current account	checking account	noughts and crosses	tick-tack-toe	timber	lumber
curtains	drapes	nursery	kindergarten	torch	flashlight
cutlery	flatware *or* silverware	off-licence	liquor store	town centre	downtown
CV	résumé	paraffin	kerosene	trainers	sneakers
dialling code	area code	pavement	sidewalk	tram	streetcar
dinner jacket	tuxedo	pepper	bell pepper	trousers	pants
double cream	heavy cream	petrol	gas *or* gasoline	turn up	cuff
drapery	dry goods	pissed	drunk	VAT	sales tax
draughts	checkers	plait	braid	vest	undershirt
drawing pin	thumb tack	plasterboard	dry lining	waistcoast	vest
dressing gown	robe	plot	lot	windscreen	windshield
dummy	pacifier *or* soother	porridge	oatmeal		
engaged tone	busy signal	postcode	zip code		
		postman	mail man		

augmentation, expatiation: *They demanded amplification of the imprecise statement.*

amplify VERB **1 = expand**, raise, extend, boost, stretch, strengthen, increase, widen, intensify, heighten, deepen, enlarge, lengthen, magnify, augment, dilate: *The music was amplified with microphones.* **OPPOSITE:** reduce **2 = go into detail**, develop, explain, expand, supplement, elaborate, augment, flesh out, round out, enlarge on, expatiate: *Intelligent guesswork must be used to amplify the facts.* **OPPOSITE:** simplify

amplitude NOUN **1 = extent**, reach, range, size, mass, sweep, dimension, bulk, scope, width, magnitude, compass, greatness, breadth, expanse, vastness, spaciousness, bigness, largeness, hugeness, capaciousness: *a man of great amplitude* **2 = fullness**, abundance, richness, plethora, profusion, completeness, plenitude, copiousness, ampleness: *The character comes to imply an amplitude of meanings.*

amply ADVERB **= fully**, well, greatly, completely, richly, liberally, thoroughly, substantially, lavishly, extensively, generously, abundantly, profusely, copiously, plentifully, unstintingly, bountifully, without stinting, plenteously, capaciously **OPPOSITE:** insufficiently

amputate VERB **= cut off**, remove, separate, sever, curtail, truncate, lop off: *To save his life, doctors amputated his legs.*

amuck *see* **amock**

amuse VERB **1 = entertain**, please, delight, charm, cheer, tickle, gratify, beguile, enliven, regale, gladden: *The thought seemed to amuse him.* **OPPOSITE:** bore **2 = occupy**, interest, involve, engage, entertain, absorb, divert, engross: *Put a selection of toys in his cot to amuse him if he wakes early.*

> QUOTATIONS
> We are not amused
> [Queen Victoria]

amusement NOUN **1 = enjoyment**, delight, entertainment, cheer, laughter, mirth, hilarity, merriment, gladdening, beguilement, regalement: *He watched with amusement to see the child so absorbed.* **OPPOSITE:** boredom **2 = diversion**, interest, sport, pleasing, fun, pleasure, recreation, entertainment, gratification: *It's unacceptable to keep animals confined for our amusement.* **3 = pastime**, game, sport, joke, entertainment, hobby, recreation, distraction, diversion, lark, prank

amusing ADJECTIVE **= funny**, humorous, gratifying, laughable, farcical, comical, droll, interesting, pleasing, charming, cheering, entertaining, comic, pleasant, lively, diverting, delightful, enjoyable, cheerful, witty, merry, gladdening, facetious, jocular, rib-tickling, waggish **OPPOSITE:** boring

anaemic ADJECTIVE **1 = pale**, weak, dull, frail, feeble, wan, sickly, bloodless, colourless, infirm, pallid, ashen, characterless, enervated, like death warmed up *(informal)*: *Losing a lot of blood makes you tired and anaemic.* **OPPOSITE:** rosy **2 = weak**, feeble: *We will see some economic recovery, but it will be very anaemic.*

anaesthetic NOUN **= painkiller**, narcotic, sedative, opiate, anodyne, analgesic, soporific, stupefacient, stupefactive: *The operation is carried out under general anaesthetic.* ▷ ADJECTIVE **= pain-killing**, dulling, numbing, narcotic, sedative, opiate, deadening, anodyne, analgesic, soporific, sleep-inducing, stupefacient, stupefactive: *They are rendered unconscious by anaesthetic darts.*

analogous ADJECTIVE **= similar**, like, related, equivalent, parallel, resembling, alike, corresponding, comparable, akin, homologous **OPPOSITE:** different

> USAGE
> The correct word to use after *analogous* is *to*, not *with*, for example: *swimming has no event that is analogous to the 100 metres in athletics* (not *analogous with the 100 metres in athletics*).

analogy NOUN **= similarity**, relation, comparison, parallel, correspondence, resemblance, correlation, likeness, equivalence, homology, similitude

analyse VERB **1 = examine**, test, study, research, judge, estimate, survey, investigate, interpret, evaluate, inspect, work over, unpack: *This book teaches you to analyse causes of stress in your life.* **2 = break down**, consider, study, separate, divide, resolve, dissolve, dissect, think through, assay, anatomize, unpack: *We haven't had time to analyse those samples yet.*

analysis NOUN **1 = study**, reasoning, opinion, judgment, interpretation, evaluation, estimation, dissection: *We did an analysis of the way they have spent money in the past.* **2 = examination**, test, division, inquiry, investigation, resolution, interpretation, breakdown, scanning, separation, evaluation, scrutiny, sifting, anatomy, dissolution, dissection, assay, perusal, anatomization: *They collect blood samples for analysis at the laboratory.*

analytic *or* **analytical** ADJECTIVE **= rational**, questioning, testing, detailed, searching, organized, exact, precise, logical, systematic, inquiring, diagnostic, investigative, dissecting, explanatory, discrete, inquisitive, interpretive, studious, interpretative, expository

anarchic ADJECTIVE **= lawless**, rioting, confused, disordered, revolutionary, chaotic, rebellious, riotous, disorganized, misruled, ungoverned, misgoverned **OPPOSITE:** law-abiding

anarchist NOUN **= revolutionary**, rebel, terrorist, insurgent, nihilist

anarchy NOUN **= lawlessness**, revolution, riot, disorder, confusion, chaos, rebellion, misrule, disorganization, misgovernment **OPPOSITE:** order

anathema NOUN **= abomination**, bête noire, enemy, pariah, bane, bugbear

ancestor NOUN **= forefather**, predecessor, precursor, forerunner, forebear, antecedent, progenitor, tupuna *or* tipuna *(N.Z.)* **OPPOSITE:** descendant

ancestral ADJECTIVE **= inherited**, hereditary, patriarchal, antecedent, forefatherly, genealogical, lineal, ancestorial

ancestry NOUN **= origin**, house, family, line, race, stock, blood, ancestors, descent, pedigree, extraction, lineage, forebears, antecedents, parentage, forefathers, genealogy, derivation, progenitors

anchor NOUN **= mooring**, hook *(Nautical)*, bower *(Nautical)*, kedge, drogue, sheet anchor: *We lost our anchor, which caused the boat to drift.* ▷ VERB **1 = moor**, harbour, dock, tie up, kedge: *The ship was anchored by the pier.* **2 = dock**, moor, harbour, drop anchor, kedge, cast anchor, drop the hook, let go the anchor, lay anchor, come to anchor: *We anchored off the beach.* **3 = secure**, tie, fix, bind, chain, attach, bolt, fasten, affix: *The child's seatbelt was not properly anchored in the car.*

anchorage NOUN **= berth**, haven, port, harbour, dock, quay, dockage, moorage, harbourage

ancient ADJECTIVE **1 = classical**, old, former, past, bygone, primordial, primeval, olden: *They believed ancient Greece and Rome were vital sources of learning.* **2 = very old**, early, aged, antique, obsolete, archaic, age-old, bygone, antiquated, hoary, olden, superannuated, antediluvian, timeworn, old as the hills: *ancient rites* **3 = old-fashioned**, dated, outdated, obsolete, out of date, unfashionable, outmoded, passé **OPPOSITE:** up-to-date

ancillary ADJECTIVE **= supplementary**, supporting, extra, additional, secondary, subsidiary, accessory, subordinate, auxiliary, contributory **OPPOSITE:** major

and CONJUNCTION **1 = also**, including, along with, together with, in addition to, as well as: *When he returned, she and her boyfriend had already gone.* **2 = moreover**, plus, furthermore: *These airlines fly to isolated places. And business travellers use them.*

> USAGE
> The forms *try and do something* and *wait and do something* should only be used in informal or spoken English. In more formal writing, use *try to* and *wait to*, for example: *we must try to prevent this happening* (not *try and prevent*).

androgynous ADJECTIVE **= hermaphrodite**, bisexual, androgyne, hermaphroditic, epicene, ambisexual

android NOUN **= robot**, automaton, humanoid, cyborg, mechanical man, bionic man *or* woman

anecdote NOUN **= story**, tale, sketch, short story, yarn, reminiscence, urban myth, urban legend

anew ADVERB **= again**, once again, once more, over again, from the beginning, from scratch, another time, afresh

angel NOUN **1 = divine messenger**, spirit, cherub, archangel, seraph,

ANGELS

Angels

Azrael, Gabriel, Michael, Raphael, Uriel

Angelic orders

angels, archangels, cherubim, dominations *or* dominions, powers, principalities *or* princedoms, seraphim, thrones, virtues spiritual being, guardian spirit: *a choir of angels* **2 = dear**, ideal, beauty, saint, treasure, darling, dream, jewel, gem, paragon: *Thank you. You're an angel.*

> QUOTATIONS
> Is man an ape or an angel? Now I am on the side of the angels
> [Benjamin Disraeli *Speech at Oxford Diocesan Conference*]

angelic ADJECTIVE **1 = pure**, beautiful, lovely, innocent, entrancing, virtuous, saintly, adorable, beatific: *an angelic little face* **2 = heavenly**, celestial, ethereal, cherubic, seraphic: *angelic choirs* **OPPOSITE:** demonic

anger NOUN **= rage**, passion, outrage, temper, fury, resentment, irritation, wrath, indignation, annoyance, agitation, ire, antagonism, displeasure, exasperation, irritability, spleen, pique, ill temper, vehemence, vexation, high dudgeon, ill humour, choler: *He cried with anger and frustration.* **OPPOSITE:** calmness
▷ VERB **= enrage**, provoke, outrage, annoy, offend, excite, irritate, infuriate, hassle *(informal)*, aggravate *(informal)*, incense, fret, gall, madden, exasperate, nettle, vex, affront, displease, rile, pique, get on someone's nerves *(informal)*, antagonize, get someone's back up, put someone's back up, nark *(Brit., Austral. & N.Z. slang)*, make someone's blood boil, get in someone's hair *(informal)*, get someone's dander up *(informal)*: *The decision to allow more construction angered the residents.* **OPPOSITE:** soothe

> QUOTATIONS
> Usually when people are sad, they don't do anything. They just cry over their condition. But when they get angry, they bring about a change
> [Malcolm X *Malcolm X Speaks*]
>
> Anger is a short madness
> [Horace *Epistles*]
> Anger and jealousy can no more bear to lose sight of their objects than love
> [George Eliot *The Mill on the Floss*]

> PROVERBS
> *Never let the sun go down on your anger*

angle NOUN **1 = gradient**, bank, slope, incline, inclination: *The boat was leaning at a 30-degree angle.* **2 = intersection**, point, edge, corner, knee, bend, elbow, crook, crotch, nook, cusp: *brackets to adjust the steering wheel's angle* **3 = point of view**, position, approach, direction, aspect, perspective, outlook, viewpoint, slant, standpoint, take *(informal)*, side: *He was considering the idea from all angles.*

angler NOUN **= fisherman**, fisher, piscator *or* piscatrix

angling NOUN **= fishing**

> QUOTATIONS
> a worm at one end and a fool at the other
> [Samuel Johnson]
>
> God never did make a more calm, quiet, innocent recreation than angling
> [Izaak Walton]
>
> Fishing is always a form of madness but happily...there is no cure
> [Alexander Douglas Home]
> an excellent angler, and now with God
> [Izaak Walton]

angry ADJECTIVE **= furious**, cross, heated, mad *(informal)*, raging, provoked, outraged, annoyed, passionate, irritated, raving, hacked (off) *(U.S. slang)*, choked, infuriated, hot, incensed, enraged, ranting, exasperated, irritable, resentful, nettled, snappy, indignant, irate, tumultuous, displeased, uptight *(informal)*, riled, up in arms, incandescent, ill-tempered, irascible, antagonized, waspish, piqued, hot under the collar *(informal)*, on the warpath, hopping mad *(informal)*, foaming at the mouth, choleric, splenetic, wrathful, at daggers drawn, in high dudgeon, as black as thunder, ireful, tooshie *(Austral. slang)*, off the air *(Austral. slang)*, aerated **OPPOSITE:** calm

angst NOUN **= anxiety**, worry, distress, torment, unease, apprehension, agitation, malaise, perturbation, vexation, fretfulness, disquietude, inquietude **OPPOSITE:** peace of mind

anguish NOUN **= suffering**, pain, torture, distress, grief, misery, agony, torment, sorrow, woe, heartache, heartbreak, pang, throe

anguished ADJECTIVE **= suffering**, wounded, tortured, distressed, tormented, afflicted, agonized, grief-stricken, wretched, brokenhearted

angular ADJECTIVE **= skinny**, spare, lean, gaunt, bony, lanky, scrawny, lank, rangy, rawboned, macilent *(rare)*

animal NOUN **1 = creature**, beast, brute: *He was attacked by wild animals.* **2 = brute**, devil, monster, savage, beast, bastard *(informal, offensive)*, villain, barbarian, swine *(informal)*, wild man: *He was an animal in his younger days.*
▷ ADJECTIVE **= physical**, gross, fleshly, bodily, sensual, carnal, brutish, bestial, animalistic: *When he was drunk, he showed his animal side.*
▸ *related prefix:* zoo-

> QUOTATIONS
> Animals, whom we have made our slaves, we do not like to consider our equal
> [Charles Darwin]
>
> The best thing about animals is that they don't talk much
> [Thornton Wilder *The Skin of Our Teeth*]
>
> If I could do anything about the way people behave towards each other, I would, but since I can't I'll stick to the animals
> [Brigitte Bardot]
>
> It's almost as if we're put here on earth to show how silly [animals] aren't
> [Russell Hoban *Turtle Diary*]

animate ADJECTIVE **= living**, live, moving, alive, breathing, alive and kicking: *the study of animate and inanimate aspects of the natural world*
▷ VERB **= enliven**, encourage, excite, urge, inspire, stir, spark, move, fire, spur, stimulate, revive, activate, rouse, prod, quicken, incite, instigate, kick-start *(informal)*, impel, energize, kindle, embolden, liven up, breathe life into, invigorate, gladden, gee up, vitalize, vivify, inspirit: *There was little about the game to animate the crowd.* **OPPOSITE:** inhibit

animated ADJECTIVE **= lively**, spirited, quick, excited, active, vital, dynamic, enthusiastic, passionate, vivid, vigorous, energetic, vibrant, brisk, buoyant, ardent, airy, fervent, zealous, elated, ebullient, sparky, sprightly, vivacious, gay, alive and kicking, full of beans *(informal)*, zestful **OPPOSITE:** listless

animation NOUN **= liveliness**, life, action, activity, energy, spirit, passion, enthusiasm, excitement, pep, sparkle, vitality, vigour, zeal, verve, zest, fervour, high spirits, dynamism, buoyancy, elation, exhilaration, gaiety, ardour, vibrancy, brio, zing *(informal)*, vivacity, ebullience, briskness, airiness, sprightliness, pizzazz *or* pizazz *(informal)*

animosity NOUN **= hostility**, hate, hatred, resentment, bitterness, malice, antagonism, antipathy, enmity, acrimony, rancour, bad blood, ill will, animus, malevolence, virulence, malignity **OPPOSITE:** friendliness

animus NOUN **= ill will**, hate, hostility, hatred, resentment, bitterness, malice, animosity, antagonism, antipathy, enmity, acrimony, rancour, bad blood, malevolence, virulence, malignity

annals PLURAL NOUN **= records**, history, accounts, registers, journals, memorials, archives, chronicles

annex VERB **1 = seize**, take over, appropriate, acquire, occupy, conquer, expropriate, arrogate: *Rome annexed the Nabatean kingdom in 106 AD.* **2 = join**, unite, add, connect, attach, tack, adjoin, fasten, affix, append, subjoin: *A gate goes through to the annexed garden.* **OPPOSITE:** detach

annexation NOUN **= seizure**, takeover, occupation, conquest, appropriation, annexing, expropriation, arrogation

annexe NOUN **1 = extension**, wing, ell, supplementary building: *They are planning to set up a museum in an annexe to the theatre.* **2 = appendix**, addition, supplement, attachment, adjunct, addendum, affixment: *The annexe lists and discusses eight titles.*

a

annihilate VERB = **destroy**, abolish, wipe out, erase, eradicate, extinguish, obliterate, liquidate, root out, exterminate, nullify, extirpate, wipe from the face of the earth, kennet *(Austral. slang)*, jeff *(Austral. slang)*

annihilation NOUN = **destruction**, wiping out, abolition, extinction, extinguishing, liquidation, rooting out, extermination, eradication, erasure, obliteration, nullification, extirpation

anniversary NOUN = **jubilee**, remembrance, commemoration

annotate VERB = **make notes on**, explain, note, illustrate, comment on, interpret, gloss, footnote, commentate, elucidate, make observations on

annotation NOUN = **note**, comment, explanation, observation, interpretation, illustration, commentary, gloss, footnote, exegesis, explication, elucidation

announce VERB 1 = **make known**, tell, report, reveal, publish, declare, advertise, broadcast, disclose, intimate, proclaim, trumpet, make public, publicize, divulge, promulgate, propound, shout *or* proclaim from the rooftops *or* housetops *(informal)*: *She was planning to announce her engagement to Peter.* **OPPOSITE:** keep secret 2 = **be a sign of**, signal, herald, warn of, signify, augur, harbinger, presage, foretell, portend, betoken: *The doorbell of the shop announced the arrival of a customer.*

announcement NOUN 1 = **statement**, communication, broadcast, explanation, publication, declaration, advertisement, testimony, disclosure, bulletin, communiqué, proclamation, utterance, intimation, promulgation, divulgence: *There has been no formal announcement by either government.* 2 = **declaration**, report, reporting, publication, revelation, disclosure, proclamation, intimation, promulgation, divulgence: *the announcement of their engagement*

announcer NOUN = **presenter**, newscaster, reporter, commentator, broadcaster, newsreader, master of ceremonies, anchor man, anchor

annoy VERB = **irritate**, trouble, bore, anger, harry, bother, disturb, provoke, get *(informal)*, bug *(informal)*, needle *(informal)*, plague, tease, harass, hassle *(informal)*, aggravate *(informal)*, badger, gall, madden, ruffle, exasperate, nettle, molest, pester, vex, displease, irk, bedevil, rile, peeve, get under your skin *(informal)*, get on your nerves *(informal)*, nark *(Brit., Austral. & N.Z. slang)*, get up your nose *(informal)*, give someone grief *(Brit. & S. African)*, make your blood boil, rub someone up the wrong way *(informal)*, get your goat *(slang)*, get in your hair *(informal)*, get on your wick *(Brit. slang)*, get your dander up *(informal)*, get your back up, incommode, put your back up, hack you off *(informal)* **OPPOSITE:** soothe

annoyance NOUN 1 = **irritation**, trouble, anger, bother, grief *(informal)*, harassment, disturbance, hassle *(informal)*, nuisance, provocation, displeasure, exasperation, aggravation, vexation, bedevilment: *To her annoyance the stranger did not go away.* 2 = **nuisance**, bother, pain *(informal)*, bind *(informal)*, bore, drag *(informal)*, plague, tease, pest, gall, pain in the neck *(informal)*: *Snoring can be more than an annoyance.*

annoyed ADJECTIVE = **irritated**, bothered, harassed, hassled *(informal)*, aggravated *(informal)*, maddened, ruffled, exasperated, nettled, vexed, miffed *(informal)*, displeased, irked, riled, harried, peeved *(informal)*, piqued, browned off *(informal)*

annoying ADJECTIVE = **irritating**, boring, disturbing, provoking, teasing, harassing, aggravating, troublesome, galling, maddening, exasperating, displeasing, bedevilling, peeving *(informal)*, irksome, bothersome, vexatious **OPPOSITE:** delightful

annual ADJECTIVE 1 = **once a year**, yearly: *the annual conference of the trade union movement* 2 = **yearlong**, yearly: *annual costs, £1,600*

annually ADVERB 1 = **once a year**, yearly, each year, every year, per year, by the year, every twelve months, per annum, year after year: *Companies report to their shareholders annually.* 2 = **per year**, yearly, each year, every year, by the year, per annum: *They hire 300 staff annually.*

annul VERB = **invalidate**, reverse, cancel, abolish, void, repeal, recall, revoke, retract, negate, rescind, nullify, obviate, abrogate, countermand, declare *or* render null and void **OPPOSITE:** restore

anodyne ADJECTIVE = **bland**, dull, boring, insipid, unexciting, uninspiring, uninteresting, mind-numbing *(informal)*: *Their quarterly meetings were anodyne affairs.* ▷ NOUN = **painkiller**, narcotic, palliative, analgesic, pain reliever: *Leisure is a kind of anodyne.*

anoint VERB 1 = **smear**, oil, rub, grease, spread over, daub, embrocate: *He anointed my forehead with oil.* 2 = **consecrate**, bless, sanctify, hallow, anele *(archaic)*: *The Pope has anointed him as Archbishop.*

anomalous ADJECTIVE = **unusual**, odd, rare, bizarre, exceptional, peculiar, eccentric, abnormal, irregular, inconsistent, off-the-wall *(slang)*, incongruous, deviating, oddball *(informal)*, atypical, aberrant, outré **OPPOSITE:** normal

anomaly NOUN = **irregularity**, departure, exception, abnormality, rarity, inconsistency, deviation, eccentricity, oddity, aberration, peculiarity, incongruity

anon ADVERB = **soon**, presently, shortly, promptly, before long, forthwith, betimes *(archaic)*, erelong *(archaic, poetic)*, in a couple of shakes *(informal)*

anonymity NOUN 1 = **namelessness**, innominateness: *Both mother and daughter have requested anonymity.* 2 = **unremarkability** *or* **unremarkableness**, characterlessness, unsingularity: *the anonymity of the rented room*

anonymous ADJECTIVE 1 = **unnamed**, unknown, unidentified, nameless, unacknowledged, incognito, unauthenticated, innominate: *You can remain anonymous if you wish.* **OPPOSITE:** identified 2 = **unsigned**, uncredited, unattributed, unattested: *I heard that an anonymous note was actually being circulated.* **OPPOSITE:** signed 3 = **nondescript**, impersonal, faceless, colourless, undistinguished, unexceptional, characterless: *It's nice to stay in a home rather than an anonymous holiday flat.*

answer VERB 1 = **reply**, explain, respond, resolve, acknowledge, react, return, retort, rejoin, refute: *He paused before answering.* **OPPOSITE:** ask 2 = **satisfy**, meet, serve, fit, fill, suit, solve, fulfil, suffice, measure up to: *We must ensure we answer real needs.* ▷ NOUN 1 = **reply**, response, reaction, resolution, explanation, plea, comeback, retort, report, return, defence, acknowledgement, riposte, counterattack, refutation, rejoinder: *Without waiting for an answer, he turned and went in.* **OPPOSITE:** question 2 = **solution**, resolution, explanation: *Simply marking an answer wrong will not help the student.* 3 = **remedy**, solution, vindication: *Prison is not the answer for most young offenders.*

answer to someone = **be responsible to**, obey, work under, be ruled by, be managed by, be subordinate to, be accountable to, be answerable to: *He answers to a boss he has met once in 18 months.*

answerable ADJECTIVE = **responsible for** *or* **to**, to blame for, liable for *or* to, accountable for *or* to, chargeable for, subject to

answer back VERB = **be impertinent**, argue, dispute, disagree, retort, contradict, rebut, talk back, be cheeky

antagonism NOUN = **hostility**, competition, opposition, conflict, rivalry, contention, friction, discord, antipathy, dissension **OPPOSITE:** friendship

antagonist NOUN = **opponent**, rival, opposer, enemy, competitor, contender, foe, adversary

antagonistic ADJECTIVE = **hostile**, opposed, resistant, at odds, incompatible, set against, averse, unfriendly, at variance, inimical, antipathetic, ill-disposed

> **USAGE**
> A useful synonym for *antagonistic*, for example in *public opinion is antagonistic to nuclear energy*, is *averse*. However, this alternative should be used with care as a very common error is to confuse it with *adverse*. *Averse* is usually followed by *to* and is meant to convey a strong dislike or hostility towards something, normally expressed by a person or people. *Adverse* is wrong in this context and should be used in relation to conditions or results: *adverse road conditions*.

antagonize VERB = **annoy**, anger, insult, offend, irritate, alienate, hassle *(informal)*, aggravate *(informal)*, gall, repel, estrange, get under your skin *(informal)*, get on your nerves *(informal)*, nark *(Brit., Austral. & N.Z. slang)*, get up your nose *(informal)*, be on your back *(slang)*, rub (someone) up the wrong way *(informal)*, disaffect, get in your hair *(informal)*, get on your wick *(Brit. slang)*, hack you off *(informal)* **OPPOSITE:** pacify

antecedent ADJECTIVE = **preceding**, earlier, former, previous, prior, preliminary, foregoing, anterior, precursory: *They were allowed to take account of antecedent legislation.* **OPPOSITE:** subsequent

anterior ADJECTIVE **1** = **front**, forward, fore, frontward: *the left anterior descending artery* **2** = **earlier**, former, previous, prior, preceding, introductory, foregoing, antecedent: *memories of our anterior existences*

anthem NOUN = **song of praise**, carol, chant, hymn, psalm, paean, chorale, canticle

anthology NOUN = **collection**, choice, selection, treasury, digest, compilation, garland, compendium, miscellany, analects

anticipate VERB **1** = **expect**, predict, forecast, prepare for, look for, hope for, envisage, foresee, bank on, apprehend, foretell, think likely, count upon: *We could not have anticipated the result of our campaigning.* **2** = **await**, look forward to, count the hours until: *We are all eagerly anticipating the next match.*

anticipation NOUN = **expectancy**, hope, expectation, apprehension, foresight, premonition, preconception, foretaste, prescience, forethought, presentiment

anticlimax NOUN = **disappointment**, letdown, comedown *(informal)*, bathos **OPPOSITE:** climax

> **QUOTATIONS**
> This is the way the world ends
> Not with a bang but a whimper
> [T.S. Eliot *The Hollow Men*]

antics PLURAL NOUN = **clowning**, tricks, stunts, mischief, larks, capers, pranks, frolics, escapades, foolishness, silliness, playfulness, skylarking, horseplay, buffoonery, tomfoolery, monkey tricks

antidote NOUN = **remedy**, cure, preventive, corrective, neutralizer, nostrum, countermeasure, antitoxin, antivenin, counteragent

antipathy NOUN = **hostility**, opposition, disgust, dislike, hatred, loathing, distaste, animosity, aversion, antagonism, enmity, rancour, bad blood, incompatibility, ill will, animus, repulsion, abhorrence, repugnance, odium, contrariety **OPPOSITE:** affinity

> **QUOTATIONS**
> I do not love thee, Dr. Fell.
> The reason why I cannot tell;
> But this I know, and know full well,
> I do not love thee, Dr. Fell
> [Thomas Brown]

antiquated ADJECTIVE = **obsolete**, old, aged, ancient, antique, old-fashioned, elderly, dated, past it *(informal)*, out-of-date, archaic, outmoded, passé, old hat, hoary, superannuated, antediluvian, outworn, cobwebby, old as the hills **OPPOSITE:** up-to-date

antique NOUN = **period piece**, relic, bygone, heirloom, collector's item, museum piece, object of virtu: *a genuine antique*
▷ ADJECTIVE **1** = **vintage**, classic, antiquarian, olden: *antique silver jewellery* **2** = **old-fashioned**, old, aged, ancient, remote, elderly, primitive, outdated, obsolete, archaic, bygone, primordial, primeval, immemorial, superannuated: *Their aim is to break taboos and change antique laws.*

antiquity NOUN **1** = **distant past**, ancient times, time immemorial, olden days: *famous monuments of classical antiquity* **2** = **old age**, age, oldness, ancientness, elderliness: *a town of great antiquity*

antiseptic ADJECTIVE = **hygienic**, clean, pure, sterile, sanitary, uncontaminated, unpolluted, germ-free, aseptic: *These herbs have strong antiseptic qualities.* **OPPOSITE:** unhygienic
▷ NOUN = **disinfectant**, purifier, bactericide, germicide: *She bathed the cut with antiseptic.*

antisocial ADJECTIVE **1** = **unsociable**, reserved, retiring, withdrawn, alienated, unfriendly, uncommunicative, misanthropic, asocial: *a generation of teenagers who will become aggressive and anti-social* **OPPOSITE:** sociable **2** = **disruptive**, disorderly, hostile, menacing, rebellious, belligerent, antagonistic, uncooperative: *Playing these games can lead to anti-social behaviour.*

antithesis NOUN **1** = **opposite**, contrast, reverse, contrary, converse, inverse, antipode: *They are the antithesis of the typical married couple.* **2** = **contrast**, opposition, contradiction, reversal, inversion, contrariety, contraposition: *the antithesis between instinct and reason*

anxiety NOUN = **uneasiness**, concern, care, worry, doubt, tension, alarm, distress, suspicion, angst, unease, apprehension, misgiving, suspense, nervousness, disquiet, trepidation, foreboding, restlessness, solicitude, perturbation, watchfulness, fretfulness, disquietude, apprehensiveness, dubiety **OPPOSITE:** confidence

anxious ADJECTIVE **1** = **eager**, keen, intent, yearning, impatient, itching, ardent, avid, expectant, desirous: *He is anxious that there should be no delay.* **OPPOSITE:** reluctant **2** = **uneasy**, concerned, worried, troubled, upset, careful, wired *(slang)*, nervous, disturbed, distressed, uncomfortable, tense, fearful, unsettled, restless, neurotic, agitated, taut, disquieted, apprehensive, edgy, watchful, jittery *(informal)*, perturbed, on edge, ill at ease, twitchy *(informal)*, solicitous, overwrought, fretful, on tenterhooks, in suspense, hot and bothered, unquiet *(chiefly literary)*, like a fish out of water, antsy *(informal)*, angsty, on pins and needles, discomposed: *He admitted he was still anxious about the situation.* **OPPOSITE:** confident

apace ADVERB = **quickly**, rapidly, swiftly, speedily, without delay, at full speed, expeditiously, posthaste, with dispatch

apart ADVERB **1** = **to pieces**, to bits, asunder, into parts: *He took the clock apart to see what was wrong with it.* **2** = **away from each other**, distant from each other: *They live 25 miles apart.* **3** = **aside**, away, alone, independently, separately, singly, excluded, isolated, cut off, to one side, to yourself, by itself, aloof, to itself, by yourself, out on a limb: *He saw her standing some distance apart.*
apart from = **except for**, excepting, other than, excluding, besides, not including, aside from, but, save, bar, not counting: *The room was empty apart from one man seated beside the fire.*

apartment NOUN **1** = **flat**, room, suite, compartment, penthouse, duplex *(U.S. & Canad.)*, crib, bachelor apartment *(Canad.)*: *She has her own apartment and her own car.* **2** = **rooms**, quarters, chambers, accommodation, living quarters: *the private apartments of the Prince of Wales at St James's Palace*

apathetic ADJECTIVE = **uninterested**, passive, indifferent, sluggish, unmoved, stoic, stoical, unconcerned, listless, cold, cool, impassive, unresponsive, phlegmatic, unfeeling, unemotional, torpid, emotionless, insensible **OPPOSITE:** interested

apathy NOUN = **lack of interest**, indifference, inertia, coolness, passivity, coldness, stoicism, nonchalance, torpor, phlegm, sluggishness, listlessness, unconcern, insensibility, unresponsiveness, impassivity, passiveness, impassibility, unfeelingness, emotionlessness, uninterestedness **OPPOSITE:** interest

ape VERB **= imitate**, copy, mirror, echo, mock, parrot, mimic, parody, caricature, affect, counterfeit

aperture NOUN **= opening**, space, hole, crack, gap, rent, passage, breach, slot, vent, rift, slit, cleft, eye, chink, fissure, orifice, perforation, eyelet, interstice

apex NOUN **1 = culmination**, top, crown, height, climax, highest point, zenith, apogee, acme: *At the apex of the party was the central committee.* **OPPOSITE:** depths **2 = highest point**, point, top, tip, summit, peak, crest, pinnacle, vertex: *She led me up a gloomy corridor to the apex of the pyramid.* **OPPOSITE:** lowest point

aphorism NOUN **= saying**, maxim, gnome, adage, proverb, dictum, precept, axiom, apothegm, saw

aphrodisiac NOUN **= love potion**, philtre: *Asparagus is reputed to be an aphrodisiac.*
▷ ADJECTIVE **= erotic** *or* **erotical**, exciting, stimulating, arousing, venereal: *plants with aphrodisiac qualities*

apiece ADVERB **= each**, individually, separately, for each, to each, respectively, from each, severally **OPPOSITE:** all together

aplenty ADJECTIVE **= in plenty**, to spare, galore, in abundance, in quantity, in profusion, à gogo (*informal*): *There were problems aplenty, and it was an uncomfortable evening.*
▷ ADVERB **= plentifully**, in abundance, abundantly, in quantity, in plenty, copiously, plenteously: *Wickets continued to fall aplenty.*

aplomb NOUN **= self-possession**, confidence, stability, self-confidence, composure, poise, coolness, calmness, equanimity, balance, self-assurance, sang-froid, level-headedness **OPPOSITE:** self-consciousness

apocalypse NOUN **= destruction**, holocaust, havoc, devastation, carnage, conflagration, cataclysm

FOUR HORSEMEN OF THE APOCALYPSE

white – Christ	black – Famine
red – War	pale – Death

apocryphal ADJECTIVE **= dubious**, legendary, doubtful, questionable, mythical, spurious, fictitious, unsubstantiated, equivocal, unverified, unauthenticated, uncanonical **OPPOSITE:** factual

apogee NOUN **= highest point**, top, tip, crown, summit, height, peak, climax, crest, pinnacle, culmination, zenith, apex, acme, vertex

apologetic ADJECTIVE **= regretful**, sorry, rueful, contrite, remorseful, penitent

apologize VERB **= say sorry**, express regret, ask forgiveness, make an apology, beg pardon, say you are sorry

apology NOUN **= regret**, explanation, excuse, confession, extenuation: *We received a letter of apology.*
apology for something *or* **someone = mockery of**, excuse for, imitation of, caricature of, travesty of, poor substitute for: *What an apology for a leader!*

apostle NOUN **1 = evangelist**, herald, missionary, preacher, messenger, proselytizer: *the twelve apostles* **2 = supporter**, champion, advocate, pioneer, proponent, propagandist, propagator: *They present themselves as apostles of free trade.*

apotheosis NOUN **= deification**, elevation, exaltation, glorification, idealization, idolization

appal VERB **= horrify**, shock, alarm, frighten, scare, terrify, outrage, disgust, dishearten, revolt, intimidate, dismay, daunt, sicken, astound, harrow, unnerve, petrify, scandalize, make your hair stand on end (*informal*)

appalled ADJECTIVE **= horrified**, shocked, stunned, alarmed, frightened, scared, terrified, outraged, dismayed, daunted, astounded, unnerved, disquieted, petrified, disheartened

appalling ADJECTIVE **1 = horrifying**, shocking, terrible, alarming, frightening, scaring, awful, terrifying, horrible, grim, dreadful, intimidating, dismaying, horrific, fearful, daunting, dire, astounding, ghastly, hideous, shameful, harrowing, vile, unnerving, petrifying, horrid, unspeakable, frightful, nightmarish, abominable, disheartening, godawful (*slang*), hellacious (*U.S. slang*): *They have been living under the most appalling conditions.* **OPPOSITE:** reassuring **2 = awful**, terrible, tremendous, distressing, horrible, dreadful, horrendous, ghastly, godawful (*slang*): *I've got the most appalling headache.*

apparatus NOUN **1 = organization**, system, network, structure, bureaucracy, hierarchy, setup (*informal*), chain of command: *a massive bureaucratic apparatus* **2 = equipment**, machine, tackle, gear, means, materials, device, tools, implements, mechanism, outfit, machinery, appliance, utensils, contraption (*informal*): *He was rescued by firemen wearing breathing apparatus.*

apparel NOUN **= clothing**, dress, clothes, equipment, gear (*informal*), habit, outfit, costume, threads (*slang*), array (*poetic*), garments, robes, trappings, attire, garb, accoutrements, vestments, raiment (*archaic, poetic*), schmutter (*slang*), habiliments

apparent ADJECTIVE **1 = seeming**, supposed, alleged, outward, exterior, superficial, ostensible, specious: *I was a bit depressed by our apparent lack of progress.* **OPPOSITE:** actual **2 = obvious**, marked, clear, plain, visible, bold, patent, evident, distinct, open, understandable, manifest, noticeable, blatant, conspicuous, overt, unmistakable, palpable, undeniable, discernible, salient, self-evident, indisputable, much in evidence, undisguised, unconcealed, indubitable, staring you in the face (*informal*), plain as the nose on your face: *The presence of a star is already apparent in the early film.* **OPPOSITE:** unclear

apparently ADVERB **= seemingly**, outwardly, ostensibly, speciously

apparition NOUN **= ghost**, spirit, shade (*literary*), phantom, spectre, spook (*informal*), wraith, chimera, revenant, visitant, eidolon, atua (*N.Z.*), kehua (*N.Z.*)

appeal VERB **= plead**, call, ask, apply, refer, request, sue, lobby, pray, beg, petition, solicit, implore, beseech, entreat, importune, adjure, supplicate: *The UN has appealed for help from the international community.* **OPPOSITE:** refuse
▷ NOUN **1 = plea**, call, application, request, prayer, petition, overture, invocation, solicitation, entreaty, supplication, suit, cry from the heart, adjuration: *The government issued a last-minute appeal to him to return.* **OPPOSITE:** refusal **2 = attraction**, charm, fascination, charisma, beauty, attractiveness, allure, magnetism, enchantment, seductiveness, interestingness, engagingness, pleasingness: *It was meant to give the party greater public appeal.* **OPPOSITE:** repulsiveness
appeal to someone = attract, interest, draw, please, invite, engage, charm, fascinate, tempt, lure, entice, enchant, captivate, allure, bewitch: *The idea appealed to him.*

> **QUOTATIONS**
> appeal: in law, to put the dice into the box for another throw
> [Ambrose Bierce *The Devil's Dictionary*]

appealing ADJECTIVE **= attractive**, inviting, engaging, charming, winning, desirable, endearing, alluring, winsome, prepossessing **OPPOSITE:** repellent

appear VERB **1 = seem**, be clear, be obvious, be evident, look (like *or* as if), be apparent, be plain, be manifest, be patent: *It appears that some missiles have been moved.* **2 = look (like** *or* **as if)**, seem, occur, look to be, come across as, strike you as: *She did her best to appear more confident than she felt.* **3 = come into view**, emerge, occur, attend, surface, come out, turn out, arise, turn up, be present, loom, show (*informal*), issue, develop, arrive, show up (*informal*), come to light, crop up (*informal*), materialize, come forth, come into sight, show your face:

The Language of Charles Kingsley

The work of Charles Kingsley (1819–75) was extensive and wide-ranging. While he is now best known for his children's fairy tale *The Water Babies*, he also produced several volumes of adult fiction, poetry, sermons, plays, and works of history. He was also a Cambridge professor and a member of the clergy whose reforming zeal is associated with Christian socialism and with the ideas that came to be known as Muscular Christianity, a movement which focused on the religious value of a fit body.

Much of Kingsley's prose is characterized by seriousness, although *The Water Babies* by contrast at times demonstrates a more playful approach to language. This is apparent in many of the names of the characters which spell out their moral nature and form a key part of Kingsley's ethical agenda. These include the fairies *Mrs Bedonebyasyoudid* and *Mrs Doasyouwouldbedoneby*, the scientist *Professor Ptthmllnsprts* (a contraction of 'put them all in spirits') and the idle *Doasyoulikes*. In this text Kingsley's writing even occasionally edges towards the kind of nonsense later to be popularized by Lewis Carroll. Describing the *Doasyoulikes*, he writes:

> They sat under the flapdoodle-trees, and let flapdoodle drop into their mouths.

An exaggerated parody of the technical language of science provides another moment of linguistic playfulness in *The Water Babies* as Kingsley produces a string of polysyllabic terms, such as *subanhypaposupernal*, *interexclusively*, and *anastomoses*.

As a man dedicated to social improvement, *reform* is a vital theme for Kingsley. In accordance with a Victorian obsession, the most salient adjective with *reform* is *sanitary*, while the most common adjective with *disease* is *preventable* (which is also, unusually, spelled *preventible*). *Health* occurs most with *moral*, *perfect*, and *public* indicating the far-reaching improvement he was aiming towards. Other recurrent collocates of *health* testify to his interest in physicality. *Robust*, *bodily*, and *animal* show that Kingsley envisioned a healthy soul in a healthy body. *Animal*, however, appears as a mixed blessing. Applied to *health* it suggests a desirable state of well-being; applied to *nature* on the other hand it signifies an inner moral weakness that mankind must battle against, as in:

> ... the temptations which all men have to yield to the low **animal nature** in them.

Other words that collocate with *animal* emphasize this negative association: *dumb*, *brute*, *mere*, and *low* all revealing Kingsley's insistence on the elevated place of humankind.

In endeavouring to persuade his readers of the vital necessity for political action to alleviate the suffering of the urban poor, Kingsley turns remarkably frequently to the verbs *forget* and *remember*. The word that most commonly modifies *forget* is *not* ('do not forget...') and in similar vein *remember* is most frequently modified by *always*, as in:

> **Remember always**, toil is the condition of our being.

Kingsley consequently gives considerable emphasis to education and his writing is also infused with a theological rhetoric. This is evident not just in the frequency of religious terms (with *God* the most salient of these, followed by *Lord* and *Christ*) but also in a verbal texture that recalls the language of the Bible and the vocal rhythm of an impassioned sermon, as in:

> ... such children as the world had never seen before, but children still: children in frankness, and purity, and affectionateness, and tenderness of conscience, and devout awe of the unseen; and children too in fancy, and silliness, and ignorance, and caprice, and jealousy, and quarrelsomeness, and love of excitement and adventure.

Central to Kingsley's effect is the use of repetition (particularly of *children*) and of an extended sequence of nouns that lifts the passage towards a moral crescendo.

A woman appeared at the far end of the street. **OPPOSITE:** disappear **4 = come into being**, come out, be published, be developed, be created, be invented, become available, come into existence: *a poem which appeared in his last collection of verse* **5 = perform**, play, act, enter, come on, take part, play a part, be exhibited, come onstage: *She appeared in several of his plays.*

appearance NOUN **1 = look**, face, form, air, figure, image, looks, bearing, aspect, manner, expression, demeanour, mien (*literary*): *He had the appearance of a college student.* **2 = arrival**, appearing, presence, turning up, introduction, showing up (*informal*), emergence, advent: *The sudden appearance of a few bags of rice could start a riot.* **3 = impression**, air, front, image, illusion, guise, façade, pretence, veneer, semblance, outward show: *They gave the appearance of being on both sides.*

> **QUOTATIONS**
> All that glisters is not gold
> [William Shakespeare *The Merchant of Venice*]
>
> Men are valued, not for what they are, but for what they seem to be
> [E.G. Bulwer-Lytton *Money*]
>
> Appearances are often deceiving
> [Aesop *The Wolf in Sheep's Clothing*]
>
> It is only shallow people who do not judge by appearances
> [Oscar Wilde *The Picture of Dorian Gray*]

> **PROVERBS**
> *You can't tell a book by its cover*

appease VERB **1 = pacify**, satisfy, calm, soothe, quiet, placate, mollify, conciliate: *The offer has not appeased separatists.* **OPPOSITE:** anger **2 = ease**, satisfy, calm, relieve, diminish, compose, quiet, blunt, soothe, subdue, lessen, alleviate, lull, quell, allay, mitigate, assuage, quench, tranquillize: *Cash is on hand to appease mounting frustration.*

appeasement NOUN **1 = pacification**, compromise, accommodation, concession, conciliation, acceding, propitiation, mollification, placation: *He denies there is a policy of appeasement.* **2 = easing**, relieving, satisfaction, softening, blunting, soothing, quieting, lessening, lulling, quelling, solace, quenching, mitigation, abatement, alleviation, assuagement, tranquillization: *the appeasement of terror*

appellation NOUN **= name**, term, style, title, address, description, designation, epithet, sobriquet

append VERB **= add**, attach, join, hang, adjoin, fasten, annex, tag on, affix, tack on, subjoin **OPPOSITE:** detach

appendage NOUN **= attachment**, addition, supplement, accessory, appendix, auxiliary, affix, ancillary, adjunct, annexe, addendum, appurtenance

appendix NOUN **= supplement**, add-on, postscript, adjunct, appendage, addendum, addition, codicil

appetite NOUN **1 = hunger**: *a slight fever, headache and loss of appetite* **2 = desire**, liking, longing, demand, taste, passion, stomach, hunger, willingness, relish, craving, yearning, inclination, zeal, zest, propensity, hankering, proclivity, appetence, appetency: *our growing appetite for scandal* **OPPOSITE:** distaste

> **QUOTATIONS**
> The appetite grows by eating
> [François Rabelais *Gargantua*]

appetizer NOUN **= hors d'oeuvre**, titbit, antipasto, canapé

applaud VERB **1 = clap**, encourage, praise, cheer, hail, acclaim, laud, give (someone) a big hand: *The audience laughed and applauded.* **OPPOSITE:** boo **2 = praise**, celebrate, approve, acclaim, compliment, salute, commend, extol, crack up (*informal*), big up (*slang*), eulogize: *He should be applauded for his courage.* **OPPOSITE:** criticize

applause NOUN **= ovation**, praise, cheering, cheers, approval, acclaim, clapping, accolade, big hand, commendation, hand-clapping, approbation, acclamation, eulogizing, plaudit

appliance NOUN **= device**, machine, tool, instrument, implement, mechanism, apparatus, gadget, waldo

applicable ADJECTIVE **= appropriate**, fitting, fit, suited, useful, suitable, relevant, to the point, apt, pertinent, befitting, apposite, apropos, germane, to the purpose **OPPOSITE:** inappropriate

applicant NOUN **= candidate**, entrant, claimant, suitor, petitioner, aspirant, inquirer, job-seeker, suppliant, postulant

application NOUN **1 = request**, claim, demand, appeal, suit, inquiry, plea, petition, requisition, solicitation: *His application for membership was rejected.* **2 = relevance**, use, value, practice, bearing, exercise, purpose, function, appropriateness, aptness, pertinence, appositeness, germaneness: *Students learned the practical application of the theory.* **3 = effort**, work, study, industry, labour, trouble, attention, struggle, pains, commitment, hard work, endeavour, dedication, toil, diligence, perseverance, travail (*literary*), attentiveness, assiduity, blood, sweat, and tears (*informal*): *his immense talent and unremitting application*

apply VERB **1 = request**, seek, appeal, put in, petition, inquire, solicit, claim, sue, requisition, make application: *I am continuing to apply for jobs.* **2 = be relevant**, concern, relate, refer, be fitting, be appropriate, be significant, fit, suit, pertain, be applicable, bear upon, appertain: *The rule applies where a person owns stock in a company.* **3 = use**, exercise, carry out, employ, engage, implement, practise, execute, assign, administer, exert, enact, utilize, bring to bear, put to use, bring into play: *The government appears to be applying the same principle.* **4 = put on**, work in, cover with, lay on, paint on, anoint, spread on, rub in, smear on, shampoo in, bring into contact with: *Applying the dye can be messy, particularly on long hair.*

apply yourself = work hard, concentrate, study, pay attention, try, commit yourself, buckle down (*informal*), be assiduous, devote yourself, be diligent, dedicate yourself, make an effort, address yourself, be industrious, persevere: *If you apply yourself, there's no reason why you shouldn't pass.*

appoint VERB **1 = assign**, name, choose, commission, select, elect, install, delegate, nominate: *It made sense to appoint a banker to this job.* **OPPOSITE:** fire **2 = decide**, set, choose, establish, determine, settle, fix, arrange, specify, assign, designate, allot: *We met at the time appointed.* **OPPOSITE:** cancel

appointed ADJECTIVE **1 = decided**, set, chosen, established, determined, settled, fixed, arranged, assigned, designated, allotted: *The appointed hour for the ceremony was drawing near.* **2 = assigned**, named, chosen, commissioned, selected, elected, installed, delegated, nominated: *The recently appointed captain led by example in the first game.* **3 = equipped**, provided, supplied, furnished, fitted out: *beautiful, well-appointed houses*

appointment NOUN **1 = selection**, naming, election, choosing, choice, commissioning, delegation, nomination, installation, assignment, allotment, designation: *his appointment as foreign minister in 1985* **2 = job**, office, position, post, situation, place, station, employment, assignment, berth (*informal*): *He is to take up an appointment as a researcher with the Society.* **3 = meeting**, interview, date, session, arrangement, consultation, engagement, fixture, rendezvous, tryst (*archaic*), assignation: *She has an appointment with her accountant.* **4 = appointee**, candidate, representative, delegate, nominee, office-holder: *He is the new appointment at RSA.*

apportion VERB **= divide**, share, deal, distribute, assign, allocate, dispense, give out, allot, mete out, dole out, measure out, parcel out, ration out

apposite ADJECTIVE **= appropriate**, fitting, suited, suitable, relevant, proper, to the point, apt, applicable, pertinent, befitting, apropos, germane, to the purpose, appertaining **OPPOSITE:** inappropriate

appraisal NOUN **1 = assessment**, opinion, estimate, judgment, evaluation, estimation, sizing up *(informal)*, recce *(slang)*: *Self-appraisal is never easy.* **2 = valuation**, pricing, rating, survey, reckoning, assay: *He has resisted being drawn into the business of cost appraisal.*

appraise VERB **= assess**, judge, review, estimate, survey, price, rate, value, evaluate, inspect, gauge, size up *(informal)*, eye up, assay, recce *(slang)*

> **USAGE**
> *Appraise* is sometimes used where *apprise* is meant: *both patients had been fully apprised* (not *appraised*) *of the situation*. This may well be due to the fact that *appraise* is considerably more common, and that people therefore tend to associate this meaning mistakenly with a word they know better.

appreciable ADJECTIVE **= significant**, marked, obvious, considerable, substantial, visible, evident, pronounced, definite, noticeable, clear-cut, discernible, measurable, material, recognizable, detectable, perceptible, distinguishable, ascertainable, perceivable **OPPOSITE:** insignificant

appreciably ADVERB **= significantly**, obviously, definitely, considerably, substantially, evidently, visibly, markedly, noticeably, palpably, perceptively, measurably, recognizably, discernibly, detectably, distinguishably, perceivably, ascertainably

appreciate VERB **1 = enjoy**, like, value, regard, respect, prize, admire, treasure, esteem, relish, cherish, savour, rate highly: *Anyone can appreciate our music.* **OPPOSITE:** scorn **2 = be aware of**, know, understand, estimate, realize, acknowledge, recognize, perceive, comprehend, take account of, be sensitive to, be conscious of, sympathize with, be alive to, be cognizant of: *She never really appreciated the depth of the conflict.* **OPPOSITE:** be unaware of **3 = be grateful for**, be obliged for, be thankful for, give thanks for, be indebted for, be in debt for, be appreciative of: *I'd appreciate it if you didn't mention that.* **OPPOSITE:** be ungrateful for **4 = increase**, rise, grow, gain, improve, mount, enhance, soar, inflate: *There is little confidence that houses will appreciate in value.* **OPPOSITE:** fall

appreciation NOUN **1 = admiration**, liking, respect, assessment, esteem, relish, valuation, enjoyment, appraisal, estimation, responsiveness: *He whistled in appreciation.* **2 = gratitude**, thanks, recognition, obligation, acknowledgment, indebtedness, thankfulness, gratefulness: *the gifts presented to them in appreciation of their work* **OPPOSITE:** ingratitude **3 = awareness**, understanding, regard, knowledge, recognition, perception, sympathy, consciousness, sensitivity, realization, comprehension, familiarity, mindfulness, cognizance: *They have a strong appreciation of the importance of economic incentives.* **OPPOSITE:** ignorance **4 = increase**, rise, gain, growth, inflation, improvement, escalation, enhancement: *You have to take capital appreciation of the property into account.* **OPPOSITE:** fall **5 = review**, report, notice, analysis, criticism, praise, assessment, recognition, tribute, evaluation, critique, acclamation: *I had written an appreciation of his work for a magazine.*

appreciative ADJECTIVE **1 = enthusiastic**, understanding, pleased, aware, sensitive, conscious, admiring, sympathetic, supportive, responsive, knowledgeable, respectful, mindful, perceptive, in the know *(informal)*, cognizant, regardful: *There is a murmur of appreciative laughter.* **2 = grateful**, obliged, thankful, indebted, beholden: *We are very appreciative of their support.*

apprehend VERB **1 = arrest**, catch, lift *(slang)*, nick *(slang, chiefly Brit.)*, capture, seize, run in *(slang)*, take, nail *(informal)*, bust *(informal)*, collar *(informal)*, pinch *(informal)*, nab *(informal)*, take prisoner, feel your collar *(slang)*: *Police have not apprehended her killer.* **OPPOSITE:** release **2 = understand**, know, think, believe, imagine, realize, recognize, appreciate, perceive, grasp, conceive, comprehend, get the message, get the picture: *Only now can I begin to apprehend the power of these forces.* **OPPOSITE:** be unaware of

apprehension NOUN **1 = anxiety**, concern, fear, worry, doubt, alarm, suspicion, dread, unease, mistrust, misgiving, disquiet, premonition, trepidation, foreboding, uneasiness, pins and needles, apprehensiveness: *It reflects real anger and apprehension about the future.* **OPPOSITE:** confidence **2 = arrest**, catching, capture, taking, seizure: *information leading to the apprehension of the alleged killer* **OPPOSITE:** release **3 = awareness**, understanding, knowledge, intelligence, ken, perception, grasp, comprehension: *the sudden apprehension of something* **OPPOSITE:** incomprehension

apprehensive ADJECTIVE **= anxious**, concerned, worried, afraid, alarmed, nervous, suspicious, doubtful, uneasy, fearful, neurotic, disquieted, foreboding, twitchy *(informal)*, mistrustful, antsy *(informal)* **OPPOSITE:** confident

apprentice NOUN **= trainee**, student, pupil, novice, beginner, learner, neophyte, tyro, probationer **OPPOSITE:** master

apprenticeship NOUN **= traineeship**, probation, studentship, novitiate *or* noviciate

apprise VERB **= make aware**, tell, warn, advise, inform, communicate, notify, enlighten, acquaint, give notice, make cognizant

approach VERB **1 = move towards**, come to, reach, near, advance, catch up, meet, come close, gain on, converge on, come near, push forward, draw near, creep up on: *When I approached them they fell silent.* **2 = make a proposal to**, speak to, apply to, appeal to, proposition, solicit, sound out, make overtures to, make advances to, broach the matter with: *When he approached me about the job, my first reaction was disbelief.* **3 = set about**, tackle, undertake, embark on, get down to, launch into, begin work on, commence on, make a start on, enter upon: *The bank has approached the issue in a practical way.* **4 = approximate**, touch, be like, compare with, resemble, come close to, border on, verge on, be comparable to, come near to: *They race at speeds approaching 200mph.*
▷ NOUN **1 = advance**, coming, nearing, appearance, arrival, advent, drawing near: *At their approach the little boy ran away and hid.* **2 = access**, way, drive, road, passage, entrance, avenue, passageway: *The path serves as an approach to the boat house.* **3** *(often plural)* **= proposal**, offer, appeal, advance, application, invitation, proposition, overture: *There had already been approaches from interested buyers.* **4 = way**, means, course, style, attitude, method, technique, manner, procedure, mode, modus operandi: *We will be exploring different approaches to information-gathering.* **5 = approximation**, likeness, semblance: *the nearest approach to an apology we have so far heard*

approachable ADJECTIVE **1 = friendly**, open, cordial, sociable, affable, congenial: *We found him very approachable and easy to talk to.* **OPPOSITE:** unfriendly **2 = accessible**, attainable, reachable, get-at-able *(informal)*, come-at-able *(informal)*: *It is approachable on foot for only a few hours a day.* **OPPOSITE:** inaccessible

appropriate ADJECTIVE **= suitable**, right, fitting, fit, suited, correct, belonging, relevant, proper, to the point, in keeping, apt, applicable, pertinent, befitting, well-suited, well-timed, apposite, apropos, opportune, becoming, seemly, felicitous, germane, to the purpose, appurtenant, congruous: *It is appropriate that Irish names dominate the list.* **OPPOSITE:** unsuitable
▷ VERB **1 = seize**, take, claim, assume, take over, acquire, confiscate, annex, usurp, impound, pre-empt, commandeer, take possession of, expropriate, arrogate: *Several other*

newspapers have appropriated the idea. **OPPOSITE:** relinquish **2 = allocate**, allow, budget, devote, assign, designate, set aside, earmark, allot, share out, apportion: *He is sceptical that Congress will appropriate more money for this.* **OPPOSITE:** withhold **3 = steal**, take, nick *(slang, chiefly Brit.)*, pocket, pinch *(informal)*, pirate, poach, swipe *(slang)*, lift *(informal)*, heist *(U.S. slang)*, embezzle, blag *(slang)*, pilfer, misappropriate, snitch *(slang)*, purloin, filch, plagiarize, thieve, peculate: *What do they think about your appropriating their music and culture?*

appropriateness NOUN **= suitability**, fitness, relevance, correctness, felicity, rightness, applicability, timeliness, aptness, pertinence, fittingness, seemliness, appositeness, properness, germaneness, opportuneness, becomingness, congruousness, felicitousness, well-suitedness

appropriation NOUN **1 = setting aside**, assignment, allocation, earmarking, allotment, apportionment: *The government raised defence appropriations by 12 per cent.* **2 = seizure**, taking, takeover, assumption, annexation, confiscation, commandeering, expropriation, pre-emption, usurpation, impoundment, arrogation: *fraud and illegal appropriation of land*

approval NOUN **1 = consent**, agreement, sanction, licence, blessing, permission, recommendation, concession, confirmation, mandate, endorsement, leave, compliance, the go-ahead *(informal)*, countenance, ratification, the green light, assent, authorization, validation, acquiescence, imprimatur, concurrence, O.K. *or* okay *(informal)*, endorsation *(Canad.)*: *The proposed modifications met with widespread approval.* **2 = favour**, liking, regard, respect, praise, esteem, acclaim, appreciation, encouragement, admiration, applause, commendation, approbation, good opinion: *an obsessive drive to win his father's approval* **OPPOSITE:** disapproval

approve VERB **= agree to**, second, allow, pass, accept, confirm, recommend, permit, sanction, advocate, bless, endorse, uphold, mandate, authorize, ratify, go along with, subscribe to, consent to, buy into *(informal)*, validate, countenance, rubber stamp, accede to, give the go-ahead to *(informal)*, give the green light to, assent to, concur in, O.K. *or* okay *(informal)*: *MPs approved the bill by a majority of 97.* **OPPOSITE:** veto **approve of something** *or* **someone = favour**, like, support, respect, praise, appreciate, agree with, admire, endorse, esteem, acclaim, applaud, commend, be pleased with, have a good opinion of, regard highly, think highly of: *Not everyone approves of the festival.*

approving ADJECTIVE **= favourable**, admiring, applauding, respectful, appreciative, commendatory, acclamatory

approximate ADJECTIVE **= rough**, close, general, near, estimated, loose, vague, hazy, sketchy, amorphous, imprecise, inexact, almost exact, almost accurate: *The times are approximate only.* **OPPOSITE:** exact **approximate to = resemble**, reach, approach, touch, come close to, border on, come near, verge on: *Something approximating a just outcome will be ensured.*

approximately ADVERB **= almost**, about, around, generally, nearly, close to, relatively, roughly, loosely, just about, more or less, in the region of, in the vicinity of, not far off, in the neighbourhood of

approximation NOUN **= guess**, estimate, conjecture, estimation, guesswork, rough idea, rough calculation, ballpark figure *(informal)*, ballpark estimate *(informal)*: *That's an approximation, but my guess is there'll be a reasonable balance.*

a priori ADJECTIVE **= deduced**, deductive, inferential

apron NOUN **= pinny**, overall, pinafore *(informal)*

apropos ADJECTIVE **= appropriate**, right, seemly, fitting, fit, related, correct, belonging, suitable, relevant, proper, to the point, apt, applicable, pertinent, befitting, apposite, opportune, germane, to the purpose: *It was a verse from the book of Job. Very apropos.* **apropos of = concerning**, about, re, regarding, respecting, on the subject of, in respect of, as to, with reference to, in re, in the matter of, as regards, in *or* with regard to: *Apropos of the party, have you had any further thoughts on a venue?*

apt ADJECTIVE **1 = appropriate**, timely, right, seemly, fitting, fit, related, correct, belonging, suitable, relevant, proper, to the point, applicable, pertinent, befitting, apposite, apropos, opportune, germane, to the purpose: *The words of this report are as apt today as they were in 1929.* **OPPOSITE:** inappropriate **2 = inclined**, likely, ready, disposed, prone, liable, given, predisposed, of a mind: *She was apt to raise her voice and wave her hands about.* **3 = gifted**, skilled, expert, quick, bright, talented, sharp, capable, smart, prompt, clever, intelligent, accomplished, ingenious, skilful, astute, adroit, teachable: *She was never a very apt student.* **OPPOSITE:** slow

aptitude NOUN **= gift**, ability, talent, capacity, intelligence, leaning, bent, tendency, faculty, capability, flair, inclination, disposition, knack, propensity, proficiency, predilection, cleverness, proclivity, quickness, giftedness, proneness, aptness

arable ADJECTIVE **= productive**, fertile, fruitful, fecund, cultivable, farmable, ploughable, tillable

arbiter NOUN **1 = judge**, referee, umpire, umpie *(Austral. slang)*, arbitrator, adjudicator: *the court's role as arbiter in the law-making process* **2 = authority**, expert, master, governor, ruler, dictator, controller, lord, pundit: *Sequins have often aroused the scorn of arbiters of taste.*

arbitrary ADJECTIVE **1 = random**, chance, optional, subjective, unreasonable, inconsistent, erratic, discretionary, personal, fanciful, wilful, whimsical, capricious: *Arbitrary arrests were common.* **OPPOSITE:** logical **2 = dictatorial**, absolute, unlimited, uncontrolled, autocratic, dogmatic, imperious, domineering, unrestrained, overbearing, tyrannical, summary, magisterial, despotic, high-handed, peremptory, tyrannous: *the virtually unlimited arbitrary power of slave owners*

arbitrate VERB **= decide**, judge, determine, settle, referee, umpire, mediate, adjudicate, adjudge, pass judgment, sit in judgment

arbitration NOUN **= decision**, settlement, judgment, determination, adjudication, arbitrament

arbitrator NOUN **= judge**, referee, umpire, umpie *(Austral. slang)*, arbiter, adjudicator

arc NOUN **= curve**, bend, bow, arch, crescent, half-moon

arcade NOUN **= gallery**, mall, cloister, portico, colonnade, covered walk, peristyle

arcane ADJECTIVE **= mysterious**, secret, hidden, esoteric, occult, recondite, cabbalistic

arch[1] NOUN **1 = archway**, curve, dome, span, vault: *The theatre is located under old railway arches in the East End.* **2 = curve**, bend, bow, crook, arc, hunch, sweep, hump, curvature, semicircle: *Train the cane supports to form an arch.*
▷ VERB **= curve**, bridge, bend, bow, span, arc: *the domed ceiling arching overhead*

arch[2] ADJECTIVE **= playful**, joking, teasing, humorous, sly, mischievous, saucy, tongue-in-cheek, jesting, jokey, pert, good-natured, roguish, frolicsome, waggish: *a slightly amused, arch expression*

archaic ADJECTIVE **1 = old**, ancient, antique, primitive, bygone, olden *(archaic)*: *archaic sculpture and porcelain* **OPPOSITE:** modern **2 = old-fashioned**, obsolete, out of date, antiquated, outmoded, passé, old hat, behind the times, superannuated: *These archaic practices are advocated by people of limited outlook.* **OPPOSITE:** up-to-date

arched ADJECTIVE = **curved**, domed, vaulted

archer NOUN = **bowman** *(archaic)*, toxophilite *(formal)*

archetypal *or* **archetypical** ADJECTIVE = **typical**, standard, model, original, normal, classic, ideal, exemplary, paradigmatic, prototypal, prototypic *or* prototypical

archetype NOUN = **prime example**, standard, model, original, pattern, classic, ideal, norm, form, prototype, paradigm, exemplar

architect NOUN **1 = designer**, planner, draughtsman, master builder: *Employ an architect to make sure the plans comply with regulations.* **2 = creator**, father, shaper, engineer, author, maker, designer, founder, deviser, planner, inventor, contriver, originator, prime mover, instigator, initiator: *the country's chief architect of economic reform*

QUOTATIONS

architect: one who drafts a plan of your house, and plans a draft of your money
[Ambrose Bierce *The Devil's Dictionary*]

archive NOUN = **record office**, museum, registry, repository: *I decided I would go to the archive and look up the issue.* ▷ PLURAL NOUN = **records**, papers, accounts, rolls, documents, files, registers, deeds, chronicles, annals: *the archives of the Imperial War Museum*

Arctic ADJECTIVE = **polar**, far-northern, hyperborean

arctic ADJECTIVE = **freezing**, cold, frozen, icy, chilly, frosty, glacial, frigid, gelid, frost-bound, cold as ice

ardent ADJECTIVE **1 = enthusiastic**, keen, eager, avid, zealous, keen as mustard: *an ardent opponent of the war* **OPPOSITE:** indifferent **2 = passionate**, warm, spirited, intense, flaming, fierce, fiery, hot, fervent, impassioned, ablaze, lusty, vehement, amorous, hot-blooded, warm-blooded, fervid: *an ardent lover* **OPPOSITE:** cold

ardour NOUN **1 = passion**, feeling, fire, heat, spirit, intensity, warmth, devotion, fervour, vehemence, fierceness: *The sexual ardour had cooled.* **2 = enthusiasm**, zeal, eagerness, earnestness, keenness, avidity: *my ardour for football*

arduous ADJECTIVE = **difficult**, trying, hard, tough, tiring, severe, painful, exhausting, punishing, harsh, taxing, heavy, steep, formidable, fatiguing, rigorous, troublesome, gruelling, strenuous, onerous, laborious, burdensome, backbreaking, toilsome **OPPOSITE:** easy

area NOUN **1 = region**, land, quarter, division, sector, district, stretch, territory, zone, plot, province, patch, neighbourhood, sphere, turf *(U.S. slang)*, realm, domain, tract, locality, neck of the woods *(informal)*: *the large number of community groups in the area* **2 = part**, section, sector, portion: *You will notice that your baby has two soft areas on its head.* **3 = range**, reach, size, sweep, extent, scope, sphere, domain, width, compass, breadth, parameters *(informal)*, latitude, expanse, radius, ambit, footprint: *Although large in area, the flat did not have many rooms.* **4 = realm**, part, department, field, province, arena, sphere, domain: *She wanted to be involved in every area of my life.*

arena NOUN **1 = ring**, ground, stage, field, theatre, bowl, pitch, stadium, enclosure, park *(U.S. & Canad.)*, coliseum, amphitheatre: *the largest indoor sports arena in the world* **2 = scene**, world, area, stage, field, theatre, sector, territory, province, forum, scope, sphere, realm, domain: *He has no intention of withdrawing from the political arena.*

arguably ADVERB = **possibly**, potentially, conceivably, plausibly, feasibly, questionably, debatably, deniably, disputably, contestably, controvertibly, dubitably, refutably

argue VERB **1 = quarrel**, fight, row, clash, dispute, disagree, feud, squabble, spar, wrangle, bicker, have an argument, cross swords, be at sixes and sevens, fight like cat and dog, go at it hammer and tongs, bandy words, altercate: *They were still arguing. I could hear them down the road.* **2 = discuss**, debate, dispute, thrash out, exchange views on, controvert: *The two of them were arguing this point.* **3 = claim**, question, reason, challenge, insist, maintain, hold, allege, plead, assert, contend, uphold, profess, remonstrate, expostulate: *His lawyers are arguing that he is unfit to stand trial.* **4 = demonstrate**, show, suggest, display, indicate, imply, exhibit, denote, evince: *I'd like to argue in a framework that is less exaggerated.*

argument NOUN **1 = reason**, case, reasoning, ground(s), defence, excuse, logic, justification, rationale, polemic, dialectic, line of reasoning, argumentation: *There's a strong argument for lowering the price.* **2 = debate**, questioning, claim, row, discussion, dispute, controversy, pleading, plea, contention, assertion, polemic, altercation, remonstrance, expostulation, remonstration: *The issue has caused heated political argument.* **3 = quarrel**, fight, row, clash, dispute, controversy, disagreement, misunderstanding, feud, barney *(informal)*, squabble, wrangle, bickering, difference of opinion, tiff, altercation: *She got into a heated argument with a stranger.* **OPPOSITE:** agreement

argumentative ADJECTIVE = **quarrelsome**, contrary, contentious, belligerent, combative, opinionated, litigious, disputatious **OPPOSITE:** easy-going

arid ADJECTIVE **1 = dry**, desert, dried up, barren, sterile, torrid, parched, waterless, moistureless: *the arid zones of the country* **OPPOSITE:** lush **2 = boring**, dull, tedious, dreary, dry, tiresome, lifeless, colourless, uninteresting, flat, uninspired, vapid, spiritless, jejune, as dry as dust: *She had given him the only joy his arid life had ever known.* **OPPOSITE:** exciting

arise VERB **1 = happen**, start, begin, follow, issue, result, appear, develop, emerge, occur, spring, set in, stem, originate, ensue, come about, commence, come to light, emanate, crop up *(informal)*, come into being, materialize: *if a problem arises later in pregnancy* **2 = get to your feet**, get up, rise, stand up, spring up, leap up: *I arose from the chair and left.* **3 = get up**, wake up, awaken, get out of bed: *He arose at 6:30 a.m. as usual.* **4 = ascend**, rise, lift, mount, climb, tower, soar, move upward: *the flat terrace, from which arises the volume of the house*

aristocracy NOUN = **upper class**, elite, nobility, gentry, peerage, ruling class, patricians, upper crust *(informal)*, noblesse *(literary)*, haut monde *(French)*, patriciate, body of nobles **OPPOSITE:** commoners

QUOTATIONS

Democracy means government by the uneducated, while aristocracy means government by the badly educated
[G.K. Chesterton *New York Times*]

An aristocracy in a republic is like a chicken whose head has been cut off; it may run about in a lively way, but in fact it is dead
[Nancy Mitford *Noblesse Oblige*]

There is a natural aristocracy among men. The grounds of this are virtue and talent
[Thomas Jefferson *Letter to John Adams*]

aristocrat NOUN = **noble**, lord, lady, peer, patrician, grandee, nobleman, aristo *(informal)*, childe *(archaic)*, noblewoman, peeress

aristocratic ADJECTIVE **1 = upper-class**, lordly, titled, gentle *(archaic)*, elite, gentlemanly, noble, patrician, blue-blooded, well-born, highborn: *a wealthy, aristocratic family* **OPPOSITE:** common **2 = refined**, fine, polished, elegant, stylish, dignified, haughty, courtly, snobbish, well-bred: *He laughed it off with aristocratic indifference.* **OPPOSITE:** vulgar

arm[1] NOUN **1 = upper limb**, limb, appendage: *She stretched her arms out.* **2 = branch**, part, office, department, division, section, wing, sector, extension, detachment, offshoot, subdivision, subsection: *the research arm of Congress* **3 = authority**, might, force, power, strength, command, sway, potency: *Local people say the long arm of the law was too heavy-handed.* **4 = inlet**, bay, passage, entrance, creek, cove, fjord, bight, ingress, sea loch *(Scot.)*, firth *or* frith *(Scot.)*

an arm and a leg = **a lot of money**,

a bomb (*Brit. slang*), a fortune, a pile (*informal*), big money, a packet (*slang*), a bundle (*slang*), big bucks (*informal, chiefly U.S.*), a tidy sum (*informal*), a king's ransom, a pretty penny (*informal*)
would give your right arm for something = would do anything for, would kill for, would sell your own grandmother for (*informal*), would give your eye teeth for

arm² VERB **1 = equip**, provide, supply, outfit, rig, array, furnish, issue with, deck out, accoutre: *She had armed herself with a loaded rifle.* **2 = provide**, prime, prepare, protect, guard, strengthen, outfit, equip, brace, fortify, forearm, make ready, gird your loins, jack up (*N.Z.*): *She armed herself with all the knowledge she could gather.*
▷ PLURAL NOUN **= weapons**, guns, firearms, weaponry, armaments, ordnance, munitions, instruments of war: *The organization has an extensive supply of arms.*

armada NOUN **= fleet**, navy, squadron, flotilla

armaments PLURAL NOUN **= weapons**, arms, guns, ammunition, weaponry, ordnance, munitions, materiel

armed ADJECTIVE **= carrying weapons**, provided, prepared, supplied, ready, protected, guarded, strengthened, equipped, primed, arrayed, furnished, fortified, in arms, forearmed, fitted out, under arms, girded, rigged out, tooled up (*slang*), accoutred

armistice NOUN **= truce**, peace, ceasefire, suspension of hostilities

armour NOUN **= protection**, covering, shield, sheathing, armour plate, chain mail, protective covering

armoured ADJECTIVE **= protected**, mailed, reinforced, toughened, bulletproof, armour-plated, steel-plated, ironclad, bombproof

armoury or (*U.S.*) **armory** NOUN **= arsenal**, magazine, ammunition dump, arms depot, ordnance depot

army NOUN **1 = soldiers**, military, troops, armed force, legions, infantry, military force, land forces, land force, soldiery: *After returning from abroad, he joined the army.* **2 = vast number**, host, gang, mob, flock, array, legion, swarm, sea, pack, horde, multitude, throng: *data collected by an army of volunteers*

> QUOTATIONS
> I don't know what effect these men will have upon the enemy, but, by God, they terrify me
> [Duke of Wellington]

> PROVERBS
> *An army marches on its stomach*

aroma NOUN **= scent**, smell, perfume, fragrance, bouquet, savour, odour, redolence

aromatic ADJECTIVE **= fragrant**, perfumed, spicy, savoury, pungent, balmy, redolent, sweet-smelling, sweet-scented, odoriferous
OPPOSITE: smelly

around PREPOSITION
1 = approximately, about, nearly, close to, roughly, just about, in the region of, circa (*of a date*), in the vicinity of, not far off, in the neighbourhood of: *My salary was around £19,000.* **2 = surrounding**, about, enclosing, encompassing, framing, encircling, on all sides of, on every side of, environing: *a prosperous suburb built around a new mosque*
▷ ADVERB **1 = everywhere**, about, throughout, all over, here and there, on all sides, in all directions, to and fro: *What are you doing following me around?* **2 = near**, close, nearby, handy, at hand, close by, close at hand: *It's important to have lots of people around.*
▸ *related prefix*: circum-

> USAGE
> In American English, *around* is used more often than *round* as an adverb and preposition, except in a few fixed phrases such as *all year round*. In British English, *round* is more commonly used as an adverb than *around*.

arousal NOUN **= stimulation**, movement, response, reaction, excitement, animation, stirring up, provocation, inflammation, agitation, exhilaration, incitement, enlivenment

arouse VERB **1 = stimulate**, encourage, inspire, prompt, spark, spur, foster, provoke, rouse, stir up, inflame, incite, instigate, whip up, summon up, whet, kindle, foment, call forth: *His work has aroused intense interest.* **OPPOSITE:** quell **2 = inflame**, move, warm, excite, spur, provoke, animate, prod, stir up, agitate, quicken, enliven, goad, foment: *He apologized, saying this subject always aroused him.* **3 = awaken**, wake up, rouse, waken: *We were aroused from our sleep by a knocking at the door.*

arraign VERB **= accuse**, charge, prosecute, denounce, indict, impeach, incriminate, call to account, take to task

arrange VERB **1 = plan**, agree, prepare, determine, schedule, organize, construct, devise, contrive, fix up, jack up (*N.Z. informal*): *She arranged an appointment for Friday afternoon.* **2 = put in order**, group, form, order, sort, class, position, range, file, rank, line up, organize, set out, sequence, exhibit, sort out (*informal*), array, classify, tidy, marshal, align, categorize, systematize, jack up (*N.Z. informal*): *He started to arrange the books in piles.* **OPPOSITE:** disorganize **3 = adapt**, score, orchestrate, harmonize, instrument: *The songs were arranged by a well-known pianist.*

arrangement NOUN **1** (*often plural*) **= plan**, planning, provision, preparation: *I am in charge of all the travel arrangements.* **2 = agreement**, contract, settlement, appointment, compromise, deal (*informal*), pact, compact, covenant: *The caves can be visited only by prior arrangement.* **3 = display**, grouping, system, order, ordering, design, ranging, structure, rank, organization, exhibition, line-up, presentation, array, marshalling, classification, disposition, alignment, setup (*informal*): *an imaginative flower arrangement* **4 = adaptation**, score, version, interpretation, instrumentation, orchestration, harmonization: *an arrangement of a well-known piece by Mozart*

array NOUN **1 = arrangement**, show, order, supply, display, collection, exhibition, line-up, mixture, parade, formation, presentation, spectacle, marshalling, muster, disposition: *the markets with their wonderful arrays of fruit and vegetables* **2 = clothing**, dress, clothes, threads (*slang*), garments, apparel, attire, garb, finery, regalia, raiment (*archaic, poetic*), schmutter (*slang*): *Bathed, dressed in his finest array, he was ready.*
▷ VERB **1 = arrange**, show, group, order, present, range, display, line up, sequence, parade, exhibit, unveil, dispose, draw up, marshal, lay out, muster, align, form up, place in order, set in line (*Military*): *Here are arrayed such 20th century relics as Madonna's bustier.* **2 = dress**, supply, clothe, wrap, deck, outfit, decorate, equip, robe, get ready, adorn, apparel (*archaic*), festoon, attire, fit out, garb, bedeck, caparison, accoutre: *a priest arrayed in white vestments*

arrest VERB **1 = capture**, catch, lift (*slang*), nick (*slang, chiefly Brit.*), seize, run in (*slang*), nail (*informal*), bust (*informal*), collar (*informal*), take, detain, pinch (*informal*), nab (*informal*), apprehend, take prisoner, take into custody, lay hold of: *Seven people were arrested for minor offences.* **OPPOSITE:** release **2 = stop**, end, hold, limit, check, block, slow, delay, halt, stall, stay, interrupt, suppress, restrain, hamper, inhibit, hinder, obstruct, retard, impede: *The new rules could arrest the development of good research.* **OPPOSITE:** speed up **3 = fascinate**, hold, involve, catch, occupy, engage, grip, absorb, entrance, intrigue, rivet, enthral, mesmerize, engross, spellbind: *As he reached the hall, he saw what had arrested her.*
▷ NOUN **1 = capture**, bust (*informal*), detention, seizure, apprehension: *information leading to the arrest of the bombers* **OPPOSITE:** release **2 = stoppage**, halt, suppression, obstruction, inhibition, blockage, hindrance: *a cardiac arrest*
OPPOSITE: acceleration

arresting ADJECTIVE **= striking**, surprising, engaging, dramatic, stunning, impressive, extraordinary, outstanding, remarkable, noticeable, conspicuous, salient, jaw-dropping **OPPOSITE:** unremarkable

arrival NOUN **1 = appearance**, coming, arriving, entrance, advent, materialization: *the day after his arrival* **2 = coming**, happening, taking place, dawn, emergence, occurrence, materialization: *They celebrated the arrival of the New Year.* **3 = newcomer**, arriver, incomer, visitor, caller, entrant, comer, visitant: *A high proportion of the new arrivals are skilled professionals.*

arrive VERB **1 = come**, appear, enter, turn up, show up *(informal)*, materialize, draw near: *Fresh groups of guests arrived.* **OPPOSITE:** depart **2 = occur**, happen, take place, ensue, transpire, fall, befall: *They needed to be much further forward before winter arrived.* **3 = succeed**, make it *(informal)*, triumph, do well, thrive, flourish, be successful, make good, prosper, cut it *(informal)*, reach the top, become famous, make the grade *(informal)*, get to the top, crack it *(informal)*, hit the jackpot *(informal)*, turn out well, make your mark *(informal)*, achieve recognition, do all right for yourself *(informal)*: *These are cars which show you've arrived.*
arrive at something = reach, make, get to, enter, land at, get as far as: *She arrived at the airport early this morning.*

arrogance NOUN **= conceit**, pride, swagger, pretension, presumption, bluster, hubris, pomposity, insolence, hauteur, pretentiousness, high-handedness, haughtiness, loftiness, imperiousness, pompousness, superciliousness, lordliness, conceitedness, contemptuousness, scornfulness, uppishness *(Brit. informal)*, disdainfulness, overweeningness **OPPOSITE:** modesty

arrogant ADJECTIVE **= conceited**, lordly, assuming, proud, swaggering, pompous, pretentious, stuck up *(informal)*, cocky, contemptuous, blustering, imperious, overbearing, haughty, scornful, puffed up, egotistical, disdainful, self-important, presumptuous, high-handed, insolent, supercilious, high and mighty *(informal)*, overweening, immodest, swollen-headed, bigheaded *(informal)*, uppish *(Brit. informal)* **OPPOSITE:** modest

arrow NOUN **1 = dart**, flight, reed *(archaic)*, bolt, shaft *(archaic)*, quarrel: *warriors armed with bows and arrows* **2 = pointer**, indicator, marker: *A series of arrows point the way to his grave.*

arsenal NOUN **1 = store**, stock, supply, magazine, stockpile **2 = armoury**, storehouse, ammunition dump, arms depot, ordnance depot: *Terrorists had broken into the arsenal and stolen a range of weapons.*

art NOUN **1 = artwork**, style of art, fine art, creativity: *the first exhibition of such art in the West* **2 = skill**, knowledge, method, facility, craft, profession, expertise, competence, accomplishment, mastery, knack, ingenuity, finesse, aptitude, artistry, artifice *(archaic)*, virtuosity, dexterity, cleverness, adroitness: *the art of seduction and romance*

artful ADJECTIVE **1 = cunning**, designing, scheming, sharp, smart, clever, subtle, intriguing, tricky, shrewd, sly, wily, politic, crafty, foxy, deceitful: *the smiles and artifices of a subtly artful woman*
OPPOSITE: straightforward **2 = skilful**, masterly, smart, clever, subtle, ingenious, adept, resourceful, proficient, adroit, dexterous: *There is also an artful contrast of shapes.*
OPPOSITE: clumsy

article NOUN **1 = feature**, story, paper, piece, item, creation, essay, composition, discourse, treatise: *a newspaper article* **2 = thing**, piece, unit, item, object, device, tool, implement, commodity, gadget, utensil: *household articles* **3 = clause**, point, part, heading, head, matter, detail, piece, particular, division, section, item, passage, portion, paragraph, proviso: *article 50 of the UN charter*

articulate ADJECTIVE **= expressive**, clear, effective, vocal, meaningful, understandable, coherent, persuasive, fluent, eloquent, lucid, comprehensible, communicative, intelligible: *She is an articulate young woman.* **OPPOSITE:** incoherent
▷ VERB **1 = express**, say, tell, state, word, speak, declare, phrase, communicate, assert, pronounce, utter, couch, put across, enunciate, put into words, verbalize, asseverate: *He failed to articulate an overall vision.* **2 = pronounce**, say, talk, speak, voice, utter, enunciate, vocalize, enounce: *He articulated each syllable.*

articulation NOUN **1 = expression**, delivery, pronunciation, saying, talking, voicing, speaking, utterance, diction, enunciation, vocalization, verbalization: *an actor able to sustain clear articulation over long periods* **2 = voicing**, statement, expression, verbalization: *a way of restricting their articulation of grievances* **3 = joint**, coupling, jointing, connection, hinge, juncture: *the articulation of different modes of production*

artifice NOUN **1 = cunning**, scheming, trick, device, craft, tactic, manoeuvre, deception, hoax, expedient, ruse, guile, trickery, duplicity, subterfuge, stratagem, contrivance, chicanery, wile, craftiness, artfulness, slyness, machination: *the artifice and illusion of sleight-of-hand card tricks* **2 = cleverness**, skill, facility, invention, ingenuity, finesse, inventiveness, deftness, adroitness: *a combination of theatrical artifice and dazzling cinematic movement*

artificial ADJECTIVE **1 = synthetic**, manufactured, plastic, man-made, non-natural: *free from artificial additives and flavours* **2 = insincere**, forced, affected, assumed, phoney or phony *(informal)*, put on, false, pretended, hollow, contrived, unnatural, feigned, spurious, meretricious: *The voice was affected, the accent artificial.*
OPPOSITE: genuine **3 = fake**, mock, imitation, bogus, simulated, phoney or phony *(informal)*, sham, pseudo *(informal)*, fabricated, counterfeit, spurious, ersatz, specious: *The sauce was glutinous and tasted artificial.*
OPPOSITE: authentic

artillery NOUN **= big guns**, battery, cannon, ordnance, gunnery, cannonry

artisan NOUN **= craftsman**, technician, mechanic, journeyman, artificer, handicraftsman, skilled workman

artist NOUN **= creator**, master, maker, craftsman, artisan *(obsolete)*, fine artist

artiste NOUN **= performer**, player, entertainer, Thespian, trouper, play-actor

artistic ADJECTIVE **1 = creative**, cultured, original, sensitive, sophisticated, refined, imaginative, aesthetic, discerning, eloquent, arty *(informal)*: *They encourage boys to be sensitive and artistic.*
OPPOSITE: untalented **2 = beautiful**, fine, pleasing, lovely, creative, elegant, stylish, cultivated, imaginative, decorative, aesthetic, exquisite, graceful, expressive, ornamental, tasteful: *an artistic arrangement* **OPPOSITE:** unattractive

artistry NOUN **= skill**, art, style, taste, talent, craft, genius, creativity, touch, flair, brilliance, sensibility, accomplishment, mastery, finesse, craftsmanship, proficiency, virtuosity, workmanship, artistic ability

artless ADJECTIVE **1 = natural**, simple, fair, frank, plain, pure, open, round, true, direct, genuine, humble, straightforward, sincere, honest, candid, unaffected, upfront *(informal)*, unpretentious, unadorned, dinkum *(Austral. & N.Z. informal)*, guileless, uncontrived, undesigning: *his artless air and charming smile*
OPPOSITE: artificial **2 = unskilled**, awkward, crude, primitive, rude, bungling, incompetent, clumsy, inept, untalented, maladroit: *a spiritless and artless display of incompetence*
OPPOSITE: artful

arty ADJECTIVE **= artistic**, arty-farty *(informal)*, arty-crafty *(informal)*

as CONJUNCTION **1 = when**, while, just as, at the time that, during the time that: *All eyes were on him as he continued.* **2 = in the way that**, like, in the manner that: *Behave towards them as you would like to be treated.* **3 = since**, because, seeing that, considering that, on account of the fact that: *This is important as it sets the mood for the day.*

a

▷ PREPOSITION = **in the role of**, being, under the name of, in the character of: *I had natural ability as a footballer.*
as for or **to** = **with regard to**, about, re, concerning, regarding, respecting, relating to, with respect to, on the subject of, with reference to, in reference to, in the matter of, apropos of, as regards, anent (*Scot.*): *As for giving them guns, I don't think that's a very good idea.*
as it were = **in a way**, to some extent, so to speak, in a manner of speaking, so to say: *I understood the words, but I didn't, as it were, understand the question.*

ascend VERB **1** = **climb**, scale, mount, go up: *I held her hand as we ascended the steps.* **OPPOSITE:** go down **2** = **slope upwards**, come up, rise up: *A number of steps ascend from the cobbled street.* **OPPOSITE:** slope downwards **3** = **move up**, rise, go up: *Keep the drill centred as it ascends and descends in the hole.* **OPPOSITE:** move down **4** = **float up**, rise, climb, tower, go up, take off, soar, lift off, fly up: *They ascended 55,900 feet in their balloon.* **OPPOSITE:** descend

ascendancy or **ascendence** NOUN = **influence**, power, control, rule, authority, command, reign, sovereignty, sway, dominance, domination, superiority, supremacy, mastery, dominion, upper hand, hegemony, prevalence, pre-eminence, predominance, rangatiratanga (*N.Z.*) **OPPOSITE:** inferiority

ascendant or **ascendent** ADJECTIVE = **influential**, controlling, ruling, powerful, commanding, supreme, superior, dominant, prevailing, authoritative, predominant, uppermost, pre-eminent: *Radical reformers are once more ascendant.*
in the ascendant = **rising**, increasing, growing, powerful, mounting, climbing, dominating, commanding, supreme, dominant, influential, prevailing, flourishing, ascending, up-and-coming, on the rise, uppermost, on the way up: *Geography, drama, art and English are in the ascendant.*

ascension NOUN **1** = **rise**, rising, mounting, climb, ascending, ascent, moving upwards: *the resurrection and ascension of Jesus Christ* **2** = **succession**, taking over, assumption, inheritance, elevation, entering upon: *fifteen years after his ascension to the throne*

ascent NOUN **1** = **climbing**, scaling, mounting, climb, clambering, ascending, ascension: *He led the first ascent of K2.* **2** = **upward slope**, rise, incline, ramp, gradient, rising ground, acclivity: *It was a tough course over a gradual ascent.* **3** = **rise**, rising, climb, ascension, upward movement: *He pressed the button and the elevator began its slow ascent.*

ascertain VERB = **find out**, learn, discover, determine, confirm, settle, identify, establish, fix, verify, make certain, suss (out) (*slang*), ferret out

ascetic NOUN = **recluse**, monk, nun, abstainer, hermit, anchorite, self-denier: *He left the luxuries of court for a life as an ascetic.* **OPPOSITE:** hedonist
▷ ADJECTIVE = **self-denying**, severe, plain, harsh, stern, rigorous, austere, Spartan, self-disciplined, celibate, puritanical, frugal, abstemious, abstinent: *priests practising an ascetic life* **OPPOSITE:** self-indulgent

ascribe VERB = **attribute**, credit, refer, charge, assign, put down, set down, impute

> **USAGE**
> *Ascribe* is sometimes used where *subscribe* is meant: *I do not subscribe* (not *ascribe*) *to this view of music.*

asexual ADJECTIVE = **sexless**, neutral, neuter

ashamed ADJECTIVE **1** = **embarrassed**, sorry, guilty, upset, distressed, shy, humbled, humiliated, blushing, self-conscious, red-faced, chagrined, flustered, mortified, sheepish, bashful, prudish, crestfallen, discomfited, remorseful, abashed, shamefaced, conscience-stricken, discountenanced: *She was ashamed that she looked so shabby.* **OPPOSITE:** proud **2** = **reluctant**, afraid, embarrassed, scared, unwilling, loath, disinclined: *Women are often ashamed to admit they are being abused.*

ashen ADJECTIVE = **pale**, white, grey, wan, livid, pasty, leaden, colourless, pallid, anaemic, ashy, like death warmed up (*informal*) **OPPOSITE:** rosy

ashore ADVERB = **on land**, on the beach, on the shore, aground, to the shore, on dry land, shorewards, landwards

aside ADVERB = **to one side**, away, alone, separately, apart, alongside, beside, out of the way, on one side, to the side, in isolation, in reserve, out of mind: *She closed the book and laid it aside.*
▷ NOUN = **interpolation**, remark, parenthesis, digression, interposition, confidential remark: *She mutters an aside to the camera.*

ask VERB **1** = **inquire**, question, quiz, query, interrogate: *'How is Frank?' he asked.* **OPPOSITE:** answer **2** = **request**, apply to, appeal to, plead with, demand, urge, sue, pray, beg, petition, crave, solicit, implore, enjoin, beseech, entreat, supplicate: *We had to ask him to leave.* **3** = **invite**, bid, summon: *She asked me back to her house.*

askance ADVERB **1** = **suspiciously**, doubtfully, dubiously, sceptically, disapprovingly, distrustfully, mistrustfully: *They have always looked askance at the western notion of democracy.* **2** = **out of the corner of your eye**, sideways, indirectly, awry, obliquely, with a side glance: *'Do you play chess?' he asked, looking askance at me.*

askew ADJECTIVE = **crooked**, awry, oblique, lopsided, off-centre, cockeyed (*informal*), skewwhiff (*Brit. informal*): *She stood there, hat askew.* **OPPOSITE:** straight
▷ ADVERB = **crookedly**, to one side, awry, obliquely, off-centre, aslant: *Some of the doors hung askew.* **OPPOSITE:** straight

asleep ADJECTIVE = **sleeping**, napping, dormant, crashed out (*slang*), dozing, slumbering, snoozing (*informal*), fast asleep, sound asleep, out for the count, dead to the world (*informal*), in a deep sleep

aspect NOUN **1** = **feature**, point, side, factor, angle, characteristic, facet: *Climate affects every aspect of our lives.* **2** = **position**, view, situation, scene, bearing, direction, prospect, exposure, point of view, outlook: *The house has a south-west aspect.* **3** = **appearance**, look, air, condition, quality, bearing, attitude, cast, manner, expression, countenance, demeanour, mien (*literary*): *The snowy tree assumed a dumb, lifeless aspect.*

aspirant NOUN = **candidate**, applicant, hopeful, aspirer, seeker, suitor, postulant: *He is among the few aspirants with administrative experience.*
▷ ADJECTIVE = **hopeful**, longing, ambitious, eager, striving, aspiring, endeavouring, wishful: *aspirant politicians*

aspiration NOUN = **aim**, longing, end, plan, hope, goal, design, dream, wish, desire, object, intention, objective, ambition, craving, endeavour, yearning, eagerness, Holy Grail (*informal*), hankering

> **QUOTATIONS**
> We are all in the gutter, but some of us are looking at the stars
> [Oscar Wilde *Lady Windermere's Fan*]
>
> An aspiration is a joy for ever, a possession as solid as a landed estate, a fortune which we can never exhaust and which gives us year by a year a revenue of pleasurable activity
> [Robert Louis Stevenson *El Dorado*]

aspire to VERB = **aim for**, desire, pursue, hope for, long for, crave, seek out, wish for, dream about, yearn for, hunger for, hanker after, be eager for, set your heart on, set your sights on, be ambitious for

aspiring ADJECTIVE = **hopeful**, longing, would-be, ambitious, eager, striving, endeavouring, wannabe (*informal*), wishful, aspirant

ass NOUN **1** = **donkey**, moke (*slang*), jennet: *She was led up to the sanctuary on an ass.* **2** = **fool**, dope (*informal*), jerk (*slang, chiefly U.S. & Canad.*), idiot, plank (*Brit. slang*), berk (*Brit. slang*), wally (*slang*), prat (*slang*), charlie (*Brit. informal*), plonker (*slang*), coot, geek (*slang*), twit (*informal, chiefly Brit.*), bonehead (*slang*), dunce, oaf, simpleton, airhead (*slang*), jackass, dipstick (*Brit. slang*), gonzo (*slang*), schmuck (*U.S. slang*), dork (*slang*), nitwit (*informal*), dolt, blockhead, ninny, divvy (*Brit. slang*), pillock (*Brit.

The Language of Catharine Parr Strickland Traill

Catharine Parr Strickland Traill (1802–99), born in Rotherhithe, England, began her career as a children's author, while her later work concerns her experiences as a settler in Canada. Her most significant works include *The Backwoods of Canada*, a collection of letters and journals detailing her observations of the life, people, and nature in Canada, and *The Female Emigrant's Guide*, a guide for new settlers. She was sister to Susanna Moodie, who also wrote about life as a Canadian settler.

Unsurprisingly, as Traill was a keen observer of nature in her new settlement, many of the nouns that she uses most frequently are those referring to nature. *Tree, lake, flower,* and *squirrel* all appear in Traill's twenty most frequently used nouns. Some other frequent nouns are those that refer to people, and *nurse, child,* and *man* are also among the twenty most frequently used nouns in Traill's work. Many of the most salient adjectives with *man,* which occurs over twice as much as *woman,* are those used to distinguish between the settlers and natives, such as *wild, civilized, white* and *Indian.* With regard to character, men are most often described as *brave, hardy,* or *wise.* On the other hand, after *Indian,* the adjectives which are most salient with *woman* include *terrible* and *dreaded,* although it should be noted that women are also described as *brave, gentle,* and *wise.*

The most frequent adjective in Traill's work is *little.* The most salient noun occurring with *little* is *squirrel,* and other prominent nouns include *creature* and *animal.* As well as being descriptive of the size of animals, *little* is used to portray affection towards them, often being modified by *dear*:

> I saw some dear little birds flying about, and I watched them perching on the dry stalks of the tall rough weeds, and they appeared to be picking seeds out of the husks.

Little also modifies people, with *little girl* occurring almost three times as much as *little boy* or *little child.* The next two most frequent adjectives are *great,* which is often used for phrases referring to degree or amount, such as *a great deal* or *a great number,* and *good,* used to modify abstract concepts (*fortune, luck*), concrete items (*food, supper*), and people, especially females (*nurse, girl, governess, mother*). Many of the other most frequently used adjectives in Traill's work are also used to modify people, such as *old* and *young,* while frequent use of adjectives such as the colours *red, black* and *white,* which are used to modify nouns such as *berry, squirrel,* and *lily,* again indicate her observations of nature.

The verbs Traill uses most frequently are similar to the most frequent verbs in the *Bank of English,* Collins' corpus of present-day English, apart from the verbs *form* and *bear* which, although not among the most frequent verbs in the *Bank of English,* appear in Traill's 100 most frequently used verbs. The most significant object of *form* is *contrast,* and the phrase *form contrast* is used to add depth to Traill's descriptions:

> The rich tint of ripened harvest formed a beautiful contrast with the azure sky and waters of the St. Laurence.

Traill uses the phrase *bear resemblance* to assist with the descriptions of her surroundings; for example:

> I do not find any description of this shrub in Pursh's Flora, but know it to be a species of honeysuckle, from the class and order, the shape and colour of the leaves, the stalks, the trumpet-shaped blossom and the fruit; all bearing a resemblance to our honeysuckles in some degree.

Some other notable features of Traill's language include the use of terms which are now considered archaic, such as *forth* and *yonder,* which are both among Traill's 100 frequently most used adverbs, and her use of punctuation marks such as the comma and the semi-colon to structure complex sentences such as the one above.

slang), halfwit, nincompoop, dweeb *(U.S. slang)*, putz *(U.S. slang)*, fathead *(informal)*, weenie *(U.S. informal)*, eejit *(Scot. & Irish)*, dumb-ass *(slang)*, numpty *(Scot. informal)*, doofus *(slang, chiefly U.S.)*, daftie *(informal)*, nerd *or* nurd *(slang)*, numbskull *or* numskull, twerp *or* twirp *(informal)*, dorba *or* dorb *(Austral. slang)*, bogan *(Austral. slang)*: *He was regarded as a pompous ass.*
▸ *related adjective:* asinine ▸ *name of male:* jack ▸ *name of female:* jenny

assail VERB **1 = criticize**, abuse, blast, put down, malign, berate, revile, vilify, tear into *(informal)*, diss *(slang, chiefly U.S.)*, impugn, go for the jugular, lambast(e): *These newspapers assail the government each day.* **2 = attack**, charge, assault, invade, set about, beset, fall upon, set upon, lay into *(informal)*, maltreat, belabour: *He was assailed by a young man with a knife.*

assailant NOUN **= attacker**, assaulter, invader, aggressor, assailer

assassin NOUN **= murderer**, killer, slayer, liquidator, executioner, hit man *(slang)*, eliminator *(slang)*, hatchet man *(slang)*

assassinate VERB **= murder**, kill, eliminate *(slang)*, take out *(slang)*, terminate, hit *(slang)*, slay, blow away *(slang, chiefly U.S.)*, liquidate

assassination NOUN **= murder**, killing, slaughter, purge, hit *(slang)*, removal, elimination *(slang)*, slaying, homicide, liquidation

> **QUOTATIONS**
> Assassination is the quickest way
> [Molière *Le Sicilien*]
>
> Assassination is the extreme form of censorship
> [George Bernard Shaw *The Rejected Statement*]

assault NOUN **= attack**, campaign, strike, rush, storm, storming, raid, invasion, charge, offensive, onset, onslaught, foray, incursion, act of aggression, inroad: *The rebels are poised for a new assault.* **OPPOSITE:** defence
▷ VERB **= strike**, attack, beat, knock, punch, belt *(informal)*, bang, batter, clip *(informal)*, slap, bash *(informal)*, deck *(slang)*, sock *(slang)*, chin *(slang)*, smack, thump, set about, lay one on *(slang)*, clout *(informal)*, cuff, flog, whack, lob, beset, clobber *(slang)*, smite *(archaic)*, wallop *(informal)*, swat, fall upon, set upon, lay into *(informal)*, tonk *(slang)*, lambast(e), belabour, beat *or* knock seven bells out of *(informal)*: *The gang assaulted him with iron bars.*

assay VERB **= analyse**, examine, investigate, assess, weigh, evaluate, inspect, try, appraise

assemblage NOUN **= group**, company, meeting, body, crowd, collection, mass, gathering, rally, assembly, flock, congregation, accumulation, multitude, throng, hui (N.Z.), conclave, aggregation, convocation, runanga (N.Z.)

assemble VERB **1 = gather**, meet, collect, rally, flock, accumulate, come together, muster, convene, congregate, foregather: *There was nowhere for students to assemble before classes.* **OPPOSITE:** scatter **2 = bring together**, collect, gather, rally, summon, accumulate, round up, marshal, come together, muster, convene, amass, congregate, call together, foregather, convoke: *The assembled multitude cheered as the leaders arrived.* **3 = put together**, make, join, set up, manufacture, build up, connect, construct, erect, piece together, fabricate, fit together: *She was trying to assemble the bomb when it went off.* **OPPOSITE:** take apart

assembly NOUN **1 = gathering**, group, meeting, body, council, conference, crowd, congress, audience, collection, mass, diet, rally, convention, flock, company, house, congregation, accumulation, multitude, throng, synod, hui (N.Z.), assemblage, conclave, aggregation, convocation, jamaat, runanga (N.Z.): *He waited until quiet settled on the assembly.* **2 = putting together**, joining, setting up, manufacture, construction, building up, connecting, erection, piecing together, fabrication, fitting together: *They are famous for their self assembly furniture range.*

assent NOUN **= agreement**, accord, sanction, approval, permission, acceptance, consent, compliance, accession, acquiescence, concurrence: *He gave his assent to the proposed legislation.* **OPPOSITE:** refusal
assent to something = agree to, allow, accept, grant, approve, permit, sanction, O.K., comply with, go along with, subscribe to, consent to, say yes to, accede to, fall in with, acquiesce in, concur with, give the green light to: *I assented to the publisher's request to write this book.*

assert VERB **1 = state**, argue, maintain, declare, allege, swear, pronounce, contend, affirm, profess, attest, predicate, postulate, avow, aver, asseverate, avouch *(archaic)*: *He asserted that the bill violated the First Amendment.* **OPPOSITE:** deny **2 = insist upon**, stress, defend, uphold, put forward, vindicate, press, stand up for: *The republics began asserting their right to govern themselves.* **OPPOSITE:** retract
assert yourself = be forceful, put your foot down *(informal)*, put yourself forward, make your presence felt, exert your influence: *He's speaking up and asserting himself much more now.*

assertion NOUN **1 = statement**, claim, allegation, profession, declaration, contention, affirmation, pronouncement, avowal, attestation, predication, asseveration: *assertions that the recession is truly over* **2 = insistence**, defence, stressing, maintenance, vindication: *They have made the assertion of ethnic identity possible.*

assertive ADJECTIVE **= confident**, firm, demanding, decided, forward, can-do *(informal)*, positive, aggressive, decisive, forceful, emphatic, insistent, feisty *(informal, chiefly U.S. & Canad.)*, pushy *(informal)*, in-your-face *(Brit. slang)*, dogmatic, strong-willed, domineering, overbearing, self-assured **OPPOSITE:** meek

assertiveness NOUN **= confidence**, insistence, aggressiveness, firmness, decisiveness, dogmatism, forcefulness, positiveness, pushiness *(informal)*, forwardness, self-assuredness, decidedness, domineeringness
OPPOSITE: meekness

assess VERB **1 = judge**, determine, estimate, fix, analyse, evaluate, rate, value, check out, compute, gauge, weigh up, appraise, size up *(informal)*, eye up: *The test was to assess aptitude rather than academic achievement.*
2 = evaluate, rate, tax, value, demand, estimate, fix, impose, levy: *What is the assessed value of the property?*

assessment NOUN **1 = judgment**, analysis, determination, evaluation, valuation, appraisal, estimation, rating, opinion, estimate, computation: *He was remanded to a mental hospital for assessment.*
2 = evaluation, rating, rate, charge, tax, demand, fee, duty, toll, levy, tariff, taxation, valuation, impost: *inflated assessments of mortgaged property*

asset NOUN **= benefit**, help, service, aid, advantage, strength, resource, attraction, blessing, boon, good point, strong point, ace in the hole, feather in your cap, ace up your sleeve
OPPOSITE: disadvantage

assiduous ADJECTIVE **= diligent**, constant, steady, hard-working, persistent, attentive, persevering, laborious, industrious, indefatigable, studious, unflagging, untiring, sedulous, unwearied **OPPOSITE:** lazy

assign VERB **1 = give**, set, grant, allocate, give out, consign, allot, apportion: *Later in the year, she'll assign them research papers.* **2 = allocate**, give, determine, fix, appoint, distribute, earmark, mete: *He assigned her all his land.* **3 = select for**, post, commission, elect, appoint, delegate, nominate, name, designate, choose for, stipulate for: *Did you choose this country or were you simply assigned here?* **4 = attribute**, credit, put down, set down, ascribe, accredit: *Assign the letters of the alphabet their numerical values.*

assignment NOUN **1 = task**, work, job, charge, position, post, commission, exercise, responsibility, duty, mission, appointment, undertaking, occupation, chore: *The course involves written assignments and practical tests.*
2 = selection, choice, option, appointment, delegation, nomination, designation: *I only ever take photos on assignment.* **3 = giving**,

issuing, grant, distribution, allocation, earmarking, allotment, designation, consignment, dealing out, assignation *(Scots Law)*, apportionment: *The state prohibited the assignment of licences to competitors.*

assimilate VERB **1 = adjust**, fit, adapt, accommodate, accustom, conform, mingle, blend in, become like, homogenize, acclimatize, intermix, become similar, acculturate: *They had been assimilated into the nation's culture.* **2 = learn**, absorb, take in, incorporate, digest, imbibe *(literary)*, ingest: *My mind could only assimilate one possibility at a time.*

assist VERB **1 = help**, back, support, further, benefit, aid, encourage, work with, work for, relieve, collaborate with, cooperate with, abet, expedite, succour, lend a hand to, lend a helping hand to, give a leg up to *(informal)*: *They decided to assist me with my chores.* **2 = facilitate**, help, further, serve, aid, forward, promote, boost, ease, sustain, reinforce, speed up, pave the way for, make easy, expedite, oil the wheels, smooth the path of, assist the progress of: *a chemical that assists in the manufacture of proteins* **OPPOSITE:** hinder

assistance NOUN **= help**, backing, service, support, benefit, aid, relief, boost, promotion, cooperation, encouragement, collaboration, reinforcement, helping hand, sustenance, succour, furtherance, abetment **OPPOSITE:** hindrance

assistant NOUN **= helper**, partner, ally, colleague, associate, supporter, deputy, subsidiary, aide, aider, second, accessory, attendant, backer, protagonist, collaborator, accomplice, confederate, auxiliary, henchman, right-hand man, adjutant, helpmate, coadjutor *(rare)*, abettor, cooperator

associate VERB **1 = connect**, couple, league, link, mix, relate, pair, ally, identify, unite, join, combine, attach, affiliate, fasten, correlate, confederate, yoke, affix, lump together, cohere, mention in the same breath, conjoin, think of together: *We've got the idea of associating progress with the future.* **OPPOSITE:** separate **2 = socialize**, mix, hang *(informal, chiefly U.S.)*, accompany, hang out *(informal)*, run around *(informal)*, mingle, be friends, befriend, consort, hang about, hobnob, fraternize: *They found out they'd been associating with a murderer.* **OPPOSITE:** avoid
▷ NOUN **= partner**, friend, ally, colleague, mate *(informal)*, companion, comrade, affiliate, collaborator, confederate, co-worker, workmate, main man *(slang, chiefly U.S.)*, cobber *(Austral. & N.Z. old-fashioned, informal)*, confrère, compeer, E hoa *(N.Z.)*: *the restaurant owner's business associates*

associated ADJECTIVE **= connected**, united, joined, leagued, linked, tied, related, allied, combined, involved, bound, syndicated, affiliated, correlated, confederated, yoked

association NOUN **1 = group**, company, club, order, union, class, society, league, band, set, troop, pack, camp, collection, gathering, organization, circle, corporation, alliance, coalition, partnership, federation, bunch, formation, faction, cluster, syndicate, congregation, batch, confederation, cooperative, fraternity, affiliation, posse *(slang)*, clique, confederacy, assemblage: *the British Olympic Association* **2 = friendship**, relationship, link, tie, relations, bond, connection, partnership, attachment, intimacy, liaison, fellowship, affinity, familiarity, affiliation, companionship, comradeship, fraternization: *The association between the two companies stretches back 30 years.* **3 = connection**, union, joining, linking, tie, mixing, relation, bond, pairing, combination, mixture, blend, identification, correlation, linkage, yoking, juxtaposition, lumping together, concomitance: *the association of the colour black with death*

assorted ADJECTIVE **= various**, different, mixed, varied, diverse, diversified, miscellaneous, sundry, motley, variegated, manifold, heterogeneous **OPPOSITE:** similar

assortment NOUN **= variety**, choice, collection, selection, mixture, diversity, array, jumble, medley, mixed bag *(informal)*, potpourri, mélange *(French)*, miscellany, mishmash, farrago, hotchpotch, salmagundi, pick 'n' mix

assuage VERB **1 = relieve**, ease, calm, moderate, temper, soothe, lessen, alleviate, lighten, allay, mitigate, quench, palliate: *She was trying to assuage her guilt.* **OPPOSITE:** increase **2 = calm**, still, quiet, relax, satisfy, soften, soothe, appease, lull, pacify, mollify, tranquillize: *The meat they'd managed to procure assuaged their hunger.* **OPPOSITE:** provoke

assume VERB **1 = presume**, think, believe, expect, accept, suppose, imagine, suspect, guess *(informal, chiefly U.S. & Canad.)*, take it, fancy, take for granted, infer, conjecture, postulate, surmise, presuppose: *It is a mistake to assume that the two are similar.* **OPPOSITE:** know **2 = take on**, begin, accept, manage, bear, handle, shoulder, take over, don, acquire, put on, take up, embrace, undertake, set about, attend to, take responsibility for, embark upon, enter upon: *He will assume the role of Chief Executive.* **3 = simulate**, affect, adopt, put on, imitate, mimic, sham, counterfeit, feign, impersonate: *He assumed an air of superiority.* **4 = take over**, take, appropriate, acquire, seize, hijack, confiscate, wrest, usurp, lay claim to, pre-empt, commandeer, requisition, expropriate, arrogate: *If there is no president, power will be assumed by extremist forces.* **OPPOSITE:** give up

assumed ADJECTIVE **= false**, affected, made-up, pretended, fake, imitation, bogus, simulated, sham, counterfeit, feigned, spurious, fictitious, make-believe, pseudonymous, phoney *or* phony *(informal)* **OPPOSITE:** real

assumption NOUN **1 = presumption**, theory, opinion, belief, guess, expectation, fancy, suspicion, premise, acceptance, hypothesis, anticipation, inference, conjecture, surmise, supposition, presupposition, premise, postulation: *They are wrong in their assumption that we are all alike.* **2 = taking on**, managing, handling, shouldering, putting on, taking up, takeover, acquisition **3 = seizure**, taking, takeover, acquisition, appropriation, wresting, confiscation, commandeering, expropriation, pre-empting, usurpation, arrogation: *the government's assumption of power*

assurance NOUN **1 = promise**, statement, guarantee, commitment, pledge, profession, vow, declaration, assertion, oath, affirmation, protestation, word, word of honour: *an assurance that other forces will not move into the territory* **OPPOSITE:** lie **2 = confidence**, conviction, courage, certainty, self-confidence, poise, assertiveness, security, faith, coolness, nerve, aplomb, boldness, self-reliance, firmness, self-assurance, certitude, sureness, self-possession, positiveness, assuredness: *He led the orchestra with assurance.* **OPPOSITE:** self-doubt

assure VERB **1 = convince**, encourage, persuade, satisfy, comfort, prove to, reassure, soothe, hearten, embolden, win someone over, bring someone round: *'Everything's going to be okay,' he assured me.* **2 = make certain**, ensure, confirm, guarantee, secure, make sure, complete, seal, clinch: *Last night's victory has assured their promotion.* **3 = promise to**, pledge to, vow to, guarantee to, swear to, attest to, confirm to, certify to, affirm to, give your word to, declare confidently to: *We can assure you of our best service at all times.*

assured ADJECTIVE **1 = confident**, certain, positive, bold, poised, assertive, complacent, fearless, audacious, pushy *(informal)*, brazen, self-confident, self-assured, self-possessed, overconfident, dauntless, sure of yourself: *He was much more assured than in recent appearances.* **OPPOSITE:** self-conscious **2 = certain**, sure, ensured, confirmed, settled, guaranteed, fixed, secure, sealed, clinched, made certain, sound, in the bag *(slang)*, dependable, beyond doubt, irrefutable,

a

unquestionable, indubitable, nailed-on *(slang)*: *Our victory is assured; nothing can stop us.* **OPPOSITE:** doubtful

astonish VERB **= amaze**, surprise, stun, stagger, bewilder, astound, daze, confound, stupefy, boggle the mind, dumbfound, flabbergast *(informal)*

astonished ADJECTIVE **= amazed**, surprised, staggered, bewildered, astounded, dazed, stunned, confounded, perplexed, gobsmacked *(informal)*, dumbfounded, flabbergasted *(informal)*, stupefied

astonishing ADJECTIVE **= amazing**, striking, surprising, brilliant, stunning, impressive, overwhelming, staggering, startling, sensational *(informal)*, bewildering, breathtaking, astounding, eye-opening, wondrous *(archaic, literary)*, jaw-dropping, stupefying

astonishment NOUN **= amazement**, surprise, wonder, confusion, awe, consternation, bewilderment, wonderment, stupefaction

astound VERB **= amaze**, surprise, overwhelm, astonish, stagger, bewilder, daze, confound, stupefy, stun, take your breath away, boggle the mind, dumbfound, flabbergast *(informal)*

astounding ADJECTIVE **= amazing**, striking, surprising, brilliant, impressive, astonishing, staggering, sensational *(informal)*, bewildering, stunning, breathtaking, wondrous *(archaic, literary)*, jaw-dropping, eye-popping *(informal)*, stupefying

astray ADJECTIVEADVERB **= off the right track**, adrift, off course, off the mark, amiss: *Many items of mail being sent to her have gone astray.*
lead someone astray = lead into sin, lead into error, lead into bad ways, lead into wrong: *The judge thought he'd been led astray by others.*

astringent ADJECTIVE **1 = contractive**, contractile, styptic: *an astringent lotion* **2 = severe**, strict, exacting, harsh, grim, stern, hard, rigid, rigorous, stringent, austere, caustic, acerbic: *an astringent satire on Hollywood*

astrology NOUN **= stargazing**, astromancy, horoscopy

astronaut NOUN **= space traveller**, cosmonaut, spaceman, spacewoman, space pilot

astronomical or **astronomic** ADJECTIVE **= huge**, great, giant, massive, vast, enormous, immense, titanic, infinite, gigantic, monumental, colossal, boundless, galactic, Gargantuan, immeasurable

astute ADJECTIVE **= intelligent**, politic, bright, sharp, keen, calculating, clever, subtle, penetrating, knowing, shrewd, cunning, discerning, sly, on the ball *(informal)*, canny, perceptive, wily, crafty, artful, insightful, foxy, adroit, sagacious **OPPOSITE:** stupid

asunder ADVERBADJECTIVE *(literary)* **= to pieces**, apart, torn, rent, to bits, to shreds, in pieces, into pieces

asylum NOUN **1 = mental hospital**, hospital, institution, psychiatric hospital, madhouse *(informal)*, funny farm *(facetious)*, loony bin *(slang)*, nuthouse *(slang)*, rubber room *(U.S. slang)*, laughing academy *(U.S. slang)*: *He spent the rest of his life in a mental asylum.* **2 = refuge**, security, haven, safety, protection, preserve, shelter, retreat, harbour, sanctuary: *He applied for asylum after fleeing his home country.*

atheism NOUN **= nonbelief**, disbelief, scepticism, infidelity, paganism, unbelief, freethinking, godlessness, irreligion, heathenism

atheist NOUN **= nonbeliever**, pagan, sceptic, disbeliever, heathen, infidel, unbeliever, freethinker, irreligionist

> **QUOTATIONS**
> An atheist is a man who has no invisible means of support
> [John Buchan *On Being a Real Person*]
>
> By night an atheist half believes a God
> [Edward Young *The Complaint: Night Thoughts*]
>
> No one has ever died an atheist
> [Plato *Laws*]
>
> There are no atheists in the foxholes
> [William Thomas Cummings *I Saw the Fall of the Philippines*]

athlete NOUN **= sportsperson**, player, runner, competitor, contender, sportsman, contestant, gymnast, games player, sportswoman

athletic ADJECTIVE **= fit**, strong, powerful, healthy, active, trim, strapping, robust, vigorous, energetic, muscular, two-fisted, sturdy, husky *(informal)*, lusty, herculean, sinewy, brawny, able-bodied, well-proportioned: *He was tall, with an athletic build.* **OPPOSITE:** feeble

athletics PLURAL NOUN **= sports**, games, races, exercises, contests, sporting events, gymnastics, track and field events, games of strength: *intercollegiate athletics*

atmosphere NOUN **1 = air**, sky, heavens, aerosphere: *These gases pollute the atmosphere of towns and cities.* **2 = feeling**, feel, air, quality, character, environment, spirit, surroundings, tone, mood, climate, flavour, aura, ambience, vibes *(slang)*: *The muted decor adds to the relaxed atmosphere.*

atom NOUN **= particle**, bit, spot, trace, scrap, molecule, grain, dot, fragment, fraction, shred, crumb, mite, jot, speck, morsel, mote, whit, tittle, iota, scintilla *(rare)*

atone VERB **= make amends**, pay, do penance, make reparation, make redress

atonement NOUN **= amends**, payment, compensation, satisfaction, redress, reparation, restitution, penance, recompense, expiation, propitiation

atrocious ADJECTIVE **1 = shocking**, terrible, appalling, horrible, godawful *(slang)*, hellacious *(U.S. slang)*, execrable, detestable: *The food here is atrocious.* **OPPOSITE:** fine **2 = cruel**, savage, brutal, vicious, ruthless, infamous, monstrous, wicked, barbaric, inhuman, diabolical, heinous, flagrant, infernal, fiendish, villainous, nefarious, horrifying, grievous: *The treatment of the prisoners was atrocious.* **OPPOSITE:** kind

atrocity NOUN **1 = act of cruelty**, wrong, crime, horror, offence, evil, outrage, cruelty, brutality, obscenity, wrongdoing, enormity, monstrosity, transgression, abomination, barbarity, villainy: *Those who committed this atrocity should be punished.* **2 = cruelty**, wrong, horror, brutality, wrongdoing, enormity, savagery, ruthlessness, wickedness, inhumanity, infamy, transgression, barbarity, viciousness, villainy, baseness, monstrousness, heinousness, nefariousness, shockingness, atrociousness, fiendishness, barbarousness, grievousness, villainousness: *stomach-churning tales of atrocity and massacre*

atrophy VERB **1 = waste away**, waste, shrink, diminish, deteriorate, decay, dwindle, wither, wilt, degenerate, shrivel: *His muscle atrophied, and he was left lame.* **2 = decline**, waste, fade, shrink, diminish, deteriorate, dwindle, wither, wilt, degenerate, shrivel, waste away: *If you let your mind stagnate, this talent will atrophy.*
▷ NOUN **1 = wasting away**, decline, wasting, decay, decaying, withering, deterioration, meltdown *(informal)*, shrivelling, degeneration, diminution: *exercises to avoid atrophy of cartilage* **2 = wasting**, decline, decay, decaying, withering, deterioration, meltdown *(informal)*, shrivelling, degeneration, diminution, wasting away: *levels of consciousness which are in danger of atrophy*

attach VERB **1 = affix**, stick, secure, bind, unite, add, join, couple, link, tie, fix, connect, lash, glue, adhere, fasten, annex, truss, yoke, append, make fast, cohere, subjoin, bootstrap (to): *Attach labels to things before you file them away.* **OPPOSITE:** detach **2 = ascribe**, connect, attribute, assign, place, associate, lay on, accredit, invest with, impute: *They have attached much significance to your visit.*
attach yourself to or **be attached to something = join**, accompany, associate with, combine with, join forces with, latch on to, unite with, sign up with, become associated with, sign on with, affiliate yourself with: *He attached himself to a group of poets known as the Martians.*

attached ADJECTIVE **= spoken for**, married, partnered, engaged, accompanied: *I wondered if he was attached.*
attached to = fond of, devoted to, affectionate towards, full of regard for: *She is very attached to her family and friends.*

attachment NOUN **1 = fondness**, liking, feeling, love, relationship, regard, bond, friendship, attraction, loyalty, affection, devotion, fidelity, affinity, tenderness, reverence, predilection, possessiveness, partiality, aroha *(N.Z.)*: *As a teenager she formed a strong attachment to one of her teachers.* **OPPOSITE:** aversion **2 = accessory**, fitting, extra, addition, component, extension, supplement, fixture, auxiliary, adaptor *or* adapter, supplementary part, add-on, adjunct, appendage, accoutrement, appurtenance: *Some models come with attachments for dusting.*

attack VERB **1 = assault**, strike (at), mug, set about, ambush, assail, tear into, fall upon, set upon, lay into *(informal)*: *He bundled her into a hallway and brutally attacked her.* **OPPOSITE:** defend **2 = invade**, occupy, raid, infringe, charge, rush, storm, encroach: *The infantry's aim was to slow attacking forces.* **3 = criticize**, blame, abuse, blast, pan *(informal)*, condemn, knock *(informal)*, slam *(slang)*, put down, slate *(informal)*, have a go (at) *(informal)*, censure, malign, berate, disparage, revile, vilify, tear into *(informal)*, slag off *(Brit. slang)*, diss *(slang, chiefly U.S.)*, find fault with, impugn, go for the jugular, lambast(e), pick holes in, excoriate, bite someone's head off, snap someone's head off, pick to pieces: *He publicly attacked the people who've been calling for a secret ballot.*
▷ NOUN **1 = assault**, charge, campaign, strike, rush, raid, invasion, offensive, aggression, blitz, onset, onslaught, foray, incursion, inroad: *a campaign of air attacks on strategic targets* **OPPOSITE:** defence **2 = criticism**, panning *(informal)*, slating *(informal)*, censure, disapproval, slagging *(slang)*, abuse, knocking *(informal)*, bad press, vilification, denigration, calumny, character assassination, disparagement, impugnment: *He launched an attack on businesses for failing to invest.* **3 = bout**, fit, access, spell, stroke, seizure, spasm, convulsion, paroxysm: *It brought on an attack of asthma.*

PROVERBS
Attack is the best form of defence

attacker NOUN **= assailant**, assaulter, raider, intruder, invader, aggressor, mugger

attain VERB **1 = obtain**, get, win, reach, effect, land, score *(slang)*, complete, gain, achieve, earn, secure, realize, acquire, fulfil, accomplish, grasp, reap, procure: *He's halfway to attaining his pilot's licence.* **2 = reach**, achieve, realize, acquire, arrive at, accomplish: *attaining a state of calmness and confidence*

attainable ADJECTIVE **= achievable**, possible, likely, potential, accessible, probable, at hand, feasible, within reach, practicable, obtainable, reachable, realizable, graspable, gettable, procurable, accomplishable **OPPOSITE:** unattainable

attainment NOUN **1 = achievement**, getting, winning, reaching, gaining, obtaining, acquisition, feat, completion, reaping, accomplishment, realization, fulfilment, arrival at, procurement, acquirement: *the attainment of independence* **2 = skill**, art, ability, talent, gift, achievement, capability, competence, accomplishment, mastery, proficiency: *their educational attainments*

attempt VERB **= try**, seek, aim, struggle, tackle, take on, experiment, venture, undertake, essay, strive, endeavour, have a go at *(informal)*, make an effort, make an attempt, have a crack at, have a shot at *(informal)*, try your hand at, do your best to, jump through hoops *(informal)*, have a stab at *(informal)*, take the bit between your teeth: *We attempted to do something like that here.*
▷ NOUN **1 = try**, go *(informal)*, shot *(informal)*, effort, trial, bid, experiment, crack *(informal)*, venture, undertaking, essay, stab *(informal)*, endeavour: *a deliberate attempt to destabilize defence* **2 = attack**, assault: *an attempt on the life of the Prime Minister*

attempted ADJECTIVE **= tried**, ventured, undertaken, endeavoured, assayed

attend VERB **1 = be present**, go to, visit, be at, be there, be here, frequent, haunt, appear at, turn up at, patronize, show up at *(informal)*, show yourself, put in an appearance at, present yourself at: *Thousands of people attended the funeral.* **OPPOSITE:** be absent **2 = pay attention**, listen, follow, hear, mark, mind, watch, note, regard, notice, observe, look on, heed, take to heart, pay heed, hearken *(archaic)*: *I'm not sure what he said – I wasn't attending.* **OPPOSITE:** ignore **3 = escort**, conduct, guard, shadow, accompany, companion, shepherd, convoy, usher, squire, chaperon: *horse-drawn coaches attended by liveried footmen*
attend to someone = look after, help, mind, aid, tend, nurse, care for, take care of, minister to, administer to: *The main thing is to attend to the injured.*
attend to something = apply yourself to, concentrate on, look after, take care of, see to, get to work on, devote yourself to, occupy yourself with: *You had better attend to the matter in hand.*

attendance NOUN **1 = presence**, being there, attending, appearance: *Her attendance at school was sporadic.* **2 = turnout**, audience, gate, congregation, house, crowd, throng, number present: *Some estimates put attendance at 60,000.*

attendant NOUN **= assistant**, guide, guard, servant, companion, aide, escort, follower, steward, waiter, usher, warden, helper, auxiliary, custodian, page, menial, concierge, underling, lackey, chaperon, flunky: *He was working as a car-park attendant.*
▷ ADJECTIVE **= accompanying**, related, associated, accessory, consequent, resultant, concomitant: *His victory, and all the attendant publicity, were deserved.*

attention NOUN **1 = thinking**, thought, mind, notice, consideration, concentration, observation, scrutiny, heed, deliberation, contemplation, thoughtfulness, attentiveness, intentness, heedfulness: *He turned his attention to the desperate state of housing in the province.* **2 = care**, support, concern, treatment, looking after, succour, ministration: *a demanding baby who wants attention 24 hours a day* **3 = awareness**, regard, notice, recognition, consideration, observation, consciousness: *Let me draw your attention to some important issues.* **OPPOSITE:** inattention
▷ PLURAL NOUN **= courtesy**, compliments, regard, respect, care, consideration, deference, politeness, civility, gallantry, mindfulness, assiduities: *He was flattered by the attentions of a younger woman.* **OPPOSITE:** discourtesy

attentive ADJECTIVE **1 = intent**, listening, concentrating, careful, alert, awake, mindful, watchful, observant, studious, on your toes, heedful, regardful: *I wish you would be more attentive to detail.* **OPPOSITE:** heedless **2 = considerate**, kind, civil, devoted, helpful, obliging, accommodating, polite, thoughtful, gracious, conscientious, respectful, courteous, gallant: *At parties he is always attentive to his wife.* **OPPOSITE:** neglectful

attenuate VERB **= weaken**, reduce, contract, lower, diminish, decrease, dilute, lessen, sap, water down, adulterate, enfeeble, enervate, devaluate

attenuated ADJECTIVE **1 = slender**, extended, thinned, slimmed, refined, stretched out, lengthened, drawn out, spun out, elongated, rarefied: *rounded arches and attenuated columns* **2 = weakened**, reduced, contracted, lowered, diminished, decreased, dilute, diluted, lessened, devalued, sapped, watered down, adulterated, enfeebled, enervated: *The vaccination contains attenuated strains of the target virus.*

attest VERB **= testify**, show, prove, confirm, display, declare, witness, demonstrate, seal, swear, exhibit, warrant, assert, manifest, give evidence, invoke, ratify, affirm, certify, verify, bear out, substantiate, corroborate, bear witness, authenticate, vouch for, evince, aver, adjure **OPPOSITE:** disprove

attic NOUN = **loft**, garret, roof space

a

attire NOUN = **clothes**, wear, dress, clothing, gear *(informal)*, habit, uniform, outfit, costume, threads *(slang)*, array *(poetic)*, garments, robes, apparel, garb, accoutrements, raiment *(archaic, poetic)*, vestment, schmutter *(slang)*, habiliments

attitude NOUN **1 = opinion**, thinking, feeling, thought, view, position, approach, belief, mood, perspective, point of view, stance, outlook, viewpoint, slant, frame of mind: *the general change in attitude towards them* **2 = manner**, air, condition, bearing, aspect, carriage, disposition, demeanour, mien *(literary)*: *He has a gentle attitude.* **3 = position**, bearing, pose, stance, carriage, posture: *scenes of the king in various attitudes of worshipping*

attorney NOUN = **lawyer**, solicitor, counsel, advocate, barrister, counsellor, legal adviser

attract VERB **1 = allure**, interest, draw, invite, persuade, engage, charm, appeal to, fascinate, win over, tempt, lure *(informal)*, induce, incline, seduce, entice, enchant, endear, lead on, coax, captivate, beguile, cajole, bewitch, decoy, inveigle, pull, catch (someone's) eye: *Summer attracts visitors to the countryside.* **OPPOSITE:** repel **2 = pull**, draw, magnetize: *Anything with strong gravity attracts other things to it.*

attraction NOUN **1 = appeal**, interest, draw, pull *(informal)*, come-on *(informal)*, charm, incentive, invitation, lure, bait, temptation, fascination, attractiveness, allure, inducement, magnetism, enchantment, endearment, enticement, captivation, temptingness, pleasingness: *It was never a physical attraction, just a meeting of minds.* **2 = pull**, draw, magnetism: *the gravitational attraction of the Sun*

attractive ADJECTIVE **1 = seductive**, charming, tempting, interesting, pleasing, pretty, fair, beautiful, inviting, engaging, likable *or* likeable, lovely, winning, sexy *(informal)*, pleasant, handsome, fetching, good-looking, glamorous, gorgeous, magnetic, cute, irresistible, enticing, provocative, captivating, beguiling, alluring, bonny, winsome, comely, prepossessing, hot *(informal)*, fit *(Brit. informal)*: *He was always very attractive to women.* **OPPOSITE:** unattractive **2 = appealing**, pleasing, inviting, fascinating, tempting, enticing, agreeable, irresistible: *Co-operation was more than just an attractive option.* **OPPOSITE:** unappealing

attributable ADJECTIVE = **ascribable**, accountable, applicable, traceable, explicable, assignable, imputable, blamable *or* blameable, placeable, referable *or* referrable

attribute VERB = **ascribe**, apply, credit, blame, refer, trace, assign, charge, allocate, put down, set down, allot, impute, reattribute: *They attribute their success to external causes such as luck.*
▷ NOUN = **quality**, point, mark, sign, note, feature, property, character, element, aspect, symbol, characteristic, indication, distinction, virtue, trait, hallmark, facet, quirk, peculiarity, idiosyncrasy: *He has every attribute a footballer could want.*

attribution NOUN = **ascription**, charge, credit, blame, assignment, attachment, placement, referral, assignation, imputation

attrition NOUN = **wearing down**, harrying, weakening, harassment, thinning out, attenuation, debilitation

attuned ADJECTIVE = **accustomed**, adjusted, coordinated, in tune, in harmony, in accord, harmonized, familiarized, acclimatized

atypical ADJECTIVE = **unusual**, exceptional, uncommon, singular, deviant, unconventional, unique, unorthodox, uncharacteristic, out of the ordinary, unrepresentative, out of keeping, uncustomary, nonconforming, unconforming **OPPOSITE:** normal

auburn ADJECTIVE = **reddish-brown**, tawny, russet, henna, rust-coloured, copper-coloured, chestnut-coloured, Titian red, nutbrown

audacious ADJECTIVE **1 = daring**, enterprising, brave, bold, risky, rash, adventurous, reckless, courageous, fearless, intrepid, valiant, daredevil, death-defying, dauntless, venturesome: *an audacious plan to win the presidency* **OPPOSITE:** timid **2 = cheeky**, presumptuous, impertinent, insolent, impudent, forward, fresh *(informal)*, assuming, rude, defiant, brazen, in-your-face *(Brit. slang)*, shameless, sassy *(U.S. informal)*, pert, disrespectful: *Audacious thieves stole her car from under her nose.* **OPPOSITE:** tactful

audacity NOUN **1 = daring**, nerve, courage, guts *(informal)*, bravery, boldness, recklessness, face *(informal)*, front, enterprise, valour, fearlessness, rashness, adventurousness, intrepidity, audaciousness, dauntlessness, venturesomeness: *I was shocked at the audacity of the gangsters.* **2 = cheek**, nerve, defiance, gall *(informal)*, presumption, rudeness, chutzpah *(U.S. & Canad. informal)*, insolence, impertinence, neck *(informal)*, impudence, effrontery, brass neck *(Brit. informal)*, shamelessness, sassiness *(U.S. informal)*, forwardness, pertness, audaciousness, disrespectfulness: *He had the audacity to look at his watch while I was talking.*

> **QUOTATIONS**
> Being tactful in audacity is knowing how far one can go too far
> [Jean Cocteau *Le Rappel à l'ordre*]

audible ADJECTIVE = **clear**, distinct, discernible, detectable, perceptible, hearable **OPPOSITE:** inaudible

audience NOUN **1 = spectators**, company, house, crowd, gathering, gallery, assembly, viewers, listeners, patrons, congregation, turnout, onlookers, throng, assemblage: *The entire audience broke into loud applause.* **2 = public**, market, following, fans, devotees, fanbase, aficionados: *She began to find a receptive audience for her work.* **3 = interview**, meeting, hearing, exchange, reception, consultation: *The Prime Minister will seek an audience with the Queen today.*

audit VERB = **inspect**, check, review, balance, survey, examine, investigate, go through, assess, go over, evaluate, vet, verify, appraise, scrutinize, inquire into: *Each year they audit our accounts and certify them as true and fair.*
▷ NOUN = **inspection**, check, checking, review, balancing, search, survey, investigation, examination, scan, scrutiny, supervision, surveillance, look-over, verification, once-over *(informal)*, checkup, superintendence: *The bank is carrying out an internal audit.*

augment VERB = **increase**, grow, raise, extend, boost, expand, add to, build up, strengthen, enhance, reinforce, swell, intensify, heighten, enlarge, multiply, inflate, magnify, amplify, dilate **OPPOSITE:** diminish

augur VERB = **bode**, promise, predict, herald, signify, foreshadow, prophesy, harbinger, presage, prefigure, portend, betoken, be an omen of

august ADJECTIVE = **noble**, great, kingly, grand, excellent, imposing, impressive, superb, distinguished, magnificent, glorious, splendid, elevated, eminent, majestic, dignified, regal, stately, high-ranking, monumental, solemn, lofty, exalted

aura NOUN = **air**, feeling, feel, quality, atmosphere, tone, suggestion, mood, scent, aroma, odour, ambience, vibes *(slang)*, vibrations *(slang)*, emanation

auspices PLURAL NOUN = **support**, backing, control, charge, care, authority, championship, influence, protection, guidance, sponsorship, supervision, patronage, advocacy, countenance, aegis

auspicious ADJECTIVE = **favourable**, timely, happy, promising, encouraging, bright, lucky, hopeful, fortunate, prosperous, rosy, opportune, propitious, felicitous **OPPOSITE:** unpromising

austere ADJECTIVE **1 = stern**, hard, serious, cold, severe, formal, grave, strict, exacting, harsh, stiff, forbidding, grim, rigorous, solemn, stringent, inflexible, unrelenting, unfeeling: *an austere, distant, cold person* **OPPOSITE:** kindly **2 = plain**, simple, severe, spare, harsh, stark, bleak, subdued, economical, Spartan, unadorned, unornamented, bare-bones: *The church was austere and simple.* **OPPOSITE:** luxurious **3 = ascetic**, strict, continent, exacting, rigid, sober, economical, solemn, Spartan, unrelenting, self-disciplined, puritanical, chaste, strait-laced, abstemious, self-denying, abstinent: *The life of the troops was comparatively austere.* **OPPOSITE:** abandoned

austerity NOUN **1 = plainness**, economy, simplicity, severity, starkness, spareness, Spartanism: *abandoned buildings with a classical austerity* **2 = asceticism**, economy, rigidity, abstinence, self-discipline, chastity, sobriety, continence, puritanism, solemnity, self-denial, strictness, abstemiousness, chasteness, exactingness, Spartanism: *the years of austerity which followed the war*

authentic ADJECTIVE **1 = real**, true, original, actual, pure, genuine, valid, faithful, undisputed, veritable, lawful, on the level *(informal)*, bona fide, dinkum *(Austral. & N.Z. informal)*, pukka, the real McCoy, true-to-life: *patterns for making authentic border-style clothing* **OPPOSITE:** fake **2 = accurate**, true, certain, reliable, legitimate, authoritative, factual, truthful, dependable, trustworthy, veracious: *authentic details about the birth of the organization* **OPPOSITE:** fictitious

authenticate VERB **1 = verify**, guarantee, warrant, authorize, certify, avouch: *All the antiques have been authenticated.* **OPPOSITE:** invalidate **2 = vouch for**, confirm, endorse, validate, attest: *He authenticated the accuracy of various details.*

authenticity NOUN **1 = genuineness**, purity, realness, veritableness: *Some factors have cast doubt on the statue's authenticity.* **2 = accuracy**, truth, certainty, validity, reliability, legitimacy, verity, actuality, faithfulness, truthfulness, dependability, trustworthiness, authoritativeness, factualness: *The film's authenticity of detail has impressed critics.*

author NOUN **1 = writer**, composer, novelist, hack, creator, columnist, scribbler, scribe, essayist, wordsmith, penpusher, littérateur, man *or* woman of letters: *She's the author of the book 'Give your Child Music'.* **2 = creator**, father, parent, mother, maker, producer, framer, designer, founder, architect, planner, inventor, mover, originator, prime mover, doer, initiator, begetter, fabricator: *the authors of the plan*

> **QUOTATIONS**
> There is probably no hell for authors in the next world – they suffer so much from critics and publishers in this
> [C.N. Bovee]

authoritarian ADJECTIVE **= strict**, severe, absolute, harsh, rigid, autocratic, dictatorial, dogmatic, imperious, domineering, unyielding, tyrannical, disciplinarian, despotic, doctrinaire: *There was a coup to restore authoritarian rule.* **OPPOSITE:** lenient
▷ NOUN **= disciplinarian**, dictator, tyrant, despot, autocrat, absolutist: *He became an overly strict authoritarian.*

authoritative ADJECTIVE **1 = commanding**, lordly, masterly, imposing, dominating, confident, decisive, imperative, assertive, autocratic, dictatorial, dogmatic, imperious, self-assured, peremptory: *He has a deep, authoritative voice.* **OPPOSITE:** timid **2 = official**, approved, sanctioned, legitimate, sovereign, authorized, commanding: *The first authoritative study was published in 1840.* **OPPOSITE:** unofficial **3 = reliable**, learned, sound, true, accurate, valid, scholarly, faithful, authentic, definitive, factual, truthful, veritable, dependable, trustworthy: *The evidence she uses is highly authoritative.* **OPPOSITE:** unreliable

authority NOUN **1** *(usually plural)* **= powers that be**, government, police, officials, the state, management, administration, the system, the Establishment, Big Brother *(informal)*, officialdom: *This was a pretext for the authorities to cancel the elections.* **2 = prerogative**, right, influence, might, force, power, control, charge, rule, government, weight, strength, direction, command, licence, privilege, warrant, say-so, sway, domination, jurisdiction, supremacy, dominion, ascendancy, mana (N.Z.): *The judge has no authority to order a second trial.* **3 = expert**, specialist, professional, master, ace *(informal)*, scholar, guru, buff *(informal)*, wizard, whizz *(informal)*, virtuoso, connoisseur, arbiter, hotshot *(informal)*, fundi *(S. African)*: *He's an authority on Russian affairs.* **4 = command**, power, control, rule, management, direction, grasp, sway, domination, mastery, dominion: *He has no natural authority.* **5 = permission**, leave, permit, sanction, licence, approval, go-ahead *(informal)*, liberty, consent, warrant, say-so, tolerance, justification, green light, assent, authorization, dispensation, carte blanche, a blank cheque, sufferance: *He must first be given authority from his own superiors.*

> **QUOTATIONS**
> Authority is never without hate
> [Euripides *Ion*]
>
> I am a man under authority, having soldiers under me; and I say to this man, Go, and he goeth; and to another, Come, and he cometh; and to my servant, Do this, and he doeth it
> [*Bible: St. Matthew*]

authorization NOUN **= permission**, right, leave, power, authority, ability, strength, permit, sanction, licence, approval, warrant, say-so, credentials, a blank cheque

authorize VERB **1 = empower**, commission, enable, entitle, mandate, accredit, give authority to: *They authorized him to use force if necessary.* **2 = permit**, allow, suffer, grant, confirm, agree to, approve, sanction, endure, license, endorse, warrant, tolerate, ratify, consent to, countenance, accredit, vouch for, give leave, give the green light for, give a blank cheque to, give authority for: *We are willing to authorize a police raid.* **OPPOSITE:** forbid

authorized ADJECTIVE **= official**, commissioned, approved, licensed, ratified, signed and sealed

autobiography NOUN **= life story**, record, history, résumé, memoirs

> **QUOTATIONS**
> An autobiography is an obituary in serial form with the last instalment missing
> [Quentin Crisp *The Naked Civil Servant*]

autocracy NOUN **= dictatorship**, tyranny, despotism, absolutism

autocrat NOUN **= dictator**, tyrant, despot, absolutist

autocratic ADJECTIVE **= dictatorial**, absolute, unlimited, all-powerful, imperious, domineering, tyrannical, despotic, tyrannous

automatic ADJECTIVE **1 = mechanical**, robot, automated, mechanized, push-button, self-regulating, self-propelling, self-activating, self-moving, self-acting, hands-off: *Modern trains have automatic doors.* **OPPOSITE:** done by hand **2 = involuntary**, natural, unconscious, mechanical, spontaneous, reflex, instinctive, instinctual, unwilled: *the automatic body functions, such as breathing* **OPPOSITE:** conscious **3 = inevitable**, certain, necessary, assured, routine, unavoidable, inescapable: *They should face an automatic charge of manslaughter.*

autonomous ADJECTIVE **= self-ruling**, free, independent, sovereign, self-sufficient, self-governing, self-determining

autonomy NOUN **= independence**, freedom, sovereignty, self-determination, self-government, self-rule, self-sufficiency, home rule, rangatiratanga (N.Z.) **OPPOSITE:** dependency

autopsy NOUN **= postmortem**, dissection, postmortem examination, necropsy

auxiliary ADJECTIVE **1 = supplementary**, reserve, emergency, substitute, secondary, back-up, subsidiary, fall-back: *auxiliary fuel tanks* **2 = supporting**, helping, aiding, assisting, accessory, ancillary: *the army and auxiliary forces* **OPPOSITE:** primary
▷ NOUN **= helper**, partner, ally, associate, supporter, assistant, companion, accessory, subordinate, protagonist, accomplice, confederate, henchman: *a nursing auxiliary*

avail NOUN **= benefit**, use, help, good, service, aid, profit, advantage, purpose, assistance, utility, effectiveness, mileage *(informal)*, usefulness, efficacy: *His efforts were to no avail.*
avail yourself of something = make use of, use, employ, exploit, take advantage of, profit from, make the most of, utilize, have recourse to, turn to account: *Guests should feel at liberty to avail themselves of your facilities.*

availability NOUN **= accessibility**, readiness, handiness, attainability, obtainability

available ADJECTIVE **= accessible**, ready, to hand, convenient, handy, vacant, on hand, at hand, free, applicable, to be had, achievable, obtainable, on tap *(informal)*, attainable, at your fingertips, at your disposal, ready for use **OPPOSITE:** in use

avalanche NOUN **1 = snow-slide**, landslide, landslip, snow-slip: *Four people died when an avalanche buried them alive last week.* **2 = large amount**, barrage, torrent, deluge, inundation: *He was greeted with an avalanche of publicity.*

avant-garde ADJECTIVE **= progressive**, pioneering, way-out *(informal)*, experimental, innovative, unconventional, far-out *(slang)*, ground-breaking, innovatory **OPPOSITE:** conservative

avarice NOUN **= greed**, meanness, penny-pinching, parsimony, acquisitiveness, rapacity, cupidity, stinginess, covetousness, miserliness, greediness, niggardliness, graspingness, close-fistedness, penuriousness **OPPOSITE:** liberality

> QUOTATIONS
> The love of money is the root of all evil
> [Bible: I Timothy]
>
> avarice, the spur of industry
> [David Hume *Essays: Moral and Political*]

avenge VERB **= get revenge for**, revenge, repay, retaliate for, take revenge for, hit back for, requite, pay (someone) back for, get even for *(informal)*, even the score for, get your own back for, take vengeance for, take satisfaction for, pay (someone) back in his *or* her own coin for

> USAGE
> In the past it was considered incorrect to use *avenge* with *yourself*, but this use is now acceptable and relatively common: *she was determined to avenge herself upon this monster.*

avenue NOUN **= street**, way, course, drive, road, pass, approach, channel, access, entry, route, path, passage, entrance, alley, pathway, boulevard, driveway, thoroughfare

average NOUN **= standard**, normal, usual, par, mode, mean, rule, medium, norm, run of the mill, midpoint: *The pay is about the average for a service industry.*
▷ ADJECTIVE **1 = usual**, common, standard, general, normal, regular, ordinary, typical, commonplace, unexceptional: *The average man burns 2000 calories a day.* **OPPOSITE:** unusual **2 = mean**, middle, medium, intermediate, median: *Of the US's million millionaires, the average age was 63.* **OPPOSITE:** minimum **3 = mediocre**, fair, ordinary, moderate, pedestrian, indifferent, not bad, middling, insignificant, so-so *(informal)*, banal, second-rate, middle-of-the-road, tolerable, run-of-the-mill, passable, undistinguished, uninspired, unexceptional, bog-standard *(Brit. & Irish slang)*, no great shakes *(informal)*, fair to middling *(informal)*: *I was only average academically.*
▷ VERB **= make on average**, be on average, even out to, do on average, balance out to: *pay increases averaging 9.75%*
on average = usually, generally, normally, typically, for the most part, as a rule: *On average we would be spending $200 a day.*

averse ADJECTIVE **= opposed**, reluctant, hostile, unwilling, backward, unfavourable, loath, disinclined, inimical, indisposed, antipathetic, ill-disposed **OPPOSITE:** favourable

aversion NOUN **= hatred**, hate, horror, disgust, hostility, opposition, dislike, reluctance, loathing, distaste, animosity, revulsion, antipathy, repulsion, abhorrence, disinclination, repugnance, odium, detestation, indisposition **OPPOSITE:** love

avert VERB **1 = ward off**, avoid, prevent, frustrate, fend off, preclude, stave off, forestall: *A fresh tragedy was narrowly averted yesterday.* **2 = turn away**, turn, turn aside: *He kept his eyes averted.*

aviation NOUN **= flying**, flight, aeronautics, powered flight

aviator NOUN **= pilot**, flyer, airman, airwoman, aeronaut

avid ADJECTIVE **1 = enthusiastic**, keen, devoted, intense, eager, passionate, ardent, fanatical, fervent, zealous, keen as mustard: *an avid collector of art* **OPPOSITE:** indifferent **2 = insatiable**, hungry, greedy, thirsty, grasping, voracious, acquisitive, ravenous, rapacious, avaricious, covetous, athirst: *He was avid for wealth.*

avoid VERB **1 = prevent**, stop, frustrate, hamper, foil, inhibit, head off, avert, thwart, intercept, hinder, obstruct, impede, ward off, stave off, forestall, defend against: *He had to take emergency action to avoid a disaster.* **2 = refrain from**, bypass, dodge, eschew, escape, duck (out of) *(informal)*, fight shy of, shirk from: *He managed to avoid giving them an idea of what he was up to.* **3 = keep away from**, dodge, shun, evade, steer clear of, sidestep, circumvent, bypass, slip through the net, body-swerve *(Scot.)*, give a wide berth to: *He had ample time to swerve and avoid the woman.*

avoidable ADJECTIVE **1 = preventable**, stoppable, avertible *or* avertable: *The tragedy was entirely avoidable.* **OPPOSITE:** unpreventable **2 = escapable**, evadable: *Smoking is an avoidable cause of disease and death.* **OPPOSITE:** inevitable

avoidance NOUN **1 = refraining**, dodging, shirking, eschewal: *tax avoidance* **2 = prevention**, safeguard, precaution, anticipation, thwarting, elimination, deterrence, forestalling, prophylaxis, preclusion, obviation: *Improve your health by stress avoidance.*

avow VERB **= state**, maintain, declare, allege, recognize, swear, assert, proclaim, affirm, profess, aver, asseverate

avowed ADJECTIVE **= declared**, open, admitted, acknowledged, confessed, sworn, professed, self-proclaimed

await VERB **1 = wait for**, expect, look for, look forward to, anticipate, stay for: *Little was said as we awaited the arrival of the chairman.* **2 = be in store for**, wait for, be ready for, lie in wait for, be in readiness for: *A nasty surprise awaited them.*

awake VERB **1 = wake up**, come to, wake, stir, awaken, rouse: *I awoke to the sound of the wind in the trees.* **2 = alert**, excite, stimulate, provoke, revive, arouse, activate, awaken, fan, animate, stir up, incite, kick-start *(informal)*, enliven, kindle, breathe life into, call forth, vivify: *He had awoken interest in the sport again.* **3 = stimulate**, excite, provoke, activate, alert, animate, fan, stir up, incite, kick-start *(informal)*, enliven, kindle, breathe life into, call forth, vivify: *The aim was to awaken an interest in foreign cultures.*
▷ ADJECTIVE **1 = not sleeping**, sleepless, wide-awake, aware, waking, conscious, aroused, awakened, restless, restive, wakeful, bright-eyed and bushy-tailed: *I don't stay awake at night worrying about that.* **OPPOSITE:** asleep **2 = alert**, aware, on the lookout, alive, attentive, on the alert, observant, watchful, on guard, on your toes, heedful, vigilant: *They are awake to the challenge of stemming the exodus.*

The Language of Edith Wharton

Edith Wharton (1862–1937) was born into a wealthy New York family, and in novels such as *The House of Mirth* (1905) and *The Age of Innocence* (1920) she writes about the upper-class society she knew well. She often visited Europe, and eventually, after her divorce in 1913, moved permanently to France. Her many novels and short stories have some similarities, both in their preoccupations and their style, with the work of Henry James, her close friend.

Unlike earlier novelists, who generally depict their characters as conversing in complete sentences, Edith Wharton reproduces the disjointed nature of real speech. Speakers in her novels often struggle to find the words they want, and break off when they fail. At other times, they break off because they do not wish to be explicit – they intend that their listener should supply the meaning they have hinted at. To render this kind of communication Wharton makes frequent use of two forms of punctuation that were used much less by 19th-century authors – the dash, and suspension points:

> 'I have done what you wished – what you advised,' she said abruptly. 'Ah – I'm glad,' he returned, embarrassed by her broaching the subject at such a moment. 'I understand – that you were right,' she went on a little breathlessly; 'but sometimes life is difficult ... perplexing ...'
>
> 'I know.'

In her narrative prose, by contrast, Wharton's sentences are often lengthy and formally structured, with subordinated clauses marked off by commas, and frequent use of relative pronouns preceded by prepositions, (*about whom*, *from which*), and conjunctions such as *but* and *and*. The following lines from *Bunner Sisters* is only part of a sentence:

> ... but gradually, as her nerves were soothed by the familiar quiet of the little shop, and the click of Evelina's pinking-machine, certain sights and sounds would detach themselves from the torrent along which she had been swept, and she would devote the rest of the day to a mental reconstruction of the different episodes of her walk, till finally it took shape in her thought as a consecutive and highly-coloured experience, from which, for weeks afterwards, she would detach some fragmentary recollection ...

Another literary feature of her narrative writing is the frequent use of abstract nouns, usually Latinate, such as *effrontery*, *felicitation*, *audacity*, *repugnance*, *conjugality*, *fatuity*. She employs many Latinate adjectives, sometimes with unexpected nouns: *inexorable* (*facts*, *punctuality*, *resolve*); *factitious* (*energy*, *exhilaration*, *complexity*); *abysmal* (*silence*, *mystery*, *purity*). This very formal diction intensifies the colloquial effect when her characters use such everyday language as phrasal verbs (eg *carry on*, *see through*, *tide over*). The first chapter of *The Age of Innocence* is an ornately phrased description of prominent figures of New York society attending an opera. The presence of a woman who has somehow flouted social conventions arouses intense disapproval, and this is voiced with harsh slanginess by a character in the final sentence of the chapter:

> 'I didn't think the Mingotts would have tried it on.'

In the narrative, this shocking woman is generally referred to as *Countess Olenska*, or *Madame Olenska*, rather than *Ellen*. *Mr* and *Mrs* are two of the words Wharton uses most, and this reflects the formality of the society she describes. However, another of her most-used words is *sense* (of *unreality*, *loneliness*, *intimacy*, *constraint*, *strangeness*). The frequency of the word is indicative both of Wharton's content, and of her style. She explores the emotional and intellectual life of people who are constrained by social conventions – but her exploration is expressed in formal language characterized by the use of nouns rather than verbs, for example '*had a sudden sense of*', rather than the more ordinary 'suddenly realized that':

> Claudia **had** in fact a **sudden sense** of deficient intuition.

award VERB **1 = present with**, give, grant, gift, distribute, render, assign, decree, hand out, confer, endow, bestow, allot, apportion, adjudge: *She was awarded the prize for both films.* **2 = grant**, give, render, assign, decree, accord, confer, adjudge: *The contract has been awarded to a British shipyard.*
▷ NOUN **1 = grant**, subsidy, scholarship, hand-out, endowment, stipend: *this year's annual pay award* **2 = prize**, gift, trophy, decoration, grant, bonsela *(S. African)*, koha (N.Z.): *She presented a bravery award to the schoolgirl.* **3 = settlement**, payment, compensation: *workmen's compensation awards*

aware ADJECTIVE **= informed**, enlightened, knowledgeable, learned, expert, versed, up to date, in the picture, in the know *(informal)*, erudite, well-read, au fait *(French)*, in the loop, well-briefed, au courant *(French)*, clued-up *(informal)*: *They are politically very aware.*
OPPOSITE: ignorant
aware of = knowing about, familiar with, conscious of, wise to *(slang)*, alert to, mindful of, acquainted with, alive to, awake to, privy to, hip to *(slang)*, appreciative of, attentive to, conversant with, apprised of, cognizant of, sensible of: *They are well aware of the dangers.*

awareness NOUN
awareness of = knowledge of, understanding of, appreciation of, recognition of, attention to, perception of, consciousness of, acquaintance with, enlightenment with, sensibility to, realization of, familiarity with, mindfulness of, cognizance of, sentience of

away ADJECTIVE **= absent**, out, gone, elsewhere, abroad, not there, not here, not present, on vacation, not at home: *She was away on a business trip.*
▷ ADVERB **1 = off**, elsewhere, abroad, hence, from here: *She drove away before he could speak again.* **2 = aside**, out of the way, to one side: *I put my journal away and prepared for bed.* **3 = at a distance**, far, apart, remote, isolated: *They live thirty miles away from town.*
4 = continuously, repeatedly, relentlessly, incessantly, interminably, unremittingly, uninterruptedly: *He would work away on his computer well into the night.*

awe NOUN **= wonder**, fear, respect, reverence, horror, terror, dread, admiration, amazement, astonishment, veneration: *She gazed in awe at the great stones.*
OPPOSITE: contempt
▷ VERB **= impress**, amaze, stun, frighten, terrify, cow, astonish, horrify, intimidate, daunt: *I am still awed by his courage.*

awed ADJECTIVE **= impressed**, shocked, amazed, afraid, stunned, frightened, terrified, cowed, astonished, horrified, intimidated, fearful, daunted, dumbfounded, wonder-struck

awe-inspiring ADJECTIVE **= impressive**, striking, wonderful, amazing, stunning *(informal)*, magnificent, astonishing, intimidating, awesome, daunting, breathtaking, eye-popping *(informal)*, fearsome, wondrous *(archaic, literary)*, jaw-dropping
OPPOSITE: unimpressive

awesome ADJECTIVE **= awe-inspiring**, striking, shocking, imposing, terrible, amazing, stunning, wonderful, alarming, impressive, frightening, awful, overwhelming, terrifying, magnificent, astonishing, horrible, dreadful, formidable, horrifying, intimidating, fearful, daunting, breathtaking, majestic, solemn, fearsome, wondrous *(archaic, literary)*, redoubtable, jaw-dropping, stupefying

awestruck *or* **awe-stricken** ADJECTIVE **= impressed**, shocked, amazed, stunned, afraid, frightened, terrified, cowed, astonished, horrified, intimidated, fearful, awed, daunted, awe-inspired, dumbfounded, struck dumb, wonder-struck

awful ADJECTIVE **1 = disgusting**, terrible, tremendous, offensive, gross, nasty, foul, horrible, dreadful, unpleasant, revolting, stinking, sickening, hideous, vulgar, vile, distasteful, horrid, frightful, nauseating, odious, repugnant, loathsome, abominable, nauseous, detestable, godawful *(slang)*, hellacious *(U.S. slang)*, festy *(Austral. slang)*, yucko *(Austral. slang)*: *an awful smell of paint* **2 = bad**, poor, terrible, appalling, foul, rubbish *(slang)*, dreadful, unpleasant, dire, horrendous, ghastly, from hell *(informal)*, atrocious, deplorable, abysmal, frightful, hellacious *(U.S. slang)*: *Even if the weather's awful there's still lots to do.* **OPPOSITE:** wonderful
3 = shocking, serious, alarming, distressing, dreadful, horrifying, horrific, hideous, harrowing, gruesome: *Her injuries were massive; it was awful.* **4 = unwell**, poorly *(informal)*, ill, terrible, sick, ugly, crook *(Austral. & N.Z. informal)*, unhealthy, unsightly, queasy, out of sorts *(informal)*, off-colour, under the weather *(informal)*, green about the gills: *I looked awful and felt quite sleepy.*

awfully ADVERB **1 = very**, extremely, terribly, exceptionally, quite, very much, seriously *(informal)*, greatly, immensely, exceedingly, excessively, dreadfully: *That caramel looks awfully good.* **2 = badly**, woefully, dreadfully, inadequately, disgracefully, wretchedly, unforgivably, shoddily, reprehensibly, disreputably: *I played awfully, and there are no excuses.*

awhile ADVERB **= for a while**, briefly, for a moment, for a short time, for a little while

> **USAGE**
> *Awhile*, written as a single word, is an adverb meaning 'for a period of time'. It can only be used with a verb, for example: *he stood awhile in thought*. It is quite commonly written by mistake instead of the noun *a while*, meaning 'a period of time', so take care not to confuse the two parts of speech: *I thought about that for a while* (not *awhile*).

awkward ADJECTIVE
1 = embarrassing, difficult, compromising, sensitive, embarrassed, painful, distressing, delicate, uncomfortable, tricky, trying, humiliating, unpleasant, sticky *(informal)*, troublesome, perplexing, disconcerting, inconvenient, thorny, untimely, ill at ease, discomfiting, ticklish, inopportune, toe-curling *(slang)*, barro *(Austral. slang)*, cringeworthy *(Brit. informal)*: *There was an awkward moment when people had to decide where to stand.* **OPPOSITE:** comfortable
2 = inconvenient, difficult, troublesome, cumbersome, unwieldy, unmanageable, clunky *(informal)*, unhandy: *It was heavy enough to make it awkward to carry.* **OPPOSITE:** convenient
3 = clumsy, stiff, rude, blundering, coarse, bungling, lumbering, inept, unskilled, bumbling, unwieldy, ponderous, ungainly, gauche, gawky, uncouth, unrefined, artless, inelegant, uncoordinated, graceless, cack-handed *(informal)*, unpolished, clownish, oafish, inexpert, maladroit, ill-bred, all thumbs, ungraceful, skill-less, unskilful, butterfingered *(informal)*, unhandy, ham-fisted *or* ham-handed *(informal)*, unco *(Austral. slang)*: *She made an awkward gesture with her hands.*
OPPOSITE: graceful
4 = uncooperative, trying, difficult, annoying, unpredictable, unreasonable, stubborn, troublesome, perverse, prickly, exasperating, irritable, intractable, vexing, unhelpful, touchy, obstinate, obstructive, bloody-minded *(Brit. informal)*, chippy *(informal)*, vexatious, hard to handle, disobliging: *She's got to an age where she's being awkward.*

awkwardness NOUN **1 = clumsiness**, stiffness, rudeness, coarseness, ineptness, ill-breeding, artlessness, gaucheness, inelegance, gaucherie, gracelessness, oafishness, gawkiness, uncouthness, maladroitness, ungainliness, clownishness, inexpertness, uncoordination, unskilfulness, unskilledness: *He displayed all the awkwardness of adolescence.* **2 = embarrassment**, difficulty, discomfort, delicacy, unpleasantness, inconvenience, stickiness *(informal)*, painfulness, ticklishness, uphill *(S. African)*, thorniness, inopportuneness, perplexingness, untimeliness: *It was* *a moment of some awkwardness in our relationship.*

awry ADVERB = **askew**, to one side, off course, out of line, obliquely, unevenly, off-centre, cockeyed *(informal)*, out of true, crookedly, skew-whiff *(informal)*: *He was concerned that his hair might go awry.*
▷ ADJECTIVE = **askew**, twisted, crooked, to one side, uneven, off course, out of line, asymmetrical, off-centre, cockeyed *(informal)*, misaligned, out of true, skew-whiff *(informal)*: *His dark hair was all awry.*
▷ ADVERB, ADJECTIVE = **wrong**, amiss: *a plan that had gone awry*

axe NOUN = **hatchet**, chopper, tomahawk, cleaver, adze: *She took an axe and wrecked the car.*
▷ VERB **1** = **abandon**, end, pull, eliminate, cancel, scrap, wind up, turn off *(informal)*, relegate, cut back, terminate, dispense with, discontinue, pull the plug on: *Community projects are being axed by the government.* **2** = **dismiss**, fire *(informal)*, sack *(informal)*, remove, get rid of, discharge, throw out, oust, give (someone) their marching orders, give the boot to *(slang)*, give the bullet to *(Brit. slang)*, give the push to, kennet *(Austral. slang)*, jeff *(Austral. slang)*: *She was axed by the Edinburgh club in October after her comments about a referee.*
an axe to grind = **pet subject**, grievance, ulterior motive, private purpose, personal consideration, private ends: *I've got no axe to grind with either of them.*
the axe = **the sack** *(informal)*, dismissal, discharge, wind-up, the boot *(slang)*, cancellation, cutback, termination, the chop *(slang)*, the (old) heave-ho *(informal)*, the order of the boot *(slang)*: *one of the four doctors facing the axe*

axiom NOUN = **principle**, fundamental, maxim, gnome, adage, postulate, dictum, precept, aphorism, truism, apophthegm

axis NOUN = **pivot**, shaft, axle, spindle, centre line

axle NOUN = **shaft**, pin, rod, axis, pivot, spindle, arbor, mandrel

azure ADJECTIVE = **sky blue**, blue, clear blue, ultramarine, cerulean, sky-coloured

Bb

baas NOUN **= master**, bo *(informal)*, chief, ruler, commander, head, overlord, overseer

babble VERB **1 = gabble**, chatter, gush, spout, waffle *(informal, chiefly Brit.)*, splutter, gaggle, burble, prattle, gibber, rabbit on *(Brit. informal)*, jabber, prate, earbash *(Austral. & N.Z. slang)*: *They all babbled simultaneously.* **2 = gurgle**, lap, bubble, splash, murmur, ripple, burble, plash: *a brook babbling only yards from the door*
▷ NOUN **1 = gabble**, chatter, burble, prattle, blabber: *He couldn't make himself heard above the babble.* **2 = gibberish**, waffle *(informal, chiefly Brit.)*, drivel, twaddle: *lots of babble about strategies and tactics*

babe NOUN **= baby**, child, innocent, infant, bairn *(Scot. & Northern English)*, tacker *(Austral. slang)*, suckling, newborn child, babe in arms, nursling

baby NOUN **= child**, infant, babe, wean *(Scot.)*, little one, bairn *(Scot. & Northern English)*, suckling, newborn child, babe in arms, sprog *(slang)*, neonate, rug rat *(U.S. & Canad. informal)*, ankle biter *(Austral. slang)*, tacker *(Austral. slang)*: *My wife has just had a baby.*
▷ ADJECTIVE **= small**, little, minute, tiny, mini, wee, miniature, dwarf, diminutive, petite, midget, teeny *(informal)*, pocket-sized, undersized, teeny-weeny *(informal)*, Lilliputian, teensy-weensy *(informal)*, pygmy *or* pigmy: *Serve with baby new potatoes.*
▷ VERB **= spoil**, pamper, cosset, coddle, pet, humour, indulge, spoon-feed, mollycoddle, overindulge, wrap up in cotton wool *(informal)*: *He'd always babied her.*

QUOTATIONS

A baby is God's opinion that life should go on
[Carl Sandburg *Remembrance Rock*]

Every baby born into the world is a finer one than the last
[Charles Dickens *Nicholas Nickleby*]

The invisible bond that gives the baby rein to discover his place in the world also brings the creeping baby back to home base
[Louise J. Kaplan *Oneness and Separateness: From Infant to Individual*]

People who say they sleep like a baby usually don't have one
[Leo Burke]

baby: a misshapen creature of no particular age, sex or condition, chiefly remarkable for the violence of the sympathies and antipathies it excites in others, itself without sentiment or emotion
[Ambrose Bierce *The Devil's Dictionary*]

back ADVERB **= ago**, before, earlier, in the past, previously
▷ NOUN **1 = spine**, backbone, vertebrae, spinal column, vertebral column: *Three of the victims were shot in the back.* **2 = rear**, other side, back end, rear side: *a room at the back of the shop* **OPPOSITE:** front **3 = end**, tail end **4 = reverse**, rear, other side, wrong side, underside, flip side, verso: *Send your answers on the back of a postcard.*
▷ ADJECTIVE **1 = rear**: *a path leading to the back garden* **OPPOSITE:** front **2 = rearmost**, hind, hindmost: *She could remember sitting in the back seat of their car.* **3 = previous**, earlier, former, past, elapsed: *A handful of back copies will give an indication of property prices.* **OPPOSITE:** future **4 = tail**, end, rear, posterior: *They had transmitters taped to their back feathers.*
▷ VERB **1 = support**, help, second, aid, champion, encourage, favour, defend, promote, sanction, sustain, assist, advocate, endorse, side with, stand up for, espouse, stand behind, countenance, abet, stick up for *(informal)*, take up the cudgels for: *He is backed by the civic movement.* **OPPOSITE:** oppose **2 = subsidize**, help, support, finance, sponsor, assist, underwrite: *Murjani backed him to start the new company.*
back down = give in, collapse, withdraw, yield, concede, submit, surrender, comply, cave in *(informal)*, capitulate, accede, admit defeat, back-pedal: *It's too late now to back down.*
back out = withdraw, retire, give up, pull out, retreat, drop out, renege, cop out *(slang)*, chicken out *(informal)*, detach yourself: *I've already promised I'll go – I can't back out now.*
back someone up = support, second, aid, assist, stand by, bolster: *The girl denied being there, and the men backed her up.*
behind someone's back = secretly, covertly, surreptitiously, furtively, conspiratorially, sneakily, deceitfully: *You enjoy her hospitality, and then criticize her behind her back.*
▸ *related adjective:* dorsal

backbone NOUN **1 = spinal column**, spine, vertebrae, vertebral column: *She doubled over, snapping her backbone and breaking her arm.* **2 = foundation**, support, base, basis, mainstay, bedrock: *the economic backbone of the nation* **3 = strength of character**, will, character, bottle *(Brit. slang)*, resolution, resolve, nerve, daring, courage, determination, guts, pluck, stamina, grit, bravery, fortitude, toughness, tenacity, willpower, mettle, boldness, firmness, spunk *(informal)*, fearlessness, steadfastness, moral fibre, hardihood, dauntlessness: *You might be taking drastic measures and you've got to have the backbone to do that.*

backer NOUN **1 = supporter**, second, ally, angel *(informal)*, patron, promoter, subscriber, underwriter, helper, benefactor: *I was looking for a backer to assist me in the attempted buy-out.* **2 = advocate**, supporter, patron, sponsor, promoter, protagonist: *He became a backer of reform at the height of the crisis.*

backfire VERB **= fail**, founder, flop *(informal)*, rebound, fall through, fall flat, boomerang, miscarry, misfire, go belly-up *(slang)*, turn out badly, meet with disaster

background NOUN **1 = upbringing**, history, culture, environment, tradition, circumstances, breeding, milieu: *Moulded by his background, he could not escape traditional values.* **2 = experience**, grounding, education, preparation, qualifications, credentials: *His background was in engineering.* **3 = circumstances**, history, conditions, situation, atmosphere, environment, framework, ambience, milieu, frame of reference: *The meeting takes place against a background of political violence.*

backing NOUN **1 = support**, seconding, championing, promotion, sanction, approval, blessing, encouragement, endorsement, patronage, accompaniment, advocacy, moral support, espousal: *He said the president had the full backing of his government.* **2 = assistance**, support, help, funds, aid, grant, subsidy, sponsorship, patronage: *She brought her action with the financial backing of the BBC.*

backlash NOUN **= reaction**, response, resistance, resentment, retaliation, repercussion, counterblast, counteraction, retroaction

backlog NOUN **= build-up**, stock, excess, accumulation, accretion

backside NOUN **= buttocks**, behind *(informal)*, seat, bottom, rear, tail *(informal)*, cheeks *(informal)*, butt *(U.S. & Canad. informal)*, bum *(Brit. slang)*, buns *(U.S. slang)*, rump, rear end, posterior, haunches, hindquarters, derrière *(euphemistic)*, tush, fundament, gluteus maximus *(Anatomy)*, coit *(Austral. slang)*, nates *(technical)*, jacksy *(Brit. slang)*, keister or keester *(slang, chiefly U.S.)*

backtrack VERB **1** *(often with* **on***)* **= retract**, withdraw, retreat, draw back, recant: *The finance minister backtracked on his decision.* **2 = retrace your steps**, go back, reverse, retreat, move back, back-pedal: *We had to backtrack to the corner and cross the street.*

backup NOUN **1 = support**, backing, help, aid, reserves, assistance, reinforcement, auxiliaries: *There's no emergency backup immediately available if something goes wrong.* **2 = substitute**, reserve, relief, stand-in, replacement, stand-by, understudy, second string, locum: *He was added to the squad as a backup.*

backward ADJECTIVE **1 = reverse**, inverted, inverse, back to front, rearward: *He did a backward flip.* **OPPOSITE:** forward
2 = underdeveloped, undeveloped: *We need to accelerate the pace of change in our backward country.* **3 = slow**, behind, stupid, retarded, deficient, underdeveloped, subnormal, half-witted, behindhand, slow-witted, intellectually handicapped *(Austral.)*: *I was slow to walk and my parents thought I was backward.*

backwardness NOUN **1 = lack of development**, underdevelopment: *I was astonished at the backwardness of our country at the time.* **2 = slowness**, learning difficulties, underdevelopment, retardation, arrested development: *Her parents were concerned about her backwardness in practical and physical activities.* **OPPOSITE:** brightness

backwards *or* **backward** ADVERB **= towards the rear**, behind you, in reverse, rearwards

backwoods PLURAL NOUN **= sticks** *(informal)*, outback, back country *(U.S.)*, back of beyond, backlands *(U.S.)*

bacteria PLURAL NOUN **= microorganisms**, viruses, bugs *(slang)*, germs, microbes, pathogens, bacilli

> **USAGE**
> *Bacteria* is a plural noun. It is therefore incorrect to talk about *a bacteria*, even though this is quite commonly heard, especially in the media. The correct singular is *a bacterium*.

bad ADJECTIVE **1 = harmful**, damaging, dangerous, disastrous, destructive, unhealthy, detrimental, hurtful, ruinous, deleterious, injurious, disadvantageous: *Divorce is bad for children.* **OPPOSITE:** beneficial
2 = severe, serious, terrible, acute, extreme, intense, painful, distressing, fierce, harsh: *The pain is often so bad she wants to scream.*
3 = unfavourable, troubling, distressing, unfortunate, grim, discouraging, unpleasant, gloomy, adverse: *The closure of the project is bad news for her staff.* **4 = inferior**, poor, inadequate, pathetic, faulty, duff *(Brit. informal)*, unsatisfactory, mediocre, defective, second-class, deficient, imperfect, second-rate, shoddy, low-grade, erroneous, substandard, low-rent *(informal, chiefly U.S.)*, two-bit *(U.S. & Canad. slang)*, crappy *(slang)*, end-of-the-pier *(Brit. informal)*, poxy *(slang)*, dime-a-dozen *(informal)*, bush-league *(Austral. & N.Z. informal)*, tinhorn *(U.S. slang)*, half-pie *(N.Z. informal)*, bodger or bodgie *(Austral. slang)*, strictly for the birds *(informal)*: *Many old people in Britain are living in bad housing.*
OPPOSITE: satisfactory
5 = incompetent, poor, useless, incapable, unfit, inexpert: *He was a bad driver.* **6 = grim**, severe, hard, tough: *Being unable to hear doesn't seem as bad as being unable to see.* **7 = wicked**, criminal, evil, corrupt, worthless, base, vile, immoral, delinquent, sinful, depraved, debased, amoral, egregious, villainous, unprincipled, iniquitous, nefarious, dissolute, maleficent: *I was selling drugs, but I didn't think I was a bad person.*
OPPOSITE: virtuous **8 = naughty**, defiant, perverse, wayward, mischievous, wicked, unruly, impish, undisciplined, roguish, disobedient: *You are a bad boy for repeating what I told you.* **OPPOSITE:** well-behaved
9 = guilty, sorry, ashamed, apologetic, rueful, sheepish, contrite, remorseful, regretful, shamefaced, conscience-stricken: *You don't have to feel bad about relaxing.* **10 = rotten**, off, rank, sour, rancid, mouldy, fetid, putrid, festy *(Austral. slang)*: *They bought so much beef that some went bad.*
not bad = O.K. *or* **okay**, fine, middling, average, fair, all right, acceptable, moderate, adequate, respectable, satisfactory, so-so, tolerable, passable, fair to middling *(informal)*: *These are not bad for cheap shoes.*

baddie *or* **baddy** NOUN *(informal)* **= villain**, criminal, rogue, bad guy, scoundrel, miscreant, antihero, evildoer, wrong 'un *(Austral. slang)*
OPPOSITE: goodie *or* goody

badge NOUN **1 = image**, brand, stamp, identification, crest, emblem, insignia: *a badge depicting a party leader*
2 = mark, sign, token: *sporting a sword as their badge of citizenship*

badger VERB **= pester**, worry, harry, bother, bug *(informal)*, bully, plague, hound, get at, harass, nag, hassle *(informal)*, chivvy, importune, bend someone's ear *(informal)*, be on someone's back *(slang)*

badly ADVERB **1 = poorly**, incorrectly, carelessly, inadequately, erroneously, imperfectly, ineptly, shoddily, defectively, faultily: *I was angry because I played so badly.* **OPPOSITE:** well
2 = severely, greatly, deeply, seriously, gravely, desperately, sorely, dangerously, intensely, painfully, acutely, exceedingly: *It was a gamble that went badly wrong.* **3 = unfavourably**, unsuccessfully: *The male sex comes out of the film very badly.*

badness NOUN **= wickedness**, wrong, evil, corruption, sin, impropriety, immorality, villainy, naughtiness, sinfulness, foulness, baseness, rottenness, vileness, shamefulness
OPPOSITE: virtue

bad-tempered ADJECTIVE **= irritable**, cross, angry, tense, crabbed, fiery, grumbling, snarling, prickly, exasperated, edgy, snappy, sullen, touchy, surly, petulant, sulky, ill-tempered, irascible, cantankerous, tetchy, ratty *(Brit. & N.Z. informal)*, tooshie *(Austral. slang)*, testy, chippy *(informal)*, fretful, grouchy *(informal)*, querulous, peevish, crabby, huffy, dyspeptic, choleric, splenetic, crotchety *(informal)*, oversensitive, snappish, ill-humoured, liverish, narky *(Brit. slang)*, out of humour
OPPOSITE: good-tempered

baffle VERB **= puzzle**, beat *(slang)*, amaze, confuse, stump, bewilder, astound, elude, confound, perplex, disconcert, mystify, flummox, boggle the mind of, dumbfound
OPPOSITE: explain

baffling ADJECTIVE **= puzzling**, strange, confusing, weird, mysterious, unclear, bewildering, elusive, enigmatic, perplexing, incomprehensible, mystifying, inexplicable, unaccountable, unfathomable
OPPOSITE: understandable

bag NOUN **= sack**, container, poke *(Scot.)*, sac, receptacle: *She left the hotel carrying a shopping bag.*
▷ VERB **1 = get**, take, land, score *(slang)*, gain, pick up, capture, acquire, get hold of, come by, procure, make sure of, win possession of: *The smart ones will have already bagged their seats.*
2 = catch, get, kill, shoot, capture, acquire, trap: *Bag a rabbit for supper.*

baggage NOUN **= luggage**, things, cases, bags, equipment, gear, trunks, suitcases, belongings, paraphernalia, accoutrements, impedimenta

baggy ADJECTIVE **= loose**, hanging, slack, loosened, bulging, not fitting, sagging, sloppy, floppy, billowing, roomy, slackened, ill-fitting, droopy, oversize, not tight **OPPOSITE:** tight

bail[1] NOUN **= security**, bond, guarantee, pledge, warranty, surety, guaranty: *He was freed on bail pending an appeal.*
bail out = escape, withdraw, get away, retreat, make your getaway, break free *or* out, make *or* effect your escape: *The pilot bailed out safely.*
bail something *or* **someone out = save**, help, free, release, aid, deliver, recover, rescue, get out, relieve, liberate, salvage, set free, save the life

b

of, extricate, save (someone's) bacon *(Brit. informal)*: *They will discuss how to bail the economy out of its slump.*

bail[2] *or* **bale** VERB **= scoop**, empty, dip, ladle, drain off: *We kept her afloat for a couple of hours by bailing frantically.*

bait NOUN **= lure**, attraction, incentive, carrot *(informal)*, temptation, bribe, magnet, snare, inducement, decoy, carrot and stick, enticement, allurement: *bait to attract audiences for advertisements*
▷ VERB **= tease**, provoke, annoy, irritate, guy *(informal)*, bother, needle *(informal)*, plague *(informal)*, mock, rag, rib *(informal)*, wind up *(Brit. slang)*, hound, torment, harass, ridicule, taunt, hassle *(informal)*, aggravate *(informal)*, badger, gall, persecute, pester, goad, irk, bedevil, take the mickey out of *(informal)*, chaff, gibe, get on the nerves of *(informal)*, nark *(Brit., Austral. & N.Z. slang)*, be on the back of *(slang)*, get in the hair of *(informal)*, get *or* take a rise out of, hack you off *(informal)*: *He delighted in baiting his mother.*

baked ADJECTIVE **= dry**, desert, seared, dried up, scorched, barren, sterile, arid, torrid, desiccated, sun-baked, waterless, moistureless

bakkie NOUN **= truck**, pick-up, van, lorry, pick-up truck

balance VERB **1 = stabilize**, level, steady: *He balanced a football on his head.* **OPPOSITE:** overbalance **2 = offset**, match, square, make up for, compensate for, counteract, neutralize, counterbalance, even up, equalize, counterpoise: *Balance spicy dishes with mild ones.* **3 = weigh**, consider, compare, estimate, contrast, assess, evaluate, set against, juxtapose: *She carefully tried to balance religious sensitivities against democratic freedom.* **4 = calculate**, rate, judge, total, determine, estimate, settle, count, square, reckon, work out, compute, gauge, tally: *He balanced his budget by rigid control over public expenditure.*
▷ NOUN **1 = equilibrium**, stability, steadiness, evenness, equipoise, counterpoise: *The medicines you are currently taking could be affecting your balance.* **OPPOSITE:** instability **2 = stability**, equanimity, constancy, steadiness: *the ecological balance of the forest* **3 = parity**, equity, fairness, impartiality, equality, correspondence, equivalence: *her ability to maintain the political balance* **4 = remainder**, rest, difference, surplus, residue: *They were due to pay the balance on delivery.* **5 = composure**, stability, restraint, self-control, poise, self-discipline, coolness, calmness, equanimity, self-restraint, steadiness, self-possession, self-mastery, strength of mind *or* will: *a balance of mind*

balance sheet NOUN **= statement**, report, account, budget, ledger, financial statement, credits and debits sheet

balcony NOUN **1 = terrace**, veranda: *He appeared on a second floor balcony to appeal to the crowd to be calm.* **2 = upper circle**, gods, gallery: *We took our seats in the balcony.*

bald ADJECTIVE **1 = hairless**, bare, shorn, clean-shaven, tonsured, depilated, glabrous *(Biology)*, baldheaded, baldpated: *The man's bald head was beaded with sweat.* **2 = plain**, direct, simple, straight, frank, severe, bare, straightforward, blunt, rude, outright, downright, forthright, unadorned, unvarnished, straight from the shoulder: *The bald truth is that he's just not happy.*

balding ADJECTIVE **= losing your hair**, receding, thin on top, becoming bald

baldness NOUN **= hairlessness**, alopecia *(Pathology)*, baldheadedness, baldpatedness, glabrousness *(Biology)*

bale *see* **bail[2]**

baleful ADJECTIVE **= menacing**, threatening, dangerous, frightening, evil, deadly, forbidding, intimidating, harmful, sinister, ominous, malignant, hurtful, vindictive, pernicious, malevolent, noxious, venomous, ruinous, intimidatory, minatory, maleficent, bodeful, louring *or* lowering, minacious **OPPOSITE:** friendly

balk *or* **baulk** VERB **= recoil**, resist, hesitate, dodge, falter, evade, shy away, flinch, quail, shirk, shrink, draw back, jib **OPPOSITE:** accept

ball NOUN **1 = sphere**, drop, globe, pellet, orb, globule, spheroid: *a golf ball* **2 = projectile**, shot, missile, bullet, ammunition, slug, pellet, grapeshot: *A cannon ball struck the ship.*

ballast NOUN **= counterbalance**, balance, weight, stability, equilibrium, sandbag, counterweight, stabilizer

balloon VERB **= expand**, rise, increase, extend, swell, blow up, enlarge, inflate, bulge, billow, dilate, be inflated, puff out, become larger, distend, bloat, grow rapidly

ballot NOUN **= vote**, election, voting, poll, polling, referendum, show of hands

balm NOUN **1 = ointment**, cream, lotion, salve, emollient, balsam, liniment, embrocation, unguent: *The balm is very soothing.* **2 = comfort**, support, relief, cheer, consolation, solace, palliative, anodyne, succour, restorative, curative: *This place is a balm to the soul.*

balmy ADJECTIVE **= mild**, warm, calm, moderate, pleasant, clement, tranquil, temperate, summery: *a balmy summer's evening* **OPPOSITE:** rough

bamboozle VERB **1 = cheat**, do *(informal)*, kid *(informal)*, skin *(slang)*, trick, fool, take in *(informal)*, con *(informal)*, stiff, sting *(informal)*, mislead, rip off *(slang)*, thwart, deceive, fleece, hoax, defraud, dupe, beguile, gull *(archaic)*, delude, swindle, stitch up *(slang)*, victimize, hoodwink, double-cross *(informal)*, diddle *(informal)*, take for a ride *(informal)*, do the dirty on *(Brit. informal)*, bilk, pull a fast one on *(informal)*, cozen: *He was bamboozled by con men.* **2 = puzzle**, confuse, stump, baffle, bewilder, confound, perplex, mystify, befuddle, flummox, nonplus: *He bamboozled Mercer into defeat.*

ban VERB **1 = prohibit**, black, bar, block, restrict, veto, forbid, boycott, suppress, outlaw, banish, disallow, proscribe, debar, blackball, interdict: *Last year arms sales were banned.* **OPPOSITE:** permit **2 = bar**, prohibit, exclude, forbid, disqualify, preclude, debar, declare ineligible: *He was banned from driving for three years.*
▷ NOUN **= prohibition**, block, restriction, veto, boycott, embargo, injunction, censorship, taboo, suppression, stoppage, disqualification, interdiction, interdict, proscription, disallowance, rahui *(N.Z.)*, restraining order *(U.S., Law)*: *The General also lifted a ban on political parties.* **OPPOSITE:** permission

banal ADJECTIVE **= unoriginal**, stock, ordinary, boring, tired, routine, dull, everyday, stereotypical, pedestrian, commonplace, mundane, tedious, vanilla *(slang)*, dreary, stale, tiresome, monotonous, humdrum, threadbare, trite, unimaginative, uneventful, uninteresting, clichéd, old hat, mind-numbing, hackneyed, ho-hum *(informal)*, vapid, repetitious, wearisome, platitudinous, cliché-ridden, unvaried **OPPOSITE:** original

banality NOUN **1 = unoriginality**, triviality, vapidity, triteness: *the banality of life* **2 = cliché**, commonplace, platitude, truism, bromide *(informal)*, trite phrase: *His ability to utter banalities never ceased to amaze me.*

band[1] NOUN **1 = ensemble**, group, orchestra, combo: *Local bands provide music for dancing.* **2 = gang**, company, group, set, party, team, lot, club, body, association, crowd, troop, pack, camp, squad, crew *(informal)*, assembly, mob, horde, troupe, posse *(informal)*, clique, coterie, bevy: *bands of government soldiers*
band together = unite, group, join, league, ally, associate, gather, pool, merge, consolidate, affiliate, collaborate, join forces, cooperate, confederate, pull together, join together, federate, close ranks, club together: *People living in a foreign city band together for company.*

band[2] NOUN **1 = headband**, tie, strip, ribbon, fillet: *She was wearing a trouser suit and a band around her forehead.* **2 = bandage**, tie, binding, strip, belt, strap, cord, swathe, fetter: *He placed a metal band around the injured kneecap.*

bandage NOUN **= dressing**, plaster, compress, gauze: *His chest was swathed in bandages.*

▷ VERB = **dress**, cover, bind, swathe: *Apply a dressing to the wound and bandage it.*

bandit NOUN = **robber**, gunman, crook, outlaw, pirate, raider, gangster, plunderer, mugger *(informal)*, hijacker, looter, highwayman, racketeer, desperado, marauder, brigand, freebooter, footpad

bandy VERB = **exchange**, trade, pass, throw, truck, swap, toss, shuffle, commute, interchange, barter, reciprocate

bane NOUN = **plague**, bête noire, trial, disaster, evil, ruin, burden, destruction, despair, misery, curse, pest, torment, woe, nuisance, downfall, calamity, scourge, affliction OPPOSITE: blessing

bang NOUN **1** = **explosion**, report, shot, pop, clash, crack, blast, burst, boom, slam, discharge, thump, clap, thud, clang, peal, detonation: *I heard four or five loud bangs.* **2** = **blow**, hit, box, knock, stroke, punch, belt *(informal)*, rap, bump, bash *(informal)*, sock *(slang)*, smack, thump, buffet, clout *(informal)*, cuff, clump *(slang)*, whack, wallop *(informal)*, slosh *(Brit. slang)*, tonk *(informal)*, clomp *(slang)*: *a nasty bang on the head*
▷ VERB **1** = **resound**, beat, crash, burst, boom, echo, drum, explode, thunder, thump, throb, thud, clang: *The engine spat and banged.* **2** = **bump**, knock, elbow, jostle: *I didn't mean to bang into you.* **3** *(often with* **on***)* = **hit**, pound, beat, strike, crash, knock, belt *(informal)*, hammer, slam, rap, bump, bash *(informal)*, thump, clatter, pummel, tonk *(informal)*, beat *or* knock seven bells out of *(informal)*: *We could bang on the desks and shout until they let us out.*
▷ ADVERB = **exactly**, just, straight, square, squarely, precisely, slap, smack, plumb *(informal)*: *bang in the middle of the track*

banish VERB **1** = **exclude**, bar, ban, dismiss, expel, throw out, oust, drive away, eject, evict, shut out, ostracize: *I was banished from the small bedroom upstairs.* **2** = **expel**, transport, exile, outlaw, deport, drive away, expatriate, excommunicate: *He was banished from England.* OPPOSITE: admit **3** = **get rid of**, remove, eliminate, eradicate, shake off, dislodge, see the back of: *a public investment programme intended to banish the recession*

banishment NOUN = **expulsion**, exile, dismissal, removal, discharge, transportation, exclusion, deportation, eviction, ejection, extrusion, proscription, expatriation, debarment

banisters PLURAL NOUN = **railing**, rail, balustrade, handrail, balusters

bank[1] NOUN **1** = **financial institution**, repository, depository: *I had money in the bank.* **2** = **store**, fund, stock, source, supply, reserve, pool, reservoir, accumulation, stockpile, hoard, storehouse: *one of the largest data banks in the world*
▷ VERB = **deposit**, keep, save: *The agency has banked your cheque.*
bank on something = **rely on**, trust (in), depend on, look to, believe in, count on, be sure of, lean on, be confident of, have confidence in, swear by, reckon on, repose trust in: *She is clearly banking on her past to be the meal ticket for her future.*

bank[2] NOUN **1** = **side**, edge, margin, shore, brink, lakeside, waterside: *an old warehouse on the banks of the canal* **2** = **mound**, banking, rise, hill, mass, pile, heap, ridge, dune, embankment, knoll, hillock, kopje *or* koppie *(S. African)*: *resting indolently upon a grassy bank*
▷ VERB = **tilt**, tip, pitch, heel, slope, incline, slant, cant, camber: *A single-engine plane took off and banked above the highway.*

bank[3] NOUN = **row**, group, line, train, range, series, file, rank, arrangement, sequence, succession, array, tier: *The typical labourer now sits in front of a bank of dials.*

bankrupt ADJECTIVE = **insolvent**, broke *(informal)*, spent, ruined, wiped out *(informal)*, impoverished, beggared, in the red, on the rocks, destitute, gone bust *(informal)*, in receivership, gone to the wall, in the hands of the receivers, on your uppers, in queer street *(informal)* OPPOSITE: solvent

bankruptcy NOUN = **insolvency**, failure, crash, disaster, ruin, liquidation, indebtedness

banner NOUN **1** = **flag**, standard, colours, jack, pennant, ensign, streamer, pennon **2** = **placard**

banquet NOUN = **feast**, spread *(informal)*, dinner, meal, entertainment, revel, blowout *(slang)*, repast, slap-up meal *(Brit. informal)*, hakari *(N.Z.)*

banter NOUN = **joking**, kidding *(informal)*, ribbing *(informal)*, teasing, jeering, mockery, derision, jesting, chaff, pleasantry, repartee, wordplay, badinage, chaffing, raillery, persiflage: *She heard them exchanging good-natured banter.*
▷ VERB = **joke**, kid *(informal)*, rib *(informal)*, tease, taunt, jeer, josh *(slang, chiefly U.S. & Canad.)*, jest, take the mickey *(informal)*, chaff: *They shared a cocktail and bantered easily.*

baptism NOUN **1** = **christening**, sprinkling, purification, immersion: *We are at a site of baptism, a place of worship.* **2** = **initiation**, beginning, debut, introduction, admission, dedication, inauguration, induction, inception, rite of passage, commencement, investiture, baptism of fire, instatement: *The new boys face a tough baptism against Leeds.*

baptize VERB **1** = **christen**, cleanse, immerse, purify, besprinkle: *I think your mother was baptized a Catholic.* **2** = **initiate**, admit, introduce, invest, recruit, enrol, induct, indoctrinate, instate: *baptized into the Church of England*

bar NOUN **1** = **public house**, pub *(informal, chiefly Brit.)*, counter, inn, local *(Brit. informal)*, lounge, saloon, tavern, canteen, watering hole *(facetious, slang)*, boozer *(Brit., Austral. & N.Z. informal)*, beer parlour *(Canad.)*, roadhouse, hostelry *(archaic, facetious)*, alehouse *(archaic)*, taproom: *the city's most popular country and western bar* **2** = **rod**, staff, stick, stake, rail, pole, paling, shaft, baton, mace, batten, palisade, crosspiece: *a crowd throwing stones and iron bars* **3** = **obstacle**, block, barrier, hurdle, hitch, barricade, snag, deterrent, obstruction, stumbling block, impediment, hindrance, interdict: *one of the fundamental bars to communication* OPPOSITE: aid
▷ VERB **1** = **lock**, block, secure, chain, attach, anchor, bolt, blockade, barricade, fortify, fasten, latch, obstruct, make firm, make fast: *For added safety, bar the door to the kitchen.* **2** = **block**, restrict, hold up, restrain, hamper, thwart, hinder, obstruct, impede, shut off: *He stepped in front of her, barring her way.* **3** = **exclude**, ban, forbid, prohibit, keep out of, disallow, shut out of, ostracize, debar, blackball, interdict, black: *They have been barred from the country since 1982.* OPPOSITE: admit

barb NOUN **1** = **point**, spur, spike, thorn, bristle, quill, prickle, tine, prong: *Apply gentle pressure on the barb with the point of the pliers.* **2** = **dig**, abuse, slight, insult, put-down, snub, sneer, scoff, rebuff, affront, slap in the face *(informal)*, gibe, aspersion: *The barb stung her exactly the way he hoped it would.*

barbarian NOUN **1** = **savage**, monster, beast, brute, yahoo, swine, ogre, sadist: *Our maths teacher was a bully and a complete barbarian.* **2** = **lout**, hooligan, illiterate, vandal, yahoo, bigot, philistine, ned *(Scot. slang)*, hoon *(Austral. & N.Z.)*, cougan *(Austral. slang)*, scozza *(Austral. slang)*, bogan *(Austral. slang)*, ruffian, ignoramus, boor, lowbrow, vulgarian: *The visitors looked upon us all as barbarians.*
▷ ADJECTIVE = **uncivilized**, wild, rough, savage, crude, primitive, vulgar, illiterate, barbaric, philistine, uneducated, unsophisticated, barbarous, boorish, uncouth, uncultivated, lowbrow, uncultured, unmannered: *rude and barbarian people* OPPOSITE: civilized

barbaric ADJECTIVE **1** = **brutal**, fierce, cruel, savage, crude, vicious, ruthless, coarse, vulgar, heartless, inhuman, merciless, bloodthirsty, remorseless, barbarous, pitiless, uncouth: *a particularly barbaric act of violence* **2** = **uncivilized**, wild, savage, primitive, rude, barbarian, barbarous: *a prehistoric and barbaric world* OPPOSITE: civilized

barbarism NOUN = **cruelty**, outrage, atrocity, brutality, savagery, ruthlessness, wickedness, inhumanity, barbarity, viciousness, coarseness, crudity, monstrousness, heinousness, fiendishness, barbarousness

barbarity NOUN **1 = viciousness**, horror, cruelty, brutality, ferocity, savagery, ruthlessness, inhumanity **2 = atrocity**, cruelty, horror, inhumanity: *the barbarities committed by the invading army*

barbarous ADJECTIVE **1 = uncivilized**, wild, rough, gross, savage, primitive, rude, coarse, vulgar, barbarian, philistine, uneducated, brutish, unsophisticated, uncouth, uncultivated, unpolished, uncultured, unmannered: *He thought the poetry of Whitman barbarous.* **2 = brutal**, cruel, savage, vicious, ruthless, ferocious, monstrous, barbaric, heartless, inhuman, merciless, remorseless, pitiless: *It was a barbarous attack on a purely civilian train.*

barbed ADJECTIVE **1 = cutting**, pointed, biting, critical, acid, hostile, nasty, harsh, savage, brutal, searing, withering, scathing, unkind, hurtful, belittling, sarcastic, caustic, scornful, vitriolic, trenchant, acrid, catty (*informal*), mordant, mordacious: *barbed comments* **2 = spiked**, pointed, toothed, hooked, notched, prickly, jagged, thorny, pronged, spiny, snaggy: *The factory was surrounded by barbed wire.*

bard NOUN = **poet**, singer, rhymer, minstrel, lyricist, troubadour

bare ADJECTIVE **1 = naked**, nude, stripped, exposed, uncovered, shorn, undressed, divested, denuded, in the raw (*informal*), disrobed, unclothed, buck naked (*slang*), unclad, scuddy (*slang*), without a stitch on (*informal*), in the bare scud (*slang*), naked as the day you were born (*informal*): *She seemed unaware that she was bare.* **OPPOSITE:** dressed **2 = simple**, basic, severe, spare, stark, austere, spartan, unadorned, unfussy, unvarnished, unembellished, unornamented, unpatterned, bare-bones: *bare wooden floors* **OPPOSITE:** adorned **3 = empty**, wanting, mean, lacking, deserted, vacant, void, scarce, barren, uninhabited, unoccupied, scanty, unfurnished: *a bare, draughty interviewing room* **OPPOSITE:** full **4 = plain**, hard, simple, cold, basic, essential, obvious, sheer, patent, evident, stark, manifest, bald, literal, overt, unembellished: *Reporters were given nothing but the bare facts.*

barely ADVERB = **only just**, just, hardly, scarcely, at a push, almost not **OPPOSITE:** completely

bargain NOUN **1 = good buy**, discount purchase, good deal, good value, steal (*informal*), snip (*informal*), giveaway, cheap purchase: *At this price the wine is a bargain.* **2 = agreement**, deal (*informal*), understanding, promise, contract, negotiation, arrangement, settlement, treaty, pledge, convention, transaction, engagement, pact, compact, covenant, stipulation: *The treaty was based on a bargain between the governments.* ▷ VERB **1 = haggle**, deal, sell, trade, traffic, barter, drive a hard bargain: *Shop in small local markets and don't be afraid to bargain.* **2 = negotiate**, deal, contract, mediate, covenant, stipulate, arbitrate, transact, cut a deal: *They prefer to bargain with individual clients, for cash.*
bargain for *or* **on something = anticipate**, expect, look for, imagine, predict, plan for, forecast, hope for, contemplate, be prepared for, foresee, foretell, count upon: *The effects of this policy were more than they had bargained for; He didn't bargain on an undercover investigation.*

barge NOUN = **canal boat**, lighter, narrow boat, scow, flatboat: *He lives on a barge and only works when he has to.*
barge in (on something *or* **someone) = interrupt**, break in (on), muscle in (on) (*informal*), intrude (on), infringe (on), burst in (on), butt in (on), impose yourself (on), force your way in (on), elbow your way in (on): *Sorry to barge in like this, but I need your advice; He just barged in on us while we were having a private conversation.*
barge into someone = bump into, drive into, press, push against, shoulder, thrust, elbow into, shove into, collide with, jostle with, cannon into: *He would barge into them and kick them in the shins.*

bark[1] VERB **1 = yap**, bay, howl, snarl, growl, yelp, woof: *Don't let the dogs bark.* **2 = shout**, snap, yell, snarl, growl, berate, bawl, bluster, raise your voice: *I didn't mean to bark at you.* ▷ NOUN = **yap**, bay, howl, snarl, growl, yelp, woof: *The Doberman let out a string of roaring barks.*

bark[2] NOUN = **covering**, casing, cover, skin, protection, layer, crust, housing, cortex (*Anatomy, Botany*), rind, husk: *The spice comes from the inner bark of the tree.* ▷ VERB = **scrape**, skin, strip, rub, scratch, shave, graze, scuff, flay, abrade: *She barked her shin off the edge of the drawer.*

barmy *or* **balmy** ADJECTIVE (*slang*) **1 = stupid**, bizarre, foolish, silly, daft (*informal*), irresponsible, irrational, senseless, preposterous, impractical, idiotic, inane, fatuous, dumb-ass (*slang*): *This policy is absolutely barmy.* **2 = insane**, odd, crazy, stupid, silly, nuts (*slang*), loony (*slang*), nutty (*slang*), goofy (*informal*), idiotic, loopy (*informal*), crackpot (*informal*), out to lunch (*informal*), dippy, out of your mind, gonzo (*slang*), doolally (*slang*), off your trolley (*slang*), round the twist (*Brit. slang*), up the pole (*informal*), off your rocker (*slang*), off the air (*Austral. slang*), wacko *or* whacko (*informal*), porangi (*N.Z.*): *He used to say I was barmy, and that really got to me.* **OPPOSITE:** sane

baroque ADJECTIVE = **ornate**, fancy, bizarre, elegant, decorated, elaborate, extravagant, flamboyant, grotesque, convoluted, flowery, rococo, florid, bedecked, overelaborate, overdecorated

barrack VERB = **heckle**, abuse, mock, bait, criticize, boo, taunt, jeer, shout down, diss (*slang, chiefly U.S.*)

barracks PLURAL NOUN = **camp**, quarters, garrison, encampment, billet, cantonment, casern

barrage NOUN **1 = bombardment**, attack, bombing, assault, shelling, battery, volley, blitz, salvo, strafe, fusillade, cannonade, curtain of fire: *a barrage of anti-aircraft fire* **2 = torrent**, attack, mass, storm, assault, burst, stream, hail, outburst, rain, spate, onslaught, deluge, plethora, profusion: *a barrage of angry questions from the floor*

barren ADJECTIVE **1 = desolate**, empty, desert, waste: *the Tibetan landscape of the high barren mountains* **2 = unproductive**, dry, useless, fruitless, arid, unprofitable, unfruitful: *He also wants to use water to irrigate barren desert land.* **OPPOSITE:** fertile **3 = dull**, boring, commonplace, tedious, dreary, stale, lacklustre, monotonous, uninspiring, humdrum, uninteresting, vapid, unrewarding, as dry as dust: *My life has become barren.* **OPPOSITE:** interesting **4 = infertile**, sterile, childless, unproductive, nonproductive, infecund, unprolific: *a three-year-old barren mare*

barricade NOUN = **barrier**, wall, railing, fence, blockade, obstruction, rampart, fortification, bulwark, palisade, stockade: *Large areas of the city have been closed off by barricades.* ▷ VERB = **bar**, block, defend, secure, lock, bolt, blockade, fortify, fasten, latch, obstruct: *The doors had been barricaded.*

barrier NOUN = **barricade**, wall, bar, block, railing, fence, pale, boundary, obstacle, ditch, blockade, obstruction, rampart, bulwark, palisade, stockade

barter VERB = **trade**, sell, exchange, switch, traffic, bargain, swap, haggle, drive a hard bargain

base[1] NOUN **1 = bottom**, floor, lowest part, deepest part: *Line the base and sides of a 20cm deep round cake tin with paper.* **OPPOSITE:** top **2 = support**, stand, foot, rest, bed, bottom, foundation, pedestal, groundwork: *The mattress is best on a solid bed base.* **3 = foundation**, institution, organization, establishment, starting point: *The family base was crucial to my development.* **4 = centre**, post, station, camp, settlement, headquarters: *Gunfire was heard at an army base close to the airport.*

The Language of Catherine Helen Spence

Catherine Helen Spence (1825–1910) was born in Scotland and emigrated to Australia when she was fourteen. There, she worked as a journalist, teacher, and author. Her writings included *Clara Morison: A Tale of South Australia During the Gold Fever,* the first novel about Australia to be written by a woman. In 1897 she became Australia's first ever female political candidate. Although she was not elected, her influence on suffrage for women led to her being commemorated on the Australian five-dollar note in 2001.

Many of the nouns that Spence uses most often are those referring to people. *Man, woman, child,* and *people* are all among her twenty most frequently used nouns. *Women* is often used as a modifier, for example in the phrases *women workers, women graduates, women lawyers,* and *women voters.* As well as adjectives such as *single, old, young,* and *poor,* many of the adjectives used to describe women are positive, for example *clever, admirable, exceptional,* and *sensible.* In contrast, the adjectives that Spence commonly associates with men include *silly, ugly,* and *plain,* although *good, honest,* and *skilful* are also salient. While the use of *women* as a modifier is more frequent, Spence also uses *men* as a modifier, such as in the phrases *men voters, men speakers,* and *men novelists.* Other frequent nouns include those that refer to family life, for example *mother, sister, family, brother, husband,* and *marriage,* and those that indicate Spence's involvement with politics, such as *society, reform, vote, right,* and *power.*

The most frequent adjective that Spence uses is *good,* which appears most often in the phrase *a good deal.* Spence usually uses *a good deal* in the phrase *a good deal of,* which is the most common use in modern English, but she also uses it before an adjective, a structure which is now rare. For example:

> Miss Rennie's verses were decidedly inferior to her own; – even her recent humiliation could not prevent her from seeing this, and she felt a good deal inspirited.

Good is also used to modify people, for example, *friend, master, husband,* and *woman*; abstract concepts, such as *fortune, luck,* and *news*; and nouns such as *work, wage,* and *education.* Another frequent adjective is *public,* which Spence uses to modify *work, conscience, ownership,* and *campaign,* again indicating her involvement with political and social issues. Other frequently occurring adjectives include those that usually relate to people, such as *old, young, poor,* and *Australian.*

Another interesting aspect of Spence's language is her use of Scots words such as *bairn, lassie, oor,* and *richts* (meaning 'child', 'girl', 'our', and 'rights', respectively), usually used to portray dialect in speech. Indeed, the speech mark is Spence's third most used punctuation mark and we see many examples of speech in her work:

> 'I talked to him for four mortal hours on the subject ... Now I don't call myself at all clever, but when Frank explained the method of voting to me, I saw it all in a minute – and you, Tom – did not you, too? but then you are rather a genius.'

Spence uses the comma over twice as much as the full stop, while in the *Bank of English,* Collins' corpus of present-day English, the full stop is used slightly more than the comma. In the above example, the comma is used in conjunction with *and* to illustrate that people do not tend to talk in short, structured sentences, and the fact that *but* is not capitalized after the question mark suggests that, in speech, people can ask a question even in the middle of a sentence.

5 = home, house, territory, pad *(slang)*, residence, home ground, abode, stamping ground, dwelling place: *For most of the spring and early summer her base was in Scotland.* **6 = essence**, source, basis, concentrate, root, core, extract: *Oils may be mixed with a base and massaged into the skin.*
▷ VERB **1 = ground**, found, build, rest, establish, depend, root, construct, derive, hinge: *He based his conclusions on the evidence given by the prisoners.*
2 = place, set, post, station, establish, fix, locate, install, garrison: *We will base ourselves in the town.*

b

base² ADJECTIVE **= dishonourable**, evil, corrupt, infamous, disgraceful, vulgar, shameful, vile, immoral, scandalous, wicked, sordid, abject, despicable, depraved, ignominious, disreputable, contemptible, villainous, ignoble, discreditable, scungy *(Austral. & N.Z.)*: *Love has the power to overcome the baser emotions.* **OPPOSITE:** honourable

baseless ADJECTIVE **= unfounded**, false, fabricated, unconfirmed, spurious, unjustified, unproven, unsubstantiated, groundless, unsupported, trumped up, without foundation, unjustifiable, uncorroborated, ungrounded, without basis **OPPOSITE:** well-founded

bash VERB **= hit**, break, beat, strike, knock, smash, punch, belt *(informal)*, crush, deck *(slang)*, batter, slap, sock *(slang)*, chin *(slang)*, smack, thump, clout *(informal)*, whack *(informal)*, biff *(slang)*, clobber *(slang)*, wallop *(informal)*, slosh *(Brit. slang)*, tonk *(informal)*, lay one on *(slang)*, beat *or* knock seven bells out of *(informal)*: *If he tries to bash you he'll have to bash me as well.*

bashful ADJECTIVE **= shy**, reserved, retiring, nervous, modest, shrinking, blushing, constrained, timid, self-conscious, coy, reticent, self-effacing, aw-shucks *(slang, chiefly U.S.)*, diffident, sheepish, mousy, timorous, abashed, shamefaced, easily embarrassed, overmodest **OPPOSITE:** forward

basic ADJECTIVE **1 = fundamental**, main, key, essential, primary, vital, principal, constitutional, cardinal, inherent, elementary, indispensable, innate, intrinsic, elemental, immanent: *Access to justice is a basic right.* **2 = vital**, needed, important, key, necessary, essential, primary, crucial, fundamental, elementary, indispensable, requisite: *shortages of even the most basic foodstuffs*
3 = essential, central, key, vital, fundamental, underlying, indispensable: *There are certain ethical principles that are basic to all the great religions.* **OPPOSITE:** secondary
4 = main, key, essential, primary: *There are three basic types of tea.* **5 = plain**, simple, classic, severe, straightforward, Spartan, uncluttered, unadorned, unfussy, bog-standard *(informal)*, unembellished, bare-bones: *the extremely basic hotel room*
▷ PLURAL NOUN **= essentials**, facts, principles, fundamentals, practicalities, requisites, nuts and bolts *(informal)*, hard facts, nitty-gritty *(informal)*, rudiments, brass tacks *(informal)*, necessaries: *Let's get down to basics and stop horsing around.*

basically ADVERB **= essentially**, firstly, mainly, mostly, principally, fundamentally, primarily, at heart, inherently, intrinsically, at bottom, in substance, au fond *(French)*

basis NOUN **1 = arrangement**, way, system, footing, agreement: *We're going to be meeting there on a regular basis.* **2 = foundation**, support, base, ground, footing, theory, bottom, principle, premise, groundwork, principal element, chief ingredient: *The UN plan is a possible basis for negotiation.*

bask VERB **= lie**, relax, lounge, sprawl, loaf, lie about, swim in, sunbathe, recline, loll, laze, outspan *(S. African)*, warm yourself, toast yourself: *Crocodiles bask on the small sandy beaches.*
bask in = enjoy, relish, delight in, savour, revel in, wallow in, rejoice in, luxuriate in, indulge yourself in, take joy in, take pleasure in *or* from: *He smiled and basked in her approval.*

bass ADJECTIVE **= deep**, low, resonant, sonorous, low-pitched, deep-toned

bastion NOUN **= stronghold**, support, defence, rock, prop, refuge, fortress, mainstay, citadel, bulwark, tower of strength, fastness

batch NOUN **= group**, set, lot, crowd, pack, collection, quantity, bunch, accumulation, assortment, consignment, assemblage, aggregation

bath NOUN **= wash**, cleaning, washing, soaping, shower, soak, cleansing, scrub, scrubbing, bathe, shampoo, sponging, douse, douche, ablution: *Have a bath every morning.*
▷ VERB **= clean**, wash, soap, shower, soak, cleanse, scrub, bathe, tub, sponge, rinse, douse, scrub down, lave *(archaic)*: *Don't feel you have to bath your child every day.*

bathe VERB **1 = swim**: *small ponds for the birds to bathe in* **2 = wash**, clean, bath, soap, shower, soak, cleanse, scrub, tub, sponge, rinse, scrub down, lave *(archaic)*: *Back home, Shirley plays with, feeds and bathes the baby.* **3 = cleanse**, clean, wash, soak, rinse: *She paused long enough to bathe her blistered feet.*
4 = cover, flood, steep, engulf, immerse, overrun, suffuse, wash over: *The arena was bathed in warm sunshine.*
▷ NOUN **= swim**, dip, dook *(Scot.)*: *an early-morning bathe*

bathroom NOUN **= lavatory**, toilet, loo *(Brit. informal)*, washroom, can *(U.S. & Canad. slang)*, john *(slang, chiefly U.S. & Canad.)*, head(s) *(Nautical, slang)*, shower, convenience *(chiefly Brit.)*, bog *(slang)*, bogger *(Austral. slang)*, brasco *(Austral. slang)*, privy, cloakroom *(Brit.)*, latrine, rest room, powder room, dunny *(Austral. & N.Z. old-fashioned)*, water closet, khazi *(slang)*, comfort station *(U.S.)*, pissoir *(French)*, Gents *or* Ladies, little boy's room *or* little girl's room *(informal)*, (public) convenience, W.C.

baton NOUN **= stick**, club, staff, stake, pole, rod, crook, cane, mace, wand, truncheon, sceptre, mere *(N.Z.)*, patu *(N.Z.)*

battalion NOUN **= company**, army, force, team, host, division, troop, brigade, regiment, legion, contingent, squadron, military force, horde, multitude, throng

batten VERB *(usually with* **down***)* **= fasten**, unite, fix, secure, lock, bind, chain, connect, attach, seal, tighten, anchor, bolt, clamp down, affix, nail down, make firm, make fast, fasten down: *The roof was never securely battened down.*

batter VERB **1 = beat**, hit, strike, knock, assault, smash, punch, belt *(informal)*, deck *(slang)*, bang, bash *(informal)*, lash, thrash, pound, lick *(informal)*, buffet, flog, maul, pelt, clobber *(slang)*, smite, wallop *(informal)*, pummel, tonk *(informal)*, cudgel, thwack, lambast(e), belabour, dash against, beat the living daylights out of, lay one on *(slang)*, drub, beat *or* knock seven bells out of *(informal)*: *He battered her around the head.*
2 = damage, destroy, hurt, injure, harm, ruin, crush, mar, wreck, total *(slang)*, shatter, weaken, bruise, demolish, shiver, trash *(slang)*, maul, mutilate, mangle, mangulate *(Austral. slang)*, disfigure, deface, play (merry) hell with *(informal)*: *a storm that's been battering the Northeast coastline*

battered ADJECTIVE **1 = beaten**, injured, harmed, crushed, bruised, squashed, beat-up *(informal)*, oppressed, manhandled, black-and-blue, ill-treated, maltreated: *research into the experiences of battered women*
2 = damaged, broken-down, wrecked, beat-up *(informal)*, ramshackle, dilapidated: *a battered leather suitcase*

battery NOUN **1 = artillery**, ordnance, gunnery, gun emplacement, cannonry: *They stopped beside a battery of abandoned guns.* **2 = series**, set, course, chain, string, sequence, suite, succession: *We give a battery of tests to each patient.* **3 = beating**, attack, assault, aggression, thumping, onslaught, physical violence: *He has served three years for assault and battery.*

battle NOUN **1 = fight**, war, attack, action, struggle, conflict, clash, set-to *(informal)*, encounter, combat, scrap *(informal)*, biffo *(Austral. slang)*, engagement, warfare, fray, duel, skirmish, head-to-head, tussle,

scuffle, fracas, scrimmage, sparring match, bagarre (*French*), melee *or* mêlée, boilover (*Austral.*): *a gun battle between police and drug traffickers* **OPPOSITE:** peace **2 = conflict**, campaign, struggle, debate, clash, dispute, contest, controversy, disagreement, crusade, strife, head-to-head, agitation: *a renewed political battle over their attitude to Europe* **3 = campaign**, drive, movement, push, struggle: *the battle against crime*
▷ VERB **1 = wrestle**, war, fight, argue, dispute, contest, combat, contend, feud, grapple, agitate, clamour, scuffle, lock horns: *Many people battled with police.* **2 = struggle**, work, labour, strain, strive, go for it (*informal*), toil, make every effort, go all out (*informal*), bend over backwards (*informal*), go for broke (*slang*), bust a gut (*informal*), give it your best shot (*informal*), break your neck (*informal*), exert yourself, make an all-out effort (*informal*), work like a Trojan, knock yourself out (*informal*), do your damnedest (*informal*), give it your all (*informal*), rupture yourself (*informal*): *Doctors battled throughout the night to save her life.*

battle cry NOUN **1 = slogan**, motto, watchword, catch phrase, tag-line, catchword, catchcry (*Austral.*): *the ideological battle cry of Hong Kong* **2 = war cry**, rallying cry, war whoop: *He screamed out a battle cry and charged.*

battlefield NOUN **= battleground**, front, field, combat zone, field of battle

battleship NOUN **= warship**, gunboat, man-of-war, ship of the line, capital ship

batty ADJECTIVE **= crazy**, odd, mad, eccentric, bats (*slang*), nuts (*slang*), barking (*slang*), peculiar, daft (*informal*), crackers (*Brit. slang*), queer (*informal*), insane, lunatic, loony (*slang*), barmy (*slang*), off-the-wall (*slang*), touched, nutty (*slang*), potty (*Brit. informal*), oddball (*informal*), off the rails, cracked (*slang*), bonkers (*slang, chiefly Brit.*), cranky (*U.S., Canad. & Irish informal*), dotty (*slang, chiefly Brit.*), loopy (*informal*), crackpot (*informal*), out to lunch (*informal*), barking mad (*slang*), out of your mind, outré, gonzo (*slang*), screwy (*informal*), doolally (*slang*), off your trolley (*slang*), off the air (*Austral. slang*), round the twist (*Brit. slang*), up the pole (*informal*), off your rocker (*slang*), not the full shilling (*informal*), as daft as a brush (*informal, chiefly Brit.*), wacko *or* whacko (*slang*), porangi (*N.Z.*), daggy (*Austral. & N.Z. informal*)

bauble NOUN **= trinket**, ornament, trifle, toy, plaything, bagatelle, gimcrack, gewgaw, knick-knack, bibelot, kickshaw

bawdy ADJECTIVE **= rude**, blue, dirty, gross, crude, erotic, obscene, coarse, filthy, indecent, vulgar, improper, steamy (*informal*), pornographic, raunchy (*U.S. slang*), suggestive, racy, lewd, risqué, X-rated (*informal*), salacious, prurient, lascivious, smutty, lustful, lecherous, ribald, libidinous, licentious, indelicate, near the knuckle (*informal*), indecorous **OPPOSITE:** clean

bawl VERB **1 = shout**, call, scream, roar, yell, howl, bellow, bay, clamour, holler (*informal*), raise your voice, halloo, hollo, vociferate: *They were shouting and bawling at each other.* **2 = cry**, weep, sob, wail, whine, whimper, whinge (*informal*), keen, greet (*Scot. archaic*), squall, blubber, snivel, shed tears, yowl, mewl, howl your eyes out: *One of the toddlers was bawling, and another had a runny nose.*

bay[1] NOUN **= inlet**, sound, gulf, entrance, creek, cove, fjord, arm (of the sea), bight, ingress, natural harbour, sea loch (*Scot.*), firth *or* frith (*Scot.*), back bay (*Canad.*): *a short ferry ride across the bay*

bay[2] NOUN **= recess**, opening, corner, niche, compartment, nook, alcove, embrasure: *Someone had placed the device in a loading bay behind the shop.*

bay[3] VERB **= howl**, cry, roar (*of a hound*), bark, lament, cry out, wail, growl, bellow, quest, bell, clamour, yelp: *A dog suddenly howled, baying at the moon.*
▷ NOUN **= cry**, bell, roar (*of a hound*), quest, bark, lament, howl, wail, growl, bellow, clamour, yelp: *She trembled at the bay of the dogs.*
at bay = away, off, at arm's length: *Eating oranges keeps colds at bay.*

bayonet VERB **= stab**, cut, wound, knife, slash, pierce, run through, spear, transfix, impale, lacerate, stick

bazaar NOUN **1 = market**, exchange, fair, marketplace, mart: *He was a vendor in Egypt's open-air bazaar.* **2 = fair**, fête, gala, festival, garden party, bring-and-buy: *a church bazaar*

be VERB **1 = be alive**, live, exist, survive, breathe, last, be present, continue, endure, be living, be extant, happen: *It hurt so badly he wished to cease to be.* **2 = take place**, happen, occur, arise, come about, transpire (*informal*), befall, come to pass: *The film's premiere is next week.*

beach NOUN **= shore**, coast, sands, margin, strand, seaside, shingle, lakeside, water's edge, lido, foreshore, seashore, plage, littoral, sea (*chiefly U.S.*)

beached ADJECTIVE **= stranded**, grounded, abandoned, deserted, wrecked, ashore, marooned, aground, high and dry

beacon NOUN **1 = signal**, sign, rocket, beam, flare, bonfire, smoke signal, signal fire **2 = lighthouse**, pharos, watchtower

bead NOUN **= drop**, tear, bubble, pearl, dot, drip, blob, droplet, globule, driblet: *beads of blood*
▷ PLURAL NOUN **= necklace**, pearls, pendant, choker, necklet, chaplet: *baubles, bangles and beads*

beady ADJECTIVE **= bright**, powerful, concentrated, sharp, intense, shining, glittering, gleaming, glinting

beak NOUN **1 = bill**, nib, neb (*archaic, dialect*), mandible: *a black bird with a yellow beak* **2 = nose**, snout, hooter (*slang*), snitch (*slang*), conk (*slang*), neb (*archaic, dialect*), proboscis, schnozzle (*slang, chiefly U.S.*): *his sharp, aristocratic beak*

beam VERB **1 = smile**, grin: *She beamed at her friend with undisguised admiration.* **2 = transmit**, show, air, broadcast, cable, send out, relay, televise, radio, emit, put on the air: *The interview was beamed live across America.* **3 = radiate**, flash, shine, glow, glitter, glare, gleam, emit light, give off light: *A sharp white spotlight beamed down on a small stage.*
▷ NOUN **1 = ray**, bar, flash, stream, glow, radiation, streak, emission, shaft, gleam, glint, glimmer: *a beam of light* **2 = rafter**, support, timber, spar, plank, girder, joist: *The ceilings are supported by oak beams.* **3 = smile**, grin: *She knew he had news, because of the beam on his face.*

beaming ADJECTIVE **1 = smiling**, happy, grinning, pleasant, sunny, cheerful, cheery, joyful, chirpy (*informal*), light-hearted: *his mother's beaming face* **2 = radiating**, bright, brilliant, flashing, shining, glowing, sparkling, glittering, gleaming, glimmering, radiant, glistening, scintillating, burnished, lustrous: *A beaming sun rose out of the sea.*

bear VERB **1 = carry**, take, move, bring, lift, transfer, conduct, transport, haul, transmit, convey, relay, tote (*informal*), hump (*Brit. slang*), lug: *a surveyor and his assistant bearing a torch* **OPPOSITE:** put down **2 = support**, shoulder, sustain, endure, uphold, withstand, bear up under: *The ice was not thick enough to bear the weight of marching men.* **OPPOSITE:** give up **3 = display**, have, show, hold, carry, possess, exhibit: *notepaper bearing the President's seal* **4 = suffer**, feel, experience, go through, sustain, stomach, endure, undergo, admit, brook, hack (*slang*), abide, put up with (*informal*): *He bore his sufferings manfully.* **5 = bring yourself to**, allow, accept, permit, endure, tolerate, hack (*informal*), countenance: *He can't bear to talk about it, even to me.* **6 = produce**, develop, generate, yield, bring forth: *The plants grow and start to bear fruit.* **7 = give birth to**, produce, deliver, breed, bring forth, beget: *She bore a son called Karl.* **8 = exhibit**, hold, maintain, entertain, harbour, cherish: *She bore no ill will. If they didn't like her, too bad.* **9 = conduct**, carry, move, deport: *There was elegance and simple dignity in the way he bore himself.*
bear down on someone = advance on, attack, approach, move towards, close in on, converge on, move in on,

b

come near to, draw near to: *A group of half a dozen men entered the pub and bore down on her.*
bear down on something *or* **someone** = **press down**, push, strain, crush, compress, weigh down, encumber: *She felt as if a great weight was bearing down on her shoulders.*
bear on something = **be relevant to**, involve, concern, affect, regard, refer to, be part of, relate to, belong to, apply to, be appropriate, befit, pertain to, touch upon, appertain to: *The remaining 32 examples do not bear on our problem.*
bear something out = **support**, prove, confirm, justify, endorse, uphold, vindicate, validate, substantiate, corroborate, legitimize: *His photographs do not quite bear this out.*
bear with someone = **be patient with**, suffer, wait for, hold on (*informal*), stand by, tolerate, put up with (*informal*), make allowances for, hang fire: *If you'll bear with me, Frank, I can explain everything.*

b

bearable ADJECTIVE = **tolerable**, acceptable, sustainable, manageable, passable, admissible, supportable, endurable, sufferable
OPPOSITE: intolerable

beard NOUN = **whiskers**, bristles, stubble, five-o'clock shadow

bearded ADJECTIVE = **unshaven**, hairy, whiskered, stubbly, bushy, shaggy, hirsute, bristly, bewhiskered

bearer NOUN **1** = **agent**, carrier, courier, herald, envoy, messenger, conveyor, emissary, harbinger: *I hate to be the bearer of bad news.* **2** = **carrier**, runner, servant, porter: *a flag bearer* **3** = **payee**, beneficiary, consignee: *the chief cashier's promise to pay the bearer*

bearing NOUN **1** (*usually with* **on** *or* **upon**) = **relevance**, relation, application, connection, import, reference, significance, pertinence, appurtenance: *My father's achievements don't have any bearing on what I do.* **OPPOSITE:** irrelevance **2** = **manner**, attitude, conduct, appearance, aspect, presence, behaviour, tone, carriage, posture, demeanour, deportment, mien (*literary*), air, comportment: *She later wrote warmly of his bearing and behaviour.* **3** = **position**, course, direction, point of compass: *I'm flying on a bearing of ninety-three degrees.*
▷ PLURAL NOUN = **way**, course, position, situation, track, aim, direction, location, orientation, whereabouts: *I lost my bearings and was just aware of cars roaring past.*

bearish ADJECTIVE = **falling**, declining, slumping

beast NOUN **1** = **animal**, creature, brute: *the threats our ancestors faced from wild beasts* **2** = **brute**, monster, savage, barbarian, fiend, swine, ogre, ghoul, sadist: *a sex beast who subjected two sisters to a terrifying ordeal*

QUOTATIONS
And what rough beast, its hour come round at last,
Slouches towards Bethlehem to be born?
[W.B. Yeats *The Second Coming*]

beastly ADJECTIVE **1** = **unpleasant**, mean, terrible, awful, nasty, foul, rotten, horrid, disagreeable, irksome: *The weather was beastly.* **OPPOSITE:** pleasant **2** = **cruel**, mean, nasty, harsh, savage, brutal, coarse, monstrous, malicious, insensitive, sadistic, unfriendly, unsympathetic, uncaring, spiteful, thoughtless, brutish, barbarous, unfeeling, inconsiderate, bestial, uncharitable, unchristian, hardhearted: *He must be wondering why everyone is being so beastly to him.* **OPPOSITE:** humane

beat VERB **1** = **batter**, break, hit, strike, knock, punch, belt (*informal*), whip, deck (*slang*), bruise, bash (*informal*), sock (*slang*), lash, chin (*slang*), pound, smack, thrash, cane, thump, lick (*informal*), buffet, clout (*informal*), flog, whack (*informal*), maul, clobber (*slang*), wallop (*informal*), tonk (*informal*), cudgel, thwack (*informal*), lambast(e), lay one on (*slang*), drub, beat *or* knock seven bells out of (*informal*): *They were beaten to death with baseball bats.* **2** = **pound**, strike, hammer, batter, thrash, pelt: *The rain was beating on the window pains.* **3** = **throb**, pulse, tick, thump, tremble, pound, quake, quiver, vibrate, pulsate, palpitate: *I felt my heart beat faster.* **4** = **hit**, strike, bang: *When you beat the drum, you feel good.* **5** = **flap**, thrash, flutter, agitate, wag, swish: *Its wings beat slowly.* **6** = **defeat**, outdo, trounce, overcome, stuff (*slang*), master, tank (*slang*), crush, overwhelm, conquer, lick (*informal*), undo, subdue, excel, surpass, overpower, outstrip, clobber (*slang*), vanquish, outrun, subjugate, run rings around (*informal*), wipe the floor with (*informal*), knock spots off (*informal*), make mincemeat of (*informal*), pip at the post, outplay, blow out of the water (*slang*), put in the shade (*informal*), bring to their knees: *She was easily beaten into third place.*
▷ NOUN **1** = **throb**, pounding, pulse, thumping, vibration, pulsating, palpitation, pulsation: *He could hear the beat of his heart.* **2** = **route**, way, course, rounds, path, circuit: *I was a relatively new PC on the beat, stationed in Hendon.*
beat it = **go away**, leave, depart, get lost (*informal*), shoo, exit, go to hell (*informal*), hook it (*slang*), scarper (*Brit. slang*), pack your bags (*informal*), make tracks, hop it (*slang*), scram (*informal*), get on your bike (*Brit. slang*), skedaddle (*informal*), sling your hook (*Brit. slang*), vamoose (*slang, chiefly U.S.*), voetsek (*S. African offensive*), rack off (*Austral. & N.Z. slang*): *Beat it before it's too late.*
beat someone up = **assault**, attack, batter, thrash, set about, do over (*Brit., Austral. & N.Z. slang*), work over (*slang*), clobber (*slang*), assail, set upon, lay into (*informal*), put the boot in (*slang*), lambast(e), duff up (*Brit. slang*), beat the living daylights out of (*informal*), knock about *or* around, fill in (*Brit. slang*), beat *or* knock seven bells out of (*informal*): *Then they actually beat her up as well.*

beaten ADJECTIVE **1** = **well-trodden**, worn, trodden, trampled, well-used, much travelled: *Before you is a well-worn path of beaten earth.* **2** = **stirred**, mixed, whipped, blended, whisked, frothy, foamy: *Cool a little and slowly add the beaten eggs.* **3** = **shaped**, worked, formed, stamped, hammered, forged: *brightly painted beaten metal* **4** = **defeated**, overcome, frustrated, overwhelmed, cowed, thwarted, vanquished, disheartened: *They had looked a beaten side with just seven minutes left.*

beating NOUN **1** = **thrashing**, hiding (*informal*), belting (*informal*), whipping (*slang*), slapping, happy slapping, tanning, lashing, smacking, caning, pasting (*slang*), flogging, drubbing, corporal punishment, chastisement: *the savage beating of a suspect by police officers* **2** = **defeat**, ruin, overthrow, pasting (*slang*), conquest, rout, downfall: *A beating at Wembley would be too much of a trauma for them.*

beau NOUN = **boyfriend**, man, guy (*informal*), date, lover, young man, steady, escort, admirer, fiancé, sweetheart, suitor, swain, toy boy, leman (*archaic*), fancy man (*slang*)

beautiful ADJECTIVE = **attractive**, pretty, lovely, stunning (*informal*), charming, tempting, pleasant, handsome, fetching, good-looking, gorgeous, fine, pleasing, fair, magnetic, delightful, cute, exquisite, enticing, seductive, graceful, captivating, appealing, radiant, alluring, drop-dead (*slang*), ravishing, bonny, winsome, comely, prepossessing, hot (*informal*), fit (*Brit. informal*) **OPPOSITE:** ugly

beautify VERB = **make beautiful**, enhance, decorate, enrich, adorn, garnish, ornament, gild, embellish, grace, festoon, bedeck, glamorize

beauty NOUN **1** = **attractiveness**, charm, grace, bloom, glamour, fairness, elegance, symmetry (*formal, literary*), allure, loveliness, handsomeness, pulchritude, comeliness, exquisiteness, seemliness: *an area of outstanding natural beauty* **OPPOSITE:** ugliness **2** = **good-looker**, looker (*informal, chiefly U.S.*), lovely (*slang*), sensation, dazzler, belle, goddess, Venus, peach (*informal*), cracker (*slang*), wow (*slang, chiefly U.S.*), dolly (*slang*), knockout (*informal*), heart-throb, stunner (*informal*), charmer, smasher (*informal*), humdinger (*slang*), glamour puss, beaut (*Austral. & N.Z. slang*): *She is known as a great beauty.* **3** = **advantage**, good, use, benefit, profit, gain, asset,

attraction, blessing, good thing, utility, excellence, boon: *the beauty of such water-based minerals*
OPPOSITE: disadvantage

becalmed ADJECTIVE = **still**, stuck, settled, stranded, motionless

because CONJUNCTION = **since**, as, in that: *They could not obey the command because they had no ammunition.*
because of = **as a result of**, on account of, by reason of, thanks to, owing to: *He failed because of a lack of money.*

> **USAGE**
> The phrase *on account of* can provide a useful alternative to *because of* in writing. It occurs relatively infrequently in spoken language, where it is sometimes followed by a clause, as in *on account of I don't do drugs*. However, this use is considered nonstandard.

beckon VERB **1** = **gesture**, sign, wave, indicate, signal, nod, motion, summon, gesticulate: *He beckoned to the waiter.* **2** = **lure**, call, draw, pull, attract, invite, tempt, entice, coax, allure: *All the attractions of the peninsula beckon.*

become VERB **1** = **come to be**, develop into, be transformed into, grow into, change into, evolve into, alter to, mature into, metamorphose into, ripen into: *After leaving school, he became a professional footballer.* **2** = **suit**, fit, enhance, flatter, ornament, embellish, grace, harmonize with, set off: *Does khaki become you?*
become of something *or* **someone** = **happen to**, befall, betide: *What will become of him?*

becoming ADJECTIVE **1** = **flattering**, pretty, attractive, enhancing, neat, graceful, tasteful, well-chosen, comely: *Softer fabrics are much more becoming than stiffer ones.*
OPPOSITE: unflattering
2 = **appropriate**, right, seemly, fitting, fit, correct, suitable, decent, proper, worthy, in keeping, compatible, befitting, decorous, comme il faut *(French)*, congruous, meet *(archaic)*: *This behaviour is not becoming among our politicians.* **OPPOSITE:** inappropriate

bed NOUN **1** = **bedstead**, couch, berth, cot, pallet, divan: *She went in to her bedroom and lay down on the bed.* **2** = **plot**, area, row, strip, patch, ground, land, garden, border: *beds of strawberries and rhubarb* **3** = **bottom**, ground, floor: *the bare bed of a dry stream* **4** = **base**, footing, basis, bottom, foundation, underpinning, groundwork, bedrock, substructure, substratum: *a sandstone bed*
▷ VERB = **fix**, set, found, base, plant, establish, settle, root, sink, insert, implant, embed: *The slabs can then be bedded on mortar to give rigid paving.*
bed down = **sleep**, lie down, retire, turn in *(informal)*, settle down, kip *(Brit. slang)*, hit the hay *(slang)*: *They bedded down in the fields.*

bedclothes PLURAL NOUN = **bedding**, covers, sheets, blankets, linen, pillow, quilt, duvet, pillowcase, bed linen, coverlet, eiderdown

bedding NOUN = **bedclothes**, covers, sheets, blankets, linen, pillow, quilt, duvet, pillowcase, bed linen, coverlet, eiderdown

bedeck VERB = **decorate**, grace, trim, array, enrich, adorn, garnish, ornament, embellish, festoon, beautify, bedight *(archaic)*, bedizen *(archaic)*, engarland

bedevil VERB = **plague**, worry, trouble, frustrate, torture, irritate, torment, harass, hassle *(informal)*, aggravate *(informal)*, afflict, pester, vex, irk

bedlam NOUN = **pandemonium**, noise, confusion, chaos, turmoil, clamour, furore, uproar, commotion, rumpus, babel, tumult, hubbub, ruction *(informal)*, hullabaloo, hue and cry, ruckus *(informal)*

bedraggled ADJECTIVE = **messy**, soiled, dirty, disordered, stained, dripping, muddied, muddy, drenched, ruffled, untidy, sodden, sullied, dishevelled, rumpled, unkempt, tousled, disarranged, disarrayed, daggy *(Austral. & N.Z. informal)*

bedridden ADJECTIVE = **confined to bed**, confined, incapacitated, laid up *(informal)*, flat on your back

bedrock NOUN **1** = **first principle**, rule, basis, basics, principle, essentials, roots, core, fundamentals, cornerstone, nuts and bolts *(informal)*, sine qua non *(Latin)*, rudiment: *Mutual trust is the bedrock of a relationship.*
2 = **bottom**, bed, foundation, underpinning, rock bottom, substructure, substratum: *It took five years to drill down to bedrock.*

bee NOUN
▸ *related adjective:* apian ▸ *collective nouns:* swarm, grist ▸ *name of home:* hive, apiary

beef NOUN = **complaint**, dispute, grievance, problem, grumble, criticism, objection, dissatisfaction, annoyance, grouse, gripe *(informal)*, protestation, grouch *(informal)*, remonstrance

beefy ADJECTIVE = **brawny**, strong, powerful, athletic, strapping, robust, hefty *(informal)*, muscular, sturdy, stalwart, bulky, burly, stocky, hulking, well-built, herculean, sinewy, thickset **OPPOSITE:** scrawny

beehive NOUN = **hive**, colony, comb, swarm, honeycomb, apiary

beer NOUN = **ale**, brew, swipes *(Brit. slang)*, wallop *(Brit. slang)*, hop juice, amber fluid *or* nectar *(Austral. informal)*, tinnie *or* tinny *(Austral. slang)*

> **QUOTATIONS**
> And malt does more than Milton can
> To justify God's ways to man
> [A. E. Housman *A Shropshire Lad*]
>
> They who drink beer will think beer
> [Washington Irving *The Sketch Book of Geoffrey Crayon*]
>
> When money's tight and is hard to get
> And your horse was also ran,
> When all you have is a heap of debt
> A pint of plain is your only man
> [Flann O'Brien *At Swim-Two-Birds*]
>
> Lo! the poor toper whose untutored sense,
> Sees bliss in ale, and can with wine dispense;
> Whose head proud fancy never taught to steer,
> Beyond the muddy ecstasies of beer
> [George Crabbe *Inebriety*]
>
> Then to the spicy nut-brown ale
> [John Milton *L'Allegro*]

beer parlour NOUN = **tavern**, inn, bar, pub *(informal, chiefly Brit.)*, public house, watering hole *(facetious, slang)*, boozer *(Brit., Austral. & N.Z. informal)*, beverage room *(Canad.)*, hostelry, alehouse *(archaic)*, taproom

befall VERB = **happen to**, fall upon, occur in, take place in, ensue in, transpire in *(informal)*, materialize in, come to pass in

befit VERB = **be appropriate for**, become, suit, be fitting for, be suitable for, be seemly for, behove *(U.S.)*

befitting ADJECTIVE = **appropriate to**, right for, suitable for, fitting for, fit for, becoming to, seemly for, proper for, apposite to, meet *(archaic)*
OPPOSITE: unsuitable for

before PREPOSITION **1** = **earlier than**, ahead of, prior to, in advance of: *Annie was born a few weeks before Christmas.*
OPPOSITE: after **2** = **in front of**, ahead of, in advance of, to the fore of: *They stopped before a large white villa.* **3** = **in the presence of**, in front of: *The Government will appear before the committee.* **4** = **ahead of**, in front of, in advance of: *I saw before me an idyllic life.*
▷ ADVERB **1** = **previously**, earlier, sooner, in advance, formerly: *The war had ended only a month or so before.*
OPPOSITE: after **2** = **in the past**, earlier, once, previously, formerly, at one time, hitherto, beforehand, a while ago, heretofore, in days *or* years gone by: *I've been here before.*

beforehand ADVERB = **in advance**, before, earlier, already, sooner, ahead, previously, in anticipation, before now, ahead of time

befriend VERB = **make friends with**, back, help, support, benefit, aid, encourage, welcome, favour, advise, sustain, assist, stand by, uphold, side with, patronize, succour

befuddle VERB = **confuse**, puzzle, baffle, bewilder, muddle, daze, perplex, mystify, disorient, faze, stupefy, flummox, bemuse, intoxicate
OPPOSITE: make clear

befuddled ADJECTIVE = **confused**, upset, puzzled, baffled, at sea, bewildered, muddled, dazed, perplexed, taken aback, intoxicated, disorientated, disorganized, muzzy (*U.S. informal*), groggy (*informal*), flummoxed, woozy (*informal*), at sixes and sevens, fuddled, inebriated, thrown off balance, discombobulated (*informal, chiefly U.S. & Canad.*), not with it (*informal*), not knowing if you are coming or going

b

beg VERB **1 = implore**, plead with, beseech, desire, request, pray, petition, conjure, crave, solicit, entreat, importune, supplicate, go on bended knee to: *I begged him to come back to England with me.* **2 = scrounge**, bum (*informal*), blag (*slang*), touch (someone) for (*slang*), mooch (*slang*), cadge, forage for, hunt around (for), sponge on (someone) for, freeload (*slang*), seek charity, call for alms, solicit charity: *I was surrounded by people begging for food.* **OPPOSITE:** give **3 = dodge**, avoid, get out of, duck (*informal*), hedge, parry, shun, evade, elude, fudge, fend off, eschew, flannel (*Brit. informal*), sidestep, shirk, equivocate, body-swerve (*Scot.*): *The research begs a number of questions.*

beget VERB **1 = cause**, bring, produce, create, effect, lead to, occasion, result in, generate, provoke, induce, bring about, give rise to, precipitate, incite, engender: *Poverty begets debt.* **2 = father**, breed, generate, sire, get, propagate, procreate: *He wanted to beget an heir.*

beggar NOUN **= tramp**, bankrupt, bum (*informal*), derelict, drifter, down-and-out, pauper, vagrant, hobo (*chiefly U.S.*), vagabond, bag lady (*chiefly U.S.*), dosser (*Brit. slang*), derro (*Austral. slang*), starveling: *Now I am a beggar, having lost everything except life.*
▷ VERB **= defy**, challenge, defeat, frustrate, foil, baffle, thwart, withstand, surpass, elude, repel: *The statistics beggar belief.*

begin VERB **1 = start**, commence, proceed: *He stood up and began to walk around the room.* **OPPOSITE:** stop **2 = commence**, start, initiate, embark on, set about, instigate, inaugurate, institute, make a beginning, set on foot: *The US wants to begin talks immediately.* **3 = start talking**, start, initiate, commence, begin business, get *or* start the ball rolling: *He didn't know how to begin.* **4 = come into existence**, start, appear, emerge, spring, be born, arise, dawn, be developed, be created, originate, commence, be invented, become available, crop up (*informal*), come into being: *It began as a local festival.* **5 = emerge**, start, spring, stem, derive, issue, originate: *The fate line begins close to the wrist.* **OPPOSITE:** end

beginner NOUN **= novice**, student, pupil, convert, recruit, amateur, initiate, newcomer, starter, trainee, apprentice, cub, fledgling, learner, freshman, neophyte, tyro, probationer, greenhorn (*informal*), novitiate, tenderfoot, proselyte **OPPOSITE:** expert

beginning NOUN **1 = start**, opening, break (*informal*), chance, source, opportunity, birth, origin, introduction, outset, starting point, onset, overture, initiation, inauguration, inception, commencement, opening move: *Think of this as a new beginning.* **OPPOSITE:** end **2 = outset**, start, opening, birth, onset, prelude, preface, commencement, kickoff (*informal*): *The question was raised at the beginning of this chapter.* **3 = origins**, family, beginnings, stock, birth, roots, heritage, descent, pedigree, extraction, ancestry, lineage, parentage, stirps: *His views come from his own humble beginnings.*

begrudge VERB **1 = resent**, envy, grudge, be jealous of: *I certainly don't begrudge him the Nobel Prize.* **2 = be bitter about**, object to, be angry about, give reluctantly, bear a grudge about, be in a huff about, give stingily, have hard feelings about: *She spends £2,000 a year on it and she doesn't begrudge a penny.*

beguile VERB **1 = charm**, please, attract, delight, occupy, cheer, fascinate, entertain, absorb, entrance, win over, amuse, divert, distract, enchant, captivate, solace, allure, bewitch, mesmerize, engross, enrapture, tickle the fancy of: *His paintings beguiled the Prince of Wales.* **2 = fool**, trick, take in, cheat, con (*informal*), mislead, impose on, deceive, dupe, gull (*archaic*), delude, bamboozle, hoodwink, take for a ride (*informal*), befool: *He used his newspapers to beguile his readers.* **OPPOSITE:** enlighten

beguiling ADJECTIVE **= charming**, interesting, pleasing, attractive, engaging, lovely, entertaining, pleasant, intriguing, diverting, delightful, irresistible, enchanting, seductive, captivating, enthralling, winning, eye-catching, alluring, bewitching, delectable, winsome, likable *or* likeable

behalf NOUN
on behalf of something *or* **someone** *or* **on something** *or* **someone's behalf** **1 = as a representative of**, representing, in the name of, as a spokesperson for: *She made an emotional public appeal on her son's behalf; On behalf of my wife and myself, I'd like to thank you all.* **2 = for the benefit of**, for the sake of, in support of, on the side of, in the interests of, on account of, for the good of, in defence of, to the advantage of, for the profit of: *The honour recognizes work done on behalf of classical theatre; The pupils were enthusiastic in their fund-raising efforts on the charity's behalf.*

> **USAGE**
> *On behalf of* is sometimes wrongly used as an alternative to *on the part of*. The distinction is that *on behalf of someone* means 'for someone's benefit' or 'representing someone', while *on the part of someone* can be roughly paraphrased as 'by someone'.

behave VERB **1 = act**, react, conduct yourself, acquit yourself, comport yourself: *He'd behaved badly.* **2** (*often reflexive*) **= be well-behaved**, be good, be polite, mind your manners, keep your nose clean, act correctly, act politely, conduct yourself properly: *You have to behave; Sit down and behave yourself.* **OPPOSITE:** misbehave

behaviour NOUN **1 = conduct**, ways, actions, bearing, attitude, manner, manners, carriage, demeanour, deportment, mien (*literary*), comportment: *He was asked to explain his extraordinary behaviour.* **2 = action**, working, running, performance, operation, practice, conduct, functioning: *This process modifies the cell's behaviour.*

> **QUOTATIONS**
> Perfect behaviour is born of complete indifference
> [Cesare Pavese *This Business of Living*]

behead VERB **= decapitate**, execute, guillotine

behest NOUN
at someone's behest = at someone's command, by someone's order, at someone's demand, at someone's wish, by someone's decree, at someone's bidding, at someone's instruction, by someone's mandate, at someone's dictate, at someone's commandment

behind PREPOSITION **1 = at the rear of**, at the back of, at the heels of: *They were parked behind the truck.* **2 = after**, following: *Keith wandered along behind him.* **3 = supporting**, for, backing, on the side of, in agreement with: *He had the state's judicial power behind him.* **4 = causing**, responsible for, the cause of, initiating, at the bottom of, to blame for, instigating: *I'd like to know who was behind this plot.* **5 = later than**, after: *The work is 22 weeks behind schedule.*
▷ ADVERB **1 = the back**, the rear: *She was attacked from behind.* **2 = after**, next, following, afterwards, subsequently, in the wake (of): *The troopers followed behind.* **OPPOSITE:** in advance of **3 = behind schedule**, delayed, running late, behind time: *The accounts are more than three months behind.* **OPPOSITE:** ahead **4 = overdue**, in debt, in arrears, behindhand: *They were falling behind with their mortgage payments.*
▷ NOUN **= bottom**, seat, bum (*Brit. slang*), butt (*U.S. & Canad. informal*), buns (*U.S. slang*), buttocks, rump, posterior, tail (*informal*), derrière (*euphemistic*), tush (*U.S. slang*), jacksy (*Brit. slang*): *jeans that actually flatter your behind*

behold VERB **= look at**, see, view, eye, consider, study, watch, check, regard, survey, witness, clock (*Brit. slang*), examine, observe, perceive, gaze, scan, contemplate, check out *(informal)*, inspect, discern, eyeball *(slang)*, scrutinize, recce *(slang)*, get a load of *(informal)*, take a gander at *(informal)*, take a dekko at *(Brit. slang)*, feast your eyes upon

beholden ADJECTIVE **= indebted**, bound, owing, grateful, obliged, in debt, obligated, under obligation

beige NOUNADJECTIVE **= fawn**, coffee, cream, sand, neutral, mushroom, tan, biscuit, camel, buff, cinnamon, khaki, oatmeal, ecru, café au lait *(French)*

being NOUN **1 = individual**, thing, body, animal, creature, human being, beast, mortal, living thing: *beings from outer space* **2 = life**, living, reality, animation, actuality: *the complex process by which the novel is brought into being* **OPPOSITE:** nonexistence **3 = soul**, spirit, presence, substance, creature, essence, organism, entity: *The music seemed to touch his very being.*

belated ADJECTIVE **= late**, delayed, overdue, late in the day, tardy, behind time, unpunctual, behindhand

belch VERB **1 = burp**, eructate, eruct: *He covered his mouth with his hand and belched discreetly.* **2 = emit**, discharge, erupt, send out, throw out, vent, vomit, issue, give out, gush, eject, diffuse, emanate, exude, give off, exhale, cast out, disgorge, give vent to, send forth, spew forth, breathe forth: *Tired old trucks belched black smoke.*

beleaguered ADJECTIVE **1 = harassed**, troubled, plagued, tormented, hassled *(informal)*, aggravated *(informal)*, badgered, persecuted, pestered, vexed, put upon: *There have been seven attempts against the beleaguered government.* **2 = besieged**, surrounded, blockaded, encompassed, beset, encircled, assailed, hemmed in, hedged in, environed: *The rebels continue to push their way towards the beleagured capital.*

belie VERB **1 = misrepresent**, disguise, conceal, distort, misinterpret, falsify, gloss over: *Her looks belie her 50 years.* **2 = disprove**, deny, expose, discredit, contradict, refute, repudiate, negate, invalidate, rebut, give the lie to, make a nonsense of, gainsay *(archaic, literary)*, prove false, blow out of the water *(slang)*, controvert, confute: *The facts of the situation belie his testimony.*

belief NOUN **1 = trust**, confidence, conviction, reliance: *a belief in personal liberty* **OPPOSITE:** disbelief **2 = faith**, principles, doctrine, ideology, creed, dogma, tenet, credence, credo: *He refuses to compete on Sundays because of his religious beliefs.* **3 = opinion**, feeling, idea, view, theory, impression, assessment, notion, judgment, point of view, sentiment, persuasion, presumption: *It is my belief that a common ground can be found.*

believable ADJECTIVE **= credible**, possible, likely, acceptable, reliable, authentic, probable, plausible, imaginable, trustworthy, creditable **OPPOSITE:** unbelievable

believe VERB **1 = think**, consider, judge, suppose, maintain, estimate, imagine, assume, gather, guess *(informal, chiefly U.S. & Canad.)*, reckon, conclude, deem, speculate, presume, conjecture, postulate, surmise: *I believe you have something of mine.* **2 = accept**, hold, buy *(slang)*, trust, credit, depend on, rely on, swallow *(informal)*, count on, buy into *(slang)*, have faith in, swear by, be certain of, be convinced of, place confidence in, presume true, take as gospel, take on *(U.S.)*: *Don't believe what you read in the papers.* **OPPOSITE:** disbelieve

believe in something = advocate, champion, approve of, swear by: *He believed in marital fidelity.*

> **QUOTATIONS**
>
> To believe with certainty we must begin with doubting
> [Stanislaus I of Poland *Maxims*]
>
> Man can believe the impossible, but man can never believe the improbable
> [Oscar Wilde *The Decay of Lying*]
>
> We can believe what we choose. We are answerable for what we choose to believe
> [Cardinal Newman *Letter to Mrs William Froude*]
>
> It is necessary to the happiness of man that he be mentally faithful to himself. Infidelity does not consist in believing, or in disbelieving, it consists in professing to believe what one does not believe
> [Thomas Paine *The Age of Reason*]
>
> I can believe anything, provided that it is incredible
> [Oscar Wilde *The Picture of Dorian Gray*]
>
> Lord, I believe; help thou mine unbelief
> [*Bible: St. Mark*]
>
> Except ye see signs and wonders, ye will not believe
> [*Bible: St. John*]
>
> Though ye believe not me, believe the works
> [*Bible: St. John*]

believer NOUN **= follower**, supporter, convert, disciple, protagonist, devotee, worshipper, apostle, adherent, zealot, upholder, proselyte **OPPOSITE:** sceptic

belittle VERB **= run down**, dismiss, diminish, put down, underestimate, discredit, ridicule, scorn, rubbish *(informal)*, degrade, minimize, downgrade, undervalue, knock *(informal)*, deride, malign, detract from, denigrate, scoff at, disparage, decry, sneer at, underrate, deprecate, depreciate, defame, derogate **OPPOSITE:** praise

belle NOUN **= beauty**, looker *(informal)*, lovely, good-looker, goddess, Venus, peach *(informal)*, cracker *(informal)*, stunner *(informal)*, charmer

bellicose ADJECTIVE **= aggressive**, offensive, hostile, destructive, defiant, provocative, belligerent, combative, antagonistic, pugnacious, hawkish, warlike, quarrelsome, militaristic, sabre-rattling, jingoistic, warmongering

belligerence NOUN **= aggressiveness**, hostility, animosity, antagonism, destructiveness, pugnacity, combativeness, offensiveness, unfriendliness

belligerent ADJECTIVE **= aggressive**, hostile, contentious, combative, unfriendly, antagonistic, pugnacious, argumentative, bellicose, quarrelsome, aggers *(Austral. slang)*, biffo *(Austral. slang)*, litigious: *He was almost back to his belligerent mood of twelve months ago.* **OPPOSITE:** friendly
▷ NOUN **= fighter**, battler, militant, contender, contestant, combatant, antagonist, warring nation, disputant: *The belligerents were due to settle their differences.*

bellow VERB **= shout**, call, cry (out), scream, roar, yell, howl, shriek, clamour, bawl, holler *(informal)*: *He bellowed the information into the telephone.*
▷ NOUN **= shout**, call, cry, scream, roar, yell, howl, shriek, bell, clamour, bawl: *a bellow of tearful rage*

belly NOUN **= stomach**, insides *(informal)*, gut, abdomen, tummy, paunch, vitals, breadbasket *(slang)*, potbelly, corporation *(informal)*, puku *(N.Z.)*

belong VERB **= go with**, fit into, be part of, relate to, attach to, be connected with, pertain to, have as a proper place

belonging NOUN **= fellowship**, relationship, association, loyalty, acceptance, attachment, inclusion, affinity, rapport, affiliation, kinship

belongings PLURAL NOUN **= possessions**, goods, things, effects, property, stuff, gear, paraphernalia, personal property, accoutrements, chattels, goods and chattels

beloved ADJECTIVE **= dear**, loved, valued, prized, dearest, sweet, admired, treasured, precious, darling, worshipped, adored, cherished, revered

below PREPOSITION **1 = under**, underneath, lower than: *The boat dipped below the surface of the water.* **2 = less than**, lower than: *Night temperatures can drop below 15 degrees Celsius.* **3 = subordinate to**, subject to, inferior to, lesser than: *white-collar staff below chief officer level*
▷ ADVERB **1 = lower**, down, under, beneath, underneath: *Spread out below was a huge crowd.* **2 = beneath**, following, at the end, underneath, at the bottom, further on: *Please write to me at the address below.*

b

belt NOUN **1 = waistband**, band, sash, girdle, girth, cummerbund, cincture: *He wore a belt with a large brass buckle.* **2 = conveyor belt**, band, loop, fan belt, drive belt: *The turning disc is connected by a drive belt to an electric motor.* **3 = zone**, area, region, section, sector, district, stretch, strip, layer, patch, portion, tract: *a belt of trees*
below the belt = unfair, foul, crooked *(informal)*, cowardly, sly, fraudulent, unjust, dishonest, deceptive, unscrupulous, devious, unethical, sneaky, furtive, deceitful, surreptitious, dishonourable, unsporting, unsportsmanlike, underhanded, not playing the game *(informal)*: *Do you think it's a bit below the belt, what they're doing?*

bemoan VERB **= lament**, regret, complain about, rue, deplore, grieve for, weep for, bewail, cry over spilt milk, express sorrow about, moan over

bemused ADJECTIVE **= puzzled**, stunned, confused, stumped, baffled, at sea, bewildered, muddled, preoccupied, dazed, perplexed, mystified, engrossed, clueless, stupefied, nonplussed, absent-minded, flummoxed, half-drunk, fuddled

bench NOUN **1 = seat**, stall, pew: *He sat down on a park bench.* **2 = worktable**, stand, table, counter, slab, trestle table, workbench: *the laboratory bench*
the bench = court, judge, judges, magistrate, magistrates, tribunal, judiciary, courtroom: *It shows how seriously the bench viewed these offences.*

benchmark NOUN **= reference point**, gauge, yardstick, measure, level, example, standard, model, reference, par, criterion, norm, touchstone

bend VERB **1 = twist**, turn, wind, lean, hook, bow, curve, arch, incline, arc, deflect, warp, buckle, coil, flex, stoop, veer, swerve, diverge, contort, inflect, incurvate: *Bend the bar into a horseshoe.* **2 = submit**, yield, bow, surrender, give in, give way, cede, capitulate, resign yourself: *Congress has to bend to his will.* **3 = force**, direct, influence, shape, persuade, compel, mould, sway: *He's very decisive. You cannot bend him.*
▷ NOUN **= curve**, turn, corner, hook, twist, angle, bow, loop, arc, zigzag, camber: *The crash occurred on a sharp bend.*

beneath PREPOSITION **1 = under**, below, underneath, lower than: *She found pleasure in sitting beneath the trees.* OPPOSITE: over **2 = inferior to**, below: *She decided he was beneath her.* **3 = unworthy of**, unfitting for, unsuitable for, inappropriate for, unbefitting: *Many find themselves having to take jobs far beneath them.*
▷ ADVERB **= underneath**, below, in a lower place: *On a shelf beneath he spotted a photo album.*
▸ *related prefix:* sub-

benefactor NOUN **= supporter**, friend, champion, defender, sponsor, angel *(informal)*, patron, promoter, contributor, backer, helper, subsidizer, philanthropist, upholder, well-wisher

beneficial ADJECTIVE **= favourable**, useful, valuable, helpful, profitable, benign, wholesome, advantageous, expedient, salutary, healthful, serviceable, salubrious, gainful OPPOSITE: harmful

beneficiary NOUN **1 = recipient**, receiver, payee, assignee, legatee: *The main beneficiaries of pension equality so far have been men.* **2 = heir**, inheritor: *a sole beneficiary of a will*

benefit NOUN **1 = good**, use, help, profit, gain, favour, utility, boon, mileage *(informal)*, avail: *I'm a great believer in the benefits of this form of therapy.* OPPOSITE: harm **2 = advantage**, interest, aid, gain, favour, assistance, betterment: *This could now work to his benefit.*
▷ VERB **1 = profit from**, make the most of, gain from, do well out of, reap benefits from, turn to your advantage: *Both sides have benefited from the talks.* **2 = help**, serve, aid, profit, improve, advance, advantage, enhance, assist, avail: *a variety of government schemes benefiting children* OPPOSITE: harm

benevolence NOUN **= kindness**, understanding, charity, grace, sympathy, humanity, tolerance, goodness, goodwill, compassion, generosity, indulgence, decency, altruism, clemency, gentleness, philanthropy, magnanimity, fellow feeling, beneficence, kindliness, kind-heartedness, aroha *(N.Z.)* OPPOSITE: ill will

benevolent ADJECTIVE **= kind**, good, kindly, understanding, caring, liberal, generous, obliging, sympathetic, humanitarian, charitable, benign, humane, compassionate, gracious, indulgent, amiable, amicable, lenient, cordial, considerate, affable, congenial, altruistic, philanthropic, bountiful, beneficent, well-disposed, kind-hearted, warm-hearted, bounteous, tender-hearted

benighted ADJECTIVE **= uncivilized**, crude, primitive, backward, uncultivated, unenlightened

benign ADJECTIVE **1 = benevolent**, kind, kindly, warm, liberal, friendly, generous, obliging, sympathetic, favourable, compassionate, gracious, amiable, genial, affable, complaisant: *Critics of the scheme take a less benign view.* OPPOSITE: unkind **2 = harmless**, innocent, superficial, innocuous, curable, inoffensive, not dangerous, remediable: *It wasn't cancer, only a benign tumour.* OPPOSITE: malignant **3 = favourable**, good, encouraging, warm, moderate, beneficial, clement, advantageous, salutary, auspicious, propitious: *relatively benign economic conditions* OPPOSITE: unfavourable

bent ADJECTIVE **1 = misshapen**, twisted, angled, bowed, curved, arched, crooked, crippled, distorted, warped, deformed, tortuous, disfigured, out of shape: *The trees were all bent and twisted from the wind.* OPPOSITE: straight **2 = stooped**, bowed, arched, hunched: *a bent, frail, old man*
▷ NOUN **= inclination**, ability, taste, facility, talent, leaning, tendency, preference, faculty, forte, flair, knack, penchant, bag *(slang)*, propensity, aptitude, predisposition, predilection, proclivity, turn of mind: *his bent for natural history*
bent on = intent on, set on, fixed on, predisposed to, resolved on, insistent on: *He's bent on suicide.*

bequeath VERB **1 = leave**, will, give, grant, commit, transmit, hand down, endow, bestow, entrust, leave to by will: *He bequeathed all his silver to his children.* **2 = give**, offer, accord, grant, afford, contribute, yield, lend, pass on, transmit, confer, bestow, impart: *It is true that colonialism did not bequeath much to Africa.*

bequest NOUN **= legacy**, gift, settlement, heritage, trust, endowment, estate, inheritance, dower, bestowal, koha *(N.Z.)*

berate VERB **= scold**, rebuke, reprimand, reproach, blast, carpet *(informal)*, put down, criticize, slate *(informal, chiefly Brit.)*, censure, castigate, revile, chide, harangue, tear into *(informal)*, tell off *(informal)*, rail at, read the riot act to, reprove, upbraid, slap on the wrist, lambast(e), bawl out *(informal)*, excoriate, rap over the knuckles, chew out *(U.S. & Canad. informal)*, tear (someone) off a strip *(Brit. informal)*, give a rocket *(Brit. & N.Z. informal)*, vituperate OPPOSITE: praise

bereavement NOUN **= loss**, death, misfortune, deprivation, affliction, tribulation

bereft ADJECTIVE
bereft of = deprived of, without, minus, lacking in, devoid of, cut off from, parted from, sans *(archaic)*, robbed of, empty of, denuded of

berg NOUN **= mountain**, peak, mount, height, ben *(Scot.)*, horn, ridge, fell *(Brit.)*, alp, pinnacle, elevation, eminence

berserk ADJECTIVE **= crazy**, wild, mad, frantic, ape *(slang)*, insane, barro *(Austral. slang)*, off the air *(Austral. slang)*, porangi *(N.Z.)*

berth NOUN **1 = bunk**, bed, cot *(Nautical)*, hammock, billet: *Golding booked a berth on the first boat he could.* **2 = anchorage**, haven, slip, port, harbour, dock, pier, wharf, quay: *A ship has applied to leave its berth.*
▷ VERB **= anchor**, land, dock, moor, tie

Bible

Books of the Bible (Old Testament)

Genesis
Exodus
Leviticus
Numbers
Deuteronomy
Joshua
Judges
Ruth
1 Samuel
2 Samuel
1 Kings
2 Kings
1 Chronicles
2 Chronicles
Ezra
Nehemiah
Esther
Job
Psalms
Proverbs
Ecclesiastes
Song of Solomon
Isaiah
Jeremiah
Lamentations
Ezekiel
Daniel
Hosea
Joel
Amos
Obadiah
Jonah
Micah
Nahum
Habakkuk
Zephaniah
Haggai
Zechariah
Malachi

Books of the Bible (New Testament)

Matthew
Mark
Luke
John
Acts
Romans
1 Corinthians
2 Corinthians
Galatians
Ephesians
Philippians
Colossians
1 Thessalonians
2 Thessalonians
1 Timothy
2 Timothy
Titus
Philemon
Hebrews
James
1 Peter
2 Peter
1 John
2 John
3 John
Jude
Revelation

Books of the Bible (Apocrypha)

Tobit
Judith
1 Maccabees
2 Maccabees
Wisdom
Ecclesiasticus
Baruch
Daniel and Susanna
Daniel, Bel and the Snake
Song of the Three
Esdras
Manasseh

Characters in the Bible

Aaron
Abednego
Abel
Abigail
Abraham
Absalom
Achitophel *or* Ahithophel
Adam
Ahab
Ahasuerus
Ammon
Amos
Ananias
Andrew
Asher
Balaam
Balthazar
Barabbas
Bartholomew
Baruch
Bathsheba
Beelzebub
Belial
Belshazzar
Benjamin
Boanerges
Boaz
Caiaphas
Cain
Caspar
Cush *or* Kush
Dan
Daniel
David
Deborah
Delilah
Dinah
Dives
Dorcas
Elias
Elijah
Elisha
Enoch
Enos
Ephraim
Esau
Esther
Eve
Ezekiel
Ezra
Gabriel
Gad
Gideon
Gilead
Gog and Magog
Goliath
Good Samaritan
Habakkuk
Hagar
Haggai
Ham
Hannah
Herod
Hezekiah
Hiram
Holofernes
Hosea
Isaac
Isaiah
Ishmael
Issachar
Jacob
Jael
James
Japheth
Jehoshaphat
Jehu
Jephthah or Jephte
Jeremiah
Jeroboam
Jesse
Jesus Christ
Jethro
Jezebel
Joab
Job
Joel
John
John the Baptist
Jonah *or* Jonas
Jonathan
Joseph
Joshua
Josiah
Jubal
Judah
Judas Iscariot
Jude
Judith
Laban
Lazarus
Leah
Levi
Lot
Lot's wife
Luke
Magus
Malachi
Manasseh
Mark
Martha
Mary
Mary Magdalene
Matthew
Matthias
Melchior
Melchizedek *or* Melchisedech
Meshach
Methuselah
Micah
Midian
Miriam
Mordecai
Moses
Nabonidus
Naboth
Nahum
Naomi
Naphtali
Nathan
Nathanael
Nebuchadnezzar *or* Nebuchadrezzar
Nehemiah
Nicodemus
Nimrod
Noah
Obadiah
Paul
Peter
Philip
Potiphar
Prodigal Son
Queen of Sheba
Rachel
Rebecca
Reuben
Ruth
Salome
Samson
Samuel
Sarah
Saul
Seth
Shadrach
Shem
Simeon
Simon
Solomon
Susanna
Tetragrammaton
Thaddeus *or* Thadeus
Thomas
Tobit
Tubal-cain
Uriah
Virgin Mary
Zacharias, Zachariah, *or* Zachary
Zebedee
Zebulun
Zechariah
Zedekiah
Zephaniah
Zilpah

Place names in the Bible

Aceldama
Antioch
Aram
Ararat
Arimathaea *or* Arimathea
Babel
Bashan
Bethesda
Bethlehem
Calvary
Cana
Canaan
Capernaum
Eden
Galilee
Garden of Eden
Gath
Gaza
Gehenna
Gethsemane
Golgotha
Gomorrah *or* Gomorrha
Goshen
Horeb
Jericho
Jerusalem
Judaea *or* Judea
Judah
land of milk and honey
land of Nod
Moab
Nazareth
On
Ophir
Rabbath Ammon
Samaria
Shiloh
Shinar
Shittim
Sodom
Tadmor
Tophet *or* Topheth
wilderness

up, drop anchor: *The ship berthed in New York.*

beseech VERB = **beg**, ask, petition, call upon, plead with, solicit, implore, entreat, importune, adjure, supplicate

beset VERB = **plague**, trouble, embarrass, torture, haunt, torment, harass, afflict, badger, perplex, pester, vex, entangle, bedevil

b

besetting ADJECTIVE = **chronic**, persistent, long-standing, prevalent, habitual, ingrained, deep-seated, incurable, deep-rooted, inveterate, incorrigible, ineradicable

beside PREPOSITION = **next to**, near, close to, neighbouring, alongside, overlooking, next door to, adjacent to, at the side of, abreast of, cheek by jowl with: *On the table beside an empty plate was a pile of books.*
beside yourself = **distraught**, desperate, mad, distressed, frantic, frenzied, hysterical, insane, crazed, demented, unbalanced, uncontrolled, deranged, berserk, delirious, unhinged, very anxious, overwrought, apoplectic, out of your mind, at the end of your tether: *He was beside himself with anxiety.*

> **USAGE**
> People occasionally confuse *beside* and *besides*. *Besides* is used for mentioning something that adds to what you have already said, for example: *I didn't feel like going and besides, I had nothing to wear. Beside* usually means *next to* or *at the side of something or someone*, for example: *he was standing beside me* (not *besides me*).

besides PREPOSITION = **apart from**, barring, excepting, other than, excluding, as well (as), in addition to, over and above: *I think she has many good qualities besides being beautiful.*
▷ ADVERB = **also**, too, further, otherwise, in addition, as well, moreover, furthermore, what's more, into the bargain: *Besides, today's young people have grown up knowing only a Conservative government.*

besiege VERB **1** = **harass**, worry, trouble, harry, bother, disturb, plague, hound, hassle (*informal*), badger, pester, importune, bend someone's ear (*informal*), give someone grief (*Brit. & S. African*), beleaguer: *She was besieged by the press and the public.* **2** = **surround**, confine, enclose, blockade, encompass, beset, encircle, close in on, hem in, shut in, lay siege to, hedge in, environ, beleaguer, invest (*rare*): *The main part of the army moved to besiege the town.*

besotted ADJECTIVE = **infatuated**, charmed, captivated, beguiled, doting, smitten, bewitched, bowled over (*informal*), spellbound, enamoured, hypnotized, swept off your feet

bespeak VERB = **engage**, solicit, prearrange, order beforehand: *I'm already bespoken to take you tomorrow morning.*

best ADJECTIVE **1** = **finest**, leading, chief, supreme, principal, first, foremost, superlative, pre-eminent, unsurpassed, most accomplished, most skilful, most excellent: *He was the best player in the world for most of the 1950s.* **2** = **most fitting**, right, most desirable, most apt, most advantageous, most correct: *the best way to end the long-running war*
▷ NOUN = **utmost**, most, greatest, hardest, highest endeavour: *You must do your best to protect yourselves.*
▷ ADVERB = **most highly**, most fully, most deeply: *The thing I liked best about the show was the music.*
the best = **the finest**, the pick, the choice, the flower, the cream, the elite, the crème de la crème: *We only offer the best to our clients.*

bestow VERB = **present**, give, accord, award, grant, commit, hand out, lavish, confer, endow, entrust, impart, allot, honour with, apportion **OPPOSITE:** obtain

bestseller NOUN = **success**, hit (*informal*), winner, smash (*informal*), belter (*slang*), sensation, blockbuster (*informal*), wow (*slang*), market leader, smash hit (*informal*), chart-topper (*informal*), runaway success, number one **OPPOSITE:** failure

bestselling ADJECTIVE = **successful**, top, hit (*informal*), smash (*informal*), flourishing, lucrative, smash-hit (*informal*), chart-topping (*informal*), moneymaking, number one, highly successful

bet VERB = **gamble**, chance, stake, venture, hazard, speculate, punt (*chiefly Brit.*), wager, put money, risk money, pledge money, put your shirt on: *I bet on a horse called Premonition.*
▷ NOUN = **gamble**, risk, stake, venture, pledge, speculation, hazard, flutter (*informal*), ante, punt, wager, long shot: *He made a 30 mile trip to the casino to place a bet.*

betray VERB **1** = **be disloyal to**, break with, grass on (*Brit. slang*), dob in (*Austral. slang*), double-cross (*informal*), stab in the back, be unfaithful to, sell down the river (*informal*), grass up (*slang*), shop (*slang, chiefly Brit.*), put the finger on (*informal*), inform on or against: *He might be seen as having betrayed his mother.* **2** = **give away**, tell, show, reveal, expose, disclose, uncover, manifest, divulge, blurt out, unmask, lay bare, tell on, let slip, evince: *She studied his face, but it betrayed nothing.*

betrayal NOUN = **disloyalty**, sell-out (*informal*), deception, treason, treachery, trickery, duplicity, double-cross (*informal*), double-dealing, breach of trust, perfidy, unfaithfulness, falseness, inconstancy **OPPOSITE:** loyalty

better ADVERB **1** = **to a greater degree**, more completely, more thoroughly: *I like your interpretation better than the one I was taught.* **2** = **in a more excellent manner**, more effectively, more attractively, more advantageously, more competently, in a superior way: *If we had played better we might have won.* **OPPOSITE:** worse
▷ ADJECTIVE **1** = **well**, stronger, improving, progressing, recovering, healthier, cured, mending, fitter, fully recovered, on the mend (*informal*), more healthy, less ill: *He is better now.* **OPPOSITE:** worse **2** = **superior**, finer, worthier, higher-quality, surpassing, preferable, more appropriate, more useful, more valuable, more suitable, more desirable, streets ahead, more fitting, more expert: *I've been able to have a better car than I otherwise could have.* **OPPOSITE:** inferior
▷ VERB **1** = **beat**, top, exceed, excel, surpass, outstrip, outdo, improve on or upon, cap (*informal*): *He bettered the old record of 4 minutes 24.* **2** = **improve**, forward, reform, advance, promote, correct, amend, mend, rectify, augment, ameliorate, meliorate: *Our parents came here with the hope of bettering themselves.* **OPPOSITE:** worsen
get the better of someone = **defeat**, beat, surpass, triumph over, outdo, trounce, outwit, best, subjugate, prevail over, outsmart (*informal*), get the upper hand, score off, run rings around (*informal*), wipe the floor with (*informal*), make mincemeat of (*informal*), blow out of the water (*slang*): *He usually gets the better of them.*

betterment NOUN = **improvement**, gain, advancement, enhancement, edification, amelioration, melioration

between PREPOSITION = **amidst**, among, mid, in the middle of, betwixt

beverage NOUN = **drink**, liquid, liquor, refreshment, draught, bevvy (*dialect*), libation (*facetious*), thirst quencher, potable, potation

beverage room NOUN = **tavern**, inn, bar, pub (*informal, chiefly Brit.*), public house, watering hole (*facetious, slang*), boozer (*Brit., Austral. & N.Z. informal*), beer parlour (*Canad.*), hostelry, alehouse (*archaic*), taproom

bevy NOUN = **group**, company, set, party, band, crowd, troop, pack, collection, gathering, gang, bunch (*informal*), cluster, congregation, clump, troupe, posse (*slang*), clique, coterie, assemblage

beware VERB **1** = **be careful**, look out, watch out, be wary, be cautious, take heed, guard against something: *Beware, this recipe is not for slimmers.* **2** = **avoid**, mind, shun, refrain from, steer clear of, guard against: *Beware using plastic cards in foreign cash machines.*

bewilder VERB = **confound**, surprise, stun, confuse, puzzle, baffle, mix up, daze, perplex, mystify, stupefy, befuddle, flummox, bemuse, dumbfound, nonplus, flabbergast (*informal*)

bewildered ADJECTIVE = **confused**, surprised, stunned, puzzled, uncertain, startled, baffled, at sea, awed, muddled, dizzy, dazed, perplexed, disconcerted, at a loss, mystified, taken aback, speechless, giddy, disorientated, bamboozled *(informal)*, nonplussed, flummoxed, at sixes and sevens, thrown off balance, discombobulated *(informal, chiefly U.S. & Canad.)*

bewildering ADJECTIVE = **confusing**, surprising, amazing, stunning, puzzling, astonishing, staggering, eye-popping *(informal)*, baffling, astounding, perplexing, mystifying, stupefying

bewitch VERB = **enchant**, attract, charm, fascinate, absorb, entrance, captivate, beguile, allure, ravish, mesmerize, hypnotize, cast a spell on, enrapture, spellbind
OPPOSITE: repulse

bewitched ADJECTIVE = **enchanted**, charmed, transformed, fascinated, entranced, possessed, captivated, enthralled, beguiled, ravished, spellbound, mesmerized, enamoured, hypnotized, enraptured, under a spell

beyond PREPOSITION **1 = on the other side of**, outwith *(Scot.)*: *They heard footsteps in the main room, beyond a door.* **2 = after**, over, past, above: *Few jockeys continue riding beyond the age of forty.* **3 = past**, outwith *(Scot.)*: *His interests extended beyond the fine arts.* **4 = except for**, but, save, apart from, other than, excluding, besides, aside from: *I knew nothing beyond a few random facts.* **5 = exceeding**, surpassing, superior to, out of reach of: *What he had done was beyond my comprehension.* **6 = outside**, over, above, outwith *(Scot.)*: *The situation was beyond her control.*

bias NOUN **1 = prejudice**, leaning, bent, tendency, inclination, penchant, intolerance, bigotry, propensity, favouritism, predisposition, nepotism, unfairness, predilection, proclivity, partiality, narrow-mindedness, proneness, one-sidedness: *There were fierce attacks on the BBC for alleged political bias.* **OPPOSITE:** impartiality **2 = slant**, cross, angle, diagonal line: *The fabric, cut on the bias, hangs as light as a cobweb.*
▷ VERB = **influence**, colour, weight, prejudice, distort, sway, warp, slant, predispose: *We mustn't allow it to bias our teaching.*

biased ADJECTIVE = **prejudiced**, weighted, one-sided, partial, distorted, swayed, warped, slanted, embittered, predisposed, jaundiced

bicker VERB = **quarrel**, fight, argue, row *(informal)*, clash, dispute, scrap *(informal)*, disagree, fall out *(informal)*, squabble, spar, wrangle, cross swords, fight like cat and dog, go at it hammer and tongs, altercate
OPPOSITE: agree

bid NOUN **1 = attempt**, try, effort, venture, undertaking, go *(informal)*, shot *(informal)*, stab *(informal)*, crack *(informal)*, endeavour: *a bid to silence its critics* **2 = offer**, price, attempt, amount, advance, proposal, sum, tender, proposition, counterbid, submission: *He made an agreed takeover bid of £351 million.*
▷ VERB **1 = make an offer**, offer, propose, submit, tender, proffer, counterbid: *She wanted to bid for it.* **2 = wish**, say, call, tell, greet: *I bade her goodnight.* **3 = tell**, call, ask, order, charge, require, direct, desire, invite, command, summon, instruct, solicit, enjoin: *I dare say he did as he was bidden.*

bidding NOUN **1 = order**, call, charge, demand, request, command, instruction, invitation, canon, beck, injunction, summons, behest, beck and call: *the bidding of his backbenchers* **2 = offer**, proposal, auction, tender: *The bidding starts at £2 million.*

big ADJECTIVE **1 = large**, great, huge, giant, massive, vast, enormous, considerable, substantial, extensive, immense, spacious, gigantic, monumental, mammoth, bulky, burly, colossal, stellar *(informal)*, prodigious, hulking, ponderous, voluminous, elephantine, ginormous *(informal)*, humongous *or* humungous *(U.S. slang)*, sizable *or* sizeable, supersize: *Australia's a big country.* **OPPOSITE:** small **2 = important**, serious, significant, grave, urgent, paramount, big-time *(informal)*, far-reaching, momentous, major league *(informal)*, weighty: *Her problem was just too big for her to tackle on her own.* **OPPOSITE:** unimportant **3 = powerful**, important, prime, principal, prominent, dominant, influential, paramount, eminent, puissant, skookum *(Canad.)*: *Their father was very big in the army.* **4 = grown-up**, adult, grown, mature, elder, full-grown: *He's a big boy now.* **OPPOSITE:** young **5 = generous**, good, princely, noble, heroic, gracious, benevolent, disinterested, altruistic, unselfish, magnanimous, big-hearted: *They describe him as an idealist with a big heart.*

bighead NOUN = **boaster**, know-all *(informal)*, swaggerer, self-seeker, egomaniac, egotist, braggart, braggadocio, narcissist, swell-head *(informal)*, blowhard *(informal)*, self-admirer, figjam *(Austral. slang)*

bigheaded ADJECTIVE = **boastful**, arrogant, swaggering, bragging, cocky, vaunting, conceited, puffed-up, bumptious, immodest, crowing, overconfident, vainglorious, swollen-headed, egotistic, full of yourself, too big for your boots *or* breeches

bigot NOUN = **fanatic**, racist, extremist, sectarian, maniac, fiend *(informal)*, zealot, persecutor, dogmatist

> **QUOTATIONS**
> There is nothing more dangerous than the conscience of a bigot
> [George Bernard Shaw]
>
> bigot: one who is obstinately and zealously attached to an opinion that you do not entertain
> [Ambrose Bierce *The Devil's Dictionary*]

bigoted ADJECTIVE = **intolerant**, twisted, prejudiced, biased, warped, sectarian, dogmatic, opinionated, narrow-minded, obstinate, illiberal
OPPOSITE: tolerant

bigotry NOUN = **intolerance**, discrimination, racism, prejudice, bias, ignorance, injustice, sexism, unfairness, fanaticism, sectarianism, racialism, dogmatism, faith hate, provincialism, narrow-mindedness, mindlessness, pig-ignorance *(slang)*
OPPOSITE: tolerance

> **QUOTATIONS**
> Bigotry may roughly be defined as the anger of men who have no opinions
> [G.K. Chesterton *Heretics*]
>
> Bigotry tries to keep truth safe in its hand
> With a grip that kills it
> [Rabindranath Tagore *Fireflies*]

bigwig NOUN = **important person**, somebody, celebrity, heavyweight *(informal)*, notable, big name, mogul, big gun *(informal)*, dignitary, celeb *(informal)*, big shot *(informal)*, personage, nob *(slang)*, big cheese *(old-fashioned, slang)*, big noise *(informal)*, big hitter *(informal)*, heavy hitter *(informal)*, panjandrum, notability, V.I.P. **OPPOSITE:** nonentity

bile NOUN = **bitterness**, anger, hostility, resentment, animosity, venom, irritability, spleen, acrimony, pique, nastiness, rancour, virulence, asperity, ill humour, irascibility, peevishness, churlishness

bill[1] NOUN **1 = charges**, rate, costs, score, account, damage *(informal)*, statement, reckoning, expense, tally, invoice, note of charge: *They couldn't afford to pay the bills.* **2 = act of parliament**, measure, proposal, piece of legislation, projected law: *The bill was opposed by a large majority.* **3 = list**, listing, programme, card, schedule, agenda, catalogue, inventory, roster, syllabus: *He is topping the bill at a dusk-to-dawn party.* **4 = advertisement**, notice, poster, leaflet, bulletin, circular, handout, placard, handbill, playbill: *A sign forbids the posting of bills.*
▷ VERB **1 = charge**, debit, invoice, send a statement to, send an invoice to: *Are you going to bill me for this?* **2 = advertise**, post, announce, push *(informal)*, declare, promote, plug *(informal)*, proclaim, tout, flaunt, publicize, crack up *(informal)*, give advance notice of: *They bill it as Britain's most exciting museum.*

bill[2] NOUN = **beak**, nib, neb *(archaic, dialect)*, mandible: *Its legs and feet are grey, its bill brownish-yellow.*

billet VERB = **quarter**, post, station, locate, install, accommodate, berth, garrison: *The soldiers were billeted in private homes.*

▷ NOUN **= quarters**, accommodation, lodging, barracks: *We hid the radio in Hut 10, which was our billet.*

billow VERB **= surge**, roll, expand, swell, balloon, belly, bulge, dilate, puff up, bloat: *the billowing sails*
▷ NOUN **= surge**, wave, flow, rush, flood, cloud, gush, deluge, upsurge, outpouring, uprush: *billows of almost solid black smoke*

b

bind VERB **1 = oblige**, make, force, require, engage, compel, prescribe, constrain, necessitate, impel, obligate: *The treaty binds them to respect their neighbour's independence.* **2 = tie**, unite, join, stick, secure, attach, wrap, rope, knot, strap, lash, glue, tie up, hitch, paste, fasten, truss, make fast: *Bind the ends of the card together with thread.* **OPPOSITE:** untie **3 = restrict**, limit, handicap, confine, detain, restrain, hamper, inhibit, hinder, impede, hem in, keep within bounds or limits: *All are bound by the same strict etiquette.* **4 = fuse**, join, stick, bond, cement, adhere: *These compounds bind with genetic material in the liver.* **5 = bandage**, cover, dress, wrap, swathe, encase: *Her mother bound the wound with a rag soaked in iodine.*
▷ NOUN **= nuisance**, inconvenience, hassle *(informal)*, drag *(informal)*, spot *(informal)*, difficulty, bore, dilemma, pest, hot water *(informal)*, uphill *(S. African)*, predicament, annoyance, quandary, pain in the neck *(informal)*, pain in the backside *(informal)*, pain in the butt *(informal)*: *It is expensive to buy and a bind to carry home.*

binding ADJECTIVE **= compulsory**, necessary, mandatory, imperative, obligatory, conclusive, irrevocable, unalterable, indissoluble
OPPOSITE: optional

binge NOUN **= bout**, session, spell, fling, feast, stint, spree, orgy, bender *(informal)*, jag *(slang)*, beano *(Brit. slang)*, blind *(slang)*

biography NOUN **= life story**, life, record, account, profile, memoir, CV, life history, curriculum vitae

QUOTATIONS

Biography is all about cutting people down to size. Getting an unruly quart into a pint pot
[Alan Bennett]

Biography is: a system in which the contradictions of a human life are unified
[José Ortega y Gasset *The Dehumanization of Art and Other Essays*]

Read no history: nothing but biography, for that is life without theory
[Benjamin Disraeli *Contarini Fleming*]

Discretion is not the better part of biography
[Lytton Strachey]

The Art of Biography
Is different from Geography
Geography is about Maps,
But Biography is about Chaps
[Edmund Clerihew Bentley *Biography for Beginners*]

bird NOUN **= feathered friend**, fowl, songbird
▸ *related adjective:* avian ▸ *name of male:* cock ▸ *name of female:* hen ▸ *name of young:* chick, fledgeling, fledgling, nestling ▸ *collective nouns:* flock, flight ▸ *name of home:* nest

QUOTATIONS

Be ye therefore wise as serpents, and harmless as doves
[*Bible: St. Matthew*]

magpie: a bird whose thievish disposition suggested to someone that it might be taught to talk
[Ambrose Bierce *The Devil's Dictionary*]

Oh, a wondrous bird is the pelican!
His beak can hold more than his belican.
He takes in his beak
Food enough for a week.
But I'll be darned if I know how the helican
[Dixon Lanier Merritt]

No ladder needs the bird but skies
To situate its wings,
Nor any leader's grim baton
Arraigns it as it sings
[Emily Dickinson]

Who wills devoutly to absorb, contain,
birds give him pain
[Richard Wilbur *The Beautiful Changes*]

I know what the caged bird feels, alas!
[Paul Lawrence Dunbar *Sympathy*]

PROVERBS

A bird in the hand is worth two in the bush
Birds of a feather flock together

bird of prey NOUN
▸ *related adjective:* raptorial

birth NOUN **1 = childbirth**, delivery, nativity, parturition: *She weighed 5lb 7oz at birth.* **OPPOSITE:** death **2 = beginning**, start, rise, source, origin, emergence, outset, genesis, initiation, inauguration, inception, commencement, fountainhead: *the birth of popular democracy* **3 = ancestry**, line, race, stock, blood, background, breeding, strain, descent, pedigree, extraction, lineage, forebears, parentage, genealogy, derivation: *men of low birth*
▸ *related adjective:* natal

QUOTATIONS

Our birth is but a sleep and a forgetting:
The Soul that rises with us, our life's Star,
Hath had elsewhere its setting,
And cometh from afar
[William Wordsworth *Ode: Intimations of Immortality*]

Birth, and copulation, and death.
That's all the facts when you come to brass tacks:
Birth, and copulation and death.
I've been born, and once is enough.
[T.S. Eliot *Sweeney Agonistes*]

It is as natural to die as to be born; and to a little infant, perhaps, the one is as painful as the other
[Francis Bacon *On Death*]

There is no cure for birth and death save to enjoy the interval
[George Santayana *Soliloquies in England*]

bisect VERB **= cut in two**, cross, separate, split, halve, cut across, intersect, cut in half, split down the middle, divide in two, bifurcate

bisexual ADJECTIVE **= bi** *(slang)*, ambisexual, ambidextrous *(slang)*, swinging both ways *(slang)*, AC/DC *(slang)*

bit[1] NOUN **1 = slice**, segment, fragment, crumb, mouthful, small piece, morsel: *a bit of cake* **2 = piece**, scrap, small piece: *crumpled bits of paper* **3 = jot**, whit, tittle, iota: *All it required was a bit of work.* **4 = part**, moment, period: *The best bit was the car chase.* **5 = little while**, time, second, minute, moment, spell, instant, tick *(Brit. informal)*, jiffy *(informal)*: *Let's wait a bit.*

bit[2] NOUN **= curb**, check, brake, restraint, snaffle: *The horse can be controlled by a snaffle bit and reins.*

bitchy ADJECTIVE **= spiteful**, mean, nasty, cruel, vicious, malicious, barbed, vindictive, malevolent, venomous, snide, rancorous, catty *(informal)*, backbiting, shrewish, ill-natured, vixenish, snarky *(informal)*
OPPOSITE: nice

bite VERB **1 = nip**, cut, tear, wound, grip, snap, crush, rend, pierce, champ, pinch, chew, crunch, clamp, nibble, gnaw, masticate: *Llamas won't bite or kick.* **2 = eat**, burn, smart, sting, erode, tingle, eat away, corrode, wear away: *nylon biting into the flesh*
▷ NOUN **1 = snack**, food, piece, taste, refreshment, mouthful, morsel, titbit, light meal: *a bite to eat* **2 = wound**, sting, pinch, nip, prick: *The boy had suffered a snake bite but he made a quick recovery.* **3 = edge**, interest, force, punch *(informal)*, sting, zest, sharpness, keenness, pungency, incisiveness, acuteness: *The novel seems to lack bite and tension.* **4 = kick** *(informal)*, edge, punch *(informal)*, spice, relish, zest, tang, sharpness, piquancy, pungency, spiciness: *I'd have preferred a bit more bite and not so much sugar.*

biting ADJECTIVE **1 = piercing**, cutting, cold, sharp, freezing, frozen, bitter, raw, chill, harsh, penetrating, arctic, nipping, icy, blighting, chilly, wintry, gelid, cold as ice: *a raw, biting northerly wind* **2 = sarcastic**, cutting, sharp, severe, stinging, withering, scathing, acrimonious, incisive, virulent, caustic, vitriolic, trenchant, mordant, mordacious: *This was the most biting criticism made against her.*

bitter ADJECTIVE **1 = grievous**, hard, severe, distressing, fierce, harsh, cruel, savage, ruthless, dire, relentless, poignant, ferocious, galling, unrelenting, merciless, remorseless, gut-wrenching, vexatious, hard-hearted: *the scene of bitter fighting* **OPPOSITE:** pleasant **2 = resentful**, hurt, wounded, angry, offended, sour, put out, sore, choked, crabbed, acrimonious, aggrieved, sullen, miffed *(informal)*, embittered, begrudging, peeved *(informal)*, piqued, rancorous: *She is said to be very bitter about the way she was sacked.* **OPPOSITE:** happy **3 = freezing**, biting, severe, intense, raw, fierce, chill, stinging, penetrating, arctic, icy, polar, Siberian, glacial, wintry: *a night in the bitter cold* **OPPOSITE:** mild **4 = sour**, biting, sharp, acid, harsh, unpleasant, tart, astringent, acrid, unsweetened, vinegary, acidulated, acerb: *The leaves taste rather bitter.* **OPPOSITE:** sweet

bitterly ADVERB **1 = resentfully**, sourly, sorely, tartly, grudgingly, sullenly, testily, acrimoniously, caustically, mordantly, irascibly: *They bitterly resented their loss of power.* **2 = intensely**, freezing, severely, fiercely, icy, bitingly: *It's been bitterly cold here in Moscow.*

bitterness NOUN **1 = resentment**, hurt, anger, hostility, indignation, animosity, venom, acrimony, pique, rancour, ill feeling, bad blood, ill will, umbrage, vexation, asperity: *I still feel bitterness and anger.* **2 = sourness**, acidity, sharpness, tartness, acerbity, vinegariness: *the strength and bitterness of the drink*

bizarre ADJECTIVE **= strange**, odd, unusual, extraordinary, fantastic, curious, weird, way-out *(informal)*, peculiar, eccentric, abnormal, ludicrous, queer *(informal)*, irregular, rum *(Brit. slang)*, uncommon, singular, grotesque, perplexing, uncanny, mystifying, off-the-wall *(slang)*, outlandish, comical, oddball *(informal)*, off the rails, zany, unaccountable, off-beat, left-field *(informal)*, freakish, wacko *(slang)*, outré, cockamamie *(slang, chiefly U.S.)*, daggy *(Austral. & N.Z. informal)* **OPPOSITE:** normal

black ADJECTIVE **1 = dark**, raven, ebony, sable, jet, dusky, pitch-black, inky, swarthy, stygian, coal-black, pitchy, murky: *He had thick black hair.* **OPPOSITE:** light **2 = gloomy**, sad, depressing, distressing, horrible, grim, bleak, hopeless, dismal, ominous, sombre, morbid, mournful, morose, lugubrious, joyless, funereal, doleful, cheerless: *After the tragic death of her son, she fell into a black depression.* **OPPOSITE:** happy **3 = terrible**, bad, devastating, tragic, fatal, unfortunate, dreadful, destructive, unlucky, harmful, adverse, dire, catastrophic, hapless, detrimental, untoward, ruinous, calamitous, cataclysmic, ill-starred, unpropitious, ill-fated, cataclysmal: *He had just undergone one of the blackest days of his political career.* **4 = wicked**, bad, evil, corrupt, vicious, immoral, depraved, debased, amoral, villainous, unprincipled, nefarious, dissolute, iniquitous, irreligious, impious, unrighteous: *the blackest laws in the country's history* **OPPOSITE:** good **5 = cynical**, weird, ironic, pessimistic, morbid, misanthropic, mordacious **6 = angry**, cross, furious, hostile, sour, menacing, moody, resentful, glowering, sulky, baleful, louring *or* lowering: *a black look on your face* **OPPOSITE:** happy **7 = dirty**, soiled, stained, filthy, muddy, blackened, grubby, dingy, grimy, sooty, mucky, scuzzy *(slang, chiefly U.S.)*, begrimed, festy *(Austral. slang)*, mud-encrusted, miry: *The whole front of him was black with dirt.* **OPPOSITE:** clean

black out = pass out, drop, collapse, faint, swoon, lose consciousness, keel over *(informal)*, flake out *(informal)*, become unconscious: *He felt so ill that he blacked out.*

black something out = darken, cover, shade, conceal, obscure, eclipse, dim, blacken, obfuscate, make dark, make darker, make dim: *The whole city is blacked out at night.*

in the black = in credit, solid, solvent, in funds, financially sound, without debt, unindebted: *Until he's in the black we certainly can't afford to get married.*

> **USAGE**
> When referring to people with dark skin, the adjective *black* or *Black* is widely used. For people of the US whose origins lie in Africa, the preferred term is *African-American*. To use *a Black* or *Blacks* as a noun is considered offensive, and it is better to talk about *a Black person* and *Black people*.

blacken VERB **1 = darken**, deepen, grow black: *He watched the blackening clouds move in.* **2 = make dark**, shadow, shade, obscure, overshadow, make darker, make dim: *The smoke blackened the sky like the apocalypse.* **3 = discredit**, stain, disgrace, smear, knock *(informal)*, degrade, rubbish *(informal)*, taint, tarnish, censure, slur, slag (off) *(slang)*, malign, reproach, denigrate, disparage, decry, vilify, slander, sully, dishonour, defile, defame, bad-mouth *(slang, chiefly U.S. & Canad.)*, traduce, bring into disrepute, smirch, calumniate: *They're trying to blacken our name.*

blacklist VERB **= exclude**, bar, ban, reject, rule out, veto, boycott, embargo, expel, vote against, preclude, disallow, repudiate, proscribe, ostracize, debar, blackball

black magic NOUN **= witchcraft**, magic, witching, voodoo, the occult, wizardry, enchantment, sorcery, occultism, incantation, black art, witchery, necromancy, diabolism, sortilege, makutu *(N.Z.)*

blackmail NOUN **= threat**, intimidation, ransom, compulsion, protection *(informal)*, coercion, extortion, pay-off *(informal)*, shakedown, hush money *(slang)*, exaction: *It looks like the pictures were being used for blackmail.*
▷ VERB **= threaten**, force, squeeze, compel, exact, intimidate, wring, coerce, milk, wrest, dragoon, extort, bleed *(informal)*, press-gang, hold to ransom: *I thought he was trying to blackmail me into saying whatever he wanted.*

blackness NOUN **= darkness**, shade, gloom, dusk, obscurity, nightfall, murk, dimness, murkiness, duskiness, shadiness, melanism, swarthiness, inkiness, nigrescence, nigritude *(rare)* **OPPOSITE:** light

blackout NOUN
1 = noncommunication, secrecy, censorship, suppression, radio silence: *a media blackout* **2 = power cut**, power failure: *an electricity blackout* **3 = unconsciousness**, collapse, faint, oblivion, swoon *(literary)*, loss of consciousness, syncope *(Pathology)*: *I suffered a blackout which lasted for several minutes.*

black sheep NOUN **= disgrace**, rebel, maverick, outcast, renegade, dropout, prodigal, individualist, nonconformist, ne'er-do-well, reprobate, wastrel, bad egg *(old-fashioned, informal)*

blame VERB **1 = hold responsible**, accuse, denounce, indict, impeach, incriminate, impute, recriminate, point a *or* the finger at: *They blamed the army for most of the atrocities.* **OPPOSITE:** absolve **2 = attribute to**, credit to, assign to, put down to, impute to: *The police blamed the explosion on terrorists.* **3** *(used in negative constructions)* **= criticize**, charge, tax, blast, condemn, put down, disapprove of, censure, reproach, chide, admonish, tear into *(informal)*, find fault with, reprove, upbraid, lambast(e), reprehend, express disapprobation of: *I do not blame them for trying to make some money.* **OPPOSITE:** praise
▷ NOUN **= responsibility**, liability, rap *(slang)*, accountability, onus, culpability, answerability: *Bad women never take the blame for anything.* **OPPOSITE:** praise

blameless ADJECTIVE **= innocent**, clear, clean, upright, stainless, honest, immaculate, impeccable, virtuous, faultless, squeaky-clean, unblemished, unsullied, uninvolved, unimpeachable, untarnished, above suspicion, irreproachable, guiltless, unspotted, unoffending **OPPOSITE:** guilty

blanch VERB **= turn pale**, fade, pale, drain, bleach, wan, whiten, go white, become pallid, become *or* grow white

b

bland ADJECTIVE **1 = dull**, boring, weak, plain, flat, commonplace, tedious, vanilla *(informal)*, dreary, tiresome, monotonous, run-of-the-mill, uninspiring, humdrum, unimaginative, uninteresting, insipid, unexciting, ho-hum *(informal)*, vapid, unstimulating, undistinctive: *It's easy on the ear but bland and forgettable.* **OPPOSITE:** exciting **2 = tasteless**, weak, watered-down, insipid, flavourless, thin, unstimulating, undistinctive: *It tasted bland and insipid, like warmed card.*

blank ADJECTIVE **1 = unmarked**, white, clear, clean, empty, plain, bare, void, spotless, unfilled, uncompleted: *He tore a blank page from his notebook.* **OPPOSITE:** marked **2 = expressionless**, empty, dull, vague, hollow, vacant, lifeless, deadpan, straight-faced, vacuous, impassive, inscrutable, inane, wooden, poker-faced *(informal)*: *He gave him a blank look.* **OPPOSITE:** expressive **3 = puzzled**, lost, confused, stumped, doubtful, baffled, stuck, at sea, bewildered, muddled, mixed up, confounded, perplexed, disconcerted, at a loss, mystified, clueless, dumbfounded, nonplussed, uncomprehending, flummoxed: *Abbot looked blank. 'I don't follow, sir.'* **4 = absolute**, complete, total, utter, outright, thorough, downright, consummate, unqualified, out and out, unmitigated, unmixed: *a blank refusal to attend*
▷ NOUN **1 = empty space**, space, gap: *Put a word in each blank to complete the sentence.* **2 = void**, vacuum, vacancy, emptiness, nothingness, vacuity, tabula rasa: *Everything was a complete blank.*

blanket NOUN **1 = cover**, rug, coverlet, afghan: *There was an old blanket in the trunk of my car.* **2 = covering**, cover, bed, sheet, coating, coat, layer, film, carpet, cloak, mantle, thickness: *The mud disappeared under a blanket of snow.*
▷ VERB **= coat**, cover, hide, surround, cloud, mask, conceal, obscure, eclipse, cloak: *More than a foot of snow blanketed parts of Michigan.*
▷ ADJECTIVE **= comprehensive**, full, complete, wide, sweeping, broad, extensive, wide-ranging, thorough, inclusive, exhaustive, all-inclusive, all-embracing: *the blanket coverage of the Olympics*

blare VERB **= blast**, scream, boom, roar, thunder, trumpet, resound, hoot, toot, reverberate, sound out, honk, clang, peal

blarney NOUN **= flattery**, coaxing, exaggeration, fawning, adulation, wheedling, spiel, sweet talk *(informal)*, flannel *(Brit. informal)*, soft soap *(informal)*, sycophancy, servility, obsequiousness, cajolery, blandishment, fulsomeness, toadyism, overpraise, false praise, honeyed words

blasé ADJECTIVE **= nonchalant**, cool, bored, distant, regardless, detached, weary, indifferent, careless, lukewarm, glutted, jaded, unmoved, unconcerned, impervious, uncaring, uninterested, apathetic, offhand, world-weary, heedless, satiated, unexcited, surfeited, cloyed **OPPOSITE:** interested

blasphemous ADJECTIVE **= irreverent**, cheeky *(informal)*, contemptuous, profane, disrespectful, godless, ungodly, sacrilegious, irreligious, impious **OPPOSITE:** reverent

blasphemy NOUN **= irreverence**, swearing, cursing, indignity *(to God)*, desecration, sacrilege, profanity, impiety, profanation, execration, profaneness, impiousness

blast NOUN **1 = explosion**, crash, burst, discharge, blow-up, eruption, detonation: *250 people were killed in the blast.* **2 = gust**, rush, storm, breeze, puff, gale, flurry, tempest, squall, strong breeze: *Blasts of cold air swept down from the mountains.* **3 = blare**, blow, scream, trumpet, wail, resound, clamour, hoot, toot, honk, clang, peal: *The buzzer suddenly responded in a long blast of sound.*
▷ VERB **1 = blow up**, bomb, destroy, burst, ruin, break up, explode, shatter, demolish, rupture, dynamite, put paid to, blow sky-high: *The explosion blasted out the external supporting wall.* **2 = criticize**, attack, put down, censure, berate, castigate, tear into *(informal)*, flay, rail at, lambast(e), chew out *(U.S. & Canad. informal)*: *They have blasted the report.*

blasted ADJECTIVE **= damned**, confounded, hateful, infernal, detestable

blastoff NOUN **= launch**, launching, take off, discharge, projection, lift-off, propelling, sendoff

blatant ADJECTIVE **= obvious**, open, clear, plain, naked, sheer, patent, evident, pronounced, straightforward, outright, glaring, manifest, bald, transparent, noticeable, conspicuous, overt, unmistakable, flaunting, palpable, undeniable, brazen, flagrant, indisputable, ostentatious, unmitigated, cut-and-dried *(informal)*, undisguised, obtrusive, unsubtle, unconcealed **OPPOSITE:** subtle

blaze VERB **1 = burn**, glow, flare, flicker, be on fire, go up in flames, be ablaze, fire, flash, flame: *The log fire was blazing merrily.* **2 = shine**, flash, beam, glow, flare, glare, gleam, shimmer, radiate: *The gardens blazed with colour.* **3 = flare up**, rage, boil, explode, fume, seethe, be livid, be incandescent: *His dark eyes were blazing with anger.*
▷ NOUN **1 = inferno**, fire, flames, bonfire, combustion, conflagration: *Two firemen were hurt in a blaze which swept through a tower block.* **2 = flash**, glow, glitter, flare, glare, gleam, brilliance, radiance: *I wanted the front garden to be a blaze of colour.*

bleach VERB **= lighten**, wash out, blanch, peroxide, whiten, blench, etiolate

bleak ADJECTIVE **1 = dismal**, black, dark, depressing, grim, discouraging, gloomy, hopeless, dreary, sombre, unpromising, disheartening, joyless, cheerless, comfortless: *The immediate outlook remains bleak.* **OPPOSITE:** cheerful **2 = exposed**, open, empty, raw, bare, stark, barren, desolate, gaunt, windswept, weather-beaten, unsheltered: *The island's pretty bleak.* **OPPOSITE:** sheltered **3 = stormy**, cold, severe, bitter, rough, harsh, chilly, windy, tempestuous, intemperate: *The weather can be quite bleak on the coast.*

bleary ADJECTIVE **= dim**, blurred, fogged, murky, fuzzy, watery, misty, hazy, foggy, blurry, ill-defined, indistinct, rheumy

bleed VERB **1 = lose blood**, flow, weep, trickle, gush, exude, spurt, shed blood: *The wound was bleeding profusely.* **2 = blend**, run, meet, unite, mix, combine, flow, fuse, mingle, converge, ooze, seep, amalgamate, meld, intermix: *The two colours will bleed into each other.* **3 = extort**, milk, squeeze, drain, exhaust, fleece: *They mean to bleed the British to the utmost.*

blemish NOUN **1 = mark**, line, spot, scratch, bruise, scar, blur, defect, flaw, blot, smudge, imperfection, speck, blotch, disfigurement, pock, smirch: *the blemish on his face* **OPPOSITE:** perfection **2 = defect**, fault, weakness, stain, disgrace, deficiency, shortcoming, taint, inadequacy, dishonour, demerit: *the one blemish on an otherwise resounding success*
▷ VERB **= dishonour**, mark, damage, spot, injure, ruin, mar, spoil, stain, blur, disgrace, impair, taint, tarnish, blot, smudge, disfigure, sully, deface, blotch, besmirch, smirch: *He wasn't about to blemish that pristine record; Nobody wanted to blemish his reputation at that time.* **OPPOSITE:** enhance

blend VERB **1 = mix**, join, combine, compound, incorporate, merge, put together, fuse, unite, mingle, alloy, synthesize, amalgamate, interweave, coalesce, intermingle, meld, intermix, commingle, commix: *Blend the ingredients until you have a smooth cream.* **2 = go well**, match, fit, suit, go with, correspond, complement, coordinate, tone in, harmonize, cohere: *Make sure all the patches blend together* **3 = combine**, mix, link, integrate, merge, put together, fuse, unite, synthesize, marry, amalgamate: *a band that blended jazz, folk and classical music*
▷ NOUN **= mixture**, cross, mix, combination, compound, brew, composite, union, fusion, synthesis, alloy, medley, concoction, amalgam, amalgamation, meld, mélange *(French)*, conglomeration, admixture: *He makes up his own blends of flour.*

bless VERB **1 = sanctify**, dedicate, ordain, exalt, anoint, consecrate, hallow, invoke happiness on: *Bless this couple and their loving commitment to one another.* **OPPOSITE:** curse **2 = endow**, give to, provide for, grant for, favour, grace, bestow to: *If God has seen fit to bless you with this gift, you should use it.* **OPPOSITE:** afflict **3 = praise**, thank, worship, glorify, magnify, exalt, extol, pay homage to, give thanks to: *Let us bless God for so uniting our hearts.*

blessed ADJECTIVE **1 = endowed**, supplied, granted, favoured, lucky, fortunate, furnished, bestowed, jammy (*Brit. slang*): *He's the son of a doctor, and well blessed with money.* **2 = happy**, contented, glad, merry, heartening, joyous, joyful, blissful: *The birth of a healthy baby is a truly blessed event.* **3 = holy**, sacred, divine, adored, revered, hallowed, sanctified, beatified: *After the ceremony, they were declared 'blessed'.*

blessing NOUN **1 = benefit**, help, service, profit, gain, advantage, favour, gift, windfall, kindness, boon, good fortune, bounty, godsend, manna from heaven: *the blessings of prosperity* **OPPOSITE:** disadvantage **2 = approval**, backing, support, agreement, regard, favour, sanction, go-ahead (*informal*), permission, leave, consent, mandate, endorsement, green light, ratification, assent, authorization, good wishes, acquiescence, approbation, concurrence, O.K. *or* okay (*informal*): *They gave their formal blessing to the idea.* **OPPOSITE:** disapproval **3 = benediction**, grace, dedication, thanksgiving, invocation, commendation, consecration, benison: *He said the blessing after taking the bread.* **OPPOSITE:** curse

blight NOUN **1 = curse**, suffering, evil, depression, corruption, distress, pollution, misery, plague, hardship, woe, misfortune, contamination, adversity, scourge, affliction, bane, wretchedness: *urban blight and unacceptable poverty* **OPPOSITE:** blessing **2 = disease**, plague, pest, fungus, contamination, mildew, contagion, infestation, pestilence, canker, cancer: *the worst year of the potato blight* ▷ VERB **= frustrate**, destroy, ruin, crush, mar, dash, wreck, spoil, crool *or* cruel (*Austral. slang*), scar, undo, mess up, annihilate, nullify, put a damper on: *families whose lives were blighted by unemployment*

blind ADJECTIVE **1 = sightless**, unsighted, unseeing, eyeless, visionless, stone-blind: *How would you describe colour to a blind person?* **OPPOSITE:** sighted **2** (*usually followed by* **to**) **= unaware of**, unconscious of, deaf to, ignorant of, indifferent to, insensitive to, oblivious of, unconcerned about, inconsiderate of, neglectful of, heedless of, insensible of, unmindful of, disregardful of: *All the time I was blind to your suffering.* **OPPOSITE:** aware **3 = unquestioning**, prejudiced, wholesale, indiscriminate, uncritical, unreasoning, undiscriminating: *her blind faith in the wisdom of the church* **4 = hidden**, concealed, obscured, dim, unseen, tucked away: *a blind corner* **OPPOSITE:** open **5 = dead-end**, closed, dark, obstructed, leading nowhere, without exit: *a dusty hotel room overlooking a blind alley* **6 = unthinking**, wild, violent, rash, reckless, irrational, hasty, senseless, mindless, uncontrollable, uncontrolled, unchecked, impetuous, intemperate, unconstrained: *The poor man went into a blind panic.*

blinding ADJECTIVE **1 = bright**, brilliant, intense, shining, glowing, blazing, dazzling, vivid, glaring, gleaming, beaming, effulgent, bedazzling: *the blinding lights of the delivery room* **2 = amazing**, striking, surprising, stunning, impressive, astonishing, eye-popping (*informal*), staggering, sensational (*informal*), breathtaking, wondrous (*archaic, literary*), jaw-dropping, gee-whizz (*slang*): *waiting for a blinding revelation that never came*

blindly ADVERB **1 = thoughtlessly**, carelessly, recklessly, indiscriminately, unreasonably, impulsively, senselessly, heedlessly, regardlessly: *Don't just blindly follow what the banker says.* **2 = wildly**, aimlessly, madly, frantically, confusedly: *Panicking blindly they stumbled towards the exit.*

blink VERB **1 = flutter**, wink, bat: *She was blinking her eyes rapidly.* **2 = flash**, flicker, sparkle, wink, shimmer, twinkle, glimmer, scintillate: *Green and yellow lights blinked on the surface of the harbour.*
on the blink = not working (properly), faulty, defective, playing up, out of action, malfunctioning, out of order, on the fritz (*U.S. slang*): *an old TV that's on the blink*

blinkered ADJECTIVE **= narrow-minded**, narrow, one-sided, prejudiced, biased, partial, discriminatory, parochial, constricted, insular, hidebound, one-eyed, lopsided **OPPOSITE:** broad-minded

bliss NOUN **1 = joy**, ecstasy, euphoria, rapture, nirvana, felicity, gladness, blissfulness, delight, pleasure, heaven, satisfaction, happiness, paradise: *It was a scene of such domestic bliss.* **OPPOSITE:** misery **2 = beatitude**, ecstasy, exaltation, blessedness, felicity, holy joy: *the bliss beyond the now*

blissful ADJECTIVE **1 = delightful**, pleasing, satisfying, heavenly (*informal*), enjoyable, gratifying, pleasurable: *There's nothing more blissful than lying by that pool.* **2 = happy**, joyful, satisfied, ecstatic, joyous, euphoric, rapturous: *a blissful smile*

blister NOUN **= sore**, boil, swelling, cyst, pimple, wen, blain, carbuncle, pustule, bleb, furuncle (*Pathology*)

blitz NOUN **= attack**, strike, assault, raid, offensive, onslaught, bombardment, bombing campaign, blitzkrieg

blizzard NOUN **= snowstorm**, storm, tempest

bloated ADJECTIVE **= too full**, swollen up: *Diners do not want to leave the table feeling bloated.*

blob NOUN **= drop**, ball, mass, pearl, lump, bead, dab, droplet, globule, glob, dewdrop

bloc NOUN **= group**, union, league, ring, alliance, coalition, axis, combine

block NOUN **1 = piece**, bar, square, mass, cake, brick, lump, chunk, cube, hunk, nugget, ingot: *a block of ice* **2 = obstruction**, bar, barrier, obstacle, impediment, hindrance: *a block to peace* ▷ VERB **1 = obstruct**, close, stop, cut off, plug, choke, clog, shut off, stop up, bung up (*informal*): *When the shrimp farm is built it will block the stream.* **OPPOSITE:** clear **2 = obscure**, bar, cut off, interrupt, obstruct, get in the way of, shut off: *a row of spruce trees that blocked his view* **3 = shut off**, stop, bar, cut off, head off, hamper, obstruct, get in the way of: *The police officer blocked his path.*

blockade NOUN **= stoppage**, block, barrier, restriction, obstacle, barricade, obstruction, impediment, hindrance, encirclement

blockage NOUN **= obstruction**, block, blocking, stoppage, impediment, occlusion

bloke NOUN **= man**, person, individual, customer (*informal*), character (*informal*), guy (*informal*), fellow, punter (*informal*), chap, boy, bod (*informal*)

blonde *or* **blond** ADJECTIVE **1 = fair**, light, light-coloured, flaxen: *The baby had blonde curls.* **2 = fair-haired**, golden-haired, tow-headed: *She was tall, blonde and attractive.*

blood NOUN **1 = lifeblood**, gore, vital fluid: *an inherited defect in the blood* **2 = family**, relations, birth, descent, extraction, ancestry, lineage, kinship, kindred: *He was of noble blood, and an officer.*
bad blood = hostility, anger, offence, resentment, bitterness, animosity, antagonism, enmity, bad feeling, rancour, hard feelings, ill will, animus, dudgeon (*archaic*), disgruntlement, chip on your shoulder: *There is, it seems, some bad blood between them.*
in cold blood = without emotion, cruelly, ruthlessly, mercilessly, callously, indifferently, unmercifully

PROVERBS
You cannot get blood from a stone
Blood is thicker than water

bloodless ADJECTIVE **= pale**, white, wan, sickly, pasty, colourless, pallid, anaemic, ashen, chalky, sallow, ashy, like death warmed up (*informal*)

bloodshed NOUN = **killing**, murder, massacre, slaughter, slaying, carnage, butchery, blood-letting, blood bath

bloodthirsty ADJECTIVE = **cruel**, savage, brutal, vicious, ruthless, ferocious, murderous, heartless, inhuman, merciless, cut-throat, remorseless, warlike, barbarous, pitiless

b

bloody ADJECTIVE **1** = **cruel**, fierce, savage, brutal, vicious, ferocious, cut-throat, warlike, barbarous, sanguinary: *Forty-three demonstrators were killed in bloody chaos.* **2** = **bloodstained**, raw, bleeding, blood-soaked, blood-spattered: *His fingers were bloody and cracked.*

bloody-minded ADJECTIVE = **difficult**, contrary, annoying, awkward, unreasonable, stubborn, perverse, exasperating, intractable, unhelpful, obstructive, cussed (*informal*), uncooperative, disobliging **OPPOSITE:** helpful

bloom NOUN **1** = **flower**, bud, blossom: *Harry carefully plucked the bloom.* **2** = **prime**, flower, beauty, height, peak, flourishing, maturity, perfection, best days, heyday, zenith, full flowering: *in the full bloom of youth* **3** = **glow**, flush, blush, freshness, lustre, radiance, rosiness: *The skin loses its youthful bloom.* **OPPOSITE:** pallor
▷ VERB **1** = **flower**, blossom, open, bud: *This plant blooms between May and June.* **OPPOSITE:** wither **2** = **grow**, develop, wax: *She bloomed into an utterly beautiful creature.* **3** = **succeed**, flourish, thrive, prosper, fare well: *Not many economies bloomed in 1990.* **OPPOSITE:** fail

blossom NOUN = **flower**, bloom, bud, efflorescence, floret: *the blossoms of plants, shrubs and trees*
▷ VERB **1** = **develop**, bloom, grow, mature: *Why do some people take longer than others to blossom?* **2** = **succeed**, progress, thrive, flourish, prosper: *His musical career blossomed.* **3** = **flower**, bloom, bud: *Rain begins to fall and peach trees blossom.*

blot NOUN **1** = **disgrace**, spot, fault, stain, scar, defect, flaw, taint, blemish, demerit, smirch, blot on your escutcheon: *a blot on the reputation of the architectural profession* **2** = **spot**, mark, patch, smear, smudge, speck, blotch, splodge, stain: *an ink blot*
▷ VERB = **soak up**, take up, absorb, dry up: *Blot any excess oils with a tissue.*
blot something out 1 = **obliterate**, hide, shadow, disguise, obscure, blur, eclipse, block out, efface, obfuscate: *The victim's face was blotted out by a camera blur.* **2** = **erase**, cancel, excise, obliterate, expunge: *He is blotting certain memories out.*

blotch NOUN = **mark**, spot, patch, splash, stain, blot, smudge, blemish, splodge, smirch, smutch

blow[1] VERB **1** = **move**, carry, drive, bear, sweep, fling, whisk, buffet, whirl, waft: *The wind blew her hair back from her forehead.* **2** = **be carried**, hover, flutter, flit, flitter: *Leaves were blowing around in the wind.* **3** = **exhale**, breathe, pant, puff, breathe out, expel air: *Take a deep breath and blow.* **4** = **play**, sound, pipe, trumpet, blare, toot: *A saboteur blew a horn to distract the hounds.*
blow over = **die down**, end, pass, finish, cease, be forgotten, subside: *Wait, and it'll blow over.*
blow someone away 1 = **bowl over**, amaze, stun, stagger, astound, electrify (*informal*), stupefy, flabbergast: *She just totally blew me away with her singing.* **2** = **open fire on**, kill, blast (*slang*), bring down, zap (*slang*), pick off, pump full of lead (*slang*): *He'd like to get hold of a gun and blow them all away.*
blow something out = **put out**, extinguish, snuff out: *I blew out the candle.*
blow something up 1 = **explode**, bomb, blast, dynamite, detonate, blow sky-high: *He was jailed for forty-five years for trying to blow up a plane.* **2** = **inflate**, pump up, fill, expand, swell, enlarge, puff up, distend: *Other than blowing up a tyre I haven't done any car maintenance.* **3** = **exaggerate**, heighten, enlarge on, inflate, embroider, magnify, amplify, overstate, embellish, blow out of (all) proportion, make a mountain out of a molehill, make a production out of, make a federal case of (*U.S. informal*), hyperbolize: *Newspapers blew up the story.* **4** = **magnify**, increase, extend, stretch, expand, widen, broaden, lengthen, amplify, elongate, dilate, make larger: *The image is blown up on a large screen.*
blow up 1 = **explode**, burst, go off, shatter, erupt, detonate: *The bomb blew up as they slept.* **2** = **lose your temper**, rage, erupt, lose it (*informal*), crack up (*informal*), see red (*informal*), lose the plot (*informal*), become angry, go ballistic (*slang, chiefly U.S.*), hit the roof (*informal*), blow a fuse (*slang, chiefly U.S.*), fly off the handle (*informal*), become enraged, go off the deep end (*informal*), wig out (*slang*), go up the wall (*slang*), go crook (*Austral. & N.Z. slang*), flip your lid (*slang*), blow your top: *I'm sorry I blew up at you.* **3** = **flare up**, widen, heighten, enlarge, broaden, magnify: *The scandal blew up into a major political furore.*
blow your top = **lose your temper**, explode, blow up (*informal*), lose it (*informal*), see red (*informal*), lose the plot (*informal*), have a fit (*informal*), throw a tantrum, fly off the handle (*informal*), go spare (*Brit. slang*), fly into a temper, flip your lid (*slang*), do your nut (*Brit. slang*): *I just asked him why he was late and he blew his top.*

blow[2] NOUN **1** = **knock**, stroke, punch, belt (*informal*), bang, rap, bash (*informal*), sock (*slang*), smack, thump, buffet, clout (*informal*), whack (*informal*), wallop (*informal*), slosh (*Brit. slang*), tonk (*informal*), clump (*slang*), clomp (*slang*): *He went off to hospital after a blow to the face.* **2** = **setback**, shock, upset, disaster, reverse, disappointment, catastrophe, misfortune, jolt, bombshell, calamity, affliction, whammy (*informal, chiefly U.S.*), choker (*informal*), sucker punch, bummer (*slang*), bolt from the blue, comedown (*informal*): *The ruling comes as a blow to environmentalists.*

blowout NOUN **1** = **binge** (*informal*), party, feast, rave (*Brit. slang*), spree, beano (*Brit. slang*), rave-up (*Brit. slang*), carousal, carouse, hooley *or* hoolie (*chiefly Irish & N.Z.*): *Once in a while we had a major blow-out.* **2** = **puncture**, burst, flat, flat tyre, flattie (*N.Z.*): *A lorry travelling south had a blow-out and crashed.*

bludge VERB = **slack**, skive (*Brit. informal*), idle, shirk, gold-brick (*U.S. slang*), bob off (*Brit. slang*), scrimshank (*Brit. Military slang*)

bludgeon VERB **1** = **club**, batter, beat, strike, belt (*informal*), clobber (*slang*), pound, cosh (*Brit.*), cudgel, beat *or* knock seven bells out of (*informal*): *A wealthy businessman has been found bludgeoned to death.* **2** = **bully**, force, cow, intimidate, railroad (*informal*), hector, coerce, bulldoze (*informal*), dragoon, steamroller, browbeat, tyrannize: *His relentless aggression bludgeons you into seeing his point.*
▷ NOUN = **club**, stick, baton, truncheon, cosh (*Brit.*), cudgel, shillelagh, bastinado, mere (*N.Z.*), patu (*N.Z.*): *I rather feel that the bludgeon has replaced the rapier.*

blue ADJECTIVE **1** = **depressed**, low, sad, unhappy, fed up, gloomy, dismal, melancholy, glum, dejected, despondent, downcast, down in the

SHADES OF BLUE

aqua	clear blue	duck-egg blue	lapis lazuli	peacock blue	royal blue	teal
aquamarine	cobalt blue	electric blue	midnight blue	periwinkle	sapphire	turquoise
azure	Copenhagen blue	gentian blue	navy blue	perse	saxe blue	ultramarine
Cambridge blue	cyan	heliotrope	Nile blue	petrol blue	sky blue	Wedgwood blue
cerulean		indigo	Oxford blue	pewter	steel blue	

The Language of Elizabeth Cleghorn Gaskell

Elizabeth Cleghorn Gaskell (1810–65) was an English essayist, short-story writer, and novelist. Some of her most significant works include the novel *Mary Barton: a tale of Manchester life*, and the first biography of Charlotte Brontë, entitled *The Life of Charlotte Brontë*. Her novels handled controversial issues of the Victorian era, such as the poor working conditions and poverty of the working classes.

One of the most frequent nouns that Gaskell uses is *man*. The most salient verb with *man* is *marry*, and after *young, old*, and *poor*, many of the adjectives used to describe *man* are positive, for example, *handsome, clever, honest, brave*, and *wise*. *Good man* appears over five times as often as *bad man*, and *man* appears over twice as often as *woman*. The adjectives used to describe women (again, after *old, young* and *poor*) are also positive, but tend to describe more typically feminine qualities; for example, *motherly, pretty, gentle*, and *beautiful*. Some of the adjectives that occur with *lady*, which Gaskell uses slightly more often than *woman*, include *grand, fine, sweet, vivacious*, and *lovely*.

Gaskell's use of language illustrates that death is an important topic in her work. *Death* appears in her 100 most frequently used nouns, and *dead* is one of the most salient adjectives modifying *man*. *Dead* also appears in her 100 most frequently used adjectives, and *die* appears in her 100 most frequently used verbs. Furthermore, *word* is among Gaskell's ten most frequently used nouns, and collocates most often with the adjective *last*. Gaskell often uses the phrase *last words* in reference to someone's final utterance before they die:

> She read the last words over again, once more: 'From my death-bed I adjure you to stand her friend; I will beg pardon on my knees for anything.'

The most frequent adjective that Gaskell uses is *little*, which is used to modify people (*girl, boy, child*), animals (*creature, bird*), periods of time (*while, pause, time*) and places (*town, room*). Another much-used noun with *little* is *bit*, and the construction *a little bit of* appears in expressions like *a little bit of business, a little bit of village gossip*, and *a little bit of nonsense*. The phrase *a little bit* appears before adjectives describing emotions, for example in *a little bit sadder, a little bit fearful* and *a little bit mortified*. Some other prevalent adjectives are also those that concern emotions: *happy, glad, afraid, anxious*, and *angry* are all among Gaskell's 100 most frequently used adjectives.

Gaskell's use of verbs also indicates that emotions are a prominent issue in her work, with *feel, cry*, and *love* all appearing in her 100 most frequently used verbs. Many of the most salient adjectives used in conjunction with *feel* include negative emotions such as *ashamed, guilty, irritated, lonely, depressed* and *sad*, although adjectives such as *grateful, proud*, and *glad* also stand out. *Love* is often modified by adverbs such as *dearly, passionately, deeply*, and *fondly*. *Cry* is also often modified by *passionately*, as well as adverbs such as *pitifully, bitterly, sadly* and *heartily*.

Another feature of Gaskell's language is her frequent use of the semicolon, for example:

> He would give the most unpalatable advice, if need were; would counsel an unsparing reduction of expenditure to an extravagant man; would recommend such an abatement of family pride as paved the way for one or two happy marriages in some instances; nay, what was the most likely piece of conduct of all to give offence forty years ago, he would speak up for an unjustly-used tenant; and that with so much temperate and well-timed wisdom and good feeling, that he more than once gained his point.

Long, complex sentences are common in Gaskell's work and she uses techniques such as repetition and the use of the semicolon to balance and structure these.

b

dumps (*informal*), down in the mouth, low-spirited, down-hearted: *There's no earthly reason for me to feel so blue.* **OPPOSITE:** happy **2 = smutty**, dirty, naughty, obscene, indecent, vulgar, lewd, risqué, X-rated (*informal*), bawdy, page-three, near the knuckle (*informal*): *a secret stash of porn mags and blue movies* **OPPOSITE:** respectable
▷ PLURAL NOUN **= depression**, gloom, melancholy, unhappiness, despondency, the hump (*Brit. informal*), dejection, moodiness, low spirits, the dumps (*informal*), doldrums, gloominess, glumness: *Interfering in-laws are the prime sources of the blues.*

blue-collar ADJECTIVE **= manual**, industrial, physical, manufacturing, labouring: *The plant employed more than a thousand blue-collar workers.*

blueprint NOUN **1 = scheme**, plan, design, system, idea, programme, proposal, strategy, pattern, suggestion, procedure, plot, draft, outline, sketch, proposition, prototype, layout, pilot scheme: *the blueprint of a new plan of economic reform* **2 = plan**, scheme, project, pattern, draft, outline, sketch, layout: *The documents contain a blueprint for a nuclear device.*

bluff[1] NOUN **= deception**, show, lie, fraud, fake, sham, pretence, deceit, bravado, bluster, humbug, subterfuge, feint, mere show: *The letter was a bluff.*
▷ VERB **= deceive**, lie, trick, fool, pretend, cheat, con, fake, mislead, sham, dupe, feign, delude, humbug, bamboozle (*informal*), hoodwink, double-cross (*informal*), pull the wool over someone's eyes: *He tried to bluff his way through another test and failed it.*

bluff[2] NOUN **= precipice**, bank, peak, cliff, ridge, crag, escarpment, promontory, scarp: *a high bluff over the Congaree River*
▷ ADJECTIVE **= hearty**, open, frank, blunt, sincere, outspoken, honest, downright, cordial, genial, affable, ebullient, jovial, plain-spoken, good-natured, unreserved, back-slapping: *a man with a bluff exterior* **OPPOSITE:** tactful

blunder NOUN **= mistake**, slip, fault, error, boob (*Brit. slang*), oversight, gaffe, slip-up (*informal*), indiscretion, impropriety, howler (*informal*), bloomer (*Brit. informal*), clanger (*informal*), faux pas, boo-boo (*informal*), gaucherie, barry *or* Barry Crocker (*Austral. slang*): *I think he made a tactical blunder.* **OPPOSITE:** correctness
▷ VERB **1 = make a mistake**, blow it (*slang*), err, slip up (*informal*), cock up (*Brit. slang*), miscalculate, foul up, drop a clanger (*informal*), put your foot in it (*informal*), drop a brick (*Brit. informal*), screw up (*informal*): *No doubt I had blundered again.* **OPPOSITE:** be correct **2 = stumble**, fall, reel, stagger, flounder, lurch, lose your balance: *He had blundered into the table, upsetting the flowers.*

blunt ADJECTIVE **1 = frank**, forthright, straightforward, explicit, rude, outspoken, bluff, downright, upfront (*informal*), trenchant, brusque, plain-spoken, tactless, impolite, discourteous, unpolished, uncivil, straight from the shoulder: *She is blunt about her personal life.* **OPPOSITE:** tactful **2 = dull**, rounded, dulled, edgeless, unsharpened: *a blunt object* **OPPOSITE:** sharp
▷ VERB **= dull**, weaken, soften, numb, dampen, water down, deaden, take the edge off: *Our appetite was blunted by the beer.* **OPPOSITE:** stimulate

blur NOUN **= haze**, confusion, fog, obscurity, dimness, cloudiness, blear, blurredness, indistinctness: *Her face is a blur.*
▷ VERB **1 = become indistinct**, soften, become vague, become hazy, become fuzzy: *If you move your eyes and your head, the picture will blur.* **2 = obscure**, make indistinct, mask, soften, muddy, obfuscate, make vague, befog, make hazy: *Scientists are trying to blur the distinction between these questions.*

blurred ADJECTIVE **= indistinct**, faint, vague, unclear, dim, fuzzy, misty, hazy, foggy, blurry, out of focus, ill-defined, lacking definition

blush VERB **= turn red**, colour, burn, flame, glow, flush, crimson, redden, go red (as a beetroot), turn scarlet: *I blushed scarlet at my stupidity.* **OPPOSITE:** turn pale
▷ NOUN **= reddening**, colour, glow, flush, pink tinge, rosiness, ruddiness, rosy tint: *A blush spread over Brenda's cheeks.*

> **QUOTATIONS**
> Man is the Only Animal that Blushes. Or needs to.
> [Mark Twain *Following the Equator*]

bluster VERB **= boast**, swagger, talk big (*slang*): *He was still blustering, but there was panic in his eyes.*
▷ NOUN **= hot air**, boasting, bluff, swagger, swaggering (*informal*), bravado, bombast: *the bluster of their campaign*

blustery ADJECTIVE **= gusty**, wild, violent, stormy, windy, tempestuous, inclement, squally, blusterous

board NOUN **1 = plank**, panel, timber, slat, piece of timber: *The floor was draughty bare boards.* **2 = council**, directors, committee, congress, ministry, advisers, panel, assembly, chamber, trustees, governing body, synod, directorate, quango, advisory group, conclave: *the US National Transportation Safety Board* **3 = meals**, provisions, victuals, daily meals: *Free room and board are provided for all hotel staff.*
▷ VERB **= get on**, enter, mount, embark, entrain, embus, enplane: *I boarded the plane bound for England.* **OPPOSITE:** get off

boast VERB **1 = brag**, crow, vaunt, bluster, talk big (*slang*), blow your own trumpet, show off, be proud of, flaunt, congratulate yourself on, flatter yourself, pride yourself on, skite (*Austral. & N.Z. informal*): *She boasted about her achievements.* **OPPOSITE:** cover up **2 = possess**, offer, present, exhibit: *The houses boast the latest energy-saving technology.*
▷ NOUN **= bragging**, vaunting, rodomontade (*literary*), gasconade (*rare*): *He was asked about earlier boasts of a quick victory.* **OPPOSITE:** disclaimer

boat NOUN **= vessel**, ship, craft, barge (*informal*), barque (*poetic*): *One of the best ways to see the area is in a small boat.*
in the same boat = in the same situation, alike, even, together, equal, on a par, on equal *or* even terms, on the same *or* equal footing: *The police and I were in the same boat.*
miss the boat = miss your chance *or* **opportunity**, miss out, be too late, lose out, blow your chance (*informal*): *Big name companies have missed the boat.*
rock the boat = cause trouble, protest, object, dissent, make waves (*informal*), throw a spanner in the works, upset the apple cart: *I said I didn't want to rock the boat in any way.*

> **QUOTATIONS**
> There is nothing – absolutely nothing – half so much worth doing as simply messing about in boats
> [Kenneth Grahame *The Wind in the Willows*]

bob VERB **= bounce**, duck, leap, hop, weave, skip, jerk, wobble, quiver, oscillate, waggle: *Balloons bobbed about in the sky.*
bob up = spring up, rise, appear, emerge, surface, pop up, jump up, bounce up: *They will bob up like corks as they cook.*

bode VERB **= augur**, portend, threaten, predict, signify, foreshadow, presage, betoken, be an omen, forebode

bodily ADJECTIVE **= physical**, material, actual, substantial, fleshly, tangible, corporal, carnal, corporeal

body NOUN **1 = physique**, build, form, figure, shape, make-up, frame, constitution: *The largest organ in the body is the liver.* **2 = torso**, trunk: *Cross your upper leg over your body.* **3 = corpse**, dead body, remains, stiff (*slang*), relics, carcass, cadaver: *His body lay in state.* **4 = organization**, company, group, society, league, association, band, congress, institution, corporation, federation, outfit (*informal*), syndicate, bloc, confederation: *the police representative body* **5 = main part**, matter, material, mass, substance, bulk, essence: *the preface, followed by the main body of the article* **6 = expanse**, mass, sweep: *It is probably the most polluted body of water in the world.* **7 = mass**, company, press, army, host, crowd, majority, assembly, mob, herd, swarm, horde, multitude, throng, bevy: *The great body of people moved slowly forward.* **8 = consistency**, substance, texture, density, richness, firmness, solidity, viscosity: *a dry wine, with good body*

boffin NOUN = **expert**, authority, brain(s) *(informal)*, intellectual, genius, guru, inventor, thinker, wizard, mastermind, intellect, egghead, wonk *(informal)*, brainbox, bluestocking *(usually derogatory)*, maven *(U.S.)*, fundi *(S. African)*

bog NOUN = **marsh**, moss *(Scot. & Northern English dialect)*, swamp, slough, wetlands, fen, mire, quagmire, morass, marshland, peat bog, pakihi *(N.Z.)*, muskeg *(Canad.)*: *We walked steadily across moor and bog.*
bog something *or* **someone down** = **hold up**, stick, delay, halt, stall, slow down, impede, slow up: *The talks have become bogged down with the issue of military reform.*

bogey NOUN **1** = **bugbear**, bête noire, horror, nightmare, bugaboo: *Age is another bogey for actresses.* **2** = **spirit**, ghost, phantom, spectre, spook *(informal)*, apparition, imp, sprite, goblin, bogeyman, hobgoblin, eidolon, atua *(N.Z.)*, kehua *(N.Z.)*: *It was no bogey, no demon.*

boggle VERB = **confuse**, surprise, shock, amaze, stun, stagger, bewilder, astound, daze, confound, stupefy, dumbfound

bogus ADJECTIVE = **fake**, false, artificial, forged, dummy, imitation, sham, fraudulent, pseudo *(informal)*, counterfeit, spurious, ersatz, phoney *or* phony *(informal)*, assumed
OPPOSITE: genuine

Bohemian ADJECTIVE *(often not cap.)* = **unconventional**, alternative, artistic, exotic, way-out *(informal)*, eccentric, avant-garde, off-the-wall *(slang)*, unorthodox, arty *(informal)*, oddball *(informal)*, offbeat, left bank, nonconformist, outré: *bohemian pre-war poets* **OPPOSITE:** conventional
▷ NOUN *(often not cap.)* = **nonconformist**, rebel, radical, eccentric, maverick, hippy, dropout, individualist, beatnik, iconoclast: *I am a bohemian. I have no roots.*

boil[1] VERB **1** = **simmer**, bubble, foam, churn, seethe, fizz, froth, effervesce: *I stood in the kitchen, waiting for the water to boil.* **2** = **be furious**, storm, rage, rave, fume, be angry, crack up *(informal)*, see red *(informal)*, go ballistic *(slang, chiefly U.S.)*, be indignant, fulminate, foam at the mouth *(informal)*, blow a fuse *(slang, chiefly U.S.)*, fly off the handle *(informal)*, go off the deep end *(informal)*, wig out *(slang)*, go up the wall *(slang)*: *She was boiling with anger.*
boil something down = **reduce**, concentrate, precipitate *(Chemistry)*, thicken, condense, decoct: *He boils down red wine and uses what's left.*

boil[2] NOUN = **pustule**, gathering, swelling, blister, blain, carbuncle, furuncle *(Pathology)*: *a boil on his nose*

boisterous ADJECTIVE **1** = **unruly**, wild, disorderly, loud, noisy, wayward, rowdy, wilful, riotous, unrestrained, rollicking, impetuous, rumbustious, uproarious, obstreperous, clamorous: *a boisterous but good-natured crowd* **OPPOSITE:** self-controlled **2** = **stormy**, rough, raging, turbulent, tumultuous, tempestuous, blustery, gusty, squally: *The boisterous wind had been making the sea increasingly choppy.* **OPPOSITE:** calm

bold ADJECTIVE **1** = **fearless**, enterprising, brave, daring, heroic, adventurous, courageous, gritty, gallant, gutsy *(slang)*, audacious, intrepid, valiant, plucky, undaunted, unafraid, unflinching, dauntless, lion-hearted, valorous: *She becomes a bold, daring rebel.* **OPPOSITE:** timid
2 = **impudent**, forward, fresh *(informal)*, confident, rude, cheeky, brash, feisty *(informal, chiefly U.S. & Canad.)*, saucy, pushy *(informal)*, brazen, in-your-face *(Brit. slang)*, shameless, sassy *(U.S. informal)*, unabashed, pert, insolent, barefaced, spirited, forceful: *Men do not like girls who are too bold.* **OPPOSITE:** shy
3 = **bright**, conspicuous, strong, striking, loud, prominent, lively, pronounced, colourful, vivid, flashy, eye-catching, salient, showy: *bold, dramatic colours* **OPPOSITE:** soft

bolster VERB = **support**, help, aid, maintain, boost, strengthen, assist, prop, reinforce, hold up, cushion, brace, shore up, augment, buttress, buoy up, give a leg up to *(informal)*

bolt NOUN **1** = **pin**, rod, peg, rivet: *details right down to the dimensions of nuts and bolts* **2** = **bar**, catch, lock, latch, fastener, sliding bar: *I heard him slide the bolt across the door.* **3** = **arrow**, missile, shaft, dart, projectile: *He pulled the crossbow bolt from his head.* **4** = **dash**, race, flight, spring, rush, rush, bound, sprint, dart, spurt: *a bolt for freedom*
▷ VERB **1** = **lock**, close, bar, secure, fasten, latch: *He reminded her to lock and bolt the kitchen door behind her.* **2** = **dash**, run, fly, spring, jump, rush, bound, leap, sprint, hurtle: *I made some excuse and bolted towards the exit.* **3** = **gobble**, stuff, wolf, cram, gorge, devour, gulp, guzzle, swallow whole: *Don't bolt your food.*

bomb NOUN = **explosive**, charge, mine, shell, missile, device, rocket, grenade, torpedo, bombshell, projectile: *There were two bomb explosions in the city overnight.*
▷ VERB = **blow up**, attack, destroy, assault, shell, blast, blitz, bombard, torpedo, open fire on, strafe, firebomb, fire upon, blow sky-high: *Airforce jets bombed the city at night.*

bombard VERB **1** = **attack**, assault, batter, barrage, besiege, beset, assail: *The media bombards all of us with images of violence and drugs and sex.* **2** = **bomb**, shell, blast, blitz, open fire, strafe, fire upon: *Rebel artillery units have regularly bombarded the airport.*

bombardment NOUN = **bombing**, attack, fire, assault, shelling, blitz, barrage, flak, strafe, fusillade, cannonade

bombast NOUN = **pomposity**, ranting, bragging, hot air *(informal)*, bluster, grandiosity, braggadocio, grandiloquence, rodomontade *(literary)*, gasconade *(rare)*, extravagant boasting, magniloquence

bombastic ADJECTIVE = **grandiloquent**, inflated, ranting, windy, high-flown, pompous, grandiose, histrionic, wordy, verbose, declamatory, fustian, magniloquent

bona fide ADJECTIVE = **genuine**, real, true, legal, actual, legitimate, authentic, honest, veritable, lawful, on the level *(informal)*, kosher *(informal)*, dinkum *(Austral. & N.Z. informal)*, the real McCoy
OPPOSITE: bogus

bond NOUN **1** = **tie**, union, coupling, link, association, relation, connection, alliance, attachment, affinity, affiliation: *the bond that linked them* **2** = **fastening**, band, tie, binding, chain, cord, shackle, fetter, manacle: *He managed to break free of his bonds.*
3 = **agreement**, word, promise, contract, guarantee, pledge, obligation, compact, covenant: *I'm not about to betray my bond with my brother.*
▷ VERB **1** = **form friendships**, connect: *They all bonded while working together.*
2 = **fix**, hold, bind, connect, glue, gum, fuse, stick, paste, fasten: *Strips of wood are bonded together.*

bondage NOUN = **slavery**, imprisonment, captivity, confinement, yoke, duress, servitude, enslavement, subjugation, serfdom, subjection, vassalage, thraldom, enthralment

bonny ADJECTIVE = **beautiful**, pretty, fair, sweet, appealing, attractive, lovely, charming, handsome, good-looking, gorgeous, radiant, alluring, comely, fit *(Brit. informal)*

bonus NOUN **1** = **extra**, benefit, commission, prize, gift, reward, premium, dividend, hand-out, perk *(Brit. informal)*, bounty, gratuity, honorarium: *a special end-of-year bonus*
2 = **advantage**, benefit, gain, extra, plus, asset, perk *(Brit. informal)*, icing on the cake: *Anything else would be a bonus.*

bony ADJECTIVE = **thin**, lean, skinny, angular, gaunt, skeletal, haggard, emaciated, scrawny, undernourished, cadaverous, rawboned, macilent *(rare)*

book NOUN **1** = **work**, title, volume, publication, manual, paperback, textbook, tract, hardback, tome: *a book about witches* **2** = **notebook**, album, journal, diary, pad, record book, Filofax®, notepad, exercise book, jotter, memorandum book: *I had several names in my little black book that I called regularly.*
▷ VERB = **reserve**, schedule, engage, line up, organize, charter, arrange for, procure, make reservations: *She booked herself a flight home last night.*
book in = **register**, enter, enrol: *He was happy to book in at the Royal Pavilion Hotel.*
▷ *See themed panel* **Books** *on page 76*

b

BOOKS

TYPES OF BOOK

album, almanac, anatomy, annual, anthology, armorial, A to Z, atlas, audio book, autobiography, Baedeker, bestiary, bibelot, Bible, biography, blook, breviary, brochure, casebook, catalogue, catechism, coffee-table book, comic book, commonplace book, companion, compendium, concordance, confessional, cookery book, copybook, diary, dictionary, directory, dispensatory, e-book, encyclopedia *or* encyclopaedia, e-reader, exercise book, formulary, gazetteer, gradus, grammar, graphic novel, grimoire, guidebook, handbook, hymn book, jotter, journal, Kindle *(trademark)*, lectionary, ledger, lexicon, log *or* logbook, manual, miscellany, missal, monograph, notebook, novel, novelette, novella, ordinal, peerage, pharmacopoeia, phrase book, prayer book, primer, prospectus, psalter, reader, reference book, register, road book, score, scrapbook, service book, sketchbook, song book, speller, statute book, storybook, telephone directory, textbook, thesaurus, vade mecum, who's who, wordbook, workbook, yearbook

PARTS OF A BOOK

acknowledgments, addendum, afterword, appendix, back, back matter, bibliography, binding, blurb, chapter, contents, corrigenda, cover, dedication, dust jacket *or* cover, endpaper, epigraph, epilogue, errata, flyleaf, folio, fore-edge, foreword, frontispiece, front matter, glossary, gutter, half-title, illustration, index, interleaf, introduction, leaf, margin, page, plate, postscript, preface, prelims, proem, prolegomenon, prologue, recto, rubric, running head, slipcase, spine, tail, title page, verso, wrapper

QUOTATIONS

A good book is the precious life-blood of a master spirit, embalmed and treasured up on purpose to a life beyond life
[John Milton *Areopagitica*]

All books are divisible into two classes, the books of the hour, and the books of all time
[John Ruskin *Sesame and Lilies*]

There is no such thing as a moral or an immoral book. Books are well written, or badly written
[Oscar Wilde *The Picture of Dorian Gray*]

Style and Structure are the essence of a book; great ideas are hogwash
[Vladimir Nabokov]

All books are either dreams or swords,
You can cut, or you can drug, with words
[Amy Lowell *Sword Blades and Poppy Seeds*]

Some books are to be tasted, others to be swallowed, and some few to be chewed and digested
[Francis Bacon *Essays*]

The reading of all good books is like conversation with the finest men of past centuries
[René Descartes *Discourse on Method*]

All good books are alike in that they are truer than if they had really happened
[Ernest Hemingway]

Books succeed,
And lives fail
[Elizabeth Barrett Browning *Aurora Leigh*]

Books are where things are explained to you; life is where things aren't
[Julian Barnes *Flaubert's Parrot*]

Even bad books are books and therefore sacred
[Günter Grass *The Tin Drum*]

I never read a book before reviewing it; it prejudices a man so
[Revd Sidney Smith]
A room without books is as a body without a soul
[John Lubbock]

When I am dead, I hope it may be said:
'His sins were scarlet, but his books were read.'
[Hilaire Belloc *On His Books*]

No furniture so charming as books
[Revd Sidney Smith]

Books will speak plain when counsellors blanch
[Francis Bacon *Essays*]

Of making many books there is no end; and much study is a weariness of the flesh
[*Bible: Ecclesiastes*]

booking NOUN **= reservation**, date, appointment

bookish ADJECTIVE **= studious**, learned, academic, intellectual, literary, scholarly, erudite, pedantic, well-read, donnish

booklet NOUN **= brochure**, leaflet, hand-out, pamphlet, folder, mailshot, handbill

boom NOUN **1 = expansion**, increase, development, growth, advance, jump, boost, improvement, spurt, upsurge, upturn, upswing: *an economic boom* **OPPOSITE:** decline **2 = bang**, report, shot, crash, clash, blast, burst, explosion, roar, thunder, rumble, clap, peal, detonation: *The stillness of the night was broken by the boom of a cannon.*
▷ VERB **1 = increase**, flourish, grow, develop, succeed, expand, strengthen, do well, swell, thrive, intensify, prosper, burgeon, spurt: *Lipstick sales have boomed even more.* **OPPOSITE:** fall **2 = bang**, roll, crash, blast, echo, drum, explode, roar, thunder, rumble, resound, reverberate, peal: *Thunder boomed like battlefield cannons over Crooked Mountain.*

boomerang VERB **= rebound**, backfire, come home to roost

boon NOUN **1 = benefit**, advantage, blessing, godsend, gift: *This battery booster is a boon for photographers.* **2 = gift**, present, grant, favour, donation, hand-out, gratuity, benefaction: *She begged him to grant her one boon.*

boorish ADJECTIVE **= loutish**, gross, crude, rude, hick *(informal, chiefly U.S. & Canad.)*, coarse, vulgar, rustic, barbaric, churlish, uneducated, bearish, uncouth, unrefined, uncivilized, clownish, oafish, ill-bred, lubberly **OPPOSITE:** refined

boost VERB **= increase**, develop, raise, expand, add to, build up, heighten, enlarge, inflate, magnify, amplify, augment, jack up: *They need to take action to boost sales.* **OPPOSITE:** decrease
▷ NOUN **1 = rise**, increase, advance,

jump, addition, improvement, expansion, upsurge, upturn, increment, upswing, upward turn: *The paper is enjoying a boost in circulation.* **OPPOSITE:** fall **2 = encouragement**, help: *It did give me a boost to win such an event.*

boot VERB **= kick**, punt, put the boot in(to) *(slang)*, drop-kick: *One guy booted the door down.*
boot someone out = dismiss, sack *(informal)*, expel, throw out, oust, relegate, kick out, eject, kiss off *(slang, chiefly U.S. & Canad.)*, show someone the door, give someone the boot *(slang)*, give someone their marching orders, give someone the bullet *(Brit. slang)*, give someone the bum's rush *(slang)*, throw out on your ear *(informal)*, give someone the heave *or* push *(informal)*: *Schools are booting out record numbers of unruly pupils.*

bootleg ADJECTIVE **= illicit**, illegal, outlawed, pirate, unofficial, black-market, unlicensed, under-the-table, unauthorized, contraband, hooky *(slang)*, under-the-counter **OPPOSITE:** official

booty NOUN **= plunder**, winnings, gains, haul, spoils, prey, loot, takings, pillage, swag *(slang)*, boodle *(slang, chiefly U.S.)*

booze VERB **= drink**, indulge, get drunk, tipple, imbibe, tope, carouse, bevvy *(dialect)*, get plastered, drink like a fish, get soused, get tanked up *(informal)*, go on a binge *or* bender *(informal)*, hit the booze *or* bottle *(informal)*: *a load of drunken businessmen who had been boozing all afternoon*

boozer NOUN **1 = pub**, local *(Brit. informal)*, bar *(informal, chiefly Brit.)*, inn, tavern, beer parlour *(Canad.)*, beverage room *(Canad.)*, public house, watering hole *(facetious, slang)*, roadhouse, hostelry, alehouse *(archaic)*, taproom: *She once caught him in a boozer with another woman.* **2 = drinker**, toper, drunk, soak *(slang)*, alcoholic, lush *(slang)*, drunkard, sot, tippler, wino *(informal)*, alko *or* alco *(Austral. slang)*, inebriate: *We always thought he was a bit of a boozer.*

border NOUN **1 = frontier**, line, marches, limit, bounds, boundary, perimeter, borderline, borderland: *Clifford is enjoying life north of the border.* **2 = edge**, lip, margin, skirt, verge, rim, hem, brim, flange: *pillowcases trimmed with a hand-crocheted border*
▷ VERB **= edge**, bound, decorate, trim, fringe, rim, hem: *white sand bordered by palm trees and tropical flowers*
border on something = come close to, approach, be like, resemble, be similar to, approximate, come near: *The atmosphere borders on the surreal.*

borderline ADJECTIVE **= marginal**, bordering, doubtful, peripheral, indefinite, indeterminate, equivocal, inexact, unclassifiable

bore[1] VERB **= drill**, mine, sink, tunnel, pierce, penetrate, burrow, puncture, perforate, gouge out: *Get the special drill bit to bore the correct-size hole.*

bore[2] VERB **= tire**, exhaust, annoy, fatigue, weary, wear out, jade, wear down, be tedious, pall on, send to sleep: *Dickie bored him all through the meal with stories of the Navy.* **OPPOSITE:** excite
▷ NOUN **= nuisance**, pain *(informal)*, drag *(informal)*, headache *(informal)*, yawn *(informal)*, anorak *(informal)*, pain in the neck *(informal)*, dullard, dull person, tiresome person, wearisome talker: *He's a bore and a fool.*

> **QUOTATIONS**
> Bore: a person who talks when you wish him to listen
> [Ambrose Bierce *The Devil's Dictionary*]
>
> The way to be a bore is to say everything
> [Voltaire *Sept Discours en vers sur l'Homme*]
>
> He was not only a bore; he bored for England
> [Malcolm Muggeridge *Tread Softly (writing of Sir Anthony Eden)*]
>
> A bore is a man who, when you ask him how he is, tells you
> [Bert Leston Taylor *The So-Called Human Race*]
>
> A healthy male adult bore consumes each year one and a half times his own weight in other people's patience
> [John Updike *Confessions of a Wild Bore*]
>
> Some people can stay longer in an hour than others can in a week
> [W.D. Howells]

bored ADJECTIVE **= fed up**, tired, hacked (off) *(U.S. slang)*, wearied, weary, uninterested, sick and tired *(informal)*, listless, browned-off *(informal)*, brassed off *(Brit. slang)*, ennuied, hoha *(N.Z.)*

boredom NOUN **= tedium**, apathy, doldrums, weariness, monotony, dullness, sameness, ennui, flatness, world-weariness, tediousness, irksomeness **OPPOSITE:** excitement

> **QUOTATIONS**
> Boredom: the desire for desires
> [Leo Tolstoy *Anna Karenina*]
>
> Boredom is a sign of satisfied ignorance, blunted apprehension, crass sympathies, dull understanding, feeble powers of attention and irreclaimable weakness of character
> [James Bridie *Mr. Bolfry*]
>
> One can be bored until boredom becomes the most sublime of all emotions
> [Logan Pearsall Smith *Afterthoughts*]
>
> Boredom is...a vital problem for the moralist, since half the sins of mankind are caused by the fear of it
> [Bertrand Russell *The Conquest of Happiness*]

boring ADJECTIVE **= uninteresting**, dull, tedious, stale, tiresome, monotonous, old, dead, flat, routine, humdrum, insipid, mind-numbing, unexciting, ho-hum *(informal)*, repetitious, wearisome, unvaried, yawnsome *(slang)*, meh *(slang)*

born VERB **= brought into this world**, delivered: *She was born in London on April 29, 1923.*

> **USAGE**
> This word is spelled without an *e*: *a new baby was born*. The word *borne*, spelled with an *e*, is the past participle of the verb *bear*: *he had borne his ordeal with great courage*, not *he had born his ordeal with great courage*.

borrow VERB **1 = take on loan**, touch (someone) for *(slang)*, scrounge *(informal)*, blag *(slang)*, mooch *(slang)*, cadge, use temporarily, take and return: *Can I borrow a pen please?* **OPPOSITE:** lend **2 = steal**, take, use, copy, adopt, appropriate, acquire, pinch *(informal)*, pirate, poach, pilfer, filch, plagiarize: *I borrowed his words for my book's title.*

> **QUOTATIONS**
> Neither a borrower nor a lender be
> [William Shakespeare *Hamlet*]

bosom NOUN **1 = breast**, chest, front, bust, teats, thorax: *On my bosom laid her weeping head.* **2 = midst**, centre, heart, protection, circle, shelter: *He went back to the snug bosom of his family.* **3 = heart**, feelings, spirit, soul, emotions, sympathies, sentiments, affections: *Something gentle seemed to move in her bosom.*
▷ ADJECTIVE **= intimate**, close, warm, dear, friendly, confidential, cherished, boon, very dear: *They were bosom friends.*

boss NOUN **= manager**, head, leader, director, chief, executive, owner, master, governor *(informal)*, employer, administrator, supervisor, superintendent, gaffer *(informal, chiefly Brit.)*, foreman, overseer, kingpin, big cheese *(old-fashioned, slang)*, baas *(S. African)*, numero uno *(informal)*, Mister Big *(slang, chiefly U.S.)*, sherang *(Austral. & N.Z.)*: *He cannot stand his boss.*
boss someone around = order around, dominate, bully, intimidate, oppress, dictate to, terrorize, put upon, push around *(slang)*, browbeat, ride roughshod over, tyrannize, rule with an iron hand: *He started bossing people around and I didn't like it.*

bossy ADJECTIVE **= domineering**, lordly, arrogant, authoritarian, oppressive, hectoring, autocratic, dictatorial, coercive, imperious, overbearing, tyrannical, despotic, high-handed

botch VERB **= spoil**, mar, bungle, fumble, screw up *(informal)*, mess up, cock up *(Brit. slang)*, mismanage, muff, make a nonsense of *(informal)*, bodge *(informal)*, make a pig's ear of *(informal)*, flub *(U.S. slang)*, crool *or* cruel *(Austral. slang)*: *It's a silly idea, and he has botched it.*
▷ NOUN **= mess**, failure, blunder, miscarriage, bungle, bungling, fumble, hash, cock-up *(Brit. slang)*, pig's ear *(informal)*, pig's breakfast *(informal)*: *I rather made a botch of that whole thing.*

b

b

bother VERB **1 = trouble**, concern, worry, upset, alarm, disturb, distress, annoy, dismay, gall, disconcert, vex, perturb, faze, put *or* get someone's back up: *That kind of jealousy doesn't bother me.* **2 = pester**, plague, irritate, put out, harass, nag, hassle *(informal)*, inconvenience, molest, breathe down someone's neck, get on your nerves *(informal)*, nark *(Brit., Austral. & N.Z. slang)*, bend someone's ear *(informal)*, give someone grief *(Brit. & S. African)*, get on your wick *(Brit. slang)*: *I don't know why he bothers me with this kind of rubbish.* **OPPOSITE:** help
▷ NOUN **= trouble**, problem, worry, difficulty, strain, grief *(Brit. & S. African)*, fuss, pest, irritation, hassle *(informal)*, nuisance, flurry, uphill *(S. African)*, inconvenience, annoyance, aggravation, vexation: *Most men hate the bother of shaving.* **OPPOSITE:** help

bottleneck NOUN **= block**, hold-up, obstacle, congestion, obstruction, impediment, blockage, snarl-up *(informal, chiefly Brit.)*, (traffic) jam

bottle shop NOUN **= off-licence** *(Brit.)*, liquor store *(U.S. & Canad.)*, bottle store *(S. African)*, package store *(U.S. & Canad.)*, offie *or* offy *(Brit. informal)*

bottle store NOUN **= off-licence** *(Brit.)*, liquor store *(U.S. & Canad.)*, bottle shop *(Austral. & N.Z.)*, package store *(U.S. & Canad.)*, offie *or* offy *(Brit. informal)*

bottom NOUN **1 = lowest part**, base, foot, bed, floor, basis, foundation, depths, support, pedestal, deepest part: *He sat at the bottom of the stairs.* **OPPOSITE:** top **2 = underside**, sole, underneath, lower side: *the bottom of their shoes* **3 = buttocks**, behind *(informal)*, rear, butt *(U.S. & Canad. informal)*, bum *(Brit. slang)*, buns *(U.S. slang)*, backside, rump, seat, tail *(informal)*, rear end, posterior, derrière *(euphemistic)*, tush *(U.S. slang)*, fundament, jacksy *(Brit. slang)*: *She moved her large bottom on the window-seat.*
▷ ADJECTIVE **= lowest**, last, base, ground, basement, undermost: *the bottom drawer of the cupboard* **OPPOSITE:** higher

bottomless ADJECTIVE **1 = unlimited**, endless, infinite, limitless, boundless, inexhaustible, immeasurable, unbounded, illimitable: *She does not have a bottomless purse.* **2 = deep**, profound, yawning, boundless, unfathomable, immeasurable, fathomless, abyssal: *His eyes were like bottomless brown pools.*

bounce VERB **1 = rebound**, return, thump, recoil, ricochet, spring back, resile: *The ball bounced past the right-hand post.* **2 = bound**, spring, jump, leap, skip, caper, prance, gambol, jounce: *Moira bounced into the office.* **3 = throw out**, fire *(informal)*, turn out, expel, oust, relegate, kick out *(informal)*, drive out, eject, evict, boot out *(informal)*, show someone the door, give someone the bum's rush *(slang)*, throw out on your ear *(informal)*: *He was bounced from two programmes for unbecoming conduct.*
▷ NOUN **1 = springiness**, give, spring, bound, rebound, resilience, elasticity, recoil: *the pace and steep bounce of the pitch* **2 = life**, go *(informal)*, energy, pep, sparkle, zip *(informal)*, vitality, animation, vigour, exuberance, dynamism, brio, vivacity, liveliness, vim *(slang)*, lustiness, vivaciousness: *the natural bounce of youth*

bouncing ADJECTIVE **= lively**, healthy, thriving, blooming, robust, vigorous, energetic, perky, sprightly, alive and kicking, fighting fit, full of beans *(informal)*, fit as a fiddle *(informal)*, bright-eyed and bushy-tailed

bouncy ADJECTIVE **1 = lively**, active, enthusiastic, energetic, bubbly, exuberant, irrepressible, ebullient, perky, chirpy *(informal)*, sprightly, vivacious, effervescent, chipper *(informal)*, full of beans *(informal)*, zestful, full of pep *(informal)*, bright-eyed and bushy-tailed: *She was bouncy and full of energy.* **OPPOSITE:** listless **2 = springy**, flexible, elastic, resilient, rubbery, spongy: *a bouncy chair* **OPPOSITE:** flat

bound[1] ADJECTIVE **1 = compelled**, obliged, forced, committed, pledged, constrained, obligated, beholden, duty-bound: *All members are bound by an oath of secrecy.* **2 = tied**, fixed, secured, attached, lashed, tied up, fastened, trussed, pinioned, made fast: *Her arms were bound to her sides.* **3 = certain**, sure, fated, doomed, destined: *There are bound to be price increases next year.*

bound[2] VERB **= leap**, bob, spring, jump, bounce, skip, vault, pounce: *He bounded up the steps and pushed the bell of the door.*
▷ NOUN **= leap**, bob, spring, jump, bounce, hurdle, skip, vault, pounce, caper, prance, lope, frisk, gambol: *With one bound Jack was free.*

bound[3] VERB **1 = surround**, confine, enclose, terminate, encircle, circumscribe, hem in, demarcate, delimit: *the trees that bounded the car park* **2 = limit**, fix, define, restrict, confine, restrain, circumscribe, demarcate, delimit: *Our lives are bounded by work, family and television.*

boundary NOUN **1 = frontier**, edge, border, march, barrier, margin, brink: *Drug traffickers operate across national boundaries.* **2 = edges**, limits, bounds, pale, confines, fringes, verges, precinct, extremities: *the western boundary of the wood* **3 = dividing line**, borderline: *the boundary between childhood and adulthood*

boundless ADJECTIVE **= unlimited**, vast, endless, immense, infinite, untold, limitless, unending, inexhaustible, incalculable, immeasurable, unbounded, unconfined, measureless, illimitable **OPPOSITE:** limited

bounds PLURAL NOUN **= boundary**, line, limit, edge, border, march, margin, pale, confine, fringe, verge, rim, perimeter, periphery: *The bounds of the empire continued to expand.*

bountiful ADJECTIVE **1 = plentiful**, generous, lavish, ample, prolific, abundant, exuberant, copious, luxuriant, bounteous, plenteous: *The land is bountiful and no one starves.* **2 = generous**, kind, princely, liberal, charitable, hospitable, prodigal, open-handed, unstinting, beneficent, bounteous, munificent, ungrudging: *Their bountiful host was bringing brandy, whisky and liqueurs.*

bounty NOUN **1 = generosity**, charity, assistance, kindness, philanthropy, benevolence, beneficence, liberality, almsgiving, open-handedness, largesse *or* largess: *The aid organization would not allow such bounty.* **2 = abundance**, plenty, exuberance, profusion, affluence, plenitude, copiousness, plenteousness: *autumn's bounty of fruits, seeds and berries* **3 = reward**, present, grant, prize, payment, gift, compensation, bonus, premium, donation, recompense, gratuity, meed *(archaic)*, largesse *or* largess, koha *(N.Z.)*: *They paid bounties for people to give up their weapons.*

bouquet NOUN **1 = bunch of flowers**, spray, garland, wreath, posy, buttonhole, corsage, nosegay, boutonniere: *a bouquet of dried violets* **2 = aroma**, smell, scent, perfume, fragrance, savour, odour, redolence: *a Sicilian wine with a light red colour and a bouquet of cloves*

bourgeois ADJECTIVE **= middle-class**, traditional, conventional, materialistic, hidebound, Pooterish

> **QUOTATIONS**
> The bourgeois treasures nothing more highly than the self
> [Hermann Hesse *Steppenwolf*]
>
> Destroy him as you will, the bourgeois always bounces up – execute him, expropriate him, starve him out en masse, and he reappears in your children
> [Cyril Connolly]
>
> How beastly the bourgeois is
> Especially the male of the species
> [D.H. Lawrence *How Beastly the Bourgeois Is*]

bout NOUN **1 = period**, time, term, fit, session, stretch, spell, turn, patch, interval, stint: *I was suffering with a bout of nerves.* **2 = round**, run, course, series, session, cycle, sequence, stint, spree: *The latest bout of violence has claimed ten lives.* **3 = fight**, match, battle, competition, struggle, contest, set-to, encounter, engagement, head-to-head, boxing match: *This will be his eighth title bout in 19 months.*

bovine ADJECTIVE **= dull**, heavy, slow, thick, stupid, dense, sluggish, lifeless, inactive, inert, lethargic, dozy *(Brit. informal)*, listless, unresponsive, stolid, torpid, slothful

bow[1] VERB = **bend**, bob, nod, incline, stoop, droop, genuflect, make obeisance: *He bowed slightly before taking her bag.*
▷ NOUN = **bending**, bob, nod, inclination, salaam, obeisance, kowtow, genuflection: *I gave a theatrical bow and waved.*
bow out = **give up**, retire, withdraw, get out, resign, quit, pull out, step down (*informal*), back out, throw in the towel, cop out (*slang*), throw in the sponge, call it a day or night: *He bowed out gracefully when his successor was appointed.*
bow to something *or* **someone** = **give in to**, accept, comply with, succumb to, submit to, surrender to, yield to, defer to, concede to, acquiesce to, kowtow to: *She is having to bow to their terms.*

bow[2] NOUN = **prow**, head, stem, fore, beak: *spray from the ship's bow*

bowels PLURAL NOUN **1** = **guts**, insides (*informal*), intestines, innards (*informal*), entrails, viscera, vitals: *Snatched sandwiches and junk food had cemented his bowels.* **2** = **depths**, hold, middle, inside, deep, interior, core, belly, midst, remotest part, deepest part, furthest part, innermost part: *deep in the bowels of the earth*

> **QUOTATIONS**
> A good reliable set of bowels is worth more to a man than any quantity of brains
> [Josh Billings]

bower NOUN = **arbour**, grotto, alcove, summerhouse, shady recess, leafy shelter

bowl[1] NOUN = **basin**, plate, dish, vessel: *Put all the ingredients into a large bowl.*

bowl[2] VERB **1** = **throw**, hurl, launch, cast, pitch, toss, fling, chuck (*informal*), lob (*informal*): *He bowled each ball so well that we won two matches.*
2 (*often with* **along**) = **drive**, shoot, speed, tear, barrel (along) (*informal, chiefly U.S. & Canad.*), trundle: *It felt just like old times, to bowl down to Knightsbridge.*
bowl someone over 1 = **knock down**, fell, floor, deck (*slang*), overturn, overthrow, bring down: *People clung to trees as the flash flood bowled them over.*
2 = **surprise**, amaze, stun, overwhelm, astonish, stagger, startle, astound, take (someone) aback, stupefy, strike (someone) dumb, throw off balance, sweep off your feet, dumbfound: *I was bowled over by India.*

box[1] NOUN = **container**, case, chest, trunk, pack, package, carton, casket, receptacle, ark (*dialect*), portmanteau, coffret, kist (*Scot. & Northern English dialect*): *They sat on wooden boxes.*
▷ VERB = **pack**, package, wrap, encase, bundle up: *He boxed the test pieces and shipped them back to Berlin.*
box something *or* **someone in** = **confine**, contain, surround, trap, restrict, isolate, cage, enclose, restrain, imprison, shut up, incarcerate, hem in, shut in, coop up: *He was boxed in with 300 metres to go.*

box[2] VERB **1** = **fight**, spar, exchange blows: *At school I boxed and played rugby.* **2** = **punch**, hit, strike, belt (*informal*), deck (*slang*), slap, sock (*slang*), buffet, clout (*informal*), cuff, whack (*informal*), wallop (*informal*), chin (*slang*), tonk (*informal*), thwack (*informal*), lay one on (*slang*): *They slapped my face and boxed my ears.*

boxer NOUN = **fighter**, pugilist, prizefighter, sparrer

boxing NOUN = **prizefighting**, the ring, sparring, fisticuffs, the fight game (*informal*), pugilism

boy NOUN = **lad**, kid (*informal*), youth, fellow, youngster, chap (*informal*), schoolboy, junior, laddie (*Scot.*), stripling

boycott VERB = **embargo**, reject, snub, refrain from, spurn, blacklist, black, cold-shoulder, ostracize, blackball **OPPOSITE:** support

boyfriend NOUN = **sweetheart**, man, lover, young man, steady, beloved, valentine, admirer, suitor, beau, date, swain, toy boy, truelove, leman (*archaic*), inamorato

boyish ADJECTIVE = **youthful**, young, innocent, adolescent, juvenile, childish, immature

brace VERB **1** = **steady**, support, balance, secure, stabilize: *He braced his back against the wall.* **2** = **support**, strengthen, steady, prop, reinforce, hold up, tighten, shove, bolster, fortify, buttress, shove up: *The lights showed the old timbers, used to brace the roof.*
▷ NOUN = **support**, stay, prop, bracer, bolster, bracket, reinforcement, strut, truss, buttress, stanchion: *She wears a neck brace.*

bracing ADJECTIVE = **refreshing**, fresh, cool, stimulating, reviving, lively, crisp, vigorous, rousing, brisk, uplifting, exhilarating, fortifying, chilly, rejuvenating, invigorating, energizing, healthful, restorative, tonic, rejuvenative **OPPOSITE:** tiring

brag VERB = **boast**, crow, swagger, vaunt, bluster, talk big (*slang*), blow your own trumpet, blow your own horn (*U.S. & Canad.*)

braid VERB = **interweave**, weave, lace, intertwine, plait, entwine, twine, ravel, interlace

brain NOUN **1** = **cerebrum**, mind, grey matter (*informal*): *The eye grows independently of the brain.*
2 = **intellectual**, genius, scholar, sage, pundit, mastermind, intellect, prodigy, highbrow, egghead (*informal*), brainbox, bluestocking (*usually derogatory*): *I've never been much of a brain myself.*
▷ PLURAL NOUN = **intelligence**, mind, reason, understanding, sense, capacity, smarts (*slang, chiefly U.S.*), wit, intellect, savvy (*slang*), nous (*Brit. slang*), suss (*slang*), shrewdness, sagacity: *They were not the only ones to have brains and ambition.*

brainwashing NOUN = **indoctrination**, conditioning, persuasion, re-education

brainwave NOUN = **idea**, thought, bright idea, stroke of genius

brainy ADJECTIVE = **intelligent**, quick, bright, sharp, brilliant, acute, smart, alert, clever, rational, knowing, quick-witted

brake NOUN = **control**, check, curb, restraint, constraint, rein: *Illness had put a brake on his progress.*
▷ VERB = **slow**, decelerate, reduce speed: *She braked to a halt and switched off.*

branch NOUN **1** = **bough**, shoot, arm, spray, limb, sprig, offshoot, prong, ramification: *the low, overhanging branches of a giant pine tree* **2** = **office**, department, unit, wing, chapter, bureau, local office: *The local branch is handling the accounts.* **3** = **division**, part, section, subdivision, subsection: *He had a fascination for submarines and joined this branch of the service.* **4** = **discipline**, section, subdivision: *an experimental branch of naturopathic medicine*
branch out = **expand**, diversify: *I continued studying moths, and branched out to other insects.*

brand NOUN **1** = **trademark**: *a supermarket's own brand* **2** = **label**, mark, sign, stamp, symbol, logo, trademark, marker, hallmark, emblem: *The brand on the barrel stood for Elbert Anderson and Uncle Sam.* **3** = **stigma**, mark, stain, disgrace, taint, slur, blot, infamy, smirch: *the brand of shame*
▷ VERB **1** = **stigmatize**, mark, label, expose, denounce, disgrace, discredit, censure, pillory, defame: *I was instantly branded as a rebel.* **2** = **mark**, burn, label, stamp, scar: *The owner couldn't be bothered to brand the cattle.*

brandish VERB = **wave**, raise, display, shake, swing, exhibit, flourish, wield, flaunt

brash ADJECTIVE = **bold**, forward, rude, arrogant, cocky, pushy (*informal*), brazen, presumptuous, impertinent, insolent, impudent, bumptious, cocksure, overconfident, hubristic, full of yourself **OPPOSITE:** timid

brassy ADJECTIVE **1** = **strident**, loud, harsh, piercing, jarring, noisy, grating, raucous, blaring, shrill, jangling, dissonant, cacophonous: *Musicians blast their brassy jazz from street corners.* **2** = **brazen**, forward, bold, brash, saucy, pushy (*informal*), pert, insolent, impudent, loud-mouthed, barefaced: *Alec and his brassy blonde wife* **3** = **flashy**, loud, blatant, vulgar, gaudy, garish, jazzy (*informal*), showy, obtrusive: *a woman with big brassy ear-rings* **OPPOSITE:** discreet

brat NOUN = **youngster**, kid (*informal*), urchin, imp, rascal, spoilt child, devil, puppy (*informal*), cub, scallywag (*informal*), whippersnapper, guttersnipe

bravado NOUN = **swagger**, boast, boasting, swaggering, vaunting, bluster, swashbuckling, bombast, braggadocio, boastfulness, fanfaronade (*rare*)

brave ADJECTIVE = **courageous**, daring, bold, heroic, adventurous, gritty, fearless, resolute, gallant, gutsy *(slang)*, audacious, intrepid, valiant, plucky, undaunted, unafraid, unflinching, dauntless, lion-hearted, valorous: *brave people who dare to challenge the tyrannical regimes* **OPPOSITE:** timid
▷ VERB = **confront**, face, suffer, challenge, bear, tackle, dare, endure, defy, withstand, stand up to: *She had to brave his anger and confess.*
OPPOSITE: give in to

> **QUOTATIONS**
> None but the brave deserves the fair
> [John Dryden *Alexander's Feast*]
>
> Fortune assists the bold
> [Virgil *Aeneid*]

bravery NOUN = **courage**, nerve, daring, pluck, spirit, bottle *(Brit. slang)*, guts *(informal)*, grit, fortitude, heroism, mettle, boldness, bravura, gallantry, valour, spunk *(informal)*, hardiness, fearlessness, intrepidity, indomitability, hardihood, dauntlessness, doughtiness, pluckiness, lion-heartedness
OPPOSITE: cowardice

> **QUOTATIONS**
> They are surely to be esteemed the bravest spirits who, having the clearest sense of both the pains and pleasures of life, do not on that account shrink from danger
> [Thucydides *The Peloponnesian War*]

bravo NOUN = **congratulations**, well done

bravura NOUN = **brilliance**, energy, spirit, display, punch *(informal)*, dash, animation, vigour, verve, panache, boldness, virtuosity, élan, exhibitionism, brio, ostentation

brawl NOUN = **fight**, battle, row *(informal)*, clash, disorder, scrap *(informal)*, fray, squabble, wrangle, skirmish, scuffle, punch-up *(Brit. informal)*, free-for-all *(informal)*, fracas, altercation, rumpus, broil, tumult, affray *(Law)*, shindig *(informal)*, donnybrook, ruckus *(informal)*, scrimmage, shindy *(informal)*, biffo *(Austral. slang)*, bagarre *(French)*, melee *or* mêlée: *He had been in a drunken street brawl.*
▷ VERB = **fight**, battle, scrap *(informal)*, wrestle, wrangle, tussle, scuffle, go at it hammer and tongs, fight like Kilkenny cats, altercate: *Gangs of youths brawled in the street.*

brawn NOUN = **muscle**, might, power, strength, muscles, beef *(informal)*, flesh, vigour, robustness, muscularity, beefiness *(informal)*, brawniness

bray VERB **1** = **neigh**, bellow, screech, heehaw: *The donkey brayed and tried to bolt.* **2** = **roar**, trumpet, bellow, hoot: *Neil brayed with angry laughter.*
▷ NOUN **1** = **neigh**, bellow, screech, heehaw: *It was a strange laugh, like the bray of a donkey.* **2** = **roar**, cry, shout, bellow, screech, hoot, bawl, harsh sound: *She cut him off with a bray of laughter.*

brazen ADJECTIVE = **bold**, forward, defiant, brash, saucy, audacious, pushy *(informal)*, shameless, unabashed, pert, unashamed, insolent, impudent, immodest, barefaced, brassy *(informal)*: *She's just a brazen hussy.* **OPPOSITE:** shy
brazen it out = **be unashamed**, persevere, be defiant, confront something, be impenitent, outface, outstare: *As for the scandal, he is as determined as ever to brazen it out.*

breach NOUN **1** = **nonobservance**, abuse, violation, infringement, trespass, disobedience, transgression, contravention, infraction, noncompliance: *The congressman was accused of a breach of secrecy laws.*
OPPOSITE: compliance
2 = **disagreement**, difference, division, separation, falling-out *(informal)*, quarrel, alienation, variance, severance, disaffection, schism, parting of the ways, estrangement, dissension: *the breach between Tito and Stalin* **3** = **opening**, crack, break, hole, split, gap, rent, rift, rupture, aperture, chasm, cleft, fissure: *A large battering ram hammered a breach in the wall.*

> **QUOTATIONS**
> Once more unto the breach, dear friends, once more
> [William Shakespeare *Henry V*]

bread NOUN **1** = **food**, provisions, fare, necessities, subsistence, kai *(N.Z. informal)*, nourishment, sustenance, victuals, nutriment, viands, aliment: *I go to work, I put bread on the table, I pay the mortgage.* **2** = **money**, funds, cash, finance, necessary *(informal)*, silver, tin *(slang)*, brass *(Northern English dialect)*, dough *(slang)*, dosh *(Brit. & Austral. slang)*, needful *(informal)*, shekels *(informal)*, dibs *(slang)*, ackers *(slang)*, spondulicks *(slang)*, rhino *(Brit. slang)*: *a period in which you could earn your bread by the sweat of your brow*

breadth NOUN **1** = **width**, spread, beam, span, latitude, broadness, wideness: *The breadth of the whole camp was 400 metres.* **2** = **extent**, area, reach, range, measure, size, scale, spread, sweep, scope, magnitude, compass, expanse, vastness, amplitude, comprehensiveness, extensiveness: *The breadth of his knowledge filled me with admiration.*

break VERB **1** = **shatter**, separate, destroy, split, divide, crack, snap, smash, crush, fragment, demolish, sever, trash *(slang)*, disintegrate, splinter, smash to smithereens, shiver: *He fell through the window, breaking the glass.* **OPPOSITE:** repair
2 = **fracture**, crack, smash: *She broke her leg in a skiing accident.* **3** = **burst**, tear, split: *The bandage must be put on when the blister breaks.* **4** = **disobey**, breach, defy, violate, disregard, flout, infringe, contravene, transgress, go counter to, infract *(Law)*: *We didn't know we were breaking the law.* **OPPOSITE:** obey
5 = **stop**, cut, check, suspend, interrupt, cut short, discontinue: *He aims to break the vicious cycle.*
6 = **disturb**, interrupt: *The noise broke my concentration.* **7** = **end**, stop, cut, drop, give up, abandon, suspend, interrupt, terminate, put an end to, discontinue, pull the plug on: *They have yet to break the link with the trade unions.* **8** = **weaken**, undermine, cow, tame, subdue, demoralize, dispirit: *He never let his jailers break him.* **9** = **ruin**, destroy, crush, humiliate, bring down, bankrupt, degrade, impoverish, demote, make bankrupt, bring to ruin: *The newspapers can make or break you.* **10** = **pause**, stop briefly, stop, rest, halt, cease, take a break, have a breather *(informal)*: *They broke for lunch.*
11 = **interrupt**, stop, suspend: *We broke our journey at a small country hotel.*
12 = **cushion**, reduce, ease, moderate, diminish, temper, soften, lessen, alleviate, lighten: *She was saved by bushes which broke her fall.* **13** = **be revealed**, come out, be reported, be published, be announced, be made public, be proclaimed, be let out, be imparted, be divulged, come out in the wash: *He resigned his post as Bishop when the scandal broke.* **14** = **reveal**, tell, announce, declare, disclose, proclaim, divulge, make known: *I worried for ages and decided I had better break the news.*
15 = **beat**, top, better, exceed, go beyond, excel, surpass, outstrip, outdo, cap *(informal)*: *The film has broken all box office records.* **16** = **happen**, appear, emerge, occur, erupt, burst out, come forth suddenly: *They continued their search as dawn broke.*
▷ NOUN **1** = **fracture**, opening, tear, hole, split, crack, gap, rent, breach, rift, rupture, gash, cleft, fissure: *a break in the earth's surface* **2** = **interval**, pause, recess, interlude, intermission, entr'acte: *They always play that music during the break.* **3** = **holiday**, leave, vacation, time off, recess, awayday, schoolie *(Austral.)*, accumulated day off or ADO *(Austral.)*: *They are currently taking a short break in Spain.* **4** = **stroke of luck**, chance, opportunity, advantage, fortune, opening: *The rain was a lucky break for the American.* **5** = **breach**, split, dispute, separation, rift, rupture, alienation, disaffection, schism, estrangement: *There is some threat of a break in relations between them.*
break away = **get away**, escape, flee, run away, break free, break loose, make your escape: *I broke away from him and rushed out into the hall.*
break down 1 = **stop working**, stop, seize up, conk out *(informal)*, go kaput *(informal)*, go phut, cark it *(Austral. & N.Z. slang)*: *Their car broke down.* **2** = **fail**, collapse, fall through, be unsuccessful, come unstuck, run aground, come to grief, come a cropper *(informal)*, turn out badly: *Paola's marriage broke down.*
3 = **be overcome**, crack up *(informal)*, go to pieces: *The young woman broke down and cried.*

The Language of Harriet Beecher Stowe

The American writer Harriet Beecher Stowe (1811–96) was born in Litchfield, Connecticut, the daughter of a clergyman. She wrote prolifically, supplying short stories and articles to various periodicals throughout her life. While she published several novels, none was more successful and enduringly popular than her first, *Uncle Tom's Cabin* (1852), which was a bestseller not only in America but throughout Europe. This was a sentimental tale of a virtuous black slave and his undeserved sufferings at the hands of a cruel white master, and it was credited with greatly popularizing the cause of Abolitionism in the USA leading up to the Civil War. Indeed, President Abraham Lincoln is supposed to have referred to her as 'the little lady who wrote the book that made this great war.'

Much of Stowe's typical language is centred on her main theme of the evils of slavery, and some of her most frequently used nouns are *slavery, master, Mas'r* (a colloquial form of 'Master'), *mistress,* and *labor.*

> We cannot be silent on those laws which deny, in effect, to the **slave** the sanctity of marriage, with all its joys, rights, and obligations; which separate, at the will of the **master**, the wife from the husband, and the children from the parents.

Especially in *Uncle Tom's Cabin,* Stowe is at pains to reproduce the typical everyday speech of uneducated Americans, both slaves and white. In this way, she frequently uses pseudo-phonetic transcriptions of dialogue, such as *Mas'r* and *de* (for 'the'), some of which, even though they may be both accurate and written with the best intentions, tend to sound patronizing to the 21st-century reader:

> Bery nice man, **de** Gineral! He comes of one of **de** bery fustest families in Old Virginny!

The great importance of religion in Stowe's life is shown in the marked prevalence of religious terms in her writing, not least in her theological works such as *Bible Heroines* (1878). Most common are nouns, and proper nouns, like *God, church, Bible, Christ,* and *spirit.* Similarly, two of her most recurrent adjectives are *Christian* and *religious.* Common collocations for *Christian* include *house, family, woman, community, church,* and *religion.*

> In laboring for the overthrow of American slavery you are pursuing a course of **Christian** duty as legitimate as in laboring to suppress the suttees of India, the cannibalism of the Fejee Islands, and other barbarities of heathenism.

Morality in general is also a dominant topic in Stowe's works, especially with a view to upholding what is right and setting a good example in the way one conducts one's everyday affairs. For example, the adjective *good* is almost ten times more common than *bad* or *evil,* and other adjectives such as *true* and *noble* have greater prominence than their opposites. *Hope, duty,* and *respect* are other frequently-met examples of this moralistic vein of writing.

Stowe was a great advocate of the importance of the family unit in the community, and her language clearly shows her respect for domesticity, and particularly the place of a married woman in creating and running a virtuous household. This can be seen in the many related nouns that she typically uses, including *child, house, family, mother, wife,* and *husband:*

> There is no more important duty devolving upon a **mother**, than the cultivation of habits of modesty and propriety in young **children**.

b

break in 1 = break and enter, enter, gain access: *The thief had broken in through a first-floor window.* **2 = interrupt**, intervene, interfere, intrude, burst in, interject, butt in, barge in, interpose, put your oar in, put your two cents in (*U.S. slang*): *Suddenly, O'Leary broke in with a suggestion.*
break off = stop talking, pause, stumble, falter, fumble, hem and haw *or* hum and haw: *He broke off in mid-sentence.*
break out 1 = begin, start, happen, occur, arise, set in, commence, spring up: *He was 29 when war broke out.* **2 = escape**, flee, bolt, burst out, get free, break loose, abscond, do a bunk (*Brit. slang*), do a Skase (*Austral. informal*): *The two men broke out and cut through a perimeter fence.* **3 = erupt**, gush, flare up, burst out, burst forth, pour forth: *A line of sweat broke out on her forehead.*
break someone in = initiate, train, accustom, habituate: *The band are breaking in a new backing vocalist.*
break something in = prepare, condition, tame: *I'm breaking in these new boots.*
break something off = detach, separate, divide, cut off, pull off, sever, part, remove, splinter, tear off, snap off: *He broke off a large piece of the clay.*
break something up = stop, end, suspend, disrupt, dismantle, disperse, terminate, disband, diffuse: *Police used tear gas to break up a demonstration.*
break through = succeed, make it (*informal*), achieve, do well, flourish, cut it (*informal*), get to the top, crack it (*informal*), make your mark (*informal*), shine forth: *There is still scope for new writers to break through.*
break through something = penetrate, go through, get past, burst through: *Protesters tried to break through a police cordon.*
break up 1 = finish, be suspended, adjourn, recess: *The meeting broke up half an hour later.* **2 = split up**, separate, part, divorce, end a relationship: *My girlfriend and I have broken up.* **3 = scatter**, separate, divide, dissolve: *The crowd broke up reluctantly.*
break with something *or* **someone = separate from**, drop (*informal*), reject, ditch (*slang*), renounce, depart from, break away from, part company with, repudiate, jilt: *It was a tough decision for him to break with Leeds.*

breakage NOUN **= break**, cut, tear, crack, rent, breach, fracture, rift, rupture, cleft, fissure

breakaway ADJECTIVE **= rebel**, revolutionary, rebellious, dissenting, insurgent, seceding, secessionist, heretical, mutinous, insubordinate, insurrectionary, schismatic

breakdown NOUN **1 = collapse**, crackup (*informal*): *They often seem depressed and close to breakdown.* **2 = analysis**, classification, dissection, categorization, detailed list, itemization: *The organisers were given a breakdown of the costs.*

breaker NOUN **= wave**, roller, comber, billow, white horse, whitecap

break-in NOUN **= burglary**, robbery, breaking and entering, home invasion (*Austral. & N.Z.*)

breakneck ADJECTIVE **= dangerous**, rapid, excessive, rash, reckless, precipitate, headlong, express

breakthrough NOUN **= development**, advance, progress, improvement, discovery, find, finding, invention, step forward, leap forwards, turn of events, quantum leap

break-up NOUN **1 = separation**, split, divorce, breakdown, ending, parting, breaking, splitting, wind-up, rift, disintegration, dissolution, termination: *a marital break-up* **2 = dissolution**, division, splitting, disintegration: *the break-up of British Rail*

breakwater NOUN **= sea wall**, spur, mole, jetty, groyne

breast NOUN **1 = heart**, feelings, thoughts, soul, being, emotions, core, sentiments, seat of the affections: *Happiness flowered in her breast.* **2 = bosom**, boobs *or* boobies, man boobs, moobs *or* moobies: *a skimpy top which barely covered her breasts*
▸ *related adjective:* mammary

breath NOUN **1 = inhalation**, breathing, pant, gasp, gulp, wheeze, exhalation, respiration: *He took a deep breath and began to climb the stairs.* **2 = gust**, sigh, puff, flutter, flurry, whiff, draught, waft, zephyr, slight movement, faint breeze: *Not even a breath of wind stirred the pine branches.* **3 = trace**, suggestion, hint, whisper, suspicion, murmur, undertone, intimation: *It was left to her to add a breath of common sense.* **4 = rest**, breather: *He had to stop for breath.* **5 = life**, energy, existence, vitality, animation, life force, lifeblood, mauri (*N.Z.*): *Here is no light, no breath, no warm flesh.*

breathe VERB **1 = inhale and exhale**, pant, gasp, puff, gulp, wheeze, respire, draw in breath: *Always breathe through your nose.* **2 = whisper**, say, voice, express, sigh, utter, articulate, murmur: *He never breathed a word about our conversation.* **3 = instil**, inspire, pass on, inject, impart, infuse, imbue: *It is the readers who breathe life into a newspaper.*

breather NOUN **= rest**, break, halt, pause, recess, breathing space, breath of air

breathless ADJECTIVE **1 = out of breath**, winded, exhausted, panting, gasping, choking, gulping, wheezing, out of whack (*informal*), short-winded: *I was a little breathless and my heartbeat was fast.* **2 = excited**, anxious, curious, eager, enthusiastic, impatient, agog, on tenterhooks, in suspense: *We were breathless with anticipation.*

breathtaking ADJECTIVE **= amazing**, striking, exciting, brilliant, dramatic, stunning (*informal*), impressive, thrilling, overwhelming, magnificent, astonishing, sensational, eye-popping (*informal*), awesome, wondrous (*archaic, literary*), awe-inspiring, jaw-dropping, heart-stirring

breed NOUN **1 = variety**, race, stock, type, species, strain, pedigree: *rare breeds of cattle* **2 = kind**, sort, type, variety, brand, stamp: *the new breed of walking holidays*
▹ VERB **1 = rear**, tend, keep, raise, maintain, farm, look after, care for, bring up, nurture, nourish: *He lived alone, breeding horses and dogs.* **2 = reproduce**, multiply, propagate, procreate, produce offspring, bear young, bring forth young, generate offspring, beget offspring, develop: *Frogs will usually breed in any convenient pond.* **3 = produce**, cause, create, occasion, generate, bring about, arouse, originate, give rise to, stir up: *If they are unemployed it's bound to breed resentment.*

breeding NOUN **= refinement**, style, culture, taste, manners, polish, grace, courtesy, elegance, sophistication, delicacy, cultivation, politeness, civility, gentility, graciousness, urbanity, politesse

breeze NOUN **= light wind**, air, whiff, draught, gust, waft, zephyr, breath of wind, current of air, puff of air, capful of wind: *a cool summer breeze*
▹ VERB **= sweep**, move briskly, pass, trip, sail, hurry, sally, glide, flit: *Lopez breezed into the room.*

breezy ADJECTIVE **1 = carefree**, casual, lively, sparkling, sunny, informal, cheerful, animated, upbeat (*informal*), buoyant, airy, easy-going, genial, jaunty, chirpy (*informal*), sparky, sprightly, vivacious, debonair, blithe, free and easy, full of beans (*informal*), light, light-hearted: *his bright and breezy personality* **OPPOSITE:** serious **2 = windy**, fresh, airy, blustery, blowing, gusty, squally, blowy, blusterous: *The day was breezy and warm.* **OPPOSITE:** calm

brevity NOUN **1 = shortness**, transience, impermanence, ephemerality, briefness, transitoriness: *The bonus of this homely soup is the brevity of its cooking time.* **2 = conciseness**, economy, crispness, concision, terseness, succinctness, curtness, pithiness: *The brevity of the letter concerned me.*
OPPOSITE: wordiness

> **QUOTATIONS**
> Brevity is the soul of wit
> [William Shakespeare *Hamlet*]
>
> I strive to be brief, and I become obscure
> [Horace *Ars Poetica*]

brew VERB **1 = boil**, make, soak, steep, stew, infuse (*tea*): *He brewed a pot of coffee.* **2 = make**, ferment, prepare by fermentation: *I brew my own beer.* **3 = start**, develop, gather, foment: *At home a crisis was brewing.* **4 = develop**,

form, gather, foment: *We'd seen the storm brewing when we were out on the boat.*
▷ NOUN = **drink**, preparation, mixture, blend, liquor, beverage, infusion, concoction, fermentation, distillation: *a mild herbal brew*

bribe NOUN = **inducement**, incentive, pay-off *(informal)*, graft *(informal)*, sweetener *(slang)*, kickback *(U.S.)*, sop, backhander *(slang)*, enticement, hush money *(slang)*, payola *(informal)*, allurement, corrupting gift, reward for treachery: *He was being investigated for receiving bribes.*
▷ VERB = **buy off**, reward, pay off *(informal)*, lure, corrupt, get at, square, suborn, grease the palm *or* hand of *(slang)*, influence by gifts, oil the palm of *(informal)*: *The company bribed the workers to be quiet.*

bribery NOUN = **corruption**, graft *(informal)*, inducement, buying off, payola *(informal)*, crookedness *(informal)*, palm-greasing *(slang)*, subornation

bric-a-brac NOUN = **knick-knacks**, ornaments, trinkets, baubles, curios, objets d'art *(French)*, gewgaws, bibelots, kickshaws, objects of virtu

bridal ADJECTIVE = **matrimonial**, marriage, wedding, marital, bride's, nuptial, conjugal, spousal, connubial, hymeneal

bride NOUN = **wife**, newly-wed, marriage partner, wifey *(informal)*

bridegroom NOUN = **husband**, groom, newly-wed, marriage partner

bridge NOUN **1** = **arch**, span, viaduct, flyover, overpass, fixed link *(Canad.)*: *He walked over the railway bridge.* **2** = **link**, tie, bond, connection: *They saw themselves as a bridge to peace.*
▷ VERB **1** = **span**, cross, go over, cross over, traverse, reach across, extend across, arch over: *a tree used to bridge the river* **2** = **reconcile**, unite, resolve: *She bridged the gap between pop music and opera.*
OPPOSITE: divide

bridle NOUN = **rein**, curb, control, check, restraint, trammels: *She dismounted and took her horse's bridle.*
▷ VERB **1** = **get angry**, draw (yourself) up, bristle, seethe, see red, be infuriated, rear up, be indignant, be maddened, raise your hackles, get your dander up *(slang)*, get your back up: *He bridled at the shortness of her tone.*
2 = **curb**, control, master, govern, moderate, restrain, rein, subdue, repress, constrain, keep in check, check, keep a tight rein on, keep on a string: *I must learn to bridle my tongue.*

brief ADJECTIVE **1** = **short**, fast, quick, temporary, fleeting, swift, short-lived, little, hasty, momentary, ephemeral, quickie *(informal)*, transitory: *This time their visit is brief.*
OPPOSITE: long **2** = **concise**, short, limited, to the point, crisp, compressed, terse, curt, laconic, succinct, clipped, pithy, thumbnail, monosyllabic: *Write a very brief description of a typical problem.*
OPPOSITE: long **3** = **curt**, short, sharp, blunt, abrupt, brusque: *He was brief, rapid, decisive.*
▷ VERB = **inform**, prime, prepare, advise, fill in *(informal)*, instruct, clue in *(informal)*, gen up *(Brit. informal)*, put in the picture *(informal)*, give a rundown, keep (someone) posted, give the gen *(Brit. informal)*: *A spokesman briefed reporters.*
▷ NOUN **1** = **summary**, résumé, outline, sketch, abstract, summing-up, digest, epitome, rundown, synopsis, précis, recapitulation, abridgment: *He gives me my first brief of the situation.* **2** = **case**, defence, argument, data, contention: *a lawyer's brief*

briefing NOUN **1** = **conference**, meeting, priming: *They're holding a press briefing tomorrow.* **2** = **instructions**, information, priming, directions, instruction, preparation, guidance, preamble, rundown: *The Chancellor gives a twenty-minute briefing to his backbenchers.*

briefly ADVERB **1** = **quickly**, shortly, precisely, casually, temporarily, abruptly, hastily, briskly, momentarily, hurriedly, curtly, summarily, fleetingly, cursorily: *He smiled briefly.* **2** = **in outline**, in brief, in passing, in a nutshell, concisely, in a few words: *There are four alternatives; they are described briefly below.*

brigade NOUN **1** = **corps**, company, force, unit, division, troop, squad, crew, team, outfit, regiment, contingent, squadron, detachment: *the men of the Seventh Armoured Brigade*
2 = **group**, party, body, band, camp, squad, organization, crew, bunch *(informal)*: *the healthy-eating brigade*

bright ADJECTIVE **1** = **vivid**, rich, brilliant, intense, glowing, colourful, highly-coloured: *a bright red dress*
2 = **shining**, flashing, beaming, glowing, blazing, sparkling, glittering, dazzling, illuminated, gleaming, shimmering, twinkling, radiant, luminous, glistening, resplendent, scintillating, lustrous, lambent, effulgent: *Newborns hate bright lights and loud noises.*
3 = **intelligent**, smart, clever, knowing, thinking, quick, aware, sharp, keen, acute, alert, rational, penetrating, enlightened, apt, astute, brainy, wide-awake, clear-headed, perspicacious, quick-witted: *I was convinced that he was brighter than average.*
OPPOSITE: stupid **4** = **clever**, brilliant, smart, sensible, cunning, ingenious, inventive, canny: *There are lots of books crammed with bright ideas.* **5** = **cheerful**, happy, glad, lively, jolly, merry, upbeat *(informal)*, joyous, joyful, genial, chirpy *(informal)*, sparky, vivacious, full of beans *(informal)*, gay, light-hearted: *The boy was so bright and animated.* **6** = **promising**, good, encouraging, excellent, golden, optimistic, hopeful, favourable, prosperous, rosy, auspicious, propitious, palmy: *Both had successful careers and the future looked bright.*
7 = **sunny**, clear, fair, pleasant, clement, lucid, cloudless, unclouded, sunlit: *the bright winter sky*
OPPOSITE: cloudy

brighten VERB **1** = **cheer up**, rally, take heart, perk up, buck up *(informal)*, become cheerful: *Seeing him, she seemed to brighten a little.* **OPPOSITE:** become gloomy **2** = **light up**, shine, glow, gleam, clear up, lighten, enliven: *Her tearful eyes brightened with interest.*
OPPOSITE: dim **3** = **enliven**, animate, make brighter, vitalize: *Planted tubs*

BRIDGES

BRIDGES

Brooklyn Bridge
Clifton Suspension Bridge
Forth Railway Bridge
Forth Road Bridge
Gateshead Millennium Bridge
Golden Gate Bridge
Halfpenny Bridge
Humber Bridge
London Bridge
Millennium Bridge
Oakland Bay Bridge
Rainbow Bridge
Rialto Bridge
Severn Bridge
Bridge of Sighs
Skye Bridge
Sydney Harbour Bridge
Tower Bridge
Tyne Bridge
Waterloo Bridge
Westminster Bridge

TYPES OF BRIDGE

aqueduct
Bailey bridge
balance, bascule, *or* counterpoise bridge
box-girder bridge
cable-stayed bridge
cantilever bridge
clapper bridge
deck bridge
drawbridge
flyover
footbridge
pivot, swing, *or* turn bridge
pontoon bridge
snow bridge
suspension bridge
truss bridge
turn bridge
viaduct

brightened the area outside the door. **4 = become brighter**, light up, glow, gleam, clear up: *The sky above the ridge of the mountains brightened.*

brightness NOUN **1 = vividness**, intensity, brilliance, splendour, resplendence: *You'll be impressed with the brightness of the colours.* **2 = intelligence**, intellect, brains *(informal)*, awareness, sharpness, alertness, cleverness, quickness, acuity, brain power, smarts *(slang, chiefly U.S.)*, smartness: *Her brightness seemed quite intimidating to me.*

b

brilliance *or* **brilliancy** NOUN **1 = cleverness**, talent, wisdom, distinction, genius, excellence, greatness, aptitude, inventiveness, acuity, giftedness, braininess: *His brilliance and genius will always remain.* **OPPOSITE:** stupidity **2 = brightness**, blaze, intensity, sparkle, glitter, dazzle, gleam, sheen, lustre, radiance, luminosity, vividness, resplendence, effulgence, refulgence: *the brilliance of the sun on the water* **OPPOSITE:** darkness **3 = splendour**, glamour, grandeur, magnificence, éclat, gorgeousness, illustriousness, pizzazz *or* pizazz *(informal)*, gilt: *The opera house was perfection, all brilliance and glamour.*

brilliant ADJECTIVE **1 = intelligent**, sharp, intellectual, alert, clever, quick, acute, profound, rational, penetrating, discerning, inventive, astute, brainy, perspicacious, quick-witted: *She had a brilliant mind.* **OPPOSITE:** stupid **2 = expert**, masterly, talented, gifted, accomplished: *a brilliant pianist* **OPPOSITE:** untalented **3 = splendid**, grand, famous, celebrated, rare, supreme, outstanding, remarkable, superb, magnificent, sterling, glorious, exceptional, notable, renowned, heroic, admirable, eminent, sublime, illustrious: *a brilliant success* **4 = bright**, shining, intense, sparkling, glittering, dazzling, vivid, radiant, luminous, ablaze, resplendent, scintillating, lustrous, coruscating, refulgent, lambent: *The event was held in brilliant sunshine.* **OPPOSITE:** dark

brim NOUN **= rim**, edge, border, lip, margin, verge, brink, flange: *The toilet was full to the brim with insects.*
▷ VERB **1 = be full**, spill, well over, run over, overflow, spill over, brim over: *They are brimming with confidence.* **2 = fill**, well over, fill up, overflow: *Michael looked at him imploringly, his eyes brimming with tears.*

brine NOUN **= salt water**, saline solution, pickling solution

bring VERB **1 = fetch**, take, carry, bear, transfer, deliver, transport, import, convey: *My father brought home a book for me.* **2 = take**, guide, conduct, accompany, escort, usher: *I brought him inside and dried him off.* **3 = cause**, produce, create, effect, occasion, result in, contribute to, inflict, wreak, engender: *The revolution brought more trouble than it was worth.* **4 = make**, force, influence, convince, persuade, prompt, compel, induce, move, dispose, sway, prevail on *or* upon: *I could not even bring myself to enter the house.*
bring someone up = rear, raise, support, train, develop, teach, nurse, breed, foster, educate, care for, nurture: *She brought up four children.*
bring something about = cause, produce, create, effect, manage, achieve, occasion, realize, generate, accomplish, give rise to, make happen, effectuate, bring to pass: *The two sides are attempting to bring about fundamental changes.*
bring something down 1 = overturn, reduce, undermine, overthrow, abase: *They were threatening to bring down the government.* **2 = reduce**, cut, drop, lower, slash, decrease: *The air fares war will bring down prices.* **3 = cut down**, level, fell, hew, lop, raze: *The lumberjacks brought the tree down.* **4 = demolish**, level, destroy, dismantle, flatten, knock down, pull down, tear down, bulldoze, raze, kennet *(Austral. slang)*, jeff *(Austral. slang)*: *Such forces would normally bring the building down.*
bring something in 1 = introduce, start, found, launch, establish, set up, institute, organize, pioneer, initiate, usher in, inaugurate: *They brought in a controversial law.* **2 = produce**, return, net, realize, generate, be worth, yield, gross, fetch, accrue: *The business brings in about £24,000 a year.*
bring something off = accomplish, achieve, perform, carry out, succeed, execute, discharge, pull off, carry off, bring to pass: *They were about to bring off an even bigger coup.*
bring something up = mention, raise, introduce, point out, refer to, allude to, broach, call attention to, speak about *or* of: *Why are you bringing that up now?*

brink NOUN **= edge**, point, limit, border, lip, margin, boundary, skirt, frontier, fringe, verge, threshold, rim, brim

brio NOUN **= energy**, spirit, enthusiasm, dash, pep, zip *(informal)*, animation, vigour, verve, zest, panache, gusto, get-up-and-go *(informal)*, élan, vivacity, liveliness

brisk ADJECTIVE **1 = quick**, lively, energetic, active, vigorous, animated, bustling, speedy, nimble, agile, sprightly, vivacious, spry: *The horse broke into a brisk trot.* **OPPOSITE:** slow **2 = short**, sharp, brief, blunt, rude, tart, abrupt, no-nonsense, terse, gruff, pithy, brusque, offhand, monosyllabic, ungracious, uncivil, snappish: *She attempted to reason with him in a rather brisk fashion.* **3 = invigorating**, fresh, biting, sharp, keen, stimulating, crisp, bracing, refreshing, exhilarating, nippy: *The breeze was cool, brisk and invigorating.* **OPPOSITE:** tiring

briskly ADVERB **1 = quickly**, smartly, promptly, rapidly, readily, actively, efficiently, vigorously, energetically, pronto *(informal)*, nimbly, posthaste: *Eve walked briskly down the corridor.* **2 = rapidly**, quickly, apace, pdq *(slang)*: *A trader said gold was selling briskly on the local market.* **3 = brusquely**, firmly, decisively, incisively: *'Anyhow,' she added briskly, 'it's none of my business.'*

bristle NOUN **= hair**, spine, thorn, whisker, barb, stubble, prickle: *two days' growth of bristles*
▷ VERB **1 = stand up**, rise, prickle, stand on end, horripilate: *It makes the hair on the nape of my neck bristle.* **2 = be angry**, rage, seethe, flare up, bridle, see red, be infuriated, spit *(informal)*, go ballistic *(slang, chiefly U.S.)*, be maddened, wig out *(slang)*, get your dander up *(slang)*: *He bristled with indignation.* **3 = abound**, crawl, be alive, hum, swarm, teem, be thick: *The country bristles with armed groups.*

Briton NOUN **= Brit** *(informal)*, limey *(U.S. & Canad. slang)*, Britisher, pommy *or* pom *(Austral. & N.Z. slang)*, Anglo-Saxon

brittle ADJECTIVE **1 = fragile**, delicate, crisp, crumbling, frail, crumbly, breakable, shivery, friable, frangible, shatterable: *Pine is brittle and breaks easily.* **OPPOSITE:** tough **2 = tense**, nervous, edgy, stiff, wired *(slang)*, irritable, curt: *a brittle man*

broach VERB **1 = bring up**, approach, introduce, mention, speak of, talk of, open up, hint at, touch on, raise the subject of: *Eventually I broached the subject of her early life.* **2 = open**, crack, pierce, puncture, uncork: *He would ask the landlord to broach a new barrel of wine.*

broad ADJECTIVE **1 = wide**, large, ample, generous, expansive: *His shoulders were broad and his waist narrow.* **2 = large**, huge, comfortable, vast, extensive, ample, spacious, expansive, roomy, voluminous, capacious, uncrowded, commodious, beamy *(of a ship)*, sizable *or* sizeable: *a broad expanse of lawn* **OPPOSITE:** narrow **3 = full**, general, comprehensive, complete, wide, global, catholic, sweeping, extensive, wide-ranging, umbrella, thorough, unlimited, inclusive, far-reaching, exhaustive, all-inclusive, all-embracing, overarching, encyclopedic: *A broad range of issues was discussed.* **4 = universal**, general, common, wide, sweeping, worldwide, widespread, wide-ranging, far-reaching: *a film with broad appeal* **5 = general**, loose, vague, approximate, indefinite, ill-defined, inexact, nonspecific, unspecific, undetailed: *a broad outline of the Society's development* **6 = clear**, open, full, plain: *Militants shot a man dead in broad daylight today.* **7 = vulgar**, blue, dirty, gross, crude, rude, naughty, coarse, indecent, improper, suggestive, risqué, boorish, uncouth, unrefined, ribald, indelicate, near the knuckle *(informal)*, indecorous, unmannerly: *Use wit rather than broad humour.*

broadcast NOUN = **transmission**, show, programme, telecast, podcast, open-line *(Canad.)*: *a broadcast on the national radio*
▷ VERB **1 = transmit**, show, send, air, radio, cable, beam, send out, relay, televise, disseminate, put on the air, podcast: *CNN also broadcasts programmes in Europe.* **2 = make public**, report, announce, publish, spread, advertise, proclaim, circulate, disseminate, promulgate, shout from the rooftops *(informal)*: *Don't broadcast your business outside the family.*

broaden VERB = **expand**, increase, develop, spread, extend, stretch, open up, swell, supplement, widen, enlarge, augment OPPOSITE: restrict

broadly ADVERB **1 = widely**, greatly, hugely, vastly, extensively, expansively: *Charles grinned broadly.* **2 = generally**, commonly, widely, universally, popularly: *This gives children a more broadly based education.* OPPOSITE: narrowly

broadside NOUN = **attack**, criticism, censure, swipe, denunciation, diatribe, philippic

brochure NOUN = **booklet**, advertisement, leaflet, hand-out, circular, pamphlet, folder, mailshot, handbill

broekies PLURAL NOUN = **underpants**, pants, briefs, drawers, knickers, panties, boxer shorts, Y-fronts®, underdaks *(Austral. slang)*

broke ADJECTIVE = **penniless**, short, ruined, bust *(informal)*, bankrupt, impoverished, in the red, cleaned out *(slang)*, insolvent, down and out, skint *(Brit. slang)*, strapped for cash *(informal)*, dirt-poor *(informal)*, flat broke *(informal)*, penurious, on your uppers, stony-broke *(Brit. slang)*, in queer street *(informal)*, without two pennies to rub together *(informal)*, without a penny to your name OPPOSITE: rich

broken ADJECTIVE **1 = interrupted**, disturbed, incomplete, erratic, disconnected, intermittent, fragmentary, spasmodic, discontinuous: *nights of broken sleep* **2 = imperfect**, halting, hesitating, stammering, disjointed: *Eric could only respond in broken English.* **3 = smashed**, destroyed, burst, shattered, fragmented, fractured, demolished, severed, ruptured, rent, separated, shivered: *Damp air came through the broken window.* **4 = defective**, not working, ruined, imperfect, out of order, not functioning, on the blink *(slang)*, on its last legs, kaput *(informal)*: *a broken guitar and a rusty snare drum* **5 = violated**, forgotten, ignored, disregarded, not kept, infringed, retracted, disobeyed, dishonoured, transgressed, traduced: *History is made up of broken promises.* **6 = defeated**, beaten, crushed, humbled, crippled, tamed, subdued, oppressed, overpowered, vanquished, demoralized, browbeaten: *He looked a broken man.*

broken-down ADJECTIVE = **not in working order**, old, worn out, out of order, dilapidated, not functioning, out of commission, on the blink *(slang)*, inoperative, kaput *(informal)*, in disrepair, on the fritz *(U.S. slang)*

brokenhearted ADJECTIVE = **heartbroken**, devastated, disappointed, despairing, miserable, choked, desolate, mournful, prostrated, grief-stricken, sorrowful, wretched, disconsolate, inconsolable, crestfallen, down in the dumps *(informal)*, heart-sick

broker NOUN = **dealer**, marketer, agent, trader, supplier, merchant, entrepreneur, negotiator, chandler, mediator, intermediary, wholesaler, middleman, factor, purveyor, go-between, tradesman, merchandiser

bronze ADJECTIVE = **reddish-brown**, copper, tan, rust, chestnut, brownish, copper-coloured, yellowish-brown, reddish-tan, metallic brown

brood NOUN **1 = offspring**, young, issue, breed, infants, clutch, hatch, litter, chicks, progeny: *The last brood of the pair was hatched.* **2 = children**, family, offspring, progeny, nearest and dearest, flesh and blood, ainga *(N.Z.)*: *She flew to the defence of her brood.*
▷ VERB = **think**, obsess, muse, ponder, fret, meditate, agonize, mull over, mope, ruminate, eat your heart out, dwell upon, repine: *She constantly broods about her family.*

brook[1] NOUN = **stream**, burn *(Scot. & Northern English)*, rivulet, gill *(dialect)*, beck, watercourse, rill, streamlet, runnel *(literary)*: *He threw the hatchet in the brook.*

brook[2] VERB = **tolerate**, stand, allow, suffer, accept, bear, stomach, endure, swallow, hack *(slang)*, abide, put up with *(informal)*, withstand, countenance, support, thole *(dialect)*: *The army will brook no weakening of its power.*

brothel NOUN = **whorehouse**, red-light district, bordello, cathouse *(U.S. slang)*, house of ill repute, knocking shop *(slang)*, bawdy house *(archaic)*, house of prostitution, bagnio, house of ill fame, stews *(archaic)*

> QUOTATIONS
> Prisons are built with stones of Law, brothels with bricks of Religion [William Blake *The Marriage of Heaven and Hell*]

brother NOUN **1 = male sibling**: *Have you got any brothers and sisters?* **2 = comrade**, partner, colleague, associate, mate, pal *(informal)*, companion, cock *(Brit. informal)*, chum *(informal)*, fellow member, confrère, compeer: *their freedom-loving brothers* **3 = monk**, cleric, friar, monastic, religious, regular: *priests and religious brothers*
▸ *related adjective:* fraternal

brotherhood NOUN **1 = fellowship**, kinship, companionship, comradeship, friendliness, camaraderie, brotherliness: *He believed in socialism and the brotherhood of man.* **2 = association**, order, union, community, society, league, alliance, clan, guild, fraternity, clique, coterie: *a secret international brotherhood*

brotherly ADJECTIVE = **fraternal**, friendly, neighbourly, sympathetic, affectionate, benevolent, kind, amicable, altruistic, philanthropic

brow NOUN **1 = forehead**, temple: *She wrinkled her brow inquisitively.* **2 = top**, summit, peak, edge, tip, crown, verge, brink, rim, crest, brim: *He climbed to the brow of the hill.*

brown ADJECTIVE **1 = brunette**, dark, bay, coffee, chocolate, brick, toasted, ginger, rust, chestnut, hazel, dun, auburn, tawny, umber, donkey

SHADES OF BROWN

almond	burnt sienna	coffee	khaki	oxblood	taupe
amber	burnt umber	copper	liver	russet	tawny
auburn	butternut	cream	mahogany	rust	teak
bay	café au lait	drab	mocha	sable	terracotta
beige	camel	dun	mousy	sand	tortoiseshell
biscuit	chestnut	ecru	mushroom	seal brown	umber
bisque	chocolate	fawn	neutral	sepia	walnut
bistre	cinnabar	ginger	nutbrown	sienna	
bronze	cinnamon	hazel	nutmeg	sorrel	
buff	cocoa	henna	oatmeal	tan	

brown, fuscous: *her deep brown eyes* **2 = tanned**, browned, bronze, bronzed, tan, dusky, sunburnt: *rows of bodies slowly going brown in the sun*
▷ VERB **= fry**, cook, grill, sear, sauté: *He browned the chicken in a frying pan.*

browse VERB **1 = skim**, scan, glance at, survey, look through, look round, dip into, leaf through, peruse, flip through, examine cursorily: *There are plenty of biographies for him to browse.* **2 = graze**, eat, feed, crop, pasture, nibble: *three red deer stags browsing 50 yards from my lodge*

bruise NOUN **= discoloration**, mark, injury, trauma *(Pathology)*, blemish, black mark, contusion, black-and-blue mark: *How did you get that bruise on your cheek?*
▷ VERB **1 = hurt**, injure, mark, blacken: *I had only bruised my knee.* **2 = damage**, mark, mar, blemish, discolour: *Be sure to store them carefully or they'll get bruised.* **3 = injure**, hurt, pain, wound, slight, insult, sting, offend, grieve, displease, rile, pique: *Men's egos are so easily bruised.*

bruiser NOUN **= tough**, heavy *(slang)*, rough *(informal)*, bully, thug, gorilla *(informal)*, hard man, rowdy, tough guy, hoodlum, bully boy, ruffian, roughneck *(slang)*

brunt NOUN **= full force**, force, pressure, violence, shock, stress, impact, strain, burden, thrust

brush[1] NOUN **1 = broom**, sweeper, besom: *Scrub lightly with a brush, then rinse.* **2 = conflict**, fight, clash, set-to *(informal)*, scrap *(informal)*, confrontation, skirmish, tussle, fracas, spot of bother *(informal)*, slight engagement: *It is his third brush with the law in less than a year.* **3 = encounter**, meeting, confrontation, rendezvous: *the trauma of a brush with death*
▷ VERB **1 = clean**, wash, polish, buff: *Have you brushed your teeth?* **2 = touch**, come into contact with, sweep, kiss, stroke, glance, flick, scrape, graze, caress: *I felt her hair brushing the back of my shoulder.*
brush someone off = ignore, cut, reject, dismiss, slight, blank *(slang)*, put down, snub, disregard, scorn, disdain, spurn, rebuff, repudiate, disown, cold-shoulder, kiss off *(slang, chiefly U.S. & Canad.)*, send to Coventry: *She just brushed me off.*
brush something aside = dismiss, ignore, discount, override, disregard, sweep aside, have no time for, kiss off *(slang, chiefly U.S. & Canad.)*: *He brushed aside my views on politics.*
brush something up *or* **brush up on something = revise**, study, go over, cram, polish up, read up on, relearn, bone up on *(informal)*, refresh your memory: *I had hoped to brush up my Spanish.*

brush[2] NOUN **= shrubs**, bushes, scrub, underwood, undergrowth, thicket, copse, brushwood: *a meadow of low brush and grass*

brusque ADJECTIVE **= curt**, short, sharp, blunt, tart, abrupt, hasty, terse, surly, gruff, impolite, monosyllabic, discourteous, unmannerly **OPPOSITE:** polite

brutal ADJECTIVE **1 = cruel**, harsh, savage, grim, vicious, ruthless, ferocious, callous, sadistic, heartless, atrocious, inhuman, merciless, cold-blooded, inhumane, brutish, bloodthirsty, remorseless, barbarous, animalistic, pitiless, uncivilized, hard-hearted: *He was the victim of a very brutal murder.* **OPPOSITE:** kind **2 = harsh**, tough, severe, rough, rude, indifferent, insensitive, callous, merciless, unconcerned, uncaring, gruff, bearish, tactless, unfeeling, impolite, uncivil, unmannerly: *She spoke with a brutal honesty.* **OPPOSITE:** sensitive

brutality NOUN **= cruelty**, atrocity, ferocity, savagery, ruthlessness, barbarism, inhumanity, barbarity, viciousness, brutishness, bloodthirstiness, savageness

brutally ADVERB **= cruelly**, fiercely, savagely, ruthlessly, viciously, mercilessly, ferociously, remorselessly, in cold blood, callously, murderously, pitilessly, heartlessly, inhumanly, barbarously, brutishly, barbarically, hardheartedly

brute NOUN **1 = savage**, devil, monster, beast, barbarian, fiend, swine, ogre, ghoul, sadist: *a drunken brute* **2 = beast**, animal, creature, wild animal: *a big brute of a dog*
▷ ADJECTIVE **= physical**, bodily, mindless, instinctive, senseless, unthinking: *He used brute force to take control.*

brutish ADJECTIVE **= coarse**, stupid, gross, cruel, savage, crude, vulgar, barbarian, crass, boorish, uncouth, loutish, subhuman, swinish

bubble NOUN **= air ball**, drop, bead, blister, blob, droplet, globule, vesicle: *a bubble of gas trapped under the surface*
▷ VERB **1 = boil**, seethe: *Heat the seasoned stock until it is bubbling.* **2 = foam**, fizz, froth, churn, agitate, percolate, effervesce: *The fermenting wine bubbled over the top.* **3 = gurgle**, splash, murmur, trickle, ripple, babble, trill, burble, lap, purl, plash: *He looked at the stream bubbling through the trees nearby.*

bubbly ADJECTIVE **1 = lively**, happy, excited, animated, merry, bouncy, elated, sparky, alive and kicking, full of beans *(informal)*: *a bubbly girl who likes to laugh* **2 = frothy**, sparkling, fizzy, effervescent, carbonated, foamy, sudsy, lathery: *a nice hot bubbly bath*

buccaneer NOUN **= pirate**, privateer, corsair, freebooter, sea-rover

buckle NOUN **= fastener**, catch, clip, clasp, hasp: *He wore a belt with a large brass buckle.*
▷ VERB **1 = fasten**, close, secure, hook, clasp: *A man came out buckling his belt.* **2 = distort**, bend, warp, crumple, contort: *A freak wave had buckled the deck.* **3 = collapse**, bend, twist, fold, give way, subside, cave in, crumple: *His right leg buckled under him.*
buckle down = apply yourself, set to, fall to, pitch in, get busy, get cracking *(informal)*, exert yourself, put your shoulder to the wheel: *I just buckled down and got on with playing.*

bud NOUN **= shoot**, branch, sprout, twig, sprig, offshoot, scion: *The first buds appeared on the trees.*
▷ VERB **= develop**, grow, shoot, sprout, burgeon, burst forth, pullulate: *The leaves were budding on the trees now.*

budding ADJECTIVE **= developing**, beginning, growing, promising, potential, burgeoning, fledgling, embryonic

buddy NOUN **= friend**, mate *(informal)*, pal, companion, comrade, chum *(informal)*, crony, main man *(slang, chiefly U.S.)*, homeboy *(slang, chiefly U.S.)*, cobber *(Austral. & N.Z. old-fashioned, informal)*, E hoa *(N.Z.)*

budge VERB **1 = yield**, change, bend, concede, surrender, comply, give way, capitulate: *Both sides say they will not budge.* **2 = persuade**, influence, convince, sway: *The Prime Minister was not to be budged by the verbal assault.* **3 = move**, roll, slide, stir, give way, change position: *The snake still refused to budge.* **4 = dislodge**, move, push, roll, remove, transfer, shift, slide, stir, propel: *I pulled and pulled but I couldn't budge it.*

budget NOUN **= allowance**, means, funds, income, finances, resources, allocation: *A designer would be beyond their budget.*
▷ VERB **= plan**, estimate, allocate, cost, ration, apportion, cost out: *I'm learning how to budget my finances.*

buff[1] ADJECTIVE **= fawn**, cream, tan, beige, yellowish, ecru, straw-coloured, sand-coloured, yellowish-brown, biscuit-coloured, camel-coloured, oatmeal-coloured: *a buff envelope*
▷ VERB **= polish**, clean, smooth, brush, shine, rub, wax, brighten, burnish: *He was already buffing the car's hubs.*
in the buff = naked, bare, nude, in the raw *(informal)*, unclothed, in the altogether *(informal)*, buck naked *(slang)*, unclad, in your birthday suit *(informal)*, scuddy *(slang)*, without a stitch on *(informal)*, with bare skin, in the bare scud *(slang)*: *My character had to appear in the buff for some scenes.*

buff[2] NOUN **= expert**, fan, addict, enthusiast, freak *(informal)*, admirer, whizz *(informal)*, devotee, connoisseur, fiend *(informal)*, grandmaster, hotshot *(informal)*, aficionado, wonk *(informal)*, maven *(U.S.)*, fundi *(S. African)*: *She is a real film buff.*

buffer NOUN **= safeguard**, screen, shield, cushion, intermediary, bulwark

buffet[1] NOUN **1 = smorgasbord**, counter, cold table: *A cold buffet had been laid out in the dining room.* **2 = snack bar**, café, cafeteria, brasserie, salad bar, refreshment counter: *We sat in the station buffet sipping tea.*

buffet[2] VERB **= knock**, push, bang, rap, slap, bump, smack, shove, thump, cuff, jolt, wallop *(informal)*, box: *Their plane had been severely buffeted by storms.*

buffoon NOUN **= clown**, fool, comic, comedian, wag, joker, jester, dag *(N.Z. informal)*, harlequin, droll, silly billy *(informal)*, joculator *or (fem.)* joculatrix

bug NOUN **1 = illness**, disease, complaint, virus, infection, disorder, disability, sickness, ailment, malaise, affliction, malady, lurgy *(informal)*: *I think I've got a bit of a stomach bug.* **2 = fault**, failing, virus, error, defect, flaw, blemish, imperfection, glitch, gremlin: *There is a bug in the software.* **3 = mania**, passion, rage, obsession, craze, fad, thing *(informal)*: *I've definitely been bitten by the gardening bug.*
▷ VERB **1 = tap**, eavesdrop, listen in on, wiretap: *He heard they were planning to bug his office.* **2 = annoy**, bother, disturb, needle *(informal)*, plague, irritate, harass, hassle *(informal)*, aggravate *(informal)*, badger, gall, nettle, pester, vex, irk, get under your skin *(informal)*, get on your nerves *(informal)*, nark *(Brit., Austral. & N.Z. slang)*, get up your nose *(informal)*, be on your back *(slang)*, get in your hair *(informal)*, get on your wick *(Brit. slang)*, hack you off *(informal)*: *I only did it to bug my parents.*

build VERB **1 = construct**, make, raise, put up, assemble, erect, fabricate, form: *Developers are now proposing to build a hotel on the site.* **OPPOSITE:** demolish **2 = establish**, start, begin, found, base, set up, institute, constitute, initiate, originate, formulate, inaugurate: *I wanted to build a relationship with my team.* **OPPOSITE:** finish **3 = develop**, increase, improve, extend, strengthen, intensify, enlarge, amplify, augment: *Diplomats hope the meetings will build mutual trust.* **OPPOSITE:** decrease
▷ NOUN **= physique**, form, body, figure, shape, structure, frame: *the smallness of his build*

building NOUN **= structure**, house, construction, dwelling, erection, edifice, domicile, pile

build-up NOUN **1 = increase**, development, growth, expansion, accumulation, enlargement, escalation, upsurge, intensification, augmentation: *a build-up of troops* **2 = accumulation**, accretion: *a build-up of gases in the city's sewers* **3 = hype**, promotion, publicity, plug *(informal)*, puff, razzmatazz *(slang)*, brouhaha, ballyhoo *(informal)*: *the build-up for the film*

built-in ADJECTIVE **= essential**, integral, included, incorporated, inherent, implicit, in-built, intrinsic, inseparable, immanent

bulbous ADJECTIVE **= bulging**, rounded, swelling, swollen, bloated, convex

bulge VERB **1 = swell out**, project, expand, swell, stand out, stick out, protrude, puff out, distend, bag: *He bulges out of his black T-shirt.* **2 = stick out**, stand out, protrude: *His eyes seemed to bulge like those of a toad.*
▷ NOUN **1 = lump**, swelling, bump, projection, hump, protuberance, protrusion: *Why won't those bulges on your hips and thighs go?* **OPPOSITE:** hollow **2 = increase**, rise, boost, surge, intensification: *a bulge in aircraft sales*

bulk NOUN **1 = size**, volume, dimensions, magnitude, substance, vastness, amplitude, immensity, bigness, largeness, massiveness: *the shadowy bulk of an ancient barn* **2 = weight**, size, mass, heaviness, poundage, portliness: *Despite his bulk he moved lightly on his feet.* **3 = majority**, mass, most, body, quantity, best part, major part, lion's share, better part, generality, preponderance, main part, plurality, nearly all, greater number: *The vast bulk of imports and exports is carried by sea.*
bulk large = be important, dominate, loom, stand out, loom large, carry weight, preponderate, threaten: *Propaganda bulks large in their plans.*

> **USAGE**
> The use of a plural noun after *bulk*, when it has the meaning 'majority', although common, is considered by some to be incorrect and should be avoided. This usage is most commonly encountered, according to the Bank of English, when referring to *funds* and *profits*: *the bulk of our profits stem from the sale of beer*. The synonyms *majority* and *most* would work better in this context.

bulky ADJECTIVE **= large**, big, huge, heavy, massive, enormous, substantial, immense, mega *(slang)*, very large, mammoth, colossal, cumbersome, weighty, hulking, unwieldy, ponderous, voluminous, unmanageable, elephantine, massy, ginormous *(informal)*, humongous *or* humungous *(U.S. slang)* **OPPOSITE:** small

bulldoze VERB **1 = demolish**, level, destroy, flatten, knock down, tear down, raze, kennet *(Austral. slang)*, jeff *(Austral. slang)*: *She defeated developers who wanted to bulldoze her home.* **2 = push**, force, drive, thrust, shove, propel: *He bulldozed through the Tigers' defence.* **3 = force**, bully, intimidate, railroad *(informal)*, cow, hector, coerce, dragoon, browbeat, put the screws on: *My parents tried to bulldoze me into going to college.*

bullet NOUN **= projectile**, ball, shot, missile, slug, pellet

bulletin NOUN **= report**, account, statement, message, communication, announcement, dispatch, communiqué, notification, news flash

bully NOUN **= persecutor**, tough, oppressor, tormentor, bully boy, browbeater, coercer, ruffian, intimidator: *I fell victim to the office bully.*
▷ VERB **1 = persecute**, intimidate, torment, hound, oppress, pick on, victimize, terrorize, push around *(slang)*, ill-treat, ride roughshod over, maltreat, tyrannize, overbear: *I wasn't going to let him bully me.* **2 = force**, coerce, railroad *(informal)*, bulldoze *(informal)*, dragoon, pressurize, browbeat, cow, hector, press-gang, domineer, bullyrag: *She used to bully me into doing my schoolwork.*

bulwark NOUN **1 = fortification**, defence, bastion, buttress, rampart, redoubt, outwork: *a bulwark against the English* **2 = defence**, support, safeguard, security, guard, buffer, mainstay: *a bulwark of democracy*

BUILDINGS AND MONUMENTS

Admiralty House
Althorp House
Alhambra
Angel of the North
Arc de Triomphe
Barbican
Beehive
Big Ben
Blenheim Palace
Buckingham Palace
Burj Dubai
Cenotaph
Charminar
Cleopatra's Needle
Crystal Palace
Edinburgh Castle
Eiffel Tower
Elysées Palace
Empire State Building
Forbidden City
Hampton Court Palace
Hermitage
Holyroodhouse
Houses of Parliament
Kaaba
Kensington Palace
Knossos
Kremlin
Lambeth Palace
Lateran
Leaning Tower of Pisa
Longleat House
Louvre
Masada
Mansion House
Monument
Nelson's Column
Pentagon
Saint James's Palace
Scone Palace
Taj Mahal
Tower of London
Vatican
Palace of Versailles
Westminster Abbey
White House

b

bumbling ADJECTIVE **= clumsy**, awkward, blundering, bungling, incompetent, inefficient, lumbering, inept, maladroit, unco *(Austral. slang)* **OPPOSITE:** efficient

bump VERB **1 = knock**, hit, strike, crash, smash, slam, bang: *He bumped his head on the low beam.* **2 = jerk**, shake, bounce, rattle, jar, jog, lurch, jolt, jostle, jounce: *We left the road again and bumped over the mountainside.*
▷ NOUN **1 = knock**, hit, blow, shock, impact, rap, collision, thump: *Small children often cry after a minor bump.* **2 = thud**, crash, knock, smash, bang, smack, thump, clump, wallop *(informal)*, clunk, clonk: *I felt a little bump and knew instinctively what had happened.* **3 = lump**, swelling, bulge, hump, node, nodule, protuberance, contusion: *She got a large bump on her forehead.*
bump into someone = meet, encounter, come across, run into, run across, meet up with, chance upon, happen upon, light upon: *I happened to bump into Mervyn Johns in the hallway.*
bump someone off = murder, kill, assassinate, remove, do in *(slang)*, eliminate, take out *(slang)*, wipe out *(informal)*, dispatch, finish off, do away with, blow away *(slang, chiefly U.S.)*, knock off *(slang)*, liquidate, rub out *(U.S. slang)*: *They will probably bump you off anyway.*

bumper ADJECTIVE **= exceptional**, excellent, exo *(Austral. slang)*, massive, unusual, mega *(slang)*, jumbo *(informal)*, abundant, whacking *(informal, chiefly Brit.)*, spanking *(informal)*, whopping *(informal)*, bountiful

bumpy ADJECTIVE **1 = uneven**, rough, pitted, irregular, rutted, lumpy, potholed, knobby: *bumpy cobbled streets* **2 = jolting**, jarring, bouncy, choppy, jerky, bone-breaking, jolty: *a hot and bumpy journey across the desert*

bunch NOUN **1 = group**, band, crowd, party, team, troop, gathering, crew *(informal)*, gang, knot, mob, flock, swarm, multitude, posse *(informal)*, bevy: *The players were a great bunch.* **2 = bouquet**, spray, sheaf: *He had left a huge bunch of flowers in her hotel room.* **3 = cluster**, clump: *She had fallen asleep clutching a fat bunch of grapes.*
bunch together *or* **up = group**, crowd, mass, collect, assemble, cluster, flock, herd, huddle, congregate: *People bunched up at all the exits.*

bundle NOUN **= bunch**, group, collection, mass, pile, quantity, stack, heap, rick, batch, accumulation, assortment: *He gathered the bundles of clothing into his arms.*
▷ VERB **= push**, thrust, shove, throw, rush, hurry, hasten, jostle, hustle: *They bundled him into a taxi.*
bundle someone up = wrap up, swathe, muffle up, clothe warmly: *Harry greeted them bundled up in a long coat and a fur hat.*
bundle something up = package, tie, pack, bind, wrap, tie up, bale, fasten, truss, tie together, palletize: *possessions bundled up and carried in weary arms*

bungle VERB **= mess up**, blow *(slang)*, ruin, spoil, blunder, fudge, screw up *(informal)*, botch, cock up *(Brit. slang)*, miscalculate, make a mess of, mismanage, muff, foul up, make a nonsense of *(informal)*, bodge *(informal)*, make a pig's ear of *(informal)*, flub *(U.S. slang)*, bitch (up), crool *or* cruel *(Austral. slang)*, louse up *(slang)* **OPPOSITE:** accomplish

bungling ADJECTIVE **= incompetent**, blundering, awkward, clumsy, inept, botching, cack-handed *(informal)*, maladroit, ham-handed *(informal)*, unskilful, ham-fisted *(informal)*, unco *(Austral. slang)*

bunk[1] NOUN
do a bunk = run away, flee, bolt, clear out *(informal)*, beat it *(slang)*, abscond, decamp, do a runner *(slang)*, run for it *(informal)*, cut and run *(informal)*, scram *(informal)*, fly the coop *(U.S. & Canad. informal)*, skedaddle *(informal)*, take a powder *(U.S. & Canad. slang)*, take it on the lam *(U.S. & Canad. slang)*, do a Skase *(Austral. informal)*: *His live-in lover has done a bunk because he won't marry her.*

bunk[2] *or* **bunkum** NOUN **= nonsense**, rubbish, rot, crap *(slang)*, garbage *(informal)*, trash, hot air *(informal)*, tosh *(slang, chiefly Brit.)*, bilge *(informal)*, twaddle, tripe *(informal)*, guff *(slang)*, havers *(Scot.)*, moonshine, malarkey, baloney *(informal)*, hogwash, bizzo *(Austral. slang)*, bull's wool *(Austral. & N.Z. slang)*, hokum *(slang, chiefly U.S. & Canad.)*, piffle *(informal)*, tomfoolery, poppycock *(informal)*, balderdash, bosh *(informal)*, eyewash *(informal)*, kak *(S. African taboo)*, stuff and nonsense, hooey *(slang)*, tommyrot, horsefeathers *(U.S. slang)*, tarradiddle: *Henry Ford's opinion that 'history is bunk'*

buoy NOUN **= float**, guide, signal, marker, beacon: *We released the buoy and drifted back on the tide.*
buoy someone up = encourage, support, boost, cheer, sustain, hearten, cheer up, keep afloat, gee up: *They are buoyed up by a sense of hope.*

buoyancy NOUN **1 = floatability**, lightness, weightlessness: *Air can be pumped into the diving suit to increase buoyancy.* **2 = cheerfulness**, bounce *(informal)*, pep, animation, good humour, high spirits, zing *(informal)*, liveliness, spiritedness, cheeriness, sunniness: *a mood of buoyancy and optimism*

buoyant ADJECTIVE **1 = cheerful**, happy, bright, lively, sunny, animated, upbeat *(informal)*, joyful, carefree, bouncy, breezy, genial, jaunty, chirpy *(informal)*, sparky, vivacious, debonair, blithe, full of beans *(informal)*, peppy *(informal)*, light-hearted: *She was in a buoyant mood.* **OPPOSITE:** gloomy **2 = floating**, light, floatable: *a small and buoyant boat*

burden NOUN **1 = trouble**, care, worry, trial, weight, responsibility, stress, strain, anxiety, sorrow, grievance, affliction, onus, albatross, millstone, encumbrance: *Her illness will be an impossible burden on him.* **2 = load**, weight, cargo, freight, bale, consignment, encumbrance: *She heaved her burden into the back.*
▷ VERB **= weigh down**, worry, load, tax, strain, bother, overwhelm, handicap, oppress, inconvenience, overload, saddle with, encumber, trammel, incommode: *We decided not to burden him with the news.*
▸ *related adjective:* onerous

burdensome ADJECTIVE **= troublesome**, trying, taxing, difficult, heavy, crushing, exacting, oppressive, weighty, onerous, irksome

bureau NOUN **1 = agency**: *the foreign employment bureau* **2 = office**, department, section, branch, station, unit, division, subdivision: *the paper's Washington bureau* **3 = desk**, writing desk: *A simple writing bureau sat in front of the window.*

bureaucracy NOUN **1 = government**, officials, authorities, administration, ministry, the system, civil service, directorate, officialdom, corridors of power: *State bureaucracies tend to stifle enterprise and initiative.* **2 = red tape**, regulations, officialdom, officialese, bumbledom: *People complain about having to deal with too much bureaucracy.*

bureaucrat NOUN **= official**, minister, officer, administrator, civil servant, public servant, functionary, apparatchik, office-holder, mandarin

burglar NOUN **= housebreaker**, thief, robber, pilferer, filcher, cat burglar, sneak thief, picklock

burglary NOUN **= breaking and entering**, housebreaking, break-in, home invasion *(Austral. & N.Z.)*

burial NOUN **= funeral**, interment, burying, obsequies, entombment, inhumation, exequies, sepulture

burial ground NOUN **= graveyard**, cemetery, churchyard, necropolis, God's acre

burlesque NOUN **= parody**, mockery, satire, caricature, send-up *(Brit. informal)*, spoof *(informal)*, travesty, takeoff *(informal)*: *The book read like a black comic burlesque.*
▷ ADJECTIVE **= satirical**, comic, mocking, mock, farcical, travestying, ironical, parodic, mock-heroic, caricatural, hudibrastic: *a trio of burlesque stereotypes*

burly ADJECTIVE **= brawny**, strong, powerful, big, strapping, hefty, muscular, sturdy, stout, bulky, stocky, hulking, beefy *(informal)*, well-built, thickset **OPPOSITE:** scrawny

burn VERB **1 = be on fire**, blaze, be ablaze, smoke, flame, glow, flare, flicker, go up in flames: *I suddenly realized the blanket was burning.* **2 = set on fire**, light, ignite, kindle, incinerate,

How to Use a Thesaurus

One of the worst sins that a writer can commit is to be dull, and a major source of dullness is the unimaginative repetition of words or phrases. Some people are blessed with an extensive vocabulary and can readily think up different words that have roughly similar meaning. For most people who are not professional writers the obvious resource is a thesaurus. The premise of a thesaurus is that it will offer lists of synonyms from which the user can make the choices that seem most appropriate for their particular needs.

Thesauruses come in two main forms. The first is the thematic type, of which *Roget's Thesaurus* is the original and still best-known example. Peter Mark Roget first published his opus in 1852, and his full title makes perfectly clear the use for which he intended it: *Thesaurus of English Words and Phrases Classified and Arranged so as to Facilitate the Expression of Ideas and Assist in Literary Composition.* In a thematic thesaurus, the idea is not so much to give directly substitutable synonyms as to gather together related terms that will suggest what the user is looking for. For example, a user may have a noun in mind and would like to know the appropriate related verb. The reader can either look up the general theme or consult the index for a link to a chosen word.

The other main kind of thesaurus is constructed more like a dictionary, in that it presents words (ie the words that are to be replaced) in alphabetical order followed by lists of synonyms for each, assuming that the reader wants to quickly find an alternative for an individual word rather than explore its more general associations. Any word that has a range of senses, or different parts of speech, will have separate synonym lists for each nuance of meaning, and it is up to the user to identify the specific meaning required. For example, the headword *army* may be broken down as follows:

1. soldiers, military, troops, armed force, legions, infantry, military force...

2. vast number, host, gang, mob, flock, array, legion, swarm, sea, pack, horde...

It's easy to spot the difference between the two areas of meaning: one is about a bunch of armed fighters, and the other just means a large number of particular things. It should also be clear that not many of the terms supplied are truly synonyms, in that one could be substituted for the other with no change of meaning. It would be silly, for example, to replace 'join the army' with 'join the legions' ('military' would be more appropriate). Similarly, while one might refer to 'an army of assistants' this couldn't sensibly be changed to 'a sea of assistants' ('vast number' would be better).

Thus, when using this kind of thesaurus it is vital to recognize and stick to a precise shade of meaning. Often, as an aid to doing this, a thesaurus will label individual synonyms as a guide to the user, indicating that some are, say, informal, technical, American, old-fashioned, etc.

It doesn't do to become too reliant on a thesaurus and assume that a particular word must never be repeated within the next few lines. Here is an example of over-enthusiastic quarrying of a thesaurus:

> I have always been interested in sport. I am a keen participant in *physical activity*, and I love to watch *play* on TV. My favourite *game* is boxing.

As you can see, none of the words in italics carries exactly the same meaning, and using them simply to avoid repeating *sport* detracts from clarity and makes the series of statements look ridiculous. There would actually be nothing wrong in repeating *sport* here as no other word will do. A writer who is stuck with such a pedestrian piece of prose would do better to restructure it completely rather than reach for woolly synonyms. For example, a revised version might be along these lines:

> I have always been interested in sport, both as a participant and as a spectator, and boxing is what I like best.

b

reduce to ashes: *He found out he'd won the Lottery, but he'd burnt the ticket.* **3 = scorch**, toast, sear, char, singe, brand: *I burnt the toast.* **4 = sting**, hurt, smart, tingle, bite, pain: *When you go to the toilet, it burns and stings.* **5 = be passionate**, blaze, be excited, be aroused, be inflamed: *The young boy was burning with a fierce ambition.* **6 = seethe**, fume, be angry, simmer, smoulder: *He was burning with rage.*

burning ADJECTIVE **1 = intense**, passionate, earnest, eager, frantic, frenzied, ardent, fervent, impassioned, zealous, vehement, all-consuming, fervid: *I had a burning ambition to become a journalist.* **OPPOSITE:** mild **2 = crucial**, important, pressing, significant, essential, vital, critical, acute, compelling, urgent: *a burning question*

burnish VERB **= polish**, shine, buff, brighten, rub up, furbish: *His shoes were burnished, his shirt perfectly pressed.* **OPPOSITE:** scuff

burrow NOUN **= hole**, shelter, tunnel, den, lair, retreat: *a rabbit's burrow*
▷ VERB **1 = dig**, tunnel, excavate: *The larvae burrow into cracks in the floor.* **2 = delve**, search, dig, probe, ferret, rummage, forage, fossick *(Austral. & N.Z.)*: *He burrowed into the pile of charts.*

burst VERB **1 = explode**, blow up, break, split, crack, shatter, fragment, shiver, disintegrate, puncture, rupture, rend asunder: *The driver lost control when a tyre burst; She burst the balloon with a pin.* **2 = rush**, run, break, break out, erupt, spout, gush forth: *Water burst through the dam and flooded their villages.* **3 = barge**, charge, rush, shove: *Gunmen burst into his home and opened fire.*
▷ NOUN **1 = rush**, surge, fit, outbreak, outburst, spate, gush, torrent, eruption, spurt, outpouring: *short bursts of activity* **2 = explosion**, crack, blast, blasting, bang, discharge: *a burst of machine-gun fire*

bury VERB **1 = inter**, lay to rest, entomb, sepulchre, consign to the grave, inearth, inhume, inurn: *soldiers who helped to bury the dead* **OPPOSITE:** dig up **2 = hide**, cover, conceal, stash *(informal)*, secrete, cache, stow away: *She buried it under some leaves.* **OPPOSITE:** uncover **3 = sink**, embed, immerse, enfold: *She buried her face in the pillows.* **4 = forget**, draw a veil over, think no more of, put in the past, not give another thought to: *It is time to bury our past misunderstandings.* **5 = engross**, involve, occupy, interest, busy, engage, absorb, preoccupy, immerse: *His reaction was to withdraw, to bury himself in work.*

bush NOUN **= shrub**, plant, hedge, thicket, shrubbery: *Trees and bushes grow down to the water's edge.*
the bush = the wilds, brush, scrub, woodland, backwoods, back country *(U.S.)*, scrubland, backlands *(U.S.)*: *He was shot dead while travelling in the bush.*

bushy ADJECTIVE **= thick**, bristling, spreading, rough, stiff, fuzzy, fluffy, unruly, shaggy, wiry, luxuriant, bristly

busily ADVERB **= actively**, briskly, intently, earnestly, strenuously, speedily, purposefully, diligently, energetically, assiduously, industriously

business NOUN **1 = trade**, selling, trading, industry, manufacturing, commerce, dealings, merchandising: *young people seeking a career in business* **2 = establishment**, company, firm, concern, organization, corporation, venture, enterprise: *The company was a family business.* **3 = profession**, work, calling, job, line, trade, career, function, employment, craft, occupation, pursuit, vocation, métier: *May I ask what business you are in?* **4 = matter**, issue, subject, point, problem, question, responsibility, task, duty, function, topic, assignment: *Parenting can be a stressful business.* **5 = concern**, affair: *My sex life is my own business.*

businesslike ADJECTIVE **= efficient**, professional, practical, regular, correct, organized, routine, thorough, systematic, orderly, matter-of-fact, methodical, well-ordered, workaday **OPPOSITE:** inefficient

businessman *or* **businesswoman** NOUN **= executive**, director, manager, merchant, capitalist, administrator, entrepreneur, tycoon, industrialist, financier, tradesman, homme d'affaires *(French)*

bust[1] NOUN **= bosom**, breasts, chest, front: *Good posture also helps your bust look bigger.*

bust[2] VERB **1 = break**, smash, split, burst, shatter, fracture, rupture, break into fragments: *They will have to bust the door to get him out.* **2 = arrest**, catch, lift *(slang)*, raid, cop *(slang)*, nail *(informal)*, collar *(informal)*, nab *(informal)*, feel your collar *(slang)*: *They were busted for possession of cannabis.*
▷ NOUN **= arrest**, capture, raid, cop *(slang)*: *He was imprisoned after a drug bust.*
go bust = go bankrupt, fail, break, be ruined, become insolvent: *Hundreds of restaurants went bust last year.*

bustle VERB **= hurry**, tear, rush, dash, scramble, fuss, flutter, beetle, hasten, scuttle, scurry, scamper: *My mother bustled around the kitchen.* **OPPOSITE:** idle
▷ NOUN **= activity**, to-do, stir, excitement, hurry, fuss, flurry, haste, agitation, commotion, ado, tumult, hurly-burly, pother: *the hustle and bustle of modern life* **OPPOSITE:** inactivity

bustling ADJECTIVE **= busy**, full, crowded, rushing, active, stirring, lively, buzzing, energetic, humming, swarming, thronged, hustling, teeming, astir

busy ADJECTIVE **1 = active**, brisk, diligent, industrious, assiduous, rushed off your feet: *He's a very busy man.* **OPPOSITE:** idle **2 = occupied with**, working, engaged in, on duty, employed in, hard at work, engrossed in, in harness, on active service: *Life is what happens to you while you're busy making other plans.* **OPPOSITE:** unoccupied **3 = hectic**, full, active, tiring, exacting, energetic, strenuous, on the go *(informal)*: *I'd had a busy day and was rather tired.*
busy yourself = occupy yourself, be engrossed, immerse yourself, involve yourself, amuse yourself, absorb yourself, employ yourself, engage yourself, keep busy *or* occupied: *He busied himself with the camera.*

but CONJUNCTION **= however**, still, yet, nevertheless: *'But,' he added, 'the vast majority must accept a common future.'*
▷ PREPOSITION **= except (for)**, save, bar, barring, excepting, excluding, with the exception of: *He was forced to wind up everything but the hotel business.*
▷ ADVERB **= only**, just, simply, merely: *St Anton is but a snowball's throw away from Lech.*

butcher NOUN **= murderer**, killer, slaughterer, slayer, destroyer, liquidator, executioner, cut-throat, exterminator: *Klaus Barbie was known in France as the Butcher of Lyon.*
▷ VERB **1 = slaughter**, prepare, carve, cut up, dress, cut, clean, joint: *Pigs were butchered, hams were hung to dry from the ceiling.* **2 = kill**, slaughter, massacre, destroy, cut down, assassinate, slay, liquidate, exterminate, put to the sword: *Our people are being butchered in their own homes.* **3 = mess up**, destroy, ruin, wreck, spoil, mutilate, botch, bodge *(informal)*: *I am not in Cannes because they butchered my film.*

butchery NOUN **= slaughter**, killing, murder, massacre, bloodshed, carnage, mass murder, blood-letting, blood bath

butt[1] NOUN **1 = end**, handle, shaft, stock, shank, hilt, haft: *Troops used tear gas and rifle butts to break up the protests.* **2 = stub**, end, base, foot, tip, tail, leftover, fag end *(informal)*: *He paused to stub out the butt of his cigar.*

butt[2] NOUN **= target**, victim, object, point, mark, subject, dupe, laughing stock, Aunt Sally: *He is still the butt of cruel jokes about his humble origins.*

butt[3] VERB **= knock**, push, bump, punch, buck, thrust, ram, shove, poke, buffet, prod, jab, bunt: *The male butted me.*
butt in 1 = interfere, meddle, intrude, heckle, barge in *(informal)*, stick your nose in, put your oar in: *Nobody asked you to butt in.* **2 = interrupt**, cut in, break in, chip in *(informal)*, put your two cents in *(U.S. slang)*: *Could I just butt in here and say something?*

butt[4] NOUN **= cask**, drum, barrel, cylinder: *The hose is great for watering your garden from your water butt.*

butter VERB
butter someone up = flatter, coax, cajole, pander to, blarney, wheedle,

suck up to *(informal)*, soft-soap, fawn on *or* upon

butterfly NOUN
▸ *name of young:* caterpillar, chrysalis, chrysalid ▸ *related enthusiast:* lepidopterist

buttocks NOUN = **bottom**, behind *(informal)*, bum *(Brit. slang)*, backside *(informal)*, seat, rear, tail *(informal)*, butt *(U.S. & Canad. informal)*, buns *(U.S. slang)*, rump, posterior, haunches, hindquarters, derrière *(euphemistic)*, tush *(U.S. slang)*, fundament, gluteus maximus *(Anatomy)*, jacksy *(Brit. slang)*

buttonhole VERB = **detain**, catch, grab, intercept, accost, waylay, take aside

buttress NOUN = **support**, shore, prop, brace, pier, reinforcement, strut, mainstay, stanchion, stay, abutment: *a buttress of rock*
▷ VERB = **support**, sustain, strengthen, shore, prop, reinforce, back up, brace, uphold, bolster, prop up, shore up, augment: *His tough line is buttressed by a democratic mandate.*

buxom ADJECTIVE = **plump**, ample, voluptuous, busty, well-rounded, curvaceous, comely, bosomy, full-bosomed **OPPOSITE:** slender

buy VERB = **purchase**, get, score *(slang)*, secure, pay for, obtain, acquire, invest in, shop for, procure: *He could not afford to buy a house.* **OPPOSITE:** sell
▷ NOUN = **purchase**, deal, bargain, acquisition, steal *(informal)*, snip *(informal)*, giveaway: *a good buy*
buy someone off = **bribe**, square, fix *(informal)*, pay off *(informal)*, lure, corrupt, get at, suborn, grease someone's palm *(slang)*, influence by gifts, oil the palm of *(informal)*: *policies designed to buy off the working-class*

buzz VERB = **hum**, whizz, drone, whir: *Attack helicopters buzzed across the city.*
▷ NOUN **1** = **hum**, buzzing, murmur, drone, whir, bombilation *or* bombination *(literary)*: *the irritating buzz of an insect* **2** = **gossip**, news, report, latest *(informal)*, word, scandal, rumour, whisper, dirt *(U.S. slang)*, gen *(Brit. informal)*, hearsay, scuttlebutt *(U.S. slang)*, goss *(informal)*: *The buzz is that she knows something.*

by PREPOSITION **1** = **through**, under the aegis of, through the agency of: *The feast was served by his mother and sisters.* **2** = **via**, over, by way of: *The train passes by Oxford.* **3** = **near**, past, along, close to, closest to, neighbouring, next to, beside, nearest to, adjoining, adjacent to: *She was sitting in a rocking chair by the kitchen window.*
▷ ADVERB = **nearby**, close, handy, at hand, within reach: *Large numbers of security police stood by.*
by and by = **presently**, shortly, soon, eventually, one day, before long, in a while, anon, in the course of time, erelong *(archaic, poetic)*: *By and by the light gradually grew fainter.*

bygone ADJECTIVE = **past**, former, previous, lost, forgotten, ancient, of old, one-time, departed, extinct, gone by, erstwhile, antiquated, of yore, olden, past recall, sunk in oblivion **OPPOSITE:** future

bypass VERB **1** = **get round**, avoid, evade, circumvent, outmanoeuvre, body-swerve *(Scot.)*: *Regulators worry that controls could easily be bypassed.* **2** = **go round**, skirt, circumvent, depart from, deviate from, pass round, detour round: *Money for new roads to bypass cities.* **OPPOSITE:** cross

bystander NOUN = **onlooker**, passer-by, spectator, witness, observer, viewer, looker-on, watcher, eyewitness **OPPOSITE:** participant

byword NOUN = **saying**, slogan, motto, maxim, gnome, adage, proverb, epithet, dictum, precept, aphorism, saw, apophthegm

Cc

C

cab NOUN **= taxi**, minicab, taxicab, hackney, hackney carriage

cabal NOUN **1 = clique**, set, party, league, camp, coalition, faction, caucus, junta, coterie, schism, confederacy, conclave: *He had been chosen by a cabal of fellow senators.* **2 = plot**, scheme, intrigue, conspiracy, machination: *The left saw it as a bourgeois cabal.*

cabin NOUN **1 = room**, berth, quarters, compartment, deckhouse: *The steward showed her to a small cabin.* **2 = hut**, shed, cottage, lodge, cot *(archaic)*, shack, chalet, shanty, hovel, bothy, whare *(N.Z.)*: *a log cabin in the woods*

Cabinet NOUN **= council**, committee, administration, ministry, assembly, board

cabinet NOUN **= cupboard**, case, locker, dresser, closet, press, chiffonier

cache NOUN **= store**, fund, supply, reserve, treasury, accumulation, stockpile, hoard, stash *(informal)*

cackle VERB **= laugh**, giggle, chuckle: *The old lady cackled with glee.*
▷ NOUN **= laugh**, giggle, chuckle: *He let out a brief cackle of triumph.*

cacophony NOUN **= discord**, racket, din, dissonance, disharmony, stridency

cad NOUN **= scoundrel** *(slang)*, rat *(informal)*, bounder *(Brit. old-fashioned, slang)*, cur, knave, rotter *(slang, chiefly Brit.)*, heel, scumbag *(slang)*, churl, dastard *(archaic)*, wrong 'un *(Austral. slang)*

cadence NOUN **1 = intonation**, accent, inflection, modulation: *He recognised the Polish cadences in her voice.*
2 = rhythm, beat, measure *(Prosody)*, metre, pulse, throb, tempo, swing, lilt: *There was a sudden shift in the cadence of the music.*

café NOUN **= snack bar**, restaurant, cafeteria, coffee shop, brasserie, coffee bar, tearoom, lunchroom, eatery *or* eaterie

cage NOUN **= enclosure**, pen, coop, hutch, pound, corral *(U.S.)*: *I hate to see animals being kept in cages.*
▷ VERB **= shut up**, confine, restrain, imprison, lock up, mew, incarcerate, fence in, impound, coop up, immure, pound: *Don't you think it's cruel to cage wild creatures?*

cagey *or* **cagy** ADJECTIVE **= guarded**, reserved, careful, cautious, restrained, wary, discreet, shrewd, wily, reticent, noncommittal, chary
OPPOSITE: careless

cajole VERB **= persuade**, tempt, lure, flatter, manoeuvre, seduce, entice, coax, beguile, wheedle, sweet-talk *(informal)*, inveigle

cake NOUN **= block**, bar, slab, lump, cube, loaf, mass: *He bought a cake of soap.*
▷ VERB **= solidify**, dry, consolidate, harden, thicken, congeal, coagulate, ossify, encrust: *The blood had begun to cake and turn brown.*

calamitous ADJECTIVE **= disastrous**, terrible, devastating, tragic, fatal, deadly, dreadful, dire, catastrophic, woeful, ruinous, cataclysmic
OPPOSITE: fortunate

calamity NOUN **= disaster**, tragedy, ruin, distress, reversal of fortune, hardship, catastrophe, woe, misfortune, downfall, adversity, scourge, mishap, affliction, trial, tribulation, misadventure, cataclysm, wretchedness, mischance
OPPOSITE: benefit

> **QUOTATIONS**
> Calamities are of two kinds: misfortune to ourselves, and good fortune to others
> [Ambrose Bierce *The Devil's Dictionary*]

calculate VERB **1 = work out**, value, judge, determine, estimate, count, reckon, weigh, consider, compute, rate, gauge, enumerate, figure: *From this we can calculate the total mass in the galaxy.* **2 = plan**, design, aim, intend, frame, arrange, formulate, contrive: *Its twin engines were calculated to give additional safety.*

calculated ADJECTIVE **= deliberate**, planned, considered, studied, intended, intentional, designed, aimed, purposeful, premeditated
OPPOSITE: unplanned

calculating ADJECTIVE **= scheming**, designing, sharp, shrewd, cunning, contriving, sly, canny, devious, manipulative, crafty, Machiavellian
OPPOSITE: direct

calculation NOUN **1 = computation**, working out, reckoning, figuring, estimate, forecast, judgment, estimation, result, answer: *He made a quick calculation on a scrap of paper.*
2 = planning, intention, deliberation, foresight, contrivance, forethought, circumspection, premeditation: *an act of cold, unspeakably cruel calculation*

calibrate VERB **= measure**, gauge

calibre *or (U.S.)* **caliber** NOUN
1 = worth, quality, ability, talent, gifts, capacity, merit, distinction, faculty, endowment, stature: *I was impressed by the high calibre of the candidates.* **2 = diameter**, bore, gauge, measure: *Next morning she was arrested and a .44 calibre revolver was found under the front seat of her car.*

call VERB **1 = name**, entitle, dub, designate, term, style, label, describe as, christen, denominate: *They called their daughter Mischa.* **2 = consider**, think, judge, estimate, describe as, refer to as, regard as: *His own party called him a traitor.* **3 = cry**, announce, shout, scream, proclaim, yell, cry out, whoop: *'Boys!' she called, 'Dinner's ready!'*
OPPOSITE: whisper **4 = phone**, contact, telephone, ring (up) *(informal, chiefly Brit.)*, give (someone) a bell *(Brit. slang)*: *Will you call me as soon as you hear anything?* **5 = hail**, address, summon, contact, halloo: *He called me over the tannoy.* **6 = summon**, gather, invite, rally, assemble, muster, convene, convoke, collect: *The group promised to call a meeting of shareholders.*
OPPOSITE: dismiss **7 = waken**, arouse, awaken, rouse: *I'm late for work! Why didn't you call me earlier?*
▷ NOUN **1 = visit**: *He decided to pay a call on Mr Cummings.* **2 = request**, order, demand, appeal, notice, command, announcement, invitation, plea, summons, supplication: *There was a call by the trade unions for members to stay home for the duration of the strike.* **3** *(used in negative constructions)* **= need**, cause, reason, grounds, occasion, excuse, justification, claim: *There was no call for him to talk to you like he did.*
4 = attraction, draw, pull *(informal)*, appeal, lure, attractiveness, allure, magnetism: *a sailor who could not resist the call of the sea* **5 = cry**, shout, scream, yell, whoop: *He heard calls coming from the cellar.* **OPPOSITE:** whisper

call for someone = fetch, pick up, collect, uplift *(Scot.)*: *I shall call for you at 7 o'clock.*

call for something 1 = demand, order, request, insist on, cry out for: *They angrily called for his resignation.*
2 = require, need, involve, demand, occasion, entail, necessitate: *It's a situation that calls for a blend of delicacy and force.*

call on someone 1 = request, ask, bid, invite, appeal to, summon, invoke, call upon, entreat, supplicate: *He was frequently called on to resolve conflicts.*
2 = visit, look up, drop in on, look in on, see: *I'm leaving early tomorrow to call on a friend.*

call someone up 1 = telephone, phone, ring *(chiefly Brit.)*, buzz *(informal)*, dial, call up, give (someone) a ring *(informal, chiefly Brit.)*, put a call through to, give (someone) a call, give (someone) a buzz *(informal)*, give (someone) a bell *(Brit. slang)*, give (someone) a tinkle *(Brit. informal)*, get on the blower to *(informal)*: *He called me up to ask how I was.* **2 = enlist**, draft, recruit, muster: *The United States has called up some 150,000 military reservists.*

calling NOUN **= profession**, work, business, line, trade, career, mission, employment, province, occupation, pursuit, vocation, walk of life, life's work, métier

callous ADJECTIVE **= heartless**, cold, harsh, hardened, indifferent, insensitive, hard-boiled *(informal)*, unsympathetic, uncaring, soulless, hard-bitten, unfeeling, obdurate, case-hardened, hardhearted
OPPOSITE: compassionate

callousness NOUN **= heartlessness**, insensitivity, hardness, coldness, harshness, obduracy, soullessness, hardheartedness, obdurateness

callow ADJECTIVE **= inexperienced**, juvenile, naïve, immature, raw, untried, green, unsophisticated, puerile, guileless, jejune, unfledged

calm ADJECTIVE **1 = cool**, relaxed, composed, sedate, undisturbed, collected, unmoved, dispassionate, unfazed *(informal)*, impassive, unflappable *(informal)*, unruffled, unemotional, self-possessed, imperturbable, equable, keeping your cool, unexcited, unexcitable, as cool as a cucumber, chilled *(informal)*: *Try to keep calm and just tell me what happened.*
OPPOSITE: excited **2 = still**, quiet, smooth, peaceful, mild, serene, tranquil, placid, halcyon, balmy, restful, windless, pacific: *The normally calm waters of Mururoa lagoon heaved and frothed.* **OPPOSITE:** rough
▷ NOUN **1 = peacefulness**, peace, serenity, calmness: *He felt a sudden sense of calm and contentment.* **2 = stillness**, peace, quiet, hush, serenity, tranquillity, repose, calmness, peacefulness: *the rural calm of Grand Rapids, Michigan* **3 = peace**, calmness: *Church leaders have appealed for calm.*
OPPOSITE: disturbance
▷ VERB **1 = soothe**, settle, quiet, relax, appease, still, allay, assuage, quieten: *She had a drink to calm her nerves.*
OPPOSITE: excite **2 = placate**, hush, pacify, mollify: *Officials hoped this action would calm the situation.*
OPPOSITE: aggravate

calmly ADVERB **= coolly**, casually, sedately, serenely, nonchalantly, impassively, dispassionately, placidly, unflinchingly, equably, imperturbably, tranquilly, composedly, collectedly, self-possessedly

camaraderie NOUN **= comradeship**, fellowship, brotherhood, companionship, togetherness, esprit de corps, good-fellowship, companionability

camouflage NOUN **1 = protective colouring**, mimicry, false appearance, deceptive markings: *Many animals employ camouflage to hide from predators.* **2 = disguise**, front, cover, screen, blind, mask, cloak, guise, masquerade, subterfuge, concealment: *Her merrymaking was only a camouflage to disguise her grief.*
▷ VERB **= disguise**, cover, screen, hide, mask, conceal, obscure, veil, cloak, obfuscate: *This is another clever attempt to camouflage reality.* **OPPOSITE:** reveal

camp¹ NOUN **1 = camp site**, tents, encampment, camping ground: *The camp was in a densely-forested area.* **2 = bivouac**, cantonment *(Military)*: *He was held in a military camp for three days.*

camp² ADJECTIVE **1 = effeminate**, campy *(informal)*, camped up *(informal)*, poncy *(slang)*: *an outrageously camp comedian* **2 = affected**, mannered, artificial, posturing, ostentatious, campy *(informal)*, camped up *(informal)*: *All the characters are either too camp or too dull.*

campaign NOUN **1 = drive**, appeal, movement, push *(informal)*, offensive, crusade: *A new campaign has begun to encourage more people to become blood donors.* **2 = operation**, drive, attack, movement, push, offensive, expedition, crusade, jihad: *The General's campaign against the militia has so far failed.*

campaigner NOUN **= demonstrator**, champion, advocate, activist, reformer, crusader

canal NOUN **= waterway**, channel, passage, conduit, duct, watercourse

cancel VERB **1 = call off**, drop, abandon, forget about: *The foreign minister has cancelled his visit to Washington.* **2 = annul**, abolish, repeal, abort, quash, do away with, revoke, repudiate, rescind, obviate, abrogate, countermand, eliminate: *Her insurance had been cancelled by the company.*
cancel something out = counterbalance, offset, make up for, compensate for, redeem, neutralize, nullify, obviate, balance out: *These two opposing factors tend to cancel each other out.*

cancellation NOUN **1 = abandonment**, abandoning: *No reason has been given for the cancellation of the event.* **2 = annulment**, abolition, repeal, elimination, quashing, revocation: *a march by groups calling for the cancellation of Third World debt*

cancer NOUN **1 = growth**, tumour, carcinoma *(Pathology)*, malignancy: *Ninety percent of lung cancers are caused by smoking.* **2 = evil**, corruption, rot, sickness, blight, pestilence, canker: *There's a cancer in the system.*
▸ *related prefix:* carcino-

candid ADJECTIVE **1 = honest**, just, open, truthful, fair, plain, straightforward, blunt, sincere, outspoken, downright, impartial, forthright, upfront *(informal)*, unequivocal, unbiased, guileless, unprejudiced, free, round, frank: *a candid account of her life as a drug addict*
OPPOSITE: diplomatic **2 = informal**, impromptu, uncontrived, unposed: *There are also some candid pictures taken when he was young.*

candidate NOUN **= contender**, competitor, applicant, nominee, entrant, claimant, contestant, suitor, aspirant, possibility, runner

candour NOUN **= honesty**, simplicity, fairness, sincerity, impartiality, frankness, directness, truthfulness, outspokenness, forthrightness, straightforwardness, ingenuousness, artlessness, guilelessness, openness, unequivocalness, naïveté
OPPOSITE: dishonesty

cannabis NOUN **= marijuana**, pot *(slang)*, dope *(slang)*, hash *(slang)*, blow *(slang)*, smoke *(informal)*, stuff *(slang)*, leaf *(slang)*, tea *(U.S. slang)*, grass *(slang)*, chronic *(U.S. slang)*, weed *(slang)*, hemp, gage *(U.S. obsolete, slang)*, hashish, mary jane *(U.S. slang)*, ganja, bhang, kif, sinsemilla, dagga *(S. African)*, charas

cannon NOUN **= gun**, big gun, artillery piece, field gun, mortar

canny ADJECTIVE **= shrewd**, knowing, sharp, acute, careful, wise, clever, subtle, cautious, prudent, astute, on the ball *(informal)*, artful, judicious, circumspect, perspicacious, sagacious, worldly-wise
OPPOSITE: inept

canon NOUN **1 = rule**, standard, principle, regulation, formula, criterion, dictate, statute, yardstick, precept: *These measures offended all the accepted canons of political economy.* **2 = list**, index, catalogue, syllabus, roll: *the body of work which constitutes the canon of English literature as taught in schools*

canopy NOUN **= awning**, covering, shade, shelter, sunshade

CANALS

Berezina Canal	Grand Union Canal	Canal do Norte
Bridgewater Canal	Houston Ship Canal	Panama Canal
Caledonian Canal	Kiel Canal	Rhine-Herne Canal
Champlain Canal	Manchester Ship Canal	Canal de São Gonçalo
Corinth Canal	Canal du Midi	Suez Canal
Dortmund-Ems Canal	Mittelland Canal	Twente Canal
Erie Canal	Moscow Canal	Welland Canal
Göta Canal	New York State Barge Canal	
Grand Canal		

C

cant[1] NOUN **1 = hypocrisy**, pretence, lip service, humbug, insincerity, pretentiousness, sanctimoniousness, pious platitudes, affected piety, sham holiness: *Politicians are holding forth with their usual hypocritical cant.* **2 = jargon**, slang, vernacular, patter, lingo, argot: *He resorted to a lot of pseudo-psychological cant to confuse me.*

cant[2] VERB **= tilt**, angle, slope, incline, slant, bevel, rise: *The helicopter canted inward towards the landing area.*

cantankerous ADJECTIVE **= bad-tempered**, contrary, perverse, irritable, crusty, grumpy, disagreeable, cranky (*U.S., Canad. & Irish informal*), irascible, tetchy, ratty (*Brit. & N.Z. informal*), testy, quarrelsome, waspish, grouchy (*informal*), peevish, crabby, choleric, crotchety (*informal*), ill-humoured, captious, difficult **OPPOSITE:** cheerful

canter VERB **= jog**, lope: *The competitors cantered into the arena.*
▷ NOUN **= jog**, lope, easy gait, dogtrot: *He set off at a canter.*

canvass VERB **1 = campaign**, solicit votes, electioneer: *I'm canvassing for the Labour Party.* **2 = poll**, study, examine, investigate, analyse, scan, inspect, sift, scrutinize: *The survey canvassed the views of almost 80 economists.*

canyon NOUN **= gorge**, pass, gulf, valley, clough (*dialect*), gully, ravine, defile, gulch (*U.S. & Canad.*), coulee (*U.S.*)

cap VERB **1 = beat**, top, better, exceed, eclipse, lick (*informal*), surpass, transcend, outstrip, outdo, run rings around (*informal*), put in the shade, overtop: *He always has to cap everyone else's achievements.* **2 = top**, cover, crown: *home-made scones capped with cream*

capability NOUN **= ability**, means, power, potential, facility, capacity, qualification(s), faculty, competence, proficiency, wherewithal, potentiality **OPPOSITE:** inability

capable ADJECTIVE **1 = able**, fitted, suited, adapted, adequate: *Such a weapon would be capable of firing conventional or nuclear shells.* **OPPOSITE:** incapable
2 = accomplished, experienced, masterly, qualified, talented, gifted, efficient, clever, intelligent, competent, apt, skilful, adept, proficient: *She's a very capable administrator.* **OPPOSITE:** incompetent

capacious ADJECTIVE **= spacious**, wide, broad, vast, substantial, comprehensive, extensive, generous, ample, expansive, roomy, voluminous, commodious, sizable *or* sizeable **OPPOSITE:** limited

capacity NOUN **1 = ability**, power, strength, facility, gift, intelligence, efficiency, genius, faculty, capability, forte, readiness, aptitude, aptness, competence *or* competency: *Our capacity for giving care, love and attention is limited.* **2 = size**, room, range, space, volume, extent, dimensions, scope, magnitude, compass, amplitude: *an aircraft with a bomb-carrying capacity of 454 kg* **3 = function**, position, role, post, appointment, province, sphere, service, office: *She was visiting in her official capacity as co-chairperson.*

cape NOUN **= headland**, point, head, peninsula, ness (*archaic*), promontory

caper VERB **= dance**, trip, spring, jump, bound, leap, bounce, hop, skip, romp, frolic, cavort, frisk, gambol: *The children were capering about, shouting and laughing.*
▷ NOUN **= escapade**, sport, stunt, mischief, lark (*informal*), prank, jest, practical joke, high jinks, antic, jape, shenanigan (*informal*): *Jack would have nothing to do with such childish capers.*

capital NOUN **= money**, funds, stock, investment(s), property, cash, finance, finances, financing, resources, assets, wealth, principal, means, wherewithal: *The company is having difficulties in raising capital.*
▷ ADJECTIVE **= first-rate**, fine, excellent, superb, sterling, splendid, world-class: *They had a capital time in London.*

capitalism NOUN **= private enterprise**, free enterprise, private ownership, laissez faire *or* laisser faire

> **QUOTATIONS**
> I think that Capitalism, wisely managed, can probably be made more efficient for attaining economic ends than any alternative system yet in sight, but that in itself it is in many ways extremely objectionable
> [John Maynard Keynes *The End of Laissez-Faire*]
>
> You show me a capitalist, and I'll show you a bloodsucker
> [Malcolm X]

capitalize VERB **= sell**, put up for sale, trade, dispose of: *The company will be capitalized at £2 million.*
capitalize on something = take advantage of, exploit, benefit from, profit from, make the most of, gain from, cash in on (*informal*): *The rebels seemed to be trying to capitalize on the public's discontent.*

capitulate VERB **= give in**, yield, concede, submit, surrender, comply, give up, come to terms, succumb, cave in (*informal*), relent **OPPOSITE:** resist

capitulation NOUN **= surrender**, yielding, submission, cave-in (*informal*)

caprice NOUN **= whim**, notion, impulse, freak, fad, quirk, vagary, whimsy, humour, fancy, fickleness, inconstancy, fitfulness, changeableness

capricious ADJECTIVE **= unpredictable**, variable, unstable, inconsistent, erratic, quirky, fickle, impulsive, mercurial, freakish, fitful, inconstant **OPPOSITE:** consistent

capsize VERB **= overturn**, turn over, invert, tip over, keel over, turn turtle, upset

capsule NOUN **1 = pill**, tablet, lozenge, bolus: *You can also take red ginseng in convenient capsule form.* **2 = pod**, case, shell, vessel, sheath, receptacle, seed case: *Each flower is globular, with an egg-shaped capsule.*

captain NOUN **1 = leader**, boss, master, skipper, chieftain, head, number one (*informal*), chief: *He is a former English cricket captain.*
2 = commander, officer, skipper, (senior) pilot: *a beefy German sea captain*

captivate VERB **= charm**, attract, fascinate, absorb, entrance, dazzle, seduce, enchant, enthral, beguile, allure, bewitch, ravish, enslave, mesmerize, ensnare, hypnotize, enrapture, sweep off your feet, enamour, infatuate **OPPOSITE:** repel

captive ADJECTIVE **= confined**, caged, imprisoned, locked up, enslaved, incarcerated, ensnared, subjugated, penned, restricted: *Her heart had begun to pound inside her chest like a captive animal.*
▷ NOUN **= prisoner**, hostage, convict, prisoner of war, detainee, internee: *He described the difficulties of surviving for four months as a captive.*

captivity NOUN **= confinement**, custody, detention, imprisonment, incarceration, internment, durance (*archaic*), restraint

> **QUOTATIONS**
> A robin red breast in a cage
> Puts all Heaven in a rage
> [William Blake *Auguries of Innocence*]

captor NOUN **= jailer** *or* **gaoler**, guard, keeper, custodian

capture VERB **= catch**, arrest, take, bag, secure, seize, nail (*informal*), collar (*informal*), nab (*informal*), apprehend, lift (*slang*), take prisoner, take into custody, feel your collar (*slang*): *The police gave chase and captured him as he was trying to escape.*
OPPOSITE: release
▷ NOUN **= arrest**, catching, trapping, imprisonment, seizure, apprehension, taking, taking captive: *The shooting happened while the man was trying to evade capture.*

car NOUN **1 = vehicle**, motor, wheels (*informal*), auto (*U.S.*), automobile, jalopy (*informal*), motorcar, machine: *They arrived by car.* **2 = (railway) carriage**, coach, cable car, dining car, sleeping car, buffet car, van: *Tour buses have replaced railway cars.*

carcass NOUN **1 = body**, remains, corpse, skeleton, dead body, cadaver (*Medical*): *A cluster of vultures crouched on the carcass of a dead buffalo.* **2 = remains**, shell, framework, debris, remnants, hulk: *At one end of the camp lies the carcass of an aircraft which crashed in the mountains.*

cardinal ADJECTIVE **= principal**, first, highest, greatest, leading, important, chief, main, prime, central, key, essential, primary, fundamental,

paramount, foremost, pre-eminent
OPPOSITE: secondary

care VERB **= be concerned**, mind, bother, be interested, be bothered, give a damn, concern yourself: *a company that cares about the environment*
▷ NOUN **1 = custody**, keeping, control, charge, management, protection, supervision, guardianship, safekeeping, ministration: *the orphans who were in her care* **2 = caution**, attention, regard, pains, consideration, heed, prudence, vigilance, forethought, circumspection, watchfulness, meticulousness, carefulness: *I chose my words with care.*
OPPOSITE: carelessness **3 = worry**, concern, pressure, trouble, responsibility, stress, burden, anxiety, hardship, woe, disquiet, affliction, tribulation, perplexity, vexation: *He never seemed to have a care in the world.*
OPPOSITE: pleasure
care for someone 1 = look after, mind, tend, attend, nurse, minister to, watch over: *They hired a nurse to care for her.* **2 = love**, desire, be fond of, want, prize, find congenial: *He wanted me to know that he still cared for me.*
care for something *or* **someone = like**, enjoy, take to, relish, be fond of, be keen on, be partial to: *I don't care for seafood very much.*
take care of something *or* **someone 1 = look after**, mind, watch, protect, tend, nurse, care for, provide for **2 = deal with**, manage, cope with, see to, handle

QUOTATIONS
What is this life if, full of care,
We have no time to stand and stare?
[W.H. Davies *Leisure*]

career NOUN **1 = occupation**, calling, employment, pursuit, vocation, livelihood, life's work: *She is now concentrating on a career as a fashion designer.* **2 = progress**, course, path, procedure, passage: *The club has had an interesting, if chequered, career.*
▷ VERB **= rush**, race, speed, tear, dash, barrel (along) (*informal, chiefly U.S. & Canad.*), bolt, hurtle, burn rubber (*informal*): *The car went careering off down the track.*

carefree ADJECTIVE **= untroubled**, happy, cheerful, careless, buoyant, airy, radiant, easy-going, cheery, breezy, halcyon, sunny, jaunty, chirpy (*informal*), happy-go-lucky, blithe, insouciant, light-hearted
OPPOSITE: unhappy

careful ADJECTIVE **1 = cautious**, painstaking, scrupulous, fastidious, circumspect, punctilious, chary, heedful, thoughtful, discreet: *One has to be extremely careful when dealing with these people.* **OPPOSITE:** careless **2 = thorough**, full, particular, accurate, precise, intensive, in-depth, meticulous, conscientious, attentive, exhaustive, painstaking, scrupulous, assiduous: *He decided to prosecute her after careful consideration of all the facts.*
OPPOSITE: casual **3 = prudent**, sparing, economical, canny, provident, frugal, thrifty: *Train your children to be careful with their pocket-money.*

PROVERBS
Softly, softly, catchee monkey

careless ADJECTIVE **1 = slapdash**, irresponsible, sloppy (*informal*), cavalier, offhand, neglectful, slipshod, lackadaisical, inattentive: *He pleaded guilty to careless driving.*
OPPOSITE: careful **2 = negligent**, hasty, unconcerned, cursory, perfunctory, thoughtless, indiscreet, unthinking, forgetful, absent-minded, inconsiderate, heedless, remiss, incautious, unmindful: *She's careless about her personal hygiene.*
OPPOSITE: careful **3 = nonchalant**, casual, offhand, artless, unstudied: *With a careless flip of his wrists, he sent the ball on its way.* **OPPOSITE:** careful

carelessness NOUN **= negligence**, neglect, omission, indiscretion, inaccuracy, irresponsibility, slackness, inattention, sloppiness (*informal*), laxity, thoughtlessness, laxness, remissness

QUOTATIONS
To lose one parent, Mr. Worthing, may be regarded as a misfortune; to lose both looks like carelessnesss
[Oscar Wilde *The Importance of Being Earnest*]

PROVERBS
Don't throw out the baby with the bathwater

caress NOUN **= stroke**, pat, kiss, embrace, hug, cuddle, fondling: *Margaret held my arm in a gentle caress.*
▷ VERB **= stroke**, cuddle, fondle, pet, embrace, hug, nuzzle, neck (*informal*), kiss: *They kissed and caressed one another.*

caretaker NOUN **= warden**, keeper, porter, superintendent, curator, custodian, watchman, janitor, concierge: *The caretaker sleeps in the building all night.*
▷ ADJECTIVE **= temporary**, holding, short-term, interim: *The administration intends to hand over power to a caretaker government.*

cargo NOUN **= load**, goods, contents, shipment, freight, merchandise, baggage, ware, consignment, tonnage, lading

caricature NOUN **= parody**, cartoon, distortion, satire, send-up (*Brit. informal*), travesty, takeoff (*informal*), lampoon, burlesque, mimicry, farce: *The poster showed a caricature of Hitler with a devil's horns and tail.*
▷ VERB **= parody**, take off (*informal*), mock, distort, ridicule, mimic, send up (*Brit. informal*), lampoon, burlesque, satirize: *Her political career has been caricatured in the newspapers.*

caring ADJECTIVE **= compassionate**, loving, kindly, warm, soft, sensitive, tender, sympathetic, responsive, receptive, considerate, warmhearted, tenderhearted, softhearted, touchy-feely (*informal*)

carnage NOUN **= slaughter**, murder, massacre, holocaust, havoc, bloodshed, shambles, mass murder, butchery, blood bath

carnal ADJECTIVE **= sexual**, animal, sexy (*informal*), fleshly, erotic, sensual, randy (*informal, chiefly Brit.*), steamy (*informal*), raunchy (*slang*), sensuous, voluptuous, lewd, wanton, amorous, salacious, prurient, impure, lascivious, lustful, lecherous, libidinous, licentious, unchaste

carnival NOUN **= festival**, fair, fête, celebration, gala, jubilee, jamboree, Mardi Gras, revelry, merrymaking, fiesta, holiday

carol NOUN **= song**, noel, hymn, Christmas song, canticle

carouse VERB **= drink**, booze (*informal*), revel, imbibe, quaff, pub-crawl (*informal, chiefly Brit.*), bevvy (*dialect*), make merry, bend the elbow (*informal*), roister

carp VERB **= find fault**, complain, beef (*slang*), criticize, nag, censure, reproach, quibble, cavil, pick holes, kvetch (*U.S. slang*), nit-pick (*informal*)
OPPOSITE: praise

carpenter NOUN **= joiner**, cabinet-maker, woodworker

carping ADJECTIVE **= fault-finding**, critical, nagging, picky (*informal*), nit-picking (*informal*), hard to please, cavilling, captious, nit-picky (*informal*)

carriage NOUN **1 = vehicle**, coach, trap, gig, cab, wagon, hackney, conveyance: *He followed in an open carriage drawn by six grey horses.*
2 = transportation, transport, delivery, conveying, freight, conveyance, carrying: *It costs £10.86 for one litre, including carriage.* **3 = bearing**, posture, gait, deportment, air: *Her legs were long and fine, her hips slender, her carriage graceful.*

carry VERB **1 = convey**, take, move, bring, bear, lift, transfer, conduct, transport, haul, transmit, fetch, relay, cart, tote (*informal*), hump (*Brit. slang*), lug: *He carried the plate through to the dining room.* **2 = transport**, take, transfer, transmit: *The ship can carry seventy passengers.* **3 = support**, stand, bear, maintain, shoulder, sustain, hold up, suffer, uphold, bolster, underpin: *This horse can't carry your weight.* **4 = transmit**, transfer, spread, pass on: *Frogs eat pests which carry diseases.* **5 = publish**, include, release, display, print, broadcast, communicate, disseminate, give: *Several magazines carried the story.*
6 = win, gain, secure, capture, accomplish: *It was this point of view that carried the day.*
carry on 1 = continue, last, endure, persist, keep going, persevere, crack on (*informal*): *Her bravery has given him the will to carry on.* **2 = make a fuss**, act up

(informal), misbehave, create *(slang)*, raise Cain: *She was yelling and screaming and carrying on like an idiot.*
carry something on = **engage in**, conduct, carry out, undertake, embark on, enter into: *The consulate will carry on a political dialogue.*
carry something out = **perform**, effect, achieve, realize, implement, fulfil, accomplish, execute, discharge, consummate, carry through: *Commitments have been made with very little intention of carrying them out.*

C

carry-on NOUN = **fuss**, disturbance, racket, fracas, commotion, rumpus, tumult, hubbub, shindy *(informal)*

carton NOUN = **box**, case, pack, package, container

cartoon NOUN **1** = **drawing**, parody, satire, caricature, comic strip, takeoff *(informal)*, lampoon, sketch: *The newspaper printed a cartoon depicting the president as a used car salesman.* **2** = **animation**, animated film, animated cartoon: *the X-rated TV cartoon, South Park*

cartridge NOUN **1** = **shell**, round, charge: *Gun and cartridge manufacturers will lose money if the game laws are amended.* **2** = **container**, case, magazine, cassette, cylinder, capsule: *Change the filter cartridge as often as instructed by the manufacturer.*

carve VERB **1** = **sculpt**, form, cut, chip, sculpture, whittle, chisel, hew, fashion: *One of the prisoners has carved a beautiful chess set.* **2** = **etch**, engrave, inscribe, fashion, slash: *He carved his name on his desk.*

carving NOUN = **sculpture**

cascade NOUN = **waterfall**, falls, torrent, flood, shower, fountain, avalanche, deluge, downpour, outpouring, cataract: *She stood still for a moment under the cascade of water.*
▷ VERB = **flow**, fall, flood, pour, plunge, surge, spill, tumble, descend, overflow, gush, teem, pitch: *A waterfall cascades down the cliff from the hills.*

case[1] NOUN **1** = **situation**, event, circumstance(s), state, position, condition, context, dilemma, plight, contingency, predicament: *In extreme cases, insurance companies can prosecute for fraud.* **2** = **instance**, example, occasion, specimen, occurrence: *Some cases of arthritis respond to a gluten-free diet.* **3** = **lawsuit**, process, trial, suit, proceedings, dispute, cause, action: *He lost his case at the European Court of Human Rights.*

case[2] NOUN **1** = **cabinet**, box, chest, holder: *There was a ten-foot long stuffed alligator in a glass case.* **2** = **container**, compact, capsule, carton, cartridge, canister, casket, receptacle: *She held up a blue spectacle case.* **3** = **suitcase**, bag, grip, trunk, holdall, portmanteau, valise: *The porter brought my cases down and called for a taxi.* **4** = **crate**, box: *The winner will receive a case of champagne.* **5** = **covering**, casing, cover, shell, wrapping, jacket, envelope, capsule, folder, sheath, wrapper, integument: *Vanilla is the seed case of a South American orchid.*

cash NOUN = **money**, change, funds, notes, ready *(informal)*, the necessary *(informal)*, resources, currency, silver, bread *(slang)*, coin, tin *(slang)*, brass *(Northern English dialect)*, dough *(slang)*, rhino *(Brit. slang)*, banknotes, bullion, dosh *(Brit. & Austral. slang)*, wherewithal, coinage, needful *(informal)*, specie, shekels *(informal)*, dibs *(slang)*, ready money, ackers *(slang)*, spondulicks *(slang)*

cashier[1] NOUN = **teller**, accountant, clerk, treasurer, bank clerk, purser, bursar, banker: *The cashier said that he would fetch the manager.*

cashier[2] VERB = **dismiss**, discharge, expel, cast off, drum out, give the boot to *(slang)*: *Many officers were cashiered on political grounds.*

casing NOUN = **covering**, case, cover, shell, container, integument

cask NOUN = **barrel**, drum, cylinder, keg

casket NOUN = **box**, case, chest, coffer, ark *(dialect)*, jewel box, kist *(Scot. & Northern English dialect)*

cast NOUN **1** = **actors**, company, players, characters, troupe, dramatis personae: *The show is very amusing and the cast are excellent.* **2** = **type**, turn, sort, kind, style, stamp: *Hers was an essentially optimistic cast of mind.*
▷ VERB **1** = **choose**, name, pick, select, appoint, assign, allot: *He has been cast in the lead role of the new Pinter play.* **2** = **bestow**, give, level, accord, direct, confer: *He cast a stern glance at the two men.* **3** = **give out**, spread, deposit, shed, distribute, scatter, emit, radiate, bestow, diffuse: *The moon cast a bright light over the yard.* **4** = **throw**, project, launch, pitch, shed, shy, toss, thrust, hurl, fling, chuck *(informal)*, sling, lob, impel, drive, drop: *She took a pebble and cast it into the water.* **5** = **mould**, set, found, form, model, shape: *This statue of Neptune is cast in bronze.*
cast someone down = **discourage**, depress, desolate, dishearten, dispirit, deject: *I am not too easily cast down by changes of fortune.*

caste NOUN = **class**, order, race, station, rank, status, stratum, social order, lineage

castigate VERB = **reprimand**, blast, carpet *(informal)*, put down, criticize, lash, slate *(informal, chiefly Brit.)*, censure, rebuke, scold, berate, dress down *(informal)*, chastise, chasten, tear into *(informal)*, diss *(slang, chiefly U.S.)*, read the riot act, slap on the wrist, lambast(e), bawl out *(informal)*, excoriate, rap over the knuckles, haul over the coals *(informal)*, chew out *(U.S. & Canad. informal)*, tear (someone) off a strip *(Brit. informal)*, give a rocket *(Brit. & N.Z. informal)*

cast-iron ADJECTIVE = **certain**, established, settled, guaranteed, fixed, definite, copper-bottomed, idiot-proof, nailed-on *(slang)*

castle NOUN = **fortress**, keep, palace, tower, peel, chateau, stronghold, citadel, fastness

castrate VERB = **neuter**, unman, emasculate, geld

casual ADJECTIVE **1** = **careless**, relaxed, informal, indifferent, unconcerned, apathetic, blasé, offhand, nonchalant, insouciant,

CASTLES

Aberystwyth
Amboise
Arundel
Ashby de la Zouch
Ashford
Aydon
Ballindalloch
Balmoral
Balvenie
Barnard
Beaumaris
Beeston
Belvoir
Berkeley
Berkhamstead
Berwick-upon-Tweed
Blarney
Blois
Braemar
Brodie
Bunraity
Cabra
Caerlaverock
Caernarfon
Caerphilly
Cahir
Canossa
Carisbrooke
Carmarthen
Carrickfergus
Château-Raoul
Cheb
Chillon
Colditz
Conwy
Crathes
Culzean
Darnaway
Dinan
Drum
Dublin
Dunnottar
Dunsinane
Dunstaffnage
Durham
Edinburgh
Eilean Donan
Esterháza
Farney
Forfar
Fotheringhay
Glamis
Harlech
Heidelberg
Herstmonceux
Inverness
Kenilworth
Kilkea
Kilkenny
Killaghy
Kilravock
Lancaster
Launceston
Leamaneh
Leeds
Leicester
Lincoln
Ludlow
Malahide
Monmouth
Otranto
Pembroke
Pendennis
Pontefract
Portlick
Rait
Restormel
Richmond
Rithes
Rock of Cashel
St Mawes
Scarborough
Sherborne
Skipton
Stirling
Stuart
Taymouth
Tintagel
Torún
Trausnitz
Trim
Urquhart
Vaduz
Vincennes
Wartburg
Warwick

The Language of James Hogg

Scottish poet and novelist James Hogg (1770–1835) worked as a shepherd in the small village of Ettrick before embarking on his literary career. One of his most notable poems is *The Queen's Wake*, a book-length work concerning the return of Mary Queen of Scots to Scotland after her exile in France, while his most famous novel is *The Private Memoirs and Confessions of a Justified Sinner.* Important themes in this work include religious fanaticism and national identity. Hogg wrote in both Scots and English.

The noun that Hogg uses most frequently is *man,* which appears over four times as often as *woman.* After *young,* the most salient adjective with *man* is *wicked,* pointing to the significance of the themes of religion and sin in Hogg's work. For example:

> It is our duty, however, to shun the society of **wicked men** as much as possible, lest we partake of their sins, and become sharers with them in punishment.

God, sin, soul, prayer, and *Heaven* all appear in Hogg's 100 most frequently used nouns, also indicating the importance of religion in his work. Hogg's use of adjectives emphasizes this further, with *wicked, religious, sinful, Christian,* and *evil* appearing in his 100 most frequent adjectives. *Religious* is used to modify nouns such as *devotion, maniac, principle,* and *scruple,* whereas *evil* is used to modify *genius* and *deed. Christian* modifies *reverence* and *resentment,* while *sinful* modifies *doubtings, pastime,* and *associate.*

Evidence of vocabulary associated with religion also surfaces in Hogg's use of verbs, with *pray* being very frequent. *Pray* is often modified by adverbs, for example *fervently, lustily,* and *inwardly.* The verb *save* also appears in Hogg's 100 most frequently used verbs and is often used in a religious context:

> Is there not enough of merit in the blood of Jesus to **save** thousands of worlds, if it was for these worlds that he died?

Interestingly, Hogg also often uses *save* as a preposition, in the sense 'except' or 'apart from'. For example:

> I was struck speechless, and could make no answer **save** by looks of surprise.

Hogg uses *save* as a preposition four times as frequently as *except*, and there are no instances of *apart.* In the *Bank of English,* Collins' corpus of present-day English, *except* as a preposition appears over twenty-four times as often as *save* as a preposition.

Another interesting feature of Hogg's language is his use of Scots vocabulary such as *laird,* and *lad* (*lord* and *boy*). *Laird* appears slightly more often than *lord,* while *boy* appears over twice as often as *lad.* With the exception of *lad* and *laird,* many of the Scots words Hogg uses appear exclusively in speech, for example *ye, wi, ain, sae, aye, canna, gie, baith, muckle,* and *deil* (*you, with, own, so, yes, can't, give, both, much,* and *devil*). This shows that Hogg most often uses Scots words to present the dialect of characters in his work:

> ...in the height of his caprice, he said to his wife: 'Whan focks are sae keen of a chance o' entertaining angels, gude-wife, it wad maybe be worth their while to tak tent what kind o' angels they are. It wadna wonder me vera muckle an ye had entertained your friend the Deil the night, for aw thought aw fand a saur o' reek an' brimstane about him. He's nane o' the best o' angels, an focks winna hae muckle credit by entertaining him.'

The passage above reflects the importance of dialogue in Hogg's work; many characters make long speeches like this one and Hogg uses devices like the use of Scots dialect or English to suggest class or lifestyle. Furthermore, the significance of religion is again evident.

lackadaisical: *an easy-going young man with a casual approach to life* **OPPOSITE:** serious **2 = chance**, unexpected, random, accidental, incidental, unforeseen, unintentional, fortuitous *(informal)*, serendipitous, unpremeditated: *It was just a casual meeting.* **OPPOSITE:** planned **3 = informal**, leisure, sporty, non-dressy: *I bought casual clothes for the weekend.* **OPPOSITE:** formal

C

casualty NOUN **1 = fatality**, death, loss, wounded: *Troops fired on the demonstrators, causing many casualties.* **2 = victim**, sufferer: *The company has been one of the greatest casualties of the recession.*

cat NOUN **= feline**, pussy *(informal)*, moggy *(slang)*, puss *(informal)*, ballarat *(Austral. informal)*, tabby ▸ *related adjective:* feline ▸ *name of male:* tom ▸ *name of female:* queen ▸ *name of young:* kitten

> **QUOTATIONS**
> cat: a soft, indestructible automaton provided by nature to be kicked when things go wrong in the domestic circle
> [Ambrose Bierce *The Devil's Dictionary*]
>
> Cats seem to go on the principle that it never does any harm to ask for what you want
> [Joseph Wood Krutch *The Twelve Seasons*]
>
> When I play with my cat, who knows whether she isn't amusing herself with me more than I am with her?
> [Montaigne *Essais*]

> **PROVERBS**
> *When the cat's away, the mice will play*
> *The cat would eat fish, but would not wet her feet*
> *All cats are grey in the dark*

cataclysm NOUN **= disaster**, collapse, catastrophe, upheaval, debacle, devastation, calamity

cataclysmic ADJECTIVE **= disastrous**, devastating, catastrophic, calamitous

catalogue *or (U.S.)* **catalog** NOUN **= list**, record, schedule, index, register, directory, inventory, gazetteer: *One of the authors of the catalogue is the Professor of Art History.* ▹ VERB **= list**, file, index, register, classify, inventory, tabulate, alphabetize: *The Royal Greenwich Observatory was founded to observe and catalogue the stars.*

catapult NOUN **= sling**, slingshot *(U.S.)*, trebuchet, ballista: *They were hit twice by missiles fired from a catapult.* ▹ VERB **= shoot**, pitch, plunge, toss, hurl, propel, hurtle, heave: *He was catapulted into the side of the van.*

cataract NOUN **1 = opacity** *(of the eye)*: *a battle with blindness caused by cataracts* **2 = waterfall**, falls, rapids, cascade, torrent, deluge, downpour, Niagara: *There was an impressive cataract at the end of the glen.*

catastrophe NOUN **= disaster**, tragedy, calamity, meltdown *(informal)*, cataclysm, trouble, trial, blow, failure, reverse, misfortune, devastation, adversity, mishap, affliction, whammy *(informal, chiefly U.S.)*, bummer *(slang)*, mischance, fiasco

catastrophic ADJECTIVE **= disastrous**, devastating, tragic, calamitous, cataclysmic

catch VERB **1 = capture**, arrest, trap, seize, nail *(informal)*, nab *(informal)*, snare, lift *(slang)*, apprehend, ensnare, entrap, feel your collar *(slang)*: *Police say they are confident of catching the killer.* **OPPOSITE:** free **2 = trap**, capture, snare, entangle, ensnare, entrap: *The locals were encouraged to catch and kill the birds.* **3 = seize**, get, grab, snatch: *I jumped up to catch the ball and fell over.* **4 = grab**, take, grip, seize, grasp, clutch, lay hold of: *He knelt beside her and caught her hand in both of his.* **OPPOSITE:** release **5 = discover**, surprise, find out, expose, detect, catch in the act, take unawares: *He caught a youth breaking into his car.* **6 = contract**, get, develop, suffer from, incur, succumb to, go down with: *The more stress you are under, the more likely you are to catch a cold.* **OPPOSITE:** escape ▹ NOUN **1 = fastener**, hook, clip, bolt, latch, clasp, hasp, hook and eye, snib *(Scot.)*, sneck *(dialect, chiefly Scot. & Northern English)*: *Always fit windows with safety locks or catches.* **2 = drawback**, trick, trap, disadvantage, hitch, snag, stumbling block, fly in the ointment: *It sounds too good to be true – what's the catch?* **OPPOSITE:** advantage
catch on 1 = understand, see, find out, grasp, see through, comprehend, twig *(Brit. informal)*, get the picture, see the light of day: *He tried to explain it to me, but it took me a while to catch on.* **2 = become popular**, take off, become trendy, come into fashion: *The idea has been around for ages without catching on.*

catchcry *(Austral.)* NOUN **= catch phrase**, slogan, saying, quotation, motto

catching ADJECTIVE **= infectious**, contagious, transferable, communicable, infective, transmittable **OPPOSITE:** non-infectious

catch phrase NOUN **= slogan**, saying, quotation, motto, catchword, catchcry *(Austral.)*

catchy ADJECTIVE **= memorable**, haunting, unforgettable, captivating

categorical ADJECTIVE **= absolute**, direct, express, positive, explicit, unconditional, emphatic, downright, unequivocal, unqualified, unambiguous, unreserved **OPPOSITE:** vague

category NOUN **= class**, grouping, heading, head, order, sort, list, department, type, division, section, rank, grade, classification, genre, subgenre

cater VERB
cater for something *or* **someone 1 = provide for**, supply, provision, purvey, victual: *Thirty restaurants and hotels catered for the event.* **2 = take into account**, consider, bear in mind, make allowance for, have regard for: *We have to cater for the demands of the marketplace.*
cater to something *or* **someone = indulge**, spoil, minister to, pamper, gratify, pander to, coddle, mollycoddle: *His parents spoil him and cater to his every whim.*

catharsis NOUN **= release**, cleansing, purging, purification

catholic ADJECTIVE **= wide**, general, liberal, global, varied, comprehensive, universal, world-wide, tolerant, eclectic, all-inclusive, ecumenical, all-embracing, broad-minded, unbigoted, unsectarian, multiculti *(informal)* **OPPOSITE:** limited

cattle PLURAL NOUN **= cows**, stock, beasts, livestock, bovines ▸ *related adjective:* bovine ▸ *collective nouns:* drove, herd

> **QUOTATIONS**
> The cow is of the bovine ilk;
> One end is moo, the other, milk
> [Ogden Nash *The Cow*]

caucus NOUN **= group**, division, section, camp, sector, lobby, bloc, contingent, pressure group, junta, public-interest group *(U.S. & Canad.)*

cause NOUN **1 = origin**, source, agency, spring, agent, maker, producer, root, beginning, creator, genesis, originator, prime mover, mainspring: *Smoking is the biggest preventable cause of death and disease.* **OPPOSITE:** result **2 = reason**, call, need, grounds, basis, incentive, motive, motivation, justification, inducement: *There is obvious cause for concern.* **3 = aim**, movement, purpose, principle, object, ideal, enterprise, end: *His comments have done nothing to help the cause of peace.* ▹ VERB **= produce**, begin, create, effect, lead to, occasion, result in, generate, provoke, compel, motivate, induce, bring about, give rise to, precipitate, incite, engender: *I don't want to cause any trouble.* **OPPOSITE:** prevent

caustic ADJECTIVE **1 = burning**, corrosive, corroding, astringent, vitriolic, acrid: *This substance is caustic; use gloves when handling it.* **2 = sarcastic**, biting, keen, cutting, severe, stinging, scathing, acrimonious, pungent, vitriolic, trenchant, mordant: *He was well known for his abrasive wit and caustic comments.* **OPPOSITE:** kind

caution NOUN **1 = care**, discretion, heed, prudence, vigilance, alertness, forethought, circumspection, watchfulness, belt and braces, carefulness, heedfulness: *Drivers are urged to exercise extreme caution in icy*

weather. **OPPOSITE:** carelessness
2 = reprimand, warning, injunction, admonition: *The others got off with a caution but I was fined.*
▷ VERB **1 = warn**, urge, advise, alert, tip off, forewarn, put you on your guard: *Banks caution young couples against opening joint bank accounts.*
2 = reprimand, warn, admonish, give an injunction to: *The two men were cautioned but the police say they will not be charged.*

> **PROVERBS**
> *You should know a man seven years before you stir his fire*
> *Once bitten, twice shy*

cautious ADJECTIVE **= careful**, guarded, alert, wary, discreet, tentative, prudent, vigilant, watchful, judicious, circumspect, cagey *(informal)*, on your toes, chary, belt-and-braces, keeping a weather eye on **OPPOSITE:** careless

cautiously ADVERB **= carefully**, alertly, discreetly, tentatively, warily, prudently, judiciously, guardedly, circumspectly, watchfully, vigilantly, cagily *(informal)*, mindfully

cavalcade NOUN **= parade**, train, procession, march-past

cavalier ADJECTIVE **= offhand**, lordly, arrogant, lofty, curt, condescending, haughty, scornful, disdainful, insolent, supercilious

cavalry NOUN **= horsemen**, horse, mounted troops
OPPOSITE: infantrymen

cave NOUN **= hollow**, cavern, grotto, den, cavity

> **QUOTATIONS**
> Caves: Usually inhabited by thieves. Always full of snakes
> [Gustave Flaubert *The Dictionary of Received Ideas*]

caveat NOUN **= warning**, caution, admonition, qualification, proviso, reservation, condition

cavern NOUN **= cave**, hollow, grotto, underground chamber

cavernous ADJECTIVE **= vast**, wide, huge, enormous, extensive, immense, spacious, expansive, capacious, commodious

cavity NOUN **= hollow**, hole, gap, pit, dent, crater

cavort VERB **= frolic**, sport, romp, caper, prance, frisk, gambol

cease VERB **1 = stop**, end, finish, be over, come to an end, peter out, die away: *Almost miraculously, the noise ceased.* **OPPOSITE:** start
2 = discontinue, end, stop, fail, finish, give up, conclude, suspend, halt, terminate, break off, refrain, leave off, give over *(informal)*, bring to an end, desist, belay *(Nautical)*: *A small number of firms have ceased trading.*
OPPOSITE: begin

ceaseless ADJECTIVE **= continual**, constant, endless, continuous, eternal, perennial, perpetual, never-ending, interminable, incessant, everlasting, unending, unremitting, nonstop, untiring
OPPOSITE: occasional

cede VERB **= surrender**, grant, transfer, abandon, yield, concede, hand over, relinquish, renounce, make over, abdicate

celebrate VERB **1 = rejoice**, party, enjoy yourself, carouse, live it up *(informal)*, whoop it up *(informal)*, make merry, paint the town red *(informal)*, go on a spree, put the flags out, roister, kill the fatted calf: *I was in a mood to celebrate.* **2 = commemorate**, honour, observe, toast, drink to, keep: *Tom celebrated his birthday two days ago.* **3 = perform**, observe, preside over, officiate at, solemnize: *Pope John Paul celebrated mass today in a city in central Poland.* **4 = praise**, honour, commend *(informal)*, glorify, publicize, exalt, laud, extol, eulogize: *a festival to celebrate the life and work of this great composer*

celebrated ADJECTIVE **= renowned**, popular, famous, outstanding, distinguished, well-known, prominent, glorious, acclaimed, notable, eminent, revered, famed, illustrious, pre-eminent, lionized
OPPOSITE: unknown

celebration NOUN **1 = party**, festival, gala, jubilee, festivity, rave *(Brit. slang)*, beano *(Brit. slang)*, revelry, red-letter day, rave-up *(Brit. slang)*, merrymaking, carousal, -fest *(in combination)*, hooley or hoolie *(chiefly Irish & N.Z.)*: *There was a celebration in our house that night.* **2 = commemoration**, honouring, remembrance: *This was not a memorial service but a celebration of his life.* **3 = performance**, observance, solemnization: *the celebration of Mass in Latin*

celebrity NOUN **1 = personality**, name, star, superstar, big name, dignitary, luminary, bigwig *(informal)*, celeb *(informal)*, face *(informal)*, big shot *(informal)*, personage, megastar *(informal)*, V.I.P.: *At the age of twelve, he was already a celebrity.* **OPPOSITE:** nobody
2 = fame, reputation, honour, glory, popularity, distinction, prestige, prominence, stardom, renown, pre-eminence, repute, éclat, notability: *She has finally achieved celebrity after 25 years as an actress.*
OPPOSITE: obscurity

> **QUOTATIONS**
> A celebrity is a person who works hard all his life to become known, then wears dark glasses to avoid being recognized
> [Fred Allen *Treadmill to Oblivion*]
>
> The celebrity is a person who is known for his well-knownness
> [Daniel Boorstin *The Image*]
>
> Celebrity: the advantage of being known by those who don't know you
> [Chamfort *Maximes et pensées*]

celestial ADJECTIVE **1 = astronomical**, planetary, stellar, astral, extraterrestrial: *the clusters of celestial bodies in the ever-expanding universe*
2 = heavenly, spiritual, divine, eternal, sublime, immortal, supernatural, astral, ethereal, angelic, godlike, seraphic: *gods and other celestial beings*

celibacy NOUN **= chastity**, purity, virginity, continence, singleness

> **QUOTATIONS**
> Marriage has many pains, but celibacy has no pleasures
> [Samuel Johnson *Rasselas*]
>
> Marriage may often be a stormy lake, but celibacy is almost always a muddy horsepond
> [Thomas Love Peacock *Melincourt*]

celibate ADJECTIVE **= chaste**, single, pure, virgin, continent

cell NOUN **1 = room**, chamber, lock-up, compartment, cavity, cubicle, dungeon, stall: *They took her back to the cell, and just left her there to die.* **2 = unit**, group, section, core, nucleus, caucus, coterie: *the abolition of Communist Party cells in all work places*

cement NOUN **1 = mortar**, plaster, paste: *The stone work has all been pointed with cement.* **2 = sealant**, glue, gum, adhesive, binder: *Stick the pieces on with tile cement.*
▷ VERB **= stick**, join, bond, attach, seal, glue, plaster, gum, weld, solder: *Most artificial joints are cemented into place.*

cemetery NOUN **= graveyard**, churchyard, burial ground, necropolis, God's acre

censor VERB **= expurgate**, cut, blue-pencil, bowdlerize

censorship NOUN **= expurgation**, blue pencil, purgation, bowdlerization *or* bowdlerisation, sanitization *or* sanitisation

> **QUOTATIONS**
> Censorship is never over for those who have experienced it
> [Nadine Gordimer *Censorship and Its Aftermath*]
>
> God forbid that any book should be banned. The practice is as indefensible as infanticide
> [Rebecca West *The Strange Necessity*]
>
> Wherever books are burned, in the end people too will be burned
> [Heinrich Heine *Almansor*]
>
> Where there is official censorship it is a sign that speech is serious
> [Paul Goodman *Growing Up Absurd*]
>
> Is it a book you would even wish your wife or your servants to read?
> [Mervyn Griffith-Jones (of D.H. Lawrence's *Lady Chatterley's Lover*)]

censure VERB **= criticize**, blame, abuse, condemn, carpet *(informal)*, denounce, put down, slate *(informal, chiefly U.S.)*, rebuke, reprimand, reproach, scold, berate, castigate,

chide, tear into *(informal)*, diss *(slang, chiefly U.S.)*, blast, read the riot act, reprove, upbraid, slap on the wrist, lambast(e), bawl out *(informal)*, excoriate, rap over the knuckles, chew out *(U.S. & Canad. informal)*, tear (someone) off a strip *(Brit. informal)*, give (someone) a rocket *(Brit. & N.Z. informal)*, reprehend: *I would not presume to censure him for his views.*
OPPOSITE: applaud
▷ NOUN **= disapproval**, criticism, blame, condemnation, rebuke, reprimand, reproach, dressing down *(informal)*, stick *(slang)*, stricture, reproof, castigation, obloquy, remonstrance: *It is a controversial policy which has attracted international censure.*
OPPOSITE: approval

C

central ADJECTIVE **1 = inner**, middle, mid, interior: *She had a house in central London.* **OPPOSITE:** outer **2 = main**, chief, key, essential, primary, principal, fundamental, focal: *The Poll Tax was a central part of Mrs Thatcher's reform of local government.*
OPPOSITE: minor

centralize VERB **= unify**, concentrate, incorporate, compact, streamline, converge, condense, amalgamate, rationalize

centre NOUN **= middle**, heart, focus, core, nucleus, hub, pivot, kernel, crux, bull's-eye, midpoint: *A large wooden table dominates the centre of the room.* **OPPOSITE:** edge
centre on something *or* **someone = focus**, concentrate, cluster, revolve, converge: *Our efforts centre on helping patients to overcome illness; All his thoughts are centred on himself.*

centrepiece NOUN **= focus**, highlight, hub, star

ceremonial ADJECTIVE **= formal**, public, official, ritual, stately, solemn, liturgical, courtly, ritualistic: *He represented the nation on ceremonial occasions.* **OPPOSITE:** informal
▷ NOUN **= ritual**, ceremony, rite, formality, solemnity: *It is difficult to imagine a more impressive ceremonial.*

ceremony NOUN **1 = ritual**, service, rite, observance, commemoration, solemnities: *The flag was blessed in a ceremony in the local cathedral.*
2 = formality, ceremonial, propriety, decorum, formal courtesy: *He was crowned with great ceremony.*

certain ADJECTIVE **1 = sure**, convinced, positive, confident, satisfied, assured, free from doubt: *She's absolutely certain she's going to make it as a singer.*
OPPOSITE: unsure **2 = bound**, sure, fated, destined: *They say he's certain to get a nomination for best supporting actor.*
OPPOSITE: unlikely **3 = inevitable**, unavoidable, inescapable, inexorable, ineluctable: *They intervened to save him from certain death.* **4 = known**, true, positive, plain, ascertained, unmistakable, conclusive, undoubted, unequivocal, undeniable, irrefutable, unquestionable, incontrovertible, indubitable, nailed-on *(slang)*: *One thing is certain – they have the utmost respect for each other.*
OPPOSITE: doubtful **5 = fixed**, decided, established, settled, definite: *He has to pay a certain sum in child support every month.* **OPPOSITE:** indefinite
6 = particular, special, individual, specific: *A certain person has been looking for you.*

certainly ADVERB **= definitely**, surely, truly, absolutely, undoubtedly, positively, decidedly, without doubt, unquestionably, undeniably, without question, unequivocally, indisputably, assuredly, indubitably, doubtlessly, come hell or high water, irrefutably

certainty NOUN **1 = confidence**, trust, faith, conviction, assurance, certitude, sureness, positiveness: *I have said with absolute certainty that there will be no change of policy.*
OPPOSITE: doubt **2 = inevitability**: *There is too little certainty about the outcome yet.* **OPPOSITE:** uncertainty **3 = fact**, truth, reality, sure thing *(informal)*, surety, banker: *A general election became a certainty three weeks ago.*

> **QUOTATIONS**
> In this world nothing is certain but death and taxes
> [Benjamin Franklin]
>
> If a man will begin with certainties, he shall end in doubts; but if he will be content to begin with doubts, he shall end in certainties
> [Francis Bacon *The Advancement of Learning*]

certificate NOUN **= document**, licence, warrant, voucher, diploma, testimonial, authorization, credential(s)

certify VERB **= confirm**, show, declare, guarantee, witness, assure, endorse, testify, notify, verify, ascertain, validate, attest, corroborate, avow, authenticate, vouch for, aver

cessation NOUN **= ceasing**, ending, break, halt, halting, pause, suspension, interruption, respite, standstill, stoppage, termination, let-up *(informal)*, remission, abeyance, discontinuance, stay

chafe VERB **1 = rub**, scratch, scrape, rasp, abrade: *The shorts were chafing my thighs.* **2 = be annoyed**, rage, fume, be angry, fret, be offended, be irritated, be incensed, be impatient, be exasperated, be inflamed, be ruffled, be vexed, be narked *(Brit., Austral. & N.Z. slang)*: *He chafed at having to take orders from someone else.*

chaff NOUN **= husks**, remains, refuse, waste, hulls, rubbish, trash, dregs

chagrin NOUN **= annoyance**, embarrassment, humiliation, dissatisfaction, disquiet, displeasure, mortification, discomfiture, vexation, discomposure: *Much to his chagrin, she didn't remember him at all.*
▷ VERB **= annoy**, embarrass, humiliate, disquiet, vex, displease, mortify, discomfit, dissatisfy, discompose: *He was chagrined at missing such an easy goal.*

chain NOUN **1 = tether**, coupling, link, bond, shackle, fetter, manacle: *The dogs were growling and pulling at their chains.* **2 = series**, set, train, string, sequence, succession, progression, concatenation: *a horrific chain of events*
▷ VERB **= bind**, confine, restrain, handcuff, shackle, tether, fetter, manacle: *We were kept in a cell, chained to the wall.*

chairman *or* **chairwoman** NOUN **1 = director**, president, chief, executive, chairperson: *I had done business with the company's chairman.* **2 = master of ceremonies**, spokesman, chair, speaker, MC, chairperson: *The chairman declared the meeting open.*

> **USAGE**
> The general trend of nonsexist language is to find a term which can apply to both sexes equally, as in the use of *actor* to refer to both men and women. *Chairman* can seem inappropriate when applied to a woman, while *chairwoman* specifies gender; therefore, the terms *chair* and *chairperson* are often preferred as alternatives.

chalk up VERB **1 = score**, win, gain, achieve, accumulate, attain: *The team chalked up one win after another.*
2 = record, mark, enter, credit, register, log, tally: *I just chalked his odd behaviour up to midlife crisis.*

challenge NOUN **1 = dare**, provocation, summons to contest, wero *(N.Z.)*: *I like a challenge, and they don't come much bigger than this.* **2 = test**, trial, opposition, confrontation, defiance, ultimatum, face-off *(slang)*: *In December, she saw off the first challenge to her leadership.*
▷ VERB **1 = dispute**, question, tackle, confront, defy, object to, disagree with, take issue with, impugn, throw down *(U.S. slang)*: *The move was immediately challenged by the opposition.*
2 = dare, invite, provoke, defy, summon, call out, throw down the gauntlet: *He left a note at the crime scene, challenging detectives to catch him.*
3 = test, try, tax: *a task that would challenge his courage* **4 = question**, interrogate, accost: *The men opened fire after they were challenged by the guard.*

chamber NOUN **1 = hall**, room: *We are going to be in the council chamber when he speaks.* **2 = council**, assembly, legislature, legislative body: *the main political chamber of the Slovenian parliament*
3 = room, bedroom, apartment, enclosure, cubicle: *We shall dine together in my chamber.* **4 = compartment**, hollow, cavity: *The incinerator works by focusing the sun's rays onto a cylindrical glass chamber.*

champion NOUN **1 = winner**, hero, victor, conqueror, title holder,

warrior: *Kasparov became a world chess champion.* **2 = defender**, guardian, patron, backer, protector, upholder, vindicator: *He received acclaim as a champion of the oppressed.*
▷ VERB **= support**, back, defend, promote, advocate, fight for, uphold, espouse, stick up for *(informal)*: *He passionately championed the poor.*

chance NOUN **1 = probability**, odds, possibility, prospect, liability, likelihood: *This partnership has a good chance of success.* **OPPOSITE:** certainty **2 = opportunity**, opening, occasion, time, scope, window: *All eligible people will get a chance to vote.* **3 = accident**, fortune, luck, fate, destiny, coincidence, misfortune, providence: *I met him quite by chance.* **OPPOSITE:** design **4 = risk**, speculation, gamble, hazard: *I certainly think it's worth taking a chance.*
▷ ADJECTIVE **= accidental**, random, casual, incidental, unforeseen, unintentional, fortuitous, inadvertent, serendipitous, unforeseeable, unlooked-for: *He describes their chance meeting as intense.* **OPPOSITE:** planned
▷ VERB **1 = happen**: *A man I chanced to meet proved to be a most unusual character.* **2 = risk**, try, stake, venture, gamble, hazard, wager: *No sniper would chance a shot from amongst that crowd.*
▶ *related adjective:* fortuitous

change NOUN **1 = alteration**, innovation, transformation, modification, mutation, metamorphosis, permutation, transmutation, difference, revolution, transition: *They are going to have to make some drastic changes.* **2 = variety**, break *(informal)*, departure, variation, novelty, diversion, whole new ball game *(informal)*: *It makes a nice change to see you in a good mood for once.* **OPPOSITE:** monotony **3 = exchange**, trade, conversion, swap, substitution, interchange: *He stuffed a bag with a few changes of clothing.*
▷ VERB **1 = alter**, reform, transform, adjust, moderate, revise, modify, remodel, reorganize, restyle, convert: *They should change the law to make it illegal to own replica weapons.* **OPPOSITE:** keep **2 = shift**, vary, transform, alter, modify, diversify, fluctuate, mutate, metamorphose, transmute: *We are trying to detect and understand how the climate changes.* **OPPOSITE:** stay **3 = exchange**, trade, replace, substitute, swap, interchange: *Can we change it for another if it doesn't work properly?*

QUOTATIONS

A state without the means of some change is without the means of its conservation
[Edmund Burke *Reflections on the Revolution in France*]

Can the Ethiopian change his skin, or the leopard his spots?
[*Bible: Jeremiah*]

The more things change, the more they are the same
[Alphonse Karr *Les Guêpes*]

Change is not made without inconvenience, even from worse to better
[Samuel Johnson *Dictionary of the English Language*]

The old order changeth, yielding place to new
[Alfred, Lord Tennyson *The Passing of Arthur*]

Philosophers have only interpreted the world in various ways; the point, however, is to change it
[Karl Marx *Theses on Feuerbach*]

When it is not necessary to change, it is necessary not to change
[Lucius Cary *Discourses of Infallibility*]

PROVERBS

Don't change horses in midstream
A change is as good as a rest
A new broom sweeps clean

changeable ADJECTIVE **= variable**, shifting, mobile, uncertain, volatile, unsettled, unpredictable, versatile, unstable, irregular, erratic, wavering, uneven, unreliable, fickle, temperamental, whimsical, mercurial, capricious, unsteady, protean, vacillating, fitful, mutable, inconstant **OPPOSITE:** constant

channel NOUN **1 = means**, way, course, approach, medium, route, path, avenue: *We'll be lodging a complaint through the official channels.* **2 = strait**, sound, route, passage, canal, waterway, main: *Oil spilled into the channel following a collision between a tanker and a trawler.* **3 = duct**, chamber, artery, groove, gutter, furrow, conduit: *Keep the drainage channel clear.*
▷ VERB **= direct**, guide, conduct, transmit, convey: *Stephen is channelling all his energies into his novel.*

chant NOUN **= song**, carol, chorus, melody, psalm: *We were listening to a CD of Gregorian chant.*
▷ VERB **= sing**, chorus, recite, intone, carol: *Muslims chanted and prayed in the temple.*

chaos NOUN **= disorder**, confusion, mayhem, anarchy, lawlessness, pandemonium, entropy, bedlam, tumult, disorganization
OPPOSITE: orderliness

QUOTATIONS

The whole worl's in a state o' chassis!
[Sean O'Casey *Juno and the Paycock*]

Chaos is a name for any order that produces confusion in our minds
[George Santayana *Dominations and Powers*]

Chaos often breeds life, when order breeds habit
[Henry Brooks Adams *The Education of Henry Adams*]

chaotic ADJECTIVE **= disordered**, confused, uncontrolled, anarchic, tumultuous, lawless, riotous, topsy-turvy, disorganized, purposeless

chap NOUN **= fellow**, man, person, individual, type, sort, customer *(informal)*, character, guy *(informal)*, bloke *(Brit. informal)*, cove *(slang)*, dude *(U.S. & Canad. informal)*, boykie *(S. African informal)*

chapter NOUN **1 = section**, part, stage, division, episode, topic, segment, instalment: *I took the title of this chapter from one of my favorite songs.* **2 = period**, time, stage, phase: *It was one of the most dramatic chapters of recent British politics.*

char VERB **= scorch**, sear, singe

character NOUN **1 = personality**, nature, make-up, cast, constitution, bent, attributes, temper, temperament, complexion, disposition, individuality, marked traits: *There is a side to his character which you haven't seen yet.* **2 = nature**, kind, quality, constitution, calibre: *Moscow's reforms were socialist in character.* **3 = person**, sort, individual, type, guy *(informal)*, fellow: *What an unpleasant character he is!* **4 = reputation**, honour, integrity, good name, rectitude: *He's begun a series of attacks on my character.* **5 = role**, part, persona: *He plays the film's central character.* **6 = eccentric**, card *(informal)*, original, nut *(slang)*, flake *(slang, chiefly U.S.)*, oddity, oddball *(informal)*, odd bod *(informal)*, queer fish *(Brit. informal)*, wacko or whacko *(informal)*: *He'll be sadly missed. He was a real character.* **7 = symbol**, mark, sign, letter, figure, type, device, logo, emblem, rune, cipher, hieroglyph: *Chinese characters inscribed on a plaque*

QUOTATIONS

Genius is formed in quiet, character in the stream of human life
[Goethe *Torquato Tasso*]

Character is much easier kept than recovered
[Thomas Paine *The American Crisis*]

A man's character is his fate
[Heraclitus *On the Universe*]

You can tell a lot about a fellow's character by the way he eats jelly beans
[Ronald Reagan]

Character is like a tree and reputation like its shadow. The shadow is what we think of it; the tree is the real thing
[Abraham Lincoln]

Fate and character are the same concept
[Novalis *Heinrich von Ofterdingen*]

characteristic NOUN **= feature**, mark, quality, property, attribute, faculty, trait, quirk, peculiarity, idiosyncrasy: *Genes determine the characteristics of every living thing.*
▷ ADJECTIVE **= typical**, special, individual, specific, representative, distinguishing, distinctive, peculiar,

singular, idiosyncratic, symptomatic: *Windmills are a characteristic feature of the landscape.* **OPPOSITE:** rare

characterize VERB **= distinguish**, mark, identify, brand, inform, stamp, typify

charade NOUN **= pretence**, farce, parody, pantomime, fake

charge VERB **1 = accuse**, indict, impeach, incriminate, arraign: *They have all the evidence required to charge him.* **OPPOSITE:** acquit **2 = attack**, assault, assail: *Our general ordered us to charge the enemy.* **OPPOSITE:** retreat **3 = rush**, storm, stampede: *He charged into the room.* **4 = fill**, load, instil, suffuse, lade: *a performance that was charged with energy* ▷ NOUN **1 = price**, rate, cost, amount, payment, expense, toll, expenditure, outlay, damage *(informal)*: *We can arrange this for a small charge.* **2 = accusation**, allegation, indictment, imputation: *They appeared at court to deny charges of murder.* **OPPOSITE:** acquittal **3 = care**, trust, responsibility, custody, safekeeping: *I have been given charge of this class.* **4 = duty**, office, concern, responsibility, remit: *I did not consider it any part of my charge to come up with marketing ideas.* **5 = ward**, pupil, protégé, dependant: *The coach tried to get his charges motivated.* **6 = attack**, rush, assault, onset, onslaught, stampede, sortie: *He led the bayonet charge from the front.* **OPPOSITE:** retreat

charisma NOUN **= charm**, appeal, personality, attraction, lure, allure, magnetism, force of personality, mojo *(U.S. slang)*

charismatic ADJECTIVE **= charming**, appealing, attractive, influential, magnetic, enticing, alluring

charitable ADJECTIVE **1 = benevolent**, liberal, generous, lavish, philanthropic, bountiful, beneficent: *He made large donations to numerous charitable organizations.* **OPPOSITE:** mean **2 = kind**, understanding, forgiving, sympathetic, favourable, tolerant, indulgent, lenient, considerate, magnanimous, broad-minded: *Some people take a less charitable view of his behaviour.* **OPPOSITE:** unkind

charity NOUN **1 = charitable organization**, fund, movement, trust, endowment: *The National Trust is a registered charity.* **2 = donations**, help, relief, gift, contributions, assistance, hand-out, philanthropy, alms-giving, benefaction, largesse *or* largess, koha *(N.Z.)*: *My mum was very proud. She wouldn't accept charity.* **OPPOSITE:** meanness **3 = kindness**, love, pity, humanity, affection, goodness, goodwill, compassion, generosity, indulgence, bounty, altruism, benevolence, fellow feeling, bountifulness, tenderheartedness, aroha *(N.Z.)*: *He had no sense of right and wrong, no charity, no humanity.* **OPPOSITE:** ill will

QUOTATIONS

The living need more charity than the dead
[George Arnold *The Jolly Old Pedagogue*]

Knowledge puffeth up, but charity edifieth
[*Bible: 1 Corinthians*]

And now abideth faith, hope, charity, these three: but the greatest of these is charity
[*Bible: 1 Corinthians*]

Charity. To love human beings in so far as they are nothing. That is to love them as God does
[Simone Weil *The New York Notebook*]

Though I speak with the tongues of men and of angels, and have not charity, I am become as sounding brass, or a tinkling cymbal. And though I have the gift of prophecy, and understand all mysteries, and all knowledge; and though I have all faith; so that I could remove mountains; and have not charity, I am nothing
[*Bible: 1 Corinthians*]

Charity begins at home, but should not end there
[Thomas Fuller *Gnomologia*]

Charity suffereth long, and is kind; charity envieth not; charity vaunteth not itself, is not puffed up... Beareth all things, believeth all things, hopeth all things, endureth all things. Charity never faileth
[*Bible: 1 Corinthians*]

Charity shall cover the multitude of sins
[*Bible: 1 Peter*]

He gives the poor man twice as much good who gives quickly
[Publilius Syrus]

PROVERBS

Charity begins at home

charlatan NOUN **= fraud**, cheat, fake, sham, pretender, quack, con man *(informal)*, impostor, fraudster, swindler, mountebank, grifter *(slang, chiefly U.S. & Canad.)*, phoney *or* phony *(informal)*, rorter *(Austral. slang)*, rogue trader

charm NOUN **1 = attraction**, appeal, fascination, allure, magnetism, desirability, allurement: *He was a man of great distinction and charm.* **OPPOSITE:** repulsiveness **2 = trinket**: *She wore a silver bracelet hung with charms.* **3 = talisman**, amulet, lucky piece, good-luck piece, mojo *(U.S. slang)*, fetish: *He carried a rabbit's foot as a good luck charm.* **4 = spell**, magic, enchantment, sorcery, makutu *(N.Z.)*: *They cross their fingers and spit over their shoulders as a charm against the evil eye.* ▷ VERB **1 = attract**, win, please, delight, fascinate, absorb, entrance, win over, enchant, captivate, beguile, allure, bewitch, ravish, mesmerize, enrapture, enamour: *My brother charms everyone he meets.* **OPPOSITE:** repel **2 = persuade**, seduce, coax, beguile, cajole, sweet-talk *(informal)*: *I'm sure you'll be able to charm him into taking you.*

QUOTATIONS

You know what charm is: a way of getting the answer yes without having asked any clear question
[Albert Camus *The Fall*]

Charm ... it's a sort of bloom on a woman. If you have it, you don't need to have anything else; and if you don't have it, it doesn't much matter what else you have
[J.M. Barrie *What Every Woman Knows*]

charming ADJECTIVE **= attractive**, pleasing, appealing, engaging, lovely, winning, pleasant, fetching, delightful, cute, irresistible, seductive, captivating, eye-catching, bewitching, delectable, winsome, likable *or* likeable **OPPOSITE:** unpleasant

chart NOUN **= table**, diagram, blueprint, graph, tabulation, plan, map: *The chart below shows the results of our survey.* ▷ VERB **1 = plot**, map out, delineate, sketch, draft, graph, tabulate: *These seas have been well charted.* **2 = monitor**, follow, record, note, document, register, trace, outline, log, graph, tabulate: *Bulletin boards charted each executive's progress.*

charter NOUN **1 = document**, right, contract, bond, permit, licence, concession, privilege, franchise, deed, prerogative, indenture: *In Britain, city status is granted by royal charter.* **2 = constitution**, laws, rules, code: *The Prime Minister also attacked the social charter.* ▷ VERB **1 = hire**, commission, employ, rent, lease: *He chartered a jet to fly her home.* **2 = authorize**, permit, sanction, entitle, license, empower, give authority: *The council is chartered to promote the understanding of British culture throughout the world.*

chase VERB **1 = pursue**, follow, track, hunt, run after, course: *She chased the thief for 100 yards.* **2 = drive away**, drive, expel, hound, send away, send packing, put to flight: *Some farmers chase you off their land quite aggressively.* **3 = rush**, run, race, shoot, fly, speed, dash, sprint, bolt, dart, hotfoot: *They chased down the stairs into the alley.* ▷ NOUN **= pursuit**, race, hunt, hunting: *He was arrested after a car chase.*

chasm NOUN **1 = gulf**, opening, crack, gap, rent, hollow, void, gorge, crater, cavity, abyss, ravine, cleft, fissure, crevasse: *The chasm was deep and its sides almost vertical.* **2 = gap**, division, gulf, split, breach, rift, alienation, hiatus: *the chasm that separates the rich from the poor*

chassis NOUN **= frame**, framework, fuselage, bodywork, substructure

chaste ADJECTIVE **1 = pure**, moral, decent, innocent, immaculate, wholesome, virtuous, virginal, unsullied, uncontaminated, undefiled, incorrupt: *Her character was pure, her thoughts chaste.*
OPPOSITE: promiscuous **2 = simple**, quiet, elegant, modest, refined, restrained, austere, unaffected, decorous: *Beyond them she could see the dim, chaste interior of the room.*

chasten VERB **= subdue**, discipline, cow, curb, humble, soften, humiliate, tame, afflict, repress, put in your place

chastise VERB **= scold**, blame, correct, discipline, lecture, carpet *(informal)*, nag, censure, rebuke, reprimand, reproach, berate, tick off *(informal)*, castigate, chide, tell off *(informal)*, find fault with, remonstrate with, bring (someone) to book, take (someone) to task, reprove, upbraid, bawl out *(informal)*, give (someone) a talking-to *(informal)*, haul (someone) over the coals *(informal)*, chew (someone) out *(U.S. & Canad. informal)*, give (someone) a dressing-down, give (someone) a rocket *(Brit. & N.Z. informal)*, give (someone) a row **OPPOSITE:** praise

chastity NOUN **= purity**, virtue, innocence, modesty, virginity, celibacy, continence, maidenhood
OPPOSITE: promiscuity

> **QUOTATIONS**
> Give me chastity and continence, but not just now
> [St. Augustine of Hippo *Confessions*]
>
> chastity – the most unnatural of all the sexual perversions
> [Aldous Huxley *Eyeless in Gaza*]
>
> I'd the upbringing a nun would envy...Until I was fifteen I was more familiar with Africa than my own body
> [Joe Orton *Entertaining Mr Sloane*]
>
> The essence of chastity is not the suppression of lust, but the total orientation of one's life towards a goal
> [Dietrich Bonhoeffer *Letters and Papers from Prison*]
>
> 'Tis chastity, my brother, chastity;
> She that has that, is clad in complete steel
> [John Milton *Comus*]

chat VERB **= talk**, gossip, jaw *(slang)*, natter, blather, schmooze *(slang)*, blether *(Scot.)*, shoot the breeze *(U.S. slang)*, chew the rag *or* fat *(slang)*: *I was just chatting to him the other day.*
▷ NOUN **= talk**, tête-à-tête, conversation, gossip, heart-to-heart, natter, blather, schmooze *(slang)*, blether *(Scot.)*, chinwag *(Brit. informal)*, confab *(informal)*, craic *(Irish informal)*, korero *(N.Z.)*: *She asked me into her office for a chat.*

chatter VERB **= prattle**, chat, rabbit on *(Brit. informal)*, babble, gab *(informal)*, natter, tattle, jabber, blather, schmooze *(slang)*, blether *(Scot.)*, run off at the mouth *(U.S. slang)*, prate, gossip: *Everyone was chattering away in different languages.*
▷ NOUN **= prattle**, chat, rabbit *(Brit. informal)*, gossip, babble, twaddle, gab *(informal)*, natter, tattle, jabber, blather, blether *(Scot.)*: *She kept up a steady stream of chatter the whole time.*

chatty ADJECTIVE **= talkative**, informal, effusive, garrulous, gabby *(informal)*, gossipy, newsy *(informal)*
OPPOSITE: quiet

cheap ADJECTIVE **1 = inexpensive**, sale, economy, reduced, keen, reasonable, bargain, low-priced, low-cost, cut-price, economical, cheapo *(informal)*: *Smoke detectors are cheap and easy to put up; People want good service at a cheap price.* **OPPOSITE:** expensive
2 = inferior, poor, worthless, second-rate, shoddy, tawdry, tatty, trashy, substandard, low-rent *(informal, chiefly U.S.)*, two-bit *(U.S. & Canad. slang)*, crappy *(slang)*, two a penny, rubbishy, dime-a-dozen *(informal)*, tinhorn *(U.S. slang)*, bodger *or* bodgie *(Austral. slang)*: *Don't resort to cheap copies; save up for the real thing.* **OPPOSITE:** good
3 = despicable, mean, low, base, vulgar, sordid, contemptible, scurvy, scungy *(Austral. & N.Z.)*: *That was a cheap trick to play on anyone.* **OPPOSITE:** decent

cheapen VERB **= degrade**, lower, discredit, devalue, demean, belittle, depreciate, debase, derogate

cheat VERB **1 = deceive**, skin *(slang)*, trick, fool, take in *(informal)*, con *(informal)*, stiff *(slang)*, sting *(informal)*, mislead, rip off *(slang)*, fleece, hoax, defraud, dupe, beguile, gull *(archaic)*, do *(informal)*, swindle, stitch up *(slang)*, victimize, bamboozle *(informal)*, hoodwink, double-cross *(informal)*, diddle *(informal)*, take for a ride *(informal)*, bilk, pull a fast one on *(informal)*, screw *(informal)*, finagle *(informal)*, scam *(slang)*: *He cheated an old woman out of her life savings.* **2 = foil**, check, defeat, prevent, frustrate, deprive, baffle, thwart: *He cheated death when he was rescued from the blazing cottage.*
▷ NOUN **= deceiver**, sharper, cheater, shark, charlatan, trickster, con man *(informal)*, impostor, fraudster, double-crosser *(informal)*, swindler, grifter *(slang, chiefly U.S. & Canad.)*, rorter *(Austral. slang)*, chiseller *(informal)*, rogue trader: *He's nothing but a rotten cheat.*

check VERB **1** *(often with* **out***)* **= examine**, test, study, look at, research, note, confirm, investigate, monitor, probe, tick, vet, inspect, look over, verify, work over, scrutinize, make sure of, inquire into, take a dekko at *(Brit. slang)*: *Check the accuracy of every detail in your CV; Get a mechanic to check the car out for you before you buy it.*
OPPOSITE: overlook **2 = stop**, control, limit, arrest, delay, halt, curb, bar, restrain, inhibit, rein, thwart, hinder, repress, obstruct, retard, impede, bridle, stem the flow of, nip in the bud, put a spoke in someone's wheel: *Sex education is expected to help check the spread of Aids.*
OPPOSITE: further
▷ NOUN **1 = examination**, test, research, investigation, inspection, scrutiny, once-over *(informal)*: *He is being constantly monitored with regular checks on his blood pressure.* **2 = control**, limitation, restraint, constraint, rein, obstacle, curb, obstruction, stoppage, inhibition, impediment, hindrance, damper: *There is no check on the flood of new immigrants arriving in the country.*

cheek NOUN **= impudence**, face *(informal)*, front, nerve, sauce *(informal)*, gall *(informal)*, disrespect, audacity, neck *(informal)*, lip *(slang)*, temerity, chutzpah *(U.S. & Canad. informal)*, insolence, impertinence, effrontery, brass neck *(Brit. informal)*, brazenness, sassiness *(U.S. informal)*

cheeky ADJECTIVE **= impudent**, rude, forward, fresh *(informal)*, insulting, saucy, audacious, sassy *(U.S. informal)*, pert, disrespectful, impertinent, insolent, lippy *(U.S. & Canad. slang)*
OPPOSITE: respectful

cheer VERB **1 = applaud**, hail, acclaim, clap, hurrah: *Cheering crowds lined the route.* **OPPOSITE:** boo **2 = hearten**, encourage, warm, comfort, elevate, animate, console, uplift, brighten, exhilarate, solace, enliven, cheer up, buoy up, gladden, elate, inspirit: *The people around him were cheered by his presence.* **OPPOSITE:** dishearten
▷ NOUN **1 = applause**, ovation: *The colonel was rewarded by a resounding cheer from his men.* **2 = cheerfulness**, comfort, joy, optimism, animation, glee, solace, buoyancy, mirth, gaiety, merriment, liveliness, gladness, hopefulness, merry-making: *This news did not bring them much cheer.*
cheer someone up = comfort, encourage, brighten, hearten, enliven, gladden, gee up, jolly along *(informal)*: *She chatted away brightly, trying to cheer him up.*
cheer up = take heart, rally, perk up, buck up *(informal)*: *Cheer up, things could be a lot worse.*

cheerful ADJECTIVE **1 = happy**, bright, contented, glad, optimistic, bucked *(informal)*, enthusiastic, sparkling, gay, sunny, jolly, animated, merry, upbeat *(informal)*, buoyant, hearty, cheery, joyful, jovial, genial, jaunty, chirpy *(informal)*, sprightly, blithe, light-hearted: *They are both very cheerful in spite of their circumstances.*
OPPOSITE: sad **2 = pleasant**, bright, sunny, gay, enlivening: *The room is bright and cheerful.* **OPPOSITE:** gloomy

cheerfulness NOUN **= happiness**, good humour, exuberance, high spirits, buoyancy, gaiety, good cheer, gladness, geniality, light-heartedness, jauntiness, joyousness

cheery ADJECTIVE **= cheerful**, happy, pleasant, lively, sunny, upbeat (*informal*), good-humoured, carefree, breezy, genial, chirpy (*informal*), jovial, full of beans (*informal*)

chemical NOUN = **compound**, drug, substance, synthetic substance, potion

chemist NOUN = **pharmacist**, apothecary (*obsolete*), pharmacologist, dispenser

cherish VERB **1** = **cling to**, prize, treasure, hold dear, cleave to: *I will cherish the memory of that visit for many years to come.* **OPPOSITE:** despise **2** = **care for**, love, support, comfort, look after, shelter, treasure, nurture, cosset, hold dear: *He genuinely loved and cherished his children.* **OPPOSITE:** neglect **3** = **harbour**, nurse, sustain, foster, entertain: *He cherished an ambition to be an actor.*

chest NOUN **1** = **breast**, front: *He crossed his arms over his chest.* **2** = **box**, case, trunk, crate, coffer, ark (*dialect*), casket, strongbox: *At the very bottom of the chest were his carving tools.*
▸ *related adjective:* pectoral

chew VERB = **munch**, bite, grind, champ, crunch, gnaw, chomp, masticate: *Be careful to eat slowly and chew your food well.*
chew something over = **consider**, weigh up, ponder, mull (over), meditate on, reflect upon, muse on, ruminate, deliberate upon: *You might want to sit back and chew things over for a while.*

chewy ADJECTIVE = **tough**, fibrous, leathery, as tough as old boots

chic ADJECTIVE = **stylish**, smart, elegant, fashionable, trendy (*Brit. informal*), up-to-date, modish, à la mode, voguish (*informal*), schmick (*Austral. informal*)
OPPOSITE: unfashionable

chide VERB = **scold**, blame, lecture, carpet (*informal*), put down, criticize, slate (*informal, chiefly Brit.*), censure, rebuke, reprimand, reproach, berate, tick off (*informal*), admonish, tear into (*informal*), blast, tell off (*informal*), find fault, diss (*slang, chiefly U.S.*), read the riot act, reprove, upbraid, slap on the wrist, lambast(e), bawl out (*informal*), rap over the knuckles, chew out (*U.S. & Canad. informal*), tear (someone) off a strip (*Brit. informal*), give (someone) a rocket (*Brit. & N.Z. informal*), reprehend, give (someone) a row (*Scot. informal*)

chief NOUN = **head**, leader, director, manager, lord, boss (*informal*), captain, master, governor, commander, principal, superior, ruler, superintendent, chieftain, ringleader, baas (*S. African*), ariki (*N.Z.*), sherang (*Austral. & N.Z.*): *The new leader is the deputy chief of the territory's defence force.* **OPPOSITE:** subordinate
▹ ADJECTIVE = **primary**, highest, leading, main, prime, capital, central, key, essential, premier, supreme, most important, outstanding, principal, prevailing, cardinal, paramount, big-time (*informal*), foremost, major league (*informal*), predominant, uppermost, pre-eminent, especial: *Financial stress is acknowledged as a chief reason for divorce; The job went to one of his chief rivals.*
OPPOSITE: minor

chiefly ADVERB **1** = **especially**, essentially, principally, primarily, above all: *We are chiefly concerned with the welfare of the children.* **2** = **mainly**, largely, usually, mostly, in general, on the whole, predominantly, in the main: *a committee composed chiefly of grey-haired old gentlemen*

child NOUN **1** = **youngster**, baby, kid (*informal*), minor, infant, babe, juvenile, toddler, tot, wean (*Scot.*), little one, brat, bairn (*Scot.*), suckling, nipper (*informal*), chit, babe in arms, sprog (*slang*), munchkin (*informal, chiefly U.S.*), rug rat (*slang*), nursling, littlie (*Austral. informal*), ankle-biter (*Austral. & U.S. slang*), tacker (*Austral. slang*): *This film is not suitable for children.* **2** = **offspring**, issue, descendant, progeny: *How many children do you have?*
▸ *related adjective:* filial ▸ *related prefix:* paedo-

> **QUOTATIONS**
> Children are the anchors that hold a mother to life
> [Sophocles *Phaedra*]
>
> The child is father of the man
> [William Wordsworth *My Heart Leaps Up*]
>
> I love children. Especially when they cry – for then someone takes them away
> [Nancy Mitford]
>
> The first half of our life is ruined by our parents and the second half by our children
> [Clarence Darrow]
>
> Your children are not your children.
> They are the sons and daughters of life's longing for itself.
> They came through you but not from you
> And though they are with you yet they belong not to you
> [Kahlil Gibran *The Prophet*]
>
> Children are completely egoistic; they feel their needs intensely and strive ruthlessly to satisfy them
> [Sigmund Freud *The Interpretation of Dreams*]
>
> Making terms with reality, with things as they are, is a full-time business for the child
> [Milton R. Sapirstein *Paradoxes of Everyday Life*]
>
> **PROVERBS**
> *Children should be seen and not heard*
> *Little children, little sorrows; big children, great sorrows*

childbirth NOUN = **child-bearing**, labour, delivery, lying-in, confinement, parturition
▸ *related adjectives:* natal, obstetric

> **QUOTATIONS**
> In sorrow thou shalt bring forth children
> [*Bible: Genesis*]
>
> Death and taxes and childbirth! There's never any convenient time for any of them
> [Margaret Mitchell *Gone with the Wind*]

childhood NOUN = **youth**, minority, infancy, schooldays, immaturity, boyhood *or* girlhood

> **QUOTATIONS**
> Childhood is the kingdom where nobody dies.
> Nobody that matters, that is
> [Edna St. Vincent Millay *Childhood is the Kingdom where Nobody Dies*]
>
> One of the great pleasures of childhood is found in the mysteries which it hides from the skepticism of the elders, and works up into small mythologies of its own
> [Oliver Wendell Holmes Sr. *The Poet at the Breakfast-Table*]

childish ADJECTIVE **1** = **youthful**, young, boyish *or* girlish: *One of his most appealing qualities is his childish enthusiasm.* **2** = **immature**, silly, juvenile, foolish, trifling, frivolous, infantile, puerile: *I've never seen such selfish and childish behaviour.*
OPPOSITE: mature

childlike ADJECTIVE = **innocent**, trusting, simple, naive, credulous, artless, ingenuous, guileless, unfeigned, trustful

chill VERB **1** = **cool**, refrigerate, freeze: *Chill the fruit salad until serving time.* **2** = **dishearten**, depress, discourage, dismay, dampen, deject: *There was a coldness in her voice which chilled him.*
▹ NOUN **1** = **coldness**, bite, nip, sharpness, coolness, rawness, crispness, frigidity: *September is here, bringing with it a chill in the mornings.* **2** = **shiver**, frisson, goose pimples, goose flesh: *He smiled an odd smile that sent a chill through me.*
▹ ADJECTIVE = **chilly**, biting, sharp, freezing, raw, bleak, wintry, frigid, parky (*Brit. informal*): *A chill wind was blowing.*

chilly ADJECTIVE **1** = **cool**, fresh, sharp, crisp, penetrating, brisk, breezy, draughty, nippy, parky (*Brit. informal*), blowy: *It was a chilly afternoon.*
OPPOSITE: warm **2** = **unfriendly**, hostile, unsympathetic, frigid, unresponsive, unwelcoming, cold as ice: *I was slightly afraid of his chilly, distant politeness.* **OPPOSITE:** friendly

chime VERB = **ring**: *The Guildhall clock chimed three o'clock.*
▹ NOUN = **sound**, boom, toll, jingle, dong, tinkle, clang, peal: *the chime of the Guildhall clock*

chimera NOUN = **illusion**, dream, fantasy, delusion, spectre, snare, hallucination, figment, ignis fatuus, will-o'-the-wisp

The Language of L Frank Baum

L Frank Baum (1856–1919) was an American playwright, filmmaker, poet, and novelist. His best-known work is the children's classic *The Wonderful Wizard of Oz*. Baum aimed to tell entertaining children's tales similar to those of the Brothers Grimm and Hans Christian Andersen, but without the violence typical of their stories.

Dialogue forms a major part of Baum's work. This is evidenced by the fact that apart from the comma, the punctuation mark Baum uses most frequently is the speech mark. Furthermore, *say, ask, tell, reply, answer, declare,* and *exclaim* all appear in Baum's fifty most frequently used verbs. These are often modified by adverbs such as *anxiously, sternly, joyfully, angrily, indignantly, earnestly,* and *proudly*:

> 'But it's all rubbish about there being danger in Taormina,' **declared** Patsy, **indignantly**.
>
> 'Oh, Louise,' **exclaimed** Patsy, reproachfully, 'why didn't you let me see the thing?'

Current literary tastes hold that modifying verbs of speech with a single adverb is overly simplistic, but this practice is appropriate to Baum's tone and audience.

Visual description is also important in Baum's work. While many of his most frequent adjectives are generic 'telling' ones such as *little, big, beautiful,* and *pretty,* colour-terms such as *red, white, black, yellow,* and *green* also frequently occur. As so much of Baum's work concerns things that are imaginary, detailed visual descriptions are necessary in order to create a vivid image in the mind's eye. *Beautiful* is used to modify many fantastical items, such as *fairy, fairyland,* and *mermaid,* as well as other nouns usually associated with fairytales like *palace, princess,* and *castle. Pretty* also modifies *mermaid* and *princess,* as well as *creature.* Baum uses the phrase *pretty creature* to refer to imaginary beings:

> They all looked downward and found a sky-blue rabbit had stuck his head out of a burrow in the ground. The rabbit's eyes were a deeper blue than his fur, and the **pretty creature** seemed friendly and unafraid.

As in the above example, colour is an important part of Baum's fantastical descriptions, as they are often applied to creatures or objects that would be coloured differently in the real world: as well as *rabbit, blue* is used to modify *carrot* and *cat,* while *green* modifies *monkey* and *maiden.* There is more evidence of the importance of the fantastical with the word *magic. Magic* appears in Baum's fifty most frequent adjectives and is used to modify items as diverse as *charm, spyglass, beanstalk,* and *dishpan* (the latter being another example of Baum making a commonplace object magical).

Baum aimed to entertain rather than frighten children with his stories and this is evident in his use of language. *Good* is his most frequently used adjective and appears over twelve times as often as *wicked.* However, *good* is often used in common phrases like *good deal, good fortune* and *good thing,* while *wicked* usually modifies 'bad' characters: *wicked witch, wicked magician, wicked giantess,* and *wicked daemon.* Good does also modify 'good' characters, for example in *good sorceress. Creature* also occurs slightly more frequently than *beast. Creature* can refer to 'good' or 'bad' characters; as well as being modified by *pretty,* it is modified by *beautiful, wicked, remarkable,* and *evil.* On the other hand, *beast* is usually modified by negative adjectives such as *terrible, ferocious, fierce,* and *savage.* But although one may think that a creature such as a *savage beast* would be frightening, in Baum's work this is not necessarily the case:

> 'For my part, I'm a **savage beast**, and have an appetite for all sorts of poor little living creatures, from a chipmunk to fat babies.'
> 'How dreadful!' said Dorothy. 'Isn't it, though?' returned the Hungry Tiger, licking his lips with his long red tongue. 'Fat babies! Don't they sound delicious? But I've never eaten any, because my conscience tells me it is wrong.'

This shows that in Baum's work, things that would usually be frightening are often made to seem less so, which correlates with his view that children's stories should, above all, entertain.

china¹ NOUN **= pottery**, ceramics, ware, porcelain, crockery, tableware, service: *She collects blue and white china.*

china² NOUN **= friend**, pal, mate *(informal)*, buddy *(informal)*, companion, best friend, intimate, cock *(Brit. informal)*, close friend, comrade, chum *(informal)*, crony, main man *(slang, chiefly U.S.)*, soul mate, homeboy *(slang, chiefly U.S.)*, cobber *(Austral. & N.Z. old-fashioned, informal)*, bosom friend, boon companion, E hoa *(N.Z.)*: *How are you, my old china?*

Chinese ADJECTIVE
▸ *related prefix:* Sino-

chink NOUN **= opening**, crack, gap, rift, aperture, cleft, crevice, fissure, cranny

chip NOUN **1 = fragment**, scrap, shaving, flake, paring, wafer, sliver, shard: *His eyes gleamed like chips of blue glass.* **2 = scratch**, nick, flaw, notch, dent: *The washbasin had a small chip in it.* **3 = counter**, disc, token: *He gambled all his chips on one number.*
▹ VERB **1 = nick**, damage, gash: *The blow chipped the woman's tooth; Steel baths are light, but they chip easily.* **2 = chisel**, whittle: *a sculptor chipping at a block of marble*
chip in 1 = contribute, pay, donate, subscribe, go Dutch *(informal)*: *We'll all chip in for the petrol and food.* **2 = interpose**, put in, interrupt, interject, butt in, put your oar in: *He chipped in, 'That's right,' before she could answer.*

chirp VERB **= chirrup**, pipe, peep, warble, twitter, cheep, tweet

chirpy ADJECTIVE **= cheerful**, happy, bright, enthusiastic, lively, sparkling, sunny, jolly, animated, buoyant, radiant, jaunty, sprightly, in high spirits, blithe, full of beans *(informal)*, light-hearted

chivalry NOUN **1 = courtesy**, politeness, gallantry, courtliness, gentlemanliness: *He always treated women with old-fashioned chivalry.* **2 = knight-errantry**, knighthood, gallantry, courtliness: *Our story is set in England, in the age of chivalry.*

choice NOUN **1 = range**, variety, selection, assortment: *It's available in a choice of colours.* **2 = selection**, preference, election, pick: *His choice of words made Rodney angry.* **3 = option**, say, alternative: *If I had any choice in the matter, I wouldn't have gone.*
▹ ADJECTIVE **= best**, bad *(slang)*, special, prime, nice, prize, select, excellent, elect, crucial *(slang)*, exclusive, elite, superior, exquisite, def *(slang)*, booshit *(Austral. slang)*, exo *(Austral. slang)*, sik *(Austral. slang)*, hand-picked, dainty, rad *(informal)*, phat *(slang)*, schmick *(Austral. informal)*: *The finest array of choicest foods is to be found within their Food Hall.*

> **QUOTATIONS**
> You pays your money and you takes your choice
> [*Punch*]
>
> We human beings do have some genuine freedom of choice and therefore some effective control over our own destinies
> [A.J.Toynbee *Some Great 'Ifs' of History*]
>
> We often experience more regret over the part we have left, than pleasure over the part we have preferred
> [Joseph Roux *Meditations of a Parish Priest*]
>
> As a man thinketh, so is he, and as a man chooseth so is he
> [Ralph Waldo Emerson *Spiritual Laws*]

choke VERB **1 = suffocate**, stifle, smother, overpower, asphyxiate: *Dense smoke swirled and billowed, its fumes choking her.* **2 = strangle**, throttle, asphyxiate: *They choked him with his tie.* **3 = block**, dam, clog, obstruct, bung, constrict, occlude, congest, close, stop, bar: *The village roads are choked with traffic.*

choose VERB **1 = pick**, take, prefer, select, elect, adopt, opt for, designate, single out, espouse, settle on, fix on, cherry-pick, settle upon, predestine: *I chose him to accompany me on my trip.* **OPPOSITE:** reject **2 = wish**, want, desire, see fit: *You can just take out the interest every year, if you choose.*

> **PROVERBS**
> *If you run after two hares you will catch neither*

choosy ADJECTIVE **= fussy**, particular, exacting, discriminating, selective, fastidious, picky *(informal)*, finicky, faddy, nit-picky *(informal)*
OPPOSITE: indiscriminating

chop VERB **= cut**, fell, axe, slash, hack, sever, shear, cleave, hew, lop, truncate: *We were set to work chopping wood.*
chop something up = cut up, divide, fragment, cube, dice, mince: *Chop up three firm tomatoes.*
the chop = the sack, sacking *(informal)*, dismissal, the boot *(slang)*, your cards *(informal)*, the axe *(informal)*, termination, the (old) heave-ho *(informal)*, the order of the boot *(slang)*: *I was amazed when I got the chop from the team.*

choppy ADJECTIVE **= rough**, broken, ruffled, tempestuous, blustery, squally **OPPOSITE:** calm

chore NOUN **= task**, job, duty, burden, hassle *(informal)*, fag *(informal)*, errand, no picnic, joe job *(Canad. informal)*

chortle VERB **= chuckle**, laugh, cackle, guffaw: *He began chortling like an idiot.*
▹ NOUN **= chuckle**, laugh, cackle, guffaw: *The old man broke into a wheezy chortle of amusement.*

chorus NOUN **1 = refrain**, response, strain, burden: *Everyone joined in the chorus.* **2 = choir**, singers, ensemble, vocalists, choristers: *The chorus was singing 'The Ode to Joy'.*
in chorus = in unison, as one, all together, in concert, in harmony, in accord, with one voice: *'Let us in,' they all wailed in chorus.*

christen VERB **1 = baptize**, name: *She was born in March and christened in June.* **2 = name**, call, term, style, title, dub, designate: *a boat which he christened 'the Stray Cat'*

Christmas NOUN **= the festive season**, Noël, Xmas *(informal)*, Yule *(archaic)*, Yuletide *(archaic)*

chronic ADJECTIVE **1 = persistent**, constant, continual, deep-seated, incurable, deep-rooted, ineradicable: *His drinking has led to chronic cirrhosis of the liver.* **2 = dreadful**, awful, appalling, atrocious, abysmal: *The programme was chronic, all banal dialogue and canned laughter.*

chronicle VERB **= record**, tell, report, enter, relate, register, recount, set down, narrate, put on record: *The rise of collectivism in Britain has been chronicled by several historians.*
▹ NOUN **= record**, story, history, account, register, journal, diary, narrative, annals, blog *(informal)*: *this vast chronicle of Napoleonic times*

chronicler NOUN **= recorder**, reporter, historian, narrator, scribe, diarist, annalist

chronological ADJECTIVE **= sequential**, ordered, historical, progressive, consecutive, in sequence
OPPOSITE: random

chubby ADJECTIVE **= plump**, stout, fleshy, tubby, flabby, portly, buxom, roly-poly, rotund, round, podgy
OPPOSITE: skinny

chuck VERB **1 = throw**, cast, pitch, shy, toss, hurl, fling, sling, heave: *Someone chucked a bottle and it caught me on the side of the head.* **2** *(often with* **away** *or* **out**, *informal)* **= throw out**, dump *(informal)*, scrap, get rid of, bin *(informal)*, ditch *(slang)*, junk *(informal)*, discard, dispose of, dispense with, jettison: *I chucked a whole lot of old magazines and papers; Don't just chuck your bottles away – recycle them.* **3 = give up** *or* **over**, leave, stop, abandon, cease, resign from, pack in, jack in: *Last summer, he chucked his job and went on the road.* **4 = vomit**, throw up *(informal)*, spew, heave *(slang)*, puke *(slang)*, barf *(U.S. slang)*, chunder *(slang, chiefly Austral.)*, upchuck *(U.S. slang)*, do a technicolour yawn, toss your cookies *(U.S. slang)*: *It smelt so bad I thought I was going to chuck.*

chuckle VERB **= laugh**, giggle, snigger, chortle, titter: *He chuckled appreciatively at her riposte.*
▹ NOUN **= laugh**, giggle, snigger, chortle, titter: *She gave a soft chuckle and said, "No chance."*

chum NOUN **= friend**, mate *(informal)*, pal *(informal)*, companion, cock *(Brit. informal)*, comrade, crony, main man *(slang, chiefly U.S.)*, cobber *(Austral. & N.Z. old-fashioned, informal)*, E hoa *(N.Z.)*

chummy ADJECTIVE **= friendly**, close, thick *(informal)*, pally *(informal)*, intimate, affectionate, buddy-buddy *(slang, chiefly U.S. & Canad.)*, palsy-walsy *(informal)*, matey or maty *(Brit. informal)*

chunk NOUN = **piece**, block, mass, portion, lump, slab, hunk, nugget, wad, dollop *(informal)*, wodge *(Brit. informal)*

chunky ADJECTIVE = **thickset**, stocky, beefy *(informal)*, stubby, dumpy: *The sergeant was a chunky man in his late twenties.*

church NOUN = **chapel**, temple, cathedral, kirk *(Scot.)*, minster, tabernacle, place of worship, house of God, megachurch *(U.S.)*

churlish ADJECTIVE = **rude**, harsh, vulgar, sullen, surly, morose, brusque, ill-tempered, boorish, uncouth, impolite, loutish, oafish, uncivil, unmannerly **OPPOSITE:** polite

churn VERB **1** = **stir up**, beat, disturb, swirl, agitate: *The powerful thrust of the boat's engine churned the water.* **2** = **swirl**, boil, toss, foam, seethe, froth: *Churning seas smash against the steep cliffs.*

cigarette NOUN = **fag** *(Brit. slang)*, smoke, gasper *(slang)*, ciggy *(informal)*, coffin nail *(slang)*, cancer stick *(slang)*

cinema NOUN **1** = **pictures**, movies, picture-house, flicks *(slang)*: *They decided to spend an evening at the cinema.* **2** = **films**, pictures, movies, the big screen *(informal)*, motion pictures, the silver screen: *Contemporary African cinema has much to offer in its vitality and freshness.*

QUOTATIONS

Photography is truth. The cinema is truth 24 times per second
[Jean-Luc Godard *Le Petit Soldat*]

A film must have a beginning, a middle and an end. But not necessarily in that order
[Jean-Luc Godard]

To wish the movies to be articulate is about as sensible as wishing the drama to be silent
[George Jean Nathan]

Pictures are for entertainment, messages should be delivered by Western Union
[Sam Goldwyn]

Cinema is a matter of what's in the frame and what's out
[Martin Scorsese]

cipher NOUN **1** = **code**, coded message, cryptogram: *The codebreakers cracked the cipher.* **2** = **nobody**, nonentity: *They were little more than ciphers who faithfully carried out the Fuehrer's commands.*

circa PREPOSITION = **approximately**, about, around, roughly, in the region of, round about

circle NOUN **1** = **ring**, round, band, disc, loop, hoop, cordon, perimeter, halo: *The flag was red with a large white circle; The monument consists of a circle of gigantic stones.* **2** = **group**, company, set, school, club, order, class, society, crowd, assembly, fellowship, fraternity, clique, coterie: *a small circle of friends* **3** = **sphere**, world, area, range, field, scene, orbit, realm, milieu: *She moved only in the most exalted circles.*
▷ VERB **1** = **go round**, ring, surround, belt, curve, enclose, encompass, compass, envelop, encircle, circumscribe, hem in, gird, circumnavigate, enwreath: *This is the ring road that circles the city.* **2** = **wheel**, spiral, revolve, rotate, whirl, pivot: *There were two helicopters circling around.*

circuit NOUN **1** = **course**, round, tour, track, route, journey: *I get asked this question a lot when I'm on the lecture circuit.* **2** = **racetrack**, course, track, racecourse: *the historic racing circuit at Brooklands* **3** = **lap**, round, tour, revolution, orbit, perambulation: *She made a slow circuit of the room.*

circuitous ADJECTIVE **1** = **indirect**, winding, rambling, roundabout, meandering, tortuous, labyrinthine: *They were taken on a circuitous route home.* **OPPOSITE:** direct **2** = **oblique**, indirect: *He has a pedantic and circuitous writing style.*

circular ADJECTIVE **1** = **round**, ring-shaped, discoid: *The car turned into a spacious, circular courtyard.* **2** = **circuitous**, cyclical, orbital: *Both sides of the river can be explored on this circular walk.*
▷ NOUN = **advertisement**, notice, ad *(informal)*, announcement, advert *(Brit. informal)*, press release: *A circular has been sent to 1,800 newspapers.*

circulate VERB **1** = **spread**, issue, publish, broadcast, distribute, diffuse, publicize, propagate, disseminate, promulgate, make known: *Public employees are circulating a petition calling for his reinstatement.* **2** = **flow**, revolve, rotate, radiate: *Cooking odours can circulate throughout the entire house.*

circulation NOUN **1** = **distribution**, currency, readership: *The paper once had the highest circulation of any daily in the country.* **2** = **bloodstream**, blood flow: *Anyone with circulation problems should seek medical advice before flying.* **3** = **flow**, circling, motion, rotation: *Fit a ventilated lid to allow circulation of air.* **4** = **spread**, distribution, transmission, dissemination: *measures inhibiting the circulation of useful information*

circumference NOUN = **edge**, limits, border, bounds, outline, boundary, fringe, verge, rim, perimeter, periphery, extremity

circumscribe VERB = **restrict**, limit, define, confine, restrain, delineate, hem in, demarcate, delimit, straiten

circumspect ADJECTIVE = **cautious**, politic, guarded, careful, wary, discriminating, discreet, sage, prudent, canny, attentive, vigilant, watchful, judicious, observant, sagacious, heedful **OPPOSITE:** rash

circumstance NOUN **1** *(usually plural)* = **condition**, situation, scenario, contingency, state of affairs, lie of the land: *They say they will never, under any circumstances, be the first to use force.* **2** *(usually plural)* = **detail**, fact, event, particular, respect, factor: *I'm making inquiries about the circumstances of her murder.* **3** *(usually plural)* = **situation**, state, means, position, station, resources, status, lifestyle: *help and support for the single mother, whatever her circumstances* **4** = **chance**, the times, accident, fortune, luck, fate, destiny, misfortune, providence: *These people are innocent victims of circumstance.*

circumstantial ADJECTIVE **1** = **indirect**, contingent, incidental, inferential, presumptive, conjectural, founded on circumstances: *He was convicted on purely circumstantial evidence.* **2** = **detailed**, particular, specific: *The reasons for the project collapsing were circumstantial.*

circumvent VERB **1** = **evade**, bypass, elude, steer clear of, sidestep: *Military rulers tried to circumvent the treaty.* **2** = **outwit**, trick, mislead, thwart, deceive, dupe, beguile, outflank, hoodwink

cistern NOUN = **tank**, vat, basin, reservoir, sink

citadel NOUN = **fortress**, keep, tower, stronghold, bastion, fortification, fastness

citation NOUN **1** = **commendation**, award, mention: *His citation says he showed outstanding and exemplary courage.* **2** = **quotation**, quote, reference, passage, illustration, excerpt: *The text is full of Biblical citations.*

cite VERB **1** = **quote**, name, evidence, advance, mention, extract, specify, allude to, enumerate, adduce: *She cites a favourite poem by George Herbert.* **2** = **summon**, call, subpoena: *The judge ruled a mistrial and cited the prosecutors for gross misconduct.*

citizen NOUN = **inhabitant**, resident, dweller, ratepayer, denizen, subject, freeman, burgher, townsman
▸ *related adjective:* civil

city NOUN = **town**, metropolis, municipality, conurbation, megalopolis

civic ADJECTIVE = **public**, community, borough, municipal, communal, local

civil ADJECTIVE **1** = **civic**, home, political, domestic, interior, municipal: *This civil unrest threatens the economy.* **OPPOSITE:** state **2** = **polite**, obliging, accommodating, civilized, courteous, considerate, affable, courtly, well-bred, complaisant, well-mannered: *He couldn't even bring himself to be civil to Pauline.* **OPPOSITE:** rude

civility NOUN = **politeness**, consideration, courtesy, tact, good manners, graciousness, cordiality, affability, amiability, complaisance, courteousness

QUOTATIONS
Civility costs nothing and buys everything
[Mary Wortley Montagu *Letter to her daughter*]

PROVERBS
A civil question deserves a civil answer

civilization NOUN **1 = society**, people, community, nation, polity: *He believed Western civilization was in grave economic and cultural danger.* **2 = culture**, development, education, progress, enlightenment, sophistication, advancement, cultivation, refinement: *a race with an advanced state of civilization*

civilize VERB **= cultivate**, improve, polish, educate, refine, tame, enlighten, humanize, sophisticate

civilized ADJECTIVE **1 = cultured**, educated, sophisticated, enlightened, humane: *All truly civilized countries must deplore torture.* **OPPOSITE:** primitive
2 = polite, mannerly, tolerant, gracious, courteous, affable, well-behaved, well-mannered: *Our divorce was conducted in a very civilized manner.*

clad ADJECTIVE **= dressed**, clothed, arrayed, draped, fitted out, decked out, attired, rigged out *(informal)*, covered

claim VERB **1 = assert**, insist, maintain, allege, uphold, profess, hold: *He claimed that it was a conspiracy against him.* **2 = take**, receive, pick up, collect, lay claim to: *Now they are returning to claim what is theirs.*
3 = demand, call for, ask for, insist on: *They intend to claim for damages against the three doctors.*
▷ NOUN **1 = assertion**, statement, allegation, declaration, contention, pretension, affirmation, protestation: *He rejected claims that he had had an affair.*
2 = demand, application, request, petition, call: *The office has been dealing with their claim for benefits.* **3 = right**, title, entitlement: *The Tudors had a tenuous claim to the monarchy.*

claimant NOUN **= applicant**, pretender, petitioner, supplicant, suppliant

clairvoyant ADJECTIVE **= psychic**, visionary, prophetic, prescient, telepathic, fey, second-sighted, extrasensory, oracular, sibylline: *a fortune-teller who claims to have clairvoyant powers*
▷ NOUN **= psychic**, diviner, prophet, visionary, oracle, seer, augur, fortune-teller, soothsayer, sibyl, prophetess, telepath: *You don't need to be a clairvoyant to see how this is going to turn out.*

QUOTATIONS
clairvoyant: a person, commonly a woman, who has the power of seeing that which is invisible to her patron – namely, that he is a blockhead
[Ambrose Bierce *The Devil's Dictionary*]

clamber VERB **= climb**, scale, scramble, claw, shin, scrabble

clammy ADJECTIVE **1 = moist**, sweating, damp, sticky, sweaty, slimy: *My shirt was clammy with sweat.*
2 = damp, humid, dank, muggy, close: *As you peer down into this pit, the clammy atmosphere rises to meet your skin.*

clamour NOUN **= noise**, shouting, racket, outcry, din, uproar, agitation, blare, commotion, babel, hubbub, brouhaha, hullabaloo, shout

clamp NOUN **= vice**, press, grip, bracket, fastener: *This clamp is ideal for holding frames and other items.*
▷ VERB **= fasten**, fix, secure, clinch, brace, make fast: *U-bolts are used to clamp the microphones to the pole.*

clan NOUN **1 = family**, house, group, order, race, society, band, tribe, sept, fraternity, brotherhood, sodality, ainga *(N.Z.)*, ngai *or* ngati *(N.Z.)*: *A clash had taken place between rival clans.*
2 = group, set, crowd, circle, crew *(informal)*, gang, faction, coterie, schism, cabal: *a powerful clan of industrialists from Monterrey*

clandestine ADJECTIVE **= secret**, private, hidden, underground, concealed, closet, covert, sly, furtive, underhand, surreptitious, stealthy, cloak-and-dagger, under-the-counter

clang VERB **= ring**, toll, resound, chime, reverberate, jangle, clank, bong, clash: *A little later the church bell clanged.*
▷ NOUN **= ringing**, clash, jangle, knell, clank, reverberation, ding-dong, clangour: *He pulled the gates shut with a clang.*

clap VERB **1 = applaud**, cheer, acclaim, give (someone) a big hand: *The men danced and the women clapped; People lined the streets to clap the marchers.*
OPPOSITE: boo **2 = strike**, pat, punch, bang, thrust, slap, whack, wallop *(informal)*, thwack: *He clapped me on the back and boomed, 'Well done.'*

clarification NOUN **= explanation**, interpretation, exposition, illumination, simplification, elucidation

clarify VERB **1 = explain**, resolve, interpret, illuminate, clear up, simplify, make plain, elucidate, explicate, clear the air about, throw *or* shed light on: *A bank spokesman was unable to clarify the situation.* **2 = refine**, cleanse, purify: *Clarify the butter by bringing it to a simmer in a small pan.*

clarity NOUN **1 = clearness**, precision, simplicity, transparency, lucidity, explicitness, intelligibility, obviousness, straightforwardness, comprehensibility: *the clarity with which the author explains this technical subject* **OPPOSITE:** obscurity
2 = transparency, clearness: *The first thing to strike me was the incredible clarity of the water.* **OPPOSITE:** cloudiness

QUOTATIONS
Everything that can be said can be said clearly
[Ludwig Wittgenstein *Tractatus Logico-Philosophicus*]

clash VERB **1 = conflict**, grapple, wrangle, lock horns, cross swords, war, feud, quarrel: *A group of 400 demonstrators clashed with police.*
2 = disagree, conflict, vary, counter, differ, depart, contradict, diverge, deviate, run counter to, be dissimilar, be discordant: *Don't make policy decisions which clash with company thinking.* **3 = not go**, jar, not match, be discordant: *The red door clashed with the pink walls.*
4 = crash, bang, rattle, jar, clatter, jangle, clang, clank: *The golden bangles on her arms clashed and jangled.*
▷ NOUN **1 = conflict**, fight, brush, confrontation, collision, showdown *(informal)*, boilover *(Austral.)*: *There are reports of clashes between militants and the security forces in the city.*
2 = disagreement, difference, division, argument, dispute, dissent, difference of opinion: *Inside government, there was a clash of views.*

clasp VERB **= grasp**, hold, press, grip, seize, squeeze, embrace, clutch, hug, enfold: *Mary clasped the children to her desperately.*
▷ NOUN **1 = grasp**, hold, grip, embrace, hug: *He gripped my hand in a strong clasp.*
2 = fastening, catch, grip, hook, snap, pin, clip, buckle, brooch, fastener, hasp, press stud: *She undid the clasp of the hooded cloak she was wearing.*

class NOUN **1 = group**, grouping, set, order, league, division, rank, caste, status, sphere: *the relationship between different social classes* **2 = type**, set, sort, kind, collection, species, grade, category, stamp, genre, classification, denomination, genus: *The navy is developing a new class of nuclear-powered submarine.*
▷ VERB **= classify**, group, rate, rank, brand, label, grade, designate, categorize, codify: *I would class my garden as being medium in size.*

classic ADJECTIVE **1 = typical**, standard, model, regular, usual, ideal, characteristic, definitive, archetypal, exemplary, quintessential, time-honoured, paradigmatic, dinki-di *(Austral. informal)*: *This is a classic example of media hype.* **2 = masterly**, best, finest, master, world-class, consummate, first-rate: *Aldous Huxley's classic work, The Perennial Philosophy* **OPPOSITE:** second-rate **3 = lasting**, enduring, abiding, immortal, undying, ageless, deathless: *These are classic designs which will fit in well anywhere.*
▷ NOUN **= standard**, masterpiece, prototype, paradigm, exemplar, masterwork, model: *The album is one of the classics of modern popular music.*

QUOTATIONS
A classic is something that everybody wants to have read and nobody wants to read
[Mark Twain]

Every man with a bellyful of the classics is an enemy to the human race
[Henry Miller *Tropic of Cancer*]

classification NOUN **1 = categorization**, grading, cataloguing, taxonomy, codification, sorting, analysis, arrangement, profiling: *the accepted classification of the animal and plant kingdoms* **2 = class**, grouping, heading, head, order, sort, list, department, type, division, section, rank, grade: *several different classifications of vehicles*

classify VERB **= categorize**, sort, file, rank, arrange, grade, catalogue, codify, pigeonhole, tabulate, systematize

classy ADJECTIVE **= high-class**, select, exclusive, superior, elegant, stylish, posh (*informal, chiefly Brit.*), swish (*informal, chiefly Brit.*), up-market, urbane, swanky (*informal*), top-drawer, ritzy (*slang*), high-toned, schmick (*Austral. informal*)

clause NOUN **= section**, condition, article, item, chapter, rider, provision, passage, point, part, heading, paragraph, specification, proviso, stipulation

claw NOUN **1 = nail**, talon: *The cat's claws got caught in my clothes.* **2 = pincer**, nipper: *The lobster has two large claws.*
▷ VERB **= scratch**, tear, dig, rip, scrape, graze, maul, scrabble, mangle, mangulate (*Austral. slang*), lacerate: *She struck back at him and clawed his arm with her hand.*

clean ADJECTIVE **1 = hygienic**, natural, fresh, sterile, pure, purified, antiseptic, sterilized, unadulterated, uncontaminated, unpolluted, decontaminated: *Disease is not a problem because clean water is available.* **OPPOSITE:** contaminated **2 = spotless**, fresh, washed, immaculate, laundered, impeccable, flawless, sanitary, faultless, squeaky-clean, hygienic, unblemished, unsullied, unstained, unsoiled, unspotted: *He wore his cleanest slacks and a navy blazer.* **OPPOSITE:** dirty **3 = moral**, good, pure, decent, innocent, respectable, upright, honourable, impeccable, exemplary, virtuous, chaste, undefiled: *I want to live a clean life, a life without sin.* **OPPOSITE:** immoral **4 = complete**, final, whole, total, perfect, entire, decisive, thorough, conclusive, unimpaired: *It is time for a clean break with the past.* **5 = neat**, simple, elegant, trim, delicate, tidy, graceful, uncluttered: *I admire the clean lines of Shaker furniture.* **OPPOSITE:** untidy
▷ VERB **= cleanse**, wash, bath, sweep, dust, wipe, vacuum, scrub, sponge, rinse, mop, launder, scour, purify, do up, swab, disinfect, deodorize, sanitize, deep clean: *Her father cleaned his glasses with a paper napkin; It took half an hour to clean the orange powder off the bath.* **OPPOSITE:** dirty

clean-cut ADJECTIVE **= neat**, trim, tidy, chiselled

cleanliness NOUN **= cleanness**, purity, freshness, whiteness, sterility, spotlessness

> **PROVERBS**
> *Cleanliness is next to godliness*

cleanse VERB **1 = purify**, clear, purge: *Your body is beginning to cleanse itself of tobacco toxins.* **2 = absolve**, clear, purge, purify: *Confession cleanses the soul.* **3 = clean**, wash, scrub, rinse, scour: *She demonstrated the proper way to cleanse the face.*

cleanser NOUN **= detergent**, soap, solvent, disinfectant, soap powder, purifier, scourer, wash

clear ADJECTIVE **1 = comprehensible**, explicit, articulate, understandable, coherent, lucid, user-friendly, intelligible: *The book is clear, readable and amply illustrated.* **OPPOSITE:** confused **2 = distinct**, audible, perceptible: *He repeated his answer in a clear, firm voice.* **OPPOSITE:** indistinct **3 = obvious**, plain, apparent, bold, patent, evident, distinct, pronounced, definite, manifest, blatant, conspicuous, unmistakable, express, palpable, unequivocal, recognizable, unambiguous, unquestionable, cut-and-dried (*informal*), incontrovertible: *It was a clear case of homicide.* **OPPOSITE:** ambiguous **4 = certain**, sure, convinced, positive, satisfied, resolved, explicit, definite, decided: *It is important to be clear on what the author is saying here.* **OPPOSITE:** confused **5 = transparent**, see-through, translucent, crystalline, glassy, limpid, pellucid: *The water is clear and plenty of fish are visible.* **OPPOSITE:** opaque **6 = unobstructed**, open, free, empty, unhindered, unimpeded, unhampered: *All exits must be kept clear in case of fire or a bomb scare.* **OPPOSITE:** blocked **7 = bright**, fine, fair, shining, sunny, luminous, halcyon, cloudless, undimmed, light, unclouded: *Most places will be dry with clear skies.* **OPPOSITE:** cloudy **8 = untroubled**, clean, pure, innocent, stainless, immaculate, unblemished, untarnished, guiltless, sinless, undefiled: *I can look back on things with a clear conscience.*
▷ VERB **1 = unblock**, unclog, free, loosen, extricate, disengage, open, disentangle: *We called in a plumber to clear our blocked sink.* **2 = remove**, clean, wipe, cleanse, tidy (up), sweep away: *Firemen were still clearing rubble from the scene of the explosion.* **3 = brighten**, break up, lighten: *As the weather cleared, helicopters began to ferry the injured to hospital.* **4 = pass over**, jump, leap, vault, miss: *The horse cleared the fence by several inches.* **5 = absolve**, acquit, vindicate, exonerate: *In a final effort to clear her name, she is writing a book.* **OPPOSITE:** blame
clear out = go away, leave, retire, withdraw, depart, beat it (*slang*), decamp, hook it (*slang*), slope off, pack your bags (*informal*), make tracks, take yourself off, make yourself scarce, rack off (*Austral. & N.Z. slang*): *'Clear out!' he bawled, 'This is private property.'*
clear something out 1 = empty, sort, tidy up: *I took the precaution of clearing out my desk before I left.* **2 = get rid of**, remove, dump, dispose of, throw away or out: *It'll take you a month just to clear out all this rubbish.*
clear something up 1 = tidy (up), order, straighten, rearrange, put in order: *I told you to clear up your room.* **2 = solve**, explain, resolve, clarify, unravel, straighten out, elucidate: *During dinner the confusion was cleared up.*

clearance NOUN **1 = evacuation**, emptying, withdrawal, removal, eviction, depopulation: *By the late fifties, slum clearance was the watchword in town planning.* **2 = permission**, consent, endorsement, green light, authorization, blank cheque, go-ahead (*informal*), leave, sanction, O.K. or okay (*informal*): *He has a security clearance that allows him access to classified information.* **3 = space**, gap, margin, allowance, headroom: *The lowest fixed bridge has 12.8m clearance.*

clear-cut ADJECTIVE **= straightforward**, specific, plain, precise, black-and-white, explicit, definite, unequivocal, unambiguous, cut-and-dried (*informal*)

clearing NOUN **= glade**, space, dell

clearly ADVERB **1 = obviously**, undoubtedly, evidently, distinctly, markedly, overtly, undeniably, beyond doubt, incontrovertibly, incontestably, openly: *He clearly believes that he is in the right.* **2 = legibly**, distinctly: *Write your address clearly on the back of the envelope.* **3 = audibly**, distinctly, intelligibly, comprehensibly: *Please speak clearly after the tone.*

cleave VERB **= split**, open, divide, crack, slice, rend, sever, part, hew, tear asunder, sunder: *The axe had cleaved open the back of his skull.*

cleft NOUN **= opening**, break, crack, gap, rent, breach, fracture, rift, chink, crevice, fissure, cranny

clemency NOUN **= mercy**, pity, humanity, compassion, kindness, forgiveness, indulgence, leniency, forbearance, quarter

clement ADJECTIVE **= mild**, fine, fair, calm, temperate, balmy

clergy NOUN **= priesthood**, ministry, clerics, clergymen, churchmen, the cloth, holy orders, ecclesiastics
▸ *related adjectives:* clerical, pastoral

> **QUOTATIONS**
> I remember the average curate at home as something between a eunuch and a snigger
> [Ronald Firbank *The Flower Beneath the Foot*]
>
> Clergy are men as well as other folks
> [Henry Fielding *Joseph Andrews*]

clergyman NOUN **= minister**, priest, vicar, parson, reverend (*informal*), rabbi, pastor, chaplain, cleric, rector, curate, father, churchman, padre, man of God, man of the cloth, divine

> **QUOTATIONS**
> The clergyman is expected to be a kind of human Sunday
> [Samuel Butler *The Way of All Flesh*]

clerical ADJECTIVE **1 = administrative**, office, bureaucratic, secretarial, book-keeping, stenographic: *The hospital blamed the mix-up on a clerical error.* **2 = ecclesiastical**, priestly, pastoral, sacerdotal: *a clergyman who had failed to carry out his clerical duties*

C

clever ADJECTIVE **1 = intelligent**, quick, bright, talented, gifted, keen, capable, smart, sensible, rational, witty, apt, discerning, knowledgeable, astute, brainy *(informal)*, quick-witted, sagacious, knowing, deep, expert: *My sister has always been the clever one in our family.* **OPPOSITE:** stupid **2 = shrewd**, bright, cunning, ingenious, inventive, astute, resourceful, canny: *It's a very clever idea.* **OPPOSITE:** unimaginative **3 = skilful**, able, talented, gifted, capable, inventive, adroit, dexterous: *My father was very clever with his hands.* **OPPOSITE:** inept

cleverness NOUN **1 = intelligence**, sense, brains, wit, brightness, nous *(Brit. slang)*, suss *(slang)*, quickness, gumption *(Brit. informal)*, sagacity, smartness, astuteness, quick wits, smarts *(slang, chiefly U.S.)*: *He congratulated himself on his cleverness.* **2 = shrewdness**, sharpness, resourcefulness, canniness: *a policy almost Machiavellian in its cleverness* **3 = dexterity**, ability, talent, gift, flair, ingenuity, adroitness: *The artist demonstrates a cleverness with colours and textures.*

cliché NOUN **= platitude**, stereotype, commonplace, banality, truism, bromide, old saw, hackneyed phrase, chestnut *(informal)*

click NOUN **= snap**, beat, tick, clack: *I heard a click and then the telephone message started to play.*
▷ VERB **1 = snap**, beat, tick, clack: *Camera shutters clicked all around me.* **2 = become clear**, come home (to), make sense, fall into place: *When I saw the TV report, it all suddenly clicked.* **3 = get on**, be compatible, hit it off *(informal)*, be on the same wavelength, get on like a house on fire *(informal)*, take to each other, feel a rapport: *They clicked immediately; they liked all the same things.*

client NOUN **= customer**, consumer, buyer, patron, shopper, habitué, patient

clientele NOUN **= customers**, market, business, following, trade, regulars, clients, patronage

cliff NOUN **= rock face**, overhang, crag, precipice, escarpment, face, scar, bluff

climactic ADJECTIVE **= crucial**, central, critical, peak, decisive, paramount, pivotal

> **USAGE**
> *Climatic* is sometimes wrongly used where *climactic* is meant. *Climatic* should be used to talk about things relating to climate; *climactic* is used to describe something which forms a climax: *the climactic moment of the Revolution.*

climate NOUN **1 = weather**, country, region, temperature, clime: *the hot and humid climate of Cyprus* **2 = atmosphere**, environment, spirit, surroundings, tone, mood, trend, flavour, feeling, tendency, temper, ambience, vibes *(slang)*: *A major change of political climate is unlikely.*

> **QUOTATIONS**
> You don't need a weatherman to know which way the wind blows
> [Bob Dylan *Subterranean Homesick Blues*]

climax NOUN **= culmination**, head, top, summit, height, highlight, peak, pay-off *(informal)*, crest, high point, zenith, apogee, high spot *(informal)*, acme, ne plus ultra *(Latin)*: *Reaching the Olympics was the climax of her career.*
▷ VERB **= culminate**, end, finish, conclude, peak, come to a head: *They did a series of charity events climaxing in a millennium concert.*

climb VERB **1 = ascend**, scale, mount, go up, clamber, shin up: *Climbing the first hill took half an hour.* **2 = clamber**, descend, scramble, dismount: *He climbed down from the cab.* **3 = rise**, go up, soar, ascend, fly up: *The plane took off, lost an engine as it climbed, and crashed just off the runway.*
climb down = back down, withdraw, yield, concede, retreat, surrender, give in, cave in *(informal)*, retract, admit defeat, back-pedal, eat your words, eat crow *(U.S. informal)*: *He has climbed down on pledges to reduce capital gains tax.*

clinch VERB **1 = secure**, close, confirm, conclude, seal, verify, sew up *(informal)*, set the seal on: *He is about to clinch a deal with an American engine manufacturer.* **2 = settle**, decide, determine, tip the balance: *Evidently this information clinched the matter.*

cling VERB **1 = clutch**, grip, embrace, grasp, hug, hold on to, clasp: *She had to cling onto the door handle until the pain passed.* **2 = stick to**, attach to, adhere to, fasten to, twine round: *His sodden trousers were clinging to his shins.*
cling to something = adhere to, maintain, stand by, cherish, abide by, be true to, be loyal to, be faithful to, cleave to: *They still cling to their beliefs.*

clinical ADJECTIVE **= unemotional**, cold, scientific, objective, detached, analytic, impersonal, antiseptic, disinterested, dispassionate, emotionless

clip[1] VERB **1 = trim**, cut, crop, dock, prune, shorten, shear, cut short, snip, pare: *I saw an old man out clipping his hedge.* **2 = smack**, strike, box, knock, punch, belt *(informal)*, thump, clout *(informal)*, cuff, whack, wallop *(informal)*, skelp *(dialect)*: *I'd have clipped his ear for him if he'd been my kid.*
▷ NOUN **1 = smack**, strike, box, knock, punch, belt *(informal)*, thump, clout *(informal)*, cuff, whack, wallop *(informal)*, skelp *(dialect)*: *The boy was later given a clip round the ear by his father.* **2 = speed**, rate, pace, gallop, lick *(informal)*, velocity: *They trotted along at a brisk clip.*

clip[2] VERB **= attach**, fix, secure, connect, pin, staple, fasten, affix, hold: *He clipped his flashlight to his belt.*

clipping NOUN **= cutting**, passage, extract, excerpt, piece, article

clique NOUN **= group**, set, crowd, pack, circle, crew *(informal)*, gang, faction, mob, clan, posse *(informal)*, coterie, schism, cabal

cloak NOUN **1 = cape**, coat, wrap, mantle: *She set out, wrapping her cloak about her.* **2 = covering**, layer, blanket, shroud: *Today most of England will be under a cloak of thick mist.* **3 = disguise**, front, cover, screen, blind, mask, shield, cover-up, façade, pretext, smoke screen: *Individualism is sometimes used as a cloak for self-interest.*
▷ VERB **1 = cover**, coat, wrap, blanket, shroud, envelop: *The coastline was cloaked in fog.* **2 = hide**, cover, screen, mask, disguise, conceal, obscure, veil, camouflage: *He uses jargon to cloak his inefficiency.*

clobber[1] VERB **= batter**, beat, assault, smash, bash *(informal)*, lash, thrash, pound, beat up *(informal)*, wallop *(informal)*, pummel, rough up *(informal)*, lambast(e), belabour, duff up *(informal)*, beat *or* knock seven bells out of *(informal)*: *She clobbered him with a vase.*

clobber[2] NOUN **= belongings**, things, effects, property, stuff, gear, possessions, paraphernalia, accoutrements, chattels: *His house is filled with a load of old clobber.*

clog VERB **= obstruct**, block, jam, hamper, hinder, impede, bung, stop up, dam up, occlude, congest

cloistered ADJECTIVE **= sheltered**, protected, restricted, shielded, confined, insulated, secluded, reclusive, shut off, sequestered, withdrawn, cloistral
OPPOSITE: public

close[1] VERB **1 = shut**, lock, push to, fasten, secure: *If you are cold, close the window.* **OPPOSITE:** open **2 = shut down**, finish, cease, discontinue: *Many enterprises will be forced to close because of the recession.* **3 = wind up**, finish, axe *(informal)*, shut down, terminate, discontinue, mothball: *There are rumours of plans to close the local college.* **4 = block up**, bar, seal, shut up: *The government has closed the border crossing.* **OPPOSITE:** open **5 = end**, finish, complete, conclude, wind up, culminate, terminate: *He closed the meeting with his customary address.*

OPPOSITE: begin **6 = clinch**, confirm, secure, conclude, seal, verify, sew up *(informal)*, set the seal on: *He needs another $30,000 to close the deal.* **7 = come together**, join, connect: *His fingers closed around her wrist.*
OPPOSITE: separate
▷ NOUN **= end**, ending, finish, conclusion, completion, finale, culmination, denouement: *His retirement brings to a close a glorious chapter in British football history.*

close² ADJECTIVE **1 = near**, neighbouring, nearby, handy, adjacent, adjoining, hard by, just round the corner, within striking distance *(informal)*, cheek by jowl, proximate, within spitting distance *(informal)*, within sniffing distance, a hop, skip and a jump away: *The plant is close to Sydney airport.* **OPPOSITE:** far **2 = intimate**, loving, friendly, familiar, thick *(informal)*, attached, devoted, confidential, inseparable, dear: *She and Linda became very close.* **OPPOSITE:** distant **3 = noticeable**, marked, strong, distinct, pronounced: *There is a close resemblance between them.* **4 = careful**, detailed, searching, concentrated, keen, intense, minute, alert, intent, thorough, rigorous, attentive, painstaking, assiduous: *His recent actions have been the subject of close scrutiny.* **5 = even**, level, neck and neck, fifty-fifty *(informal)*, evenly matched, equally balanced: *It is still a close contest between the two leading parties.* **6 = imminent**, near, approaching, impending, at hand, upcoming, nigh, just round the corner: *A White House official said an agreement is close.* **OPPOSITE:** far away **7 = stifling**, confined, oppressive, stale, suffocating, stuffy, humid, sweltering, airless, muggy, unventilated, heavy, thick: *They sat in that hot, close room for two hours.* **OPPOSITE:** airy **8 = accurate**, strict, exact, precise, faithful, literal, conscientious: *The poem is a close translation from the original Latin.*

closed ADJECTIVE **1 = shut**, locked, sealed, fastened: *Her bedroom door was closed.* **OPPOSITE:** open **2 = shut down**, out of business, out of service: *The airport shop was closed.* **3 = exclusive**, select, restricted: *No-one was admitted to this closed circle of elite students.* **4 = finished**, over, ended, decided, settled, concluded, resolved, terminated: *I now consider the matter closed.*

closet NOUN **= cupboard**, cabinet, recess, cubicle, cubbyhole: *Perhaps there's room in the broom closet.*
▷ ADJECTIVE **= secret**, private, hidden, unknown, concealed, covert, unrevealed: *He is a closet Fascist.*

closure NOUN **= closing**, end, finish, conclusion, stoppage, termination, cessation

clot VERB **= congeal**, thicken, curdle, coalesce, jell, coagulate: *The patient's blood refused to clot.*

cloth NOUN **= fabric**, material, textiles, dry goods, stuff

clothe VERB **= dress**, outfit, rig, array, robe, drape, get ready, swathe, apparel, attire, fit out, garb, doll up *(slang)*, accoutre, cover, deck
OPPOSITE: undress

clothes PLURAL NOUN **= clothing**, wear, dress, gear *(informal)*, habits, get-up *(informal)*, outfit, costume, threads *(slang)*, wardrobe, ensemble, garments, duds *(informal)*, apparel, clobber *(Brit. slang)*, attire, garb, togs *(informal)*, vestments, glad rags *(informal)*, raiment *(archaic, poetic)*, rigout *(informal)*

clothing NOUN **= clothes**, wear, dress, gear *(informal)*, habits, get-up *(informal)*, outfit, costume, threads *(slang)*, wardrobe, ensemble, garments, duds *(informal)*, apparel, clobber *(Brit. slang)*, attire, garb, togs *(informal)*, vestments, glad rags *(informal)*, raiment *(archaic, poetic)*, rigout *(informal)*

> **QUOTATIONS**
> The origins of clothing are not practical. They are mystical and erotic. The primitive man in the wolf-pelt was not keeping dry; he was saying: 'Look what I killed. Aren't I the best?'
> [Katherine Hamnett]
>
> The apparel oft proclaims the man
> [William Shakespeare *Hamlet*]
>
> Clothes make the man. Naked people have little or no influence in society
> [Mark Twain]
>
> Beware of all enterprises that require new clothes, and not rather a new wearer of clothes
> [Henry David Thoreau *Walden*]
>
> Thou shalt not wear a garment of divers sort, as of woollen and linen together
> [*Bible: Deuteronomy*]
>
> kilt: a costume sometimes worn by Scotchmen in America and Americans in Scotland
> [Ambrose Bierce *The Devil's Dictionary*]
>
> Sure, deck your lower limbs in pants;
> Yours are the limbs, my sweeting.
> You look divine as you advance -
> Have you seen yourself retreating?
> [Ogden Nash *What's the Use?*]

cloud NOUN **1 = mist**, fog, haze, obscurity, vapour, nebula, murk, darkness, gloom: *The sun was almost entirely obscured by cloud.* **2 = billow**, mass, shower, puff: *The hens darted away on all sides, raising a cloud of dust.*
▷ VERB **1 = confuse**, obscure, distort, impair, muddle, disorient: *Perhaps anger has clouded his vision.* **2 = darken**, dim, be overshadowed, be overcast: *The sky clouded and a light rain began to fall.*

cloudy ADJECTIVE **1 = dull**, dark, dim, gloomy, dismal, sombre, overcast, leaden, sunless, louring *or* lowering: *It was a cloudy, windy day.*
OPPOSITE: clear **2 = opaque**, muddy, murky: *She could just barely see him through the cloudy water.* **3 = vague**, confused, obscure, blurred, unclear, hazy, indistinct: *The legal position on this issue is very cloudy.* **OPPOSITE:** plain

clout VERB **= hit**, strike, punch, deck *(slang)*, slap, sock *(slang)*, chin *(slang)*, smack, thump, cuff, clobber *(slang)*, wallop *(informal)*, box, wham, lay one on *(slang)*, skelp *(dialect)*: *The officer clouted him on the head.*
▷ NOUN **1 = thump**, blow, crack, punch, slap, sock *(slang)*, cuff, wallop *(informal)*, skelp *(dialect)*: *I was half tempted to give them a clout myself.* **2 = influence**, power, standing, authority, pull, weight, bottom, prestige, mana *(N.Z.)*: *The two firms wield enormous clout in financial markets.*

cloven ADJECTIVE **= split**, divided, cleft, bisected

clown NOUN **1 = comedian**, fool, harlequin, jester, buffoon, pierrot, dolt: *a classic circus clown with a big red nose and baggy suit* **2 = joker**, comic, prankster: *He gained a reputation as the class clown.* **3 = fool**, dope *(informal)*, jerk *(slang, chiefly U.S. & Canad.)*, idiot, ass, berk *(Brit. slang)*, prat *(slang)*, moron, twit *(informal, chiefly Brit.)*, imbecile *(informal)*, ignoramus, jackass, dolt, blockhead, ninny, putz *(U.S. slang)*, eejit *(Scot. & Irish)*, doofus *(slang, chiefly U.S.)*, dorba *or* dorb *(Austral. slang)*, bogan *(Austral. slang)*, lamebrain *(informal)*, numbskull *or* numskull: *I could do a better job than those clowns in Washington.*
▷ VERB *(usually with* **around***)* **= play the fool**, mess about, jest, act the fool, act the goat, play the goat: *He clowned a lot and anatagonized his workmates; Stop clowning around and get some work done.*

cloying ADJECTIVE **1 = sickly**, nauseating, icky *(informal)*, treacly, oversweet, excessive: *Her cheap, cloying scent enveloped him.* **2 = over-sentimental**, sickly, nauseating, mushy, twee, slushy, mawkish, icky *(informal)*, treacly, oversweet: *The film is sentimental but rarely cloying.*

club NOUN **1 = association**, company, group, union, society, circle, lodge, guild, fraternity, set, order, sodality: *He was a member of the local youth club.* **2 = stick**, bat, bludgeon, truncheon, cosh *(Brit.)*, cudgel: *Men armed with knives and clubs attacked his home.*
▷ VERB **= beat**, strike, hammer, batter, bash, clout *(informal)*, bludgeon, clobber *(slang)*, pummel, cosh *(Brit.)*, beat *or* knock seven bells out of *(informal)*: *Two thugs clubbed him with baseball bats.*

> **QUOTATIONS**
> I don't want to belong to any club that will accept me as a member
> [Groucho Marx]

C

clue NOUN **= indication**, lead, sign, evidence, tip, suggestion, trace, hint, suspicion, pointer, tip-off, inkling, intimation

clueless ADJECTIVE **= stupid**, thick, dull, naive, dim, dense, dumb *(informal)*, simple-minded, dozy *(Brit. informal)*, simple, slow, witless, dopey *(informal)*, moronic, unintelligent, half-witted, slow on the uptake *(informal)*

clump NOUN **= cluster**, group, bunch, bundle, shock: *There was a clump of trees bordering the side of the road.*
▷ VERB **= stomp**, stamp, stump, thump, lumber, tramp, plod, thud, clomp: *They went clumping up the stairs to bed.*

clumsiness NOUN **= insensitivity**, heavy-handedness, tactlessness, gaucheness, lack of tact, uncouthness

clumsy ADJECTIVE **1 = awkward**, blundering, bungling, lumbering, inept, bumbling, ponderous, ungainly, gauche, accident-prone, gawky, heavy, uncoordinated, cack-handed *(informal)*, inexpert, maladroit, ham-handed *(informal)*, like a bull in a china shop, klutzy *(U.S. & Canad. slang)*, unskilful, butterfingered *(informal)*, ham-fisted *(informal)*, unco *(Austral. slang)*: *I'd never seen a clumsier, less coordinated boxer.* **OPPOSITE:** skilful **2 = unwieldy**, ill-shaped, unhandy, clunky *(informal)*: *The keyboard is a large and clumsy instrument.*

cluster NOUN **= gathering**, group, collection, bunch, knot, clump, assemblage: *A cluster of men blocked the doorway.*
▷ VERB **= gather**, group, collect, bunch, assemble, flock, huddle: *The passengers clustered together in small groups.*

clutch VERB **1 = hold**, grip, embrace, grasp, cling to, clasp: *She was clutching a photograph in her hand.* **2 = seize**, catch, grab, grasp, snatch: *I staggered and had to clutch at a chair for support.*
▷ PLURAL NOUN **= power**, hands, control, grip, possession, grasp, custody, sway, keeping, claws: *He escaped his captors' clutches by jumping from a moving vehicle.*

clutter NOUN **= untidiness**, mess, disorder, confusion, litter, muddle, disarray, jumble, hotchpotch: *She preferred her work area to be free of clutter.* **OPPOSITE:** order
▷ VERB **= litter**, scatter, strew, mess up: *I don't want to clutter the room up with too much junk.* **OPPOSITE:** tidy

cluttered ADJECTIVE **= untidy**, confused, disordered, littered, messy, muddled, jumbled, disarrayed

coach NOUN **1 = instructor**, teacher, trainer, tutor, handler: *He has joined the team as a coach.* **2 = bus**, charabanc: *I hate travelling by coach.*
▷ VERB **= instruct**, train, prepare, exercise, drill, tutor, cram: *He coached me for my French A levels.*

coalesce VERB **= blend**, unite, mix, combine, incorporate, integrate, merge, consolidate, come together, fuse, amalgamate, meld, cohere

coalition NOUN **= alliance**, union, league, association, combination, merger, integration, compact, conjunction, bloc, confederation, fusion, affiliation, amalgam, amalgamation, confederacy

coarse ADJECTIVE **1 = rough**, crude, unfinished, homespun, impure, unrefined, rough-hewn, unprocessed, unpolished, coarse-grained, unpurified: *He wore a shepherd's tunic of coarse cloth; a tablespoon of coarse sea salt* **OPPOSITE:** smooth **2 = vulgar**, offensive, rude, indecent, improper, raunchy *(slang)*, earthy, foul-mouthed, bawdy, impure, smutty, impolite, ribald, immodest, indelicate: *He has a very coarse sense of humour.* **3 = loutish**, rough, brutish, boorish, uncivil: *They don't know how to behave, and are coarse and insulting.* **OPPOSITE:** well-mannered

coast NOUN **= shore**, border, beach, strand, seaside, coastline, seaboard: *Camp sites are usually situated along the coast.*
▷ VERB **= cruise**, sail, drift, taxi, glide, freewheel: *I slipped into neutral gear and coasted down the slope.*
▸ *related adjective:* littoral

coat NOUN **1 = fur**, hair, skin, hide, wool, fleece, pelt: *Vitamin B6 is great for improving the condition of dogs' and horses' coats.* **2 = layer**, covering, coating, overlay: *The front door needs a new coat of paint.*
▷ VERB **= cover**, spread, plaster, smear: *Coat the fish with seasoned flour.*

coating NOUN **= layer**, covering, finish, skin, sheet, coat, dusting, blanket, membrane, glaze, film, varnish, veneer, patina, lamination

coat of arms NOUN **= heraldry**, crest, insignia, escutcheon, blazonry

coax VERB **= persuade**, cajole, talk into, wheedle, sweet-talk *(informal)*, prevail upon, inveigle, soft-soap *(informal)*, twist (someone's) arm, flatter, entice, beguile, allure **OPPOSITE:** bully

cobber NOUN **= friend**, pal, mate *(informal)*, buddy *(informal)*, china *(Brit. & S. African informal)*, best friend, intimate, cock *(Brit. informal)*, close friend, comrade, chum *(informal)*, crony, alter ego, main man *(slang, chiefly U.S.)*, soul mate, homeboy *(slang, chiefly U.S.)*, bosom friend, boon companion, E hoa *(N.Z.)*

cock NOUN **= cockerel**, rooster, chanticleer: *We heard the sound of a cock crowing in the yard.*
▷ VERB **= raise**, prick up, perk up: *He suddenly cocked an ear and listened.*

cocktail NOUN **= mixture**, combination, compound, blend, concoction, mix, amalgamation, admixture

cocky[1] ADJECTIVE **= overconfident**, arrogant, brash, swaggering, conceited, egotistical, cocksure, swollen-headed, vain, full of yourself: *He was a little cocky because he was winning all the time.* **OPPOSITE:** modest

cocky[2] *or* **cockie** NOUN **= farmer**, smallholder, crofter *(Scot.)*, grazier, agriculturalist, rancher, husbandman: *He got some casual work with the cane cockies on Maroochy River.*

cocoon VERB **1 = wrap**, swathe, envelop, swaddle, pad: *She lay on the sofa, cocooned in blankets.* **2 = protect**, shelter, cushion, insulate, screen: *I was cocooned in my own safe little world.*

coddle VERB **= pamper**, spoil, indulge, cosset, baby, nurse, pet, wet-nurse *(informal)*, mollycoddle

code NOUN **1 = principles**, rules, manners, custom, convention, ethics, maxim, etiquette, system, kawa *(N.Z.)*, tikanga *(N.Z.)*: *Writers are expected to observe journalistic ethics and code of conduct.* **2 = cipher**, cryptograph: *They used elaborate secret codes.*

codify VERB **= systematize**, catalogue, classify, summarize, tabulate, collect, organize

coerce VERB **= force**, compel, bully, intimidate, railroad *(informal)*, constrain, bulldoze *(informal)*, dragoon, pressurize, browbeat, press-gang, twist (someone's) arm *(informal)*, drive

coercion NOUN **= force**, pressure, threats, bullying, constraint, intimidation, compulsion, duress, browbeating, strong-arm tactics *(informal)*

cogent ADJECTIVE **= convincing**, strong, powerful, effective, compelling, urgent, influential, potent, irresistible, compulsive, forceful, conclusive, weighty, forcible

cognition NOUN **= perception**, reasoning, understanding, intelligence, awareness, insight, comprehension, apprehension, discernment

coherence NOUN **= consistency**, rationality, concordance, consonance, congruity, union, agreement, connection, unity, correspondence

coherent ADJECTIVE **1 = consistent**, reasoned, organized, rational, logical, meaningful, systematic, orderly: *He has failed to work out a coherent strategy for modernising the service.* **OPPOSITE:** inconsistent **2 = articulate**, lucid, comprehensible, intelligible: *He's so calm when he speaks in public. I wish I could be that coherent.* **OPPOSITE:** unintelligible

cohort NOUN **= group**, set, band, contingent, batch: *We now have results for the first cohort of pupils to be assessed.*

coil VERB **1 = wind**, twist, curl, loop, spiral, twine: *He turned off the water and began to coil the hose.* **2 = curl**, wind, twist, snake, loop, entwine, twine, wreathe, convolute: *A python had coiled itself around the branch of the tree.*

coin NOUN **= money**, change, cash, silver, copper, dosh *(Brit. & Austral. slang)*, specie, kembla *(Austral. slang)*: *His pocket was full of coins.*
▷ VERB **= invent**, create, make up,

Creative Word Formation

There are three main types of word formation in English: affixation, compounding, and conversion. Writers coining new words may exploit these, or the more unusual processes of backformation, reduplication, and blending. When a new word is used once but does not pass into common parlance, it is termed a 'nonce word'. If it becomes sufficiently frequent to be codified in a dictionary, the new word is technically a neologism until it is so commonplace that it simply becomes part of the language. Writers who have become famous for their lexical inventiveness include Lewis Carroll, James Joyce, and George Orwell; they are all credited with first citations for many words in the *Oxford English Dictionary*.

Affixation is the process of adding a prefix or suffix to an existing lexeme to create a new word, often in a different word class. Joyce coined many words in *Ulysses* by creative use of affixes, for example 'toyable' meaning 'fit for toying with'; 'pussful' meaning 'mouthful'; 'inexquisite' meaning 'not exquisite':

> Phedo's **toyable** fair hair.
>
> The drouthy clerics do be fainting for a **pussful**.
>
> The bar where bald stood by sister gold,
> **inexquisite** contrast.

The process of conversion is also very common, changing the word class but not the form of a word. The process of verbalizing nouns is considered typical of American English (eg 'to reference' from the noun 'reference'; 'to action' from the noun 'action'; 'to transition' from the noun 'transition'), however Shakespeare also famously used nouns as verbs, eg in *Cymbeline*, where the noun 'partner' is used for the first time as a verb meaning 'to be joined or associated with someone':

> A Lady, So faire,..to be **partner'd** With
> Tomboyes.

Compounding takes two or more lexemes and puts them together to make a new lexical unit. The resulting lexical unit may be more or less transparent (eg on a spectrum from 'blackbird' to 'breakfast'). Orwell coined several compound words in *Nineteen Eighty-Four* which have become evocative of political dystopia, eg 'doublethink' and 'Newspeak'.

Other processes of word formation in English such as blending, backformation, and reduplication may be less common but allow for even greater experimentation. Lewis Carroll was a great exponent of blending, producing such delightful coinages as 'chortle' (a blend of 'chuckle' and 'snort') and 'frumious' (a blend of 'fuming' and 'furious'). Blending is extensively used in journalism and advertising as well as in literature, eg the film star couplings dubbed 'Brangelina' and 'TomKat'. Backformation is the opposite of affixation, so that real or imaginary affixes are removed from the original item, eg the verb 'edit' is derived from the noun 'editor' by removing the '-or' ending. Writers can use backformation to humorous effect by saying that they are 'ruth' not 'ruthless' or 'couth' not 'uncouth'. Reduplication is one of the most unusual types of word formation in English, forming new lexemes out of two of the same or similar elements, eg 'bling-bling', 'sing-song'. Some literary examples are: 'spillspilling', 'roocoocoo', 'ripripple' (Joyce) and 'snickersnack', 'jubjub' (Carroll). These have a range of effects from childlike or imitative to dismissive or intensifying.

It is, of course, possible to make up words which are complete nonsense. Depending on the larger textual context and their sonorousness, they may be interpreted and adopted by other writers, as has happened with items from Lewis Carroll's nonsense verse *Jabberwocky*:

> 'Twas brillig, and the slithy toves
> Did gyre and gimble in the wabe;
> All mimsy were the borogoves,
> And the mome raths outgrabe.

frame, forge, conceive, originate, formulate, fabricate, think up: *The phrase 'cosmic ray' was coined by R. A. Millikan in 1925.*

coincide VERB **1 = occur simultaneously**, coexist, synchronize, be concurrent: *The exhibition coincides with the 50th anniversary of his death.* **2 = agree**, match, accord, square, correspond, tally, concur, harmonize: *a case in which public and private interests coincide* **OPPOSITE:** disagree

C

coincidence NOUN **= chance**, accident, luck, fluke, eventuality, stroke of luck, happy accident, fortuity

coincidental ADJECTIVE **= accidental**, unintentional, unintended, unplanned, fortuitous, fluky (*informal*), chance, casual **OPPOSITE:** deliberate

cold ADJECTIVE **1 = chilly**, biting, freezing, bitter, raw, chill, harsh, bleak, arctic, icy, frosty, wintry, frigid, inclement, parky (*Brit. informal*), cool: *It was bitterly cold outside.* **OPPOSITE:** hot **2 = freezing**, frozen, chilled, numb, chilly, shivery, benumbed, frozen to the marrow: *I'm hungry, I'm cold and I have nowhere to sleep.* **3 = distant**, reserved, indifferent, aloof, glacial, cold-blooded, apathetic, frigid, unresponsive, unfeeling, passionless, undemonstrative, standoffish: *His wife is a cold, unfeeling woman.* **OPPOSITE:** emotional **4 = unfriendly**, indifferent, stony, lukewarm, glacial, unmoved, unsympathetic, apathetic, frigid, inhospitable, unresponsive: *The president is likely to receive a cold reception when he speaks today.* **OPPOSITE:** friendly
▷ NOUN **= coldness**, chill, frigidity, chilliness, frostiness, iciness: *He must have come inside to get out of the cold.*

cold-blooded ADJECTIVE **= callous**, cruel, savage, brutal, ruthless, steely, heartless, inhuman, merciless, unmoved, dispassionate, barbarous, pitiless, unfeeling, unemotional, stony-hearted **OPPOSITE:** caring

collaborate VERB **1 = work together**, team up, join forces, cooperate, play ball (*informal*), participate: *The two men collaborated on an album in 1986.* **2 = conspire**, cooperate, collude, fraternize: *He was accused of having collaborated with the secret police.*

collaboration NOUN **1 = teamwork**, partnership, cooperation, association, alliance, concert: *There is substantial collaboration with neighbouring departments.* **2 = conspiring**, cooperation, collusion, fraternization: *rumours of his collaboration with the occupying forces during the war*

collaborator NOUN **1 = co-worker**, partner, colleague, associate, team-mate, confederate: *My wife was an important collaborator on the novel.* **2 = traitor**, turncoat, quisling, collaborationist, fraternizer: *Two alleged collaborators were shot dead by masked activists.*

collapse VERB **1 = fall down**, fall, give way, subside, cave in, crumple, fall apart at the seams: *A section of the Bay Bridge had collapsed.* **2 = fail**, fold, founder, break down, fall through, come to nothing, go belly-up (*informal*): *His business empire collapsed under a massive burden of debt.* **3 = faint**, break down, pass out, black out, swoon (*literary*), crack up (*informal*), keel over (*informal*), flake out (*informal*): *It's common to see people in the streets collapsing from hunger.*
▷ NOUN **1 = falling down**, ruin, falling apart, cave-in, disintegration, subsidence: *Floods and a collapse of the tunnel roof were a constant risk.* **2 = failure**, slump, breakdown, flop, downfall: *Their economy is teetering on the edge of collapse.* **3 = faint**, breakdown, blackout, prostration: *A few days after his collapse he was sitting up in bed.*

collar VERB **= seize**, catch, arrest, appropriate, grab, capture, nail (*informal*), nab (*informal*), apprehend, lay hands on

collate VERB **= collect**, gather, organize, assemble, compose, adduce, systematize

collateral NOUN **= security**, guarantee, deposit, assurance, surety, pledge

colleague NOUN **= fellow worker**, partner, ally, associate, assistant, team-mate, companion, comrade, helper, collaborator, confederate, auxiliary, workmate, confrère

collect VERB **1 = gather**, save, assemble, heap, accumulate, aggregate, amass, stockpile, hoard: *Two young girls were collecting firewood.* **OPPOSITE:** scatter **2 = raise**, secure, gather, obtain, acquire, muster, solicit: *They collected donations for a fund to help the earthquake victims.* **3 = assemble**, meet, rally, cluster, come together, convene, converge, congregate, flock together: *A crowd collected outside.* **OPPOSITE:** disperse

collected ADJECTIVE **= calm**, together (*slang*), cool, confident, composed, poised, serene, sedate, self-controlled, unfazed (*informal*), unperturbed, unruffled, self-possessed, keeping your cool, unperturbable, as cool as a cucumber, chilled (*informal*) **OPPOSITE:** nervous

collection NOUN **1 = accumulation**, set, store, mass, pile, heap, stockpile, hoard, congeries: *He has gathered a large collection of prints and paintings over the years.* **2 = compilation**, accumulation, anthology: *Two years ago he published a collection of short stories.* **3 = group**, company, crowd, gathering, assembly, cluster, congregation, assortment, assemblage: *A collection of people of all ages assembled to pay their respects.* **4 = gathering**, acquisition, accumulation: *computer systems designed to speed up the collection of information* **5 = contribution**, donation, alms: *I asked my headmaster if we could arrange a collection for the refugees.* **6 = offering**, offertory: *I put a five-pound note in the church collection.*

collective ADJECTIVE **1 = joint**, united, shared, common, combined, corporate, concerted, unified, cooperative: *It was a collective decision taken by the full board.* **OPPOSITE:** individual **2 = combined**, aggregate, composite, cumulative: *Their collective volume wasn't very large.* **OPPOSITE:** separate

collide VERB **1 = crash**, clash, meet head-on, come into collision: *Two trains collided head-on early this morning.* **2 = conflict**, clash, be incompatible, be at variance: *It is likely that their interests will collide.*

collision NOUN **1 = crash**, impact, accident, smash, bump, pile-up (*informal*), prang (*informal*): *Their van was involved in a collision with a car.* **2 = conflict**, opposition, clash, clashing, encounter, disagreement, incompatibility: *a collision between two strong personalities*

colloquial ADJECTIVE **= informal**, familiar, everyday, vernacular, conversational, demotic, idiomatic

collude VERB **= conspire**, scheme, plot, intrigue, collaborate, contrive, abet, connive, be in cahoots (*informal*), machinate

collusion NOUN **= conspiracy**, intrigue, deceit, complicity, connivance, secret understanding

colonist NOUN **= settler**, immigrant, pioneer, colonial, homesteader (*U.S.*), colonizer, frontiersman

colonize VERB **= settle**, populate, put down roots in, people, pioneer, open up

colonnade NOUN **= cloisters**, arcade, portico, covered walk

colony NOUN **= settlement**, territory, province, possession, dependency, outpost, dominion, satellite state, community

colossal ADJECTIVE **= huge**, massive, vast, enormous, immense, titanic, gigantic, monumental, monstrous, mammoth, mountainous, stellar (*informal*), prodigious, gargantuan, herculean, elephantine, humongous or humungous (*U.S. slang*), supersize **OPPOSITE:** tiny

colour or (*U.S.*) **color** NOUN **1 = hue**, tone, shade, tint, tinge, tincture, colourway: *The badges come in twenty different colours and shapes.* **2 = paint**, stain, dye, tint, pigment, tincture, coloration, colourwash, colorant: *the latest range of lip and eye colours* **3 = liveliness**, life, interest, excitement, animation, zest: *The ceremony brought a touch of colour to the normally drab proceedings.*
▷ PLURAL NOUN **1 = flag**, standard, banner, emblem, ensign: *Troops raised*

the country's colours in a special ceremony. **2 = nature**, quality, character, aspect, personality, stamp, traits, temperament: *After we were married, he showed his true colours.*
▷ VERB **1 = blush**, flush, crimson, redden, go crimson, burn, go as red as a beetroot: *He couldn't help noticing that she coloured slightly.* **2 = influence**, affect, prejudice, distort, pervert, taint, slant: *The attitude of parents colours the way their children behave.* **3 = exaggerate**, disguise, embroider, misrepresent, falsify, gloss over: *He wrote a highly coloured account of his childhood.*

colourful ADJECTIVE **1 = bright**, rich, brilliant, intense, vivid, vibrant, psychedelic, motley, variegated, jazzy *(informal)*, multicoloured, Day-glo®, kaleidoscopic: *Everyone was dressed in colourful clothes.* **OPPOSITE:** drab **2 = interesting**, rich, unusual, stimulating, graphic, lively, distinctive, vivid, picturesque, characterful: *an irreverent and colourful tale of Restoration England* **OPPOSITE:** boring

colourless ADJECTIVE **1 = uncoloured**, faded, neutral, bleached, washed out, achromatic: *a colourless, almost odourless liquid* **2 = ashen**, washed out, wan, sickly, anaemic: *Her face was colourless, and she was shaking.* **OPPOSITE:** radiant **3 = uninteresting**, dull, tame, dreary, drab, lacklustre, vacuous, insipid, vapid, characterless, unmemorable: *His wife is a drab, colourless little woman.* **OPPOSITE:** interesting

column NOUN **1 = pillar**, support, post, shaft, upright, obelisk: *Great stone steps led past Greek columns to the main building.* **2 = line**, train, row, file, rank, string, queue, procession, cavalcade: *There were reports of columns of military vehicles appearing on the streets.*

columnist NOUN **= journalist**, correspondent, editor, reporter, critic, reviewer, gossip columnist, journo *(slang)*

coma NOUN **= unconsciousness**, trance, oblivion, lethargy, stupor, torpor, insensibility

comatose ADJECTIVE **1 = unconscious**, in a coma, out cold, insensible: *The right side of my brain had been so severely bruised that I was comatose for a month.* **2 = inert**, stupefied, out cold, somnolent, torpid, insensible, dead to the world *(informal)*, drugged: *Granpa lies comatose on the sofa.*

comb VERB **1 = untangle**, arrange, groom, dress: *Her reddish hair was cut short and neatly combed.* **2 = search**, hunt through, sweep, rake, sift, scour, rummage, ransack, forage, fossick *(Austral. & N.Z.)*, go through with a fine-tooth comb: *Officers combed the woods for the murder weapon.*

combat NOUN **= fight**, war, action, battle, conflict, engagement, warfare, skirmish: *Over 16 million men died in combat during the war.* **OPPOSITE:** peace
▷ VERB **= fight**, battle against, oppose, contest, engage, cope with, resist, defy, withstand, struggle against, contend with, do battle with, strive against: *new government measures to combat crime* **OPPOSITE:** support

combatant NOUN **= fighter**, soldier, warrior, contender, gladiator, belligerent, antagonist, fighting man, serviceman *or* servicewoman: *His grandfather was a Boer war combatant.*
▷ ADJECTIVE **= fighting**, warring, battling, conflicting, opposing, contending, belligerent, combative: *the monitoring of ceasefires between combatant states*

combative ADJECTIVE **= aggressive**, militant, contentious, belligerent, antagonistic, pugnacious, warlike, bellicose, truculent, quarrelsome **OPPOSITE:** nonaggressive

combination NOUN **1 = mixture**, mix, compound, blend, composite, amalgam, amalgamation, meld, coalescence: *A combination of factors are to blame.* **2 = association**, union, alliance, coalition, merger, federation, consortium, unification, syndicate, confederation, cartel, confederacy, cabal: *The company's chairman has proposed a merger or other business combination.*

combine VERB **1 = amalgamate**, marry, mix, bond, bind, compound, blend, incorporate, integrate, merge, put together, fuse, synthesize: *Combine the flour with water to make a paste; Her tale combines a strong storyline with sly humour.* **OPPOSITE:** separate **2 = join together**, link, connect, integrate, merge, fuse, amalgamate, meld: *Disease and starvation are combining to kill thousands.* **3 = unite**, associate, team up, unify, get together, collaborate, join forces, cooperate, join together, pool resources: *Different states or groups can combine to enlarge their markets.* **OPPOSITE:** split up

combustible ADJECTIVE **= flammable**, explosive, incendiary, inflammable

come VERB **1 = approach**, near, advance, move towards, draw near: *We heard the train coming; Tom, come here and look at this.* **2 = arrive**, move, appear, enter, turn up *(informal)*, show up *(informal)*, materialize: *Two police officers came into the hall; My brother's coming from Canada tomorrow.* **3 = reach**, extend: *The water came to his chest.* **4 = happen**, fall, occur, take place, come about, come to pass: *Saturday's fire-bombing came without warning.* **5 = be available**, be made, be offered, be produced, be on offer: *The wallpaper comes in black and white only.*
come about = happen, result, occur, take place, arise, transpire *(informal)*, befall, come to pass: *Any possible solution to the Irish question can only come about through dialogue.*
come across as something *or* **someone = seem**, look, seem to be, appear to be, give the impression of being
come across someone = meet, encounter, run into, bump into *(informal)*: *I recently came across a college friend in New York.*
come across something = find, discover, notice, unearth, stumble upon, hit upon, chance upon, happen upon, light upon: *He came across the jawbone of a 4.5 million-year-old marsupial.*
come at someone = attack, charge, rush, go for, assault, fly at, assail, fall upon, rush at: *A madman came at him with an axe.*
come back = return, reappear, re-enter: *She came back half an hour later.*
come between people = separate, part, divide, alienate, estrange, set at odds: *It's difficult to imagine anything coming between them.*
come by something = get, win, land, score *(slang)*, secure, obtain, acquire, get hold of, procure, take possession of: *How did you come by that cheque?*
come down 1 = decrease, fall, drop, reduce, go down, diminish, lessen, become lower: *Interest rates are coming down.* **2 = fall**, descend: *The rain began to come down.*
come down on someone = reprimand, blast, carpet *(informal)*, put down, criticize, jump on *(informal)*, rebuke, dress down *(informal)*, tear into *(informal)*, diss *(slang, chiefly U.S.)*, read the riot act, lambast(e), bawl out *(informal)*, rap over the knuckles, chew out *(U.S. & Canad. informal)*, tear (someone) off a strip *(Brit. informal)*, give (someone) a rocket *(Brit. & N.Z. informal)*: *If she came down too hard on him, he would rebel.*
come down on something = decide on, choose, favour: *He clearly came down on the side of the President.*
come down to something = amount to, boil down to: *In the end it all comes down to a matter of personal preference.*
come down with something = catch, get, take, contract, fall victim to, fall ill, be stricken with, take sick, sicken with: *He came down with chickenpox.*
come forward = volunteer, step forward, present yourself, offer your services: *A witness came forward to say that she had seen him that night.*
come from something 1 = be from, originate, hail from, be a native of: *Nearly half the students come from France.* **2 = be obtained**, be from, issue, emerge, flow, arise, originate, emanate: *Chocolate comes from the cacao tree.*
come in 1 = arrive, enter, appear, show up *(informal)*, cross the threshold: *They were scared when they first came in.* **2 = finish**: *My horse came in third in the second race.*
come in for something = receive, get, suffer, endure, be subjected to, bear the brunt of, be the object of: *The plans have already come in for fierce criticism.*
come into something = inherit, be left, acquire, succeed to, be

C

bequeathed, fall heir to: *My father has just come into a fortune.*
come off = **succeed**, work out, be successful, pan out (*informal*), turn out well: *It was a good try but it didn't quite come off.*
come on 1 = **progress**, develop, improve, advance, proceed, make headway: *He is coming on very well at the violin.* 2 = **begin**, appear, take place: *Winter is coming on.*
come out 1 = **be published**, appear, be released, be issued, be launched: *The book comes out this week.* 2 = **be revealed**, emerge, be reported, be announced, become apparent, come to light, be divulged: *The truth is beginning to come out now.* 3 = **turn out**, result, end up, work out, pan out (*informal*): *I'm sure it will come out all right in the end.*
come out with something = **say**, speak, utter, let out: *Everyone burst out laughing when he came out with this remark.*
come round *or* **around** 1 = **call**, visit, drop in, stop by, pop in: *Beryl came round last night to apologize.* 2 = **change your opinion**, yield, concede, mellow, relent, accede, acquiesce: *It looks like they're coming around to our way of thinking; Don't worry, she'll come round eventually.* 3 = **regain consciousness**, come to, recover, rally, revive: *When I came round I was on the kitchen floor.*
come through = **succeed**, triumph, prevail, make the grade (*informal*): *He's putting his job at risk if he doesn't come through.*
come through something = **survive**, overcome, endure, withstand, weather, pull through: *We've come through some rough times.*
come to = **revive**, recover, rally, come round, regain consciousness: *When he came to and raised his head he saw Barney.*
come to something = **amount to**, total, add up to: *The bill came to over a hundred pounds.*
come up = **happen**, occur, arise, turn up, spring up, crop up: *Sorry I'm late – something came up at home.*
come up to something = **measure up to**, meet, match, approach, rival, equal, compare with, resemble, admit of comparison with, stand *or* bear comparison with: *Her work did not come up to his exacting standards.*
come up with something = **produce**, offer, provide, present, suggest, advance, propose, submit, furnish: *Several members have come up with suggestions of their own.*

comeback NOUN 1 = **return**, revival, rebound, resurgence, rally, recovery, triumph: *Sixties singing star Petula Clark is making a comeback.* 2 = **response**, reply, retort, retaliation, riposte, rejoinder: *I tried to think of a witty comeback.*

comedian NOUN = **comic**, laugh (*informal*), wit, clown, funny man, humorist, wag, joker, jester, dag (*N.Z. informal*), card (*informal*)

comedy NOUN 1 = **light entertainment**, sitcom (*informal*), soap opera (*slang*), soapie *or* soapy (*Austral.*): *Channel Four's comedy, 'Father Ted'* **OPPOSITE:** tragedy 2 = **humour**, fun, joking, farce, jesting, slapstick, wisecracking, hilarity, witticisms, facetiousness, chaffing: *He and I provided the comedy with songs and monologues.* **OPPOSITE:** seriousness

QUOTATIONS

Comedy is an imitation of the common errors of our life
[Sir Philip Sidney *The Defence of Poetry*]

The world is a comedy to those that think, a tragedy to those that feel
[Horace Walpole *Letters*]

All tragedies are finish'd by a death,
All comedies are ended by a marriage
[Lord Byron *Don Juan*]

You can't be beautiful and sexy forever. You can be funny
[Diane Keaton]

comfort NOUN 1 = **ease**, luxury, wellbeing, opulence: *She had enough money to live in comfort for the rest of her life.* 2 = **consolation**, cheer, encouragement, succour, help, support, aid, relief, ease, compensation, alleviation: *I tried to find some words of comfort to offer her.* **OPPOSITE:** annoyance
▷ VERB = **console**, encourage, ease, cheer, strengthen, relieve, reassure, soothe, hearten, solace, assuage, gladden, commiserate with: *He put his arm round her, trying to comfort her.* **OPPOSITE:** distress

comfortable ADJECTIVE 1 = **loose-fitting**, loose, adequate, ample, snug, roomy, commodious: *Dress in loose comfortable clothes that do not make you feel restricted.* **OPPOSITE:** tight-fitting 2 = **pleasant**, homely, easy, relaxing, delightful, enjoyable, cosy, agreeable, restful: *A home should be comfortable and friendly.* **OPPOSITE:** unpleasant 3 = **at ease**, happy, at home, contented, relaxed, serene: *Lie down on your bed and make yourself comfortable.* **OPPOSITE:** uncomfortable 4 = **well-off**, prosperous, affluent, well-to-do, comfortably-off, in clover (*informal*): *She came from a stable, comfortable, middle-class family.*

comforting ADJECTIVE = **consoling**, encouraging, cheering, reassuring, soothing, heart-warming, inspiriting **OPPOSITE:** upsetting

comic ADJECTIVE = **funny**, amusing, witty, humorous, farcical, comical, light, joking, droll, facetious, jocular, waggish: *The novel is both comic and tragic.* **OPPOSITE:** sad
▷ NOUN = **comedian**, funny man, humorist, wit, clown, wag, jester, dag (*N.Z. informal*), buffoon: *At that time he was still a penniless, unknown comic.*

comical ADJECTIVE = **funny**, entertaining, comic, silly, amusing, ridiculous, diverting, absurd, hilarious, ludicrous, humorous, priceless, laughable, farcical, whimsical, zany, droll, risible, side-splitting

coming ADJECTIVE 1 = **approaching**, next, future, near, due, forthcoming, imminent, in store, impending, at hand, upcoming, on the cards, in the wind, nigh, just round the corner: *This obviously depends on the weather in the coming months.* 2 = **up-and-coming**, future, promising, aspiring: *He is widely regarded as the coming man of Scottish rugby.*
▷ NOUN = **arrival**, approach, advent, accession: *Most of us welcome the coming of summer.*

command VERB 1 = **order**, tell, charge, demand, require, direct, bid, compel, enjoin: *He commanded his troops to attack.* **OPPOSITE:** beg 2 = **have authority over**, lead, head, control, rule, manage, handle, dominate, govern, administer, supervise, be in charge of, reign over: *the French general who commands the UN troops in the region* **OPPOSITE:** be subordinate to
▷ NOUN 1 = **order**, demand, direction, instruction, requirement, decree, bidding, mandate, canon, directive, injunction, fiat, ultimatum, commandment, edict, behest, precept: *The tanker failed to respond to a command to stop.* 2 = **domination**, control, rule, grasp, sway, mastery, dominion, upper hand, power, government: *the struggle for command of the air* 3 = **management**, power, control, charge, authority, direction, supervision: *In 1942 he took command of 108 Squadron.*

commandeer VERB = **seize**, appropriate, hijack, confiscate, requisition, sequester, expropriate, sequestrate

commander NOUN = **leader**, director, chief, officer, boss, head, captain, baas (*S. African*), ruler, commander-in-chief, commanding officer, C in C, C.O., sherang (*Austral. & N.Z.*)

commanding ADJECTIVE 1 = **dominant**, controlling, dominating, superior, decisive, advantageous: *Right now you're in a very commanding position.* 2 = **authoritative**, imposing, impressive, compelling, assertive, forceful, autocratic, peremptory: *The voice at the other end of the line was serious and commanding.* **OPPOSITE:** unassertive

commemorate VERB = **celebrate**, remember, honour, recognize, salute, pay tribute to, immortalize, memorialize **OPPOSITE:** ignore

commemoration NOUN 1 = **ceremony**, tribute, memorial service, testimonial: *A special commemoration for her will be held next week.* 2 = **remembrance**, honour, tribute: *a march in commemoration of Malcolm X*

commemorative ADJECTIVE = **memorial**, celebratory

commence VERB 1 = **embark on**, start, open, begin, initiate, originate, instigate, inaugurate, enter upon:

They commenced a systematic search of the area. **OPPOSITE:** stop **2 = start**, open, begin, go ahead: *The academic year commences at the beginning of October.* **OPPOSITE:** end

commencement NOUN **= beginning**, start, opening, launch, birth, origin, dawn, outset, onset, initiation, inauguration, inception, embarkation

commend VERB **1 = praise**, acclaim, applaud, compliment, extol, approve, big up *(slang)*, eulogize, speak highly of: *She was highly commended for her bravery.* **OPPOSITE:** criticize **2 = recommend**, suggest, approve, advocate, endorse, vouch for, put in a good word for: *I can commend it to you as a sensible course of action.*

commendable ADJECTIVE **= praiseworthy**, deserving, worthy, admirable, exemplary, creditable, laudable, meritorious, estimable

commendation NOUN **= praise**, credit, approval, acclaim, encouragement, Brownie points, approbation, acclamation, good opinion, panegyric, encomium

> **QUOTATIONS**
> commendation: the tribute that we pay to achievements that resemble, but do not equal, our own
> [Ambrose Bierce *The Devil's Dictionary*]

commensurate ADJECTIVE **1 = equivalent**, consistent, corresponding, comparable, compatible, in accord, proportionate, coextensive: *Employees are paid salaries commensurate with those of teachers.* **2 = appropriate**, fitting, fit, due, sufficient, adequate: *The resources available are in no way commensurate to the need.*

comment VERB **1 = remark**, say, note, mention, point out, observe, utter, opine, interpose: *Stuart commented that this was very true.* **2** *(usually with* **on***)* **= remark on**, explain, talk about, discuss, speak about, say something about, allude to, elucidate, make a comment on: *So far Mr Cook has not commented on these reports.*
▷ NOUN **1 = remark**, statement, observation: *He made these comments at a news conference.* **2 = note**, criticism, explanation, illustration, commentary, exposition, annotation, elucidation: *He had added a few comments in the margin.*

commentary NOUN **1 = narration**, report, review, explanation, description, voice-over: *He gave the listening crowd a running commentary on the game.* **2 = analysis**, notes, review, critique, treatise: *He will be writing a twice-weekly commentary on American society and culture.*

commentator NOUN **1 = reporter**, special correspondent, sportscaster, commenter: *a sports commentator* **2 = critic**, interpreter, annotator: *He is a commentator on African affairs.*

commercial ADJECTIVE **1 = mercantile**, business, trade, trading, sales: *In its heyday it was a major centre of commercial activity.* **2 = profitable**, popular, in demand, marketable, saleable: *Whether the project will be a commercial success is still uncertain.* **3 = materialistic**, mercenary, profit-making, venal, monetary, exploited, pecuniary: *There's a feeling among a lot of people that music has become too commercial.*

commiserate VERB *(often with* **with***)* **= sympathize**, pity, feel for, console, condole

commission VERB **= appoint**, order, contract, select, engage, delegate, nominate, authorize, empower, depute: *You can commission them to paint something especially for you.*
▷ NOUN **1 = duty**, authority, trust, charge, task, function, mission, employment, appointment, warrant, mandate, errand: *She approached him with a commission to write the screen play for the film.* **2 = fee**, cut, compensation, percentage, allowance, royalties, brokerage, rake-off *(slang)*: *He got a commission for bringing in new clients.* **3 = committee**, board, representatives, commissioners, delegation, deputation, body of commissioners: *The authorities have been asked to set up a commission to investigate the murders.*

commit VERB **1 = do**, perform, carry out, execute, enact, perpetrate: *I have never committed any crime.* **2 = give**, deliver, engage, deposit, hand over, commend, entrust, consign: *The government have committed billions of pounds for a programme to reduce acid rain.* **OPPOSITE:** withhold **3 = put in custody**, confine, imprison, consign: *His drinking caused him to be committed to a psychiatric hospital.* **OPPOSITE:** release
commit yourself to something = pledge to, promise to, bind yourself to, make yourself liable for, obligate yourself to: *She didn't want to commit herself to working at weekends.*

commitment NOUN **1 = dedication**, loyalty, devotion, adherence: *a commitment to the ideals of Bolshevism* **OPPOSITE:** indecisiveness **2 = responsibility**, tie, duty, obligation, liability, engagement: *I've got too many commitments to take on anything more right now.* **3 = pledge**, promise, guarantee, undertaking, vow, assurance, word: *We made a commitment to keep working together.* **OPPOSITE:** disavowal

> **PROVERBS**
> *In for a penny, in for a pound*
> *One might as well be hanged for a sheep as a lamb*

committee NOUN **= group**, commission, panel, delegation, subcommittee, deputation

> **QUOTATIONS**
> a group of men who individually can do nothing but as a group decide that nothing can be done
> [attributed to Fred Allen]
>
> a group of the unwilling, chosen from the unfit, to do the unnecessary
> [Richard Harkness]
>
> Committees are to get everybody together and homogenize their thinking
> [Art Linkletter *A Child's Garden of Misinformation*]

> **PROVERBS**
> *A committee is a group of men who keep minutes and waste hours*

commodity NOUN *(usually plural)* **= goods**, produce, stock, products, merchandise, wares

common ADJECTIVE **1 = usual**, standard, daily, regular, ordinary, familiar, plain, conventional, routine, frequent, everyday, customary, commonplace, vanilla *(slang)*, habitual, run-of-the-mill, humdrum, stock, workaday, bog-standard *(Brit. & Irish slang)*, a dime a dozen: *Earthquakes are fairly common in this part of the world.* **OPPOSITE:** rare **2 = popular**, general, accepted, standard, routine, widespread, universal, prevailing, prevalent: *It is common practice these days to administer vitamin K during childbirth.* **3 = shared**, collective: *They share a common language.* **4 = ordinary**, average, simple, typical, undistinguished, dinki-di *(Austral. informal)*: *He proclaims himself to be the voice of the common man.* **OPPOSITE:** important **5 = vulgar**, low, inferior, coarse, plebeian: *She might be a little common at times, but she was certainly not boring.* **OPPOSITE:** refined **6 = collective**, public, community, social, communal: *social policies which promote the common good* **OPPOSITE:** personal

commonplace ADJECTIVE **= everyday**, common, ordinary, widespread, pedestrian, customary, mundane, vanilla *(slang)*, banal, run-of-the-mill, humdrum, dime-a-dozen *(informal)*: *Foreign vacations have become commonplace nowadays.* **OPPOSITE:** rare
▷ NOUN **= cliché**, platitude, banality, truism: *It is a commonplace to say that the poetry of the first world war was greater than that of the second.*

common sense NOUN **= good sense**, sound judgment, level-headedness, practicality, prudence, nous *(Brit. slang)*, soundness, reasonableness, gumption *(Brit. informal)*, horse sense, native intelligence, mother wit, smarts *(slang, chiefly U.S.)*, wit

common-sense ADJECTIVE **= sensible**, sound, practical, reasonable, realistic, shrewd, down-to-earth, matter-of-fact, sane, astute, judicious, level-headed, hard-headed, grounded **OPPOSITE:** foolish

commotion NOUN **= disturbance**, to-do, riot, disorder, excitement, fuss, turmoil, racket, upheaval, bustle, furore, uproar, ferment, agitation, ado, rumpus, tumult, hubbub, hurly-burly, brouhaha, hullabaloo, hue and cry

communal ADJECTIVE **1 = community**, neighbourhood: *Communal violence broke out in different parts of the country* **2 = public**, shared, general, joint, collective, communistic: *The inmates ate in a communal dining room.* **OPPOSITE:** private

commune NOUN **= community**, collective, cooperative, kibbutz

commune with VERB **1 = contemplate**, ponder, reflect on, muse on, meditate on: *He set off from the lodge to commune with nature.* **2 = talk to**, communicate with, discuss with, confer with, converse with, discourse with, parley with, korero (N.Z.): *You can now commune with people from the safety of your PC.*

communicable ADJECTIVE **= infectious**, catching, contagious, transferable, transmittable

communicate VERB **1 = contact**, talk, speak, phone, correspond, make contact, be in touch, ring up *(informal, chiefly Brit.)*, be in contact, get in contact, e-mail, text: *My natural mother has never communicated with me; They communicated in sign language.* **2 = make known**, report, announce, reveal, publish, declare, spread, disclose, pass on, proclaim, transmit, convey, impart, divulge, disseminate: *The result will be communicated to parents.* **OPPOSITE:** keep secret **3 = pass on**, transfer, spread, transmit: *typhus, a disease communicated by body lice*

communication NOUN **1 = contact**, conversation, correspondence, intercourse, link, relations, connection: *The problem is a lack of real communication between you.* **2 = passing on**, spread, circulation, transmission, disclosure, imparting, dissemination, conveyance: *Treatment involves the communication of information.* **3 = message**, news, report, word, information, statement, intelligence, announcement, disclosure, dispatch, e-mail, text: *The ambassador has brought with him a communication from the President.* ▷ PLURAL NOUN **= connections**, travel, links, transport, routes: *Violent rain has caused flooding and cut communications between neighbouring towns.*

TELECOMMUNICATION TERMS

Blackberry	mobile phone
Bluetooth	MSN
e-mail	pager
IM *or* instant messaging	Skype
MMS	SMS *or* text messaging

communicative ADJECTIVE **= talkative**, open, frank, forthcoming, outgoing, informative, candid, expansive, chatty, voluble, loquacious, unreserved **OPPOSITE:** reserved

Communion NOUN **= Eucharist**, Mass, Sacrament, Lord's Supper

communion NOUN **= affinity**, accord, agreement, unity, sympathy, harmony, intercourse, fellowship, communing, closeness, rapport, converse, togetherness, concord

communiqué NOUN **= announcement**, report, bulletin, dispatch, news flash, official communication

communism NOUN *(usually cap.)* **= socialism**, Marxism, Stalinism, collectivism, Bolshevism, Marxism-Leninism, state socialism, Maoism, Trotskyism, Eurocommunism, Titoism

QUOTATIONS

We Communists are like seeds and the people are like the soil. Wherever we go, we must unite with the people, take root and blossom among them
[Mao Tse-tung]

A spectre is haunting Europe – the spectre of Communism
[Karl Marx *The Communist Manifesto*]

[Russian Communism is] the illegitimate child of Karl Marx and Catherine the Great
[Clement Attlee]

Communism is Soviet power plus the electrification of the whole country
[Lenin]

One strength of the communist system of the East is that it has some of the character of a religion and inspires the emotions of a religion
[Albert Einstein *Out of My Later Life*]

Far from being a classless society, Communism is governed by an elite as steadfast in its determination to maintain its prerogatives as any oligarchy known to history
[Robert F. Kennedy *The Pursuit of Justice*]

Under capitalism, man exploits man. Under communism, it's just the opposite
[John Kenneth Galbraith]

communist NOUN *(often cap.)* **= socialist**, Red *(informal)*, Marxist, Bolshevik, collectivist

QUOTATIONS

What is a communist? One who hath yearnings
For equal division of unequal earnings
[Ebenezer Elliot *Epigram*]

community NOUN **1 = society**, people, public, association, population, residents, commonwealth, general public, populace, body politic, state, company: *He's well liked by the local community.* **2 = district**, area, quarter, region, sector, parish, neighbourhood, vicinity, locality, locale, neck of the woods *(informal)*: *a black township on the outskirts of the mining community*

commute VERB **1 = travel**: *He commutes to London every day.* **2 = reduce**, cut, modify, shorten, alleviate, curtail, remit, mitigate: *His death sentence was commuted to life imprisonment.*

commuter NOUN **= daily traveller**, passenger, suburbanite

compact[1] ADJECTIVE **1 = closely packed**, firm, solid, thick, dense, compressed, condensed, impenetrable, impermeable, pressed together: *a thick, bare trunk crowned by a compact mass of dark-green leaves* **OPPOSITE:** loose **2 = concise**, brief, to the point, succinct, terse, laconic, pithy, epigrammatic, pointed: *The strength of the series is in its concise, compact short-story quality.* **OPPOSITE:** lengthy ▷ VERB **= pack closely**, stuff, cram, compress, condense, tamp: *The soil settles and is compacted by the winter rain.* **OPPOSITE:** loosen

compact[2] NOUN **= agreement**, deal, understanding, contract, bond, arrangement, alliance, treaty, bargain, pact, covenant, entente, concordat: *The Pilgrims signed a democratic compact aboard the Mayflower.*

companion NOUN **1 = friend**, partner, ally, colleague, associate, mate *(informal)*, gossip *(archaic)*, buddy *(informal)*, comrade, accomplice, crony, confederate, consort, main man *(slang, chiefly U.S.)*, homeboy *(slang, chiefly U.S.)*, cobber *(Austral. & N.Z. old-fashioned, informal)*: *He has been her constant companion for the last six years.* **2 = assistant**, aide, escort, attendant: *She was employed as companion to a wealthy old lady.* **3 = complement**, match, fellow, mate, twin, counterpart: *The book was written as the companion to a trilogy of television documentaries.*

companionship NOUN **= fellowship**, company, friendship, fraternity, rapport, camaraderie, togetherness, comradeship, amity, esprit de corps, conviviality

company NOUN **1 = business**, firm, association, corporation, partnership, establishment, syndicate, house, concern: *She worked as a secretary in an insurance company.* **2 = group**, troupe, set, community, league, band, crowd, camp, collection, gathering, circle, crew, assembly, convention, ensemble, throng, coterie, bevy, assemblage, party, body: *He was a notable young actor in a company of rising stars.* **3 = troop**, unit, squad, team: *The division consists of two tank companies and one infantry company.* **4 = companionship**, society, presence, fellowship: *I would be grateful for your company on the drive back.* **5 = guests**, party, visitors, callers: *Oh, I'm sorry, I didn't realise you had company.*

QUOTATIONS
Every man is like the company he is wont to keep
[Euripides *Phoenix*]

A wise man may look ridiculous in the company of fools
[Thomas Fuller *Gnomologia*]

Tell me thy company, and I'll tell thee what thou art
[Miguel de Cervantes *Don Quixote*]

PROVERBS
A man is known by the company he keeps
Two is company, three's a crowd

comparable ADJECTIVE **1 = equal**, equivalent, on a par, tantamount, a match, proportionate, commensurate, as good: *They should be paid the same wages for work of comparable value; Farmers were meant to get an income comparable with that of townspeople.* **OPPOSITE:** unequal **2 = similar**, related, alike, corresponding, akin, analogous, of a piece, cognate, cut from the same cloth: *The scoring systems used in the two studies are not directly comparable.*

comparative ADJECTIVE **= relative**, qualified, by comparison, approximate

compare VERB **= contrast**, balance, weigh, set against, collate, juxtapose: *Compare the two illustrations in Fig 60.*
compare to something = liken to, parallel, identify with, equate to, correlate to, mention in the same breath as: *Commentators compared his work to that of James Joyce.*
compare with something = be as good as, match, approach, equal, compete with, come up to, vie, be on a par with, be the equal of, approximate to, hold a candle to, bear comparison, be in the same class as: *The flowers here do not compare with those at home.*

comparison NOUN **1 = contrast**, distinction, differentiation, juxtaposition, collation: *There are no previous statistics for comparison.* **2 = similarity**, analogy, resemblance, correlation, likeness, comparability: *There is no comparison between the picture quality of a video and that of a DVD.*

QUOTATIONS
Comparisons are odious
[John Fortescue *De Laudibus Legum Angliae*]

Comparisons are odorous
[William Shakespeare *Much Ado About Nothing*]

compartment NOUN **1 = section**, carriage, berth: *We shared our compartment with a group of businessmen.* **2 = bay**, chamber, booth, locker, niche, cubicle, alcove, pigeonhole, cubbyhole, cell: *I put the vodka in the freezer compartment of the fridge.* **3 = category**, area, department, division, section, subdivision: *We usually put the mind, the body and the spirit into three separate compartments.*

compass NOUN **= range**, field, area, reach, scope, sphere, limit, stretch, bound, extent, zone, boundary, realm: *Within the compass of a book of this size, such a comprehensive survey is not practicable.*

compassion NOUN **= sympathy**, understanding, charity, pity, humanity, mercy, heart, quarter, sorrow, kindness, tenderness, condolence, clemency, commiseration, fellow feeling, soft-heartedness, tender-heartedness, aroha (N.Z.)
OPPOSITE: indifference

compassionate ADJECTIVE **= sympathetic**, kindly, understanding, tender, pitying, humanitarian, charitable, humane, indulgent, benevolent, lenient, merciful, kind-hearted, tender-hearted **OPPOSITE:** uncaring

compatibility NOUN **1 = agreement**, consistency, accordance, affinity, conformity, concord, congruity, accord: *National courts can freeze any law while its compatibility with European Community legislation is tested.* **2 = like-mindedness**, harmony, empathy, rapport, single-mindedness, amity, sympathy, congeniality: *Dating allows people to check out their compatibility before making a commitment to one another.*

compatible ADJECTIVE **1 = consistent**, in keeping, consonant, congenial, congruent, reconcilable, congruous, accordant, agreeable: *Free enterprise, he argued, was compatible with Russian values and traditions.* **OPPOSITE:** inappropriate **2 = like-minded**, harmonious, in harmony, in accord, of one mind, of the same mind, en rapport (*French*): *She and I are very compatible – we're interested in all the same things.*
OPPOSITE: incompatible

compatriot NOUN **= fellow countryman**, countryman, fellow citizen

compel VERB **= force**, make, urge, enforce, railroad (*informal*), drive, oblige, constrain, hustle (*slang*), necessitate, coerce, bulldoze (*informal*), impel, dragoon

compelling ADJECTIVE **1 = convincing**, telling, powerful, forceful, conclusive, weighty, cogent, irrefutable: *He puts forward a compelling argument against the culling of badgers.* **2 = fascinating**, gripping, irresistible, enchanting, enthralling, hypnotic, spellbinding, mesmeric: *Her eyes were her best feature, wide-set and compelling; a violent yet compelling film*
OPPOSITE: boring

compendium NOUN **= collection**, summary, abstract, digest, compilation, epitome, synopsis, précis

compensate VERB **1 = recompense**, repay, refund, reimburse, indemnify, make restitution, requite, remunerate, satisfy, make good: *To ease financial difficulties, farmers could be compensated for their loss of subsidies.* **2 = make amends for**, make up for, atone for, pay for, do penance for, cancel out, make reparation for, make redress for: *She compensated for her burst of anger by doing even more for the children.* **3 = balance**, cancel (out), offset, make up for, redress, counteract, neutralize, counterbalance: *The rewards more than compensated for the inconveniences involved in making the trip.*

PROVERBS
What you lose on the swings you gain on the roundabouts

compensation NOUN **1 = reparation**, damages, payment, recompense, indemnification, offset, remuneration, indemnity, restitution, reimbursement, requital: *He received one year's salary as compensation for loss of office.* **2 = recompense**, amends, reparation, restitution, atonement: *The present she left him was no compensation for her absence.*

compete VERB **1 = contend**, fight, rival, vie, challenge, struggle, contest, strive, pit yourself against: *The stores will inevitably end up competing with each other for increased market shares.* **2 = take part**, participate, be in the running, be a competitor, be a contestant, play: *He has competed twice in the London marathon.*

competence NOUN **1 = ability**, skill, talent, capacity, expertise, proficiency, competency, capability: *I regard him as a man of integrity and high professional competence.*
OPPOSITE: incompetence **2 = fitness**, suitability, adequacy, appropriateness: *They questioned her competence as a mother.*
OPPOSITE: inadequacy

QUOTATIONS
He has, indeed, done it very well; but it is a foolish thing well done
[Samuel Johnson]

competent ADJECTIVE **1 = able**, skilled, capable, clever, endowed, proficient: *He was a loyal and very competent civil servant.*
OPPOSITE: incompetent **2 = fit**, qualified, equal, appropriate, suitable, sufficient, adequate: *I don't feel competent to deal with a medical emergency.* **OPPOSITE:** unqualified

competition NOUN **1 = rivalry**, opposition, struggle, contest, contention, strife, one-upmanship (*informal*): *There's been some fierce competition for the title.* **2 = opposition**, field, rivals, challengers: *In this business you have to stay one step ahead of the competition.* **3 = contest**, event, championship, tournament, head-to-head: *He will be banned from international competitions for four years.*

QUOTATIONS
A horse never runs so fast as when he has other horses to catch up and outpace
[Ovid *The Art of Love*]

C

competitive ADJECTIVE **1 = cut-throat**, aggressive, fierce, ruthless, relentless, antagonistic, dog-eat-dog: *Modelling is a tough, competitive world.* **2 = ambitious**, pushing, opposing, aggressive, two-fisted, vying, contentious, combative: *He has always been a fiercely competitive player.*

competitor NOUN **1 = rival**, competition, opposition, adversary, antagonist: *The bank isn't performing as well as some of its competitors.* **2 = contestant**, participant, contender, challenger, entrant, player, opponent: *One of the oldest competitors in the race won the silver medal.*

C

compilation NOUN **= collection**, treasury, accumulation, anthology, assortment, assemblage

compile VERB **= put together**, collect, gather, organize, accumulate, marshal, garner, amass, cull, anthologize

complacency NOUN **= smugness**, satisfaction, gratification, contentment, self-congratulation, self-satisfaction

complacent ADJECTIVE **= smug**, self-satisfied, pleased with yourself, resting on your laurels, pleased, contented, satisfied, gratified, serene, unconcerned, self-righteous, self-assured, self-contented **OPPOSITE:** insecure

complain VERB **= find fault**, moan, grumble, whinge *(informal)*, beef *(slang)*, carp, fuss, bitch *(slang)*, groan, grieve, lament, whine, growl, deplore, grouse, gripe *(informal)*, bemoan, bleat, put the boot in *(slang)*, bewail, kick up a fuss *(informal)*, grouch *(informal)*, bellyache *(slang)*, kvetch *(U.S. slang)*, nit-pick *(informal)*

complaint NOUN **1 = protest**, accusation, objection, grievance, remonstrance, charge: *There have been a number of complaints about the standard of service.* **2 = grumble**, criticism, beef *(slang)*, moan, bitch *(slang)*, lament, grievance, wail, dissatisfaction, annoyance, grouse, gripe *(informal)*, grouch *(informal)*, plaint, fault-finding: *I don't have any complaints about the way I've been treated.* **3 = disorder**, problem, trouble, disease, upset, illness, sickness, ailment, affliction, malady, indisposition: *Eczema is a common skin complaint.*

complement VERB **= enhance**, complete, improve, boost, crown, add to, set off, heighten, augment, round off: *Nutmeg complements the flavour of these beans perfectly.*
▷ NOUN **1 = accompaniment**, companion, accessory, completion, finishing touch, rounding-off, adjunct, supplement: *The green wallpaper is the perfect complement to the old pine of the dresser.* **2 = total**, capacity, quota, aggregate, contingent, entirety: *Each ship had a complement of around a dozen officers and 250 men.*

> **USAGE**
> This is sometimes confused with *compliment* but the two words have very different meanings. As the synonyms show, the verb form of *complement* means 'to enhance' and 'to complete' something. In contrast, common synonyms of *compliment* as a verb are *praise*, *commend*, and *flatter*.

complementary ADJECTIVE **= matching**, companion, corresponding, compatible, reciprocal, interrelating, interdependent, harmonizing **OPPOSITE:** incompatible

complete ADJECTIVE **1 = total**, perfect, absolute, utter, outright, thorough, consummate, out-and-out, unmitigated, dyed-in-the-wool, thoroughgoing, deep-dyed *(usually derogatory)*: *He made me look like a complete idiot.* **2 = whole**, full, entire: *A complete tenement block was burnt to the ground.* **OPPOSITE:** partial **3 = entire**, full, whole, intact, unbroken, faultless, undivided, unimpaired: *Scientists have found the oldest complete skeleton of an ape-like man.* **OPPOSITE:** incomplete **4 = unabridged**, full, entire: *the complete works of Shakespeare* **5 = finished**, done, ended, completed, achieved, concluded, fulfilled, accomplished: *The work of restoring the farmhouse is complete.* **OPPOSITE:** unfinished
▷ VERB **1 = perfect**, accomplish, finish off, round off, crown, cap: *the stickers needed to complete the collection* **OPPOSITE:** spoil **2 = finish**, conclude, fulfil, accomplish, do, end, close, achieve, perform, settle, realize, execute, discharge, wrap up *(informal)*, terminate, finalize: *He had just completed his first novel.* **OPPOSITE:** start

completely ADVERB **= totally**, entirely, wholly, utterly, quite, perfectly, fully, solidly, absolutely, altogether, thoroughly, in full, every inch, en masse, heart and soul, a hundred per cent, one hundred per cent, from beginning to end, down to the ground, root and branch, in toto *(Latin)*, from A to Z, hook, line and sinker, lock, stock and barrel

completion NOUN **= finishing**, end, close, conclusion, accomplishment, realization, fulfilment, culmination, attainment, fruition, consummation, finalization

complex ADJECTIVE **1 = compound**, compounded, multiple, composite, manifold, heterogeneous, multifarious: *His complex compositions are built up of many overlapping layers.* **2 = complicated**, difficult, involved, mixed, elaborate, tangled, mingled, intricate, tortuous, convoluted, knotty, labyrinthine, circuitous: *in-depth coverage of today's complex issues* **OPPOSITE:** simple
▷ NOUN **1 = structure**, system, scheme, network, organization, aggregate, composite, synthesis: *Our philosophy is a complex of many tightly interrelated ideas.* **2 = obsession**, preoccupation, phobia, fixation, fixed idea, idée fixe *(French)*: *I have never had a complex about my weight.*

> **USAGE**
> Although *complex* and *complicated* are close in meaning, care should be taken when using one as a synonym of the other. *Complex* should be used to say that something consists of several parts rather than that it is difficult to understand, analyse, or deal with, which is what *complicated* inherently means. In the following real example a clear distinction is made between the two words: *the British benefits system is phenomenally complex and is administered by a complicated range of agencies.*

complexion NOUN **1 = skin**, colour, colouring, hue, skin tone, pigmentation: *She had short brown hair and a pale complexion.* **2 = nature**, character, make-up, cast, stamp, disposition: *The political complexion of the government has changed.*

complexity NOUN **= complication**, involvement, intricacy, entanglement, convolution

compliance NOUN **1 = conformity**, agreement, obedience, assent, observance, concurrence: *The company says it is in full compliance with US labor laws.* **OPPOSITE:** disobedience **2 = submissiveness**, yielding, submission, obedience, deference, passivity, acquiescence, complaisance, consent: *Suddenly, he hated her for her compliance and passivity.* **OPPOSITE:** defiance

compliant ADJECTIVE **= obedient**, willing, accepting, yielding, obliging, accommodating, passive, cooperative, agreeable, submissive, conformist, deferential, acquiescent, complaisant, conformable

complicate VERB **= make difficult**, confuse, muddle, embroil, entangle, make intricate, involve **OPPOSITE:** simplify

complicated ADJECTIVE **1 = involved**, difficult, puzzling, troublesome, problematic, perplexing: *The situation in Lebanon is very complicated.* **OPPOSITE:** simple **2 = complex**, involved, elaborate, intricate, Byzantine: *a complicated voting system* **OPPOSITE:** understandable **3 = convoluted**, labyrinthine: *the workings of his his complicated mind*

complication NOUN **1 = problem**, difficulty, obstacle, drawback, snag, uphill *(S. African)*, stumbling block, aggravation: *The age difference was a complication to the relationship.* **2 = complexity**, combination, mixture, web, confusion, intricacy, entanglement: *His poetry was characterised by a complication of imagery and ideas.*

The Language of LM Montgomery

LM Montgomery (1874–1942) was a Canadian author, best known for the popular novel *Anne of Green Gables,* which began a series of other novels about the same protagonist, the orphaned girl Anne. *Anne of Green Gables* was originally intended for readers of all ages but is now viewed mainly as a children's book. As well as publishing several novels, Montgomery wrote many short stories and poems.

Montgomery's physical descriptions of her characters are an important part of her work. Many of the words she uses most often are those concerning physical qualities: *eye, face, head,* and *hair* all appear in her fifty most frequently used nouns. *Eye* is modified by adjectives such as *blue, green,* and *brown,* as well as *beady, sharp,* and *piercing,* while *face* is modified by *pretty, pale, handsome, ugly, weathered,* and *craggy. Head* is modified by *bald, massive,* and *shapely. Hair* is modified by *curly, brown, thick, golden, glossy,* and, of course, *red*; it is not surprising that Anne, plagued by the red hair which she despises, is often described in these terms. Interestingly, Montgomery often uses adjectives that would usually modify *hair* to modify *head,* for example, *curly, brown, glossy, silky,* and *golden*:

> Felicity tossed her **golden head** and shot an unsisterly glance at Dan.

In Montgomery's work, there is one more instance of *curly head* than there is of *curly hair,* while *golden hair* appears almost three times as often as *golden head.* However, the attribution of qualities to *head* that would usually describe *hair* is much rarer in modern English. In the *Bank of English,* Collins' corpus of modern day English, *golden hair* appears over six times as frequently as *golden head* and *curly hair* appears over twenty times as frequently as *curly head.* But the adjectives that Montgomery uses to modify *head* do not just concern physical qualities. For example, in the phrases 'her tired curly head' or 'her jaunty brown head', the mood of the characters as well as their appearance is illustrated.

Indeed, Montgomery often uses physical descriptions of her characters to portray, not only how they look, but also their emotional state. Some of the other adjectives Montgomery uses with *eye* include *bloodshot* and *red-rimmed,* while salient verbs include *flash, twinkle, water,* and *glisten*:

> Hurt, Katrina's eyes **glistened** with tears.

Adjectives revealing of emotion used to modify *face* include *taut, radiant, solemn,* and *crimson,* while salient verbs include *flush, crumple, relax, contort,* and *smile*:

> A match flared, a hand lit a small candle and Tenzin's face smiled reassuringly at me as though he sensed my fear of the darkness.

Many of the adjectives that Montgomery uses are positive. After *little,* the most frequent adjective she uses is *good*; *sweet, lovely, splendid,* and *delightful* also appear in her 100 most frequently used adjectives. *Jolly* and *gay,* which may be considered more old-fashioned, are also fairly frequent. *Jolly* modifies *playmate, chum* and *laugh*; *gay,* which is of course used in its original sense 'happy', modifies *laugh, reveller,* and *chatter.*

Negative terms also appear in Montgomery's 100 most frequently used adjectives, for example *bad, awful, dreadful,* and *terrible. Awful* modifies *temper, failure, dream,* and *feeling,* while *dreadful* modifies *mischief, predicament,* and *foolishness. Terrible* modifies *mess, blow,* and *mood.* It is interesting that the positive adjectives are often used to modify people, or things closely associated with them, such as their laugh or voice, while the negative adjectives tend to modify more abstract concepts. Further evidence of this is that *good* often modifies *friend, girl,* and *fellow,* while *bad* tends to modify *temper, dream,* and *habit.*

C

complicity NOUN = **collusion**, conspiracy, collaboration, connivance, abetment

compliment NOUN = **praise**, honour, tribute, courtesy, admiration, bouquet, flattery, eulogy: *She blushed, but accepted the compliment with good grace.* **OPPOSITE:** criticism
▷ PLURAL NOUN **1 = greetings**, regards, respects, good wishes, salutation: *Give my compliments to your lovely wife when you write home.* **OPPOSITE:** insult
2 = congratulations, praise, commendation: *That was an excellent meal – my compliments to the chef.*
▷ VERB = **praise**, flatter, salute, congratulate, pay tribute to, commend, laud, extol, crack up *(informal)*, pat on the back, sing the praises of, wax lyrical about, big up *(slang)*, speak highly of: *They complimented me on my performance.*
OPPOSITE: criticize

> **USAGE**
> *Compliment* is sometimes confused with *complement*.

complimentary ADJECTIVE
1 = flattering, approving, appreciative, congratulatory, eulogistic, commendatory: *We often get complimentary remarks regarding the quality of our service.* **OPPOSITE:** critical
2 = free, donated, courtesy, honorary, free of charge, on the house, gratuitous, gratis: *He had complimentary tickets for the show.*

comply VERB = **obey**, follow, respect, agree to, satisfy, observe, fulfil, submit to, conform to, adhere to, abide by, consent to, yield to, defer to, accede to, act in accordance with, perform, acquiesce with **OPPOSITE:** defy

component NOUN = **part**, piece, unit, item, element, ingredient, constituent: *Enriched uranium is a key component of nuclear weapons.*
▷ ADJECTIVE = **constituent**, composing, inherent, intrinsic: *Polish workers will now be making component parts for Boeing 757s.*

compose VERB **1 = put together**, make up, constitute, comprise, make, build, form, fashion, construct, compound: *They agreed to form a council composed of leaders of the rival factions.*
OPPOSITE: destroy **2 = create**, write, produce, imagine, frame, invent, devise, contrive: *He started at once to compose a reply to her letter.* **3 = arrange**, make up, construct, put together, order, organize: *The drawing is beautifully composed.*
compose yourself = **calm yourself**, be still, control yourself, settle yourself, collect yourself, pull yourself together: *She quickly composed herself before she entered the room.*

composed ADJECTIVE = **calm**, together *(slang)*, cool, collected, relaxed, confident, poised, at ease, laid-back *(informal)*, serene, tranquil, sedate, self-controlled, level-headed, unfazed *(informal)*, unflappable, unruffled, self-possessed, imperturbable, unworried, keeping your cool, as cool as a cucumber, chilled *(informal)*, grounded **OPPOSITE:** agitated

composite ADJECTIVE = **compound**, mixed, combined, complex, blended, conglomerate, synthesized: *The chassis is made of a complex composite structure incorporating carbon fibre.*
▷ NOUN = **compound**, blend, conglomerate, fusion, synthesis, amalgam, meld: *Spain is a composite of diverse traditions and people.*

composition NOUN **1 = design**, form, structure, make-up, organization, arrangement, constitution, formation, layout, configuration: *Materials of different composition absorb and reflect light differently.* **2 = creation**, work, piece, production, opus, masterpiece, chef-d'oeuvre *(French)*: *Bach's compositions are undoubtedly among the greatest ever written.* **3 = essay**, writing, study, exercise, treatise, literary work: *Write a composition on the subject 'What I Did on My Holidays'.*
4 = arrangement, balance, proportion, harmony, symmetry, concord, consonance, placing: *Let us study the composition of this painting.*
5 = production, creation, making, fashioning, formation, putting together, invention, compilation, formulation: *These plays are arranged in order of their composition.*

> **QUOTATIONS**
> At school, composition tests your stamina, whereas translation requires intelligence. But in later life you can scoff at those who did well in composition
> [Gustave Flaubert *The Dictionary of Received Ideas*]

compost NOUN = **fertilizer**, mulch, humus

composure NOUN = **calmness**, calm, poise, self-possession, cool *(slang)*, ease, dignity, serenity, tranquillity, coolness, aplomb, equanimity, self-assurance, sang-froid, placidity, sedateness **OPPOSITE:** agitation

compound NOUN = **combination**, mixture, blend, composite, conglomerate, fusion, synthesis, alloy, medley, amalgam, meld, composition: *Organic compounds contain carbon in their molecules.*
OPPOSITE: element
▷ ADJECTIVE = **complex**, multiple, composite, conglomerate, intricate, not simple: *a tall shrub with shiny compound leaves* **OPPOSITE:** simple
▷ VERB **1 = intensify**, add to, complicate, worsen, heighten, exacerbate, aggravate, magnify, augment, add insult to injury: *Additional bloodshed will only compound the misery.* **OPPOSITE:** lessen **2 = combine**, unite, mix, blend, fuse, mingle, synthesize, concoct, amalgamate, coalesce, intermingle, meld: *An emotion oddly compounded of pleasure and bitterness flooded over me.* **OPPOSITE:** divide

comprehend VERB = **understand**, see, take in, perceive, grasp, conceive, make out, discern, assimilate, see the light, fathom, apprehend, get the hang of *(informal)*, get the picture, know **OPPOSITE:** misunderstand

comprehensible ADJECTIVE = **understandable**, clear, plain, explicit, coherent, user-friendly, intelligible

comprehension NOUN = **understanding**, grasp, conception, realization, sense, knowledge, intelligence, judgment, perception, discernment
OPPOSITE: incomprehension

comprehensive ADJECTIVE = **broad**, full, complete, wide, catholic, sweeping, extensive, blanket, umbrella, thorough, inclusive, exhaustive, all-inclusive, all-embracing, overarching, encyclopedic **OPPOSITE:** limited

compress VERB **1 = squeeze**, crush, squash, constrict, press, crowd, wedge, cram: *Poor posture can compress the body's organs.* **2 = condense**, contract, concentrate, compact, shorten, summarize, abbreviate: *Textbooks compressed six millennia of Egyptian history into a few pages.*

compressed ADJECTIVE **1 = squeezed**, concentrated, compact, compacted, consolidated, squashed, flattened, constricted: *a biodegradable product made from compressed peat and cellulose*
2 = reduced, compacted, shortened, abridged: *All those three books are compressed into one volume.*

compression NOUN = **squeezing**, pressing, crushing, consolidation, condensation, constriction

comprise VERB **1 = be composed of**, include, contain, consist of, take in, embrace, encompass, comprehend: *The exhibition comprises 50 oils and watercolours.* **2 = make up**, form, constitute, compose: *Women comprise 44% of hospital medical staff.*

> **USAGE**
> The use of *of* after *comprise* should be avoided: *the library comprises* (not *comprises of) 6,500,000 books and manuscripts*. *Consist*, however, should be followed by *of* when used in this way: *Her crew consisted of children from Devon and Cornwall.*

compromise NOUN = **give-and-take**, agreement, settlement, accommodation, concession, adjustment, trade-off, middle ground, half measures: *Be willing to make compromises between what your partner wants and what you want.*
OPPOSITE: disagreement
▷ VERB **1 = meet halfway**, concede, make concessions, give and take, strike a balance, strike a happy medium, go fifty-fifty *(informal)*: *I don't think we can compromise on fundamental principles.* **OPPOSITE:** disagree
2 = undermine, expose, embarrass, weaken, prejudice, endanger,

discredit, implicate, jeopardize, dishonour, imperil: *He had compromised himself by accepting the money.* **OPPOSITE:** support

PROVERBS
If the mountain will not come to Mahomet, Mahomet must go to the mountain

compulsion NOUN **1 = urge**, need, obsession, necessity, preoccupation, drive: *He felt a compulsion to talk about his ex-wife all the time.* **2 = force**, pressure, obligation, constraint, urgency, coercion, duress, demand: *Students learn more when they are in classes out of choice rather than compulsion.*

compulsive ADJECTIVE **1 = obsessive**, confirmed, chronic, persistent, addictive, uncontrollable, incurable, inveterate, incorrigible: *He is a compulsive liar.* **2 = fascinating**, gripping, absorbing, compelling, captivating, enthralling, hypnotic, engrossing, spellbinding: *This really is compulsive reading.* **3 = irresistible**, overwhelming, compelling, urgent, neurotic, besetting, uncontrollable, driving: *He seems to have an almost compulsive desire to play tricks.*

compulsory ADJECTIVE **= obligatory**, forced, required, binding, mandatory, imperative, requisite, de rigueur *(French)* **OPPOSITE:** voluntary

compute VERB **= calculate**, rate, figure, total, measure, estimate, count, reckon, sum, figure out, add up, tally, enumerate

comrade NOUN **= companion**, friend, partner, ally, colleague, associate, fellow, mate *(informal)*, pal *(informal)*, buddy *(informal)*, compatriot, crony, confederate, co-worker, main man *(slang, chiefly U.S.)*, homeboy *(slang, chiefly U.S.)*, cobber *(Austral. & N.Z. old-fashioned, informal)*, compeer

comradeship NOUN **= fellowship**, solidarity, fraternity, brotherhood, companionship, camaraderie, kotahitanga *(N.Z.)*

con VERB **= swindle**, trick, cheat, rip off *(slang)*, kid *(informal)*, skin *(slang)*, stiff *(slang)*, mislead, deceive, hoax, defraud, dupe, gull *(archaic)*, rook *(slang)*, humbug, bamboozle *(informal)*, hoodwink, double-cross *(informal)*, diddle *(informal)*, take for a ride *(informal)*, inveigle, do the dirty on *(Brit. informal)*, bilk, sell a pup, pull a fast one on *(informal)*, scam *(slang)*: *He claimed that the businessman had conned him out of his life savings; The British motorist has been conned by the government.*
▷ NOUN **= swindle**, trick, fraud, deception, scam *(slang)*, sting *(informal)*, bluff, fastie *(Austral. slang)*: *I am afraid you have been the victim of a con.*

concave ADJECTIVE **= hollow**, cupped, depressed, scooped, hollowed, excavated, sunken, indented **OPPOSITE:** convex

conceal VERB **1 = hide**, bury, stash *(informal)*, secrete, cover, screen, disguise, obscure, camouflage: *The device, concealed in a dustbin, was defused by police.* **OPPOSITE:** reveal **2 = keep secret**, hide, disguise, mask, suppress, veil, dissemble, draw a veil over, keep dark, keep under your hat: *Robert could not conceal his relief.* **OPPOSITE:** show

concealed ADJECTIVE **= hidden**, covered, secret, screened, masked, obscured, covert, unseen, tucked away, secreted, under wraps, inconspicuous

concealment NOUN **1 = cover**, hiding, camouflage, hiding place: *The criminals vainly sought concealment from the searchlight.* **2 = cover-up**, disguise, keeping secret: *His concealment of his true motives was masterly.* **OPPOSITE:** disclosure

concede VERB **1 = admit**, allow, accept, acknowledge, own, grant, confess: *She finally conceded that he was right.* **OPPOSITE:** deny **2 = give up**, yield, hand over, surrender, relinquish, cede: *The central government has never conceded that territory to the Kurds.* **OPPOSITE:** conquer

conceit NOUN **1 = self-importance**, vanity, arrogance, complacency, pride, swagger, narcissism, egotism, self-love, amour-propre, vainglory: *He knew, without conceit, that he was considered a genius.* **2 = image**, idea, concept, metaphor, imagery, figure of speech, trope: *Critics may complain that the novel's central conceit is rather simplistic.*

conceited ADJECTIVE **= self-important**, vain, arrogant, stuck up *(informal)*, cocky, narcissistic, puffed up, egotistical, overweening, immodest, vainglorious, swollen-headed, bigheaded *(informal)*, full of yourself, too big for your boots *or* breeches **OPPOSITE:** modest

conceivable ADJECTIVE **= imaginable**, possible, credible, believable, thinkable **OPPOSITE:** inconceivable

conceive VERB **1 = imagine**, envisage, comprehend, visualize, think, believe, suppose, fancy, appreciate, grasp, apprehend: *We now cannot conceive of a world without electricity.* **2 = think up**, form, produce, create, develop, design, project, purpose, devise, formulate, contrive: *I began to conceive a plan of attack.* **3 = become pregnant**, get pregnant, become impregnated: *Women should give up alcohol before they plan to conceive.*

concentrate VERB **1 = focus your attention**, focus, pay attention, be engrossed, apply yourself: *Try to concentrate on what you're doing.* **OPPOSITE:** pay no attention **2 = focus**, centre, converge, bring to bear: *We should concentrate our efforts on tackling crime in the inner cities.* **3 = gather**, collect, cluster, accumulate, congregate: *Most poor people are concentrated in this area.* **OPPOSITE:** scatter

concentrated ADJECTIVE **1 = condensed**, rich, undiluted, reduced, evaporated, thickened, boiled down: *Sweeten dishes with honey or concentrated apple juice.* **2 = intense**, hard, deep, intensive, all-out *(informal)*: *She makes a concentrated effort to keep her feet on the ground.*

concentration NOUN **1 = attention**, application, absorption, single-mindedness, intentness: *His talking kept breaking my concentration.* **OPPOSITE:** inattention **2 = focusing**, centring, consolidation, convergence, bringing to bear, intensification, centralization: *This concentration of effort and resources should not be to the exclusion of everything else.* **3 = convergence**, collection, mass, cluster, accumulation, aggregation: *The area has one of the world's greatest concentrations of wildlife.* **OPPOSITE:** scattering

concept NOUN **= idea**, view, image, theory, impression, notion, conception, hypothesis, abstraction, conceptualization

conception NOUN **1 = understanding**, idea, picture, impression, perception, clue, appreciation, comprehension, inkling: *He doesn't have the slightest conception of teamwork.* **2 = idea**, plan, design, image, concept, notion: *The symphony is admirable in its conception.* **3 = impregnation**, insemination, fertilization, germination: *Six weeks after conception your baby is the size of your little fingernail.* **4 = origin**, beginning, launching, birth, formation, invention, outset, initiation, inception: *It is six years since the project's conception.*

concern NOUN **1 = anxiety**, fear, worry, distress, unease, apprehension, misgiving, disquiet: *The move follows growing public concern over the spread of the disease.* **2 = worry**, care, anxiety: *His concern was that people would know that he was responsible.* **3 = affair**, issue, matter, consideration: *Feminism must address issues beyond the concerns of middle-class whites.* **4 = care**, interest, regard, consideration, solicitude, attentiveness: *He had only gone along out of concern for his two grandsons.* **5 = business**, job, charge, matter, department, field, affair, responsibility, task, mission, pigeon *(informal)*: *The technical aspects are not my concern.* **6 = company**, house, business, firm, organization, corporation, enterprise, establishment: *If not a large concern, his business was at least a successful one.* **7 = importance**, interest, bearing, relevance: *The survey's findings are a matter of great concern.*
▷ VERB **1 = worry**, trouble, bother, disturb, distress, disquiet, perturb, make uneasy, make anxious: *It concerned her that Bess was developing a crush on Max.* **2 = be about**, cover, deal with, go into, relate to, have to do with: *The bulk of the book concerns the author's childhood.* **3 = be relevant to**, involve, affect, regard, apply to, bear

C

on, have something to do with, pertain to, interest, touch: *This matter doesn't concern you, so stay out of it.*

concerned ADJECTIVE **1 = involved**, interested, active, mixed up, implicated, privy to: *I believe he was concerned in all those matters you mention; It's been a difficult time for all concerned.* **2 = worried**, troubled, upset, bothered, disturbed, anxious, distressed, uneasy: *I've been very concerned about the situation.* **OPPOSITE:** indifferent **3 = caring**, attentive, solicitous: *A concerned friend put a comforting arm around her shoulder.*

concerning PREPOSITION **= regarding**, about, re, touching, respecting, relating to, on the subject of, as to, with reference to, in the matter of, apropos of, as regards

concert
in concert = together, jointly, unanimously, in unison, in league, in collaboration, shoulder to shoulder, concertedly

concerted ADJECTIVE **= coordinated**, united, joint, combined, collaborative **OPPOSITE:** separate

concession NOUN **1 = compromise**, agreement, settlement, accommodation, adjustment, trade-off, give-and-take, half measures: *Britain has made sweeping concessions to China in order to reach a settlement.* **2 = privilege**, right, permit, licence, franchise, entitlement, indulgence, prerogative: *The government has granted concessions to three private telephone companies.* **3 = reduction**, saving, grant, discount, allowance: *tax concessions for mothers who choose to stay at home with their children* **4 = surrender**, yielding, conceding, renunciation, relinquishment: *He said there'd be no concession of territory.*

conciliation NOUN **= pacification**, reconciliation, disarming, appeasement, propitiation, mollification, soothing, placation

conciliatory ADJECTIVE **= pacifying**, pacific, disarming, appeasing, mollifying, peaceable, placatory, soothing

concise ADJECTIVE **= brief**, short, to the point, compact, summary, compressed, condensed, terse, laconic, succinct, pithy, synoptic, epigrammatic, compendious **OPPOSITE:** rambling

conclave NOUN **= secret** *or* **private meeting**, council, conference, congress, session, cabinet, assembly, parley, runanga *(N.Z.)*

conclude VERB **1 = decide**, judge, establish, suppose, determine, assume, gather, reckon *(informal)*, work out, infer, deduce, surmise: *We concluded that he was telling the truth.* **2 = come to an end**, end, close, finish, wind up, draw to a close: *The evening concluded with dinner and speeches.* **OPPOSITE:** begin **3 = bring to an end**, end, close, finish, complete, wind up, terminate, round off: *They concluded their annual summit meeting today.* **OPPOSITE:** begin **4 = accomplish**, effect, settle, bring about, fix, carry out, resolve, clinch, pull off, bring off *(informal)*: *If the clubs cannot conclude a deal, an independent tribunal will decide.*

conclusion NOUN **1 = decision**, agreement, opinion, settlement, resolution, conviction, verdict, judgment, deduction, inference: *We came to the conclusion that it was too difficult to combine the two techniques.* **2 = end**, ending, close, finish, completion, finale, termination, bitter end, result: *At the conclusion of the programme, viewers were invited to phone in.* **3 = outcome**, result, upshot, consequence, sequel, culmination, end result, issue: *Executives said it was the logical conclusion of a process started in 1987.*
in conclusion = finally, lastly, in closing, to sum up: *In conclusion, walking is a cheap, safe form of exercise.*

conclusive ADJECTIVE **= decisive**, final, convincing, clinching, definite, definitive, irrefutable, unanswerable, unarguable, ultimate **OPPOSITE:** inconclusive

concoct VERB **= make up**, design, prepare, manufacture, plot, invent, devise, brew, hatch, formulate, contrive, fabricate, think up, cook up *(informal)*, trump up, project

concoction NOUN **= mixture**, preparation, compound, brew, combination, creation, blend

concord NOUN **= treaty**, agreement, convention, compact, protocol, entente, concordat: *The Concord of Wittenberg was agreed in 1536.*

concourse NOUN **= crowd**, collection, gathering, assembly, crush, multitude, throng, convergence, hui *(N.Z.)*, assemblage, meeting, runanga *(N.Z.)*: *The streets were filled with a fair concourse of people that night.*

concrete NOUN **= cement** *(not in technical usage)*: *The posts have to be set in concrete.* ▷ ADJECTIVE **1 = specific**, precise, explicit, definite, clear-cut, unequivocal, unambiguous: *He had no concrete evidence.* **OPPOSITE:** vague **2 = real**, material, actual, substantial, sensible, tangible, factual: *using concrete objects to teach addition and subtraction* **OPPOSITE:** abstract

concubine NOUN **= mistress**, courtesan, kept woman

concur VERB **= agree**, accord, approve, assent, accede, acquiesce

concurrent ADJECTIVE **= simultaneous**, coexisting, concomitant, contemporaneous, coincident, synchronous, concerted

concussion NOUN **1 = shock**, brain injury: *She fell off a horse and suffered a concussion.* **2 = impact**, crash, shaking, clash, jarring, collision, jolt, jolting: *I was blown off the deck by the concussion of the torpedoes.*

condemn VERB **1 = denounce**, damn, criticize, disapprove, censure, reprove, upbraid, excoriate, reprehend, blame: *Political leaders united yesterday to condemn the latest wave of violence.* **OPPOSITE:** approve **2 = sentence**, convict, damn, doom, pass sentence on: *He was condemned to life imprisonment.* **OPPOSITE:** acquit

> QUOTATIONS
> Society needs to condemn a little more and understand a little less
> [John Major]

condemnation NOUN **= denunciation**, blame, censure, disapproval, reproach, stricture, reproof, denouncement

condensation NOUN **1 = distillation**, precipitation, liquefaction: *The surface refrigeration allows the condensation of water.* **2 = abridgment**, summary, abstract, digest, contraction, synopsis, précis, encapsulation: *a condensation of a book that offers ten ways to be a better manager*

condense VERB **1 = abridge**, contract, concentrate, compact, shorten, summarize, compress, encapsulate, abbreviate, epitomize, précis: *The English translation has been condensed into a single more readable book.* **OPPOSITE:** expand **2 = concentrate**, reduce, precipitate *(Chemistry)*, thicken, boil down, solidify, coagulate: *The compressed gas is cooled and condenses into a liquid.* **OPPOSITE:** dilute

condensed ADJECTIVE **1 = abridged**, concentrated, compressed, potted, shortened, summarized, slimmed-down, encapsulated: *I also produced a condensed version of the paper.* **2 = concentrated**, reduced, thickened, boiled down, precipitated *(Chemistry)*: *condensed milk*

condescend VERB **1 = patronize**, talk down to, treat like a child, treat as inferior, treat condescendingly: *a writer who does not condescend to his readers* **2 = deign**, see fit, lower yourself, be courteous enough, bend, submit, stoop, unbend *(informal)*, vouchsafe, come down off your high horse *(informal)*, humble *or* demean yourself: *He never condescended to notice me.*

condescending ADJECTIVE **= patronizing**, lordly, superior, lofty, snooty *(informal)*, snobbish, disdainful, supercilious, toffee-nosed *(slang, chiefly Brit.)*, on your high horse *(informal)*

condescension NOUN **= patronizing attitude**, superiority, disdain, haughtiness, loftiness, superciliousness, lordliness, airs

condition NOUN **1 = state**, order, shape, nick *(Brit. informal)*, trim: *The two-bedroom chalet is in good condition.* **2 = situation**, state, position, status, circumstances, plight, status quo *(Latin)*, case, predicament: *The government has to encourage people to better their condition.* **3 = requirement**, terms, rider, provision, restriction, qualification, limitation, modification, requisite, prerequisite, proviso, stipulation, rule, demand: *They had agreed to a summit subject to certain conditions.* **4 = health**, shape, fitness, trim, form, kilter, state of health, fettle, order: *She was in fine condition for a woman of her age.* **5 = ailment**, problem, complaint, weakness, malady, infirmity: *Doctors suspect he may have a heart condition.* ▷ PLURAL NOUN **= circumstances**, situation, environment, surroundings, way of life, milieu: *The conditions in the camp are just awful.* ▷ VERB **= train**, teach, educate, adapt, accustom, inure, habituate: *We have been conditioned to believe that it is weak to be scared.*

conditional ADJECTIVE **= dependent**, limited, qualified, contingent, provisional, with reservations **OPPOSITE:** unconditional

conditioning NOUN **= training**, education, teaching, accustoming, habituation

condom NOUN **= sheath**, safe *(U.S. & Canad. slang)*, rubber *(U.S. slang)*, blob *(Brit. slang)*, scumbag *(U.S. slang)*, Frenchie *(slang)*, flunky *(slang)*, French letter *(slang)*, rubber johnny *(Brit. slang)*, French tickler *(slang)*

condone VERB **= overlook**, excuse, forgive, pardon, disregard, turn a blind eye to, wink at, look the other way, make allowance for, let pass **OPPOSITE:** condemn

conducive ADJECTIVE **= favourable**, helpful, productive, contributory, calculated to produce, leading, tending

conduct VERB **1 = carry out**, run, control, manage, direct, handle, organize, govern, regulate, administer, supervise, preside over: *I decided to conduct an experiment.* **2 = accompany**, lead, escort, guide, attend, steer, convey, usher, pilot: *He asked if he might conduct us to the ball.* ▷ NOUN **1 = management**, running, control, handling, administration, direction, leadership, organization, guidance, supervision: *Also up for discussion will be the conduct of free and fair elections.* **2 = behaviour**, ways, bearing, attitude, manners, carriage, demeanour, deportment, mien *(literary)*, comportment: *Other people judge you by your conduct.*
conduct yourself = behave yourself, act, carry yourself, acquit yourself, deport yourself, comport yourself: *The way he conducts himself reflects on the party.*

conduit NOUN **= passage**, channel, tube, pipe, canal, duct, main

confederacy NOUN **= union**, league, alliance, coalition, federation, compact, confederation, covenant, bund

confederate NOUN **= associate**, partner, ally, colleague, accessory, accomplice, abettor: *The conspirators were joined by their confederates.* ▷ ADJECTIVE **= allied**, federal, associated, combined, federated, in alliance: *We want a confederate Europe.*

confer VERB **1 = discuss**, talk, consult, deliberate, discourse, converse, parley: *He conferred with Hill and the others in his office.* **2 = grant**, give, present, accord, award, hand out, bestow, vouchsafe: *An honorary degree was conferred on him by Newcastle University in 1976.*

conference NOUN **= meeting**, congress, discussion, convention, forum, consultation, seminar, symposium, hui *(N.Z.)*, convocation, colloquium

confess VERB **1 = admit**, acknowledge, disclose, confide, own up, come clean *(informal)*, divulge, blurt out, come out of the closet, make a clean breast of, get (something) off your chest *(informal)*, spill your guts *(slang)*, 'fess up *(U.S.)*, sing *(slang, chiefly U.S.)*: *He has confessed to seventeen murders; She confesses that she only wrote those books for the money.* **OPPOSITE:** cover up **2 = declare**, own up, allow, prove, reveal, grant, confirm, concede, assert, manifest, affirm, profess, attest, evince, aver: *I must confess I'm not a great sports enthusiast.*

confession NOUN **= admission**, revelation, disclosure, acknowledgment, avowal, divulgence, exposure, unbosoming

PROVERBS
Confession is good for the soul

confidant *or* **confidante** NOUN **= close friend**, familiar, intimate, crony, alter ego, bosom friend

confide VERB **= tell**, admit, reveal, confess, whisper, disclose, impart, divulge, breathe

confidence NOUN **1 = trust**, belief, faith, dependence, reliance, credence: *I have every confidence in you.* **OPPOSITE:** distrust **2 = self-assurance**, courage, assurance, aplomb, boldness, self-reliance, self-possession, nerve: *She always thinks the worst of herself and has no confidence whatsoever.* **OPPOSITE:** shyness **3 = secret**: *I'm not in the habit of exchanging confidences with her.*
in confidence = in secrecy, privately, confidentially, between you and me (and the gatepost), (just) between ourselves: *I'm telling you all these things in confidence.*

confident ADJECTIVE **1 = certain**, sure, convinced, positive, secure, satisfied, counting on: *I am confident that everything will come out right in time.* **OPPOSITE:** unsure **2 = self-assured**, positive, assured, bold, self-confident, self-reliant, self-possessed, sure of yourself, can-do *(informal)*: *In time he became more confident and relaxed.* **OPPOSITE:** insecure

confidential ADJECTIVE **1 = secret**, private, intimate, classified, privy, off the record, hush-hush *(informal)*: *She accused them of leaking confidential information.* **2 = secretive**, low, soft, hushed: *He adopted a confidential tone of voice.*

confidentially ADVERB **= in secret**, privately, personally, behind closed doors, in confidence, in camera, between ourselves, sub rosa

configuration NOUN **= arrangement**, form, shape, cast, outline, contour, conformation, figure

confine VERB **1 = imprison**, enclose, shut up, intern, incarcerate, circumscribe, hem in, immure, keep, cage: *He has been confined to his barracks.* **2 = restrict**, limit: *She had largely confined her activities to the world of big business.* ▷ PLURAL NOUN **= limits**, bounds, boundaries, compass, precincts, circumference, edge, pale: *The movie is set entirely within the confines of the abandoned factory.*

confined ADJECTIVE **= restricted**, small, limited, narrow, enclosed, cramped

confinement NOUN **1 = imprisonment**, custody, detention, incarceration, internment, porridge *(slang)*: *She had been held in solitary confinement for four months.* **2 = childbirth**, labour, travail, childbed, accouchement *(French)*, time: *His pregnant wife is near her confinement.*

confirm VERB **1 = prove**, support, establish, back up, verify, validate, bear out, substantiate, corroborate, authenticate: *This confirms what I suspected all along.* **2 = ratify**, establish, approve, sanction, endorse, authorize, certify, validate, authenticate: *He is due to be confirmed as President on Friday.* **3 = strengthen**, establish, settle, fix, secure, assure, reinforce, clinch, verify, fortify: *He has confirmed his position as the world's number one snooker player.*

confirmation NOUN **1 = proof**, evidence, testimony, verification, ratification, validation, corroboration, authentication, substantiation: *He took her resignation as confirmation of their suspicions.* **OPPOSITE:** repudiation **2 = affirmation**, approval, acceptance, endorsement, ratification, assent, agreement: *She glanced over at James for confirmation of what she'd said.* **OPPOSITE:** disapproval

confirmed ADJECTIVE **= long-established**, seasoned, rooted, chronic, hardened, habitual, ingrained, inveterate, inured, dyed-in-the-wool

confiscate VERB **= seize**, appropriate, impound, commandeer, sequester, expropriate **OPPOSITE:** give back

confiscation NOUN **= seizure**, appropriation, impounding, forfeiture, expropriation, sequestration, takeover

C

conflagration NOUN **= fire**, blaze, holocaust, inferno, wildfire

conflict NOUN **1 = dispute**, difference, opposition, hostility, disagreement, friction, strife, fighting, antagonism, variance, discord, bad blood, dissension, divided loyalties: *Try to keep any conflict between you and your ex-partner to a minimum.* **OPPOSITE:** agreement **2 = struggle**, battle, clash, strife: *the anguish of his own inner conflict* **3 = battle**, war, fight, clash, contest, set-to *(informal)*, encounter, combat, engagement, warfare, collision, contention, strife, head-to-head, fracas, boilover *(Austral.)*: *The National Security Council has met to discuss ways of preventing a military conflict.* **OPPOSITE:** peace
▷ VERB **= be incompatible**, clash, differ, disagree, contend, strive, collide, be at variance: *He held firm opinions which sometimes conflicted with my own.* **OPPOSITE:** agree

conflicting ADJECTIVE **= incompatible**, opposed, opposing, clashing, contrary, contradictory, inconsistent, paradoxical, discordant **OPPOSITE:** agreeing

conform VERB **1 = fit in**, follow, yield, adjust, adapt, comply, obey, fall in, toe the line, follow the crowd, run with the pack, follow convention: *Children who can't or won't conform are often bullied.* **2** *(with* **with***)* **= fulfil**, meet, match, suit, satisfy, agree with, obey, abide by, accord with, square with, correspond with, tally with, harmonize with: *These activities do not conform with diplomatic rules and regulations.*

conformation NOUN **= shape**, build, form, structure, arrangement, outline, framework, anatomy, configuration

conformist NOUN **= traditionalist**, conservative, reactionary, Babbitt *(U.S.)*, stickler, yes man, stick-in-the-mud *(informal)*, conventionalist

conformity NOUN **1 = compliance**, agreement, accordance, observance, conformance, obedience: *The prime minister is, in conformity with the constitution, chosen by the president.* **2 = conventionality**, compliance, allegiance, orthodoxy, observance, traditionalism, Babbittry *(U.S.)*: *Excessive conformity is usually caused by fear of disapproval.*

confound VERB **1 = bewilder**, baffle, amaze, confuse, astonish, startle, mix up, astound, perplex, surprise, mystify, flummox, boggle the mind, be all Greek to *(informal)*, dumbfound, nonplus, flabbergast *(informal)*: *For many years medical scientists were confounded by these seemingly contradictory facts.* **2 = disprove**, contradict, refute, negate, destroy, ruin, overwhelm, explode, overthrow, demolish, annihilate, give the lie to, make a nonsense of, prove false, blow out of the water *(slang)*, controvert, confute: *The findings confound all the government's predictions.*

confront VERB **1 = tackle**, deal with, cope with, brave, beard, face up to, meet head-on: *We are learning how to confront death.* **2 = trouble**, face, afflict, perplex, perturb, bedevil: *the environmental crisis which confronts us all* **3 = challenge**, face, oppose, tackle, encounter, defy, call out, stand up to, come face to face with, accost, face off *(slang)*: *She pushed her way through the mob and confronted him face to face.* **OPPOSITE:** evade

confrontation NOUN **= conflict**, fight, crisis, contest, set-to *(informal)*, encounter, showdown *(informal)*, head-to-head, face-off *(slang)*, boilover *(Austral.)*

confuse VERB **1 = mix up with**, take for, mistake for, muddle with: *I can't see how anyone could confuse you two with each other.* **2 = bewilder**, puzzle, baffle, perplex, mystify, fluster, faze, flummox, bemuse, be all Greek to *(informal)*, nonplus: *Politics just confuses me.* **3 = obscure**, cloud, complicate, muddle, darken, make more difficult, muddy the waters: *His critics accused him of trying to confuse the issue.*

confused ADJECTIVE **1 = bewildered**, puzzled, baffled, at sea, muddled, dazed, perplexed, at a loss, taken aback, disorientated, muzzy *(U.S. informal)*, nonplussed, flummoxed, at sixes and sevens, thrown off balance, discombobulated *(informal, chiefly U.S. & Canad.)*, not with it *(informal)*, not knowing if you are coming or going: *People are confused about what they should eat to stay healthy.* **OPPOSITE:** enlightened **2 = disorderly**, disordered, chaotic, mixed up, jumbled, untidy, out of order, in disarray, topsy-turvy, disorganized, higgledy-piggledy *(informal)*, at sixes and sevens, disarranged, disarrayed: *The situation remains confused as both sides claim victory; Everything lay in a confused heap on the floor.* **OPPOSITE:** tidy

> QUOTATIONS
> If you are sure you understand everything that is going on, you are hopelessly confused
> [Walter Mondale]
>
> Anyone who isn't confused doesn't really understand the situation
> [Ed Murrow (on the Vietnam War)]

confusing ADJECTIVE **= bewildering**, complicated, puzzling, misleading, unclear, baffling, muddling, contradictory, ambiguous, inconsistent, perplexing, clear as mud *(informal)* **OPPOSITE:** clear

confusion NOUN **1 = bewilderment**, doubt, uncertainty, puzzlement, perplexity, mystification, bafflement, perturbation: *Omissions in my recent article may have caused some confusion.* **OPPOSITE:** enlightenment **2 = disorder**, chaos, turmoil, upheaval, muddle, bustle, shambles, disarray, commotion, disorganization, disarrangement: *The rebel leader seems to have escaped in the confusion.* **OPPOSITE:** order **3 = puzzlement**, bewilderment, perplexity, bafflement, mystification, perturbation: *I left his office in a state of confusion.*

congeal VERB **= thicken**, set, freeze, harden, clot, stiffen, condense, solidify, curdle, jell, coagulate

congenial ADJECTIVE **= pleasant**, kindly, pleasing, friendly, agreeable, cordial, sociable, genial, affable, convivial, companionable, favourable, complaisant

congenital ADJECTIVE **1 = inborn**, innate, inherent, hereditary, natural, constitutional, inherited, inbred: *When he was 17, he died of congenital heart disease.* **2 = complete**, confirmed, chronic, utter, hardened, thorough, habitual, incurable, inveterate, incorrigible, deep-dyed *(usually derogatory)*: *He is a congenital liar.*

congested ADJECTIVE **1 = packed (out)**, crowded, overcrowded, teeming: *Some areas are congested with both cars and people.* **OPPOSITE:** empty **2 = clogged**, jammed, blocked-up, overfilled, stuffed, packed, crammed, overflowing, stuffed-up: *The arteries in his neck had become fatally congested.* **OPPOSITE:** clear

congestion NOUN **= overcrowding**, crowding, mass, jam, clogging, bottleneck, snarl-up *(informal, chiefly Brit.)*

conglomerate NOUN **= corporation**, multinational, corporate body, business, association, consortium, aggregate, agglomerate

congratulate VERB **= compliment**, pat on the back, wish joy to

congratulations PLURAL NOUN **= good wishes**, greetings, compliments, best wishes, pat on the back, felicitations: *I offer you my congratulations on your appointment as chairman.*
▷ INTERJECTION **= good wishes**, greetings, compliments, best wishes, felicitations: *Congratulations! You have a healthy baby boy.*

> QUOTATIONS
> congratulation: the civility of envy
> [Ambrose Bierce *The Devil's Dictionary*]

congregate VERB **= come together**, meet, mass, collect, gather, concentrate, rally, assemble, flock, muster, convene, converge, throng, rendezvous, foregather, convoke **OPPOSITE:** disperse

congregation NOUN **= parishioners**, host, brethren, crowd, assembly, parish, flock, fellowship, multitude, throng, laity, flock

congress NOUN **1 = meeting**, council, conference, diet, assembly, convention, conclave, legislative assembly, convocation, hui *(N.Z.)*, runanga *(N.Z.)*: *A lot has changed since the party congress.* **2 = legislature**, house, council, parliament, representatives, delegates, quango, legislative assembly, chamber of deputies, House of Representatives (N.Z.): *It's far from certain that the congress will approve them.*

conical *or* **conic** ADJECTIVE **= cone-shaped**, pointed, tapered, tapering, pyramidal, funnel-shaped

conjecture NOUN **= guess**, theory, fancy, notion, speculation, assumption, hypothesis, inference, presumption, surmise, theorizing, guesswork, supposition, shot in the dark, guesstimate *(informal)*: *Your assertion is merely a conjecture, not a fact.* ▷ VERB **= guess**, speculate, surmise, theorize, suppose, imagine, assume, fancy, infer, hypothesize: *This may or may not be true; we are all conjecturing here.*

conjunction NOUN **= combination**, union, joining, association, coincidence, juxtaposition, concurrence

conjure VERB **1 = produce**, generate, bring about, give rise to, make, create, effect, produce as if by magic: *They managed to conjure an impressive victory.* **2** *(often with* **up***)* **= summon up**, raise, invoke, rouse, call upon: *The ouija board is used to conjure up spirits and communicate with them.*
conjure something up = bring to mind, recall, evoke, recreate, recollect, produce as if by magic: *When he closed his eyes, he could conjure up almost every event of his life.*

conjuring NOUN **= magic**, juggling, trickery, sleight of hand

connect VERB **1 = link**, join, couple, attach, fasten, affix, unite: *You can connect the machine to your hi-fi.* **OPPOSITE:** separate **2 = associate**, unite, join, couple, league, link, mix, relate, pair, ally, identify, combine, affiliate, correlate, confederate, lump together, mention in the same breath, think of together: *There is no evidence to connect him to the robberies; I wouldn't have connected the two events if you hadn't said that.*

connected ADJECTIVE **= linked**, united, joined, coupled, related, allied, associated, combined, bracketed, affiliated, akin, banded together

connection NOUN **1 = association**, relationship, link, relation, bond, correspondence, relevance, tie-in, correlation, interrelation: *There is no evidence of any connection between BSE and the brain diseases recently confirmed in cats.* **2 = communication**, alliance, commerce, attachment, intercourse, liaison, affinity, affiliation, union: *I no longer have any connection with my ex-husband's family.* **3 = link**, coupling, junction, fastening, tie: *Check radiators for small leaks, especially round pipework connections.* **4 = contact**, friend, relation, ally, associate, relative, acquaintance, kin, kindred, kinsman, kith: *She used her connections to full advantage.* **5 = context**, relation, reference, frame of reference: *13 men have been questioned in connection with the murder.*

connivance NOUN **= collusion**, intrigue, conspiring, complicity, abetting, tacit consent, abetment

connive VERB **= conspire**, scheme, plot, intrigue, collude: *Senior politicians connived to ensure that he was not released.*

connoisseur NOUN **= expert**, authority, judge, specialist, buff *(informal)*, devotee, whiz *(informal)*, arbiter, aficionado, savant, maven *(U.S.)*, appreciator, cognoscente, fundi *(S. African)*

> **QUOTATIONS**
> connoisseur: a specialist who knows everything about something and nothing about anything else
> [Ambrose Bierce *The Devil's Dictionary*]

connotation NOUN **= implication**, colouring, association, suggestion, significance, nuance, undertone

connote VERB **= imply**, suggest, indicate, intimate, signify, hint at, betoken, involve

conquer VERB **1 = seize**, obtain, acquire, occupy, overrun, annex, win: *Early in the eleventh century the whole of England was again conquered by the Vikings.* **2 = defeat**, overcome, overthrow, beat, stuff *(slang)*, master, tank *(slang)*, triumph, crush, humble, lick *(informal)*, undo, subdue, rout, overpower, quell, get the better of, clobber *(slang)*, vanquish, subjugate, prevail over, checkmate, run rings around *(informal)*, wipe the floor with *(informal)*, make mincemeat of *(informal)*, put in their place, blow out of the water *(slang)*, bring to their knees: *a Navajo myth about a great warrior who conquers the spiritual enemies of his people* **OPPOSITE:** lose to **3 = overcome**, beat, defeat, master, rise above, overpower, get the better of, surmount, best: *I had learned to conquer my fear of spiders.*

> **QUOTATIONS**
> I came, I saw, I conquered (veni, vidi, vici)
> [Julius Caesar]
>
> To conquer with arms is to make only a temporary conquest; to conquer the world by earning its esteem is to make a permanent conquest
> [Woodrow Wilson *Address to Congress*]

conqueror NOUN **= winner**, champion, master, victor, conquistador, lord

conquest NOUN **1 = takeover**, coup, acquisition, invasion, occupation, appropriation, annexation, subjugation, subjection: *He had led the conquest of southern Poland in 1939.* **2 = defeat**, victory, triumph, overthrow, pasting *(slang)*, rout, mastery, vanquishment: *This hidden treasure charts the brutal Spanish conquest of the Aztecs.* **3 = seduction**: *people who boast about their sexual conquests* **4 = catch**, prize, supporter, acquisition, follower, admirer, worshipper, adherent, fan, feather in your cap: *He was a womaniser whose conquests included everyone from prostitutes to princesses.*

conscience NOUN **1 = principles**, scruples, moral sense, sense of right and wrong, still small voice: *I have battled with my conscience over whether I should send this letter or not.* **2 = guilt**, shame, regret, remorse, contrition, self-reproach, self-condemnation: *She was suffering terrible pangs of conscience about what she had done.*
in all conscience = in fairness, rightly, certainly, fairly, truly, honestly, in truth, assuredly: *She could not, in all conscience, back out on her deal with him.*

> **QUOTATIONS**
> Conscience: the inner voice which warns us that someone may be looking
> [H.L. Mencken *A Little Book in C Major*]
>
> Thus conscience does make cowards of us all
> [William Shakespeare *Hamlet*]
>
> Conscience is thoroughly well-bred and soon leaves off talking to those who do not wish to hear it
> [Samuel Butler]

> **PROVERBS**
> *A guilty conscience needs no accuser*

conscientious ADJECTIVE **= thorough**, particular, careful, exact, faithful, meticulous, painstaking, diligent, punctilious **OPPOSITE:** careless

conscious ADJECTIVE **1** *(often with* **of***)* **= aware of**, wise to *(slang)*, alert to, responsive to, cognizant of, sensible of, clued-up on *(informal)*, percipient of: *She was very conscious of Max studying her.* **OPPOSITE:** unaware **2 = deliberate**, knowing, reasoning, studied, responsible, calculated, rational, reflective, self-conscious, intentional, wilful, premeditated: *Make a conscious effort to relax your muscles.* **OPPOSITE:** unintentional **3 = awake**, wide-awake, sentient, alive: *She was fully conscious throughout the operation.* **OPPOSITE:** asleep

consciousness NOUN **= awareness**, understanding, knowledge, recognition, enlightenment, sensibility, realization, apprehension

consecrate VERB **= sanctify**, dedicate, ordain, exalt, venerate, set apart, hallow, devote

consecutive ADJECTIVE **= successive**, running, following, succeeding, in turn, uninterrupted, chronological, sequential, in sequence, seriatim

consensus NOUN **= agreement**, general agreement, unanimity, common consent, unity, harmony, assent, concord, concurrence, kotahitanga *(N.Z.)*

USAGE
The original meaning of the word *consensus is a collective opinion*. Because the concept of 'opinion' is contained within this word, a few people argue that the phrase *a consensus of opinion* is incorrect and should be avoided. However, this common use of the word is unlikely to jar with the majority of speakers.

C

consent NOUN **= agreement**, sanction, approval, go-ahead *(informal)*, permission, compliance, green light, assent, acquiescence, concurrence, O.K. *or* okay *(informal)*: *Can my child be medically examined without my consent?* **OPPOSITE:** refusal
▷ VERB **= agree**, approve, yield, permit, comply, concur, assent, accede, acquiesce, play ball *(informal)*: *I was a little surprised when she consented to my proposal.* **OPPOSITE:** refuse

consequence NOUN **1 = result**, effect, outcome, repercussion, end, issue, event, sequel, end result, upshot: *Her lawyers said she understood the consequences of her actions.* **2 = importance**, interest, concern, moment, value, account, note, weight, import, significance, portent: *This question is of little consequence.* **3 = status**, standing, bottom, rank, distinction, eminence, repute, notability: *He was a sad little man of no consequence.*
in consequence = consequently, as a result, so, then, thus, therefore, hence, accordingly, for that reason, thence, ergo: *His death was totally unexpected and, in consequence, no plans had been made for his replacement.*

PROVERBS
As you sow, so shall you reap

consequent ADJECTIVE **= following**, resulting, subsequent, successive, ensuing, resultant, sequential

consequential ADJECTIVE
1 = resulting, subsequent, successive, ensuing, indirect, consequent, resultant, sequential, following: *The company disclaims any liability for incidental or consequential damages.* **2 = important**, serious, significant, grave, far-reaching, momentous, weighty, eventful: *From a medical standpoint, a week is usually not a consequential delay.*

consequently ADVERB **= as a result**, thus, therefore, necessarily, hence, subsequently, accordingly, for that reason, thence, ergo

conservation NOUN
1 = preservation, saving, protection, maintenance, custody, safeguarding, upkeep, guardianship, safekeeping: *Attention must be paid to the conservation of the environment.* **2 = economy**, saving, thrift, husbandry, careful management, thriftiness: *projects aimed at energy conservation*

Conservative ADJECTIVE **= Tory**, Republican *(U.S.)*, right-wing: *Even among Conservative voters, more than a third disapprove of the tax.*
▷ NOUN **= Tory**, Republican *(U.S.)*, right-winger: *Up to eighty Conservatives are expected to vote against the bill.*

QUOTATIONS
No amount of cajolery, and no attempts at ethical or social seduction, can eradicate from my heart a deep burning hatred for the Tory Party... So far as I am concerned they are lower than vermin
[Aneurin Bevan]

Conservative: a statesman who is enamoured of existing evils, as distinguished from the Liberal, who wishes to replace them with others
[Ambrose Bierce *The Devil's Dictionary*]

I've got money so I'm a Conservative
[Lord Thomson of Fleet]

I am driven into grudging toleration of the Conservative Party because it is the party of non-politics, of resistance to politics
[Kingsley Amis]

conservative ADJECTIVE
= traditional, guarded, quiet, conventional, moderate, cautious, sober, reactionary, die-hard, middle-of-the-road, hidebound: *People tend to be more adventurous when they're young and more conservative as they get older.* **OPPOSITE:** radical
▷ NOUN **= traditionalist**, moderate, reactionary, die-hard, middle-of-the-roader, stick-in-the-mud *(informal)*: *The new judge is regarded as a conservative.* **OPPOSITE:** radical

QUOTATIONS
We know what happens to people who stay in the middle of the road. They get run down
[Aneurin Bevan]

The most conservative man in this world is the British Trade Unionist when you want to change him
[Ernest Bevin]

I do not know which makes a man more conservative – to know nothing but the present, or nothing but the past
[John Maynard Keynes *The End of Laissez-Faire*]

A man who is determined never to move out of the beaten road cannot lose his way
[William Hazlitt *The Round Table*]

A conservative is a man with two perfectly good legs who, however, has never learned to walk forward
[Franklin D. Roosevelt]

The most radical revolutionary will become a conservative the day after the revolution
[Hannah Arendt]

conservatory NOUN **= greenhouse**, hothouse, glasshouse

conserve VERB **1 = save**, husband, take care of, hoard, store up, go easy on, use sparingly: *The factory has closed over the weekend to conserve energy.* **OPPOSITE:** waste **2 = protect**, keep, save, preserve: *an increase in US aid to help developing countries conserve their forests*

consider VERB **1 = think**, see, believe, rate, judge, suppose, deem, view as, look upon, regard as, hold to be, adjudge: *I had always considered myself a strong, competent woman.* **2 = think about**, study, reflect on, examine, weigh, contemplate, deliberate, muse, ponder, revolve, meditate, work over, mull over, eye up, ruminate, chew over, cogitate, turn over in your mind: *Consider how much you can afford to pay.* **3 = bear in mind**, remember, regard, respect, think about, care for, take into account, reckon with, take into consideration, make allowance for, keep in view: *Y ou have to consider the feelings of those around you.*

considerable ADJECTIVE **= large**, goodly, much, great, marked, comfortable, substantial, reasonable, tidy, lavish, ample, noticeable, abundant, plentiful, tolerable, appreciable, sizable *or* sizeable: *We have already spent a considerable amount of money on repairs.* **OPPOSITE:** small

considerably ADVERB **= greatly**, very much, seriously *(informal)*, significantly, remarkably, substantially, markedly, noticeably, appreciably

considerate ADJECTIVE **= thoughtful**, kind, kindly, concerned, obliging, attentive, mindful, unselfish, solicitous **OPPOSITE:** inconsiderate

consideration NOUN **1 = thought**, study, review, attention, regard, analysis, examination, reflection, scrutiny, deliberation, contemplation, perusal, cogitation: *He said there should be careful consideration of the company's future role.*
2 = thoughtfulness, concern, respect, kindness, friendliness, tact, solicitude, kindliness, considerateness: *Show consideration for other rail travellers.*
3 = factor, point, issue, concern, element, aspect, determinant: *Price was a major consideration in our choice of house.* **4 = payment**, fee, reward, remuneration, recompense, perquisite, tip: *He does odd jobs for a consideration.*
take something into consideration = bear in mind, consider, remember, think about, weigh, take into account, make allowance for, keep in view: *Other factors must also be taken into consideration.*

considering PREPOSITION **= taking into account**, in the light of, bearing in mind, in view of, keeping in mind, taking into consideration: *The former hostage is in remarkably good shape considering his ordeal.*
▷ ADVERB **= all things considered**, all in all, taking everything into consideration, taking everything into account: *I think you've got off very lightly, considering.*

Punctuation

Punctuation is a set of symbols used in written language to present and break up a text and convey meaning. Unlike conventions of spelling and grammar, which are fairly fixed in modern English, some points of punctuation allow a great deal of stylistic variation. A writer may explore and exploit these different styles, creating a range of effects.

Accepted style in punctuation has changed over time. In the past, for example, longer sentences and a greater use of commas were *de rigueur*, as is evidenced in the works of Jane Austen and Charles Dickens. Nowadays we usually find shorter sentences and fewer commas more appealing, as in this example from Charles Dickens:

> So, the Phoenicians, coasting about the Islands, would come, without much difficulty, to where the tin and lead were.
>
> So the Phoenicians, coasting about the Islands, would come without much difficulty to where the tin and lead were.

The second version of the sentence has three fewer commas than the first but would probably be preferred today because it looks simple and uncluttered.

Today commas are added only if needed to aid understanding of the text or to avoid ambiguity, and can be left out when this helps the flow of the piece. One type of ambiguity is shown in the following example:

> I would like to thank my parents, God and Janet.

This sentence requires a further comma after *God* in order to clarify that the writer's parents, God, and Janet are four separate entities.

Another powerful piece of punctuation is the semi-colon. Henry James used a great number where other writers might have put a full stop or a comma. Semi-colons often join clauses of related meaning, and show linkage where a full stop would be too abrupt. In the first example below, we would probably still use a semi-colon today, but in the second a comma or no punctuation mark at all:

> I didn't come to Europe to lead a merely conventional life; I could do that at Bangor.
>
> It is a peasant's landscape; not, as in England, a landlord's.

The colon can be an elegant punctuation mark if used correctly and sparingly. It can present an example:

> 'But this evening you are a different person: new thoughts – even a new voice.'

It can point the reader's attention forward:

> For there was one quality in Henry for which she was never prepared, however much she reminded herself of it: his obtuseness.

And it can also link contrasting statements:

> For her no love could be degrading: she stood outside all degradation.
>
> (Examples from EM Forster)

Commas, dashes, or brackets can be used to add a comment, qualification, or a digression in a text. This can create a chatty effect:

> Before I was eight I used to write stories – or dictate them at least – and I had produced an excellent history of Moses ...
>
> And then I read (for the first time – I know not how) the Window in Thrums.
>
> I never, or almost never, saw two pages of his work that I could not have put in one without the smallest loss of material.
>
> (Examples from Robert Louis Stevenson's correspondence)

One punctuation mark which must be handled with great care is the exclamation mark. A useful rule of thumb is to try to substitute full stops for the exclamation marks. If there is no loss in meaning, then full stops may be preferable (example from Anthony Trollope):

> Not to believe in him would be the foulest treason! To lose him would be to die! To deny him would be to deny her God!

Although they are useful for creating a sense of drama and heightening emotion, the effect of too many exclamation marks may be to irritate the reader.

consign VERB **1 = put away**, commit, deposit, relegate: *For decades, many of his works were consigned to the basements of museums.* **2 = deliver**, ship, transfer, transmit, convey: *He had managed to obtain arms in France and have them safely consigned to America.*

consignment NOUN **= shipment**, delivery, batch, goods

consist VERB

consist in something = lie in, involve, reside in, be expressed by, subsist in, be found *or* contained in: *His work as a consultant consists in advising foreign companies.*

consist of something = be made up of, include, contain, incorporate, amount to, comprise, be composed of: *My diet consisted almost exclusively of fruit.*

consistency NOUN **1 = agreement**, harmony, correspondence, accordance, regularity, coherence, compatibility, uniformity, constancy, steadiness, steadfastness, evenness, congruity: *There's always a lack of consistency in matters of foreign policy.* **2 = texture**, density, thickness, firmness, viscosity, compactness: *I added a little milk to mix the dough to the right consistency.*

QUOTATIONS

Consistency is the last refuge of the unimaginative
[Oscar Wilde]

A foolish consistency is the hobgoblin of little minds
[Ralph Waldo Emerson *Essays: Self-Reliance*]

consistent ADJECTIVE **1 = steady**, even, regular, stable, constant, persistent, dependable, unchanging, true to type, undeviating: *He has never been the most consistent of players.* **OPPOSITE:** erratic **2 = compatible**, agreeing, in keeping, harmonious, in harmony, consonant, in accord, congruent, congruous, accordant: *These new goals are not consistent with the existing policies.* **OPPOSITE:** incompatible **3 = coherent**, logical, compatible, harmonious, consonant, all of a piece: *A theory should be internally consistent.* **OPPOSITE:** contradictory

QUOTATIONS

We cannot remain consistent with the world save by growing inconsistent with our past selves
[Havelock Ellis *The Dance of Life*]

consolation NOUN **= comfort**, help, support, relief, ease, cheer, encouragement, solace, succour, alleviation, assuagement

console VERB **= comfort**, cheer, relieve, soothe, support, encourage, calm, solace, assuage, succour, express sympathy for
OPPOSITE: distress

QUOTATIONS

Isn't everyone consoled when faced with a trouble or fact he doesn't understand, by a word, some simple word, which tells us nothing and yet calms us?
[Luigi Pirandello *Six Characters in Search of an Author*]

Anything that consoles is fake
[Iris Murdoch *Prayer and the Pursuit of Happiness*]

consolidate VERB **1 = strengthen**, secure, reinforce, cement, fortify, stabilize: *The Prime Minister hopes to consolidate existing trade ties between the two countries.* **2 = combine**, unite, join, marry, merge, unify, amalgamate, federate, conjoin: *The state's four higher education boards are to be consolidated.*

consolidation NOUN **1 = strengthening**, reinforcement, fortification, stabilization: *Change brought about the growth and consolidation of the working class.* **2 = combination**, union, association, alliance, merger, federation, amalgamation: *Further consolidations in the industry may follow.*

consort VERB **= associate with**, mix with, mingle with, hang with (*informal, chiefly U.S.*), go around with, keep company with, fraternize with, hang about, around *or* out with: *He regularly consorted with drug-dealers.*
▷ NOUN **= spouse**, wife, husband, partner, associate, fellow, companion, significant other (*U.S. informal*), wahine (*N.Z.*), wifey (*informal*): *Queen Victoria's consort, Prince Albert*

conspicuous ADJECTIVE **= obvious**, clear, apparent, visible, patent, evident, manifest, noticeable, blatant, discernible, salient, perceptible, easily seen **OPPOSITE:** inconspicuous

conspiracy NOUN **= plot**, scheme, intrigue, collusion, confederacy, cabal, frame-up (*slang*), machination, league, golden circle

conspirator NOUN **= plotter**, intriguer, conspirer, traitor, schemer

conspire VERB **1 = plot**, scheme, intrigue, devise, manoeuvre, contrive, machinate, plan, hatch treason: *I had a persecution complex and thought people were conspiring against me.* **2 = work together**, combine, contribute, cooperate, concur, tend, conduce: *History and geography have conspired to bring Greece to a moment of decision.*

constancy NOUN **1 = steadiness**, stability, regularity, uniformity, perseverance, firmness, permanence: *Climate reflects a basic struggle between constancy and change.* **2 = faithfulness**, loyalty, devotion, fidelity, dependability, trustworthiness, steadfastness: *Even before they were married, she had worried about his constancy.*

QUOTATIONS

But I am constant as the northern star
Of whose true-fixed and resting quality
There is no fellow in the firmament
[William Shakespeare *Julius Caesar*]

constant ADJECTIVE **1 = continuous**, sustained, endless, persistent, eternal, relentless, perpetual, continual, never-ending, habitual, uninterrupted, interminable, unrelenting, incessant, everlasting, ceaseless, unremitting, nonstop: *Women are under constant pressure to be thin.* **OPPOSITE:** occasional **2 = unchanging**, even, fixed, regular, permanent, stable, steady, uniform, continual, unbroken, immutable, immovable, invariable, unalterable, unvarying, firm: *The temperature should be kept more or less constant.* **OPPOSITE:** changing **3 = faithful**, true, devoted, loyal, stalwart, staunch, dependable, trustworthy, trusty, steadfast, unfailing, tried-and-true: *She couldn't bear the thought of losing her constant companion.*
OPPOSITE: undependable

constantly ADVERB **= continuously**, always, all the time, invariably, continually, aye (*Scot.*), endlessly, relentlessly, persistently, perpetually, night and day, incessantly, nonstop, interminably, everlastingly, morning, noon and night
OPPOSITE: occasionally

consternation NOUN **= dismay**, shock, alarm, horror, panic, anxiety, distress, confusion, terror, dread, fright, amazement, fear, bewilderment, trepidation

constituent NOUN **1 = voter**, elector, member of the electorate: *They plan to consult their constituents before taking action.* **2 = component**, element, ingredient, part, unit, factor, principle: *Caffeine is the active constituent of drinks such as tea and coffee.*
▷ ADJECTIVE **= component**, basic, essential, integral, elemental: *The fuel is dissolved in nitric acid and separated into its constituent parts.*

constitute VERB **1 = represent**, be, consist of, embody, exemplify, be equivalent to: *The result of the vote hardly constitutes a victory.* **2 = make up**, make, form, compose, comprise: *The country's ethnic minorities constitute 7 per cent of its total population.* **3 = set up**, found, name, create, commission, establish, appoint, delegate, nominate, enact, authorize, empower, ordain, depute: *On 6 July a People's Revolutionary Government was constituted.*

constitution NOUN **1 = state of health**, build, body, make-up, frame, physique, physical condition: *He must have an extremely strong constitution.* **2 = structure**, form, nature, make-up, organization, establishment, formation, composition, character, temper, temperament, disposition: *He ran a small research team looking into the chemical constitution of coal.*

constitutional ADJECTIVE **= legitimate**, official, legal, chartered, statutory, vested

constrain VERB **1 = restrict**, confine, curb, restrain, rein, constrict, hem in, straiten, check, chain: *Women are too often constrained by family commitments.* **2 = force**, pressure, urge, bind, compel, oblige, necessitate, coerce, impel, pressurize, drive: *Individuals will be constrained to make many sacrifices for the greater good.*

constraint NOUN **1 = restriction**, limitation, curb, rein, deterrent, hindrance, damper, check: *Their decision to abandon the trip was made because of financial constraints.* **2 = force**, pressure, necessity, restraint, compulsion, coercion: *People are not morally responsible for that which they do under constraint or compulsion.* **3 = repression**, reservation, embarrassment, restraint, inhibition, timidity, diffidence, bashfulness: *She feels no constraint in discussing sexual matters.*

constrict VERB **1 = squeeze**, contract, narrow, restrict, shrink, tighten, pinch, choke, cramp, strangle, compress, strangulate: *Severe migraine can be treated with a drug which constricts the blood vessels.* **2 = limit**, restrict, confine, curb, inhibit, delimit, straiten: *Senators crafting the bill were frequently constricted by budget limits.*

constriction NOUN **= tightness**, pressure, narrowing, reduction, squeezing, restriction, constraint, cramp, compression, blockage, limitation, impediment, stricture

construct VERB **1 = build**, make, form, create, design, raise, establish, set up, fashion, shape, engineer, frame, manufacture, put up, assemble, put together, erect, fabricate: *The boxes should be constructed from rough-sawn timber.* **OPPOSITE:** demolish **2 = create**, make, form, set up, organize, compose, put together, formulate: *You will find it difficult to construct a spending plan without first recording your outgoings.*

construction NOUN **1 = building**, assembly, creation, formation, composition, erection, fabrication: *With the exception of teak, this is the finest wood for boat construction.* **2 = structure**, building, edifice, form, figure, shape: *The British pavilion is an impressive steel and glass construction.* **3 = interpretation**, meaning, reading, sense, explanation, rendering, take *(informal, chiefly U.S.)*, inference: *He put the wrong construction on what he saw.*

constructive ADJECTIVE **= helpful**, positive, useful, practical, valuable, productive **OPPOSITE:** unproductive

construe VERB **= interpret**, take, read, explain

consult VERB **1 = ask**, refer to, turn to, interrogate, take counsel, ask advice of, pick (someone's) brains, question: *Consult your doctor before undertaking a strenuous exercise programme.* **2 = confer**, talk, debate, deliberate, commune, compare notes, consider: *The umpires consulted quickly.* **3 = refer to**, check in, look in: *He had to consult a pocket dictionary.*

consultant NOUN **= specialist**, adviser, counsellor, authority

consultation NOUN **1 = discussion**, talk, council, conference, dialogue: *Next week he'll be in Florida for consultations with President Mitterrand.* **2 = meeting**, interview, session, appointment, examination, deliberation, hearing: *A personal diet plan is devised after a consultation with a nutritionist.*

consume VERB **1 = eat**, swallow, devour, put away, gobble (up), eat up, guzzle, polish off *(informal)*: *Andrew would consume nearly two pounds of cheese per day.* **2 = use up**, use, spend, waste, employ, absorb, drain, exhaust, deplete, squander, utilize, dissipate, expend, eat up, fritter away: *Some of the most efficient refrigerators consume 70 percent less electricity than traditional models.* **3 = destroy**, devastate, demolish, ravage, annihilate, lay waste: *Fire consumed the building.* **4** *(often passive)* **= obsess**, dominate, absorb, preoccupy, devour, eat up, monopolize, engross: *I was consumed by fear.*

consumer NOUN **= buyer**, customer, user, shopper, purchaser

> **QUOTATIONS**
> The consumer, so it is said, is the king ... each is a voter who uses his money as votes to get the things done that he wants done
> [Paul A. Samuelson *Economics*]
> Every man is a consumer, and ought to be a producer ... He is by constitution expensive, and needs to be rich
> [Ralph Waldo Emerson *Wealth*]
>
> The consumer isn't a moron; she is your wife
> [David Ogilvy *Confessions of an Advertising Man*]

consuming ADJECTIVE **= overwhelming**, gripping, absorbing, compelling, devouring, engrossing, immoderate

consummate ADJECTIVE **1 = skilled**, perfect, supreme, polished, superb, practised, accomplished, matchless: *He acted the part with consummate skill.* **2 = complete**, total, supreme, extreme, ultimate, absolute, utter, conspicuous, unqualified, deep-dyed *(usually derogatory)*: *He was a consummate liar and exaggerator.*
▷ VERB **= complete**, finish, achieve, conclude, perform, perfect, carry out, crown, fulfil, end, accomplish, effectuate, put the tin lid on: *No one has yet been able to consummate a deal.* **OPPOSITE:** initiate

consummation NOUN **= completion**, end, achievement, perfection, realization, fulfilment, culmination

consumption NOUN **1 = using up**, use, loss, waste, drain, consuming, expenditure, exhaustion, depletion, utilization, dissipation: *The laws have led to a reduction in fuel consumption.* **2 = tuberculosis**, atrophy, T.B., emaciation: *an opera about a prostitute dying of consumption in a garret*

contact NOUN **1 = communication**, link, association, connection, correspondence, intercourse: *Opposition leaders are denying any contact with the government in Kabul.* **2 = touch**, contiguity: *Hepatitis B virus is spread by contact with infected blood.* **3 = connection**, colleague, associate, liaison, acquaintance, confederate: *Her business contacts described her as 'a very determined lady'.*
▷ VERB **= get** *or* **be in touch with**, call, reach, approach, phone, ring (up) *(informal, chiefly Brit.)*, write to, speak to, communicate with, get hold of, touch base with *(U.S. & Canad. informal)*, e-mail, text: *When she first contacted me, she was upset.*

contagion NOUN **= spread**, spreading, communication, passage, proliferation, diffusion, transference, dissemination, dispersal, transmittal: *He continues to isolate his country from the contagion of foreign ideas.*

contagious ADJECTIVE **= infectious**, catching, spreading, epidemic, communicable, transmissible

contain VERB **1 = hold**, incorporate, accommodate, enclose, have capacity for: *Factory shops contain a wide range of cheap furnishings.* **2 = include**, consist of, embrace, comprise, embody, comprehend: *The committee contains 11 Democrats and nine Republicans.* **3 = restrain**, control, hold in, curb, suppress, hold back, stifle, repress, keep a tight rein on: *The city authorities said the curfew had contained the violence.*

container NOUN **= holder**, vessel, repository, receptacle

contaminate VERB **= pollute**, infect, stain, corrupt, taint, sully, defile, adulterate, befoul, soil **OPPOSITE:** purify

contaminated ADJECTIVE **= polluted**, dirtied, poisoned, infected, stained, corrupted, tainted, sullied, defiled, soiled, adulterated

contamination NOUN **= pollution**, dirtying, infection, corruption, poisoning, decay, taint, filth, impurity, contagion, adulteration, foulness, defilement

contemplate VERB **1 = consider**, plan, think of, propose, intend, envisage, foresee, have in view or in mind: *He contemplated a career as an army medical doctor.* **2 = think about**, consider, ponder, mull over, reflect upon, ruminate (upon), meditate on, brood over, muse over, deliberate over, revolve or turn over in your mind: *He lay in his hospital bed and cried as he contemplated his future.* **3 = look at**, examine, observe, check out *(informal)*, inspect, gaze at, behold, eye up, view, study, regard, survey, stare at, scrutinize, eye: *He contemplated his hands thoughtfully.*

contemplation NOUN **1 = thought**, consideration, reflection, musing, meditation, pondering, deliberation, reverie, rumination, cogitation: *The garden is a place of quiet contemplation.* **2 = observation**, viewing, looking at,

C

survey, examination, inspection, scrutiny, gazing at: *He was lost in contemplation of the landscape.*

contemplative ADJECTIVE = **thoughtful**, reflective, introspective, rapt, meditative, pensive, ruminative, in a brown study, intent, musing, deep *or* lost in thought

contemporary ADJECTIVE **1 = modern**, latest, recent, current, with it *(informal)*, trendy *(Brit. informal)*, up-to-date, present-day, in fashion, up-to-the-minute, à la mode, newfangled, happening *(informal)*, present, ultramodern: *The gallery holds regular exhibitions of contemporary art, sculpture and photography.* **OPPOSITE:** old-fashioned **2 = coexisting**, concurrent, contemporaneous, synchronous, coexistent: *The book draws upon official records and the reports of contemporary witnesses.*
▷ NOUN = **peer**, fellow, equal: *a glossary of terms used by Shakespeare and his contemporaries*

USAGE
Since *contemporary* can mean either 'of the present period' or 'of the same period', it is best to avoid it where ambiguity might arise, as in *a production of Othello in contemporary dress*. A synonym such as *modern* or *present-day* would clarify if the sense 'of the present period' were being used, while a specific term, such as *Elizabethan*, would be appropriate if the sense 'of the same period' were being used.

contempt NOUN = **scorn**, disdain, mockery, derision, disrespect, disregard **OPPOSITE:** respect

contemptible ADJECTIVE = **despicable**, mean, low, base, cheap, worthless, shameful, shabby, vile, degenerate, low-down *(informal)*, paltry, pitiful, abject, ignominious, measly, scurvy, detestable, odious **OPPOSITE:** admirable

contemptuous ADJECTIVE = **scornful**, insulting, arrogant, withering, sneering, cavalier, condescending, haughty, disdainful, insolent, derisive, supercilious, high and mighty, on your high horse *(informal)* **OPPOSITE:** respectful

contend VERB **1 = argue**, hold, maintain, allege, assert, affirm, avow, aver: *The government contends that he is a fundamentalist.* **2 = compete**, fight, struggle, clash, contest, strive, vie, grapple, jostle, skirmish: *The two main groups contended for power.*

contender NOUN = **competitor**, rival, candidate, applicant, hopeful, contestant, aspirant

content[1] NOUN **1 = subject matter**, ideas, matter, material, theme, text, substance, essence, gist: *She is reluctant to discuss the content of the play.* **2 = amount**, measure, size, load, volume, capacity: *Sunflower margarine has the same fat content as butter.*
▷ PLURAL NOUN **1 = constituents**, elements, load, ingredients: *Empty the contents of the pan into the sieve.* **2 = subjects**, chapters, themes, topics, subject matter, divisions: *There is no initial list of contents at the start of the book.*

content[2] ADJECTIVE = **satisfied**, happy, pleased, contented, comfortable, fulfilled, at ease, gratified, agreeable, willing to accept: *I'm perfectly content with the way the campaign has gone.*
▷ NOUN = **satisfaction**, peace, ease, pleasure, comfort, peace of mind, gratification, contentment: *Once he'd retired, he could potter about the garden to his heart's content.*
content yourself with something = **satisfy yourself with**, be happy with, be satisfied with, be content with: *He had to content himself with the knowledge that he had been right.*

contented ADJECTIVE = **satisfied**, happy, pleased, content, comfortable, glad, cheerful, at ease, thankful, gratified, serene, at peace **OPPOSITE:** discontented

contention NOUN **1 = assertion**, claim, stand, idea, view, position, opinion, argument, belief, allegation, profession, declaration, thesis, affirmation: *Sufficient research evidence exists to support this contention.* **2 = dispute**, hostility, disagreement, feuding, strife, wrangling, discord, enmity, dissension: *They generally tried to avoid subjects of contention between them.*

contentious ADJECTIVE = **argumentative**, wrangling, perverse, bickering, combative, pugnacious, quarrelsome, litigious, querulous, cavilling, disputatious, factious, captious

contentment NOUN = **satisfaction**, peace, content, ease, pleasure, comfort, happiness, fulfilment, gratification, serenity, equanimity, gladness, repletion, contentedness **OPPOSITE:** discontent

QUOTATIONS
Poor and content is rich and rich enough
[William Shakespeare *Othello*]

contest NOUN **1 = competition**, game, match, trial, tournament, head-to-head: *Few contests in the recent history of British boxing have been as thrilling.* **2 = struggle**, fight, battle, debate, conflict, dispute, encounter, controversy, combat, discord: *a bitter contest over who should control the state's future*
▷ VERB **1 = compete in**, take part in, fight in, go in for, contend for, vie in: *He quickly won his party's nomination to contest the elections.* **2 = oppose**, question, challenge, argue, debate, dispute, object to, litigate, call in *or* into question: *Your former employer has to reply within 14 days in order to contest the case.*

contestant NOUN = **competitor**, candidate, participant, contender, entrant, player, aspirant

context NOUN **1 = circumstances**, times, conditions, situation, ambience: *the historical context in which Chaucer wrote* **2 = frame of reference**, background, framework, relation, connection: *Without a context, I would have assume it was written by a man.*

contingency NOUN = **possibility**, happening, chance, event, incident, accident, emergency, uncertainty, eventuality, juncture

contingent NOUN = **group**, detachment, deputation, set, body, section, bunch *(informal)*, quota, batch: *There were contingents from the navies of virtually all EC countries.*
▷ ADJECTIVE = **chance**, random, casual, uncertain, accidental, haphazard, fortuitous: *these apparently random, contingent and unexplained phenomena*
contingent on = **dependent on**, subject to, controlled by, conditional on: *Growth is contingent on improved incomes.*

continual ADJECTIVE **1 = constant**, endless, continuous, eternal, perpetual, uninterrupted, interminable, incessant, everlasting, unremitting, unceasing: *Despite continual pain, he refused all drugs.* **OPPOSITE:** erratic **2 = frequent**, regular, repeated, repetitive, recurrent, oft-repeated: *She suffered continual police harassment.* **OPPOSITE:** occasional

continually ADVERB **1 = constantly**, always, all the time, forever, aye *(Scot.)*, endlessly, eternally, incessantly, nonstop, interminably, everlastingly: *The large rotating fans whirred continually.* **2 = repeatedly**, often, frequently, many times, over and over, again and again, time and (time) again, persistently, time after time, many a time and oft *(archaic, poetic)*: *He continually changed his mind.*

continuance NOUN = **perpetuation**, lasting, carrying on, keeping up, endurance, continuation, prolongation

continuation NOUN **1 = continuing**, lasting, carrying on, maintenance, keeping up, endurance, perpetuation, prolongation: *What we'll see in the future is a continuation of this trend.* **2 = addition**, extension, supplement, sequel, resumption, postscript: *This chapter is a continuation of Chapter 8.*

continue VERB **1 = keep on**, go on, maintain, pursue, sustain, carry on, stick to, keep up, prolong, persist in, keep at, persevere, stick at, press on with: *Outside the hall, people continued their vigil.* **OPPOSITE:** stop **2 = go on**, advance, progress, proceed, carry on, keep going, crack on *(informal)*: *As the investigation continued, the plot began to thicken.* **3 = resume**, return to, take up again, proceed, carry on, recommence, pick up where you left off: *She looked up for a moment, then continued drawing.* **OPPOSITE:** stop **4 = remain**, last, stay, rest, survive, carry on, live on, endure, stay on, persist, abide: *For ten days I continued in this state; He had hoped to continue as a full-time career officer.* **OPPOSITE:** quit

continuing ADJECTIVE **= lasting**, sustained, enduring, ongoing, in progress

continuity NOUN **= cohesion**, flow, connection, sequence, succession, progression, wholeness, interrelationship

continuous ADJECTIVE **= constant**, continued, extended, prolonged, unbroken, uninterrupted, unceasing **OPPOSITE:** occasional

contort VERB **= twist**, knot, distort, warp, deform, misshape

contortion NOUN **= twist**, distortion, deformity, convolution, bend, knot, warp

contour NOUN **= outline**, profile, lines, form, figure, shape, relief, curve, silhouette

contraband ADJECTIVE **= smuggled**, illegal, illicit, black-market, hot (*informal*), banned, forbidden, prohibited, unlawful, bootleg, bootlegged, interdicted

contract NOUN **= agreement**, deal (*informal*), commission, commitment, arrangement, understanding, settlement, treaty, bargain, convention, engagement, pact, compact, covenant, bond, stipulation, concordat: *The company won a prestigious contract for work on the building.*
▷ VERB **1 = agree**, arrange, negotiate, engage, pledge, bargain, undertake, come to terms, shake hands, covenant, make a deal, commit yourself, enter into an agreement: *He has contracted to lease part of the collection to a museum in Japan.* **OPPOSITE:** refuse **2 = constrict**, confine, tighten, shorten, wither, compress, condense, shrivel: *New research shows that an excess of meat and salt can contract muscles.* **3 = tighten**, narrow, knit, purse, shorten, pucker: *As we move our bodies, our muscles contract and relax.* **OPPOSITE:** stretch **4 = lessen**, reduce, shrink, diminish, decrease, dwindle: *Output fell last year and is expected to contract further this year.* **OPPOSITE:** increase **5 = catch**, get, develop, acquire, incur, be infected with, go down with, be afflicted with: *He contracted AIDS from a blood transfusion.* **OPPOSITE:** avoid

contraction NOUN **1 = tightening**, narrowing, tensing, shortening, drawing in, constricting, shrinkage: *Cramp is caused by contraction of the muscles.* **2 = abbreviation**, reduction, shortening, compression, diminution, constriction, elision: *'It's' is a contraction of 'it is'.*

contradict VERB **1 = dispute**, deny, challenge, belie, fly in the face of, make a nonsense of, be at variance with: *We knew she was wrong, but nobody liked to contradict her; His comments contradict remarks he made earlier that day.* **2 = negate**, deny, oppose, counter, contravene, rebut, impugn, controvert: *The result appears to contradict a major study carried out last December.* **OPPOSITE:** confirm

contradiction NOUN **1 = conflict**, inconsistency, contravention, incongruity, confutation: *They see no contradiction in using violence to bring about a religious state.* **2 = negation**, opposite, denial, antithesis: *What he does is a contradiction of what he says.*

contradictory ADJECTIVE **= inconsistent**, conflicting, opposed, opposite, contrary, incompatible, paradoxical, irreconcilable, antithetical, discrepant

contraption NOUN **= device**, instrument, mechanism, apparatus, gadget, contrivance, rig

contrary ADJECTIVE **1 = opposite**, different, opposed, clashing, counter, reverse, differing, adverse, contradictory, inconsistent, diametrically opposed, antithetical: *His sister was of the contrary opinion to his.* **OPPOSITE:** in agreement **2 = perverse**, difficult, awkward, wayward, intractable, wilful, obstinate, cussed (*informal*), stroppy (*Brit. slang*), cantankerous, disobliging, unaccommodating, thrawn (*Scot. & Northern English dialect*): *Why must she always be so contrary?* **OPPOSITE:** cooperative
▷ NOUN **= opposite**, reverse, converse, antithesis: *Let me assure you that the contrary is, in fact, the case.*
on the contrary = quite the opposite *or* **reverse**, on the other hand, in contrast, conversely: *The government must, on the contrary, re-establish its authority.*

contrast NOUN **= difference**, opposition, comparison, distinction, foil, disparity, differentiation, divergence, dissimilarity, contrariety: *The two women provided a startling contrast in appearance.*
▷ VERB **1 = differentiate**, compare, oppose, distinguish, set in opposition: *She contrasted the situation then with the present crisis.* **2 = differ**, be contrary, be distinct, be at variance, be dissimilar: *Johnstone's easy charm contrasted with the prickliness of his boss.*

contravene VERB **1 = break**, violate, go against, infringe, disobey, transgress: *He said the article did not contravene the industry's code of conduct.* **2 = conflict with**, cross, oppose, interfere with, thwart, contradict, hinder, go against, refute, counteract: *This deportation order contravenes basic human rights.*

contravention NOUN **1 = breach**, violation, infringement, trespass, disobedience, transgression, infraction: *They are in direct contravention of the law.* **2 = conflict**, interference, contradiction, hindrance, rebuttal, refutation, disputation, counteraction: *He denied that the new laws were a contravention of fundamental rights.*

contribute VERB **= give**, provide, supply, donate, furnish, subscribe, chip in (*informal*), bestow: *They say they would like to contribute more to charity.*
contribute to something = be partly responsible for, lead to, be instrumental in, be conducive to, conduce to, help: *Design faults in the boat contributed to the tragedy.*

contribution NOUN **= gift**, offering, grant, donation, input, subscription, bestowal, koha (*N.Z.*)

contributor NOUN **1 = donor**, supporter, patron, subscriber, backer, bestower, giver: *Redford is the institute's leading financial contributor and is active in fund-raising.* **2 = writer**, correspondent, reporter, journalist, freelance, freelancer, journo (*slang*): *All of the pieces by the magazine's contributors appear anonymously.*

contrite ADJECTIVE **= sorry**, humble, chastened, sorrowful, repentant, remorseful, regretful, penitent, conscience-stricken, in sackcloth and ashes

contrition NOUN **= regret**, sorrow, remorse, repentance, compunction, penitence, self-reproach

contrivance NOUN **1 = device**, machine, equipment, gear, instrument, implement, mechanism, invention, appliance, apparatus, gadget, contraption: *They wear simple clothes and shun modern contrivances.* **2 = stratagem**, plan, design, measure, scheme, trick, plot, dodge, expedient, ruse, artifice, machination: *It is nothing more than a contrivance to raise prices.*

contrive VERB **1 = devise**, plan, fabricate, create, design, scheme, engineer, frame, manufacture, plot, construct, invent, improvise, concoct, wangle (*informal*): *The oil companies were accused of contriving a shortage of gasoline to justify price increases.* **2 = manage**, succeed, arrange, manoeuvre: *Somehow he contrived to pass her a note without her chaperone seeing it.*

contrived ADJECTIVE **= forced**, planned, laboured, strained, artificial, elaborate, unnatural, overdone, recherché **OPPOSITE:** natural

control NOUN **1 = power**, government, rule, authority, management, direction, command, discipline, guidance, supervision, jurisdiction, supremacy, mastery, superintendence, charge: *The first aim of his government would be to establish control over the republic's territory.* **2 = restraint**, check, regulation, brake, limitation, curb: *There are to be tighter controls on land speculation.* **3 = self-discipline**, cool, calmness, self-restraint, restraint, coolness, self-mastery, self-command: *He had a terrible temper, and sometimes lost control completely.* **4 = switch**, instrument, button, dial, lever, knob, remote

C

control: *He adjusted the temperature control.* ▷ PLURAL NOUN = **instruments**, dash, dials, console, dashboard, control panel, remote control: *He died of a heart attack while at the controls of the plane.* ▷ VERB **1** = **have power over**, lead, rule, manage, boss *(informal)*, direct, handle, conduct, dominate, command, pilot, govern, steer, administer, oversee, supervise, manipulate, call the shots, call the tune, reign over, keep a tight rein on, have charge of, superintend, have (someone) in your pocket, keep on a string: *He now controls the largest retail development empire in southern California; My husband tried to control me in every way.* **2** = **limit**, restrict, curb, delimit: *The government tried to control rising health-care costs.* **3** = **restrain**, limit, check, contain, master, curb, hold back, subdue, repress, constrain, bridle, rein in: *Try to control that temper of yours.*

QUOTATIONS

> Who controls the past controls the future: who controls the present controls the past
> [George Orwell *Nineteen Eighty-Four*]
>
> Who can control his fate?
> [William Shakespeare *Othello*]

controversial ADJECTIVE = **disputed**, contended, contentious, at issue, debatable, polemic, under discussion, open to question, disputable, third rail *(U.S. politics)*

controversy NOUN = **argument**, debate, row, discussion, dispute, contention, quarrel, squabble, strife, wrangle, wrangling, polemic, wedge issue, third rail *(U.S. politics)*, altercation, dissension, barbecue stopper *(Austral. informal)*

conundrum NOUN = **puzzle**, problem, riddle, enigma, teaser, poser, brain-teaser *(informal)*

convalesce VERB = **recover**, rest, rally, rehabilitate, recuperate, improve

convalescence NOUN = **recovery**, rehabilitation, recuperation, return to health, improvement

convalescent ADJECTIVE = **recovering**, getting better, recuperating, on the mend, improving, mending

convene VERB **1** = **call**, gather, assemble, summon, bring together, muster, convoke: *He convened a meeting of all the managers.* **2** = **meet**, gather, rally, assemble, come together, muster, congregate: *Senior officials convened in London for an emergency meeting.*

convenience NOUN **1** = **benefit**, good, interest, advantage: *He was happy to make a detour for her convenience.* **2** = **suitability**, fitness, appropriateness, opportuneness: *She was delighted with the convenience of this arrangement.* **3** = **usefulness**, utility, serviceability, handiness: *The convenience of digital cameras means that more and more people are buying them nowadays.* **OPPOSITE:** uselessness **4** = **accessibility**, availability, nearness, handiness: *They miss the convenience of London's tubes and buses.* **5** = **appliance**, facility, comfort, amenity, labour-saving device, help: *The chalets have all the modern conveniences.*

at your convenience = **at a suitable time**, at your leisure, in your own time, whenever you like, in your spare time, in a spare moment: *Please call me to set up an appointment at your convenience.*

convenient ADJECTIVE **1** = **suitable**, fitting, fit, handy, satisfactory: *The family found it more convenient to eat in the kitchen.* **2** = **useful**, practical, handy, serviceable, labour-saving: *Pre-prepared foods are a tempting and convenient option.* **OPPOSITE:** useless **3** = **nearby**, available, accessible, handy, at hand, within reach, close at hand, just round the corner: *The town is convenient for Heathrow Airport.* **OPPOSITE:** inaccessible **4** = **appropriate**, timely, suited, suitable, beneficial, well-timed, opportune, seasonable, helpful: *She will try to arrange a mutually convenient time for an interview.*

convent NOUN = **nunnery**, religious community, religious house

QUOTATIONS

> The convent, which belongs to the West as it does to the East, to antiquity as it does to the present time, to Buddhism and Muhammadanism as it does to Christianity, is one of the optical devices whereby man gains a glimpse of infinity
> [Victor Hugo *Les Misérables*]
>
> I like convents, but I wish they would not admit anyone under the age of fifty
> [Napoleon Bonaparte]

convention NOUN **1** = **custom**, practice, tradition, code, usage, protocol, formality, etiquette, propriety, kawa *(N.Z.)*, tikanga *(N.Z.)*, rule: *It's just a social convention that men don't wear skirts.* **2** = **agreement**, contract, treaty, bargain, pact, compact, protocol, stipulation, concordat: *the importance of observing the Geneva convention on human rights* **3** = **assembly**, meeting, council, conference, congress, convocation, hui *(N.Z.)*, runanga *(N.Z.)*: *I flew to Boston to attend the annual convention of the Parapsychological Association.*

conventional ADJECTIVE **1** = **proper**, conservative, correct, formal, respectable, bourgeois, genteel, staid, conformist, decorous, Pooterish: *a respectable married woman with conventional opinions* **2** = **ordinary**, standard, normal, regular, usual, vanilla *(slang)*, habitual, bog-standard *(Brit. & Irish slang)*, common: *the cost of fuel and electricity used by a conventional system* **3** = **traditional**, accepted, prevailing, orthodox, customary, prevalent, hidebound, wonted: *The conventional wisdom on these matters is being challenged.* **4** = **unoriginal**, routine, stereotyped, pedestrian, commonplace, banal, prosaic, run-of-the-mill, hackneyed, vanilla *(slang)*: *This is a rather conventional work by a mediocre author.* **OPPOSITE:** unconventional

converge VERB = **come together**, meet, join, combine, gather, merge, coincide, mingle, intersect: *As they flow south, the five rivers converge.*

converge on something = **close in on**, arrive at, move towards, home in on, come together at: *Hundreds of coaches will converge on the capital.*

convergence NOUN = **meeting**, junction, intersection, confluence, concentration, blending, merging, coincidence, conjunction, mingling, concurrence, conflux

conversation NOUN = **talk**, exchange, discussion, dialogue, tête-à-tête, conference, communication, chat, gossip, intercourse, discourse, communion, converse, powwow, colloquy, chinwag *(Brit. informal)*, confabulation, confab *(informal)*, craic *(Irish informal)*, korero *(N.Z.)* ▸ *related adjective:* colloquial

QUOTATIONS

> The art of conversation is the art of hearing as well as being heard
> [William Hazlitt *The Plain Speaker*]
>
> That is the happiest conversation where there is no competition, no vanity, but a calm quiet interchange of sentiments
> [Samuel Johnson]
>
> In conversation discretion is more important than eloquence
> [Baltasar Gracián *The Art of Worldly Wisdom*]
>
> Conversation is the enemy of good wine and food
> [Alfred Hitchcock]

conversational ADJECTIVE = **chatty**, informal, communicative, colloquial

converse[1] VERB = **talk**, speak, chat, communicate, discourse, confer, commune, exchange views, shoot the breeze *(slang, chiefly U.S. & Canad.)*, korero *(N.Z.)*: *They were conversing in German, their only common language.*

converse[2] NOUN = **opposite**, reverse, contrary, other side of the coin, obverse, antithesis: *If that is true, the converse is equally so.* ▷ ADJECTIVE = **opposite**, counter, reverse, contrary: *Stress reduction techniques have the converse effect on the immune system.*

conversion NOUN **1** = **change**, transformation, metamorphosis, transfiguration, transmutation, transmogrification *(humorous)*: *the conversion of disused rail lines into cycle* *routes* **2 = adaptation**, reconstruction, modification, alteration, remodelling, reorganization: *A loft conversion can add considerably to the value of a house.* **3 = reformation**, rebirth, change of heart, proselytization: *his conversion to Christianity*

convert VERB **1 = change**, turn, transform, alter, metamorphose, transpose, transmute, transmogrify *(humorous)*: *a handy table which converts into an ironing board* **2 = adapt**, modify, remodel, reorganize, customize, restyle: *By converting the loft, they were able to have two extra bedrooms.* **3 = reform**, save, convince, proselytize, bring to God: *I resent religious people who insist on trying to convert others.*
▷ NOUN **= neophyte**, disciple, proselyte, catechumen: *She was a recent convert to Roman Catholicism.*

convertible ADJECTIVE **= changeable**, interchangeable, exchangeable, adjustable, adaptable

convex ADJECTIVE **= rounded**, bulging, protuberant, gibbous, outcurved **OPPOSITE:** concave

convey VERB **1 = communicate**, impart, reveal, relate, disclose, make known, tell: *I tried to convey the wonder of the experience to my husband.* **2 = carry**, transport, move, bring, support, bear, conduct, transmit, fetch: *They borrowed our boats to convey themselves across the river.*

conveyance NOUN **1 = vehicle**, transport: *He had never travelled in such a strange conveyance before.*
2 = transportation, movement, transfer, transport, transmission, carriage, transference: *the conveyance of bicycles on Regional Railway trains*

convict VERB **= find guilty**, sentence, condemn, imprison, pronounce guilty: *There was sufficient evidence to convict him.*
▷ NOUN **= prisoner**, criminal, con *(slang)*, lag *(slang)*, villain, felon, jailbird, malefactor: *The prison houses only lifers and convicts on death row.*

conviction NOUN **1 = belief**, view, opinion, principle, faith, persuasion, creed, tenet, kaupapa *(N.Z.)*: *Their religious convictions prevented them from taking up arms.* **2 = certainty**, confidence, assurance, fervour, firmness, earnestness, certitude: *He preaches with conviction.*

convince VERB **1 = assure**, persuade, satisfy, prove to, reassure: *I soon convinced him of my innocence.*
2 = persuade, induce, coax, talk into, prevail upon, inveigle, twist (someone's) arm, bring round to the idea of: *He convinced her to go ahead and marry Bud.*

> **USAGE**
> The use of *convince* to talk about persuading someone to do something is considered by many British speakers to be wrong or unacceptable. It would be preferable to use an alternative such as *persuade* or *talk into*.

convincing ADJECTIVE **= persuasive**, credible, conclusive, incontrovertible, telling, likely, powerful, impressive, probable, plausible, cogent
OPPOSITE: unconvincing

convivial ADJECTIVE **= sociable**, friendly, lively, cheerful, jolly, merry, festive, hearty, genial, fun-loving, jovial, back-slapping, gay, partyish *(informal)*

convocation NOUN **= meeting**, congress, convention, synod, diet, assembly, concourse, council, assemblage, conclave, hui *(N.Z.)*, runanga *(N.Z.)*

convoy VERB **= escort**, conduct, accompany, shepherd, protect, attend, guard, pilot, usher

convulse VERB **1 = shake**, twist, agitate, contort: *He let out a cry that convulsed his whole body.* **2 = twist**, contort, work: *Olivia's face convulsed in a series of spasms.*

convulsion NOUN **1 = spasm**, fit, shaking, seizure, contraction, tremor, cramp, contortion, paroxysm: *He fell to the floor in the grip of an epileptic convulsion.*
2 = upheaval, disturbance, furore, turbulence, agitation, commotion, tumult: *It was a decade that saw many great social, economic and political convulsions.*

cool ADJECTIVE **1 = cold**, chilled, chilling, refreshing, chilly, nippy: *I felt a current of cool air.* **OPPOSITE:** warm **2 = calm**, together *(slang)*, collected, relaxed, composed, laid-back *(informal)*, serene, sedate, self-controlled, placid, level-headed, dispassionate, unfazed *(informal)*, unruffled, unemotional, self-possessed, imperturbable, unexcited, chilled *(informal)*: *He was marvellously cool, smiling as if nothing had happened.*
OPPOSITE: agitated **3 = unfriendly**, reserved, distant, indifferent, aloof, lukewarm, unconcerned, uninterested, frigid, unresponsive, offhand, unenthusiastic, uncommunicative, unwelcoming, standoffish: *People found him too cool, aloof and arrogant.* **OPPOSITE:** friendly
4 = unenthusiastic, indifferent, lukewarm, uninterested, apathetic, unresponsive, unwelcoming: *The idea met with a cool response.* **5 = fashionable**, with it *(informal)*, hip *(slang)*, stylish, trendy *(Brit. informal)*, chic, up-to-date, urbane, up-to-the-minute, voguish *(informal)*, trendsetting, nang *(Brit. slang)*, schmick *(Austral. informal)*, funky: *He was trying to be really cool and trendy.* **6 = impudent**, bold, cheeky, audacious, brazen, shameless, presumptuous, impertinent: *He displayed a cool disregard for the rules.*
▷ VERB **1 = lose heat**, cool off: *Drain the meat and allow it to cool.*
OPPOSITE: warm (up) **2 = make cool**, freeze, chill, refrigerate, cool off: *Huge fans are used to cool the factory.*
OPPOSITE: warm (up) **3 = calm (down)**, lessen, abate: *Within a few minutes their tempers had cooled.*
4 = lessen, calm (down), quiet, moderate, temper, dampen, allay, abate, assuage: *His strange behaviour had cooled her passion.*
▷ NOUN **1 = coldness**, chill, coolness: *She walked into the cool of the hallway.*
2 = calmness, control, temper, composure, self-control, poise, self-discipline, self-possession: *She kept her cool and managed to get herself out of the situation.*

coolness NOUN **1 = coldness**, freshness, chilliness, nippiness: *He felt the coolness of the tiled floor.*
OPPOSITE: warmness **2 = calmness**, control, composure, self-control, self-discipline, self-possession, level-headedness, imperturbability, sedateness, placidness: *They praised him for his coolness under pressure.*
OPPOSITE: agitation
3 = unfriendliness, reserve, distance, indifference, apathy, remoteness, aloofness, frigidity, unconcern, unresponsiveness, frostiness, offhandedness: *She seemed quite unaware of the sudden coolness of her friend's manner.*
OPPOSITE: friendliness
4 = impudence, audacity, boldness, insolence, impertinence, shamelessness, cheekiness, brazenness, presumptuousness, audaciousness: *The coolness of his suggestion took her breath away.*

coop NOUN **= pen**, pound, box, cage, enclosure, hutch, corral *(chiefly U.S. & Canad.)*: *Behind the house, the pair set up a chicken coop.*
coop someone up = confine, imprison, shut up, impound, pound, pen, cage, immure: *He was cooped up in a cell with ten other inmates.*

cooperate VERB **1 = work together**, collaborate, coordinate, join forces, conspire, concur, pull together, pool resources, combine your efforts: *The two parties are cooperating more than they have done in years.* **OPPOSITE:** conflict
2 = help, contribute to, assist, go along with, aid, pitch in, abet, play ball *(informal)*, lend a helping hand: *He agreed to cooperate with the police investigation.* **OPPOSITE:** oppose

cooperation NOUN **1 = teamwork**, concert, unity, collaboration, give-and-take, combined effort, esprit de corps, concurrence, kotahitanga *(N.Z.)*: *A deal with Japan could open the door to economic cooperation with East Asia.* **OPPOSITE:** opposition
2 = help, assistance, participation, responsiveness, helpfulness: *The police asked for the public's cooperation in their hunt for the killer.* **OPPOSITE:** hindrance

> **PROVERBS**
> *Two heads are better than one*

cooperative ADJECTIVE **1 = shared**, united, joint, combined, concerted, collective, unified, coordinated, collaborative: *The visit was intended to develop cooperative relations between the countries.* **2 = helpful**, obliging, accommodating, supportive,

C

responsive, onside *(informal)*: *I made every effort to be co-operative.*

coordinate VERB **1 = organize**, synchronize, integrate, bring together, mesh, correlate, systematize: *Officials visited the earthquake zone to coordinate the relief effort.* **2 = match**, blend, harmonize: *She'll show you how to coordinate pattern and colours.*
coordinate with = go with, match, blend with, harmonize with: *Choose a fabric that co-ordinates with your colour scheme.*

C

cope VERB **= manage**, get by *(informal)*, struggle through, rise to the occasion, survive, carry on, make out *(informal)*, make the grade, hold your own: *It was amazing how my mother coped after my father died.*
cope with something = deal with, handle, struggle with, grapple with, wrestle with, contend with, tangle with, tussle with, weather: *She has had to cope with losing all her previous status and money.*

copious ADJECTIVE **= abundant**, liberal, generous, lavish, full, rich, extensive, ample, overflowing, plentiful, exuberant, bountiful, luxuriant, profuse, bounteous, superabundant, plenteous

cop out VERB **= avoid**, dodge, abandon, withdraw from, desert, quit, skip, renounce, revoke, renege, skive *(Brit. slang)*, bludge *(Austral. & N.Z. informal)*

cop-out NOUN **= pretence**, dodge, pretext, fraud, alibi

copulate VERB **= have intercourse**, have sex

copy NOUN **= reproduction**, duplicate, photocopy, carbon copy, image, print, fax, representation, fake, replica, imitation, forgery, counterfeit, Xerox®, transcription, likeness, replication, facsimile, Photostat®: *Always keep a copy of everything in your own files.* **OPPOSITE:** original
▷ VERB **1 = reproduce**, replicate, duplicate, photocopy, transcribe, counterfeit, Xerox®, Photostat®: *She never participated in copying classified documents for anyone.* **OPPOSITE:** create **2 = imitate**, act like, emulate, behave like, follow, repeat, mirror, echo, parrot, ape, mimic, simulate, follow suit, follow the example of: *We all tend to copy people we admire; coquettish gestures which she had copied from actresses in soap operas*

cord NOUN **= rope**, line, string, twine

cordial ADJECTIVE **1 = warm**, welcoming, friendly, cheerful, affectionate, hearty, agreeable, sociable, genial, affable, congenial, warm-hearted: *I had never known him to be so chatty and cordial.* **OPPOSITE:** unfriendly **2 = wholehearted**, earnest, sincere, heartfelt: *She didn't bother to hide her cordial dislike of him.*

cordon NOUN **= chain**, line, ring, barrier, picket line: *Police formed a cordon between the two crowds.*
cordon something off = surround, isolate, close off, fence off, separate, enclose, picket, encircle: *The police cordoned the area off.*

core NOUN **1 = centre**: *Lava is molten rock from the earth's core* **2 = heart**, essence, nucleus, kernel, crux, gist, nub, pith: *He has the ability to get straight to the core of a problem.*

corner NOUN **1 = angle**, joint, crook: *the corner of a door* **2 = bend**, curve: *He waited until the man had turned the corner.* **3 = space**, hole, niche, recess, cavity, hideaway, nook, cranny, hide-out, hidey-hole *(informal)*: *She hid it away in a corner of her room.* **4 = tight spot**, predicament, tricky situation, spot *(informal)*, hole *(informal)*, hot water *(informal)*, pickle *(informal)*: *He appears to have got himself into a tight corner.*
▷ VERB **1 = trap**, catch, run to earth, bring to bay: *The police moved in with tear gas and cornered him.* **2 = monopolize**, take over, dominate, control, hog *(slang)*, engross, exercise *or* have a monopoly of: *This restaurant has cornered the market for specialist paellas.*

cornerstone NOUN **= basis**, key, premise, starting point, bedrock

corny ADJECTIVE **1 = unoriginal**, banal, trite, hackneyed, dull, old-fashioned, stereotyped, commonplace, feeble, stale, old hat: *I know it sounds corny, but I'm not motivated by money.*
2 = sentimental, mushy *(informal)*, maudlin, slushy *(informal)*, mawkish, schmaltzy *(slang)*: *a corny old love song*

corollary NOUN **= consequence**, result, effect, outcome, sequel, end result, upshot

corporal ADJECTIVE **= bodily**, physical, fleshly, anatomical, carnal, corporeal *(archaic)*, material

corporate ADJECTIVE **= collective**, collaborative, united, shared, allied, joint, combined, pooled, merged, communal

corporation NOUN **1 = business**, company, concern, firm, society, association, organization, enterprise, establishment, corporate body: *chairman of a huge multi-national corporation* **2 = town council**, council, municipal authorities, civic authorities: *The local corporation has given permission for the work to proceed.*

corps NOUN **= team**, unit, regiment, detachment, company, body, band, division, troop, squad, crew, contingent, squadron

corpse NOUN **= body**, remains, carcass, cadaver, stiff *(slang)*

corpus NOUN **= collection**, body, whole, compilation, entirety, oeuvre *(French)*, complete works

corral VERB **= enclose**, confine, cage, fence in, impound, pen in, coop up: *The men were corralled into a hastily constructed concentration camp.*

correct ADJECTIVE **1 = accurate**, right, true, exact, precise, flawless, faultless, on the right lines, O.K. *or* okay *(informal)*: *The information was correct at the time of going to press.* **OPPOSITE:** inaccurate **2 = right**, standard, regular, appropriate, acceptable, strict, proper, precise: *The use of the correct procedure is vital.* **3 = proper**, seemly, standard, fitting, diplomatic, kosher *(informal)*: *They refuse to adopt the rules of correct behaviour.* **OPPOSITE:** inappropriate
▷ VERB **1 = rectify**, remedy, redress, right, improve, reform, cure, adjust, regulate, amend, set the record straight, emend: *He may need surgery to correct the problem.* **OPPOSITE:** spoil **2 = rebuke**, discipline, reprimand, chide, admonish, chastise, chasten, reprove, punish: *He gently corrected me for taking the Lord's name in vain.* **OPPOSITE:** praise

> **QUOTATIONS**
> For whom the Lord loveth he correcteth
> [*Bible: Proverbs*]

correction NOUN **1 = rectification**, improvement, amendment, adjustment, modification, alteration, emendation: *He has made several corrections and additions to the document.* **2 = punishment**, discipline, reformation, admonition, chastisement, reproof, castigation: *jails and other places of correction*

corrective ADJECTIVE **1 = remedial**, therapeutic, palliative, restorative, rehabilitative: *He has received extensive corrective surgery to his skull.* **2 = disciplinary**, punitive, penal, reformatory: *He was placed in a corrective institution for children.*

correctly ADVERB **= rightly**, right, perfectly, properly, precisely, accurately, aright

correctness NOUN **1 = truth**, accuracy, precision, exactitude, exactness, faultlessness: *Please check the correctness of the details on this form.* **2 = decorum**, propriety, good manners, civility, good breeding, bon ton *(French)*: *He conducted himself with formal correctness at all times.*

correlate VERB **1 = correspond**, parallel, be connected, equate, tie in, match: *Obesity correlates with increased risk of heart disease and stroke.* **2 = connect**, compare, associate, tie in, coordinate, match: *attempts to correlate specific language functions with particular parts of the brain*

correlation NOUN **= correspondence**, link, relation, connection, equivalence

correspond VERB **1 = be consistent**, match, agree, accord, fit, square, coincide, complement, be related, tally, conform, correlate, dovetail, harmonize: *The two maps of London correspond closely.* **OPPOSITE:** differ **2 = communicate**, write, keep in touch, exchange letters, e-mail, text: *We corresponded regularly for years.*

correspondence NOUN **1 = communication**, writing, contact:

The Language of Nathaniel Hawthorne

Nathaniel Hawthorne (1804–64) is one of America's most important antebellum authors. Initially a short-story writer, he later moved on to novels, the most famous of which is the romance *The Scarlet Letter.* His work is known for its symbolism and darkness and for the themes of religion and guilt. Evidence of archaic vocabulary in Hawthorne's work is extensive. For example, *forth, hither, whence, thither, thence,* and *yonder* all appear in his 100 most frequently used adverbs. *Forth* modifies a range of verbs including *set, stretch, burst, thrust,* and *shadow*:

> It might **shadow forth** his own fate, – he having made himself one of the personages.

The phrase *shadow forth* is frequent in Hawthorne's work, but in modern English it is fairly uncommon. Other archaic adverbs that Hawthorne uses to modify verbs include *hither*, which modifies *come, bring, lure,* and *trundle*, while *come, originate,* and *ooze* occur with *whence. Thither* modifies *come, go, voyage,* and *transplant,* and *thence* modifies *summon, spread,* and *descend. Lie, hang,* and *descend* occur with *yonder.*

This dated vocabulary is crucial to Hawthorne's style. Hawthorne considered his books to be not novels but *romances*, meaning the heroic narrative genre which originated in the Middle Ages, rather than the class of contemporary fiction about two people falling in love. The romance genre was already antiquated by the 19th century, and Hawthorne's vocabulary is one means of evoking it for his contemporary audience.

Other adverbs Hawthorne uses frequently provide emphasis to a sentence. *Indeed, certainly, doubtless, moreover,* and *exceedingly* all appear in his 100 most frequently used adverbs:

> Well, Mrs. Hutchinson's lectures soon caused a great disturbance; for the ministers of Boston did not think it safe and proper that a woman should publicly instruct the people in religious doctrines. **Moreover**, she made the matter worse by declaring that the Rev. Mr. Cotton was the only sincerely pious and holy clergyman in New England.

The above reflects the themes of religion and morality in Hawthorne's work. Some of the 100 most frequently used nouns he uses include *church, spirit,* and *soul.* Also, *minister* is fairly frequent. In addition to adjectives such as *Gothic, Catholic, English,* and *Christian,* many of the words which modify *church* are positive (*magnificent, picturesque,* and *noble*). Adjectives which modify *minister* may be positive (*godly, celebrated,* and *eminent*); however, *minister* is also modified by negative adjectives like *unkind* and *wretched.* Adjectives such as *immortal, sinful, devout,* and *Christian* modify *soul.* Hawthorne's 100 most frequently used adjectives also include *moral, spiritual,* and *holy. Moral* most frequently modifies *sense, atmosphere,* and *force. Spiritual* modifies *existence, influence,* and *communication,* while *holy* modifies *water, apostle,* and *symbol. Pray* appears in Hawthorne's most frequently used verbs and is modified by adverbs such as *internally, earnestly,* and *fervently*:

> Sometimes she heard the Doctor muttering, as was his wont; once she fancied he was **praying**, and dropping on her knees, she also **prayed fervently** ....And then there was an utter silence, unbroken forevermore by the lips that had uttered so many objectionable things.

Death is an important theme of Hawthorne's work, and *dead, die,* and *death* occur frequently in his work, the latter modified by both negative adjectives (*violent, awful,* and *ugly*) and positive ones (*peaceful* and *beautiful*).

Another of Hawthorne's major themes is love, and *love* appears in both his 100 most frequently used verbs and nouns. The adjectives which frequently modify *love* include *passionate, genuine,* and *earnest,* as well as *brotherly, holy,* and *pure.* Similarly, the verb *love* is often modified by adverbs including *dearly, passionately, deeply,* and *devoutly.*

The judges' decision is final and no correspondence will be entered into. **2 = letters**, post, mail: *He always replied to his correspondence promptly.* **3 = relation**, match, agreement, fitness, comparison, harmony, coincidence, similarity, analogy, correlation, conformity, comparability, concurrence, congruity: *correspondences between Eastern religions and Christianity*

C

correspondent NOUN **1 = reporter**, journalist, contributor, special correspondent, journo *(slang)*, hack: *Here is a special report from our Europe correspondent.* **2 = letter writer**, pen friend *or* pen pal: *He wasn't a good correspondent and only wrote to me once a year.*

corresponding ADJECTIVE **= equivalent**, matching, similar, related, correspondent, identical, complementary, synonymous, reciprocal, analogous, interrelated, correlative

corridor NOUN **= passage**, alley, aisle, hallway, passageway

corroborate VERB **= support**, establish, confirm, document, sustain, back up, endorse, ratify, validate, bear out, substantiate, authenticate **OPPOSITE:** contradict

corrode VERB **= eat away**, waste, consume, corrupt, deteriorate, erode, rust, gnaw, oxidize

corrosive ADJECTIVE **= corroding**, wasting, caustic, vitriolic, acrid, erosive: *Sodium and sulphur are highly corrosive elements.*

corrugated ADJECTIVE **= furrowed**, channelled, ridged, grooved, wrinkled, creased, fluted, rumpled, puckered, crinkled

corrupt ADJECTIVE **1 = dishonest**, bent *(slang)*, crooked *(informal)*, rotten, shady *(informal)*, fraudulent, unscrupulous, unethical, venal, unprincipled: *corrupt police officers who took bribes* **OPPOSITE:** honest **2 = depraved**, abandoned, vicious, degenerate, debased, demoralized, profligate, dishonoured, defiled, dissolute: *the flamboyant and morally corrupt court of Charles the Second* **3 = distorted**, doctored, altered, falsified: *a corrupt text of a poem by Milton*
▷ VERB **1 = bribe**, square, fix *(informal)*, buy off, suborn, grease (someone's) palm *(slang)*: *The ability to corrupt politicians, policemen, and judges was fundamental to Mafia operations.* **2 = deprave**, pervert, subvert, debase, demoralize, debauch: *Cruelty depraves and corrupts.* **OPPOSITE:** reform **3 = distort**, doctor, tamper with: *Computer hackers often break into important sites to corrupt files.*

corruption NOUN **1 = dishonesty**, fraud, fiddling *(informal)*, graft *(informal)*, bribery, extortion, profiteering, breach of trust, venality, shady dealings *(informal)*, shadiness: *He faces 54 charges of corruption and tax evasion.* **2 = depravity**, vice, evil, degradation, perversion, decadence, impurity, wickedness, degeneration, immorality, iniquity, profligacy, viciousness, sinfulness, turpitude, baseness: *It was a society sinking into corruption and vice.* **3 = distortion**, doctoring, falsification: *The name 'Santa Claus' is a corruption of 'Saint Nicholas'.*

corset NOUN **= girdle**, bodice, foundation garment, panty girdle, stays *(rare)*

cortege NOUN **= procession**, train, entourage, cavalcade, retinue, suite

cosmetic ADJECTIVE **= superficial**, surface, touching-up, nonessential

cosmic ADJECTIVE **1 = extraterrestrial**, stellar: *Inside the heliosphere we are screened from cosmic rays.* **2 = universal**, general, omnipresent, all-embracing, overarching: *There are cosmic laws governing our world.* **3 = vast**, huge, immense, infinite, grandiose, limitless, measureless: *It was an understatement of cosmic proportions.*

cosmonaut NOUN **= astronaut**, spaceman, space pilot, space cadet

cosmopolitan ADJECTIVE **= sophisticated**, worldly, cultured, refined, cultivated, urbane, well-travelled, worldly-wise **OPPOSITE:** unsophisticated

cosmos NOUN **= universe**, world, creation, macrocosm

cosset VERB **= pamper**, baby, pet, coddle, mollycoddle, wrap up in cotton wool *(informal)*

cost NOUN **1 = price**, worth, expense, rate, charge, figure, damage *(informal)*, amount, payment, expenditure, outlay: *The cost of a loaf of bread has increased five-fold.* **2 = loss**, suffering, damage, injury, penalty, hurt, expense, harm, sacrifice, deprivation, detriment: *a man who always looks after 'number one', whatever the cost to others*
▷ PLURAL NOUN **= expenses**, spending, expenditure, overheads, outgoings, outlay, budget: *The company admits its costs are still too high.*
▷ VERB **1 = sell at**, come to, set (someone) back *(informal)*, be priced at, command a price of: *The course is limited to 12 people and costs £50.* **2 = lose**, deprive of, cheat of: *The operation saved his life, but cost him his sight.*
at all costs = no matter what, regardless, whatever happens, at any price, come what may, without fail: *We must avoid any further delay at all costs.*

costly ADJECTIVE **1 = expensive**, dear, stiff, excessive, steep *(informal)*, highly-priced, exorbitant, extortionate: *Having curtains professionally made can be costly.* **OPPOSITE:** inexpensive **2 = splendid**, rich, valuable, precious, gorgeous, lavish, luxurious, sumptuous, priceless, opulent: *the exceptionally beautiful and costly cloths made in northern Italy* **3 = damaging**, disastrous, harmful, catastrophic, loss-making, ruinous, deleterious: *If you follow the procedures correctly you will avoid costly mistakes.*

costume NOUN **= outfit**, dress, clothing, get-up *(informal)*, uniform, ensemble, robes, livery, apparel, attire, garb, national dress

cosy ADJECTIVE **1 = comfortable**, homely, warm, intimate, snug, comfy *(informal)*, sheltered: *Guests can relax in the cosy bar before dinner.* **2 = snug**, warm, secure, comfortable, sheltered, comfy *(informal)*, tucked up, cuddled up, snuggled down: *I was lying cosy in bed with the Sunday papers.* **3 = intimate**, friendly, informal: *a cosy chat between friends*

coterie NOUN **= clique**, group, set, camp, circle, gang, outfit *(informal)*, posse *(informal)*, cabal

cottage NOUN **= cabin**, lodge, hut, shack, chalet, but-and-ben *(Scot.)*, cot, whare *(N.Z.)*

couch NOUN **= sofa**, bed, chesterfield, ottoman, settee, divan, chaise longue, day bed: *He lay down on the couch.*
▷ VERB **= express**, word, frame, phrase, utter, set forth: *This time his proposal was couched as an ultimatum.*

cough VERB **= clear your throat**, bark, hawk, hack, hem: *He began to cough violently.*
▷ NOUN **= frog** *or* **tickle in your throat**, bark, hack: *He put a hand over his mouth to cover a cough.*
cough up = fork out, deliver, hand over, surrender, come across *(informal)*, shell out *(informal)*, ante up *(informal, chiefly U.S.)*: *I'll have to cough up $10,000 a year for private tuition.*

council NOUN **1 = committee**, governing body, board, panel, quango, jamaat: *The city council has voted almost unanimously in favour of the proposal.* **2 = governing body**, house, parliament, congress, cabinet, ministry, diet, panel, assembly, chamber, convention, synod, conclave, convocation, conference, jamaat, runanga *(N.Z.)*: *The powers of the King had been handed over temporarily to a council of ministers.*

counsel NOUN **1 = advice**, information, warning, direction, suggestion, recommendation, caution, guidance, admonition: *He had always been able to count on her wise counsel.* **2 = legal adviser**, lawyer, attorney, solicitor, advocate, barrister: *The defence counsel warned that the judge should stop the trial.*
▷ VERB **= advise**, recommend, advocate, prescribe, warn, urge, caution, instruct, exhort, admonish: *My advisors counselled me to do nothing.*

count VERB **1** *(often with* **up***)* **= add (up)**, total, reckon (up), tot up, score, check, estimate, calculate, compute, tally, number, enumerate, cast up: *I counted the money. It came to more than five hundred*

pounds. **2 = matter**, be important, cut any ice *(informal)*, carry weight, tell, rate, weigh, signify, enter into consideration: *It's as if your opinions just don't count.* **3 = consider**, judge, regard, deem, think of, rate, esteem, look upon, impute: *I count him as one of my best friends.* **4 = include**, number among, take into account *or* consideration: *The years before their arrival in prison are not counted as part of their sentence.*
▷ NOUN **= calculation**, poll, reckoning, sum, tally, numbering, computation, enumeration: *At the last count the police had 247 people in custody.*
count on *or* **upon something** *or* **someone = depend on**, trust, rely on, bank on, take for granted, lean on, reckon on, take on trust, believe in, pin your faith on: *I'm counting on your support; We're all counting on you to do the right thing.*
count someone out = leave out, except, exclude, disregard, pass over, leave out of account: *If it means working extra hours, you can count me out.*

countenance NOUN **= face**, features, expression, look, appearance, aspect, visage, mien *(literary)*, physiognomy: *He met each inquiry with an impassive countenance.*
▷ VERB **= tolerate**, sanction, endorse, condone, support, encourage, approve, endure, brook, stand for *(informal)*, hack *(slang)*, put up with *(informal)*: *He would not countenance his daughter marrying while she was still a student.*

counter VERB **1 = oppose**, meet, block, resist, offset, parry, deflect, repel, rebuff, fend off, counteract, ward off, stave off, repulse, obviate, hold at bay: *They discussed a plan to counter the effects of such a blockade.* **2 = retaliate**, return, answer, reply, respond, come back, retort, hit back, rejoin, strike back: *The union countered with letters rebutting the company's claim.* **OPPOSITE:** yield
▷ ADVERB **= opposite to**, against, versus, conversely, in defiance of, at variance with, contrarily, contrariwise: *Their findings ran counter to all expectations.* **OPPOSITE:** in accordance with
▷ ADJECTIVE **= opposing**, conflicting, opposed, contrasting, opposite, contrary, adverse, contradictory, obverse, against: *These charges and counter charges are being exchanged at an important time.* **OPPOSITE:** similar

counteract VERB **1 = act against**, check, defeat, prevent, oppose, resist, frustrate, foil, thwart, hinder, cross: *Many countries within the region are planning measures to counteract a missile attack.* **2 = offset**, negate, neutralize, invalidate, counterbalance, annul, obviate, countervail: *pills to counteract high blood pressure*

counterbalance VERB **= offset**, balance out, compensate for, make up for, counterpoise, countervail

counterfeit ADJECTIVE **= fake**, copied, false, forged, imitation, bogus, simulated, sham, fraudulent, feigned, spurious, ersatz, phoney *or* phony *(informal)*, pseud *or* pseudo *(informal)*: *He admitted possessing and delivering counterfeit currency.*
OPPOSITE: genuine
▷ NOUN **= fake**, copy, reproduction, imitation, sham, forgery, phoney *or* phony *(informal)*, fraud: *Levi Strauss says counterfeits of the company's jeans are flooding Europe.* **OPPOSITE:** the real thing
▷ VERB **= fake**, copy, forge, imitate, simulate, sham, fabricate, feign: *He is alleged to have counterfeited video cassettes.*

counterpart NOUN **= opposite number**, equal, twin, equivalent, peer, match, fellow, mate

countless ADJECTIVE **= innumerable**, legion, infinite, myriad, untold, limitless, incalculable, immeasurable, numberless, uncounted, multitudinous, endless, measureless **OPPOSITE:** limited

country NOUN **1 = nation**, state, land, commonwealth, kingdom, realm, sovereign state, people: *the disputed boundary between the two countries* **2 = people**, community, nation, society, citizens, voters, inhabitants, grass roots, electors, populace, citizenry, public: *Seventy per cent of this country is opposed to blood sports.* **3 = countryside**, rural areas, provinces, outdoors, sticks *(informal)*, farmland, outback *(Austral. & N.Z.)*, the middle of nowhere, green belt, wide open spaces *(informal)*, backwoods, back country *(U.S.)*, the back of beyond, bush *(N.Z. & S. African)*, backlands *(U.S.)*, boondocks *(U.S. slang)*: *They live somewhere way out in the country.* **OPPOSITE:** town **4 = territory**, part, land, region, terrain: *This is some of the best walking country in the district.* **5 = native land**, nationality, homeland, motherland, fatherland, patria *(Latin)*, Hawaiki (N.Z.), Godzone *(Austral. informal)*: *I am willing to serve my country.*
▷ ADJECTIVE **= rural**, pastoral, rustic, agrarian, bucolic, Arcadian: *I want to live a simple country life.* **OPPOSITE:** urban
▸ *related adjectives:* pastoral, rural

countryman NOUN **1 = compatriot**, fellow citizen: *He beat his fellow countryman in the final.* **2 = yokel**, farmer, peasant, provincial, hick *(informal, chiefly U.S. & Canad.)*, rustic, swain, hillbilly, bucolic, country dweller, hayseed *(U.S. & Canad. informal)*, clodhopper *(informal)*, cockie *(N.Z.)*, (country) bumpkin: *He had the red face of a countryman.*

countryside NOUN **= country**, rural areas, outdoors, farmland, outback *(Austral. & N.Z.)*, green belt, wide open spaces *(informal)*, sticks *(informal)*

county NOUN **= province**, district, shire: *He is living now in his mother's home county of Oxfordshire.*
▷ ADJECTIVE **= upper-class**, upper-crust *(informal)*, tweedy, plummy *(informal)*, green-wellie, huntin', shootin', and fishin' *(informal)*: *They were all upper-crust ladies, pillars of the county set.*

coup NOUN **= masterstroke**, feat, stunt, action, stroke, exploit, manoeuvre, deed, accomplishment, tour de force *(French)*, stratagem, stroke of genius

coup d'état NOUN **= overthrow**, takeover, coup, rebellion, putsch, seizure of power, palace revolution

couple NOUN **= pair**, two, brace, span *(of horses or oxen)*, duo, twain *(archaic)*, twosome: *There are a couple of police officers standing guard.*
couple something to something = link to, connect to, pair with, unite with, join to, hitch to, buckle to, clasp to, yoke to, conjoin to: *The engine is coupled to a semiautomatic gearbox.*

coupon NOUN **= slip**, ticket, certificate, token, voucher, card, detachable portion

courage NOUN **= bravery**, nerve, fortitude, boldness, balls *(taboo)*, bottle *(Brit. slang)*, resolution, daring, guts *(informal)*, pluck, grit, heroism, mettle, firmness, gallantry, valour, spunk *(informal)*, fearlessness, intrepidity **OPPOSITE:** cowardice

> **QUOTATIONS**
> No one can answer for his courage when he has never been in danger
> [Duc de la Rochefoucauld *Maxims*]
>
> Sometimes even to live is an act of courage
> [Seneca *Letters to Lucilius*]
>
> Courage is not simply one of the virtues but the form of every virtue at the testing point
> [C.S. Lewis]
>
> Screw your courage to the sticking place
> [William Shakespeare *Macbeth*]
>
> As to moral courage, I have very rarely met with two o'clock in the morning courage: I mean instantaneous courage
> [Napoleon Bonaparte]

courageous ADJECTIVE **= brave**, daring, bold, plucky, hardy, heroic, gritty, stalwart, fearless, resolute, gallant, audacious, intrepid, valiant, indomitable, dauntless, ballsy *(taboo)*, lion-hearted, valorous, stouthearted **OPPOSITE:** cowardly

courier NOUN **1 = messenger**, runner, carrier, bearer, herald, envoy, emissary: *The cheques were delivered to the bank by a private courier.* **2 = guide**, representative, escort, conductor, chaperon, cicerone, dragoman: *He was a travel courier.*

course NOUN **1 = route**, way, line, road, track, channel, direction, path, passage, trail, orbit, tack, trajectory: *For nearly four hours we maintained our course northwards.* **2 = procedure**, plan, policy, programme, method, conduct,

behaviour, manner, mode, regimen: *Resignation is the only course left open to him.* **3 = progression**, order, unfolding, development, movement, advance, progress, flow, sequence, succession, continuity, advancement, furtherance, march: *a series of naval battles which altered the course of history* **4 = classes**, course of study, programme, schedule, lectures, curriculum, studies: *I'll shortly be beginning a course on the modern novel.* **5 = racecourse**, race, circuit, cinder track, lap: *On the Tour de France, 200 cyclists cover a course of 2,000 miles.* **6 = period**, time, duration, term, passing, sweep, passage, lapse: *In the course of the 1930s steel production in Britain approximately doubled.*
▷ VERB **1 = run**, flow, stream, gush, race, speed, surge, dash, tumble, scud, move apace: *The tears coursed down his cheeks.* **2 = hunt**, follow, chase, pursue: *New muzzling regulations for dogs coursing hares have been introduced.*
in due course = in time, finally, eventually, in the end, sooner or later, in the course of time: *I hope that it will be possible in due course.*
of course = naturally, certainly, obviously, definitely, undoubtedly, needless to say, without a doubt, indubitably: *There'll be the usual inquiry, of course.*

court NOUN **1 = law court**, bar, bench, tribunal, court of justice, seat of judgment: *At this rate, you could find yourself in court for assault.* **2 = palace**, hall, castle, manor: *She came to visit England, where she was presented at the court of James I.* **3 = royal household**, train, suite, attendants, entourage, retinue, cortege: *tales of King Arthur and his court*
▷ VERB **1 = cultivate**, seek, flatter, solicit, pander to, curry favour with, fawn upon: *Britain's political parties are courting the vote of the lesbian and gay community.* **2 = invite**, seek, attract, prompt, provoke, bring about, incite: *If he thinks he can remain in power by force he is courting disaster.* **3 = woo**, go (out) with, go steady with *(informal)*, date, chase, pursue, take out, make love to, run after, walk out with, keep company with, pay court to, set your cap at, pay your addresses to, step out with *(informal)*: *I was courting him at 19 and married him when I was 21.*

courteous ADJECTIVE **= polite**, civil, respectful, mannerly, polished, refined, gracious, gallant, affable, urbane, courtly, well-bred, well-mannered **OPPOSITE:** discourteous

courtesan NOUN **= mistress**, prostitute, whore, call girl, working girl *(facetious, slang)*, kept woman, harlot, paramour, scarlet woman, fille de joie *(French)*

courtesy NOUN **1 = politeness**, grace, good manners, civility, gallantry, good breeding, graciousness, affability, urbanity, courtliness: *He is a gentleman who behaves with the utmost courtesy towards ladies.* **2 = favour**, consideration, generosity, kindness, indulgence, benevolence: *If you're not coming, at least do me the courtesy of letting me know.*

courtier NOUN **= attendant**, follower, squire, train-bearer

> **QUOTATIONS**
> The two maxims of any great man at court are, always to keep his countenance, and never to keep his word
> [Jonathan Swift *Thoughts on Various Subjects*]

courtly ADJECTIVE **= ceremonious**, civil, formal, obliging, refined, polite, dignified, stately, aristocratic, gallant, affable, urbane, decorous, chivalrous, highbred

courtship NOUN **= wooing**, courting, suit, romance, engagement, keeping company

courtyard NOUN **= yard**, square, piazza, quadrangle, area, plaza, enclosure, cloister, quad *(informal)*, peristyle

cove NOUN **= bay**, sound, creek, inlet, bayou, firth *or* frith *(Scot.)*, anchorage

covenant NOUN **1 = promise**, contract, agreement, commitment, arrangement, treaty, pledge, bargain, convention, pact, compact, concordat, trust: *the United Nations covenant on civil and political rights* **2 = deed**, contract, bond: *If you make regular gifts through a covenant we can reclaim the income tax.*

cover VERB **1 = conceal**, cover up, screen, hide, shade, curtain, mask, disguise, obscure, hood, veil, cloak, shroud, camouflage, enshroud: *the black patch which covered his left eye* **OPPOSITE:** reveal **2 = clothe**, invest, dress, wrap, envelop: *He covered his head with a turban.* **OPPOSITE:** uncover **3 = overlay**, blanket, eclipse, mantle, canopy, overspread, layer: *The clouds had spread and nearly covered the entire sky.* **4 = coat**, cake, plaster, smear, envelop, spread, encase, daub, overspread: *She was soaking wet and covered with mud.* **5 = submerge**, flood, engulf, overrun, wash over: *Nearly a foot of water covered the streets.* **6 = travel over**, cross, traverse, pass through *or* over, range: *It would not be easy to cover ten miles on that amount of petrol.* **7 = protect**, guard, defend, shelter, shield, watch over: *You make a run for it and I'll cover you.* **8 = insure**, compensate, provide for, offset, balance, make good, make up for, take account of, counterbalance: *These items are not covered by your medical insurance.* **9 = deal with**, refer to, provide for, take account of, include, involve, contain, embrace, incorporate, comprise, embody, encompass, comprehend: *The law covers four categories of experiments.* **OPPOSITE:** exclude **10 = consider**, deal with, examine, investigate, detail, describe, survey, refer to, tell of, recount: *In this lecture, I aim to cover several topics.* **11 = report on**, write about, commentate on, give an account of, relate, tell of, narrate, write up: *He was sent to Italy to cover the World Cup.* **12 = pay for**, fund, provide for, offset, be enough for: *Please send £1.50 to cover postage.*
▷ NOUN **1 = protection**, shelter, shield, refuge, defence, woods, guard, sanctuary, camouflage, hiding place, undergrowth, concealment: *There were barren wastes of field with no trees and no cover.* **2 = insurance**, payment, protection, compensation, indemnity, reimbursement: *Make sure that the firm's accident cover is adequate.* **3 = covering**, case, top, cap, coating, envelope, lid, canopy, sheath, wrapper, awning: *Put a polythene cover over it to protect it from dust.* **4 = bedclothes**, bedding, sheet, blanket, quilt, duvet, eiderdown: *He groaned and slid farther under the covers.* **5 = jacket**, case, binding, wrapper: *a small book with a green cover* **6 = disguise**, front, screen, mask, cover-up, veil, cloak, façade, pretence, pretext, window-dressing, smoke screen: *The grocery store was just a cover for their betting shop.*
cover for someone = stand in for, take over, substitute, relieve, double for, fill in for, hold the fort for *(informal)*: *She did not have enough nurses to cover for those who were off sick.*
cover something up = conceal, hide, suppress, repress, keep secret, whitewash *(informal)*, hush up, sweep under the carpet, draw a veil over, keep silent about, cover your tracks, keep dark, feign ignorance about, keep under your hat *(informal)*: *They knew they had done something wrong and lied to cover it up.*

coverage NOUN **= reporting**, treatment, analysis, description, reportage

covering NOUN **= cover**, coating, casing, wrapping, layer, blanket: *Sawdust was used as a hygienic floor covering.*
▷ ADJECTIVE **= explanatory**, accompanying, introductory, descriptive: *Include a covering letter with your CV.*

covert ADJECTIVE **= secret**, private, hidden, disguised, concealed, veiled, sly, clandestine, underhand, unsuspected, surreptitious, stealthy

cover-up NOUN **= concealment**, conspiracy, whitewash *(informal)*, complicity, front, smoke screen

covet VERB **= long for**, desire, fancy *(informal)*, envy, crave, aspire to, yearn for, thirst for, begrudge, hanker after, lust after, set your heart on, have your eye on, would give your eyeteeth for

cow VERB **= intimidate**, daunt, frighten, scare, bully, dismay, awe, subdue, unnerve, overawe, terrorize, browbeat, psych out *(informal)*, dishearten

coward NOUN **= wimp**, chicken *(slang)*, scaredy-cat *(informal)*, sneak, pussy *(slang, chiefly U.S.)*, yellow-belly *(slang)*

QUOTATIONS

Cowards die many times before their deaths
[William Shakespeare *Julius Caesar*]

coward: one who in a perilous emergency thinks with his legs
[Ambrose Bierce *The Devil's Dictionary*]

May coward shame distain his name,
The wretch that dares not die!
[Robert Burns *McPherson's Farewell*]

All men would be cowards if they durst
[John Wilmot *A Satire against Mankind*]

cowardice NOUN **= faint-heartedness**, weakness, softness, fearfulness, pusillanimity, spinelessness, timorousness

QUOTATIONS

To know what is right and not to do it is the worst cowardice
[Confucius *Analects*]

'I cannot do this. This is too much for me. I shall ruin myself if I take this risk. I cannot take the leap, it's impossible. All of me will be gone if I do this, and I cling to myself'
[J.N.Figgis]

cowardly ADJECTIVE **= faint-hearted**, scared, spineless, gutless (*informal*), base, soft, yellow (*informal*), weak, chicken (*slang*), shrinking, fearful, craven, abject, dastardly, timorous, weak-kneed (*informal*), pusillanimous, chicken-hearted, lily-livered, white-livered, sookie (*N.Z.*) **OPPOSITE:** brave

cowboy NOUN **= cowhand**, drover, herder, rancher, stockman, cattleman, herdsman, gaucho, buckaroo (*U.S.*), ranchero (*U.S.*), cowpuncher (*U.S. informal*), broncobuster (*U.S.*), wrangler (*U.S.*)

cower VERB **= cringe**, shrink, tremble, crouch, flinch, quail, draw back, grovel

coy ADJECTIVE **1 = modest**, retiring, shy, shrinking, arch, timid, self-effacing, demure, flirtatious, bashful, prudish, aw-shucks, skittish, coquettish, kittenish, overmodest: *She was demure without being coy.* **OPPOSITE:** bold **2 = uncommunicative**, mum, secretive, reserved, quiet, silent, evasive, taciturn, unforthcoming, tight-lipped, close-lipped: *The hotel are understandably coy about the incident.*

crack VERB **1 = break**, split, burst, snap, fracture, splinter, craze, rive: *A gas main had cracked under my neighbour's garage; Crack the salt crust and you will find the skin just peels off the fish.* **2 = snap**, ring, crash, burst, explode, crackle, pop, detonate: *Thunder cracked in the sky.* **3 = hit**, clip (*informal*), slap, smack, thump, buffet, clout (*informal*), cuff, whack, wallop (*informal*), chop: *She drew back her fist and cracked him on the jaw; He cracked his head on the pavement and was knocked out.* **4 = cleave**, break: *Crack the eggs into a bowl.* **5 = solve**, work out, resolve, interpret, clarify, clear up, fathom, decipher, suss (out) (*slang*), get to the bottom of, disentangle, elucidate, get the answer to: *He has finally cracked the code after years of painstaking research.* **6 = break down**, collapse, yield, give in, give way, succumb, lose control, be overcome, go to pieces: *She's calm and strong, and will not crack under pressure.*
▷ NOUN **1 = break**, chink, gap, breach, fracture, rift, cleft, crevice, fissure, cranny, interstice: *She watched him though a crack in the curtains.* **2 = split**, break, chip, breach, fracture, rupture, cleft: *The plate had a crack in it.* **3 = snap**, pop, crash, burst, explosion, clap, report: *Suddenly there was a loud crack and glass flew into the air.* **4 = blow**, slap, smack, thump, buffet, clout (*informal*), cuff, whack, wallop (*informal*), clip (*informal*): *He took a crack on the head during the game.* **5 = attempt**, go (*informal*), try, shot, opportunity, stab (*informal*): *I'd love to have a crack at the title next year.* **6 = joke**, dig, insult, gag (*informal*), quip, jibe, wisecrack, witticism, funny remark, smart-alecky remark: *He made a nasty crack about her weight.*
▷ ADJECTIVE **= first-class**, choice, excellent, ace, elite, superior, world-class, first-rate, hand-picked: *He is said to be a crack shot.*
crack up 1 = have a breakdown, collapse, break down, go crazy (*informal*), go berserk, freak out (*informal*), go to pieces, go ape (*slang*), fly off the handle (*informal*), come apart at the seams (*informal*), throw a wobbly (*slang*), go off the deep end (*informal*), go out of your mind, flip your lid (*slang*), go off your rocker (*slang*), go off your head (*slang*): *He's going to crack up if he doesn't take a break soon.* **2 = burst out laughing**, laugh, fall about (laughing), guffaw, roar with laughter, be in stitches, split your sides: *We all just cracked up when he told us.*

crackdown NOUN **= clampdown**, crushing, repression, suppression

cracked ADJECTIVE **1 = broken**, damaged, split, chipped, flawed, faulty, crazed, defective, imperfect, fissured: *a cracked mirror* **2 = crazy**, nuts (*slang*), eccentric, nutty (*slang*), touched, bats (*slang*), daft (*informal*), batty (*slang*), insane, loony (*slang*), off-the-wall (*slang*), oddball (*informal*), loopy (*informal*), crackpot (*informal*), out to lunch (*informal*), round the bend (*slang*), out of your mind, gonzo (*slang*), doolally (*slang*), off your trolley (*slang*), off the air (*Austral. slang*), round the twist (*Brit. slang*), up the pole (*informal*), off your rocker (*slang*), crackbrained, off your head *or* nut (*slang*), wacko *or* whacko (*informal*), porangi (*N.Z.*), daggy (*Austral. & N.Z. informal*): *Everyone in our family's a bit cracked.*

cradle NOUN **1 = crib**, cot, Moses basket, bassinet: *The baby sleeps in the cradle upstairs.* **2 = birthplace**, beginning, source, spring, origin, fount, fountainhead, wellspring: *New York is the cradle of capitalism.*
▷ VERB **= hold**, support, rock, nurse, nestle: *I cradled her in my arms.*

craft NOUN **1 = vessel**, boat, ship, plane, aircraft, spacecraft, barque: *Cannabis smuggling by small craft to remote sites is rising.* **2 = occupation**, work, calling, business, line, trade, employment, pursuit, vocation, handiwork, handicraft: *All kinds of traditional crafts are preserved here.* **3 = skill**, art, ability, technique, know-how (*informal*), expertise, knack, aptitude, artistry, dexterity, workmanship: *Lilyanne learned her craft of cooking from her grandmother.* **4 = cunning**, ingenuity, guile, cleverness, scheme, subtlety, deceit, ruse, artifice, trickery, wiles, duplicity, subterfuge, contrivance, shrewdness, artfulness: *They defeated their enemies through craft and cunning.*

craftsman NOUN **= skilled worker**, artisan, master, maker, wright, technician, artificer, smith

craftsmanship NOUN **= workmanship**, technique, expertise, mastery, artistry

crafty ADJECTIVE **= cunning**, scheming, sly, devious, knowing, designing, sharp, calculating, subtle, tricky, shrewd, astute, fraudulent, canny, wily, insidious, artful, foxy, deceitful, duplicitous, tricksy, guileful **OPPOSITE:** open

crag NOUN **= rock**, peak, bluff, pinnacle, tor, aiguille

craggy ADJECTIVE **= rocky**, broken, rough, rugged, uneven, jagged, stony, precipitous, jaggy (*Scot.*)

cram VERB **1 = stuff**, force, jam, ram, shove, compress, compact: *She pulled off her school hat and crammed it into a wastebasket.* **2 = pack**, fill, stuff: *She crammed her mouth with nuts.* **3 = squeeze**, press, crowd, pack, crush, pack in, fill to overflowing, overfill, overcrowd: *We crammed into my car and set off.* **4 = study**, revise, swot, bone up (*informal*), grind, swot up, mug up (*slang*): *She was cramming hard for her exam.*

cramp¹ NOUN **= spasm**, pain, ache, contraction, pang, stiffness, stitch, convulsion, twinge, crick, shooting pain: *She started getting stomach cramps this morning.*

cramp² VERB **= restrict**, hamper, inhibit, hinder, check, handicap, confine, hamstring, constrain, obstruct, impede, shackle, circumscribe, encumber: *Like more and more women, she believes wedlock would cramp her style.*

cramped ADJECTIVE **= restricted**, confined, overcrowded, crowded, packed, narrow, squeezed, uncomfortable, awkward, closed in, congested, circumscribed, jammed in, hemmed in **OPPOSITE:** spacious

C

crank NOUN **= eccentric**, freak *(informal)*, oddball *(informal)*, weirdo *or* weirdie *(informal)*, case *(informal)*, character *(informal)*, nut *(slang)*, flake *(slang, chiefly U.S.)*, screwball *(slang, chiefly U.S. & Canad.)*, odd fish *(informal)*, kook *(U.S. & Canad. informal)*, queer fish *(Brit. informal)*, rum customer *(Brit. slang)*, wacko *or* whacko *(informal)*

cranky ADJECTIVE **= eccentric**, wacky *(slang)*, oddball *(informal)*, freakish, odd, strange, funny *(informal)*, bizarre, peculiar, queer *(informal)*, rum *(Brit. slang)*, quirky, idiosyncratic, off-the-wall *(slang)*, freaky *(slang)*, outré, wacko *or* whacko *(informal)*, daggy *(Austral. & N.Z. informal)*

C

cranny NOUN **= crevice**, opening, hole, crack, gap, breach, rift, nook, cleft, chink, fissure, interstice

crash NOUN **1 = collision**, accident, smash, wreck, prang *(informal)*, bump, pile-up *(informal)*, smash-up: *His elder son was killed in a car crash a few years ago.* **2 = smash**, clash, boom, smashing, bang, thunder, thump, racket, din, clatter, clattering, thud, clang: *Two people in the flat recalled hearing a loud crash about 1.30am.* **3 = collapse**, failure, depression, ruin, bankruptcy, downfall: *He predicted correctly that there was going to be a stock market crash.*
▷ VERB **1 = fall**, pitch, plunge, sprawl, topple, lurch, hurtle, come a cropper *(informal)*, overbalance, fall headlong: *He lost his balance and crashed to the floor.* **2 = plunge**, hurtle, precipitate yourself: *We heard the sound of an animal crashing through the undergrowth.* **3 = smash**, break, break up, shatter, fragment, fracture, shiver, disintegrate, splinter, dash to pieces: *Her glass fell on the floor and crashed into a thousand pieces* **4 = collapse**, fail, go under, be ruined, go bust *(informal)*, fold up, go broke *(informal)*, go to the wall, go belly up *(informal)*, smash, fold: *When the market crashed they assumed the deal would be cancelled.*
▷ ADJECTIVE **= intensive**, concentrated, immediate, urgent, round-the-clock, emergency: *I might take a crash course in typing.*
crash into = collide with, hit, bump into, bang into, run into, drive into, plough into, hurtle into: *His car crashed into the rear of a van.*

crass ADJECTIVE **= insensitive**, stupid, gross, blundering, dense, coarse, witless, boorish, obtuse, unrefined, asinine, indelicate, oafish, lumpish, doltish **OPPOSITE:** sensitive

crate NOUN **= container**, case, box, packing case, tea chest: *A crane was already unloading crates and pallets.*
▷ VERB **= box**, pack, enclose, pack up, encase, case: *The plane had been dismantled, crated, and shipped to London.*

crater NOUN **= hollow**, hole, depression, dip, cavity, shell hole

crave VERB **1 = long for**, yearn for, hanker after, be dying for, want, need, require, desire, fancy *(informal)*, hope for, cry out for *(informal)*, thirst for, pine for, lust after, pant for, sigh for, set your heart on, hunger after, eat your heart out over, would give your eyeteeth for: *There may be certain times of day when smokers crave a cigarette.* **2 = beg**, ask for, seek, petition, pray for, plead for, solicit, implore, beseech, entreat, supplicate: *If I may crave your lordship's indulgence, I would like to consult my client.*

craven ADJECTIVE **= cowardly**, weak, scared, fearful, abject, dastardly, mean-spirited, timorous, pusillanimous, chicken-hearted, yellow *(informal)*, lily-livered

craving NOUN **= longing**, hope, desire, urge, yen *(informal)*, hunger, appetite, ache, lust, yearning, thirst, hankering

crawl VERB **1 = creep**, slither, go on all fours, move on hands and knees, inch, drag, wriggle, writhe, move at a snail's pace, worm your way, advance slowly, pull *or* drag yourself along: *I began to crawl on my hands and knees towards the door.* **OPPOSITE:** run **2 = grovel**, creep, cringe, humble yourself, abase yourself: *I'll apologize to him, but I won't crawl.*
be crawling with something = be full of, teem with, be alive with, swarm with, be overrun with *(slang)*, be lousy with: *This place is crawling with police.*
crawl to someone = fawn on, pander to, suck up to *(slang)*, toady to, truckle to, lick someone's boots *(slang)*: *I'd have to crawl to her to keep my job.*

craze NOUN **= fad**, thing, fashion, trend, passion, rage, enthusiasm, mode, vogue, novelty, preoccupation, mania, infatuation, the latest thing *(informal)*

crazed ADJECTIVE **= mad**, crazy, raving, insane, lunatic, demented, unbalanced, deranged, berserk, unhinged, berko *(Austral. slang)*, off the air *(Austral. slang)*, porangi *(N.Z.)*

crazy ADJECTIVE **1 = strange**, odd, bizarre, fantastic, silly, weird, ridiculous, outrageous, peculiar, eccentric, rum *(Brit. slang)*, oddball *(informal)*, cockamamie *(slang, chiefly U.S.)*, wacko *or* whacko *(informal)*, off the air *(Austral. slang)*, porangi *(N.Z.)*, daggy *(Austral. & N.Z. informal)*: *I ignored the crazy guy seated beside me on the bus.* **OPPOSITE:** normal **2 = ridiculous**, wild, absurd, inappropriate, foolish, ludicrous, irresponsible, unrealistic, unwise, senseless, preposterous, potty *(Brit. informal)*, short-sighted, unworkable, foolhardy, idiotic, nonsensical, half-baked *(informal)*, inane, fatuous, ill-conceived, quixotic, imprudent, impracticable, cockeyed *(informal)*, cockamamie *(slang, chiefly U.S.)*, porangi *(N.Z.)*: *I know it sounds a crazy idea, but hear me out.* **OPPOSITE:** sensible **3 = insane**, mad, unbalanced, deranged, touched, cracked *(slang)*, mental *(slang)*, nuts *(slang)*, barking *(slang)*, daft *(informal)*, batty *(slang)*, crazed, lunatic, demented, cuckoo *(informal)*, barmy *(slang)*, off-the-wall *(slang)*, off the air *(Austral. slang)*, nutty *(slang)*, potty *(Brit. informal)*, berserk, delirious, bonkers *(slang, chiefly Brit.)*, idiotic, unhinged, loopy *(informal)*, crackpot *(informal)*, out to lunch *(informal)*, round the bend *(slang)*, barking mad *(slang)*, out of your mind, maniacal, not all there *(informal)*, doolally *(slang)*, off your head *(slang)*, off your trolley *(slang)*, round the twist *(Brit. slang)*, up the pole *(informal)*, of unsound mind, not right in the head, off your rocker *(slang)*, not the full shilling *(informal)*, a bit lacking upstairs *(informal)*, as daft as a brush *(informal, chiefly Brit.)*, mad as a hatter, mad as a March hare, nutty as a fruitcake *(slang)*, porangi *(N.Z.)*: *If I think about it too much, I'll go crazy; some crazy man who had killed his wife and family before committing suicide* **OPPOSITE:** sane **4 = fanatical**, wild *(informal)*, mad, devoted, enthusiastic, passionate, hysterical, ardent, very keen, zealous, smitten, infatuated, enamoured: *He's crazy about football.* **OPPOSITE:** uninterested

creak VERB **= squeak**, grind, scrape, groan, grate, screech, squeal, scratch, rasp

creaky ADJECTIVE **= squeaky**, creaking, squeaking, unoiled, grating, rusty, rasping, raspy: *She pushed open the creaky door.*

cream NOUN **1 = lotion**, ointment, oil, essence, cosmetic, paste, emulsion, salve, liniment, unguent: *Gently apply the cream to the affected areas.* **2 = best**, elite, prime, pick, flower, the crème de la crème: *The event was attended by the cream of Hollywood society.*
▷ ADJECTIVE **= off-white**, ivory, yellowish-white: *cream silk stockings*

creamy ADJECTIVE **1 = milky**, buttery: *creamy mashed potato* **2 = smooth**, soft, creamed, lush, oily, velvety, rich: *Whisk the mixture until it is smooth and creamy.*

crease NOUN **1 = fold**, ruck, line, tuck, ridge, groove, pucker, corrugation: *She frowned at the creases in her silk dress.* **2 = wrinkle**, line, crow's-foot: *There were tiny creases at the corner of his eyes.*
▷ VERB **1 = crumple**, rumple, pucker, crinkle, fold, ridge, double up, crimp, ruck up, corrugate: *Most outfits crease a bit when you're travelling; Liz sat down carefully, so as not to crease her skirt.* **2 = wrinkle**, crumple, screw up: *His face creased with mirth.*

create VERB **1 = cause**, lead to, occasion, bring about: *Criticism will only create feelings of failure.* **2 = make**, form, produce, develop, design, generate, invent, coin, compose, devise, initiate, hatch, originate, formulate, give birth to, spawn, dream up *(informal)*, concoct, beget, give life to, bring into being *or* existence, architect: *He's creating a whole new language of painting* **OPPOSITE:** destroy

3 = **appoint**, make, found, establish, set up, invest, install, constitute: *They are about to create a scholarship fund for black students.*

creation NOUN 1 = **universe**, world, life, nature, cosmos, natural world, living world, all living things: *the origin of all creation* 2 = **invention**, production, concept, achievement, brainchild *(informal)*, concoction, handiwork, pièce de résistance *(French)*, magnum opus, chef-d'oeuvre *(French)*: *The bathroom is entirely my own creation.* 3 = **making**, generation, formation, conception, genesis: *the time and effort involved in the creation of a work of art* 4 = **setting up**, development, production, institution, foundation, constitution, establishment, formation, laying down, inception, origination: *He said all sides were committed to the creation of a democratic state.*

creative ADJECTIVE = **imaginative**, gifted, artistic, inventive, original, inspired, clever, productive, fertile, ingenious, visionary

creativity NOUN = **imagination**, talent, inspiration, productivity, fertility, ingenuity, originality, inventiveness, cleverness, fecundity

creator NOUN 1 = **maker**, father, author, framer, designer, architect, inventor, originator, initiator, begetter: *George Lucas, the creator of the Star Wars films* 2 *(usually with cap.)* = **God**, Maker: *This was the first object placed in the heavens by the Creator.*

creature NOUN 1 = **living thing**, being, animal, beast, brute, critter *(U.S. dialect)*, quadruped, dumb animal, lower animal: *Many cultures believe that every living creature possesses a spirit.* 2 = **person**, man, woman, individual, character, fellow, soul, human being, mortal, body: *He is one of the most amiable creatures in existence.* 3 = **minion**, tool, instrument *(informal)*, puppet, cohort *(chiefly U.S.)*, dependant, retainer, hanger-on, lackey: *We are not merely creatures of our employers.*

credence NOUN 1 = **credibility**, credit, plausibility, believability: *Further studies are needed to lend credence to this notion.* 2 = **belief**, trust, confidence, faith, acceptance, assurance, certainty, dependence, reliance: *Seismologists give this idea little credence.*

credentials PLURAL NOUN 1 = **qualifications**, ability, skill, capacity, fitness, attribute, capability, endowment(s), accomplishment, eligibility, aptitude, suitability: *He has the right credentials for the job.* 2 = **certification**, document, reference(s), papers, title, card, licence, recommendation, passport, warrant, voucher, deed, testament, diploma, testimonial, authorization, missive, letters of credence, attestation, letter of recommendation *or* introduction: *He called at Government House to present his credentials.*

credibility NOUN = **believability**, reliability, plausibility, trustworthiness, tenability

credible ADJECTIVE 1 = **believable**, possible, likely, reasonable, probable, plausible, conceivable, imaginable, tenable, verisimilar: *This claim seems perfectly credible to me.* **OPPOSITE:** unbelievable 2 = **reliable**, honest, dependable, trustworthy, sincere, trusty: *the evidence of credible witnesses* **OPPOSITE:** unreliable

credit NOUN 1 = **praise**, honour, recognition, glory, thanks, approval, fame, tribute, merit, acclaim, acknowledgment, kudos, commendation, Brownie points: *It would be wrong of us to take all the credit for this result.* 2 = **source of satisfaction** *or* **pride**, asset, honour, feather in your cap: *He is a credit to his family.* 3 = **prestige**, reputation, standing, position, character, influence, regard, status, esteem, clout *(informal)*, good name, estimation, repute: *His remarks lost him credit with many people.* 4 = **belief**, trust, confidence, faith, reliance, credence: *At first this theory met with little credit.*
▷ VERB = **believe**, rely on, have faith in, trust, buy *(slang)*, accept, depend on, swallow *(informal)*, fall for, bank on: *You can't credit anything he says.*
credit someone with something = **attribute to**, assign to, ascribe to, accredit to, impute to, chalk up to *(informal)*: *You don't credit me with any intelligence at all, do you?*
credit something to someone = **attribute to**, ascribe to, accredit to, impute to, chalk up to *(informal)*: *Although the song is usually credited to Lennon and McCartney, it was written by McCartney alone.*
on credit = **on account**, by instalments, on tick *(informal)*, on hire-purchase, on the slate *(informal)*, by deferred payment, on (the) H.P.: *They bought most of their furniture on credit.*

PROVERBS
credit where credit is due

creditable ADJECTIVE = **praiseworthy**, worthy, respectable, admirable, honourable, exemplary, reputable, commendable, laudable, meritorious, estimable

credulity NOUN = **gullibility**, naïveté *or* naivety, blind faith, credulousness

creed NOUN = **belief**, principles, profession *(of faith)*, doctrine, canon, persuasion, dogma, tenet, credo, catechism, articles of faith

creek NOUN 1 = **inlet**, bay, cove, bight, firth *or* frith *(Scot.)*: *The offshore fishermen took shelter from the storm in a creek.* 2 = **stream**, brook, tributary, bayou, rivulet, watercourse, streamlet, runnel: *Follow Austin Creek for a few miles.*

creep VERB 1 = **crawl**, worm, wriggle, squirm, slither, writhe, drag yourself, edge, inch, crawl on all fours: *The rabbit crept off and hid in a hole.* 2 = **sneak**, steal, tiptoe, slink, skulk, approach unnoticed: *I went back to the hotel and crept up to my room.*
▷ NOUN = **bootlicker** *(informal)*, sneak, sycophant, crawler *(slang)*, toady: *He's a smug, sanctimonious little creep.*
give someone the creeps = **disgust**, frighten, scare, repel, repulse, make your hair stand on end, make you squirm

creeper NOUN = **climbing plant**, runner, vine *(chiefly U.S.)*, climber, rambler, trailing plant

creepy ADJECTIVE = **disturbing**, threatening, frightening, terrifying, weird, forbidding, horrible, menacing, unpleasant, scary *(informal)*, sinister, ominous, eerie, macabre, nightmarish, hair-raising, awful

crescent NOUN = **meniscus**, sickle, new moon, half-moon, old moon, sickle-shape: *a flag with a white crescent on a red ground*

crest NOUN 1 = **top**, summit, peak, ridge, highest point, pinnacle, apex, head, crown, height: *He reached the crest of the hill.* 2 = **tuft**, crown, comb, plume, mane, tassel, topknot, cockscomb: *Both birds had a dark blue crest.* 3 = **emblem**, badge, symbol, insignia, charge, bearings, device: *On the wall is the family crest.*

crestfallen ADJECTIVE = **disappointed**, depressed, discouraged, dejected, despondent, downcast, disheartened, disconsolate, downhearted, sick as a parrot *(informal)*, choked
OPPOSITE: elated

crevice NOUN = **gap**, opening, hole, split, crack, rent, fracture, rift, slit, cleft, chink, fissure, cranny, interstice

crew NOUN 1 = **(ship's) company**, hands, (ship's) complement: *These vessels carry small crews of around twenty men.* 2 = **team**, company, party, squad, gang, corps, working party, posse: *a two-man film crew making a documentary* 3 = **crowd**, set, lot, bunch *(informal)*, band, troop, pack, camp, gang, mob, herd, swarm, company, horde, posse *(informal)*, assemblage: *a motley crew of college friends*

crib NOUN 1 = **cradle**, bed, cot, bassinet, Moses basket: *She placed the baby back in its crib.* 2 = **translation**, notes, key, trot *(U.S. slang)*: *Only desperate students take cribs into the exam with them.* 3 = **manger**, box, stall, rack, bunker: *He claimed the cribs in which the calves were kept had been approved by the RSPCA.*
▷ VERB = **copy**, cheat, pirate, pilfer, purloin, plagiarize, pass off as your own work: *He had been caught cribbing in an exam.*

crick NOUN = **spasm**, cramp, convulsion, twinge: *I've got a crick in my neck from looking up at the screen.*
▷ VERB = **rick**, jar, wrench: *I cricked my back from sitting in the same position for too long.*

C

crime NOUN **1 = offence**, job *(informal)*, wrong, fault, outrage, atrocity, violation, trespass, felony, misdemeanour, misdeed, transgression, unlawful act: *He has committed no crime and poses no danger to the public.* **2 = lawbreaking**, corruption, delinquency, illegality, wrong, vice, sin, guilt, misconduct, wrongdoing, wickedness, iniquity, villainy, unrighteousness, malefaction: *Much of the city's crime revolves around protection rackets.*

criminal NOUN **= lawbreaker**, convict, con *(slang)*, offender, crook *(informal)*, lag *(slang)*, villain, culprit, sinner, delinquent, felon, con man *(informal)*, rorter *(Austral. slang)*, jailbird, malefactor, evildoer, transgressor, skelm *(S. African)*, rogue trader, perp *(U.S. & Canad. informal)*: *He was put in a cell with several hardened criminals.*
▷ ADJECTIVE **1 = unlawful**, illicit, lawless, wrong, illegal, corrupt, crooked *(informal)*, vicious, immoral, wicked, culpable, under-the-table, villainous, nefarious, iniquitous, indictable, felonious, bent *(slang)*: *The entire party cannot be blamed for the criminal actions of a few members.*
OPPOSITE: lawful **2 = disgraceful**, ridiculous, foolish, senseless, scandalous, preposterous, deplorable: *This project is a criminal waste of time and resources.*

criminality NOUN **= illegality**, crime, corruption, delinquency, wrongdoing, lawlessness, wickedness, depravity, culpability, villainy, sinfulness, turpitude

cringe VERB **1 = shrink**, flinch, quail, recoil, start, shy, tremble, quiver, cower, draw back, blench: *I cringed in horror.* **2 = wince**, squirm, writhe: *The idea makes me cringe.*

crinkle NOUN **= crease**, wrinkle, crumple, ruffle, twist, fold, curl, rumple, pucker, crimp: *The fabric was smooth, without a crinkle.*

cripple VERB **1 = disable**, paralyse, lame, debilitate, mutilate, maim, incapacitate, enfeeble, weaken, hamstring: *He had been warned that another bad fall could cripple him for life.* **2 = damage**, destroy, ruin, bring to a standstill, halt, spoil, cramp, impair, put paid to, vitiate, put out of action: *A total cut-off of supplies would cripple the country's economy.* **OPPOSITE:** help

crippled ADJECTIVE **= disabled**, handicapped, challenged, paralysed, lame, deformed, incapacitated, bedridden, housebound, enfeebled

crisis NOUN **1 = emergency**, plight, catastrophe, predicament, pass, trouble, disaster, mess, dilemma, strait, deep water, meltdown *(informal)*, extremity, quandary, dire straits, exigency, critical situation: *Strikes worsened the country's economic crisis.* **2 = critical point**, climax, point of no return, height, confrontation, crunch *(informal)*, turning point, culmination, crux, moment of truth, climacteric, tipping point: *The anxiety that had been building within him reached a crisis.*

crisp ADJECTIVE **1 = firm**, crunchy, crispy, crumbly, fresh, brittle, unwilted: *Bake the potatoes till they're nice and crisp.* **OPPOSITE:** soft **2 = bracing**, fresh, refreshing, brisk, invigorating: *a crisp autumn day* **OPPOSITE:** warm **3 = clean**, smart, trim, neat, tidy, orderly, spruce, snappy, clean-cut, well-groomed, well-pressed: *He wore a panama hat and a crisp white suit.* **4 = brief**, clear, short, tart, incisive, terse, succinct, pithy, brusque: *In a clear, crisp voice, he began his speech.*

criterion NOUN **= standard**, test, rule, measure, principle, proof, par, norm, canon, gauge, yardstick, touchstone, bench mark

> **USAGE**
> The word *criteria* is the plural of *criterion* and it is incorrect to use it as an alternative singular form; *these criteria are not valid* is correct, and so is *this criterion is not valid*, but not *this criteria is not valid*.

critic NOUN **1 = judge**, authority, expert, analyst, commentator, pundit, reviewer, connoisseur, arbiter, expositor: *The New York critics had praised her performance.* **2 = fault-finder**, attacker, detractor, knocker *(informal)*: *He became a fierce critic of the tobacco industry.*

> **QUOTATIONS**
> It's not the critic who counts. Not the man who points out where the strong man stumbled or where the doer of great deeds could have done them better
> [Theodore Roosevelt]
>
> The proper function of the critic is to save the tale from the artist who created it
> [D.H. Lawrence]
>
> A critic is a man who knows the way but can't drive the car
> [Kenneth Tynan]
>
> critic: a person who boasts himself hard to please because nobody tries to please him
> [Ambrose Bierce *The Devil's Dictionary*]
>
> A critic is a bundle of biases held loosely together by a sense of taste
> [Whitney Balliet *Dinosaurs in the Morning*]

critical ADJECTIVE **1 = crucial**, decisive, momentous, deciding, pressing, serious, vital, psychological, urgent, all-important, pivotal, high-priority, now or never: *The incident happened at a critical point in the campaign.* **OPPOSITE:** unimportant **2 = grave**, serious, dangerous, acute, risky, hairy *(slang)*, precarious, perilous: *Ten of the injured are said to be in a critical condition.* **OPPOSITE:** safe **3 = disparaging**, disapproving, scathing, derogatory, nit-picking *(informal)*, censorious, cavilling, fault-finding, captious, carping, niggling, nit-picky *(informal)*: *He has apologized for critical remarks he made about the referee.* **OPPOSITE:** complimentary **4 = analytical**, penetrating, discriminating, discerning, diagnostic, perceptive, judicious, accurate, precise: *What is needed is a critical analysis of the evidence.* **OPPOSITE:** undiscriminating

criticism NOUN **1 = fault-finding**, censure, disapproval, disparagement, stick *(slang)*, knocking *(informal)*, panning *(informal)*, slamming *(slang)*, slating *(informal)*, flak *(informal)*, slagging *(slang)*, strictures, bad press, denigration, brickbats *(informal)*, character assassination, critical remarks, animadversion: *The policy had repeatedly come under strong criticism.* **2 = analysis**, review, notice, assessment, judgment, commentary, evaluation, appreciation, appraisal, critique, elucidation: *Her work includes novels, poetry and literary criticism.*

criticize VERB **= find fault with**, censure, disapprove of, knock *(informal)*, blast, pan *(informal)*, condemn, slam *(slang)*, carp, put down, slate *(informal)*, have a go (at) *(informal)*, disparage, tear into *(informal)*, diss *(slang, chiefly U.S.)*, nag at, lambast(e), pick holes in, pick to pieces, give (someone *or* something) a bad press, pass strictures upon, nit-pick *(informal)* **OPPOSITE:** praise

critique NOUN **= essay**, review, analysis, assessment, examination, commentary, appraisal, treatise

croak VERB **1 = grunt**, squawk, caw: *Frogs croaked in the reeds.* **2 = rasp**, gasp, grunt, wheeze, utter *or* speak harshly, utter *or* speak huskily, utter *or* speak throatily: *Daniel managed to croak, 'Help me.'* **3 = die**, expire, pass away, perish, buy it *(U.S. slang)*, check out *(U.S. slang)*, kick it *(slang)*, go belly-up *(slang)*, peg out *(informal)*, kick the bucket *(informal)*, buy the farm *(U.S. slang)*, peg it *(informal)*, cark it *(Austral. & N.Z. slang)*, pop your clogs *(informal)*, hop the twig *(informal)*: *The old man finally croaked at the age of 92.*

crone NOUN **= old woman**, witch, hag, old bag *(derogatory, slang)*, old bat *(slang)*, kuia *(N.Z.)*

crony NOUN **= friend**, china *(Brit. slang)*, colleague, associate, mate *(informal)*, pal *(informal)*, companion, cock *(Brit. informal)*, buddy *(informal)*, comrade, chum *(informal)*, accomplice, ally, sidekick *(slang)*, main man *(slang, chiefly U.S.)*, homeboy *(slang, chiefly U.S.)*, cobber *(Austral. & N.Z. old-fashioned, informal)*

crook NOUN **= criminal**, rogue, cheat, thief, shark, lag *(slang)*, villain, robber, racketeer, fraudster, swindler, knave *(archaic)*, grifter *(slang, chiefly U.S. & Canad.)*, chiseller *(informal)*, skelm *(S. African)*: *The man is a crook and a liar.*
▷ VERB **= bend**, hook, angle, bow,

The Language of Stephen Crane

The American novelist, short-story writer, and journalist Stephen Crane (1871–1900) was born in Newark, New Jersey, and packed an impressive variety of experience into his short life, He worked as a war correspondent in Greece and Cuba and after a shipwreck spent several days lost at sea in a small open boat. However, it is for his fiction, specifically his novel of the American Civil War, *The Red Badge of Courage* (1895), that he is best remembered. This highly popular novel was considered so true to life that much of the reading public felt that its author must really have served in the conflict.

His writing style is plain and direct, without great use of adjectives, as one might expect from a journalist, but he carries this style into his fiction too, which has often been described as naturalistic. In this he was somewhat ahead of his time, but later writers with similarly direct styles, such as Joseph Conrad and Ernest Hemingway, readily acknowledged their admiration of and debt to Crane.

This realism can be seen in his depiction of the speech of his characters, in which he tries to give a flavour of the actual everyday conversational American English of the times. For example, many colloquialisms are to be regularly found in his work, such as *yeh*, *git*, and *yer*, as well as *damn* being used as a curse word:

> 'I'll club hell outa **yeh** when I ketch **yeh**,' he shouted, and disappeared.

> 'Come on! We'll all **git** killed if we stay here.'

Being so much concerned with war, it is no surprise that Crane's writing abounds in nouns relating to this subject, such as *soldier*, *captain*, *regiment*, *battle*, *officer*, *sword*, *war*, *wound*, and *blood:*

> At times he regarded the wounded **soldiers** in an envious way. He conceived persons with torn bodies to be peculiarly happy. He wished that he, too, had a **wound**, a red badge of courage.

Crane's typical use of verbs also illustrates his major theme of warfare, with among his most common being *fight*, *run*, *fall*, and *kill*. As the title of his most famous novel shows, Crane was very much interested in what constitutes true bravery, what distinguishes a hero from a coward, and the effects of fear on the human spirit. The protagonist in *The Red Badge of Courage* is at heart no coward but, infected with the panic of his comrades, he runs away from the enemy. For Crane there was a fine line between courage and fear, and he makes it clear that a person may embody both emotions, either of which may become predominant at any time, without this meaning that the individual must be branded forever by the behaviour of a moment:

> Since he had turned his back upon the fight his fears had been wondrously magnified. Death about to thrust him between the shoulder blades was far more dreadful than death about to smite him between the eyes.

Dying of tuberculosis at the age of 28, Crane never lived to see the world through the eyes of middle age, let alone old age, and his writing essentially reflects a young man's view of life. His main characters are young and impressionable, and *youth*, *boy*, and *girl* appear regularly among his most frequently used nouns. Similarly, *young* is one of his predominant adjectives.

curve, curl, cock, flex: *He crooked his finger at her and said, 'Come here.'*
▷ ADJECTIVE **= ill**, sick, poorly (*informal*), funny (*informal*), weak, ailing, queer, frail, feeble, unhealthy, seedy (*informal*), sickly, unwell, laid up (*informal*), queasy, infirm, out of sorts (*informal*), dicky (*Brit. informal*), nauseous, off-colour, under the weather (*informal*), at death's door, indisposed, peaky, on the sick list (*informal*), green about the gills: *He admitted to feeling a bit crook.*
go (off) crook = lose your temper, be furious, rage, go mad, lose it (*informal*), seethe, crack up (*informal*), see red (*informal*), lose the plot (*informal*), go ballistic (*slang, chiefly U.S.*), blow a fuse (*slang, chiefly U.S.*), fly off the handle (*informal*), be incandescent, go off the deep end (*informal*), throw a fit (*informal*), wig out (*slang*), go up the wall (*slang*), blow your top, lose your rag (*slang*), be beside yourself, flip your lid (*slang*): *She went crook when I confessed.*

crooked ADJECTIVE **1 = bent**, twisted, bowed, curved, irregular, warped, deviating, out of shape, misshapen: *the crooked line of his broken nose* **OPPOSITE:** straight **2 = deformed**, crippled, distorted, disfigured: *Whole families went about with crooked legs or twisted shoulders.* **3 = at an angle**, angled, tilted, to one side, uneven, slanted, slanting, squint, awry, lopsided, askew, asymmetric, off-centre, skewwhiff (*Brit. informal*), unsymmetrical: *He gave her a crooked grin.* **4 = dishonest**, criminal, illegal, corrupt, dubious, questionable, unlawful, shady (*informal*), fraudulent, unscrupulous, under-the-table, bent (*slang*), shifty, deceitful, underhand, unprincipled, dishonourable, nefarious, knavish: *She might expose his crooked business deals to the authorities.* **OPPOSITE:** honest

croon VERB **1 = sing**, warble: *a nightclub singer who crooned romantic songs* **2 = say softly**, breathe, hum, purr: *The man was crooning soft words of encouragement to his wife.*

crop NOUN **= yield**, produce, gathering, fruits, harvest, vintage, reaping, season's growth: *a fine crop of apples*
▷ VERB **1 = harvest**, pick, collect, gather, bring in, reap, bring home, garner, mow: *I started cropping my beans in July.* **2 = graze**, eat, browse, feed on, nibble: *I let the horse drop his head to crop the grass.* **3 = cut**, reduce, trim, clip, dock, prune, shorten, shear, snip, pare, lop: *She cropped her hair and dyed it blonde.*
crop up = happen, appear, emerge, occur, arise, turn up, spring up: *As we get older health problems often crop up.*

cross VERB **1 = go across**, pass over, traverse, cut across, move across, travel across: *She was partly to blame for failing to look as she crossed the road.* **2 = span**, bridge, ford, go across, extend over: *A bridge crosses the river about half a mile outside the village.* **3 = intersect**, meet, intertwine, crisscross: *The two roads cross at this junction.* **4 = oppose**, interfere with, hinder, obstruct, deny, block, resist, frustrate, foil, thwart, impede: *He was not a man to cross.* **5 = interbreed**, mix, blend, cross-pollinate, crossbreed, hybridize, cross-fertilize, intercross: *These small flowers were later crossed with a white flowering species.*
▷ NOUN **1 = crucifix**: *She wore a cross on a silver chain.* **2 = trouble**, worry, trial, load, burden, grief, misery, woe, misfortune, affliction, tribulation: *My wife is much cleverer than I am; it is a cross I have to bear.* **3 = mixture**, combination, blend, amalgam, amalgamation: *The noise that came out was a cross between a laugh and a bark.* **4 = crossbreed**, hybrid: *a cross between a collie and a poodle*
▷ ADJECTIVE **= angry**, impatient, irritable, annoyed, put out, hacked (off) (*informal*), crusty, snappy, grumpy, vexed, sullen, surly, fractious, petulant, disagreeable, short, churlish, peeved (*informal*), ill-tempered, irascible, cantankerous, tetchy, ratty (*Brit. & N.Z. informal*), tooshie (*Austral. slang*), testy, fretful, waspish, in a bad mood, grouchy (*informal*), querulous, shirty (*slang, chiefly Brit.*), peevish, splenetic, crotchety (*informal*), snappish, ill-humoured, captious, pettish, out of humour, hoha (*N.Z.*): *Everyone was getting bored and cross.* **OPPOSITE:** good-humoured
cross something out *or* **off = strike off** *or* **out**, eliminate, cancel, delete, blue-pencil, score off *or* out: *He crossed her name off the list.*

cross-examine VERB **= question**, grill (*informal*), quiz, interrogate, catechize, pump

crotch NOUN **= groin**, lap, crutch

crouch VERB **= bend down**, kneel, squat, stoop, bow, duck, hunch

crow VERB **= gloat**, triumph, boast, swagger, brag, vaunt, bluster, exult, blow your own trumpet

crowd NOUN **1 = multitude**, mass, assembly, throng, company, press, army, host, pack, mob, flock, herd, swarm, horde, rabble, concourse, bevy: *It took some two hours before the crowd was fully dispersed.* **2 = group**, set, lot, circle, gang, bunch (*informal*), clique: *All the old crowd from my university days were there.* **3 = audience**, spectators, house, gate, attendance: *When the song finished, the crowd went wild.*
▷ VERB **1 = flock**, press, push, mass, collect, gather, stream, surge, cluster, muster, huddle, swarm, throng, congregate, foregather: *The hungry refugees crowded around the lorries.* **2 = squeeze**, pack, pile, bundle, cram: *A group of journalists were crowded into a minibus; Hundreds of people crowded into the building.* **3 = congest**, pack, cram: *Demonstrators crowded the streets shouting slogans.* **4 = jostle**, batter, butt, push, elbow, shove: *It had been a tense, restless day with people crowding her all the time.*
the crowd = the masses, the people, the public, the mob, the rank and file, the populace, the rabble, the proletariat, the hoi polloi, the riffraff, the vulgar herd: *You can learn to stand out from the crowd.*

crowded ADJECTIVE **= packed**, full, busy, mobbed, cramped, swarming, overflowing, thronged, teeming, congested, populous, jam-packed, crushed

crown NOUN **1 = coronet**, tiara, diadem, circlet, coronal (*poetic*), chaplet: *a beautiful woman wearing a golden crown* **2 = laurel wreath**, trophy, distinction, prize, honour, garland, laurels, wreath, kudos: *He won the middleweight crown in 1947.* **3 = high point**, head, top, tip, summit, crest, pinnacle, apex: *We stood on the crown of the hill.*
▷ VERB **1 = install**, invest, honour, dignify, ordain, inaugurate: *He had himself crowned as Emperor.* **2 = top**, cap, be on top of, surmount: *A rugged castle crowns the cliffs.* **3 = cap**, finish, complete, perfect, fulfil, consummate, round off, put the finishing touch to, put the tin lid on, be the climax *or* culmination of: *The summit was crowned by the signing of the historical treaty.* **4 = strike**, belt (*informal*), bash, hit over the head, box, punch, cuff, biff (*slang*), wallop: *I felt like crowning him with the frying pan.*
the Crown 1 = monarch, ruler, sovereign, rex *or* regina (*Latin*), emperor *or* empress, king *or* queen: *loyal subjects of the Crown* **2 = monarchy**, sovereignty, royalty: *All treasure trove is the property of the Crown.*

crucial ADJECTIVE **1 = vital**, important, pressing, essential, urgent, momentous, high-priority: *the most crucial election campaign in years* **2 = critical**, central, key, psychological, decisive, pivotal, now or never: *At the crucial moment, his nerve failed.*

crucify VERB **1 = execute**, put to death, nail to a cross: *the day that Christ was crucified* **2 = pan** (*informal*), rubbish (*informal*), ridicule, slag (off) (*slang*), lampoon, wipe the floor with (*informal*), tear to pieces: *She was crucified by the critics for her performance.* **3 = torture**, rack, torment, harrow: *He had been crucified by guilt ever since his child's death.*

crude ADJECTIVE **1 = rough**, undeveloped, basic, outline, unfinished, makeshift, sketchy, unformed: *a crude way of assessing the risk of heart disease* **2 = simple**, rudimentary, basic, primitive, coarse, clumsy, rough-and-ready, rough-hewn: *crude wooden carvings* **3 = vulgar**, dirty, rude, obscene, coarse, indecent, crass, tasteless, lewd, X-rated (*informal*), boorish, smutty, uncouth, gross: *a crude sense of humour*

OPPOSITE: tasteful **4 = unrefined**, natural, raw, unprocessed, unpolished, unprepared: *8.5 million tonnes of crude steel* **OPPOSITE:** processed

crudely ADVERB **1 = roughly**, basically, sketchily: *The donors can be split – a little crudely – into two groups.* **2 = simply**, roughly, basically, coarsely, clumsily: *a crudely carved wooden form* **3 = vulgarly**, rudely, coarsely, crassly, indecently, obscenely, lewdly, impolitely, tastelessly: *and yet she spoke so crudely*

cruel ADJECTIVE **1 = brutal**, ruthless, callous, sadistic, inhumane, hard, fell *(archaic)*, severe, harsh, savage, grim, vicious, relentless, murderous, monstrous, unnatural, unkind, heartless, atrocious, inhuman, merciless, cold-blooded, malevolent, hellish, depraved, spiteful, brutish, bloodthirsty, remorseless, barbarous, pitiless, unfeeling, hard-hearted, stony-hearted: *the cruel practice of bullfighting; the persecution of prisoners by cruel officers* **OPPOSITE:** kind **2 = bitter**, severe, painful, ruthless, traumatic, grievous, unrelenting, merciless, pitiless: *Fate dealt him a cruel blow.*

> **QUOTATIONS**
> I must be cruel, only to be kind
> [William Shakespeare *Hamlet*]

cruelly ADVERB **1 = brutally**, severely, savagely, viciously, mercilessly, in cold blood, callously, monstrously, unmercifully, sadistically, pitilessly, spitefully, heartlessly, barbarously: *Douglas was often treated cruelly by his fellow-pupils.* **2 = bitterly**, deeply, severely, mortally, painfully, ruthlessly, mercilessly, grievously, pitilessly, traumatically: *His life has been cruelly shattered by an event not of his own making.*

cruelty NOUN **= brutality**, spite, severity, savagery, ruthlessness, sadism, depravity, harshness, inhumanity, barbarity, callousness, viciousness, bestiality, heartlessness, spitefulness, bloodthirstiness, mercilessness, fiendishness, hardheartedness

cruise NOUN **= sail**, voyage, boat trip, sea trip: *He and his wife were planning to go on a world cruise.*
▷ VERB **1 = sail**, coast, voyage: *She wants to cruise the canals of France in a barge.* **2 = travel along**, coast, drift, keep a steady pace: *A black and white police car cruised past.*

crumb NOUN **1 = bit**, grain, particle, fragment, shred, speck, sliver, morsel: *I stood up, brushing crumbs from my trousers.* **2 = morsel**, scrap, atom, shred, mite, snippet, sliver, soupçon *(French)*: *There is one crumb of comfort – at least we've still got each other.*

crumble VERB **1 = disintegrate**, collapse, break up, deteriorate, decay, fall apart, perish, degenerate, decompose, tumble down, moulder, go to pieces: *Under the pressure, the flint crumbled into fragments; The chalk cliffs are crumbling.* **2 = crush**, fragment, crumb, pulverize, pound, grind, powder, granulate: *Roughly crumble the cheese into a bowl.* **3 = collapse**, break down, deteriorate, decay, fall apart, degenerate, go to pieces, go to rack and ruin: *Their economy crumbled under the weight of United Nations sanctions.*

crummy ADJECTIVE **= second-rate**, cheap, inferior, substandard, poor, pants *(informal)*, miserable, rotten *(informal)*, duff *(Brit. informal)*, lousy *(slang)*, shoddy, trashy, low-rent *(informal, chiefly U.S.)*, for the birds *(informal)*, third-rate, contemptible, two-bit *(U.S. & Canad. slang)*, crappy *(slang)*, rubbishy, poxy *(slang)*, dime-a-dozen *(informal)*, bodger or bodgie *(Austral. slang)*, bush-league *(Austral. & N.Z. informal)*, tinhorn *(U.S. slang)*, of a sort or of sorts, strictly for the birds *(informal)*

crumple VERB **1 = crush**, squash, screw up, scrumple: *She crumpled the paper in her hand.* **2 = crease**, wrinkle, rumple, ruffle, pucker: *She sat down carefully, so as not to crumple her skirt.* **3 = collapse**, sink, go down, fall: *He crumpled to the floor in agony.* **4 = break down**, fall, collapse, give way, cave in, go to pieces: *Sometimes we just crumpled under our grief.* **5 = screw up**, pucker: *She faltered, and then her face crumpled once more.*

crunch VERB **= chomp**, champ, munch, masticate, chew noisily, grind
the crunch = critical point, test, crisis, emergency, crux, moment of truth, hour of decision: *He can rely on my support when the crunch comes.*

crusade NOUN **1 = campaign**, drive, movement, cause, push: *a crusade against racism on the football terraces* **2 = holy war**, jihad: *He was leading a religious crusade that did not respect national boundaries.*
▷ VERB **= campaign**, fight, push, struggle, lobby, agitate, work: *a newspaper that has crusaded against drug traffickers*

crusader NOUN **= campaigner**, champion, advocate, activist, reformer

crush VERB **1 = squash**, pound, break, smash, squeeze, crumble, crunch, mash, compress, press, crumple, pulverize: *Their vehicle was crushed by an army tank.* **2 = crease**, wrinkle, crumple, rumple, scrumple, ruffle: *I don't want to crush my skirt.* **3 = overcome**, overwhelm, put down, subdue, overpower, quash, quell, extinguish, stamp out, vanquish, conquer: *The military operation was the first step in a plan to crush the uprising.* **4 = demoralize**, depress, devastate, discourage, humble, put down *(slang)*, humiliate, squash, flatten, deflate, mortify, psych out *(informal)*, dishearten, dispirit, deject: *Listen to criticism but don't be crushed by it.* **5 = squeeze**, press, embrace, hug, enfold: *He crushed her in his arms.*
▷ NOUN **= crowd**, mob, horde, throng, press, pack, mass, jam, herd, huddle, swarm, multitude, rabble: *They got separated from each other in the crush.*

crust NOUN **= layer**, covering, coating, incrustation, film, outside, skin, surface, shell, coat, caking, scab, concretion

crusty ADJECTIVE **1 = crispy**, well-baked, crisp, well-done, brittle, friable, hard, short: *crusty french loaves* **2 = irritable**, short, cross, prickly, touchy, curt, surly, gruff, brusque, cantankerous, tetchy, ratty *(Brit. & N.Z. informal)*, testy, chippy *(informal)*, short-tempered, peevish, crabby, choleric, splenetic, ill-humoured, captious, snappish or snappy: *a crusty old colonel with a gruff manner*

crux NOUN **= crucial point**, heart, core, essence, nub, decisive point

cry VERB **1 = weep**, sob, bawl, shed tears, keen, greet *(Scot. archaic)*, wail, whine, whimper, whinge *(informal)*, blubber, snivel, yowl, howl your eyes out: *I hung up the phone and started to cry.* **OPPOSITE:** laugh **2 = shout**, call, scream, roar, hail, yell, howl, call out, exclaim, shriek, bellow, whoop, screech, bawl, holler *(informal)*, ejaculate, sing out, halloo, vociferate: *'You're under arrest!' he cried.* **OPPOSITE:** whisper **3 = announce**, hawk, advertise, proclaim, bark *(informal)*, trumpet, shout from the rooftops *(informal)*: *In the street below, a peddler was crying his wares.*
▷ NOUN **1 = weep**, greet *(Scot. archaic)*, sob, howl, bawl, blubber, snivel: *Have a good cry if you want to.* **2 = shout**, call, scream, roar, yell, howl, shriek, bellow, whoop, screech, hoot, ejaculation, bawl, holler *(informal)*, exclamation, squawk, yelp, yoo-hoo: *Her brother gave a cry of recognition.* **3 = weeping**, sobbing, blubbering, snivelling
cry off = back out, withdraw, quit, cop out *(slang)*, beg off, excuse yourself: *She caught flu and had to cry off at the last minute.*

crypt NOUN **= vault**, tomb, catacomb

cryptic ADJECTIVE **= mysterious**, dark, coded, puzzling, obscure, vague, veiled, ambiguous, enigmatic, perplexing, arcane, equivocal, abstruse, Delphic, oracular

crystallize VERB **= harden**, solidify, coalesce, form crystals: *Keep stirring the mixture or the sugar will crystallize.*

cub NOUN **= young**, baby, offspring, whelp

cuddle VERB **1 = hug**, embrace, clasp, fondle, cosset: *He cuddled their newborn baby.* **2 = pet**, hug, canoodle *(slang)*, bill and coo: *They used to kiss and cuddle in front of everyone.*
cuddle up = snuggle, nestle: *My cat cuddled up to me.*

cuddly ADJECTIVE **= soft**, plump, buxom, curvaceous, warm

cue NOUN **= signal**, sign, nod, hint, prompt, reminder, suggestion

C

C

cuff[1] NOUN
off the cuff 1 = **impromptu**, spontaneous, improvised, offhand, unrehearsed, extempore: *I didn't mean any offence. It was just an off-the-cuff remark.* 2 = **without preparation**, spontaneously, impromptu, offhand, on the spur of the moment, ad lib, extempore, off the top of your head: *He was speaking off the cuff when he made this suggestion.*

cuff[2] NOUN = **smack**, blow, knock, punch, thump, box, belt *(informal)*, rap, slap, clout *(informal)*, whack, biff *(slang)*: *He gave the dog a cuff.*

cul-de-sac NOUN = **dead end**, blind alley

cull VERB = **select**, collect, gather, amass, choose, pick, pick up, pluck, glean, cherry-pick

culminate VERB = **end up**, end, close, finish, conclude, wind up, climax, terminate, come to a head, come to a climax, rise to a crescendo

culmination NOUN = **climax**, conclusion, completion, finale, consummation

culpability NOUN = **fault**, blame, responsibility, liability, accountability

culpable ADJECTIVE = **blameworthy**, wrong, guilty, to blame, liable, in the wrong, at fault, sinful, answerable, found wanting, reprehensible
OPPOSITE: blameless

culprit NOUN = **offender**, criminal, villain, sinner, delinquent, felon, person responsible, guilty party, wrongdoer, miscreant, evildoer, transgressor, perp *(U.S. & Canad. informal)*

cult NOUN 1 = **sect**, following, body, faction, party, school, church, faith, religion, denomination, clique, hauhau *(N.Z.)*: *The teenager may have been abducted by a religious cult.* 2 = **craze**, fashion, trend, fad: *The programme has become something of a cult among thirty-somethings.* 3 = **obsession**, worship, admiration, devotion, reverence, veneration, idolization: *The cult of personality surrounding pop stars leaves me cold.*

cultivate VERB 1 = **farm**, work, plant, tend, till, harvest, plough, bring under cultivation: *She cultivated a small garden of her own.* 2 = **develop**, establish, acquire, foster, devote yourself to, pursue: *Try to cultivate a positive mental attitude.* 3 = **court**, associate with, seek out, run after, consort with, butter up, dance attendance upon, seek someone's company or friendship, take trouble or pains with: *He only cultivates people who may be of use to him.* 4 = **foster**, further, forward, encourage: *She went out of her way to cultivate his friendship.*
5 = **improve**, better, train, discipline, polish, refine, elevate, enrich, civilize: *My father encouraged me to cultivate my mind.*

cultivated ADJECTIVE = **refined**, cultured, advanced, polished, educated, sophisticated, accomplished, discriminating, enlightened, discerning, civilized, genteel, well-educated, urbane, erudite, well-bred

cultivation NOUN 1 = **farming**, working, gardening, tilling, ploughing, husbandry, agronomy: *environments where aridity makes cultivation of the land difficult* 2 = **growing**, planting, production, farming: *groups that want a ban on the cultivation of GM crops* 3 = **development**, fostering, pursuit, devotion to: *the cultivation of a positive approach to life and health*
4 = **promotion**, support, encouragement, nurture, patronage, advancement, advocacy, enhancement, furtherance: *those who devote themselves to the cultivation of the arts* 5 = **refinement**, letters, learning, education, culture, taste, breeding, manners, polish, discrimination, civilization, enlightenment, sophistication, good taste, civility, gentility, discernment: *He was a man of cultivation and scholarship.*

cultural ADJECTIVE 1 = **ethnic**, national, native, folk, racial: *a deep sense of honour which was part of his cultural heritage*
2 = **artistic**, educational, elevating, aesthetic, enriching, broadening, enlightening, developmental, civilizing, edifying, educative: *This holiday was a rich cultural experience.*

culture NOUN 1 = **the arts**: *France's Minister of Culture and Education*
2 = **civilization**, society, customs, way of life: *people of different cultures*
3 = **lifestyle**, habit, way of life, mores: *Social workers say this has created a culture of dependency.* 4 = **refinement**, education, breeding, polish, enlightenment, accomplishment, sophistication, good taste, erudition, gentility, urbanity: *He was a well-travelled man of culture and breeding.*

cultured ADJECTIVE = **refined**, advanced, polished, intellectual, educated, sophisticated, accomplished, scholarly, enlightened, knowledgeable, well-informed, genteel, urbane, erudite, highbrow, well-bred, well-read OPPOSITE: uneducated

culvert NOUN = **drain**, channel, gutter, conduit, watercourse

cumbersome ADJECTIVE
1 = **awkward**, heavy, hefty *(informal)*, clumsy, bulky, weighty, impractical, inconvenient, burdensome, unmanageable, clunky *(informal)*: *Although the machine looks cumbersome, it is easy to use.* OPPOSITE: easy to use
2 = **inefficient**, unwieldy, badly organized: *an old and cumbersome computer system* OPPOSITE: efficient

cumulative ADJECTIVE = **collective**, increasing, aggregate, amassed, accruing, snowballing, accumulative

cunning ADJECTIVE 1 = **crafty**, sly, devious, artful, sharp, subtle, tricky, shrewd, astute, canny, wily, Machiavellian, shifty, foxy, guileful: *He's a cunning, devious, good-for-nothing so-and-so.* OPPOSITE: frank
2 = **ingenious**, subtle, imaginative, shrewd, sly, astute, devious, artful, Machiavellian: *I came up with a cunning plan.* 3 = **skilful**, clever, deft, adroit, dexterous: *The artist's cunning use of light and shadow creates perspective.*
OPPOSITE: clumsy
▷ NOUN 1 = **craftiness**, guile, trickery, shrewdness, deviousness, artfulness, slyness, wiliness: *an example of the cunning of modern art thieves*
OPPOSITE: candour 2 = **skill**, art, ability, craft, subtlety, ingenuity, finesse, artifice, dexterity, cleverness, deftness, astuteness, adroitness: *He tackled the problem with skill and cunning.*
OPPOSITE: clumsiness

> QUOTATIONS
> Cunning is the dark sanctuary of incapacity
> [Lord Chesterfield *Letters...to his Godson and Successor*]

cup NOUN 1 = **mug**, goblet, chalice, teacup, beaker, demitasse, bowl: *a set of matching cups and saucers* 2 = **trophy**: *First prize is a silver cup and a scroll.*

cupboard NOUN = **cabinet**, closet, locker, press

curative ADJECTIVE = **restorative**, healing, therapeutic, tonic, corrective, medicinal, remedial, salutary, healthful, health-giving

curb VERB = **restrain**, control, check, contain, restrict, moderate, suppress, inhibit, subdue, hinder, repress, constrain, retard, impede, stem the flow of, keep a tight rein on: *He must learn to curb that temper of his.*
▷ NOUN = **restraint**, control, check, brake, limitation, rein, deterrent, bridle: *He called for much stricter curbs on immigration.*

curdle VERB = **congeal**, clot, thicken, condense, turn sour, solidify, coagulate OPPOSITE: dissolve

cure VERB 1 = **make better**, correct, heal, relieve, remedy, mend, rehabilitate, help, ease: *An operation finally cured his shin injury.* 2 = **restore to health**, restore, heal: *I was cured almost overnight.* 3 = **preserve**, smoke, dry, salt, pickle, kipper: *Legs of pork were cured and smoked over the fire.*
▷ NOUN = **remedy**, treatment, medicine, healing, antidote, corrective, panacea, restorative, nostrum: *There is still no cure for the common cold.*

> QUOTATIONS
> It is part of the cure to wish to be cured
> [Seneca *Phaedra*]
> The cure is worse than the disease
> [Philip Massinger *The Bondman*]

cure-all NOUN = **panacea**, elixir, nostrum, elixir vitae *(Latin)*

curio NOUN **= collector's item**, antique, trinket, knick-knack, bibelot

curiosity NOUN **1 = inquisitiveness**, interest, prying, snooping *(informal)*, nosiness *(informal)*, infomania: *Mr Lim was a constant source of curiosity to his neighbours.* **2 = oddity**, wonder, sight, phenomenon, spectacle, freak, marvel, novelty, rarity: *The company is a curiosity in the world of publishing.* **3 = collector's item**, trinket, curio, knick-knack, objet d'art *(French)*, bibelot: *The mantelpieces and windowsills are adorned with curiosities.*

PROVERBS
Curiosity killed the cat

curious ADJECTIVE **1 = inquisitive**, interested, questioning, searching, inquiring, peering, puzzled, peeping, meddling, prying, snoopy *(informal)*, nosy *(informal)*: *He was intensely curious about the world around him.* **OPPOSITE:** uninterested **2 = strange**, unusual, bizarre, odd, novel, wonderful, rare, unique, extraordinary, puzzling, unexpected, exotic, mysterious, marvellous, peculiar, queer *(informal)*, rum *(Brit. slang)*, singular, unconventional, quaint, unorthodox: *A lot of curious things have happened here in the past few weeks.* **OPPOSITE:** ordinary

curl NOUN **1 = ringlet**, lock: *a little girl with blonde curls* **2 = twist**, spiral, coil, kink, whorl, curlicue: *A thick curl of smoke rose from the rusty stove.*
▷ VERB **1 = crimp**, wave, perm, frizz: *She had curled her hair for the event.* **2 = twirl**, turn, bend, twist, curve, loop, spiral, coil, meander, writhe, corkscrew, wreathe: *Smoke was curling up the chimney.* **3 = wind**, entwine, twine: *She curled her fingers round his wrist.*

curly ADJECTIVE **= wavy**, waved, curled, curling, fuzzy, kinky, permed, corkscrew, crimped, frizzy

currency NOUN **1 = money**, coinage, legal tender, medium of exchange, bills, notes, coins: *More people favour a single European currency than oppose it.* **2 = acceptance**, exposure, popularity, circulation, vogue, prevalence: *His theory has gained wide currency in America.*

current NOUN **1 = flow**, course, undertow, jet, stream, tide, progression, river, tideway: *The swimmers were swept away by the strong current.* **2 = draught**, flow, breeze, puff: *I felt a current of cool air blowing in my face.* **3 = mood**, feeling, spirit, atmosphere, trend, tendency, drift, inclination, vibe *(slang)*, undercurrent: *A strong current of nationalism is running through the country.*
▷ ADJECTIVE **1 = present**, fashionable, ongoing, up-to-date, in, now *(informal)*, happening *(informal)*, contemporary, in the news, sexy *(informal)*, trendy *(Brit. informal)*, topical, present-day, in fashion, in vogue, up-to-the-minute: *current trends in the music scene* **OPPOSITE:** out-of-date **2 = prevalent**, general, common, accepted, popular, widespread, in the air, prevailing, circulating, going around, customary, rife, in circulation: *the prevailing tide of current opinion*

curse VERB **1 = swear**, cuss *(informal)*, blaspheme, use bad language, turn the air blue *(informal)*, be foul-mouthed, take the Lord's name in vain: *He was obviously very drunk and cursed continuously at passers-by.* **2 = abuse**, damn, scold, swear at, revile, vilify, fulminate, execrate, vituperate, imprecate: *He cursed her for having been so careless.* **3 = put a curse on**, damn, doom, jinx, excommunicate, execrate, put a jinx on, accurse, imprecate, anathematize: *I began to think that I was cursed.* **4 = afflict**, trouble, burden: *He's always been cursed with a bad memory.*
▷ NOUN **1 = oath**, obscenity, blasphemy, expletive, profanity, imprecation, swearword: *He shot her an angry look and a curse.* **2 = malediction**, jinx, anathema, hoodoo *(informal)*, evil eye, excommunication, imprecation, execration: *He believes someone has put a curse on him.* **3 = affliction**, evil, plague, scourge, cross, trouble, disaster, burden, ordeal, torment, hardship, misfortune, calamity, tribulation, bane, vexation: *The curse of alcoholism is a huge problem in Britain.*

QUOTATIONS
A plague o' both your houses
[William Shakespeare *Romeo and Juliet*]

How comes it that you curse, Frère Jean? It's only, said the monk, in order to embellish my language
[François Rabelais *Gargantua*]

[Cursing] is an operation which in literature, particularly in the drama, is commonly fatal to the victim. Nevertheless, the liability to a cursing is a risk that cuts but a small figure in fixing the rates of life insurance
[Ambrose Bierce *The Devil's Dictionary*]

PROVERBS
Curses, like chickens, come home to roost

cursed ADJECTIVE **= under a curse**, damned, doomed, jinxed, bedevilled, fey *(Scot.)*, star-crossed, accursed, ill-fated

cursory ADJECTIVE **= brief**, passing, rapid, casual, summary, slight, hurried, careless, superficial, hasty, perfunctory, desultory, offhand, slapdash

curt ADJECTIVE **= terse**, short, brief, sharp, summary, blunt, rude, tart, abrupt, gruff, brusque, offhand, ungracious, uncivil, unceremonious, snappish

curtail VERB **= reduce**, cut, diminish, decrease, dock, cut back, shorten, lessen, cut short, pare down, retrench

curtain NOUN **= hanging**, drape *(chiefly U.S.)*, portière: *Her bedroom curtains were drawn.*

curtain something off = conceal, screen, hide, veil, drape, shroud, shut off: *The bed was a massive four-poster, curtained off by ragged draperies.*

curvaceous ADJECTIVE **= shapely**, voluptuous, curvy, busty, well-rounded, buxom, full-figures, bosomy, well-stacked *(Brit. slang)*, Rubenesque

curvature NOUN **= curving**, bend, curve, arching, arc

curve NOUN **= bend**, turn, loop, arc, curvature, camber: *a curve in the road*
▷ VERB **= bend**, turn, wind, twist, bow, arch, snake, arc, coil, swerve: *The track curved away below him.*
▸ *related adjective:* sinuous

curved ADJECTIVE **= bent**, rounded, sweeping, twisted, bowed, arched, arced, humped, serpentine, sinuous, twisty

cushion NOUN **= pillow**, pad, bolster, headrest, beanbag, scatter cushion, hassock: *Her leg was propped up on two cushions.*
▷ VERB **1 = protect**, support, bolster, cradle, buttress: *The suspension is designed to cushion passengers from the effects of riding over rough roads.* **2 = soften**, dampen, muffle, mitigate, deaden, suppress, stifle: *He spoke gently, trying to cushion the blow of rejection.*

cushy ADJECTIVE **= easy**, soft, comfortable, undemanding, jammy *(Brit. slang)*

custodian NOUN **= keeper**, guardian, superintendent, warden, caretaker, curator, protector, warder, watchman, overseer

custody NOUN **1 = care**, charge, protection, supervision, preservation, auspices, aegis, tutelage, guardianship, safekeeping, keeping, trusteeship, custodianship: *I'm taking him to court to get custody of the children.* **2 = imprisonment**, detention, confinement, incarceration: *Three people appeared in court and two of them were remanded in custody.*

custom NOUN **1 = tradition**, practice, convention, ritual, form, policy, rule, style, fashion, usage, formality, etiquette, observance, praxis, unwritten law, kaupapa *(N.Z.)*: *The custom of lighting the Olympic flame goes back centuries.* **2 = habit**, way, practice, manner, procedure, routine, mode, wont: *It was his custom to approach every problem cautiously.* **3 = customers**, business, trade, patronage: *Providing discounts is not the only way to win custom.*

QUOTATIONS
Custom reconciles us to everything
[Edmund Burke *The Origin of our Ideas of the Sublime and Beautiful*]

a custom
More honoured in the breach than the observance
[William Shakespeare *Hamlet*]

customarily ADVERB **= usually**, generally, commonly, regularly, normally, traditionally, ordinarily, habitually, in the ordinary way, as a rule

customary ADJECTIVE **1 = usual**, general, common, accepted, established, traditional, normal, ordinary, familiar, acknowledged, conventional, routine, everyday: *It is customary to offer a drink or a snack to guests.* **OPPOSITE:** unusual **2 = accustomed**, regular, usual, habitual, wonted: *She took her customary seat behind her desk.*

customer NOUN **= client**, consumer, regular *(informal)*, buyer, patron, shopper, purchaser, habitué

customs PLURAL NOUN **= import charges**, tax, duty, toll, tariff

cut VERB **1 = slit**, saw, score, nick, slice, slash, pierce, hack, penetrate, notch: *Thieves cut a hole in the fence; You can hear the saw as it cuts through the bone.* **2 = chop**, split, divide, slice, segment, dissect, cleave, part: *Cut the tomatoes into small pieces.* **3 = carve**, slice: *Mr Long was cutting himself a piece of the cake.* **4 = sever**, cut in two, sunder: *I cut the rope with scissors.* **5 = shape**, carve, engrave, chisel, form, score, fashion, chip, sculpture, whittle, sculpt, inscribe, hew: *Geometric motifs are cut into the stone walls.* **6 = slash**, nick, wound, lance, gash, lacerate, incise: *I cut myself shaving.* **7 = clip**, mow, trim, dock, prune, snip, pare, lop: *The previous tenants hadn't even cut the grass.* **8 = trim**, shave, hack, snip: *She cut his ragged hair and shaved off his beard.* **9 = reduce**, lower, slim (down), diminish, slash, decrease, cut back, rationalize, ease up on, downsize, kennet *(Austral. slang)*, jeff *(Austral. slang)*: *The first priority is to cut costs.* **OPPOSITE:** increase **10 = abridge**, edit, shorten, curtail, condense, abbreviate, précis: *He has cut the play judiciously.* **OPPOSITE:** extend **11 = delete**, take out, expurgate **12 = hurt**, wound, upset, sting, grieve, pain, hurt someone's feelings: *The personal criticism has cut him deeply.* **13 = ignore**, avoid, slight, blank *(slang)*, snub, spurn, freeze (someone) out *(informal)*, cold-shoulder, turn your back on, send to Coventry, look straight through (someone): *She just cut me in the street.* **OPPOSITE:** greet **14 = cross**, interrupt, intersect, bisect: *a straight line that cuts the vertical axis*

▷ NOUN **1 = incision**, nick, rent, stroke, rip, slash, groove, slit, snip: *The operation involves making several cuts in the cornea.* **2 = gash**, nick, wound, slash, graze, laceration: *He had sustained a cut on his left eyebrow.* **3 = reduction**, fall, lowering, slash, decrease, cutback, diminution: *The economy needs an immediate 2 per cent cut in interest rates.* **4 = share**, piece, slice, percentage, portion, kickback *(chiefly U.S.)*, rake-off *(slang)*: *The lawyers, of course, will take their cut of the profits.* **5 = style**, look, form, fashion, shape, mode, configuration: *The cut of her clothes made her look slimmer and taller.*

a cut above something *or* **someone = superior to**, better than, more efficient than, more reliable than, streets ahead of, more useful than, more capable than, more competent than: *He's a cut above the usual boys she goes out with.*

be cut out for something = be suited for, be designed for, be fitted for, be suitable for, be adapted for, be equipped for, be adequate for, be eligible for, be competent for, be qualified for: *She wasn't cut out for motherhood.*

cut in = interrupt, break in, butt in, interpose: *'That's not true,' the duchess cut in suddenly.*

cut someone down to size = make (someone) look small, humble, humiliate, bring (someone) low, take (someone) down a peg *(informal)*, abash, crush, put (someone) in their place, take the wind out of (someone's) sails: *It's high time someone cut that arrogant little creep down to size.*

cut someone off 1 = separate, isolate, sever, keep apart: *The exiles had been cut off from all contact with their homeland.* **2 = interrupt**, stop, break in, butt in, interpose: *'But sir, I'm under orders to -' Clark cut him off. 'Don't argue with me.'* **3 = disinherit**, renounce, disown: *His father cut him off without a penny.*

cut someone out = exclude, eliminate, oust, displace, supersede, supplant: *He felt that he was being cut out of the decision-making process completely.*

cut someone up = slash, injure, wound, knife, lacerate: *They cut him up with a razor.*

cut something back 1 = reduce, check, lower, slash, decrease, curb, lessen, economize, downsize, retrench, draw *or* pull in your horns *(informal)*, kennet *(Austral. slang)*, jeff *(Austral. slang)*: *The government has cut back on defence spending.* **2 = trim**, prune, shorten: *Cut back the root of the bulb to within half an inch of the base.*

cut something down 1 = reduce, moderate, decrease, lessen, lower: *Car owners were asked to cut down their travel.* **2 = fell**, level, hew, lop: *A vandal with a chainsaw cut down several trees in the park.*

cut something off = discontinue, disconnect, suspend, halt, obstruct, bring to an end: *The rebels have cut off the electricity supply from the capital.*

cut something out 1 = remove, extract, censor, delete, edit out: *All the violent scenes had been cut out of the film.* **2 = stop**, cease, refrain from, pack in, kick *(informal)*, give up, sever: *You can cut that behaviour out right now.*

be cut up = be upset, be disturbed, be distressed, be stricken, be agitated, be heartbroken, be desolated, be dejected, be wretched: *Terry was very cut up by Jim's death.*

cut something up = chop, divide, slice, carve, dice, mince: *Cut the sausages up and cook them over a medium heat.*

cutback NOUN **= reduction**, cut, retrenchment, economy, decrease, lessening

cute ADJECTIVE **= appealing**, sweet, attractive, engaging, charming, delightful, lovable, winsome, winning, cutesy *(informal, chiefly U.S.)*

cut-price ADJECTIVE **= cheap**, sale, reduced, bargain, cut-rate *(chiefly U.S.)*, cheapo *(informal)*

cut-throat ADJECTIVE **1 = competitive**, fierce, ruthless, relentless, unprincipled, dog-eat-dog: *the cut-throat world of international finance* **2 = murderous**, violent, bloody, cruel, savage, ferocious, bloodthirsty, barbarous, homicidal, thuggish, death-dealing: *Captain Hook and his band of cut-throat pirates*

cutting ADJECTIVE **1 = hurtful**, wounding, severe, acid, bitter, malicious, scathing, acrimonious, barbed, sarcastic, sardonic, caustic, vitriolic, trenchant, pointed: *People make cutting remarks to help themselves feel superior to others.* **OPPOSITE:** kind **2 = piercing**, biting, sharp, keen, bitter, raw, chilling, stinging, penetrating, numbing: *a cutting wind* **OPPOSITE:** pleasant

cycle NOUN **= series of events**, round *(of years)*, circle, revolution, rotation

cyclone NOUN **= typhoon**, hurricane, tornado, whirlwind, tempest, twister *(U.S. informal)*, storm

cynic NOUN **= sceptic**, doubter, pessimist, misanthrope, misanthropist, scoffer

> **QUOTATIONS**
>
> A cynic is a man who knows the price of everything and the value of nothing
> [Oscar Wilde *Lady Windermere's Fan*]
>
> The cynic is one who never sees a good quality in a man, and never fails to see a bad one
> [H.W. Beecher *Proverbs from Plymouth Pulpit*]
>
> cynic: a blackguard whose faulty vision sees things as they are, not as they ought to be
> [Ambrose Bierce *The Devil's Dictionary*]

cynical ADJECTIVE **1 = sceptical**, mocking, ironic, sneering, pessimistic, scoffing, contemptuous, sarcastic, sardonic, scornful, distrustful, derisive, misanthropic: *He has a very cynical view of the world.* **OPPOSITE:** trusting **2 = unbelieving**, sceptical, disillusioned, pessimistic, disbelieving, mistrustful: *My experiences have made me cynical about relationships.* **OPPOSITE:** optimistic

cynicism NOUN **1 = scepticism**, pessimism, sarcasm, misanthropy, sardonicism: *I found Ben's cynicism wearing at times.* **2 = disbelief**, doubt, scepticism, mistrust: *This talk betrays a certain cynicism about free trade.*

> **QUOTATIONS**
>
> Cynicism is intellectual dandyism without the coxcomb's feathers
> [George Meredith *The Egoist*]

cyst NOUN **= sac**, growth, blister, wen, vesicle

Dd

dab VERB **1 = pat**, touch, tap, wipe, blot, swab: *dabbing her eyes with a tissue* **2 = apply**, daub, stipple: *She dabbed iodine on the cuts.*
▷ NOUN **1 = spot**, bit, drop, pat, fleck, smudge, speck, dollop *(informal)*, smidgen *or* smidgin *(informal, chiefly U.S. & Canad.)*: *a dab of glue* **2 = touch**, stroke, flick, smudge: *just one dab of the right fragrance*

dabble VERB **= play (at** *or* **with)**, potter, tinker (with), trifle (with), dip into, dally (with)

daft ADJECTIVE **1 = stupid**, simple, crazy, silly, absurd, foolish, giddy, goofy, idiotic, inane, loopy *(informal)*, witless, crackpot *(informal)*, out to lunch *(informal)*, dopey *(informal)*, scatty *(Brit. informal)*, asinine, gonzo *(slang)*, doolally *(slang)*, off your head *(informal)*, off your trolley *(slang)*, up the pole *(informal)*, dumb-ass *(slang)*, wacko *or* whacko *(slang)*, off the air *(Austral. slang)*: *I wasn't so daft as to believe him.* **2 = crazy**, mad, mental *(slang)*, touched, nuts *(slang)*, barking *(slang)*, crackers *(Brit. slang)*, insane, lunatic, demented, nutty *(slang)*, deranged, unhinged, round the bend *(Brit. slang)*, barking mad *(slang)*, not right in the head, not the full shilling *(informal)*, off the air *(Austral. slang)*, porangi *(N.Z.)*: *It either sends you daft or kills you.*
daft about = enthusiastic about, mad about, crazy about *(informal)*, doting on, besotted with, sweet on, nuts about *(slang)*, potty about *(Brit. informal)*, infatuated by, dotty about *(slang, chiefly Brit.)*, nutty about *(informal)*: *He's just daft about her.*

dag NOUN **= joker**, comic, wag, wit, comedian, clown, kidder *(informal)*, jester, humorist, prankster: *He does all these great impersonations – he's such a dag.*
rattle your dags = hurry up, get a move on, step on it *(informal)*, get your skates on *(informal)*, make haste: *You'd better rattle your dags and get on with this before the boss gets back.*

dagga NOUN **= cannabis**, marijuana, pot *(slang)*, dope *(slang)*, hash *(slang)*, black *(slang)*, blow *(slang)*, smoke *(informal)*, stuff *(slang)*, leaf *(slang)*, tea *(U.S. slang)*, grass *(slang)*, chronic *(U.S. slang)*, weed *(slang)*, hemp, gage *(U.S. obsolete, slang)*, hashish, mary jane *(U.S. slang)*, ganja, bhang, kif, wacky baccy *(slang)*, sinsemilla, charas

dagger NOUN **= knife**, bayonet, dirk, stiletto, poniard, skean: *The man raised his arm and plunged a dagger into her back.*
at daggers drawn = on bad terms, at odds, at war, at loggerheads, up in arms, at enmity: *She and her supervisor are always at daggers drawn.*
look daggers at someone = glare, frown, scowl, glower, look black, lour *or* lower: *The girls looked daggers at me.*

QUOTATIONS
Is this a dagger which I see before me
The handle toward my hand?
[William Shakespeare *Macbeth*]

daggy ADJECTIVE **1 = untidy**, unkempt, dishevelled, tousled, disordered, messy, ruffled, scruffy, rumpled, bedraggled, ratty *(informal)*, straggly, windblown, disarranged, mussed up *(informal)* **2 = eccentric**, odd, strange, bizarre, weird, peculiar, abnormal, queer *(informal)*, irregular, uncommon, quirky, singular, unconventional, idiosyncratic, off-the-wall *(slang)*, outlandish, whimsical, rum *(Brit. slang)*, capricious, anomalous, freakish, aberrant, wacko *(slang)*, outré

daily ADJECTIVE **1 = everyday**, regular, circadian *(Biology)*, diurnal, quotidian: *the company's daily turnover* **2 = day-to-day**, common, ordinary, routine, everyday, commonplace, quotidian: *factors which deeply influence daily life*
▷ ADVERB **= every day**, day by day, day after day, once a day, per diem: *The shop is open daily.*

dainty ADJECTIVE **1 = delicate**, pretty, charming, fine, elegant, neat, exquisite, graceful, petite: *The girls were dainty and feminine.*
OPPOSITE: clumsy **2 = delectable**, choice, delicious, tender, tasty, savoury, palatable, toothsome: *a dainty morsel* **3 = particular**, nice, refined, fussy, scrupulous, fastidious, choosy, picky *(informal)*, finicky, finical: *They cater for a range of tastes, from the dainty to the extravagant.*

dais NOUN **= platform**, stage, podium, rostrum, estrade *(rare)*

dale NOUN **= valley**, glen, vale, dell, dingle, strath *(Scot.)*, coomb

dalliance NOUN **= dabbling**, playing, toying, trifling: *a fashionable dalliance with ideas of liberty and reason*

dally VERB **= waste time**, delay, fool (about *or* around), linger, hang about, loiter, while away, dawdle, fritter away, procrastinate, tarry, dilly-dally *(informal)*, drag your feet *or* heels: *He did not dally long over his meal.*
OPPOSITE: hurry (up)
dally with someone = flirt with, tease, lead on, toy with, play around with, fool (about *or* around) with, trifle with, play fast and loose with *(informal)*, frivol with *(informal)*: *He was dallying with some floosie.*

dam NOUN **= barrier**, wall, barrage, obstruction, embankment, hindrance: *They went ahead with plans to build a dam across the river.*
▷ VERB **= block up**, block, hold in, restrict, check, confine, choke, hold back, barricade, obstruct: *The reservoir was formed by damming the River Blith.*

damage NOUN **1 = destruction**, harm, loss, injury, suffering, hurt, ruin, crushing, wrecking, shattering, devastation, detriment, mutilation, impairment, annihilation, ruination: *There have been many reports of minor damage to buildings.*
OPPOSITE: improvement **2 = cost**, price, charge, rate, bill, figure, amount, total, payment, expense, outlay: *What's the damage for these tickets?*
▷ VERB **= spoil**, hurt, injure, smash, harm, ruin, crush, devastate, mar, wreck, shatter, weaken, gut, demolish, undo, trash *(slang)*, total *(slang)*, impair, ravage, mutilate, annihilate, incapacitate, raze, deface, play (merry) hell with *(informal)*: *He damaged the car with a baseball bat.*
OPPOSITE: fix
▷ PLURAL NOUN **= compensation**, fine, payment, satisfaction, amends, reparation, indemnity, restitution, reimbursement, atonement, recompense, indemnification, meed *(archaic)*, requital: *He was vindicated in court and damages were awarded.*

damaging ADJECTIVE **= harmful**, detrimental, hurtful, ruinous, prejudicial, deleterious, injurious, disadvantageous **OPPOSITE:** helpful

dame NOUN **1** *(with cap.)* **= lady**, baroness, dowager, grande dame *(French)*, noblewoman, peeress: *a Dame of the British Empire* **2 = woman**, girl, lady, female, bird *(slang)*, maiden *(archaic)*, miss, chick *(slang)*, maid *(archaic)*, gal *(slang)*, lass, lassie *(informal)*, wench *(facetious)*, charlie *(Austral. slang)*, chook *(Austral. slang)*, wahine *(N.Z.)*: *This is one classy dame you've got yourself here.*

damn VERB **= criticize**, condemn, blast, pan *(informal)*, slam *(slang)*, denounce, put down, slate *(informal)*, censure, castigate, tear into *(informal)*, diss *(slang, chiefly U.S.)*, inveigh against, lambast(e), excoriate, denunciate: *You can't damn him for his beliefs.* **OPPOSITE:** praise
not give a damn = not care, not mind, be indifferent, not give a hoot, not care a jot, not give two hoots, not care a whit, not care a brass farthing, not give a tinker's curse *or* damn *(slang)*: *Frankly, my dear, I don't give a damn.*

damnation NOUN = **condemnation**, damning, sending to hell, consigning to perdition

> QUOTATIONS
> For what shall it profit a man, if he shall gain the whole world, and lose his own soul?
> [*Bible: St. Mark*]

damned ADJECTIVE = **infernal**, accursed, detestable, revolting, infamous, confounded, despicable, abhorred, hateful, loathsome, abominable, freaking *(slang, chiefly U.S.)*

d

damning ADJECTIVE = **incriminating**, implicating, condemnatory, dooming, accusatorial, damnatory, implicative

damp ADJECTIVE = **moist**, wet, dripping, soggy, humid, sodden, dank, sopping, clammy, dewy, muggy, drizzly, vaporous: *She wiped the table with a damp cloth; damp weather*
OPPOSITE: dry
▷ NOUN = **moisture**, liquid, humidity, drizzle, dew, dampness, wetness, dankness, clamminess, mugginess: *There was damp everywhere in the house.*
OPPOSITE: dryness
▷ VERB = **moisten**, wet, soak, dampen, lick, moisturize, humidify: *She damped a hand towel and laid it across her head.*
damp something down = **curb**, reduce, check, cool, moderate, dash, chill, dull, diminish, discourage, restrain, inhibit, stifle, allay, deaden, pour cold water on: *He tried to damp down his panic.*

dampen VERB **1** = **reduce**, check, moderate, dash, dull, restrain, deter, stifle, lessen, smother, muffle, deaden: *Nothing seemed to dampen his enthusiasm.* **2** = **moisten**, wet, spray, make damp, bedew, besprinkle: *She took the time to dampen a cloth and wash her face.*

damper NOUN = **discouragement**, cloud, chill, curb, restraint, gloom, cold water *(informal)*, pall

dampness NOUN = **moistness**, damp, moisture, humidity, wetness, sogginess, dankness, clamminess, mugginess **OPPOSITE:** dryness

dance VERB **1** = **prance**, rock, trip, swing, spin, hop, skip, sway, whirl, caper, jig, frolic, cavort, gambol, bob up and down, cut a rug *(informal)*: *They like to dance to the music on the radio.* **2** = **caper**, trip, spring, jump, bound, leap, bounce, hop, skip, romp, frolic, cavort, gambol: *He danced off down the road.*
▷ NOUN = **ball**, social, hop *(informal)*, disco, knees-up *(Brit. informal)*, discotheque, dancing party, B and S *(Austral. informal)*: *She often went to dances and parties in the village.*

> QUOTATIONS
> You should make a point of trying everything once, excepting incest and folk-dancing
> [Arnold Bax *Farewell My Youth*]
>
> There are many kinds of dances, but all those requiring the participation of the two sexes have two characteristics in common; they are conspicuously innocent, and warmly loved by the vicious
> [Ambrose Bierce *The Devil's Dictionary*]
>
> Come, knit hands, and beat the ground,
> In a light fantastic round
> [John Milton *Comus*]
>
> Dancing is the loftiest, the most moving, the most beautiful of the arts, because it is no mere translation or abstraction from life; it is life itself
> [Havelock Ellis *The Dance of Life*]
>
> On with the dance! Let joy be unconfined;
> No sleep till morn, when Youth and Pleasure meet
> To chase the glowing hours with flying feet
> [Lord Byron *Childe Harold's Pilgrimage*]
>
> No sober man dances, unless he happens to be mad
> [Cicero *Pro Murena*]

dancer NOUN = **ballerina**, hoofer *(slang)*, Terpsichorean

dandy NOUN = **fop**, beau, swell *(informal)*, blood *(rare)*, buck *(archaic)*, blade *(archaic)*, peacock, dude *(U.S. & Canad. informal)*, toff *(Brit. slang)*, macaroni *(obsolete)*, man about town, popinjay, coxcomb: *a handsome young dandy*
▷ ADJECTIVE = **excellent**, great, fine, capital, splendid, first-rate: *Everything's fine and dandy.*

danger NOUN **1** = **jeopardy**, vulnerability, insecurity, precariousness, endangerment: *Your life is in danger.* **2** = **hazard**, risk, threat, menace, peril, pitfall: *These roads are a danger to cyclists.*

dangerous ADJECTIVE = **perilous**, threatening, risky, hazardous, exposed, alarming, vulnerable, nasty, ugly, menacing, insecure, hairy *(slang)*, unsafe, precarious, treacherous, breakneck, parlous *(archaic)*, fraught with danger, chancy *(informal)*, unchancy *(Scot.)*
OPPOSITE: safe

> QUOTATIONS
> mad, bad, and dangerous to know
> [Caroline Lamb (of Byron)]

dangerously ADVERB = **perilously**, alarmingly, carelessly, precariously, recklessly, daringly, riskily, harmfully, hazardously, unsafely, unsecurely: *He rushed downstairs dangerously fast.*

dangle VERB **1** = **hang**, swing, trail, sway, flap, hang down, depend: *A gold bracelet dangled from his left wrist.* **2** = **offer**, flourish, brandish, flaunt, tempt someone with, lure someone with, entice someone with, tantalize someone with: *They dangled rich rewards before me.*

dangling ADJECTIVE = **hanging**, swinging, loose, trailing, swaying, disconnected, drooping, unconnected

dank ADJECTIVE = **damp**, dripping, moist, soggy, clammy, dewy

dapper ADJECTIVE = **neat**, nice, smart, trim, stylish, spruce, dainty, natty *(informal)*, well-groomed, well turned out, trig *(archaic, dialect)*, soigné
OPPOSITE: untidy

dappled ADJECTIVE = **mottled**, spotted, speckled, pied, flecked, variegated, checkered, freckled, stippled, piebald, brindled

dare VERB **1** = **risk doing**, venture, presume, make bold *(archaic)*, hazard doing, brave doing: *I didn't dare to tell my uncle what had happened.* **2** = **challenge**, provoke, defy, taunt, goad, throw down the gauntlet: *She dared me to ask him out.*

daredevil NOUN = **adventurer**, show-off *(informal)*, madcap, desperado, exhibitionist, stunt man, hot dog *(chiefly U.S.)*, adrenalin junky *(slang)*: *a tragic ending for a daredevil whose luck ran out*
▷ ADJECTIVE = **daring**, bold, adventurous, reckless, audacious, madcap, death-defying: *He gets his kicks from daredevil car-racing.*

daring ADJECTIVE = **brave**, bold, adventurous, rash, have-a-go *(informal)*, reckless, fearless, audacious, intrepid, impulsive, valiant, plucky, game *(informal)*, daredevil, venturesome, (as) game as Ned Kelly *(Austral. slang)*: *a daring rescue attempt* **OPPOSITE:** timid
▷ NOUN = **bravery**, nerve *(informal)*, courage, face *(informal)*, spirit, bottle *(Brit. slang)*, guts *(informal)*, pluck, grit, audacity, boldness, temerity, derring-do *(archaic)*, spunk *(informal)*, fearlessness, rashness, intrepidity: *His daring may have cost him his life.*
OPPOSITE: timidity

dark ADJECTIVE **1** = **dim**, murky, shady, shadowy, grey, cloudy, dingy, overcast, dusky, unlit, pitch-black, indistinct, poorly lit, sunless, tenebrous, darksome *(literary)*, pitchy, unilluminated: *It was a dark and stormy night.* **2** = **black**, brunette, ebony, dark-skinned, sable, dusky, swarthy: *a tall, dark and handsome stranger*
OPPOSITE: fair **3** = **evil**, foul, horrible, sinister, infamous, vile, satanic, wicked, atrocious, sinful, hellish, infernal, nefarious, damnable: *magicians who harnessed dark powers* **4** = **secret**, deep, hidden, mysterious, concealed, obscure, mystic, enigmatic, puzzling, occult, arcane, cryptic, abstruse, recondite, Delphic: *the dark recesses of the mind* **5** = **gloomy**, sad, grim, miserable, low, bleak, moody, dismal, pessimistic, melancholy, sombre, morbid, glum, mournful, morose, joyless, doleful, cheerless: *His endless chatter kept me from thinking dark thoughts.*

The Brontës' Use of Nouns

One of the commonest nouns in the writings of the Brontë sisters is *eye*. Characters look intently at the world and other people; they respond to the beauty and expression in others' eyes; their eyes show their feelings, and they communicate by their looks:

> She looked at me; her eye said most plainly, 'I cannot follow you.'

In *Jane Eyre* there are a number of powerful descriptions of the sensation of being looked at. For example, the young Jane, in disgrace at Mr Brocklehurst's school feels the burning gaze of the other girls:

> I felt their **eyes** directed like burning-glasses against my scorched skin.

The second time that Jane meets Mr Rochester, he keeps his eyes turned away when she enters the room; she is acutely aware that he is not looking at her, and tension mounts until he does, with eyes that were *dark, irate and piercing*. In Brontë novels, people with deep emotions generally have dark eyes: Heathcliff in *Wuthering Heights* has black eyes, while feeble, timid Edgar Linton has *great blue eyes*, and in *Jane Eyre* the eye of the impassive St John Rivers is *a cold, bright, blue gem*.

It is remarkable that *eye* is used more than *word* by the Brontës, but *word* is another of their top ten most frequently used nouns. Drama in their novels arises less from events than from dialogue, memory, or thought; words are intensely exciting and often violent:

> ... their conversation, was recent, raw, and stinging in my mind; I had felt every **word** as acutely as I had heard it plainly ...

Not surprisingly, given the emotional nature of the sisters' writings, *heart* is another of the words they use most. Hearts occasionally *rejoice*, but much more often they *break, ache, throb*, or *quake*. Such violently physical verbs convey how the effect of strong emotion permeates the whole body:

> My **heart** beat thick, my head grew hot.

While the Brontës make frequent use of common nouns to convey strong emotion, they also have a decided taste for literary words, such as *couch* for bed, *raiment, dress*, or *attire* for clothes, *apartment* for room, and *physiognomy* for face. Even after the thrillingly horrifying description of Lockwood reaching through the broken glass to find his hand taken by a little ice-cold hand, Emily makes Lockwood describe Heathcliff grinding his teeth to subdue the *maxillary convulsions*. The meeting between Jane and Mr Rochester, mentioned above, is full of subtle, intense feeling – yet the darkly fascinating hero ponderously asks Mrs Fairfax to serve as Adèle's *auditress* and *interlocutrice*. Great variation in register is particularly marked in Charlotte's writing: one minute Mr Rochester addresses Adèle as a *genuine daughter of Paris*, the next he declares how intolerable it would be to him to spend an evening with a *brat*.

Another element in Charlotte's varied language is her use of French, without translation. This is found particularly in *Villette* and *The Professor*, both set in Belgium – but in *Jane Eyre* too, Adèle speaks her native French, and Jane (and occasionally Mr Rochester) speaks to her in that language.

OPPOSITE: cheerful **6 = angry**, threatening, forbidding, frowning, ominous, dour, scowling, sullen, glum, glowering, sulky: *He shot her a dark glance.*
▷ NOUN **1 = darkness**, shadows, gloom, dusk, obscurity, murk, dimness, semi-darkness, murkiness: *I've always been afraid of the dark.*
2 = night, twilight, evening, evo (*Austral. slang*), dusk, night-time, nightfall: *after dark*

darken VERB **1 = cloud**, shadow, shade, obscure, eclipse, dim, deepen, overshadow, blacken, becloud: *A storm darkened the sky.* OPPOSITE: brighten
2 = make dark, shade, blacken, make darker, deepen: *She darkened her eyebrows with mascara.* **3 = become gloomy**, blacken, become angry, look black, go crook (*Austral. & N.Z. slang*), grow troubled: *His face suddenly darkened.*
OPPOSITE: become cheerful
4 = sadden, upset, cloud, blacken, cast a pall over, cast a gloom upon: *Nothing was going to darken his mood today.*

darkness NOUN **= dark**, shadows, shade, gloom, obscurity, blackness, murk, dimness, murkiness, duskiness, shadiness

darling NOUN **1 = beloved**, love, dear, dearest, angel, treasure, precious, loved one, sweetheart, sweetie, truelove, dear one: *Hello, darling!*
2 = favourite, pet, spoilt child, apple of your eye, blue-eyed boy, fair-haired boy (*U.S.*): *He was the darling of the family.*
▷ ADJECTIVE **1 = beloved**, dear, dearest, sweet, treasured, precious, adored, cherished, revered: *my darling baby boy*
2 = adorable, sweet, attractive, lovely, charming, cute, enchanting, captivating: *a perfectly darling little house*

darn VERB **= mend**, repair, patch, stitch, sew up, cobble up: *His aunt darned his old socks.*
▷ NOUN **= mend**, patch, reinforcement, invisible repair: *blue woollen stockings with untidy darns*

dart VERB **= dash**, run, race, shoot, fly, speed, spring, tear, rush, bound, flash, hurry, sprint, bolt, hasten, whizz, haste, flit, scoot: *She darted away through the trees.*

dash VERB **1 = rush**, run, race, shoot, fly, career, speed, spring, tear, bound, hurry, barrel (along) (*informal, chiefly U.S. & Canad.*), sprint, bolt, dart, hasten, scurry, haste, stampede, burn rubber (*informal*), make haste, hotfoot: *Suddenly she dashed out into the garden.*
OPPOSITE: dawdle **2 = throw**, cast, pitch, slam, toss, hurl, fling, chuck (*informal*), propel, project, sling, lob (*informal*): *She dashed the doll against the stone wall.* **3 = crash**, break, smash, shatter, shiver, splinter: *The waves dashed against the side of the ship.*
4 = disappoint, ruin, frustrate, spoil, foil, undo, thwart, dampen, confound, crool *or* cruel (*Austral. slang*): *They had their hopes raised and then dashed.*
▷ NOUN **1 = rush**, run, race, sprint, bolt, dart, spurt, sortie: *a 160-mile dash to hospital* **2 = drop**, little, bit, shot (*informal*), touch, spot, suggestion, trace, hint, pinch, sprinkling, tot, trickle, nip, tinge, soupçon (*French*): *Add a dash of balsamic vinegar.*
OPPOSITE: lot **3 = style**, spirit, flair, flourish, vigour, verve, panache, élan, brio, vivacity: *He played with great fire and dash.*

dashing ADJECTIVE **= stylish**, smart, elegant, dazzling, flamboyant, sporty, swish (*informal, chiefly Brit.*), urbane, jaunty, dapper, showy

dastardly ADJECTIVE **= despicable**, mean, low, base, sneaking, cowardly, craven, vile, abject, sneaky, contemptible, underhand, weak-kneed (*informal*), faint-hearted, spiritless, recreant (*archaic*), caitiff (*archaic*), niddering (*archaic*)

data NOUN **1 = details**, facts, figures, materials, documents, intelligence, statistics, gen (*Brit. informal*), dope (*informal*), info (*informal*)
2 = information, input

> **USAGE**
> From a historical point of view only, the word *data* is a plural. In fact, in many cases it is not clear from context if it is being used as a singular or plural, so there is no issue: *when next needed the data can be accessed very quickly*. When it is necessary to specify, the preferred usage nowadays in general language is to treat it as singular, as in: *this data is useful to the government in the planning of housing services*. There are rather more examples in the Bank of English of *these data* than *this data*, with a marked preference for the plural in academic and scientific writing. As regards *data is* versus *data are*, the preference for the plural form overall is even more marked in that kind of writing. When speaking, however, it is best to opt for treating the word as singular, except in precise scientific contexts. The singular form *datum* is comparatively rare in the sense of a single item of data.

date NOUN **1 = time**, stage, period: *An inquest will be held at a later date.*
2 = appointment, meeting, arrangement, commitment, engagement, rendezvous, tryst, assignation: *He had made a date with the girl.* **3 = partner**, escort, friend, steady (*informal*), plus-one (*informal*): *She is his date for the dance.*
▷ VERB **1 = put a date on**, determine the date of, assign a date to, fix the period of: *It is difficult to date the relic.*
2 = become dated, become old-fashioned, obsolesce: *It always looks smart and will never date.*
date from *or* **date back to = come from**, belong to, originate in, exist from, bear a date of: *The imperial palace dates back to the 16th century.*
to date = up to now, yet, so far, until now, now, as yet, thus far, up to this point, up to the present: *This is the band's fourth top twenty single to date.*

dated ADJECTIVE **= old-fashioned**, outdated, out of date, obsolete, archaic, unfashionable, antiquated, outmoded, passé, out, old hat, untrendy (*Brit. informal*), démodé (*French*), out of the ark (*informal*)
OPPOSITE: modern

daub VERB **= smear**, dirty, splatter, stain, spatter, sully, deface, smirch, begrime, besmear, bedaub, paint, coat, stain, plaster, slap on (*informal*): *They daubed his home with slogans.*
▷ NOUN **= smear**, spot, stain, blot, blotch, splodge, splotch, smirch: *Apply an extra daub of colour.*

daughter NOUN **1 = female child**, girl
2 = descendant, girl
▸ *related adjective:* filial

> **QUOTATIONS**
> As is the mother, so is her daughter
> [*Bible: Ezekiel*]
>
> A daughter is an embarrassing and ticklish possession
> [Menander *Perinthis*]
>
> Marry your son when you will; your daughter when you can
> [George Herbert *Jacula Prudentum*]

daunt VERB **= discourage**, alarm, shake, frighten, scare, terrify, cow, intimidate, deter, dismay, put off, subdue, overawe, frighten off, dishearten, dispirit
OPPOSITE: reassure

daunted ADJECTIVE **= intimidated**, alarmed, shaken, frightened, overcome, cowed, discouraged, deterred, dismayed, put off, disillusioned, unnerved, demoralized, dispirited, downcast

daunting ADJECTIVE **= intimidating**, alarming, frightening, discouraging, awesome, unnerving, disconcerting, demoralizing, off-putting (*Brit. informal*), disheartening
OPPOSITE: reassuring

dawdle VERB **1 = waste time**, potter, trail, lag, idle, loaf, hang about, dally, loiter, dilly-dally (*informal*), drag your feet *or* heels: *They dawdled arm in arm past the shopfronts.* OPPOSITE: hurry
2 = linger, idle, dally, take your time, procrastinate, drag your feet *or* heels: *I dawdled over a beer.*

dawn NOUN **1 = daybreak**, morning, sunrise, dawning, daylight, aurora (*poetic*), crack of dawn, sunup, cockcrow, dayspring (*poetic*): *She woke at dawn.*
2 = beginning, start, birth, rise, origin, dawning, unfolding, emergence, outset, onset, advent, genesis, inception: *the dawn of the radio age*
▷ VERB **1 = begin**, start, open, rise, develop, emerge, unfold, originate: *A new era seemed about to dawn.* **2 = grow light**, break, brighten, lighten: *The next day dawned.*

dawn on *or* **upon someone = hit**, strike, occur to, register *(informal)*, become apparent, come to mind, cross your mind, come into your head, flash across your mind: *Then the chilling truth dawned on me.*

> **QUOTATIONS**
> rosy-fingered dawn
> [Homer *Iliad*]
>
> For what human ill does not dawn seem to be an alleviation?
> [Thornton Wilder *The Bridge of San Luis Rey*]

day NOUN **1 = twenty-four hours**, working day: *The conference is on for three days.* **2 = daytime**, daylight, daylight hours: *They sleep during the day.* **3 = date**, particular day: *What day are you leaving?* **4 = time**, age, era, prime, period, generation, heyday, epoch: *In my day we treated our elders with more respect.*
call it a day = stop, finish, cease, pack up *(informal)*, leave off, knock off *(informal)*, desist, pack it in *(slang)*, shut up shop, jack it in, chuck it in *(informal)*, give up *or* over: *Faced with such opposition, he had no choice but to call it a day.*
day after day = continually, regularly, relentlessly, persistently, incessantly, nonstop, unremittingly, monotonously, unfalteringly: *In this job I just do the same thing day after day.*
day by day = gradually, slowly, progressively, daily, steadily, bit by bit, little by little, by degrees: *Day by day, he got weaker.*
▸ *related adjective:* diurnal

daybreak NOUN **= dawn**, morning, sunrise, first light, crack of dawn, break of day, sunup, cockcrow, dayspring *(poetic)*

daydream NOUN **= fantasy**, dream, imagining, fancy, reverie, figment of the imagination, wish, pipe dream, fond hope, castle in the air *or* in Spain: *He escaped into daydreams of heroic men and beautiful women.*
▹ VERB **= fantasize**, dream, imagine, envision, stargaze: *He daydreams of being a famous journalist.*

daylight NOUN **1 = sunlight**, sunshine, light of day: *Lack of daylight can make people feel depressed.*
2 = daytime, broad daylight, daylight hours: *It was still daylight but many cars had their headlamps on.*

day-to-day ADJECTIVE **= everyday**, regular, usual, routine, accustomed, customary, habitual, run-of-the-mill, wonted

daze VERB **1 = stun**, shock, paralyse, numb, stupefy, benumb: *The blow caught me on the temple and dazed me.*
2 = confuse, surprise, amaze, blind, astonish, stagger, startle, dazzle, bewilder, astound, perplex, flummox, dumbfound, nonplus, flabbergast *(informal)*, befog: *We were dazed by the sheer size of the spectacle.*
▹ NOUN **= shock**, confusion, distraction, trance, bewilderment, stupor, trancelike state: *I was walking around in a daze.*

dazed ADJECTIVE **= shocked**, stunned, confused, staggered, baffled, at sea, bewildered, muddled, numbed, dizzy, bemused, perplexed, disorientated, flabbergasted *(informal)*, dopey *(slang)*, groggy *(informal)*, stupefied, nonplussed, light-headed, flummoxed, punch-drunk, woozy *(informal)*, fuddled

dazzle VERB **1 = impress**, amaze, fascinate, overwhelm, astonish, awe, overpower, bowl over *(informal)*, overawe, hypnotize, stupefy, take your breath away, strike dumb: *He dazzled her with his knowledge of the world.*
2 = blind, confuse, daze, bedazzle: *She was dazzled by the lights.*
▹ NOUN **= splendour**, sparkle, glitter, flash, brilliance, magnificence, razzmatazz *(slang)*, razzle-dazzle *(slang)*, éclat: *The dazzle of stardom and status attracts them.*

dazzling ADJECTIVE **= splendid**, brilliant, stunning, superb, divine, glorious, sparkling, glittering, sensational *(informal)*, sublime, virtuoso, drop-dead *(slang)*, ravishing, scintillating **OPPOSITE:** ordinary

dead ADJECTIVE **1 = deceased**, gone, departed, late, perished, extinct, defunct, passed away, pushing up (the) daisies: *My husband's been dead for a year now.* **OPPOSITE:** alive
2 = inanimate, still, barren, sterile, stagnant, lifeless, inert, uninhabited: *The polluted and stagnant water seems dead.* **3 = boring**, dull, dreary, flat, plain, stale, tasteless, humdrum, uninteresting, insipid, ho-hum *(informal)*, vapid, dead-and-alive: *It was a horrible, dead little town.* **4 = not working**, useless, inactive, inoperative: *This battery's dead.* **OPPOSITE:** working **5 = obsolete**, old, antique, discarded, extinct, archaic, disused: *dead languages* **6 = spiritless**, cold, dull, wooden, glazed, indifferent, callous, lukewarm, inhuman, unsympathetic, apathetic, frigid, glassy, unresponsive, unfeeling, torpid: *He watched the procedure with cold, dead eyes.* **OPPOSITE:** lively **7 = numb**, frozen, paralysed, insensitive, inert, deadened, immobilized, unfeeling, torpid, insensible, benumbed: *My arm had gone dead.* **8 = total**, complete, perfect, entire, absolute, utter, outright, thorough, downright, unqualified: *They hurried about in dead silence.* **9 = exhausted**, tired, worn out, spent, wasted, done in *(informal)*, all in *(slang)*, drained, wiped out *(informal)*, sapped, knackered *(slang)*, prostrated, clapped out *(Brit., Austral. & N.Z. informal)*, tired out, ready to drop, dog-tired *(informal)*, zonked *(slang)*, dead tired, dead beat *(informal)*, shagged out *(Brit. slang)*, worn to a frazzle *(informal)*, on your last legs *(informal)*, creamcrackered *(Brit. slang)*: *I must get some sleep – I'm absolutely dead.*
▹ NOUN **= middle**, heart, depth, thick, midst: *in the dead of night*
▹ ADVERB **= exactly**, quite, completely, totally, directly, perfectly, fully, entirely, absolutely, thoroughly, wholly, utterly, consummately, wholeheartedly, unconditionally, to the hilt, one hundred per cent, unmitigatedly: *You're dead right.*

> **PROVERBS**
> *Dead men tell no tales*
> *Never speak ill of the dead*

deadbeat NOUN **= layabout**, bum *(informal)*, waster, lounger, piker *(Austral. & N.Z. slang)*, sponge *(informal)*, parasite, drone, loafer, slacker *(informal)*, scrounger *(informal)*, skiver *(Brit. slang)*, idler, freeloader *(slang)*, good-for-nothing, sponger *(informal)*, wastrel, bludger *(Austral. & N.Z. informal)*, cadger, quandong *(Austral. slang)*

deaden VERB **1 = reduce**, dull, diminish, check, weaken, cushion, damp, suppress, blunt, paralyse, impair, numb, lessen, alleviate, smother, dampen, anaesthetize, benumb: *He needs morphine to deaden the pain in his chest.* **2 = suppress**, reduce, dull, diminish, cushion, damp, mute, stifle, hush, lessen, smother, dampen, muffle, quieten: *They managed to deaden the sound.*

deadline NOUN **= time limit**, cutoff point, target date *or* time, limit

deadlock NOUN **1 = impasse**, stalemate, standstill, halt, cessation, gridlock, standoff, full stop: *Peace talks ended in a deadlock last month.* **2 = tie**, draw, stalemate, impasse, standstill, gridlock, standoff, dead heat: *Larkham broke the deadlock with a late goal.*

deadly ADJECTIVE **1 = lethal**, fatal, deathly, dangerous, devastating, destructive, mortal, murderous, poisonous, malignant, virulent, pernicious, noxious, venomous, baleful, death-dealing, baneful: *a deadly disease currently affecting dolphins*
2 = boring, dull, tedious, flat, monotonous, uninteresting, mind-numbing, unexciting, ho-hum *(informal)*, wearisome, as dry as dust: *She found the party deadly.* **3 = deathly**, white, pale, ghostly, ghastly, wan, pasty, colourless, pallid, anaemic, ashen, sallow, whitish, cadaverous, waxen, ashy, deathlike, wheyfaced: *The deadly pallor of her skin.*

deadpan ADJECTIVE **= expressionless**, empty, blank, wooden, straight-faced, vacuous, impassive, inscrutable, poker-faced, inexpressive

deaf ADJECTIVE **1 = hard of hearing**, without hearing, stone deaf: *She is now profoundly deaf.* **2 = oblivious**, indifferent, unmoved, unconcerned, unsympathetic, impervious, unresponsive, heedless, unhearing: *The assembly were deaf to all pleas for financial help.*

PROVERBS
There's none so deaf as those that will not hear

deafen VERB **= make deaf**, split *or* burst the eardrums

deafening ADJECTIVE **= ear-splitting**, intense, piercing, ringing, booming, overpowering, resounding, dinning, thunderous, ear-piercing

deal NOUN **1 = agreement**, understanding, contract, business, negotiation, arrangement, bargain, transaction, pact: *Japan has done a deal with America on rice exports.* **2 = amount**, quantity, measure, degree, mass, volume, share, portion, bulk: *a great deal of money*
deal in something = sell, trade in, stock, traffic in, buy and sell: *The company deals in antiques.*
deal something out = distribute, give, administer, share, divide, assign, allocate, dispense, bestow, allot, mete out, dole out, apportion: *a failure to deal out effective punishments to offenders*
deal with something = be concerned with, involve, concern, touch, regard, apply to, bear on, pertain to, be relevant to, treat of: *the parts of the book which deal with events in Florence*
deal with something *or* **someone**
1 = handle, manage, treat, cope with, take care of, see to, attend to, get to grips with, come to grips with: *the way in which the company deals with complaints* **2 = behave towards**, act towards, conduct yourself towards: *He's a hard man to deal with.*

dealer NOUN **= trader**, marketer, merchant, supplier, wholesaler, purveyor, tradesman, merchandiser

dealings PLURAL NOUN **= business**, selling, trading, trade, traffic, truck, bargaining, commerce, transactions, business relations

dear ADJECTIVE **1 = beloved**, close, valued, favourite, respected, prized, dearest, sweet, treasured, precious, darling, intimate, esteemed, cherished, revered: *Mrs Cavendish is a dear friend of mine.* OPPOSITE: hated **2 = expensive**, costly, high-priced, excessive, pricey *(informal)*, at a premium, overpriced, exorbitant: *Don't buy that one – it's too dear.*
OPPOSITE: cheap
▷ NOUN **= darling**, love, dearest, sweet, angel, treasure, precious, beloved, loved one, sweetheart, truelove: *Yes, my dear.*

dearly ADVERB **1 = very much**, greatly, extremely, profoundly: *She would dearly love to marry.* **2 = at great cost**, dear, at a high price, at a heavy cost: *He is paying dearly for his folly.*

dearth NOUN **= lack**, want, need, absence, poverty, shortage, deficiency, famine, inadequacy, scarcity, paucity, insufficiency, sparsity, scantiness, exiguousness

death NOUN **1 = dying**, demise, bereavement, end, passing, release, loss, departure, curtains *(informal)*, cessation, expiration, decease, quietus: *There had been a death in the family.* OPPOSITE: birth
2 = destruction, ending, finish, ruin, wiping out, undoing, extinction, elimination, downfall, extermination, annihilation, obliteration, ruination: *the death of everything he had ever hoped for*
OPPOSITE: beginning **3** *(sometimes capital)* **= the Grim Reaper**, the Dark Angel: *Carrying a long scythe is the hooded figure of Death.*
▸ *related adjectives:* fatal, lethal, mortal

QUOTATIONS

Dust thou art, and unto dust shalt thou return
[*Bible: Genesis*]

Any man's death diminishes me, because I am involved in Mankind; And therefore never send to know for whom the bell tolls; it tolls for thee
[John Donne *LXXX Sermons*]

To die completely, a person must not only forget but be forgotten, and he who is not forgotten is not dead
[Samuel Butler *Notebooks*]

Death, the most dreaded of evils, is therefore of no concern to us; for while we exist death is not present, and when death is present we no longer exist
[Epicurus *letter to Menoeceus*]

Death hath so many doors to let out life
[John Fletcher *The Custom of the Country*]

I could not look on Death, which being known,
Men led me to him, blindfold and alone
[Rudyard Kipling *Epitaphs of the War*]

One dies only once, and it's for such a long time
[Molière *Le Dépit Amoureux*]

I want death to find me planting my cabbages, but caring little for it, and even less for the imperfections of my garden
[Montaigne *Essais*]

Anyone can stop a man's life, but no one his death; a thousand doors open on to it
[Seneca *Phoenissae*]

Death hath ten thousand doors
For men to take their exits
[John Webster *The Duchess of Malfi*]

After the first death, there is no other
[Dylan Thomas *A refusal to mourn the death, by fire, of a child in London*]

Revenge triumphs over death; love slights it; honour aspireth to it; grief flieth to it
[Francis Bacon *Essays*]

Fear death? – to feel the fog in my throat,
The mist in my face
[Robert Browning *Prospice*]

Death never takes the wise man by surprise; he is always ready to go
[Jean de la Fontaine *Fables*]

If there wasn't death, I think you couldn't go on
[Stevie Smith]

My name is Death: the last best friend am I
[Robert Southey *The Curse of Kehama*]

O death, where is thy sting? O grave, where is thy victory?
[*Bible: I Corinthians*]

It is good to die before one has done anything deserving death
[Anaxandrides *fragment*]

Fear of death is worse than death itself
[William Shakespeare *King Lear*]

I have been half in love with easeful death
[John Keats *Ode to a Nightingale*]

How wonderful is death,
Death and his brother sleep!
[Percy Bysshe Shelley *Queen Mab*]

Though I walk through the valley of the shadow of death, I will fear no evil
[*Bible: Psalm 23*]

Death be not proud, though some have called thee
Mighty and dreadful, for thou art not so
[John Donne *Holy Sonnets*]

We all labour against our own cure, for death is the cure of all diseases
[Thomas Browne *Religio Medici*]

Death is nature's way of telling you to slow down
[Anon.]

Men fear death as children fear to go in the dark; and as that natural fear in children is increased with tales, so is the other
[Francis Bacon *Essays*]

Death and taxes and childbirth! There's never any convenient time for any of them
[Margaret Mitchell *Gone with the Wind*]

There is no cure for birth and death save to enjoy the interval
[George Santayana *Soliloquies in England*]

In this world nothing can be said to be certain, except death and taxes
[Benjamin Franklin *letter to Jean Baptiste Le Roy*]

PROVERBS
Death is the great leveller

deathly ADJECTIVE **1 = deathlike**, white, pale, ghastly, wan, gaunt, haggard, bloodless, pallid, ashen, sallow, cadaverous, ashy, like death warmed up (*informal*): *the deathly pallor of her cheeks* **2 = fatal**, terminal, deadly, terrible, destructive, lethal, mortal, malignant, incurable, pernicious: *a deathly illness*

debacle or **débâcle** NOUN = **disaster**, catastrophe, fiasco

debar VERB = **bar**, exclude, prohibit, black, stop, keep out, preclude, shut out, blackball, interdict, refuse admission to

debase VERB **1 = corrupt**, contaminate, devalue, pollute, impair, taint, depreciate, defile, adulterate, vitiate, bastardize: *He claims that advertising debases the English language.* **OPPOSITE:** purify **2 = degrade**, reduce, lower, shame, humble, disgrace, humiliate, demean, drag down, dishonour, cheapen, abase: *I won't debase myself by answering that question.* **OPPOSITE:** exalt

debased ADJECTIVE **1 = corrupt**, devalued, reduced, lowered, mixed, contaminated, polluted, depreciated, impure, adulterated: *a debased form of Buddhism* **2 = degraded**, corrupt, fallen, low, base, abandoned, perverted, vile, sordid, depraved, debauched, scungy (*Austral. & N.Z.*): *Such women were seen as morally debased.* **OPPOSITE:** virtuous

debatable ADJECTIVE = **doubtful**, uncertain, dubious, controversial, unsettled, questionable, undecided, borderline, in dispute, moot, arguable, iffy (*informal*), open to question, disputable

debate NOUN = **discussion**, talk, argument, dispute, analysis, conversation, consideration, controversy, dialogue, contention, deliberation, polemic, altercation, disputation: *There has been a lot of debate about this point.*
▷ VERB **1 = discuss**, question, talk about, argue about, dispute, examine, contest, deliberate, contend, wrangle, thrash out, controvert: *The causes of depression are much debated.* **2 = consider**, reflect, think about, weigh, contemplate, deliberate, ponder, revolve, mull over, ruminate, give thought to, cogitate, meditate upon: *He debated whether to have yet another double vodka.*

debauched ADJECTIVE = **corrupt**, abandoned, perverted, degraded, degenerate, immoral, dissipated, sleazy, depraved, wanton, debased, profligate, dissolute, licentious, pervy (*slang*)

debauchery NOUN = **depravity**, excess, lust, revel, indulgence, orgy, incontinence, gluttony, dissipation, licentiousness, intemperance, overindulgence, lewdness, dissoluteness, carousal

debilitate VERB = **weaken**, exhaust, wear out, sap, incapacitate, prostrate, enfeeble, enervate, devitalize **OPPOSITE:** invigorate

debilitating ADJECTIVE = **weakening**, tiring, exhausting, draining, fatiguing, wearing, sapping, incapacitating, enervating, enfeebling, devitalizing **OPPOSITE:** invigorating

debonair ADJECTIVE = **elegant**, charming, dashing, smooth, refined, courteous, affable, suave, urbane, well-bred

debrief VERB = **interrogate**, question, examine, probe, quiz, cross-examine

debris NOUN = **remains**, bits, pieces, waste, ruins, wreck, rubbish, fragments, litter, rubble, wreckage, brash, detritus, dross

debt NOUN = **debit**, bill, score, due, duty, commitment, obligation, liability, arrears: *He is still paying off his debts.*
in debt = owing, liable, accountable, in the red (*informal*), in arrears, beholden, in hock (*informal, chiefly U.S.*): *You shouldn't borrow more money if you're already in debt.*

debtor NOUN = **borrower**, mortgagor

debunk VERB = **expose**, show up, mock, ridicule, puncture, deflate, disparage, lampoon, cut down to size

debut NOUN **1 = entrance**, beginning, launch, launching, introduction, first appearance, inauguration **2 = presentation**, coming out, introduction, first appearance, launching, initiation

decadence NOUN = **degeneration**, decline, corruption, fall, decay, deterioration, dissolution, perversion, dissipation, debasement, retrogression

decadent ADJECTIVE = **degenerate**, abandoned, corrupt, degraded, immoral, self-indulgent, depraved, debased, debauched, dissolute **OPPOSITE:** moral

decamp VERB = **make off**, fly, escape, desert, flee, bolt, run away, flit (*informal*), abscond, hook it (*slang*), sneak off, do a runner (*slang*), scarper (*Brit. slang*), steal away, do a bunk (*Brit. slang*), fly the coop (*U.S. & Canad. informal*), skedaddle (*informal*), hightail it (*informal, chiefly U.S.*), take a powder (*U.S. & Canad. slang*), take it on the lam (*U.S. & Canad. slang*), do a Skase (*Austral. informal*)

decant VERB = **transfer**, tap, drain, pour out, draw off, let flow

decapitate VERB = **behead**, execute, guillotine

decay VERB **1 = rot**, break down, disintegrate, spoil, crumble, deteriorate, perish, degenerate, fester, decompose, mortify, moulder, go bad, putrefy: *The bodies buried in the fine ash slowly decayed.* **2 = decline**, sink, break down, diminish, dissolve, crumble, deteriorate, fall off, dwindle, lessen, wane, disintegrate, degenerate: *The work ethic in this country has decayed over the past 30 years.* **OPPOSITE:** grow
▷ NOUN **1 = rot**, rotting, deterioration, corruption, mould, blight, perishing, disintegration, corrosion, decomposition, gangrene, mortification, canker, caries, putrefaction, putrescence, cariosity, putridity: *Plaque causes tooth decay and gum disease.* **2 = decline**, collapse, deterioration, failing, fading, decadence, degeneration, degeneracy: *problems of urban decay and gang violence* **OPPOSITE:** growth

decayed ADJECTIVE = **rotten**, bad, decaying, wasted, spoiled, perished, festering, decomposed, corroded, unsound, putrid, putrefied, putrescent, carrion, carious

decaying ADJECTIVE = **rotting**, deteriorating, disintegrating, crumbling, perishing, wasting away, wearing away, gangrenous, putrefacient

deceased ADJECTIVE = **dead**, late, departed, lost, gone, expired, defunct, lifeless, pushing up daisies (*informal*)

deceit NOUN = **lying**, fraud, cheating, deception, hypocrisy, cunning, pretence, treachery, dishonesty, guile, artifice, trickery, misrepresentation, duplicity, subterfuge, feint, double-dealing, chicanery, wile, dissimulation, craftiness, imposture, fraudulence, slyness, deceitfulness, underhandedness **OPPOSITE:** honesty

deceitful ADJECTIVE = **dishonest**, false, deceiving, fraudulent, treacherous, deceptive, hypocritical, counterfeit, crafty, sneaky, illusory, two-faced, disingenuous, untrustworthy, underhand, insincere, double-dealing, duplicitous, fallacious, guileful, knavish (*archaic*)

deceive VERB = **take in**, trick, fool (*informal*), cheat, con (*informal*), kid (*informal*), stiff (*slang*), sting (*informal*), mislead, betray, lead (someone) on (*informal*), hoax, dupe, beguile, delude, swindle, outwit, ensnare, bamboozle (*informal*), hoodwink, entrap, double-cross (*informal*), take for a ride (*informal*), pull a fast one on (*slang*), cozen, scam (*slang*), pull the wool over (someone's) eyes: *He has deceived and disillusioned us all.*

decency NOUN **1 = propriety**, correctness, decorum, fitness, good form, respectability, etiquette, appropriateness, seemliness: *His sense of decency forced him to resign.* **2 = courtesy**, grace, politeness, good manners, civility, good breeding, graciousness, urbanity, courteousness, gallantness: *He did not have the decency to inform me of his plans.*

decent ADJECTIVE **1 = satisfactory**, average, fair, all right, reasonable, suitable, sufficient, acceptable, good enough, adequate, competent, ample, tolerable, up to scratch, passable, up to standard, up to the mark: *Nearby there is a village with a decent pub.*

OPPOSITE: unsatisfactory **2 = proper**, becoming, seemly, fitting, fit, appropriate, suitable, respectable, befitting, decorous, comme il faut *(French)*: *They married after a decent interval.* OPPOSITE: improper **3 = good**, kind, friendly, neighbourly, generous, helpful, obliging, accommodating, sympathetic, comradely, benign, gracious, benevolent, courteous, amiable, amicable, sociable, genial, peaceable, companionable, well-disposed: *Most people around here are decent folk.* **4 = respectable**, nice, pure, proper, modest, polite, chaste, presentable, decorous: *He wanted to marry a decent woman.*

d

deception NOUN **1 = trickery**, fraud, deceit, hypocrisy, cunning, treachery, guile, duplicity, insincerity, legerdemain, dissimulation, craftiness, fraudulence, deceitfulness, deceptiveness: *He admitted conspiring to obtain property by deception.* OPPOSITE: honesty **2 = trick**, lie, fraud, cheat, bluff, sham, snare, hoax, decoy, ruse, artifice, subterfuge, canard, feint, stratagem, porky *(Brit. slang)*, pork pie *(Brit. slang)*, wile, hokum *(slang, chiefly U.S. & Canad.)*, leg-pull *(Brit. informal)*, imposture, snow job *(slang, chiefly U.S. & Canad.)*, fastie *(Austral. slang)*: *You've been the victim of a rather cruel deception.*

QUOTATIONS

Deceive boys with toys, but men with oaths
[Lysander]

O what a tangled web we weave,
When first we practise to deceive!
[Walter Scott *Marmion*]

You can fool some of the people all of the time, and all of the people some of the time, but you cannot fool all of the people all of the time
[ascribed to Abraham Lincoln]

One may smile, and smile, and be a villain
[William Shakespeare *Hamlet*]

We are never so easily deceived as when we imagine we are deceiving others
[Duc de la Rochefoucauld *Maxims*]

deceptive ADJECTIVE **1 = misleading**, false, fake, mock, ambiguous, unreliable, spurious, illusory, specious, fallacious, delusive: *Appearances can be deceptive.* **2 = dishonest**, deceiving, fraudulent, treacherous, hypocritical, crafty, sneaky, two-faced, disingenuous, deceitful, untrustworthy, underhand, insincere, duplicitous, guileful: *Her worst fault is a strongly deceptive streak.*

decide VERB **1 = make a decision**, make up your mind, reach *or* come to a decision, end, choose, determine, purpose, elect, conclude, commit yourself, come to a conclusion: *I can't decide what to do.* OPPOSITE: hesitate **2 = resolve**, answer, determine, settle, conclude, decree, clear up, ordain, adjudicate, adjudge, arbitrate: *This is a question that should be decided by government.* **3 = settle**, determine, conclude, resolve: *The goal that decided the match came just before half-time.*

decided ADJECTIVE **1 = definite**, certain, positive, absolute, distinct, pronounced, clear-cut, undisputed, unequivocal, undeniable, unambiguous, indisputable, categorical, unquestionable: *We were at a decided disadvantage.* OPPOSITE: doubtful **2 = determined**, firm, decisive, assertive, emphatic, resolute, strong-willed, unhesitating, unfaltering: *a man of very decided opinions* OPPOSITE: irresolute

decidedly ADVERB **= definitely**, clearly, certainly, absolutely, positively, distinctly, downright, decisively, unequivocally, unmistakably

deciding ADJECTIVE **= determining**, chief, prime, significant, critical, crucial, principal, influential, decisive, conclusive

decimate VERB **= destroy**, devastate, wipe out, ravage, eradicate, annihilate, put paid to, lay waste, wreak havoc on

decipher VERB **1 = decode**, crack, solve, understand, explain, reveal, figure out *(informal)*, unravel, suss (out) *(slang)*: *I'm still no closer to deciphering the code.* **2 = figure out**, read, understand, interpret *(informal)*, make out, unravel, deduce, construe, suss (out) *(slang)*: *I can't decipher these notes.*

decision NOUN **1 = judgment**, finding, ruling, order, result, sentence, settlement, resolution, conclusion, outcome, verdict, decree, arbitration: *The judge's decision was greeted with dismay.* **2 = decisiveness**, purpose, resolution, resolve, determination, firmness, forcefulness, purposefulness, resoluteness, strength of mind *or* will: *He is very much a man of decision and action.*

decisive ADJECTIVE **1 = crucial**, significant, critical, final, positive, absolute, influential, definite, definitive, momentous, conclusive, fateful: *his decisive victory in the elections* OPPOSITE: uncertain **2 = resolute**, decided, firm, determined, forceful, uncompromising, incisive, trenchant, strong-minded: *Firm decisive action will be taken to end the incident.* OPPOSITE: indecisive

deck VERB **= decorate**, dress, trim, clothe, grace, array, garland, adorn, ornament, embellish, apparel *(archaic)*, festoon, attire, bedeck, beautify, bedight *(archaic)*, bedizen *(archaic)*, engarland: *The house was decked with flowers.*
deck someone *or* **something out = dress up**, doll up *(slang)*, prettify, trick out, rig out, pretty up, prink, tog up *or* out: *She had decked him out in expensive clothes.*

declaim VERB **= speak**, lecture, proclaim, recite, rant, harangue, hold forth, spiel *(informal)*, orate, perorate: *He used to declaim verse to us with immense energy.*
declaim against something *or* **someone = protest against**, attack, rail at *or* against, denounce, decry, inveigh against: *He declaimed against the injustice of his treatment.*

declaration NOUN **1 = announcement**, proclamation, decree, notice, manifesto, notification, edict, pronouncement, promulgation, pronunciamento: *The two countries will sign the declaration of peace tomorrow.* **2 = affirmation**, profession, assertion, revelation, disclosure, acknowledgment, protestation, avowal, averment: *declarations of undying love* **3 = statement**, testimony, deposition, attestation: *I signed a declaration allowing my doctor to disclose my medical details.*

declare VERB **1 = state**, claim, announce, voice, express, maintain, confirm, assert, proclaim, pronounce, utter, notify, affirm, profess, avow, aver, asseverate: *He declared his intention to become the best golfer in the world.* **2 = testify**, state, witness, swear, assert, affirm, certify, attest, bear witness, vouch, give testimony, asseverate: *They declare that there is no lawful impediment to the marriage.* **3 = make known**, tell, reveal, show, broadcast, confess, communicate, disclose, convey, manifest, make public: *Anyone carrying money into or out of the country must declare it.*

decline VERB **1 = fall**, fail, drop, contract, lower, sink, flag, fade, shrink, diminish, decrease, slow down, fall off, dwindle, lessen, wane, ebb, slacken: *a declining birth rate* OPPOSITE: rise **2 = deteriorate**, fade, weaken, pine, decay, worsen, lapse, languish, degenerate, droop: *Her father's health has declined significantly in recent months.* OPPOSITE: improve **3 = refuse**, reject, turn down, avoid, deny, spurn, abstain, forgo, send your regrets, say 'no': *He declined their invitation.* OPPOSITE: accept
▷ NOUN **1 = depression**, recession, slump, falling off, downturn, dwindling, lessening, diminution, abatement: *The first signs of economic decline became visible.* OPPOSITE: rise **2 = deterioration**, fall, failing, slump, weakening, decay, worsening, descent, downturn, disintegration, degeneration, atrophy, decrepitude, retrogression, enfeeblement: *Rome's decline in the fifth century.* OPPOSITE: improvement

decode VERB **1 = decipher**, crack, work out, solve, interpret, unscramble, decrypt, descramble: *The secret documents were intercepted and decoded.* OPPOSITE: encode **2 = understand**, explain, interpret, make sense of, construe, decipher, elucidate, throw light on, explicate: *You don't need to be a genius to decode his work.*

decompose VERB **1 = rot**, spoil, corrupt, crumble, decay, perish, fester, corrode, moulder, go bad, putrefy: *foods which decompose and rot* **2 = break down**, break up, crumble, deteriorate, fall apart, disintegrate, degenerate: *Plastics take years to decompose.*

decomposition NOUN **= rot**, corruption, decay, rotting, perishing, mortification, putrefaction, putrescence, putridity: *The bodies were in an advanced state of decomposition.*

decor or **décor** NOUN **= decoration**, colour scheme, ornamentation, furnishing style

decorate VERB **1 = adorn**, deck, trim, embroider, garnish, ornament, embellish, festoon, bedeck, beautify, grace, engarland: *He decorated the box with glitter and ribbons.* **2 = do up**, paper, paint, wallpaper, renovate *(informal)*, furbish: *a small, badly decorated office* **3 = pin a medal on**, cite, confer an honour on *or* upon: *He was decorated for his services to the nation.*

decoration NOUN **1 = adornment**, trimming, garnishing, enhancement, elaboration, embellishment, ornamentation, beautification: *He played a part in the decoration of the tree.* **2 = ornament**, trimmings, garnish, frill, scroll, spangle, festoon, trinket, bauble, flounce, arabesque, curlicue, furbelow, falderal, cartouch(e): *We were putting the Christmas decorations up.* **3 = medal**, award, order, star, colours, ribbon, badge, emblem, garter: *He was awarded several military decorations.*

decorative ADJECTIVE **= ornamental**, fancy, pretty, attractive, enhancing, adorning, for show, embellishing, showy, beautifying, nonfunctional, arty-crafty

decorum NOUN **= propriety**, decency, etiquette, breeding, protocol, respectability, politeness, good manners, good grace, gentility, deportment, courtliness, politesse, punctilio, seemliness
OPPOSITE: impropriety

decoy NOUN **= lure**, attraction, bait, trap, inducement, enticement, ensnarement

decrease VERB **1 = drop**, decline, lessen, contract, lower, ease, shrink, diminish, fall off, dwindle, wane, subside, abate, peter out, slacken: *Population growth is decreasing each year.* **2 = reduce**, cut, lower, contract, depress, moderate, weaken, diminish, turn down, slow down, cut down, shorten, dilute, impair, lessen, curtail, wind down, abate, tone down, truncate, abridge, downsize: *Regular doses of aspirin decrease the risk of heart attack.* **OPPOSITE:** increase
▷ NOUN **= lessening**, decline, reduction, loss, falling off, downturn, dwindling, contraction, ebb, cutback, subsidence, curtailment, shrinkage, diminution, abatement: *There has been a decrease in the number of young unemployed people.* **OPPOSITE:** growth

decree NOUN **1 = law**, order, ruling, act, demand, command, regulation, mandate, canon, statute, covenant, ordinance, proclamation, enactment, edict, dictum, precept: *He issued a decree ordering all unofficial armed groups to disband.* **2 = judgment**, finding, order, result, ruling, decision, award, conclusion, verdict, arbitration: *court decrees relating to marital property*
▷ VERB **= order**, rule, command, decide, demand, establish, determine, proclaim, dictate, prescribe, pronounce, lay down, enact, ordain: *He got the two men off the hook by decreeing a general amnesty.*

decrepit ADJECTIVE **1 = ruined**, broken-down, battered, crumbling, rundown, deteriorated, decaying, beat-up *(informal)*, shabby, worn-out, ramshackle, dilapidated, antiquated, rickety, weather-beaten, tumbledown: *The film was shot in a decrepit police station.* **2 = weak**, aged, frail, wasted, fragile, crippled, feeble, past it, debilitated, incapacitated, infirm, superannuated, doddering: *a decrepit old man*

decry VERB **= condemn**, blame, abuse, blast, denounce, put down, criticize, run down, discredit, censure, detract, denigrate, belittle, disparage, rail against, depreciate, tear into *(informal)*, diss *(slang, chiefly U.S.)*, lambast(e), traduce, excoriate, derogate, cry down, asperse

dedicate VERB **1 = devote**, give, apply, commit, concern, occupy, pledge, surrender, give over to: *He dedicated himself to politics.* **2 = offer**, address, assign, inscribe: *This book is dedicated to the memory of my sister.* **3 = consecrate**, bless, sanctify, set apart, hallow: *The church is dedicated to a saint.*

dedicated ADJECTIVE **= committed**, devoted, sworn, enthusiastic, single-minded, zealous, purposeful, given over to, wholehearted
OPPOSITE: indifferent

dedication NOUN **1 = commitment**, loyalty, devotion, allegiance, adherence, single-mindedness, faithfulness, wholeheartedness, devotedness: *To be successful takes hard work and dedication.*
OPPOSITE: indifference
2 = inscription, message, address: *His book contains a dedication to his parents.*

deduce VERB **= work out**, reason, understand, gather, conclude, derive, infer, glean

deduct VERB **= subtract**, remove, take off, withdraw, take out, take from, take away, reduce by, knock off *(informal)*, decrease by **OPPOSITE:** add

deduction NOUN **1 = conclusion**, finding, verdict, judgment, assumption, inference, corollary: *It was a pretty astute deduction.* **2 = reasoning**, thinking, thought, reason, analysis, logic, cogitation, ratiocination: *'How did you guess?' 'Deduction,' he replied.* **3 = discount**, reduction, cut, concession, allowance, decrease, rebate, diminution: *your gross income, before tax and insurance deductions* **4 = subtraction**, reduction, allowance, concession: *the deduction of tax at 20%*

deed NOUN **1 = action**, act, performance, achievement, exploit, feat: *His heroic deeds were celebrated in every corner of the country.* **2 = document**, title, contract, title deed, indenture: *He asked if I had the deeds to his father's property.*

deem VERB **= consider**, think, believe, hold, account, judge, suppose, regard, estimate, imagine, reckon, esteem, conceive

deep ADJECTIVE **1 = big**, wide, broad, profound, yawning, cavernous, bottomless, unfathomable, fathomless, abyssal: *The workers had dug a deep hole in the centre of the garden.*
OPPOSITE: shallow **2 = intense**, great, serious *(informal)*, acute, extreme, grave, profound, heartfelt, unqualified, abject, deeply felt, heartrending: *a period of deep personal crisis* **OPPOSITE:** superficial **3 = sound**, peaceful, profound, unbroken, undisturbed, untroubled: *He fell into a deep sleep.* **4** *(with* **in***)* **= absorbed in**, lost in, gripped by, intent on, preoccupied with, carried away by, immersed in, engrossed in, rapt by: *Before long we were deep in conversation.* **5 = wise**, learned, searching, keen, critical, acute, profound, penetrating, discriminating, shrewd, discerning, astute, perceptive, incisive, perspicacious, sagacious: *She gave him a long deep look.* **OPPOSITE:** simple
6 = dark, strong, rich, warm, intense, vivid: *rich, deep colours* **OPPOSITE:** light
7 = low, booming, bass, full, mellow, resonant, sonorous, mellifluous, dulcet, low-pitched, full-toned: *His voice was deep and mellow.*
OPPOSITE: high **8 = astute**, knowing, clever, designing, scheming, sharp, smart, intelligent, discriminating, shrewd, cunning, discerning, canny, devious, perceptive, insidious, artful, far-sighted, far-seeing, perspicacious, sagacious: *a very deep individual*
OPPOSITE: simple **9 = secret**, hidden, unknown, mysterious, concealed, obscure, abstract, veiled, esoteric, mystifying, impenetrable, arcane, abstruse, recondite: *a deep, dark secret*
▷ NOUN **= middle**, heart, midst, dead, thick, culmination: *in the deep of night*
▷ ADVERB **1 = far**, a long way, a good way, miles, deeply, far down, a great distance: *They travelled deep into the forest.* **2 = far**, late: *We talked deep into the night.*
the deep = the ocean, the sea, the waves, the main, the drink *(informal)*,

the high seas, the briny *(informal)*: *whales and other creatures of the deep*

PROVERBS
Still waters run deep

deepen VERB **1 = intensify**, increase, grow, strengthen, reinforce, escalate, magnify, augment: *Sloane's uneasiness deepened; Further job losses deepened the gloom.* **2 = dig out**, excavate, scoop out, hollow out, scrape out: *The tunnels have been widened and deepened.*

deeply ADVERB **= thoroughly**, completely, seriously, sadly, severely, gravely, profoundly, intensely, to the heart, passionately, acutely, to the core, feelingly, movingly, distressingly, to the quick, affectingly

deep-rooted *or* **deep-seated** ADJECTIVE **= fixed**, confirmed, rooted, settled, entrenched, ingrained, inveterate, dyed-in-the-wool, ineradicable **OPPOSITE:** superficial

deface VERB **= vandalize**, damage, destroy, total *(slang)*, injure, mar, spoil, trash *(slang)*, impair, tarnish, obliterate, mutilate, deform, blemish, disfigure, sully

de facto ADVERB **= in fact**, really, actually, in effect, in reality: *Unification has now de facto replaced the signing of such a treaty.*
▷ ADJECTIVE **= actual**, real, existing: *a de facto recognition of the republic's independence*

defamation NOUN **= slander**, smear, libel, scandal, slur, vilification, opprobrium, denigration, calumny, character assassination, disparagement, obloquy, aspersion, traducement

defamatory ADJECTIVE **= slanderous**, insulting, abusive, denigrating, disparaging, vilifying, derogatory, injurious, libellous, vituperative, calumnious, contumelious

defame VERB **= slander**, smear, libel, discredit, knock *(informal)*, rubbish *(informal)*, disgrace, blacken, slag (off) *(slang)*, detract, malign, denigrate, disparage, vilify, dishonour, stigmatize, bad-mouth *(slang, chiefly U.S. & Canad.)*, besmirch, traduce, cast aspersions on, speak evil of, cast a slur on, calumniate, vituperate, asperse

default NOUN **1 = failure**, want, lack, fault, absence, neglect, defect, deficiency, lapse, omission, dereliction: *The other team failed to turn up so we won by default.*
2 = nonpayment, evasion: *The country can't pay its foreign debts and default is inevitable.*
▷ VERB **= fail to pay**, dodge, evade, rat *(informal)*, neglect, levant *(Brit.)*, welch or welsh *(slang)*: *Many borrowers are defaulting on loans.*

defeat VERB **1 = beat**, crush, overwhelm, conquer, stuff *(slang)*, master, worst, tank *(slang)*, overthrow, lick *(informal)*, undo, subdue, rout, overpower, quell, trounce, clobber *(slang)*, vanquish, repulse, subjugate, run rings around *(informal)*, wipe the floor with *(informal)*, make mincemeat of *(informal)*, pip at the post, outplay, blow out of the water *(slang)*, murk *(slang)*: *His guerrillas defeated the colonial army.* **OPPOSITE:** surrender
2 = frustrate, foil, thwart, ruin, baffle, confound, balk, get the better of, forestall, stymie: *The challenges of constructing such a huge novel almost defeated her.*
▷ NOUN **1 = conquest**, beating, overthrow, pasting *(slang)*, rout, debacle, trouncing, repulse, vanquishment: *The vote was seen as something of a defeat for the lobbyists.*
OPPOSITE: victory **2 = frustration**, failure, reverse, disappointment, setback, thwarting: *the final defeat of all his hopes*

QUOTATIONS
How are the mighty fallen, and the weapons of war perished!
[*Bible: II Samuel*]

Defeat is a thing of weariness, of incoherence, of boredom. And above all futility
[Antoine de Saint-Exupéry *Flight to Arras*]

Victory has a hundred fathers, but defeat is an orphan
[Count Galeazzo Giano *Diary*]

defeated ADJECTIVE **= beaten**, crushed, conquered, worsted, routed, overcome, overwhelmed, thrashed, licked *(informal)*, thwarted, overpowered, balked, trounced, vanquished, checkmated, bested **OPPOSITE:** victorious

defeatist NOUN **= pessimist**, sceptic, scoffer, doubter, quitter, prophet of doom, yielder: *a defeatist might give up at this point*
▷ ADJECTIVE **= pessimistic**, resigned, despairing, hopeless, foreboding, despondent, fatalistic: *Don't go out there with a defeatist attitude.*

defecate VERB **= excrete**, eliminate, discharge, evacuate *(Physiology)*, dump *(slang, chiefly U.S.)*, pass a motion, move the bowels, empty the bowels, open the bowels, egest, void excrement

defect NOUN **= deficiency**, want, failing, lack, mistake, fault, error, absence, weakness, flaw, shortcoming, inadequacy, imperfection, frailty, foible: *The report pointed out the defects in the present system.*
▷ VERB **= desert**, rebel, quit, revolt, change sides, apostatize, tergiversate: *a KGB official who defected in 1963*

defection NOUN **= desertion**, revolt, rebellion, abandonment, dereliction, backsliding, apostasy

defective ADJECTIVE **1 = faulty**, broken, not working, flawed, imperfect, out of order, on the blink *(slang)*: *Retailers can return defective merchandise.* **OPPOSITE:** perfect
2 = deficient, lacking, short, inadequate, insufficient, incomplete, scant: *food which is defective in nutritional quality* **OPPOSITE:** adequate

defector NOUN **= deserter**, renegade, turncoat, apostate, recreant *(archaic)*, runagate *(archaic)*, tergiversator

defence *or (U.S.)* **defense** NOUN
1 = protection, cover, security, guard, shelter, refuge, resistance, safeguard, immunity: *The land was flat, giving no scope for defence.* **2 = armaments**, weapons: *Twenty-eight per cent of the federal budget is spent on defense.*
3 = argument, explanation, excuse, plea, apology, justification, vindication, rationalization, apologia, exoneration, exculpation, extenuation: *a spirited defence of the government's economic progress* **4 = plea** *(Law)*, case, claim, pleading, declaration, testimony, denial, alibi, vindication, rebuttal: *His defence was that records were fabricated by the police.*
▷ PLURAL NOUN **= shield**, barricade, fortification, bastion, buttress, rampart, bulwark, fastness, fortified pa *(N.Z.)*: *Soldiers are beginning to strengthen the city's defences.*

defenceless *or (U.S.)* **defenseless** ADJECTIVE **= helpless**, exposed, vulnerable, naked, endangered, powerless, wide open, unarmed, unprotected, unguarded
OPPOSITE: safe

defend VERB **1 = protect**, cover, guard, screen, secure, preserve, look after, shelter, shield, harbour, safeguard, fortify, ward off, watch over, stick up for *(informal)*, keep safe, give sanctuary: *They defended themselves against some racist thugs.* **2 = support**, champion, justify, maintain, sustain, plead for, endorse, assert, stand by, uphold, vindicate, stand up for, espouse, speak up for, stick up for *(informal)*: *Police chiefs strongly defended police conduct.*

defendant NOUN **= accused**, respondent, appellant, litigant, prisoner at the bar

defender NOUN **1 = supporter**, champion, advocate, sponsor, follower, patron, apologist, upholder, vindicator: *a strong defender of human rights* **2 = protector**, guard, guardian, escort, bodyguard, guardian angel: *He proclaims himself a defender of the environment.*

defensible ADJECTIVE **= justifiable**, right, sound, reasonable, acceptable, sensible, valid, legitimate, plausible, permissible, well-founded, tenable, excusable, pardonable, vindicable: *Her reasons for action are morally defensible.*
OPPOSITE: unjustifiable

defensive ADJECTIVE **1 = protective**, defending, opposing, safeguarding, watchful, on the defensive, on guard: *hastily organized defensive measures*
2 = oversensitive, uptight *(informal)*: *She heard the blustering, defensive note in his voice.*

defensively ADVERB **= in self-defence**, in defence, suspiciously, on the defensive

The Brontës' Use of Verbs

Of the three Brontë sisters, Charlotte (1816–55) was the one who lived longest, and was most prolific. The best known of her novels is *Jane Eyre*; she also wrote *Villette* and *The Professor*. Emily (1818–48) wrote *Wuthering Heights*, and Anne (1820–49) wrote *The Tenant of Wildfell Hall* and *Agnes Grey*. All the sisters also wrote poetry. Anne spent her life in Yorkshire; her sisters spent some time in Brussels, and spoke French fluently. All worked as governesses and teachers.

The three women had different characters, as is clear from their novels, but their works have in common a powerful emotional quality. *Feel* and *love* are very frequently used verbs. Their writing is dramatic, sometimes melodramatic, with a great deal of direct speech: verbs to do with speaking, such as *say*, *speak*, *ask*, and *answer* are very common in all their books. Often *say* is replaced by a livelier synonym, such as *exclaim* or *cry*. All the sisters made heavy use of the exclamation mark, not only in spoken dialogue, but also in internal monologue:

'Oh! that that some kind spirit would whisper those words in his ear,' I inwardly **exclaimed**.

The novels have first person narrators, who tell their story and report dialogue, either to other characters, or to the reader, who is sometimes invited into the drama. Anne begins *The Tenant of Wildfell Hall* with the word *You* (*'You must go back with me to the autumn of 1829'*), and Jane Eyre announces her climactic decision directly to the reader:

Reader, I married him!

As we have seen, the Brontës often prefer to use a synonym for the common verb *say*. The synonym may be more dramatic, such as *whisper*, *murmur*, *thunder*, or simply less common, such as *utter*, *observe*, *remark*, *inquire*; sometimes the choice is extremely formal, such as *vociferate* or *asseverate*. The use of literary or formal words is a marked characteristic of their writing – thus *endeavour* is used almost as much as *try*; *cease* almost as much as *stop*. Characters invariably *descend*, rather than *go down*, stairs; they *rise* rather than *stand up*; *seek* is preferred to *look for*. *Continue* is used much more frequently than *go on*. *Resume* is used transitively to mean *continue with*, or *go back to*, as in current usage, but with a much wider variety of objects; people resume their seat, position, tone, manner – even their bonnets.

At the opposite extreme from this high-flown language, however, is the Yorkshire dialect that the sisters grew up surrounded by. Emily makes use of it for some of the characters in *Wuthering Heights*. Joseph, for example, uses the dialect verbs *mun* (must), *dee* (die), and *brust* (burst). Emily also represents the Yorkshire pronunciation of such words as *have, had, go*, and *serve*:

I mun hev' my wage, and I mun goa! I hed aimed to dee wheare I'd sarved.

When they write in dialect the Brontës' grammar is natural and colloquial, but elsewhere it can be very formal and literary. Verb and pronoun are often inverted:

'No, indeed, Mrs Fairfax!' **exclaimed** I, nettled; 'he is nothing like my father!'

They sometimes use formal subjunctive constructions, such as *God grant he be not disappointed!* Also, instead of making verbs negative by the use of the *do* auxiliary (*I do not know, he did not heed*), they often place *not* after the verb, in the manner of Shakespeare or the Bible, eg *I know not how he would bear it; Mr Rochester heard but heeded not*. Similarly there is a tendency to use the verb followed by *no* (*I felt no fear; I saw no change; she gained no precise knowledge)* rather than, for example, *I didn't feel any fear*.

The Brontës (daughters of a vicar, and committed Anglicans) were of course extremely familiar with the language of the Bible. Their writing shows its influence in various ways, including their use of archaic verb forms, such as *thou hast, he hath, thou standest*, and *thou shalt*.

d

defer[1] VERB **= postpone**, delay, put off, suspend, shelve, set aside, adjourn, hold over, procrastinate, put on ice *(informal)*, put on the back burner *(informal)*, protract, take a rain check on *(U.S. & Canad. informal)*, prorogue

defer[2] VERB *(with* **to***)* **= comply with**, give way to, submit to, bow to, give in to, yield to, accede to, capitulate to

deference NOUN **1 = respect**, regard, consideration, attention, honour, esteem, courtesy, homage, reverence, politeness, civility, veneration, thoughtfulness: *Out of deference to his feelings, I refrained from commenting.* **OPPOSITE:** disrespect **2 = obedience**, yielding, submission, compliance, capitulation, acquiescence, obeisance, complaisance: *a chain of social command linked by deference to authority* **OPPOSITE:** disobedience

deferential ADJECTIVE **= respectful**, civil, polite, courteous, considerate, obedient, submissive, dutiful, ingratiating, reverential, obsequious, complaisant, obeisant, regardful

defiance NOUN **= resistance**, challenge, opposition, confrontation, contempt, disregard, provocation, disobedience, insolence, insubordination, rebelliousness, recalcitrance, contumacy **OPPOSITE:** obedience

defiant ADJECTIVE **= resisting**, challenging, rebellious, daring, aggressive, bold, provocative, audacious, recalcitrant, antagonistic, insolent, mutinous, disobedient, refractory, insubordinate, contumacious **OPPOSITE:** obedient

deficiency NOUN **1 = lack**, want, deficit, absence, shortage, deprivation, inadequacy, scarcity, dearth, privation, insufficiency, scantiness: *They did tests for signs of vitamin deficiency.* **OPPOSITE:** sufficiency **2 = failing**, fault, weakness, defect, flaw, drawback, shortcoming, imperfection, frailty, demerit: *the most serious deficiency in their air defence*

deficient ADJECTIVE **1 = lacking**, wanting, needing, short, inadequate, insufficient, scarce, scant, meagre, skimpy, scanty, exiguous: *a diet deficient in vitamins* **2 = unsatisfactory**, weak, flawed, inferior, impaired, faulty, incomplete, defective, imperfect: *deficient landing systems*

deficit NOUN **= shortfall**, shortage, deficiency, loss, default, arrears

defile VERB **1 = degrade**, stain, disgrace, sully, debase, dishonour, besmirch, smirch: *He felt his father's memory had been defiled by the article.* **2 = desecrate**, violate, contaminate, abuse, pollute, profane, dishonour, despoil, treat sacrilegiously: *Who gave you permission to defile this sacred place?* **3 = dirty**, soil, contaminate, smear, pollute, taint, tarnish, make foul, smirch, befoul: *piles of old clothes defiled with excrement*

define VERB **1 = mark out**, outline, limit, bound, delineate, circumscribe, demarcate, delimit: *Armed forces were deployed to define military zones.* **2 = describe**, interpret, characterize, explain, spell out, expound: *How exactly do you define reasonable behaviour?* **3 = establish**, detail, determine, specify, designate: *The Court must define the limits of its authority.*

definite ADJECTIVE **1 = specific**, exact, precise, clear, particular, express, determined, fixed, black-and-white, explicit, clear-cut, cut-and-dried *(informal)*, clearly defined: *It's too soon to give a definite answer.* **OPPOSITE:** vague **2 = clear**, explicit, black-and-white, clear-cut, unequivocal, unambiguous, guaranteed, cut-and-dried *(informal)*: *We didn't have any definite proof.* **3 = noticeable**, marked, clear, decided, striking, noted, particular, obvious, dramatic, considerable, remarkable, apparent, evident, distinct, notable, manifest, conspicuous: *There has been a definite improvement.* **4 = certain**, decided, sure, settled, convinced, positive, confident, assured: *She is very definite about her feelings.* **OPPOSITE:** uncertain

> **USAGE**
> *Definite* and *definitive* should be carefully distinguished. *Definite* indicates precision and firmness, as in *a definite decision*. *Definitive* includes these senses but also indicates conclusiveness. *A definite answer* indicates a clear and firm answer to a particular question; *a definitive answer* implies an authoritative resolution of a complex question.

definitely ADVERB **= certainly**, clearly, obviously, surely, easily, plainly, absolutely, positively, decidedly, needless to say, without doubt, unquestionably, undeniably, categorically, without question, unequivocally, unmistakably, far and away, without fail, beyond any doubt, indubitably, defo *(Brit. informal)*, come hell or high water *(informal)*

definition NOUN **1 = description**, interpretation, explanation, clarification, exposition, explication, elucidation, statement of meaning: *There is no general agreement on a standard definition of sanity.* **2 = sharpness**, focus, clarity, contrast, precision, distinctness: *This printer has excellent definition.*

definitive ADJECTIVE **1 = final**, convincing, absolute, clinching, decisive, definite, conclusive, irrefutable: *No one has come up with a definitive answer to that question.* **2 = authoritative**, greatest, ultimate, reliable, most significant, exhaustive, superlative, mother of all *(informal)*: *It is still the definitive book on the islands.*

deflate VERB **1 = humiliate**, humble, squash, put down *(slang)*, disconcert, chasten, mortify, dispirit: *Her comments deflated him a bit.* **2 = puncture**, flatten, empty: *The vandals had deflated his car's tyres.* **OPPOSITE:** inflate **3 = collapse**, go down, contract, empty, shrink, void, flatten: *The balloon began to deflate.* **OPPOSITE:** expand **4 = reduce**, depress, decrease, diminish, devalue, depreciate: *artificially deflated prices*

deflect VERB **= turn aside**, turn, bend, twist, sidetrack

deflection NOUN **= deviation**, bending, veering, swerving, divergence, turning aside, refraction, declination

deform VERB **1 = disfigure**, twist, injure, cripple, ruin, mar, spoil, mutilate, maim, deface: *Severe rheumatoid arthritis deforms limbs.* **2 = distort**, twist, warp, buckle, mangle, contort, gnarl, misshape, malform: *Plastic deforms when subjected to heat.*

deformation NOUN **= distortion**, warping, contortion, malformation, disfiguration, misshapenness

deformed ADJECTIVE **= distorted**, bent, twisted, crooked, crippled, warped, maimed, marred, mangled, disfigured, misshapen, malformed, misbegotten

deformity NOUN **1 = abnormality**, defect, malformation, disfigurement: *facial deformities in babies* **2 = distortion**, irregularity, misshapenness, misproportion: *Bones grind against each other, leading to pain and deformity.*

defraud VERB **= cheat**, rob, con *(informal)*, do *(slang)*, skin *(slang)*, stiff *(slang)*, rip off *(slang)*, fleece, swindle, stitch up *(slang)*, rook *(slang)*, diddle *(informal)*, bilk, gyp *(slang)*, pull a fast one on *(informal)*, cozen, scam *(slang)*

defray VERB **= pay**, meet, cover, clear, settle, discharge

deft ADJECTIVE **= skilful**, able, expert, clever, neat, handy, adept, nimble, proficient, agile, adroit, dexterous **OPPOSITE:** clumsy

defunct ADJECTIVE **1 = dead**, extinct, gone, departed, expired, deceased, bygone, nonexistent: *the leader of the now defunct Social Democratic Party* **2 = not functioning**, obsolete, out of commission, inoperative: *He looked at the defunct apparatus and diagnosed the problem.*

defuse VERB **1 = calm**, settle, cool, contain, smooth, stabilize, damp down, take the heat *or* sting out of: *Officials will hold talks aimed at defusing tensions over trade.* **OPPOSITE:** aggravate **2 = deactivate**, disable, disarm, make safe: *Police have defused a bomb.* **OPPOSITE:** activate

defy VERB **1 = resist**, oppose, confront, face, brave, beard, disregard, stand up to, spurn, flout, disobey, hold out against, put up a fight (against), hurl defiance at, contemn: *This was the first time that I had dared to defy her.*

2 = challenge, dare, provoke: *He defied me to come up with a better idea.* **3 = foil**, defeat, escape, frustrate, be beyond, baffle, thwart, elude, confound: *a fragrance that defies description*

degenerate VERB **= decline**, slip, sink, decrease, deteriorate, worsen, rot, decay, lapse, fall off, regress, go to pot, retrogress: *He degenerated into drug and alcohol abuse.*
▷ ADJECTIVE **= depraved**, base, corrupt, fallen, low, perverted, degraded, degenerated, immoral, decadent, debased, debauched, dissolute, pervy (*slang*): *the degenerate attitudes he found among some of his fellow officers*

degeneration NOUN **= deterioration**, decline, dissolution, descent, regression, dissipation, degeneracy, debasement

degradation NOUN **1 = disgrace**, shame, humiliation, discredit, ignominy, dishonour, mortification: *scenes of misery and degradation* **2 = deterioration**, decline, decadence, degeneration, perversion, degeneracy, debasement, abasement: *the progressive degradation of the state*

degrade VERB **1 = demean**, disgrace, humiliate, injure, shame, corrupt, humble, discredit, pervert, debase, dishonour, cheapen: *Pornography degrades women.* **OPPOSITE:** ennoble **2 = demote**, reduce, lower, downgrade, depose, cashier: *He was degraded to a lower rank.* **OPPOSITE:** promote

degraded ADJECTIVE **1 = humiliated**, embarrassed, shamed, mortified, debased, discomfited, abased: *I felt cheap and degraded by his actions.* **2 = corrupt**, low, base, abandoned, vicious, vile, sordid, decadent, despicable, depraved, debased, profligate, disreputable, debauched, dissolute, scungy (*Austral. & N.Z.*): *morally degraded individuals*

degrading ADJECTIVE **= demeaning**, lowering, humiliating, disgraceful, shameful, unworthy, debasing, undignified, contemptible, cheapening, dishonourable, infra dig (*informal*)

degree NOUN **1 = amount**, measure, rate, stage, extent, grade, proportion, gradation: *They achieved varying degrees of success.* **2 = rank**, order, standing, level, class, position, station, status, grade, caste, nobility, echelon: *the fall of a man of high degree and noble character*
by degrees = little by little, slowly, gradually, moderately, gently, piecemeal, bit by bit, imperceptibly, inch by inch, unhurriedly: *The crowd was thinning, but only by degrees.*

dehydrate VERB **= dry**, evaporate, parch, desiccate, exsiccate

deign VERB **= condescend**, consent, stoop, see fit, think fit, lower yourself, deem it worthy

deity NOUN **= god**, goddess, immortal, divinity, godhead, divine being, supreme being, celestial being, atua (*N.Z.*)

dejected ADJECTIVE **= downhearted**, down, low, blue, sad, depressed, miserable, gloomy, dismal, melancholy, glum, despondent, downcast, morose, disheartened, wretched, disconsolate, crestfallen, doleful, down in the dumps (*informal*), cast down, sick as a parrot (*informal*), woebegone, low-spirited
OPPOSITE: cheerful

delay VERB **1 = put off**, suspend, postpone, stall, shelve, prolong, defer, hold over, temporize, put on the back burner (*informal*), protract, take a rain check on (*U.S. & Canad. informal*): *I delayed my departure until she could join me.* **2 = hold up**, detain, hold back, stop, arrest, halt, hinder, obstruct, retard, impede, bog down, set back, slow up: *The passengers were delayed by bad weather.* **OPPOSITE:** speed (up) **3 = linger**, lag, loiter, dawdle, tarry, dilly-dally (*informal*), drag your feet *or* heels (*informal*): *If he delayed any longer, the sun would be up.*
▷ NOUN **1 = hold-up**, wait, check, setback, interruption, obstruction, stoppage, impediment, hindrance: *Air restrictions might mean delays for Easter holidaymakers.* **2 = dawdling**, lingering, loitering, procrastination, tarrying, dilly-dallying (*informal*): *We'll send you a quote without delay.*

delectable ADJECTIVE **1 = delicious**, tasty, luscious, inviting, satisfying, pleasant, delightful, enjoyable, lush, enticing, gratifying, dainty, yummy (*slang*), scrumptious (*informal*), appetizing, toothsome, lekker (*S. African slang*), yummo (*Austral. slang*): *a delectable dessert* **OPPOSITE:** disgusting **2 = charming**, pleasant, delightful, agreeable, adorable: *a delectable young woman in a swimsuit*

delegate NOUN **= representative**, agent, deputy, ambassador, commissioner, envoy, proxy, depute (*Scot.*), legate, spokesman *or* spokeswoman: *The rebels' chief delegate repeated their demands.*
▷ VERB **1 = entrust**, transfer, hand over, give, pass on, assign, relegate, consign, devolve: *Many employers find it hard to delegate duties.* **2 = appoint**, commission, select, contract, engage, nominate, designate, mandate, authorize, empower, accredit, depute: *Officials have been delegated to start work on a settlement.*

delegation NOUN **1 = deputation**, envoys, contingent, commission, embassy, legation: *They sent a delegation to the talks.* **2 = commissioning**, relegation, assignment, devolution, committal, deputizing, entrustment: *the delegation of his responsibilities to his assistant*

delete VERB **= remove**, cancel, cut out, erase, edit, excise, strike out, obliterate, efface, blot out, cross out, expunge, dele, rub out, edit out, blue-pencil

deliberate ADJECTIVE **1 = intentional**, meant, planned, considered, studied, designed, intended, conscious, calculated, thoughtful, wilful, purposeful, premeditated, prearranged, done on purpose: *The attack was deliberate and unprovoked.* **OPPOSITE:** accidental **2 = careful**, measured, slow, cautious, wary, thoughtful, prudent, circumspect, methodical, unhurried, heedful: *His movements were gentle and deliberate.* **OPPOSITE:** hurried
▷ VERB **= consider**, think, ponder, discuss, debate, reflect, consult, weigh, meditate, mull over, ruminate, cogitate: *The jury deliberated for two hours before returning with the verdict.*

deliberately ADVERB **= intentionally**, on purpose, consciously, emphatically, knowingly, resolutely, pointedly, determinedly, wilfully, by design, studiously, in cold blood, wittingly, calculatingly

deliberation NOUN **1 = consideration**, thought, reflection, study, speculation, calculation, meditation, forethought, circumspection, cogitation: *His decision was the result of great deliberation.* **2** (*usually plural*) **= discussion**, talk, conference, exchange, debate, analysis, conversation, dialogue, consultation, seminar, symposium, colloquy, confabulation: *The outcome of the deliberations was inconclusive.*

> **QUOTATIONS**
> deliberation: the act of examining your bread to determine which side it is buttered on
> [Ambrose Bierce *The Devil's Dictionary*]

delicacy NOUN **1 = fragility**, frailty, brittleness, flimsiness, frailness, frangibility: *the delicacy of the crystal glasses* **2 = daintiness**, charm, grace, elegance, neatness, prettiness, slenderness, exquisiteness: *a country where the feminine ideal is delicacy and grace* **3 = difficulty**, sensitivity, stickiness (*informal*), precariousness, critical nature, touchiness, ticklishness: *the delicacy of the political situation* **4 = sensitivity**, understanding, consideration, judgment, perception, diplomacy, discretion, skill, finesse, tact, thoughtfulness, savoir-faire, adroitness, sensitiveness: *He's shown considerable delicacy and tact.* **5 = treat**, luxury, goody, savoury, dainty, morsel, titbit, choice item, juicy bit, bonne bouche (*French*): *course after course of mouthwatering delicacies* **6 = lightness**, accuracy, precision, elegance, sensibility, purity, subtlety, refinement, finesse, nicety, fineness, exquisiteness: *He played with a superb delicacy of touch.*

delicate ADJECTIVE **1 = fine**, detailed, elegant, exquisite, graceful: *china with a delicate design* **2 = subtle**, fine, nice, soft, delicious, faint, refined, muted, subdued, pastel, understated, dainty:

The colours are delicate and tasteful. **OPPOSITE:** bright **3 = fragile**, weak, frail, brittle, tender, flimsy, dainty, breakable, frangible: *Although the material looks tough, it is very delicate.* **4 = difficult**, critical, sensitive, complicated, sticky *(informal)*, problematic, precarious, thorny, touchy, knotty, ticklish: *the delicate issue of adoption* **5 = skilled**, accurate, precise, deft: *A cosmetic surgeon performed the delicate operation.* **6 = fastidious**, nice, critical, pure, Victorian, proper, refined, discriminating, stuffy, scrupulous, prim, puritanical, squeamish, prudish, prissy *(informal)*, strait-laced, schoolmarmish *(Brit. informal)*, old-maidish *(informal)*: *He didn't want to offend his mother's delicate sensibilities.* **OPPOSITE:** crude **7 = diplomatic**, sensitive, careful, subtle, thoughtful, discreet, prudent, considerate, judicious, tactful: *a situation which requires delicate handling* **OPPOSITE:** insensitive

delicately ADVERB **1 = finely**, lightly, subtly, softly, carefully, precisely, elegantly, gracefully, deftly, exquisitely, skilfully, daintily: *soup delicately flavoured with nutmeg* **2 = tactfully**, carefully, subtly, discreetly, thoughtfully, diplomatically, sensitively, prudently, judiciously, considerately: *a delicately-worded memo*

delicious ADJECTIVE **1 = delectable**, tasty, luscious, choice, savoury, palatable, dainty, mouthwatering, yummy *(slang)*, scrumptious *(informal)*, appetizing, toothsome, ambrosial, lekker *(S. African slang)*, nectareous, yummo *(Austral. slang)*: *a wide selection of delicious meals to choose from* **OPPOSITE:** unpleasant **2 = delightful**, pleasing, charming, heavenly, thrilling, entertaining, pleasant, enjoyable, exquisite, captivating, agreeable, pleasurable, rapturous, delectable: *a delicious feeling of anticipation* **OPPOSITE:** unpleasant

delight VERB **= please**, satisfy, content, thrill, charm, cheer, amuse, divert, enchant, rejoice, gratify, ravish, gladden, give pleasure to, tickle pink *(informal)*: *The report has delighted environmentalists.* **OPPOSITE:** displease
▷ NOUN **= pleasure**, joy, satisfaction, comfort, happiness, ecstasy, enjoyment, bliss, felicity, glee, gratification, rapture, gladness: *To my delight, the plan worked perfectly.* **OPPOSITE:** displeasure
delight in *or* **take a delight in something** *or* **someone = like**, love, enjoy, appreciate, relish, indulge in, savour, revel in, take pleasure in, glory in, luxuriate in: *He delighted in sharing his news.*

delighted ADJECTIVE **= pleased**, happy, charmed, thrilled, enchanted, ecstatic, captivated, jubilant, joyous, elated, over the moon *(informal)*, overjoyed, rapt, gladdened, cock-a-hoop, blissed out, in seventh heaven, sent, stoked *(Austral. & N.Z. informal)*

delightful ADJECTIVE **= pleasant**, pleasing, charming, engaging, heavenly, thrilling, fascinating, entertaining, amusing, enjoyable, enchanting, captivating, gratifying, agreeable, pleasurable, ravishing, rapturous **OPPOSITE:** unpleasant

delineate VERB **= outline**, describe, draw, picture, paint, chart, trace, portray, sketch, render, depict, characterize, map out: *The relationship between Church and State was delineated in a formal agreement.*

delinquency NOUN **= crime**, misconduct, wrongdoing, fault, offence, misdemeanour, misdeed, misbehaviour, villainy, lawbreaking

delinquent NOUN **= criminal**, offender, villain, culprit, young offender, wrongdoer, juvenile delinquent, miscreant, malefactor, lawbreaker

delirious ADJECTIVE **1 = mad**, crazy, raving, insane, demented, deranged, incoherent, unhinged, light-headed: *I was delirious and blacked out several times.* **OPPOSITE:** rational **2 = ecstatic**, wild, excited, frantic, frenzied, hysterical, carried away, blissed out, beside yourself, sent, Corybantic: *He was delirious with joy.* **OPPOSITE:** calm

delirium NOUN **1 = madness**, raving, insanity, lunacy, derangement: *In her delirium, she fell to the floor.* **2 = frenzy**, passion, rage, fever, fury, ecstasy, hysteria: *She was in a delirium of panic.*

deliver VERB **1 = bring**, carry, bear, transport, distribute, convey, cart: *The pizza will be delivered in 20 minutes.* **2** *(sometimes with* **over** *or* **up***)* **= hand over**, present, commit, give up, yield, surrender, turn over, relinquish, make over: *He was led in handcuffs and delivered over to me.* **3 = give**, read, present, announce, publish, declare, proclaim, pronounce, utter, give forth: *He will deliver a speech about schools.* **4 = strike**, give, deal, launch, throw, direct, aim, administer, inflict: *A single blow had been delivered to the head.* **5 = release**, free, save, rescue, loose, discharge, liberate, acquit, redeem, ransom, emancipate: *I thank God for delivering me from that pain.*

deliverance NOUN **= release**, rescue, liberation, salvation, redemption, ransom, emancipation

delivery NOUN **1 = handing over**, transfer, distribution, transmission, dispatch, consignment, conveyance, transmittal: *the delivery of goods and resources* **2 = consignment**, goods, shipment, batch: *a delivery of fresh eggs* **3 = speech**, speaking, expression, pronunciation, utterance, articulation, intonation, diction, elocution, enunciation, vocalization: *His speeches were magnificent but his delivery was hopeless.* **4 = childbirth**, labour, confinement, parturition: *She had an easy delivery.*

delude VERB **= deceive**, kid *(informal)*, fool, trick, take in *(informal)*, cheat, con *(informal)*, mislead, impose on, hoax, dupe, beguile, gull *(archaic)*, bamboozle *(informal)*, hoodwink, take for a ride *(informal)*, pull the wool over someone's eyes, lead up the garden path *(informal)*, cozen, misguide, scam *(slang)*

deluge NOUN **1 = rush**, flood, avalanche, barrage, spate, torrent: *a deluge of criticism* **2 = flood**, spate, overflowing, torrent, downpour, cataclysm, inundation: *A dozen homes were damaged in the deluge.*
▷ VERB **1 = overwhelm**, swamp, engulf, overload, overrun, inundate: *The office was deluged with complaints.* **2 = flood**, drown, swamp, submerge, soak, drench, inundate, douse: *Torrential rain deluged the capital.*

delusion NOUN **= misconception**, mistaken idea, misapprehension, fancy, illusion, deception, hallucination, fallacy, self-deception, false impression, phantasm, misbelief

deluxe *or* **de luxe** ADJECTIVE **= luxurious**, grand, select, special, expensive, rich, exclusive, superior, elegant, costly, splendid, gorgeous, sumptuous, plush *(informal)*, opulent, palatial, splendiferous *(facetious)*

delve VERB **1 = research**, investigate, explore, examine, probe, look into, burrow into, dig into: *She delved into her mother's past.* **2 = rummage**, search, look, burrow, ransack, forage, dig, fossick *(Austral. & N.Z.)*: *He delved into his rucksack and pulled out a folder.*

demagogue NOUN **= agitator**, firebrand, haranguer, rabble-rouser, soapbox orator

demand VERB **1 = request**, ask (for), order, expect, claim, seek, call for, insist on, exact, appeal for, solicit: *She demanded an immediate apology.* **2 = challenge**, ask, question, inquire: *'What do you expect me to do about it?' she demanded.* **3 = require**, take, want, need, involve, call for, entail, necessitate, cry out for: *The task demands much patience and hard work.* **OPPOSITE:** provide
▷ NOUN **1 = request**, order, charge, bidding: *He grew ever more fierce in his demands.* **2 = need**, want, call, market, claim, requirement, necessity: *The demand for coal is down.*
in demand = sought after, needed, popular, favoured, requested, in favour, fashionable, well-liked, in vogue, like gold dust: *He was much in demand as a lecturer.*

demanding ADJECTIVE **= difficult**, trying, hard, taxing, wearing, challenging, tough, exhausting, exacting, exigent: *It is a demanding job.* **OPPOSITE:** easy

demarcation NOUN **1 = limit**, bound, margin, boundary, confine, enclosure, pale: *The demarcation of the border between the two countries.* **2 = delimitation**, division, distinction, separation, differentiation: *The demarcation of duties became more blurred.*

demean VERB **= degrade**, lower, debase, humble, abase: *Pornography demeans women.*
demean yourself = lower yourself, humiliate yourself, humble yourself, debase yourself, downgrade yourself, abase yourself, belittle yourself, degrade yourself: *I wasn't going to demean myself by answering him.*

demeanour *or (U.S.)* **demeanor** NOUN **1 = behaviour**, conduct, manner **2 = bearing**, air, manner, carriage, deportment, mien *(literary)*, comportment

demented ADJECTIVE **= mad**, crazy, foolish, daft *(informal)*, frenzied, distraught, manic, insane, crazed, lunatic, unbalanced, deranged, idiotic, unhinged, dotty *(slang, chiefly Brit.)*, loopy *(informal)*, crackpot *(informal)*, out to lunch *(informal)*, barking mad *(slang)*, barking *(slang)*, maniacal, gonzo *(slang)*, doolally *(slang)*, off your trolley *(slang)*, up the pole *(informal)*, non compos mentis *(Latin)*, not the full shilling *(informal)*, crackbrained, wacko *or* whacko *(slang)*, off the air *(Austral. slang)*, porangi *(N.Z.)* **OPPOSITE:** sane

demise NOUN **1 = failure**, end, fall, defeat, collapse, ruin, breakdown, overthrow, downfall, dissolution, termination: *the demise of the reform movement* **2 = death**, end, dying, passing, departure, expiration, decease: *Smoking was the cause of his early demise.*

democracy NOUN **= self-government**, republic, commonwealth, representative government, government by the people

QUOTATIONS

To give victory to the right, not bloody bullets, but peaceful ballots only, are necessary
[Abraham Lincoln *speech*]

My notion of democracy is that under it the weakest should have the same opportunity as the strongest
[Gandhi *Non-Violence in Peace and War*]

Democracy ... is a charming form of government, full of variety and disorder, and dispensing a sort of equality to equals and unequals alike
[Plato *The Republic*]

Man's capacity for justice makes democracy possible; but man's inclination to injustice makes democracy necessary
[Reinhold Niebuhr *The Children of Light and the Children of Darkness*]

After each war there is a little less democracy to save
[Brooks Atkinson *Once Around the Sun*]

Democracy is the superior form of government, because it is based on a respect for man as a reasonable being
[John F. Kennedy *Why England Slept*]

Democracy means government by discussion, but it is only effective if you can stop people talking
[Clement Atlee *Anatomy of Britain*]

Democracy is the worst form of Government except all those other forms that have been tried from time to time
[Winston Churchill *speech*]

Democracy is the name we give the people whenever we need them
[Robert, Marquis de Flers and Arman de Caillavet *L'habit vert*]

Democracy substitutes election by the incompetent many for appointment by the corrupt few
[George Bernard Shaw *Man and Superman*]

All the ills of democracy can be cured by more democracy
[Alfred Emanuel Smith]

government of the people, by the people, and for the people
[Abraham Lincoln *Gettysburg Address*]

Democratic nations care but little for what has been, but they are haunted by visions of what will be
[Alexis de Tocqueville *Democracy in America*]

Two Cheers for Democracy: one because it admits variety and two because it permits criticism. Two cheers are quite enough: there is no occasion to give three
[E.M. Forster *Two Cheers for Democracy*]

Democracy means government by the uneducated, while aristocracy means government by the badly educated
[G.K. Chesterton *New York Times*]

Democrat NOUN **= left-winger**: *The director of the company has links to the Democrats.*

democratic ADJECTIVE **= self-governing**, popular, republican, representative, autonomous, populist, egalitarian

demolish VERB **1 = knock down**, level, destroy, ruin, overthrow, dismantle, flatten, trash *(slang)*, total *(slang)*, tear down, bulldoze, raze, pulverize: *The building is being demolished to make way for a motorway.* **OPPOSITE:** build **2 = destroy**, wreck, overturn, overthrow, undo, blow out of the water *(slang)*: *Their intention was to demolish his reputation.* **3 = devour**, eat, consume, swallow, bolt, gorge, put away, gobble up, guzzle, polish off *(informal)*, gulp down, wolf down, pig out on *(slang)*: *We demolished a six-pack of beer.*

demolition NOUN **= knocking down**, levelling, destruction, explosion, wrecking, tearing down, bulldozing, razing

demon NOUN **1 = evil spirit**, devil, fiend, goblin, ghoul, malignant spirit, atua *(N.Z.)*, wairua *(N.Z.)*: *a woman possessed by evil demons* **2 = wizard**, master, ace *(informal)*, addict, fanatic, fiend: *He is a demon for discipline.* **3 = monster**, beast, villain, rogue, barbarian, brute, ogre: *He was a dictator and a demon.*

demonic, demoniac *or* **demoniacal** ADJECTIVE **1 = devilish**, satanic, diabolical, hellish, infernal, fiendish, diabolic: *demonic forces* **2 = frenzied**, mad, furious, frantic, hectic, manic, crazed, frenetic, maniacal, like one possessed: *a demonic drive to succeed*

demonstrable ADJECTIVE **= provable**, obvious, evident, certain, positive, unmistakable, palpable, undeniable, self-evident, verifiable, irrefutable, incontrovertible, axiomatic, indubitable, attestable, evincible

demonstrate VERB **1 = prove**, show, establish, indicate, make clear, manifest, evidence, testify to, evince, show clearly, flag up: *You have to demonstrate that you are reliable.* **2 = show**, evidence, express, display, indicate, exhibit, manifest, make clear *or* plain, flag up: *Have they demonstrated a commitment to democracy?* **3 = march**, protest, rally, object, parade, picket, say no to, remonstrate, take up the cudgels, express disapproval, hikoi *(N.Z.)*: *Vast crowds have been demonstrating against the reforms.* **4 = describe**, show, explain, teach, illustrate: *He demonstrated how to peel and chop garlic.*

demonstration NOUN **1 = march**, protest, rally, sit-in, parade, procession, demo *(informal)*, picket, mass lobby, hikoi *(N.Z.)*: *Riot police broke up the demonstration.* **2 = display**, show, performance, explanation, description, presentation, demo *(informal)*, exposition: *a cookery demonstration* **3 = indication**, proof, testimony, confirmation, affirmation, validation, substantiation, attestation: *an unprecedented demonstration of people power* **4 = exhibition**, display, expression, illustration: *physical demonstrations of affection*

demoralize VERB **= dishearten**, undermine, discourage, shake, depress, weaken, rattle *(informal)*, daunt, unnerve, disconcert, psych out *(informal)*, dispirit, deject **OPPOSITE:** encourage

demoralized ADJECTIVE **= disheartened**, undermined, discouraged, broken, depressed, crushed, weakened, subdued, unnerved, unmanned, dispirited, downcast, sick as a parrot *(informal)*

demoralizing ADJECTIVE **= disheartening**, discouraging, depressing, crushing, disappointing, daunting, dampening, dispiriting **OPPOSITE:** encouraging

demote VERB **= downgrade**, relegate, degrade, kick downstairs *(slang)*, declass, disrate *(Naval)*, lower in rank **OPPOSITE:** promote

demur VERB **= object**, refuse, protest, doubt, dispute, pause, disagree, hesitate, waver, balk, take exception, cavil: *At first I demurred when he asked me to do it.*
▷ NOUN **= objection**, protest, dissent, hesitation, misgiving, qualm, scruple, compunction, demurral, demurrer: *She entered without demur.*

d

demure ADJECTIVE **= shy**, reserved, modest, retiring, reticent, unassuming, diffident, decorous **OPPOSITE:** brazen

den NOUN **1 = lair**, hole, shelter, cave, haunt, cavern, hide-out: *The skunk makes its den in burrows and hollow logs.* **2 = study**, retreat, sanctuary, hideaway, cloister, sanctum, cubbyhole, snuggery: *The walls of his den were covered in posters.*

denial NOUN **1 = negation**, dismissal, contradiction, dissent, disclaimer, retraction, repudiation, disavowal, adjuration: *their previous denial that chemical weapons were being used* **OPPOSITE:** admission **2 = refusal**, veto, rejection, prohibition, rebuff, repulse: *the denial of visas to international workers*

denigrate VERB **= disparage**, run down, slag (off) *(slang)*, knock *(informal)*, rubbish *(informal)*, blacken, malign, belittle, decry, revile, vilify, slander, defame, bad-mouth *(slang, chiefly U.S. & Canad.)*, besmirch, impugn, calumniate, asperse **OPPOSITE:** praise

denizen NOUN **= inhabitant**, resident, citizen, occupant, dweller

denomination NOUN **1 = religious group**, belief, sect, persuasion, creed, school, hauhau *(N.Z.)*: *Acceptance of women preachers varies from one denomination to another.* **2 = unit**, value, size, grade: *a pile of bank notes, mostly in small denominations*

denote VERB **= indicate**, show, mean, mark, express, import, imply, designate, signify, typify, betoken

denouement *or* **dénouement** NOUN **= outcome**, end, result, consequence, resolution, conclusion, end result, upshot: *an unexpected denouement to the affair*

denounce VERB **1 = condemn**, attack, censure, decry, castigate, revile, vilify, proscribe, stigmatize, impugn, excoriate, declaim against: *The leaders took the opportunity to denounce the attacks.* **2 = report**, dob in *(Austral. slang)*: *Informers might at any moment denounce them to the authorities.*

dense ADJECTIVE **1 = thick**, close, heavy, solid, substantial, compact, compressed, condensed, impenetrable, close-knit, thickset: *a large, dense forest* **OPPOSITE:** thin **2 = heavy**, thick, substantial, opaque, impenetrable: *a dense column of smoke* **3 = stupid** *(informal)*, slow, thick, dull, dumb *(informal)*, crass, dozy *(Brit. informal)*, stolid, dopey *(informal)*, moronic, obtuse, brainless, blockheaded, braindead *(informal)*, dumb-ass *(informal)*, dead from the neck up *(informal)*, thickheaded, blockish, dim-witted *(informal)*, slow-witted, thick-witted: *He's not a bad man, just a bit dense.* **OPPOSITE:** bright

density NOUN **1 = tightness**, closeness, thickness, compactness, impenetrability, denseness, crowdedness: *The region has a high population density.* **2 = mass**, body, bulk, consistency, solidity: *Jupiter's moon Io has a density of 3.5 grams per cubic centimetre.*

dent NOUN **= hollow**, chip, indentation, depression, impression, pit, dip, crater, ding *(Austral. & N.Z. obsolete, informal)*, dimple, concavity: *There was a dent in the bonnet of the car.*
▷ VERB **= make a dent in**, press in, gouge, depress, hollow, imprint, push in, dint, make concave: *The table's brass feet dented the carpet's thick pile.*

denude VERB **= strip**, expose, bare, uncover, divest, lay bare

denunciation NOUN **1 = condemnation**, criticism, accusation, censure, stick *(slang)*, invective, character assassination, stigmatization, castigation, obloquy, denouncement, fulmination: *a stinging denunciation of his critics* **2 = implication**, accusation, indictment, incrimination, denouncement, inculpation: *Denunciation by family, friends and colleagues inevitably sowed distrust.*

deny VERB **1 = contradict**, oppose, counter, disagree with, rebuff, negate, rebut, refute, gainsay *(archaic, literary)*: *She denied the accusations.* **OPPOSITE:** admit **2 = renounce**, reject, discard, revoke, retract, repudiate, renege, disown, rebut, disavow, recant, disclaim, abjure, abnegate, refuse to acknowledge *or* recognize: *I denied my parents because I wanted to become someone else.* **3 = refuse**, decline, forbid, reject, rule out, veto, turn down, prohibit, withhold, preclude, disallow, negate, begrudge, interdict: *His ex-wife denies him access to his children.* **OPPOSITE:** permit

deodorant NOUN **1 = antiperspirant**, deodorizer: *He took a can of deodorant and sprayed his armpits.* **2 = deodorizer**, disinfectant, air freshener, fumigant: *She didn't like the smell of the carpet deodorant in the limousine.*

depart VERB **1 = leave**, go, withdraw, retire, disappear, quit, retreat, exit, go away, vanish, absent (yourself), start out, migrate, set forth, take (your) leave, decamp, hook it *(slang)*, slope off, pack your bags *(informal)*, make tracks, rack off *(Austral. & N.Z. slang)*: *In the morning Mr McDonald departed for Sydney.* **OPPOSITE:** arrive **2 = deviate**, vary, differ, stray, veer, swerve, diverge, digress, turn aside: *It takes a brave cook to depart radically from the traditional menu.* **3 = resign**, leave, quit, step down *(informal)*, give in your notice, call it a day *or* night, vacate your post: *A number of staff departed during her reign as manager.*

departed ADJECTIVE **= dead**, late, deceased, expired, perished

department NOUN **1 = section**, office, unit, station, division, branch, bureau, subdivision: *He worked in the sales department.* **2 = area**, line, responsibility, function, province, sphere, realm, domain, speciality: *Sorry, I don't know – that's not my department.*

departure NOUN **1 = leaving**, going, retirement, withdrawal, exit, going away, removal, exodus, leave-taking: *The airline has more than 90 scheduled departures from here each day.* **OPPOSITE:** arrival **2 = retirement**, going, withdrawal, exit, going away, removal: *This would inevitably involve his departure from the post.* **3 = shift**, change, difference, variation, innovation, novelty, veering, deviation, branching out, divergence, digression: *This album is a considerable departure from her previous work.*

dependable ADJECTIVE **= reliable**, sure, responsible, steady, faithful, staunch, reputable, trustworthy, trusty, go-to, unfailing **OPPOSITE:** undependable

dependant NOUN **= relative**, rellie *(Austral. slang)*, child, minor, subordinate, cohort *(chiefly U.S.)*, protégé, henchman, retainer, hanger-on, minion, vassal

> **USAGE**
> *Dependant* is the generally accepted correct spelling in British usage for the noun and always refers to people: *if you are single and have no dependants*. The adjective should be spelt *dependent*: *tax allowance for dependent* (not *dependant*) *children*. American usage spells both adjective and noun with an *e* in the last syllable.

dependence *or (sometimes U.S.)* **dependance** NOUN **= reliance**, trust, hope, confidence, belief, faith, expectation, assurance: *the city's traditional dependence on tourism*

dependency *or (sometimes U.S.)* **dependancy** NOUN **1 = overreliance**, attachment: *I am concerned by his dependency on his mother.* **2 = addiction**, dependence, craving, need, habit, obsession, enslavement, overreliance: *He began to show signs of alcohol and drug dependency.*

dependent *or (sometimes U.S.)* **dependant** ADJECTIVE **1 = reliant**, vulnerable, helpless, powerless,

weak, defenceless: *I refuse to be dependent, despite having a baby to care for.* **OPPOSITE:** independent
2 = determined by, depending on, subject to, influenced by, relative to, liable to, conditional on, contingent on: *companies whose earnings are largely dependent on foreign economies*
dependent on *or* **upon = reliant on**, relying on, counting on: *He was dependent on his parents for everything.*

depend on VERB **1 = be determined by**, be based on, be subject to, hang on, rest on, revolve around, hinge on, be subordinate to, be contingent on: *What happened later would depend on his talk with her.* **2 = count on**, turn to, trust in, bank on, lean on, rely upon, confide in, build upon, calculate on, reckon on: *She assured him that he could depend on her.*

depict VERB **1 = illustrate**, portray, picture, paint, outline, draw, sketch, render, reproduce, sculpt, delineate, limn: *a gallery of pictures depicting famous battles* **2 = describe**, present, represent, detail, outline, sketch, characterize: *Children's books often depict animals as gentle creatures.*

depiction NOUN **1 = picture**, drawing, image, outline, illustration, sketch, likeness, delineation: *The vase has a depiction of a man playing a lyre.*
2 = representation, description, portrait, illustration, sketch, portrayal: *the depiction of socialists as Utopian dreamers*

deplete VERB **= use up**, reduce, drain, exhaust, consume, empty, decrease, evacuate, lessen, impoverish, expend **OPPOSITE:** increase

depleted ADJECTIVE **= used (up)**, drained, exhausted, consumed, spent, reduced, emptied, weakened, decreased, lessened, worn out, depreciated

depletion NOUN **= using up**, reduction, drain, consumption, lowering, decrease, expenditure, deficiency, dwindling, lessening, exhaustion, diminution

deplorable ADJECTIVE **1 = terrible**, distressing, dreadful, sad, unfortunate, disastrous, miserable, dire, melancholy, heartbreaking, grievous, regrettable, lamentable, calamitous, wretched, pitiable: *Many of them work under deplorable conditions.* **OPPOSITE:** excellent **2 = disgraceful**, shameful, scandalous, reprehensible, disreputable, dishonourable, execrable, blameworthy, opprobrious: *Sexual harassment is deplorable.* **OPPOSITE:** admirable

deplore VERB **1 = disapprove of**, condemn, object to, denounce, censure, abhor, deprecate, take a dim view of, excoriate: *He says he deplores violence.* **2 = lament**, regret, mourn, rue, bemoan, grieve for, bewail, sorrow over: *They deplored the heavy loss of life in the earthquake.*

deploy VERB **= use**, station, set up, position, arrange, set out, dispose, utilize, spread out, distribute

deployment NOUN **= use**, stationing, spread, organization, arrangement, positioning, disposition, setup, utilization

deport VERB **= expel**, exile, throw out, oust, banish, expatriate, extradite, evict, send packing, show you the door

deportation NOUN **= expulsion**, exile, removal, transportation, exclusion, extradition, eviction, ejection, banishment, expatriation, debarment

depose VERB **= oust**, dismiss, displace, degrade, downgrade, cashier, demote, dethrone, remove from office

deposit VERB **1 = put**, place, lay, drop, settle: *The barman deposited a glass and two bottles of beer in front of him.* **2 = store**, keep, put, bank, save, lodge, entrust, consign, hoard, stash *(informal)*, lock away, put in storage: *You are advised to deposit valuables in the hotel safe.*
▷ NOUN **1 = down payment**, security, stake, pledge, warranty, instalment, retainer, part payment: *A deposit of £20 is required when ordering.*
2 = accumulation, growth, mass, build-up, layer: *underground deposits of gold and diamonds* **3 = sediment**, grounds, residue, lees, precipitate, deposition, silt, dregs, alluvium, settlings: *A powdery deposit had settled at the bottom of the glass.*

deposition NOUN **1 = sworn statement** *(Law)*, evidence, testimony, declaration, affidavit: *The material would be checked against depositions from other witnesses.*
2 = removal, dismissal, ousting, toppling, expulsion, displacement, unseating, dethronement: *It was this issue which led to the deposition of the leader.*

depository NOUN **= storehouse**, store, warehouse, depot, repository, safe-deposit box

depot NOUN **1 = arsenal**, warehouse, storehouse, repository, depository, dump: *a government arms depot* **2 = bus station**, station, garage, terminus: *She was reunited with her boyfriend in the bus depot.*

deprave VERB **= corrupt**, pervert, degrade, seduce, subvert, debase, demoralize, debauch, brutalize, lead astray, vitiate

depraved ADJECTIVE **= corrupt**, abandoned, perverted, evil, vicious, degraded, vile, degenerate, immoral, wicked, shameless, sinful, lewd, debased, profligate, debauched, lascivious, dissolute, licentious, pervy *(slang)* **OPPOSITE:** moral

> **QUOTATIONS**
> No one ever suddenly became depraved
> [Juvenal *Satires*]

depravity NOUN **= corruption**, vice, evil, criminality, wickedness, immorality, iniquity, profligacy, debauchery, viciousness, degeneracy, sinfulness, debasement, turpitude, baseness, depravation, vitiation

deprecate VERB **= disparage**, criticize, run down, discredit, scorn, deride, detract, malign, denigrate, belittle, vilify, knock *(informal)*, diss *(slang, chiefly U.S.)*, bad-mouth *(slang, chiefly U.S. & Canad.)*, lambast(e): *They deprecate him and refer to him as 'a bit of a red'.*

depreciate VERB **1 = decrease**, reduce, lessen, devalue, deflate, lower in value, devaluate: *The demand for foreign currency depreciates the real value of local currencies.* **OPPOSITE:** augment
2 = lose value, devalue, devaluate: *Inflation is rising rapidly and the yuan is depreciating.* **OPPOSITE:** appreciate

depreciation NOUN **= devaluation**, fall, drop, depression, slump, deflation

depress VERB **1 = sadden**, upset, distress, chill, discourage, grieve, daunt, oppress, desolate, weigh down, cast down, bring tears to your eyes, make sad, dishearten, dispirit, make your heart bleed, aggrieve, deject, make despondent, cast a gloom upon, harsh someone's mellow *or* buzz: *The state of the country depresses me.* **OPPOSITE:** cheer
2 = lower, cut, reduce, diminish, decrease, impair, lessen: *The stronger currency depressed sales.* **OPPOSITE:** raise
3 = devalue, depreciate, cheapen, devaluate: *A dearth of buyers has depressed prices* **4 = press down**, push, squeeze, lower, flatten, compress, push down, bear down on: *He depressed the pedal that lowered the chair.*

depressed ADJECTIVE **1 = sad**, down, low, blue, unhappy, discouraged, fed up, moody, gloomy, pessimistic, melancholy, sombre, glum, mournful, dejected, despondent, dispirited, downcast, morose, disconsolate, crestfallen, doleful, downhearted, heavy-hearted, down in the dumps *(informal)*, cheerless, woebegone, down in the mouth *(informal)*, low-spirited: *He seemed somewhat depressed.* **2 = poverty-stricken**, poor, deprived, distressed, disadvantaged, rundown, impoverished, needy, destitute, down at heel: *attempts to encourage investment in depressed areas* **3 = lowered**, devalued, weakened, impaired, depreciated, cheapened: *We need to prevent further falls in already depressed prices.* **4 = sunken**, hollow, recessed, set back, indented, concave: *Manual pressure is applied to a depressed point on the body.*

depressing ADJECTIVE **= bleak**, black, sad, distressing, discouraging, gloomy, daunting, hopeless, dismal, melancholy, dreary, harrowing, saddening, sombre, heartbreaking, dispiriting, disheartening, funereal, dejecting

depression NOUN **1 = despair**, misery, sadness, dumps *(informal)*, the blues, melancholy, unhappiness, hopelessness, despondency, the hump *(Brit. informal)*, bleakness, melancholia, dejection, wretchedness, low spirits, gloominess, dolefulness, cheerlessness, downheartedness: *I slid into a depression and became morbidly fascinated with death.* **2 = recession**, slump, economic decline, credit crunch, stagnation, inactivity, hard *or* bad times: *He never forgot the hardships he witnessed during the depression.* **3 = hollow**, pit, dip, bowl, valley, sink, impression, dent, sag, cavity, excavation, indentation, dimple, concavity: *an area pockmarked by rainfilled depressions*

> **QUOTATIONS**
> It's a recession when your neighbour loses his job; it's a depression when you lose yours [Harry S. Truman]

deprivation NOUN **1 = lack**, denial, withdrawal, removal, expropriation, divestment, dispossession, deprival: *Millions suffer from sleep deprivation caused by long work hours.* **2 = want**, need, hardship, suffering, distress, disadvantage, oppression, detriment, privation, destitution: *Single women with children are likely to suffer financial deprivation.*

deprive VERB **= dispossess**, rob, strip, divest, expropriate, despoil, bereave

deprived ADJECTIVE **= poor**, disadvantaged, needy, in need, lacking, bereft, destitute, in want, denuded, down at heel, necessitous **OPPOSITE:** prosperous

depth NOUN **1 = deepness**, drop, measure, extent, profundity, profoundness: *The fish were detected at depths of more than a kilometre.* **2 = strength**, intensity, seriousness, severity, extremity, keenness, intenseness: *I am well aware of the depth of feeling that exists in the town* **3 = insight**, intelligence, wisdom, penetration, profundity, acuity, discernment, perspicacity, sagacity, astuteness, profoundness, perspicuity: *His writing has a depth that will outlast him.* **OPPOSITE:** superficiality **4 = breadth**, degree, magnitude, amplitude: *We were impressed with the depth of her knowledge.* **5 = intensity**, strength, warmth, richness, brightness, vibrancy, vividness: *The blue base gives the red paint more depth.* **6 = complexity**, intricacy, elaboration, obscurity, abstruseness, reconditeness: *His music lacks depth.*
▷ PLURAL NOUN **1 = deepest part**, middle, midst, remotest part, furthest part, innermost part: *A sound came from the depths of the forest.* **2 = most intense part**, pit, void, abyss, chasm, deepest part, furthest part, bottomless depth: *a man who had plumbed the depths of despair*

deputy NOUN **= substitute**, representative, ambassador, agent, commissioner, delegate, lieutenant, proxy, surrogate, second-in-command, nuncio, legate, vicegerent, number two: *France's minister for culture and his deputy attended the meeting.*
▷ MODIFIER **= assistant**, subordinate, depute *(Scot.)*: *the academy's deputy director*

deranged ADJECTIVE **= mad**, crazy, insane, distracted, frantic, frenzied, irrational, maddened, crazed, lunatic, demented, unbalanced, berserk, delirious, unhinged, loopy *(informal)*, crackpot *(informal)*, out to lunch *(informal)*, barking mad *(slang)*, barking *(slang)*, gonzo *(slang)*, doolally *(slang)*, off your trolley *(slang)*, up the pole *(informal)*, not the full shilling *(informal)*, wacko *or* whacko *(slang)*, berko *(Austral. slang)*, off the air *(Austral. slang)*, porangi *(N.Z.)* **OPPOSITE:** sane

derelict ADJECTIVE **1 = abandoned**, deserted, ruined, neglected, discarded, forsaken, dilapidated: *His body was found dumped in a derelict warehouse.* **2 = negligent**, slack, irresponsible, careless, lax, remiss: *They would be derelict in their duty not to pursue it.*
▷ NOUN **= tramp**, bum *(informal)*, outcast, drifter, down-and-out, vagrant, hobo *(chiefly U.S.)*, vagabond, bag lady, dosser *(Brit. slang)*, derro *(Austral. slang)*: *a confused and wizened derelict wandered in off the street*

dereliction NOUN **1 = abandonment**, desertion, renunciation, relinquishment: *The previous owners had rescued the building from dereliction.* **2 = negligence**, failure, neglect, evasion, delinquency, abdication, faithlessness, nonperformance, remissness: *He pleaded guilty to wilful dereliction of duty.*

deride VERB **= mock**, ridicule, scorn, knock *(informal)*, insult, taunt, sneer, jeer, disdain, scoff, detract, flout, disparage, chaff, gibe, pooh-pooh, contemn

derision NOUN **= mockery**, laughter, contempt, ridicule, scorn, insult, sneering, disdain, scoffing, disrespect, denigration, disparagement, contumely, raillery

derisory ADJECTIVE **= ridiculous**, insulting, outrageous, ludicrous, preposterous, laughable, contemptible

derivation NOUN **= origin**, source, basis, beginning, root, foundation, descent, ancestry, genealogy, etymology

derivative ADJECTIVE **= unoriginal**, copied, second-hand, rehashed, imitative, plagiarized, uninventive, plagiaristic: *their dull, derivative debut album* **OPPOSITE:** original
▷ NOUN **= by-product**, spin-off, offshoot, descendant, derivation, outgrowth: *a poppy-seed derivative similar to heroin*

derive VERB **= obtain**, get, receive, draw, gain, collect, gather, extract, elicit, glean, procure: *He is one of those people who derives pleasure from helping others.*
derive from something = come from, stem from, arise from, flow from, spring from, emanate from, proceed from, descend from, issue from, originate from: *The word Druid may derive from 'drus', meaning 'oak tree'.*

derogatory ADJECTIVE **= disparaging**, damaging, offensive, slighting, detracting, belittling, unfavourable, unflattering, dishonouring, defamatory, injurious, discreditable, uncomplimentary, depreciative **OPPOSITE:** complimentary

descend VERB **1 = fall**, drop, sink, go down, plunge, dive, tumble, plummet, subside, move down: *Disaster struck as the plane descended through the mist.* **OPPOSITE:** rise= **get off** **2 = go down**, come down, walk down, move down, climb down: *Things are cooler and more damp as we descend to the cellar.* **3 = slope**, dip, incline, slant, gravitate: *The path descended steeply to the rushing river.*
be descended from = originate from, derive from, spring from, proceed from, issue from: *He was proud to be descended from tradesmen.*
descend on something *or* **someone = attack**, assault, raid, invade, swoop, pounce, assail, arrive, come in force: *Drunken mobs descended on their homes.*
descend to something = lower yourself to, stoop to, condescend to, abase yourself by: *She's got too much dignity to descend to writing anonymous letters.*

descendant NOUN **= successor**, child, issue, son, daughter, heir, offspring, progeny, scion, inheritor **OPPOSITE:** ancestor

descent NOUN **1 = fall**, drop, plunge, coming down, swoop: *The airplane crashed on its descent into the airport.* **2 = slope**, drop, dip, incline, slant, declination, declivity: *On the descents, cyclists freewheel past cars.* **3 = decline**, deterioration, degradation, decadence, degeneration, debasement: *his swift descent from respected academic to homeless derelict* **4 = origin**, extraction, ancestry, lineage, family tree, parentage, heredity, genealogy, derivation: *All the contributors were of foreign descent.*

describe VERB **1 = relate**, tell, report, present, detail, explain, express, illustrate, specify, chronicle, recount, recite, impart, narrate, set forth, give an account of: *We asked her to describe what she had seen.* **2 = portray**, depict, characterize, define, sketch: *Even his allies describe him as forceful, aggressive and determined.* **3 = trace**, draw, outline, mark out, delineate: *The ball described a perfect arc across the field.*

description NOUN **1 = account**, report, explanation, representation,

The Brontës' Use of Adjectives

Charlotte uses adjectives profusely to fine-tune the meaning of nouns. She uses them singly, in pairs or even in threes, fours, fives, or sixes: *a metallic clatter; some low-ceiled oaken chamber; a still, hot, perfect day; a handsome, heroic-looking young gentleman; a sanguine, brilliant, careless, exacting, handsome, romping child.* She forms adjectives from nouns (*fur collared, steel clasped*), and makes frequent use of compounds formed with *-less* and *-ful*: *fathomless depth and measureless distance; a still, dark day, equally beamless and breezeless; an ireful glance*. She combines common and extremely uncommon words: *the grey and battlemented hall; a bad, mad, embruted partner; his once brilliant and now rayless eyes.* She harnesses the energy of verbs by using participles adjectivally: *my ever-torturing pain; the low-gliding and pale-beaming sun; a heaving, stamping, clattering process.* The texture of her writing is generally so densely descriptive that when simple adjectives appear singly they have particular weight:

> The ground was **hard**, the air was **still**, my road was **lonely**.

Two adjectives that Charlotte uses frequently - *dark* and *strange* - are particularly characteristic of her romantic vision. Both words have can have negative or positive connotations: the young Jane is terrified when, as a punishment, she is locked in a *dark and haunted chamber*, but she is strongly attracted by Mr Rochester's face, which is *dark, strong, and stern.* The laugh she hears from the attic is strange, and so too is Mr Rochester's rough, unconventional demeanour. However, she sets no store by politeness and restraint, and thrills to the *strange energy* of his voice, and *strange fire* in his voice. In his declaration of love, he applies the adjective to her;

> You - you **strange**, you almost unearthly thing!

By comparison, Emily's use of adjectives is sparing, especially at climactic moments. Lockwood uses the pompous word *importunate* to describe the branch he thinks is knocking against the window of the room he has been given for the night. This pomposity throws into startling relief what follows:

> 'I must stop it, nevertheless!', I muttered, knocking my knuckles through the glass, and stretching an arm out to seize the importunate branch; instead of which, my fingers closed on the fingers of a little, ice-cold hand!

Nelly Deane's description of Heathcliff on the morning after Cathy dies is wonderful - and almost devoid of adjectives. His devastation is conveyed by his motionless indifference to his surroundings: his hair soaked with dew because he has spent the whole night standing outside, so still that a pair of ousels fly to and fro past him, building their nest. When later he bursts into furious speech, it is all the more shocking, and the words *frightful* and *ungovernable* are scarcely necessary:

> 'May she wake in torment!' he cried, with **frightful** vehemence, stamping his foot, and groaning in a sudden paroxysm of **ungovernable** passion.

The dialect adjectives used by some characters in *Wuthering Heights* are generally terms of abuse, or commendation, rather than mere description. Joseph rails against the wickedness of those who surround him, speaking of *ill childer* (bad children), and *ill ways*. He calls Heathcliff *that fahl* and *flaysome* (wicked and dreadful) *divil of a gypsy*. When he uses the word *bonny* (fine or pretty) it is ironical. He speaks mainly in dialect; other characters use dialect words occasionally. Mr Earnshaw affectionately calls his son *my bonny man*, and Nelly speaks of Cathy's *bonny hair*. She recalls how she'd been called a *cant lass* (good girl) when she did her work well. Catherine tells Heathcliff he's played her an *ill turn*. When she is sick she asks Nelly to shut the window because she is *starving* (freezing cold).

sketch, narrative, portrayal, depiction, narration, characterization, delineation: *He gave a description of the surgery he was about to perform.* **2 = calling**, naming, branding, labelling, dubbing, designation: *his description of the country as a 'police state'* **3 = kind**, sort, type, order, class, variety, brand, species, breed, category, kidney, genre, genus, ilk: *Events of this description occurred daily.*

descriptive ADJECTIVE **= graphic**, vivid, expressive, picturesque, detailed, explanatory, pictorial, illustrative, depictive

d

desecrate VERB **= profane**, dishonour, defile, violate, contaminate, pollute, pervert, despoil, blaspheme, commit sacrilege
OPPOSITE: revere

desert NOUN
just deserts = due, payment, reward, punishment, right, return, retribution, recompense, come-uppance *(slang)*, meed *(archaic)*, requital, guerdon *(poetic)*

desert[1] NOUN **= wilderness**, waste, wilds, wasteland: *The vehicles have been modified to suit conditions in the desert.*
▷ ADJECTIVE **= barren**, dry, waste, wild, empty, bare, lonely, solitary, desolate, arid, unproductive, infertile, uninhabited, uncultivated, unfruitful, untilled: *the desert wastes of Mexico*

desert[2] VERB **1 = abandon**, leave, give up, quit *(informal)*, withdraw from, move out of, relinquish, renounce, vacate, forsake, go away from, leave empty, relinquish possession of: *Poor farmers are deserting their fields and looking for jobs.* **2 = leave**, abandon, strand, betray, maroon, walk out on *(informal)*, forsake, jilt, run out on *(informal)*, throw over, leave stranded, leave high and dry, leave (someone) in the lurch: *Her husband deserted her years ago.*
OPPOSITE: take care of **3 = abscond**, defect, decamp, go over the hill *(Military, slang)*: *He deserted from the army last month.*

deserted ADJECTIVE **1 = empty**, abandoned, desolate, neglected, lonely, vacant, derelict, bereft, unoccupied, godforsaken: *a deserted town* **2 = abandoned**, neglected, forsaken, lonely, forlorn, cast off, left stranded, left in the lurch, unfriended: *the image of a wronged and deserted wife*

deserter NOUN **= defector**, runaway, fugitive, traitor, renegade, truant, escapee, absconder, apostate

desertion NOUN **1 = abandonment**, betrayal, forsaking, dereliction, relinquishment: *It was a long time since she'd referred to her father's desertion of them.* **2 = defection**, apostasy: *mass desertion by the electorate*
3 = absconding, flight, escape *(informal)*, evasion, truancy: *The high rate of desertion has added to the army's woes.*

deserve VERB **= merit**, warrant, be entitled to, have a right to, win, rate, earn, justify, be worthy of, have a claim to

deserved ADJECTIVE **= well-earned**, just, right, meet *(archaic)*, fitting, due, fair, earned, appropriate, justified, suitable, merited, proper, warranted, rightful, justifiable, condign

deservedly ADVERB **= rightly**, fittingly, fairly, appropriately, properly, duly, justifiably, justly, by rights, rightfully, according to your due, condignly
OPPOSITE: undeservedly

deserving ADJECTIVE **= worthy**, righteous, commendable, laudable, praiseworthy, meritorious, estimable
OPPOSITE: undeserving

desiccate VERB **= dry**, drain, evaporate, dehydrate, parch, exsiccate

design VERB **1 = plan**, describe, draw, draft, trace, outline, invent, devise, sketch, formulate, contrive, think out, delineate: *They have designed a machine that is both attractive and practical.*
2 = create, make, plan, project, fashion, scheme, propose, invent, devise, tailor, draw up, conceive, originate, contrive, fabricate, think up: *We may be able to design a course to suit your particular needs.* **3 = intend**, mean, plan, aim, purpose: *a compromise designed to please everyone*
▷ NOUN **1 = pattern**, form, figure, style, shape, organization, arrangement, construction, motif, configuration: *The pictures are based on simple geometric designs.* **2 = plan**, drawing, model, scheme, draft, outline, sketch, blueprint, delineation: *They drew up the design in a week.* **3 = intention**, end, point, aim, goal, target, purpose, object, objective, intent: *Is there some design in having him here?*

designate VERB **1 = name**, call, term, style, label, entitle, dub, nominate, christen: *one man interviewed in our study, whom we shall designate as 'Mr E'*
2 = specify, describe, indicate, define, characterize, stipulate, denote: *I live in Exmoor, which is designated as a national park.* **3 = choose**, reserve, select, label, flag, assign, allocate, set aside
4 = appoint, name, choose, commission, select, elect, delegate, nominate, assign, depute: *We need to designate someone as our spokesperson.*

designation NOUN **1 = name**, title, label, description, denomination, epithet: *Level 4 alert is a designation reserved for very serious incidents.*
2 = appointment, specification, classification: *the designation of the city as a centre of culture* **3 = election**, choice, selection, appointment, nomination: *the designation of Ali as Prophet Muhammad's successor*

designer NOUN **1 = couturier**, stylist: *She is a fashion designer.* **2 = producer**, architect, deviser, creator, planner, inventor, artificer, originator: *Designer Harvey Postlethwaite has rejoined Ferrari.*

designing ADJECTIVE **= scheming**, plotting, intriguing, crooked *(informal)*, shrewd, conspiring, cunning, sly, astute, treacherous, unscrupulous, devious, wily, crafty, artful, conniving, Machiavellian, deceitful

desirability NOUN **= worth**, value, benefit, profit, advantage, merit, usefulness

desirable ADJECTIVE
1 = advantageous, useful, valuable, helpful, profitable, of service, convenient, worthwhile, beneficial, preferable, advisable: *Prolonged negotiation was not desirable.*
OPPOSITE: disadvantageous= **popular**
OPPOSITE: unpopular **2 = attractive**, appealing, beautiful, winning, interesting, pleasing, pretty, fair, inviting, engaging, lovely, charming, fascinating, sexy *(informal)*, handsome, fetching, good-looking, eligible, glamorous, gorgeous, magnetic, cute, enticing, seductive, captivating, alluring, adorable, bonny, winsome, comely, prepossessing: *the young women whom his classmates thought most desirable*
OPPOSITE: unattractive

desire VERB **1 = want**, long for, crave, fancy, hope for, ache for, covet, aspire to, wish for, yearn for, thirst for, hanker after, set your heart on, desiderate: *He was bored and desired change in his life.* **2 = request**, ask, petition, solicit, entreat, importune: *His Majesty desires me to make his wishes known to you.*
▷ NOUN **1 = wish**, want, longing, need, hope, urge, yen *(informal)*, hunger, appetite, aspiration, ache, craving, yearning, inclination, thirst, hankering: *I had a strong desire to help and care for people* **2 = lust**, passion, libido, appetite, lechery, carnality, lasciviousness, concupiscence, randiness *(informal, chiefly Brit.)*, lustfulness: *Teenage sex may not always come out of genuine desire.*

desired ADJECTIVE **= required**, necessary, correct, appropriate, right,

DESERTS

Arabian	Gibson	Kalahari	Mojave	Taklimakan
Atacama	Gobi	Kara Kum	Nubian	Shama
Dasht-i-Lut	Great Sandy	Kyzyl Kum	Rub'al Khali	Thar
Death Valley	Great Victoria	Libyan	Sahara	

expected, fitting, particular, express, accurate, proper, exact

desist VERB **= stop**, cease, refrain from, end, kick *(informal)*, give up, suspend, break off, abstain, discontinue, leave off, have done with, give over *(informal)*, forbear, belay *(Nautical)*

desolate ADJECTIVE **1 = uninhabited**, deserted, bare, waste, wild, ruined, bleak, solitary, barren, dreary, godforsaken, unfrequented: *a desolate, godforsaken place* **OPPOSITE:** inhabited **2 = miserable**, depressed, lonely, lonesome *(chiefly U.S. & Canad.)*, gloomy, dismal, melancholy, forlorn, bereft, dejected, despondent, downcast, wretched, disconsolate, down in the dumps *(informal)*, cheerless, comfortless, companionless: *He was desolate without her.* **OPPOSITE:** happy
▷ VERB **1 = deject**, depress, distress, discourage, dismay, grieve, daunt, dishearten: *I was desolated by the news.* **OPPOSITE:** cheer **2 = destroy**, ruin, devastate, ravage, lay low, lay waste, despoil, depopulate: *A great famine desolated the country.*

desolation NOUN **1 = misery**, distress, despair, gloom, sadness, woe, anguish, melancholy, unhappiness, dejection, wretchedness, gloominess: *He expresses his sense of desolation without self-pity.* **2 = bleakness**, isolation, loneliness, solitude, wildness, barrenness, solitariness, forlornness, desolateness: *We looked out upon a scene of utter desolation.* **3 = ruin**, destruction, havoc, devastation, ruination: *The army left a trail of desolation and death in its wake.*

despair VERB **= lose hope**, give up, lose heart, be despondent, be dejected: *He despairs at much of the press criticism.*
▷ NOUN **= despondency**, depression, misery, gloom, desperation, anguish, melancholy, hopelessness, dejection, wretchedness, disheartenment: *She shook her head in despair at the futility of it all.*

despairing ADJECTIVE **= hopeless**, desperate, depressed, anxious, miserable, frantic, dismal, suicidal, melancholy, dejected, broken-hearted, despondent, downcast, grief-stricken, wretched, disconsolate, inconsolable, down in the dumps *(informal)*, at the end of your tether

despatch *see* **dispatch**

desperado NOUN **= criminal**, thug, outlaw, villain, gangster, gunman, bandit, mugger *(informal)*, cut-throat, hoodlum *(chiefly U.S.)*, ruffian, heavy *(slang)*, lawbreaker, skelm *(S. African)*

desperate ADJECTIVE **1 = hopeless**, despairing, in despair, forlorn, abject, dejected, despondent, demoralized, wretched, disconsolate, inconsolable, downhearted, at the end of your tether: *Her people were poor, desperate and starving.* **2 = grave**, great, pressing, serious, critical, acute, severe, extreme, urgent, dire, drastic, very grave: *Troops are needed to get food to people in desperate need.* **3 = last-ditch**, dangerous, daring, determined, wild, violent, furious, risky, frantic, rash, hazardous, precipitate, hasty, audacious, madcap, foolhardy, headstrong, impetuous, death-defying: *a desperate rescue attempt*

desperately ADVERB **= gravely**, badly, seriously, severely, dangerously, perilously

desperation NOUN **1 = misery**, worry, trouble, pain, anxiety, torture, despair, agony, sorrow, distraction, anguish, unhappiness, heartache, hopelessness, despondency: *this feeling of desperation and helplessness* **2 = recklessness**, madness, defiance, frenzy, impetuosity, rashness, foolhardiness, heedlessness: *It was an act of sheer desperation.*

QUOTATIONS

The mass of men lead lives of quiet desperation
[Henry David Thoreau *Walden*]

PROVERBS

Beggars can't be choosers
A drowning man will clutch at a straw

despicable ADJECTIVE **= contemptible**, mean, low, base, cheap, infamous, degrading, worthless, disgraceful, shameful, vile, sordid, pitiful, abject, hateful, reprehensible, ignominious, disreputable, wretched, scurvy, detestable, scungy *(Austral. & N.Z.)*, beyond contempt **OPPOSITE:** admirable

despise VERB **= look down on**, loathe, scorn, disdain, spurn, undervalue, deride, detest, revile, abhor, have a down on *(informal)*, contemn **OPPOSITE:** admire

despite PREPOSITION **= in spite of**, in the face of, regardless of, even with, notwithstanding, in defiance of, in the teeth of, undeterred by, in contempt of

despondency NOUN **= dejection**, depression, despair, misery, gloom, sadness, desperation, melancholy, hopelessness, the hump *(Brit. informal)*, discouragement, wretchedness, low spirits, disconsolateness, dispiritedness, downheartedness

despondent ADJECTIVE **= dejected**, sad, depressed, down, low, blue, despairing, discouraged, miserable, gloomy, hopeless, dismal, melancholy, in despair, glum, dispirited, downcast, morose, disheartened, sorrowful, wretched, disconsolate, doleful, downhearted, down in the dumps *(informal)*, sick as a parrot *(informal)*, woebegone, low-spirited **OPPOSITE:** cheerful

despot NOUN **= tyrant**, dictator, oppressor, autocrat, monocrat

despotic ADJECTIVE **= tyrannical**, authoritarian, dictatorial, absolute, arrogant, oppressive, autocratic, imperious, domineering, monocratic

despotism NOUN **= tyranny**, dictatorship, oppression, totalitarianism, autocracy, absolutism, autarchy, monocracy

dessert NOUN **= pudding**, sweet *(informal)*, afters *(Brit. informal)*, second course, last course, sweet course

destination NOUN **= stop**, station, haven, harbour, resting-place, terminus, journey's end, landing-place

d

destined ADJECTIVE **= fated**, meant, intended, designed, certain, bound, doomed, ordained, predestined, foreordained: *He feels that he was destined to become a musician.*
destined for = bound for, booked for, directed towards, scheduled for, routed for, heading for, assigned to, en route to, on the road to: *products destined for the south*

destiny NOUN **1 = fate**, fortune, lot, portion, doom, nemesis, divine decree: *We are masters of our own destiny.* **2** *(usually cap.)* **= fortune**, chance, karma, providence, kismet, predestination, divine will: *Is it Destiny or accident that brings people together?*

QUOTATIONS

destiny: a tyrant's authority for crime and a fool's excuse for failure
[Ambrose Bierce *The Devil's Dictionary*]

Everything comes gradually and at its appointed hour
[Ovid *The Art of Love*]

Thy lot or portion of life is seeking after thee; therefore be at rest from seeking after it
[Ali Ibn-Abi-Talib]

PROVERBS

What must be, must be

destitute ADJECTIVE **= penniless**, poor, impoverished, distressed, needy, on the rocks, insolvent, poverty-stricken, down and out, indigent, impecunious, dirt-poor *(informal)*, on the breadline *(informal)*, flat broke *(informal)*, short, penurious, on your uppers, necessitous, in queer street *(informal)*, moneyless, without two pennies to rub together *(informal)*: *destitute children who live on the streets*
destitute of = lacking, wanting, without, in need of, deprived of, devoid of, bereft of, empty of, drained of, deficient in, depleted in: *a country destitute of natural resources*

destroy VERB **1 = ruin**, smash, crush, waste, devastate, break down, wreck, shatter, gut, wipe out, dispatch, dismantle, demolish, trash *(slang)*, total *(slang)*, ravage, slay, eradicate, torpedo, extinguish, desolate, annihilate, put paid to, raze, blow to bits, extirpate, blow sky-high: *The building was completely destroyed.* **2 = slaughter**, kill, exterminate: *The horse had to be destroyed.*

destruction NOUN **1 = ruin**, havoc, wreckage, crushing, wrecking, shattering, undoing, demolition, devastation, annihilation, ruination: *the extensive destruction caused by the rioters* **2 = massacre**, overwhelming, slaughter, overthrow, extinction, end, downfall, liquidation, obliteration, extermination, eradication: *Our objective was the destruction of the enemy forces.* **3 = slaughter**: *the destruction of animals infected with foot-and-mouth disease*

destructive ADJECTIVE **1 = devastating**, fatal, deadly, lethal, harmful, damaging, catastrophic, detrimental, hurtful, pernicious, noxious, ruinous, calamitous, cataclysmic, baleful, deleterious, injurious, baneful, maleficent: *the awesome destructive power of nuclear weapons* **2 = negative**, hostile, discouraging, undermining, contrary, vicious, adverse, discrediting, disparaging, antagonistic, derogatory: *Try to give constructive rather than destructive criticism.*

desultory ADJECTIVE **= random**, vague, irregular, loose, rambling, inconsistent, erratic, disconnected, haphazard, cursory, aimless, off and on, fitful, spasmodic, discursive, unsystematic, inconstant, maundering, unmethodical

detach VERB **1 = separate**, free, remove, divide, isolate, cut off, sever, loosen, segregate, disconnect, tear off, disengage, disentangle, unfasten, disunite, uncouple, unhitch, disjoin, unbridle: *Detach the bottom part from the form and keep it for reference.* **OPPOSITE:** attach **2 = free**, remove, separate, isolate, cut off, segregate, disengage: *Gradually my husband detached me from all my friends.*

detached ADJECTIVE **1 = objective**, neutral, impartial, reserved, aloof, impersonal, disinterested, unbiased, dispassionate, uncommitted, uninvolved, unprejudiced: *The piece is written in a detached, precise style.* **OPPOSITE:** subjective **2 = separate**, free, severed, disconnected, loosened, discrete, unconnected, undivided, disjoined: *He lost his sight because of a detached retina.*

detachment NOUN **1 = indifference**, fairness, neutrality, objectivity, impartiality, coolness, remoteness, nonchalance, aloofness, unconcern, disinterestedness, nonpartisanship: *her professional detachment* **2 = unit**, party, force, body, detail, squad, patrol, task force: *a detachment of marines*

detail NOUN **1 = point**, fact, feature, particular, respect, factor, count, item, instance, element, aspect, specific, component, facet, technicality: *I recall every detail of the party.* **2 = fine point**, part, particular, nicety, minutiae, triviality: *Only minor details now remain to be settled.* **3 = party**, force, body, duty, squad, assignment, fatigue, detachment: *His personal detail totalled sixty men.* ▷ VERB **1 = list**, describe, relate, catalogue, portray, specify, depict, recount, rehearse, recite, narrate, delineate, enumerate, itemize, tabulate, particularize: *The report detailed the human rights abuses committed.* **2 = appoint**, name, choose, commission, select, elect, delegate, nominate, assign, allocate, charge: *He detailed someone to take it to the Incident Room.* **in detail = comprehensively**, completely, fully, thoroughly, extensively, inside out, exhaustively, point by point, item by item: *Examine the wording in detail before deciding on the final text.*

detailed ADJECTIVE **1 = comprehensive**, full, complete, minute, particular, specific, extensive, exact, thorough, meticulous, exhaustive, all-embracing, itemized, encyclopedic, blow-by-blow, particularized: *a detailed account of the discussions* **OPPOSITE:** brief **2 = complicated**, involved, complex, fancy, elaborate, intricate, meticulous, convoluted: *detailed line drawings*

detain VERB **1 = hold**, arrest, confine, restrain, imprison, intern, take prisoner, take into custody, hold in custody: *He was arrested and detained for questioning.* **2 = delay**, keep, stop, hold up, hamper, hinder, retard, impede, keep back, slow up *or* down: *We won't detain you any further.*

detect VERB **1 = discover**, find, reveal, catch, expose, disclose, uncover, track down, unmask: *equipment used to detect radiation* **2 = notice**, see, spot, catch, note, identify, observe, remark, recognize, distinguish, perceive, scent, discern, ascertain, descry: *He could detect a certain sadness in her face.*

detection NOUN **= discovery**, exposure, uncovering, tracking down, unearthing, unmasking, ferreting out

detective NOUN **= investigator**, cop *(slang)*, copper *(slang)*, dick *(slang, chiefly U.S.)*, constable, tec *(slang)*, private eye, sleuth *(informal)*, private investigator, gumshoe *(U.S. slang)*, bizzy *(slang)*, C.I.D. man

detention NOUN **= imprisonment**, custody, restraint, keeping in, quarantine, confinement, porridge *(slang)*, incarceration **OPPOSITE:** release

deter VERB **1 = discourage**, inhibit, put off, frighten, intimidate, daunt, hinder, dissuade, talk out of: *Jail sentences have done nothing to deter the offenders.* **2 = prevent**, stop, check, curb, damp, restrain, prohibit, hinder, debar: *Capital punishment does not deter crime.*

detergent NOUN **= cleaner**, cleanser: *He squeezed some detergent over the dishes.* ▷ ADJECTIVE **= cleansing**, cleaning, purifying, abstergent, detersive: *low-lather detergent powders*

deteriorate VERB **1 = decline**, worsen, degenerate, slump, degrade, depreciate, go downhill, go to the dogs *(informal)*, go to pot: *There are fears that the situation may deteriorate.* **OPPOSITE:** improve **2 = disintegrate**, decay, spoil, fade, break down, weaken, crumble, fall apart, ebb, decompose, wear away, retrogress: *X-rays are used to prevent fresh food from deteriorating.*

deterioration NOUN **1 = decline**, fall, drop, slump, worsening, downturn, depreciation, degradation, degeneration, debasement, retrogression, vitiation, dégringolade *(French)*: *the rapid deterioration in relations between the two countries* **2 = disintegration**, corrosion, atrophy: *enzymes that cause the deterioration of food*

determination NOUN **1 = resolution**, purpose, resolve, drive, energy, conviction, courage, dedication, backbone, fortitude, persistence, tenacity, perseverance, willpower, boldness, firmness, staying power, stubbornness, constancy, single-mindedness, earnestness, obstinacy, steadfastness, doggedness, relentlessness, resoluteness, indomitability, staunchness: *They acted with great courage and determination.* **OPPOSITE:** indecision **2 = decision**, ruling, settlement, resolution, resolve, conclusion, verdict, judgment: *A determination will be made as to the future of the treaty.*

> **QUOTATIONS**
> Nil carborundum illegitimi (Don't let the bastards grind you down)
> *[cod Latin slogan in circulation during the Second World War]*

> **PROVERBS**
> *When the going gets tough, the tough get going*

determine VERB **1 = affect**, control, decide, rule, condition, direct, influence, shape, govern, regulate, ordain: *What determines whether you are a success or a failure?* **2 = settle**, learn, establish, discover, check, find out, work out, detect, certify, verify, ascertain: *The investigation will determine what really happened.* **3 = decide on**, choose, establish, purpose, fix, elect, resolve: *The people have a right to determine their own future.* **4 = decide**, purpose, conclude, resolve, make up your mind: *I determined that I would ask him outright.*

determined ADJECTIVE **= resolute**, firm, dogged, fixed, constant, bold, intent, persistent, relentless, stalwart, persevering, single-minded, purposeful, tenacious, undaunted, strong-willed, steadfast, unwavering, immovable, unflinching, strong-minded: *He is making a determined effort to regain lost ground.*

determining ADJECTIVE = **deciding**, important, settling, essential, critical, crucial, decisive, final, definitive, conclusive

deterrent NOUN = **discouragement**, obstacle, curb, restraint, impediment, check, hindrance, disincentive, defensive measures, determent **OPPOSITE:** incentive

detest VERB = **hate**, loathe, despise, abhor, be hostile to, recoil from, be repelled by, have an aversion to, abominate, dislike intensely, execrate, feel aversion towards, feel disgust towards, feel hostility towards, feel repugnance towards **OPPOSITE:** love

dethrone VERB = **depose**, overthrow, oust, unseat, uncrown

detonate VERB = **set off**, trigger, explode, discharge, blow up, touch off: *The terrorists planted and detonated the bomb.*

detonation NOUN = **explosion**, blast, bang, report, boom, discharge, fulmination

detour NOUN = **diversion**, bypass, deviation, circuitous route, roundabout way, indirect course

detract from VERB **1 = lessen**, reduce, diminish, lower, take away from, derogate, devaluate: *Her faults did not seem to detract from her appeal.* **OPPOSITE:** enhance **2 = divert**, shift, distract, deflect, draw *or* lead away from: *They can only detract attention from the serious issues.*

USAGE
Detract is sometimes wrongly used where *distract* is meant: *a noise distracted* (not *detracted*) *my attention.*

detractor NOUN = **slanderer**, belittler, disparager, defamer, traducer, muckraker, scandalmonger, denigrator, backbiter, derogator *(rare)*

detriment NOUN = **damage**, loss, harm, injury, hurt, prejudice, disadvantage, impairment, disservice

detrimental ADJECTIVE = **damaging**, destructive, harmful, adverse, pernicious, unfavourable, prejudicial, baleful, deleterious, injurious, inimical, disadvantageous **OPPOSITE:** beneficial

devastate VERB **1 = destroy**, waste, ruin, sack, wreck, spoil, demolish, trash *(slang)*, level, total *(slang)*, ravage, plunder, desolate, pillage, raze, lay waste, despoil: *A fire devastated large parts of the castle.* **2 = shatter**, overwhelm, confound, floor *(informal)*: *If word of this gets out, it will devastate his family.*

devastating ADJECTIVE **1 = destructive**, damaging, catastrophic, harmful, detrimental, pernicious, ruinous, calamitous, cataclysmic, deleterious, injurious, maleficent: *the devastating force of the floods* **2 = traumatic**, shocking, upsetting, disturbing, painful, scarring: *The diagnosis was devastating. She had cancer.* **3 = savage**, cutting, overwhelming, withering, overpowering, satirical, incisive, sardonic, caustic, vitriolic, trenchant, mordant: *his devastating criticism of the Prime Minister*

devastation NOUN = **destruction**, ruin, havoc, ravages, demolition, plunder, pillage, desolation, depredation, ruination, spoliation

develop VERB **1 = grow**, advance, progress, mature, evolve, flourish, blossom, ripen: *Children develop at different rates.* **2 = result**, follow, arise, issue, happen, spring, stem, derive, break out, ensue, come about, be a direct result of: *a problem which developed from a leg injury* **3 = establish**, set up, promote, generate, undertake, initiate, embark on, cultivate, instigate, inaugurate, set in motion: *her dreams of developing her own business* **4 = form**, start, begin, contract, establish, pick up, breed, acquire, generate, foster, originate: *She developed a taste for expensive nightclubs.* **5 = expand**, extend, work out, elaborate, unfold, enlarge, broaden, amplify, augment, dilate upon: *They allowed me to develop their original idea.*

development NOUN **1 = growth**, increase, growing, advance, progress, spread, expansion, extension, evolution, widening, maturing, unfolding, unravelling, advancement, progression, thickening, enlargement: *the development of the embryo* **2 = establishment**, forming, generation, institution, invention, initiation, inauguration, instigation, origination: *the development of new and innovative services* **3 = event**, change, happening, issue, result, situation, incident, circumstance, improvement, outcome, phenomenon, evolution, unfolding, occurrence, upshot, turn of events, evolvement: *There has been a significant development in the case.*

deviant ADJECTIVE = **perverted**, sick *(informal)*, twisted, bent *(slang)*, abnormal, queer *(informal, derogatory)*, warped, perverse, wayward, kinky *(slang)*, devious, deviate, freaky *(slang)*, aberrant, pervy *(slang)*, sicko *(informal)*: *social reactions to deviant and criminal behaviour* **OPPOSITE:** normal
▷ NOUN = **pervert**, freak, queer *(informal, derogatory)*, misfit, sicko *(informal)*, odd type: *a dangerous deviant who lived rough*

deviate VERB = **differ**, vary, depart, part, turn, bend, drift, wander, stray, veer, swerve, meander, diverge, digress, turn aside

deviation NOUN = **departure**, change, variation, shift, alteration, discrepancy, inconsistency, disparity, aberration, variance, divergence, fluctuation, irregularity, digression

device NOUN **1 = gadget**, machine, tool, instrument, implement, invention, appliance, apparatus, gimmick, utensil, contraption, contrivance, waldo, gizmo *or* gismo *(slang, chiefly U.S. & Canad.)*: *This device can measure minute quantities of matter.* **2 = ploy**, scheme, strategy, plan, design, project, shift, trick, manoeuvre, stunt, dodge, expedient, ruse, artifice, gambit, stratagem, wile: *His actions are obviously a device to buy time.*

devil NOUN **1 = evil spirit**, demon, fiend, ghoul, hellhound, atua *(N.Z.)*, wairua *(N.Z.)*: *the image of devils with horns and cloven hoofs* **2 = brute**, monster, savage, beast, villain, rogue, barbarian, fiend, terror, swine, ogre: *the savage devils who mugged a helpless old woman* **3 = person**, individual, soul, creature, thing, human being, beggar: *I feel sorry for the poor devil who marries you.* **4 = scamp**, monkey *(informal)*, rogue, imp, rascal, tyke *(informal)*, scoundrel, scallywag *(informal)*, mischief-maker, whippersnapper, toerag *(slang)*, pickle *(Brit. informal)*, nointer *(Austral. slang)*: *You cheeky little devil!*
the Devil = **Satan**, Lucifer, Prince of Darkness, Old One, Deuce, Old Gentleman *(informal)*, Lord of the Flies, Old Harry *(informal)*, Mephistopheles, Evil One, Beelzebub, Old Nick *(informal)*, Mephisto, Belial, Clootie *(Scot.)*, deil *(Scot.)*, Apollyon, Old Scratch *(informal)*, Foul Fiend, Wicked One, archfiend, Old Hornie *(informal)*, Abbadon: *the eternal conflict between God and the Devil*

QUOTATIONS

If the devil doesn't exist, but man has created him, he has created him in his own image and likeness
[Fyodor Dostoevsky *The Brothers Karamazov*]

How art thou fallen from heaven,
O Lucifer, son of the morning!
[*Bible: Isaiah*]

Be sober, be vigilant; because your adversary the devil, as a roaring lion, walketh about, seeking whom he may devour
[*Bible: I Peter*]

The serpent subtlest beast of all the field,
Of huge extent sometimes, with brazen eyes
And hairy mane terrific
[John Milton *Paradise Lost*]

The devil's most devilish when respectable
[Elizabeth Barrett Browning *Aurora Leigh*]

An apology for the Devil; It must be remembered that we have only heard one side of the case. God has written all the books
[Samuel Butler]

PROVERBS

Better the devil you know than the devil you don't know
The devil looks after his own

d

d

> *He who sups with the devil should have a long spoon*
> *Talk of the devil, and he shall appear*

devilish ADJECTIVE **1 = fiendish**, diabolical, wicked, satanic, atrocious, hellish, infernal, accursed, execrable, detestable, damnable, diabolic: *devilish instruments of torture* **2 = difficult**, involved, complex, complicated, baffling, intricate, perplexing, thorny, knotty, problematical, ticklish: *It was a devilish puzzle to solve.*

devious ADJECTIVE **1 = sly**, scheming, calculating, tricky, crooked (*informal*), indirect, treacherous, dishonest, wily, insidious, evasive, deceitful, underhand, insincere, surreptitious, double-dealing, not straightforward: *She tracked down the other woman by devious means.*
OPPOSITE: straightforward
2 = indirect, roundabout, wandering, crooked, rambling, tortuous, deviating, circuitous, excursive: *He followed a devious route.* **OPPOSITE:** direct

devise VERB **= work out**, plan, form, design, imagine, frame, arrange, plot, construct, invent, conceive, formulate, contrive, dream up, concoct, think up

devoid ADJECTIVE (*with* **of**) **= lacking in**, without, free from, wanting in, sans (*archaic*), bereft of, empty of, deficient in, denuded of, barren of

devolution NOUN **= transfer of power**, decentralization, distribution of power, surrender of power, relinquishment of power

devolve VERB **= transfer**, entrust, consign, depute

devote VERB **= dedicate**, give, commit, apply, reserve, pledge, surrender, assign, allot, give over, consecrate, set apart

devoted ADJECTIVE **= dedicated**, loving, committed, concerned, caring, true, constant, loyal, faithful, fond, ardent, staunch, devout, steadfast **OPPOSITE:** disloyal

devotee NOUN **1 = enthusiast**, fan, supporter, follower, addict, admirer, buff (*informal*), fanatic, adherent, aficionado: *She is a devotee of Bach's music.*
2 = follower, student, supporter, pupil, convert, believer, partisan, disciple, learner, apostle, adherent, votary, proselyte, catechumen: *devotees of the Hare Krishna movement*

devotion NOUN **1 = love**, passion, affection, intensity, attachment, zeal, fondness, fervour, adoration, ardour, earnestness: *She was flattered by his devotion.* **2 = dedication**, commitment, loyalty, allegiance, fidelity, adherence, constancy, faithfulness: *devotion to the cause*
OPPOSITE: indifference **3 = worship**, reverence, spirituality, holiness, piety, sanctity, adoration, godliness, religiousness, devoutness: *He was kneeling by his bed in an attitude of devotion.*
OPPOSITE: irreverence
▷ PLURAL NOUN **= prayers**, religious observance, church service, divine office: *He performs his devotions twice a day.*

devotional ADJECTIVE **= religious**, spiritual, holy, sacred, devout, pious, reverential

devour VERB **1 = eat**, consume, swallow, bolt, dispatch, cram, stuff, wolf, gorge, gulp, gobble, guzzle, polish off (*informal*), pig out on (*slang*): *She devoured half an apple pie.* **2 = enjoy**, go through, absorb, appreciate, take in, relish, drink in, delight in, revel in, be preoccupied with, feast on, be engrossed by, read compulsively *or* voraciously: *He devoured 17 novels during his tour of India.*

devouring ADJECTIVE **= overwhelming**, powerful, intense, flaming, consuming, excessive, passionate, insatiable

devout ADJECTIVE **1 = religious**, godly, pious, pure, holy, orthodox, saintly, reverent, prayerful: *She was a devout Christian.* **OPPOSITE:** irreverent
2 = sincere, serious, deep, earnest, genuine, devoted, intense, passionate, profound, ardent, fervent, heartfelt, zealous, dinkum (*Austral. & N.Z. informal*): *a devout opponent of racism* **OPPOSITE:** indifferent

dexterity NOUN **1 = skill**, expertise, mastery, touch, facility, craft, knack, finesse, artistry, proficiency, smoothness, neatness, deftness, nimbleness, adroitness, effortlessness, handiness: *He showed great dexterity on the guitar.*
OPPOSITE: incompetence
2 = cleverness, art, ability, ingenuity, readiness, aptitude, adroitness, aptness, expertness, skilfulness: *the wit and verbal dexterity of the script*

diabolical ADJECTIVE **1 = dreadful**, shocking, terrible, appalling, nasty, tricky, unpleasant, outrageous, vile, excruciating, atrocious, abysmal, damnable: *the diabolical treatment of their prisoners* **2 = wicked**, cruel, savage, monstrous, malicious, satanic, from hell (*informal*), malignant, unspeakable, inhuman, implacable, malevolent, hellish, devilish, infernal, fiendish, ungodly, black-hearted, demoniac, hellacious (*U.S. slang*): *sins committed in a spirit of diabolical enjoyment*

diagnose VERB **= identify**, determine, recognize, distinguish, interpret, pronounce, pinpoint

diagnosis NOUN **1 = identification**, discovery, recognition, detection: *Diagnosis of this disease can be very difficult.* **2 = opinion**, conclusion, interpretation, pronouncement: *She needs to have a second test to confirm the diagnosis.*

diagnostic ADJECTIVE **= symptomatic**, particular, distinguishing, distinctive, peculiar, indicative, idiosyncratic, recognizable, demonstrative

diagonal ADJECTIVE **= slanting**, angled, oblique, cross, crosswise, crossways, cater-cornered (*U.S. informal*), cornerways

diagonally ADVERB **= aslant**, obliquely, on the cross, at an angle, crosswise, on the bias, cornerwise

diagram NOUN **= plan**, figure, drawing, chart, outline, representation, sketch, layout, graph

dialect NOUN **= language**, speech, tongue, jargon, idiom, vernacular, brogue, lingo (*informal*), patois, provincialism, localism

> QUOTATIONS
> Dialect words – those terrible marks of the beast to the truly genteel [Thomas Hardy *The Mayor of Casterbridge*]

dialectic NOUN **= debate**, reasoning, discussion, logic, contention, polemics, disputation, argumentation, ratiocination

dialogue NOUN **1 = discussion**, conference, exchange, debate, confabulation: *He wants to open a dialogue with the protesters.*
2 = conversation, discussion, communication, discourse, converse, colloquy, confabulation, duologue, interlocution: *Those who witnessed their dialogue spoke of high emotion.* **3 = script**, conversation, lines, spoken part: *The play's dialogue is sharp and witty.*

diametrically ADVERB **= completely**, totally, entirely, absolutely, utterly

diarrhoea *or* (*U.S.*) **diarrhea** NOUN **= the runs**, the trots (*informal*), dysentery, looseness, the skits (*informal*), Montezuma's revenge (*informal*), gippy tummy, holiday tummy, Spanish tummy, the skitters (*informal*)

diary NOUN **1 = journal**, chronicle, day-to-day account, blog (*informal*): *the most famous descriptive passage in his diary* **2 = engagement book**, Filofax®, appointment book: *My diary is pretty full next week.*

DIARISTS

Marie Bashkirtseff (*Russian*)
Fanny Burney (*English*)
E.M. Delafield (*English*)
John Evelyn (*English*)
Helen Fielding (Bridget Jones) (*English*)
Anne Frank (*Dutch*)
André Gide (*French*)
George and Weedon Grossmith (Charles Pooter) (*English*)
Francis Kilvert (*British*)
Samuel Pepys (*English*)
Marion Rivers-Moore (*English*)
Sue Townsend (Adrian Mole) (*English*)
Anaïs Nin (*French-U.S.*)
Dorothy Wordsworth (*English*)

QUOTATIONS
Keep a diary and someday it'll keep you
[Mae West *Every Day's a Holiday*]

Only good girls keep diaries. Bad girls don't have the time
[Tallulah Bankhead]

diatribe NOUN = **tirade**, abuse, criticism, denunciation, reviling, stricture, harangue, invective, vituperation, stream of abuse, verbal onslaught, philippic

dicey ADJECTIVE = **dangerous**, difficult, tricky, risky, hairy *(slang)*, ticklish, chancy *(informal)*

dichotomy NOUN = **division**, split, separation, disjunction

dicky ADJECTIVE = **weak**, queer *(informal)*, shaky, unreliable, unsteady, unsound, fluttery

dictate VERB = **speak**, say, utter, read out: *He dictates his novels to his secretary.*
▷ NOUN **1** = **command**, order, decree, word, demand, direction, requirement, bidding, mandate, injunction, statute, fiat, ultimatum, ordinance, edict, behest: *They must abide by the dictates of the new government.* **2** = **principle**, law, rule, standard, code, criterion, ethic, canon, maxim, dictum, precept, axiom, moral law: *We have followed the dictates of our consciences.*
dictate to someone = **order (about)**, direct, lay down the law, pronounce to: *What gives them the right to dictate to us?*

dictator NOUN = **absolute ruler**, tyrant, despot, oppressor, autocrat, absolutist, martinet

dictatorial ADJECTIVE **1** = **absolute**, unlimited, totalitarian, autocratic, unrestricted, tyrannical, despotic: *He suspended the constitution and assumed dictatorial powers.* **OPPOSITE:** democratic **2** = **domineering**, authoritarian, oppressive, bossy *(informal)*, imperious, overbearing, magisterial, iron-handed, dogmatical: *his dictatorial management style* **OPPOSITE:** servile

dictatorship NOUN = **absolute rule**, tyranny, totalitarianism, authoritarianism, reign of terror, despotism, autocracy, absolutism

diction NOUN = **pronunciation**, speech, articulation, delivery, fluency, inflection, intonation, elocution, enunciation

dictionary NOUN = **wordbook**, vocabulary, glossary, encyclopedia, lexicon, concordance

QUOTATIONS
Dictionaries are like watches; the worst is better than none, and the best cannot be expected to go quite true
[Samuel Johnson]

When I feel inclined to read poetry I take down my Dictionary. The poetry of words is quite as beautiful as that of sentences. The author may arrange the gems effectively, but their shape and lustre have been given by the attrition of the ages
[Oliver Wendell Holmes Sr. *The Autocrat's Autobiography*]

To make dictionaries is dull work
[Dr. Johnson *Dictionary*]

dictionary: a malevolent literary device for cramping the growth of a language and making it hard and inelastic. This dictionary, however, is a most useful work
[Ambrose Bierce *The Devil's Dictionary*]

dictum NOUN **1** = **saying**, saw, maxim, adage, proverb, precept, axiom, gnome: *the dictum that it is preferable to be roughly right than precisely wrong* **2** = **decree**, order, demand, statement, command, dictate, canon, fiat, edict, pronouncement: *his dictum that the priority of the government must be the health of the people*

didactic ADJECTIVE **1** = **instructive**, educational, enlightening, moral, edifying, homiletic, preceptive: *In totalitarian societies, art exists solely for didactic purposes.* **2** = **pedantic**, academic, formal, pompous, schoolmasterly, erudite, bookish, abstruse, moralizing, priggish, pedagogic: *He adopts a lofty, didactic tone when addressing women.*

die VERB **1** = **pass away**, depart, expire, perish, buy it *(U.S. slang)*, check out *(U.S. slang)*, kick it *(slang)*, croak *(slang)*, give up the ghost, go belly-up *(slang)*, snuff it *(slang)*, peg out *(informal)*, kick the bucket *(slang)*, buy the farm *(U.S. slang)*, peg it *(informal)*, decease, cark it *(Austral. & N.Z. slang)*, pop your clogs *(informal)*, breathe your last, hop the twig *(slang)*: *His mother died when he was a child.* **OPPOSITE:** live **2** = **stop**, fail, halt, break down, run down, stop working, peter out, fizzle out, lose power, seize up, conk out *(informal)*, go kaput *(informal)*, go phut, fade out *or* away: *The engine coughed, spluttered, and died.* **3** = **dwindle**, end, decline, pass, disappear, sink, fade, weaken, diminish, vanish, decrease, decay, lapse, wither, wilt, lessen, wane, subside, ebb, die down, die out, abate, peter out, die away, grow less: *My love for you will never die.* **OPPOSITE:** increase
be dying for something = **long for**, want, desire, crave, yearn for, hunger for, pine for, hanker after, be eager for, ache for, swoon over, languish for, set your heart on: *I'm dying for a cigarette.*
be dying of something = **be overcome with**, succumb to, collapse with: *I'm dying of thirst.*

die-hard *or* **diehard** NOUN = **reactionary**, fanatic, zealot, intransigent, stick-in-the-mud *(informal)*, old fogey, ultraconservative: *He has links with former Communist diehards.*

diet[1] NOUN **1** = **food**, provisions, fare, rations, subsistence, kai *(N.Z. informal)*, nourishment, sustenance, victuals, commons, edibles, comestibles, nutriment, viands, aliment: *Watch your diet – you need plenty of fruit and vegetables.* **2** = **fast**, regime, abstinence, regimen, dietary regime: *Have you been on a diet? You've lost a lot of weight.*
▷ VERB = **slim**, fast, lose weight, abstain, eat sparingly: *Most of us have dieted at some time in our lives.*
OPPOSITE: overindulge

QUOTATIONS
with cheesecake you've got a choice: Either EAT it or BE it
[Liz Lochhead *Fat Girl's Confession*]

all [diets] blur together, leaving you with only one definite piece of information: french-fried potatoes are out
[Jean Kerr *Please Don't Eat the Daisies*]

Diets are like boyfriends – it never really works to go back to them
[Nigella Lawson]

diet[2] NOUN *(often cap.)* = **council**, meeting, parliament, sitting, congress, chamber, convention, legislature, legislative assembly: *The Diet has time to discuss the bill only until the 10th November.*

dieter NOUN = **slimmer**, weight watcher, calorie counter, faster, reducer

differ VERB **1** = **be dissimilar**, contradict, contrast with, vary, counter, belie, depart from, diverge, negate, fly in the face of, run counter to, be distinct, stand apart, make a nonsense of, be at variance with: *His story differed from his mother's in several respects.* **OPPOSITE:** accord **2** = **disagree**, clash, dispute, dissent: *The two leaders have differed on the issue of sanctions.* **OPPOSITE:** agree

difference NOUN **1** = **dissimilarity**, contrast, variation, change, variety, exception, distinction, diversity, alteration, discrepancy, disparity, deviation, differentiation, peculiarity, divergence, singularity, particularity, distinctness, unlikeness: *the vast difference in size* **OPPOSITE:** similarity **2** = **remainder**, rest, balance, remains, excess: *They pledge to refund the difference within 48 hours.* **3** = **disagreement**, conflict, argument, row, clash, dispute, set-to *(informal)*, controversy, contention, quarrel, strife, wrangle, tiff, contretemps, discordance, contrariety: *They are learning how to resolve their differences.*
OPPOSITE: agreement

different ADJECTIVE **1** = **dissimilar**, opposed, contrasting, changed, clashing, unlike, altered, diverse, at odds, inconsistent, disparate, deviating, divergent, at variance, discrepant, streets apart: *We have totally different views.* **2** = **various**, some, many, several, varied, numerous, diverse, divers *(archaic)*, assorted, miscellaneous, sundry, manifold, multifarious: *Different countries specialise in different products.* **3 = unusual**, unique, special, strange, rare, extraordinary, bizarre, distinctive, something else, peculiar, uncommon, singular, unconventional, out of the ordinary, left-field *(informal)*, atypical: *Try to think of a menu that is interesting and different.* **4 = other**, another, separate, individual, distinct, discrete: *What you do in the privacy of your own home is a different matter.*

d

QUOTATIONS

And now for something completely different
[*Monty Python's Flying Circus*]

If a man does not keep pace with his companions, perhaps it is because he hears a different drummer
[Henry David Thoreau *Walden*]

USAGE

On the whole, *different from* is preferable to *different to* and *different than*, both of which are considered unacceptable by some people. *Different to* is often heard in British English, but is thought by some people to be incorrect; and *different than*, though acceptable in American English, is often regarded as unacceptable in British English. This makes *different from* the safest option: *this result is only slightly different from that obtained in the US* – or you can rephrase the sentence: *this result differs only slightly from that obtained in the US.*

differential ADJECTIVE **= distinctive**, distinguishing, discriminative, diacritical: *They may be forced to eliminate differential voting rights.*
▷ NOUN **= difference**, discrepancy, disparity, amount of difference: *Industrial wage differentials widened.*

differentiate VERB **1 = distinguish**, separate, discriminate, contrast, discern, mark off, make a distinction, tell apart, set off *or* apart: *He cannot differentiate between his imagination and the real world.* **2 = make different**, separate, distinguish, characterize, single out, segregate, individualize, mark off, set apart, set off: *distinctive policies that differentiate them from the other parties* **3 = become different**, change, convert, transform, alter, adapt, modify: *These ectodermal cells differentiate into two cell types.*

differently ADVERB **= dissimilarly**, otherwise, in another way, in contrary fashion **OPPOSITE:** similarly

difficult ADJECTIVE **1 = hard**, tough, taxing, demanding, challenging, painful, exacting, formidable, uphill, strenuous, problematic, arduous, onerous, laborious, burdensome, wearisome, no picnic *(informal)*, toilsome, like getting blood out of a stone: *It is difficult for single mothers to get jobs.* **OPPOSITE:** easy **2 = problematical**, involved, complex, complicated, delicate, obscure, abstract, baffling, intricate, perplexing, thorny, knotty, abstruse, ticklish, enigmatical: *It was a very difficult decision to make.* **OPPOSITE:** simple **3 = troublesome**, trying, awkward, demanding, rigid, stubborn, perverse, fussy, tiresome, intractable, fastidious, fractious, unyielding, obstinate, intransigent, unmanageable, unbending, uncooperative, hard to please, refractory, obstreperous, pig-headed, bull-headed, unaccommodating, unamenable: *I had a feeling you were going to be difficult about this.* **OPPOSITE:** cooperative **4 = tough**, trying, hard, dark, grim, straitened, full of hardship: *These are difficult times.* **OPPOSITE:** easy

difficulty NOUN **1 = problem**, trouble, obstacle, hurdle, dilemma, hazard, complication, hassle *(informal)*, snag, uphill *(S. African)*, predicament, pitfall, stumbling block, impediment, hindrance, tribulation, quandary, can of worms *(informal)*, point at issue, disputed point: *There is only one difficulty. The hardest thing is to leave.* **2 = hardship**, labour, pain, strain, awkwardness, painfulness, strenuousness, arduousness, laboriousness: *The injured man mounted his horse with difficulty.*

diffident ADJECTIVE **= shy**, reserved, withdrawn, reluctant, modest, shrinking, doubtful, backward, unsure, insecure, constrained, timid, self-conscious, hesitant, meek, unassuming, unobtrusive, self-effacing, sheepish, aw-shucks, bashful, timorous, unassertive

diffuse VERB **= spread**, distribute, scatter, circulate, disperse, dispense, dispel, dissipate, propagate, disseminate: *Our aim is to diffuse new ideas obtained from elsewhere.*
▷ ADJECTIVE **1 = spread-out**, scattered, dispersed, unconcentrated: *a diffuse community* **OPPOSITE:** concentrated **2 = rambling**, loose, vague, meandering, waffling *(informal)*, long-winded, wordy, discursive, verbose, prolix, maundering, digressive, diffusive, circumlocutory: *His writing is so diffuse that it is almost impossible to understand.* **OPPOSITE:** concise

USAGE

This word is quite commonly misused instead of *defuse*, when talking about calming down a situation. However, the words are very different in meaning and should never be used as alternatives to each other.

diffusion NOUN **= spreading**, distribution, scattering, circulation, expansion, propagation, dissemination, dispersal, dispersion, dissipation

dig VERB **1 = hollow out**, mine, pierce, quarry, excavate, gouge, scoop out: *Dig a large hole and bang the stake in.* **2 = delve**, tunnel, burrow, grub: *I changed into clothes more suited to digging.* **3 = turn over**, till, break up, hoe: *He was outside digging the garden.* **4 = search**, hunt, root, delve, forage, dig down, fossick *(Austral. & N.Z.)*: *He dug around in his pocket for his keys.* **5 = poke**, drive, push, stick, punch, stab, thrust, shove, prod, jab: *She dug her nails into his flesh.* **6 = like**, enjoy, go for, appreciate, groove *(obsolete, slang)*, delight in, be fond of, be keen on, be partial to: *I really dig this band's energy.* **7 = understand**, follow: *Can you dig what I'm trying to say?*
▷ NOUN **1 = cutting remark**, crack *(slang)*, insult, taunt, sneer, jeer, quip, barb, wisecrack *(informal)*, gibe: *She couldn't resist a dig at him after his unfortunate performance.* **2 = poke**, thrust, butt, nudge, prod, jab, punch: *She silenced him with a sharp dig in the small of the back.*
dig in = begin *or* **start eating**, tuck in *(informal)*: *Pull up a chair and dig in.*

digest VERB **1 = ingest**, absorb, incorporate, dissolve, assimilate: *She couldn't digest food properly.* **2 = take in**, master, absorb, grasp, drink in, soak up, devour, assimilate: *She read everything, digesting every fragment of news.*
▷ NOUN **= summary**, résumé, abstract, epitome, condensation, compendium, synopsis, précis, abridgment: *a regular digest of environmental statistics*

digestion NOUN **= ingestion**, absorption, incorporation, assimilation
▸ *related adjective:* peptic

digit NOUN **= finger**, toe: *Many animals have five digits.*

dignified ADJECTIVE **= distinguished**, august, reserved, imposing, formal, grave, noble, upright, stately, solemn, lofty, exalted, decorous
OPPOSITE: undignified

dignify VERB **= distinguish**, honour, grace, raise, advance, promote, elevate, glorify, exalt, ennoble, aggrandize

dignitary NOUN **= public figure**, worthy, notable, high-up *(informal)*, bigwig *(informal)*, celeb *(informal)*, personage, pillar of society, pillar of the church, notability, pillar of the state, V.I.P.

dignity NOUN **1 = decorum**, breeding, gravity, majesty, grandeur, respectability, nobility, propriety, solemnity, gentility, courtliness, loftiness, stateliness: *Everyone admired her extraordinary dignity and composure.* **2 = self-importance**, pride, self-esteem, self-respect, self-regard, self-possession, amour-propre *(French)*: *Admit that you were wrong. You won't lose dignity.*

digress VERB **= wander**, drift, stray, depart, ramble, meander, diverge, deviate, turn aside, be diffuse, expatiate, go off at a tangent, get off the point *or* subject

The Brontës' Use of Adverbs

The highly literary character of the Brontës' language shows in their frequent use of adverbs such as *whither, hither,* and *thither*; *whence, hence,* and *thence.* These words were not generally used in the colloquial language of the early nineteenth century, except in dialect. Thus when Joseph says *Maister, coom hither!*, this is his normal speech. When Mr Rochester says *Come, Jane - come hither*, the poetic word communicates more feeling than *here* would have done.

When used by Anne and Charlotte, the word *scarce* is hardly ever an adjective. It is a literary form of *scarcely*, and modifies adjectives (*scarce intelligible; scarce articulate*), other adverbs (*scarce palpably; scarce ever*) and clauses (*scarce knowing what to answer*). It is indicative of the more natural style of Emily's writing that she uses *hardly* in this context:

> I give you what I have: the present is **hardly** worth accepting; but I have nothing else to offer.

Another archaic adverb used particularly by Anne and Charlotte is *fain* (gladly), as in:

> I would **fain** have put it off till the morrow.

In modern usage the adverb *much* is almost always qualified by words such as *not, too, how,* or *so*. The Brontës' use of the word is often literary: *much vexed; too much excited; I marvelled much; many pity you much*. Similarly *ever*, which now is mainly restricted to questions and negative statements, is used positively to mean 'always':

> She had **ever** hated me; It was and **ever** must be an enigma.

Some common adverbs can have unexpected meanings in the Brontës' writing. As in modern usage, *quite* sometimes means 'fairly' (*quite young; quite hot*), and sometimes 'entirely' (*quite possible; quite true*). The first meaning is the main modern sense, whereas the Brontës more often use the word with the second sense (*Thornfield Hall is quite a ruin; It is quite a right thing; She is quite grieved about you*). In modern English *quite a good...* very often precedes a noun, to indicate that the noun is moderately good, but this is not the usage of the Brontës. In the following, we are told that the churchgoer is an impeccable Christian, not a mediocre one:

> He has been a most exemplary attendant at church these last few Sundays: you would think he was **quite** a good Christian.

When reporting speech, the Brontës use a wide variety of synonyms for *say*. These verbs are very often modified by an adverb - examples are *calmly, dolefully, decisively, impatiently, pettishly, meekly, peremptorily, shiveringly, contemptuously*.

Charlotte is almost as profuse in her use of descriptive adverbs as of adjectives, and has an obvious liking for groups of three:

> They fear ...to smile too **gaily**, speak too **freely**, or move too **quickly**.

In the quotation above each adverb modifies a verb, and the sentence is rhythmical and easily comprehensible. This is not always the case when one verb is burdened by three adverbs, as in *The voice spoke in pain and woe, **wildly, eerily, urgently**; He looked down at her **gravely, kindly**, yet **commandingly**. Other eyes ... watched them **closely, keenly, shrewdly***. A single adverb can be much more telling, as when Jane imagines Grace Poole laughing *drearily* to herself.

d

dilapidated ADJECTIVE **= ruined**, fallen in, broken-down, battered, neglected, crumbling, rundown, decayed, decaying, falling apart, beat-up *(informal)*, shaky, shabby, worn-out, ramshackle, in ruins, rickety, decrepit, tumbledown, uncared for, gone to rack and ruin

dilate VERB **= enlarge**, extend, stretch, expand, swell, widen, broaden, puff out, distend **OPPOSITE:** contract

dilemma NOUN **= predicament**, problem, difficulty, spot *(informal)*, fix *(informal)*, mess, puzzle, jam *(informal)*, embarrassment, plight, strait, pickle *(informal)*, how-do-you-do *(informal)*, quandary, perplexity, tight corner *or* spot

on the horns of a dilemma = between the devil and the deep blue sea, between a rock and a hard place *(informal)*, between Scylla and Charybdis: *I found myself on the horns of a dilemma – whatever I did, it would be wrong.*

> **USAGE**
> The use of *dilemma* to refer to a problem that seems incapable of solution is considered by some people to be incorrect. To avoid this misuse of the word, an appropriate alternative such as *predicament* could be used.

dilettante NOUN **= amateur**, aesthete, dabbler, trifler, nonprofessional

diligence NOUN **= application**, industry, care, activity, attention, perseverance, earnestness, attentiveness, assiduity, intentness, assiduousness, laboriousness, heedfulness, sedulousness

diligent ADJECTIVE **= hard-working**, careful, conscientious, earnest, active, busy, persistent, attentive, persevering, tireless, painstaking, laborious, industrious, indefatigable, studious, assiduous, sedulous **OPPOSITE:** indifferent

dilute VERB **1 = water down**, thin (out), weaken, adulterate, make thinner, cut *(informal)*: *Dilute the syrup well with cooled, boiled water.* **OPPOSITE:** condense **2 = reduce**, weaken, diminish, temper, decrease, lessen, diffuse, mitigate, attenuate: *It was a clear attempt to dilute black voting power.* **OPPOSITE:** intensify

diluted ADJECTIVE **= watered down**, thinned, weak, weakened, dilute, watery, adulterated, cut *(informal)*, wishy-washy *(informal)*

dim ADJECTIVE **1 = dull**, weak, pale, muted, subdued, feeble, murky, opaque, dingy, subfusc: *She stood waiting in the dim light.* **2 = poorly lit**, dark, gloomy, murky, shady, shadowy, dusky, crepuscular, darkish, tenebrous, unilluminated, caliginous *(archaic)*: *The room was dim and cool and quiet.* **3 = cloudy**, grey, gloomy, dismal, overcast, leaden: *a dim February day* **OPPOSITE:** bright **4 = unclear**, obscured, faint, blurred, fuzzy, shadowy, hazy, indistinguishable, bleary, undefined, out of focus, ill-defined, indistinct, indiscernible: *His torch picked out the dim figures.* **OPPOSITE:** distinct **5 = obscure**, remote, vague, confused, shadowy, imperfect, hazy, intangible, indistinct: *The era of social activism is all but a dim memory.* **6 = unfavourable**, bad, black, depressing, discouraging, gloomy, dismal, sombre, unpromising, dispiriting, disheartening: *The prospects for a peaceful solution are dim.* **7** *(informal)* **= stupid**, slow, thick, dull, dense, dumb *(informal)*, daft *(informal)*, dozy *(Brit. informal)*, obtuse, unintelligent, asinine, slow on the uptake *(informal)*, braindead *(informal)*, doltish: *She's not as dim as she seems.* **OPPOSITE:** bright
▷ VERB **1 = turn down**, lower, fade, dull, bedim: *Dim the overhead lights.* **2 = grow** *or* **become faint**, fade, dull, grow *or* become dim: *The houselights dimmed.* **3 = darken**, dull, cloud over: *The dusk sky dims to a chilly indigo.*

dimension NOUN **1 = aspect**, side, feature, angle, facet: *This adds a new dimension to our work.* **2 = extent**, size, magnitude, importance, scope, greatness, amplitude, largeness: *She did not understand the dimension of her plight.*
▷ PLURAL NOUN **= proportions**, range, size, scale, measure, volume, capacity, bulk, measurement, amplitude, bigness: *the grandiose dimensions of the room*

diminish VERB **1 = decrease**, decline, lessen, contract, weaken, shrink, dwindle, wane, recede, subside, ebb, taper, die out, fade away, abate, peter out: *The threat of war has diminished.* **OPPOSITE:** grow **2 = reduce**, cut, decrease, lessen, contract, lower, weaken, curtail, abate, retrench: *Federalism is intended to diminish the power of the central state.* **OPPOSITE:** increase **3 = belittle**, scorn, devalue, undervalue, deride, demean, denigrate, scoff at, disparage, decry, sneer at, underrate, deprecate, depreciate, cheapen, derogate: *He never diminished her in front of other people.*

diminution NOUN **1 = decrease**, decline, lessening, weakening, decay, contraction, abatement: *a slight diminution in asset value* **2 = reduction**, cut, decrease, weakening, deduction, contraction, lessening, cutback, retrenchment, abatement, curtailment: *The president has accepted a diminution of his original powers.*

diminutive ADJECTIVE **= small**, little, tiny, minute, pocket(-sized), mini, wee, miniature, petite, midget, undersized, teeny-weeny, Lilliputian, bantam, teensy-weensy, pygmy *or* pigmy **OPPOSITE:** giant

din NOUN **= noise**, row, racket, crash, clash, shout, outcry, clamour, clatter, uproar, commotion, pandemonium, babel, hubbub, hullabaloo, clangour **OPPOSITE:** silence

dine VERB **= eat**, lunch, feast, sup, chow down *(slang)*: *He dines alone most nights.*
dine on *or* **off something = eat**, consume, feed on: *I could dine on caviar and champagne for the rest of my life.*

dingy ADJECTIVE **= discoloured**, soiled, dirty, shabby, faded, seedy, grimy: *wallpaper with dingy yellow stripes*

dinkum ADJECTIVE **= genuine**, honest, natural, frank, sincere, candid, upfront *(informal)*, artless, guileless

dinky ADJECTIVE **= cute**, small, neat, mini, trim, miniature, petite, dainty, natty *(informal)*, cutesy *(informal, chiefly U.S.)*

dinner NOUN **1 = meal**, main meal, spread *(informal)*, repast, blowout *(slang)*, collation, refection: *Would you like to stay and have dinner?* **2 = banquet**, feast, blowout *(slang)*, repast, beanfeast *(Brit. informal)*, carousal, hakari *(N.Z.)*: *The annual dinner was held in the spring.*

dinosaur NOUN **= fuddy-duddy**, anachronism, dodo *(informal)*, stick-in-the-mud *(informal)*, antique *(informal)*, fossil *(informal)*, relic *(informal)*, back number *(informal)*

dint
by dint of = by means of, using, by virtue of, by force of

diocese NOUN **= bishopric**, see

dip VERB **1 = plunge**, immerse, bathe, duck, rinse, douse, dunk, souse: *Dip the food into the sauce.* **2 = drop (down)**, set, fall, lower, disappear, sink, fade, slump, descend, tilt, subside, sag, droop: *The sun dipped below the horizon.* **3 = slope**, drop (down), descend, fall, decline, pitch, sink, incline, drop away: *a path which suddenly dips down into a tunnel*
▷ NOUN **1 = plunge**, ducking, soaking, drenching, immersion, douche, submersion: *Freshen the salad leaves with a quick dip into cold water.* **2 = nod**, drop, lowering, slump, sag: *She acknowledged me with a slight dip of the head.* **3 = hollow**, hole, depression, pit, basin, dent, trough, indentation, concavity: *Turn right where the road makes a dip.* **4 = mixture**, solution, preparation, suspension, infusion, concoction, dilution: *sheep dip*
dip into something 1 = sample, try, skim, play at, glance at, run over, browse, dabble, peruse, surf *(Computing)*: *a chance to dip into a wide selection of books* **2 = draw upon**, use, employ, extract, take from, make use of, fall back on, reach into, have recourse to: *She was forced to dip into her savings.*

diplomacy NOUN **1 = statesmanship**, statecraft, international negotiation: *Today's resolution is significant for American diplomacy.* **2 = tact**, skill, sensitivity, craft, discretion, subtlety, delicacy, finesse, soft power, savoir-faire, artfulness: *It took all his powers of diplomacy to get her to return.* **OPPOSITE:** tactlessness

QUOTATIONS

Diplomacy is to do and say
The nastiest thing in the nicest way
[Isaac Goldberg *The Reflex*]

A soft answer turneth away wrath
[*Bible: Proverbs*]

A word spoken in due season, how good is it!
[*Bible: Proverbs*]

A word fitly spoken is like apples of gold in pictures of silver
[*Bible: Proverbs*]

diplomacy: the patriotic art of lying for one's country
[Ambrose Bierce *The Devil's Dictionary*]

diplomat NOUN **= official**, ambassador, envoy, statesman, consul, attaché, emissary, chargé d'affaires

diplomatic ADJECTIVE **1 = consular**, official, foreign-office, ambassadorial, foreign-politic: *The two countries have resumed full diplomatic relations.* **2 = tactful**, politic, sensitive, subtle, delicate, polite, discreet, prudent, adept, considerate, judicious, treating with kid gloves: *She is very direct. I tend to be more diplomatic.* **OPPOSITE:** tactless

dire ADJECTIVE **= desperate**, pressing, crying, critical, terrible, crucial, alarming, extreme, awful, appalling, urgent, cruel, horrible, disastrous, grim, dreadful, gloomy, fearful, dismal, drastic, catastrophic, ominous, horrid, woeful, ruinous, calamitous, cataclysmic, portentous, godawful (*slang*), exigent, bodeful

direct VERB **1 = aim**, point, turn, level, train, focus, fix, cast: *He directed the tiny beam of light at the roof.* **2 = guide**, show, lead, point the way, point in the direction of: *A guard directed them to the right.* **3 = control**, run, manage, lead, rule, guide, handle, conduct, advise, govern, regulate, administer, oversee, supervise, dispose, preside over, mastermind, call the shots, call the tune, superintend: *He will direct day-to-day operations.* **4 = order**, command, instruct, charge, demand, require, bid, enjoin, adjure: *They have been directed to give special attention to poverty.* **5 = address**, send, mail, route, label, superscribe: *Please direct your letters to me at this address.*
▷ ADJECTIVE **1 = quickest**, shortest: *They took the direct route.* **2 = straight**, through: *a direct flight from Glasgow* **OPPOSITE:** circuitous **3 = first-hand**, personal, immediate: *He has direct experience of the process.* **OPPOSITE:** indirect **4 = clear**, specific, plain, absolute, distinct, definite, explicit, downright, point-blank, unequivocal, unqualified, unambiguous, categorical: *He denied there was a direct connection between the two cases.* **OPPOSITE:** ambiguous **5 = straightforward**, open, straight, frank, blunt, sincere, outspoken, honest, matter-of-fact, downright, candid, forthright, truthful, upfront (*informal*), man-to-man, plain-spoken: *He avoided giving a direct answer.* **OPPOSITE:** indirect **6 = verbatim**, exact, word-for-word, strict, accurate, faithful, letter-for-letter: *It was a direct quotation from his earlier speech.*
▷ ADVERB **= non-stop**, straight: *You can fly there direct from Glasgow.*

direction NOUN **1 = way**, course, line, road, track, bearing, route, path: *We drove ten miles in the opposite direction.* **2 = tendency**, bent, current, trend, leaning, drift, bias, orientation, tack, tenor, proclivity: *They threatened a mass walk-out if the party did not change direction.* **3 = management**, government, control, charge, administration, leadership, command, guidance, supervision, governance, oversight, superintendence: *The house was built under the direction of his partner.*

directions PLURAL NOUN **= instructions**, rules, information, plan, briefing, regulations, recommendations, indication, guidelines, guidance: *Don't throw away the directions until we've finished cooking.*

directive NOUN **= order**, ruling, regulation, charge, notice, command, instruction, dictate, decree, mandate, canon, injunction, imperative, fiat, ordinance, edict

directly ADVERB **1 = straight**, unswervingly, without deviation, by the shortest route, in a beeline: *The plane will fly the hostages directly back home.* **2 = immediately**, promptly, instantly, right away, straightaway, speedily, instantaneously, pronto (*informal*), pdq (*slang*): *Directly after the meeting, an official appealed on television* **3 = at once**, presently, soon, quickly, as soon as possible, in a second, straightaway, forthwith, posthaste: *He'll be there directly.* **4 = honestly**, openly, frankly, plainly, face-to-face, overtly, point-blank, unequivocally, truthfully, candidly, unreservedly, straightforwardly, straight from the shoulder (*informal*), without prevarication: *She explained simply and directly what she hoped to achieve.*

directness NOUN **= honesty**, candour, frankness, sincerity, plain speaking, bluntness, outspokenness, forthrightness, straightforwardness

director NOUN **= controller**, head, leader, manager, chief, executive, chairman, boss (*informal*), producer, governor, principal, administrator, supervisor, organizer, baas (*S. African*), helmer, sherang (*Austral. & N.Z.*)

dirge NOUN **= lament**, requiem, elegy, death march, threnody, dead march, funeral song, coronach (*Scot. & Irish*)

dirt NOUN **1 = filth**, muck, grime, dust, mud, stain, crap (*taboo, slang*), tarnish, smudge, mire, impurity, slob (*Irish*), crud (*slang*), kak (*S. African taboo, slang*), grot (*slang*): *I started to scrub off the dirt.* **2 = soil**, ground, earth, clay, turf, clod, loam, loam: *They all sit on the dirt in the shade of a tree.*

dirty ADJECTIVE **1 = filthy**, soiled, grubby, nasty, foul, muddy, polluted, messy, sullied, grimy, unclean, mucky, grotty (*slang*), grungy (*slang, chiefly U.S. & Canad.*), scuzzy (*slang, chiefly U.S.*), begrimed, festy (*Austral. slang*): *The woman had matted hair and dirty fingernails.* **OPPOSITE:** clean **2 = dishonest**, illegal, unfair, cheating, corrupt, crooked, deceiving, fraudulent, treacherous, deceptive, unscrupulous, crafty, deceitful, double-dealing, unsporting, knavish (*archaic*): *Their opponents used dirty tactics.* **OPPOSITE:** honest **3 = obscene**, rude, coarse, indecent, blue, offensive, gross, filthy, vulgar, pornographic, sleazy, suggestive, lewd, risqué, X-rated (*informal*), bawdy, salacious, smutty, off-colour, unwholesome, page-three: *He laughed at their dirty jokes.* **OPPOSITE:** decent **4 = despicable**, mean, low, base, cheap, nasty, cowardly, beggarly, worthless, shameful, shabby, vile, sordid, low-down (*informal*), abject, squalid, ignominious, contemptible, wretched, scurvy, detestable, scungy (*Austral. & N.Z.*): *That was a dirty trick to play.*
▷ VERB **= soil**, foul, stain, spoil, smear, muddy, pollute, blacken, mess up, smudge, sully, defile, smirch, begrime: *He was afraid the dog's hairs might dirty the seats.* **OPPOSITE:** clean

disability NOUN **= handicap**, affliction, disorder, defect, impairment, disablement, infirmity

disable VERB **= handicap**, weaken, cripple, damage, hamstring, paralyse, impair, debilitate, incapacitate, prostrate, unman, immobilize, put out of action, enfeeble, render inoperative, render *hors de combat*

disabled ADJECTIVE **= differently abled**, physically challenged, handicapped, challenged, weakened, crippled, paralysed, lame, mutilated, maimed, incapacitated, infirm, bedridden **OPPOSITE:** able-bodied

USAGE

Referring to people with disabilities as *the disabled* can cause offence and should be avoided. Instead, refer to them as people *with disabilities* or *who are physically challenged*, or, possibly, *disabled people* or *differently abled people*. In general, the terms used for disabilities or medical conditions should be avoided as collective nouns for people who have them – so, for example, instead of *the blind*, it is preferable to refer to *sightless people*, *vision-impaired people*, or *partially-sighted people*, depending on the degree of their condition.

d

disabuse VERB **= enlighten**, correct, set right, open the eyes of, set straight, shatter (someone's) illusions, free from error, undeceive

disadvantage NOUN **1 = drawback**, trouble, burden, weakness, handicap, liability, minus *(informal)*, flaw, hardship, nuisance, snag, inconvenience, downside, impediment, hindrance, privation, weak point, fly in the ointment *(informal)*: *They suffer the disadvantage of having been political exiles.* **OPPOSITE:** advantage **2 = harm**, loss, damage, injury, hurt, prejudice, detriment, disservice: *An attempt to prevent an election would be to their disadvantage.* **OPPOSITE:** benefit **at a disadvantage = exposed**, vulnerable, wide open, unprotected, defenceless, open to attack, assailable: *Children from poor families were at a distinct disadvantage.*

d

disadvantaged ADJECTIVE **= deprived**, struggling, impoverished, discriminated against, underprivileged

disaffected ADJECTIVE **= alienated**, resentful, discontented, hostile, estranged, dissatisfied, rebellious, antagonistic, disloyal, seditious, mutinous, uncompliant, unsubmissive

disaffection NOUN **= alienation**, resentment, discontent, hostility, dislike, disagreement, dissatisfaction, animosity, aversion, antagonism, antipathy, disloyalty, estrangement, ill will, repugnance, unfriendliness

disagree VERB **1 = differ (in opinion)**, argue, debate, clash, dispute, contest, fall out *(informal)*, contend, dissent, quarrel, wrangle, bicker, take issue with, have words *(informal)*, cross swords, be at sixes and sevens: *The two men disagreed about what to do next.* **OPPOSITE:** agree **2 = make ill**, upset, sicken, trouble, hurt, bother, distress, discomfort, nauseate, be injurious: *Orange juice seems to disagree with some babies.* **disagree with something** *or* **someone = oppose**, object to, dissent from: *I disagree with drug laws in general.*

disagreeable ADJECTIVE **1 = nasty**, offensive, disgusting, unpleasant, distasteful, horrid, repellent, unsavoury, obnoxious, unpalatable, displeasing, repulsive, objectionable, repugnant, uninviting, yucky *or* yukky *(slang)*, yucko *(Austral. slang)*: *a disagreeable odour* **OPPOSITE:** pleasant **2 = ill-natured**, difficult, nasty, cross, contrary, unpleasant, rude, irritable, unfriendly, bad-tempered, surly, churlish, brusque, tetchy, ratty *(Brit. & N.Z. informal)*, peevish, ungracious, disobliging, unlikable *or* unlikeable: *He's a shallow, disagreeable man.* **OPPOSITE:** good-natured

disagreement NOUN **= argument**, row, difference, division, debate, conflict, clash, dispute, falling out, misunderstanding, dissent, quarrel, squabble, strife, wrangle, discord, tiff, altercation: *My instructor and I had a brief disagreement.* **OPPOSITE:** agreement

disallow VERB **= reject**, refuse, ban, dismiss, cancel, veto, forbid, embargo, prohibit, rebuff, repudiate, disown, proscribe, disavow, disclaim, abjure

disappear VERB **1 = vanish**, recede, drop out of sight, vanish off the face of the earth, evanesce, be lost to view or sight: *The car drove off and disappeared from sight.* **OPPOSITE:** appear **2 = pass**, wane, ebb, fade away: *The problem should disappear altogether by the age of five.* **3 = flee**, bolt, run away, fly, escape, split *(slang)*, retire, withdraw, take off *(informal)*, get away, vanish, depart, go, make off, abscond, take flight, do a runner *(slang)*, scarper *(Brit. slang)*, slope off, cut and run *(informal)*, beat a hasty retreat, make your escape, make your getaway: *The prisoner disappeared after being released on bail.* **4 = be lost**, be taken, be stolen, go missing, be mislaid: *My wallet seems to have disappeared.* **5 = cease**, end, fade, vanish, dissolve, expire, evaporate, perish, die out, pass away, cease to exist, melt away, leave no trace, cease to be known: *The immediate threat has disappeared.*

disappearance NOUN **1 = vanishing**, going, passing, disappearing, fading, melting, eclipse, evaporation, evanescence: *the gradual disappearance of the pain* **2 = flight**, departure, desertion, disappearing trick: *his disappearance while out on bail* **3 = loss**, losing, mislaying: *Police are investigating the disappearance of confidential files.*

disappoint VERB **1 = let down**, dismay, fail, dash, disillusion, sadden, vex, chagrin, dishearten, disenchant, dissatisfy, disgruntle: *He said that he was surprised and disappointed by the decision.* **2 = frustrate**, foil, thwart, defeat, baffle, balk: *His hopes have been disappointed many times before.*

disappointed ADJECTIVE **= let down**, upset, distressed, discouraged, depressed, choked, disillusioned, discontented, dejected, disheartened, disgruntled, dissatisfied, downcast, saddened, disenchanted, despondent, downhearted, cast down **OPPOSITE:** satisfied

disappointing ADJECTIVE **= unsatisfactory**, inadequate, discouraging, sorry, upsetting, sad, depressing, unhappy, unexpected, pathetic, inferior, insufficient, lame, disconcerting, second-rate, unworthy, not much cop *(Brit. slang)*

disappointment NOUN **1 = regret**, distress, discontent, dissatisfaction, disillusionment, displeasure, chagrin, disenchantment, dejection, despondency, discouragement, mortification, unfulfilment: *They expressed their disappointment at what had happened.* **2 = letdown**, blow, disaster, failure, setback, fiasco, misfortune, calamity, whammy *(informal, chiefly U.S.)*, choker *(informal)*, washout *(informal)*: *The defeat was a bitter disappointment.* **3 = frustration**, failure, ill-success: *There was resentment among the people at the disappointment of their hopes.*

disapproval NOUN **= displeasure**, criticism, objection, condemnation, dissatisfaction, censure, reproach, denunciation, deprecation, disapprobation, stick *(slang)*

disapprove VERB **1 = condemn**, object to, dislike, censure, deplore, deprecate, frown on, take exception to, take a dim view of, find unacceptable, have a down on *(informal)*, discountenance, look down your nose at *(informal)*, raise an *or* your eyebrow: *My mother disapproved of my working in a pub.* **OPPOSITE:** approve **2 = turn down**, reject, veto, set aside, spurn, disallow: *The judge disapproved the adoption because of my criminal record.* **OPPOSITE:** endorse

disapproving ADJECTIVE **= critical**, discouraging, frowning, disparaging, censorious, reproachful, deprecatory, condemnatory, denunciatory, disapprobatory, boot-faced *(informal)* **OPPOSITE:** approving

disarm VERB **1 = demilitarize**, disband, demobilize, deactivate: *The forces in the territory should disarm.* **2 = win over**, persuade: *She did her best to disarm her critics.*

disarmament NOUN **= arms reduction**, demobilization, arms limitation, demilitarization, de-escalation

disarming ADJECTIVE **= charming**, winning, irresistible, persuasive, likable *or* likeable

disarray NOUN **1 = confusion**, upset, disorder, indiscipline, disunity, disharmony, disorganization, unruliness, discomposure, disorderliness: *The feud has plunged the country into political disarray.* **OPPOSITE:** order **2 = untidiness**, state, mess, chaos, tangle, mix-up, muddle, clutter, shambles, jumble, hotchpotch, hodgepodge *(U.S.)*, dishevelment, pig's breakfast *(informal)*: *He found the room in disarray.* **OPPOSITE:** tidiness

disaster NOUN **1 = catastrophe**, trouble, blow, accident, stroke, reverse, tragedy, ruin, misfortune, adversity, calamity, mishap, whammy *(informal, chiefly U.S.)*, misadventure, cataclysm, act of God, bummer *(slang)*, ruination, car crash *(informal)*, train wreck *(informal)*, perfect storm, mischance: *the second air disaster in less than two months* **2 = failure**, mess, flop *(informal)*, catastrophe, rout, debacle, cock-up *(Brit. slang)*, washout *(informal)*: *The whole production was a disaster.*

disastrous ADJECTIVE **1 = terrible**, devastating, tragic, fatal, unfortunate, dreadful, destructive, unlucky, harmful, adverse, dire, catastrophic, detrimental, untoward, ruinous, calamitous, cataclysmic, ill-starred, unpropitious, ill-fated, cataclysmal: *the recent, disastrous earthquake* **2 = unsuccessful**, devastating, tragic, calamitous, cataclysmic: *The team has had another disastrous day.*

disavow VERB **= deny**, reject, contradict, retract, repudiate, disown, rebut, disclaim, forswear, gainsay *(archaic, literary)*, abjure

disband VERB **1 = dismiss**, separate, break up, scatter, dissolve, let go, disperse, send home, demobilize: *All the armed groups will be disbanded.* **2 = break up**, separate, scatter, disperse, part company, go (their) separate ways: *The rebels have agreed to disband by the end of the month.*

disbelief NOUN **= scepticism**, doubt, distrust, mistrust, incredulity, unbelief, dubiety **OPPOSITE:** belief

disbelieve VERB **= doubt**, reject, discount, suspect, discredit, not accept, mistrust, not buy *(slang)*, repudiate, scoff at, not credit, not swallow *(informal)*, give no credence to

disburse VERB **= pay out**, spend, lay out, fork out *(slang)*, expend, shell out *(informal)*

> **USAGE**
> *Disburse* is sometimes wrongly used where *disperse* is meant: *the police used water cannons to disperse* (not *disburse*) *the crowd.*

disbursement NOUN **= payment**, spending, expenditure, disposal, outlay

disc NOUN **1 = circle**, plate, saucer, discus: *a revolving disc with replaceable blades* **2 = record**, vinyl, gramophone record, phonograph record *(U.S. & Canad.)*, platter *(U.S. slang)*: *This disc includes the piano sonata in C minor.*

> **USAGE**
> In British English, the spelling *disc* is generally preferred, except when using the word in its computer senses, where *disk* is preferred. In US English, the spelling *disk* is used for all senses.

discard VERB **= get rid of**, drop, remove, throw away *or* out, reject, abandon, dump *(informal)*, shed, scrap, axe *(informal)*, ditch *(slang)*, junk *(informal)*, chuck *(informal)*, dispose of, relinquish, dispense with, jettison, repudiate, cast aside **OPPOSITE:** keep

discern VERB **= see**, perceive, make out, notice, observe, recognize, behold, catch sight of, suss (out) *(slang)*, espy, descry: *Under the bridge we could just discern a shadowy figure.*

discernible ADJECTIVE **= clear**, obvious, apparent, plain, visible, distinct, noticeable, recognizable, detectable, observable, perceptible, distinguishable, appreciable, discoverable

discerning ADJECTIVE **= discriminating**, knowing, sharp, critical, acute, sensitive, wise, intelligent, subtle, piercing, penetrating, shrewd, ingenious, astute, perceptive, judicious, clear-sighted, percipient, perspicacious, sagacious

discharge VERB **1 = release**, free, clear, liberate, pardon, let go, acquit, allow to go, set free, exonerate, absolve: *You are being discharged on medical grounds.* **2 = dismiss**, sack *(informal)*, fire *(informal)*, remove, expel, discard, oust, eject, cashier, give (someone) the boot *(slang)*, give (someone) the sack *(informal)*, kennet *(Austral. slang)*, jeff *(Austral. slang)*: *the regulation that gay people should be discharged from the military* **3 = carry out**, perform, fulfil, accomplish, do, effect, realize, observe, implement, execute, carry through: *the quiet competence with which he discharged his many duties* **4 = pay**, meet, clear, settle, square (up), honour, satisfy, relieve, liquidate: *The goods will be sold in order to discharge the debt.* **5 = pour forth**, release, empty, leak, emit, dispense, void, gush, ooze, exude, give off, excrete, disembogue: *The resulting salty water will be discharged at sea.* **6 = fire**, shoot, set off, explode, let off, detonate, let loose *(informal)*: *He was tried for unlawfully and dangerously discharging a weapon.*
▷ NOUN **1 = release**, liberation, clearance, pardon, acquittal, remittance, exoneration: *The doctors began to discuss his discharge from hospital.* **2 = dismissal**, notice, removal, the boot *(slang)*, expulsion, the sack *(informal)*, the push *(slang)*, marching orders *(informal)*, ejection, demobilization, kiss-off *(slang, chiefly U.S. & Canad.)*, the bum's rush *(slang)*, the (old) heave-ho *(informal)*, the order of the boot *(slang)*, congé, your books *or* cards *(informal)*: *They face receiving a dishonourable discharge from the Army.* **3 = emission**, flow, ooze, secretion, excretion, pus, seepage, suppuration: *They develop a fever and a watery discharge from the eyes.* **4 = firing**, report, shot, blast, burst, explosion, discharging, volley, salvo, detonation, fusillade: *Where firearms are kept at home, the risk of accidental discharge is high.* **5 = carrying out**, performance, achievement, execution, accomplishment, fulfilment, observance: *free of any influence which might affect the discharge of his duties*

disciple NOUN **1 = apostle**: *Jesus and his disciples* **2 = follower**, student, supporter, pupil, convert, believer, partisan, devotee, apostle, adherent, proselyte, votary, catechumen: *a major intellectual figure with disciples throughout Europe* **OPPOSITE:** teacher

> **THE DISCIPLES OF JESUS**
>
> | | |
> |---|---|
> | Andrew | Jude |
> | Bartholomew | Matthew |
> | James | Peter |
> | James | Philip |
> | John | Simon |
> | Judas | Thomas |

disciplinarian NOUN **= authoritarian**, tyrant, despot, stickler, taskmaster, martinet, drill sergeant, strict teacher, hard master

discipline NOUN **1 = control**, rule, authority, direction, regulation, supervision, orderliness, strictness: *the need for strict discipline in military units* **2 = self-control**, control, restraint, self-discipline, coolness, cool, willpower, calmness, self-restraint, orderliness, self-mastery, strength of mind *or* will: *His image of calm, control and discipline that appealed to voters.* **3 = training**, practice, exercise, method, regulation, drill, regimen: *inner disciplines like transcendental meditation* **4 = field of study**, area, subject, theme, topic, course, curriculum, speciality, subject matter, branch of knowledge, field of inquiry *or* reference: *appropriate topics for the new discipline of political science*
▷ VERB **1 = punish**, correct, reprimand, castigate, chastise, chasten, penalize, bring to book, reprove: *He was disciplined by his company, but not dismissed.* **2 = train**, control, govern, check, educate, regulate, instruct, restrain: *I'm very good at disciplining myself.*

> **PROVERBS**
> *Spare the rod and spoil the child*

disclaim VERB **1 = deny**, decline, reject, disallow, retract, repudiate, renege, rebut, disavow, abnegate, disaffirm: *She disclaims any knowledge of her husband's business activities.* **2 = renounce**, reject, abandon, relinquish, disown, abdicate, forswear, abjure: *the legislation which enabled him to disclaim his title*

disclaimer NOUN **= denial**, rejection, renunciation, retraction, repudiation, disavowal, abjuration

disclose VERB **1 = make known**, tell, reveal, publish, relate, broadcast, leak, confess, communicate, unveil, utter, make public, impart, divulge, out *(informal)*, let slip, spill the beans about *(informal)*, blow wide open *(slang)*, get off your chest *(informal)*, spill your guts about *(slang)*: *Neither side would disclose details of the transaction.* **OPPOSITE:** keep secret **2 = show**, reveal, expose, discover, exhibit, unveil, uncover, lay bare, bring to light, take the wraps off: *clapboard façades that revolve to disclose snug interiors* **OPPOSITE:** hide

disclosure NOUN **1 = revelation**, exposé, announcement, publication, leak, admission, declaration, confession, acknowledgment: *unauthorised newspaper disclosures* **2 = uncovering**, publication, exposure, revelation, divulgence: *The disclosure of his marriage proposal was badly-timed.*

discolour or (U.S.) **discolor** VERB **1 = mark**, soil, mar, fade, stain, streak, tinge: *Test first as this cleaner may discolour the fabric.* **2 = stain**, fade, streak, rust, tarnish: *A tooth which has been hit hard may discolour.*

d

discoloured or (U.S.) **discolored** ADJECTIVE **= stained**, tainted, tarnished, faded, pale, washed out, wan, blotched, besmirched, foxed, etiolated

discomfort NOUN **1 = pain**, suffering, hurt, smarting, ache, throbbing, irritation, tenderness, pang, malaise, twinge, soreness: *He suffered some discomfort, but no real pain.* **OPPOSITE:** comfort **2 = uneasiness**, worry, anxiety, doubt, alarm, distress, suspicion, apprehension, misgiving, nervousness, disquiet, agitation, qualms, trepidation, perturbation, apprehensiveness, dubiety, inquietude: *She heard the discomfort in his voice as he reluctantly agreed.* **OPPOSITE:** reassurance **3 = inconvenience**, trouble, difficulty, bother, hardship, irritation, hassle (informal), nuisance, uphill (S. African), annoyance, awkwardness, unpleasantness, vexation: *the hazards and discomforts of primitive continental travel* ▷ VERB **= make uncomfortable**, worry, trouble, shake, alarm, disturb, distress, unsettle, ruffle, unnerve, disquiet, perturb, discomfit, discompose: *World leaders will have been greatly discomforted by these events.* **OPPOSITE:** reassure

disconcert VERB **= disturb**, worry, trouble, upset, confuse, rattle (informal), baffle, put off, unsettle, bewilder, shake up (informal), undo, flurry, agitate, ruffle, perplex, unnerve, unbalance, take aback, fluster, perturb, faze, flummox, throw off balance, nonplus, abash, discompose, put out of countenance

disconcerted ADJECTIVE **= disturbed**, worried, troubled, thrown (informal), upset, confused, embarrassed, annoyed, rattled (informal), distracted, at sea, unsettled, bewildered, shook up (informal), flurried, ruffled, taken aback, flustered, perturbed, fazed, nonplussed, flummoxed, caught off balance, out of countenance

disconcerting ADJECTIVE **= disturbing**, upsetting, alarming, confusing, embarrassing, awkward, distracting, dismaying, baffling, bewildering, perplexing, off-putting (Brit. informal), bothersome

disconnect VERB **1 = cut off**: *The company has disconnected our electricity for non-payment.* **2 = detach**, separate, part, divide, sever, disengage, take apart, uncouple: *He disconnected the bottle from the overhead hook.*

disconnected ADJECTIVE **1 = unrelated**: *a sequence of utterly disconnected events* **2 = confused**, mixed-up, rambling, irrational, jumbled, unintelligible, illogical, incoherent, disjointed, garbled, uncoordinated: *a meaningless jumble of disconnected words*

disconsolate ADJECTIVE **1 = inconsolable**, crushed, despairing, miserable, hopeless, heartbroken, desolate, forlorn, woeful, grief-stricken, wretched: *She was disconsolate when her husband left her.* **2 = sad**, low, unhappy, miserable, gloomy, dismal, melancholy, forlorn, woeful, dejected, wretched, down in the dumps (informal): *He was looking increasingly disconsolate.*

discontent NOUN **= dissatisfaction**, unhappiness, displeasure, regret, envy, restlessness, uneasiness, vexation, discontentment, fretfulness

discontented ADJECTIVE **= dissatisfied**, complaining, unhappy, miserable, fed up, disgruntled, disaffected, vexed, displeased, fretful, cheesed off (Brit. slang), brassed off (Brit. slang), with a chip on your shoulder (informal) **OPPOSITE:** satisfied

discontinue VERB **= stop**, end, finish, drop, kick (informal), give up, abandon, suspend, quit, halt, pause, cease, axe (informal), interrupt, terminate, break off, put an end to, refrain from, leave off, pull the plug on, belay (Nautical)

discontinued ADJECTIVE **= stopped**, ended, finished, abandoned, halted, terminated, no longer made, given up or over

discontinuity NOUN **= lack of unity**, disconnection, incoherence, disunion, lack of coherence, disjointedness, disconnectedness

discord NOUN **= disagreement**, division, conflict, difference, opposition, row, clashing, dispute, contention, friction, strife, wrangling, variance, disunity, dissension, incompatibility, discordance, lack of concord **OPPOSITE:** agreement

discordant ADJECTIVE **1 = disagreeing**, conflicting, clashing, different, opposite, contrary, at odds, contradictory, inconsistent, incompatible, incongruous, divergent: *He displays attitudes and conduct discordant with his culture.* **2 = harsh**, jarring, grating, strident, shrill, jangling, dissonant, cacophonous, inharmonious, unmelodious: *They produced a discordant sound.*

discount VERB **1 = mark down**, reduce, lower: *Tour prices are being discounted.* **2 = disregard**, reject, ignore, overlook, discard, set aside, dispel, pass over, repudiate, disbelieve, brush off (slang), lay aside, pooh-pooh: *His theory was discounted immediately.* ▷ NOUN **= deduction**, cut, reduction, concession, allowance, rebate, cut price: *You often get a discount on discontinued goods.*

discourage VERB **1 = dishearten**, daunt, deter, crush, put off, depress, cow, dash, intimidate, dismay, unnerve, unman, overawe, demoralize, cast down, put a damper on, psych out (informal), dispirit, deject: *Don't let this setback discourage you.* **OPPOSITE:** hearten **2 = put off**, deter, prevent, dissuade, talk out of, discountenance: *a campaign to discourage children from smoking* **OPPOSITE:** encourage

discouraged ADJECTIVE **= put off**, deterred, daunted, dashed, dismayed, pessimistic, dispirited, downcast, disheartened, crestfallen, sick as a parrot (informal)

discouragement NOUN **1 = deterrent**, opposition, obstacle, curb, check, setback, restraint, constraint, impediment, hindrance, damper, disincentive: *Uncertainty is one of the major discouragements to investment.* **2 = depression**, disappointment, despair, pessimism, hopelessness, despondency, loss of confidence, dejection, discomfiture, low spirits, downheartedness: *There's a sense of discouragement creeping into the workforce.*

discouraging ADJECTIVE **= disheartening**, disappointing, depressing, daunting, dampening, unfavourable, off-putting (Brit. informal), dispiriting, unpropitious

discourse NOUN **1 = conversation**, talk, discussion, speech, communication, chat, dialogue, converse: *a tradition of political discourse* **2 = speech**, talk, address, essay, lecture, sermon, treatise, dissertation, homily, oration, disquisition, whaikorero (N.Z.): *He responds with a lengthy discourse on deployment strategy.*

discover VERB **1 = find out**, see, learn, reveal, spot, determine, notice, realize, recognize, perceive, detect, disclose, uncover, discern, ascertain, suss (out) (slang), get wise to (informal): *As he discovered, she had a brilliant mind.* **2 = find**, come across, uncover, unearth, turn up, dig up, come upon, bring to light, light upon: *His body was discovered on a roadside outside the city.* **3 = invent**, design, pioneer, devise, originate, contrive, conceive of: *Scientists discovered a way of forming the image in a thin layer on the surface.*

discoverer NOUN **1 = explorer**, pioneer: *the myth of the heroic discoverer* **2 = inventor**, author, originator, initiator: *the discoverer of carbon-dioxide lasers*

discovery NOUN **1 = finding out**, news, announcement, revelation, disclosure, realization: *the discovery that his wife was HIV positive* **2 = invention**, launch, institution, introduction, pioneering, innovation, initiation, inauguration, induction, coinage, origination: *the discovery of new forensic techniques* **3 = breakthrough**, find, finding, development, advance, leap, coup, invention, step forward, godsend, quantum leap: *In that year, two momentous discoveries were made.* **4 = finding**, turning up, locating, revelation, uncovering, disclosure, detection, espial: *the discovery of a mass grave in the south-west of the country*

> QUOTATIONS
> Discovery consists of seeing what everybody has seen and thinking what nobody has thought
> [Albert von Szent-Györgyi *The Scientist Speculates*]

discredit VERB **1 = disgrace**, blame, shame, smear, stain, humiliate, degrade, taint, slur, detract from, disparage, vilify, slander, sully, dishonour, stigmatize, defame, bring into disrepute, bring shame upon: *He says his accusers are trying to discredit him.* **OPPOSITE:** honour **2 = dispute**, question, challenge, deny, reject, discount, distrust, mistrust, repudiate, cast doubt on *or* upon, disbelieve, pooh-pooh: *They realized there would be problems in discrediting the evidence.*
▷ NOUN **= disgrace**, scandal, shame, disrepute, smear, stigma, censure, slur, ignominy, dishonour, imputation, odium, ill-repute, aspersion: *His actions have brought discredit on the whole regiment.* **OPPOSITE:** honour

discredited ADJECTIVE **= rejected**, exposed, exploded, discarded, obsolete, refuted, debunked, outworn

discreet ADJECTIVE **= tactful**, diplomatic, politic, reserved, guarded, careful, sensible, cautious, wary, discerning, prudent, considerate, judicious, circumspect, sagacious: *He followed at a discreet distance.* **OPPOSITE:** tactless

discrepancy NOUN **= disagreement**, difference, variation, conflict, contradiction, inconsistency, disparity, variance, divergence, dissonance, incongruity, dissimilarity, discordance, contrariety

discrete ADJECTIVE **= separate**, individual, distinct, detached, disconnected, unattached, discontinuous

> USAGE
> This word is quite often used by mistake where *discreet* is intended: *reading is a set of discrete skills; she was discreet (not discrete) about the affair.*

discretion NOUN **1 = tact**, care, consideration, judgment, caution, diplomacy, good sense, prudence, acumen, wariness, discernment, circumspection, sagacity, carefulness, judiciousness, heedfulness: *He conducted the whole affair with the utmost discretion.* **OPPOSITE:** tactlessness **2 = choice**, will, wish, liking, mind, option, pleasure, preference, inclination, disposition, predilection, volition: *She was given the money to use at her own discretion.*

> PROVERBS
> *Discretion is the better part of valour*

discretionary ADJECTIVE **= optional**, arbitrary *(Law)*, unrestricted, elective, open to choice, nonmandatory

discriminate VERB **= differentiate**, distinguish, discern, separate, assess, evaluate, tell the difference, draw a distinction: *He is incapable of discriminating between a good idea and a bad one.*
discriminate against someone = treat differently, single out, victimize, disfavour, treat as inferior, show bias against, show prejudice against: *They believe the law discriminates against women.*

discriminating ADJECTIVE **= discerning**, particular, keen, critical, acute, sensitive, refined, cultivated, selective, astute, tasteful, fastidious **OPPOSITE:** undiscriminating

discrimination NOUN **1 = prejudice**, bias, injustice, intolerance, bigotry, favouritism, unfairness, inequity: *measures to counteract racial discrimination* **2 = discernment**, taste, judgment, perception, insight, penetration, subtlety, refinement, acumen, keenness, sagacity, acuteness, clearness: *He praised our taste and discrimination.*

discriminatory ADJECTIVE **= prejudiced**, biased, partial, weighted, favouring, one-sided, partisan, unjust, preferential, prejudicial, inequitable

discuss VERB **= talk about**, consider, debate, review, go into, examine, argue about, thrash out, ventilate, reason about, exchange views on, deliberate about, weigh up the pros and cons of, converse about, confer about

discussion NOUN **1 = talk**, debate, argument, conference, exchange, review, conversation, consideration, dialogue, consultation, seminar, discourse, deliberation, symposium, colloquy, confabulation, korero *(N.Z.)*: *There was a discussion about the wording of the report.* **2 = examination**, investigation, analysis, scrutiny, dissection: *For a discussion of biology and sexual politics, see chapter 4.*

> QUOTATIONS
> To jaw-jaw is better than to war-war
> [Winston Churchill]
>
> The aim of argument, or of discussion, should be not victory, but progress
> [Joseph Joubert *Pensées*]

disdain NOUN **= contempt**, dislike, scorn, arrogance, indifference, sneering, derision, hauteur, snobbishness, contumely, haughtiness, superciliousness: *She looked at him with disdain.*
▷ VERB **= scorn**, reject, despise, slight, disregard, spurn, undervalue, deride, look down on, belittle, sneer at, pooh-pooh, contemn, look down your nose at *(informal)*, misprize: *a political leader who disdained the compromises of politics*

> QUOTATIONS
> A little disdain is not amiss; a little scorn is alluring
> [William Congreve *The Way of the World*]

disdainful ADJECTIVE **= contemptuous**, scornful, arrogant, superior, proud, sneering, aloof, haughty, derisive, supercilious, high and mighty *(informal)*, hoity-toity *(informal)*, turning up your nose (at), on your high horse *(informal)*, looking down your nose (at)

disease NOUN **1 = illness**, condition, complaint, upset, infection, disorder, sickness, ailment, affliction, malady, infirmity, indisposition, lurgy *(informal)*, lifestyle disease: *illnesses such as heart disease* **2 = evil**, disorder, plague, curse, cancer, blight, contamination, scourge, affliction, bane, contagion, malady, canker: *the disease of racism eating away at the core of our society*

diseased ADJECTIVE **= unhealthy**, sick, infected, rotten, ailing, tainted, sickly, unwell, crook *(Austral. & N.Z. informal)*, unsound, unwholesome

disembark VERB **= land**, get off, alight, arrive, step out, go ashore

disembodied ADJECTIVE **= ghostly**, phantom, spectral

disenchanted ADJECTIVE **= disillusioned**, disappointed, soured, cynical, indifferent, sick, let down, blasé, jaundiced, undeceived

disenchantment NOUN **= disillusionment**, disappointment, disillusion, rude awakening

disengage VERB **1 = release**, free, separate, ease, liberate, loosen, set free, extricate, untie, disentangle, unloose, unbridle: *He gently disengaged himself from his sister's tearful embrace.* **2 = detach**, withdraw: *More vigorous action is needed to force the army to disengage.*

disengaged ADJECTIVE **= unconnected**, separate, apart, detached, unattached

disengagement NOUN **= disconnection**, withdrawal, separation, detachment, disentanglement

disentangle VERB **1 = resolve**, clear (up), work out, sort out, clarify,

d

simplify: *The author brilliantly disentangles complex debates.* **2 = free**, separate, loose, detach, sever, disconnect, extricate, disengage: *They are looking at ways to disentangle him from this situation.* **3 = untangle**, unravel, untwist, unsnarl: *The rope could not be disentangled and had to be cut.*

disfigure VERB **1 = damage**, scar, mutilate, maim, injure, wound, deform: *These items could be used to injure or disfigure someone.* **2 = mar**, distort, blemish, deface, make ugly, disfeature: *ugly new houses which disfigure the countryside*

d

disgorge VERB **= emit**, discharge, send out, expel, throw out, vent, throw up, eject, spout, spew, belch, send forth

disgrace NOUN **1 = shame**, contempt, discredit, degradation, disrepute, ignominy, dishonour, infamy, opprobrium, odium, disfavour, obloquy, disesteem: *I have brought disgrace upon my family.*
OPPOSITE: honour **2 = scandal**, stain, stigma, blot, blemish: *the disgrace of having an illegitimate child*
▷ VERB **= shame**, stain, humiliate, discredit, degrade, taint, sully, dishonour, stigmatize, defame, abase, bring shame upon: *These soldiers have disgraced their regiment.*
OPPOSITE: honour

disgraced ADJECTIVE **= shamed**, humiliated, discredited, branded, degraded, mortified, in disgrace, dishonoured, stigmatized, under a cloud, in the doghouse *(informal)*

disgraceful ADJECTIVE **= shameful**, shocking, scandalous, mean, low, infamous, degrading, unworthy, ignominious, disreputable, contemptible, dishonourable, detestable, discreditable, blameworthy, opprobrious

disgruntled ADJECTIVE **= discontented**, dissatisfied, annoyed, irritated, put out, hacked (off) *(U.S. slang)*, grumpy, vexed, sullen, displeased, petulant, sulky, peeved, malcontent, testy, peevish, huffy, cheesed off *(Brit. slang)*, hoha *(N.Z.)*

disguise VERB **= hide**, cover, conceal, screen, mask, suppress, withhold, veil, cloak, shroud, camouflage, keep secret, hush up, draw a veil over, keep dark, keep under your hat: *He made no attempt to disguise his contempt.*
▷ NOUN **= costume**, get-up *(informal)*, mask, camouflage, false appearance: *a ridiculous disguise.*

disguised ADJECTIVE **1 = in disguise**, masked, camouflaged, undercover, incognito, unrecognizable: *a disguised bank robber* **2 = false**, assumed, pretend, artificial, forged, fake, mock, imitation, sham, pseudo *(informal)*, counterfeit, feigned, phoney *or* phony *(informal)*: *Their HQ used to be a disguised builders' yard.*

disgust VERB **= sicken**, outrage, offend, revolt, put off, repel, nauseate, gross out *(U.S. slang)*, turn your stomach, fill with loathing, cause aversion: *He disgusted everyone with his boorish behaviour.*
OPPOSITE: delight
▷ NOUN **= outrage**, shock, anger, hurt, fury, resentment, wrath, indignation: *Colleagues last night spoke of their disgust at the decision.*

disgusted ADJECTIVE **1 = outraged**, appalled, offended, sickened, scandalized: *I'm disgusted with the way that he was treated.* **2 = sickened**, repelled, repulsed, nauseated: *squeamish men who are disgusted by the idea of menstruation*

disgusting ADJECTIVE **1 = sickening**, foul, revolting, gross, repellent, nauseating, repugnant, loathsome, festy *(Austral. slang)*, yucko *(Austral. slang)* **2 = appalling**, shocking, awful, offensive, dreadful, horrifying

dish NOUN **1 = bowl**, plate, platter, salver: *Pile the potatoes into a warm serving dish.* **2 = food**, fare, recipe: *There are plenty of vegetarian dishes to choose from.*
dish something out = distribute, assign, allocate, designate, set aside, hand out, earmark, inflict, mete out, dole out, share out, apportion: *The council wants to dish the money out to specific projects.*
dish something up = serve up, serve, produce, present, hand out, ladle out, spoon out: *They dished up the next course.*

disharmony NOUN **= discord**, conflict, clash, friction, discordance, disaccord, inharmoniousness

disheartened ADJECTIVE **= discouraged**, depressed, crushed, dismayed, choked, daunted, dejected, dispirited, downcast, crestfallen, downhearted, sick as a parrot *(informal)*

dishevelled *or (U.S.)* **disheveled** ADJECTIVE **= untidy**, disordered, messy, ruffled, rumpled, bedraggled, unkempt, tousled, hanging loose, blowsy, uncombed, disarranged, disarrayed, frowzy, daggy *(Austral. & N.Z. informal)* **OPPOSITE:** tidy

dishonest ADJECTIVE **= deceitful**, corrupt, crooked *(informal)*, designing, lying, bent *(slang)*, false, unfair, cheating, deceiving, shady *(informal)*, fraudulent, treacherous, deceptive, unscrupulous, crafty, swindling, disreputable, untrustworthy, double-dealing, unprincipled, mendacious, perfidious, untruthful, guileful, knavish *(archaic)*
OPPOSITE: honest

dishonesty NOUN **= deceit**, fraud, corruption, cheating, graft *(informal)*, treachery, trickery, criminality, duplicity, falsehood, chicanery, falsity, sharp practice, perfidy, mendacity, fraudulence, crookedness, wiliness, unscrupulousness, improbity

> **QUOTATIONS**
> Dishonesty is the raw material not of quacks only, but also in great part of dupes
> [Thomas Carlyle *Count Cagliostro*]
>
> Thou shalt not steal; an empty feat
> When it's so lucrative to cheat
> [Arthur Hugh Clough *The Latest Decalogue*]

dishonour *or (U.S.)* **dishonor** VERB **= disgrace**, shame, discredit, corrupt, degrade, blacken, sully, debase, debauch, defame, abase: *It would dishonour my family if I didn't wear the veil.*
OPPOSITE: respect
▷ NOUN **= disgrace**, scandal, shame, discredit, degradation, disrepute, reproach, ignominy, infamy, opprobrium, odium, disfavour, abasement, obloquy: *You have brought dishonour on a fine and venerable institution.*
OPPOSITE: honour

disillusion VERB **= shatter the illusions of**, disabuse, bring down to earth, open the eyes of, disenchant, undeceive

disillusioned ADJECTIVE **= disenchanted**, disappointed, enlightened, indifferent, disabused, sadder and wiser, undeceived

disillusionment NOUN **= disenchantment**, disappointment, disillusion, enlightenment, rude awakening, lost innocence

disincentive NOUN **= discouragement**, deterrent, impediment, damper, dissuasion, determent

disinclined ADJECTIVE **= reluctant**, unwilling, averse, opposed, resistant, hesitant, balking, loath, not in the mood, indisposed, antipathetic

disinfect VERB **= sterilize**, purify, decontaminate, clean, cleanse, fumigate, deodorize, sanitize
OPPOSITE: contaminate

disinfectant NOUN **= antiseptic**, sterilizer, germicide, sanitizer

disintegrate VERB **= break up**, crumble, fall apart, separate, shatter, splinter, break apart, fall to pieces, go to pieces, disunite

disinterest NOUN **= indifference**, apathy, lack of interest, disregard, detachment, absence of feeling

disinterested ADJECTIVE **1 = impartial**, objective, neutral, detached, equitable, impersonal, unbiased, even-handed, unselfish, uninvolved, unprejudiced, free from self-interest: *Scientists are expected to be impartial and disinterested.*
OPPOSITE: biased **2 = indifferent**, apathetic, uninterested: *We had become jaded, disinterested and disillusioned.*

> **USAGE**
> *Disinterested* is now so commonly used to mean 'not interested' that to avoid ambiguity it is often advisable to replace it by a synonym when the meaning

The Language of John Buchan

The Scottish author John Buchan (1875–1940) was multi-faceted both as a writer and as a man. A son of the manse, his career included working as a lawyer, publisher, journalist, and editor, before he was appointed Governor-General of Canada (as Lord Tweedsmuir) in 1935. He wrote many short stories, well-received biographies of Scott and Montrose, as well as historical novels such as *John Burnet of Barns* (1898) and *Witch Wood* (1927), but it is as the writer of popular thrillers (which he referred to as his 'shockers') that he is most widely known. Several of these featured the same hero, the adventurous Richard Hannay, from *The Thirty-Nine Steps* (1915) to *The Island of Sheep* (1936).

Buchan's language in his fiction is predominantly direct and shorn of excessive ornamentation. Especially in his thrillers, he is too concerned with communicating the essential facts and story elements and keeping up a suspenseful pace to linger much on description. Thus his most commonly used adjectives are the brief and basic *white, black, wild,* and *queer.* The latter, of course, is chiefly used in a sense that is now largely outdated, that of 'odd, strange', and would strike quite another note to modern ears:

> But I've got a notion that some devilish **queer** things will happen before to-morrow morning.

Like Buchan's adjectives, his most frequently used nouns tend to be short and plain, such as *friend, heart, war,* and *enemy*. Like many of his contemporaries, Buchan's narrators and characters very much frame their lives in terms of 'the war' (meaning the First World War), measuring eras as 'before the war' or 'after the war'. War changed everything for these generations:

> I learned in the **war** that civilization anywhere is a very thin crust.

Unlike those of many of his contemporary writers, Buchan's novels have much less to do with witty conversation in drawing-rooms and distracting affairs of the heart than with the physically demanding world of the adventurer. Nature and the untamed countryside, whether in the rugged Highlands of Scotland or the plains of Africa, are the setting for the elements of plot that drive the stories. It is therefore no surprise that landscape nouns such as *hill, mountain, earth,* and *stream* predominate.

> After that I crossed a low **pass** to the head of another **sea-loch**, and, following the map, struck over the shoulder of a great **hill** and ate my luncheon far up on its side, with a wonderful vista of wood and water below me.

As might be expected from a Scottish writer who set many of his works in his homeland, Buchan's language typically contains a leavening of Scots vocabulary, including such terms as *ye, glen, wi',* and *ken*:

> I'm no' going to let **ye** into this business till I **ken** that **ye**'ll help.

However, Buchan essentially confines his use of Scotticisms to the dialogue of Scots characters; his narration is couched in the standard literary English of his time. For this reason critics have long debated the 'Scottishness' of Buchan as a writer. Buchan was above all a popular writer, with his thrillers especially being bestsellers throughout the English-speaking world. As a Scot, he was formed by the country that bore him, and when he reproduced the Scots language he knew what he was talking about, but the tenor of his writing was international.

intended is 'impartial, unbiased'. In the Bank of English about 10% of the examples of the word occur followed by *in*, and overall about a third of examples are of this usage.

disjointed ADJECTIVE **1 = incoherent**, confused, disordered, rambling, disconnected, unconnected, loose, aimless, fitful, spasmodic: *his disjointed drunken ramblings* **2 = disconnected**, separated, divided, split, displaced, dislocated, disunited: *our increasingly fragmented and disjointed society*

d

dislike VERB **= hate**, object to, loathe, despise, shun, scorn, disapprove of, detest, abhor, recoil from, take a dim view of, be repelled by, be averse to, disfavour, have an aversion to, abominate, have a down on *(informal)*, disrelish, have no taste *or* stomach for, not be able to bear *or* abide *or* stand: *We don't serve liver often because so many people dislike it.* **OPPOSITE:** like
▷ NOUN **= hatred**, disgust, hostility, loathing, disapproval, distaste, animosity, aversion, antagonism, displeasure, antipathy, enmity, animus, disinclination, repugnance, odium, detestation, disapprobation: *The two women viewed each other with dislike and suspicion.* **OPPOSITE:** liking

dislocate VERB **1 = put out of joint**, disconnect, disengage, unhinge, disunite, disjoint, disarticulate: *She had dislocated her shoulder in the fall.* **2 = disrupt**, disturb, disorder: *The strike was designed to dislocate the economy.*

dislocation NOUN **1 = disruption**, disorder, disturbance, disarray, disorganization: *The refugees have suffered a total dislocation of their lives.* **2 = putting out of joint**, unhinging, disengagement, disconnection, disarticulation: *He suffered a double dislocation of his left ankle.*

dislodge VERB **1 = displace**, remove, disturb, dig out, uproot, extricate, disentangle, knock loose: *Use a hoof pick to dislodge stones and dirt from your horse's feet.* **2 = oust**, remove, expel, throw out, displace, topple, force out, eject, depose, unseat: *The leader cannot dislodge her this time.*

disloyal ADJECTIVE **= treacherous**, false, unfaithful, subversive, two-faced, faithless, untrustworthy, perfidious, apostate, traitorous **OPPOSITE:** loyal

disloyalty NOUN **= treachery**, infidelity, breach of trust, double-dealing, falsity, perfidy, unfaithfulness, falseness, betrayal of trust, inconstancy, deceitfulness, breaking of faith, Punic faith

dismal ADJECTIVE **1 = bad**, awful, dreadful, rotten *(informal)*, terrible, poor, dire, duff *(Brit. informal)*, abysmal, frightful, godawful *(slang)*: *the country's dismal record in the Olympics* **2 = sad**, gloomy, melancholy, black, dark, depressing, discouraging, bleak, dreary, sombre, forlorn, despondent, lugubrious, sorrowful, wretched, funereal, cheerless, dolorous: *You can't occupy yourself with dismal thoughts all the time.* **OPPOSITE:** happy **3 = gloomy**, depressing, dull, dreary, lugubrious, cheerless: *The main part of the hospital is pretty dismal.* **OPPOSITE:** cheerful

dismantle VERB **= take apart**, strip, demolish, raze, disassemble, unrig, take to pieces *or* bits

dismay VERB **1 = alarm**, frighten, scare, panic, distress, terrify, appal, startle, horrify, paralyse, unnerve, put the wind up (someone) *(informal)*, give (someone) a turn *(informal)*, affright, fill with consternation: *The committee was dismayed by what it had been told.* **2 = disappoint**, upset, sadden, dash, discourage, put off, daunt, disillusion, let down, vex, chagrin, dishearten, dispirit, disenchant, disgruntle: *He was dismayed to learn that she was already married.*
▷ NOUN **1 = alarm**, fear, horror, panic, anxiety, distress, terror, dread, fright, unease, apprehension, nervousness, agitation, consternation, trepidation, uneasiness: *They reacted to the news with dismay.* **2 = disappointment**, upset, distress, frustration, dissatisfaction, disillusionment, chagrin, disenchantment, discouragement, mortification: *Much to her dismay, he did not call.*

dismember VERB **= cut into pieces**, divide, rend, sever, mutilate, dissect, dislocate, amputate, disjoint, anatomize, dislimb

dismiss VERB **1 = reject**, disregard, spurn, repudiate, pooh-pooh: *He dismissed the reports as mere speculation.* **2 = banish**, drop, dispel, shelve, discard, set aside, eradicate, cast out, lay aside, put out of your mind: *I dismissed the thought from my mind.* **3 = sack**, fire *(informal)*, remove *(informal)*, axe *(informal)*, discharge, oust, lay off, kick out *(informal)*, cashier, send packing *(informal)*, give (someone) notice, kiss off *(slang, chiefly U.S. & Canad.)*, give (someone) their marching orders, give (someone) the push *(informal)*, give (someone) the elbow, give (someone) the boot *(slang)*, give (someone) the bullet *(Brit. slang)*, kennet *(Austral. slang)*, jeff *(Austral. slang)*: *the power to dismiss civil servants who refuse to work* **4 = let go**, free, release, discharge, dissolve, liberate, disperse, disband, send away: *Two more witnesses were called, heard and dismissed.*

dismissal NOUN **= the sack**, removal, discharge, notice, the boot *(slang)*, expulsion *(informal)*, the push *(slang)*, marching orders *(informal)*, kiss-off *(slang, chiefly U.S. & Canad.)*, the bum's rush *(slang)*, the (old) heave-ho *(informal)*, the order of the boot *(slang)*, your books *or* cards *(informal)*

dismount VERB **= get off**, descend, get down, alight, light

disobedience NOUN **= defiance**, mutiny, indiscipline, revolt, insubordination, waywardness, infraction, recalcitrance, noncompliance, unruliness, nonobservance

disobey VERB **1 = defy**, ignore, rebel, resist, disregard, refuse to obey, dig your heels in *(informal)*, go counter to: *a naughty boy who often disobeyed his mother* **2 = infringe**, defy, refuse to obey, flout, violate, contravene, overstep, transgress, go counter to: *He was forever disobeying the rules.*

disorder NOUN **1 = illness**, disease, complaint, condition, sickness, ailment, affliction, malady, infirmity, indisposition: *a rare nerve disorder that can cause paralysis of the arms* **2 = untidiness**, mess, confusion, chaos, muddle, state, clutter, shambles, disarray, jumble, irregularity, disorganization, hotchpotch, derangement, hodgepodge *(U.S.)*, pig's breakfast *(informal)*, disorderliness: *The emergency room was in disorder.* **3 = disturbance**, fight, riot, turmoil, unrest, quarrel, upheaval, brawl, clamour, uproar, turbulence, fracas, commotion, rumpus, tumult, hubbub, shindig *(informal)*, hullabaloo, scrimmage, unruliness, shindy *(informal)*, bagarre *(French)*, biffo *(Austral. slang)*: *He called on the authorities to stop public disorder.*

disorderly ADJECTIVE **1 = untidy**, confused, chaotic, messy, irregular, jumbled, indiscriminate, shambolic *(informal)*, disorganized, higgledy-piggledy *(informal)*, unsystematic: *The desk was covered in a disorderly jumble of old papers.* **OPPOSITE:** tidy **2 = unruly**, disruptive, rowdy, turbulent, unlawful, stormy, rebellious, boisterous, tumultuous, lawless, riotous, unmanageable, ungovernable, refractory, obstreperous, indisciplined: *disorderly conduct*

disorganized ADJECTIVE **= muddled**, confused, disordered, shuffled, chaotic, jumbled, haphazard, unorganized, unsystematic, unmethodical

disorientate *or* **disorient** VERB **= confuse**, upset, perplex, dislocate, cause to lose your bearings

disorientated *or* **disoriented** ADJECTIVE **= confused**, lost, unsettled, bewildered, mixed up, perplexed, all at sea

disown VERB **= deny**, reject, abandon, renounce, disallow, retract, repudiate, cast off, rebut, disavow, disclaim, abnegate, refuse to acknowledge *or* recognize

disparage VERB **= run down**, dismiss, put down, criticize, underestimate, discredit, ridicule, scorn, minimize, disdain, undervalue, deride, slag (off) *(slang)*, knock *(informal)*, blast, rubbish *(informal)*, malign, detract from, denigrate, belittle, decry, underrate, vilify, slander, deprecate, tear into *(informal)*, diss *(slang, chiefly U.S.)*, defame, bad-mouth *(slang, chiefly U.S. & Canad.)*, lambast(e), traduce, derogate, asperse

disparaging ADJECTIVE **= contemptuous**, damaging, critical, slighting, offensive, insulting, abusive, scathing, dismissive, belittling, unfavourable, derogatory, unflattering, scornful, disdainful, defamatory, derisive, libellous, slanderous, deprecatory, uncomplimentary, fault-finding, contumelious
OPPOSITE: complimentary

disparate ADJECTIVE **= different**, contrasting, unlike, contrary, distinct, diverse, at odds, dissimilar, discordant, at variance, discrepant

disparity NOUN **= difference**, gap, inequality, distinction, imbalance, discrepancy, incongruity, unevenness, dissimilarity, disproportion, unlikeness, dissimilitude

dispassionate ADJECTIVE **1 = unemotional**, cool, collected, calm, moderate, composed, sober, serene, unmoved, temperate, unfazed *(informal)*, unruffled, imperturbable, unexcited, unexcitable: *He spoke in a flat dispassionate tone.*
OPPOSITE: emotional **2 = objective**, fair, neutral, detached, indifferent, impartial, impersonal, disinterested, unbiased, uninvolved, unprejudiced: *We try to be dispassionate about the cases we bring.* **OPPOSITE:** biased

dispatch *or* **despatch** VERB **1 = send**, transmit, forward, express, communicate, consign, remit: *He dispatched a telegram.* **2 = kill**, murder, destroy, do in *(slang)*, eliminate *(slang)*, take out *(slang)*, execute, butcher, slaughter, assassinate, slay, finish off, put an end to, do away with, blow away *(slang, chiefly U.S.)*, liquidate, annihilate, exterminate, take (someone's) life, bump off *(slang)*: *They may catch him and dispatch him immediately.* **3 = carry out**, perform, fulfil, effect, finish, achieve, settle, dismiss, conclude, accomplish, execute, discharge, dispose of, expedite, make short work of *(informal)*: *He dispatched his business.*
▷ NOUN **1 = message**, news, report, story, letter, account, piece, item, document, communication, instruction, bulletin, communiqué, missive: *This dispatch from our West Africa correspondent.* **2 = speed**, haste, promptness, alacrity, rapidity, quickness, swiftness, briskness, expedition, celerity, promptitude, precipitateness: *He feels we should act with despatch.*

dispel VERB **= drive away**, dismiss, eliminate, resolve, scatter, expel, disperse, banish, rout, allay, dissipate, chase away

dispensation NOUN **1 = exemption**, licence, exception, permission, privilege, relaxation, immunity, relief, indulgence, reprieve, remission: *The committee were not prepared to grant special dispensation.* **2 = distribution**, supplying, dealing out, appointment, endowment, allotment, consignment, disbursement, apportionment, bestowal, conferment: *the dispensation of justice*

dispense VERB **1 = distribute**, assign, allocate, allot, mete out, dole out, share out, apportion, deal out, disburse: *They had already dispensed £40,000 in grants.* **2 = prepare**, measure, supply, mix: *a store licensed to dispense prescriptions* **3 = administer**, direct, operate, carry out, implement, undertake, enforce, execute, apply, discharge: *High Court judges dispensing justice round the country* **4 = exempt**, except, excuse, release, relieve, reprieve, let off *(informal)*, exonerate: *No-one is dispensed from collaborating in this task.*
dispense with something *or* **someone 1 = do away with**, ignore, give up, cancel, abolish, omit, disregard, pass over, brush aside, forgo, render needless: *We'll dispense with formalities.* **2 = do without**, get rid of, dispose of, relinquish, shake off: *Up at the lectern he dispensed with his notes.*

dispersal NOUN **1 = scattering**, spread, distribution, dissemination, dissipation: *the plants' mechanisms of dispersal of their spores* **2 = spread**, broadcast, circulation, diffusion, dissemination: *the dispersal of this notably negative attitude*

disperse VERB **1 = scatter**, spread, distribute, circulate, strew, diffuse, dissipate, disseminate, throw about: *Intense currents disperse the sewage.* **2 = break up**, separate, dismiss, disappear, send off, vanish, scatter, dissolve, rout, dispel, disband, part company, demobilize, go (their) separate ways: *The crowd dispersed peacefully.* **OPPOSITE:** gather **3 = dissolve**, disappear, vanish, evaporate, break up, dissipate, melt away, evanesce: *The fog dispersed and I became aware of the sun.*

dispirited ADJECTIVE **= disheartened**, depressed, discouraged, down, low, sad, gloomy, glum, dejected, in the doldrums, despondent, downcast, morose, crestfallen, sick as a parrot *(informal)*

dispiriting ADJECTIVE **= disheartening**, disappointing, depressing, crushing, discouraging, daunting, sickening, saddening, demoralizing **OPPOSITE:** reassuring

displace VERB **1 = replace**, succeed, take over from, supersede, oust, usurp, supplant, take the place of, crowd out, fill *or* step into (someone's) boots: *These factories have displaced tourism.* **2 = force out**, turn out, expel, throw out, oust, unsettle, kick out *(informal)*, eject, evict, dislodge, boot out *(informal)*, dispossess, turf out *(informal)*: *In Europe alone, 30 million people were displaced.* **3 = move**, shift, disturb, budge, misplace, disarrange, derange: *A strong wind is all it would take to displace the stones.* **4 = remove**, fire *(informal)*, dismiss, sack *(informal)*, discharge, oust, depose, cashier, dethrone, remove from office: *They displaced him in a coup.*

display VERB **1 = show**, present, exhibit, unveil, open to view, take the wraps off, put on view: *The cabinets display seventeenth-century porcelain.* **OPPOSITE:** conceal **2 = expose**, show, reveal, bare, exhibit, uncover, lay bare, expose to view: *She displayed her wound.* **3 = demonstrate**, show, reveal, register, expose, disclose, betray, manifest, divulge, make known, evidence, evince: *It was unlike him to display his feelings.* **4 = show off**, parade, exhibit, sport *(informal)*, flash *(informal)*, boast, flourish, brandish, flaunt, vaunt, make a (great) show of, disport, make an exhibition of: *She does not have to display her charms.*
▷ NOUN **1 = proof**, exhibition, demonstration, evidence, expression, exposure, illustration, revelation, testimony, confirmation, manifestation, affirmation, substantiation: *an outward display of affection* **2 = exhibition**, show, demonstration, presentation, showing, array, expo *(informal)*, exposition: *a display of your work* **3 = ostentation**, show, dash, flourish, fanfare, pomp: *He embraced it with such confidence and display.* **4 = show**, exhibition, demonstration, parade, spectacle, pageant, pageantry: *a dazzling dance display*

displease VERB **= annoy**, upset, anger, provoke, offend, irritate, put out, hassle *(informal)*, aggravate *(informal)*, incense, gall, exasperate, nettle, vex, irk, rile, pique, nark *(Brit., Austral. & N.Z. slang)*, dissatisfy, put your back up, hack you off *(informal)*

displeasure NOUN **= annoyance**, anger, resentment, irritation, offence, dislike, wrath, dissatisfaction, disapproval, indignation, distaste, pique, vexation, disgruntlement, disfavour, disapprobation
OPPOSITE: satisfaction

disposable ADJECTIVE **1 = throwaway**, paper, nonreturnable: *disposable nappies for babies up to 8lb* **2 = available**, expendable, free for use, consumable, spendable, at your service: *He had little disposable income.*

disposal NOUN **= throwing away**, dumping *(informal)*, scrapping, removal, discarding, clearance, jettisoning, ejection, riddance, relinquishment: *the disposal of radioactive waste*
at your disposal = available, ready, to hand, accessible, convenient, handy,

on hand, at hand, obtainable, on tap, expendable, at your fingertips, at your service, free for use, ready for use, consumable, spendable: *Do you have this information at your disposal?*

dispose VERB **1 = arrange**, put, place, group, set, order, stand, range, settle, fix, rank, distribute, array: *He was preparing to dispose his effects about the room.* **2 = lead**, move, condition, influence, prompt, tempt, adapt, motivate, bias, induce, incline, predispose, actuate: *theologies which dispose their adherents to fanaticism*
dispose of someone = kill, murder, destroy, do in *(slang)*, take out *(slang)*, execute, slaughter, dispatch, assassinate, slay, do away with, knock off *(slang)*, liquidate, neutralize, exterminate, take (someone's) life, bump off *(slang)*, wipe (someone) from the face of the earth *(informal)*: *They had hired an assassin to dispose of him.*
dispose of something 1 = get rid of, destroy, dump *(informal)*, scrap, bin *(informal)*, junk *(informal)*, chuck *(informal)*, discard, unload, dispense with, jettison, get shot of, throw out *or* away: *Fold up the nappy and dispose of it.* **2 = deal with**, manage, treat, handle, settle, cope with, take care of, see to, finish with, attend to, get to grips with: *the manner in which you disposed of that problem* **3 = give**, give up, part with, bestow, transfer, make over: *He managed to dispose of more money and goods.*

disposed ADJECTIVE **= inclined**, given, likely, subject, ready, prone, liable, apt, predisposed, tending towards, of a mind to

disposition NOUN **1 = character**, nature, spirit, make-up, constitution, temper, temperament: *his friendly and cheerful disposition* **2 = tendency**, inclination, propensity, habit, leaning, bent, bias, readiness, predisposition, proclivity, proneness: *They show no disposition to take risks.* **3 = arrangement**, grouping, ordering, organization, distribution, disposal, placement: *the disposition of walls and entrances*

dispossess VERB **= strip**, deprive

dispossessed ADJECTIVE **= destitute**, landless

disproportionate ADJECTIVE **= excessive**, too much, unreasonable, uneven, unequal, unbalanced, out of proportion, inordinate, incommensurate

disprove VERB **= prove false**, discredit, refute, contradict, negate, invalidate, rebut, give the lie to, make a nonsense of, blow out of the water *(slang)*, controvert, confute
OPPOSITE: prove

dispute VERB **1 = contest**, question, challenge, deny, doubt, oppose, object to, contradict, rebut, impugn, controvert, call in *or* into question: *He disputed the allegations.* **2 = argue**, fight, clash, row, disagree, fall out *(informal)*, contend, feud, quarrel, brawl, squabble, spar, wrangle, bicker, have an argument, cross swords, be at sixes and sevens, fight like cat and dog, go at it hammer and tongs, altercate: *Whole towns disputed with neighboring villages over boundaries.*
▷ NOUN **1 = disagreement**, conflict, argument, falling out, dissent, friction, strife, discord, altercation: *There has been much dispute over the ownership of the lease.* **2 = argument**, row, clash, controversy, disturbance, contention, feud, quarrel, brawl, squabble, wrangle, difference of opinion, tiff, dissension, shindig *(informal)*, shindy *(informal)*, bagarre *(French)*: *The dispute between them is settled.*

disqualification NOUN **= ban**, exclusion, elimination, rejection, ineligibility, debarment, disenablement, disentitlement

disqualified ADJECTIVE **= eliminated**, knocked out, out of the running, debarred, ineligible

disqualify VERB **= ban**, rule out, prohibit, preclude, debar, declare ineligible, disentitle

disquiet NOUN **= uneasiness**, concern, fear, worry, alarm, anxiety, distress, unrest, angst, nervousness, trepidation, foreboding, restlessness, fretfulness, disquietude: *There is growing public disquiet.*
▷ VERB **= make uneasy**, concern, worry, trouble, upset, bother, disturb, distress, annoy, plague, unsettle, harass, hassle *(informal)*, agitate, vex, perturb, discompose, incommode: *He's obviously disquieted by the experience.*

disquieting ADJECTIVE **= worrying**, troubling, upsetting, disturbing, distressing, annoying, irritating, unsettling, harrowing, unnerving, disconcerting, vexing, perturbing, bothersome

disregard VERB **= ignore**, discount, take no notice of, overlook, neglect, pass over, turn a blind eye to, disobey, laugh off, make light of, pay no attention to, pay no heed to, leave out of account, brush aside *or* away: *He disregarded the advice of his executives.*
OPPOSITE: pay attention to
▷ NOUN **= ignoring**, neglect, contempt, indifference, negligence, disdain, disrespect, heedlessness: *a callous disregard for human life*

disrepair NOUN **= dilapidation**, collapse, decay, deterioration, ruination: *The house was in a bad state of disrepair.*
in disrepair = out of order, broken, decayed, worn-out, decrepit, not functioning, out of commission, on the blink *(slang)*, bust *(informal)*, kaput *(informal)*: *Everything was in disrepair.*

disreputable ADJECTIVE **= discreditable**, mean, low, base, shocking, disorderly, notorious, vicious, infamous, disgraceful, shameful, vile, shady *(informal)*, scandalous, ignominious, contemptible, louche, unprincipled, dishonourable, opprobrious
OPPOSITE: respectable

disrepute NOUN **= discredit**, shame, disgrace, unpopularity, ignominy, dishonour, infamy, disfavour, ill repute, obloquy, ill favour, disesteem

disrespect NOUN **= contempt**, cheek, disregard, rudeness, lack of respect, irreverence, insolence, impertinence, impudence, discourtesy, incivility, impoliteness, lese-majesty, unmannerliness OPPOSITE: respect

disrespectful ADJECTIVE **= contemptuous**, insulting, rude, cheeky, irreverent, bad-mannered, impertinent, insolent, impolite, impudent, discourteous, uncivil, ill-bred

disrupt VERB **1 = interrupt**, stop, upset, hold up, interfere with, unsettle, obstruct, cut short, intrude on, break up *or* into: *Anti-war protests disrupted the debate.* **2 = disturb**, upset, confuse, disorder, spoil, unsettle, agitate, disorganize, disarrange, derange, throw into disorder: *The drought has disrupted agricultural production.*

disruption NOUN **= disturbance**, disorder, confusion, interference, disarray, interruption, stoppage, disorderliness

disruptive ADJECTIVE **= disturbing**, upsetting, disorderly, unsettling, troublesome, unruly, obstreperous, troublemaking OPPOSITE: well-behaved

dissatisfaction NOUN **= discontent**, frustration, resentment, regret, distress, disappointment, dismay, irritation, unhappiness, annoyance, displeasure, exasperation, chagrin

> PROVERBS
> *The grass is always greener on the other side of the fence*

dissatisfied ADJECTIVE **= discontented**, frustrated, unhappy, disappointed, fed up, disgruntled, not satisfied, unfulfilled, displeased, unsatisfied, ungratified
OPPOSITE: satisfied

dissect VERB **1 = cut up** *or* **apart**, dismember, lay open, anatomize: *We dissected a frog in biology.* **2 = analyse**, study, investigate, research, explore, break down, inspect, scrutinize: *People want to dissect his work.*

dissection NOUN **1 = cutting up**, anatomy, autopsy, dismemberment, postmortem (examination), necropsy, anatomization: *a growing supply of corpses for dissection* **2 = analysis**, examination, breakdown, research, investigation, inspection, scrutiny: *the dissection of my proposals*

disseminate VERB **= spread**, publish, broadcast, distribute, scatter, proclaim, circulate, sow, disperse, diffuse, publicize, dissipate, propagate, promulgate

dissemination NOUN = **spread**, publishing, broadcasting, publication, distribution, circulation, diffusion, propagation, promulgation

dissension NOUN = **disagreement**, conflict, dissent, dispute, contention, quarreling, friction, strife, discord, discordance, conflict of opinion

dissent NOUN = **disagreement**, opposition, protest, resistance, refusal, objection, discord, demur, dissension, dissidence, nonconformity, remonstrance: *He has responded harshly to any dissent.* **OPPOSITE:** assent

dissent from something = **disagree with**, object to, protest against, refuse to accept: *No one dissents from the decision to unify.*

dissenter NOUN = **objector**, dissident, nonconformist, protestant, disputant

dissenting ADJECTIVE = **disagreeing**, protesting, opposing, conflicting, differing, dissident

dissertation NOUN = **thesis**, essay, discourse, critique, exposition, treatise, disquisition

disservice NOUN = **wrong**, injury, harm, injustice, disfavour, unkindness, bad turn, ill turn **OPPOSITE:** good turn

dissident ADJECTIVE = **dissenting**, disagreeing, nonconformist, heterodox, schismatic, dissentient: *links with a dissident group*
▷ NOUN = **protester**, rebel, dissenter, demonstrator, agitator, recusant, protest marcher: *political dissidents*

dissimilar ADJECTIVE = **different**, unlike, various, varied, diverse, assorted, unrelated, disparate, miscellaneous, sundry, divergent, manifold, heterogeneous, mismatched, multifarious, not similar, not alike, not capable of comparison **OPPOSITE:** alike

dissipate VERB = **disappear**, fade, vanish, dissolve, disperse, evaporate, diffuse, melt away, evanesce: *The tension in the room had dissipated.*

dissipated ADJECTIVE **1** = **debauched**, abandoned, self-indulgent, profligate, intemperate, dissolute, rakish: *He was still handsome though dissipated.* **2** = **squandered**, spent, wasted, exhausted, consumed, scattered: *A lot of it has simply been dissipated.*

dissociate or **disassociate** VERB = **separate**, distance, divorce, isolate, detach, segregate, disconnect, set apart: *how to dissociate emotion from reason*

dissociate yourself from something or **someone** = **break away from**, part company with, break off relations with: *He dissociated himself from his former friends.*

dissociation NOUN = **separation**, break, division, distancing, divorce, isolation, segregation, detachment, severance, disengagement, disconnection, disunion

dissolution NOUN **1** = **ending**, end, finish, conclusion, suspension, dismissal, termination, adjournment, disbandment, discontinuation: *He stayed on until the dissolution of the firm.* **OPPOSITE:** union **2** = **breaking up**, parting, divorce, separation, disintegration: *the dissolution of a marriage*

dissolve VERB **1** = **melt**, soften, thaw, flux, liquefy, deliquesce: *Heat gently until the sugar dissolves.* **2** = **end**, dismiss, suspend, axe (*informal*), break up, wind up, overthrow, terminate, discontinue, dismantle, disband, disunite: *The King agreed to dissolve the present commission.* **3** = **disappear**, fade, vanish, break down, crumble, disperse, dwindle, evaporate, disintegrate, perish, diffuse, dissipate, decompose, melt away, waste away, evanesce: *His new-found optimism dissolved.*

dissolve into or **in something** = **break into**, burst into, give way to, launch into: *She dissolved into tears.*

dissonance or **dissonancy** NOUN = **discordance**, discord, jangle, cacophony, jarring, harshness, lack of harmony, unmelodiousness: *a jumble of silence and dissonance*

distance NOUN **1** = **space**, length, extent, range, stretch, gap, interval, separation, span, width: *They measured the distance between the island and the shore.* **2** = **remoteness**: *The distance wouldn't be a problem.* **3** = **aloofness**, reserve, detachment, restraint, indifference, stiffness, coolness, coldness, remoteness, frigidity, uninvolvement, standoffishness: *There were periods of distance, of coldness.*

go the distance = **finish**, stay the course, complete, see through, bring to an end: *Riders are determined to go the distance.*

in the distance = **far off**, far away, on the horizon, afar, yonder: *We suddenly saw her in the distance.*

> **QUOTATIONS**
> distance: the only thing that the rich are willing for the poor to call theirs and keep
> [Ambrose Bierce *The Devil's Dictionary*]
>
> 'Tis distance lends enchantment to the view
> [Thomas Campbell *Pleasures of Hope*]
>
> Distance has the same effect on the mind as on the eye
> [Samuel Johnson *Rasselas*]

distant ADJECTIVE **1** = **far-off**, far, remote, removed, abroad, out-of-the-way, far-flung, faraway, outlying, afar: *the war in that distant land* **OPPOSITE:** close **2** = **remote**, slight: *He's a distant relative.* **3** = **reserved**, cold, withdrawn, cool, formal, remote, stiff, restrained, detached, indifferent, aloof, unfriendly, reticent, haughty, unapproachable, standoffish: *He's direct and courteous, but distant.* **OPPOSITE:** friendly **4** = **faraway**, blank, abstracted, vague, absorbed, distracted, unaware, musing, vacant, preoccupied, bemused, oblivious, dreamy, daydreaming, absent-minded, inattentive: *There was a distant look in her eyes.*

distaste NOUN = **dislike**, horror, disgust, loathing, aversion, revulsion, displeasure, antipathy, abhorrence, disinclination, repugnance, odium, disfavour, detestation, disrelish

distasteful ADJECTIVE = **unpleasant**, offensive, obscene, undesirable, unsavoury, obnoxious, unpalatable, displeasing, repulsive, objectionable, disagreeable, repugnant, loathsome, abhorrent, nauseous, uninviting **OPPOSITE:** enjoyable

distil VERB **1** = **purify**, refine, evaporate, condense, sublimate, vaporize: *When water is used it must be distilled* **2** = **extract**, express, squeeze, obtain, take out, draw out, separate out, press out: *The oil is distilled from the berries.*

distillation NOUN = **essence**, extract, elixir, spirit, quintessence

distinct ADJECTIVE **1** = **different**, individual, separate, disconnected, discrete, dissimilar, unconnected, unattached: *The book is divided into two distinct parts.* **OPPOSITE:** similar **2** = **striking**, sharp, dramatic, stunning (*informal*), outstanding, bold, noticeable, well-defined: *to impart a distinct flavour with a minimum of cooking fat* **3** = **definite**, marked, clear, decided, obvious, sharp, plain, apparent, patent, evident, black-and-white, manifest, noticeable, conspicuous, clear-cut, unmistakable, palpable, recognizable, unambiguous, observable, perceptible, appreciable: *There was a distinct change in her attitude.* **OPPOSITE:** vague

distinction NOUN **1** = **difference**, contrast, variation, differential, discrepancy, disparity, deviation, differentiation, fine line, distinctness, dissimilarity: *There were obvious distinctions between the two.* **2** = **excellence**, note, quality, worth, account, rank, reputation, importance, consequence, fame, celebrity, merit, superiority, prominence, greatness, eminence, renown, repute: *He is a composer of distinction and sensitivity.* **3** = **feature**, quality, characteristic, name, mark, individuality, peculiarity, singularity, distinctiveness, particularity: *He has the distinction of being their greatest living writer.* **4** = **merit**, credit, honour, integrity, excellence, righteousness, rectitude, uprightness: *She had served her country with distinction and strength.*

distinctive ADJECTIVE = **characteristic**, special, individual, specific, unique, typical, extraordinary, distinguishing, peculiar, singular, idiosyncratic **OPPOSITE:** ordinary

distinctly ADVERB **1 = definitely**, clearly, obviously, sharply, plainly, patently, manifestly, decidedly, markedly, noticeably, unmistakably, palpably: *two distinctly different sectors* **2 = clearly**, plainly, precisely: *'If I may speak, gentlemen,' he said distinctly.*

distinguish VERB **1 = differentiate**, determine, separate, discriminate, decide, judge, discern, ascertain, tell the difference, make a distinction, tell apart, tell between: *Could he distinguish right from wrong?* **2 = characterize**, mark, separate, single out, individualize, set apart: *one of the things that distinguishes artists from other people* **3 = make out**, recognize, perceive, know, see, tell, pick out, discern: *He could distinguish voices.*

distinguishable ADJECTIVE **1 = recognizable**, noticeable, conspicuous, discernible, obvious, evident, manifest, perceptible, well-marked: *This port is distinguishable by its colour.* **2 = conspicuous**, clear, strong, bright, plain, bold, pronounced, colourful, vivid, eye-catching, salient: *Already shapes were more distinguishable.*

distinguished ADJECTIVE **= eminent**, great, important, noted, famous, celebrated, well-known, prominent, esteemed, acclaimed, notable, renowned, prestigious, elevated, big-time *(informal)*, famed, conspicuous, illustrious, major league *(informal)* **OPPOSITE:** unknown

distinguishing ADJECTIVE **= characteristic**, marked, distinctive, typical, peculiar, differentiating, individualistic

distort VERB **1 = misrepresent**, twist, bias, disguise, pervert, slant, colour, misinterpret, falsify, garble: *The media distorts reality.* **2 = deform**, bend, twist, warp, buckle, mangle, mangulate *(Austral. slang)*, disfigure, contort, gnarl, misshape, malform: *Make sure the image isn't distorted by lumps and bumps.*

distorted ADJECTIVE **= deformed**, bent, twisted, crooked, irregular, warped, buckled, disfigured, contorted, misshapen: *His face was distorted but recognizable.*

distortion NOUN **1 = misrepresentation**, bias, slant, perversion, falsification, colouring: *He accused reporters of wilful distortion.* **2 = deformity**, bend, twist, warp, buckle, contortion, malformation, crookedness, twistedness: *the gargoyle-like distortion of her face*

distract VERB **1 = divert**, sidetrack, draw away, turn aside, lead astray, draw or lead away from: *Video games sometimes distract him from his homework.* **2 = amuse**, occupy, entertain, beguile, engross: *I took out a book and tried to distract myself.* **3 = agitate**, trouble, disturb, confuse, puzzle, torment, bewilder, madden, confound, perplex, disconcert, derange, discompose: *Another story of hers distracts me.*

distracted ADJECTIVE **1 = agitated**, troubled, confused, puzzled, at sea, bewildered, bemused, confounded, perplexed, flustered, in a flap *(informal)*: *At work, he thought about her all day. He was distracted.* **2 = frantic**, wild, mad, crazy, desperate, raving, frenzied, distraught, insane, deranged, grief-stricken, overwrought, at the end of your tether: *My father was distracted by grief.*

distraction NOUN **1 = disturbance**, interference, diversion, interruption: *Total concentration is required with no distractions.* **2 = entertainment**, recreation, amusement, diversion, pastime, divertissement, beguilement: *every conceivable distraction from shows to bouncy castles* **3 = frenzy**, desperation, mania, insanity, delirium, derangement: *A very clingy child can drive a parent to distraction.*

distraught ADJECTIVE **= frantic**, wild, desperate, mad, anxious, distressed, raving, distracted, hysterical, worked-up, agitated, crazed, overwrought, out of your mind, at the end of your tether, wrought-up, beside yourself

distress VERB **= upset**, worry, trouble, pain, wound, bother, disturb, dismay, grieve, torment, harass, afflict, harrow, agitate, sadden, perplex, disconcert, agonize, fluster, perturb, faze, throw (someone) off balance: *I did not want to frighten or distress her.*
▷ NOUN **1 = suffering**, pain, worry, anxiety, torture, grief, misery, agony, sadness, discomfort, torment, sorrow, woe, anguish, heartache, affliction, desolation, wretchedness: *Her mouth grew stiff with pain and distress.* **2 = need**, suffering, trouble, trial, difficulties, poverty, misery, hard times, hardship, straits, misfortune, adversity, calamity, affliction, privation, destitution, ill-fortune, ill-luck, indigence: *There was little support to help them in their distress.*

distressed ADJECTIVE **1 = upset**, worried, troubled, anxious, distracted, tormented, distraught, afflicted, agitated, saddened, wretched: *I felt distressed about my problem.* **2 = poverty-stricken**, poor, impoverished, needy, destitute, indigent, down at heel, straitened, penurious: *investment in the nation's distressed areas*

distressing ADJECTIVE **= upsetting**, worrying, disturbing, painful, affecting, sad, afflicting, harrowing, grievous, hurtful, lamentable, heart-breaking, nerve-racking, gut-wrenching, distressful

distribute VERB **1 = hand out**, dispense, give out, dish out *(informal)*, disseminate, deal out, disburse, pass round: *Students shouted slogans and distributed leaflets.* **2 = circulate**, deliver, convey: *to distribute a national newspaper* **3 = share**, give, deal, divide, assign, administer, allocate, dispose, dispense, allot, mete out, dole out, apportion, measure out: *He began to distribute jobs among his friends.* **4 = spread**, scatter, disperse, diffuse, disseminate, strew: *Break the exhibition up and distribute it around existing museums.*

distribution NOUN **1 = delivery**, mailing, transport, transportation, handling: *He admitted there had been problems with distribution.* **2 = sharing**, division, assignment, rationing, allocation, partition, allotment, dispensation, apportionment: *a more equitable distribution of wealth* **3 = spreading**, circulation, diffusion, scattering, propagation, dissemination, dispersal, dispersion: *There will be a widespread distribution of leaflets.* **4 = spread**, organization, arrangement, location, placement, disposition: *those who control the distribution of jobs*

district NOUN **= area**, community, region, sector, quarter, ward, parish, neighbourhood, vicinity, locality, locale, neck of the woods *(informal)*

distrust VERB **= suspect**, doubt, discredit, be wary of, wonder about, mistrust, disbelieve, be suspicious of, be sceptical of, misbelieve: *I don't have any reason to distrust them.*
OPPOSITE: trust
▷ NOUN **= suspicion**, question, doubt, disbelief, scepticism, mistrust, misgiving, qualm, wariness, lack of faith, dubiety: *an atmosphere of distrust*
OPPOSITE: trust

> **QUOTATIONS**
> Trust him no further than you can throw him
> [Thomas Fuller *Gnomologia*]

distrustful ADJECTIVE **= suspicious**, doubting, wary, cynical, doubtful, sceptical, uneasy, dubious, distrusting, disbelieving, leery *(slang)*, mistrustful, chary

disturb VERB **1 = interrupt**, trouble, bother, startle, plague, disrupt, put out, interfere with, rouse, hassle, inconvenience, pester, intrude on, butt in on: *I didn't want to disturb you.* **2 = upset**, concern, worry, trouble, shake, excite, alarm, confuse, distress, distract, dismay, unsettle, agitate, ruffle, confound, unnerve, vex, fluster, perturb, derange, discompose: *He had been disturbed by the news of the attack.* **OPPOSITE:** calm **3 = muddle**, disorder, mix up, mess up, disorganize, jumble up, disarrange, muss *(U.S. & Canad.)*: *His notes had not been disturbed.*

disturbance NOUN **1 = disorder**, bother *(informal)*, turmoil, riot, upheaval, fray, brawl, uproar, agitation, fracas, commotion, rumpus, tumult, hubbub, shindig *(informal)*, ruction *(informal)*, ruckus *(informal)*, shindy *(informal)*: *During the disturbance, three men were hurt.* **2 = upset**, bother, disorder, confusion, distraction, intrusion, interruption, annoyance, agitation, hindrance, perturbation, derangement: *The home would cause less disturbance than a school.* **3 = problem**, disorder, upset, trouble: *Poor educational performance is linked to emotional disturbances.*

disturbed ADJECTIVE **1 = unbalanced**, troubled, disordered, unstable, neurotic, upset, deranged, unsound, maladjusted: *The murderer was apparently mentally disturbed.* **OPPOSITE:** balanced **2 = worried**, concerned, troubled, upset, bothered, nervous, anxious, uneasy **OPPOSITE:** calm

disturbing ADJECTIVE **= worrying**, troubling, upsetting, alarming, frightening, distressing, startling, discouraging, dismaying, unsettling, harrowing, agitating, disconcerting, disquieting, perturbing

ditch NOUN **= channel**, drain, trench, dyke, furrow, gully, moat, watercourse: *The car went out of control and ended up in a ditch.*
▷ VERB **1 = get rid of**, dump *(informal)*, scrap, discard, dispose of, dispense with, jettison, throw out *or* overboard **2 = leave**, drop, abandon, dump *(informal)*, axe *(informal)*, get rid of, bin *(informal)*, chuck *(informal)*, forsake, jilt: *I can't bring myself to ditch him.*

dither VERB **= vacillate**, hesitate, waver, haver, falter, hum and haw, faff about *(Brit. informal)*, shillyshally *(informal)*, swither *(Scot.)*: *We're still dithering over whether to get married.* **OPPOSITE:** decide
▷ NOUN **= flutter**, flap *(informal)*, fluster, bother, stew *(informal)*, twitter *(informal)*, tizzy *(informal)*, pother, tiz-woz *(informal)*: *I am in such a dither I forget to put the water in.*

diva NOUN **= singer**, opera singer, prima donna

dive VERB **1 = plunge**, drop, jump, pitch, leap, duck, dip, descend, plummet: *He tried to escape by diving into a river.* **2 = go underwater**, submerge: *They are diving to collect marine organisms.* **3 = nose-dive**, fall, plunge, crash, pitch, swoop, plummet: *His monoplane stalled and dived into the ground.*
▷ NOUN **1 = plunge**, spring, jump, leap, dash, header *(informal)*, swoop, lunge, nose dive: *He made a sudden dive for his legs.* **2 = sleazy bar**, joint *(slang)*, honky-tonk *(U.S. slang)*: *We've played in all the dives about here.*

diverge VERB **1 = separate**, part, split, branch, divide, fork, divaricate: *The aims of the partners began to diverge.* **2 = conflict**, differ, disagree, dissent, be at odds, be at variance: *Theory and practice sometimes diverged.* **3 = deviate**, depart, stray, wander, meander, turn aside: *a course that diverged from the coastline*

divergence NOUN **= difference**, varying, departure, disparity, deviation, separation

divergent ADJECTIVE **= different**, conflicting, differing, disagreeing, diverse, separate, varying, variant, diverging, dissimilar, deviating

> **USAGE**
> Some people dislike the use of *divergent* in this sense, preferring synonyms such as *different* or *differing*.

diverse ADJECTIVE **1 = various**, mixed, varied, diversified, assorted, miscellaneous, several, sundry, motley, manifold, heterogeneous, of every description: *shops selling a diverse range of gifts* **2 = different**, contrasting, unlike, varying, differing, separate, distinct, disparate, discrete, dissimilar, divergent, discrepant: *Their attitudes were refreshingly diverse.*

diversify VERB **= vary**, change, expand, transform, alter, spread out, branch out

diversion NOUN **1 = distraction**, deviation, deflection, digression: *The whole argument is a diversion.* **2 = pastime**, play, game, sport, delight, pleasure, entertainment, hobby, relaxation, recreation, enjoyment, distraction, amusement, gratification, divertissement, beguilement: *Finger-painting is an excellent diversion.* **3 = detour**, deviation, circuitous route, roundabout way, indirect course: *They turned back because of traffic diversions.* **4 = deviation**, departure, straying, divergence, digression

diversity NOUN **1 = difference**, diversification, variety, divergence, multiplicity, heterogeneity, variegation, diverseness: *the cultural diversity of British society* **2 = range**, variety, scope, sphere

> **PROVERBS**
> *It takes all sorts to make a world*

divert VERB **1 = redirect**, switch, avert, deflect, deviate, sidetrack, turn aside: *A new bypass will divert traffic from the A13.* **2 = distract**, shift, deflect, detract, sidetrack, lead astray, draw *or* lead away from: *They want to divert the attention of the people from the real issues.* **3 = entertain**, delight, amuse, please, charm, gratify, beguile, regale: *diverting her with jokes and fiery arguments*

diverting ADJECTIVE **= entertaining**, amusing, enjoyable, fun, pleasant, humorous, beguiling

divest VERB **1 = deprive**, strip, dispossess, despoil: *They were divested of all their personal possessions.* **2 = strip**, remove, take off, undress, denude, disrobe, unclothe: *the formalities of divesting her of her coat*

divide VERB **1 = separate**, part, split, cut (up), sever, shear, segregate, cleave, subdivide, bisect, sunder: *the artificial line that divided the city* **OPPOSITE:** join **2 = share**, distribute, allocate, portion, dispense, allot, mete, dole out, apportion, deal out, measure out, divvy (up) *(informal)*: *Divide the soup among four bowls.* **3 = split**, break up, alienate, embroil, come between, disunite, estrange, sow dissension, cause to disagree, set at variance *or* odds, set *or* pit against one another: *She has divided the group.*
divide something up = group, sort, separate, arrange, grade, classify, categorize: *The idea is to divide up the country into four sectors.*

> **QUOTATIONS**
> Divide and rule
> [Philip of Macedon]

dividend NOUN **= bonus**, share, cut *(informal)*, gain, extra, plus, portion, divvy *(informal)*

divination NOUN **= prediction**, divining, prophecy, presage, foretelling, clairvoyance, fortune-telling, prognostication, augury, soothsaying, sortilege ▷ *See themed panel* **Divination** *on page 192*

> **QUOTATIONS**
> divination: the art of nosing out the occult. Divination is of as many kinds as there are fruit-bearing varieties of the flowering dunce and the early fool
> [Ambrose Bierce *The Devil's Dictionary*]

divine ADJECTIVE **1 = heavenly**, spiritual, holy, immortal, supernatural, celestial, angelic, superhuman, godlike, cherubic, seraphic, supernal *(literary)*, paradisaical: *a gift from divine beings* **2 = sacred**, religious, holy, spiritual, blessed, revered, venerable, hallowed, consecrated, sanctified: *the message of the Divine Book* **3 = wonderful**, perfect, beautiful, excellent, lovely, stunning *(informal)*, glorious, marvellous, splendid, gorgeous, delightful, exquisite, radiant, superlative, ravishing: *You look simply divine.*
▷ NOUN **= priest**, minister, vicar, reverend, pastor, cleric, clergyman, curate, churchman, padre *(informal)*, holy man, man of God, man of the cloth, ecclesiastic, father confessor: *He had the air of a divine.*
▷ VERB **1 = guess**, understand, suppose, suspect, perceive, discern, infer, deduce, apprehend, conjecture, surmise, foretell, intuit, prognosticate: *He had tried to divine her intentions.* **2 = dowse** *(for water or minerals)*: *I was divining for water.*

divinity NOUN **1 = theology**, religion, religious studies: *He entered university to study arts and divinity* **2 = godliness**, holiness, sanctity, godhead, divine nature, godhood: *a lasting faith in the divinity of Christ's word* **3 = deity**, spirit, genius, guardian spirit, daemon, god *or* goddess, atua (N.Z.): *The three statues are Roman divinities.*

division NOUN **1 = separation**, dividing, splitting up, detaching, partition, cutting up, bisection:

DIVINATION

Methods of divination

astrology	crystal gazing	dowsing	numerology	runes	sortilege	tea leaves
clairvoyance	dice	I Ching	palmistry	scrying	tarot	

Means of divination

ailuromancy	cats	crithomancy	freshly baked bread	necromancy	the dead
alphitomancy	wheat *or* barley cakes	cromniomancy	onions	oneiromancy	dreams
arachnomancy	spiders	crystallomancy	crystal ball	ornithomancy	birds
astragalomancy	dice	dactylomancy	suspended ring	pegomancy	sacred pool
bibliomancy	passages from books	geomancy	earth, sand, *or* dust	pyromancy	fire *or* flames
cartomancy	cards	hippomancy	horses	radiesthesia	pendulum
catoptromancy	mirror	hydromancy	water	rhabdomancy	rod *or* wand
ceromancy	melted wax	lampadomancy	oil lamps	sciomancy	ghosts
chiromancy	hands	lithomancy	precious stones	tasseography	tea leaves
cleidomancy	suspended key	lychnomancy	flames of wax candles	theomancy	god
		molybdomancy	molten lead	tyromancy	cheese

a division into two independent factions **2 = sharing**, distribution, assignment, rationing, allocation, allotment, apportionment: *the division of labour between workers and management* **3 = disagreement**, split, breach, feud, rift, rupture, abyss, chasm, variance, discord, difference of opinion, estrangement, disunion: *the division between the prosperous west and the impoverished east* **opposite:** unity **4 = dividing line**, border, boundary, divide, partition, demarcation, divider: *the division between North and South Korea* **5 = department**, group, head, sector, branch, subdivision: *the sales division* **6 = part**, bit, piece, section, sector, class, category, segment, portion, fraction, compartment: *Each was divided into several divisions.*

QUOTATIONS
If a house be divided against itself, that house cannot stand
[Bible: St. Mark]

PROVERBS
He who divides gets the worst share

divisive adjective **= disruptive**, unsettling, alienating, troublesome, controversial, contentious

divorce noun **1 = separation**, split, break-up, parting, split-up, rift, dissolution, severance, estrangement, annulment, decree nisi, disunion: *Numerous marriages now end in divorce.* **2 = breach**, break, split, falling-out *(informal)*, disagreement, feud, rift, bust-up *(informal)*, rupture, abyss, chasm, schism, estrangement: *a divorce between the government and trade unions*
▷ verb **1 = split up**, separate, part company, annul your marriage, dissolve your marriage: *My parents divorced when I was young.* **2 = separate**, divide, isolate, detach, distance, sever, disconnect, dissociate, set apart, disunite, sunder: *We have been able to divorce sex from reproduction.*

divulge verb **= make known**, tell, reveal, publish, declare, expose, leak, confess, exhibit, communicate, spill *(informal)*, disclose, proclaim, betray, uncover, impart, promulgate, let slip, blow wide open *(slang)*, get off your chest *(informal)*, cough *(slang)*, out *(informal)*, spill your guts about *(slang)* **opposite:** keep secret

dizzy adjective **1 = giddy**, faint, light-headed, swimming, reeling, staggering, shaky, wobbly, off balance, unsteady, vertiginous, woozy *(informal)*, weak at the knees: *She felt slightly dizzy.* **2 = confused**, dazzled, at sea, bewildered, muddled, bemused, dazed, disorientated, befuddled, light-headed, punch-drunk, fuddled: *Her wonderful dark good looks and wit made me dizzy.* **3 = scatterbrained**, silly, foolish, frivolous, giddy, capricious, forgetful, flighty, light-headed, scatty *(Brit. informal)*, empty-headed, bird-brained *(informal)*, featherbrained, ditzy *or* ditsy *(slang)*: *a charmingly dizzy grandmother* **4 = steep**, towering, soaring, lofty, sky-high, vertiginous: *I escalated to the dizzy heights.*

do verb **1 = perform**, work, achieve, carry out, produce, effect, complete, conclude, undertake, accomplish, execute, discharge, pull off, transact: *I was trying to do some work.* **2 = behave**, act, conduct yourself, deport yourself, bear yourself, acquit yourself: *I go where I will and I do as I please.* **3 = make**, prepare, fix, arrange, look after, organize, be responsible for, see to, get ready, make ready: *I'll do the dinner, you can help.* **4 = solve**, work out, resolve, figure out, decode, decipher, puzzle out: *I could have done the crossword.* **5 = get on**, manage, fare, proceed, make out, prosper, get along: *She did well at school.* **6 = present**, give, show, act, produce, stage, perform, mount, put on: *I've always wanted to do a show on his life.* **7 = be adequate**, be enough, be sufficient, answer, serve, suit, content, satisfy, suffice, be of use, pass muster, cut the mustard, fill the bill *(informal)*, meet requirements: *A plain old 'I love you' won't do.* **8 = cheat**, trick, con *(informal)*, skin *(slang)*, stiff *(slang)*, deceive, fleece, hoax, defraud, dupe, swindle, diddle *(informal)*, take (someone) for a ride *(informal)*, pull a fast one on *(informal)*, cozen, scam *(slang)*: *I'll tell you how they did me.* **9 = produce**, make, create, develop, manufacture, construct, invent, fabricate **10 = visit**, tour in *or* around, look at, cover, explore, take in *(informal)*, stop in, journey through *or* around, travel in *or* around: *Families doing Europe can hire one of these motor-homes.*
▷ noun **= party**, gathering, function, social, event, affair, at-home, occasion, celebration, reception, bash *(informal)*, rave *(Brit. slang)*, get-together *(informal)*, festivity, knees-up *(Brit. informal)*, beano *(Brit. slang)*, social gathering, shindig *(informal)*, soirée, rave-up *(Brit. slang)*, hooley *or* hoolie *(chiefly Irish & N.Z.)*: *They always have all-night dos there.*

do away with someone = kill, murder, do in *(slang)*, destroy, take out *(slang)*, dispatch, slay, blow away *(slang, chiefly U.S.)*, knock off *(slang)*, liquidate, exterminate, take (someone's) life, bump off *(slang)*: *He tried to do away with her.*

do away with something = get rid of, remove, eliminate, axe *(informal)*, abolish, junk *(informal)*, pull, chuck *(informal)*, discard, put an end to, dispense with, discontinue, put paid to, pull the plug on: *They must do away with nuclear weapons altogether.*

do's and don'ts = rules, code, regulations, standards, instructions, customs, convention, usage, protocol, formalities, etiquette, p's and q's, good *or* proper behaviour: *Please advise me on the do's and dont's.*

do someone in 1 = kill, murder, destroy, eliminate *(slang)*, take out *(slang)*, execute, butcher, slaughter, dispatch, assassinate, slay, do away with, blow away *(slang, chiefly U.S.)*, knock off *(slang)*, liquidate,

The Language of Rolf Boldrewood

The pseudonym 'Rolf Boldrewood' was the pen name of Thomas Alexander Browne (1826–1915), an Australian romance writer whose best known work is *Robbery Under Arms*, a novel about bushrangers (robbers living in the Australian bush). Boldrewood's writings are celebrated for their portrayal of pioneer life in Australia.

The two nouns that Boldrewood uses most frequently are *man* and *horse*. Each is modified by *old* more times than any other adjective. Most occurrences of *old man* have the meaning 'father', although Boldrewood's characters also sometimes affably refer to each other as 'old man', as in:

I was just in time – eh, Jim, **old man**?

Most occurrences of *old horse* also demonstrate this affectionate use of 'old', with only a few occurrences referring to the age of the animal. *Good*, the adjective Boldrewood uses most frequently, is also a significant modifier of both *man* and *horse*. It is interesting that Boldrewood uses these two adjectives in similar ways to describe both men and horses. However, the verbs that Boldrewood uses with *man* and *horse* are quite different. *Sell, lead, ride, train, shoe, hobble, feed*, and *saddle* are the most salient verbs occurring with *horse*, whereas, after *see* and *say, kill* and *shoot* are the most salient verbs to take *man* as their object.

The verb Boldrewood uses most frequently is *see*, and *man* and *horse* are the two nouns with which it is most frequently used. However, Boldrewood also uses *see* with *cattle, horseman* and *bull*. *Horse* and *cattle* are also salient subjects of Boldrewood's second most frequent verb, *come*. The frequency with which horses and cattle are mentioned in Boldrewood's writings is indicative of their importance in early colonial Australia.

The noun *work* is another word that occurs frequently in Boldrewood's writings, particularly in *Robbery Under Arms*. The adjectives that most frequently collocate with *work* in this novel are *hard, steady*, and *honest*. This reflects the constant regret of the narrator, Dick, that he gave up the opportunity of a regular job and a normal life for the criminal life of a bushranger.

Boldrewood sometimes uses as adverbs words which, in modern English, we can only use as adjectives. Two such words are *sudden* and *regular*; in modern English, we would have to add '-ly' to each of these words to use them as adverbs. The following examples demonstrate Boldrewood's use of *sudden* and *regular* as adverbs:

... I saw two horsemen pop up **sudden** round the back of the house and ride towards the front gate.

No wonder it **regular** broke my heart to leave it.

The use of words such as *sudden* and *regular* as adverbs is a literary usage not uncommon in the 19th century. It is interesting to note, however, that both *suddenly* and *regularly* also occur in Boldrewood's writings:

... said Aileen, **suddenly** taking both my hands in hers.

I don't say we **regularly** went in for drinking; but we began to want it by twelve o'clock every day ...

Another literary use of language found commonly in Boldrewood's texts is the construction 'the tears come into somebody's eyes', as in:

Her lips shook and trembled and **the tears came into** her **eyes**.

This construction is found predominantly in 19th-century and early-20th-century literary texts. In modern English we would not include the definite article when using this construction.

annihilate, neutralize, take (someone's) life, bump off *(slang)*: *Whoever did him in removed a brave man.* **2 = exhaust**, tire, drain, shatter *(informal)*, weaken, fatigue, weary, fag *(informal)*, sap, wear out, tire out, knacker *(slang)*: *The Christmas thing kind of did me in.*
do without something *or* **someone = manage without**, give up, dispense with, forgo, kick *(informal)*, sacrifice, abstain from, get along without: *This is something we cannot do without.*

> **PROVERBS**
> *Do unto others what you would they should do unto you*

docile ADJECTIVE **= obedient**, manageable, compliant, amenable, submissive, pliant, tractable, biddable, ductile, teachable *(rare)*
OPPOSITE: difficult

dock[1] NOUN **= port**, haven, harbour, pier, wharf, quay, waterfront, anchorage: *He brought his boat right into the dock at Southampton.*
▷ VERB **1 = moor**, land, anchor, put in, tie up, berth, drop anchor: *The vessel is about to dock in Singapore* **2 = link up**, unite, join, couple, rendezvous, hook up: *The shuttle is scheduled to dock with the space station.*

dock[2] VERB **1 = cut**, reduce, decrease, diminish, lessen: *He threatened to dock her fee.* **OPPOSITE:** increase **2 = deduct**, subtract: *He had a point docked for insulting his opponent.* **3 = cut off**, crop, clip, shorten, curtail, cut short: *It is an offence for an unqualified person to dock a dog's tail.*

docket NOUN **1 = label**, bill, ticket, certificate, tag, voucher, tab, receipt, tally, chit, chitty, counterfoil: *The clerk asked me to sign the docket.* **2 = file**, index, register: *The Court has 1,400 appeals on its docket.*

doctor NOUN **= physician**, medic *(informal)*, general practitioner, medical practitioner, G.P.: *Do not stop the treatment without consulting your doctor.*
▷ VERB **1 = change**, alter, interfere with, disguise, pervert, fudge, tamper with, tinker with, misrepresent, falsify, meddle with, mess about with: *They doctored the photograph.*
2 = add to, spike, cut, mix something with something, dilute, water down, adulterate: *He had doctored her milk.*

> **QUOTATIONS**
> God heals, and the doctor takes the fee
> [Benjamin Franklin *Poor Richard's Almanack*]
>
> Men who are occupied in the restoration of health to other men, by the joint exertion of skill and humanity, are above all the great of the earth
> [Voltaire *Philosophical Dictionary*]
>
> The best doctors in the world are Doctor Diet, Doctor Quiet, and Doctor Merryman
> [Jonathan Swift *Polite Conversation*]
>
> I am simply in Hell, where there are no doctors – at least, not in a professional capacity
> [T.S. Eliot *The Cocktail Party*]
>
> One finger in the throat and one in the rectum makes a good diagnostician
> [William Osler *Aphorisms from his Bedside Teachings*]
>
> God and the doctor we alike adore
> But only when in danger, not before;
> The danger o'er, both are alike requited,
> God is forgotten, and the Doctor slighted
> [John Owen *Epigrams*]

doctrinaire ADJECTIVE **1 = dogmatic**, rigid, fanatical, inflexible: *forty-five years of doctrinaire Stalinism*
2 = impractical, theoretical, speculative, ideological, unrealistic, hypothetical, unpragmatic: *It is a doctrinaire scheme.*

doctrine NOUN **= teaching**, principle, belief, opinion, article, concept, conviction, canon, creed, dogma, tenet, precept, article of faith, kaupapa *(N.Z.)*

document NOUN **= paper**, form, certificate, report, record, testimonial, authorization, legal form: *The foreign minister signed the document today.*
▷ VERB **= support**, back up, certify, verify, detail, instance, validate, substantiate, corroborate, authenticate, give weight to, particularize: *The effects of smoking have been well documented.*

doddle NOUN **= piece of cake**, picnic *(informal)*, child's play *(informal)*, pushover *(slang, informal)*, no sweat *(slang)*, cinch *(slang)*, cakewalk *(informal)*, money for old rope, bludge *(Austral. & N.Z. informal)*

dodge VERB **1 = duck**, dart, swerve, sidestep, shoot, shift, turn aside, body-swerve *(Scot.)*: *We dodged behind a pillar.* **2 = evade**, avoid, escape, get away from, elude, body-swerve *(Scot.)*, slip through the net of: *Thieves dodged the security system in the shop.* **3 = avoid**, hedge, parry, get out of, evade, shirk: *He has repeatedly dodged the question.*
▷ NOUN **= trick**, scheme, ploy, trap, device, fraud, con *(slang)*, manoeuvre, deception, scam *(slang)*, gimmick, hoax, wheeze *(Brit. slang)*, deceit, ruse, artifice, subterfuge, canard, feint, stratagem, contrivance, machination, fastie *(Austral. slang)*: *It was probably just a dodge to stop you going away.*

dodgy ADJECTIVE **1 = nasty**, offensive, unpleasant, revolting, distasteful, repellent, unsavoury, obnoxious, repulsive, objectionable, repugnant, shonky *(Austral. & N.Z. informal)*: *He was a bit of a dodgy character.* **2 = risky**, difficult, tricky, dangerous, delicate, uncertain, problematic(al), unreliable, dicky *(Brit. informal)*, dicey *(informal, chiefly Brit.)*, ticklish, chancy *(informal)*, shonky *(Austral. & N.Z. informal)*: *Predicting voting trends is a dodgy business.*

doer NOUN **= achiever**, organizer, powerhouse *(slang)*, dynamo, live wire *(slang)*, go-getter *(informal)*, active person, wheeler-dealer *(informal)*

doff VERB **1 = tip**, raise, remove, lift, take off: *The peasants doffed their hats.*
2 = take off, remove, shed, discard, throw off, cast off, slip out of, slip off: *He doffed his shirt and jeans.*

dog NOUN **1 = hound**, canine, bitch, puppy, pup, mongrel, tyke, mutt *(slang)*, pooch *(slang)*, cur, man's best friend, kuri *or* goorie *(N.Z.)*, brak *(S. African)*: *Outside a dog was barking.*
2 = scoundrel, villain, cur, heel *(slang)*, knave *(archaic)*, blackguard: *Out of my sight, you dog!*
▷ VERB **1 = plague**, follow, trouble, haunt, hound, torment, afflict: *His career has been dogged by bad luck.*
2 = pursue, follow, track, chase, shadow, harry, tail *(informal)*, trail, hound, stalk, go after, give chase to: *The three creatures had dogged him from hut to hut.*
dog-eat-dog = ruthless, fierce, vicious, ferocious, cut-throat, with no holds barred: *TV is a dog-eat-dog business.*
▸ *related adjective:* canine ▸ *name of female:* bitch ▸ *name of young:* pup, puppy

> **QUOTATIONS**
> Love me, love my dog
> [St. Bernard]
>
> The more one gets to know of men, the more one values dogs
> [A. Toussenel]
>
> Dogs live with man as courtiers round a monarch, steeped in the flattery of his notice and enriched with sinecures
> [Robert Louis Stevenson *The Character of Dogs*]
>
> The great pleasure of a dog is that you may make a fool of yourself with him and not only will he not scold you, but he will make a fool of himself too
> [Samuel Butler *Notebooks*]
>
> Histories are more full of examples of the fidelity of dogs than of friends
> [Alexander Pope]

> **PROVERBS**
> *Every dog has its day*
> *Why keep a dog and bark yourself?*
> *If you lie down with dogs, you will get up with fleas*
> *A live dog is better than a dead lion*
> *Let sleeping dogs lie*

dogged ADJECTIVE **= determined**, steady, persistent, stubborn, firm, staunch, persevering, resolute, single-minded, tenacious, steadfast, unyielding, obstinate, indefatigable, immovable, stiff-necked, unshakable, unflagging, pertinacious **OPPOSITE:** irresolute

dogma NOUN **= doctrine**, teachings, principle, opinion, article, belief, creed, tenet, precept, credo, article of faith, kaupapa *(N.Z.)*

dogmatic ADJECTIVE **1 = opinionated**, arrogant, assertive, arbitrary, emphatic, downright, dictatorial, imperious, overbearing, categorical, magisterial, doctrinaire, obdurate, peremptory: *His dogmatic style deflects opposition.* **2 = doctrinal**, authoritative, categorical, canonical, oracular, ex cathedra: *Dogmatic socialism does not offer a magic formula.*

doing NOUN **1 = carrying out** *or* **through**, performance, execution, implementation: *Nothing deflates impossibility like the doing of it.* **2 = handiwork**, act, action, achievement, exploit, deed: *It was all her doing.*

doings PLURAL NOUN **= deeds**, actions, exploits, concerns, events, affairs, happenings, proceedings, transactions, dealings, goings-on *(informal)*: *the everyday doings of a group of schoolchildren*

doldrums
the doldrums = blues, depression, dumps *(informal)*, gloom, boredom, apathy, inertia, stagnation, inactivity, tedium, dullness, the hump *(Brit. informal)*, ennui, torpor, lassitude, listlessness: *He had been through the doldrums.*

dole NOUN **= share**, grant, gift, allowance, portion, donation, quota, parcel, handout, modicum, pittance, alms, gratuity, koha *(N.Z.)*: *They hold out fragile arms for a dole of food.*
dole something out = give out, share, deal out, distribute, divide, assign, administer, allocate, hand out, dispense, allot, mete, apportion: *I began to dole out the money.*

dollop NOUN **1 = lump**, blob **2 = helping**, serving, portion, scoop, gob

dolphin NOUN
▸ *collective noun:* school

domain NOUN **= area**, field, department, discipline, sphere, realm, speciality: *the great experimenters in the domain of art*

domestic ADJECTIVE **1 = home**, internal, native, indigenous, not foreign: *sales in the domestic market* **2 = household**, home, family, private, domiciliary: *a plan for sharing domestic chores* **3 = home-loving**, homely, housewifely, stay-at-home, domesticated: *She was kind and domestic.* **4 = domesticated**, trained, tame, house, pet, house-trained: *a domestic cat*
▷ NOUN **= servant**, help, maid, woman *(informal)*, daily, char *(informal)*, charwoman, daily help: *She worked for 10 or 15 years as a domestic.*

domesticate *or (sometimes U.S.)* **domesticize** VERB **1 = tame**, break, train, house-train, gentle: *We domesticated the dog.* **2 = naturalize**, accustom, familiarize, habituate, acclimatize: *New World peoples domesticated a cornucopia of plants.*

domesticated ADJECTIVE **1 = tame**, broken (in), tamed: *our domesticated animals and plants* **OPPOSITE:** wild **2 = home-loving**, homely, domestic, housewifely, house-trained *(humorous)*: *I have never been very domesticated.*

domesticity NOUN **= home life**, housekeeping, domestication, homemaking, housewifery, home-lovingness

dominance NOUN **= control**, government, power, rule, authority, command, sway, domination, supremacy, mastery, ascendancy, paramountcy

dominant ADJECTIVE **1 = main**, chief, primary, outstanding, principal, prominent, influential, prevailing, paramount, prevalent, predominant, pre-eminent: *She was a dominant figure in the film industry.* **OPPOSITE:** minor **2 = controlling**, leading, ruling, commanding, supreme, governing, superior, presiding, authoritative, ascendant: *controlled by the dominant class*

dominate VERB **1 = control**, lead, rule, direct, master, govern, monopolize, tyrannize, have the upper hand over, lead by the nose *(informal)*, overbear, have the whip hand over, domineer, keep under your thumb: *He denied that his country wants to dominate Europe.* **2 = tower above**, overlook, survey, stand over, loom over, stand head and shoulders above, bestride: *The building dominates this whole place.*

domination NOUN **= control**, power, rule, authority, influence, command, sway, dictatorship, repression, oppression, suppression, supremacy, mastery, tyranny, ascendancy, subordination, despotism, subjection

domineering ADJECTIVE **= overbearing**, arrogant, authoritarian, oppressive, autocratic, masterful, dictatorial, coercive, bossy *(informal)*, imperious, tyrannical, magisterial, despotic, high-handed, iron-handed **OPPOSITE:** submissive

dominion NOUN **1 = control**, government, power, rule, authority, command, sovereignty, sway, domination, jurisdiction, supremacy, mastery, ascendancy, mana *(N.Z.)*: *They believe they have dominion over us.* **2 = kingdom**, territory, province, country, region, empire, patch, turf *(U.S. slang)*, realm, domain: *The Republic is a dominion of the Brazilian people.*

don VERB **= put on**, get into, dress in, pull on, change into, get dressed in, clothe yourself in, slip on *or* into

donate VERB **= give**, present, contribute, grant, commit, gift, hand out, subscribe, endow, chip in *(informal)*, bestow, entrust, impart, bequeath, make a gift of

donation NOUN **= contribution**, gift, subscription, offering, present, grant, hand-out, boon, alms, stipend, gratuity, benefaction, largesse *or* largess, koha *(N.Z.)*

done INTERJECTION **= agreed**, you're on *(informal)*, O.K. *or* okay *(informal)*, it's a bargain, it's a deal, ka pai *(N.Z.)*: *'You lead and we'll look for it.' – 'Done.'*
▷ ADJECTIVE **1 = finished**, completed, accomplished, over, through, ended, perfected, realized, concluded, executed, terminated, consummated, in the can *(informal)*: *By evening the work is done, and just in time.* **2 = cooked**, ready, cooked enough, cooked to a turn, cooked sufficiently: *When the cake is done, remove it from the oven.* **3 = acceptable**, proper, conventional, protocol, de rigueur *(French)*: *It simply isn't done.*
done for = finished *(informal)*, lost, beaten, defeated, destroyed, ruined, broken, dashed, wrecked, doomed, foiled, undone: *I thought we were all done for.*
done in *or* **up = exhausted**, bushed *(informal)*, all in *(slang)*, worn out, dead *(informal)*, knackered *(slang)*, clapped out *(Austral. & N.Z. informal)*, tired out, ready to drop, dog-tired *(informal)*, zonked *(slang)*, dead beat *(informal)*, fagged out *(informal)*, worn to a frazzle *(informal)*, on your last legs, creamcrackered *(Brit. slang)*: *You must be really done in.*
have *or* **be done with something** *or* **someone = be through with**, give up, be finished with, throw over, wash your hands of, end relations with: *Let us have done with him.*

donor NOUN **= giver**, contributor, benefactor, philanthropist, grantor *(Law)*, donator, almsgiver **OPPOSITE:** recipient

doom NOUN **= destruction**, ruin, catastrophe, death, downfall: *his warnings of impending doom*
▷ VERB **= condemn**, sentence, consign, foreordain, destine, predestine, preordain: *Some suggest the leisure park is doomed to failure.*

doomed ADJECTIVE **= hopeless**, condemned, ill-fated, fated, unhappy, unfortunate, cursed, unlucky, blighted, hapless, bedevilled, luckless, ill-starred, star-crossed, ill-omened

door NOUN **= opening**, entry, entrance, exit, doorway, ingress, egress: *I was knocking at the front door.*
out of doors = in the open air, outside, outdoors, out, alfresco: *The weather was fine for working out of doors.*
show someone the door = throw out, remove, eject, evict, turn out, bounce *(slang)*, oust, drive out, boot out *(informal)*, ask to leave, show out, throw out on your ear *(informal)*: *Would they forgive him or show him the door?*

do-or-die ADJECTIVE **= desperate**, risky, hazardous, going for broke, win-or-bust, death-or-glory, kill-or-cure

d

dope NOUN **1 = drugs**, narcotics, opiates, dadah (*Austral. slang*): *A man asked them if they wanted to buy some dope.* **2 = idiot**, fool, jerk (*slang, chiefly U.S. & Canad.*), plank (*Brit. slang*), charlie (*Brit. informal*), berk (*Brit. slang*), wally (*slang*), prat (*slang*), plonker (*slang*), coot, geek (*slang*), twit (*informal, chiefly Brit.*), dunce, oaf, simpleton, dimwit (*informal*), dipstick (*Brit. slang*), gonzo (*slang*), schmuck (*U.S. slang*), dork (*slang*), nitwit (*informal*), dolt, blockhead, divvy (*Brit. slang*), pillock (*Brit. slang*), dweeb (*U.S. slang*), putz (*U.S. slang*), fathead (*informal*), eejit (*Scot. & Irish*), dumb-ass (*slang*), numpty (*Scot. informal*), lamebrain (*informal*), nerd *or* nurd (*slang*), numbskull *or* numskull, dorba *or* dorb (*Austral. slang*), bogan (*Austral. slang*): *I don't feel I'm such a dope.* **3 = information**, facts, details, material, news, intelligence, gen (*Brit. informal*), info (*informal*), inside information, lowdown (*informal*): *They had plenty of dope on him.*
▷ VERB **= drug**, doctor, knock out, inject, sedate, stupefy, anaesthetize, narcotize: *I'd been doped with Somnolin.*

dopey *or* **dopy** ADJECTIVE **1 = drowsy**, dazed, groggy (*informal*), drugged, muzzy, stupefied, half-asleep, woozy (*informal*): *The medicine always made him feel dopey.* **2 = stupid**, simple, slow, thick, silly, foolish, dense, dumb (*informal*), senseless, goofy (*informal*), idiotic, dozy (*Brit. informal*), asinine, dumb-ass (*slang*): *I was so dopey I believed him.*

dormant ADJECTIVE **= latent**, inactive, lurking, quiescent, unrealized, unexpressed, inoperative

dorp NOUN **= town**, village, settlement, municipality, kainga *or* kaika (*N.Z.*)

dose NOUN **1 = measure**, amount, allowance, portion, prescription, ration, draught, dosage, potion: *A dose of penicillin can wipe out infection.* **2 = quantity**, measure, supply, portion

dot NOUN **= spot**, point, mark, circle, atom, dab, mite, fleck, jot, speck, full stop, speckle, mote, iota: *a small black dot in the middle*
▷ VERB **= spot**, stud, fleck, speckle: *Small coastal towns dotted the area.*
on the dot = on time, promptly, precisely, exactly (*informal*), to the minute, on the button (*informal*), punctually: *At nine o'clock on the dot, they arrived.*

dote (*with* **on** *or* **upon**) VERB **= adore**, prize, treasure, admire, hold dear, idolize, lavish affection on

doting ADJECTIVE **= adoring**, devoted, fond, foolish, indulgent, lovesick

dotty ADJECTIVE **= crazy**, touched, peculiar, eccentric, batty (*slang*), off-the-wall (*slang*), potty (*Brit. informal*), oddball (*informal*), loopy (*informal*), crackpot (*informal*), out to lunch (*informal*), outré, doolally (*slang*), off your trolley (*slang*), up the pole (*informal*), wacko *or* whacko (*slang*), off the air (*Austral. slang*), porangi (*N.Z.*), daggy (*Austral. & N.Z. informal*)

double ADJECTIVE **1 = matching**, coupled, doubled, paired, twin, duplicate, in pairs, binate (*Botany*): *a pair of double doors into the room* **2 = deceitful**, false, fraudulent, deceiving, treacherous, dishonest, deceptive, hypocritical, counterfeit, two-faced, disingenuous, insincere, double-dealing, duplicitous, perfidious, knavish (*archaic*), Janus-faced: *a woman who had lived a double life* **3 = dual**, enigmatic, cryptic, twofold, Delphic, enigmatical: *The book has a double meaning.*
▷ NOUN **= twin**, lookalike, spitting image, copy, fellow, mate, counterpart, clone, replica, ringer (*slang*), impersonator (*informal*), dead ringer (*slang*), Doppelgänger, duplicate: *Your mother sees you as her double.*
▷ VERB **1 = multiply by two**, duplicate, increase twofold, repeat, enlarge, magnify: *They need to double the number of managers.* **2 = fold up** *or* **over**: *He doubled the sheet back upon itself.* **3** (*with* **as**) **= function as**, serve as: *The military greatcoat doubled as a bedroll.*
at *or* **on the double = at once**, now, immediately, directly, quickly, promptly, right now, straight away, right away, briskly, without delay, pronto (*informal*), at full speed, in double-quick time, this instant, this very minute, pdq (*slang*), posthaste, tout de suite (*French*): *Come to my office, please, on the double.*

double-cross VERB **= betray**, trick, cheat, mislead, two-time (*informal*), defraud, swindle, hoodwink, sell down the river (*informal*), cozen

doubly ADVERB **= twice as**, in two ways, twofold, as much again, in double measure

doubt NOUN **1 = uncertainty**, confusion, hesitation, dilemma, scepticism, misgiving, suspense, indecision, bewilderment, lack of confidence, hesitancy, perplexity, vacillation, lack of conviction, irresolution, dubiety: *They were troubled and full of doubt.* **OPPOSITE:** certainty **2 = suspicion**, scepticism, distrust, fear, apprehension, mistrust, misgivings, disquiet, qualms, incredulity, lack of faith: *Where there is doubt, may we bring faith.*
OPPOSITE: belief
▷ VERB **1 = be uncertain**, be sceptical, be dubious: *They doubted whether that could happen.* **2 = waver**, hesitate, vacillate, sway, fluctuate, dither (*chiefly Brit.*), haver, oscillate, chop and change, blow hot and cold (*informal*), keep changing your mind, shillyshally (*informal*), be irresolute *or* indecisive, swither (*Scot.*): *Stop doubting and start loving.* **3 = disbelieve**, question, suspect, query, distrust, mistrust, lack confidence in, misgive: *I have no reason to doubt his word.*
OPPOSITE: believe
no doubt = certainly, surely, probably, admittedly, doubtless, assuredly, doubtlessly: *No doubt I'm biased.*

QUOTATIONS

There lives more faith in honest doubt,
Believe me, than in half the creeds
[Alfred Tennyson *In Memoriam A.H.H.*]

I show you doubt, to prove that faith exists
[Robert Browning *Balaustion's Adventure*]

If a man will begin with certainties, he shall end in doubts; but if he will be content to begin with doubts, he shall end in certainties
[Francis Bacon *The Advancement of Learning*]

Ten thousand difficulties do not make one doubt
[Cardinal Newman *Apologia pro Vita Sua*]

Our doubts are traitors
And make us lose the good we oft might win
By fearing to attempt
[William Shakespeare *Measure for Measure*]

Doubt of the reality of love ends by making us doubt everything
[Henri Frédéric Amiel *Journal*]

USAGE

In affirmative sentences, *whether* was in the past the only word considered acceptable for linking the verb *doubt* to a following clause, for example *I doubt whether he will come*. Nowadays, *doubt if* and *doubt that* are both considered acceptable alternatives to *doubt whether*. In negative sentences, use *that* after *doubt*, for example *I don't doubt that he is telling the truth*. The old-fashioned form *not doubt but that*, as in *I do not doubt but that he is telling the truth*, is now rarely used and sounds very stiff and formal.

doubter NOUN **= sceptic**, questioner, disbeliever, agnostic, unbeliever, doubting Thomas

doubtful ADJECTIVE **1 = unlikely**, unclear, dubious, unsettled, dodgy (*Brit., Austral. & N.Z. informal*), questionable, ambiguous, improbable, indefinite, unconfirmed, inconclusive, debatable, indeterminate, iffy (*informal*), equivocal, inexact: *It seemed doubtful that he would move at all.*
OPPOSITE: certain **2 = unsure**, uncertain, hesitant, suspicious, hesitating, sceptical, unsettled, tentative, wavering, unresolved, perplexed, undecided, unconvinced, vacillating, leery (*slang*), distrustful, in two minds (*informal*), irresolute: *Why did he sound so doubtful?*
OPPOSITE: certain **3 = questionable**, suspect, suspicious, crooked, dubious,

dodgy (*Brit., Austral. & N.Z. informal*), slippery, shady (*informal*), unscrupulous, fishy (*informal*), shifty, disreputable, untrustworthy, shonky (*Austral. & N.Z. informal*): *They all seemed of very doubtful character.*

USAGE
In the past, *whether* was the only word considered acceptable for linking the adjective *doubtful* in the sense of 'improbable' to a following clause, for example *it is doubtful whether he will come*. Nowadays, however, *doubtful if* and *doubtful that* are also considered acceptable.

doubtless ADVERB **= probably**, presumably, most likely

doughty ADJECTIVE **= intrepid**, brave, daring, bold, hardy, heroic, courageous, gritty, fearless, resolute, gallant, valiant, redoubtable, dauntless, valorous, stouthearted

dour ADJECTIVE **= gloomy**, forbidding, grim, sour, dismal, dreary, sullen, unfriendly, morose **OPPOSITE:** cheery

douse *or* **dowse** VERB **1 = put out**, smother, blow out, extinguish, snuff (out): *The crew began to douse the fire.* **2 = drench**, soak, steep, saturate, duck, submerge, immerse, dunk, souse, plunge into water: *They doused him in petrol.*

dovetail VERB **= correspond**, match, agree, accord, coincide, tally, conform, harmonize

dowdy ADJECTIVE **= frumpy**, old-fashioned, shabby, drab, tacky (*U.S. informal*), unfashionable, dingy, frumpish, ill-dressed, frowzy **OPPOSITE:** chic

down ADJECTIVE **= depressed**, low, sad, blue, unhappy, discouraged, miserable, fed up, dismal, pessimistic, melancholy, glum, dejected, despondent, dispirited, downcast, morose, disheartened, crestfallen, downhearted, down in the dumps (*informal*), sick as a parrot (*informal*), low-spirited: *The old man sounded really down.*
▷ VERB **1 = swallow**, drink (down), drain, gulp (down), put away (*informal*), toss off: *We downed several bottles of local wine.* **2 = bring down**, fell, knock down, throw, trip, floor, tackle, deck (*slang*), overthrow, prostrate: *A bank guard shot him and downed him.*

down-and-out ADJECTIVE **= destitute**, ruined, impoverished, derelict, penniless, dirt-poor (*informal*), flat broke (*informal*), on your uppers (*informal*), without two pennies to rub together (*informal*): *He looked unshaven, shabby and down-and-out.*
▷ NOUN **= tramp**, bum (*informal*), beggar, derelict, outcast, pauper, vagrant, vagabond, bag lady, dosser (*Brit. slang*), derro (*Austral. slang*): *some poor down-and-out in need of a meal*

downbeat ADJECTIVE **1 = low-key**, muted, subdued, sober, sombre: *The headlines were suitably downbeat.* **2 = gloomy**, negative, depressed, pessimistic, unfavourable: *They found him in gloomy, downbeat mood.* **OPPOSITE:** cheerful

downcast ADJECTIVE **= dejected**, sad, depressed, unhappy, disappointed, discouraged, miserable, dismayed, choked, daunted, dismal, despondent, dispirited, disheartened, disconsolate, crestfallen, down in the dumps (*informal*), cheerless, sick as a parrot (*informal*) **OPPOSITE:** cheerful

downfall NOUN **= ruin**, fall, destruction, collapse, breakdown, disgrace, overthrow, descent, undoing, comeuppance (*slang*), comedown

downgrade VERB **1 = demote**, degrade, take down a peg (*informal*), lower *or* reduce in rank: *His superiors downgraded him.* **OPPOSITE:** promote **2 = run down**, denigrate, disparage, detract from, decry: *He was never one to downgrade his talents.*

down-market ADJECTIVE **= second-rate**, cheap, inferior, tacky (*informal*), shoddy, low-grade, tawdry, low-quality, downscale, two-bit (*U.S. & Canad. slang*), cheap and nasty (*informal*), lowbrow, bush-league (*Austral. & N.Z. informal*), bodger *or* bodgie (*Austral. slang*) **OPPOSITE:** first-rate

downpour NOUN **= rainstorm**, flood, deluge, torrential rain, cloudburst, inundation

downright ADJECTIVE **= complete**, absolute, utter, total, positive, clear, plain, simple, explicit, outright, blatant, unequivocal, unqualified, out-and-out, categorical, undisguised, thoroughgoing, arrant, deep-dyed (*usually derogatory*)

downside NOUN **= drawback**, disadvantage, snag, problem, trouble, minus (*informal*), flip side, other side of the coin (*informal*), bad *or* weak point **OPPOSITE:** benefit

down-to-earth ADJECTIVE **= sensible**, practical, realistic, common-sense, matter-of-fact, sane, no-nonsense, hard-headed, unsentimental, plain-spoken, grounded

downtrodden ADJECTIVE **= oppressed**, abused, exploited, subservient, subjugated, tyrannized

downward ADJECTIVE **= descending**, declining, heading down, earthward

doze VERB **= nap**, sleep, slumber, nod, kip (*Brit. slang*), snooze (*informal*), catnap, drowse, sleep lightly, zizz (*Brit. informal*): *For a while she dozed fitfully.*
▷ NOUN **= nap**, kip (*Brit. slang*), snooze (*informal*), siesta, little sleep, catnap, forty winks (*informal*), shuteye (*slang*), zizz (*Brit. informal*): *After lunch I had a doze.*

dozy ADJECTIVE **= stupid**, simple, slow, silly, daft (*informal*), senseless, goofy (*informal*), witless, not all there, slow-witted

drab ADJECTIVE **= dull**, grey, gloomy, dismal, dreary, shabby, sombre, lacklustre, flat, dingy, colourless, uninspired, vapid, cheerless **OPPOSITE:** bright

Draconian ADJECTIVE (*sometimes not cap.*) **= severe**, hard, harsh, stern, drastic, stringent, punitive, austere, pitiless

draft NOUN **1 = outline**, plan, sketch, version, rough, abstract, delineation, preliminary form: *I rewrote his first draft.* **2 = money order**, bill (of exchange), cheque, postal order: *The money was payable by a draft.*
▷ VERB **= outline**, write, plan, produce, create, design, draw, frame, compose, devise, sketch, draw up, formulate, contrive, delineate: *He drafted a standard letter.*

drag VERB **1 = pull**, draw, haul, trail, tow, tug, jerk, yank, hale, lug: *He got up and dragged his chair towards the table.* **2 = lag**, trail, linger, loiter, straggle, dawdle, hang back, tarry, draggle: *I was dragging behind* **3 = go slowly**, inch, creep, crawl, advance slowly: *The minutes dragged past.*
▷ NOUN **= nuisance**, pain (*informal*), bore, bother, pest, hassle (*informal*), inconvenience, annoyance, pain in the neck, pain in the backside (*informal*), pain in the butt (*informal*): *Shopping for clothes is a drag.*
drag on = last, continue, carry on, remain, endure, persist, linger, abide: *The conflict has dragged on for two years.*
drag yourself = go slowly, creep, crawl, inch, shuffle, shamble, limp along, move at a snail's pace, advance slowly: *I managed to drag myself to the surgery.*

dragoon VERB **= force**, drive, compel, bully, intimidate, railroad (*informal*), constrain, coerce, impel, strong-arm (*informal*), browbeat

drain NOUN **1 = sewer**, channel, pipe, sink, outlet, ditch, trench, conduit, duct, culvert, watercourse: *He built his own house and laid his own drains.* **2 = reduction**, strain, drag, expenditure, exhaustion, sapping, depletion: *This has been a big drain on resources.*
▷ VERB **1 = remove**, draw, empty, withdraw, milk, tap, pump, bleed, evacuate: *machines to drain water out of the mines* **2 = empty**: *I didn't know what we would find when we drained the pool.* **3 = flow out**, leak, discharge, trickle, ooze, seep, exude, well out, effuse: *The water drained away.* **4 = drink up**, swallow, finish, put away (*informal*), quaff, gulp down: *She drained the contents of her glass and refilled it.* **5 = exhaust**, tire, wear out, strain, weaken, fatigue, weary, debilitate, prostrate, tax, tire out, enfeeble, enervate: *My emotional turmoil has drained me.* **6 = consume**, waste, exhaust, empty, deplete, use up, sap, dissipate, swallow up: *Deficits drain resources from the pool of national savings.*

d

down the drain = **gone**, lost, wasted, ruined, gone for good: *His public image is down the drain.*

drainage NOUN = **sewerage**, waste, sewage

dram NOUN = **measure**, shot *(informal)*, drop, glass, tot, slug, snort *(slang)*, snifter *(informal)*

drama NOUN **1** = **play**, show, stage show, stage play, dramatization, theatrical piece: *He acted in radio dramas.* **2** = **theatre**, acting, dramatic art, stagecraft, dramaturgy, Thespian art: *He knew nothing of Greek drama.* **3** = **excitement**, crisis, dramatics, spectacle, turmoil, histrionics, theatrics: *the drama of a hostage release*

QUOTATIONS

Drama is life with the dull bits cut out
[Alfred Hitchcock]

The drama is make-believe. It does not deal with the truth but with effect
[W. Somerset Maugham *The Summing Up*]

Life is full of internal dramas, instantaneous and sensational, played to an audience of one
[Anthony Powell]

pantomime: a play in which the story is told without violence to the language. The least disagreeable form of dramatic action
[Ambrose Bierce *The Devil's Dictionary*]

for what's a play without a woman in it?
[Thomas Kyd *The Spanish Tragedy*]

dramatic ADJECTIVE **1** = **exciting**, emotional, thrilling, tense, startling, sensational, breathtaking, electrifying, melodramatic, climactic, high-octane *(informal)*, shock-horror *(facetious)*, suspenseful: *He witnessed many dramatic escapes.* **2** = **theatrical**, Thespian, dramaturgical, dramaturgic: *a dramatic arts major in college* **3** = **expressive**: *She lifted her hands in a dramatic gesture.* **4** = **powerful**, striking, stunning *(informal)*, impressive, effective, vivid, jaw-dropping: *The film's dramatic special effects impressed the audience.*
OPPOSITE: ordinary

dramatist NOUN = **playwright**, screenwriter, scriptwriter, dramaturge

dramatize *or* **dramatise** VERB = **exaggerate**, overdo, overstate, lay it on (thick) *(slang)*, play-act, play to the gallery, make a performance of: *The novel has been dramatised.*

drape VERB **1** = **cover**, wrap, fold, array, adorn, swathe: *He draped himself in the flag.* **2** = **hang**, drop, dangle, suspend, lean, droop, let fall: *She draped her arm over the back of the couch.*

drastic ADJECTIVE = **extreme**, strong, radical, desperate, severe, harsh, dire, forceful

draught *or (U.S.)* **draft** NOUN **1** = **breeze**, current, movement, flow, puff, influx, gust, current of air: *Block draughts around doors and windows.* **2** = **drink**: *He took a draught of beer.*

draw VERB **1** = **sketch**, design, outline, trace, portray, paint, depict, mark out, map out, delineate: *Draw a rough design for a logo.* **2** = **pull**, drag, haul, tow, tug: *He drew his chair nearer the fire.* **3** = **inhale**, breathe in, pull, inspire, suck, respire: *He paused, drawing a deep breath.* **4** = **extract**, take, remove, drain: *They still have to draw their water from wells.* **5** = **choose**, pick, select, take, single out: *We drew the winning name.* **6** = **deduce**, make, get, take, derive, infer: *He draws two conclusions from this.* **7** = **attract**, engage: *He wanted to draw attention to their plight.* **8** = **entice**, bring in: *The game is drawing huge crowds.*
▷ NOUN **1** = **tie**, deadlock, stalemate, impasse, dead heat: *The game ended in a draw.* **2** = **appeal**, interest, pull *(informal)*, charm, attraction, lure, temptation, fascination, attractiveness, allure, magnetism, enchantment, enticement, captivation, temptingness: *The draw of India lies in its beauty.*
draw back = **recoil**, withdraw, retreat, shrink, falter, back off, shy away, flinch, retract, quail, start back: *I drew back with a horrified scream.*
draw on *or* **upon something** = **make use of**, use, employ, rely on, exploit, extract, take from, fall back on, have recourse to: *He drew on his experience as a yachtsman.*
draw something out = **stretch out**, extend, lengthen, elongate, attenuate: *She drew the speech out interminably.*
draw something up = **draft**, write, produce, create, prepare, frame, compose, devise, formulate, contrive: *They drew up a formal agreement.*
draw up = **halt**, stop, pull up, stop short, come to a stop: *A police car drew up at the gate.*

drawback NOUN = **disadvantage**, trouble, difficulty, fault, handicap, obstacle, defect, deficiency, flaw, hitch, nuisance, snag, downside, stumbling block, impediment, detriment, imperfection, hindrance, fly in the ointment *(informal)*
OPPOSITE: advantage

drawing NOUN = **picture**, illustration, representation, cartoon, sketch, portrayal, depiction, study, outline, delineation

drawl VERB = **speak** *or* say slowly

drawn ADJECTIVE = **tense**, worn, strained, stressed, tired, pinched, fatigued, harassed, fraught, sapped, harrowed, haggard

dread VERB = **fear**, shrink from, cringe at the thought of, quail from, shudder to think about, have cold feet about *(informal)*, anticipate with horror, tremble to think about: *I'm dreading Christmas this year.*
▷ NOUN = **fear**, alarm, horror, terror, dismay, fright, apprehension, consternation, trepidation, apprehensiveness, affright: *She thought with dread of the cold winters to come.*

dreadful ADJECTIVE **1** = **terrible**, shocking, awful, alarming, distressing, appalling, tragic, horrible, formidable, fearful, dire, horrendous, hideous, monstrous, from hell *(informal)*, grievous, atrocious, frightful, godawful *(slang)*, hellacious *(U.S. slang)*: *They told us the dreadful news.* **2** = **serious**, terrible, awful, appalling, horrendous, monstrous, unspeakable, abysmal: *We've made a dreadful mistake* **3** = **awful**, terrible, horrendous, frightful

dream NOUN **1** = **vision**, illusion, delusion, hallucination, reverie: *I had a dream that I was in an old house.* **2** = **ambition**, wish, fantasy, desire, Holy Grail *(informal)*, pipe dream: *My dream is to have a house in the country.* **3** = **daydream**: *I wandered around in a kind of dream.* **4** = **delight**, pleasure, joy, beauty, treasure, gem, marvel, pearler *(Austral. slang)*, beaut *(Austral. & N.Z. slang)*: *This cart really is a dream to drive.*
▷ VERB **1** = **have dreams**, hallucinate: *She dreamt about her baby.* **2** = **daydream**, stargaze, build castles in the air *or* in Spain: *She spent most of her time looking out of the window and dreaming.*
dream of something *or* **someone** = **daydream about**, fantasize about: *She dreamed of going to work overseas.*
dream something up = **invent**, create, imagine, devise, hatch, contrive, concoct, think up, cook up *(informal)*, spin: *I dreamed up a plan.*

DRAMA

TYPES OF DRAMA

comedy
comedy of manners
commedia dell'arte
costume piece *or* costume drama
farce
Grand Guignol
Jacobean
kabuki
Kathakali
kitchen sink
melodrama
morality play
mystery play
No *or* Noh
passion play
Restoration Comedy
revenge tragedy
shadow play
situation comedy *or* sitcom
sketch
soap opera
street theatre
theatre of cruelty
theatre of the absurd
tragedy
tragicomedy

QUOTATIONS

Your old men shall dream dreams, your young men shall see visions
[*Bible: Joel*]

We are such stuff
As dreams are made on, and our little life
Is rounded with a sleep
[William Shakespeare *The Tempest*]

I talk of dreams;
Which are the children of an idle brain,
Begot of nothing but vain fantasy
[William Shakespeare *Romeo and Juliet*]

Judge of your natural character by what you do in your dreams
[Ralph Waldo Emerson *Journals*]

I have a dream that one day on the red hills of Georgia the sons of former slaves and the sons of former slave owners will be able to sit down together at the table of brotherhood
[Martin Luther King *speech at 1963 Civil Rights March*]

dreamer NOUN = **idealist**, visionary, daydreamer, utopian, theorizer, fantasizer, romancer, Don Quixote, escapist, Walter Mitty, fantasist, fantast

dreamy ADJECTIVE **1 = vague**, abstracted, absent, musing, preoccupied, daydreaming, faraway, pensive, in a reverie, with your head in the clouds: *His face assumed a dreamy expression.* **2 = relaxing**, calming, romantic, gentle, soothing, lulling: *a dreamy, delicate song* **3 = impractical**, vague, imaginary, speculative, visionary, fanciful, quixotic, dreamlike, airy-fairy: *full of dreamy ideals* **OPPOSITE:** realistic

dreary ADJECTIVE **1 = dull**, boring, tedious, routine, drab, tiresome, lifeless, monotonous, humdrum, colourless, uneventful, uninteresting, mind-numbing, ho-hum *(informal)*, wearisome, as dry as dust: *They live such dreary lives.* **OPPOSITE:** exciting **2 = dismal**, depressing, bleak, sad, lonely, gloomy, solitary, melancholy, sombre, forlorn, glum, mournful, lonesome *(chiefly U.S. & Canad.)*, downcast, sorrowful, wretched, joyless, funereal, doleful, cheerless, drear, comfortless: *A dreary little town in the Midwest*

dredge up VERB = **dig up**, raise, rake up, discover, uncover, draw up, unearth, drag up, fish up

dregs PLURAL NOUN = **sediment**, grounds, lees, waste, deposit, trash, residue, scum, dross, residuum, scourings, draff

the dregs = **scum**, outcasts, rabble, down-and-outs, good-for-nothings, riffraff, canaille *(French)*, ragtag and bobtail: *the dregs of society*

drench VERB = **soak**, flood, wet, duck, drown, steep, swamp, saturate, inundate, souse, imbrue

dress NOUN **1 = frock**, gown, garment, robe: *She was wearing a black dress.* **2 = clothing**, clothes, gear *(informal)*, costume, threads *(slang)*, garments, apparel, attire, garb, togs, raiment *(archaic, poetic)*, vestment, schmutter *(slang)*, habiliment: *a well-groomed gent in smart dress and specs*
▷ VERB **1 = put on clothes**, don clothes, slip on *or* into something: *He told her to wait while he dressed.* **OPPOSITE:** undress **2 = clothe**: *We dressed the baby in a warm outfit.* **3 = bandage**, treat, plaster, bind up: *I dressed her wounds.* **4 = decorate**, deck, adorn, trim, array, drape, ornament, embellish, festoon, bedeck, furbish, rig out: *advice on how to dress a Christmas tree* **5 = arrange**, do (up), groom, set, prepare, comb (out), get ready: *He's so careless about dressing his hair.*

dress someone down = **reprimand**, rebuke, scold, berate, castigate, tear into *(informal)*, tell off *(informal)*, read the riot act, reprove, upbraid, slap on the wrist, carpet *(informal)*, bawl out *(informal)*, rap over the knuckles, haul over the coals, chew out *(U.S. & Canad. informal)*, tear (someone) off a strip *(Brit. informal)*, give a rocket *(Brit. & N.Z. informal)*: *He dressed them down in public.*

dress up 1 = put on fancy dress, wear a costume, disguise yourself: *She dressed up as a witch.* **2 = dress formally**, dress for dinner, doll yourself up *(slang)*, put on your best bib and tucker *(informal)*, put on your glad rags *(informal)*: *She did not feel obliged to dress up for the cameras.*

QUOTATIONS

When you're all dressed up and have no place to go
[George Whiting *song title*]

Singularity in dress is ridiculous; in fact it is generally looked upon as a proof that the mind is somewhat deranged
[St. John Baptist de la Salle *The Rules of Christian Manners and Civility*]

Eat to please thyself, but dress to please others
[Benjamin Franklin *Poor Richard's Almanack*]

dressmaker NOUN = **seamstress**, tailor, couturier, sewing woman, modiste

dribble VERB **1 = run**, drip, trickle, drop, leak, ooze, seep, fall in drops: *Sweat dribbled down his face.* **2 = drool**, drivel, slaver, slobber, drip saliva: *She's dribbling on her collar.*

drift VERB **1 = float**, go (aimlessly), bob, coast, slip, sail, slide, glide, meander, waft, be carried along, move gently: *We proceeded to drift along the river.* **2 = wander**, stroll, stray, roam, meander, rove, range, straggle, traipse *(informal)*, stravaig *(Scot. & Northern English dialect)*, peregrinate: *People drifted around the room.* **3 = stray**, wander, roam, meander, digress, get sidetracked, go off at a tangent, get off the point: *I let my attention drift.* **4 = pile up**, gather, accumulate, amass, bank up: *The snow, except where it drifted, was only calf-deep.*
▷ NOUN **1 = pile**, bank, mass, heap, mound, accumulation: *A boy was trapped in a snow drift.* **2 = meaning**, point, gist, aim, direction, object, import, intention, implication, tendency, significance, thrust, tenor, purport: *She was beginning to get his drift.*

drifter NOUN = **wanderer**, bum *(informal)*, tramp, itinerant, vagrant, hobo *(U.S.)*, vagabond, rolling stone, bag lady *(chiefly U.S.)*, derro *(Austral. slang)*

drill NOUN **1 = bit**, borer, gimlet, rotary tool, boring tool: *pneumatic drills* **2 = training**, exercise, discipline, instruction, preparation, repetition: *A local army base teaches them military drill.* **3 = practice**: *a fire drill*
▷ VERB **1 = bore**, pierce, penetrate, sink in, puncture, perforate: *I drilled five holes at equal distance.* **2 = train**, coach, teach, exercise, discipline, practise, instruct, rehearse: *He drills the choir to a high standard.*

drink VERB **1 = swallow**, drain, sip, suck, gulp, sup, swig *(informal)*, swill, guzzle, imbibe, quaff, partake of, toss off: *He drank his cup of tea.* **2 = booze** *(informal)*, tipple, tope, hit the bottle *(informal)*, bevvy *(dialect)*, bend the elbow *(informal)*, go on a binge *or* bender *(informal)*: *He was smoking and drinking too much.*
▷ NOUN **1 = glass**, cup, swallow, sip, draught, gulp, swig *(informal)*, taste, tipple, snifter *(informal)*, noggin: *a drink of water.* **2 = beverage**, refreshment, potion, liquid, thirst quencher: *Can I offer you a drink?* **3 = alcohol**, booze *(informal)*, liquor, spirits, the bottle *(informal)*, Dutch courage, hooch *or* hootch *(informal, chiefly U.S. & Canad.)*: *Too much drink is bad for your health.*

drink something in = **absorb**, take in, digest, pay attention to, soak up, devour, assimilate, be fascinated by, imbibe: *She stood drinking in the view.*

drink to something = **toast**, salute, pledge the health of: *Let's drink to his memory.*

the drink = **the sea**, the main, the deep, the ocean, the briny *(informal)*: *His plane went down in the drink.*

QUOTATIONS

Let us eat and drink; for tomorrow we shall die
[*Bible: Isaiah*]

Take thine ease, eat, drink, and be merry
[*Bible: St. Luke*]

I drink when I have occasion for it, and sometimes when I have not
[Miguel de Cervantes *Don Quixote*]

Drink to me only with thine eyes
[Ben Jonson *To Celia*]

It's all right to drink like a fish – if you drink what a fish drinks
[Mary Pettibone Poole *A Glass Eye at the Keyhole*]

One reason I don't drink is that I want to know when I'm having a good time
[Nancy Astor]

I wasna fou, but just had plenty
[Robert Burns *Death and Dr. Hornbook*]

I have taken more out of alcohol than alcohol has taken out of me
[Winston Churchill]

Man wants little drink below,
But wants that little strong
[Oliver Wendell Holmes *A Song of other Days*]

d

Give strong drink unto him that is ready to perish, and wine unto those that be of heavy hearts
[*Bible: Proverbs*]

Let schoolmasters puzzle their brain,
With grammar, and nonsense, and learning,
Good liquor, I stoutly maintain,
Gives genius a better discerning
[Oliver Goldsmith *She Stoops to Conquer*]

Candy
Is dandy
But liquor
Is quicker
[Ogden Nash *Reflections on Ice-breaking*]

I arrived on the job in what I considered to be a perfect state of equilibrium, half man and half alcohol
[Eddie Condon *We Called it Music*]

Wine is the drink of the gods, milk the drink of babies, tea the drink of women, and water the drink of beasts
[John Stuart Blackie]

Drink moderately, for drunkenness neither keeps a secret, nor observes a promise
[Miguel de Cervantes *Don Quixote*]

We drink one another's healths and spoil our own
[Jerome K. Jerome *The Idle Thoughts of an Idle Fellow*]

Drink! for you know not whence you came, nor why:
Drink! for you know not why you go, nor where
[Omar Khayyám *Rubáiyát*]

I will drink Life to the lees:
all times I have enjoyed greatly, have suffered greatly
[Alfred, Lord Tennyson *Ulysses*]

A little learning is a dangerous thing;
Drink deep, or taste not the Pierian spring:
There shallow draughts intoxicate the brain,
And drinking largely sobers us again
[Alexander Pope *An Essay on Criticism*]

brandy: a cordial composed of one part thunder-and-lightning, one part remorse, two parts bloody murder, one part death-hell-and-the-grave and four parts clarified Satan
[Ambrose Bierce *The Devil's Dictionary*]

Claret is the liquor for boys; port, for men; but he who aspires to be a hero must drink brandy
[Dr. Johnson]

rum: generically, fiery liquors that produce madness in total abstainers
[Ambrose Bierce *The Devil's Dictionary*]

Cocktails have all the disagreeability without the utility of a disinfectant
[Shane Leslie *The Observer*]

The proper union of gin and vermouth is a great and sudden glory; it is one of the happiest marriages on earth, and one of the shortest lived
[Bernard De Voto]

drinker NOUN **= alcoholic**, drunk, boozer *(informal)*, soak *(slang)*, lush *(slang)*, toper, sponge *(informal)*, guzzler, drunkard, sot, tippler, wino *(informal)*, inebriate, dipsomaniac, bibber, alko *or* alco *(Austral. slang)*

drip VERB **= drop**, splash, sprinkle, trickle, dribble, exude, drizzle, plop: *a cloth that dripped pink drops upon the floor*
▷ NOUN **1 = drop**, bead, trickle, dribble, droplet, globule, pearl, driblet: *Drips of water rolled down his uniform.* **2 = weakling**, wet *(Brit. informal)*, weed *(informal)*, softie *(informal)*, mummy's boy *(informal)*, namby-pamby, ninny, milksop: *The kid is a drip!*

drive VERB **1 = go (by car)**, ride (by car), motor, travel by car: *I drove into town and went for dinner.* **2 = operate**, manage, direct, guide, handle, steer: *Don't expect to be able to drive a car or operate machinery.* **3 = push**, propel: *pistons that drive the wheels* **4 = thrust**, push, sink, dig, hammer, plunge, stab, ram: *I used the sledgehammer to drive the pegs in.* **5 = herd**, urge, impel: *The shepherds drove the sheep up to pasture.* **6 = force**, press, prompt, spur, compel, motivate, oblige, railroad *(informal)*, prod, constrain, prick, coerce, goad, impel, dragoon, actuate: *Depression drove him to attempt suicide.* **7 = work**, overwork, overburden: *For the next six years he drove himself mercilessly.*
▷ NOUN **1 = run**, ride, trip, journey, spin *(informal)*, hurl *(Scot.)*, outing, excursion, jaunt: *We might go for a drive on Sunday.* **2 = initiative**, push *(informal)*, energy, enterprise, ambition, pep, motivation, zip *(informal)*, vigour, get-up-and-go *(informal)*: *He is best remembered for his drive and enthusiasm.* **3 = campaign**, push *(informal)*, crusade, action, effort, appeal, advance, surge: *the drive towards democracy*
drive at something = mean, suggest, intend, refer to, imply, intimate, get at, hint at, have in mind, allude to, insinuate: *He wasn't sure what she was driving at.*

drivel VERB **= babble**, ramble, waffle *(informal, chiefly Brit.)*, gab *(informal)*, gas *(informal)*, maunder, blether, prate: *I drivelled on about the big race that day.*
▷ NOUN **= nonsense**, rubbish, garbage, malarkey *(informal)*, rot, crap *(slang)*, trash, bunk *(informal)*, blah *(slang)*, hot air *(informal)*, tosh *(slang, chiefly Brit.)*, waffle *(informal, chiefly Brit.)*, prating, pap, bilge *(informal)*, twaddle, tripe *(informal)*, dross, gibberish, guff *(slang)*, moonshine, hogwash, hokum *(slang, chiefly U.S. & Canad.)*, piffle *(informal)*, poppycock *(informal)*, balderdash, bosh *(informal)*, eyewash *(informal)*, tommyrot, horsefeathers *(U.S. slang)*, bunkum *or* buncombe *(chiefly U.S.)*, bizzo *(Austral. slang)*, bull's wool *(Austral. & N.Z. slang)*: *What absolute drivel!*

drizzle NOUN **= fine rain**, Scotch mist, smir *(Scot.)*: *The drizzle had stopped and the sun was breaking through.*
▷ VERB **= rain**, shower, spit, spray, sprinkle, mizzle *(dialect)*, spot *or* spit with rain: *It was starting to drizzle.*

droll ADJECTIVE **= amusing**, odd, funny, entertaining, comic, ridiculous, diverting, eccentric, ludicrous, humorous, quaint, off-the-wall *(slang)*, laughable, farcical, whimsical, comical, oddball *(informal)*, risible, jocular, clownish, waggish

drone[1] NOUN **= parasite**, skiver *(Brit. slang)*, idler, lounger, leech, loafer, couch potato *(slang)*, scrounger *(informal)*, sponger *(informal)*, sluggard, bludger *(Austral. & N.Z. informal)*, quandong *(Austral. slang)*

drone[2] VERB **1 = hum**, buzz, vibrate, purr, whirr, thrum: *An invisible plane drones through the night sky.* **2** *(often with* **on**) **= speak monotonously**, drawl, chant, spout, intone, talk interminably: *Her voice droned on.*
▷ NOUN **= hum**, buzz, purr, vibration, whirr, whirring, thrum: *the constant drone of the motorway*

droning ADJECTIVE **= monotonous**, boring, tedious, drawling, soporific: *the minister's relentlessly droning voice*

drool VERB **1 = drivel**, dribble, salivate, slaver, slobber, water at the mouth: *The dog was drooling on my shoulder*
2 *(often with* **over**) **= gloat over**, pet, gush, make much of, rave about *(informal)*, dote on, slobber over: *Fashion editors drooled over every item.*

droop VERB **= sag**, drop, hang (down), sink, bend, dangle, fall down: *a young man with a drooping moustache*

droopy ADJECTIVE **= sagging**, limp, wilting, stooped, floppy, drooping, languid, flabby, languorous, pendulous, lassitudinous

drop VERB **1 = fall**, lower, decline, diminish: *Temperatures can drop to freezing at night.* **2** *(often with* **away**)

Clichés

What exactly is a cliché? According to the *Collins English Dictionary* definition it is:

a word or expression that has lost much of its force through overexposure.

How does this 'overexposure' come about? Quite simply, an expression that is now commonly identified as a cliché started out as an original turn of phrase dreamt up by some writer, whether unknown or still famous, to perfectly express what he or she wanted to say. The expression was picked up by others who immediately appreciated its aptness or memorableness, and in time it became for many the form of words that sprang automatically to mind whenever a given topic was being broached. This is why things always *grind to a halt*, why searchers always *leave no stone unturned*, and why a predictable outcome is always *a foregone conclusion*. The point is that the cliché is the easy option; using it makes it unnecessary to have to exercise the brain too much.

Is this necessarily a bad thing? Many people would argue that when an expression is obviously right then it would be perverse not to make use of it. No-one can be original all of the time, and if a phrase is familiar it is because it does its job well. However, the main drawback with the use of too many clichés is that it suggests that the writer or speaker has been too lazy to think deeply about the subject. It is akin to choosing the convenience meal over something you have taken the time and trouble to cook yourself. As a writer you don't want to be thought of as someone who is merely regurgitating other people's ideas or insights; you don't want your content to come across as dull and hackneyed. If much of what you have to say has the ring of familiarity about it, a reader or listener is entitled to assume that you have nothing new to offer. If you can only express yourself in clichéd terms, then you shouldn't be surprised if you are dismissed as second-rate, offering only second-hand ideas.

While you might want to cultivate an informal style and present a non-stuffy image, it should be remembered that the proper use of colloquial expressions is, as the term suggests, in the spoken rather than the written word. A few clichés strewn throughout a speech, for example, may put the listeners at ease, help eke out material that is unfortunately pretty thin, or establish a common ground. They will soon be forgotten about anyway. It is different in print, however, where a certain permanence comes into play, and few readers will want to plough through a lot of hackneyed stuff, involving expressions that have lost their original power through being *past their sell-by date*.

It would be a mistake to assume that all clichés are old and hoary echoes of classic literature. New examples are being coined all the time, and it can be surprising how quickly someone's smart turn of phrase becomes so much copied that it very soon becomes over-familiar. Happy people have not been describing themselves as *over the moon* for very long; nor have the disappointed felt entitled to call themselves *gutted* until relatively recently. However, both expressions are undoubtedly clichés. Reality television and man-in-the-street interviews have much to asnwer for.

How, then, to avoid using clichés? A simple test is to consider whether or not an expression comes into your head automatically and fully-formed. The chances are that it is so reassuringly familiar because it has been used far too many times before. Think about what the words actually mean. Could the same meaning be conveyed by putting it another way? This is not to say that you must take something simple and deliberately make it more elaborate or twist its meaning. Often clichés are memorable because they are fairly fancy turns of phrase, and using plainer, more direct language instead may be the ideal way to communicate your meaning. For example, saying *when all is said and done* is really only a long-winded alternative for *finally, ultimately*, or *in the end*. Similarly, why insist that you are going to *go through something with a fine-tooth comb* when you can *investigate thoroughly* or *examine it carefully*? Is there really any need to describe the ultimate entry in a list as *last, but not least*? Most people would thank you for simply saying *finally* or *in conclusion*, or some other plain turn of phrase that doesn't smack of phoney even-handedness or an unnecessary effort at avoiding offending anyone.

= **decline**, fall, sink: *The ground dropped away steeply.* **3 = plunge**, fall, dive, tumble, descend, plummet: *Part of an aeroplane had dropped out of the sky and hit me.* **4 = drip**, trickle, dribble, fall in drops: *He felt hot tears dropping onto his fingers.* **5 = sink**, fall, descend, droop: *She let her head drop.* **6 = set down**, leave, deposit, unload, let off: *He dropped me outside the hotel.* **7 = quit**, give up, abandon, cease, axe *(informal)*, kick *(informal)*, terminate, relinquish, remit, discontinue, forsake: *He was told to drop the idea.* **8 = abandon**, desert, forsake, repudiate, leave, jilt, throw over: *He has dropped those friends who used to drink with him.*
▷ NOUN **1 = decrease**, fall, cut, lowering, decline, reduction, slump, fall-off, downturn, deterioration, cutback, diminution, decrement: *He was prepared to take a drop in wages.*
2 = droplet, bead, globule, bubble, pearl, drip, driblet: *a drop of blue ink*
3 = dash, shot *(informal)*, spot, taste, trace, pinch, sip, tot, trickle, nip, dab, mouthful: *I'll have a drop of that milk.*
4 = fall, plunge, descent, abyss, chasm, precipice: *There was a sheer drop just outside my window.*
drop in = visit, call, stop, turn up, look up, call in, look in, pop in *(informal)*, swing by *(informal)*: *I'll drop in on my way home.*
drop off 1 = fall asleep, nod (off), doze (off), snooze *(informal)*, catnap, drowse, have forty winks *(informal)*: *I was just dropping off.* **2 = decrease**, lower, decline, shrink, diminish, fall off, dwindle, lessen, wane, subside, slacken: *The toll of casualties has dropped off sharply.*
drop out = leave, stop, give up, withdraw, quit, pull out, back out, renege, throw in the towel, cop out *(slang)*, fall by the wayside: *He went to university, but dropped out after a year.*
drop out of something = discontinue, give up, abandon, quit, cease, terminate, forsake: *She had a troubled childhood and dropped out of high school.*
drop someone off = set down, leave, deliver, let off, allow to alight: *I'm going to drop you off and pick you up myself.*

droppings PLURAL NOUN = **excrement**, stool, manure, dung, faeces, guano, excreta, doo-doo *(informal)*, ordure, kak *(S. African taboo)*

dross NOUN **1** rubbish, remains, refuse, lees, waste, debris, dregs **2 = nonsense**, garbage *(chiefly U.S.)*, drivel, twaddle, pants *(slang)*, rot, crap *(slang)*, trash, hot air *(informal)*, tosh *(slang, chiefly Brit.)*, pap, bilge *(informal)*, tripe *(informal)*, gibberish, guff *(slang)*, havers *(Scot.)*, moonshine, claptrap *(informal)*, hogwash, hokum *(slang, chiefly U.S. & Canad.)*, codswallop *(Brit. slang)*, piffle *(informal)*, poppycock *(informal)*, balderdash, bosh *(informal)*, wack *(U.S. slang)*, eyewash *(informal)*, stuff and nonsense, flapdoodle *(slang)*, tommyrot, horsefeathers *(U.S. slang)*, bunkum *or* buncombe *(chiefly U.S.)*, bizzo *(Austral. slang)*, bull's wool *(Austral. & N.Z. slang)*: *Why are you wasting your time reading that dross?*

drought NOUN **1 = water shortage**, dryness, dry weather, dry spell, aridity, drouth *(Scot.)*, parchedness: *Drought and famines have killed up to two million people.* **OPPOSITE:** flood
2 = shortage, lack, deficit, deficiency, want, need, shortfall, scarcity, dearth, insufficiency: *The Western world was suffering through the oil drought.*
OPPOSITE: abundance

drove NOUN *(often plural)* = **herd**, company, crowds, collection, gathering, mob, flocks, swarm, horde, multitude, throng

drown VERB **1 = go down**, go under: *He drowned during a storm.* **2 = drench**, flood, soak, steep, swamp, saturate, engulf, submerge, immerse, inundate, deluge: *The country would be drowned in blood.* **3** *(often with* **out***)* **= overwhelm**, overcome, wipe out, overpower, obliterate, swallow up: *His words were soon drowned by amplified police sirens.*

> **QUOTATIONS**
> I was much farther out than you
> thought
> And not waving but drowning
> [Stevie Smith *Not Waving But Drowning*]

drowsiness NOUN = **sleepiness**, tiredness, lethargy, torpor, sluggishness, languor, somnolence, heavy eyelids, doziness, torpidity
OPPOSITE: wakefulness

drowsy ADJECTIVE **1 = sleepy**, tired, lethargic, heavy, nodding, dazed, dozy, comatose, dopey *(slang)*, half asleep, somnolent, torpid: *He felt pleasantly drowsy.* **OPPOSITE:** awake
2 = peaceful, quiet, sleepy, soothing, lulling, dreamy, restful, soporific: *The drowsy air hummed with bees.*

drubbing NOUN = **beating**, defeat, hammering *(informal)*, pounding, whipping, thrashing, licking *(informal)*, pasting *(slang)*, flogging, trouncing, clobbering *(slang)*, walloping *(informal)*, pummelling

drudge NOUN = **menial**, worker, servant, slave, toiler, dogsbody *(informal)*, plodder, factotum, scullion *(archaic)*, skivvy *(chiefly Brit.)*, maid *or* man of all work

drudgery NOUN = **labour**, grind *(informal)*, sweat *(informal)*, hard work, slavery, chore, fag *(informal)*, toil, slog, donkey-work, sweated labour, menial labour, skivvying *(Brit.)*

drug NOUN **1 = medication**, medicine, remedy, physic, medicament: *The drug will treat those infected* **2 = dope** *(slang)*, narcotic *(slang)*, stimulant, opiate, dadah *(Austral. slang)*: *the problem of drug abuse*
▷ VERB = **knock out**, dope *(slang)*, numb, deaden, stupefy, anaesthetize: *They drugged the guard dog.*

drug addict NOUN = **junkie** *(informal)*, tripper *(informal)*, crack-head *(informal)*, acid head *(informal)*, dope-fiend *(slang)*, hop-head *(informal)*, head *(informal)*

drugged ADJECTIVE = **stoned**, high *(informal)*, flying *(slang)*, bombed *(slang)*, tripping *(informal, slang)*, wasted *(slang)*, smashed *(slang)*, wrecked *(slang)*, turned on *(slang)*, out of it *(slang)*, doped *(slang)*, under the influence *(informal)*, on a trip *(informal)*, spaced out *(slang)*, comatose, stupefied, out of your mind *(slang)*, zonked *(slang)*, out to it *(Austral. & N.Z. slang)*

drum VERB = **pound**, beat, tap, rap, lash, thrash, tattoo, throb, pulsate, reverberate: *Rain drummed on the roof of the car.*
drum something into someone = drive, hammer, instil, din, harp on about: *Examples were drummed into students' heads.*
drum something up = seek, attract, request, ask for, obtain, bid for, petition, round up, solicit, canvass: *drumming up business*

drunk ADJECTIVE = **intoxicated**, loaded *(slang, chiefly U.S. & Canad.)*, tight *(informal)*, canned *(slang)*, flying *(slang)*, bombed *(slang)*, stoned *(slang)*, wasted *(slang)*, smashed *(slang)*, steaming *(slang)*, wrecked *(slang)*, soaked *(informal)*, out of it *(slang)*, plastered *(slang)*, drunken, blitzed *(slang)*, lit up *(slang)*, merry *(Brit. informal)*, stewed *(slang)*, pickled *(informal)*, bladdered *(slang)*, under the influence *(informal)*, sloshed *(slang)*, tipsy, maudlin, well-oiled *(slang)*, legless *(informal)*, paralytic *(informal)*, tired and emotional *(euphemistic)*, steamboats *(Scot. slang)*, tiddly *(slang, chiefly Brit.)*, zonked *(slang)*, blotto *(slang)*, fuddled, inebriated, out to it *(Austral. & N.Z. slang)*, sottish, tanked up *(slang)*, bacchic, half seas over *(informal)*, bevvied *(dialect)*, babalas *(S. African)*, fu' *(Scot.)*, pie-eyed *(slang)*: *I got drunk and had to be carried home.*
▷ NOUN = **drunkard**, alcoholic, lush *(slang)*, boozer *(informal)*, toper, sot, soak *(slang)*, wino *(informal)*, inebriate, alko *or* alco *(Austral. slang)*: *A drunk lay in the alley.*

> **QUOTATIONS**
> Man, being reasonable, must get drunk;
> The best of Life is but intoxication
> [Lord Byron *Don Juan*]
>
> It's the wise man who stays home when he's drunk
> [Euripides *The Cyclops*]
>
> Two things a man cannot hide: that he is drunk, and that he is in love
> [Antiphanes]
>
> A man who exposes himself when he is intoxicated has not the art of getting drunk
> [Samuel Johnson]

drunkard NOUN = **drunk**, alcoholic, soak *(slang)*, drinker, lush *(slang)*, carouser, sot, tippler, toper, wino *(informal)*, dipsomaniac, alko *or* alco *(Austral. slang)*

drunken ADJECTIVE **1 = intoxicated**, smashed *(slang)*, drunk, flying *(slang)*, bombed *(slang)*, wasted *(slang)*, steaming *(slang)*, wrecked *(slang)*, out of it *(slang)*, boozing *(informal)*, blitzed *(slang)*, lit up *(slang)*, bladdered *(slang)*, under the influence *(informal)*, tippling, toping, red-nosed, legless *(informal)*, paralytic *(informal)*, steamboats *(Scot. slang)*, zonked *(slang)*, bibulous, blotto *(slang)*, inebriate, out to it *(Austral. & N.Z. slang)*, sottish, bevvied *(dialect)*, (gin-)sodden: *Drunken yobs smashed shop windows.* **2 = boozy**, dissipated *(informal)*, riotous, debauched, dionysian, orgiastic, bacchanalian, bacchic, saturnalian: *A loud, drunken party was raging nearby.*

drunkenness NOUN **= intoxication**, alcoholism, intemperance, inebriation, dipsomania, tipsiness, insobriety, bibulousness, sottishness

QUOTATIONS

Drink moderately, for drunkenness neither keeps a secret, nor observes a promise
[Miguel de Cervantes *Don Quixote*]

What does drunkenness not accomplish? It unlocks secrets, confirms our hopes, urges the indolent into battle, lifts the burden from anxious minds, teaches new arts
[Horace *Epistles*]

dry ADJECTIVE **1 = dehydrated**, dried-up, arid, torrid, parched, desiccated, waterless, juiceless, sapless, moistureless: *a hard, dry desert landscape* **OPPOSITE:** wet **2 = dried**, crisp, withered, brittle, shrivelled, crispy, parched, desiccated, sun-baked: *She heard the rustle of dry leaves.* **3 = thirsty**, parched: *She was suddenly dry.* **4 = sarcastic**, cutting, sharp, keen, cynical, low-key, sly, sardonic, deadpan, droll, ironical, quietly humorous: *He is renowned for his dry wit.* **5 = dull**, boring, tedious, commonplace, dreary, tiresome, monotonous, run-of-the-mill, humdrum, unimaginative, uninteresting, mind-numbing, ho-hum *(informal)*: *The work was very dry and dull* **OPPOSITE:** interesting **6 = plain**, simple, bare, basic, pure, stark, unembellished: *an infuriating list of dry facts and dates*
▷ VERB **1 = drain**, make dry: *Wash and dry the lettuce.* **2** *(often with* **out***)* **= dehydrate**, make dry, desiccate, sear, parch, dehumidify: *They bought a machine to dry the wood and cut costs.* **OPPOSITE:** wet
dry out *or* **up = become dry**, harden, wither, mummify, shrivel up, wizen: *The pollen dries up and becomes hard.*

dryness NOUN **1 = aridity**, drought, dehydration, aridness, dehumidification, waterlessness, moisturelessness, parchedness: *the parched dryness of the air* **2 = thirstiness**, thirst, parchedness: *Symptoms include dryness of the mouth.*

dual ADJECTIVE **= twofold**, double, twin, matched, coupled, paired, duplicate, binary, duplex

duality NOUN **= dualism**, dichotomy, polarity, doubleness, biformity, duplexity

dub VERB **= name**, call, term, style, label, nickname, designate, christen, denominate

dubious ADJECTIVE **1 = suspect**, suspicious, crooked, dodgy *(Brit., Austral. & N.Z. informal)*, questionable, unreliable, shady *(informal)*, unscrupulous, fishy *(informal)*, disreputable, untrustworthy, undependable: *dubious business dealings* **OPPOSITE:** trustworthy **2 = unsure**, uncertain, suspicious, hesitating, doubtful, sceptical, tentative, wavering, hesitant, undecided, unconvinced, iffy *(informal)*, leery *(slang)*, distrustful, in two minds *(informal)*: *My parents were a bit dubious about it all.* **OPPOSITE:** sure **3 = doubtful**, questionable, ambiguous, debatable, moot, arguable, equivocal, open to question, disputable: *This is a very dubious honour.*

duck VERB **1 = bob**, drop, lower, bend, bow, dodge, crouch, stoop: *He ducked in time to save his head from the blow.* **2 = dodge**, avoid, escape, evade, elude, sidestep, circumvent, shirk, body-swerve *(Scot.)*: *He had ducked the confrontation.* **3 = dunk**, wet, plunge, dip, submerge, immerse, douse, souse: *She splashed around in the pool trying to duck him.*

duct NOUN **= pipe**, channel, passage, tube, canal, funnel, conduit

dud NOUN **= failure**, flop *(informal)*, washout *(informal)*, clinker *(slang, chiefly U.S.)*, clunker *(informal)*: *He's been a dud from day one.*
▷ ADJECTIVE **= faulty**, broken, failed, damaged, bust *(informal)*, not working, useless, flawed, impaired, duff *(Brit. informal)*, worthless, defective, imperfect, malfunctioning, out of order, unsound, not functioning, valueless, on the blink, inoperative, kaput *(informal)*: *He replaced a dud valve.*

due ADJECTIVE **1 = expected**, scheduled, expected to arrive: *The results are due at the end of the month.* **2 = fitting**, deserved, appropriate, just, right, becoming, fit, justified, suitable, merited, proper, obligatory, rightful, requisite, well-earned, bounden: *Treat them with due attention.* **3 = payable**, outstanding, owed, owing, unpaid, in arrears: *I've got a tax rebate due.*
▷ NOUN **= right(s)**, privilege, deserts, merits, prerogative, comeuppance *(informal)*: *No doubt he felt it was his due.*
▷ ADVERB **= directly**, dead, straight, exactly, undeviatingly: *They headed due north.*

USAGE

For years people have been debating the use of *due to* in the sense 'because of'. Purists claimed that a sentence such as *the late arrival of the 10.15 train from Guildford is due to snow on the lines* was correct, while *the trains are running late due to snow on the lines* was incorrect. Their reasoning was that as an adjective, *due* should modify a noun, as it does in the first sentence (the train's late *arrival* was *due to* the snow); but in the second sentence there is no specific noun that the word *due* can be said to modify. Few people nowadays would object strongly to the use of *due* in the second sentence, but if you want to avoid any possibility of this, you may find it preferable to replace it with an alternative that is not the subject of debate, such as *because of*.

duel NOUN **1 = single combat**, affair of honour: *He killed a man in a duel.* **2 = contest**, fight, competition, clash, encounter, engagement, rivalry: *sporadic artillery duels*
▷ VERB **= fight**, struggle, clash, compete, contest, contend, vie with, lock horns: *We duelled for two years.*

dues PLURAL NOUN **= membership fee**, charges, fee, contribution, levy

duff ADJECTIVE **= bad**, poor, useless, pathetic, inferior, worthless, unsatisfactory, defective, deficient, imperfect, substandard, low-rent *(informal, chiefly U.S.)*, poxy *(slang)*, pants *(informal)*, bodger *or* bodgie *(Austral. slang)*

duffer NOUN **= clot**, blunderer *(Brit. informal)*, booby, clod, oaf, bungler, galoot *(slang, chiefly U.S.)*, lubber, lummox *(informal)*

dulcet ADJECTIVE **= sweet**, pleasing, musical, charming, pleasant, honeyed, delightful, soothing, agreeable, harmonious, melodious, mellifluous, euphonious, mellifluent

dull ADJECTIVE **1 = boring**, tedious, dreary, flat, dry, plain, commonplace, tiresome, monotonous, prosaic, run-of-the-mill, humdrum, unimaginative, dozy, uninteresting, mind-numbing, ho-hum *(informal)*, vapid, as dry as dust: *They can both be rather dull.* **OPPOSITE:** exciting **2 = lifeless**, dead, heavy, slow, indifferent, sluggish, insensitive, apathetic, listless, unresponsive, passionless, insensible: *We all feel dull and sleepy between 1 and 3pm.* **OPPOSITE:** lively **3 = drab**, faded, muted, subdued, feeble, murky, sombre, toned-down, subfusc: *The stamp was a dull blue colour.* **4 = cloudy**, dim, gloomy, dismal, overcast, leaden, turbid: *It's always dull and raining.* **OPPOSITE:** bright **5 = muted**, faint, suppressed, subdued, stifled, indistinct: *The coffin was closed with a dull thud.* **6 = blunt**, dulled, blunted,

not keen, not sharp, edgeless, unsharpened: *using the dull edge of her knife* **OPPOSITE:** sharp
▷ VERB **1 = relieve**, blunt, lessen, moderate, soften, alleviate, allay, mitigate, assuage, take the edge off, palliate: *They gave him morphine to dull the pain.* **2 = cloud over**, darken, grow dim, become cloudy: *Her eyes dulled and she gazed blankly.* **3 = dampen**, reduce, check, depress, moderate, discourage, stifle, lessen, smother, sadden, dishearten, dispirit, deject: *Her illness failed to dull her optimism.*

d

dullness NOUN **1 = tediousness**, monotony, banality, flatness, dreariness, vapidity, insipidity: *the dullness of their routine life* **OPPOSITE:** interest **2 = stupidity**, thickness, slowness, dimness, obtuseness, doziness *(Brit. informal)*, dim-wittedness, dopiness *(slang)*: *his dullness of mind* **OPPOSITE:** intelligence **3 = drabness**, greyness, dimness, gloominess, dinginess, colourlessness: *the dullness of an old painting* **OPPOSITE:** brilliance

duly ADVERB **1 = properly**, fittingly, correctly, appropriately, accordingly, suitably, deservedly, rightfully, decorously, befittingly: *He duly apologized for his behaviour.* **2 = on time**, promptly, in good time, punctually, at the proper time: *The engineer duly arrived, expecting to have to repair the boiler.*

dumb ADJECTIVE **1 = unable to speak**, mute: *a young deaf and dumb man* **OPPOSITE:** articulate **2 = silent**, mute, speechless, inarticulate, tongue-tied, wordless, voiceless, soundless, at a loss for words, mum: *We were all struck dumb for a minute.* **3 = stupid**, thick, dull, foolish, dense, dozy *(Brit. informal)*, dim, obtuse, unintelligent, asinine, braindead *(informal)*, dim-witted *(informal)*: *I came up with this dumb idea.* **OPPOSITE:** clever

dumbfounded ADJECTIVE **= amazed**, stunned, astonished, confused, overcome, overwhelmed, staggered, thrown, startled, at sea, dumb, bewildered, astounded, breathless, confounded, taken aback, speechless, bowled over *(informal)*, gobsmacked *(Brit. slang)*, flabbergasted *(informal)*, nonplussed, lost for words, flummoxed, thunderstruck, knocked sideways *(informal)*, knocked for six *(informal)*

dummy NOUN **1 = model**, figure, mannequin, form, manikin, lay figure: *a shop-window dummy* **2 = imitation**, copy, duplicate, sham, counterfeit, replica: *The police video camera was a dummy.* **3 = fool**, jerk *(slang, chiefly U.S. & Canad.)*, idiot, plank *(Brit. slang)*, charlie *(Brit. informal)*, berk *(Brit. slang)*, wally *(slang)*, prat *(slang)*, plonker *(slang)*, coot, geek *(slang)*, dunce, oaf, simpleton, dullard, dimwit *(informal)*, dipstick *(Brit. slang)*, gonzo *(slang)*, schmuck *(U.S. slang)*, dork *(slang)*, nitwit *(informal)*, dolt, blockhead, divvy *(Brit. slang)*, pillock *(Brit. slang)*, dweeb *(U.S. slang)*, fathead *(informal)*, weenie *(U.S. informal)*, eejit *(Scot. & Irish)*, dumb-ass *(slang)*, numpty *(Scot. informal)*, doofus *(slang, chiefly U.S.)*, lamebrain *(informal)*, nerd or nurd *(slang)*, numbskull or numskull, dorba or dorb *(Austral. slang)*, bogan *(Austral. slang)*: *He's no dummy, this guy.*
▷ ADJECTIVE **= imitation**, false, fake, artificial, mock, bogus, simulated, sham, phoney or phony *(informal)*: *Soldiers were still using dummy guns.*

dummy run NOUN **= practice**, trial, dry run: *They do a dummy run with the brakes.*

dump VERB **1 = drop**, deposit, throw down, let fall, fling down: *We dumped our bags on the table.* **2 = get rid of**, tip, discharge, dispose of, unload, jettison, empty out, coup *(Scot.)*, throw away or out: *Untreated sewage is dumped into the sea.* **3 = scrap**, axe *(informal)*, get rid of, abolish, junk *(informal)*, put an end to, discontinue, jettison, put paid to: *Ministers believed it was vital to dump the tax.*
▷ NOUN **1 = rubbish tip**, tip, junkyard, rubbish heap, refuse heap: *The walled garden was used as a dump.* **2 = pigsty**, hole *(informal)*, joint *(slang)*, slum, shack, shanty, hovel: *'What a dump!' she said.*

dumps PLURAL NOUN
down in the dumps = down, low, blue, sad, unhappy, low-spirited, discouraged, fed up, moody, pessimistic, melancholy, glum, dejected, despondent, dispirited, downcast, morose, crestfallen, downhearted

dumpy ADJECTIVE **= podgy**, homely, short, plump, squat, stout, chunky, chubby, tubby, roly-poly, pudgy, squab, fubsy *(archaic, dialect)*

dunce NOUN **= simpleton**, moron, duffer *(informal)*, bonehead *(slang)*, loon *(informal)*, goose *(informal)*, ass, donkey, oaf, dullard, dimwit *(informal)*, ignoramus, nitwit *(informal)*, dolt, blockhead, halfwit, nincompoop, fathead *(informal)*, dunderhead, lamebrain *(informal)*, thickhead, numbskull or numskull

dungeon NOUN **= prison**, cell, cage, vault, lockup, oubliette, calaboose *(U.S. informal)*, donjon, boob *(Austral. slang)*

dunny NOUN **= toilet**, lavatory, bathroom, loo *(Brit. informal)*, W.C., bog *(slang)*, Gents or Ladies, can *(U.S. & Canad. slang)*, john *(slang, chiefly U.S. & Canad.)*, head(s) *(Nautical, slang)*, throne *(informal)*, closet, privy, cloakroom *(Brit.)*, urinal, latrine, washroom, powder room, crapper *(taboo, slang)*, water closet, khazi *(slang)*, pissoir *(French)*, little boy's room or little girl's room *(informal)*, (public) convenience, bogger *(Austral. slang)*, brasco *(Austral. slang)*

dupe NOUN **= victim**, mug *(Brit. slang)*, sucker *(slang)*, pigeon *(slang)*, sap *(slang)*, gull, pushover *(slang)*, fall guy *(informal)*, simpleton: *an innocent dupe in a political scandal*
▷ VERB **= deceive**, trick, cheat, con *(informal)*, kid *(informal)*, rip off *(slang)*, hoax, defraud, beguile, gull *(archaic)*, delude, swindle, outwit, bamboozle *(informal)*, hoodwink, take for a ride *(informal)*, pull a fast one on *(informal)*, cozen, scam *(slang)*: *Some of the offenders duped the psychologists.*

duplicate ADJECTIVE **= identical**, matched, matching, twin, corresponding, twofold: *a duplicate copy*
▷ NOUN **1 = copy**, facsimile: *I've lost my card and have to get a duplicate.* **2 = photocopy**, copy, reproduction, replica, Xerox®, carbon copy, Photostat®: *Enclosed is a duplicate of the invoice we sent you last month.*
▷ VERB **1 = repeat**, reproduce, echo, copy, clone, replicate: *Scientists hope the work done can be duplicated elswhere.* **2 = copy**, photocopy, Xerox®, Photostat®: *He was duplicating some articles.*

duplicity NOUN **= deceit**, fraud, deception, hypocrisy, dishonesty, guile, artifice, falsehood, double-dealing, chicanery, perfidy, dissimulation **OPPOSITE:** honesty

durable ADJECTIVE **1 = hard-wearing**, strong, tough, sound, substantial, reliable, resistant, sturdy, long-lasting: *Fine bone china is strong and durable.* **OPPOSITE:** fragile **2 = enduring**, lasting, permanent, continuing, firm, fast, fixed, constant, abiding, dependable, unwavering, unfaltering: *We were unable to establish any durable agreement.*

duration NOUN **= length**, time, period, term, stretch, extent, spell, span, time frame, timeline

duress NOUN **= pressure**, threat, constraint, compulsion, coercion

dusk NOUN **1 = twilight**, evening, evo *(Austral. slang)*, nightfall, sunset, dark, sundown, eventide, gloaming *(Scot. poetic)*: *We arrived home at dusk.* **OPPOSITE:** dawn **2 = shade**, darkness, gloom, obscurity, murk, shadowiness: *She turned and disappeared into the dusk.*

dusky ADJECTIVE **1 = dim**, twilight, shady, shadowy, gloomy, murky, cloudy, overcast, crepuscular, darkish, twilit, tenebrous, caliginous *(archaic)*: *He was walking down the road one dusky evening.* **2 = dark**, swarthy, dark-complexioned: *I could see dusky girls with flowers about their necks.*

dust NOUN **1 = grime**, grit, powder, powdery dirt: *I could see a thick layer of dust on the stairs.* **2 = earth**, ground, soil, dirt: *Your trousers will get dirty if you sit down in the dust.* **3 = particles**, fine fragments: *The air was black with coal dust.*
▷ VERB **= sprinkle**, cover, powder, spread, spray, scatter, sift, dredge: *Lightly dust the fish with flour.*

dusty ADJECTIVE **1 = dirty**, grubby, unclean, unswept, undusted: *The books looked dusty and unused.*
2 = powdery, sandy, chalky, crumbly, granular, friable: *Inside the box was only a dusty substance.*

dutiful ADJECTIVE **= conscientious**, devoted, obedient, respectful, compliant, submissive, docile, deferential, reverential, filial, punctilious, duteous *(archaic)*: *The days of the dutiful wife are over.*
OPPOSITE: disrespectful

duty NOUN **1 = responsibility**, job, task, work, calling, business, service, office, charge, role, function, mission, province, obligation, assignment, pigeon *(informal)*, onus: *My duty is to look after the animals.* **2 = tax**, customs, toll, levy, tariff, excise, due, impost: *Duty on imports would also be reduced.*
off duty = off work, off, free, on holiday, at leisure: *I'm off duty.*
on duty = at work, busy, engaged, on active service: *Extra staff had been put on duty.*

QUOTATIONS

Our duty is to be useful, not according to our desires but according to our powers
[Henri Frédéric Amiel *Journal*]

Without duty, life is soft and boneless; it cannot hold itself together
[Joseph Joubert *Pensées*]

When a stupid man is doing something that he is ashamed of, he always declares that it is his duty
[George Bernard Shaw *Caesar and Cleopatra*]

Do your duty, and leave the outcome to the Gods
[Pierre Corneille *Horace*]

England expects that every man will do his duty
[Horatio Nelson *signal at the Battle of Trafalgar*]

Duty, honour! We make these words say whatever we want, the same as we do with parrots
[Alfred Capus *Mariage Bourgeois*]

dwarf NOUN **= gnome**, midget, Lilliputian, Tom Thumb, munchkin *(informal, chiefly U.S.)*, homunculus, manikin, hop-o'-my-thumb, pygmy or pigmy: *With the aid of magic the dwarfs created a wonderful rope.*
▷ ADJECTIVE **= miniature**, small, baby, tiny, pocket, dwarfed, diminutive, petite, bonsai, pint-sized, undersized, teeny-weeny, Lilliputian, teensy-weensy: *dwarf shrubs*
▷ VERB **1 = tower above** *or* **over**, dominate, overlook, stand over, loom over, stand head and shoulders above: *The huge sign dwarfed his figure.*
2 = eclipse, tower above *or* over, put in the shade, diminish: *completely dwarfing the achievements of others*

SNOW WHITE'S SEVEN DWARFS

Bashful	Grumpy	Sneezy
Doc	Happy	
Dopey	Sleepy	

dwell VERB **= live**, stay, reside, rest, quarter, settle, lodge, abide, hang out *(informal)*, sojourn, establish yourself
dwell on *or* **upon something = go on about**, emphasize *(informal)*, elaborate on, linger over, harp on about, be engrossed in, expatiate on, continue to think about, tarry over: *I'd rather not dwell on the past.*

dwelling NOUN **= home**, house, residence, abode, quarters, establishment, lodging, pad *(slang)*, habitation, domicile, dwelling house, whare *(N.Z.)*

dwindle VERB **= lessen**, fall, decline, contract, sink, fade, weaken, shrink, diminish, decrease, decay, wither, wane, subside, ebb, die down, die out, abate, shrivel, peter out, die away, waste away, taper off, grow less
OPPOSITE: increase

dye NOUN **= colouring**, colour, pigment, stain, tint, tinge, colorant: *bottles of hair dye*
▷ VERB **= colour**, stain, tint, tinge, pigment, tincture: *The woman spun and dyed the wool.*

dying ADJECTIVE **1 = near death**, going, failing, fading, doomed, expiring, ebbing, near the end, moribund, fading fast, in extremis *(Latin)*, at death's door, not long for this world, on your deathbed, breathing your last: *He is a dying man.*
2 = final, last, parting, departing: *the dying wishes of her mother* **3 = failing**, declining, sinking, foundering, diminishing, decreasing, dwindling, subsiding: *Shipbuilding is a dying business.*

dynamic ADJECTIVE **= energetic**, spirited, powerful, active, vital, driving, electric, go-ahead, lively, magnetic, vigorous, animated, high-powered, forceful, go-getting *(informal)*, tireless, indefatigable, high-octane *(informal)*, zippy *(informal)*, full of beans *(informal)*
OPPOSITE: apathetic

dynamism NOUN **= energy**, go *(informal)*, drive, push *(informal)*, initiative, enterprise, pep, zip *(informal)*, vigour, zap *(slang)*, get-up-and-go *(informal)*, brio, liveliness, forcefulness

dynasty NOUN **= empire**, house, rule, regime, sovereignty

d

Ee

e

each ADJECTIVE **= every**, every single: *Each book is beautifully illustrated.*
▷ PRONOUN **= every one**, all, each one, each and every one, one and all: *Three doctors each had a different diagnosis.*
▷ ADVERB **= apiece**, individually, singly, for each, to each, respectively, per person, from each, per head, per capita: *The children were given one each.*

> **USAGE**
> *Each* is a singular pronoun and should be used with a singular verb – for example, *each of the candidates was interviewed separately* (not *were interviewed separately*).

eager ADJECTIVE **1** *(often with* **to** *or* **for***)* **= anxious**, keen, raring, hungry, intent, yearning, impatient, itching, thirsty, zealous: *Robert was eager to talk about life in the Army.*
OPPOSITE: unenthusiastic **2 = keen**, interested, earnest, intense, enthusiastic, passionate, ardent, avid *(informal)*, fervent, zealous, fervid, keen as mustard, bright-eyed and bushy-tailed *(informal)*: *He looked at the crowd of eager faces around him.*
OPPOSITE: uninterested

eagerness NOUN **1 = longing**, anxiety, hunger, yearning, zeal, impatience, impetuosity, avidity: *an eagerness to learn* **2 = passion**, interest, enthusiasm, intensity, fervour, ardour, earnestness, keenness, heartiness, thirst, intentness: *the voice of a woman speaking with breathless eagerness*

ear NOUN **1 = sensitivity**, taste, discrimination, appreciation, musical perception: *He has a fine ear for music.* **2 = attention**, hearing, regard, notice, consideration, observation, awareness, heed: *The lobbyists have the ear of influential western leaders.*
lend an ear = listen, pay attention, heed, take notice, pay heed, hearken *(archaic)*, give ear: *Please lend an ear for a moment or two.*
turn a deaf ear to something = ignore, reject, overlook, neglect, disregard, pass over, take no notice of, be oblivious to, pay no attention to, give the cold shoulder to
▸ *related adjective:* aural

early ADVERB **1 = in good time**, beforehand, ahead of schedule, in advance, with time to spare, betimes *(archaic)*: *She arrived early to get a good seat.*
OPPOSITE: late **2 = too soon**, before the usual time, prematurely, ahead of time: *The snow came early that year.*
OPPOSITE: late
▷ ADJECTIVE **1 = first**, opening, earliest, initial, introductory: *the book's early chapters* **2 = premature**, forward, advanced, untimely, unseasonable: *I decided to take early retirement.* **OPPOSITE:** belated
3 = primitive, first, earliest, young, original, undeveloped, primordial, primeval: *early man's cultural development*
OPPOSITE: developed

> **PROVERBS**
> *The early bird catches the worm*
> *Early to bed and early to rise, makes a man healthy, wealthy, and wise*

earmark VERB **1 = set aside**, reserve, label, flag, tag, allocate, designate, mark out, keep back: *Extra money has been earmarked for the new projects.*
2 = mark out, identify, designate: *The pit was one of the 31 earmarked for closure by the Trade and Industry Secretary.*

earn VERB **1 = be paid**, make, get, receive, draw, gain, net, collect, bring in, gross, procure, clear, get paid, take home: *The dancers can earn up to £130 for each session.* **2 = deserve**, win, gain, attain, justify, merit, warrant, be entitled to, reap, be worthy of: *Companies must earn a reputation for honesty.*

earnest ADJECTIVE **1 = serious**, keen, grave, intense, steady, dedicated, eager, enthusiastic, passionate, sincere, thoughtful, solemn, ardent, fervent, impassioned, zealous, staid, keen as mustard: *Ella was a pious, earnest young woman.*
OPPOSITE: frivolous **2 = determined**, firm, dogged, constant, urgent, intent, persistent, ardent, persevering, resolute, heartfelt, zealous, vehement, wholehearted: *Despite their earnest efforts, they failed to win support.* **OPPOSITE:** half-hearted

earnestness NOUN **1 = seriousness**, resolution, passion, enthusiasm, warmth, gravity, urgency, zeal, sincerity, fervour, eagerness, ardour, keenness: *He spoke with intense earnestness.* **2 = determination**, resolve, urgency, zeal, ardour, vehemence: *the earnestness of their struggle for freedom*

earnings PLURAL NOUN **= income**, pay, wages, revenue, reward, proceeds, salary, receipts, return, remuneration, takings, stipend, take-home pay, emolument, gross pay, net pay

earth NOUN **1 = world**, planet, globe, sphere, orb, earthly sphere, terrestrial sphere: *The space shuttle returned safely to earth today.* **2 = ground**, land, dry land, terra firma: *The earth shook under our feet.*
3 = soil, ground, land, dust, mould, clay, dirt, turf, sod, silt, topsoil, clod, loam: *The road winds through parched earth, scrub and cactus.*
▸ *related adjective:* terrestrial

> **QUOTATIONS**
> To see the earth as we now see it, small and beautiful in that eternal silence where it floats, is to see ourselves as riders on the earth together, brothers on that bright loveliness in the unending night
> [Archibald MacLeish *Riders on Earth*]

earthenware NOUN **= crockery**, pots, ceramics, pottery, terracotta, crocks, faience, maiolica

earthly ADJECTIVE **1 = worldly**, material, physical, secular, mortal, mundane, terrestrial, temporal, human, materialistic, profane, telluric, sublunary, non-spiritual, tellurian, terrene: *They lived in an earthly paradise.* **OPPOSITE:** spiritual
2 = sensual, worldly, base, physical, gross, low, fleshly, bodily, vile, sordid, carnal: *He has forsworn all earthly pleasures for the duration of a season.*
3 = possible, likely, practical, feasible, conceivable, imaginable: *What earthly reason would they have for lying?*

earthy ADJECTIVE **1 = crude**, coarse, raunchy *(slang)*, lusty, bawdy, ribald: *his extremely earthy brand of humour*
2 = claylike, soil-like: *Strong, earthy colours add to the effect.*

ease NOUN **1 = straightforwardness**, simplicity, readiness: *For ease of reference, only the relevant extracts of the regulations are included.* **2 = comfort**, luxury, leisure, relaxation, prosperity, affluence, rest, repose, restfulness: *She lived a life of ease.*
OPPOSITE: hardship **3 = peace of mind**, peace, content, quiet, comfort, happiness, enjoyment, serenity, tranquillity, contentment, calmness, quietude: *Qigong exercises promote ease of mind and body.* **OPPOSITE:** agitation
4 = naturalness, informality, freedom, liberty, unaffectedness, unconstraint, unreservedness, relaxedness: *Co-stars particularly appreciate his ease on the set.*
OPPOSITE: awkwardness
▷ VERB **1 = relieve**, calm, moderate, soothe, lessen, alleviate, appease, lighten, lower, allay, relax, still, mitigate, assuage, pacify, mollify, tranquillize, palliate: *I gave him some brandy to ease the pain.*
OPPOSITE: aggravate **2** *(often with* **off** *or* **up***)* **= reduce**, moderate, weaken, diminish, decrease, slow down, dwindle, lessen, die down, abate,

slacken, grow less, de-escalate: *The heavy snow had eased a little.* **3 = move carefully**, edge, guide, slip, inch, slide, creep, squeeze, steer, manoeuvre: *I eased my way towards the door.* **4 = facilitate**, further, aid, forward, smooth, assist, speed up, simplify, make easier, expedite, lessen the labour of: *The information pack is designed to ease the process of making a will.* OPPOSITE: hinder

easily ADVERB **1 = without a doubt**, clearly, surely, certainly, obviously, definitely, plainly, absolutely, undoubtedly, unquestionably, undeniably, unequivocally, far and away, indisputably, beyond question, indubitably, doubtlessly: *It could easily be another year before we see any change.* **2 = without difficulty**, smoothly, readily, comfortably, effortlessly, simply, with ease, straightforwardly, without trouble, standing on your head, with your eyes closed *or* shut: *Wear clothes you can remove easily.*

easy ADJECTIVE **1 = simple**, straightforward, no trouble, not difficult, effortless, painless, clear, light, uncomplicated, child's play *(informal)*, plain sailing, undemanding, a pushover *(slang)*, a piece of cake *(informal)*, no bother, a bed of roses, easy-peasy *(slang)*: *This is not an easy task.* OPPOSITE: hard **2 = untroubled**, contented, relaxed, satisfied, calm, peaceful, serene, tranquil, quiet, undisturbed, unworried: *I was not altogether easy in my mind about this decision.* **3 = relaxed**, friendly, open, natural, pleasant, casual, informal, laid-back *(informal)*, graceful, gracious, unaffected, easy-going, affable, unpretentious, unforced, undemanding, unconstrained, unceremonious: *She laughed and joked and made easy conversation with everyone.* OPPOSITE: stiff **4 = carefree**, comfortable, leisurely, trouble-free, untroubled, cushy *(informal)* OPPOSITE: difficult **5 = tolerant**, light, liberal, soft, flexible, mild, laid-back *(informal)*, indulgent, easy-going, lenient, permissive, unoppressive: *I guess we've always been too easy with our children.* OPPOSITE: strict **6 = accommodating**, yielding, manageable, easy-going, compliant, amenable, submissive, docile, pliant, tractable, biddable: *'Your father was not an easy child,' she told me.* OPPOSITE: difficult **7 = vulnerable**, soft, naive, susceptible, gullible, exploitable: *She was an easy target for con-men.* **8 = leisurely**, relaxed, comfortable, moderate, unhurried, undemanding: *the easy pace set by pilgrims heading to Canterbury*

> PROVERBS
> *Easy come, easy go*

easy-going ADJECTIVE **= relaxed**, easy, liberal, calm, flexible, mild, casual, tolerant, laid-back *(informal)*, indulgent, serene, lenient, carefree, placid, unconcerned, amenable, permissive, happy-go-lucky, unhurried, nonchalant, insouciant, even-tempered, easy-peasy *(slang)*, chilled *(informal)* OPPOSITE: tense

eat VERB **1 = consume**, swallow, chew, scoff *(slang)*, devour, munch, tuck into *(informal)*, put away, gobble, polish off *(informal)*, wolf down: *She was eating a sandwich.* **2 = have a meal**, lunch, breakfast, dine, snack, feed, graze *(informal)*, have lunch, have dinner, have breakfast, nosh *(slang)*, take food, have supper, break bread, chow down *(slang)*, take nourishment: *Let's go out to eat.*

> QUOTATIONS
> One should eat to live, and not live to eat
> [Molière *L'Avare*]
> Most vegetarians I ever see looked enough like their food to be classed as cannibals
> [Finley Peter Donne]

eavesdrop VERB **= listen in**, spy, overhear, bug *(informal)*, pry, tap in, snoop *(informal)*, earwig *(informal)*

ebb VERB **1 = flow back**, go out, withdraw, sink, retreat, fall back, wane, recede, fall away: *We hopped from rock to rock as the tide ebbed from the causeway.* **2 = decline**, drop, sink, flag, weaken, shrink, diminish, decrease, deteriorate, decay, dwindle, lessen, subside, degenerate, fall away, fade away, abate, peter out, slacken: *There were occasions when my enthusiasm ebbed.*
▷ NOUN **= flowing back**, going out, withdrawal, retreat, wane, waning, regression, low water, low tide, ebb tide, outgoing tide, falling tide, receding tide: *We decided to leave on the ebb at six o'clock next morning.*

ebony ADJECTIVE **= black**, dark, jet, raven, sable, pitch-black, jet-black, inky, swarthy, coal-black

ebullient ADJECTIVE **= exuberant**, excited, enthusiastic, buoyant, exhilarated, elated, irrepressible, vivacious, effervescent, effusive, in high spirits, zestful

eccentric ADJECTIVE **= odd**, strange, bizarre, weird, peculiar, abnormal, queer *(informal)*, irregular, uncommon, quirky, singular, unconventional, idiosyncratic, off-the-wall *(slang)*, outlandish, whimsical, rum *(Brit. slang)*, capricious, anomalous, freakish, aberrant, wacko *(slang)*, outré, daggy *(Austral. & N.Z. informal)*: *an eccentric character who wears a beret and sunglasses* OPPOSITE: normal
▷ NOUN **= crank** *(informal)*, character *(informal)*, nut *(slang)*, freak *(informal)*, flake *(slang, chiefly U.S.)*, oddity, oddball *(informal)*, loose cannon, nonconformist, wacko *(slang)*, case *(informal)*, screwball *(slang, chiefly U.S. & Canad.)*, card *(informal)*, odd fish *(informal)*, kook *(U.S. & Canad. informal)*, queer fish *(Brit. informal)*, rum customer *(Brit. slang)*, weirdo *or* weirdie *(informal)*, gink *(slang)*: *My other friend was a real English eccentric.*

eccentricity NOUN **1 = oddity**, peculiarity, strangeness, irregularity, weirdness, singularity, oddness, waywardness, nonconformity, capriciousness, unconventionality, queerness *(informal)*, bizarreness, whimsicality, freakishness, outlandishness: *She is unusual to the point of eccentricity.* **2 = foible**, anomaly, abnormality, quirk, oddity, aberration, peculiarity, idiosyncrasy: *We all have our little eccentricities.*

ecclesiastical ADJECTIVE **= clerical**, religious, church, churchly, priestly, spiritual, holy, divine, pastoral, sacerdotal

echelon NOUN **= level**, place, office, position, step, degree, rank, grade, tier, rung

echo NOUN **1 = reverberation**, ringing, repetition, answer, resonance, resounding: *He heard nothing but the echoes of his own voice in the cave.* **2 = copy**, reflection, clone, reproduction, imitation, duplicate, double, reiteration: *Their cover version is just a pale echo of the real thing.* **3 = reminder**, suggestion, trace, hint, recollection, vestige, evocation, intimation: *The accident has echoes of past disasters.*
▷ VERB **1 = reverberate**, repeat, resound, ring, resonate: *The distant crash of bombs echoes through the whole city.* **2 = recall**, reflect, copy, mirror, resemble, reproduce, parrot, imitate, reiterate, ape: *Many phrases in the last chapter echo earlier passages.*

eclectic ADJECTIVE **= diverse**, general, broad, varied, comprehensive, extensive, wide-ranging, selective, diversified, manifold, heterogeneous, catholic, all-embracing, liberal, many-sided, multifarious, dilettantish

eclipse NOUN **1 = obscuring**, covering, blocking, shading, dimming, extinction, darkening, blotting out, occultation: *a total eclipse of the sun* **2 = decline**, fall, loss, failure, weakening, deterioration, degeneration, diminution: *the eclipse of the influence of the Republican party in West Germany*
▷ VERB **1 = surpass**, exceed, overshadow, excel, transcend, outdo, outclass, outshine, leave *or* put in the shade *(informal)*: *The gramophone was eclipsed by the compact disc.* **2 = obscure**, cover, block, cloud, conceal, dim, veil, darken, shroud, extinguish, blot out: *The sun was eclipsed by the moon.*

economic ADJECTIVE **1 = financial**, business, trade, industrial, commercial, mercantile: *The pace of economic growth is picking up.* **2 = monetary**, financial, material, fiscal, budgetary, bread-and-butter *(informal)*, pecuniary: *Their country faces an economic crisis.* **3 = profitable**, successful, commercial, rewarding, productive, lucrative, worthwhile, viable, solvent, cost-effective, money-making, profit-making, remunerative: *The service will make surfing the Web an economic proposition.* **4 = economical**, fair, cheap, reasonable, modest, low-priced, inexpensive: *The new process is more economic but less environmentally friendly.*

economical ADJECTIVE **1 = economic**, fair, cheap, reasonable, modest, low-priced, inexpensive: *It is more economical to wash a full load.* **OPPOSITE:** expensive **2 = thrifty**, sparing, careful, prudent, provident, frugal, parsimonious, scrimping, economizing: *ideas for economical housekeeping* **OPPOSITE:** extravagant **3 = efficient**, sparing, cost-effective, money-saving, time-saving, work-saving, unwasteful: *the practical, economical virtues of a small hatchback* **OPPOSITE:** wasteful

economics NOUN **= finance**, commerce, the dismal science

> **QUOTATIONS**
> We have always known that heedless self-interest was bad morals; we know now that it is bad economics
> [Franklin Delano Roosevelt *First Inaugural Address*]
>
> The Dismal Science
> [Thomas Carlyle *Latter-Day Pamphlets*]

economy NOUN **1 = financial system**, financial state: *Africa's most industrialized economy* **2 = thrift**, saving, restraint, prudence, providence, husbandry, retrenchment, frugality, parsimony, thriftiness, sparingness: *They have achieved quite remarkable effects with great economy of means.*

> **QUOTATIONS**
> Economy is going without something you do want in case you should, some day, want something you probably won't want
> [Anthony Hope *The Dolly Dialogues*]
>
> Everybody is always in favour of general economy and particular expenditure
> [Anthony Eden]
>
> Take care of the pence, and the pounds will take care of themselves
> [William Lowndes]

> **PROVERBS**
> *Cut your coat according to your cloth*

ecstasy NOUN **= rapture**, delight, joy, enthusiasm, frenzy, bliss, trance, euphoria, fervour, elation, rhapsody, exaltation, transport, ravishment **OPPOSITE:** agony

> **QUOTATIONS**
> To burn always with this hard, gemlike flame, to maintain this ecstasy, is success in life
> [Walter Pater *Studies in the History of the Renaissance*]
> Take all away from me, but leave me Ecstasy,
> And I am richer then than all my Fellow Men
> [Emily Dickinson]
>
> To be bewitched is not to be saved, though all the magicians and aesthetes in the world should pronounce it to be so
> [George Santayana *The Life of Reason: Reason in Art*]

ecstatic ADJECTIVE **= rapturous**, entranced, enthusiastic, frenzied, joyous, fervent, joyful, elated, over the moon *(informal)*, overjoyed, blissful, delirious, euphoric, enraptured, on cloud nine *(informal)*, cock-a-hoop, blissed out, transported, rhapsodic, sent, walking on air, in seventh heaven, floating on air, in exaltation, in transports of delight, stoked *(Austral. & N.Z. informal)*

ecumenical, oecumenical, ecumenic *or* **oecumenic** ADJECTIVE **= unifying**, universal, non-denominational, non-sectarian, general

eddy NOUN **= swirl**, whirlpool, vortex, undertow, tideway, counter-current, counterflow: *the swirling eddies of the fast-flowing river*
▷ VERB **= swirl**, turn, roll, spin, twist, surge, revolve, whirl, billow: *The dust whirled and eddied in the sunlight.*

edge NOUN **1 = border**, side, line, limit, bound, lip, margin, outline, boundary, fringe, verge, brink, threshold, rim, brim, perimeter, contour, periphery, flange: *She was standing at the water's edge.* **2 = verge**, point, brink, threshold: *They have driven the rhino to the edge of extinction.* **3 = advantage**, lead, dominance, superiority, upper hand, head start, ascendancy, whip hand: *This could give them the edge over their oppponents.* **4 = power**, interest, force, bite, effectiveness, animation, zest, incisiveness, powerful quality: *Featuring new bands gives the show an edge.* **5 = sharpness**, point, sting, urgency, bitterness, keenness, pungency, acuteness: *There was an unpleasant edge to her voice.*
▷ VERB **1 = inch**, ease, creep, worm, slink, steal, sidle, work, move slowly: *He edged closer to the door.* **2 = border**, shape, bind, trim, fringe, rim, hem, pipe: *a chocolate brown jacket edged with yellow*
on edge = tense, excited, wired *(slang)*, nervous, eager, impatient, irritable, apprehensive, edgy, uptight *(informal)*, ill at ease, twitchy *(informal)*, tetchy, on tenterhooks, keyed up, antsy *(informal)*, adrenalized: *Ever since their arrival she had felt on edge.*

edgy ADJECTIVE **= nervous**, wired *(slang)*, anxious, tense, neurotic, irritable, touchy, uptight *(informal)*, on edge, nervy *(Brit. informal)*, ill at ease, restive, twitchy *(informal)*, irascible, tetchy, chippy *(informal)*, on tenterhooks, keyed up, antsy *(informal)*, on pins and needles, adrenalized

edible ADJECTIVE **= safe to eat**, harmless, wholesome, palatable, digestible, eatable, comestible *(rare)*, fit to eat, good **OPPOSITE:** inedible

edict NOUN **= decree**, law, act, order, ruling, demand, command, regulation, dictate, mandate, canon, manifesto, injunction, statute, fiat, ordinance, proclamation, enactment, dictum, pronouncement, ukase *(rare)*, pronunciamento

edifice NOUN **= building**, house, structure, construction, pile, erection, habitation

edify VERB **= instruct**, school, teach, inform, guide, improve, educate, nurture, elevate, enlighten, uplift

edifying ADJECTIVE **= instructive**, improving, inspiring, elevating, enlightening, uplifting, instructional

edit VERB **1 = revise**, check, improve, correct, polish, adapt, rewrite, censor, condense, annotate, rephrase, redraft, copy-edit, emend, prepare for publication, redact: *The publisher has the right to edit the book once it has been written.* **2 = put together**, select, arrange, organize, assemble, compose, rearrange, reorder: *She has edited a collection of essays.* **3 = be in charge of**, control, direct, be responsible for, be the editor of: *I used to edit the college paper in the old days.*

edition NOUN **1 = printing**, publication: *a rare first edition of a Dickens novel* **2 = copy**, impression, number: *The Christmas edition of the catalogue is out now.* **3 = version**, volume, issue **4 = programme** *(TV, Radio)*: *We'll be back in our next edition in a week's time.*

educate VERB **= teach**, school, train, coach, develop, improve, exercise, inform, discipline, rear, foster, mature, drill, tutor, instruct, cultivate, enlighten, civilize, edify, indoctrinate

educated ADJECTIVE **1 = cultured**, lettered, intellectual, learned, informed, experienced, polished, literary, sophisticated, refined, cultivated, enlightened, knowledgeable, civilized, tasteful, urbane, erudite, well-bred: *He is an educated, amiable and decent man.* **OPPOSITE:** uncultured **2 = taught**, schooled, coached, informed, tutored, instructed, nurtured, well-informed, well-read, well-taught: *The country's workforce is well educated and diligent.* **OPPOSITE:** uneducated

education NOUN **1 = teaching**, schooling, training, development, coaching, improvement, discipline, instruction, drilling, tutoring, nurture, tuition, enlightenment, erudition, indoctrination, edification: *institutions for the care and education of children* **2 = learning**, schooling, culture, breeding,

The Language of Rudyard Kipling

Rudyard Kipling (1865–1936) was a prolific author of fiction and poetry, famous for such classics as his Indian novel *Kim* and the short story collections *The Jungle Books* and the *Just So Stories*. Kipling was born in India, and much of his work is concerned with the British Empire. While his writing is at times jingoistic, there are also elements of sharp critique in his representation of imperial themes.

Many of Kipling's most famous works are considered children's classics. By far the most frequent adjective with *child* and *children* is *little*. Often *little child* is used in a simile, such as:

... as soft as the heart of a **little child**...

Likewise, *boy* appears often with *small* or *little*. *Bad* and *good* are also frequent adjectives with numerous other indicators of behaviour also appearing, in many cases as compound adjectives: *pure-souled*, *high-minded*, *pure-minded*, *right-minded* and *well-behaved*. This emphasis on rightness and purity indicates a public-school ethos common in the literature of the period. Chiming with Kipling's association with Victorian 'Boy's-own' writing and with Baden-Powell's scout movement, the usage of *girl* is far less frequent. Where *girl* appears *little* is again the most prominent modifying adjective. Others that occur emphasize appearance rather than behaviour: *red-haired* and *pretty* are the most frequent after *little*.

British is used most commonly in Kipling's work in the context of the army with *soldier*, *regiment*, and *infantry* being the nouns usually modified by it. Such a pattern reflects Kipling's recurrent focus on the military, most notable in *Kim* and in his short stories. *Indian* by contrast appears most commonly with *government*. *Imperial* is used not simply to designate something that pertains to the Empire, but also frequently as an adjective suggesting excellence, as in:

'What luck! What stupendous and **imperial** luck!' said Dick.

This usage was common in Victorian and Edwardian Britain and reveals how deeply-ingrained the idea of Empire was in the national consciousness. Interestingly, by far the most salient modifier of *country* in Kipling is *own*, illustrating both a sense of belonging and the idea of exile that often saw Kipling's characters thinking back to their *own country*.

There are numerous examples of words of Indian origin occurring in Kipling's work, many of which remain in common usage in English. *Bungalow* and *veranda* describe the architecture of the Anglo-India where much of Kipling's writing is set. *Polo* was the game of choice for the British officer class but was Asian in origin. Other Indian words that Kipling often uses have largely disappeared from English. *Sahib* and *Memsahib* were familiar designations of seniority in the context of the British Empire in India that are no longer current in the postcolonial era. Kipling often uses the archaic *thee* for 'you', a usage that was already dated by the late 19th century. This is used most regularly in Kipling's representation of the speech of his Indian characters, both human and in *The Jungle Books*, his Indian animal characters. It suggests an elaborate formality that these figures often demonstrate.

Kipling's writing is also notable for its use of colloquialism and dialect. His poetry in particular aims to catch the voices of working-class soldiers through adapting grammar and spelling to the vernacular rhythms of cockney speech. Apostrophes indicating the omission of characters, usually consonants, are consequently a recurrent feature:

'E rushes at the smoke when we let drive
An' before we know, 'e's 'acking at our 'ead;
'E's all 'ot sand an' ginger when alive,
An' 'e's generally shammin' when 'e's dead.

In a perhaps similar way, his animal stories contain many examples of onomatopoeia as Kipling aims to reproduce the texture of animal sounds, calls and movements: *ahoo*, *tunk-a-tunk*, *ngaayah!*

scholarship, civilization, cultivation, refinement

> **QUOTATIONS**
> The roots of education are bitter, but the fruit is sweet
> [Aristophanes]
>
> Education makes a people easy to lead, but difficult to drive; easy to govern, but impossible to enslave
> [Lord Henry Brougham *speech to the House of Commons*]
>
> To live for a time close to great minds is the best education
> [John Buchan *Memory Hold the Door*]
>
> Education is simply the soul of a society as it passes from one generation to another
> [G.K. Chesterton]
>
> Education made us what we are
> [C.A. Helvétus *Discours XXX*]
>
> 'Tis education forms the common mind,
> Just as the twig is bent, the tree's inclined
> [Alexander Pope *Epistles to Several Persons*]
>
> Education is something that tempers the young and consoles the old, gives wealth to the poor and adorns the rich
> [Diogenes (The Cynic)]
>
> Even while they teach, men learn
> [Seneca *Letters*]
>
> Education is what survives when what has been learnt has been forgotten
> [B.F. Skinner *Education in 1984*]
>
> To me education is a leading out of what is already there in the pupil's soul
> [Muriel Spark *The Prime of Miss Jean Brodie*]
>
> Anyone who has passed through the regular gradations of a classical education, and is not made a fool by it, may consider himself as having had a very narrow escape
> [William Hazlitt *The Ignorance of the Learned*]
>
> When you educate a man you educate an individual; when you educate a woman you educate a whole family
> [Charles D. McIver]
>
> Men must be born free; they cannot be born wise, and it is the duty of any university to make free men wise
> [Adlai Stevenson]
>
> There is no such whetstone, to sharpen a good wit and encourage a will to learning, as is praise
> [Roger Ascham *The Schoolmaster*]
>
> Education: that which discloses to the wise and disguises from the foolish their lack of understanding
> [Ambrose Bierce *The Devil's Dictionary*]
>
> Better build schoolrooms for 'the boy' than cells and gibbets for 'the man'
> [Eliza Cook *A Song for the Ragged Schools*]
>
> Man is the only creature which must be educated
> [Immanuel Kant]
>
> Ask me my three main priorities for government and I tell you: education, education, education
> [Tony Blair]
>
> Education is the most powerful weapon which you can use to change the world
> [Nelson Mandela]

educational ADJECTIVE **1 = academic**, school, learning, teaching, scholastic, pedagogical, pedagogic: *the British educational system* **2 = instructive**, useful, cultural, illuminating, enlightening, informative, instructional, didactic, edifying, educative, heuristic: *The kids had an enjoyable and educational day.*

educator NOUN **= teacher**, professor, lecturer, don, coach, guide, fellow, trainer, tutor, instructor, mentor, schoolteacher, pedagogue, edifier, educationalist *or* educationist, schoolmaster *or* schoolmistress, master *or* mistress

eerie ADJECTIVE **= uncanny**, strange, frightening, ghostly, weird, mysterious, scary *(informal)*, sinister, uneasy, fearful, awesome, unearthly, supernatural, unnatural, spooky *(informal)*, creepy *(informal)*, spectral, eldritch *(poetic)*, preternatural

efface VERB **= obliterate**, remove, destroy, cancel, wipe out, erase, eradicate, excise, delete, annihilate, raze, blot out, cross out, expunge, rub out, extirpate

effect NOUN **1 = result**, consequence, conclusion, outcome, event, issue, aftermath, fruit, end result, upshot: *the psychological effects of head injuries* **2 = impression**, feeling, impact, influence: *The whole effect is cool, light and airy* **3 = purpose**, meaning, impression, sense, import, drift, intent, essence, thread, tenor, purport: *He told me to get lost, or words to that effect.* **4 = implementation**, force, action, performance, operation, enforcement, execution: *We are now resuming diplomatic relations with Syria with immediate effect.*
▷ VERB **= bring about**, make, cause, produce, create, complete, achieve, perform, carry out, fulfil, accomplish, execute, initiate, give rise to, consummate, actuate, effectuate: *Prospects for effecting real political change have taken a step backward.*
in effect = in fact, really, actually, essentially, virtually, effectively, in reality, in truth, as good as, in actual fact, to all intents and purposes, in all but name, in actuality, for practical purposes: *The deal would create, in effect, the world's biggest airline.*
put, bring *or* **carry into effect = implement**, perform, carry out, fulfil, enforce, execute, bring about, put into action, put into operation, bring into force: *a decree bringing these political reforms into effect*
take effect = produce results, work, begin, come into force, become operative: *The ban takes effect from July.*

> **USAGE**
> It is quite common for the verb *effect* to be mistakenly used where *affect* is intended. *Effect* is relatively uncommon and rather formal, and is a synonym of 'bring about'. Conversely, the noun *effect* is quite often mistakenly written with an initial *a*. The following are correct: *the group is still recovering from the effects of the recession; they really are powerless to effect any change*. The next two examples are incorrect: *the full affects of the shutdown won't be felt for several more days; men whose lack of hair doesn't effect their self-esteem.*

effective ADJECTIVE **1 = efficient**, successful, useful, active, capable, valuable, helpful, adequate, productive, operative, competent, serviceable, efficacious, effectual: *Antibiotics are effective against this organism.* **OPPOSITE:** ineffective **2 = powerful**, strong, convincing, persuasive, telling, impressive, compelling, potent, forceful, striking, emphatic, weighty, forcible, cogent: *You can't make an effective argument if all you do is stridently voice your opinion.* **OPPOSITE:** weak **3 = virtual**, essential, practical, implied, implicit, tacit, unacknowledged: *They have had effective control of the area.* **4 = in operation**, official, current, legal, real, active, actual, in effect, valid, operative, in force, in execution: *The new rules will become effective in the next few days.* **OPPOSITE:** inoperative

effectiveness NOUN **= power**, effect, efficiency, success, strength, capability, use, validity, usefulness, potency, efficacy, fruitfulness, productiveness

effects PLURAL NOUN **= belongings**, goods, things, property, stuff, gear, furniture, possessions, trappings, paraphernalia, personal property, accoutrements, chattels, movables: *His daughters came to collect his effects.*

effeminate ADJECTIVE **= womanly**, affected, camp *(informal)*, soft, weak, feminine, unmanly, sissy, effete, foppish, womanish, wussy *(slang)*, womanlike, poofy *(slang)*, wimpish *or* wimpy *(informal)* **OPPOSITE:** manly

effervescent ADJECTIVE **1 = fizzy**, bubbling, sparkling, bubbly, foaming, fizzing, fermenting, frothing, frothy, aerated, carbonated, foamy, gassy: *an effervescent mineral water* **OPPOSITE:** still **2 = lively**, excited, dynamic, enthusiastic, sparkling, energetic, animated, merry, buoyant, exhilarated, bubbly, exuberant, high-spirited, irrepressible, ebullient, chirpy, vital, scintillating, vivacious, zingy *(informal)*: *an effervescent blonde actress* **OPPOSITE:** dull

effete ADJECTIVE **= weak**, cowardly, feeble, ineffectual, decrepit, spineless, enfeebled, weak-kneed *(informal)*, enervated, overrefined, chicken-hearted, wimpish *or* wimpy *(informal)*

efficacy NOUN **= effectiveness**, efficiency, power, value, success, strength, virtue, vigour, use, usefulness, potency, fruitfulness, productiveness, efficaciousness

efficiency NOUN **1 = effectiveness**, power, economy, productivity, organization, efficacy, cost-effectiveness, orderliness: *ways to increase agricultural efficiency* **2 = competence**, ability, skill, expertise, capability, readiness, professionalism, proficiency, adeptness, skilfulness: *her efficiency as a manager*

efficient ADJECTIVE **1 = effective**, successful, structured, productive, powerful, systematic, streamlined, cost-effective, methodical, well-organized, well-planned, labour-saving, effectual: *an efficient form of contraception* **OPPOSITE:** inefficient **2 = competent**, able, professional, capable, organized, productive, skilful, adept, ready, proficient, businesslike, well-organized, workmanlike: *a highly efficient worker* **OPPOSITE:** incompetent

effigy NOUN **= likeness**, figure, image, model, guy, carving, representation, statue, icon, idol, dummy, statuette

effluent NOUN **= waste**, discharge, flow, emission, sewage, pollutant, outpouring, outflow, exhalation, issue, emanation, liquid waste, efflux, effluvium, effluence

effort NOUN **1 = attempt**, try, endeavour, shot *(informal)*, bid, essay, go *(informal)*, stab *(informal)*: *He made no effort to hide.* **2 = exertion**, work, labour, trouble, force, energy, struggle, stress, application, strain, striving, graft, toil, hard graft, travail *(literary)*, elbow grease *(facetious)*, blood, sweat, and tears *(informal)*: *A great deal of effort had been put into the planning.* **3 = achievement**, act, performance, product, job, production, creation, feat, deed, accomplishment, attainment: *The gallery is showcasing her latest efforts.*

QUOTATIONS

Effort is only effort when it begins to hurt
[José Ortega y Gasset *In Search of Goethe From Within, Letter to a German*]

Lovely it is, when the winds are churning up the waves on the great sea, to gaze out from the land on the great efforts of someone else
[Lucretius *De Rerum Natura*]

Whatever is worth doing at all is worth doing well
[Lord Chesterfield *Letters to His Son*]

Whatsoever thy hand findeth to do, do it with thy might
[*Bible: Ecclesiastes*]

effortless ADJECTIVE **1 = easy**, simple, flowing, smooth, graceful, painless, uncomplicated, trouble-free, facile, undemanding, easy-peasy *(slang)*, untroublesome, unexacting: *In a single effortless motion, he scooped Frannie into his arms.* **OPPOSITE:** difficult **2 = natural**, simple, spontaneous, instinctive, intuitive: *She liked him above all for his effortless charm.*

effusive ADJECTIVE **= demonstrative**, enthusiastic, lavish, extravagant, overflowing, gushing, exuberant, expansive, ebullient, free-flowing, unrestrained, talkative, fulsome, profuse, unreserved

egg NOUN **= ovum**, gamete, germ cell: *a baby bird hatching from its egg*
egg someone on = incite, push, encourage, urge, prompt, spur, provoke, prod, goad, exhort: *She was egging him on to fight.*

egocentric ADJECTIVE **= self-centred**, vain, selfish, narcissistic, self-absorbed, egotistical, inward looking, self-important, self-obsessed, self-seeking, egoistic, egoistical

egotism *or* **egoism** NOUN **= self-centredness**, self-esteem, vanity, superiority, self-interest, selfishness, narcissism, self-importance, self-regard, self-love, self-seeking, self-absorption, self-obsession, egocentricity, egomania, self-praise, vainglory, self-conceit, self-admiration, conceitedness

ejaculate VERB **1 = have an orgasm**, come *(taboo, slang)*, climax, emit semen: *a tendency to ejaculate too quickly* **2 = discharge**, release, emit, shoot out, eject, spurt: *sperm ejaculated by the male during sexual intercourse* **3 = exclaim**, declare, shout, call out, cry out, burst out, blurt out: *'Good God!' Liz ejaculated.*

ejaculation NOUN **= discharge**, release, emission, ejection

eject VERB **1 = throw out**, remove, turn out, expel *(slang)*, exile, oust, banish, deport, drive out, evict, boot out *(informal)*, force to leave, chuck out *(informal)*, bounce, turf out *(informal)*, give the bum's rush *(slang)*, show someone the door, throw someone out on their ear *(informal)*: *He was forcibly ejected from the restaurant.* **2 = dismiss**, sack *(informal)*, fire *(informal)*, remove, get rid of, discharge, expel, throw out, oust, kick out *(informal)*, kennet *(Austral. slang)*, jeff *(Austral. slang)*: *He was ejected from his first job for persistent latecoming.* **3 = discharge**, expel, emit, give off: *He fired a single shot, then ejected the spent cartridge.* **4 = bail out**, escape, get out: *The pilot ejected from the plane and escaped injury.*

ejection NOUN **1 = expulsion**, removal, ouster *(Law)*, deportation, eviction, banishment, exile: *the ejection of hecklers at the meeting* **2 = dismissal**, sacking *(informal)*, firing *(informal)*, removal, discharge, the boot *(slang)*, expulsion, the sack *(informal)*, dislodgement: *These actions led to his ejection from office.* **3 = emission**, throwing out, expulsion, spouting, casting out, disgorgement: *the ejection of an electron by an atomic nucleus*

eke out VERB **= be sparing with**, stretch out, be economical with, economize on, husband, be frugal with: *I had to eke out my redundancy money for about ten weeks.*
eke out a living = support yourself, survive, get by, make ends meet, scrimp, save, scrimp and save: *people trying to eke out a living in forest areas*

elaborate ADJECTIVE **1 = complicated**, detailed, studied, laboured, perfected, complex, careful, exact, precise, thorough, intricate, skilful, painstaking: *an elaborate research project* **2 = ornate**, detailed, involved, complex, fancy, complicated, decorated, extravagant, intricate, baroque, ornamented, fussy, embellished, showy, ostentatious, florid: *a designer known for his elaborate costumes* **OPPOSITE:** plain
▷ VERB **1 = develop**, improve, enhance, polish, complicate, decorate, refine, garnish, ornament, flesh out: *The plan was elaborated by five members of the council.* **2** *(usually with* **on** *or* **upon***)* **= expand upon**, extend upon, enlarge on, amplify upon, embellish, flesh out, add detail to: *A spokesman declined to elaborate on the statement.* **OPPOSITE:** simplify

élan NOUN **= style**, spirit, dash, flair, animation, vigour, verve, zest, panache, esprit, brio, vivacity, impetuosity

elapse VERB **= pass**, go, go by, lapse, pass by, slip away, roll on, slip by, roll by, glide by

elastic ADJECTIVE **1 = flexible**, yielding, supple, rubbery, pliable, plastic, springy, pliant, tensile, stretchy, ductile, stretchable: *Work the dough until it is slightly elastic.* **OPPOSITE:** rigid **2 = adaptable**, yielding, variable, flexible, accommodating, tolerant, adjustable, supple, complaisant: *an elastic interpretation of the rules* **OPPOSITE:** inflexible

elasticity NOUN **1 = flexibility**, suppleness, plasticity, give *(informal)*, pliability, ductility, springiness, pliancy, stretchiness, rubberiness: *Daily facial exercises help to retain the skin's elasticity.* **2 = adaptability**, accommodation, flexibility, tolerance, variability, suppleness, complaisance, adjustability, compliantness: *the elasticity of demand for this commodity*

elated ADJECTIVE = **joyful**, excited, delighted, proud, cheered, thrilled, elevated, animated, roused, exhilarated, ecstatic, jubilant, joyous, over the moon *(informal)*, overjoyed, blissful, euphoric, rapt, gleeful, sent, puffed up, exultant, in high spirits, on cloud nine *(informal)*, cock-a-hoop, blissed out, in seventh heaven, floating *or* walking on air, stoked *(Austral. & N.Z. informal)*
OPPOSITE: dejected

elation NOUN = **joy**, delight, thrill, excitement, ecstasy, bliss, euphoria, glee, rapture, high spirits, exhilaration, jubilation, exaltation, exultation, joyfulness, joyousness

elbow NOUN = **joint**, turn, corner, bend, angle, curve: *The boat was moored at the elbow of the river.*
▷ VERB = **push**, force, crowd, shoulder, knock, bump, shove, nudge, jostle, hustle: *They elbowed me out of the way.*
at your elbow = **within reach**, near, to hand, handy, at hand, close by: *the whisky glass that was forever at his elbow*

elder ADJECTIVE = **older**, first, senior, first-born, earlier born: *the elder of her two daughters*
▷ NOUN **1** = **older person**, senior: *Nowadays the young have no respect for their elders.* **2** = **church official**, leader, office bearer, presbyter: *He is now an elder of the village church.*

elect VERB **1** = **vote for**, choose, pick, determine, select, appoint, opt for, designate, pick out, settle on, decide upon: *The people have voted to elect a new president.* **2** = **choose**, decide, prefer, select, opt: *Those electing to smoke will be seated at the rear.*
▷ ADJECTIVE **1** = **selected**, chosen, picked, choice, preferred, select, elite, hand-picked: *one of the elect few permitted to enter* **2** = **future**, to-be, coming, next, appointed, designate, prospective: *the date when the president-elect takes office*

election NOUN **1** = **vote**, poll, ballot, determination, referendum, franchise, plebiscite, show of hands: *Poland's first fully free elections for more than fifty years* **2** = **appointment**, choosing, picking, choice, selection: *the election of the Labour government in 1964*

> **QUOTATIONS**
> Elections are won by men and women chiefly because most people vote against somebody rather than for somebody
> [Franklin P. Adams *Nods and Becks*]

elector NOUN = **voter**, chooser, selector, constituent, member of the electorate, member of a constituency, enfranchised person

electric ADJECTIVE **1** = **electric-powered**, powered, cordless, battery-operated, electrically-charged, mains-operated: *her electric guitar* **2** = **charged**, exciting, stirring, thrilling, stimulating, dynamic, tense, rousing, electrifying, adrenalized: *The atmosphere in the hall was electric.*

electrify VERB **1** = **thrill**, shock, excite, amaze, stir, stimulate, astonish, startle, arouse, animate, rouse, astound, jolt, fire, galvanize, take your breath away: *The spectators were electrified by his courage.* **OPPOSITE:** bore **2** = **wire up**, wire, supply electricity to, convert to electricity: *The west-coast line was electrified as long ago as 1974.*

elegance NOUN = **style**, taste, beauty, grace, dignity, sophistication, grandeur, refinement, polish, gentility, sumptuousness, courtliness, gracefulness, tastefulness, exquisiteness

> **QUOTATIONS**
> To me, elegance is not to pass unnoticed but to get to the very soul of what one is
> [Christian Lacroix]

elegant ADJECTIVE **1** = **stylish**, fine, beautiful, sophisticated, delicate, artistic, handsome, fashionable, refined, cultivated, chic, luxurious, exquisite, nice, discerning, graceful, polished, sumptuous, genteel, choice, tasteful, urbane, courtly, modish, comely, à la mode, schmick *(Austral. informal)*: *Patricia looked as beautiful and elegant as always.* **OPPOSITE:** inelegant **2** = **ingenious**, simple, effective, appropriate, clever, neat, apt: *The poem impressed me with its elegant simplicity.*

elegiac ADJECTIVE = **lamenting**, sad, melancholy, nostalgic, mournful, plaintive, melancholic, sorrowful, funereal, valedictory, keening, dirgeful, threnodial, threnodic

elegy NOUN = **lament**, requiem, dirge, plaint *(archaic)*, threnody, keen, funeral song, coronach *(Scot. & Irish)*, funeral poem

element NOUN **1** = **component**, part, feature, unit, section, factor, principle, aspect, foundation, ingredient, constituent, subdivision: *one of the key elements of the UN's peace plan* **2** = **group**, faction, clique, set, party, circle: *The government must weed out criminal elements from the security forces.* **3** = **trace**, suggestion, hint, dash, suspicion, tinge, smattering, soupçon: *There is an element of truth in his accusation.*
▷ PLURAL NOUN = **weather conditions**, climate, the weather, wind and rain, atmospheric conditions, powers of nature, atmospheric forces: *The area is exposed to the elements.*
in your element = **in a situation you enjoy**, in your natural environment, in familiar surroundings: *My stepmother was in her element, organizing everyone.*

elemental ADJECTIVE **1** = **primal**, original, primitive, primordial: *the elemental powers of the universe* **2** = **atmospheric**, natural, meteorological: *the elemental forces that shaped this rugged Atlantic coast*

elementary ADJECTIVE **1** = **basic**, essential, primary, initial, fundamental, introductory, preparatory, rudimentary, elemental, bog-standard *(informal)*: *Literacy now includes elementary computer skills.*
OPPOSITE: advanced **2** = **simple**, clear, easy, plain, straightforward, rudimentary, uncomplicated, facile, undemanding, unexacting: *elementary questions designed to test numeracy*
OPPOSITE: complicated

elevate VERB **1** = **promote**, raise, advance, upgrade, exalt, kick upstairs *(informal)*, aggrandize, give advancement to: *He was elevated to the post of Prime Minister.* **2** = **increase**, lift, raise, step up, intensify, move up, hoist, raise high: *Emotional stress can elevate blood pressure.* **3** = **raise**, lift, heighten, uplift, hoist, lift up, raise up, hike up, upraise: *Jack elevated the gun at the sky.* **4** = **cheer**, raise, excite, boost, animate, rouse, uplift, brighten, exhilarate, hearten, lift up, perk up, buoy up, gladden, elate: *She bought some new clothes, but they failed to elevate her spirits.*

elevated ADJECTIVE **1** = **exalted**, high, important, august, grand, superior, noble, dignified, high-ranking, lofty: *His new job has given him a certain elevated status.* **2** = **high-minded**, high, fine, grand, noble, inflated, dignified, sublime, lofty, high-flown, pompous, exalted, bombastic: *the magazine's elevated tone* **OPPOSITE:** humble **3** = **raised**, high, lifted up, upraised: *an elevated platform on the stage*

elevation NOUN **1** = **side**, back, face, front, aspect: *the addition of a two-storey wing on the north elevation* **2** = **altitude**, height: *We're at an elevation of about 13,000 feet above sea level.* **3** = **promotion**, upgrading, advancement, exaltation, preferment, aggrandizement: *celebrating his elevation to the rank of Prime Minister* **4** = **rise**, hill, mountain, height, mound, berg *(S. African)*, high ground, higher ground, eminence, hillock, rising ground, acclivity: *The resort is built on an elevation overlooking the sea.*

elicit VERB **1** = **bring about**, cause, derive, bring out, evoke, give rise to, draw out, bring forth, bring to light, call forth: *He was hopeful that his request would elicit a positive response.* **2** = **obtain**, extract, exact, evoke, wrest, draw out, extort, educe: *the question of how far police should go to elicit a confession*

eligible ADJECTIVE **1** = **entitled**, fit, qualified, suited, suitable: *You could be eligible for a university scholarship.*
OPPOSITE: ineligible **2** = **available**, free, single, unmarried, unattached: *Britain's most eligible bachelor*

eliminate VERB **1** = **remove**, end, stop, withdraw, get rid of, abolish, cut out, dispose of, terminate, banish, eradicate, put an end to, do away with, dispense with, stamp out, exterminate, get shot of, wipe from the face of the earth: *The Act has not eliminated discrimination in employment.* **2 = knock out**, drop, reject, exclude, axe *(informal)*, get rid of, expel, leave out, throw out, omit, put out, eject: *I was eliminated from the 400 metres in the semifinals.* **3 = murder**, kill, do in *(slang)*, take out *(slang)*, terminate, slay, blow away *(slang, chiefly U.S.)*, liquidate, annihilate, exterminate, bump off *(slang)*, rub out *(U.S. slang)*, waste *(informal)*: *They claimed that 87,000 'reactionaries' had been eliminated.*

elite NOUN **= aristocracy**, best, pick, elect, cream, upper class, nobility, gentry, high society, the crème de la crème, flower, nonpareil: *a government comprised mainly of the elite*
OPPOSITE: rabble
▷ ADJECTIVE **= leading**, best, finest, pick, choice, selected, elect, crack *(slang)*, supreme, exclusive, privileged, first-class, foremost, first-rate, pre-eminent, most excellent: *the elite troops of the President's bodyguard*

elitist ADJECTIVE **= snobbish**, exclusive, superior, arrogant, selective, pretentious, stuck-up *(informal)*, patronizing, condescending, snooty *(informal)*, uppity, high and mighty *(informal)*, hoity-toity *(informal)*, high-hat *(informal, chiefly U.S.)*, uppish *(Brit. informal)*: *He described skiing as an elitist sport.*

elixir NOUN **1 = panacea**, cure-all, nostrum, sovereign remedy: *a magical elixir of eternal youth* **2 = syrup**, essence, solution, concentrate, mixture, extract, potion, distillation, tincture, distillate: *For severe teething pains, try an infant paracetamol elixir.*

elliptical ADJECTIVE **= oblique**, concentrated, obscure, compact, indirect, ambiguous, concise, condensed, terse, cryptic, laconic, abstruse, recondite: *elliptical references to matters best not discussed in public*

elongate VERB **= lengthen**, extend, stretch (out), make longer

elongated ADJECTIVE **= extended**, long, stretched

elope VERB **= run away**, leave, escape, disappear, bolt, run off, slip away, abscond, decamp, sneak off, steal away, do a bunk *(informal)*

eloquence NOUN **1 = fluency**, effectiveness, oratory, expressiveness, persuasiveness, forcefulness, gracefulness, powerfulness, whaikorero *(N.Z.)*: *the eloquence with which he delivered his message*
2 = expressiveness, significance, meaningfulness, pointedness: *the eloquence of his gestures*

eloquent ADJECTIVE **1 = silver-tongued**, moving, powerful, effective, stirring, articulate, persuasive, graceful, forceful, fluent, expressive, well-expressed: *He made a very eloquent speech at the dinner.*
OPPOSITE: inarticulate **2 = expressive**, telling, pointed, revealing, significant, pregnant, vivid, meaningful, indicative, suggestive: *Her only reply was an eloquent glance at the clock.*

elsewhere ADVERB **= in** *or* **to another place**, away, abroad, hence *(archaic)*, somewhere else, not here, in other places, in *or* to a different place

elucidate VERB **= clarify**, explain, illustrate, interpret, make clear, unfold, illuminate, spell out, clear up, gloss, expound, make plain, annotate, explicate, shed *or* throw light upon

elude VERB **1 = evade**, escape, lose, avoid, flee, duck *(informal)*, dodge, get away from, shake off, run away from, circumvent, outrun, body-swerve *(Scot.)*: *The thieves managed to elude the police for months.* **2 = escape**, baffle, frustrate, puzzle, stump, be beyond (someone), confound: *The appropriate word eluded him.*

> **USAGE**
> *Elude* is sometimes wrongly used where *allude* is meant: *he was alluding* (not *eluding*) *to his previous visit to the city.*

elusive ADJECTIVE **1 = difficult to catch**, tricky, slippery, difficult to find, evasive, shifty: *I had no luck in tracking down this elusive man.*
2 = indefinable, puzzling, fleeting, subtle, baffling, indefinite, transient, intangible, indescribable, transitory, indistinct: *an attempt to recapture an elusive memory*

emaciated ADJECTIVE **= skeletal**, thin, weak, lean, pinched, skinny, wasted, gaunt, bony, haggard, atrophied, scrawny, attenuate, attenuated, undernourished, scraggy, half-starved, cadaverous, macilent *(rare)*

emanate VERB **1 = give out**, send out, emit, radiate, exude, issue, give off, exhale, send forth: *He emanated sympathy.* **2** *(often with* **from***)* **= flow**, emerge, spring, proceed, arise, stem, derive, originate, issue, come forth: *The aroma of burning wood emanated from the stove.*

emancipate VERB **= free**, release, liberate, set free, deliver, discharge, let out, let loose, untie, unchain, enfranchise, unshackle, disencumber, unfetter, unbridle, disenthral, manumit
OPPOSITE: enslave

emancipation NOUN **= liberation**, freedom, freeing, release, liberty, discharge, liberating, setting free, letting loose, untying, deliverance, unchaining, manumission, enfranchisement, unshackling, unfettering **OPPOSITE:** slavery

emasculate VERB **= weaken**, soften, cripple, impoverish, debilitate, reduce the power of, enfeeble, make feeble, enervate, deprive of force

embalm VERB **= preserve**, lay out, mummify

embargo NOUN **= ban**, bar, block, barrier, restriction, boycott, restraint, check, prohibition, moratorium, stoppage, impediment, blockage, hindrance, interdiction, interdict, proscription, rahui *(N.Z.)*: *The UN has imposed an arms embargo against the country.*
▷ VERB **= block**, stop, bar, ban, restrict, boycott, check, prohibit, impede, blacklist, proscribe, ostracize, debar, interdict: *They embargoed oil shipments to the US.*

embark VERB **= go aboard**, climb aboard, board ship, step aboard, go on board, take ship: *They embarked on the battle cruiser HMS Renown.* **OPPOSITE:** get off
embark on something = begin, start, launch, enter, engage, take up, set out, undertake, initiate, set about, plunge into, commence, broach: *He is embarking on a new career as a writer.*

embarrass VERB **= shame**, distress, show up *(informal)*, humiliate, disconcert, chagrin, fluster, mortify, faze, discomfit, make uncomfortable, make awkward, discountenance, nonplus, abash, discompose, make ashamed, put out of countenance

embarrassed ADJECTIVE **= ashamed**, upset, shamed, uncomfortable, shown-up, awkward, abashed, humiliated, uneasy, unsettled, self-conscious, thrown, disconcerted, red-faced, chagrined, flustered, mortified, sheepish, discomfited, discountenanced, caught with egg on your face, not know where to put yourself, put out of countenance

embarrassing ADJECTIVE **= humiliating**, upsetting, compromising, shaming, distressing, delicate, uncomfortable, awkward, tricky, sensitive, troublesome, shameful, disconcerting, touchy, mortifying, discomfiting, toe-curling *(slang)*, cringe-making *(Brit. informal)*, cringeworthy *(Brit. informal)*, barro *(Austral. slang)*

embarrassment NOUN **1 = shame**, distress, showing up *(informal)*, humiliation, discomfort, unease, chagrin, self-consciousness, awkwardness, mortification, discomfiture, bashfulness, discomposure: *We apologize for any embarrassment this statement may have caused.* **2 = problem**, difficulty, nuisance, source of trouble, thorn in your flesh: *The poverty figures were an embarrassment to the president.*
3 = predicament, problem, difficulty *(informal)*, mess, jam *(informal)*, plight, scrape *(informal)*, pickle *(informal)*: *He is in a state of temporary financial embarrassment.*

embed *or* **imbed** VERB *(often with* **in***)* **= fix**, set, plant, root, sink, lodge, insert, implant, drive in, dig in, hammer in, ram in

e

embellish VERB **1 = decorate**, enhance, adorn, dress, grace, deck, trim, dress up, enrich, garnish, ornament, gild, festoon, bedeck, tart up *(slang)*, beautify: *The boat was embellished with red and blue carvings.* **2 = elaborate**, colour, exaggerate, dress up, embroider, varnish: *He embellished the story with invented dialogue and extra details.*

embellishment NOUN **1 = decoration**, garnishing, ornament, gilding, enhancement, enrichment, adornment, ornamentation, trimming, beautification: *Florence is full of buildings with bits of decoration and embellishment.* **2 = elaboration**, exaggeration, embroidery: *I lack the story-teller's gift of embellishment.*

ember NOUN *(usually plural)* **= cinders**, ashes, residue, live coals

embezzle VERB **= misappropriate**, steal, appropriate, rob, pocket, nick *(slang, chiefly Brit.)*, pinch *(informal)*, rip off *(slang)*, siphon off, pilfer, purloin, filch, help yourself to, thieve, defalcate *(Law)*, peculate

embezzlement NOUN **= misappropriation**, stealing, robbing, fraud, pocketing, theft, robbery, nicking *(slang, chiefly Brit.)*, pinching *(informal)*, appropriation, siphoning off, thieving, pilfering, larceny, purloining, filching, pilferage, peculation, defalcation *(Law)*

embittered ADJECTIVE **= resentful**, angry, acid, bitter, sour, soured, alienated, disillusioned, disaffected, venomous, rancorous, at daggers drawn *(informal)*, nursing a grudge, with a chip on your shoulder *(informal)*

emblazon VERB **= decorate**, show, display, present, colour, paint, illuminate, adorn, ornament, embellish, blazon

emblem NOUN **1 = crest**, mark, design, image, figure, seal, shield, badge, insignia, coat of arms, heraldic device, sigil *(rare)*: *the emblem of the Red Cross* **2 = representation**, symbol, mark, sign, type, token: *The eagle was an emblem of strength and courage.*

emblematic *or* **emblematical** ADJECTIVE **1 = symbolic**, significant, figurative, allegorical: *Dogs are emblematic of faithfulness.* **2 = characteristic**, representative, typical, symptomatic: *This comment is emblematic of his no-nonsense approach to life.*

embodiment NOUN **= personification**, example, model, type, ideal, expression, symbol, representation, manifestation, realization, incarnation, paradigm, epitome, incorporation, paragon, perfect example, exemplar, quintessence, actualization, exemplification, reification

embody VERB **1 = personify**, represent, express, realize, incorporate, stand for, manifest, exemplify, symbolize, typify, incarnate, actualize, reify, concretize: *Jack Kennedy embodied all the hopes of the 1960s.* **2** *(often with* **in***)* **= incorporate**, include, contain, combine, collect, concentrate, organize, take in, integrate, consolidate, bring together, encompass, comprehend, codify, systematize: *The proposal has been embodied in a draft resolution.*

embolden VERB **= encourage**, cheer, stir, strengthen, nerve, stimulate, reassure, fire, animate, rouse, inflame, hearten, invigorate, gee up, make brave, give courage, vitalize, inspirit

embrace VERB **1 = hug**, hold, cuddle, seize, squeeze, grasp, clasp, envelop, encircle, enfold, canoodle *(slang)*, take or hold in your arms: *Penelope came forward and embraced her sister.* **2 = accept**, support, receive, welcome, adopt, grab, take up, seize, make use of, espouse, take on board, welcome with open arms, avail yourself of, receive enthusiastically: *He embraces the new information age.* **3 = include**, involve, cover, deal with, contain, take in, incorporate, comprise, enclose, provide for, take into account, embody, encompass, comprehend, subsume: *a theory that would embrace the whole field of human endeavour*
▷ NOUN **= hug**, hold, cuddle, squeeze, clinch *(slang)*, clasp, canoodle *(slang)*: *a young couple locked in a passionate embrace*

embroil VERB **= involve**, complicate, mix up, implicate, entangle, mire, ensnare, encumber, enmesh

embryo NOUN **1 = fetus**, unborn child, fertilized egg: *The embryo lives in the amniotic cavity.* **2 = germ**, beginning, source, root, seed, nucleus, rudiment: *The League of Nations was the embryo of the UN.*

embryonic *or* **embryonal** ADJECTIVE **= rudimentary**, early, beginning, primary, budding, fledgling, immature, seminal, nascent, undeveloped, incipient, inchoate, unformed, germinal
OPPOSITE: advanced

emerge VERB **1 = come out**, appear, come up, surface, rise, proceed, arise, turn up, spring up, emanate, materialize, issue, come into view, come forth, become visible, manifest yourself: *He was waiting outside as she emerged from the building.*
OPPOSITE: withdraw **2 = become apparent**, develop, come out, turn up, become known, come to light, crop up, transpire, materialize, become evident, come out in the wash: *Several interesting facts emerged from his story.*

emergence NOUN **1 = coming**, development, arrival, surfacing, rise, appearance, arising, turning up, issue, dawn, advent, emanation, materialization: *the emergence of new democracies in Central Europe* **2 = disclosure**, publishing, broadcasting, broadcast, publication, declaration, revelation, becoming known, becoming apparent, coming to light, becoming evident: *Following the emergence of new facts, the conviction was quashed.*

emergency NOUN **= crisis**, danger, difficulty, accident, disaster, necessity, pinch, plight, scrape *(informal)*, strait, catastrophe, predicament, calamity, extremity, quandary, exigency, critical situation, urgent situation: *He has the ability to deal with emergencies quickly.*
▷ ADJECTIVE **1 = urgent**, crisis, immediate: *She made an emergency appointment.* **2 = alternative**, extra, additional, substitute, replacement, temporary, makeshift, stopgap: *The plane is carrying emergency supplies.*

emergent ADJECTIVE **= developing**, coming, beginning, rising, appearing, budding, burgeoning, fledgling, nascent, incipient

emigrate VERB **= move abroad**, move, relocate, migrate, remove, resettle, leave your country

emigration NOUN **= departure**, removal, migration, exodus, relocation, resettlement

> **QUOTATIONS**
> Emigration, forced or chosen, across national frontiers or from village to metropolis, is the quintessential experience of our time
> [John Berger *And Our Faces, My Heart, Brief as Photos*]

eminence NOUN **1 = prominence**, reputation, importance, fame, celebrity, distinction, note, esteem, rank, dignity, prestige, superiority, greatness, renown, pre-eminence, repute, notability, illustriousness: *pilots who achieved eminence in the aeronautical world* **2 = high ground**, bank, rise, hill, summit, height, mound, elevation, knoll, hillock, kopje or koppie *(S. African)*: *The house is built on an eminence, and has a pleasing prospect.*

eminent ADJECTIVE **= prominent**, high, great, important, noted, respected, grand, famous, celebrated, outstanding, distinguished, well-known, superior, esteemed, notable, renowned, prestigious, elevated, paramount, big-time *(informal)*, foremost, high-ranking, conspicuous, illustrious, major league *(informal)*, exalted, noteworthy, pre-eminent **OPPOSITE:** unknown

emissary NOUN **= envoy**, agent, deputy, representative, ambassador, diplomat, delegate, courier, herald, messenger, consul, attaché, go-between, legate

emission NOUN **= giving off** *or* **out**, release, shedding, leak, radiation, discharge, transmission, venting, issue, diffusion, utterance, ejaculation, outflow, issuance, ejection, exhalation, emanation, exudation

emit VERB **1 = give off**, release, shed, leak, transmit, discharge, send out, throw out, vent, issue, give out, radiate, eject, pour out, diffuse, emanate, exude, exhale, breathe out, cast out, give vent to, send forth: *The stove emitted a cloud of evil-smelling smoke.* **OPPOSITE:** absorb **2 = utter**, produce, voice, give out, let out: *Polly blinked and emitted a small cry.*

emotion NOUN **1 = feeling**, spirit, soul, passion, excitement, sensation, sentiment, agitation, fervour, ardour, vehemence, perturbation: *Her voice trembled with emotion.* **2 = instinct**, sentiment, sensibility, intuition, tenderness, gut feeling, soft-heartedness: *the split between reason and emotion*

emotional ADJECTIVE **1 = psychological**, private, personal, hidden, spiritual, inner: *Victims are left with emotional problems that can last for life.* **2 = moving**, touching, affecting, exciting, stirring, thrilling, sentimental, poignant, emotive, heart-rending, heart-warming, tear-jerking (*informal*): *It was a very emotional moment.* **3 = emotive**, sensitive, controversial, delicate, contentious, heated, inflammatory, touchy: *Selling ivory from elephants is a very emotional issue.* **4 = passionate**, enthusiastic, sentimental, fiery, feeling, susceptible, responsive, ardent, fervent, zealous, temperamental, excitable, demonstrative, hot-blooded, fervid, touchy-feely (*informal*): *I don't get as emotional as I once did.* **OPPOSITE:** dispassionate

USAGE
Although *emotive* can be used as a synonym of *emotional*, there are differences in meaning that should first be understood. *Emotional* is the more general and neutral word for referring to anything to do with the emotions and emotional states. *Emotive* has the more restricted meaning of 'tending to arouse emotion', and is often associated with issues, subjects, language, and words. However, since *emotional* can also mean 'arousing emotion', with certain nouns it is possible to use either word, depending on the slant one wishes to give: *an emotive/emotional appeal on behalf of the disadvantaged young.*

emotive ADJECTIVE **1 = sensitive**, controversial, delicate, contentious, inflammatory, touchy: *Embryo research is an emotive subject.* **2 = moving**, touching, affecting, emotional, exciting, stirring, thrilling, sentimental, poignant, heart-rending, heart-warming, tear-jerking (*informal*): *He made an emotive speech to his fans.*

empathize
empathize with = identify with, understand, relate to, feel for, sympathize with, have a rapport with, feel at one with, be on the same wavelength as

emphasis NOUN **1 = importance**, attention, weight, significance, stress, strength, priority, moment, intensity, insistence, prominence, underscoring, pre-eminence: *Too much emphasis is placed on research.* **2 = stress**, accent, accentuation, force, weight: *The emphasis is on the first syllable of the word.*

emphasize VERB **1 = highlight**, stress, insist, underline, draw attention to, flag up, dwell on, underscore, weight, play up, make a point of, give priority to, press home, give prominence to, prioritize: *I should emphasize that nothing has been finally decided as yet.* **OPPOSITE:** minimize **2 = stress**, accent, accentuate, lay stress on, put the accent on: *'That's up to you,' I said, emphasizing the 'you'.*

emphatic ADJECTIVE **1 = forceful**, decided, certain, direct, earnest, positive, absolute, distinct, definite, vigorous, energetic, unmistakable, insistent, unequivocal, vehement, forcible, categorical: *His response was immediate and emphatic.* **OPPOSITE:** hesitant **2 = significant**, marked, strong, striking, powerful, telling, storming (*informal*), impressive, pronounced, decisive, resounding, momentous, conclusive: *Yesterday's emphatic victory was their fifth in succession.* **OPPOSITE:** insignificant

empire NOUN **1 = kingdom**, territory, province, federation, commonwealth, realm, domain, imperium (*rare*): *the fall of the Roman empire* **2 = organization**, company, business, firm, concern, corporation, consortium, syndicate, multinational, conglomeration: *control of a huge publishing empire*

empirical ADJECTIVE **= first-hand**, direct, observed, practical, actual, experimental, pragmatic, factual, experiential **OPPOSITE:** hypothetical

employ VERB **1 = hire**, commission, appoint, take on, retain, engage, recruit, sign up, enlist, enrol, have on the payroll: *The company employs 18 staff.* **2 = use**, apply, exercise, exert, make use of, utilize, ply, bring to bear, put to use, bring into play, avail yourself of: *the approaches and methods we employed in this study* **3 = spend**, fill, occupy, involve, engage, take up, make use of, use up: *Your time could be usefully employed in attending to business matters.*

employed ADJECTIVE **1 = working**, in work, having a job, in employment, in a job, earning your living: *He was employed on a part-time basis.* **OPPOSITE:** out of work **2 = busy**, active, occupied, engaged, hard at work, in harness, rushed off your feet: *You have enough work to keep you fully employed.* **OPPOSITE:** idle

employee or (*U.S.*) **employe** NOUN **= worker**, labourer, workman, staff member, member of staff, hand, wage-earner, white-collar worker, blue-collar worker, hired hand, job-holder, member of the workforce

employer NOUN **1 = boss** (*informal*), manager, head, leader, director, chief, executive, owner, owner, master, chief executive, governor (*informal*), skipper, managing director, administrator, patron, supervisor, superintendent, gaffer (*informal, chiefly Brit.*), foreman, proprietor, manageress, overseer, kingpin, honcho (*informal*), big cheese (*slang, old-fashioned*), baas (*S. African*), numero uno (*informal*), Mister Big (*slang, chiefly U.S.*), sherang (*Austral. & N.Z.*): *It is a privilege to work for such an excellent employer.* **2 = company**, business, firm, organization, establishment, outfit (*informal*): *Shorts is Ulster's biggest private-sector employer*

employment NOUN **1 = job**, work, business, position, trade, post, situation, employ, calling, profession, occupation, pursuit, vocation, métier: *She was unable to find employment in the area.* **2 = taking on**, commissioning, appointing, hire, hiring, retaining, engaging, appointment, recruiting, engagement, recruitment, enlisting, enrolling, enlistment, enlrolment: *a ban on the employment of children under the age of nine* **3 = use**, application, exertion, exercise, utilization: *the widespread employment of 'smart' bombs in this war*

emporium NOUN **= shop**, market, store, supermarket, outlet, warehouse, department store, mart, boutique, bazaar, retail outlet, superstore, hypermarket

empower VERB **1 = authorize**, allow, commission, qualify, permit, sanction, entitle, delegate, license, warrant, give power to, give authority to, invest with power: *The army is now empowered to operate on a shoot-to-kill basis.* **2 = enable**, equip, emancipate, give means to, enfranchise: *empowering the underprivileged by means of education*

emptiness NOUN **1 = futility**, banality, worthlessness, hollowness, pointlessness, meaninglessness, barrenness, senselessness, aimlessness, purposelessness, unsatisfactoriness, valuelessness: *suffering from feelings of emptiness and depression* **2 = meaninglessness**, vanity, banality, frivolity, idleness, unreality, silliness, triviality, ineffectiveness, cheapness, insincerity, worthlessness, hollowness, inanity,

e

unsubstantiality, trivialness, vainness: *the unsoundness and emptiness of his beliefs* **3 = void**, gap, vacuum, empty space, nothingness, blank space, free space, vacuity: *She wanted a man to fill the emptiness in her life.* **4 = bareness**, waste, desolation, destitution, blankness, barrenness, desertedness, vacantness: *the emptiness of the desert* **5 = blankness**, vacancy, vacuity, impassivity, vacuousness, expressionlessness, stoniness, unintelligence, absentness, vacantness: *There was an emptiness about her eyes, as if she were in a state of shock.*

e

empty ADJECTIVE **1 = bare**, clear, abandoned, deserted, vacant, free, void, desolate, destitute, uninhabited, unoccupied, waste, unfurnished, untenanted, without contents: *The room was bare and empty.* **OPPOSITE:** full **2 = meaningless**, cheap, hollow, vain, idle, trivial, ineffective, futile, insubstantial, insincere: *His father said he was going to beat him, but he knew it was an empty threat.* **3 = worthless**, meaningless, hollow, pointless, unsatisfactory, futile, unreal, senseless, frivolous, fruitless, aimless, inane, valueless, purposeless, otiose, bootless (*old-fashioned*): *My life was hectic but empty before I met him.* **OPPOSITE:** meaningful **4 = blank**, absent, vacant, stony, deadpan, vacuous, impassive, expressionless, unintelligent: *She saw the empty look in his eyes as he left.*
▷ VERB **1 = clear**, drain, gut, void, unload, pour out, unpack, unburden, remove the contents of: *I emptied the ashtray.* **OPPOSITE:** fill **2 = exhaust**, consume the contents of, void, deplete, use up: *Cross emptied his glass with one swallow.* **OPPOSITE:** replenish **3 = evacuate**, clear, vacate: *a bore who could empty a room in two minutes just by talking about his therapy*

emulate VERB **= imitate**, follow, copy, mirror, echo, mimic, take after, follow in the footsteps of, follow the example of, take a leaf out of someone's book, model yourself on

emulation NOUN **= imitation**, following, copying, mirroring, reproduction, mimicry

enable VERB **1 = allow**, permit, facilitate, empower, give someone the opportunity, give someone the means: *The new test should enable doctors to detect the disease early.* **OPPOSITE:** prevent **2 = authorize**, allow, commission, permit, qualify, sanction, entitle, license, warrant, empower, give someone the right: *The authorities have refused visas to enable them to enter the country.* **OPPOSITE:** stop

enact VERB **1 = establish**, order, pass, command, approve, sanction, proclaim, decree, authorize, ratify, ordain, validate, legislate, make law: *The bill would be submitted for discussion before being enacted as law.* **2 = perform**, play, act, present, stage, represent, put on, portray, depict, act out, play the part of, appear as *or* in, personate: *She enacted the stories told to her by her father.*

enactment *or* **enaction** NOUN **1 = passing**, legislation, sanction, approval, establishment, proclamation, ratification, authorization, validation, making law: *the enactment of a Bill of Rights* **2 = decree**, order, law, act, ruling, bill, measure, command, legislation, regulation, resolution, dictate, canon, statute, ordinance, commandment, edict, bylaw: *enactments which empowered the court to require security to be given* **3 = portrayal**, staging, performance, playing, acting, performing, representation, depiction, play-acting, personation: *The building was also used for the enactment of plays.*

enamoured
enamoured with *or* **of = in love with**, taken with, charmed by, fascinated by, entranced by, fond of, enchanted by, captivated by, enthralled by, smitten with, besotted with, bewitched by, crazy about (*informal*), infatuated with, enraptured by, wild about (*informal*), swept off your feet by, nuts on *or* about (*slang*)

encampment NOUN **= camp**, base, post, station, quarters, campsite, bivouac, camping ground, cantonment

encapsulate *or* **incapsulate** VERB **= sum up**, digest, summarize, compress, condense, abbreviate, epitomize, abridge, précis

enchant VERB **= fascinate**, delight, charm, entrance, dazzle, captivate, enthral, beguile, bewitch, ravish, mesmerize, hypnotize, cast a spell on, enrapture, enamour, spellbind

enchanting ADJECTIVE **= delightful**, fascinating, appealing, attractive, lovely, charming, entrancing, pleasant, endearing, captivating, alluring, bewitching, ravishing, winsome, Orphean

enchantment NOUN **1 = charm**, fascination, delight, beauty, joy, attraction, bliss, allure, transport, rapture, mesmerism, ravishment, captivation, beguilement, allurement: *The campsite had its own peculiar enchantment.* **2 = spell**, magic, charm, witchcraft, voodoo, wizardry, sorcery, occultism, incantation, necromancy, conjuration, makutu (*N.Z.*): *an effective countercharm against enchantment by the faerie folk*

encircle VERB **= surround**, ring, circle, enclose, encompass, compass, envelop, girdle, circumscribe, hem in, enfold, environ, gird in, begird (*poetic*), enwreath

enclose *or* **inclose** VERB **1 = surround**, cover, circle, bound, wrap, fence, pound, pen, hedge, confine, close in, encompass, wall in, encircle, encase, fence in, impound, circumscribe, hem in, shut in, environ: *The land was enclosed by an eight-foot wire fence.* **2 = send with**, include, put in, insert: *I enclose a cheque for £10.*

encompass VERB **1 = include**, hold, involve, cover, admit, deal with, contain, take in, embrace, incorporate, comprise, embody, comprehend, subsume: *His repertoire encompassed everything from Bach to Scott Joplin.* **2 = surround**, circle, enclose, close in, envelop, encircle, fence in, ring, girdle, circumscribe, hem in, shut in, environ, enwreath: *Egypt is encompassed by the Mediterranean, Sudan, the Red Sea and Libya.*

encounter VERB **1 = experience**, meet, face, suffer, have, go through, sustain, endure, undergo, run into, live through: *Every day we encounter stresses of one kind or another.* **2 = meet**, confront, come across, run into (*informal*), bump into (*informal*), run across, come upon, chance upon, meet by chance, happen on *or* upon: *Did you encounter anyone on your walk?* **3 = battle with**, attack, fight, oppose, engage with, confront, combat, clash with, contend with, strive against, struggle with, grapple with, face off (*slang*), do battle with, cross swords with, come into conflict with, meet head on: *They were about to cross the border and encounter Iraqi troops.*
▷ NOUN **1 = meeting**, brush, confrontation, rendezvous, chance meeting: *an encounter with a remarkable man* **2 = battle**, fight, action, conflict, clash, dispute, contest, set to (*informal*), run-in (*informal*), combat, confrontation, engagement, collision, skirmish, head-to-head, face-off (*slang*): *They were killed in an encounter with security forces near the border.*

encourage VERB **1 = inspire**, comfort, rally, cheer, stimulate, reassure, animate, console, rouse, hearten, cheer up, embolden, buoy up, pep up, boost someone's morale, give hope to, buck up (*informal*), gee up, lift the spirits of, give confidence to, inspirit: *When things aren't going well, he always encourages me.* **OPPOSITE:** discourage **2 = urge**, persuade, prompt, spur, coax, incite, egg on, abet: *He encouraged her to quit her job.* **OPPOSITE:** dissuade **3 = promote**, back, help, support, increase, further, aid, forward, advance, favour, boost, strengthen, foster, advocate, stimulate, endorse, commend, succour: *Their task is to encourage private investment in Russia.* **OPPOSITE:** prevent

encouragement NOUN
1 = inspiration, help, support, aid, favour, comfort, comforting, cheer, cheering, consolation, reassurance, morale boosting, succour: *Thanks for all your advice and encouragement.* **2 = urging**, prompting, stimulus, persuasion, coaxing, egging on, incitement: *She had needed no*

The Language of James Fenimore Cooper

James Fenimore Cooper (1789–1851) was an American novelist best known for his Leatherstocking Tales and in particular the second of that sequence, *The Last of the Mohicans*. He also produced numerous volumes of travel writing and fiction set at sea. Although his work has often been thought of simplistically as romantic adventure, it is widely acknowledged to be a significant part of American literary history.

Wilderness is a key note in Cooper's representation of early 19th-century America. Many of the adjectives he attaches to it express the substantial dimensions of the uncultivated land that was central to American national consciousness at the time. *Unexplored*, *primeval*, *virgin* are all commonplace expressions for the vast tracts of land still uninhabited by settlers. *Virgin* is used much more frequently, however, with *forest* of which it is the most salient modifier, followed by *American* and *interminable*. *Woods*, which occurs slightly more frequently than *forest*, are more often *open*, *boundless*, *dark*, or *dense*. A more unusual locution with *wilderness* in Cooper's writing is *howling*, as in:

> I travelled seventy miles alone in the **howling wilderness**, with a rifle bullet in my thigh.

Another prominent term in this context is *frontier*, indicating the point at which settlement meets with *wilderness*. In Cooper's work this appears most commonly with words with a military resonance. The most salient is *warfare* and second most frequent is *post*, referring to the garrisons positioned along the *frontier*. Given the steady movement of the *frontier* into the *wilderness*, it is unsurprising that the most salient adjective with *settlement* in Cooper's writing should be *new*, occurring three times more frequently than *distant*.

The *adventures* that occur against this backdrop have a broader range of meanings than they have today. The sense of *adventure* as a dramatic narrative, involving challenges, mishaps, and usually a journey, is present in Cooper's writing and most saliently appears with *wild*, alongside indicators of hazard such as *perilous* or *desperate*. In addition to this *adventure* also evokes an economic endeavour: a *pecuniary* or *profitable adventure*. At other times, adventure is used more generally to denote a mission or undertaking, as in:

> I come on a private **adventure**.

A specifically literary *adventure* is more likely to be referred to by Cooper as *romance*, which signifies more than a text that deals with notions of romantic love. *Romance*, in opposition to *adventure*, is seen to be inherently untrue: an *adventure* could have a strong factual basis. *Tale* occurs commonly, while *novel* much less so, largely because Cooper's texts deal with oral storytelling much more than with written narratives as his characters relate their stories to one another.

Cooper's rendering of dialogue has been criticized for its stiff and unnatural language. Certainly, there is a notable formality to this aspect of his texts. *Sir* is a favoured term of address between Cooper's characters, often with *my good*, as in:

> Why, **my good sir**, the sea has unsettled your brain!

The use of *do* as an auxiliary verb in dialogue is another characteristic of this formal register, as *I believe*, for example, is extended to *I do believe*. To the modern reader the inevitable alterations in language and culture since Cooper was writing accentuate this rather awkward feel. Some favourite usages of Cooper's that are now significantly dated include, *seemeth* for *seems*, as in:

> Come, there **seemeth** yet some hope left for us, boy.

Another now archaic term that appears with frequency in Cooper's work is *countenance*. This corresponds to the modern *face*, which appears almost twice as often. There is little difference in their usage in Cooper's writing with *pale* (or *pallid*) and *sweet* featuring recurrently with each.

encouragement to accept his invitation. **3 = promotion**, backing, support, boost, endorsement, stimulation, advocacy, furtherance: *The encouragement of trade will benefit the process of economic reform in China.*

> **QUOTATIONS**
> It's a good thing to shoot an admiral now and then to encourage the others
> [Voltaire *Candide*]

encouraging ADJECTIVE **= promising**, good, bright, comforting, cheering, stimulating, reassuring, hopeful, satisfactory, cheerful, favourable, rosy, heartening, auspicious, propitious **OPPOSITE:** discouraging

encroach VERB *(often with* **on** *or* **upon***)* **= intrude**, invade, trespass, infringe, usurp, impinge, trench, overstep, make inroads, impose yourself

encroachment NOUN **= intrusion**, invasion, violation, infringement, trespass, incursion, usurpation, inroad, impingement

encumber VERB **1 = burden**, load, embarrass, saddle, oppress, obstruct, retard, weigh down: *The company is still labouring under the debt burden that it was encumbered with in the 1980s.* **2 = hamper**, restrict, handicap, slow down, cramp, inhibit, clog, hinder, inconvenience, overload, impede, weigh down, trammel, incommode: *fishermen encumbered with bulky clothing and boots*

encyclopedic *or* **encyclopaedic** ADJECTIVE **= comprehensive**, full, complete, vast, universal, wide-ranging, thorough, in-depth, exhaustive, all-inclusive, all-embracing, all-encompassing, thoroughgoing

end NOUN **1 = close**, ending, finish, expiry, expiration: *The report is expected by the end of the year.* **OPPOSITE:** beginning **2 = conclusion**, ending, climax, completion, finale, culmination, denouement, consummation: *His big scene comes towards the end of the film.* **OPPOSITE:** start **3 = finish**, close, stop, resolution, conclusion, closure, wind-up, completion, termination, cessation: *She brought the interview to an abrupt end.* **4 = extremity**, limit, edge, border, bound, extent, extreme, margin, boundary, terminus: *Surveillance equipment is placed at both ends of the tunnel.* **5 = tip**, point, head, peak, extremity: *He tapped the ends of his fingers together.* **6 = purpose**, point, reason, goal, design, target, aim, object, mission, intention, objective, drift, intent, aspiration: *another policy designed to achieve the same end* **7 = outcome**, result, consequence, resolution, conclusion, completion, issue, sequel, end result, attainment, upshot, consummation: *The end justifies the means.* **8 = death**, dying, ruin, destruction, passing on, doom, demise, extinction, dissolution, passing away, extermination, annihilation, expiration, ruination: *Soon after we spoke to him, he met a violent end.* **9 = remnant**, butt, bit, stub, scrap, fragment, stump, remainder, leftover, tail end, oddment, tag end: *an ashtray overflowing with cigarette ends*
▷ VERB **1 = stop**, finish, complete, resolve, halt, cease, axe *(informal)*, dissolve, wind up, terminate, call off, discontinue, put paid to, bring to an end, pull the plug on, call a halt to, nip in the bud, belay *(Nautical)*: *Talks have resumed to try to end the fighting.* **OPPOSITE:** start **2 = finish**, close, conclude, wind up, culminate, terminate, come to an end, draw to a close: *The book ends on a lengthy description of Hawaii.* **OPPOSITE:** begin **3 = destroy**, take, kill, abolish, put an end to, do away with, extinguish, annihilate, exterminate, put to death: *I believe you should be free to end your own life.*
end up 1 = finish up, stop, wind up, come to a halt, fetch up *(informal)*: *The car ended up at the bottom of the river.* **2 = turn out to be**, finish as, finish up, pan out *(informal)*, become eventually: *She could have ended up a millionairess.*
▸ *related adjectives*: final, terminal, ultimate

> **QUOTATIONS**
> The end must justify the means
> [Matthew Prior *Hans Carvel*]

> **PROVERBS**
> *All good things must come to an end*
> *All's well that ends well*

endanger VERB **= put at risk**, risk, threaten, compromise, hazard, jeopardize, imperil, put in danger, expose to danger **OPPOSITE:** save

endear VERB **= attract**, draw, bind, engage, charm, attach, win, incline, captivate

endearing ADJECTIVE **= attractive**, winning, pleasing, appealing, sweet, engaging, charming, pleasant, cute, enticing, captivating, lovable, alluring, adorable, winsome, cutesy *(informal, chiefly U.S.)*

endeavour VERB **= try**, labour, attempt, aim, struggle, venture, undertake, essay, strive, aspire, have a go, go for it *(informal)*, make an effort, have a shot *(informal)*, have a crack *(informal)*, take pains, bend over backwards *(informal)*, do your best, go for broke *(slang)*, bust a gut *(informal)*, give it your best shot *(informal)*, jump through hoops *(informal)*, have a stab *(informal)*, break your neck *(informal)*, make an all-out effort *(informal)*, knock yourself out *(informal)*, do your damnedest *(informal)*, give it your all *(informal)*, rupture yourself *(informal)*: *I will endeavour to rectify the situation.*
▷ NOUN **= attempt**, try, shot *(informal)*, effort, trial, go *(informal)*, aim, bid, crack *(informal)*, venture, enterprise, undertaking, essay, stab *(informal)*: *His first endeavours in the field were wedding films.*

ended ADJECTIVE **= finished**, done, over, through, closed, past, complete, done with, settled, all over (bar the shouting), no more, concluded, accomplished, wrapped-up *(informal)*, at an end, finis

ending NOUN **= finish**, end, close, resolution, conclusion, summing up, wind-up, completion, finale, termination, culmination, cessation, denouement, last part, consummation **OPPOSITE:** start

endless ADJECTIVE **1 = eternal**, constant, infinite, perpetual, continual, immortal, unbroken, unlimited, uninterrupted, limitless, interminable, incessant, boundless, everlasting, unending, ceaseless, inexhaustible, undying, unceasing, unbounded, measureless, unfading: *causing over 25,000 deaths in a seemingly endless war* **OPPOSITE:** temporary **2 = interminable**, constant, persistent, perpetual, never-ending, incessant, monotonous, overlong: *I am sick to death of your endless complaints.* **3 = continuous**, unbroken, uninterrupted, undivided, without end: *an endless conveyor belt*

endorse *or* **indorse** VERB **1 = approve**, back, support, champion, favour, promote, recommend, sanction, sustain, advocate, warrant, prescribe, uphold, authorize, ratify, affirm, approve of, subscribe to, espouse, vouch for, throw your weight behind: *I can endorse this statement wholeheartedly.* **2 = sign**, initial, countersign, sign on the back of, superscribe, undersign: *The payee must endorse the cheque.*

endorsement *or* **indorsement** NOUN **= approval**, backing, support, championing, favour, promotion, sanction, recommendation, acceptance, agreement, warrant, confirmation, upholding, subscription, fiat, advocacy, affirmation, ratification, authorization, seal of approval, approbation, espousal, O.K. *or* okay *(informal)*, endorsation *(Canad.)*

endow VERB **1 = finance**, fund, pay for, award, grant, invest in, confer, settle on, bestow, make over, bequeath, purvey, donate money to: *The ambassador has endowed a public-service fellowship programme.* **2 = imbue**, steep, bathe, saturate, pervade, instil, infuse, permeate, impregnate, inculcate: *Herbs have been used for centuries to endow a whole range of foods with subtle flavours.*

endowed ADJECTIVE *(usually with* **with***)* **= provided**, favoured, graced, blessed, supplied, furnished, enriched

endowment NOUN **1 = provision**, fund, funding, award, income, grant, gift, contribution, revenue, subsidy, presentation, donation, legacy, hand-out, boon, bequest, stipend, bestowal, benefaction, largesse *or* largess, koha *(N.Z.)*: *The company gave the Oxford Union a generous £1m endowment.* **2** *(usually plural)* **= talent**, power, feature, quality, ability, gift, capacity, characteristic, attribute, qualification, genius, faculty, capability, flair, aptitude: *individuals with higher-than-average intellectual endowments*

endurance NOUN **1 = staying power**, strength, resolution, resignation, determination, patience, submission, stamina, fortitude, persistence, tenacity, perseverance, toleration, sufferance, doggedness, stickability *(informal)*, pertinacity: *a test of endurance* **2 = permanence**, stability, continuity, duration, continuation, longevity, durability, continuance, immutability, lastingness: *The book is about the endurance of the class system in Britain.*

endure VERB **1 = experience**, suffer, bear, weather, meet, go through, encounter, cope with, sustain, brave, undergo, withstand, live through, thole *(Scot.)*: *He'd endured years of pain and sleepless nights because of arthritis.* **2 = put up with**, stand, suffer, bear, allow, accept, stick *(slang)*, take *(informal)*, permit, stomach, swallow, brook, tolerate, hack *(slang)*, abide, submit to, countenance, stick out *(informal)*, take patiently: *I simply can't endure another moment of her company.* **3 = last**, live, continue, remain, stay, hold, stand, go on, survive, live on, prevail, persist, abide, be durable, wear well: *Somehow the language endures and continues to survive to this day.*

PROVERBS
What can't be cured must be endured

enduring ADJECTIVE **= long-lasting**, lasting, living, continuing, remaining, firm, surviving, permanent, constant, steady, prevailing, persisting, abiding, perennial, durable, immortal, steadfast, unwavering, immovable, imperishable, unfaltering
OPPOSITE: brief

enemy NOUN **= foe**, rival, opponent, the opposition, competitor, the other side, adversary, antagonist
OPPOSITE: friend
▸ *related adjective:* inimical

QUOTATIONS
Pay attention to your enemies, for they are the first to discover your mistakes
[Antisthenes]

You can discover what your enemy fears most by observing the means he uses to frighten you
[Eric Hoffer *The Passionate State of Mind*]

A man cannot be too careful in the choice of his enemies
[Oscar Wilde *Lady Windermere's Fan*]

A very great man once said you should love your enemies, and that's not a bad piece of advice. We can love them, but, by God, that doesn't mean we're not going to fight them
[Norman Schwarzkopf]

The enemy advances, we retreat.
The enemy camps, we harass.
The enemy tires, we attack.
The enemy retreats, we pursue
[Mao Zedong *slogan for his troops*]

We have met the enemy and he is us
[Walt Kelly *Pogo*]

Yet is every man his own greatest enemy, and as it were his own executioner
[Thomas Browne *Religio Medici*]

If we could read the secret history of our enemies, we should find in each man's life sorrow and suffering enough to disarm all hostility
[Henry Wadsworth Longfellow *Driftwood*]

energetic ADJECTIVE **1 = forceful**, strong, determined, powerful, storming *(informal)*, active, aggressive, dynamic, vigorous, potent, hard-hitting, high-powered, strenuous, punchy *(informal)*, forcible, high-octane *(informal)*: *an energetic public-relations campaign* **2 = lively**, spirited, active, dynamic, vigorous, animated, brisk, tireless, bouncy, indefatigable, alive and kicking, zippy *(informal)*, full of beans *(informal)*, bright-eyed and bushy-tailed *(informal)*: *Two-year-olds can be incredibly energetic.*
OPPOSITE: lethargic **3 = strenuous**, hard, taxing, demanding, tough, exhausting, vigorous, arduous: *an energetic exercise routine*

energize *or* **energise** VERB
1 = stimulate, drive, stir, motivate, activate, animate, enthuse, quicken, enliven, galvanize, liven up, pep up, invigorate, vitalize, inspirit: *their ability to energize their followers*
2 = stimulate, operate, trigger, turn on, start up, activate, switch on, kick-start, electrify, actuate: *When energized, the coil creates an electromagnetic force.*

energy NOUN **1 = strength**, might, force, power, activity, intensity, stamina, exertion, forcefulness: *He was saving his energy for the big race in Belgium.* **2 = liveliness**, life, drive, fire, spirit, determination, pep, go *(informal)*, zip *(informal)*, vitality, animation, vigour, verve, zest, resilience, get-up-and-go *(informal)*, élan, brio, vivacity, vim *(slang)*: *At 65 years old, her energy and looks are wonderful.* **3 = power**: *Oil shortages have brought an energy crisis.*

enfold *or* **infold** VERB **1 = wrap**, surround, enclose, wrap up, encompass, shroud, immerse, swathe, envelop, sheathe, enwrap: *Wood was comfortably enfolded in a woolly dressing-gown.* **2 = embrace**, hold, fold, hug, cuddle, clasp: *He enfolded her gently in his arms.*

enforce VERB **1 = carry out**, apply, implement, fulfil, execute, administer, put into effect, put into action, put into operation, put in force: *The measures are being enforced by Interior Ministry troops.* **2 = impose**, force, require, urge, insist on, compel, exact, oblige, constrain, coerce: *They tried to limit the cost by enforcing a low-tech specification.*

enforced ADJECTIVE **= imposed**, required, necessary, compelled, dictated, prescribed, compulsory, mandatory, constrained, ordained, obligatory, unavoidable, involuntary

enforcement NOUN
1 = administration, carrying out, application, prosecution, execution, implementation, reinforcement, fulfilment: *the adequate enforcement of the law* **2 = imposition**, requirement, obligation, insistence, exaction: *the stricter enforcement of speed limits for vehicles*

engage VERB **1 = participate in**, join in, take part in, undertake, practise, embark on, enter into, become involved in, set about, partake of: *They continue to engage in terrorist activities.*
2 = captivate, win, draw, catch, arrest, fix, attract, capture, charm, attach, fascinate, enchant, allure, enamour: *He engaged us with tales of his adventures.* **3 = occupy**, involve, draw, busy, grip, absorb, tie up, preoccupy, immerse, engross: *He tried to engage me in conversation.* **4 = employ**, commission, appoint, take on, hire, retain, recruit, enlist, enrol, put on the payroll: *We have been able to engage some staff.* **OPPOSITE:** dismiss **5 = book**, reserve, secure, hire, rent, charter, lease, prearrange: *He managed to engage a room for the night.* **6 = interlock**, join, interact, mesh, interconnect, dovetail: *Press the lever until you hear the catch engage.* **7 = set going**, apply, trigger, activate, switch on, energize, bring into operation: *Show me how to engage the four-wheel drive.* **8 = begin battle with**, attack, take on, encounter, combat, fall on, battle with, meet, fight with, assail, face off *(slang)*, wage war on, join battle with, give battle to, come to close quarters with: *They could engage the enemy beyond the range of the torpedoes.*

engaged ADJECTIVE **1 = occupied**, working, involved, committed, employed, busy, absorbed, tied up, preoccupied, engrossed: *the various projects he was engaged on* **2 = betrothed**, promised, pledged, affianced, promised in marriage: *He was engaged to Miss Julia Boardman.*
OPPOSITE: unattached **3 = in use**, busy, tied up, unavailable: *We tried to phone you back but the line was engaged.*
OPPOSITE: free

engagement NOUN **1 = appointment**, meeting, interview, date, commitment, arrangement, rendezvous: *He had an engagement at a* *restaurant in Greek Street at eight.* **2 = betrothal**, marriage contract, troth *(archaic)*, agreement to marry: *I've broken off my engagement to Arthur.* **3 = battle**, fight, conflict, action, struggle, clash, contest, encounter, combat, confrontation, skirmish, face-off *(slang)*: *The constitution prevents them from military engagement on foreign soil.* **4 = participation**, joining, taking part, involvement: *his proactive engagement in the peace process* **5 = job**, work, post, situation, commission, employment, appointment, gig *(informal)*, stint: *her first official engagement as Miss World*

engaging ADJECTIVE **= charming**, interesting, pleasing, appealing, attractive, lovely, fascinating, entertaining, winning, pleasant, fetching *(informal)*, delightful, cute, enchanting, captivating, agreeable, lovable, winsome, cutesy *(informal, chiefly U.S.)*, likable *or* likeable **OPPOSITE:** unpleasant

engender VERB **= produce**, make, cause, create, lead to, occasion, excite, result in, breed, generate, provoke, induce, bring about, arouse, give rise to, precipitate, incite, instigate, foment, beget: *Insults engender hatred against those who indulge in them.*

engine NOUN **= machine**, motor, mechanism, generator, dynamo

engineer NOUN **1 = designer**, producer, architect, developer, deviser, creator, planner, inventor, stylist, artificer, originator, couturier: *He is a fully qualified civil engineer.* **2 = worker**, specialist, operator, practitioner, operative, driver, conductor, technician, handler, skilled employee: *They sent a service engineer to repair the disk drive.* ▷ VERB **1 = design**, plan, create, construct, devise, originate: *Many of Kuwait's freeways were engineered by W. S. Atkins.* **2 = bring about**, plan, control, cause, effect, manage, set up *(informal)*, scheme, arrange, plot, manoeuvre, encompass, mastermind, orchestrate, contrive, concoct, wangle *(informal)*, finagle *(informal)*: *Some people believe that his murder was engineered by Stalin.*

engrave VERB **= carve**, cut, etch, inscribe, chisel, incise, chase, enchase *(rare)*, grave *(archaic)*

engraved ADJECTIVE **= fixed**, set, printed, impressed, lodged, embedded, imprinted, etched, ingrained, infixed

engraving NOUN **1 = print**, block, impression, carving, etching, inscription, plate, woodcut, dry point: *the engraving of Shakespeare at the front of the book* **2 = cutting**, carving, etching, inscribing, chiselling, inscription, chasing, dry point, enchasing *(rare)*: *Glass engraving has increased in popularity over recent years.*

engrossed ADJECTIVE **= absorbed**, lost, involved, occupied, deep, engaged, gripped, fascinated, caught up, intrigued, intent, preoccupied, immersed, riveted, captivated, enthralled, rapt

engrossing ADJECTIVE **= absorbing**, interesting, arresting, engaging, gripping, fascinating, compelling, intriguing, riveting, captivating, enthralling

engulf *or* **ingulf** VERB **1 = immerse**, bury, flood (out), plunge, consume, drown, swamp, encompass, submerge, overrun, inundate, deluge, envelop, swallow up: *The flat was engulfed in flames.* **2 = overwhelm**, overcome, crush, absorb, swamp, engross: *He was engulfed by a feeling of emptiness.*

enhance VERB **= improve**, better, increase, raise, lift, boost, add to, strengthen, reinforce, swell, intensify, heighten, elevate, magnify, augment, exalt, embellish, ameliorate **OPPOSITE:** reduce

enhancement NOUN **= improvement**, strengthening, heightening, enrichment, increment, embellishment, boost, betterment, augmentation, amelioration

enigma NOUN **= mystery**, problem, puzzle, riddle, paradox, conundrum, teaser

enigmatic *or* **enigmatical** ADJECTIVE **= mysterious**, puzzling, obscure, baffling, ambiguous, perplexing, incomprehensible, mystifying, inexplicable, unintelligible, paradoxical, cryptic, inscrutable, unfathomable, indecipherable, recondite, Delphic, oracular, sphinxlike **OPPOSITE:** straightforward

enjoin VERB **1 = order**, charge, warn, urge, require, direct, bid, command, advise, counsel, prescribe, instruct, call upon: *She enjoined me strictly not to tell anyone else.* **2 = prohibit**, bar, ban, forbid, restrain, preclude, disallow, proscribe, interdict, place an injunction on: *the government's attempt to enjoin the publication of the book*

enjoy VERB **1 = take pleasure in** *or* **from**, like, love, appreciate, relish, delight in, revel in, be pleased with, be fond of, be keen on, rejoice in, be entertained by, find pleasure in, find satisfaction in, take joy in: *He enjoys playing cricket.* **OPPOSITE:** hate **2 = have**, use, own, experience, possess, have the benefit of, reap the benefits of, have the use of, be blessed *or* favoured with: *The average German will enjoy 40 days' paid holiday this year.* **enjoy yourself = have a good time**, be happy, have fun, have a field day *(informal)*, have a ball *(informal)*, live life to the full, make merry, let your hair down: *He's too busy enjoying himself to get much work done.*

PROVERBS
Make hay while the sun shines

enjoyable ADJECTIVE **= pleasurable**, good, great, fine, pleasing, nice, satisfying, lovely, entertaining, pleasant, amusing, delicious, delightful, gratifying, agreeable, delectable, to your liking **OPPOSITE:** unpleasant

enjoyment NOUN **1 = pleasure**, liking, fun, delight, entertainment, joy, satisfaction, happiness, relish, recreation, amusement, indulgence, diversion, zest, gratification, gusto, gladness, delectation, beer and skittles *(informal)*: *She ate with great enjoyment.* **2 = benefit**, use, advantage, favour, possession, blessing: *the enjoyment of equal freedom by all*

enlarge VERB **1 = expand**, increase, extend, add to, build up, widen, intensify, blow up *(informal)*, heighten, broaden, inflate, lengthen, magnify, amplify, augment, make bigger, elongate, make larger: *plans to enlarge the park into a 30,000 all-seater stadium* **OPPOSITE:** reduce **2 = grow**, increase, extend, stretch, expand, swell, wax, multiply, inflate, lengthen, diffuse, elongate, dilate, become bigger, puff up, grow larger, grow bigger, become larger, distend, bloat: *The glands in the neck may enlarge.* **enlarge on something = expand on**, develop, add to, fill out, elaborate on, flesh out, expatiate on, give further details about: *I wish to enlarge on the statement I made yesterday.*

enlighten VERB **= inform**, tell, teach, advise, counsel, educate, instruct, illuminate, make aware, edify, apprise, let know, cause to understand

enlightened ADJECTIVE **= informed**, aware, liberal, reasonable, educated, sophisticated, refined, cultivated, open-minded, knowledgeable, literate, broad-minded **OPPOSITE:** ignorant

enlightenment NOUN **= understanding**, information, learning, education, teaching, knowledge, instruction, awareness, wisdom, insight, literacy, sophistication, comprehension, cultivation, refinement, open-mindedness, edification, broad-mindedness

enlist VERB **1 = join up**, join, enter (into), register, volunteer, sign up, enrol: *He enlisted as a private in the Mexican War.* **2 = obtain**, get, gain, secure, engage, procure: *I had to enlist the help of several neighbours to clear the mess.*

enliven VERB **= cheer up**, excite, inspire, cheer, spark, enhance, stimulate, wake up, animate, fire, rouse, brighten, exhilarate, quicken, hearten, perk up, liven up, buoy up, pep up, invigorate, gladden, vitalize, vivify, inspirit, make more exciting, make more lively **OPPOSITE:** subdue

en masse ADVERB **= all together**, together, as one, as a whole, ensemble, as a group, in a group, all at once, in a mass, as a body, in a body

enmity NOUN = **hostility**, hate, spite, hatred, bitterness, friction, malice, animosity, aversion, venom, antagonism, antipathy, acrimony, rancour, bad blood, ill will, animus, malevolence, malignity **OPPOSITE:** friendship

ennoble VERB **1 = dignify**, honour, enhance, elevate, magnify, raise, glorify, exalt, aggrandize: *the fundamental principles of life which ennoble mankind* **2 = raise to the peerage**, kick upstairs *(informal)*, make noble: *He had been ennobled for arranging a government loan in 1836.*

ennui NOUN = **boredom**, dissatisfaction, tiredness, the doldrums, lethargy, tedium, lassitude, listlessness

enormity NOUN **1 = hugeness**, extent, magnitude, greatness, vastness, immensity, massiveness, enormousness, extensiveness: *He was appalled by the enormity of the task ahead of him.* **2 = wickedness**, disgrace, atrocity, depravity, viciousness, villainy, turpitude, outrageousness, baseness, vileness, evilness, monstrousness, heinousness, nefariousness, atrociousness: *the enormity of the crime they had committed* **3 = atrocity**, crime, horror, evil, outrage, disgrace, monstrosity, abomination, barbarity, villainy: *the horrific enormities perpetrated on the islanders*

enormous ADJECTIVE = **huge**, massive, vast, extensive, tremendous, gross, excessive, immense, titanic, jumbo *(informal)*, gigantic, monstrous, mammoth, colossal, mountainous, stellar *(informal)*, prodigious, gargantuan, elephantine, astronomic, ginormous *(informal)*, Brobdingnagian, humongous *or* humungous *(U.S. slang)*, supersize **OPPOSITE:** tiny

enough ADJECTIVE = **sufficient**, adequate, ample, abundant, as much as you need, as much as is necessary: *They had enough money for a one-way ticket.*
▷ PRONOUN = **sufficiency**, plenty, sufficient, abundance, adequacy, right amount, ample supply: *I hope you brought enough for everyone.*
▷ ADVERB = **sufficiently**, amply, fairly, moderately, reasonably, adequately, satisfactorily, abundantly, tolerably, passably: *Do you think sentences for criminals are tough enough already?*

> **PROVERBS**
> *Enough is as good as a feast*

enquire *see* **inquire**

enquiry *see* **inquiry**

enrage VERB = **anger**, provoke, irritate, infuriate, aggravate *(informal)*, incense, gall, madden, inflame, exasperate, incite, antagonize, make you angry, nark *(Brit., Austral. & N.Z. slang)*, make your blood boil, get your back up, make you see red *(informal)*, put your back up **OPPOSITE:** calm

enraged ADJECTIVE = **furious**, cross, wild, angry, angered, mad *(informal)*, raging, irritated, fuming, choked, infuriated, aggravated *(informal)*, incensed, inflamed, exasperated, very angry, irate, livid *(informal)*, incandescent, on the warpath, fit to be tied *(slang)*, boiling mad, raging mad, tooshie *(Austral. slang)*, off the air *(Austral. slang)*

enraptured ADJECTIVE = **enchanted**, delighted, charmed, fascinated, absorbed, entranced, captivated, transported, enthralled, beguiled, bewitched, ravished, spellbound, enamoured

enrich VERB **1 = enhance**, develop, improve, boost, supplement, refine, cultivate, heighten, endow, augment, ameliorate, aggrandize: *Vivid fantasies can enrich your sex life.* **2 = make rich**, make wealthy, make affluent, make prosperous, make well-off: *He enriched himself at the expense of others.*

enrol *or (U.S.)* **enroll** VERB **1 = enlist**, register, be accepted, be admitted, join up, matriculate, put your name down for, sign up *or* on: *To enrol for the conference, fill in the attached form.* **2 = recruit**, take on, engage, enlist: *I thought I'd enrol you with an art group at the school.*

enrolment *or (U.S.)* **enrollment** NOUN = **enlistment**, admission, acceptance, engagement, registration, recruitment, matriculation, signing on *or* up

en route ADVERB = **on** *or* along the way, travelling, on the road, in transit, on the journey

ensemble NOUN **1 = group**, company, band, troupe, cast, orchestra, chorus, supporting cast: *an ensemble of young musicians* **2 = collection**, set, body, whole, total, sum, combination, entity, aggregate, entirety, totality, assemblage, conglomeration: *The state is an ensemble of political and social structures.* **3 = outfit**, suit, get-up *(informal)*, costume: *a dashing ensemble in navy and white*

enshrine VERB = **preserve**, protect, treasure, cherish, revere, exalt, consecrate, embalm, sanctify, hallow, apotheosize

ensign NOUN = **flag**, standard, colours, banner, badge, pennant, streamer, jack, pennon

enslave VERB = **subjugate**, bind, dominate, trap, suppress, enthral, yoke, tyrannize, sell into slavery, reduce to slavery, enchain

ensnare VERB = **trap**, catch, capture, seize, snarl, embroil, net, snare, entangle, entrap, enmesh

ensue VERB = **follow**, result, develop, succeed, proceed, arise, stem, derive, come after, issue, befall, flow, come next, come to pass *(archaic)*, supervene, be consequent on, turn out *or* up **OPPOSITE:** come first

ensure *or (esp. U.S.)* **insure** VERB **1 = make certain**, guarantee, secure, make sure, confirm, warrant, certify: *Steps must be taken to ensure this never happens again.* **2 = protect**, defend, secure, safeguard, guard, make safe: *The plan is aimed at ensuring the future of freshwater fish species.*

entail VERB = **involve**, require, cause, produce, demand, lead to, call for, occasion, need, impose, result in, bring about, give rise to, encompass, necessitate

entangle VERB **1 = tangle**, catch, trap, twist, knot, mat, mix up, snag, snarl, snare, jumble, ravel, trammel, enmesh: *The door handle had entangled itself with the strap of her bag.* **OPPOSITE:** disentangle **2 = embroil**, involve, complicate, mix up, muddle, implicate, bog down, enmesh: *Bureaucracy can entangle ventures for months.*

entanglement NOUN = **becoming entangled**, mix-up, becoming enmeshed, becoming ensnared, becoming jumbled, entrapment, snarl-up *(informal, chiefly Brit.)*, ensnarement: *Many dolphins are accidentally killed through entanglement in fishing equipment.*

enter VERB **1 = come** *or* **go in** *or* **into**, arrive, set foot in somewhere, cross the threshold of somewhere, make an entrance: *He entered and stood near the door.* **OPPOSITE:** exit **2 = penetrate**, get in, insert into, pierce, pass into, perforate: *The bullet entered his right eye.* **3 = join**, start work at, begin work at, sign up for, enrol in, become a member of, enlist in, commit yourself to: *He entered the company as a junior trainee.* **OPPOSITE:** leave **4 = participate in**, join (in), be involved in, get involved in, play a part in, partake in, associate yourself with, start to be in: *A million young people enter the labour market each year.* **5 = begin**, start, take up, move into, set about, commence, set out on, embark upon: *I have entered a new phase in my life.* **6 = compete in**, contest, take part in, join in, fight, sign up for, go in for: *As a boy he entered many music competitions.* **7 = record**, note, register, log, list, write down, take down, inscribe, set down, put in writing: *Prue entered the passage in her notebook, then read it aloud again.* **8 = submit**, offer, present, table, register, lodge, tender, put forward, proffer: *I entered a plea of guilty to the charges.*

enterprise NOUN **1 = firm**, company, business, concern, operation, organization, establishment, commercial undertaking: *There are plenty of small industrial enterprises.* **2 = venture**, operation, project, adventure, undertaking, programme, pursuit, endeavour: *Horse breeding is a risky enterprise.* **3 = initiative**, energy, spirit, resource, daring, enthusiasm, push *(informal)*, imagination, drive, pep, readiness, vigour, zeal, ingenuity, originality, eagerness, audacity, boldness, get-up-and-go *(informal)*, alertness, resourcefulness, gumption *(informal)*, adventurousness, imaginativeness: *His trouble is that he lacks enterprise.*

enterprising ADJECTIVE = **resourceful**, original, spirited, keen, active, daring, alert, eager, bold, enthusiastic, vigorous, imaginative, energetic, adventurous, ingenious, up-and-coming, audacious, zealous, intrepid, venturesome

entertain VERB **1 = amuse**, interest, please, delight, occupy, charm, enthral, cheer, divert, recreate *(rare)*, regale, give pleasure to: *He entertained us with anecdotes about his job.* **2 = show hospitality to**, receive, accommodate, treat, put up, lodge, be host to, have company of, invite round, ask round, invite to a meal, ask for a meal: *I don't really like to entertain guests any more.* **3 = consider**, support, maintain, imagine, think about, hold, foster, harbour, contemplate, conceive of, ponder, cherish, bear in mind, keep in mind, think over, muse over, give thought to, cogitate on, allow yourself to consider: *I wouldn't entertain the idea of doing such a job.*

entertaining ADJECTIVE = **enjoyable**, interesting, pleasing, funny, charming, cheering, pleasant, amusing, diverting, delightful, witty, humorous, pleasurable, recreative *(rare)*

entertainment NOUN **1 = enjoyment**, fun, pleasure, leisure, satisfaction, relaxation, recreation, enjoyment, distraction, amusement, diversion: *I play the piano purely for my own entertainment.* **2 = pastime**, show, sport, performance, play, treat, presentation, leisure activity, beer and skittles: *He organized entertainments and events for elderly people.*

> **QUOTATIONS**
> I believe entertainment can aspire to be art, and can become art, but if you set out to make art you're an idiot
> [Steve Martin]
> This day my wife made it appear to me that my late entertainment this week cost me above £12, an expense which I am almost ashamed of, though it is but once in a great while, and it is the end for which, in the most part, we live, to have such a merry day once or twice in a man's life
> [Samuel Pepys *Diary*]

enthral *or (U.S.)* **enthrall** VERB = **engross**, charm, grip, fascinate, absorb, entrance, intrigue, enchant, rivet, captivate, beguile, ravish, mesmerize, hypnotize, enrapture, hold spellbound, spellbind

enthralling ADJECTIVE = **engrossing**, charming, gripping, fascinating, entrancing, compelling, intriguing, compulsive, enchanting, riveting, captivating, beguiling, mesmerizing, hypnotizing, spellbinding

enthusiasm NOUN **1 = keenness**, interest, passion, excitement, warmth, motivation, relish, devotion, zeal, zest, fervour, eagerness, ardour, vehemence, earnestness, zing *(informal)*, avidity: *Her lack of enthusiasm filled me with disappointment.* **2 = interest**, passion, rage, hobby, obsession, craze, fad *(informal)*, mania, hobbyhorse: *the current enthusiasm for skateboarding*

enthusiast NOUN = **fan**, supporter, lover, follower, addict, freak *(informal)*, admirer, buff *(informal)*, fanatic, devotee, fiend *(informal)*, adherent, zealot, aficionado, groupie *(slang)*

COLLECTORS AND ENTHUSIASTS

ailurophile	cats
arctophile	teddy bears
audiophile	high-fidelity sound reproduction
automobilist	cars
bibliophile	books
brolliologist	umbrellas
campanologist	bell-ringing
cartophilist	cigarette cards
cruciverbalist	crosswords
deltiologist	picture postcards
discophile	gramophone records
fusilatelist	phonecards
herbalist	herbs
lepidopterist	moths and butterflies
medallist	medals
numismatist	coins
oenophile	wine
paranumismatist	coin-like objects
philatelist	stamps
phillumenist	matchbox labels
phraseologist	phrases
scripophile	share certificates
vexillologist	flags
zoophile	animals

enthusiastic ADJECTIVE = **keen**, earnest, spirited, committed, excited, devoted, warm, eager, lively, passionate, vigorous, ardent, hearty, exuberant, avid, fervent, zealous, ebullient, vehement, wholehearted, full of beans *(informal)*, fervid, keen as mustard, bright-eyed and bushy-tailed *(informal)* **OPPOSITE:** apathetic

entice VERB = **lure**, attract, invite, persuade, draw, tempt, induce, seduce, lead on, coax, beguile, allure, cajole, decoy, wheedle, prevail on, inveigle, dangle a carrot in front of

enticing ADJECTIVE = **attractive**, appealing, inviting, charming, fascinating, tempting, intriguing, irresistible, persuasive, seductive, captivating, beguiling, alluring **OPPOSITE:** unattractive

entire ADJECTIVE **1 = continuous**, unified, unbroken, uninterrupted, undivided: *He had spent his entire life in China as a doctor.* **2 = whole**, full, complete, total: *The entire family was killed in the crash.* **3 = absolute**, full, total, utter, outright, thorough, unqualified, unrestricted, undiminished, unmitigated, unreserved: *He assured me of his entire confidence in me.* **4 = intact**, whole, perfect, unmarked, unbroken, sound, unharmed, undamaged, without a scratch, unmarred: *No document is entire, and it is often unclear in what order the pieces fit together.*

entirely ADVERB **1 = completely**, totally, perfectly, absolutely, fully, altogether, thoroughly, wholly, utterly, every inch, without exception, unreservedly, in every respect, without reservation, lock, stock and barrel: *The two cases are entirely different.* **OPPOSITE:** partly **2 = only**, exclusively, solely: *The whole episode was entirely my fault.*

entirety NOUN = **whole**, total, sum, unity, aggregate, totality

entitle VERB **1 = give the right to**, allow, enable, permit, sanction, license, qualify for, warrant, authorize, empower, enfranchise, make eligible: *Your contract entitles you to a full refund.* **2 = call**, name, title, term, style, label, dub, designate, characterize, christen, give the title of, denominate: *an instrumental piece entitled 'Changing States'*

entity NOUN **1 = thing**, being, body, individual, object, presence, existence, substance, quantity, creature, organism: *the concept of the earth as a living entity* **2 = essential nature**, being, existence, essence, quintessence, real nature, quiddity *(Philosophy)*: *key periods of national or cultural entity and development*

entomb VERB = **bury**, inter, lay to rest, sepulchre, place in a tomb, inhume, inurn

entourage NOUN = **retinue**, company, following, staff, court, train, suite, escort, cortege

entrails PLURAL NOUN = **intestines**, insides *(informal)*, guts, bowels, offal, internal organs, innards *(informal)*, vital organs, viscera

entrance[1] NOUN **1 = way in**, opening, door, approach, access, entry, gate, passage, avenue, doorway, portal, inlet, ingress, means of access: *He drove in through a side entrance.* **OPPOSITE:** exit **2 = appearance**, coming in, entry, arrival, introduction, ingress: *The audience chanted his name as he made his entrance.* **OPPOSITE:** exit **3 = admission**, access, entry, entrée, admittance, permission to enter, ingress, right of entry: *Hewitt gained entrance to the house by pretending to be a heating engineer.*

entrance[2] VERB **1 = enchant**, delight, charm, absorb, fascinate, dazzle, captivate, transport, enthral, beguile, bewitch, ravish, gladden, enrapture, spellbind: *She entranced the audience with her classical Indian singing.* OPPOSITE: bore **2 = mesmerize**, bewitch, hypnotize, put a spell on, cast a spell on, put in a trance: *The sailors were entranced by the voices of the sirens.*

entrant NOUN **1 = newcomer**, novice, initiate, beginner, trainee, apprentice, convert, new member, fresher, neophyte, tyro, probationer: *the newest entrant to the political scene* **2 = competitor**, player, candidate, entry, participant, applicant, contender, contestant: *All items submitted for the competition must be the entrant's own work.*

entrap NOUN **= trick**, lure, seduce, entice, deceive, implicate, lead on, embroil, beguile, allure, entangle, ensnare, inveigle, set a trap for, enmesh: *She was trying to entrap him into marriage.*
▷ VERB **= catch**, net, capture, trap, snare, entangle, ensnare: *The whale's mouth contains filters which entrap plankton.*

entreaty NOUN **= plea**, appeal, suit, request, prayer, petition, exhortation, solicitation, supplication, importunity, earnest request

entrench *or* **intrench** VERB **= fix**, set, establish, plant, seat, settle, root, install, lodge, anchor, implant, embed, dig in, ensconce, ingrain

entrenched *or* **intrenched** ADJECTIVE **= fixed**, set, firm, rooted, well-established, ingrained, deep-seated, deep-rooted, indelible, unshakeable *or* unshakable, ineradicable

entrepreneur NOUN **= businessman** *or* **businesswoman**, tycoon, director, executive, contractor, industrialist, financier, speculator, magnate, impresario, business executive

entrust *or* **intrust** VERB **1 = give custody of**, trust, deliver, commit, delegate, hand over, turn over, confide, commend, consign: *her reluctance to entrust her children to the care of someone else* **2** *(usually with* **with***)* **= assign**, charge, trust, invest, authorize: *They are prepared to entrust him with the leadership of the party.*

entry NOUN **1 = admission**, access, entrance, admittance, entrée, permission to enter, right of entry: *Entry to the museum is free.* **2 = coming in**, entering, appearance, arrival, entrance: *He made his triumphal entry into Mexico.* OPPOSITE: exit **3 = introduction**, presentation, initiation, inauguration, induction, debut, investiture: *The time has come to prepare her for her entry into society.* **4 = record**, listing, account, note, minute, statement, item, registration, memo, memorandum, jotting: *Her diary entry for that day records his visit.* **5 = competitor**, player, attempt, effort, candidate, participant, challenger, submission, entrant, contestant: *The winner was selected from hundreds of entries.* **6 = way in**, opening, door, approach, access, gate, passage, entrance, avenue, doorway, portal, inlet, passageway, ingress, means of access: *A lorry blocked the entry to the school.*

entwine *or* **intwine** VERB **= twist**, surround, embrace, weave, knit, braid, encircle, wind, intertwine, interweave, plait, twine, ravel, interlace, entwist *(archaic)* OPPOSITE: disentangle

enumerate VERB **1 = list**, tell, name, detail, relate, mention, quote, cite, specify, spell out, recount, recite, itemize, recapitulate: *She enumerated all the reasons why she wanted to leave him.* **2 = count**, calculate, sum up, total, reckon, compute, add up, tally, number: *They enumerated the casualties.*

enunciate VERB **1 = pronounce**, say, speak, voice, sound, utter, articulate, vocalize, enounce *(formal)*: *She enunciated each word slowly and carefully.* **2 = state**, declare, proclaim, pronounce, publish, promulgate, propound: *He was always ready to enunciate his views to anyone who would listen.*

envelop VERB **= enclose**, cover, hide, surround, wrap around, embrace, blanket, conceal, obscure, veil, encompass, engulf, cloak, shroud, swathe, encircle, encase, swaddle, sheathe, enfold, enwrap

envelope NOUN **= wrapping**, casing, case, covering, cover, skin, shell, coating, jacket, sleeve, sheath, wrapper

enviable ADJECTIVE **= desirable**, favoured, privileged, fortunate, lucky, blessed, advantageous, to die for *(informal)*, much to be desired, covetable OPPOSITE: undesirable

envious ADJECTIVE **= covetous**, jealous, grudging, malicious, resentful, green-eyed, begrudging, spiteful, jaundiced, green with envy

environment NOUN **1 = surroundings**, setting, conditions, situation, medium, scene, circumstances, territory, background, atmosphere, context, habitat, domain, milieu, locale: *The children were brought up in completely different environments.* **2 = habitat**, home, surroundings, territory, terrain, locality, natural home: *the maintenance of a safe environment for marine mammals*

environmental ADJECTIVE **= ecological**, green, eco-friendly

environmentalist NOUN **= conservationist**, ecologist, green, friend of the earth

environs PLURAL NOUN **= surrounding area**, surroundings, district, suburbs, neighbourhood, outskirts, precincts, vicinity, locality, purlieus

envisage VERB **1 = imagine**, contemplate, conceive (of), visualize, picture, fancy, think up, conceptualize: *I can't envisage being married to someone like him.* **2 = foresee**, see, expect, predict, anticipate, envision: *Scientists envisage a major breakthrough in the next few years.*

envision VERB **= conceive of**, expect, imagine, predict, anticipate, see, contemplate, envisage, foresee, visualize

envoy NOUN **1 = ambassador**, minister, diplomat, emissary, legate, plenipotentiary: *A French envoy arrived in Beirut on Sunday.* **2 = messenger**, agent, deputy, representative, delegate, courier, intermediary, emissary: *the Secretary General's personal envoy*

envy NOUN **= covetousness**, spite, hatred, resentment, jealousy, bitterness, malice, ill will, malignity, resentfulness, enviousness *(informal)*: *He admitted his feelings of envy towards his brother.*
▷ VERB **1 = be jealous (of)**, resent, begrudge, be envious (of): *I have a famous brother and a lot of people envy me for that.* **2 = covet**, desire, crave, aspire to, yearn for, hanker after: *He envied her peace of mind.*

QUOTATIONS

Nothing sharpens sight like envy
[Thomas Fuller *Gnomologia*]

Our envy always lasts much longer than the happiness of those we envy
[Duc de la Rochefoucauld *Maxims*]

Even success softens not the heart of the envious
[Pindar *Odes*]

ephemeral ADJECTIVE **= transient**, short, passing, brief, temporary, fleeting, short-lived, fugitive, flitting, momentary, transitory, evanescent, impermanent, fugacious OPPOSITE: eternal

epidemic ADJECTIVE **= widespread**, wide-ranging, general, sweeping, prevailing, rampant, prevalent, rife, pandemic: *The abuse of crack has reached epidemic proportions in the US in recent years.*
▷ NOUN **1 = outbreak**, plague, growth, spread, scourge, contagion: *A flu epidemic is sweeping through Britain.* **2 = spate**, plague, outbreak, wave, rash, eruption, upsurge: *an epidemic of racist crimes*

epilogue NOUN **= conclusion**, postscript, coda, afterword, concluding speech OPPOSITE: prologue

episode NOUN **1 = event**, experience, happening, matter, affair, incident, circumstance, adventure, business, occurrence, escapade: *an unfortunate and rather sordid episode in my life* **2 = instalment**, part, act, scene, section, chapter, passage: *The final episode will be shown next Saturday.*

episodic *or* **episodical** ADJECTIVE **1 = irregular**, occasional, sporadic, intermittent: *episodic attacks of fever* **2 = irregular**, rambling, disconnected, anecdotal, disjointed, wandering, discursive, digressive: *an episodic narrative of unrelated characters*

epistle NOUN **= letter**, note, message, communication, missive

epitaph NOUN **1 = commemoration**, elegy, obituary: *a fitting epitaph for a great man* **2 = inscription**, engraving: *His words are carved as his epitaph on the headstone of his grave.*

e

epithet NOUN **1 = name**, title, description, tag, nickname, designation, appellation, sobriquet, moniker *or* monicker *(slang)*: *players who fitted their manager's epithet of 'headless chickens'* **2 = curse**, obscenity, blasphemy, swear word, imprecation: *a stream of obscene epithets*

epitome NOUN **= personification**, essence, embodiment, type, representation, norm, archetype, exemplar, typical example, quintessence

epitomize *or* **epitomise** VERB **= typify**, represent, illustrate, embody, exemplify, symbolize, personify, incarnate

epoch NOUN **= era**, time, age, period, date, aeon

equal ADJECTIVE **1** *(often with* **to** *or* **with***)* **= identical**, the same, matched, matching, like, equivalent, uniform, alike, corresponding, tantamount, one and the same, proportionate, commensurate: *a population having equal numbers of men and women* **OPPOSITE:** unequal **2 = fair**, just, impartial, egalitarian, unbiased, even-handed, equable: *Women demand equal rights with men.* **OPPOSITE:** unfair **3 = even**, balanced, fifty-fifty *(informal)*, evenly matched, evenly balanced, evenly proportioned: *an equal contest* **OPPOSITE:** uneven **4** *(with* **to***)* **= capable of**, adequate for: *She wanted to show she was equal to any test they gave her.*
▷ NOUN **= match**, equivalent, fellow, twin, mate, peer, parallel, counterpart, compeer: *She was one of the boys, their equal.*
▷ VERB **1 = amount to**, make, come to, total, balance, agree with, level, parallel, tie with, equate, correspond to, be equal to, square with, be tantamount to, equalize, tally with, be level with, be even with: *The average pay rise equalled 1.41 times inflation.* **OPPOSITE:** be unequal to **2 = be equal to**, match, reach, rival, come up to, be level with, be even with: *The victory equalled Scotland's best in history.* **3 = be as good as**, match, compare with, equate with, measure up to, be as great as: *No amount of money can equal memories like that.*

equality NOUN **1 = fairness**, equal opportunity, equal treatment, egalitarianism, fair treatment, justness: *the principle of racial equality* **OPPOSITE:** inequality **2 = sameness**, balance, identity, similarity, correspondence, parity, likeness, uniformity, equivalence, evenness, coequality, equatability: *They advocate the unconditional equality of incomes.* **OPPOSITE:** disparity

> **QUOTATIONS**
>
> We hold these truths to be self-evident, that all men are created equal, that they are endowed by their Creator with certain unalienable rights, that among these are life, liberty, and the pursuit of happiness
> [Thomas Jefferson *The Declaration of Independence*]
>
> I have a dream that my four little children will one day live in a nation where they will not be judged by the color of their skin but by the content of their character
> [Martin Luther King Jr. *speech at civil rights march*]
>
> The defect of equality is that we only desire it with our superiors
> [Henry Becque *Querelles littéraires*]
>
> All animals are equal but some animals are more equal than others
> [George Orwell *Animal Farm*]
>
> Even the president of the United States sometimes must have to stand naked
> [Bob Dylan *It's Alright, Ma (I'm Only Bleeding)*]

equalize *or* **equalise** VERB **1 = make equal**, match, level, balance, square, equal, smooth, equate, standardize, even out, even up, regularize, make level: *Such measures are needed to equalize wage rates between countries.* **2 = draw level**, level the score, square the score, make the score level: *Brazil equalized with only 16 minutes remaining.*

equanimity NOUN **= composure**, peace, calm, poise, serenity, tranquillity, coolness, aplomb, calmness, phlegm, steadiness, presence of mind, sang-froid, self-possession, placidity, level-headedness, imperturbability

equate VERB **1 = identify**, associate, connect, compare, relate, mention in the same breath, think of in connection with, think of together: *I equate suits with power and authority.* **2 = make equal**, match, balance, square, even up, equalize: *relying on arbitrage to equate prices between the various stock exchanges*

equation NOUN **= equating**, match, agreement, balancing, pairing, comparison, parallel, equality, correspondence, likeness, equivalence, equalization

equestrian ADJECTIVE **= riding**, mounted, horse riding

equilibrium NOUN **1 = stability**, balance, symmetry, steadiness, evenness, equipoise, counterpoise: *For the economy to be in equilibrium, income must equal expenditure.* **2 = composure**, calm, stability, poise, serenity, coolness, calmness, equanimity, steadiness, self-possession, collectedness: *I paused and took deep breaths to restore my equilibrium.*

equip VERB **1 = supply**, provide, stock, dress, outfit, arm, rig, array, furnish, endow, attire, fit out, deck out, kit out, fit up, accoutre: *The country did not have the funds to equip the reserve army properly.* **2 = prepare**, qualify, educate, get ready, endow: *Our aim is to provide courses which equip students for future employment.*

equipment NOUN **= apparatus**, stock, supplies, material, stuff, tackle, gear, tools, provisions, kit, rig, baggage, paraphernalia, accoutrements, appurtenances, equipage

equitable ADJECTIVE **= even-handed**, just, right, fair, due, reasonable, proper, honest, impartial, rightful, unbiased, dispassionate, proportionate, unprejudiced, nondiscriminatory

equity NOUN **= fairness**, justice, integrity, honesty, fair play, righteousness, impartiality, rectitude, reasonableness, even-handedness, fair-mindedness, uprightness, equitableness **OPPOSITE:** unfairness

equivalence *or* **equivalency** NOUN **= equality**, correspondence, agreement, similarity, identity, parallel, match, parity, conformity, likeness, sameness, parallelism, evenness, synonymy, alikeness, interchangeableness

equivalent ADJECTIVE **= equal**, even, same, comparable, parallel, identical, alike, corresponding, correspondent, synonymous, of a kind, tantamount, interchangeable, of a piece with, commensurate, homologous: *A unit of alcohol is equivalent to a glass of wine.* **OPPOSITE:** different
▷ NOUN **= equal**, counterpart, correspondent, twin, peer, parallel, match, opposite number: *the civil administrator of the West Bank and his equivalent in Gaza*

equivocal ADJECTIVE **= ambiguous**, uncertain, misleading, obscure, suspicious, vague, doubtful, dubious, questionable, ambivalent, indefinite, evasive, oblique, indeterminate, prevaricating, oracular **OPPOSITE:** clear

era NOUN **= age**, time, period, stage, date, generation, cycle, epoch, aeon, day *or* days

eradicate VERB **= wipe out**, eliminate, remove, destroy, get rid of, abolish, erase, excise, extinguish, stamp out, obliterate, uproot, weed out, annihilate, put paid to, root out,

The Language of George Eliot

'George Eliot' was the pen-name of Mary Ann Evans (1819–1880), the author of Victorian classics including *Adam Bede*, *The Mill on the Floss*, *Middlemarch* and *Daniel Deronda*. Eliot's novels are celebrated for their psychological depth and their portrayal of contemporary rural society.

Eliot's most frequent noun is *man*, usually collocating with adjectives such as *wise*, *clever*, *strong*, and *honest*. *Women*, on the other hand, tend to be described as *pretty*, *fine*, *sweet*, *loving*, and *little*. Even in those passages where women are described as *clever*, this is filtered through the negative perceptions of such qualities in Victorian society:

> 'But I shall be a **clever woman**,' said Maggie, with a toss. 'Oh, I dare say, and a nasty, conceited thing. Everybody'll hate you.'

Eliot often uses the phrase *a man of*, for example *a man of sober passions*, *men of duller fibre* and *a man of family* (meaning 'a man from a reputable family'). *Man of business* occurs several times, and there are no instances of the form *business man*, which was just coming into use in Eliot's time. Lydgate, the doctor in *Middlemarch*, is often referred to (and refers to himself) by the now archaic phrase *medical man*, whereas the other doctors are simply *doctors*. The synonyms are nicely distinguished: Lydgate is more than a doctor; he is a man who identifies himself with his profession, and *medical man* captures this:

> 'Do you know, Tertius, I often wish you had not been a **medical man**.' 'Nay, Rosy, don't say that... That is like saying you wish you had married another man.'

Another of Eliot's five most frequent nouns is *life*, often modified by an adjective which describes a role: *married life*, *domestic life*, *private life*, *public life*, and *religious life*. This reflects the centrality of society and community in Eliot's novels: people don't simply have *lives*; they have lives which interconnect with others and which enforce upon them certain roles and duties. These roles are often stifling: indeed, *married life* is most frequently used in phases such as *the duties/trials/troubles* of married life. *Middlemarch* was described by Virginia Woolf as 'one of the few English novels written for grown-up people', and one aspect of this is Eliot's portrayal of marriage, not as a happy ending as it often was in other Victorian women's novels, but as a complex and difficult reality.

The theme of limitation can also be seen in Eliot's use of adjectives relating to space. In particular, she often uses *narrow* in the metaphorical sense 'constrained, limited', for example:

> Grandcourt discerned the signs of Gwendolen's expectation, interpreting them with the **narrow correctness** which leaves a world of unknown feeling behind.

Broad tends to be used in the physical sense, but *wide* is also used metaphorically to express the themes of provincialism and limitation that are central Eliot's novels, especially when it is used as a comparative in phrases such as *wider relations*, *wider knowledge*, and *wider life*.

A prominent aspect of Eliot's language is her use of words in the semantic field of vision: both *see* and *eye* are among the hundred most frequent words in her novels. *See* frequently collocates with negative words, and Eliot often writes that characters *do not see*, *never see*, or *only see*, as in the following example from *Scenes of Clerical Life*:

> ... which made her feel as if she had **only seen** life through a dim haze before.

The frequency of these phrases is significant in light of Eliot's repeated use of physical vision as a metaphor for understanding: in *Middlemarch*, for example, Dorothea's self-delusion is shown through her physical short-sightedness. Related to this is the frequency of words referring to knowledge, such as *mind*, *conscious*, and *consciousness*. The most frequent collocate of *mind* is *fill* or *full* (in 'his mind was full of happy visions'), but it is notable that there are several examples of the mind *glancing* over thoughts or memories, again indicating the interconnectedness of vision and knowledge in Eliot's novels.

efface, exterminate, expunge, extirpate, wipe from the face of the earth

eradication NOUN **= wiping out**, abolition, destruction, elimination, removal, extinction, extermination, annihilation, erasure, obliteration, effacement, extirpation, expunction

erase VERB **1 = delete**, cancel out, wipe out, remove, eradicate, excise, obliterate, efface, blot out, expunge: *They are desperate to erase the memory of their defeat.* **2 = rub out**, remove, wipe out, delete, scratch out: *She erased the words from the blackboard.*

e

erect ADJECTIVE **= upright**, raised, straight, standing, stiff, firm, rigid, vertical, elevated, perpendicular, pricked-up: *Her head was erect and her back was straight.* **OPPOSITE:** bent
▷ VERB **1 = build**, raise, set up, lift, pitch, mount, stand up, rear, construct, put up, assemble, put together, elevate: *Demonstrators have erected barricades in the roads.* **OPPOSITE:** demolish **2 = found**, establish, form, create, set up, institute, organize, put up, initiate: *the edifice of free trade which has been erected since the war*

erection NOUN **1 = hard-on** *(slang)*, erect penis: *As he disrobed, his erection became obvious.* **2 = building**, setting-up, manufacture, construction, assembly, creation, establishment, elevation, fabrication: *the erection of temporary fencing to protect hedges under repair*

ergo CONJUNCTION **= therefore**, so, then, thus, hence, consequently, accordingly, for that reason, in consequence

erode VERB **1 = disintegrate**, crumble, deteriorate, corrode, break up, grind down, waste away, wear down *or* away: *By 1980, Miami beach had all but totally eroded.* **2 = destroy**, consume, spoil, crumble, eat away, corrode, break up, grind down, abrade, wear down *or* away: *Once exposed, soil is quickly eroded by wind and rain.* **3 = weaken**, destroy, undermine, diminish, impair, lessen, wear away: *His fumbling of the issue of reform has eroded his authority.*

erosion NOUN **1 = disintegration**, deterioration, corrosion, corrasion, wearing down *or* away, grinding down: *erosion of the river valleys* **2 = deterioration**, wearing, undermining, destruction, consumption, weakening, spoiling, attrition, eating away, abrasion, grinding down, wearing down *or* away: *an erosion of moral standards*

erotic ADJECTIVE **= sexual**, sexy *(informal)*, crude, explicit, rousing, sensual, seductive, vulgar, stimulating, steamy *(informal)*, suggestive, aphrodisiac, voluptuous, carnal, titillating, bawdy, lustful, sexually arousing, erogenous, amatory

err VERB **1 = make a mistake**, mistake, go wrong, blunder, slip up *(informal)*, misjudge, be incorrect, be inaccurate, miscalculate, go astray, be in error, put your foot in it *(informal)*, misapprehend, blot your copybook *(informal)*, drop a brick *or* clanger *(informal)*: *The contractors seriously erred in their original estimates.* **2 = sin**, fall, offend, lapse, trespass, do wrong, deviate, misbehave, go astray, transgress, be out of order, blot your copybook *(informal)*: *If he errs again, he will be severely punished.*

QUOTATIONS
To err is human, to forgive divine
[Alexander Pope *An Essay on Criticism*]

errand NOUN **= job**, charge, commission, message, task, mission

errant ADJECTIVE **= sinning**, offending, straying, wayward, deviant, erring, aberrant

erratic ADJECTIVE **= unpredictable**, variable, unstable, irregular, shifting, eccentric, abnormal, inconsistent, uneven, unreliable, wayward, capricious, desultory, changeable, aberrant, fitful, inconstant **OPPOSITE:** regular

erroneous ADJECTIVE **= incorrect**, wrong, mistaken, false, flawed, faulty, inaccurate, untrue, invalid, unfounded, spurious, amiss, unsound, wide of the mark, inexact, fallacious **OPPOSITE:** correct

error NOUN **= mistake**, slip, fault, blunder, flaw, boob *(Brit. slang)*, delusion, oversight, misconception, fallacy, inaccuracy, howler *(informal)*, bloomer *(Brit. informal)*, boner *(slang)*, miscalculation, misapprehension, solecism, erratum, barry *or* Barry Crocker *(Austral. slang)*

ersatz ADJECTIVE **= artificial**, substitute, pretend, fake, imitation, synthetic, bogus, simulated, sham, counterfeit, spurious, phoney *or* phony *(informal)*

erstwhile ADJECTIVE **= former**, old, late, previous, once, past, ex *(informal)*, one-time, sometime, bygone, quondam

erudite ADJECTIVE **= learned**, lettered, cultured, educated, scholarly, cultivated, knowledgeable, literate, well-educated, well-read **OPPOSITE:** uneducated

erudition NOUN **= learning**, education, knowledge, scholarship, letters, lore, academic knowledge

erupt VERB **1 = explode**, blow up, flare up, emit lava: *The volcano erupted in 1980.* **2 = gush**, burst out, be ejected, burst forth, pour forth, belch forth, spew forth *or* out: *Lava erupted from the volcano and flowed over the ridge.* **3 = start**, break out, begin, explode, flare up, burst out, boil over: *Heavy fighting erupted again two days after the cease-fire.* **4 = break out**, appear, flare up: *My skin erupted in pimples.*

eruption NOUN **1 = explosion**, discharge, outburst, venting, ejection: *the volcanic eruption of Tambora in 1815* **2 = flare-up**, outbreak, sally: *the sudden eruption of violence on the streets of the city* **3 = inflammation**, outbreak, rash, flare-up: *an unpleasant eruption of boils*

escalate VERB **1 = grow**, increase, extend, intensify, expand, surge, be increased, mount, heighten: *Unions and management fear the dispute could escalate.* **OPPOSITE:** decrease **2 = increase**, develop, extend, intensify, expand, build up, step up, heighten, enlarge, magnify, amplify: *Defeat could cause one side or the other to escalate the conflict.* **OPPOSITE:** lessen

escalation NOUN **= increase**, rise, build-up, expansion, heightening, developing, acceleration, upsurge, intensification, amplification

escapade NOUN **= adventure**, fling, stunt, romp, trick, scrape *(informal)*, spree, mischief, lark *(informal)*, caper, prank, antic

escape VERB **1 = get away**, flee, take off, fly, bolt, skip, slip away, abscond, decamp, hook it *(slang)*, do a runner *(slang)*, do a bunk *(Brit. slang)*, fly the coop *(U.S. & Canad. informal)*, make a break for it, slip through your fingers, skedaddle *(informal)*, take a powder *(U.S. & Canad. slang)*, make your getaway, take it on the lam *(U.S. & Canad. slang)*, break free *or* out, make *or* effect your escape, run away *or* off, do a Skase *(Austral. informal)*: *A prisoner has escaped from a jail in Northern England.* **2 = avoid**, miss, evade, dodge, shun, elude, duck, steer clear of, circumvent, body-swerve *(Scot.)*: *He was lucky to escape serious injury.* **3 = be forgotten by**, be beyond (someone), baffle, elude, puzzle, stump: *an actor whose name escapes me for the moment* **4** *(usually with* **from***)* **= leak out**, flow out, drain away, discharge, gush out, emanate, seep out, exude, spurt out, spill out, pour forth: *Leave a vent open to let some of the moist air escape.*
▷ NOUN **1 = getaway**, break, flight, break-out, bolt, decampment: *He made his escape from the country.* **2 = avoidance**, evasion, circumvention, elusion: *his narrow escape from bankruptcy* **3 = relaxation**, relief, recreation, distraction, diversion, pastime: *For me television is an escape.* **4 = leak**, emission, discharge, outpouring, gush, spurt, outflow, leakage, drain, seepage, issue, emanation, efflux, effluence, outpour: *You should report any suspected gas escape immediately.*

eschew VERB **= avoid**, give up, abandon, have nothing to do with, shun, elude, renounce, refrain from, forgo, abstain from, fight shy of, forswear, abjure, kick *(informal)*, swear off, give a wide berth to, keep *or* steer clear of

escort NOUN **1 = guard**, protection, safeguard, bodyguard, company, train, convoy, entourage, retinue, cortege: *He arrived with a police escort.* **2 = companion**, partner, attendant, guide, squire *(rare)*, protector, beau, chaperon, plus-one *(informal)*: *My sister needed an escort for a company dinner.* ▷ VERB **= accompany**, lead, partner, conduct, guide, guard, shepherd, convoy, usher, squire, hold (someone's) hand, chaperon: *I escorted him to the door.*

esoteric ADJECTIVE **= obscure**, private, secret, hidden, inner, mysterious, mystical, mystic, occult, arcane, Hermetic, cryptic, inscrutable, abstruse, recondite, cabbalistic

especially ADVERB **1 = notably**, largely, chiefly, mainly, mostly, principally, strikingly, conspicuously, outstandingly: *The group is said to be gaining support, especially in the rural areas.* **2 = very**, specially, particularly, signally, extremely, remarkably, unusually, exceptionally, extraordinarily, markedly, supremely, uncommonly: *Giving up smoking can be especially difficult.* **3 = particularly**, expressly, exclusively, precisely, specifically, uniquely, peculiarly, singularly: *The system we design will be especially for you.*

espionage NOUN **= spying**, intelligence, surveillance, counter-intelligence, undercover work

espouse VERB **= support**, back, champion, promote, maintain, defend, adopt, take up, advocate, embrace, uphold, stand up for

espy VERB **= catch sight of**, see, discover, spot, notice, sight, observe, spy, perceive, detect, glimpse, make out, discern, behold, catch a glimpse of, descry

essay NOUN **1 = composition**, study, paper, article, piece, assignment, discourse, tract, treatise, dissertation, disquisition: *He was asked to write an essay about his home town.* **2 = attempt**, go *(informal)*, try, effort, shot *(informal)*, trial, struggle, bid, test, experiment, crack *(informal)*, venture, undertaking, stab *(informal)*, endeavour, exertion: *His first essay in running a company was a disaster.* ▷ VERB **= attempt**, try, test, take on, undertake, strive for, endeavour, have a go at, try out, have a shot at *(informal)*, have a crack at *(informal)*, have a bash at *(informal)*: *He essayed a smile, but it was a dismal failure.*

essence NOUN **1 = fundamental nature**, nature, being, life, meaning, heart, spirit, principle, soul, core, substance, significance, entity, bottom line, essential part, kernel, crux, lifeblood, pith, quintessence, basic characteristic, quiddity: *Some claim that Ireland's very essence is expressed through its language.* **2 = concentrate**, spirits, extract, elixir, tincture, distillate: *Add a few drops of vanilla essence.*
in essence = essentially, materially, virtually, basically, fundamentally, in effect, substantially, in the main, to all intents and purposes, in substance: *In essence, we share the same ideology.*
of the essence = vitally important, essential, vital, critical, crucial, key, indispensable, of the utmost importance: *Time is of the essence with this project.*

essential ADJECTIVE **1 = vital**, important, needed, necessary, critical, crucial, key, indispensable, requisite, vitally important, must-have: *It is absolutely essential that we find this man quickly.* **OPPOSITE:** unimportant **2 = fundamental**, main, basic, radical, key, principal, constitutional, cardinal, inherent, elementary, innate, hard-wired, intrinsic, elemental, immanent: *Two essential elements must be proven: motive and opportunity.* **OPPOSITE:** secondary **3 = concentrated**, extracted, refined, volatile, rectified, distilled: *essential oils used in aromatherapy* ▷ NOUN **= prerequisite**, principle, fundamental, necessity, must, basic, requisite, vital part, sine qua non *(Latin)*, rudiment, must-have: *the essentials of everyday life, such as food and water*

establish VERB **1 = set up**, found, start, create, institute, organize, install, constitute, inaugurate: *They established the school in 1989.* **2 = prove**, show, confirm, demonstrate, ratify, certify, verify, validate, substantiate, corroborate, authenticate: *An autopsy was being done to establish the cause of death.* **3 = secure**, form, base, ground, plant, settle, fix, root, implant, entrench, ensconce, put down roots: *He has established himself as a pivotal figure in US politics.*

Establishment NOUN
the Establishment = the authorities, the system, the powers that be, the ruling class, the established order, institutionalized authority: *the revolution against the Establishment*

establishment NOUN **1 = creation**, founding, setting up, foundation, institution, organization, formation, installation, inauguration, enactment: *discussions to explore the establishment of diplomatic relations* **2 = organization**, company, business, firm, house, concern, operation, structure, institution, institute, corporation, enterprise, outfit *(informal)*, premises, setup *(informal)*: *Shops and other commercial establishments remained closed today.* **3 = office**, house, building, plant, quarters, factory: *a scientific research establishment*

estate NOUN **1 = lands**, property, area, grounds, domain, manor, holdings, demesne, homestead *(U.S. & Canad.)*: *a shooting party on his estate in Yorkshire* **2 = area**, centre, park, development, site, zone, plot: *an industrial estate* **3 = property**, capital, assets, fortune, goods, effects, wealth, possessions, belongings: *His estate was valued at £100,000.*

esteem VERB **= respect**, admire, think highly of, like, love, value, prize, honour, treasure, cherish, revere, reverence, be fond of, venerate, regard highly, take off your hat to: *a scholar whom he highly esteemed* ▷ NOUN **= respect**, regard, honour, consideration, admiration, reverence, estimation, veneration: *He is held in high esteem by his colleagues.*

estimate VERB **1 = calculate roughly**, value, guess, judge, reckon, assess, evaluate, gauge, number, appraise: *His personal riches were estimated at over £8 million.* **2 = think**, believe, consider, rate, judge, hold, rank, guess, reckon, assess, conjecture, surmise: *Officials estimate it will be two days before electricity is restored to the island.* ▷ NOUN **1 = approximate calculation**, guess, reckoning, assessment, judgment, evaluation, valuation, appraisal, educated guess, guesstimate *(informal)*, rough calculation, ballpark figure *(informal)*, approximate cost, approximate price, appraisement: *This figure is five times the original estimate.* **2 = assessment**, opinion, belief, appraisal, evaluation, conjecture, appraisement, judgment, estimation, surmise: *I was wrong in my estimate of his capabilities.*

estimation NOUN **1 = opinion**, view, regard, belief, honour, credit, consideration, judgment, esteem, evaluation, admiration, reverence, veneration, good opinion, considered opinion: *He has gone down considerably in my estimation.* **2 = estimate**, reckoning, assessment, appreciation, valuation, appraisal, guesstimate *(informal)*, ballpark figure *(informal)*: *estimations of pre-tax profits of £12.5 million*

estrangement NOUN **= alienation**, parting, division, split, withdrawal, break-up, breach, hostility, separation, withholding, disaffection, disunity, dissociation, antagonization

estuary NOUN **= inlet**, mouth, creek, firth, fjord

et cetera *or* **etcetera** ADVERB **= and so on**, and so forth, etc.

etch VERB **1 = engrave**, cut, impress, stamp, carve, imprint, inscribe, furrow, incise, ingrain: *a simple band of heavy gold etched with runes* **2 = corrode**, eat into, burn into: *The acid etched holes in the surface.*

etching NOUN **= print**, impression, carving, engraving, imprint, inscription

eternal ADJECTIVE **1 = everlasting**, lasting, permanent, enduring, endless, perennial, perpetual, timeless, immortal, unending, unchanging, immutable, indestructible, undying, without end, unceasing, imperishable,

e

deathless, sempiternal *(literary)*: *the quest for eternal youth*
OPPOSITE: transitory
2 = interminable, constant, endless, abiding, infinite, continual, immortal, never-ending, everlasting, ceaseless, unremitting, deathless: *In the background was that eternal humming noise.* **OPPOSITE:** occasional

eternity NOUN **1 = the afterlife**, heaven, paradise, the next world, the hereafter: *I have always found the thought of eternity terrifying.* **2 = perpetuity**, immortality, infinity, timelessness, endlessness, infinitude, time without end: *the idea that our species will survive for all eternity* **3 = ages**, years, an age, centuries, for ever *(informal)*, aeons, donkey's years *(informal)*, yonks *(informal)*, a month of Sundays *(informal)*, a long time *or* while, an age *or* eternity: *The war went on for an eternity.*

> **QUOTATIONS**
> Eternity's a terrible thought.
> I mean, where's it all going to end?
> [Tom Stoppard *Rosencrantz and Guildenstern are Dead*]
>
> Eternity! thou pleasing, dreadful thought!
> [Joseph Addison *Cato*]
>
> Every instant of time is a pinprick of eternity
> [Marcus Aurelius *Meditations*]
>
> Eternity is in love with the productions of time
> [William Blake *The Marriage of Heaven and Hell*]

ethereal ADJECTIVE **1 = insubstantial**, light, fairy, aerial, airy, intangible, rarefied, impalpable: *the ethereal world of romantic fiction* **2 = spiritual**, heavenly, unearthly, sublime, celestial, unworldly, empyreal: *the ethereal realm of the divine*

ethical ADJECTIVE **1 = moral**, behavioural: *the ethical dilemmas of genetic engineering* **2 = right**, morally right, morally acceptable, good, just, fitting, fair, responsible, principled, correct, decent, proper, upright, honourable, honest, righteous, virtuous: *Would it be ethical to lie to save a person's life?* **OPPOSITE:** unethical

ethics PLURAL NOUN **= moral code**, standards, principles, morals, conscience, morality, moral values, moral principles, moral philosophy, rules of conduct, moral beliefs, tikanga *(N.Z.)*

> **QUOTATIONS**
> True ethics begin where the use of language ceases
> [Albert Schweitzer *Civilization and Ethics*]

ethnic *or* **ethnical** ADJECTIVE **= cultural**, national, traditional, native, folk, racial, genetic, indigenous

ethos NOUN **= spirit**, character, attitude, beliefs, ethic, tenor, disposition

etiquette NOUN **= good** *or* **proper behaviour**, manners, rules, code, customs, convention, courtesy, usage, protocol, formalities, propriety, politeness, good manners, decorum, civility, politesse, p's and q's, polite behaviour, kawa *(N.Z.)*, tikanga *(N.Z.)*

eulogy NOUN **= praise**, tribute, acclaim, compliment, applause, accolade, paean, commendation, exaltation, glorification, acclamation, panegyric, encomium, plaudit, laudation

euphoria NOUN **= elation**, joy, ecstasy, bliss, glee, rapture, high spirits, exhilaration, jubilation, intoxication, transport, exaltation, joyousness
OPPOSITE: despondency

euthanasia NOUN **= mercy killing**, assisted suicide

evacuate VERB **1 = remove**, clear, withdraw, expel, move out, send to a safe place: *18,000 people have been evacuated from the city.* **2 = abandon**, leave, clear, desert, quit, depart (from), withdraw from, pull out of, move out of, relinquish, vacate, forsake, decamp from: *The residents have evacuated the area.*

evacuation NOUN **1 = removal**, departure, withdrawal, clearance, flight, expulsion, exodus: *an evacuation of the city's four million inhabitants*
2 = abandonment, withdrawal from, pulling out, moving out, clearance from, vacation from: *the mass evacuation of Srebrenica*

evade VERB **1 = avoid**, escape, dodge, get away from, shun, elude, eschew, steer clear of, sidestep, circumvent, duck, shirk, slip through the net of, escape the clutches of, body-swerve *(Scot.)*: *He managed to evade the police for six months.* **OPPOSITE:** face **2 = avoid answering**, parry, circumvent, fend off, balk, cop out of *(slang)*, fence, fudge, hedge, prevaricate, flannel *(Brit. informal)*, beat about the bush about, equivocate: *Mr Archer denied that he was evading the question.*

evaluate VERB **= assess**, rate, value, judge, estimate, rank, reckon, weigh, calculate, gauge, weigh up, appraise, size up *(informal)*, assay

evaluation NOUN **= assessment**, rating, judgment, calculation, valuation, appraisal, estimation

evangelical ADJECTIVE **= crusading**, converting, missionary, zealous, revivalist, proselytizing, propagandizing

evaporate VERB **1 = disappear**, vaporize, dematerialize, evanesce, melt, vanish, dissolve, disperse, dry up, dispel, dissipate, fade away, melt away: *Moisture is drawn to the surface of the fabric so that it evaporates.* **2 = dry up**, dry, dehydrate, vaporize, desiccate: *The water is evaporated by the sun.* **3 = fade away**, disappear, fade, melt, vanish, dissolve, disperse, dissipate, melt away: *My anger evaporated and I wanted to cry.*

evaporation NOUN **1 = vaporization**, vanishing, disappearance, dispelling, dissolution, fading away, melting away, dispersal, dissipation, evanescence, dematerialization: *The cooling effect is caused by the evaporation of sweat on the skin.* **2 = drying up**, drying, dehydration, desiccation, vaporization: *an increase in evaporation of both lake and ground water*

evasion NOUN **1 = avoidance**, escape, dodging, shirking, cop-out *(slang)*, circumvention, elusion: *an evasion of responsibility* **2 = deception**, shuffling, cunning, fudging, pretext, ruse, artifice, trickery, subterfuge, equivocation, prevarication, sophistry, evasiveness, obliqueness, sophism: *They face accusations from the Opposition Party of evasion and cover-up.*

evasive ADJECTIVE **1 = deceptive**, misleading, indirect, cunning, slippery, tricky, shuffling, devious, oblique, shifty, cagey *(informal)*, deceitful, dissembling, prevaricating, equivocating, sophistical, casuistic, casuistical: *He was evasive about the circumstances of their first meeting.*
OPPOSITE: straightforward
2 = avoiding, escaping, circumventing: *Four high-flying warplanes had to take evasive action.*

eve NOUN **1 = night before**, day before, vigil: *the eve of his 27th birthday* **2 = brink**, point, edge, verge, threshold: *when Europe stood on the eve of war in 1914*

even ADJECTIVE **1 = regular**, stable, constant, steady, smooth, uniform, unbroken, uninterrupted, unwavering, unvarying, metrical: *It is important to have an even temperature when you work.* **OPPOSITE:** variable **2 = level**, straight, flat, plane, smooth, true, steady, uniform, parallel, flush, horizontal, plumb: *The tables are fitted with a glass top to provide an even surface.*
OPPOSITE: uneven **3 = equal**, like, the same, matching, similar, uniform, parallel, identical, comparable, commensurate, coequal: *Divide the dough into 12 even pieces.*
OPPOSITE: unequal **4 = equally matched**, level, tied, drawn, on a par, neck and neck, fifty-fifty *(informal)*, equalized, all square, equally balanced: *It was an even game.*
OPPOSITE: ill-matched **5 = square**, quits, on the same level, on an equal footing: *You don't owe me anything now. We're even.* **6 = calm**, stable, steady, composed, peaceful, serene, cool, tranquil, well-balanced, placid, undisturbed, unruffled, imperturbable, equable, even-tempered, unexcitable, equanimous: *Normally Rose had an even temper; she was rarely irritable.* **OPPOSITE:** excitable
7 = fair, just, balanced, equitable, impartial, disinterested, unbiased, dispassionate, fair and square, unprejudiced: *We all have an even chance of winning.* **OPPOSITE:** unfair
▷ ADVERB **1 = despite**, in spite of,

disregarding, notwithstanding, in spite of the fact that, regardless of the fact that: *He kept calling me, even though he was married.* **2 = all the more**, much, still, yet, to a greater extent, to a greater degree: *Stan was speaking even more slowly than usual.*
even as = while, just as, whilst, at the time that, at the same time as, exactly as, during the time that: *Even as she said this, she knew it was not quite true.*
even so = nevertheless, still, however, yet, despite that, in spite of (that), nonetheless, all the same, notwithstanding that, be that as it may: *The bus was half empty. Even so, he came and sat next to me.*
even something out = make *or* **become level**, align, level, square, smooth, steady, flatten, stabilize, balance out, regularize: *Rates of house price inflation have evened out between the North and South of the country.*
even something up = equalize, match, balance, equal: *These missiles would help to even up the balance of power.*
get even (with) = pay back, repay, reciprocate, even the score, requite, get your own back, settle the score, take vengeance, take an eye for an eye, be revenged *or* revenge yourself, give tit for tat, pay (someone) back in their own coin, return like for like: *I'm going to get even if it's the last thing I do.*

even-handed ADJECTIVE **= fair**, just, balanced, equitable, impartial, disinterested, unbiased, fair and square, unprejudiced

evening NOUN **= dusk** *(archaic)*, night, sunset, twilight, sundown, eve, vesper *(archaic)*, eventide *(archaic, poetic)*, gloaming *(Scot., poetic)*, e'en *(archaic, poetic)*, close of day, crepuscule, even, evo *(Austral. slang)*

> **QUOTATIONS**
> It is a beauteous evening, calm and free,
> The holy time is quiet as a nun,
> Breathless with adoration
> [William Wordsworth *It is a Beauteous Evening*]
>
> The curfew tolls the knell of passing day
> [Thomas Gray *Elegy Written in a Country Churchyard*]
>
> Let us go then, you and I
> When the evening is spread out against the sky
> Like a patient etherized upon a table
> [T.S. Eliot *Love Song of J. Alfred Prufrock*]

event NOUN **1 = incident**, happening, experience, matter, affair, occasion, proceeding, fact, business, circumstance, episode, adventure, milestone, occurrence, escapade: *in the wake of recent events in Europe* **2 = competition**, game, tournament, contest, bout: *major sporting events*
in any event *or* **at all events = whatever happens**, regardless, in any case, no matter what, at any rate, come what may: *It is not going to be an easy decision, in any event.*
in the event of = in the eventuality of, in the situation of, in the likelihood of: *The bank will make an immediate refund in the event of any error.*

eventful ADJECTIVE **= exciting**, active, busy, dramatic, remarkable, historic, full, lively, memorable, notable, momentous, fateful, noteworthy, consequential **OPPOSITE:** dull

eventual ADJECTIVE **= final**, later, resulting, future, overall, concluding, ultimate, prospective, ensuing, consequent

eventuality NOUN **= possibility**, event, likelihood, probability, case, chance, contingency

eventually ADVERB **= in the end**, finally, one day, after all, some time, ultimately, at the end of the day, in the long run, sooner or later, some day, when all is said and done, in the fullness of time, in the course of time

ever ADVERB **1 = at any time**, at all, in any case, at any point, by any chance, on any occasion, at any period: *Don't you ever talk to me like that again!* **2 = always**, for ever, at all times, relentlessly, eternally, evermore, unceasingly, to the end of time, everlastingly, unendingly, aye *(Scot.)*: *Mother, ever the peacemaker, told us to stop fighting.* **3 = constantly**, continually, endlessly, perpetually, incessantly, unceasingly, unendingly: *They grew ever further apart as time went on.*

everlasting ADJECTIVE **1 = eternal**, endless, abiding, infinite, perpetual, timeless, immortal, never-ending, indestructible, undying, imperishable, deathless: *The icon embodies a potent symbol of everlasting life.* **OPPOSITE:** transitory **2 = continual**, constant, endless, continuous, never-ending, interminable, incessant, ceaseless, unremitting, unceasing: *I'm tired of your everlasting bickering.*

every ADJECTIVE **= each**, each and every, every single

everybody PRONOUN **= everyone**, each one, the whole world, each person, every person, all and sundry, one and all

everyday ADJECTIVE **1 = daily**, day-to-day, diurnal, quotidian: *opportunities for improving fitness in your everyday routine* **OPPOSITE:** occasional **2 = ordinary**, common, usual, familiar, conventional, routine, dull, stock, accustomed, customary, commonplace, mundane, vanilla *(slang)*, banal, habitual, run-of-the-mill, unimaginative, workaday, unexceptional, bog-standard *(Brit. & Irish slang)*, common or garden *(informal)*, dime-a-dozen *(informal)*, wonted: *an exhilarating escape from the drudgery of everyday life* **OPPOSITE:** unusual

everyone PRONOUN **= everybody**, each one, the whole world, each person, every person, all and sundry, one and all

> **USAGE**
> *Everyone* and *everybody* are interchangeable, and can be used as synonyms of each other in any context. Care should be taken, however, to distinguish between *everyone* as a single word and *every one* as two words, the latter form correctly being used to refer to each individual person or thing in a particular group: *every one of them is wrong.*

everything PRONOUN **= all**, the whole, the total, the lot, the sum, the whole lot, the aggregate, the entirety, each thing, the whole caboodle *(informal)*, the whole kit and caboodle *(informal)*

everywhere ADVERB **1 = all over**, all around, the world over, high and low, in each place, in every nook and cranny, far and wide *or* near, to *or* in every place: *I looked everywhere but I couldn't find him.* **2 = all around**, all over, in each place, in every nook and cranny, ubiquitously, far and wide *or* near, to *or* in every place: *There were clothes scattered around everywhere.*

evict VERB **= expel**, remove, turn out, put out, throw out, oust, kick out *(informal)*, eject, dislodge, boot out *(informal)*, force to leave, dispossess, chuck out *(informal)*, show the door (to), turf out *(informal)*, throw on to the streets

eviction NOUN **= expulsion**, removal, clearance, ouster *(Law)*, ejection, dispossession, dislodgement

evidence NOUN **1 = proof**, grounds, data, demonstration, confirmation, verification, corroboration, authentication, substantiation: *There is no evidence to support this theory.* **2 = sign(s)**, mark, suggestion, trace, indication, token, manifestation: *Police said there was no evidence of a struggle.* **3 = testimony**, statement, witness, declaration, submission, affirmation, deposition, avowal, attestation, averment: *Forensic scientists will be called to give evidence.*
▷ VERB **= show**, prove, reveal, display, indicate, witness, demonstrate, exhibit, manifest, signify, denote, testify to, evince: *He still has a lot to learn, as is evidenced by his recent behaviour.*

evident ADJECTIVE **= obvious**, clear, plain, apparent, visible, patent, manifest, tangible, noticeable, blatant, conspicuous, unmistakable, palpable, salient, indisputable, perceptible, incontrovertible, incontestable, plain as the nose on your face **OPPOSITE:** hidden

evidently ADVERB **1 = obviously**, clearly, plainly, patently, undoubtedly, manifestly, doubtless, without question, unmistakably, indisputably, doubtlessly, incontrovertibly, incontestably: *He had evidently just woken up.* **2 = apparently**, it seems, seemingly, outwardly, it would seem, ostensibly, so it seems, to all appearances: *Ellis evidently wished to negotiate downwards, after Atkinson had set the guidelines.*

evil ADJECTIVE **1 = wicked**, bad, wrong, corrupt, vicious, vile, malicious, base, immoral, malignant, sinful, unholy, malevolent, heinous, depraved, villainous, nefarious, iniquitous, reprobate, maleficent: *the country's most evil criminals* **2 = harmful**, painful, disastrous, destructive, dire, catastrophic, mischievous, detrimental, hurtful, woeful, pernicious, ruinous, sorrowful, deleterious, injurious, baneful (*archaic*): *Few people would not condemn slavery as evil.* **3 = demonic**, satanic, diabolical, hellish, devilish, infernal, fiendish: *This place is said to be haunted by an evil spirit.* **4 = offensive**, nasty, foul, unpleasant, vile, noxious, disagreeable, putrid, pestilential, mephitic: *There was an evil stench in the room.* **5 = unfortunate**, unlucky, unfavourable, ruinous, calamitous, inauspicious: *people of honour who happen to have fallen upon evil times*
▷ NOUN **1 = wickedness**, bad, wrong, vice, corruption, sin, wrongdoing, depravity, immorality, iniquity, badness, viciousness, villainy, sinfulness, turpitude, baseness, malignity, heinousness, maleficence: *We are being attacked by the forces of evil.* **2 = harm**, suffering, pain, hurt, misery, sorrow, woe: *those who see television as the root of all evil* **3 = act of cruelty**, crime, ill, horror, outrage, cruelty, brutality, misfortune, mischief, affliction, monstrosity, abomination, barbarity, villainy: *Racism is one of the greatest evils in the world.*

QUOTATIONS

So farewell hope, and with hope farewell fear,
Farewell remorse: all good to me is lost;
Evil be thou my Good
[John Milton *Paradise Lost*]

Evil be to him who evil thinks (Honi soit qui mal y pense)
[*Motto of the Order of the Garter*]

What we call evil is simply ignorance bumping its head in the dark
[Henry Ford]

The evil that men do lives after them
[William Shakespeare *Julius Caesar*]

Evil alone has oil for every wheel
[Edna St. Vincent Millay *Mine the Harvest*]

Sufficient unto the day is the evil thereof
[*Bible: St. Matthew*]

PROVERBS

Choose the lesser of two evils
See no evil, hear no evil, speak no evil

evince VERB **= show**, evidence, reveal, establish, express, display, indicate, demonstrate, exhibit, make clear, manifest, signify, attest, bespeak, betoken, make evident

evoke VERB **1 = arouse**, cause, excite, stimulate, induce, awaken, give rise to, stir up, rekindle, summon up: *The programme has evoked a storm of protest.* **OPPOSITE:** suppress **2 = provoke**, produce, elicit, call to mind, call forth, educe (*rare*): *Hearing these songs can still evoke strong memories and emotions.*

evolution NOUN **1 = rise**, development, adaptation, natural selection, Darwinism, survival of the fittest, evolvement: *the evolution of plants and animals* **2 = development**, growth, advance, progress, working out, expansion, extension, unfolding, progression, enlargement, maturation, unrolling: *a crucial period in the evolution of modern physics*

evolve VERB **1 = develop**, metamorphose, adapt yourself: *Modern birds evolved from dinosaurs.* **2 = grow**, develop, advance, progress, mature: *Popular music evolved from folk songs.* **3 = work out**, develop, progress, expand, elaborate, unfold, enlarge, unroll: *He evolved a working method from which he has never departed.*

exacerbate VERB **= irritate**, excite, provoke, infuriate, aggravate (*informal*), enrage, madden, inflame, exasperate, vex, embitter, add insult to injury, fan the flames of, envenom

exact ADJECTIVE **1 = accurate**, very, correct, true, particular, right, express, specific, careful, precise, identical, authentic, faithful, explicit, definite, orderly, literal, unequivocal, faultless, on the money (*U.S.*), unerring, veracious: *I can't remember the exact words he used.* **OPPOSITE:** approximate **2 = meticulous**, severe, careful, strict, exacting, precise, rigorous, painstaking, scrupulous, methodical, punctilious: *She is very punctual and very exact in her duties.*
▷ VERB **1 = demand**, claim, require, call for, force, impose, command, squeeze, extract, compel, wring, wrest, insist upon, extort: *He has exacted a high price for his co-operation.* **2 = inflict**, apply, impose, administer, mete out, deal out: *She exacted a terrible revenge on her attackers.*

exacting ADJECTIVE **1 = demanding**, hard, taxing, difficult, tough, painstaking: *He was not well enough to carry out such an exacting task.* **OPPOSITE:** easy **2 = strict**, severe, harsh, stern, rigid, rigorous, stringent, oppressive, imperious, unsparing: *Our new manager has very exacting standards.*

exactly ADVERB **1 = accurately**, correctly, definitely, truly, precisely, strictly, literally, faithfully, explicitly, rigorously, unequivocally, scrupulously, truthfully, methodically, unerringly, faultlessly, veraciously: *Can you describe exactly what he looked like?* **2 = precisely**, just, expressly, prompt (*informal*), specifically, bang on (*informal*), to the letter, on the button (*informal*): *He arrived at exactly five o'clock.*
▷ SENTENCE SUBSTITUTE **= precisely**, yes, quite, of course, certainly, indeed, truly, that's right, absolutely, spot-on (*Brit. informal*), just so, quite so, ya (*S. African*), as you say, you got it (*informal*), assuredly, yebo (*S. African informal*): *'We don't know the answer to that.' – 'Exactly. So shut up and stop speculating.'*
not exactly = not at all, hardly, not really, not quite, certainly not, by no means, in no way, not by any means, in no manner: *Sailing is not exactly a cheap hobby.*

exaggerate VERB **= overstate**, emphasize, enlarge, inflate, embroider, magnify, overdo, amplify, exalt, embellish, overestimate, overemphasize, pile it on about (*informal*), blow up out of all proportion, lay it on thick about (*informal*), lay it on with a trowel about (*informal*), make a production (out) of (*informal*), make a federal case of (*U.S. informal*), hyperbolize

exaggerated ADJECTIVE **= overstated**, extreme, excessive, over the top (*informal*), inflated, extravagant, overdone, tall (*informal*), amplified, hyped, pretentious, exalted, overestimated, overblown, fulsome, hyperbolic, highly coloured, O.T.T. (*slang*)

exaggeration NOUN **= overstatement**, inflation, emphasis, excess, enlargement, pretension, extravagance, hyperbole, magnification, amplification, embellishment, exaltation, pretentiousness, overemphasis, overestimation
OPPOSITE: understatement

QUOTATIONS

The report of my death was an exaggeration
[Mark Twain]

An exaggeration is a truth that has lost its temper
[Kahlil Gibran *Sand and Foam*]

exalt VERB **1 = praise**, acclaim, applaud, pay tribute to, bless, worship, magnify (*archaic*), glorify, reverence, laud, extol, crack up (*informal*), pay homage to, idolize, apotheosize, set on a pedestal: *This book exalts her as a genius.* **2 = uplift**, raise, lift, excite, delight, inspire, thrill, stimulate, arouse, heighten, elevate, animate, exhilarate, electrify, fire the imagination of, fill with joy, elate, inspirit: *Great music exalts the human spirit.*

exaltation NOUN **1 = elation**, delight, joy, excitement, inspiration, ecstasy, stimulation, bliss, transport, animation, elevation, rapture, exhilaration, jubilation, exultation, joyousness: *The city was swept up in the mood of exaltation.* **2 = praise**, tribute, worship, acclaim, applause, glory, blessing, homage, reverence, magnification, apotheosis, glorification, acclamation, panegyric, idolization, extolment, lionization, laudation: *The poem is an exaltation of love.*

exalted ADJECTIVE **1 = high-ranking**, high, grand, honoured, intellectual, noble, prestigious, august, elevated, eminent, dignified, lofty: *I seldom move in such exalted circles.* **2 = noble**, ideal, superior, elevated, intellectual, uplifting, sublime, lofty, high-minded: *I don't think of poetry as an exalted calling, as some poets do.* **3 = elated**, excited, inspired, stimulated, elevated, animated, uplifted, transported, exhilarated, ecstatic, jubilant, joyous, joyful, over the moon (*informal*), blissful, rapturous, exultant, in high spirits, on cloud nine (*informal*), cock-a-hoop, in seventh heaven, inspirited, stoked (*Austral. & N.Z. informal*): *She had the look of someone exalted by an excess of joy.*

examination NOUN **1 = checkup**, analysis, going-over (*informal*), exploration, health check, check, medical, once-over (*informal*): *a routine medical examination* **2 = exam**, test, research, paper, investigation, practical, assessment, quiz, evaluation, oral, appraisal, catechism: *accusations of cheating in school examinations*

examine VERB **1 = inspect**, test, consider, study, check, research, review, survey, investigate, explore, probe, analyse, scan, vet, check out, ponder, look over, look at, sift through, work over, pore over, appraise, scrutinize, peruse, take stock of, assay, recce (*slang*), look at carefully, go over *or* through: *He examined her passport and stamped it.* **2 = check**, analyse, check over: *The doctor examined her, but could find nothing wrong.* **3 = test**, question, assess, quiz, evaluate, appraise, catechize: *the pressures of being judged and examined by our teachers* **4 = question**, quiz, interrogate, cross-examine, grill (*informal*), give the third degree to (*informal*): *I was called and examined as a witness.*

example NOUN **1 = instance**, specimen, case, sample, illustration, case in point, particular case, particular instance, typical case, exemplification, representative case: *examples of sexism and racism in the police force* **2 = illustration**, model, ideal, standard, norm, precedent, pattern, prototype, paradigm, archetype, paragon, exemplar: *This piece is a perfect example of symphonic construction.* **3 = warning**, lesson, caution, deterrent, admonition: *We were punished as an example to others.*

for example = as an illustration, like, such as, for instance, to illustrate, by way of illustration, exempli gratia (*Latin*), e.g., to cite an instance: *You could, for example, walk instead of taking the car.*

> **PROVERBS**
> *Practise what you preach*

exasperate VERB **= irritate**, anger, provoke, annoy, rouse, infuriate, hassle (*informal*), exacerbate, aggravate (*informal*), incense, enrage, gall, madden, inflame, bug (*informal*), nettle, get to (*informal*), vex, embitter, irk, rile (*informal*), pique, rankle, peeve (*informal*), needle (*informal*), get on your nerves (*informal*), try the patience of, nark (*Brit., Austral. & N.Z. slang*), get in your hair (*informal*), get on your wick (*Brit. slang*), hack you off (*informal*) **OPPOSITE:** calm

exasperating ADJECTIVE **= irritating**, provoking, annoying, infuriating, aggravating (*informal*), galling, maddening, vexing, irksome, enough to drive you up the wall (*informal*), enough to try the patience of a saint

exasperation NOUN **= irritation**, anger, rage, fury, wrath, provocation, passion, annoyance, ire (*literary*), pique, aggravation (*informal*), vexation, exacerbation

excavate VERB **1 = dig up**, mine, dig, tunnel, scoop, cut, hollow, trench, burrow, quarry, delve, gouge: *A team of archaeologists is excavating the site.* **2 = unearth**, expose, uncover, dig out, exhume, lay bare, bring to light, bring to the surface, disinter: *They have excavated the fossil remains of a prehistoric man.*

excavation NOUN **= hole**, mine, pit, ditch, shaft, cutting, cut, hollow, trench, burrow, quarry, dig, trough, cavity, dugout, diggings

exceed VERB **1 = surpass**, better, pass, eclipse, beat, cap (*informal*), top, be over, be more than, overtake, go beyond, excel, transcend, be greater than, outstrip, outdo, outreach, be larger than, outshine, surmount, be superior to, outrun, run rings around (*informal*), outdistance, knock spots off (*informal*), put in the shade (*informal*): *His performance exceeded all expectations.* **2 = go over the limit of**, go beyond, overstep, go beyond the bounds of: *This programme exceeded the bounds of taste and decency.*

exceeding ADJECTIVE **= extraordinary**, great, huge, vast, enormous, superior, excessive, exceptional, surpassing, superlative, pre-eminent, streets ahead

exceedingly ADVERB **= extremely**, very, highly, greatly, especially, hugely, seriously (*informal*), vastly, unusually, enormously, exceptionally, extraordinarily, excessively, superlatively, inordinately, to a fault, to the nth degree, surpassingly

excel VERB **= be superior**, better, pass, eclipse, beat, top, cap (*informal*), exceed, go beyond, surpass, transcend, outdo, outshine, surmount, run rings around (*informal*), put in the shade (*informal*), outrival: *Few dancers have excelled her in virtuosity.*

excel in *or* **at something = be good at**, be master of, predominate in, shine at, be proficient in, show talent in, be skilful at, have (something) down to a fine art, be talented at: *She excelled at outdoor sports.*

excellence NOUN **= high quality**, worth, merit, distinction, virtue, goodness, perfection, superiority, purity, greatness, supremacy, eminence, virtuosity, transcendence, pre-eminence, fineness

excellent ADJECTIVE **= outstanding**, good, great, fine, prime, capital, noted, choice, champion, cool (*informal*), select, brilliant, very good, cracking (*Brit. informal*), crucial (*slang*), mean (*slang*), superb, distinguished, fantastic, magnificent, superior, sterling, worthy, first-class, marvellous, exceptional, terrific, splendid, notable, mega (*slang*), topping (*Brit. slang*), sovereign, dope (*slang*), world-class, exquisite, admirable, exemplary, wicked (*slang*), first-rate, def (*slang*), superlative, top-notch (*informal*), brill (*informal*), nang (*Brit. slang*), pre-eminent, meritorious, estimable, tiptop, bodacious (*slang, chiefly U.S.*), boffo (*slang*), jim-dandy (*slang*), A1 *or* A-one (*informal*), bitchin' (*U.S. slang*), chillin' (*U.S. slang*), booshit (*Austral. slang*), exo (*Austral. slang*), sik (*Austral. slang*), rad (*informal*), phat (*slang*), schmick (*Austral. informal*), beaut (*informal*), barrie (*Scot. slang*), belting (*Brit. slang*), pearler (*Austral. slang*), bakgat (*S. African*) **OPPOSITE:** terrible

except PREPOSITION (*often with* **for**) **= apart from**, but for, saving, bar, barring, excepting, other than, excluding, omitting, with the exception of, aside from, save (*archaic*), not counting, exclusive of: *I don't drink, except for the occasional glass of wine.*
▷ VERB **= exclude**, rule out, leave out, omit, disregard, pass over: *Men are such swine (present company excepted, of course).*

exception NOUN **= special case**, departure, freak, anomaly, inconsistency, deviation, quirk, oddity, peculiarity, irregularity: *an exception to the usual rule*

take exception (*usually with* **to**) **= object to**, disagree with, take offence at, take umbrage at, be resentful of, be offended at, demur at, quibble at: *I take exception to being checked up on like this.*

exceptional ADJECTIVE **1 = remarkable**, special, excellent, extraordinary, outstanding, superior, first-class, marvellous, notable, phenomenal, first-rate, prodigious, unsurpassed, one in a million, bodacious *(slang, chiefly U.S.)*, unexcelled: *His piano playing is exceptional.* **OPPOSITE:** average **2 = unusual**, special, odd, strange, rare, extraordinary, unprecedented, peculiar, abnormal, irregular, uncommon, inconsistent, singular, deviant, anomalous, atypical, aberrant: *The courts hold that this case is exceptional.* **OPPOSITE:** ordinary

excerpt NOUN **= extract**, part, piece, section, selection, passage, portion, fragment, quotation, citation, pericope: *an excerpt from Tchaikovsky's 'Nutcracker'*
▷ VERB **= extract**, take, select, quote, cite, pick out, cull: *The readings were excerpted from his autobiography.*

e

excess NOUN **1 = surfeit**, surplus, overdose, overflow, overload, plethora, glut, overabundance, superabundance, superfluity: *Avoid an excess of sugar in your diet.* **OPPOSITE:** shortage **2 = overindulgence**, extravagance, profligacy, debauchery, dissipation, intemperance, indulgence, prodigality, extreme behaviour, immoral behaviour, dissoluteness, immoderation, exorbitance, unrestraint: *He had led a life of excess.* **OPPOSITE:** moderation
▷ ADJECTIVE **= spare**, remaining, extra, additional, surplus, unwanted, redundant, residual, leftover, superfluous, unneeded: *After cooking the fish, pour off any excess fat.*

excessive ADJECTIVE **1 = immoderate**, too much, enormous, extreme, exaggerated, over the top *(slang)*, extravagant, needless, unreasonable, disproportionate, undue, uncontrolled, superfluous, prodigal, unrestrained, profligate, inordinate, fulsome, intemperate, unconscionable, overmuch, O.T.T. *(slang)*: *the alleged use of excessive force by police* **2 = inordinate**, unfair, unreasonable, disproportionate, undue, unwarranted, exorbitant, over the odds, extortionate, immoderate: *banks which cripple their customers with excessive charges*

exchange VERB **= interchange**, change, trade, switch, swap, truck, barter, reciprocate, bandy, give to each other, give to one another: *We exchanged addresses.*
▷ NOUN **1 = conversation**, talk, word, discussion, chat, dialogue, natter, powwow: *I had a brief exchange with him before I left.* **2 = interchange**, dealing, trade, switch, swap, traffic, trafficking, truck, swapping, substitution, barter, bartering, reciprocity, tit for tat, quid pro quo: *a free exchange of information* **3 = market**, money market, Bourse: *the Stock Exchange*

excise¹ NOUN **= tax**, duty, customs, toll, levy, tariff, surcharge, impost: *Smokers will be hit by increases in tax and excise.*

excise² VERB **1 = delete**, cut, remove, erase, destroy, eradicate, strike out, exterminate, cross out, expunge, extirpate, wipe from the face of the earth: *a crusade to excise racist and sexist references in newspapers* **2 = cut off** *or* **out** *or* **away**, remove, take out, extract: *She has already had one skin cancer excised.*

excitable ADJECTIVE **= nervous**, emotional, violent, sensitive, tense, passionate, volatile, hasty, edgy, temperamental, touchy, mercurial, uptight *(informal)*, irascible, testy, hot-headed, chippy *(informal)*, hot-tempered, quick-tempered, highly strung, adrenalized **OPPOSITE:** calm

excite VERB **1 = thrill**, inspire, stir, stimulate, provoke, awaken, animate, move, fire, rouse, exhilarate, agitate, quicken, inflame, enliven, galvanize, foment: *I only take on work that excites me.* **2 = arouse**, stimulate, provoke, evoke, rouse, stir up, fire, elicit, work up, incite, instigate, whet, kindle, waken: *The proposal failed to excite our interest.* **3 = titillate**, thrill, stimulate, turn on *(slang)*, arouse, get going *(informal)*, electrify: *Try exciting your partner with a little bondage.*

excited ADJECTIVE **1 = thrilled**, stirred, stimulated, enthusiastic, high *(informal)*, moved, wild, aroused, awakened, animated, roused, tumultuous, aflame: *He was so excited he could hardly speak.* **2 = agitated**, worried, stressed, alarmed, nervous, disturbed, tense, flurried, worked up, feverish, overwrought, hot and bothered *(informal)*, discomposed, adrenalized: *There's no need to get so excited.*

excitement NOUN **1 = exhilaration**, action, activity, passion, heat, thrill, adventure, enthusiasm, fever, warmth, flurry, animation, furore, ferment, agitation, commotion, elation, ado, tumult, perturbation, discomposure: *The audience was in a state of great excitement.* **2 = pleasure**, thrill, sensation, stimulation, tingle, kick *(informal)*: *The game had its challenges, excitements and rewards.*

exciting ADJECTIVE **1 = stimulating**, inspiring, dramatic, gripping, stirring, thrilling, moving, sensational, rousing, exhilarating, electrifying, intoxicating, rip-roaring *(informal)*: *the most exciting adventure of their lives* **OPPOSITE:** boring **2 = titillating**, stimulating, sexy *(informal)*, arousing, erotic, provocative: *fantasizing about a sexually exciting scene*

exclaim VERB **= cry out**, call, declare, cry, shout, proclaim, yell, utter, call out, ejaculate, vociferate

exclamation NOUN **= cry**, call, shout, yell, outcry, utterance, ejaculation, expletive, interjection, vociferation

exclude VERB **1 = keep out**, bar, ban, veto, refuse, forbid, boycott, embargo, prohibit, disallow, shut out, proscribe, black, refuse to admit, ostracize, debar, blackball, interdict, prevent from entering: *The Academy excluded women from its classes.* **OPPOSITE:** let in **2 = omit**, reject, eliminate, rule out, miss out, leave out, preclude, repudiate: *Vegetarians exclude meat products from their diet.* **OPPOSITE:** include **3 = eliminate**, reject, ignore, rule out, except, leave out, set aside, omit, pass over, not count, repudiate, count out: *We can't exclude the possibility of suicide.*

exclusion NOUN **1 = ban**, bar, veto, refusal, boycott, embargo, prohibition, disqualification, interdict, proscription, debarment, preclusion, forbiddance, nonadmission: *They demand the exclusion of former communists from political life.* **2 = elimination**, exception, missing out, rejection, leaving out, omission, repudiation: *the exclusion of dairy products from your diet*

exclusive ADJECTIVE **1 = select**, fashionable, stylish, private, limited, choice, narrow, closed, restricted, elegant, posh *(informal, chiefly Brit.)*, chic, selfish, classy *(slang)*, restrictive, aristocratic, high-class, swish *(informal, chiefly Brit.)*, up-market, snobbish, top-drawer, ritzy *(slang)*, high-toned, clannish, discriminative, cliquish: *He is a member of Britain's most exclusive club.* **OPPOSITE:** unrestricted **2 = sole**, only, full, whole, single, private, complete, total, entire, unique, absolute, undivided, unshared: *We have exclusive use of a 60-foot boat.* **OPPOSITE:** shared **3 = entire**, full, whole, complete, total, absolute, undivided: *She wants her father's exclusive attention.* **4 = limited**, unique, restricted, confined, peculiar: *Infatuations are not exclusive to the very young.*
exclusive of = except for, excepting, excluding, ruling out, not including, omitting, not counting, leaving aside, debarring: *All charges are exclusive of value added tax.*

excommunicate VERB **= expel**, ban, remove, exclude, denounce, banish, eject, repudiate, proscribe, cast out, unchurch, anathematize

excrement NOUN **= faeces**, dung, stool, droppings, motion, mess *(of a domestic animal)*, defecation, excreta, ordure, kak *(S. African taboo)*, night soil

excrete VERB **= defecate**, discharge, expel, evacuate, eliminate, void, eject, exude, egest

excruciating ADJECTIVE **= agonizing**, acute, severe, extreme, burning, violent, intense, piercing, racking, searing, tormenting, exquisite, harrowing, unbearable, insufferable, torturous, unendurable

Adverbs in 'The Times' and 'The Sun'

One of the most striking differences between the two newspapers is their use of connective adverbs, which are much more frequent in *The Times. However* occurs more than three times as often in *The Times* as in *The Sun*; *nevertheless* eleven times as often. *The Times* is also thirty-six times more likely to use *moreover*, twenty times more likely to use *thus*, eight times more likely to use *furthermore*, four times more likely to use *therefore*, and twice as likely to use *on the other hand*.

Another evident difference is in the use of 'hedging' adverbs such as *perhaps* and *rather*. *Perhaps* occurs more than three times as often in *The Times* as in *The Sun*, and one of the main differences is its more frequent use as a modifier of another adverb in phrases such as *perhaps surprisingly* and *perhaps understandably*, which occur quite rarely in *The Sun*. *Rather* occurs two and a half times more frequently in *The Times* than in *The Sun*. In both newspapers, most of the uses are of the form *rather than* meaning 'instead of', but it is in their use of *rather* as a modifier meaning 'quite' that the papers differ most. This form of *rather* occurs seven times more frequently in *The Times*, often modifying *more* and *less*:

The truth was **rather less** prosaic. (*The Times*)

Redman's position, like that of so many of his peers, is **rather more** ambiguous. (*The Times*)

There are also differences in the use of emphatic adverbs. Both use *very* and *certainly* with similar frequency, but *The Times* uses *particularly* two and a half times more often than *The Sun* does, in phrases such as *particularly well* and *particularly impressive*. *The Times* also uses *highly* twice as often, for example in *highly unlikely*, *highly successful*, and *highly regarded*. On the other hand, *The Sun* is over twice as likely to use *definitely*, usually in sentences such as 'he definitely deserved to win'. *Amazingly* is two and a half times more frequent in *The Sun*, occurring both as a modifier of adjectives (*amazingly clever, amazingly calm*) and as a sentence adverb, for example:

Amazingly, Thompson survived the blast. (*The Sun*)

Terribly meaning 'very' is slightly more frequent in *The Times*, in phrases such as 'terribly clever'. There are more occurrences of *seriously* in *The Sun*, especially in the sense 'very', with none of the original sense of weightiness:

And already we've seen some **seriously stylish** red carpet appearances. (*The Sun*)

The Sun is almost four times more likely to use the adverb *hopefully*. *The Times* has slightly more examples of *hopefully* meaning 'in a hopeful manner', as below:

They will have the belief that one **hopefully** thrown bomb will explode on Khan's vulnerable chin. (*The Times*)

However, in both newspapers the majority of uses are as a sentence adverb meaning 'it is hoped that', for example:

Pope John Paul II is expected to return to Ireland in the spring and **hopefully** will visit the North. (*The Sun*)

The next generation ... will **hopefully** be better at creating national wealth than we were. (*The Times*)

Although this sense of *hopefully* has long been criticized by purists, it is clearly becoming the most widely used sense.

excursion NOUN **= trip**, airing, tour, journey, outing, expedition, ramble, day trip, jaunt, pleasure trip

excuse VERB **1 = justify**, explain, defend, vindicate, condone, mitigate, apologize for, make excuses for: *I know you're upset but that doesn't excuse your behaviour.* **OPPOSITE:** blame **2 = forgive**, pardon, overlook, tolerate, indulge, acquit, pass over, turn a blind eye to, exonerate, absolve, bear with, wink at, make allowances for, extenuate, exculpate: *He's a total bastard – excuse me for swearing.* **3 = free**, relieve, liberate, exempt, release, spare, discharge, let off, absolve: *She was excused from her duties for the day.* **OPPOSITE:** convict
▷ NOUN **1 = justification**, reason, explanation, defence, grounds, plea, apology, pretext, vindication, mitigation, mitigating circumstances, extenuation: *There is no excuse for what he did.* **OPPOSITE:** accusation **2 = pretext**, evasion, pretence, cover-up, expedient, get-out, cop-out *(slang)*, subterfuge: *It was just an excuse to get out of going to school.* **3 = poor substitute**, apology, mockery, travesty: *He is a pathetic excuse for a father.*

e

execute VERB **1 = put to death**, kill, shoot, hang, behead, decapitate, guillotine, electrocute: *His father had been executed for treason.* **2 = carry out**, effect, finish, complete, achieve, realize, do, implement, fulfil, enforce, accomplish, render, discharge, administer, prosecute, enact, consummate, put into effect, bring off: *We are going to execute our campaign plan to the letter.* **3 = perform**, do, carry out, accomplish: *The landing was skilfully executed.*

execution NOUN **1 = killing**, hanging, the death penalty, the rope, capital punishment, beheading, the electric chair, the guillotine, the noose, the scaffold, electrocution, decapitation, the firing squad, necktie party *(informal)*: *He was sentenced to execution by lethal injection.* **2 = carrying out**, performance, operation, administration, achievement, effect, prosecution, rendering, discharge, enforcement, implementation, completion, accomplishment, realization, enactment, bringing off, consummation: *the unquestioning execution of his orders* **3 = performance**, style, delivery, manner, technique, mode, presentation, rendition: *his masterly execution of a difficult piece*

executioner NOUN **= hangman**, firing squad, headsman, public executioner, Jack Ketch

executive NOUN **1 = administrator**, official, director, manager, chairman, managing director, controller, chief executive officer, senior manager, chairwoman, chairperson: *Her husband is a senior bank executive.* **2 = administration**, government, directors, management, leadership, hierarchy, directorate: *the executive of the National Union of Students*
▷ ADJECTIVE **= administrative**, controlling, directing, governing, regulating, decision-making, managerial: *He sits on the executive committee of the company.*

exemplar NOUN **1 = model**, example, standard, ideal, criterion, paradigm, epitome, paragon: *They viewed their new building as an exemplar of taste.* **2 = example**, instance, illustration, type, specimen, prototype, typical example, representative example, exemplification: *One of the wittiest exemplars of the technique was M.C. Escher.*

exemplary ADJECTIVE **1 = ideal**, good, fine, model, excellent, sterling, admirable, honourable, commendable, laudable, praiseworthy, meritorious, estimable, punctilious: *He showed outstanding and exemplary courage in the face of danger.* **2 = typical**, representative, characteristic, illustrative: *an exemplary case of how issues of this sort can be resolved* **3 = warning**, harsh, cautionary, admonitory, monitory: *He demanded exemplary sentences for those behind the violence.*

exemplify VERB **= show**, represent, display, demonstrate, instance, illustrate, exhibit, depict, manifest, evidence, embody, serve as an example of

exempt VERB **= grant immunity**, free, except, excuse, release, spare, relieve, discharge, liberate, let off, exonerate, absolve: *Companies with fewer than 55 employees would be exempted from these requirements.*
▷ ADJECTIVE **= immune**, free, excepted, excused, released, spared, clear, discharged, liberated, not subject to, absolved, not liable to: *Men in college were exempt from military service.* **OPPOSITE:** liable

exemption NOUN **= immunity**, freedom, privilege, relief, exception, discharge, release, dispensation, absolution, exoneration

exercise VERB **1 = put to use**, use, apply, employ, practise, exert, enjoy, wield, utilize, bring to bear, avail yourself of: *They are merely exercising their right to free speech.* **2 = train**, work out, practise, drill, keep fit, inure, do exercises: *She exercises two or three times a week.* **3 = worry**, concern, occupy, try, trouble, pain, disturb, burden, distress, preoccupy, agitate, perplex, vex, perturb: *an issue that has long exercised the finest scientific minds*
▷ NOUN **1 = use**, practice, application, operation, employment, discharge, implementation, enjoyment, accomplishment, fulfilment, exertion, utilization: *Leadership does not rest on the exercise of force alone.* **2 = exertion**, training, activity, action, work, labour, effort, movement, discipline, toil, physical activity: *Lack of exercise can lead to feelings of depression and exhaustion.* **3 = manoeuvre**, campaign, operation, movement, deployment: *a missile being used in a military exercise* **4 = task**, problem, lesson, assignment, work, schooling, practice, schoolwork: *Try working through the opening exercises in this chapter.*

exert VERB **= apply**, use, exercise, employ, wield, make use of, utilize, expend, bring to bear, put forth, bring into play: *He exerted all his considerable charm to get her to agree.*
exert yourself = make an effort, work, labour, struggle, strain, strive, endeavour, go for it *(informal)*, try hard, toil, bend over backwards *(informal)*, do your best, go for broke *(slang)*, bust a gut *(informal)*, spare no effort, make a great effort, give it your best shot *(informal)*, break your neck *(informal)*, apply yourself, put yourself out, make an all-out effort *(informal)*, get your finger out *(Brit. informal)*, pull your finger out *(Brit. informal)*, knock yourself out *(informal)*, do your damnedest *(informal)*, give it your all *(informal)*, rupture yourself *(informal)*: *He never exerts himself for other people.*

exertion NOUN **1 = effort**, action, exercise, struggle, industry, labour, trial, pains, stretch, strain, endeavour, toil, travail *(literary)*, elbow grease *(facetious)*: *panting from the exertion of climbing the stairs* **2 = use**, exercise, application, employment, bringing to bear, utilization: *the exertion of legislative power*

exhale VERB **= give off**, emit, steam, discharge, send out, evaporate, issue, eject, emanate: *The craters exhale water, carbon dioxide, and sulphur dioxide.*

exhaust VERB **1 = tire out**, tire, fatigue, drain, disable, weaken, cripple, weary, sap, wear out, debilitate, prostrate, enfeeble, make tired, enervate: *The effort of speaking had exhausted him.* **2 = use up**, spend, finish, consume, waste, go through, run through, deplete, squander, dissipate, expend: *We have exhausted almost all our food supplies.*

exhausted ADJECTIVE **1 = worn out**, tired out, drained, spent, beat *(slang)*, bushed *(informal)*, dead *(informal)*, wasted, done in *(informal)*, weak, all in *(slang)*, disabled, crippled, fatigued, wiped out *(informal)*, sapped, debilitated, jaded, knackered *(slang)*, prostrated, clapped out *(Brit., Austral. & N.Z. informal)*, effete, enfeebled, enervated, ready to drop, dog-tired *(informal)*, zonked *(slang)*, dead tired, dead beat *(informal)*, shagged out *(Brit. slang)*, fagged out *(informal)*, worn to a frazzle *(informal)*, on your last legs *(informal)*, creamcrackered *(Brit. slang)*, out on your feet *(informal)*: *She was too exhausted even to think clearly.* **OPPOSITE:** invigorated **2 = used up**, consumed, spent, finished, gone, depleted, dissipated, expended, at an end: *Mining companies are shutting down* *operations as the coal supply is exhausted.* **OPPOSITE:** replenished

exhausting ADJECTIVE **= tiring**, hard, testing, taxing, difficult, draining, punishing, crippling, fatiguing, wearying, gruelling, sapping, debilitating, strenuous, arduous, laborious, enervating, backbreaking

exhaustion NOUN **1 = tiredness**, fatigue, weariness, lassitude, feebleness, prostration, debilitation, enervation: *He is suffering from nervous exhaustion.* **2 = depletion**, emptying, consumption, using up: *the exhaustion of the country's resources*

exhaustive ADJECTIVE **= thorough**, detailed, complete, full, total, sweeping, comprehensive, extensive, intensive, full-scale, in-depth, far-reaching, all-inclusive, all-embracing, encyclopedic, thoroughgoing **OPPOSITE:** superficial

exhibit VERB **1 = show**, reveal, display, demonstrate, air, evidence, express, indicate, disclose, manifest, evince, make clear *or* plain: *He has exhibited signs of anxiety and stress.* **2 = display**, show, present, set out, parade, unveil, flaunt, put on view: *Her work was exhibited in the best galleries in Europe.*
▷ NOUN **= object**, piece, model, article, illustration: *He showed me round the exhibits in the museum.*

exhibition NOUN **1 = show**, display, exhibit, showing, fair, representation, presentation, spectacle, showcase, expo *(informal)*, exposition, ex *(Canad. informal)*: *an exhibition of expressionist art* **2 = display**, show, performance, demonstration, airing, revelation, manifestation: *He treated the fans to an exhibition of power and speed.*

exhilarate VERB **= excite**, delight, cheer, thrill, stimulate, animate, exalt, lift, enliven, invigorate, gladden, elate, inspirit, pep *or* perk up

exhilarating ADJECTIVE **= exciting**, thrilling, stimulating, breathtaking, cheering, exalting, enlivening, invigorating, gladdening, vitalizing, exhilarant

exhilaration NOUN **= excitement**, delight, joy, happiness, animation, high spirits, elation, mirth, gaiety, hilarity, exaltation, cheerfulness, vivacity, liveliness, gladness, joyfulness, sprightliness, gleefulness **OPPOSITE:** depression

exhort VERB **= urge**, warn, encourage, advise, bid, persuade, prompt, spur, press, counsel, caution, call upon, incite, goad, admonish, enjoin, beseech, entreat

exhortation NOUN **= urging**, warning, advice, counsel, lecture, caution, bidding, encouragement, sermon, persuasion, goading, incitement, admonition, beseeching, entreaty, clarion call, enjoinder *(rare)*

exhume VERB **= dig up**, unearth, disinter, unbury, disentomb **OPPOSITE:** bury

exile NOUN **1 = banishment**, expulsion, deportation, eviction, separation, ostracism, proscription, expatriation: *During his exile, he began writing books.* **2 = expatriate**, refugee, outcast, émigré, deportee: *the release of all political prisoners and the return of exiles*
▷ VERB **= banish**, expel, throw out, deport, oust, drive out, eject, expatriate, proscribe, cast out, ostracize: *Dante was exiled from Florence in 1302 because of his political activities.*

exiled ADJECTIVE **= banished**, deported, expatriate, outcast, refugee, ostracized, expat

exist VERB **1 = live**, be present, be living, last, survive, breathe, endure, be in existence, be, be extant, have breath: *Many people believe that the Loch Ness Monster does exist.* **2 = occur**, happen, stand, remain, obtain, be present, prevail, abide: *the social climate which existed 20 years ago* **3 = survive**, stay alive, make ends meet, subsist, eke out a living, scrape by, scrimp and save, support yourself, keep your head above water, get along *or* by: *the problems of having to exist on unemployment benefit*

> **USAGE**
> Although *be extant* is given as a synonym of *exist*, according to some, *extant* should properly be used only where there is a connotation of survival, often against all odds: *the oldest extant document dates from 1492*. Using *extant* where the phrase *in existence* can be substituted would in this view be incorrect: *in existence* (not *extant*) *for nearly 15 years, they have been consistently one of the finest rock bands on the planet*. In practice, however, the distinct meanings of the two phrases often overlap: *these beasts, the largest primates on the planet and the greatest of the great apes, are man's closest living relatives and the only extant primates with which we share close physical characteristics*.

existence NOUN **1 = reality**, being, life, survival, duration, endurance, continuation, subsistence, actuality, continuance: *Public worries about accidents are threatening the very existence of the nuclear power industry.* **2 = life**, situation, way of life, lifestyle: *the man who rescued her from her wretched existence* **3 = creation**, life, the world, reality, the human condition, this mortal coil: *pondering the mysteries of existence*

existent ADJECTIVE **= in existence**, living, existing, surviving, around, standing, remaining, present, current, alive, enduring, prevailing, abiding, to the fore *(Scot.)*, extant

existing ADJECTIVE **= in existence**, living, present, surviving, remaining, available, alive, in operation, extant, alive and kicking **OPPOSITE:** gone

exit NOUN **1 = way out**, door, gate, outlet, doorway, vent, gateway, escape route, passage out, egress: *We headed quickly for the fire exit.* **OPPOSITE:** entry **2 = departure**, withdrawal, retreat, farewell, going, retirement, goodbye, exodus, evacuation, decamping, leave-taking, adieu: *She made a dignified exit.*
▷ VERB **= depart**, leave, go out, withdraw, retire, quit, retreat, go away, say goodbye, bid farewell, make tracks, take your leave, go offstage *(Theatre)*: *He exited without saying goodbye.* **OPPOSITE:** enter

exodus NOUN **= departure**, withdrawal, retreat, leaving, flight, retirement, exit, migration, evacuation

exonerate VERB **= acquit**, clear, excuse, pardon, justify, discharge, vindicate, absolve, exculpate

exorbitant ADJECTIVE **= excessive**, high, expensive, extreme, ridiculous, outrageous, extravagant, unreasonable, undue, preposterous, unwarranted, inordinate, extortionate, unconscionable, immoderate **OPPOSITE:** reasonable

exorcise *or* **exorcize** VERB **1 = drive out**, expel, cast out, adjure: *He tried to exorcise the pain of his childhood trauma.* **2 = purify**, free, cleanse: *They came to our house and exorcized me.*

exorcism NOUN **= driving out**, cleansing, expulsion, purification, deliverance, casting out, adjuration

exotic ADJECTIVE **1 = unusual**, different, striking, strange, extraordinary, bizarre, fascinating, curious, mysterious, colourful, glamorous, peculiar, unfamiliar, outlandish: *his striking and exotic appearance* **OPPOSITE:** ordinary **2 = foreign**, alien, tropical, external, extraneous, naturalized, extrinsic, not native: *travelling around the globe to collect rare and exotic plant species*

expand VERB **1 = get bigger**, increase, grow, extend, swell, widen, blow up, wax, heighten, enlarge, multiply, inflate, thicken, fill out, lengthen, fatten, dilate, become bigger, puff up, become larger, distend: *Water expands as it freezes.* **OPPOSITE:** contract **2 = make bigger**, increase, develop, extend, widen, blow up, heighten, enlarge, multiply, broaden, inflate, thicken, fill out, lengthen, magnify, amplify, augment, dilate, make larger, distend, bloat, protract: *We can expand the size of the image.* **OPPOSITE:** reduce **3 = spread (out)**, open (out), stretch (out), unfold, unravel, diffuse, unfurl, unroll, outspread: *The flowers fully expand at night.*
expand on something = go into detail about, embellish, elaborate on, develop, flesh out, expound on, enlarge on, expatiate on, add detail to: *He expanded on some remarks he made in his last speech.*

expanse NOUN **= area**, range, field, space, stretch, sweep, extent, plain, tract, breadth

e

expansion NOUN **1 = increase**, development, growth, spread, diffusion, magnification, multiplication, amplification, augmentation: *the rapid expansion of private health insurance* **2 = enlargement**, inflation, increase, growth, swelling, unfolding, expanse, unfurling, opening out, distension: *Slow breathing allows for full expansion of the lungs.*

expansive ADJECTIVE **1 = wide**, broad, extensive, spacious, sweeping: *an expansive grassy play area* **2 = comprehensive**, extensive, broad, wide, widespread, wide-ranging, thorough, inclusive, far-reaching, voluminous, all-embracing: *the book's expansive coverage of this period* **3 = talkative**, open, friendly, outgoing, free, easy, warm, sociable, genial, affable, communicative, effusive, garrulous, loquacious, unreserved: *He became more expansive as he began to relax.*

expatriate ADJECTIVE **= exiled**, refugee, banished, emigrant, émigré, expat: *The military is preparing to evacuate women and children of expatriate families.* ▷ NOUN **= exile**, refugee, emigrant, émigré: *British expatriates in Spain*

expect VERB **1 = think**, believe, suppose, assume, trust, imagine, reckon, forecast, calculate, presume, foresee, conjecture, surmise, think likely: *We expect the talks will continue until tomorrow.* **2 = anticipate**, look forward to, predict, envisage, await, hope for, contemplate, bargain for, look ahead to: *I wasn't expecting to see you today.* **3 = require**, demand, want, wish, look for, call for, ask for, hope for, insist on, count on, rely upon: *He expects total obedience and blind loyalty from his staff.*

expectancy NOUN **1 = likelihood**, prospect, tendency, outlook, probability: *the average life expectancy of the British male* **2 = expectation**, hope, anticipation, waiting, belief, looking forward, assumption, prediction, probability, suspense, presumption, conjecture, surmise, supposition: *The atmosphere here at the stadium is one of expectancy.*

expectant ADJECTIVE **1 = expecting**, excited, anticipating, anxious, ready, awaiting, eager, hopeful, apprehensive, watchful, in suspense: *She turned to me with an expectant look on her face.* **2 = pregnant**, expecting (*informal*), gravid, enceinte: *antenatal classes for expectant mothers*

expectation NOUN **1** (*usually plural*) **= projection**, supposition, assumption, calculation, belief, forecast, assurance, likelihood, probability, presumption, conjecture, surmise, presupposition: *Sales of the car have far exceeded expectations.* **2 = anticipation**, hope, possibility, prospect, chance, fear, promise, looking forward, excitement, prediction, outlook, expectancy, apprehension, suspense: *His nerves tingled with expectation.* **3** (*usually plural*) **= requirement**, demand, want, wish, insistence, reliance: *Sometimes people have unreasonable expectations of the medical profession.*

> QUOTATIONS
> Blessed is the man who expects nothing, for he shall never be disappointed
> [Alexander Pope *letter to Fortescue*]

expected ADJECTIVE **= anticipated**, wanted, promised, looked-for, predicted, forecast, awaited, hoped-for, counted on, long-awaited

expecting ADJECTIVE **= pregnant**, with child, expectant, in the club (*Brit. slang*), in the family way (*informal*), gravid, enceinte

expediency *or* **expedience** NOUN **= suitability**, benefit, fitness, utility, effectiveness, convenience, profitability, practicality, usefulness, prudence, pragmatism, propriety, desirability, appropriateness, utilitarianism, helpfulness, advisability, aptness, judiciousness, properness, meetness, advantageousness

expedient ADJECTIVE **= advantageous**, effective, useful, profitable, fit, politic, appropriate, practical, suitable, helpful, proper, convenient, desirable, worthwhile, beneficial, pragmatic, prudent, advisable, utilitarian, judicious, opportune: *It might be expedient to keep this information to yourself.* **OPPOSITE:** unwise ▷ NOUN **= means**, measure, scheme, method, resource, resort, device, manoeuvre, expediency, stratagem, contrivance, stopgap: *I reduced my spending by the simple expedient of destroying my credit cards.*

expedite VERB **= speed (up)**, forward, promote, advance, press, urge, rush, assist, hurry, accelerate, dispatch, facilitate, hasten, precipitate, quicken **OPPOSITE:** hold up

expedition NOUN **1 = journey**, exploration, mission, voyage, tour, enterprise, undertaking, quest, trek: *Byrd's 1928 expedition to Antarctica* **2 = team**, crew, party, group, company, travellers, explorers, voyagers, wayfarers: *Forty-three members of the expedition were killed.* **3 = trip**, tour, outing, excursion, jaunt: *We went on a shopping expedition.*

expel VERB **1 = throw out**, exclude, ban, bar, dismiss, discharge, relegate, kick out (*informal*), ask to leave, send packing, turf out (*informal*), black, debar, drum out, blackball, give the bum's rush (*slang*), show you the door, throw out on your ear (*informal*): *secondary school students expelled for cheating in exams* **OPPOSITE:** let in **2 = banish**, exile, oust, deport, expatriate, evict, force to leave, proscribe: *An American academic was expelled from the country yesterday.* **OPPOSITE:** take in **3 = drive out**, discharge, throw out, force out, let out, eject, issue, dislodge, spew, belch, cast out: *Poisonous gas is expelled into the atmosphere.*

expend VERB **1 = use (up)**, employ, go through (*informal*), exhaust, consume, dissipate: *the number of calories you expend through exercise* **2 = spend**, pay out, lay out (*informal*), fork out (*slang*), shell out, disburse: *the amount of money expended on this project so far*

expendable ADJECTIVE **= dispensable**, unnecessary, unimportant, replaceable, nonessential, inessential **OPPOSITE:** indispensable

expenditure NOUN **1 = spending**, payment, expense, outgoings, cost, charge, outlay, disbursement: *The government should reduce their expenditure on defence.* **2 = consumption**, use, using, application, output: *The rewards justified the expenditure of effort.*

> QUOTATIONS
> Expenditure rises to meet income
> [C. Northcote Parkinson *The Law and the Profits*]

expense NOUN **= cost**, charge, expenditure, payment, spending, output, toll, consumption, outlay, disbursement: *She has refurbished the whole place at vast expense.* **at the expense of = with the sacrifice of**, with the loss of, at the cost of, at the price of: *The company has increased productivity at the expense of safety.*

expensive ADJECTIVE **= costly**, high-priced, lavish, extravagant, rich, dear, stiff, excessive, steep (*informal*), pricey, overpriced, exorbitant **OPPOSITE:** cheap

experience NOUN **1 = knowledge**, understanding, practice, skill, evidence, trial, contact, expertise, know-how (*informal*), proof, involvement, exposure, observation, participation, familiarity, practical knowledge: *He lacks experience of international rugby.* **2 = event**, affair, incident, happening, test, trial, encounter, episode, adventure, ordeal, occurrence: *It was an experience I would not like to go through again.* ▷ VERB **= undergo**, have, know, feel, try, meet, face, suffer, taste, go through, observe, sample, encounter, sustain, perceive, endure, participate in, run into, live through, behold, come up against, apprehend, become familiar with: *couples who have experienced the trauma of divorce*

> QUOTATIONS
> Trust one who has gone through it
> [Virgil *Aeneid*]
>
> Experience is not what happens to a man. It is what a man does with what happens to him
> [Aldous Huxley *Texts and Pretexts*]

Experience is the name everyone gives to their mistakes
[Oscar Wilde *Lady Windermere's Fan*]

All experience is an arch to build upon
[Henry Brooks Adams *The Education of Henry Adams*]

What poor education I have received has been gained in the University of Life
[Horatio Bottomley]

If you have lived one day you have seen everything; one day is the same as all the others
[Montaigne *Essais*]

Nothing ever becomes real till it is experienced
–Even a Proverb is no proverb to you till your Life has illustrated it
[John Keats *letter to George and Georgiana Keats*]

PROVERBS
Experience is the mother of wisdom
Experience is the best teacher

experienced ADJECTIVE **1 = knowledgeable**, trained, professional, skilled, tried, tested, seasoned, expert, master, qualified, familiar, capable, veteran, practised, accomplished, competent, skilful, adept, well-versed: *a team made up of experienced professionals* **OPPOSITE:** inexperienced **2 = worldly-wise**, knowing, worldly, wise, mature, sophisticated: *Perhaps I'm a bit more experienced about life than you are.*

experiment NOUN **1 = test**, trial, investigation, examination, venture, procedure, demonstration, observation, try-out, assay, trial run, scientific test, dummy run: *a proposed new law banning animal experiments* **2 = research**, investigation, analysis, observation, research and development, experimentation, trial and error: *The only way to find out is by experiment.*
▷ VERB **= test**, investigate, trial, research, try, examine, pilot, sample, verify, put to the test, assay: *Scientists have been experimenting with a new drug.*

experimental ADJECTIVE **1 = test**, trial, pilot, preliminary, provisional, tentative, speculative, empirical, exploratory, trial-and-error, fact-finding, probationary: *The technique is still in the experimental stages.* **2 = innovative**, new, original, radical, creative, ingenious, avant-garde, inventive, ground-breaking: *He writes bizarre and highly experimental music.*

expert NOUN **= specialist**, authority, professional, master, pro *(informal)*, ace *(informal)*, genius, guru, pundit, buff *(informal)*, wizard, adept, whizz *(informal)*, maestro, virtuoso, connoisseur, hotshot *(informal)*, past master, dab hand *(Brit. informal)*, wonk *(informal)*, maven *(U.S.)*, fundi *(S. African)*: *an expert in computer graphics* **OPPOSITE:** amateur
▷ ADJECTIVE **= skilful**, trained, experienced, able, professional, skilled, master, masterly, qualified, talented, outstanding, clever, practised, accomplished, handy, competent, apt, adept, knowledgeable, virtuoso, deft, proficient, facile, adroit, dexterous: *The faces of the waxworks are modelled by expert sculptors.* **OPPOSITE:** unskilled

QUOTATIONS
An expert is a man who has made all the mistakes which can be made in a very narrow field
[Niels Henrik David Bohr]

An expert is one who knows more and more about less and less
[Nicholas Murray Butler]

An expert is someone who knows some of the worst mistakes that can be made in his subject and who manages to avoid them
[Werner Heisenberg *Der Teil und das Ganze*]

expertise NOUN **= skill**, knowledge, know-how *(informal)*, facility, grip, craft, judgment, grasp, mastery, knack, proficiency, dexterity, cleverness, deftness, adroitness, aptness, expertness, knowing inside out, ableness, masterliness, skilfulness

expiration NOUN **= expiry**, end, finish, conclusion, close, termination, cessation

expire VERB **1 = become invalid**, end, finish, conclude, close, stop, run out, cease, lapse, terminate, come to an end, be no longer valid: *He continued to live in the States after his visa had expired.* **2 = die**, decease, depart, buy it *(U.S. slang)*, check out *(U.S. slang)*, perish, kick it *(slang)*, croak *(slang)*, go belly-up *(slang)*, snuff it *(informal)*, peg out *(informal)*, kick the bucket *(informal)*, peg it *(informal)*, depart this life, meet your maker, cark it *(Austral. & N.Z. slang)*, pop your clogs *(informal)*, pass away or on: *He expired in excruciating agony.*

expiry NOUN **= expiration**, ending, end, conclusion, close, demise, lapsing, lapse, termination, cessation

explain VERB **1 = make clear** or **plain**, describe, demonstrate, illustrate, teach, define, solve, resolve, interpret, disclose, unfold, clarify, clear up, simplify, expound, elucidate, put into words, throw light on, explicate *(formal)*, give the details of, unpack: *He explained the process to us in simple terms.* **2 = account for**, excuse, justify, give a reason for, give an explanation for: *Can you explain why you didn't telephone me?*

QUOTATIONS
Never explain – your friends do not need it and your enemies will not believe you anyway
[Elbert Hubbard *The Motto Book*]

explanation NOUN **1 = reason**, meaning, cause, sense, answer, account, excuse, motive, justification, vindication, mitigation, the why and wherefore: *The president has given no explanation for his behaviour.* **2 = description**, report, definition, demonstration, teaching, resolution, interpretation, illustration, clarification, exposition, simplification, explication, elucidation: *his lucid explanation of the mysteries of cricket*

explanatory *or* **explanative** ADJECTIVE **= descriptive**, interpretive, illustrative, interpretative, demonstrative, justifying, expository, illuminative, elucidatory, explicative

explicit ADJECTIVE **1 = clear**, obvious, specific, direct, certain, express, plain, absolute, exact, precise, straightforward, definite, overt, unequivocal, unqualified, unambiguous, categorical: *He left explicit instructions on how to set the video timer.* **OPPOSITE:** vague **2 = frank**, direct, open, specific, positive, plain, patent, graphic, distinct, outspoken, upfront *(informal)*, unambiguous, unrestricted, unrestrained, uncensored, unreserved: *songs containing explicit references to sexual activity* **OPPOSITE:** indirect

explode VERB **1 = blow up**, erupt, burst, go off, shatter, shiver: *They were clearing up when the second bomb exploded.* **2 = detonate**, set off, discharge, let off: *The first test atomic bomb was exploded in the New Mexico desert.* **3 = lose your temper**, rage, erupt, blow up *(informal)*, lose it *(informal)*, crack up *(informal)*, see red *(informal)*, lose the plot *(informal)*, become angry, have a fit *(informal)*, go ballistic *(slang, chiefly U.S.)*, hit the roof *(informal)*, throw a tantrum, blow a fuse *(slang, chiefly U.S.)*, go berserk *(slang)*, go mad *(slang)*, fly off the handle *(informal)*, go spare *(Brit. slang)*, become enraged, go off the deep end *(informal)*, go up the wall *(slang)*, blow your top *(informal)*, go crook *(Austral. & N.Z. slang)*, fly into a temper, flip your lid *(slang)*, do your nut *(Brit. slang)*: *He exploded with rage at the accusation.* **4 = increase**, grow, develop, extend, advance, shoot up, soar, boost, expand, build up, swell, step up *(informal)*, escalate, multiply, proliferate, snowball, aggrandize: *The population has exploded in the last twenty years.* **5 = disprove**, discredit, refute, belie, demolish, repudiate, put paid to, invalidate, debunk, prove impossible, prove wrong, give the lie to, blow out of the water *(slang)*: *an article which explodes the myth that thin equals sexy*

exploit NOUN **= feat**, act, achievement, enterprise, adventure, stunt, deed, accomplishment, attainment, escapade: *His wartime exploits were made into a TV series.*
▷ VERB **1 = take advantage of**, abuse,

e

use, manipulate, milk, misuse, dump on *(slang, chiefly U.S.)*, ill-treat, play on *or* upon: *Casual workers are being exploited for slave wages.* **2 = make the best use of**, use, make use of, utilize, cash in on *(informal)*, capitalize on, put to use, make capital out of, use to advantage, use to good advantage, live off the backs of, turn to account, profit by *or* from: *The opposition are exploiting the situation to their advantage.*

exploitation NOUN **1 = misuse**, abuse, manipulation, imposition, using, ill-treatment: *the exploitation of working women* **2 = capitalization**, utilization, using to good advantage, trading upon: *the exploitation of the famine by local politicians*

e

exploration NOUN **1 = expedition**, tour, trip, survey, travel, journey, reconnaissance, recce *(slang)*: *We devoted a week to the exploration of the Mayan sites of Copan.* **2 = investigation**, study, research, survey, search, inquiry, analysis, examination, probe, inspection, scrutiny, once-over *(informal)*: *an exploration of Celtic mythology*

exploratory ADJECTIVE **= investigative**, trial, searching, probing, experimental, analytic, fact-finding

explore VERB **1 = travel around**, tour, survey, scout, traverse, range over, recce *(slang)*, reconnoitre, case *(slang)*, have *or* take a look around: *We explored the old part of the town.* **2 = investigate**, consider, research, survey, search, prospect, examine, probe, analyse, look into, inspect, work over, scrutinize, inquire into: *The film explores the relationship between artist and instrument.*

explosion NOUN **1 = blast**, crack, burst, bang, discharge, report, blowing up, outburst, clap, detonation: *Three people were killed in a bomb explosion in London today.* **2 = increase**, rise, development, growth, boost, expansion, enlargement, escalation, upturn: *a population explosion* **3 = outburst**, fit, storm, attack, surge, flare-up, eruption, paroxysm: *His reaction was an explosion of anger.* **4 = outbreak**, flare-up, eruption, upsurge: *an explosion of violence in the country's capital*

explosive ADJECTIVE **1 = unstable**, dangerous, volatile, hazardous, unsafe, perilous, combustible, inflammable: *Highly explosive gas is naturally found in coal mines.* **2 = dangerous**, worrying, strained, anxious, charged, ugly, tense, hazardous, stressful, perilous, nerve-racking, overwrought: *a potentially explosive situation* **3 = fiery**, violent, volatile, stormy, touchy, vehement, chippy *(informal)*: *He inherited his father's explosive temper.*
▷ NOUN **= bomb**, mine, shell, missile, rocket, grenade, charge, torpedo, incendiary: *A large quantity of arms and explosives was seized.*

exponent NOUN **1 = advocate**, champion, supporter, defender, spokesman, spokeswoman, promoter, backer, spokesperson, proponent, propagandist, upholder: *a leading exponent of genetic engineering* **2 = performer**, player, interpreter, presenter, executant: *the great exponent of Bach, Glenn Gould*

expose VERB **1 = uncover**, show, reveal, display, exhibit, present, unveil, manifest, lay bare, take the wraps off, put on view: *He pulled up his T-shirt, exposing his white belly.*
OPPOSITE: hide **2 = reveal**, disclose, uncover, air, detect, betray, show up, denounce, unearth, let out, divulge, unmask, lay bare, make known, bring to light, out *(informal)*, smoke out, blow wide open *(slang)*: *After the scandal was exposed, he committed suicide.*
OPPOSITE: keep secret **3 = make vulnerable**, subject, leave open, lay open: *people exposed to high levels of radiation*
expose someone to something = introduce to, acquaint with, bring into contact with, familiarize with, make familiar with, make conversant with: *when women from these societies become exposed to Western culture*

exposé NOUN **= exposure**, revelation, uncovering, disclosure, divulgence

exposed ADJECTIVE **1 = unconcealed**, revealed, bare, exhibited, unveiled, shown, uncovered, on display, on show, on view, laid bare, made manifest: *Skin cancer is most likely to occur on exposed parts of the body.* **2 = unsheltered**, open, unprotected, open to the elements: *This part of the coast is very exposed.* **3 = vulnerable**, open, subject, in danger, liable, susceptible, wide open, left open, laid bare, in peril, laid open: *The troops are exposed to attack by the enemy.*

exposition NOUN **1 = explanation**, account, description, interpretation, illustration, presentation, commentary, critique, exegesis, explication, elucidation: *Her speech was an exposition of her beliefs in freedom and justice.* **2 = exhibition**, show, fair, display, demonstration, presentation, expo *(informal)*: *an art exposition*

exposure NOUN **1 = vulnerability**, subjection, susceptibility, laying open: *Exposure to lead is known to damage the brains of young children.* **2 = hypothermia**, frostbite, extreme cold, intense cold: *Two people died of exposure in Chicago overnight.* **3 = revelation**, exposé, uncovering, disclosure, airing, manifestation, detection, divulging, denunciation, unmasking, divulgence: *the exposure of Anthony Blunt as a former Soviet spy* **4 = publicity**, promotion, attention, advertising, plugging *(informal)*, propaganda, hype, pushing, media hype: *The candidates have been getting a lot of exposure on TV.* **5 = uncovering**, showing, display, exhibition, baring, revelation, presentation, unveiling, manifestation: *a bodice allowing full exposure of the breasts* **6 = contact**, experience, awareness, acquaintance, familiarity: *Repeated exposure to the music reveals its hidden depths.*

expound VERB **= explain**, describe, illustrate, interpret, unfold, spell out, set forth, elucidate, explicate *(formal)*

express VERB **1 = state**, communicate, convey, articulate, say, tell, put, word, speak, voice, declare, phrase, assert, pronounce, utter, couch, put across, enunciate, put into words, give voice to, verbalize, asseverate: *He expressed grave concern at their attitude.* **2 = show**, indicate, exhibit, demonstrate, reveal, disclose, intimate, convey, testify to, depict, designate, manifest, embody, signify, symbolize, denote, divulge, bespeak, make known, evince: *He expressed his anger in a destructive way.*
▷ ADJECTIVE **1 = explicit**, clear, direct, precise, pointed, certain, plain, accurate, exact, distinct, definite, outright, unambiguous, categorical: *The ship was sunk on express orders from the Prime Minister.* **2 = specific**, exclusive, particular, sole, special, deliberate, singular, clear-cut, especial: *I bought the camera with the express purpose of taking nature photos.* **3 = fast**, direct, quick, rapid, priority, prompt, swift, high-speed, speedy, quickie *(informal)*, nonstop, expeditious: *A special express service is available.*

expression NOUN **1 = statement**, declaration, announcement, communication, mention, assertion, utterance, articulation, pronouncement, enunciation, verbalization, asseveration: *From Cairo came expressions of regret at the attack.* **2 = indication**, demonstration, exhibition, display, showing, show, sign, symbol, representation, token, manifestation, embodiment: *We attended as an expression of solidarity.* **3 = look**, countenance, face, air, appearance, aspect, mien *(literary)*: *He sat there with a sad expression on his face.* **4 = intonation**, style, delivery, phrasing, emphasis, execution, diction: *She puts a lot of expression into her playing.* **5 = phrase**, saying, word, wording, term, language, speech, remark, maxim, idiom, adage, choice of words, turn of phrase, phraseology, locution, set phrase: *He uses some remarkably coarse expressions.*

expressionless ADJECTIVE **= blank**, empty, deadpan, straight-faced, wooden, dull, vacuous, inscrutable, poker-faced *(informal)*

expressive ADJECTIVE **1 = vivid**, strong, striking, telling, moving, lively, sympathetic, energetic, poignant, emphatic, eloquent, forcible: *She had a small, expressive face.*
OPPOSITE: impassive **2** *(with* **of)** **= meaningful**, indicative, suggestive, demonstrative, revealing,

significant, allusive: *All his poems are expressive of his love for nature.*

expressly ADVERB **1 = explicitly**, clearly, plainly, absolutely, positively, definitely, outright, manifestly, distinctly, decidedly, categorically, pointedly, unequivocally, unmistakably, in no uncertain terms, unambiguously: *He had expressly forbidden her to go out on her own.* **2 = specifically**, specially, especially, particularly, purposely, exclusively, precisely, solely, exactly, deliberately, intentionally, on purpose: *Bleasdale had written the role expressly for this actor.*

expropriate VERB **= seize**, take, appropriate, confiscate, assume, take over, take away, commandeer, requisition, arrogate

expropriation NOUN **= seizure**, takeover, impounding, confiscation, commandeering, requisitioning, sequestration, disseisin *(Law)*

expulsion NOUN **1 = ejection**, exclusion, dismissal, removal, exile, discharge, eviction, banishment, extrusion, proscription, expatriation, debarment, dislodgment: *Her behaviour led to her expulsion from school.* **2 = discharge**, emptying, emission, voiding, spewing, secretion, excretion, ejection, seepage, suppuration: *the expulsion of waste products from the body*

expunge VERB **= erase**, remove, destroy, abolish, cancel, get rid of, wipe out, eradicate, excise, delete, extinguish, strike out, obliterate, annihilate, efface, exterminate, annul, raze, blot out, extirpate

exquisite ADJECTIVE **1 = beautiful**, elegant, graceful, pleasing, attractive, lovely, charming, comely: *She has exquisite manners.* **OPPOSITE:** unattractive **2 = fine**, beautiful, lovely, elegant, precious, delicate, dainty: *The natives brought exquisite beadwork to sell.* **3 = intense**, acute, severe, sharp, keen, extreme, piercing, poignant, excruciating: *His words gave her exquisite pain.* **4 = refined**, cultivated, discriminating, sensitive, polished, selective, discerning, impeccable, meticulous, consummate, appreciative, fastidious: *The house was furnished with exquisite taste.* **5 = excellent**, fine, outstanding, superb, choice, perfect, select, delicious, divine, splendid, admirable, consummate, flawless, superlative, incomparable, peerless, matchless: *The hotel features friendly staff and exquisite cuisine.* **OPPOSITE:** imperfect

extant ADJECTIVE **= in existence**, existing, remaining, surviving, living, existent, subsisting, undestroyed

> **USAGE**
> Used carefully, the word *extant* describes something that has survived, often against all odds. It therefore carries a slightly more specific meaning than *in existence*, and should not be considered as being automatically interchangeable with this phrase. For example, you might say *the oldest extant document dates from 1492*; but *in existence* (not *extant*) *for 15 years, they are still one of the most successful bands in the world*. In many contexts, however, these ideas overlap, leaving the writer to decide whether *extant* or *in existence* best expresses the intended meaning.

extend VERB **1 = spread out**, reach, stretch, continue, carry on: *The territory extends over one fifth of Canada's land mass.* **2 = stretch**, stretch out, spread out, unfurl, straighten out, unroll: *Stand straight with your arms extended at your sides.* **3 = last**, continue, go on, stretch, carry on: *His playing career extended from 1894 to 1920.* **4 = protrude**, project, stand out, bulge, stick out, hang, overhang, jut out: *His legs extended from the bushes.* **5 = reach**, spread, go as far as: *His possessiveness extends to people as well as property.* **6 = widen**, increase, develop, expand, spread, add to, enhance, supplement, enlarge, broaden, diversify, amplify, augment: *They have added three new products to extend their range.* **OPPOSITE:** reduce **7 = make longer**, prolong, lengthen, draw out, spin out, elongate, drag out, protract: *They have extended the deadline by 24 hours.* **OPPOSITE:** shorten **8 = offer**, give, hold out, present, grant, advance, yield, reach out, confer, stretch out, stick out, bestow, impart, proffer, put forth: *'I'm Chuck,' the man said, extending his hand.* **OPPOSITE:** withdraw

extended ADJECTIVE **1 = lengthened**, long, prolonged, protracted, stretched out, drawn-out, unfurled, elongated, unrolled: *He and Naomi spent an extended period getting to know one another.* **2 = broad**, wide, expanded, extensive, widespread, comprehensive, large-scale, enlarged, far-reaching: *a tribal society grouped in huge extended families* **3 = outstretched**, conferred, stretched out, proffered: *She found herself kissing the old lady's extended hand.*

extension NOUN **1 = annexe**, wing, addition, supplement, branch, appendix, add-on, adjunct, appendage, ell, addendum: *the new extension to London's National Gallery* **2 = lengthening**, extra time, continuation, postponement, prolongation, additional period of time, protraction: *He has been granted a six-month extension to his visa.* **3 = development**, expansion, widening, increase, stretching, broadening, continuation, enlargement, diversification, amplification, elongation, augmentation: *Russia is contemplating the extension of its territory*

extensive ADJECTIVE **1 = large**, considerable, substantial, spacious, wide, sweeping, broad, expansive, capacious, commodious: *This 18th-century manor house is set in extensive grounds.* **OPPOSITE:** confined **2 = comprehensive**, complete, thorough, lengthy, long, wide, wholesale, pervasive, protracted, all-inclusive: *The story received extensive coverage in The Times.* **OPPOSITE:** restricted **3 = great**, large, huge, extended, vast, widespread, comprehensive, universal, large-scale, far-reaching, prevalent, far-flung, all-inclusive, voluminous, humongous *or* humungous *(U.S. slang)*: *The blast caused extensive damage.* **OPPOSITE:** limited

extent NOUN **1 = magnitude**, amount, degree, scale, level, measure, stretch, quantity, bulk, duration, expanse, amplitude: *The full extent of the losses was revealed yesterday.* **2 = size**, area, range, length, reach, bounds, sweep, sphere, width, compass, breadth, ambit: *an estate about seven or eight acres in extent*

exterior NOUN **= outside**, face, surface, covering, finish, skin, appearance, aspect, shell, coating, façade, outside surface: *The exterior of the building was a masterpiece of architecture.* ▷ ADJECTIVE **= outer**, outside, external, surface, outward, superficial, outermost: *The exterior walls were made of pre-formed concrete.* **OPPOSITE:** inner

exterminate VERB **= destroy**, kill, eliminate, abolish, eradicate, annihilate, extirpate

extermination NOUN **= destruction**, murder, massacre, slaughter, killing, wiping out, genocide, elimination, mass murder, annihilation, eradication, extirpation

> **QUOTATIONS**
> We seem to be in the midst of an era of delirious ferocity, with half of mankind hell bent upon exterminating the other half
> [H.L. Mencken]

external ADJECTIVE **1 = outer**, outside, surface, apparent, visible, outward, exterior, superficial, outermost: *the external surface of the wall* **OPPOSITE:** internal **2 = foreign**, international, alien, exotic, exterior, extraneous, extrinsic: *the commissioner for external affairs* **OPPOSITE:** domestic **3 = outside**, visiting, independent, extramural: *The papers are checked by external examiners.* **OPPOSITE:** inside

extinct ADJECTIVE **1 = dead**, lost, gone, vanished, defunct: *It is 250 years since the wolf became extinct in Britain.* **OPPOSITE:** living **2 = inactive**, extinguished, doused, out, snuffed out, quenched: *The island's tallest volcano is long extinct.*

extinction NOUN **= dying out**, death, destruction, abolition, oblivion, extermination, annihilation, eradication, obliteration, excision, extirpation

extinguish VERB **1 = put out**, stifle, smother, blow out, douse, snuff out, quench: *It took about 50 minutes to extinguish the fire.* **2 = destroy**, end, kill, remove, eliminate, obscure, abolish, suppress, wipe out, erase, eradicate, annihilate, put paid to, exterminate, expunge, extirpate: *The message extinguished her hopes of Richard's return.*

extol VERB **= praise**, acclaim, applaud, pay tribute to, celebrate, commend, magnify *(archaic)*, glorify, exalt, laud, crack up *(informal)*, sing the praises of, eulogize, cry up, panegyrize

extort VERB **= extract**, force, squeeze, exact, bully, bleed *(informal)*, blackmail, wring, coerce, wrest

extortion NOUN **= blackmail**, force, oppression, compulsion, coercion, shakedown *(U.S. slang)*, rapacity, exaction

extortionate ADJECTIVE **= exorbitant**, excessive, outrageous, unreasonable, inflated, extravagant, preposterous, sky-high, inordinate, immoderate: *the extortionate price of designer clothes* **OPPOSITE:** reasonable

extra ADJECTIVE **1 = additional**, more, new, other, added, further, fresh, accessory, supplementary, auxiliary, add-on, supplemental, ancillary: *Extra staff have been taken on to cover busy periods.* **OPPOSITE:** vital **2 = surplus**, excess, reserve, spare, unnecessary, redundant, needless, unused, leftover, superfluous, extraneous, unneeded, inessential, supernumerary, supererogatory: *This exercise will help you burn up any extra calories.*
▷ NOUN **= addition**, bonus, supplement, accessory, complement, add-on, affix, adjunct, appendage, addendum, supernumerary, appurtenance: *Optional extras including cooking tuition.* **OPPOSITE:** necessity
▷ ADVERB **1 = in addition**, additionally, over and above: *You may be charged extra for this service.* **2 = exceptionally**, very, specially, especially, particularly, extremely, remarkably, unusually, extraordinarily, uncommonly: *Try extra hard to be nice to him.*

extract VERB **1 = obtain**, take out, distil, squeeze out, draw out, express, separate out, press out: *Citric acid can be extracted from the juice of oranges.* **2 = take out**, draw, pull, remove, withdraw, pull out, bring out: *He extracted a small notebook from his pocket.* **3 = pull out**, remove, take out, draw, uproot, pluck out, extirpate: *She has to have a tooth extracted at 3 today.* **4 = elicit**, get, obtain, force, draw, gather, derive, exact, bring out, evoke, reap, wring, glean, coerce, wrest: *He tried to extract further information from the witness.* **5 = select**, quote, cite, abstract, choose, cut out, reproduce, cull, copy out: *material extracted from a range of texts*
▷ NOUN **1 = passage**, selection, excerpt, cutting, clipping, abstract, quotation, citation: *He read us an extract from his latest novel.* **2 = essence**, solution, concentrate, juice, distillation, decoction, distillate: *fragrances taken from plant extracts*

> **USAGE**
> People sometimes use *extract* where *extricate* would be better. Although both words can refer to a physical act of removal from a place, *extract* has a more general sense than *extricate*. *Extricate* has additional overtones of 'difficulty', and is most commonly used with reference to getting a person – particularly *yourself* – out of a situation. So, for example, you might say *he will find it difficult to extricate himself* (not *extract himself*) *from this situation.*

extraction NOUN **1 = origin**, family, ancestry, descent, race, stock, blood, birth, pedigree, lineage, parentage, derivation: *He married a young lady of Indian extraction.* **2 = taking out**, drawing, pulling, withdrawal, removal, uprooting, extirpation: *the extraction of wisdom teeth* **3 = distillation**, separation, derivation: *High temperatures are used during the extraction of cooking oils.*

extraneous ADJECTIVE
1 = nonessential, unnecessary, extra, additional, redundant, needless, peripheral, supplementary, incidental, superfluous, unneeded, inessential, adventitious, unessential: *Just give me the basic facts, with no extraneous details.* **2 = irrelevant**, inappropriate, unrelated, unconnected, immaterial, beside the point, impertinent, inadmissible, off the subject, inapplicable, inapt, inapposite: *Let's not allow ourselves to be sidetracked by extraneous questions.*

extraordinary ADJECTIVE
1 = remarkable, special, wonderful, outstanding, rare, amazing, fantastic, astonishing, marvellous, eye-popping *(informal)*, exceptional, notable, serious *(informal)*, phenomenal, singular, wondrous *(archaic, literary)*, out of this world *(informal)*, extremely good: *He is an extraordinary musician.*
OPPOSITE: unremarkable **2 = unusual**, surprising, odd, strange, unique, remarkable, bizarre, curious, weird, unprecedented, peculiar, unfamiliar, uncommon, unheard-of, unwonted: *What an extraordinary thing to happen!*
OPPOSITE: ordinary

extravagance NOUN
1 = overspending, squandering, profusion, profligacy, wastefulness, waste, lavishness, prodigality, improvidence: *He was accused of gross mismanagement and financial extravagance.* **2 = luxury**, treat, indulgence, extra, frill, nonessential: *Her only extravagance was shoes.* **3 = excess**, folly, exaggeration, absurdity, recklessness, wildness, dissipation, outrageousness, unreasonableness, preposterousness, immoderation, exorbitance, unrestraint: *the ridiculous extravagance of his claims*

extravagant ADJECTIVE **1 = wasteful**, excessive, lavish, prodigal, profligate, spendthrift, imprudent, improvident: *his extravagant lifestyle* **OPPOSITE:** economical **2 = overpriced**, expensive, costly: *Her aunt gave her an uncharacteristically extravagant gift.* **3 = exorbitant**, excessive, steep *(informal)*, unreasonable, inordinate, extortionate: *hotels charging extravagant prices* **OPPOSITE:** reasonable
4 = excessive, exaggerated, outrageous, wild, fantastic, absurd, foolish, over the top *(slang)*, unreasonable, preposterous, fanciful, unrestrained, inordinate, outré, immoderate, O.T.T. *(slang)*: *He was extravagant in his admiration of Lillie.*
OPPOSITE: moderate **5 = showy**, elaborate, flamboyant, impressive, fancy, flashy, ornate, pretentious, grandiose, gaudy, garish, ostentatious: *The couple wed in extravagant style in 1995.*
OPPOSITE: restrained

extravaganza NOUN **= spectacular**, show, spectacle, display, pageant, flight of fancy

extreme ADJECTIVE **1 = great**, high, highest, greatest, worst, supreme, acute, severe, maximum, intense, ultimate, utmost, mother of all *(informal)*, uttermost: *people living in extreme poverty* **OPPOSITE:** mild
2 = severe, radical, strict, harsh, stern, rigid, dire, drastic, uncompromising, unbending: *The scheme was rejected as being too extreme.*
3 = radical, unusual, excessive, exceptional, exaggerated, outrageous, over the top *(slang)*, unreasonable, uncommon, unconventional, fanatical, zealous, out-and-out, inordinate, egregious, intemperate, immoderate, O.T.T. *(slang)*: *his extreme political views*
OPPOSITE: moderate **4 = farthest**, furthest, far, final, last, ultimate, remotest, terminal, utmost, far-off, faraway, outermost, most distant, uttermost: *the room at the extreme end of the corridor* **OPPOSITE:** nearest
▷ NOUN **= limit**, end, edge, opposite, pole, ultimate, boundary, antithesis, extremity, acme: *a 'middle way' between the extremes of success and failure*

extremely ADVERB **= very**, highly, greatly, particularly, severely, terribly, ultra, utterly, unusually, exceptionally, extraordinarily, intensely, tremendously, markedly, awfully *(informal)*, acutely, exceedingly, excessively, inordinately, uncommonly, to a fault, to the nth degree, to *or* in the extreme

extremist NOUN **= radical**, activist, militant, enthusiast, fanatic, devotee, die-hard, bigot, zealot, energumen: *Police believe the bombing*

The Language of Henry David Thoreau

Henry David Thoreau (1817–62) was an American naturalist and philosopher. He is best known for *Walden*, his autobiographical reflections on two years he spent living self-sufficiently in a cabin near Walden Pond. *Walden* offers a critique of contemporary society and a philosophy of simple living; it is both a work of philosophy and a prose-poem celebrating nature. Thoreau's other major work was *Civil Disobedience*, an essay on the human right to oppose an unjust government.

Thoreau uses adjectives sparsely. His most frequent is *good*, often in the phrase *as good as* meaning 'nearly', for example 'a Blue-Pearmain tree... almost as good as wild.' Other adjectives are used to describe the natural world: *wild apples; the high banks of the river; a long woodland lake.* Also among Thoreau's top twenty adjectives is *true*. Whereas in modern English the most prominent sense of *true* is 'not false', used in phrases such as 'it is true', Thoreau almost always uses it before a noun to mean 'genuine', for example in *true enjoyment, true culture,* and *true poem.* Thoreau's use of *very* is also striking. In modern English, it is usually used as an adverb, for example in *very sad* or *very fast*; it is occasionally used as an adjective to emphasise the truth or importance of something, usually in set phrases such as *his very nature* and *the very idea of it.* The latter usage is about seven times more frequent in Thoreau's works than in the *Bank of English,* Collins' corpus of present-day English, and Thoreau uses it in a much wider variety of contexts, such as:

> The **very** cows are driven to their country
> pastures before the end of May.

Thoreau's most frequent noun is *man,* which he often uses generically in phrases such as *the thoughtful man, the civilized man,* and *the wise man*, for example in 'Go where he will, the wise man is at home'. This usage reflects Thoreau's philosophical interest in the abstract and the universal. Another feature of Thoreau's language which shows this is his frequent use of aphoristic statements beginning with infinitive verbs, such as:

> **To be** in company, even with the best, is soon
> wearisome and dissipating. I love to be alone.

The balance of these two sentences – the universal aphorism about solitude paralleled by the simple assertion of his own love for it – encapsulates the essence of Thoreau's style, which is both abstract and personal.

After *man,* the three most frequent nouns in Thoreau's works are *day, life,* and *time,* indicating his concern with the passing of time, both in his immediate descriptions of the world around him, and in his larger reflections on life:

> **Time** is but the stream I go a-fishing in. I drink
> at it; but while I drink I see the sandy bottom
> and detect how shallow it is.

Other frequent nouns are those describing the natural world, such as *tree, wood,* and *water. Nature* is also frequent. It is sometime lower-case, where it means either 'fundamental qualities', as in *the fisherman's nature*, or 'the natural world', as in *the ordinary decay of nature*. More often, though, *Nature* is capitalized and personified:

> Look up at the tree-tops and see how finely
> **Nature** finishes off **her** work there.

Indeed, Thoreau often presents the natural world around him as sentient: trees *permit* cows to stand beside them; the earth *slumbers* while the air is *alive*; the wind *murmurs*; the *unsympathizing river* does not allow travellers to cross. Natural phenomena are often given as the subjects of sentences – for example, 'It is rare that the summer lets an apple go without streaking or spotting it on some part of its sphere' – thus creating a sense of nature (or Nature) as active and powerful.

Government is also among Thoreau's top one hundred nouns, particularly frequent in *Civil Disobedience.* Unsurprisingly, *government* often collocates with negative words such as *unjust* and *oppress.*

was the work of left-wing extremists.
▷ ADJECTIVE = **extreme**, wild, mad, enthusiastic, passionate, frenzied, obsessive, fanatical, fervent, zealous, bigoted, rabid, immoderate, overenthusiastic: *The riots were organized by extremist groups.*

extremity NOUN **1 = limit**, end, edge, border, top, tip, bound, minimum, extreme, maximum, pole, margin, boundary, terminal, frontier, verge, brink, rim, brim, pinnacle, termination, nadir, zenith, apex, terminus, apogee, farthest point, furthest point, acme: *a small port on the north-western extremity of the island*
2 = depth, height, excess, climax, consummation, acuteness: *his lack of restraint in the extremity of his grief*
3 = crisis, trouble, emergency, disaster, setback, pinch, plight, hardship, adversity, dire straits, exigency, extreme suffering: *Even in extremity, she never lost her sense of humour.*
▷ PLURAL NOUN = **hands and feet**, limbs, fingers and toes: *Rheumatoid arthritis affects the extremities and limbs.*

extricate VERB **1 = withdraw**, relieve, free, clear, deliver, liberate, wriggle out of, get (someone) off the hook *(slang)*, disembarrass: *an attempt to extricate himself from his financial difficulties* **2 = free**, clear, release, remove, rescue, get out, disengage, disentangle: *Emergency workers tried to extricate the survivors from the wreckage.*

extrovert *or* **extravert** NOUN = **outgoing person**, mingler, socializer, mixer, life and soul of the party: *He was a showman, an extrovert who revelled in controversy.*
OPPOSITE: introvert
▷ ADJECTIVE = **sociable**, social, lively, outgoing, hearty, exuberant, amiable, gregarious: *His extrovert personality won him many friends.* **OPPOSITE:** introverted

exuberance NOUN **1 = high spirits**, energy, enthusiasm, vitality, life, spirit, excitement, pep, animation, vigour, zest, eagerness, buoyancy, exhilaration, cheerfulness, brio, vivacity, ebullience, liveliness, effervescence, sprightliness: *Her burst of exuberance overwhelmed me.*
2 = luxuriance, abundance, richness, profusion, plenitude, lushness, superabundance, lavishness, rankness, copiousness: *the exuberance of plant life in the region*

exuberant ADJECTIVE **1 = high-spirited**, spirited, enthusiastic, lively, excited, eager, sparkling, vigorous, cheerful, energetic, animated, upbeat *(informal)*, buoyant, exhilarated, elated, ebullient, chirpy *(informal)*, sprightly, vivacious, effervescent, full of life, full of beans *(informal)*, zestful: *Our son was a highly active and exuberant little person.* **OPPOSITE:** subdued
2 = luxuriant, rich, lavish, abundant, lush, overflowing, plentiful, teeming, copious, profuse, superabundant, plenteous: *hillsides ablaze with exuberant flowers and shrubs*
3 = fulsome, excessive, exaggerated, lavish, overdone, superfluous, prodigal, effusive: *exuberant praise*

exude VERB **1 = radiate**, show, display, exhibit, manifest, emanate: *She exudes an air of confidence.* **2 = emit**, leak, discharge, ooze, emanate, issue, secrete, excrete: *Nearby was a factory which exuded a pungent smell.* **3 = seep**, leak, sweat, bleed, weep, trickle, ooze, emanate, issue, filter through, well forth: *the fluid that exudes from the cane toad's back*

exult VERB **1 = be joyful**, be delighted, rejoice, be overjoyed, celebrate, be elated, be jubilant, jump for joy, make merry, be in high spirits, jubilate: *He seemed calm, but inwardly he exulted.* **2** *(often with* **over**) **= revel**, glory in, boast, crow, taunt, brag, vaunt, drool, gloat, take delight in: *He was still exulting over his victory.*

exultant ADJECTIVE = **joyful**, delighted, flushed, triumphant, revelling, rejoicing, jubilant, joyous, transported, elated, over the moon *(informal)*, overjoyed, rapt, gleeful, exulting, cock-a-hoop, stoked *(Austral. & N.Z. informal)*

eye NOUN **1 = eyeball**, optic *(informal)*, peeper *(slang)*, orb *(poetic)*, organ of vision, organ of sight: *He is blind in one eye.* **2** *(often plural)* **= eyesight**, sight, vision, observation, perception, ability to see, range of vision, power of seeing: *her sharp eyes and acute hearing*
3 = appreciation, taste, recognition, judgment, discrimination, perception, discernment: *He has an eye for talent.* **4 = observance**, observation, supervision, surveillance, attention, notice, inspection, heed, vigil, watch, lookout, vigilance, alertness, watchfulness: *He played under his grandmother's watchful eye.* **5 = centre**, heart, middle, mid, core, nucleus: *the eye of the hurricane*
▷ VERB = **look at**, view, study, watch, check, regard, survey, clock *(Brit. slang)*, observe, stare at, scan, contemplate, check out *(informal)*, inspect, glance at, gaze at, behold *(archaic, literary)*, eyeball *(slang)*, scrutinize, peruse, get a load of *(informal)*, take a dekko at *(Brit. slang)*, have *or* take a look at: *We eyed each other thoughtfully.*
an eye for an eye = retaliation, justice, revenge, vengeance, reprisal, retribution, requital, lex talionis: *His philosophy was an eye for an eye and a tooth for a tooth.*
turn a blind eye to *or* **close your eyes to = ignore**, reject, overlook, disregard, pass over, take no notice of, be oblivious to, pay no attention to, turn your back on, turn a deaf ear to, bury your head in the sand: *They just closed their eyes to what was going on.*
eye something *or* **someone up = ogle**, leer at, make eyes at, give (someone) the (glad) eye: *My brother is forever eyeing up women in the street.*
in *or* **to someone's eyes = in the opinion of**, in the mind of, from someone's viewpoint, in the judgment of, in someone's point of view, in the belief of
see eye to eye (with) = agree (with), accord (with), get on (with), fall in (with), coincide (with), go along (with), subscribe (to), be united (with), concur (with), harmonize (with), speak the same language (as), be on the same wavelength (as), be of the same mind (as), be in unison (with): *They saw eye to eye on almost every aspect of the production.*
set, clap *or* **lay eyes on someone = see**, meet, notice, observe, encounter, come across, run into, behold: *I haven't set eyes on him for years.*
up to your eyes (in) = very busy (with), overwhelmed (with), caught up (in), inundated (by), wrapped up (in), engaged (in), flooded out (by), fully occupied (with), up to here (with), up to your elbows (in): *I am up to my eyes in work just now.*
▸ *related adjectives:* ocular, ophthalmic, optic

> **QUOTATIONS**
> If thy right eye offend thee, pluck it out
> [*Bible: St. Matthew*]
>
> The sight of you is good for sore eyes
> [Jonathan Swift *Polite Conversation*]

> **PROVERBS**
> *The eyes are the windows of the soul*

eye-catching ADJECTIVE = **striking**, arresting, attractive, dramatic, spectacular, captivating, showy

eyesight NOUN = **vision**, sight, observation, perception, ability to see, range of vision, power of seeing, power of sight

eyesore NOUN = **mess**, blight, blot, blemish, sight *(informal)*, horror, disgrace, atrocity, ugliness, monstrosity, disfigurement

eyewitness NOUN = **observer**, witness, spectator, looker-on, viewer, passer-by, watcher, onlooker, bystander

Ff

fable NOUN **1 = legend**, myth, parable, allegory, story, tale, apologue: *Each tale has the timeless quality of fable.* **2 = fiction**, lie, fantasy, myth, romance, invention, yarn *(informal)*, fabrication, falsehood, fib, figment, untruth, fairy story *(informal)*, urban myth, white lie, tall story *(informal)*, urban legend: *Is reincarnation fact or fable?* **OPPOSITE:** fact

fabled ADJECTIVE **= legendary**, fictional, famed, mythical, storied, famous, fabulous

fabricate VERB **1 = make up**, invent, concoct, falsify, form, coin, devise, forge, fake, feign, trump up: *All four claim that officers fabricated evidence against them.* **2 = manufacture**, make, build, form, fashion, shape, frame, construct, assemble, erect: *All the tools are fabricated from high-quality steel.*

fabrication NOUN **1 = forgery**, lie, fiction, myth, fake, invention, fable, concoction, falsehood, figment, untruth, porky *(Brit. slang)*, fairy story *(informal)*, pork pie *(Brit. slang)*, cock-and-bull story *(informal)*: *She described the interview with her as a 'complete fabrication'.* **2 = manufacture**, production, construction, assembly, erection, assemblage, building: *More than 200 improvements were made in the design and fabrication of the shuttle.*

fabulous ADJECTIVE **1 = wonderful**, excellent, brilliant, superb, spectacular, fantastic *(informal)*, marvellous, sensational *(informal)*, first-rate, brill *(informal)*, magic *(informal)*, out-of-this-world *(informal)*: *The scenery and weather were fabulous.* **OPPOSITE:** ordinary **2 = astounding**, amazing, extraordinary, remarkable, incredible, astonishing, eye-popping *(informal)*, legendary, immense, unbelievable, breathtaking, phenomenal, inconceivable: *You'll be entered in our free draw to win this fabulous prize.* **3 = legendary**, imaginary, mythical, fictitious, made-up, fantastic, invented, unreal, mythological, apocryphal: *The chimaera of myth is a fabulous beast made up of the parts of other animals.*

façade NOUN **1 = front**, face, exterior, frontage: *the façade of the building* **2 = show**, front, appearance, mask, exterior, guise, pretence, veneer, semblance: *They hid the troubles plaguing their marriage behind a façade of family togetherness.*

face NOUN **1 = countenance**, features, kisser *(slang)*, profile, dial *(Brit. slang)*, mug *(slang)*, visage, physiognomy, lineaments, phiz *or* phizog *(slang)*: *She had a beautiful face.* **2 = expression**, look, air, appearance, aspect, countenance: *He was walking around with a sad face.* **3 = side**, front, cover, outside, surface, aspect, exterior, right side, elevation, facet, vertical surface: *He climbed 200 feet up the cliff face.* **4 = dial**, display **5 = nature**, image, character, appearance, concept, conception, make-up **6 = self-respect**, respect, reputation, dignity, standing, authority, image, regard, status, honour, esteem, prestige, self-image, mana *(N.Z.)* **7 = impudence**, front, confidence, audacity, nerve, neck *(informal)*, sauce *(informal)*, cheek *(informal)*, assurance, gall *(informal)*, presumption, boldness, chutzpah *(U.S. & Canad. informal)*, sass *(U.S. & Canad. informal)*, effrontery, brass neck *(Brit. informal)*, sassiness *(U.S. informal)*: *I haven't the face to borrow off him.*
▷ VERB **1** *(often with* **to, towards,** *or* **on***)* **= look onto**, overlook, be opposite, look out on, front onto, give towards *or* onto: *The garden faces south.* **2 = confront**, meet, encounter, deal with, oppose, tackle, cope with, experience, brave, defy, come up against, be confronted by, face off *(slang)*: *He looked relaxed and calm as he faced the press.*
face someone down = intimidate, defeat, confront, subdue, disconcert
make *or* **pull a face at someone = scowl**, frown, pout, grimace, smirk, moue *(French)*: *She made a face at him behind his back.*
on the face of it = to all appearances, apparently, seemingly, outwardly, at first sight, at face value, to the eye: *On the face of it, that seems to make sense.*
show your face = turn up, come, appear, be seen, show up *(informal)*, put in *or* make an appearance, approach: *I felt I ought to show my face at her father's funeral.*

faceless ADJECTIVE **= impersonal**, remote, unknown, unidentified, anonymous

face-lift NOUN **1 = renovation**, improvement, restoration, refurbishing, modernization, redecoration: *Nothing gives a room a faster face-lift than a coat of paint.* **2 = cosmetic surgery**, plastic surgery: *She once threw a party to celebrate her face-lift.*

facet NOUN **1 = aspect**, part, face, side, phase, angle: *The caste system shapes nearly every facet of Indian life.* **2 = face**, side, surface, plane, slant: *The stones shone back at her, a thousand facets of light in their white-gold settings.*

face up to VERB **= accept**, deal with, tackle, acknowledge, cope with, confront, come to terms with, meet head-on, reconcile yourself to: *You must face the truth that the relationship has ended.*

facile ADJECTIVE **1 = superficial**, shallow, slick, glib, hasty, cursory: *I hated him making facile suggestions when I knew the problem was extremely complex.* **2 = effortless**, easy, simple, quick, ready, smooth, skilful, adept, fluent, uncomplicated, proficient, adroit, dexterous, light: *His facile win tells us he's in form.* **OPPOSITE:** difficult

facilitate VERB **= further**, help, forward, promote, ease, speed up, pave the way for, make easy, expedite, oil the wheels of, smooth the path of, assist the progress of **OPPOSITE:** hinder

facility NOUN **1** *(often plural)* **= amenity**, means, aid, opportunity, advantage, resource, equipment, provision, convenience, appliance: *What recreational facilities are now available?* **2 = opportunity**, possibility, convenience: *The bank will not extend the borrowing facility.* **3 = ability**, skill, talent, gift, craft, efficiency, knack, fluency, proficiency, dexterity, quickness, adroitness, expertness, skilfulness: *They shared a facility for languages.* **4 = ease**, readiness, fluency, smoothness, effortlessness: *He had always spoken with facility.* **OPPOSITE:** difficulty

facsimile NOUN **= copy**, print, carbon, reproduction, replica, transcript, duplicate, photocopy, Xerox®, carbon copy, Photostat®, fax

fact NOUN **1 = truth**, reality, gospel (truth), certainty, verity, actuality, naked truth: *How much was fact and how much fancy no one knew.* **OPPOSITE:** fiction **2 = detail**, point, feature, particular, item, specific, circumstance: *The lorries always left in the dead of night when there were few witnesses around to record the fact.* **3 = event**, happening, act, performance, incident, deed, occurrence, fait accompli *(French)*: *He was sure the gun was planted after the fact.*
▷ PLURAL NOUN **= information**, details, data, the score *(informal)*, gen *(Brit. informal)*, info *(informal)*, the whole story, ins and outs, the lowdown *(informal)*: *There is so much information you can find the facts for yourself.*
as a matter of fact *or* **in fact** *or* **in point of fact = actually**, really,

indeed, truly, in reality, in truth, to tell the truth, in actual fact: *That sounds rather simple, but in fact it's very difficult.*

> **QUOTATIONS**
> In this life we want nothing but facts, sir; nothing but facts
> [Charles Dickens *Hard Times*]

faction NOUN **1 = group**, set, party, division, section, camp, sector, minority, combination, coalition, gang, lobby, bloc, contingent, pressure group, caucus, junta, clique, coterie, schism, confederacy, splinter group, cabal, ginger group, public-interest group *(U.S. & Canad.)*: *A peace agreement will be signed by the leaders of the country's warring factions.* **2 = dissension**, division, conflict, rebellion, disagreement, friction, strife, turbulence, variance, discord, infighting, disunity, sedition, tumult, disharmony, divisiveness: *Faction and self-interest appear to be the norm.* **OPPOSITE:** agreement

factor NOUN **= element**, thing, point, part, cause, influence, item, aspect, circumstance, characteristic, consideration, component, determinant

factory NOUN **= works**, plant, mill, workshop, assembly line, shop floor, manufactory *(obsolete)*

factual ADJECTIVE **= true**, objective, authentic, unbiased, close, real, sure, correct, genuine, accurate, exact, precise, faithful, credible, matter-of-fact, literal, veritable, circumstantial, unadorned, dinkum *(Austral. & N.Z. informal)*, true-to-life
OPPOSITE: fictitious

faculty NOUN **1 = ability**, power, skill, facility, talent, gift, capacity, bent, capability, readiness, knack, propensity, aptitude, dexterity, cleverness, adroitness, turn: *A faculty for self-preservation is necessary when you have friends like hers.* **OPPOSITE:** failing **2 = department**, school, discipline, profession, branch of learning: *the Faculty of Social and Political Sciences* **3 = teaching staff**, staff, teachers, professors, lecturers *(chiefly U.S.)*: *The faculty agreed on a change in the requirements.* **4 = power**, reason, sense, intelligence, mental ability, physical ability: *He was drunk and not in control of his faculties.*

fad NOUN **= craze**, fashion, trend, fancy, rage, mode, vogue, whim, mania, affectation

fade VERB **1 = become pale**, dull, dim, bleach, wash out, blanch, discolour, blench, lose colour, lose lustre, decolour: *All colour fades, especially under the impact of direct sunlight.* **2 = make pale**, dull, dim, bleach, wash out, blanch, discolour, decolour: *Even a soft light fades the carpets in a room.* **3 = grow dim**, dim, fade away, become less loud: *The sound of the last bomber's engines faded into the distance.* **4** *(usually with* **away** *or* **out***)* **= dwindle**, disappear, vanish, melt away, fall, fail, decline, flag, dissolve, dim, disperse, wither, wilt, wane, perish, ebb, languish, die out, droop, shrivel, die away, waste away, vanish into thin air, become unimportant, evanesce, etiolate: *She had a way of fading into the background when things got rough.*

faded ADJECTIVE **= discoloured**, pale, bleached, washed out, dull, dim, indistinct, etiolated, lustreless

fading ADJECTIVE **= declining**, dying, disappearing, vanishing, decreasing, on the decline

faeces *or (esp. U.S.)* **feces** PLURAL NOUN **= excrement**, stools, excreta, bodily waste, dung, droppings, ordure

fail VERB **1 = be unsuccessful**, founder, fall flat, come to nothing, fall, miss, go down, break down, flop *(informal)*, be defeated, fall short, fall through, fall short of, fizzle out *(informal)*, come unstuck, run aground, miscarry, be in vain, misfire, fall by the wayside, go astray, come to grief, come a cropper *(informal)*, bite the dust, go up in smoke, go belly-up *(slang)*, come to naught, lay an egg *(slang, chiefly U.S. & Canad.)*, go by the board, not make the grade *(informal)*, go down like a lead balloon *(informal)*, turn out badly, fall flat on your face, meet with disaster, be found lacking *or* wanting: *He was afraid the revolution they had started would fail.* **OPPOSITE:** succeed **2 = disappoint**, abandon, desert, neglect, omit, let down, forsake, turn your back on, be disloyal to, break your word, forget: *We waited twenty-one years; don't fail us now.* **3 = stop working**, stop, die, give up, break down, cease, stall, cut out, malfunction, conk out *(informal)*, go on the blink *(informal)*, go phut: *The lights mysteriously failed.* **4 = wither**, perish, sag, droop, waste away, shrivel up: *In fact many food crops failed because of the drought* **5 = go bankrupt**, crash, collapse, fold *(informal)*, close down, go under, go bust *(informal)*, go out of business, be wound up, go broke *(informal)*, go to the wall, go into receivership, go into liquidation, become insolvent, smash: *So far this year, 104 banks have failed.* **6 = decline**, fade, weaken, deteriorate, dwindle, sicken, degenerate, fall apart at the seams, be on your last legs *(informal)*: *He was 58 and his health was failing rapidly.* **7 = give out**, disappear, fade, dim, dwindle, wane, gutter, languish, peter out, die away, grow dim, sink: *Here in the hills, the light failed more quickly*
without fail = without exception, regularly, constantly, invariably, religiously, unfailingly, conscientiously, like clockwork, punctually, dependably: *He attended every meeting without fail.*

failing NOUN **= shortcoming**, failure, fault, error, weakness, defect, deficiency, lapse, flaw, miscarriage, drawback, misfortune, blemish, imperfection, frailty, foible, blind spot: *He had invented an imaginary son, in order to make up for his real son's failings.*
OPPOSITE: strength
▷ PREPOSITION **= in the absence of**, lacking, in default of: *Find someone who will let you talk things through, or failing that, write down your thoughts.*

failure NOUN **1 = lack of success**, defeat, collapse, abortion, wreck, frustration, breakdown, overthrow, miscarriage, fiasco, downfall: *The policy is doomed to failure.*
OPPOSITE: success **2 = loser**, disappointment, no-good, flop *(informal)*, write-off, incompetent, no-hoper *(chiefly Austral.)*, dud *(informal)*, clinker *(slang, chiefly U.S.)*, black sheep, washout *(informal)*, clunker *(informal)*, dead duck *(slang)*, ne'er-do-well, nonstarter: *I just felt I had been a failure in my personal life.* **3 = negligence**, neglect, deficiency, default, shortcoming, omission, oversight, dereliction, nonperformance, nonobservance, nonsuccess, remissness: *They didn't prove his case of a failure of duty.*
OPPOSITE: observance **4 = breakdown**, stalling, cutting out, malfunction, crash, disruption, stoppage, mishap, conking out *(informal)*: *There were also several accidents mainly caused by engine failures on take-off.* **5 = failing**, deterioration, decay, loss, decline: *He was being treated for kidney failure.* **6 = bankruptcy**, crash, collapse, ruin, folding *(informal)*, closure, winding up, downfall, going under, liquidation, insolvency: *Business failures rose 16% last month.*
OPPOSITE: prosperity

> **QUOTATIONS**
> There's many a slip 'twixt the cup and the lip
> [R.B. Barham *The Ingoldsby Legends*]
>
> A failure is a stranger in his own house
> [Eric Hoffer *The Passionate State of Mind*]
>
> There is not a fiercer hell than the failure in a great object
> [John Keats *Endymion*]
>
> There is no failure except in no longer trying
> [Elbert Hubbard *The Note Book*]

faint ADJECTIVE **1 = dim**, low, light, soft, thin, faded, whispered, distant, dull, delicate, vague, unclear, muted, subdued, faltering, hushed, bleached, feeble, indefinite, muffled, hazy, ill-defined, indistinct: *He became aware of the soft, faint sounds of water dripping.*
OPPOSITE: clear **2 = slight**, weak, feeble, unenthusiastic, remote, slim, vague, slender: *She made a faint attempt at a laugh.* **3 = timid**, weak, feeble, lame, unconvincing, unenthusiastic, timorous, faint-hearted, spiritless, half-hearted, lily-livered: *He let his arm flail out in a faint attempt to strike her.*
OPPOSITE: brave **4 = dizzy**, giddy, light-headed, vertiginous, weak,

exhausted, fatigued, faltering, wobbly, drooping, languid, lethargic, muzzy, woozy *(informal)*, weak at the knees, enervated: *Other signs of angina are nausea, feeling faint and shortness of breath.* **OPPOSITE:** energetic
▷ VERB **= pass out**, black out, lose consciousness, keel over *(informal)*, fail, go out, collapse, fade, weaken, languish, swoon *(literary)*, flake out *(informal)*: *I thought he'd faint when I kissed him.*
▷ NOUN **= blackout**, collapse, coma, swoon *(literary)*, unconsciousness, syncope *(Pathology)*: *She slumped on the ground in a faint.*

faintly ADVERB **1 = slightly**, rather, a little, somewhat, dimly: *She felt faintly ridiculous.* **2 = softly**, weakly, feebly, in a whisper, indistinctly, unclearly: *The voice came faintly back to us across the water.*

fair¹ ADJECTIVE **1 = unbiased**, impartial, even-handed, unprejudiced, just, clean, square, equal, objective, reasonable, proper, legitimate, upright, honourable, honest, equitable, lawful, trustworthy, on the level *(informal)*, disinterested, dispassionate, above board, according to the rules: *I wanted them to get a fair deal.* **OPPOSITE:** unfair **2 = respectable**, middling, average, reasonable, decent, acceptable, moderate, adequate, satisfactory, not bad, mediocre, so-so *(informal)*, tolerable, passable, O.K. *or* okay *(informal)*, all right: *He had a fair command of English.* **3 = light**, golden, blonde, blond, yellowish, fair-haired, light-coloured, flaxen-haired, towheaded, tow-haired: *She had bright eyes and fair hair.* **4 = light-complexioned**, white, pale: *It's important to protect my fair skin from the sun.* **5 = fine**, clear, dry, bright, pleasant, sunny, favourable, clement, cloudless, unclouded, sunshiny: *Weather conditions were fair.* **6 = beautiful**, pretty, attractive, lovely, handsome, good-looking, bonny, comely, beauteous, well-favoured, fit *(Brit. informal)*: *Faint heart never won fair lady.* **OPPOSITE:** ugly
fair and square = honestly, straight, legally, on the level *(informal)*, by the book, lawfully, above board, according to the rules, without cheating: *We were beaten fair and square.*

fair² NOUN **1 = carnival**, fête, gala, bazaar: *I used to love going to the fair when I was young.* **2 = exhibition**, show, market, festival, mart, expo *(informal)*, exposition: *The date for the book fair has been changed.*

fairly ADVERB **1 = equitably**, objectively, legitimately, honestly, justly, lawfully, without prejudice, dispassionately, impartially, even-handedly, without bias: *They solved their problems quickly and fairly.* **2 = moderately**, rather, quite, somewhat, reasonably, adequately, pretty well, tolerably, passably: *We did fairly well.* **3 = positively**, really, simply, absolutely, in a manner of speaking, veritably: *He fairly flew across the room.* **4 = deservedly**, objectively, honestly, justifiably, justly, impartially, equitably, without fear or favour, properly: *It can no doubt be fairly argued that he is entitled to every penny.*

fair-minded ADJECTIVE **= impartial**, just, fair, reasonable, open-minded, disinterested, unbiased, even-handed, unprejudiced

fairness NOUN **= impartiality**, justice, equity, legitimacy, decency, disinterestedness, uprightness, rightfulness, equitableness

> **QUOTATIONS**
> One should always play fairly when one has the winning cards
> [Oscar Wilde *An Ideal Husband*]

fairy NOUN **= sprite**, elf, brownie, hob, pixie, puck, imp, leprechaun, peri, Robin Goodfellow

fairy tale *or* **fairy story** NOUN **1 = folk tale**, romance, traditional story: *She was like a princess in a fairy tale.* **2 = lie**, fantasy, fiction, invention, fabrication, untruth, porky *(Brit. slang)*, pork pie *(Brit. slang)*, urban myth, tall story, urban legend, cock-and-bull story *(informal)*: *Many of those who write books lie much more than those who tell fairy tales.*

faith NOUN **1 = confidence**, trust, credit, conviction, assurance, dependence, reliance, credence: *She had placed a great deal of faith in him.* **OPPOSITE:** distrust **2 = religion**, church, belief, persuasion, creed, communion, denomination, dogma: *England shifted officially from a Catholic to a Protestant faith in the 16th century.* **OPPOSITE:** agnosticism

faithful ADJECTIVE **1 = loyal**, true, committed, constant, attached, devoted, dedicated, reliable, staunch, truthful, dependable, trusty, steadfast, unwavering, true-blue, immovable, unswerving: *Older Americans are among this country's most faithful voters; She had remained faithful to her husband.* **OPPOSITE:** disloyal **2 = accurate**, just, close, true, strict, exact, precise: *His screenplay is faithful to the novel.*
the faithful = believers, brethren, followers, congregation, adherents, the elect, communicants: *The faithful revered him then as a prophet.*

faithfulness NOUN **= loyalty**, devotion, fidelity, constancy, dependability, trustworthiness, fealty, adherence

faithless ADJECTIVE **= disloyal**, unreliable, unfaithful, untrustworthy, doubting, false, untrue, treacherous, dishonest, fickle, perfidious, untruthful, traitorous, unbelieving, inconstant, false-hearted, recreant *(archaic)*

fake VERB **1 = forge**, copy, reproduce, fabricate, counterfeit, falsify: *Did they fake this evidence?* **2 = sham**, affect, assume, put on, pretend, simulate, feign, go through the motions of: *He faked nonchalance.*
▷ NOUN **1 = forgery**, copy, fraud, reproduction, dummy, imitation, hoax, counterfeit: *It is filled with famous works of art, and every one of them is a fake.* **2 = charlatan**, deceiver, sham, quack, mountebank, phoney *or* phony *(informal)*: *She denied claims that she is a fake.*
▷ ADJECTIVE **= artificial**, false, forged, counterfeit, affected, assumed, put-on, pretend *(informal)*, mock, imitation, sham, pseudo *(informal)*, feigned, pinchbeck, phoney *or* phony *(informal)*: *The bank manager is said to have issued fake certificates.*
OPPOSITE: genuine

fall VERB **1 = drop**, plunge, tumble, plummet, trip, settle, crash, collapse, pitch, sink, go down, come down, dive, stumble, descend, topple, subside, cascade, trip over, drop down, nose-dive, come a cropper *(informal)*, keel over, face-plant *(informal)*, go head over heels: *Her father fell into the sea after a massive heart attack.* **OPPOSITE:** rise **2 = decrease**, drop, decline, go down, flag, slump, diminish, fall off, dwindle, lessen, subside, ebb, abate, depreciate, become lower: *Her weight fell to under seven stones.* **OPPOSITE:** increase **3 = be overthrown**, be taken, surrender, succumb, yield, submit, give way, capitulate, be conquered, give in *or* up, pass into enemy hands: *The town fell to Croatian forces.* **OPPOSITE:** triumph **4 = be killed**, die, be lost, perish, be slain, be a casualty, meet your end: *Another wave of troops followed the first, running past those who had fallen.* **OPPOSITE:** survive **5 = occur**, happen, come about, chance, take place, fall out, befall, come to pass: *Easter falls in early April.*
▷ NOUN **1 = drop**, slip, plunge, dive, spill, tumble, descent, plummet, nose dive, face-plant *(informal)*: *The helmets are designed to withstand impacts equivalent to a fall from a bicycle.* **2 = decrease**, drop, lowering, decline, reduction, slump, dip, falling off, dwindling, lessening, diminution, cut: *There was a sharp fall in the value of the pound.* **3 = collapse**, defeat, surrender, downfall, death, failure, ruin, resignation, destruction, overthrow, submission, capitulation: *the fall of Rome* **4 = slope**, incline, descent, downgrade, slant, declivity: *a fall of 3.5 kilometres*
▷ PLURAL NOUN **= waterfall**, rapids, cascade, cataract, linn *(Scot.)*, force *(Northern English dialect)*: *The falls have always been an insurmountable obstacle for salmon and sea trout.*
fall apart 1 = break up, crumble, disintegrate, fall to bits, go to seed, come apart at the seams, break into pieces, go *or* come to pieces, shatter: *The work was never finished and bit by bit the building fell apart.* **2 = break down**,

dissolve, disperse, disband, lose cohesion: *The national coalition fell apart five weeks ago.* **3 = go to pieces**, break down, crack up (*informal*), have a breakdown, crumble: *I was falling apart.*
fall away **1 = slope**, drop, go down, incline, incline downwards: *On either side of the tracks the ground fell away sharply.* **2 = decrease**, drop, diminish, fall off, dwindle, lessen: *Demand began to fall away.*
fall back **= retreat**, retire, withdraw, move back, recede, pull back, back off, recoil, draw back: *The congregation fell back from them as they entered.*
fall back on something *or* **someone** **= resort to**, have recourse to, employ, turn to, make use of, call upon, press into service: *When necessary, instinct is the most reliable resource you can fall back on.*
fall behind **1 = lag**, trail, be left behind, drop back, get left behind, lose your place: *The horse fell behind on the final furlong.* **2 = be in arrears**, be late, not keep up: *He faces losing his home after falling behind with the payments.*
fall down (*often with* **on**) **= fail**, disappoint, go wrong, fall short, fail to make the grade, prove unsuccessful: *That is where his argument falls down.*
fall for someone **= fall in love with**, become infatuated with, be smitten by, be swept off your feet by, desire, fancy (*Brit. informal*), succumb to the charms of, lose your head over: *I just fell for him right away.*
fall for something **= be fooled by**, be deceived by, be taken in by, be duped by, buy (*slang*), accept, swallow (*informal*), take on board, give credence to: *It was just a line to get you out of here, and you fell for it!*
fall in **= collapse**, sink, cave in, crash in, fall to the ground, fall apart at the seams, come down about your ears: *Part of my bedroom ceiling has fallen in.*
fall in with someone **= make friends with**, go around with, become friendly with, hang about with (*informal*): *At University he had fallen in with a small clique of literature students.*
fall in with something **= go along with**, support, accept, agree with, comply with, submit to, yield to, buy into (*informal*), cooperate with, assent, take on board, concur with: *Her reluctance to fall in with his plans led to trouble.*
fall off **1 = tumble**, topple, plummet, be unseated, come a cropper *or* purler (*informal*), take a fall *or* tumble: *He fell off at the second fence.* **2 = decrease**, drop, reduce, decline, fade, slump, weaken, shrink, diminish, dwindle, lessen, wane, subside, fall away, peter out, slacken, tail off (*informal*), ebb away, go down *or* downhill: *Unemployment is rising again and retail buying has fallen off.*
fall on *or* **upon something** *or* **someone** **= attack**, assault, snatch, assail, tear into (*informal*), lay into, descend upon, pitch into (*informal*), belabour, let fly at, set upon *or* about: *They fell upon the enemy from the rear.*
fall out **1 = argue**, fight, row, clash, differ, disagree, quarrel, squabble, have a row, have words, come to blows, cross swords, altercate: *She fell out with her husband.*
fall short (*often with* **of**) **= be lacking**, miss, fail, disappoint, be wanting, be inadequate, be deficient, fall down on (*informal*), prove inadequate, not come up to expectations *or* scratch (*informal*): *His achievements are bound to fall short of his ambitions.*
fall through **= fail**, be unsuccessful, come to nothing, fizzle out (*informal*), miscarry, go awry, go by the board: *The deal fell through.*
fall to someone **= be the responsibility of**, be up to, come down to, devolve upon: *It fell to me to get rid of them.*
fall to something **= begin**, start, set to, set about, commence, apply yourself to: *They fell to fighting among themselves.*

fallacy NOUN **= error**, mistake, illusion, flaw, deception, delusion, inconsistency, misconception, deceit, falsehood, untruth, misapprehension, sophistry, casuistry, sophism, faultiness

fallen ADJECTIVE **1 = killed**, lost, dead, slaughtered, slain, perished: *Work began on establishing the cemeteries as permanent memorials to our fallen servicemen.* **2 = dishonoured**, lost, loose, shamed, ruined, disgraced, immoral, sinful, unchaste: *She would be thought of as a fallen woman.*

fallible ADJECTIVE **= imperfect**, weak, uncertain, ignorant, mortal, frail, erring, prone to error
OPPOSITE: infallible

fallow ADJECTIVE **1 = uncultivated**, unused, undeveloped, unplanted, untilled: *The fields lay fallow.* **2 = inactive**, resting, idle, dormant, inert: *There followed something of a fallow period.*

false ADJECTIVE **1 = incorrect**, wrong, mistaken, misleading, faulty, inaccurate, invalid, improper, unfounded, erroneous, inexact: *This resulted in false information being entered.* **OPPOSITE:** correct **2 = untrue**, fraudulent, unreal, concocted, fictitious, trumped up, fallacious, untruthful, truthless: *You do not know whether what you are told is true or false.* **OPPOSITE:** true **3 = artificial**, forged, fake, mock, reproduction, synthetic, replica, imitation, bogus, simulated, sham, pseudo (*informal*), counterfeit, feigned, spurious, ersatz, pretended: *He paid for a false passport.* **OPPOSITE:** real **4 = treacherous**, lying, deceiving, unreliable, two-timing (*informal*), dishonest, deceptive, hypocritical, unfaithful, two-faced, disloyal, unsound, deceitful, faithless, untrustworthy, insincere, double-dealing, dishonourable, duplicitous, mendacious, perfidious, treasonable, traitorous, inconstant, delusive, false-hearted: *She was a false friend, envious of her lifestyle and her life with her husband.* **OPPOSITE:** loyal

falsehood NOUN **1 = untruthfulness**, deception, deceit, dishonesty, prevarication, mendacity, dissimulation, perjury, inveracity (*rare*): *She called the verdict a victory of truth over falsehood.* **2 = lie**, story, fiction, fabrication, fib, untruth, porky (*Brit. slang*), pork pie (*Brit. slang*), misstatement: *He accused them of knowingly spreading falsehoods about him.*

> **QUOTATIONS**
> The most dangerous of all falsehoods is a slightly distorted truth
> [G.C. Lichtenberg]

falsify VERB **= alter**, forge, fake, tamper with, doctor, cook (*slang*), distort, pervert, belie, counterfeit, misrepresent, garble, misstate

falter VERB **1 = hesitate**, delay, waver, vacillate, break: *I have not faltered in my quest for a new future.* **OPPOSITE:** persevere **2 = tumble**, shake, tremble, totter: *As he neared the house, he faltered.* **3 = stutter**, pause, stumble, hesitate, stammer, speak haltingly: *Her voice faltered and she had to stop a moment to control it.*

faltering ADJECTIVE **= hesitant**, broken, weak, uncertain, stumbling, tentative, stammering, timid, irresolute

fame NOUN **= prominence**, glory, celebrity, stardom, name, credit, reputation, honour, prestige, stature, eminence, renown, repute, public esteem, illustriousness
OPPOSITE: obscurity

> **QUOTATIONS**
> If fame is to come only after death,
> I am in no hurry for it
> [Martial *Epigrams*]
>
> In the future everybody will be world famous for fifteen minutes
> [Andy Warhol *exhibition catalogue*]
>
> Fame is the spur that the clear spirit doth raise
> (That last infirmity of noble mind)
> To scorn delights, and live laborious days
> [John Milton *Lycidas*]
>
> Fame is like a river, that beareth up things light and swollen, and drowns things heavy and solid
> [Francis Bacon *Essays*]
>
> Fame is a food that dead men eat –
> I have no stomach for such meat
> [Henry Austin Dobson *Fame is a Food*]
>
> Famous men have the whole earth as their memorial
> [Pericles]

famed ADJECTIVE **= renowned**, celebrated, recognized, well-known, acclaimed, widely-known

familiar ADJECTIVE **1 = well-known**, household, everyday, recognized, common, stock, domestic, repeated,

ordinary, conventional, routine, frequent, accustomed, customary, mundane, recognizable, common or garden *(informal)*: *They are already familiar faces on our TV screens.* **OPPOSITE:** unfamiliar **2 = friendly**, close, dear, intimate, confidential, amicable, chummy *(informal)*, buddy-buddy *(slang, chiefly U.S. & Canad.)*, palsy-walsy *(informal)*: *the old familiar relationship* **OPPOSITE:** formal **3 = relaxed**, open, easy, friendly, free, near, comfortable, intimate, casual, informal, amicable, cordial, free-and-easy, unreserved, unconstrained, unceremonious, hail-fellow-well-met: *the comfortable, familiar atmosphere* **4 = disrespectful**, forward, bold, presuming, intrusive, presumptuous, impudent, overfamiliar, overfree: *The driver of that taxi-cab seemed to me familiar to the point of impertinence.*
familiar with = acquainted with, aware of, introduced to, conscious of, at home with, no stranger to, informed about, abreast of, knowledgeable about, versed in, well up in, proficient in, conversant with, on speaking terms with, in the know about, *au courant* with, *au fait* with: *only too familiar with the problems*

familiarity NOUN **1 = acquaintance**, experience, understanding, knowledge, awareness, grasp, acquaintanceship: *The enemy would always have the advantage of familiarity with the rugged terrain.* **OPPOSITE:** unfamiliarity **2 = friendliness**, friendship, intimacy, closeness, freedom, ease, openness, fellowship, informality, sociability, naturalness, absence of reserve, unceremoniousness: *Close personal familiarity between councillors and staff can prove embarrassing.* **OPPOSITE:** formality **3 = disrespect**, forwardness, overfamiliarity, liberties, liberty, cheek, presumption, boldness: *He had behaved with undue and oily familiarity.* **OPPOSITE:** respect

PROVERBS
Familiarity breeds contempt

familiarize *or* **familiarise** VERB **= accustom**, instruct, habituate, make used to, school, season, train, prime, coach, get to know (about), inure, bring into common use, make conversant

family NOUN **1 = relations**, people, children, issue, relatives, household, folk *(informal)*, offspring, descendants, brood, kin, nuclear family, progeny, kindred, next of kin, kinsmen, ménage, kith and kin, your nearest and dearest, kinsfolk, your own flesh and blood, ainga *(N.Z.)*, cuzzies or cuzzie-bros *(N.Z.)*, rellies *(Austral. slang)*: *His family are completely behind him, whatever he decides.* **2 = children**, kids *(informal)*, offspring, little ones, munchkins *(informal, chiefly U.S.)*, littlies *(Austral. informal)*: *Are you going to have a family?* **3 = ancestors**, forebears, parentage, forefathers, house, line, race, blood, birth, strain, tribe, sept, clan, descent, dynasty, pedigree, extraction, ancestry, lineage, genealogy, line of descent, stemma, stirps: *Her family came to Los Angeles at the turn of the century.* **4 = species**, group, class, system, order, kind, network, genre, classification, subdivision, subclass: *foods in the cabbage family, such as Brussels sprouts*
▸ *related adjective:* familial

QUOTATIONS
You don't choose your family. They are God's gift to you, as you are to them
[Desmond Tutu *address at enthronement as archbishop of Cape Town*]

The family – that dear octopus from whose tentacles we never quite escape
[Dodie Smith *Dear Octopus*]

All happy families are alike, but every unhappy one is unhappy in its own way
[Leo Tolstoy *Anna Karenina*]

PROVERBS
Blood is thicker than water

USAGE
Some careful writers insist that a singular verb should always be used with collective nouns such as *government, team, family, committee,* and *class*, for example: *the class is doing a project on Vikings; the company is mounting a big sales campaign*. In British usage, however, a plural verb is often used with a collective noun, especially where the emphasis is on a collection of individual objects or people rather than a group regarded as a unit: *the family are all on holiday*. The most important thing to remember is never to treat the same collective noun as both singular and plural in the same sentence: *the family is well and sends its best wishes* or *the family are well and send their best wishes*, but not *the family is well and send their best wishes*.

family tree NOUN **= lineage**, genealogy, line of descent, ancestral tree, line, descent, pedigree, extraction, ancestry, blood line, stemma, stirps, whakapapa *(N.Z.)*

famine NOUN **= hunger**, want, starvation, deprivation, scarcity, dearth, destitution

QUOTATIONS
They that die by famine die by inches
[Matthew Henry *Expositions on the Old and New Testament*]

famous ADJECTIVE **= well-known**, celebrated, acclaimed, notable, noted, excellent, signal, honoured, remarkable, distinguished, prominent, glorious, legendary, renowned, eminent, conspicuous, illustrious, much-publicized, lionized, far-famed **OPPOSITE:** unknown

fan[1] NOUN **= blower**, ventilator, air conditioner, vane, punkah *(in India)*, blade, propeller: *He cools himself with an electric fan.*
▹ VERB **1 = blow**, cool, refresh, air-condition, ventilate, air-cool, winnow *(rare)*: *She fanned herself with a piece of cardboard.* **2 = stimulate**, increase, excite, provoke, arouse, rouse, stir up, work up, agitate, whip up, add fuel to the flames, impassion, enkindle: *economic problems which often fan hatred* **3** *(often with* **out***)* **= spread out**, spread, lay out, disperse, unfurl, open out, space out: *The main body of troops fanned out to the west.*

fan[2] NOUN **1 = supporter**, lover, follower, enthusiast, admirer, groupie *(slang)*, rooter *(U.S.)*: *As a boy he was a Manchester United fan.* **2 = devotee**, addict, freak *(informal)*, buff *(informal)*, fiend *(informal)*, adherent, zealot, aficionado, groupie *(slang)*

fanatic NOUN **= extremist**, activist, militant, addict, enthusiast, buff *(informal)*, visionary, devotee, bigot, zealot, energumen

QUOTATIONS
A fanatic is one who can't change his mind and won't change the subject
[Winston Churchill]

fanatical ADJECTIVE **= obsessive**, burning, wild, mad, extreme, enthusiastic, passionate, frenzied, visionary, fervent, zealous, bigoted, rabid, immoderate, overenthusiastic

fanaticism NOUN **= immoderation**, enthusiasm, madness, devotion, dedication, zeal, bigotry, extremism, infatuation, single-mindedness, zealotry, obsessiveness, monomania, overenthusiasm

QUOTATIONS
Fanaticism is the wisdom of the spirit
[Eva Perón]

Fanaticism consists in redoubling your effort when you have forgotten your aim
[George Santayana *The Life of Reason*]

fancier NOUN **= expert**, amateur, breeder, connoisseur, aficionado

fanciful ADJECTIVE **= unreal**, wild, ideal, romantic, fantastic, curious, fabulous, imaginative, imaginary, poetic, extravagant, visionary, fairy-tale, mythical, whimsical, capricious, chimerical **OPPOSITE:** unimaginative

fancy ADJECTIVE **1 = elaborate**, decorated, decorative, extravagant, intricate, baroque, ornamented, ornamental, ornate, elegant, fanciful, embellished: *It was packaged in a fancy plastic case with attractive graphics.* **OPPOSITE:** plain **2 = expensive**, high-quality, classy, flashy, swish *(informal)*, showy,

f

ostentatious: *They sent me to a fancy private school.*
▷ NOUN **1 = whim**, thought, idea, desire, urge, notion, humour, impulse, inclination, caprice: *His interest was just a passing fancy.* **2 = delusion**, dream, vision, fantasy, nightmare, daydream, chimera, phantasm: *His book is a bold surrealist mixture of fact and fancy.*
▷ VERB **1 = wish for**, want, desire, would like, hope for, dream of, relish, long for, crave, be attracted to, yearn for, thirst for, hanker after, have a yen for: *I just fancied a drink.* **2 = be attracted to**, find attractive, desire, lust after, like, prefer, favour, take to, go for, be captivated by, have an eye for, have a thing about *(informal)*, have eyes for, take a liking to: *I think he thinks I fancy him.* **3 = suppose**, think, believe, imagine, guess *(informal, chiefly U.S. & Canad.)*, reckon, conceive, infer, conjecture, surmise, think likely, be inclined to think: *She fancied he was trying to hide a smile.*
fancy yourself = think you are God's gift, have a high opinion of yourself, think you are the cat's whiskers: *She really fancies herself in that new outfit.*
take a fancy to something *or* **someone = start liking**, like, want, be fond of, hanker after, have a partiality for: *Sylvia took quite a fancy to him.*

> **QUOTATIONS**
> Ever let the fancy roam,
> Pleasure never is at home
> [John Keats *Fancy*]
>
> Tell me where is fancy bred,
> Or in the heart or in the head?
> [William Shakespeare *The Merchant of Venice*]

fanfare NOUN **= trumpet call**, flourish, trump *(archaic)*, tucket *(archaic)*, fanfaronade

fang NOUN **= tooth**, tusk

fantasize *or* **fantasise** VERB **= daydream**, imagine, invent, romance, envision, hallucinate, see visions, live in a dream world, build castles in the air, give free rein to the imagination

fantastic ADJECTIVE **1 = wonderful**, great, excellent, very good, mean *(slang)*, topping *(Brit. slang)*, cracking *(Brit. informal)*, crucial *(slang)*, smashing *(informal)*, superb, tremendous *(informal)*, magnificent, marvellous, terrific *(informal)*, sensational *(informal)*, mega *(slang)*, awesome *(slang)*, dope *(slang)*, world-class, first-rate, def *(slang)*, brill *(informal)*, out of this world *(informal)*, boffo *(slang)*, jim-dandy *(slang)*, bitchin' *(U.S. slang)*, chillin' *(U.S. slang)*, booshit *(Austral. slang)*, exo *(Austral. slang)*, sik *(Austral. slang)*, rad *(informal)*, phat *(slang)*, schmick *(Austral. informal)*, beaut *(informal)*, barrie *(Scot. slang)*, belting *(Brit. slang)*, pearler *(Austral. slang)*: *I have a fantastic social life.*
OPPOSITE: ordinary **2 = enormous**, great, huge, vast, severe, extreme, overwhelming, tremendous, immense: *fantastic amounts of money* **3 = strange**, bizarre, weird, exotic, peculiar, imaginative, queer, grotesque, quaint, unreal, fanciful, outlandish, whimsical, freakish, chimerical, phantasmagorical: *outlandish and fantastic images* **4 = implausible**, unlikely, incredible, absurd, irrational, preposterous, capricious, cock-and-bull *(informal)*, cockamamie *(slang, chiefly U.S.)*, mad: *He had cooked up some fantastic story about how the ring had come into his possession.*

fantasy *or* **phantasy** NOUN **1 = daydream**, dream, wish, fancy, delusion, reverie, flight of fancy, pipe dream: *Everyone's had a fantasy about winning the lottery* **2 = imagination**, fancy, invention, creativity, originality: *a world of imagination and fantasy*

far ADVERB **1 = a long way**, miles, deep, a good way, afar, a great distance: *They came from far away.* **2 = much**, greatly, very much, extremely, significantly, considerably, decidedly, markedly, incomparably: *He was a far better cook than Amy.*
▷ ADJECTIVE *(often with* **off***)* **= remote**, distant, far-flung, faraway, long, removed, out-of-the-way, far-removed, outlying, off the beaten track: *people in far-off lands*
OPPOSITE: near
by far *or* **far and away = very much**, easily, immeasurably, by a long way, incomparably, to a great degree, by a long shot, by a long chalk *(informal)*, by a great amount: *by far the most successful*
far and wide = extensively, everywhere, worldwide, far and near, widely, broadly, in all places, in every nook and cranny, here, there and everywhere: *His fame spread far and wide.*
far from = not at all, not, by no means, absolutely not: *She is far from happy.*
so far 1 = up to a point, to a certain extent, to a limited extent: *Their loyalty only went so far.* **2 = up to now**, to date, until now, thus far, up to the present: *So far, they have had no success.*

faraway ADJECTIVE **1 = distant**, far, remote, far-off, far-removed, far-flung, outlying, beyond the horizon: *They had just returned from faraway places.* **2 = dreamy**, lost, distant, abstracted, vague, absent: *She smiled with a faraway look in her eyes.*

farce NOUN **1 = comedy**, satire, slapstick, burlesque, buffoonery, broad comedy: *The plot often borders on farce.* **2 = mockery**, joke, nonsense, parody, shambles, sham, absurdity, malarkey, travesty, ridiculousness: *The election was a farce, as only 22% of voters cast their ballots.*

farcical ADJECTIVE **1 = ludicrous**, ridiculous, absurd, preposterous, laughable, nonsensical, derisory, risible: *a farcical nine months' jail sentence* **2 = comic**, funny, amusing, slapstick, droll, custard-pie, diverting: *from farcical humour to deepest tragedy*

fare NOUN **1 = charge**, price, ticket price, transport cost, ticket money, passage money: *He could barely afford the railway fare.* **2 = food**, meals, diet, provisions, board, commons, table, feed, menu, rations, tack *(informal)*, kai *(N.Z. informal)*, nourishment, sustenance, victuals, nosebag *(slang)*, nutriment, vittles *(obsolete, dialect)*, eatables: *traditional Portuguese fare* **3 = passenger**, customer, pick-up *(informal)*, traveller: *The taxi driver picked up a fare.*
▷ VERB **1 = get on**, do, manage, make out, prosper, get along: *He was not faring well.* **2** *(used impersonally)* **= happen**, go, turn out, proceed, pan out *(informal)*: *The show fared quite well.*

farewell INTERJECTION **= goodbye**, bye *(informal)*, so long, see you, take care, good morning, bye-bye *(informal)*, good day, all the best, good night, good evening, good afternoon, see you later, ciao *(Italian)*, have a nice day *(U.S.)*, adieu *(French)*, au revoir *(French)*, be seeing you, auf Wiedersehen *(German)*, adios *(Spanish)*, mind how you go, haere ra *(N.Z.)*: *'Farewell, lad, and may we meet again soon.'*
▷ NOUN **= goodbye**, parting, departure, leave-taking, adieu, valediction, sendoff *(informal)*, adieux *or* adieus: *a touching farewell*

far-fetched ADJECTIVE **= unconvincing**, unlikely, strained, fantastic, incredible, doubtful, unbelievable, dubious, unrealistic, improbable, unnatural, preposterous, implausible, hard to swallow *(informal)*, cock-and-bull *(informal)*
OPPOSITE: believable

farm NOUN **= smallholding**, holding, ranch *(chiefly U.S. & Canad.)*, farmstead, land, station *(Austral. & N.Z.)*, acres, vineyard, plantation, croft *(Scot.)*, grange, homestead, acreage: *We have a small farm.*
▷ VERB **= cultivate**, work, plant, operate, till the soil, grow crops on, bring under cultivation, keep animals on, practise husbandry: *They had farmed the same land for generations.*

farmer NOUN **= agriculturist**, yeoman, smallholder, crofter *(Scot.)*, grazier, agriculturalist, rancher, agronomist, husbandman, cockie *or* cocky *(Austral. & N.Z. informal)*

farming NOUN **= agriculture**, cultivation, husbandry, land management, agronomy, tilling

far-out ADJECTIVE **= strange**, wild, unusual, bizarre, weird, avant-garde, unconventional, off-the-wall *(slang)*, outlandish, outré, advanced

far-reaching ADJECTIVE **= extensive**, important, significant, sweeping, broad, widespread, pervasive, momentous

The Language of Samuel Johnson

Samuel Johnson (1709–84) was an English poet, essayist, literary critic, and lexicographer, whose *A Dictionary of the English Language* (1755) set the standard for English lexicography throughout the 18th and 19th centuries. His distinctive prose style, particularly his complex clauses and abundant use of Latinate words, led to the coinage of the adjective *Johnsonian.*

Johnson's preference for Latinate vocabulary is evident in the fact that he uses *receive* approximately seven times as often as *get.* This is particularly striking in comparison with modern usage: in the *Bank of English*, Collins' corpus of present-day English, it is *get* that is the preferred form, more than eight times as frequent as *receive.* The most significant collocate of *receive* in Johnson's works is *advantage*; other recurrent phrases include *receive a visit, receive pleasure,* and *receive improvement.* Similarly, the verb *endeavour* is nearly three times as frequent as *try* in Johnson's works. In modern English, the verb *endeavour* is much less frequent, occurring 350 times less often than *try* in the *Bank of English.* Furthermore, in modern English, *endeavour* is usually used as a noun (in, for example, 'her artistic endeavours'), whereas Johnson uses the verb form more often. Frequent phrases are *endeavour to recommend* and *endeavour to gain.*

Another of Johnson's Latinisms is *procure.* This occurs over 200 times per million words in Johnson; in the *Bank of English* it occurs twice per million words. Johnson often uses it in the sense 'get possession of' (for example, he refers to people procuring camels, guns and provisions), although also in the now obsolete sense 'cause, bring about':

> I stayed two months in the province of Ligonus, and during that time **procured** a church to be built of hewn stone.

However, it is easy to ignore the non-Latinate words that also constitute Johnson's core vocabulary. Although he rarely uses *get, give* is one of the verbs he uses most frequently. It is often used as a semantically empty verb with an accompanying noun, as in *give account, give encouragement, give proof* and *give occasion.* Unlike in modern English, it is rarely used as part of a phrasal verb; there are only a few examples of such combinations (mostly *give up*) in Johnson's works. His most frequent adjective is also non-Latinate: *great,* always in the sense 'large' or 'important'. One of the most salient collocates is *part*, in phrases such as:

> To **the greater part of** mankind the duties of life are inconsistent with much study.

Another frequent adjective is *common* in its various senses: 'joint' ('the common interest of Britain and Europe'), 'public' ('common policy'), 'frequent' ('roving pirates [which] must have been very common') and 'ordinary' ('common sense', 'common prudence'). However, the newer pejorative sense 'low, base' which we find in modern English (in, for example, 'common gossip' and 'common accent') is not evident in Johnson.

One of the most interesting features of Johnson's language is his frequent use of the semi-colon, which he uses to balance and control complex sentences such as the following:

> But it must be remembered, that life consists not of a series of illustrious actions, or elegant enjoyments; the greater part of our time passes in compliance with necessities, in the performance of daily duties, in the removal of small inconveniences, in the procurement of petty pleasures; and we are well or ill at ease, as the main stream of life glides on smoothly, or is ruffled by small obstacles and frequent interruption.

Also notable in this sentence is the placement of commas; a modern writer who inserted a comma into 'it must be remembered, that' would be censured for incorrect usage. Johnson's style combines two functions of punctuation: its grammatical function in combining clauses; and its rhetorical function in marking pauses. Modern punctuation is largely grammatical, but rhetorical use was still prevalent in the 18th century.

far-sighted ADJECTIVE = **prudent**, acute, wise, cautious, sage, shrewd, discerning, canny, provident, judicious, prescient, far-seeing, politic

fascinate VERB = **entrance**, delight, charm, absorb, intrigue, enchant, rivet, captivate, enthral, beguile, allure, bewitch, ravish, transfix, mesmerize, hypnotize, engross, enrapture, interest greatly, enamour, hold spellbound, spellbind, infatuate **OPPOSITE:** bore

fascinated ADJECTIVE = **entranced**, charmed, absorbed, very interested, captivated, hooked on, enthralled, beguiled, smitten, bewitched, engrossed, spellbound, infatuated, hypnotized, under a spell

fascinating ADJECTIVE = **captivating**, engaging, gripping, compelling, intriguing, very interesting, irresistible, enticing, enchanting, seductive, riveting, alluring, bewitching, ravishing, engrossing **OPPOSITE:** boring

fascination NOUN = **attraction**, pull, spell, magic, charm, lure, glamour, allure, magnetism, enchantment, sorcery

Fascism NOUN *(sometimes not cap.)* = **authoritarianism**, dictatorship, totalitarianism, despotism, autocracy, absolutism, Hitlerism

fashion NOUN **1** = **style**, look, trend, rage, custom, convention, mode, vogue, usage, craze, fad, latest style, prevailing taste, latest: *I wore short skirts, as was the fashion.* **2** = **method**, way, style, approach, manner, mode: *We must go about this in an organized fashion.*
▷ VERB **1** = **make**, shape, cast, construct, work, form, create, design, manufacture, forge, mould, contrive, fabricate: *The desk was fashioned out of oak.* **2** = **fit**, adapt, tailor, suit, adjust, accommodate: *dresses fashioned to hide the bulges*
after a fashion = **to some extent**, somehow, in a way, moderately, to a certain extent, to a degree, somehow or other, in a manner of speaking: *He knew the way, after a fashion.*

fashionable ADJECTIVE = **popular**, in fashion, trendy *(Brit. informal)*, cool *(slang)*, designer, in *(informal)*, latest, happening *(informal)*, current, modern, with it *(informal)*, usual, smart, hip *(slang)*, prevailing, stylish, chic, up-to-date, customary, genteel, in vogue, all the rage, up-to-the-minute, modish, à la mode, voguish *(informal)*, trendsetting, all the go *(informal)*, schmick *(Austral. informal)*, funky, page-three *(Indian)*
OPPOSITE: unfashionable

fast[1] ADJECTIVE **1** = **quick**, flying, winged, rapid, fleet, hurried, accelerated, swift, speedy, brisk, hasty, nimble, mercurial, sprightly, nippy *(Brit. informal)*: *She walked at a fast pace.* **OPPOSITE:** slow **2** = **fixed**, firm, sound, stuck, secure, tight, jammed, fortified, fastened, impregnable, immovable: *He held the gate fast.* **OPPOSITE:** unstable **3** = **dissipated**, wild, exciting, loose, extravagant, reckless, immoral, promiscuous, giddy, self-indulgent, wanton, profligate, impure, intemperate, dissolute, rakish, licentious, gadabout *(informal)*: *He experimented with drugs and the fast life.* **4** = **close**, lasting, firm, permanent, constant, devoted, loyal, faithful, stalwart, staunch, steadfast, unwavering: *The men had always been fast friends.*
▷ ADVERB **1** = **quickly**, rapidly, swiftly, hastily, hurriedly, speedily, presto, apace, in haste, like a shot *(informal)*, at full speed, hell for leather *(informal)*, like lightning, hotfoot, like a flash, at a rate of knots, like the clappers *(Brit. informal)*, like a bat out of hell *(slang)*, pdq *(slang)*, like nobody's business *(informal)*, posthaste, like greased lightning *(informal)*, with all haste: *He drives terrifically fast.* **OPPOSITE:** slowly **2** = **firmly**, staunchly, resolutely, steadfastly, determinedly, unwaveringly, unchangeably: *We can only try to hold fast to our principles.* **3** = **securely**, firmly, tightly, fixedly: *She held fast to the stair rail.* **4** = **fixedly**, firmly, soundly, deeply, securely, tightly: *The tanker is stuck fast on the rocks.* **5** = **recklessly**, wildly, loosely, extravagantly, promiscuously, rakishly, intemperately: *He lived fast and died young.*

fast[2] VERB = **go hungry**, abstain, go without food, deny yourself, practise abstention, refrain from food or eating: *She had fasted to lose weight.*
▷ NOUN = **fasting**, diet, abstinence: *The fast is broken, traditionally with dates and water.*

fasten VERB **1** = **secure**, close, lock, chain, seal, bolt, do up: *He fastened the door behind him.* **2** = **tie**, bind, lace, tie up: *The dress fastens down the back.* **3** = **fix**, join, link, connect, grip, attach, anchor, affix, make firm, make fast: *Use screws to fasten the shelf to the wall.* **4** *(often with* **on** *or* **upon**) = **concentrate**, focus, fix: *Her thoughts fastened on one event.* **5** = **direct**, aim, focus, fix, concentrate, bend, rivet: *They fastened their gaze on the table and did not look up.*

fastening NOUN = **tie**, union, coupling, link, linking, bond, joint, binding, connection, attachment, junction, zip, fusion, clasp, concatenation, ligature, affixation

fastidious ADJECTIVE = **particular**, meticulous, fussy, overdelicate, difficult, nice, critical, discriminating, dainty, squeamish, choosy, picky *(informal)*, hard to please, finicky, punctilious, pernickety, hypercritical, overnice, nit-picky *(informal)*
OPPOSITE: careless

fat NOUN = **fatness**, flesh, bulk, obesity, cellulite, weight problem, flab, blubber, paunch, fatty tissue, adipose tissue, corpulence, beef *(informal)*: *ways of reducing body fat*
▷ ADJECTIVE **1** = **overweight**, large, heavy, plump, gross, stout, obese, fleshy, beefy *(informal)*, tubby, portly, roly-poly, rotund, podgy, corpulent, elephantine, broad in the beam *(informal)*, solid: *I can eat what I like without getting fat.* **OPPOSITE:** thin **2** = **large**, rich, substantial, thriving, flourishing, profitable, productive, lucrative, fertile, lush, prosperous, affluent, fruitful, cushy *(slang)*, jammy *(Brit. slang)*, remunerative: *They are set to make a fat profit.* **OPPOSITE:** scanty **3** = **fatty**, greasy, lipid, adipose, oleaginous, suety, oily: *Most heart cases are the better for cutting out fat meat.* **OPPOSITE:** lean
a fat chance = **no chance**, (a) slim chance, very little chance, not much chance: *You've got a fat chance of getting there on time.*

> **QUOTATIONS**
>
> I'm fat, but I'm thin inside. Has it ever struck you that there's a thin man inside every fat man, just as they say there's a statue inside every block of stone?
> [George Orwell *Coming Up for Air*]
>
> Imprisoned in every fat man a thin one is wildly signalling to be let out
> [Cyril Connolly *The Unquiet Grave*]
>
> Let me have men about me that are fat
> [William Shakespeare *Julius Caesar*]
>
> Some people are born to fatness. Others have to get there
> [Les Murray]
>
> I'm built for comfort, I ain't built for speed
> [Willie Dixon *Built for Comfort*]
>
> Fat is a social disease, and fat is a feminist issue
> [Susie Orbach *Fat is a Feminist Issue*]

fatal ADJECTIVE **1** = **disastrous**, devastating, crippling, lethal, catastrophic, ruinous, calamitous, baleful, baneful: *It dealt a fatal blow to his chances.* **OPPOSITE:** minor **2** = **decisive**, final, determining, critical, crucial, fateful: *putting off that fatal moment* **3** = **lethal**, deadly, mortal, causing death, final, killing, terminal, destructive, malignant, incurable, pernicious: *She had suffered a fatal heart attack.* **OPPOSITE:** harmless

fatalism NOUN = **resignation**, acceptance, passivity, determinism, stoicism, necessitarianism, predestinarianism

fatality NOUN = **casualty**, death, loss, victim

fate NOUN **1** = **destiny**, chance, fortune, luck, the stars, weird *(archaic)*, providence, nemesis, kismet, predestination, divine will: *I see no use* *quarrelling with fate.* **2 = fortune**, destiny, lot, portion, cup, horoscope: *No man chooses his fate.* **3 = outcome**, future, destiny, end, issue, upshot: *What will be the fate of the elections?* **4 = downfall**, end, death, ruin, destruction, doom, demise: *This new proposal seems doomed to the same fate.*

QUOTATIONS

Fate keeps on happening
[Anita Loos *Gentlemen Prefer Blondes*]

Fate is not an eagle, it creeps like a rat
[Elizabeth Bowen *The House in Paris*]

... to deny fate is arrogance, to declare that we are the sole shapers of our existence is madness
[Oriana Fallaci *A Man*]

We may become the makers of our fate when we have ceased to pose as its prophets
[Karl Popper *The Open Society and its Enemies*]

Fate and character are the same concept
[Novalis *Heinrich von Ofterdingen*]

PROVERBS

Man proposes, God disposes
What must be, must be (Italian, Che sera, sera)

fated ADJECTIVE **= destined**, doomed, predestined, preordained, foreordained, pre-elected

fateful ADJECTIVE **1 = crucial**, important, significant, critical, decisive, momentous, portentous: *What changed for him in that fateful year?* **OPPOSITE:** unimportant **2 = disastrous**, fatal, deadly, destructive, lethal, ominous, ruinous: *He had sailed on his third and fateful voyage.*

Father NOUN **= priest**, minister, vicar, parson, pastor, cleric, churchman, padre *(informal)*, confessor, abbé, curé, man of God: *The prior, Father Alessandro, came over to talk to them.*

father NOUN **1 = daddy** *(informal)*, dad *(informal)*, male parent, patriarch, pop *(U.S. informal)*, governor *(informal)*, old man *(Brit. informal)*, pa *(informal)*, old boy *(informal)*, papa *(old-fashioned, informal)*, sire, pater, biological father, foster father, begetter, paterfamilias, birth father: *He was a good father to my children.* **2 = founder**, author, maker, architect, creator, inventor, originator, prime mover, initiator: *He was the father of modern photography.* **3** *(often plural)* **= forefather**, predecessor, ancestor, forebear, progenitor, tupuna *or* tipuna *(N.Z.)*: *land of my fathers* **4** *(usually plural)* **= leader**, senator, elder, patron, patriarch, guiding light, city father, kaumatua *(N.Z.)*: *City fathers tried to revive the town's economy.*
▷ VERB **1 = sire**, parent, conceive, bring to life, beget, procreate, bring into being, give life to, get: *He fathered at least three children.* **2 = originate**, found, create, establish, author, institute, invent, engender: *He fathered the modern computer.*
▸ *related adjective:* paternal

QUOTATIONS

Honour thy father and thy mother
[*Bible: Exodus*]

'Tis happy for him, that his father was before him
[Jonathan Swift *Polite Conversation*]

No man is responsible for his father. That is entirely his mother's affair
[Margaret Turnbull *Alabaster Lamps*]

No man can know who was his father
[Homer *Odyssey*]

It's all any reasonable child can expect if the dad is present at the conception
[Joe Orton *Entertaining Mr. Sloane*]

It is a wise father that knows his own child
[William Shakespeare *The Merchant of Venice*]

PROVERBS

Like father like son

fatherland NOUN **= homeland**, motherland, old country, native land, land of your birth, land of your fathers, whenua *(N.Z.)*, Godzone *(Austral. informal)*

fatherly ADJECTIVE **= paternal**, kind, kindly, tender, protective, supportive, benign, affectionate, indulgent, patriarchal, benevolent, forbearing

fathom VERB **= understand**, grasp, comprehend, interpret, get to the bottom of

fatigue NOUN **= tiredness**, lethargy, weariness, ennui, heaviness, debility, languor, listlessness, overtiredness: *Those affected suffer extreme fatigue.* **OPPOSITE:** freshness
▷ VERB **= tire**, exhaust, weaken, weary, drain, fag (out) *(informal)*, whack *(Brit. informal)*, wear out, jade, take it out of *(informal)*, poop *(informal)*, tire out, knacker *(slang)*, drain of energy, overtire: *It fatigues me to list them all.* **OPPOSITE:** refresh

fatigued ADJECTIVE **= tired**, exhausted, weary, tired out, bushed *(informal)*, wasted, all in *(slang)*, fagged (out) *(informal)*, whacked *(Brit. informal)*, jaded, knackered *(slang)*, clapped out *(Austral. & N.Z. informal)*, overtired, zonked *(slang)*, dead beat *(informal)*, jiggered *(informal)*, on your last legs, creamcrackered *(Brit. informal)*

fatten VERB **1 = grow fat**, spread, expand, swell, thrive, broaden, thicken, put on weight, gain weight, coarsen, become fat, become fatter: *The creature continued to grow and fatten.* **2 = feed up**, feed, stuff, build up, cram, nourish, distend, bloat, overfeed: *They fattened up ducks and geese.*

fatty ADJECTIVE **= greasy**, fat, creamy, oily, adipose, oleaginous, suety, rich

fatuous ADJECTIVE **= foolish**, stupid, silly, dull, absurd, dense, ludicrous, lunatic, mindless, idiotic, vacuous, inane, witless, puerile, moronic, brainless, asinine, weak-minded, dumb-ass *(slang)*

faucet NOUN **= tap**, spout, spigot, stopcock, valve

fault NOUN **1 = responsibility**, liability, guilt, accountability, culpability: *It was all my fault we quarrelled.* **2 = mistake**, slip, error, offence, blunder, lapse, negligence, omission, boob *(Brit. slang)*, oversight, slip-up, indiscretion, inaccuracy, howler *(informal)*, glitch *(informal)*, error of judgment, boo-boo *(informal)*, barry *or* Barry Crocker *(Austral. slang)*: *It was a genuine fault.* **3 = failing**, lack, weakness, defect, deficiency, flaw, drawback, shortcoming, snag, blemish, imperfection, Achilles heel, weak point, infirmity, demerit: *His manners always made her blind to his faults.* **OPPOSITE:** strength
▷ VERB **= criticize**, blame, complain, condemn, moan about, censure, hold (someone) responsible, hold (someone) accountable, find fault with, call to account, impugn, find lacking, hold (someone) to blame: *You can't fault them for lack of invention.*
at fault = guilty, responsible, to blame, accountable, in the wrong, culpable, answerable, blamable: *He didn't accept that he was at fault.*
find fault with something *or* **someone = criticize**, complain about, whinge about *(informal)*, whine about *(informal)*, quibble, diss *(slang, chiefly U.S.)*, carp at, take to task, pick holes in, grouse about *(informal)*, haul over the coals *(informal)*, pull to pieces, nit-pick *(informal)*: *I do tend to find fault with everybody.*
to a fault = excessively, overly *(U.S.)*, unduly, ridiculously, in the extreme, needlessly, out of all proportion, preposterously, overmuch, immoderately: *He was generous to a fault.*

QUOTATIONS

The fault, dear Brutus, is not in our stars,
But in ourselves
[William Shakespeare *Julius Caesar*]

faultless ADJECTIVE **= flawless**, model, perfect, classic, correct, accurate, faithful, impeccable, exemplary, foolproof, unblemished

faulty ADJECTIVE **1 = defective**, damaged, not working, malfunctioning, broken, bad, flawed, impaired, imperfect, blemished, out of order, on the blink, buggy *(informal)*: *They will repair the faulty equipment.* **2 = incorrect**, wrong, flawed, inaccurate, bad, weak, invalid, erroneous, unsound, imprecise, fallacious: *Their interpretation was faulty.*

faux pas NOUN **= gaffe**, blunder, indiscretion, impropriety, bloomer *(Brit. informal)*, boob *(Brit. slang)*, clanger *(informal)*, solecism, breach of etiquette, gaucherie, barbecue stopper *(Austral. informal)*

f

favour *or (U.S.)* **favor** NOUN
1 = approval, grace, esteem, goodwill, kindness, friendliness, commendation, partiality, approbation, kind regard: *They viewed him with favour.* **OPPOSITE:** disapproval **2 = favouritism**, preference, bias, nepotism, preferential treatment, partisanship, jobs for the boys *(informal)*, partiality, one-sidedness: *employers to show favour to women and racial minorities* **3 = support**, backing, aid, championship, promotion, assistance, patronage, espousal, good opinion: *He wanted to win the favour of the voters.* **4 = good turn**, service, benefit, courtesy, kindness, indulgence, boon, good deed, kind act, obligement *(Scot. archaic)*: *I've come to ask for a favour.* **OPPOSITE:** wrong **5 = memento**, present, gift, token, souvenir, keepsake, love-token: *place cards and wedding favours*
▷ VERB **1 = prefer**, opt for, like better, incline towards, choose, pick, desire, select, elect, adopt, go for, fancy, single out, plump for, be partial to: *She favours community activism over legislation.* **OPPOSITE:** object to **2 = indulge**, reward, spoil, esteem, side with, pamper, befriend, be partial to, smile upon, pull strings for *(informal)*, have in your good books, treat with partiality, value: *There was good reason for favouring him.* **3 = support**, like, back, choose, champion, encourage, approve, fancy, advocate, opt for, subscribe to, commend, stand up for, espouse, be in favour of, countenance, patronize: *He favours greater protection of the environment.* **OPPOSITE:** oppose **4 = help**, benefit, aid, advance, promote, assist, accommodate, facilitate, abet, succour, do a kindness to: *Circumstances favoured them.* **5 = oblige**, please, honour, accommodate, benefit: *The beautiful girls would favour me with a look.*
in favour of = for, backing, supporting, behind, pro, all for *(informal)*, on the side of, right behind: *They were in favour of the decision.*

> **QUOTATIONS**
> One good turn deserves another
> [John Fletcher & Philip Massinger *The Little French Lawyer*]

favourable *or (U.S.)* **favorable**
ADJECTIVE **1 = positive**, kind, understanding, encouraging, welcoming, friendly, approving, praising, reassuring, enthusiastic, sympathetic, benign, commending, complimentary, agreeable, amicable, well-disposed, commendatory: *He made favourable comments about her work.* **OPPOSITE:** disapproving **2 = affirmative**, agreeing, confirming, positive, assenting, corroborative: *He expects a favourable reply.* **3 = advantageous**, timely, good, promising, fit, encouraging, fair, appropriate, suitable, helpful, hopeful, convenient, beneficial, auspicious, opportune, propitious: *favourable weather conditions* **OPPOSITE:** disadvantageous

favourably *or (U.S.)* **favorably**
ADVERB **1 = positively**, well, enthusiastically, helpfully, graciously, approvingly, agreeably, with approval, without prejudice, genially, with approbation, in a kindly manner, with cordiality: *He responded favourably to my suggestions.* **2 = advantageously**, well, fortunately, conveniently, profitably, to your advantage, auspiciously, opportunely: *They are far more favourably placed than their opponents.*

favourite *or (U.S.)* **favorite** ADJECTIVE **= preferred**, favoured, best-loved, most-liked, special, choice, dearest, pet, esteemed, fave *(informal)*: *Her favourite writer is Charles Dickens.*
▷ NOUN **= darling**, pet, preference, blue-eyed boy *(informal)*, pick, choice, dear, beloved, idol, fave *(informal)*, teacher's pet, the apple of your eye: *He was a favourite of the king.*

favouritism *or (U.S.)* **favoritism**
NOUN **= bias**, preference, nepotism, preferential treatment, partisanship, jobs for the boys *(informal)*, partiality, one-sidedness **OPPOSITE:** impartiality

fawn[1] ADJECTIVE **= beige**, neutral, buff, yellowish-brown, greyish-brown: *She put on a light fawn coat.*

fawn[2] VERB *(usually with* **on** *or* **upon***)* **= ingratiate yourself**, court, flatter, pander to, creep, crawl, kneel, cringe, grovel, curry favour, toady, pay court, kowtow, bow and scrape, dance attendance, truckle, be obsequious, be servile, lick (someone's) boots: *People fawn on you when you're famous.*

fawning ADJECTIVE **= obsequious**, crawling, flattering, cringing, abject, grovelling, prostrate, deferential, sycophantic, servile, slavish, bowing and scraping, bootlicking *(informal)*

fear NOUN **1 = dread**, horror, panic, terror, dismay, awe, fright, tremors, qualms, consternation, alarm, trepidation, timidity, fearfulness, blue funk *(informal)*, apprehensiveness, cravenness: *I shivered with fear at the sound of gunfire.* **2 = bugbear**, bête noire, horror, nightmare, anxiety, terror, dread, spectre, phobia, bogey, thing *(informal)*: *Flying was his greatest fear.* **3 = anxiety**, concern, worry, doubt, nerves *(informal)*, distress, suspicion, willies *(informal)*, creeps *(informal)*, butterflies *(informal)*, funk *(informal)*, angst, unease, apprehension, misgiving(s), nervousness, agitation, foreboding(s), uneasiness, solicitude, blue funk *(informal)*, heebie-jeebies *(informal)*, collywobbles *(informal)*, disquietude: *His fear might be groundless.* **4 = awe**, wonder, respect, worship, dread, reverence, veneration: *There is no fear of God before their eyes.*
▷ VERB **1 = be afraid of**, dread, be scared of, be frightened of, shudder at, be fearful of, be apprehensive about, tremble at, be terrified by, have a horror of, take fright at, have a phobia about, have qualms about, live in dread of, be in a blue funk about *(informal)*, have butterflies in your stomach about *(informal)*, shake in your shoes about: *If people fear you they respect you.* **2 = revere**, respect, reverence, venerate, stand in awe of: *They feared God in a way which most modern men can hardly imagine.* **3 = regret**, feel, suspect, have a feeling, have a hunch, have a sneaking suspicion, have a funny feeling: *I fear that a land war now looks probable.*
fear for something *or* **someone = worry about**, be concerned about, be anxious about, tremble for, be distressed about, feel concern for, be disquieted over: *He fled, saying he feared for his life.*

> **QUOTATIONS**
> Let me assert my firm belief that the only thing we have to fear is fear itself
> [Franklin D. Roosevelt *Inaugural Address*]
>
> I cannot do this. This is too much for me. I shall ruin myself if I take this risk. I cannot take the leap, it's impossible. All of me will be gone if I do this and I cling to myself
> [J.N. Figgis]
>
> Let them hate, so long as they fear
> [Accius]
>
> Perfect love casteth out fear
> [*Bible: 1 John*]
>
> Perfect fear casteth out love
> [Cyril Connolly]

fearful ADJECTIVE **1 = scared**, afraid, alarmed, frightened, nervous, terrified, apprehensive, petrified, jittery *(informal)*: *They were fearful that the fighting might spread.* **OPPOSITE:** unafraid **2 = timid**, afraid, frightened, scared, alarmed, wired *(slang)*, nervous, anxious, shrinking, tense, intimidated, uneasy, neurotic, hesitant, apprehensive, jittery *(informal)*, panicky, nervy *(Brit. informal)*, diffident, jumpy, timorous, pusillanimous, faint-hearted: *I had often been very fearful and isolated.* **OPPOSITE:** brave **3 = frightful**, shocking, terrible, awful, distressing, appalling, horrible, grim, dreadful, horrific, dire, horrendous, ghastly, hideous, monstrous, harrowing, gruesome, grievous, unspeakable, atrocious, hair-raising, hellacious *(U.S. slang)*: *The earthquake was a fearful disaster.*

fearfully ADVERB **1 = nervously**, uneasily, timidly, apprehensively, diffidently, in fear and trembling, timorously, with bated breath, with many misgivings *or* forebodings, with your heart in your mouth: *Softly, fearfully, he stole from the room.* **2 = very**, terribly, horribly, tremendously, awfully, exceedingly, excessively, dreadfully, frightfully: *This dress is fearfully expensive.*

fearless ADJECTIVE = **intrepid**, confident, brave, daring, bold, heroic, courageous, gallant, gutsy *(slang)*, valiant, plucky, game *(informal)*, doughty, undaunted, indomitable, unabashed, unafraid, unflinching, dauntless, lion-hearted, valorous, (as) game as Ned Kelly *(Austral. slang)*

fearsome ADJECTIVE = **formidable**, alarming, frightening, awful, terrifying, appalling, horrifying, menacing, dismaying, awesome, daunting, horrendous, unnerving, hair-raising, awe-inspiring, baleful, hellacious *(U.S. slang)*

feasibility NOUN = **possibility**, viability, usefulness, expediency, practicability, workability

feasible ADJECTIVE = **practicable**, possible, reasonable, viable, workable, achievable, attainable, realizable, likely
OPPOSITE: impracticable

feast NOUN **1 = banquet**, repast, spread *(informal)*, dinner, entertainment, barbecue, revel, junket, beano *(Brit. slang)*, blowout *(slang)*, carouse, slap-up meal *(Brit. informal)*, beanfeast *(Brit. informal)*, jollification, carousal, festive board, treat, hakari *(N.Z.)*: *Lunch was a feast of meat, vegetables, cheese, and wine.*
2 = festival, holiday, fête, celebration, holy day, red-letter day, religious festival, saint's day, -fest, gala day: *The feast of Passover began last night.*
3 = treat, delight, pleasure, enjoyment, gratification, cornucopia: *Chicago provides a feast for the ears of any music lover.*
▷ VERB = **eat your fill**, wine and dine, overindulge, eat to your heart's content, stuff yourself, consume, indulge, gorge, devour, pig out *(slang)*, stuff your face *(slang)*, fare sumptuously, gormandize: *We feasted on cakes and ice cream.*
feast your eyes on something = look at with delight, gaze at, devour with your eyes: *She stood feasting her eyes on the view.*

feat NOUN = **accomplishment**, act, performance, achievement, enterprise, undertaking, exploit, deed, attainment, feather in your cap

feather NOUN = **plume**

feathery ADJECTIVE = **downy**, soft, feathered, fluffy, plumed, wispy, plumy, plumate *or* plumose *(Botany, Zoology)*, light

feature NOUN **1 = aspect**, quality, characteristic, attribute, point, mark, property, factor, trait, hallmark, facet, peculiarity: *The gardens are a special feature of this property.* **2 = article**, report, story, piece, comment, item, column: *a special feature on breast cancer research*
3 = highlight, draw, attraction, innovation, speciality, specialty, main item, crowd puller *(informal)*, special attraction, special: *the most striking feature of the whole garden*
4 = face, countenance, physiognomy, lineaments: *She arranged her features in a bland expression.*
▷ VERB **1 = spotlight**, present, promote, set off, emphasize, play up, accentuate, foreground, call attention to, give prominence to, give the full works *(slang)*: *This event features a stunning catwalk show.* **2 = star**, appear, headline, participate, play a part: *She featured in a Hollywood film.*

febrile ADJECTIVE = **feverish**, hot, fevered, flushed, fiery, inflamed, delirious, pyretic *(Medical)*

feckless ADJECTIVE = **irresponsible**, useless, hopeless, incompetent, feeble, worthless, futile, ineffectual, aimless, good-for-nothing, shiftless, weak

federation NOUN = **union**, league, association, alliance, combination, coalition, partnership, consortium, syndicate, confederation, amalgamation, confederacy, entente, Bund *(German)*, copartnership, federacy

fed up ADJECTIVE = **cheesed off**, down, depressed, bored, tired, annoyed, hacked (off) *(U.S. slang)*, weary, gloomy, blue, dismal, discontented, dissatisfied, glum, sick and tired *(informal)*, browned-off *(informal)*, down in the mouth *(informal)*, brassed off *(Brit. slang)*, hoha *(N.Z.)*

fee NOUN = **charge**, pay, price, cost, bill, account, payment, wage, reward, hire, salary, compensation, toll, remuneration, recompense, emolument, honorarium, meed *(archaic)*

feeble ADJECTIVE **1 = weak**, failing, exhausted, weakened, delicate, faint, powerless, frail, debilitated, sickly, languid, puny, weedy *(informal)*, infirm, effete, enfeebled, doddering, enervated, etiolated, shilpit *(Scot.)*: *He was old and feeble.* **OPPOSITE:** strong
2 = inadequate, weak, pathetic, insufficient, incompetent, ineffective, inefficient, lame, insignificant, ineffectual, indecisive: *He said the Government had been feeble.*
3 = unconvincing, poor, thin, weak, slight, tame, pathetic, lame, flimsy, paltry, flat: *This is a feeble argument.*
OPPOSITE: effective

feed VERB **1 = cater for**, provide for, nourish, provide with food, supply, sustain, nurture, cook for, wine and dine, victual, provision: *Feeding a hungry family is expensive.* **2 = graze**, eat, browse, pasture: *The cows stopped feeding.* **3 = eat**, drink milk, take nourishment: *When a baby is thirsty, it feeds more often.* **4 = supply**, take, send, carry, convey, impart: *blood vessels that feed blood to the brain* **5 = disclose**, give, tell, reveal, supply, communicate, pass on, impart, divulge, make known: *He fed information to a rival company.* **6 = encourage**, boost, fuel, strengthen, foster, minister to, bolster, fortify, augment, make stronger: *Wealth is feeding our obsession with house prices.*
▷ NOUN **1 = food**, fodder, forage, silage, provender, pasturage: *a crop grown for animal feed* **2 = meal**, spread *(informal)*, dinner, lunch, tea, breakfast, feast, supper, tuck-in *(informal)*, nosh *(slang)*, repast, nosh-up *(Brit. slang)*: *She's had a good feed.*
feed on something = live on, depend on, devour, exist on, partake of, subsist on: *The insects breed and feed on particular cacti.*

feel VERB **1 = experience**, suffer, bear, go through, endure, undergo, have a sensation of, have: *He was still feeling pain from a stomach injury.* **2 = touch**, handle, manipulate, run your hands over, finger, stroke, paw, maul, caress, fondle: *The doctor felt his head.* **3 = be aware of**, have a sensation of, be sensible of, enjoy: *He felt her leg against his.* **4 = perceive**, sense, detect, discern, know, experience, notice, observe: *He felt something was nearby.*
5 = grope, explore, fumble, sound: *He felt his way down the wooden staircase.*
6 = sense, be aware, be convinced, have a feeling, have the impression, intuit, have a hunch, feel in your bones: *I feel that he still misses her.*
7 = believe, consider, judge, deem, think, hold, be of the opinion that: *They felt that the police could not guarantee their safety.* **8 = seem**, appear, strike you as: *The air feels wet and cold on these evenings.* **9 = notice**, note, observe, perceive, detect, discern: *The charity is still feeling the effects of revelations about its former president.*
▷ NOUN **1 = texture**, finish, touch, surface, surface quality: *a crisp papery feel* **2 = impression**, feeling, air, sense, quality, atmosphere, mood, aura, ambience, vibes *(slang)*: *He wanted to get the feel of the place.*
feel for someone = feel compassion for, pity, feel sorry for, sympathize with, be moved by, be sorry for, empathize, commiserate with, bleed for, feel sympathy for, condole with: *I really felt for her.*
feel like something = want, desire, would like, fancy, wish for, could do with, feel the need for, feel inclined, feel up to, have the inclination for: *I feel like a little exercise.*

feeler
put out feelers = approach, probe, test of the waters, overture, trial, launch a trial balloon

feeling NOUN **1 = emotion**, sentiment: *Strong feelings of pride welled up in me.*
2 = opinion, view, attitude, belief, point of view, instinct, inclination: *She has strong feelings about the growth in violence.* **3 = passion**, heat, emotion, intensity, warmth, sentimentality: *a voice that trembles with feeling* **4 = ardour**,

love, care, affection, warmth, tenderness, fondness, fervour: *He never lost his feeling for her.* **5 = sympathy**, understanding, concern, pity, appreciation, sensitivity, compassion, sorrow, sensibility, empathy, fellow feeling: *He felt a rush of feeling for the woman.* **6 = sensation**, sense, impression, awareness: *Focus on the feeling of relaxation.* **7 = sense of touch**, sense, perception, sensation, feel, touch: *After the accident he had no feeling in his legs.* **8 = impression**, idea, sense, notion, suspicion, consciousness, hunch, apprehension, inkling, presentiment: *I have a feeling that everything will come right for us.* **9 = atmosphere**, mood, aura, ambience, feel, air, quality, vibes *(slang)*: *a feeling of opulence and grandeur*
▷ PLURAL NOUN **= emotions**, ego, self-esteem, sensibilities, susceptibilities, sensitivities: *He was afraid of hurting my feelings.*
bad feeling = hostility, anger, dislike, resentment, bitterness, distrust, enmity, ill feeling, ill will, upset: *There's been some bad feeling between them.*

feign VERB **= pretend**, affect, assume, put on, devise, forge, fake, imitate, simulate, sham, act, fabricate, counterfeit, give the appearance of, dissemble, make a show of

feigned ADJECTIVE **= pretended**, affected, assumed, false, artificial, fake, imitation, simulated, sham, pseudo *(informal)*, fabricated, counterfeit, spurious, ersatz, insincere

feint NOUN **= bluff**, manoeuvre, dodge, mock attack, play, blind, distraction, pretence, expedient, ruse, artifice, gambit, subterfuge, stratagem, wile

feisty ADJECTIVE **= fiery**, spirited, bold, plucky, vivacious, (as) game as Ned Kelly *(Austral. slang)*

felicity NOUN **1 = happiness**, joy, ecstasy, bliss, delectation, blessedness, blissfulness: *a period of domestic felicity* **2 = aptness**, grace, effectiveness, suitability, propriety, appropriateness, applicability, becomingness, suitableness: *his felicity of word and phrase*

feline ADJECTIVE **1 = catlike**, leonine: *a black, furry, feline creature* **2 = graceful**, flowing, smooth, elegant, sleek, slinky, sinuous, stealthy: *He moves with feline pace.*

fell VERB **1 = cut down**, cut, level, demolish, flatten, knock down, hew, raze: *Badly infected trees should be felled.* **2 = knock down**, floor, flatten, strike down, prostrate, deck *(slang)*: *A blow on the head felled him.*

fellow NOUN **1 = man**, boy, person, individual, customer *(informal)*, character, guy *(informal)*, bloke *(Brit. informal)*, punter *(informal)*, chap *(informal)*, boykie *(S. African informal)*: *He appeared to be a fine fellow.* **2 = associate**, colleague, peer, co-worker, member, friend, partner, equal, companion, comrade, crony, compeer: *He stood out from all his fellows at work.*
▷ MODIFIER **= co-**, similar, related, allied, associate, associated, affiliated, akin, like: *My fellow inmates treated me with kindness.*

fellowship NOUN **1 = society**, club, league, association, organization, guild, fraternity, brotherhood, sisterhood, order, sodality: *the National Youth Fellowship* **2 = camaraderie**, intimacy, communion, familiarity, brotherhood, companionship, sociability, amity, kindliness, fraternization, companionability, intercourse: *a sense of community and fellowship*

> **QUOTATIONS**
> Fellowship is heaven, and lack of fellowship is hell
> [William Morris *A Dream of John Ball*]

feminine ADJECTIVE **1 = womanly**, pretty, soft, gentle, tender, modest, delicate, graceful, girlie, girlish, ladylike: *the ideal of feminine beauty* **OPPOSITE:** masculine **2 = effeminate**, camp *(informal)*, weak, unmanly, effete, womanish, unmasculine: *men with feminine gestures*

femininity NOUN **= womanliness**, delicacy, softness, womanhood, gentleness, girlishness, feminineness, muliebrity

fen NOUN **= marsh**, moss *(Scot.)*, swamp, bog, slough, quagmire, holm *(dialect)*, morass, pakihi *(N.Z.)*, muskeg *(Canad.)*

fence NOUN **= barrier**, wall, defence, guard, railings, paling, shield, hedge, barricade, hedgerow, rampart, palisade, stockade, barbed wire: *They climbed over the fence into the field.*
sit on the fence = be uncommitted, be uncertain, be undecided, vacillate, be in two minds, blow hot and cold *(informal)*, be irresolute, avoid committing yourself: *He is sitting on the fence, refusing to commit himself.*
▷ VERB (*with* **in** *or* **off**) **= enclose**, surround, bound, hedge, pound, protect, separate, guard, defend, secure, pen, restrict, confine, fortify, encircle, coop, impound, circumscribe: *He intends to fence in about 100 acres of land.*

fend
fend for yourself = look after yourself, support yourself, sustain yourself, take care of yourself, provide for yourself, make do, make provision for yourself, shift for yourself: *He was just left to fend for himself.*
fend something *or* **someone off 1 = deflect**, resist, parry, avert, ward off, stave off, turn aside, hold *or* keep at bay: *He fended off questions from the Press.* **2 = beat off**, resist, parry, avert, deflect, repel, drive back, ward off, stave off, repulse, keep off, turn aside, hold *or* keep at bay: *He raised his hand to fend off the blow.*

feral ADJECTIVE **1 = wild**, untamed, uncultivated, undomesticated, unbroken: *There are many feral cats roaming the area.* **2 = savage**, fierce, brutal, ferocious, fell, wild, vicious, bestial: *the feral scowl of the young street mugger*

ferment NOUN **= commotion**, turmoil, unrest, turbulence, trouble, heat, excitement, glow, fever, disruption, frenzy, stew, furore, uproar, agitation, tumult, hubbub, brouhaha, imbroglio, state of unrest: *The country is in a state of political ferment.* **OPPOSITE:** tranquillity
▷ VERB **1 = brew**, froth, concoct, effervesce, work, rise, heat, boil, bubble, foam, seethe, leaven: *red wine made from grapes left to ferment for three weeks* **2 = stir up**, excite, provoke, rouse, agitate, inflame, incite: *They tried to ferment political unrest.*

ferocious ADJECTIVE **1 = fierce**, violent, savage, ravening, predatory, feral, rapacious, wild: *By its nature a lion is ferocious.* **OPPOSITE:** gentle **2 = cruel**, bitter, brutal, vicious, ruthless, relentless, barbaric, merciless, brutish, bloodthirsty, barbarous, pitiless, tigerish: *Fighting has been ferocious.*

ferocity NOUN **= savagery**, violence, cruelty, brutality, ruthlessness, inhumanity, wildness, barbarity, viciousness, fierceness, rapacity, bloodthirstiness, savageness, ferociousness

ferry NOUN **= ferry boat**, boat, ship, passenger boat, packet boat, packet: *They crossed the river by ferry.*
▷ VERB **= transport**, bring, carry, ship, take, run, shuttle, convey, chauffeur: *They ferried in more soldiers to help with the search.*

fertile ADJECTIVE **= productive**, rich, flowering, lush, fat, yielding, prolific, abundant, plentiful, fruitful, teeming, luxuriant, generative, fecund, fruit-bearing, flowing with milk and honey, plenteous **OPPOSITE:** barren

fertility NOUN **= fruitfulness**, abundance, richness, fecundity, luxuriance, productiveness

fertilization *or* **fertilisation** NOUN **= insemination**, propagation, procreation, implantation, pollination, impregnation

fertilize *or* **fertilise** VERB **1 = inseminate**, impregnate, pollinate, make pregnant, fructify, make fruitful, fecundate: *sperm levels needed to fertilize the egg* **2 = enrich**, feed, compost, manure, mulch, top-dress, dress, fertigate *(Austral.)*: *grown in recently fertilized soil*

fertilizer *or* **fertiliser** NOUN **= compost**, muck, manure, dung, guano, marl, bone meal, dressing, toad juice *(Austral.)*

fervent ADJECTIVE **= ardent**, earnest, enthusiastic, fervid, passionate, warm, excited, emotional, intense, flaming, eager, animated, fiery, ecstatic, devout, heartfelt, impassioned, zealous, vehement, perfervid *(literary)* **OPPOSITE:** apathetic

USAGE
Care should be taken when using *fervid* as an alternative to *fervent*. Although both come from the same root and share the meaning 'intense, ardent', *fervent* has largely positive connotations, and is associated with hopes, wishes, and beliefs, or admirers, supporters, and fans. Apart from being used less often than *fervent*, *fervid* is chiefly negative: *in the fervid politics of New York city*. A *fervent* kiss from an admirer would probably be welcome; a *fervid* one would not.

fervour *or (U.S.)* **fervor** NOUN **= ardour**, passion, enthusiasm, excitement, intensity, warmth, animation, zeal, eagerness, vehemence, earnestness, fervency

QUOTATIONS
Fervour is the weapon of choice of the impotent
[Frantz Fanon *Black Skins White Masks*]

fester VERB **1 = intensify**, gall, smoulder, chafe, irk, rankle, aggravate: *Resentments are starting to fester.* **2 = putrefy**, decay, become infected, become inflamed, suppurate, ulcerate, maturate, gather: *The wound is festering and gangrene has set in.*

festering ADJECTIVE **= septic**, infected, poisonous, inflamed, pussy, suppurating, ulcerated, purulent, maturating, gathering: *afflicted by festering sores*

festival NOUN **1 = celebration**, fair, carnival, gala, treat, fête, entertainment, jubilee, fiesta, festivities, jamboree, -fest, field day: *The Festival will provide spectacles like river pageants.* **2 = holy day**, holiday, feast, commemoration, feast day, red-letter day, saint's day, fiesta, fête, anniversary: *the Jewish festival of the Passover*

festive ADJECTIVE **= celebratory**, happy, holiday, carnival, jolly, merry, gala, hearty, jubilant, cheery, joyous, joyful, jovial, convivial, gleeful, back-slapping, Christmassy, mirthful, sportive, light-hearted, festal, gay **OPPOSITE:** mournful

festivity NOUN **1 = merrymaking**, fun, pleasure, amusement, mirth, gaiety, merriment, revelry, conviviality, joviality, joyfulness, jollification, sport: *There was a general air of festivity and abandon.* **2** *(often plural)* **= celebration**, party, festival, entertainment, rave *(Brit. slang)*, beano *(Brit. slang)*, fun and games, rave-up *(Brit. slang)*, jollification, festive event, carousal, festive proceedings, hooley *or* hoolie *(chiefly Irish & N.Z.)*: *The festivities included a firework display.*

festoon NOUN **= decoration**, garland, swathe, wreath, swag, lei, chaplet: *festoons of laurel and magnolia*
▷ VERB **= decorate**, deck, array, drape, garland, swathe, bedeck, wreathe, beribbon, engarland, hang: *The temples are festooned with lights.*

fetch VERB **1 = bring**, pick up, collect, go and get, get, carry, deliver, conduct, transport, go for, obtain, escort, convey, retrieve: *She fetched a towel from the bathroom.* **2 = sell for**, make, raise, earn, realize, go for, yield, bring in: *The painting is expected to fetch two million pounds.*
fetch up = end up, reach, arrive, turn up, come, stop, land, halt, finish up: *We eventually fetched up at their house.*

fetching ADJECTIVE **= attractive**, sweet, charming, enchanting, fascinating, intriguing, cute, enticing, captivating, alluring, winsome

fête *or* **fete** NOUN **= fair**, festival, gala, bazaar, garden party, sale of work: *The Vicar is organizing a church fete.*
▷ VERB **= entertain**, welcome, honour, make much of, wine and dine, hold a reception for (someone), lionize, bring out the red carpet for (someone), kill the fatted calf for (someone), treat: *The actress was fêted at a special dinner.*

fetish NOUN **1 = fixation**, obsession, mania, thing *(informal)*, idée fixe *(French)*: *I've got a bit of a shoe fetish.* **2 = talisman**, amulet, cult object: *Tribal elders carried the sacred fetishes.*

fetter PLURAL NOUN **1 = restraints**, checks, curbs, constraints, captivity, obstructions, bondage, hindrances: *without the fetters of restrictive rules* **2 = chains**, bonds, irons, shackles, manacles, leg irons, gyves *(archaic)*, bilboes: *He saw a boy in fetters in the dungeon.*
▷ VERB **1 = restrict**, bind, confine, curb, restrain, hamstring, hamper, encumber, clip someone's wings, trammel, straiten: *He would not be fettered by bureaucracy.* **2 = chain**, tie, tie up, shackle, hobble, hold captive, manacle, gyve *(archaic)*, put a straitjacket on: *My foes fettered me hand and foot.*

feud NOUN **= hostility**, row, conflict, argument, faction, falling out, disagreement, rivalry, contention, quarrel, grudge, strife, bickering, vendetta, discord, enmity, broil, bad blood, estrangement, dissension: *a long and bitter feud between families*
▷ VERB **= quarrel**, row, clash, dispute, fall out, contend, brawl, war, squabble, duel, bicker, be at odds, be at daggers drawn: *He feuded with his ex-wife.*

fever NOUN **1 = ague**, high temperature, feverishness, pyrexia *(Medical)*: *Symptoms of the disease include fever and weight loss.* **2 = excitement**, heat, passion, intensity, flush, turmoil, ecstasy, frenzy, ferment, agitation, fervour, restlessness, delirium: *I got married in a fever of excitement.*
▸ *related adjective:* febrile

PROVERBS
Feed a cold and starve a fever

fevered ADJECTIVE **= frantic**, excited, desperate, distracted, frenzied, impatient, obsessive, restless, agitated, frenetic, overwrought

feverish *or* **fevorous** ADJECTIVE **1 = frantic**, excited, desperate, distracted, frenzied, impatient, obsessive, restless, agitated, frenetic, overwrought: *a state of feverish excitement* **OPPOSITE:** calm **2 = hot**, burning, flaming, fevered, flushed, hectic, inflamed, febrile, pyretic *(Medical)*: *She looked feverish; her eyes glistened.*

few ADJECTIVE **= not many**, one or two, hardly any, scarcely any, rare, thin, scattered, insufficient, scarce, scant, meagre, negligible, sporadic, sparse, infrequent, scanty, inconsiderable: *In some districts there are few survivors.* **OPPOSITE:** many
▷ PRONOUN **= a small number**, a handful, a sprinkling, a scattering, some, scarcely any: *A strict diet is appropriate for only a few.*
few and far between = scarce, rare, unusual, scattered, irregular, uncommon, in short supply, hard to come by, infrequent, thin on the ground, widely spaced, seldom met with: *Successful women politicians were few and far between.*

fiancé *or* **fiancée** NOUN **= husband-** *or* **wife-to-be**, intended, betrothed, prospective spouse, future husband *or* wife

fiasco NOUN **= flop**, failure, disaster, ruin, mess *(informal)*, catastrophe, rout, debacle, cock-up *(Brit. slang)*, washout *(informal)*

fib NOUN **= lie**, story, fiction, untruth, whopper *(informal)*, porky *(Brit. slang)*, pork pie *(Brit. slang)*, white lie, prevarication

fibre *or (U.S.)* **fiber** NOUN **= thread**, strand, filament, tendril, pile, texture, staple, wisp, fibril: *a variety of coloured fibres*
moral fibre = strength of character, strength, resolution, resolve, stamina, backbone, toughness: *They all lacked courage, backbone or moral fibre.*

fickle ADJECTIVE **= capricious**, variable, volatile, unpredictable, unstable, unfaithful, temperamental, mercurial, unsteady, faithless, changeable, quicksilver, vacillating, fitful, flighty, blowing hot and cold, mutable, irresolute, inconstant **OPPOSITE:** constant

QUOTATIONS
The fickleness of the women I love is matched only by the infernal constancy of the women who love me
[George Bernard Shaw *The Philanderer*]

f

fiction NOUN **1 = tale**, story, novel, legend, myth, romance, fable, storytelling, narration, creative writing, work of imagination: *She is a writer of historical fiction.* **2 = imagination**, fancy, fantasy, creativity: *a story of truth or fiction* **3 = lie**, fancy, fantasy, invention, improvisation, fabrication, concoction, falsehood, untruth, porky *(Brit. slang)*, pork pie *(Brit. slang)*, urban myth, tall story, urban legend, cock and bull story *(informal)*, figment of the imagination: *Total recycling is a fiction.*

> QUOTATIONS
> 'Tis strange – but true; for truth is always strange;
> Stranger than fiction
> [Lord Byron *Don Juan*]
>
> Truth may be stranger than fiction, but fiction is truer
> [Frederic Raphael *Contemporary Novelists*]
>
> Literature is a luxury. Fiction is a necessity
> [G.K. Chesterton *The Defendant*]

f

fictional ADJECTIVE **= imaginary**, made-up, invented, legendary, unreal, nonexistent

fictitious ADJECTIVE **1 = false**, made-up, bogus, untrue, non-existent, fabricated, counterfeit, feigned, spurious, apocryphal: *a source of fictitious rumours* OPPOSITE: true **2 = imaginary**, imagined, made-up, assumed, invented, artificial, improvised, mythical, unreal, fanciful, make-believe: *Persons portrayed in this production are fictitious.*

fiddle NOUN **1 = fraud**, racket, scam *(slang)*, piece of sharp practice, fix, sting *(informal)*, graft *(informal)*, swindle, wangle *(informal)*: *legitimate businesses that act as a cover for tax fiddles* **2 = violin**: *He played the fiddle at local dances.*
▷ VERB **1** *(often with* **with***)* **= fidget**, play, finger, toy, tamper, trifle, mess about *or* around: *She fiddled with a pen on the desk.* **2** *(often with* **with***)* **= tinker**, adjust, interfere, mess about *or* around: *He fiddled with the radio dial.* **3 = cheat**, cook *(informal)*, fix, manoeuvre *(informal)*, graft *(informal)*, diddle *(informal)*, wangle *(informal)*, gerrymander, finagle *(informal)*: *Stop fiddling your expenses account.*

fiddling ADJECTIVE **= trivial**, small, petty, trifling, insignificant, unimportant, pettifogging, futile

fidelity NOUN **1 = loyalty**, faith, integrity, devotion, allegiance, constancy, faithfulness, dependability, trustworthiness, troth *(archaic)*, fealty, staunchness, devotedness, lealty *(archaic, Scot.)*, true-heartedness: *I had to promise fidelity to the Queen.* OPPOSITE: disloyalty **2 = accuracy**, precision, correspondence, closeness, adherence, faithfulness, exactitude, exactness, scrupulousness, preciseness: *the fidelity of these early documents* OPPOSITE: inaccuracy

> QUOTATIONS
> Histories are more full of examples of the fidelity of dogs than of friends
> [Alexander Pope]

fidget VERB **= move restlessly**, fiddle *(informal)*, bustle, twitch, fret, squirm, chafe, jiggle, jitter *(informal)*, be like a cat on hot bricks *(informal)*, worry

field NOUN **1 = meadow**, land, green, lea *(poetic)*, pasture, mead *(archaic)*, greensward *(archaic, literary)*: *They went for walks together in the fields.* **2 = speciality**, line, area, department, environment, territory, discipline, province, pale, confines, sphere, domain, specialty, sphere of influence, purview, metier, sphere of activity, bailiwick, sphere of interest, sphere of study: *They are both experts in their field.* **3 = line**, reach, range, limits, bounds, sweep, scope: *Our field of vision is surprisingly wide.* **4 = competitors**, competition, candidates, runners, applicants, entrants, contestants: *The two most experienced athletes led the field.*
▷ VERB **1 = deal with**, answer, handle, respond to, reply to, deflect, turn aside: *He fielded questions from journalists.* **2 = retrieve**, return, stop, catch, pick up: *He fielded the ball and threw it at the wicket.*

fiend NOUN **1 = brute**, monster, savage, beast, degenerate, barbarian, ogre, ghoul: *a saint to his parents and a fiend to his children* **2 = enthusiast**, fan, addict, freak *(informal)*, fanatic, maniac, energumen: *a strong-tea fiend* **3 = demon**, devil, evil spirit, hellhound, atua *(N.Z.)*: *She is a fiend incarnate, leading these people to eternal damnation.*

fiendish ADJECTIVE **1 = difficult**, involved, complex, puzzling, baffling, intricate, thorny, knotty: *It is a fiendish question without an easy answer.* **2 = wicked**, cruel, savage, monstrous, malicious, satanic, malignant, unspeakable, atrocious, inhuman, diabolical, implacable, malevolent, hellish, devilish, infernal, accursed, ungodly, black-hearted, demoniac: *a fiendish act of wickedness*

fierce ADJECTIVE **1 = ferocious**, wild, dangerous, cruel, savage, brutal, aggressive, menacing, vicious, fiery, murderous, uncontrollable, feral, untamed, barbarous, fell *(archaic)*, threatening, baleful, truculent, tigerish, aggers *(Austral. slang)*, biffo *(Austral. slang)*: *the teeth of some fierce animal* OPPOSITE: gentle **2 = intense**, strong, keen, passionate, relentless, cut-throat: *He inspires fierce loyalty in his friends.* **3 = stormy**, strong, powerful, violent, intense, raging, furious, howling, uncontrollable, boisterous, tumultuous, tempestuous, blustery, inclement: *Two climbers were trapped by a fierce storm.* OPPOSITE: tranquil

fiercely ADVERB **= ferociously**, savagely, passionately, furiously, viciously, menacingly, tooth and nail, in a frenzy, like cat and dog, frenziedly, tigerishly, with no holds barred, tempestuously, with bared teeth, uncontrolledly

fiery ADJECTIVE **1 = burning**, flaming, glowing, blazing, on fire, red-hot, ablaze, in flames, aflame, afire: *People set up fiery barricades.* **2 = excitable**, violent, fierce, passionate, irritable, impetuous, irascible, peppery, hot-headed, choleric: *a red-head's fiery temper*

fiesta NOUN **= carnival**, party, holiday, fair, fête, festival, celebration, feast, revel, jubilee, festivity, jamboree, Mardi Gras, revelry, Saturnalia, saint's day, merrymaking, carousal, bacchanal *or* bacchanalia, gala

fight VERB **1 = oppose**, campaign against, dispute, contest, resist, defy, contend, withstand, stand up to, take issue with, make a stand against: *She devoted her life to fighting poverty.* **2 = strive**, battle, push, struggle, contend: *He had to fight hard for his place in the team.* **3 = battle**, assault, combat, war with, go to war, do battle, wage war, take up arms, bear arms against, engage in hostilities, carry on war, engage: *The Sioux fought other tribes for territorial rights.* **4 = engage in**, conduct, wage, pursue, carry on: *They fought a war against injustice.* **5 = take the field**, cross swords, taste battle: *He fought in the war and was taken prisoner.* **6 = brawl**, clash, scrap *(informal)*, exchange blows, struggle, row, tilt, wrestle, feud, grapple, tussle, joust, come to blows, lock horns, throw down *(U.S. slang)*, fight like Kilkenny cats: *a lot of unruly drunks fighting* **7 = box**, spar with, exchange blows with, throw down *(U.S. slang)*: *I'd like to fight him for the title.*
▷ NOUN **1 = battle**, campaign, movement, struggle: *I will continue the fight for justice.* **2 = conflict**, war, action, clash, contest, encounter, brush, combat, engagement, hostilities, skirmish, passage of arms: *They used to be allies in the fight against the old Communist regime.* **3 = brawl**, set-to *(informal)*, riot, scrap *(informal)*, confrontation, rumble *(U.S. & N.Z. slang)*, slugfest *(informal)*, throwdown *(U.S. slang)*, fray, duel, skirmish, head-to-head, tussle, scuffle, free-for-all *(informal)*, fracas, altercation, dogfight, joust, dissension, affray *(Law)*, shindig *(informal)*, scrimmage, sparring match, exchange of blows, shindy *(informal)*, melee *or* mêlée, biffo *(Austral. slang)*, boilover *(Austral.)*: *He got a bloody nose in a fight.* **4 = row**, argument, dispute, quarrel, squabble: *He had a big fight with his dad last night.* **5 = match**, contest, bout, battle, competition, struggle, set-to, encounter, engagement, head-to-head, boxing match: *The referee stopped the fight in the second round.*

Nouns, Pronouns, and Determiners in 'The Times' and 'The Sun'

An area of usage which has been changing in recent years is the treatment of plural nouns. One aspect of this is the choice of *less* or *fewer* before a plural noun, and usage in *The Times* and *The Sun* is very similar in this respect: both use *fewer* very infrequently, and *less* about forty times more frequently, in examples such as:

> Of course, taking on board **less toxins** in the first place might be a smart move. (*The Times*)

> Another advantage of the new system is that there are far **less errors** than in the past. (*The Sun*)

On the other hand, *The Times* is more likely than *The Sun* to treat Latinate plural nouns as plurals. All of the examples with *data* in *The Sun* use a singular verb or determiner, as in -

> **This data is** uploaded to the database. (*The Sun*)

- whereas usage in *The Times* is evenly divided between plural and singular verbs following *data*. Another interesting area of difference is the use of plural or singular verbs with collective nouns such as *government*, *family*, and *group*. Both newspapers tend to use singular verbs, but to differing degrees. *The Sun* uses a singular form with *government* twice as often as a plural, but still uses plural forms fairly frequently, as in -

> ...the **government are** more obsessed with league tables than catching the Mr Bigs. (*The Sun*)

> - while The Times is eighteen times more likely to use a singular verb, as in

> The **government hopes** the tax will raise £70m over the next two years. (*The Times*)

Similarly, *The Sun* uses singular verbs with *group* just under three times more often than plural verbs, while *The Times* is more than eleven times more likely to use a singular verb. On the other hand, *family* is more frequently presented as a collection of individuals (therefore plural) rather than a unit. In *The Times*, singular and plural verbs with *family* are evenly divided; in *The Sun*, plural forms are almost twice as frequent.

A notable difference in pronoun and determiner usage is that, while *it* occurs with equal frequency in the two newspapers, *its* is almost four times as frequent, and *itself* over three times as frequent, in *The Times* as in *The Sun*. The case with *its* is not because *The Sun* uses *it's*: *it's* is always used in *The Sun* as a contraction of *it is*. It is not clear why *The Times* uses *its* more often, although perhaps it is related to its focus on abstract concepts and institutions, or to its use of *its* where *The Sun* would use *their* or *of it*. The more frequent use of *itself* in *The Times* might also be explained by its use as an emphatic, as in:

> Wild-eyed youths... eager to undermine our society, Parliament and democracy **itself**. (*The Times*)

Whom is five times more frequent in *The Times* than in *The Sun*. Furthermore, most of the uses of *whom* in *The Sun* follow a preposition, where *whom* is the only option, eg:

> ... a further 390 missing, the vast majority **of whom** are feared to have died. (*The Sun*)

Whom used without a preceding preposition is over seven times more frequent in *The Times*, in sentences such as:

> ... it is Gordon Brown **whom** Mr. Darling can curse for his gaffe. (*The Times*)

Such cases are much more likely to be expressed by *who* or *that* in *The Sun*, as in:

> I have a girlfriend **who** I have known for years. (*The Sun*)

6 = resistance, spirit, pluck, militancy, mettle, belligerence, will to resist, gameness, pluckiness: *We had a lot of fight in us.*
fight shy of something = avoid, shun, steer clear of, duck out of *(informal)*, keep at arm's length, hang back from, keep aloof from: *It's no use fighting shy of publicity.*

fighter NOUN **1 = combatant**, battler, militant, contender, contestant, belligerent, antagonist, disputant: *She's a real fighter and has always defied the odds.* **2 = boxer**, wrestler, bruiser *(informal)*, pugilist, prize fighter: *a tough little street fighter* **3 = soldier**, warrior, fighting man, man-at-arms: *His guerrillas are widely accepted as some of the best fighters in the Afghan resistance.*

f

figment NOUN **= invention**, production, fancy, creation, fiction, fable, improvisation, fabrication, falsehood

figurative ADJECTIVE **= symbolical**, representative, abstract, allegorical, typical, tropical *(Rhetoric)*, imaginative, ornate, descriptive, fanciful, pictorial, metaphorical, flowery, florid, poetical, emblematical **OPPOSITE:** literal

figure NOUN **1 = digit**, character, symbol, number, numeral, cipher: *deduct the second figure from the first* **2 = outline**, form, shape, shadow, profile, silhouette: *A figure appeared in the doorway.* **3 = shape**, build, body, frame, proportions, chassis *(slang)*, torso, physique: *Take pride in your health and your figure.* **4 = personage**, force, face *(informal)*, leader, person, individual, character, presence, somebody, personality, celebrity, worthy, notable, big name, dignitary, notability: *The movement is supported by key figures.* **5 = diagram**, drawing, picture, illustration, representation, sketch, emblem: *Figure 26 shows a small circular garden of herbs.* **6 = design**, shape, pattern, device, motif, depiction: *The impulsive singer had the figure cut into his shaven hair.* **7 = price**, cost, value, amount, total, sum: *It's hard to put a figure on the damage.*
▷ VERB **1 = make sense**, follow, be expected, add up, go without saying, seem reasonable: *When I finished, he said, 'Yeah. That figures'.* **2** *(usually with* **in***)* **= feature**, act, appear, contribute to, be included, be mentioned, play a part, be featured, have a place in, be conspicuous: *I didn't figure in his plans.* **3 = calculate**, work out, compute, tot up, add, total, count, reckon, sum, tally: *Figure the interest rate.*
figure on something = plan on, depend on, rely on, count on, bargain on: *I never figured on that scenario.*
figure something out = calculate, reckon, work out, compute: *I want to figure out how much it'll cost.*
figure something *or* **someone out = understand**, make out, fathom, make head or tail of *(informal)*, see, solve, resolve, comprehend, make sense of, decipher, think through, suss (out) *(slang)*: *How do you figure that out?; I can't figure that guy out at all.*

figurehead NOUN **= nominal head**, leader in name only, titular head, front man, name, token, dummy, puppet, mouthpiece, cipher, nonentity, straw man *(chiefly U.S.)*, man of straw

figure of speech NOUN **= expression**, image, turn of phrase, trope

filament NOUN **= strand**, string, wire, fibre, thread, staple, wisp, cilium *(Biology, Zoology)*, fibril, pile

file[1] NOUN **1 = folder**, case, portfolio, binder: *a file of insurance papers* **2 = dossier**, record, information, data, documents, case history, report, case: *We have files on people's tax details.* **3 = line**, row, chain, string, column, queue, procession: *A file of soldiers, spaced and on both sides.*
▷ VERB **1 = arrange**, order, classify, put in place, slot in *(informal)*, categorize, pigeonhole, put in order: *Papers are filed alphabetically.* **2 = register**, record, enter, log, put on record: *They have filed formal complaints.* **3 = march**, troop, parade, walk in line, walk behind one another: *They filed into the room and sat down.*

file[2] VERB **= smooth**, shape, polish, rub, refine, scrape, rasp, burnish, rub down, abrade: *shaping and filing nails*

filibuster NOUN **= obstruction**, delay, postponement, hindrance, procrastination: *The Senator used a filibuster to stop the bill.*
▷ VERB **= obstruct**, prevent, delay, put off, hinder, play for time, procrastinate: *They threatened to filibuster until Senate adjourns.*

filigree NOUN **= wirework**, lace, lattice, tracery, lacework

fill VERB **1 = top up**, fill up, make full, become full, brim over: *While the bath was filling, he undressed.* **2 = swell**, expand, inflate, become bloated, extend, balloon, fatten: *Your lungs fill with air.* **3 = pack**, crowd, squeeze, cram, throng: *Thousands of people filled the streets.* **4 = stock**, supply, store, pack, load, furnish, replenish: *I fill the shelves in a supermarket until 12pm.* **5 = plug**, close, stop, seal, cork, bung, block up, stop up: *Fill the holes with plaster.* **6 = saturate**, charge, pervade, permeate, imbue, impregnate, suffuse, overspread: *The barn was filled with the smell of hay.* **7 = fulfil**, hold, perform, carry out, occupy, take up, execute, discharge, officiate: *She filled the role of diplomat's wife for many years.* **8** *(often with* **up***)* **= satisfy**, stuff, gorge, glut, satiate, sate: *They filled themselves with chocolate cake.*
fill in for someone = replace, represent, substitute for, cover for, take over from, act for, stand in for, sub for, deputize for: *relief employees who fill in for workers while on break*
fill someone in = inform, acquaint, advise of, apprise of, bring up to date with, update with, put wise to *(slang)*, give the facts *or* background of: *I'll fill him in on the details.*
fill something in = complete, answer, fill up, fill out *(U.S.)*: *Fill in the coupon and send it to the above address.*
your fill = sufficient, enough, plenty, ample, all you want, a sufficiency: *We have had our fill of disappointments.*

filling NOUN **= stuffing**, padding, filler, wadding, inside, insides, contents, innards *(informal)*: *Make the filling from down or feathers.*
▷ ADJECTIVE **= satisfying**, heavy, square, substantial, ample: *a well-spiced and filling meal*

fillip NOUN **= boost**, push, spur, spice, incentive, stimulus, prod, zest, goad

film NOUN **1 = movie**, picture, flick *(slang)*, motion picture: *He appeared in the star role of the film.* **2 = cinema**, the movies: *Film is a business with limited opportunities for actresses.* **3 = layer**, covering, cover, skin, coating, coat, dusting, tissue, membrane, scum, gauze, integument, pellicle: *The sea is coated with a film of sewage.* **4 = haze**,

FIGURES OF SPEECH

alliteration
allusion
anacoluthia
anadiplosis
analogy
anaphora
anastrophe
antiphrasis
antithesis
antonomasia
apophasis
aporia
aposiopesis
apostrophe
catachresis
chiasmus
circumlocution
climax
emphasis
epanaphora
epanorthosis
exclamation
gemination
hendiadys
hypallage
hyperbaton
hyperbole
hysteron proteron
inversion
irony
kenning
litotes
malapropism
meiosis
metaphor
metonymy
onomatopoeia
oxymoron
paralipsis
parenthesis
periphrasis
personification
pleonasm
polysyndeton
prolepsis
prosopopoeia
repetition
rhetorical question
sarcasm
simile
snowclone
spoonerism
syllepsis
synechdoche
tmesis
zeugma

cloud, blur, mist, veil, opacity, haziness, mistiness: *There was a sort of film over my eyes.*
▷ VERB **1 = photograph**, record, shoot, video, videotape, take: *We filmed the scene in one hour.* **2 = adapt for the screen**, make into a film: *He filmed her life story.*
▶ *related adjective*: cinematic

filter NOUN **= sieve**, mesh, gauze, strainer, membrane, riddle, sifter: *a paper coffee filter*
▷ VERB **1 = trickle**, leach, seep, percolate, well, escape, leak, penetrate, ooze, dribble, exude: *Water filtered through the peat.* **2** (*with* **through**) **= purify**, treat, strain, refine, riddle, sift, sieve, winnow, filtrate, screen: *The best prevention for cholera is to filter water.*

filth NOUN **1 = dirt**, refuse, pollution, muck, garbage, sewage, contamination, dung, sludge, squalor, grime, faeces, slime, excrement, nastiness, carrion, excreta, crud (*slang*), foulness, putrefaction, ordure, defilement, kak (*S. African taboo slang*), grot (*slang*), filthiness, uncleanness, putrescence, foul matter: *tons of filth and sewage*
2 = obscenity, corruption, pornography, indecency, impurity, vulgarity, smut, vileness, dirty-mindedness: *The dialogue was all filth and innuendo.*

filthy ADJECTIVE **1 = dirty**, nasty, foul, polluted, vile, squalid, slimy, unclean, putrid, faecal, scummy, scuzzy (*slang, chiefly U.S.*), feculent, festy (*Austral. slang*): *The water looks stale and filthy.*
2 = grimy, black, muddy, smoky, blackened, grubby, sooty, unwashed, mucky, scuzzy (*slang, chiefly U.S.*), begrimed, mud-encrusted, miry, festy (*Austral. slang*): *He always wore a filthy old jacket.* **3 = obscene**, foul, corrupt, coarse, indecent, pornographic, suggestive, lewd, depraved, foul-mouthed, X-rated (*informal*), bawdy, impure, smutty, licentious, dirty-minded: *The play was full of filthy foul language.* **4 = despicable**, mean, low, base, offensive, vicious, vile, contemptible, scurvy: *'You filthy swine!' Penelope shouted.*

final ADJECTIVE **1 = last**, latest, end, closing, finishing, concluding, ultimate, terminal, last-minute, eventual, terminating: *the final book in the series* **OPPOSITE:** first
2 = irrevocable, absolute, decisive, definitive, decided, finished, settled, definite, conclusive, irrefutable, incontrovertible, unalterable, determinate, net-net (*informal*): *The judge's decision is final.*

finale NOUN **= climax**, ending, close, conclusion, culmination, denouement, last part, epilogue, last act, crowning glory, finis
OPPOSITE: opening

finality NOUN **= conclusiveness**, resolution, decisiveness, certitude, definiteness, irrevocability, inevitableness, unavoidability, decidedness

finalize *or* **finalise** VERB **= complete**, settle, conclude, tie up, decide, agree, work out, clinch, wrap up (*informal*), shake hands, sew up (*informal*), complete the arrangements for

finally ADVERB **1 = eventually**, at last, in the end, ultimately, at the last, at the end of the day, in the long run, at length, at the last moment, at long last, when all is said and done, in the fullness of time, after a long time: *The food finally arrived at the end of the week.*
2 = lastly, in the end, ultimately: *Finally came the dessert trolley* **3 = in conclusion**, lastly, in closing, to conclude, to sum up, in summary: *Finally, a word or two of advice.*
4 = conclusively, for good, permanently, for ever, completely, definitely, once and for all, decisively, convincingly, inexorably, irrevocably, for all time, inescapably, beyond the shadow of a doubt: *Finally they are drawing a line under the affair.*

finance NOUN **= economics**, business, money, banking, accounts, investment, commerce, financial affairs, money management: *a major player in the world of high finance*
▷ PLURAL NOUN **= resources**, money, funds, capital, cash, affairs, budgeting, assets, cash flow, financial affairs, money management, wherewithal, financial condition: *Women manage the day-to-day finances.*
▷ VERB **= fund**, back, support, pay for, guarantee, float, invest in, underwrite, endow, subsidize, bankroll (*U.S.*), set up in business, provide security for, provide money for: *new taxes to finance increased military expenditure*

financial ADJECTIVE **= economic**, business, money, budgeting, budgetary, commercial, monetary, fiscal, pecuniary, pocketbook

find VERB **1 = discover**, turn up, uncover, unearth, spot, expose, come up with, locate, detect, come across, track down, catch sight of, stumble upon, hit upon, espy, ferret out, chance upon, light upon, put your finger on, lay your hand on, run to ground, run to earth, descry: *The police also found a pistol.* **OPPOSITE:** lose
2 = regain, recover, get back, retrieve, repossess: *Luckily she found her bag.*
3 = obtain, get, come by, procure, win, gain, achieve, earn, acquire, attain: *Many people here cannot find work.*
4 = encounter, meet, recognize: *They found her walking alone on the beach.*
5 = observe, learn, note, discover, notice, realize, remark, come up with, arrive at, perceive, detect, become aware, experience, ascertain: *The study found that heart disease can begin in childhood.* **6 = feel**, have, experience, sense, obtain, know: *Could anyone find pleasure in killing this creature?*
7 = provide, supply, contribute, furnish, cough up (*informal*), purvey, be responsible for, bring: *Their parents can usually find the money for them.*
▷ NOUN **= discovery**, catch, asset, bargain, acquisition, good buy: *Another lucky find was a pair of candle-holders.*
find someone out = detect, catch, unmask, rumble (*Brit. informal*), reveal, expose, disclose, uncover, suss (out) (*slang*), bring to light: *I wondered for a moment if she'd found me out.*
find something out = learn, discover, realize, observe, perceive, detect, become aware, come to know, note: *It was such a relief to find out that the boy was normal.*

PROVERBS
finders keepers

finding NOUN **= judgment**, ruling, decision, award, conclusion, verdict, recommendation, decree, pronouncement

fine[1] ADJECTIVE **1 = excellent**, good, great, striking, choice, beautiful, masterly, select, rare, very good, supreme, impressive, outstanding, magnificent, superior, accomplished, sterling, first-class, divine, exceptional, splendid, world-class, exquisite, admirable, skilful, ornate, first-rate, showy, bakgat (*S. African*): *This is a fine book.* **OPPOSITE:** poor
2 = satisfactory, good, all right, suitable, acceptable, convenient, agreeable, hunky-dory (*informal*), fair, O.K. *or* okay (*informal*): *It's fine to ask questions as we go along.* **3 = thin**, small, light, narrow, wispy: *The heat scorched the fine hairs on her arms.* **4 = delicate**, light, thin, sheer, lightweight, flimsy, wispy, gossamer, diaphanous, gauzy, chiffony: *Her suit was of a pale grey fine material.* **OPPOSITE:** coarse
5 = stylish, expensive, elegant, refined, tasteful, quality, schmick (*Austral. informal*): *We waited in our fine clothes.* **6 = exquisite**, delicate, fragile, dainty: *She wears fine jewellery wherever she goes.* **7 = minute**, exact, precise, nice: *They are reserving judgement on the fine detail.* **8 = keen**, minute, nice, quick, sharp, critical, acute, sensitive, subtle, precise, refined, discriminating, tenuous, fastidious, hairsplitting: *She has a fine eye for detail.*
9 = brilliant, quick, keen, alert, clever, intelligent, penetrating, astute: *He had a fine mind and excellent knowledge.*
10 = sharp, keen, polished, honed, razor-sharp, cutting: *tapering to a fine point* **11 = good-looking**, striking, pretty, attractive, lovely, smart, handsome, stylish, bonny, well-favoured, fit (*Brit. informal*): *You're a very fine woman.* **12 = sunny**, clear, fair, dry, bright, pleasant, clement, balmy, cloudless: *I'll do the garden if the weather is fine.* **OPPOSITE:** cloudy **13 = pure**, clear, refined, unadulterated, unalloyed, unpolluted, solid, sterling: *a light, fine oil, high in vitamin content*

fine² NOUN **= penalty**, damages, punishment, forfeit, financial penalty, amercement *(obsolete)*: *If convicted he faces a fine of one million dollars.*
▷ VERB **= penalize**, charge, punish: *She was fined £300 and banned from driving.*

finery NOUN **= splendour**, trappings, frippery, glad rags *(informal)*, gear *(informal)*, decorations, ornaments, trinkets, Sunday best, gewgaws, showiness, best bib and tucker *(informal)*, bling *(slang)*

finesse NOUN **1 = skill**, style, know-how *(informal)*, polish, craft, sophistication, cleverness, quickness, adroitness, adeptness **2 = diplomacy**, discretion, subtlety, delicacy, tact, savoir-faire, artfulness, adeptness: *handling diplomatic challenges with finesse*
▷ VERB **= manoeuvre**, steer, manipulate, bluff: *a typical politician trying to finesse a sticky situation*

finger NOUN **1 = digit**, thumb, forefinger, little finger, index finger, middle finger, ring finger, third finger, first finger, second finger, fourth finger **2 = strip**, piece, band, sliver, bit
▷ VERB **= touch**, feel, handle, play with, manipulate, paw *(informal)*, maul, toy with, fiddle with *(informal)*, meddle with, play about with: *He fingered the few coins in his pocket.*
= inform on, shop *(slang, chiefly Brit.)*, grass *(Brit. slang)*, rat *(informal)*, betray, notify, peach *(slang)*, tip off, squeal *(slang)*, leak to, incriminate, tell on *(informal)*, blow the whistle on *(informal)*, snitch *(slang)*, blab, nark *(Brit., Austral. & N.Z. slang)*, inculpate, dob in *(Austral. slang)*
put your finger on something = identify, place, remember, discover, indicate, recall, find out, locate, pin down, bring to mind, hit upon, hit the nail on the head: *She couldn't quite put her finger on the reason.*
▸ *related adjective:* digital

finish VERB **1 = stop**, close, complete, achieve, conclude, cease, accomplish, execute, discharge, culminate, wrap up *(informal)*, terminate, round off, bring to a close *or* conclusion: *He was cheered when he finished his speech.* **OPPOSITE:** start **2 = get done**, complete, put the finishing touch(es) to, finalize, do, deal with, settle, conclude, fulfil, carry through, get out of the way, make short work of: *They've been working to finish a report this week.* **3 = end**, stop, conclude, wind up, terminate: *The teaching day finished at around 4pm.* **4 = consume**, dispose of, devour, polish off, drink, eat, drain, get through, dispatch, deplete: *He finished his dinner and left.* **5 = use up**, use, spend, empty, exhaust, expend: *Once you have finished all 21 pills, stop for seven days.* **6 = coat**, polish, stain, texture, wax, varnish, gild, veneer, lacquer, smooth off, face: *The bowl is finished in a pearlized lustre.* **7** *(often with* **off**) **= destroy**, defeat, overcome, bring down, best, worst, ruin, get rid of, dispose of, rout, put an end to, overpower, annihilate, put paid to, move in for the kill, drive to the wall, administer *or* give the coup de grâce: *I played well but I didn't finish him off.*
8 *(often with* **off**) **= kill**, murder, destroy, do in *(slang)*, take out *(slang)*, massacre, butcher, slaughter, dispatch, slay, eradicate, do away with, blow away *(slang, chiefly U.S.)*, knock off *(slang)*, annihilate, exterminate, take (someone's) life, bump off *(slang)*: *She finished him off with an axe.*
▷ NOUN **1 = end**, ending, close, closing, conclusion, run-in, winding up *(informal)*, wind-up, completion, finale, termination, culmination, cessation, last stage(s), denouement, finalization: *I intend to see the job through to the finish.* **OPPOSITE:** beginning
2 = surface, appearance, polish, shine, grain, texture, glaze, veneer, lacquer, lustre, smoothness, patina: *The finish of the woodwork was excellent.*

finished ADJECTIVE **1 = over**, done, completed, achieved, through, ended, closed, full, final, complete, in the past, concluded, shut, accomplished, executed, tied up, wrapped up *(informal)*, terminated, sewn up *(informal)*, finalized, over and done with: *Finally, last spring, the film was finished.* **OPPOSITE:** begun **2 = ruined**, done for *(informal)*, doomed, bankrupt, through, lost, gone, defeated, devastated, wrecked, wiped out, undone, washed up *(informal, chiefly U.S.)*, wound up, liquidated: *'This business is finished,' he said sadly.*

finite ADJECTIVE **= limited**, bounded, restricted, demarcated, conditioned, circumscribed, delimited, terminable, subject to limitations
OPPOSITE: infinite

fire NOUN **1 = flames**, blaze, combustion, inferno, conflagration, holocaust: *A forest fire is sweeping across the country.* **2 = passion**, force, light, energy, heat, spirit, enthusiasm, excitement, dash, intensity, sparkle, life, vitality, animation, vigour, zeal, splendour, verve, fervour, eagerness, dynamism, lustre, radiance, virtuosity, élan, ardour, brio, vivacity, impetuosity, burning passion, scintillation, fervency, pizzazz *or* pizazz *(informal)*: *His punishing schedule seemed to dim his fire at times.*
3 = bombardment, shooting, firing, shelling, hail, volley, barrage, gunfire, sniping, flak, salvo, fusillade, cannonade: *His car was raked with fire from automatic weapons.*
▷ VERB **1 = let off**, shoot, launch, shell, loose, set off, discharge, hurl, eject, detonate, let loose *(informal)*, touch off: *a huge gun designed to fire nuclear or chemical shells* **2 = shoot**, explode, discharge, detonate, pull the trigger: *Soldiers fired rubber bullets to disperse crowds.* **3 = dismiss**, sack *(informal)*, get rid of, discharge, lay off, make redundant, cashier, give notice, show the door, give the boot *(slang)*, kiss off *(slang, chiefly U.S. & Canad.)*, give the push, give the bullet *(Brit. slang)*, give marching orders, give someone their cards, give the sack to *(informal)*, kennet *(Austral. slang)*, jeff *(Austral. slang)*: *She was sent a letter saying she was fired from her job.* **4 = inspire**, excite, stir, stimulate, motivate, irritate, arouse, awaken, animate, rouse, stir up, quicken, inflame, incite, electrify, enliven, spur on, galvanize, inspirit, impassion: *They were fired with an enthusiasm for public speaking.* **5 = set fire to**, torch, ignite, set on fire, kindle, set alight, set ablaze, put a match to, set aflame, enkindle, light: *matches, turpentine and cotton, with which they fired the houses*
on fire 1 = burning, flaming, blazing, alight, ablaze, in flames, aflame, fiery: *The captain radioed that the ship was on fire.* **2 = ardent**, excited, inspired, eager, enthusiastic, passionate, fervent: *He was on fire, youthfully impatient.*
▸ *related mania:* pyromania

> **PROVERBS**
> *Fight fire with fire*
> *Fire is a good servant but a bad master*
> *If you play with fire you get burnt*
> *Out of the frying pan, into the fire*

firearm NOUN **= gun**, weapon, handgun, revolver, shooter *(slang)*, piece *(slang)*, rod *(slang)*, pistol, heater *(U.S. slang)*

firebrand NOUN **= rabble-rouser**, activist, incendiary, fomenter, instigator, agitator, demagogue, tub-thumper, soapbox orator

fireworks PLURAL NOUN
1 = pyrotechnics, illuminations, feux d'artifice: *The rally ended with spectacular fireworks and band music.* **2 = trouble**, row, storm, rage, temper, wax *(informal, chiefly Brit.)*, uproar, hysterics, paroxysms, fit of rage: *The big media companies will be forced to compete, and we should see some fireworks.*

firm¹ ADJECTIVE **1 = hard**, solid, compact, dense, set, concentrated, stiff, compacted, rigid, compressed, inflexible, solidified, unyielding, congealed, inelastic, jelled, close-grained, jellified: *Fruit should be firm and excellent in condition.* **OPPOSITE:** soft
2 = secure, strong, fixed, secured, rooted, stable, steady, anchored, braced, robust, cemented, fast, sturdy, embedded, fastened, riveted, taut, stationary, motionless, immovable, unmoving, unshakeable, unfluctuating: *use a firm platform or a sturdy ladder* **OPPOSITE:** unstable
3 = strong, close, tight, steady: *The quick handshake was firm and cool.*
4 = strict, unwavering, unswerving, unshakeable, constant, stalwart, resolute, inflexible, steadfast, unyielding, immovable, unflinching,

unbending, obdurate, unalterable, unfaltering: *They needed the guiding hand of a firm father figure.* **5 = determined**, true, settled, fixed, resolved, strict, definite, set on, adamant, stalwart, staunch, resolute, inflexible, steadfast, unyielding, unwavering, immovable, unflinching, unswerving, unbending, obdurate, unshakeable, unalterable, unshaken, unfaltering: *He held a firm belief in the afterlife.* **OPPOSITE:** wavering **6 = definite**, hard, clear, confirmed, settled, fixed, hard-and-fast, cut-and-dried *(informal)*: *firm evidence*

firm² NOUN **= company**, business, concern, association, organization, house, corporation, venture, enterprise, partnership, establishment, undertaking, outfit *(informal)*, consortium, conglomerate: *The firm's employees were expecting large bonuses.*

firmament NOUN **= sky**, skies, heaven, heavens, the blue, vault, welkin *(archaic)*, empyrean *(poetic)*, vault of heaven, rangi *(N.Z.)*

firmly ADVERB **1 = securely**, safely, tightly: *The door is locked and the windows are firmly shut.* **2 = immovably**, securely, steadily, like a rock, unflinchingly, enduringly, motionlessly, unshakeably: *boards firmly fixed to metal posts in the ground* **3 = steadily**, securely, tightly, unflinchingly: *She held me firmly by the elbow.* **4 = resolutely**, strictly, staunchly, steadfastly, determinedly, through thick and thin, with decision, with a rod of iron, definitely, unwaveringly, unchangeably: *Political opinions are firmly held.*

firmness NOUN **1 = hardness**, resistance, density, rigidity, stiffness, solidity, inflexibility, compactness, fixedness, inelasticity: *the firmness of the ground* **2 = steadiness**, tension, stability, tightness, soundness, tautness, tensile strength, immovability: *testing the firmness of the nearest stakes* **3 = strength**, tightness, steadiness: *He was surprised at the firmness of her grip.* **4 = resolve**, resolution, constancy, inflexibility, steadfastness, obduracy, strictness, strength of will, fixity, fixedness, staunchness: *There was no denying his considerable firmness of purpose.*

first ADJECTIVE **1 = earliest**, initial, opening, introductory, original, maiden, primitive, primordial, primeval, pristine: *The first men of this race lived like gods; the first few flakes of snow* **2 = top**, best, winning, premier: *The first prize is thirty-one thousand pounds.* **3 = elementary**, key, basic, primary, fundamental, cardinal, rudimentary, elemental: *It is time to go back to first principles.* **4 = foremost**, highest, greatest, leading, head, ruling, chief, prime, supreme, principal, paramount, overriding, pre-eminent: *The first priority for development is to defeat inflation.*
▷ NOUN **= novelty**, innovation, originality, new experience: *It is a first for New York.*
▷ ADVERB **= to begin with**, firstly, initially, at the beginning, in the first place, beforehand, to start with, at the outset, before all else: *I do not remember who spoke first.*
from the first = start, beginning, outset, the very beginning, introduction, starting point, inception, commencement, the word 'go' *(informal)*: *You knew about me from the first, didn't you?*

> **QUOTATIONS**
> Many that are first shall be last; and the last shall be first
> [*Bible: St. Mark*]

> **PROVERBS**
> *First come, first served*
> *First things first*

first class *or* **first-class** ADJECTIVE **= excellent**, great, very good, superb, topping *(Brit. slang)*, top, tops *(slang)*, bad *(slang)*, prime, capital, choice, champion, cool *(informal)*, brilliant, crack *(slang)*, mean *(slang)*, cracking *(Brit. informal)*, crucial *(slang)*, outstanding, premium, ace *(informal)*, marvellous, exceptional, mega *(slang)*, sovereign, dope *(slang)*, world-class, blue-chip, top-flight, top-class, five-star, exemplary, wicked *(slang)*, first-rate, def *(slang)*, superlative, second to none, top-notch *(informal)*, brill *(informal)*, top-drawer, matchless, tiptop, boffo *(slang)*, jim-dandy *(slang)*, twenty-four carat, A1 *or* A-one *(informal)*, bitchin' *(U.S. slang)*, chillin' *(U.S. slang)*, booshit *(Austral. slang)*, exo *(Austral. slang)*, sik *(Austral. slang)*, rad *(informal)*, phat *(slang)*, schmick *(Austral. informal)*, beaut *(informal)*, barrie *(Scot. slang)*, belting *(Brit. slang)*, pearler *(Austral. slang)*
OPPOSITE: terrible

first-hand ADJECTIVE **= direct**, personal, immediate, face-to-face, straight from the horse's mouth: *He'll get a first-hand briefing on the emergency.*
at first hand = directly, personally, immediately, face-to-face, straight from the horse's mouth: *I heard all about it first-hand.*

first-rate ADJECTIVE **= excellent**, outstanding, first class, exceptional, mean *(slang)*, topping *(Brit. slang)*, top, tops *(slang)*, prime, cool *(informal)*, crack *(slang)*, cracking *(Brit. informal)*, crucial *(slang)*, exclusive, superb, mega *(slang)*, sovereign, dope *(slang)*, world-class, admirable, wicked *(slang)*, def *(slang)*, superlative, second to none, top-notch *(informal)*, brill *(informal)*, tiptop, bodacious *(slang, chiefly U.S.)*, boffo *(slang)*, jim-dandy *(slang)*, A1 *or* A-one *(informal)*, bitchin' *(U.S. slang)*, chillin' *(U.S. slang)*, booshit *(Austral. slang)*, exo *(Austral. slang)*, sik *(Austral. slang)*, rad *(informal)*, phat *(slang)*, schmick *(Austral. informal)*

fiscal ADJECTIVE **= financial**, money, economic, monetary, budgetary, pecuniary, tax

fish VERB **1 = angle**, net, cast, trawl: *He learnt to fish in the River Cam.* **2 = look (for)**, search, delve, ferret, rummage, fossick *(Austral. & N.Z.)*: *He fished in his pocket for the key.*
fish for something = seek, look for, angle for, try to get, hope for, hunt for, hint at, elicit, solicit, invite, search for: *She may be fishing for a compliment.*
fish something out = pull out, produce, take out, extract, bring out, extricate, haul out, find: *She fished out a pair of his socks.*
▸ *related adjectives:* piscine, ichthyoid
▸ *name of young:* fry ▸ *collective noun:* shoal

fishy ADJECTIVE **1 = fishlike**, piscine, piscatorial, piscatory: *It hasn't a very strong fishy flavour.* **2 = suspicious**, odd, suspect, unlikely, funny *(informal)*, doubtful, dubious, dodgy *(Brit., Austral. & N.Z. informal)*, queer, rum *(Brit. slang)*, questionable, improbable, implausible, cock-and-bull *(informal)*, shonky *(Austral. & N.Z. informal)*: *There seems to be something fishy going on.*

fission NOUN **= splitting**, parting, breaking, division, rending, rupture, cleavage, schism, scission

fissure NOUN **= crack**, opening, hole, split, gap, rent, fault, breach, break, fracture, rift, slit, rupture, cleavage, cleft, chink, crevice, cranny, interstice

fit¹ VERB **1 = adapt**, fashion, shape, arrange, alter, adjust, modify, tweak *(informal)*, customize: *She was having her wedding dress fitted.* **2 = place**, position, insert: *She fitted her key in the lock.* **3 = attach**, join, connect, interlock: *Fit hinge bolts to give support to the door lock.* **4 = suit**, meet, match, belong to, agree with, go with, conform to, correspond to, accord with, be appropriate to, concur with, tally with, dovetail with, be consonant with: *Her daughter doesn't fit the current feminine ideal.* **5 = equip**, provide, arm, prepare, outfit, accommodate, fit out, kit out, rig out, accoutre: *The bombs were fitted with time devices.*
▷ ADJECTIVE **1 = appropriate**, qualified, suitable, competent, right, becoming, meet *(archaic)*, seemly, trained, able, prepared, fitting, fitted, ready, skilled, correct, deserving, capable, adapted, proper, equipped, good enough, adequate, worthy, convenient, apt, well-suited, expedient, apposite: *You're not fit to be a mother!* **OPPOSITE:** inappropriate **2 = healthy**, strong, robust, sturdy, well, trim, strapping, hale, in good shape, in good condition, in good health, toned up, as right as rain, in good trim, able-bodied: *It will take a very fit person to beat me.* **OPPOSITE:** unfit

f

fit[2] NOUN **1 = seizure**, attack, bout, spasm, convulsion, paroxysm: *Once a fit has started there's nothing you can do to stop it.* **2 = bout**, burst, outbreak, outburst, spell: *I broke into a fit of giggles.*
have a fit = go mad, explode, blow up (*informal*), lose it (*informal*), see red (*informal*), lose the plot (*informal*), throw a tantrum, fly off the handle (*informal*), go spare (*Brit. slang*), blow your top (*informal*), fly into a temper, flip your lid (*slang*), do your nut (*Brit. slang*): *He'd have a fit if he knew what we were up to!*
in *or* **by fits and starts = spasmodically**, sporadically, erratically, fitfully, on and off, irregularly, intermittently, off and on, unsystematically: *Military technology advances by fits and starts.*

fitful ADJECTIVE **= irregular**, broken, disturbed, erratic, variable, flickering, unstable, uneven, fluctuating, sporadic, intermittent, impulsive, haphazard, desultory, spasmodic, inconstant
OPPOSITE: regular

fitfully ADVERB **= irregularly**, on and off, intermittently, sporadically, off and on, erratically, in fits and starts, spasmodically, in snatches, desultorily, by fits and starts, interruptedly

fitness NOUN **1 = appropriateness**, qualifications, adaptation, competence, readiness, eligibility, suitability, propriety, preparedness, applicability, aptness, pertinence, seemliness: *There is a debate about his fitness for the job.* **2 = health**, strength, good health, vigour, good condition, wellness, robustness: *Squash was thought to offer all-round fitness.*

fitted ADJECTIVE **= built-in**, permanent: *I've recarpeted our bedroom and added fitted wardrobes.*

fitting ADJECTIVE **= appropriate**, suitable, proper, apt, right, becoming, meet (*archaic*), seemly, correct, decent, desirable, apposite, decorous, comme il faut (*French*): *The President's address was a fitting end to the campaign.*
OPPOSITE: unsuitable
▷ NOUN **= accessory**, part, piece, unit, connection, component, attachment: *brass light fittings*
▷ PLURAL NOUN **= furnishings**, extras, equipment, fixtures, appointments, furniture, trimmings, accessories, conveniences, accoutrements, bells and whistles, fitments, appurtenances: *He has made fittings for antique cars.*

fix VERB **1 = place**, join, stick, attach, set, position, couple, plant, link, establish, tie, settle, secure, bind, root, connect, locate, pin, install, anchor, glue, cement, implant, embed, fasten, make fast: *Fix the photo to the card using double-sided tape* **2** (*often with* **up**) **= decide**, set, name, choose, limit, establish, determine, settle, appoint, arrange, define, conclude, resolve, arrive at, specify, agree on: *He's fixed a time when I can see him.* **3** (*often with* **up**) **= arrange**, organize, sort out, see to, make arrangements for: *I've fixed it for you to see them.* **4 = repair**, mend, service, sort, correct, restore, adjust, regulate, see to, overhaul, patch up, get working, put right, put to rights: *If something is broken, we fix it.* **5 = focus**, direct at, level at, fasten on, rivet on: *Attention is fixed on the stock market.* **6 = rig**, set up (*informal*), influence, manipulate, bribe, manoeuvre, fiddle (*informal*), pull strings (*informal*): *They offered players bribes to fix a league match.* **7 = stabilize**, set, consolidate, harden, thicken, stiffen, solidify, congeal, rigidify: *Egg yolk is used to fix the pigment.*
▷ NOUN **= mess**, spot (*informal*), corner, hole (*slang*), difficulty, jam (*informal*), dilemma, embarrassment, plight, hot water (*informal*), pickle (*informal*), uphill (*S. African*), predicament, difficult situation, quandary, tight spot, ticklish situation: *The government has got itself in a fix.*
fix someone up (*often with* **with**) **= provide**, supply, accommodate, bring about, furnish, lay on, arrange for: *We'll fix him up with a job.*
fix something up = arrange, plan, settle, fix, organize, sort out, agree on, make arrangements for: *I fixed up an appointment to see her.*

> **PROVERBS**
> *If it ain't broke, don't fix it*

fixated ADJECTIVE **= obsessed**, fascinated, preoccupied, captivated, attached, devoted, absorbed, caught up in, single-minded, smitten, taken up with, besotted, wrapped up in, engrossed, spellbound, infatuated, mesmerized, hypnotized, hung up on (*slang*), monomaniacal, prepossessed
OPPOSITE: uninterested

fixation NOUN **= obsession**, complex, addiction, hang-up (*informal*), preoccupation, mania, infatuation, idée fixe (*French*), thing (*informal*)

fixed ADJECTIVE **1 = inflexible**, set, steady, resolute, unwavering, unflinching, unblinking, unbending, undeviating: *people who have fixed ideas about things* **OPPOSITE:** wavering **2 = immovable**, set, established, secure, rooted, permanent, attached, anchored, rigid, made fast: *Nato was concentrating on hitting buildings and other fixed structures.* **OPPOSITE:** mobile **3 = agreed**, set, planned, decided, established, settled, arranged, resolved, specified, definite: *The deal was settled at a prearranged fixed price* **4 = rigged**, framed, put-up, manipulated, packed: *Some races are fixed.*

fizz VERB **1 = bubble**, froth, fizzle, effervesce, produce bubbles: *She was holding a tray of glasses that fizzed.* **2 = sputter**, buzz, sparkle, hiss, crackle: *The engine fizzed and went dead.*

fizzle VERB (*often with* **out**) **= die away**, fail, collapse, fold (*informal*), abort, fall through, peter out, come to nothing, miss the mark, end in disappointment

fizzy ADJECTIVE **= bubbly**, bubbling, sparkling, effervescent, carbonated, gassy

flab NOUN **= fat**, flesh, flabbiness, fleshiness, weight, beef (*informal*), heaviness, slackness, plumpness, loose flesh

flabbergasted ADJECTIVE **= astonished**, amazed, stunned, overcome, overwhelmed, staggered, astounded, dazed, confounded, disconcerted, speechless, bowled over (*informal*), gobsmacked (*Brit. slang*), dumbfounded, nonplussed, lost for words, struck dumb, abashed, rendered speechless

flabby ADJECTIVE **1 = limp**, hanging, loose, slack, unfit, sagging, sloppy, baggy, floppy, lax, drooping, flaccid, pendulous, toneless, yielding: *bulging thighs and flabby stomach* **OPPOSITE:** firm **2 = weak**, ineffective, feeble, impotent, wasteful, ineffectual, disorganized, spineless, effete, boneless, nerveless, enervated, wussy (*slang*), wimpish *or* wimpy (*informal*): *Many signs of flabby management remain.*

flaccid ADJECTIVE **= limp**, soft, weak, loose, slack, lax, drooping, flabby, nerveless

flag[1] NOUN **= banner**, standard, colours, jack, pennant, ensign, streamer, pennon, banderole, gonfalon: *They raised the white flag in surrender.*
▷ VERB **1 = mark**, identify, indicate, label, tab, pick out, note, docket: *I promise to flag these things more clearly.* **2** (*often with* **down**) **= hail**, stop, signal, salute, wave down: *They flagged a car down.*

> **QUOTATIONS**
> Then raise the scarlet standard high!
> Within its folds we'll live or die
> Tho' cowards flinch and traitors sneer
> We'll keep the red flag flying here
> [James M. Connell *The Red Flag*]

flag[2] VERB **= weaken**, fall, die, fail, decline, sink, fade, slump, pine, faint, weary, fall off, succumb, falter, wilt, wane, ebb, sag, languish, abate, droop, peter out, taper off, feel the pace, lose your strength: *His enthusiasm was in no way flagging.*

flagging ADJECTIVE **= weakening**, failing, declining, waning, giving up, tiring, sinking, fading, decreasing, slowing down, deteriorating, wearying, faltering, wilting, ebbing

flagrant ADJECTIVE **= outrageous**, open, blatant, barefaced, shocking, crying, enormous, awful, bold, dreadful, notorious, glaring, infamous, scandalous, flaunting, atrocious, brazen, shameless, out-and-out, heinous, ostentatious, egregious, undisguised, immodest, arrant, flagitious **OPPOSITE:** slight

flagstone NOUN **= paving stone**, flag, slab, block

flail VERB **= thrash**, beat, windmill, thresh

flair NOUN **1 = ability**, feel, talent, gift, genius, faculty, accomplishment, mastery, knack, aptitude: *She has a flair for languages.* **2 = style**, taste, dash, chic, elegance, panache, discernment, stylishness: *the panache and flair you'd expect*

flak NOUN **= criticism**, stick *(slang)*, opposition, abuse, complaints, hostility, condemnation, censure, disapproval, bad press, denigration, brickbats *(informal)*, disparagement, fault-finding, disapprobation

flake NOUN **= chip**, scale, layer, peeling, shaving, disk, wafer, sliver, lamina, squama *(Biology)*: *flakes of paint*
▷ VERB **= chip**, scale (off), peel (off), blister, desquamate: *Some of the shell had flaked away.*

flamboyance NOUN **= showiness**, show, style, dash, sparkle, chic, flair, verve, swagger, extravagance, panache, pomp, glitz *(informal)*, élan, bravura, swank *(informal)*, theatricality, exhibitionism, brio, ostentation, stylishness, flashiness, flamboyancy, floridity, pizzazz *or* pizazz *(informal)* **OPPOSITE:** restraint

flamboyant ADJECTIVE **1 = camp** *(informal)*, dashing, theatrical: *He was a flamboyant personality.* **2 = showy**, rich, elaborate, over the top *(informal)*, extravagant, baroque, ornate, ostentatious, rococo: *flamboyant architectural paint effects* **3 = colourful**, striking, exciting, brilliant, glamorous, stylish, dazzling, glitzy *(slang)*, showy, florid, bling *(slang)*, swashbuckling: *He wears flamboyant clothes.*

flame NOUN **1 = fire**, light, spark, glow, blaze, brightness, inferno: *a huge ball of flame* **2 = passion**, fire, enthusiasm, intensity, affection, warmth, fervour, ardour, keenness, fervency: *that burning flame of love* **3 = sweetheart**, partner, lover, girlfriend, boyfriend, beloved, heart-throb *(Brit.)*, beau, ladylove: *She kept inviting his old flame round to their house.*
▷ VERB **= burn**, flash, shine, glow, blaze, flare, glare: *His dark eyes flamed with rage.*

flaming ADJECTIVE **1 = burning**, blazing, fiery, ignited, red, brilliant, raging, glowing, red-hot, ablaze, in flames, afire: *A group followed carrying flaming torches.* **2 = intense**, angry, raging, impassioned, hot, aroused, vivid, frenzied, ardent, scintillating, vehement: *She had a flaming row with her lover.*

flammable ADJECTIVE **= combustible**, incendiary, inflammable, ignitable

> **USAGE**
> *Flammable* and *inflammable* are interchangeable when used of the properties of materials. *Flammable* is, however, often preferred for warning labels as there is less likelihood of misunderstanding (*inflammable* being sometimes taken to mean *not flammable*). *Inflammable* is preferred in figurative contexts: *this could prove to be an inflammable situation.*

flank NOUN **1 = side**, quarter, hip, thigh, loin, haunch, ham: *He put his hand on the dog's flank.* **2 = wing**, side, sector, aspect: *The assault element opened up from their right flank.*
▷ VERB **= border**, line, wall, screen, edge, circle, bound, skirt, fringe, book-end: *The altar was flanked by two Christmas trees.*

flannel NOUN **= waffle** *(Brit. informal)*, flattery, blarney, sweet talk *(U.S. informal)*, baloney *(informal)*, equivocation, hedging, prevarication, weasel words *(informal, chiefly U.S.)*, soft soap *(informal)*: *He gave me a lot of flannel.*
▷ VERB **= prevaricate**, hedge, flatter, waffle *(informal, chiefly Brit.)*, blarney, sweet-talk *(informal)*, soft-soap *(informal)*, equivocate, butter up, pull the wool over (someone's) eyes: *He flannelled and prevaricated.*

flap VERB **1 = flutter**, wave, swing, swish, flail: *Sheets flapped on the clothes line.* **2 = beat**, wave, thrash, flutter, agitate, wag, vibrate, shake, thresh: *The bird flapped its wings furiously.* **3 = panic**, fuss, dither *(chiefly Brit.)*: *There's no point in you flapping around in the kitchen, making your guest feel uneasy.*
▷ NOUN **1 = cover**, covering, tail, fold, skirt, tab, overlap, fly, apron, lapel, lappet: *He drew back the tent flap and strode out.* **2 = flutter**, beating, waving, shaking, swinging, bang, banging, swish: *the gunshot flap of a topsail* **3 = panic**, state *(informal)*, agitation, commotion, sweat *(informal)*, stew *(informal)*, dither *(chiefly Brit.)*, fluster, twitter *(informal)*, tizzy *(informal)*: *Wherever he goes, there's always a flap.*

flare VERB **1 = blaze**, flame, dazzle, glare, flicker, flutter, waver, burn up: *Camp fires flared like beacons in the dark.* **2 = widen**, spread, broaden, spread out, dilate, splay: *a dress cut to flare from the hips*
▷ NOUN **= flame**, burst, flash, blaze, dazzle, glare, flicker: *The flare of fires lights up the blacked-out streets.*
flare up = burn, explode, blaze, be on fire, go up in flames, be alight, flame: *The fire flared up again.*
▷ VERB **= lose your temper**, explode, lose it *(informal)*, lose control, lose the plot *(informal)*, throw a tantrum, fly off the handle *(informal)*, lose your cool *(informal)*, blow your top *(informal)*, fly into a temper: *She suddenly lost her temper with me and flared up.*

flash NOUN **1 = blaze**, ray, burst, spark, beam, sparkle, streak, flare, dazzle, shaft, glare, gleam, flicker, shimmer, twinkle, scintillation, coruscation: *a sudden flash of lightning* **2 = burst**, show, sign, touch, display, rush, demonstration, surge, outbreak, outburst, manifestation: *The essay could do with a flash of wit.*
▷ VERB **1 = blaze**, shine, beam, sparkle, glitter, flare, glare, gleam, light up, flicker, shimmer, twinkle, glint, glisten, scintillate, coruscate: *Lightning flashed among the distant dark clouds.* **2 = speed**, race, shoot, fly, tear, sweep, dash, barrel (along) *(informal, chiefly U.S. & Canad.)*, whistle, sprint, bolt, streak, dart, zoom, burn rubber *(informal)*: *Cars flashed by every few minutes.* **3 = show quickly**, display, expose, exhibit, flourish, show off, flaunt: *He flashed his official card.*
▷ ADJECTIVE **= ostentatious**, smart, glamorous, trendy, showy, cheap, bling *(slang)*: *flash jewellery and watches*
in a flash = in a moment, in a second, in an instant, in a split second, in a trice, in a jiffy *(informal)*, in the twinkling of an eye, in a twinkling, in two shakes of a lamb's tail *(informal)*, in the bat of an eye *(informal)*: *The answer came to him in a flash.*

flashy ADJECTIVE **= showy**, loud, over the top *(informal)*, flamboyant, brash, tacky *(informal)*, flaunting, glitzy *(slang)*, tasteless, naff *(Brit. slang)*, gaudy, garish, jazzy *(informal)*, tawdry, ostentatious, snazzy *(informal)*, glittery, meretricious, cheap and nasty, in poor taste, tinselly, bling *(slang)* **OPPOSITE:** plain

flat[1] ADJECTIVE **1 = even**, level, levelled, plane, smooth, uniform, horizontal, unbroken, planar: *Sit the cup on a flat surface while measuring.* **OPPOSITE:** uneven **2 = horizontal**, prone, outstretched, reclining, prostrate, laid low, supine, recumbent, lying full length: *Two men near him threw themselves flat.* **OPPOSITE:** upright **3 = punctured**, collapsed, burst, blown out, deflated, empty: *It was impossible to ride with a flat tyre.* **4 = used up**, finished, empty, drained, expired: *The battery was flat.* **5 = absolute**, firm, direct, straight, positive, fixed, plain, final, explicit, definite, outright, unconditional, downright, unmistakable, unequivocal, unqualified, out-and-out, categorical, peremptory: *She is likely to give you a flat refusal.* **6 = dull**, dead, empty, boring, depressing, pointless, tedious, stale, lacklustre, tiresome, lifeless, monotonous, uninteresting, insipid, unexciting, spiritless: *The past few days have been flat and empty.* **OPPOSITE:** exciting **7 = without energy**, empty, weak, tired, depressed, drained, weary, worn out, dispirited, downhearted, tired out: *I've been feeling flat at times.* **8 = monotonous**, boring, uniform, dull, tedious, droning, tiresome, unchanging, colourless, toneless, samey *(informal)*, uninflected, unvaried: *Her voice was flat, with no hope in it.*

f

▷ NOUN *(often plural)* = **plain**, strand, shallow, marsh, swamp, shoal, lowland, mud flat: *salt marshes and mud flats*
▷ ADVERB = **completely**, directly, absolutely, categorically, precisely, exactly, utterly, outright, point blank, unequivocally: *He had turned her down flat.*
flat out = **at full speed**, all out, to the full, hell for leather *(informal)*, as hard as possible, at full tilt, at full gallop, posthaste, for all you are worth, under full steam: *Everyone is working flat out.*

flat[2] NOUN = **apartment**, rooms, quarters, digs, suite, penthouse, living quarters, duplex *(U.S. & Canad.)*, bachelor apartment *(Canad.)*: *She lives with her husband in a flat.*

f

flatly ADVERB = **absolutely**, completely, positively, categorically, unequivocally, unhesitatingly

flatten VERB **1** *(sometimes with* **out***)* = **level**, roll, plaster, squash, compress, trample, iron out, even out, smooth off: *How do you put enough pressure on to the metal to flatten it?* **2** *(sometimes with* **out***)* = **destroy**, level, ruin, demolish, knock down, pull down, tear down, throw down, bulldoze, raze, remove, kennet *(Austral. slang)*, jeff *(Austral. slang)*: *Bombing raids flattened much of the area.* **3** = **knock down**, fell, floor, deck *(slang)*, bowl over, prostrate, knock off your feet: *I've never seen a woman flatten someone like that!* **4** = **crush**, beat, defeat, trounce, master, worst, overwhelm, conquer, lick *(informal)*, undo, subdue, rout, overpower, quell, clobber *(slang)*, vanquish, run rings around *(informal)*, wipe the floor with *(informal)*, make mincemeat of *(informal)*, blow out of the water *(slang)*: *In the squash court his aim is to flatten me.*

flatter VERB **1** = **praise**, compliment, pander to, sweet-talk *(informal)*, court, humour, puff, flannel *(Brit. informal)*, fawn, cajole, lay it on (thick) *(slang)*, wheedle, inveigle, soft-soap *(informal)*, butter up, blandish: *I knew he was just flattering me.* **2** = **suit**, become, enhance, set off, embellish, do something for, show to advantage: *Orange flatters those with golden skin tones.*

flattering ADJECTIVE **1** = **becoming**, kind, effective, enhancing, well-chosen: *It wasn't a very flattering photograph.* **OPPOSITE:** unflattering **2** = **ingratiating**, complimentary, gratifying, fawning, sugary, fulsome, laudatory, adulatory, honeyed, honey-tongued: *The press was flattering.* **OPPOSITE:** uncomplimentary

flattery NOUN = **obsequiousness**, fawning, adulation, sweet-talk *(informal)*, flannel *(Brit. informal)*, blarney, soft-soap *(informal)*, sycophancy, servility, cajolery, blandishment, fulsomeness, toadyism, false praise, honeyed words

QUOTATIONS

I suppose flattery hurts no one, that is, if he doesn't inhale
[Adlai Stevenson]

Everyone likes flattery; and when you come to Royalty you should lay it on with a trowel
[Benjamin Disraeli]

flatulence NOUN = **wind**, borborygmus *(Medical)*, eructation: *Avoid any food that causes flatulence.*

flaunt VERB = **show off**, display, boast, parade, exhibit, flourish, brandish, vaunt, make a (great) show of, sport *(informal)*, disport, make an exhibition of, flash about

USAGE
Flaunt is sometimes wrongly used where *flout* is meant: *they must be prevented from flouting* (not *flaunting*) *the law.*

flavour *or* **flavor** NOUN **1** = **taste**, seasoning, flavouring, savour, extract, essence, relish, smack, aroma, odour, zest, tang, zing *(informal)*, piquancy, tastiness: *The cheese has a strong flavour.* **OPPOSITE:** blandness **2** = **quality**, feeling, feel, style, property, touch, character, aspect, tone, suggestion, stamp, essence, tinge, soupçon *(French)*: *clothes with a nostalgic Forties flavour*
▷ VERB = **season**, spice, add flavour to, enrich, infuse, imbue, pep up, leaven, ginger up, lace: *Flavour dishes with exotic herbs and spices.*

flavouring *or* **flavoring** NOUN = **essence**, extract, zest, tincture, spirit

flaw NOUN **1** = **weakness**, failing, defect, weak spot, spot, fault, scar, blemish, imperfection, speck, disfigurement, chink in your armour: *The only flaw in his character is a short temper.* **2** = **crack**, break, split, breach, tear, rent, fracture, rift, cleft, crevice, fissure, scission: *a flaw in the rock wide enough for a foot*

flawed ADJECTIVE **1** = **damaged**, defective, imperfect, blemished, broken, cracked, chipped, faulty: *the unique beauty of a flawed object* **2** = **erroneous**, incorrect, inaccurate, invalid, wrong, mistaken, false, faulty, untrue, unfounded, spurious, amiss, unsound, wide of the mark, inexact, fallacious: *The tests were seriously flawed.*

flawless ADJECTIVE = **perfect**, impeccable, faultless, spotless, unblemished, unsullied: *She has a flawless complexion.*

flay VERB **1** = **skin**, strip, peel, scrape, excoriate, remove the skin from: *to flay the flesh away from his muscles* **2** = **upbraid**, slam *(slang)*, castigate, revile, tear into *(informal)*, diss *(slang, chiefly U.S.)*, excoriate, tear a strip off, execrate, pull to pieces *(informal)*, give a tongue-lashing, criticize severely: *The critics flayed him with accusations of misanthropy.*

fleck NOUN = **mark**, speck, streak, spot, dot, pinpoint, speckle: *His hair is dark grey with flecks of ginger.*
▷ VERB = **speckle**, mark, spot, dust, dot, streak, dapple, stipple, mottle, variegate, bespeckle, besprinkle: *patches of red paint which flecked her blouse*

fledgling *or* **fledgeling** NOUN = **chick**, nestling, young bird: *The fathers of these fledglings are all dead.*

flee VERB = **run away**, leave, escape, bolt, fly, avoid, split *(slang)*, take off *(informal)*, get away, vanish, depart, run off, shun, make off, abscond, decamp, take flight, hook it *(slang)*, do a runner *(slang)*, scarper *(Brit. slang)*, slope off, cut and run *(informal)*, make a run for it, beat a hasty retreat, turn tail, fly the coop *(U.S. & Canad. informal)*, make a quick exit, skedaddle *(informal)*, make yourself scarce *(informal)*, take a powder *(U.S. & Canad. slang)*, make your escape, make your getaway, take it on the lam *(U.S. & Canad. slang)*, take to your heels

fleece NOUN = **wool**, hair, coat, fur, coat of wool: *a blanket of lamb's fleece*
▷ VERB = **cheat**, skin *(slang)*, steal, rob, con *(informal)*, rifle, stiff *(slang)*, soak *(U.S. & Canad. slang)*, bleed *(informal)*, rip off *(slang)*, plunder, defraud, overcharge, swindle, rook *(slang)*, diddle *(informal)*, take for a ride *(informal)*, despoil, take to the cleaners *(slang)*, sell a pup, cozen, mulct, scam *(slang)*: *She claims he fleeced her out of thousands of pounds.*

fleet[1] NOUN = **navy**, vessels, task force, squadron, warships, flotilla, armada, naval force, sea power, argosy: *damage inflicted upon the British fleet*

fleet[2] ADJECTIVE = **swift**, flying, fast, quick, winged, rapid, speedy, nimble, mercurial, meteoric, nimble-footed: *He was fleet as a deer.*

fleeting ADJECTIVE = **momentary**, short, passing, flying, brief, temporary, short-lived, fugitive, transient, flitting, ephemeral, transitory, evanescent, fugacious, here today, gone tomorrow **OPPOSITE:** lasting

flesh NOUN **1** = **fat**, muscle, beef *(informal)*, tissue, body, brawn: *Illness had wasted the flesh from her body.* **2** = **fatness**, fat, adipose tissue, corpulence, weight: *porcine wrinkles of flesh* **3** = **meat**, food: *the pale pink flesh of trout and salmon* **4** = **physical nature**, sensuality, physicality, carnality, body, human nature, flesh and blood, animality, sinful nature: *the sins of the flesh*
your own flesh and blood = **family**, blood, relations, relatives, kin, kindred, kith and kin, blood relations, kinsfolk, ainga *(N.Z.)*, rellies *(Austral. slang)*: *The kid was his own flesh and blood.*
▸ *related adjective:* carnal

The Language of JM Barrie

Scottish writer and playwright JM Barrie (1860–1937) is best known for creating Peter Pan, the central figure in both the play *Peter Pan, or The Boy Who Wouldn't Grow Up* and the novelized version, *Peter Pan and Wendy*, which tells more or less the same story. He also wrote other works about Peter Pan as well as a number of plays and novels on different subjects. *The Admirable Crichton*, for instance, is a comic play about the class system.

It is clear from *Peter Pan and Wendy* that Barrie was fond of children and knew exactly what was required to entertain them. He often builds up a picture of what seems to be normal everyday reality before suddenly transforming it into something quite different and very unexpected. He juxtaposes words (often formal and difficult ones) that suggest real-world normality with flights of fancy and ridiculous childlike behaviour in grown-ups so as to create a surreal and humorous whole, details of which would often have a particular appeal for adults:

> Mrs. Darling loved to have everything just so, and Mr. Darling had a passion for being exactly like his neighbours; so, of course, they had a nurse. As they were poor, owing to the amount of milk the children drank, this nurse was a prim Newfoundland dog, called Nana, who had belonged to no one in particular until the Darlings engaged her.
>
> 'No doubt, but I have an uneasy feeling at times that she looks upon the children as puppies.'
>
> 'Oh no, dear one, I feel sure she knows they have souls.'

In the same book Barrie uses personification to add to the sense of the surreal, with night-lights that *yawn* and can't *keep awake* and stars that are *fond of fun* and call out to Peter. Barrie makes sure he excites and maintains his reader's interest by posing questions about what will happen and hinting at terrible or exciting events in the future:

> Such is the terrible man against whom Peter Pan is pitted. Which will win?
>
> The opportunity came a week later, on that never-to-be-forgotten Friday.

In *Peter Pan and Wendy*, the female characters within Peter's orbit are shown to love him in a way he does not understand and to see themselves in competition with one another. The use of the harsh adjectives *cheap* and *abandoned* with reference to little Wendy and fairy Tinker Bell seems to hint at an underlying demanding but unwanted and incomprehensible female sexuality that may perhaps reflect some of Barrie's fears about women. Because Peter is young and uncomprehending, still with his baby *little pearls*, he does not have to confront these situations:

> She made herself rather **cheap** by inclining her face toward him, but he merely dropped an acorn button into her hand; so she slowly returned her face to where it had been before ...
>
> 'Oh yes, Tinker Bell will tell you,' Wendy retorted scornfully. 'She is an **abandoned** little creature.'

Barrie's interest in characters that remain young in this and other works may be linked to the tragic and deeply affecting death of an older brother when the writer was a child. Dead at 14, this boy would remain forever young in everyone's memory.

In some of his earliest published writings, *Auld Licht Idylls, A Window in Thrums*, and *The Little Minister* (those dealing with small-town Scottish life), Barrie draws on his Scottish upbringing in Kirriemuir, which becomes *Thrums* in his books. The style of these books is notably different: Barrie writes the dialogue of the local people in their native Scots, includes many Scots words in the narrative, and uses the *not* negative forms in the conversation of locals, where non-Scots would favour *n't*:

> 'If ye go on like that,' he said, 'I'll gang awa oot an' droon mysel, or be a sojer.'
>
> It climbs from a shallow **burn**, and we used to sit on the **brig** a long time before venturing to climb. As boys we ran up the **brae**.
>
> 'Why did you not kiss me?'

> QUOTATIONS
> Bone of my bones, and flesh of my flesh
> [*Bible: Genesis*]
>
> I saw him now going the way of all flesh
> [John Webster *Westward Hoe*]
>
> The spirit indeed is willing, but the flesh is weak
> [*Bible: St. Matthew*]

fleshy ADJECTIVE = **plump**, fat, chubby, obese, hefty, overweight, ample, stout, chunky, meaty, beefy *(informal)*, tubby, podgy, brawny, corpulent, well-padded

flex VERB = **bend**, contract, stretch, angle, curve, tighten, crook, move

f

flexibility NOUN **1 = elasticity**, pliability, springiness, pliancy, tensility, give *(informal)*: *The flexibility of the lens decreases with age.* **2 = adaptability**, openness, versatility, adjustability: *the flexibility of distance learning* **3 = complaisance**, accommodation, give and take, amenability: *They should be ready to show some flexibility.*

flexible ADJECTIVE **1 = pliable**, plastic, yielding, elastic, supple, lithe, limber, springy, willowy, pliant, tensile, stretchy, whippy, lissom(e), ductile, bendable, mouldable: *brushes with long, flexible bristles* **OPPOSITE:** rigid **2 = adaptable**, open, variable, adjustable, discretionary: *flexible working hours* **OPPOSITE:** inflexible **3 = compliant**, accommodating, manageable, amenable, docile, tractable, biddable, complaisant, responsive, gentle: *Their boss was flexible and lenient.* **OPPOSITE:** unyielding

flick VERB **1 = jerk**, pull, tug, lurch, jolt: *The man flicked his gun up from beside his thigh.* **2 = strike**, tap, jab, remove quickly, hit, touch, stroke, rap, flip, peck, whisk, dab, fillip: *She flicked a speck of fluff from her sleeve.*
▷ NOUN = **tap**, touch, sweep, stroke, rap, flip, peck, whisk, jab: *a flick of a paintbrush*
flick through something = **browse**, glance at, skim, leaf through, flip through, thumb through, skip through: *She flicked through some magazines.*

flicker VERB **1 = twinkle**, flash, sparkle, flare, shimmer, gutter, glimmer: *Firelight flickered on the faded furnishings.* **2 = flutter**, waver, quiver, vibrate: *Her eyelids flickered then opened.*
▷ NOUN **1 = glimmer**, flash, spark, flare, gleam: *I saw the flicker of flames.* **2 = trace**, drop, breath, spark, atom, glimmer, vestige, iota: *He felt a flicker of regret.*

flier *see* **flyer**

flight[1] NOUN **1 = journey**, trip, voyage: *The flight will take four hours.* **2 = aviation**, flying, air transport, aeronautics, aerial navigation: *Supersonic flight could become a routine form of travel.* **3 = flying**, winging, mounting, soaring, ability to fly: *These hawks are magnificent in flight.* **4 = flock**, group, unit, cloud, formation, squadron, swarm, flying group: *a flight of green parrots*

flight[2] NOUN = **escape**, fleeing, departure, retreat, exit, running away, exodus, getaway, absconding: *his secret flight into exile*
put to flight = **drive off**, scatter, disperse, rout, stampede, scare off, send packing, chase off: *We were put to flight by a herd of bullocks.*
take (to) flight = **run away** *or* **off**, flee, bolt, abscond, decamp, do a runner *(slang)*, turn tail, do a bunk *(Brit. slang)*, fly the coop *(U.S. & Canad. informal)*, beat a retreat, light out *(informal)*, skedaddle *(informal)*, make a hasty retreat, take a powder *(U.S. & Canad. slang)*, withdraw hastily, take it on the lam *(U.S. & Canad. slang)*, do a Skase *(Austral. informal)*: *He decided to take flight immediately.*

flighty ADJECTIVE = **frivolous**, wild, volatile, unstable, irresponsible, dizzy, fickle, unbalanced, impulsive, mercurial, giddy, capricious, unsteady, thoughtless, changeable, impetuous, skittish, light-headed, harebrained, scatterbrained, ditzy *or* ditsy *(slang)*

flimsy ADJECTIVE **1 = fragile**, weak, slight, delicate, shallow, shaky, frail, superficial, makeshift, rickety, insubstantial, gimcrack, unsubstantial: *a flimsy wooden door* **OPPOSITE:** sturdy **2 = thin**, light, sheer, transparent, chiffon, gossamer, gauzy: *a flimsy pink chiffon nightgown* **3 = unconvincing**, poor, thin, weak, inadequate, pathetic, transparent, trivial, feeble, unsatisfactory, frivolous, tenuous, implausible: *The charges were based on flimsy evidence.*

flinch VERB **1 = wince**, start, duck, shrink, cringe, quail, recoil, cower, blench: *The slightest pressure made her flinch.* **2** *(often with* **from***)* **= shy away**, shrink, withdraw, flee, retreat, back off, swerve, shirk, draw back, baulk: *He has never flinched from harsh decisions.*

fling VERB = **throw**, toss, hurl, chuck *(informal)*, launch, cast, pitch, send, shy, jerk, propel, sling, precipitate, lob *(informal)*, catapult, heave, let fly: *The woman flung the cup at him.*
▷ NOUN **1 = binge**, good time, bash, bit of fun, party, rave *(Brit. slang)*, spree, indulgence *(informal)*, beano *(Brit. slang)*, night on the town, rave-up *(Brit. slang)*, hooley *or* hoolie *(chiefly Irish & N.Z.)*: *the last fling before you take up a job* **2 = try**, go *(informal)*, attempt, shot *(informal)*, trial, crack *(informal)*, venture, gamble, stab *(informal)*, bash *(informal)*, whirl *(informal)*: *the England bowler's chance of a fling at South Africa in the second Test today*

flip VERB **1 = flick**, switch, snap, slick, jerk: *He walked out, flipping off the lights.* **2 = spin**, turn, overturn, turn over, roll over, twist: *The plane flipped over and burst into flames.* **3 = toss**, throw, cast, pitch, flick, fling, sling: *I flipped a cigarette butt out of the window.*
▷ NOUN = **toss**, throw, cast, pitch, spin, snap, twist, flick, jerk: *having gambled all on the flip of a coin*

flippant ADJECTIVE = **frivolous**, rude, cheeky, irreverent, flip *(informal)*, superficial, saucy, glib, pert, disrespectful, offhand, impertinent, impudent **OPPOSITE:** serious

flirt VERB **1 = chat up**, lead on *(informal)*, dally with, make advances at, make eyes at, coquet, philander, make sheep's eyes at: *He's flirting with all the ladies.* **2** *(usually with* **with***)* **= toy with**, consider, entertain, play with, dabble in, trifle with, give a thought to, expose yourself to: *My mother used to flirt with nationalism.*
▷ NOUN = **tease**, philanderer, coquette, heart-breaker, wanton, trifler: *She's a born flirt.*

flirtation NOUN = **teasing**, philandering, dalliance, coquetry, toying, intrigue, trifling

> QUOTATIONS
> Merely innocent flirtation,
> Not quite adultery, but adulteration
> [Lord Byron *Don Juan*]
>
> Coquetry whets the appetite; flirtation depraves it. Coquetry is the thorn that guards the rose – easily trimmed off when once plucked. Flirtation is like the slime on water-plants, making them hard to handle, and when caught, only to be cherished in slimy waters
> [Donald Grant Mitchell *Reveries of a Bachelor*]
>
> Is that a gun in your pocket, or are you just glad to see me?
> [Mae West *Diamond Lil*]

flirtatious ADJECTIVE = **teasing**, flirty, coquettish, amorous, come-on *(informal)*, arch, enticing, provocative, coy, come-hither, sportive

flit VERB = **fly**, dash, dart, skim, pass, speed, wing, flash, fleet, whisk, flutter

float VERB **1 = glide**, sail, drift, move gently, bob, coast, slide, be carried, slip along: *barges floating quietly by the grassy river banks* **2 = be buoyant**, stay afloat, be *or* lie on the surface, rest on water, hang, hover, poise, displace water: *Empty things float.* **OPPOSITE:** sink **3 = launch**, offer, sell, set up, promote, get going, push off: *He floated his firm on the Stock Market.* **OPPOSITE:** dissolve

floating ADJECTIVE **1 = uncommitted**, wavering, undecided, indecisive, vacillating, sitting on the fence *(informal)*, unaffiliated, independent: *floating voters appear to have deserted the party* **2 = free**, wandering, variable, fluctuating, unattached, migratory, movable, unfixed: *a house I shared with a floating population of others*

flock NOUN **1 = herd**, group, flight, drove, colony, gaggle, skein: *They kept a small flock of sheep.* **2 = crowd**, company, group, host, collection, mass, gathering, assembly, convoy, herd, congregation, horde, multitude, throng, bevy: *his flock of advisors*
▷ VERB **1 = stream**, crowd, mass, swarm, throng: *The public have flocked to the show.* **2 = gather**, group, crowd, mass, collect, assemble, herd, huddle, converge, throng, congregate, troop: *The crowds flocked around her.*

flog VERB **= beat**, whip, lash, thrash, whack, scourge, hit hard, trounce, castigate, chastise, flay, lambast(e), flagellate, punish severely, beat *or* knock seven bells out of *(informal)*

flogging NOUN **= beating**, hiding *(informal)*, whipping, lashing, thrashing, caning, scourging, trouncing, flagellation, horsewhipping

flood NOUN **1 = deluge**, downpour, flash flood, inundation, tide, overflow, torrent, spate, freshet: *This is the sort of flood dreaded by cavers.* **2 = torrent**, flow, rush, stream, tide, abundance, multitude, glut, outpouring, profusion: *The administration is trying to stem the flood of refugees.* **3 = series**, stream, avalanche, barrage, spate, torrent: *He received a flood of complaints.* **4 = outpouring**, rush, stream, surge, torrent: *She broke into a flood of tears.*
▷ VERB **1 = immerse**, swamp, submerge, inundate, deluge, drown, cover with water: *The house was flooded.* **2 = pour over**, swamp, run over, overflow, inundate, brim over: *Many streams have flooded their banks.* **3 = engulf**, flow into, rush into, sweep into, overwhelm, surge into, swarm into, pour into, gush into: *Large numbers of immigrants flooded the area.* **4 = saturate**, fill, choke, swamp, glut, oversupply, overfill: *a policy aimed at flooding Europe with exports* **5 = stream**, flow, rush, pour, surge: *Enquiries flooded in from all over the world.*
▸ *related adjectives:* fluvial, diluvial

floor NOUN **1 = ground**: *He's sitting on the floor watching TV.* **2 = storey**, level, stage, tier: *It's on the fifth floor of the hospital.*
▷ VERB **1 = disconcert**, stump, baffle, confound, beat, throw *(informal)*, defeat, puzzle, conquer, overthrow, bewilder, perplex, bowl over *(informal)*, faze, discomfit, bring up short, dumbfound, nonplus: *He was floored by the announcement.* **2 = knock down**, fell, knock over, prostrate, deck *(slang)*: *He was floored twice in the second round.*

flop VERB **1 = slump**, fall, drop, collapse, sink, tumble, topple: *She flopped, exhausted, on to a sofa.* **2 = hang down**, hang, dangle, sag, droop, hang limply: *His hair flopped over his left eye.* **3 = fail**, close, bomb *(U.S. & Canad. slang)*, fold *(informal)*, founder, fall short, fall flat, come to nothing, come unstuck, misfire, go belly-up *(slang)*, go down like a lead balloon *(informal)*: *The film flopped badly at the box office.* **OPPOSITE:** succeed
▷ NOUN **= failure**, disaster, loser, fiasco, debacle, washout *(informal)*, cockup *(Brit. slang)*, nonstarter: *The public decide whether a film is a hit or a flop.* **OPPOSITE:** success

floppy ADJECTIVE **= droopy**, soft, loose, hanging, limp, flapping, sagging, baggy, flip-flop, flaccid, pendulous

floral ADJECTIVE **= flowery**, flower-patterned

florid ADJECTIVE **1 = flowery**, high-flown, figurative, grandiloquent, euphuistic: *a liking for florid writing* **2 = ornate**, busy, flamboyant, baroque, fussy, embellished, flowery, overelaborate: *the cast-iron fireplace and the florid ceiling* **OPPOSITE:** plain **3 = flushed**, ruddy, rubicund, high-coloured, high-complexioned, blowsy: *He was a stout, florid man.* **OPPOSITE:** pale

flotsam NOUN **1 = debris**, rubbish, wreckage, detritus, jetsam **2 = debris**, sweepings, rubbish, junk, odds and ends

flounce VERB *(often with* **out**, **away**, **off**, *etc)* **= bounce**, storm, stamp, go quickly, throw, spring, toss, fling, jerk

flounder VERB **1 = falter**, struggle, stall, slow down, run into trouble, come unstuck *(informal)*, be in difficulties, hit a bad patch: *The economy was floundering.* **2 = dither**, struggle, blunder, be confused, falter, be in the dark, be out of your depth: *The president is floundering, trying to jump-start his campaign.* **3 = struggle**, toss, thrash, plunge, stumble, tumble, muddle, fumble, grope, wallow: *men floundering about in the water*

> **USAGE**
> Flounder is sometimes wrongly used where founder is meant: *the project foundered* (not *floundered*) *because of lack of funds.*

flourish VERB **1 = thrive**, increase, develop, advance, progress, boom, bloom, blossom, prosper, burgeon: *Business soon flourished.* **OPPOSITE:** fail **2 = succeed**, do well, be successful, move ahead, get ahead, go places *(informal)*, go great guns *(slang)*, go up in the world: *On graduation he flourished as a journalist.* **3 = grow**, thrive, develop, flower, succeed, get on, bloom, blossom, prosper, bear fruit, be vigorous, be in your prime: *The plant is flourishing particularly well.* **4 = wave**, brandish, sweep, swish, display, shake, swing, wield, flutter, wag, flaunt, vaunt, twirl: *He flourished his glass to make the point.*
▷ NOUN **1 = wave**, sweep, brandish, swish, shaking, swing, dash, brandishing, twirling, twirl, showy gesture: *with a flourish of his hand* **2 = show**, display, parade, fanfare: *with a flourish of church bells* **3 = curlicue**, sweep, decoration, swirl, plume, embellishment, ornamentation: *He underlined his name with a showy flourish.*

flourishing ADJECTIVE **= thriving**, successful, doing well, blooming, mushrooming, prospering, rampant, burgeoning, on a roll, going places, going strong, in the pink, in top form, on the up and up *(informal)*

flout VERB **= defy**, scorn, spurn, scoff at, outrage, insult, mock, scout *(archaic)*, ridicule, taunt, deride, sneer at, jeer at, laugh in the face of, show contempt for, gibe at, treat with disdain **OPPOSITE:** respect

flow VERB **1 = run**, course, rush, sweep, move, issue, pass, roll, flood, pour, slide, proceed, stream, run out, surge, spill, go along, circulate, swirl, glide, ripple, cascade, whirl, overflow, gush, inundate, deluge, spurt, teem, spew, squirt, purl, well forth: *A stream flowed down into the valley.* **2 = pour**, move, sweep, flood, stream, overflow: *Large numbers of refugees continue to flow into the country.* **3 = issue**, follow, result, emerge, spring, pour, proceed, arise, derive, ensue, emanate: *Undesirable consequences flow from these misconceptions.*
▷ NOUN **1 = stream**, current, movement, motion, course, issue, flood, drift, tide, spate, gush, flux, outpouring, outflow, undertow, tideway: *watching the quiet flow of the olive-green water* **2 = outpouring**, flood, stream, succession, train, plenty, abundance, deluge, plethora, outflow, effusion, emanation: *the opportunity to control the flow of information*

flower NOUN **1 = bloom**, blossom, efflorescence: *Each individual flower is tiny.* **2 = elite**, best, prime, finest, pick, choice, cream, height, the crème de la crème, choicest part: *the flower of American manhood* **3 = height**, prime, peak, vigour, freshness, greatest *or* finest point: *You are hardly in the first flower of youth.*
▷ VERB **1 = bloom**, open, mature, flourish, unfold, blossom, burgeon, effloresce: *Several of these plants will flower this year.* **2 = blossom**, grow, develop, progress, mature, thrive, flourish, bloom, bud, prosper: *Their relationship flowered.*
▸ *related adjective:* floral ▸ *related prefix:* antho-

> **QUOTATIONS**
> 'Tis the last rose of summer
> Left blooming alone;
> All her lovely companions
> Are faded and gone
> [Thomas Moore *'Tis the last rose of Summer*]
>
> There is no 'Why' about the rose,
> it blossoms because it blossoms
> It pays no heed to itself, and does
> not care whether it is seen
> [Angelus Silesius]
>
> The flower is the poetry of
> reproduction. It is an example of

> the eternal seductiveness of life [Jean Giraudoux *The Enchanted*]
>
> When you take a flower in your hand and really look at it, it's your world for the moment [Georgia O'Keeffe]
>
> O my love's like a red, red rose [Robert Burns *A Red, Red Rose*]

flowering ADJECTIVE **= blooming**, in flower, in bloom, in blossom, out, open, ready, blossoming, florescent, abloom

flowery ADJECTIVE **1 = floral**, flower-patterned: *The baby was dressed in a flowery jumpsuit.* **2 = ornate**, fancy, rhetorical, high-flown, embellished, figurative, florid, overwrought, euphuistic, baroque: *They were using uncommonly flowery language.*
OPPOSITE: plain

flowing ADJECTIVE **1 = streaming**, rushing, gushing, teeming, falling, full, rolling, sweeping, flooded, fluid, prolific, abundant, overrun, brimming over: *fragrance borne by the swiftly flowing stream* **2 = sleek**, smooth, fluid, unbroken, uninterrupted: *a smooth flowing line against a cloudless sky* **3 = fluent**, easy, natural, continuous, effortless, uninterrupted, free-flowing, cursive, rich: *his own rhetoric and flowing style of delivery*

fluctuate VERB **1 = change**, swing, vary, alter, hesitate, alternate, waver, veer, rise and fall, go up and down, ebb and flow, seesaw: *Body temperatures can fluctuate when you are ill.* **2 = shift**, undulate, oscillate, vacillate: *the constantly fluctuating price of crude oil*

fluctuation NOUN **= change**, shift, swing, variation, instability, alteration, wavering, oscillation, alternation, vacillation, unsteadiness, inconstancy

fluency NOUN **= ease**, control, facility, command, assurance, readiness, smoothness, slickness, glibness, volubility, articulateness

fluent ADJECTIVE **= effortless**, natural, articulate, well-versed, glib, facile, voluble, smooth-spoken

fluff NOUN **= fuzz**, down, pile, dust, fibre, threads, nap, lint, oose (*Scot.*), dustball: *bits of fluff on the sleeve of her jumper*
▷ VERB **= mess up**, spoil, bungle, screw up (*informal, informal*), cock up (*Brit. slang*), foul up (*informal*), make a nonsense of, be unsuccessful in, make a mess off, muddle, crool *or* cruel (*Austral. slang*): *She fluffed her interview at Oxford.*

fluffy ADJECTIVE **= soft**, fuzzy, feathery, downy, fleecy, flossy

fluid NOUN **= liquid**, solution, juice, liquor, sap: *Make sure that you drink plenty of fluids.*
▷ ADJECTIVE **1 = changeable**, mobile, flexible, volatile, unstable, adjustable, fluctuating, indefinite, shifting, floating, adaptable, mercurial, protean, mutable: *The situation is extremely fluid.*
OPPOSITE: fixed **2 = liquid**, running, flowing, watery, molten, melted, runny, liquefied, in solution, aqueous: *List the fluid and cellular components of blood.* **OPPOSITE:** solid

fluke NOUN **= stroke of luck**, accident, coincidence, chance occurrence, chance, stroke, blessing, freak, windfall, quirk, lucky break, serendipity, quirk of fate, fortuity, break: *The discovery was something of a fluke.*

flunk VERB **= fail**, screw up (*informal*), flop in (*informal*), plough (*Brit. slang*), be unsuccessful in, not make the grade at (*informal*), not come up to scratch in (*informal*), not come up to the mark in (*informal*)

flurry NOUN **1 = commotion**, stir, bustle, flutter, to-do, excitement, hurry, fuss, disturbance, flap, whirl, furore, ferment, agitation, fluster, ado, tumult: *There was a flurry of excitement.* **2 = burst**, spell, bout, outbreak, spurt: *a flurry of diplomatic activity* **3 = gust**, shower, gale, swirl, squall, storm: *A flurry of snowflakes was scudding by the window.*

flush[1] VERB **1 = blush**, colour, burn, flame, glow, crimson, redden, suffuse, turn red, go red, colour up, go as red as a beetroot: *He turned away, his face flushing.* **2 = cleanse**, wash out, swab, rinse out, flood, drench, syringe, swill, hose down, douche: *Flush the eye with clean cold water.* **3 = expel**, drive, eject, dislodge: *Flush the contents down the lavatory.*
▷ NOUN **1 = blush**, colour, glow, reddening, redness, rosiness: *There was a slight flush on his cheeks.* **2 = bloom**, glow, vigour, freshness: *the first flush of young love*

flush[2] ADJECTIVE **1 = level**, even, true, flat, square, plane: *Make sure the tile is flush with the surrounding tiles.* **2 = wealthy**, rich, rolling (*slang*), well-off, in the money (*informal*), in funds, well-heeled (*informal*), replete, moneyed, well-supplied, minted (*Brit. slang*): *Many developing countries were flush with dollars.* **3 = affluent**, liberal, generous, lavish, abundant, overflowing, plentiful, prodigal, full: *If we're feeling flush we'll give them champagne.*
▷ ADVERB **= level**, even, touching, squarely, in contact, hard (against): *The edges fit flush with the walls.*

flush[3] VERB (*often with* **out**) **= drive out**, force, dislodge, put to flight, start, discover, disturb, uncover, rouse: *They flushed them out of their hiding places.*

flushed ADJECTIVE **1** (*often with* **with**) **= exhilarated**, excited, aroused, elated, high (*informal*), inspired, thrilled, animated, enthused, intoxicated, stoked (*Austral. & N.Z. informal*): *She was flushed with the success of the venture.* **2 = blushing**, red, hot, burning, embarrassed, glowing, rosy, crimson, feverish, ruddy, rubicund: *Young girls with flushed faces pass by.*

fluster VERB **= upset**, bother, disturb, ruffle, heat, excite, confuse, hurry, rattle (*informal*), bustle, hassle (*informal*), flurry, agitate, confound, unnerve, perturb, throw off balance, make nervous

fluted ADJECTIVE **= grooved**, channelled, furrowed, corrugated

flutter VERB **1 = beat**, bat, flap, tremble, shiver, flicker, ripple, waver, fluctuate, agitate, ruffle, quiver, vibrate, palpitate: *a butterfly fluttering its wings* **2 = flit**, hover, flitter: *The birds were fluttering among the trees.*
▷ NOUN **1 = tremor**, tremble, shiver, shudder, palpitation: *She felt a flutter of trepidation in her stomach.* **2 = vibration**, twitching, quiver, quivering: *loud twittering and a desperate flutter of wings* **3 = agitation**, state (*informal*), confusion, excitement, flap (*informal*), tremble, flurry, dither (*chiefly Brit.*), commotion, fluster, tumult, perturbation, state of nervous excitement: *She was in a flutter.*

flux NOUN **1 = instability**, change, transition, unrest, modification, alteration, mutation, fluctuation, mutability: *a period of economic flux* **2 = flow**, movement, motion, fluidity: *the flux of cosmic rays*

fly[1] VERB **1 = take wing**, soar, glide, take to the air, wing, mount, sail, hover, flutter, flit: *The bird flew away.* **2 = pilot**, control, operate, steer, manoeuvre, navigate, be at the controls, aviate: *He flew a small plane to Cuba.* **3 = airlift**, send by plane, take by plane, take in an aircraft: *The relief supples are being flown from Pisa.* **4 = flutter**, wave, float, flap: *A flag was flying on the new HQ.* **5 = display**, show, flourish, brandish: *He sailed in a ship flying a red flag.* **6 = rush**, race, shoot, career, speed, tear, dash, hurry, barrel (along) (*informal, chiefly U.S. & Canad.*), sprint, bolt, dart, zoom, hare (*Brit. informal*), hasten, whizz (*informal*), scoot, scamper, burn rubber (*informal*), be off like a shot (*informal*): *I flew downstairs.* **7 = pass swiftly**, pass, glide, slip away, roll on, flit, elapse, run its course, go quickly: *We walked and the time flew by.* **8 = leave**, disappear, get away, depart, run, escape, flee, take off, run from, shun, clear out (*informal*), light out (*informal*), abscond, decamp, take flight, do a runner (*slang*), run for it, cut and run (*informal*), fly the coop (*U.S. & Canad. informal*), beat a retreat, make a quick exit, make a getaway, show a clean pair of heels, skedaddle (*informal*), hightail (*informal, chiefly U.S.*), take a powder (*U.S. & Canad. slang*), hasten away, make your escape, take it on the lam (*U.S. & Canad. slang*), take to your heels: *I'll have to fly.*

let fly = lose your temper, lash out, burst forth, keep nothing back, give free rein, let (someone) have it: *She let fly with a string of obscenities.*

let something fly = throw, launch, cast, hurl, shoot, fire, fling, chuck (*informal*), sling, lob (*informal*), hurtle, let off, heave: *The midfielder let fly a powerful shot.*

fly² NOUN
fly in the ointment = problem, difficulty, rub, flaw, hitch, drawback, snag, small problem

fly³ ADJECTIVE **= cunning**, knowing, sharp, smart, careful, shrewd, astute, on the ball (*informal*), canny, wide-awake, nobody's fool, not born yesterday: *He is devious and very fly.*

flyer *or* **flier** NOUN **1 = pilot**, aeronaut, airman *or* airwoman, aviator *or* aviatrix: *escape lines for shot-down allied flyers* **2 = air traveller**, air passenger: *regular business flyers* **3 = handbill**, bill, notice, leaf, release, literature (*informal*), leaflet, advert (*Brit. informal*), circular, booklet, pamphlet, handout, throwaway (*U.S.*), promotional material, publicity material: *posters, newsletters and flyers* **4 = jump**, spring, bound, leap, hurdle, vault, jeté, flying *or* running jump: *At this point he took a flyer off the front.*

flying ADJECTIVE **1 = airborne**, waving, winging, floating, streaming, soaring, in the air, hovering, flapping, gliding, fluttering, wind-borne, volitant: *a species of flying insect* **2 = fast**, running, express, speedy, winged, mobile, rapid, fleet, mercurial: *He made a flying start to the final.* **3 = hurried**, brief, rushed, fleeting, short-lived, hasty, transitory, fugacious: *I paid a flying visit to the capital.*

foam NOUN **= froth**, spray, bubbles, lather, suds, spume, head: *The water curved round the rock in bursts of foam.*
▷ VERB **= bubble**, boil, fizz, froth, lather, effervesce: *We watched the water foam and bubble.*

fob
fob someone off = put off, deceive, appease, flannel (*Brit. informal*), give (someone) the run-around (*informal*), stall, equivocate with: *I've asked her but she fobs me off with excuses.*
fob something off on someone = pass off, dump, get rid of, inflict, unload, foist, palm off: *He likes to fob his work off on others.*

focus NOUN **1 = centre**, focal point, central point, core, bull's eye, centre of attraction, centre of activity, cynosure: *The children are the focus of her life.* **2 = focal point**, heart, target, headquarters, hub, meeting place: *the focus of the campaign for Black rights*
▷ VERB **1** (*often with* **on**) **= concentrate**, centre, spotlight, zero in on (*informal*), meet, join, direct, aim, pinpoint, converge, rivet, bring to bear, zoom in: *The summit is expected to focus on arms control.* **2 = fix**, train, direct, aim: *He focused the binoculars on the boat.*

fodder NOUN **= feed**, food, rations, tack (*informal*), foodstuff, kai (*N.Z. informal*), forage, victuals, provender, vittles (*obsolete, dialect*)

foe NOUN **= enemy**, rival, opponent, adversary, antagonist, foeman (*archaic*) **OPPOSITE:** friend

fog NOUN **1 = mist**, gloom, haze, smog, murk, miasma, murkiness, peasouper (*informal*): *The crash happened in thick fog.* **2 = stupor**, confusion, trance, daze, haze, disorientation: *He was in a fog when he got up.*
▷ VERB **1 = mist over** *or* **up**, cloud over, steam up, become misty: *The windows fogged immediately.* **2 = daze**, cloud, dim, muddle, blind, confuse, obscure, bewilder, darken, perplex, stupefy, befuddle, muddy the waters, obfuscate, blear, becloud, bedim: *His mind was fogged with fatigue.*

foggy ADJECTIVE **1 = misty**, grey, murky, cloudy, obscure, blurred, dim, hazy, nebulous, indistinct, soupy, smoggy, vaporous, brumous (*rare*): *Conditions were damp and foggy this morning.* **OPPOSITE:** clear **2 = unclear**, confused, clouded, stupid, obscure, vague, dim, bewildered, muddled, dazed, cloudy, stupefied, indistinct, befuddled, dark: *My foggy brain sifted through the possibilities.* **OPPOSITE:** sharp

foible NOUN **= idiosyncrasy**, failing, fault, weakness, defect, quirk, imperfection, peculiarity, weak point, infirmity

foil¹ VERB **= thwart**, stop, check, defeat, disappoint, counter, frustrate, hamper, baffle, elude, balk, circumvent, outwit, nullify, checkmate, nip in the bud, put a spoke in (someone's) wheel (*Brit.*): *A brave police chief foiled an armed robbery.*

foil² NOUN **= complement**, setting, relief, contrast, background, antithesis: *A cold beer is the perfect foil for a curry.*

foist
foist something on *or* **upon someone = force**, impose: *I don't foist my beliefs on other people.*

fold VERB **1 = bend**, double, gather, tuck, overlap, crease, pleat, intertwine, double over, turn under: *He folded the paper carefully.* **2** (*often with* **up**, *informal*) **= go bankrupt**, close, fail, crash, collapse, founder, shut down, go under, be ruined, go bust (*informal*), go to the wall, go belly-up (*slang*): *The company folded in 1990.* **3** (*with* **in**) **= wrap**, envelop, entwine, enfold: *He folded her in his arms.* **4** (*often with* **up** or **in**) **= wrap up**, wrap, enclose, envelop, do up, enfold: *an object folded neatly in tissue-paper*
▷ NOUN **= crease**, turn, gather, bend, layer, overlap, wrinkle, pleat, ruffle, furrow, knife-edge, double thickness, folded portion: *Make another fold and turn the ends together.*

folder NOUN **= file**, portfolio, envelope, dossier, binder

folk NOUN **1 = people**, persons, humans, individuals, men and women, human beings, humanity, inhabitants, mankind, mortals: *the innate reserve of country folk* **2** (*usually plural, informal*) **= family**, parents, relations, relatives, tribe, clan, kin, kindred, ainga (*N.Z.*), rellies (*Austral. slang*): *I've been avoiding my folks lately.*

PROVERBS
There's nowt so queer as folk

follow VERB **1 = accompany**, attend, escort, come after, go behind, tag along behind, bring up the rear, come behind, come *or* go with, tread on the heels of: *Please follow me, madam.* **2 = pursue**, track, dog, hunt, chase, shadow, tail (*informal*), trail, hound, stalk, run after: *I think we're being followed.* **OPPOSITE:** avoid **3 = come after**, go after, come next: *the rioting and looting that followed the verdict* **OPPOSITE:** precede **4 = result**, issue, develop, spring, flow, proceed, arise, ensue, emanate, be consequent, supervene: *If the explanation is right, two things will follow.* **5 = obey**, observe, comply with, adhere to, mind, watch, note, regard, stick to, heed, conform to, keep to, pay attention to, be guided by, toe the line, act according to, act in accordance with, give allegiance to: *Take care to follow the instructions.* **OPPOSITE:** ignore **6 = copy**, imitate, emulate, mimic, model, adopt, live up to, take a leaf out of someone's book, take as an example, pattern yourself upon: *He did not follow his example in taking drugs.* **7 = succeed**, replace, come after, take over from, come next, supersede, supplant, take the place of, step into the shoes of: *He followed his father and became a surgeon.* **8 = understand**, get, see, catch, realize, appreciate, take in, grasp, catch on (*informal*), keep up with, comprehend, fathom, get the hang of (*informal*), get the picture: *Can you follow the plot so far?* **9 = keep up with**, support, be interested in, cultivate, be devoted to, be a fan of, keep abreast of, be a devotee *or* supporter of: *the millions of people who follow football*
follow something through = complete, conclude, pursue, see through, consummate, bring to a conclusion: *They have been unwilling to follow through their ideas.*

follower NOUN **1 = supporter**, fan, representative, convert, believer, admirer, backer, partisan, disciple, protagonist, devotee, worshipper, apostle, pupil, cohort (*chiefly U.S.*), adherent, henchman, groupie (*slang*), habitué, votary: *violent clashes between followers of the two organizations* **OPPOSITE:** leader **2 = attendant**, assistant, companion, helper, sidekick (*slang*), henchman, retainer (*History*), hanger-on, minion, lackey: *a London gangster and his two thuggish followers* **OPPOSITE:** opponent

following ADJECTIVE **1 = next**, subsequent, successive, ensuing, coming, later, succeeding, specified,

consequent, consequential: *We went to dinner the following evening.* **2 = coming**, about to be mentioned: *Write down the following information.*
▷ NOUN **= supporters**, backing, public, support, train, fans, audience, circle, suite, patronage, clientele, entourage, coterie, retinue: *Rugby League enjoys a huge following.*

folly NOUN **= foolishness**, bêtise *(rare)*, nonsense, madness, stupidity, absurdity, indiscretion, lunacy, recklessness, silliness, idiocy, irrationality, imprudence, rashness, imbecility, fatuity, preposterousness, daftness *(informal)*, desipience
OPPOSITE: wisdom

QUOTATIONS
As a dog returneth to his vomit, so a fool returneth to his folly
[*Bible: Proverbs*]

foment VERB **= stir up**, raise, encourage, promote, excite, spur, foster, stimulate, provoke, brew, arouse, rouse, agitate, quicken, incite, instigate, whip up, goad, abet, sow the seeds of, fan the flames

USAGE
Both *foment* and *ferment* can be used to talk about stirring up trouble: *he was accused of fomenting/fermenting unrest*. Only *ferment* can be used intransitively or as a noun: *his anger continued to ferment* (not *foment*); *rural areas were unaffected by the ferment in the cities*.

fond ADJECTIVE **1 = loving**, caring, warm, devoted, tender, adoring, affectionate, indulgent, doting, amorous: *She gave him a fond smile.*
OPPOSITE: indifferent **2 = unrealistic**, empty, naive, vain, foolish, deluded, indiscreet, credulous, overoptimistic, delusive, delusory, absurd: *My fond hope is that we'll be ready on time.*
OPPOSITE: sensible
fond of 1 = attached to, in love with, keen on, attracted to, having a soft spot for, enamoured of: *I am very fond of Michael.* **2 = keen on**, into *(informal)*, hooked on, partial to, having a soft spot for, having a taste for, addicted to, having a liking for, predisposed towards, having a fancy for: *He was fond of marmalade.*

fondle VERB **= caress**, pet, cuddle, touch gently, pat, stroke, dandle

fondly ADVERB **1 = lovingly**, tenderly, affectionately, amorously, dearly, possessively, with affection, indulgently, adoringly: *Their eyes met fondly across the table.*
2 = unrealistically, stupidly, vainly, foolishly, naively, credulously: *I fondly imagined my life could be better.*

fondness NOUN **1 = devotion**, love, affection, warmth, attachment, kindness, tenderness, care, aroha *(N.Z.)*: *a great fondness for children*
OPPOSITE: dislike **2 = liking**, love, taste, fancy, attraction, weakness, preference, attachment, penchant, susceptibility, predisposition, soft spot, predilection, partiality: *I've always had a fondness for jewels.*

food NOUN **= nourishment**, cooking, provisions, fare, board, commons, table, eats *(slang)*, stores, feed, diet, meat, bread, menu, tuck *(informal)*, tucker *(Austral. & N.Z. informal)*, rations, nutrition, cuisine, tack *(informal)*, refreshment, scoff *(slang)*, nibbles, grub *(slang)*, foodstuffs, subsistence, kai *(N.Z. informal)*, larder, chow *(informal)*, sustenance, nosh *(slang)*, daily bread, victuals, edibles, comestibles, provender, nosebag *(slang)*, pabulum *(rare)*, nutriment, vittles *(obsolete, dialect)*, viands, aliment, eatables *(slang)*, survival rations
▸ *related adjective:* alimentary ▸ *related noun:* gastronomy

QUOTATIONS
A cucumber should be well sliced, and dressed with pepper and vinegar, and then thrown out, as good for nothing
[Dr. Johnson]

We lived for days on nothing but food and water
[W.C. Fields]

Food first, then morality
[Bertolt Brecht *The Threepenny Opera*]

Tell me what you eat and I will tell you what you are
[Anthelme Brillat-Savarin *Physiologie du Gout*]

There is not one kind of food for all men. You must and you will feed those faculties which you exercise. The laborer whose body is weary does not require the same food with the scholar whose brain is weary
[Henry David Thoreau *letter to Harrison Blake*]

After a good dinner one can forgive anybody, even one's own relatives
[Oscar Wilde]

There is no love sincerer than the love of food
[George Bernard Shaw *Man and Superman*]

Sharing food with another human being is an intimate act that should not be indulged in lightly
[M.F.K. Fisher *An Alphabet for Gourmets*]

On the Continent people have good food; in England people have good table manners
[George Mikes *How to be an Alien*]

Stands the church clock at ten to three?
And is there honey still for tea?
[Rupert Brooke *Grantchester*]

Dinner at the Huntercombes' possessed only two dramatic features – the wine was a farce and the food a tragedy
[Anthony Powell *The Acceptance World*]

The healsome porritch, chief of Scotia's food
[Robert Burns *The Cotter's Saturday Night*]

Fair fa' your honest, sonsie face,
Great chieftain o' the puddin'-race!
[Robert Burns *To a Haggis*]

Doubtless God could have made a better berry, but doubtless God never did
[William Butler (on the strawberry)]

Mayonnaise: one of the sauces which serve the French in place of a state religion
[Ambrose Bierce *The Devil's Dictionary*]

Milk's leap towards immortality
[Clifford Fadiman (of cheese) *Any Number Can Play*]

Sauce: the one infallible sign of civilization and enlightenment. A people with no sauces has one thousand vices; a people with one sauce has only nine hundred and ninety-nine. For every sauce invented and accepted a vice is renounced and forgiven
[Ambrose Bierce *The Devil's Dictionary*]

[If the people have no bread] let them eat cake
[Marie-Antoinette]

Man shall not live by bread alone, but by every word that proceedeth out of the mouth of God
[*Bible: St. Matthew*]

PROVERBS
Half a loaf is better than no bread
You cannot have your cake and eat it
What's sauce for the goose is sauce for the gander
An apple a day keeps the doctor away

fool NOUN **1 = simpleton**, idiot, mug *(Brit. slang)*, berk *(Brit. slang)*, charlie *(Brit. informal)*, silly, goose *(informal)*, dope *(informal)*, jerk *(slang, chiefly U.S. & Canad.)*, dummy *(slang)*, ass *(U.S. & Canad. taboo)*, clot *(Brit. informal)*, plank *(Brit. slang)*, sap *(slang)*, wally *(slang)*, illiterate, prat *(slang)*, plonker *(slang)*, coot, moron, nit *(informal)*, git *(Brit. slang)*, geek *(slang)*, twit *(informal, chiefly Brit.)*, bonehead *(slang)*, chump *(informal)*, dunce, imbecile *(informal)*, loon, clod, cretin, oaf, bozo *(U.S. slang)*, dullard, dimwit *(informal)*, ignoramus, dumbo *(slang)*, jackass, dipstick *(Brit. slang)*, gonzo *(slang)*, schmuck *(U.S. slang)*, dork *(slang)*, nitwit *(informal)*, dolt, blockhead, ninny, divvy *(Brit. slang)*, bird-brain *(informal)*, pillock *(Brit. slang)*, halfwit, nincompoop, dweeb *(U.S. slang)*, putz *(U.S. slang)*, fathead *(informal)*, weenie *(U.S. informal)*, schlep *(U.S. slang)*, eejit *(Scot. & Irish)*, dumb-ass *(slang)*, pea-brain *(slang)*, dunderhead, numpty *(Scot. informal)*, doofus *(slang, chiefly U.S.)*, lamebrain *(informal)*, mooncalf, thickhead, clodpate *(archaic)*, nerd *or* nurd *(slang)*, numbskull *or* numskull, twerp *or* twirp *(informal)*, dorba *or* dorb

(*Austral. slang*), bogan (*Austral. slang*), dill (*Austral. & N.Z. informal*): *He'd been a fool to get involved with her.* **OPPOSITE:** genius **2 = dupe**, butt, mug (*Brit. slang*), sucker (*slang*), gull (*archaic*), stooge (*slang*), laughing stock, pushover (*informal*), fall guy (*informal*), chump (*informal*), greenhorn (*informal*), easy mark (*informal*): *He feels she has made a fool of him.* **3 = jester**, comic, clown, harlequin, motley, buffoon, pierrot, court jester, punchinello, joculator *or* (*fem.*) joculatrix, merry-andrew: *Every good court has its resident fool.*
▷ VERB **= deceive**, cheat, mislead, delude, kid (*informal*), trick, take in, con (*informal*), stiff (*slang*), have (someone) on, bluff, hoax, dupe, beguile, gull (*archaic*), swindle, make a fool of, bamboozle, hoodwink, take for a ride (*informal*), put one over on (*informal*), play a trick on, pull a fast one on (*informal*), scam (*slang*): *Art dealers fool a lot of people.*
fool around with something = play around with, play with, tamper with, toy with, mess around with, meddle with, trifle with, fiddle around with (*informal*), monkey around with: *He was fooling around with his cot, and he fell out of bed.*

foolhardy ADJECTIVE **= rash**, risky, irresponsible, reckless, precipitate, unwise, impulsive, madcap, impetuous, hot-headed, imprudent, incautious, venturesome, venturous, temerarious **OPPOSITE:** cautious

foolish ADJECTIVE **1 = unwise**, silly, absurd, rash, unreasonable, senseless, short-sighted, ill-advised, foolhardy, nonsensical, inane, indiscreet, ill-judged, ill-considered, imprudent, unintelligent, asinine, injudicious, incautious: *It would be foolish to raise hopes unnecessarily.* **OPPOSITE:** sensible **2 = silly**, stupid, mad, daft (*informal*), simple, weak, crazy, ridiculous, dumb (*informal*), ludicrous, senseless, barmy (*slang*), potty (*Brit. informal*), goofy (*informal*), idiotic, half-baked (*informal*), dotty (*slang*), inane, fatuous, loopy (*informal*), witless, crackpot (*informal*), moronic, brainless, half-witted, imbecilic, off your head (*informal*), braindead (*informal*), harebrained, as daft as a brush (*informal, chiefly Brit.*), dumb-ass (*slang*), doltish: *How foolish I was not to have seen my doctor earlier.*

foolishly ADVERB **= unwisely**, stupidly, mistakenly, absurdly, like a fool, idiotically, incautiously, imprudently, ill-advisedly, indiscreetly, short-sightedly, injudiciously, without due consideration

foolishness NOUN **1 = stupidity**, irresponsibility, recklessness, idiocy, weakness, absurdity, indiscretion, silliness, inanity, imprudence, rashness, foolhardiness, folly, bêtise (*rare*): *the foolishness of dangerously squabbling politicians* **2 = nonsense**, carrying-on (*informal, chiefly Brit.*), rubbish, trash, bunk, malarkey (*informal*), claptrap (*informal*), rigmarole, foolery, bunkum *or* buncombe (*chiefly U.S.*): *I don't have time to listen to this foolishness.*

> **QUOTATIONS**
> Mix a little foolishness with your prudence; it's good to be silly at the right moment
> [Horace *Odes*]

foolproof ADJECTIVE **= infallible**, certain, safe, guaranteed, never-failing, unassailable, sure-fire (*informal*), unbreakable

foot PLURAL NOUN **= tootsies** (*informal*)
▷ NOUN **1 = paw**, pad, trotter, hoof **2 = bottom**, end, base, foundation, lowest part
drag your feet = stall, procrastinate, block, hold back, obstruct

foothold NOUN **1 = basis**, standing, base, position, foundation **2 = toehold**, hold, support, footing, grip

footing NOUN **1 = basis**, foundation, foothold, base position, ground, settlement, establishment, installation, groundwork: *a sounder financial footing for the future* **2 = relationship**, terms, position, basis, state, standing, condition, relations, rank, status, grade: *They are trying to compete on an equal footing.* **3 = foothold**, hold, grip, toehold, support: *He lost his footing and slid into the water.*

footpath NOUN **= pavement**, sidewalk (*U.S. & Canad.*)

footstep NOUN **1 = step**, tread, footfall: *I heard footsteps outside.* **2 = footprint**, mark, track, trace, outline, imprint, indentation, footmark: *people's footsteps in the snow*

footwear NOUN **= footgear**, boots, shoes, slippers, sandals

forage NOUN (*for cattle*) **= fodder**, food, feed, foodstuffs, provender: *forage needed to feed one cow and its calf*
▷ VERB **= search**, hunt, scavenge, cast about, seek, explore, raid, scour, plunder, look round, rummage, ransack, scrounge (*informal*), fossick (*Austral. & N.Z.*): *They were forced to forage for clothes and fuel.*

foray NOUN **= raid**, sally, incursion, inroad, attack, assault, invasion, swoop, reconnaissance, sortie, irruption

forbearance NOUN **1 = patience**, resignation, restraint, tolerance, indulgence, long-suffering, moderation, self-control, leniency, temperance, mildness, lenity, longanimity (*rare*): *a high degree of tolerance and forbearance* **OPPOSITE:** impatience **2 = abstinence**, refraining, avoidance: *forbearance from military action*

forbid VERB **= prohibit**, ban, disallow, proscribe, exclude, rule out, veto, outlaw, inhibit, hinder, preclude, make illegal, debar, interdict **OPPOSITE:** permit

> **QUOTATIONS**
> God forbid
> [*Bible: Romans*]
>
> It is forbidden to forbid
> [*French student graffiti*]

> **USAGE**
> Traditionally, it has been considered more correct to talk about *forbidding someone to do something*, rather than *forbidding someone from doing something*. Recently, however, the *from* option has become generally more acceptable, so that *he was forbidden to come in* and *he was forbidden from coming in* may both now be considered correct.

forbidden ADJECTIVE **= prohibited**, banned, vetoed, outlawed, taboo, out of bounds, proscribed, verboten (*German*)

> **QUOTATIONS**
> There is a charm about the forbidden that makes it unspeakably desirable
> [Mark Twain *Notebook*]

> **PROVERBS**
> *Stolen fruit is sweet*

forbidding ADJECTIVE **= threatening**, severe, frightening, hostile, grim, menacing, sinister, daunting, ominous, unfriendly, foreboding, baleful, bodeful **OPPOSITE:** inviting

force NOUN **1 = compulsion**, pressure, violence, enforcement, constraint, oppression, coercion, duress, arm-twisting (*informal*): *calls for the siege to be ended by force* **2 = power**, might, pressure, hard power, energy, stress, strength, impact, muscle, momentum, impulse, stimulus, vigour, potency, dynamism, life: *slamming the door behind her with all her force* **OPPOSITE:** weakness **3 = influence**, power, effect, authority, weight, strength, punch (*informal*), significance, effectiveness, validity, efficacy, soundness, persuasiveness, cogency, bite: *He changed our world through the force of his ideas.* **4 = intensity**, vigour, vehemence, fierceness, drive, emphasis, persistence: *She took a step back from the force of his rage.* **5 = army**, unit, division, corps, company, body, host, troop, squad, patrol, regiment, battalion, legion, squadron, detachment: *a pan-European peace-keeping force*
▷ VERB **1 = compel**, make, drive, press, pressure, urge, overcome, oblige, railroad (*informal*), constrain, necessitate, coerce, impel, strong-arm (*informal*), dragoon, pressurize, press-gang, put the squeeze on (*informal*), obligate, twist (someone's) arm, put the screws on (*informal*), bring pressure to bear upon: *They forced him to work for them at gun point.* **2 = impose**, foist: *To force this agreement*

f

on the nation is wrong. **3 = push**, thrust, propel: *They forced her head under the icy waters, drowning her.* **4 = break open**, blast, wrench, prise, wrest, use violence on: *The police forced the door of the flat and arrested him.* **5 = extort**, drag, exact, wring: *using torture to force a confession out of a suspect* **OPPOSITE:** coax
in force 1 = valid, working, current, effective, binding, operative, operational, in operation, on the statute book: *The new tax is already in force.* **2 = in great numbers**, all together, in full strength: *Voters turned out in force.*

QUOTATIONS
Force without reason falls of its own weight
[Horace *Odes*]

There is no real force without justice
[Napoleon *Maxims*]

Where force is necessary, there it must be applied boldly, decisively and completely. But one must know the limitations of force; one must know when to blend force with a manoeuvre, a blow with an agreement
[Leon Trotsky *What Next?*]

Who overcomes
By force, hath overcome but half his foe
[John Milton *Paradise Lost*]

Force is as pitiless to the man who possesses it, or thinks he does, as it is to its victims; the second it crushes, the first it intoxicates. The truth is, nobody really possesses it
[Simone Weil *The Iliad or the Poem of Force*]

forced ADJECTIVE **1 = compulsory**, enforced, slave, unwilling, mandatory, obligatory, involuntary, conscripted: *a system of forced labour* **OPPOSITE:** voluntary **2 = false**, affected, strained, wooden, stiff, artificial, contrived, unnatural, insincere, laboured: *a forced smile* **OPPOSITE:** natural

forceful ADJECTIVE **1 = dynamic**, powerful, vigorous, potent, assertive: *He was a man of forceful character.* **OPPOSITE:** weak **2 = powerful**, strong, convincing, effective, compelling, persuasive, weighty, pithy, cogent, telling: *This is a forceful argument for joining them.*

forcible ADJECTIVE **1 = violent**, armed, aggressive, compulsory, drastic, coercive: *forcible resettlement of villagers* **2 = compelling**, strong, powerful, effective, active, impressive, efficient, valid, mighty, potent, energetic, forceful, weighty, cogent: *He is a forcible advocate for the arts.*

forcibly ADVERB **= by force**, compulsorily, under protest, against your will, under compulsion, by main force, willy-nilly

forebear *or* **forbear** NOUN **= ancestor**, father, predecessor, forerunner, forefather, progenitor, tupuna *or* tipuna (N.Z.)

foreboding NOUN **1 = dread**, fear, anxiety, chill, unease, apprehension, misgiving, premonition, presentiment, apprehensiveness: *an uneasy sense of foreboding* **2 = omen**, warning, prediction, portent, sign, token, foreshadowing, presage, prognostication, augury, foretoken: *No one paid any attention to their gloomy forebodings.*

forecast VERB **= predict**, anticipate, foresee, foretell, call, plan, estimate, calculate, divine, prophesy, augur, forewarn, prognosticate, vaticinate *(rare)*: *They forecast a defeat for the Prime Minister.*
▷ NOUN **= prediction**, projection, anticipation, prognosis, planning, guess, outlook, prophecy, foresight, conjecture, forewarning, forethought: *He delivered his election forecast.*

forefather NOUN **= ancestor**, father, predecessor, forerunner, forebear, progenitor, procreator, primogenitor, tupuna *or* tipuna (N.Z.)

forefront NOUN **= lead**, centre, front, fore, spearhead, prominence, vanguard, foreground, leading position, van

forego *see* **forgo**

foregoing ADJECTIVE **= preceding**, former, above, previous, prior, antecedent, anterior, just mentioned, previously stated

foreground NOUN **1 = front**, focus, forefront: *the foreground of this boldly painted landscape* **2 = prominence**, limelight, fore, forefront: *This worry has come to the foreground in recent years.*

foreign ADJECTIVE **1 = alien**, overseas, exotic, unknown, outside, strange, imported, borrowed, remote, distant, external, unfamiliar, far off, outlandish, beyond your ken: *a foreign language* **OPPOSITE:** native **2 = unassimilable**, external, extraneous, outside: *rejected the transplanted organ as a foreign object* **3 = uncharacteristic**, inappropriate, unrelated, incongruous, inapposite, irrelevant: *He fell into a gloomy mood that was usually so foreign to him.*

foreigner NOUN **= alien**, incomer, immigrant, non-native, stranger, newcomer, settler, outlander
▸ *related phobia:* xenophobia

foremost ADJECTIVE **= leading**, best, first, highest, front, chief, prime, primary, supreme, initial, most important, principal, paramount, inaugural, pre-eminent, headmost

forerunner NOUN **1 = omen**, sign, indication, token, premonition, portent, augury, prognostic, foretoken, harbinger: *Some respiratory symptoms can be the forerunners of asthma.* **2 = precursor**, predecessor, ancestor, prototype, forebear, progenitor, herald: *the forerunners of those who were to support the Nazis*

foresee VERB **= predict**, forecast, anticipate, envisage, prophesy, foretell, forebode, vaticinate *(rare)*, divine

foreshadow VERB **= predict**, suggest, promise, indicate, signal, imply, bode, prophesy, augur, presage, prefigure, portend, betoken, adumbrate, forebode

foresight NOUN **= forethought**, prudence, circumspection, far-sightedness, care, provision, caution, precaution, anticipation, preparedness, prescience, premeditation, prevision *(rare)*
OPPOSITE: hindsight

forestall VERB **= prevent**, stop, frustrate, anticipate, head off, parry, thwart, intercept, hinder, preclude, balk, circumvent, obviate, nip in the bud, provide against

forestry NOUN **= woodcraft**, silviculture, arboriculture, dendrology *(Botany)*, woodmanship

foretaste NOUN **= sample**, example, indication, preview, trailer, prelude, whiff, foretoken, warning

foretell VERB **= predict**, forecast, prophesy, portend, call, signify, bode, foreshadow, augur, presage, forewarn, prognosticate, adumbrate, forebode, foreshow, soothsay, vaticinate *(rare)*

forever *or* **for ever** ADVERB **1 = evermore**, always, ever, for good, for keeps, for all time, in perpetuity, for good and all *(informal)*, till the cows come home *(informal)*, world without end, till the end of time, till Doomsday: *We will live together forever.* **2 = constantly**, always, all the time, continually, endlessly, persistently, eternally, perpetually, incessantly, interminably, unremittingly, everlastingly: *He was forever attempting to arrange deals.*

USAGE
Forever and *for ever* can both be used to say that something is without end. For all other meanings, *forever* is the preferred form.

forewarn VERB **= alert**, advise, caution, tip off, apprise, give fair warning, put on guard, put on the qui vive

PROVERBS
Forewarned is forearmed

foreword NOUN **= introduction**, preliminary, preface, preamble, prologue, prolegomenon

forfeit NOUN **= penalty**, fine, damages, forfeiture, loss, mulct, amercement *(obsolete)*: *That is the forfeit he must pay.*
▷ VERB **= relinquish**, lose, give up, surrender, renounce, be deprived of, say goodbye to, be stripped of: *He was ordered to forfeit more than £1.5m in profits.*

The Language of Anthony Trollope

Anthony Trollope (1815–82) was one of the most prolific and successful English novelists of the Victorian era. His most celebrated works are his series of novels set in the fictional county of Barsetshire, collectively known as 'The Chronicles of Barsetshire' (which include his comic masterpiece *Barchester Towers*), his series of 'Palliser novels', and his satire *The Way We Live Now*.

The most immediately striking aspect of Trollope's language is his preference for words of only one or two syllables. Trollope achieved his prodigious output (a total of 47 novels, plus a number of travel books, biographies, and short stories) by writing to a strict daily quota, beginning on a new book as soon as he had finished the one before, and shorter, simpler, and less Latinate words presumably came more naturally to him as he wrote with such speed and in such volume. Thus he uses *ask* nearly 11,000 times – twice as often as *question*, and thirty times more often than *inquire*; *need* is used twice as often as *require*; and *try* and *attempt* are used twice as often as *endeavour*.

On the other hand, Trollope uses the Latinate verb *occur* slightly more often than the non-Latinate *happen*; this is striking in comparison with modern fiction in Collins' corpus, the *Bank of English*, where *happen* is almost nine times as frequent as *occur*. Trollope sometimes uses *occur* in the sense 'suggest itself' especially in phrases such as 'an idea occurred to me', where it is not synonymous with *happen*. Equally frequent, though, are sentences such as the following, which in modern fiction would be more likely to be expressed with *happen*:

> Nothing had since **occurred** which had created any suspicion in Mrs. Robarts's mind.

Another difference from modern English is that Trollope uses the adjective *pleasant* almost twice as often as he does *nice*. *Smiles, places, companions,* and *evenings* are *pleasant*, often *very pleasant*. *Girls*, on the other hand, are more likely to be *nice*, suggesting a slight difference in sense; *pleasant* is used in the sense 'enjoyable', while *nice* has the additional sense 'good, respectable'. There are also a few instances of *nice* in the sense 'subtle', for example:

> He had that **nice appreciation** of the feelings of others which belongs of right exclusively to women.

Conversation is an important feature in Trollope's works, as is shown by the over 140,000 sets of opening and closing quotation marks appearing throughout them, with exclamation marks also figuring largely. Apart from the auxiliary verbs *be* and *do*, the most commonly-found verb in his works is *say*, with other speech-act verbs, such as *speak, ask, talk, declare, explain, admit, answer, assure, reply, mention,* and *discuss* making up a sizeable percentage of his verbs. *Express* is nearly ten times more frequent in Trollope's works than in modern fiction, often in the phrases *express an opinion/wish/regret*.

Trollope's novels deal largely with relationships and interactions between his characters; thus many of his most commonly-used nouns are 'familial' ones such as *father, mother, child, son, daughter, brother, sister, uncle, aunt, cousin,* and *niece*. Interestingly, *friend* occurs nine times more frequently than *enemy*, perhaps indicating that Trollope's characters were in general more amiable than otherwise. *Lover* is more frequent than in modern fiction (240 times per million words in Trollope compared to less than 50 times per million words in the *Bank of English* fiction section) although in the more innocent sense 'suitor'; salient collocates are *rejected, accepted,* and *favoured*:

> The **accepted lover** came over to lunch, and was made as much of as though the Whitstables had always kept a town house.

forfeiture NOUN = **loss**, giving up, surrender, forfeiting, confiscation, sequestration *(Law)*, relinquishment

forge VERB **1 = form**, build, create, establish, set up, fashion, shape, frame, construct, invent, devise, mould, contrive, fabricate, hammer out, make, work: *They agreed to forge closer economic ties.* **2 = fake**, copy, reproduce, imitate, counterfeit, feign, falsify, coin: *They discovered forged dollar notes.* **3 = create**, make, work, found, form, model, fashion, shape, cast, turn out, construct, devise, mould, contrive, fabricate, hammer out, beat into shape: *To forge a blade takes great skill.*

f

forged ADJECTIVE **1 = fake**, copy, false, counterfeit, pretend, artificial, mock, pirated, reproduction, synthetic, imitation, bogus, simulated, duplicate, quasi, sham, fraudulent, pseudo, fabricated, copycat *(informal)*, falsified, ersatz, unoriginal, ungenuine, phony *or* phoney *(informal)*: *She was carrying a forged American passport.* **OPPOSITE:** genuine **2 = formed**, worked, founded, modelled, fashioned, shaped, cast, framed, stamped, crafted, moulded, minted, hammered out, beat out, beaten into shape: *fifteen tons of forged steel parts*

forger NOUN = **counterfeiter**, copier, copyist, falsifier, coiner

forgery NOUN **1 = falsification**, faking, pirating, counterfeiting, fraudulence, fraudulent imitation, coining: *He was found guilty of forgery.* **2 = fake**, imitation, sham, counterfeit, falsification, phoney *or* phony *(informal)*: *The letter was a forgery.*

forget VERB **1 = fail to remember**, not remember, not recollect, let slip from the memory, fail to bring to mind: *She forgot where she left the car.* **OPPOSITE:** remember **2 = neglect**, overlook, omit, not remember, be remiss, fail to remember: *Don't forget that all dogs need a supply of water.* **3 = leave behind**, lose, lose sight of, mislay: *I forgot my passport.* **4 = dismiss from your mind**, ignore, overlook, stop thinking about, let bygones be bygones, consign to oblivion, put out of your mind: *I can't forget what happened today.*

forgetful ADJECTIVE = **absent-minded**, vague, careless, neglectful, oblivious, lax, negligent, dreamy, slapdash, heedless, slipshod, inattentive, unmindful, apt to forget, having a memory like a sieve **OPPOSITE:** mindful

forgetfulness NOUN = **absent-mindedness**, oblivion, inattention, carelessness, abstraction, laxity, laxness, dreaminess, obliviousness, lapse of memory, heedlessness, woolgathering

forgive VERB = **excuse**, pardon, bear no malice towards, not hold something against, understand, acquit, condone, remit, let off *(informal)*, turn a blind eye to, exonerate, absolve, bury the hatchet, let bygones be bygones, turn a deaf ear to, accept (someone's) apology **OPPOSITE:** blame

> **QUOTATIONS**
> To err is human, to forgive, divine
> [Alexander Pope *An Essay on Criticism*]

forgiveness NOUN = **pardon**, mercy, absolution, exoneration, overlooking, amnesty, acquittal, remission, condonation

> **QUOTATIONS**
> Resist not evil; but whosoever shall smite thee on thy right cheek, turn to him the other also
> [*Bible: St. Matthew*]
>
> We read that we ought to forgive our enemies; but we do not read that we ought to forgive our friends
> [Cosimo de Medici]
>
> Always forgive your enemies; nothing annoys them so much
> [Oscar Wilde]
>
> The stupid neither forgive nor forget; the naïve forgive and forget; the wise forgive but do not forget
> [Thomas Szasz *The Second Sin*]
>
> God will forgive me; that is His business
> [Heinrich Heine]
>
> Father, forgive them; for they know not what they do
> [*Bible: St. Luke*]
>
> Lord, how oft shall my brother sin against me, and I forgive him? till seven times? Jesus said unto him, I say not unto thee, Until seven times; but Until seventy times seven
> [*Bible: St. Matthew*]

forgiving ADJECTIVE = **lenient**, tolerant, compassionate, clement, patient, mild, humane, gracious, long-suffering, merciful, magnanimous, forbearing, willing to forgive, soft-hearted

forgo *or* **forego** VERB = **give up**, sacrifice, surrender, do without, kick *(informal)*, abandon, resign, yield, relinquish, renounce, waive, say goodbye to, cede, abjure, leave alone *or* out

fork VERB = **branch**, part, separate, split, divide, diverge, subdivide, branch off, go separate ways, bifurcate

forked ADJECTIVE = **branching**, split, branched, divided, angled, pronged, zigzag, tined, Y-shaped, bifurcate(d)

forlorn ADJECTIVE **1 = miserable**, helpless, pathetic, pitiful, lost, forgotten, abandoned, unhappy, lonely, lonesome *(chiefly U.S. & Canad.)*, homeless, forsaken, bereft, destitute, wretched, disconsolate, friendless, down in the dumps *(informal)*, pitiable, cheerless, woebegone, comfortless: *He looked a forlorn figure as he limped off.* **OPPOSITE:** cheerful **2 = abandoned**, deserted, ruined, bleak, dreary, desolate, godforsaken, waste: *The once glorious palaces stood empty and forlorn.* **3 = hopeless**, useless, vain, pointless, futile, no-win, unattainable, impracticable, unachievable, impossible, not having a prayer: *a forlorn effort to keep from losing my mind*

form NOUN **1 = type**, sort, kind, variety, way, system, order, class, style, practice, method, species, manner, stamp, description: *He contracted a rare form of cancer.* **2 = shape**, formation, configuration, construction, cut, model, fashion, structure, pattern, cast, appearance, stamp, mould: *Valleys often take the form of deep canyons.* **3 = structure**, plan, order, organization, arrangement, construction, proportion, format, framework, harmony, symmetry, orderliness: *the sustained narrative form of the novel* **4 = build**, being, body, figure, shape, frame, outline, anatomy, silhouette, physique, person: *her petite form and delicate features* **5 = condition**, health, shape, nick *(informal)*, fitness, trim, good condition, good spirits, fettle: *He's now fighting his way back to top form.* **6 = document**, paper, sheet, questionnaire, application: *You will be asked to fill in an application form.* **7 = procedure**, behaviour, manners, etiquette, use, rule, conduct, ceremony, custom, convention, ritual, done thing, usage, protocol, formality, wont, right practice, kawa *(N.Z.)*, tikanga *(N.Z.)*: *a frequent broadcaster on correct form and dress* **8 = class**, year, set, rank, grade, stream: *I was going into the sixth form at school.* **9 = mode**, character, shape, appearance, arrangement, manifestation, guise, semblance, design: *The rejoicing took the form of exuberant masquerades.*

▷ VERB **1 = arrange**, combine, line up, organize, assemble, dispose, draw up: *He gave orders for the cadets to form into lines.* **2 = make**, produce, model, fashion, build, create, shape, manufacture, stamp, construct, assemble, forge, mould, fabricate: *The bowl was formed out of clay.* **3 = constitute**, make up, compose, comprise, serve as, make: *Children form the majority of dead and injured.* **4 = establish**, start, found, launch, set up, invent, devise, put together, bring about, contrive: *You may want to form a company to buy a joint freehold.* **5 = take shape**, grow, develop, materialize, rise, appear, settle, show up *(informal)*, accumulate, come into being, crystallize, become visible: *Stalactites and stalagmites began to form.* **6 = draw up**, design, devise, formulate, plan, pattern, frame, organize, think up: *She rapidly formed a plan.* **7 = develop**, pick up, acquire, cultivate, contract, get into *(informal)*: *It is easier to form good* *habits than to break bad ones.* **8 = train**, develop, shape, mould, school, teach, guide, discipline, rear, educate, bring up, instruct: *Anger at injustice formed his character.*

formal ADJECTIVE **1 = serious**, stiff, detached, aloof, official, reserved, correct, conventional, remote, exact, precise, starched, prim, unbending, punctilious, ceremonious: *He wrote a very formal letter of apology.* **OPPOSITE:** informal **2 = official**, express, explicit, authorized, set, legal, fixed, regular, approved, strict, endorsed, prescribed, rigid, certified, solemn, lawful, methodical, pro forma *(Latin)*: *No formal announcement has been made.* **3 = ceremonial**, traditional, solemn, ritualistic, dressy: *They arranged a formal dinner after the play.* **4 = conventional**, established, traditional: *He didn't have any formal dance training.*

formality NOUN **1 = correctness**, seriousness, decorum, ceremoniousness, protocol, etiquette, politesse, p's and q's, punctilio: *Her formality and seriousness amused him.* **2 = convention**, form, conventionality, matter of form, procedure, ceremony, custom, gesture, ritual, rite: *The will was read, but it was a formality.*

format NOUN **= arrangement**, form, style, make-up, look, plan, design, type, appearance, construction, presentation, layout

formation NOUN **1 = establishment**, founding, forming, setting up, starting, production, generation, organization, manufacture, constitution: *the formation of a new government* **2 = development**, shaping, constitution, evolution, moulding, composition, compilation, accumulation, genesis, crystallization: *The formation of my character and temperament.* **3 = arrangement**, grouping, figure, design, structure, pattern, rank, organization, array, disposition, configuration: *He was flying in formation with seven other jets.*

formative ADJECTIVE **1 = developmental**, sensitive, susceptible, impressionable, malleable, pliant, mouldable: *She spent her formative years growing up in London.* **2 = influential**, determinative, controlling, important, shaping, significant, moulding, decisive, developmental: *a formative influence on his life*

former ADJECTIVE **1 = previous**, one-time, erstwhile, ex-, late, earlier, prior, sometime, foregoing, antecedent, anterior, quondam, whilom *(archaic)*, ci-devant *(French)*: *He pleaded not guilty to murdering his former wife.* **OPPOSITE:** current **2 = past**, earlier, long ago, bygone, old, ancient, departed, old-time, long gone, of yore: *Remember him as he was in former years.* **OPPOSITE:** present **3 = aforementioned**, above, first mentioned, aforesaid, preceding, foregoing: *Most people can be forgiven for choosing the former.*

formerly ADVERB **= previously**, earlier, in the past, at one time, before, lately, once, already, heretofore, aforetime *(archaic)*

formidable ADJECTIVE **1 = difficult**, taxing, challenging, overwhelming, staggering, daunting, mammoth, colossal, arduous, very great, onerous, toilsome: *We have a formidable task ahead of us.* **OPPOSITE:** easy **2 = impressive**, great, powerful, tremendous, mighty, terrific, awesome, invincible, indomitable, redoubtable, puissant: *She looked every bit as formidable as her mother.* **3 = intimidating**, threatening, dangerous, terrifying, appalling, horrible, dreadful, menacing, dismaying, fearful, daunting, frightful, baleful, shocking: *a formidable, well-trained, well-equipped fighting force* **OPPOSITE:** encouraging

formula NOUN **1 = method**, plan, policy, rule, principle, procedure, recipe, prescription, blueprint, precept, modus operandi, way: *The new peace formula means hostilities have ended.* **2 = form of words**, code, phrase, formulary, set expression: *He developed a mathematical formula.* **3 = mixture**, preparation, compound, composition, concoction, tincture, medicine: *bottles of formula*

formulate VERB **1 = devise**, plan, develop, prepare, work out, invent, evolve, coin, forge, draw up, originate, map out: *He formulated his plan for escape.* **2 = express**, detail, frame, define, specify, articulate, set down, codify, put into words, systematize, particularize, give form to: *I was impressed by how he formulated his ideas.*

forsake VERB **1 = desert**, leave, abandon, quit, strand, jettison, repudiate, cast off, disown, jilt, throw over, leave in the lurch: *I still love him and would never forsake him.* **2 = give up**, set aside, relinquish, forgo, kick *(informal)*, yield, surrender, renounce, have done with, stop using, abdicate, stop having, turn your back on, forswear: *She forsook her notebook for new technology.* **3 = abandon**, leave, go away from, take your leave of: *He has no plans to forsake the hills.*

forsaken ADJECTIVE **1 = abandoned**, ignored, lonely, lonesome *(chiefly U.S. & Canad.)*, stranded, ditched, left behind, marooned, outcast, forlorn, cast off, jilted, friendless, left in the lurch: *She felt forsaken and gave up any attempt at order.* **2 = deserted**, abandoned, isolated, solitary, desolate, forlorn, destitute, disowned, godforsaken: *a forsaken church and a derelict hotel*

fort NOUN **= fortress**, keep, station, camp, tower, castle, garrison, stronghold, citadel, fortification, redoubt, fastness, blockhouse, fortified pa *(N.Z.)*: *Soldiers inside the fort are under sustained attack.* **hold the fort = take responsibility**, cover, stand in, carry on, take over the reins, maintain the status quo, deputize, keep things moving, keep things on an even keel: *His partner is holding the fort while he is away.*

forte NOUN **= speciality**, strength, talent, strong point, métier, long suit *(informal)*, gift **OPPOSITE:** weak point

forth ADVERB **1 = forward**, out, away, ahead, onward, outward: *Go forth into the desert.* **2 = out**, into the open, out of concealment: *He brought forth a small gold amulet.*

f

forthcoming ADJECTIVE **1 = approaching**, coming, expected, future, imminent, prospective, impending, upcoming: *his opponents in the forthcoming election* **2 = available**, ready, accessible, at hand, in evidence, obtainable, on tap *(informal)*: *They promised that the money would be forthcoming.* **3 = communicative**, open, free, informative, expansive, sociable, chatty, talkative, unreserved: *He was very forthcoming in court.*

forthright ADJECTIVE **= outspoken**, open, direct, frank, straightforward, blunt, downright, candid, upfront *(informal)*, plain-spoken, straight from the shoulder *(informal)* **OPPOSITE:** secretive

forthwith ADVERB **= immediately**, directly, instantly, at once, right away, straightaway, without delay, tout de suite *(French)*, quickly

fortification NOUN **1 = reinforcement**, protecting, securing, protection, strengthening, reinforcing, embattlement: *Europe's fortification of its frontiers* **2 = defence**, keep, protection, castle, fort, fortress, stronghold, bastion, citadel, bulwark, fastness, fortified pa *(N.Z.)*: *troops stationed just behind the fortification* **3 = strengthening**, supplementing, reinforcement: *nutrient fortification of food*

fortify VERB **1 = protect**, defend, secure, strengthen, reinforce, support, brace, garrison, shore up, augment, buttress, make stronger, embattle: *British soldiers working to fortify an airbase* **2 = strengthen**, add alcohol to: *All sherry is made from wine fortified with brandy.* **3 = sustain**, encourage, confirm, cheer, strengthen, reassure, brace, stiffen, hearten, embolden, invigorate: *The volunteers were fortified by their patriotic belief.* **OPPOSITE:** dishearten

fortitude NOUN **= courage**, strength, resolution, determination, guts *(informal)*, patience, pluck, grit, endurance, bravery, backbone, perseverance, firmness, staying power, valour, fearlessness, strength of mind, intrepidity, hardihood, dauntlessness, stoutheartedness

fortress NOUN **= castle**, fort, stronghold, citadel, redoubt, fastness, fortified pa *(N.Z.)*

fortuitous ADJECTIVE **1 = chance**, lucky, random, casual, contingent, accidental, arbitrary, incidental, unforeseen, unplanned: *a fortuitous quirk of fate* **2 = lucky**, happy, fortunate, serendipitous, providential, fluky *(informal)*: *It was a fortuitous discovery.*

fortunate ADJECTIVE **1 = lucky**, happy, favoured, bright, golden, rosy, on a roll, jammy *(Brit. slang)*, in luck, having a charmed life, born with a silver spoon in your mouth: *He has had a very fortunate life.* **OPPOSITE:** unfortunate **2 = providential**, auspicious, fortuitous, felicitous, timely, promising, encouraging, helpful, profitable, convenient, favourable, advantageous, expedient, opportune, propitious: *It was fortunate that the water was shallow.*

f

fortunately ADVERB **= luckily**, happily, as luck would have it, providentially, by good luck, by a happy chance

fortune NOUN **1 = large sum of money**, bomb *(Brit. slang)*, packet *(slang)*, bundle *(slang)*, big money, big bucks *(informal, chiefly U.S.)*, megabucks *(U.S. & Canad. slang)*, an arm and a leg *(informal)*, king's ransom, pretty penny *(informal)*, top whack *(informal)*: *Eating out all the time costs a fortune.* **2 = wealth**, means, property, riches, resources, assets, pile *(informal)*, possessions, treasure, prosperity, mint, gold mine, wad *(U.S. & Canad. slang)*, affluence, opulence, tidy sum *(informal)*: *He made his fortune in car sales.* **OPPOSITE:** poverty **3 = luck**, accident, fluke *(informal)*, stroke of luck, serendipity, hap *(archaic)*, twist of fate, run of luck: *Such good fortune must be shared with my friends.* **4 = chance**, fate, destiny, providence, the stars, Lady Luck, kismet, fortuity: *He is certainly being smiled on by fortune.* **5** *(often plural)* **= destiny**, life, lot, experiences, history, condition, success, means, circumstances, expectation, adventures: *She kept up with the fortunes of the family.*

QUOTATIONS

Fortune, that favours fools
[Ben Jonson *The Alchemist*]

No woman can be a beauty without a fortune
[George Farquhar *The Beaux' Stratagem*]

The slings and arrows of outrageous fortune
[William Shakespeare *Hamlet*]

Base Fortune, now I see, that in thy wheel
There is a point, to which when men aspire,
They tumble headlong down
[Christopher Marlowe *Edward II*]

forum NOUN **1 = meeting**, conference, assembly, meeting place, court, body, council, parliament, congress, gathering, diet, senate, rally, convention, tribunal *(archaic, literary)*, seminar, get-together *(informal)*, congregation, caucus *(chiefly U.S. & Canad.)*, synod, convergence, symposium, hui *(N.Z.)*, moot, assemblage, conclave, convocation, consistory *(in various Churches)*, ecclesia *(in Church use)*, colloquium, folkmoot *(in medieval England)*, runanga *(N.Z.)*: *a forum where problems could be discussed* **2 = public square**, court, square, chamber, platform, arena, pulpit, meeting place, amphitheatre, stage, rostrum, agora *(in ancient Greece)*: *Generals appeared before the excited crowds in the Forum.*

forward ADJECTIVE **1 = leading**, first, head, front, advance, foremost, fore: *to allow more troops to move to forward positions* **2 = future**, early, advanced, progressive, premature, prospective, onward, forward-looking: *The University system requires more forward planning.* **3 = presumptuous**, confident, familiar, bold, fresh *(informal)*, assuming, presuming, cheeky, brash, pushy *(informal)*, brazen, shameless, sassy *(U.S. informal)*, pert, impertinent, impudent, bare-faced, overweening, immodest, brass-necked *(Brit. informal)*, overfamiliar, brazen-faced, overassertive: *He's very forward and confident.* **OPPOSITE:** shy
▷ ADVERB **= into the open**, out, to light, to the front, to the surface, into consideration, into view, into prominence: *Over the years similar theories have been put forward.*
▷ VERB **1 = further**, back, help, support, aid, encourage, speed, advance, favour, promote, foster, assist, hurry, hasten, expedite: *He forwarded their cause with courage, skill and humour.* **OPPOSITE:** retard **2 = send on**, send, post, pass on, ship, route, transmit, dispatch, freight, redirect: *The document was forwarded to the President.*

forwards *or* **forward** ADVERB **1 = forth**, on, ahead, onwards: *He walked forward into the room.* **OPPOSITE:** backward(s) **2 = on**, onward, onwards: *His work from that time forward was confined to portraits.*

fossick VERB **= search**, hunt, explore, ferret, check, forage, rummage

foster VERB **1 = bring up**, mother, raise, nurse, look after, rear, care for, take care of, nurture: *She has fostered more than 100 children.* **2 = develop**, support, further, encourage, feed, promote, stimulate, uphold, nurture, cultivate, foment: *They are keen to foster trading links with the West.* **OPPOSITE:** suppress **3 = cherish**, sustain, entertain, harbour, accommodate, nourish: *She fostered a fierce ambition.*

foul ADJECTIVE **1 = dirty**, rank, offensive, nasty, disgusting, unpleasant, revolting, contaminated, rotten, polluted, stinking, filthy, tainted, grubby, repellent, squalid, repulsive, sullied, grimy, nauseating, loathsome, unclean, impure, grotty *(slang)*, fetid, grungy *(slang, chiefly U.S. & Canad.)*, putrid, malodorous, noisome, scuzzy *(slang, chiefly U.S.)*, mephitic, olid, yucky *or* yukky *(slang)*, festy *(Austral. slang)*, yucko *(Austral. slang)*: *foul, polluted water* **OPPOSITE:** clean **2 = obscene**, crude, indecent, foul-mouthed, low, blue, dirty, gross, abusive, coarse, filthy, vulgar, lewd, profane, blasphemous, scurrilous, smutty, scatological: *He was sent off for using foul language.* **3 = stormy**, bad, wild, rough, wet, rainy, murky, foggy, disagreeable, blustery: *The weather was foul, with heavy hail and snow.* **4 = unfair**, illegal, dirty, crooked, shady *(informal)*, fraudulent, unjust, dishonest, unscrupulous, underhand, inequitable, unsportsmanlike: *a foul tackle* **5 = offensive**, bad, base, wrong, evil, notorious, corrupt, vicious, infamous, disgraceful, shameful, vile, immoral, scandalous, wicked, sinful, despicable, heinous, hateful, abhorrent, egregious, abominable, dishonourable, nefarious, iniquitous, detestable: *He is accused of all manner of foul deeds.* **OPPOSITE:** admirable
▷ VERB **1 = dirty**, soil, stain, contaminate, smear, pollute, taint, sully, defile, besmirch, smirch, begrime, besmear: *sea grass fouled with black tar* **OPPOSITE:** clean **2 = clog**, block, jam, choke: *The pipe was fouled with grain.* **3 = entangle**, catch, twist, snarl, ensnare, tangle up: *The freighter fouled its propeller in fishing nets.*

foul play NOUN **= crime**, fraud, corruption, deception, treachery, criminal activity, duplicity, dirty work, double-dealing, skulduggery, chicanery, villainy, sharp practice, perfidy, roguery, dishonest behaviour

foul something up VERB **= bungle**, spoil, botch, mess up, cock up *(Brit. slang)*, make a mess of, mismanage, make a nonsense of, muck up *(slang)*, bodge *(informal)*, make a pig's ear of *(informal)*, put a spanner in the works *(Brit. informal)*, flub *(U.S. slang)*, crool *or* cruel *(Austral. slang)*: *There are risks that laboratories may foul up these tests.*

found VERB **1 = establish**, start, set up, begin, create, institute, organize, construct, constitute, originate, endow, inaugurate, bring into being: *He founded the Centre for Journalism Studies.* **2 = erect**, build, construct, raise, settle: *The town was founded in 1610.*

foundation NOUN **1 = basis**, heart, root, mainstay, beginning, support, ground, rest, key, principle, fundamental, premise, starting point, principal element: *Best friends are the foundation of my life.* **2** *(often plural)* **= substructure**, underpinning, groundwork, bedrock, base, footing, bottom: *vertical or lateral support for building foundations* **3 = setting up**, institution, instituting, organization, settlement, establishment, initiating, originating, starting, endowment, inauguration: *the foundation of the modern welfare state*

founded ADJECTIVE
founded on = based on, built on, rooted in, grounded on, established on

founder[1] NOUN **= initiator**, father, establisher, author, maker, framer, designer, architect, builder, creator, beginner, generator, inventor, organizer, patriarch, benefactor, originator, constructor, institutor: *He was the founder of the medical faculty.*

founder[2] VERB **1 = fail**, collapse, break down, abort, fall through, be unsuccessful, come to nothing, come unstuck, miscarry, misfire, fall by the wayside, come to grief, bite the dust, go belly-up *(slang)*, go down like a lead balloon *(informal)*: *The talks have foundered.* **2 = sink**, go down, be lost, submerge, capsize, go to the bottom: *Three ships foundered in heavy seas.*

fountain NOUN **1 = font**, spring, reservoir, spout, fount, water feature, well: *In the centre of the courtyard was a round fountain.* **2 = jet**, stream, spray, gush: *The volcano spewed a fountain of molten rock.* **3 = source**, fount, wellspring, wellhead, beginning, rise, cause, origin, genesis, commencement, derivation, fountainhead: *You are a fountain of ideas.*

fowl NOUN **= poultry**
▸ *name of male:* cock ▸ *name of female:* hen

foxy ADJECTIVE **= crafty**, knowing, sharp, tricky, shrewd, cunning, sly, astute, canny, devious, wily, artful, guileful

foyer NOUN **= entrance hall**, lobby, reception area, vestibule, anteroom, antechamber

fracas NOUN **= brawl**, fight, trouble, row, riot, disturbance, quarrel, uproar, skirmish, scuffle, free-for-all *(informal)*, rumpus, aggro *(slang)*, affray *(Law)*, shindig *(informal)*, donnybrook, scrimmage, shindy *(informal)*, bagarre *(French)*, melee or mêlée, biffo *(Austral. slang)*

fraction NOUN **1 = bit**, little bit, mite, jot, tiny amount, iota, scintilla: *I opened my eyes a fraction.* **2 = percentage**, share, cut, division, section, proportion, slice, ratio, portion, quota, subdivision, moiety: *only a small fraction of the cost* **3 = fragment**, part, piece, section, sector, selection, segment: *You will find only a fraction of the collection on display.*

fractious ADJECTIVE **= irritable**, cross, awkward, unruly, touchy, recalcitrant, petulant, tetchy, ratty *(Brit. & N.Z. informal)*, testy, chippy *(informal)*, fretful, grouchy *(informal)*, querulous, peevish, refractory, crabby, captious, froward *(archaic)*, pettish
OPPOSITE: affable

fracture NOUN **1 = break**, split, crack: *a double fracture of the right arm* **2 = cleft**, opening, split, crack, gap, rent, breach, rift, rupture, crevice, fissure, schism: *large fractures in the crust creating the valleys*
▷ VERB **1 = break**, crack: *You've fractured a rib.* **2 = split**, separate, divide, rend, fragment, splinter, rupture: *a society that could fracture along class lines*

fragile ADJECTIVE **1 = unstable**, weak, vulnerable, delicate, uncertain, insecure, precarious, flimsy: *The fragile government was on the brink of collapse.* **2 = fine**, weak, delicate, frail, feeble, brittle, flimsy, dainty, easily broken, breakable, frangible: *Coffee was served to them in cups of fragile china.*
OPPOSITE: durable **3 = unwell**, poorly, weak, delicate, crook *(Austral. & N.Z. informal)*, shaky, frail, feeble, sickly, unsteady, infirm: *He felt irritated and strangely fragile.*

fragility NOUN **= weakness**, delicacy, frailty, infirmity, feebleness, brittleness, frangibility

fragment NOUN **= piece**, part, bit, scrap, particle, portion, fraction, shiver, shred, remnant, speck, sliver, wisp, morsel, oddment, chip: *She read everything, digesting every fragment of news.*
▷ VERB **1 = break**, split, shatter, crumble, shiver, disintegrate, splinter, come apart, break into pieces, come to pieces: *It's an exploded fracture – the bones have fragmented.*
OPPOSITE: fuse **2 = break up**, divide, split up, disunite: *Their country's government has fragmented into disarray.*

fragmentary ADJECTIVE
= incomplete, broken, scattered, partial, disconnected, discrete, sketchy, piecemeal, incoherent, scrappy, disjointed, bitty, unsystematic

fragrance or **fragrancy** NOUN
1 = scent, smell, perfume, bouquet, aroma, balm, sweet smell, sweet odour, redolence, fragrancy: *A shrubby plant with a strong fragrance.*
OPPOSITE: stink **2 = perfume**, scent, cologne, eau de toilette, eau de Cologne, toilet water, Cologne water: *The advertisement is for a male fragrance.*

fragrant ADJECTIVE **= aromatic**, perfumed, balmy, redolent, sweet-smelling, sweet-scented, odorous, ambrosial, odoriferous
OPPOSITE: stinking

frail ADJECTIVE **1 = feeble**, weak, puny, decrepit, infirm: *She lay in bed looking particularly frail.* **OPPOSITE:** strong **2 = flimsy**, weak, vulnerable, delicate, fragile, brittle, unsound, wispy, insubstantial, breakable, frangible, slight: *The frail craft rocked as he clambered in.*

frailty NOUN **1 = weakness**, susceptibility, fallibility, peccability: *a triumph of will over human frailty*
OPPOSITE: strength **2 = infirmity**, poor health, feebleness, puniness, frailness: *She died after a long period of increasing frailty.* **3 = fault**, failing, vice, weakness, defect, deficiency, flaw, shortcoming, blemish, imperfection, foible, weak point, peccadillo, chink in your armour: *She is aware of his faults and frailties.* **OPPOSITE:** strong point

frame NOUN **1 = mounting**, setting, surround, mount: *She kept a picture of her mother in a silver frame.* **2 = casing**, framework, structure, shell, system, form, construction, fabric, skeleton, chassis: *He supplied housebuilders with modern timber frames.* **3 = physique**, build, form, body, figure, skeleton, anatomy, carcass, morphology: *belts pulled tight against their bony frames*
▷ VERB **1 = mount**, case, enclose: *The picture is now ready to be framed.* **2 = surround**, ring, enclose, close in, encompass, envelop, encircle, fence in, hem in: *The swimming pool is framed by tropical gardens.* **3 = devise**, plan, form, shape, institute, draft, compose, sketch, forge, put together, conceive, hatch, draw up, formulate, contrive, map out, concoct, cook up, block out: *A convention was set up to frame a constitution.*
frame of mind = mood, state, spirit, attitude, humour, temper, outlook, disposition, mind-set, fettle: *He was not in the right frame of mind to continue.*

framework NOUN **1 = system**, plan, order, scheme, arrangement, fabric, schema, frame of reference, the bare bones: *within the framework of federal regulations* **2 = structure**, body, frame, foundation, shell, fabric, skeleton: *wooden shelves on a steel framework*

franchise NOUN **1 = authorization**, right, permit, licence, charter, privilege, prerogative: *the franchise to build and operate the tunnel* **2 = vote**, voting rights, suffrage: *the introduction of universal franchise*

frank ADJECTIVE **1 = candid**, open, free, round, direct, plain, straightforward, blunt, outright, sincere, outspoken, honest, downright, truthful, forthright, upfront *(informal)*, unrestricted, plain-spoken, unreserved, artless, ingenuous, straight from the shoulder *(informal)*: *They had a frank discussion about the issue.*
OPPOSITE: secretive **2 = unconcealed**, open, undisguised, dinkum *(Austral. & N.Z. informal)*: *with frank admiration on his face*

frankly ADVERB **1 = honestly**, sincerely, in truth, candidly, to tell (you) the truth, to be frank (with you), to be honest: *Quite frankly, I don't care.* **2 = openly**, freely, directly, straight, plainly, bluntly, overtly, candidly, without reserve, straight from the shoulder: *The leaders have been speaking frankly about their problems.*

frankness NOUN **= outspokenness**, openness, candour, truthfulness, plain speaking, bluntness, forthrightness, laying it on the line, ingenuousness, absence of reserve

frantic ADJECTIVE **1 = frenzied**, wild, mad, raging, furious, raving, distracted, distraught, berserk, uptight *(informal)*, overwrought, at the end of your tether, beside yourself, at your wits' end, berko *(Austral. slang)*: *A bird had been locked in and was now quite frantic.* **OPPOSITE:** calm **2 = hectic**, desperate, frenzied, fraught *(informal)*, frenetic: *A busy night in the restaurant is frantic in the kitchen.*

fraternity NOUN **1 = companionship**, fellowship, brotherhood, kinship, camaraderie, comradeship: *He needs the fraternity of others.* **2 = circle**, company, set, order, clan, guild: *the spread of stolen guns among the criminal fraternity* **3 = brotherhood**, club, union, society, league, association, sodality: *He joined a college fraternity.*

fraud NOUN **1 = deception**, deceit, treachery, swindling, guile, trickery, duplicity, double-dealing, chicanery, sharp practice, imposture, fraudulence, spuriousness: *He was jailed for two years for fraud.* **OPPOSITE:** honesty **2 = scam**, craft, cheat, sting *(informal)*, deception *(slang)*, artifice, humbug, canard, stratagems, chicane: *a fraud involving pension and social security claims* **3 = hoax**, trick, cheat, con *(informal)*, deception, sham, spoof *(informal)*, prank, swindle, ruse, practical joke, joke, fast one *(informal)*, imposture, fastie *(Austral. slang)*: *He never wrote the letter; it was a fraud.* **4 = impostor**, cheat, fake, bluffer, sham, hoax, hoaxer, forgery, counterfeit, pretender, charlatan, quack, fraudster, swindler, mountebank, grifter *(slang, chiefly U.S. & Canad.)*, double-dealer, phoney *or* phony *(informal)*: *He believes many psychics are frauds.*

fraudulent ADJECTIVE **= deceitful**, false, crooked *(informal)*, untrue, sham, treacherous, dishonest, deceptive, counterfeit, spurious, crafty, swindling, double-dealing, duplicitous, knavish, phoney *or* phony *(informal)*, criminal **OPPOSITE:** genuine

fraught ADJECTIVE **1 = tense**, trying, difficult, distressing, tricky, emotionally charged: *It has been a somewhat fraught day.* **2 = agitated**, wired *(slang)*, anxious, distressed, tense, distracted, emotive, uptight *(informal)*, emotionally charged, strung-up, on tenterhooks, hag-ridden, adrenalized: *She's depressed, fraught, and exhausted.*
fraught with = filled with, full of, charged with, accompanied by, attended by, stuffed with, laden with, heavy with, bristling with, replete with, abounding with: *The production has been fraught with problems.*

fray[1] NOUN **= fight**, battle, row, conflict, clash, set-to *(informal)*, riot, combat, disturbance, rumble *(U.S. & N.Z. slang)*, quarrel, brawl, skirmish, scuffle, rumpus, broil, affray *(Law)*, shindig *(informal)*, donnybrook, battle royal, ruckus *(informal)*, scrimmage, shindy *(informal)*, bagarre *(French)*, melee *or* mêlée, biffo *(Austral. slang)*, boilover *(Austral.)*: *Today he entered the fray on the side of the moderates.*

fray[2] VERB **= wear thin**, wear, rub, fret, wear out, chafe, wear away, become threadbare: *The stitching had begun to fray at the edges.*

frayed ADJECTIVE **1 = worn**, ragged, worn out, tattered, threadbare, worn thin, out at elbows: *a shapeless and frayed jumper* **2 = strained**, stressed, tense, edgy, uptight *(informal)*, frazzled: *Nerves are frayed all round.*

freak MODIFIER **= abnormal**, chance, unusual, unexpected, exceptional, unpredictable, queer, erratic, unparalleled, unforeseen, fortuitous, unaccountable, atypical, aberrant, fluky *(informal)*, odd, bizarre: *The ferry was hit by a freak wave off the coast.*
▷ NOUN **1 = enthusiast**, fan, nut *(slang)*, addict, buff *(informal)*, fanatic, devotee, fiend *(informal)*, aficionado: *He's a self-confessed computer freak.* **2 = aberration**, eccentric, anomaly, abnormality, sport *(Biology)*, monster, mutant, oddity, monstrosity, malformation, rara avis *(Latin)*, queer fish *(Brit. informal)*, teratism: *Not so long ago, transsexuals were regarded as freaks.* **3 = weirdo** *or* **weirdie** *(informal)*, eccentric, oddity, case *(informal)*, character *(informal)*, nut *(slang)*, flake *(slang, chiefly U.S.)*, oddball *(informal)*, nonconformist, screwball *(slang, chiefly U.S. & Canad.)*, odd fish *(informal)*, kook *(U.S. & Canad. informal)*, queer fish *(Brit. informal)*: *The cast consisted of a bunch of freaks and social misfits.*

freakish ADJECTIVE **= odd**, strange, fantastic, weird, abnormal, monstrous, grotesque, unnatural, unconventional, outlandish, freaky *(slang)*, aberrant, outré, malformed, preternatural, teratoid *(Biology)*: *a freakish monstrous thing, something out of a dream*

freaky ADJECTIVE **= weird**, odd, wild, strange, crazy, bizarre, abnormal, queer, rum *(Brit. slang)*, unconventional, far-out *(slang)*, freakish

free ADJECTIVE **1 = complimentary**, for free *(informal)*, for nothing, unpaid, for love, free of charge, on the house, without charge, gratuitous, at no cost, gratis, buckshee *(Brit. slang)*: *The seminars are free, with lunch provided.* **2 = allowed**, permitted, unrestricted, unimpeded, open, clear, able, loose, unattached, unregulated, disengaged, untrammelled, unobstructed, unhampered, unengaged: *The government will be free to pursue its economic policies.* **3 = at liberty**, loose, liberated, at large, off the hook *(slang)*, on the loose: *All the hostages are free.* **OPPOSITE:** confined **4 = independent**, unfettered, unrestrained, uncommitted, footloose, unconstrained, unengaged, not tied down: *I was young, free and single at the time.* **5 = available**, extra, empty, spare, vacant, unused, uninhabited, unoccupied, untaken: *There's only one seat free on the train.* **6** *(often with* **of** *or* **with***)* **= generous**, willing, liberal, eager, lavish, charitable, hospitable, prodigal, bountiful, open-handed, unstinting, unsparing, bounteous, munificent, big *(informal)*: *They weren't always so free with their advice.* **OPPOSITE:** mean **7 = autonomous**, independent, democratic, sovereign, self-ruling, self-governing, emancipated, self-determining, autarchic: *We cannot survive as a free nation.* **8 = relaxed**, open, easy, forward, natural, frank, liberal, familiar, loose, casual, informal, spontaneous, laid-back *(informal)*, easy-going *(informal)*, lax, uninhibited, unforced, free and easy, unbidden, unconstrained, unceremonious: *a confidential but free manner* **OPPOSITE:** formal
▷ ADVERB **= freely**, easily, loosely, smoothly, idly: *Two stubby legs swing free.*
▷ VERB **1** *(often with* **of** *or* **from***)* **= clear**, deliver, disengage, cut loose, release, rescue, rid, relieve, exempt, undo, redeem, ransom, extricate, unburden, unshackle: *It will free us of a whole lot of debt.* **2 = release**, liberate, let out, set free, deliver, loose, discharge, unleash, let go, untie, emancipate, unchain, turn loose, uncage, set at liberty, unfetter, disenthrall, unbridle, manumit: *They are going to free more prisoners.* **OPPOSITE:** confine **3 = disentangle**, extricate, disengage, detach, separate, loose, unfold, unravel, disconnect, untangle, untwist, unsnarl: *It took firemen two hours to free him.*
free and easy = relaxed, liberal, casual, informal, tolerant, laid-back *(informal)*, easy-going, lax, lenient, uninhibited, unceremonious: *He had a free and easy approach.*
free of *or* **from = unaffected by**, without, above, lacking (in), beyond, clear of, devoid of, exempt from, immune to, sans *(archaic)*, safe from, untouched by, deficient in, unencumbered by, not liable to: *She retains her slim figure and is free of wrinkles.*

QUOTATIONS

Free at last, Free at last
Thank God Almighty
I'm Free at last
[Martin Luther King Jr. *Spiritual, quoted on his tomb*]

The free way of life proposes ends, but it does not prescribe means
[Robert F. Kennedy *The Pursuit of Justice*]

I am condemned to be free
[Jean-Paul Sartre *L'Être et le néant*]

The thoughts of a prisoner – they're not free either. They keep returning to the same things
[Alexander Solzhenitsyn *One Day in the Life of Ivan Denisovich*]

PROVERBS
The best things in life are free
There's no such thing as a free lunch

freedom NOUN **1 = independence**, democracy, sovereignty, autonomy, self-determination, emancipation, self-government, home rule, autarchy, rangatiratanga *(N.Z.)*: *They want greater political freedom.* **2 = liberty**, release, discharge, emancipation, deliverance, manumission: *All hostages and detainees would gain their freedom.* **OPPOSITE:** captivity **3** *(usually with* **from***)* **= exemption**, release, relief, privilege, immunity, impunity: *freedom from government control* **4 = licence**, latitude, a free hand, free rein, play, power, range, opportunity, ability, facility, scope, flexibility, discretion, leeway, carte blanche, blank cheque, elbowroom: *freedom to buy and sell at the best price* **OPPOSITE:** restriction **5 = openness**, ease, directness, naturalness, abandon, familiarity, candour, frankness, informality, casualness, ingenuousness, lack of restraint *or* reserve, unconstraint: *His freedom of manner ran contrary to the norm.* **OPPOSITE:** restraint

free-for-all NOUN **= fight**, row, riot, brawl, fracas, affray *(Law)*, dust-up *(informal)*, shindig *(informal)*, donnybrook, scrimmage, shindy *(informal)*, bagarre *(French)*, melee *or* mêlée, biffo *(Austral. slang)*

freely ADVERB **1 = abundantly**, liberally, lavishly, like water, extravagantly, copiously, unstintingly, with a free hand, bountifully, open-handedly, amply: *He was spending very freely.* **2 = openly**, frankly, plainly, candidly, unreservedly, straightforwardly, without reserve: *He had someone to whom he could talk freely.* **3 = willingly**, readily, voluntarily, spontaneously, without prompting, of your own free will, of your own accord: *He freely admits he lives for racing.* **4 = easily**, cleanly, loosely, smoothly, readily: *You must allow the clubhead to swing freely.* **5 = without restraint**, voluntarily, willingly, unchallenged, as you please, without being forced, without let or hindrance: *They cast their votes freely.*

freeway NOUN **= motorway** *(Brit.)*, autobahn *(German)*, autoroute *(French)*, autostrada *(Italian)*

freewheel VERB **= coast**, drift, glide, relax your efforts, rest on your oars, float

freeze VERB **1 = ice over** *or* **up**, harden, stiffen, solidify, congeal, become solid, glaciate: *The ground froze solid.* **2 = chill**, benumb: *The cold morning froze my fingers.* **3 = fix**, hold, limit, hold up, peg: *Wages have been frozen and workers laid off.* **4 = suspend**, stop, shelve, curb, cut short, discontinue: *They have already frozen their aid programme.*

freezing ADJECTIVE **1 = icy**, biting, bitter, raw, chill, chilled, penetrating, arctic, numbing, polar, Siberian, frosty, glacial, wintry, parky *(Brit. informal)*, cold as ice, frost-bound, cutting: *a freezing January afternoon* **2 = frozen**, chilled, numb, chilly, very cold, shivery, benumbed, frozen to the marrow: *You must be freezing!*

freight NOUN **1 = transportation**, traffic, delivery, carriage, shipment, haulage, conveyance, transport: *France derives 16% of revenue from air freight.* **2 = cargo**, goods, contents, load, lading, delivery, burden, haul, bulk, shipment, merchandise, bales, consignment, payload, tonnage: *26 tonnes of freight*

French ADJECTIVE **= Gallic**: *All the staff are French.*
▸ *related prefixes:* Franco-, Gallo-

frenetic ADJECTIVE **= frantic**, wild, excited, crazy, frenzied, distraught, obsessive, fanatical, demented, unbalanced, overwrought, maniacal

frenzied ADJECTIVE **= uncontrolled**, wild, excited, mad, crazy, furious, frantic, distraught, hysterical, agitated, frenetic, feverish, rabid, maniacal

frenzy NOUN **1 = fit**, burst, bout, outburst, spasm, convulsion, paroxysm: *The country was gripped by a frenzy of nationalism.* **2 = fury**, transport, passion, rage, madness, turmoil, distraction, seizure, hysteria, mania, insanity, agitation, aberration, lunacy, delirium, paroxysm, derangement: *Something like a frenzy enveloped them.* **OPPOSITE:** calm

frequency NOUN **= recurrence**, repetition, constancy, periodicity, commonness, frequentness, prevalence

frequent ADJECTIVE **= common**, repeated, usual, familiar, constant, everyday, persistent, reiterated, recurring, customary, continual, recurrent, habitual, incessant: *He is a frequent visitor to the house.* **OPPOSITE:** infrequent
▷ VERB **= visit**, attend, haunt, be found at, patronize, hang out at *(informal)*, visit often, go to regularly, be a regular customer of: *I hear he frequents that restaurant.* **OPPOSITE:** keep away

frequently ADVERB **= often**, commonly, repeatedly, many times, very often, oft *(archaic, poetic)*, over and over again, habitually, customarily, oftentimes *(archaic)*, not infrequently, many a time, much **OPPOSITE:** infrequently

fresh ADJECTIVE **1 = additional**, more, new, other, added, further, extra, renewed, supplementary, auxiliary: *He asked the police to make fresh enquiries.* **2 = natural**, raw, crude, unsalted, unprocessed, uncured, unpreserved, undried, green: *A meal with fresh ingredients doesn't take long to prepare.* **OPPOSITE:** preserved **3 = new**, original, novel, unusual, latest, different, recent, modern, up-to-date, this season's, unconventional, unorthodox, ground-breaking, left-field *(informal)*, new-fangled, modernistic: *These designers are full of fresh ideas.* **OPPOSITE:** old **4 = invigorating**, clear, clean, bright, sweet, pure, stiff, crisp, sparkling, bracing, refreshing, brisk, spanking, unpolluted: *The air was fresh and she felt revived.* **OPPOSITE:** stale **5 = cool**, cold, refreshing, brisk, chilly, nippy: *The breeze was fresh and from the north.* **6 = vivid**, bright, verdant, undimmed, unfaded: *a semi-circular mosaic, its colours still fresh* **OPPOSITE:** old **7 = rosy**, clear, fair, bright, healthy, glowing, hardy, blooming, wholesome, ruddy, florid, dewy, good: *His fresh complexion made him look young.* **OPPOSITE:** pallid **8 = lively**, rested, bright, keen, vital, restored, alert, bouncing, revived, refreshed, vigorous, energetic, sprightly, invigorated, spry, chipper *(informal)*, full of beans *(informal)*, like a new man, full of vim and vigour *(informal)*, unwearied, bright-eyed and bushy-tailed *(informal)*: *I nearly always wake up fresh and rested.* **OPPOSITE:** weary **9 = inexperienced**, new, young, green, natural, raw, youthful, unqualified, callow, untrained, untried, artless, uncultivated, wet behind the ears: *The soldiers were fresh recruits.* **OPPOSITE:** experienced **10 = cheeky** *(informal)*, bold, brazen, impertinent, forward, familiar, flip *(informal)*, saucy, audacious, sassy *(U.S. informal)*, pert, disrespectful, presumptuous, insolent, impudent, smart-alecky *(informal)*: *Don't get fresh with me.* **OPPOSITE:** well-mannered

freshen VERB **= refresh**, restore, rouse, enliven, revitalize, spruce up, liven up, freshen up, titivate

freshness NOUN **1 = novelty**, creativity, originality, inventiveness, newness, innovativeness: *They have a freshness and individuality that others lack.* **2 = cleanness**, shine, glow, bloom, sparkle, vigour, brightness, wholesomeness, clearness, dewiness: *the freshness of early morning*

fret VERB **1 = worry**, anguish, brood, agonize, obsess, lose sleep, upset yourself, distress yourself: *I was constantly fretting about others' problems.* **2 = annoy**, trouble, bother, disturb, distress, provoke, irritate, grieve, torment, harass, nag, gall, agitate, ruffle, nettle, vex, goad, chagrin, irk, rile, pique, peeve *(informal)*, rankle with: *The quickening of time frets me.*

friction NOUN **1 = conflict**, opposition, hostility, resentment, disagreement, rivalry, discontent, wrangling, bickering, animosity, antagonism, discord, bad feeling, bad blood,

f

dissension, incompatibility, disharmony, dispute: *There was friction between the children.* **2 = resistance**, rubbing, scraping, grating, irritation, erosion, fretting, attrition, rasping, chafing, abrasion, wearing away: *The pistons are graphite-coated to prevent friction.* **3 = rubbing**, scraping, grating, fretting, rasping, chafing, abrasion: *the friction of his leg against hers*

friend NOUN **1 = companion**, pal, mate *(informal)*, buddy *(informal)*, partner, china *(Brit. & S. African informal)*, familiar, best friend, intimate, close friend, comrade, chum *(informal)*, crony, alter ego, confidant, playmate, confidante, main man *(slang, chiefly U.S.)*, soul mate, homeboy *(slang, chiefly U.S.)*, cobber *(Austral. & N.Z.)*, cuzzie *or* cuzzie-bro *(N.Z.)*, E hoa *(N.Z. old-fashioned, informal)*, bosom friend, boon companion, Achates: *I had a long talk with my best friend.* **OPPOSITE:** foe **2 = supporter**, ally, associate, sponsor, advocate, patron, backer, partisan, protagonist, benefactor, adherent, well-wisher: *the Friends of Birmingham Royal Ballet*

QUOTATIONS

A friend should bear his friend's infirmities
[William Shakespeare *Julius Caesar*]

The belongings of friends are common
[Aristotle]

My best friend is the man who in wishing me well wishes it for my sake
[Aristotle *Nicomachean Ethics*]

Friends are born, not made
[Henry Adams *The Education of Henry Adams*]

I count myself nothing else so happy
As in a soul remembering my good friends
[William Shakespeare *Richard II*]

True happiness
Consists not in the multitude of friends,
But in the worth and choice
[Ben Jonson *Cynthia's Revels*]

Friends are God's apology for relatives
[Hugh Kingsmill]

Old friends are the best. King James used to call for his old shoes; for they were easiest for his feet
[John Seldon *Table Talk*]

Old friends are the blessing of one's later years – half a word conveys one's meaning
[Horace Walpole]

The only way to have a friend is to be one
[Ralph Waldo Emerson *Essays: First Series*]

When your friend holds you affectionately by both hands you are safe, for you can watch both his
[Ambrose Bierce]

Of two close friends, one is always the slave of the other
[Mikhail Lermontov *A Hero of Our Time*]

PROVERBS

A friend in need is a friend indeed

friendliness NOUN **= amiability**, warmth, sociability, conviviality, neighbourliness, affability, geniality, kindliness, congeniality, companionability, mateyness *or* matiness *(Brit. informal)*, open arms

friendly ADJECTIVE **1 = amiable**, kind, kindly, welcoming, warm, neighbourly, thick *(informal)*, attached, pally *(informal)*, helpful, sympathetic, fond, outgoing, comradely, confiding, affectionate, receptive, benevolent, attentive, sociable, genial, affable, fraternal, good, close, on good terms, chummy *(informal)*, peaceable, companionable, clubby, well-disposed, buddy-buddy *(slang, chiefly U.S. & Canad.)*, palsy-walsy *(informal)*, matey *or* maty *(Brit. informal)*, down with *(informal)*, on visiting terms: *He has been friendly to me.* **2 = amicable**, warm, familiar, pleasant, intimate, informal, benign, conciliatory, cordial, congenial, convivial: *a friendly atmosphere* **OPPOSITE:** unfriendly

friendship NOUN **1 = attachment**, relationship, bond, alliance, link, association, tie: *They struck up a close friendship.* **2 = friendliness**, affection, harmony, goodwill, intimacy, affinity, familiarity, closeness, rapport, fondness, companionship, concord, benevolence, comradeship, amity, good-fellowship: *a whole new world of friendship and adventure* **OPPOSITE:** unfriendliness **3 = closeness**, love, regard, affection, intimacy, fondness, companionship, comradeship: *He really values your friendship.*

QUOTATIONS

Friendship is a single soul dwelling in two bodies
[Aristotle]

Friendship makes prosperity more brilliant, and lightens adversity by dividing and sharing it
[Cicero *De Amicitia*]

Friendship admits of difference of character, as love does that of sex
[Joseph Roux *Meditations of a Parish Priest*]

Men seem to kick friendship around like a football, but it doesn't seem to crack. Women treat it as glass and it goes to pieces
[Anne Morrow Lindburgh]

Friendship: a ship big enough to carry two in fair weather, but only one in foul
[Ambrose Bierce *The Devil's Dictionary*]

fright NOUN **1 = fear**, shock, alarm, horror, panic, terror, dread, dismay, quaking, apprehension, consternation, trepidation, cold sweat, fear and trembling, (blue) funk *(informal)*: *To hide my fright I asked a question.* **OPPOSITE:** courage **2 = scare**, start, turn, surprise, shock, jolt, the creeps *(informal)*, the shivers, the willies *(slang)*, the heebie-jeebies *(slang)*: *The snake gave everyone a fright.* **3 = sight** *(informal)*, mess *(informal)*, eyesore, scarecrow, frump: *She looked a fright in a long dark wig.*

frighten VERB **= scare**, shock, alarm, terrify, cow, appal, startle, intimidate, dismay, daunt, unnerve, petrify, unman, terrorize, scare (someone) stiff, put the wind up (someone) *(informal)*, scare the living daylights out of (someone) *(informal)*, make your hair stand on end *(informal)*, get the wind up, make your blood run cold, throw into a panic, affright *(archaic)*, freeze your blood, make (someone) jump out of his skin *(informal)*, throw into a fright **OPPOSITE:** reassure

frightened ADJECTIVE **= afraid**, alarmed, scared, terrified, shocked, frozen, cowed, startled, dismayed, unnerved, petrified, flustered, panicky, terrorized, in a panic, scared stiff, in a cold sweat, abashed, terror-stricken, affrighted *(archaic)*, in fear and trepidation, numb with fear

frightening ADJECTIVE **= terrifying**, shocking, alarming, appalling, startling, dreadful, horrifying, menacing, intimidating, dismaying, scary *(informal)*, fearful, daunting, fearsome, unnerving, spooky *(informal)*, hair-raising, baleful, spine-chilling, bloodcurdling

frightful ADJECTIVE **1 = terrible**, shocking, alarming, awful, appalling, horrible, grim, terrifying, dreadful, dread, fearful, traumatic, dire, horrendous, ghastly, hideous, harrowing, gruesome, unnerving, lurid, from hell *(informal)*, grisly, macabre, petrifying, horrid, unspeakable, godawful *(slang)*, hellacious *(U.S. slang)*: *refugees trapped in frightful conditions* **OPPOSITE:** pleasant **2 = dreadful**, great, terrible, extreme, awful, annoying, unpleasant, disagreeable, insufferable: *He got himself into a frightful muddle.* **OPPOSITE:** slight

frigid ADJECTIVE **1 = freezing**, cold, frozen, icy, chill, arctic, Siberian, frosty, cool, glacial, wintry, gelid, frost-bound, hyperboreal: *The water was too frigid to allow him to remain submerged.* **OPPOSITE:** hot **2 = chilly**, formal, stiff, forbidding, rigid, passive, icy, austere, aloof, lifeless, repellent, unresponsive, unfeeling, unbending, unapproachable, passionless, unloving, cold as ice, cold-hearted: *She replied with a frigid smile.* **OPPOSITE:** warm

Charles Dickens' Use of Nouns

Charles Dickens (1812–70) was one of the most popular English authors of the 19th century, perhaps of all time. His novels – among which are the classics *Great Expectations, Oliver Twist, A Christmas Carol* and *David Copperfield* – combine social commentary with vivid characters and memorable plots.

One of the central aspects of Dickens' novels is a sense of place, and this is reflected in the words *house, home,* and *room,* all of which are among his forty most frequent nouns. *Houses* are frequently *old, empty,* and occasionally *haunted* in his ghost stories. *Homes*, on the other hand, are *happy* and *comfortable,* and there are frequent references to one's 'own home' as a place of sanctuary. *Rooms* are often *little,* and conjure up a sense of safety and belonging:

> I... passed the night at Peggotty's, in a **little room** in the roof (with the Crocodile Book on a shelf by the bed's head) which was to be always mine, Peggotty said, and should always be kept for me in exactly the same state.

The safety and comfort of homes is set against the solitariness and destitution of those who have *no home,* or less frequently, are *homeless.*

Another aspect of the importance of place is the centrality of London, which has been described as almost like a character in Dickens' novels. Dickens spent most of his life in London as it grew and changed through the Industrial Revolution to become, by the middle of the 19th century, a city where all classes and types of people – wealthy gentleman, prostitutes, beggars, and pickpockets – lived in close proximity. His descriptions bring to life the sights, smells, and sounds of this teeming city. *London* is often used as a noun modifier in his works, for example in *a London fog, a London summer's day* and *London life.* The name *London* itself holds a mysterious sense of awe for the young orphan Oliver Twist as he sees the word on a signpost:

> The name awakened a new train of ideas in the boy's mind. **London**! – that great place! – nobody – not even Mr. Bumble – could ever find him there!

Dickens' novels are primarily about people, and *man, woman,* and *child* are among his most frequent nouns. Children are viewed sympathetically as *poor, innocent, precious,* and *neglected.* And, of course, there are several references to *dead children,* who carry a special quality of preserved innocence in Dickens' novels, although this feature of his work has often been derided as overly sentimental: in Oscar Wilde's famous words, 'You would need to have a heart of stone not to laugh at the death of Little Nell'.

Among Dickens' hundred most frequent nouns is *love,* both as a form of address in the affectionate 'My love' and 'My dearest love', and as an abstract noun. Frequent adjectives which modify *love* include *devoted, undying, maternal,* and *faithful. Love* also appears in phrases such as *love affair, love letter, love story,* and the now obsolete *love passage* meaning 'romantic interlude':

> 'Augustus!' said Miss Pecksniff, in a low voice. 'I verily believe you have said that fifty thousand times, in my hearing. What a Prose you are!' This was succeeded by some trifling **love passages**, which appeared to originate with, if not to be wholly carried on by Miss Pecksniff....

One of the most inventive features of Dickens' nouns is his use of proper nouns, or names. Dickens created some of the most memorable names in literature, such as *Ebenezer Scrooge, Mr Micawber, Samuel Pickwick,* and *Uriah Heep*. The names that Dickens coins often fit their characters perfectly; for example, *Miss Havisham*, the wealthy but bitter spinster in *Great Expectations,* reminds us that *having* is a *sham.* Several of Dickens' names have passed into general usage: there is a medical term *Pickwickian syndrome* meaning 'obesity'; *Micawberism* is used to refer to unwarranted optimism; and, perhaps most widespread, *Scrooge* can refer to any miser or to miserly qualities: in the *Bank of English,* Collins' corpus of present-day English, there are references to 'Scrooge employers' and people who 'play Scrooge with travel expenses'.

frill NOUN **1 = ruffle**, gathering, tuck, ruff, flounce, ruche, ruching, furbelow, purfle: *net curtains with frills* **2** *(often plural)* **= trimmings**, extras, additions, fuss, jazz *(slang)*, dressing up, decoration(s), bits and pieces, icing on the cake, finery, embellishments, affectation(s), ornamentation, ostentation, frippery, bells and whistles, tomfoolery, gewgaws, superfluities, fanciness, frilliness, fandangles: *The booklet restricts itself to facts without frills.*

frilly ADJECTIVE **= ruffled**, fancy, lacy, frothy, ruched, flouncy

fringe NOUN **1 = border**, edging, edge, binding, trimming, hem, frill, tassel, flounce: *The jacket had leather fringes.* **2 = edge**, limits, border, margin, march, marches, outskirts, perimeter, periphery, borderline: *They lived together on the fringe of the campus.*
▷ MODIFIER **= unofficial**, alternative, radical, innovative, avant-garde, unconventional, unorthodox: *numerous fringe meetings held during the conference*
▷ VERB **= border**, edge, surround, bound, skirt, trim, enclose, flank: *Swampy islands of vegetation fringe the coastline.*

f

fringed ADJECTIVE **1 = bordered**, edged, befringed: *She wore a fringed scarf.* **2 = edged**, bordered, margined, outlined: *tiny islands fringed with golden sand*

frisk VERB **1 = search**, check, inspect, run over, shake down *(U.S. slang)*, body-search: *He pushed him against the wall and frisked him.* **2 = frolic**, play, sport, dance, trip, jump, bounce, hop, skip, romp, caper, prance, cavort, gambol, rollick, curvet: *creatures that grunted and frisked about*

frisky ADJECTIVE **= lively**, spirited, romping, playful, bouncy, high-spirited, rollicking, in high spirits, full of beans *(informal)*, coltish, kittenish, frolicsome, ludic *(literary)*, sportive, full of joie de vivre **OPPOSITE:** sedate

fritter VERB *(usually with* **away***)* **= squander**, waste, run through, dissipate, misspend, idle away, fool away, spend like water

frivolous ADJECTIVE **1 = flippant**, foolish, dizzy, superficial, silly, flip *(informal)*, juvenile, idle, childish, giddy, puerile, flighty, ill-considered, empty-headed, light-hearted, nonserious, light-minded, ditzy *or* ditsy *(slang)*: *I was a bit too frivolous to be a doctor.* **OPPOSITE:** serious **2 = trivial**, petty, trifling, unimportant, light, minor, shallow, pointless, extravagant, peripheral, niggling, paltry, impractical, nickel-and-dime *(U.S. slang)*, footling *(informal)*: *wasting money on frivolous projects* **OPPOSITE:** important

frivolousness *or* **frivolity** NOUN **= flippancy**, fun, nonsense, folly, trifling, lightness, jest, gaiety, silliness, triviality, superficiality, levity, shallowness, childishness, giddiness, flummery, light-heartedness, puerility, flightiness, frivolousness **OPPOSITE:** seriousness

frizzy ADJECTIVE **= tight-curled**, crisp, corrugated, wiry, crimped, frizzed

frog NOUN
▸ *name of young:* tadpole

frolic NOUN **= merriment**, sport, fun, amusement, gaiety, fun and games, skylarking *(informal)*, high jinks, drollery: *Their relationship is never short on fun and frolic.*
▷ VERB **= play**, romp, lark, caper, cavort, frisk, gambol, make merry, rollick, cut capers, sport: *Tourists sunbathe and frolic in the ocean.*

front NOUN **1 = head**, start, lead, beginning, top, fore, forefront: *Stand at the front of the line.* **2 = exterior**, facing, face, façade, frontage, anterior, obverse, forepart: *Attached to the front of the house was a veranda.* **3 = foreground**, fore, forefront, nearest part: *the front of the picture* **4 = front line**, trenches, vanguard, firing line, van: *Her husband is fighting at the front.* **5 = appearance**, show, face, air, bearing, aspect, manner, expression, exterior, countenance, demeanour, mien: *He kept up a brave front.* **6 = disguise**, cover, blind, mask, cover-up, cloak, façade, pretext: *a front for crime syndicates*
▷ ADJECTIVE **1 = foremost**, at the front: *She is still missing her front teeth.* **OPPOSITE:** back **2 = leading**, first, lead, head, foremost, topmost, headmost: *He is the front runner for the star role.*
▷ VERB *(often with* **on** *or* **onto***)* **= face onto**, overlook, look out on, have a view of, look over *or* onto: *Victorian houses fronting onto the pavement*

frontier NOUN **= border**, limit, edge, bound, boundary, confines, verge, perimeter, borderline, dividing line, borderland, marches

frost NOUN **= hoarfrost**, freeze, freeze-up, Jack Frost, rime

frosty ADJECTIVE **1 = cold**, frozen, icy, chilly, wintry, parky *(Brit. informal)*: *sharp, frosty nights* **2 = icy**, ice-capped, icicled, hoar *(rare)*, rimy: *a cat lifting its paws off the frosty stones* **3 = unfriendly**, discouraging, icy, frigid, off-putting *(Brit. informal)*, unenthusiastic, unwelcoming, standoffish, cold as ice: *He may get a frosty reception.*

froth NOUN **= foam**, head, bubbles, lather, suds, spume, effervescence, scum: *the froth on the top of a glass of beer*
▷ VERB **= fizz**, foam, come to a head, lather, bubble over, effervesce: *The sea froths over my feet.*

frothy ADJECTIVE **1 = foamy**, foaming, bubbly, effervescent, sudsy, spumous, spumescent, spumy: *frothy milk shakes* **2 = trivial**, light, empty, slight, unnecessary, vain, petty, trifling, frivolous, frilly, unsubstantial: *the kind of frothy songs one hears*

frown VERB **= glare**, scowl, glower, make a face, look daggers, knit your brows, give a dirty look, lour *or* lower: *He frowned at her anxiously.*
frown on = disapprove of, dislike, discourage, take a dim view of, look askance at, discountenance, view with disfavour, not take kindly to, show disapproval *or* displeasure: *This practice is frowned upon as being wasteful.*
▷ NOUN **= scowl**, glare, glower, dirty look: *a deep frown on the boy's face*

frozen ADJECTIVE **1 = icy**, hard, solid, frosted, arctic, ice-covered, icebound: *the frozen bleakness of the Far North* **2 = chilled**, cold, iced, refrigerated, ice-cold: *frozen desserts like ice cream* **3 = ice-cold**, freezing, numb, very cold, frigid, frozen stiff, chilled to the marrow: *I'm frozen out here.* **4 = motionless**, rooted, petrified, stock-still, turned to stone, stopped dead in your tracks: *She was frozen in horror.* **5 = fixed**, held, stopped, limited, suspended, pegged *(of a price)*: *Prices would be frozen and wages raised.*

frugal ADJECTIVE **1 = thrifty**, sparing, careful, prudent, provident, parsimonious, abstemious, penny-wise, saving, cheeseparing: *She lives a frugal life.* **OPPOSITE:** wasteful **2 = meagre**, economical, niggardly: *Her diet was frugal.*

fruit NOUN **1 = produce**, crop, yield, harvest: *The fruit has got a long storage life.* **2** *(often plural)* **= result**, reward, outcome, end result, return, effect, benefit, profit, advantage, consequence: *The findings are the fruit of more than three years' research.*

> **QUOTATIONS**
> A good tree cannot bring forth evil fruit, neither can a corrupt tree bring forth good fruit
> [*Bible: St. Matthew*]

> **PROVERBS**
> *He that would eat the fruit must climb the tree*

fruitful ADJECTIVE **1 = useful**, successful, effective, rewarding, profitable, productive, worthwhile, beneficial, advantageous, well-spent, gainful: *We had a long, fruitful relationship.* **OPPOSITE:** useless **2 = fertile**, fecund, fructiferous: *a landscape that was fruitful and lush* **OPPOSITE:** barren **3 = productive**, prolific, abundant, plentiful, rich, flush, spawning, copious, profuse, plenteous: *blossoms on a fruitful tree*

fruition NOUN **= fulfilment**, maturity, completion, perfection, enjoyment, realization, attainment, maturation, consummation, ripeness, actualization, materialization

fruitless ADJECTIVE **= useless**, vain, unsuccessful, in vain, pointless, futile, unproductive, abortive, to no avail, ineffectual, unprofitable, to no effect, unavailing, unfruitful, profitless, bootless **OPPOSITE:** fruitful

fruity ADJECTIVE **1 = rich**, full, mellow: *a lovely, fruity wine* **2 = resonant**, full, deep, rich, vibrant, mellow: *He had a solid, fruity laugh.* **3 = risqué**, indecent, suggestive, racy, blue, hot, sexy, ripe, spicy *(informal)*, vulgar, juicy, titillating, bawdy, salacious, smutty, indelicate, near the knuckle *(informal)*: *She clearly enjoyed the fruity joke.*

frumpy *or* **frumpish** ADJECTIVE **= dowdy**, dated, dreary, out of date, drab, unfashionable, dingy, mumsy, badly-dressed

frustrate VERB **1 = discourage**, anger, depress, annoy, infuriate, exasperate, dishearten, dissatisfy: *These questions frustrated me.* **OPPOSITE:** encourage **2 = thwart**, stop, check, block, defeat, disappoint, counter, confront, spoil, foil, baffle, inhibit, hobble, balk, circumvent, forestall, neutralize, stymie, nullify, render null and void, crool *or* cruel *(Austral. slang)*: *The government has deliberately frustrated his efforts.* **OPPOSITE:** further

frustrated ADJECTIVE **= disappointed**, discouraged, infuriated, discontented, exasperated, resentful, embittered, irked, disheartened, carrying a chip on your shoulder *(informal)*

frustration NOUN **1 = annoyance**, disappointment, resentment, irritation, grievance, dissatisfaction, exasperation, vexation: *a man fed up with the frustrations of everyday life* **2 = obstruction**, blocking, curbing, foiling, failure, spoiling, thwarting, contravention, circumvention, nonfulfilment, nonsuccess: *the frustration of their plan*

fudge VERB **= misrepresent**, avoid, dodge, evade, hedge, stall, fake, flannel *(Brit. informal)*, patch up, falsify, equivocate

fuel NOUN **1 = nourishment**, food, kai *(N.Z. informal)*, sustenance: *Babies and toddlers need fuel for growth.* **2 = incitement**, encouragement, ammunition, provocation, food, material, incentive, fodder: *His comments are bound to add fuel to the debate.* ▷ VERB **= inflame**, power, charge, fire, fan, encourage, feed, boost, sustain, stimulate, nourish, incite, whip up, stoke up: *The economic boom was fuelled by easy credit.*

fugitive NOUN **= runaway**, refugee, deserter, escapee, runagate *(archaic)*

fulfil *or (U.S.)* **fullfil** VERB **1 = carry out**, perform, execute, discharge, keep, effect, finish, complete, achieve, conclude, accomplish, bring to completion: *He is too ill to fulfil his duties.* **OPPOSITE:** neglect **2 = achieve**, realize, satisfy, attain, consummate, bring to fruition, perfect: *He decided to fulfil his dream and go to college.* **3 = satisfy**, please, content, cheer, refresh, gratify, make happy: *After the war, nothing quite fulfilled her.* **4 = comply with**, meet, fill, satisfy, observe, obey, conform to, answer: *All the necessary conditions were fulfilled.*

fulfilment *or (U.S.)* **fullfilment** NOUN **= achievement**, effecting, implementation, carrying out *or* through, end, crowning, discharge, discharging, completion, perfection, accomplishment, realization, attainment, observance, consummation

full ADJECTIVE **1 = filled**, stocked, brimming, replete, complete, entire, loaded, sufficient, intact, gorged, saturated, bursting at the seams, brimful: *Repeat the layers until the terrine is full.* **2 = crammed**, crowded, packed, crushed, jammed, in use, congested, chock-full, chock-a-block: *The centre is full beyond capacity.* **OPPOSITE:** empty **3 = occupied**, taken, in use, unavailable: *The cheap seats were all full.* **4 = satiated**, satisfied, having had enough, replete, sated: *It's healthy to stop eating when I'm full.* **5 = extensive**, detailed, complete, broad, generous, adequate, ample, abundant, plentiful, copious, plenary, plenteous: *Full details will be sent to you.* **OPPOSITE:** incomplete **6 = comprehensive**, complete, thorough, exhaustive, all-inclusive, all-embracing, unabridged: *They can now publish a full list of candidates.* **7 = rounded**, strong, rich, powerful, intense, pungent: *Italian plum tomatoes have a full flavour.* **8 = plump**, rounded, voluptuous, shapely, well-rounded, buxom, curvaceous: *large sizes for ladies with a fuller figure* **9 = voluminous**, large, loose, baggy, billowing, puffy, capacious, loose-fitting, balloon-like: *My wedding dress has a very full skirt.* **OPPOSITE:** tight **10 = rich**, strong, deep, loud, distinct, resonant, sonorous, clear: *She has a full voice; mine is a bit lighter.* **OPPOSITE:** thin
in full = completely, fully, in total, without exception, in its entirety, in toto *(Latin)*: *We will refund your money in full.*
to the full = thoroughly, completely, fully, entirely, to the limit, without reservation, to the utmost: *She has a good mind which should be used to the full.*

full-blooded ADJECTIVE **= wholehearted**, full, complete, sweeping, thorough, uncompromising, exhaustive, all-embracing

full-blown ADJECTIVE **1 = fully developed**, total, full-scale, fully fledged, full, whole, developed, complete, advanced, entire, full-sized, fully grown, fully formed: *You're talking this thing up into a full-blown conspiracy.* **OPPOSITE:** undeveloped **2 = in full bloom**, full, flowering, unfolded, blossoming, opened out: *the faded hues of full-blown roses*

full-bodied ADJECTIVE **= rich**, strong, big, heavy, heady, mellow, fruity, redolent, full-flavoured, well-matured

fullness *or (U.S.)* **fulness** NOUN **1 = plenty**, glut, saturation, sufficiency, profusion, satiety, repletion, copiousness, ampleness, adequateness: *High-fibre diets give the feeling of fullness.* **2 = completeness**, wealth, entirety, totality, wholeness, vastness, plenitude, comprehensiveness, broadness, extensiveness: *She displayed the fullness of her cycling talent.* **3 = roundness**, voluptuousness, curvaceousness, swelling, enlargement, dilation, distension, tumescence: *I accept my body with all its womanly fullness.* **4 = richness**, strength, resonance, loudness, clearness: *with modest riffs and a fullness in sound*

full-scale ADJECTIVE **= major**, extensive, wide-ranging, all-out, sweeping, comprehensive, proper, thorough, in-depth, exhaustive, all-encompassing, thoroughgoing, full-dress

fully ADVERB **1 = completely**, totally, perfectly, entirely, absolutely, altogether, thoroughly, intimately, wholly, positively, utterly, every inch, heart and soul, to the hilt, one hundred per cent, in all respects, from first to last, lock, stock and barrel: *She was fully aware of my thoughts.* **2 = in all respects**, completely, totally, entirely, altogether, thoroughly, wholly: *He had still not fully recovered.* **3 = adequately**, amply, comprehensively, sufficiently, enough, satisfactorily, abundantly, plentifully: *These debates are discussed fully later in the book.* **4 = at least**, quite, without (any) exaggeration, without a word of a lie *(informal)*: *He set his sights and let fly from fully 35 yards.*

fully-fledged *or* **full-fledged** ADJECTIVE **= experienced**, trained, senior, professional, qualified, mature, proficient, time-served

fulsome ADJECTIVE **= extravagant**, excessive, over the top, sickening, overdone, fawning, nauseating, inordinate, ingratiating, cloying, insincere, saccharine, sycophantic, unctuous, smarmy *(Brit. informal)*, immoderate, adulatory, gross

> **USAGE**
> In journalism, *fulsome* is often used simply to mean 'extremely complimentary' or 'full, rich, or abundant'. In other kinds of writing, however, this word should only be used if you intend to suggest negative overtones of excess or insincerity.

fumble VERB **1** *(often with* **for** *or* **with***)* **= grope**, flounder, paw *(informal)*, scrabble, feel around: *She crept from the bed and fumbled for her dressing gown.* **2 = bungle**, spoil, botch, mess up, cock up *(Brit. slang)*, mishandle, mismanage, muff, make a hash of *(informal)*, make a nonsense of, bodge *(informal)*, misfield, crool *or* cruel

f

(Austral. slang): *I'd hate to fumble a chance like this.*

fume VERB = **rage**, boil, seethe, see red *(informal)*, storm, rave, rant, smoulder, crack up *(informal)*, go ballistic *(slang, chiefly U.S.)*, champ at the bit *(informal)*, blow a fuse *(slang, chiefly U.S.)*, fly off the handle *(informal)*, get hot under the collar *(informal)*, go off the deep end *(informal)*, wig out *(slang)*, go up the wall *(slang)*, get steamed up about *(slang)*: *I fumed when these women did not respond.*
▷ NOUN **1** *(often plural)* = **smoke**, gas, exhaust, pollution, haze, vapour, smog, miasma, exhalation, effluvium: *car exhaust fumes* **2** = **stench**, stink, whiff *(Brit. slang)*, reek, pong *(Brit. informal)*, foul smell, niff *(Brit. slang)*, malodour, mephitis, fetor, noisomeness: *stale alcohol fumes*

f

fuming ADJECTIVE = **furious**, angry, raging, choked, roused, incensed, enraged, seething, up in arms, incandescent, in a rage, on the warpath *(informal)*, foaming at the mouth, at boiling point *(informal)*, all steamed up *(slang)*, tooshie *(Austral. slang)*

fun NOUN **1** = **amusement**, sport, treat, pleasure, entertainment, cheer, good time, recreation, enjoyment, romp, distraction, diversion, frolic, junketing, merriment, whoopee *(informal)*, high jinks, living it up, jollity, beer and skittles *(informal)*, merrymaking, jollification: *You still have time to join in the fun.* **2** = **joking**, clowning, merriment, playfulness, play, game, sport, nonsense, teasing, jesting, skylarking *(informal)*, horseplay, buffoonery, tomfoolery, jocularity, foolery: *There was lots of fun going on last night.* **3** = **enjoyment**, pleasure, joy, cheer, mirth, gaiety: *She had a great sense of fun.*
OPPOSITE: gloom
▷ MODIFIER = **enjoyable**, entertaining, pleasant, amusing, lively, diverting, witty, convivial: *It was a fun evening.*
for *or* **in fun** = **for a joke**, tongue in cheek, jokingly, playfully, for a laugh, mischievously, in jest, teasingly, with a straight face, facetiously, light-heartedly, roguishly, with a gleam *or* twinkle in your eye: *Don't say such things, even in fun.*
make fun of something *or* **someone** = **mock**, tease, ridicule, poke fun at, take off, rag, rib *(informal)*, laugh at, taunt, mimic, parody, deride, send up *(Brit. informal)*, scoff at, sneer at, lampoon, make a fool of, pour scorn on, take the mickey out of *(Brit. informal)*, satirize, pull someone's leg, hold up to ridicule, make a monkey of, make sport of, make the butt of, make game of: *Don't make fun of me!*

> **QUOTATIONS**
> That [sex] was the most fun I've ever had without laughing
> [Woody Allen *Annie Hall*]
>
> People must not do things for fun. We are not here for fun. There is no reference to fun in any Act of Parliament
> [A.P. Herbert *Uncommon Law*]

function NOUN **1** = **purpose**, business, job, concern, use, part, office, charge, role, post, operation, situation, activity, exercise, responsibility, task, duty, mission, employment, capacity, province, occupation, raison d'être *(French)*: *The main function of merchant banks is to raise capital.* **2** = **reception**, party, affair, gathering, bash *(informal)*, lig *(Brit. slang)*, social occasion, soiree, do *(informal)*: *We were going down to a function in London.*
▷ VERB **1** = **work**, run, operate, perform, be in business, be in running order, be in operation *or* action, go: *The authorities say the prison is now functioning properly.* **2** *(with* **as***)* = **act**, serve, operate, perform, behave, officiate, act the part of, do duty, have the role of, be in commission, be in operation *or* action, serve your turn: *On weekdays, one third of the room functions as a workspace.*

functional ADJECTIVE **1** = **practical**, utility, utilitarian, serviceable, hard-wearing, useful: *The decor is functional.* **2** = **working**, operative, operational, in working order, going, prepared, ready, viable, up and running, workable, usable: *We have fully functional smoke alarms on all staircases.*

functionary NOUN = **officer**, official, dignitary, office holder, office bearer, employee

fund NOUN **1** = **reserve**, stock, supply, store, collection, pool, foundation, endowment, tontine: *a scholarship fund for undergraduate students* **2** = **store**, stock, source, supply, mine, reserve, treasury, vein, reservoir, accumulation, hoard, repository: *He has an extraordinary fund of energy.*
▷ VERB = **finance**, back, support, pay for, promote, float, endow, subsidize, stake, capitalize, provide money for, put up the money for: *The foundation has funded a variety of faculty programs.*

fundamental ADJECTIVE **1** = **central**, first, most important, prime, key, necessary, basic, essential, primary, vital, radical, principal, cardinal, integral, indispensable, intrinsic: *the fundamental principles of democracy*
OPPOSITE: incidental **2** = **basic**, essential, underlying, organic, profound, elementary, rudimentary: *The two leaders have very fundamental differences.*

fundamentally ADVERB **1** = **basically**, at heart, at bottom: *Fundamentally, women like him for his sensitivity.*
2 = **essentially**, radically, basically, primarily, profoundly, intrinsically: *He disagreed fundamentally with her judgment.*

fundi NOUN = **expert**, authority, specialist, professional, master, pro *(informal)*, ace *(informal)*, genius, guru, pundit, buff *(informal)*, maestro, virtuoso, boffin *(Brit. informal)*, hotshot *(informal)*, past master, dab hand *(Brit. informal)*, wonk *(informal)*, maven *(U.S.)*

funds PLURAL NOUN = **money**, capital, cash, finance, means, savings, necessary *(informal)*, resources, assets, silver, bread *(slang)*, wealth, tin *(slang)*, brass *(Northern English dialect)*, dough *(slang)*, rhino *(Brit. slang)*, the ready *(informal)*, dosh *(Brit. & Austral. slang)*, hard cash, the wherewithal, needful *(informal)*, shekels *(informal)*, dibs *(slang)*, ready money, ackers *(slang)*, spondulicks *(slang)*: *The concert will raise funds for AIDS research.*

funeral NOUN = **burial**, committal, laying to rest, cremation, interment, obsequies, entombment, inhumation

funereal ADJECTIVE = **gloomy**, dark, sad, grave, depressing, dismal, lamenting, solemn, dreary, sombre, woeful, mournful, lugubrious, sepulchral, dirge-like, deathlike

funk VERB = **chicken out of**, dodge, recoil from, take fright, flinch from, duck out of *(informal)*, turn tail *(informal)*

funnel VERB **1** = **conduct**, direct, channel, convey, move, pass, pour, filter: *This device funnels the water from a downpipe into a butt.* **2** = **channel**, direct, pour, filter, convey: *The centre will funnel money into research.*

funny ADJECTIVE **1** = **humorous**, amusing, comical, entertaining, killing *(informal)*, rich, comic, silly, ridiculous, diverting, absurd, jolly, witty, hilarious, ludicrous, laughable, farcical, slapstick, riotous, droll, risible, facetious, jocular, side-splitting, waggish, jocose: *I'll tell you a funny story.* **OPPOSITE:** unfunny
2 = **comic**, comical, a scream, a card *(informal)*, a caution *(informal)*: *He could be funny when he wanted to be.*
3 = **peculiar**, odd, strange, unusual, remarkable, bizarre, puzzling, curious, weird, mysterious, suspicious, dubious, queer, rum *(Brit. slang)*, quirky, perplexing: *There's something funny about him.* **4** = **ill**, poorly *(informal)*, queasy, sick, odd, crook *(Austral. & N.Z. informal)*, ailing, queer, unhealthy, seedy *(informal)*, unwell, out of sorts *(informal)*, off-colour *(informal)*, under the weather *(informal)*: *My head ached and my stomach felt funny.*

furious ADJECTIVE **1** = **angry**, mad, raging, boiling, fuming, choked, frantic, frenzied, infuriated, incensed, enraged, maddened, inflamed, very angry, cross, livid *(informal)*, up in arms, incandescent, on the warpath *(informal)*, foaming at the mouth, wrathful, in high dudgeon, wroth *(archaic)*, fit to be tied *(slang)*, beside yourself, tooshie *(Austral. slang)*: *He is furious at the way his wife has been treated.* **OPPOSITE:** pleased
2 = **violent**, wild, intense, fierce,

savage, turbulent, stormy, agitated, boisterous, tumultuous, vehement, unrestrained, tempestuous, impetuous, ungovernable: *A furious gunbattle ensued.*

furnish VERB **1 = decorate**, fit, fit out, appoint, provide, stock, supply, store, provision, outfit, equip, fit up, purvey: *Many proprietors try to furnish their hotels with antiques.* **2 = supply**, give, offer, provide, present, reveal, grant, afford, hand out, endow, bestow: *They'll be able to furnish you with the details.*

furniture NOUN **= household goods**, furnishings, fittings, house fittings, goods, things *(informal)*, effects, equipment, appointments, possessions, appliances, chattels, movable property, movables

furore *or (U.S.)* **furor** NOUN **= commotion**, to-do, stir, excitement, fury, disturbance, flap *(informal)*, outburst, frenzy, outcry, uproar, brouhaha, hullabaloo

furrow NOUN **1 = groove**, line, channel, hollow, trench, seam, crease, fluting, rut, corrugation: *Bike trails crisscrossed the grassy furrows.* **2 = wrinkle**, line, crease, crinkle, crow's-foot, gather, fold, crumple, rumple, pucker, corrugation: *Deep furrows marked the corner of his mouth.*
▷ VERB **= wrinkle**, knit, draw together, crease, seam, flute, corrugate: *My bank manager furrowed his brow.*

further ADVERB **= in addition**, moreover, besides, furthermore, also, yet, on top of, what's more, to boot, additionally, over and above, as well as, into the bargain: *Further, losing one day doesn't mean you won't win the next.*
▷ ADJECTIVE **= additional**, more, new, other, extra, fresh, supplementary: *There was nothing further to be done.*
▷ VERB **= promote**, help, develop, aid, forward, champion, push, encourage, speed, advance, work for, foster, contribute to, assist, plug *(informal)*, facilitate, pave the way for, hasten, patronize, expedite, succour, lend support to: *Education needn't only be about furthering your career.*
OPPOSITE: hinder

furthermore ADVERB **= moreover**, further, in addition, besides, too, as well, not to mention, what's more, to boot, additionally, into the bargain

furthest ADJECTIVE **= most distant**, extreme, ultimate, remotest, outermost, uttermost, furthermost, outmost

furtive ADJECTIVE **= sly**, secret, hidden, sneaking, covert, cloaked, behind someone's back, secretive, clandestine, sneaky, under-the-table, slinking, conspiratorial, skulking, underhand, surreptitious, stealthy
OPPOSITE: open

fury NOUN **1 = anger**, passion, rage, madness, frenzy, wrath, ire, red mist *(informal)*, impetuosity: *She screamed, her face distorted with fury.*
OPPOSITE: calmness **2 = violence**, force, power, intensity, severity, turbulence, ferocity, savagery, vehemence, fierceness, tempestuousness: *We were lashed by the full fury of the elements.* **OPPOSITE:** peace

fuse VERB **1 = join**, unite, combine, blend, integrate, merge, put together, dissolve, amalgamate, federate, coalesce, intermingle, meld, run together, commingle, intermix, agglutinate: *Conception occurs when a single sperm fuses with an egg.*
OPPOSITE: separate **2 = bond**, join, stick, melt, weld, smelt, solder: *They all fuse into a glassy state.*

fusion NOUN **= merging**, uniting, union, merger, federation, mixture, blend, blending, integration, synthesis, amalgamation, coalescence, commingling, commixture

fuss NOUN **1 = commotion**, to-do, worry, upset, bother, stir, confusion, excitement, hurry, flap *(informal)*, bustle, flutter, flurry, agitation, fidget, fluster, ado, hue and cry, palaver, storm in a teacup *(Brit.)*, pother: *I don't know what all the fuss is about.* **2 = bother**, trouble, struggle, hassle *(informal)*, nuisance, inconvenience, hindrance: *He gets down to work without any fuss.*
3 = complaint, row, protest, objection, trouble, display, argument, difficulty, upset, bother, unrest, hassle *(informal)*, squabble, furore, altercation: *We kicked up a fuss and got an apology.*
▷ VERB **= worry**, flap *(informal)*, bustle, fret, niggle, fidget, chafe, take pains, make a meal of *(informal)*, be agitated, labour over, get worked up, get in a stew *(informal)*, make a thing of *(informal)*: *She fussed about getting me a drink.*

fussy ADJECTIVE **1 = particular**, difficult, exacting, discriminating, fastidious, dainty, squeamish, choosy *(informal)*, picky *(informal)*, nit-picking *(informal)*, hard to please, finicky, pernickety, faddish, faddy, old-maidish, old womanish, overparticular, nit-picky *(informal)*: *She's not fussy about her food.*
2 = overelaborate, busy, cluttered, rococo, overdecorated, overembellished: *We are not keen on floral patterns and fussy designs.*

futile ADJECTIVE **1 = useless**, vain, unsuccessful, pointless, empty, hollow, in vain, worthless, barren, sterile, fruitless, forlorn, unproductive, abortive, to no avail, ineffectual, unprofitable, valueless, unavailing, otiose, profitless, nugatory, without rhyme or reason, bootless: *a futile attempt to ward off the blow* **OPPOSITE:** useful **2 = trivial**, pointless, trifling, unimportant: *She doesn't want to comment. It's too futile.*
OPPOSITE: important

futility NOUN **1 = uselessness**, ineffectiveness, pointlessness, fruitlessness, emptiness, hollowness, spitting in the wind, bootlessness: *the injustice and futility of terrorism*
2 = triviality, vanity, pointlessness, unimportance: *a sense of the emptiness and futility of life*

> **QUOTATIONS**
> As futile as a clock in an empty house
> [James Thurber]

future NOUN **1 = time to come**, hereafter, what lies ahead: *He made plans for the future.* **2 = prospect**, expectation, outlook: *She has a splendid future in the police force.*
▷ ADJECTIVE **= forthcoming**, to be, coming, later, expected, approaching, to come, succeeding, fated, ultimate, subsequent, destined, prospective, eventual, ensuing, impending, unborn, in the offing: *the future King and Queen* **OPPOSITE:** past

fuzz NOUN **= fluff**, down, hair, pile, fibre, nap, floss, lint

fuzzy ADJECTIVE **1 = frizzy**, fluffy, woolly, downy, flossy, down-covered, linty, napped: *He is a fierce bearded character with fuzzy hair.* **2 = indistinct**, faint, blurred, vague, distorted, unclear, shadowy, bleary, unfocused, out of focus, ill-defined: *a couple of fuzzy pictures* **OPPOSITE:** distinct

Gg

gadget NOUN **= device**, thing, appliance, machine, tool, implement, invention, instrument, novelty, apparatus, gimmick, utensil, contraption *(informal)*, gizmo *(slang, chiefly U.S. & Canad.)*, contrivance

gaffe NOUN **= blunder**, mistake, error, indiscretion, lapse, boob *(Brit. slang)*, slip-up *(informal)*, slip, howler, bloomer *(informal)*, clanger *(informal)*, faux pas, boo-boo *(informal)*, solecism, gaucherie, barry or Barry Crocker *(Austral. slang)*

> **QUOTATIONS**
> A gaffe is when a politician tells the truth
> [Michael Kinsley]

gag[1] NOUN **= muzzle**, tie, restraint: *His captors had put a gag of thick leather in his mouth.*
▷ VERB **1 = suppress**, silence, subdue, muffle, curb, stifle, muzzle, quieten: *a journalist who claimed he was gagged by his bosses* **2 = retch**, choke, heave: *I knelt by the toilet and gagged.*

gag[2] NOUN **= joke**, crack *(slang)*, funny *(informal)*, quip, pun, jest, wisecrack *(informal)*, sally, witticism: *He made a gag about bald men.*

gaiety NOUN **1 = cheerfulness**, glee, good humour, buoyancy, happiness, animation, exuberance, high spirits, elation, exhilaration, hilarity, merriment, joie de vivre *(French)*, good cheer, vivacity, jollity, liveliness, gladness, effervescence, light-heartedness, joyousness: *There was a bright, infectious gaiety in the children's laughter.* **OPPOSITE:** misery **2 = merrymaking**, celebration, revels, festivity, fun, mirth, revelry, conviviality, jollification, carousal: *The mood was one of laughter and gaiety.*

gaily ADVERB **1 = cheerfully**, happily, gleefully, brightly, blithely, merrily, joyfully, cheerily, jauntily, light-heartedly, chirpily *(informal)*: *She laughed gaily.* **2 = colourfully**, brightly, vividly, flamboyantly, gaudily, brilliantly, flashily, showily: *gaily painted front doors*

gain VERB **1 = acquire**, get, receive, achieve, earn, pick up, win, secure, collect, gather, obtain, build up, attain, glean, procure: *Students can gain valuable experience doing part-time work.* **2 = profit**, make, earn, get, win, clear, land, score *(slang)*, achieve, net, bag, secure, collect, gather, realize, obtain, capture, acquire, bring in, harvest, attain, reap, glean, procure: *The company didn't disclose how much it expects to gain from the deal.* **OPPOSITE:** lose **3 = put on**, increase in, gather, build up: *Some people gain weight after they give up smoking.* **4 = attain**, earn, get, achieve, win, reach, get to, secure, obtain, acquire, arrive at, procure: *Passing exams is no longer enough to gain a place at university.*
▷ NOUN **1 = rise**, increase, growth, advance, improvement, upsurge, upturn, increment, upswing: *House prices showed a gain of nearly 8% in June.* **2 = profit**, income, earnings, proceeds, winnings, return, produce, benefit, advantage, yield, dividend, acquisition, attainment, lucre, emolument: *He buys art solely for financial gain.* **OPPOSITE:** loss
▷ PLURAL NOUN **= profits**, earnings, revenue, proceeds, winnings, takings, pickings, booty: *Investors will have their gains taxed as income in future.*
gain on something or **someone = get nearer to**, close in on, approach, catch up with, narrow the gap on: *The car began to gain on the van.*

gainful ADJECTIVE **= profitable**, rewarding, productive, lucrative, paying, useful, valuable, worthwhile, beneficial, fruitful, advantageous, expedient, remunerative, moneymaking

gainsay VERB **= deny**, dispute, disagree with, contradict, contravene, rebut, controvert **OPPOSITE:** confirm

gait NOUN **= walk**, step, bearing, pace, stride, carriage, tread, manner of walking

gala NOUN **= festival**, party, fête, celebration, carnival, festivity, pageant, jamboree: *a gala at the Royal Opera House*
▷ ADJECTIVE **= festive**, merry, joyous, joyful, celebratory, convivial, gay, festal: *I want to make her birthday a gala occasion.*

galaxy NOUN **= star system**, solar system, nebula

gale NOUN **1 = storm**, hurricane, tornado, cyclone, whirlwind, blast, gust, typhoon, tempest, squall: *forecasts of fierce gales over the next few days* **2 = outburst**, scream, roar, fit, storm, shout, burst, explosion, outbreak, howl, shriek, eruption, peal, paroxysm: *gales of laughter from the audience*

gall[1] NOUN **= growth**, lump, excrescence: *The mites live within the galls that are formed on the plant.*

gall[2] VERB **= annoy**, provoke, irritate, aggravate *(informal)*, get *(informal)*, trouble, bother, disturb, plague, madden, ruffle, exasperate, nettle, vex, displease, irk, rile *(informal)*, peeve *(informal)*, get under your skin *(informal)*, get on your nerves *(informal)*, nark *(Brit., Austral. & N.Z. slang)*, get up your nose *(informal)*, make your blood boil, rub up the wrong way, get on your wick *(Brit. slang)*, get your back up, put your back up, hack you off *(informal)*: *It was their smugness that galled her most.*

gallant ADJECTIVE **1 = brave**, daring, bold, heroic, courageous, dashing, noble, manly, gritty, fearless, intrepid, valiant, plucky, doughty, dauntless, lion-hearted, valorous, manful, mettlesome: *gallant soldiers who gave their lives* **OPPOSITE:** cowardly **2 = courteous**, mannerly, gentlemanly, polite, gracious, attentive, courtly, chivalrous: *He was a thoughtful, gallant and generous man.* **OPPOSITE:** discourteous

gallantry NOUN **1 = bravery**, spirit, daring, courage, nerve, guts *(informal)*, pluck, grit, heroism, mettle, boldness, manliness, valour, derring-do *(archaic)*, fearlessness, intrepidity, valiance, courageousness, dauntlessness, doughtiness: *He was awarded a medal for his gallantry.* **OPPOSITE:** cowardice **2 = courtesy**, politeness, chivalry, attentiveness, graciousness, courtliness, gentlemanliness, courteousness: *He kissed her hand with old-fashioned gallantry.* **OPPOSITE:** discourtesy

galling ADJECTIVE **= annoying**, provoking, irritating, aggravating *(informal)*, disturbing, humiliating, maddening, exasperating, vexing, displeasing, rankling, irksome, vexatious, nettlesome

gallop VERB **1 = run**, race, shoot, career, speed, bolt, stampede: *The horses galloped away.* **2 = dash**, run, race, shoot, fly, career, speed, tear, rush, barrel (along) *(informal, chiefly U.S. & Canad.)*, sprint, dart, zoom: *They were galloping around the garden playing football.*

galore ADVERB **= in abundance**, everywhere, to spare, all over the place, aplenty, in great numbers, in profusion, in great quantity, à gogo *(informal)*

galvanize VERB **= stimulate**, encourage, inspire, prompt, move, fire, shock, excite, wake, stir, spur, provoke, startle, arouse, awaken, rouse, prod, jolt, kick-start, electrify, goad, impel, invigorate

gamble NOUN **1 = risk**, chance, venture, lottery, speculation, uncertainty, leap in the dark: *the*

President's risky gamble in calling an election **OPPOSITE:** certainty **2 = bet**, flutter (*informal*), punt (*chiefly Brit.*), wager: *My father-in-law likes a drink and the odd gamble.*
▷ VERB **1** (*often with* **on**) **= take a chance**, back, speculate, take the plunge, stick your neck out (*informal*), put your faith *or* trust in: *Few firms will be prepared to gamble on new products.* **2 = risk**, chance, stake, venture, hazard, wager: *Are you prepared to gamble your career on this matter?* **3 = bet**, play, game, stake, speculate, back, punt, wager, put money on, have a flutter (*informal*), try your luck, put your shirt on, lay *or* make a bet: *John gambled heavily on the horses.*

game[1] NOUN **1 = pastime**, sport, activity, entertainment, recreation, distraction, amusement, diversion: *the game of hide-and-seek* **OPPOSITE:** job **2 = match**, meeting, event, competition, tournament, clash, contest, round, head-to-head: *We won three games against Australia.* **3 = amusement**, joke, entertainment, diversion, lark: *Some people simply regard life as a game.* **4 = activity**, business, line, situation, proceeding, enterprise, undertaking, occupation, pursuit: *She's new to this game, so go easy on her.* **5 = wild animals** *or* **birds**, prey, quarry: *men who shoot game for food* **6 = scheme**, plan, design, strategy, trick, plot, tactic, manoeuvre, dodge, ploy, scam, stratagem, fastie (*Austral. slang*): *All right, what's your little game?*
▷ ADJECTIVE **1 = willing**, prepared, ready, keen, eager, interested, inclined, disposed, up for it (*informal*), desirous: *He said he's game for a similar challenge next year.* **2 = brave**, courageous, dogged, spirited, daring, bold, persistent, gritty, fearless, feisty (*informal, chiefly U.S. & Canad.*), persevering, intrepid, valiant, plucky, unflinching, dauntless, (as) game as Ned Kelly (*Austral. slang*): *They were the only ones game enough to give it a try.* **OPPOSITE:** cowardly

> **QUOTATIONS**
>
> Play for more than you can afford to lose, and you will learn the game
> [Winston Churchill]
>
> It should be noted that children at play are not playing about; their games should be seen as their most serious-minded activity
> [Montaigne *Essais*]
>
> Die: the singular of 'dice'. We seldom hear the word, because there is a prohibitory proverb, 'Never say die.'
> [Ambrose Bierce *The Devil's Dictionary*]
>
> I am sorry I have not learned to play at cards. It is very useful in life; it generates kindness and consolidates society
> [Dr. Johnson]
>
> It's just a game – baseball – an amusement, a marginal thing, not an art, not a consequential metaphor for life, not a public trust
> [Richard Ford *Stop Blaming Baseball*]
>
> Life is a game in which the rules are constantly changing; nothing spoils a game more than those who take it seriously
> [Quentin Crisp *Manners From Heaven*]

game[2] ADJECTIVE **= lame**, injured, disabled, crippled, defective, bad, maimed, deformed, gammy (*Brit. slang*): *a game leg*

gamut NOUN **= range**, series, collection, variety, lot, field, scale, sweep, catalogue, scope, compass, assortment

gang NOUN **= group**, crowd, pack, company, party, lot, band, crew (*informal*), bunch, mob, horde

gangster NOUN **= hoodlum** (*chiefly U.S.*), crook (*informal*), thug, bandit, heavy (*slang*), tough, hood (*U.S. slang*), robber, gang member, mobster (*U.S. slang*), racketeer, desperado, ruffian, brigand, wise guy (*U.S.*), tsotsi (*S. African*)

gaol *see* **jail**

gap NOUN **1 = opening**, space, hole, break, split, divide, crack, rent, breach, slot, vent, rift, aperture, cleft, chink, crevice, fissure, cranny, perforation, interstice: *the wind tearing through gaps in the window frames* **2 = interval**, pause, recess, interruption, respite, lull, interlude, breathing space, hiatus, intermission, lacuna, entr'acte: *There followed a gap of four years.* **3 = difference**, gulf, contrast, disagreement, discrepancy, inconsistency, disparity, divergence: *the gap between the poor and the well-off*

gape VERB **1 = stare**, wonder, goggle, gawp (*Brit. slang*), gawk: *She stopped what she was doing and gaped at me.* **2 = open**, split, crack, yawn: *A hole gaped in the roof.*

gaping ADJECTIVE **= wide**, great, open, broad, vast, yawning, wide open, cavernous

garb NOUN **= clothes**, dress, clothing, gear (*slang*), wear, habit, get-up (*informal*), uniform, outfit, costume, threads (*slang*), array, ensemble, garments, robes, duds (*informal*), apparel, clobber (*Brit. slang*), attire, togs (*informal*), vestments, raiment (*archaic*), rigout (*informal*), bling (*slang*)

garbage NOUN **1 = junk**, rubbish, litter, trash (*chiefly U.S.*), refuse, waste, sweepings, scraps, debris, muck, filth, swill, slops, offal, detritus, dross, odds and ends, flotsam and jetsam, grot (*slang*), leavings, dreck (*slang, chiefly U.S.*), scourings, offscourings: *rotting piles of garbage* **2 = nonsense**, rot, crap (*slang*), trash, hot air (*informal*), tosh (*informal*), pap, bilge (*informal*), drivel, twaddle, tripe (*informal*), gibberish, malarkey, guff (*slang*), moonshine, claptrap (*informal*), hogwash, hokum (*slang, chiefly U.S. & Canad.*), codswallop (*Brit. slang*), piffle (*informal*), poppycock (*informal*), balderdash, bosh (*informal*), eyewash (*informal*), kak (*S. African slang*), stuff and nonsense, bunkum *or* buncombe (*chiefly U.S.*), bizzo (*Austral. slang*), bull's wool (*Austral. & N.Z. slang*): *I personally think the story is complete garbage.*

garbled ADJECTIVE **= jumbled**, confused, distorted, mixed up, muddled, incomprehensible, unintelligible

garden NOUN **= grounds**, park, plot, patch, lawn, allotment, yard (*U.S. & Canad.*), forest park (*N.Z.*)
▸ *related adjective:* horticultural

> **QUOTATIONS**
>
> We must cultivate our gardens
> [Voltaire *Candide*]
>
> God Almighty first planted a garden, and, indeed, it is the purest of human pleasures
> [Francis Bacon *Essays*]
>
> The kiss of the sun for pardon,
> The song of the birds for mirth,
> One is nearer God's Heart in a garden
> Than anywhere else on earth
> [Dorothy Frances Gurney *God's Garden*]
>
> Paradise haunts gardens, and some gardens are paradises
> [Derek Jarman *Derek Jarman's Garden*]
>
> If you would be happy for a week, take a wife; if you would be happy for a month, kill your pig; but if you would be happy all your life, plant a garden
> [*Chinese proverb*]

gargantuan ADJECTIVE **= huge**, big, large, giant, massive, towering, vast, enormous, extensive, tremendous, immense, mega (*slang*), titanic, jumbo (*informal*), gigantic, monumental, monstrous, mammoth, colossal, mountainous, prodigious, stupendous, elephantine, ginormous (*informal*), Brobdingnagian, humongous *or* humungous (*U.S. slang*) **OPPOSITE:** tiny

> **USAGE**
>
> Some people think that *gargantuan* should only be used to describe things connected with food: *a gargantuan meal*; *his gargantuan appetite*. Nevertheless, the word is now widely used as a synonym of *colossal* or *massive*.

garish ADJECTIVE **= gaudy**, bright, glaring, vulgar, brilliant, flash (*informal*), loud, brash, tacky (*informal*), flashy, tasteless, naff (*Brit. slang*), jazzy (*informal*), tawdry, showy, brassy, raffish **OPPOSITE:** dull

garland NOUN **= wreath**, band, bays, crown, honours, loop, laurels, festoon, coronet, coronal, chaplet: *They wore garlands of summer flowers in their hair.*
▷ VERB **= adorn**, crown, deck, festoon, wreathe: *Players were garlanded with flowers.*

g

garment NOUN *(often plural)* = **clothes**, wear, dress, clothing, gear *(slang)*, habit, get-up *(informal)*, uniform, outfit, costume, threads *(slang)*, array, robes, duds *(informal)*, apparel, clobber *(Brit. slang)*, attire, garb, togs, vestments, articles of clothing, raiment *(archaic)*, rigout *(informal)*, habiliment

garnish NOUN = **decoration**, ornament, embellishment, adornment, ornamentation, trimming, trim: *Reserve some watercress for garnish.*
▷ VERB = **decorate**, adorn, ornament, embellish, deck, festoon, trim, bedeck: *She had prepared the vegetables and was garnishing the roast.*
OPPOSITE: strip

g

garrison NOUN **1** = **troops**, group, unit, section, command, armed force, detachment: *a five-hundred-man garrison* **2** = **fort**, fortress, camp, base, post, station, stronghold, fortification, encampment, fortified pa *(N.Z.)*: *The approaches to the garrison have been heavily mined.*
▷ VERB = **station**, position, post, mount, install, assign, put on duty: *No other soldiers were garrisoned there.*

garrulous ADJECTIVE **1** = **talkative**, gossiping, chattering, babbling, gushing, chatty, long-winded, effusive, gabby *(informal)*, prattling, voluble, gossipy, loquacious, verbose, mouthy: *a garrulous old woman*
OPPOSITE: taciturn **2** = **rambling**, lengthy, diffuse, long-winded, wordy, discursive, windy, overlong, verbose, prolix, prosy: *boring, garrulous prose*
OPPOSITE: concise

gas NOUN **1** = **fumes**, vapour: *Exhaust gases contain many toxins.* **2** = **petrol**, gasoline: *a tank of gas*

gash NOUN = **cut**, tear, split, wound, rent, slash, slit, gouge, incision, laceration: *a long gash just above his right eye*
▷ VERB = **cut**, tear, split, wound, rend, slash, slit, gouge, lacerate: *He gashed his leg while felling trees.*

gasp VERB = **pant**, blow, puff, choke, gulp, fight for breath, catch your breath: *He gasped for air before being pulled under again.*
▷ NOUN = **pant**, puff, gulp, intake of breath, sharp intake of breath: *She gave a small gasp of pain.*

gate NOUN = **barrier**, opening, door, access, port *(Scot.)*, entrance, exit, gateway, portal, egress

gather VERB **1** = **congregate**, assemble, get together, collect, group, meet, mass, rally, flock, come together, muster, convene, converge, rendezvous, foregather: *In the evenings, we gathered round the fire and talked.*
OPPOSITE: scatter **2** = **assemble**, group, collect, round up, marshal, bring together, muster, convene, call together: *He called to her to gather the children together.* **OPPOSITE:** disperse **3** = **collect**, assemble, accumulate, round up, mass, heap, marshal, bring together, muster, pile up, garner, amass, stockpile, hoard, stack up: *She started gathering up her things.* **4** = **pick**, harvest, pluck, reap, garner, glean: *The people lived by fishing, gathering nuts and fruits, and hunting.* **5** = **build up**, rise, increase, grow, develop, expand, swell, intensify, wax, heighten, deepen, enlarge, thicken: *Storm clouds were gathering in the distance.*
6 = **understand**, believe, hear, learn, assume, take it, conclude, presume, be informed, infer, deduce, surmise, be led to believe: *I gather his report is highly critical of the project.* **7** = **fold**, tuck, pleat, ruffle, pucker, shirr: *Gather the skirt at the waist.*

gathering NOUN = **assembly**, group, crowd, meeting, conference, company, party, congress, mass, rally, convention, knot, flock, get-together *(informal)*, congregation, muster, turnout, multitude, throng, hui *(N.Z.)*, concourse, assemblage, conclave, convocation, runanga *(N.Z.)*: *He spoke today before a large gathering of world leaders.*

gauche ADJECTIVE = **awkward**, clumsy, inept, unsophisticated, inelegant, graceless, unpolished, uncultured, maladroit, ill-bred, ill-mannered, lacking in social graces
OPPOSITE: sophisticated

gaudy ADJECTIVE = **garish**, bright, glaring, vulgar, brilliant, flash *(informal)*, loud, brash, tacky *(informal)*, flashy, tasteless, jazzy *(informal)*, tawdry, showy, gay, ostentatious, raffish **OPPOSITE:** dull

gauge VERB **1** = **measure**, calculate, evaluate, value, size, determine, count, weigh, compute, ascertain, quantify: *He gauged the wind at over thirty knots.* **2** = **judge**, estimate, guess, assess, evaluate, rate, appraise, reckon, adjudge: *See if you can gauge his reaction to the offer.*
▷ NOUN = **meter**, indicator, dial, measuring instrument: *a temperature gauge*

gaunt ADJECTIVE **1** = **thin**, lean, skinny, skeletal, wasted, drawn, spare, pinched, angular, bony, lanky, haggard, emaciated, scrawny, skin and bone, scraggy, cadaverous, rawboned: *Looking gaunt and tired, he denied there was anything to worry about.*
OPPOSITE: plump **2** = **bleak**, bare, harsh, forbidding, grim, stark, dismal, dreary, desolate, forlorn: *a large, gaunt, grey house*
OPPOSITE: inviting

gawky ADJECTIVE = **awkward**, clumsy, lumbering, ungainly, gauche, uncouth, loutish, graceless, clownish, oafish, maladroit, lumpish, ungraceful, unco *(Austral. slang)* **OPPOSITE:** graceful

gay ADJECTIVE **1** = **homosexual**, camp *(informal)*, lesbian, pink *(informal)*, queer *(informal, derogatory)*, same-sex, sapphic, moffie *(S. African slang)*: *The quality of life for gay men has improved over the last decade.* **2** = **cheerful**, happy, bright, glad, lively, sparkling, sunny, jolly, animated, merry, upbeat *(informal)*, buoyant, cheery, joyous, joyful, carefree, jaunty, chirpy *(informal)*, vivacious, jovial, gleeful, debonair, blithe, insouciant, full of beans *(informal)*, light-hearted: *I am in good health, gay and cheerful.*
OPPOSITE: sad **3** = **colourful**, rich, bright, brilliant, vivid, flamboyant, flashy, gaudy, garish, showy: *I like gay, vibrant posters.* **OPPOSITE:** drab
▷ NOUN = **homosexual**, lesbian, fairy *(slang)*, queer *(informal, derogatory)*, faggot *(slang, chiefly U.S. & Canad.)*, auntie *or* aunty *(Austral. slang)*, lily *(Austral. slang)*: *Gays have proved themselves to be style leaders.*
OPPOSITE: heterosexual

> **USAGE**
> By far the most common and up-to-date use of the word *gay* is in reference to being homosexual. Other senses of the word have become uncommon and dated.

gaze VERB = **stare**, look, view, watch, regard, contemplate, gape, eyeball *(slang)*, ogle, look fixedly: *He gazed reflectively at the fire.*
▷ NOUN = **stare**, look, fixed look: *She felt uncomfortable under the woman's steady gaze.*

gazette NOUN = **newspaper**, paper, journal, organ, periodical, news-sheet

g'day *or* **gidday** INTERJECTION = **hello**, hi *(informal)*, greetings, how do you do?, good morning, good evening, good afternoon, welcome, kia ora *(N.Z.)*: *Gidday, mate!*

gear NOUN **1** = **mechanism**, works, action, gearing, machinery, cogs, cogwheels, gearwheels: *The boat's steering gear failed.* **2** = **equipment**, supplies, tackle, tools, instruments, outfit, rigging, rig, accessories, apparatus, trappings, paraphernalia, accoutrements, appurtenances, equipage: *fishing gear* **3** = **possessions**, things, effects, stuff, kit, luggage, baggage, belongings, paraphernalia, personal property, chattels: *They helped us put our gear in the van.* **4** = **clothing**, wear, dress, clothes, habit, outfit, costume, threads *(slang)*, array, garments, apparel, attire, garb, togs, rigout: *I used to wear trendy gear but it just looked ridiculous.*
▷ VERB *(with* **to** *or* **towards***)* = **equip**, fit, suit, adjust, adapt, rig, tailor: *Colleges are not always geared towards the needs of mature students.*

gem NOUN **1** = **precious stone**, jewel, stone, semiprecious stone: *The mask is inset with emeralds and other gems.* **2** = **treasure**, pick, prize, jewel, flower, pearl, masterpiece, paragon, humdinger *(slang)*, taonga *(N.Z.)*: *Castel Clara was a gem of a hotel.*

Charles Dickens' Use of Verbs

Given the importance of dialogue in Dickens' novels, it is not surprising that speech-act verbs such as *say, ask,* and *reply* are among Dickens' most frequent verbs. He also uses other verbs such as *believe* and *hope* to report speech, indirectly stating what a character says so as to avoid the overuse of *said* and *replied*:

> Was his face at all disfigured? No, he **believed** not.
>
> Young John replied, with acknowledgments, that he only **hoped** he did what was right, and what showed how entirely he was devoted to Miss Dorrit. He wished to be unselfish; and he **hoped** he was.

These are more effective and punchy than the alternatives 'he said that he believed it was not' or 'he said he hoped he was unselfish'.

Other frequent verbs indicate the centrality of human suffering in Dickens' work: *cry, suffer,* and *die.* Adverbs such as *bitterly, piteously,* and *heartily* occur with *cry,* while people *suffer severely, greatly,* and *intensely.* Objects of *suffer* include *pain, loss, torture, distress,* and *death.* The verb *die* occurs with adverbs such as *suddenly, miserably,* and *slowly,* and Dickens' characters most frequently *die in* places such as the *street, prison,* or *workhouse* and *die of* conditions such as *fever, rheumatism,* and *consumption*. Extended senses of *die* are also used, such as the colloquial sense 'long to' in 'Poor Mr. Toots, who was dying to accept the invitation.' Other frequent verbs concern human relationships, for example *marry* and *love.* The phrases *marry for money* and *marry for love* both appear, although it is notable that the former is about twice as frequent as the latter in Dickens' works, perhaps reflecting the realities of Victorian society, where marriage was a much more practical affair than it is nowadays.

Dickens also makes frequent use of phrasal verbs. The ones he uses most frequently are those which are still very common in modern English, such as *sit down, turn up,* and *make up.* However, he also uses more inventive combinations such as *colour up* ('blush'), which give a colloquial and vivid flavour to his prose:

> The girl **colours up**, and puts out her hand with a very awkward affectation of indifference.

We are also reminded of the way that phrasal verbs change over time. For example, Dickens uses the now-rare *face out* – for example in 'ready to face out the worst' – which would now be expressed by *face up to,* or perhaps *face down.* Also, Dickens makes more use of prefixed verbs, which have now largely been replaced by phrasal verbs. For example, in modern English, prefixed verbs with *out* almost always have the meaning 'more than' or 'better than': *outdo, outnumber, outrun* and so on. In Dickens, however, we find prefixed forms such as *outlaugh* and *outface* which would now be expressed as *laugh out (loud)* and *face up to.*

Dickens' inventiveness can also be seen in the verbs he uses infrequently. In particular, he often converts nouns or adjectives to verbs in an effective way: we read, for example, of someone who *sicks* ('acts as a sick-nurse'); someone *cornering out* ('going round a corner'); and someone *rose-pinking for a character* ('putting on rose-pink colour to dress up as a character').

Some of the most striking passages in Dickens' novels are those where he does *not* use verbs, or uses very few of them. Perhaps the most famous of these is in the opening chapter of *Bleak House*:

> Fog everywhere. Fog up the river, where it flows among green aits and meadows; fog down the river... Fog on the Essex marshes, fog on the Kentish heights. Fog creeping into the cabooses of collier-brigs; fog lying out on the yards and hovering in the rigging of great ships...

The lack of verbs in some of these sentences, and the use of non-finite verbs such as *lying* and *creeping* in others, creates a kind of telegraphic, descriptive style, heightened by the lack of conjunctions and the repetition of the pervasive *fog.*

genealogy NOUN **= ancestry**, descent, pedigree, line, origin, extraction, lineage, family tree, parentage, derivation, blood line

general ADJECTIVE **1 = widespread**, accepted, popular, public, common, broad, extensive, universal, prevailing, prevalent: *Contrary to general opinion, Wiccans are not devil-worshippers.* **OPPOSITE:** individual **2 = overall**, complete, total, global, comprehensive, blanket, inclusive, all-embracing, overarching: *His firm took over general maintenance of the park last summer.* **OPPOSITE:** restricted **3 = universal**, overall, widespread, collective, across-the-board, all-inclusive: *The figures represent a general decline in unemployment.* **OPPOSITE:** exceptional **4 = vague**, broad, loose, blanket, sweeping, unclear, inaccurate, approximate, woolly, indefinite, hazy, imprecise, ill-defined, inexact, unspecific, undetailed: *chemicals called by the general description 'flavour enhancer'* **OPPOSITE:** specific

g

generality NOUN **1 = generalization**, abstraction, sweeping statement, vague notion, loose statement: *He avoided this tricky question and talked in generalities.* **2 = impreciseness**, vagueness, looseness, lack of detail, inexactitude, woolliness, indefiniteness, approximateness, inexactness, lack of preciseness: *There are problems with this definition, given its level of generality.*

generally ADVERB **1 = broadly**, mainly, mostly, principally, on the whole, predominantly, in the main, for the most part: *University teachers generally have admitted a lack of enthusiasm about their subjects.* **2 = usually**, commonly, typically, regularly, normally, on average, on the whole, for the most part, almost always, in most cases, by and large, ordinarily, as a rule, habitually, conventionally, customarily: *As women we generally say and feel too much about these things.* **OPPOSITE:** occasionally **3 = commonly**, widely, publicly, universally, extensively, popularly, conventionally, customarily: *It is generally believed that drinking red wine in moderation is beneficial.* **OPPOSITE:** individually

generate VERB **= produce**, create, make, form, cause, initiate, bring about, originate, give rise to, engender, whip up **OPPOSITE:** end

generation NOUN **1 = age group**, peer group: *He's the leading American playwright of his generation.* **2 = age**, period, era, time, days, lifetime, span, epoch: *Within a generation, flight has become popular with many travellers.*

generic ADJECTIVE **= collective**, general, common, wide, sweeping, comprehensive, universal, blanket, inclusive, all-encompassing **OPPOSITE:** specific

generosity NOUN **1 = liberality**, charity, bounty, munificence, beneficence, largesse *or* largess: *There are many stories of his generosity.* **2 = magnanimity**, goodness, kindness, benevolence, selflessness, charity, unselfishness, high-mindedness, nobleness: *his moral decency and generosity of spirit*

> QUOTATIONS
> Generosity knows how to count, but refrains
> [Mason Cooley *City Aphorisms*]

generous ADJECTIVE **1 = liberal**, lavish, free, charitable, free-handed, hospitable, prodigal, bountiful, open-handed, unstinting, beneficent, princely, bounteous, munificent, ungrudging: *He's very generous with his money.* **OPPOSITE:** mean **2 = magnanimous**, kind, noble, benevolent, good, big, high-minded, unselfish, big-hearted, ungrudging: *He was not generous enough to congratulate his successor.* **3 = plentiful**, lavish, ample, abundant, full, rich, liberal, overflowing, copious, bountiful, unstinting, profuse, bounteous *(literary)*, plenteous: *a room with a generous amount of storage space* **OPPOSITE:** meagre

> PROVERBS
> *It is easy to be generous with other people's property*

genesis NOUN **= beginning**, source, root, origin, start, generation, birth, creation, dawn, formation, outset, starting point, engendering, inception, commencement, propagation **OPPOSITE:** end

genial ADJECTIVE **= friendly**, kind, kindly, pleasant, warm, cheerful, jolly, hearty, agreeable, cheery, amiable, cordial, affable, congenial, jovial, convivial, good-natured, warm-hearted **OPPOSITE:** unfriendly

genitals PLURAL NOUN **= sex organs**, privates, loins, genitalia, private parts, reproductive organs, pudenda ▸ *related adjective:* venereal

genius NOUN **1 = brilliance**, ability, talent, capacity, gift, bent, faculty, excellence, endowment, flair, inclination, knack, propensity, aptitude, cleverness, creative power: *This is the mark of her genius as a designer.* **2 = master**, expert, mastermind, brain *(informal)*, buff *(informal)*, intellect *(informal)*, adept, maestro, virtuoso, whiz *(informal)*, hotshot *(informal)*, rocket scientist *(informal, chiefly U.S.)*, wonk *(informal)*, brainbox, maven *(U.S.)*, master-hand, fundi *(S. African)*: *a 14-year-old mathematical genius* **OPPOSITE:** dunce

> QUOTATIONS
> Genius is one per cent inspiration and ninety-nine per cent perspiration
> [Thomas Alva Edison *Life*]
>
> When a true genius appears in the world, you may know him by this sign, that the dunces are all in confederacy against him
> [Jonathan Swift *Thoughts on Various Subjects*]
>
> The true genius is a mind of large general powers, accidentally determined to some particular direction
> [Dr. Johnson *Lives of the English Poets*]
>
> Genius is ... the child of imitation
> [Joshua Reynolds *Discourses on Art*]
>
> If I have seen further [than other men] it is by standing upon the shoulders of giants
> [Isaac Newton *letter to Robert Hooke*]
>
> Genius must be born, and never can be taught
> [John Dryden *To Mr. Congreve*]
>
> In every work of genius we recognize our own rejected thoughts
> [Ralph Waldo Emerson *Self-Reliance*]
>
> I have nothing to declare but my genius
> [Oscar Wilde]
>
> Every man of genius is considerably helped by being dead
> [Robert Lynd]
>
> Genius does what it must,
> And Talent does what it can
> [Owen Meredith *Last Words of a Sensitive Second-rate Poet*]
>
> It takes a lot of time to be a genius, you have to sit around so much doing nothing, really doing nothing
> [Gertrude Stein *Everybody's Autobiography*]
>
> Genius is only a greater aptitude for patience
> [Comte de Buffon]

genre NOUN **= type**, group, school, form, order, sort, kind, class, style, character, fashion, brand, species, category, stamp, classification, genus, subdivision

genteel ADJECTIVE **= refined**, cultured, mannerly, elegant, formal, gentlemanly, respectable, polite, cultivated, courteous, courtly, well-bred, ladylike, well-mannered **OPPOSITE:** unmannerly

gentility NOUN **1 = refinement**, culture, breeding, courtesy, elegance, formality, respectability, cultivation, politeness, good manners, courtliness **2 = blue blood**, high birth, rank, good family, good breeding, gentle birth

gentle ADJECTIVE **1 = kind**, loving, kindly, peaceful, soft, quiet, pacific, tender, mild, benign, humane, compassionate, amiable, meek, lenient, placid, merciful, kind-hearted, sweet-tempered, tender-hearted: *a quiet and gentle man who liked sports and enjoyed life* **OPPOSITE:** unkind **2 = slow**, easy, slight, deliberate, moderate, gradual, imperceptible: *His movements were gentle and deliberate.* **3 = moderate**, low, light, easy, soft, calm, slight, mild, soothing, clement, temperate, balmy: *The wind had dropped to a gentle breeze.* **OPPOSITE:** violent

gentlemanly ADJECTIVE **= chivalrous**, mannerly, obliging, refined, polite, civil, cultivated, courteous, gallant, genteel, suave, well-bred, well-mannered

> **QUOTATIONS**
> Anyone can be heroic from time to time, but a gentleman is something you have to be all the time
> [Luigi Pirandello *The Pleasure of Honesty*]

gentleness NOUN **= tenderness**, compassion, kindness, consideration, sympathy, sweetness, softness, mildness, kindliness

gentry NOUN **= nobility**, lords, elite, nobles, upper class, aristocracy, peerage, ruling class, patricians, upper crust *(informal)*, gentility, gentlefolk

genuine ADJECTIVE **1 = authentic**, real, original, actual, sound, true, pure, sterling, valid, legitimate, honest, veritable, bona fide, dinkum *or* dinky-di *(Austral. & N.Z. informal)*, the real McCoy: *They are convinced the painting is genuine.* **OPPOSITE:** counterfeit **2 = heartfelt**, sincere, honest, earnest, real, true, frank, unaffected, wholehearted, unadulterated, unalloyed, unfeigned: *There was genuine joy in the room.* **OPPOSITE:** affected **3 = sincere**, straightforward, honest, natural, frank, candid, upfront *(informal)*, dinkum *or* dinky-di *(Austral. & N.Z. informal)*, artless, guileless: *She is a very caring and genuine person.* **OPPOSITE:** hypocritical

> **QUOTATIONS**
> Genuineness only thrives in the dark. Like celery
> [Aldous Huxley *Those Barren Leaves*]

genus NOUN **= type**, sort, kind, group, set, order, race, class, breed, category, genre, classification

germ NOUN **1 = microbe**, virus, bug *(informal)*, bacterium, bacillus, microorganism: *a germ that destroyed hundreds of millions of lives* **2 = beginning**, root, seed, origin, spark, bud, embryo, rudiment: *The germ of an idea took root in her mind.*

German NOUN
▸ *related prefixes:* Germano-, Teuto-

germinate VERB **= sprout**, grow, shoot, develop, generate, swell, bud, vegetate

gestation NOUN **= incubation**, development, growth, pregnancy, evolution, ripening, maturation

gesticulate VERB **= signal**, sign, wave, indicate, motion, gesture, beckon, make a sign

gesture NOUN **= sign**, action, signal, motion, indication, gesticulation: *She made a menacing gesture with her fist.*
▹ VERB **= signal**, sign, wave, indicate, motion, beckon, gesticulate: *I gestured towards the boathouse and he looked inside.*

get VERB **1 = become**, grow, turn, wax, come to be: *The boys were getting bored.* **2 = persuade**, convince, win over, induce, influence, sway, entice, coax, incite, impel, talk into, wheedle, prevail upon: *How did you get him to pose for this picture?* **3 = arrive**, come, reach, make it *(informal)*: *It was dark by the time she got home.* **4 = manage**, fix, succeed, arrange, contrive, wangle *(informal)*: *How did he get to be the boss of a major company?* **5 = annoy**, upset, anger, bother, disturb, trouble, bug *(informal)*, irritate, aggravate *(informal)*, gall, madden, exasperate, nettle, vex, irk, rile, pique, get on your nerves *(informal)*, nark *(Brit., Austral. & N.Z. slang)*, get up your nose *(informal)*, give someone grief *(Brit. & S. African)*, make your blood boil, get your goat *(slang)*, get on your wick *(Brit. slang)*, get your back up, hack you off *(informal)*: *What gets me is the attitude of these people.* **6 = obtain**, receive, gain, acquire, win, land, score *(slang)*, achieve, net, pick up, bag, secure, attain, reap, get hold of, come by, glean, procure, get your hands on, come into possession of: *The problem was how to get enough food.* **7 = fetch**, bring, collect: *Go and get your Daddy for me.* **8 = understand**, follow, catch, see, notice, realize, appreciate, be aware of, take in, perceive, grasp, comprehend, fathom, apprehend, suss (out) *(slang)*, get the hang of *(informal)*, get your head round: *You don't seem to get the point.* **9 = catch**, develop, contract, succumb to, fall victim to, go down with, come down with, become infected with, be afflicted with, be smitten by: *When I was five I got measles.* **10 = arrest**, catch, grab, capture, trap, seize, take, nail *(informal)*, collar *(informal)*, nab *(informal)*, apprehend, take prisoner, take into custody, lay hold of: *The police have got the killer.* **11 = contact**, reach, communicate with, get hold of, get in touch with: *We've been trying to get you on the phone all day.* **12 = puzzle**, confuse, baffle, bewilder, confound, perplex, mystify, stump, beat *(slang)*, flummox, nonplus: *No, I can't answer that question – you've got me there.* **13 = move**, touch, affect, excite, stir, stimulate, arouse, have an impact on, have an effect on, tug at (someone's) heartstrings *(often facetious)*: *I don't know what it is about that song, it just gets me.*

get across something = cross, negotiate, pass over, traverse, ford: *When we got across the beach, we saw some Spanish guys waiting for us.*

get at someone 1 = criticize, attack, blame, put down, knock *(informal)*, carp, have a go (at) *(informal)*, taunt, nag, hassle *(informal)*, pick on, disparage, diss *(slang, chiefly U.S.)*, find fault with, put the boot into *(slang)*, nark *(Brit., Austral. & N.Z. slang)*, be on your back *(slang)*: *His mother doesn't like me, and she gets at me all the time.* **2 = corrupt**, influence, bribe, tamper with, buy off, fix *(informal)*, suborn: *He claims these government officials have been got at.*

get at something 1 = reach, touch, grasp, get (a) hold of, stretch to: *The goat was on its hind legs trying to get at the leaves.* **2 = find out**, get, learn, reach, reveal, discover, acquire, detect, uncover, attain, get hold of, gain access to, come to grips with: *We're only trying to get at the truth.* **3 = imply**, mean, suggest, hint, intimate, lead up to, insinuate: *'What are you getting at now?' demanded Rick.*

get away = escape, leave, disappear, flee, depart, fly, slip away, abscond, decamp, hook it *(slang)*, do a runner *(slang)*, slope off, do a bunk *(Brit. slang)*, fly the coop *(U.S. & Canad. informal)*, skedaddle *(informal)*, take a powder *(U.S. & Canad. slang)*, make good your escape, make your getaway, take it on the lam *(U.S. & Canad. slang)*, break free *or* out, run away *or* off, do a Skase *(Austral. informal)*: *They tried to stop him but he got away.*

get back = return, arrive home, come back *or* home: *It was late when we got back from the hospital.*

get back at someone = retaliate, pay (someone) back, hit back at, take revenge on, get even with, strike back at, even the score with, exact retribution on, get your own back on, make reprisal with, be avenged on, settle the score with, give (someone) a taste of his *or* her own medicine, give tit for tat, take *or* wreak vengeance on: *My wife had left me and I wanted to get back at her.*

get by = manage, survive, cope, fare, get through, exist, make out, get along, make do, subsist, muddle through, keep your head above water, make both ends meet: *I'm a survivor. I'll get by.*

get in = arrive, come in, appear, land: *Our flight got in late.*

get off 1 = be absolved, be acquitted, escape punishment, walk *(slang, chiefly U.S.)*: *He is likely to get off with a small fine.* **2 = leave**, go, move, take off *(informal)*, depart, slope off, make tracks, set out *or* off: *I'd like to get off before it begins to get dark.* **3 = descend**, leave, exit, step down, alight, disembark, dismount: *We got off at the next stop.*

get on 1 = be friendly, agree, get along, concur, be compatible, hit it off *(informal)*, harmonize, be on good terms: *Do you get on with your neighbours?* **2 = progress**, manage, cope, fare, advance, succeed, make out *(informal)*, prosper, cut it *(informal)*, get along: *I asked how he was getting on.* **3 = board**, enter, mount, climb, embark, ascend: *The bus stopped to let the passengers get on.*

get out 1 = leave, escape, withdraw, quit, take off *(informal)*, exit, go, break out, go away, depart, evacuate, vacate,

clear out (*informal*), abscond, decamp, hook it (*slang*), free yourself, do a bunk (*Brit. slang*), extricate yourself, sling your hook (*Brit. slang*), rack off (*Austral. & N.Z. slang*), do a Skase (*Austral. informal*): *I think we should get out while we still can.*
get out of something = **avoid**, dodge, evade, escape, shirk, body-swerve (*Scot.*): *It's amazing what people will do to get out of paying taxes.*
get over something **1** = **recover from**, survive, get better from, come round, bounce back, mend, get well, recuperate, turn the corner, pull through, get back on your feet, feel yourself again, regain your health *or* strength: *It took me a very long time to get over the shock of her death.* **2** = **overcome**, deal with, solve, resolve, defeat, master, lick (*informal*), shake off, rise above, get the better of, surmount: *How would they get over that problem, he wondered?* **3** = **cross**, pass, pass over, traverse, get across, move across, ford, go across: *The travellers were trying to get over the river.*
get round someone = **win over**, persuade, charm, influence, convince, convert, sway, coax, cajole, wheedle, prevail upon, bring round, talk round: *Max could always get round his mother.*
get round something = **overcome**, deal with, solve, resolve, defeat, master, bypass, lick (*informal*), shake off, rise above, get the better of, circumvent, surmount: *No one has found a way of getting round the problem.*
get something across = **communicate**, publish, spread, pass on, transmit, convey, impart, get (something) through, disseminate, bring home, make known, put over, make clear *or* understood: *I need a better way of getting my message across to people.*
get something back = **regain**, recover, retrieve, take back, recoup, repossess: *You have 14 days in which to cancel and get your money back.*
get something over = **communicate**, spread, pass on, convey, impart, make known, get *or* put across, make clear *or* understood: *We have got the message over to young people that smoking isn't cool.*
get together = **meet**, unite, join, collect, gather, rally, assemble, muster, convene, converge, congregate: *This is the only forum where East and West can get together.*
get up = **arise**, stand (up), rise, get to your feet: *I got up and walked over to the door.*

getaway NOUN = **escape**, break, flight, break-out, decampment

get-together NOUN = **gathering**, party, celebration, reception, meeting, social, function, bash (*informal*), rave (*Brit. slang*), festivity, do (*informal*), knees-up (*Brit. informal*), beano (*Brit. slang*), social gathering, shindig (*informal*), soirée, rave-up (*Brit. slang*), hooley *or* hoolie (*chiefly Irish & N.Z.*)

ghastly ADJECTIVE = **horrible**, shocking, terrible, awful, grim, dreadful, horrendous, hideous, from hell (*informal*), horrid (*informal*), repulsive, frightful, loathsome, godawful (*slang*) **OPPOSITE:** lovely

ghost NOUN **1** = **spirit**, soul, phantom, spectre, spook (*informal*), apparition, wraith, shade (*literary*), phantasm, atua (*N.Z.*), kehua (*N.Z.*), wairua (*N.Z.*): *The village is said to be haunted by the ghosts of the dead children.* **2** = **trace**, shadow, suggestion, hint, suspicion, glimmer, semblance: *He gave the ghost of a smile.*
▸ *related adjective:* spectral

QUOTATIONS
Ghost stories appeal to our craving for immortality. If you can be afraid of a ghost, then you have to believe that a ghost may exist. And if a ghost exists then oblivion might not be the end
[Stanley Kubrick]
Even the living were only ghosts in the making
[Pat Barker *The Ghost Road*]

ghostly ADJECTIVE = **unearthly**, weird, phantom, eerie, supernatural, uncanny, spooky (*informal*), spectral, eldritch (*poetic*), phantasmal

ghoulish ADJECTIVE = **macabre**, sick (*informal*), disgusting, hideous, gruesome, grisly, horrid, morbid, unwholesome

giant ADJECTIVE = **huge**, great, large, vast, enormous, extensive, tremendous, immense, titanic, jumbo (*informal*), gigantic, monumental, monstrous, mammoth, colossal, mountainous, stellar (*informal*), prodigious, stupendous, gargantuan, elephantine, ginormous (*informal*), Brobdingnagian, humongous *or* humungous (*U.S. slang*), supersize: *a giant oak table; a giant step towards unification* **OPPOSITE:** tiny
▷ NOUN = **ogre**, monster, titan, colossus, leviathan, behemoth: *a Nordic saga of giants and monsters*

gibber VERB = **gabble**, chatter, babble, waffle (*informal, chiefly Brit.*), prattle, jabber, blab, rabbit on (*Brit. informal*), blather, blabber, earbash (*Austral. & N.Z. slang*)

gibberish NOUN = **nonsense**, crap (*slang*), garbage (*informal*), hot air (*informal*), tosh (*slang, chiefly Brit.*), babble, pap, bilge (*informal*), drivel, malarkey, twaddle, tripe (*informal*), guff (*slang*), prattle, mumbo jumbo, moonshine, jabber, gabble, gobbledegook (*informal*), hogwash, hokum (*slang, chiefly U.S. & Canad.*), blather, double talk, piffle (*informal*), all Greek (*informal*), poppycock (*informal*), balderdash, bosh (*informal*), yammer (*informal*), eyewash (*informal*), tommyrot, horsefeathers (*U.S. slang*), bunkum *or* buncombe (*chiefly U.S.*), bizzo (*Austral. slang*), bull's wool (*Austral. & N.Z. slang*)

gibe *see* jibe

giddy ADJECTIVE **1** = **dizzy**, reeling, faint, unsteady, light-headed, vertiginous: *He felt giddy and light-headed.* **2** = **flighty**, silly, volatile, irresponsible, reckless, dizzy, careless, frivolous, impulsive, capricious, thoughtless, impetuous, skittish, heedless, scatterbrained, ditzy *or* ditsy (*slang*): *Man is a giddy creature.* **OPPOSITE:** serious

gift NOUN **1** = **donation**, offering, present, contribution, grant, legacy, hand-out, endowment, boon, bequest, gratuity, prezzie (*informal*), bonsela (*S. African*), largesse *or* largess, koha (*N.Z.*): *a gift of $50,000* **2** = **talent**, ability, capacity, genius, power, bent, faculty, capability, forte, flair, knack, aptitude: *As a youth he discovered a gift for teaching.*

gifted ADJECTIVE = **talented**, able, skilled, expert, masterly, brilliant, capable, clever, accomplished, proficient, adroit
OPPOSITE: talentless

gigantic ADJECTIVE = **huge**, great, large, giant, massive, vast, enormous, extensive, tremendous, immense, titanic, jumbo (*informal*), monumental, monstrous, mammoth, colossal, mountainous, stellar (*informal*), prodigious, stupendous, gargantuan, herculean, elephantine, ginormous (*informal*), Brobdingnagian, humongous *or* humungous (*U.S. slang*), supersize
OPPOSITE: tiny

giggle VERB = **laugh**, chuckle, snigger, chortle, titter, twitter, tee-hee: *Both girls began to giggle*
▷ NOUN = **laugh**, chuckle, snigger, chortle, titter, twitter: *She gave a little giggle.*

gimmick NOUN = **stunt**, trick, device, scheme, manoeuvre, dodge, ploy, gambit, stratagem, contrivance

gingerly ADVERB = **cautiously**, carefully, reluctantly, suspiciously, tentatively, warily, hesitantly, timidly, circumspectly, cagily (*informal*), charily **OPPOSITE:** carelessly

gird VERB **1** = **girdle**, bind, belt: *The other knights urged Galahad to gird on his sword.* **2** = **surround**, ring, pen, enclose, encompass, encircle, hem in, enfold, engird: *a proposal to gird the river with a series of small hydroelectric dams* **3** = **prepare**, ready, steel, brace, fortify, make *or* get ready: *They are girding themselves for battle against a new enemy.*

girdle NOUN = **belt**, band, sash, waistband, cummerbund: *These muscles hold in the waist like an invisible girdle.*
▷ VERB = **surround**, ring, bound, enclose, encompass, hem, encircle, fence in, gird: *The old town centre is girdled by a boulevard lined with trees.*

girl NOUN = **female child**, schoolgirl, lass, lassie (*informal*), miss, maiden (*archaic*), maid (*archaic*)

girth NOUN **= size**, measure, proportions, dimensions, bulk, measurement(s), circumference

gist NOUN **= essence**, meaning, point, idea, sense, import, core, substance, drift, significance, nub, pith, quintessence

give VERB **1 = perform**, do, carry out, execute: *She stretched her arms out and gave a great yawn.* **2 = communicate**, announce, publish, transmit, pronounce, utter, emit, issue, be a source of, impart: *He gave no details of his plans.* **3 = produce**, make, cause, occasion, engender: *Her visit gave great pleasure to the children.* **4 = present**, contribute, donate, provide, supply, award, grant, deliver, commit, administer, furnish, confer, bestow, entrust, consign, make over, hand over *or* out: *This recipe was given to me years ago; They still give to charity despite hard economic times.* **OPPOSITE:** take **5 = collapse**, fall, break, sink, bend: *My knees gave under me.* **6 = concede**, allow, grant: *You're a bright enough kid, I'll give you that.* **7 = surrender**, yield, devote, hand over, relinquish, part with, cede: *a memorial to a man who gave his life for his country* **8 = demonstrate**, show, offer, provide, evidence, display, indicate, manifest, set forth: *The handout gives all the times of the performances.*
give in = admit defeat, yield, concede, collapse, quit, submit, surrender, comply, succumb, cave in *(informal)*, capitulate: *My parents gave in and let me go to the camp.*
give something away = reveal, expose, leak, disclose, betray, uncover, let out, divulge, let slip, let the cat out of the bag *(informal)*: *They were giving away company secrets.*
give something off *or* **out = emit**, produce, release, discharge, send out, throw out, vent, exude, exhale: *Natural gas gives off less carbon dioxide than coal.*
give something out 1 = distribute, issue, deliver, circulate, hand out, dispense, dole out, pass round: *There were people at the entrance giving out leaflets.* **2 = make known**, announce, publish, broadcast, communicate, transmit, utter, notify, impart, disseminate, shout from the rooftops *(informal)*: *He wouldn't give out any information.*
give something up 1 = abandon, stop, quit, kick *(informal)*, cease, cut out, renounce, leave off, say goodbye to, desist, kiss (something) goodbye, forswear: *I'm trying to give up smoking.* **2 = quit**, leave, resign, step down from *(informal)*: *She gave up her job to join her husband's campaign.* **3 = hand over**, yield, surrender, relinquish, waive: *The government refused to give up any territory.*

given ADJECTIVE **1 = specified**, particular, specific, designated, stated, predetermined: *the number of accidents at this spot in a given period* **2 = inclined**, addicted, disposed, prone, liable: *I am not very given to emotional displays.*

glacial ADJECTIVE **1 = icy**, biting, cold, freezing, frozen, bitter, raw, chill, piercing, arctic, polar, chilly, frosty, wintry: *The air from the sea felt glacial.* **2 = unfriendly**, hostile, cold, icy, frosty, antagonistic, frigid, inimical: *The Duchess gave him a glacial look and moved on.*

glad ADJECTIVE **1 = happy**, pleased, delighted, contented, cheerful, gratified, joyful, overjoyed, chuffed *(slang)*, gleeful: *I'm glad I decided to go after all.* **OPPOSITE:** unhappy **2 = pleasing**, happy, cheering, pleasant, delightful, cheerful, merry, gratifying, cheery, joyous, felicitous: *the bringer of glad tidings*

gladly ADVERB **1 = happily**, cheerfully, gleefully, merrily, gaily, joyfully, joyously, jovially: *He gladly accepted my invitation.* **2 = willingly**, freely, happily, readily, cheerfully, with pleasure, with (a) good grace: *The counsellors will gladly baby-sit during their free time.* **OPPOSITE:** reluctantly

glamorous ADJECTIVE **1 = attractive**, beautiful, lovely, charming, entrancing, elegant, dazzling, enchanting, captivating, alluring, bewitching, page-three *(Indian)*: *some of the world's most beautiful and glamorous women* **OPPOSITE:** unglamorous **2 = exciting**, glittering, prestigious, glossy, glitzy *(slang)*, bling *(slang)*, page-three *(Indian)*: *his glamorous playboy lifestyle* **OPPOSITE:** unglamorous

glamour NOUN **1 = charm**, appeal, beauty, attraction, fascination, allure, magnetism, enchantment, bewitchment, page-three *(Indian)*: *Her air of mystery only added to her glamour.* **2 = excitement**, magic, thrill, romance, prestige, glitz *(slang)*: *the glamour of showbiz*

glance VERB **1 = peek**, look, view, check, clock *(Brit. informal)*, gaze, glimpse, check out *(informal)*, peep, take a dekko at *(Brit. slang)*: *He glanced at his watch.* **OPPOSITE:** scrutinize **2** *(with* **over, through,** *etc.)* **= scan**, browse, dip into, leaf through, flip through, thumb through, skim through, riffle through, run over *or* through, surf *(Computing)*: *I picked up the book and glanced through it.*
▷ NOUN **= peek**, look, glimpse, peep, squint, butcher's *(Brit. slang)*, quick look, gander *(informal)*, brief look, dekko *(slang)*, shufti *(Brit. slang)*, gink *(N.Z. slang)*: *She stole a quick glance at her watch.* **OPPOSITE:** good look

glare VERB **1 = scowl**, frown, glower, look daggers, stare angrily, give a dirty look, lour *or* lower: *He glared and muttered something.* **2 = dazzle**, blaze, flare, flame: *The light was glaring straight into my eyes.*
▷ NOUN **1 = scowl**, frown, glower, dirty look, black look, angry stare, lour *or* lower: *His glasses magnified his irritable glare.* **2 = dazzle**, glow, blaze, flare, flame, brilliance: *the glare of a car's headlights*

glaring ADJECTIVE **= obvious**, open, outstanding, patent, visible, gross, outrageous, manifest, blatant, conspicuous, overt, audacious, flagrant, rank, egregious, unconcealed: *I never saw such a glaring example of misrepresentation.* **OPPOSITE:** inconspicuous

glassy ADJECTIVE **1 = smooth**, clear, slick, shiny, glossy, transparent, slippery: *glassy green pebbles* **2 = expressionless**, cold, fixed, empty, dull, blank, glazed, vacant, dazed, lifeless: *There was a remote, glassy look in his eyes.*

glaze NOUN **= coat**, finish, polish, shine, gloss, varnish, enamel, lacquer, lustre, patina: *hand-painted tiles with decorative glazes*
▷ VERB **= coat**, polish, gloss, varnish, enamel, lacquer, burnish, furbish: *After the pots are fired, they are glazed in a variety of colours.*

gleam VERB **= shine**, flash, glow, sparkle, glitter, flare, shimmer, glint, glimmer, glisten, scintillate: *His red sports car gleamed in the sun.*
▷ NOUN **1 = glimmer**, flash, beam, glow, sparkle: *the gleam of the headlights* **2 = trace**, ray, suggestion, hint, flicker, glimmer, inkling: *There was a gleam of hope for a peaceful settlement.*

gleaming ADJECTIVE **= shining**, bright, brilliant, glowing, sparkling, glimmering, glistening, scintillating, burnished, lustrous **OPPOSITE:** dull

glean VERB **= gather**, learn, pick up, collect, harvest, accumulate, reap, garner, amass, cull

glee NOUN **= delight**, joy, triumph, exuberance, elation, exhilaration, mirth, hilarity, merriment, exultation, gladness, joyfulness, joyousness **OPPOSITE:** gloom

gleeful ADJECTIVE **= delighted**, happy, pleased, cheerful, merry, triumphant, gratified, exuberant, jubilant, joyous, joyful, elated, overjoyed, chirpy *(informal)*, exultant, cock-a-hoop, mirthful, stoked *(Austral. & N.Z. informal)*

glib ADJECTIVE **= smooth**, easy, ready, quick, slick, plausible, slippery, fluent, suave, artful, insincere, fast-talking, smooth-tongued **OPPOSITE:** sincere

glide VERB **= slip**, sail, slide, skim

glimmer VERB **= gleam**, shine, glow, sparkle, glitter, blink, flicker, shimmer, twinkle, glisten: *The moon glimmered faintly through the mists.*
▷ NOUN **1 = glow**, ray, sparkle, gleam, blink, flicker, shimmer, twinkle: *In the east there is the faintest glimmer of light.* **2 = trace**, ray, suggestion, hint, grain, gleam, flicker, inkling: *Our last glimmer of hope faded.*

glimpse NOUN **= look**, sighting, sight, glance, peep, peek, squint, butcher's *(Brit. slang)*, quick look, gander *(informal)*, brief view, shufti *(Brit.*

g

slang): *The fans waited outside the hotel to get a glimpse of their heroine.*
▷ VERB **= catch sight of**, spot, sight, view, clock *(Brit. informal)*, spy, espy: *She glimpsed a group of people standing on the bank of a river.*

glint VERB **= gleam**, flash, shine, sparkle, glitter, twinkle, glimmer: *The sea glinted in the sun.*
▷ NOUN **= gleam**, flash, shine, sparkle, glitter, twinkle, twinkling, glimmer: *glints of sunlight*

glisten VERB **= gleam**, flash, shine, sparkle, glitter, shimmer, twinkle, glint, glimmer, scintillate

glitch NOUN **= problem**, difficulty, fault, flaw, bug *(informal)*, hitch, snag, uphill *(S. African)*, interruption, blip, malfunction, kink, gremlin, fly in the ointment

g

glitter VERB **= shine**, flash, sparkle, flare, glare, gleam, shimmer, twinkle, glint, glimmer, glisten, scintillate: *The palace glittered with lights.*
▷ NOUN **1 = glamour**, show, display, gilt, splendour, tinsel, pageantry, gaudiness, showiness: *all the glitter and glamour of a Hollywood premiere* **2 = sparkle**, flash, shine, beam, glare, gleam, brilliance, sheen, shimmer, brightness, lustre, radiance, scintillation: *the glitter of strobe lights and mirror balls*

gloat VERB **= relish**, triumph, glory, crow, revel in, vaunt, drool, exult, rub your hands

global ADJECTIVE **1 = worldwide**, world, international, universal, planetary: *a global ban on nuclear testing* **2 = comprehensive**, general, total, thorough, unlimited, exhaustive, all-inclusive, all-encompassing, encyclopedic, unbounded: *a global vision of contemporary society* **OPPOSITE:** limited

globe NOUN **= planet**, world, earth, sphere, orb

gloom NOUN **1 = darkness**, dark, shadow, cloud, shade, twilight, dusk, obscurity, blackness, dullness, murk, dimness, murkiness, cloudiness, gloominess, duskiness: *the gloom of a foggy November morning* **OPPOSITE:** light **2 = depression**, despair, misery, sadness, sorrow, blues, woe, melancholy, unhappiness, desolation, despondency, dejection, low spirits, downheartedness: *the deepening gloom over the economy* **OPPOSITE:** happiness

gloomy ADJECTIVE **1 = dark**, dull, dim, dismal, black, grey, obscure, murky, dreary, sombre, shadowy, overcast, dusky: *Inside it's gloomy after all that sunshine.* **OPPOSITE:** light **2 = miserable**, down, sad, dismal, low, blue, pessimistic, melancholy, glum, dejected, despondent, dispirited, downcast, joyless, downhearted, down in the dumps *(informal)*, cheerless, down in the mouth, in low spirits: *He is gloomy about the fate of the economy.* **OPPOSITE:** happy **3 = depressing**, bad, dismal, dreary, black, saddening, sombre, dispiriting, disheartening, funereal, cheerless, comfortless: *Officials say the outlook for next year is gloomy.*

glorify VERB **1 = praise**, celebrate, magnify, laud, extol, crack up *(informal)*, eulogize, sing *or* sound the praises of: *the banning of songs glorifying war* **OPPOSITE:** condemn **2 = worship**, honour, bless, adore, revere, exalt, pay homage to, venerate, sanctify, immortalize: *We are committed to serving the Lord and glorifying his name.* **OPPOSITE:** dishonour **3 = enhance**, raise, elevate, adorn, dignify, magnify, augment, lift up, ennoble, add lustre to, aggrandize: *They've glorified his job with an impressive title, but he's still just a salesman.* **OPPOSITE:** degrade

glorious ADJECTIVE **1 = splendid**, beautiful, bright, brilliant, shining, superb, divine, gorgeous, dazzling, radiant, resplendent, splendiferous *(facetious)*: *a glorious Edwardian opera house* **OPPOSITE:** dull **2 = delightful**, fine, wonderful, excellent, heavenly *(informal)*, marvellous, splendid, gorgeous, pleasurable, splendiferous *(facetious)*: *We opened the window and let in the glorious evening air.* **3 = illustrious**, famous, celebrated, distinguished, noted, grand, excellent, honoured, magnificent, noble, renowned, elevated, eminent, triumphant, majestic, famed, sublime: *He had a glorious career spanning more than six decades.* **OPPOSITE:** ordinary

glory NOUN **1 = honour**, praise, fame, celebrity, distinction, acclaim, prestige, immortality, eminence, kudos, renown, exaltation, illustriousness: *He had his moment of glory when he won the London Marathon.* **OPPOSITE:** shame **2 = splendour**, majesty, greatness, grandeur, nobility, pomp, magnificence, pageantry, éclat, sublimity: *the glory of the royal court* **3 = beauty**, brilliance, lustre, radiance, gorgeousness, resplendence: *the glory of an autumn sunset* **4 = worship**, praise, blessing, gratitude, thanksgiving, homage, adoration, veneration: *Glory be to God.*
▷ VERB **= triumph**, boast, relish, revel, crow, drool, gloat, exult, take delight, pride yourself: *The workers were glorying in their new-found freedom.*

QUOTATIONS

We are all motivated by a keen desire for praise, and the better a man is, the more he is inspired by glory. The very philosophers themselves, even in those books which they write on contempt of glory, inscribe their names
[Cicero *Pro Archia*]

The paths of glory lead but to the grave
[Thomas Gray *Elegy Written in a Country Churchyard*]

Not in utter nakedness,
But trailing clouds of glory do we come
[William Wordsworth *Intimations of Immortality*]

To the greater glory of God (ad majorem Dei gloriam)
[*Motto of the Society of Jesus*]

Thus passes the glory of the world (sic transit gloria mundi)
[*Anon.*]

gloss[1] NOUN **1 = shine**, gleam, sheen, polish, brilliance, varnish, brightness, veneer, lustre, burnish, patina: *The rain produced a black gloss on the asphalt.* **2 = façade**, show, front, surface, appearance, mask, semblance: *He tried to put a gloss of respectability on the horrors the regime perpetrated.*

gloss[2] NOUN **= interpretation**, comment, note, explanation, commentary, translation, footnote, elucidation: *A gloss in the margin explains this unfamiliar word.*
▷ VERB **= interpret**, explain, comment, translate, construe, annotate, elucidate: *Earlier editors glossed 'drynke' as 'love-potion'.*

glossy ADJECTIVE **= shiny**, polished, shining, glazed, bright, brilliant, smooth, sleek, silky, burnished, glassy, silken, lustrous **OPPOSITE:** dull

glow NOUN **1 = light**, gleam, splendour, glimmer, brilliance, brightness, radiance, luminosity, vividness, incandescence, phosphorescence: *The rising sun cast a golden glow over the fields.* **OPPOSITE:** dullness **2 = colour**, bloom, flush, blush, reddening, rosiness: *The moisturiser gave my face a healthy glow that lasted all day.* **OPPOSITE:** pallor
▷ VERB **1 = shine**, burn, gleam, brighten, glimmer, smoulder: *The night lantern glowed softly in the darkness.* **2 = be pink**, colour, flush, blush: *Her freckled skin glowed with health.* **3 = be suffused**, thrill, radiate, tingle: *The expectant mothers positively glowed with pride.*

glower VERB **= scowl**, glare, frown, look daggers, give a dirty look, lour *or* lower: *He glowered at me but said nothing.*
▷ NOUN **= scowl**, glare, frown, dirty look, black look, angry stare, lour *or* lower: *His frown deepened into a glower of resentment.*

glowing ADJECTIVE **1 = complimentary**, enthusiastic, rave *(informal)*, ecstatic, rhapsodic, laudatory, adulatory: *The premiere of his play received glowing reviews.* **OPPOSITE:** scathing **2 = bright**, vivid, vibrant, rich, warm, radiant, luminous: *stained glass in rich, glowing colours* **OPPOSITE:** dull

glue NOUN **= adhesive**, cement, gum, paste: *a tube of glue*
▷ VERB **= stick**, fix, seal, cement, gum, paste, affix: *Glue the fabric around the window and leave to dry.*

glum ADJECTIVE **= gloomy**, miserable, dismal, down, low, melancholy, dejected, downcast, morose, doleful, downhearted, down in the dumps *(informal)*, down in the mouth, in low spirits **OPPOSITE:** cheerful

glut NOUN **= surfeit**, excess, surplus, plethora, saturation, oversupply, overabundance, superabundance: *There's a glut of agricultural products in Western Europe.* **OPPOSITE:** scarcity
▷ VERB **1 = saturate**, flood, choke, clog, overload, inundate, deluge, oversupply: *Soldiers returning from war had glutted the job market.* **2 = overfill**, fill, stuff, cram, satiate: *The pond was glutted with fish.*

glutinous ADJECTIVE **= sticky**, adhesive, cohesive, gooey, viscous, gummy, gluey, viscid

glutton NOUN **= gourmand**, gorger, gannet *(slang)*, gobbler, pig *(informal)*

gluttonous ADJECTIVE **= greedy**, insatiable, voracious, ravenous, rapacious, piggish, hoggish

gluttony NOUN **= greed**, rapacity, voracity, greediness, voraciousness, piggishness

gnarled ADJECTIVE **1 = twisted**, knotted, contorted, knotty: *a garden full of ancient gnarled trees* **2 = wrinkled**, rough, rugged, leathery: *an old man with gnarled hands*

gnaw VERB **1 = bite**, chew, nibble, munch: *Woodlice attack living plants and gnaw at the stems.* **2 = distress**, worry, trouble, harry, haunt, plague, nag, fret: *Doubts were already gnawing away at the back of his mind.* **3 = erode**, consume, devour, eat away *or* into, wear away *or* down: *This run of bad luck has gnawed away at his usually optimistic character.*

go VERB **1 = move**, travel, advance, journey, proceed, pass, fare *(archaic)*, set off: *It took us an hour to go three miles.* **OPPOSITE:** stay **2 = leave**, withdraw, depart, move out, decamp, slope off, make tracks: *Come on, let's go.* **3 = lead**, run, reach, spread, extend, stretch, connect, span, give access: *There's a mountain road that goes from Blairstown to Millbrook Village.* **4 = elapse**, pass, flow, fly by, expire, lapse, slip away: *The week has gone so quickly!* **5 = be given**, be spent, be awarded, be allotted: *The money goes to projects chosen by the Board.* **6 = die**, perish, pass away, buy it *(U.S. slang)*, expire, check out *(U.S. slang)*, kick it *(slang)*, croak *(slang)*, give up the ghost, snuff it *(informal)*, peg out *(informal)*, kick the bucket *(slang)*, peg it *(informal)*, cark it *(Austral. & N.Z. slang)*, pop your clogs *(informal)*: *I want you to have my jewellery after I've gone.* **7 = proceed**, develop, turn out, work out, fare, fall out, pan out *(informal)*: *She says everything is going smoothly.* **8 = function**, work, run, move, operate, perform: *My car isn't going very well at the moment.* **OPPOSITE:** fail **9 = match**, blend, correspond, fit, suit, chime, harmonize: *That jacket and those trousers don't really go.* **10 = serve**, help, tend: *It just goes to prove you can't trust anyone.*
▷ NOUN **1 = attempt**, try, effort, bid, shot *(informal)*, crack *(informal)*, essay, stab *(informal)*, whirl *(informal)*, whack *(informal)*: *It took us two goes to get the colour right.* **2 = turn**, shot *(informal)*, spell, stint: *Whose go is it next?* **3 = energy**, life, drive, spirit, pep, vitality, vigour, verve, force, get-up-and-go *(informal)*, oomph *(informal)*, brio, vivacity: *For an old woman she still has a lot of go in her.*

go about something 1 = tackle, begin, approach, undertake, set about: *I want him back, but I just don't know how to go about it.* **2 = engage in**, perform, conduct, pursue, practise, ply, carry on with, apply yourself to, busy *or* occupy yourself with: *We were simply going about our business when we were pounced on by the police.*

go along with something = agree, follow, cooperate, concur, assent, acquiesce: *Whatever the majority decision, I'm prepared to go along with it.*

go at something = set about, start, begin, tackle, set to, get down to, wade into, get to work on, make a start on, get cracking on *(informal)*, address yourself to, get weaving on *(informal)*: *He went at this unpleasant task with grim determination.*

go away = leave, withdraw, exit, depart, move out, go to hell *(informal)*, decamp, hook it *(slang)*, slope off, pack your bags *(informal)*, make tracks, get on your bike *(Brit. slang)*, bog off *(Brit. slang)*, sling your hook *(Brit. slang)*, rack off *(Austral. & N.Z. slang)*: *I wish he'd just go away and leave me alone.*

go back = return: *I decided to go back to bed.*

go back on something *(often with* **on**) **= repudiate**, break, forsake, retract, renege on, desert, back out of, change your mind about: *The budget crisis has forced the President to go back on his word.*

go by = pass, proceed, elapse, flow on, move onward: *My grandmother was becoming more and more frail as time went by.*

go by something = obey, follow, adopt, observe, comply with, heed, submit to, be guided by, take as guide: *If they can prove that I'm wrong, then I'll go by what they say.*

go down 1 = fall, drop, decline, slump, decrease, fall off, dwindle, lessen, ebb, depreciate, become lower: *Crime has gone down 70 per cent.* **2 = set**, sink: *the glow left in the sky after the sun has gone down* **3 = sink**, founder, go under, be submerged: *The ship went down during a training exercise.*

go for someone 1 = prefer, like, choose, favour, admire, be attracted to, be fond of, hold with: *I tend to go for large dark men.* **2 = attack**, assault, assail, spring upon, rush upon, launch yourself at, set about *or* upon: *Patrick went for him, grabbing him by the throat.* **3 = scold**, attack, blast, criticize, flame *(informal)*, put down, tear into *(informal)*, diss *(slang, chiefly U.S.)*, impugn, lambast(e): *My mum went for me because I hadn't told her where I was going.*

go in for something = participate in, pursue, take part in, undertake, embrace, practise, engage in: *They go in for tennis and bowls.*

go into something 1 = investigate, consider, study, research, discuss, review, examine, pursue, probe, analyse, look into, delve into, work over, scrutinize, inquire into: *I'd like to go into this matter in a bit more detail.* **2 = enter**, begin, participate in: *He has decided to go into the tourism business.*

go off 1 = depart, leave, quit, go away, move out, decamp, hook it *(slang)*, slope off, pack your bags *(informal)*, rack off *(Austral. & N.Z. slang)*: *She just went off without saying a word to anyone.* **2 = explode**, fire, blow up, detonate: *A gun went off somewhere in the distance.* **3 = sound**, ring, toll, chime, peal: *The fire alarm went off.* **4 = take place**, happen, occur, come off *(informal)*, come about: *The meeting went off all right.* **5 = go bad**, turn, spoil, rot, go stale: *Don't eat that! It's gone off!*

go on 1 = happen, occur, take place: *I don't know what's going on.* **2 = continue**, last, stay, proceed, carry on, keep going: *the necessity for the war to go on* **3** *(often with* **about**) **= ramble on**, carry on, chatter, waffle *(informal, chiefly Brit.)*, witter (on) *(informal)*, rabbit on *(Brit. informal)*, prattle, blether, earbash *(Austral. & N.Z. slang)*: *They're always going on about choice and market forces.*

go on doing something *or* **go on with something = continue**, pursue, proceed, carry on, stick to, persist, keep on, keep at, persevere, stick at: *Go on with your work.*

go out *(informal)* **= see someone**, court, date *(chiefly U.S.)*, woo, go steady, be romantically involved with, step out with: *They've been going out for six weeks now.*
▷ VERB **= be extinguished**, die out, fade out: *The bedroom light went out after a moment.*

go over something 1 = examine, study, review, revise, inspect, work over: *An accountant has gone over the books.* **2 = rehearse**, read, scan, reiterate, skim over, peruse: *We went over our lines together before the show.*

go through something 1 = suffer, experience, bear, endure, brave, undergo, tolerate, withstand: *He was going through a very difficult time.* **2 = search**, look through, rummage through, rifle through, hunt through, fossick through *(Austral. & N.Z.)*, ferret about in: *It was evident that someone had been going through my possessions.* **3 = examine**, check, search, explore, look through, work over: *Going through his list of customers is a massive job.* **4 = use up**, exhaust, consume, squander: *He goes through*

around £500 in an average week.
go through with something = **carry on**, continue, pursue, keep on, persevere: *Richard pleaded with Belinda not to go through with the divorce.*
go together **1** = **harmonize**, match, agree, accord, fit, make a pair: *Red wine and oysters don't really go together.* **2** = **go out**, court, date (*informal, chiefly U.S.*), go steady (*informal*): *We've been going together for a month.*
go under **1** = **fail**, die, sink, go down, fold (*informal*), founder, succumb, go bankrupt: *If one firm goes under it could provoke a cascade of bankruptcies.* **2** = **sink**, go down, founder, submerge: *The ship went under, taking with her all her crew.*
go up = **increase**, rise, mount, soar, get higher: *Interest rates have gone up again.*
go with something = **match**, suit, blend, correspond with, agree with, fit, complement, harmonize: *Does this tie go with this shirt?*
go without something = **be deprived of**, want, lack, be denied, do without, abstain, go short, deny yourself: *I have known what it is like to go without food for days.*
no go = **impossible**, not on (*informal*), vain, hopeless, futile: *I tried to get him to change his mind, but it was no go.*

goad VERB = **urge**, drive, prompt, spur, stimulate, provoke, arouse, propel, prod, prick, incite, instigate, egg on, exhort, impel: *He goaded me into taking direct action.*
▷ NOUN = **incentive**, urge, spur, motivation, pressure, stimulus, stimulation, impetus, incitement: *His distrust only acted as a goad to me to prove him wrong.*

go-ahead NOUN = **permission**, consent, green light, assent, leave, authorization, O.K. *or* okay (*informal*): *Don't do any major repair work until you get the go-ahead from your insurers.*
▷ ADJECTIVE = **enterprising**, pioneering, ambitious, progressive, go-getting (*informal*), up-and-coming: *The estate is one of the most go-ahead wine producers in South Africa.*

goal NOUN = **aim**, end, target, purpose, object, intention, objective, ambition, destination, Holy Grail (*informal*)

goat NOUN
▸ *related adjective:* caprine ▸ *name of male:* billy, buck ▸ *name of female:* nanny ▸ *name of young:* kid, yeanling ▸ *collective nouns:* herd, tribe

gob NOUN = **piece**, lump, chunk, hunk, nugget, blob, wad, clod, wodge (*Brit. informal*)

gobble VERB = **devour**, swallow, gulp, guzzle, wolf, bolt, cram in, gorge on, pig out on (*slang*), stuff yourself with

go-between NOUN = **intermediary**, agent, medium, broker, factor, dealer, liaison, mediator, middleman

god NOUN = **deity**, immortal, divinity, divine being, supreme being, atua (*N.Z.*)
▷ *See themed panel* **Gods and Godesses** *on page 298*

QUOTATIONS

As flies to wanton boys are we to the gods;
They kill us for their sport
[William Shakespeare *King Lear*]

Heaven always bears some proportion to earth. The god of the cannibal will be a cannibal, of the crusader a crusader, and of the merchants a merchant
[Ralph Waldo Emerson *The Conduct of Life*]

If the triangles were to make a god, he would have three sides
[Montesquieu *Lettres Persanes*]

Bacchus: a convenient deity invented by the ancients as an excuse for getting drunk
[Ambrose Bierce *The Devil's Dictionary*]

It is convenient that there be gods, and, as it is convenient, let us believe that there are
[Ovid *Ars Amatoria*]

godforsaken ADJECTIVE = **desolate**, abandoned, deserted, remote, neglected, lonely, bleak, gloomy, backward, dismal, dreary, forlorn, wretched

godless ADJECTIVE = **wicked**, depraved, profane, unprincipled, atheistic, ungodly, irreligious, impious, unrighteous

godlike ADJECTIVE = **divine**, heavenly, celestial, superhuman

godly ADJECTIVE = **devout**, religious, holy, righteous, pious, good, saintly, god-fearing

godsend NOUN = **blessing**, help, benefit, asset, boon

gogga NOUN = **insect**, bug, creepy-crawly (*Brit. informal*)

goggle VERB = **stare**, gape, gawp (*slang*), gawk

going-over NOUN **1** = **examination**, study, check, review, survey, investigation, analysis, inspection, scrutiny, perusal: *Michael was given a complete going-over and was diagnosed with hay fever.* **2** = **thrashing**, attack, beating, whipping, thumping, pasting (*slang*), buffeting, drubbing (*informal*): *The bouncers took him outside and gave him a thorough going-over.* **3** = **dressing-down**, talking-to (*informal*), lecture, rebuke, reprimand, scolding, chiding, tongue-lashing, chastisement, castigation: *Our manager gave us a right going-over in the changing room after the game.*

golden ADJECTIVE **1** = **yellow**, bright, brilliant, blonde, blond, flaxen: *She combed and arranged her golden hair.* **OPPOSITE:** dark **2** = **successful**, glorious, prosperous, best, rich, flourishing, halcyon: *the golden age of American moviemaking* **OPPOSITE:** worst **3** = **promising**, excellent, valuable, favourable, advantageous, auspicious, opportune, propitious: *There's a golden opportunity for peace which must be seized.* **OPPOSITE:** unfavourable **4** = **favourite**, favoured, most popular, best-loved

gone ADJECTIVE **1** = **missing**, lost, away, vanished, absent, astray: *He's already been gone four hours!* **2** = **used up**, spent, finished, consumed: *After two years, all her money was gone.* **3** = **past**, over, ended, finished, elapsed: *Those happy times are gone forever.*

good ADJECTIVE **1** = **excellent**, great, fine, pleasing, capital, choice, crucial (*slang*), acceptable, pleasant, worthy, first-class, divine, splendid, satisfactory, superb, enjoyable, awesome (*slang*), dope (*slang*), world-class, admirable, agreeable, super (*informal*), pleasurable, wicked (*slang*), bad (*slang*), first-rate, tiptop, bitchin' (*U.S. slang*), booshit (*Austral. slang*), exo (*Austral. slang*), sik (*Austral. slang*), rad (*informal*), phat (*slang*), schmick (*Austral. informal*), beaut (*informal*), barrie (*Scot. slang*), belting (*Brit. slang*), pearler (*Austral. slang*): *You should read this book – it's really good.* **OPPOSITE:** bad **2** = **proficient**, able, skilled, capable, expert, talented, efficient, clever, accomplished, reliable, first-class, satisfactory, competent, thorough, adept, first-rate, adroit, dexterous: *He is very good at his job.* **OPPOSITE:** bad **3** = **beneficial**, useful, healthy, helpful, favourable, wholesome, advantageous, salutary, salubrious: *Rain water was once considered to be good for the complexion.* **OPPOSITE:** harmful **4** = **honourable**, moral, worthy, ethical, upright, admirable, honest, righteous, exemplary, right, virtuous, trustworthy, altruistic, praiseworthy, estimable: *The president is a good man.* **OPPOSITE:** bad **5** = **well-behaved**, seemly, mannerly, proper, polite, orderly, obedient, dutiful, decorous, well-mannered: *The children have been very good all day.* **OPPOSITE:** naughty **6** = **kind**, kindly, friendly, obliging, charitable, humane, gracious, benevolent, merciful, beneficent, well-disposed, kind-hearted: *It's very good of you to help out at such short notice.* **OPPOSITE:** unkind **7** = **true**, real, genuine, proper, reliable, dependable, sound, trustworthy, dinkum (*Austral. & N.Z. informal*): *She's been a good friend to me over the years.* **8** = **full**, long, whole, complete, entire, solid, extensive: *The film lasts a good two and a half hours.* **OPPOSITE:** scant **9** = **considerable**, large, substantial, sufficient, adequate, ample: *A good number of people agree with me.* **10** = **valid**, convincing, compelling, legitimate, authentic, persuasive, sound, bona fide: *Can you think of one good reason why I should tell you?* **OPPOSITE:** invalid **11** = **best**, newest, special, finest, nicest, smartest, fancy, most valuable, most precious: *Try not to get paint on your good clothes.* **12** = **edible**, untainted, uncorrupted, eatable, fit to eat: *Is this fish still good, or has it gone off?*

Charles Dickens' Use of Adjectives

Many of the adjectives that Dickens uses most often are those that concern emotions. For example, *happy, anxious, miserable,* and *cheerful* all appear in his hundred most frequent adjectives. *Happy* often modifies nouns referring to time: characters remember *those happy days* and *the happiest hours. Happy* is also frequently used in greetings and toasts: as in modern English, *Many happy returns* and *Happy New Year* are found, but there are also collocations which have since fallen out of use, for example:

> A hundred happy returns of this auspicious day, Mr. Heathfield!

> 'Oh dear, Mrs Kenwigs', said Miss Petowker, 'while Mr Noggs is making that punch to drink happy returns in, do let Morleena go through that figure dance before Mr Lillyvick.'

Cheerful often modifies nouns relating to people, such as *face, voice,* and *smile.* It is also particularly associated with light and warmth: there are frequent references to *cheerful fires,* and several to the sun's *cheerful rays. Miserable* mostly co-occurs with *creature, wretch,* and *man,* while *anxious* collocates with *face, eye,* and *look.*

Many of Dickens' favoured adjectives are those that indicate the recurrent theme of social status. We read of *rich relations, rich heiresses,* and *rich debtors*; of *poor children* and *poor people. Poor* is also often used in the extended sense 'deserving sympathy' rather than 'lacking money', although these uses are often hard to distinguish, as in 'the poor child, who was one of the dirtiest little unfortunates I ever saw...' The phrase *rich and poor* also appears, as Dickens describes the bustling city of London with its mixture of characters from every walk of life:

> The streets are thronged with a vast concourse of people, gay and shabby, **rich and poor**, idle and industrious...

High and *low* are among Dickens' forty most frequent adjectives, and although these usually refer to space, there are also references to social status, such as *high connexions* and *low standings.* There are several instances of *lower classes*, but only one of *higher classes*, and a handful of *upper classes. Married* co-occurs with adverbs such as *happily, newly,* and *fast,* and nouns such as *couple, lady, sister,* and *daughter. Lady* is qualified by *married* almost twenty times more frequently than *man* is. On the other hand, *single gentleman* appears thirteen times as often as *single lady*: the latter are more likely to be referred to as *spinsters.*

Dickens had a predilection for Latinate terms such as *commodious, obdurate, pecuniary, remunerative, prodigious,* and *matrimonial.* However, he also satirizes the excessive use of such language in the character of Mr. Micawber, and occasionally contrasts Latinate and plain language to comic effect:

> It is not an avocation of a remunerative description - in other words, it does not pay - and some temporary embarrassments of a pecuniary nature have been the consequence...

Perhaps most interesting are Dickens' least frequent adjectives, which are wonderful examples of his linguistic inventiveness. Dickens liked to coin new adjectives from existing nouns, for example *cellarous, streety,* and *prisonous.* Innovative compounds include *pleasantest-situated, whimsically-twisted, plague-beleaguered, fruit-smeared, grateful-tempered, sweat-bedabbled, hitherto-bottled-up, turned-up-nosed,* and *proud-stomached.* These allow Dickens to sketch characters and scenes in a few words:

> Mr Tapley suppressed his own inclination to laugh; and with one of his most **whimsically-twisted** looks, replied...

> He darted swiftly from the room with every particle of his **hitherto-bottled-up** indignation effervescing, from all parts of his countenance, in a perspiration of passion.

GODS AND GODDESSES

Aztec

Acolmiztli
Acolnahuacatl
Amimitl
Atl
Atlaua
Camaxtli
Centeotl
Centzonuitznaua
Chalchiuhtlatonal
Chalchiuhtlicue
Chalchiutotolin
Chalmecacihuilt
Chantico
Chicomecoatl
Chicomexochtli
Chiconahui
Cihuacoatl
Coatlicue
Cochimetl
Coyolxauhqui
Ehecatl
Huehueteotl
Huitzilopochtli
Huixtocihuatl
Ilamatecuhtli
Innan
Itzlacoliuhque
Itzli
Itzpapalotl
Ixtlilton
Macuilxochitl
Malinalxochi
Mayahuel
Mictlantecihuatl
Mictlantecutli
Mixcoatl
Nanauatzin
Omacatl
Omecihuatl
Ometecuhtli
Patecatl
Paynal
Quetzalcoatl
Tecciztecatl
Techalotl
Techlotl
Tepeyollotl
Teteo
Tezcatlipoca
Tlahuixcalpantecuhtli
Tlaloc
Tlaltecuhtli
Tlazolteotl
Tonacatecuhtli
Tonatiuh
Tzapotla
Tena
Tzintetol
Tzontemoc
Uixtociuatl
Xilonen
Xipe Totec
Xippilli
Xiuhcoatl
Xiuhteuctli
Xochipilli
Xochiquetzal
Xolotl
Yacatecuhtli

Celtic

Áine
Anu
Arianhrod
Artio
Badb
Balor
Banba
Bécuma
Belenus
Bíle
Blodeuedd
Bóand
Bodb
Brigid
Ceridwen
Cernunnos
Dagda
Dana
Danu
Dôn
Donn
Epona
Ériu
Esus
Fand
Lir
Lleu Llaw Gyffes
Llyr
Lugh
Mabon
Macha
Manannán
Manawydan
Medb
Midir
Morrígan
Nantosuelta
Nechtan
Nemain
Nemetona
Núadu
Ogma
Óengus Mac Óc
Rhiannon
Rosmerta
Sequana
Sirona
Sucellus
Taranis
Teutates
Vagdavercustis

Egyptian

Anubis
Hathor
Horus
Isis
Maat
Osiris
Ptah
Ra *or* Amen-Ra
Re
Serapis
Set
Thoth

Greek

Aeolus	winds
Aphrodite	love and beauty
Apollo	light, youth, and music
Ares	war
Artemis	hunting and the moon
Asclepius	healing
Athene *or* Pallas Athene	wisdom
Bacchus	wine
Boreas	north wind
Cronos	fertility of the earth
Demeter	agriculture
Dionysus	wine
Eos	dawn
Eris	discord
Eros	love
Fates	destiny
Gaea	the earth
Graces	charm and beauty
Hades	underworld
Hebe	youth and spring
Hecate	underworld
Helios	sun
Hephaestus	fire and metalworking
Hera	queen of the gods
Hermes	messenger of the gods
Horae *or* the Hours	seasons
Hymen	marriage
Hyperion	sun
Hypnos	sleep
Iris	rainbow
Momus	blame and mockery
Morpheus	sleep and dreams
Nemesis	vengeance
Nike	victory
Pan	woods and shepherds
Poseidon	sea and earthquakes
Rhea	fertility
Selene	moon
Uranus	sky
Zephyrus	west wind
Zeus	king of the gods

Hindu

Agni
Brahma
Devi
Durga
Ganesa
Hanuman
Indra
Kali
Kama
Krishna
Lakshmi
Maya
Rama
Siva
Ushas
Varuna
Vishnu

Incan

Apo
Apocatequil
Apu Illapu
Apu Punchau
Catequil
Cavillaca
Chasca
Chasca Coyllur
Cocomama
Coniraya
Copacati
Ekkeko
Huaca
Illapa
Inti
Ka-Ata-Killa Kon
Mama Allpa
Mama Cocha
Mama Oello
Mama Pacha
Mama Quilla
Manco Capac
Pachacamac
Pariacaca
Paricia
Punchau
Supay
Urcaguary
Vichama
Viracocha
Zaramama

Norse

Aegir
Aesir
Balder
Bragi
Frey
Freya
Frigg
Hel
Heimdall
Idun
Loki
Njord
Norns
Odin
Thor
Tyr
Vanir

GODS AND GODDESSES (CONTINUED)

Mayan

Ac Yanto	Ah Peku	Bitol	Colel Cab	Ix	Nohochacyum
Acan	Ah Puch	Buluc Chabtan	Colop U Uichkin	Ixchel *or* Ix Chebel Yax	Tlacolotl
Acat	Ah Tabai	Cabaguil	Coyopa	Ixtab	Tohil
Ah Bolom Tzacab	Ah Uincir Dz'acab	Cakulha	Cum Hau	Ixzaluoh	Tzakol
Ah Cancum	Ah Uuc Ticab	Camaxtli	Ekchuah	Kan	Votan
Ah Chun Caan	Ahau-Kin	Camazotz	Ghanan	Kan-u-Uayeyab	Xaman Ek
Ah Chuy Kak	Ahmakiq	Caprakan	Gucumatz	Kan-xib-yui	Yaluk
Ah Ciliz	Ahulane	Cauac	Hacha'kyum	Kianto	Yum Caax
Ah Cun Can	Ajbit	Chac	Hun Came	K'in	Zotz
Ah Cuxtal	Akhushtal	Chac Uayab Xoc	Hun Hunahpu	Kinich Ahau	
Ah Hulneb	Alaghom Naom	Chamer	Hunab Ku	Kukulcan	
Ah Kin	Alom	Chibirias	Hurakan	Mulac	
Ah Mun	Backlum Chaam	Cit Bolon Tum	Itzamna	Naum	
Ah Muzencab	Balam	Cizin	Itzananohk'u		

Roman

Aesculapius	medicine	Flora	flowers	Pluto	underworld
Apollo	light, youth, and music	Janus	doors and beginnings	Quirinus	war
Aurora	dawn	Juno	queen of the gods	Saturn	agriculture and vegetation
Bacchus	wine	Jupiter *or* Jove	king of the gods	Sol	sun
Bellona	war	Lares	household	Somnus	sleep
Bona Dea	fertility	Luna	moon	Trivia	crossroads
Ceres	agriculture	Mars	war	Venus	love
Cupid	love	Mercury	messenger of the gods	Victoria	victory
Cybele	nature	Minerva	wisdom	Vulcan	fire and metalworking
Diana	hunting and the moon	Neptune	sea		
Faunus	forests	Penates	storeroom		
		Phoebus	sun		

opposite: bad **13 = convenient**, timely, fitting, fit, appropriate, suitable, well-timed, opportune: *Is this a good time for us to discuss our plans?* **opposite:** inconvenient
▷ NOUN **1 = benefit**, interest, gain, advantage, use, service, profit, welfare, behalf, usefulness, wellbeing: *I'm only doing all this for your own good.* **opposite:** disadvantage **2 = virtue**, goodness, righteousness, worth, merit, excellence, morality, probity, rectitude, uprightness: *Good and evil may co-exist within one family.* **opposite:** evil
for good = permanently, finally, for ever, once and for all, irrevocably, never to return, sine die *(Latin)*: *A few shots of this drug cleared up the disease for good.*

goodbye NOUN **= farewell**, parting, leave-taking: *It was a very emotional goodbye.*
▷ INTERJECTION **= farewell**, see you, see you later, ciao *(Italian)*, cheerio, adieu, ta-ta, au revoir *(French)*, auf Wiedersehen *(German)*, adios *(Spanish)*, haere ra *(N.Z.)*: *Well, goodbye and good luck.*

good-humoured ADJECTIVE **= genial**, happy, pleasant, cheerful, amiable, affable, congenial, good-tempered

good-looking ADJECTIVE **= attractive**, pretty, fair, beautiful, lovely, handsome, gorgeous, bonny, personable, comely, well-favoured, hot *(informal)*, fit *(Brit. informal)*

good-natured ADJECTIVE **= amiable**, kind, kindly, friendly, generous, helpful, obliging, tolerant, agreeable, benevolent, good-hearted, magnanimous, well-disposed, warm-hearted

goodness NOUN **1 = virtue**, honour, merit, integrity, morality, honesty, righteousness, probity, rectitude, uprightness: *He retains his faith in human goodness.* **opposite:** badness **2 = excellence**, value, quality, worth, merit, superiority: *his total belief in the goodness of socialist society* **3 = nutrition**, benefit, advantage, nourishment, wholesomeness, salubriousness: *drinks full of natural goodness* **4 = kindness**, charity, humanity, goodwill, mercy, compassion, generosity, friendliness, benevolence, graciousness, beneficence, kindliness, humaneness, kind-heartedness: *performing actions of goodness towards the poor*

QUOTATIONS

Goodness is easier to recognise than to define
[W.H. Auden *I Believe*]

Nobody deserves to be praised for his goodness if he has not the power to be wicked. All other goodness is often only weakness and impotence of the will
[Duc de la Rochefoucauld *Maxims*]

Goodness is not achieved in a vacuum, but in the company of other men, attended by love
[Saul Bellow *Dangling Man*]

goods PLURAL NOUN **1 = merchandise**, stock, products, stuff, commodities, wares: *a wide range of consumer goods* **2 = property**, things, effects, gear, furniture, movables, possessions, furnishings, belongings, trappings, paraphernalia, chattels, appurtenances: *You can give all your unwanted goods to charity.*

goodwill NOUN **= friendliness**, favour, friendship, benevolence, amity, kindliness

gooey ADJECTIVE **1 = sticky**, soft, tacky, viscous, glutinous, gummy, icky *(informal)*, gluey, gloopy, gungy: *a lovely gooey, sticky mess* **2 = sentimental**, romantic, sloppy, soppy, maudlin, syrupy *(informal)*, slushy *(informal)*, mawkish, tear-jerking *(informal)*, icky *(informal)*: *He wrote me a long, gooey love letter.*

gore[1] NOUN **= blood**, slaughter, bloodshed, carnage, butchery: *video nasties full of blood and gore*

gore[2] VERB **= pierce**, wound, stab, spit, transfix, impale: *He was gored to death by a rhinoceros.*

gorge NOUN **= ravine**, canyon, pass, clough *(dialect)*, chasm, cleft, fissure, defile, gulch *(U.S. & Canad.)*: *a steep path into Crete's Samaria Gorge*
▷ VERB **1 = overeat**, bolt, devour, gobble, wolf, swallow, gulp, guzzle, pig out *(slang)*: *I could spend all day gorging on chocolate.* **2** *(usually reflexive)* **= stuff**, fill, feed, cram, glut, surfeit,

satiate, sate: *Three men were gorging themselves on grouse and watermelon.*

gorgeous ADJECTIVE **1 = magnificent**, grand, beautiful, superb, spectacular, splendid, glittering, dazzling, luxurious, sumptuous, opulent: *Some of these Renaissance buildings are absolutely gorgeous.* **OPPOSITE:** shabby **2 = beautiful**, attractive, lovely, stunning *(informal)*, elegant, handsome, good-looking, exquisite, drop-dead *(slang)*, ravishing, hot *(informal)*, fit *(Brit. informal)*: *The cosmetics industry uses gorgeous women to sell its products.* **OPPOSITE:** ugly **3 = fine**, glorious, sunny: *It's a gorgeous day.* **OPPOSITE:** dull

gory ADJECTIVE **1 = grisly**, bloody, murderous, bloodthirsty: *The film is full of gory death scenes.* **2 = bloody**, bloodstained, blood-soaked: *The ambulanceman carefully stripped off his gory clothes.*

g

gospel NOUN **1 = doctrine**, news, teachings, message, revelation, creed, credo, tidings: *He visited the sick and preached the gospel.* **2 = truth**, fact, certainty, the last word, verity: *The results were not to be taken as gospel.*

gossip NOUN **1 = idle talk**, scandal, hearsay, tittle-tattle, buzz, dirt *(U.S. slang)*, goss *(informal)*, jaw *(slang)*, gen *(Brit. informal)*, small talk, chitchat, blether, scuttlebutt *(U.S. slang)*, chinwag *(Brit. informal)*: *There has been a lot of gossip about the reasons for his absence; a magazine packed with celebrity gossip* **2 = busybody**, babbler, prattler, chatterbox *(informal)*, blether, chatterer, scandalmonger, gossipmonger, tattletale *(chiefly U.S. & Canad.)*: *She was a vicious old gossip.* ▷ VERB **= chat**, chatter, blather, schmooze *(slang)*, jaw *(slang)*, dish the dirt *(informal)*, blether, shoot the breeze *(slang, chiefly U.S.)*, chew the fat *or* rag *(slang)*: *We gossiped well into the night.*

> **QUOTATIONS**
> There is only one thing in the world worse than being talked about, and that is not being talked about
> [Oscar Wilde *The Picture of Dorian Gray*]
> Gossip is a sort of smoke that comes from the dirty tobacco-pipes of those that diffuse it; it proves nothing but the bad taste of the smoker
> [George Eliot *Daniel Deronda*]

gouge VERB **= scoop**, cut, score, dig (out), scratch, hollow (out), claw, chisel, gash, incise: *quarries which have gouged great holes in the hills* ▷ NOUN **= gash**, cut, scratch, hollow, score, scoop, notch, groove, trench, furrow, incision: *iron-rimmed wheels digging great gouges into the road's surface*

gourmet NOUN **= connoisseur**, foodie *(informal)*, bon vivant *(French)*, epicure, gastronome

govern VERB **1 = rule**, lead, control, command, manage, direct, guide, handle, conduct, order, reign over, administer, oversee, supervise, be in power over, call the shots, call the tune, hold sway over, superintend: *They go to the polls on Friday to choose the people they want to govern their country.* **2 = determine**, decide, guide, rule, influence, underlie, sway: *Marine insurance is governed by a strict series of rules and regulations.* **3 = restrain**, control, check, contain, master, discipline, regulate, curb, inhibit, tame, subdue, get the better of, bridle, hold in check, keep a tight rein on: *Try to govern your temper.*

government NOUN **1 = administration**, executive, ministry, regime, governing body, powers-that-be: *The Government has insisted that confidence is needed before the economy can improve.* **2 = rule**, state, law, authority, administration, sovereignty, governance, dominion, polity, statecraft: *our system of government*

governmental ADJECTIVE **= administrative**, state, political, official, executive, ministerial, sovereign, bureaucratic

governor NOUN **= leader**, administrator, ruler, head, minister, director, manager, chief, officer, executive, boss *(informal)*, commander, controller, supervisor, superintendent, mandarin, comptroller, functionary, overseer, baas *(S. African)*
▸ *related adjective:* gubernatorial

gown NOUN **= dress**, costume, garment, robe, frock, garb, habit

grab VERB **= snatch**, catch, seize, capture, bag, grip, grasp, clutch, snap up, pluck, latch on to, catch *or* take hold of

grace NOUN **1 = elegance**, finesse, poise, ease, polish, refinement, fluency, suppleness, gracefulness: *He moved with the grace of a trained dancer.* **OPPOSITE:** ungainliness **2 = manners**, decency, cultivation, etiquette, breeding, consideration, propriety, tact, decorum, mannerliness: *He hadn't even the grace to apologize for what he'd done.* **OPPOSITE:** bad manners **3 = indulgence**, mercy, pardon, compassion, quarter, charity, forgiveness, reprieve, clemency, leniency: *He was granted four days' grace to be with his family.* **4 = benevolence**, favour, goodness, goodwill, generosity, kindness, beneficence, kindliness: *It was only by the grace of God that no one died.* **OPPOSITE:** ill will **5 = prayer**, thanks, blessing, thanksgiving, benediction: *Leo, will you say grace?* **6 = favour**, regard, respect, approval, esteem, approbation, good opinion: *The reasons for his fall from grace are not clear.* **OPPOSITE:** disfavour ▷ VERB **1 = adorn**, enhance, decorate, enrich, set off, garnish, ornament, deck, embellish, bedeck, beautify: *the beautiful old Welsh dresser that graced this homely room* **2 = honour**, favour, distinguish, elevate, dignify, glorify: *He graced our ceremony with his distinguished presence.* **OPPOSITE:** insult

> **QUOTATIONS**
> Some hae meat and canna eat,
> Some wad eat that want it;
> But we hae meat, and we can eat,
> Sae let the Lord be thankit
> [Robert Burns *Grace Before Meat*]

graceful ADJECTIVE **= elegant**, easy, flowing, smooth, fine, pleasing, beautiful, agile, symmetrical, gracile *(rare)*: *Her movements were so graceful they seemed effortless.* **OPPOSITE:** inelegant

graceless ADJECTIVE **1 = inelegant**, forced, awkward, clumsy, ungainly, unco *(Austral. slang)*: *a graceless pirouette* **2 = ill-mannered**, crude, rude, coarse, vulgar, rough, improper, shameless, unsophisticated, gauche, barbarous, boorish, gawky, uncouth, loutish, indecorous, unmannerly: *She couldn't stand his blunt, graceless manner.*

gracious ADJECTIVE **= courteous**, polite, civil, accommodating, kind, kindly, pleasing, friendly, obliging, amiable, cordial, hospitable, courtly, chivalrous, well-mannered: *He is always a gracious host.* **OPPOSITE:** ungracious

grade VERB **= classify**, rate, order, class, group, sort, value, range, rank, brand, arrange, evaluate: *The college does not grade the children's work.* ▷ NOUN **1 = class**, condition, quality, brand: *a good grade of plywood* **2 = mark**, degree, place, order: *pressure on students to obtain good grades* **3 = level**, position, rank, group, order, class, stage, step, station, category, rung, echelon: *Staff turnover is high among junior grades.*
make the grade = succeed, measure up, win through, pass muster, come up to scratch *(informal)*, come through with flying colours, prove acceptable, measure up to expectations: *She had a strong desire to be a dancer, but failed to make the grade.*

gradient NOUN **= slope**, hill, rise, grade, incline, bank

gradual ADJECTIVE **= steady**, even, slow, regular, gentle, moderate, progressive, piecemeal, unhurried **OPPOSITE:** sudden

gradually ADVERB **= steadily**, slowly, moderately, progressively, gently, step by step, evenly, piecemeal, bit by bit, little by little, by degrees, piece by piece, unhurriedly, drop by drop

graduate VERB **1 = mark off**, grade, proportion, regulate, gauge, calibrate, measure out: *The volume control knob is graduated from 1 to 11.* **2 = classify**, rank, grade, group, order, sort, range, arrange, sequence: *proposals to introduce an income tax which is graduated*

graft[1] NOUN **= shoot**, bud, implant, sprout, splice, scion: *These plants are*

propagated by grafts, buds or cuttings.
▷ VERB **= join**, insert, transplant, implant, splice, affix: *Pear trees are grafted on quince root-stocks.*

graft[2] NOUN **= labour**, work, industry, effort, struggle, sweat, toil, slog, exertion, blood, sweat, and tears (*informal*): *His career has been one of hard graft.*
▷ VERB **= work**, labour, struggle, sweat (*informal*), grind (*informal*), slave, strive, toil, drudge: *I really don't enjoy grafting away in a stuffy office all day.*

grain NOUN **1 = seed**, kernel, grist: *a grain of wheat* **2 = cereal**, corn: *a bag of grain* **3 = bit**, piece, trace, spark, scrap, suspicion, molecule, particle, fragment, atom, ounce, crumb, mite, jot, speck, morsel, granule, modicum, mote, whit, iota: *a grain of sand* **4 = texture**, pattern, surface, fibre, weave, nap: *Brush the paint over the wood in the direction of the grain.*

grammar NOUN **= syntax**, rules of language

> **QUOTATIONS**
> When I split an infinitive, God damn it, I split it so it will stay split
> [Raymond Chandler *Letter to Edward Weeks*]
>
> This is the sort of English up with which I will not put
> [Winston Churchill]

GRAMMATICAL CASES

ablative	instrumental
accusative	locative
agentive	nominative
dative	objective
elative	oblique
ergative	possessive
genitive	subjective
illative	vocative

grammatical ADJECTIVE **= syntactic**, linguistic

grand ADJECTIVE **1 = impressive**, great, large, magnificent, striking, fine, princely, imposing, superb, glorious, noble, splendid, gorgeous, luxurious, eminent, majestic, regal, stately, monumental, sublime, sumptuous, grandiose, opulent, palatial, ostentatious, splendiferous (*facetious*): *a grand building in the centre of town* **OPPOSITE:** unimposing **2 = ambitious**, great, glorious, lofty, grandiose, exalted, ostentatious: *He arrived in America full of grand schemes and lofty dreams.* **3 = superior**, great, lordly, noble, elevated, eminent, majestic, dignified, stately, lofty, august, illustrious, pompous, pretentious, haughty: *She's too busy with her grand new friends to bother with us now.* **4 = excellent**, great (*informal*), fine, wonderful, very good, brilliant, outstanding, smashing (*informal*), superb, first-class, divine, marvellous (*informal*), terrific (*informal*), splendid, awesome (*slang*), world-class, admirable, super (*informal*), first-rate, splendiferous (*facetious*): *He was having a grand time meeting new people.* **OPPOSITE:** bad **5 = chief**, highest, lead, leading, head, main, supreme, principal, big-time (*informal*), major league (*informal*), pre-eminent: *the federal grand jury* **OPPOSITE:** inferior

grandeur NOUN **= splendour**, glory, majesty, nobility, pomp, state, magnificence, sumptuousness, sublimity, stateliness

grandiose ADJECTIVE **1 = pretentious**, ambitious, extravagant, flamboyant, high-flown, pompous, showy, ostentatious, bombastic: *Not one of his grandiose plans has ever come to anything.* **OPPOSITE:** unpretentious **2 = imposing**, grand, impressive, magnificent, majestic, stately, monumental, lofty: *the grandiose building which housed the mayor's offices* **OPPOSITE:** humble

grant NOUN **= award**, allowance, donation, endowment, gift, concession, subsidy, hand-out, allocation, bounty, allotment, bequest, stipend: *My application for a grant has been rejected.*
▷ VERB **1 = give**, allow, present, award, accord, permit, assign, allocate, hand out, confer on, bestow on, impart, allot, vouchsafe: *France has agreed to grant him political asylum.* **2 = accept**, allow, admit, acknowledge, concede, cede, accede: *The magistrates granted that the charity was justified in bringing the action.*

granule NOUN **= grain**, scrap, molecule, particle, fragment, atom, crumb, jot, speck, iota

graphic ADJECTIVE **1 = vivid**, clear, detailed, striking, telling, explicit, picturesque, forceful, expressive, descriptive, illustrative, well-drawn: *graphic descriptions of violence* **OPPOSITE:** vague **2 = pictorial**, seen, drawn, visible, visual, representational, illustrative, diagrammatic: *a graphic representation of how the chemical acts on the body* **OPPOSITE:** impressionistic

grapple VERB **1 = deal**, tackle, cope, face, fight, battle, struggle, take on, engage, encounter, confront, combat, contend, wrestle, tussle, get to grips, do battle, address yourself to: *The economy is just one of the problems that the country is grappling with.* **2 = struggle**, fight, combat, wrestle, battle, clash, contend, strive, tussle, scuffle, come to grips: *He grappled desperately with Holmes for control of the weapon.*

grasp VERB **1 = grip**, hold, catch, grab, seize, snatch, clutch, clinch, clasp, lay *or* take hold of: *He grasped both my hands.* **2 = understand**, realize, take in, get, see, follow, catch on, comprehend, get the message about, get the picture about, catch *or* get the drift of: *The Government has not yet grasped the seriousness of the crisis.*
▷ NOUN **1 = grip**, hold, possession, embrace, clutches, clasp: *She slipped her hand from his grasp.* **2 = understanding**, knowledge, grip, perception, awareness, realization, mastery, comprehension: *They have a good grasp of foreign languages.* **3 = reach**, power, control, range, sweep, capacity, scope, sway, compass, mastery: *Peace is now within our grasp.*

grasping ADJECTIVE **= greedy**, acquisitive, rapacious, mean, selfish, stingy, penny-pinching (*informal*), venal, miserly, avaricious, niggardly, covetous, tightfisted, close-fisted, snoep (*S. African informal*) **OPPOSITE:** generous

grate VERB **1 = shred**, mince, pulverize: *Grate the cheese into a mixing bowl.* **2 = scrape**, grind, rub, scratch, creak, rasp: *His chair grated as he got to his feet.*
grate on someone *or* **grate on someone's nerves = annoy**, irritate, aggravate (*informal*), gall, exasperate, nettle, jar, vex, chafe, irk, rankle, peeve, get under your skin (*informal*), get up your nose (*informal*), get on your nerves (*informal*), nark (*Brit., Austral. & N.Z. slang*), set your teeth on edge, get on your wick (*Brit. slang*), rub you up the wrong way, hack you off (*informal*): *His manner always grated on me.*

grateful ADJECTIVE **= thankful**, obliged, in (someone's) debt, indebted, appreciative, beholden

gratification NOUN **1 = satisfaction**, delight, pleasure, joy, thrill, relish, enjoyment, glee, kick *or* kicks (*informal*): *Eventually they recognized him, much to his gratification.* **OPPOSITE:** disappointment **2 = indulgence**, satisfaction, fulfilment: *the gratification of his every whim* **OPPOSITE:** denial

gratify VERB **= please**, delight, satisfy, thrill, give pleasure, gladden

grating[1] NOUN **= grille**, grid, grate, lattice, trellis, gridiron: *an open grating in the sidewalk*

grating[2] ADJECTIVE **= irritating**, grinding, harsh, annoying, jarring, unpleasant, scraping, raucous, strident, squeaky, rasping, discordant, disagreeable, irksome: *I can't stand that grating voice of his.* **OPPOSITE:** pleasing

gratitude NOUN **= thankfulness**, thanks, recognition, obligation, appreciation, indebtedness, sense of obligation, gratefulness **OPPOSITE:** ingratitude

gratuitous ADJECTIVE **= unjustified**, unnecessary, needless, unfounded, unwarranted, superfluous, wanton, unprovoked, groundless, baseless, uncalled-for, unmerited, causeless **OPPOSITE:** justifiable

gratuity NOUN **= tip**, present, gift, reward, bonus, donation, boon, bounty, recompense, perquisite, baksheesh, benefaction, pourboire *(French)*, bonsela *(S. African)*, largesse *or* largess

grave[1] NOUN = **tomb**, vault, crypt, mausoleum, sepulchre, pit, last resting place, burying place: *They used to visit her grave twice a year.*
▸ *related adjective:* sepulchral

> **QUOTATIONS**
> The grave's a fine and private place,
> But none do there, I think, embrace
> [Andrew Marvell *To his Coy Mistress*]

grave[2] ADJECTIVE **1 = serious**, important, significant, critical, pressing, threatening, dangerous, vital, crucial, acute, severe, urgent, hazardous, life-and-death, momentous, perilous, weighty, leaden, of great consequence: *He says the situation in his country is very grave.* **OPPOSITE:** trifling **2 = solemn**, sober, gloomy, dull, thoughtful, subdued, sombre, dour, grim-faced, long-faced, unsmiling: *She could tell by his grave expression that something terrible had happened.* **OPPOSITE:** carefree

graveyard NOUN = **cemetery**, churchyard, burial ground, charnel house, necropolis, boneyard *(informal)*, God's acre *(literary)*

gravitas NOUN = **seriousness**, gravity, solemnity

gravitate VERB = **be drawn**, move, tend, lean, be pulled, incline, be attracted, be influenced

gravity NOUN **1 = seriousness**, importance, consequence, significance, urgency, severity, acuteness, moment, weightiness, momentousness, perilousness, hazardousness: *You don't seem to appreciate the gravity of this situation.* **OPPOSITE:** triviality **2 = solemnity**, gloom, seriousness, gravitas, thoughtfulness, grimness: *There was an appealing gravity to everything she said.* **OPPOSITE:** frivolity

graze[1] VERB = **feed**, crop, browse, pasture: *cows grazing in a field*

graze[2] VERB **1 = scratch**, skin, bark, scrape, chafe, abrade: *I had grazed my knees a little.* **2 = touch**, brush, rub, scrape, shave, skim, kiss, glance off: *A bullet had grazed his arm.*
▹ NOUN = **scratch**, scrape, abrasion: *He just has a slight graze.*

greasy ADJECTIVE **1 = fatty**, slick, slippery, oily, slimy, oleaginous: *He propped his elbows upon the greasy counter.* **2 = sycophantic**, fawning, grovelling, ingratiating, smooth, slick, oily, unctuous, smarmy *(Brit. informal)*, toadying: *She called him 'a greasy little Tory sycophant'.*

great ADJECTIVE **1 = large**, big, huge, vast, enormous, extensive, tremendous, immense, gigantic, mammoth, bulky, colossal, prodigious, stupendous, voluminous, elephantine, ginormous *(informal)*, humongous *or* humungous *(U.S. slang)*, supersize: *a great hall as long and high as a church* **OPPOSITE:** small **2 = extreme**, considerable, excessive, high, decided, pronounced, extravagant, prodigious, inordinate: *I'll take great care of it; That must have taken a great effort on his part.* **3 = major**, lead, leading, chief, main, capital, grand, primary, principal, prominent, superior, paramount, big-time *(informal)*, major league *(informal)*: *the great cultural achievements of the past* **4 = important**, serious, significant, critical, crucial, heavy, grave, momentous, weighty, consequential: *his pronouncements on the great political matters of the age* **OPPOSITE:** unimportant **5 = famous**, celebrated, outstanding, excellent, remarkable, distinguished, prominent, glorious, notable, renowned, eminent, famed, illustrious, exalted, noteworthy: *the great American president, Abraham Lincoln* **6 = expert**, skilled, talented, skilful, good, able, masterly, crack *(slang)*, superb, world-class, adept, stellar *(informal)*, superlative, proficient, adroit: *He was one of the West Indies' greatest cricketers.* **OPPOSITE:** unskilled **7 = excellent**, good, fine, wonderful, mean *(slang)*, topping *(Brit. slang)*, cracking *(Brit. informal)*, superb, fantastic *(informal)*, tremendous *(informal)*, marvellous *(informal)*, terrific *(informal)*, mega *(slang)*, sovereign, awesome *(slang)*, dope *(slang)*, admirable, first-rate, def *(informal)*, brill *(informal)*, boffo *(slang)*, bitchin', chillin' *(U.S. slang)*, booshit *(Austral. slang)*, exo *(Austral. slang)*, sik *(Austral. slang)*, rad *(informal)*, phat *(slang)*, schmick *(Austral. informal)*, beaut *(informal)*, barrie *(Scot. slang)*, belting *(Brit. slang)*, pearler *(Austral. slang)*: *It's a great film; you must see it.* **OPPOSITE:** poor **8 = very**, really, particularly, truly, extremely, awfully *(informal)*, exceedingly: *He gave me a great big smile.* **9 = enthusiastic**, keen, active, devoted, zealous: *I'm not a great fan of football.*

greatly ADVERB = **very much**, much, hugely, vastly, extremely, highly, seriously *(informal)*, notably, considerably, remarkably, enormously, immensely, tremendously, markedly, powerfully, exceedingly, mightily, abundantly, by much, by leaps and bounds, to the nth degree

greatness NOUN **1 = grandeur**, glory, majesty, splendour, power, pomp, magnificence: *the greatness of ancient Rome* **2 = fame**, glory, celebrity, distinction, eminence, note, lustre, renown, illustriousness: *Abraham Lincoln achieved greatness.*

greed *or* **greediness** NOUN **1 = gluttony**, voracity, insatiableness, ravenousness: *He ate too much out of sheer greed.* **2 = avarice**, longing, desire, hunger, craving, eagerness, selfishness, acquisitiveness, rapacity, cupidity, covetousness, insatiableness: *an insatiable greed for power* **OPPOSITE:** generosity

> **QUOTATIONS**
> There is enough in the world for everyone's need, but not enough for everyone's greed
> [Frank Buchman *Remaking the World*]

> **PROVERBS**
> *The more you get, the more you want*
> *The pitcher will go to the well once too often*

greedy ADJECTIVE **1 = gluttonous**, insatiable, voracious, ravenous, piggish, hoggish, hungry *(Austral. & N.Z. informal)*: *a greedy little boy who ate too many sweets* **2 = avaricious**, grasping, selfish, insatiable, acquisitive, rapacious, materialistic, desirous, covetous, hungry *(Austral. & N.Z. informal)*: *He attacked greedy bosses for awarding themselves big pay rises.* **OPPOSITE:** generous

Greek ADJECTIVE = **Hellenic**: *his extensive knowledge of Greek antiquity*
▹ NOUN = **Hellene**: *The ancient Greeks referred to themselves as Hellenes.*

> **QUOTATIONS**
> I fear the Greeks, even when they are bearing gifts
> [Virgil *Aeneid*]

green ADJECTIVE **1 = verdant**, leafy, grassy: *The city has only thirteen square centimetres of green space for each inhabitant.* **2 = ecological**, conservationist, environment-friendly, ecologically sound, eco-friendly, ozone-friendly, non-polluting, green-collar: *trying to persuade governments to adopt greener policies* **3 = unripe**, fresh, raw, immature: *Pick and ripen any green fruits in a warm dark place.* **4 = inexperienced**, new, innocent, raw, naive, ignorant, immature, gullible, callow, untrained, unsophisticated, credulous, ingenuous, unpolished, wet behind the ears *(informal)*: *He was a young lad, very green and immature.* **5 = jealous**, grudging, resentful, envious, covetous: *Collectors worldwide will turn green with envy.* **6 = nauseous**, ill, sick, pale, unhealthy, wan, under

SHADES OF GREEN

almond green	celadon	emerald green	olive	teal
apple green	chartreuse	jade	pea green	turquoise
aqua	citron	lime green	pine green	
aquamarine	cyan	Lincoln green	pistachio	
avocado	eau de nil	Nile green	sea green	

the weather: *By the end of the race the runners would be green with sickness.*
▷ NOUN **1** *(with capital)* = **environmentalist**, conservationist: *The Greens see themselves as a radical alternative to the two major parties.*
2 = **lawn**, common, turf, sward, grassplot: *a pageant on the village green*
▸ *related adjective:* verdant

green light NOUN = **authorization**, sanction, approval, go-ahead *(informal)*, blessing, permission, confirmation, clearance, imprimatur, O.K. *or* okay *(informal)*

greet VERB **1** = **salute**, hail, nod to, say hello to, address, accost, tip your hat to: *He greeted us with a smile.*
2 = **welcome**, meet, receive, karanga (N.Z.), mihi (N.Z.), haeremai (N.Z.): *She was waiting at the door to greet her guests.*
3 = **receive**, take, respond to, react to: *The European Court's decision has been greeted with dismay.*

greeting NOUN = **welcome**, reception, hail, salute, address, salutation, hongi (N.Z.), kia ora (N.Z.): *His greeting was familiar and friendly.*
▷ PLURAL NOUN = **best wishes**, regards, respects, compliments, good wishes, salutations: *They exchanged hearty Christmas greetings.*

gregarious ADJECTIVE = **outgoing**, friendly, social, cordial, sociable, affable, convivial, companionable
OPPOSITE: unsociable

grey ADJECTIVE **1** = **dull**, dark, dim, gloomy, cloudy, murky, drab, misty, foggy, overcast, sunless: *It was a grey, wet April Sunday.* **2** = **boring**, dull, anonymous, faceless, colourless, nondescript, characterless: *little grey men in suits* **3** = **old**, aged, ancient, mature, elderly, venerable, hoary: *a grey old man* **4** = **pale**, wan, livid, bloodless, colourless, pallid, ashen, like death warmed up *(informal)*: *His face was grey with pain.* **5** = **ambiguous**, uncertain, neutral, unclear, debatable: *The whole question of refugees is something of a grey area.*

SHADES FROM BLACK TO WHITE

ash	ivory	putty
black	jet	raven
charcoal	off-white	sable
cream	oyster	silver
ebony	white	slate
eggshell	pearl	steel grey
grey	pewter	stone
gunmetal	pitch-black	white
iron	platinum	

gridlock NOUN **1** = **traffic jam**: *The streets are wedged solid with the traffic gridlock.* **2** = **deadlock**, halt, stalemate, impasse, standstill, full stop: *He agreed that these policies will lead to a gridlock in the future.*

grief NOUN = **sadness**, suffering, pain, regret, distress, misery, agony, mourning, sorrow, woe, anguish, remorse, bereavement, heartache, heartbreak, mournfulness: *Their grief soon gave way to anger.* **OPPOSITE:** joy
come to grief = **fail**, founder, break down, come unstuck, miscarry, fall flat on your face, meet with disaster: *So many marriages have come to grief over lack of money.*

QUOTATIONS
Grief is a species of idleness
[Dr. Johnson *letter to Mrs Thrale*]

grievance NOUN = **complaint**, protest, beef *(slang)*, gripe *(informal)*, axe to grind, chip on your shoulder *(informal)*

grieve VERB **1** = **mourn**, suffer, weep, ache, lament, sorrow, wail: *He's grieving over his dead wife and son.*
2 = **sadden**, hurt, injure, distress, wound, crush, pain, afflict, upset, agonize, break the heart of, make your heart bleed: *It grieved me to see him in such distress.* **OPPOSITE:** gladden

grievous ADJECTIVE **1** = **deplorable**, shocking, appalling, dreadful, outrageous, glaring, intolerable, monstrous, shameful, unbearable, atrocious, heinous, lamentable, egregious: *Their loss would be a grievous blow to our engineering industries.*
OPPOSITE: pleasant **2** = **severe**, damaging, heavy, wounding, grave, painful, distressing, dreadful, harmful, calamitous, injurious: *He survived in spite of suffering grievous injuries.*
OPPOSITE: mild

grim ADJECTIVE = **terrible**, shocking, severe, harsh, forbidding, horrible, formidable, sinister, ghastly, hideous, gruesome *(slang)*, grisly, horrid, frightful, godawful

grimace VERB = **scowl**, frown, sneer, wince, lour *or* lower, make a face *or* faces: *She started to sit up, grimaced with pain, and sank back.*
▷ NOUN = **scowl**, frown, sneer, wince, face, wry face: *He took another drink of his coffee. 'Awful,' he said with a grimace.*

grime NOUN = **dirt**, filth, soot, smut, grot *(slang)*

grimy ADJECTIVE = **dirty**, polluted, filthy, soiled, foul, grubby, sooty, unclean, grotty *(slang)*, smutty, scuzzy *(slang)*, begrimed, festy *(Austral. slang)*

grind VERB **1** = **crush**, mill, powder, grate, pulverize, pound, kibble, abrade, granulate: *Grind the pepper in a pepper mill.* **2** = **press**, push, crush, jam, mash, force down: *He ground his cigarette under his heel.* **3** = **grate**, scrape, grit, gnash: *If you grind your teeth at night, see your dentist.* **4** = **sharpen**, file, polish, sand, smooth, whet: *The tip can be ground to a much sharper edge.*
▷ NOUN = **hard work** *(informal)*, labour, effort, task, sweat *(informal)*, chore, toil, drudgery: *Life continues to be a terrible grind for the ordinary person.*
grind someone down = **oppress**, suppress, harass, subdue, hound, bring down, plague, persecute, subjugate, trample underfoot, tyrannize (over): *There will always be some bosses who want to grind you down.*

grip VERB **1** = **grasp**, hold, catch, seize, clutch, clasp, latch on to, take hold of: *She gripped his hand tightly.* **2** = **engross**, fascinate, absorb, entrance, hold, catch up, compel, rivet, enthral, mesmerize, spellbind: *The whole nation was gripped by the dramatic story.*
▷ NOUN **1** = **clasp**, hold, grasp, handclasp (U.S.): *His strong hand eased the bag from her grip.* **2** = **control**, rule, influence, command, power, possession, sway, dominance, domination, mastery: *The president maintains an iron grip on his country.*
3 = **hold**, purchase, friction, traction: *a new kind of rubber which gives tyres a better grip* **4** = **understanding**, sense, command, perception, awareness, grasp, appreciation, mastery, comprehension, discernment: *He has lost his grip on reality.*
come *or* **get to grips with something** = **tackle**, deal with, handle, take on, meet, encounter, cope with, confront, undertake, grasp, face up to, grapple with, close with, contend with: *The government's first task is to get to grips with the economy.*

gripe VERB = **complain**, moan, groan, grumble, beef *(slang)*, carp, bitch *(slang)*, nag, whine, grouse, bleat, grouch *(informal)*, bellyache *(slang)*, kvetch (U.S. *slang*): *He started griping about the prices they were charging.*
▷ NOUN = **complaint**, protest, objection, beef *(slang)*, moan, grumble, grievance, grouse, grouch *(informal)*: *My only gripe is that just one main course and one dessert were available.*

gripping ADJECTIVE = **fascinating**, exciting, thrilling, entrancing, compelling, compulsive, riveting, enthralling, engrossing, spellbinding, unputdownable *(informal)*

grisly ADJECTIVE = **gruesome**, shocking, terrible, awful, terrifying, appalling, horrible, grim, dreadful, sickening, ghastly, hideous, macabre, horrid, frightful, abominable, hellacious (U.S. *slang*)
OPPOSITE: pleasant

USAGE
Note the spelling of *grisly* (as in *a grisly murder*). It should be carefully distinguished from the word *grizzly* (as in *a grizzly bear*), which means 'greyish in colour'.

grit NOUN **1** = **gravel**, sand, dust, pebbles: *He felt tiny bits of grit and sand peppering his knees.* **2** = **courage**, spirit, resolution, determination, nerve, guts *(informal)*, balls *(taboo, slang)*, pluck, backbone, fortitude, toughness, tenacity, perseverance, mettle, doggedness, hardihood: *He showed grit and determination in his fight back to health.*
▷ VERB = **clench**, grind, grate, gnash: *Gritting my teeth, I did my best to stifle a sharp retort.*

gritty ADJECTIVE **1 = rough**, sandy, dusty, abrasive, rasping, grainy, gravelly, granular: *She threw a handful of gritty dust into his eyes.* **2 = courageous**, game, dogged, determined, tough, spirited, brave, hardy, feisty *(informal, chiefly U.S. & Canad.)*, resolute, tenacious, plucky, steadfast, mettlesome, (as) game as Ned Kelly *(Austral. slang)*: *a gritty determination to get to the top*

grizzle VERB **= whine**, fret, whimper, whinge *(informal)*, snivel, girn *(Scot.)*

grizzled ADJECTIVE **= grey**, greying, grey-haired, grizzly, hoary, grey-headed

groan VERB **1 = moan**, cry, sigh: *The man on the floor began to groan with pain.* **2 = complain**, object, moan, grumble, gripe *(informal)*, beef *(slang)*, carp, bitch *(slang)*, lament, whine, grouse, bemoan, whinge *(informal)*, grouch *(informal)*, bellyache *(slang)*: *His parents were beginning to groan about the cost of it all.*
▷ NOUN **1 = moan**, cry, sigh, whine: *She heard him let out a pitiful, muffled groan.* **2 = complaint**, protest, objection, grumble, beef *(slang)*, grouse, gripe *(informal)*, grouch *(informal)*: *I don't have time to listen to your moans and groans.*

groggy ADJECTIVE **= dizzy**, faint, stunned, confused, reeling, shaky, dazed, wobbly, weak, unsteady, muzzy, stupefied, befuddled, punch-drunk, woozy *(informal)*

groom NOUN **1 = stableman**, stableboy, hostler *or* ostler *(archaic)*: *He worked as a groom at a stables on Dartmoor.* **2 = newly-wed**, husband, bridegroom, marriage partner: *We toasted the bride and groom.*
▷ VERB **1 = brush**, clean, tend, rub down, curry: *The horses were exercised and groomed with special care.* **2 = smarten up**, dress, clean, turn out, get up *(informal)*, tidy, preen, spruce up, primp, gussy up *(slang, chiefly U.S.)*: *She always appeared perfectly groomed.* **3 = train**, prime, prepare, coach, ready, educate, drill, nurture, make ready: *He was already being groomed for a top job.*

groove NOUN **= indentation**, cut, hollow, score, channel, trench, flute, gutter, trough, furrow, rut

grope VERB **= feel**, search, fumble, flounder, fish, finger, scrabble, cast about, fossick *(Austral. & N.Z.)*

gross ADJECTIVE **1 = flagrant**, obvious, glaring, blatant, serious, shocking, rank, plain, sheer, utter, outrageous, manifest, shameful, downright, grievous, unqualified, heinous, egregious, unmitigated, arrant: *The company were found guilty of gross negligence.* **OPPOSITE:** qualified **2 = vulgar**, offensive, crude, rude, obscene, low, coarse, indecent, improper, unseemly, lewd, X-rated *(informal)*, impure, smutty, ribald, indelicate: *That's a disgusting thing to say – you're so gross!* **OPPOSITE:** decent **3 = coarse**, crass, tasteless, unsophisticated, ignorant, insensitive, callous, boorish, unfeeling, unrefined, uncultured, undiscriminating, imperceptive: *He is a gross and boorish individual.* **OPPOSITE:** cultivated **4 = fat**, obese, overweight, great, big, large, heavy, massive, dense, bulky, hulking, corpulent, lumpish: *I've put on so much weight I look totally gross.* **OPPOSITE:** slim **5 = total**, whole, entire, aggregate, before tax, before deductions: *Gross sales in June totalled 270 million pounds.* **OPPOSITE:** net
▷ VERB **= earn**, make, take, bring in, rake in *(informal)*: *So far the films have grossed nearly £290 million.*

grotesque ADJECTIVE **1 = unnatural**, bizarre, weird, odd, strange, fantastic, distorted, fanciful, deformed, outlandish, whimsical, freakish, misshapen, malformed: *statues of grotesque mythical creatures* **OPPOSITE:** natural **2 = absurd**, ridiculous, ludicrous, preposterous, incongruous: *the grotesque disparities between the rich and the poor* **OPPOSITE:** natural

grouch VERB **= complain**, moan, grumble, beef *(slang)*, carp, bitch *(slang)*, whine, grouse, gripe *(informal)*, whinge *(informal)*, bleat, find fault, bellyache *(slang)*, kvetch *(U.S. slang)*: *They grouched about how hard-up they were.*
▷ NOUN **1 = moaner**, complainer, grumbler, whiner, grouser, malcontent, curmudgeon, crosspatch *(informal)*, crab *(informal)*, faultfinder: *He's an old grouch but she puts up with him.* **2 = complaint**, protest, objection, grievance, moan, grumble, beef *(slang)*, grouse, gripe *(informal)*: *One of their biggest grouches is the new system of payment.*

grouchy ADJECTIVE **= bad-tempered**, cross, irritable, grumpy, discontented, grumbling, surly, petulant, sulky, ill-tempered, irascible, cantankerous, tetchy, ratty *(Brit. & N.Z. informal)*, testy, querulous, peevish, huffy, liverish

ground NOUN **1 = earth**, land, dry land, terra firma: *We slid down the roof and dropped to the ground.* **2 = arena**, pitch, stadium, park *(informal)*, field, enclosure: *the city's football ground*
▷ PLURAL NOUN **1 = estate**, holding, land, fields, gardens, property, district, territory, domain: *the palace grounds* **2 = reason**, cause, basis, argument, call, base, occasion, foundation, excuse, premise, motive, justification, rationale, inducement: *In the interview he gave some grounds for optimism.* **3 = dregs**, lees, deposit, sediment: *Place the coffee grounds in the bottom and pour hot water over them.*
▷ VERB **1 = base**, found, establish, set, settle, fix: *Her argument was grounded in fact.* **2 = instruct**, train, prepare, coach, teach, inform, initiate, tutor, acquaint with, familiarize with: *Make sure the children are properly grounded in the basics.*

groundless ADJECTIVE **= baseless**, false, unfounded, unjustified, unproven, empty, unauthorized, unsubstantiated, unsupported, uncorroborated **OPPOSITE:** well-founded

groundwork NOUN **= preliminaries**, basis, foundation, base, footing, preparation, fundamentals, cornerstone, underpinnings, spadework

group NOUN **1 = crowd**, company, party, band, troop, pack, gathering, gang, bunch, congregation, posse *(slang)*, bevy, assemblage: *The trouble involved a small group of football supporters.* **2 = cluster**, formation, clump, aggregation: *a small group of islands off northern Japan*
▷ VERB **1 = arrange**, order, sort, class, range, gather, organize, assemble, put together, classify, marshal, bracket, assort: *The fact sheets are grouped into seven sections.* **2 = unite**, associate, gather, cluster, get together, congregate, band together: *We want to encourage them to group together as one big purchaser.*

grouse VERB **= complain**, moan, grumble, gripe *(informal)*, beef *(slang)*, carp, bitch *(slang)*, whine, whinge *(informal)*, bleat, find fault, grouch *(informal)*, bellyache *(slang)*, kvetch *(U.S. slang)*: *'How come they never tell us what's going on?' he groused.*
▷ NOUN **= complaint**, protest, objection, moan, grievance, grumble, gripe *(informal)*, beef *(slang)*, grouch *(informal)*: *There have been grouses about the economy, interest rates and house prices.*

grove NOUN **= wood**, woodland, plantation, covert, thicket, copse, brake, coppice, spinney

grovel VERB **= humble yourself**, creep, crawl, flatter, fawn, pander, cower, toady, kowtow, bow and scrape, lick someone's boots, demean yourself, abase yourself **OPPOSITE:** hold your head high

grow VERB **1 = develop**, fill out, get bigger, get taller: *We stop growing once we reach maturity.* **OPPOSITE:** shrink **2 = get bigger**, spread, swell, extend, stretch, expand, widen, enlarge, multiply, thicken: *An inoperable tumour was growing in his brain.* **3 = spring up**, shoot up, develop, flourish, sprout, germinate, vegetate: *The station had roses growing at each end of the platform.* **4 = cultivate**, produce, raise, farm, breed, nurture, propagate: *I always grow a few red onions in my allotment.* **5 = become**, get, turn, come to be: *He's growing old.* **6 = originate**, spring, arise, stem, issue: *The idea for this book grew out of conversations with Philippa Brewster.* **7 = improve**, advance, progress, succeed, expand, thrive, flourish, prosper: *The economy continues to grow.*

grown-up NOUN **= adult**, man, woman: *Tell a grown-up if you're being bullied.*
▷ ADJECTIVE **= mature**, adult, of age, fully-grown: *Her grown-up children are all doing well in their chosen careers.*

g

Charles Dickens' Use of Adverbs

Many of the adverbs that Dickens uses most frequently are those which provide emphasis, such as *perfectly, extremely,* and *wholly*; also frequent are *undoubtedly, unquestionably, entirely,* and *absolutely.* Characters are not just good, but *unquestionably good;* they are not just silent, but *entirely silent.* As in modern English, *wholly* is used most often to modify negative adjectives such as *unable, unconscious, unexpected, indescribable, unnecessary,* and *uninformed. Perfectly,* on the other hand, has shifted in usage slightly over the last century and a half. In modern English, it is almost always used with positive adjectives such as *good, normal,* and *happy*; in Dickens, however, we often find negative combinations such as *a perfectly incapable king* and *a perfectly unreasonable man.*

Another adverb which has narrowed in meaning is *happily,* which now almost always means *contentedly*; Dickens uses it more frequently in the sense 'fortunately, luckily':

> But **happily** for her, she was quite complacent again now and beamed with nods and smiles.

There are also several adverbs which have since become archaic, for example *forth* in phrasal verbs such as *issue forth, set forth* and *go forth*; and *yonder* in phrases such as *lie yonder* and *over yonder.* Another frequent adverb which would now be thought of as somewhat old-fashioned is *gaily,* which occurs with verbs such as *sing, laugh, flutter, dress,* and *talk.*

Dialogue is an important aspect of Dickens' novels, and his characters do not simply *say* and *reply*: they say things *quietly, politely, abruptly, thoughtfully, cheerfully, impatiently,* and *composedly.* This kind of usage is often derided in modern fiction: Stephen King, for example, wrote scathingly that JK Rowling 'never met an adverb she didn't like', referring to the frequent use of phrases such as *said nervously, replied angrily* and so on in the *Harry Potter* series. But, characteristic of the rich abundant style of so much 19th-century prose, Dickens had no objection to flavouring his verbs with descriptive adverbs. Indeed, we often find adverb piled upon adverb:

> The truth is, he wrote to me under a sort of protest while unable to write to you with any hope of an answer – wrote **coldly**, **haughtily**, **distantly**, **resentfully**.

> And I laughed, **frantically**, **wildly**, **gloomily**, **incoherently**, **disagreeably**.

However, while it must be admitted that the overuse of adverbs can be trite, Dickens' style is often inventive and highly effective, reminding us that they are not always to be avoided:

> The moaning water cast its seaweed **duskily** at their feet...

> the driving rain, which now poured down more **soakingly** than ever...

> the pupils formed in line and **buzzingly** passed a ragged book from hand to hand...

Dickens himself was aware of the potential misuse of adverbs; in *A Tale of Two Cities* he satirizes a pompous legal document which accuses Charles Darnay of spying 'wickedly, falsely, traitorously, and otherwise evil-adverbiously'. He also describes one of his characters as an adverb, noting the unfavourable qualities of both:

> Miss Brook Dingwall was one of that numerous class of young ladies, who, like adverbs, may be known by their answering to a commonplace question, and doing nothing else.

Although he is referring to *yes/no* type of adverb here, the comparison does indicate that Dickens was aware that adverbs are not the most necessary parts of speech.

growth NOUN **1 = increase**, development, expansion, extension, growing, heightening, proliferation, enlargement, multiplication: *the unchecked growth of the country's population* **OPPOSITE:** decline **2 = progress**, success, improvement, expansion, advance, prosperity, advancement: *enormous economic growth* **OPPOSITE:** failure **3 = vegetation**, development, production, sprouting, germination, shooting: *This helps to encourage new growth and makes the plant flower profusely.* **4 = tumour**, cancer, swelling, lump, carcinoma *(Pathology)*, sarcoma *(Medical)*, excrescence: *This type of surgery could even be used to extract cancerous growths.*

> **PROVERBS**
> *Great oaks from little acorns grow*

g

grub NOUN **1 = larva**, maggot, caterpillar: *The grubs do their damage by tunnelling through ripened fruit.* **2 = food**, feed, rations, tack *(informal)*, eats *(slang)*, kai *(N.Z. informal)*, sustenance, nosh *(slang)*, victuals, nosebag *(slang)*, vittles *(obsolete, dialect)*: *Get yourself some grub and come and sit down.*
▷ VERB **1 = search**, hunt, scour, ferret, rummage, forage, fossick *(Austral. & N.Z.)*: *grubbing through piles of paper for his address* **2 = dig**, search, root *(informal)*, probe, burrow, rootle *(Brit.)*: *chickens grubbing around in the dirt for food*

grubby ADJECTIVE **= dirty**, soiled, filthy, squalid, messy, shabby, seedy, scruffy, sordid, untidy, grimy, unwashed, unkempt, mucky, smutty, grungy *(slang, chiefly U.S. & Canad.)*, slovenly, manky *(Scot. dialect)*, scuzzy *(slang)*, scungy *(Austral. & N.Z.)*, frowzy, besmeared, festy *(Austral. slang)*

grudge NOUN **= resentment**, bitterness, grievance, malice, hate, spite, dislike, animosity, aversion, venom, antipathy, enmity, rancour, hard feelings, ill will, animus, malevolence: *It was an accident and I bear him no grudge.* **OPPOSITE:** goodwill
▷ VERB **= resent**, mind, envy, covet, begrudge: *Few seem to grudge him his good fortune.* **OPPOSITE:** welcome

gruelling ADJECTIVE **= exhausting**, demanding, difficult, tiring, trying, hard, taxing, grinding, severe, crushing, fierce, punishing, harsh, stiff, brutal, fatiguing, strenuous, arduous, laborious, backbreaking **OPPOSITE:** easy

gruesome ADJECTIVE **= horrific**, shocking, terrible, awful, horrible, grim, horrifying, fearful, obscene, horrendous, ghastly, hideous, from hell *(informal)*, grisly, macabre, horrid, repulsive, repugnant, loathsome, abominable, spine-chilling, hellacious *(U.S. slang)* **OPPOSITE:** pleasant

gruff ADJECTIVE **1 = hoarse**, rough, harsh, rasping, husky, low, croaking, throaty, guttural: *He picked up the phone expecting to hear the chairman's gruff voice.* **OPPOSITE:** mellifluous **2 = surly**, rough, rude, grumpy, blunt, crabbed, crusty, sullen, bad-tempered, curt, churlish, brusque, impolite, grouchy *(informal)*, ungracious, discourteous, uncivil, ill-humoured, unmannerly, ill-natured: *His gruff exterior concealed a kind heart.* **OPPOSITE:** polite

grumble VERB **1 = complain**, moan, gripe *(informal)*, whinge *(informal)*, beef *(slang)*, carp, bitch *(slang)*, whine, grouse, bleat, grouch *(informal)*, bellyache *(slang)*, kvetch *(U.S. slang)*, repine: *'This is very inconvenient,' he grumbled.* **2 = rumble**, growl, gurgle: *His stomach grumbled loudly.*
▷ NOUN **1 = complaint**, protest, objection, moan, grievance, grouse, gripe *(informal)*, grouch *(informal)*, beef *(slang)*: *My grumble is with the structure and organisation of his material.* **2 = rumble**, growl, gurgle: *One could hear, far to the east, a grumble of thunder.*

grumpy ADJECTIVE **= irritable**, cross, bad-tempered, grumbling, crabbed, edgy, surly, petulant, ill-tempered, cantankerous, tetchy, ratty *(Brit. & N.Z. informal)*, testy, grouchy *(informal)*, querulous, peevish, huffy, crotchety *(informal)*, liverish

guarantee VERB **1 = ensure**, secure, assure, warrant, insure, make certain: *Surplus resources alone do not guarantee growth.* **2 = promise**, pledge, undertake, swear: *We guarantee to refund your money if you are not delighted with your purchase.*
▷ NOUN **1 = promise**, word, pledge, undertaking, assurance, certainty, covenant, word of honour: *We can give no guarantee that their demands will be met.* **2 = warranty**, contract, bond, guaranty: *The goods were still under guarantee.*

guarantor NOUN **= underwriter**, guarantee, supporter, sponsor, backer, surety, warrantor

guard VERB **= protect**, watch, defend, secure, police, mind, cover, screen, preserve, shelter, shield, patrol, oversee, safeguard, watch over: *Gunmen guarded homes near the cemetery.*
▷ NOUN **1 = sentry**, warder, warden, custodian, watch, patrol, lookout, watchman, sentinel: *The prisoners overpowered their guards and locked them in a cell.* **2 = escort**, patrol, convoy: *a heavily armed guard of police* **3 = shield**, security, defence, screen, protection, pad, safeguard, bumper, buffer, rampart, bulwark: *The heater should have a safety guard fitted.*
off guard = unprepared, napping, unwary, unready, with your defences down: *His question had caught me off guard.*
on (your) guard = vigilant, cautious, wary, prepared, ready, alert, watchful, on the lookout, circumspect, on the alert, on the qui vive: *Be on your guard against crooked car dealers.*
▸ *related adjective:* custodial

guarded ADJECTIVE **= cautious**, reserved, careful, suspicious, restrained, wary, discreet, prudent, reticent, circumspect, cagey *(informal)*, leery *(slang)*, noncommittal

guardian NOUN **= keeper**, champion, defender, guard, trustee, warden, curator, protector, warder, custodian, preserver

guerrilla NOUN **= freedom fighter**, partisan, irregular, underground fighter, member of the underground *or* resistance

guess VERB **1 = estimate**, predict, work out, speculate, fathom, conjecture, postulate, surmise, hazard a guess, hypothesize: *I can only guess what it cost him to tell you the truth.* **OPPOSITE:** know **2 = suppose**, think, believe, suspect, judge, imagine, reckon, fancy, conjecture, dare say: *I guess I'm just being paranoid.*
▷ NOUN **1 = estimate**, reckoning, speculation, judgment, hypothesis, conjecture, surmise, shot in the dark, ballpark figure *(informal)*: *He took her pulse and made a guess at her blood pressure.* **OPPOSITE:** certainty **2 = supposition**, feeling, idea, theory, notion, suspicion, hypothesis: *My guess is that she's waiting for you to make the first move.*

> **QUOTATIONS**
> The shrewd guess, the fertile hypothesis, the courageous leap to a tentative conclusion – these are the most valuable coin of the thinker at work
> [Jerome S. Bruner *The Process of Education*]
>
> I never guess. It is a shocking habit – destructive to the logical faculty
> [Sir Arthur Conan Doyle *The Sign of Four*]

guesswork NOUN **= speculation**, theory, presumption, conjecture, estimation, surmise, supposition

guest NOUN **= visitor**, company, caller, manu(w)hiri *(N.Z.)*

guff NOUN **= nonsense**, rubbish, malarkey, rot, crap *(slang)*, garbage *(informal)*, trash, hot air *(informal)*, tosh *(slang, chiefly Brit.)*, pap, bilge *(informal)*, humbug, drivel, tripe *(informal)*, moonshine, hogwash, hokum *(slang, chiefly U.S. & Canad.)*, piffle *(informal)*, poppycock *(informal)*, balderdash, bosh *(informal)*, eyewash *(informal)*, kak *(S. African taboo, slang)*, empty talk, tommyrot, horsefeathers *(U.S. slang)*, bunkum *or* buncombe *(chiefly U.S.)*, bizzo *(Austral. slang)*, bull's wool *(Austral. & N.Z. slang)*

guidance NOUN **= advice**, direction, leadership, instruction, government, help, control, management, teaching, counsel, counselling, auspices

guide NOUN **1 = handbook**, manual, guidebook, instructions, catalogue: *Our 10-page guide will help you change your life for the better.* **2 = directory**, street map: *The Rough Guide to Paris lists accommodation for as little as £25 a night.* **3 = escort**, leader, controller, attendant, usher, chaperon, torchbearer, dragoman: *With guides, the*

journey can be done in fourteen days. **4 = pointer**, sign, signal, mark, key, clue, landmark, marker, beacon, signpost, guiding light, lodestar: *His only guide was the stars overhead.* **5 = model**, example, standard, ideal, master, inspiration, criterion, paradigm, exemplar, lodestar: *The checklist serves as a guide to students, teachers, and parents.*
▷ VERB **1 = lead**, direct, escort, conduct, pilot, accompany, steer, shepherd, convoy, usher, show the way: *He took the bewildered man by the arm and guided him out.* **2 = steer**, control, manage, direct, handle, command, manoeuvre: *He guided his plane down the runway and took off.* **3 = supervise**, train, rule, teach, influence, advise, counsel, govern, educate, regulate, instruct, oversee, sway, superintend: *He should have let his instinct guide him.*

guild NOUN **= society**, union, league, association, company, club, order, organization, corporation, lodge, fellowship, fraternity, brotherhood

guile NOUN **= cunning**, craft, deception, deceit, trickery, duplicity, cleverness, art, gamesmanship (*informal*), craftiness, artfulness, slyness, trickiness, wiliness **OPPOSITE:** honesty

guilt NOUN **1 = shame**, regret, remorse, contrition, guilty conscience, bad conscience, self-reproach, self-condemnation, guiltiness: *Her emotions went from anger to guilt in the space of a few seconds.* **OPPOSITE:** pride **2 = culpability**, blame, responsibility, misconduct, delinquency, criminality, wickedness, iniquity, sinfulness, blameworthiness, guiltiness: *You were never convinced of his guilt, were you?* **OPPOSITE:** innocence

> **QUOTATIONS**
> This is his first punishment, that by the verdict of his own heart no guilty man is acquitted
> [Juvenal *Satires*]
>
> So full of artless jealousy is guilt
> It spills itself in fearing to be spilt
> [William Shakespeare *Hamlet*]

guilty ADJECTIVE **1 = ashamed**, sorry, rueful, sheepish, contrite, remorseful, regretful, shamefaced, hangdog, conscience-stricken: *When she saw me, she looked extremely guilty.* **OPPOSITE:** proud **2 = culpable**, responsible, convicted, to blame, offending, erring, at fault, reprehensible, iniquitous, felonious, blameworthy: *They were found guilty of manslaughter; The guilty pair were caught red-handed.* **OPPOSITE:** innocent

guise NOUN **1 = form**, appearance, dress, fashion, shape, aspect, mode, semblance: *He claimed the Devil had appeared to him in the guise of a goat.* **2 = pretence**, show, mask, disguise, face, front, aspect, façade, semblance: *Fascism is on the rise under the guise of conservative politics.*

gulch NOUN **= ravine**, canyon, defile, gorge, gully, pass

gulf NOUN **1 = bay**, bight, sea inlet: *Hurricane Andrew was last night heading into the Gulf of Mexico.* **2 = chasm**, opening, split, gap, rent, breach, separation, void, rift, abyss, cleft: *the gulf between rural and urban life*

gullible ADJECTIVE **= trusting**, innocent, naive, unsuspecting, green, simple, silly, foolish, unsophisticated, credulous, born yesterday, wet behind the ears (*informal*), easily taken in, unsceptical, as green as grass **OPPOSITE:** suspicious

gully NOUN **= ravine**, canyon, gorge, chasm, channel, fissure, defile, watercourse

gulp VERB **1 = swallow**, bolt, devour, gobble, knock back (*informal*), wolf, swig (*informal*), swill, guzzle, quaff: *She quickly gulped her tea.* **2 = gasp**, swallow, choke: *He slumped back, gulping for air.*
▷ NOUN **= swallow**, draught, mouthful, swig (*informal*): *He drank half of his whisky in one gulp.*

gum NOUN **= glue**, adhesive, resin, cement, paste: *a pound note that had been torn in half and stuck together with gum*
▷ VERB **= stick**, glue, affix, cement, paste, clog: *a mild infection in which the baby's eyelashes can become gummed together*

gun NOUN **= firearm**, shooter (*slang*), piece (*slang*), rod (*slang*), heater (*U.S. slang*), handgun

> **QUOTATIONS**
> They hesitate
> We hesitate.
> They have a gun.
> We have no gun
> [D.H. Lawrence *Mountain Lion*]
>
> God, Guts, and Guns made America Great
> [U.S.bumper sticker]

gunman NOUN **= armed man**, hit man (*slang*), gunslinger (*U.S. slang*)

gurgle VERB **= ripple**, lap, bubble, splash, murmur, babble, burble, purl, plash: *a narrow channel along which water gurgles*
▷ NOUN **= burble**, chuckle, ripple, babble: *There was a gurgle of laughter on the other end of the line*

guru NOUN **1 = authority**, expert, leader, master, pundit, arbiter, Svengali, torchbearer, fundi (*S. African*): *Fashion gurus dictate crazy ideas such as puffball skirts.* **2 = teacher**, mentor, sage, master, tutor, mahatma, guiding light, swami, maharishi: *He set himself up as a faith healer and spiritual guru.*

gush VERB **1 = flow**, run, rush, flood, pour, jet, burst, stream, cascade, issue, spurt, spout: *Piping hot water gushed out of the tap.* **2 = enthuse**, rave, spout, overstate, rhapsodize, effuse: *'Oh, you were just brilliant,' she gushed.*
▷ NOUN **= stream**, flow, rush, flood, jet, burst, issue, outburst, cascade, torrent, spurt, spout, outflow: *I heard a gush of water.*

gust NOUN **1 = blast**, blow, rush, breeze, puff, gale, flurry, squall: *A gust of wind drove down the valley.* **2 = surge**, fit, storm, burst, explosion, gale, outburst, eruption, paroxysm: *A gust of laughter greeted him as he walked into the room.*
▷ VERB **= blow**, blast, puff, squall: *strong winds gusting up to 164 miles an hour*

gusto NOUN **= relish**, enthusiasm, appetite, appreciation, liking, delight, pleasure, enjoyment, savour, zeal, verve, zest, fervour, exhilaration, brio, zing (*informal*) **OPPOSITE:** apathy

gusty ADJECTIVE **= windy**, stormy, breezy, blustering, tempestuous, blustery, inclement, squally, blowy

gut NOUN **= paunch** (*informal*), belly, spare tyre (*Brit. slang*), potbelly, puku (*N.Z.*): *His gut sagged over his belt.*
▷ VERB **1 = disembowel**, draw, dress, clean, eviscerate: *It is not always necessary to gut the fish prior to freezing.* **2 = ravage**, strip, empty, sack, rifle, plunder, clean out, ransack, pillage, despoil: *The church had been gutted by vandals.*
▷ ADJECTIVE **= instinctive**, natural, basic, emotional, spontaneous, innate, intuitive, hard-wired, involuntary, heartfelt, deep-seated, unthinking: *At first my gut reaction was to simply walk out of there.*
▸ *technical name:* viscera ▸ *related adjective:* visceral

guts PLURAL NOUN **1 = intestines**, insides (*informal*), stomach, belly, bowels, inwards, innards (*informal*), entrails: *The crewmen were standing ankle-deep in fish guts.* **2 = courage**, spirit, nerve, daring, pluck, grit, backbone, willpower, bottle (*slang*), audacity, mettle, boldness, spunk (*informal*), forcefulness, hardihood: *The new Chancellor has the guts to push through unpopular tax increases.*

gutsy ADJECTIVE **= brave**, determined, spirited, bold, have-a-go (*informal*), courageous, gritty, staunch, feisty (*informal, chiefly U.S. & Canad.*), game (*informal*), resolute, gallant, plucky, indomitable, mettlesome, (as) game as Ned Kelly (*Austral. slang*)

gutter NOUN **= drain**, channel, tube, pipe, ditch, trench, trough, conduit, duct, sluice

guy NOUN **= man**, person, fellow, lad, cat (*obsolete, slang*), bloke (*Brit. informal*), chap

guzzle VERB **= devour**, drink, bolt, wolf, cram, gorge, gobble, knock back (*informal*), swill, quaff, tope, pig out on (*slang*), stuff yourself with

Gypsy or **Gipsy** NOUN **= traveller**, roamer, wanderer, Bohemian, rover, rambler, nomad, vagrant, Romany, vagabond: *the largest community of Gypsies of any country*

gyrate VERB **= rotate**, circle, spin, spiral, revolve, whirl, twirl, pirouette

g

Hh

habit NOUN **1 = mannerism**, custom, way, practice, manner, characteristic, tendency, quirk, propensity, foible, proclivity: *He has an endearing habit of licking his lips.* **2 = custom**, rule, practice, tradition, routine, convention, mode, usage, wont, second nature: *It had become a habit with her to annoy him.* **3 = addiction**, weakness, obsession, dependence, compulsion, fixation: *After twenty years as a chain smoker, he has given up the habit.* **4 = dress**, costume, garment, apparel, garb, habiliment, riding dress: *She emerged having changed into her riding habit.*

habitat NOUN **= home**, environment, surroundings, element, territory, domain, terrain, locality, home ground, abode, habitation, natural home

habitation NOUN **1 = occupation**, living in, residence, tenancy, occupancy, residency, inhabitance, inhabitancy: *20 percent of private-rented dwellings are unfit for human habitation.* **2 = dwelling**, home, house, residence, quarters, lodging, pad *(slang)*, abode, living quarters, domicile, dwelling house: *Behind the habitations, the sandstone cliffs rose abruptly.*

habitual ADJECTIVE **1 = customary**, normal, usual, common, standard, natural, traditional, fixed, regular, ordinary, familiar, routine, accustomed, wonted: *He soon recovered his habitual geniality.* **OPPOSITE:** unusual **2 = persistent**, established, confirmed, constant, frequent, chronic, hardened, recurrent, ingrained, inveterate: *three out of four of them would become habitual criminals* **OPPOSITE:** occasional

hack[1] VERB **1** *(sometimes with* **away***)* **= cut**, chop, slash, mutilate, mangle, mangulate *(Austral. slang)*, gash, hew, lacerate: *He desperately hacked through the undergrowth; Some were hacked to death with machetes.* **2 = cough**, bark, wheeze, rasp: *The patients splutter and hack.*
▷ NOUN **= cough**, bark, wheeze, rasp: *smoker's hack*

hack[2] NOUN **1 = reporter**, writer, correspondent, journalist, scribbler, contributor, literary hack, penny-a-liner, Grub Street writer: *tabloid hacks, always eager to find victims* **2 = yes-man**, lackey, toady, flunky: *Party hacks from the old days still hold influential jobs.*
▷ ADJECTIVE **= unoriginal**, pedestrian, mediocre, poor, tired, stereotyped, banal, undistinguished, uninspired: *ill-paid lectureships and hack writing*

hackles PLURAL NOUN
raise someone's hackles *or* **make someone's hackles rise = anger**, annoy, infuriate, cause resentment, rub someone up the wrong way, make someone see red *(informal)*, get someone's dander up *(slang)*, hack you off *(informal)*

hackneyed ADJECTIVE **= clichéd**, stock, tired, common, stereotyped, pedestrian, played out *(informal)*, commonplace, worn-out, stale, overworked, banal, run-of-the-mill, threadbare, trite, unoriginal, timeworn **OPPOSITE:** original

Hades NOUN **= underworld**, hell, nether regions, lower world, infernal regions, realm of Pluto, (the) inferno

haemorrhage NOUN **= drain**, outpouring, rapid loss
▷ VERB **= drain**, bleed, flow rapidly

hag NOUN **= witch**, virago, shrew, vixen, crone, fury, harridan, beldam *(archaic)*, termagant

haggard ADJECTIVE **= gaunt**, wasted, drawn, thin, pinched, wrinkled, ghastly, wan, emaciated, shrunken, careworn, hollow-eyed **OPPOSITE:** robust

haggle VERB **1 = bargain**, barter, beat down, drive a hard bargain, dicker *(chiefly U.S.)*, chaffer, palter, higgle: *Ella taught her how to haggle with used furniture dealers.* **2 = wrangle**, dispute, quarrel, squabble, bicker: *As the politicians haggle, the violence worsens.*

hail[1] NOUN **1 = hailstones**, sleet, hailstorm, frozen rain: *a short-lived storm with heavy hail* **2 = shower**, rain, storm, battery, volley, barrage, bombardment, pelting, downpour, salvo, broadside: *The victim was hit by a hail of bullets.*
▷ VERB **1 = rain**, shower, pelt: *It started to hail, huge great stones.* **2 = batter**, rain, barrage, bombard, pelt, rain down on, beat down upon: *Shellfire was hailing down on the city's edge.*

hail[2] VERB **1 = acclaim**, honour, acknowledge, cheer, applaud, glorify, exalt: *hailed as the greatest American novelist of his generation* **OPPOSITE:** condemn **2 = salute**, call, greet, address, welcome, speak to, shout to, say hello to, accost, sing out, halloo: *I saw him and hailed him.* **OPPOSITE:** snub **3 = flag down**, summon, signal to, wave down: *I hurried away to hail a taxi.*
hail from somewhere = come from, be born in, originate in, be a native of, have your roots in: *The band members hail from Glasgow and Edinburgh.*

hair NOUN **= locks**, mane, tresses, shock, mop, head of hair: *a girl with long blonde hair*
by a hair = by a narrow margin, by a whisker, by a hair's-breadth, by a split second, by a fraction of an inch, by the skin of your teeth
get in someone's hair = annoy, plague, irritate, harass, hassle *(informal)*, aggravate *(informal)*, exasperate, pester, be on someone's back *(slang)*, get on someone's nerves *(informal)*, nark *(Brit., Austral. & N.Z. slang)*, get up your nose *(informal)*, piss you off *(taboo, slang)*, get on your wick *(Brit. slang)*, hack you off *(informal)*
let your hair down = let yourself go, relax, chill out *(slang, chiefly U.S.)*, let off steam *(informal)*, let it all hang out *(informal)*, mellow out *(informal)*, veg out *(slang, chiefly U.S.)*, outspan *(S. African)*: *a time when everyone really lets their hair down*
make someone's hair stand on end = terrify, shock, scare, appal, horrify, make someone's hair curl, freeze someone's blood, scare the bejesus out of *(informal)*
not turn a hair = remain calm, keep your cool *(slang)*, not bat an eyelid, keep your hair on *(Brit. informal)*: *The man didn't turn a hair.*
split hairs = quibble, find fault, cavil, overrefine, pettifog, nit-pick *(informal)*: *Don't split hairs. You know what I'm getting at.*

> **QUOTATIONS**
> Doth not even nature itself teach you, that if a man have long hair, it is a shame unto him? But if a woman have long hair, it is a glory to her
> [*Bible: I Corinthians*]

hairdresser NOUN **= stylist**, barber, coiffeur *or* coiffeuse, friseur, snipper *(informal)*

hair-raising ADJECTIVE **= frightening**, shocking, alarming, thrilling, exciting, terrifying, startling, horrifying, scary, breathtaking, creepy, petrifying, spine-chilling, bloodcurdling

hairstyle NOUN **= haircut**, hairdo, coiffure, cut, style

hairy ADJECTIVE **1 = shaggy**, woolly, furry, stubbly, bushy, bearded, unshaven, hirsute, fleecy, bewhiskered, pileous *(Biology)*, pilose *(Biology)*: *I don't mind having a hairy chest, but the stuff on my back is really thick.* **2 = dangerous**, scary, risky, unpredictable, hazardous, perilous: *His driving was a bit hairy.*

halcyon ADJECTIVE **1 = happy**, golden, flourishing, prosperous, carefree, palmy: *It was all a far cry from those halcyon days in 1990.* **2 = peaceful**, still, quiet, calm, gentle, mild, serene, tranquil, placid, pacific, undisturbed, unruffled: *The next day dawned sunny with a halcyon blue sky.*

hale ADJECTIVE **= healthy**, well, strong, sound, fit, flourishing, blooming, robust, vigorous, hearty, in the pink, in fine fettle, right as rain (*Brit. informal*), able-bodied

half NOUN **= fifty per cent**, equal part: *A half of the voters have not made up their minds.*
▷ ADJECTIVE **= partial**, limited, fractional, divided, moderate, halved, incomplete: *Children received only a half portion.*
▷ ADVERB **= partially**, partly, incompletely, slightly, all but, barely, in part, inadequately, after a fashion, pretty nearly: *The vegetables are only half cooked.*
▸ *related prefixes:* bi-, hemi-, demi-, semi-

PROVERBS
The half is better than the whole
Half a loaf is better than no bread

half-baked ADJECTIVE **= stupid**, impractical, crazy, silly, foolish, senseless, short-sighted, inane, loopy (*informal*), ill-conceived, crackpot (*informal*), ill-judged, brainless, unformed, poorly planned, harebrained, dumb-ass (*slang*), unthought out *or* through

half-hearted ADJECTIVE **= unenthusiastic**, indifferent, apathetic, cool, neutral, passive, lacklustre, lukewarm, uninterested, perfunctory, listless, spiritless **OPPOSITE:** enthusiastic

halfway ADVERB **1 = midway**, to the midpoint, to *or* in the middle: *He was halfway up the ladder.* **2 = partially**, partly, moderately, rather, nearly: *You need hard currency to get anything halfway decent.*
▷ ADJECTIVE **= midway**, middle, mid, central, intermediate, equidistant: *He was third fastest at the halfway point.*
meet someone halfway = compromise, accommodate, come to terms, reach a compromise, strike a balance, trade off with, find the middle ground: *The Democrats are willing to meet the president halfway.*

hall NOUN **1 = passage**, lobby, corridor, hallway, foyer, entry, passageway, entrance hall, vestibule: *The lights were on in the hall and in the bedroom.* **2 = meeting place**, chamber, auditorium, concert hall, assembly room: *We filed into the lecture hall.*

hallmark NOUN **1 = trademark**, indication, badge, emblem, sure sign, telltale sign: *a technique that has become the hallmark of their films* **2 = mark**, sign, device, stamp, seal, symbol, signet, authentication: *He uses a hallmark on the base of his lamps to distinguish them.*

hallowed ADJECTIVE **= sanctified**, holy, blessed, sacred, honoured, dedicated, revered, consecrated, sacrosanct, inviolable, beatified

hallucinate VERB **= imagine**, trip (*informal*), envision, daydream, fantasize, freak out (*informal*), have hallucinations

hallucination NOUN **= illusion**, dream, vision, fantasy, delusion, mirage, apparition, phantasmagoria, figment of the imagination

hallucinogenic ADJECTIVE **= psychedelic**, mind-blowing (*informal*), psychoactive, hallucinatory, psychotropic, mind-expanding

halo NOUN **= ring of light**, aura, corona, radiance, nimbus, halation (*Photography*), aureole *or* aureola

halt VERB **1 = stop**, draw up, pull up, break off, stand still, wait, rest, call it a day, belay (*Nautical*): *They halted at a short distance from the house.* **OPPOSITE:** continue **2 = come to an end**, stop, cease: *The flow of assistance to refugees has virtually halted.* **3 = hold back**, end, check, block, arrest, stem, curb, terminate, obstruct, staunch, cut short, impede, bring to an end, stem the flow, nip in the bud: *Striking workers halted production at the auto plant yesterday.* **OPPOSITE:** aid
▷ NOUN **= stop**, end, close, break, stand, arrest, pause, interruption, impasse, standstill, stoppage, termination: *Air traffic has been brought to a halt.* **OPPOSITE:** continuation

halting ADJECTIVE **= faltering**, stumbling, awkward, hesitant, laboured, stammering, imperfect, stuttering

halve VERB **1 = cut in half**, reduce by fifty per cent, decrease by fifty per cent, lessen by fifty per cent: *The work force has been halved in two years.* **2 = split in two**, cut in half, bisect, divide in two, share equally, divide equally: *Halve the pineapple and scoop out the inside.*

hammer VERB **1 = hit**, drive, knock, beat, strike, tap, bang: *Hammer a wooden peg into the hole.* **2** (*often with* **into**) **= impress upon**, repeat, drive home, drum into, grind into, din into, drub into: *He hammered it into me that I had not become a rotten goalkeeper.* **3 = defeat**, beat, thrash, stuff (*slang*), master, worst, tank (*slang*), lick (*informal*), slate (*informal*), trounce, clobber (*slang*), run rings around (*informal*), wipe the floor with (*informal*), blow out of the water (*slang*), drub: *He hammered the young left-hander in four straight sets.*
hammer away at something = work, keep on, persevere, grind, persist, stick at, plug away (*informal*), drudge, pound away, peg away (*chiefly Brit.*), beaver away (*Brit. informal*): *Palmer kept hammering away at his report.*

hamper VERB **= hinder**, handicap, hold up, prevent, restrict, frustrate, curb, slow down, restrain, hamstring, interfere with, cramp, thwart, obstruct, impede, hobble, fetter, encumber, trammel **OPPOSITE:** help

hamstring VERB **= thwart**, stop, block, prevent, ruin, frustrate, handicap, curb, foil, obstruct, impede, balk, fetter

hamstrung ADJECTIVE **= incapacitated**, disabled, crippled, helpless, paralysed, at a loss, hors de combat (*French*)

hand NOUN **1 = palm**, fist, paw (*informal*), mitt (*slang*), hook, meathook (*slang*): *I put my hand into my pocket.* **2 = influence**, part, share, agency, direction, participation: *Did you have a hand in his downfall?* **3 = assistance**, help, aid, support, helping hand: *Come and give me a hand in the garden.* **4 = worker**, employee, labourer, workman, operative, craftsman, artisan, hired man, hireling: *He now works as a farm hand.* **5 = round of applause**, clap, ovation, big hand: *Let's give 'em a big hand.* **6 = writing**, script, handwriting, calligraphy, longhand, penmanship, chirography: *written in the composer's own hand*
▷ VERB **1 = give**, pass, hand over, present to, deliver: *He handed me a little rectangle of white paper.* **2 = help**, guide, conduct, lead, aid, assist, convey: *He handed her into his old Alfa Romeo sports car.*
at *or* **on hand = within reach**, nearby, handy, close, available, ready, on tap (*informal*), at your fingertips: *Having the right equipment on hand is enormously helpful.*
hand in glove = in association, in partnership, in league, in collaboration, in cooperation, in cahoots (*informal*): *They work hand in glove with the western intelligence agencies.*
hand over fist = swiftly, easily, steadily, by leaps and bounds: *Investors would lose money hand over fist if a demerger went ahead.*
hand something down = pass on *or* **down**, pass, transfer, bequeath, will, give, grant, gift, endow: *a family heirloom handed down from generation to generation*
hand something on = pass on *or* **down**, pass, transfer, bequeath, will, give, grant, relinquish: *His chauffeur-driven car will be handed on to his successor.*
hand something out = distribute, give out, issue, pass out, dish out, dole out, deal out, hand round, pass round, give round
hand something *or* **someone in = give**, turn in, turn over
hand something *or* **someone over 1 = give**, present, deliver, donate: *He handed over a letter of apology.* **2 = turn over**, release, transfer, deliver, yield, surrender: *The American was formally handed over to the ambassador.*
hands down = easily, effortlessly, with ease, comfortably, without difficulty, with no trouble, standing on your head, with one hand tied behind your back, with no contest, with your eyes closed *or* shut: *We*

h

should have won hands down.
in hand 1 = in reserve, ready, put by, available for use: *I'll pay now as I have the money in hand.* **2 = under control**, in order, receiving attention: *The organizers say that matters are well in hand.*
lay hands on someone 1 = attack, assault, set on, beat up, work over *(slang)*, lay into *(informal)*: *The crowd laid hands on him.* **2 = bless** *(Christianity)*, confirm, ordain, consecrate: *The bishop laid hands on the sick.*
lay hands on something = get hold of, get, obtain, gain, grab, acquire, seize, grasp: *the ease with which prisoners can lay hands on drugs*
▸ *related adjective:* manual

PROVERBS
One hand washes the other
Many hands make light work
A bird in the hand is worth two in the bush

handbook NOUN **= guidebook**, guide, manual, instruction book, Baedeker, vade mecum

handcuff VERB **= shackle**, secure, restrain, fetter, manacle: *They tried to handcuff him but he fought his way free.*
▹ PLURAL NOUN **= shackles**, cuffs *(informal)*, fetters, manacles, bracelets *(slang)*: *He was led away to jail in handcuffs.*

handful NOUN **= few**, sprinkling, small amount, small quantity, smattering, small number
OPPOSITE: a lot

handgun NOUN **= pistol**, automatic, revolver, shooter *(informal)*, piece *(U.S. slang)*, rod *(U.S. slang)*, derringer

handicap NOUN **1 = disability**, defect, impairment, physical abnormality: *a child with a medically recognized handicap* **2 = disadvantage**, block, barrier, restriction, obstacle, limitation, hazard, drawback, shortcoming, stumbling block, impediment, albatross, hindrance, millstone, encumbrance: *Being a foreigner was not a handicap.* **OPPOSITE:** advantage
3 = advantage, penalty, head start: *I see your handicap is down from 16 to 12.*
▹ VERB **= hinder**, limit, restrict, burden, hamstring, hamper, hold back, retard, impede, hobble, encumber, place at a disadvantage: *Greater levels of stress may seriously handicap some students.* **OPPOSITE:** help

handicraft NOUN **= skill**, art, craft, handiwork

handily ADVERB **1 = conveniently**, readily, suitably, helpfully, advantageously, accessibly: *He was handily placed to slip the ball home at the far post.* **2 = skilfully**, expertly, cleverly, deftly, adroitly, capably, proficiently, dexterously: *In the November election Nixon won handily.*

handiwork NOUN **= creation**, product, production, achievement, result, design, invention, artefact, handicraft, handwork

handkerchief NOUN **= hanky**, tissue *(informal)*, mouchoir, snot rag *(slang)*, nose rag *(slang)*

handle NOUN **= grip**, knob, hilt, haft, stock, handgrip, helve: *The handle of a cricket bat protruded from under his arm.*
▹ VERB **1 = manage**, deal with, tackle, cope with: *I don't know if I can handle the job.* **2 = deal with**, manage, take care of, administer, conduct, supervise: *She handled travel arrangements for the press corps.* **3 = control**, manage, direct, operate, guide, use, steer, manipulate, manoeuvre, wield: *One report said the aircraft would become difficult to handle.* **4 = hold**, feel, touch, pick up, finger, grasp, poke, paw *(informal)*, maul, fondle: *Be careful when handling young animals.* **5 = deal in**, market, sell, trade in, carry, stock, traffic in: *Japanese dealers won't handle US cars.*
6 = discuss, report, treat, review, tackle, examine, discourse on: *I think we should handle the story very sensitively.*
fly off the handle = lose your temper, explode, lose it *(informal)*, lose the plot *(informal)*, let fly *(informal)*, go ballistic *(slang, chiefly U.S.)*, fly into a rage, have a tantrum, wig out *(slang)*, lose your cool *(slang)*, blow your top, flip your lid *(slang)*, hit *or* go through the roof *(informal)*: *He flew off the handle at the slightest thing.*

handling NOUN **= management**, running, treatment, approach, administration, conduct, manipulation

hand-out NOUN **1** *(often plural)* **= charity**, dole, alms, pogey *(Canad.)*: *They depended on handouts from the state.* **2 = press release**, bulletin, circular, mailshot, press kit: *Official handouts described the couple as elated.* **3 = leaflet**, literature *(informal)*, bulletin, flyer, pamphlet, printed matter: *lectures, handouts, slides and videos* **4 = giveaway**, freebie *(informal)*, free gift, free sample: *advertised with publicity handouts*

hand-picked ADJECTIVE **= selected**, chosen, choice, select, elect, elite, recherché **OPPOSITE:** random

handsome ADJECTIVE **1 = good-looking**, attractive, gorgeous, fine, stunning, elegant, personable, nice-looking, dishy *(informal, chiefly Brit.)*, comely, fanciable, well-proportioned, hot *(informal)*, fit *(Brit. informal)*: *a tall, dark, handsome farmer*
OPPOSITE: ugly **2 = generous**, large, princely, liberal, considerable, lavish, ample, abundant, plentiful, bountiful, sizable *or* sizeable: *They will make a handsome profit on the property.*
OPPOSITE: mean

PROVERBS
Handsome is as handsome does

handsomely ADVERB **= generously**, amply, richly, liberally, lavishly, abundantly, plentifully, bountifully, munificently

handwriting NOUN **= writing**, hand, script, fist, scrawl, calligraphy, longhand, penmanship, chirography
▸ *related noun:* graphology

handy ADJECTIVE **1 = useful**, practical, helpful, neat, convenient, easy to use, manageable, user-friendly, serviceable: *handy hints on looking after indoor plants; a handy little device*
OPPOSITE: useless **2 = convenient**, close, near, available, nearby, accessible, on hand, at hand, within reach, just round the corner, at your fingertips: *This lively town is handy for Londoners; Keep a pencil and paper handy.*
OPPOSITE: inconvenient **3 = skilful**, skilled, expert, clever, adept, ready, deft, nimble, proficient, adroit, dexterous: *Are you handy with a needle?*
OPPOSITE: unskilled

handyman NOUN **= odd-jobman**, jack-of-all-trades, handy Andy *(informal)*, DIY expert

hang VERB **1 = dangle**, swing, suspend, be pendent: *I was left hanging by my fingertips.* **2 = lower**, suspend, dangle, let down, let droop: *I hung the sheet out of the window at 6am.* **3 = lean**, incline, loll, bend forward, bow, bend downward: *He hung over the railing and kicked out with his feet.* **4 = droop**, drop, dangle, trail, sag: *the shawl hanging loose from her shoulders* **5 = decorate**, cover, fix, attach, deck, furnish, drape, fasten: *The walls were hung with huge modern paintings.* **6 = execute**, lynch, string up *(informal)*, gibbet, send to the gallows: *The five were expected to be hanged at 7 am on Tuesday.* **7 = hover**, float, drift, linger, remain: *A haze of expensive perfume hangs around her.*
get the hang of something = grasp, understand, learn, master, comprehend, catch on to, acquire the technique of, get the knack *or* technique: *It's a bit tricky at first till you get the hang of it.*
hang about *or* **around = loiter**, frequent, haunt, linger, roam, loaf, waste time, dally, dawdle, skulk, tarry, dilly-dally *(informal)*: *On Saturdays we hang about in the park.*
hang around with someone = associate, go around with, mix, hang *(informal, chiefly U.S.)*, hang out *(informal)*: *She used to hang around with the boys.*
hang back = be reluctant, hesitate, hold back, recoil, demur, be backward: *His closest advisors believe he should hang back no longer.*
hang fire = put off, delay, stall, be slow, vacillate, hang back, procrastinate: *I've got to hang fire on that one.*
hang on 1 = wait, stop, hold on, hold the line, remain: *Hang on a sec. I'll come with you.* **2 = continue**, remain, go on, carry on, endure, hold on, persist, hold out, persevere, stay the course: *Manchester United hung on to take the Cup.*
3 = grasp, grip, clutch, cling, hold fast: *He hangs on tightly, his arms around my neck.*
hang on *or* **upon something**
1 = depend on, turn on, rest on, be subject to, hinge on, be determined by, be dependent on, be conditional on, be contingent on: *Much hangs on the success of the collaboration.* **2 = listen**

attentively to, pay attention to, be rapt, give ear to: *a man who knew his listeners were hanging on his every word*

hanger-on NOUN **= parasite**, follower, cohort *(chiefly U.S.)*, leech, dependant, minion, lackey, sycophant, freeloader *(slang)*, sponger *(informal)*, ligger *(slang)*, quandong *(Austral. slang)*

hanging ADJECTIVE **= suspended**, swinging, dangling, loose, flopping, flapping, floppy, drooping, unattached, unsupported, pendent

hang-out NOUN **= haunt**, joint *(slang)*, resort, dive *(slang)*, den

hangover NOUN **= aftereffects**, morning after *(informal)*, head *(informal)*, crapulence

hang-up NOUN **= preoccupation**, thing *(informal)*, problem, block, difficulty, obsession, mania, inhibition, phobia, fixation

hank NOUN **= coil**, roll, length, bunch, piece, loop, clump, skein

hanker after *or* **hanker for** VERB **= desire**, want, long for, hope for, crave, covet, wish for, yearn for, pine for, lust after, eat your heart out, ache for, yen for *(informal)*, itch for, set your heart on, hunger for *or* after, thirst for *or* after

hankering NOUN **= desire**, longing, wish, hope, urge, yen *(informal)*, pining, hunger, ache, craving, yearning, itch, thirst

haphazard ADJECTIVE
1 = unsystematic, disorderly, disorganized, casual, careless, indiscriminate, aimless, slapdash, slipshod, hit or miss *(informal)*, unmethodical: *The investigation does seem haphazard.* **OPPOSITE:** systematic
2 = random, chance, accidental, arbitrary, fluky *(informal)*: *She was trying to connect her life's seemingly haphazard events.* **OPPOSITE:** planned

hapless ADJECTIVE **= unlucky**, unfortunate, cursed, unhappy, miserable, jinxed, luckless, wretched, ill-starred, ill-fated

happen VERB **1 = occur**, take place, come about, follow, result, appear, develop, arise, come off *(informal)*, ensue, crop up *(informal)*, transpire *(informal)*, materialize, present itself, come to pass, see the light of day, eventuate: *We cannot say for sure what will happen.* **2 = chance**, turn out *(informal)*, have the fortune to be: *I looked in the nearest paper, which happened to be the Daily Mail.* **3 = befall**, overtake, become of, betide: *It's the best thing that ever happened to me.*

happen on *or* **upon something = find**, encounter, run into, come upon, turn up, stumble on, hit upon, chance upon, light upon, blunder on, discover unexpectedly: *He just happened upon a charming guest house.*

happening NOUN **= event**, incident, occasion, case, experience, chance, affair, scene, accident, proceeding, episode, adventure, phenomenon, occurrence, escapade

happily ADVERB **1 = luckily**, fortunately, providentially, favourably, auspiciously, opportunely, propitiously, seasonably: *Happily, his neck injuries were not serious.* **2 = joyfully**, cheerfully, gleefully, blithely, merrily, gaily, joyously, delightedly: *Albert leaned back happily and lit a cigarette.*
3 = willingly, freely, gladly, enthusiastically, heartily, with pleasure, contentedly, lief *(rare)*: *If I've caused any offence, I will happily apologize.*

happiness NOUN **= pleasure**, delight, joy, cheer, satisfaction, prosperity, ecstasy, enjoyment, bliss, felicity, exuberance, contentment, wellbeing, high spirits, elation, gaiety, jubilation, merriment, cheerfulness, gladness, beatitude, cheeriness, blessedness, light-heartedness
OPPOSITE: unhappiness

QUOTATIONS

Perfect happiness, even in memory, is not common
[Jane Austen *Emma*]

A lifetime of happiness! No man alive could bear it: it would be hell on earth
[George Bernard Shaw *Man and Superman*]

The world of the happy is quite another than the world of the unhappy
[Ludwig Wittgenstein *Tractatus Logico-Philosophicus*]

The search for happiness is one of the chief sources of unhappiness
[Eric Hoffer *The Passionate State of Mind*]

Unbroken happiness is a bore: it should have ups and downs
[Molière *Les fourberies de Scapin*]

It is not enough to be happy, it is also necessary that others not be
[Jules Renard *Journal*]

Happiness depends upon ourselves
[Aristotle *Nicomachean Ethics*]

Happiness to me is wine,
Effervescent, superfine.
Full of tang and fiery pleasure,
Far too hot to leave me leisure
For a single thought beyond it
[Amy Lowell *Sword Blades and Poppy Seeds*]

Happiness is a matter of one's most ordinary everyday mode of consciousness being busy and lively and unconcerned with self
[Iris Murdoch *The Nice and the Good*]

To be happy, we must not be too concerned with others
[Albert Camus *The Fall*]

I am happy and content because I think I am
[Alain René Lesage *Histoire de Gil Blas de Santillane*]

Ask yourself whether you are happy, and you cease to be so
[John Stuart Mill *Autobiography*]

Happiness does not lie in happiness, but in the achievement of it
[Fyodor Dostoevsky *A Diary of a Writer*]

In theory there is a possibility of perfect happiness: To believe in the indestructible element within one, and not to strive towards it
[Franz Kafka *The Collected Aphorisms*]

Happiness is not an ideal of reason but of imagination
[Immanuel Kant *Fundamental Principles of the Metaphysics of Ethics*]

Happiness is in the taste, and not in the things
[La Rochefoucauld *Maxims*]

Shall I give you my recipe for happiness? I find everything useful and nothing indispensable. I find everything wonderful and nothing miraculous. I reverence the body. I avoid first causes like the plague
[Norman Douglas *South Wind*]

Happiness lies in the fulfilment of the spirit through the body
[Cyril Connolly *The Unquiet Grave*]

We have no more right to consume happiness without producing it than to consume wealth without producing it
[George Bernard Shaw *Candida*]

What we call happiness in the strictest sense comes from the (preferably sudden) satisfaction of needs which have been dammed up to a high degree
[Sigmund Freud *Civilization and its Discontents*]

Happiness is an imaginary condition, formerly often attributed by the living to the dead, now usually attributed by adults to children, and by children to adults
[Thomas Szasz *The Second Sin*]

Nothing ages like happiness
[Oscar Wilde *An Ideal Husband*]

Happiness is no laughing matter
[Richard Whately *Apophthegms*]

Happiness is enjoyed only in proportion as it is known; and such is the state or folly of man, that it is known only by experience of its contrary
[Samuel Johnson *The Adventurer*]

happiness: an agreeable sensation arising from contemplating the misery of another
[Ambrose Bierce *The Devil's Dictionary*]

Happiness makes up in height for what it lacks in length
[Robert Frost *The Witness Tree*]

happy ADJECTIVE **1 = pleased**, delighted, content, contented, thrilled, glad, blessed, blest, sunny, cheerful, jolly, merry, ecstatic, gratified, jubilant, joyous, joyful, elated, over the moon *(informal)*, overjoyed, blissful, rapt, blithe, on cloud nine *(informal)*, cock-a-hoop, walking on air *(informal)*, floating on air, stoked *(Austral. & N.Z. informal)*: *I'm just happy to be back running.* **2 = contented**, blessed, blest, joyful, blissful, blithe: *We have a very happy marriage.* **OPPOSITE:** sad **3 = fortunate**, lucky, timely, appropriate, convenient, favourable, auspicious, propitious, apt, befitting, advantageous, well-timed, opportune, felicitous, seasonable: *a happy coincidence* **OPPOSITE:** unfortunate

> **QUOTATIONS**
>
> Happy the man, and happy he alone
> He who can call today his own;
> He who, secure within, can say,
> Tomorrow, do thy worst, for I have lived today
> [John Dryden *Imitation of Horace*]
>
> The happy man is not he who seems thus to others, but who seems thus to himself
> [Publilius Syrus *Moral Sayings*]
>
> Call no man happy till he dies, he is at best but fortunate
> [Solon]
>
> Happy men are grave. They carry their happiness cautiously, as they would a glass filled to the brim which the slightest movement could cause to spill over, or break
> [Jules Barbey D'Aurevilly *Les Diaboliques*]
>
> No one can be perfectly free till all are free; no one can be perfectly moral till all are moral; no one can be perfectly happy till all are happy
> [Herbert Spencer *Social Statics*]
>
> We are never happy: we can only remember that we were so once
> [Alexander Smith]

happy-go-lucky ADJECTIVE **= carefree**, casual, easy-going, irresponsible, unconcerned, untroubled, nonchalant, blithe, heedless, insouciant, devil-may-care, improvident, light-hearted **OPPOSITE:** serious

harangue VERB **= rant at**, address, lecture, exhort, preach to, declaim, hold forth, spout at *(informal)*: *haranguing her furiously in words she didn't understand*
▷ NOUN **= rant**, address, speech, lecture, tirade, polemic, broadside, diatribe, homily, exhortation, oration, spiel *(informal)*, declamation, philippic: *a political harangue*

harass VERB **= annoy**, trouble, bother, worry, harry, disturb, devil *(informal)*, plague, bait, hound, torment, hassle *(informal)*, badger, persecute, exasperate, pester, vex, breathe down someone's neck, chivvy *(Brit.)*, give someone grief *(Brit. & S. African)*, be on your back *(slang)*, beleaguer

harassed ADJECTIVE **= hassled**, worried, troubled, strained, harried, under pressure, plagued, tormented, distraught *(informal)*, vexed, under stress, careworn

harassment NOUN **= hassle**, trouble, bother, grief *(informal)*, torment, irritation, persecution *(informal)*, nuisance, badgering, annoyance, pestering, aggravation *(informal)*, molestation, vexation, bedevilment

harbinger NOUN **= sign**, indication, herald, messenger, omen, precursor, forerunner, portent, foretoken

harbour NOUN **1 = port**, haven, dock, mooring, marina, pier, wharf, anchorage, jetty, pontoon, slipway: *The ship was allowed to tie up in the harbour.* **2 = sanctuary**, haven, shelter, retreat, asylum, refuge, oasis, covert, safe haven, sanctum: *a safe harbour for music rejected by the mainstream*
▷ VERB **1 = hold**, bear, maintain, nurse, retain, foster, entertain, nurture, cling to, cherish, brood over: *He might have been murdered by someone harbouring a grudge.* **2 = shelter**, protect, hide, relieve, lodge, shield, conceal, secrete, provide refuge, give asylum to: *harbouring terrorist suspects*

hard ADJECTIVE **1 = tough**, strong, firm, solid, stiff, compact, rigid, resistant, dense, compressed, stony, impenetrable, inflexible, unyielding, rocklike: *He stamped his feet on the hard floor.* **OPPOSITE:** soft **2 = difficult**, involved, complex, complicated, puzzling, tangled, baffling, intricate, perplexing, impenetrable, thorny, knotty, unfathomable, ticklish: *That's a very hard question.* **OPPOSITE:** easy **3 = exhausting**, tough, exacting, formidable, fatiguing, wearying, rigorous, uphill, gruelling, strenuous, arduous, laborious, burdensome, Herculean, backbreaking, toilsome: *Coping with three babies is very hard work.* **OPPOSITE:** easy **4 = forceful**, strong, powerful, driving, heavy, sharp, violent, smart, tremendous, fierce, vigorous, hefty: *He gave her a hard push which toppled her backwards.* **5 = harsh**, severe, strict, cold, exacting, cruel, grim, stern, ruthless, stubborn, unjust, callous, unkind, unrelenting, implacable, unsympathetic, pitiless, unfeeling, obdurate, unsparing, affectless, hardhearted: *His father was a hard man.* **OPPOSITE:** kind **6 = grim**, dark, painful, distressing, harsh, disastrous, unpleasant, intolerable, grievous, disagreeable, calamitous: *Those were hard times.* **7 = definite**, reliable, verified, cold, plain, actual, bare, undeniable, indisputable, verifiable, unquestionable, unvarnished: *He wanted more hard evidence.*
▷ ADVERB **1 = strenuously**, steadily, persistently, earnestly, determinedly, doggedly, diligently, energetically, assiduously, industriously, untiringly, flatstick *(S. African slang)*: *I'll work hard. I don't want to let him down.* **2 = intently**, closely, carefully, sharply, keenly: *You had to listen hard to hear him.* **3 = forcefully**, strongly, heavily, sharply, severely, fiercely, vigorously, intensely, violently, powerfully, forcibly, with all your might, with might and main: *I kicked a dustbin very hard and broke my toe.* **OPPOSITE:** softly **4 = with difficulty**, painfully, laboriously: *the hard won rights of the working woman*

hard-bitten ADJECTIVE **= tough**, realistic, cynical, practical, shrewd, down-to-earth, matter-of-fact, hard-nosed *(informal)*, hard-headed, unsentimental, hard-boiled *(informal)*, case-hardened, badass *(slang, chiefly U.S.)* **OPPOSITE:** idealistic

hard-boiled ADJECTIVE **= tough**, practical, realistic, cynical, shrewd, down-to-earth, matter-of-fact, hard-nosed *(informal)*, hard-headed, hard-bitten *(informal)*, unsentimental, case-hardened, badass *(slang, chiefly U.S.)* **OPPOSITE:** idealistic

hard-core ADJECTIVE **1 = dyed-in-the-wool**, extreme, dedicated, rigid, staunch, die-hard, steadfast, obstinate, intransigent: *a hard-core group of right-wing senators* **2 = explicit**, obscene, pornographic, X-rated *(informal)*: *jailed for peddling hard-core porn videos through the post*

harden VERB **1 = solidify**, set, freeze, cake, bake, clot, thicken, stiffen, crystallize, congeal, coagulate, anneal: *Mould the mixture into shape before it hardens.* **2 = accustom**, season, toughen, train, brutalize, inure, habituate, case-harden: *hardened by the rigours of the Siberian steppes* **3 = reinforce**, strengthen, fortify, steel, nerve, brace, toughen, buttress, gird, indurate: *Their action can only serve to harden the attitude of landowners.*

hardened ADJECTIVE **1 = habitual**, set, fixed, chronic, shameless, inveterate, incorrigible, reprobate, irredeemable, badass *(slang, chiefly U.S.)*: *hardened criminals* **OPPOSITE:** occasional **2 = seasoned**, experienced, accustomed, toughened, inured, habituated: *hardened politicians* **OPPOSITE:** naive

hard-headed ADJECTIVE **= shrewd**, tough, practical, cool, sensible, realistic, pragmatic, astute, hard-boiled *(informal)*, hard-bitten, level-headed, unsentimental, badass *(slang, chiefly U.S.)* **OPPOSITE:** idealistic

hard-hearted ADJECTIVE **= unsympathetic**, hard, cold, cruel, indifferent, insensitive, callous, stony, unkind, heartless, inhuman, merciless, intolerant, uncaring, pitiless, unfeeling, unforgiving, hard as nails, affectless **OPPOSITE:** kind

The Language of Kenneth Grahame

Best known for his children's classic, *The Wind in the Willows,* Kenneth Grahame (1859–1932) had previously written, amongst other things, a collection of essays entitled *Pagan Papers* and two episodic books featuring five orphaned children, *The Golden Age* and *Dream Days*, the latter containing another well-known and attractive Grahame tale, *The Reluctant Dragon*.

Although often poetic, appealing and witty, *Pagan Papers* is perhaps too literary in style and too full of classical allusions and Latin quotes to be an easy read. In *The Lost Centaur*, for example, Grahame imagines how Achilles sees himself in relation to his centaur teacher, Cheiron, and uses this as a basis for discussing Man's break from the rest of the Animal Kingdom in a text full of literary constructions such as *and yet* and *nay*.

Lyrical and poetic, *The Wind in the Willows* is evocative as well as beautifully and creatively written, conjuring up the magic of countryside, river, and changing Nature. The range of words used makes it a challenging read for children (*cellarage, panoply, expatiate, raiment, habiliments, runnels, provender, corsair, valorous* ...), but the engaging animal characters and the flowing, appealing story pull the reader in. While clearly written, it also contains allusions likely to pass over audience heads:

> ... a picked body of Toads, known at the Die-hards, or the Death-or-Glory Toads ...

One of Grahame's techniques for bringing Nature and the surroundings to life in *The Wind in the Willows* is to personify them, especially using happy verbs: flowers *smile* from banks; the floor *smiles* at the ceiling; plates *grin* at pots; the corn ripples and *laughs*; and the river *chuckles*. Onomatopoeia and visual words that evoke bursts of light also come into play to convey the sounds and reflective quality of the flowing river that is central to the story:

> All was a-shake and a-shiver – glints and gleams and sparkles, rustle and swirl, chatter and bubble.

Rhetorical devices abound in Grahame: metaphors, similes, irony, repetition, antithesis, hyperbole, climax, and so on:

> 'I should like to say one word about our kind host, Mr. Toad. We all know Toad!' – (great laughter) – 'GOOD Toad, MODEST Toad, HONEST Toad!'

> The rusty key creaked in the lock, the great door clanged behind them; and Toad was a helpless prisoner in the remotest dungeon of the best-guarded keep of the stoutest castle in all the length and breadth of Merry England.

Presented with warmth and affection, the miscreant character of Toad steals the show. One minute he's 'a very limp and dejected Toad', with his skin hanging 'baggily about him', and the next 'Toad the terror, the traffic-queller' is being irrepressible in his enthusiasm for his supposed folly. He hops speedily from 'unhappy Toad', 'the miserable Toad', 'the hapless Toad' to, in his own estimation, 'clever Toad, great Toad, GOOD Toad!'. Grahame makes us share in Toad's joyous and childlike 'O bliss! O poop-poop! O my! O my!' And he juxtaposes Toad's frequent puffed-up vain and deluded views of himself with reality to humorous effect:

> Toad, of course, in his vanity, thought that her interest in him proceeded from a growing tenderness; and he could not help half-regretting that the social gulf between them was so very wide, for she was a comely lass, and evidently admired him very much.

The world of *The Wind in the Willows* may also have been a place of fantasy escape for the adult author, and, with its dearth of female characters, a place of refuge from 'the clash of sex' that his unhappy marriage perhaps represented. It offered places 'where two or three friends of simple tastes could sit about as they pleased and eat and smoke and talk in comfort and contentment', where homes were appealingly described in best estate-agent terms ('what a nice snug dwelling-place it would make for an animal with few wants and fond of a bijou riverside residence') and where there was 'NOTHING – absolutely nothing – half so much worth doing as simply messing about in boats'.

hardly ADVERB **1 = barely**, only just, scarcely, just, faintly, with difficulty, infrequently, with effort, at a push (*Brit. informal*), almost not: *Nick, on the sofa, hardly slept.* **OPPOSITE:** completely **2 = only just**, just, only, barely, not quite, scarcely: *I could hardly see the garden for the fog.* **3 = not at all**, not, no way, by no means: *It's hardly surprising his ideas didn't catch on.*

hard-nosed ADJECTIVE **= tough**, practical, realistic, shrewd, pragmatic, down-to-earth, hardline, uncompromising, businesslike, hard-headed, unsentimental, badass (*slang, chiefly U.S.*)

hard-pressed ADJECTIVE **1 = under pressure**, pushed (*informal*), harried, in difficulties, up against it (*informal*), with your back to the wall: *Hard-pressed consumers are spending less on luxuries.* **2 = pushed** (*informal*), in difficulties, up against it (*informal*): *This year the airline will be hard-pressed to make a profit.*

h

hardship NOUN **= suffering**, want, need, trouble, trial, difficulty, burden, misery, torment, oppression, persecution, grievance, misfortune, austerity, adversity, calamity, affliction, tribulation, privation, destitution **OPPOSITE:** ease

hard up ADJECTIVE **= poor**, broke (*informal*), short, bust (*informal*), bankrupt, impoverished, in the red (*informal*), cleaned out (*slang*), penniless, out of pocket, down and out, skint (*Brit. slang*), strapped for cash (*informal*), impecunious, dirt-poor (*informal*), on the breadline, flat broke (*informal*), on your uppers (*informal*), in queer street, without two pennies to rub together (*informal*), short of cash *or* funds **OPPOSITE:** wealthy

hardy ADJECTIVE **1 = strong**, tough, robust, sound, fit, healthy, vigorous, rugged, sturdy, hale, stout, stalwart, hearty, lusty, in fine fettle: *They grew up to be farmers, round-faced and hardy.* **OPPOSITE:** frail **2 = courageous**, brave, daring, bold, heroic, manly, gritty, feisty (*informal, chiefly U.S. & Canad.*), resolute, intrepid, valiant, plucky, valorous, stouthearted: *A few hardy souls leapt into the encircling seas.* **OPPOSITE:** feeble

hare NOUN
▸ *related adjective:* leporine ▸ *name of male:* buck ▸ *name of female:* doe ▸ *name of young:* leveret ▸ *name of home:* down, husk

harem NOUN **= women's quarters**, seraglio, zenana (*in eastern countries*), gynaeceum (*in ancient Greece*)

hark VERB **= listen**, attend, pay attention, hearken (*archaic*), give ear, hear, mark, notice, give heed: *Hark. I hear the returning footsteps of my love.*
hark back to something 1 = recall, recollect, call to mind, cause you to remember, cause you to recollect: *pitched roofs, which hark back to the Victorian era* **2 = return to**, remember, recall, revert to, look back to, think back to, recollect, regress to: *The result devastated me at the time. Even now I hark back to it.*

harlot NOUN **= prostitute**, tart (*informal*), whore, slag, pro (*slang*), tramp (*slang*), call girl, working girl (*facetious, slang*), slapper (*Brit. slang*), hussy, streetwalker, loose woman, fallen woman, scrubber (*Brit. & Austral. slang*), strumpet

harm VERB **1 = injure**, hurt, wound, abuse, molest, ill-treat, maltreat, lay a finger on, ill-use: *The hijackers seemed anxious not to harm anyone.* **OPPOSITE:** heal **2 = damage**, hurt, ruin, mar, spoil, impair, blemish: *a warning that the product may harm the environment*
▷ NOUN **1 = injury**, suffering, damage, ill, hurt, distress: *a release of radioactivity which would cause harm* **2 = damage**, loss, ill, hurt, misfortune, mischief, detriment, impairment, disservice: *It would probably do the economy more harm than good.* **OPPOSITE:** good **3 = sin**, wrong, evil, wickedness, immorality, iniquity, sinfulness, vice: *There was no harm in keeping the money.* **OPPOSITE:** goodness

harmful ADJECTIVE **= damaging**, dangerous, negative, evil, destructive, hazardous, unhealthy, detrimental, hurtful, pernicious, noxious, baleful, deleterious, injurious, unwholesome, disadvantageous, baneful, maleficent **OPPOSITE:** harmless

harmless ADJECTIVE **1 = safe**, benign, wholesome, innocuous, not dangerous, nontoxic, innoxious: *working at developing harmless substitutes for these gases* **OPPOSITE:** dangerous **2 = inoffensive**, innocent, innocuous, gentle, tame, unobjectionable: *He seemed harmless enough.*

harmonious ADJECTIVE **1 = friendly**, amicable, cordial, sympathetic, compatible, agreeable, in harmony, in unison, fraternal, congenial, in accord, concordant, of one mind, en rapport (*French*): *the most harmonious European Community summit for some time* **OPPOSITE:** unfriendly **2 = compatible**, matching, coordinated, correspondent, agreeable, consistent, consonant, congruous: *a harmonious blend of colours* **OPPOSITE:** incompatible **3 = melodious**, musical, harmonic, harmonizing, tuneful, concordant, mellifluous, dulcet, sweet-sounding, euphonious, euphonic, symphonious (*literary*): *producing harmonious sounds* **OPPOSITE:** discordant

harmonize VERB **1 = match**, accord, suit, blend, correspond, tally, chime, coordinate, go together, tone in, cohere, attune, be of one mind, be in unison: *The music had to harmonize with the seasons.* **2 = coordinate**, match, agree, blend, tally, reconcile, attune: *members have progressed towards harmonizing their economies*

harmony NOUN **1 = accord**, order, understanding, peace, agreement, friendship, unity, sympathy, consensus, cooperation, goodwill, rapport, conformity, compatibility, assent, unanimity, concord, amity, amicability, like-mindedness: *a future in which humans live in harmony with nature* **OPPOSITE:** conflict **2 = tune**, melody, unison, tunefulness, euphony, melodiousness: *singing in harmony* **OPPOSITE:** discord **3 = balance**, consistency, fitness, correspondence, coordination, symmetry, compatibility, suitability, concord, parallelism, consonance, congruity: *the ordered harmony of the universe* **OPPOSITE:** incongruity

harness VERB **1 = exploit**, control, channel, apply, employ, utilize, mobilize, make productive, turn to account, render useful: *the movement's ability to harness the anger of all Ukrainians* **2 = put in harness**, couple, saddle, yoke, hitch up, inspan (*S. African*): *the horses were harnessed to a heavy wagon*
▷ NOUN **= equipment**, tackle, gear, tack, trappings: *Always check that the straps of the harness are properly adjusted.*
in harness 1 = working, together, in a team: *At Opera North he will be in harness with Paul Daniel.* **2 = at work**, working, employed, active, busy, in action: *The longing for work will return and you will be right back in harness.*

harp VERB **= go on**, reiterate, dwell on, labour, press, repeat, rub in

harried ADJECTIVE **= harassed**, worried, troubled, bothered, anxious, distressed, plagued, tormented, hassled (*informal*), agitated, beset, hard-pressed, hag-ridden

harrowing ADJECTIVE **= distressing**, disturbing, alarming, frightening, painful, terrifying, chilling, traumatic, tormenting, heartbreaking, excruciating, agonizing, nerve-racking, heart-rending, gut-wrenching

harry VERB **= pester**, trouble, bother, disturb, worry, annoy, plague, tease, torment, harass, hassle (*informal*), badger, persecute, molest, vex, bedevil, breathe down someone's neck, chivvy, give someone grief (*Brit. & S. African*), be on your back (*slang*), get in your hair (*informal*)

harsh ADJECTIVE **1 = severe**, hard, tough, grim, stark, stringent, austere, Spartan, inhospitable, comfortless, bare-bones: *Hundreds of political detainees were held under harsh conditions.* **2 = bleak**, cold, freezing, severe, bitter, icy: *The weather grew harsh and unpredictable.* **3 = cruel**, savage, brutal, ruthless, relentless, unrelenting, barbarous, pitiless: *the harsh experience of war* **4 = hard**, sharp, severe, bitter, cruel, stern, unpleasant, abusive, unkind, pitiless, unfeeling: *He said many harsh and unkind things.* **OPPOSITE:** kind **5 = drastic**, hard, severe, stringent, punitive, austere, Draconian, punitory: *more harsh laws governing the behaviour, status and even clothes of women* **6 = raucous**, rough, jarring, grating, strident, rasping, discordant, croaking, guttural, dissonant, unmelodious: *It's a pity she has such a loud harsh voice.* **OPPOSITE:** soft

harshly ADVERB **= severely**, roughly, cruelly, strictly, grimly, sternly, brutally

harshness NOUN **= bitterness**, acrimony, ill-temper, sourness, asperity, acerbity

harvest NOUN **1 = harvesting**, picking, gathering, collecting, reaping, harvest-time: *300 million tons of grain in the fields at the start of the harvest* **2 = crop**, yield, year's growth, produce: *a bumper potato harvest*
▷ VERB **1 = gather**, pick, collect, bring in, pluck, reap: *Many farmers are refusing to harvest the sugar cane.* **2 = collect**, get, gain, earn, obtain, acquire, accumulate, garner, amass: *In his new career he has blossomed and harvested many awards.*

hash NOUN
make a hash of = mess up, muddle, bungle, botch, cock up (*Brit. slang*), mishandle, mismanage, make a nonsense of (*informal*), bodge (*informal*), make a pig's ear of (*informal*), flub (*U.S. slang*)

hassle NOUN **= trouble**, problem, difficulty, upset, bother, grief (*informal*), trial, struggle, uphill (*S. African*), inconvenience: *I don't think it's worth the money or the hassle.*
▷ VERB **= bother**, bug (*informal*), annoy, harry, hound, harass, badger, pester, get on your nerves (*informal*), be on your back (*slang*), get in your hair (*informal*), breath down someone's neck: *My husband started hassling me.*

hassled ADJECTIVE **= bothered**, pressured, worried, stressed, under pressure, hounded, uptight, browbeaten, hunted, hot and bothered

haste NOUN **= speed**, rapidity, urgency, expedition, dispatch, velocity, alacrity, quickness, swiftness, briskness, nimbleness, fleetness, celerity, promptitude, rapidness: *Authorities appear to be moving with haste against the three dissidents.* **OPPOSITE:** slowness

hasten VERB **1 = hurry (up)**, speed (up), advance, urge, step up (*informal*), accelerate, press, dispatch, precipitate, quicken, push forward, expedite: *He may hasten the collapse of his own country.* **OPPOSITE:** slow down **2 = rush**, run, race, fly, speed, tear (along), dash, hurry (up), barrel (along) (*informal, chiefly U.S. & Canad.*), sprint, bolt, beetle, scuttle, scurry, haste, burn rubber (*informal*), step on it (*informal*), make haste, get your skates on (*informal*): *He hastened along the landing to her room.* **OPPOSITE:** dawdle

hastily ADVERB **1 = quickly**, fast, rapidly, promptly, straightaway, speedily, apace, pronto (*informal*), double-quick, hotfoot, pdq (*slang*), posthaste: *He said goodnight hastily.* **2 = hurriedly**, rashly, precipitately, recklessly, too quickly, on the spur of the moment, impulsively, impetuously, heedlessly: *I decided that nothing should be done hastily.*

hasty ADJECTIVE **1 = speedy**, fast, quick, prompt, rapid, fleet, hurried, urgent, swift, brisk, expeditious: *They need to make a hasty escape.* **OPPOSITE:** leisurely **2 = brief**, short, quick, passing, rushed, fleeting, superficial, cursory, perfunctory, transitory: *After the hasty meal, they took up their positions.* **OPPOSITE:** long **3 = rash**, premature, reckless, precipitate, impulsive, headlong, foolhardy, thoughtless, impetuous, indiscreet, imprudent, heedless, incautious, unduly quick: *Let's not be hasty.* **OPPOSITE:** cautious

hatch VERB **1 = incubate**, breed, sit on, brood, bring forth: *I transferred the eggs to a hen canary to hatch and rear.* **2 = devise**, plan, design, project, scheme, manufacture, plot, invent, put together, conceive, brew, formulate, contrive, dream up (*informal*), concoct, think up, cook up (*informal*), trump up: *accused of hatching a plot to assassinate the Pope*

hatchet NOUN **= axe**, machete, tomahawk, cleaver

hate VERB **1 = detest**, loathe, despise, dislike, be sick of, abhor, be hostile to, recoil from, be repelled by, have an aversion to, abominate, not be able to bear, execrate: *Most people hate him, but I don't.* **OPPOSITE:** love **2 = dislike**, detest, shrink from, recoil from, have no stomach for, not be able to bear: *She hated hospitals and dreaded the operation.* **OPPOSITE:** like **3 = be unwilling**, regret, be reluctant, hesitate, be sorry, be loath, feel disinclined: *I hate to admit it, but you were right.*
▷ NOUN **= dislike**, hostility, hatred, loathing, animosity, aversion, antagonism, antipathy, enmity, abomination, animus, abhorrence, odium, detestation, execration: *eyes that held a look of hate* **OPPOSITE:** love

hateful ADJECTIVE **= horrible**, despicable, offensive, foul, disgusting, forbidding, revolting, obscene, vile, repellent, obnoxious, repulsive, heinous, odious, repugnant, loathsome, abhorrent, abominable, execrable, detestable

hatred NOUN **= hate**, dislike, animosity, aversion, revulsion, antagonism, antipathy, enmity, abomination, ill will, animus, repugnance, odium, detestation, execration **OPPOSITE:** love

QUOTATIONS
Hatred, for the man who is not engaged in it, is a little like the odour of garlic for one who hasn't eaten any
[Jean Rostand *Pensées d'un Biologiste*]

haughty ADJECTIVE **= proud**, arrogant, lofty, high, stuck-up (*informal*), contemptuous, conceited, imperious, snooty (*informal*), scornful, snobbish, disdainful, supercilious, high and mighty (*informal*), overweening, hoity-toity (*informal*), on your high horse (*informal*), uppish (*Brit. informal*) **OPPOSITE:** humble

haul VERB **1 = drag**, draw, pull, hale, heave: *He hauled himself to his feet.* **2 = pull**, trail, convey, tow, move, carry, transport, tug, cart, hump (*Brit. slang*), lug: *A crane hauled the car out of the stream.*
▷ NOUN **= yield**, gain, spoils, find, catch, harvest, loot, takings, booty: *The haul was worth £4,000.*

haunt VERB **1 = plague**, trouble, obsess, torment, come back to, possess, stay with, recur, beset, prey on, weigh on: *The decision to leave her children now haunts her.* **2 = visit**, hang around *or* about, frequent, linger in, resort to, patronize, repair to, spend time in, loiter in, be a regular in: *During the day he haunted the town's cinemas.* **3 = appear in**, materialize in: *His ghost is said to haunt some of the rooms.*
▷ NOUN **= meeting place**, resort, hangout (*informal*), den, rendezvous, stamping ground, gathering place: *a favourite summer haunt for yachtsmen*

haunted ADJECTIVE **1 = possessed**, ghostly, cursed, eerie, spooky (*informal*), jinxed: *a haunted castle* **2 = preoccupied**, worried, troubled, plagued, obsessed, tormented: *She looked so haunted, I almost didn't recognise her.*

haunting ADJECTIVE **= evocative**, poignant, unforgettable, indelible

have VERB **1 = own**, keep, possess, hold, retain, occupy, boast, be the owner of: *I want to have my own business.* **2 = get**, obtain, take, receive, accept, gain, secure, acquire, procure, take receipt of: *When can I have the new car?* **3 = suffer**, experience, undergo, sustain, endure, be suffering from: *He might be having a heart attack.* **4 = give birth to**, bear, deliver, bring forth, beget, bring into the world: *My wife has just had a baby boy.* **5 = put up with** (*informal*), allow, permit, consider, think about, entertain, tolerate: *I'm not having any of that nonsense.* **6 = experience**, go through, undergo, meet with, come across, run into, be faced with: *Did you have some trouble with your neighbours?*
have had it = be exhausted, be knackered (*Brit. informal*), be finished, be pooped (*U.S. slang*): *I've had it. Let's call it a day.*
have someone on = tease, kid (*informal*), wind up (*Brit. slang*), trick, deceive, take the mickey, pull someone's leg, play a joke on, jerk *or* yank someone's chain (*informal*): I

thought he was just having me on.
have something on 1 = wear, be wearing, be dressed in, be clothed in, be attired in: *She had on new black shoes.* **2 = have something planned**, be committed to, be engaged to, have something on the agenda: *We have a meeting on that day.*
have to 1 = must, should, be forced, ought, be obliged, be bound, have got to, be compelled: *Now, you have to go into town.* **2 = have got to**, must: *That has to be the biggest lie ever told.*

haven NOUN **1 = sanctuary**, shelter, retreat, asylum, refuge, oasis, sanctum: *a real haven at the end of a busy working day* **2 = harbour**, port, anchorage, road *(Nautical)*: *She lay alongside in Largs Yacht Haven for a few days.*

havoc NOUN **1 = devastation**, damage, destruction, waste, ruin, wreck, slaughter, ravages, carnage, desolation, rack and ruin, despoliation: *Rioters caused havoc in the centre of the town.* **2 = disorder**, confusion, chaos, disruption, mayhem, shambles: *A single mare running loose could cause havoc among otherwise reliable stallions.*
play havoc with something = wreck, destroy, devastate, disrupt, demolish, disorganize, bring into chaos: *Drug addiction soon played havoc with his career.*

hawk VERB **= peddle**, market, sell, push, traffic, tout *(informal)*, vend

hawker NOUN **= pedlar**, tout, vendor, travelling salesman, crier, huckster, barrow boy *(Brit.)*, door-to-door salesman

haywire ADJECTIVE **1 = out of order**, out of commission, on the blink *(slang)*, on the fritz *(slang)*: *Her pacemaker went haywire near hand dryers.* **2 = crazy**, wild, mad, potty *(Brit. informal)*, berserk, bonkers *(slang, chiefly Brit.)*, loopy *(informal)*, mad as a hatter, berko *(Austral. slang)*, off the air *(Austral. slang)*, porangi *(N.Z.)*: *I went haywire in our first few weeks on holiday.*

hazard NOUN **= danger**, risk, threat, problem, menace, peril, jeopardy, pitfall, endangerment, imperilment: *a sole that reduces the hazard of slipping on slick surfaces*
▷ VERB **= jeopardize**, risk, endanger, threaten, expose, imperil, put in jeopardy: *He could not believe that the man would have hazarded his grandson.*
hazard a guess = guess, conjecture, suppose, speculate, presume, take a guess: *I would hazard a guess that they'll do fairly well.*

hazardous ADJECTIVE **= dangerous**, risky, difficult, uncertain, unpredictable, insecure, hairy *(slang)*, unsafe, precarious, perilous, parlous *(archaic, humorous)*, dicey *(informal, chiefly Brit.)*, fraught with danger, chancy *(informal)* **OPPOSITE:** safe

haze NOUN **= mist**, film, cloud, steam, fog, obscurity, vapour, smog, dimness, smokiness

hazy ADJECTIVE **1 = misty**, faint, dim, dull, obscure, veiled, smoky, cloudy, foggy, overcast, blurry, nebulous: *The air was filled with hazy sunshine and frost.* **OPPOSITE:** bright **2 = vague**, uncertain, unclear, muddled, fuzzy, indefinite, loose, muzzy, nebulous, ill-defined, indistinct: *I have only a hazy memory of what he was like.* **OPPOSITE:** clear

head NOUN **1 = skull**, crown, pate, bean *(U.S. & Canad. slang)*, nut *(slang)*, loaf *(slang)*, cranium, conk *(slang)*, noggin, noddle *(informal, chiefly Brit.)*: *She turned her head away from him.* **2 = mind**, reasoning, understanding, thought, sense, brain, brains *(informal)*, intelligence, wisdom, wits, common sense, loaf *(Brit. informal)*, intellect, rationality, grey matter, brainpower, mental capacity: *He was more inclined to use his head.* **3 = ability**, mind, talent, capacity, faculty, flair, mentality, aptitude: *I don't have a head for business.* **4 = front**, beginning, top, first place, fore, forefront: *the head of the queue* **5 = forefront**, cutting edge, vanguard, van: *his familiar position at the head of his field* **6 = top**, crown, summit, height, peak, crest, pinnacle, apex, vertex: *the head of the stairs* **7 = head teacher**, principal, headmaster *or* headmistress: *full of admiration for the head and teachers* **8 = leader**, president, director, manager, chief, boss *(informal)*, captain, master, premier, commander, principal, supervisor, superintendent, chieftain, sherang *(Austral. & N.Z.)*: *heads of government from more than 100 countries* **9 = climax**, crisis, turning point, culmination, end, conclusion, tipping point: *These problems came to a head in September.* **10 = source**, start, beginning, rise, origin, commencement, well head: *the head of the river* **11 = headland**, point, cape, promontory, foreland: *a ship off the beach head*
▷ ADJECTIVE **= chief**, main, leading, first, highest, front, prime, premier, supreme, principal, arch, foremost, pre-eminent, topmost: *I had the head man out from the gas company.*
▷ VERB **1 = lead**, precede, be the leader of, be *or* go first, be *or* go at the front of, lead the way: *The parson, heading the procession, had just turned right.* **2 = top**, lead, crown, cap: *Running a business heads the list of ambitions among interviewees.* **3 = be in charge of**, run, manage, lead, control, rule, direct, guide, command, govern, supervise: *He heads the department's Office of Civil Rights.*
go to your head 1 = intoxicate, befuddle, inebriate, addle, stupefy, fuddle, put (someone) under the table *(informal)*: *That wine was strong, it went to your head.* **2 = make someone conceited**, puff someone up, make someone full of themselves: *not a man to let a little success go to his head*
head for something *or* **someone = make for**, aim for, set off for, go to, turn to, set out for, make a beeline for, start towards, steer for: *He headed for the bus stop.*
head over heels = completely, thoroughly, utterly, intensely, wholeheartedly, uncontrollably: *head over heels in love*
head someone off = intercept, divert, deflect, cut someone off, interpose, block someone off: *He turned into the hallway and headed her off.*
head something off = prevent, stop, avert, parry, fend off, ward off, forestall: *good at spotting trouble on the way and heading it off*
put your heads together = consult, confer, discuss, deliberate, talk (something) over, powwow, confab *(informal)*, confabulate: *Everyone put their heads together and reached an arrangement.*
▸ *related adjectives:* capital, cephalic

headache NOUN **1 = migraine**, head *(informal)*, neuralgia, cephalalgia *(Medical)*: *I have had a terrible headache for the past two days.* **2** *(informal)* **= problem**, worry, trouble, bother, nuisance, inconvenience, bane, vexation: *Their biggest headache is the increase in the price of fuel.*

headfirst *or* **head first** ADVERB **1 = headlong**, head foremost: *He has apparently fallen headfirst down the stairwell.* **2 = recklessly**, rashly, hastily, precipitately, without thinking, carelessly, heedlessly, without forethought: *On arrival he plunged head first into these problems.*

heading NOUN **1 = title**, name, caption, headline, rubric: *helpful chapter headings* **2 = category**, class, section, division: *There, under the heading of wholesalers, he found it.*

headland NOUN **= promontory**, point, head, cape, cliff, bluff, mull *(Scot.)*, foreland, bill

headlong ADVERB **1 = hastily**, hurriedly, helter-skelter, pell-mell, heedlessly: *He ran headlong for the open door.* **2 = headfirst**, head-on, headforemost: *She missed her footing and fell headlong down the stairs.* **3 = rashly**, wildly, hastily, precipitately, head first, thoughtlessly, impetuously, heedlessly, without forethought: *Do not leap headlong into decisions.*
▷ ADJECTIVE **= hasty**, reckless, precipitate, dangerous, impulsive, thoughtless, breakneck, impetuous, inconsiderate: *a headlong rush for the exit*

headmaster *or* **headmistress** NOUN **= principal**, head, head teacher, rector

> **USAGE**
> The general trend of nonsexist language is to find a term which can apply to both sexes equally, as in the use of *actor* to refer to both men and women. This being so, *head teacher* is usually preferable to the gender-specific terms *headmaster* and *headmistress.*

headstrong ADJECTIVE **= stubborn**, wilful, obstinate, contrary, perverse, unruly, intractable, stiff-necked, ungovernable, self-willed, pig-headed, mulish, froward *(archaic)* **OPPOSITE:** manageable

headway NOUN **= progress**, ground, inroads, strides

heady ADJECTIVE **1 = exciting**, thrilling, stimulating, exhilarating, overwhelming, intoxicating: *in the heady days just after their marriage* **2 = intoxicating**, strong, potent, inebriating, spirituous: *The wine is a heady blend of claret and aromatic herbs.*

heal VERB **1** *(sometimes with* **up***)* **= mend**, get better, get well, cure, regenerate, show improvement: *The bruising had gone, but it was six months before it all healed.* **2 = cure**, restore, mend, make better, remedy, make good, make well: *No doctor has ever healed a broken bone. They just set them.* **OPPOSITE:** injure **3 = patch up**, settle, reconcile, put right, harmonize, conciliate: *Sophie and her sister have healed the family rift.*

healing ADJECTIVE **= restoring**, medicinal, therapeutic, remedial, restorative, curative, analeptic, sanative: *Get in touch with the body's own healing abilities.*

health NOUN **1 = condition**, state, form, shape, tone, constitution, fettle: *Although he's old, he's in good health.* **2 = wellbeing**, strength, fitness, vigour, good condition, wellness, soundness, robustness, healthiness, salubrity, haleness: *In hospital they nursed me back to health.* **OPPOSITE:** illness **3 = state**, condition, shape: *There's no way to predict the future health of the banking industry.*

QUOTATIONS

Health is a state of complete physical, mental and social well-being, and not merely the absence of disease or infirmity [*Constitution of the World Health Organization*]

Objection, evasion, happy distrust, pleasure in mockery are signs of health: everything unconditional belongs in pathology [Friedrich Nietzsche *Beyond Good and Evil*]

PROVERBS

An apple a day keeps the doctor away

healthful ADJECTIVE **= healthy**, beneficial, good for you, bracing, nourishing, wholesome, nutritious, invigorating, salutary, salubrious, health-giving

healthy ADJECTIVE **1 = well**, sound, fit, strong, active, flourishing, hardy, blooming, robust, vigorous, sturdy, hale, hearty, in good shape *(informal)*, in good condition, in the pink, alive and kicking, fighting fit, in fine form, in fine fettle, hale and hearty, fit as a fiddle *(informal)*, right as rain *(Brit. informal)*, physically fit, in fine feather: *She had a normal pregnancy and delivered a healthy child.* **OPPOSITE:** ill **2 = wholesome**, beneficial, nourishing, good for you, nutritious, salutary, hygienic, healthful, salubrious, health-giving: *a healthy diet* **OPPOSITE:** unwholesome **3 = invigorating**, bracing, beneficial, good for you, salutary, healthful, salubrious: *a healthy outdoor pursuit*

heap NOUN **1 = pile**, lot, collection, store, mountain, mass, stack, rick, mound, accumulation, stockpile, hoard, aggregation: *a heap of bricks* **2** *(often plural, informal)* **= a lot**, lots *(informal)*, plenty, masses, load(s) *(informal)*, ocean(s), great deal, quantities, tons, stack(s), lashings *(Brit. informal)*, abundance, oodles *(informal)*: *You have heaps of time.*
▷ VERB *(sometimes with* **up***)* **= pile**, store, collect, gather, stack, accumulate, mound, amass, stockpile, hoard, bank: *They were heaping up wood for a bonfire.*
heap something on someone *(with* **on***)* **= load with**, burden with, confer on, assign to, bestow on, shower upon: *He heaped scorn on both their methods and motives.*

hear VERB **1 = overhear**, catch, detect: *She heard no further sounds.* **2 = listen to**, heed, attend to, eavesdrop on, listen in to, give attention to, hearken to *(archaic)*, hark to, be all ears for *(informal)*: *You can hear commentary on the match in about half an hour.* **3 = try**, judge, examine, investigate: *He had to wait months before his case was heard.* **4 = learn**, discover, find out, understand, pick up, gather, be informed, ascertain, be told of, get wind of *(informal)*, hear tell *(dialect)*: *He had heard that the trophy had been sold.*

hearing NOUN **1 = sense of hearing**, auditory perception, ear, aural faculty: *His mind still seemed clear and his hearing was excellent.* **2 = inquiry**, trial, investigation, industrial tribunal: *The judge adjourned the hearing until next Tuesday.* **3 = chance to speak**, interview, audience, audition: *a means of giving a candidate a fair hearing* **4 = earshot**, reach, range, hearing distance, auditory range: *No one spoke disparagingly of her father in her hearing.*
▸ *related adjective:* audio

hearsay NOUN **= rumour**, talk, gossip, report, buzz, dirt *(U.S. slang)*, goss *(informal)*, word of mouth, tittle-tattle, talk of the town, scuttlebutt *(slang, chiefly U.S.)*, idle talk, mere talk, on dit *(French)*

heart NOUN **1 = emotions**, feelings, sentiments, love, affection: *I phoned him up and poured out my heart; The beauty quickly captured his heart.* **2 = nature**, character, soul, constitution, essence, temperament, inclination, disposition: *She loved his brilliance and his generous heart.* **3 = tenderness**, feeling(s), love, understanding, concern, sympathy, pity, humanity, affection, compassion, kindness, empathy, benevolence, concern for others: *They are ruthless, formidable, without heart.* **4 = root**, core, essence, centre, nucleus, marrow, hub, kernel, crux, gist, central part, nitty-gritty *(informal)*, nub, pith, quintessence: *The heart of the problem is supply and demand.* **5 = courage**, will, spirit, mind, purpose, bottle *(Brit. informal)*, resolution, resolve, nerve, stomach, enthusiasm, determination, guts *(informal)*, spine, pluck, bravery, backbone, fortitude, mettle, boldness, spunk *(informal)*: *I did not have the heart or spirit left to jog back to my hotel.*
at heart = fundamentally, essentially, basically, really, actually, in fact, truly, in reality, in truth, in essence, deep down, at bottom, au fond *(French)*
by heart = from *or* **by memory**, verbatim, word for word, pat, word-perfect, by rote, off by heart, off pat, parrot-fashion *(informal)*: *Mack knew this passage by heart.*
from (the bottom of) your heart = deeply, heartily, fervently, heart and soul, devoutly, with all your heart: *thanking you from the bottom of my heart*
from the heart = sincerely, earnestly, in earnest, with all your heart, in all sincerity
heart and soul = completely, entirely, absolutely, wholeheartedly, to the hilt, devotedly
lose heart = give up, despair, lose hope, become despondent, give up the ghost *(informal)*
take heart = be encouraged, be comforted, cheer up, perk up, brighten up, be heartened, buck up *(informal)*, derive comfort: *Investors failed to take heart from the stronger yen.*
▸ *related adjectives:* cardiac, cardiothoracic

heartache NOUN **= sorrow**, suffering, pain, torture, distress, despair, grief, agony, torment, bitterness, anguish, remorse, heartbreak, affliction, heartsickness

heartbreak NOUN **= grief**, suffering, pain, despair, misery, sorrow, anguish, desolation

heartbreaking ADJECTIVE **= sad**, distressing, tragic, bitter, poignant, harrowing, desolating, grievous, pitiful, agonizing, heart-rending, gut-wrenching **OPPOSITE:** happy

hearten VERB **= encourage**, inspire, cheer, comfort, assure, stimulate, reassure, animate, console, rouse, incite, embolden, buoy up, buck up *(informal)*, raise someone's spirits, revivify, gee up, inspirit

heartfelt ADJECTIVE **= sincere**, deep, earnest, warm, genuine, profound, honest, ardent, devout, hearty, fervent, cordial, wholehearted, dinkum *(Austral. & N.Z. informal)*, unfeigned **OPPOSITE:** insincere

heartily ADVERB **1 = sincerely**, feelingly, deeply, warmly, genuinely,

h

profoundly, cordially, unfeignedly: *He laughed heartily.* **2 = enthusiastically**, vigorously, eagerly, resolutely, earnestly, zealously: *I heartily agree with her comments.* **3 = thoroughly**, very, completely, totally, absolutely: *We're all heartily sick of all the aggravation.*

heartless ADJECTIVE **= cruel**, hard, callous, cold, harsh, brutal, unkind, inhuman, merciless, cold-blooded, uncaring, pitiless, unfeeling, cold-hearted, affectless, hardhearted **OPPOSITE:** compassionate

heart-rending ADJECTIVE **= moving**, sad, distressing, affecting, tragic, pathetic, poignant, harrowing, heartbreaking, pitiful, gut-wrenching, piteous

heart-to-heart ADJECTIVE **= intimate**, honest, candid, open, personal, sincere, truthful, unreserved: *I had a heart-to-heart talk with my mother.*
▷ NOUN **= tête-à-tête**, cosy chat, one-to-one, private conversation, private chat: *I've had a heart-to-heart with him.*

heart-warming ADJECTIVE **= moving**, touching, affecting, pleasing, encouraging, warming, rewarding, satisfying, cheering, gratifying, heartening

hearty ADJECTIVE **1 = friendly**, genial, warm, generous, eager, enthusiastic, ardent, cordial, affable, ebullient, jovial, effusive, unreserved, back-slapping: *He was a hearty, bluff, athletic sort of guy.* **OPPOSITE:** cool **2 = wholehearted**, sincere, heartfelt, real, true, earnest, genuine, honest, unfeigned: *With the last sentiment, Arnold was in hearty agreement.* **OPPOSITE:** insincere **3 = substantial**, filling, ample, square, solid, nourishing, sizable *or* sizeable: *The men ate a hearty breakfast.* **4 = healthy**, well, strong, sound, active, hardy, robust, vigorous, energetic, hale, alive and kicking, right as rain (*Brit. informal*): *She was still hearty and strong at 120 years and married a third husband at 92.* **OPPOSITE:** frail

heat VERB **1** (*sometimes with* **up**) **= warm (up)**, cook, boil, roast, reheat, make hot: *Meanwhile, heat the tomatoes and oil in a pan.* **OPPOSITE:** chill **2 = intensify**, increase, heighten, deepen, escalate: *The war of words continues to heat up.*
▷ NOUN **1 = warmth**, hotness, temperature, swelter, sultriness, fieriness, torridity, warmness, calefaction: *Leaves drooped in the fierce heat of the sun.* **OPPOSITE:** cold **2 = hot weather**, warmth, closeness, high temperature, heatwave, warm weather, hot climate, hot spell, mugginess: *The heat is killing me.* **3 = passion**, excitement, intensity, violence, fever, fury, warmth, zeal, agitation, fervour, ardour, vehemence, earnestness, impetuosity: *It was all done in the heat of the moment.* **OPPOSITE:** calmness

heat up = warm up, get hotter, become hot, rise in temperature, become warm, grow hot: *In the summer her mobile home heats up like an oven.*
▶ *related adjective:* thermal

PROVERBS
If you can't stand the heat get out of the kitchen

heated ADJECTIVE **1 = impassioned**, intense, spirited, excited, angry, violent, bitter, raging, furious, fierce, lively, passionate, animated, frenzied, fiery, stormy, vehement, tempestuous: *It was a very heated argument.* **OPPOSITE:** calm **2 = wound up**, worked up, keyed up, het up (*informal*): *Most people tend to get a bit heated about issues like these.*

heathen NOUN **1 = pagan**, infidel, unbeliever, idolater, idolatress: *the condescending air of missionaries seeking to convert the heathen* **2 = barbarian**, savage, philistine, oaf, ignoramus, boor: *She called us all heathens and hypocrites.*
▷ ADJECTIVE **1 = pagan**, infidel, godless, irreligious, idolatrous, heathenish: *a heathen temple* **2 = uncivilized**, savage, primitive, barbaric, brutish, unenlightened, uncultured: *to disappear into the cold heathen north*

QUOTATIONS
heathen: a benighted creature who has the folly to worship something that he can see and feel
[Ambrose Bierce *The Devil's Dictionary*]

heave VERB **1 = lift**, raise, pull (up), drag (up), haul (up), tug, lever, hoist, heft (*informal*): *He heaved Barney to his feet.* **2 = throw**, fling, toss, send, cast, pitch, hurl, sling: *Heave a brick at the telly.* **3 = surge**, rise, swell, billow: *The grey seas heaved.* **4 = vomit**, be sick, throw up (*informal*), chuck (up) (*slang, chiefly U.S.*), chuck (*Austral. & N.Z. informal*), gag, spew, retch, barf (*U.S. slang*), chunder (*slang, chiefly Austral.*), upchuck (*U.S. slang*), do a technicolour yawn (*slang*), toss your cookies (*U.S. slang*): *He gasped and heaved and vomited.* **5 = breathe**, sigh, puff, groan, sob, breathe heavily, suspire (*archaic*), utter wearily: *Mr Collier heaved a sigh and got to his feet.*

heaven NOUN **1 = paradise**, next world, hereafter, nirvana (*Buddhism, Hinduism*), bliss, Zion (*Christianity*), Valhalla (*Norse myth*), Happy Valley, happy hunting ground (*Native American legend*), life to come, life everlasting, abode of God, Elysium *or* Elysian fields (*Greek myth*): *I believed that when I died I would go to heaven.* **2 = happiness**, paradise, ecstasy, bliss, felicity, utopia, contentment, rapture, enchantment, dreamland, seventh heaven, transport, sheer bliss: *My idea of heaven is drinking champagne with friends on a sunny day.* **the heavens = sky**, ether, firmament, celestial sphere, welkin (*archaic*), empyrean (*poetic*): *a map of the heavens*

QUOTATIONS
In my father's house are many mansions
[*Bible: St. John*]

Work and pray
Live on hay
You'll get pie in the sky when you die
[Joe Hill *The Preacher and the Slave*]

The kingdom of heaven is like to a grain of mustard seed
[*Bible: St. Matthew*]

The kingdom of heaven is like unto a merchant man, seeking goodly pearls; who, when he had found one pearl of great price, went and sold all that he had, and bought it
[*Bible: St. Matthew*]

The heaven of each is but what each desires
[Thomas Moore *Lalla Rookh*]

heaven: a place where the wicked cease from troubling you with talk of their personal affairs, and the good listen with attention while you expound your own
[Ambrose Bierce *The Devil's Dictionary*]

heavenly ADJECTIVE **1 = celestial**, holy, divine, blessed, blest, immortal, supernatural, angelic, extraterrestrial, superhuman, godlike, beatific, cherubic, seraphic, supernal (*literary*), empyrean (*poetic*), paradisaical: *heavenly beings whose function it is to serve God* **OPPOSITE:** earthly **2 = wonderful**, lovely, delightful, beautiful, entrancing, divine (*informal*), glorious, exquisite, sublime, alluring, blissful, ravishing, rapturous: *The idea of spending two weeks with him seems heavenly.* **OPPOSITE:** awful

heavily ADVERB **1 = excessively**, to excess, very much, a great deal, frequently, considerably, copiously, without restraint, immoderately, intemperately: *Her husband drank heavily and beat her.* **2 = densely**, closely, thickly, compactly: *They can be found in grassy and heavily wooded areas.* **3 = hard**, clumsily, awkwardly, weightily: *A man stumbled heavily against the car.*

heaviness NOUN **1 = weight**, gravity, ponderousness, heftiness: *the heaviness of earthbound matter* **2 = sadness**, depression, gloom, seriousness, melancholy, despondency, dejection, gloominess, glumness: *a heaviness in his reply which discouraged further questioning*

heavy ADJECTIVE **1 = weighty**, large, massive, hefty, bulky, ponderous: *He was carrying a very heavy load.* **OPPOSITE:** light **2 = intensive**, severe, serious, concentrated, fierce, excessive, relentless: *Heavy fighting has been going on.* **3 = considerable**, large, huge, substantial, abundant, copious, profuse: *There was a heavy amount of traffic on the roads.* **OPPOSITE:** slight **4 = onerous**, hard, difficult, severe, harsh, tedious, intolerable, oppressive, grievous, burdensome, wearisome, vexatious: *They bear a heavy burden of responsibility.* **OPPOSITE:** easy **5 = sluggish**, slow, dull, wooden, stupid, inactive, inert, apathetic, drowsy, listless, indolent, torpid: *I struggle to raise eyelids still heavy with sleep.* **OPPOSITE:** alert **6 = hard**, demanding, difficult, physical, strenuous, laborious: *They employ two full-timers to do the heavy work.* **7 = overcast**, dull, gloomy, cloudy, leaden, louring *or* lowering: *The night sky was heavy with rain clouds.* **8 = sad**, depressed, gloomy, grieving, melancholy, dejected, despondent, downcast, sorrowful, disconsolate, crestfallen: *My parents' faces were heavy with fallen hope.* **OPPOSITE:** happy **9 = serious**, grave, solemn, difficult, deep, complex, profound, weighty: *I don't want any more of that heavy stuff.* **OPPOSITE:** trivial

heavy-handed ADJECTIVE **1 = oppressive**, harsh, Draconian, autocratic, domineering, overbearing: *heavy-handed police tactics* **2 = clumsy**, awkward, bungling, inept, graceless, inexpert, maladroit, ham-handed *(informal)*, like a bull in a china shop *(informal)*, ham-fisted *(informal)*: *She tends to be a little heavy-handed.* **OPPOSITE:** skilful

heckle VERB **= jeer**, interrupt, shout down, disrupt, bait, barrack *(informal)*, boo, taunt, pester

hectic ADJECTIVE **= frantic**, chaotic, frenzied, heated, wild, excited, furious, fevered, animated, turbulent, flurrying, frenetic, boisterous, feverish, tumultuous, flustering, riotous, rumbustious **OPPOSITE:** peaceful

hector VERB **= bully**, harass, browbeat, worry, threaten, menace, intimidate, ride roughshod over, bullyrag

hedge NOUN **= guard**, cover, protection, compensation, shield, safeguard, counterbalance, insurance cover: *Gold is traditionally a hedge against inflation.*
▷ VERB **1 = prevaricate**, evade, sidestep, duck, dodge, flannel *(Brit. informal)*, waffle *(informal, chiefly Brit.)*, quibble, beg the question, pussyfoot *(informal)*, equivocate, temporize, be noncommittal: *When asked about his involvement, he hedged.* **2 = enclose**, edge, border, surround, fence: *sweeping lawns hedged with floribundas*
hedge against something = protect, insure, guard, safeguard, shield, cover, fortify: *You can hedge against redundancy or illness with insurance.*
hedge someone in = hamper, restrict, handicap, hamstring, hinder, hem in: *He was hedged in by his own shyness.*
hedge something in = surround, enclose, encompass, encircle, ring, fence in, girdle, hem in: *a steep and rocky footpath hedged in by the shadowy green forest*
hedge something *or* **someone about = restrict**, confine, hinder, hem in, hem around, hem about: *The offer was hedged about by conditions.*

hedonism NOUN **= pleasure-seeking**, gratification, sensuality, self-indulgence, dolce vita, pursuit of pleasure, luxuriousness, sensualism, sybaritism, epicureanism, epicurism

hedonistic ADJECTIVE **= pleasure-seeking**, self-indulgent, luxurious, voluptuous, sybaritic, epicurean, bacchanalian

heed VERB **= pay attention to**, listen to, take notice of, follow, mark, mind, consider, note, regard, attend, observe, obey, bear in mind, be guided by, take to heart, give ear to: *Few at the conference in London last week heeded his warning.* **OPPOSITE:** ignore
▷ NOUN **= thought**, care, mind, note, attention, regard, respect, notice, consideration, watchfulness: *He pays too much heed these days to my nephew Tom.* **OPPOSITE:** disregard

heedless ADJECTIVE **= careless**, reckless, negligent, rash, precipitate, oblivious, foolhardy, thoughtless, unthinking, imprudent, neglectful, inattentive, incautious, unmindful, unobservant **OPPOSITE:** careful

heel NOUN **1 = end**, stump, remainder, crust, rump, stub: *the heel of a loaf of bread* **2 = swine**, cad *(Brit. informal)*, scoundrel, scally *(Northwest English dialect)*, bounder *(Brit. old-fashioned, slang)*, rotter *(slang, chiefly Brit.)*, scumbag *(slang)*, blackguard, wrong 'un *(Austral. slang)*: *Suddenly I feel like a total heel.*
take to your heels = flee, escape, run away *or* off, take flight, hook it *(slang)*, turn tail, show a clean pair of heels, skedaddle *(informal)*, vamoose *(slang, chiefly U.S.)*: *He stood, for a moment, then took to his heels.*

hefty ADJECTIVE **1 = big**, strong, massive, strapping, robust, muscular, burly, husky *(informal)*, hulking, beefy *(informal)*, brawny: *She was quite a hefty woman.* **OPPOSITE:** small **2 = forceful**, heavy, powerful, vigorous *(slang)*: *Lambert gave him a hefty shove to send him on his way.* **OPPOSITE:** gentle **3 = heavy**, large, massive, substantial, tremendous, awkward, ample, bulky, colossal, cumbersome, weighty, unwieldy, ponderous: *The gritty foursome took turns shouldering the hefty load every five minutes.* **OPPOSITE:** light **4 = large**, massive, substantial, excessive, inflated, sizeable, astronomical *(informal)*, extortionate: *A long-distance romance followed with hefty phone bills.*

height NOUN **1 = tallness**, stature, highness, loftiness: *Her height is intimidating for some men.* **OPPOSITE:** shortness **2 = altitude**, measurement, highness, elevation, tallness: *build a wall up to a height of 2 metres* **OPPOSITE:** depth **3 = peak**, top, hill, mountain, crown, summit, crest, pinnacle, elevation, apex, apogee, vertex: *From a height, it looks like a desert.* **OPPOSITE:** valley **4 = culmination**, climax, zenith, limit, maximum, ultimate, extremity, uttermost, ne plus ultra *(Latin)*, utmost degree: *He was struck down at the height of his career.* **OPPOSITE:** low point
▸ *related phobia:* acrophobia

heighten VERB **= intensify**, increase, add to, improve, strengthen, enhance, sharpen, aggravate, magnify, amplify, augment

heinous ADJECTIVE **= shocking**, evil, monstrous, grave, awful, vicious, outrageous, revolting, infamous, hideous, unspeakable, atrocious, flagrant, odious, hateful, abhorrent, abominable, villainous, nefarious, iniquitous, execrable

heir NOUN **= successor**, beneficiary, inheritor, heiress *(fem.)*, scion, next in line, inheritress *or* inheritrix *(fem.)*

hell NOUN **1 = the underworld**, the abyss, Hades *(Greek myth)*, hellfire, the inferno, fire and brimstone, the bottomless pit, Gehenna *(New Testament, Judaism)*, the nether world, the lower world, Tartarus *(Greek myth)*, the infernal regions, the bad fire *(informal)*, Acheron *(Greek myth)*, Abaddon, the abode of the damned: *Don't worry about going to Hell, just be good.* **2 = torment**, suffering, agony, trial, nightmare, misery, ordeal, anguish, affliction, martyrdom, wretchedness: *the hell of grief and lost love*
hell for leather = headlong, speedily, quickly, swiftly, hurriedly, at the double, full-tilt, pell-mell, hotfoot, at a rate of knots, like a bat out of hell *(slang)*, posthaste: *The first horse often goes hell for leather.*

QUOTATIONS

Hell is paved with the skulls of priests
[St. John Chrysostom *De Sacerdotio*]

Let none admire
The riches that grow in hell; that soil may best
Deserve the precious bane
[John Milton *Paradise Lost*]

There is a dreadful Hell,
And everlasting pains;
There sinners must with devils dwell
In darkness, fire, and chains
[Isaac Watts *Divine Songs for Children*]

Hell hath no limits nor is circumscribed
In one self place, where we are is Hell,
And to be short, when all the world dissolves
And every creature shall be purified
All places shall be Hell that are not Heaven
[Christopher Marlowe *Doctor Faustus*]

h

> But wherefore thou alone?
> Wherefore with thee
> Came not all hell broke loose?
> [John Milton *Paradise Lost*]
>
> Hell is other people
> [Jean-Paul Sartre *Huis Clos*]
>
> A perpetual holiday is a good
> working definition of hell
> [George Bernard Shaw *Parents and Children*]
>
> Hell is a city much like London -
> A populous and smoky city
> [Percy Bysshe Shelley *Peter Bell the Third*]
>
> Hell is not to love any more,
> madame. Not to love any more!
> [Georges Bernanos *The Diary of a Country Priest*]
>
> What is hell?
> Hell is yourself,
> Hell is alone, the other figures in it
> Merely projections
> [T.S. Eliot *The Cocktail Party*]
>
> If there is no Hell, a good many
> preachers are obtaining money
> under false pretenses
> [William A. Sunday]

hellbent ADJECTIVE = **intent** *(informal)*, set, determined, settled, fixed, resolved, bent

hellish ADJECTIVE **1 = atrocious**, terrible, dreadful, cruel, vicious, monstrous, wicked, inhuman, barbarous, abominable, nefarious, accursed, execrable, detestable: *He was held for three years in hellish conditions.* **OPPOSITE:** wonderful **2 = devilish**, fiendish, diabolical, infernal, damned, damnable, demoniacal: *They began to pray, making devilish gestures with a hellish noise.*

hello INTERJECTION = **hi** *(informal)*, greetings, how do you do?, good morning, good evening, good afternoon, welcome, kia ora *(N.Z.)*, gidday or g'day *(Austral. & N.Z.)*

helm NOUN = **tiller**, wheel, rudder, steering gear: *I got into our dinghy while Willis took the helm.*
at the helm = **in charge**, in control, in command, directing, at the wheel, in the saddle, in the driving seat: *He has been at the helm of Lonrho for 31 years.*

help VERB **1** *(sometimes with* **out**) = **aid**, back, support, second, encourage, promote, assist, relieve, stand by, befriend, cooperate with, abet, lend a hand, succour, lend a helping hand, give someone a leg up *(informal)*: *If you're not willing to help me, I'll find somebody who will.* **OPPOSITE:** hinder **2 = improve**, ease, heal, cure, relieve, remedy, facilitate, alleviate, mitigate, ameliorate: *A cosmetic measure which will do nothing to help the situation long term.* **OPPOSITE:** make worse **3 = assist**, aid, support, give a leg up *(informal)*: *Martin helped Tanya over the rail.* **4 = resist**, refrain from, avoid, control, prevent, withstand, eschew, keep from, abstain from, forbear: *I can't help feeling sorry for the poor man.*
▷ NOUN **1 = assistance**, aid, support, service, advice, promotion, guidance, cooperation, helping hand: *Thanks very much for your help.* **OPPOSITE:** hindrance **2 = remedy**, cure, relief, corrective, balm, salve, succour, restorative: *There is no help for him and no doctor on this earth could save him.* **3 = assistant**, hand, worker, employee, helper: *a hired help*

helper NOUN = **assistant**, partner, ally, colleague, supporter, mate, deputy, second, subsidiary, aide, aider, attendant, collaborator, auxiliary, henchman, right-hand man, adjutant, helpmate, coadjutor, abettor

helpful ADJECTIVE **1 = cooperative**, accommodating, kind, caring, friendly, neighbourly, sympathetic, supportive, benevolent, considerate, beneficent: *The staff in the London office are helpful.* **2 = useful**, practical, productive, profitable, constructive, serviceable: *The catalogue includes helpful information.* **3 = beneficial**, advantageous, expedient, favourable: *It is often helpful to have someone with you when you get bad news.*

helpfulness NOUN **1 = cooperation**, kindness, support, assistance, sympathy, friendliness, rallying round, neighbourliness, good neighbourliness: *The level of expertise and helpfulness is higher in small shops.* **2 = usefulness**, benefit, advantage: *the helpfulness of the information pack*

helping NOUN = **portion**, serving, ration, piece, dollop *(informal)*, plateful

helpless ADJECTIVE **1 = vulnerable**, exposed, unprotected, defenceless, abandoned, dependent, stranded, wide open, forlorn, destitute: *The children were left helpless.* **OPPOSITE:** invulnerable **2 = powerless**, weak, disabled, incapable, challenged, paralysed, incompetent, unfit, feeble, debilitated, impotent, infirm: *Since the accident I am completely helpless.* **OPPOSITE:** powerful

helplessness NOUN = **vulnerability**, weakness, impotence, powerlessness, disability, infirmity, feebleness, forlornness, defencelessness

helter-skelter ADJECTIVE = **haphazard**, confused, disordered, random, muddled, jumbled, topsy-turvy, hit-or-miss, higgledy-piggledy *(informal)*: *another crisis in his helter-skelter existence*
▷ ADVERB = **wildly**, rashly, anyhow, headlong, recklessly, carelessly, pell-mell: *a panic-stricken crowd running helter-skelter*

hem NOUN = **edge**, border, margin, trimming, fringe: *Cut a jagged edge along the hem to give a ragged look.*
hem something or **someone in 1 = surround**, edge, border, skirt, confine, enclose, shut in, hedge in, environ: *Manchester is hemmed in by greenbelt countryside.* **2 = restrict**, confine, beset, circumscribe: *hemmed in by rigid, legal contracts*

hence ADVERB = **therefore**, thus, consequently, for this reason, in consequence, ergo, on that account

henceforth ADVERB = **from now on**, in the future, hereafter, hence, hereinafter, from this day forward

henchman NOUN = **attendant**, supporter, heavy *(slang)*, associate, aide, follower, subordinate, bodyguard, minder *(slang)*, crony, sidekick *(slang)*, cohort *(chiefly U.S.)*, right-hand man, minion, satellite, myrmidon

henpecked ADJECTIVE = **dominated**, subjugated, browbeaten, subject, bullied, timid, cringing, meek, treated like dirt, led by the nose, tied to someone's apron strings **OPPOSITE:** domineering

herald VERB **1 = indicate**, promise, precede, pave the way, usher in, harbinger, presage, portend, foretoken: *Their discovery could herald a cure for some forms of impotence.* **2 = announce**, publish, advertise, proclaim, broadcast, trumpet, publicize: *Tonight's clash is being heralded as the match of the season.*
▷ NOUN **1 = forerunner**, sign, signal, indication, token, omen, precursor, harbinger: *I welcome the report as the herald of more freedom, not less.* **2 = messenger**, courier, proclaimer, announcer, crier, town crier, bearer of tidings: *Jill hovered by the hearth while the herald delivered his news.*

herculean ADJECTIVE **1 = arduous**, hard, demanding, difficult, heavy, tough, exhausting, formidable, gruelling, strenuous, prodigious, onerous, laborious, toilsome: *Finding a lawyer may seem like a Herculean task.* **2 = strong**, muscular, powerful, athletic, strapping, mighty, rugged, sturdy, stalwart, husky *(informal)*, sinewy, brawny: *His shoulders were Herculean with long arms.*

herd NOUN **1 = flock**, crowd, collection, mass, drove, crush, mob, swarm, horde, multitude, throng, assemblage, press: *large herds of elephant and buffalo* **2 = mob**, the masses, rabble, populace, the hoi polloi, the plebs, riffraff: *They are individuals; they will not follow the herd.*
▷ VERB **1 = lead**, drive, force, direct, guide, shepherd: *The group was herded onto a bus.* **2 = drive**, lead, force, guide, shepherd: *A boy herded sheep down towards the lane.*

hereafter ADVERB = **in future**, after this, from now on, henceforth, henceforward, hence: *Hereafter for three years my name will not appear at all.*
the hereafter = **afterlife**, next world, life after death, future life, the beyond: *belief in the hereafter*

hereditary ADJECTIVE **1 = genetic**, inborn, inbred, transmissible,

The Language of Edith Nesbit

Edith Nesbit (married name, Edith Bland, 1858–1924) was the author of a large number of successful children's stories, including *The Railway Children, The Story of the Treasure Seekers,* and *Five Children and It.* She was also the writer of *Beautiful Stories from Shakespeare,* a child-friendly retelling of plays by the Bard. Some of her books are grounded in the reality of everyday life while others soar into the realms of fantasy and magic. Some have since been adapted for the screen.

Nesbit's writing style is very approachable, conversational and surprisingly fresh and modern. She favours natural, ordinary words over more formal Latinate ones. For her there is no reluctance about using *get*, for instance. In *The Story of the Treasure Seekers*, the young narrator tells his tale in a chatty, exuberant manner, including little details and usages that one wouldn't normally expect to see in a final, edited text, a carefully crafted technique that lends freshness, pace, and immediacy, for example, 'recover his equi-what's-its-name'. He makes comments that reveal facts he is apparently blind to, and this helps to engage the reader, whom he addresses as *you* in a sometimes rather belligerent manner:

> Albert's uncle says I ought to have put this in the preface, but I never read prefaces, and it is not much good writing things just for people to skip.
>
> Our Mother is dead, and if you think we don't care because I don't tell you much about her you only show that you do not understand people at all.

Even though she was writing at a time when many had a very orthodox attitude to grammar and word choice, Nesbit is no pedant about usage; at times she uses natural, everyday words and constructions that some people even now would consider incorrect: *aggravating* in the sense of *annoying*; *like* as a conjunction; *if* followed by the indicative, *was,* rather than by the subjunctive, *were*:

> She had never felt quite so spiteful before, but, then, Harry had never before been quite so **aggravating**.
>
> You never crossed it out like you did his address.
>
> I feel as if I was in a lunatic asylum.

Where the stories have dated is in the choice of informal words and expressions that have not survived the passage of time. *What rot,* people say. Things are *simply ripping* or *rather decent.* People are *bricks* or *muffs*. And your family are *your people*. *Jolly* makes an appearance 382 times in Nesbit's books (for example, *jolly hungry; jolly careful; jolly well*).

Nesbit sometimes uses *shall* and *should* in the first person where nowadays we would tend to use *will* or *'ll* and *would* or *'d.* These sound rather formal to the modern ear although that would not have been the case at the time of writing:

> 'I don't believe we **shall** turn to stone,' said Robert, breaking a long miserable silence ...

In her work we occasionally encounter superlatives formed with an '-est' ending even though the root adjective is a long one not ending in '-y' (*miserablest, wonderfullest, perfectest, curiousest*). This has a livelier feel than the more standard construction with *most.*

There is sometimes a barely concealed didactic element in Nesbit's stories, something that may jar with some readers, and the tales are clearly written in the era of the stiff upper lip, when manliness was a virtue and crying, especially in a male, was not:

> This was very wrong, for you should always speak the truth, however unhappy it makes people.
>
> Thinking of other people's comfort makes them like you.
>
> I will say for you you're more like a man and less like a snivelling white rabbit now ...

Even though Edith Nesbit was a forward-thinking political activist who co-founded the Fabian Society, occasionally the social attitudes of her day, as displayed in her stories, grate a little in our more heterogeneous, multicultural times:

> They're only savages, and they don't know any better.

inheritable: *In men, hair loss is hereditary.* **2 = inherited**, handed down, passed down, willed, family, traditional, transmitted, ancestral, bequeathed, patrimonial: *hereditary peerages*

heredity NOUN **= genetics**, inheritance, genetic make-up, congenital traits

heresy NOUN **= unorthodoxy**, apostasy, dissidence, impiety, revisionism, iconoclasm, heterodoxy

> **QUOTATIONS**
> The heresy of one age becomes the orthodoxy of the next
> [Helen Keller *Optimism*]
>
> They that approve a private opinion, call it opinion; but they that mislike it, heresy; and yet heresy signifies no more than private opinion
> [Thomas Hobbes *Leviathan*]

h

heretic NOUN **= nonconformist**, dissident, separatist, sectarian, renegade, revisionist, dissenter, apostate, schismatic

heretical ADJECTIVE **1 = controversial**, unorthodox, revisionist, freethinking: *I made a heretical suggestion.* **2 = unorthodox**, revisionist, iconoclastic, heterodox, impious, idolatrous, schismatic, freethinking: *The Church regards spirit mediums as heretical.*

heritage NOUN **= inheritance**, legacy, birthright, lot, share, estate, tradition, portion, endowment, bequest, patrimony

hermit NOUN **= recluse**, monk, loner *(informal)*, solitary, anchorite, anchoress, stylite, eremite

hero NOUN **1 = protagonist**, leading man, lead actor, male lead, principal male character: *The hero of Doctor Zhivago dies in 1929.* **2 = star**, champion, celebrity, victor, superstar, great man, heart-throb *(Brit.)*, conqueror, exemplar, celeb *(informal)*, megastar *(informal)*, popular figure, man of the hour: *the goalscoring hero of the British hockey team* **3 = idol**, favourite, pin-up *(slang)*, fave *(informal)*: *I still remember my boyhood heroes.*

> **QUOTATIONS**
> Unhappy the land that is in need of heroes
> [Bertolt Brecht *Galileo*]
>
> If I was to stumble upon Jesus Christ I'd say 'Good Afternoon' and then walk on. But if I met Robert Burns or Shakespeare, well, that would be a different matter. I'd stop and talk for a wee while
> [Robin Jenkins]
>
> See, the conquering hero comes! Sound the trumpets, beat the drums!
> [Thomas Morell *Judas Maccabeus*]
>
> Ultimately a hero is a man who would argue with the gods, and so awakens devils to contest his vision
> [Norman Mailer *The Presidential Papers*]

heroic ADJECTIVE **1 = courageous**, brave, daring, bold, fearless, gallant, intrepid, valiant, doughty, undaunted, dauntless, lion-hearted, valorous, stouthearted: *The heroic sergeant risked his life to rescue 29 fishermen.* **OPPOSITE:** cowardly **2 = legendary**, classical, mythological, Homeric: *another in an endless series of man's heroic myths of his own past* **3 = epic**, grand, classic, extravagant, exaggerated, elevated, inflated, high-flown, grandiose: *a heroic style, with a touch of antiquarian realism* **OPPOSITE:** simple

> **QUOTATIONS**
> The high sentiments always win in the end, the leaders who offer blood, toil, tears and sweat always get more out of their followers than those who offer safety and a good time. When it comes to the pinch, human beings are heroic
> [George Orwell *The Art of Donald McGill*]

heroine NOUN **1 = protagonist**, leading lady, diva, prima donna, female lead, lead actress, principal female character: *The heroine is a senior TV executive.* **2 = star**, celebrity, goddess, celeb *(informal)*, megastar *(informal)*, woman of the hour: *The heroine of the day was the winner of the Gold medal.* **3 = idol**, favourite, pin-up *(slang)*, fave *(informal)*: *I still remember my childhood heroines.*

> **USAGE**
> Note that the word *heroine*, meaning 'a female hero', has an *e* at the end. The drug *heroin* is spelled without a final *e*.

heroism NOUN **= bravery**, daring, courage, spirit, fortitude, boldness, gallantry, valour, fearlessness, intrepidity, courageousness

hero-worship NOUN **= admiration**, idolization, adulation, adoration, veneration, idealization, putting on a pedestal

hesitant ADJECTIVE **= uncertain**, reluctant, shy, halting, doubtful, sceptical, unsure, hesitating, wavering, timid, diffident, lacking confidence, vacillating, hanging back, irresolute, half-hearted **OPPOSITE:** confident

hesitate VERB **1 = waver**, delay, pause, haver *(Brit.)*, wait, doubt, falter, be uncertain, dither *(chiefly Brit.)*, vacillate, equivocate, temporize, hum and haw, shillyshally *(informal)*, swither *(Scot. dialect)*: *She hesitated, debating whether to answer the phone.* **OPPOSITE:** be decisive **2 = be reluctant**, be unwilling, shrink from, think twice, boggle, scruple, demur, hang back, be disinclined, balk *or* baulk: *I will not hesitate to take unpopular decisions.* **OPPOSITE:** be determined

hesitation NOUN **1 = delay**, pausing, uncertainty, stalling, dithering, indecision, hesitancy, doubt, vacillation, temporizing, shilly-shallying, irresolution, hemming and hawing, dubiety: *After some hesitation, he answered her question.* **2 = reluctance**, reservation(s), misgiving(s), ambivalence, qualm(s), unwillingness, scruple(s), compunction, demurral: *The board said it had no hesitation in rejecting the offer.*

heterogeneous ADJECTIVE **= varied**, different, mixed, contrasting, unlike, diverse, diversified, assorted, unrelated, disparate, miscellaneous, motley, incongruous, dissimilar, divergent, manifold, discrepant

hew VERB **1 = cut**, chop, axe, hack, split, lop: *He felled, peeled and hewed his own timber.* **2 = carve**, make, form, fashion, shape, model, sculpture, sculpt: *medieval monasteries hewn out of the rockface*

heyday NOUN **= prime**, time, day, flowering, pink, bloom, high point, zenith, salad days, prime of life

hiatus NOUN **= pause**, break, interval, space, gap, breach, blank, lapse, interruption, respite, chasm, discontinuity, lacuna, entr'acte

hibernate VERB **= sleep**, lie dormant, winter, overwinter, vegetate, remain torpid, sleep snug

hidden ADJECTIVE **1 = secret**, veiled, dark, mysterious, obscure, mystical, mystic, shrouded, occult, latent, cryptic, hermetic, ulterior, abstruse, recondite, hermetic *or* hermetical: *Uncover hidden meanings and discover special messages.* **2 = concealed**, covered, secret, covert, unseen, clandestine, secreted, under wraps, unrevealed: *The pictures had obviously been taken by a hidden camera.*

hide¹ VERB **1 = conceal**, stash *(informal)*, secrete, cache, put out of sight: *He hid the bicycle in the hawthorn hedge.* **OPPOSITE:** display **2 = go into hiding**, take cover, keep out of sight, hole up, lie low, go underground, go to ground, go to earth: *They hid behind a tree.* **3 = keep secret**, suppress, withhold, keep quiet about, hush up, draw a veil over, keep dark, keep under your hat: *I have absolutely nothing to hide, I have done nothing wrong.* **OPPOSITE:** disclose **4 = obscure**, cover, screen, bury, shelter, mask, disguise, conceal, eclipse, veil, cloak, shroud, camouflage, blot out: *The compound was hidden by trees and shrubs.* **OPPOSITE:** reveal

hide² NOUN **= skin**, fell, leather, pelt: *the process of tanning animal hides*

hideaway NOUN **= hiding place**, haven, retreat, refuge, sanctuary, hide-out, nest, sequestered nook

hidebound ADJECTIVE **= conventional**, set, rigid, narrow, puritan, narrow-minded, strait-laced, brassbound, ultraconservative, set in your ways **OPPOSITE:** broad-minded

hideous ADJECTIVE **1 = ugly**, revolting, ghastly, monstrous, grotesque, gruesome, grisly, unsightly,

repulsive: *She saw a hideous face at the window and screamed.*
OPPOSITE: beautiful **2 = terrifying**, shocking, terrible, awful, appalling, disgusting, horrible, dreadful, horrific, obscene, sickening, horrendous, macabre, horrid, odious, loathsome, abominable, detestable, godawful *(slang)*: *His family was subjected to a hideous attack.*

hide-out NOUN **= hiding place**, shelter, den, hideaway, lair, secret place

hiding NOUN **= beating**, whipping, thrashing, tanning *(slang)*, caning, licking *(informal)*, flogging, spanking, walloping *(informal)*, drubbing, lathering *(informal)*, whaling, larruping *(Brit. dialect)*

hierarchy NOUN **= grading**, ranking, social order, pecking order, class system, social stratum

> **QUOTATIONS**
> We rank ourselves by the familiar dog system, a ladderlike social arrangement wherein one individual outranks all others, the next outranks all but the first, and so on down the hierarchy
> [Elizabeth Marshall Thomas *Strong and Sensitive Cats*]
>
> In a hierarchy every employee tends to rise to his level of incompetence
> [Laurence Peter *The Peter Principle*]

higgledy-piggledy ADJECTIVE **= haphazard**, muddled, jumbled, indiscriminate, topsy-turvy, helter-skelter, pell-mell: *books stacked in higgledy-piggledy piles on the floor*
▷ ADVERB **= haphazardly**, all over the place, anyhow, topsy-turvy, helter-skelter, all over the shop *(informal)*, pell-mell, confusedly, any old how: *boulders tossed higgledy-piggledy as though by some giant*

high ADJECTIVE **1 = tall**, towering, soaring, steep, elevated, lofty: *A house with a high wall around it.*
OPPOSITE: short **2 = extreme**, great, acute, severe, extraordinary, excessive: *Officials said casualties were high.* **OPPOSITE:** low **3 = strong**, violent, extreme, blustery, squally, sharp: *High winds have knocked down trees and power lines.* **4 = expensive**, dear, steep *(informal)*, costly, stiff, high-priced, exorbitant: *I think it's a good buy overall, despite the high price.*
5 = important, leading, ruling, chief, powerful, significant, distinguished, prominent, superior, influential, notable, big-time *(informal)*, eminent, major league *(informal)*, exalted, consequential, skookum *(Canad.)*: *Every one of them is controlled by the families of high officials.* **OPPOSITE:** lowly
6 = notable, leading, famous, significant, celebrated, distinguished, renowned, eminent, pre-eminent: *She has always had a high reputation for her excellent stories.* **7 = high-pitched**, piercing, shrill, penetrating, treble, soprano, strident, sharp, acute, piping: *Her high voice really irritated Maria.* **OPPOSITE:** deep
8 = cheerful, excited, merry, exhilarated, exuberant, joyful, bouncy *(informal)*, boisterous, elated, light-hearted, stoked *(Austral. & N.Z. informal)*: *Her spirits were high with the hope of seeing Nick.* **OPPOSITE:** dejected
9 = intoxicated, stoned *(slang)*, spaced out *(slang)*, tripping *(informal)*, turned on *(slang)*, on a trip *(informal)*, delirious, euphoric, freaked out *(informal)*, hyped up *(slang)*, zonked *(slang)*, inebriated: *He was too high on drugs and alcohol to remember them.*
10 = luxurious, rich, grand, lavish, extravagant, opulent, hedonistic: *an emphatic contrast to his Park Avenue high life*
▷ ADVERB **= way up**, aloft, far up, to a great height: *on combat patrol flying high above the landing sites*
▷ NOUN **1 = peak**, height, top, summit, crest, record level, apex: *Sales of Russian vodka have reached an all-time high.* **2 = intoxication**, trip *(informal)*, euphoria, delirium, ecstasy: *The 'thrill' sought is said to be similar to a drug high.*
high and dry = abandoned, stranded, helpless, forsaken, bereft, destitute, in the lurch: *You could be left high and dry in a strange town.*
high and mighty = self-important, superior, arrogant, stuck-up *(informal)*, conceited, imperious, overbearing, haughty, snobbish, disdainful: *I think you're a bit too high and mighty yourself.*

highbrow ADJECTIVE **= intellectual**, cultured, sophisticated, deep, cultivated, brainy *(informal)*, highbrowed, bookish: *He presents his own highbrow literary programme.*
OPPOSITE: unintellectual
▷ NOUN **= intellectual**, scholar, egghead *(informal)*, brain *(informal)*, mastermind, Brahmin *(U.S.)*, aesthete, savant, brainbox *(slang)*: *the sniggers of the highbrows*
OPPOSITE: philistine

> **QUOTATIONS**
> A highbrow is a kind of person who looks at a sausage and thinks of Picasso
> [A.P. Herbert *The Highbrow*]

high-class ADJECTIVE **= high-quality**, top *(slang)*, choice, select, exclusive, elite, superior, posh *(informal, chiefly Brit.)*, classy *(slang)*, top-flight, upper-class, swish *(informal, chiefly Brit.)*, first-rate, up-market, top-drawer, ritzy *(slang)*, tip-top, high-toned, A1 or A-one *(informal)*
OPPOSITE: inferior

higher-up NOUN **= superior**, senior, manager, director, executive, boss, gaffer *(informal, chiefly Brit.)*, baas *(S. African)*, sherang *(Austral. & N.Z.)*

high-flown ADJECTIVE **= extravagant**, elaborate, pretentious, exaggerated, inflated, lofty, grandiose, overblown, florid, high-falutin *(informal)*, arty-farty *(informal)*, magniloquent
OPPOSITE: straightforward

high-handed ADJECTIVE **= dictatorial**, domineering, overbearing, arbitrary, oppressive, autocratic, bossy *(informal)*, imperious, tyrannical, despotic, peremptory

highlight VERB **= emphasize**, stress, accent, feature, set off, show up, underline, spotlight, play up, accentuate, flag, foreground, focus attention on, call attention to, give prominence to, bring to the fore: *Two events have highlighted the tensions in recent days.* **OPPOSITE:** play down
▷ NOUN **= high point**, peak, climax, feature, focus, best part, focal point, main feature, high spot, memorable part: *one of the highlights of the tournament*
OPPOSITE: low point

highly ADVERB **1 = extremely**, very, greatly, seriously *(informal)*, vastly, exceptionally, extraordinarily, immensely, decidedly, tremendously, supremely, eminently: *He was a highly successful salesman.* **2 = favourably**, well, warmly, enthusiastically, approvingly, appreciatively: *one of the most highly regarded chefs in the French capital*

highly-strung ADJECTIVE **= nervous**, stressed, tense, sensitive, wired *(slang)*, restless, neurotic, taut, edgy, temperamental, excitable, nervy *(Brit. informal)*, twitchy *(informal)*, on tenterhooks, easily upset, on pins and needles, adrenalized
OPPOSITE: relaxed

high-minded ADJECTIVE **= principled**, moral, worthy, noble, good, fair, pure, ethical, upright, elevated, honourable, righteous, idealistic, virtuous, magnanimous
OPPOSITE: dishonourable

high-powered ADJECTIVE **= dynamic**, driving, powerful, enterprising, effective, go-ahead, aggressive, vigorous, energetic, forceful, fast-track, go-getting *(informal)*, high-octane *(informal)*, highly capable

high-pressure ADJECTIVE **= forceful**, aggressive, compelling, intensive, persistent, persuasive, high-powered, insistent, bludgeoning, pushy *(informal)*, in-your-face *(slang)*, coercive, importunate

high-spirited ADJECTIVE **= lively**, spirited, vivacious, vital, daring, dashing, bold, energetic, animated, vibrant, exuberant, bouncy, boisterous, fun-loving, ebullient, sparky, effervescent, alive and kicking, full of life, spunky *(informal)*, full of beans *(informal)*, frolicsome, mettlesome

hijack or **highjack** VERB **= seize**, take over, commandeer, expropriate, skyjack

hike NOUN **= walk**, march, trek, ramble, tramp, traipse, journey on foot: *a hike around the cluster of hills*
▷ VERB **= walk**, march, trek, ramble, tramp, leg it *(informal)*, back-pack, hoof it *(slang)*: *You could hike through the Fish River Canyon.*

hike something up = hitch up, raise, lift, pull up, jack up: *He hiked up his trouser legs.*

hiker NOUN **= walker**, rambler, backpacker, wayfarer, hillwalker

hilarious ADJECTIVE **1 = funny**, entertaining, amusing, hysterical, humorous, exhilarating, comical, side-splitting: *He had a fund of hilarious tales.* **2 = merry**, uproarious, happy, gay, noisy, jolly, joyous, joyful, jovial, rollicking, convivial, mirthful: *Everyone had a hilarious time.*
OPPOSITE: serious

hilarity NOUN **= merriment**, high spirits, mirth, gaiety, laughter, amusement, glee, exuberance, exhilaration, cheerfulness, jollity, levity, conviviality, joviality, boisterousness, joyousness, jollification

h

hill NOUN **1 = mount**, down *(archaic)*, fell, height, mound, prominence, elevation, eminence, hilltop, tor, knoll, hillock, brae *(Scot.)*, kopje *or* koppie *(S. African)*: *They climbed to the top of the hill.* **2 = slope**, incline, gradient, rise, climb, brae *(Scot.)*, acclivity: *the shady street that led up the hill to the office building*

THE SEVEN HILLS OF ROME

Aventine	Palatine
Caelian	Quirinal
Capitoline	Viminal
Esquiline	

hilly ADJECTIVE **= mountainous**, rolling, steep, undulating

hilt NOUN **= handle**, grip, haft, handgrip, helve: *the hilt of the small, sharp knife*
to the hilt = fully, completely, totally, entirely, wholly: *James was overdrawn and mortgaged to the hilt.*

hind ADJECTIVE **= back**, rear, hinder, posterior, caudal *(Anatomy)*

hinder VERB **= obstruct**, stop, check, block, prevent, arrest, delay, oppose, frustrate, handicap, interrupt, slow down, deter, hamstring, hamper, thwart, retard, impede, hobble, stymie, encumber, throw a spanner in the works, trammel, hold up *or* back **OPPOSITE:** help

hindrance NOUN **= obstacle**, check, bar, block, difficulty, drag, barrier, restriction, handicap, limitation, hazard, restraint, hitch, drawback, snag, deterrent, interruption, obstruction, stoppage, stumbling block, impediment, encumbrance, trammel **OPPOSITE:** help

hinge on VERB **= depend on**, be subject to, hang on, turn on, rest on, revolve around, be contingent on, pivot on

hint NOUN **1 = clue**, mention, suggestion, implication, indication, reminder, tip-off, pointer, allusion, innuendo, inkling, intimation, insinuation, word to the wise: *I'd dropped a hint about having an exhibition of his work.* **2 = advice**, help, tip(s), suggestion(s), pointer(s): *I'm hoping to get some fashion hints.* **3 = trace**, touch, suggestion, taste, breath, dash, whisper, suspicion, tinge, whiff, speck, undertone, soupçon *(French)*: *I glanced at her and saw no hint of irony on her face.*
▷ VERB *(sometimes with* **at***)* **= suggest**, mention, indicate, imply, intimate, tip off, let it be known, insinuate, allude to the fact, tip the wink *(informal)*: *The President hinted he might make some changes in the government.*

hip ADJECTIVE **= trendy** *(Brit. informal)*, with it, fashionable, in, aware, informed, wise *(slang)*, clued-up *(informal)*, funky

hippy *or* **hippie** NOUN **= flower child**, bohemian, dropout, free spirit, beatnik, basketweaver *(Austral. derogatory, slang)*

hire VERB **1 = employ**, commission, take on, engage, appoint, sign up, enlist: *hired on short-term contracts* **2 = rent**, charter, lease, let, engage: *To hire a car you must produce a current driving licence.*
▷ NOUN **1 = rental**, hiring, rent, lease: *Fishing tackle is available for hire.* **2 = charge**, rental, price, cost, fee: *Surf board hire is $12 per day.*

hirsute ADJECTIVE **= hairy**, bearded, shaggy, unshaven, bristly, bewhiskered, hispid *(Biology)*

hiss VERB **1 = whistle**, wheeze, rasp, whiz, whirr, sibilate: *The air hissed out of the pipe.* **2 = jeer**, mock, ridicule, deride, decry, revile: *The delegates booed and hissed him.*
▷ NOUN **= fizz**, buzz, hissing, fizzing, sibilance, sibilation: *the hiss of a beer bottle opening*

historian NOUN **= chronicler**, recorder, biographer, antiquarian, historiographer, annalist, chronologist

> **QUOTATIONS**
> Historians are left forever chasing shadows, painfully aware of their inability ever to reconstruct a dead world in its completeness
> [Simon Schama *Dead Certainties*]
>
> History repeats itself. Historians repeat each other
> [Philip Guedalla *Supers and Supermen*]
>
> historian: a broad-gauge gossip
> [Ambrose Bierce *The Devil's Dictionary*]

historic ADJECTIVE **= significant**, notable, momentous, famous, celebrated, extraordinary, outstanding, remarkable, ground-breaking, consequential, red-letter, epoch-making
OPPOSITE: unimportant

> **USAGE**
> Although *historic* and *historical* are similarly spelt they are very different in meaning and should not be used interchangeably. A distinction is usually made between *historic*, which means 'important' or 'significant', and *historical*, which means 'pertaining to history': *a historic decision; a historical perspective*.

historical ADJECTIVE **= factual**, real, documented, actual, authentic, chronicled, attested, archival, verifiable **OPPOSITE:** contemporary

history NOUN **1 = the past**, the old days, antiquity, yesterday, the good old days, yesteryear, ancient history, olden days, days of old, days of yore, bygone times: *Is history about to repeat itself?* **2 = chronicle**, record, story, account, relation, narrative, saga, recital, narration, annals, recapitulation: *his magnificent history of broadcasting in Canada*

histrionic ADJECTIVE **= theatrical**, affected, dramatic, forced, camp *(informal)*, actorly, artificial, unnatural, melodramatic, actressy: *Dorothea let out a histrionic groan.*
▷ PLURAL NOUN **= dramatics**, scene, tantrums, performance, temperament, theatricality, staginess, hissy fit *(informal)*: *When I explained everything, there were no histrionics.*

hit VERB **1 = strike**, beat, knock, punch, belt *(informal)*, deck *(slang)*, bang, batter, clip *(informal)*, slap, bash *(informal)*, sock *(slang)*, chin *(slang)*, smack, thump, clout *(informal)*, cuff, flog, whack, clobber *(slang)*, smite *(archaic)*, wallop *(informal)*, swat, lay one on *(slang)*, beat *or* knock seven bells out of *(informal)*: *She hit him hard across his left arm.* **2 = collide with**, run into, bump into, clash with, smash into, crash against, bang into, meet head-on: *The car hit a traffic sign before skidding out of control.* **3 = affect**, damage, harm, ruin, devastate, overwhelm, touch, impact on, impinge on, leave a mark on, make an impact *or* impression on: *The big cities have been hit by a wave of panic-buying; the earthquake which hit northern Peru* **4 = reach**, strike, gain, achieve, secure, arrive at, accomplish, attain: *Oil prices hit record levels yesterday.*
▷ NOUN **1 = shot**, blow, impact, collision: *The house took a direct hit then the rocket exploded.* **2 = blow**, knock, stroke, belt *(informal)*, rap, slap, bump, smack, clout *(informal)*, cuff, swipe *(informal)*, wallop *(informal)*: *a hit on the head* **3 = success**, winner, triumph, smash *(informal)*, sensation, sellout, smasheroo *(informal)*: *The song became a massive hit in 1945.*
hit it off = get on (well) with, take to, click *(slang)*, warm to, be on good terms, get on like a house on fire *(informal)*: *How well did you hit it off with one another?*
hit on *or* **upon something = think up**, discover, arrive at, guess, realize, invent, come upon, stumble on,

chance upon, light upon, strike upon: *We finally hit on a solution.*
hit out at someone = **attack**, condemn, denounce, lash out, castigate, rail against, assail, inveigh against, strike out at: *The President hit out at what he sees as foreign interference.*

> **QUOTATIONS**
> A hit, a very palpable hit
> [William Shakespeare *Hamlet*]

hit-and-miss *or* **hit-or-miss** ADJECTIVE = **haphazard**, random, uneven, casual, indiscriminate, cursory, perfunctory, aimless, disorganized, undirected, scattershot **OPPOSITE:** systematic

hitch NOUN = **problem**, catch, trouble, check, difficulty, delay, hold-up, obstacle, hazard, drawback, hassle *(informal)*, snag, uphill *(S. African)*, stoppage, mishap, impediment, hindrance: *The five-hour operation went without a hitch.*
▷ VERB **1** = **hitchhike**, thumb a lift: *I hitched a lift into town.* **2** = **fasten**, join, attach, unite, couple, tie, connect, harness, tether, yoke, make fast: *We hitched the horse to the cart.*
hitch something up = **pull up**, tug, jerk, yank, hoick: *He hitched his trousers up over his potbelly.*

hither ADVERB = **here**, over here, to this place, close, closer, near, nearer, nigh *(archaic)*

hitherto ADVERB = **previously**, so far, until now, thus far, up to now, till now, heretofore

hive NOUN **1** = **colony**, swarm: *the dance performed by honeybees as they returned to the hive* **2** = **centre**, hub, powerhouse *(slang)*: *In the morning the house was a hive of activity.*

hoard VERB = **save**, store, collect, gather, treasure, accumulate, garner, amass, stockpile, buy up, put away, hive, cache, lay up, put by, stash away *(informal)*: *They've begun to hoard food and gasoline.*
▷ NOUN = **store**, fund, supply, reserve, mass, pile, heap, fall-back, accumulation, stockpile, stash, cache, treasure-trove: *a hoard of silver and jewels*

hoarse ADJECTIVE = **rough**, harsh, husky, grating, growling, raucous, rasping, gruff, throaty, gravelly, guttural, croaky **OPPOSITE:** clear

hoary ADJECTIVE **1** = **old**, aged, ancient, antique, venerable, antiquated: *the hoary old myth that women are unpredictable* **2** = **white-haired**, white, grey, silvery, frosty, grey-haired, grizzled, hoar: *hoary beards*

hoax NOUN = **trick**, joke, fraud, con *(informal)*, deception, spoof *(informal)*, prank, swindle, ruse, practical joke, canard, fast one *(informal)*, imposture, fastie *(Austral. slang)*: *His claim to have a bomb was a hoax.*
▷ VERB = **deceive**, trick, fool, take in *(informal)*, con *(slang)*, wind up *(Brit. slang)*, kid *(informal)*, bluff, dupe, gull *(archaic)*, delude, swindle, bamboozle *(informal)*, gammon *(Brit. informal)*, hoodwink, take (someone) for a ride *(informal)*, befool, hornswoggle *(slang)*, scam *(slang)*: *He recently hoaxed Nelson Mandela by pretending to be Tony Blair.*

hobble VERB **1** = **limp**, stagger, stumble, shuffle, falter, shamble, totter, dodder, halt: *He got up slowly and hobbled over to the table.* **2** = **restrict**, hamstring, shackle, fetter: *The poverty of 10 million citizens hobbles our economy.*

hobby NOUN = **pastime**, relaxation, leisure pursuit, sideline, diversion, avocation, favourite occupation, (leisure) activity

hobnob VERB = **socialize**, mix, associate, hang out *(informal)*, mingle, consort, hang about, keep company, fraternize

hog VERB = **monopolize**, dominate, tie up, corner, corner the market in, be a dog in the manger

hoist VERB = **raise**, lift, erect, elevate, heave, upraise: *He hoisted himself to a sitting position.*
▷ NOUN = **lift**, crane, elevator, winch, tackle: *It takes three nurses and a hoist to get me into this chair.*

hold VERB **1** = **carry**, keep, grip, grasp, cling to, clasp: *Hold the baby while I load the car.* **2** = **support**, take, bear, shoulder, sustain, prop, brace: *Hold the weight with a straight arm above your head.* **OPPOSITE:** give way **3** = **embrace**, grasp, clutch, hug, squeeze, cradle, clasp, enfold: *If only he would hold her close to him.* **4** = **restrain**, constrain, check, bind, curb, hamper, hinder: *He was held in an arm lock.* **OPPOSITE:** release **5** = **detain**, arrest, confine, imprison, impound, pound, hold in custody, put in jail: *the return of two seamen held on spying charges* **OPPOSITE:** release **6** = **accommodate**, take, contain, seat, comprise, have a capacity for: *The small bottles don't seem to hold much.* **7** = **consider**, think, believe, view, judge, regard, maintain, assume, reckon, esteem, deem, presume, entertain the idea: *She holds that it is not admissible to ordain women.* **OPPOSITE:** deny **8** = **occupy**, have, fill, maintain, retain, possess, hold down *(informal)*: *She has never held a ministerial post.* **9** = **conduct**, convene, have, call, run, celebrate, carry on, assemble, preside over, officiate at, solemnize: *They held frequent consultations concerning technical problems.* **OPPOSITE:** cancel **10** *(sometimes with* **up***)* = **continue**, last, remain, stay, wear, resist, endure, persist, persevere: *Our luck couldn't hold for ever.* **11** = **apply**, exist, be the case, stand up, operate, be in force, remain true, hold good, remain valid: *Today, most people think that argument no longer holds.*
▷ NOUN **1** = **grip**, grasp, clutch, clasp: *He released his hold on the camera.* **2** = **foothold**, footing, purchase, leverage, vantage, anchorage: *The idea didn't really get a hold in this country.* **3** = **control**, authority, influence, pull *(informal)*, sway, dominance, clout *(informal)*, mastery, dominion, ascendancy, mana *(N.Z.)*: *It's always useful to have a hold over people.*
hold back = **desist**, forbear, hesitate, stop yourself, restrain yourself, refrain from doing something: *She wanted to say something but held back.*
hold forth = **speak**, go on, discourse, lecture, preach, spout *(informal)*, harangue, declaim, spiel *(informal)*, descant, orate, speechify, korero *(N.Z.)*: *He is capable of holding forth with great eloquence.*
hold off = **put off**, delay, postpone, defer, avoid, refrain, keep from: *The hospital staff held off taking him in for an X-ray.*
hold on = **wait (a minute)**, hang on *(informal)*, sit tight *(informal)*, hold your horses *(informal)*, just a moment *or* second: *Hold on while I have a look.*
hold onto something *or* **someone** **1** = **grab**, hold, grip, clutch, cling to: *He was struggling to hold onto the rock above his head.* **2** = **retain**, keep, hang onto, not give away, keep possession of: *to enable Spurs to hold onto their striker*
hold out = **last**, continue, carry on, endure, hang on, persist, persevere, stay the course, stand fast: *He can only hold out for a few more weeks.*
hold out against something *or* **someone** = **withstand**, resist, fend off, keep at bay, fight: *They held out against two companies of troops.*
hold someone back = **hinder**, prevent, restrain, check, hamstring, hamper, inhibit, thwart, obstruct, impede: *Does her illness hold her back from making friends or enjoying life?*
hold someone up = **delay**, slow down, hinder, stop, detain, retard, impede, set back: *Why were you holding everyone up?*
hold something back **1** = **restrain**, check, curb, control, suppress, rein (in), repress, stem the flow of: *Stagnation in home sales is holding back economic recovery.* **2** = **withhold**, hold in, suppress, stifle, repress, keep the lid on *(informal)*, keep back: *You seem to be holding something back.*
hold something out = **offer**, give, present, extend, proffer: *Max held out his cup for a refill.*
hold something over = **postpone**, delay, suspend, put off, defer, adjourn, waive, take a rain check on *(U.S. & Canad. informal)*: *Further voting might be held over until tomorrow.*
hold something up **1** = **display**, show, exhibit, flourish, show off, hold aloft, present: *Hold it up so we can see it.* **2** = **support**, prop, brace, bolster, sustain, shore up, buttress, jack up: *Mills have iron pillars holding up the roof.* **3** = **rob**, mug *(informal)*, stick up *(slang, chiefly U.S.)*, waylay: *A thief ran off with hundreds of pounds after holding up a petrol station.*
hold something *or* **someone off** = **fend off**, repel, rebuff, stave off, repulse, keep off: *holding off*

a tremendous challenge
hold up = last, survive, endure, bear up, wear: *Children's wear is holding up well in the recession.*
hold with something = approve of, be in favour of, support, subscribe to, countenance, agree to *or* with, take kindly to: *I don't hold with the way they do things nowadays.*

holder NOUN **1 = owner**, bearer, possessor, keeper, purchaser, occupant, proprietor, custodian, incumbent: *the holders of the Championship; the club has 73,500 season-ticket holders* **2 = case**, cover, container, sheath, receptacle, housing: *a toothbrush holder*

holding *(often plural)* NOUN **= property**, securities, investments, resources, estate, assets, possessions, stocks and shares, land interests

h

hold-up NOUN **1 = robbery**, theft, mugging *(informal)*, stick-up *(slang, chiefly U.S.)*: *an armed hold-up at a National Australia bank* **2 = delay**, wait, hitch, trouble, difficulty, setback, snag, traffic jam, obstruction, stoppage, bottleneck: *They arrived late due to a motorway hold-up.*

hole NOUN **1 = cavity**, depression, pit, hollow, pocket, chamber, cave, shaft, cavern, excavation: *He took a shovel, dug a hole, and buried his possessions.* **2 = opening**, split, crack, break, tear, gap, rent, breach, outlet, vent, puncture, aperture, fissure, orifice, perforation: *They got in through a hole in the wall; kids with holes in the knees of their jeans* **3 = burrow**, nest, den, earth, shelter, retreat, covert, lair: *a rabbit hole* **4 = fault**, error, flaw, defect, loophole, discrepancy, inconsistency, fallacy: *There were some holes in that theory.* **5 = hovel**, dump *(informal)*, dive *(slang)*, slum, joint *(slang)*: *Why don't you leave this awful hole and come to live with me?* **6 = predicament**, spot *(informal)*, fix *(informal)*, mess, jam *(informal)*, dilemma, scrape *(informal)*, tangle, hot water *(informal)*, quandary, tight spot, imbroglio: *He admitted that the government was in 'a dreadful hole'.*
hole up = hide, shelter, take refuge, go into hiding, take cover, go to earth: *holing up in his Paris flat with the phone off the hook*

holiday NOUN **1 = vacation**, leave, break, time off, recess, away day, schoolie *(Austral.)*, accumulated day off *or* ADO *(Austral.)*, staycation *or* stacation *(informal)*: *I've just come back from a holiday in the United States.* **2 = festival**, bank holiday, festivity, public holiday, fête, celebration, anniversary, feast, red-letter day, name day, saint's day, gala: *New Year's Day is a public holiday throughout Britain.*

QUOTATIONS
He capers, he dances, he has eyes of youth; he writes verses, he speaks of holiday, he smells April and May
[William Shakespeare *The Merry Wives of Windsor*]

A perpetual holiday is a good working definition of hell
[George Bernard Shaw *Parents and Children*]

holiness NOUN **= sanctity**, spirituality, sacredness, purity, divinity, righteousness, piety, godliness, saintliness, blessedness, religiousness, devoutness, virtuousness

holler VERB *(sometimes with* **out***)* **= yell**, call, cry, shout, cheer, roar, hail, bellow, whoop, clamour, bawl, hurrah, halloo, huzzah *(archaic)*: *He hollered for help.*
▷ NOUN **= yell**, call, cry, shout, cheer, roar, hail, bellow, whoop, clamour, bawl, hurrah, halloo, huzzah *(archaic)*: *The men were celebrating with drunken whoops and hollers.*

hollow ADJECTIVE **1 = empty**, vacant, void, unfilled, not solid: *a hollow cylinder* **OPPOSITE:** solid **2 = sunken**, depressed, cavernous, indented, concave, deep-set: *hollow cheeks* **OPPOSITE:** rounded **3 = worthless**, empty, useless, vain, meaningless, pointless, futile, fruitless, specious, Pyrrhic, unavailing: *Any threat to bring in the police is a hollow one.* **OPPOSITE:** meaningful **4 = insincere**, false, artificial, cynical, hypocritical, hollow-hearted: *His hollow laugh had no mirth in it.* **5 = dull**, low, deep, flat, rumbling, muted, muffled, expressionless, sepulchral, toneless, reverberant: *the hollow sound of a gunshot* **OPPOSITE:** vibrant
▷ NOUN **1 = cavity**, cup, hole, bowl, depression, pit, cave, den, basin, dent, crater, trough, cavern, excavation, indentation, dimple, concavity: *where water gathers in a hollow and forms a pond* **OPPOSITE:** mound **2 = valley**, dale, glen, dell, dingle: *Locals in the sleepy hollow peered out of their country cottages.* **OPPOSITE:** hill
▷ VERB *(often followed by* **out***)* **= scoop out**, dig out, excavate, gouge out, channel, groove, furrow: *Someone had hollowed out a large block of stone.*

holocaust NOUN **1 = devastation**, destruction, carnage, genocide, inferno, annihilation, conflagration: *A nuclear holocaust seemed a very real possibility in the '50s.* **2 = genocide**, massacre, carnage, mass murder, annihilation, pogrom: *a fund for survivors of the holocaust and their families*

holy ADJECTIVE **1 = sacred**, blessed, hallowed, dedicated, venerable, consecrated, venerated, sacrosanct, sanctified: *To them, as to all Tibetans, this is a holy place.* **OPPOSITE:** unsanctified **2 = devout**, godly, religious, pure, divine, faithful, righteous, pious, virtuous, hallowed, saintly, god-fearing: *The Indians think of him as a holy man.* **OPPOSITE:** sinful

QUOTATIONS
Is that which is holy loved by the gods because it is holy, or is it holy because it is loved by the gods?
[Plato *Euthyphro*]

homage NOUN **1 = respect**, honour, worship, esteem, admiration, awe, devotion, reverence, duty, deference, adulation, adoration: *two marvellous films that pay homage to our literary heritage* **OPPOSITE:** contempt **2 = allegiance**, service, tribute, loyalty, devotion, fidelity, faithfulness, obeisance, troth *(archaic)*, fealty: *At his coronation he received the homage of kings.*

home NOUN **1 = dwelling**, house, residence, abode, habitation, pad *(slang)*, domicile, dwelling place: *the allocation of land for new homes* **2 = birthplace**, household, homeland, home town, homestead, native land, Godzone *(Austral. informal)*: *She was told to leave home by her father; His father worked away from home for many years.* **3 = territory**, environment, habitat, range, element, haunt, home ground, abode, habitation, stamping ground: *threatening the home of the famous African mountain gorillas*
▷ ADJECTIVE **= domestic**, national, local, central, internal, native, inland: *Europe's software companies still have a growing home market.*
at home 1 = in, present, available: *Remember I'm not at home to callers.* **2 = at ease**, relaxed, comfortable, content, at peace: *We soon felt quite at home.*
at home in, on, *or* **with = familiar with**, experienced in, skilled in, proficient in, conversant with, au fait with, knowledgeable of, well-versed in: *Graphic artists will feel at home with Photoshop.*
bring something home to someone = make clear, emphasize, drive home, press home, impress upon: *It was to bring home to Americans the immediacy of the crisis.*

QUOTATIONS
Mid pleasures and palaces though
we may roam,
Be it ever so humble, there's no
place like home.
Home, home, sweet, sweet home!
There's no place like home! There's
no place like home!
[J.H. Payne *Clari, the Maid of Milan*]

Home is where the heart is
[Pliny the Elder]

Home is the place where, when you
have to go there,
They have to take you in
[Robert Frost *The Death of the Hired Man*]

PROVERBS
East, west, home's best
An Englishman's home is his castle

homeland NOUN **= native land**, birthplace, motherland, fatherland, country of origin, mother country, Godzone *(Austral. informal)*

homeless ADJECTIVE **= destitute**, exiled, displaced, dispossessed, unsettled, outcast, abandoned, down-and-out

homely ADJECTIVE **1 = comfortable**, welcoming, friendly, domestic, familiar, informal, cosy, comfy (*informal*), homespun, downhome (*slang, chiefly U.S.*), homelike, homy: *We try and provide a very homely atmosphere.* **2 = plain**, simple, natural, ordinary, modest, everyday, down-to-earth, unaffected, unassuming, unpretentious, unfussy: *Scottish baking is homely, comforting and truly good.* **OPPOSITE:** elaborate **3 = unattractive**, plain, ugly, not striking, unprepossessing, not beautiful, no oil painting (*informal*), ill-favoured: *The man was homely and overweight.*

homespun ADJECTIVE **= unsophisticated**, homely, plain, rough, rude, coarse, home-made, rustic, artless, inelegant, unpolished

homicidal ADJECTIVE **= murderous**, deadly, lethal, maniacal, death-dealing

homicide NOUN **= murder**, killing, manslaughter, slaying, bloodshed

homily NOUN **= sermon**, talk, address, speech, lecture, preaching, discourse, oration, declamation

homogeneous *or* **homogenous** ADJECTIVE **= uniform**, similar, consistent, identical, alike, comparable, akin, analogous, kindred, unvarying, cognate **OPPOSITE:** diverse

homosexual ADJECTIVE **= gay**, lesbian, queer (*informal, derogatory*), camp (*informal*), pink (*informal*), same-sex, homoerotic, sapphic, moffie (*S. African slang*): *a homosexual relationship*
▷ NOUN **= gay**, lesbian, queer (*informal, derogatory*), moffie (*S. African slang*), auntie *or* aunty (*Austral. slang*), lily (*Austral. slang*): *You didn't tell me he was a homosexual.*
▸ *related phobia:* homophobia

QUOTATIONS

I am the Love that dare not speak its name
[Lord Alfred Douglas *Two Loves*]

In homosexual sex you know exactly what the other person is feeling
[William Burroughs]

These names: gay, queer, homosexual, are limiting. I would love to finish with them
[Derek Jarman *At Your Own Risk*]

I have heard some say... [homosexual] practices are allowed in France and in other NATO countries. We are not French, and we are not other nationals. We are British, thank God!
[Field Marshal Montgomery]

homy *or* **homey** ADJECTIVE **= homely**, comfortable, welcoming, domestic, friendly, familiar, cosy, comfy (*informal*), homespun, downhome (*slang, chiefly U.S.*), homelike

hone VERB **1 = improve**, better, polish, enhance, upgrade, refine, sharpen, augment, help: *honing the skills of senior managers* **2 = sharpen**, point, grind, edge, file, polish, whet, strop: *four grinding wheels for honing fine-edged tools*

USAGE
Hone is sometimes wrongly used where *home* is meant: *this device makes it easier to home in on* (not *hone in on*) *the target*.

honest ADJECTIVE **1 = trustworthy**, decent, upright, reliable, ethical, honourable, conscientious, reputable, truthful, virtuous, law-abiding, trusty, scrupulous, high-minded, veracious: *My dad was the most honest man I have ever met.* **OPPOSITE:** dishonest **2 = open**, direct, frank, plain, straightforward, outright, sincere, candid, forthright, upfront (*informal*), undisguised, round, ingenuous, unfeigned: *I was honest about what I was doing.* **OPPOSITE:** secretive **3 = genuine**, real, true, straight, fair, proper, authentic, equitable, impartial, on the level (*informal*), bona fide, dinkum (*Austral. & N.Z. informal*), above board, fair and square, on the up and up, honest to goodness: *It was an honest mistake on his part.* **OPPOSITE:** false

QUOTATIONS

To be honest, as this world goes, is to be one man picked out of ten thousand
[William Shakespeare *Hamlet*]

An honest man's the noblest work of God
[Alexander Pope *An Essay on Man*]

An honest man's word is as good as his bond
[Cervantes *Don Quixote*]

honestly ADVERB **1 = ethically**, legitimately, legally, in good faith, on the level (*informal*), lawfully, honourably, by fair means, with clean hands: *charged with failing to act honestly in his duties as an officer* **2 = frankly**, plainly, candidly, straight (out), truthfully, to your face, in plain English, in all sincerity: *It came as a shock to hear him talk so honestly about an old friend.*

honesty NOUN **1 = integrity**, honour, virtue, morality, fidelity, probity, rectitude, veracity, faithfulness, truthfulness, trustworthiness, straightness, incorruptibility, scrupulousness, uprightness, reputability: *It's time for complete honesty from political representatives.* **2 = frankness**, openness, sincerity, candour, bluntness, outspokenness, genuineness, plainness, straightforwardness: *Good communication encourages honesty in a relationship.*

QUOTATIONS

The surest way to remain poor is to be an honest man
[Napoleon Bonaparte *Maxims*]

No legacy is so rich as honesty
[William Shakespeare *All's Well That Ends Well*]

Honesty's a fool
[William Shakespeare *Othello*]

Honesty is a fine jewel, but much out of fashion
[Thomas Fuller *Gnomologia*]

Honesty is praised, then left to shiver
[Juvenal *Satires*]

PROVERBS
Honesty is the best policy

honeyed ADJECTIVE **1 = flattering**, sweet, soothing, enticing, mellow, seductive, agreeable, sweetened, cajoling, alluring, melodious, unctuous, dulcet: *His gentle manner and honeyed tones reassured Andrew.* **2 = sweet**, sweetened, luscious, sugary, syrupy, toothsome: *I could smell the honeyed ripeness of melons and peaches.*

honorary ADJECTIVE **= nominal**, unofficial, titular, ex officio, honoris causa (*Latin*), in name *or* title only

honour NOUN **1 = integrity**, principles, morality, honesty, goodness, fairness, decency, righteousness, probity, rectitude, trustworthiness, uprightness: *I can no longer serve with honour as a member of your government.* **OPPOSITE:** dishonour **2 = prestige**, credit, reputation, glory, fame, distinction, esteem, dignity, elevation, eminence, renown, repute, high standing: *He brought honour and glory to his country.* **OPPOSITE:** disgrace **3 = reputation**, standing, prestige, image, status, stature, good name, kudos, cachet: *Britain's national honour was at stake.* **4 = acclaim**, regard, respect, praise, recognition, compliments, homage, accolades, reverence, deference, adoration, commendation, veneration: *One grand old English gentleman at least will be received with honour.* **OPPOSITE:** contempt **5 = privilege**, credit, favour, pleasure, compliment, source of pride *or* satisfaction: *Five other cities had been competing for the honour of staging the Games.* **6 = virginity**, virtue, innocence, purity, modesty, chastity: *He had fell designs on her honour.*
▷ VERB **1 = acclaim**, celebrate, praise, decorate, compliment, commemorate, dignify, commend, glorify, exalt, laud, lionize: *Two American surgeons were honoured with the Nobel Prize.* **2 = respect**, value, esteem, prize, appreciate, admire, worship, adore, revere, glorify, reverence, exalt, venerate, hallow: *Honour your parents, that's what the Bible says.* **OPPOSITE:** scorn **3 = fulfil**, keep, carry out, observe, discharge, live up to, be true to, be as good as (*informal*), be faithful to: *He had failed to honour his word.* **4 = pay**, take, accept, clear, pass, cash, credit, acknowledge: *The bank refused to honour his cheque.* **OPPOSITE:** refuse

h

QUOTATIONS

Duty, honour! We make these words say whatever we want, the same as we do with parrots
[Alfred Capus *Mariage Bourgeois*]

If I lose mine honour,
I lose myself
[William Shakespeare *Antony and Cleopatra*]

Remember, you're fighting for this woman's honour....which is probably more than she ever did
[Groucho Marx *Duck Soup (film)*]

The louder he talked of his honour, the faster we counted our spoons
[Ralph Waldo Emerson *The Conduct of Life*]

PROVERBS

There is no honour among thieves

honourable ADJECTIVE **1 = principled**, moral, ethical, just, true, fair, upright, honest, virtuous, trustworthy, trusty, high-minded, upstanding: *I believe he was an honourable man.* **2 = proper**, right, respectable, righteous, virtuous, creditable: *However, their intentions are honourable.* **3 = prestigious**, great, noble, noted, distinguished, notable, renowned, eminent, illustrious, venerable: *an honourable profession*

QUOTATIONS

For Brutus is an honourable man
[William Shakespeare *Julius Caesar*]

hoodoo NOUN **= jinx**, curse, bad luck, voodoo, nemesis, hex *(U.S. & Canad. informal)*, evil eye, evil star

hoodwink VERB **= deceive**, trick, fool, cheat, con *(informal)*, kid *(informal)*, mislead, hoax, dupe, gull *(archaic)*, delude, swindle, rook *(slang)*, bamboozle *(informal)*, take (someone) for a ride *(informal)*, lead up the garden path *(informal)*, sell a pup, pull a fast one on *(informal)*, cozen, befool, scam *(slang)*

hook NOUN **= fastener**, catch, link, lock, holder, peg, clasp, hasp: *One of his jackets hung from a hook.*
▷ VERB **1 = fasten**, fix, secure, catch, clasp, hasp: *one of those can openers you hook onto the wall* **2 = catch**, land, trap, entrap: *Whenever one of us hooked a fish, we moved on.*
by hook or by crook = by any means, somehow, somehow or other, someway, by fair means or foul: *They intend to get their way, by hook or by crook.*
hook, line, and sinker = completely, totally, entirely, thoroughly, wholly, utterly, through and through, lock, stock and barrel: *We fell for it hook, line, and sinker.*
off the hook = let off, cleared, acquitted, vindicated, in the clear, exonerated, under no obligation, allowed to walk *(slang, chiefly U.S.)*: *Officials accused of bribery always seem to get off the hook.*

hooked ADJECTIVE **1 = bent**, curved, beaked, aquiline, beaky, hook-shaped, hamate *(rare)*, hooklike, falcate *(Biology)*, unciform *(Anatomy)*, uncinate *(Biology)*: *He was tall and thin, with a hooked nose.* **2 = obsessed**, addicted, taken, devoted, turned on *(slang)*, enamoured: *Open this book and read a few pages and you will be hooked.* **3 = addicted**, dependent, using *(informal)*, having a habit: *He spent a number of years hooked on cocaine, heroin and alcohol.*

hooligan NOUN **= delinquent**, tough, vandal, casual, ned *(Scot. slang)*, rowdy, hoon *(Austral. & N.Z.)*, hoodlum *(chiefly U.S.)*, ruffian, lager lout, yob *or* yobbo *(Brit. slang)*, cougan *(Austral. slang)*, scozza *(Austral. slang)*, bogan *(Austral. slang)*, hoodie *(informal)*

hooliganism NOUN **= delinquency**, violence, disorder, vandalism, rowdiness, loutishness, yobbishness

hoop NOUN **= ring**, band, loop, wheel, round, girdle, circlet

hoot NOUN **1 = cry**, shout, howl, scream, shriek, whoop: *the hoots of night birds* **2 = toot**, beep, honk: *He strode on, ignoring the car, in spite of a further warning hoot.* **3 = jeer**, yell, boo, catcall: *His confession was greeted with derisive hoots.* **4 = laugh**, scream *(informal)*, caution *(informal)*, card *(informal)*: *He's a hoot, a real character.*
▷ VERB **1 = jeer**, boo, howl, yell, catcall: *The protesters chanted, blew whistles and hooted.* **2 = cry**, call, screech, tu-whit tu-whoo: *Out in the garden an owl hooted suddenly.* **3 = toot**, sound, blast, blare, beep, honk: *Somewhere in the distance a siren hooted.* **4 = shout**, cry, yell, scream, shriek, whoop: *Bev hooted with laughter.*

hop VERB **= jump**, spring, bound, leap, skip, vault, caper: *I hopped down three steps.*
▷ NOUN **= jump**, step, spring, bound, leap, bounce, skip, vault: *'This is a catchy rhythm,' he added with a few hops.*

hope VERB **= believe**, expect, trust, rely, look forward to, anticipate, contemplate, count on, foresee, keep your fingers crossed, cross your fingers: *I hope that the police will take the strongest action against them.*
▷ NOUN **= belief**, confidence, expectation, longing, dream, desire, faith, ambition, assumption, anticipation, expectancy, light at the end of the tunnel: *Kevin hasn't given up hope of being fit.* OPPOSITE: despair

hopeful ADJECTIVE **1 = optimistic**, confident, assured, looking forward to, anticipating, buoyant, sanguine, expectant: *Surgeons were hopeful of saving her sight.* OPPOSITE: despairing **2 = promising**, encouraging, bright, reassuring, cheerful, rosy, heartening, auspicious, propitious: *hopeful forecasts that the economy will improve* OPPOSITE: unpromising

hopefully ADVERB **1 = optimistically**, confidently, expectantly, with anticipation, sanguinely: *'Am I welcome?' he smiled hopefully.* **2 = it is hoped**, probably, all being well, God willing, conceivably, feasibly, expectedly: *Hopefully, you won't have any problems after reading this.*

USAGE

Some people object to the use of *hopefully* as a synonym for the phrase 'it is hoped that' in a sentence such as *hopefully I'll be able to attend the meeting*. This use of the adverb first appeared in America in the 1960s, but it has rapidly established itself elsewhere. There are really no strong grounds for objecting to it, since we accept other sentence adverbials that fulfil a similar function, for example *unfortunately*, which means 'it is unfortunate that' in a sentence such as *unfortunately I won't be able to attend the meeting*.

hopeless ADJECTIVE **1 = pessimistic**, desperate, despairing, forlorn, in despair, abject, dejected, despondent, demoralized, defeatist, disconsolate, downhearted: *Even able pupils feel hopeless about job prospects.* OPPOSITE: hopeful **2 = impossible**, pointless, futile, useless, vain, forlorn, no-win, unattainable, impracticable, unachievable, not having a prayer: *I don't believe your situation is as hopeless as you think.* **3 = no good**, inadequate, useless *(informal)*, poor, pants *(informal)*, pathetic, inferior, incompetent, ineffectual: *I'd be hopeless at working for somebody else.* **4 = incurable**, irreversible, irreparable, lost, helpless, irremediable, past remedy, remediless: *a hopeless mess* OPPOSITE: curable

hopelessly ADVERB **1 = without hope**, desperately, in despair, despairingly, irredeemably, irremediably, beyond all hope: *hopelessly in love* **2 = completely**, totally, extremely, desperately, terribly, utterly, tremendously, awfully, impossibly, frightfully: *The story is hopelessly confusing.*

horde NOUN **= crowd**, mob, swarm, press, host, band, troop, pack, crew, drove, gang, multitude, throng

horizon NOUN **1 = skyline**, view, vista, field *or* range of vision: *The sun had already sunk below the horizon.* **2 = scope**, perspective, range, prospect, stretch, ken, sphere, realm, compass, ambit, purview: *By embracing other cultures, we actually broaden our horizons.*

horizontal ADJECTIVE **= level**, flat, plane, parallel, supine

horny ADJECTIVE **= aroused**, excited, turned on *(slang)*, randy *(informal, chiefly Brit.)*, raunchy *(slang)*, amorous, lustful

horrible ADJECTIVE **1 = dreadful**, terrible, awful, nasty, cruel, beastly *(informal)*, mean, unpleasant, ghastly *(informal)*, unkind, horrid, disagreeable: *a horrible little boy* OPPOSITE: wonderful **2 = terrible**,

'Less' and 'fewer' in Classic Literature

The controversy over *less* and *fewer* is a favourite one amongst grammatical purists. The distinction is clear, they say: *less* should only be used with uncountable nouns, which have no plural form (*less time, less money, less sense*); *fewer* should be used when the noun is countable and plural (*fewer people, fewer bananas, fewer ideas*). However, as anyone knows who has seen a '10 items or less' sign at a supermarket checkout, the distinction is often ignored in real English. Since *items* is countable and plural, the grammatically correct form of this phrase would be '10 items or fewer'. Yet speakers – and writers – often prefer *less.*

In classic literature of the eighteenth to early twentieth century, plural nouns are over three times more likely to be preceded by *fewer* than by *less*. Today's purists would find the following perfectly respectable:

> But Harriet was less humble, had **fewer scruples** than formerly. (Jane Austen)
>
> She asked **fewer questions** than before. (Henry James)
>
> There were noticeably **fewer omnibuses** and less road traffic generally. (HG Wells)

Yet there are also quite frequent examples of *less* used before a plural noun, which would be perceived as incorrect by grammatical purists:

> I have a few more sins on my soul and a few **less crowns** in my pouch. (Arthur Conan Doyle)
>
> The Honourable Mrs. Morton was now seventy, but no old lady ever showed **less signs** of advanced age. (Anthony Trollope)
>
> They had better food to eat, **less hours** of labor, more holidays ... (Jack London)

Certain plurals are more likely to be preceded by *less*; others by *fewer.* Several nineteenth-century authors (including Charles Dickens, RL Stevenson, and William Makepeace Thackeray) refer to some people or books having 'less pretensions' than others; none uses the phrase 'fewer pretensions'. On the other hand, several authors write about ideas being expressed in 'fewer words'; none uses the phrase 'less words'. One plural that is often used with *less* in modern English is *people,* perhaps because it is an irregular, and therefore less obvious, plural. However, classic writers such as Dickens, Thackeray, and Wilkie Collins always use the form *fewer people.*

In eighteenth- and nineteenth-century literature we also find evidence of a sense of *less* which has now been lost. In many cases, it means 'smaller, inferior' rather than 'fewer', and writers perceive a subtle distinction between the two:

> Many men with **fewer sympathies** for the distressed and needy, with less abilities and harder hearts ... (Charles Dickens)
>
> I went into the country ... with **no fewer or less diseases** than a jaundice, a dropsy, and an asthma (Henry Fielding)

Indeed, in some cases it is difficult to tell the difference between the two senses: the following might be interpreted as meaning either 'fewer provisions' or 'inferior provisions':

> We all approved this advice, and immediately resolved to go back that one day's journey, resolving, though we carried **less provisions**. (Daniel Defoe)

This sense of *less* is now obsolete, and has been replaced by *smaller* or *lesser*, perhaps because of possible confusion with the stigmatized use of *less* meaning 'fewer'.

awful, appalling, terrifying, shocking, grim, dreadful, revolting, fearful, obscene, ghastly, hideous, shameful, gruesome, from hell *(informal)*, grisly, horrid, repulsive, frightful, heinous, loathsome, abhorrent, abominable, hellacious *(U.S. slang)*: *Still the horrible shrieking came out of his mouth.*

horrid ADJECTIVE **1 = unpleasant**, terrible, awful, offensive, nasty, disgusting, horrible, dreadful, obscene, disagreeable, yucky *or* yukky *(slang)*, yucko *(Austral. slang)*: *What a horrid smell!* **2 = nasty**, dreadful, horrible, mean, unkind, cruel, beastly *(informal)*: *I must have been a horrid little girl.*

horrific ADJECTIVE **= horrifying**, shocking, appalling, frightening, awful, terrifying, grim, dreadful, horrendous, ghastly, from hell *(informal)*, grisly, frightful, hellacious *(U.S. slang)*

horrify VERB **1 = terrify**, alarm, frighten, scare, intimidate, petrify, terrorize, put the wind up *(informal)*, make your hair stand on end, affright: *a crime trend that will horrify all parents* **OPPOSITE:** comfort **2 = shock**, appal, disgust, dismay, sicken, outrage, gross out *(U.S. slang)*: *When I saw these figures I was horrified.* **OPPOSITE:** delight

horror NOUN **1 = terror**, fear, alarm, panic, dread, dismay, awe, fright, apprehension, consternation, trepidation: *I felt numb with horror.* **2 = hatred**, disgust, loathing, aversion, revulsion, antipathy, abomination, abhorrence, repugnance, odium, detestation: *his horror of death* **OPPOSITE:** love

horse NOUN **= nag**, mount, mare, colt, filly, stallion, gelding, jade, pony, yearling, steed *(archaic, literary)*, dobbin, moke *(Austral. slang)*, hobby *(archaic, dialect)*, yarraman *or* yarramin *(Austral.)*, gee-gee *(slang)*, cuddy *or* cuddie *(dialect, chiefly Scot.)*, studhorse *or* stud: *A small man on a grey horse had appeared.*

horse around *or* **about = play around** *or* **about**, fool about *or* around, clown, misbehave, play the fool, roughhouse *(slang)*, play the goat, monkey about *or* around, indulge in horseplay, lark about *or* around: *Later that day I was horsing around with Katie.*

▸ *related adjectives:* equestrian, equine, horsey ▸ *related noun:* equitation ▸ *name of male:* stallion ▸ *name of female:* mare ▸ *name of young:* foal, colt, filly ▸ *related mania:* hippomania ▸ *related phobia:* hippophobia

> **QUOTATIONS**
> A horse! a horse! my kingdom for a horse!
> [William Shakespeare *Richard III*]
>
> A horse is dangerous at both ends and uncomfortable in the middle
> [Ian Fleming]

> **PROVERBS**
> *Don't change horses in midstream*
> *You can take a horse to water but you cannot make him drink*
> *A nod's as good as a wink to a blind horse*
> *Nothing is so good for the inside of a man as the outside of a horse*

horseman NOUN **= rider**, equestrian

hospitable ADJECTIVE **= welcoming**, kind, friendly, liberal, generous, gracious, amicable, cordial, sociable, genial, bountiful **OPPOSITE:** inhospitable

hospitality NOUN **= welcome**, warmth, kindness, friendliness, sociability, conviviality, neighbourliness, cordiality, heartiness, hospitableness

> **QUOTATIONS**
> Be not forgetful to entertain strangers; for thereby some have entertained angels unawares
> [*Bible: Hebrews*]
>
> hospitality: the virtue which induces us to feed and lodge certain persons who are not in need of food and lodging
> [Ambrose Bierce *The Devil's Dictionary*]
>
> Welcome the coming, speed the going guest
> [Alexander Pope *Imitations of Horace*]
>
> When hospitality becomes an art, it loses its very soul
> [Max Beerbohm *And Even Now*]

host[1] *or* **hostess** NOUN **1 = master of ceremonies**, proprietor, innkeeper, landlord *or* landlady: *We were greeted by our host, a courteous man in a formal suit.* **2 = presenter**, compere *(Brit.)*, anchorman *or* anchorwoman: *I am host of a live radio programme.*
▹ VERB **= present**, introduce, compere *(Brit.)*, front *(informal)*: *She also hosts a show on St Petersburg Radio.*

> **QUOTATIONS**
> A host is like a general; it takes a mishap to reveal his genius
> [Horace *Satires*]
>
> Mankind is divisible into two great classes: hosts and guests
> [Max Beerbohm *Hosts and Guests*]

host[2] NOUN **1 = multitude**, lot, load *(informal)*, wealth, array, myriad, great quantity, large number: *a whole host of gadgets* **2 = crowd**, army, pack, drove, mob, herd, legion, swarm, horde, throng: *A host of stars from British stage and screen attended the awards ceremony.*

hostage NOUN **= captive**, prisoner, pledge, pawn, security, surety

hostile ADJECTIVE **1 = antagonistic**, anti *(informal)*, opposed, opposite, contrary, inimical, ill-disposed: *hostile to the idea of foreign intervention* **2 = unfriendly**, belligerent, antagonistic, unkind, malevolent, warlike, bellicose, inimical, rancorous, ill-disposed: *The Governor faced hostile crowds when he visited the town.* **OPPOSITE:** friendly **3 = inhospitable**, adverse, alien, uncongenial, unsympathetic, unwelcoming, unpropitious: *some of the most hostile climatic conditions in the world* **OPPOSITE:** hospitable

hostility NOUN **1 = unfriendliness**, hatred, animosity, spite, bitterness, malice, venom, antagonism, enmity, abhorrence, malevolence, detestation: *She looked at Ron with open hostility.* **OPPOSITE:** friendliness **2 = opposition**, resentment, antipathy, aversion, antagonism, ill feeling, bad blood, ill-will, animus: *hostility among traditionalists to this method of teaching history* **OPPOSITE:** approval
▹ PLURAL NOUN **= warfare**, war, fighting, conflict, combat, armed conflict, state of war: *Military chiefs agreed to cease hostilities throughout the country.* **OPPOSITE:** peace

hot ADJECTIVE **1 = heated**, burning, boiling, steaming, flaming, roasting, searing, blistering, fiery, scorching, scalding, piping hot: *Cook the meat quickly on a hot barbecue plate.* **2 = warm**, close, stifling, humid, torrid, sultry, sweltering, balmy, muggy: *It was too hot even for a gentle stroll.* **OPPOSITE:** cold **3 = spicy**, pungent, peppery, piquant, biting, sharp, acrid: *He loved hot curries.* **OPPOSITE:** mild **4 = intense**, passionate, heated, spirited, excited, fierce, lively, animated, ardent, inflamed, fervent, impassioned, fervid: *The nature of Scottishness is a matter of hot debate in Scotland.* **5 = new**, latest, fresh, recent, up to date, just out, up to the minute, bang up to date *(informal)*, hot off the press: *If you hear any hot news, tell me, won't you?* **OPPOSITE:** old **6 = popular**, hip, fashionable, cool, in demand, sought-after, must-see, in vogue: *a ticket for the hottest show in town* **OPPOSITE:** unpopular **7 = fierce**, intense, strong, keen, competitive, cut-throat: *hot competition from abroad* **8 = fiery**, violent, raging, passionate, stormy, touchy, vehement, impetuous, irascible: *His hot temper was making it difficult for others to work with him.* **OPPOSITE:** calm

hot air NOUN **= empty talk**, rant, guff *(slang)*, bombast, wind, gas *(informal)*, verbiage, claptrap *(informal)*, blather, bunkum *(chiefly U.S.)*, blether, bosh *(informal)*, tall talk *(informal)*

hotbed NOUN **= breeding ground**, nest, den

hot-headed ADJECTIVE **= volatile**, rash, fiery, reckless, precipitate, hasty, unruly, foolhardy, impetuous, hot-tempered, quick-tempered

hothouse NOUN **= greenhouse**, conservatory, glasshouse, orangery

hotly ADVERB **1 = fiercely**, passionately, angrily, vehemently, indignantly, with indignation, heatedly, impetuously: *The bank hotly denies any wrongdoing.* **2 = closely**, enthusiastically, eagerly, with enthusiasm, hotfoot: *He'd sneaked out of America hotly pursued by the CIA.*

hound VERB **1 = harass**, harry, bother, provoke, annoy, torment, hassle *(informal)*, prod, badger, persecute, pester, goad, keep after: *hounded by the press* **2 = force**, drive, pressure, push, chase, railroad *(informal)*, propel, impel, pressurize: *hounded out of office*

house NOUN **1 = home**, residence, dwelling, building, pad *(slang)*, homestead, edifice, abode, habitation, domicile, whare *(N.Z.)*: *her parents' house in Warwickshire* **2 = household**, family, ménage: *If he set his alarm clock, it would wake the whole house.* **3 = firm**, company, business, concern, organization, partnership, establishment, outfit *(informal)*: *the world's top fashion houses* **4 = assembly**, parliament, Commons, legislative body: *the joint sessions of the two parliamentary houses* **5 = restaurant**, inn, hotel, pub *(Brit. informal)*, tavern, public house, hostelry: *The house offers a couple of freshly prepared à la carte dishes.* **6 = dynasty**, line, race, tribe, clan, ancestry, lineage, family tree, kindred: *the Saudi Royal House*
▷ VERB **1 = accommodate**, board, quarter, take in, put up, lodge, harbour, billet, domicile: *Regrettably we have to house families in these inadequate flats.* **2 = contain**, keep, hold, cover, store, protect, shelter: *The building houses a collection of motorcycles and cars.* **3 = take**, accommodate, sleep, provide shelter for, give a bed to: *The building will house twelve boys and eight girls.*
on the house = free, for free *(informal)*, for nothing, free of charge, gratis, without expense: *He brought them glasses of champagne on the house.*

> **QUOTATIONS**
> A house is a machine for living in
> [Le Corbusier *Vers une architecture*]

household NOUN **= family**, home, house, ménage, family circle, ainga *(N.Z.)*: *growing up in a male-only household*
▷ MODIFIER **= domestic**, family, domiciliary: *I always do the household chores first.*

householder NOUN **= occupant**, resident, tenant, proprietor, homeowner, freeholder, leaseholder

housekeeping NOUN **= household management**, homemaking *(U.S.)*, home economy, housewifery, housecraft

housing NOUN **1 = accommodation**, homes, houses, dwellings, domiciles: *a shortage of affordable housing* **2 = case**, casing, covering, cover, shell, jacket, holder, container, capsule, sheath, encasement: *Both housings are waterproof to a depth of two metres.*

hovel NOUN **= hut**, hole, shed, cabin, den, slum, shack, shanty, whare *(N.Z.)*

hover VERB **1 = float**, fly, hang, drift, be suspended, flutter, poise: *Beautiful butterflies hovered above the wild flowers.* **2 = linger**, loiter, wait nearby, hang about *or* around *(informal)*: *Judith was hovering in the doorway.* **3 = waver**, alternate, fluctuate, haver *(Brit.)*, falter, dither *(chiefly Brit.)*, oscillate, vacillate, seesaw, swither *(Scot. dialect)*: *We hover between great hopes and great fears.*

however ADVERB **= but**, nevertheless, still, though, yet, even though, on the other hand, nonetheless, notwithstanding, anyhow, be that as it may

howl VERB **1 = bay**, cry, bark, yelp, quest *(of a hound)*: *A dog suddenly howled, baying at the moon.* **2 = cry**, shout, scream, roar, weep, yell, cry out, wail, shriek, bellow, bawl, yelp: *The baby was howling for her 3am feed.*
▷ NOUN **1 = baying**, cry, bay, bark, barking, yelp, yelping, yowl: *It was the howl of an animal crying out in hunger.* **2 = cry**, scream, roar, bay, wail, outcry, shriek, bellow, clamour, hoot, bawl, yelp, yowl: *a howl of rage*

howler NOUN **= mistake**, error, blunder, boob *(Brit. slang)*, bloomer *(Brit. informal)*, clanger *(informal)*, malapropism, schoolboy howler, booboo *(informal)*, barry *or* Barry Crocker *(Austral. slang)*

hub NOUN **= centre**, heart, focus, core, middle, focal point, pivot, nerve centre

hubbub NOUN **1 = noise**, racket, din, uproar, cacophony, pandemonium, babel, tumult, hurly-burly: *a hubbub of excited conversation from over a thousand people* **2 = hue and cry**, confusion, disturbance, riot, disorder, clamour, rumpus, bedlam, brouhaha, ruction *(informal)*, hullabaloo, ruckus *(informal)*: *the hubbub over the election*

hubris NOUN **= pride**, vanity, arrogance, conceit, self-importance, haughtiness, conceitedness

huddle VERB **1 = curl up**, crouch, hunch up, nestle, snuggle, make yourself small: *She sat huddled on the side of the bed, weeping.* **2 = crowd**, press, gather, collect, squeeze, cluster, flock, herd, throng: *strangers huddling together for warmth*
▷ NOUN **1 = crowd**, mass, bunch, cluster, heap, muddle, jumble: *a huddle of bodies, gasping for air* **2 = discussion**, conference, meeting, hui *(N.Z.)*, powwow, confab *(informal)*, korero *(N.Z.)*: *He went into a huddle with his lawyers to consider an appeal.*

hue NOUN **1 = colour**, tone, shade, dye, tint, tinge, tincture: *The same hue will look different in different lights.* **2 = aspect**, light, cast, complexion: *a comeback of such theatrical hue*

huff NOUN **= sulk**, temper, bad mood, passion, rage, pet, pique, foulie *(Austral. slang)*: *He went into a huff because he lost the game.*

hug VERB **1 = embrace**, hold (onto), cuddle, squeeze, cling, clasp, enfold, hold close, take in your arms: *They hugged each other like a couple of lost children.* **2 = follow closely**, keep close, stay near, cling to, follow the course of: *The road hugs the coast for hundreds of miles.*
▷ NOUN **= embrace**, squeeze, bear hug, clinch *(slang)*, clasp: *She leapt out of the seat, and gave him a hug.*

huge ADJECTIVE **= enormous**, great, giant, large, massive, vast, extensive, tremendous, immense, mega *(slang)*, titanic, jumbo *(informal)*, gigantic, monumental, mammoth, bulky, colossal, mountainous, stellar *(informal)*, prodigious, stupendous, gargantuan, elephantine, ginormous *(informal)*, Brobdingnagian, humongous *or* humungous *(U.S. slang)*
OPPOSITE: tiny

hugely ADVERB **= immensely**, enormously, massively, prodigiously, monumentally, stupendously

hui NOUN **= meeting**, gathering, assembly, meet, conference, congress, session, rally, convention, get-together *(informal)*, reunion, congregation, conclave, convocation, powwow

hulk NOUN **= wreck**, shell, hull, shipwreck, frame

hulking ADJECTIVE **= ungainly**, massive, lumbering, gross, awkward, clumsy, bulky, cumbersome, overgrown, unwieldy, ponderous, clunky *(informal)*, oafish, lumpish, lubberly, unco *(Austral. slang)*

hull NOUN **1 = framework**, casing, body, covering, frame, skeleton: *The hull had suffered extensive damage to the starboard side.* **2 = husk**, skin, shell, peel, pod, rind, shuck: *I soaked the hulls off lima beans.*
▷ VERB **= trim**, peel, skin, shell, husk, shuck: *Soak them in water with lemon juice for 30 minutes before hulling.*

hum VERB **1 = drone**, buzz, murmur, throb, vibrate, purr, croon, thrum, whir: *We could hear a buzz, like a bee humming.* **2 = be busy**, buzz, bustle, move, stir, pulse, be active, vibrate, pulsate: *On Saturday morning, the town hums with activity.*

human ADJECTIVE **1 = mortal**, anthropoid, manlike: *the human body*
OPPOSITE: nonhuman **2 = kind**, natural, vulnerable, kindly, understandable, humane, compassionate, considerate, approachable: *Singapore has a human side too, beside the relentless efficiency.*
OPPOSITE: inhuman
▷ NOUN **= human being**, person, individual, body, creature, mortal, man *or* woman: *The drug has not yet been tested on humans.* **OPPOSITE:** nonhuman
▸ *related prefix:* anthropo-

> **QUOTATIONS**
> Drinking when we are not thirsty and making love all year round, madam; that is all there is to distinguish us from other animals
> [Pierre-Augustin Caron de Beaumarchais *The Marriage of Figaro*]

h

> Being human signifies, for each one of us, belonging to a class, a society, a country, a continent and a civilization [Claude Lévi-Strauss *Tristes Tropiques*]

humane ADJECTIVE **= kind**, compassionate, good, kindly, understanding, gentle, forgiving, tender, mild, sympathetic, charitable, benign, clement, benevolent, lenient, merciful, good-natured, forbearing, kind-hearted **OPPOSITE:** cruel

humanitarian ADJECTIVE **1 = compassionate**, charitable, humane, benevolent, altruistic, beneficent: *They will be released as a humanitarian act.* **2 = charitable**, philanthropic, public-spirited: *a convoy of humanitarian aid from Britain*
▷ NOUN **= philanthropist**, benefactor, Good Samaritan, altruist: *I like to think of myself as a humanitarian.*

h

humanity NOUN **1 = the human race**, man, mankind, people, men, mortals, humankind, Homo sapiens: *They face charges of committing crimes against humanity.* **2 = human nature**, mortality, humanness: *It made him feel deprived of his humanity.* **3 = kindness**, charity, compassion, understanding, sympathy, mercy, tolerance, tenderness, philanthropy, benevolence, fellow feeling, benignity, brotherly love, kind-heartedness: *His speech showed great humility and humanity.*
▷ PLURAL NOUN **= arts**, liberal arts, classics, classical studies, literae humaniores: *The number of students majoring in the humanities has declined.*

> **QUOTATIONS**
> Out of the crooked timber of humanity no straight thing can ever be made
> [Immanuel Kant *Idee zu einer allgemeinen Geschichte in welt bürgerlicher Absicht*]
>
> We're all of us guinea pigs in the laboratory of God. Humanity is just a work in progress
> [Tennessee Williams *Camino Real*]

humble ADJECTIVE **1 = modest**, meek, unassuming, unpretentious, submissive, self-effacing, unostentatious: *Andy was a humble, courteous and gentle man.*
OPPOSITE: proud **2 = lowly**, common, poor, mean, low, simple, ordinary, modest, obscure, commonplace, insignificant, unimportant, unpretentious, undistinguished, plebeian, low-born: *He came from a fairly humble, poor background.*
OPPOSITE: distinguished
▷ VERB **= humiliate**, shame, disgrace, break, reduce, lower, sink, crush, put down *(slang)*, bring down, subdue, degrade, demean, chagrin, chasten, mortify, debase, put (someone) in their place, abase, take down a peg *(informal)*, abash: *the little car company that humbled the industry giants*
OPPOSITE: exalt

humbly ADVERB **= meekly**, modestly, respectfully, cap in hand, diffidently, deferentially, submissively, unassumingly, obsequiously, subserviently, on bended knee, servilely

humbug NOUN **= nonsense**, rubbish, trash, hypocrisy, cant, malarkey, baloney *(informal)*, claptrap *(informal)*, quackery, eyewash *(informal)*, charlatanry

humdrum ADJECTIVE **= dull**, ordinary, boring, routine, commonplace, mundane, tedious, dreary, banal, tiresome, monotonous, uneventful, uninteresting, mind-numbing, ho-hum *(informal)*, repetitious, wearisome, unvaried
OPPOSITE: exciting

humid ADJECTIVE **= damp**, sticky, moist, wet, steamy, sultry, dank, clammy, muggy **OPPOSITE:** dry

humidity NOUN **= damp**, moisture, dampness, wetness, moistness, sogginess, dankness, clamminess, mugginess, humidness

humiliate VERB **= embarrass**, shame, humble, crush, disgrace, put down, subdue, degrade, chagrin, chasten, mortify, debase, discomfit, bring low, put (someone) in their place, take the wind out of someone's sails, abase, take down a peg *(informal)*, abash, make (someone) eat humble pie
OPPOSITE: honour

humiliating ADJECTIVE
= embarrassing, shaming, humbling, mortifying, crushing, disgracing, degrading, ignominious, toe-curling *(slang)*, cringe-making *(Brit. informal)*, cringeworthy *(Brit. informal)*, barro *(Austral. slang)*

humiliation NOUN
= embarrassment, shame, disgrace, humbling, put-down, degradation, affront, indignity, chagrin, ignominy, dishonour, mortification, loss of face, abasement, self-abasement

humility NOUN **= modesty**, diffidence, meekness, submissiveness, servility, self-abasement, humbleness, lowliness, unpretentiousness, lack of pride **OPPOSITE:** pride

> **QUOTATIONS**
> Humility is the first of the virtues – for other people
> [Oliver Wendell Holmes *The Professor at the Breakfast Table*]
>
> One may be humble out of pride
> [Montaigne *Essais*]
>
> He that humbleth himself wishes to be exalted
> [Friedrich Nietzsche *Human, All Too Human*]
>
> The first test of a truly great man is his humility
> [John Ruskin *Modern Painters*]
>
> For whosoever exalteth himself shall be abased; and he that humbleth himself shall be exalted
> [*Bible: St. Luke*]

humorist NOUN **= comedian**, comic, wit, eccentric, wag, joker, card *(informal)*, jester, dag *(N.Z. informal)*, funny man

humorous ADJECTIVE **= funny**, comic, amusing, entertaining, witty, merry, hilarious, ludicrous, laughable, farcical, whimsical, comical, droll, facetious, jocular, side-splitting, waggish, jocose **OPPOSITE:** serious

humour NOUN **1 = comedy**, funniness, fun, amusement, funny side, jocularity, facetiousness, ludicrousness, drollery, comical aspect: *She couldn't ignore the humour of the situation.* **OPPOSITE:** seriousness **2 = mood**, spirits, temper, disposition, frame of mind: *Could that have been the source of his good humour?* **3 = joking**, jokes, comedy, wit, gags *(informal)*, farce, jesting, jests, wisecracks *(informal)*, witticisms, wittiness: *The film has lots of adult humour.*
▷ VERB **= indulge**, accommodate, go along with, spoil, flatter, pamper, gratify, pander to, mollify, cosset, fawn on: *Most of the time he humoured her for an easy life.* **OPPOSITE:** oppose

BODILY HUMOURS

black bile	blood
yellow bile	phlegm

> **QUOTATIONS**
> Humour is by far the most significant activity of the human brain
> [Edward De Bono]
>
> Humor brings insight and tolerance. Irony brings a deeper and less friendly understanding
> [Agnes Repplier *In Pursuit of Laughter*]
>
> The secret source of humor itself is not joy but sorrow. There is no humor in heaven
> [Mark Twain *Following the Equator*]
>
> There are men so philosophical that they can see humor in their own toothaches. But there has never lived a man so philosophical that he could see the toothache in his own humor
> [H.L. Mencken *A Mencken Chrestomathy*]
>
> There seems to be no lengths to which humorless people will not go to analyze humor. It seems to worry them
> [Robert Benchley *What Does It Mean?*]
>
> Humour is falling downstairs if you do it while in the act of warning your wife not to
> [Kenneth Bird]
>
> Humour is emotional chaos remembered in tranquillity
> [James Thurber]

humourless ADJECTIVE **= serious**, intense, solemn, straight, dry, dour, unfunny, po-faced, unsmiling, heavy-going, unamused, unamusing

hump NOUN **= lump**, bump, projection, bulge, mound, hunch, knob, protuberance, protrusion: *The path goes over a large hump by a tree.*
▷ VERB **= carry**, lug, heave, hoist, shoulder: *Charlie humped his rucksack up the stairs.*

hunch NOUN **= feeling**, idea, impression, suspicion, intuition, premonition, inkling, presentiment: *I had a hunch that we would work well together.*
▷ VERB **= crouch**, bend, stoop, curve, arch, huddle, draw in, squat, hump: *He hunched over the map to read the small print.*

hunger NOUN **1 = appetite**, emptiness, voracity, hungriness, ravenousness: *Hunger is the body's sign that blood sugar is too low.* **2 = starvation**, famine, malnutrition, undernourishment: *Three hundred people are dying of hunger every day.* **3 = desire**, appetite, craving, yen *(informal)*, ache, lust, yearning, itch, thirst, greediness: *He has a hunger for success that seems bottomless.*
hunger for *or* **after something = want**, desire, crave, hope for, long for, wish for, yearn for, pine for, hanker after, ache for, thirst after, itch after: *He hungered for adventure.*

> **QUOTATIONS**
> There's no sauce in the world like hunger
> [Miguel de Cervantes *Don Quixote*]

> **PROVERBS**
> *Hunger drives the wolf from the wood*

hungry ADJECTIVE **1 = starving**, ravenous, famished, starved, empty, hollow, voracious, peckish *(informal, chiefly Brit.)*, famishing: *My friend was hungry, so we went to get some food.* **2 = eager**, keen, craving, yearning, greedy, avid, desirous, covetous, athirst: *I left Oxford in 1961 hungry to be a critic.*

hunk NOUN **= lump**, piece, chunk, block, mass, wedge, slab, nugget, wodge *(Brit. informal)*, gobbet

hunt VERB **= stalk**, track, chase, pursue, trail, hound, gun for: *Her irate husband was hunting her lover with a gun.*
▷ NOUN **= search**, hunting, investigation, chase, pursuit, quest: *The couple had helped in the hunt for the toddlers.*
hunt for something *or* **someone = search for**, look for, try to find, seek for, forage for, rummage for, scour for, look high and low, fossick for *(Austral. & N.Z.)*, go in quest of, ferret about for: *A forensic team was hunting for clues.*

hunted ADJECTIVE **= harassed**, desperate, harried, tormented, stricken, distraught, persecuted, terror-stricken

hunter NOUN **= huntsman** *or* **huntress**, Diana, Herne, Orion, Nimrod, jaeger *(rare)*, Artemis, sportsman *or* sportswoman

hurdle NOUN **1 = obstacle**, block, difficulty, barrier, handicap, hazard, complication, snag, uphill *(S. African)*, obstruction, stumbling block, impediment, hindrance: *The weather will be the biggest hurdle.* **2 = fence**, wall, hedge, block, barrier, barricade: *The horse dived at the hurdle and clipped the top.*

hurl VERB **= throw**, fling, chuck *(informal)*, send, fire, project, launch, cast, pitch, shy, toss, propel, sling, heave, let fly (with)

hurly-burly NOUN **= commotion**, confusion, chaos, turmoil, disorder, upheaval, furore, uproar, turbulence, pandemonium, bedlam, tumult, hubbub, brouhaha **OPPOSITE:** order

hurricane NOUN **= storm**, gale, tornado, cyclone, typhoon, tempest, twister *(U.S. informal)*, windstorm, willy-willy *(Austral.)*

hurried ADJECTIVE **1 = hasty**, quick, brief, rushed, short, swift, speedy, precipitate, quickie *(informal)*, breakneck: *They had a hurried breakfast, then left.* **2 = rushed**, perfunctory, hectic, speedy, superficial, hasty, cursory, slapdash: *a hurried overnight redrafting of the text*

hurriedly ADVERB **= hastily**, quickly, briskly, speedily, in a rush, at the double, hurry-scurry

hurry VERB **1 = rush**, fly, dash, barrel (along) *(informal, chiefly U.S. & Canad.)*, scurry, scoot, burn rubber *(informal)*: *Claire hurried along the road.* **OPPOSITE:** dawdle **2 = make haste**, rush, lose no time, get a move on *(informal)*, step on it *(informal)*, get your skates on *(informal)*, crack on *(informal)*: *There was no longer any reason to hurry.* **3** *(sometimes with* **up***)* **= speed (up)**, accelerate, hasten, quicken, hustle, urge, push on, goad, expedite: *The President's attempt to hurry the process of independence.* **OPPOSITE:** slow down
▷ NOUN **= rush**, haste, speed, urgency, bustle, flurry, commotion, precipitation, quickness, celerity, promptitude: *the hurry of people wanting to get home* **OPPOSITE:** slowness

hurt VERB **1 = injure**, damage, wound, cut, disable, bruise, scrape, impair, gash: *He had hurt his back in an accident.* **OPPOSITE:** heal **2 = ache**, be sore, be painful, burn, smart, sting, throb, be tender: *His collar bone only hurt when he lifted his arm.* **3 = harm**, injure, molest, ill-treat, maltreat, lay a finger on: *Did they hurt you?* **4 = upset**, distress, pain, wound, annoy, sting, grieve, afflict, sadden, cut to the quick, aggrieve: *I'll go. I've hurt you enough.*
▷ NOUN **1 = distress**, suffering, pain, grief, misery, agony, sadness, sorrow, woe, anguish, heartache, wretchedness: *I was full of jealousy and hurt.* **OPPOSITE:** happiness **2 = harm**, trouble, damage, wrong, loss, injury, misfortune, mischief, affliction: *I am sorry for any hurt that it may have caused.*
▷ ADJECTIVE **1 = injured**, wounded, damaged, harmed, cut, scratched, bruised, scarred, scraped, grazed: *They were dazed but did not seem to be badly hurt.* **OPPOSITE:** healed **2 = upset**, pained, injured, wounded, sad, crushed, offended, aggrieved, miffed *(informal)*, rueful, piqued, tooshie *(Austral. slang)*: *He gave me a slightly hurt look.* **OPPOSITE:** calmed

hurtful ADJECTIVE **= unkind**, upsetting, distressing, mean, cutting, damaging, wounding, nasty, cruel, destructive, harmful, malicious, mischievous, detrimental, pernicious, spiteful, prejudicial, injurious, disadvantageous, maleficent

hurtle VERB **= rush**, charge, race, shoot, fly, speed, tear, crash, plunge, barrel (along) *(informal, chiefly U.S. & Canad.)*, scramble, spurt, stampede, scoot, burn rubber *(informal)*, rush headlong, go hell for leather *(informal)*

husband NOUN **= partner**, man *(informal)*, spouse, hubby *(informal)*, mate, old man *(informal)*, bridegroom, significant other *(U.S. informal)*, better half *(humorous)*: *Eva married her husband Jack in 1957.*
▷ VERB **= conserve**, budget, use sparingly, save, store, hoard, economize on, use economically, manage thriftily: *Husbanding precious resources was part of rural life.*
OPPOSITE: squander

> **QUOTATIONS**
> Thy husband is thy lord, thy life, thy keeper,
> Thy head, thy sovereign; one that cares for thee,
> And for thy maintenance commits his body
> To painful labour both by sea and land
> [William Shakespeare *The Taming of the Shrew*]
>
> An archaeologist is the best husband any woman can have; the older she gets, the more interested he is in her
> [Agatha Christie]
>
> Being a husband is a full-time job. That is why so many husbands fail. They cannot give their entire attention to it
> [Arnold Bennett *The Title*]
>
> An early-rising man ... a good spouse but a bad husband
> [Gabriel García Márquez *In Evil Hour*]
>
> A husband is what is left of the lover after the nerve has been extracted
> [Helen Rowland *A Guide to Men*]
>
> The majority of husbands remind me of an orang-utan trying to play the violin
> [Honoré de Balzac *The Physiology of Marriage*]

h

> A good husband should be deaf and a good wife blind
> [*French proverb*]

husbandry NOUN **1 = farming**, agriculture, cultivation, land management, tillage, agronomy: *The current meagre harvest suggests poor husbandry.* **2 = thrift**, economy, good housekeeping, frugality, careful management: *These people consider themselves adept at financial husbandry.*

hush VERB **= quieten**, still, silence, suppress, mute, muzzle, shush: *She tried to hush her noisy father.*
▷ NOUN **= quiet**, silence, calm, still (*poetic*), peace, tranquillity, stillness, peacefulness: *A hush fell over the crowd.*
hush something up = cover up, conceal, suppress, sit on (*informal*), squash, smother, keep secret, sweep under the carpet (*informal*), draw a veil over, keep dark: *The authorities have tried to hush it up.*

hush-hush ADJECTIVE **= secret**, confidential, classified, top-secret, restricted, under wraps

husk NOUN **= rind**, shell, hull, covering, bark, chaff, shuck

husky ADJECTIVE **1 = hoarse**, rough, harsh, raucous, rasping, croaking, gruff, throaty, guttural, croaky: *His voice was husky with grief.* **2 = muscular**, powerful, strapping, rugged, hefty, burly, stocky, beefy (*informal*), brawny, thickset: *a very husky young man, built like a football player*

hustle VERB **1 = jostle**, force, push, crowd, rush, hurry, thrust, elbow, shove, jog, bustle, impel: *The guards hustled Harry out of the car.* **2 = hurry**, hasten, get a move on (*informal*): *You'll have to hustle if you're to get home for supper.*

hut NOUN **1 = cabin**, shack, shanty, hovel, whare (*N.Z.*): *a mud hut with no electricity, gas, or running water* **2 = shed**, outhouse, lean-to, lockup: *Never leave a garage or garden hut unlocked.*

hybrid NOUN **1 = crossbreed**, cross, mixture, compound, composite, mule, amalgam, mongrel, half-breed, half-blood: *a hybrid between watermint and spearmint; best champion Mule or Hybrid* **2 = mixture**, compound, composite, amalgam: *a hybrid of solid and liquid fuel*

hygiene NOUN **= cleanliness**, sanitation, disinfection, sterility, sanitary measures, hygienics

hygienic ADJECTIVE **= clean**, healthy, sanitary, pure, sterile, salutary, disinfected, germ-free, aseptic **OPPOSITE:** dirty

hymn NOUN **1 = religious song**, song of praise, carol, chant, anthem, psalm, paean, canticle, doxology: *Readings were accompanied by an old Irish hymn.* **2 = song of praise**, anthem, paean: *a hymn to freedom and rebellion*

hype NOUN **= publicity**, promotion, build-up, plugging (*informal*), puffing, racket, razzmatazz (*slang*), brouhaha, ballyhoo (*informal*)

hyperbole NOUN **= exaggeration**, hype (*informal*), overstatement, enlargement, magnification, amplification

hypnotic ADJECTIVE **= mesmeric**, soothing, narcotic, opiate, soporific, sleep-inducing, somniferous

hypnotize VERB **1 = mesmerize**, put in a trance, put to sleep: *The ability to hypnotize yourself can be learnt in a single session.* **2 = fascinate**, absorb, entrance, magnetize, spellbind: *He's hypnotized by that black hair and that white face.*

hypochondriac NOUN **= neurotic**, valetudinarian, cyberchondriac

hypocrisy NOUN **= insincerity**, pretence, deceit, deception, cant, duplicity, dissembling, falsity, imposture, sanctimoniousness, phoniness (*informal*), deceitfulness, pharisaism, speciousness, two-facedness, phariseeism
OPPOSITE: sincerity

> **QUOTATIONS**
> Hypocrisy is a tribute which vice pays to virtue
> [Duc de la Rochefoucauld *Réflexions ou Sentences et Maximes Morales*]
>
> I hope you have not been leading a double life, pretending to be wicked and being really good all the time. That would be hypocrisy
> [Oscar Wilde *The Importance of Being Earnest*]
>
> Why beholdest thou the mote that is in thy brother's eye, but considerest not the beam that is in thine own eye?
> [*Bible: St. Matthew*]
>
> hypocrisy, the only evil that walks
> Invisible, except to God alone
> [John Milton *Paradise Lost*]

hypocrite NOUN **= fraud**, deceiver, pretender, charlatan, impostor, pharisee, dissembler, Tartuffe, Pecksniff, Holy Willie, whited sepulchre, phoney *or* phony (*informal*)

> **QUOTATIONS**
> No man is a hypocrite in his pleasures
> [Dr. Johnson]
>
> Ye are like unto whited sepulchres
> [*Bible: St. Matthew*]
>
> Their sighan', cantan', grace-proud faces,
> Their three-mile prayers, and half-mile graces
> [Robert Burns *To the Rev. John M'Math*]

hypocritical ADJECTIVE **= insincere**, false, fraudulent, hollow, deceptive, spurious, two-faced, deceitful, sanctimonious, specious, duplicitous, dissembling, canting, Janus-faced, pharisaical, phoney *or* phony (*informal*)

hypodermic NOUN **= syringe**, needle, works (*slang*)

hypothesis NOUN **= theory**, premise, proposition, assumption, thesis, postulate, supposition, premiss

> **QUOTATIONS**
> It is a good morning exercise for a research scientist to discard a pet hypothesis every day before breakfast
> [Konrad Lorenz *On Aggression*]

hypothetical ADJECTIVE **= theoretical**, supposed, academic, assumed, imaginary, speculative, putative, conjectural **OPPOSITE:** real

hysteria NOUN **= frenzy**, panic, madness, agitation, delirium, hysterics, unreason

hysterical ADJECTIVE **1 = frenzied**, mad, frantic, raving, distracted, distraught, crazed, uncontrollable, berserk, overwrought, convulsive, beside yourself, berko (*Austral. slang*): *I slapped her because she became hysterical.* **OPPOSITE:** calm **2 = hilarious**, uproarious, side-splitting, farcical, comical, wildly funny: *a hysterical, satirical revue* **OPPOSITE:** serious

Ii

ice NOUN
break the ice = **kick off** *(informal)*, lead the way, take the plunge *(informal)*, make a start, begin a relationship, initiate the proceedings, start *or* set the ball rolling *(informal)*: *The main purpose of his trip was to break the ice.*
skate on thin ice = **be at risk**, be vulnerable, be unsafe, be in jeopardy, be out on a limb, be open to attack, be sticking your neck out *(informal)*: *I had skated on thin ice for long enough.*

icy ADJECTIVE **1** = **cold**, freezing, bitter, biting, raw, chill, chilling, arctic, chilly, frosty, glacial, ice-cold, frozen over, frost-bound: *An icy wind blew across the moor.* **OPPOSITE:** hot **2** = **slippery**, glassy, slippy *(informal, dialect)*, like a sheet of glass, rimy: *an icy road*
3 = **unfriendly**, cold, distant, hostile, forbidding, indifferent, aloof, stony, steely, frosty, glacial, frigid, unwelcoming: *His response was icy.*
OPPOSITE: friendly

idea NOUN **1** = **plan**, scheme, proposal, design, theory, strategy, method, solution, suggestion, recommendation, proposition: *It's a good idea to keep a stock of tins in the cupboard.* **2** = **notion**, thought, view, understanding, teaching, opinion, belief, conclusion, hypothesis, impression, conviction, judgment, interpretation, sentiment, doctrine, conception, viewpoint: *Some of his ideas about democracy are entirely his own.*
3 = **impression**, estimate, guess, hint, notion, clue, conjecture, surmise, inkling, approximation, intimation, ballpark figure: *This graph will give you some idea of levels of ability.*
4 = **understanding**, thought, view, sense, opinion, concept, impression, judgment, perception, conception, abstraction, estimation: *By the end of the week you will have a clearer idea of the system.* **5** = **intention**, aim, purpose, object, end, plan, reason, goal, design, objective, motive: *The idea is to help lower-income families to buy their homes.*

QUOTATIONS
Nothing is more dangerous than an idea, when you have only one idea
[Alain *Propos sur la religion*]

A stand can be made against invasion by an army; no stand can be made against invasion by an idea
[Victor Hugo *Histoire d'une Crime*]

It is better to entertain an idea than to take it home to live with you for the rest of your life
[Randall Jarrell *Pictures from an Institution*]

Right now it's only a notion, but I think I can get the money to make it into a concept, and later turn it into an idea
[Woody Allen *Annie Hall*]

USAGE
It is usually considered correct to say that someone has *the idea of doing something*, rather than *the idea to do something*. For example, you would say *he had the idea of taking a holiday*, not *he had the idea to take a holiday*.

ideal NOUN **1** *(often plural)* = **principle**, standard, ideology, morals, conviction, integrity, scruples, probity, moral value, rectitude, sense of duty, sense of honour, uprightness: *The party has drifted too far from its socialist ideals.* **2** = **epitome**, standard, dream, pattern, perfection, last word, paragon, nonpareil, standard of perfection: *Throughout his career she remained his feminine ideal.* **3** = **model**, example, criterion, prototype, paradigm, archetype, exemplar: *the ideal of beauty in those days*
▷ ADJECTIVE **1** = **perfect**, best, model, classic, supreme, ultimate, archetypal, exemplary, consummate, optimal, quintessential: *She decided I was the ideal person to take over this job.*
OPPOSITE: imperfect **2** = **imaginary**, impractical, Utopian, romantic, fantastic, fabulous, poetic, visionary, fairy-tale, mythical, unreal, fanciful, unattainable, ivory-towered, imagal *(Psychoanalysis)*: *Their ideal society collapsed around them in revolution.*
OPPOSITE: actual **3** = **hypothetical**, academic, intellectual, abstract, theoretical, speculative, conceptual, metaphysical, transcendental, notional: *an ideal economic world*

QUOTATIONS
The ideal has many names, and beauty is but one of them
[W. Somerset Maugham *Cakes and Ale*]

idealist NOUN = **romantic**, visionary, dreamer, Utopian

idealistic ADJECTIVE = **perfectionist**, romantic, optimistic, visionary, Utopian, quixotic, impracticable, starry-eyed **OPPOSITE:** realistic

idealize VERB = **romanticize**, glorify, exalt, worship, magnify, ennoble, deify, put on a pedestal, apotheosize

ideally ADVERB = **in a perfect world**, in theory, preferably, if possible, all things being equal, under the best of circumstances, if you had your way, in a Utopia

identical ADJECTIVE = **alike**, like, the same, matching, equal, twin, equivalent, corresponding, duplicate, synonymous, indistinguishable, analogous, interchangeable, a dead ringer *(slang)*, the dead spit *(informal)*, like two peas in a pod
OPPOSITE: different

identifiable ADJECTIVE
= **recognizable**, noticeable, known, unmistakable, discernible, detectable, distinguishable, ascertainable

identification NOUN **1** = **discovery**, recognition, determining, establishment, diagnosis, confirmation, detection, divination: *Early identification of the disease can prevent death.* **2** = **recognition**, naming, labelling, distinguishing, cataloguing, classifying, confirmation, pinpointing, establishment of identity: *Officials are awaiting positive identification before proceeding.* **3** = **connection**, relationship, link, association, tie, partnership, affinity, familiarity, interconnection, interrelation: *There is a close identification of nationhood with language.* **4** = **understanding**, relationship, involvement, unity, sympathy, empathy, rapport, fellow feeling: *She had an intense identification with animals.* **5** = **ID**, papers, credentials, licence, warrant, identity card, proof of identity, photocard, letters of introduction: *I'll need to see some identification.*

identify VERB **1** = **recognize**, place, name, remember, spot, label, flag, catalogue, tag, diagnose, classify, make out, pinpoint, recollect, put your finger on *(informal)*: *I tried to identify her perfume.* **2** = **establish**, spot, confirm, finger *(informal, chiefly U.S.)*, demonstrate, pick out, single out, certify, verify, validate, mark out, substantiate, corroborate, flag up: *Police have already identified around ten suspects.*
identify something *or* **someone with something** *or* **someone** = **equate with**, associate with, think of in connection with, put in the same category as: *Audiences identify her with roles depicting sweet, passive women.*
identify with someone = **relate to**, understand, respond to, feel for, ally with, empathize with, speak the same language as, put yourself in the place *or* shoes of, see through another's eyes, be on the same wavelength as: *She would only play the role if she could identify with the character.*

identity NOUN **= individuality**, self, character, personality, existence, distinction, originality, peculiarity, uniqueness, oneness, singularity, separateness, distinctiveness, selfhood, particularity

ideology NOUN **= belief(s)**, ideas, principles, ideals, opinion, philosophy, doctrine, creed, dogma, tenets, world view, credence, articles of faith, Weltanschauung *(German)*

idiocy NOUN **= foolishness**, insanity, lunacy, tomfoolery, inanity, imbecility, senselessness, cretinism, fatuity, abject stupidity, asininity, fatuousness **OPPOSITE:** wisdom

idiom NOUN **1 = phrase**, expression, turn of phrase, locution, set phrase: *Proverbs and idioms may become worn with over-use.* **2 = language**, talk, style, usage, jargon, vernacular, parlance, mode of expression: *I was irritated by his use of archaic idiom.*

i

idiosyncrasy NOUN **= peculiarity**, habit, characteristic, quirk, eccentricity, oddity, mannerism, affectation, trick, singularity, personal trait

idiosyncratic ADJECTIVE **= distinctive**, special, individual, typical, distinguishing, distinct, peculiar, individualistic

idiot NOUN **= fool**, jerk *(slang, chiefly U.S. & Canad.)*, ass, plank *(Brit. slang)*, charlie *(Brit. informal)*, berk *(Brit. slang)*, wally *(slang)*, prat *(slang)*, plonker *(slang)*, moron, geek *(slang)*, twit *(informal, chiefly Brit.)*, chump, imbecile, cretin, oaf, simpleton, airhead *(slang)*, dimwit *(informal)*, dipstick *(Brit. slang)*, gonzo *(slang)*, schmuck *(U.S. slang)*, dork *(slang)*, nitwit *(informal)*, blockhead, divvy *(Brit. slang)*, pillock *(Brit. slang)*, halfwit, nincompoop, dweeb *(U.S. slang)*, putz *(U.S. slang)*, eejit *(Scot. & Irish)*, dumb-ass *(slang)*, dunderhead, numpty *(Scot. informal)*, doofus *(slang, chiefly U.S.)*, lamebrain *(informal)*, mooncalf, nerd *or* nurd *(slang)*, numbskull *or* numskull, galah *(Austral. & N.Z. informal)*, dorba *or* dorb *(Austral. slang)*, bogan *(Austral. slang)*, dill *(Austral. & N.Z. informal)*

idiotic ADJECTIVE **= foolish**, crazy, stupid, dumb *(informal)*, daft *(informal)*, insane, lunatic, senseless, foolhardy, inane, fatuous, loopy *(informal)*, crackpot *(informal)*, moronic, imbecile, unintelligent, asinine, imbecilic, braindead *(informal)*, harebrained, dumb-ass *(slang)*, halfwitted **OPPOSITE:** wise

idle ADJECTIVE **1 = unoccupied**, unemployed, redundant, jobless, out of work, out of action, inactive, at leisure, between jobs, unwaged, at a loose end: *Employees have been idle for almost a month now.* **OPPOSITE:** occupied **2 = unused**, stationary, inactive, out of order, ticking over, gathering dust, mothballed, out of service, out of action *or* operation: *Now the machine is lying idle.* **3 = lazy**, slow, slack, sluggish, lax, negligent, inactive, inert, lethargic, indolent, lackadaisical, good-for-nothing, remiss, workshy, slothful, shiftless: *I've never met such an idle bunch of workers!* **OPPOSITE:** busy **4 = useless**, vain, pointless, hopeless, unsuccessful, ineffective, worthless, futile, fruitless, unproductive, abortive, ineffectual, groundless, of no use, valueless, disadvantageous, unavailing, otiose, of no avail, profitless, bootless: *It would be idle to pretend the system is worthless.* **OPPOSITE:** useful **5 = trivial**, superficial, insignificant, frivolous, silly, unnecessary, irrelevant, foolish, unhelpful, flippant, puerile, flighty, ill-considered, empty-headed, nugatory: *He kept up the idle chatter for another five minutes.* **OPPOSITE:** meaningful
▷ VERB *(often with* **away***)* **= fritter**, while, waste, fool, lounge, potter, loaf, dally, loiter, dawdle, laze: *He idled the time away in dreamy thought.*

idleness NOUN **1 = inactivity**, unemployment, leisure, inaction, time on your hands: *Idleness is a very bad thing for human nature.* **2 = loafing**, inertia, sloth, pottering, trifling, laziness, time-wasting, lazing, torpor, sluggishness, skiving *(Brit. slang)*, vegetating, dilly-dallying *(informal)*, shiftlessness: *Idleness and incompetence are not inbred in our workers.*

> **QUOTATIONS**
> Idleness is the only refuge of weak minds
> [Lord Chesterfield *Letters to his Son*]

idly ADVERB **= lazily**, casually, passively, languidly, unthinkingly, sluggishly, languorously, lethargically, apathetically, indolently, inertly, lackadaisically, inactively, shiftlessly, slothfully **OPPOSITE:** energetically

idol NOUN **1 = hero**, superstar, pin-up, favourite, pet, darling, beloved *(slang)*, fave *(informal)*: *They cheered as they caught sight of their idol.* **2 = graven image**, god, image, deity, pagan symbol: *They shaped the substance into idols that were eaten ceremoniously.*

idolize VERB **= worship**, love, adore, admire, revere, glorify, exalt, look up to, venerate, hero-worship, deify, bow down before, dote upon, apotheosize, worship to excess

idyllic ADJECTIVE **= heavenly**, idealized, ideal, charming, peaceful, pastoral, picturesque, rustic, Utopian, halcyon, out of this world, unspoiled, arcadian

if CONJUNCTION **1 = provided**, assuming, given that, providing, allowing, admitting, supposing, granting, in case, presuming, on the assumption that, on condition that, as long as: *If you would like to make a donation, please enclose a cheque.* **2 = when**, whenever, every time, any time: *She gets very upset if I exclude her from anything.* **3 = whether**: *He asked if I had left with you, and I said no.*
▷ NOUN **= doubt**, condition, uncertainty, provision, constraint, hesitation, vagueness, stipulation: *This business is full of ifs.*

> **PROVERBS**
> *If ifs and ands were pots and pans there'd be no need for tinkers*

iffy ADJECTIVE **= uncertain**, doubtful, unpredictable, conditional, undecided, up in the air, problematical, chancy *(informal)*, in the lap of the gods

ignite VERB **1 = catch fire**, burn, burst into flames, fire, inflame, flare up, take fire: *The blast was caused by pockets of methane gas which ignited.* **2 = set fire to**, light, set alight, torch, kindle, touch off, put a match to *(informal)*: *The bombs ignited a fire which destroyed some 60 houses.*

ignoble ADJECTIVE **1 = dishonourable**, low, base, mean, petty, infamous, degraded, craven, disgraceful, shabby, vile, degenerate, abject, unworthy, shameless, despicable, heinous, dastardly, contemptible, wretched: *an ignoble episode from their country's past* **2 = lowly**, mean, low, base, common, peasant, vulgar, plebeian, humble, lowborn *(rare)*, baseborn *(archaic)*: *They wanted to spare him the shame of an ignoble birth.*

ignominious ADJECTIVE **= humiliating**, disgraceful, shameful, sorry, scandalous, abject, despicable, mortifying, undignified, disreputable, dishonourable, inglorious, discreditable, indecorous **OPPOSITE:** honourable

ignominy NOUN **= disgrace**, shame, humiliation, contempt, discredit, stigma, disrepute, dishonour, infamy, mortification, bad odour **OPPOSITE:** honour

ignorance NOUN **1 = lack of education**, stupidity, foolishness, blindness, illiteracy, benightedness, unenlightenment, unintelligence, mental darkness: *In my ignorance, I had never heard of R and B music.* **OPPOSITE:** knowledge **2** *(with* **of***)* **= unawareness of**, inexperience of, unfamiliarity with, innocence of, unconsciousness of, greenness about, oblivion about, nescience of *(literary)*: *a complete ignorance of non-European history*

> **QUOTATIONS**
> No more; where ignorance is bliss,
> 'Tis folly to be wise
> [Thomas Gray *Ode on a Distant Prospect of Eton College*]
>
> If ignorance is indeed bliss, it is a very low grade of the article
> [Tehyi Hsieh *Chinese Epigrams Inside Out and Proverbs*]
>
> Ignorance is not bliss – it is oblivion
> [Philip Wylie *Generation of Vipers*]

The Language of Louisa May Alcott

American novelist Louisa May Alcott (1832–88) is best known for writing the children's novel *Little Women* and its sequels. But she also wrote other, quite different works; at the time, one of those written under the pen name AM Barnard was thought too sensationalist for publication.

Alcott came from an unconventional family that had strong moral and philosophical ideas about society, responsible living, the rights of women, and the wrongness of slavery, many of which they tried to put into effect in their lives and in the schools set up by her philosopher father. He had a particular enthusiasm for Bunyan's *Pilgrim's Progress*, a work to which many allusions are made in *Little Women* as the characters strive to become better people. *Little Women* draws strongly and appealingly on Louisa May Alcott's home life, on the life lessons she learnt in it, and on the characters of her, her mother, and sisters.

Written in normal, everyday English with few occurrences of obvious Americanisms such as *gotten*, and a good deal of natural-sounding conversation advancing the story, *Little Women* and Alcott's other children's books contain little lessons in good living, moral values, striving to overcome one's faults, and the importance of fairness, unselfishness, and work for the benefit of all. With all these lofty aims, it is no accident that *try* and *help* are common verbs in Alcott:

> I resolved if I lived I'd **try** at least to be less selfish, and make some one happier for my being in the world.

> Don't you feel that it is pleasanter to **help** one another, to have daily duties which make leisure sweet when it comes, and to bear and forbear, that home may be comfortable and lovely to us all?

Although the Alcotts lived in poverty much of the time and the young Louisa, like *Little Women*'s Jo and Meg, had to work to bring money into the coffers, in her books there are many references to money and possessions not bringing happiness, to the importance of work and using time well, and to the desirability of counting one's blessings:

> Have regular hours for work and play, make each day both useful and pleasant, and prove that you understand the worth of time by employing it well. Then youth will be delightful, old age will bring few regrets, and life become a beautiful success, in spite of poverty.

> So they asked an old woman what spell they could use to make them happy, and she said, 'When you feel discontented, think over your blessings, and be grateful.'

Many of the books contain negative references to smoking and drinking – in real life Alcott campaigned for temperance – and there are numerous references to temptation:

> You know as well as I do; your mother doesn't like it [smoking], and it's a bad habit, for it wastes money and does you no good.

> But **drinking** is a more serious thing, and leads to worse harm than any that can afflict your body alone.

Plain is a common adjective in Alcott's work, whether it is describing clothes, food, furniture, surroundings, or people. It is never negative and usually very positive. Plain faces are made beautiful by their expressions, while people look attractive in their plain clothes. *Simple*, too, occurs often and with similar positive connotations; in a description of another author's work Alcott writes:

> ... suggestive, pleasing thoughts are unfolded on every page; the reflective and descriptive passages are natural, **simple**, and exquisitely finished.

Interestingly, Amy's malapropistic and inaccurate attempts at using *good words* in *Little Women* draw the following reaction from Meg:

> 'I like your nice manners and refined ways of speaking, when you don't try to be elegant. But your absurd words are as bad as Jo's slang.'

The plain, readable style of Louisa May Alcott's work is clearly exactly what she was aiming at.

Ignorance, the stem and root of all evil
[Plato]

What we call evil is simply ignorance bumping its head in the dark
[Henry Ford]

We live and learn, but not the wiser grow
[John Pomfret *Reason*]

To be conscious that you are ignorant is a great step to knowledge
[Benjamin Disraeli *Sybil*]

Nothing in all the world is more dangerous than sincere ignorance and conscientious stupidity
[Martin Luther King *Strength to Love*]

Ignorance is not innocence but sin
[Robert Browning *The Inn Album*]

Ignorance itself is without a doubt a sin for those who do not wish to understand; for those who, however, cannot understand, it is the punishment of sin
[St Augustine]

Ignorance is the curse of God,
Knowledge the wing wherewith we fly to heaven
[William Shakespeare *Henry VI*]

I know nothing except the fact of my ignorance
[Socrates]

If you think education is expensive – try ignorance
[Derek Bok]

He who knows and knows he knows,
He is a wise man; seek him.
He who knows and knows not he knows,
He is asleep; wake him.
He who knows not and knows he knows not,
He is a child; teach him.
He who knows not and knows not he knows not,
He is a fool; shun him!
[Anon.]

PROVERBS
One half of the world does not know how the other half lives

ignorant ADJECTIVE **1 = uneducated**, unaware, naive, green, illiterate, inexperienced, innocent, untrained, unlearned, unread, untutored, uncultivated, wet behind the ears *(informal)*, unlettered, untaught, unknowledgeable, uncomprehending, unscholarly, as green as grass: *They don't ask questions for fear of appearing ignorant.* **OPPOSITE:** educated **2 = insensitive**, gross, crude, rude, shallow, superficial, crass: *Some very ignorant people called me all kinds of names.* **3** (with **of**) **= uninformed of**, unaware of, oblivious to, blind to, innocent of, in the dark about, unconscious of, unschooled in, out of the loop of, inexperienced of, uninitiated about, unknowing of, unenlightened about: *Many people are worryingly ignorant of the facts.* **OPPOSITE:** informed

ignore VERB **1 = pay no attention to**, neglect, disregard, slight, overlook, scorn, spurn, rebuff, take no notice of, be oblivious to, dinghy *(Brit. slang)*: *She said her husband ignored her.* **OPPOSITE:** pay attention to **2 = overlook**, discount, disregard, reject, neglect, shrug off, pass over, brush aside, turn a blind eye to, turn a deaf ear to, shut your eyes to: *Such arguments ignore the important issues.* **3 = snub**, cut *(informal)*, slight, blank *(slang)*, rebuff, cold-shoulder, turn your back on, give (someone) the cold shoulder, send (someone) to Coventry, give (someone) the brush-off, dinghy *(Brit. slang)*: *I kept sending letters and cards but he just ignored me.*

ilk NOUN **= type**, sort, kind, class, style, character, variety, brand, breed, stamp, description, kidney, disposition

> **USAGE**
> Some people object to the use of the phrase *of that ilk* to mean 'of that type or class', claiming that it arises from a misunderstanding of the original Scottish expression. The Scottish phrase *of that ilk* has a very specific meaning, indicating that the person mentioned is laird of an estate with the same name as his family, for example *Moncrieff of that ilk* (that is, 'Moncrieff, laird of Moncrieff estate'). The more general use is, however, well established and is now generally regarded as acceptable.

ill ADJECTIVE **1 = unwell**, sick, poorly *(informal)*, diseased, funny *(informal)*, weak, crook *(Austral. & N.Z. slang)*, ailing, queer, frail, feeble, unhealthy, seedy *(informal)*, sickly, laid up *(informal)*, queasy, infirm, out of sorts *(informal)*, dicky *(Brit. informal)*, nauseous, off-colour, under the weather *(informal)*, at death's door, indisposed, peaky, on the sick list *(informal)*, valetudinarian, green about the gills, not up to snuff *(informal)*: *He was seriously ill with pneumonia.* **OPPOSITE:** healthy **2 = harmful**, bad, damaging, evil, foul, unfortunate, destructive, unlucky, vile, detrimental, hurtful, pernicious, noxious, ruinous, deleterious, injurious, iniquitous, disadvantageous, maleficent: *ill effects from the contamination of the water* **OPPOSITE:** favourable **3 = hostile**, malicious, acrimonious, cross, harsh, adverse, belligerent, unkind, hurtful, unfriendly, malevolent, antagonistic, hateful, bellicose, cantankerous, inimical, rancorous, ill-disposed: *He bears no ill feelings towards you.* **OPPOSITE:** kind **4 = bad**, threatening, disturbing, menacing, unlucky, sinister, gloomy, dire, ominous, unhealthy, unfavourable, foreboding, unpromising, inauspicious, unwholesome, unpropitious, bodeful: *His absence preyed on her mind like an ill omen.*
▷ NOUN **1 = problem**, trouble, suffering, worry, trial, injury, pain, hurt, strain, harm, distress, misery, hardship, woe, misfortune, affliction, tribulation, unpleasantness: *He is responsible for many of the country's ills.* **2 = harm**, suffering, damage, hurt, evil, destruction, grief, trauma, anguish, mischief, malice: *I know it will be difficult for them but I wish them no ill.* **OPPOSITE:** good
▷ ADVERB **1 = badly**, unfortunately, unfavourably, inauspiciously: *This development may bode ill for the government.* **2 = hardly**, barely, scarcely, just, only just, by no means, at a push: *We can ill afford another scandal.* **OPPOSITE:** well **3 = illegally**, criminally, unlawfully, fraudulently, dishonestly, illicitly, illegitimately, unscrupulously, foully: *He used his ill-gotten gains to pay for a £360,000 house.* **4 = insufficiently**, badly, poorly, inadequately, imperfectly, deficiently: *We were ill-prepared for last year's South Africa tour.*

ill-advised ADJECTIVE **= misguided**, inappropriate, foolish, rash, reckless, unwise, short-sighted, unseemly, foolhardy, thoughtless, indiscreet, ill-judged, ill-considered, imprudent, wrong-headed, injudicious, incautious, impolitic, overhasty **OPPOSITE:** wise

ill at ease ADJECTIVE **= uncomfortable**, nervous, tense, strange, wired *(slang)*, disturbed, anxious, awkward, uneasy, unsettled, faltering, unsure, restless, out of place, neurotic, self-conscious, hesitant, disquieted, edgy, on edge, twitchy *(informal)*, on tenterhooks, fidgety, unquiet, like a fish out of water, antsy *(informal)*, unrelaxed, on pins and needles *(informal)* **OPPOSITE:** comfortable

ill-considered ADJECTIVE **= unwise**, rash, imprudent, careless, precipitate, hasty, heedless, injudicious, improvident, overhasty

ill-defined ADJECTIVE **= unclear**, vague, indistinct, blurred, dim, fuzzy, shadowy, woolly, nebulous **OPPOSITE:** clear

illegal ADJECTIVE **= unlawful**, banned, forbidden, prohibited, criminal, outlawed, unofficial, illicit, unconstitutional, lawless, wrongful, off limits, unlicensed, under-the-table, unauthorized, proscribed, under-the-counter, actionable *(Law)*, felonious **OPPOSITE:** legal

illegality NOUN **= crime**, wrong, felony, criminality, lawlessness, illegitimacy, wrongness, unlawfulness, illicitness

illegible ADJECTIVE **= indecipherable**, unreadable, faint, crabbed, scrawled, hieroglyphic, hard to make out, undecipherable, obscure **OPPOSITE:** legible

illegitimacy NOUN **1 = bastardy**, bastardism: *Divorce and illegitimacy lead to millions of one-parent families.* **2 = illegality**, unconstitutionality, unlawfulness, illicitness, irregularity: *They denounced the illegitimacy and oppressiveness of the regime.*

illegitimate ADJECTIVE **1 = born out of wedlock**, natural, bastard, love, misbegotten *(literary)*, baseborn *(archaic)*: *In 1985 the news of his illegitimate child came out.* **2 = unlawful**, illegal, illicit, improper, unconstitutional, under-the-table, unauthorized, unsanctioned: *a ruthless and illegitimate regime* **OPPOSITE:** legal **3 = invalid**, incorrect, illogical, spurious, unsound: *It is not illegitimate to seek a parallel between the two events.*

> **QUOTATIONS**
> There are no illegitimate children – only illegitimate parents
> [Judge Léon R. Yankwich]

ill-fated ADJECTIVE **= doomed**, unfortunate, unlucky, unhappy, blighted, hapless, luckless, ill-starred, star-crossed, ill-omened

ill feeling NOUN **= hostility**, resentment, bitterness, offence, indignation, animosity, antagonism, enmity, rancour, bad blood, hard feelings, ill will, animus, dudgeon *(archaic)*, chip on your shoulder **OPPOSITE:** goodwill

illiberal ADJECTIVE **= intolerant**, prejudiced, bigoted, narrow-minded, small-minded, reactionary, hidebound, uncharitable, ungenerous **OPPOSITE:** tolerant

illicit ADJECTIVE **1 = illegal**, criminal, prohibited, unlawful, black-market, illegitimate, off limits, unlicensed, unauthorized, bootleg, contraband, felonious: *information about the use of illicit drugs* **OPPOSITE:** legal **2 = forbidden**, improper, immoral, wrong, guilty, clandestine, furtive: *He clearly condemns illicit love.*

illiteracy NOUN **= lack of education**, ignorance, benightedness, illiterateness

illiterate ADJECTIVE **= uneducated**, ignorant, unlettered, unable to read and write, analphabetic **OPPOSITE:** educated

ill-judged ADJECTIVE **= misguided**, foolish, rash, unwise, short-sighted, ill-advised, ill-considered, wrong-headed, injudicious, overhasty

ill-mannered ADJECTIVE **= rude**, impolite, discourteous, coarse, churlish, boorish, insolent, uncouth, loutish, uncivil, ill-bred, badly behaved, ill-behaved, unmannerly **OPPOSITE:** polite

illness NOUN **= sickness**, ill health, malaise, attack, disease, complaint, infection, disorder, bug *(informal)*, disability, ailment, affliction, poor health, malady, infirmity, indisposition, lurgy *(informal)*

illogical ADJECTIVE **= irrational**, absurd, unreasonable, meaningless, incorrect, faulty, inconsistent, invalid, senseless, spurious, inconclusive, unsound, unscientific, specious, fallacious, sophistical **OPPOSITE:** logical

ill-tempered ADJECTIVE **= cross**, irritable, grumpy, irascible, sharp, annoyed, impatient, touchy, bad-tempered, curt, spiteful, tetchy, ratty *(Brit. & N.Z. informal)*, testy, chippy *(informal)*, choleric, ill-humoured, liverish **OPPOSITE:** good-natured

ill-treat VERB **= abuse**, injure, harm, wrong, damage, harry, harass, misuse, oppress, dump on *(slang, chiefly U.S.)*, mishandle, maltreat, ill-use, handle roughly, knock about *or* around

ill-treatment NOUN **= abuse**, harm, mistreatment, damage, injury, misuse, ill-use, rough handling

illuminate VERB **1 = light up**, light, brighten, irradiate, illumine *(literary)*: *No streetlights illuminate the street.* **OPPOSITE:** darken **2 = explain**, interpret, make clear, clarify, clear up, enlighten, shed light on, elucidate, explicate, give insight into: *The instructors use games to illuminate the subject.* **OPPOSITE:** obscure **3 = decorate**, illustrate, adorn, ornament: *medieval illuminated manuscripts*

illuminating ADJECTIVE **= informative**, revealing, enlightening, helpful, explanatory, instructive **OPPOSITE:** confusing

illumination NOUN **1 = light**, lighting, lights, ray, beam, lighting up, brightening, brightness, radiance: *The only illumination came from a small window above.* **2 = enlightenment**, understanding, insight, perception, awareness, revelation, inspiration, clarification, edification: *No further illumination can be had from this theory.* ▷ PLURAL NOUN **= lights**, decorations, fairy lights: *the famous Blackpool illuminations*

illusion NOUN **1 = delusion**, misconception, misapprehension, fancy, deception, fallacy, self-deception, false impression, false belief, misbelief: *No one really has any illusions about winning the war.* **2 = false impression**, feeling, appearance, impression, fancy, deception, imitation, sham, pretence, semblance, fallacy: *Floor-to-ceiling windows give the illusion of extra space.* **OPPOSITE:** reality **3 = fantasy**, vision, hallucination, trick, spectre, mirage, semblance, daydream, apparition, chimera, figment of the imagination, phantasm, ignis fatuus, will-o'-the-wisp: *It creates the illusion of moving around in the computer's graphic environment.*

illusory *or* **illusive** ADJECTIVE **= unreal**, false, misleading, untrue, seeming, mistaken, apparent, sham, deceptive, deceitful, hallucinatory, fallacious, chimerical, delusive **OPPOSITE:** real

illustrate VERB **1 = demonstrate**, show, exhibit, emphasize, exemplify, explicate: *The example of the United States illustrates this point.* **2 = explain**, describe, interpret, sum up, make clear, clarify, summarize, bring home, point up, make plain, elucidate: *She illustrates her analysis with extracts from interviews and discussions.* **3 = adorn**, ornament, embellish: *He has illustrated the book with black-and-white photographs.*

illustrated ADJECTIVE **= pictured**, decorated, illuminated, embellished, pictorial, with illustrations

illustration NOUN **1 = example**, case, instance, sample, explanation, demonstration, interpretation, specimen, analogy, clarification, case in point, exemplar, elucidation, exemplification: *These figures are an illustration of the country's dynamism.* **2 = picture**, drawing, painting, image, print, plate, figure, portrait, representation, sketch, decoration, portrayal, likeness, adornment: *She looked like a princess in a nineteenth century illustration.*

illustrative ADJECTIVE **1 = representative**, typical, descriptive, explanatory, interpretive, expository, explicatory, illustrational: *The following excerpt is illustrative of her interaction with students.* **2 = pictorial**, graphic, diagrammatic, delineative: *an illustrative guide to the daily activities of the football club*

illustrious ADJECTIVE **= famous**, great, noted, celebrated, signal, brilliant, remarkable, distinguished, prominent, glorious, noble, splendid, notable, renowned, eminent, famed, exalted **OPPOSITE:** obscure

ill will NOUN **= hostility**, spite, dislike, hatred, envy, resentment, grudge, malice, animosity, aversion, venom, antagonism, antipathy, enmity, acrimony, rancour, bad blood, hard feelings, animus, malevolence, unfriendliness **OPPOSITE:** goodwill

image NOUN **1 = thought**, idea, vision, concept, impression, perception, conception, mental picture, conceptualization: *The words 'Côte d'Azur' conjure up images of sun, sea and sand.* **2 = figure of speech**, metaphor, simile, conceit, trope: *The images in the poem illustrate the poet's frame of mind.* **3 = reflection**, appearance, likeness, mirror image: *I peered at my image in the mirror.* **4 = figure**, idol, icon, fetish, talisman: *The polished stone bore the graven image of a snakebird.* **5 = replica**, copy, reproduction, counterpart, spit *(informal, chiefly Brit.)*, clone, facsimile, spitting image *(informal)*, similitude,

Doppelgänger, (dead) ringer *(slang)*, double: *The boy is the image of his father.* **6 = picture**, photo, photograph, representation, reproduction, snapshot: *A computer creates an image on the screen.*

imaginable ADJECTIVE **= possible**, conceivable, likely, credible, plausible, believable, under the sun, comprehensible, thinkable, within the bounds of possibility, supposable **OPPOSITE:** unimaginable

imaginary ADJECTIVE **= fictional**, made-up, invented, supposed, imagined, assumed, ideal, fancied, legendary, visionary, shadowy, unreal, hypothetical, fanciful, fictitious, mythological, illusory, nonexistent, dreamlike, hallucinatory, illusive, chimerical, unsubstantial, phantasmal, suppositious, imagal *(Psychoanalysis)* **OPPOSITE:** real

imagination NOUN **1 = creativity**, vision, invention, ingenuity, enterprise, insight, inspiration, wit, originality, inventiveness, resourcefulness: *He has a logical mind and a little imagination.* **2 = mind's eye**, fancy: *Long before I went there, the place was alive in my imagination.*

imaginative ADJECTIVE **= creative**, original, inspired, enterprising, fantastic, clever, stimulating, vivid, ingenious, visionary, inventive, fanciful, dreamy, whimsical, poetical **OPPOSITE:** unimaginative

imagine VERB **1 = envisage**, see, picture, plan, create, project, think of, scheme, frame, invent, devise, conjure up, envision, visualize, dream up *(informal)*, think up, conceive of, conceptualize, fantasize about, see in the mind's eye, form a mental picture of, ideate: *He could not imagine a more peaceful scene.* **2 = believe**, think, suppose, assume, suspect, gather, guess *(informal, chiefly U.S. & Canad.)*, realize, take it, reckon, fancy, deem, speculate, presume, take for granted, infer, deduce, apprehend, conjecture, surmise: *I imagine you're referring to me.*

imbalance NOUN **= unevenness**, bias, inequality, unfairness, partiality, disproportion, lopsidedness, top-heaviness, lack of proportion

imbed *see* embed

imbibe VERB **1 = drink**, consume, knock back *(informal)*, sink *(informal)*, swallow, suck, swig *(informal)*, quaff: *They were used to imbibing enormous quantities of alcohol.* **2 = absorb**, receive, take in, gain, gather, acquire, assimilate, ingest: *He'd imbibed a set of mystical beliefs from the cradle.*

imbue VERB **= instil**, infuse, steep, bathe, saturate, pervade, permeate, impregnate, inculcate

imitate VERB **1 = copy**, follow, repeat, echo, emulate, ape, simulate, mirror, follow suit, duplicate, counterfeit, follow in the footsteps of, take a leaf out of (someone's) book: *a precedent which may be imitated by other activists* **2 = do an impression of**, take off *(informal)*, mimic, do *(informal)*, affect, copy, mock, parody, caricature, send up *(Brit. informal)*, spoof *(informal)*, impersonate, burlesque, personate: *He screwed up his face and imitated the Colonel.*

imitation NOUN **1 = replica**, fake, reproduction, sham, forgery, carbon copy *(informal)*, counterfeit, counterfeiting, likeness, duplication: *the most accurate imitation of Chinese architecture in Europe* **2 = copying**, echoing, resemblance, aping, simulation, mimicry: *She learned her golf by imitation.* **3 = impression**, parody, mockery, takeoff *(informal)*, impersonation: *I could do a pretty good imitation of him.*
▷ ADJECTIVE **= artificial**, mock, reproduction, dummy, synthetic, man-made, simulated, sham, pseudo *(informal)*, ersatz, repro, phoney *or* phony *(informal)*: *a set of Dickens bound in imitation leather* **OPPOSITE:** real

> **QUOTATIONS**
> Almost all absurdity of conduct arises from the imitation of those whom we cannot resemble
> [Dr. Johnson *The Rambler*]
>
> Imitation is the sincerest flattery
> [Charles Colton *Lacon*]
>
> To do the opposite of something is also a form of imitation, namely an imitation of its opposite
> [G.C. Lichtenberg *Aphorisms*]

imitator NOUN **= impersonator**, mimic, impressionist, copycat, echo, follower, parrot *(informal)*, copier, carbon copy *(informal)*

immaculate ADJECTIVE **1 = clean**, impeccable, spotless, trim, neat, spruce, squeaky-clean, spick-and-span, neat as a new pin: *Her front room was kept immaculate.* **OPPOSITE:** dirty **2 = pure**, perfect, innocent, impeccable, virtuous, flawless, faultless, squeaky-clean, guiltless, above reproach, sinless, incorrupt: *her immaculate reputation* **OPPOSITE:** corrupt **3 = perfect**, flawless, impeccable, stainless, faultless, unblemished, unsullied, uncontaminated, unpolluted, untarnished, unexceptionable, undefiled: *My car's in absolutely immaculate condition.* **OPPOSITE:** tainted

immaterial ADJECTIVE **= irrelevant**, insignificant, unimportant, unnecessary, trivial, trifling, inconsequential, extraneous, inconsiderable, of no importance, of no consequence, inessential, a matter of indifference, of little account, inapposite **OPPOSITE:** significant

immature ADJECTIVE **1 = young**, adolescent, undeveloped, green, raw, premature, unfinished, imperfect, untimely, unripe, unformed, unseasonable, unfledged: *The birds were in immature plumage.* **2 = childish**, juvenile, infantile, puerile, callow, babyish, wet behind the ears *(informal)*, jejune: *You're just being childish and immature.* **OPPOSITE:** adult

immaturity NOUN **1 = rawness**, imperfection, greenness, unpreparedness, unripeness: *In spite of some immaturity of style, it showed real imagination.* **2 = childishness**, puerility, callowness, juvenility, babyishness: *his immaturity and lack of social skills*

immeasurable ADJECTIVE **= incalculable**, vast, immense, endless, unlimited, infinite, limitless, boundless, bottomless, inexhaustible, unfathomable, unbounded, inestimable, measureless, illimitable **OPPOSITE:** finite

immediate ADJECTIVE **1 = instant**, prompt, instantaneous, quick, on-the-spot, split-second: *My immediate reaction was one of digust.* **OPPOSITE:** later **2 = current**, present, pressing, existing, actual, urgent, on hand, extant: *The immediate problem is not lack of food, but transportation.* **3 = nearest**, next, direct, close, near, adjacent, contiguous, proximate: *I was seated at his immediate left.* **OPPOSITE:** far

immediately ADVERB **= at once**, now, instantly, straight away, directly, promptly, right now, right away, there and then, speedily, without delay, without hesitation, instantaneously, forthwith, pronto *(informal)*, unhesitatingly, this instant, on the nail, this very minute, posthaste, tout de suite *(French)*, before you could say Jack Robinson *(informal)*

immemorial ADJECTIVE **= age-old**, ancient, long-standing, traditional, fixed, rooted, archaic, time-honoured, of yore, olden *(archaic)*

immense ADJECTIVE **= huge**, great, massive, vast, large, giant, enormous, extensive, tremendous, mega *(slang)*, titanic, infinite, jumbo *(informal)*, very big, gigantic, monumental, monstrous, mammoth, colossal, mountainous, stellar *(informal)*, prodigious, interminable, stupendous, king-size, king-sized, immeasurable, elephantine, ginormous *(informal)*, Brobdingnagian, illimitable, humongous *or* humungous *(U.S. slang)*, supersize **OPPOSITE:** tiny

immerse VERB **1 = engross**, involve, absorb, busy, occupy, engage: *His commitments did not allow him to immerse himself in family life.* **2 = plunge**, dip, submerge, sink, duck, bathe, douse, dunk, submerse: *The electrodes are immersed in liquid.*

immersed ADJECTIVE **= engrossed**, involved, absorbed, deep, busy, occupied, taken up, buried, consumed, wrapped up, bound up, rapt, spellbound, mesmerized, in a brown study

immersion NOUN **1 = involvement**, concentration, preoccupation, absorption: *long-term assignments that allowed them total immersion in their subjects* **2 = dipping**, submerging, plunging, ducking, dousing, dunking: *The wood had become swollen from prolonged immersion.*

immigrant NOUN **= settler**, incomer, alien, stranger, outsider, newcomer, migrant, emigrant

imminent ADJECTIVE **= near**, coming, close, approaching, threatening, gathering, on the way, in the air, forthcoming, looming, menacing, brewing, impending, at hand, upcoming, on the cards, on the horizon, in the pipeline, nigh *(archaic)*, in the offing, fast-approaching, just round the corner, near-at-hand **OPPOSITE:** remote

immobile ADJECTIVE **= motionless**, still, stationary, fixed, rooted, frozen, stable, halted, stiff, rigid, static, riveted, lifeless, inert, at rest, inanimate, immovable, immobilized, at a standstill, unmoving, stock-still, like a statue, immotile **OPPOSITE:** mobile

immobility NOUN **= stillness**, firmness, steadiness, stability, fixity, inertness, immovability, motionlessness, absence of movement

immobilize VERB **= paralyse**, stop, freeze, halt, disable, cripple, lay up *(informal)*, bring to a standstill, put out of action, render inoperative

immoral ADJECTIVE **= wicked**, bad, wrong, abandoned, evil, corrupt, vicious, obscene, indecent, vile, degenerate, dishonest, pornographic, sinful, unethical, lewd, depraved, impure, debauched, unprincipled, nefarious, dissolute, iniquitous, reprobate, licentious, of easy virtue, unchaste **OPPOSITE:** moral

immorality NOUN **= wickedness**, wrong, vice, evil, corruption, sin, depravity, iniquity, debauchery, badness, licentiousness, turpitude, dissoluteness **OPPOSITE:** morality

immortal ADJECTIVE **1 = timeless**, eternal, everlasting, lasting, traditional, classic, constant, enduring, persistent, abiding, perennial, ageless, unfading: *Wuthering Heights – that immortal love story.* **OPPOSITE:** ephemeral **2 = undying**, eternal, perpetual, indestructible, death-defying, imperishable, deathless: *They were considered gods and therefore immortal.* **OPPOSITE:** mortal
▷ NOUN **1 = hero**, genius, paragon, great: *They had paid £50 a head just to be in the presence of an immortal.* **2 = god**, goddess, deity, Olympian, divine being, immortal being, atua *(N.Z.)*: *In the legend, the fire is supposed to turn him into an immortal.*

immortality NOUN **1 = eternity**, perpetuity, everlasting life, timelessness, incorruptibility, indestructibility, endlessness, deathlessness: *belief in the immortality of the soul* **2 = fame**, glory, celebrity, greatness, renown, glorification, gloriousness: *Some people want to achieve immortality through their works.*

QUOTATIONS

No young man believes he shall ever die
[William Hazlitt *Uncollected Essays*]

I have good hope that there is something after death
[Plato *Phaedo*]

Should this my firm persuasion of the soul's immortality prove to be a mere delusion, it is at least a pleasing delusion, and I will cherish it to my last breath
[Cicero *De Senectute*]

Immortality is health; this life is a long sickness
[St Augustine *Sermons*]

Unable are the Loved to die
For Love is Immortality
[Emily Dickinson]

Children endow their parents with a vicarious immortality
[George Santayana *The Life of Reason: Reason in Society*]

I don't want to achieve immortality through my work ... I want to achieve it through not dying
[Woody Allen]

All the doctrines that have flourished in the world about immortality have hardly affected men's natural sentiment in the face of death
[George Santayana *The Life of Reason: Reason in Religion*]

Our Creator would never have made such lovely days, and given us the deep hearts to enjoy them, unless we were meant to be immortal
[Nathaniel Hawthorne *The Old Manse*]

Do not try to live forever. You will not succeed
[George Bernard Shaw *The Doctor's Dilemma*]

Millions long for immortality who don't know what to do with themselves on a rainy Saturday afternoon
[Susan Ertz *Anger in the Sky*]

immovable ADJECTIVE **1 = fixed**, set, fast, firm, stuck, secure, rooted, stable, jammed, stationary, immutable, unbudgeable: *It was declared unsafe because the support bars were immovable.* **2 = inflexible**, adamant, resolute, steadfast, constant, unyielding, unwavering, impassive, obdurate, unshakable, unchangeable, unshaken, stony-hearted, unimpressionable: *On one issue, however, she was immovable.*
OPPOSITE: flexible

immune
immune from = exempt from, free from, let off *(informal)*, not subject to, not liable to: *Members are immune from prosecution for corruption.*
immune to 1 = resistant to, free from, protected from, safe from, not open to, spared from, secure against, invulnerable to, insusceptible to: *The blood test will tell whether you are immune to the disease.* **2 = unaffected by**, not affected by, invulnerable to, insusceptible to: *He never became immune to the sight of death.*

immunity NOUN **1 = exemption**, amnesty, indemnity, release, freedom, liberty, privilege, prerogative, invulnerability, exoneration: *The police are offering immunity to witnesses who can help them.* **2** *(with* **to***)* **= resistance**, protection, resilience, inoculation, immunization: *immunity to airborne bacteria* **OPPOSITE:** susceptibility

immunize VERB **= vaccinate**, inoculate, protect, safeguard

immutable ADJECTIVE **= unchanging**, fixed, permanent, stable, constant, enduring, abiding, perpetual, inflexible, steadfast, sacrosanct, immovable, ageless, invariable, unalterable, unchangeable, changeless

imp NOUN **1 = demon**, devil, sprite: *He sees the devil as a little imp with horns.* **2 = rascal**, rogue, brat, urchin, minx, scamp, pickle *(Brit. informal)*, gamin, nointer *(Austral. slang)*: *I didn't say that, you little imp!*

impact NOUN **1 = effect**, influence, consequences, impression, repercussions, ramifications: *They expect the meeting to have a marked impact on the country's future.* **2 = collision**, force, contact, shock, crash, knock, stroke, smash, bump, thump, jolt: *The pilot must have died on impact.*
▷ VERB **= hit**, strike, crash, clash, crush, ram, smack, collide: *the sharp tinkle of metal impacting on stone*

impair VERB **= worsen**, reduce, damage, injure, harm, mar, undermine, weaken, spoil, diminish, decrease, blunt, deteriorate, lessen, hinder, debilitate, vitiate, enfeeble, enervate **OPPOSITE:** improve

impaired ADJECTIVE **= damaged**, flawed, faulty, defective, imperfect, unsound

impale VERB **= pierce**, stick, run through, spike, lance, spear, skewer, spit, transfix

impart VERB **1 = communicate**, pass on, convey, tell, reveal, discover, relate, disclose, divulge, make known: *the ability to impart knowledge and command respect* **2 = give**, accord, lend, bestow, offer, grant, afford, contribute, yield, confer: *She managed to impart great elegance to the dress she wore.*

impartial ADJECTIVE **= neutral**, objective, detached, just, fair, equal, open-minded, equitable, disinterested, unbiased, even-handed, nonpartisan, unprejudiced, without fear or favour, nondiscriminating **OPPOSITE:** unfair

impartiality NOUN **= neutrality**, equity, fairness, equality, detachment, objectivity, disinterest, open-mindedness, even-handedness, disinterestedness, dispassion, nonpartisanship, lack of bias **OPPOSITE:** unfairness

impassable ADJECTIVE **= blocked**, closed, obstructed, impenetrable, unnavigable

impasse NOUN **= deadlock**, stalemate, standstill, dead end, standoff, blind alley *(informal)*

impassioned ADJECTIVE **= intense**, heated, passionate, warm, excited, inspired, violent, stirring, flaming, furious, glowing, blazing, vivid, animated, rousing, fiery, worked up, ardent, inflamed, fervent, ablaze, vehement, fervid **OPPOSITE:** cool

impassive ADJECTIVE **= unemotional**, unmoved, emotionless, reserved, cool, calm, composed, indifferent, self-contained, serene, callous, aloof, stoical, unconcerned, apathetic, dispassionate, unfazed *(informal)*, inscrutable, stolid, unruffled, phlegmatic, unfeeling, poker-faced *(informal)*, imperturbable, insensible, impassible *(rare)*, unexcitable, insusceptible, unimpressible

impatience NOUN **1 = irritability**, shortness, edginess, intolerance, quick temper, snappiness, irritableness: *There was a hint of impatience in his tone.* **OPPOSITE:** patience **2 = eagerness**, longing, enthusiasm, hunger, yearning, thirst, zeal, fervour, ardour, vehemence, earnestness, keenness, impetuosity, heartiness, avidity, intentness, greediness: *She showed impatience to continue the climb.* **3 = haste**, hurry, impetuosity, rashness, hastiness: *They visited a fertility clinic in their impatience to have a child.*

> **QUOTATIONS**
> All human errors are impatience, a premature breaking off of methodical procedure, an apparent fencing-in of what is apparently at issue
> [Franz Kafka *The Collected Aphorisms*]

impatient ADJECTIVE **1 = cross**, tense, annoyed, irritated, prickly, edgy, touchy, bad-tempered, intolerant, petulant, ill-tempered, cantankerous, ratty *(Brit. & N.Z. informal)*, chippy *(informal)*, hot-tempered, quick-tempered, crotchety *(informal)*, ill-humoured, narky *(Brit. slang)*, out of humour: *He becomes impatient as the hours pass.* **2 = irritable**, fiery, abrupt, hasty, snappy, indignant, curt, vehement, brusque, irascible, testy: *Beware of being too impatient with others.* **OPPOSITE:** easy-going **3 = eager**, longing, keen, hot, earnest, raring, anxious, hungry, intent, enthusiastic, yearning, greedy, restless, ardent, avid, fervent, zealous, chafing, vehement, fretful, straining at the leash, fervid, keen as mustard, like a cat on hot bricks *(informal)*, athirst: *They are impatient for jobs and security.* **OPPOSITE:** calm

impeach VERB **= charge**, accuse, prosecute, blame, denounce, indict, censure, bring to trial, arraign

impeachment NOUN **= accusation**, prosecution, indictment, arraignment

impeccable ADJECTIVE **= faultless**, perfect, pure, exact, precise, exquisite, stainless, immaculate, flawless, squeaky-clean, unerring, unblemished, unimpeachable, irreproachable, sinless, incorrupt **OPPOSITE:** flawed

impede VERB **= hinder**, stop, slow (down), check, bar, block, delay, hold up, brake, disrupt, curb, restrain, hamper, thwart, clog, obstruct, retard, encumber, cumber, throw a spanner in the works of *(Brit. informal)* **OPPOSITE:** help

impediment NOUN **= obstacle**, barrier, check, bar, block, difficulty, hazard, curb, snag, obstruction, stumbling block, hindrance, encumbrance, fly in the ointment, millstone around your neck **OPPOSITE:** aid

impel VERB **= force**, move, compel, drive, require, push, influence, urge, inspire, prompt, spur, stimulate, motivate, oblige, induce, prod, constrain, incite, instigate, goad, actuate **OPPOSITE:** discourage

impending ADJECTIVE **= looming**, coming, approaching, near, nearing, threatening, forthcoming, brewing, imminent, hovering, upcoming, on the horizon, in the pipeline, in the offing

impenetrable ADJECTIVE **1 = impassable**, solid, impervious, thick, dense, hermetic, impermeable, inviolable, unpierceable: *The range forms an impenetrable barrier between Europe and Asia.* **OPPOSITE:** passable **2 = incomprehensible**, obscure, baffling, dark, hidden, mysterious, enigmatic, arcane, inexplicable, unintelligible, inscrutable, unfathomable, indiscernible, cabbalistic, enigmatical: *His philosophical work is notoriously impenetrable.* **OPPOSITE:** understandable

imperative ADJECTIVE **= urgent**, essential, pressing, vital, crucial, compulsory, indispensable, obligatory, exigent **OPPOSITE:** unnecessary

imperceptible ADJECTIVE **= undetectable**, slight, subtle, small, minute, fine, tiny, faint, invisible, gradual, shadowy, microscopic, indistinguishable, inaudible, infinitesimal, teeny-weeny, unnoticeable, insensible, impalpable, indiscernible, teensy-weensy, inappreciable **OPPOSITE:** perceptible

imperceptibly ADVERB **= invisibly**, slowly, subtly, little by little, unobtrusively, unseen, by a hair's-breadth, unnoticeably, indiscernibly, inappreciably

imperfect ADJECTIVE **= flawed**, impaired, faulty, broken, limited, damaged, partial, unfinished, incomplete, defective, patchy, immature, deficient, rudimentary, sketchy, undeveloped, inexact **OPPOSITE:** perfect

imperfection NOUN **1 = blemish**, fault, defect, flaw, stain: *Scanners locate imperfections in the cloth.* **2 = fault**, failing, weakness, defect, deficiency, flaw, shortcoming, inadequacy, frailty, foible, weak point: *He concedes that there are imperfections in the socialist system.* **3 = incompleteness**, deficiency, inadequacy, frailty, insufficiency: *It is its imperfection that gives it its beauty.* **OPPOSITE:** perfection

imperial ADJECTIVE **= royal**, regal, kingly, queenly, princely, sovereign, majestic, monarchial, monarchal

imperil VERB **= endanger**, risk, hazard, jeopardize **OPPOSITE:** protect

imperious ADJECTIVE **= domineering**, dictatorial, bossy *(informal)*, haughty, lordly, commanding, arrogant, authoritative, autocratic, overbearing, tyrannical, magisterial, despotic, high-handed, overweening, tyrannous

impermanent ADJECTIVE **= temporary**, passing, brief, fleeting, elusive, mortal, short-lived, flying, fugitive, transient, momentary, ephemeral, transitory, perishable, fly-by-night *(informal)*, evanescent, inconstant, fugacious, here today, gone tomorrow *(informal)*

impersonal ADJECTIVE **1 = inhuman**, cold, remote, bureaucratic: *a large impersonal orphanage* **2 = detached**, neutral, dispassionate, cold, formal, aloof, businesslike: *We must be as impersonal as a surgeon with a knife.* **OPPOSITE:** intimate

impersonate VERB **1 = imitate**, pose as *(informal)*, masquerade as, enact, ape, act out, pass yourself off as: *He was returned to prison for impersonating a police officer.* **2 = mimic**, take off *(informal)*, do *(informal)*, ape, parody, caricature, do an impression of, personate: *He was a brilliant mimic who could impersonate most of the staff.*

impersonation NOUN **= imitation**, impression, parody, caricature, takeoff *(informal)*, mimicry

impertinent ADJECTIVE **1 = rude**, forward, cheeky *(informal)*, saucy *(informal)*, fresh *(informal)*, bold, flip *(informal)*, brazen, sassy *(U.S. informal)*, pert, disrespectful, presumptuous, insolent, impolite, impudent, lippy *(U.S. & Canad. slang)*, discourteous, uncivil, unmannerly: *I don't like strangers who ask impertinent questions.* **OPPOSITE:** polite **2 = inappropriate**, irrelevant, incongruous, inapplicable: *Since we already knew this, to tell us again seemed impertinent.* **OPPOSITE:** appropriate

imperturbable ADJECTIVE **= calm**, cool, collected, composed, complacent, serene, tranquil, sedate, undisturbed, unmoved, stoic, stoical, unfazed *(informal)*, unflappable *(informal)*, unruffled, self-possessed, nerveless, unexcitable, equanimous **OPPOSITE:** agitated

impervious ADJECTIVE **1 = unaffected**, immune, unmoved, closed, untouched, proof, invulnerable, unreceptive, unswayable: *They are impervious to all suggestion of change.* **2 = resistant**, sealed, impenetrable, invulnerable, impassable, hermetic, impermeable, imperviable: *The floorcovering will need to be impervious to water.*

impetuous ADJECTIVE **= rash**, hasty, impulsive, violent, furious, fierce, eager, passionate, spontaneous, precipitate, ardent, impassioned, headlong, unplanned, unbridled, vehement, unrestrained, spur-of-the-moment, unthinking, unpremeditated, unreflecting **OPPOSITE:** cautious

impetus NOUN **1 = incentive**, push, spur, motivation, impulse, stimulus, catalyst, goad, impulsion: *She needed a new impetus for her talent.* **2 = force**, power, energy, momentum: *This decision will give renewed impetus to economic regeneration.*

impinge
impinge on *or* **upon something = invade**, violate, encroach on, trespass on, infringe on, make inroads on, obtrude on: *If he were at home all the time he would impinge on my space.*
impinge on *or* **upon something** *or* **someone = affect**, influence, relate to, impact on, touch, touch upon, have a bearing on, bear upon: *These cuts have impinged on the region's largest employers.*

impish ADJECTIVE **= mischievous**, devilish, roguish, rascally, elfin, puckish, waggish, sportive, prankish

implacable ADJECTIVE **= ruthless**, cruel, relentless, uncompromising, intractable, inflexible, unrelenting, merciless, unforgiving, inexorable, unyielding, remorseless, pitiless, unbending, unappeasable **OPPOSITE:** merciful

implant VERB **1 = insert**, place, plant, fix, root, sow, graft, embed, ingraft: *Doctors have implanted an artificial heart into a 46-year-old man.* **2 = instil**, sow, infuse, inculcate, infix: *His father had implanted in him an ambition to obtain an education.*

implausible ADJECTIVE **= improbable**, unlikely, weak, incredible, unbelievable, dubious, suspect, unreasonable, flimsy, unconvincing, far-fetched, cock-and-bull *(informal)*

implement VERB **= carry out**, effect, carry through, complete, apply, perform, realize, fulfil, enforce, execute, discharge, bring about, enact, put into action *or* effect: *The government promised to implement a new system to control loan institutions.* **OPPOSITE:** hinder
▷ NOUN **= tool**, machine, device, instrument, appliance, apparatus, gadget, utensil, contraption, contrivance, agent: *writing implements*

implementation NOUN **= carrying out**, effecting, execution, performance, performing, discharge, enforcement, accomplishment, realization, fulfilment

implicate VERB **= incriminate**, involve, compromise, embroil, entangle, inculpate: *He didn't find anything in the notebooks to implicate her.* **OPPOSITE:** dissociate
implicate something *or* **someone in something = involve in**, associate with, connect with, tie up with: *This particular system has been implicated in alcohol effects.*

implicated ADJECTIVE **= involved**, suspected, incriminated, under suspicion

implication NOUN **1 = suggestion**, hint, inference, meaning, conclusion, significance, presumption, overtone, innuendo, intimation, insinuation, signification: *The implication was obvious: vote for us or you'll be sorry.* **2 = involvement**, association, connection, incrimination, entanglement: *Implication in a murder finally brought him to the gallows.* **3 = consequence**, result, development, ramification, complication, upshot: *He was acutely aware of the political implications of his decision.*

implicit ADJECTIVE **1 = implied**, understood, suggested, hinted at, taken for granted, unspoken, inferred, tacit, undeclared, insinuated, unstated, unsaid, unexpressed: *He wanted to make explicit in the film what was implicit in the play.* **OPPOSITE:** explicit **2 = inherent**, contained, underlying, intrinsic, latent, ingrained, inbuilt: *Implicit in snobbery is a certain timidity.* **3 = absolute**, full, complete, total, firm, fixed, entire, constant, utter, outright, consummate, unqualified, out-and-out, steadfast, wholehearted, unadulterated, unreserved, unshakable, unshaken, unhesitating: *He had implicit faith in the noble intentions of the Emperor.*

implicitly ADVERB **= absolutely**, completely, utterly, unconditionally, unreservedly, firmly, unhesitatingly, without reservation

implied ADJECTIVE **= suggested**, inherent, indirect, hinted at, implicit, unspoken, tacit, undeclared, insinuated, unstated, unexpressed

implore VERB **= beg**, beseech, entreat, conjure, plead with, solicit, pray to, importune, crave of, supplicate, go on bended knee to

imply VERB **1 = suggest**, hint, insinuate, indicate, signal, intimate, signify, connote, give (someone) to understand: *Are you implying that I had something to do with this?* **2 = involve**, mean, entail, include, require, indicate, import, point to, signify, denote, presuppose, betoken: *The meeting in no way implies a resumption of contact with the terrorists.*

impolite ADJECTIVE **= bad-mannered**, rude, disrespectful, rough, churlish, boorish, insolent, uncouth, unrefined, loutish, ungentlemanly, ungracious, discourteous, indelicate, uncivil, unladylike, indecorous, ungallant, ill-bred, unmannerly, ill-mannered **OPPOSITE:** polite

import VERB **= bring in**, buy in, ship in, land, introduce: *We spent $5000 million more on importing food than on selling abroad.*
▷ NOUN **1 = significance**, concern, value, worth, weight, consequence, substance, moment, magnitude, usefulness, momentousness: *Such arguments are of little import.* **2 = meaning**, implication, significance, sense, message, bearing, intention, explanation, substance, drift, interpretation, thrust, purport, upshot, gist, signification: *I have already spoken about the import of his speech.*

importance NOUN **1 = significance**, interest, concern, matter, moment, value, worth, weight, import, consequence, substance, relevance, usefulness, momentousness: *Safety is of paramount importance.* **2 = prestige**, standing, status, rule, authority, influence, distinction, esteem, prominence, supremacy, mastery, dominion, eminence, ascendancy, pre-eminence, mana *(N.Z.)*: *He was too puffed up with his own importance to accept the verdict.*

important ADJECTIVE **1 = significant**, critical, substantial, grave, urgent, serious, material, signal, primary, meaningful, far-reaching, momentous, seminal, weighty, of substance, salient, noteworthy: *an important economic challenge to the government* **OPPOSITE:** unimportant **2** *(often with* **to***)* **= valued**, loved, prized, dear, essential, valuable, of interest, treasured, precious, esteemed, cherished, of concern, highly regarded: *Her sons are the most important* *thing in her life.* **3 = powerful**, leading, prominent, commanding, supreme, outstanding, high-level, dominant, influential, notable, big-time (*informal*), foremost, eminent, high-ranking, authoritative, major league (*informal*), of note, noteworthy, pre-eminent, skookum (*Canad.*): *an important figure in the media world*

impose

impose on someone = intrude on, exploit, take advantage of, use, trouble, abuse, bother, encroach on, horn in (*informal*), trespass on, gate-crash (*informal*), take liberties with, butt in on, presume upon, force yourself on, obtrude on: *I was afraid you'd think we were imposing on you.*

impose something on *or* **upon someone 1 = levy**, apply, introduce, put, place, set, charge, establish, lay, fix, institute, exact, decree, ordain: *They impose fines on airlines who bring in illegal immigrants.* **2 = inflict**, force, enforce, visit, press, apply, thrust, dictate, saddle (someone) with, foist: *Beware of imposing your own tastes on your children.*

imposing ADJECTIVE **= impressive**, striking, grand, august, powerful, effective, commanding, awesome, majestic, dignified, stately, forcible **OPPOSITE:** unimposing

imposition NOUN **1 = application**, introduction, levying, decree, laying on: *the imposition of VAT on fuel bills* **2 = intrusion**, liberty, presumption, cheek (*informal*), encroachment: *I know this is an imposition, but please hear me out.* **3 = charge**, tax, duty, burden, levy: *the Poll Tax and other local government impositions*

impossibility NOUN **= hopelessness**, inability, impracticability, inconceivability

> **QUOTATIONS**
> Probable impossibilities are to be preferred to improbable possibilities
> [Aristotle *Poetics*]

impossible ADJECTIVE **1 = not possible**, out of the question, impracticable, unfeasible, beyond the bounds of possibility: *It was impossible to get in because no one knew the password.* **2 = unachievable**, hopeless, out of the question, vain, unthinkable, inconceivable, far-fetched, unworkable, implausible, unattainable, unobtainable, beyond you, not to be thought of: *You shouldn't promise what's impossible.* **OPPOSITE:** possible **3 = absurd**, crazy (*informal*), ridiculous, unacceptable, outrageous, ludicrous, unreasonable, unsuitable, intolerable, preposterous, laughable, farcical, illogical, insoluble, unanswerable, inadmissible, ungovernable: *The Government was now in an impossible situation.*

impostor NOUN **= fraud**, cheat, fake, impersonator, rogue, deceiver, sham, pretender, hypocrite, charlatan, quack, trickster, knave (*archaic*), phoney *or* phony (*informal*)

impotence NOUN **= powerlessness**, inability, helplessness, weakness, disability, incompetence, inadequacy, paralysis, inefficiency, frailty, incapacity, infirmity, ineffectiveness, uselessness, feebleness, enervation, inefficacy **OPPOSITE:** powerfulness

impotent ADJECTIVE **= powerless**, weak, helpless, unable, disabled, incapable, paralysed, frail, incompetent, ineffective, feeble, incapacitated, unmanned, infirm, emasculate, nerveless, enervated **OPPOSITE:** powerful

impoverish VERB **1 = bankrupt**, ruin, beggar, break, pauperize: *a society impoverished by wartime inflation* **2 = deplete**, drain, exhaust, diminish, use up, sap, wear out, reduce: *Mint impoverishes the soil quickly.*

impoverished ADJECTIVE **1 = poor**, needy, destitute, ruined, distressed, bankrupt, poverty-stricken, indigent, impecunious, straitened, penurious, necessitous, in reduced *or* straitened circumstances: *The goal is to lure businesses into impoverished areas.* **OPPOSITE:** rich **2 = depleted**, spent, reduced, empty, drained, exhausted, played out, worn out, denuded: *Against the impoverished defence, he poached an early goal.*

impracticable ADJECTIVE **= unfeasible**, impossible, out of the question, unworkable, unattainable, unachievable **OPPOSITE:** practicable

impractical ADJECTIVE **1 = unworkable**, impracticable, unrealistic, inoperable, impossible, unserviceable, nonviable: *With regularly scheduled airlines, sea travel became impractical.* **OPPOSITE:** practical **2 = idealistic**, wild, romantic, unrealistic, visionary, unbusinesslike, starry-eyed: *He's full of wacky, weird and impractical ideas.* **OPPOSITE:** realistic

imprecise ADJECTIVE **= indefinite**, estimated, rough, vague, loose, careless, ambiguous, inaccurate, sloppy (*informal*), woolly, hazy, indeterminate, wide of the mark, equivocal, ill-defined, inexact, inexplicit, blurred round the edges **OPPOSITE:** precise

impregnable ADJECTIVE **= invulnerable**, strong, secure, unbeatable, invincible, impenetrable, unassailable, indestructible, immovable, unshakable, unconquerable **OPPOSITE:** vulnerable

impregnate VERB **1 = saturate**, soak, steep, fill, seep, pervade, infuse, permeate, imbue, suffuse, percolate, imbrue (*rare*): *plastic impregnated with a light-absorbing dye* **2 = inseminate**, fertilize, make pregnant, fructify, fecundate, get with child: *War entailed killing the men and impregnating the women.*

impress VERB **= excite**, move, strike, touch, affect, influence, inspire, grab (*informal*), amaze, overcome, stir, overwhelm, astonish, dazzle, sway, awe, overawe, make an impression on, rock (*slang, chiefly U.S.*): *What impressed him most was their speed.*

impress something on *or* **upon someone = stress**, bring home to, instil in, drum into, knock into, emphasize to, fix in, inculcate in, ingrain in: *I've impressed on them the need for professionalism.*

impression NOUN **1 = idea**, feeling, thought, sense, opinion, view, assessment, judgment, reaction, belief, concept, fancy, notion, conviction, suspicion, hunch, apprehension, inkling, funny feeling (*informal*): *My impression is that they are totally out of control.* **2 = effect**, influence, impact, sway: *She gave no sign that his charm had made any impression on her.* **3 = imitation**, parody, impersonation, mockery, send-up (*Brit. informal*), takeoff (*informal*): *He amused us doing impressions of film actors.* **4 = mark**, imprint, stamp, stamping, depression, outline, hollow, dent, impress, indentation: *the world's oldest fossil impressions of plant life*

make an impression = cause a stir, stand out, make an impact, be conspicuous, find favour, make a hit (*informal*), arouse comment, excite notice: *He's certainly made an impression on the interviewing board.*

> **PROVERBS**
> *First impressions are the most lasting*

impressionable ADJECTIVE **= suggestible**, vulnerable, susceptible, open, sensitive, responsive, receptive, gullible, ingenuous **OPPOSITE:** blasé

impressive ADJECTIVE **= grand**, striking, splendid, good, great (*informal*), fine, affecting, powerful, exciting, wonderful, excellent, dramatic, outstanding, stirring, superb, first-class, marvellous (*informal*), terrific (*informal*), awesome, world-class, admirable, first-rate, crash-hot (*Austral.*), forcible **OPPOSITE:** unimpressive

imprint NOUN **= mark**, print, impression, stamp, indentation: *the imprint of his little finger*
▷ VERB **= engrave**, print, stamp, impress, etch, emboss: *a racket with the club's badge imprinted on the strings*

imprison VERB **= jail**, confine, detain, lock up, constrain, put away, intern, incarcerate, send down (*informal*), send to prison, impound, put under lock and key, immure **OPPOSITE:** free

imprisoned ADJECTIVE **= jailed**, confined, locked up, inside (*slang*), in jail, captive, behind bars, put away, interned, incarcerated, in irons, under lock and key, immured

imprisonment NOUN **= confinement**, custody, detention, captivity, incarceration, internment, duress

The Language of Jack London

Jack London (1876–1916) was an American novelist most famous for his canine tales *White Fang* and *The Call of the Wild* though he also produced a broad range of other work, including short stories, journalism, and memoirs. After humble beginnings in California, his flamboyant life was filled with a remarkable array of jobs from a poacher of oysters to war-correspondent before he finally became one of the most successful writers of his generation.

Among London's numerous careers was a period spent trying to make his fortune as a prospector in the Klondike gold rush. *Gold* is consequently a prominent feature of his writing and is accompanied by a specialized vocabulary. The self-explanatory *coarse* is the most salient adjective with *gold*, though other lexical choices are more unusual. *Flour gold* indicates small particles of the precious metal mingled with other substances, as in:

> **Flour gold** was in this gravel, and after two feet it gave away again to muck.

Bonanza is another recurrent term in London's work that is associated primarily with the gold rush. While it predominantly features as a place name (Bonanza Creek in *Burning Daylight*, for example), it also appears as a noun indicating a stroke of good fortune and as an adjective describing someone who has profited from such success, most commonly a *bonanza farmer*. More generally the semantic field of *money* and *wealth* is important in London's writing with verbs denoting various forms of acquisition appearing often with *money*, particularly *get*, *make*, *borrow*, and *earn*. *Wealth* is modified most frequently by *great*, while *poverty*, conversely, appears rarely in London's work.

The Pacific islands, where London spent some months aboard a yacht, feature as the setting for many of his texts. This strand of his writing leads him to depict the Pidgin English adopted by the indigenous inhabitants. A prominent word in this context is *fella*, evidently a contracted version of fellow. This appears most often with *boy*, followed by another of London's renderings of Pidgin, *marster*. Frequently, this is extended into a longer, more elaborate description of a man that emphasizes the imperialist context of London and his characters' contact with Pacific islanders. *Big fella white marster* is the most recurrent such term, while *fella dog* occurs on several occasions as a term of abuse. Other features of this language include the addition of *'m* to verbs, as in:

> One fella boy hurt'm that fella dog – my word!

Savve meaning understand is a word recurring in London's Pidgin that has some currency in modern English, more usually as savvy, connoting shrewdness or wisdom.

Alcohol formed the subject of London's autobiographical 'Alcoholic Memoirs', *John Barleycorn* and features in much of his writing. When *drink* appears as a verb it is most likely to refer to *beer*, with *cocktail* the second most common tipple. More soberly, however, *coffee* features before both *whiskey* and *wine*. As a noun *drink* is considerably more frequently accompanied by *strong* than by anything else. *Smoking* is also a consistent element of London's writing with *cigar* more salient than *cigarette* or *pipe*.

A notable part of London's popular literary style is his use of punchy openings that immediately grab the reader's attention. One especially prominent strategy is the use of *it* as the first word of the story. *The Cruise of the Snark*, for instance begins:

> It began in the swimming pool at Glen Ellen.

Also among London's favourite devices is starting with a proper noun, usually the name of the main character, and/or beginning with dialogue. The majority of his first sentences are short and consist of only one clause.

improbable ADJECTIVE **1 = doubtful**, unlikely, uncertain, unbelievable, dubious, questionable, fanciful, far-fetched, implausible: *It seems improbable that this year's figure will show a drop.* **OPPOSITE:** probable **2 = unconvincing**, weak, unbelievable, preposterous: *Their marriage seems an improbable alliance.* **OPPOSITE:** convincing

impromptu ADJECTIVE **= spontaneous**, improvised, unprepared, off-the-cuff *(informal)*, offhand, ad-lib, unscripted, unrehearsed, unpremeditated, extempore, unstudied, extemporaneous, extemporized **OPPOSITE:** rehearsed

improper ADJECTIVE **1 = inappropriate**, unfit, unsuitable, out of place, unwarranted, incongruous, unsuited, ill-timed, uncalled-for, inopportune, inapplicable, unseasonable, inapt, infelicitous, inapposite, malapropos: *He maintained that he had done nothing improper.* **OPPOSITE:** appropriate **2 = indecent**, vulgar, suggestive, unseemly, untoward, risqué, smutty, unbecoming, unfitting, impolite, off-colour, indelicate, indecorous: *He would never be improper; he is always the perfect gentleman.* **OPPOSITE:** decent **3 = incorrect**, wrong, inaccurate, false, irregular, erroneous: *The improper use of medicine can lead to severe adverse reactions.*

impropriety NOUN **1 = indecency**, vulgarity, immodesty, bad taste, incongruity, unsuitability, indecorum: *Inviting him up to your hotel room would smack of impropriety.* **OPPOSITE:** propriety **2 = lapse**, mistake, slip, blunder, gaffe, bloomer *(Brit. informal)*, faux pas, solecism, gaucherie: *He resigned amid allegations of financial impropriety.*

> **QUOTATIONS**
> Impropriety is the soul of wit
> [W. Somerset Maugham *The Moon and Sixpence*]

improve VERB **1 = enhance**, better, add to, upgrade, amend, mend, augment, embellish, touch up, ameliorate, polish up: *He improved their house.* **OPPOSITE:** worsen **2 = get better**, pick up, look up *(informal)*, develop, advance, perk up, take a turn for the better *(informal)*: *The weather is beginning to improve.* **3 = recuperate**, recover, rally, mend, make progress, turn the corner, gain ground, gain strength, convalesce, be on the mend, grow better, make strides, take on a new lease of life *(informal)*: *He had improved so much the doctor cut his dosage.*

improvement NOUN **1 = enhancement**, increase, gain, boost, amendment, correction, heightening, advancement, enrichment, face-lift, embellishment, betterment, rectification, augmentation, amelioration: *the dramatic improvements in conditions* **2 = advance**, development, progress, recovery, reformation, upswing, furtherance: *The system we've just introduced has been a great improvement.*

improvisation NOUN **1 = invention**, spontaneity, ad-libbing, extemporizing: *Funds were not abundant, and clever improvisation was necessary.* **2 = ad-lib**: *an improvisation on 'Jingle Bells'*

improvise VERB **1 = devise**, contrive, make do, concoct, throw together: *If you don't have a wok, improvise one.* **2 = ad-lib**, invent, vamp, busk, wing it *(informal)*, play it by ear *(informal)*, extemporize, speak off the cuff *(informal)*: *Take the story and improvise on it.*

improvised ADJECTIVE **= unprepared**, spontaneous, makeshift, spur-of-the-moment, off-the-cuff *(informal)*, ad-lib, unrehearsed, extempore, extemporaneous, extemporized

imprudent ADJECTIVE **= unwise**, foolish, rash, irresponsible, reckless, careless, ill-advised, foolhardy, indiscreet, unthinking, ill-judged, ill-considered, inconsiderate, heedless, injudicious, incautious, improvident, impolitic, overhasty, temerarious **OPPOSITE:** prudent

impudence NOUN **= boldness**, nerve *(informal)*, cheek *(informal)*, face *(informal)*, front, neck *(informal)*, gall *(informal)*, lip *(slang)*, presumption, audacity, rudeness, chutzpah *(U.S. & Canad. informal)*, insolence, impertinence, effrontery, brass neck *(Brit. informal)*, shamelessness, sauciness, brazenness, sassiness *(U.S. informal)*, pertness, bumptiousness

impudent ADJECTIVE **= bold**, rude, cheeky *(informal)*, forward, fresh *(informal)*, saucy *(informal)*, cocky *(informal)*, audacious, brazen, shameless, sassy *(U.S. informal)*, pert, presumptuous, impertinent, insolent, lippy *(U.S. & Canad. slang)*, bumptious, immodest, bold-faced **OPPOSITE:** polite

impulse NOUN **1 = urge**, longing, desire, drive, wish, fancy, notion, yen *(informal)*, instinct, yearning, inclination, itch, whim, compulsion, caprice: *He resisted an impulse to smile.* **2 = force**, pressure, push, movement, surge, motive, thrust, momentum, stimulus, catalyst, impetus: *Their impulse of broadcasting was for human rights.*
on impulse = impulsively, of your own accord, freely, voluntarily, instinctively, impromptu, off the cuff *(informal)*, in the heat of the moment, off your own bat, quite unprompted: *After lunch she decided, on impulse, to take a bath.*

> **QUOTATIONS**
> I am the very slave of circumstance
> And impulse – borne away with every breath!
> [Lord Byron *Sardanapalus*]
>
> To our strongest impulse, to the tyrant in us, not only our reason but also our conscience yields
> [Friedrich Nietzsche *Beyond Good and Evil*]
>
> Have no truck with first impulses for they are always generous ones
> [Casimir, Comte de Montrond]

impulsive ADJECTIVE **= instinctive**, emotional, unpredictable, quick, passionate, rash, spontaneous, precipitate, intuitive, hasty, headlong, impetuous, devil-may-care, unconsidered, unpremeditated **OPPOSITE:** cautious

impunity NOUN **= immunity**, freedom, licence, permission, liberty, security, exemption, dispensation, nonliability

impure ADJECTIVE **1 = unrefined**, mixed, alloyed, debased, adulterated, admixed: *impure diamonds* **2 = immoral**, corrupt, obscene, indecent, gross, coarse, lewd, carnal, X-rated *(informal)*, salacious, unclean, prurient, lascivious, smutty, lustful, ribald, immodest, licentious, indelicate, unchaste: *They say such behaviour might lead to impure temptations.* **OPPOSITE:** moral **3 = unclean**, dirty, foul, infected, contaminated, polluted, filthy, tainted, sullied, defiled, unwholesome, vitiated, festy *(Austral. slang)*: *They were warned against drinking the impure water from the stream.* **OPPOSITE:** clean

impurity NOUN **1** *(often plural)* **= dirt**, pollutant, scum, grime, contaminant, dross, bits, foreign body, foreign matter: *The air is filtered to remove impurities.* **2 = contamination**, infection, pollution, taint, filth, foulness, defilement, dirtiness, uncleanness, befoulment: *The soap is boiled to remove all traces of impurity.* **3 = immorality**, corruption, obscenity, indecency, vulgarity, prurience, coarseness, licentiousness, immodesty, carnality, lewdness, grossness, salaciousness, lasciviousness, unchastity, smuttiness: *impurity, lust and evil desires*

impute VERB **= attribute**, assign, ascribe, credit, refer, accredit

inaccessible ADJECTIVE **= out-of-reach**, remote, out-of-the-way, unattainable, impassable, unreachable, unapproachable, un-get-at-able *(informal)* **OPPOSITE:** accessible

inaccuracy NOUN **1 = imprecision**, unreliability, incorrectness, unfaithfulness, erroneousness, inexactness: *He was disturbed by the inaccuracy of the answers.* **2 = error**, mistake, slip, fault, defect, blunder, lapse, boob *(Brit. slang)*, literal *(Printing)*, howler *(informal)*, miscalculation, typo *(informal, Printing)*, erratum, corrigendum, barry *or* Barry Crocker *(Austral. slang)*: *Guard against inaccuracies by checking with a variety of sources.*

inaccurate ADJECTIVE **= incorrect**, wrong, mistaken, wild, faulty, careless, unreliable, defective, unfaithful, erroneous, unsound, imprecise, wide of the mark, out, inexact, off-base (*U.S. & Canad. informal*), off-beam (*informal*), discrepant, way off-beam (*informal*) **OPPOSITE:** accurate

inaction NOUN **= inactivity**, inertia, idleness, immobility, torpor, dormancy, torpidity

> **QUOTATIONS**
> The only thing necessary for the triumph of evil is for good men to do nothing
> [Edmund Burke]

inactive ADJECTIVE **1 = unused**, idle, dormant, latent, inert, immobile, mothballed, out of service, inoperative, abeyant: *The satellite has been inactive since its launch two years ago.* **OPPOSITE:** used **2 = idle**, unemployed, out of work, jobless, unoccupied, kicking your heels: *He has been inactive since last year.* **OPPOSITE:** employed **3 = lazy**, passive, slow, quiet, dull, low-key (*informal*), sluggish, lethargic, sedentary, indolent, somnolent, torpid, slothful: *He certainly was not politically inactive.* **OPPOSITE:** active

inactivity NOUN **1 = immobility**, unemployment, inaction, passivity, hibernation, dormancy **OPPOSITE:** mobility

inadequacy NOUN **1 = shortage**, poverty, dearth, paucity, insufficiency, incompleteness, meagreness, skimpiness, scantiness, inadequateness: *the inadequacy of the water supply* **2 = incompetence**, inability, deficiency, incapacity, ineffectiveness, incompetency, unfitness, inefficacy, defectiveness, inaptness, faultiness, unsuitableness: *his deep-seated sense of inadequacy* **3 = shortcoming**, failing, lack, weakness, shortage, defect, imperfection: *He drank heavily in an effort to forget his own inadequacies.*

inadequate ADJECTIVE **1 = insufficient**, short, scarce, meagre, poor, lacking, incomplete, scant, sparse, skimpy, sketchy, insubstantial, scanty, niggardly, incommensurate: *Supplies of food and medicine are inadequate.* **OPPOSITE:** adequate **2 = incapable**, incompetent, pathetic, faulty, unfitted, defective, unequal, deficient, imperfect, unqualified, not up to scratch (*informal*), inapt: *She felt quite painfully inadequate in the crisis.* **OPPOSITE:** capable

inadequately ADVERB **= insufficiently**, poorly, thinly, sparsely, scantily, imperfectly, sketchily, skimpily, meagrely

inadvertent ADJECTIVE **= unintentional**, accidental, unintended, chance, careless, negligent, unwitting, unplanned, thoughtless, unthinking, heedless, unpremeditated, unheeding

inadvertently ADVERB **= unintentionally**, accidentally, by accident, mistakenly, unwittingly, by mistake, involuntarily **OPPOSITE:** deliberately

inalienable ADJECTIVE **= sacrosanct**, absolute, unassailable, inherent, entailed (*Law*), non-negotiable, inviolable, nontransferable, untransferable

inane ADJECTIVE **= senseless**, stupid, silly, empty, daft (*informal*), worthless, futile, trifling, frivolous, mindless, goofy (*informal*), idiotic, vacuous, fatuous, puerile, vapid, unintelligent, asinine, imbecilic, devoid of intelligence **OPPOSITE:** sensible

inanimate ADJECTIVE **= lifeless**, inert, dead, cold, extinct, defunct, inactive, soulless, quiescent, spiritless, insensate, insentient **OPPOSITE:** animate

inaugural ADJECTIVE **= first**, opening, initial, maiden, introductory, dedicatory

inaugurate VERB **1 = invest**, install, induct, instate: *The new president will be inaugurated on January 20.* **2 = open**, commission, dedicate, ordain: *A new centre for research was inaugurated today.* **3 = launch**, begin, introduce, institute, set up, kick off (*informal*), initiate, originate, commence, get under way, usher in, set in motion: *They inaugurated the first ever scheduled flights.*

inauguration NOUN **1 = investiture**, installation, induction: *the inauguration of the new Governor* **2 = opening**, launch, birth, inception, commencement: *They later attended the inauguration of the University.* **3 = launch**, launching, setting up, institution, initiation: *the inauguration of monetary union*

inborn ADJECTIVE **= natural**, inherited, inherent, hereditary, instinctive, innate, intuitive, ingrained, congenital, inbred, native, immanent, in your blood, connate

inbred ADJECTIVE **= innate**, natural, constitutional, native, ingrained, inherent, deep-seated, immanent

inbuilt ADJECTIVE **= integral**, built-in, incorporated, component

incalculable ADJECTIVE **= vast**, enormous, immense, countless, infinite, innumerable, untold, limitless, boundless, inestimable, numberless, uncountable, measureless, without number, incomputable

incandescent ADJECTIVE **= glowing**, brilliant, shining, red-hot, radiant, luminous, white-hot, Day-Glo, phosphorescent

incantation NOUN **= chant**, spell, charm, formula, invocation, hex (*U.S. & Canad. informal*), abracadabra, conjuration

incapacitate VERB **= disable**, cripple, paralyse, scupper (*Brit. slang*), prostrate, immobilize, put someone out of action (*informal*), lay someone up (*informal*)

incapacitated ADJECTIVE **= disabled**, challenged, unfit, out of action (*informal*), laid up (*informal*), immobilized, indisposed, hors de combat (*French*)

incapacity NOUN **= inability**, weakness, inadequacy, impotence, powerlessness, ineffectiveness, feebleness, incompetency, unfitness, incapability

incapsulate *see* **encapsulate**

incarcerate VERB **= imprison**, confine, detain, lock up, restrict, restrain, intern, send down (*Brit.*), impound, coop up, throw in jail, put under lock and key, immure, jail *or* gaol

incarceration NOUN **= confinement**, restraint, imprisonment, detention, captivity, bondage, internment

incarnate ADJECTIVE **1 = personified**, embodied, typified: *He referred to her as evil incarnate.* **2 = made flesh**, in the flesh, in human form, in bodily form: *Why should God become incarnate as a male?*

incarnation NOUN **= embodiment**, manifestation, epitome, type, impersonation, personification, avatar, exemplification, bodily form

incendiary ADJECTIVE **= inflammatory**, provocative, subversive, seditious, rabble-rousing, dissentious

incense[1] NOUN **= perfume**, scent, fragrance, bouquet, aroma, balm, redolence: *an atmospheric place, pungent with incense*

incense[2] VERB **= anger**, infuriate, enrage, excite, provoke, irritate, gall, madden, inflame, exasperate, rile (*informal*), raise the hackles of, nark (*Brit., Austral. & N.Z. slang*), make your blood boil (*informal*), rub you up the wrong way, make your hackles rise, get your hackles up, make you see red (*informal*): *This proposal will incense conservation campaigners.*

incensed ADJECTIVE **= angry**, mad (*informal*), furious, cross, fuming, choked, infuriated, enraged, maddened, exasperated, indignant, irate, up in arms, incandescent, steamed up (*slang*), hot under the collar (*informal*), on the warpath (*informal*), wrathful, ireful (*literary*), tooshie (*Austral. slang*), off the air (*Austral. slang*)

incentive NOUN **= inducement**, motive, encouragement, urge, come-on (*informal*), spur, lure, bait, motivation, carrot (*informal*), impulse, stimulus, impetus, stimulant, goad, incitement, enticement **OPPOSITE:** disincentive

inception NOUN **= beginning**, start, rise, birth, origin, dawn, outset, initiation, inauguration, commencement, kickoff *(informal)* **OPPOSITE:** end

incessant ADJECTIVE = **constant**, endless, continuous, persistent, eternal, relentless, perpetual, continual, unbroken, never-ending, interminable, unrelenting, everlasting, unending, ceaseless, unremitting, nonstop, unceasing **OPPOSITE:** intermittent

incessantly ADVERB = **all the time**, constantly, continually, endlessly, persistently, eternally, perpetually, nonstop, ceaselessly, without a break, interminably, everlastingly

incidence NOUN = **prevalence**, frequency, occurrence, rate, amount, degree, extent

incident NOUN **1** = **disturbance**, scene, clash, disorder, confrontation, brawl, uproar, skirmish, mishap, fracas, commotion, contretemps: *Safety chiefs are investigating the incident.* **2** = **happening**, event, affair, business, fact, matter, occasion, circumstance, episode, occurrence, escapade: *They have not based it on any incident from the past.* **3** = **adventure**, drama, excitement, crisis, spectacle, theatrics: *The birth was not without incident.*

incidental ADJECTIVE **1** = **secondary**, subsidiary, subordinate, minor, occasional, ancillary, nonessential: *The playing of music proved to be incidental to the main business.* **OPPOSITE:** essential **2** = **accompanying**, related, attendant, contingent, contributory, concomitant: *At the bottom of the bill were various incidental expenses.*

incidentally ADVERB **1** = **by the way**, in passing, en passant, parenthetically, by the bye: *The tower, incidentally, dates from the twelfth century.* **2** = **accidentally**, casually, by chance, coincidentally, fortuitously, by happenstance: *In her denunciation, she incidentally shed some light on another mystery.*

incinerate VERB **1** = **burn up**, carbonize: *The government is trying to stop them incinerating their own waste.* **2** = **cremate**, burn up, reduce to ashes, consume by fire: *Some of the victims were incinerated.*

incipient ADJECTIVE = **beginning**, starting, developing, originating, commencing, embryonic, nascent, inchoate, inceptive

incision NOUN = **cut**, opening, slash, notch, slit, gash

incisive ADJECTIVE = **penetrating**, sharp, keen, acute, piercing, trenchant, perspicacious **OPPOSITE:** dull

incite VERB = **provoke**, encourage, drive, excite, prompt, urge, spur, stimulate, set on, animate, rouse, prod, stir up, inflame, instigate, whip up, egg on, goad, impel, foment, put up to, agitate for *or* against **OPPOSITE:** discourage

incitement NOUN = **provocation**, prompting, encouragement, spur, motive, motivation, impulse, stimulus, impetus, agitation, inducement, goad, instigation, clarion call

inclination NOUN **1** = **desire**, longing, wish, need, aspiration, craving, yearning, hankering: *He had neither the time nor the inclination to think about it.* **2** = **tendency**, liking, taste, turn, fancy, leaning, bent, stomach, prejudice, bias, affection, thirst, disposition, penchant, fondness, propensity, aptitude, predisposition, predilection, proclivity, partiality, turn of mind, proneness: *He set out to follow his artistic inclinations.* **OPPOSITE:** aversion **3** = **bow**, bending, nod, bowing: *a polite inclination of his head*

incline VERB **1** = **predispose**, influence, tend, persuade, prejudice, bias, sway, turn, dispose: *the factors which incline us towards particular beliefs* **2** = **bend**, lower, nod, bow, stoop, nutate *(rare)*: *He inclined his head very slightly.*
▷ NOUN = **slope**, rise, dip, grade, descent, ramp, ascent, gradient, declivity, acclivity: *He came to a halt at the edge of a steep incline.*

inclined ADJECTIVE **1** = **disposed**, given, prone, likely, subject, liable, apt, predisposed, tending towards: *He was inclined to self-pity.* **2** = **willing**, minded, ready, disposed, of a mind *(informal)*: *I am inclined to agree with Alan.*

inclose *see* **enclose**

include VERB **1** = **contain**, involve, incorporate, cover, consist of, take in, embrace, comprise, take into account, embody, encompass, comprehend, subsume: *The trip was extended to include a few other events.* **OPPOSITE:** exclude **2** = **count**, introduce, make a part of, number among: *I had worked hard to be included in a project like this.* **3** = **add**, enter, put in, insert: *You should include details of all your benefits.*

including PREPOSITION = **containing**, with, counting, plus, together with, as well as, inclusive of

inclusion NOUN = **addition**, incorporation, introduction, insertion **OPPOSITE:** exclusion

inclusive ADJECTIVE = **comprehensive**, full, overall, general, global, sweeping, all-in, blanket, umbrella, across-the-board, all-together, catch-all *(chiefly U.S.)*, all-embracing, overarching, in toto *(Latin)* **OPPOSITE:** limited

incognito ADJECTIVE = **in disguise**, unknown, disguised, unrecognized, under an assumed name

incoherent ADJECTIVE = **unintelligible**, wild, confused, disordered, wandering, muddled, rambling, inconsistent, jumbled, stammering, disconnected, stuttering, unconnected, disjointed, inarticulate, uncoordinated **OPPOSITE:** coherent

income NOUN = **revenue**, gains, earnings, means, pay, interest, returns, profits, wages, rewards, yield, proceeds, salary, receipts, takings

> **QUOTATIONS**
>
> A large income is the best recipe for happiness I ever heard of. It certainly may secure all the myrtle and turkey part of it
> [Jane Austen *Mansfield Park*]
>
> There are few sorrows, however poignant, in which a good income is of no avail
> [Logan Pearsall Smith]

incoming ADJECTIVE **1** = **arriving**, landing, approaching, entering, returning, homeward: *The airport was closed to incoming flights.* **OPPOSITE:** departing **2** = **new**, next, succeeding, elected, elect: *the problems confronting the incoming government*

incomparable ADJECTIVE = **unequalled**, supreme, unparalleled, paramount, superlative, transcendent, unrivalled, inimitable, unmatched, peerless, matchless, beyond compare

incompatibility NOUN = **inconsistency**, conflict, discrepancy, antagonism, incongruity, irreconcilability, disparateness, uncongeniality

incompatible ADJECTIVE = **inconsistent**, conflicting, contradictory, unsuitable, disparate, incongruous, discordant, antagonistic, irreconcilable, unsuited, mismatched, discrepant, uncongenial, antipathetic, ill-assorted, inconsonant **OPPOSITE:** compatible

incompetence NOUN = **ineptitude**, inability, inadequacy, incapacity, ineffectiveness, uselessness, insufficiency, ineptness, incompetency, unfitness, incapability, skill-lessness

incompetent ADJECTIVE = **inept**, useless, incapable, unable, cowboy *(informal)*, floundering, bungling, unfit, unfitted, ineffectual, incapacitated, inexpert, skill-less, unskilful **OPPOSITE:** competent

incomplete ADJECTIVE = **unfinished**, partial, insufficient, wanting, short, lacking, undone, defective, deficient, imperfect, undeveloped, fragmentary, unaccomplished, unexecuted, half-pie *(N.Z. informal)* **OPPOSITE:** complete

incomprehensible ADJECTIVE **1** = **unintelligible**: *Her speech was almost incomprehensible.* **OPPOSITE:** comprehensible **2** = **obscure**, puzzling, mysterious, baffling, enigmatic, perplexing, opaque, impenetrable, inscrutable, unfathomable, above your head, beyond comprehension, all Greek to you *(informal)*, beyond your grasp:

incomprehensible mathematics puzzles
OPPOSITE: understandable

inconceivable ADJECTIVE
= **unimaginable**, impossible, incredible, staggering *(informal)*, unbelievable, unthinkable, out of the question, incomprehensible, unheard-of, mind-boggling *(informal)*, beyond belief, unknowable, not to be thought of **OPPOSITE:** conceivable

inconclusive ADJECTIVE = **uncertain**, vague, ambiguous, open, indecisive, unsettled, undecided, unconvincing, up in the air *(informal)*, indeterminate

incongruity NOUN
= **inappropriateness**, discrepancy, inconsistency, disparity, incompatibility, unsuitability, inaptness, inharmoniousness

incongruous ADJECTIVE
= **inappropriate**, absurd, out of place, conflicting, contrary, contradictory, inconsistent, unsuitable, improper, incompatible, discordant, incoherent, extraneous, unsuited, unbecoming, out of keeping, inapt, disconsonant **OPPOSITE:** appropriate

inconsequential ADJECTIVE
= **unimportant**, trivial, insignificant, minor, petty, trifling, negligible, paltry, immaterial, measly, inconsiderable, nickel-and-dime *(U.S. slang)*, of no significance

inconsiderable ADJECTIVE
= **insignificant**, small, slight, light, minor, petty, trivial, trifling, negligible, unimportant, small-time *(informal)*, inconsequential, exiguous

inconsiderate ADJECTIVE = **selfish**, rude, insensitive, self-centred, careless, unkind, intolerant, thoughtless, unthinking, tactless, uncharitable, ungracious, indelicate **OPPOSITE:** considerate

inconsistency NOUN
1 = unreliability, instability, unpredictability, fickleness, unsteadiness: *His worst fault was his inconsistency.* **2 = incompatibility**, paradox, discrepancy, disparity, disagreement, variance, divergence, incongruity, contrariety, inconsonance: *the alleged inconsistencies in his evidence*

inconsistent ADJECTIVE
1 = changeable, variable, unpredictable, unstable, irregular, erratic, uneven, fickle, capricious, unsteady, inconstant: *You are inconsistent and unpredictable.*
OPPOSITE: consistent
2 = incompatible, conflicting, contrary, at odds, contradictory, in conflict, incongruous, discordant, incoherent, out of step, irreconcilable, at variance, discrepant, inconstant: *The outburst was inconsistent with the image he had cultivated.* **OPPOSITE:** compatible

inconsolable ADJECTIVE
= **heartbroken**, devastated, despairing, desolate, wretched, heartsick, brokenhearted, sick at heart, prostrate with grief

inconspicuous ADJECTIVE
1 = unobtrusive, hidden, unnoticeable, retiring, quiet, ordinary, plain, muted, camouflaged, insignificant, unassuming, unostentatious: *I'll try to be as inconspicuous as possible.*
OPPOSITE: noticeable **2 = plain**, ordinary, modest, unobtrusive, unnoticeable: *The studio is an inconspicuous grey building.*

incontrovertible ADJECTIVE
= **indisputable**, sure, certain, established, positive, undeniable, irrefutable, unquestionable, unshakable, beyond dispute, incontestable, indubitable, nailed-on *(slang)*

inconvenience NOUN **1 = trouble**, difficulty, bother, upset, fuss, disadvantage, disturbance, disruption, drawback, hassle *(informal)*, nuisance, downside, annoyance, hindrance, awkwardness, vexation, uphill *(S. African)*: *We apologize for any inconvenience caused during the repairs.*
2 = awkwardness, unfitness, unwieldiness, cumbersomeness, unhandiness, unsuitableness, untimeliness: *The expense and inconvenience of PCs means that they will be replaced.*
▷ VERB = **trouble**, bother, disturb, upset, disrupt, put out, hassle *(informal)*, irk, discommode, give (someone) bother *or* trouble, make (someone) go out of his way, put to trouble: *He promised not to inconvenience them any further.*

> **QUOTATIONS**
> An adventure is only an inconvenience rightly considered. An inconvenience is only an adventure wrongly considered
> [G.K. Chesterton *All Things Considered*]

inconvenient ADJECTIVE
1 = troublesome, annoying, awkward, embarrassing, disturbing, unsuitable, tiresome, untimely, bothersome, vexatious, inopportune, disadvantageous, unseasonable: *It's very inconvenient to have to wait so long.*
OPPOSITE: convenient **2 = difficult**, awkward, unmanageable, cumbersome, unwieldy, unhandy: *This must be the most inconvenient house ever built.*

incorporate VERB **1 = include**, contain, take in, embrace, integrate, embody, encompass, assimilate, comprise of: *The new cars will incorporate a number of major improvements.*
2 = integrate, include, absorb, unite, merge, accommodate, knit, fuse, assimilate, amalgamate, subsume, coalesce, harmonize, meld: *The agreement allowed the rebels to be incorporated into the police force.* **3 = blend**, mix, combine, compound, consolidate, fuse, mingle, meld: *Gradually incorporate the olive oil into the dough.*

incorporation NOUN = **merger**, federation, blend, integration, unifying, inclusion, fusion, absorption, assimilation, amalgamation, coalescence

incorrect ADJECTIVE = **false**, wrong, mistaken, flawed, faulty, unfitting, inaccurate, untrue, improper, erroneous, out, wide of the mark *(informal)*, specious, inexact, off-base *(U.S. & Canad. informal)*, off-beam *(informal)*, way off-beam *(informal)*
OPPOSITE: correct

incorrigible ADJECTIVE = **incurable**, hardened, hopeless, intractable, inveterate, unreformed, irredeemable

increase VERB **1 = raise**, extend, boost, expand, develop, advance, add to, strengthen, enhance, step up *(informal)*, widen, prolong, intensify, heighten, elevate, enlarge, multiply, inflate, magnify, amplify, augment, aggrandize, upscale: *The company has increased the price of its cars.*
OPPOSITE: decrease **2 = grow**, develop, spread, mount, expand, build up, swell, wax, enlarge, escalate, multiply, fill out, get bigger, proliferate, snowball, dilate: *The population continues to increase.*
OPPOSITE: shrink
▷ NOUN = **growth**, rise, boost, development, gain, addition, expansion, extension, heightening, proliferation, enlargement, escalation, upsurge, upturn, bounce, increment, intensification, step-up *(informal)*, augmentation, aggrandizement: *a sharp increase in productivity*
on the increase = growing, increasing, spreading, expanding, escalating, multiplying, developing, on the rise, proliferating: *Crime is on the increase.*

increasingly ADVERB = **progressively**, more and more, to an increasing extent, continuously more

incredible ADJECTIVE **1 = amazing**, great, wonderful, brilliant, stunning, extraordinary, overwhelming, ace *(informal)*, astonishing, staggering, marvellous, sensational *(informal)*, mega *(slang)*, breathtaking, astounding, far-out *(slang)*, eye-popping *(informal)*, prodigious, awe-inspiring, superhuman, rad *(informal)*: *Thanks, I had an incredible time.*
2 = unbelievable, impossible, absurd, unthinkable, questionable, improbable, inconceivable, preposterous, unconvincing, unimaginable, outlandish, far-fetched, implausible, beyond belief, cock-and-bull *(informal)*, not able to hold water: *Do not dismiss as incredible the stories your children tell you.*

incredulity NOUN = **disbelief**, doubt, scepticism, distrust, unbelief

incredulous ADJECTIVE
= **disbelieving**, doubting, sceptical, suspicious, doubtful, dubious,

i

unconvinced, distrustful, mistrustful, unbelieving
OPPOSITE: credulous

increment NOUN **= increase**, gain, addition, supplement, step up, advancement, enlargement, accretion, accrual, augmentation, accruement

incriminate VERB **= implicate**, involve, accuse, blame, indict, point the finger at *(informal)*, stigmatize, arraign, blacken the name of, inculpate

incumbent NOUN **= holder**, keeper, bearer, custodian: *The previous incumbent led the party for eleven years.* ▷ ADJECTIVE **= obligatory**, required, necessary, essential, binding, compulsory, mandatory, imperative: *It is incumbent upon all of us to make an extra effort.*

incur VERB **= sustain**, experience, suffer, gain, earn, collect, meet with, provoke, run up, induce, arouse, expose yourself to, lay yourself open to, bring upon yourself

i

incurable ADJECTIVE **1 = fatal**, terminal, inoperable, irrecoverable, irremediable, remediless: *He is suffering from an incurable skin disease.* **2 = incorrigible**, hopeless, inveterate, dyed-in-the-wool: *He's an incurable romantic.*

incursion NOUN **= foray**, raid, invasion, penetration, infiltration, inroad, irruption

indebted ADJECTIVE **= grateful**, obliged, in debt, obligated, beholden, under an obligation

indecency NOUN **= obscenity**, impurity, lewdness, impropriety, pornography, vulgarity, coarseness, crudity, licentiousness, foulness, outrageousness, immodesty, grossness, vileness, bawdiness, unseemliness, indelicacy, smuttiness, indecorum
OPPOSITE: decency

indecent ADJECTIVE **1 = obscene**, lewd, dirty, blue, offensive, outrageous, inappropriate, rude, gross, foul, crude, coarse, filthy, vile, improper, pornographic, salacious, impure, smutty, immodest, licentious, scatological, indelicate: *She accused him of making indecent suggestions.* **OPPOSITE:** decent **2 = unbecoming**, unsuitable, vulgar, improper, tasteless, unseemly, undignified, disreputable, unrefined, discreditable, indelicate, indecorous, unbefitting: *The legislation was drafted with indecent haste.* **OPPOSITE:** proper

indecision NOUN **= hesitation**, doubt, uncertainty, wavering, ambivalence, dithering *(chiefly Brit.)*, hesitancy, indecisiveness, vacillation, shilly-shallying *(informal)*, irresolution

QUOTATIONS
There is no more miserable human being than one in whom nothing is habitual but indecision, and for whom the lighting of every cigar, the drinking of every cup, the time of rising and going to bed every day, and the beginning of every bit of work, are subjects of express volitional deliberation
[William James *Varieties of Religious Experience*]

PROVERBS
The cat would eat fish, but would not wet her feet

indecisive ADJECTIVE **1 = hesitating**, uncertain, wavering, doubtful, faltering, tentative, undecided, dithering *(chiefly Brit.)*, vacillating, in two minds *(informal)*, undetermined, pussyfooting *(informal)*, irresolute: *He was criticised as a weak and indecisive leader.* **OPPOSITE:** decisive **2 = inconclusive**, unclear, undecided, indefinite, indeterminate: *An indecisive vote would force a second round of voting.*
OPPOSITE: conclusive

indeed ADVERB **1 = certainly**, yes, definitely, surely, truly, absolutely, undoubtedly, positively, decidedly, without doubt, undeniably, without question, unequivocally, indisputably, assuredly, doubtlessly: *'Did you know him?' 'I did indeed.'* **2 = really**, actually, in fact, certainly, undoubtedly, genuinely, in reality, to be sure, in truth, categorically, verily *(archaic)*, in actuality, in point of fact, veritably: *Later he admitted that the payments had indeed been made.*

indefatigable ADJECTIVE **= tireless**, dogged, persevering, patient, relentless, diligent, inexhaustible, unremitting, assiduous, unflagging, untiring, sedulous, pertinacious, unwearying, unwearied

indefensible ADJECTIVE **= unforgivable**, wrong, inexcusable, unjustifiable, untenable, unpardonable, insupportable, unwarrantable **OPPOSITE:** defensible

indefinite ADJECTIVE **1 = uncertain**, general, vague, unclear, unsettled, loose, unlimited, evasive, indeterminate, imprecise, undefined, equivocal, ill-defined, indistinct, undetermined, inexact, unfixed, oracular: *The trial was adjourned for an indefinite period.* **OPPOSITE:** settled **2 = unclear**, unknown, uncertain, obscure, doubtful, ambiguous, indeterminate, imprecise, undefined, ill-defined, indistinct, undetermined, inexact, unfixed: *a handsome woman of indefinite age*
OPPOSITE: specific

indefinitely ADVERB **= endlessly**, continually, for ever, ad infinitum, sine die *(Latin)*, till the cows come home *(informal)*

indelible ADJECTIVE **= permanent**, lasting, enduring, ingrained, indestructible, ineradicable, ineffaceable, inexpungible, inextirpable **OPPOSITE:** temporary

indemnify VERB **1 = insure**, protect, guarantee, secure, endorse, underwrite: *They agreed to indemnify the taxpayers against any loss.* **2 = compensate**, pay, reimburse, satisfy, repair, repay, requite, remunerate: *They don't have the money to indemnify everybody.*

indemnity NOUN **1 = insurance**, security, guarantee, protection: *They had failed to take out full indemnity cover.* **2 = compensation**, remuneration, reparation, satisfaction, redress, restitution, reimbursement, requital: *The government paid the family an indemnity for the missing pictures.* **3 = exemption**, immunity, impunity, privilege: *He was offered indemnity from prosecution in return for his evidence.*

indent VERB **1 = notch**, cut, score, mark, nick, pink, scallop, dint, serrate: *the country's heavily indented coastline* **2 = order**, request, ask for, requisition: *We had to indent for hatchets and torches.*

indentation NOUN **= notch**, cut, nick, depression, pit, dip, bash *(informal)*, hollow, dent, jag, dimple

independence NOUN **= freedom**, liberty, autonomy, separation, sovereignty, self-determination, self-government, self-rule, self-sufficiency, self-reliance, home rule, autarchy, rangatiratanga *(N.Z.)*
OPPOSITE: subjugation

independent ADJECTIVE **1 = separate**, unrelated, unconnected, unattached, uncontrolled, unconstrained: *Two independent studies have been carried out.* **OPPOSITE:** controlled **2 = self-sufficient**, free, liberated, unconventional, self-contained, individualistic, unaided, self-reliant, self-supporting: *There were benefits to being a single, independent woman.* **3 = self-governing**, free, autonomous, separated, liberated, sovereign, self-determining, nonaligned, decontrolled, autarchic: *a fully independent state* **OPPOSITE:** subject

independently ADVERB **= separately**, alone, solo, on your own, by yourself, unaided, individually, autonomously, under your own steam

indescribable ADJECTIVE **= unutterable**, indefinable, beyond words, ineffable, inexpressible, beyond description, incommunicable, beggaring description

indestructible ADJECTIVE **= permanent**, durable, unbreakable, lasting, enduring, abiding, immortal, everlasting, indelible, incorruptible, imperishable, indissoluble, unfading, nonperishable
OPPOSITE: breakable

indeterminate ADJECTIVE **= uncertain**, indefinite, unspecified, vague, inconclusive, imprecise, undefined, undetermined, inexact, unfixed, unstipulated
OPPOSITE: fixed

index NOUN = **indication**, guide, sign, mark, note, evidence, signal, symptom, hint, clue, token

indicate VERB 1 = **show**, suggest, reveal, display, signal, demonstrate, point to, imply, disclose, manifest, signify, denote, bespeak, make known, be symptomatic of, evince, betoken, flag up: *The survey indicated that most old people are independent.* 2 = **imply**, suggest, hint, intimate, signify, insinuate, give someone to understand: *He has indicated that he might resign.* 3 = **point to**, point out, specify, gesture towards, designate: *'Sit down,' he said, indicating a chair.* 4 = **register**, show, record, mark, read, express, display, demonstrate: *The gauge indicated that it was boiling.*

indication NOUN = **sign**, mark, evidence, warning, note, signal, suggestion, symptom, hint, clue, manifestation, omen, inkling, portent, intimation, forewarning, wake-up call

indicative ADJECTIVE = **suggestive**, significant, symptomatic, pointing to, exhibitive, indicatory, indicial

indicator NOUN = **sign**, mark, measure, guide, display, index, signal, symbol, meter, gauge, marker, benchmark, pointer, signpost, barometer

indict VERB = **charge**, accuse, prosecute, summon, impeach, arraign, serve with a summons

indictment NOUN = **charge**, allegation, prosecution, accusation, impeachment, summons, arraignment

indifference NOUN 1 = **disregard**, apathy, lack of interest, negligence, detachment, coolness, carelessness, coldness, nonchalance, callousness, aloofness, inattention, unconcern, absence of feeling, heedlessness: *his callous indifference to the plight of his son* **OPPOSITE:** concern 2 = **irrelevance**, insignificance, triviality, unimportance: *They regard dress as a matter of indifference.*

indifferent ADJECTIVE 1 = **unconcerned**, distant, detached, cold, cool, regardless, careless, callous, aloof, unimpressed, unmoved, unsympathetic, impervious, uncaring, uninterested, apathetic, unresponsive, heedless, inattentive: *People have become indifferent to the suffering of others.* **OPPOSITE:** concerned 2 = **mediocre**, middling, average, fair, ordinary, moderate, insignificant, unimportant, so-so *(informal)*, immaterial, passable, undistinguished, uninspired, of no consequence, no great shakes *(informal)*, half-pie *(N.Z. informal)*: *She had starred in several indifferent movies.* **OPPOSITE:** excellent

indigenous ADJECTIVE = **native**, original, aboriginal, home-grown, autochthonous

indigent ADJECTIVE = **destitute**, poor, impoverished, needy, penniless, poverty-stricken, down and out, in want, down at heel *(informal)*, impecunious, dirt-poor, straitened, on the breadline, short, flat broke *(informal)*, penurious, necessitous **OPPOSITE:** wealthy

indigestion NOUN = **upset stomach**, heartburn, dyspepsia, dyspepsy

indignant ADJECTIVE = **resentful**, angry, mad *(informal)*, heated, provoked, furious, annoyed, hacked (off) *(U.S. slang)*, sore *(informal)*, fuming *(informal)*, choked, incensed, disgruntled, exasperated, irate, livid *(informal)*, seeing red *(informal)*, miffed *(informal)*, riled, up in arms *(informal)*, peeved *(informal)*, in a huff, hot under the collar *(informal)*, huffy *(informal)*, wrathful, narked *(Brit., Austral. & N.Z. slang)*, in high dudgeon, tooshie *(Austral. slang)*, off the air *(Austral. slang)*

indignation NOUN = **resentment**, anger, rage, fury, wrath, ire *(literary)*, exasperation, pique, umbrage, righteous anger

indignity NOUN = **humiliation**, abuse, outrage, injury, slight, insult, snub, reproach, affront, disrespect, dishonour, opprobrium, obloquy, contumely

indirect ADJECTIVE 1 = **related**, accompanying, secondary, subsidiary, contingent, collateral, incidental, unintended, ancillary, concomitant: *They are feeling the indirect effects of the recession elsewhere.* 2 = **circuitous**, winding, roundabout, curving, wandering, rambling, deviant, meandering, tortuous, zigzag, long-drawn-out, circumlocutory: *The goods went by a rather indirect route.* **OPPOSITE:** direct

indirectly ADVERB 1 = **by implication**, in a roundabout way, circumlocutorily: *Drugs are indirectly responsible for the violence.* 2 = **obliquely**, in a roundabout way, evasively, not in so many words, circuitously, periphrastically: *He referred indirectly to the territorial dispute.*

indiscreet ADJECTIVE = **tactless**, foolish, rash, reckless, unwise, hasty, ill-advised, unthinking, ill-judged, ill-considered, imprudent, heedless, injudicious, incautious, undiplomatic, impolitic **OPPOSITE:** discreet

indiscretion NOUN 1 = **folly**, foolishness, recklessness, imprudence, rashness, tactlessness, gaucherie: *Occasionally they paid for their indiscretion with their lives.* 2 = **mistake**, slip, error, lapse, folly, boob *(Brit. slang)*, gaffe, bloomer *(Brit. informal)*, faux pas, barry *or* Barry Crocker *(Austral. slang)*: *rumours of his mother's youthful indiscretions*

> **QUOTATIONS**
> Careless talk costs lives
> [*Second World War security slogan*]

indiscriminate ADJECTIVE = **random**, general, wholesale, mixed, sweeping, confused, chaotic, careless, mingled, jumbled, miscellaneous, promiscuous, motley, haphazard, uncritical, aimless, desultory, hit or miss *(informal)*, higgledy-piggledy *(informal)*, undiscriminating, unsystematic, unselective, undistinguishable, unmethodical, scattershot **OPPOSITE:** systematic

indispensable ADJECTIVE = **essential**, necessary, needed, key, vital, crucial, imperative, requisite, needful, must-have **OPPOSITE:** dispensable

indistinct ADJECTIVE 1 = **unclear**, confused, obscure, faint, blurred, vague, doubtful, ambiguous, fuzzy, shadowy, indefinite, misty, hazy, unintelligible, indistinguishable, indeterminate, bleary, undefined, out of focus, ill-defined, indiscernible: *The lettering is fuzzy and indistinct.* **OPPOSITE:** distinct 2 = **muffled**, confused, faint, dim, weak, indistinguishable, indiscernible: *the indistinct murmur of voices*

indistinguishable ADJECTIVE = **identical**, the same, cut from the same cloth, like as two peas in a pod *(informal)*

individual ADJECTIVE 1 = **separate**, single, independent, isolated, lone, solitary, discrete: *waiting for the group to decide rather than making individual decisions* **OPPOSITE:** collective 2 = **unique**, special, fresh, novel, exclusive, distinct, singular, idiosyncratic, unorthodox: *It was all part of her very individual personality.* **OPPOSITE:** conventional ▷ NOUN = **person**, being, human, party, body *(informal)*, type, unit, character, soul, creature, human being, mortal, personage, living soul: *the rights and responsibilities of the individual*

individualism NOUN = **independence**, self-interest, originality, self-reliance, egoism, egocentricity, self-direction, freethinking

individualist NOUN = **maverick**, nonconformist, independent, original, loner, lone wolf, freethinker

individuality NOUN = **character**, personality, uniqueness, distinction, distinctiveness, originality, peculiarity, singularity, separateness, discreteness

individually ADVERB = **separately**, independently, singly, one by one, one at a time, severally

indoctrinate VERB = **brainwash**, school, train, teach, drill, initiate, instruct, imbue

indoctrination NOUN = **brainwashing**, schooling, training, instruction, drilling, inculcation

indomitable ADJECTIVE = **invincible**, resolute, steadfast, set, staunch, unbeatable, unyielding, unflinching, unconquerable, untameable **OPPOSITE:** weak

indorse *see* **endorse**

indorsement *see* **endorsement**

induce VERB **1 = cause**, produce, create, begin, effect, lead to, occasion, generate, provoke, motivate, set off, bring about, give rise to, precipitate, incite, instigate, engender, set in motion: *an economic crisis induced by high oil prices* **OPPOSITE:** prevent **2 = persuade**, encourage, influence, get, move, press, draw, convince, urge, prompt, sway, entice, coax, incite, impel, talk someone into, prevail upon, actuate: *I would do anything to induce them to stay.* **OPPOSITE:** dissuade

inducement NOUN **= incentive**, motive, cause, influence, reward, come-on *(informal)*, spur, consideration, attraction, lure, bait, carrot *(informal)*, encouragement, impulse, stimulus, incitement, clarion call

i

induct VERB **= install**, admit, introduce, allow, swear, initiate, inaugurate

induction NOUN **= installation**, institution, introduction, initiation, inauguration, investiture

indulge VERB **1 = gratify**, satisfy, fulfil, feed, give way to, yield to, cater to, pander to, regale, gladden, satiate: *His success has let him indulge his love of expensive cars.* **2 = spoil**, pamper, cosset, baby, favour, humour, give in to, coddle, spoon-feed, mollycoddle, fawn on, overindulge: *He did not agree with indulging children.*
indulge yourself = treat yourself, splash out, spoil yourself, luxuriate in something, overindulge yourself: *You can indulge yourself without spending a fortune.*

indulgence NOUN **1 = luxury**, treat, extravagance, favour, privilege: *The car is one of my few indulgences.* **2 = leniency**, pampering, spoiling, kindness, fondness, permissiveness, partiality: *The king's indulgence towards his sons angered them.* **3 = intemperance**, excess, extravagance, debauchery, dissipation, overindulgence, prodigality, immoderation, dissoluteness, intemperateness: *Sadly, constant indulgence can be a costly affair.* **OPPOSITE:** temperance **4 = gratification**, satisfaction, fulfilment, appeasement, satiation: *his indulgence of his gross appetites*

indulgent ADJECTIVE **= lenient**, liberal, kind, kindly, understanding, gentle, tender, mild, fond, favourable, tolerant, gratifying, easy-going, compliant, permissive, forbearing **OPPOSITE:** strict

industrialist NOUN **= capitalist**, tycoon, magnate, boss, producer, manufacturer, baron, financier, captain of industry, big businessman

industrious ADJECTIVE **= hard-working**, diligent, active, busy, steady, productive, energetic, conscientious, tireless, zealous, laborious, assiduous, sedulous **OPPOSITE:** lazy

industry NOUN **1 = business**, production, manufacturing, trade, trading, commerce, commercial enterprise: *countries where industry is developing rapidly* **2 = trade**, world, business, service, line, field, craft, profession, occupation: *the textile industry* **3 = diligence**, effort, labour, hard work, trouble, activity, application, striving, endeavour, toil, vigour, zeal, persistence, assiduity, tirelessness: *No one doubted his industry or his integrity.*

> **QUOTATIONS**
> Go to the ant, thou sluggard; consider her ways, and be wise
> [*Bible: Proverbs*]
>
> Where there is no desire, there will be no industry
> [John Locke *Some Thoughts Concerning Education*]
>
> Avarice, the spur of industry
> [David Hume *Essays, Moral and Political: Of Civil Liberty*]
>
> If you have great talents, industry will improve them; if you have but moderate abilities, industry will supply their deficiency
> [Joshua Reynolds *Discourses on Art*]

ineffable ADJECTIVE **= indescribable**, unspeakable, indefinable, beyond words, unutterable, inexpressible, incommunicable

ineffective ADJECTIVE **1 = unproductive**, useless, futile, vain, unsuccessful, pointless, fruitless, to no avail, ineffectual, unprofitable, to no effect, unavailing, unfruitful, profitless, bootless, inefficacious: *Reform will continue to be painful and ineffective.* **OPPOSITE:** effective **2 = inefficient**, inadequate, useless, poor, weak, pathetic, powerless, unfit, feeble, worthless, inept, impotent, ineffectual: *They are burdened with an ineffective leader.*

ineffectual ADJECTIVE **1 = unproductive**, useless, ineffective, vain, unsuccessful, pointless, futile, fruitless, to no avail, unprofitable, to no effect, unavailing, unfruitful, profitless, bootless, inefficacious: *the well-meaning but ineffectual jobs programs of the past* **2 = inefficient**, useless, powerless, poor, weak, inadequate, pathetic, unfit, ineffective, feeble, worthless, inept, impotent: *The mayor had become ineffectual in the war against drugs.*

inefficiency NOUN **= incompetence**, slackness, sloppiness, disorganization, carelessness

inefficient ADJECTIVE **1 = wasteful**, uneconomical, profligate, ruinous, improvident, unthrifty, inefficacious: *the inefficient use of funds* **2 = incompetent**, incapable, inept, weak, bungling, feeble, sloppy, ineffectual, disorganized, slipshod, inexpert: *Some people are very inefficient workers.* **OPPOSITE:** efficient

ineligible ADJECTIVE **= unqualified**, ruled out, unacceptable, disqualified, incompetent *(Law)*, unfit, unfitted, unsuitable, undesirable, objectionable, unequipped

inept ADJECTIVE **1 = incompetent**, bungling, clumsy, cowboy *(informal)*, awkward, bumbling, gauche, cack-handed *(informal)*, inexpert, maladroit, unskilful, unhandy, unworkmanlike: *He was inept and lacked the intelligence to govern.* **OPPOSITE:** competent **2 = unsuitable**, inappropriate, out of place, ridiculous, absurd, meaningless, pointless, unfit, improper, inapt, infelicitous, malapropos: *The Government's inept response turned this into a crisis.* **OPPOSITE:** appropriate

ineptitude NOUN **= incompetence**, inefficiency, inability, incapacity, clumsiness, unfitness, gaucheness, inexpertness, unhandiness

inequality NOUN **= disparity**, prejudice, difference, bias, diversity, irregularity, unevenness, lack of balance, disproportion, imparity, preferentiality

> **QUOTATIONS**
> All animals are equal but some animals are more equal than others
> [George Orwell *Animal Farm*]
>
> Whatever may be the general endeavor of a community to render its members equal and alike, the personal pride of individuals will always seek to rise above the line, and to form somewhere an inequality to their own advantage
> [Alexis de Tocqueville *Democracy in America*]
>
> The worker is the slave of capitalist society, the female worker the slave of that slave
> [James Connolly *The Re-conquest of Ireland*]

inert ADJECTIVE **= inactive**, still, motionless, dead, passive, slack, static, dormant, lifeless, leaden, immobile, inanimate, unresponsive, unmoving, quiescent, torpid, unreactive, slumberous *(chiefly poetic)*: *He covered the inert body with a blanket* **OPPOSITE:** moving

inertia NOUN **= inactivity**, apathy, lethargy, passivity, stillness, laziness, sloth, idleness, stupor, drowsiness, dullness, immobility, torpor, sluggishness, indolence, lassitude, languor, listlessness, deadness, unresponsiveness **OPPOSITE:** activity

inescapable ADJECTIVE **= unavoidable**, inevitable, certain, sure, fated, destined, inexorable, ineluctable, ineludible *(rare)*

inevitable ADJECTIVE **= unavoidable**, inescapable, inexorable, sure, certain, necessary, settled, fixed, assured,

The Language of Henry Fielding

Henry Fielding (1707–54) was a novelist and comic dramatist. He is known particularly for his picaresque novel *Tom Jones* (1749), and for *Joseph Andrews*, which started as a parody of Richardson's *Pamela*. He is also noted as an enlightened magistrate and founder of the Bow Street runners (1749).

The noun that occurs most frequently in Fielding's writing is *man*, as is the case for many authors; it occurs more than twice as often as *woman*. More exceptional is the high frequency of *lady* and *gentleman*. A *lady* is a person of some social status: the fact that *lady* occurs more often than *woman* suggests the social milieu that Fielding focuses on. If a character is described as *a poor woman*, she may either be unfortunate or short of money, while *a poor lady* is invariably an unfortunate one. *Lady* is also used to mean *wife*, as in *Mr Booth and his lady*. *Woman* sometimes means *maid*, as in *Neither the lady nor her woman*.

In modern usage a *gentleman* may be a man who behaves well, but in the 18th century, being a *gentleman* is a matter of birth, education, manner, and appearance:

> if you wear but the appearance of a **gentleman**, they never suspect you are not one.

Another salient noun is *person*. In modern English *people*, rather than *person*, is generally used for the plural of *person*, except in some formal contexts, such as legal language. Fielding uses both *people* and *persons*, but the latter is much more frequent – *two persons* occurs more than twice as often as *two people*. The usage is not formal:

> she was one of the merriest **persons** in the whole prison.

In the 18th century it was normal to use *sir* and *madam* in the way that *monsieur* and *madame* are used in modern French – that is, everyday forms of address that are lacking in modern English, which can call attention, or punctuate a dialogue. Samuel Johnson, a contemporary of Fielding, often begins a remark with *Sir*, or *Madam* – which may seem pompous to a modern reader, but was actually quite unremarkable. *Sir* and *Madam* are among Fielding's most frequently used nouns because much of his writing is dialogue, and his characters speak in the manner of their time:

> 'I presume you are a lawyer, **sir**?' 'No, indeed, **sir**,' answered Booth.

It is not only the characters who speak in Fielding's novels: his authorial voice is ever-present, humorously addressing the reader: *Here, reader, give me leave to stop a minute; Here possibly the reader will blame Mrs Bennet; Some readers may perhaps think...* As well as intervening in the narrative, Fielding prefaces each chapter of *Tom Jones* and *Joseph Andrews* with some comment on what it contains – remarking for example, that it is *a little chapter in which is contained a little incident*.

The prefaces are often funny, but they also function as constant reminders that we are active participants in the process of reading a novel, and that novels are constructs that can be analysed and categorized: thus one chapter is billed as

> shewing what kind of history this is; what it is like, and what it is not like

The prefaces are written like notes, or headlines – they provide a piquant stylistic contrast to the prose of the chapters, which often contains long, Latinate sentences. In the 18th century such sentences were normal in serious writing. Fielding humorously employs them to describe mundane things such as a sister's view that her brother is a silly idiot whom she's kindly humouring:

> With reflections of this nature she usually, as has been hinted, accompanied every act of compliance with her brother's inclinations; and surely nothing could more contribute to heighten the merit of this compliance than a declaration that she knew, at the same time, the folly and unreasonableness of those inclinations to which she submitted.

fated, decreed, destined, ordained, predetermined, predestined, preordained, ineluctable, unpreventable **OPPOSITE:** avoidable

inevitably ADVERB **= unavoidably**, naturally, necessarily, surely, certainly, as a result, automatically, consequently, of necessity, perforce, inescapably, as a necessary consequence

inexcusable ADJECTIVE **= unforgivable**, indefensible, unjustifiable, outrageous, unpardonable, unwarrantable, inexpiable **OPPOSITE:** excusable

inexhaustible ADJECTIVE **1 = endless**, infinite, never-ending, limitless, boundless, bottomless, unbounded, measureless, illimitable: *They seem to have an inexhaustible supply of ammunition.* **OPPOSITE:** limited **2 = tireless**, undaunted, indefatigable, unfailing, unflagging, untiring, unwearying, unwearied: *the sound of his inexhaustible voice, still talking* **OPPOSITE:** tiring

i

inexorable ADJECTIVE **= unrelenting**, relentless, implacable, hard, severe, harsh, cruel, adamant, inescapable, inflexible, merciless, unyielding, immovable, remorseless, pitiless, unbending, obdurate, ineluctable, unappeasable **OPPOSITE:** relenting

inexorably ADVERB **= relentlessly**, inevitably, irresistibly, remorselessly, implacably, unrelentingly

inexpensive ADJECTIVE **= cheap**, reasonable, low-priced, budget, bargain, modest, low-cost, economical **OPPOSITE:** expensive

inexperience NOUN **= unfamiliarity**, ignorance, newness, rawness, greenness, callowness, unexpertness

> **PROVERBS**
> *You cannot put an old head on young shoulders*

inexperienced ADJECTIVE **= new**, unskilled, untrained, green, fresh, amateur, raw, unfamiliar, unused, callow, immature, unaccustomed, untried, unschooled, wet behind the ears *(informal)*, unacquainted, unseasoned, unpractised, unversed, unfledged **OPPOSITE:** experienced

inexplicable ADJECTIVE **= unaccountable**, strange, mysterious, baffling, enigmatic, incomprehensible, mystifying, unintelligible, insoluble, inscrutable, unfathomable, beyond comprehension **OPPOSITE:** explicable

inextricably ADVERB **= inseparably**, totally, intricately, irretrievably, indissolubly, indistinguishably

infallibility NOUN **1 = supremacy**, perfection, omniscience, impeccability, faultlessness, irrefutability, unerringness: *exaggerated views of the infallibility of science* **2 = reliability**, safety, dependability, trustworthiness, sureness: *The technical infallibility of their systems is without doubt.*

infallible ADJECTIVE **1 = perfect**, impeccable, faultless, unerring, omniscient, unimpeachable: *She had an infallible eye for style.* **OPPOSITE:** fallible **2 = sure**, certain, reliable, unbeatable, dependable, trustworthy, foolproof, sure-fire *(informal)*, unfailing: *She hit on an infallible way of staying sober amid a flood of toasts.* **OPPOSITE:** unreliable

infamous ADJECTIVE **= notorious**, base, shocking, outrageous, disgraceful, monstrous, shameful, vile, scandalous, wicked, atrocious, heinous, odious, hateful, loathsome, ignominious, disreputable, egregious, abominable, villainous, dishonourable, nefarious, iniquitous, detestable, opprobrious, ill-famed, flagitious **OPPOSITE:** esteemed

infamy NOUN **= notoriety**, scandal, shame, disgrace, atrocity, discredit, stigma, disrepute, ignominy, dishonour, abomination, opprobrium, villainy, odium, outrageousness, obloquy

infancy NOUN **1 = early childhood**, babyhood: *the development of the mind from infancy onwards* **2 = beginnings**, start, birth, roots, seeds, origins, dawn, early stages, emergence, outset, cradle, inception: *the infancy of the electronic revolution* **OPPOSITE:** end

> **QUOTATIONS**
> Heaven lies about us in our infancy
> [William Wordsworth *Intimations of Immortality*]

infant NOUN **= baby**, child, babe, toddler, tot, wean *(Scot.)*, little one, bairn *(Scot.)*, suckling, newborn child, babe in arms, sprog *(slang)*, munchkin *(informal, chiefly U.S.)*, neonate, rug rat *(slang)*, littlie *(Austral. informal)*, ankle-biter *(Austral. slang)*, tacker *(Austral. slang)*: *young mums with infants in prams*
▷ ADJECTIVE **= early**, new, developing, young, growing, initial, dawning, fledgling, newborn, immature, embryonic, emergent, nascent, unfledged: *The infant company was based in Germany.*

> **QUOTATIONS**
> At first the infant,
> Mewling and puking in the nurse's arms
> [William Shakespeare *As You Like It*]

infantile ADJECTIVE **= childish**, immature, puerile, babyish, young, weak **OPPOSITE:** mature

infatuated ADJECTIVE **= obsessed**, fascinated, captivated, possessed, carried away, inflamed, beguiled, smitten *(informal)*, besotted, bewitched, intoxicated, crazy about *(informal)*, spellbound, enamoured, enraptured, under the spell of, head over heels in love with, swept off your feet

infatuation NOUN **= obsession**, thing *(informal)*, passion, crush *(informal)*, madness, folly, fixation, foolishness

infect VERB **1 = contaminate**, transmit disease to, spread disease to *or* among: *A single mosquito can infect a large number of people.* **2 = pollute**, dirty, poison, foul, corrupt, contaminate, taint, defile, vitiate: *The birds infect the milk.* **3 = affect**, move, touch, influence, upset, overcome, stir, disturb: *I was infected by her fear.*

infection NOUN **= disease**, condition, complaint, illness, virus, disorder, corruption, poison, pollution, contamination, contagion, defilement, septicity

infectious ADJECTIVE **= catching**, spreading, contagious, communicable, poisoning, corrupting, contaminating, polluting, virulent, defiling, infective, vitiating, pestilential, transmittable

infer VERB **= deduce**, understand, gather, conclude, derive, presume, conjecture, surmise, read between the lines, put two and two together

> **USAGE**
> The use of *infer* to mean *imply* is becoming more and more common in both speech and writing. There is nevertheless a useful distinction between the two which many people would be in favour of maintaining. To *infer* means 'to deduce', and is used in the construction 'to infer something from something': *I inferred from what she said that she had not been well.* To *imply* means 'to suggest, to insinuate' and is normally followed by a clause: *are you implying that I was responsible for the mistake?*

inference NOUN **= deduction**, conclusion, assumption, reading, consequence, presumption, conjecture, surmise, corollary

inferior ADJECTIVE **1 = lower**, junior, minor, secondary, subsidiary, lesser, humble, subordinate, lowly, less important, menial: *the inferior status of women in many societies* **OPPOSITE:** superior **2 = substandard**, bad, poor, mean, worse, poorer, pants *(informal)*, flawed, rotten, dire, indifferent, duff *(Brit. informal)*, mediocre, second-class, deficient, imperfect, second-rate, shoddy, low-grade, unsound, downmarket, low-rent *(informal, chiefly U.S.)*, for the birds *(informal)*, wretched, two-bit *(U.S. & Canad. slang)*, crappy *(slang)*, no great shakes *(informal)*, poxy *(slang)*, dime-a-dozen *(informal)*, bush-league *(Austral. & N.Z. informal)*, not much cop *(Brit. slang)*, tinhorn *(U.S. slang)*, half-pie *(N.Z. informal)*, of a sort *or* of sorts, strictly for the birds *(informal)*, bodger *or* bodgie *(Austral. slang)*: *The cassettes were of inferior quality.* **OPPOSITE:** excellent
▷ NOUN **= underling**, junior, subordinate, lesser, menial, minion:

It was a gentleman's duty to be civil, even to his inferiors.

> **QUOTATIONS**
> No-one can make you feel inferior without your consent
> [Eleanor Roosevelt]

inferiority NOUN **= subservience**, subordination, lowliness, servitude, abasement, inferior status *or* standing **OPPOSITE:** superiority

infernal ADJECTIVE **1 = damned**, malevolent, hellish, devilish, accursed, damnable: *The post office is shut, which is an infernal bore.* **2 = hellish**, lower, underworld, nether, Stygian, Hadean, Plutonian, chthonian, Tartarean *(literary)*: *the goddess of the infernal regions* **OPPOSITE:** heavenly

infertile ADJECTIVE **1 = sterile**, barren, infecund: *According to one survey, one woman in eight is infertile.* **2 = barren**, unproductive, nonproductive, unfruitful, infecund: *The waste is dumped, making the surrounding land infertile.* **OPPOSITE:** fertile

infertility NOUN **= sterility**, barrenness, unproductiveness, unfruitfulness, infecundity

infest VERB **= overrun**, flood, invade, penetrate, ravage, swarm, throng, beset, permeate

infested ADJECTIVE **= overrun**, plagued, crawling, swarming, ridden, alive, ravaged, lousy *(slang)*, beset, pervaded, teeming, buggy

infidel NOUN **= unbeliever**, sceptic, atheist, heretic, agnostic, heathen, nonconformist, freethinker, nonbeliever

infidelity NOUN **= unfaithfulness**, cheating *(informal)*, adultery, betrayal, duplicity, disloyalty, bad faith, perfidy, falseness, faithlessness, false-heartedness

infiltrate VERB **= penetrate**, pervade, permeate, creep in, percolate, filter through to, make inroads into, sneak into *(informal)*, insinuate yourself, work *or* worm your way into

infinite ADJECTIVE **1 = vast**, enormous, immense, wide, countless, innumerable, untold, stupendous, incalculable, immeasurable, inestimable, numberless, uncounted, measureless, uncalculable: *an infinite variety of landscapes* **2 = enormous**, total, supreme, absolute, all-embracing, unbounded: *With infinite care, he shifted positions.* **3 = limitless**, endless, unlimited, eternal, perpetual, never-ending, interminable, boundless, everlasting, bottomless, unending, inexhaustible, immeasurable, without end, unbounded, numberless, measureless, illimitable, without number: *There is an infinite number of atoms.* **OPPOSITE:** finite

> **QUOTATIONS**
> What you see, yet cannot see over, is as good as infinite
> [Thomas Carlyle *Sartor Resartus*]

infinity NOUN **= eternity**, vastness, immensity, perpetuity, endlessness, infinitude, boundlessness

> **QUOTATIONS**
> I can't help it:- in spite of myself, infinity torments me
> [Alfred de Musset *L'Espoir en Dieu*]
>
> The eternal silence of these infinite spaces frightens me
> [Pascal *Pensées*]
>
> Suffering is permanent, obscure and dark,
> And shares the nature of infinity
> [William Wordsworth *The Borderers*]

infirm ADJECTIVE **1 = frail**, weak, feeble, failing, ailing, debilitated, decrepit, enfeebled, doddery, doddering: *her ageing, infirm husband* **OPPOSITE:** robust **2 = irresolute**, weak, faltering, unstable, shaky, insecure, wavering, wobbly, indecisive, unsound, vacillating: *She has little patience with the 'infirm of purpose'.*

inflame VERB **1 = enrage**, stimulate, provoke, fire, heat, excite, anger, arouse, rouse, infuriate, ignite, incense, madden, agitate, kindle, rile, foment, intoxicate, make your blood boil, impassion: *They hold the rebels responsible for inflaming the villagers.* **OPPOSITE:** calm **2 = aggravate**, increase, intensify, worsen, exacerbate, fan: *The shooting has only inflamed passions further.*

inflamed ADJECTIVE **= swollen**, sore, red, hot, angry, infected, fevered, festering, chafing, septic

inflammable ADJECTIVE **= flammable**, explosive, volatile, incendiary, combustible

inflammation NOUN **= swelling**, soreness, burning, heat, sore, rash, tenderness, redness, painfulness

inflammatory ADJECTIVE **= provocative**, incendiary, explosive, fiery, inflaming, insurgent, anarchic, rabid, riotous, intemperate, seditious, rabble-rousing, demagogic, like a red rag to a bull, instigative

inflate VERB **1 = blow up**, pump up, swell, balloon, dilate, distend, aerate, bloat, puff up *or* out: *He jumped into the sea and inflated the liferaft.* **OPPOSITE:** deflate **2 = increase**, boost, expand, enlarge, escalate, amplify: *Promotion can inflate a film's final cost.* **OPPOSITE:** diminish **3 = exaggerate**, embroider, embellish, emphasize, enlarge, magnify, overdo, amplify, exalt, overstate, overestimate, overemphasize, blow out of all proportion, aggrandize, hyperbolize: *Even his war record was fraudulently inflated.*

inflated ADJECTIVE **= exaggerated**, excessive, swollen, amplified, hyped, exalted, overblown

inflation NOUN **= increase**, expansion, extension, swelling, escalation, enlargement, intensification

inflection NOUN **1 = intonation**, stress, emphasis, beat, measure, rhythm, cadence, modulation, accentuation: *His voice was devoid of inflection.* **2 = conjugation**, declension: *At around 2 years, the child adds many grammatical inflections.*

inflexibility NOUN **= obstinacy**, persistence, intransigence, obduracy, fixity, steeliness

inflexible ADJECTIVE **1 = fixed**, set, established, rooted, rigid, immovable, unadaptable: *He was a man of unchanging habits and an inflexible routine.* **2 = obstinate**, strict, relentless, firm, fixed, iron, adamant, rigorous, stubborn, stringent, uncompromising, resolute, steely, intractable, inexorable, implacable, steadfast, hard and fast, unyielding, immutable, immovable, unbending, obdurate, stiff-necked, dyed-in-the-wool, unchangeable, brassbound, set in your ways: *They viewed him as stubborn, inflexible and dogmatic.* **OPPOSITE:** flexible **3 = stiff**, hard, rigid, hardened, taut, inelastic, nonflexible: *The boot is too inflexible to be comfortable.* **OPPOSITE:** pliable

inflict VERB **= impose**, exact, administer, visit, apply, deliver, levy, wreak, mete *or* deal out

influence NOUN **1 = control**, power, authority, direction, command, domination, supremacy, mastery, ascendancy, mana *(N.Z.)*: *As he grew older, she had less influence and couldn't control him.* **2 = power**, force, authority, pull *(informal)*, weight, strength, connections, importance, prestige, clout *(informal)*, leverage, good offices: *They should continue to use their influence for the release of all hostages.* **3 = spell**, hold, power, rule, weight, magic, sway, allure, magnetism, enchantment: *I fell under the influence of a history master.*
▷ VERB **1 = affect**, have an effect on, have an impact on, control, concern, direct, guide, impact on, modify, bear upon, impinge upon, act *or* work upon: *What you eat may influence your risk of getting cancer.* **2 = persuade**, move, prompt, urge, counsel, induce, incline, dispose, arouse, sway, rouse, entice, coax, incite, instigate, predispose, impel, prevail upon: *The conference influenced us to launch the campaign.* **3 = carry weight with**, cut any ice with *(informal)*, pull strings with *(informal)*, bring pressure to bear upon, make yourself felt with: *Her attempt to influence the Press rebounded.*

influential ADJECTIVE **1 = important**, powerful, moving, telling, leading, strong, guiding, inspiring, prestigious, meaningful, potent, persuasive, authoritative, momentous, weighty: *one of the most influential books ever written* **OPPOSITE:** unimportant **2 = instrumental**, important, significant, controlling, guiding,

i

effective, crucial, persuasive, forcible, efficacious: *He had been influential in shaping economic policy.*

influx NOUN = **arrival**, flow, rush, invasion, convergence, inflow, incursion, inundation, inrush

infold *see* **enfold**

inform VERB **1** = **tell**, advise, let someone know, notify, brief, instruct, enlighten, acquaint, leak to, communicate to, fill someone in, keep someone posted, apprise, clue someone in *(informal)*, put someone in the picture *(informal)*, tip someone off, send word to, give someone to understand, make someone conversant (with): *They would inform him of any progress they had made.* **2** = **infuse**, characterize, permeate, animate, saturate, typify, imbue, suffuse: *All great songs are informed by a certain sadness and tension.*
inform on someone = **betray**, report, denounce, shop *(slang, chiefly Brit.)*, peach *(slang)*, give someone away, incriminate, tell on *(informal)*, blow the whistle on *(informal)*, grass on *(Brit. slang)*, double-cross *(informal)*, rat on *(informal)*, spill the beans on *(informal)*, stab someone in the back, nark *(Brit., Austral. & N.Z. slang)*, blab about, squeal on *(slang)*, snitch on *(slang)*, put the finger on *(informal)*, sell someone down the river *(informal)*, blow the gaff on *(Brit. slang)*, tell all on, inculpate, dob someone in *(Austral. & N.Z. slang)*: *Somebody must have informed on us.*

PROVERBS
Never tell tales out of school

informal ADJECTIVE **1** = **natural**, relaxed, casual, familiar, unofficial, laid-back, easy-going, colloquial, unconstrained, unceremonious: *She is refreshingly informal.* **2** = **relaxed**, easy, comfortable, simple, natural, casual, cosy, laid-back *(informal)*, mellow, leisurely, easy-going: *The house has an informal atmosphere.* OPPOSITE: formal **3** = **casual**, comfortable, leisure, everyday, simple: *Most of the time she needs informal clothes.* **4** = **unofficial**, irregular, unconstrained, unceremonious: *an informal meeting of EU ministers* OPPOSITE: official

informality NOUN = **familiarity**, naturalness, casualness, ease, relaxation, simplicity, lack of ceremony

information NOUN = **facts**, details, material, news, latest *(informal)*, report, word, message, notice, advice, knowledge, data, intelligence, instruction, counsel, the score *(informal)*, gen *(Brit. informal)*, dope *(informal)*, info *(informal)*, inside story, blurb, lowdown *(informal)*, tidings, drum *(Austral. informal)*, heads up *(U.S. & Canad.)*

informative ADJECTIVE = **instructive**, revealing, educational, forthcoming, illuminating, enlightening, chatty, communicative, edifying, gossipy, newsy

informed ADJECTIVE = **knowledgeable**, up to date, enlightened, learned, primed, posted, expert, briefed, familiar, versed, acquainted, in the picture, up, abreast, in the know *(informal)*, erudite, well-read, conversant, au fait *(French)*, in the loop, genned up *(Brit. informal)*, au courant *(French)*, keeping your finger on the pulse

informer NOUN = **betrayer**, grass *(Brit. slang)*, sneak, squealer *(slang)*, Judas, accuser, stool pigeon, nark *(Brit., Austral. & N.Z. slang)*, fizgig *(Austral. slang)*

infrequent ADJECTIVE = **occasional**, rare, uncommon, unusual, sporadic, few and far between, once in a blue moon OPPOSITE: frequent

infringe VERB = **break**, violate, contravene, disobey, transgress: *The film exploited his image and infringed his copyright.*
infringe on *or* **upon** = **intrude on**, compromise, undermine, limit, weaken, diminish, disrupt, curb, encroach on, trespass on: *It's starting to infringe on our personal liberties.*

infringement NOUN = **contravention**, breach, violation, trespass, transgression, infraction, noncompliance, nonobservance

infuriate VERB = **enrage**, anger, provoke, irritate, incense, gall, madden, exasperate, rile, nark *(Brit., Austral. & N.Z. slang)*, be like a red rag to a bull, make your blood boil, get your goat *(slang)*, make your hackles rise, raise your hackles, get your back up, make you see red *(informal)*, put your back up OPPOSITE: soothe

infuriating ADJECTIVE = **annoying**, irritating, aggravating *(informal)*, provoking, galling, maddening, exasperating, irksome, vexatious, pestilential

infuse VERB = **brew**, soak, steep, saturate, immerse, macerate: *teas made by infusing the roots of herbs*

ingenious ADJECTIVE = **creative**, original, brilliant, clever, masterly, bright, subtle, fertile, shrewd, inventive, skilful, crafty, resourceful, adroit, dexterous OPPOSITE: unimaginative

ingenuity NOUN = **originality**, genius, inventiveness, skill, gift, faculty, flair, knack, sharpness, cleverness, resourcefulness, shrewdness, adroitness, ingeniousness OPPOSITE: dullness

ingrained *or* **engrained** ADJECTIVE = **fixed**, rooted, deep-seated, fundamental, constitutional, inherent, hereditary, in the blood, intrinsic, deep-rooted, indelible, inveterate, inborn, inbred, inbuilt, ineradicable, brassbound

ingratiate VERB
ingratiate yourself with someone = **get on the right side of**, court, win over, flatter, pander to, crawl to, play up to, get in with, suck up to *(informal)*, curry favour with, grovel to, keep someone sweet, lick someone's boots, fawn to, toady to, seek someone's favour, rub someone up the right way *(informal)*, be a yes man to, insinuate yourself with

ingratiating ADJECTIVE = **sycophantic**, servile, obsequious, crawling, humble, flattering, fawning, unctuous, toadying, bootlicking *(informal)*, timeserving

ingredient NOUN = **component**, part, element, feature, piece, unit, item, aspect, attribute, constituent

inhabit VERB = **live in**, people, occupy, populate, reside in, tenant, lodge in, dwell in, colonize, take up residence in, abide in, make your home in

inhabitant NOUN = **occupant**, resident, citizen, local, native, tenant, inmate, dweller, occupier, denizen, indigene, indweller

inhabited ADJECTIVE = **populated**, peopled, occupied, held, developed, settled, tenanted, colonized

inhalation NOUN = **breathing**, breath, inspiration, inhaling

inhale VERB = **breathe in**, gasp, draw in, suck in, respire OPPOSITE: exhale

inherent ADJECTIVE = **intrinsic**, natural, basic, central, essential, native, fundamental, underlying, hereditary, instinctive, innate, ingrained, elemental, congenital, inborn, inbred, inbuilt, immanent, connate OPPOSITE: extraneous

inherit VERB = **be left**, come into, be willed, accede to, succeed to, be bequeathed, fall heir to

inheritance NOUN = **legacy**, estate, heritage, provision, endowment, bequest, birthright, patrimony

inheritor NOUN = **heir**, successor, recipient, beneficiary, legatee

inhibit VERB **1** = **hinder**, stop, prevent, check, bar, arrest, frustrate, curb, restrain, constrain, obstruct, impede, bridle, stem the flow of, throw a spanner in the works of, hold back *or* in: *Sugary drinks inhibit digestion.* OPPOSITE: further **2** = **prevent**, stop, bar, frustrate, forbid, prohibit, debar: *The poor will be inhibited from getting the medical care they need.* OPPOSITE: allow

inhibited ADJECTIVE = **shy**, reserved, guarded, withdrawn, frustrated, subdued, repressed, constrained, self-conscious, reticent, uptight *(informal)* OPPOSITE: uninhibited

inhibition NOUN **1** = **shyness**, reserve, restraint, hang-up *(informal)*, modesty, nervousness, reticence, self-consciousness, timidity, diffidence, bashfulness, mental blockage, timidness: *They behave with a total lack of inhibition.* **2** = **obstacle**, check, bar, block, barrier, restriction, hazard, restraint, hitch, drawback, snag, deterrent, obstruction, stumbling block, impediment, hindrance, encumbrance, interdict: *They cited security fears as a major inhibition to internet shopping.*

inhospitable ADJECTIVE **1 = bleak**, empty, bare, hostile, lonely, forbidding, barren, sterile, desolate, unfavourable, uninhabitable, godforsaken: *the earth's most inhospitable regions* **2 = unfriendly**, unwelcoming, uncongenial, cool, unkind, xenophobic, ungenerous, unsociable, unreceptive: *He believed the province to be inhabited by a mean, inhospitable people.* **OPPOSITE:** hospitable

inhuman ADJECTIVE **= cruel**, savage, brutal, vicious, ruthless, barbaric, heartless, merciless, diabolical, cold-blooded, remorseless, barbarous, fiendish, pitiless, unfeeling, bestial **OPPOSITE:** humane

inhumane ADJECTIVE **= cruel**, savage, brutal, severe, harsh, grim, unkind, heartless, atrocious, unsympathetic, hellish, depraved, barbarous, pitiless, unfeeling, uncompassionate

inhumanity NOUN **= cruelty**, atrocity, brutality, ruthlessness, barbarism, viciousness, heartlessness, unkindness, brutishness, cold-bloodedness, pitilessness, cold-heartedness, hardheartedness

> **QUOTATIONS**
> Man's inhumanity to man
> Makes countless thousands mourn
> [Robert Burns *Man was Made to Mourn*]
>
> The worst sin towards our fellow creatures is not to hate them, but to be indifferent to them: that's the essence of inhumanity
> [George Bernard Shaw *The Devil's Disciple*]

inimical ADJECTIVE **= hostile**, opposed, contrary, destructive, harmful, adverse, hurtful, unfriendly, unfavourable, antagonistic, injurious, unwelcoming, ill-disposed **OPPOSITE:** helpful

inimitable ADJECTIVE **= unique**, unparalleled, unrivalled, incomparable, supreme, consummate, unmatched, peerless, unequalled, matchless, unsurpassable, nonpareil, unexampled

iniquity NOUN **= wickedness**, wrong, crime, evil, sin, offence, injustice, wrongdoing, misdeed, infamy, abomination, sinfulness, baseness, unrighteousness, heinousness, evildoing **OPPOSITE:** goodness

initial ADJECTIVE **= opening**, first, early, earliest, beginning, primary, maiden, inaugural, commencing, introductory, embryonic, incipient, inchoate, inceptive **OPPOSITE:** final

initially ADVERB **= at first**, first, firstly, originally, primarily, at the start, in the first place, to begin with, at the outset, in the beginning, in the early stages, at *or* in the beginning

initiate VERB **1 = begin**, start, open, launch, establish, institute, pioneer, kick off *(informal)*, bring about, embark on, originate, set about, get under way, instigate, kick-start, inaugurate, set in motion, trigger off, lay the foundations of, commence on, set going, break the ice on, set the ball rolling on: *They wanted to initiate a discussion on economics.* **2 = introduce**, admit, enlist, enrol, launch, establish, invest, recruit, induct, instate: *She was initiated as a member of the secret society.*
▷ NOUN **= novice**, member, pupil, convert, amateur, newcomer, beginner, trainee, apprentice, entrant, learner, neophyte, tyro, probationer, novitiate, proselyte: *He was an initiate of a Chinese spiritual discipline.*
initiate someone into something = instruct in, train in, coach in, acquaint with, drill in, make aware of, teach about, tutor in, indoctrinate, prime in, familiarize with: *I was initiated into the darker side of the work.*

initiation NOUN **1 = introduction**, installation, inauguration, inception, commencement: *They announced the initiation of a rural development programme.* **2 = entrance**, debut, introduction, admission, inauguration, induction, inception, enrolment, investiture, baptism of fire, instatement: *This was my initiation into the peace movement.*

initiative NOUN **1 = advantage**, start, lead, upper hand: *We have the initiative and we intend to keep it.* **2 = enterprise**, drive, push *(informal)*, energy, spirit, resource, leadership, ambition, daring, enthusiasm, pep, vigour, zeal, originality, eagerness, dynamism, boldness, inventiveness, get-up-and-go *(informal)*, resourcefulness, gumption *(informal)*, adventurousness: *He was disappointed by her lack of initiative.*

inject VERB **1 = vaccinate**, shoot *(informal)*, administer, jab *(informal)*, shoot up *(informal)*, mainline *(informal)*, inoculate: *His son was injected with strong drugs.* **2 = introduce**, bring in, insert, instil, infuse, breathe, interject: *She kept trying to inject a little fun into their relationship.*

injection NOUN **1 = vaccination**, shot *(informal)*, jab *(informal)*, dose, vaccine, booster, immunization, inoculation: *They gave me an injection to help me sleep.* **2 = introduction**, investment, insertion, advancement, dose, infusion, interjection: *An injection of cash is needed to fund some of these projects.*

injunction NOUN **= order**, ruling, command, instruction, dictate, mandate, precept, exhortation, admonition

injure VERB **1 = hurt**, wound, harm, break, damage, smash, crush, mar, disable, shatter, bruise, impair, mutilate, maim, mangle, mangulate *(Austral. slang)*, incapacitate: *A bomb exploded, seriously injuring five people.* **2 = damage**, harm, ruin, wreck, weaken, spoil, impair, crool *or* cruel *(Austral. slang)*: *Too much stress can injure your health.* **3 = undermine**, damage, mar, blight, tarnish, blacken, besmirch, vitiate: *an attempt to injure another trader's business*

injured ADJECTIVE **1 = hurt**, damaged, wounded, broken, cut, crushed, disabled, challenged, weakened, bruised, scarred, crook *(Austral. & N.Z. slang)*, fractured, lamed, mutilated, maimed, mangled: *The injured man had a superficial stomach wound.* **2 = wronged**, abused, harmed, insulted, offended, tainted, tarnished, blackened, maligned, vilified, mistreated, dishonoured, defamed, ill-treated, maltreated, ill-used: *As yet, there has been no complaint from the injured party.* **3 = upset**, hurt, wounded, troubled, bothered, undermined, distressed, unhappy, stung, put out, grieved, hassled *(informal)*, disgruntled, displeased, reproachful, cut to the quick: *compensation for injured feelings*

injurious ADJECTIVE **= harmful**, bad, damaging, corrupting, destructive, adverse, unhealthy, detrimental, hurtful, pernicious, noxious, ruinous, deleterious, iniquitous, disadvantageous, baneful *(archaic)*, maleficent, unconducive

injury NOUN **1 = wound**, cut, damage, slash, trauma *(Pathology)*, sore, gash, lesion, abrasion, laceration: *Four police officers sustained serious injuries in the explosion.* **2 = harm**, suffering, damage, ill, hurt, disability, misfortune, affliction, impairment, disfigurement: *The two other passengers escaped serious injury.* **3 = wrong**, abuse, offence, insult, injustice, grievance, affront, detriment, disservice: *She was awarded £3,500 for injury to her feelings.*

injustice NOUN **1 = unfairness**, discrimination, prejudice, bias, inequality, oppression, intolerance, bigotry, favouritism, inequity, chauvinism, iniquity, partisanship, partiality, narrow-mindedness, one-sidedness, unlawfulness, unjustness: *They will continue to fight injustice.* **OPPOSITE:** justice **2 = wrong**, injury, crime, abuse, error, offence, sin, grievance, infringement, trespass, misdeed, transgression, infraction, bad *or* evil deed: *I don't want to do an injustice to what I've recorded.*

inkling NOUN **= suspicion**, idea, hint, suggestion, notion, indication, whisper, clue, conception, glimmering, intimation, faintest *or* foggiest idea

inland ADJECTIVE **= interior**, internal, upcountry

inlet NOUN **= bay**, creek, cove, passage, entrance, fjord, bight, ingress, sea loch *(Scot.)*, arm of the sea, firth *or* frith *(Scot.)*

innards PLURAL NOUN **1 = intestines**, insides *(informal)*, guts, entrails, viscera, vitals: *What happens to the innards of a carcass hung up for butchery?* **2 = works**, mechanism, guts *(informal)*: *The innards of the PC are built into the desk.*

innate ADJECTIVE **= inborn**, natural, inherent, essential, native, constitutional, inherited, indigenous, instinctive, intuitive, intrinsic, ingrained, congenital, inbred, immanent, in your blood, connate **OPPOSITE:** acquired

inner ADJECTIVE **1 = inside**, internal, interior, inward: *She got up and went into an inner office.* **OPPOSITE:** outer **2 = central**, middle, internal, interior: *I've always taught in inner London.* **3 = intimate**, close, personal, near, private, friendly, confidential, cherished, bosom: *He was part of the Francoist inner circle.* **4 = hidden**, deep, secret, underlying, obscure, repressed, esoteric, unrevealed: *He loves studying chess and discovering its inner secrets.* **OPPOSITE:** obvious

i

innkeeper NOUN **= publican**, hotelier, mine host, host *or* hostess, landlord *or* landlady

innocence NOUN **1 = naiveté**, simplicity, inexperience, freshness, credulity, gullibility, ingenuousness, artlessness, unworldliness, guilelessness, credulousness, simpleness, trustfulness, unsophistication, naiveness: *the sweet innocence of youth* **OPPOSITE:** worldliness **2 = blamelessness**, righteousness, clean hands, uprightness, sinlessness, irreproachability, guiltlessness: *He claims to have evidence which could prove his innocence.* **OPPOSITE:** guilt **3 = chastity**, virtue, purity, modesty, virginity, celibacy, continence, maidenhood, stainlessness: *She can still evoke the innocence of 14-year-old Juliet.* **4 = ignorance**, oblivion, lack of knowledge, inexperience, unfamiliarity, greenness, unawareness, nescience *(literary)*: *'Maybe innocence is bliss,' he suggested.*

innocent ADJECTIVE **1 = not guilty**, in the clear, blameless, clear, clean, honest, faultless, squeaky-clean, uninvolved, irreproachable, guiltless, unoffending: *The police knew from day one that I was innocent.* **OPPOSITE:** guilty **2 = naive**, open, trusting, simple, natural, frank, confiding, candid, unaffected, childlike, gullible, unpretentious, unsophisticated, unworldly, credulous, artless, ingenuous, guileless, wet behind the ears *(informal)*, unsuspicious: *They seemed so young and innocent.* **OPPOSITE:** worldly **3 = harmless**, innocuous, inoffensive, well-meant, unobjectionable, unmalicious, well-intentioned: *It was probably an innocent question, but he got very flustered.* **OPPOSITE:** malicious **4 = pure**, stainless, immaculate, moral, virgin, decent, upright, impeccable, righteous, pristine, wholesome, spotless, demure, chaste, unblemished, virginal, unsullied, sinless, incorrupt: *that innocent virgin, Clarissa* **OPPOSITE:** impure
▷ NOUN **= child**, novice, greenhorn *(informal)*, babe in arms *(informal)*, ingénue *or (masc.)* ingénu: *He was a hopeless innocent where women were concerned.*
innocent of = free from, clear of, unaware of, ignorant of, untouched by, unfamiliar with, empty of, lacking, unacquainted with, nescient of: *She was completely natural and innocent of any airs and graces.*

innocuous ADJECTIVE **= harmless**, safe, innocent, inoffensive, innoxious

innovation NOUN **1 = change**, revolution, departure, introduction, variation, transformation, upheaval, alteration: *technological innovations of the industrial age* **2 = newness**, novelty, originality, freshness, modernism, modernization, uniqueness: *We must promote originality and encourage innovation.*

innovative ADJECTIVE **= novel**, new, original, different, fresh, unusual, unfamiliar, uncommon, inventive, singular, ground-breaking, left-field *(informal)*, transformational, variational

innovator NOUN **= modernizer**, introducer, inventor, changer, transformer

innuendo NOUN **= insinuation**, suggestion, hint, implication, whisper, overtone, intimation, imputation, aspersion

innumerable ADJECTIVE **= countless**, many, numerous, infinite, myriad, untold, incalculable, numberless, unnumbered, multitudinous, beyond number **OPPOSITE:** limited

inoculation NOUN **= injection**, shot *(informal)*, jab *(informal)*, vaccination, dose, vaccine, booster, immunization

inordinate ADJECTIVE **= excessive**, unreasonable, disproportionate, extravagant, undue, preposterous, unwarranted, exorbitant, unrestrained, intemperate, unconscionable, immoderate **OPPOSITE:** moderate

inorganic ADJECTIVE **= artificial**, chemical, man-made, mineral

inquest NOUN **= inquiry**, investigation, probe, inquisition

inquire *or* **enquire** VERB **= ask**, question, query, quiz, seek information of, request information of: *He inquired whether there had been any messages left for him.*
inquire into = investigate, study, examine, consider, research, search, explore, look into, inspect, probe into, scrutinize, make inquiries into: *Inspectors inquired into the affairs of the company.*

inquiry *or* **enquiry** NOUN **1 = question**, query, investigation: *He made some inquiries and discovered she had gone abroad.* **2 = investigation**, hearing, study, review, search, survey, analysis, examination, probe, inspection, exploration, scrutiny, inquest: *a murder inquiry* **3 = research**, investigation, analysis, examination, inspection, exploration, scrutiny, interrogation: *The investigation has switched to a new line of inquiry.*

inquisition NOUN **= investigation**, questioning, examination, inquiry, grilling *(informal)*, quizzing, inquest, cross-examination, third degree *(informal)*

inquisitive ADJECTIVE **= curious**, questioning, inquiring, peering, probing, intrusive, prying, snooping *(informal)*, scrutinizing, snoopy *(informal)*, nosy *(informal)*, nosy-parkering *(informal)* **OPPOSITE:** uninterested

insane ADJECTIVE **1 = mad**, crazy, nuts *(slang)*, cracked *(slang)*, mental *(slang)*, barking *(slang)*, crackers *(Brit. slang)*, mentally ill, crazed, demented, cuckoo *(informal)*, deranged, loopy *(informal)*, round the bend *(informal)*, barking mad *(slang)*, out of your mind, gaga *(informal)*, screwy *(informal)*, doolally *(slang)*, off your trolley *(slang)*, round the twist *(informal)*, of unsound mind, not right in the head, non compos mentis *(Latin)*, off your rocker *(slang)*, not the full shilling *(informal)*, mentally disordered, buggy *(U.S. slang)*, off the air *(Austral. slang)*, porangi *(N.Z.)*: *Some people simply can't take it and they go insane.* **OPPOSITE:** sane **2 = stupid**, foolish, daft *(informal)*, bizarre, irresponsible, irrational, lunatic, senseless, preposterous, impractical, idiotic, inane, fatuous, dumb-ass *(slang)*: *Listen, this is completely insane.* **OPPOSITE:** reasonable

insanity NOUN **1 = madness**, mental illness, dementia, aberration, mental disorder, delirium, craziness, mental derangement: *a powerful study of a woman's descent into insanity* **OPPOSITE:** sanity **2 = stupidity**, folly, lunacy, irresponsibility, senselessness, preposterousness: *the final financial insanity of the decade* **OPPOSITE:** sense

> **USAGE**
> The word *insane* has a specific legal use, as in *insane and unfit to plead.* The word *insanity*, however, is not acceptable in general mental health contexts, and many of its synonyms, for example *mental derangement*, are also considered inappropriate or offensive. Acceptable terms are *psychiatric disorder* or *psychiatric illness.*

insatiable ADJECTIVE **= unquenchable**, greedy, voracious, ravenous, rapacious, intemperate, gluttonous, unappeasable, insatiate, quenchless, edacious **OPPOSITE:** satiable

inscribe VERB **1 = carve**, cut, etch, engrave, impress, imprint: *They read the words inscribed on the walls of the monument.* **2 = dedicate**, sign, address: *The book is inscribed: To John Arlott from Laurie Lee.*

inscription NOUN **= engraving**, words, lettering, label, legend, saying

inscrutable ADJECTIVE **1 = enigmatic**, blank, impenetrable, deadpan, unreadable, poker-faced *(informal)*, sphinxlike: *It is important to keep a straight face and remain inscrutable.* **OPPOSITE:** transparent **2 = mysterious**, incomprehensible, inexplicable, hidden, unintelligible, unfathomable, unexplainable, undiscoverable: *Even when opened the contents of the package were as inscrutable as ever.* **OPPOSITE:** comprehensible

insect NOUN **= bug**, creepy-crawly *(Brit. informal)*, gogga *(S. African informal)* ▸ *related adjective:* entomic ▸ *collective noun:* swarm

insecure ADJECTIVE **1 = unconfident**, worried, anxious, afraid, shy, uncertain, unsure, timid, self-conscious, hesitant, meek, self-effacing, diffident, unassertive: *Many women are insecure about their performance as mothers.* **OPPOSITE:** confident **2 = unsafe**, dangerous, exposed, vulnerable, hazardous, wide-open, perilous, unprotected, defenceless, unguarded, open to attack, unshielded, ill-protected: *Mobile phones are inherently insecure, as anyone can listen in.* **OPPOSITE:** safe **3 = unreliable**, unstable, unsafe, precarious, unsteady, unsound: *low-paid, insecure jobs* **OPPOSITE:** secure

insecurity NOUN **1 = anxiety**, fear, worry, uncertainty, unsureness: *She is always assailed by emotional insecurity.* **OPPOSITE:** confidence **2 = vulnerability**, risk, danger, weakness, uncertainty, hazard, peril, defencelessness: *The increase in crime has created feelings of insecurity.* **OPPOSITE:** safety **3 = instability**, uncertainty, unreliability, precariousness, weakness, shakiness, unsteadiness, dubiety, frailness: *the harshness and insecurity of agricultural life* **OPPOSITE:** stability

insensitive ADJECTIVE **= unfeeling**, indifferent, unconcerned, uncaring, tough, hardened, callous, crass, unresponsive, thick-skinned, obtuse, tactless, imperceptive, unsusceptible: *My husband is very insensitive about my problem.* **OPPOSITE:** sensitive **insensitive to = unaffected by**, immune to, impervious to, dead to, unmoved by, proof against: *He had become insensitive to cold.*

inseparable ADJECTIVE **1 = devoted**, close, intimate, bosom: *The two girls were inseparable.* **2 = indivisible**, inalienable, conjoined, indissoluble, inseverable: *He believes liberty is inseparable from social justice.*

insert VERB **= put**, place, set, position, work in, slip, slide, slot, thrust, stick in, wedge, tuck in

insertion NOUN **1 = inclusion**, introduction, interpolation: *the first experiment involving the insertion of a new gene* **2 = insert**, addition, inclusion, supplement, implant, inset: *The correction to the text may involve an insertion or a deletion.*

inside NOUN **= interior**, contents, core, nucleus, inner part, inner side: *Cut off the top and scoop out the inside with a teaspoon.*
▷ PLURAL NOUN **= stomach**, gut, guts, belly, bowels, internal organs, innards *(informal)*, entrails, viscera, vitals: *My insides ached from eating too much.*
▷ ADJECTIVE **1 = inner**, internal, interior, inward, innermost: *four-berth inside cabins with en suite bathrooms* **OPPOSITE:** outside **2 = confidential**, private, secret, internal, exclusive, restricted, privileged, classified: *The editor denies he had any inside knowledge.*
▷ ADVERB **= indoors**, in, within, under cover: *They chatted briefly on the doorstep before going inside.*

insidious ADJECTIVE **= stealthy**, subtle, cunning, designing, smooth, tricky, crooked, sneaking, slick, sly, treacherous, deceptive, wily, crafty, artful, disingenuous, Machiavellian, deceitful, surreptitious, duplicitous, guileful **OPPOSITE:** straightforward

insight NOUN **1 = understanding**, intelligence, perception, sense, knowledge, vision, judgment, awareness, grasp, appreciation, intuition, penetration, comprehension, acumen, discernment, perspicacity: *He was a man of considerable insight and diplomatic skills.* **2** *(with* **into***)* **= understanding**, perception, awareness, experience, description, introduction, observation, judgment, revelation, comprehension, intuitiveness: *The talk gave us some insight into the work they were doing.*

insightful ADJECTIVE **= perceptive**, shrewd, discerning, understanding, wise, penetrating, knowledgeable, astute, observant, perspicacious, sagacious

insignia NOUN **= badge**, symbol, decoration, crest, earmark, emblem, ensign, distinguishing mark

insignificance NOUN **= unimportance**, irrelevance, triviality, pettiness, worthlessness, meaninglessness, inconsequence, immateriality, paltriness, negligibility **OPPOSITE:** importance

insignificant ADJECTIVE **= unimportant**, minor, irrelevant, petty, trivial, meaningless, trifling, meagre, negligible, flimsy, paltry, immaterial, inconsequential, nondescript, measly, scanty, inconsiderable, of no consequence, nonessential, small potatoes, nickel-and-dime *(U.S. slang)*, of no account, nugatory, unsubstantial, not worth mentioning, of no moment **OPPOSITE:** important

insincere ADJECTIVE **= deceitful**, lying, false, pretended, hollow, untrue, dishonest, deceptive, devious, hypocritical, unfaithful, evasive, two-faced, disingenuous, faithless, double-dealing, duplicitous, dissembling, mendacious, perfidious, untruthful, dissimulating, Janus-faced **OPPOSITE:** sincere

insinuate VERB **= imply**, suggest, hint, indicate, intimate, allude

insipid ADJECTIVE **1 = tasteless**, bland, flavourless, watered down, watery, wishy-washy *(informal)*, unappetizing, savourless: *It tasted bland and insipid, like warm cardboard.* **OPPOSITE:** tasty **2 = bland**, boring, dull, flat, dry, weak, stupid, limp, tame, pointless, tedious, stale, drab, banal, tiresome, lifeless, prosaic, trite, unimaginative, colourless, uninteresting, anaemic, wishy-washy *(informal)*, ho-hum *(informal)*, vapid, wearisome, characterless, spiritless, jejune, prosy: *On the surface she seemed meek, rather bland and insipid; They gave an insipid opening performance in a nil-nil draw.* **OPPOSITE:** exciting

insist VERB **1 = persist**, press (someone), be firm, stand firm, stand your ground, lay down the law, put your foot down *(informal)*, not take no for an answer, brook no refusal, take or make a stand: *I didn't want to join in, but he insisted.* **2 = demand**, order, urge, require, command, dictate, entreat: *I insisted that the fault be repaired.* **3 = assert**, state, maintain, hold, claim, declare, repeat, vow, swear, contend, affirm, reiterate, profess, avow, aver, asseverate: *He insisted that he was acting out of compassion.*

insistence NOUN **1 = demand**, urging, command, pressing, dictate, entreaty, importunity, insistency: *She had attended an interview at his insistence.* **2 = assertion**, claim, statement, declaration, contention, persistence, affirmation, pronouncement, reiteration, avowal, attestation: *her insistence that she wanted to dump her raunchy image*

insistent ADJECTIVE **1 = emphatic**, persistent, demanding, pressing, dogged, urgent, forceful, persevering, unrelenting, peremptory, importunate, exigent: *He is most insistent on this point.* **2 = persistent**, repeated, constant, repetitive, incessant, unremitting: *the insistent rhythms of dance music*

insolence NOUN **= rudeness**, cheek *(informal)*, disrespect, front, abuse, sauce *(informal)*, gall *(informal)*, audacity, boldness, chutzpah *(U.S. &*

Canad. informal), insubordination, impertinence, impudence, effrontery, backchat *(informal)*, incivility, sassiness *(U.S. informal)*, pertness, contemptuousness
OPPOSITE: politeness

insolent ADJECTIVE **= rude**, cheeky, impertinent, fresh *(informal)*, bold, insulting, abusive, saucy, contemptuous, pert, impudent, uncivil, insubordinate, brazen-faced
OPPOSITE: polite

insoluble ADJECTIVE **= inexplicable**, mysterious, baffling, obscure, mystifying, impenetrable, unaccountable, unfathomable, indecipherable, unsolvable
OPPOSITE: explicable

insolvency NOUN **= bankruptcy**, failure, ruin, liquidation

insolvent ADJECTIVE **= bankrupt**, ruined, on the rocks *(informal)*, broke *(informal)*, failed, gone bust *(informal)*, in receivership, gone to the wall, in the hands of the receivers, in queer street *(informal)*

insomnia NOUN **= sleeplessness**, restlessness, wakefulness

insouciance NOUN **= nonchalance**, light-heartedness, jauntiness, airiness, breeziness, carefreeness

inspect VERB **1 = examine**, check, look at, view, eye, survey, observe, scan, check out *(informal)*, look over, eyeball *(slang)*, scrutinize, give (something *or* someone) the once-over *(informal)*, take a dekko at *(Brit. slang)*, go over *or* through: *Cut the fruit in half and inspect the pips.* **2 = check**, examine, investigate, study, look at, research, search, survey, assess, probe, audit, vet, oversee, supervise, check out *(informal)*, look over, work over, superintend, give (something *or* someone) the once-over *(informal)*, go over *or* through: *Each hotel is inspected once a year.*

inspection NOUN **1 = examination**, investigation, scrutiny, scan, look-over, once-over *(informal)*: *Closer inspection reveals that they are banded with yellow.* **2 = check**, search, investigation, review, survey, examination, scan, scrutiny, supervision, surveillance, look-over, once-over *(informal)*, checkup, recce *(slang)*, superintendence: *A routine inspection of the vessel turned up 50 kg of the drug.*

inspector NOUN **= examiner**, investigator, supervisor, monitor, superintendent, auditor, censor, surveyor, scrutinizer, checker, overseer, scrutineer

inspiration NOUN **1 = imagination**, creativity, ingenuity, talent, insight, genius, productivity, fertility, stimulation, originality, inventiveness, cleverness, fecundity, imaginativeness: *A good way of getting inspiration is by looking at others' work.* **2 = motivation**, example, influence, model, boost, spur, incentive, revelation, encouragement, stimulus, catalyst, stimulation, inducement, incitement, instigation, afflatus: *She was very impressive and a great inspiration to all.* **OPPOSITE:** deterrent **3 = influence**, spur, stimulus, muse: *India's myths and songs are the inspiration for her books.*

inspire VERB **1 = motivate**, move, cause, stimulate, encourage, influence, persuade, spur, be responsible for, animate, rouse, instil, infuse, hearten, enliven, imbue, spark off, energize, galvanize, gee up, inspirit, fire *or* touch the imagination of: *What inspired you to change your name?* **OPPOSITE:** discourage **2 = give rise to**, cause, produce, result in, prompt, stir, spawn, engender: *His legend would even inspire a song by Simon and Garfunkel.*

inspired ADJECTIVE **1 = brilliant**, wonderful, impressive, exciting, outstanding, thrilling, memorable, dazzling, enthralling, superlative, of genius: *She produced an inspired performance.* **2 = stimulated**, possessed, aroused, uplifted, exhilarated, stirred up, enthused, exalted, elated, galvanized: *Garcia played like a man inspired.*

inspiring ADJECTIVE **= uplifting**, encouraging, exciting, moving, affecting, stirring, stimulating, rousing, exhilarating, heartening
OPPOSITE: uninspiring

instability NOUN **1 = uncertainty**, insecurity, weakness, imbalance, vulnerability, wavering, volatility, unpredictability, restlessness, fluidity, fluctuation, disequilibrium, transience, impermanence, precariousness, mutability, shakiness, unsteadiness, inconstancy: *unpopular policies which resulted in political instability*
OPPOSITE: stability **2 = imbalance**, weakness, volatility, variability, frailty, unpredictability, oscillation, vacillation, capriciousness, unsteadiness, flightiness, fitfulness, changeableness: *Caligula's inherent mental instability*

install VERB **1 = set up**, put in, place, position, station, establish, lay, fix, locate, lodge: *They had installed a new phone line in the apartment.* **2 = institute**, establish, introduce, invest, ordain, inaugurate, induct, instate: *A new Catholic bishop was installed yesterday.* **3 = settle**, position, plant, establish, lodge, ensconce: *Before her husband's death she had installed herself in a modern villa.*

installation NOUN **1 = setting up**, fitting, instalment, placing, positioning, establishment: *Lives could be saved if installation of alarms was stepped up.* **2 = appointment**, ordination, inauguration, induction, investiture, instatement: *He invited her to attend his installation as chief of his tribe.* **3 = base**, centre, post, station, camp, settlement, establishment, headquarters: *a secret military installation*

instalment NOUN **1 = payment**, repayment, part payment: *The first instalment is payable on application.* **2 = part**, section, chapter, episode, portion, division: *The next instalment deals with the social impact of the war.*

instance NOUN **1 = example**, case, occurrence, occasion, sample, illustration, precedent, case in point, exemplification: *a serious instance of corruption* **2 = insistence**, demand, urging, pressure, stress, application, request, prompting, impulse, behest, incitement, instigation, solicitation, entreaty, importunity: *The meeting was organized at the instance of two senior ministers.*
▷ VERB **= name**, mention, identify, point out, advance, quote, finger *(informal, chiefly U.S.)*, refer to, point to, cite, specify, invoke, allude to, adduce, namedrop: *She could have instanced many women who fitted this description.*

instant NOUN **1 = moment**, second, minute, shake *(informal)*, flash, tick *(Brit. informal)*, no time, twinkling, split second, jiffy *(informal)*, trice, twinkling of an eye *(informal)*, two shakes *(informal)*, two shakes of a lamb's tail *(informal)*, bat of an eye *(informal)*: *The pain disappeared in an instant.* **2 = time**, point, hour, moment, stage, occasion, phase, juncture: *At the same instant, he flung open the car door.*
▷ ADJECTIVE **1 = immediate**, prompt, instantaneous, direct, quick, urgent, on-the-spot, split-second: *He had taken an instant dislike to her.* **2 = ready-made**, fast, convenience, ready-mixed, ready-cooked, precooked: *He was stirring instant coffee into two mugs of hot water.*

instantaneous ADJECTIVE **= immediate**, prompt, instant, direct, on-the-spot

instantaneously ADVERB **= immediately**, instantly, at once, straight away, promptly, on the spot, forthwith, in the same breath, then and there, pronto *(informal)*, in the twinkling of an eye *(informal)*, on the instant, in a fraction of a second, posthaste, quick as lightning, in the bat of an eye *(informal)*

instantly ADVERB **= immediately**, at once, straight away, now, directly, on the spot, right away, there and then, without delay, instantaneously, forthwith, this minute, pronto *(informal)*, posthaste, instanter *(Law)*, tout de suite *(French)*

instead ADVERB **= rather**, alternatively, preferably, in preference, in lieu, on second thoughts: *Forget about dieting and eat normally instead.*
instead of = in place of, rather than, in preference to, in lieu of, in contrast with, as an alternative *or* equivalent to: *She had to spend four months away, instead of the usual two.*

instigate VERB **= provoke**, start, encourage, move, influence, prompt,

Phrasal verbs in 'The Times' and 'The Sun'

Phrasal verbs are one of the most intrinsic and idiomatic features of the English language. They are found in all genres and registers: some are literary (*mete out, set forth*); others are colloquial (*listen up, check it out*); and some are so entrenched in the language (*look up a word, set off on a journey*) that they are the most natural way of expressing a concept. Phrasal verbs are very frequent in both *The Times* and *The Sun*, but slightly more so in *The Sun*, where they occur approximately 40 times per thousand words, compared to *The Times*, where there are approximately 30 phrasal verbs per thousand words. Typical examples are:

> Dave Shrigley **stepped down** as Wolfson's chief executive. (*The Times*)

> The Limerick-based entrepreneur **set up** his company in 2001. (*The Times*)

> Dancing **broke out** in the streets of Sri Lanka last night. (*The Sun*)

> But while his career **takes off**, his mother and sister struggle to cope in his absence. (*The Sun*)

However, while idiomatic phrasal verbs such as those above are highly frequent in both newspapers, there are other differences in usage. One is that *The Sun* is almost twice as likely to convert phrasal verbs into nouns or adjectives. Both newspapers use combinations such as *back-up, line-up*, and *runner-up*, but *The Sun* uses more combinations referring to fights, such as *bust-up, shoot-up*, and *punch-up*. Combinations with *off* tend to relate to football in both newspapers: *kick-off, play-off*, and *sending-off*. *Down* is frequently used in *dressing-down, dumbed-down, let-down*, and *put-down*, but *The Sun* also has several uses of *shut-down*, which does not appear in *The Times:*

> US-based Twitter bosses delayed a planned **shut-down** for maintenance. (*The Sun*)

The Times, on the other hand, uses the combination *trickle-down*, a usage not found in *The Sun*:

> There was a **trickle-down** strategy: throwing money at the banks would trickle down to the rest of the economy. (*The Times*)

Out is used in both newspapers in *bail-out, buy-out sell-out*, and *shoot-out* (usually in the phrase *penalty shoot-out*), but *The Sun* also has more usages of *cop-out* and *chill-out*, as in:

> You can drive, but for the ultimate **chill-out** the train is a great way to appreciate the scenery. (*The Sun*)

Variation can also be found in the senses of individual phrasal verbs. In *The Times, make up* is almost always used in sense 'supply what is lacking', as in *make up the shortfall*, or 'constitute', as in *make up the bulk of something*. In *The Sun*, on the other hand, *make up* is also frequently used in the sense 'invent', as in *make up an excuse*.

Furthermore, *The Sun* is more likely to use phrasal verbs where the adverbial particle does not add much meaning to the verb. *Meet up (with)* is almost four times as frequent in *The Sun*; *kill off* is over three times as frequent; and *check up (on)* is twice as frequent. Examples include:

> About 150 MPs pledged continued loyalty to the PM if he **killed off** the proposal. (*The Sun*)

> Also, remember to **check up on** the game rules and scoring details. (*The Sun*)

This type of phrasal verb has long been condemned by purists as verbose; it seems that while *The Times* is quite accepting of phrasal verbs in general, it is more resistant to these redundant combinations.

trigger, spur, stimulate, set off, initiate, bring about, rouse, prod, stir up, get going, incite, kick-start, whip up, impel, kindle, foment, actuate **OPPOSITE:** suppress

instigation NOUN = **prompting**, urging, bidding, incentive, encouragement, behest, incitement

instigator NOUN = **ringleader**, inciter, motivator, leader, spur, goad, troublemaker, incendiary, firebrand, prime mover, fomenter, agitator, stirrer *(informal)*, mischief-maker

instil *or* **instill** VERB = **introduce**, implant, engender, infuse, imbue, impress, insinuate, sow the seeds, inculcate, engraft, infix

instinct NOUN **1** = **natural inclination**, feeling, urge, talent, tendency, faculty, inclination, intuition, knack, aptitude, predisposition, sixth sense, proclivity, gut reaction *(informal)*, second sight: *I didn't have a strong maternal instinct.* **2** = **talent**, skill, gift, capacity, bent, genius, faculty, knack, aptitude: *She has a natural instinct to perform.* **3** = **intuition**, feeling, impulse, gut feeling *(informal)*, sixth sense: *I should have gone with my first instinct.*

instinctive ADJECTIVE = **natural**, inborn, automatic, unconscious, mechanical, native, inherent, spontaneous, reflex, innate, intuitive, subconscious, involuntary, visceral, unthinking, instinctual, unlearned, unpremeditated, intuitional **OPPOSITE:** acquired

instinctively ADVERB = **intuitively**, naturally, automatically, without thinking, involuntarily, by instinct, in your bones

institute NOUN = **establishment**, body, centre, school, university, society, association, college, institution, organization, foundation, academy, guild, conservatory, fellowship, seminary, seat of learning: *a research institute devoted to software programming*
▷ VERB = **establish**, start, begin, found, launch, set up, introduce, settle, fix, invest, organize, install, pioneer, constitute, initiate, originate, enact, commence, inaugurate, set in motion, bring into being, put into operation: *We will institute a number of methods to improve safety.* **OPPOSITE:** end

institution NOUN **1** = **establishment**, body, centre, school, university, society, association, college, institute, organization, foundation, academy, guild, conservatory, fellowship, seminary, seat of learning: *Class size varies from one type of institution to another.* **2** = **custom**, practice, tradition, law, rule, procedure, convention, ritual, fixture, rite: *I believe in the institution of marriage.* **3** = **creation**, introduction, establishment, investment, debut, foundation, formation, installation, initiation, inauguration, enactment, inception, commencement, investiture: *the institution of the forty-hour week*

institutional ADJECTIVE = **conventional**, accepted, established, formal, establishment *(informal)*, organized, routine, orthodox, bureaucratic, procedural, societal

instruct VERB **1** = **order**, tell, direct, charge, bid, command, mandate, enjoin: *They have instructed solicitors to sue for compensation.* **2** = **teach**, school, train, direct, coach, guide, discipline, educate, drill, tutor, enlighten, give lessons in: *He instructs family members in nursing techniques.* **3** = **tell**, advise, inform, counsel, notify, brief, acquaint, apprise: *Instruct them that they've got three months to get it sorted out.*

instruction NOUN **1** = **order**, ruling, command, rule, demand, direction, regulation, dictate, decree, mandate, directive, injunction, behest: *No reason for this instruction was given.*
2 = **teaching**, schooling, training, classes, grounding, education, coaching, lesson(s), discipline, preparation, drilling, guidance, tutoring, tuition, enlightenment, apprenticeship, tutorials, tutelage: *Each candidate is given instruction in safety.*
▷ PLURAL NOUN = **information**, rules, advice, directions, recommendations, guidance, specifications: *This book gives instructions for making a variety of hand creams.*

instructive ADJECTIVE = **informative**, revealing, useful, educational, helpful, illuminating, enlightening, instructional, cautionary, didactic, edifying

instructor NOUN = **teacher**, coach, guide, adviser, trainer, demonstrator, tutor, guru, mentor, educator, pedagogue, preceptor *(rare)*, master *or* mistress, schoolmaster *or* schoolmistress

instrument NOUN **1** = **tool**, device, implement, mechanism, appliance, apparatus, gadget, utensil, contraption *(informal)*, contrivance, waldo: *a thin tube-like optical instrument*
2 = **agent**, means, force, cause, medium, agency, factor, channel, vehicle, mechanism, organ: *The veto is a traditional instrument for diplomacy.*
3 = **puppet**, tool, pawn, toy, creature, dupe, stooge *(slang)*, plaything, cat's-paw: *The Council was an instrument of Government.*

instrumental ADJECTIVE = **active**, involved, influential, useful, helpful, conducive, contributory, of help *or* service

insubstantial ADJECTIVE **1** = **flimsy**, thin, weak, slight, frail, feeble, tenuous: *Her limbs were insubstantial, almost transparent.*
OPPOSITE: substantial **2** = **imaginary**, unreal, fanciful, immaterial, ephemeral, illusory, incorporeal, chimerical: *Their thoughts seemed as insubstantial as smoke.*

insufferable ADJECTIVE = **unbearable**, impossible, intolerable, dreadful, outrageous, unspeakable, detestable, insupportable, unendurable, past bearing, more than flesh and blood can stand, enough to test the patience of a saint, enough to try the patience of Job **OPPOSITE:** bearable

insufficient ADJECTIVE = **inadequate**, incomplete, scant, meagre, short, sparse, deficient, lacking, unqualified, insubstantial, incommensurate **OPPOSITE:** ample

insular ADJECTIVE = **narrow-minded**, prejudiced, provincial, closed, limited, narrow, petty, parochial, blinkered, circumscribed, inward-looking, illiberal, parish-pump **OPPOSITE:** broad-minded

insulate VERB = **isolate**, protect, screen, defend, shelter, shield, cut off, cushion, cocoon, close off, sequester, wrap up in cotton wool

insult VERB = **offend**, abuse, injure, wound, slight, outrage, put down, humiliate, libel, snub, slag (off) *(slang)*, malign, affront, denigrate, disparage, revile, slander, displease, defame, hurt (someone's) feelings, call names, give offence to: *I didn't mean to insult you.* **OPPOSITE:** praise
▷ NOUN **1** = **jibe**, slight, put-down, abuse, snub, barb, affront, indignity, contumely, abusive remark, aspersion: *Some of the officers shouted insults at prisoners on the roof.* **2** = **offence**, slight, outrage, snub, slur, affront, rudeness, slap in the face *(informal)*, kick in the teeth *(informal)*, insolence, aspersion: *Their behaviour was an insult to the people they represented.* ▷ *See themed panel* **Insults and Terms of Abuse** *on facing page*

> **QUOTATIONS**
> This is adding insult to injuries
> [Edward Moore *The Foundling*]

insulting ADJECTIVE = **offensive**, rude, abusive, slighting, degrading, affronting, contemptuous, disparaging, scurrilous, insolent **OPPOSITE:** complimentary

insuperable ADJECTIVE = **insurmountable**, invincible, impassable, unconquerable **OPPOSITE:** surmountable

insurance NOUN **1** = **assurance**, cover, security, protection, coverage, safeguard, indemnity, indemnification: *You are advised to take out insurance on your lenses.*
2 = **protection**, security, guarantee, provision, shelter, safeguard, warranty: *Put something away as insurance against failure of the business.*

insure VERB **1** = **assure**, cover, protect, guarantee, warrant, underwrite, indemnify: *We automatically insure your furniture and belongings against fire.*
2 = **protect**, cover, safeguard: *He needs to insure himself against ambitious party rivals.*

INSULTS AND TERMS OF ABUSE

airhead	chuckie	doofus	galah	mong	ogre	slag
article	chump	dope	geek	moron	pea-brain	slapper
berk	clod	dork	git	mug	pillock	tart
bird-brain	clot	doughnut	goose	muppet	plank	thickhead
bitch	clown	drip	halfwit	nerd *or* nurd	plonker	thicko
blockhead	coot	dumb-ass	heifer	nincompoop	prat	twerp *or* twirp
bonehead	cow	dumbo	idiot	ninny	rascal	twit
bozo	cretin	dummy	imbecile	nit	rogue	wally
bushpig	devil	dunce	jerk	nitwit	scab	whore *or* 'ho
cabbage	dimwit	dweeb	lamebrain	numbskull *or* numskull	scoundrel	wimp
charlie	dipstick	eejit	loon	numpty	scrubber	wretch
cheeky monkey	divvy	fathead	mincer	oaf	scutter	wuss
chicken	donkey	fool	minger		simpleton	

insurgent NOUN **= rebel**, revolutionary, revolter, rioter, resister, mutineer, revolutionist, insurrectionist: *The insurgents took control of the main military air base.*
▷ ADJECTIVE **= rebellious**, revolutionary, mutinous, revolting, riotous, seditious, disobedient, insubordinate, insurrectionary: *The insurgent leaders were publicly executed.*

insurmountable ADJECTIVE **= insuperable**, impossible, overwhelming, hopeless, invincible, impassable, unconquerable

insurrection NOUN **= rebellion**, rising, revolution, riot, coup, revolt, uprising, mutiny, insurgency, putsch, sedition

intact ADJECTIVE **= undamaged**, whole, complete, sound, perfect, entire, virgin, untouched, unscathed, unbroken, flawless, unhurt, faultless, unharmed, uninjured, unimpaired, undefiled, all in one piece, together, scatheless, unviolated **OPPOSITE:** damaged

intangible ADJECTIVE **= abstract**, vague, invisible, dim, elusive, shadowy, airy, unreal, indefinite, ethereal, evanescent, incorporeal, impalpable, unsubstantial

integral ADJECTIVE **1 = essential**, basic, fundamental, necessary, component, constituent, indispensable, intrinsic, requisite, elemental: *Rituals form an integral part of any human society.* **OPPOSITE:** inessential **2 = whole**, full, complete, entire, intact, undivided: *This is meant to be an integral service.* **OPPOSITE:** partial

integrate VERB **= join**, unite, combine, blend, incorporate, merge, accommodate, knit, fuse, mesh, assimilate, amalgamate, coalesce, harmonize, meld, intermix **OPPOSITE:** separate

integrity NOUN **1 = honesty**, principle, honour, virtue, goodness, morality, purity, righteousness, probity, rectitude, truthfulness, trustworthiness, incorruptibility, uprightness, scrupulousness, reputability: *I have always regarded him as a man of integrity.* **OPPOSITE:** dishonesty **2 = unity**, unification, cohesion, coherence, wholeness, soundness, completeness: *Separatist movements are a threat to the integrity of the nation.* **OPPOSITE:** fragility

> QUOTATIONS
> This above all: to thine own self be true
> [William Shakespeare *Hamlet*]

intellect NOUN **1 = intelligence**, mind, reason, understanding, sense, brains (*informal*), judgment: *Do the emotions develop in parallel with the intellect?* **2 = thinker**, intellectual, genius, mind, brain (*informal*), intelligence, rocket scientist (*informal, chiefly U.S.*), egghead (*informal*): *My boss isn't a great intellect.*

> QUOTATIONS
> We should take care not to make the intellect our god; it has, of course, powerful muscles, but no personality
> [Albert Einstein *Out of My Later Years*]
>
> I care not whether a man is good or evil; all that I care
> Is whether he is a wise man or a fool. Go! put off holiness
> And put on intellect
> [William Blake *Jerusalem*]

intellectual ADJECTIVE **= scholarly**, learned, academic, lettered, intelligent, rational, cerebral, erudite, scholastic, highbrow, well-read, studious, bookish: *They were very intellectual and witty.* **OPPOSITE:** stupid
▷ NOUN **= academic**, expert, genius, thinker, master, brain (*informal*), mastermind, maestro, highbrow, rocket scientist (*informal, chiefly U.S.*), egghead (*informal*), brainbox, bluestocking (*usually derogatory*), pointy-head (*informal, chiefly U.S.*), master-hand, fundi (*S. African*), acca (*Austral. slang*): *teachers, artists and other intellectuals* **OPPOSITE:** idiot

> QUOTATIONS
> An intellectual is someone whose mind watches itself
> [Albert Camus *Notebooks 1935-42*]
>
> To the man-in-the-street, who, I'm sorry to say
> Is a keen observer of life
> The word 'Intellectual' suggests straight away
> A man who's untrue to his wife
> [W.H. Auden *New Year Letter*]

intelligence NOUN **1 = intellect**, understanding, brains (*informal*), mind, reason, sense, knowledge, capacity, smarts (*slang, chiefly U.S.*), judgment, wit, perception, awareness, insight, penetration, comprehension, brightness, aptitude, acumen, nous (*Brit. slang*), alertness, cleverness, quickness, discernment, grey matter (*informal*), brain power: *She's a woman of exceptional intelligence.* **OPPOSITE:** stupidity **2 = information**, news, facts, report, findings, word, notice, advice, knowledge, data, disclosure, gen (*Brit. informal*), tip-off, low-down (*informal*), notification, heads up (*U.S. & Canad.*): *a senior officer involved in gathering intelligence* **OPPOSITE:** misinformation

intelligent ADJECTIVE **= clever**, bright, smart, knowing, quick, sharp, acute, alert, rational, penetrating, enlightened, apt, discerning, knowledgeable, astute, well-informed, brainy (*informal*), perspicacious, quick-witted, sagacious **OPPOSITE:** stupid

intelligentsia NOUN **= intellectuals**, highbrows, literati, masterminds, the learned, eggheads (*informal*), illuminati

intelligible ADJECTIVE **= understandable**, clear, distinct, lucid, comprehensible **OPPOSITE:** unintelligible

intemperate ADJECTIVE **= excessive**, extreme, over the top (*slang*), wild, violent, severe, passionate, extravagant, uncontrollable, self-indulgent, unbridled, prodigal, unrestrained, tempestuous, profligate, inordinate, incontinent, ungovernable, immoderate, O.T.T. (*slang*) **OPPOSITE:** temperate

intend VERB **1 = plan**, mean, aim, determine, scheme, propose, purpose, contemplate, envisage, foresee, be resolved *or* determined, have in mind *or* view: *She intends to do A levels and go to university.* **2** *(often with* **for***)* = **destine**, mean, design, earmark, consign, aim, mark out, set apart: *This money is intended for the development of the tourist industry.*

intended ADJECTIVE = **planned**, proposed: *He hoped the sarcasm would have its intended effect.*
▷ NOUN = **betrothed**, fiancé *or* fiancée, future wife *or* husband, husband- *or* wife-to-be: *Attention is turned to the Queen's youngest son and his intended.*

intense ADJECTIVE **1** = **extreme**, great, severe, fierce, serious *(informal)*, deep, powerful, concentrated, supreme, acute, harsh, intensive, excessive, profound, exquisite, drastic, forceful, protracted, unqualified, agonizing, mother of all *(informal)*: *He was sweating from the intense heat.* **OPPOSITE:** mild **2** = **fierce**, close, tough: *The battle for third place was intense.* **3** = **passionate**, burning, earnest, emotional, keen, flaming, consuming, fierce, eager, enthusiastic, heightened, energetic, animated, ardent, fanatical, fervent, heartfelt, impassioned, vehement, forcible, fervid: *She is more adult, and more intense than I had imagined.* **OPPOSITE:** indifferent

> **USAGE**
> *Intense* is sometimes wrongly used where *intensive* is meant: *the land is under intensive* (not *intense*) *cultivation*. *Intensely* is sometimes wrongly used where *intently* is meant: *he listened intently* (not *intensely*).

intensely ADVERB **1** = **very**, highly, extremely, greatly, strongly, severely, terribly, ultra, utterly, unusually, exceptionally, extraordinarily, markedly, awfully *(informal)*, acutely, exceedingly, excessively, inordinately, uncommonly, to the nth degree, to *or* in the extreme: *The fast-food business is intensely competitive.* **2** = **intently**, deeply, seriously *(informal)*, profoundly, passionately: *He sipped his drink, staring intensely at me.*

intensify VERB **1** = **increase**, boost, raise, extend, concentrate, add to, strengthen, enhance, compound, reinforce, step up *(informal)*, emphasize, widen, heighten, sharpen, magnify, amplify, augment, redouble: *They are intensifying their efforts to secure the release of the hostages.* **OPPOSITE:** decrease **2** = **escalate**, increase, extend, widen, heighten, deepen, quicken: *The conflict is almost bound to intensify.*

intensity NOUN **1** = **force**, power, strength, severity, extremity, fierceness: *The attack was anticipated, but its intensity came as a shock.* **2** = **passion**, emotion, fervour, force, power, fire, energy, strength, depth, concentration, excess, severity, vigour, potency, extremity, fanaticism, ardour, vehemence, earnestness, keenness, fierceness, fervency, intenseness: *His intensity, and the ferocity of his feelings alarmed me.*

intensive ADJECTIVE = **concentrated**, thorough, exhaustive, full, demanding, detailed, complete, serious, concerted, intense, comprehensive, vigorous, all-out, in-depth, strenuous, painstaking, all-embracing, assiduous, thoroughgoing

intent ADJECTIVE = **absorbed**, focused, fixed, earnest, committed, concentrated, occupied, intense, fascinated, steady, alert, wrapped up, preoccupied, enthralled, attentive, watchful, engrossed, steadfast, rapt, enrapt: *She looked from one intent face to another.* **OPPOSITE:** indifferent
▷ NOUN = **intention**, aim, purpose, meaning, end, plan, goal, design, target, object, resolution, resolve, objective, ambition, aspiration: *a statement of intent on arms control* **OPPOSITE:** chance
intent on something = **set on**, committed to, eager to, bent on, fixated on, hellbent on *(informal)*, insistent about, determined about, resolute about, inflexible about, resolved about: *The rebels are obviously intent on stepping up the pressure.*
to all intents and purposes = **in effect**, essentially, effectively, really, actually, in fact, virtually, in reality, in truth, in actuality, for practical purposes: *To all intents and purposes he was my father.*

intention NOUN = **aim**, plan, idea, goal, end, design, target, wish, scheme, purpose, object, objective, determination, intent

> **PROVERBS**
> *The road to hell is paved with good intentions*

intentional ADJECTIVE = **deliberate**, meant, planned, studied, designed, purposed, intended, calculated, wilful, premeditated, prearranged, done on purpose, preconcerted **OPPOSITE:** unintentional

intentionally ADVERB = **deliberately**, on purpose, wilfully, by design, designedly

intently ADVERB = **attentively**, closely, hard, keenly, steadily, fixedly, searchingly, watchfully

inter VERB = **bury**, lay to rest, entomb, sepulchre, consign to the grave, inhume, inurn

intercede VERB = **mediate**, speak, plead, intervene, arbitrate, advocate, interpose

intercept VERB = **catch**, take, stop, check, block, arrest, seize, cut off, interrupt, head off, deflect, obstruct

interchange NOUN = **exchange**, give and take, alternation, reciprocation: *the interchange of ideas from different disciplines*
▷ VERB = **exchange**, switch, swap, alternate, trade, barter, reciprocate, bandy: *She likes to interchange furniture at home with stock from the shop.*

interchangeable ADJECTIVE = **identical**, the same, equivalent, synonymous, reciprocal, exchangeable, transposable, commutable

intercourse NOUN **1** = **sexual intercourse**, sex *(informal)*, lovemaking, the other *(informal)*, congress, screwing *(taboo, slang)*, intimacy, shagging *(Brit. taboo, slang)*, sexual relations, sexual act, nookie *(slang)*, copulation, coitus, carnal knowledge, intimate relations, rumpy-pumpy *(slang)*, legover *(slang)*, coition, rumpo *(slang)*: *I did not have intercourse with that woman.* **2** = **contact**, relationships, communication, association, relations, trade, traffic, connection, truck, commerce, dealings, correspondence, communion, converse, intercommunication: *There was social intercourse between the old and the young.*

interest NOUN **1** = **importance**, concern, significance, moment, note, weight, import, consequence, substance, relevance, momentousness: *Food was of no interest to her at all.* **OPPOSITE:** insignificance **2** = **attention**, regard, curiosity, notice, suspicion, scrutiny, heed, absorption, attentiveness, inquisitiveness, engrossment: *They will follow the political crisis with interest.* **OPPOSITE:** disregard **3** *(often plural)* = **hobby**, activity, pursuit, entertainment, relaxation, recreation, amusement, preoccupation, diversion, pastime, leisure activity: *He developed a wide range of sporting interests.* **4** *(often plural)* = **advantage**, good, benefit, profit, gain, boot *(dialect)*: *Did the Directors act in the best interests of their club?* **5** *(often plural)* = **business**, concern, matter, affair: *The family controls large dairy interests.* **6** = **stake**, investment: *The West has an interest in promoting democratic forces.*
▷ VERB **1** = **arouse your curiosity**, engage, appeal to, fascinate, move, involve, touch, affect, attract, grip, entertain, absorb, intrigue, amuse, divert, rivet, captivate, catch your eye, hold the attention of, engross: *This part of the book interests me in particular.* **OPPOSITE:** bore **2** *(with* **in***)* = **sell**, persuade to buy: *In the meantime, can I interest you in a new car?*
in the interest(s) of = **for the sake of**, on behalf of, on the part of, to the advantage of: *We must all work together in the interest of national stability.*

interested ADJECTIVE **1** = **curious**, into *(informal)*, moved, affected, attracted, excited, drawn, keen, gripped, fascinated, stimulated, intent, responsive, riveted, captivated, attentive: *He did not look interested.* **OPPOSITE:** uninterested

2 = involved, concerned, affected, prejudiced, biased, partial, partisan, implicated, predisposed: *All the interested parties finally agreed to the idea.*

interesting ADJECTIVE **= intriguing**, fascinating, absorbing, pleasing, appealing, attractive, engaging, unusual, gripping, stirring, entertaining, entrancing, stimulating, curious, compelling, amusing, compulsive, riveting, captivating, enthralling, beguiling, thought-provoking, engrossing, spellbinding **OPPOSITE:** uninteresting

interface NOUN **= connection**, link, boundary, border, frontier: *the interface between bureaucracy and the working world*
▷ VERB **= connect**, couple, link, combine, join together: *the way we interface with the environment*

interfere VERB **= meddle**, intervene, intrude, butt in, get involved, tamper, pry, encroach, intercede, stick your nose in *(informal)*, stick your oar in *(informal)*, poke your nose in *(informal)*, intermeddle, put your two cents in *(U.S. slang)*: *Stop interfering and leave me alone!*
interfere with something or someone = conflict with, affect, get in the way of, check, block, clash, frustrate, handicap, hamper, disrupt, cramp, inhibit, thwart, hinder, obstruct, impede, baulk, trammel, be a drag upon *(informal)*: *Drug problems frequently interfered with his work.*

interference NOUN **= intrusion**, intervention, meddling, opposition, conflict, obstruction, prying, impedance, meddlesomeness, intermeddling

interfering ADJECTIVE **= meddling**, intrusive, prying, obtrusive, meddlesome, interruptive

interim ADJECTIVE **= temporary**, provisional, makeshift, acting, passing, intervening, caretaker, improvised, transient, stopgap, pro tem: *an interim report*
▷ NOUN **= interval**, meanwhile, meantime, respite, interregnum, entr'acte: *He was to remain in jail in the interim.*

interior NOUN **1 = inside**, centre, heart, middle, contents, depths, core, belly, nucleus, bowels, bosom, innards *(informal)*: *The boat's interior badly needed painting.* **2 = heartland**, centre, hinterland, upcountry: *a 5-day hike into the interior*
▷ ADJECTIVE **1 = inside**, internal, inner: *He turned on the interior light and examined the map.* **OPPOSITE:** exterior **2 = mental**, emotional, psychological, private, personal, secret, hidden, spiritual, intimate, inner, inward, instinctive, impulsive: *the interior life of human beings* **3 = domestic**, home, national, civil, internal: *The French Interior Minister has intervened over the scandal.*

interject VERB **= interrupt with**, put in, interpose, introduce, throw in, interpolate

interjection NOUN **= exclamation**, cry, ejaculation, interpolation, interposition

interloper NOUN **= trespasser**, intruder, gate-crasher *(informal)*, uninvited guest, meddler, unwanted visitor, intermeddler

interlude NOUN **= interval**, break, spell, stop, rest, halt, episode, pause, respite, stoppage, breathing space, hiatus, intermission, entr'acte

intermediary NOUN **= mediator**, agent, middleman, broker, entrepreneur, go-between

intermediate ADJECTIVE **= middle**, mid, halfway, in-between *(informal)*, midway, intervening, transitional, intermediary, median, interposed

interminable ADJECTIVE **= endless**, long, never-ending, dragging, unlimited, infinite, perpetual, protracted, limitless, boundless, everlasting, ceaseless, long-winded, long-drawn-out, immeasurable, wearisome, unbounded
OPPOSITE: limited

intermission NOUN **= interval**, break, pause, stop, rest, suspension, recess, interruption, respite, lull, stoppage, interlude, cessation, let-up *(informal)*, breathing space, entr'acte

intermittent ADJECTIVE **= periodic**, broken, occasional, recurring, irregular, punctuated, sporadic, recurrent, stop-go *(informal)*, fitful, spasmodic, discontinuous
OPPOSITE: continuous

intern VERB **= imprison**, hold, confine, detain, hold in custody

internal ADJECTIVE **1 = domestic**, home, national, local, civic, in-house, intramural: *The country stepped up internal security.* **2 = inner**, inside, interior: *Some of the internal walls are made of plasterboard.* **OPPOSITE:** external **3 = emotional**, mental, private, secret, subjective: *The personal, internal battle is beautifully portrayed.* **OPPOSITE:** revealed

international ADJECTIVE **= global**, world, worldwide, universal, cosmopolitan, planetary, intercontinental

Internet NOUN
the Internet = the information superhighway, the net *(informal)*, the web *(informal)*, the World Wide Web, cyberspace, blogosphere, the interweb *(facetious)*

interplay NOUN **= interaction**, give-and-take, reciprocity, reciprocation, meshing

interpret VERB **1 = take**, understand, read, explain, regard, construe: *The speech might be interpreted as a coded message.* **2 = translate**, convert, paraphrase, adapt, transliterate: *She spoke little English, so her husband interpreted.* **3 = explain**, define, clarify, spell out, make sense of, decode, decipher, expound, elucidate, throw light on, explicate: *The judge has to interpret the law as it's being passed.* **4 = understand**, read, explain, crack, solve, figure out *(informal)*, comprehend, decode, deduce, decipher, suss out *(slang)*: *The pictures are often difficult to interpret.* **5 = portray**, present, perform, render, depict, enact, act out: *Shakespeare, marvellously interpreted by Orson Welles*

interpretation NOUN
1 = explanation, meaning, reading, understanding, sense, analysis, construction, exposition, explication, elucidation, signification: *The Opposition put a different interpretation on the figures.* **2 = performance**, portrayal, presentation, rendering, reading, execution, rendition, depiction: *her full-bodied interpretation of the role of Micaela* **3 = reading**, study, review, version, analysis, explanation, examination, diagnosis, evaluation,

i

INTERNET TERMS

BitTorrent	cookie	hotpsot	podcast	Twitterverse	web directory
blog, blogger, *or* blogging	domain name	ISP *or* Internet service provider	portal	upload	weblog
blogosphere	download	leetspeak *or* 1337speak	RSS	URL *or* universe resource locator	webmail
blogstream	eBay *(trademark)*	lurk	search engine	voip	webmaster
bookmark	e-book	message board	search engine optimization *or* SEO	VPN	webpage
broadband	FTP *or* ftp	netiquette	Skype *(trademark)*	Web 2.0	website
browse	Generation C	newsgroup	spam	web address	Wi-Fi
browser	Google *(trademark)*	offline	spoofing	WebBoard	wiki
bulletin board	guestbook	online	surf	webcam	wikitorial
chatroom	hit			webcast	Yahoo *(trademark)*
	home page				

exposition, exegesis, explication, elucidation: *the interpretation of the scriptures*

interpreter NOUN **= translator**, linguist, metaphrast, paraphrast

interrogate VERB **= question**, ask, examine, investigate, pump, grill *(informal)*, quiz, cross-examine, cross-question, put the screws on *(informal)*, catechize, give (someone) the third degree *(informal)*

interrogation NOUN **= questioning**, inquiry, examination, probing, grilling *(informal)*, cross-examination, inquisition, third degree *(informal)*, cross-questioning

interrupt VERB **1 = intrude**, disturb, intervene, interfere (with), break in, heckle, butt in, barge in *(informal)*, break (someone's) train of thought: *'Sorry to interrupt, Colonel.'* **2 = suspend**, break, stop, end, cut, stay, check, delay, cease, cut off, postpone, shelve, put off, defer, break off, adjourn, cut short, discontinue: *He has interrupted his holiday to return to London.*

interruption NOUN **1 = disruption**, break, halt, obstacle, disturbance, hitch, intrusion, obstruction, impediment, hindrance: *The sudden interruption stopped her in mid-flow.* **2 = stoppage**, stop, pause, suspension, cessation, severance, hiatus, disconnection, discontinuance: *interruptions in the supply of food and fuel*

intersect VERB **= cross**, meet, cut, divide, cut across, bisect, crisscross

intersection NOUN **= junction**, crossing, crossroads

intersperse VERB **= scatter**, sprinkle, intermix, pepper, interlard, bestrew

interval NOUN **1 = period**, time, spell, term, season, space, stretch, pause, span: *There was a long interval of silence.* **2 = break**, interlude, intermission, rest, gap, pause, respite, lull, entr'acte: *During the interval, wine was served.* **3 = delay**, wait, gap, interim, hold-up, meanwhile, meantime, stoppage, hiatus: *the interval between her arrival and lunch* **4 = stretch**, area, space, distance, gap: *figures separated by intervals of pattern and colour*

intervene VERB **1 = step in** *(informal)*, interfere, mediate, intrude, intercede, arbitrate, interpose, take a hand *(informal)*: *The situation calmed down when police intervened.* **2 = interrupt**, involve yourself, put your oar in, interpose yourself, put your two cents in *(U.S. slang)*: *She intervened and told me to stop it.* **3 = happen**, occur, take place, follow, succeed, arise, ensue, befall, materialize, come to pass, supervene: *The mailboat comes weekly unless bad weather intervenes.*

intervention NOUN **= mediation**, involvement, interference, intrusion, arbitration, conciliation, intercession, interposition, agency

interview NOUN **1 = meeting**, examination, evaluation, oral (examination), interrogation: *When I went for my first job interview I arrived extremely early.* **2 = audience**, talk, conference, exchange, dialogue, consultation, press conference: *There'll be an interview with the Chancellor after the break.*
▷ VERB **1 = examine**, talk to, sound out: *He was among three candidates interviewed for the job.* **2 = question**, interrogate, examine, investigate, ask, pump, grill *(informal)*, quiz, cross-examine, cross-question, put the screws on *(informal)*, catechize, give (someone) the third degree *(informal)*: *The police interviewed the driver, but they had no evidence to go on.*

interviewer NOUN **= questioner**, reporter, investigator, examiner, interrogator, interlocutor

intestinal ADJECTIVE **= abdominal**, visceral, duodenal, gut *(informal)*, inner, coeliac, stomachic

intestine NOUN *(usu pl)* **= guts**, insides *(informal)*, bowels, internal organs, innards *(informal)*, entrails, vitals
▸ *technical name:* viscera

intimacy NOUN **= familiarity**, closeness, understanding, confidence, confidentiality, fraternization **OPPOSITE:** aloofness

intimate[1] ADJECTIVE **1 = close**, dear, loving, near, warm, friendly, familiar, thick *(informal)*, devoted, confidential, cherished, bosom, inseparable, nearest and dearest: *I discussed this only with my intimate friends.* **OPPOSITE:** distant **2 = private**, personal, confidential, special, individual, particular, secret, exclusive, privy: *He wrote about the intimate details of his family life.* **OPPOSITE:** public **3 = detailed**, minute, full, experienced, personal, deep, particular, specific, immediate, comprehensive, exact, elaborate, profound, penetrating, thorough, in-depth, intricate, first-hand, exhaustive: *He surprised me with his intimate knowledge of the situation.* **4 = cosy**, relaxed, friendly, informal, harmonious, snug, comfy *(informal)*, warm: *an intimate candlelit dinner for two*
▷ NOUN **= friend**, close friend, buddy *(informal)*, mate *(informal)*, pal, comrade, chum *(informal)*, mucker *(Brit. slang)*, crony, main man *(slang, chiefly U.S.)*, china *(Brit. slang)*, homeboy *(slang, chiefly U.S.)*, cobber *(Austral. & N.Z. old-fashioned, informal)*, bosom friend, familiar, confidant or confidante, (constant) companion, E hoa *(N.Z.)*: *They are to have an autumn wedding, an intimate of the couple confides.* **OPPOSITE:** stranger

intimate[2] VERB **1 = suggest**, indicate, hint, imply, warn, allude, let it be known, insinuate, give (someone) to understand, drop a hint, tip (someone) the wink *(Brit. informal)*: *He intimated that he was contemplating leaving the company.* **2 = announce**, state, declare, communicate, impart, make known: *He had intimated to them his readiness to come to a settlement.*

intimately ADVERB **1 = closely**, very well, personally, warmly, familiarly, tenderly, affectionately, confidentially, confidingly: *You have to be willing to get to know your partner intimately.* **2 = fully**, very well, thoroughly, in detail, inside out, to the core, through and through: *a golden age of musicians whose work she knew intimately*

intimation NOUN **1 = hint**, warning, suggestion, indication, allusion, inkling, insinuation: *I did not have any intimation that he was going to resign.* **2 = announcement**, notice, communication, declaration: *their first public intimation of how they will spend the budget*

intimidate VERB **= frighten**, pressure, threaten, alarm, scare, terrify, cow, bully, plague, menace, hound, awe, daunt, harass, subdue, oppress, persecute, lean on *(informal)*, coerce, overawe, scare off *(informal)*, terrorize, pressurize, browbeat, twist someone's arm *(informal)*, tyrannize, dishearten, dispirit, affright *(archaic)*, domineer

intimidation NOUN **= bullying**, pressure, threat(s), menaces, coercion, arm-twisting *(informal)*, browbeating, terrorization

intonation NOUN **1 = tone**, inflection, cadence, modulation, accentuation: *His voice had a very slight German intonation.* **2 = incantation**, spell, charm, formula, chant, invocation, hex *(U.S. & Canad. informal)*, conjuration: *They could hear strange music and chanting intonations.*

intone VERB **= chant**, sing, recite, croon, intonate

intoxicating ADJECTIVE **1 = alcoholic**, strong, intoxicant, spirituous, inebriant: *intoxicating liquor* **2 = exciting**, thrilling, stimulating, sexy *(informal)*, heady, exhilarating: *The music is pulsating and the atmosphere intoxicating.*

intoxication NOUN **1 = drunkenness**, inebriation, tipsiness, inebriety, insobriety: *Intoxication interferes with memory and thinking.* **2 = excitement**, euphoria, elation, exhilaration, infatuation, delirium, exaltation: *the intoxication of greed and success*

intractable ADJECTIVE **= difficult**, contrary, awkward, wild, stubborn, perverse, wayward, unruly, uncontrollable, wilful, incurable, fractious, unyielding, obstinate, intransigent, headstrong, unmanageable, undisciplined, cantankerous, unbending, obdurate, uncooperative, stiff-necked, ungovernable, self-willed, refractory, pig-headed, bull-headed

intransigent ADJECTIVE **= uncompromising**, intractable, tough, stubborn, hardline, tenacious, unyielding, obstinate, immovable, unbending, obdurate, stiff-necked, inflexible, unbudgeable **OPPOSITE:** compliant

intrenched *see* **entrenched**

intrepid ADJECTIVE = **fearless**, brave, daring, bold, heroic, game *(informal)*, have-a-go *(informal)*, courageous, stalwart, resolute, gallant, audacious, valiant, plucky, doughty, undaunted, unafraid, unflinching, nerveless, dauntless, lion-hearted, valorous, stouthearted, (as) game as Ned Kelly *(Austral. slang)* **OPPOSITE:** fearful

intricacy NOUN = **complexity**, involvement, complication, elaborateness, obscurity, entanglement, convolutions, involution, intricateness, knottiness

intricate ADJECTIVE = **complicated**, involved, complex, difficult, fancy, sophisticated, elaborate, obscure, tangled, baroque, perplexing, tortuous, Byzantine, convoluted, rococo, knotty, labyrinthine, daedal *(literary)* **OPPOSITE:** simple

intrigue NOUN **1** = **plot**, scheme, conspiracy, manoeuvre, manipulation, collusion, ruse, trickery, cabal, stratagem, double-dealing, chicanery, sharp practice, wile, knavery, machination: *the plots and intrigues in the novel* **2** = **affair**, romance, intimacy, liaison, amour: *She detected her husband in an intrigue with a prostitute.*
▷ VERB **1** = **interest**, fascinate, arouse the curiosity of, attract, charm, rivet, titillate, pique, tickle your fancy: *The novelty of the situation intrigued him.*
2 = **plot**, scheme, manoeuvre, conspire, connive, machinate: *The main characters spend their time intriguing for control.*

intriguing ADJECTIVE = **interesting**, fascinating, absorbing, exciting, engaging, gripping, stirring, stimulating, curious, compelling, amusing, diverting, provocative, beguiling, thought-provoking, titillating, engrossing, tantalizing

intrinsic ADJECTIVE = **essential**, real, true, central, natural, basic, radical, native, genuine, fundamental, constitutional, built-in, underlying, inherent, elemental, congenital, inborn, inbred **OPPOSITE:** extrinsic

intrinsically ADVERB = **essentially**, basically, fundamentally, constitutionally, as such, in itself, at heart, by definition, per se

introduce VERB **1** = **bring in**, establish, set up, start, begin, found, develop, launch, institute, organize, pioneer, initiate, originate, commence, get going, instigate, phase in, usher in, inaugurate, set in motion, bring into being: *The Government has introduced a number of other money-saving ideas.*
2 = **present**, acquaint, make known, familiarize, do the honours, make the introduction: *Someone introduced us and I sat next to him.* **3** = **announce**, present, open, launch, precede, lead into, preface, lead off: *'Health Matters' is introduced by Dick Oliver on the World Service.* **4** = **suggest**, offer, air, table, advance, propose, recommend, float, submit, bring up, put forward, set forth, ventilate, broach, moot: *She does not abandon her responsibility to introduce new ideas.* **5** = **add**, insert, inject, throw in *(informal)*, infuse, interpose, interpolate: *I wish to introduce a note of cool reason to the discussion.*

introduction NOUN **1** = **launch**, institution, establishment, start, opening, beginning, pioneering, presentation, initiation, inauguration, induction, commencement, instigation: *He is remembered for the introduction of the moving assembly line.*
OPPOSITE: elimination **2** = **opening**, prelude, preface, lead-in, preliminaries, overture, preamble, foreword, prologue, intro *(informal)*, commencement, opening remarks, proem, opening passage, prolegomena, prolegomenon, exordium: *In her introduction to the book she provides a summary of the ideas.*
OPPOSITE: conclusion **3** = **insertion**, addition, injection, interpolation: *the introduction of air bubbles into the veins*
OPPOSITE: extraction

introductory ADJECTIVE
1 = **preliminary**, elementary, first, early, initial, inaugural, preparatory, initiatory, prefatory, precursory: *an introductory course in religion and theology*
OPPOSITE: concluding **2** = **starting**, opening, initial, early: *out on the shelves at an introductory price of £2.99*

introspection NOUN = **self-examination**, brooding, self-analysis, navel-gazing *(slang)*, introversion, heart-searching

introspective ADJECTIVE = **inward-looking**, introverted, brooding, contemplative, meditative, subjective, pensive, inner-directed

introverted ADJECTIVE
= **introspective**, withdrawn, inward-looking, self-contained, self-centred, indrawn, inner-directed

intrude VERB = **butt in**, encroach, push in, obtrude, thrust yourself in *or* forward, put your two cents in *(U.S. slang)*: *He kept intruding with personal questions.*
intrude on something *or* **someone**
1 = **interfere with**, interrupt, impinge on, encroach on, meddle with, infringe on: *It's annoying when unforeseen events intrude on your day.* **2** = **trespass on**, invade, infringe on, obtrude on: *They intruded on to the field of play.*

intruder NOUN = **trespasser**, burglar, invader, squatter, prowler, interloper, infiltrator, gate-crasher *(informal)*

intrusion NOUN **1** = **interruption**, interference, infringement, trespass, encroachment: *I hope you don't mind this intrusion.* **2** = **invasion**, breach, infringement, infiltration, encroachment, infraction, usurpation: *I felt it was a grotesque intrusion into our lives.*

intrusive ADJECTIVE **1** = **interfering**, disturbing, invasive, unwanted, presumptuous, uncalled-for, importunate: *The cameras were not an intrusive presence.* **2** = **pushy** *(informal)*, forward, interfering, unwanted, impertinent, nosy *(informal)*, officious, meddlesome: *Her bodyguards were less than gentle with intrusive journalists.*

intrust *see* **entrust**

intuition NOUN **1** = **instinct**, perception, insight, sixth sense, discernment: *Her intuition was telling her that something was wrong.* **2** = **feeling**, idea, impression, suspicion, premonition, inkling, presentiment: *You can't make a case on intuitions, you know.*

intuitive ADJECTIVE = **instinctive**, spontaneous, innate, involuntary, instinctual, untaught, unreflecting

intuitively ADVERB = **instinctively**, automatically, spontaneously, involuntarily, innately, instinctually

intwine *see* **entwine**

inundate VERB **1** = **overwhelm**, flood, swamp, engulf, overflow, overrun, glut: *Her office was inundated with requests for tickets.* **2** = **flood**, engulf, submerge, drown, overflow, immerse, deluge: *Their neighbourhood is being inundated by the rising waters.*

invade VERB **1** = **attack**, storm, assault, capture, occupy, seize, raid, overwhelm, violate, conquer, overrun, annex, march into, assail, descend upon, infringe on, burst in on, make inroads on: *In 1944 the allies invaded the Italian mainland.* **2** = **infest**, swarm, overrun, flood, infect, ravage, beset, pervade, permeate, overspread: *Every so often the kitchen would be invaded by ants.*

invader NOUN = **attacker**, raider, plunderer, aggressor, looter, trespasser

invalid¹ NOUN = **patient**, sufferer, convalescent, valetudinarian: *I hate being treated as an invalid.*
▷ ADJECTIVE = **disabled**, challenged, ill, sick, poorly *(informal)*, weak, ailing, frail, feeble, sickly, infirm, bedridden, valetudinarian: *I have an invalid wife and am labelled as a carer.*

invalid² ADJECTIVE **1** = **null and void**, void, worthless, untrue, null, not binding, inoperative, nugatory: *The trial was stopped and the results declared invalid.* **OPPOSITE:** valid
2 = **unfounded**, false, untrue, illogical, irrational, unsound, unscientific, baseless, fallacious, ill-founded: *Those arguments are rendered invalid by the hard facts.* **OPPOSITE:** sound

invalidate VERB = **nullify**, cancel, annul, undermine, weaken, overthrow, undo, quash, overrule,

i

rescind, abrogate, render null and void **OPPOSITE:** validate

invalidity NOUN **= falsity**, fallacy, unsoundness, inconsistency, irrationality, illogicality, speciousness, sophism, fallaciousness

invaluable ADJECTIVE **= precious**, valuable, priceless, costly, inestimable, beyond price, worth your *or* its weight in gold **OPPOSITE:** worthless

invariably ADVERB **= always**, regularly, constantly, every time, inevitably, repeatedly, consistently, ever, continually, aye *(Scot.)*, eternally, habitually, perpetually, without exception, customarily, unfailingly, on every occasion, unceasingly, day in, day out

invasion NOUN **1 = attack**, assault, capture, takeover, raid, offensive, occupation, conquering, seizure, onslaught, foray, appropriation, sortie, annexation, incursion, expropriation, inroad, irruption, arrogation: *seven years after the Roman invasion of Britain* **2 = intrusion**, breach, violation, disturbance, disruption, infringement, overstepping, infiltration, encroachment, infraction, usurpation: *Is reading a child's diary a gross invasion of privacy?*

invective NOUN **= abuse**, censure, tirade, reproach, berating, denunciation, diatribe, vilification, tongue-lashing, billingsgate, vituperation, castigation, obloquy, contumely, philippic(s), revilement

invent VERB **1 = create**, make, produce, develop, design, discover, imagine, manufacture, generate, come up with *(informal)*, coin, devise, conceive, originate, formulate, spawn, contrive, improvise, dream up *(informal)*, concoct, think up: *He invented the first electric clock.* **2 = make up**, devise, concoct, forge, fake, fabricate, feign, falsify, cook up *(informal)*, trump up: *I stood there, trying to invent a plausible excuse.*

invention NOUN **1 = creation**, machine, device, design, development, instrument, discovery, innovation, gadget, brainchild *(informal)*, contraption, contrivance: *It's been tricky marketing his new invention.* **2 = development**, design, production, setting up, foundation, construction, constitution, creation, discovery, introduction, establishment, pioneering, formation, innovation, conception, masterminding, formulation, inception, contrivance, origination: *fifty years after the invention of the printing press* **3 = fiction**, story, fantasy, lie, yarn, fabrication, concoction, falsehood, fib *(informal)*, untruth, urban myth, prevarication, tall story *(informal)*, urban legend, figment *or* product of (someone's) imagination: *The story was undoubtedly pure invention.* **4 = creativity**, vision, imagination, initiative, enterprise, inspiration, genius, brilliance, ingenuity, originality, inventiveness, resourcefulness, creativeness, ingeniousness, imaginativeness: *powers of invention and mathematical ability*

inventive ADJECTIVE **= creative**, original, innovative, imaginative, gifted, inspired, fertile, ingenious, ground-breaking, resourceful **OPPOSITE:** uninspired

inventor NOUN **= creator**, father, maker, author, framer, designer, architect, coiner, originator

inventory NOUN **= list**, record, catalogue, listing, account, roll, file, schedule, register, description, log, directory, tally, roster, stock book

inverse ADJECTIVE **1 = opposite**, reverse, reversed, contrary, inverted, converse, transposed: *The tension grew in inverse proportion to the distance from their destination.* **2 = reverse**, opposite, reversed, inverted, transposed: *The hologram can be flipped to show the inverse image.*

inversion NOUN **= reversal**, opposite, antithesis, transposition, contrary, contrariety, contraposition, transposal, antipode

invert VERB **= overturn**, upturn, turn upside down, upset, reverse, capsize, transpose, introvert, turn inside out, turn turtle, invaginate *(Pathology)*, overset, intussuscept *(Pathology)*

invest VERB **1 = spend**, expend, advance, venture, put in, devote, lay out, sink in, use up, plough in: *When people buy houses they're investing a lot of money.* **2 = charge**, fill, steep, saturate, endow, pervade, infuse, imbue, suffuse, endue: *The buildings are invested with a nations's history.* **3 = empower**, provide, charge, sanction, license, authorize, vest: *The constitution had invested him with certain powers.* **4 = install**, establish, ordain, crown, inaugurate, anoint, consecrate, adopt, induct, enthrone, instate: *He was invested as a paramount chief of a district tribe.*
invest in something = buy, get, purchase, score *(slang)*, pay for, obtain, acquire, procure: *Why don't you invest in an ice cream machine?*

investigate VERB **= examine**, study, research, consider, go into, explore, search for, analyse, look into, inspect, look over, sift, probe into, work over, scrutinize, inquire into, make inquiries about, enquire into

investigation NOUN **= examination**, study, inquiry, hearing, research, review, search, survey, analysis, probe, inspection, exploration, scrutiny, inquest, fact finding, recce *(slang)*

investigative ADJECTIVE **= fact-finding**, researching, investigating, research, inspecting

investigator NOUN **= examiner**, researcher, inspector, monitor, detective, analyser, explorer, reviewer, scrutinizer, checker, inquirer, scrutineer

investment NOUN **1 = investing**, backing, funding, financing, contribution, speculation, transaction, expenditure, outlay: *The government introduced tax incentives to encourage investment.* **2 = stake**, interest, share, concern, portion, ante *(informal)*: *an investment of £28 million* **3 = buy**, asset, acquisition, venture, risk, speculation, gamble: *A small-screen portable TV can be a good investment.*

inveterate ADJECTIVE **1 = chronic**, confirmed, incurable, hardened, established, long-standing, hard-core, habitual, obstinate, incorrigible, dyed-in-the-wool, ineradicable, deep-dyed *(usually derogatory)*: *an inveterate gambler* **2 = deep-rooted**, entrenched, ingrained, deep-seated, incurable, established: *the inveterate laziness of these boys* **3 = staunch**, long-standing, dyed-in-the-wool, deep-dyed *(usually derogatory)*: *the spirit of an inveterate Tory*

invidious ADJECTIVE **= undesirable**, unpleasant, hateful, thankless **OPPOSITE:** pleasant

invigorating ADJECTIVE **= refreshing**, stimulating, bracing, fresh, tonic, uplifting, exhilarating, rejuvenating, energizing, healthful, restorative, salubrious, rejuvenative

invincible ADJECTIVE **= unbeatable**, unassailable, indomitable, unyielding, indestructible, impregnable, insuperable, invulnerable, unconquerable, unsurmountable **OPPOSITE:** vulnerable

invisible ADJECTIVE **1 = unseen**, imperceptible, indiscernible, unseeable, unperceivable: *The lines were so fine as to be nearly invisible.* **OPPOSITE:** visible **2 = hidden**, concealed, obscured, secret, disguised, inconspicuous, unobserved, unnoticeable, inappreciable: *The problems of the poor are largely invisible.*

invitation NOUN **1 = request**, call, invite *(informal)*, bidding, summons: *He received an invitation to lunch.* **2 = inducement**, come-on *(informal)*, temptation, challenge, provocation, open door, overture, incitement, enticement, allurement: *Don't leave your bag there – it's an invitation to a thief.*

invite VERB **1 = ask**, bid, summon, request the pleasure of (someone's) company: *She invited him to her birthday party.* **2 = request**, seek, look for, call for, ask for, bid for, appeal for, petition, solicit: *The Department is inviting applications from local groups.* **3 = encourage**, attract, cause, draw, lead to, court, ask for *(informal)*, generate, foster, tempt, provoke, induce, bring on, solicit, engender, allure, call forth, leave the door open

The Language of Katherine Mansfield

Katherine Mansfield (née Kathleen Mansfield Beauchamp) was born in Wellington, New Zealand, in 1888. She went to London in 1903 to study at Queen's College, and also spent some time in Germany. She moved permanently to England in 1908. Her first published book was *In a German Pension* (1911), a collection of maliciously humorous depictions of the guests at the pension of the title. Mansfield later disowned it, and refused to let it be re-published during the First World War. Two more collections of short stories, *Bliss* (1921) and *The Garden Party* (1922) were published before her death from TB in 1923.

Xenophobia is not the only aspect of her early stories that Katherine Mansfield later rejected: another is their language. Her early work is at times somewhat literary, with a scattering of Latinate phrases, such *the masculine element* (ie 'the men'), or children described as lying together *in mutual amity*. Dialogue is introduced by bookish synonyms for *say*, eg *murmur, cry, protest, retort, urge*. In later years Mansfield made less use of these. In the following passage from *Life of Ma Parker*, for example, speech is presented with a minimum of introductory verbs, and is simple and colloquial:

> But he put his arms round her neck and rubbed his cheek against hers. 'Gran, gi' us a penny!' he coaxed. 'Be off with you; Gran ain't got no pennies.' 'Yes, you 'ave.' 'No, I ain't.' 'Yes, you 'ave . Gi' us one!' Already she was feeling for the old, squashed, black leather purse.

Non-standard language is often presented in novels as laughable, but here it is not; the grandmother's feeling for her grandson is tenderly conveyed, and contrasts with the crassness of the utterances of the literary gentleman whose flat Ma Parker cleans. Women are generally the focus of sympathy in Mansfield's writing: *she* occurs a good deal more often than *he*.

In the dialogue between Ma Parker and the little boy, every word is of Old English, rather than Latin, origin. This preference for Anglo-Saxon language is found throughout Mansfield's later work - not just in the speech of uneducated people. The nouns she uses most are predominantly Anglo-Saxon, and concrete - words for people (*man, child, girl, woman*); parts of the body (*hand, head, eye*); domestic things (*room, bed, window*), clothes (*hat, coat*). Among the hundred verbs she uses most frequently, only four are of Latin origin (*turn, suppose, expect,* and *decide*), and these too are common, everyday words.

The energy of verbs of movement is very important in Mansfield's lively descriptions:

> On the veranda there hung a long string of bathing-dresses, **clinging** together as though they'd just been rescued from the sea ...

> The sunlight **pressed** through the windows, **thieved** its way in, **flashed** its light over the furniture and the photographs.

Such verbs require no adverbs. Descriptive adverbs (as opposed to adverbs such as *never, so, very*) are not particularly frequent in her later stories; the ones that occur most frequently are *quickly, slowly*, and *gently*. Several times she intensifies the effect of the adverb by repeating it: *quickly, quickly, like a rat; She jerked slowly, slowly up the steps; ...gently, very gently, she bit her mother's ear.*

The most salient adjectives in the stories describe size (*little, long, big*); colour (*white, black, blue*); and other physical characteristics (*cold, warm, soft, wet*). They are common, often monosyllabic words, but with them Mansfield conveys an acute sense of how things look and feel:

> The shepherd stopped whistling; he rubbed his **red** nose and **wet** beard on his **wet** sleeve and, screwing up his eyes, glanced in the direction of the sea.

to: *Their refusal to compromise will invite more criticism from the UN.*

inviting ADJECTIVE = **tempting**, appealing, attractive, pleasing, welcoming, warm, engaging, fascinating, intriguing, magnetic, delightful, enticing, seductive, captivating, beguiling, alluring, mouthwatering **OPPOSITE:** uninviting

invocation NOUN **1 = appeal**, request, petition, beseeching, solicitation, entreaty: *an invocation for divine guidance* **2 = prayer**, chant, supplication, orison, karakia *(N.Z.)*: *Please stand for the invocation.*

invoke VERB **1 = apply**, use, implement, call in, initiate, resort to, put into effect: *The judge invoked an international law that protects refugees.* **2 = call upon**, appeal to, pray to, petition, conjure, solicit, beseech, entreat, adjure, supplicate: *The great magicians of old invoked their gods with sacrifice.*

involuntary ADJECTIVE = **unintentional**, automatic, unconscious, spontaneous, reflex, instinctive, uncontrolled, unthinking, instinctual, blind, unconditioned **OPPOSITE:** voluntary

involve VERB **1 = entail**, mean, demand, require, call for, occasion, result in, imply, give rise to, encompass, necessitate: *Running a kitchen involves a great deal of discipline and speed.* **2 = include**, contain, take in, embrace, cover, incorporate, draw in, comprise, number among: *The cover-up involved people at the very highest level.* **3 = implicate**, tangle, mix up, embroil, link, entangle, incriminate, mire, stitch up *(slang)*, enmesh, inculpate *(formal)*: *I seem to have involved myself in something I don't understand.* **4 = concern**, draw in, associate, connect, bear on: *He started involving me in the more confidential aspects of the job.*

involved ADJECTIVE = **complicated**, complex, intricate, hard, difficult, confused, confusing, sophisticated, elaborate, tangled, bewildering, jumbled, entangled, tortuous, Byzantine, convoluted, knotty, unfathomable, labyrinthine: *The operation can be quite involved, requiring special procedures.* **OPPOSITE:** straightforward

involvement NOUN = **connection**, interest, relationship, concern, association, commitment, friendship, attachment: *He has always felt a deep involvement with animals.*

invulnerable ADJECTIVE = **safe**, secure, invincible, impenetrable, unassailable, indestructible, insusceptible **OPPOSITE:** vulnerable

inward ADJECTIVE **1 = incoming**, entering, penetrating, inbound, inflowing, ingoing, inpouring: *a sharp, inward breath like a gasp* **2 = internal**, inner, private, personal, inside, secret, hidden, interior, confidential, privy, innermost, inmost: *a glow of inward satisfaction* **OPPOSITE:** outward

inwardly ADVERB = **privately**, secretly, to yourself, within, inside, at heart, deep down, in your head, in your inmost heart

iota NOUN = **bit**, particle, atom, trace, hint, scrap, grain, mite, jot, speck, whit, tittle

irascible ADJECTIVE = **bad-tempered**, cross, irritable, crabbed, touchy, cantankerous, peppery, tetchy, ratty *(Brit. & N.Z. informal)*, testy, chippy *(informal)*, short-tempered, hot-tempered, quick-tempered, choleric, narky *(Brit. slang)*

irate ADJECTIVE = **angry**, cross, furious, angered, mad *(informal)*, provoked, annoyed, irritated, fuming *(informal)*, choked, infuriated, incensed, enraged, worked up, exasperated, indignant, livid, riled, up in arms, incandescent, hacked off *(U.S. slang)*, piqued, hot under the collar *(informal)*, wrathful, fit to be tied *(slang)*, as black as thunder, tooshie *(Austral. slang)*, off the air *(Austral. slang)*

ire NOUN *(Literary)* = **anger**, rage, fury, wrath, passion, indignation, annoyance, displeasure, exasperation, choler

iridescent ADJECTIVE = **shimmering**, pearly, opalescent, shot, opaline, prismatic, rainbow-coloured, polychromatic, nacreous

irk VERB = **irritate**, annoy, aggravate *(informal)*, provoke, bug *(informal)*, put out *(informal)*, gall, ruffle, nettle, vex, rile, peeve *(informal)*, get on your nerves *(informal)*, nark *(Brit., Austral. & N.Z. slang)*, miff *(informal)*, be on your back *(slang)*, get in your hair *(informal)*, rub you up the wrong way *(informal)*, put your nose out of joint *(informal)*, get your back up, put your back up, hack you off *(informal)*

irksome ADJECTIVE = **irritating**, trying, annoying, aggravating, troublesome, unwelcome, exasperating, tiresome, vexing, disagreeable, burdensome, wearisome, bothersome, vexatious **OPPOSITE:** pleasant

iron MODIFIER = **ferrous**, ferric, irony: *The huge iron gate was locked.*
▷ ADJECTIVE = **inflexible**, hard, strong, tough, steel, rigid, adamant, unconditional, steely, implacable, indomitable, unyielding, immovable, unbreakable, unbending, obdurate: *a man of icy nerve and iron will* **OPPOSITE:** weak
iron something out = **settle**, resolve, sort out, eliminate, get rid of, reconcile, clear up, simplify, unravel, erase, eradicate, put right, straighten out, harmonize, expedite, smooth over: *The various groups had managed to iron out their differences.*
▸ *related adjectives:* ferric, ferrous
▸ *related prefix:* ferro-

ironic *or* **ironical** ADJECTIVE **1 = sarcastic**, dry, sharp, acid, bitter, stinging, mocking, sneering, scoffing, wry, scathing, satirical, tongue-in-cheek, sardonic, caustic, double-edged, acerbic, trenchant, mordant, mordacious: *At the most solemn moments he would make an ironic remark.* **2 = paradoxical**, absurd, contradictory, puzzling, baffling, ambiguous, inconsistent, confounding, enigmatic, illogical, incongruous: *It's ironic that the sort of people this film celebrates would never watch it.*

irons PLURAL NOUN = **chains**, shackles, fetters, manacles, bonds: *These people need to be clapped in irons themselves.*

irony NOUN **1 = sarcasm**, mockery, ridicule, bitterness, scorn, satire, cynicism, derision, causticity, mordancy: *She examined his face for a hint of irony, but found none.* **2 = paradox**, ambiguity, absurdity, incongruity, contrariness: *Opposition parties wasted no time in stressing the irony of the situation.*

irrational ADJECTIVE **1 = illogical**, crazy, silly, absurd, foolish, unreasonable, unwise, preposterous, idiotic, nonsensical, unsound, unthinking, injudicious, unreasoning: *an irrational fear of science* **OPPOSITE:** rational **2 = senseless**, wild, crazy, unstable, insane, mindless, demented, aberrant, brainless, off the air *(Austral. slang)*: *They behaved in such a bizarre and irrational manner.*

irrationality NOUN = **senselessness**, madness, insanity, absurdity, lunacy, lack of judgment, illogicality, unreasonableness, preposterousness, unsoundness, brainlessness

irreconcilable ADJECTIVE **1 = implacable**, uncompromising, inflexible, inexorable, intransigent, unappeasable: *an irreconcilable clash of personalities* **2 = incompatible**, conflicting, opposed, inconsistent, incongruous, diametrically opposed: *their irreconcilable points of view*

irrefutable ADJECTIVE = **undeniable**, sure, certain, irresistible, invincible, unassailable, indisputable, unanswerable, unquestionable, incontrovertible, beyond question, incontestable, indubitable, apodictic, irrefragable

irregular ADJECTIVE **1 = variable**, inconsistent, erratic, shifting, occasional, random, casual, shaky, wavering, uneven, fluctuating, eccentric, patchy, sporadic, intermittent, haphazard, unsteady, desultory, fitful, spasmodic, unsystematic, inconstant, nonuniform, unmethodical, scattershot: *She was suffering from an irregular heartbeat.* **OPPOSITE:** steady **2 = uneven**, broken, rough, twisted, twisting, curving, pitted, ragged, crooked, unequal, jagged, bumpy, lumpy, serpentine, contorted, lopsided, craggy, indented, asymmetrical, serrated, holey, unsymmetrical: *He had bad teeth, irregular and discoloured.* **OPPOSITE:** even **3 = inappropriate**, unconventional, improper, unethical, odd, unusual, extraordinary, disorderly, exceptional, peculiar, unofficial, abnormal, queer, rum *(Brit. slang)*, back-door, unsuitable, unorthodox, out-of-order, unprofessional, anomalous: *The minister was accused of irregular business practices.* **4 = unofficial**, underground, guerrilla, volunteer, resistance, partisan, rogue, paramilitary, mercenary: *At least 17 irregular units are involved in the war.*

irregularity NOUN **1 = inconsistency**, randomness, disorganization, unsteadiness, unpunctuality, haphazardness, disorderliness, lack of method, desultoriness: *a dangerous irregularity in her heartbeat* **2 = unevenness**, deformity, asymmetry, crookedness, contortion, patchiness, lopsidedness, raggedness, lack of symmetry, spottiness, jaggedness: *treatment of irregularities of the teeth* **3 = malpractice**, anomaly, breach, abnormality, deviation, oddity, aberration, malfunction, peculiarity, singularity, unorthodoxy, unconventionality: *charges arising from alleged financial irregularities*

irregularly ADVERB **= erratically**, occasionally, now and again, intermittently, off and on, anyhow, unevenly, fitfully, haphazardly, eccentrically, spasmodically, jerkily, in snatches, out of sequence, by fits and starts, disconnectedly, unmethodically, unpunctually

irrelevance *or* **irrelevancy** NOUN **= inappropriateness**, inapplicability, inaptness, unconnectedness, pointlessness, non sequitur, inconsequence, extraneousness, inappositeness **OPPOSITE:** relevance

irrelevant ADJECTIVE **= unconnected**, unrelated, unimportant, inappropriate, peripheral, insignificant, negligible, immaterial, extraneous, beside the point, impertinent, neither here nor there, inapplicable, inapt, inapposite, inconsequent **OPPOSITE:** relevant

irreparable ADJECTIVE **= beyond repair**, irreversible, incurable, irretrievable, irrecoverable, irremediable

irreplaceable ADJECTIVE **= indispensable**, unique, invaluable, priceless

irrepressible ADJECTIVE **= unstoppable**, buoyant, uncontrollable, boisterous, ebullient, effervescent, unmanageable, unquenchable, bubbling over, uncontainable, unrestrainable, insuppressible

irresistible ADJECTIVE **1 = overwhelming**, compelling, overpowering, urgent, potent, imperative, compulsive, uncontrollable, overmastering: *It proved an irresistible temptation to go back.* **2 = seductive**, inviting, tempting, enticing, provocative, fascinating, enchanting, captivating, beguiling, alluring, bewitching, ravishing: *The music is irresistible.* **3 = inescapable**, inevitable, unavoidable, sure, certain, fated, destined, inexorable, ineluctable: *They feel the case for change is irresistible.*

irrespective of PREPOSITION **= despite**, in spite of, regardless of, discounting, notwithstanding, without reference to, without regard to

irresponsible ADJECTIVE **= thoughtless**, reckless, careless, wild, unreliable, giddy, untrustworthy, flighty, ill-considered, good-for-nothing, shiftless, harebrained, undependable, harum-scarum, scatterbrained, featherbrained **OPPOSITE:** responsible

irreverence NOUN **= disrespect**, cheek *(informal)*, impertinence, sauce *(informal)*, mockery, derision, lack of respect, impudence, flippancy, cheekiness *(informal)*

irreverent ADJECTIVE **= disrespectful**, cheeky *(informal)*, impertinent, fresh *(informal)*, mocking, flip *(informal)*, saucy, contemptuous, tongue-in-cheek, sassy *(U.S. informal)*, flippant, iconoclastic, derisive, impudent **OPPOSITE:** reverent

irreversible ADJECTIVE **= irrevocable**, incurable, irreparable, final, unalterable

irrevocable ADJECTIVE **= fixed**, settled, irreversible, fated, predetermined, immutable, invariable, irretrievable, predestined, unalterable, unchangeable, changeless, irremediable, unreversible

> **QUOTATIONS**
>
> The moving finger writes; and having writ,
> Moves on; nor all thy piety nor wit
> Shall lure it back to cancel half a line,
> Nor all thy tears wash out a word of it.
> [Edward Fitzgerald *Rubaiyat of Omar Khayyam*]
>
> One cannot step twice into the same river
> [Heraclitus]

irrigate VERB **= water**, wet, moisten, flood, inundate, fertigate *(Austral.)*

irritability NOUN **= bad temper**, impatience, ill humour, prickliness, tetchiness, irascibility, peevishness, testiness, touchiness **OPPOSITE:** good humour

irritable ADJECTIVE **= bad-tempered**, cross, snappy, hot, tense, crabbed, fiery, snarling, prickly, exasperated, edgy, touchy, petulant, ill-tempered, irascible, cantankerous, tetchy, ratty *(Brit. & N.Z. informal)*, testy, chippy *(informal)*, fretful, peevish, crabby, dyspeptic, choleric, crotchety *(informal)*, oversensitive, snappish, ill-humoured, narky *(Brit. slang)*, out of humour **OPPOSITE:** even-tempered

irritate VERB **1 = annoy**, anger, bother, provoke, offend, needle *(informal)*, harass, infuriate, aggravate *(informal)*, incense, fret, enrage, gall, ruffle, inflame, exasperate, nettle, pester, vex, irk, pique, rankle with, get under your skin *(informal)*, get on your nerves *(informal)*, nark *(Brit., Austral. & N.Z. slang)*, drive you up the wall *(slang)*, rub you up the wrong way *(informal)*, get your goat *(slang)*, try your patience, get in your hair *(informal)*, get on your wick *(informal)*, get your dander up *(informal)*, raise your hackles, get your back up, get your hackles up, put your back up, hack you off *(informal)*: *Their attitude irritates me.* **OPPOSITE:** placate **2 = inflame**, pain, rub, scratch, scrape, grate, graze, fret, gall, chafe, abrade: *Chillies can irritate the skin.*

irritated ADJECTIVE **= annoyed**, cross, angry, bothered, put out, hacked (off) *(U.S. slang)*, harassed, impatient, ruffled, exasperated, irritable, nettled, vexed, displeased, flustered, peeved *(informal)*, piqued, out of humour, tooshie *(Austral. slang)*, hoha *(N.Z.)*

irritating ADJECTIVE **= annoying**, trying, provoking, infuriating, upsetting, disturbing, nagging, aggravating *(informal)*, troublesome, galling, maddening, disquieting, displeasing, worrisome, irksome, vexatious, pestilential **OPPOSITE:** pleasing

irritation NOUN **1 = annoyance**, anger, fury, resentment, wrath, gall, indignation, impatience, displeasure, exasperation, chagrin, irritability, ill temper, shortness, vexation, ill humour, testiness, crossness, snappiness, infuriation: *For the first time he felt irritation at her methods.* **OPPOSITE:** pleasure **2 = nuisance**, annoyance, irritant, pain *(informal)*, drag *(informal)*, bother, plague, menace, tease, pest, hassle, provocation, gall, goad, aggravation *(informal)*, pain in the neck *(informal)*, thorn in your flesh: *Don't allow a minor irritation to mar your ambitions.*

island NOUN **= isle**, inch *(Scot. & Irish)*, atoll, holm *(dialect)*, islet, ait *or* eyot *(dialect)*, cay *or* key
▸ *related adjective:* insular

isolate VERB **1 = separate**, break up, cut off, detach, split up, insulate, segregate, disconnect, divorce, sequester, set apart, disunite, estrange: *This policy could isolate members* *from the UN security council.* **2 = quarantine**, separate, exclude, cut off, detach, keep in solitude: *Patients will be isolated for one month after treatment.*

isolated ADJECTIVE **= remote**, far, distant, lonely, out-of-the-way, hidden, retired, far-off, secluded, inaccessible, faraway, outlying, in the middle of nowhere, off the beaten track, backwoods, godforsaken, incommunicado, unfrequented: *Many of the refugee areas are in isolated areas.*

isolation NOUN **= separation**, withdrawal, loneliness, segregation, detachment, quarantine, solitude, exile, self-sufficiency, seclusion, remoteness, disconnection, insularity

issue NOUN **1 = topic**, point, matter, problem, business, case, question, concern, subject, affair, argument, theme, controversy, can of worms (*informal*): *Is it right for the Church to express a view on political issues?* **2 = point**, question, concern, bone of contention, matter of contention, point in question: *I wasn't earning much money, but that was not the issue.* **3 = edition**, printing, copy, impression, publication, number, instalment, imprint, version: *The problem is underlined in the latest issue of the Lancet.* **4 = children**, young, offspring, babies, kids (*informal*), seed (*chiefly biblical*), successors, heirs, descendants, progeny, scions: *He died without issue in 1946.* **OPPOSITE:** parent **5 = distribution**, issuing, supply, supplying, delivery, publication, circulation, sending out, dissemination, dispersal, issuance: *the issue of supplies to refugees*
▷ VERB **1 = give out**, release, publish, announce, deliver, spread, broadcast, distribute, communicate, proclaim, put out, circulate, emit, impart, disseminate, promulgate, put in circulation: *He issued a statement denying the allegations.* **2 = emerge**, come out, proceed, rise, spring, flow, arise, stem, originate, emanate, exude, come forth, be a consequence of: *A tinny voice issued from a speaker.*
at issue = under discussion, in question, in dispute, under consideration, to be decided, for debate: *The problems of immigration were not the question at issue.*
take issue with something or **someone = disagree with**, question, challenge, oppose, dispute, object to, argue with, take exception to, raise an objection to: *She might take issue with you on that matter.*

itch VERB **1 = prickle**, tickle, tingle, crawl: *When you have hayfever, your eyes and nose stream and itch.* **2 = long**, ache, crave, burn, pine, pant, hunger, lust, yearn, hanker: *I was itching to get involved.*
▷ NOUN **1 = irritation**, tingling, prickling, itchiness: *Scratch my back – I've got an itch.* **2 = desire**, longing, craving, passion, yen (*informal*), hunger, lust, yearning, hankering, restlessness: *an insatiable itch to switch from channel to channel*

itchy ADJECTIVE **= impatient**, eager, restless, unsettled, edgy, restive, fidgety

item NOUN **1 = article**, thing, object, piece, unit, component: *The most valuable item on show will be a Picasso.* **2 = matter**, point, issue, case, question, concern, detail, subject, feature, particular, affair, aspect, entry, theme, consideration, topic: *The other item on the agenda is the tour.* **3 = report**, story, piece, account, note, feature, notice, article, paragraph, bulletin, dispatch, communiqué, write-up: *There was an item in the paper about him.*

itemize VERB **= list**, record, detail, count, document, instance, set out, specify, inventory, number, enumerate, particularize

itinerant ADJECTIVE **= wandering**, travelling, journeying, unsettled, Gypsy, roaming, roving, nomadic, migratory, vagrant, peripatetic, vagabond, ambulatory, wayfaring **OPPOSITE:** settled

itinerary NOUN **= schedule**, line, programme, tour, route, journey, circuit, timetable

ivory tower NOUN **= seclusion**, remoteness, unreality, retreat, refuge, cloister, sanctum, splendid isolation, world of your own

Jj

jab VERB = **poke**, dig, punch, thrust, tap, stab, nudge, prod, lunge: *a needle was jabbed into the baby's arm*
▷ NOUN = **poke**, dig, punch, thrust, tap, stab, nudge, prod, lunge: *He gave me a jab in the side.*

jacket NOUN = **covering**, casing, case, cover, skin, shell, coat, wrapping, envelope, capsule, folder, sheath, wrapper, encasement, housing

jackpot NOUN = **prize**, winnings, award, pool, reward, pot, kitty, bonanza, pot of gold at the end of the rainbow

jack up VERB **1 = hoist**, raise, elevate, winch up, lift, rear, uplift, lift up, heave, haul up, hike up, upraise: *They jacked up the car.* **2 = increase**, raise, put up, augment, advance, boost, expand, add to, enhance, step up *(informal)*, intensify, enlarge, escalate, inflate, amplify: *The company would have to jack up its prices.*

jaded ADJECTIVE **1 = tired**, bored, weary, worn out, done in *(informal)*, clapped out *(Brit., Austral. & N.Z. informal)*, spent, drained, exhausted, shattered, dulled, fatigued, fed up, wearied, fagged (out) *(informal)*, sapped, uninterested, listless, tired-out, enervated, zonked *(slang)*, over-tired, ennuied, hoha *(N.Z.)*: *We had both become jaded, disinterested and disillusioned.* **OPPOSITE:** fresh
2 = satiated, sated, surfeited, cloyed, gorged, glutted: *scrumptious little things to tickle my jaded palate*

jagged ADJECTIVE = **uneven**, pointed, craggy, broken, toothed, rough, ragged, ridged, spiked, notched, barbed, cleft, indented, serrated, snaggy, denticulate **OPPOSITE:** rounded

jail *or* **gaol** NOUN = **prison**, penitentiary *(U.S.)*, jailhouse *(Southern U.S.)*, penal institution, can *(slang)*, inside, cooler *(slang)*, confinement, dungeon, clink *(slang)*, glasshouse *(Military, informal)*, brig *(chiefly U.S.)*, borstal, calaboose *(U.S. informal)*, choky *(slang)*, pound, nick *(Brit. slang)*, stir *(slang)*, jug *(slang)*, slammer *(slang)*, lockup, reformatory, quod *(slang)*, poky *or* pokey *(U.S. & Canad. slang)*, boob *(Austral. slang)*: *Three prisoners escaped from a jail.*
▷ VERB = **imprison**, confine, detain, lock up, constrain, put away, intern, incarcerate, send down, send to prison, impound, put under lock and key, immure: *He was jailed for twenty years.*

> **QUOTATIONS**
> Go to jail. Go directly to jail. Do not pass go. Do not collect $200.
> [Charles Brace Darrow *Instructions for Monopoly*]

jailbird *or* **gaolbird** NOUN = **prisoner**, convict, con *(slang)*, lag *(slang)*, trusty, felon, malefactor, ticket-of-leave man *(archaic)*

jailer *or* **gaoler** NOUN = **guard**, keeper, warden, screw *(slang)*, captor, warder, turnkey *(archaic)*

jam NOUN **1 = tailback**, queue, hold-up, bottleneck, snarl-up, line, chain, congestion, obstruction, stoppage, gridlock: *a nine-mile traffic jam*
2 = predicament, tight spot, scrape *(informal)*, corner, state, situation, trouble, spot *(informal)*, hole *(slang)*, fix *(informal)*, bind, emergency, mess, dilemma, pinch, plight, strait, hot water, pickle *(informal)*, deep water, quandary: *It could get the government out of a jam.*
▷ VERB **1 = pack**, force, press, stuff, squeeze, compact, ram, wedge, cram, compress: *He jammed his hands into his pockets.* **2 = crowd**, cram, throng, crush, press, mass, surge, flock, swarm, congregate: *In summer, the beach is jammed with day-trippers.* **3 = congest**, block, clog, stick, halt, stall, obstruct: *The phone lines are jammed. Everybody wants to talk about it.*

> **QUOTATIONS**
> The rule is, jam tomorrow and jam yesterday – but never jam today
> [Lewis Carroll *Alice Through the Looking Glass*]

jamboree NOUN = **festival**, party, fête, celebration, blast *(U.S. slang)*, rave *(Brit. slang)*, carnival, spree, jubilee, festivity, beano *(Brit. slang)*, merriment, revelry, carouse, rave-up *(Brit. slang)*, carousal, frolic, hooley *or* hoolie *(chiefly Irish & N.Z.)*

jangle VERB = **rattle**, ring, clash, clatter, chime, ping, vibrate, jingle, ding, clank: *Her necklaces and bracelets jangled as she walked.*
▷ NOUN = **clash**, clang, cacophony, reverberation, rattle, jar, racket, din, dissonance, clangour: *a jangle of bells*
OPPOSITE: quiet

janitor NOUN = **caretaker**, porter, custodian, concierge, doorkeeper

jar[1] NOUN = **pot**, container, flask, receptacle, vessel, drum, vase, jug, pitcher, urn, crock, canister, repository, decanter, carafe, flagon: *We saved each season's harvest in clear glass jars.*

jar[2] VERB **1** *(usually with* **on***)* **= irritate**, grind, clash, annoy, offend, rattle, gall, nettle, jangle, irk, grate on, get on your nerves *(informal)*, nark *(Brit., Austral. & N.Z. slang)*, discompose: *The least bit of discord seemed to jar on his nerves.*
2 *(sometimes with* **with***)* **= clash**, conflict, contrast, differ, disagree, interfere, contend, collide, oppose: *They had always been complementary and their temperaments seldom jarred.* **3 = jolt**, rock, shake, disturb, bump, rattle, grate, agitate, vibrate, rasp, convulse: *The impact jarred his arm, right up to the shoulder.*

jargon NOUN = **parlance**, slang, idiom, patter, tongue, usage, dialect, cant, lingo *(informal)*, patois, argot

jaundiced ADJECTIVE = **cynical**, bitter, hostile, prejudiced, biased, suspicious, partial, jealous, distorted, sceptical, resentful, envious, bigoted, spiteful, preconceived
OPPOSITE: optimistic

jaunt NOUN = **outing**, tour, trip, stroll, expedition, excursion, ramble, promenade, airing

jaunty ADJECTIVE **1 = sprightly**, buoyant, carefree, high-spirited, gay, lively, airy, breezy, perky, sparky, self-confident: *The novel is altogether jauntier than these quotations imply.*
OPPOSITE: serious **2 = smart**, trim, gay, dapper, spruce, showy: *a jaunty little hat*

jaw PLURAL NOUN = **opening**, gates, entrance, aperture, mouth, abyss, maw, orifice, ingress: *He opens the jaws of the furnace with the yank of a lever.*
▷ VERB = **talk**, chat, rabbit (on) *(Brit. informal)*, gossip, chatter, spout, babble, natter, schmooze *(slang)*, shoot the breeze *(U.S. slang)*, run off at the mouth *(slang)*, chew the fat *or* rag *(slang)*: *jawing for half an hour with the very affable waiter*
▸ *technical names:* maxilla *(upper)*, mandible *(lower)*

jealous ADJECTIVE **1 = suspicious**, suspecting, guarded, protective, wary, doubtful, sceptical, attentive, anxious, apprehensive, vigilant, watchful, zealous, possessive, solicitous, distrustful, mistrustful, unbelieving: *She got insanely jealous and there was a terrible fight.*
OPPOSITE: trusting **2 = envious**, grudging, resentful, begrudging, green, intolerant, green-eyed, invidious, green with envy, desirous, covetous, emulous: *I have never sought to make my readers jealous of my megastar lifestyle.* **OPPOSITE:** satisfied

jealousy NOUN = **suspicion**, distrust, mistrust, possessiveness, doubt, spite, resentment, wariness, ill-will, dubiety

jeer VERB = **mock**, hector, deride, heckle, knock *(informal)*, barrack,

ridicule, taunt, sneer, scoff, banter, flout, gibe, cock a snook at (*Brit.*), contemn (*formal*): *His motorcade was jeered by angry residents.* **OPPOSITE:** cheer
▷ NOUN = **mockery**, abuse, ridicule, taunt, sneer, hiss, boo, scoff, hoot, derision, gibe, catcall, obloquy, aspersion: *the heckling and jeers of his audience* **OPPOSITE:** applause

jeopardize VERB = **endanger**, threaten, put at risk, put in jeopardy, risk, expose, gamble, hazard, menace, imperil, put on the line

jeopardy NOUN = **danger**, risk, peril, vulnerability, venture, exposure, liability, hazard, insecurity, pitfall, precariousness, endangerment

jerk VERB = **jolt**, bang, bump, lurch, shake: *The car jerked to a halt.*
▷ NOUN = **lurch**, movement, thrust, twitch, jolt, throw: *He indicated the bedroom with a jerk of his head.*

jerky ADJECTIVE = **bumpy**, rough, jolting, jumpy, shaky, bouncy, uncontrolled, twitchy, fitful, spasmodic, convulsive, tremulous **OPPOSITE:** smooth

jest NOUN = **joke**, play, crack (*slang*), sally, gag (*informal*), quip, josh (*slang, chiefly U.S. & Canad.*), banter, hoax, prank, wisecrack (*informal*), pleasantry, witticism, jape, bon mot: *It was a jest rather than a reproach.*
▷ VERB = **joke**, kid (*informal*), mock, tease, sneer, jeer, quip, josh (*slang, chiefly U.S. & Canad.*), scoff, banter, deride, chaff, gibe: *He enjoyed drinking and jesting with his cronies.*

jester NOUN = **fool**, clown, harlequin, zany, madcap, prankster, buffoon, pantaloon, mummer: *a chap dressed as a court jester*

jet NOUN = **stream**, current, spring, flow, rush, flood, burst, spray, fountain, cascade, gush, spurt, spout, squirt: *benches equipped with water jets to massage your back and feet*
▷ VERB **1 = fly**, wing, cruise, soar, zoom: *They spend a great deal of time jetting around the world.* **2 = stream**, course, issue, shoot, flow, rush, surge, spill, gush, emanate, spout, spew, squirt: *a cloud of white smoke jetted out from the trees*

jet-black ADJECTIVE = **black**, jet, raven, ebony, sable, pitch-black, inky, coal-black

jet-setting ADJECTIVE = **fashionable**, rich, sophisticated, trendy (*Brit. informal*), cosmopolitan, well-off, high-society, ritzy (*slang*), trendsetting

jettison VERB **1 = abandon**, reject, desert, dump, shed, scrap, throw out, discard, throw away, relinquish, forsake, slough off, throw on the scrapheap: *The government seems to have jettisoned the plan.* **2 = expel**, dump, unload, throw overboard, eject, heave: *The crew jettisoned excess fuel and made an emergency landing.*

jetty NOUN = **pier**, dock, wharf, mole, quay, breakwater, groyne

jewel NOUN **1 = gemstone**, gem, precious stone, brilliant, ornament, trinket, sparkler (*informal*), rock (*slang*): *a golden box containing precious jewels*
2 = treasure, wonder, prize, darling, pearl, gem, paragon, pride and joy, taonga (*N.Z.*): *Barbados is a perfect jewel of an island.*

jewellery NOUN = **jewels**, treasure, gems, trinkets, precious stones, ornaments, finery, regalia, bling (*slang*)

> QUOTATIONS
> I never hated a man enough to give him his diamonds back
> [Zsa Zsa Gabor]

jibe *or* **gibe** NOUN = **jeer**, sneer, dig (*informal*), crack, taunt, snide remark: *a cruel jibe about her weight*
▷ VERB = **jeer**, mock, sneer, taunt: *'What's the matter, can't you read?' she jibed.*

jig VERB = **skip**, bob, prance, jiggle, shake, bounce, twitch, wobble, caper, wiggle, jounce

jiggle VERB **1 = shake**, jerk, agitate, joggle: *He jiggled the doorknob noisily.*
2 = jerk, bounce, jog, fidget, shake, twitch, wiggle, jig, shimmy, joggle

jilt VERB = **reject**, drop, disappoint, abandon, desert, ditch (*slang*), betray, discard, deceive, forsake, throw over, coquette, leave (someone) in the lurch

> QUOTATIONS
> Say what you will, 'tis better to be left than never to have been loved
> [William Congreve *The Way of the World*]

jingle VERB = **ring**, rattle, clatter, chime, jangle, tinkle, clink, clank, tintinnabulate: *Her bracelets jingled like bells.*
▷ NOUN **1 = rattle**, ringing, tinkle, clang, clink, reverberation, clangour: *the jingle of money in a man's pocket*
2 = song, tune, melody, ditty, chorus, slogan, verse, limerick, refrain, doggerel: *advertising jingles*

jinx NOUN = **curse**, plague, voodoo, nemesis, black magic, hoodoo (*informal*), hex (*U.S. & Canad. informal*), evil eye: *Someone had put a jinx on him.*
▷ VERB = **curse**, bewitch, hex (*U.S. & Canad. informal*): *He's trying to rattle me, he said to himself, trying to jinx me so I can't succeed.*

jitters PLURAL NOUN = **nerves**, anxiety, butterflies (in your stomach) (*informal*), nervousness, the shakes (*informal*), fidgets, cold feet (*informal*), the willies (*informal*), tenseness, heebie-jeebies (*slang*)

jittery ADJECTIVE = **nervous**, anxious, jumpy, twitchy (*informal*), wired (*slang*), trembling, shaky, neurotic, agitated, quivering, hyper (*informal*), fidgety, antsy (*informal*)
OPPOSITE: calm

job NOUN **1 = position**, post, function, capacity, work, posting, calling, place, business, office, trade, field, career, situation, activity, employment, appointment, craft, profession, occupation, placement, vocation, livelihood, métier: *the pressure of being the first woman in the job* **2 = task**, concern, duty, charge, work, business, role, operation, affair, responsibility, function, contribution, venture, enterprise, undertaking, pursuit, assignment, stint, chore, errand: *Their main job is to preserve health rather than treat illness.*

jobless ADJECTIVE = **unemployed**, redundant, out of work, on the dole (*Brit. informal*), inactive, out of a job, unoccupied, idle

jockey VERB = **manoeuvre**, manage, engineer, negotiate, trim, manipulate, cajole, insinuate, wheedle, finagle (*informal*)

jog VERB **1 = run**, trot, canter, lope, dogtrot: *He could scarcely jog around the block that first day.* **2 = nudge**, push, shake, prod: *Avoid jogging the camera.*
3 = stimulate, remind, prompt, stir, arouse, activate, nudge, prod: *Keep a card file on the books you have read to jog your memory later.*

join VERB **1 = enrol in**, enter, sign up for, become a member of, enlist in: *He joined the Army five years ago.*
2 = connect, unite, couple, link, marry, tie, combine, attach, knit, cement, adhere, fasten, annex, add, splice, yoke, append: *The opened link is used to join the two ends of the chain.*
OPPOSITE: detach **3 = meet**, touch, border, extend, butt, adjoin, conjoin, reach: *Allahabad, where the Ganges and the Yamuna rivers join* **OPPOSITE:** part

joint ADJECTIVE = **shared**, mutual, collective, communal, united, joined, allied, combined, corporate, concerted, consolidated, cooperative, reciprocal, collaborative: *They came to a joint decision as to where they would live.*
▷ NOUN = **junction**, union, link, connection, knot, brace, bracket, seam, hinge, weld, linkage, intersection, node, articulation, nexus: *Cut the stem just below a leaf joint.*
▸ *related adjective:* articular

jointly ADVERB = **collectively**, together, in conjunction, as one, in common, mutually, in partnership, in league, unitedly
OPPOSITE: separately

joke NOUN **1 = jest**, gag (*informal*), wisecrack (*informal*), witticism, crack (*informal*), sally, quip, josh (*slang, chiefly U.S. & Canad.*), pun, quirk, one-liner (*informal*), jape: *No one told worse jokes than Claus.* **2 = laugh**, jest, fun, josh (*slang, chiefly U.S. & Canad.*), lark, sport, frolic, whimsy, jape: *It was probably just a joke to them, but it wasn't funny to me.*
3 = prank, trick, practical joke, lark (*informal*), caper, frolic, escapade, antic, jape: *I thought she was playing a joke on me at first but she wasn't.*
4 = laughing stock, butt, clown, buffoon, simpleton: *That man is just a complete joke.*
▷ VERB = **jest**, kid (*informal*), fool, mock, wind up (*Brit. slang*), tease,

ridicule, taunt, quip, josh *(slang, chiefly U.S. & Canad.)*, banter, deride, frolic, chaff, gambol, play the fool, play a trick: *Don't get defensive, Charlie. I was only joking.*

joker NOUN **= comedian**, comic, wit, clown, wag, kidder *(informal)*, jester, prankster, buffoon, trickster, humorist

jokey ADJECTIVE **= playful**, funny, amusing, teasing, humorous, mischievous, jesting, wisecracking, droll, facetious, waggish, prankish, nonserious **OPPOSITE:** humourless

jolly ADJECTIVE **= happy**, bright, funny, lively, hopeful, sunny, cheerful, merry, vibrant, hilarious, festive, upbeat *(informal)*, bubbly, gay, airy, playful, exuberant, jubilant, cheery, good-humoured, joyous, joyful, carefree, breezy, genial, ebullient, chirpy *(informal)*, sprightly, jovial, convivial, effervescent, frolicsome, ludic *(literary)*, mirthful, sportive, light-hearted, jocund, gladsome *(archaic)*, blithesome
OPPOSITE: miserable

jolt VERB **1 = jerk**, push, shake, knock, jar, shove, jog, jostle: *The train jolted into motion.* **2 = surprise**, upset, stun, disturb, astonish, stagger, startle, perturb, discompose: *He was momentarily jolted by the news.*
▷ NOUN **1 = jerk**, start, jump, shake, bump, jar, jog, lurch, quiver: *One tiny jolt could worsen her injuries.* **2 = surprise**, blow, shock, setback, reversal, bombshell, thunderbolt, whammy *(informal, chiefly U.S.)*, bolt from the blue: *The campaign came at a time when America needed such a jolt.*

jostle VERB **= push**, press, crowd, shake, squeeze, thrust, butt, elbow, bump, scramble, shove, jog, jolt, throng, hustle, joggle

jot VERB *(usually with* **down***)* **= note down**, record, list, note, register, tally, scribble: *Listen carefully to the instructions and jot them down.*
▷ NOUN **= bit**, detail, ace, scrap, grain, particle, atom, fraction, trifle, mite, tad *(informal, chiefly U.S.)*, speck, morsel, whit, tittle, iota, scintilla, smidgen *or* smidgin *(informal, chiefly U.S. & Canad.)*: *It doesn't affect my judgement one jot.*

journal NOUN **1 = magazine**, record, review, register, publication, bulletin, chronicle, gazette, periodical, zine *(informal)*: *All our results are published in scientific journals.* **2 = newspaper**, paper, daily, weekly, monthly, tabloid: *He was a spokesperson for The New York Times and some other journals.* **3 = diary**, record, history, log, notebook, chronicle, annals, yearbook, commonplace book, daybook, blog *(informal)*: *On the plane he wrote in his journal.*

journalist NOUN **= reporter**, writer, correspondent, newsman *or* newswoman, stringer, commentator, broadcaster, hack *(derogatory)*, columnist, contributor, scribe *(informal)*, pressman, journo *(slang)*, newshound *(informal)*, newspaperman *or* newspaperwoman

> **QUOTATIONS**
> Journalists say a thing that they know isn't true, in the hope that if they keep on saying it long enough it will be true
> [Arnold Bennett *The Title*]

journey NOUN **1 = trip**, drive, tour, flight, excursion, progress, cruise, passage, trek, outing, expedition, voyage, ramble, jaunt, peregrination, travel: *a journey from Manchester to Plymouth* **2 = progress**, passage, voyage, pilgrimage, odyssey: *My films try to describe a journey of discovery.*
▷ VERB **= travel**, go, move, walk, fly, range, cross, tour, progress, proceed, fare, wander, trek, voyage, roam, ramble, traverse, rove, wend, go walkabout *(Austral.)*, peregrinate: *She has journeyed on horseback through Africa and Turkey.*

> **QUOTATIONS**
> A journey of a thousand miles must begin with a single step
> [Lao-tze *Tao Te Ching*]
>
> A journey is like marriage. The certain way to be wrong is to think you control it
> [John Steinbeck *Travels With Charley*]
>
> Whenever I prepare for a journey I prepare as though for death. Should I never return, all is in order
> [Katherine Mansfield]

jovial ADJECTIVE **= cheerful**, happy, jolly, animated, glad, merry, hilarious, buoyant, airy, jubilant, cheery, cordial, convivial, blithe, gay, mirthful, jocund, jocose
OPPOSITE: solemn

joy NOUN **1 = delight**, pleasure, triumph, satisfaction, happiness, ecstasy, enjoyment, bliss, transport, euphoria, festivity, felicity, glee, exuberance, rapture, elation, exhilaration, radiance, gaiety, jubilation, hilarity, exaltation, ebullience, exultation, gladness, joyfulness, ravishment: *Salter shouted with joy.* **OPPOSITE:** sorrow
2 = treasure, wonder, treat, prize, delight, pride, charm, thrill: *one of the joys of being a chef*

joyful ADJECTIVE **1 = pleasing**, satisfying, engaging, charming, delightful, enjoyable, gratifying, agreeable, pleasurable: *Giving birth to a child is both painful and joyful.*
2 = delighted, happy, satisfied, glad, jolly, merry, gratified, pleased, jubilant, elated, over the moon *(informal)*, jovial, rapt, enraptured, on cloud nine *(informal)*, cock-a-hoop, floating on air, light-hearted, jocund, gladsome *(archaic)*, blithesome, stoked *(Austral. & N.Z. informal)*: *We're a very joyful people.*

joyless ADJECTIVE **= unhappy**, sad, depressing, miserable, gloomy, dismal, dreary, dejected, dispirited, downcast, down in the dumps *(informal)*, cheerless

joyous ADJECTIVE **= joyful**, cheerful, merry, festive, heartening, rapturous, blithe

jubilant ADJECTIVE **= overjoyed**, excited, thrilled, glad, triumphant, rejoicing, exuberant, joyous, elated, over the moon *(informal)*, euphoric, triumphal, enraptured, exultant, cock-a-hoop, rhapsodic, stoked *(Austral. & N.Z. informal)*
OPPOSITE: downcast

jubilation NOUN **= joy**, triumph, celebration, excitement, ecstasy, jubilee, festivity, elation, jamboree, exultation

jubilee NOUN **= celebration**, holiday, fête, festival, carnival, festivity, gala

judge NOUN **1 = magistrate**, justice, beak *(Brit. slang)*, His, Her *or* Your Honour: *The judge adjourned the hearing until next Tuesday.* **2 = referee**, expert, specialist, umpire, umpie *(Austral. slang)*, mediator, examiner, connoisseur, assessor, arbiter, appraiser, arbitrator, moderator, adjudicator, evaluator, authority: *A panel of judges is now selecting the finalists.*
3 = critic, assessor, arbiter, appraiser, evaluator: *I'm a pretty good judge of character.*
▷ VERB **1 = adjudicate**, referee, umpire, mediate, officiate, adjudge, arbitrate: *Entries will be judged in two age categories.* **2 = evaluate**, rate, consider, appreciate, view, class, value, review, rank, examine, esteem, criticize, ascertain, surmise: *It will take a few more years to judge the impact of these ideas.*
3 = estimate, guess, assess, calculate, evaluate, gauge, appraise: *It is important to judge the weight of your washing load.* **4 = find**, rule, pass, pronounce, decree, adjudge: *He was judged guilty and burned at the stake.*
▸ *related adjective:* judicial

> **QUOTATIONS**
> He who has the judge for his father goes into court with an easy mind
> [Miguel de Cervantes *Don Quixote*]
>
> A judge is not supposed to know anything about the facts of life until they have been presented in evidence and explained to him at least three times
> [Lord Parker]
>
> Forbear to judge, for we are sinners all
> [William Shakespeare *Henry VI, part II*]
>
> Judge not, that ye be not judged
> [*Bible: St. Matthew*]

> **PROVERBS**
> *No one should be judge in his own cause*

judgment NOUN **1 = opinion**, view, estimate, belief, assessment, conviction, diagnosis, valuation, deduction, appraisal: *In your judgment, what has changed over the past few years?*
2 = verdict, finding, result, ruling, decision, sentence, conclusion,

determination, decree, order, arbitration, adjudication, pronouncement: *The Court is expected to give its judgment within the next ten days.* **3 = sense**, common sense, good sense, judiciousness, reason, understanding, taste, intelligence, smarts *(slang, chiefly U.S.)*, discrimination, perception, awareness, wisdom, wit, penetration, prudence, sharpness, acumen, shrewdness, discernment, perspicacity, sagacity, astuteness, percipience: *Publication of the information was a serious error in judgment.*

judgmental ADJECTIVE **= condemnatory**, self-righteous, censorious, pharisaic, critical

judicial ADJECTIVE **= legal**, official, judiciary, juridical

judicious ADJECTIVE **= sensible**, considered, reasonable, discerning, sound, politic, acute, informed, diplomatic, careful, wise, cautious, rational, sober, discriminating, thoughtful, discreet, sage, enlightened, shrewd, prudent, sane, skilful, astute, expedient, circumspect, well-advised, well-judged, sagacious, sapient **OPPOSITE:** injudicious

j

jug NOUN **= container**, pitcher, urn, carafe, creamer *(U.S. & Canad.)*, vessel, jar, crock, ewer

juggle VERB **= manipulate**, change, doctor *(informal)*, fix *(informal)*, alter, modify, disguise, manoeuvre, tamper with, misrepresent, falsify

juice NOUN **1 = liquid**, extract, fluid, liquor, sap, nectar: *the juice of about six lemons* **2 = secretion**, serum: *the digestive juices of the human intestinal tract*

juicy ADJECTIVE **1 = moist**, lush, watery, succulent, sappy: *a thick, juicy steak* **2 = interesting**, colourful, sensational, vivid, provocative, spicy *(informal)*, suggestive, racy, risqué: *It provided some juicy gossip for a few days.*

jumble NOUN **= muddle**, mixture, mess, disorder, confusion, chaos, litter, clutter, disarray, medley, mélange *(French)*, miscellany, mishmash, farrago, hotchpotch *(U.S.)*, hodgepodge, gallimaufry, pig's breakfast *(informal)*, disarrangement: *a meaningless jumble of words*
▷ VERB **= mix**, mistake, confuse, disorder, shuffle, tangle, muddle, confound, entangle, ravel, disorganize, disarrange, dishevel: *animals whose remains were jumbled together by scavengers and floods*

jumbo ADJECTIVE **= giant**, large, huge, immense, mega *(informal)*, gigantic, oversized, elephantine, ginormous *(informal)*, humongous *or* humungous *(U.S. slang)*, supersize **OPPOSITE:** tiny

jump VERB **1 = leap**, dance, spring, bound, bounce, hop, skip, caper, prance, gambol: *stamping their boots and jumping up and down to knock the snow off* **2 = vault**, clear, hurdle, go over, sail over, hop over: *He jumped the first fence beautifully.* **3 = spring**, bound, leap, bounce: *She jumped to her feet and ran downstairs.* **4 = recoil**, start, jolt, flinch, shake, jerk, quake, shudder, twitch, wince: *The phone shrilled, making her jump.* **5 = increase**, rise, climb, escalate, gain, advance, boost, mount, soar, surge, spiral, hike, ascend: *The number of crimes jumped by ten per cent last year.* **6 = miss**, avoid, skip, omit, evade, digress: *He refused to jump the queue for treatment at the local hospital.*
▷ NOUN **1 = leap**, spring, skip, bound, buck, hop, vault, caper: *With a few hops and a jump they launched themselves into the air.* **2 = rise**, increase, escalation, upswing, advance, boost, elevation, upsurge, upturn, increment, augmentation: *an eleven per cent jump in profits* **3 = jolt**, start, movement, shock, shake, jar, jerk, lurch, twitch, swerve, spasm: *When Spider tapped on a window, Miguel gave an involuntary jump.* **4 = hurdle**, gate, barrier, fence, obstacle, barricade, rail: *Hurdlers need to have unnaturally over-flexible knees to clear the jump.*

jumped-up ADJECTIVE **= conceited**, arrogant, pompous, stuck-up, cocky, overbearing, puffed up, presumptuous, insolent, immodest, toffee-nosed, self-opinionated, too big for your boots *or* breeches

jumper NOUN **= sweater**, top, jersey, cardigan, woolly, pullover

jumpy ADJECTIVE **= nervous**, anxious, tense, shaky, restless, neurotic, agitated, hyper *(informal)*, apprehensive, jittery *(informal)*, on edge, twitchy *(informal)*, fidgety, timorous, antsy *(informal)*, wired *(slang)* **OPPOSITE:** calm

juncture NOUN **= moment**, time, point, crisis, occasion, emergency, strait, contingency, predicament, crux, exigency, conjuncture

junior ADJECTIVE **1 = minor**, lower, secondary, lesser, subordinate, inferior: *a junior minister attached to the prime minister's office* **2 = younger**: *junior pupils* **OPPOSITE:** senior

junk NOUN **= rubbish**, refuse, waste, scrap, litter, debris, crap *(slang)*, garbage *(chiefly U.S.)*, trash, clutter, rummage, dross, odds and ends, space junk, oddments, flotsam and jetsam, leavings, dreck *(slang, chiefly U.S.)*

junkie *or* **junky** NOUN **= addict**, user, drug addict, druggie *(informal)*, head *(slang)*, freak *(informal)*, mainliner *(slang)*, smackhead *(slang)*, pill-popper *(slang)*, pothead *(slang)*, cokehead *(slang)*, acidhead *(slang)*, hashhead *(slang)*, weedhead *(slang)*

junta NOUN **= cabal**, council, faction, league, set, party, ring, camp, crew, combination, assembly, gang, clique, coterie, schism, confederacy, convocation

jurisdiction NOUN **1 = authority**, say, power, control, rule, influence, command, sway, dominion, prerogative, mana *(N.Z.)*: *The British police have no jurisdiction over foreign bank accounts.* **2 = range**, area, field, district, bounds, zone, province, circuit, scope, orbit, sphere, compass, dominion: *matters which lie within his own jurisdiction*

just ADVERB **1 = recently**, lately, only now: *The two had only just met.* **2 = merely**, but, only, simply, solely, no more than, nothing but: *It's just a suggestion.* **3 = barely**, hardly, only just, scarcely, at most, by a whisker, at a push, by the skin of your teeth: *He could just reach the man's head with his right hand.* **4 = exactly**, really, quite, completely, totally, perfectly, entirely, truly, absolutely, precisely, altogether, positively: *Kiwi fruit are just the thing for a healthy snack.*
▷ ADJECTIVE **1 = fair**, good, legitimate, honourable, right, square, pure, decent, upright, honest, equitable, righteous, conscientious, impartial, virtuous, lawful, blameless, unbiased, fair-minded, unprejudiced: *She fought honestly for a just cause and for freedom.* **OPPOSITE:** unfair **2 = fitting**, due, correct, deserved, appropriate, justified, reasonable, suitable, decent, sensible, merited, proper, legitimate, desirable, apt, rightful, well-deserved, condign: *This cup final is a just reward for all the efforts they have put in.* **OPPOSITE:** inappropriate
just about = practically, almost, nearly, close to, virtually, all but, not quite, well-nigh: *He is just about the best golfer in the world.*

QUOTATIONS
Thrice is he arm'd that hath his quarrel just
[William Shakespeare *Henry VI, part II*]

USAGE
The expression *just exactly* is considered to be poor style because, since both words mean the same thing, only one or the other is needed. Use *just – it's just what they want* – or *exactly – it's exactly what they want*, but not both together.

justice NOUN **1 = fairness**, equity, integrity, honesty, decency, impartiality, rectitude, reasonableness, uprightness, justness, rightfulness, right: *There is no justice in this world!* **OPPOSITE:** injustice **2 = justness**, fairness, legitimacy, reasonableness, right, integrity, honesty, legality, rectitude, rightfulness: *We must win people round to the justice of our cause.* **3 = judge**, magistrate, beak *(Brit. slang)*, His, Her *or* Your Honour: *a justice on the Supreme Court*

justifiable ADJECTIVE **= reasonable**, right, sound, fit, acceptable, sensible, proper, valid, legitimate, understandable, lawful, well-founded, defensible, tenable, excusable, warrantable, vindicable **OPPOSITE:** indefensible

The Language of Bram Stoker

Abraham ('Bram') Stoker (1847–1912) was born in Dublin. He worked first as a civil servant, but he was always drawn to the theatre, and soon became a drama critic. In time he became personal manager to the great actor Sir Henry Irving, but he is best known for his novel *Dracula* (1897), which introduced the the idea of the vampire to the horror genre.

Stoker's language is on the whole rather plain; he tends to avoid long, Latinate words in favour of direct Anglo-Saxon. Surprisingly enough, given the evil and horror with which he deals, the adjective he uses most commonly is *good*, even putting it into the mouth of his eponymous villain:

> I pray you, my **good** young friend, that you will not discourse of things other than business in your letters.

The next most common adjective in Stoker's writing is *long*. This word he uses in purely physical description, particularly in relation to Count Dracula himself, who is 'a long figure' and whose fingernails and remarkably canine teeth are both long and sharp. However, the most characteristic use is in terms of duration; the book is full of long spells, long nights, and long years. This, of course, is perfectly in keeping with one of the major themes of *Dracula*, that of being immortal, or at least unable to die. The Count has endured an existence longer than many normal human generations and knows what it means for time to seem interminable.

Also consonant with what the reader would expect from a novel about a great evil, Stoker's next most frequently used adjectives are *strange*, *dark* and *terrible*. Common collocates with *strange* include *things*, giving overtones of the indescribable, as in:

> I asked him of some of the **strange things** of the preceding night.

Dark appears most often with *figures* and *forms*, suggesting something evil but not quite within the bounds of human perception, something mysterious and threatening. All of this tends towards building up a picture of a world in which inexplicable dangers surround the characters.

Terrible is most often paired with *experience, shock, fear, strain* and *task* It is used in its true, literal sense of 'inspiring terror' rather than in the more informal and looser use as a mere intensifier, a use which would certainly have been known to contemporaries of Stoker.

Some of the most frequent nouns that Stoker uses are *love, fear, sleep, power,* and *danger,* all of which are, perhaps surprisingly in a novel about a vampire, much more common than *blood*! In keeping with his more predominant use of *good* rather than *evil*, *love* seems to have been at the forefront of Stoker's mind.

> 'Jonathan,' she said, and the word sounded like music on her lips it was so full of **love** and tenderness.

Fear is experienced by almost all of the characters in *Dracula*, and as the novel is firmly placed within the genre of horror, this is precisely the emotion that the author wishes to inspire in his readers. Stoker's characters are right to be afraid, not just of the death, physical pain, injury, loss, and grief that threaten to afflict them, but also of the peril to their immortal souls if they should become, like the Count or his creatures, one of the undead.

> I am in **fear**, in awful **fear**, and there is no escape for me.

One of the most frightening aspects of Dracula is his *power*. He is described as being physically very strong, but above all he is able to exert an indefinable power over ordinary mortals, almost hypnotizing them into doing his will, even over great distances. And, of course, to those who have had their blood sucked by this monster, he becomes the Master, whom they are unable to disobey, even if they could summon the will to resist his commands and desires.

justification NOUN = **reason**, grounds, defence, basis, excuse, approval, plea, warrant, apology, rationale, vindication, rationalization, absolution, exoneration, explanation, exculpation, extenuation

justify VERB = **explain**, support, warrant, bear out, legitimize, establish, maintain, confirm, defend, approve, excuse, sustain, uphold, acquit, vindicate, validate, substantiate, exonerate, legalize, absolve, exculpate

justly ADVERB = **justifiably**, rightly, correctly, properly, legitimately, rightfully, with good reason, lawfully

jut VERB = **stick out**, project, extend, protrude, poke, bulge, overhang, impend

juvenile NOUN = **child**, youth, minor, girl, boy, teenager, infant, adolescent: *The number of juveniles in the general population has fallen.* **OPPOSITE:** adult
▷ ADJECTIVE **1** = **young**, junior, adolescent, youthful, immature: *a scheme to lock up persistent juvenile offenders* **OPPOSITE:** adult **2** = **immature**, childish, infantile, puerile, young, youthful, inexperienced, boyish, callow, undeveloped, unsophisticated, girlish, babyish, jejune: *As he gets older he becomes more juvenile.*

juxtaposition NOUN = **proximity**, adjacency, contact, closeness, vicinity, nearness, contiguity, propinquity

Kk

kai NOUN **= food**, grub *(slang)*, provisions, fare, board, commons, eats *(slang)*, feed, diet, meat, bread, tuck *(informal)*, tucker *(Austral. & N.Z. informal)*, rations, nutrition, tack *(informal)*, refreshment, scoff *(slang)*, nibbles, foodstuffs, nourishment, chow *(informal)*, sustenance, nosh *(slang)*, daily bread, victuals, edibles, comestibles, provender, nosebag *(slang)*, pabulum *(rare)*, nutriment, vittles *(obsolete, dialect)*, viands, aliment, eatables *(slang)*

kak NOUN **1 = faeces**, excrement, stool, muck, manure, dung, droppings, waste matter: *His shoes were covered in kak.* **2 = rubbish**, nonsense, malarkey, garbage *(informal)*, rot, crap *(taboo, slang)*, drivel, tripe *(informal)*, claptrap *(informal)*, poppycock *(informal)*, pants, bizzo *(Austral. slang)*, bull's wool *(Austral. & N.Z. slang)*: *Now you're just talking kak.*

kaleidoscopic ADJECTIVE **1 = many-coloured**, multi-coloured, harlequin, psychedelic, motley, variegated, prismatic, varicoloured: *a kaleidoscopic set of bright images* **2 = changeable**, shifting, varied, mobile, variable, fluid, uncertain, volatile, unpredictable, unstable, fluctuating, indefinite, unsteady, protean, mutable, impermanent, inconstant: *a kaleidoscopic world of complex relationships* **3 = complicated**, complex, confused, confusing, disordered, puzzling, unclear, baffling, bewildering, chaotic, muddled, intricate, jumbled, convoluted, disorganized, disarranged: *a kaleidoscopic and fractured view of Los Angeles*

kamikaze MODIFIER **= self-destructive**, suicidal, foolhardy

keel over VERB **1 = collapse**, faint, pass out, black out *(informal)*, swoon *(literary)*: *He keeled over and fell flat on his back.* **2 = capsize**, list, upset, founder, overturn, turn over, lean over, tip over, topple over, turn turtle: *The vessel keeled over towards the murky water.*

keen[1] ADJECTIVE **1 = eager**, earnest, spirited, devoted, intense, fierce, enthusiastic, passionate, ardent, avid, fervent, impassioned, zealous, ebullient, wholehearted, fervid, bright-eyed and bushy-tailed *(informal)*: *a keen amateur photographer* **OPPOSITE:** unenthusiastic **2 = earnest**, fierce, intense, vehement, burning, flaming, consuming, eager, passionate, heightened, energetic, ardent, fanatical, fervent, impassioned, fervid: *his keen sense of loyalty* **3 = sharp**, satirical, incisive, trenchant, pointed, cutting, biting, edged, acute, acid, stinging, piercing, penetrating, searing, tart, withering, scathing, pungent, sarcastic, sardonic, caustic, astringent, vitriolic, acerbic, mordant, razor-like, finely honed: *a keen sense of humour* **OPPOSITE:** dull **4 = perceptive**, quick, sharp, brilliant, acute, smart, wise, clever, subtle, piercing, penetrating, discriminating, shrewd, discerning, ingenious, astute, intuitive, canny, incisive, insightful, observant, perspicacious, sapient: *a man of keen intellect* **OPPOSITE:** obtuse **5 = penetrating**, clear, powerful, sharp, acute, sensitive, piercing, discerning, perceptive, observant: *a keen eye for detail* **6 = intense**, strong, fierce, relentless, cut-throat: *Competition is keen for these awards.*

keen[2] VERB **= lament**, cry, weep, sob, mourn, grieve, howl, sorrow, wail, whine, whimper, bewail: *He tossed back his head and keened.*

keep VERB **1** *(usually with* **from***)* **= prevent**, hold back, deter, inhibit, block, stall, restrain, hamstring, hamper, withhold, hinder, retard, impede, shackle, keep back: *Embarrassment has kept me from doing all sorts of things.* **2** *(sometimes with* **on***)* **= continue**, go on, carry on, persist in, persevere in, remain: *I turned back after a while, but he kept walking.* **3 = hold on to**, maintain, retain, keep possession of, save, preserve, nurture, cherish, conserve: *We want to keep as many players as we can.* **OPPOSITE:** lose **4 = store**, put, place, house, hold, deposit, pile, stack, heap, amass, stow: *She kept her money under the mattress.* **5 = carry**, stock, have, hold, sell, supply, handle, trade in, deal in: *The shop keeps specialized books on various aspects of the collection.* **6 = comply with**, carry out, honour, fulfil, hold, follow, mind, respect, observe, respond to, embrace, execute, obey, heed, conform to, adhere to, abide by, act upon: *I'm hoping you'll keep your promise to come for a long visit.* **OPPOSITE:** disregard **7 = support**, maintain, sustain, provide for, mind, fund, board, finance, feed, look after, foster, shelter, care for, take care of, nurture, safeguard, cherish, nourish, subsidize: *She could just about afford to keep her five kids.* **8 = raise**, own, maintain, tend, farm, breed, look after, rear, care for, bring up, nurture, nourish: *This mad writer kept a lobster as a pet.* **9 = manage**, run, administer, be in charge (of), rule, direct, handle, govern, oversee, supervise, preside over, superintend: *His father kept a village shop.* **10 = delay**, detain, hinder, impede, stop, limit, check, arrest, curb, constrain, obstruct, retard, set back: *'Sorry to keep you, Jack.'* **OPPOSITE:** release **11 = associate with**, mix with, mingle with, hang out with *(informal)*, hang with *(informal, chiefly U.S.)*, be friends with, consort with, run around with *(informal)*, hobnob with, socialize with, hang about with, fraternize with: *I don't like the company you keep.*

▷ NOUN **1 = board**, food, maintenance, upkeep, means, living, support, nurture, livelihood, subsistence, kai *(N.Z. informal)*, nourishment, sustenance: *I need to give my parents money for my keep.* **2 = tower**, castle, stronghold, dungeon, citadel, fastness, donjon: *the parts of the keep open to visitors*

keep at it = persist, continue, carry on, keep going, stick with it, stay with it, be steadfast, grind it out, persevere, remain with it: *'Keep at it!' Thade encouraged me.*

keep something back 1 = hold back, hold, save, set aside, husband, store, retain, preserve, hang on to, conserve, stockpile, hoard, lay up, put by: *Roughly chop the vegetables, and keep back a few for decoration.* **2 = suppress**, hide, reserve, conceal, restrain, cover up, withhold, stifle, censor, repress, smother, muffle, muzzle, keep something under your hat: *Neither of them is telling the whole truth. They're both keeping something back.* **3 = restrain**, control, limit, check, delay, restrict, curb, prohibit, withhold, hold back, constrain, retard, keep a tight rein on: *I can no longer keep back my tears.*

keep something up 1 = continue, make, maintain, carry on, persist in, persevere with: *They can no longer keep up the repayments.* **2 = maintain**, sustain, uphold, perpetuate, retain, preserve, prolong: *keeping up the pressure against the government*

keep up = keep pace, match, compete, contend, emulate, persevere: *Things are changing so fast, it's hard to keep up.*

keeper NOUN **= curator**, guardian, steward, superintendent, attendant, caretaker, overseer, preserver: *the keeper of the library at the V&A*

keeping NOUN **= care**, keep, charge, trust, protection, possession, maintenance, custody, patronage, guardianship, safekeeping: *It has been handed over for safe keeping.*

in keeping with = in agreement with, consistent with, in harmony with, in accord with, in compliance with, in conformity with, in balance with, in correspondence with, in proportion with, in congruity with, in observance with: *His office was in keeping with his station and experience.*

keepsake NOUN **= souvenir**, symbol, token, reminder, relic, remembrance, emblem, memento, favour

keg NOUN **= barrel**, drum, vat, cask, firkin, tun, hogshead

ken NOUN
beyond someone's ken = beyond the knowledge of, beyond the comprehension of, beyond the understanding of, beyond the acquaintance of, beyond the awareness of, beyond the cognizance of

kernel NOUN **= essence**, core, substance, gist, grain, marrow, germ, nub, pith

key NOUN **1 = opener**, door key, latchkey: *She reached for her coat and car keys.* **2 = answer**, means, secret, solution, path, formula, passage, clue, cue, pointer, sign: *The key to success is to be ready from the start.*
▷ MODIFIER **= essential**, leading, major, main, important, chief, necessary, basic, vital, crucial, principal, fundamental, decisive, indispensable, pivotal, must-have: *He is expected to be the key witness at the trial.* **OPPOSITE:** minor

k

keynote NOUN **= heart**, centre, theme, core, substance, essence, marrow, kernel, gist, pith

keystone NOUN **= basis**, principle, core, crux, ground, source, spring, root, motive, cornerstone, lynchpin, mainspring, fundament, quoin

kia ora INTERJECTION **= hello**, hi (*informal*), greetings, gidday *or* g'day (*Austral. & N.Z.*), how do you do?, good morning, good evening, good afternoon, welcome

kick VERB **1 = boot**, strike, knock, punt, put the boot in(to) (*slang*): *The fiery actress kicked him in the shins.* **2 = give up**, break, stop, abandon, quit, cease, eschew, leave off, desist from, end: *She's kicked her drug habit.*
▷ NOUN **1 = thrill**, glow, buzz (*slang*), tingle, high (*slang*), sensation: *I got a kick out of seeing my name in print.* **2 = pungency**, force, power, edge, strength, snap (*informal*), punch, intensity, pep, sparkle, vitality, verve, zest, potency, tang, piquancy: *The coffee had more of a kick than it seemed on first tasting.*
kick someone out = dismiss, remove, reject, get rid of, discharge, expel, oust, eject, evict, toss out, give the boot (*slang*), sack (*informal*), kiss off (*slang, chiefly U.S. & Canad.*), give (someone) their marching orders, give the push, give the bum's rush (*slang*), show someone the door, throw someone out on their ear (*informal*), kennet (*Austral. slang*), jeff (*Austral. slang*): *They kicked five foreign journalists out of the country.*
kick something off = begin, start, open, commence, launch, initiate, get under way, kick-start, get on the road: *We kicked off the meeting with a song.*

kickback NOUN **= bribe**, payoff, backhander (*slang*), enticement, share, cut (*informal*), payment, gift, reward, incentive, graft (*informal*), sweetener (*slang*), inducement, sop, recompense, hush money (*slang*), payola (*informal*), allurement

kick-off NOUN **= start**, opening, beginning, commencement, outset, starting point, inception

kid[1] NOUN **= child**, girl, boy, baby, lad, teenager, youngster, infant, adolescent, juvenile, toddler, tot, lass, wean, little one, bairn, stripling, sprog (*slang*), munchkin (*informal, chiefly U.S.*), rug rat (*U.S. & Canad. informal*), littlie (*Austral. informal*), ankle-biter (*Austral. slang*), tacker (*Austral. slang*)

kid[2] VERB **= tease**, joke, trick, fool, pretend, mock, rag (*Brit.*), wind up (*Brit. slang*), ridicule, hoax, beguile, gull (*archaic*), delude, jest, bamboozle, hoodwink, cozen, jerk *or* yank someone's chain (*informal*): *I'm just kidding.*

kidnap VERB **= abduct**, remove, steal, capture, seize, snatch (*slang*), hijack, run off with, run away with, make off with, hold to ransom

kill VERB **1 = slay**, murder, execute, slaughter, destroy, waste (*informal*), do in (*slang*), take out (*slang*), massacre, butcher, wipe out (*informal*), dispatch, cut down, erase, assassinate, eradicate, whack (*informal*), do away with, blow away (*slang, chiefly U.S.*), obliterate, knock off (*slang*), liquidate, decimate, annihilate, neutralize, exterminate, terminate (*slang*), croak, mow down, take (someone's) life, bump off (*slang*), extirpate, wipe from the face of the earth (*informal*): *More than 1,000 people have been killed by the armed forces.* **2 = destroy**, defeat, crush, scotch, still, stop, total (*slang*), ruin, halt, cancel, wreck, shatter, veto, suppress, dismantle, stifle, trash (*slang*), ravage, eradicate, smother, quash, quell, extinguish, annihilate, put paid to: *Public opinion may yet kill the proposal.*

killer NOUN **= murderer**, slaughterer, slayer, hit man (*slang*), butcher, gunman, assassin, destroyer, liquidator, terminator, executioner, exterminator, genocidaire

killing NOUN **= murder**, massacre, slaughter, execution, dispatch, manslaughter, elimination, slaying, homicide, bloodshed, carnage, fatality, liquidation, extermination, annihilation, eradication, butchery: *This is a brutal killing.*
▷ ADJECTIVE **1 = tiring**, hard, testing, taxing, difficult, draining, exhausting, punishing, crippling, fatiguing, gruelling, sapping, debilitating, strenuous, arduous, laborious, enervating, backbreaking: *He covered the last 300 metres in around 41sec, a killing pace.* **2 = deadly**, deathly, dangerous, fatal, destructive, lethal, mortal, murderous, death-dealing: *Diphtheria was a killing disease.*
make a killing = profit, gain, clean up (*informal*), be lucky, be successful, make a fortune, strike it rich (*informal*), make a bomb (*slang*), rake it in (*informal*), have a windfall: *They have made a killing on the deal.*

killjoy NOUN **= spoilsport**, dampener, damper, wet blanket (*informal*)

kin NOUN **= family**, people, relations, relatives, connections, kindred, kinsmen, kith, kinsfolk, ainga (*N.Z.*), rellies (*Austral. slang*)

kind[1] ADJECTIVE **= considerate**, good, loving, kindly, understanding, concerned, friendly, neighbourly, gentle, generous, mild, obliging, sympathetic, charitable, thoughtful, benign, humane, affectionate, compassionate, clement, gracious, indulgent, benevolent, attentive, amiable, courteous, amicable, lenient, cordial, congenial, philanthropic, unselfish, propitious, beneficent, kind-hearted, bounteous, tender-hearted: *He was a very kind man, full of common sense.* **OPPOSITE:** unkind

kind[2] NOUN **1 = class**, sort, type, variety, brand, grade, category, genre, classification, league: *They developed a new kind of film-making.* **2 = sort**, set, type, ilk, family, race, species, breed, genus: *I hate Lewis and his kind just as much as you do.* **3 = nature**, sort, type, manner, style, quality, character, make-up, habit, stamp, description, mould, essence, temperament, persuasion, calibre, disposition: *Donations came in from all kinds of people.*

> **USAGE**
> It is common in informal speech to combine singular and plural in sentences like *children enjoy those kind of stories*. However, this is not acceptable in careful writing, where the plural must be used consistently: *children enjoy those kinds of stories*.

kind-hearted ADJECTIVE **= sympathetic**, kind, generous, helpful, tender, humane, compassionate, gracious, amicable, considerate, altruistic, good-natured, tender-hearted **OPPOSITE:** hard-hearted

kindle VERB **1 = arouse**, excite, inspire, stir, thrill, stimulate, provoke, induce, awaken, animate, rouse, sharpen, inflame, incite, foment, bestir, enkindle: *These poems have helped kindle the imagination of generations of children.* **2 = light**, start, ignite, fire, spark, torch, inflame, set fire to, set a match to: *I came in and kindled a fire in the stove.* **OPPOSITE:** extinguish

kindly ADJECTIVE = **benevolent**, kind, caring, nice, warm, gentle, helpful, pleasant, mild, sympathetic, beneficial, polite, favourable, benign, humane, compassionate, hearty, cordial, considerate, genial, affable, good-natured, beneficent, well-disposed, kind-hearted, warm-hearted: *He was a stern critic but an extremely kindly man.* **OPPOSITE:** cruel
▷ ADVERB = **benevolently**, politely, generously, thoughtfully, tenderly, lovingly, cordially, affectionately, helpfully, graciously, obligingly, agreeably, indulgently, selflessly, unselfishly, compassionately, considerately: *He kindly carried our picnic in a rucksack.* **OPPOSITE:** unkindly

kindness NOUN **1** = **goodwill**, understanding, charity, grace, humanity, affection, patience, tolerance, goodness, compassion, hospitality, generosity, indulgence, decency, tenderness, clemency, gentleness, philanthropy, benevolence, magnanimity, fellow-feeling, amiability, beneficence, kindliness: *We have been treated with such kindness by everybody.* **OPPOSITE:** malice **2** = **good deed**, help, service, aid, favour, assistance, bounty, benefaction: *It would be a kindness to leave her alone.*

QUOTATIONS

Kindness acts
Not always as you think; a hated hand
Renders it odious
[Corneille *Cinna*]

Kindness effects more than severity
[Aesop *Fables: The Wind and the Sun*]

True kindness presupposes the faculty of imagining as one's own the suffering and joys of others
[André Gide *Portraits and Aphorisms*]

That best portion of a good man's life,
His little, nameless, unremembered acts
Of kindness and of love
[William Wordsworth *Lines Composed a Few Miles Above Tintern Abbey*]

Yet I do fear thy nature;
It is too full o' the milk of human kindness
To catch the nearest way
[William Shakespeare *Macbeth*]

kindred NOUN = **family**, relations, relatives, connections, flesh, kin, lineage, kinsmen, kinsfolk, ainga (*N.Z.*), rellies (*Austral. slang*): *The offender made proper restitution to the victim's kindred.*
▷ ADJECTIVE **1** = **similar**, like, related, allied, corresponding, affiliated, akin, kin, cognate, matching: *I recall discussions with her on these and kindred topics.* **2** = **like-minded**, similar, compatible, understanding, similar, friendly, sympathetic, responsive, agreeable, in tune, congenial, like, companionable: *We're sort of kindred spirits.*

king NOUN = **ruler**, monarch, sovereign, crowned head, leader, lord, prince, Crown, emperor, majesty, head of state, consort, His Majesty, overlord

kingdom NOUN **1** = **country**, state, nation, land, division, territory, province, empire, commonwealth, realm, domain, tract, dominion, sovereign state: *the Kingdom of Denmark* **2** = **domain**, territory, province, realm, area, department, field, zone, arena, sphere: *nature study trips to the kingdom of the polar bear*

kink NOUN **1** = **twist**, bend, wrinkle, knot, tangle, coil, corkscrew, entanglement, crimp, frizz: *a tiny black kitten with tufted ears and a kink in her tail* **2** = **quirk**, eccentricity, foible, idiosyncrasy, whim, fetish, vagary, singularity, crotchet: *What kink did he have in his character?* **3** = **flaw**, difficulty, defect, complication, tangle, knot, hitch, imperfection: *working out the kinks of a potential trade agreement*

kinky ADJECTIVE **1** = **perverted**, warped, deviant, unnatural, degenerated, unsavoury, unhealthy, depraved, licentious, pervy (*slang*): *engaging in some kind of kinky sexual activity* **2** = **weird**, odd, strange, bizarre, peculiar, eccentric, queer, quirky, unconventional, off-the-wall (*slang*), outlandish, oddball (*informal*), wacko (*slang*), outré: *kinky behaviour* **3** = **twisted**, curled, curly, frizzy, tangled, coiled, crimped, frizzled: *He had red kinky hair.*

kinship NOUN **1** = **relationship**, kin, family ties, consanguinity, ties of blood, blood relationship: *the ties of kinship* **2** = **similarity**, relationship, association, bearing, connection, alliance, correspondence, affinity: *She evidently felt a sense of kinship with the woman.*

kinsman *or* **kinswoman** NOUN = **relative**, relation, blood relative, fellow tribesman, fellow clansman, rellie (*Austral. slang*)

kiosk NOUN = **booth**, stand, counter, stall, newsstand, bookstall

kiss VERB **1** = **peck** (*informal*), osculate, snog (*Brit. slang*), neck (*informal*), smooch (*informal*), canoodle (*slang*): *She kissed me hard on the mouth.* **2** = **brush**, touch, shave, scrape, graze, caress, glance off, stroke: *The wheels of the aircraft kissed the runway.*
▷ NOUN = **peck** (*informal*), snog (*Brit. slang*), smacker (*slang*), smooch (*informal*), French kiss, osculation: *I put my arms around her and gave her a kiss.*

QUOTATIONS

You must not kiss and tell
[William Congreve *Love for Love*]

When women kiss it always reminds one of prize-fighters shaking hands
[H.L. Mencken *A Mencken Chrestomathy*]

The kiss originated when the first male reptile licked the first female reptile, implying in a subtle, complimentary way that she was as succulent as the small reptile he had for dinner the night before
[F. Scott Fitzgerald *The Crack-Up*]

You must remember this, a kiss is still a kiss,
A sigh is just a sigh;
The fundamental things apply,
As time goes by
[Herman Hupfeld *As Time Goes By*]

kit NOUN **1** = **equipment**, supplies, materials, tackle, tools, instruments, provisions, implements, rig, apparatus, trappings, utensils, paraphernalia, accoutrements, appurtenances: *The kit consisted of about twenty cosmetic items.* **2** = **gear**, things, effects, dress, clothes, clothing, stuff, equipment, uniform, outfit, rig, costume, garments, baggage, equipage: *I forgot my gym kit.*
kit something *or* **someone out** *or* **up** = **equip**, fit, supply, provide with, arm, stock, outfit, costume, furnish, fix up, fit out, deck out, accoutre: *kitted out with winter coat, skirts, jumpers, nylon stockings*

kitchen NOUN = **cookhouse**, galley, kitchenette, scullery

knack NOUN = **skill**, art, ability, facility, talent, gift, capacity, trick, bent, craft, genius, expertise, forte, flair, competence, ingenuity, propensity, aptitude, dexterity, cleverness, quickness, adroitness, expertness, handiness, skilfulness **OPPOSITE:** ineptitude

knackered ADJECTIVE **1** = **exhausted**, worn out, tired out, drained, beat (*slang*), done in (*informal*), all in (*slang*), debilitated, prostrated, enervated, ready to drop, dog-tired (*informal*), zonked (*slang*), dead tired, dead beat (*slang*) **2** = **broken**, not working, out of order, not functioning, done in (*informal*), ruined, worn out, on the blink (*slang*), on its last legs

knavish ADJECTIVE = **dishonest**, tricky, fraudulent, deceptive, unscrupulous, rascally, scoundrelly, deceitful, villainous, unprincipled, dishonourable, roguish **OPPOSITE:** honourable

knead VERB = **squeeze**, work, massage, manipulate, form, press, shape, stroke, blend, rub, mould

kneel VERB = **genuflect**, bow, stoop, curtsy *or* curtsey, bow down, kowtow, get down on your knees, make obeisance

knell NOUN = **ring**, sound, toll, chime, clang, peal

knickers PLURAL NOUN = **underwear**, smalls, briefs, drawers, panties, bloomers

knife NOUN = **blade**, carver, cutter, cutting tool: *a knife and fork*
▷ VERB = **cut**, wound, stab, slash, thrust, gore, pierce, spear, jab,

bayonet, impale, lacerate: *She was knifed in the back six times.*

knit VERB **1 = join**, unite, link, tie, bond, ally, combine, secure, bind, connect, merge, weave, fasten, meld: *Sport knits the whole family close together.* **2 = heal**, unite, join, link, bind, connect, loop, mend, fasten, intertwine, interlace: *broken bones that have failed to knit* **3 = furrow**, tighten, knot, wrinkle, crease, screw up, pucker, scrunch up: *They knitted their brows and started to grumble.*

knob NOUN **= ball**, stud, nub, protuberance, boss, bunch, swell, knot, bulk, lump, bump, projection, snag, hump, protrusion, knurl

knock VERB **1 = bang**, beat, strike, tap, rap, bash *(informal)*, thump, buffet, pummel: *Knock at my window at eight o'clock and I'll be ready.* **2 = hit**, strike, punch, belt *(informal)*, slap, chin *(slang)*, smack, thump, clap, cuff, smite *(archaic)*, thwack, lay one on *(slang)*, beat *or* knock seven bells out of *(informal)*: *He was mucking around and he knocked her in the stomach.* **3 = criticize**, condemn, put down, run down, abuse, blast, pan *(informal)*, slam *(slang)*, slate *(informal)*, have a go (at) *(informal)*, censure, slag (off) *(slang)*, denigrate, belittle, disparage, deprecate, diss *(slang, chiefly U.S.)*, find fault with, carp at, lambast(e), pick holes in, cast aspersions on, cavil at, pick to pieces, give (someone *or* something) a bad press, nit-pick *(informal)*: *I'm not knocking them: if they want to do it, it's up to them.*

▷ NOUN **1 = knocking**, pounding, beating, tap, hammering, bang, banging, rap, thump, thud: *They heard a knock at the front door.* **2 = bang**, blow, impact, jar, collision, jolt, smash: *The bags have tough exterior materials to protect against knocks.* **3 = blow**, hit, punch, crack, belt *(informal)*, clip, slap, bash, smack, thump, clout *(informal)*, cuff, box: *He had taken a knock on the head in training.* **4 = setback**, check, defeat, blow, upset, reverse, disappointment, hold-up, hitch, reversal, misfortune, rebuff, whammy *(informal, chiefly U.S.)*, bummer *(slang)*: *The art market has suffered some severe knocks.*

knock about *or* **around = wander**, travel, roam, rove, range, drift, stray, ramble, straggle, traipse, go walkabout *(Austral.)*, stravaig *(Scot. & Northern English dialect)*: *reporters who knock around in troubled parts of the world*

knock about *or* **around with someone = mix with**, associate with, mingle with, hang out with *(informal)*, hang with *(informal, chiefly U.S.)*, be friends with, consort with, run around with *(informal)*, hobnob with, socialize with, accompany, hang about with, fraternize with: *I used to knock about with all the lads.*

knock off = stop work, get out, conclude, shut down, terminate, call it a day *(informal)*, finish work, clock off, clock out: *What time do you knock off?*

knock someone about *or* **around = hit**, attack, beat, strike, damage, abuse, hurt, injure, wound, assault, harm, batter, slap, bruise, thrash, beat up *(informal)*, buffet, maul, work over *(slang)*, clobber *(slang)*, mistreat, manhandle, maltreat, lambast(e), slap around *(informal)*, beat *or* knock seven bells out of *(informal)*: *He started knocking me around.*

knock someone down = run over, hit, run down, knock over, mow down: *He died in hospital after being knocked down by a car.*

knock someone off = kill, murder, do in *(slang)*, slaughter, destroy, waste *(informal)*, take out *(slang)*, execute, massacre, butcher, wipe out *(informal)*, dispatch, cut down, erase, assassinate, slay, eradicate, whack *(informal)*, do away with, blow away *(slang, chiefly U.S.)*, obliterate, liquidate, decimate, annihilate, neutralize, exterminate, croak, mow down, take (someone's) life, bump off *(slang)*, extirpate, wipe from the face of the earth *(informal)*: *Several people had a motive to knock him off.*

knock someone out 1 = floor, knock unconscious, knock senseless, render unconscious, level, stun, daze: *He had never been knocked out in a professional fight.* **2 = eliminate**, beat, defeat, trounce, vanquish: *We were knocked out in the quarter-finals.* **3 = impress**, move, strike, touch, affect, influence, excite, inspire, grab *(informal)*, stir, overwhelm, sway, make an impression on: *That performance knocked me out.*

knock something down 1 = demolish, destroy, flatten, tear down, level, total *(slang)*, fell, ruin, dismantle, trash *(slang)*, bulldoze, raze, pulverize, kennet *(Austral. slang)*, jeff *(Austral. slang)*: *Why doesn't he just knock the wall down?*

knock something off 1 = steal, take, nick *(slang, chiefly Brit.)*, thieve, rob, pinch, cabbage *(Brit. slang)*, blag *(slang)*, pilfer, purloin, filch: *Cars can be stolen almost as easily as knocking off a bike.* **2 = remove**, take away, deduct, debit, subtract: *I'll knock off another £100 if you pay in cash.*

knockabout ADJECTIVE **= boisterous**, riotous, rollicking, rough-and-tumble, rumbustious, rambunctious *(informal)*, harum-scarum, farcical, slapstick

knockout NOUN **1 = killer blow**, coup de grâce *(French)*, kayo *(slang)*, KO *or* K.O. *(slang)*: *a first-round knockout in Las Vegas* **2 = success**, hit, winner, triumph, smash, sensation, smash hit, stunner *(informal)*, smasheroo *(informal)*: *The first story is a knockout.* OPPOSITE: failure

knoll NOUN **= hillock**

knot NOUN **1 = connection**, tie, bond, joint, bow, loop, braid, splice, rosette, ligature: *One lace had broken and been tied in a knot.* **2 = group**, company, set, band, crowd, pack, squad, circle, crew *(informal)*, gang, mob, clique, assemblage: *A little knot of men stood clapping.*

▷ VERB **= tie**, secure, bind, complicate, weave, loop, knit, tether, entangle: *He knotted the bandanna around his neck.*

knotty ADJECTIVE **1 = puzzling**, hard, difficult, complex, complicated, tricky, baffling, intricate, troublesome, perplexing, mystifying, thorny, problematical: *The new management team faces some knotty problems.* **2 = knotted**, rough, rugged, bumpy, gnarled, knobby, nodular: *the knotty trunk of a hawthorn tree*

know VERB **1 = have knowledge of**, see, understand, recognize, perceive, be aware of, be conscious of: *I don't know the name of the place; I think I know the answer.* **2 = be acquainted with**, recognize, associate with, be familiar with, be friends with, be friendly with, have knowledge of, have dealings with, socialize with, fraternize with, be pals with: *Do you two know each other?* OPPOSITE: be unfamiliar with **3** *(sometimes with* **about** *or* **of***)* **= be familiar with**, experience, understand, ken *(Scot.)*, comprehend, fathom, apprehend, have knowledge of, be acquainted with, feel certain of, have dealings in, be versed in: *Hire someone with experience, someone who knows about real estate.* OPPOSITE: be ignorant of **4 = recognize**, remember, identify, recall, place, spot, notice, distinguish, perceive, make out, discern, differentiate, recollect: *Would she know you if she saw you on the street?*

> QUOTATIONS
> To really know someone is to have loved and hated him in turn
> [Marcel Jouhandeau]

> PROVERBS
> *What you don't know can't hurt you*
> *Know thyself*

know-all NOUN **= smart aleck**, wise guy *(informal)*, smarty *(informal)*, clever-clogs *(informal)*, clever Dick *(informal)*, smarty-pants *(informal)*, smartarse *(slang)*, wiseacre, smarty-boots *(informal)*

know-how NOUN **= expertise**, experience, ability, skill, knowledge, facility, talent, command, craft, grasp, faculty, capability, flair, knack, ingenuity, aptitude, proficiency, dexterity, cleverness, deftness, savoir-faire, adroitness, ableness

knowing ADJECTIVE **= meaningful**, significant, expressive, eloquent, enigmatic, suggestive

knowingly ADVERB **= deliberately**, purposely, consciously, intentionally, on purpose, wilfully, wittingly

knowledge NOUN **1 = understanding**, sense, intelligence, judgment, perception, awareness, insight, grasp, appreciation, penetration,

comprehension, discernment: *the quest for scientific knowledge* **2 = learning**, schooling, education, science, intelligence, instruction, wisdom, scholarship, tuition, enlightenment, erudition: *She didn't intend to display her knowledge, at least not yet.*
OPPOSITE: ignorance
3 = consciousness, recognition, awareness, apprehension, cognition, discernment: *taken without my knowledge or consent*
OPPOSITE: unawareness
4 = acquaintance, information, notice, intimacy, familiarity, cognizance: *She disclaims any knowledge of her husband's business concerns.*
OPPOSITE: unfamiliarity

QUOTATIONS

Knowledge is power
[Francis Bacon *Meditationes Sacrae*]

Knowledge is power. Unfortunate dupes of this saying will keep on reading, ambitiously, till they have stunned their native initiative, and made their thoughts weak
[Clarence Day *This Simian World*]

Knowledge is power, if you know it about the right person
[Ethel Watts Mumford]

All I know is that I know nothing
[Socrates]

That knowledge which stops at what it does not know, is the highest knowledge
[Chang Tzu *The Music of Heaven and Earth*]

No man's knowledge here can go beyond his experience
[John Locke *Essay concerning Human Understanding*]

Nothing that is worth knowing can be taught
[Oscar Wilde *The Critic as Artist*]

Knowledge is not knowledge until someone else knows that one knows
[Lucilius *fragment*]

He that increaseth knowledge increaseth sorrow
[*Bible: Ecclesiastes*]

Knowledge is of two kinds. We know a subject ourselves, or we know where we can find information upon it
[Dr. Johnson]

Knowledge puffeth up, but charity edifieth
[*Bible: I Corinthians*]

It is the province of knowledge to speak and it is the privilege of wisdom to listen
[Oliver Wendell Holmes *The Poet at the Breakfast-Table*]

If a little knowledge is dangerous, where is the man who has so much as to be out of danger?
[T.H. Huxley *Collected Essays*]

Owl hasn't exactly got Brain, but he Knows Things
[A.A. Milne *Winnie-the-Pooh*]

Knowledge in the end is based on acknowledgement
[Ludwig Wittgenstein *On Certainty*]

There are known knowns – there are things we know that we know. There are known unknowns – that is to say, there are things that we now know we don't know. But there are also unknown unknowns – there are things we do not know we don't know
[Donald Rumsfeld]

PROVERBS

A little knowledge is a dangerous thing
An old poacher makes the best gamekeeper

knowledgeable ADJECTIVE **1 = well-informed**, acquainted, conversant, au fait *(French)*, experienced, understanding, aware, familiar, conscious, in the know *(informal)*, cognizant, in the loop, au courant *(French)*, clued-up *(informal)*, across, down with: *school-age children who were very knowledgeable about soccer*
2 = intelligent, lettered, learned, educated, scholarly, erudite: *He was a knowledgeable and well-read man.*

known ADJECTIVE **= famous**, well-known, celebrated, popular, common, admitted, noted, published, obvious, familiar, acknowledged, recognized, plain, confessed, patent, manifest, avowed **OPPOSITE:** unknown

koppie *or* **kopje** NOUN **= hill**, down *(archaic)*, fell, mount, height, mound, prominence, elevation, eminence, hilltop, tor, knoll, hillock, brae *(Scot.)*

kudos NOUN **= prestige**, regard, honour, praise, glory, fame, distinction, esteem, acclaim, applause, plaudits, renown, repute, notability, laudation

k

L

label NOUN **1 = tag**, ticket, tab, marker, flag, tally, sticker, docket *(chiefly Brit.)*: *He peered at the label on the bottle.* **2 = epithet**, description, classification, characterization: *Her treatment of her husband earned her the label of the most hated woman in America.* **3 = brand**, company, mark, trademark, brand name, trade name: *designer labels*
▷ VERB **1 = tag**, mark, stamp, ticket, flag, tab, tally, sticker, docket *(chiefly Brit.)*: *The produce was labelled 'Made in China'.* **2 = brand**, classify, describe, class, call, name, identify, define, designate, characterize, categorize, pigeonhole: *Too often the press are labelled as bad boys.*

laborious ADJECTIVE **1 = hard**, difficult, tiring, exhausting, wearing, tough, fatiguing, uphill, strenuous, arduous, tiresome, onerous, burdensome, herculean, wearisome, backbreaking, toilsome: *Keeping the garden tidy all year round can be a laborious task.* **OPPOSITE:** easy **2 = industrious**, hard-working, diligent, tireless, persevering, painstaking, indefatigable, assiduous, unflagging, sedulous: *He was gentle and kindly, living a laborious life in his Paris flat.* **3 = forced**, laboured, strained, ponderous, not fluent: *a laborious prose style* **OPPOSITE:** natural

labour NOUN **1 = toil**, effort, industry, grind *(informal)*, pains, sweat *(informal)*, slog *(informal)*, exertion, drudgery, travail, donkey-work: *the labour of seeding, planting and harvesting* **OPPOSITE:** leisure **2 = workers**, employees, workforce, labourers, hands, workmen: *The country lacked skilled labour.* **3 = work**, effort, employment, toil, industry: *Every man should receive a fair price for the product of his labour.* **4 = childbirth**, birth, delivery, contractions, pains, throes, travail, labour pains, parturition: *By the time she realised she was in labour, it was too late.* **5 = chore**, job, task, undertaking: *The chef looked up from his labours.*
▷ VERB **1 = work**, toil, strive, work hard, grind *(informal)*, sweat *(informal)*, slave, endeavour, plod away, drudge, travail, slog away *(informal)*, exert yourself, peg along *or* away *(chiefly Brit.)*, plug along *or* away *(informal)*: *peasants labouring in the fields* **OPPOSITE:** rest **2 = struggle**, work, strain, work hard, strive, go for it *(informal)*, grapple, toil, make an effort, make every effort, do your best, exert yourself, work like a Trojan: *For years he laboured to build a religious community.* **3 = overemphasize**, stress, elaborate, exaggerate, strain, dwell on, overdo, go on about, make a production (out) of *(informal)*, make a federal case of *(U.S. informal)*: *I don't want to labour the point, but there it is.* **4** *(usually with* **under***)* **= be disadvantaged by**, suffer from, be a victim of, be burdened by: *She laboured under the illusion that I knew what I was doing.*

laboured ADJECTIVE **1 = difficult**, forced, strained, heavy, awkward: *From his slow walk and laboured breathing, she realized he was not well.* **2 = contrived**, studied, affected, awkward, unnatural, overdone, ponderous, overwrought: *The prose of his official communications was so laboured, pompous and verbose.*

labourer NOUN **= worker**, workman, working man, manual worker, hand, blue-collar worker, drudge, unskilled worker, navvy *(Brit. informal)*, labouring man

> **PROVERBS**
> *The labourer is worthy of his hire*

Labour Party ADJECTIVE **= left-wing**, Democrat *(U.S.)*

labyrinth NOUN **= maze**, jungle, tangle, coil, snarl, entanglement

labyrinthine ADJECTIVE **= mazelike**, winding, tangled, intricate, tortuous, convoluted, mazy

lace NOUN **1 = netting**, net, filigree, tatting, meshwork, openwork: *a plain white lace bedspread* **2 = cord**, tie, string, lacing, thong, shoelace, bootlace: *He was sitting on the bed, tying the laces of an old pair of running shoes.*
▷ VERB **1 = fasten**, tie, tie up, do up, secure, bind, close, attach, thread: *No matter how tightly I lace these shoes, my ankles wobble.* **2 = mix**, drug, doctor, add to, spike, contaminate, fortify, adulterate: *She laced his food with sleeping pills.* **3 = intertwine**, interweave, entwine, twine, interlink: *He took to lacing his fingers together in an attempt to keep his hands still.*

lacerate VERB **1 = tear**, cut, wound, rend, rip, slash, claw, maim, mangle, mangulate *(Austral. slang)*, gash, jag: *Its claws lacerated his thighs.* **2 = hurt**, wound, rend, torture, distress, torment, afflict, harrow: *He was born into a family already lacerated with tensions and divisions.*

laceration NOUN **= cut**, injury, tear, wound, rent, rip, slash, trauma *(Pathology)*, gash, mutilation

lack NOUN **= shortage**, want, absence, deficiency, need, shortcoming, deprivation, inadequacy, scarcity, dearth, privation, shortness, destitution, insufficiency, scantiness, debt: *Despite his lack of experience, he got the job.* **OPPOSITE:** abundance
▷ VERB **= miss**, want, need, require, not have, be without, be short of, be in need of, be deficient in: *It lacked the power of the Italian cars.* **OPPOSITE:** have

lackey NOUN **= hanger-on**, fawner, pawn, attendant, tool, instrument, parasite, cohort *(chiefly U.S.)*, valet, menial, minion, footman, sycophant, yes-man, manservant, toady, flunky, flatterer, varlet *(archaic)*

lacking ADJECTIVE **= deficient**, wanting, needing, missing, inadequate, minus *(informal)*, flawed, impaired, sans *(archaic)*

lacklustre ADJECTIVE **= flat**, boring, dull, dim, dry, muted, sombre, drab, lifeless, prosaic, leaden, unimaginative, uninspired, unexciting, vapid, lustreless

laconic ADJECTIVE **= terse**, short, brief, clipped, to the point, crisp, compact, concise, curt, succinct, pithy, monosyllabic, sententious **OPPOSITE:** long-winded

lacy ADJECTIVE **= filigree**, open, fine, sheer, delicate, frilly, gossamer, gauzy, net-like, lace-like, meshy

lad NOUN **= boy**, kid *(informal)*, guy *(informal)*, youth, fellow, youngster, chap *(informal)*, juvenile, shaver *(informal)*, nipper *(informal)*, laddie *(Scot.)*, stripling

laden ADJECTIVE **= loaded**, burdened, hampered, weighted, full, charged, taxed, oppressed, fraught, weighed down, encumbered

lady NOUN **1 = gentlewoman**, duchess, noble, dame, baroness, countess, aristocrat, viscountess, noblewoman, peeress: *Our governess was told to make sure we knew how to talk like English ladies.* **2 = woman**, female, girl, miss, maiden *(archaic)*, maid *(archaic)*, lass, damsel, lassie *(informal)*, charlie *(Austral. slang)*, chook *(Austral. slang)*, wahine *(N.Z.)*: *She's a very sweet old lady.*

ladylike ADJECTIVE **= refined**, cultured, sophisticated, elegant, proper, modest, respectable, polite, genteel, courtly, well-bred, decorous **OPPOSITE:** unladylike

lag VERB **1 = hang back**, delay, drag (behind), trail, linger, be behind, idle, saunter, loiter, straggle, dawdle, tarry, drag your feet *(informal)*: *The boys crept forward, Roger lagging a little.* **2 = drop**, fail, diminish, decrease, flag, fall off, wane, ebb, slacken, lose strength: *Trade has lagged since the embargo.*

Collective Nouns in Classic Literature

A problematic set of words in English are the collective nouns such as *family, group, team, government,* and *staff,* which are grammatically singular but refer to a group. In British English they are often followed by a plural verb; in American English, they tend to be treated as singular nouns. In some cases, the choice of plural or singular depends on the way the group is perceived: for example, if we think of the government as a unified whole, we might say that 'the government **is** responsible'; if we think of it as a collection of individuals with different aims, we might say 'the government **are** responsible'.

In classic literature of the eighteenth to early twentieth century, *government* is almost always treated as a singular. Abraham Lincoln and Thomas Jefferson, who, unsurprisingly, use the word *government* frequently in their speeches and letters, always use it with a singular verb:

> Although the **government has** no official information upon this subject ...
> (Abraham Lincoln)

Other writers also tend to treat *government* as singular, with a few exceptions such as:

> The French **government are** also fortifying other points along the coast.
> (Nathaniel Hawthorne)

Team is a much less frequent word in classic literature, but when it does occur, it is almost always treated as singular. There are a few exceptions in the reported speech in PG Wodehouse's novels. In the following example, the natural inconsistency of speech is reflected in the movement from collective noun (*team*) to plural verb (*are*) to singular pronoun (*it*):

> 'And the school **team aren't** such a lot of flyers that you can afford to go chucking people out of it whenever you want to ...' (PG Wodehouse)

This shows the way that collective nouns are variably interpreted: in the first part of the sentence the team is thought of as a collection of people (who aren't flyers); towards the end of the sentence the team is though of as a unit (which can throw its members out).

Family is more variable in classic literature. Some writers, including William Thackeray and Anthony Trollope, tend to use *family* with a singular verb; others, including Charles Dickens, use it with a plural verb more often. Examples include:

> You know how terribly the **family is** cut up by this great misfortune to our cousin Mountjoy.
> (Anthony Trollope)

> ... this is the first night in many on which the **family have** been alone. (Charles Dickens)

Another noun which causes problems in modern English is *number*, which is occasionally treated as plural in sentences such as '**The number of** units to be charged **are** recorded automatically' (from the *Bank of English*, Collins' corpus of present-day English). This is often considered incorrect because *number* is grammatically singular; arguably, though, 'number of units' is a conceptual plural, similar to *family* and *team*. In classic literature, *number* is almost always treated as singular, although there are a few exceptions which indicate that the troublesome nature of the word has a long history:

> ... **the number of** claims **are** so uncertain that nobody knows what they engage in when they subscribe. (Daniel Defoe)

laggard NOUN **= straggler**, lounger, lingerer, piker *(Austral. & N.Z. slang)*, snail, saunterer, loafer, loiterer, dawdler, skiver *(Brit. slang)*, idler, slowcoach *(Brit. informal)*, sluggard, bludger *(Austral. & N.Z. informal)*, slowpoke *(U.S. & Canad. informal)*

laid-back ADJECTIVE **= relaxed**, calm, casual, together *(slang)*, at ease, easy-going, unflappable *(informal)*, unhurried, free and easy, easy-peasy *(slang)*, chilled *(informal)*
OPPOSITE: tense

lair NOUN **1 = nest**, den, hole, burrow, resting place: *a fox's lair* **2 = hide-out** *(informal)*, retreat, refuge, den, sanctuary: *The village was once a pirate's lair.*

laissez faire *or* **laisser faire** NOUN **= nonintervention**, free trade, individualism, free enterprise, live and let live

lake NOUN **= pond**, pool, reservoir, loch *(Scot.)*, lagoon, mere, lough *(Irish)*, tarn

lame ADJECTIVE **1 = disabled**, handicapped, crippled, limping, defective, hobbling, game, halt *(archaic)*: *He had to pull out of the Championships when his horse went lame.* **2 = unconvincing**, poor, pathetic, inadequate, thin, weak, insufficient, feeble, unsatisfactory, flimsy: *He mumbled some lame excuse about having gone to sleep.*

lament VERB **= bemoan**, grieve, mourn, weep over, complain about, regret, wail about, deplore, bewail: *Ken began to lament the death of his only son.*
▷ NOUN **1 = complaint**, moaning, moan, keening, wail, wailing, lamentation, plaint, ululation: *the professional woman's lament that a woman's judgment is questioned more than a man's* **2 = dirge**, requiem, elegy, threnody, monody, coronach *(Scot. & Irish)*: *a lament for the late, great Buddy Holly*

lamentable ADJECTIVE
1 = regrettable, distressing, tragic, unfortunate, harrowing, grievous, woeful, deplorable, mournful, sorrowful, gut-wrenching: *This lamentable state of affairs lasted until 1947.* **2 = disappointing**, poor, miserable, unsatisfactory, mean, low quality, meagre, pitiful, wretched, not much cop *(Brit. slang)*: *He admitted he was partly to blame for England's lamentable performance.*

lamentation NOUN **= sorrow**, grief, weeping, mourning, moan, grieving, sobbing, keening, lament, wailing, dirge, plaint, ululation

laminated ADJECTIVE **= covered**, coated, overlaid, veneered, faced

lampoon VERB **= ridicule**, mock, mimic, parody, caricature, send up *(Brit. informal)*, take off *(informal)*, make fun of, squib, burlesque, satirize, pasquinade: *He was lampooned for his short stature and political views.*
▷ NOUN **= satire**, parody, caricature, send-up *(Brit. informal)*, takeoff *(informal)*, skit, squib, burlesque, pasquinade, piss-take *(informal)*: *his scathing lampoons of consumer culture*

land NOUN **1 = ground**, earth, dry land, terra firma: *It isn't clear whether the plane went down over land or sea.* **2 = soil**, ground, earth, clay, dirt, sod, loam: *a small piece of grazing land* **3 = countryside**, farming, farmland, rural districts: *Living off the land was hard enough at the best of times.* **4 = property**, grounds, estate, acres, real estate, realty, acreage, real property, homestead *(U.S. & Canad.)*: *Good agricultural land is in short supply.* **5 = country**, nation, region, state, district, territory, province, kingdom, realm, tract, motherland, fatherland: *America, land of opportunity*
▷ VERB **1 = arrive**, dock, put down, moor, berth, alight, touch down, disembark, come to rest, debark: *The jet landed after a flight of just under three hours.* **2 = gain**, get, win, score *(slang)*, secure, obtain, acquire: *He landed a place on the graduate training scheme.*
land up = end up, arrive, turn up, wind up, finish up, fetch up *(informal)*: *We landed up at the Las Vegas at about 6.30.*
▸ *related adjective:* terrestrial

landing NOUN **1 = coming in**, arrival, touchdown, disembarkation, disembarkment: *I had to make a controlled landing into the sea.* **2 = platform**, jetty, quayside, landing stage: *Take the bus to the landing.*

landlord NOUN **1 = owner**, landowner, proprietor, freeholder, lessor, landholder: *His landlord doubled the rent.* **2 = innkeeper**, host, hotelier, hotel-keeper: *The landlord refused to serve him because he considered him too drunk.*

landmark NOUN **1 = feature**, spectacle, monument: *The Ambassador Hotel is a Los Angeles landmark.* **2 = milestone**, turning point, watershed, critical point, tipping point: *a landmark in world history* **3 = boundary marker**, cairn, benchmark, signpost, milepost: *an abandoned landmark on top of Townsville's Castle Hill*

landscape NOUN **= scenery**, country, view, land, scene, prospect, countryside, outlook, terrain, panorama, vista

landslide NOUN **= landslip**, avalanche, mudslide, rockfall

lane NOUN **= road**, street, track, path, strip, way, passage, trail, pathway, footpath, passageway, thoroughfare

language NOUN **1 = tongue**, speech, vocabulary, dialect, idiom, vernacular, patter, lingo *(informal)*, patois, lingua franca: *the English language* **2 = speech**, communication, expression, speaking, talk, talking, conversation, discourse, interchange, utterance, parlance, vocalization, verbalization: *Students examined how children acquire language.* **3 = style**, wording, expression, phrasing, vocabulary, usage, parlance, diction, phraseology: *a booklet summarising it in plain language*

QUOTATIONS

Language is the dress of thought
[Samuel Johnson *Lives of the English Poets: Cowley*]

After all, when you come right down to it, how many people speak the same language even when they speak the same language?
[Russell Hoban *The Lion of Boaz-Jachin and Jachin-Boaz*]

Languages are the pedigrees of nations
[Samuel Johnson]

We've come intil a gey queer time
Whan scrievin Scots is near a crime
"There's no-one speaks like that",
they fleer
But wha the deil spoke like King
Lear?
[Sydney Goodsir Smith *Epistle to John Guthrie*]

A language is a dialect with an army and a navy
[Max Weinrich]

One does not inhabit a country; one inhabits a language. That is our country, our fatherland – and no other
[E.M. Cioran *Anathemas and Admirations*]

Everything can change, but not the language that we carry inside us, like a world more exclusive and final than one's mother's womb
[Italo Calvino *By Way of an Autobiography*]

To God I speak Spanish, to women Italian, to men French, and to my horse – German
[attributed to Emperor Charles V]

In language, the ignorant have prescribed laws to the learned
[Richard Duppa *Maxims*]

Language is fossil poetry
[Ralph Waldo Emerson *Essays: Nominalist and Realist*]

Political language... is designed to make lies sound truthful and murder respectable, and to give an appearance of solidity to pure wind
[George Orwell *Shooting an Elephant*]

languid ADJECTIVE **= inactive**, lazy, indifferent, lethargic, weary, sluggish, inert, uninterested, listless, unenthusiastic, languorous, lackadaisical, torpid, spiritless
OPPOSITE: energetic

languish VERB **1 = decline**, waste away, fade away, wither away, flag, weaken, wilt, sicken: *He continues to languish in prison.* **OPPOSITE:** flourish **2 = waste away**, suffer, rot, be abandoned, be neglected, be disregarded: *New products languish on the drawing board.* **OPPOSITE:** thrive **3** *(often with* **for***)* = **pine**, want, long, desire, sigh, hunger, yearn, hanker, eat your heart out over, suspire: *a bride languishing for a kiss that never comes*

languishing ADJECTIVE = **fading**, failing, declining, flagging, sinking, weakening, deteriorating, withering, wilting, sickening, drooping, droopy, wasting away

lank ADJECTIVE **1** = **limp**, lifeless, long, dull, straggling, lustreless: *She ran her fingers through her hair; it felt lank and dirty.* **2** = **thin**, lean, slim, slender, skinny, spare, gaunt, lanky, emaciated, scrawny, attenuated, scraggy, rawboned: *a lank youth with a ponytail*

lanky ADJECTIVE = **gangling**, thin, tall, spare, angular, gaunt, bony, weedy *(informal)*, scrawny, rangy, scraggy, rawboned, loose-jointed
OPPOSITE: chubby

lap¹ NOUN = **circuit**, course, round, tour, leg, distance, stretch, circle, orbit, loop: *the last lap of the race*

lap² VERB **1** = **ripple**, wash, splash, slap, swish, gurgle, slosh, purl, plash: *the water that lapped against the pillars of the pier* **2** = **drink**, sip, lick, swallow, gulp, sup: *The kitten lapped milk from a dish.*
lap something up = **relish**, like, enjoy, appreciate, delight in, savour, revel in, wallow in, accept eagerly: *They're eager to learn, so they lap it up.*

lapse NOUN **1** = **decline**, fall, drop, descent, deterioration, relapse, backsliding: *His behaviour showed neither decency or dignity. It was an uncommon lapse.* **2** = **mistake**, failing, fault, failure, error, slip, negligence, omission, oversight, indiscretion: *The incident was being seen as a serious security lapse.* **3** = **interval**, break, gap, passage, pause, interruption, lull, breathing space, intermission: *a time lapse between receipt of new information and its publication*
▷ VERB **1** = **slip**, fall, decline, sink, drop, slide, deteriorate, degenerate: *Teenagers occasionally find it all too much to cope with and lapse into bad behaviour.* **2** = **end**, stop, run out, expire, terminate, become obsolete, become void: *Her membership of the Labour Party has lapsed.*

lapsed ADJECTIVE **1** = **expired**, ended, finished, run out, invalid, out of date, discontinued, unrenewed: *He returned to the Party after years of lapsed membership.* **2** = **backsliding**, uncommitted, lacking faith, nonpractising: *She calls herself a lapsed Catholic.*

large ADJECTIVE **1** = **big**, great, huge, heavy, giant, massive, vast, enormous, tall, considerable, substantial, strapping, immense *(informal)*, hefty, gigantic, monumental, bulky, chunky, burly, colossal, hulking, goodly, man-size, brawny, elephantine, thickset, ginormous *(informal)*, humongous *or* humungous *(U.S. slang)*, sizable *or* sizeable, supersize: *He was a large man with a thick square head.* **OPPOSITE:** small **2** = **massive**, great, big, huge, giant, vast, enormous, considerable, substantial, immense, tidy *(informal)*, jumbo *(informal)*, gigantic, monumental, mammoth, colossal, gargantuan, stellar *(informal)*, king-size, ginormous *(informal)*, humongous *or* humungous *(U.S. slang)*, sizable *or* sizeable, supersize: *In a large room about a dozen children are sitting on the carpet.* **OPPOSITE:** small **3** = **plentiful**, full, grand, liberal, sweeping, broad, comprehensive, extensive, generous, lavish, ample, spacious, abundant, grandiose, copious, roomy, bountiful, capacious, profuse: *The gang finally left with a large amount of cash and jewellery.*
OPPOSITE: scanty
at large 1 = **in general**, generally, chiefly, mainly, as a whole, in the main: *The public at large does not seem to want any change.* **2** = **free**, roaming, on the run, fugitive, at liberty, on the loose, unchained, unconfined: *The man who tried to have her killed is still at large.*
by and large = **on the whole**, generally, mostly, in general, all things considered, predominantly, in the main, for the most part, all in all, as a rule, taking everything into consideration: *By and large, the papers greet the government's new policy with scepticism.*

largely ADVERB = **mainly**, generally, chiefly, widely, mostly, principally, primarily, considerably, predominantly, extensively, by and large, as a rule, to a large extent, to a great extent

large-scale ADJECTIVE = **wide-ranging**, global, sweeping, broad, wide, vast, extensive, wholesale, far-reaching

largesse *or* **largess** NOUN **1** = **generosity**, charity, bounty, philanthropy, munificence, liberality, alms-giving, benefaction, open-handedness: *his most recent act of largesse* **2** = **gift**, present, grant, donation, endowment, bounty, bequest: *The president has been travelling around the country distributing largesse.*

lark NOUN = **prank**, game, fun, fling, romp, spree, revel, mischief, caper, frolic, escapade, skylark, gambol, antic, jape, rollick: *The children thought it was a great lark.*
lark about = **fool around**, play around, romp around, have fun, caper, frolic, cavort, gambol, muck around, make mischief, lark around, rollick, cut capers: *They complained about me larking about when they were trying to concentrate.*

lascivious ADJECTIVE **1** = **lustful**, sensual, immoral, randy *(informal, chiefly Brit.)*, horny *(slang)*, voluptuous, lewd, wanton, salacious, prurient, lecherous, libidinous, licentious, unchaste: *The man was lascivious, sexually perverted and insatiable.* **2** = **bawdy**, dirty, offensive, crude, obscene, coarse, indecent, blue, vulgar, immoral, pornographic, suggestive, X-rated *(informal)*, scurrilous, smutty, ribald: *their lewd and lascivious talk*

lash¹ VERB **1** = **pound**, beat, strike, hammer, drum, smack *(dialect)*: *The rain was absolutely lashing down.* **2** = **censure**, attack, blast, put down, criticize, slate *(informal, chiefly Brit.)*, ridicule, scold, berate, castigate, lampoon, tear into *(informal)*, flay, upbraid, satirize, lambast(e), belabour: *The report lashes into police commanders for failing to act on intelligence information.* **3** = **whip**, beat, thrash, birch, flog, lam *(slang)*, scourge, chastise, lambast(e), flagellate, horsewhip: *They snatched up whips and lashed the backs of those who had fallen.*
▷ NOUN = **blow**, hit, strike, stroke, stripe, swipe *(informal)*: *They sentenced him to five lashes for stealing a ham from his neighbour.*

lash² VERB = **fasten**, join, tie, secure, bind, rope, strap, make fast: *Secure the anchor by lashing it to the rail.*

lass NOUN = **girl**, young woman, miss, bird *(slang)*, maiden, chick *(slang)*, maid, damsel, colleen *(Irish)*, lassie *(informal)*, wench *(facetious)*, charlie *(Austral. slang)*, chook *(Austral. slang)*

last¹ ADJECTIVE **1** = **most recent**, latest, previous: *Much has changed since my last visit.* **2** = **hindmost**, furthest, final, at the end, remotest, furthest behind, most distant, rearmost, aftermost: *She said it was the very last house on the road.* **OPPOSITE:** foremost **3** = **final**, closing, concluding, ultimate, utmost: *the last three pages of the chapter*
OPPOSITE: first
▷ ADVERB = **in** *or* **at the end**, after, behind, in the rear, bringing up the rear: *I testified last.*
▷ NOUN = **end**, ending, close, finish, conclusion, completion, finale, termination: *a thriller with plenty of twists to keep you guessing to the last*
at last = **finally**, eventually, in the end, ultimately, at the end of the day, at length, at long last, in conclusion, in the fullness of time: *'All right,' he said at last. 'You may go.'*
the last word 1 = **final decision**, final say, final statement, conclusive comment: *She likes to have the last word in any discussion.* **2** = **leading**, best, first, highest, finest, cream, supreme, elite, first-class, foremost, first-rate, superlative, pre-eminent, unsurpassed, the crème de la crème, most excellent: *a venue that is the last word in trendiness*

> QUOTATIONS
> Many that are first shall be last; and the last shall be first
> [Bible: St. Mark]

USAGE
Since *last* can mean either *after all others* or *most recent*, it is better to avoid using this word where ambiguity might arise, as in *her last novel*. *Final* or *latest* should be used as alternatives in such contexts to avoid any possible confusion.

last² VERB **= continue**, keep, remain, survive, wear, carry on, endure, hold on, persist, keep on, hold out, abide: *You only need a very small amount, so the tube lasts for ages.* **OPPOSITE:** end

last-ditch ADJECTIVE **= final**, frantic, desperate, struggling, straining, heroic, all-out *(informal)*

lasting ADJECTIVE **= continuing**, long-term, permanent, enduring, remaining, eternal, abiding, long-standing, perennial, lifelong, durable, perpetual, long-lasting, deep-rooted, indelible, unending, undying, unceasing
OPPOSITE: passing

lastly CONJUNCTION **= finally**, to conclude, at last, in the end, ultimately, all in all, to sum up, in conclusion

latch NOUN **= fastening**, catch, bar, lock, hook, bolt, clamp, hasp, sneck *(dialect)*: *You left the latch off the gate and the dog escaped.*
▷ VERB **= fasten**, bar, secure, lock, bolt, make fast, sneck *(dialect)*: *He latched the door, tested it and turned round to speak to us.*

late ADJECTIVE **1 = overdue**, delayed, last-minute, belated, tardy, behind time, unpunctual, behindhand: *A few late arrivals were still straggling in.* **OPPOSITE:** early **2 = dead**, deceased, departed, passed on, old, former, previous, preceding, defunct: *my late husband* **OPPOSITE:** alive **3 = recent**, new, advanced, fresh: *some late news just in for the people of Merseyside*
OPPOSITE: old
▷ ADVERB **= behind time**, belatedly, tardily, behindhand, dilatorily, unpunctually: *The talks began some fifteen minutes late.* **OPPOSITE:** early

lately ADVERB **= recently**, of late, just now, in recent times, not long ago, latterly

lateness NOUN **= delay**, late date, retardation, tardiness, unpunctuality, belatedness, advanced hour

latent ADJECTIVE **= hidden**, secret, concealed, invisible, lurking, veiled, inherent, unseen, dormant, undeveloped, quiescent, immanent, unrealized, unexpressed
OPPOSITE: obvious

later ADVERB **= afterwards**, after, next, eventually, in time, subsequently, later on, thereafter, in a while, in due course, at a later date, by and by, at a later time: *I'll join you later.*
▷ ADJECTIVE **= subsequent**, next, following, ensuing: *at a later news conference*

lateral ADJECTIVE **= sideways**, side, flanking, edgeways, sideward

latest ADJECTIVE **= up-to-date**, current, fresh, newest, happening *(informal)*, modern, most recent, up-to-the-minute

lather NOUN **1 = froth**, soap, bubbles, foam, suds, soapsuds: *He wiped off the lather with a towel.* **2 = fluster**, state *(informal)*, sweat, fever, fuss, flap *(informal)*, stew *(informal)*, dither *(chiefly Brit.)*, twitter *(informal)*, tizzy *(informal)*, pother: *'I'm not going to get into a lather over this defeat,' said the manager.*
▷ VERB **= froth**, soap, foam: *The shampoo lathers so much it's difficult to rinse it all out.*

latitude NOUN **= scope**, liberty, indulgence, freedom, play, room, space, licence, leeway, laxity, elbowroom, unrestrictedness

latter NOUN **= second**, last, last-mentioned, second-mentioned: *He tracked down his cousin and uncle. The latter was sick.*
▷ ADJECTIVE **= last**, later, latest, ending, closing, final, concluding: *The latter part of the debate concentrated on abortion.* **OPPOSITE:** earlier

USAGE
The latter should only be used to specify the second of two items, for example in *if I had to choose between the hovercraft and the ferry, I would opt for the latter*. Where there are three or more items, the last can be referred to as *the last-named*, but not *the latter*.

latterly ADVERB **= recently**, lately, of late, hitherto

lattice NOUN **= grid**, network, web, grating, mesh, grille, trellis, fretwork, tracery, latticework, openwork, reticulation

laud VERB **= praise**, celebrate, honour, acclaim, approve, magnify *(archaic)*, glorify, extol, sing *or* sound the praises of

laudable ADJECTIVE **= praiseworthy**, excellent, worthy, admirable, of note, commendable, creditable, meritorious, estimable
OPPOSITE: blameworthy

laugh VERB **= chuckle**, giggle, snigger, crack up *(informal)*, cackle, chortle, guffaw, titter, roar, bust a gut *(informal)*, be convulsed *(informal)*, be in stitches, crease up *(informal)*, split your sides, be rolling in the aisles *(informal)*: *He laughed with pleasure when people said he looked like his Dad.*
▷ NOUN **1 = chortle**, giggle, chuckle, snigger, guffaw, titter, belly laugh, roar, shriek: *He gave a deep rumbling laugh at his own joke.* **2 = joke**, scream *(informal)*, hoot *(informal)*, lark, prank: *Working there's great. It's quite a good laugh actually.* **3 = clown**, character *(informal)*, scream *(informal)*, comic, caution *(informal)*, wit, comedian, entertainer, card *(informal)*, wag, joker, hoot *(informal)*, humorist: *He was a good laugh and great to have in the dressing room.*

laugh at something *or* **someone = make fun of**, mock, tease, ridicule, taunt, jeer, deride, scoff at, belittle, lampoon, take the mickey out of *(informal)*, pour scorn on, make a mock of: *I thought people were laughing at me because I was ugly.*

laugh something off = disregard, ignore, dismiss, overlook, shrug off, minimize, brush aside, make light of, pooh-pooh: *While I used to laugh it off, I'm now getting irritated by it.*

QUOTATIONS
Laugh and the world laughs with you;
Weep, and you weep alone;
For the sad old earth must borrow its mirth,
But has enough trouble of its own
[Ella Wheeler Wilcox *Solitude*]

One can know a man from his laugh, and if you like a man's laugh before you know anything of him, you may confidently say that he is a good man
[Fyodor Dostoevsky *The House of the Dead*]

PROVERBS
He who laughs last, laughs longest

laughable ADJECTIVE **1 = ridiculous**, absurd, ludicrous, preposterous, farcical, nonsensical, derisory, risible, derisive, worthy of scorn: *He claimed that the allegations were 'laughable'.*
2 = funny, amusing, hilarious, humorous, diverting, comical, droll, mirthful: *Groucho's laughable view of human pomp*

laughing stock NOUN **= figure of fun**, target, victim, butt, fair game, Aunt Sally *(Brit.)*, everybody's fool

laughter NOUN **1 = chuckling**, laughing, giggling, chortling, guffawing, tittering, cachinnation: *Their laughter filled the corridor.*
2 = amusement, entertainment, humour, glee, fun, mirth, hilarity, merriment: *Pantomime is about bringing laughter to thousands.*

QUOTATIONS
Laughter is pleasant, but the exertion is too much for me
[Thomas Love Peacock *Nightmare Abbey*]

Delight hath a joy in it either permanent or pleasant. Laughter hath only a scornful tickling
[Sir Philip Sidney *The Defence of Poetry*]

If we may believe our logicians, man is distinguished from all other creatures by the faculty of laughter
[Joseph Addison]

The only honest art form is laughter, comedy. You can't fake it ... try to fake three laughs in an hour – ha ha ha ha ha – they'll take you away, man. You can't
[Lenny Bruce *Performing and the Art of Comedy*]

As the crackling of thorns under a pot, so is the laughter of a fool
[*Bible: Ecclesiastes*]

launch VERB **1 = propel**, fire, dispatch, discharge, project, send off, set in motion, send into orbit: *A Delta II rocket was launched from Cape Canaveral early this morning.* **2 = begin**, start, open, initiate, introduce, found, set up, originate, commence, get under way, instigate, inaugurate, embark upon: *The police have launched an investigation into the incident.*
▷ NOUN **1 = propelling**, projection, sendoff: *This morning's launch of the space shuttle Columbia has been delayed.* **2 = beginning**, start, introduction, initiation, opening, founding, setting-up, inauguration, commencement, instigation: *the launch of a campaign to restore law and order*
launch into something = start enthusiastically, begin, initiate, embark on, instigate, inaugurate, embark upon: *He launched into a speech about the importance of new products.*

launder VERB **1 = wash**, clean, dry-clean, tub, wash and iron, wash and press: *She wore a freshly laundered and starched white shirt.* **2 = process**, doctor, manipulate: *The House voted today to crack down on banks that launder drug money.*

laurel NOUN
rest on your laurels = sit back, relax, take it easy, relax your efforts

lavatory NOUN **= toilet**, bathroom, loo (*Brit. informal*), bog (*slang*), can (*U.S. & Canad. slang*), john (*slang, chiefly U.S. & Canad.*), head(s) (*Nautical, slang*), throne (*informal*), closet, privy, cloakroom (*Brit.*), urinal, latrine, washroom, powder room, ablutions (*Military, informal*), crapper (*taboo, slang*), water closet, khazi (*slang*), pissoir (*French*), Gents *or* Ladies, little boy's room *or* little girl's room (*informal*), (public) convenience, W.C., dunny (*Austral. & N.Z. old-fashioned, informal*), bogger (*Austral. slang*), brasco (*Austral. slang*)

lavish ADJECTIVE **1 = grand**, magnificent, splendid, lush, abundant, sumptuous, exuberant, opulent, copious, luxuriant, profuse: *a lavish party to celebrate his fiftieth birthday* **OPPOSITE:** stingy **2 = extravagant**, wild, excessive, exaggerated, unreasonable, wasteful, prodigal, unrestrained, intemperate, immoderate, improvident, thriftless: *Critics attack his lavish spending and flamboyant style.* **OPPOSITE:** thrifty **3 = generous**, free, liberal, bountiful, effusive, open-handed, unstinting, munificent: *American reviewers are lavish in their praise of this book.* **OPPOSITE:** stingy
▷ VERB **= shower**, pour, heap, deluge, dissipate: *The emperor promoted the general and lavished him with gifts.* **OPPOSITE:** stint

law NOUN **1 = constitution**, code, legislation, charter, jurisprudence: *Obscene and threatening phone calls are against the law.* **2 = statute**, act, bill, rule, demand, order, command, code, regulation, resolution, decree, canon, covenant, ordinance, commandment, enactment, edict: *The law was passed on a second vote.* **3 = principle**, standard, code, formula, criterion, canon, precept, axiom, kaupapa (*N.Z.*): *inflexible moral laws* **4 = the legal profession**, the bar, barristers: *a career in law*
lay down the law = be dogmatic, call the shots (*informal*), pontificate, rule the roost, crack the whip, boss around, dogmatize, order about *or* around: *traditional parents who believed in laying down the law for their offspring*
▸ *related adjectives:* legal, judicial

QUOTATIONS

The end of the law is, not to abolish or restrain, but to preserve and enlarge freedom
[John Locke *Second Treatise of Civil Government*]

It may be true that the law cannot make a man love me, but it can keep him from lynching me, and I think that's pretty important
[Martin Luther King Jr.]

The law is a causeway upon which so long as he keeps to it a citizen may walk safely
[Robert Bolt *A Man For All Seasons*]

No brilliance is needed in the law. Nothing but common sense, and relatively clean finger nails
[John Mortimer *A Voyage Round My Father*]

A jury consists of twelve persons chosen to decide who has the better lawyer
[Robert Frost]

Laws were made to be broken
[John Wilson *Noctes Ambrosianae*]

The Common Law of England has been laboriously built about a mythical figure – the figure of "The Reasonable Man"
[A.P. Herbert *Uncommon Law*]

We do not get good laws to restrain bad people. We get good people to restrain bad laws
[G.K. Chesterton *All Things Considered*]

The law is a ass – a idiot
[Charles Dickens *Oliver Twist*]

Ignorance of the law excuses no man; not that all men know the law, but because 'tis an excuse every man will plead, and no man can tell how to confute him
[John Selden *Table Talk*]

Written laws are like spider's webs; they will catch, it is true, the weak and poor, but would be torn in pieces by the rich and powerful
[Anacharsis]

Law is a bottomless pit
[Dr. Arbuthnot *The History of John Bull*]

It is better that ten guilty persons escape than one innocent suffer
[William Blackstone *Commentaries on the Laws of England*]

The one great principle of the English law is to make business for itself
[Charles Dickens *Bleak House*]

No poet ever interpreted nature as freely as a lawyer interprets the truth
[Jean Giraudoux *La Guerre de Troie n'aura pas lieu*]

The laws of most countries are far worse than the people who execute them, and many of them are only able to remain laws by being seldom or never carried into effect
[John Stuart Mill *The Subjection of Women*]

PROVERBS

Hard cases make bad laws
One law for the rich, and another for the poor

law-abiding ADJECTIVE **= obedient**, good, peaceful, honourable, orderly, honest, lawful, compliant, dutiful, peaceable

lawful ADJECTIVE **= legal**, constitutional, just, proper, valid, warranted, legitimate, authorized, rightful, permissible, legalized, allowable, licit **OPPOSITE:** unlawful

lawless ADJECTIVE **= disorderly**, wild, unruly, rebellious, chaotic, reckless, insurgent, anarchic, riotous, unrestrained, seditious, mutinous, insubordinate, ungoverned **OPPOSITE:** law-abiding

lawlessness NOUN **= anarchy**, disorder, chaos, reign of terror, mob rule, mobocracy, ochlocracy

lawsuit NOUN **= case**, cause, action, trial, suit, argument, proceedings, dispute, contest, prosecution, legal action, indictment, litigation, industrial tribunal, legal proceedings

lawyer NOUN **= legal adviser**, attorney, solicitor, counsel, advocate, barrister, counsellor, legal representative

QUOTATIONS

The laws I love; the lawyers I suspect
[Charles Churchill *The Farewell*]

If there were no bad people there would be no good lawyers
[Charles Dickens *The Old Curiosity Shop*]

I'm trusting in the Lord and a good lawyer
[Oliver North]

I don't want a lawyer to tell me what I cannot do; I hire him to tell me how to do what I want to do
[J. Pierpont Morgan]

Woe unto you, lawyers! For ye have taken away the key of knowledge
[*Bible: St. Luke*]

lawyer: one skilled in circumvention of the law
[Ambrose Bierce *The Devil's Dictionary*]

A lawyer with his briefcase can steal more than a hundred men with guns
[Mario Puzo *The Godfather*]

PROVERBS

A man who is his own lawyer has a fool for a client

lax ADJECTIVE **= slack**, casual, careless, sloppy *(informal)*, easy-going, negligent, lenient, slapdash, neglectful, slipshod, remiss, easy-peasy *(slang)*, overindulgent
OPPOSITE: strict

laxative NOUN **= purgative**, salts, purge, cathartic, physic *(rare)*, aperient

lay[1] VERB **1 = place**, put, set, spread, plant, establish, settle, leave, deposit, put down, set down, posit: *Lay a sheet of newspaper on the floor.* **2 = devise**, plan, design, prepare, work out, plot, hatch, contrive, concoct: *They were laying a trap for the kidnapper.*
3 = produce, bear, deposit: *Freezing weather hampered the hen's ability to lay eggs.* **4 = arrange**, prepare, make, organize, position, locate, set out, devise, put together, dispose, draw up: *The organisers meet in March to lay plans.* **5 = attribute**, charge, assign, allocate, allot, ascribe, impute: *She refused to lay the blame on any one party.*
6 = put forward, offer, present, advance, lodge, submit, bring forward: *Police have decided not to lay charges over allegations of phone tapping.*
7 = bet, stake, venture, gamble, chance, risk, hazard, wager, give odds: *I wouldn't lay bets on his remaining manager after the spring.*
lay into someone = attack, hit, set about, hit out at, assail, tear into, pitch into *(informal)*, go for the jugular, lambast(e), belabour, lash into, let fly at: *A mob of women laid into him with handbags and pointed shoes.*
lay off = stop, give up, quit, cut it out, leave alone, pack in, abstain, leave off, give over *(informal)*, let up, get off someone's back *(informal)*, give it a rest *(informal)*: *He went on attacking her until other passengers arrived and told him to lay off.*
lay someone off = dismiss, fire *(informal)*, release, drop, sack *(informal)*, pay off, discharge, oust, let go, make redundant, give notice to, give the boot to *(slang)*, give the sack to *(informal)*, give someone their cards, kennet *(Austral. slang)*, jeff *(Austral. slang)*: *100,000 federal workers will be laid off to reduce the deficit.*
lay someone out = knock out, fell, floor, knock unconscious, knock for six, kayo *(slang)*: *He turned round, marched over to the man, and just laid him out.*
lay someone up = confine (to bed), hospitalize, incapacitate: *He was recovering from a knee injury that laid him up for six months.*
lay something aside = abandon, reject, dismiss, postpone, shelve, put off, renounce, put aside, cast aside: *All animosities were laid aside for the moment.*
lay something bare = reveal, show, expose, disclose, unveil, divulge: *The clearing out of disused workshops laid bare thousands of glazed tiles.*
lay something down 1 = stipulate, state, establish, prescribe, assume, formulate, affirm, ordain, set down, postulate: *The Companies Act lays down a set of minimum requirements.*
2 = sacrifice, give up, yield, surrender, turn over, relinquish: *The drug traffickers have offered to lay down their arms.*
lay something in = store (up), collect, build up, accumulate, buy in, amass, stockpile, hoard, stock up, heap up: *They began to lay in extensive stores of food supplies.*
lay something on = provide, prepare, supply, organize, give, cater (for), furnish, purvey: *They laid on a superb meal.*
lay something out 1 = arrange, order, design, display, exhibit, put out, spread out: *She took a deck of cards and began to lay them out.* **2 = spend**, pay, invest, fork out *(slang)*, expend, shell out *(informal)*, disburse: *You won't have to lay out a fortune for this dining table.*

USAGE

In standard English, the verb *to lay* (meaning 'to put something somewhere') always needs an object, for example *the Queen laid a wreath*. By contrast, the verb *to lie* is always used without an object, for example *he was just lying there*.

lay[2] ADJECTIVE **1 = nonclerical**, secular, non-ordained, laic, laical: *He is a Methodist lay preacher and social worker.*
2 = nonspecialist, amateur, unqualified, untrained, inexpert, nonprofessional: *It is difficult for a lay person to gain access to medical libraries.*

layer NOUN **1 = covering**, film, cover, sheet, coating, coat, blanket, mantle: *A fresh layer of snow covered the street.*
2 = tier, level, seam, stratum: *Critics and the public puzzle out the layers of meaning in his photos.*

layman NOUN **= nonprofessional**, amateur, outsider, lay person, non-expert, nonspecialist

lay-off NOUN **= unemployment**, firing *(informal)*, sacking *(informal)*, dismissal, discharge

layout NOUN **= arrangement**, design, draft, outline, format, plan, formation, geography

laze VERB **1 = idle**, lounge, hang around, loaf, stand around, loll: *Fred lazed in an easy chair.* **2** *(often with* **away***)* **= kill time**, waste time, fritter away, pass time, while away the hours, veg out *(slang, chiefly U.S.)*, fool away: *She lazed away most of the morning.*

laziness NOUN **= idleness**, negligence, inactivity, slowness, sloth, sluggishness, slackness, indolence, tardiness, dilatoriness, slothfulness, do-nothingness, faineance

lazy ADJECTIVE **1 = idle**, inactive, indolent, slack, negligent, inert, remiss, workshy, slothful, shiftless: *I was too lazy to learn how to read music.*
OPPOSITE: industrious **2 = lethargic**, languorous, slow-moving, languid, sleepy, sluggish, drowsy, somnolent, torpid: *We would have a lazy lunch and then lie on the beach in the sun.*
OPPOSITE: quick

leach VERB **= extract**, strain, drain, filter, seep, percolate, filtrate, lixiviate *(Chemistry)*

lead VERB **1 = go in front (of)**, head, be in front, be at the head (of), walk in front (of): *Tom was leading, a rifle slung over his back.* **2 = guide**, conduct, steer, escort, precede, usher, pilot, show the way: *He led him into the house.*
3 = connect to, link, open onto: *the doors that led to the yard* **4 = be ahead (of)**, be first, exceed, be winning, excel, surpass, come first, transcend, outstrip, outdo, blaze a trail: *So far he leads by five games to two.* **5 = command**, rule, govern, preside over, head, control, manage, direct, supervise, be in charge of, head up: *He led the country between 1949 and 1984.* **6 = live**, have, spend, experience, pass, undergo: *She led a normal happy life with her sister and brother.* **7 = result in**, cause, produce, contribute, generate, bring about, bring on, give rise to, conduce: *He warned that a pay rise would lead to job cuts.*
8 = cause, prompt, persuade, move, draw, influence, motivate, prevail, induce, incline, dispose: *It was not as straightforward as we were led to believe.*
▷ NOUN **1 = first place**, winning position, primary position, vanguard, van: *Labour are still in the lead in the opinion polls.* **2 = advantage**, start, advance, edge, margin, winning margin: *He now has a lead of 30 points.* **3 = example**, direction, leadership, guidance, model, pattern: *the need for the president to give a moral lead* **4 = clue**, tip, suggestion, trace, hint, guide, indication, pointer, tip-off: *The inquiry team is following up possible leads.*
5 = leading role, principal, protagonist, title role, star part, principal part: *Two dancers from the Bolshoi Ballet dance the leads.* **6 = leash**, line, cord, rein, tether: *He came out with a little dog on a lead.*
▷ ADJECTIVE **= main**, prime, top, leading, first, head, chief, premier, primary, most important, principal, foremost: *Cossiga's reaction is the lead story in the Italian press.*
lead off = begin, start, open, set out, kick off *(informal)*, initiate, commence, get going, get under way, inaugurate, start the ball rolling *(informal)*: *Whenever there was a dance he and I led off.*
lead someone on = entice, tempt, lure, mislead, draw on, seduce, deceive, beguile, delude, hoodwink, inveigle, string along *(informal)*: *I bet she led him on, but how could he be so weak?*
lead up to something = introduce,

approach, prepare for, intimate, pave the way for, prepare the way, make advances, make overtures, work round to: *I'm leading up to something quite important.*

leaden ADJECTIVE 1 = **grey**, dingy, overcast, sombre, lacklustre, dark grey, greyish, lustreless, louring *or* lowering: *The weather was bitterly cold, with leaden skies.* 2 = **laboured**, wooden, stiff, sluggish, plodding, stilted, humdrum: *a leaden English translation from the Latin* 3 = **lifeless**, dull, gloomy, dismal, dreary, languid, listless, spiritless: *the leaden boredom of the Victorian marriage* 4 = **heavy**, lead, crushing, oppressive, cumbersome, inert, onerous, burdensome: *The dull, leaden sickly feeling returned.*

leader NOUN = **principal**, president, head, chief, boss *(informal)*, director, manager, chairman, captain, chair, premier, governor, commander, superior, ruler, conductor, controller, counsellor, supervisor, superintendent, big name, big gun *(informal)*, chairwoman, chieftain, bigwig *(informal)*, ringleader, chairperson, big shot *(informal)*, overseer, big cheese *(slang, old-fashioned)*, big noise *(informal)*, big hitter *(informal)*, baas *(S. African)*, torchbearer, number one, sherang *(Austral. & N.Z.)* **OPPOSITE:** follower

leadership NOUN 1 = **authority**, control, influence, command, premiership, captaincy, governance, headship, superintendency: *He praised her leadership during the crisis.*
2 = **guidance**, government, authority, management, administration, direction, supervision, domination, directorship, superintendency: *What most people want to see is determined, decisive action and firm leadership.*

> **QUOTATIONS**
> The art of leadership is saying no, not saying yes. It is very easy to say yes.
> [Tony Blair]

leading ADJECTIVE = **principal**, top, major, main, first, highest, greatest, ruling, chief, prime, key, primary, supreme, most important, outstanding, governing, superior, dominant, foremost, pre-eminent, unsurpassed, number one **OPPOSITE:** minor

leaf NOUN 1 = **frond**, flag, needle, pad, blade, bract, cotyledon, foliole: *The leaves of the horse chestnut had already fallen.* 2 = **page**, sheet, folio: *He flattened the wrappers and put them between the leaves of his book.*
leaf through something = **skim**, glance, scan, browse, look through, dip into, flick through, flip through, thumb through, riffle: *Most patients derive enjoyment from leafing through old picture albums.*
turn over a new leaf = **reform**, change, improve, amend, make a fresh start, begin anew, change your ways, mend your ways: *He realized he was in the wrong and promised to turn over a new leaf.*

leaflet NOUN = **booklet**, notice, advert *(Brit. informal)*, brochure, bill, circular, flyer, tract, pamphlet, handout, mailshot, handbill

leafy ADJECTIVE = **green**, leaved, leafed, shaded, shady, summery, verdant, bosky *(literary)*, springlike, in foliage

league NOUN 1 = **association**, union, alliance, coalition, group, order, band, corporation, combination, partnership, federation, compact, consortium, guild, confederation, fellowship, fraternity, confederacy: *the League of Nations* 2 = **class**, group, level, category, ability group: *Her success has taken her out of my league.*
in league with someone = **collaborating with**, leagued with, allied with, conspiring with, working together with, in cooperation with, in cahoots with *(informal)*, hand in glove with: *He accused the President of being in league with the terrorists.*

leak VERB 1 = **escape**, pass, spill, release, discharge, drip, trickle, ooze, seep, exude, percolate: *The pool's sides had cracked and the water had leaked out.*
2 = **disclose**, tell, reveal, pass on, give away, make public, divulge, let slip, make known, spill the beans *(informal)*, blab *(informal)*, let the cat out of the bag, blow wide open *(slang)*: *He revealed who had leaked a confidential police report.*
▷ NOUN 1 = **leakage**, leaking, discharge, drip, oozing, seepage, percolation: *It's thought a gas leak may have caused the blast.* 2 = **hole**, opening, crack, puncture, aperture, chink, crevice, fissure, perforation: *a leak in the radiator* 3 = **disclosure**, exposé, exposure, admission, revelation, uncovering, betrayal, unearthing, divulgence: *Serious leaks involving national security are likely to be investigated.*

leaky ADJECTIVE = **leaking**, split, cracked, punctured, porous, waterlogged, perforated, holey, not watertight

lean[1] VERB 1 = **bend**, tip, slope, incline, tilt, heel, slant: *He leaned forward to give her a kiss.* 2 = **rest**, prop, be supported, recline, repose: *She was feeling tired and was glad to lean against him.* 3 = **tend**, prefer, favour, incline, be prone to, gravitate, be disposed to, have a propensity to: *Politically, I lean towards the right.*
lean on someone = **depend on**, trust, rely on, cling to, count on, confide in, have faith in: *She leaned on him to help her solve her problems.*

lean[2] ADJECTIVE = **thin**, slim, slender, skinny, angular, trim, spare, gaunt, bony, lanky, wiry, emaciated, scrawny, svelte, lank, rangy, scraggy, macilent *(rare)*: *She watched the tall, lean figure step into the car.* **OPPOSITE:** fat

leaning NOUN = **tendency**, liking for, bias, inclination, taste, bent, disposition, penchant, propensity, aptitude, predilection, proclivity, partiality, proneness

leap VERB 1 = **jump**, spring, bound, bounce, hop, skip, caper, cavort, frisk, gambol: *The newsreels show him leaping into the air.* 2 = **vault**, clear, jump, bound, spring: *He leapt over a wall brandishing a weapon.*
▷ NOUN 1 = **jump**, spring, bound, hop, skip, vault, caper, frisk: *He took Britain's fifth medal with a leap of 2.37 metres.*
2 = **rise**, change, increase, soaring, surge, escalation, upsurge, upswing: *The result has been a giant leap in productivity.*
leap at something = **accept eagerly**, seize on, jump at: *They leapt at the chance of a cheap holiday in Italy.*

learn VERB 1 = **master**, grasp, acquire, pick up, take in, attain, become able, familiarize yourself with: *Their children were going to learn English.* 2 = **discover**, hear, understand, gain knowledge, find out about, become aware, discern, ascertain, come to know, suss (out) *(slang)*: *It was only after his death that she learned of his affair.*
3 = **memorize**, commit to memory, learn by heart, learn by rote, get (something) word-perfect, learn parrot-fashion, get off pat, con *(archaic)*: *He learned this song as an inmate in a Texas prison.*

learned ADJECTIVE = **scholarly**, experienced, lettered, cultured, skilled, expert, academic, intellectual, versed, literate, well-informed, erudite, highbrow, well-read **OPPOSITE:** uneducated

learner NOUN = **student**, pupil, scholar, novice, beginner, trainee, apprentice, disciple, neophyte, tyro **OPPOSITE:** expert

learning NOUN = **knowledge**, study, education, schooling, research, scholarship, tuition, enlightenment

> **QUOTATIONS**
> Much learning doth make thee mad
> [*Bible: Acts*]
>
> The further one goes, the less one knows
> [Lao-tze *Tao Te Ching*]
>
> Try to learn something about everything and everything about something
> [Thomas Henry Huxley *memorial stone*]
>
> Learning without thought is labour lost; thought without learning is perilous
> [Confucius *Analects*]
>
> A little learning is a dangerous thing;
> Drink deep, or taste not the Pierian spring:
> There shallow draughts intoxicate the brain,
> And drinking largely sobers us again
> [Alexander Pope *An Essay on Criticism*]

> That one gets used to everything -
> One gets used to that.
> The usual name for it is
> A learning process
> [Hans Magnus Enzensberger *The Force of Habit*]
>
> The bookful blockhead, ignorantly read,
> With loads of learned lumber in his head
> [Alexander Pope *An Essay on Criticism*]

lease VERB **= hire**, rent, let, loan, charter, rent out, hire out

leash NOUN **1 = lead**, line, restraint, cord, rein, tether: *All dogs should be on a leash.* **2 = restraint**, hold, control, check, curb: *They have kept the company on a tight leash.*
▷ VERB **= tether**, control, secure, restrain, tie up, hold back, fasten: *Make sure your dog is leashed and muzzled.*

least ADJECTIVE **= smallest**, meanest, fewest, minutest, lowest, tiniest, minimum, slightest, minimal: *If you like cheese, go for the ones with the least fat.*
at least = at the minimum, at the very least, not less than: *Aim to have at least half a pint of milk a day.*

leathery ADJECTIVE **= tough**, hard, rough, hardened, rugged, wrinkled, durable, leathern *(archaic)*, coriaceous, leatherlike

1

leave[1] VERB **1 = depart from**, withdraw from, go from, escape from, desert, quit, flee, exit, pull out of, retire from, move out of, disappear from, run away from, forsake, flit *(informal)*, set out from, go away from, hook it *(slang)*, pack your bags *(informal)*, make tracks, abscond from, decamp from, sling your hook *(Brit. slang)*, slope off from, take your leave of, do a bunk from *(Brit. slang)*, take yourself off from *(informal)*: *Just pack your bags and leave; He was not allowed to leave the country.* **OPPOSITE:** arrive
2 = quit, give up, get out of, resign from, drop out of: *He left school with no qualifications.* **3 = give up**, abandon, desert, dump *(informal)*, drop, surrender, ditch *(informal)*, chuck *(informal)*, discard, relinquish, renounce, jilt *(informal)*, cast aside, forbear, leave in the lurch: *He left me for another woman.* **OPPOSITE:** stay with
4 = entrust, commit, delegate, refer, hand over, assign, consign, allot, cede, give over: *For the moment, I leave you to make all the decisions.*
5 = bequeath, will, transfer, endow, transmit, confer, hand down, devise *(Law)*, demise: *He died two years later, leaving everything to his wife.* **6 = forget**, lay down, leave behind, mislay: *I'd left my raincoat in the restaurant.* **7 = cause**, produce, result in, generate, deposit: *Abuse always leaves emotional scars.*
leave off something = stop, end, finish, give up, cease, halt, break off, refrain from, abstain from, discontinue, knock off *(informal)*, give over *(informal)*, kick *(informal)*, desist, keep off, belay *(Nautical)*: *We all left off eating and stood about with bowed heads.*
leave something or **someone out = omit**, exclude, miss out, forget, except, reject, ignore, overlook, neglect, skip, disregard, bar, cast aside, count out: *If you prefer mild flavours, leave out the chilli.*

leave[2] NOUN **1 = holiday**, break, vacation, time off, sabbatical, leave of absence, furlough, schoolie *(Austral.)*, accumulated day off or ADO *(Austral.)*: *Why don't you take a few days' leave?*
2 = permission, freedom, sanction, liberty, concession, consent, allowance, warrant, authorization, dispensation: *an application for leave to appeal against the judge's order*
OPPOSITE: refusal **3 = departure**, parting, withdrawal, goodbye, farewell, retirement, leave-taking, adieu, valediction: *He thanked them for the pleasure of their company and took his leave.* **OPPOSITE:** arrival

leave-taking NOUN **= departure**, going, leaving, parting, goodbye, farewell, valediction, sendoff *(informal)*

lecherous ADJECTIVE **= lustful**, randy *(informal, chiefly Brit.)*, raunchy *(slang)*, lewd, wanton, carnal, salacious, prurient, lascivious, libidinous, licentious, lubricious *(literary)*, concupiscent, goatish *(archaic, literary)*, unchaste, ruttish
OPPOSITE: puritanical

lechery NOUN **= lustfulness**, lust, licentiousness, salaciousness, sensuality, profligacy, debauchery, prurience, womanizing, carnality, lewdness, wantonness, lasciviousness, libertinism, concupiscence, randiness *(informal, chiefly Brit.)*, leching *(informal)*, rakishness, lubricity, libidinousness, lecherousness

lecture NOUN **1 = talk**, address, speech, lesson, instruction, presentation, discourse, sermon, exposition, harangue, oration, disquisition: *In his lecture he covered an enormous variety of topics.* **2 = telling-off** *(informal)*, rebuke, reprimand, talking-to *(informal)*, heat *(slang, chiefly U.S. & Canad.)*, going-over *(informal)*, wigging *(Brit. slang)*, censure, scolding, chiding, dressing-down *(informal)*, reproof, castigation: *Our captain gave us a stern lecture on safety.*
▷ VERB **1 = talk**, speak, teach, address, discourse, spout, expound, harangue, give a talk, hold forth, expatiate: *She has lectured and taught all over the world.*
2 = tell off *(informal)*, berate, scold, reprimand, carpet *(informal)*, censure, castigate, chide, admonish, tear into *(informal)*, read the riot act, reprove, bawl out *(informal)*, chew out *(U.S. & Canad. informal)*, tear (someone) off a strip *(Brit. informal)*, give a rocket *(Brit. & N.Z. informal)*, give someone a talking-to *(informal)*, give someone a dressing-down *(informal)*, give someone a telling-off *(informal)*: *He used to lecture me about getting too much sun.*

ledge NOUN **= shelf**, step, ridge, projection, mantle, sill

lee NOUN **= shelter**, cover, screen, protection, shadow, shade, shield, refuge

leech NOUN **= parasite**, hanger-on, sycophant, freeloader *(slang)*, sponger *(informal)*, ligger *(slang)*, bloodsucker *(informal)*, quandong *(Austral. slang)*

leer VERB **= grin**, eye, stare, wink, squint, goggle, smirk, drool, gloat, ogle: *men standing around, leering at passing females*
▷ NOUN **= grin**, stare, wink, squint, smirk, drool, gloat, ogle: *When I asked the clerk for my room key, he gave it to me with a leer.*

leery ADJECTIVE **= wary**, cautious, uncertain, suspicious, doubting, careful, shy, sceptical, dubious, unsure, distrustful, on your guard, chary

lees PLURAL NOUN **= sediment**, grounds, refuse, deposit, precipitate, dregs, settlings

leeway NOUN **= room**, play, space, margin, scope, latitude, elbowroom

left ADJECTIVE **1 = left-hand**, port, larboard *(Nautical)*: *She had a pain in her chest, on the left side.* **2 = socialist**, liberal, radical, progressive, left-wing, leftist: *The play offers a new perspective on left politics.*
▸ *related adjectives:* sinister, sinistral

leftover NOUN **= remnant**, leaving, remains, scrap, oddment: *Refrigerate any leftovers.*
▷ ADJECTIVE **= surplus**, remaining, extra, excess, unwanted, unused, uneaten: *Leftover chicken makes a wonderful salad.*

left-wing ADJECTIVE **= socialist**, communist, red *(informal)*, radical, leftist, liberal, revolutionary, militant, Marxist, Bolshevik, Leninist, collectivist, Trotskyite

left-winger NOUN **= socialist**, communist, red *(informal)*, pinko *(derogatory, chiefly U.S.)*, radical, revolutionary, militant, Marxist, Bolshevik, Leninist, Trotskyite

leg NOUN **1 = limb**, member, shank, lower limb, pin *(informal)*, stump *(informal)*: *He was tapping his walking stick against his leg.* **2 = support**, prop, brace, upright: *His ankles were tied to the legs of the chair.* **3 = stage**, part, section, stretch, lap, segment, portion: *The first leg of the journey was by boat.*
a leg up = boost, help, support, push, assistance, helping hand
leg it = run, walk, escape, flee, hurry, run away, make off, make tracks, hotfoot, go on foot, skedaddle *(informal)*: *He was legging it across the field.*
not have a leg to stand on = have no basis, be vulnerable, be undermined, be invalid, be illogical, be defenceless, lack support, be full of holes: *It's only*

The Language of Susan Coolidge

'Susan Coolidge' is the pen-name of Sarah Woolsey (1835–1905). She was born in Cleveland, Ohio and worked as a nurse in the American Civil War, after which she began writing. She is best known for her 'Katy' series of children's books; the first, *What Katy Did* appeared in 1872. In them she describes a large, happy family (the Carrs) modelled on the one she grew up in. As was normal for children's books in the 19th century, there is a strong element of moral instruction in her books, but this is made very palatable by the vitality of her depiction of her characters – their physical energy, acute sensations, and warm feelings.

The most important characters in the Katy books are female – the word *girl* is used four times more often than *boy*, and they are not at all girly; Katy likes to be outdoors, climbs fences, slides down roofs, rages about and fights girls in another school. Animals often figure in Coolidge's descriptions; the noise of a wild game invented by Katy was:

> ...like the bellowing of the bulls of Bashan, the squeaking of pigs, the cackle of turkey-cocks, and the laugh of wild hyenas all at once.

The Carr children learn Bible verses every Sunday, as well as going to church and Sunday school. Dorry is too young to spell correctly, but his letter to Santa Claus requests *a new Bibel* as well as a *Kellidescope*. Thus *the bulls of Bashan* (mentioned in the Old Testament in the Book of Ezekiel) are as much part of their world as pigs and kittens. When Katy is seriously injured, Cousin Helen suggests that her sufferings are *The School of Pain*, in which God will teach her the lessons of *Patience, Cheerfulness, Making the Best of Things, Hopefulness and Neatness*. The importance of these virtues is marked by their capitals. Following this conversation Katy dreams that God helps her read a book:

> ...stooping over her was a great beautiful Face.

Coolidge certainly set out to morally improve her readers – but she also appeals to more earthly instincts. The verbs *love* and *eat* are used with equal frequency in her work. Like later writers such as Enid Blyton and JK Rowling, she provides many detailed descriptions of food:

> The corn-bread and fresh mountain trout and the ham and eggs were savory to the last degree, and the flapjacks... which were eaten with a sauce of melted raspberry jelly, deserved even higher encomium.

Her writing has great warmth, and is full of lively dialogue peppered with exclamation marks, fun, and excitement. Characters frequently express affection; *my darling; my pet; come here and kiss me*, and Coolidge herself, or her narrative persona, also speaks lovingly of the children:

> Clover, a fair, sweet dumpling of a girl; pretty little Phil; poor little Elsie; my poor Katy.

Coolidge's English of course has American features, as regards vocabulary and spelling: *pout* (sulk), *bureau* (chest of drawers), *candy, biscuits* (bread rolls), *sidewalk, I guess, backward, toward, savory, color* etc. In the 19th century, however, *fellow* (often used by Coolidge's characters) had not yet been replaced by *guy* as the common American informal term for *man*, so here her usage is indistinguishable from British English.

The language of a modern American book would differ much more from British English than hers does, because of grammatical differences that have developed since her time. In modern British usage *have you got?; I haven't got* etc are often used when Americans would say *do you have?; I don't have* etc. Coolidge does not use *do* as an auxiliary with *have;* instead she uses older constructions: inversion for questions, as in *Have you a partner?* and the addition of *no* or *not* after the verb for negatives, as in *I have no mother or sister.*

Another divergence between modern American and British grammar is the American preference for the simple past, rather than the perfect tense, for recent actions, eg *Did you have dinner?* instead of *Have you had dinner?* – ie when the question is asked around dinner time. Coolidge uses the perfect tense in such contexts:

> What sort of a day have you had, little daughter?

my word against his, so I don't have a leg to stand on.
on its *or* **your last legs = worn out**, dying, failing, exhausted, giving up the ghost, at death's door, about to collapse, about to fail, about to break down: *By the mid-1980s the copper industry in the US was on its last legs.*
pull someone's leg = tease, joke, trick, fool, kid *(informal)*, have (someone) on, rag, rib *(informal)*, wind up *(Brit. slang)*, deceive, hoax, make fun of, poke fun at, twit, chaff, lead up the garden path, jerk *or* yank someone's chain *(informal)*: *Of course I won't tell them; I was only pulling your leg.*
shake a leg = hurry, rush, move it, hasten, get cracking *(informal)*, get a move on *(informal)*, look lively *(informal)*, stir your stumps *(informal)*: *Come on, shake a leg! We've got loads to do today.*
stretch your legs = take a walk, exercise, stroll, promenade, move about, go for a walk, take the air: *Take regular breaks to stretch your legs.*

legacy NOUN **= bequest**, inheritance, endowment, gift, estate, devise *(Law)*, heirloom

legal ADJECTIVE **1 = judicial**, judiciary, forensic, juridical, jurisdictive: *the British legal system* **2 = lawful**, allowed, sanctioned, constitutional, proper, valid, legitimate, authorized, rightful, permissible, legalized, allowable, within the law, licit: *What I did was perfectly legal.*

legalistic ADJECTIVE **= hairsplitting**, narrow, strict, contentious, literal, narrow-minded, polemical, litigious, disputatious

legality NOUN **= lawfulness**, validity, legitimacy, accordance with the law, permissibility, rightfulness, admissibleness

legalize *or* **legalise** VERB **= permit**, allow, approve, sanction, license, legitimate, authorize, validate, legitimize, make legal, decriminalize

legal tender NOUN **= currency**, money, medium, payment, specie

legend NOUN **1 = myth**, story, tale, fiction, narrative, saga, fable, folk tale, urban myth, urban legend, folk story: *the legends of ancient Greece* **2 = celebrity**, star, phenomenon, genius, spectacle, wonder, big name, marvel, prodigy, luminary, celeb *(informal)*, megastar *(informal)*: *the blues legend, B.B. King* **3 = inscription**, title, caption, device, device, motto, rubric: *a banner bearing the following legend*

legendary ADJECTIVE **1 = famous**, celebrated, well-known, acclaimed, renowned, famed, immortal, illustrious: *His political skill is legendary.* **OPPOSITE:** unknown **2 = mythical**, fabled, traditional, romantic, fabulous, fanciful, fictitious, storybook, apocryphal: *The hill is supposed to be the resting place of the legendary King Lud.* **OPPOSITE:** factual

legible ADJECTIVE **= readable**, clear, plain, bold, neat, distinct, easy to read, easily read, decipherable

legion NOUN **1 = army**, company, force, division, troop, brigade: *The last of the Roman legions left Britain in AD 410.* **2 = multitude**, host, mass, drove, number, horde, myriad, throng: *His sense of humour won him a legion of friends.*
▷ ADJECTIVE **= very many**, numerous, countless, myriad, numberless, multitudinous: *Books on this subject are legion.*

legislate VERB **= make laws**, establish laws, prescribe, enact laws, pass laws, ordain, codify laws, put laws in force

legislation NOUN **1 = law**, act, ruling, rule, bill, measure, regulation, charter, statute: *legislation to protect women's rights* **2 = lawmaking**, regulation, prescription, enactment, codification: *This can be put right through positive legislation.*

legislative ADJECTIVE **= law-making**, parliamentary, congressional, judicial, ordaining, law-giving, juridical, jurisdictive

legislator NOUN **= lawmaker**, parliamentarian, lawgiver

legislature NOUN **= parliament**, house, congress, diet, senate, assembly, chamber, law-making body

legitimate ADJECTIVE **1 = lawful**, real, true, legal, acknowledged, sanctioned, genuine, proper, authentic, statutory, authorized, rightful, kosher *(informal)*, dinkum *(Austral. & N.Z. informal)*, legit *(slang)*, licit: *They have demanded the restoration of the legitimate government.* **OPPOSITE:** unlawful **2 = reasonable**, just, correct, sensible, valid, warranted, logical, justifiable, well-founded, admissible: *That's a perfectly legitimate fear.* **OPPOSITE:** unreasonable
▷ VERB **= legitimize**, allow, permit, sanction, authorize, legalize, give the green light to, legitimatize, pronounce lawful: *We want to legitimate this process by passing a law.*

legitimize *or* **legitimise** VERB **= legalize**, permit, sanction, legitimate, authorize, give the green light to, pronounce lawful

leisure NOUN **= spare time**, free time, rest, holiday, quiet, ease, retirement, relaxation, vacation, recreation, time off, breathing space, spare moments: *I was working constantly, with little or no leisure.* **OPPOSITE:** work
at one's leisure = in your own (good) time, in due course, at your convenience, unhurriedly, when it suits you, without hurry, at an unhurried pace, when you get round to it *(informal)*: *He could read through all the national papers at his leisure.*

> **QUOTATIONS**
> All intellectual improvement arises from leisure
> [Dr. Johnson]
>
> Leisure contains the future, it is the new horizon
> [Henri Lefebvre *Everyday Life in the Modern World*]

leisurely ADJECTIVE **= unhurried**, relaxed, slow, easy, comfortable, gentle, lazy, laid-back *(informal)*, restful: *Lunch was a leisurely affair.* **OPPOSITE:** hurried
▷ ADVERB **= unhurriedly**, slowly, easily, comfortably, lazily, at your leisure, at your convenience, lingeringly, indolently, without haste: *We walked leisurely into the hotel.* **OPPOSITE:** hurriedly

lekker ADJECTIVE **= delicious**, tasty, luscious, choice, savoury, palatable, dainty, delectable, mouthwatering, yummy *(slang)*, scrumptious *(informal)*, appetizing, toothsome, ambrosial, yummo *(Austral. slang)*

lemon NOUN
▶ *related adjectives:* citric, citrine, citrous

lend VERB **1 = loan**, advance, sub *(Brit. informal)*, accommodate one with: *I lent him ten pounds to go to the pictures.* **2 = give**, provide, add, present, supply, grant, afford, contribute, hand out,

ARTHURIAN LEGEND

Characters in Arthurian legend

Arthur, Bedivere, Bors, Caradoc, Elaine, Galahad, Gareth (of Orkney), Gawain *or* Gawayne, Guinevere, Igraine, Lancelot *or* Launcelot du Lac, Launfal, Merlin, Modred, Morgan Le Fay, Nimue, Parsifal *or* Perceval, Tristan *or* Tristram, Uther Pendragon, Viviane *or* the Lady of the Lake

Places in Arthurian legend

Astolat, Avalon, Camelot, Glastonbury, Lyonnesse, Tintagel

furnish, confer, bestow, impart: *He attended the news conference to lend his support.*
lend itself to something = be appropriate for, suit, be suitable for, fit, be appropriate to, be adaptable to, present opportunities of, be serviceable for: *The room itself lends itself well to summer eating with its light airy atmosphere.*

> QUOTATIONS
> Neither a borrower nor a lender be
> [William Shakespeare *Hamlet*]

length NOUN **1 = distance**, reach, measure, extent, span, longitude: *It is about a metre in length.* **2 = duration**, term, period, space, stretch, span, expanse: *His film is over two hours in length.* **3 = piece**, measure, section, segment, portion: *a 30ft length of rope* **4 = lengthiness**, extent, elongation, wordiness, verbosity, prolixity, long-windedness, extensiveness, protractedness: *I hope the length of this letter will make up for my not having written earlier.*
at length 1 = at last, finally, eventually, in time, in the end, at long last: *At length, my father went into the house.* **2 = for a long time**, completely, fully, thoroughly, for hours, in detail, for ages, in depth, to the full, exhaustively, interminably: *They spoke at length, reviewing the entire incident.*

lengthen VERB **1 = extend**, continue, increase, stretch, expand, elongate, make longer: *The runway had to be lengthened.* OPPOSITE: shorten **2 = protract**, extend, prolong, draw out, spin out, make longer: *They want to lengthen the school day.* OPPOSITE: cut down

lengthy ADJECTIVE **1 = protracted**, long, prolonged, very long, tedious, lengthened, diffuse, drawn-out, interminable, long-winded, long-drawn-out, overlong, verbose, prolix: *the lengthy process of filling out forms* **2 = very long**, rambling, interminable, long-winded, wordy, discursive, extended, overlong, verbose, prolix: *a lengthy article in the newspaper* OPPOSITE: brief

leniency *or* **lenience** NOUN **= mercy**, compassion, clemency, quarter, pity, tolerance, indulgence, tenderness, moderation, gentleness, forbearance, mildness, lenity

lenient ADJECTIVE **= merciful**, sparing, gentle, forgiving, kind, tender, mild, tolerant, compassionate, clement, indulgent, forbearing
OPPOSITE: severe

leper NOUN **= outcast**, reject, untouchable, pariah, lazar *(archaic)*

lesbian ADJECTIVE **= homosexual**, gay, les *(slang)*, butch *(slang)*, sapphic, lesbo *(slang)*, tribadic: *Many of her best friends were lesbian.*
▷ NOUN **= lezzie** *(slang)*, les *(slang)*, butch *(slang)*, lesbo *(slang)*: *a youth group for lesbians, gays and bisexuals*

lesion NOUN **= injury**, hurt, wound, bruise, trauma *(Pathology)*, sore, impairment, abrasion, contusion

less ADJECTIVE **= smaller**, shorter, slighter, not so much: *Eat less fat to reduce the risk of heart disease.*
▷ ADVERB **= to a smaller extent**, little, barely, not much, not so much, meagrely: *We are eating more and exercising less.*
▷ PREPOSITION **= minus**, without, lacking, excepting, subtracting: *Company car drivers will pay ten percent, less tax.*

> QUOTATIONS
> Less is more
> [Ludwig Mies van der Rohe]

> USAGE
> *Less* should not be confused with *fewer*. *Less* refers strictly only to quantity and not to number: *there is less water than before*. *Fewer* means smaller in number: *there are fewer people than before*.

lessen VERB **1 = reduce**, lower, diminish, decrease, relax, ease, narrow, moderate, dial down, weaken, erode, impair, degrade, minimize, curtail, lighten, wind down, abridge, de-escalate: *Keep immunisations up to date to lessen the risk of serious illness.* OPPOSITE: increase **2 = grow less**, diminish, decrease, contract, ease, weaken, shrink, slow down, dwindle, lighten, wind down, die down, abate, slacken: *The attention she gives him will certainly lessen once the baby is born.*

lesser ADJECTIVE **= lower**, slighter, secondary, subsidiary, subordinate, inferior, less important
OPPOSITE: greater

lesson NOUN **1 = class**, schooling, period, teaching, coaching, session, instruction, lecture, seminar, tutoring, tutorial: *She took piano lessons.* **2 = example**, warning, model, message, moral, deterrent, precept, exemplar: *There is one lesson to be learned from this crisis.* **3 = exercise**, reading, practice, task, lecture, drill, assignment, homework, recitation: *Now let's look at lesson one.* **4 = Bible reading**, reading, text, Bible passage, Scripture passage: *The Rev. Nicola Judd read the lesson.*

let VERB **1 = enable**, make, allow, cause, grant, permit: *They let him talk.* **2 = allow**, grant, permit, warrant, authorize, give the go-ahead, give permission, suffer *(archaic)*, give the green light, give leave, give the O.K. *or* okay *(informal)*: *Mum didn't let us have sweets very often.* **3 = lease**, hire, rent, rent out, hire out, sublease: *The reasons for letting a house, or part of one, are varied.*
let on 1 = reveal, disclose, say, tell, admit, give away, divulge, let slip, make known, let the cat out of the bag *(informal)*: *He knows who the culprit is, but he is not letting on.* **2 = pretend**, make out, feign, simulate, affect, profess, counterfeit, make believe, dissemble, dissimulate: *He's been knocking on doors, letting on he's selling encyclopedias.*
let someone down = disappoint, fail, abandon, desert, disillusion, fall short, leave stranded, leave in the lurch, disenchant, dissatisfy: *Don't worry, I won't let you down.*
let someone off = excuse, release, discharge, pardon, spare, forgive, exempt, dispense, exonerate, absolve, grant an amnesty to: *The police let him off with a warning.*
let something down = deflate, empty, exhaust, flatten, puncture: *I let the tyres down on his car.*
let something off 1 = fire, explode, set off, discharge, detonate: *He had let off fireworks to celebrate the Revolution.* **2 = emit**, release, leak, exude, give off: *They must do it without letting off any fumes.*
let something out 1 = release, discharge: *He let out his breath in a long sigh.* **2 = emit**, make, produce, give vent to: *When she saw him, she let out a cry of horror.* **3 = reveal**, tell, make known, let slip, leak, disclose, betray, let fall, take the wraps off: *She let out that she had seen him the night before.*
let something *or* **someone in = admit**, include, receive, welcome, greet, take in, incorporate, give access to, allow to enter: *The lattice-work lets in air, but not light.*
let up = stop, diminish, decrease, subside, relax, ease (up), moderate, lessen, abate, slacken: *The rain had let up.*

> PROVERBS
> *Let sleeping dogs lie*

letdown NOUN **= disappointment**, disillusionment, frustration, anticlimax, setback, washout *(informal)*, comedown *(informal)*, disgruntlement

lethal ADJECTIVE **= deadly**, terminal, fatal, deathly, dangerous, devastating, destructive, mortal, murderous, poisonous, virulent, pernicious, noxious, baneful
OPPOSITE: harmless

lethargic ADJECTIVE **= sluggish**, slow, lazy, sleepy, heavy, dull, indifferent, debilitated, inactive, inert, languid, apathetic, drowsy, listless, comatose, stupefied, unenthusiastic, somnolent, torpid, slothful, enervated, unenergetic
OPPOSITE: energetic

lethargy NOUN **= sluggishness**, inertia, inaction, slowness, indifference, apathy, sloth, stupor, drowsiness, dullness, torpor, sleepiness, lassitude, languor, listlessness, torpidity, hebetude *(rare)*
OPPOSITE: energy

letter NOUN **1 = message**, line, answer, note, reply, communication, dispatch, acknowledgment, billet *(archaic)*, missive, epistle, e-mail: *I had received a letter from a very close friend.* **2 = character**, mark, sign, symbol: *the letters of the alphabet*
to the letter = precisely, strictly, literally, exactly, faithfully,

accurately, word for word, punctiliously: *She obeyed his instructions to the letter.*
▸ *related adjective:* epistolary

> **QUOTATIONS**
> Sir, more than kisses, letters mingle souls
> [John Donne *To Sir Henry Wotton*]
>
> All letters, methinks, should be free and easy as one's discourse, not studied as an oration, not made up of hard words like a charm
> [Dorothy Osborne *Letter to William Temple*]
>
> I have made this [letter] longer than usual, only because I have not had the time to make it shorter
> [Blaise Pascal *Lettres Provinciales*]

letters PLURAL NOUN = **learning**, education, culture, literature, humanities, scholarship, erudition, belles-lettres: *bon viveur, man of letters and long-time party supporter*

let-up NOUN = **lessening**, break, pause, interval, recess, respite, lull, cessation, remission, breathing space, slackening, abatement

level NOUN **1 = position**, standard, degree, grade, standing, stage, rank, status: *in order according to their level of difficulty* **2 = height**, altitude, elevation, vertical position: *The water came up to her chin and the bubbles were at eye level.* **3 = flat surface**, plane, horizontal: *The horse showed good form on the level.*
▷ ADJECTIVE **1 = equal**, in line, aligned, balanced, on a line, at the same height: *She knelt down so that their eyes were level.* **2 = horizontal**, even, flat, plane, smooth, uniform, as flat as a pancake: *a plateau of level ground* **OPPOSITE:** slanted **3 = even**, tied, equal, drawn, neck and neck, all square, level pegging: *The teams were level at the end of extra time.*
▷ VERB **1 = equalize**, balance, even up: *He got two goals to level the score.* **2 = destroy**, devastate, wreck, demolish, flatten, knock down, pull down, tear down, bulldoze, raze, lay waste to, kennet *(Austral. slang)*, jeff *(Austral. slang)*: *Further tremors could level yet more buildings.* **OPPOSITE:** build **3 = direct**, point, turn, train, aim, focus, beam: *The soldiers level guns at each other along the border.* **4 = flatten**, plane, smooth, make flat, even off *or* out: *He'd been levelling off the ground before putting up the shed.*
level with someone = be honest, be open, be frank, come clean *(informal)*, be straightforward, be up front *(slang)*, be above board, keep nothing back: *Levelling with you, I was in two minds before this happened.*
on the level = honest, genuine, sincere, open, straight, fair, square, straightforward, up front *(slang)*, dinkum *(Austral. & N.Z. informal)*, above board: *There were moments where you wondered if anyone was on the level.*

level-headed ADJECTIVE **= calm**, balanced, reasonable, composed, together *(slang)*, cool, collected, steady, sensible, sane, dependable, unflappable *(informal)*, self-possessed, even-tempered, grounded

lever NOUN **= handle**, bar, crowbar, jemmy, handspike: *Robert leaned lightly on the lever and the rock groaned.*
▷ VERB **= prise**, move, force, raise, pry *(U.S.)*, jemmy: *Neighbours eventually levered the door open with a crowbar.*

leverage NOUN **1 = influence**, authority, pull *(informal)*, weight, rank, clout *(informal)*, purchasing power, ascendancy: *His position affords him the leverage to get things done through committees.* **2 = force**, hold, pull, strength, grip, grasp: *The spade and fork have longer shafts, providing better leverage.*

leviathan NOUN **= monster**, whale, mammoth, Titan, hulk, colossus, behemoth

levy NOUN **= tax**, fee, toll, tariff, duty, assessment, excise, imposition, impost, exaction: *an annual motorway levy on all drivers*
▷ VERB **= impose**, charge, tax, collect, gather, demand, exact: *Taxes should not be levied without the authority of Parliament.*

lewd ADJECTIVE **= indecent**, obscene, vulgar, dirty, blue, loose, vile, pornographic, wicked, wanton, X-rated *(informal)*, profligate, bawdy, salacious, impure, lascivious, smutty, lustful, libidinous, licentious, unchaste

lexicon NOUN **= vocabulary**, dictionary, glossary, word list, wordbook

liabilities PLURAL NOUN **= debts**, expenditure, debit, arrears, obligations, accounts payable: *The company had liabilities of $250 million.*

liability NOUN **1 = disadvantage**, burden, drawback, inconvenience, drag, handicap, minus *(informal)*, nuisance, impediment, albatross, hindrance, millstone, encumbrance: *What was once a vote-catching policy is now a political liability.* **2 = responsibility**, accountability, culpability, obligation, onus, answerability: *They admit liability, but dispute the amount of his claim.*

liable ADJECTIVE **1 = likely**, tending, inclined, disposed, prone, apt: *Only a small number are liable to harm themselves or others.* **2 = vulnerable**, subject, exposed, prone, susceptible, open, at risk of: *These women are particularly liable to depression.* **3 = responsible**, accountable, amenable, answerable, bound, obligated, chargeable: *The airline's insurer is liable for damages.*

> **USAGE**
> In the past, it was considered incorrect to use *liable* to mean 'probable' or 'likely', as in *it's liable to happen soon*. However, this usage is now generally considered acceptable.

liaise VERB **= communicate**, link up, connect, intermediate, mediate, interchange, hook up, keep contact

liaison NOUN **1 = contact**, communication, connection, interchange: *Liaison between the police and the art world is vital to combat art crime.* **2 = intermediary**, contact, hook-up, go-between: *She acts as a liaison between patients and staff.* **3 = affair**, romance, intrigue, fling, love affair, amour, entanglement, illicit romance: *She embarked on a series of sexual liaisons with society figures.*

liar NOUN **= falsifier**, storyteller *(informal)*, perjurer, fibber, fabricator, prevaricator

> **QUOTATIONS**
> A liar should have a good memory
> [Quintilian *Institutio Oratoria*]

libel NOUN **= defamation**, slander, misrepresentation, denigration, smear, calumny, vituperation, obloquy, aspersion: *He sued them for libel over the remarks.*
▷ VERB **= defame**, smear, slur, blacken, malign, denigrate, revile, vilify, slander, traduce, derogate, calumniate, drag (someone's) name through the mud: *The newspaper which libelled him had already offered him compensation.*

liberal ADJECTIVE **1 = tolerant**, enlightened, open-minded, permissive, advanced, catholic, humanitarian, right-on *(informal)*, indulgent, easy-going, unbiased, high-minded, broad-minded, unprejudiced, unbigoted, politically correct *or* PC: *She is known to have liberal views on abortion and contraception.* **OPPOSITE:** intolerant **2 = progressive**, radical, reformist, libertarian, advanced, right-on *(informal)*, forward-looking, humanistic, free-thinking, latitudinarian, politically correct *or* PC: *a liberal democracy with a multiparty political system* **OPPOSITE:** conservative **3 = abundant**, generous, handsome, lavish, ample, rich, plentiful, copious, bountiful, profuse, munificent: *She made liberal use of her older sister's make-up and clothes.* **OPPOSITE:** limited **4 = generous**, kind, charitable, extravagant, free-handed, prodigal, altruistic, open-hearted, bountiful, magnanimous, open-handed, unstinting, beneficent, bounteous: *They thanked him for his liberal generosity.* **OPPOSITE:** stingy **5 = flexible**, general, broad, rough, free, loose, lenient, not close, inexact, not strict, not literal: *a liberal translation* **OPPOSITE:** strict

> **QUOTATIONS**
> conservative: a statesman who is enamoured of existing evils, as distinguished from the Liberal, who wishes to replace them with others
> [Ambrose Bierce *The Devil's Dictionary*]

liberalism NOUN **= progressivism**, radicalism, humanitarianism, libertarianism, freethinking, latitudinarianism

QUOTATIONS

By liberalism I don't mean the creed of any party or any century. I mean a generosity of spirit, a tolerance of others, an attempt to comprehend otherness, a commitment to the rule of law, a high ideal of the worth and dignity of man, a repugnance for authoritarianism and a love of freedom
[Alan Paton *Lecture at Yale University*]

liberalize VERB **= relax**, ease, moderate, modify, stretch, soften, broaden, loosen, mitigate, slacken, ameliorate

liberate VERB **= free**, release, rescue, save, deliver, discharge, redeem, let out, set free, let loose, untie, emancipate, unchain, unbind, manumit **OPPOSITE:** imprison

liberator NOUN **= deliverer**, saviour, rescuer, redeemer, freer, emancipator, manumitter

liberty NOUN **1 = independence**, sovereignty, liberation, autonomy, immunity, self-determination, emancipation, self-government, self-rule: *Such a system would be a blow to the liberty of the people.* **2 = freedom**, liberation, redemption, emancipation, deliverance, manumission, enfranchisement, unshackling, unfettering: *Three convictions meant three months' loss of liberty.* **OPPOSITE:** restraint
at liberty 1 = free, escaped, unlimited, at large, not confined, untied, on the loose, unchained, unbound: *There is no confirmation that he is at liberty.* **2 = able**, free, allowed, permitted, entitled, authorized: *I'm not at liberty to say where it is, because the deal hasn't gone through yet.*
take liberties or **a liberty = not show enough respect**, show disrespect, act presumptuously, behave too familiarly, behave impertinently: *She knew she was taking a big liberty in doing this for him without his knowledge.*

QUOTATIONS

I know not what course others may take; but as for me, give me liberty, or give me death!
[Patrick Henry]

Liberty is liberty, not equality or fairness or justice or human happiness or a quiet conscience
[Isaiah Berlin *Two Concepts of Liberty*]

The tree of liberty must be refreshed from time to time with the blood of patriots and tyrants. It is its natural manure
[Thomas Jefferson]

Liberty is precious – so precious that it must be rationed
[Lenin]

Liberty means responsibility. That is why most men dread it
[George Bernard Shaw *Man and Superman*]

Liberty too must be limited in order to be possessed
[Edmund Burke *Letter to the Sheriffs of Bristol*]

The liberty of the individual must be thus far limited; he must not make himself a nuisance to other people
[John Stuart Mill *On Liberty*]

libretto NOUN **= words**, book, lines, text, script, lyrics

licence NOUN **1 = certificate**, document, permit, charter, warrant: *The painting was returned on a temporary import licence.* **2 = permission**, the right, authority, leave, sanction, liberty, privilege, immunity, entitlement, exemption, prerogative, authorization, dispensation, a free hand, carte blanche, blank cheque: *The curfew gave the police licence to hunt people as if they were animals.* **OPPOSITE:** denial **3 = freedom**, creativity, latitude, independence, liberty, deviation, leeway, free rein, looseness: *All that stuff about catching a giant fish was just a bit of poetic licence.* **OPPOSITE:** restraint **4 = laxity**, abandon, disorder, excess, indulgence, anarchy, lawlessness, impropriety, irresponsibility, profligacy, licentiousness, unruliness, immoderation: *a world of licence and corruption* **OPPOSITE:** moderation

license VERB **= permit**, commission, enable, sanction, allow, entitle, warrant, authorize, empower, certify, accredit, give a blank cheque to **OPPOSITE:** forbid

lick VERB **1 = taste**, lap, tongue, touch, wash, brush: *The dog licked the man's hand excitedly.* **2 = beat**, defeat, overcome, best, top, stuff *(slang)*, tank *(slang)*, undo, rout, excel, surpass, outstrip, outdo, trounce, clobber *(slang)*, vanquish, run rings around *(informal)*, wipe the floor with *(informal)*, blow out of the water *(slang)*: *He might be able to lick us all in a fair fight.* **3 = flicker**, touch, flick, dart, ripple, ignite, play over, kindle: *The fire sent its red tongues licking into the hallway.*
▷ NOUN **1 = dab**, little bit, touch, taste, sample, stroke, brush, speck: *It could do with a lick of paint to brighten up its premises.* **2 = pace**, rate, speed, clip *(informal)*: *an athletic cyclist travelling at a fair lick*

licking NOUN **= thrashing**, beating, hiding *(informal)*, whipping, tanning *(slang)*, flogging, spanking, drubbing: *If Dad came home and found us, we could expect a licking.*

lie[1] NOUN **= falsehood**, deceit, fabrication, fib, fiction, invention, deception, untruth, porky *(Brit. slang)*, pork pie *(Brit. slang)*, white lie, falsification, prevarication, falsity, mendacity: *I've had enough of your lies.*
▷ VERB **= fib**, fabricate, invent, misrepresent, falsify, tell a lie, prevaricate, perjure, not tell the truth, equivocate, dissimulate, tell untruths, not speak the truth, say something untrue, forswear yourself: *If asked, he lies about his age.*
give the lie to something = disprove, expose, discredit, contradict, refute, negate, invalidate, rebut, make a nonsense of, prove false, controvert, confute: *This survey gives the lie to the idea that Britain is moving towards economic recovery.*
▸ *related adjective:* mendacious

QUOTATIONS

There is no worse lie than a truth misunderstood by those who hear it
[William James *Varieties of Religious Experience*]

Whoever would lie usefully should lie seldom
[Lord Hervey *Memoirs of the Reign of George II*]

The lie in the soul is a true lie
[Benjamin Jowett *Introduction to his translation of Plato's Republic*]

I can't tell a lie, Pa; you know I can't tell a lie
[George Washington]

The broad mass of a nation.... will more easily fall victim to a big lie than to a small one
[Adolf Hitler *Mein Kampf*]

Every word she writes is a lie, including 'and' and 'the'
[Mary McCarthy (on Lillian Hellman)]

It contains a misleading impression, not a lie. It was being economical with the truth
[Sir Robert Armstrong (during the 'Spycatcher' trial)]

A lie will easily get you out of a scrape, and yet, strangely and beautifully, rapture possesses you when you have taken the scrape and left out the lie
[C.E. Montague *Disenchantment*]

lie[2] VERB **1 = recline**, rest, lounge, couch, sprawl, stretch out, be prone, loll, repose, be prostrate, be supine, be recumbent: *He was lying motionless on his back.* **2 = be placed**, be, rest, exist, extend, be situated: *a newspaper lying on a nearby couch* **3 = be situated**, sit, be located, be positioned: *The islands lie at the southern end of the mountain range.* **4** *(usually with* **in**) **= exist**, be present, consist, dwell, reside, pertain, inhere: *The problem lay in the large amounts spent on defence.* **5 = be buried**, remain, rest, be, be found, belong, be located, be interred, be entombed: *Here lies Catin, son of Magarus.* **6** *(usually with* **on** *or* **upon**) **= weigh**, press, rest, burden, oppress: *The pain of losing his younger brother still lies heavy on his mind.*

liege NOUN **= feudal lord**, master, superior, sovereign, chieftain, overlord, seigneur, suzerain

l

lieu NOUN
in lieu of = instead of, in place of

life NOUN **1 = being**, existence, breath, entity, vitality, animation, viability, sentience: *a newborn baby's first minutes of life* **2 = living things**, creatures, wildlife, organisms, living beings: *Is there life on Mars?* **3 = existence**, being, lifetime, time, days, course, span, duration, continuance: *He spent the last fourteen years of his life in retirement.* **4 = way of life**, situation, conduct, behaviour, life style: *How did you adjust to college life?* **5 = liveliness**, activity, energy, spirit, go *(informal)*, pep, sparkle, vitality, animation, vigour, verve, zest, high spirits, get-up-and-go *(informal)*, oomph *(informal)*, brio, vivacity: *The town itself was full of life and character.* **6 = biography**, story, history, career, profile, confessions, autobiography, memoirs, life story: *It was his aim to write a life of John Paul Jones.* **7 = spirit**, heart, soul, essence, core, lifeblood, moving spirit, vital spark, animating spirit, élan vital *(French)*: *He's sucked the life out of her.* **8 = person**, human, individual, soul, human being, mortal: *a war in which thousands of lives were lost*
▸ *related adjectives*: animate, vital

QUOTATIONS

Life's but a walking shadow, a poor player,
That struts and frets his hour upon the stage,
And then is heard no more; it is a tale
Told by an idiot, full of sound and fury,
Signifying nothing
[William Shakespeare *Macbeth*]

The unexamined life is not worth living
[Socrates]

Life can only be understood backwards; but it must be lived forwards
[Søren Kierkegaard]

Life is a comedy to those that think, and a tragedy to those that feel
[Horace Walpole *Letter to Anne, Countess of Upper Ossory*]

Life is a tragedy when seen in close-up, but a comedy in long-shot
[Charlie Chaplin]

Life is long to the miserable, but short to the happy
[Publilius Syrus *Sententiae*]

The essence of life is statistical improbability on a colossal scale
[Richard Dawkins *The Blind Watchmaker*]

Life exists in the universe only because the carbon atom possesses certain exceptional qualities
[James Jeans *The Mysterious Universe*]

Life is an abnormal business
[Eugène Ionesco *The Rhinoceros*]

Life is fired at us point blank
[José Ortega y Gasset]

There is only one minute in which you are alive, *this minute* – here and now. The only way to live is by accepting each minute as an unrepeatable miracle. Which is exactly what it is – a miracle and unrepeatable
[Storm Jameson]

Look to this day
For it is life, the very life of life
[*The Sufi*]

In the time of your life, live – so that in that wondrous time you shall not add to the misery and sorrow of the world – but shall smile at the infinite delight and mystery of it
[William Saroyan]

Man is born to live, not to prepare for life
[Boris Pasternak *Doctor Zhivago*]

What is life? It is the flash of a firefly in the night. It is the breath of a buffalo in the winter time; it is the little shadow which runs across the grass and loses itself in the sunset
[Crowfoot, a great hunter of the Blackfoot *Last words*]

Oh, what a day-to-day business life is
[Jules Laforgue *Complainte sur certains ennuis*]

Believe me! The secret of reaping the greatest fruitfulness and the greatest enjoyment from life is to live dangerously!
[Friedrich Nietzsche *Die fröhliche Wissenschaft*]

Life is just one damned thing after another
[Frank Ward O'Malley]

Life doesn't imitate art, it imitates bad television
[Woody Allen *Husbands and Wives*]

Lift not the painted veil which those who live
Call Life
[Percy Bysshe Shelley *Sonnet*]

Life is one long process of getting tired
[Samuel Butler *Notebooks*]

There is no wealth but life
[John Ruskin *Unto This Last*]

Every man regards his own life as the New Year's Eve of time
[Jean Paul Richter *Levana*]

Life isn't all beer and skittles
[Thomas Hughes *Tom Brown's Schooldays*]

Life is far too important a thing ever to talk seriously about
[Oscar Wilde *Lady Windermere's Fan*]

The meaning of life is that it stops
[Franz Kafka]

It is the essence of life that it exists for its own sake
[A.N. Whitehead *Nature and Life*]

Old and young, we are all on our last cruise
[Robert Louis Stevenson *Virginibus Puerisque*]

Human life is everywhere a state in which much is to be endured, and little to be enjoyed
[Dr. Johnson *Rasselas*]

'Tis all a chequer-board of nights and days
Where Destiny with men for pieces plays;
Hither and thither moves, and mates, and slays,
And one by one back in the closet lays
[Edward Fitzgerald *The Rubáiyát of Omar Khayyám*]

Life is real! Life is earnest!
And the grave is not its goal;
Dust thou art, to dust returnest,
Was not spoken of the soul
[Henry Wadsworth Longfellow *A Psalm of Life*]

PROVERBS

Life begins at forty

lifeblood NOUN **= animating force**, life, heart, inspiration, guts *(informal)*, essence, stimulus, driving force, vital spark

lifeless ADJECTIVE **1 = dead**, unconscious, extinct, deceased, cold, defunct, inert, inanimate, comatose, out cold, out for the count, insensible, in a faint, insensate, dead to the world *(informal)*: *There was no breathing or pulse and he was lifeless.* **OPPOSITE:** alive **2 = barren**, empty, desert, bare, waste, sterile, unproductive, uninhabited: *They may appear lifeless, but they provide a valuable habitat for plants and animals.* **3 = dull**, cold, flat, hollow, heavy, slow, wooden, stiff, passive, static, pointless, sluggish, lacklustre, lethargic, colourless, listless, torpid, spiritless: *His novels are shallow and lifeless.* **OPPOSITE:** lively

lifelike ADJECTIVE **= realistic**, faithful, authentic, natural, exact, graphic, vivid, photographic, true-to-life, undistorted

lifelong ADJECTIVE **= long-lasting**, enduring, lasting, permanent, constant, lifetime, for life, persistent, long-standing, perennial, deep-rooted, for all your life

lifetime NOUN **= existence**, time, day(s), course, period, span, life span, your natural life, all your born days

lift VERB **1 = raise**, pick up, hoist, draw up, elevate, uplift, heave up, buoy up, raise high, bear aloft, upheave, upraise: *Curious shoppers lifted their children to take a closer look at the parade.* **OPPOSITE:** lower **2 = revoke**, end, remove, withdraw, stop, relax, cancel, terminate, rescind, annul, countermand: *The Commission has urged them to lift their ban on imports.* **OPPOSITE:** impose **3 = exalt**, raise, improve, advance, promote, boost, enhance, upgrade, elevate, dignify,

cheer up, perk up, ameliorate, buoy up: *A brisk walk in the fresh air can lift your mood.* **OPPOSITE:** depress **4 = disappear**, clear, vanish, disperse, dissipate, rise, be dispelled: *The fog had lifted and revealed a warm sunny day.* **5 = steal**, take, copy, appropriate, nick *(slang, chiefly Brit.)*, pocket, pinch *(informal)*, pirate, cabbage *(Brit. slang)*, crib *(informal)*, half-inch *(old-fashioned, slang)*, blag *(slang)*, pilfer, purloin, plagiarize, thieve: *The line could have been lifted from a Woody Allen film.*
▷ NOUN **1 = boost**, encouragement, stimulus, reassurance, uplift, pick-me-up, fillip, shot in the arm *(informal)*, gee-up: *My selection for the team has given me a tremendous lift.* **OPPOSITE:** blow **2 = elevator** *(chiefly U.S.)*, hoist, paternoster: *They took the lift to the fourth floor.* **3 = ride**, run, drive, transport, hitch *(informal)*, car ride: *He had a car and often gave me a lift home.*
lift off = take off, be launched, blast off, take to the air: *The plane lifted off and climbed steeply into the night sky.*

light[1] NOUN **1 = brightness**, illumination, luminosity, luminescence, ray of light, flash of light, shining, glow, blaze, sparkle, glare, gleam, brilliance, glint, lustre, radiance, incandescence, phosphorescence, scintillation, effulgence, lambency, refulgence: *Cracks of light filtered through the shutters.* **OPPOSITE:** dark **2 = lamp**, bulb, torch, candle, flare, beacon, lighthouse, lantern, taper: *You get into the music and lights, and the people around you.* **3 = match**, spark, flame, lighter: *Have you got a light, anybody?* **4 = aspect**, approach, attitude, context, angle, point of view, interpretation, viewpoint, slant, standpoint, vantage point: *He has worked hard to portray New York in a better light.* **5 = understanding**, knowledge, awareness, insight, information, explanation, illustration, enlightenment, comprehension, illumination, elucidation: *At last the light dawned. He was going to get married!* **OPPOSITE:** mystery **6 = daybreak**, morning, dawn, sun, sunrise, sunshine, sunlight, daylight, daytime, sunbeam, morn *(poetic)*, cockcrow, broad day: *Three hours before first light, he gave orders for the evacuation of the camp.*
▷ ADJECTIVE **1 = bright**, brilliant, shining, glowing, sunny, illuminated, luminous, well-lighted, well-lit, lustrous, aglow, well-illuminated: *Her house is light and airy, crisp and clean.* **OPPOSITE:** dark **2 = pale**, fair, faded, blonde, blond, bleached, pastel, light-coloured, whitish, light-toned, light-hued: *The walls are light in colour.* **OPPOSITE:** dark
▷ VERB **1 = illuminate**, light up, brighten, lighten, put on, turn on, clarify, switch on, floodlight, irradiate, illumine, flood with light: *The giant moon lit the road brightly.* **OPPOSITE:** darken **2 = ignite**, inflame, fire, torch, kindle, touch off, set alight, set a match to: *He hunched down to light a cigarette.* **OPPOSITE:** put out
bring something to light = reveal, expose, unveil, show, discover, disclose, show up, uncover, unearth, lay bare: *The truth is unlikely to be brought to light by this enquiry.*
come to light = be revealed, appear, come out, turn up, be discovered, become known, become apparent, be disclosed, transpire: *Nothing about this sum has come to light.*
in the light of something = considering, because of, taking into account, bearing in mind, in view of, taking into consideration, with knowledge of: *In the light of this information, we can now identify a number of issues.*
light up 1 = cheer, shine, blaze, sparkle, animate, brighten, lighten, irradiate: *Sue's face lit up with surprise.* **2 = shine**, flash, beam, blaze, sparkle, flare, glare, gleam, flicker: *a keypad that lights up when you pick up the handset*

> **QUOTATIONS**
> And God said, Let there be light; and there was light
> [Bible: Genesis]

light[2] ADJECTIVE **1 = insubstantial**, thin, delicate, lightweight, easy, slight, portable, buoyant, airy, flimsy, underweight, not heavy, transportable, lightsome, imponderous: *Try to wear light, loose clothes.* **OPPOSITE:** heavy **2 = weak**, soft, gentle, moderate, slight, mild, faint, indistinct: *a light breeze* **OPPOSITE:** strong **3 = crumbly**, loose, sandy, porous, spongy, friable: *light, tropical soils* **OPPOSITE:** hard **4 = digestible**, small, restricted, modest, frugal, not rich, not heavy: *wine and cheese or other light refreshment* **OPPOSITE:** substantial **5 = undemanding**, easy, simple, moderate, manageable, effortless, cushy *(informal)*, untaxing, unexacting: *He was on the training field for some light work yesterday.* **OPPOSITE:** strenuous **6 = insignificant**, small, minute, tiny, slight, petty, trivial, trifling, inconsequential, inconsiderable, unsubstantial: *She confessed her astonishment at her light sentence.* **OPPOSITE:** serious **7 = light-hearted**, pleasing, funny, entertaining, amusing, diverting, witty, trivial, superficial, humorous, gay, trifling, frivolous, unserious: *a light entertainment programme* **OPPOSITE:** serious **8 = carefree**, happy, bright, lively, sunny, cheerful, animated, merry, gay, airy, frivolous, cheery, untroubled, blithe, light-hearted: *to finish on a lighter note* **9 = nimble**, graceful, airy, deft, agile, sprightly, lithe, limber, lissom, light-footed, sylphlike: *the light steps of a ballet dancer* **OPPOSITE:** clumsy **10 = dizzy**, reeling, faint, volatile, giddy, unsteady, light-headed: *Her head felt light, and a serene confidence came over her.*
light on or **upon something 1 = settle**, land, perch, alight: *Her eyes lit on the brandy that he had dropped on the floor.* **2 = come across**, find, discover, encounter, stumble on, hit upon, happen upon: *the kind of thing that philosophers lighted upon.*
light out = run away, escape, depart, make off, abscond, quit, do a runner *(slang)*, scarper *(Brit. slang)*, do a bunk *(Brit. slang)*, fly the coop *(U.S. & Canad. informal)*, skedaddle *(informal)*, take a powder *(U.S. & Canad. slang)*, take it on the lam *(U.S. & Canad. slang)*, do a Skase *(Austral. informal)*: *I lit out of the door and never went back again.*

lighten[1] VERB **= brighten**, flash, shine, illuminate, gleam, light up, irradiate, become light, make bright: *The sky began to lighten.*

lighten[2] VERB **1 = ease**, relieve, alleviate, allay, reduce, facilitate, lessen, mitigate, assuage: *He felt the need to lighten the atmosphere.* **OPPOSITE:** intensify **2 = cheer**, lift, revive, brighten, hearten, perk up, buoy up, gladden, elate: *Here's a little something to lighten your spirits.* **OPPOSITE:** depress **3 = make lighter**, ease, disburden, reduce in weight: *Blending with a food processor lightens the mixture.*

light-headed ADJECTIVE **1 = faint**, dizzy, hazy, giddy, delirious, unsteady, vertiginous, woozy *(informal)*: *Your blood pressure will drop and you may feel light-headed.* **2 = frivolous**, silly, shallow, foolish, superficial, trifling, inane, flippant, flighty, bird-brained *(informal)*, featherbrained, rattlebrained *(slang)*: *a light-headed girl*

light-hearted ADJECTIVE **= carefree**, happy, bright, glad, sunny, cheerful, jolly, merry, upbeat *(informal)*, playful, joyous, joyful, genial, chirpy *(informal)*, jovial, untroubled, gleeful, happy-go-lucky, gay, effervescent, blithe, insouciant, frolicsome, ludic *(literary)*, jocund, blithesome *(literary)* **OPPOSITE:** gloomy

lightly ADVERB **1 = moderately**, thinly, slightly, sparsely, sparingly: *a small and lightly armed UN contingent* **OPPOSITE:** heavily **2 = gently**, softly, slightly, faintly, delicately, gingerly, airily, timidly: *He kissed her lightly on the mouth.* **OPPOSITE:** forcefully **3 = carelessly**, indifferently, breezily, thoughtlessly, flippantly, frivolously, heedlessly, slightingly: *'Once a detective always a detective,' he said lightly.* **OPPOSITE:** seriously **4 = easily**, simply, readily, effortlessly, unthinkingly, without thought, flippantly, heedlessly: *His allegations cannot be dismissed lightly.* **OPPOSITE:** with difficulty

lightweight ADJECTIVE **1 = thin**, fine, delicate, sheer, flimsy, gossamer, diaphanous, filmy, unsubstantial: *lightweight denim* **2 = unimportant**,

L

shallow, trivial, insignificant, slight, petty, worthless, trifling, flimsy, paltry, inconsequential, undemanding, insubstantial, nickel-and-dime (*U.S. slang*), of no account: *Some of the discussion in the book is lightweight and unconvincing.* **OPPOSITE:** significant

like[1] ADJECTIVE **= similar to**, same as, allied to, equivalent to, parallel to, resembling, identical to, alike, corresponding to, comparable to, akin to, approximating, analogous to, cognate to: *She's a great friend; we are like sisters.* **OPPOSITE:** different
▷ NOUN **= equal**, equivalent, parallel, match, twin, counterpart: *We are dealing with an epidemic the like of which we have never seen.* **OPPOSITE:** opposite

PROVERBS
Like breeds like

USAGE
The use of *like* to mean 'such as' was in the past considered undesirable in formal writing, but has now become acceptable, for example in *I enjoy team sports like football and rugby*. However, the common use of *look like* and *seem like* to mean 'look or seem as if' is thought by many people to be incorrect or nonstandard. You might say *it looks as if* (or *as though*) *he's coming*, but it is still wise to avoid *it looks like he's coming*, particularly in formal or written contexts.

like[2] VERB **1 = enjoy**, love, adore (*informal*), delight in, go for, dig (*slang*), relish, savour, revel in, be fond of, be keen on, be partial to, have a preference for, have a weakness for: *He likes baseball.* **OPPOSITE:** dislike **2 = admire**, approve of, appreciate, prize, take to, esteem, cherish, hold dear, take a shine to (*informal*), think well of: *I like the way this book is set out.* **OPPOSITE:** dislike **3 = wish**, want, choose, prefer, desire, select, fancy, care, feel inclined: *Would you like to come back for coffee?*
▷ NOUN (*usually plural*) **= liking**, favourite, preference, cup of tea (*informal*), predilection, partiality: *I know all her likes and dislikes, and her political viewpoints.*

likelihood NOUN **= probability**, chance, possibility, prospect, liability, good chance, strong possibility, reasonableness, likeliness

likely ADJECTIVE **1 = inclined**, disposed, prone, liable, tending, apt: *People are more likely to accept change if they understand it.* **2 = probable**, expected, anticipated, odds-on, on the cards, to be expected: *A 'yes' vote is the likely outcome.* **3 = plausible**, possible, reasonable, credible, feasible, believable, verisimilar: *It's likely that he still loves her.* **4 = appropriate**, promising, pleasing, fit, fair, favourite, qualified, suitable, acceptable, proper, hopeful, agreeable, up-and-coming, befitting: *He seemed a likely candidate to become Prime Minister.*
▷ ADVERB **= probably**, no doubt, presumably, in all probability, like enough (*informal*), doubtlessly, like as not (*informal*): *Very likely he'd told them of his business interest.*

USAGE
When using *likely* as an adverb, it is usual to precede it by another, intensifying, adverb such as *very* or *most*, for example *it will most likely rain*. The use of *likely* as an adverb without an intensifier, for example *it will likely rain*, is considered nonstandard in British English, though it is common in colloquial U.S. English.

like-minded ADJECTIVE **= agreeing**, compatible, harmonious, in harmony, unanimous, in accord, of one mind, of the same mind, en rapport (*French*)

liken VERB **= compare**, match, relate, parallel, equate, juxtapose, mention in the same breath, set beside

likeness NOUN **1 = resemblance**, similarity, correspondence, affinity, similitude: *These stories have a startling likeness to one another.* **2 = portrait**, study, picture, model, image, photograph, copy, counterpart, representation, reproduction, replica, depiction, facsimile, effigy, delineation: *The museum displays wax likenesses of every U.S. president.* **3 = appearance**, form, guise, semblance: *a disservice in the likeness of a favour*

likewise ADVERB **1 = also**, too, as well, further, in addition, moreover, besides, furthermore: *All their attempts were spurned. Similar offers from the right were likewise rejected.* **2 = similarly**, the same, in the same way, in similar fashion, in like manner: *He made donations and encouraged others to do likewise.*

liking NOUN **= fondness**, love, taste, desire, bent, stomach, attraction, weakness, tendency, preference, bias, affection, appreciation, inclination, thirst, affinity, penchant, propensity, soft spot, predilection, partiality, proneness **OPPOSITE:** dislike

lilt NOUN **= rhythm**, intonation, cadence, beat, pitch, swing, sway

limb NOUN **1 = part**, member, arm, leg, wing, extension, extremity, appendage: *She stretched out her cramped limbs.* **2 = branch**, spur, projection, offshoot, bough: *the limb of an enormous leafy tree*

limber ADJECTIVE **= pliant**, flexible, supple, agile, plastic, graceful, elastic, lithe, pliable, lissom(e), loose-jointed, loose-limbed: *He bent at the waist to show how limber his long back was.*
limber up = loosen up, prepare, exercise, warm up, get ready: *The dancers were limbering up at the back of the hall; some exercises to limber up the legs*

limelight NOUN **= publicity**, recognition, fame, the spotlight, attention, prominence, stardom, public eye, public notice, glare of publicity

limit NOUN **1 = end**, bound, ultimate, deadline, utmost, breaking point, termination, extremity, greatest extent, the bitter end, end point, cutoff point, furthest bound: *Her love for him was being tested to its limits.* **2 = boundary**, end, edge, border, extent, pale, confines, frontier, precinct, perimeter, periphery: *the city limits* **3 = limitation**, maximum, restriction, ceiling, restraint: *He outlined the limits of British power.*
▷ VERB **= restrict**, control, check, fix, bound, confine, specify, curb, restrain, ration, hinder, circumscribe, hem in, demarcate, delimit, put a brake on, keep within limits, straiten: *He limited payments on the country's foreign debt.*
the limit = the end, it (*informal*), enough, the last straw, the straw that broke the camel's back: *Really, Mark, you are the limit!*

limitation NOUN **1 = restriction**, control, check, block, curb, restraint, constraint, obstruction, impediment: *There is to be no limitation on the number of opposition parties.* **2 = weakness**, failing, qualification, reservation, defect, disadvantage, flaw, drawback, shortcoming, snag, imperfection: *This drug has one important limitation.*

limited ADJECTIVE **1 = restricted**, controlled, fixed, defined, checked, bounded, confined, curbed, hampered, constrained, finite, circumscribed: *They have a limited amount of time to get their point across.* **OPPOSITE:** unlimited **2 = narrow**, little, small, restricted, slight, inadequate, minimal, insufficient, unsatisfactory, scant: *The shop has a very limited selection.*

limitless ADJECTIVE **= infinite**, endless, unlimited, never-ending, vast, immense, countless, untold, boundless, unending, inexhaustible, undefined, immeasurable, unbounded, numberless, measureless, illimitable, uncalculable

limp[1] VERB **= hobble**, stagger, stumble, shuffle, halt (*archaic*), hop, falter, shamble, totter, dodder, hirple (*Scot.*): *He limped off with a leg injury.*
▷ NOUN **= lameness**, hobble, hirple (*Scot.*): *A stiff knee forced her to walk with a limp.*

limp[2] ADJECTIVE **1 = floppy**, soft, relaxed, loose, flexible, slack, lax, drooping, flabby, limber, pliable, flaccid: *The residue can leave the hair limp and dull looking.* **OPPOSITE:** stiff **2 = weak**, tired, exhausted, worn out, spent, debilitated, lethargic, enervated: *He carried her limp body into the room and laid her on the bed.* **OPPOSITE:** strong

The Language of Willa Cather

Willa Cather (1873–1947) was a journalist, editor, and novelist. She was born into a farming family in Virginia. When she was eight the family moved west to Nebraska. Several of her best-known novels, such as *O Pioneers!* (1913) and *My Ántonia* (1918) are based on the experience of living there. She won the Pulitzer Prize for *One of Ours* (1922), a remarkable book about American soldiers in World War 1.

In the extreme conditions of the prairies, survival depended on practical skills – pioneers needed to know how to build their own houses, till the unbroken land, cook what they grew, and kill rattlesnakes. In Cather's novels about this challenging existence, how people do things and how things are made are of great importance. In *My Ántonia*, Jimmy, the ten-year-old orphan who comes to live in Nebraska with his grandparents, notices every detail of their house: the plaster laid directly on the earth walls, the hard cement floor, the wooden ceiling. *Watch*, *look*, and *see* are frequently used verbs:

> I **watched** Mrs. Shimerda at her work. She took from the oven a coffee-cake which she wanted to keep warm for supper, and wrapped it in a quilt stuffed with feathers. I have seen her put even a roast goose in this quilt to keep it hot.

This thorough observation possibly stems from Cather's work as a journalist, and indeed her cataloguing of details often comes across more as reportage than as evocative description.

On the other hand, as well as observing such practical details, Jimmy looks with fascination at the country surrounding him, the moving, endless expanse of red grass; he feels the wind and the sun and is 'entirely happy'. *Country* is a frequently used noun in Cather's writing; *the country* , as well as its everyday meaning of 'rural areas', as in *boys from the country*; *a day in the country*, also has a more spiritual significance:

> Even Carl, never a very cheerful boy, and considerably darkened by these last two bitter years, loved the **country** on days like this, felt something strong and young and wild come out of it, that laughed at care.

Cather spent much of her adult life in cities, but the noun *city* does not have the positive connotations of *country*. Some of her characters are repelled by city life – a woman in Chicago sees it as *a wilderness*; she is wearied by the *crash and scramble of that big, rich, appetent Western city*.

Nouns relating to the seasons and the weather, such as *winter, summer, sun, wind*, and *snow* are salient in Cather's work. In the extreme climate of the prairies, summer and winter are contrasting worlds: summer a time of warmth, flowers and plenty, winter a time when people are in danger of dying of hunger and cold, and when a dead body needs to be cut loose from the pool of blood that freezes it fast to the ground. In an autumn storm Jimmy hears the ominous sound of coyotes:

> Presently, in one of those sobbing intervals between the blasts, the coyotes tuned up with their whining howl; one, two, three, then all together – to tell us that winter was coming.

The English of Cather's narrative prose is not markedly different from the British English of her time. In describing country life, she necessarily uses local words relating to farming, such as *lariat* and *corral*, and the names of the plants and animals of the prairie, such as *catalpa, smartweed, earth-owl, bull-snake, gopher*, and *possum*. Her characters, of course, use American words such as *drugstore, depot* (station), *station agent* (station master), *sidewalk, recess* (school break), *smart* (clever), *mad* (angry) – but these make up a very small proportion of her total vocabulary. Some non-standard grammar in dialogue is typically American, eg *He ain't mad about nothin', is he?* Cather also records the faulty English of recent immigrants:

> You know I ain't no spy nor nodding, like what dem boys say.

limpid ADJECTIVE **1 = clear**, bright, pure, transparent, translucent, crystal-clear, crystalline, pellucid: *limpid rock-pools* **2 = understandable**, clear, lucid, unambiguous, comprehensible, intelligible, perspicuous: *The speech was a model of its kind – limpid and unaffected.*

line[1] NOUN **1 = stroke**, mark, rule, score, bar, band, channel, dash, scratch, slash, underline, streak, stripe, groove: *Draw a line down the centre of the page.* **2 = wrinkle**, mark, crease, furrow, crow's foot: *He has a large, generous face with deep lines.* **3 = row**, queue, rank, file, series, column, sequence, convoy, procession, crocodile (*Brit.*): *Children clutching empty bowls form a line.* **4 = string**, cable, wire, strand, rope, thread, cord, filament, wisp: *a piece of fishing line* **5 = trajectory**, way, course, track, channel, direction, route, path, axis: *Walk in a straight line.* **6 = outline**, shape, figure, style, cut, features, appearance, profile, silhouette, configuration, contour: *a dress that follows the line of the body* **7 = boundary**, mark, limit, edge, border, frontier, partition, borderline, demarcation: *the California state line* **8 = formation**, front, position, front line, trenches, firing line: *the fortification they called the Maginot Line* **9 = approach**, policy, position, way, course, practice, scheme, method, technique, procedure, tactic, avenue, ideology, course of action: *The government promised to take a hard line on terrorism.* **10 = occupation**, work, calling, interest, business, job, area, trade, department, field, career, activity, bag (*slang*), employment, province, profession, pursuit, forte, vocation, specialization: *What was your father's line of business?* **11 = lineage**, family, breed, succession, race, stock, strain, descent, ancestry, parentage: *We were part of a long line of artists.* **12 = note**, message, letter, memo, report, word, card, e-mail, postcard, text: *My phone doesn't work, so drop me a line.*
▷ VERB **1 = border**, edge, bound, fringe, rank, skirt, verge, rim: *Thousands of people lined the streets as the procession went by.* **2 = mark**, draw, crease, furrow, cut, rule, score, trace, underline, inscribe: *Her face was lined with concern.*
draw the line at something = object to, prohibit, stop short at, set a limit at, put your foot down over: *He declared that he would draw the line at hitting a woman.*
in line for = due for, being considered for, a candidate for, shortlisted for, in the running for, on the short list for, next in succession to: *He must be in line for a place in the Guinness Book of Records.*
in line with = in accord, in agreement, in harmony, in step, in conformity: *This is in line with medical opinion.*
line something up 1 = align, order, range, arrange, sequence, array, regiment, dispose, marshal, straighten, straighten up, put in a line: *He lined the glasses up behind the bar.* **2 = prepare**, schedule, organize, secure, obtain, come up with, assemble, get together, lay on, procure, jack up (*N.Z. informal*): *He's lining up a two-week tour for the New Year.*
line up = queue up, file, fall in, form a queue, form ranks: *The senior leaders lined up behind him in orderly rows.*

line[2] VERB **= fill**, face, cover, reinforce, encase, inlay, interline, ceil: *They line their dens with leaves or grass.*

lineage NOUN **= descent**, family, line, succession, house, stock, birth, breed, pedigree, extraction, ancestry, forebears, progeny, heredity, forefathers, genealogy

lined ADJECTIVE **1 = wrinkled**, worn, furrowed, wizened: *His lined face was that of an old man.* **2 = ruled**, feint: *Take a piece of lined paper.*

lines PLURAL NOUN **= principle**, plan, example, model, pattern, procedure, convention: *so-called autonomous republics based on ethnic lines*

line-up NOUN **= arrangement**, team, row, selection, array

linger VERB **1 = continue**, last, remain, stay, carry on, endure, persist, abide: *The guilty feelings lingered.* **2 = hang on**, last, survive, cling to life, die slowly: *He lingered for weeks in a coma.* **3 = stay**, remain, stop, wait, delay, lag, hang around, idle, dally, loiter, take your time, wait around, dawdle, hang in the air, procrastinate, tarry, drag your feet *or* heels: *Customers are welcome to linger over coffee until midnight.*

lingering ADJECTIVE **= slow**, prolonged, protracted, long-drawn-out, remaining, dragging, persistent: *He died a lingering death.*

lingo NOUN **= language**, jargon, dialect, talk, speech, tongue, idiom, vernacular, patter, cant, patois, argot

link NOUN **1 = connection**, relationship, association, tie-up, affinity, affiliation, vinculum: *the link between smoking and lung cancer* **2 = relationship**, association, tie, bond, connection, attachment, liaison, affinity, affiliation: *They hope to cement close links with Moscow.* **3 = component**, part, piece, division, element, constituent: *Seafood is the first link in a chain of contaminations.*
▷ VERB **1 = associate**, relate, identify, connect, bracket: *Liver cancer is linked to the hepatitis B virus.* **2 = connect**, join, unite, couple, tie, bind, attach, fasten, yoke: *the Channel Tunnel linking Britain and France* **OPPOSITE:** separate

lion NOUN **= hero**, champion, fighter, warrior, conqueror, lionheart, brave person

lip NOUN **1 = edge**, rim, brim, margin, brink, flange: *the lip of the jug* **2 = impudence**, rudeness, insolence, impertinence, sauce (*informal*), cheek (*informal*), effrontery, backchat (*informal*), brass neck (*informal*): *Enough of that lip if you want me to help you!*
pay lip service to something *or* **someone = pretend to support**, support insincerely, support hypocritically
smack *or* **lick your lips = gloat**, drool, slaver: *They licked their lips in anticipation.*
▸ *related adjective:* labial

liquefy VERB **= melt**, dissolve, thaw, liquidize, run, fuse, flux, deliquesce

liquid NOUN **= fluid**, solution, juice, liquor, sap: *Drink plenty of liquid.*
▷ ADJECTIVE **1 = fluid**, running, flowing, wet, melted, thawed, watery, molten, runny, liquefied, aqueous: *Wash in warm water with liquid detergent.* **2 = clear**, bright, brilliant, shining, transparent, translucent, limpid: *a mosaic of liquid cobalts and greens* **3 = smooth**, clear, soft, flowing, sweet, pure, melting, fluent, melodious, mellifluous, dulcet, mellifluent: *He had a deep liquid voice.* **4 = convertible**, disposable, negotiable, realizable: *The bank had sufficient liquid assets to continue operating.*

liquidate VERB **1 = dissolve**, cancel, abolish, terminate, annul: *A unanimous vote was taken to liquidate the company.* **2 = convert to cash**, cash, realize, sell off, sell up: *The company closed down operations and began liquidating its assets.* **3 = kill**, murder, remove, destroy, do in (*slang*), silence, eliminate, take out (*slang*), get rid of, wipe out (*informal*), dispatch, finish off, do away with, blow away (*slang, chiefly U.S.*), annihilate, exterminate, bump off (*slang*), rub out (*U.S. slang*): *They have not hesitated in the past to liquidate their rivals.*

liquor NOUN **1 = alcohol**, drink, spirits, booze (*informal*), grog, hard stuff (*informal*), strong drink, Dutch courage (*informal*), intoxicant, juice (*informal*), hooch *or* hootch (*informal, chiefly U.S. & Canad.*): *The room was filled with cases of liquor.* **2 = juice**, stock, liquid, extract, gravy, infusion, broth: *Drain the oysters and retain the liquor.*

list[1] NOUN **= inventory**, record, listing, series, roll, file, schedule, index, register, catalogue, directory, tally, invoice, syllabus, tabulation, leet (*Scot.*): *There were six names on the list.*
▷ VERB **= itemize**, record, note, enter, file, schedule, index, register, catalogue, write down, enrol, set down, enumerate, note down, tabulate: *The students were asked to list their favourite sports.*

list[2] VERB **= lean**, tip, heel, incline, tilt, cant, heel over, careen: *The ship listed again, and she was thrown back.*
▷ NOUN **= tilt**, leaning, slant, cant: *The ship's list was so strong that she stumbled.*

listen VERB **1 = hear**, attend, pay attention, hark, be attentive, be all ears, lend an ear, hearken (*archaic*), prick up your ears, give ear, keep your ears open, pin back your ears (*informal*): *He spent his time listening to the radio.* **2 = pay attention**, observe, obey, mind, concentrate, heed, take notice, take note of, take heed of, do as you are told, give heed to: *When I asked him to stop, he wouldn't listen.*

listless ADJECTIVE **= languid**, sluggish, lifeless, lethargic, heavy, limp, vacant, indifferent, languishing, inert, apathetic, lymphatic, impassive, supine, indolent, torpid, inattentive, enervated, spiritless, mopish **OPPOSITE:** energetic

litany NOUN **1 = recital**, list, tale, catalogue, account, repetition, refrain, recitation, enumeration: *She listened to the litany of complaints against her client.* **2 = prayer**, petition, invocation, supplication, set words: *She recited a litany in an unknown tongue.*

literacy NOUN **= education**, learning, knowledge, scholarship, cultivation, proficiency, articulacy, ability to read and write, articulateness

literal ADJECTIVE **1 = exact**, close, strict, accurate, faithful, verbatim, word for word: *a literal translation* **2 = unimaginative**, boring, dull, down-to-earth, matter-of-fact, factual, prosaic, colourless, uninspired, prosy: *He is a very literal person.* **3 = actual**, real, true, simple, plain, genuine, gospel, bona fide, unvarnished, unexaggerated: *He was saying no more than the literal truth.*

literally ADVERB **= exactly**, really, closely, actually, simply, plainly, truly, precisely, strictly, faithfully, to the letter, verbatim, word for word

literary ADJECTIVE **= well-read**, lettered, learned, formal, intellectual, scholarly, literate, erudite, bookish

literate ADJECTIVE **= educated**, lettered, learned, cultured, informed, scholarly, cultivated, knowledgeable, well-informed, erudite, well-read

literature NOUN **1 = writings**, letters, compositions, lore, creative writing, written works, belles-lettres: *classic works of literature* **2 = information**, publicity, leaflet, brochure, circular, pamphlet, handout, mailshot, handbill: *I'm sending you literature from two other companies.*

QUOTATIONS

It takes a great deal of history to produce a little literature
[Henry James *Hawthorne*]

Remarks are not literature
[Gloria Steinem *Autobiography of Alice B. Toklas*]

Literature is mostly about having sex and not much about children; life is the other way around
[David Lodge *The British Museum is Falling Down*]

Literature is news that STAYS news
[Ezra Pound *ABC of Reading*]

Literature is a luxury. Fiction is a necessity
[G.K. Chesterton *The Defendant*]

Literature is where I go to explore the highest and lowest places in human society and in the human spirit, where I hope to find not absolute truth but the truth of the tale, of the imagination and of the heart
[Salman Rushdie]

Our American professors like their literature clear and cold and pure and very dead
[Sinclair Lewis *The American Fear of Literature*]

When once the itch of literature comes over a man, nothing can cure it but the scratching of a pen
[Samuel Lover *Handy Andy*]

lithe ADJECTIVE **= supple**, flexible, agile, limber, pliable, pliant, lissom(e), loose-jointed, loose-limbed

litigant NOUN **= claimant**, party, plaintiff, contestant, litigator, disputant

litigation NOUN **= lawsuit**, case, action, process, disputing, prosecution, contending

litigious ADJECTIVE **= contentious**, belligerent, argumentative, quarrelsome, disputatious

litter NOUN **1 = rubbish**, refuse, waste, fragments, junk, debris, shreds, garbage *(chiefly U.S.)*, trash, muck,

LITERARY TERMS

allegory
alliteration
allusion
amphigory
Angry Young Men
anti-hero
antinovel
anti-roman
aphorism
archaism
Augustan
Bakhtinian
bathos
Beat Generation
belles-lettres
belletrist
bibliography
Bildungsroman
black comedy
Bloomsbury group
bodice-ripper
bombast
bowdlerization
Brechtian
bricolage
Byronic
carnivalesque
campus novel
causerie
Celtic Revival
cento
chiller
Ciceronian
classicism
coda
colloquialism
comedy
comedy of manners
commedia dell'arte
conceit
courtly love
cultural materialism
cut-up technique
cyberpunk
death of the author
decadence
deconstruction
denouement
Derridian
dialectic
dialogue
Dickensian
discourse
double entendre
drama
epic
epilogue
epistle
epistolary novel
epitaph
erasure
essay
exegesis
expressionism
fable
fabulist
faction
fantastique
fantasy
feminist theory
festschrift
figure of speech
fin de siècle
foreword
Foucauldian
Futurism
gloss
Gongorism
Gothic
hagiography
Hellenism
hermeneutics
historical novel
historicism
Homeric
Horatian
hudibrastic verse
imagery
interior monologue
intertextuality
invective
Jacobean
Janeite
Johnsonian
journalese
Joycean
Juvenalian
Kafkaesque
kailyard
kenning
kiddy lit
lampoon
Laurentian *or* Lawrentian
legend
literary criticism
littérateur
locus classicus
Lost Generation
magic realism *or* magical realism
marxist theory
maxim
melodrama
metafiction
metalanguage
metanarrative
metaphor
mock-heroic
modernism
motif
myth
mythopoeia
narrative
narratology
narrator
naturalism
new criticism
new historicism
nom de plume
nouveau roman
novel
novelette
novella
onomatopoeia
oxymoron
palindrome
paraphrase
parody
pastiche
pastoral
pathos
picaresque
plagiarism
plot
polemic
pornography
post-colonialism
postmodernism
post-structuralism
post-theory
pot-boiler
queer theory
realism
Restoration comedy
roman
roman à clef
Romanticism
saga
samizdat
satire
science fiction *or* SF
sentimental novel
shopping-and-fucking *or* S & F novel
short story
signifier and signified
simile
sketch
socialist realism
Southern Gothic
splatterpunk
Spoonerism
story
stream of consciousness
structuralism
Sturm und Drang
subplot
subtext
Surrealism
Swiftian
theme
theory
thesis
tragedy
tragicomedy
trope
verse
vignette

detritus, grot *(slang)*: *If you see litter in the corridor, pick it up.* **2 = jumble**, mess, disorder, confusion, scatter, tangle, muddle, clutter, disarray, untidiness: *He pushed aside the litter of books.* **3 = brood**, family, young, offspring, progeny: *a litter of puppies* **4 = bedding**, couch, mulch, floor cover, straw-bed: *The birds scratch through leaf litter on the forest floor.* **5 = stretcher**, palanquin: *The Colonel winced as the porters jolted the litter.*
▷ VERB **1 = clutter**, mess up, clutter up, be scattered about, disorder, disarrange, derange, muss *(U.S. & Canad.)*: *Glass from broken bottles litters the pavement.* **2 = scatter**, spread, shower, strew: *Concrete holiday resorts are littered across the mountainside.*

little ADJECTIVE **1 = not much**, small, insufficient, scant, meagre, sparse, skimpy, measly, hardly any: *I had little money and little free time.* **OPPOSITE:** ample **2 = small**, minute, short, tiny, mini, wee, compact, miniature, dwarf, slender, diminutive, petite, dainty, elfin, bijou, infinitesimal, teeny-weeny, Lilliputian, munchkin *(informal, chiefly U.S.)*, teensy-weensy, pygmy *or* pigmy: *We sat round a little table.* **OPPOSITE:** big **3 = young**, small, junior, infant, immature, undeveloped, babyish: *When I was little, I was hyperactive.* **4 = unimportant**, minor, petty, trivial, trifling, insignificant, negligible, paltry, inconsiderable: *He found himself getting angry over little things.* **OPPOSITE:** important **5 = mean**, base, cheap, petty, narrow-minded, small-minded, illiberal: *I won't play your little mind-games.*
▷ ADVERB **1 = hardly**, barely, not quite, not much, only just, scarcely: *On the way back they spoke very little.* **OPPOSITE:** much **2 = rarely**, seldom, scarcely, not often, infrequently, hardly ever: *We go there very little nowadays.* **OPPOSITE:** always
▷ NOUN **= bit**, touch, spot, trace, hint, dash, particle, fragment, pinch, small amount, dab, trifle, tad *(informal, chiefly U.S.)*, snippet, speck, modicum: *Don't give me too much. Just a little.* **OPPOSITE:** lot
a little = to a small extent, slightly, to some extent, to a certain extent, to a small degree: *I'm getting a little tired of having to correct your mistakes.*

liturgical ADJECTIVE **= ceremonial**, ritual, solemn, sacramental, formal, eucharistic

liturgy NOUN **= ceremony**, service, ritual, services, celebration, formula, worship, rite, sacrament, form of worship

live[1] VERB **1 = dwell**, board, settle, lodge, occupy, abide, inhabit, hang out *(informal)*, stay *(chiefly Scot.)*, reside, have as your home, have your home in: *She has lived here for 10 years.* **2 = exist**, last, prevail, be, have being, breathe, persist, be alive, have life, draw breath, remain alive: *He's got a terrible disease and will not live long.* **3 = survive**, remain alive, feed yourself, get along, make a living, earn a living, make ends meet, subsist, eke out a living, support yourself, maintain yourself: *the last indigenous people to live by hunting* **4 = thrive**, be happy, flourish, prosper, have fun, enjoy life, enjoy yourself, luxuriate, live life to the full, make the most of life: *My friends told me to get out and live a bit.*

live[2] ADJECTIVE **1 = living**, alive, breathing, animate, existent, vital, quick *(archaic)*: *tests on live animals* **2 = active**, connected, switched on, unexploded: *A live bomb had earlier been defused.* **3 = topical**, important, pressing, current, hot, burning, active, vital, controversial, unsettled, prevalent, pertinent: *Directors' remuneration looks set to become a live issue.*
live wire = dynamo, hustler *(U.S. & Canad. slang)*, ball of fire *(informal)*, life and soul of the party, go-getter *(informal)*, self-starter: *My sister's a real live wire, and full of fun.*

livelihood NOUN **= occupation**, work, employment, means, living, job, maintenance, subsistence, bread and butter *(informal)*, sustenance, (means of) support, (source of) income

lively ADJECTIVE **1 = animated**, spirited, quick, keen, active, alert, dynamic, sparkling, vigorous, cheerful, energetic, outgoing, merry, upbeat *(informal)*, brisk, bubbly, nimble, agile, perky, chirpy *(informal)*, sparky, sprightly, vivacious, frisky, gay, alive and kicking, spry, chipper *(informal)*, blithe, full of beans *(informal)*, frolicsome, full of pep *(informal)*, blithesome, bright-eyed and bushy-tailed: *She had a sweet, lively personality.* **OPPOSITE:** dull **2 = busy**, crowded, stirring, buzzing, bustling, moving, eventful: *lively streets full of bars and cafés* **OPPOSITE:** slow **3 = vivid**, strong, striking, bright, exciting, stimulating, bold, colourful, refreshing, forceful, racy, invigorating: *toys made with bright and lively colours* **OPPOSITE:** dull **4 = enthusiastic**, strong, keen, stimulating, eager, formidable, vigorous, animated, weighty: *The newspapers showed a lively interest in European developments.*

liven up VERB **1 = stir**, brighten, hot up *(informal)*, cheer up, perk up, buck up *(informal)*: *He livened up after midnight, relaxing a little.* **2 = cheer up**, animate, rouse, enliven, perk up, brighten up, pep up, buck up *(informal)*, put life into, vitalize, vivify: *How could we decorate the room to liven it up?*

livery NOUN **= costume**, dress, clothing, suit, uniform, attire, garb, regalia, vestments, raiment *(archaic, poetic)*

livid ADJECTIVE **1 = angry**, cross, furious, outraged, mad *(informal)*, boiling, fuming, choked, infuriated, incensed, enraged, exasperated, indignant, incandescent, hot under the collar *(informal)*, fit to be tied *(slang)*, beside yourself, as black as thunder, tooshie *(Austral. slang)*, off the air *(Austral. slang)*: *I am absolutely livid about it.* **OPPOSITE:** delighted **2 = discoloured**, angry, purple, bruised, black-and-blue, contused: *The scarred side of his face was a livid red.*

living NOUN **1 = livelihood**, work, job, maintenance, occupation, subsistence, bread and butter *(informal)*, sustenance, (means of) support, (source of) income: *He earns his living doing all kinds of things.* **2 = lifestyle**, ways, situation, conduct, behaviour, customs, way of life, mode of living: *the stresses of modern living*
▷ ADJECTIVE **1 = alive**, existing, moving, active, vital, breathing, lively, vigorous, animated, animate, alive and kicking, in the land of the living *(informal)*, quick *(archaic)*: *All things, whether living or dead, are believed to influence each other.* **OPPOSITE:** dead **2 = current**, continuing, present, developing, active, contemporary, persisting, ongoing, operative, in use, extant: *a living language* **OPPOSITE:** obsolete

> **QUOTATIONS**
> The living are the dead on holiday
> [Maurice Maeterlinck]

load VERB **1 = fill**, stuff, pack, pile, stack, heap, cram, freight, lade: *The three men had finished loading the truck.* **2 = make ready**, charge, prime, prepare to fire: *I knew how to load and handle a gun.*
▷ NOUN **1 = cargo**, lading, delivery, haul, shipment, batch, freight, bale, consignment: *He drove by with a big load of hay.* **2 = oppression**, charge, pressure, worry, trouble, weight, responsibility, burden, affliction, onus, albatross, millstone, encumbrance, incubus: *High blood pressure imposes an extra load on the heart.*
load someone down = burden, worry, trouble, hamper, oppress, weigh down, saddle with, encumber, snow under: *I'm loaded down with work at the moment.*

loaded ADJECTIVE **1 = laden**, full, charged, filled, weighted, burdened, freighted: *shoppers loaded with bags* **2 = charged**, armed, primed, at the ready, ready to shoot *or* fire: *He turned up on her doorstep with a loaded gun.* **3 = tricky**, charged, sensitive, delicate, manipulative, emotive, insidious, artful, prejudicial, tendentious: *That's a loaded question.* **4 = biased**, weighted, rigged, distorted: *The press is loaded in favour of the government.* **5 = rich**, wealthy, affluent, well off, rolling *(slang)*, flush *(informal)*, well-heeled *(informal)*, well-to-do, moneyed, minted *(Brit. slang)*: *Her new boyfriend's absolutely loaded.*

loaf[1] NOUN **1 = lump**, block, cake, cube, slab: *a loaf of crusty bread* **2 = head**, mind, sense, common sense, block *(informal)*, nous *(Brit. slang)*, chump *(Brit. slang)*, gumption *(Brit. informal)*, noddle *(informal, chiefly Brit.)*: *You've got to use your loaf in this game.*

loaf² VERB **= idle**, hang around, take it easy, lie around, loiter, loll, laze, lounge around, veg out *(slang, chiefly U.S.)*, be indolent: *She studied, and I just loafed around.*

loafer NOUN **= idler**, lounger, bum *(informal)*, piker *(Austral. & N.Z. slang)*, drone *(Brit.)*, shirker, couch potato *(slang)*, time-waster, layabout, skiver *(Brit. slang)*, ne'er-do-well, wastrel, bludger *(Austral. & N.Z. informal)*, lazybones *(informal)*

loan NOUN **= advance**, credit, mortgage, accommodation, allowance, touch *(slang)*, overdraft: *They want to make it easier for people to get a loan.*
▷ VERB **= lend**, allow, credit, advance, accommodate, let out: *They asked us to loan our boat to them.*

loath *or* **loth** ADJECTIVE **= unwilling**, against, opposed, counter, resisting, reluctant, backward, averse, disinclined, indisposed
OPPOSITE: willing

loathe VERB **= hate**, dislike, despise, detest, abhor, abominate, have a strong aversion to, find disgusting, execrate, feel repugnance towards, not be able to bear *or* abide

loathing NOUN **= hatred**, hate, horror, disgust, aversion, revulsion, antipathy, abomination, repulsion, abhorrence, repugnance, odium, detestation, execration

loathsome ADJECTIVE **= hateful**, offensive, nasty, disgusting, horrible, revolting, obscene, vile, obnoxious, repulsive, nauseating, odious, repugnant, abhorrent, abominable, execrable, detestable, yucky *or* yukky *(slang)*, yucko *(Austral. slang)*
OPPOSITE: delightful

lob VERB **= throw**, launch, toss, hurl, lift, pitch, shy *(informal)*, fling, loft

lobby VERB **= campaign**, press, pressure, push, influence, promote, urge, persuade, appeal, petition, pull strings *(Brit. informal)*, exert influence, bring pressure to bear, solicit votes: *Gun control advocates are lobbying hard for new laws.*
▷ NOUN **1 = pressure group**, group, camp, faction, lobbyists, interest group, special-interest group, ginger group, public-interest group *(U.S. & Canad.)*: *Agricultural interests are some of the most powerful lobbies there.*
2 = corridor, hall, passage, entrance, porch, hallway, foyer, passageway, entrance hall, vestibule: *I met her in the lobby of the museum.*

lobola NOUN **= dowry**, portion, marriage settlement, dot *(archaic)*

local ADJECTIVE **1 = community**, district, regional, provincial, parish, neighbourhood, small-town *(chiefly U.S.)*, parochial, parish pump: *I was going to pop up to the local library.*
2 = confined, limited, narrow, restricted: *The blockage caused a local infection.*
▷ NOUN **= resident**, native, inhabitant, character *(informal)*, local yokel *(derogatory)*: *That's what the locals call the place.*

locale NOUN **= site**, place, setting, position, spot, scene, location, venue, locality, locus

locality NOUN **1 = neighbourhood**, area, region, district, vicinity, neck of the woods *(informal)*: *Details of the drinking water quality in your locality can be obtained.* **2 = site**, place, setting, position, spot, scene, location, locale: *Such a locality is popularly referred to as a 'hot spot'.*

localize VERB **= restrict**, limit, contain, concentrate, confine, restrain, circumscribe, delimit: *There was an attempt to localize the benefits of the university's output.*

locate VERB **1 = find**, discover, detect, come across, track down, pinpoint, unearth, pin down, lay your hands on, run to earth *or* ground: *We've simply been unable to locate him.* **2 = place**, put, set, position, seat, site, establish, settle, fix, situate: *It was voted the best city to locate a business.*

location NOUN **= place**, point, setting, position, situation, spot, venue, whereabouts, locus, locale

lock¹ VERB **1 = fasten**, close, secure, shut, bar, seal, bolt, latch, sneck *(dialect)*: *Are you sure you locked the front door?* **2 = unite**, join, link, engage, mesh, clench, entangle, interlock, entwine: *He locked his fingers behind his head.* **3 = embrace**, press, grasp, clutch, hug, enclose, grapple, clasp, encircle: *He locked her in a passionate clinch.*
▷ NOUN **= fastening**, catch, bolt, clasp, padlock: *He heard her key turning in the lock.*
lock someone out = shut out, bar, ban, exclude, keep out, debar, refuse admittance to: *My husband's locked me out.*
lock someone up = imprison, jail, confine, cage, detain, shut up, incarcerate, send down *(informal)*, send to prison, put behind bars: *You're mad. You should be locked up.*

lock² NOUN **= strand**, curl, tuft, tress, ringlet: *She brushed a lock of hair off his forehead.*

lodge NOUN **1 = cabin**, house, shelter, cottage, hut, chalet, gatehouse, hunting lodge: *a ski lodge* **2 = society**, group, club, association, section, wing, chapter, branch, assemblage: *My father would occasionally go to his Masonic lodge.*
▷ VERB **1 = register**, put, place, set, lay, enter, file, deposit, submit, put on record: *He has four weeks in which to lodge an appeal.* **2 = stay**, room, stop *(Brit. informal)*, board, reside, sojourn: *She lodged with a farming family.* **3 = accommodate**, house, shelter, put up, entertain, harbour, quarter, billet: *They questioned me, then lodged me in a children's home.* **4 = stick**, remain, catch, implant, come to rest, become fixed, imbed: *The bullet lodged in the sergeant's leg.*

lodger NOUN **= tenant**, roomer, guest, resident, boarder, paying guest

lodging NOUN *(often plural)* **= accommodation**, rooms, boarding, apartments, quarters, digs *(Brit. informal)*, shelter, residence, dwelling, abode, habitation, bachelor apartment *(Canad.)*

lofty ADJECTIVE **1 = noble**, grand, distinguished, superior, imposing, renowned, elevated, majestic, dignified, stately, sublime, illustrious, exalted: *Amid the chaos, he had lofty aims.* **OPPOSITE:** humble
2 = high, raised, towering, tall, soaring, elevated, sky-high: *a light, lofty apartment* **OPPOSITE:** low
3 = haughty, lordly, proud, arrogant, patronizing, condescending, snooty *(informal)*, disdainful, supercilious, high and mighty *(informal)*, toffee-nosed *(slang, chiefly Brit.)*: *the lofty disdain he often expresses for his profession*
OPPOSITE: modest

l

log NOUN **1 = stump**, block, branch, chunk, trunk, bole, piece of timber: *He dumped the logs on the big stone hearth.*
2 = record, listing, account, register, journal, chart, diary, tally, logbook, daybook, blog *(informal)*: *The complaint was recorded in the ship's log.*
▷ VERB **= record**, report, enter, book, note, register, chart, put down, tally, set down, make a note of: *Details of the crime are logged in the computer.*

loggerhead NOUN
at loggerheads = quarrelling, opposed, feuding, at odds, estranged, in dispute, at each other's throats, at daggers drawn, at enmity

logic NOUN **1 = science of reasoning**, deduction, dialectics, argumentation, ratiocination, syllogistic reasoning: *Students learn philosophy and logic.*
2 = connection, rationale, coherence, relationship, link, chain of thought: *I don't follow the logic of your argument.*
3 = reason, reasoning, sense, good reason, good sense, sound judgment: *The plan was based on sound commercial logic.*

logical ADJECTIVE **1 = rational**, clear, reasoned, reasonable, sound, relevant, consistent, valid, coherent, pertinent, well-organized, cogent, well-reasoned, deducible: *a logical argument* **OPPOSITE:** illogical
2 = reasonable, obvious, sensible, most likely, natural, necessary, wise, plausible, judicious: *There was a logical explanation.* **OPPOSITE:** unlikely

logistics NOUN **= organization**, management, strategy, engineering, plans, masterminding, coordination, orchestration

loiter VERB **= linger**, idle, loaf, saunter, delay, stroll, lag, dally, loll, dawdle, skulk, dilly-dally *(informal)*, hang about *or* around

loll VERB **1 = lounge**, relax, lean, slump, flop, sprawl, loaf, slouch, recline, outspan *(S. African)*: *He lolled back in his comfortable chair.* **2 = droop**, drop, hang, flop, flap, dangle, sag, hang loosely: *his tongue lolling out of the side of his mouth*

lone ADJECTIVE **1 = solitary**, single, separate, one, only, sole, by yourself, unaccompanied: *a lone woman motorist* **2 = isolated**, deserted, remote, secluded, lonesome *(chiefly U.S. & Canad.)*, godforsaken: *a lone tree on a hill*

loneliness NOUN **= solitude**, isolation, desolation, seclusion, aloneness, dreariness, solitariness, forlornness, lonesomeness *(chiefly U.S. & Canad.)*, desertedness

> **QUOTATIONS**
> Alone, alone, all, all alone,
> Alone on a wide wide sea!
> And never a saint took pity on
> My soul in agony
> [Samuel Taylor Coleridge *The Ancient Mariner*]

lonely ADJECTIVE **1 = solitary**, alone, isolated, abandoned, lone, withdrawn, single, estranged, outcast, forsaken, forlorn, destitute, by yourself, lonesome *(chiefly U.S. & Canad.)*, friendless, companionless: *lonely people who just want to talk* **OPPOSITE:** accompanied **2 = desolate**, deserted, remote, isolated, solitary, out-of-the-way, secluded, uninhabited, sequestered, off the beaten track *(informal)*, godforsaken, unfrequented: *dark, lonely streets* **OPPOSITE:** crowded

loner NOUN **= individualist**, outsider, solitary, maverick, hermit, recluse, misanthrope, lone wolf

lonesome ADJECTIVE **= lonely**, deserted, isolated, lone, gloomy, dreary, desolate, forlorn, friendless, cheerless, companionless

long[1] ADJECTIVE **1 = elongated**, extended, stretched, expanded, extensive, lengthy, far-reaching, spread out: *Her legs were long and thin.* **OPPOSITE:** short **2 = prolonged**, slow, dragging, sustained, lengthy, lingering, protracted, interminable, spun out, long-drawn-out: *This is a long film, three hours and seven minutes.* **OPPOSITE:** brief

long[2] VERB **= desire**, want, wish, burn, dream of, pine, hunger, ache, lust, crave, yearn, covet, itch, hanker, set your heart on, eat your heart out over: *He longed for the good old days.*

long-drawn-out ADJECTIVE **= prolonged**, marathon, lengthy, protracted, interminable, spun out, dragged out, overlong, overextended

longing NOUN **= desire**, hope, wish, burning, urge, ambition, hunger, yen *(informal)*, hungering, aspiration, ache, craving, yearning, coveting, itch, thirst, hankering: *He felt a longing for the familiar.* **OPPOSITE:** indifference
▷ ADJECTIVE **= yearning**, anxious, eager, burning, hungry, pining, craving, languishing, ardent, avid, wishful, wistful, desirous: *sharp intakes of breath and longing looks* **OPPOSITE:** indifferent

long-lived ADJECTIVE **= long-lasting**, enduring, full of years, old as Methuselah, longevous

long-standing ADJECTIVE **= established**, fixed, enduring, abiding, long-lasting, long-lived, long-established, time-honoured

long-suffering ADJECTIVE **= uncomplaining**, patient, resigned, forgiving, tolerant, easy-going, stoical, forbearing

long-winded ADJECTIVE **= rambling**, prolonged, lengthy, tedious, diffuse, tiresome, wordy, long-drawn-out, garrulous, discursive, repetitious, overlong, verbose, prolix **OPPOSITE:** brief

look VERB **1 = see**, view, consider, watch, eye, study, check, regard, survey, clock *(Brit. slang)*, examine, observe, stare, glance, gaze, scan, check out *(informal)*, inspect, gape, peep, behold *(archaic)*, goggle, eyeball *(slang)*, scrutinize, ogle, gawp *(Brit. slang)*, gawk, recce *(slang)*, get a load of *(informal)*, take a gander at *(informal)*, rubberneck *(slang)*, take a dekko at *(Brit. slang)*, feast your eyes upon: *She turned to look at him.* **2 = search**, seek, hunt, forage, fossick *(Austral. & N.Z.)*: *Have you looked on the piano?* **3 = consider**, contemplate: *Next term we'll be looking at the Second World War period.* **4 = face**, overlook, front on, give onto: *The terrace looks onto the sea.* **5 = hope**, expect, await, anticipate, reckon on: *We're not looking to make a fortune.* **6 = seem**, appear, display, seem to be, look like, exhibit, manifest, strike you as: *She was looking miserable.*
▷ NOUN **1 = glimpse**, view, glance, observation, review, survey, sight, examination, gaze, inspection, peek, squint *(informal)*, butcher's *(Brit. slang)*, gander *(informal)*, once-over *(informal)*, recce *(slang)*, eyeful *(informal)*, look-see *(slang)*, shufti *(Brit. slang)*: *She took a last look in the mirror.* **2 = appearance**, effect, bearing, face, air, style, fashion, cast, aspect, manner, expression, impression, complexion, guise, countenance, semblance, demeanour, mien *(literary)*: *They've opted for a rustic look in the kitchen.*
look after something *or* **someone = take care of**, mind, watch, protect, tend, guard, nurse, care for, supervise, sit with, attend to, keep an eye on, take charge of: *I love looking after the children.*
look down on *or* **upon someone = disdain**, despise, scorn, sneer at, spurn, hold in contempt, treat with contempt, turn your nose up (at) *(informal)*, contemn *(formal)*, look down your nose at *(informal)*, misprize: *I wasn't successful, so they looked down on me.*
look forward to something = anticipate, expect, look for, wait for, await, hope for, long for, count on, count the days until, set your heart on: *He was looking forward to working with the new Prime Minister.*
look out for something = be careful of, beware, watch out for, pay attention to, be wary of, be alert to, be vigilant about, keep an eye out for, be on guard for, keep your eyes open for, keep your eyes peeled for, keep your eyes skinned for, be on the qui vive for: *What are the symptoms you should look out for?*
look over something = examine, view, check, monitor, scan, check out *(informal)*, inspect, look through, eyeball *(slang)*, work over, flick through, peruse, cast an eye over, take a dekko at *(Brit. slang)*: *He could have looked over the papers in less than ten minutes.*
look someone up = visit, call on, go to see, pay a visit to, drop in on *(informal)*, look in on: *She looked up some friends of bygone years.*
look something up = research, find, search for, hunt for, track down, seek out: *I looked up your name and address in the personnel file.*
look up = improve, develop, advance, pick up, progress, come along, get better, shape up *(informal)*, perk up, ameliorate, show improvement: *Things are looking up in the computer industry.*
look up to someone = respect, honour, admire, esteem, revere, defer to, have a high opinion of, regard highly, think highly of: *A lot of the younger girls look up to you.*

> **PROVERBS**
> *Look before you leap*

lookalike NOUN **= double**, twin, clone, replica, spit *(informal, chiefly Brit.)*, ringer *(slang)*, spitting image *(informal)*, dead ringer *(slang)*, living image, exact match, spit and image *(informal)*

lookout NOUN **1 = watchman**, guard, sentry, sentinel, vedette *(Military)*: *One committed the burglary and the other acted as lookout.* **2 = watch**, guard, vigil, qui vive: *He denied that he had failed to keep a proper lookout during the night.* **3 = watchtower**, post, tower, beacon, observatory, citadel, observation post: *Troops tried to set up a lookout post inside a refugee camp.* **4 = concern**, business, worry, funeral *(informal)*, pigeon *(Brit. informal)*: *It was your lookout if you put your life in danger.*

loom VERB **1 = appear**, emerge, hover, take shape, threaten, bulk, menace, come into view, become visible: *the mountains loomed out of the blackness* **2 = overhang**, rise, mount, dominate, tower, soar, overshadow, hang over, rise up, overtop: *He loomed over me.*

l

loop NOUN **= curve**, ring, circle, bend, twist, curl, spiral, hoop, coil, loophole, twirl, kink, noose, whorl, eyelet, convolution: *She reached for a loop of garden hose.*
▷ VERB **= twist**, turn, join, roll, circle, connect, bend, fold, knot, curl, spiral, coil, braid, encircle, wind round, curve round: *He looped the rope over the wood.*

loophole NOUN **= let-out**, escape, excuse, plea, avoidance, evasion, pretence, pretext, subterfuge, means of escape

loose ADJECTIVE **1 = free**, detached, insecure, unfettered, released, floating, wobbly, unsecured, unrestricted, untied, unattached, movable, unfastened, unbound, unconfined: *A page came loose and floated onto the tiles.* **2 = slack**, easy, hanging, relaxed, loosened, not fitting, sloppy, baggy, slackened, loose-fitting, not tight: *Wear loose clothes as they're more comfortable.* **OPPOSITE:** tight **3 = promiscuous**, fast, abandoned, immoral, dissipated, lewd, wanton, profligate, disreputable, debauched, dissolute, libertine, licentious, unchaste: *casual sex and loose morals* **OPPOSITE:** chaste **4 = vague**, random, inaccurate, disordered, rambling, diffuse, indefinite, disconnected, imprecise, ill-defined, indistinct, inexact: *We came to some sort of loose arrangement before he went home.* **OPPOSITE:** precise
▷ VERB **= free**, release, ease, liberate, detach, unleash, let go, undo, loosen, disconnect, set free, slacken, untie, disengage, unfasten, unbind, unloose, unbridle: *He loosed his grip on the rifle.* **OPPOSITE:** fasten

loosen VERB **= untie**, undo, release, separate, detach, let out, unstick, slacken, unbind, work free, work loose, unloose: *He loosened the scarf around his neck.*
loosen up = relax, chill *(slang)*, soften, unwind, go easy *(informal)*, lighten up *(slang)*, hang loose, outspan *(S. African)*, ease up *or* off: *Relax, smile; loosen up in mind and body.*

loot VERB **= plunder**, rob, raid, sack, rifle, ravage, ransack, pillage, despoil: *Gangs began breaking windows and looting shops.*
▷ NOUN **= plunder**, goods, prize, haul, spoils, booty, swag *(slang)*: *They steal in order to sell their loot for cash.*

lop VERB **= cut**, crop, chop, trim, clip, dock, hack, detach, prune, shorten, sever, curtail, truncate

lope VERB **= stride**, spring, bound, gallop, canter, lollop

lopsided ADJECTIVE **= crooked**, one-sided, tilting, warped, uneven, unequal, disproportionate, squint, unbalanced, off balance, awry, askew, out of shape, asymmetrical, cockeyed, out of true, skewwhiff *(Brit. informal)*

lord NOUN **1 = peer**, nobleman, count, duke, gentleman, earl, noble, baron, aristocrat, viscount, childe *(archaic)*: *She married a lord and lives in a huge house in the country.* **2 = ruler**, leader, chief, king, prince, master, governor, commander, superior, monarch, sovereign, liege, overlord, potentate, seigneur: *It was the home of the powerful lords of Baux.*
lord it over someone = boss around *or* **about** *(informal)*, order around, threaten, bully, menace, intimidate, hector, bluster, browbeat, ride roughshod over, pull rank on, tyrannize, put on airs, be overbearing, act big *(slang)*, overbear, play the lord, domineer: *Alex seemed to enjoy lording it over the three girls.*
the Lord *or* **Our Lord = Jesus Christ**, God, Christ, Messiah, Jehovah, the Almighty, the Galilean, the Good Shepherd, the Nazarene

lore NOUN **= traditions**, sayings, experience, saws, teaching, beliefs, wisdom, doctrine, mythos, folk-wisdom, traditional wisdom

lose VERB **1 = be defeated**, be beaten, lose out, be worsted, come to grief, come a cropper *(informal)*, be the loser, suffer defeat, get the worst of, take a licking *(informal)*, crash out: *The government lost the argument over the pace of reform.* **2 = mislay**, miss, drop, forget, displace, be deprived of, fail to keep, lose track of, suffer loss, misplace: *I lost my keys.* **3 = forfeit**, miss, fail, yield, default, be deprived of, pass up *(informal)*, lose out on *(informal)*: *He lost his licence.* **4 = waste**, consume, squander, drain, exhaust, lavish, deplete, use up, dissipate, expend, misspend: *He stands to lose millions of pounds.* **5 = stray from**, miss, confuse, wander from: *The men lost their way in a sandstorm.* **6 = escape from**, pass, leave behind, evade, lap, duck, dodge, shake off, elude, slip away from, outstrip, throw off, outrun, outdistance, give someone the slip: *I couldn't lose him, but he couldn't overtake.*

loser NOUN **= failure**, flop *(informal)*, underdog, also-ran, no-hoper *(Austral. slang)*, dud *(informal)*, lemon *(slang)*, clinker *(slang, chiefly U.S.)*, washout *(informal)*, non-achiever

> **QUOTATIONS**
> Show me a good loser and I will show you a loser
> [Paul Newman]

loss NOUN **1 = losing**, waste, disappearance, deprivation, squandering, drain, forfeiture: *The loss of income is about £250 million.* **OPPOSITE:** gain **2** *(sometimes plural)* **= deficit**, debt, deficiency, debit, depletion, shrinkage, losings: *The company will cease operating due to continued losses.* **OPPOSITE:** gain **3 = damage**, cost, injury, hurt, harm, disadvantage, detriment, impairment: *His death is a great loss to us.* **OPPOSITE:** advantage
▷ PLURAL NOUN **= casualties**, dead, victims, death toll, fatalities, number killed, number wounded: *Enemy losses were said to be high.*
at a loss = confused, puzzled, baffled, bewildered, stuck *(informal)*, helpless, stumped, perplexed, mystified, nonplussed, at your wits' end: *I was at a loss for what to do next.*

> **PROVERBS**
> *One man's loss is another man's gain*

lost ADJECTIVE **1 = missing**, missed, disappeared, vanished, strayed, wayward, forfeited, misplaced, mislaid: *a lost book* **2 = bewildered**, confused, puzzled, baffled, helpless, ignorant, perplexed, mystified, clueless *(slang)*: *I feel lost and lonely in a strange town alone.* **3 = wasted**, consumed, neglected, misused, squandered, forfeited, dissipated, misdirected, frittered away, misspent, misapplied: *a lost opportunity* **4 = gone**, finished, destroyed, vanished, extinct, defunct, died out: *The sense of community is lost.* **5 = past**, former, gone, dead, forgotten, lapsed, extinct, obsolete, out-of-date, bygone, unremembered: *the relics of a lost civilization* **6 = engrossed**, taken up, absorbed, entranced, abstracted, absent, distracted, preoccupied, immersed, dreamy, rapt, spellbound: *She was silent for a while, lost in thought.* **7 = fallen**, corrupt, depraved, wanton, abandoned, damned, profligate, dissolute, licentious, unchaste, irreclaimable: *without honour, without heart, without religion ... a lost woman*

lot NOUN **1 = bunch** *(informal)*, group, crowd, crew, set, band, quantity, assortment, consignment: *We've just sacked one lot of builders.* **2 = destiny**, situation, circumstances, fortune, chance, accident, fate, portion, doom, hazard, plight: *Young people are usually less contented with their lot.* **3 = share**, group, set, piece, collection, portion, parcel, batch: *The receivers are keen to sell the stores as one lot.*
a lot *or* **lots 1 = plenty**, scores, masses *(informal)*, load(s) *(informal)*, ocean(s), wealth, piles *(informal)*, a great deal, quantities, stack(s), heap(s), a good deal, large amount, abundance, reams *(informal)*, oodles *(informal)*: *A lot of our land is used to grow crops.* **2 = often**, regularly, a great deal, frequently, a good deal: *They went out a lot when they lived in the city.*
draw lots = choose, pick, select, toss up, draw straws *(informal)*, throw dice, spin a coin: *Two names were selected by drawing lots.*
throw in your lot with someone = join with, support, join forces with, make common cause with, align yourself with, ally *or* align yourself with, join fortunes with: *He has decided to throw in his lot with the far-right groups.*

lotion NOUN **= cream**, solution, balm, salve, liniment, embrocation

lottery NOUN **1 = raffle**, draw, lotto *(Brit., N.Z. & S. African)*, sweepstake: *the national lottery* **2 = gamble**, chance, risk, venture, hazard, toss-up *(informal)*: *Which judges are assigned to a case is always a bit of a lottery.*

loud ADJECTIVE **1 = noisy**, strong, booming, roaring, piercing, thundering, forte *(Music)*, turbulent, resounding, deafening, thunderous, rowdy, blaring, strident, boisterous, tumultuous, vociferous, vehement, sonorous, ear-splitting, obstreperous, stentorian, clamorous, ear-piercing, high-sounding: *Suddenly there was a loud bang.* **OPPOSITE:** quiet **2 = garish**, bold, glaring, flamboyant, vulgar, brash, tacky *(informal)*, flashy, lurid, tasteless, naff *(Brit. slang)*, gaudy, tawdry, showy, ostentatious, brassy: *He liked to shock with his gold chains and loud clothes.* **OPPOSITE:** sombre **3 = loud-mouthed**, offensive, crude, coarse, vulgar, brash, crass, raucous, brazen *(informal)*: *I like your manner; loud people are horrible.* **OPPOSITE:** quiet

loudly ADVERB **= noisily**, vigorously, vehemently, vociferously, uproariously, lustily, shrilly, fortissimo *(Music)*, at full volume, deafeningly, at the top of your voice, clamorously

lounge VERB **= relax**, pass time, hang out *(informal)*, idle, loaf, potter, sprawl, lie about, waste time, recline, take it easy, saunter, loiter, loll, dawdle, laze, kill time, make yourself at home, veg out *(slang, chiefly U.S.)*, outspan *(S. African)*, fritter time away: *They ate and drank and lounged in the shade.*
▷ NOUN **= sitting room**, living room, parlour, drawing room, front room, reception room, television room: *They sat before a roaring fire in the lounge.*

louring *or* **lowering** ADJECTIVE **1 = darkening**, threatening, forbidding, menacing, black, heavy, dark, grey, clouded, gloomy, ominous, cloudy, overcast, foreboding: *a heavy, louring sky* **2 = glowering**, forbidding, grim, frowning, brooding, scowling, sullen, surly: *We walked in fear of his lowering temperament.*

lousy ADJECTIVE **1 = inferior**, bad, poor, terrible, awful, no good, miserable, rotten *(informal)*, duff, second-rate, shoddy, low-rent *(informal, chiefly U.S.)*, for the birds *(informal)*, two-bit *(U.S. & Canad. slang)*, slovenly, poxy *(slang)*, dime-a-dozen *(informal)*, bush-league *(Austral. & N.Z. informal)*, not much cop *(Brit. slang)*, tinhorn *(U.S. slang)*, of a sort *or* of sorts, strictly for the birds *(informal)*, bodger *or* bodgie *(Austral. slang)*: *The menu is limited and the food is lousy.* **2 = mean**, low, base, dirty, vicious, rotten *(informal)*, vile, despicable, hateful, contemptible: *This is just lousy, cheap, fraudulent behaviour from the government.* **3** (with **with**) **= well-supplied with**, rolling in *(slang)*, not short of, amply supplied with: *a hotel lousy with fleas*

lout NOUN **= oaf**, boor, bear, ned *(Scot. slang)*, yahoo, hoon *(Austral. & N.Z. slang)*, clod, bumpkin, gawk, dolt, churl, lubber, lummox *(informal)*, clumsy idiot, yob *or* yobbo *(Brit. slang)*, cougan *(Austral. slang)*, scozza *(Austral. slang)*, bogan *(Austral. slang)*

lovable *or* **loveable** ADJECTIVE **= endearing**, attractive, engaging, charming, winning, pleasing, sweet, lovely, fetching *(informal)*, delightful, cute, enchanting, captivating, cuddly, amiable, adorable, winsome, likable *or* likeable **OPPOSITE:** detestable

love VERB **1 = adore**, care for, treasure, cherish, prize, worship, be devoted to, be attached to, be in love with, dote on, hold dear, think the world of, idolize, feel affection for, have affection for, adulate: *We love each other, and we want to spend our lives together.* **OPPOSITE:** hate **2 = enjoy**, like, desire, fancy, appreciate, relish, delight in, savour, take pleasure in, have a soft spot for, be partial to, have a weakness for: *We loved the food so much, especially the fish dishes.* **OPPOSITE:** dislike **3 = cuddle**, neck *(informal)*, kiss, pet, embrace, caress, fondle, canoodle *(slang)*: *the loving and talking that marked an earlier stage of the relationship*
▷ NOUN **1 = passion**, liking, regard, friendship, affection, warmth, attachment, intimacy, devotion, tenderness, fondness, rapture, adulation, adoration, infatuation, ardour, endearment, aroha *(N.Z.)*, amity: *Our love for each other has been increased by what we've been through together.* **OPPOSITE:** hatred **2 = liking**, taste, delight in, bent for, weakness for, relish for, enjoyment, devotion to, penchant for, inclination for, zest for, fondness for, soft spot for, partiality to: *a love of literature* **3 = beloved**, dear, dearest, sweet, lover, angel, darling, honey, loved one, sweetheart, truelove, dear one, leman *(archaic)*, inamorata *or* inamorato: *Don't cry, my love.* **OPPOSITE:** enemy **4 = sympathy**, understanding, heart, charity, pity, humanity, warmth, mercy, sorrow, kindness, tenderness, friendliness, condolence, commiseration, fellow feeling, soft-heartedness, tender-heartedness, aroha *(N.Z.)*: *a manifestation of his love for his fellow men*
fall in love with someone = lose your heart to, fall for, be taken with, take a shine to *(informal)*, become infatuated with, fall head over heels in love with, be swept off your feet by, bestow your affections on: *I fell in love with him the moment I saw him.*
for love = without payment, freely, for nothing, free of charge, gratis, pleasurably: *She does it for love – not money.*
for love or money = by any means, ever, under any conditions: *Replacement parts couldn't be found for love or money.*
in love = enamoured, charmed, captivated, smitten, wild *(informal)*, mad *(informal)*, crazy *(informal)*, enthralled, besotted, infatuated, enraptured: *She had never before been in love.*
make love = have sexual intercourse, have sex, go to bed, sleep together, do it *(informal)*, mate, have sexual relations, have it off *(slang)*, have it away *(slang)*: *After six months of friendship, one night, they made love.*
▸ *related adjective:* amatory

QUOTATIONS

How do I love thee? Let me count the ways
[Elizabeth Barrett Browning *Sonnets from the Portuguese*]

All that matters is love and work
[attributed to Sigmund Freud]

Money was scarce but new love has no need of money. Somewhere to go, to be together is all and we were lucky. We had that. Hell is love with no place to go
[Dilys Rose *All the Little Loved Ones*]

To be overtopped in anything else I can bear: but in the tests of generous love I defy all mankind
[Robert Burns *letter to Clarinda*]

Love's pleasure lasts but a moment; love's sorrow lasts all through life
[Jean-Pierre Claris de Florian *Celestine*]

What love is, if thou wouldst be taught,
Thy heart must teach alone -
Two souls with but a single thought,
Two hearts that beat as one
[Friedrich Halm *Der Sohn der Wildnis*]

Love is like the measles; we all have to go through it
[Jerome K. Jerome *The Idle Thoughts of an Idle Fellow*]

Love's like the measles – all the worse when it comes late in life
[Douglas Jerrold *Wit and Opinions of Douglas Jerrold*]

No, there's nothing half so sweet in life
As love's young dream
[Thomas Moore *Love's Young Dream*]

And all for love, and nothing for reward
[Edmund Spenser *The Faerie Queene*]

'Tis better to have loved and lost
Than never to have loved at all
[Alfred, Lord Tennyson *In Memoriam A.H.H.*]

Love means never having to say you're sorry
[Erich Segal *Love Story*]

In the Spring a livelier iris changes on the burnish'd dove;
In the Spring a young man's fancy lightly turns to thoughts of love
[Alfred, Lord Tennyson *Locksley Hall*]

Words for Nationalities in 'The Times' and 'The Sun'

B*ritish* is twice as frequent in *The Times* as in *The Sun*, and it also enters into different combinations. *The Sun* usually uses it to modify nouns denoting people, for example *British woman, British troops,* and *British public. The Times,* while also using phrases like these, additionally uses *British* to describe abstract concepts: *British politics, British history,* and *British society* are much more frequent than in *The Sun.* Furthermore, *The Times* modifies *British* with adverbs such as *quintessentially, uniquely,* and *very* more frequently than *The Sun* does. For example:

> The growers' association insists that the **quintessentially British** vegetable [cauliflower] must be saved. (*The Times*)

The Times also uses *English* about one and a half times more often than *The Sun* does. Both frequently use it with reference to sports (*English football, English club, English player*) but *The Times* makes more references to other aspects of Englishness, notably *English literature* and the *English countryside*. Again, *The Times* more frequently modifies *English* with adverbs such as *typically, painfully, quintessentially,* and *peculiarly*:

> ... his reliance on a **peculiarly English** sense of whimsy. (*The Times*)

Scottish is slightly more frequent in *The Sun,* but the majority of the occurrences are in reference to football, whereas *The Times* more frequently refers to politics (*Scottish parliament,* the *Scottish executive, Scottish minister*), landscape (*Scottish mountains*), and culture (*Scottish university*). It is interesting to note that, whereas one can be *peculiarly* or *typically Scottish* in *The Times,* one is much less likely to be *quintessentially Scottish.* In both newspapers, *Scotch* appears only in set phrases such as *Scotch broth, Scotch egg,* and, of course, *Scotch whisky.*

Irish and *Welsh* are also slightly more frequent in *The Sun* than in *The Times,* again usually in relation to sport. *Tycoon* is a frequent collocate of *Irish* in both newspapers, for example with reference to Sir Anthony O'Reilly and John Magnier. (In fact, *tycoons* in both are more likely to be Irish, American, or Russian than any other nationality.)

American is twice as frequent in *The Times* as in *The Sun.* Most of the occurrences in *The Sun* relate to popular culture (*American star, American charts, American TV*). *The Times,* on the other hand, tends to make references to politics (*American president*), business (*American firm, American economy*), and warfare (*American troops, American soldier*); it also uses the phrase *the American dream* about three times more often.

French is used about one and half times more often in *The Times.* Both newspapers make frequent reference to French sportspeople; additionally, *The Times* uses *French* in phrases relating to history (*French revolution, French resistance*) and cookery (*French cuisine, French chef*), whereas the more salient collocates in *The Sun* relate to holiday-making (*French tourist, French resort*).

The Times more frequently refers to these nationalities with abstract nouns. In particular, *Englishness* is seven times more frequent in *The Times* than in *The Sun*, in examples such as:

> ... a film that brilliantly captures a sense of **Englishness**. (*The Times*)

Britishness and *Irishness* are both twice as frequent in *The Times*, and they are often linked, as in:

> They did not see **Britishness** and **Irishness** as being mutually exclusive. (*The Times*)

Scottishness, Welshness, and *Frenchness* are quite rare in *The Times* and even more so in *The Sun. Americanness* occurs only once in *The Times*, and not at all in *The Sun.*

Love is like any other luxury. You have no right to it unless you can afford it
[Anthony Trollope *The Way we Live Now*]

Love conquers all things; let us too give in to love
[Virgil *Eclogue*]

Love and do what you will
[Saint Augustine of Hippo *In Epistolam Joannis ad Parthos*]

Those have most power to hurt us that we love
[Francis Beaumont and John Fletcher *The Maid's Tragedy*]

My love's a noble madness
[John Dryden *All for Love*]

And love's the noblest frailty of the mind
[John Dryden *The Indian Emperor*]

Love's tongue is in the eyes
[Phineas Fletcher *Piscatory Eclogues*]

Love is only one of many passions
[Dr. Johnson *Plays of William Shakespeare, preface*]

Where both deliberate, the love is slight;
Whoever loved that loved not at first sight?
[Christopher Marlowe *Hero and Leander*]

If love is the answer, could you rephrase the question?
[Lily Tomlin]

Men love in haste, but they detest at leisure
[Lord Byron *Don Juan*]

Men have died from time to time and worms have eaten them, but not for love
[William Shakespeare *As You Like It*]

The course of true love never did run smooth
[William Shakespeare *A Midsummer Night's Dream*]

Love is not love
Which alters when it alteration finds
[William Shakespeare *Sonnets*]

Love is like linen – often changed, the sweeter
[Phineas Fletcher *Sicelides*]

O my love's like a red, red rose
[Robert Burns *A Red, Red Rose*]

Two things a man cannot hide: that he is drunk, and that he is in love
[Antiphanes]

Every man is a poet when he is in love
[Plato *Symposium*]

one that lov'd not wisely but too well
[William Shakespeare *Othello*]

To fall in love is to create a religion that has a fallible god
[Jorge Luis Borges *The Meeting in a Dream*]

Love is like quicksilver in the hand. Leave the fingers open and it stays. Clutch it, and it darts away
[Dorothy Parker]

Love does not consist in gazing at each other, but in looking outward in the same direction
[Antoine de Saint-Exupéry]

Love ceases to be a pleasure, when it ceases to be a secret
[Aphra Behn *The Lover's Watch, Four O'Clock*]

Women who love the same man have a kind of bitter freemasonry
[Max Beerbohm *Zuleika Dobson*]

Many waters cannot quench love, neither can the floods drown it
[*Bible: Song of Solomon*]

Greater love hath no man than this, that a man lay down his life for his friends
[*Bible: St. John*]

O lyric Love, half-angel and half-bird
And all a wonder and a wild desire
[Robert Browning *The Ring and the Book*]

Man's love is of man's life a thing apart,
'Tis woman's whole existence
[Lord Byron *Don Juan*]

Whoever loves, if he do not propose
The right true end of love, he's one that goes
To sea for nothing but to make him sick
[John Donne *Love's Progress*]

I am two fools, I know,
For loving, and for saying so
In whining poetry
[John Donne *The Triple Fool*]

How alike are the groans of love to those of the dying
[Malcolm Lowry *Under the Volcano*]

Love is the delusion that one woman differs from another
[H.L. Mencken *Chrestomathy*]

After all, my erstwhile dear,
My no longer cherished,
Need we say it was not love,
Now that love has perished?
[Edna St. Vincent Millay *Passer Mortuus Est*]

If I am pressed to say why I loved him, I feel it can only be explained by replying: 'Because it was he; because it was me.'
[Montaigne *Essais*]

Love built on beauty, soon as beauty, dies
[John Donne *The Anagram*]

Love thy neighbour as thyself
[*Bible: Leviticus*]

PROVERBS

All's fair in love and war
Love is blind
One cannot love and be wise
Love makes the world go round
Love will find a way

love affair NOUN **= romance**, relationship, affair, intrigue, liaison, amour, affaire de coeur *(French)*: *a love affair with a married man*

loveless ADJECTIVE **1 = unloving**, hard, cold, icy, insensitive, unfriendly, heartless, frigid, unresponsive, unfeeling, cold-hearted: *She is in a loveless relationship.* **2 = unloved**, disliked, forsaken, lovelorn, friendless, unappreciated, unvalued, uncherished: *A busy professional life had left her loveless at the age of 30.*

lovelorn ADJECTIVE **= lovesick**, mooning, slighted, pining, yearning, languishing, spurned, jilted, moping, unrequited, crossed in love

lovely ADJECTIVE **1 = beautiful**, appealing, attractive, charming, winning, pretty, sweet, handsome, good-looking, exquisite, admirable, enchanting, graceful, captivating, amiable, adorable, comely, fit *(Brit. informal)*: *You look lovely.* **OPPOSITE:** ugly **2 = wonderful**, pleasing, nice, pleasant, engaging, marvellous, delightful, enjoyable, gratifying, agreeable: *What a lovely surprise!* **OPPOSITE:** horrible

lovemaking NOUN **= sexual intercourse**, intercourse, intimacy, sexual relations, the other *(informal)*, mating, nookie *(slang)*, copulation, coitus, act of love, carnal knowledge, rumpy-pumpy *(slang)*, coition, sexual union *or* congress, rumpo *(slang)*

lover NOUN **= sweetheart**, beloved, loved one, beau, flame *(informal)*, mistress, admirer, suitor, swain *(archaic)*, woman friend, lady friend, man friend, toy boy, paramour, leman *(archaic)*, fancy bit *(slang)*, boyfriend *or* girlfriend, fancy man *or* fancy woman *(slang)*, fiancé *or* fiancée, inamorata *or* inamorato, Wag *(Brit. informal)*

QUOTATIONS

All mankind love a lover
[Ralph Waldo Emerson *Spiritual Laws*]

loving ADJECTIVE **1 = affectionate**, kind, warm, dear, friendly, devoted, tender, fond, ardent, cordial, doting, amorous, solicitous, demonstrative, warm-hearted: *a loving husband and father* **OPPOSITE:** cruel **2 = tender**, kind, caring, warm, gentle, sympathetic, considerate: *The house has been restored with loving care.*

low[1] ADJECTIVE **1 = small**, little, short, stunted, squat, fubsy *(archaic, dialect)*: *She put it down on the low table.* **OPPOSITE:** tall **2 = low-lying**, deep, depressed, shallow, subsided, sunken, ground-level: *The sun was low in the sky.* **OPPOSITE:** high **3 = inexpensive**, cheap, reasonable, bargain, moderate, modest, cut-price, economical, bargain-basement: *The low prices and friendly service made for a*

pleasant evening out. **4 = meagre**, little, small, reduced, depleted, scant, trifling, insignificant, sparse, paltry, measly: *They are having to live on very low incomes.* **OPPOSITE:** significant **5 = inferior**, bad, poor, inadequate, pathetic, worthless, unsatisfactory, mediocre, deficient, second-rate, shoddy, low-grade, puny, substandard, low-rent *(informal, chiefly U.S.)*, half-pie *(N.Z. informal)*, bodger *or* bodgie *(Austral. slang)*: *They criticised staff for the low standard of care.* **6 = quiet**, soft, gentle, whispered, muted, subdued, hushed, muffled: *Her voice was so low he had to strain to catch it.* **OPPOSITE:** loud **7 = dejected**, down, blue, sad, depressed, unhappy, miserable, fed up, moody, gloomy, dismal, forlorn, glum, despondent, downcast, morose, disheartened, downhearted, down in the dumps *(informal)*, sick as a parrot *(informal)*, cheesed off *(informal)*, brassed off *(Brit. slang)*: *'I didn't ask for this job, you know,' he tells friends when he is low.* **OPPOSITE:** happy **8 = coarse**, common, rough, gross, crude, rude, obscene, disgraceful, vulgar, undignified, disreputable, unbecoming, unrefined, dishonourable, ill-bred: *stripteases interspersed with bits of ribald low comedy* **9 = contemptible**, mean, base, nasty, cowardly, degraded, vulgar, vile, sordid, abject, unworthy, despicable, depraved, menial, reprehensible, dastardly, scurvy, servile, unprincipled, dishonourable, ignoble: *That was a really low trick.* **OPPOSITE:** honourable **10 = lowly**, poor, simple, plain, peasant, obscure, humble, meek, unpretentious, plebeian, lowborn: *a man of low birth and no breeding* **11 = ill**, weak, exhausted, frail, dying, reduced, sinking, stricken, feeble, debilitated, prostrate: *She's still feeling a bit low after having flu.* **OPPOSITE:** strong
lie low = hide, lurk, hole up, hide away, keep a low profile, hide out, go underground, skulk, go into hiding, take cover, keep out of sight, go to earth, conceal yourself: *Far from lying low, he became more outspoken than ever.*

low² VERB **= moo**, bellow: *Cattle were lowing in the barns.*

low-down NOUN **= information**, intelligence, info *(informal)*, inside story, gen *(Brit. informal)*, dope *(informal)*: *We want you to give us the lowdown on your team-mates.*
▷ ADJECTIVE **= mean**, low, base, cheap *(informal)*, nasty, ugly, despicable, reprehensible, contemptible, underhand, scurvy: *They will stoop to every low-down trick.*

lower ADJECTIVE **1 = subordinate**, under, smaller, junior, minor, secondary, lesser, low-level, inferior, second-class: *the lower ranks of council officers* **2 = reduced**, cut, diminished, decreased, lessened, curtailed, pared down: *You may get it at a slightly lower price.* **OPPOSITE:** increased
▷ VERB **1 = drop**, sink, depress, let down, submerge, take down, let fall, make lower: *They lowered the coffin into the grave.* **OPPOSITE:** raise **2 = lessen**, cut, reduce, moderate, diminish, slash, decrease, prune, minimize, curtail, abate: *a drug which lowers cholesterol levels* **OPPOSITE:** increase **3 = demean**, humble, disgrace, humiliate, degrade, devalue, downgrade, belittle, condescend, debase, deign, abase: *Don't lower yourself. Don't be the way they are.* **4 = quieten**, soften, hush, tone down: *He moved closer, lowering his voice.*

lowering *see* **louring**

low-key ADJECTIVE **= subdued**, quiet, restrained, muted, played down, understated, muffled, toned down, low-pitched

lowly ADJECTIVE **1 = lowborn**, obscure, subordinate, inferior, mean, proletarian, ignoble, plebeian: *lowly bureaucrats pretending to be senators* **2 = unpretentious**, common, poor, average, simple, ordinary, plain, modest, homespun: *He started out as a lowly photographer.*

low-tech ADJECTIVE **= unsophisticated**, simple, basic, elementary **OPPOSITE:** high-tech *or* hi-tech

loyal ADJECTIVE **= faithful**, true, devoted, dependable, constant, attached, patriotic, staunch, trustworthy, trusty, steadfast, dutiful, unwavering, true-blue, immovable, unswerving, tried and true, true-hearted **OPPOSITE:** disloyal

loyalty NOUN **= faithfulness**, commitment, devotion, allegiance, reliability, fidelity, homage, patriotism, obedience, constancy, dependability, trustworthiness, steadfastness, troth *(archaic)*, fealty, staunchness, trueness, trustiness, true-heartedness

> **QUOTATIONS**
> No man can serve two masters
> *[Bible: St. Matthew]*

lozenge NOUN **= tablet**, pastille, troche, cough drop, jujube

lubricate VERB **= oil**, grease, smear, smooth the way, oil the wheels, make smooth, make slippery

lucid ADJECTIVE **1 = clear**, obvious, plain, evident, distinct, explicit, transparent, clear-cut, crystal clear, comprehensible, intelligible, limpid, pellucid: *His prose is always lucid and compelling.* **OPPOSITE:** vague **2 = clear-headed**, sound, reasonable, sensible, rational, sober, all there, sane, compos mentis *(Latin)*, in your right mind: *He wasn't very lucid; he didn't quite know where he was.* **OPPOSITE:** confused

luck NOUN **1 = good fortune**, success, advantage, prosperity, break *(informal)*, stroke of luck, blessing, windfall, good luck, fluke, godsend, serendipity: *I knew I needed a bit of luck to win.* **2 = fortune**, lot, stars, chance, accident, fate, hazard, destiny, hap *(archaic)*, twist of fate, fortuity: *The goal owed more to luck than good planning.*

luckily ADVERB **= fortunately**, happily, by chance, as luck would have it, fortuitously, opportunely, as it chanced

luckless ADJECTIVE **= unlucky**, unfortunate, unsuccessful, hapless, unhappy, disastrous, cursed, hopeless, jinxed, calamitous, ill-starred, star-crossed, unpropitious, ill-fated

lucky ADJECTIVE **1 = fortunate**, successful, favoured, charmed, blessed, prosperous, jammy *(Brit. slang)*, serendipitous: *I consider myself the luckiest man on the face of the earth.* **OPPOSITE:** unlucky **2 = fortuitous**, timely, fortunate, auspicious, opportune, propitious, providential, adventitious: *They are now desperate for a lucky break.* **OPPOSITE:** unlucky

> **PROVERBS**
> *Lucky at cards, unlucky in love*
> *Third time lucky*

lucrative ADJECTIVE **= profitable**, rewarding, productive, fruitful, paying, high-income, well-paid, money-making, advantageous, gainful, remunerative

ludicrous ADJECTIVE **= ridiculous**, crazy, absurd, preposterous, odd, funny, comic, silly, laughable, farcical, outlandish, incongruous, comical, zany, nonsensical, droll, burlesque, cockamamie *(slang, chiefly U.S.)* **OPPOSITE:** sensible

lug VERB **= drag**, carry, pull, haul, tow, yank, hump *(Brit. slang)*, heave

luggage NOUN **= baggage**, things, cases, bags, gear, trunks, suitcases, paraphernalia, impedimenta

lugubrious ADJECTIVE **= gloomy**, serious, sad, dismal, melancholy, dreary, sombre, woeful, mournful, morose, sorrowful, funereal, doleful, woebegone, dirgelike

lukewarm ADJECTIVE **1 = tepid**, warm, blood-warm: *Wash your face with lukewarm water.* **2 = half-hearted**, cold, cool, indifferent, unconcerned, uninterested, apathetic, unresponsive, phlegmatic, unenthusiastic, laodicean: *The study received a lukewarm response from the Home Secretary.*

lull NOUN **= respite**, pause, quiet, silence, calm, hush, tranquillity, stillness, let-up *(informal)*, calmness: *a lull in the conversation*
▷ VERB **= calm**, soothe, subdue, still, quiet, compose, hush, quell, allay, pacify, lullaby, tranquillize, rock to sleep: *It is easy to be lulled into a false sense of security.*

lullaby NOUN **= cradlesong**, berceuse

lumber¹ VERB **= burden**, land, load, saddle, impose upon, encumber: *She was lumbered with a bill for about £90.*

▷ NOUN **= junk**, refuse, rubbish, discards, trash, clutter, jumble, white elephants, castoffs, trumpery: *The wheels had been consigned to the loft as useless lumber.*

lumber[2] VERB **= plod**, shuffle, shamble, trudge, stump, clump, waddle, trundle, lump along: *He turned and lumbered back to his chair.*

lumbering ADJECTIVE **= awkward**, heavy, blundering, bumbling, hulking, unwieldy, ponderous, ungainly, elephantine, heavy-footed, lubberly

luminary NOUN **= celebrity**, star, expert, somebody, lion, worthy, notable, big name, dignitary, leading light, celeb *(informal)*, personage, megastar *(informal)*, fundi *(S. African)*, V.I.P.

luminous ADJECTIVE **= bright**, lighted, lit, brilliant, shining, glowing, vivid, illuminated, radiant, resplendent, lustrous, luminescent: *The luminous dial on the clock showed five minutes to seven.*

lump[1] NOUN **1 = piece**, group, ball, spot, block, mass, cake, bunch, cluster, chunk, wedge, dab, hunk, nugget, gob, clod, gobbet: *a lump of wood* **2 = swelling**, growth, bump, tumour, bulge, hump, protuberance, protrusion, tumescence: *I've got a lump on my shoulder.*

▷ VERB **= group**, throw, mass, combine, collect, unite, pool, bunch, consolidate, aggregate, batch, conglomerate, coalesce, agglutinate: *She felt out of place lumped together with alcoholics and hard-drug users.*

lump[2] VERB

lump it = put up with it, take it, stand it, bear it, suffer it, hack it *(slang)*, tolerate it, endure it, brook it: *He was going to kick up a fuss, but he realized he'd have to lump it.*

lumpy ADJECTIVE **= bumpy**, clotted, uneven, knobbly, grainy, curdled, granular, full of lumps

lunacy NOUN **1 = foolishness**, madness, folly, stupidity, absurdity, aberration, idiocy, craziness, tomfoolery, imbecility, foolhardiness, senselessness: *the lunacy of the tax system* **OPPOSITE:** sense **2 = insanity**, madness, mania, dementia, psychosis, idiocy, derangement: *Lunacy became the official explanation for his actions.* **OPPOSITE:** sanity

lunatic NOUN **= madman**, maniac, psychopath, nut *(slang)*, loony *(slang)*, nutter *(Brit. slang)*, nutcase *(slang)*, headcase *(informal)*, headbanger *(informal)*, crazy *(informal)*: *Her son thinks she's a raving lunatic.*

▷ ADJECTIVE **= mad**, crazy, insane, irrational, nuts *(slang)*, barking *(slang)*, daft, demented, barmy *(slang)*, deranged, bonkers *(slang, chiefly Brit.)*, unhinged, loopy *(informal)*, crackpot *(informal)*, out to lunch *(informal)*, barking mad *(slang)*, maniacal, gonzo *(slang)*, up the pole *(informal)*, crackbrained, wacko *or* whacko *(informal)*, off the air *(Austral. slang)*: *the operation of the market taken to lunatic extremes*

lunge VERB **= pounce**, charge, bound, dive, leap, plunge, dash, thrust, poke, jab: *I lunged forward to try to hit him.*

▷ NOUN **= thrust**, charge, pounce, pass, spring, swing, jab, swipe *(informal)*: *He knocked on the door and made a lunge for her when she opened it.*

lurch VERB **1 = tilt**, roll, pitch, list, rock, lean, heel: *As the car sped over a pothole, she lurched forward.* **2 = stagger**, reel, stumble, weave, sway, totter: *a drunken yob lurching out of a bar, shouting obscenities*

lure VERB **= tempt**, draw, attract, invite, trick, seduce, entice, beckon, lead on, allure, decoy, ensnare, inveigle: *They did not realise that they were being lured into a trap.*

▷ NOUN **= temptation**, attraction, incentive, bait, carrot *(informal)*, magnet, inducement, decoy, enticement, siren song, allurement: *The lure of rural life is proving as strong as ever.*

lurid ADJECTIVE **1 = sensational**, shocking, disgusting, graphic, violent, savage, startling, grim, exaggerated, revolting, explicit, vivid, ghastly, gruesome, grisly, macabre, melodramatic, yellow *(of journalism)*, gory, unrestrained, shock-horror *(facetious)*: *lurid accounts of deaths and mutilations* **OPPOSITE:** mild **2 = glaring**, bright, bloody, intense, flaming, vivid, fiery, livid, sanguine, glowering, overbright: *She always painted her toenails a lurid red or orange.* **OPPOSITE:** pale

lurk VERB **= hide**, sneak, crouch, prowl, snoop, lie in wait, slink, skulk, conceal yourself, move with stealth, go furtively

luscious ADJECTIVE **1 = sexy**, attractive, arousing, erotic, inviting, provocative, seductive, cuddly, sensuous, alluring, voluptuous, kissable, beddable: *a luscious young blonde* **2 = delicious**, sweet, juicy, rich, honeyed, savoury, succulent, palatable, mouth-watering, delectable, yummy *(slang)*, scrumptious *(informal)*, appetizing, toothsome, yummo *(Austral. slang)*: *luscious fruit*

lush ADJECTIVE **1 = abundant**, green, flourishing, lavish, dense, prolific, rank, teeming, overgrown, verdant: *the lush green meadows* **2 = luxurious**, grand, elaborate, lavish, extravagant, sumptuous, plush *(informal)*, ornate, opulent, palatial, ritzy *(slang)*: *The hotel is lush, plush and very non-backpacker.* **3 = succulent**, fresh, tender, ripe, juicy: *an unusual combination of vegetables and lush fruits*

lust NOUN **1 = lechery**, sensuality, licentiousness, carnality, the hots *(slang)*, libido, lewdness, wantonness, salaciousness, lasciviousness, concupiscence, randiness *(informal, chiefly Brit.)*, pruriency: *His lust for her grew until it was overpowering.* **2 = desire**, longing, passion, appetite, craving, greed, thirst, cupidity, covetousness, avidity, appetence: *It was his lust for glitz and glamour that was driving them apart.*

lust for *or* **after someone** *or* **something = desire**, want, crave, need, yearn for, covet, slaver over, lech after *(informal)*, be consumed with desire for, hunger for *or* after: *Half the campus is lusting after her; She lusted after the Directorship.*

QUOTATIONS

> Natural freedoms are but just;
> There's something generous in mere lust
> [John Wilmot, Earl of Rochester *A Ramble in St. James' Park*]

lustful ADJECTIVE **= lascivious**, sexy *(informal)*, passionate, erotic, craving, sensual, randy *(informal, chiefly Brit.)*, raunchy *(slang)*, horny *(slang)*, hankering, lewd, wanton, carnal, prurient, lecherous, hot-blooded, libidinous, licentious, concupiscent, unchaste

lustre NOUN **1 = sparkle**, shine, glow, glitter, dazzle, gleam, gloss, brilliance, sheen, shimmer, glint, brightness, radiance, burnish, resplendence, lambency, luminousness: *Gold retains its lustre for far longer than other metals.* **2 = glory**, honour, fame, distinction, prestige, renown, illustriousness: *The team is relying too much on names that have lost their lustre.*

lustrous ADJECTIVE **= shining**, bright, glowing, sparkling, dazzling, shiny, gleaming, glossy, shimmering, radiant, luminous, glistening, burnished

lusty ADJECTIVE **= vigorous**, strong, powerful, healthy, strapping, robust, rugged, energetic, sturdy, hale, stout, stalwart, hearty, virile, red-blooded *(informal)*, brawny

luxuriant ADJECTIVE **1 = lush**, rich, dense, abundant, excessive, thriving, flourishing, rank, productive, lavish, ample, fertile, prolific, overflowing, plentiful, exuberant, fruitful, teeming, copious, prodigal, riotous, profuse, fecund, superabundant, plenteous: *wide spreading branches and luxuriant foliage* **OPPOSITE:** sparse **2 = elaborate**, fancy, decorated, extravagant, flamboyant, baroque, sumptuous, ornate, festooned, flowery, rococo, florid, corinthian: *luxuriant draperies and soft sofas* **OPPOSITE:** plain

luxuriate VERB **1 = enjoy**, delight, indulge, relish, revel, bask, wallow: *Lie back and luxuriate in the scented oil.* **2 = live in luxury**, take it easy, live the life of Riley, have the time of your life, be in clover: *He retired to luxuriate in Hollywood.*

luxurious ADJECTIVE **1 = sumptuous**, expensive, comfortable, magnificent, costly, splendid, lavish, plush *(informal)*, opulent, ritzy *(slang)*, de luxe, well-appointed: *a luxurious hotel* **2 = self-indulgent**, pleasure-loving, sensual, pampered, voluptuous, sybaritic, epicurean: *She had come to enjoy this luxurious lifestyle.* **OPPOSITE:** austere

> **USAGE**
> *Luxurious* is sometimes wrongly used where *luxuriant* is meant: *he had a luxuriant* (not *luxurious*) *moustache*; *the walls were covered with a luxuriant growth of wisteria.*

luxury NOUN **1 = opulence**, splendour, richness, extravagance, affluence, hedonism, a bed of roses, voluptuousness, the life of Riley, sumptuousness: *She was brought up in an atmosphere of luxury and wealth.* **OPPOSITE:** poverty **2 = extravagance**, treat, extra, indulgence, frill, nonessential: *We never had money for little luxuries.* **OPPOSITE:** necessity **3 = pleasure**, delight, comfort, satisfaction, enjoyment, bliss, indulgence, gratification, wellbeing: *Relax in the luxury of a Roman-style bath.* **OPPOSITE:** discomfort

> **QUOTATIONS**
> Give us the luxuries of life, and we will dispense with its necessities
> [John Lothrop Motley]

lyric ADJECTIVE **1 = songlike**, musical, lyrical, expressive, melodic: *His splendid short stories and lyric poetry.* **2 = melodic**, clear, light, flowing, graceful, mellifluous, dulcet: *her fresh, beautiful, lyric voice*

lyrical ADJECTIVE **= enthusiastic**, emotional, inspired, poetic, carried away, ecstatic, expressive, impassioned, rapturous, effusive, rhapsodic

Mm

macabre ADJECTIVE **= gruesome**, grim, ghastly, frightening, ghostly, weird, dreadful, unearthly, hideous, eerie, grisly, horrid, morbid, frightful, ghoulish **OPPOSITE:** delightful

Machiavellian ADJECTIVE **= scheming**, cynical, shrewd, cunning, designing, intriguing, sly, astute, unscrupulous, wily, opportunist, crafty, artful, amoral, foxy, deceitful, underhand, double-dealing, perfidious

machine NOUN **1 = appliance**, device, apparatus, engine, tool, instrument, mechanism, gadget, contraption, gizmo *(informal)*, contrivance: *I put a coin in the machine and pulled the lever.* **2 = system**, agency, structure, organization, machinery, setup *(informal)*: *He has put the party publicity machine behind another candidate.*

> **QUOTATIONS**
> Machines are worshipped because they are beautiful and valued because they confer power; they are hated because they are hideous and loathed because they impose slavery [Bertrand Russell *Sceptical Essays: Machines and the Emotions*]

machinery NOUN **1 = equipment**, gear, instruments, apparatus, works, technology, tackle, tools, mechanism(s), gadgetry: *Farmers import most of their machinery and materials.* **2 = administration**, system, organization, agency, machine, structure, channels, procedure: *the government machinery and administrative procedures*

> **QUOTATIONS**
> The world is dying of machinery [George Moore *Confessions of a Young Man*]

macho ADJECTIVE **= manly**, masculine, butch *(slang)*, two-fisted, tough, chauvinist, virile, he-man

mad ADJECTIVE **1 = insane**, mental *(slang)*, crazy *(informal)*, nuts *(slang)*, bananas *(slang)*, barking *(slang)*, raving, distracted, frantic, frenzied, unstable, crackers *(Brit. slang)*, batty *(slang)*, crazed, lunatic, loony *(slang)*, psychotic, demented, cuckoo *(informal)*, unbalanced, barmy *(slang)*, nutty *(slang)*, deranged, delirious, rabid, bonkers *(slang, chiefly Brit.)*, flaky *(U.S. slang)*, unhinged, loopy *(informal)*, crackpot *(informal)*, out to lunch *(informal)*, round the bend *(Brit. slang)*, aberrant, barking mad *(slang)*, out of your mind, gonzo *(slang)*, screwy *(informal)*, doolally *(slang)*, off your head *(slang)*, off your trolley *(slang)*, round the twist *(Brit. slang)*, up the pole *(informal)*, of unsound mind, as daft as a brush *(informal, chiefly Brit.)*, lost your marbles *(informal)*, not right in the head, non compos mentis *(Latin)*, off your rocker *(slang)*, not the full shilling *(informal)*, off your nut *(slang)*, off your chump *(slang)*, wacko *or* whacko *(informal)*, off the air *(Austral. slang)*: *the mad old lady down the street* **OPPOSITE:** sane **2 = foolish**, absurd, wild, stupid, daft *(informal)*, ludicrous, unreasonable, irrational, unsafe, senseless, preposterous, foolhardy, nonsensical, unsound, inane, imprudent, asinine: *Isn't that a rather mad idea?* **OPPOSITE:** sensible **3 = angry**, cross, furious, irritated, fuming, choked, infuriated, raging, ape *(slang)*, incensed, enraged, exasperated, irate, livid *(informal)*, berserk, seeing red *(informal)*, incandescent, wrathful, fit to be tied *(slang)*, in a wax *(informal, chiefly Brit.)*, berko *(Austral. slang)*, tooshie *(Austral. slang)*, off the air *(Austral. slang)*: *I'm pretty mad about it, I can tell you.* **OPPOSITE:** calm **4** *(usually with* **about***)* **= enthusiastic**, wild, crazy *(informal)*, nuts *(slang)*, keen, hooked, devoted, in love with, fond, daft *(informal)*, ardent, fanatical, avid, impassioned, zealous, infatuated, dotty *(slang, chiefly Brit.)*, enamoured: *He's mad about you.* **OPPOSITE:** nonchalant **5 = frenzied**, wild, excited, energetic, abandoned, agitated, frenetic, uncontrolled, boisterous, full-on *(informal)*, ebullient, gay, riotous, unrestrained: *The game is a mad dash against the clock.*

> **USAGE**
> *Mad* is often used in informal speech to describe behaviour that is wild or unpredictable, or a person who is behaving in such a way. Care should be taken with this word and with all its synonyms, since many of them can cause great offence. In particular, it is important to avoid the loose use of clinical terms such as *psychotic* unless you are referring seriously to specific psychiatric disorders. In contexts where psychiatric disorders are being discussed, you should avoid labelling people with the name of their condition. For example, instead of describing someone as *psychotic*, you would say they were *having a psychotic episode*; similarly, you would say that someone is *affected by depression*, rather than labelling them *a depressive*. Note that some people also object to the phrase *suffer from* in this context, as in *he suffers from paranoia*, preferring more neutral verbs such as *experience* or *be affected by*. Also avoid using old-fashioned words such as *insane*, *demented*, and *lunatic* with reference to psychiatric disorders. In all contexts, informal and judgmental words such as *mental* and *loony* are to be avoided.

madcap ADJECTIVE **= reckless**, rash, impulsive, ill-advised, wild, crazy, foolhardy, thoughtless, crackpot *(informal)*, hot-headed, imprudent, heedless, hare-brained: *They flitted from one madcap scheme to another.*
▷ NOUN **= daredevil**, tearaway, wild man, hothead: *Madcap Mark Roberts can be seen doing dangerous stunts in the countryside.*

madden VERB **= infuriate**, irritate, incense, enrage, upset, provoke, annoy, aggravate *(informal)*, gall, craze, inflame, exasperate, vex, unhinge, drive you crazy, nark *(Brit., Austral. & N.Z. slang)*, drive you round the bend *(Brit. slang)*, make your blood boil, drive you to distraction *(informal)*, get your goat *(slang)*, drive you round the twist *(Brit. slang)*, get your dander up *(informal)*, make your hackles rise, raise your hackles, drive you off your head *(slang)*, drive you out of your mind, get your back up, get your hackles up, make you see red *(informal)*, put your back up, hack you off *(informal)* **OPPOSITE:** calm

made-up ADJECTIVE **1 = painted**, powdered, rouged, done up: *heavily made-up face* **2 = false**, invented, imaginary, fictional, untrue, mythical, unreal, fabricated, make-believe, trumped-up, specious: *It looks like a made-up word to me.*

madly ADVERB **1 = passionately**, wildly, desperately, intensely, exceedingly, extremely, excessively, to distraction, devotedly: *She has fallen madly in love with him.* **2 = foolishly**, wildly, absurdly, ludicrously, unreasonably, irrationally, senselessly, nonsensically: *This seemed madly dangerous.* **3 = energetically**, quickly, wildly, rapidly, hastily, furiously, excitedly, hurriedly, recklessly, speedily, like mad *(informal)*, hell for leather, like lightning, hotfoot, like the clappers *(Brit. informal)*, like nobody's business *(informal)*, like greased lightning *(informal)*: *Children ran madly around the tables, shouting and playing.* **4 = insanely**, frantically, hysterically, crazily, deliriously, distractedly, rabidly, frenziedly, dementedly: *He would cackle madly to himself in the small hours.*

madman *or* **madwoman** NOUN = **lunatic**, psycho *(slang)*, maniac, loony *(slang)*, nut *(slang)*, psychotic, psychopath, nutter *(Brit. slang)*, nutcase *(slang)*, headcase *(informal)*, mental case *(slang)*, headbanger *(informal)*, crazy *(informal)*

> **QUOTATIONS**
> There is only one difference between a madman and me. I am not mad
> [Salvador Dali *Diary of a Genius*]

madness NOUN **1 = insanity**, mental illness, delusion, mania, dementia, distraction, aberration, psychosis, lunacy, craziness, derangement, psychopathy: *He was driven to the brink of madness.* **2 = foolishness**, nonsense, folly, absurdity, idiocy, wildness, daftness *(informal)*, foolhardiness, preposterousness: *It is political madness.* **3 = frenzy**, riot, furore, uproar, abandon, excitement, agitation, intoxication, unrestraint: *The country was in a state of madness*

maelstrom NOUN **1 = whirlpool**, swirl, eddy, vortex, Charybdis *(literary)*: *a maelstrom of surf and confused seas* **2 = turmoil**, disorder, confusion, chaos, upheaval, uproar, pandemonium, bedlam, tumult: *Inside, she was a maelstrom of churning emotions.*

maestro NOUN = **master**, expert, genius, virtuoso, wonk *(informal)*, fundi *(S. African)*

magazine NOUN = **journal**, paper, publication, supplement, rag *(informal)*, issue, glossy *(informal)*, pamphlet, periodical, fanzine *(informal)*

magic NOUN **1 = sorcery**, wizardry, witchcraft, enchantment, occultism, black art, spells, necromancy, sortilege, theurgy: *Legends say that Merlin raised the stones by magic.* **2 = conjuring**, illusion, trickery, sleight of hand, hocus-pocus, jiggery-pokery *(informal, chiefly Brit.)*, legerdemain, prestidigitation, jugglery: *His secret hobby: performing magic.* **3 = charm**, power, glamour, fascination, magnetism, enchantment, allurement, mojo *(U.S. slang)*: *The singer believes he can still regain some of his old magic.*
▷ ADJECTIVE = **miraculous**, entrancing, charming, fascinating, marvellous, magical, magnetic, enchanting, bewitching, spellbinding, sorcerous: *Then came those magic moments in the rose-garden.*

magician NOUN **1 = conjuror**, illusionist, prestidigitator: *It was like watching a magician showing you how he performs a trick.* **2 = sorcerer**, witch, wizard, illusionist, warlock, necromancer, thaumaturge *(rare)*, theurgist, archimage *(rare)*, enchanter *or* enchantress: *Uther called on Merlin the magician to help him.* **3 = miracle-worker**, genius, marvel, wizard, virtuoso, wonder-worker, spellbinder: *He was a magician with words.*

magisterial ADJECTIVE = **authoritative**, lordly, commanding, masterful, imperious
OPPOSITE: subservient

magistrate NOUN = **judge**, justice, provost *(Scot.)*, bailie *(Scot.)*, justice of the peace, J.P.
▸ *related adjective:* magisterial

magnanimous ADJECTIVE = **generous**, kind, noble, selfless, big, free, kindly, handsome, charitable, high-minded, bountiful, unselfish, open-handed, big-hearted, unstinting, beneficent, great-hearted, munificent, ungrudging
OPPOSITE: petty

magnate NOUN = **tycoon**, leader, chief, fat cat *(slang, chiefly U.S.)*, baron, notable, mogul, bigwig *(informal)*, grandee, big shot *(informal)*, captain of industry, big wheel *(slang)*, big cheese *(slang, old-fashioned)*, plutocrat, big noise *(informal)*, big hitter *(informal)*, magnifico, heavy hitter *(informal)*, nabob *(informal)*, Mister Big *(slang, chiefly U.S.)*, V.I.P.

magnetic ADJECTIVE = **attractive**, irresistible, seductive, captivating, charming, fascinating, entrancing, charismatic, enchanting, hypnotic, alluring, mesmerizing
OPPOSITE: repulsive

magnetism NOUN = **charm**, appeal, attraction, power, draw, pull, spell, magic, fascination, charisma, attractiveness, allure, enchantment, hypnotism, drawing power, seductiveness, mesmerism, captivatingness

magnification NOUN
1 = enlargement, increase, inflation, boost, expansion, blow-up *(informal)*, intensification, amplification, dilation, augmentation: *a magnification of the human eye* **2 = exaggeration**, build-up, heightening, deepening, enhancement, aggrandizement: *the magnification of this character on the screen*

magnificence NOUN = **splendour**, glory, majesty, grandeur, brilliance, nobility, gorgeousness, sumptuousness, sublimity, resplendence

magnificent ADJECTIVE **1 = splendid**, striking, grand, impressive, august, rich, princely, imposing, elegant, divine *(informal)*, glorious, noble, gorgeous, lavish, elevated, luxurious, majestic, regal, stately, sublime, sumptuous, grandiose, exalted, opulent, transcendent, resplendent, splendiferous *(facetious)*: *a magnificent country house in wooded grounds*
OPPOSITE: ordinary **2 = brilliant**, fine, excellent, outstanding, superb, superior, splendid: *She is magnificent at making you feel able to talk.*

magnify VERB **1 = enlarge**, increase, boost, expand, intensify, blow up *(informal)*, heighten, amplify, augment, dilate: *The telescope magnifies images over 11 times.* **OPPOSITE:** reduce
2 = make worse, exaggerate, intensify, worsen, heighten, deepen, exacerbate, aggravate, increase, inflame, fan the flames of: *Poverty and human folly magnify natural disasters.*
3 = exaggerate, overdo, overstate, build up, enhance, blow up, inflate, overestimate, dramatize, overrate, overplay, overemphasize, blow up out of all proportion, aggrandize, make a production (out) of *(informal)*, make a federal case of *(U.S. informal)*: *spend their time magnifying ridiculous details*
OPPOSITE: understate

magnitude NOUN **1 = importance**, consequence, significance, mark, moment, note, weight, proportion, dimension, greatness, grandeur, eminence: *An operation of this magnitude is going to be difficult.*
OPPOSITE: unimportance
2 = immensity, size, extent, enormity, strength, volume, vastness, bigness, largeness, hugeness: *the magnitude of the task confronting them*
OPPOSITE: smallness **3 = intensity**, measure, capacity, amplitude: *a quake with a magnitude exceeding 5*

maid NOUN **1 = servant**, chambermaid, housemaid, menial, handmaiden *(archaic)*, maidservant, female servant, domestic *(archaic)*, parlourmaid, serving-maid: *A maid brought me breakfast at half past eight.*
2 = girl, maiden, lass, miss, nymph *(poetic)*, damsel, lassie *(informal)*, wench: *But can he win back the heart of this fair maid?*

maiden NOUN = **girl**, maid, lass, damsel, miss, virgin, nymph *(poetic)*, lassie *(informal)*, wench: *stories of brave princes and beautiful maidens*
▷ MODIFIER **1 = first**, initial, inaugural, introductory, initiatory: *The Titanic sank on its maiden voyage.*
2 = unmarried, pure, virgin, intact, chaste, virginal, unwed, undefiled: *An elderly maiden aunt had left him £1000.*

mail NOUN **1 = letters**, post, packages, parcels, correspondence: *She looked through the mail.* **2 = postal service**, post, postal system: *Your cheque is in the mail.*
▷ VERB **1 = post**, send, forward, dispatch, send by mail *or* post: *He mailed me the contract.* **2 = e-mail**, send, forward: *You can write or mail your CV to us.*

maim VERB = **cripple**, hurt, injure, wound, mar, disable, hamstring, impair, lame, mutilate, mangle, incapacitate, put out of action, mangulate *(Austral. slang)*

main ADJECTIVE = **chief**, leading, major, prime, head, special, central, particular, necessary, essential, premier, primary, vital, critical, crucial, supreme, outstanding, principal, cardinal, paramount, foremost, predominant, pre-

eminent, must-have: *My main concern now is to protect the children.*
OPPOSITE: minor
▷ PLURAL NOUN **1 = pipeline**, channel, pipe, conduit, duct: *the water supply from the mains* **2 = cable**, line, electricity supply, mains supply: *amplifiers which plug into the mains*
in the main = on the whole, generally, mainly, mostly, in general, for the most part: *In the main, children are taboo in the workplace.*

mainly ADVERB **= chiefly**, mostly, largely, generally, usually, principally, in general, primarily, above all, substantially, on the whole, predominantly, in the main, for the most part, most of all, first and foremost, to the greatest extent

mainstay NOUN **= pillar**, backbone, bulwark, prop, anchor, buttress, lynchpin, chief support

mainstream ADJECTIVE **= conventional**, general, established, received, accepted, central, current, core, prevailing, orthodox, lamestream *(informal)*
OPPOSITE: unconventional

maintain VERB **1 = continue**, retain, preserve, sustain, carry on, keep, keep up, prolong, uphold, nurture, conserve, perpetuate: *You should always maintain your friendships.* **OPPOSITE:** end **2 = assert**, state, hold, claim, insist, declare, allege, contend, affirm, profess, avow, aver, asseverate: *Prosecutors maintain that no deal was made.* **OPPOSITE:** disavow **3 = look after**, care for, take care of, finance, conserve, keep in good condition: *The house costs a fortune to maintain.*

maintenance NOUN **1 = upkeep**, keeping, care, supply, repairs, provision, conservation, nurture, preservation: *the maintenance of government buildings* **2 = allowance**, living, support, keep, food, livelihood, subsistence, upkeep, sustenance, alimony, aliment: *Absent fathers must pay maintenance for their children.* **3 = continuation**, carrying-on, continuance, support, perpetuation, prolongation, sustainment, retainment: *the maintenance of peace and stability in Asia*

majestic ADJECTIVE **= grand**, magnificent, impressive, superb, kingly, royal, august, princely, imposing, imperial, noble, splendid, elevated, awesome, dignified, regal, stately, monumental, sublime, lofty, pompous, grandiose, exalted, splendiferous *(facetious)*
OPPOSITE: modest

majesty NOUN **= grandeur**, glory, splendour, magnificence, dignity, nobility, sublimity, loftiness, impressiveness, awesomeness, exaltedness **OPPOSITE:** triviality

major ADJECTIVE **1 = important**, vital, critical, significant, great, serious, radical, crucial, outstanding, grave, extensive, notable, weighty, pre-eminent: *Exercise has a major part to play in combating disease.* **2 = main**, higher, greater, bigger, lead, leading, head, larger, better, chief, senior, supreme, superior, elder, uppermost: *We heard extracts from three of his major works.*
OPPOSITE: minor

majority NOUN **1 = most**, more, mass, bulk, best part, better part, lion's share, preponderance, plurality, greater number: *The majority of our customers come from out of town.* **2 = adulthood**, maturity, age of consent, seniority, manhood *or* womanhood: *Once you reach your majority, you can do what you please.*

QUOTATIONS
One, on God's side, is a majority
[Wendell Phillips]

USAGE
The majority of should always refer to a countable number of things or people. If you are talking about an amount or quantity, rather than a countable number, use *most of*, as in *most of the harvest was saved* (not *the majority of the harvest was saved*).

make VERB **1 = produce**, cause, create, effect, lead to, occasion, generate, bring about, give rise to, engender, beget: *The crash made a noise like a building coming down.* **2 = perform**, do, act out, effect, carry out, engage in, execute, prosecute: *I made a gesture at him and turned away.* **3 = force**, cause, press, compel, drive, require, oblige, induce, railroad *(informal)*, constrain, coerce, impel, dragoon, pressurize, prevail upon: *You can't make me do anything.* **4 = appoint**, name, select, elect, invest, install, nominate, assign, designate, hire as, cast as, employ as, ordain, vote in as, recruit as, engage as, enlist as: *They made him transport minister.* **5 = create**, build, produce, manufacture, form, model, fashion, shape, frame, construct, assemble, compose, forge, mould, put together, originate, fabricate: *They now make cars at two plants in Europe.* **6 = enact**, form, pass, establish, fix, institute, frame, devise, lay down, draw up: *The only person who makes rules in this house is me.* **7 = earn**, get, gain, net, win, clear, secure, realize, obtain, acquire, bring in, take in, fetch: *How much money did we make?* **8 = amount to**, total, constitute, add up to, count as, tot up to *(informal)*: *They are adding three aircraft carriers. That makes six in all.* **9 = get to**, reach, catch, arrive at, meet, arrive in time for: *We made the train, jumping aboard just as it was pulling out; We have to make New Orleans by nightfall.* **10 = calculate**, judge, estimate, determine, think, suppose, reckon, work out, compute, gauge, count up, put a figure on: *I make the total for the year £69,599.*
▷ NOUN **= brand**, sort, style, model, build, form, mark, kind, type, variety, construction, marque: *What make of car did he decide to buy?*
make as if = pretend, affect, give the impression that, feign, feint, make a show of, act as if *or* though: *He made as if to chase me.*
make away *or* **off with something = steal**, nick *(slang, chiefly Brit.)*, pinch *(informal)*, nab *(informal)*, carry off, swipe *(slang)*, knock off *(slang)*, pilfer, cart off *(slang)*, purloin, filch: *They tied her up and made away with £2000.*
make believe = pretend, play, enact, feign, play-act, act as if *or* though: *He made believe he didn't understand what I was saying.*
make do = manage, cope, improvise, muddle through, get along *or* by, scrape along *or* by: *It's not going to be easy but I can make do.*
make for something 1 = head for, aim for, head towards, set out for, be bound for, make a beeline for, steer (a course) for, proceed towards: *He rose from his seat and made for the door.* **2 = contribute to**, produce, further, forward, advance, promote, foster, facilitate, be conducive to: *A happy parent makes for a happy child.*
make it 1 = succeed, be successful, prosper, be a success, arrive *(informal)*, get on, make good, cut it *(informal)*, get ahead, make the grade *(informal)*, crack it *(informal)*, make it big, get somewhere, distinguish yourself: *I have the talent to make it.* **2 = get better**, survive, recover, rally, come through, pull through: *The nurses didn't think he was going to make it.*
make off = flee, clear out *(informal)*, abscond, fly, bolt, decamp, hook it *(slang)*, do a runner *(slang)*, run for it *(informal)*, slope off, cut and run *(informal)*, beat a hasty retreat, fly the coop *(U.S. & Canad. informal)*, make away, skedaddle *(informal)*, take a powder *(U.S. & Canad. slang)*, take to your heels, run away *or* off: *They broke free and made off in a stolen car.*
make out = fare, manage, do, succeed, cope, get on, proceed, thrive, prosper: *He wondered how they were making out.*
make something out 1 = see, observe, distinguish, perceive, recognize, detect, glimpse, pick out, discern, catch sight of, espy, descry: *I could just make out a tall pale figure.* **2 = understand**, see, work out, grasp, perceive, follow, realize, comprehend, fathom, decipher, suss (out) *(slang)*, get the drift of: *It's hard to make out what criteria are used.* **3 = write out**, complete, draft, draw up, inscribe, fill in *or* out: *I'll make out a receipt for you.* **4 = pretend**, claim, suggest, maintain, declare, allege, hint, imply, intimate, assert, insinuate, let on, make as if: *They were trying to make out that I'd done it.* **5 = prove**, show, describe, represent, demonstrate, justify: *You could certainly make out a case for this point of view.*
make something up = invent, create, construct, compose, write, frame, manufacture, coin, devise, hatch, originate, formulate, dream up,

The Language of Abraham Lincoln

Abraham Lincoln (1809–65) was the first Republican president of the United States. He led the country through the American Civil War and introduced measures that led to the abolition of slavery eight months after his assassination. Lincoln had a great love of language and literature, and his speeches and letters are recognized both for their persuasiveness and for their fluency in expressing complicated ideas.

As might be expected, the issue of slavery is at the heart of many of Lincoln's writings. In fact, after *man*, *slavery* is the noun which Lincoln uses most frequently. *Question* is a very common collocate of *slavery* in Lincoln's writings, with both *the slavery question* and *the question of slavery* occurring a significant number of times. *Wrong* and *right* are the adjectives that most frequently occur predicatively with *slavery*; however, *wrong* occurs almost twice as often as *right*, as in:

> If **slavery** is not **wrong**, nothing is **wrong**.

The verbs that most frequently take *slavery* as their object are *exclude, prohibit,* and *abolish*, while the most salient verb to have *slavery* as its subject is *exist*, as in:

> Will you please tell me by what right **slavery exists** in Texas to-day?

Slave is also within the top 100 words used by Lincoln, and this word frequently occurs as a noun modifier, with *slave state, slave trade, slave law,* and *slave property* all occurring commonly within Lincoln's letters and speeches. *Hold, take,* and *make* are the verbs that most frequently take *slave* as their object, and *fugitive* is the adjective that most commonly modifies *slave*.

After *man* and *slavery*, Lincoln's third most frequently used noun is *people*. The adjectives with which he most frequently uses *people* are *American, white, free* (or *freed*), *whole* (as in 'the whole American people'), and *plain* (in the sense 'common'). Lincoln also frequently uses the construction *the people of the state/country/nation*, as in 'the patriotic people of the whole country'. The verbs *allow* and *unite* commonly collocate with *people* in Lincoln's writings, as in:

> ... we already have an important principle to rally and **unite the people** ...

These collocations between *people* and words such as *whole* and *unite* reveal Lincoln's determination to preserve the unity of the United States, which was threatened by the Civil War. There is also in Lincoln's writings a significant collocation between the adjective *whole* and the noun *country*; again, this is not surprising, given that Lincoln was president during the most turbulent period in America's history, and that he fought to prevent the Confederate States of America from seceding from the United States.

Government and *law* are other nouns frequently used by Lincoln. The adjectives that most frequently modify *government* are *free, territorial,* and *new*, whereas *martial* and *supreme* are the most common adjectival modifiers of *law*. *Establish, sustain,* and *save* are the verbs that most commonly take *government* as their object, and *become, pass,* and *enact*, the verbs that most commonly take *law* as their object.

Lincoln also frequently uses the noun *question*. *Question* is most frequently modified by *constitutional*, and the verbs that most frequently take *question* as their object are *decide, settle, ask,* and *answer*. In the case of *answer*, when the subject is *I*, the sentence is usually positive; however, when the subject is *he*, the sentence tends to be negative, as in:

> ... he had not directly **answered that question** ...

fabricate, concoct, cook up *(informal)*, trump up: *She made up stories about him.* **make up = settle your differences**, shake hands, make peace, bury the hatchet, call it quits, forgive and forget, mend fences, become reconciled, declare a truce, be friends again: *She came back and they made up.* **make up for something = compensate for**, redress, make amends for, atone for, balance out, offset, expiate, requite, make reparation for, make recompense for: *The compensation is intended to make up for stress caused.* **make up something 1 = form**, account for, constitute, compose, comprise: *Women officers make up 13 per cent of the police force.* **2 = complete**, meet, supply, fill, round off: *Some of the money they receive is in grants; loans make up the rest.* **make up to someone = flirt with**, be all over, come on to, chase after, court, pursue, woo, run after, chat up *(informal)*, curry favour with, make overtures to, make eyes at: *She watched as her best friend made up to the man she herself loved.*

make-believe NOUN **= fantasy**, imagination, pretence, charade, unreality, dream, play-acting: *She squandered her millions on a life of make-believe.* **OPPOSITE:** reality ▷ ADJECTIVE **= imaginary**, dream, imagined, made-up, fantasy, pretend, pretended, mock, sham, unreal, fantasized: *Children withdraw at times into a make-believe world.* **OPPOSITE:** real

Maker NOUN **= God**, Creator, Prime Mover

maker NOUN **= manufacturer**, producer, builder, constructor, fabricator

makeshift ADJECTIVE **= temporary**, provisional, make-do, substitute, jury *(chiefly Nautical)*, expedient, rough and ready, stopgap

make-up NOUN **1 = cosmetics**, paint *(informal)*, powder, face *(informal)*, greasepaint *(Theatre)*, war paint *(informal)*, maquillage *(French)*: *Normally she wore little make-up, but this evening was clearly an exception.* **2 = nature**, character, constitution, temperament, make, build, figure, stamp, temper, disposition, frame of mind, cast of mind: *He became convinced that there was some fatal flaw in his make-up.* **3 = structure**, organization, arrangement, form, construction, assembly, constitution, format, formation, composition, configuration: *the chemical make-up of the atmosphere*

making NOUN **= creation**, production, manufacture, construction, assembly, forging, composition, fabrication: *a book about the making of the movie* ▷ PLURAL NOUN **= beginnings**, qualities, potential, stuff, basics, materials, capacity, ingredients, essence, capability, potentiality: *He had the makings of a successful journalist.* **in the making = budding**, potential, up and coming, emergent, coming, growing, developing, promising, burgeoning, nascent, incipient: *Her drama teacher says she is a star in the making.*

malady NOUN **= disease**, complaint, illness, disorder, sickness, ailment, affliction, infirmity, ill, indisposition, lurgy *(informal)*

malaise NOUN **= unease**, illness, depression, anxiety, weakness, sickness, discomfort, melancholy, angst, disquiet, doldrums, lassitude, enervation

malcontent NOUN **= troublemaker**, rebel, complainer, grumbler, grouser, agitator, stirrer *(informal)*, mischief-maker, grouch *(informal)*, fault-finder: *Five years ago, a band of malcontents seized power.* ▷ ADJECTIVE **= discontented**, unhappy, disgruntled, dissatisfied, disgusted, rebellious, resentful, disaffected, restive, unsatisfied, ill-disposed, factious: *The film follows three malcontent teenagers around Paris.*

male ADJECTIVE **= masculine**, manly, macho, virile, manlike, manful **OPPOSITE:** female

QUOTATIONS

The male is a domestic animal which, if treated with firmness and kindness, can be trained to do most things
[Jilly Cooper]

A man is as old as he's feeling,
A woman as old as she looks
[Mortimer Collins *The Unknown Quantity*]

malevolent ADJECTIVE **= spiteful**, hostile, vicious, malicious, malign, malignant, vindictive, pernicious, vengeful, hateful *(archaic)*, baleful, rancorous, evil-minded, maleficent, ill-natured **OPPOSITE:** benevolent

malfunction VERB **= break down**, fail, go wrong, play up *(Brit. informal)*, stop working, be defective, conk out *(informal)*, develop a fault: *Radiation can cause microprocessors to malfunction.* ▷ NOUN **= fault**, failure, breakdown, defect, flaw, impairment, glitch: *There must have been a computer malfunction.*

malice NOUN **= spite**, animosity, enmity, hate, hatred, bitterness, venom, spleen, rancour, bad blood, ill will, animus, malevolence, vindictiveness, evil intent, malignity, spitefulness, vengefulness, maliciousness

QUOTATIONS

Malice is of a low stature, but it hath very long arms
[George Savile, Marquess of Halifax *Political, Moral, and Miscellaneous Thoughts*]

Malice is only another name for mediocrity
[Patrick Kavanagh]

malicious ADJECTIVE **= spiteful**, malevolent, malignant, vicious, bitter, resentful, pernicious, vengeful, bitchy *(informal)*, hateful, baleful, injurious, rancorous, catty *(informal)*, shrewish, ill-disposed, evil-minded, ill-natured **OPPOSITE:** benevolent

malign VERB **= disparage**, abuse, run down, libel, knock *(informal)*, injure, rubbish *(informal)*, smear, blacken (someone's name), slag (off) *(slang)*, denigrate, revile, vilify, slander, defame, bad-mouth *(slang, chiefly U.S. & Canad.)*, traduce, speak ill of, derogate, do a hatchet job on *(informal)*, calumniate, asperse: *We maligned him dreadfully, assuming the very worst about him.* **OPPOSITE:** praise ▷ ADJECTIVE **= evil**, bad, destructive, harmful, hostile, vicious, malignant, wicked, hurtful, pernicious, malevolent, baleful, deleterious, injurious, baneful, maleficent: *the malign influence jealousy had on their lives* **OPPOSITE:** good

malignant ADJECTIVE **1 = uncontrollable**, dangerous, evil, fatal, deadly, cancerous, virulent, irremediable: *a malignant breast tumour* **2 = hostile**, harmful, bitter, vicious, destructive, malicious, malign, hurtful, pernicious, malevolent, spiteful, baleful, injurious, inimical, maleficent, of evil intent: *a malignant minority indulging in crime and violence* **OPPOSITE:** benign

malleable ADJECTIVE **1 = manageable**, adaptable, compliant, impressionable, pliable, tractable, biddable, governable, like putty in your hands: *She was young enough to be malleable.* **2 = workable**, soft, plastic, tensile, ductile: *Silver is the most malleable of all metals.*

malpractice NOUN **= misconduct**, abuse, negligence, mismanagement, misbehaviour, dereliction

mammal NOUN

QUOTATIONS

Tiger! Tiger! burning bright
In the forests of the night;
What immortal hand or eye,
Could frame thy fearful symmetry?
[William Blake *The Tiger*]

gnu: an animal of South Africa, which in its domesticated state resembles a horse, a buffalo, and a stag. In its wild condition it is something like a thunderbolt, an earthquake and a cyclone
[Ambrose Bierce *The Devil's Dictionary*]

nature's great masterpiece, an elephant
The only harmless great thing
[John Donne *The Progress of the Soul*]

mouse: an animal which strews its path with fainting women
[Ambrose Bierce *The Devil's Dictionary*]

PROVERBS

The leopard does not change his spots

m

mammoth ADJECTIVE = **colossal**, huge, giant, massive, vast, enormous, mighty, immense, titanic, jumbo *(informal)*, gigantic, monumental, mountainous, stellar *(informal)*, prodigious, stupendous, gargantuan, elephantine, ginormous *(informal)*, Brobdingnagian, humongous *or* humungous *(U.S. slang)*, supersize **OPPOSITE:** tiny

man NOUN **1 = male**, guy *(informal)*, fellow *(informal)*, gentleman, bloke *(Brit. informal)*, chap *(Brit. informal)*, dude *(U.S. informal)*, geezer *(informal)*, adult male: *I had not expected the young man to reappear before evening.* **2 = human**, human being, body, person, individual, adult, being, somebody, soul, personage: *a possible step to sending a man back to the moon* **3 = mankind**, humanity, people, mortals, human race, humankind, Homo sapiens: *Anxiety is modern man's natural state.* **4 = partner**, boy, husband, lover, mate, boyfriend, old man, groom, spouse, sweetheart, beau, significant other *(U.S.)*: *Does your man cuddle you enough?*
▷ VERB = **staff**, people, fill, crew, occupy, garrison, furnish with men: *Soldiers manned roadblocks in the city.*
to a man = **without exception**, as one, every one, unanimously, each and every one, one and all, bar none: *Economists, almost to a man, were sceptical.*
▸ *related adjectives:* anthropic, anthropoid, anthropoidal

QUOTATIONS

Man is only a reed, the weakest thing in nature; but he is a thinking reed
[Blaise Pascal *Pensées*]

Man is the measure of all things
[Protagoras]

Man is heaven's masterpiece
[Francis Quarles *Emblems*]

The more I see of men, the better I like dogs
[Mme Roland]

There are many wonderful things, and nothing is more wonderful than man
[Sophocles *Antigone*]

Man is a noble animal, splendid in ashes, and pompous in the grave
[Thomas Browne *Hydriotaphia*]

Man is an embodied paradox, a bundle of contradictions
[Charles Colton *Lacon*]

Man has but three events in his life: to be born, to live, and to die. He is not conscious of his birth, he suffers at his death and he forgets to live
[Jean de la Bruyère *The Characters, or the Manners of the Age*]

The four stages of man are infancy, childhood, adolescence and obsolescence
[Art Linkletter *A Child's Garden of Misinformation*]

Man is a useless passion
[Jean-Paul Sartre *L'Être et le néant*]

Glory to Man in the highest! for Man is the master of things
[Algernon Charles Swinburne *Atalanta in Calydon: Hymn of Man*]

I sometimes think that God in creating man somewhat overestimated his ability
[Oscar Wilde]

What a piece of work is man! how noble in reason! how infinite in faculty! in form, in moving, how express and admirable! in action how like an angel! in apprehension how like a god! the beauty of the world! the paragon of animals!
[William Shakespeare *Hamlet*]

Man is nature's sole mistake
[W.S. Gilbert *Princess Ida*]

Man is something to be surpassed
[Friedrich Nietzsche *Thus Spake Zarathustra*]

The human race, to which so many of my readers belong
[G.K. Chesterton *The Napoleon of Notting Hill*]

Man was formed for society
[William Blackstone *Commentaries on the Laws of England*]

man: an animal so lost in rapturous contemplation of what he thinks he is as to overlook what he indubitably ought to be
[Ambrose Bierce *The Devil's Dictionary*]

Men are but children of a larger growth
[John Dryden *All for Love*]

Man, became man through work, who stepped out of the animal kingdom as transformer of the natural into the artificial, who became therefore the magician
[Ernst Fischer *The Necessity of Art*]

Men play the game, women know the score
[Roger Woddis]

PROVERBS

The best of men are but men at best

mana NOUN = **authority**, influence, power, might, force, weight, strength, domination, sway, standing, status, importance, esteem, stature, eminence

manacle NOUN = **handcuff**, bond, chain, shackle, tie, iron, fetter, gyve *(archaic)*: *He had a steel-reinforced cell with manacles fixed to the walls.*
▷ VERB = **handcuff**, bind, confine, restrain, check, chain, curb, hamper, inhibit, constrain, shackle, fetter, tie someone's hands, put in chains, clap *or* put in irons: *His hands were manacled behind his back.*

manage VERB **1 = be in charge of**, run, handle, rule, direct, conduct, command, govern, administer, oversee, supervise, preside over, be head of, call the shots in, superintend, call the tune in: *Within two years, he was managing the store.* **2 = organize**, use, handle, govern, regulate: *Managing your time is increasingly important.* **3 = cope**, survive, shift, succeed, get on, carry on, fare, get through, make out, cut it *(informal)*, get along, make do, get by *(informal)*, crack it *(informal)*, muddle through: *How did your mother manage when he left?* **4 = perform**, do, deal with, achieve, carry out, undertake, cope with, accomplish, contrive, finish off, bring about *or* off: *those who can only manage a few hours of work* **5 = control**, influence, guide, handle, master, dominate, manipulate: *Her daughter couldn't manage the horse.* **6 = steer**, operate, pilot: *managing a car well in bad conditions*

manageable ADJECTIVE = **easy**, convenient, handy, user-friendly, wieldy **OPPOSITE:** difficult

management NOUN **1 = administration**, control, rule, government, running, charge, care, operation, handling, direction, conduct, command, guidance, supervision, manipulation, governance, superintendence: *the responsibility for its day-to-day management* **2 = directors**, board, executive(s), bosses *(informal)*, administration, employers, directorate: *The management is doing its best to control the situation.*

manager NOUN = **supervisor**, head, director, executive, boss *(informal)*, governor, administrator, conductor, controller, superintendent, gaffer *(informal, chiefly Brit.)*, proprietor, organizer, comptroller, overseer, baas *(S. African)*, sherang *(Austral. & N.Z.)*

mandate NOUN = **command**, order, charge, authority, commission, sanction, instruction, warrant, decree, bidding, canon, directive, injunction, fiat, edict, authorization, precept

mandatory ADJECTIVE = **compulsory**, required, binding, obligatory, requisite **OPPOSITE:** optional

manfully ADVERB = **bravely**, boldly, vigorously, stoutly, hard, strongly, desperately, courageously, stalwartly, powerfully, resolutely, determinedly, heroically, valiantly, nobly, gallantly, like the devil, to the best of your ability, like a Trojan, intrepidly, like one possessed, with might and main

mangle VERB = **crush**, mutilate, maim, deform, cut, total *(slang)*, tear, destroy, ruin, mar, rend, wreck, spoil, butcher, cripple, hack, distort, trash *(slang)*, maul, disfigure, lacerate, mangulate *(Austral. slang)*

manhandle VERB **1 = rough up**, pull, push, paw *(informal)*, maul, handle roughly, knock about *or* around: *Foreign journalists were manhandled by the* *police.* **2 = haul**, carry, pull, push, lift, manoeuvre, tug, shove, hump *(Brit. slang)*, heave: *The three of us manhandled the dinghy out of the shed.*

manhood NOUN **= manliness**, masculinity, spirit, strength, resolution, courage, determination, maturity, bravery, fortitude, mettle, firmness, virility, valour, hardihood, manfulness

mania NOUN **1 = obsession**, passion, thing *(informal)*, desire, rage, enthusiasm, craving, preoccupation, craze, fad *(informal)*, fetish, fixation, partiality: *They had a mania for travelling.* **2 = madness**, disorder, frenzy, insanity, dementia, aberration, lunacy, delirium, craziness, derangement: *the treatment of mania*

maniac NOUN **1 = madman** *or* **madwoman**, psycho *(slang)*, lunatic, loony *(slang)*, psychopath, nutter *(Brit. slang)*, nutcase *(slang)*, headcase *(informal)*, headbanger *(informal)*, crazy *(informal)*: *a drug-crazed maniac* **2 = fanatic**, fan, enthusiast, freak *(informal)*, fiend *(informal)*: *big spending football maniacs*

manifest ADJECTIVE **= obvious**, apparent, patent, evident, open, clear, plain, visible, bold, distinct, glaring, noticeable, blatant, conspicuous, unmistakable, palpable, salient: *cases of manifest injustice* **OPPOSITE:** concealed
▷ VERB **= display**, show, reveal, establish, express, prove, declare, demonstrate, expose, exhibit, set forth, make plain, evince: *He's only convincing when that inner fury manifests itself.* **OPPOSITE:** conceal

manifestation NOUN **1 = sign**, symptom, indication, mark, example, evidence, instance, proof, token, testimony: *Different animals have different manifestations of the disease.* **2 = display**, show, exhibition, expression, demonstration, appearance, exposure, revelation, disclosure, materialization: *the manifestation of grief*

manifold ADJECTIVE **= numerous**, many, various, varied, multiple, diverse, multiplied, diversified, abundant, assorted, copious, multifarious, multitudinous, multifold

manipulate VERB **1 = influence**, control, direct, guide, conduct, negotiate, exploit, steer, manoeuvre, do a number on *(chiefly U.S.)*, twist around your little finger: *He's a very difficult character. He manipulates people; She was unable, for once, to manipulate events.* **2 = work**, use, operate, handle, employ, wield: *The technology uses a pen to manipulate a computer.*

mankind NOUN **= people**, man, humanity, human race, humankind, Homo sapiens

QUOTATIONS

> I hate mankind, for I think myself one of the best of them, and I know how bad I am
> [Dr. Johnson]

> Mankind have been created for the sake of one another. Either instruct them, therefore, or endure them
> [Marcus Aurelius *Meditations*]

USAGE

Some people object to the use of *mankind* to refer to all human beings on the grounds that it is sexist. A preferable term is *humankind*, which refers to both men and women.

manliness NOUN **= virility**, masculinity, manhood, machismo, courage, bravery, vigour, heroism, mettle, boldness, firmness, valour, fearlessness, intrepidity, hardihood

manly ADJECTIVE **= virile**, male, masculine, macho, strong, powerful, brave, daring, bold, strapping, hardy, heroic, robust, vigorous, muscular, courageous, fearless, butch *(slang)*, resolute, gallant, valiant, well-built, red-blooded *(informal)*, dauntless, stout-hearted, valorous, manful **OPPOSITE:** effeminate

man-made ADJECTIVE **= artificial**, manufactured, plastic *(slang)*, mock, synthetic, ersatz

manner NOUN **1 = style**, way, fashion, method, means, form, process, approach, practice, procedure, habit, custom, routine, mode, genre, tack, tenor, usage, wont: *The manner in which young children are spoken to depends on who is present.* **2 = behaviour**, look, air, bearing, conduct, appearance, aspect, presence, tone, demeanour,

TYPES OF MANIA

ablutomania	washing	gamomania	marriage	nudomania	nudity
agoramania	open spaces	graphomania	writing	nymphomania	sex
ailuromania	cats	gymnomania	nakedness	ochlomania	crowds
andromania	men	gynomania	women	oikomania	home
Anglomania	England	hamartiomania	sin	oinomania	wine
anthomania	flowers	hedonomania	pleasure	ophidiomania	reptiles
apimania	bees	heliomania	sun	orchidomania	testicles
arithmomania	counting	hippomania	horses	ornithomania	birds
automania	solitude	homicidomania	murder	phagomania	eating
autophonomania	suicide	hydromania	water	pharmacomania	medicines
balletomania	ballet	hylomania	woods	phonomania	noise
ballistomania	bullets	hypnomania	sleep	photomania	light
bibliomania	books	ichthyomania	fish	plutomania	great wealth
chionomania	snow	iconomania	icons	potomania	drinking
choreomania	dancing	kinesomania	movement	pyromania	fire
chrematomania	money	kleptomania	stealing	scribomania	writing
cremnomania	cliffs	logomania	talking	siderodromomania	railway travel
cynomania	dogs	macromania	becoming larger	sitomania	food
dipsomania	alcohol	megalomania	your own importance	sophomania	your own wisdom
doramania	fur			thalassomania	the sea
dromomania	travelling	melomania	music	thanatomania	death
egomania	your self	mentulomania	penises	theatromania	theatre
eleuthromania	freedom	micromania	becoming smaller	timbromania	stamps
entheomania	religion	monomania	one thing	trichomania	hair
entomomania	insects	musicomania	music	verbomania	words
ergasiomania	work	musomania	mice	xenomania	foreigners
eroticomania	erotica	mythomania	lies	zoomania	animals
erotomania	sex	necromania	death		
florimania	plants	noctimania	night		

deportment, mien *(literary)*, comportment: *His manner was self-assured and brusque.* **3 = type**, form, sort, kind, nature, variety, brand, breed, category: *What manner of place is this?*
▷ PLURAL NOUN **1 = conduct**, bearing, behaviour, breeding, carriage, demeanour, deportment, comportment: *He dressed well and had impeccable manners.* **2 = politeness**, courtesy, etiquette, refinement, polish, decorum, p's and q's: *That should teach you some manners.* **3 = protocol**, ceremony, customs, formalities, good form, proprieties, the done thing, social graces, politesse: *the morals and manners of a society*

QUOTATIONS
Manners are love in a cool climate
[Quentin Crisp *Manners From Heaven*]
Manners are the happy ways of doing things; each once a stroke of genius or of love, now repeated and hardened into usage
[Ralph Waldo Emerson *The Conduct of Life*]
Fine manners need the support of fine manners in others
[Ralph Waldo Emerson *The Conduct of Life*]
To Americans, English manners are far more frightening than none at all
[Randall Jarrell *Pictures from an Institution*]

PROVERBS
Manners maketh man

mannered ADJECTIVE **= affected**, put-on, posed, artificial, pseudo *(informal)*, pretentious, stilted, arty-farty *(informal)* **OPPOSITE:** natural

mannerism NOUN **= habit**, characteristic, trait, quirk, peculiarity, foible, idiosyncrasy

manoeuvre VERB **1 = steer**, direct, guide, pilot, work, move, drive, handle, negotiate, jockey, manipulate, navigate: *We attempted to manoeuvre the canoe closer to him.* **2 = scheme**, plot, plan, intrigue, wangle *(informal)*, machinate: *He manoeuvred his way to the top.* **3 = manipulate**, arrange, organize, devise, manage, set up, engineer, fix, orchestrate, contrive, stage-manage: *You manoeuvred things in similar situations in the past.*
▷ NOUN **1 = stratagem**, move, plan, action, movement, scheme, trick, plot, tactic, intrigue, dodge, ploy, ruse, artifice, subterfuge, machination: *manoeuvres to block the electoral process* **2** *(often plural)* **= movement**, operation, exercise, deployment, war game: *The camp was used for military manoeuvres.*

mansion NOUN **= residence**, manor, hall, villa, dwelling, abode, habitation, seat

mantle NOUN **1 = covering**, cover, screen, cloud, curtain, envelope, blanket, veil, shroud, canopy, pall: *The park looked grim under a mantle of soot and ash.* **2 = cloak**, wrap, cape, hood, shawl: *flaxen hair that hung round her shoulders like a silken mantle*
▷ VERB **= cover**, hide, blanket, cloud, wrap, screen, mask, disguise, veil, cloak, shroud, envelop, overspread: *Many of the peaks were already mantled with snow.*

manual ADJECTIVE **1 = physical**, human, done by hand: *semi-skilled and unskilled manual work* **2 = hand-operated**, hand, non-automatic: *There is a manual pump to get rid of water.*
▷ NOUN **= handbook**, guide, instructions, bible, guidebook, workbook: *the instruction manual*

manufacture VERB **1 = make**, build, produce, construct, form, create, process, shape, turn out, assemble, compose, forge, mould, put together, fabricate, mass-produce: *The first three models are being manufactured at our factory in Manchester.* **2 = concoct**, make up, invent, devise, hatch, fabricate, think up, cook up *(informal)*, trump up: *He said the allegations were manufactured on the flimsiest evidence.*
▷ NOUN **= making**, production, construction, assembly, creation, produce, fabrication, mass-production: *the manufacture of nuclear weapons*

manufacturer NOUN **= maker**, producer, builder, creator, industrialist, factory-owner, constructor, fabricator

manure NOUN **= compost**, muck, fertilizer, dung, droppings, excrement, ordure

many ADJECTIVE **= numerous**, various, varied, countless, abundant, myriad, innumerable, sundry, copious, manifold, umpteen *(informal)*, profuse, multifarious, multitudinous, multifold, divers *(archaic)*: *He had many books and papers on the subject.*
▷ PRONOUN **= a lot**, lots *(informal)*, plenty, a mass, scores, piles *(informal)*, tons *(informal)*, heaps *(informal)*, large numbers, a multitude, umpteen *(informal)*, a horde, a thousand and one, a gazillion *(informal)*: *Many had avoided the delays by consulting the tourist office.*
the many = the masses, the people, the crowd, the majority, the rank and file, the multitude, (the) hoi polloi: *It gave power to a few to change the world for the many.*

mar VERB **1 = harm**, damage, hurt, spoil, stain, blight, taint, tarnish, blot, sully, vitiate, put a damper on: *A number of problems marred the smooth running of the event.* **2 = ruin**, injure, spoil, scar, flaw, impair, mutilate, detract from, maim, deform, blemish, mangle, disfigure, deface: *The scar was discreet enough not to mar his good looks.* **OPPOSITE:** improve

marauder NOUN **= raider**, outlaw, bandit, pirate, robber, ravager, plunderer, pillager, buccaneer, brigand, corsair, sea wolf, freebooter, reiver *(dialect)*

march VERB **1 = parade**, walk, file, pace, stride, tread, tramp, swagger, footslog: *A Scottish battalion was marching down the street.* **2 = walk**, strut, storm, sweep, stride, stalk, flounce: *She marched in without even knocking.*
▷ NOUN **1 = walk**, trek, hike, tramp, slog, yomp *(Brit. informal)*, routemarch: *After a short march, the column entered the village.* **2 = demonstration**, parade, procession, demo *(informal)*: *Organisers expect up to 3000 people to join the march.* **3 = progress**, development, advance, evolution, progression: *The relentless march of technology*

margin NOUN **1 = room**, space, surplus, allowance, scope, play, compass, latitude, leeway, extra room, elbowroom: *There is very little margin for error in the way the money is collected.* **2 = edge**, side, limit, border, bound, boundary, confine, verge, brink, rim, brim, perimeter, periphery: *These islands are on the margins of human habitation.*

marginal ADJECTIVE **1 = insignificant**, small, low, minor, slight, minimal, negligible: *This is a marginal improvement on October.* **2 = borderline**, bordering, on the edge, peripheral: *The poor are forced to cultivate marginal lands higher up the mountain.*

marijuana NOUN **= cannabis**, pot *(slang)*, weed *(slang)*, dope *(slang)*, blow *(slang)*, smoke *(informal)*, stuff *(slang)*, leaf *(slang)*, tea *(U.S. slang)*, grass *(slang)*, chronic *(U.S. slang)*, hemp, hash *(slang)*, gage *(U.S. obsolete, slang)*, hashish, mary jane *(U.S. slang)*, ganja, bhang, kif, wacky baccy *(slang)*, sinsemilla, dagga *(S. African)*, charas

QUOTATIONS
I experimented with marijuana a time or two. And I didn't like it, and I didn't inhale
[Bill Clinton]

marine ADJECTIVE **= nautical**, sea, maritime, oceanic, naval, saltwater, seafaring, ocean-going, seagoing, pelagic, thalassic

mariner NOUN **= sailor**, seaman, sea dog, seafarer, hand, salt, tar, navigator, gob *(U.S. slang)*, matelot *(slang, chiefly Brit.)*, Jack Tar, seafaring man, bluejacket

marital ADJECTIVE **= matrimonial**, married, wedded, nuptial, conjugal, spousal, connubial

maritime ADJECTIVE **1 = nautical**, marine, naval, sea, oceanic, seafaring: *the largest maritime museum of its kind* **2 = coastal**, seaside, littoral: *The country has a temperate, maritime climate.*

mark NOUN **1 = spot**, stain, streak, smudge, line, nick, impression, scratch, bruise, scar, dent, blot,

m

blemish, blotch, pock, splotch, smirch: *The dogs rub against the walls and make dirty marks.* **2 = characteristic**, feature, symptom, standard, quality, measure, stamp, par, attribute, criterion, norm, trait, badge, hallmark, yardstick, peculiarity: *The mark of a civilized society is that it looks after its weakest members.* **3 = indication**, sign, note, evidence, symbol, proof, token: *Shopkeepers closed their shutters as a mark of respect.* **4 = brand**, impression, label, stamp, print, device, flag, seal, symbol, token, earmark, emblem, insignia, signet, handprint: *Each book was adorned with the publisher's mark at the bottom of the spine.* **5 = impression**, effect, influence, impact, trace, imprint, vestiges: *A religious upbringing had left its mark on him.* **6 = target**, goal, aim, purpose, end, object, objective: *The second shot missed its mark completely.*
▷ VERB **1 = scar**, scratch, dent, imprint, nick, brand, impress, stain, bruise, streak, blot, smudge, blemish, blotch, splotch, smirch: *How do you stop the horses marking the turf?* **2 = label**, identify, brand, flag, stamp, characterize: *The bank marks the cheque 'certified'.* **3 = grade**, correct, assess, evaluate, appraise: *He was marking essays in his study.* **4 = distinguish**, show, illustrate, exemplify, denote, evince, betoken: *the river which marks the border* **5 = observe**, mind, note, regard, notice, attend to, pay attention to, pay heed to, hearken to *(archaic)*: *Mark my words. He won't last.*
make your mark = succeed, make it *(informal)*, make good, prosper, be a success, achieve recognition, get on in the world, make something of yourself, find a place in the sun, make a success of yourself: *She made her mark in the film industry in the 1960s.*

m

marked ADJECTIVE **= noticeable**, clear, decided, striking, noted, obvious, signal, dramatic, considerable, outstanding, remarkable, apparent, prominent, patent, evident, distinct, pronounced, notable, manifest, blatant, conspicuous, salient
OPPOSITE: imperceptible

markedly ADVERB **= noticeably**, greatly, clearly, obviously, seriously *(informal)*, signally, patently, notably, considerably, remarkably, evidently, manifestly, distinctly, decidedly, strikingly, conspicuously, to a great extent, outstandingly

market NOUN **= fair**, mart, bazaar, souk *(Arabic)*: *Many traders in the market have special offers today.*
▷ VERB **= sell**, promote, retail, peddle, vend, offer for sale: *These phones have been marketed here since 1963.*

marketable ADJECTIVE **= sought after**, wanted, in demand, saleable, merchantable, vendible

marksman or **markswoman** NOUN **= sharpshooter**, good shot, crack shot *(informal)*, dead shot *(informal)*, deadeye *(informal, chiefly U.S.)*

maroon VERB **= abandon**, leave, desert, strand, leave high and dry *(informal)*, cast away, cast ashore

marriage NOUN **1 = wedding**, match, nuptials, wedlock, wedding ceremony, matrimony, espousal, nuptial rites: *When did the marriage take place?* **2 = union**, coupling, link, association, alliance, merger, confederation, amalgamation: *The merger is an audacious marriage between old and new.*
▸ *related adjectives:* conjugal, connubial, marital, nuptial

QUOTATIONS

Therefore shall a man leave his father and his mother, and shall cleave unto his wife: and they shall be one flesh
[*Bible: Genesis*]

'Marriage': this I call the will that moves two to create the one which is more than those who created it
[Friedrich Nietzsche *Thus Spake Zarathustra*]

Let me not to the marriage of true minds
Admit impediments. Love is not love
Which alters when it alteration finds,
Or bends with the remover to remove
[William Shakespeare *Sonnet 116*]

A happy marriage perhaps represents the ideal of human relationship – a setting in which each partner, while acknowledging the need of the other, feels free to be what he or she by nature is
[Anthony Storr *The Integrity of the Personality*]

Marriage is an act of will that signifies and involves a mutual gift, which unites the spouses and binds them to their eventual souls, with whom they make up a sole family – a domestic church
[Pope John Paul II]

Marriage is socialism among two people
[Barbara Ehrenreich *The Worst Years of Our Lives*]

The problem with marriage is that it ends every night after making love, and it must be rebuilt every morning before breakfast
[Gabriel García Márquez *Love in the Time of Cholera*]

A journey is like marriage. The certain way to be wrong is to think you control it
[John Steinbeck *Travels With Charley: In Search of America*]

Marriage brings one into fatal connection with custom and tradition, and traditions and customs are like the wind and weather, altogether incalculable
[Søren Kierkegaard *Either/Or*]

Marriage must be a relation either of sympathy or of conquest
[George Eliot *Romola*]

A marriage is no amusement but a solemn act, and generally a sad one
[Queen Victoria *Letter to her daughter*]

Either marriage is a destiny, I believe, or there is no sense in it at all, it's a piece of humbug
[Max Frisch *I'm Not Stiller*]

Happiness in marriage is entirely a matter of chance
[Jane Austen *Pride and Prejudice*]

If there is one notion I hate more than another, it is that of marriage – I mean marriage in the vulgar, weak sense, as a mere matter of sentiment
[Charlotte Bronte *Shirley*]

Every woman should marry – and no man
[Benjamin Disraeli *Lothair*]

There are good marriages, but no delightful ones
[Duc de la Rochefoucauld *Réflexions ou Sentences et Maximes Morales*]

It doesn't much signify whom one marries, for one is sure to find next morning that it was someone else
[Samuel Rogers *Table Talk*]

It is a woman's business to get married as soon as possible, and a man's to keep unmarried as long as he can
[George Bernard Shaw *Man and Superman*]

Marriage is like life in this – that it is a field of battle, and not a bed of roses
[Robert Louis Stevenson *Virginibus Puerisque*]

If all men are born free, how is it that all women are born slaves?
[Mary Astell *Some Reflections upon Marriage*]

I married beneath me, all women do
[Nancy Astor]

Single women have a dreadful propensity for being poor – which is one very strong argument in favour of matrimony
[Jane Austen *letter*]

Marriage always demands the finest arts of insincerity possible between two human beings
[Vicki Baum *Zwischenfall in Lohwinckel*]

Marriage is the grave or tomb of wit
[Margaret Cavendish, Duchess of Newcastle *Nature's Three Daughters*]

Courtship to marriage, as a very witty prologue to a very dull play
[William Congreve *The Old Bachelor*]

I am to be married within these three days; married past redemption
[John Dryden *Marriage à la Mode*]

When I said I would die a bachelor I did not think I should live till I were married
[William Shakespeare *Much Ado About Nothing*]

Men are April when they woo,
December when they wed
[William Shakespeare *As You Like It*]

One should always be in love. That is the reason one should never marry
[Oscar Wilde *A Woman of No Importance*]

Marriage is a great institution, but I'm not ready for an institution yet
[Mae West]

Marriage has many pains, but celibacy has no pleasures
[Dr. Johnson]

Marriages are made in Heaven
[John Lyly *Euphues and his England*]

Men marry because they are tired, women because they are curious; both are disappointed
[Oscar Wilde *A Woman of No Importance*]

A man in love is incomplete until he has married. Then he's finished
[Zsa Zsa Gabor]

A happy marriage is a long conversation which always seems too short
[André Maurois *Memories*]

Marriage is three parts love and seven parts forgiveness
[Langdon Mitchell]

Marriage is a great institution – no family should be without it
[Bob Hope]

Marriage is popular because it combines the maximum of temptation with the maximum of opportunity
[George Bernard Shaw *Maxims for Revolutionists*]

Strange to say what delight we married people have to see these poor fools decoyed into our condition
[Samuel Pepys]

Bigamy is having one husband too many. Monogamy is the same thing
[Erica Jong]

No man is genuinely happy, married, who has to drink worse whisky than he used to drink when he was single
[H.L. Mencken *Selected Prejudices*]

Kissing don't last: cookery do!
[George Meredith *The Ordeal of Richard Feverel*]

It was very good of God to let Carlyle and Mrs. Carlyle marry one another and so make only two people miserable instead of four
[Samuel Butler]

one fool at least in every married couple
[Henry Fielding *Amelia*]

Hogamus, higamous
Man is polygamous
Higamus, hogamous
Woman monogamous
[William James]

There once was an old man of Lyme
Who married three wives at a time,
When asked 'Why a third?'
He replied, 'One's absurd!
And bigamy, Sir, is a crime!'
[William Cosmo Monkhouse]

Marriage may often be a stormy lake, but celibacy is almost always a muddy horsepond
[Thomas Love Peacock *Melincourt*]

Marriage is based on the theory that when man discovers a brand of beer exactly to his taste he should at once throw up his job and go work in the brewery
[George Jean Nathan]

married ADJECTIVE **1 = wedded**, one, united, joined, wed, hitched *(slang)*, spliced *(informal)*: *We have been married for 14 years.* **2 = marital**, wifely, husbandly, nuptial, matrimonial, conjugal, spousal, connubial: *the first ten years of married life*

marry VERB **1 = tie the knot** *(informal)*, wed, take the plunge *(informal)*, walk down the aisle *(informal)*, get hitched *(slang)*, get spliced *(informal)*, become man and wife, plight your troth *(old-fashioned)*: *They married a month after they met.* **2 = unite**, match, join, link, tie, bond, ally, merge, knit, unify, splice, yoke: *It will be difficult to marry his two interests – cooking and sport.*

QUOTATIONS

Thus grief still treads upon the heels of pleasure:
Marry'd in haste, we may repent at leisure
[William Congreve *The Old Bachelor*]

There is not one in a hundred of either sex who is not taken in when they marry ... it is, of all transactions, the one in which people expect most from others, and are least honest themselves
[Jane Austen *Mansfield Park*]

It is better to marry than to burn
[*Bible: I Corinthians*]

Advice for persons about to marry.
-'Don't.'
[*Punch*]

PROVERBS

Never marry for money, but marry where money is

marsh NOUN **= swamp**, moss *(Scot. & Northern English dialect)*, bog, slough, fen, quagmire, morass, muskeg *(Canad.)*

marshal VERB **1 = conduct**, take, lead, guide, steer, escort, shepherd, usher: *He was marshalling the visitors, showing them where to go.* **2 = arrange**, group, order, collect, gather, line up, organize, assemble, deploy, array, dispose, draw up, muster, align: *The government marshalled its economic resources.*

martial ADJECTIVE **= military**, soldierly, brave, heroic, belligerent, warlike, bellicose

martyrdom NOUN **= persecution**, suffering, torture, agony, ordeal, torment, anguish **OPPOSITE:** bliss

QUOTATIONS

A thing is not necessarily true because a man dies for it
[Oscar Wilde *Sebastian Melmoth*]

marvel VERB **= be amazed**, wonder, gaze, gape, goggle, be awed, be filled with surprise: *Her fellow workers marvelled at her infinite energy.*
▷ NOUN **1 = wonder**, phenomenon, miracle, portent: *A new technological marvel was invented there – the electron microscope.* **2 = genius**, whizz *(informal)*, prodigy: *Her death is a great tragedy. She really was a marvel.*

marvellous ADJECTIVE **= excellent**, great *(informal)*, mean *(slang)*, topping *(Brit. slang)*, wonderful, brilliant, bad *(slang)*, cracking *(Brit. informal)*, amazing, crucial *(slang)*, extraordinary, remarkable, smashing *(informal)*, superb, spectacular, fantastic *(informal)*, magnificent, astonishing, fabulous *(informal)*, divine *(informal)*, glorious, terrific *(informal)*, splendid, sensational *(informal)*, mega *(slang)*, sovereign, awesome *(slang)*, breathtaking, phenomenal, astounding, singular, miraculous, colossal, super *(informal)*, wicked *(informal)*, def *(slang)*, prodigious, wondrous *(archaic, literary)*, brill *(informal)*, stupendous, jaw-dropping, eye-popping, bodacious *(slang, chiefly U.S.)*, boffo *(slang)*, jim-dandy *(slang)*, chillin' *(U.S. slang)*, booshit *(Austral. slang)*, exo *(Austral. slang)*, sik *(Austral. slang)*, rad *(informal)*, phat *(slang)*, schmick *(Austral. informal)*: *He's a marvellous actor.*
OPPOSITE: terrible

masculine ADJECTIVE **1 = male**, manly, mannish, manlike, virile, manful: *masculine characteristics such as a deep voice and facial hair* **2 = strong**, powerful, bold, brave, strapping, hardy, robust, vigorous, muscular, macho, butch *(slang)*, resolute, gallant, well-built, red-blooded *(informal)*, stout-hearted, two-fisted: *an aggressive, masculine image*

mask NOUN **1 = disguise**, visor, vizard *(archaic)*, stocking mask, false face, domino *(rare)*: *a gunman wearing a mask* **2 = façade**, disguise, show, front, cover, screen, blind, cover-up, veil, cloak, guise, camouflage, veneer, semblance, concealment: *His mask cracked, and she saw an angry and violent man.*
▷ VERB **= disguise**, hide, conceal, obscure, cover (up), screen, blanket, veil, cloak, mantle, camouflage, enshroud: *A cloud masked the sun.*

masquerade VERB **= pose**, pretend to be, impersonate, profess to be, pass yourself off, simulate, disguise yourself: *He masqueraded as a doctor and fooled everyone.*
▷ NOUN **1 = pretence**, disguise, deception, front *(informal)*, cover, screen, put-on *(slang)*, mask, cover-up, cloak, guise, subterfuge, dissimulation, imposture: *He claimed that the elections would be a masquerade.* **2 = masked ball**, revel, mummery, fancy dress party, costume ball, masked party: *A man was killed at the Christmas masquerade.*

mass NOUN **1 = lot**, collection, load, combination, pile, quantity, bunch, stack, heap, rick, batch, accumulation, stockpile, assemblage, aggregation, conglomeration: *On his desk is a mass of books and papers.* **2 = piece**, block, lump, chunk, hunk, concretion: *Cut it up before it cools and sets into a solid mass.* **3 = majority**, body, bulk, best part, greater part, almost all, lion's share, preponderance: *The Second World War involved the mass of the population.* **4 = crowd**, group, body, pack, lot, army, host, band, troop, drove, crush, bunch *(informal)*, mob, flock, herd, number, horde, multitude, throng, rabble, assemblage: *A mass of excited people clogged the street.* **5 = size**, matter, weight, extent, dimensions, bulk, magnitude, greatness: *Pluto and Triton have nearly the same mass and density.*
▷ ADJECTIVE **= large-scale**, general, popular, widespread, extensive, universal, wholesale, indiscriminate, pandemic: *ideas on combating mass unemployment*
▷ VERB **= gather**, assemble, accumulate, collect, rally, mob, muster, swarm, amass, throng, congregate, foregather: *Shortly after the announcement, police began to mass at the shipyard.*
the masses = the multitude, the crowd, the mob, the common people, the great unwashed *(derogatory)*, the hoi polloi, the commonalty: *His music is commercial. It is aimed at the masses.*

massacre NOUN **= slaughter**, killing, murder, holocaust, carnage, extermination, annihilation, butchery, mass slaughter, blood bath: *She lost her mother in the massacre.*
▷ VERB **= slaughter**, kill, murder, butcher, take out *(slang)*, wipe out, slay, blow away *(slang, chiefly U.S.)*, annihilate, exterminate, mow down, cut to pieces: *Troops indiscriminately massacred the defenceless population.*

massage NOUN **= rub-down**, rubbing, manipulation, kneading, reflexology, shiatsu, acupressure, chiropractic treatment, palpation: *Massage isn't a long-term cure for stress.*
▷ VERB **1 = rub down**, rub, manipulate, knead, pummel, palpate: *She massaged her foot, which was bruised and aching.* **2 = manipulate**, alter, distort, doctor, cook *(informal)*, fix *(informal)*, rig, fiddle *(informal)*, tamper with, tinker with, misrepresent, fiddle with, falsify: *efforts to massage the unemployment figures*

massive ADJECTIVE **= huge**, great, big, heavy, imposing, vast, enormous, solid, impressive, substantial, extensive, monster, immense, hefty, titanic, gigantic, monumental, whacking *(informal)*, mammoth, bulky, colossal, whopping *(informal)*, weighty, stellar *(informal)*, hulking, ponderous, gargantuan, elephantine, ginormous *(informal)*, humongous *or* humungous *(U.S. slang)*, supersize
OPPOSITE: tiny

master NOUN **1 = lord**, ruler, commander, chief, director, manager, boss *(informal)*, head, owner, captain, governor, employer, principal, skipper *(informal)*, controller, superintendent, overlord, overseer, baas *(S. African)*: *My master ordered me to deliver the message.* **OPPOSITE:** servant **2 = expert**, maestro, pro *(informal)*, ace *(informal)*, genius, wizard, adept, virtuoso, grandmaster, doyen, past master, dab hand *(Brit. informal)*, wonk *(informal)*, maven *(U.S.)*, fundi *(S. African)*: *He is a master at blocking progress.* **OPPOSITE:** amateur **3 = teacher**, tutor, instructor, schoolmaster, pedagogue, preceptor: *a retired maths master*
OPPOSITE: student
▷ ADJECTIVE **= main**, principal, chief, prime, grand, great, foremost, predominant: *There's a Georgian four-poster in the master bedroom.*
OPPOSITE: lesser
▷ VERB **1 = learn**, understand, pick up, acquire, grasp, get the hang of *(informal)*, become proficient in, know inside out, know backwards: *Students are expected to master a second language.* **2 = overcome**, defeat, suppress, conquer, check, curb, tame, lick *(informal)*, subdue, overpower, quash, quell, triumph over, bridle, vanquish, subjugate: *He wanted to master his fears of becoming ill.* **OPPOSITE:** give in to **3 = control**, manage, direct, dominate, rule, command, govern, regulate: *His genius alone has mastered every crisis.*

masterful ADJECTIVE **1 = skilful**, skilled, expert, finished, fine, masterly, excellent, crack *(informal)*, supreme, clever, superior, world-class, exquisite, adept, consummate, first-rate, deft, superlative, adroit, dexterous: *a masterful performance of boxing* **OPPOSITE:** unskilled **2 = domineering**, authoritative, dictatorial, bossy *(informal)*, arrogant, imperious, overbearing, tyrannical, magisterial, despotic, high-handed, peremptory, overweening, self-willed: *Successful businesses need bold, masterful managers.* **OPPOSITE:** meek

USAGE
In current usage there is a lot of overlap between the meanings of *masterful* and *masterly*. According to some, the first should only be used where there is a connotation of power and domination, the second where the connotations are of great skill. Nevertheless, as the Bank of English shows, the majority of uses of *masterful* these days relate to the second meaning, as in *musically, it was a masterful display of the folk singer's art*. Anyone wishing to observe the distinction would use only *masterly* in the context just given, and *masterful* in contexts such as: *his need to be masterful with women was extreme*; *Alec was so masterful that he surprised himself*.

masterly ADJECTIVE **= skilful**, skilled, expert, finished, fine, excellent, crack *(informal)*, supreme, clever, superior, world-class, exquisite, adept, consummate, first-rate, superlative, masterful, adroit, dexterous

mastermind VERB **= plan**, manage, direct, organize, devise, conceive, be the brains behind *(informal)*: *The finance minister will continue to mastermind economic reform.*
▷ NOUN **= organizer**, director, manager, authority, engineer, brain(s) *(informal)*, architect, genius, planner, intellect, virtuoso, rocket scientist *(informal, chiefly U.S.)*, brainbox: *He was the mastermind behind the plan.*

masterpiece NOUN **= classic**, tour de force *(French)*, pièce de résistance *(French)*, magnum opus, master work, jewel, chef-d'oeuvre *(French)*

mastery NOUN **1 = understanding**, knowledge, comprehension, ability, skill, know-how, command, grip, grasp, expertise, prowess, familiarity, attainment, finesse, proficiency, virtuosity, dexterity, cleverness, deftness, acquirement: *He demonstrated his mastery of political manoeuvring.* **2 = control**, authority, command, rule, victory, triumph, sway, domination, superiority, conquest, supremacy, dominion, upper hand, ascendancy, pre-eminence, mana *(N.Z.)*, whip hand: *a region where humans have gained mastery over the major rivers*

masturbation NOUN **= self-abuse**, onanism, playing with yourself *(slang)*, autoeroticism

> **QUOTATIONS**
> Hey, don't knock masturbation! It's sex with someone I love
> [Woody Allen *Annie Hall*]

match NOUN **1 = game**, test, competition, trial, tie, contest, fixture, bout, head-to-head: *He was watching a football match.* **2 = companion**, mate, equal, equivalent, counterpart, fellow, complement: *Moira was a perfect match for him.* **3 = replica**, double, copy, twin, equal, spit *(informal, chiefly Brit.)*, duplicate, lookalike, ringer *(slang)*, spitting image *(informal)*, dead ringer

Mythology

Characters in classical mythology

Achilles
Actaeon
Adonis
Aeneas
Agamemnon
Ajax
Amazons
Andromache
Andromeda
Antigone
Arachne
Argonauts
Ariadne
Atalanta
Atlas
Callisto
Calypso
Cassandra
Cassiopeia
Castor
Charon
Circe
Clytemnestra
Daedalus
Daphne
Dido
Diomedes
Echo
Electra
Endymion
Europa
Eurydice
Galatea
Ganymede
Hector
Hecuba
Helen
Heracles
Hercules
Hermaphroditus
Hippolytus
Hyacinthus
Icarus
Io
Ixion
Jason
Jocasta
Leda
Medea
Medusa
Menelaus
Midas
Minos
Muses
Narcissus
Niobe
Odysseus
Oedipus
Orestes
Orion
Orpheus
Pandora
Paris
Penelope
Persephone
Perseus
Pleiades
Pollux
Polydeuces
Polyphemus
Priam
Prometheus
Proserpina
Psyche
Pygmalion
Pyramus
Remus
Romulus
Semele
sibyl
Silenus
Sisyphus
Tantalus
Theseus
Thisbe
Tiresias
Ulysses

Places in classical mythology

Acheron
Colchis
Elysium
Erebus
Hades
Helicon
Islands of the Blessed
Ithaca
Knossos
Lethe
Olympus
Parnassus
Phlegethon
Styx
Tartarus
Thebes
Troy

Places in Norse mythology

Asgard *or* Asgarth
Bifrost
Hel or Hela
Jotunheim
Midgard *or* Midgarth
Nidhogg
Niflheim
Svartalpheim
Utgard
Valhalla
Vanaheim

Muses

Calliope	epic poetry
Clio	history
Erato	love poetry
Euterpe	lyric poetry and music
Melpomene	tragedy
Polyhymnia	singing, mime, and sacred dance
Terpsichore	dance and choral song
Thalia	comedy and pastoral poetry
Urania	astronomy

Mythological creatures

afreet or afrit
androsphinx
banshee
basilisk
behemoth
brownie
bunyip
centaur
Cerberus
Charybdis
chimera *or* chimaera
cockatrice
Cyclops
dragon
dryad
dwarf
Echidna
elf
erlking
fairy
faun
fay
Fury
genie
Geryon
ghost
giant
goblin
Gorgon
gremlin
Grendel
griffin, griffon, *or* gryphon
hamadryad
Harpy
hippocampus
hippogriff *or* hippogryph
hobbit
hobgoblin
Hydra
impundulu
jinni, jinnee, djinni, *or* djinny
kelpie
kraken
kylin
lamia
leprechaun
leviathan
Medusa
mermaid
merman
Minotaur
naiad
Nereid
nix *or* nixie
nymph
Oceanid
orc
oread
Pegasus
peri
phoenix
pixie
roc
salamander
satyr
Scylla
Siren
Sphinx
sylph
tokoloshe
tricorn
troll
unicorn
vampire
water nymph
wood nymph

Characters in Norse mythology

Andvari
Ask
Atli
Aurvandil the Bold
Brynhild
Fafnir
Gudrun
Gunnar
Gutthorn
Hreidmar
Lif
Lifthrasir
Mimir
Regin
Sigmund
Svipdagr
Sigurd
Wayland

Labours of Hercules

the slaying of the Nemean lion
the slaying of the Lernaean hydra
the capture of the hind of Ceryneia
the capture of the wild boar of Erymanthus
the cleansing of the Augean stables
the shooting of the Stymphalian birds
the capture of the Cretan bull
the capture of the horses of Diomedes
the taking of the girdle of Hippolyte
the capture of the cattle of Geryon
the recovery of the golden apples of Hesperides
the taking of Cerberus

The Fates

Atropos
Clotho
Lachesis

The Graces

Aglaia
Euphrosyne
Thalia

(slang), spit and image *(informal)*: *He asked his assistant to look for a match of the vase he broke.* **4 = marriage**, union, couple, pair, pairing, item *(informal)*, alliance, combination, partnership, duet, affiliation: *Hollywood's favourite love match foundered on the rocks.* **5 = equal**, rival, equivalent, peer, competitor, counterpart: *I was no match for a man with such power.*
▷ VERB **1 = correspond with**, suit, go with, complement, fit with, accompany, team with, blend with, tone with, harmonize with, coordinate with: *These shoes match your dress.* **2 = tailor**, fit, suit, adapt: *You don't have to match your lipstick to your outfit.* **3 = correspond**, agree, accord, square, coincide, tally, conform, match up, be compatible, harmonize, be consonant: *Their strengths in memory and spatial skills matched.* **4 = pair**, unite, join, couple, link, marry, ally, combine, mate, yoke: *It can take time and money to match buyers and sellers.* **5 = rival**, equal, compete with, compare with, emulate, contend with, measure up to: *We matched them in every department of the game.*
match something or **someone against something** or **someone = pit against**, set against, play off against, put in opposition to: *The finals begin today, matching the United States against France.*

m

matching ADJECTIVE **= identical**, like, same, double, paired, equal, toning, twin, equivalent, parallel, corresponding, comparable, duplicate, coordinating, analogous **OPPOSITE:** different

matchless ADJECTIVE **= unequalled**, unique, unparalleled, unrivalled, perfect, supreme, exquisite, consummate, superlative, inimitable, incomparable, unmatched, peerless, unsurpassed **OPPOSITE:** average

mate NOUN **1 = friend**, pal *(informal)*, companion, buddy *(informal)*, china *(Brit. slang)*, cock *(Brit. informal)*, comrade, chum *(informal)*, mucker *(Brit. informal)*, crony, main man *(slang, chiefly U.S.)*, homeboy *(slang, chiefly U.S.)*, cobber *(Austral. & N.Z. old-fashioned, informal)*, E hoa *(N.Z.)*: *A mate of mine used to play soccer for Liverpool.* **2 = partner**, lover, companion, spouse, consort, significant other *(U.S. informal)*, better half *(humorous)*, helpmeet, husband or wife: *He has found his ideal mate.* **3 = double**, match, fellow, twin, counterpart, companion: *The guest cabin is a mirror image of its mate.* **4 = assistant**, subordinate, apprentice, helper, accomplice, sidekick *(informal)*: *The electrician's mate ignored the red-lettered warning signs.* **5 = colleague**, associate, companion, co-worker, fellow-worker, compeer: *He celebrated with work mates in the pub.*
▷ VERB **1 = pair**, couple, breed, copulate: *They want the males to mate with wild females.* **2 = marry**, match, wed, get married, shack up *(informal)*: *Women typically seek older men with which to mate.* **3 = join**, match, couple, pair, yoke: *The film tries very hard to mate modern with old.*

material NOUN **1 = substance**, body, matter, stuff, elements, constituents: *the decomposition of organic material* **2 = cloth**, stuff, fabric, textile: *the thick material of her skirt* **3 = information**, work, details, facts, notes, evidence, particulars, data, info *(informal)*, subject matter, documentation: *In my version of the story, I added some new material.*
▷ ADJECTIVE **1 = physical**, worldly, solid, substantial, concrete, fleshly, bodily, tangible, palpable, corporeal, nonspiritual: *the material world* **2 = relevant**, important, significant, essential, vital, key, serious, grave, meaningful, applicable, indispensable, momentous, weighty, pertinent, consequential, apposite, apropos, germane: *The company failed to disclose material information.*

materialize VERB **1 = occur**, happen, take place, turn up, come about, take shape, come into being, come to pass: *None of the anticipated difficulties materialized.* **2 = appear**, arrive, emerge, surface, turn up, loom, show up *(informal)*, pop up *(informal)*, put in an appearance: *He materialized at her side, notebook at the ready.*

materially ADVERB **= significantly**, much, greatly, considerably, essentially, seriously, gravely, substantially **OPPOSITE:** insignificantly

maternal ADJECTIVE **= motherly**, protective, nurturing, maternalistic

maternity NOUN **= motherhood**, parenthood, motherliness

matey ADJECTIVE **= friendly**, intimate, comradely, thick *(informal)*, pally *(informal)*, amiable, sociable, chummy *(informal)*, free-and-easy, companionable, clubby, buddy-buddy *(slang, chiefly U.S. & Canad.)*, hail-fellow-well-met, palsy-walsy *(informal)*

matrimonial ADJECTIVE **= marital**, married, wedding, wedded, nuptial, conjugal, spousal, connubial, hymeneal

matrimony NOUN **= marriage**, nuptials, wedlock, wedding ceremony, marital rites

matted ADJECTIVE **= tangled**, knotted, unkempt, knotty, tousled, ratty, uncombed

matter NOUN **1 = situation**, thing, issue, concern, business, question, event, subject, affair, incident, proceeding, episode, topic, transaction, occurrence: *It was a private matter.* **2 = substance**, material, body, stuff: *A proton is an elementary particle of matter.* **3 = content**, sense, subject, argument, text, substance, burden, thesis, purport, gist, pith: *This conflict forms the matter of the play.* **4 = pus**, discharge, secretion, suppuration, purulence: *If the wound starts to produce yellow matter, see your doctor.* **5 = importance**, interest, moment, note, weight, import, consequence, significance: *Forget it; it's of no matter.*
▷ VERB **= be important**, make a difference, count, be relevant, make any difference, mean anything, have influence, carry weight, cut any ice *(informal)*, be of consequence, be of account: *It doesn't matter how long you take.*

matter-of-fact ADJECTIVE **= unsentimental**, flat, dry, plain, dull, sober, down-to-earth, mundane, lifeless, prosaic, deadpan, unimaginative, unvarnished, emotionless, unembellished

mature VERB **= develop**, grow up, bloom, blossom, come of age, become adult, age, reach adulthood, maturate: *young girls who have not yet matured*
▷ ADJECTIVE **1 = matured**, seasoned, ripe, mellow, ripened: *grate some mature cheddar cheese* **2 = grown-up**, adult, grown, of age, full-blown, fully fledged, fully-developed, full-grown: *Here is the voice of a mature man, expressing sorrow for a lost ideal.*
OPPOSITE: immature

maturity NOUN **1 = adulthood**, majority, completion, puberty, coming of age, fullness, full bloom, full growth, pubescence, manhood or womanhood: *Humans experience a delayed maturity compared with other mammals.* **OPPOSITE:** immaturity **2 = ripeness**, perfection, maturation: *the dried seeds of peas that have been picked at maturity*

maudlin ADJECTIVE **= sentimental**, tearful, mushy *(informal)*, soppy *(Brit. informal)*, weepy *(informal)*, slushy *(informal)*, mawkish, lachrymose, icky *(informal)*, overemotional

maul VERB **1 = mangle**, claw, lacerate, tear, mangulate *(Austral. slang)*: *He had been mauled by a bear.* **2 = ill-treat**, beat, abuse, batter, thrash, beat up *(informal)*, molest, work over *(slang)*, pummel, manhandle, rough up, handle roughly, knock about or around, beat or knock seven bells out of *(informal)*: *The troops were severely mauled before evacuating the island.*

maverick NOUN **= rebel**, radical, dissenter, individualist, protester, eccentric, heretic, nonconformist, iconoclast, dissentient: *He was too much of a maverick to hold high office.*
OPPOSITE: traditionalist
▷ ADJECTIVE **= rebel**, radical, dissenting, individualistic, eccentric, heretical, iconoclastic, nonconformist: *Her maverick behaviour precluded any chance of promotion.*

maw NOUN **= mouth**, crop, throat, jaws, gullet, craw

maxim NOUN **= saying**, motto, adage, proverb, rule, saw, gnome, dictum, axiom, aphorism, byword, apophthegm

maximum ADJECTIVE **= greatest**, highest, supreme, paramount, utmost, most, maximal, topmost: *The maximum height for a fence here is 2 metres.* **OPPOSITE:** minimal
▷ NOUN **= top**, most, peak, ceiling, crest, utmost, upper limit, uttermost: *The law provides for a maximum of two years in prison.* **OPPOSITE:** minimum

maybe ADVERB **= perhaps**, possibly, it could be, conceivably, perchance (*archaic*), mayhap (*archaic*), peradventure (*archaic*)

mayhem NOUN **= chaos**, trouble, violence, disorder, destruction, confusion, havoc, fracas, commotion

maze NOUN **= web**, puzzle, confusion, tangle, snarl, mesh, labyrinth, imbroglio, convolutions, complex network: *a maze of dimly-lit corridors*

meadow NOUN **= field**, pasture, grassland, ley, lea (*poetic*)

meagre ADJECTIVE **= insubstantial**, little, small, poor, spare, slight, inadequate, pathetic, slender, scant, sparse, deficient, paltry, skimpy, puny, measly, scanty, exiguous, scrimpy

mean[1] VERB **1 = signify**, say, suggest, indicate, represent, express, stand for, convey, spell out, purport, symbolize, denote, connote, betoken: *The red signal means that you can shoot.* **2 = imply**, suggest, intend, indicate, refer to, intimate, get at (*informal*), hint at, have in mind, drive at (*informal*), allude to, insinuate: *What do you think he means by that?* **3 = presage**, promise, herald, foreshadow, augur, foretell, portend, betoken, adumbrate: *An enlarged prostate does not necessarily mean cancer.* **4 = result in**, cause, produce, effect, lead to, involve, bring about, give rise to, entail, engender, necessitate: *Trade and product discounts can mean big savings.* **5 = intend**, want, plan, expect, design, aim, wish, think, propose, purpose, desire, set out, contemplate, aspire, have plans, have in mind: *I didn't mean to hurt you.* **6 = destine**, make, design, suit, fate, predestine, preordain: *He said that we were meant to be together.*

mean[2] ADJECTIVE **1 = miserly**, stingy, parsimonious, niggardly, close (*informal*), near (*informal*), tight, selfish, beggarly, mercenary, skimpy, penny-pinching, ungenerous, penurious, tight-fisted, mingy (*Brit. informal*), hungry (*Austral. & N.Z. informal*), snoep (*S. African informal*): *Don't be mean with the fabric, or the curtains will end up looking skimpy.*
OPPOSITE: generous
2 = dishonourable, base, petty, degraded, disgraceful, shameful, shabby, vile, degenerate, callous, sordid, abject, despicable, narrow-minded, contemptible, wretched, scurvy, ignoble, hard-hearted, scungy (*Austral. & N.Z.*), low-minded: *Upstaging the bride was a particularly mean trick.* **OPPOSITE:** honourable **3 = malicious**, hostile, nasty, sour, unpleasant, rude, unfriendly, bad-tempered, disagreeable, churlish, ill-tempered, cantankerous: *The prison officer described him as the meanest man he'd ever met.* **OPPOSITE:** kind **4 = shabby**, poor, miserable, rundown, beggarly, seedy, scruffy, sordid, paltry, squalid, tawdry, low-rent (*informal, chiefly U.S.*), contemptible, wretched, down-at-heel, grungy (*slang, chiefly U.S.*), scuzzy (*slang, chiefly U.S.*): *He was raised in the mean streets of the central market district.* **OPPOSITE:** superb **5 = lowly**, low, common, ordinary, modest, base, obscure, humble, inferior, vulgar, menial, proletarian, undistinguished, servile, ignoble, plebeian, lowborn, baseborn (*archaic*): *southern opportunists of mean origins* **OPPOSITE:** noble

mean[3] NOUN **= average**, middle, balance, norm, median, midpoint: *Take a hundred and twenty values and calculate the mean.*
▷ ADJECTIVE **= average**, middle, middling, standard, medium, normal, intermediate, median, medial: *the mean score for 26-year-olds*

meander VERB **1 = wind**, turn, snake, zigzag: *The river meandered in lazy curves.* **2 = wander**, stroll, stray, ramble, stravaig (*Scot. & Northern English dialect*): *We meandered along the Irish country roads.*
▷ NOUN **= curve**, bend, turn, twist, loop, coil, zigzag: *The outer bank of a meander in the river.*

meandering ADJECTIVE **= winding**, wandering, snaking, tortuous, convoluted, serpentine, circuitous **OPPOSITE:** straight

meaning NOUN **1 = significance**, message, explanation, substance, value, import, implication, drift, interpretation, essence, purport, connotation, upshot, gist, signification: *I became more aware of the symbols and their meanings.* **2 = definition**, sense, interpretation, explication, elucidation, denotation: *arguing over the exact meaning of this word or that* **3 = purpose**, point, end, idea, goal, design, aim, object, intention: *Unsure of the meaning of this remark, he remained silent.* **4 = force**, use, point, effect, value, worth, consequence, thrust, validity, usefulness, efficacy: *a challenge that gives meaning to life*
▷ ADJECTIVE **= expressive**, meaningful, pointed, revealing, significant, speaking, pregnant, suggestive, telltale: *He nodded and gave me a meaning look.*

meaningful ADJECTIVE **1 = significant**, important, serious, material, useful, relevant, valid, worthwhile, purposeful: *a meaningful and constructive dialogue* **OPPOSITE:** trivial **2 = expressive**, suggestive, meaning, pointed, speaking, pregnant: *The two men expressed a quick, meaningful look.*

meaningless ADJECTIVE **= nonsensical**, senseless, inconsequential, inane, insubstantial **OPPOSITE:** worthwhile

meanness NOUN **1 = miserliness**, parsimony, stinginess, tight-fistedness, niggardliness, selfishness, minginess (*Brit. informal*), penuriousness: *This careful attitude to money can border on meanness.* **2 = pettiness**, degradation, degeneracy, wretchedness, narrow-mindedness, shabbiness, baseness, vileness, sordidness, shamefulness, scurviness, abjectness, low-mindedness, ignobility, despicableness, disgracefulness, dishonourableness: *Their meanness of spirit is embarrassing.* **3 = malice**, hostility, bad temper, rudeness, nastiness, unpleasantness, ill temper, sourness, unfriendliness, maliciousness, cantankerousness, churlishness, disagreeableness: *There was always a certain amount of cruelty, meanness and villainy.* **4 = shabbiness**, squalor, insignificance, pettiness, wretchedness, seediness, tawdriness, sordidness, scruffiness, humbleness, poorness, paltriness, beggarliness, contemptibleness: *the meanness of our surroundings*

means PLURAL NOUN **1 = method**, way, course, process, medium, measure, agency, channel, instrument, avenue, mode, expedient: *We do not have the means to fight such a crimewave.* **2 = money**, funds, capital, property, riches, income, resources, estate, fortune, wealth, substance, affluence, wherewithal: *He did not have the means to compensate her.*
by all means = certainly, surely, of course, definitely, absolutely, positively, doubtlessly: *'Can I come and see your house?' 'Yes, by all means.'*
by means of = by way of, using, through, via, utilizing, with the aid of, by dint of: *a course taught by means of lectures and seminars*
by no means = in no way, no way, not at all, definitely not, not in the least, on no account, not in the slightest, not the least bit, absolutely not: *This is by no means out of the ordinary.*

meantime *or* **meanwhile** ADVERB **= at the same time**, in the meantime, simultaneously, for the present, concurrently, in the meanwhile

meanwhile *or* **meantime** ADVERB **= for now**, in the meantime, for the moment, in the interim, for then, in the interval, in the meanwhile, in the intervening time

measly ADJECTIVE **= meagre**, miserable, pathetic, paltry, mean, poor, petty, beggarly, pitiful, skimpy, puny, stingy, contemptible, scanty, miserly, niggardly, ungenerous, mingy (*Brit. informal*), snoep (*S. African informal*)

measurable ADJECTIVE **1 = perceptible**, material, significant, distinct, palpable, discernible, detectable: *Both leaders expect measurable progress.* **2 = quantifiable**, material, quantitative, assessable, determinable, computable, gaugeable, mensurable: *measurable quantities such as the number of jobs*

measure VERB **= quantify**, rate, judge, determine, value, size, estimate, survey, assess, weigh, calculate, evaluate, compute, gauge, mark out, appraise, calibrate: *Measure the length and width of the gap.*
▷ NOUN **1 = quantity**, share, amount, degree, reach, range, size, capacity, extent, proportion, allowance, portion, scope, quota, ration, magnitude, allotment, amplitude: *The colonies were claiming a larger measure of self-government.* **2 = standard**, example, model, test, par, criterion, norm, benchmark, barometer, yardstick, touchstone, litmus test: *The local elections were seen as a measure of the government's success.* **3 = action**, act, step, procedure, means, course, control, proceeding, initiative, manoeuvre, legal action, deed, expedient: *He said stern measures would be taken against the rioters.* **4 = gauge**, rule, scale, metre, ruler, yardstick: *a tape measure* **5 = law**, act, bill, legislation, resolution, statute, enactment: *They passed a measure that would give small businesses more benefits.*
for good measure = in addition, as well, besides, to boot, as an extra, into the bargain, as a bonus: *For good measure, a few details of hotels were included.*
measure up = come up to standard, be fit, be adequate, be capable, be suitable, make the grade (*informal*), be suited, be satisfactory, come up to scratch (*informal*),
cut the mustard (*U.S. slang*), fulfil the expectations, fit *or* fill the bill: *I was informed that I didn't measure up.*
measure up to something *or* **someone = achieve**, meet, match, rival, equal, compare to, come up to, be equal to, vie with, be on a level with: *It was tiring, always trying to measure up to her high standards.*

measured ADJECTIVE **1 = steady**, even, slow, regular, dignified, stately, solemn, leisurely, sedate, unhurried: *They have to proceed at a measured pace.* **2 = considered**, planned, reasoned, studied, calculated, deliberate, sober, premeditated, well-thought-out: *Her more measured approach will appeal to voters.* **3 = quantified**, standard, exact, regulated, precise, gauged, verified, predetermined, modulated: *Is the difference in measured intelligence genetic or environmental?*

measurement NOUN **1 = size**, length, dimension, area, amount, weight, volume, capacity, extent, height, depth, width, magnitude, amplitude: *Some of the measurements are doubtless inaccurate.* **2 = calculation**, assessment, evaluation, estimation, survey, judgment, valuation, appraisal, computation, calibration, mensuration, metage: *Measurement of blood pressure can be undertaken by the practice nurse.*

meat NOUN **1 = food**, provisions, nourishment, sustenance, eats (*slang*), fare, flesh, rations, grub (*slang*), subsistence, kai (*N.Z. informal*), chow (*informal*), nosh (*slang*), victuals, comestibles, provender, nutriment, viands: *They gave meat and drink to the poor.* **2 = gist**, point, heart, core, substance, essence, nucleus, marrow, kernel, nub, pith: *The real meat of the conference was the attempt to agree on minimum standards.*

QUOTATIONS
If you knew how meat was made, you'd probably lose your lunch. I'm from cattle country. That's why I became a vegetarian
[K. D. Lang]

PROVERBS
The nearer the bone, the sweeter the meat

meaty ADJECTIVE **1 = substantial**, rich, nourishing, hearty: *a lasagne with a meaty sauce* **2 = brawny**, muscular, heavy, solid, strapping, sturdy, burly, husky (*informal*), fleshy, beefy (*informal*), heavily built: *a pleasant lady with meaty arms* **3 = interesting**, rich, significant, substantial, profound, meaningful, pithy: *This time she has been given a more meaty role in the film.*

mechanical ADJECTIVE **1 = automatic**, automated, mechanized, power-driven, motor-driven, machine-driven: *a small mechanical device that taps out the numbers* **OPPOSITE:** manual
2 = unthinking, routine, automatic, matter-of-fact, cold, unconscious, instinctive, lacklustre, involuntary, impersonal, habitual, cursory, perfunctory, unfeeling, machine-like, emotionless, spiritless: *His retort was mechanical.* **OPPOSITE:** conscious

mechanism NOUN **1 = workings**, motor, gears, works, action, components, machinery, innards (*informal*): *the locking mechanism*
2 = process, workings, way, means, system, performance, operation, medium, agency, method, functioning, technique, procedure, execution, methodology: *the clumsy mechanism of price controls* **3 = machine**, system, structure, device, tool, instrument, appliance, apparatus, contrivance: *The heat-producing mechanism will switch itself on automatically.*

meddle VERB **= interfere**, intervene, tamper, intrude, pry, butt in, interpose, stick your nose in (*informal*), put your oar in, intermeddle, put your two cents in (*U.S. slang*)

mediate VERB **= intervene**, moderate, step in (*informal*), intercede, settle, referee, resolve, umpire, reconcile, arbitrate, interpose, conciliate, make peace, restore harmony, act as middleman, bring to terms, bring to an agreement

mediation NOUN **= arbitration**, intervention, reconciliation, conciliation, good offices, intercession, interposition

mediator NOUN **= negotiator**, arbitrator, judge, referee, advocate, umpire, intermediary, middleman, arbiter, peacemaker, go-between, moderator, interceder, honest broker

medicinal ADJECTIVE **= therapeutic**, medical, healing, remedial, restorative, curative, analeptic, roborant, sanative

medicine NOUN **= remedy**, drug, cure, prescription, medication, nostrum, physic, medicament

QUOTATIONS
Formerly, when religion was strong and science weak, men mistook magic for medicine; now, when science is strong and religion weak, men mistake medicine for magic
[Thomas Szasz *The Second Skin*]
Nearly all men die of their medicines, not of their diseases
[Molière *Le Malade Imaginaire*]

medieval ADJECTIVE **= old-fashioned**, antique, primitive, obsolete, out-of-date, archaic, prehistoric, antiquated, anachronistic, antediluvian, unenlightened, out of the ark

mediocre ADJECTIVE **= second-rate**, average, ordinary, indifferent, middling, pedestrian, inferior, commonplace, vanilla (*slang*), insignificant, so-so (*informal*), banal, tolerable, run-of-the-mill, passable, undistinguished, uninspired, bog-standard (*Brit. & Irish slang*), no great shakes (*informal*), half-pie (*N.Z. informal*), fair to middling (*informal*), meh (*slang*) **OPPOSITE:** excellent

QUOTATIONS
Some men are born mediocre, some men achieve mediocrity, and some men have mediocrity thrust upon them. With Major it had been all three
[Joseph Heller *Catch-22*]

mediocrity NOUN **1 = insignificance**, indifference, inferiority, meanness, ordinariness, unimportance, poorness: *She lamented the mediocrity of contemporary literature.* **2 = nonentity**, nobody, lightweight (*informal*), second-rater, cipher: *Surrounded by mediocrities, he seemed a towering intellectual.*

QUOTATIONS
Mediocrity knows nothing higher than itself, but talent instantly recognizes genius
[Sir Arthur Conan Doyle *The Valley of Fear*]

meditate VERB **= reflect**, think, consider, contemplate, deliberate, muse, ponder, ruminate, cogitate, be

m

in a brown study: *I was meditating, and reached a higher state of consciousness.* **meditate on something = consider**, study, contemplate, ponder, reflect on, mull over, think over, chew over, deliberate on, weigh, turn something over in your mind: *He meditated on the problem.*

meditation NOUN **= reflection**, thought, concentration, study, musing, pondering, contemplation, reverie, ruminating, rumination, cogitation, cerebration, a brown study

meditative ADJECTIVE **= reflective**, thoughtful, contemplative, studious, pensive, deliberative, ruminative, cogitative

medium ADJECTIVE **= average**, mean, middle, middling, fair, intermediate, midway, mediocre, median, medial: *foods which contain only medium levels of sodium* **OPPOSITE:** extraordinary
▷ NOUN **1 = spiritualist**, seer, clairvoyant, fortune teller, spiritist, channeller: *Going to see a medium provided a starting point for her.* **2 = middle**, mean, centre, average, compromise, middle ground, middle way, midpoint, middle course, middle path: *It's difficult to strike a happy medium.*

medley NOUN **= mixture**, confusion, jumble, assortment, patchwork, pastiche, mixed bag *(informal)*, potpourri, mélange *(French)*, miscellany, mishmash, farrago, hotchpotch, hodgepodge, salmagundi, olio, gallimaufry, omnium-gatherum

meek ADJECTIVE **1 = submissive**, soft, yielding, gentle, peaceful, modest, mild, patient, humble, timid, long-suffering, compliant, unassuming, unpretentious, docile, deferential, forbearing, acquiescent: *He was a meek, mild-mannered fellow.* **OPPOSITE:** overbearing **2 = spineless**, weak, tame, boneless, weak-kneed *(informal)*, spiritless, unresisting, wussy *(slang)*, wimpish *or* wimpy *(informal)*: *He may be self-effacing, but he certainly isn't meek.*

> **QUOTATIONS**
> Blessed are the meek: for they shall inherit the earth
> [*Bible: St. Matthew*]
>
> It's going to be fun to watch and see how long the meek can keep the earth after they inherit it
> [Kin Hubbard]

meet VERB **1 = encounter**, come across, run into, happen on, find, contact, confront, bump into *(informal)*, run across, chance on, come face to face with: *He's the kindest person I've ever met.* **OPPOSITE:** avoid **2 = gather**, collect, assemble, get together, rally, come together, muster, convene, congregate, foregather: *The commission met four times between 1988 and 1991.* **OPPOSITE:** disperse **3 = fulfil**, match (up to), answer, perform, handle, carry out, equal, satisfy, cope with, discharge, comply with, come up to, conform to, gratify, measure up to: *The current arrangements are inadequate to meet our needs.* **OPPOSITE:** fall short of **4 = experience**, face, suffer, bear, go through, encounter, endure, undergo: *Never had she met such spite and pettiness.* **5 = converge**, unite, join, cross, touch, connect, come together, link up, adjoin, intersect, abut: *a crossing where four paths meet* **OPPOSITE:** diverge

meeting NOUN **1 = conference**, gathering, assembly, meet, congress, session, rally, convention, get-together *(informal)*, reunion, congregation, hui *(N.Z.)*, conclave, convocation, powwow: *He travels to London regularly for business meetings.* **2 = encounter**, introduction, confrontation, engagement, rendezvous, tryst, assignation: *Thirty-seven years after our first meeting I was back in his studio.* **3 = convergence**, union, crossing, conjunction, junction, intersection, concourse, confluence: *the meeting of three streams*

melancholy ADJECTIVE **= sad**, down, depressed, unhappy, low, blue, miserable, moody, gloomy, dismal, sombre, woeful, glum, mournful, dejected, despondent, dispirited, melancholic, downcast, lugubrious, pensive, sorrowful, disconsolate, joyless, doleful, downhearted, heavy-hearted, down in the dumps *(informal)*, woebegone, down in the mouth, low-spirited: *It was at this time of day that he felt most melancholy.* **OPPOSITE:** happy
▷ NOUN **= sadness**, depression, misery, gloom, sorrow, woe, blues, unhappiness, despondency, the hump *(Brit. informal)*, dejection, low spirits, gloominess, pensiveness: *He watched the process with an air of melancholy.* **OPPOSITE:** happiness

melee *or* **mêlée** NOUN **= fight**, fray, brawl, skirmish, tussle, scuffle, free-for-all *(informal)*, fracas, set-to *(informal)*, rumpus, broil, affray *(Law)*, shindig *(informal)*, donnybrook, ruction *(informal)*, battle royal, ruckus *(informal)*, scrimmage, stramash *(Scot.)*, shindy *(informal)*, bagarre *(French)*, biffo *(Austral. slang)*

mellow ADJECTIVE **1 = tuneful**, full, rich, soft, melodious, mellifluous, dulcet, well-tuned, euphonic: *the mellow background music* **2 = full-flavoured**, rounded, rich, sweet, smooth, delicate, juicy: *a mellow, well-balanced wine* **3 = ripe**, perfect, mature, ripened, well-matured: *a mellow, creamy Somerset Brie* **OPPOSITE:** unripe **4 = relaxed**, happy, cheerful, jolly, elevated, merry *(Brit. informal)*, expansive, cordial, genial, jovial: *After a few glasses, he was feeling mellow.*
▷ VERB **1 = relax**, improve, settle, calm, mature, soften, sweeten: *She has mellowed with age.* **2 = season**, develop, improve, perfect, ripen: *Long cooking mellows the flavour beautifully.*

melodramatic ADJECTIVE **= theatrical**, actorly, extravagant, histrionic, sensational, hammy *(informal)*, actressy, stagy, overemotional, overdramatic

melody NOUN **1 = tune**, song, theme, refrain, air, music, strain, descant: *a catchy melody with a frenetic beat* **2 = tunefulness**, music, harmony, musicality, euphony, melodiousness: *Her voice was full of melody.*

melt VERB **1 = dissolve**, run, soften, fuse, thaw, diffuse, flux, defrost, liquefy, unfreeze, deliquesce: *The snow had melted.* **2** *(often with* **away***)* **= disappear**, fade, vanish, dissolve, disperse, evaporate, evanesce: *When he heard these words, his inner doubts melted away.* **3 = soften**, touch, relax, disarm, mollify: *His smile is enough to melt any woman's heart.*

member NOUN **= representative**, associate, supporter, fellow, subscriber, comrade, disciple

membership NOUN **1 = participation**, belonging, fellowship, enrolment: *his membership of the Communist Party* **2 = members**, body, associates, fellows: *the recent fall in party membership*

memento NOUN **= souvenir**, trophy, memorial, token, reminder, relic, remembrance, keepsake

memoir NOUN **= account**, life, record, register, journal, essay, biography, narrative, monograph

memoirs PLURAL NOUN **= autobiography**, diary, life story, life, experiences, memories, journals, recollections, reminiscences

> **QUOTATIONS**
> To write one's memoirs is to speak ill of everybody except oneself
> [Marshal Pétain]

memorable ADJECTIVE **= noteworthy**, celebrated, impressive, historic, important, special, striking, famous, significant, signal, extraordinary, remarkable, distinguished, haunting, notable, timeless, unforgettable, momentous, illustrious, catchy, indelible, unfading **OPPOSITE:** forgettable

memorandum NOUN **= note**, minute, message, communication, reminder, memo, jotting, e-mail

> **QUOTATIONS**
> A memorandum is written not to inform the reader but to protect the writer
> [Dean Acheson]

memorial NOUN **1 = monument**, cairn, shrine, plaque, cenotaph: *Every village had its war memorial.* **2 = petition**, address, statement, memorandum: *a memorial to the Emperor written in characters of gold*
▷ ADJECTIVE **= commemorative**, remembrance, monumental:

m

A memorial service is being held at St Paul's Church.

memorize VERB **= remember**, learn, commit to memory, learn by heart, learn by rote, get by heart, con *(archaic)*

memory NOUN **1 = recall**, mind, retention, ability to remember, powers of recall, powers of retention: *He had a good memory for faces.* **2 = recollection**, reminder, reminiscence, impression, echo, remembrance: *He had happy memories of his father.* **3 = commemoration**, respect, honour, recognition, tribute, remembrance, observance: *They held a minute's silence in memory of those who had died.*

> **QUOTATIONS**
>
> The man with a good memory remembers nothing because he forgets nothing
> [Augusto Roa Bastos *I The Supreme*]
>
> The charm, one might say the genius of memory, is that it is choosy, chancy, and temperamental: it rejects the edifying cathedral and indelibly photographs the small boy outside, chewing a hunk of melon in the dust
> [Elizabeth Bowen]
>
> Our memories are card-indexes consulted, and then put back in disorder by authorities whom we do not control
> [Cyril Connolly *The Unquiet Grave*]
>
> We find a little of everything in our memory; it is a sort of pharmacy, a sort of chemical laboratory, in which our groping hand may come to rest, now on a sedative drug, now on a dangerous poison
> [Marcel Proust *Remembrance of Things Past*]

menace NOUN **1 = danger**, risk, threat, hazard, peril, jeopardy: *In my view you are a menace to the public.* **2 = nuisance**, plague, pest, annoyance, troublemaker, mischief-maker: *Don't be such a menace!* **3 = threat**, warning, intimidation, ill-omen, ominousness, commination: *a pervading sense of menace*
▷ VERB **= bully**, threaten, intimidate, terrorize, alarm, frighten, scare, browbeat, utter threats to: *She is being menaced by her sister's boyfriend.*

menacing ADJECTIVE **= threatening**, dangerous, alarming, frightening, forbidding, looming, intimidating, ominous, baleful, intimidatory, minatory, bodeful, louring *or* lowering, minacious
OPPOSITE: encouraging

mend VERB **1 = repair**, fix, restore, renew, patch up, renovate, refit, retouch: *They took a long time to mend the roof.* **2 = darn**, repair, patch, stitch, sew: *cooking their meals, mending their socks* **3 = heal**, improve, recover, cure, remedy, get better, be all right, be cured, recuperate, pull through, convalesce: *He must have an operation to mend torn knee ligaments; The arm is broken, but you'll mend.* **4 = improve**, better, reform, correct, revise, amend, rectify, ameliorate, emend: *There will be disciplinary action if you do not mend your ways.*
on the mend = convalescent, improving, recovering, getting better, recuperating, convalescing: *The baby had been poorly but was on the mend.*

menial ADJECTIVE **= low-status**, degrading, lowly, unskilled, low, base, sorry, boring, routine, dull, humble, mean, vile, demeaning, fawning, abject, grovelling, humdrum, subservient, ignominious, sycophantic, servile, slavish, ignoble, obsequious: *low-paid menial jobs such as cleaning*
OPPOSITE: high
▷ NOUN **= servant**, domestic, attendant, lackey, labourer, serf, underling, drudge, vassal *(archaic)*, dogsbody *(informal)*, flunky, skivvy *(chiefly Brit.)*, varlet *(archaic)*: *The name 'beef-eater' was aimed at any well-fed menial.* **OPPOSITE:** master

menstruation NOUN **= period**, menstrual cycle, menses, courses *(Physiology)*, flow *(informal)*, monthly *(informal)*, the curse *(informal)*, catamenia *(Physiology)*

mental ADJECTIVE **1 = intellectual**, rational, theoretical, cognitive, brain, conceptual, cerebral: *the mental development of children* **2** *(slang)* **= insane**, mad, disturbed, unstable, mentally ill, lunatic, psychotic, unbalanced, deranged, round the bend *(Brit. slang)*, as daft as a brush *(informal, chiefly Brit.)*, not right in the head: *I just said to him 'you must be mental!'*

mentality NOUN **= attitude**, character, personality, psychology, make-up, outlook, disposition, way of thinking, frame of mind, turn of mind, cast of mind

mentally ADVERB **= psychologically**, intellectually, rationally, inwardly, subjectively

mention VERB **= refer to**, point out, acknowledge, bring up, state, report, reveal, declare, cite, communicate, disclose, intimate, tell of, recount, hint at, impart, allude to, divulge, broach, call attention to, make known, touch upon, adduce, speak about *or* of: *She did not mention her mother's absence.*
▷ NOUN **1** *(often with* **of***)* **= reference**, announcement, observation, indication, remark, notification, allusion: *The statement made no mention of government casualties.* **2 = acknowledgment**, recognition, tribute, citation, honourable mention: *Two of the losers deserve special mention.*
not to mention = to say nothing of, besides, not counting, as well as: *It was both deliberate and malicious, not to mention sick.*

mentor NOUN **= guide**, teacher, coach, adviser, tutor, instructor, counsellor, guru

menu NOUN **= bill of fare**, tariff *(chiefly Brit.)*, set menu, table d'hôte, carte du jour *(French)*

mercantile ADJECTIVE **1 = commercial**, business, trade, trading, merchant: *the emergence of a new mercantile class* **2 = profit-making**, money-orientated: *the urban society and its mercantile values*

mercenary NOUN **= hireling**, freelance *(History)*, soldier of fortune, condottiere *(History)*, free companion *(History)*: *In the film he plays a brutish, trigger-happy mercenary.*
▷ ADJECTIVE **1 = greedy**, grasping, acquisitive, venal, avaricious, covetous, money-grubbing *(informal)*, bribable: *Despite his mercenary motives, he is not a cynic.* **OPPOSITE:** generous **2 = hired**, paid, bought, venal: *The mercenary soldier is not a valued creature.*

merchandise NOUN **= goods**, produce, stock, products, truck, commodities, staples, wares, stock in trade, vendibles: *25% off selected merchandise*
▷ VERB **= trade**, market, sell, retail, distribute, deal in, buy and sell, traffic in, vend, do business in: *He advises shops on how to merchandise their wares.*

merchant NOUN **= tradesman**, dealer, trader, broker, retailer, supplier, seller, salesman, vendor, shopkeeper, trafficker, wholesaler, purveyor

> **QUOTATIONS**
>
> A merchant shall hardly keep himself from doing wrong
> [*Bible: Ecclesiasticus*]

merciful ADJECTIVE **= compassionate**, forgiving, sympathetic, kind, liberal, soft, sparing, generous, mild, pitying, humane, clement, gracious, lenient, beneficent, forbearing, tender-hearted, benignant
OPPOSITE: merciless

merciless ADJECTIVE **= cruel**, ruthless, hard, severe, harsh, relentless, callous, heartless, unforgiving, fell *(archaic)*, inexorable, implacable, unsympathetic, inhumane, barbarous, pitiless, unfeeling, unsparing, hard-hearted, unmerciful, unappeasable, unpitying

mercurial ADJECTIVE **= capricious**, volatile, unpredictable, erratic, variable, unstable, fickle, temperamental, impulsive, irrepressible, changeable, quicksilver, flighty, inconstant
OPPOSITE: consistent

mercy NOUN **1 = compassion**, charity, pity, forgiveness, quarter, favour, grace, kindness, clemency, leniency, benevolence, forbearance: *Neither side*

showed its prisoners any mercy. **OPPOSITE:** cruelty **2 = blessing**, relief, boon, godsend, piece of luck, benison (*archaic*): *It was a mercy he'd gone so quickly in the end.*
at the mercy of something *or* **someone 1 = defenceless against**, subject to, open to, exposed to, vulnerable to, threatened by, susceptible to, prey to, an easy target for, naked before, unprotected against: *Buildings are left to decay at the mercy of vandals and bad weather.* **2 = in the power of**, under the control of, in the clutches of, under the heel of: *Servants or slaves were at the mercy of their masters.*

> **QUOTATIONS**
> Yet I shall temper so
> Justice with mercy
> [John Milton *Paradise Lost*]

mere ADJECTIVE **1 = simple**, merely, no more than, nothing more than, just, common, plain, pure, pure and simple, unadulterated, unmitigated, unmixed: *It proved to be a mere trick of fate.* **2 = bare**, slender, trifling, meagre, just, only, basic, no more than, minimal, scant, paltry, skimpy, scanty: *Cigarettes were a mere 2 cents a packet.*

merge VERB **1 = combine**, blend, fuse, amalgamate, unite, join, mix, consolidate, mingle, converge, coalesce, melt into, meld, intermix: *The two countries merged into one.* **OPPOSITE:** separate **2 = join**, unite, combine, consolidate, fuse: *He wants to merge the two agencies.* **OPPOSITE:** separate **3 = melt**, blend, incorporate, mingle, tone with, be swallowed up by, become lost in: *His features merged into the darkness.*

merger NOUN **= union**, fusion, consolidation, amalgamation, combination, coalition, incorporation

merit NOUN **= advantage**, value, quality, worth, strength, asset, virtue, good point, strong point, worthiness: *They have been persuaded of the merits of the scheme.*
▷ VERB **= deserve**, warrant, be entitled to, earn, incur, have a right to, be worthy of, have a claim to: *Such ideas merit careful consideration.*

> **QUOTATIONS**
> What is merit? The opinion one man entertains of another
> [Lord Palmerston]

merited ADJECTIVE **= deserved**, justified, warranted, just, earned, appropriate, entitled, rightful, condign, rightly due

merriment NOUN **= fun**, amusement, glee, mirth, sport, laughter, festivity, frolic, gaiety, hilarity, revelry, jollity, levity, liveliness, conviviality, joviality, jocularity, merrymaking

merry ADJECTIVE **1 = cheerful**, happy, upbeat (*informal*), carefree, glad, jolly, festive, joyous, joyful, genial, fun-loving, chirpy (*informal*), vivacious, rollicking, convivial, gleeful, blithe, frolicsome, mirthful, sportive, light-hearted, jocund, gay, blithesome: *He was much loved for his merry nature.* **OPPOSITE:** gloomy **2 = tipsy**, happy, elevated (*informal*), mellow, tiddly (*slang, chiefly Brit.*), squiffy (*Brit. informal*): *After a couple of glasses I was feeling a bit merry.*
make merry = have fun, celebrate, revel, have a good time, feast, frolic, enjoy yourself, carouse, make whoopee (*informal*): *Neighbours went out into the streets and made merry together.*

> **QUOTATIONS**
> A merry heart maketh a cheerful countenance
> [Bible: *Proverbs*]

mesh NOUN **1 = net**, netting, network, web, tracery: *The ground-floor windows are obscured by wire mesh.* **2 = trap**, web, tangle, toils, snare, entanglement: *He lures young talent into his mesh.*
▷ VERB **1 = engage**, combine, connect, knit, come together, coordinate, interlock, dovetail, fit together, harmonize: *Their senses of humour meshed perfectly.* **2 = entangle**, catch, net, trap, tangle, snare, ensnare, enmesh: *Limes and plane trees meshed in unpruned disorder.*

mesmerize VERB **= entrance**, fascinate, absorb, captivate, grip, enthral, hypnotize, magnetize, hold spellbound, spellbind

mess NOUN **1 = untidiness**, disorder, confusion, chaos, turmoil, litter, clutter, disarray, jumble, disorganization, grot (*slang*), dirtiness: *Linda can't stand mess.* **2 = shambles**, botch, hash, cock-up (*Brit. slang*), state, bodge (*informal*), pig's breakfast (*informal*): *I've made such a mess of my life.* **3 = difficulty**, dilemma, plight, spot (*informal*), hole (*informal*), fix (*informal*), jam (*informal*), hot water (*informal*), stew (*informal*), mix-up, muddle, pickle (*informal*), uphill (*S. African*), predicament, deep water, perplexity, tight spot, imbroglio, fine kettle of fish (*informal*): *I've got myself into a bit of a mess.*
mess about *or* **around 1 = potter about**, dabble, amuse yourself, footle (*informal*), fool about *or* around, muck about *or* around (*informal*), play about *or* around: *We were just messing around playing with paint; Stop messing about and get on with your work.* **2 = meddle**, play, interfere, toy, fiddle (*informal*), tamper, tinker, trifle, fool about *or* around: *I'd like to know who's been messing about with the pram.*
mess something up 1 = botch, bungle, make a hash of (*informal*), make a nonsense of, make a pig's ear of (*informal*), cock something up (*Brit. slang*), muck something up (*Brit. slang*), muddle something up: *If I messed it up, I would probably be fired.* **2 = dirty**, foul, litter, pollute, clutter, besmirch, disarrange, befoul, dishevel: *I hope they haven't messed up your house.*
mess with something *or* **someone = interfere with**, play with, fiddle with (*informal*), tamper with, tinker with, meddle with: *You are messing with people's religion and they don't like that.*

message NOUN **1 = communication**, note, bulletin, word, letter, notice, memo, dispatch, memorandum, communiqué, missive, intimation, tidings, e-mail, text: *Would you like to leave a message?* **2 = point**, meaning, idea, moral, theme, import, purport: *The report's message was unequivocal.*
get the message = understand, see, get it, catch on (*informal*), comprehend, twig (*Brit. informal*), get the point, take the hint: *I think they got the message that this attitude is wrong.*

messenger NOUN **= courier**, agent, runner, carrier, herald, envoy, bearer, go-between, emissary, harbinger, delivery boy, errand boy

messy ADJECTIVE **1 = disorganized**, sloppy (*informal*), untidy, slovenly: *She was a good, if messy, cook.* **2 = dirty**, grubby, grimy, scuzzy (*slang, chiefly U.S.*): *The work tends to be messy, so wear old clothes.* **3 = untidy**, disordered, littered, chaotic, muddled, cluttered, shambolic, disorganized, daggy (*Austral. & N.Z. informal*): *Mum made me clean up my messy room.* **OPPOSITE:** tidy **4 = dishevelled**, ruffled, untidy, rumpled, bedraggled, unkempt, tousled, uncombed, daggy (*Austral. & N.Z. informal*): *She's just an old woman with very messy hair.* **5 = confusing**, difficult, complex, confused, tangled, chaotic, tortuous: *Life is a messy and tangled business.*

metamorphose VERB **= transform**, change, alter, remake, convert, remodel, mutate, reshape, be reborn, transmute, transfigure, transmogrify (*humorous*), transubstantiate

metamorphosis NOUN **= transformation**, conversion, alteration, change, mutation, rebirth, changeover, transfiguration, transmutation, transubstantiation, transmogrification (*humorous*)

metaphor NOUN **= figure of speech**, image, symbol, analogy, emblem, conceit (*literary*), allegory, trope, figurative expression

metaphorical ADJECTIVE **= figurative**, symbolic, emblematic, allegorical, emblematical, tropical (*Rhetoric*)

metaphysical ADJECTIVE **1 = abstract**, intellectual, theoretical, deep, basic, essential, ideal, fundamental, universal, profound, philosophical, speculative, high-flown, esoteric, transcendental, abstruse, recondite, oversubtle: *metaphysical questions like personal responsibility for violence* **2 = supernatural**, spiritual, unreal, intangible, immaterial, incorporeal, impalpable, unsubstantial: *He was moved by a metaphysical sense quite alien to him.*

meteoric ADJECTIVE = **spectacular**, sudden, overnight, rapid, fast, brief, brilliant, flashing, fleeting, swift, dazzling, speedy, transient, momentary, ephemeral
OPPOSITE: gradual

mete out VERB = **distribute**, portion, assign, administer, ration, dispense, allot, dole out, share out, apportion, deal out, measure out, parcel out, divide out

method NOUN **1** = **manner**, process, approach, technique, way, plan, course, system, form, rule, programme, style, practice, fashion, scheme, arrangement, procedure, routine, mode, modus operandi: *new teaching methods* **2** = **orderliness**, planning, order, system, form, design, structure, purpose, pattern, organization, regularity: *They go about their work with method and common sense.*

methodical ADJECTIVE = **orderly**, planned, ordered, structured, regular, disciplined, organized, efficient, precise, neat, deliberate, tidy, systematic, meticulous, painstaking, businesslike, well-regulated
OPPOSITE: haphazard

meticulous ADJECTIVE = **thorough**, detailed, particular, strict, exact, precise, microscopic, fussy, painstaking, perfectionist, scrupulous, fastidious, punctilious, nit-picky *(informal)* **OPPOSITE:** careless

m

metropolis NOUN = **city**, town, capital, big city, municipality, conurbation, megalopolis

mettle NOUN **1** = **courage**, spirit, resolution, resolve, life, heart, fire, bottle *(Brit. slang)*, nerve, daring, guts *(informal)*, pluck, grit, bravery, fortitude, vigour, boldness, gallantry, ardour, valour, spunk *(informal)*, indomitability, hardihood, gameness: *It's the first real test of his mettle this season.* **2** = **character**, quality, nature, make-up, stamp, temper, kidney, temperament, calibre, disposition: *He is of a different mettle from the others.*

microbe NOUN = **microorganism**, virus, bug *(informal)*, germ, bacterium, bacillus

microscopic ADJECTIVE = **tiny**, minute, invisible, negligible, minuscule, imperceptible, infinitesimal, teeny-weeny, teensy-weensy **OPPOSITE:** huge

midday NOUN = **noon**, twelve o'clock, noonday, noontime, twelve noon, noontide

middle NOUN **1** = **centre**, heart, inside, thick, core, midst, nucleus, hub, halfway point, midpoint, midsection: *I was in the middle of the back row.*
2 = **waist**, gut, belly, tummy *(informal)*, waistline, midriff, paunch, midsection: *At 53, he has a few extra pounds around his middle.*
▷ ADJECTIVE **1** = **central**, medium, inside, mid, intervening, inner, halfway, intermediate, median, medial: *that crucial middle point of the picture* **2** = **intermediate**, inside, intervening, inner: *the middle level of commanding officers*

middle-class ADJECTIVE = **bourgeois**, traditional, conventional, suburban, petit-bourgeois

middleman NOUN = **intermediary**, broker, entrepreneur, distributor, go-between

middling ADJECTIVE **1** = **mediocre**, all right, indifferent, so-so *(informal)*, unremarkable, tolerable, run-of-the-mill, passable, serviceable, unexceptional, half-pie *(N.Z. informal)*, O.K. *or* okay *(informal)*: *They enjoyed only middling success until 1963.* **2** = **moderate**, medium, average, fair, ordinary, modest, adequate, bog-standard *(Brit. & Irish slang)*: *a man of middling height*

midget NOUN = **dwarf**, shrimp *(informal)*, gnome, Tom Thumb, munchkin *(informal, chiefly U.S.)*, homunculus, manikin, homuncule, pygmy *or* pigmy: *They used to call him 'midget' or 'shorty' at work.*
▷ ADJECTIVE **1** = **baby**, small, tiny, miniature, dwarf, teeny-weeny, teensy-weensy: *an accompaniment of midget roast potatoes* **2** = **diminutive**, little, pocket-sized, Lilliputian, dwarfish, pygmy *or* pigmy: *The part is played by midget actor Warwick Edwards.*

midnight NOUN = **twelve o'clock**, middle of the night, dead of night, twelve o'clock at night, the witching hour

midst NOUN = **middle**, centre, heart, interior, thick, depths, core, hub, bosom: *The organisation realised it had a traitor in its midst.*
in the midst of **1** = **during**, in the middle of, amidst: *We are in the midst of a recession.* **2** = **among**, in the middle of, surrounded by, amidst, in the thick of, enveloped by: *I was sitting in the midst of a traffic jam.*

midway ADVERB = **halfway**, in the middle of, part-way, equidistant, at the midpoint, betwixt and between

miffed ADJECTIVE = **upset**, hurt, annoyed, offended, irritated, put out, hacked (off) *(U.S. slang)*, resentful, nettled, aggrieved, vexed, displeased, irked, in a huff, piqued, narked *(Brit., Austral. & N.Z. slang)*, tooshie *(Austral. slang)*

might NOUN = **power**, force, energy, ability, strength, capacity, efficiency, capability, sway, clout *(informal)*, vigour, prowess, potency, efficacy, valour, puissance, hard power: *The might of the army could prove a decisive factor.*

mightily ADVERB **1** = **very**, highly, greatly, hugely, very much, seriously *(informal)*, extremely, intensely, decidedly, exceedingly: *He had given a mightily impressive performance.*
2 = **powerfully**, vigorously, strongly, forcefully, energetically, with all your strength, with all your might and main: *She strove mightily to put him from her thoughts.*

mighty ADJECTIVE **1** = **powerful**, strong, strapping, robust, hardy, vigorous, potent, sturdy, stout, forceful, stalwart, doughty, lusty, indomitable, manful, puissant: *a mighty young athlete* **OPPOSITE:** weak
2 = **great**, large, huge, grand, massive, towering, vast, enormous, tremendous, immense, titanic, gigantic, monumental, bulky, colossal, stellar *(informal)*, prodigious, stupendous, elephantine, ginormous *(informal)*, humongous *or* humungous *(U.S. slang)*: *a land marked with vast lakes and mighty rivers* **OPPOSITE:** tiny

> **QUOTATIONS**
> How are the mighty fallen, and the weapons of war perished
> [*Bible: II Samuel*]

migrant NOUN = **wanderer**, immigrant, traveller, gypsy, tinker, rover, transient, nomad, emigrant, itinerant, drifter, vagrant: *economic migrants and political refugees*
▷ ADJECTIVE = **itinerant**, wandering, drifting, roving, travelling, shifting, immigrant, gypsy, transient, nomadic, migratory, vagrant: *migrant workers*

migrate VERB = **move**, travel, journey, wander, shift, drift, trek, voyage, roam, emigrate, rove

migration NOUN = **wandering**, journey, voyage, travel, movement, shift, trek, emigration, roving

migratory ADJECTIVE = **nomadic**, travelling, wandering, migrant, itinerant, unsettled, shifting, gypsy, roving, transient, vagrant, peripatetic

mild ADJECTIVE **1** = **gentle**, kind, easy, soft, pacific, calm, moderate, forgiving, tender, pleasant, mellow, compassionate, indulgent, serene, easy-going, amiable, meek, placid, docile, merciful, peaceable, forbearing, equable, easy-oasy *(slang)*, chilled *(informal)*: *He is a mild man, reasonable almost to the point of blandness.*
OPPOSITE: harsh **2** = **temperate**, warm, calm, moderate, clement, tranquil, balmy: *The area is famous for its mild winters.* **OPPOSITE:** cold **3** = **bland**, thin, smooth, tasteless, insipid, flavourless: *The cheese has a soft, mild flavour.* **4** = **soothing**, mollifying, emollient, demulcent, lenitive: *Wash your face thoroughly with a mild soap.*

milieu NOUN = **surroundings**, setting, scene, environment, element, background, location, sphere, locale, mise en scène *(French)*

militant ADJECTIVE = **aggressive**, warring, fighting, active, combating, contending, vigorous, two-fisted, assertive, in arms, embattled, belligerent, combative: *one of the most active militant groups* **OPPOSITE:** peaceful
▷ NOUN = **activist**, radical, fighter, partisan, belligerent, combatant: *The militants were apparently planning a terrorist attack.*

The Language of George Washington

George Washington (1732–99) served as the commander of the Continental Army in the American Revolutionary War and, in 1789, became the first president of the newly formed United States of America.

The language of Washington's speeches is sophisticated and polished; however, it can also be heavy and difficult to read. His sentences are sometimes very long; indeed, one sentence in Washington's first State of the Union address contains 121 words! The difficulty such a style poses to modern readers is not due solely to the distance in time between the present day and the period in which Washington wrote, for the writing style of Benjamin Franklin, a contemporary of Washington, is relatively easy to read in comparison. It is possible that Washington deliberately adopted this style, perhaps believing that, as the first president of the United States, his manner of speech should be more sophisticated than that of the average man.

Although Washington's sentences are sometimes very long, his writing style is not verbose; in fact, quite the opposite is true. Washington avoided using more words than was necessary to convey his meaning. Indeed, Washington's second inaugural address, delivered in 1793, is the shortest inaugural address ever delivered by a US president, coming in at only 135 words – little longer than the longest sentence in his first State of the Union address! As well as being succinct, Washington's speeches are characterized by reason and logic; he quite deliberately does not, unlike many modern politicians, attempt to appeal to the emotions of his audience. He was a man of the Enlightenment and believed in persuading his listeners through reason alone, rather than through appeal to their emotions.

Washington's speeches demonstrate the use of various rhetorical techniques. One such technique is apophasis; this is the device of mentioning a subject by stating that it will not be mentioned. For example, in his first State of the Union address, Washington said:

> The advancement of agriculture, commerce, and manufactures by all proper means will not, I trust, need recommendation ...

Of course, by mentioning this at all, Washington *is* recommending it. Washington also makes use of rhetorical questions, as the following example, from his eighth State of the Union address, demonstrates:

> Ought our country to remain in such cases dependent on foreign supply, precarious because liable to be interrupted?

Another rhetorical technique frequently found in Washington's speeches is a tendency to list words or phrases in threes; these series of threes are, in the language of rhetoric, known as tricola. The following examples, from Washington's first State of the Union address, demonstrate Washington's use of this:

> ... the concord, peace, and plenty with which we are blessed ...

> ... your patriotism, firmness, and wisdom ...

As well as his speeches, Washington wrote many letters and also kept diaries. The style of his letters and diaries is of course less polished than that of his speeches, but they are perhaps better records of Washington's language. Whereas his diaries and letters are of his own sole composition, Washington had help with the writing of his speeches.

Perhaps the most interesting observation to be made from the vocabulary of Washington's diaries and letters is his clear interest in agriculture. In these writings, Washington often writes about Mount Vernon, the plantation established by his father. Crop-growing seems to have been the main subject of Washington's agricultural interest, judging by the high frequency of occurrence of words such as *seed, crop,* and *plow*. Words relating to livestock do, however, occur frequently too, including *cattle, sheep,* and *wool*.

military ADJECTIVE **= warlike**, armed, soldierly, martial, soldierlike: *Military action may become necessary.*
the military = the armed forces, the forces, the services, the army: *Did you serve in the military?*

militate VERB
militate against something = counteract, conflict with, contend with, count against, oppose, counter, resist, be detrimental to, weigh against, tell against

militia NOUN **= reserve(s)**, National Guard (*U.S.*), Territorial Army (*Brit.*), yeomanry (*History*), fencibles (*History*), trainband (*History*)

milk VERB **= exploit**, use, pump, squeeze, drain, take advantage of, bleed, impose on, wring, fleece, suck dry

milky ADJECTIVE **= white**, clouded, opaque, cloudy, alabaster, whitish, milk-white

mill NOUN **1 = grinder**, crusher, quern: *a pepper mill* **2 = factory**, works, shop, plant, workshop, foundry: *a textile mill*
▷ VERB **= grind**, pound, press, crush, powder, grate, pulverize, granulate, comminute: *freshly milled black pepper*
mill about *or* **around = swarm**, crowd, stream, surge, seethe, throng: *Quite a few people were milling about.*

m

millstone NOUN **= burden**, weight, load, albatross, drag, affliction, dead weight, encumbrance

mime NOUN **= dumb show**, gesture, pantomime, mummery: *Students presented a mime and a puppet show*
▷ VERB **= act out**, represent, gesture, simulate, pantomime: *She mimed getting up in the morning.*

mimic VERB **1 = imitate**, do (*informal*), take off (*informal*), ape, parody, caricature, impersonate: *He could mimic anybody, reducing his friends to helpless laughter.* **2 = resemble**, look like, mirror, echo, simulate, take on the appearance of: *Don't try to mimic anybody. Just be yourself.*
▷ NOUN **= imitator**, impressionist, copycat (*informal*), impersonator, caricaturist, parodist, parrot: *He's a very good mimic.*

mimicry NOUN **= imitation**, impression, impersonation, copying, imitating, mimicking, parody, caricature, mockery, burlesque, apery

mince VERB **1 = cut**, grind, crumble, dice, hash, chop up: *I'll buy some lean meat and mince it myself.* **2 = posture**, pose, ponce (*slang*), attitudinize: *'Ooh, a sailor!' he minced and she laughed aloud.* **3 = tone down**, spare, moderate, weaken, diminish, soften, hold back, extenuate, palliate, euphemize: *The doctors didn't mince their words, and predicted the worst.*

mincing ADJECTIVE **= affected**, nice, camp (*informal*), precious, pretentious, dainty, sissy, effeminate, foppish, poncy (*slang*), arty-farty (*informal*), lah-di-dah (*informal*), niminy-piminy

mind NOUN **1 = brain**, head, imagination, psyche, subconscious: *I'm trying to clear my mind of all this.* **2 = memory**, recollection, remembrance, powers of recollection: *He spent the next hour going over the trial in his mind.* **3 = attention**, thinking, thoughts, concentration: *My mind was never on my work.* **4 = intelligence**, reason, reasoning, understanding, sense, spirit, brain(s) (*informal*), wits, mentality, intellect, grey matter (*informal*), ratiocination: *an excellent training for the young mind* **5 = thinker**, academic, intellectual, genius, brain (*informal*), scholar, sage, intellect, rocket scientist (*informal, chiefly U.S.*), brainbox, acca (*Austral. slang*): *She moved to London, meeting some of the best minds of her time.* **6 = intention**, will, wish, desire, urge, fancy, purpose, leaning, bent, notion, tendency, inclination, disposition: *They could interpret it that way if they'd a mind to.* **7 = sanity**, reason, senses, judgment, wits, marbles (*informal*), rationality, mental balance: *Sometimes I feel I'm losing my mind.*
▷ VERB **1 = take offence at**, dislike, care about, object to, resent, disapprove of, be bothered by, look askance at, be affronted by: *I hope you don't mind me calling in like this.* **2 = be careful**, watch, take care, be wary, be cautious, be on your guard: *Mind you don't burn those sausages.* **3 = be sure**, ensure, make sure, be careful, make certain: *Mind you don't let the cat out.* **4 = look after**, watch, protect, tend, guard, take care of, attend to, keep an eye on, have *or* take charge of: *Could you mind the shop while I'm out, please?* **5 = pay attention to**, follow, mark, watch, note, regard, respect, notice, attend to, listen to, observe, comply with, obey, heed, adhere to, take heed of, pay heed to: *You mind what I say now!*
in *or* **of two minds = undecided**, uncertain, unsure, wavering, hesitant, dithering (*chiefly Brit.*), vacillating, swithering (*Scot.*), shillyshallying (*informal*): *I am in two minds about going.*
make up your mind = decide, choose, determine, resolve, reach a decision, come to a decision: *Once he made up his mind to do something, there was no stopping him.*
mind out = be careful, watch out, take care, look out, beware, pay attention, keep your eyes open, be on your guard: *Mind out. We're coming in to land!*
▸ *related adjective:* mental

QUOTATIONS
The mind is at its best about the age of forty-nine
[Aristotle *Rhetoric*]

The mind is its own place, and in itself
Can make a heaven of hell, a hell of heaven
[John Milton *Paradise Lost*]

What is matter? – Never mind.
What is mind? – No matter
[*Punch*]

PROVERBS
Great minds think alike, fools seldom differ

mindful ADJECTIVE (*with* **of**) **= aware**, careful, conscious, alert, sensible, wary, thoughtful, attentive, respectful, watchful, alive to, cognizant, chary, heedful, regardful **OPPOSITE:** heedless

mindless ADJECTIVE **1 = unthinking**, gratuitous, thoughtless, careless, oblivious, brutish, inane, witless, heedless, unmindful, dumb-ass (*slang*): *blackmail, extortion and mindless violence* **OPPOSITE:** reasoning
2 = unintelligent, stupid, foolish, careless, negligent, idiotic, thoughtless, inane, witless, forgetful, moronic, obtuse, neglectful, asinine, imbecilic, braindead (*informal*), dumb-ass (*slang*), dead from the neck up (*informal*): *She wasn't at all the mindless little wife they perceived her to be.*
3 = mechanical, automatic, monotonous, mind-numbing, brainless: *the mindless repetitiveness of some tasks*

mind's eye NOUN
in your mind's eye = in your imagination, in your head, in your mind

mine NOUN **1 = pit**, deposit, shaft, vein, colliery, excavation, coalfield, lode: *an explosion at a coal mine* **2 = source**, store, fund, stock, supply, reserve, treasury, wealth, abundance, hoard: *a mine of information*
▷ VERB **1 = dig up**, extract, quarry, unearth, delve, excavate, hew, dig for: *not enough coal to be mined economically* **2 = lay mines in** *or* **under**, sow with mines: *The approaches to the garrison have been heavily mined.*

miner NOUN **= coalminer**, pitman (*Brit.*), collier (*Brit.*)

mingle VERB **1 = mix**, combine, blend, merge, unite, join, marry, compound, alloy, interweave, coalesce, intermingle, meld, commingle, intermix, admix: *Cheers and applause mingled in a single roar.* **OPPOSITE:** separate **2 = associate**, circulate, hang out (*informal*), consort, socialize, rub shoulders (*informal*), hobnob, fraternize, hang about *or* around: *Guests ate and mingled.* **OPPOSITE:** dissociate

miniature ADJECTIVE **= small**, little, minute, baby, reduced, tiny, pocket, toy, mini, wee, dwarf, scaled-down, diminutive, minuscule, midget, teeny-weeny, Lilliputian, teensy-weensy, pygmy *or* pigmy **OPPOSITE:** giant

minimal ADJECTIVE **= minimum**, smallest, least, slightest, token, nominal, negligible, least possible, littlest

minimize VERB **1 = reduce**, decrease, shrink, diminish, prune, curtail, attenuate, downsize, miniaturize:

You can minimize these problems with sensible planning. **OPPOSITE:** increase **2 = play down**, discount, underestimate, belittle, disparage, decry, underrate, deprecate, depreciate, make light *or* little of: *Some have minimized the importance of these factors.* **OPPOSITE:** praise

minimum ADJECTIVE **= lowest**, smallest, least, slightest, minimal, least possible, littlest: *He was only five feet nine, the minimum height for a policeman.* **OPPOSITE:** maximum
▷ NOUN **= lowest**, least, depth, slightest, lowest level, nadir, bottom level: *She has cut her teaching hours to a minimum.*

minion NOUN **= follower**, henchman, underling, lackey, favourite, pet, creature, darling, parasite, cohort *(chiefly U.S.)*, dependant, hanger-on, sycophant, yes man, toady, hireling, flunky, flatterer, lickspittle, bootlicker *(informal)*

minister NOUN **1 = official**, ambassador, diplomat, delegate, executive, administrator, envoy, cabinet member, office-holder, plenipotentiary: *He concluded a deal with the Danish minister in Washington.* **2 = clergyman**, priest, divine, vicar, parson, preacher, pastor, chaplain, cleric, rector, curate, churchman, padre *(informal)*, ecclesiastic: *His father was a Baptist minister.*
minister to = attend to, serve, tend to, answer to, accommodate, take care of, cater to, pander to, administer to, be solicitous of: *For 44 years he had ministered to the poor and the sick.*

ministry NOUN **1 = department**, office, bureau, government department: *the Ministry of Justice* **2 = administration**, government, council, cabinet: *He disclosed that his ministry gave funds to parties in Namibia.* **3 = the priesthood**, the church, the cloth, the pulpit, holy orders: *So what prompted him to enter the ministry?*

minor ADJECTIVE **= small**, lesser, subordinate, smaller, light, slight, secondary, petty, inferior, trivial, trifling, insignificant, negligible, unimportant, paltry, inconsequential, inconsiderable, nickel-and-dime *(U.S. slang)* **OPPOSITE:** major

minstrel NOUN **= musician**, singer, harper, bard, troubadour, songstress, jongleur

mint VERB **1 = make**, produce, strike, cast, stamp, punch, coin: *the right to mint coins* **2 = invent**, produce, fashion, make up, construct, coin, devise, forge, fabricate, think up: *The book comprises a lexicon of freshly minted descriptions.*
▷ NOUN **= fortune**, million, bomb *(Brit. slang)*, pile *(informal)*, packet *(slang)*, bundle *(slang)*, heap *(informal)*, King's ransom, top whack *(informal)*: *They were worth a mint.*
▷ ADJECTIVE **= perfect**, excellent, first-class, brand-new, fresh, unmarked, undamaged, unblemished, untarnished: *a set of Victorian stamps in mint condition*

minuscule ADJECTIVE **= tiny**, little, minute, fine, very small, miniature, microscopic, diminutive, infinitesimal, teeny-weeny, Lilliputian, teensy-weensy

minute[1] NOUN **1 = sixty seconds**, sixtieth of an hour: *A minute later she came to the front door.* **2 = moment**, second, bit, shake *(informal)*, flash, instant, tick *(Brit. informal)*, sec *(informal)*, short time, little while, jiffy *(informal)*, trice: *I'll be with you in a minute.*
up to the minute = latest, in, newest, now *(informal)*, with it *(informal)*, smart, stylish, trendiest, trendy *(Brit. informal)*, vogue, up to date, modish, (most) fashionable, schmick *(Austral. informal)*: *a big range of up-to-the-minute appliances*

minute[2] ADJECTIVE **1 = small**, little, tiny, miniature, slender, fine, microscopic, diminutive, minuscule, infinitesimal, teeny-weeny, Lilliputian, teensy-weensy: *Only a minute amount is needed.* **OPPOSITE:** huge **2 = negligible**, slight, petty, trivial, trifling, unimportant, paltry, puny, piddling *(informal)*, inconsiderable, picayune *(U.S.)*: *gambling large sums on the minute chance of a big win* **OPPOSITE:** significant **3 = precise**, close, detailed, critical, exact, meticulous, exhaustive, painstaking, punctilious: *We will have to pore over this report in minute detail.* **OPPOSITE:** imprecise

minutely ADVERB **= precisely**, closely, exactly, in detail, critically, meticulously, painstakingly, exhaustively, with a fine-tooth comb

minutes PLURAL NOUN **= record**, notes, proceedings, transactions, transcript, memorandum: *He'd been reading the minutes of the last meeting.*

minutiae PLURAL NOUN **= details**, particulars, subtleties, trifles, trivia, niceties, finer points, ins and outs

miracle NOUN **= wonder**, phenomenon, sensation, marvel, amazing achievement, astonishing feat

miraculous ADJECTIVE **= wonderful**, amazing, extraordinary, incredible, astonishing, marvellous, magical, unbelievable, phenomenal, astounding, eye-popping *(informal)*, inexplicable, wondrous *(archaic, literary)*, unaccountable, superhuman **OPPOSITE:** ordinary

mirage NOUN **= illusion**, vision, hallucination, pipe dream, chimera, optical illusion, phantasm

mire NOUN **1 = mud**, dirt, muck, ooze, sludge, slime, slob *(Irish)*, gloop *(informal)*, grot *(slang)*: *the muck and mire of farmyards* **2 = swamp**, marsh, bog, fen, quagmire, morass, wetland, pakihi *(N.Z.)*, muskeg *(Canad.)*: *Many of those killed were buried in the mire.*
▷ VERB **1 = soil**, dirty, muddy, besmirch, begrime, bespatter: *The party has been mired by allegations of sleaze.* **2 = entangle**, involve, mix up, catch up, bog down, tangle up, enmesh: *The minister still remains mired in the controversy of the affair.*

mirror NOUN **= looking-glass**, glass *(Brit.)*, reflector, speculum: *He went into the bathroom and looked in the mirror.*
▷ VERB **= reflect**, show, follow, match, represent, copy, repeat, echo, parallel, depict, reproduce, emulate: *His own shock was mirrored in her face.*

mirror image NOUN **= reflection**, double, image, copy, twin, representation, clone, replica, likeness, spitting image *(informal)*, dead ringer *(informal)*, exact likeness

mirth NOUN **= merriment**, amusement, fun, pleasure, laughter, rejoicing, festivity, glee, frolic, sport, gaiety, hilarity, cheerfulness, revelry, jollity, levity, gladness, joviality, jocularity, merrymaking, joyousness

misadventure NOUN **= misfortune**, accident, disaster, failure, reverse, setback, catastrophe, debacle, bad luck, calamity, mishap, bad break *(informal)*, ill fortune, ill luck, mischance

misapprehension NOUN **= misunderstanding**, mistake, error, delusion, misconception, fallacy, misreading, false impression, misinterpretation, false belief, misconstruction, wrong idea *or* impression

misappropriate VERB **= steal**, embezzle, pocket, misuse, swindle, misspend, misapply, defalcate *(Law)*

misbehave VERB **= be naughty**, be bad, act up *(informal)*, muck about *(Brit. slang)*, get up to mischief *(informal)*, carry on *(informal)*, be insubordinate **OPPOSITE:** behave

misbehaviour NOUN **= misconduct**, mischief, misdemeanour, shenanigans *(informal)*, impropriety, acting up *(informal)*, bad behaviour, misdeeds, rudeness, indiscipline, insubordination, naughtiness, monkey business *(informal)*, incivility

miscalculate VERB **1 = misjudge**, get something wrong, underestimate, underrate, overestimate, overrate: *He has badly miscalculated the mood of the people.* **2 = calculate wrongly**, blunder, make a mistake, get it wrong, err, slip up: *The government seems to have miscalculated and bills are higher.*

miscarriage NOUN **1 = spontaneous abortion**, still birth: *She wanted to get pregnant again after suffering a miscarriage.* **2 = failure**, error, breakdown, mismanagement, undoing, thwarting, mishap, botch *(informal)*, perversion, misfire, mischance, nonsuccess: *The report concluded that no miscarriage of justice had taken place.*

miscarry VERB **1 = have a miscarriage**, lose your baby, have a spontaneous abortion: *Many women who miscarry eventually have healthy babies.* **2 = fail**, go wrong, fall through, come to nothing, misfire, go astray, go awry, come to grief, go amiss, go pear-shaped *(informal)*, gang agley *(Scot.)*: *My career miscarried when I thought I had everything.*

miscellaneous ADJECTIVE **= mixed**, various, varied, diverse, confused, diversified, mingled, assorted, jumbled, sundry, motley, indiscriminate, manifold, heterogeneous, multifarious, multiform

mischief NOUN **1 = misbehaviour**, trouble, naughtiness, pranks, shenanigans *(informal)*, monkey business *(informal)*, waywardness, devilment, impishness, roguishness, roguery: *The little lad was always up to some mischief.* **2 = harm**, trouble, damage, injury, hurt, evil, disadvantage, disruption, misfortune, detriment: *The conference was a platform to cause political mischief.*

mischievous ADJECTIVE **1 = naughty**, bad, troublesome, wayward, exasperating, playful, rascally, impish, roguish, vexatious, puckish, frolicsome, arch, ludic *(literary)*, sportive, badly behaved: *She rocks back and forth on her chair like a mischievous child.* **2 = malicious**, damaging, vicious, destructive, harmful, troublesome, malignant, detrimental, hurtful, pernicious, spiteful, deleterious, injurious: *a mischievous campaign by the press*

m

misconception NOUN **= delusion**, error, misunderstanding, fallacy, misapprehension, mistaken belief, wrong idea, wrong end of the stick, misconstruction

misconduct NOUN **= immorality**, wrongdoing, mismanagement, malpractice, misdemeanour, delinquency, impropriety, transgression, misbehaviour, dereliction, naughtiness, malfeasance *(Law)*, unethical behaviour, malversation *(rare)*

misconstrue VERB **= misinterpret**, misunderstand, misjudge, misread, mistake, misapprehend, get a false impression of, misconceive, mistranslate, get your lines crossed about, make a wrong interpretation of

misdeed NOUN *(often plural)* **= offence**, wrong, crime, fault, sin, misconduct, trespass, misdemeanour, transgression, villainy

misdemeanour NOUN **= offence**, misconduct, infringement, trespass, misdeed, transgression, misbehaviour, peccadillo

miserable ADJECTIVE **1 = sad**, down, low, depressed, distressed, gloomy, dismal, afflicted, melancholy, heartbroken, desolate, forlorn, mournful, dejected, broken-hearted, despondent, downcast, sorrowful, wretched, disconsolate, crestfallen, doleful, down in the dumps *(informal)*, woebegone, down in the mouth *(informal)*: *She went to bed, miserable and depressed.* **OPPOSITE:** happy **2 = pathetic**, low, sorry, disgraceful, mean, shameful, shabby, abject, despicable, deplorable, lamentable, contemptible, scurvy, pitiable, detestable, piteous: *They have so far accepted a miserable 1,100 refugees from the former Yugoslavia.* **OPPOSITE:** respectable

miserly ADJECTIVE **= mean**, stingy, penny-pinching *(informal)*, parsimonious, close, near, grasping, beggarly, illiberal, avaricious, niggardly, ungenerous, covetous, penurious, tightfisted, close-fisted, mingy *(Brit. informal)*, snoep *(S. African informal)* **OPPOSITE:** generous

misery NOUN **1 = unhappiness**, distress, despair, grief, suffering, depression, torture, agony, gloom, sadness, discomfort, torment, hardship, sorrow, woe, anguish, melancholy, desolation, wretchedness: *All that money brought nothing but misery.* **OPPOSITE:** happiness **2 = poverty**, want, need, squalor, privation, penury, destitution, wretchedness, sordidness, indigence: *An elite profited from the misery of the poor.* **OPPOSITE:** luxury **3 = moaner**, pessimist, killjoy, spoilsport, grouch *(informal)*, prophet of doom, wet blanket *(informal)*, sourpuss *(informal)*, wowser *(Austral. & N.Z. slang)*: *I'm not such a misery now. I've got things sorted out a bit.* **4 = misfortune**, trouble, trial, disaster, load, burden, curse, ordeal, hardship, catastrophe, sorrow, woe, calamity, affliction, tribulation, bitter pill *(informal)*: *There is no point dwelling on the miseries of the past.*

misfire VERB **= fail**, go wrong, fall through, miscarry, go pear-shaped *(informal)*, fail to go off, go phut *(informal)*

misfit NOUN **= nonconformist**, eccentric, flake *(slang, chiefly U.S.)*, oddball *(informal)*, fish out of water *(informal)*, square peg (in a round hole) *(informal)*

misfortune NOUN **1** *(often plural)* **= bad luck**, adversity, hard luck, ill luck, infelicity, evil fortune, bad trot *(Austral. slang)*: *She seemed to enjoy the misfortunes of others.* **2 = mishap**, loss, trouble, trial, blow, failure, accident, disaster, reverse, tragedy, harm, misery, setback, hardship, calamity, affliction, tribulation, whammy *(informal, chiefly U.S.)*, misadventure, bummer *(slang)*, mischance, stroke of bad luck, evil chance: *He had had his full share of misfortunes.* **OPPOSITE:** good luck

> **QUOTATIONS**
> In the misfortune of our best friends, we always find something which is not displeasing to us
> [Duc de la Rochefoucauld *Réflexions ou Maximes Morales*]
>
> misfortune: the kind of fortune which never misses
> [Ambrose Bierce *The Devil's Dictionary*]
>
> **PROVERBS**
> *Misfortunes never come singly*

misgiving NOUN **= unease**, worry, doubt, anxiety, suspicion, uncertainty, reservation, hesitation, distrust, apprehension, qualm, trepidation, scruple, dubiety

misguided ADJECTIVE **= unwise**, mistaken, foolish, misled, misplaced, deluded, ill-advised, imprudent, injudicious, labouring under a delusion *or* misapprehension

mishandle VERB **= mismanage**, bungle, botch, mess up *(informal)*, screw (up) *(informal)*, make a mess of, muff, make a hash of *(informal)*, make a nonsense of, bodge *(informal)*, flub *(U.S. slang)*

mishap NOUN **= accident**, disaster, misfortune, stroke of bad luck, adversity, calamity, misadventure, contretemps, mischance, infelicity, evil chance, evil fortune

misinform VERB **= mislead**, deceive, misdirect, misguide, give someone a bum steer *(informal, chiefly U.S.)*

misinterpret VERB **= misunderstand**, mistake, distort, misrepresent, misjudge, falsify, pervert, misread, misconstrue, get wrong, misapprehend, misconceive

misjudge VERB **= miscalculate**, be wrong about, underestimate, underrate, overestimate, overrate, get the wrong idea about

mislay VERB **= lose**, misplace, miss, be unable to find, lose track of, be unable to put *or* lay your hand on, forget the whereabouts of

mislead VERB **= deceive**, fool, delude, take someone in *(informal)*, bluff, beguile, misdirect, misinform, hoodwink, lead astray, pull the wool over someone's eyes *(informal)*, take someone for a ride *(informal)*, misguide, give someone a bum steer *(informal, chiefly U.S.)*

misleading ADJECTIVE **= confusing**, false, ambiguous, deceptive, spurious, evasive, disingenuous, tricky *(informal)*, deceitful, specious, delusive, delusory, sophistical, casuistical, unstraightforward **OPPOSITE:** straightforward

mismatched ADJECTIVE **= incompatible**, clashing, irregular, disparate, incongruous, discordant, unsuited, ill-assorted, unreconcilable, misallied

misogynist ADJECTIVE **= chauvinist**, sexist, patriarchal
▷ NOUN **= woman-hater**, male chauvinist, anti-feminist, MCP *(informal)*, male chauvinist pig *(informal)*, male supremacist

misquote VERB **= misrepresent**, twist, distort, pervert, muddle, mangle, falsify, garble, misreport, misstate, quote *or* take out of context

misrepresent VERB **= distort**, disguise, pervert, belie, twist, misinterpret, falsify, garble, misstate

miss[1] VERB **1 = fail to notice**, mistake, overlook, pass over: *It's the first thing you see. You can't miss it.* **2 = misunderstand**, fail to appreciate: *She seemed to have missed the point.* **3 = long for**, wish for, yearn for, want, need, hunger for, pine for, long to see, ache for, feel the loss of, regret the absence of: *Your mum and I are going to miss you at Christmas.* **4 = be late for**, fail to catch *or* get: *He missed the last bus home.* **5 = not go to**, skip, cut, omit, be absent from, fail to attend, skive off *(informal)*, play truant from, bludge *(Austral. & N.Z. informal)*, absent yourself from: *We missed our swimming lesson last week.* **6 = avoid**, beat, escape, skirt, duck, cheat, bypass, dodge, evade, get round, elude, steer clear of, sidestep, circumvent, find a way round, give a wide berth to: *We left early, hoping to miss the worst of the traffic.*
▷ NOUN **= mistake**, failure, fault, error, blunder, omission, oversight: *After several more misses, they finally got two arrows in the lion's chest.*

miss[2] NOUN **= girl**, maiden, maid, schoolgirl, young lady, lass, damsel, spinster, lassie *(informal)*: *She didn't always come over as such a shy little miss.*

misshapen ADJECTIVE **= deformed**, twisted, crippled, distorted, ugly, crooked, warped, grotesque, wry, unsightly, contorted, ungainly, malformed, ill-made, unshapely, ill-proportioned

missile NOUN **= projectile**, weapon, shell, rocket

missing ADJECTIVE **= lost**, misplaced, not present, gone, left behind, astray, unaccounted for, mislaid, nowhere to be found

mission NOUN **1 = assignment**, job, labour, operation, work, commission, trip, message *(Scot.)*, task, undertaking, expedition, chore, errand: *the most crucial stage of his latest peace mission* **2 = task**, work, calling, business, job, office, charge, goal, operation, commission, trust, aim, purpose, duty, undertaking, pursuit, quest, assignment, vocation, errand: *He viewed his mission in life as protecting the weak from evil.*

missionary NOUN **= evangelist**, preacher, apostle, converter, propagandist, proselytizer

missive NOUN **= letter**, report, note, message, communication, dispatch, memorandum, epistle

mist NOUN **= fog**, cloud, steam, spray, film, haze, vapour, drizzle, smog, dew, condensation, haar *(Eastern Brit.)*, smur *or* smir *(Scot.)*: *Thick mist made flying impossible.*
mist over *or* **up = steam (up)**, cloud, obscure, blur, fog, film, blear, becloud, befog: *The windscreen was misting over.*

mistake NOUN **1 = error**, blunder, oversight, slip, misunderstanding, boob *(Brit. slang)*, misconception, gaffe *(informal)*, slip-up *(informal)*, bloomer *(Brit. informal)*, clanger *(informal)*, miscalculation, error of judgment, faux pas, false move, boo-boo *(informal)*, barry *or* Barry Crocker *(Austral. slang)*: *He says there must have been some mistake.* **2 = oversight**, error, slip, inaccuracy, fault, slip-up *(informal)*, howler *(informal)*, goof, solecism, erratum, barry *or* Barry Crocker *(Austral. slang)*: *Spelling mistakes are often just the result of haste.*
▷ VERB **= misunderstand**, misinterpret, misjudge, misread, misconstrue, get wrong, misapprehend, misconceive: *No one should mistake how serious this issue is.*
mistake something *or* **someone for something** *or* **someone = confuse with**, accept as, take for, mix up with, misinterpret as, confound with: *Hayfever is often mistaken for a summer cold.*

> **QUOTATIONS**
> We are built to make mistakes, coded for error
> [Lewis Thomas *The Medusa and the Snail*]
>
> The man who makes no mistakes does not usually make anything
> [Edward John Phelps]

mistaken ADJECTIVE **1 = wrong**, incorrect, misled, in the wrong, misguided, off the mark, off target, wide of the mark, misinformed, off base *(U.S. & Canad. informal)*, barking up the wrong tree *(informal)*, off beam *(informal)*, getting the wrong end of the stick *(informal)*, way off beam *(informal)*, labouring under a misapprehension: *I see I was mistaken about you.* **OPPOSITE:** correct **2 = inaccurate**, false, inappropriate, faulty, unfounded, erroneous, unsound, fallacious: *She obviously had a mistaken view.* **OPPOSITE:** accurate

mistakenly ADVERB **= incorrectly**, wrongly, falsely, by mistake, inappropriately, erroneously, in error, inaccurately, misguidedly, fallaciously

mistimed ADJECTIVE **= inopportune**, badly timed, inconvenient, untimely, ill-timed, unseasonable, unsynchronized

mistreat VERB **= abuse**, injure, harm, molest, misuse, maul, manhandle, wrong, rough up, ill-treat, brutalize, maltreat, ill-use, handle roughly, knock about *or* around

mistreatment NOUN **= abuse**, ill-treatment, maltreatment, injury, harm, misuse, mauling, manhandling, roughing up, molestation, unkindness, rough handling, brutalization, ill-usage

mistress NOUN **= lover**, girlfriend, concubine, kept woman, paramour, floozy *(slang)*, fancy woman *(slang)*, inamorata, doxy *(archaic)*, fancy bit *(slang)*, ladylove *(rare)*

mistrust NOUN **= suspicion**, scepticism, distrust, doubt, uncertainty, apprehension, misgiving, wariness, dubiety: *There was mutual mistrust between the two men.*
▷ VERB **= be wary of**, suspect, beware, distrust, apprehend, have doubts about: *You should mistrust all journalists.*

misty ADJECTIVE **= foggy**, unclear, murky, fuzzy, obscure, blurred, vague, dim, opaque, cloudy, hazy, overcast, bleary, nebulous, indistinct
OPPOSITE: clear

misunderstand VERB **1 = misinterpret**, misread, get the wrong idea (about), mistake, misjudge, misconstrue, mishear, misapprehend, be at cross-purposes with, misconceive: *They simply misunderstood him.* **2 = miss the point**, get the wrong end of the stick, get your wires crossed, get your lines crossed: *I think he simply misunderstood.*

misunderstanding NOUN **1 = mistake**, error, mix-up, misconception, misreading, misapprehension, false impression, misinterpretation, misjudgment, wrong idea, misconstruction: *Tell them what you want to avoid misunderstandings.* **2 = disagreement**, difference, conflict, argument, difficulty, breach, falling-out *(informal)*, quarrel, rift, squabble, rupture, variance, discord, dissension: *a misunderstanding between friends*

misunderstood ADJECTIVE **= misjudged**, misinterpreted, misread, misconstrued, unrecognized, misheard, unappreciated

misuse NOUN **1 = waste**, embezzlement, squandering, dissipation, fraudulent use, misemployment, misusage: *the misuse of public funds* **2 = abuse**, corruption, exploitation: *the misuse of power* **3 = misapplication**, abuse, illegal use, wrong use: *the misuse of drugs in sport* **4 = perversion**, distortion, desecration, profanation: *Fundamentalism is a deplorable misuse of a faith.* **5 = misapplication**, solecism, malapropism, catachresis: *his hilarious misuse of words* **6 = mistreatment**, abuse, harm, exploitation, injury, manhandling, ill-treatment, maltreatment, rough handling, inhumane treatment, cruel treatment, ill-usage: *the history of the misuse of Aborigines*
▷ VERB **1 = abuse**, misapply, misemploy, prostitute: *She misused her position in the government.* **2 = waste**, squander, dissipate, embezzle, misappropriate: *The committee has cleared leaders of misusing funds.* **3 = mistreat**, abuse, injure, harm, exploit, wrong, molest, manhandle, ill-treat, brutalize, maltreat, ill-use, handle roughly: *His parents should not have misused him.* **OPPOSITE:** cherish **4 = profane**, corrupt, desecrate,

pervert: *breaking a taboo, misusing a sacred ceremony*

mitigate VERB = **ease**, moderate, soften, check, quiet, calm, weaken, dull, diminish, temper, blunt, soothe, subdue, lessen, appease, lighten, remit, allay, placate, abate, tone down, assuage, pacify, mollify, take the edge off, extenuate, tranquillize, palliate, reduce the force of **OPPOSITE:** intensify

> **USAGE**
> *Mitigate* is sometimes wrongly used where *militate* is meant: *his behaviour militates* (not *mitigates*) *against his chances of promotion.*

mitigation NOUN **1 = extenuation**, explanation, excuse: *In mitigation, the offences were at the lower end of the scale.* **2 = relief**, moderation, allaying, remission, diminution, abatement, alleviation, easement, extenuation, mollification, palliation, assuagement: *the mitigation or cure of a physical or mental condition*

mix VERB **1 = combine**, blend, merge, unite, join, cross, compound, incorporate, put together, fuse, mingle, jumble, alloy, amalgamate, interweave, coalesce, intermingle, meld, commingle, commix: *Oil and water don't mix; Mix the cinnamon with the sugar.* **2 = socialize**, associate, hang out *(informal)*, mingle, circulate, come together, consort, hobnob, fraternize, rub elbows *(informal)*: *He mixes with people younger than himself.* **3** *(often with* **up**) **= combine**, marry, blend, integrate, amalgamate, coalesce, meld, commix: *The plan was to mix up office and residential zones.*
▷ NOUN **= mixture**, combination, blend, fusion, compound, jumble, assortment, alloy, medley, concoction, amalgam, mixed bag *(informal)*, meld, melange, miscellany: *a magical mix of fantasy and reality*
mix someone up = bewilder, upset, confuse, disturb, puzzle, muddle, perplex, unnerve, fluster, throw into confusion: *You're not helping at all, you're just mixing me up even more.*
mix someone up in something *(usually passive)* **= entangle**, involve, implicate, embroil, rope in: *He could have got mixed up in the murder.*
mix something up 1 = confuse, scramble, muddle, confound: *Depressed people often mix up their words.* **2 = blend**, beat, mix, stir, fold: *Mix up the batter in advance.*

mixed ADJECTIVE **1 = uncertain**, conflicting, confused, doubtful, unsure, muddled, contradictory, ambivalent, indecisive, equivocal: *I came home from the meeting with mixed feelings.* **2 = varied**, diverse, different, differing, diversified, cosmopolitan, assorted, jumbled, disparate, miscellaneous, motley, haphazard, manifold, heterogeneous: *I found a very mixed group of individuals.* **OPPOSITE:** homogeneous **3 = combined**, blended, fused, alloyed, united, compound, incorporated, composite, mingled, amalgamated: *silver jewellery with mixed metals and semi-precious stones* **OPPOSITE:** pure

mixed-up ADJECTIVE **= confused**, disturbed, puzzled, bewildered, at sea, upset, distraught, muddled, perplexed, maladjusted

mixture NOUN **1 = blend**, mix, variety, fusion, assortment, combine, brew, jumble, medley, concoction, amalgam, amalgamation, mixed bag *(informal)*, meld, potpourri, mélange *(French)*, miscellany, conglomeration, hotchpotch, admixture, salmagundi: *a mixture of spiced, grilled vegetables* **2 = composite**, union, compound, alloy: *a mixture of concrete and resin* **3 = cross**, combination, blend, association: *a mixture between Reggae, Bhangra, and Soul fusion* **4 = concoction**, union, compound, blend, brew, composite, amalgam, conglomeration: *Prepare the mixture carefully.*

mix-up NOUN **= confusion**, mistake, misunderstanding, mess, tangle, muddle, jumble, fankle *(Scot.)*

moan VERB **1 = groan**, sigh, sob, whine, keen, lament, deplore, bemoan, bewail: *'My head, my head,' she moaned.* **2 = grumble**, complain, groan, whine, beef *(slang)*, carp, bitch *(slang)*, grouse, gripe *(informal)*, whinge *(informal)*, bleat, moan and groan, grouch *(informal)*: *I used to moan if I didn't get at least 8 hours' sleep.*
▷ NOUN **1 = groan**, sigh, sob, lament, wail, grunt, whine, lamentation: *She gave a low choking moan and began to tremble violently.* **2 = complaint**, protest, grumble, beef *(slang)*, bitch *(slang)*, whine, grouse, gripe *(informal)*, grouch *(informal)*, kvetch *(U.S. slang)*: *They have been listening to people's gripes and moans.*

mob NOUN **1 = crowd**, pack, collection, mass, body, press, host, gathering, drove, gang, flock, herd, swarm, horde, multitude, throng, assemblage: *a growing mob of demonstrators* **2 = masses**, rabble, hoi polloi, scum, great unwashed *(informal, derogatory)*, riffraff, canaille *(French)*, commonalty: *If they continue like this, there is a danger of the mob taking over.* **3 = gang**, company, group, set, lot, troop, crew *(informal)*: *Can you stop your mob tramping all over the place?*
▷ VERB **1 = surround**, besiege, overrun, jostle, fall on, set upon, crowd around, swarm around: *Her car was mobbed by the media.* **2 = crowd into**, fill, crowd, pack, jam, cram into, fill to overflowing: *Demonstrators mobbed the streets.*

mobile ADJECTIVE **1 = movable**, moving, travelling, wandering, portable, locomotive, itinerant, peripatetic, ambulatory, motile: *a four-hundred-seat mobile theatre* **2 = changeable**, meaning, animated, expressive, eloquent, suggestive, ever-changing: *She had a mobile, expressive face.*

mobilize VERB **1 = rally**, organize, stimulate, excite, prompt, marshal, activate, awaken, animate, muster, foment, put in motion: *We must try to mobilize international support.* **2 = deploy**, prepare, ready, rally, assemble, call up, marshal, muster, call to arms, get *or* make ready: *The government has mobilized troops to help.*

mock VERB **= laugh at**, insult, tease, ridicule, taunt, scorn, sneer, scoff, deride, flout, make fun of, wind someone up *(Brit. slang)*, poke fun at, chaff, take the mickey out of *(informal)*, jeer at, show contempt for, make a monkey out of, laugh to scorn: *I thought you were mocking me.* **OPPOSITE:** respect
▷ ADJECTIVE **= imitation**, pretended, artificial, forged, fake, false, faked, dummy, bogus, sham, fraudulent, pseudo *(informal)*, counterfeit, feigned, spurious, ersatz, phoney *or* phony *(informal)*: *'It's tragic,' he swooned in mock horror.* **OPPOSITE:** genuine
▷ NOUN **= laughing stock**, fool, dupe, sport, travesty, jest, Aunt Sally *(Brit.)*: *She found herself made a mock of.*

mockery NOUN **1 = derision**, contempt, ridicule, scorn, jeering, disdain, scoffing, disrespect, gibes, contumely: *Was there a glint of mockery in his eyes?* **2 = farce**, laughing stock, joke, apology *(informal)*, letdown: *This action makes a mockery of the government's plans.*

mocking ADJECTIVE **= scornful**, insulting, taunting, scoffing, satirical, contemptuous, irreverent, sarcastic, sardonic, derisory, disrespectful, disdainful, derisive, satiric, contumelious

mode NOUN **1 = method**, way, plan, course, system, form, state, process, condition, style, approach, quality, practice, fashion, technique, manner, procedure, custom, vein: *the capitalist mode of production* **2 = fashion**, style, trend, rage, vogue, look, craze: *Their designs were exterminated by the mode for uncluttered space.*

model NOUN **1 = representation**, image, copy, miniature, dummy, replica, imitation, duplicate, lookalike, facsimile, mock-up: *an architect's model of a wooden house* **2 = pattern**, example, design, standard, type, original, ideal, mould, norm, gauge, prototype, paradigm, archetype, exemplar, lodestar: *the Chinese model of economic reform* **3 = version**, form, kind, design, style, type, variety, stamp, mode, configuration: *To keep the cost down, opt for a basic model.* **4 = sitter**, subject, poser: *an artist's model* **5 = mannequin**, supermodel, fashion model, clothes horse *(informal)*: *a top photographic model*
▷ MODIFIER **1 = imitation**, copy, toy, miniature, dummy, duplicate, facsimile: *a model aeroplane* **2 = ideal**,

perfect, impeccable, exemplary, consummate, flawless, faultless: *At school she was a model pupil.* **OPPOSITE:** imperfect **3 = archetypal**, standard, typical, illustrative, paradigmatic: *The aim is to develop a model farm from which farmers can learn.*
▷ VERB **1 = base**, shape, plan, found, pattern, mould: *She asked if he had modelled the hero on anyone in particular.* **2 = show off** *(informal)*, wear, display, sport: *Two boys modelled a variety of clothes from Harrods.* **3 = shape**, form, design, fashion, cast, stamp, carve, mould, sculpt: *Sometimes she carved wood or modelled clay.*

> **QUOTATIONS**
> Rules and models destroy genius and art
> [William Hazlitt *Sketches and Essays*]

moderate ADJECTIVE **1 = mild**, reasonable, controlled, limited, cool, calm, steady, modest, restrained, deliberate, sober, middle-of-the-road, temperate, judicious, peaceable, equable: *He was an easy-going man of very moderate views.* **OPPOSITE:** extreme **2 = average**, middling, medium, fair, ordinary, indifferent, mediocre, so-so *(informal)*, passable, unexceptional, fairish, half-pie *(N.Z. informal)*, fair to middling *(informal)*: *The drug offered only moderate improvements.*
▷ VERB **1 = soften**, control, calm, temper, regulate, quiet, diminish, decrease, curb, restrain, tame, subdue, play down, lessen, repress, mitigate, tone down, pacify, modulate, soft-pedal *(informal)*: *They are hoping that he will be persuaded to moderate his views.* **2 = lessen**, relax, ease, wane, abate: *The crisis has moderated somewhat.* **OPPOSITE:** intensify **3 = arbitrate**, judge, chair, referee, preside, mediate, take the chair: *trying to moderate a quarrel between the two states*

moderation NOUN **= restraint**, justice, fairness, composure, coolness, temperance, calmness, equanimity, reasonableness, mildness, justness, judiciousness, sedateness, moderateness: *He called on all parties to show moderation.*
in moderation = moderately, within reason, within limits, within bounds, in moderate quantities: *Many of us are able to drink in moderation.*

> **QUOTATIONS**
> Moderation is a virtue only in those who are thought to have an alternative
> [Henry Kissinger]
>
> We know what happens to people who stay in the middle of the road. They get run down
> [Aneurin Bevan]

> **PROVERBS**
> *Moderation in all things*

modern ADJECTIVE **1 = current**, present, contemporary, recent, late, present-day, latter-day: *the problem of materialism in modern society* **2 = up-to-date**, latest, fresh, new, novel, with it *(informal)*, up-to-the-minute, newfangled, neoteric *(rare)*: *a more tailored and modern style* **OPPOSITE:** old-fashioned

modernity NOUN **= novelty**, currency, innovation, freshness, newness, contemporaneity, recentness

modernize VERB **= update**, renew, revamp, remake, renovate, remodel, rejuvenate, make over, face-lift, bring up to date, rebrand

modest ADJECTIVE **1 = moderate**, small, limited, fair, ordinary, middling, meagre, frugal, scanty, unexceptional: *You don't get rich, but you can earn a modest living from it.* **2 = unpretentious**, simple, reserved, retiring, quiet, shy, humble, discreet, blushing, self-conscious, coy, meek, reticent, unassuming, self-effacing, demure, diffident, bashful, aw-shucks: *He's modest, as well as being a great player.*

modesty NOUN **= reserve**, decency, humility, shyness, propriety, reticence, timidity, diffidence, quietness, coyness, self-effacement, meekness, lack of pretension, bashfulness, humbleness, unpretentiousness, demureness, unobtrusiveness, discreetness **OPPOSITE:** conceit

modicum NOUN **= little**, bit, drop, touch, inch, scrap, dash, grain, particle, fragment, atom, pinch, ounce, shred, small amount, crumb, tinge, mite, tad *(informal, chiefly U.S.)*, speck, iota

modification NOUN **= change**, restriction, variation, qualification, adjustment, revision, alteration, mutation, reformation, refinement, modulation

modify VERB **1 = change**, reform, vary, convert, transform, alter, adjust, adapt, revise, remodel, rework, tweak *(informal)*, reorganize, recast, reshape, redo, refashion: *They agreed to modify their recruitment policy.* **2 = tone down**, limit, reduce, lower, qualify, relax, ease, restrict, moderate, temper, soften, restrain, lessen, abate: *He had to modify his language considerably.*

modish ADJECTIVE **= fashionable**, current, smart, stylish, trendy *(Brit. informal)*, in, now *(informal)*, with it *(informal)*, contemporary, hip *(slang)*, vogue, chic, all the rage, up-to-the-minute, à la mode, voguish, schmick *(Austral. informal)*, funky

modulate VERB **= adjust**, balance, vary, tone, tune, regulate, harmonize, inflect, attune

modus operandi NOUN **= procedure**, way, system, process, operation, practice, method, technique, praxis

mogul NOUN **= tycoon**, lord, baron, notable, magnate, big gun *(informal)*, big shot *(informal)*, personage, nob *(slang, chiefly Brit.)*, potentate, big wheel *(slang)*, big cheese *(slang, old-fashioned)*, big noise *(informal)*, big hitter *(informal)*, heavy hitter *(informal)*, nabob *(informal)*, bashaw, V.I.P.

moist ADJECTIVE **= damp**, wet, dripping, rainy, soggy, humid, dank, clammy, dewy, not dry, drizzly, dampish, wettish

moisten VERB **= dampen**, water, wet, soak, damp, moisturize, humidify, bedew

moisture NOUN **= damp**, water, liquid, sweat, humidity, dew, perspiration, dampness, wetness, dankness, wateriness

molecule NOUN **= particle**, atom, mite, jot, speck, mote, iota

molest VERB **1 = abuse**, attack, hurt, injure, harm, interfere with, assail, accost, manhandle, ill-treat, maltreat: *He was accused of sexually molesting a colleague.* **2 = annoy**, worry, upset, harry, bother, disturb, bug *(informal)*, plague, irritate, tease, torment, harass, afflict, badger, persecute, beset, hector, pester, vex: *He disguised himself to avoid being molested in the street.*

mollify VERB **= pacify**, quiet, calm, compose, soothe, appease, quell, sweeten, placate, conciliate, propitiate

mom NOUN **= mum**, mother, ma

moment NOUN **1 = instant**, second, minute, flash, shake *(informal)*, tick *(Brit. informal)*, no time, twinkling, split second, jiffy *(informal)*, trice, two shakes *(informal)*, two shakes of a lamb's tail *(informal)*, bat of an eye *(informal)*: *In a moment he was gone.* **2 = time**, point, stage, instant, point in time, hour, juncture: *At this moment a car stopped outside the house.* **3 = importance**, concern, value, worth, weight, import, consequence, substance, significance, gravity, seriousness, weightiness: *I was glad I had nothing of great moment to do that afternoon.*

> **QUOTATIONS**
> in the twinkling of an eye
> [*Bible: I Corinthians*]

momentarily ADVERB **= briefly**, for a moment, temporarily, for a second, for a minute, for a short time, for an instant, for a little while, for a short while, for the nonce

momentary ADJECTIVE **= short-lived**, short, brief, temporary, passing, quick, fleeting, hasty, transitory **OPPOSITE:** lasting

momentous ADJECTIVE **= significant**, important, serious, vital, critical, crucial, grave, historic, decisive, pivotal, fateful, weighty, consequential, of moment, earth-shaking *(informal)* **OPPOSITE:** unimportant

momentum NOUN **= impetus**, force, power, drive, push, energy, strength, thrust, propulsion, go-forward

monarch NOUN = **ruler**, king *or* queen, sovereign, tsar, potentate, crowned head, emperor *or* empress, prince *or* princess

monarchy NOUN **1** = **sovereignty**, despotism, autocracy, kingship, absolutism, royalism, monocracy: *a debate on the future of the monarchy* **2** = **kingdom**, empire, realm, principality: *The country was a monarchy until 1973.*

monastery NOUN = **abbey**, house, convent, priory, cloister, religious community, nunnery, friary

monastic ADJECTIVE = **monkish**, secluded, cloistered, reclusive, withdrawn, austere, celibate, contemplative, ascetic, sequestered, hermit-like, conventual, cenobitic, coenobitic, cloistral, eremitic, monachal

monetary ADJECTIVE = **financial**, money, economic, capital, cash, fiscal, budgetary, pecuniary

money NOUN = **cash**, funds, capital, currency, hard cash, green *(slang)*, readies *(informal)*, riches, necessary *(informal)*, silver, bread *(slang)*, coin, tin *(slang)*, brass *(Northern English dialect)*, loot *(informal)*, dough *(slang)*, the ready *(informal)*, banknotes, dosh *(Brit. & Austral. slang)*, lolly *(Brit. slang)*, the wherewithal, legal tender, megabucks *(U.S. & Canad. slang)*, needful *(informal)*, specie, shekels *(informal)*, dibs *(slang)*, filthy lucre *(facetious)*, moolah *(slang)*, ackers *(slang)*, gelt *(slang, chiefly U.S.)*, spondulicks *(slang)*, pelf *(derogatory)*, mazuma *(slang, chiefly U.S.)*, kembla *(Austral. slang)*: *A lot of money that you pay goes back to the distributor.*
in the money = **rich**, wealthy, prosperous, affluent, rolling *(slang)*, loaded *(slang)*, flush *(informal)*, well-off, well-heeled *(informal)*, well-to-do, on Easy Street *(informal)*, in clover *(informal)*, minted *(Brit. slang)*: *If you are lucky, you could be in the money.*
▸ *related adjective:* pecuniary

QUOTATIONS

Money speaks sense in a language all nations understand
[Aphra Behn *The Lucky Chance*]

When a fellow says, it hain't the money but the principle of the thing, it's the money
[Kin Hubbard *Hoss Sense and Nonsense*]

Money is our madness, our vast collective madness
[D.H. Lawrence]

The almighty dollar is the only object of worship
[*Philadelphia Public Ledger*]

Wine maketh merry, but money answereth all things
[*Bible: Ecclesiastes*]

Money is coined liberty
[Fyodor Dostoevsky *House of the Dead*]

Money is the sinews of love, as of war
[George Farquhar *Love and a Bottle*]

Better authentic mammon than a bogus god
[Louis MacNiece *Autumn Journal*]

Money is like a sixth sense without which you cannot make a complete use of the other five
[W. Somerset Maugham *Of Human Bondage*]

My boy ... always try to rub up against money, for if you rub up against money long enough, some of it may rub off on you
[Damon Runyon *A Very Honorable Guy*]

but it is pretty to see what money will do
[Samuel Pepys *Diary*]

If you can actually count your money, then you are not really a rich man
[J. Paul Getty]

Money doesn't make you happy. I now have $50 million but I was just as happy when I had $48 million
[Arnold Schwarzenegger]

Money doesn't talk, it swears
[Bob Dylan *It's Alright, Ma (I'm Only Bleeding)*]

Money is like muck, not good except it be spread
[Francis Bacon *Of Seditions and Troubles*]

Money ... is none of the wheels of trade: it is the oil which renders the motion of the wheels more smooth and easy
[David Hume *Essays: Moral and Political*]

Money couldn't buy friends but you got a better class of enemy
[Spike Milligan *Puckoon*]

PROVERBS

Bad money drives out good
Money isn't everything
Money talks
Money is power
Money makes money
Shrouds have no pockets
You can't take it with you when you go

moneyed *or* **monied** ADJECTIVE = **rich**, loaded *(slang)*, wealthy, flush *(informal)*, prosperous, affluent, well-off, well-heeled *(informal)*, well-to-do, minted *(Brit. slang)*

moneymaking ADJECTIVE = **profitable**, successful, lucrative, gainful, paying, thriving, remunerative

mongrel NOUN = **hybrid**, cross, half-breed, crossbreed, mixed breed, bigener *(Biology)*: *They were walking their pet mongrel on the outskirts of the town when it happened.*
▷ ADJECTIVE = **half-breed**, hybrid, crossbred, of mixed breed: *He was determined to save his mongrel puppy.*

monitor VERB = **check**, follow, record, watch, survey, observe, scan, oversee, supervise, keep an eye on, keep track of, keep tabs on: *Officials had not been allowed to monitor the voting.*
▷ NOUN **1** = **guide**, observer, supervisor, overseer, invigilator: *Government monitors will continue to accompany reporters.* **2** = **prefect** *(Brit.)*, head girl, head boy, senior boy, senior girl: *As a school monitor he set a good example.*

monk NOUN = **friar**, brother, religious, novice, monastic, oblate
▸ *related adjective:* monastic

monkey NOUN **1** = **simian**, ape, primate, jackanapes *(archaic)*: *He walked on all fours like a monkey.* **2** = **rascal**, horror, devil, rogue, imp, tyke, scallywag, mischief maker, scamp, nointer *(Austral. slang)*: *She's such a little monkey.*
▸ *related adjective:* simian ▸ *collective noun:* troop

QUOTATIONS

monkey: an arboreal animal which makes itself at home in genealogical trees
[Ambrose Bierce *The Devil's Dictionary*]

monolithic ADJECTIVE = **huge**, giant, massive, imposing, solid, substantial, gigantic, monumental, colossal, impenetrable, intractable, immovable

monologue NOUN = **speech**, lecture, sermon, harangue, soliloquy, oration, spiel *(informal)*

monopolize VERB **1** = **control**, corner, take over, dominate, exercise *or* have a monopoly of: *They are virtually monopolizing the market.* **2** = **keep to yourself**, corner, hog *(slang)*, engross: *He monopolized her totally, to the exclusion of her brothers and sisters.*

monotonous ADJECTIVE **1** = **tedious**, boring, dull, repetitive, uniform, all the same, plodding, tiresome, humdrum, unchanging, colourless, mind-numbing, soporific, ho-hum *(informal)*, repetitious, wearisome, samey *(informal)*, unvaried: *It's monotonous work, like most factory jobs.*
OPPOSITE: interesting **2** = **toneless**, flat, uniform, droning, unchanging, uninflected: *a monotonous voice*
OPPOSITE: animated

monotony NOUN = **tedium**, routine, boredom, dullness, sameness, uniformity, flatness, repetitiveness, tediousness, repetitiousness, colourlessness, tiresomeness

monster NOUN **1** = **giant**, mammoth, titan, colossus, monstrosity, leviathan, behemoth: *He said he'd hooked a real monster of a fish.* **2** = **brute**, devil, savage, beast, demon, villain, barbarian, fiend, ogre, ghoul, bogeyman: *You make me sound like an absolute monster!*

monstrosity NOUN **1** = **freak**, horror, monster, mutant, ogre, lusus naturae *(Latin)*, miscreation, teratism: *The*

m

The Language of Susanna Moodie

Susanna Moodie (1803–85), born in Suffolk, England, began her career as a children's author before later writing about her experiences as a settler in Canada. Her memoir, *Roughing it in the Bush,* focuses on the challenges which faced new immigrants to Canada. She was sister to Catharine Parr Strickland Traill, who also wrote about life as a Canadian settler.

The fact that Moodie wrote about the hardships facing new immigrants is reflected in her use of language, with *suffer* appearing in her 100 most frequently used verbs. Some of the most salient objects used with *suffer* include *agony, hardship, punishment,* and *pain*:

> If we occasionally **suffered** severe pain, we as often experienced great pleasure, and I have contemplated a well-hoed ridge of potatoes on that bush farm, with as much delight as in years long past I had experienced in examining a fine painting in some well-appointed drawing-room.

While Moodie writes realistically about the difficulties she experienced as an immigrant, she also focuses on the positive side of life in Canada. Indeed, many of her 100 most frequently used adjectives are positive terms, for example, *good, beautiful, handsome, noble, glorious,* and *excellent. Good* appears over three times as frequently as *bad.* Some of the most salient nouns Moodie uses *good* to modify include *quality, friend,* and *farm.* The most prominent nouns modified by *bad* include *bread, beginning,* and *potato. Noble* modifies *hound, endeavour,* and *landscape,* while *glorious* modifies *privilege* and *creation. Excellent* is used to modify people, especially females in a specified role or occupation (*sempstress, dairymaid, housewife, housekeeper, wife*), as well as food and drink (*dinner, vinegar, salad, beer, meat, supper.*) Many of the most frequent nouns modified by *beautiful* include animals and other features of nature, for example *snow-bird, flower, shrub,* and *blossom. Handsome* modifies nouns as diverse as *homestead, game-cock,* and *steam-boat.*

However, negative terms such as *dreadful* also appear in Moodie's 100 most frequently used adjectives. In addition, *terrible* is fairly frequent. *Terrible* modifies *disease, thunderstorm,* and *beast,* while *dreadful* modifies *calamity, sacrifice, hardship,* and *struggles:*

> It was always a humiliating feeling to our proud minds, that hirelings should witness our **dreadful** struggles with poverty, and the strange shifts we were forced to make in order to obtain even food.

Many of the nouns that Moodie uses most frequently refer to people, such as *man, woman,* and *child,* or things that are closely associated with them, such as *heart, hand, face,* and *mind. Man* appears almost twice as much as *child* and almost three times as much as *woman. Man* is modified by a range of negative and positive adjectives such as *good, bad, clever, honest,* and *wicked.* Adjectives used to describe *child* include *neglected, ragged, spoiled,* and *dutiful.* Again, Moodie uses both positive and negative adjectives to describe women, for example, *amiable, sensible, avaricious,* and *ill-tempered.* However, Moodie usually uses negative adjectives to modify *mind,* such as *uncultivated, perverted, weak* and *disturbed,* although she also uses some positive adjectives such as *well-cultivated* and *enlightened.* Positive adjectives such as *warm* and *faithful* modify *heart,* but there are some instances of adjectives such as *stony.* The noun *hand* is often associated with verbs portraying emotion, for example, *shake, tremble,* and *clench.* Similarly, verbs associated with *face* include *flush, smile,* and *blush.*

The illustration of emotions is an important part of Moodie's work with *feel, cry,* and *love* appearing in her 100 most frequently used verbs, and *love, affection,* and *passion* appearing in her 100 most frequently used nouns. Notable adjectives associated with *feel* include *ashamed, proud, alarmed,* and *happy,* while the verb *love* is modified by adverbs such as *dearly, fiercely, fondly,* and *passionately. Cry,* is modified by *vehemently, angrily,* and *piteously.* The most striking adjectives describing the noun *love* include *maternal, earthly,* and *devoted,* while *affection* is described as *mournful* and *ardent.* Moodie describes *passion* as *evil, turbulent, sensual, sinful,* and *romantic.*

towering figure looked like some monstrosity from a sci-fi movie. **2 = hideousness**, horror, evil, atrocity, abnormality, obscenity, dreadfulness, frightfulness, heinousness, hellishness, loathsomeness: *the monstrosity of Nazism*

monstrous ADJECTIVE **1 = outrageous**, shocking, evil, horrifying, vicious, foul, cruel, infamous, intolerable, disgraceful, scandalous, atrocious, inhuman, diabolical, heinous, odious, loathsome, devilish, egregious, fiendish, villainous: *She endured his monstrous behaviour for years.* **OPPOSITE:** decent **2 = huge**, giant, massive, great, towering, vast, enormous, tremendous, immense, titanic, gigantic, mammoth, colossal, stellar *(informal)*, prodigious, stupendous, gargantuan, elephantine, ginormous *(informal)*, humongous *or* humungous *(U.S. slang)*: *They were erecting a monstrous edifice.* **OPPOSITE:** tiny **3 = unnatural**, terrible, horrible, dreadful, abnormal, obscene, horrendous, hideous, grotesque, gruesome, frightful, hellish, freakish, fiendish, miscreated: *the film's monstrous fantasy figure* **OPPOSITE:** normal

month NOUN **= four weeks**, thirty days, moon

monument NOUN **1 = memorial**, cairn, statue, pillar, marker, shrine, tombstone, mausoleum, commemoration, headstone, gravestone, obelisk, cenotaph: *He laid a wreath on a monument near Bayeux.* **2 = testament**, record, witness, token, reminder, remembrance, memento: *By his achievements he leaves a fitting monument to his beliefs.*

> **QUOTATIONS**
> If you seek a monument, look around (Si monumentum requiris, circumspice)
> [son of Sir Christopher Wren *Inscription in St. Paul's Cathedral*]

monumental ADJECTIVE **= important**, classic, significant, outstanding, lasting, enormous, historic, enduring, memorable, awesome, majestic, immortal, unforgettable, prodigious, stupendous, awe-inspiring, epoch-making: *his monumental work on Chinese astronomy* **OPPOSITE:** unimportant
▷ ADJECTIVE **= immense**, great, massive, terrible, tremendous, horrible, staggering, catastrophic, gigantic, colossal, whopping *(informal)*, indefensible, unforgivable, egregious: *It had been a monumental blunder to give him the assignment.* **OPPOSITE:** tiny
▷ ADJECTIVE **= commemorative**, memorial, monolithic, statuary, funerary: *monumental architecture*

mood NOUN **1 = state of mind**, spirit, humour, temper, vein, tenor, disposition, frame of mind: *He was clearly in a good mood today.* **2 = depression**, sulk, bad temper, blues, dumps *(informal)*, wax *(informal, chiefly Brit.)*, melancholy, doldrums, the hump *(Brit. informal)*, bate *(Brit. slang)*, fit of pique, low spirits, the sulks, grumps *(informal)*, foulie *(Austral. slang)*: *She was obviously in a mood.*
in the mood = inclined, willing, interested, minded, keen, eager, disposed towards, in the (right) frame of mind, favourable towards: *After all that activity we were in the mood for a good meal.*

moody ADJECTIVE **1 = changeable**, volatile, unpredictable, unstable, erratic, fickle, temperamental, impulsive, mercurial, capricious, unsteady, fitful, flighty, faddish, inconstant: *She was unstable and moody.* **OPPOSITE:** stable **2 = sulky**, cross, wounded, angry, offended, irritable, crabbed, crusty, temperamental, touchy, curt, petulant, ill-tempered, irascible, cantankerous, tetchy, testy, chippy *(informal)*, in a huff, short-tempered, waspish, piqued, crabby, huffy, splenetic, crotchety *(informal)*, ill-humoured, huffish, tooshie *(Austral. slang)*: *He is a moody man behind that jokey front.* **OPPOSITE:** cheerful **3 = gloomy**, sad, miserable, melancholy, frowning, dismal, dour, sullen, glum, introspective, in the doldrums, out of sorts *(informal)*, downcast, morose, lugubrious, pensive, broody, crestfallen, doleful, down in the dumps *(informal)*, saturnine, down in the mouth *(informal)*, mopish, mopy: *Don't go all moody on me!* **OPPOSITE:** cheerful **4 = sad**, gloomy, melancholy, sombre: *melancholy guitars and moody lyrics*

moon NOUN **= satellite**: *Neptune's large moon*
▷ VERB **= idle**, drift, loaf, languish, waste time, daydream, mope, mooch *(Brit. slang)*: *She was mooning around all morning, doing nothing.*
▸ *related adjective*: lunar

> **QUOTATIONS**
> Swear not by the moon, the inconstant moon
> [William Shakespeare *Romeo and Juliet*]

moor[1] NOUN **= moorland**, fell *(Brit.)*, heath, muir *(Scot.)*: *The small town is high up on the moors.*

moor[2] VERB **= tie up**, fix, secure, anchor, dock, lash, berth, fasten, make fast: *She had moored her boat on the right bank of the river.*

moot VERB **= bring up**, propose, suggest, introduce, put forward, ventilate, broach: *When the theatre idea was first mooted, I had my doubts.*
▷ ADJECTIVE **= debatable**, open, controversial, doubtful, unsettled, unresolved, undecided, at issue, arguable, open to debate, contestable, disputable: *How long he'll be able to do so is a moot point.*

mop NOUN **1 = squeegee**, sponge, swab: *She was standing outside the door with a mop and bucket.* **2 = mane**, shock, mass, tangle, mat, thatch: *He was dark-eyed with a mop of tight curls.*
▷ VERB **= clean**, wash, wipe, sponge, swab, squeegee: *There was a woman mopping the stairs.*
mop something up 1 = clean up, wash, sponge, mop, soak up, swab, wipe up, sop up: *A waiter mopped up the mess as best he could.* **2 = finish off**, clear, account for, eliminate, round up, clean out, neutralize, pacify: *The infantry divisions mopped up remaining centres of resistance.*

mope VERB **= brood**, moon, pine, hang around, idle, fret, pout, languish, waste time, sulk, be gloomy, eat your heart out, be apathetic, be dejected, be down in the mouth *(informal)*, have a long face, wear a long face, go about like a half-shut knife *(informal)*

moral ADJECTIVE **1 = ethical**, social, behavioural: *the moral issues involved in 'playing God'* **2 = psychological**, emotional, mental: *He showed moral courage in defending his ideas.* **3 = good**, just, right, principled, pure, decent, innocent, proper, noble, ethical, upright, honourable, honest, righteous, virtuous, blameless, high-minded, chaste, upstanding, meritorious, incorruptible: *The committee members are moral, competent people.* **OPPOSITE:** immoral
▷ NOUN **= lesson**, meaning, point, message, teaching, import, significance, precept: *The moral of the story is, let the buyer beware.*
▷ PLURAL NOUN **= morality**, standards, conduct, principles, behaviour, manners, habits, ethics, integrity, mores, scruples: *Western ideas and morals*

> **QUOTATIONS**
> An Englishman thinks he is moral when he is only uncomfortable
> [George Bernard Shaw *Man and Superman*]
>
> Food first, then morals
> [Bertolt Brecht *The Threepenny Opera*]

morale NOUN **= confidence**, heart, spirit, temper, self-esteem, team spirit, mettle, esprit de corps

morality NOUN **1 = virtue**, justice, principles, morals, honour, integrity, goodness, honesty, decency, fair play, righteousness, good behaviour, propriety, chastity, probity, rectitude, rightness, uprightness: *an effort to preserve traditional morality* **2 = ethics**, conduct, principles, ideals, morals, manners, habits, philosophy, mores, moral code: *aspects of Christian morality* **3 = rights and wrongs**, ethics, ethicality: *the morality of blood sports*

> **QUOTATIONS**
> Morality is the herd-instinct in the individual
> [Friedrich Nietzsche *Die fröhliche Wissenschaft*]

> Morality is a private and costly luxury
> [Henry Brooks Adams *The Education of Henry Adams*]
>
> We know no spectacle so ridiculous as the British public in one of its periodical fits of morality
> [Lord Macaulay *Essays*]
>
> One becomes moral as soon as one is unhappy
> [Marcel Proust *Within a Budding Grove*]
>
> Morality comes with the sad wisdom of age, when the sense of curiosity has withered
> [Graham Greene *A Sort of Life*]

morass NOUN **1 = mess**, confusion, chaos, jam *(informal)*, tangle, mix-up, muddle, quagmire: *I tried to drag myself out of the morass of despair.* **2 = marsh**, swamp, bog, slough, fen, moss *(Scot. & Northern English dialect)*, quagmire, marshland, muskeg *(Canad.)*: *a morass of gooey mud*

moratorium NOUN **= postponement**, stay, freeze, halt, suspension, respite, standstill

morbid ADJECTIVE **1 = gruesome**, sick, dreadful, ghastly, hideous, unhealthy, grisly, macabre, horrid, ghoulish, unwholesome: *Some people have a morbid fascination with crime.* **2 = gloomy**, brooding, pessimistic, melancholy, sombre, grim, glum, lugubrious, funereal, low-spirited: *He was in no mood for any morbid introspection.* **OPPOSITE:** cheerful **3 = diseased**, sick, infected, deadly, ailing, unhealthy, malignant, sickly, pathological, unsound: *Uraemia is a morbid condition.* **OPPOSITE:** healthy

more DETERMINER **= extra**, additional, spare, new, other, added, further, fresh, new-found, supplementary: *Give them a bit more information.*
▷ ADVERB **1 = to a greater extent**, longer, better, further, some more: *When we are tired we feel pain more.* **2 = moreover**, also, in addition, besides, furthermore, what's more, on top of that, to boot, into the bargain, over and above that: *He was blind, and more, his eyepits were scooped hollows.*

moreover ADVERB **= furthermore**, also, further, in addition, too, as well, besides, likewise, what is more, to boot, additionally, into the bargain, withal *(literary)*

moribund ADJECTIVE **= declining**, weak, waning, standing still, stagnant, stagnating, on the way out, at a standstill, obsolescent, on its last legs, forceless

morning NOUN **1 = before noon**, forenoon, morn *(poetic)*, a.m.: *On Sunday morning he was woken by the telephone ringing loudly.* **2 = dawn**, sunrise, morrow *(archaic)*, first light, daybreak, break of day: *I started to lose hope of ever seeing the morning.*

> **QUOTATIONS**
> Awake! For morning in the bowl of night
> Has flung the stone that puts the stars to flight
> And lo! the Hunter of the East has caught
> The Sultan's turret in a noose of light
> [Edward Fitzgerald *The Rubáiyát of Omar Khayyám*]

moron NOUN **= fool**, idiot, dummy *(slang)*, berk *(Brit. slang)*, charlie *(Brit. informal)*, tosser *(Brit. slang)*, dope *(informal)*, jerk *(slang, chiefly U.S. & Canad.)*, ass, plank *(Brit. slang)*, wally *(slang)*, prat *(slang)*, plonker *(slang)*, coot, geek *(slang)*, twit *(informal, chiefly Brit.)*, bonehead *(slang)*, chump, dunce, imbecile, cretin, oaf, simpleton, airhead *(slang)*, dimwit *(informal)*, dipstick *(Brit. slang)*, gonzo *(slang)*, schmuck *(U.S. slang)*, dork *(slang)*, nitwit *(informal)*, dolt, blockhead, divvy *(Brit. slang)*, pillock *(Brit. slang)*, halfwit, dweeb *(U.S. slang)*, putz *(U.S. slang)*, fathead *(informal)*, weenie *(U.S. informal)*, eejit *(Scot. & Irish)*, dumb-ass *(slang)*, dunderhead, numpty *(Scot. informal)*, doofus *(slang, chiefly U.S.)*, lamebrain *(informal)*, mental defective, thickhead, muttonhead *(slang)*, nerd *or* nurd *(slang)*, numbskull *or* numskull, dorba *or* dorb *(Austral. slang)*, bogan *(Austral. slang)*

moronic ADJECTIVE **= idiotic**, simple, foolish, mindless, thick, stupid, daft *(informal)*, retarded, gormless *(Brit. informal)*, brainless, cretinous, unintelligent, dimwitted *(informal)*, asinine, imbecilic, braindead *(informal)*, mentally defective, dumb-ass *(slang)*, doltish, dead from the neck up *(informal)*, halfwitted, muttonheaded *(slang)*

morose ADJECTIVE **= sullen**, miserable, moody, gloomy, down, low, cross, blue, depressed, sour, crabbed, pessimistic, perverse, melancholy, dour, crusty, glum, surly, mournful, gruff, churlish, sulky, taciturn, ill-tempered, in a bad mood, grouchy *(informal)*, down in the dumps *(informal)*, crabby, saturnine, ill-humoured, ill-natured
OPPOSITE: cheerful

morsel NOUN **= piece**, bite, bit, slice, scrap, part, grain, taste, segment, fragment, fraction, snack, crumb, nibble, mouthful, tad *(informal, chiefly U.S.)*, titbit, soupçon *(French)*

mortal ADJECTIVE **1 = human**, worldly, passing, earthly, fleshly, temporal, transient, ephemeral, perishable, corporeal, impermanent, sublunary: *Man is designed to be mortal.* **2 = fatal**, killing, terminal, deadly, destructive, lethal, murderous, death-dealing: *a mortal blow to terrorism* **3 = unrelenting**, bitter, sworn, deadly, relentless, to the death, implacable, out-and-out, irreconcilable, remorseless: *Broadcasting was regarded as the mortal enemy of live music.* **4 = great**, serious, terrible, enormous, severe, extreme, grave, intense, awful, dire, agonizing: *She lived in mortal fear that one day she would be found out.*
▷ NOUN **= human being**, being, man, woman, body, person, human, individual, earthling: *impossible needs for any mere mortal to meet*

> **QUOTATIONS**
> What fools these mortals be!
> [William Shakespeare *A Midsummer Night's Dream*]

mortality NOUN **1 = humanity**, transience, impermanence, ephemerality, temporality, corporeality, impermanency: *The event served as a stark reminder of our mortality.* **2 = death**, dying, fatality, loss of life: *the nation's infant mortality rate*

> **QUOTATIONS**
> Dust thou art, and unto dust thou shalt return
> [*Bible: Genesis*]
>
> Earth to earth, ashes to ashes, dust to dust
> [*Book of Common Prayer*]
>
> Old mortality, the ruins of forgotten times
> [Thomas Browne *Hydriotaphia*]
>
> All men think all men mortal but themselves
> [Edward Young *Night Thoughts*]
>
> Man that is born of a woman is of few days, and full of trouble. He cometh forth like a flower, and is cut down; he fleeth also as a shadow, and continueth not
> [*Bible: Job*]

> **PROVERBS**
> *Here today and gone tomorrow*

mortified ADJECTIVE **= humiliated**, embarrassed, shamed, crushed, annoyed, humbled, horrified, put down, put out *(informal)*, ashamed, confounded, deflated, vexed, affronted, displeased, chagrined, chastened, discomfited, abashed, put to shame, rendered speechless, made to eat humble pie *(informal)*, given a showing-up *(informal)*

mortify VERB **1 = humiliate**, disappoint, embarrass, shame, crush, annoy, humble, deflate, vex, affront, displease, chagrin, discomfit, abase, put someone to shame, abash: *She mortified her family by leaving her husband.* **2 = discipline**, control, deny, subdue, chasten, abase: *The most austere of the Christians felt the need to mortify themselves.*

mortuary NOUN **= morgue**, funeral home *(U.S.)*, funeral parlour

most PRONOUN **= nearly all**, the majority, the mass, almost all, the bulk, the lion's share, the preponderance

USAGE
More and *most* should be distinguished when used in comparisons. *More* applies to cases involving two people, objects, etc., *most* to cases involving three or more: *John is the more intelligent of the two; he is the most intelligent of the students.*

mostly ADVERB **1 = mainly**, largely, chiefly, principally, primarily, above all, on the whole, predominantly, for the most part, almost entirely: *I am working with mostly highly motivated people.* **2 = generally**, usually, on the whole, most often, as a rule, customarily: *We mostly go to clubs, or round to a friend's house.*

mote NOUN **= speck**, spot, grain, particle, fragment, atom, mite

moth NOUN
▸ *name of young:* caterpillar ▸ *related enthusiast:* lepidopterist

mother NOUN **= female parent**, mum *(Brit. informal)*, ma *(informal)*, mater, dam, old woman *(informal)*, mom *(U.S. & Canad.)*, mummy *(Brit. informal)*, old lady *(informal)*, foster mother, birth mother, biological mother: *Mother and child form a close attachment.*
▹ VERB **1 = give birth to**, produce, bear, bring forth, drop: *She had dreamed of mothering a large family.* **2 = nurture**, raise, protect, tend, nurse, rear, care for, cherish: *She felt a great need to mother him.*
▹ MODIFIER **= native**, natural, innate, inborn, connate: *He looks on Turkey as his mother country.*
▸ *related adjective:* maternal

QUOTATIONS
So for the mother's sake the child was dear
And dearer was the mother for the child
[Samuel Taylor Coleridge *'Sonnet to a Friend Who Asked How I Felt When the Nurse First Presented My Infant Child to Me'*]

Honour thy mother and thy father
[*Bible: Exodus*]

As is the mother, so is her daughter
[*Bible: Ezekiel*]

All women become like their mothers. That is their tragedy. No man does. That is his
[Oscar Wilde *The Importance of Being Earnest*]

Few misfortunes can befall a boy which bring worse consequences than to have a really affectionate mother
[W. Somerset Maugham *A Writer's Notebook*]

motherly ADJECTIVE **= maternal**, loving, kind, caring, warm, comforting, sheltering, gentle, tender, protective, fond, affectionate

motif NOUN **1 = design**, form, shape, decoration, ornament: *wallpaper with a rose motif* **2 = theme**, idea, subject, concept, leitmotif: *the motif of magical apples in fairytales*

motion NOUN **1 = movement**, action, mobility, passing, travel, progress, flow, passage, locomotion, motility, kinesics: *the laws governing light, sound and motion* **2 = gesture**, sign, wave, signal, gesticulation: *He made a neat chopping motion with his hand.* **3 = proposal**, suggestion, recommendation, proposition, submission: *The conference is now debating the motion.*
▹ VERB **= gesture**, direct, wave, signal, nod, beckon, gesticulate: *She motioned for the doors to be opened.*
in motion 1 = in progress, going on, under way, afoot, on the go *(informal)*: *His job begins in earnest now that the World Cup is in motion.* **2 = moving**, going, working, travelling, functioning, under way, operational, on the move *(informal)*: *Always stay seated while a bus is in motion.*
▸ *related adjective:* kinetic

motionless ADJECTIVE **= still**, static, stationary, standing, fixed, frozen, calm, halted, paralysed, lifeless, inert, unmoved, transfixed, at rest, immobile, inanimate, at a standstill, unmoving, stock-still
OPPOSITE: moving

motivate VERB **1 = inspire**, drive, stimulate, provoke, lead, move, cause, prompt, stir, trigger, set off, induce, arouse, prod, get going, instigate, impel, actuate, give incentive to, inspirit: *His hard work was motivated by a need to achieve.* **2 = stimulate**, drive, inspire, stir, arouse, get going, galvanize, incentivize: *How do you motivate people to work hard and efficiently?*

motivation NOUN **1 = incentive**, inspiration, motive, stimulus, reason, spur, impulse, persuasion, inducement, incitement, instigation, carrot and stick: *Money is my motivation.* **2 = inspiration**, drive, desire, ambition, hunger, interest: *The team may be lacking motivation for next week's game.*

motive NOUN **= reason**, motivation, cause, ground(s), design, influence, purpose, object, intention, spur, incentive, inspiration, stimulus, rationale, inducement, incitement, mainspring, the why and wherefore: *Police have ruled out robbery as a motive for the killing.*
▹ ADJECTIVE **= moving**, driving, motivating, operative, activating, impelling: *the motive power behind a boxer's punches*

motley ADJECTIVE **= miscellaneous**, mixed, varied, diversified, mingled, unlike, assorted, disparate, dissimilar, heterogeneous
OPPOSITE: homogeneous

mottled ADJECTIVE **= blotchy**, spotted, pied, streaked, marbled, flecked, variegated, chequered, speckled, freckled, dappled, tabby, stippled, piebald, brindled

motto NOUN **= saying**, slogan, maxim, rule, cry, formula, gnome, adage, proverb, dictum, precept, byword, watchword, tag-line

mould[1] NOUN **1 = cast**, form, die, shape, pattern, stamp, matrix: *the moulds for the foundry* **2 = design**, line, style, fashion, build, form, cut, kind, shape, structure, pattern, brand, frame, construction, stamp, format, configuration: *At first sight, he is not cast in the leading man mould.* **3 = nature**, character, sort, kind, quality, type, stamp, kidney, calibre, ilk: *every man of heroic mould who struggles up to eminence*
▹ VERB **1 = shape**, make, work, form, create, model, fashion, cast, stamp, construct, carve, forge, sculpt: *We moulded a statue out of mud.* **2 = influence**, make, form, control, direct, affect, shape: *The experience has moulded her personality.*

mould[2] NOUN **= fungus**, blight, mildew, mustiness, mouldiness: *jars of jam with mould on them*

moulder VERB **= decay**, waste, break down, crumble, rot, disintegrate, perish, decompose

mouldy ADJECTIVE **= stale**, spoiled, rotting, decaying, bad, rotten, blighted, musty, fusty, mildewed

mound NOUN **1 = heap**, bing *(Scot.)*, pile, drift, stack, rick: *huge mounds of dirt* **2 = hill**, bank, rise, dune, embankment, knoll, hillock, kopje *or* koppie *(S. African)*: *We sat on a grassy mound and had our picnic.* **3 = barrow**, tumulus: *an ancient, man-made burial mound* **4 = earthwork**, rampart, bulwark, motte *(History)*: *a rough double-moated mound earmarked as an ancient monument*

mount VERB **1 = launch**, stage, prepare, deliver, set in motion: *a security operation mounted by the army* **2 = increase**, build, grow, swell, intensify, escalate, multiply: *For several hours, tension mounted.*
OPPOSITE: decrease **3 = accumulate**, increase, collect, gather, build up, pile up, amass, cumulate: *The uncollected garbage mounts in the streets.* **4 = ascend**, scale, climb (up), go up, clamber up, make your way up: *He was mounting the stairs to the tower.* **OPPOSITE:** descend **5 = get (up) on**, jump on, straddle, climb onto, climb up on, hop on to, bestride, get on the back of, get astride: *He mounted his horse and rode away.* **OPPOSITE:** get off **6 = display**, set, frame, set off: *He mounts the work in a frame.* **7 = fit**, place, set, position, set up, fix, secure, attach, install, erect, put in place, put in position, emplace: *The fuel tank is mounted on the side of the truck.* **8 = display**, present, stage, prepare, put on, organize, get up *(informal)*, exhibit, put on display: *mounting an exhibition of historical Tiffany jewellery*
▹ NOUN **1 = horse**, steed *(literary)*: *the number of owners who care for older mounts* **2 = backing**, setting, support, stand, base, mounting, frame, fixture, foil: *Even on a solid mount, any movement nearby may shake the image.*

mountain NOUN **1 = peak**, mount, height, ben (*Scot.*), horn, ridge, fell (*Brit.*), berg (*S. African*), alp, pinnacle, elevation, Munro, eminence: *Ben Nevis, Britain's highest mountain* **2 = heap**, mass, masses, pile, a great deal, ton, stack, abundance, mound, profusion, shedload (*Brit. informal*): *They are faced with a mountain of bureaucracy.*

mountainous ADJECTIVE **1 = high**, towering, soaring, steep, rocky, highland, alpine, upland: *a mountainous region* **2 = huge**, great, enormous, mighty, immense, daunting, gigantic, monumental, mammoth, prodigious, hulking, ponderous: *a plan designed to reduce the company's mountainous debt* **OPPOSITE:** tiny

mourn VERB **1** (*often with* **for**) **= grieve for**, miss, lament, keen for, weep for, sorrow for, wail for, wear black for: *She still mourned her father.* **2 = bemoan**, rue, deplore, bewail: *We mourned the loss of our cities.*

mournful ADJECTIVE **1 = dismal**, sad, unhappy, miserable, gloomy, grieving, melancholy, sombre, heartbroken, desolate, woeful, rueful, heavy, downcast, grief-stricken, lugubrious, disconsolate, joyless, funereal, heavy-hearted, down in the dumps (*informal*), cheerless, brokenhearted: *He looked mournful, even near to tears.* **OPPOSITE:** happy **2 = sad**, distressing, unhappy, tragic, painful, afflicting, melancholy, harrowing, grievous, woeful, deplorable, lamentable, plaintive, calamitous, sorrowful, piteous: *the mournful wail of bagpipes* **OPPOSITE:** cheerful

mourning NOUN **1 = grieving**, grief, bereavement, weeping, woe, lamentation, keening: *The period of mourning and bereavement may be long.* **2 = black**, weeds, sackcloth and ashes, widow's weeds: *Yesterday the whole country was in mourning.*

mouth NOUN **1 = lips**, trap (*slang*), chops (*slang*), jaws, gob (*slang, esp. Brit.*), maw, yap (*slang*), cakehole (*Brit. slang*): *She clamped her hand against her mouth.* **2 = entrance**, opening, gateway, cavity, door, aperture, crevice, orifice: *the mouth of the tunnel* **3 = opening**, lip, rim: *a lit candle stuck in the bottle's mouth* **4 = inlet**, outlet, estuary, firth, outfall, debouchment: *the mouth of the river* **5 = boasting**, gas (*informal*), bragging, hot air (*slang*), braggadocio, idle talk, empty talk: *She is all mouth and no talent.* **6 = insolence**, lip (*slang*), sauce (*informal*), cheek (*informal*), rudeness, impudence, backchat (*informal*)
▷ VERB **= utter**, say, speak, voice, express, pronounce, articulate, enunciate, verbalize, vocalize, say insincerely, say for form's sake
down in *or* **at the mouth = depressed**, down, blue, sad, unhappy, miserable, melancholy, dejected, dispirited, downcast, disheartened, crestfallen, down in the dumps (*informal*), sick as a parrot (*informal*), in low spirits
mouth off = rant, rave, spout, sound off, declaim, jabber
▸ *related adjectives:* oral, oscular

PROVERBS
A shut mouth catches no flies

mouthful NOUN **= taste**, little, bite, bit, drop, sample, swallow, sip, sup, spoonful, morsel, forkful

mouthpiece NOUN **1 = spokesperson**, agent, representative, delegate, spokesman *or* spokeswoman: *their mouthpiece is the vice-president* **2 = publication**, journal, organ, periodical: *The newspaper is regarded as a mouthpiece of the ministry.*

movable ADJECTIVE **= portable**, mobile, transferable, detachable, not fixed, transportable, portative

move VERB **1 = transfer**, change, carry, transport, switch, shift, transpose: *She moved the sheaf of papers into position.* **2 = go**, walk, march, advance, progress, shift, proceed, stir, budge, make a move, change position: *She waited for him to get up, but he didn't move.* **3 = relocate**, leave, remove, quit, go away, migrate, emigrate, move house, flit (*Scot. & Northern English dialect*), decamp, up sticks (*Brit. informal*), pack your bags (*informal*), change residence: *My home is in Yorkshire and I don't want to move.* **4 = drive**, lead, cause, influence, persuade, push, shift, inspire, prompt, stimulate, motivate, induce, shove, activate, propel, rouse, prod, incite, impel, set going: *The hearings moved him to come up with these suggestions.* **OPPOSITE:** discourage **5 = touch**, affect, excite, impress, stir, agitate, disquiet, make an impression on, tug at your heartstrings (*often facetious*): *These stories surprised and moved me.* **6 = propose**, suggest, urge, recommend, request, advocate, submit, put forward: *I moved that the case be dismissed.*
▷ NOUN **1 = action**, act, step, movement, shift, motion, manoeuvre, deed: *Daniel's eyes followed her every move.* **2 = ploy**, action, measure, step, initiative, stroke, tactic, manoeuvre, deed, tack, ruse, gambit, stratagem: *The cut in interest rates was a wise move.* **3 = transfer**, posting, shift, removal, migration, relocation, flit (*Scot. & Northern English dialect*), flitting (*Scot. & Northern English dialect*), change of address: *He announced his move to Montparnasse in 1909.* **4 = turn**, go, play, chance, shot (*informal*), opportunity: *It's your move, chess fans tell Sports Minister.*
get a move on = speed up, hurry (up), get going, get moving, get cracking (*informal*), step on it (*informal*), make haste, shake a leg (*informal*), get your skates on (*informal*), stir yourself: *I'd better get a move on if I want to finish on time.*
on the move 1 = in transit, moving, travelling, journeying, on the road (*informal*), under way, voyaging, on the run, in motion, on the wing: *My husband and I were always on the move.* **2 = active**, moving, developing, advancing, progressing, succeeding, stirring, going forward, astir: *Aviation is on the move, and many airlines are forming alliances.*

movement NOUN **1 = group**, party, organization, grouping, front, camp, faction: *a nationalist movement that's gaining strength* **2 = campaign**, drive, push, crusade: *He contributed to the Movement for the Ordination of Women.* **3 = move**, act, action, operation, motion, gesture, manoeuvre: *He could watch her every movement.* **4 = activity**, moving, stirring, bustle, agitation: *There was movement behind the door.* **5 = advance**, progress, flow, progression: *the movement of the fish going up river* **6 = transfer**, transportation, displacement: *the movement of people, goods and services across borders* **7 = trend**, flow, swing, current, tendency: *the movement towards democracy* **8 = development**, change, shift, variation, fluctuation: *the meeting seems to have produced no movement on either side* **9 = progression**, advance, progress, breakthrough: *the participants believed movement forward was possible* **10 = section**, part, division, passage: *the first movement of Beethoven's 7th symphony*

movie NOUN **= film**, picture, feature, flick (*slang*), motion picture, moving picture (*U.S.*): *That was the first movie he ever made.*
the movies = the cinema, a film, the pictures (*informal*), the flicks (*slang*), the silver screen (*informal*): *He took her to the movies.*

moving ADJECTIVE **1 = emotional**, touching, affecting, exciting, inspiring, stirring, arousing, poignant, emotive, impelling: *It was a moving moment for them.* **OPPOSITE:** unemotional **2 = mobile**, running, active, going, operational, in motion, driving, kinetic, movable, motile, unfixed: *the moving parts in the engine* **OPPOSITE:** stationary **3 = motivating**, stimulating, dynamic, propelling, inspirational, impelling, stimulative: *He has been a moving force in the world of art criticism.*

mow VERB **= cut**, crop, trim, shear, scythe: *He mowed the lawn and did other routine chores.*
mow something *or* **someone down = massacre**, butcher, slaughter, cut down, shoot down, blow away (*slang, chiefly U.S.*), cut to pieces: *Gunmen mowed down 10 people in the attack.*

much ADVERB **1 = greatly**, a lot, considerably, decidedly, exceedingly, appreciably: *My hairstyle has never changed much.* **OPPOSITE:** hardly **2 = often**, a lot, regularly, routinely, a great deal, frequently, many times, habitually, on many occasions, customarily: *She didn't see her father much.*
▷ ADJECTIVE **= great**, a lot of, plenty

of, considerable, substantial, piles of *(informal)*, ample, abundant, copious, oodles of *(informal)*, plenteous, sizable *or* sizeable amount, shedful *(slang)*: *They are grown in full sun, without much water.* **OPPOSITE:** little
▷ PRONOUN **= a lot**, plenty, a great deal, lots *(informal)*, masses *(informal)*, loads *(informal)*, tons *(informal)*, heaps *(informal)*, a good deal, an appreciable amount: *There was so much to talk about.* **OPPOSITE:** little

QUOTATIONS
much of a muchness
[John Vanburgh & Colley Cibber *The Provok'd Husband*]

muck NOUN **1 = dirt**, mud, filth, crap *(taboo, slang)*, sewage, ooze, scum, sludge, mire, slime, slob *(Irish)*, gunk *(informal)*, gunge *(informal)*, crud *(slang)*, kak *(S. African informal)*, grot *(slang)*: *This congealed muck was interfering with the filter.* **2 = manure**, crap *(taboo, slang)*, dung, ordure: *He could smell muck and clean fresh hay.*
muck something up = ruin, bungle, botch, make a mess of, blow *(slang)*, mar, spoil, muff, make a nonsense of, bodge *(informal)*, make a pig's ear of *(informal)*, flub *(U.S. slang)*, make a muck of *(slang)*, mess something up, screw something up *(informal)*, cock something up *(Brit. slang)*, crool *or* cruel *(Austral. slang)*: *At the 13th hole, I mucked it up.*

PROVERBS
Where there's muck, there's brass

mucky ADJECTIVE **= dirty**, soiled, muddy, filthy, messy, grimy, mud-caked, bespattered, begrimed, festy *(Austral. slang)*

mud NOUN **= dirt**, clay, ooze, silt, sludge, mire, slime, slob *(Irish)*, gloop *(informal)*

muddle NOUN **= confusion**, mess, disorder, chaos, plight, tangle, mix-up, clutter, disarray, daze, predicament, jumble, ravel, perplexity, disorganization, hotchpotch, hodgepodge *(U.S.)*, pig's breakfast *(informal)*, fankle *(Scot.)*: *My thoughts are all in a muddle.*
▷ VERB **1 = jumble**, confuse, disorder, scramble, tangle, mix up, make a mess of: *Already some people have begun to muddle the two names.* **2 = confuse**, bewilder, daze, confound, perplex, disorient, stupefy, befuddle: *She felt muddled, and a wave of dizziness swept over her.*
muddle along *or* **through = scrape by**, make it, manage, cope, get along, get by *(informal)*, manage somehow: *We will muddle through and just play it day by day.*

muddled ADJECTIVE **1 = incoherent**, confused, loose, vague, unclear, woolly, muddleheaded: *the muddled thinking of the Government's transport policy* **OPPOSITE:** clear **2 = bewildered**, confused, at sea, dazed, perplexed, disoriented, stupefied, befuddled: *I'm afraid I'm a little muddled. I don't know where to begin.* **3 = jumbled**, confused, disordered, scrambled, tangled, chaotic, messy, mixed-up, disorganized, higgledy-piggledy *(informal)*, disarrayed: *a muddled pile of historical manuscripts* **OPPOSITE:** orderly

muddy ADJECTIVE **1 = boggy**, swampy, marshy, miry, quaggy: *a muddy track* **2 = dirty**, soiled, grimy, mucky, mud-caked, bespattered, clarty *(Scot. & Northern English dialect)*: *muddy boots* **3 = dull**, flat, blurred, unclear, smoky, washed-out, dingy, lustreless: *The paper has turned a muddy colour.* **4 = cloudy**, dirty, foul, opaque, impure, turbid: *He was up to his armpits in muddy water.* **5 = confused**, vague, unclear, muddled, fuzzy, woolly, hazy, indistinct: *Such muddy thinking is typical of those who have always had it easy.*
▷ VERB **= smear**, soil, dirty, smirch, begrime, bespatter: *The clothes he was wearing were all muddied.*

muffle VERB **1 = deaden**, suppress, gag, stifle, silence, dull, soften, hush, muzzle, quieten: *He held a handkerchief over the mouthpiece to muffle his voice.* **2** *(often with* **up***)* **= wrap up**, cover, disguise, conceal, cloak, shroud, swathe, envelop, swaddle: *All of us were muffled up in several layers of clothing.*

muffled ADJECTIVE **= indistinct**, suppressed, subdued, dull, faint, dim, muted, strangled, stifled

mug[1] NOUN **= cup**, pot, jug, beaker, tankard, stein, flagon, toby jug: *He had been drinking mugs of coffee to keep himself awake.*

mug[2] NOUN **1 = face**, features, countenance, visage, clock *(Brit. slang)*, kisser *(slang)*, dial *(slang)*, mush *(Brit. slang)*, puss *(slang)*, phiz *or* phizog *(Brit. slang)*: *He managed to get his ugly mug on telly.* **2 = fool**, innocent, sucker *(slang)*, charlie *(Brit. informal)*, gull *(archaic)*, chump *(informal)*, simpleton, putz *(U.S. slang)*, weenie *(U.S. informal)*, muggins *(Brit. slang)*, easy *or* soft touch *(slang)*, dorba *or* dorb *(Austral. slang)*, bogan *(Austral. slang)*: *I feel such a mug for signing the agreement.*
▷ VERB **= attack**, assault, beat up, rob, steam *(informal)*, hold up, do over *(Brit., Austral. & N.Z. slang)*, work over *(slang)*, assail, lay into *(informal)*, put the boot in *(slang)*, duff up *(Brit. slang)*, set about *or* upon, beat *or* knock seven bells out of *(informal)*: *I was getting into my car when this guy tried to mug me.*
mug up (on) something = study, cram *(informal)*, bone up on *(informal)*, swot up on *(Brit. informal)*, get up *(informal)*: *It's advisable to mug up on your Spanish before you go.*

mull over VERB **= ponder**, consider, study, think about, examine, review, weigh, contemplate, reflect on, think over, muse on, meditate on, ruminate on, deliberate on, turn something over in your mind

multiple ADJECTIVE **= many**, several, various, numerous, collective, sundry, manifold, multitudinous

multiplicity NOUN **= number**, lot, host, mass, variety, load *(informal)*, pile *(informal)*, ton, stack, diversity, heap *(informal)*, array, abundance, myriad, profusion

multiply VERB **1 = increase**, extend, expand, spread, build up, accumulate, augment, proliferate: *Her husband multiplied his demands on her time.* **OPPOSITE:** decrease **2 = reproduce**, breed, propagate: *These creatures can multiply quickly.*

multitude NOUN **1 = great number**, lot, host, collection, army, sea, mass, assembly, legion, horde, myriad, concourse, assemblage: *Addiction to drugs can bring a multitude of other problems.* **2 = crowd**, host, mass, mob, congregation, swarm, sea, horde, throng, great number: *the multitudes that surround the Pope* **3 = public**, mob, herd, populace, rabble, proletariat, common people, hoi polloi, commonalty: *The hideous truth was hidden from the multitude.*

mum ADJECTIVE **= silent**, quiet, dumb, mute, secretive, uncommunicative, unforthcoming, tight-lipped, closemouthed

mumbo jumbo NOUN **1 = gibberish**, nonsense, jargon, humbug, cant, Greek *(informal)*, claptrap *(informal)*, gobbledegook *(informal)*, rigmarole, double talk: *It's all full of psychoanalytic mumbo jumbo.* **2 = superstition**, magic, ritual, hocus-pocus: *He dabbled in all sorts of mumbo jumbo.*

munch VERB **= chew**, champ, crunch, chomp, scrunch, masticate

mundane ADJECTIVE **1 = ordinary**, routine, commonplace, banal, everyday, day-to-day, vanilla *(slang)*, prosaic, humdrum, workaday: *Be willing to do mundane tasks with good grace.* **OPPOSITE:** extraordinary **2 = earthly**, worldly, human, material, fleshly, secular, mortal, terrestrial, temporal, sublunary: *spiritual immortals who had transcended the mundane world* **OPPOSITE:** spiritual

municipal ADJECTIVE **= civic**, city, public, local, community, council, town, district, urban, metropolitan, borough

municipality NOUN **= town**, city, district, borough, township, burgh *(Scot.)*, urban community, dorp *(S. African)*

murder NOUN **1 = killing**, homicide, massacre, assassination, slaying, bloodshed, carnage, butchery: *The three accused are charged with attempted murder.* **2 = agony**, misery, hell *(informal)*: *I've taken three aspirins, but this headache's still absolute murder.*
▷ VERB **1 = kill**, massacre, slaughter, assassinate, hit *(slang)*, destroy, waste *(informal)*, do in *(informal)*, eliminate *(slang)*, take out *(slang)*, terminate *(slang)*, butcher, dispatch, slay, blow away *(slang, chiefly U.S.)*, bump off *(slang)*, rub out *(U.S. slang)*, take the life

of, do to death, murk *(slang)*: *a thriller about two men who murder a third* **2 = ruin**, destroy, mar, spoil, butcher, mangle: *She murdered the song.* **3 = beat decisively**, thrash, stuff *(slang)*, cream *(slang, chiefly U.S.)*, tank *(slang)*, hammer *(informal)*, slaughter, lick *(informal)*, wipe the floor with *(informal)*, make mincemeat of *(informal)*, blow someone out of the water *(slang)*, drub, defeat someone utterly, murk *(slang)*: *The front row murdered the Italians in the scrums.*

QUOTATIONS

Thou shalt not kill
[*Bible: Exodus*]

Murder will out
[Geoffrey Chaucer *The Nun's Priest's Tale*]

murder most foul
[William Shakespeare *Hamlet*]

murderer NOUN **= killer**, assassin, slayer, butcher, slaughterer, cut-throat, hit man *(slang)*

QUOTATIONS

Every murderer is probably somebody's old friend
[Agatha Christie *The Mysterious Affair at Styles*]

You can always count on a murderer for a fancy prose style
[Vladimir Nabokov *Lolita*]

murderous ADJECTIVE **1 = deadly**, savage, brutal, destructive, fell *(archaic)*, bloody, devastating, cruel, lethal, withering, ferocious, cut-throat, bloodthirsty, barbarous, internecine, death-dealing, sanguinary: *This murderous lunatic could kill them all.* **2 = unpleasant**, difficult, dangerous, exhausting, sapping, harrowing, strenuous, arduous, hellish *(informal)*, killing *(informal)*: *Four games in six days is murderous and most unfair.*

murky ADJECTIVE **1 = dark**, gloomy, dismal, grey, dull, obscure, dim, dreary, cloudy, misty, impenetrable, foggy, overcast, dusky, nebulous, cheerless: *Their plane crashed in murky weather.* **OPPOSITE:** bright **2 = dark**, obscure, cloudy, impenetrable: *the deep, murky waters of Loch Ness*

murmur VERB **= mumble**, whisper, mutter, drone, purr, babble, speak in an undertone: *He turned and murmured something to the professor.*
▷ NOUN **1 = whisper**, whispering, mutter, mumble, drone, purr, babble, undertone: *She spoke in a low murmur.* **2 = complaint**, word, moan *(informal)*, grumble, beef *(slang)*, grouse, gripe *(informal)*: *She was so flattered she paid up without a murmur.*

muscle NOUN **1 = tendon**, sinew, muscle tissue, thew: *He has a strained thigh muscle.* **2 = strength**, might, force, power, weight, stamina, potency, brawn, sturdiness: *The team showed more muscle than mental application.*

muscle in = impose yourself, encroach, butt in, force your way in, elbow your way in: *He complained that they were muscling in on his deal.*

muscular ADJECTIVE **= strong**, powerful, athletic, strapping, robust, vigorous, sturdy, stalwart, husky *(informal)*, beefy *(informal)*, lusty, sinewy, muscle-bound, brawny, powerfully built, thickset, well-knit

muse VERB **= ponder**, consider, reflect, contemplate, think, weigh up, deliberate, speculate, brood, meditate, mull over, think over, ruminate, cogitate, be lost in thought, be in a brown study

mush NOUN **1 = pulp**, paste, mash, purée, pap, slush, goo *(informal)*: *Over-ripe bananas will collapse into a mush in this recipe.* **2 = sentimentality**, corn *(informal)*, slush *(informal)*, schmaltz *(slang)*, mawkishness: *The lyrics are mush and the melodies banal.*

mushroom VERB **= expand**, increase, spread, boom, flourish, sprout, burgeon, spring up, shoot up, proliferate, luxuriate, grow rapidly

mushy ADJECTIVE **1 = soft**, squidgy *(informal)*, slushy, squashy, squelchy, pulpy, doughy, pappy, semi-liquid, paste-like, semi-solid: *When the fruit is mushy and cooked, remove from the heat.* **2 = sentimental**, wet *(Brit. informal)*, sloppy *(informal)*, corny *(slang)*, sugary, maudlin, weepy, saccharine, syrupy, slushy *(informal)*, mawkish, schmaltzy *(slang)*, icky *(informal)*, three-hankie *(informal)*: *Don't go getting all mushy and sentimental.*

music NOUN

QUOTATIONS

Music has charms to soothe a savage breast
[William Congreve *The Mourning Bride*]

There's no passion in the human soul,
But finds its food in music
[George Lillo *The Fatal Curiosity*]

Great music is that which penetrates the ear with facility and leaves the memory with difficulty
[Thomas Beecham]

Bach gave us God's word
Mozart gave us God's laughter
Beethoven gave us God's fire
God gave us music that we might pray without words
[*from a German Opera House poster*]

Music is a beautiful opiate, if you don't take it too seriously
[Henry Miller *The Air-Conditioned Nightmare*]

The opera ain't over till the fat lady sings
[Dan Cook]

Opera is where a guy gets stabbed in the back and, instead of bleeding, he sings
[Ed Gardner *Duffy's Tavern*]

It is cruel, you know, that music should be so beautiful. It has the beauty of loneliness and of pain: of strength and freedom. The beauty of disappointment and never-satisfied love. The cruel beauty of nature, and everlasting beauty of monotony
[Benjamin Britten *letter*]

Such sweet compulsion doth in music lie
[John Milton *Arcades*]

The greatest moments of the human spirit may be deduced from the greatest moments in music
[Aaron Copland *Music as an Aspect of the Human Spirit*]

My music is best understood by children and animals
[Igor Stravinsky]

When I get those really intense moments it doesn't feel like it's the violin that's giving them to me, it's like I'm in touch with some realm of consciousness which is much bigger than I am ... It's the music which takes over
[Nigel Kennedy]

Music is your own experience, your own thoughts, your wisdom. If you don't live it, it won't come out of your horn
[Charlie Parker]

Hell is full of musical amateurs; music is the brandy of the damned
[George Bernard Shaw *Man and Superman*]

Music is feeling, then, not sound
[Wallace Stevens *Peter Quince at the Clavier*]

MUSICAL NOTES AND RESTS

British name	American name
breve	double-whole note
semibreve	whole note
minim	half note
crotchet	quarter note
quaver	eighth note
semiquaver	sixteenth note
demisemiquaver	thirty-second note
hemidemisemiquaver	sixty-fourth note

m

Music is spiritual. The music business is not
[Van Morrison]

If music be the food of love, play on;
Give me excess of it
[William Shakespeare *Twelfth Night*]

Without music life would be a mistake
[Friedrich Nietzsche *The Twilight of the Idols*]

I have been told that Wagner's music is better than it sounds
[Mark Twain]

A musicologist is a man who can read music but can't hear it
[Thomas Beecham]

He has Van Gogh's ear for music
[Orson Welles]

Music is essentially useless, as life is
[George Santayana *Little Essays*]

Music is a memory bank for finding one's way about the world
[Bruce Chatwin *The Songlines*]

Music is the healing force of the universe
[Albert Ayler]

All music is folk music, I ain't never heard no horse sing a song
[Louis Armstrong]

The only sensual pleasure without vice
[Dr. Johnson]

The English may not like music but they absolutely love the noise it makes
[Thomas Beecham]

Classic music is th'kind that we keep thinkin'll turn into a tune
[Kin Hubbard *Comments of Abe Martin and His Neighbours*]

There are two golden rules for an orchestra: start together and finish together. The public doesn't give a damn what goes on in between
[Thomas Beecham]

two skeletons copulating on a corrugated tin roof
[Thomas Beecham (describing the harpsichord)]

too much counterpoint; what is worse, Protestant counterpoint
[Thomas Beecham (describing Bach's music)]

fiddle: an instrument to tickle human ears by friction of a horse's tail on the entrails of a cat
[Ambrose Bierce *The Devil's Dictionary*]

Some say, that Signor Bononcini,
Compared to Handel's a mere ninny;
Others aver, that to him Handel
Is scarcely fit to hold a candle.
Strange! that such high dispute should be
'Twixt Tweedledum and Tweedledee
[John Byrom *On the Feuds between Handel and Bononcini*]

If the music doesn't say it, how can the words say it for the music?
[John Coltrane]

Extraordinary how potent cheap music is
[Noël Coward *Private Lives*]

opera: a play representing life in another world, whose inhabitants have no speech but song, no motions but gestures and no postures but attitudes
[Ambrose Bierce *The Devil's Dictionary*]

What passion cannot music raise and quell?
[John Dryden *A Song for St. Cecilia's Day*]

piano: a parlor utensil for subduing the impenitent visitor. It is operated by depressing the keys of the machine and the spirits of the audience
[Ambrose Bierce *The Devil's Dictionary*]

an exotic and irrational entertainment
[Dr. Johnson (of Italian opera)]

Sing 'em muck! It's all they can understand!
[Dame Nellie Melba (of Australians)]

Music and women I cannot but give way to, whatever my business is
[Samuel Pepys *Diary*]

Music begins to atrophy when it departs too far from the dance… poetry begins to atrophy when it gets too far from music
[Ezra Pound *The ABC of Reading*]

[Rock music] is still only certain elements in the blues isolated, coarsened and amplified. It may affect audiences more strongly but this is only to say that home-distilled hooch is more affecting than château-bottled claret, or a punch on the nose than a reasoned refutation under nineteen headings
[Philip Larkin]

In memory everything seems to happen to music
[Tennessee Williams *The Glass Menagerie*]

You don't need any brains to listen to music
[Luciano Pavarotti]

musical ADJECTIVE = **melodious**, lyrical, harmonious, melodic, lilting, tuneful, dulcet, sweet-sounding, euphonious, euphonic
OPPOSITE: discordant

musing NOUN = **thinking**, reflection, meditation, abstraction, contemplation, introspection, reverie, dreaming, day-dreaming, rumination, navel gazing *(slang)*, absent-mindedness, cogitation, brown study, cerebration, woolgathering

muskeg NOUN = **swamp**, bog, marsh, quagmire, moss *(Scot. & Northern English dialect)*, slough, fen, mire, morass, everglade(s) *(U.S.)*, pakihi *(N.Z.)*

muss VERB = **mess (up)**, disarrange, dishevel, ruffle, rumple, make untidy, tumble

must[1] NOUN = **necessity**, essential, requirement, duty, fundamental, obligation, imperative, requisite, prerequisite, sine qua non *(Latin)*, necessary thing, must-have: *A visit to the motor museum is a must.*

must[2] NOUN = **mould**, rot, decay, mildew, mustiness, fustiness, fetor, mouldiness: *The air was heady with the smell of must.*

muster VERB **1 = summon up**, collect, call up, marshal: *Mustering all her strength, she pulled hard on the oars.* **2 = rally**, group, gather, assemble, round up, marshal, mobilize, call together: *The general had mustered his troops north of the border.* **3 = assemble**, meet, come together, convene, congregate, convoke: *They mustered in the open, well wrapped and saying little.*
▷ NOUN = **assembly**, meeting, collection, gathering, rally, convention, congregation, roundup, mobilization, hui *(N.Z.)*, concourse, assemblage, convocation, runanga *(N.Z.)*: *He called a general muster of all soldiers.*
pass muster = be acceptable, qualify, measure up, make the grade, fill the bill *(informal)*, be *or* come up to scratch: *I could not pass muster in this language.*

musty ADJECTIVE = **stale**, stuffy, airless, decayed, smelly, dank, mouldy, fusty, mildewed, frowsty, mildewy

mutation NOUN **1 = anomaly**, variation, deviant, freak of nature: *Scientists have found a genetic mutation that causes the disease.* **2 = change**, variation, evolution, transformation, modification, alteration, deviation, metamorphosis, transfiguration: *I was forced to watch my father's mutation from sober to drunk.*

mute ADJECTIVE **1 = close-mouthed**, silent, taciturn, tongue-tied, tight-lipped, unspeaking: *He was mute, distant and indifferent.* **2 = silent**, dumb, unspoken, tacit, wordless, voiceless, unvoiced: *I threw her a mute look of appeal.* **3 = dumb**, speechless, voiceless, unspeaking, aphasic, aphonic: *The duke's daughter became mute after a shock.*
▷ VERB **1 = tone down**, lower, moderate, subdue, dampen, soft-pedal: *Bush muted some of his more extreme views.* **2 = muffle**, subdue, moderate, lower, turn down, soften, dampen, tone down, deaden: *The wooded hillside muted the sounds.*

mutilate VERB **1 = maim**, damage, injure, disable, butcher, cripple, hack, lame, cut up, mangle, mangulate *(Austral. slang)*, dismember, disfigure, lacerate, cut to pieces: *He tortured and*

m

The Language of Thomas Jefferson

Thomas Jefferson (1743–1826) was the third president of the United States. An eloquent and respected writer on political issues, he was the principle author of the Declaration of Independence.

The noun which occurs most frequently in Jefferson's speeches, memoirs, letters and other writings is *government*. *New, British,* and *republican* are the three adjectives which most commonly collocate with *government*, and these collocations reflect Jefferson's preoccupation with the establishing of a new republican government, independent from that of Britain.

Country and *nation* are, after *government*, the nouns which Jefferson uses most commonly. Although both are often used to refer to the United States, there are a significant number of occurrences of *mother country* in Jefferson's writings; Jefferson uses *mother country* to refer to Britain. *Subject* is another noun commonly used by Jefferson, and the adjective which most saliently modifies *subject* is *British*, as in:

> It cannot admit of a doubt, but that **British subjects** in America are entitled to the same rights and privileges, as their fellow **subjects** possess in Britain ...

Again, the frequency with which these collocations are found in Jefferson's writings is indicative of Jefferson's belief in American independence from Britain.

Power, in various senses, is another of Jefferson's 100 most commonly used words. *Belligerent* and *foreign* collocate particularly frequently with *power*; when Jefferson talks about *belligerent powers*, he is referring to European nations. In these contexts, *power* is being used in the sense 'a country with political or military strength'. Other common collocates of *power* in Jefferson's writings are *executive* and *legislative*, and in these contexts, *power* means 'ability or capacity to do something'. The construction *powers of government* is also commonly found in Jefferson's writings, as in:

> They will distribute the **powers of government** into three parts, legislative, judiciary, and executive.

Law is another noun frequently used by Jefferson. The phrase *laws of nature* is found a significant number of times in his writings; Jefferson, probably influenced by the English philosopher John Locke, was interested in the differences and relations between the man-made laws of a particular community and the laws of nature, which are said to have validity everywhere. As such, it is not surprising that *the law of nations* and *laws of the land* also occur commonly in Jefferson's writings. The laws of nature were thought to be so fundamental that the second sentence of the Declaration of Independence is in fact an acknowledgment of them and the natural rights they grant:

> We hold these truths to be self-evident, that all men are created equal, that they are endowed by their Creator with certain unalienable Rights, that among these are Life, Liberty and the pursuit of Happiness.

As would be expected, some words Jefferson uses would nowadays be classified as archaic. For example, *believe* is one of the verbs Jefferson uses most frequently, and it commonly collocates with the adverb *verily* (an archaic word meaning 'in truth'), as in:

> ... those principles on which I **verily believe** the future happiness of our country essentially depends.

However, while some of Jefferson's vocabulary is certainly archaic, it is interesting to note that much of his core vocabulary is still in everyday use.

Jefferson's writing style is noted, above all else, for its power and its clarity. There is no secret behind this; as he himself commented, 'The most valuable of all talents is that of never using two words when one will do.'

mutilated six young men. **2 = distort**, cut, damage, mar, spoil, butcher, hack, censor, adulterate, expurgate, bowdlerize: *The writer's verdict was that his screenplay had been mutilated.*

mutiny NOUN **= rebellion**, revolt, uprising, insurrection, rising, strike, revolution, riot, resistance, disobedience, insubordination, refusal to obey orders: *A series of mutinies in the armed forces destabilized the regime.*
▷ VERB **= rebel**, revolt, rise up, disobey, strike, resist, defy authority, refuse to obey orders, be insubordinate: *Units around the city mutinied after receiving no pay.*

mutt NOUN **1 = mongrel**, dog, hound, tyke, pooch *(informal)*, cur: *He was being harassed by a large, off-the-leash mutt.* **2 = fool**, idiot, berk *(Brit. slang)*, moron, charlie *(Brit. informal)*, jerk *(slang, chiefly U.S. & Canad.)*, plank *(Brit. slang)*, wally *(slang)*, prat *(slang)*, plonker *(slang)*, coot, geek *(slang)*, twit *(informal, chiefly Brit.)*, imbecile *(informal)*, ignoramus, dipstick *(Brit. slang)*, gonzo *(slang)*, schmuck *(U.S. slang)*, dork *(slang)*, dolt, divvy *(Brit. slang)*, pillock *(Brit. slang)*, dweeb *(U.S. slang)*, putz *(U.S. slang)*, weenie *(U.S. informal)*, eejit *(Scot. & Irish)*, dumb-ass *(slang)*, dunderhead, numpty *(Scot. informal)*, doofus *(slang, chiefly U.S.)*, thickhead, nerd *or* nurd *(slang)*, numbskull *or* numskull, dorba *or* dorb *(Austral. slang)*, bogan *(Austral. slang)*: *'I'm the mutt of my family,' she declares.*

mutter VERB **= grumble**, complain, murmur, rumble, whine, mumble, grouse, bleat, grouch *(informal)*, talk under your breath

mutual ADJECTIVE **= shared**, common, joint, interactive, returned, communal, reciprocal, interchangeable, reciprocated, correlative, requited

USAGE
Mutual is sometimes used, as in *a mutual friend*, to mean 'common to or shared by two or more people'. This use has sometimes been frowned on in the past because it does not reflect the two-way relationship contained in the origins of the word, which comes from Latin *mutuus* meaning 'reciprocal'. However, this usage is very common and is now generally regarded as acceptable.

muzzle NOUN **1 = jaws**, mouth, nose, snout: *The dog presented its muzzle for scratching.* **2 = gag**, guard, restraint: *dogs that have to wear a muzzle*
▷ VERB **= suppress**, silence, curb, restrain, choke, gag, stifle, censor: *He complained of being muzzled by the chairman.*

myopic ADJECTIVE **1 = narrow-minded**, short-sighted, narrow, unimaginative, small-minded, unadventurous, near-sighted: *The government still has a myopic attitude to spending.* **2 = short-sighted**, near-sighted, as blind as a bat *(informal)*: *Rhinos are thick-skinned, myopic and love to wallow in mud.*

myriad NOUN **= multitude**, millions, scores, host, thousands, army, sea, mountain, flood, a million, a thousand, swarm, horde: *They face a myriad of problems bringing up children.*
▷ ADJECTIVE **= innumerable**, countless, untold, incalculable, immeasurable, a thousand and one, multitudinous: *pop culture in all its myriad forms*

mysterious ADJECTIVE **1 = strange**, unknown, puzzling, curious, secret, hidden, weird, concealed, obscure, baffling, veiled, mystical, perplexing, uncanny, incomprehensible, mystifying, impenetrable, arcane, inexplicable, cryptic, insoluble, unfathomable, abstruse, recondite: *He died in mysterious circumstances.* **OPPOSITE:** clear **2 = secretive**, enigmatic, evasive, discreet, covert, reticent, furtive, inscrutable, non-committal, surreptitious, cloak-and-dagger, sphinx-like: *As for his job – well, he was very mysterious about it.*

QUOTATIONS
God moves in a mysterious way
His wonders to perform;
He plants his footsteps in the sea,
And rides upon the storm
[William Cowper *Olney Hymns*]

mystery NOUN **1 = puzzle**, problem, question, secret, riddle, enigma, conundrum, teaser, poser *(informal)*, closed book: *The source of the gunshots still remains a mystery.* **2 = secrecy**, uncertainty, obscurity, mystique, darkness, ambiguity, ambiguousness: *It is an elaborate ceremony, shrouded in mystery.*

mystical *or* **mystic** ADJECTIVE **= supernatural**, mysterious, transcendental, esoteric, occult, arcane, metaphysical, paranormal, inscrutable, otherworldly, abstruse, cabalistic, preternatural, nonrational

mystify VERB **= puzzle**, confuse, baffle, bewilder, beat *(slang)*, escape, stump, elude, confound, perplex, bamboozle *(informal)*, flummox, be all Greek to *(informal)*, nonplus, befog

mystique NOUN **= fascination**, spell, magic, charm, glamour, awe, charisma

myth NOUN **1 = legend**, story, tradition, fiction, saga, fable, parable, allegory, fairy story, folk tale, urban myth, urban legend: *a famous Greek myth* **2 = illusion**, story, fancy, fantasy, imagination, invention, delusion, superstition, fabrication, falsehood, figment, tall story, cock and bull story *(informal)*: *Contrary to popular myth, most women are not spendthrifts.*

mythical ADJECTIVE **1 = legendary**, storied, fabulous, imaginary, fairy-tale, fabled, mythological, storybook, allegorical, folkloric, chimerical: *the mythical beast that had seven or more heads* **2 = imaginary**, made-up, fantasy, invented, pretended, untrue, unreal, fabricated, fanciful, fictitious, make-believe, nonexistent: *They are trying to preserve a mythical sense of nationhood.*

mythological ADJECTIVE **= legendary**, fabulous, fabled, traditional, invented, heroic, imaginary, mythical, mythic, folkloric

mythology NOUN **= legend**, myths, folklore, stories, tradition, lore, folk tales, mythos

m

Nn

nab VERB **= catch**, arrest, apprehend, seize, lift *(slang)*, nick *(slang, chiefly Brit.)*, grab, capture, nail *(informal)*, collar *(informal)*, snatch, catch in the act, feel your collar *(slang)*

nadir NOUN **= bottom**, depths, lowest point, rock bottom, all-time low **OPPOSITE:** height

naff ADJECTIVE **= bad**, poor, inferior, worthless, pants *(slang)*, duff *(Brit. informal)*, shabby, second-rate, shoddy, low-grade, low-quality, trashy, substandard, for the birds *(informal)*, crappy *(slang)*, valueless, rubbishy, poxy *(slang)*, strictly for the birds *(informal)*, twopenny-halfpenny, bodger or bodgie *(Austral. slang)*: *This music is really naff.* **OPPOSITE:** excellent

nag[1] VERB **= scold**, harass, badger, pester, worry, harry, plague, hassle *(informal)*, vex, berate, breathe down someone's neck, upbraid, chivvy, bend someone's ear *(informal)*, be on your back *(slang)*, henpeck: *The more Sarah nagged her, the more stubborn Cissie became.*
▷ NOUN **= scold**, complainer, grumbler, virago, shrew, tartar, moaner, harpy, harridan, termagant, fault-finder: *My husband calls me a nag if I complain about anything.*

nag[2] NOUN *(often derog.)* **= horse** (U.S.), hack, jade, plug: *a bedraggled knight riding a lame, flea-ridden old nag*

nagging ADJECTIVE **1 = continuous**, persistent, continual, niggling, repeated, constant, endless, relentless, perpetual, never-ending, interminable, unrelenting, incessant, unremitting: *He complained about a nagging pain between his shoulders.* **2 = scolding**, complaining, critical, sharp-tongued, shrewish: *He tried to ignore the screaming, nagging voice of his wife.*

> **QUOTATIONS**
> Nagging is the repetition of unpalatable truths
> [Edith Summerskill *speech to the Married Women's Association*]

nail NOUN **1 = tack**, spike, rivet, hobnail, brad *(technical)*: *A mirror hung on a nail above the washstand.* **2 = fingernail**, toenail, talon, thumbnail, claw: *Keep your nails short and your hands clean.*
▷ VERB **1 = fasten**, fix, secure, attach, pin, hammer, tack: *Frank put the first plank down and nailed it in place.* **2 = catch**, arrest, capture, apprehend, lift *(slang)*, trap, nab *(informal)*, snare, ensnare, entrap, feel your collar *(slang)*: *The police have been trying to nail him for years.*

naive, naïve or **naïf** ADJECTIVE **= gullible**, trusting, credulous, unsuspicious, green, simple, innocent, childlike, callow, unsophisticated, unworldly, artless, ingenuous, guileless, wet behind the ears *(informal)*, jejune, as green as grass **OPPOSITE:** worldly

naivety, naiveté or **naïveté** NOUN **= gullibility**, innocence, simplicity, inexperience, credulity, ingenuousness, artlessness, guilelessness, callowness

naked ADJECTIVE **1 = nude**, stripped, exposed, bare, uncovered, undressed, in the raw *(informal)*, starkers *(informal)*, stark-naked, unclothed, in the buff *(informal)*, in the altogether *(informal)*, buck naked *(slang)*, undraped, in your birthday suit *(informal)*, scuddy *(slang)*, without a stitch on *(informal)*, in the bare scud *(slang)*, naked as the day you were born *(informal)*: *They stripped him naked; A girl was lying on the rug, completely naked.* **OPPOSITE:** dressed **2 = undisguised**, open, simple, plain, patent, evident, stark, manifest, blatant, overt, unmistakable, unqualified, unadorned, unvarnished, unconcealed: *Naked aggression could not go unchallenged.* **OPPOSITE:** disguised

nakedness NOUN **1 = nudity**, undress, bareness, deshabille: *He pulled the blanket over his body to hide his nakedness.* **2 = starkness**, simplicity, openness, plainness: *the nakedness of the emotion expressed in these songs*

name NOUN **1 = title**, nickname, designation, appellation, term, handle *(slang)*, denomination, epithet, sobriquet, cognomen, moniker or monicker *(slang)*: *I don't even know if Sullivan is his real name.* **2 = reputation**, character, honour, fame, distinction, esteem, eminence, renown, repute, note: *He had made a name for himself as a musician; I was forced to pursue this litigation to protect my good name.*
▷ VERB **1 = call**, christen, baptize, dub, term, style, label, entitle, denominate: *My mother insisted on naming me Horace.* **2 = nominate**, choose, commission, mention, identify, select, appoint, specify, designate: *The Scots have yet to name their team.*
▸ *related adjective:* nominal

> **QUOTATIONS**
> What's in a name? That which we call a rose
> By any other name would smell as sweet
> [William Shakespeare *Romeo and Juliet*]

named ADJECTIVE **1 = called**, christened, known as, dubbed, termed, styled, labelled, entitled, denominated, baptized: *He was named John.* **2 = nominated**, chosen, picked, commissioned, mentioned, identified, selected, appointed, cited, specified, designated, singled out: *She has been named Business Woman of the Year.*

nameless ADJECTIVE **1 = unnamed**, unknown, obscure, anonymous, unheard-of, undistinguished, untitled: *They had their cases rejected by nameless officials.* **2 = anonymous**, unknown, unnamed, incognito: *My source of information is a judge who wishes to remain nameless.* **3 = horrible**, unspeakable, indescribable, abominable, ineffable, unutterable, inexpressible: *He was suddenly seized by a nameless dread.*

namely ADVERB **= specifically**, that is to say, to wit, i.e., viz.

nap[1] VERB **= sleep**, rest, nod, drop off *(informal)*, doze, kip *(Brit. slang)*, snooze *(informal)*, nod off *(informal)*, catnap, drowse, zizz *(Brit. informal)*: *An elderly person may nap during the day.*
▷ NOUN **= sleep**, rest, kip *(Brit. slang)*, siesta, catnap, forty winks *(informal)*, shuteye *(slang)*, zizz *(Brit. informal)*, nana nap *(informal)*: *I think I'll take a little nap for an hour or so.*

nap[2] NOUN **= pile**, down, fibre, weave, shag, grain: *She buried her face in the towel's soft nap.*

napkin NOUN **= serviette**, cloth

narcissism or **narcism** NOUN **= egotism**, vanity, self-love, self-admiration

narcotic NOUN **= drug**, anaesthetic, painkiller, sedative, opiate, tranquillizer, anodyne, analgesic: *He appears to be under the influence of some sort of narcotic.*
▷ ADJECTIVE **= sedative**, calming, dulling, numbing, hypnotic, analgesic, stupefying, soporific, painkilling: *drugs which have a narcotic effect*

narrate VERB **= tell**, recount, report, detail, describe, relate, unfold, chronicle, recite, set forth

narration NOUN **1 = storytelling**, telling, reading, relation, explanation, description **2 = account**, explanation, description, recital, voice-over *(in a film)*

narrative NOUN **= story**, report, history, detail, account, statement, tale, chronicle

narrator NOUN **= storyteller**, writer, author, reporter, commentator, chronicler, reciter, raconteur

narrow ADJECTIVE **1 = thin**, fine, slim, pinched, slender, tapering, attenuated: *a woman with a full bust and hips and a narrow waist* **OPPOSITE:** broad **2 = limited**, restricted, confined, tight, close, near, cramped, meagre, constricted, circumscribed, scanty, straitened, incapacious: *He squeezed his way along the narrow space between the crates.* **OPPOSITE:** wide **3 = insular**, prejudiced, biased, partial, reactionary, puritan, bigoted, dogmatic, intolerant, narrow-minded, small-minded, illiberal: *a narrow and outdated view of family life* **OPPOSITE:** broad-minded **4 = exclusive**, limited, select, restricted, confined: *She achieved a fame that transcended the narrow world of avant-garde theatre.*
▷ VERB **1** (*often with* **down**) **= restrict**, limit, reduce, diminish, constrict, circumscribe, straiten: *I don't want to narrow my options too early on.* **2 = get narrower**, taper, shrink, tighten, constrict: *This sign means that the road narrows on both sides.*

narrowly ADVERB **1 = just**, barely, only just, scarcely, by the skin of your teeth, by a whisker *or* hair's-breadth: *Five firemen narrowly escaped death.* **2 = closely**, keenly, carefully, intently, intensely, fixedly, searchingly: *He frowned and looked narrowly at his colleague.*

narrow-minded ADJECTIVE **= intolerant**, conservative, prejudiced, biased, provincial, petty, reactionary, parochial, short-sighted, bigoted, insular, opinionated, small-minded, hidebound, illiberal, strait-laced **OPPOSITE:** broad-minded

narrows PLURAL NOUN **= channel**, sound, gulf, passage, straits

nastiness NOUN **1 = spite**, malice, venom, unpleasantness, meanness, bitchiness (*slang*), offensiveness, spitefulness: *'You're just like your mother,' he said, with a tone of nastiness in his voice.* **2 = obscenity**, porn (*informal*), pornography, indecency, licentiousness, ribaldry, smuttiness: *Almost every page of the book was filled with this kind of nastiness.*

nasty ADJECTIVE **1 = unpleasant**, ugly, disagreeable: *This divorce could turn nasty.* **OPPOSITE:** pleasant **2 = spiteful**, mean, offensive, annoying, vicious, unpleasant, abusive, vile, malicious, bad-tempered, despicable, disagreeable: *He's only nasty to me when there's no-one around to see it.* **OPPOSITE:** pleasant **3 = disgusting**, unpleasant, dirty, offensive, foul, horrible, polluted, filthy, sickening, vile, distasteful, repellent, obnoxious, objectionable, disagreeable, nauseating, odious, repugnant, loathsome, grotty (*slang*), malodorous, noisome, unappetizing, yucky *or* yukky (*slang*), festy (*Austral. slang*), yucko (*Austral. slang*): *It's got a really nasty smell.* **4 = serious**, bad, dangerous, critical, severe, painful: *Lili had a nasty chest infection.* **5 = obscene**, blue, gross, foul, indecent, pornographic, lewd, impure, lascivious, smutty, ribald, licentious: *There's no need for such nasty language, young man.* **OPPOSITE:** clean

nation NOUN **1 = country**, state, commonwealth, realm, micronation: *Such policies would require unprecedented cooperation between nations.* **2 = public**, people, community, society, population: *It was a story that touched the nation's heart.*

> **QUOTATIONS**
>
> For nation shall rise against nation, and kingdom against kingdom
> [*Bible: St. Matthew*]
>
> No nation is fit to sit in judgement upon any other nation
> [Woodrow Wilson *speech*]
>
> A nation is the same people living in the same place
> [James Joyce *Ulysses*]
>
> Nations, like men, have their infancy
> [Viscount Henry St. John Bolingbroke *On the Study of History*]
>
> The great nations have always acted like gangsters, and the small nations like prostitutes
> [Stanley Kubrick]

national ADJECTIVE **1 = nationwide**, state, public, civil, widespread, governmental, countrywide: *major national and international issues* **2 = ethnic**, social: *the national characteristics and history of the country*
▷ NOUN **= citizen**, subject, resident, native, inhabitant: *He is in fact a British national and passport holder.*

nationalism NOUN **= patriotism**, loyalty to your country, chauvinism, jingoism, nationality, allegiance, fealty

> **QUOTATIONS**
>
> Nationalism, that magnificent song that made the people rise against their oppressors, stops short, falters and dies away on the day that independence is proclaimed
> [Frantz Fanon *The Wretched of the Earth*]
>
> While it is often the enemy of democracy, nationalism has also been democracy's handmaiden, from the time of the French Revolution
> [Francis Fukuyama]
>
> I question the right of that great Moloch, national sovereignty, to burn its children to save its pride
> [Anthony Meyer]
>
> Patriotism is a lively sense of collective responsibility. Nationalism is a silly cock crowing on its own dunghill
> [Richard Aldington *The Colonel's Daughter*]

nationalistic ADJECTIVE **= patriotic**, xenophobic, chauvinistic, jingoistic, loyal to your country

nationality NOUN **1 = citizenship**, birth: *When asked his nationality, he said, 'British'.* **2 = race**, nation, ethnic group: *the many nationalities that comprise Ethopia*

nationwide ADJECTIVE **= national**, general, widespread, countrywide, overall

native ADJECTIVE **1 = indigenous**, local, aboriginal (*often offensive*): *a spokeswoman for native peoples around the world* **2 = mother**, indigenous, vernacular: *French is not my native tongue.* **3 = domestic**, local, indigenous, home-made, home-grown, home: *Several native plants also provide edible berries.*
▷ NOUN (*usually with* **of**) **= inhabitant**, national, resident, citizen, countryman, aborigine (*often offensive*), dweller: *He was a native of France.*

Nativity NOUN **= birth of Christ**, manger scene

natter VERB **= gossip**, talk, rabbit (on) (*Brit. informal*), jaw (*slang*), chatter, witter (*informal*), prattle, jabber, gabble, blather, blether, shoot the breeze (*informal*), run off at the mouth (*slang*), prate, talk idly, chew the fat *or* rag (*slang*), earbash (*Austral. & N.Z. slang*): *His mother would natter on the phone for hours.*
▷ NOUN **= gossip**, talk, conversation, chat, jaw (*slang*), craic (*Irish informal*), gab (*informal*), prattle, jabber, gabble, palaver, blather, chitchat, blether, chinwag (*Brit. informal*), gabfest (*informal, chiefly U.S. & Canad.*), confabulation: *We must get together some time for a good natter.*

natty ADJECTIVE **= smart**, sharp, dashing, elegant, trim, neat, fashionable, stylish, trendy (*Brit. informal*), chic, spruce, well-dressed, dapper, snazzy (*informal*), well-turned-out, crucial (*slang*), schmick (*Austral. informal*)

natural ADJECTIVE **1 = logical**, reasonable, valid, legitimate: *A period of depression is a natural response to bereavement.* **2 = normal**, common, regular, usual, ordinary, typical, everyday: *It's just not natural behaviour for a child of his age.* **OPPOSITE:** abnormal **3 = innate**, native, characteristic, indigenous, inherent, instinctive, intuitive, congenital, inborn, immanent, in your blood, essential: *He has a natural flair for business.* **4 = unaffected**, open, frank, genuine, spontaneous, candid, unpretentious, unsophisticated, dinkum (*Austral. & N.Z. informal*), artless, ingenuous, real, simple, unstudied: *Jan's sister was as natural and friendly as the rest of the family.* **OPPOSITE:** affected **5 = pure**, plain, organic, whole, unrefined, unbleached, unpolished, unmixed: *He prefers to use high quality natural produce.* **OPPOSITE:** processed

naturalism NOUN **= realism**, authenticity, plausibility, verisimilitude, factualism

naturalist NOUN **= biologist**, ecologist, botanist, zoologist

naturalistic ADJECTIVE **1 = realistic**, photographic, kitchen sink, representational, lifelike, warts and all *(informal)*, true-to-life, vérité, factualistic: *These drawings are amongst his most naturalistic.* **2 = lifelike**, realistic, real-life, true-to-life: *Research is needed under rather more naturalistic conditions.*

naturally ADVERB **1 = of course**, certainly, as a matter of course, as anticipated: *We are naturally concerned about the future.* **2 = typically**, simply, normally, spontaneously, customarily: *A study of yoga leads naturally to meditation.*

nature NOUN **1 = creation**, world, earth, environment, universe, cosmos, natural world: *man's ancient sense of kinship with nature* **2 = flora and fauna**, country, landscape, countryside, scenery, natural history: *an organization devoted to the protection of nature* **3 = quality**, character, make-up, constitution, attributes, essence, traits, complexion, features: *The protests had been non-political in nature.* **4 = temperament**, character, personality, disposition, outlook, mood, humour, temper: *She trusted people. That was her nature.* **5 = kind**, sort, style, type, variety, species, category, description: *This – and other books of a similar nature – are urgently needed.*

QUOTATIONS

nature red in tooth and claw
[Alfred, Lord Tennyson *In Memoriam*]

Nature does nothing without purpose or uselessly
[Aristotle *Politics*]

You may drive out nature with a pitchfork, yet she'll be constantly running back
[Horace *Epistles*]

In nature there are neither rewards nor punishments – there are consequences
[Robert G. Ingersoll *Some Reasons Why*]

In her [Nature's] inventions nothing is lacking, and nothing is superfluous
[Leonardo da Vinci]

'I play for seasons; not eternities!'
Says Nature
[George Meredith *Modern Love*]

naughty ADJECTIVE **1 = disobedient**, bad, mischievous, badly behaved, wayward, playful, wicked, sinful, fractious, impish, roguish, refractory: *You naughty boy, you gave me such a fright.* **OPPOSITE:** good **2 = obscene**, blue, vulgar, improper, lewd, risqué, X-rated *(informal)*, bawdy, smutty, off-colour, ribald: *saucy TV shows crammed with naughty innuendo* **OPPOSITE:** clean

nausea NOUN **1 = sickness**, vomiting, retching, squeamishness, queasiness, biliousness: *I was overcome with a feeling of nausea.* **2 = disgust**, loathing, aversion, revulsion, abhorrence, repugnance, odium: *She spoke in a little-girl voice which brought on a palpable feeling of nausea.*

nauseate VERB **1 = sicken**, turn your stomach: *The smell of frying nauseated her.* **2 = disgust**, offend, horrify, revolt, repel, repulse, gross out *(U.S. slang)*: *Ugliness nauseates me. I like to have beautiful things around me.*

nauseous ADJECTIVE **1 = sick**, crook *(Austral. & N.Z. informal)*: *The drugs make me feel nauseous.* **2 = sickening**, offensive, disgusting, revolting, distasteful, repulsive, nauseating, repugnant, loathsome, abhorrent, detestable, yucky *or* yukky *(slang)*, yucko *(Austral. slang)*: *The floor was deep with bat dung giving off a nauseous smell.*

nautical ADJECTIVE **= maritime**, marine, yachting, naval, seafaring, seagoing

naval ADJECTIVE **= nautical**, marine, maritime

navel NOUN **1 = bellybutton** *(informal)*: *A small incision is made just below the navel.* **2 = centre**, middle, hub, central point: *The city was once the jewel in the navel of the Gold Coast.*
▸ *technical name:* umbilicus ▸ *related adjective:* umbilical

navigate VERB **1 = steer**, drive, direct, guide, handle, pilot, sail, skipper, manoeuvre: *He was responsible for safely navigating the ship.* **2 = manoeuvre**, drive, direct, guide, handle, pilot: *He expertly navigated the plane through 45 minutes of fog.* **3 = plot a course**, sail, find your way, plan a course: *They navigated by the sun and stars.* **4 = sail**, cruise, manoeuvre, voyage: *Such boats can be built locally and can navigate on the Nile.*

navigation NOUN **= sailing**, cruising, steering, voyaging, seamanship, helmsmanship

navigator NOUN **= helmsman**, pilot, seaman, mariner

navy NOUN **= fleet**, warships, flotilla, armada

near ADJECTIVE **1 = close**, bordering, neighbouring, nearby, beside, adjacent, adjoining, close by, at close quarters, just round the corner, contiguous, proximate, within sniffing distance *(informal)*, a hop, skip and a jump away *(informal)*: *The town is very near; Where's the nearest telephone?* **OPPOSITE:** far **2 = imminent**, forthcoming, approaching, looming, impending, upcoming, on the cards *(informal)*, nigh, in the offing, near-at-hand, next: *Departure time was near.* **OPPOSITE:** far-off **3 = intimate**, close, related, allied, familiar, connected, attached, akin: *I have no near relations.* **OPPOSITE:** distant **4 = mean**, stingy, parsimonious, miserly, niggardly, ungenerous, tightfisted, close-fisted: *They joked about him being so near with his money.*

nearby ADJECTIVE **= neighbouring**, adjacent, adjoining: *At a nearby table a man was complaining in a loud voice.*
▹ ADVERB **= close at hand**, within reach, not far away, at close quarters, just round the corner, proximate, within sniffing distance *(informal)*: *He might easily have been seen by someone who lived nearby.*

nearing ADJECTIVE **= approaching**, coming, advancing, imminent, impending, upcoming

nearly ADVERB **1 = practically**, about, almost, virtually, all but, just about, not quite, as good as, well-nigh: *The beach was nearly empty.* **2 = almost**, about, approaching, roughly, just about, approximately: *It was already nearly eight o'clock.*

neat ADJECTIVE **1 = tidy**, nice, straight, trim, orderly, spruce, uncluttered, shipshape, spick-and-span: *Her house was neat and tidy and gleamingly clean.* **OPPOSITE:** untidy **2 = methodical**, tidy, systematic, fastidious: *'It's not like Alf to leave a mess like that,' I remarked, 'He's always so neat.'* **OPPOSITE:** disorganized **3 = smart**, trim, tidy, spruce, dapper, natty *(informal)*, well-groomed, well-turned out: *She always looked neat and well groomed.* **4 = graceful**, elegant, adept, nimble, agile, adroit, efficient: *He had the neat movements of a dancer.* **OPPOSITE:** clumsy **5 = clever**, efficient, handy, apt, well-judged: *It was a neat solution to the problem.* **OPPOSITE:** inefficient **6 = cool**, great *(informal)*, excellent, brilliant, cracking *(Brit. informal)*, smashing *(informal)*, superb, fantastic *(informal)*, tremendous, ace *(informal)*, fabulous *(informal)*, marvellous, terrific, awesome *(slang)*, mean *(slang)*, super *(informal)*, brill *(informal)*, bodacious *(slang, chiefly U.S.)*, boffo *(slang)*, chillin' *(U.S. slang)*, booshit *(Austral. slang)*, exo *(Austral. slang)*, sik *(Austral. slang)*, rad *(informal)*, phat *(slang)*, schmick *(Austral. informal)*, beaut *(informal)*, barrie *(Scot. slang)*, belting *(Brit. slang)*, pearler *(Austral. slang)*: *I've just had a really neat idea.* **OPPOSITE:** terrible **7 = undiluted**, straight, pure, unmixed: *He poured himself a glass of neat brandy and swallowed it in one.*

neatly ADVERB **1 = tidily**, nicely, smartly, systematically, methodically, fastidiously: *He took off his trousers and folded them neatly.* **2 = smartly**, elegantly, stylishly, tidily, nattily: *She was neatly dressed, her hair was tidy and she carried a shoulder-bag.* **3 = gracefully**, expertly, efficiently, adeptly, skilfully, nimbly, adroitly, dexterously, agilely: *He sent the ball over the bar with a neatly executed header.* **4 = cleverly**, precisely, accurately, efficiently, aptly, elegantly: *She neatly summed up a common attitude among many teachers and parents.*

neatness NOUN **1 = order**, organization, harmony, tidiness, orderliness: *The grounds were a perfect balance between neatness and natural* *wildness.* **2 = tidiness**, niceness, orderliness, smartness, fastidiousness, trimness, spruceness: *He was a paragon of neatness and efficiency.* **3 = grace**, skill, efficiency, expertise, precision, elegance, agility, dexterity, deftness, nimbleness, adroitness, adeptness, daintiness, gracefulness, preciseness, skilfulness: *neatness of movement* **4 = cleverness**, efficiency, precision, elegance, aptness: *He appreciated the neatness of their plan.*

nebulous ADJECTIVE **1 = vague**, confused, uncertain, obscure, unclear, ambiguous, indefinite, hazy, indeterminate, imprecise, indistinct: *the nebulous concept of 'spirit'* **2 = obscure**, vague, dim, murky, shadowy, cloudy, misty, hazy, amorphous, indeterminate, shapeless, indistinct, unformed: *We glimpsed a nebulous figure through the mist.*

necessarily ADVERB **1 = automatically**, naturally, definitely, undoubtedly, accordingly, by definition, of course, certainly: *A higher price does not necessarily guarantee a better product.* **2 = inevitably**, of necessity, unavoidably, perforce, incontrovertibly, nolens volens *(Latin)*: *In any policy area, a number of ministries is necessarily involved.*

necessary ADJECTIVE **1 = needed**, required, essential, vital, compulsory, mandatory, imperative, indispensable, obligatory, requisite, de rigueur *(French)*, needful, must-have: *Is your journey really necessary?; Please make all the necessary arrangements.* **OPPOSITE:** unnecessary **2 = inevitable**, certain, unavoidable, inescapable: *Wastage was no doubt a necessary consequence of war.* **OPPOSITE:** avoidable

necessitate VERB **= compel**, force, demand, require, call for, oblige, entail, constrain, impel, make necessary

necessity NOUN **1 = need**, demand, requirement, exigency, indispensability, needfulness: *There is agreement on the necessity of reforms.* **2 = essential**, need, necessary, requirement, fundamental, requisite, prerequisite, sine qua non *(Latin)*, desideratum, want, must-have: *Water is a basic necessity of life.* **3 = inevitability**, certainty: *the ultimate necessity of death* **4 = poverty**, need, privation, penury, destitution, extremity, indigence: *They were reduced to begging through economic necessity.* **5 = essential**, need, requirement, fundamental: *They sometimes had to struggle to pay for necessities.*

necropolis NOUN **= cemetery**, graveyard, churchyard, burial ground

need VERB **1 = want**, miss, require, lack, have to have, demand: *He desperately needed money.* **2 = require**, want, demand, call for, entail, necessitate, have occasion to *or* for: *The building needs quite a few repairs.* **3 = have to**, be obliged to: *You needn't bother, I'll do it myself.*

▷ NOUN **1 = requirement**, demand, essential, necessity, requisite, desideratum, must-have: *the special nutritional needs of children* **2 = necessity**, call, demand, requirement, obligation: *There's no need to call the police.* **3 = emergency**, want, necessity, urgency, exigency: *In her moment of need, her mother was nowhere to be seen.* **4 = poverty**, deprivation, destitution, neediness, distress, extremity, privation, penury, indigence, impecuniousness: *the state of need in Third World countries*

needed ADJECTIVE **= necessary**, wanted, required, lacked, called for, desired

needle VERB **= irritate**, provoke, annoy, sting, bait, harass, taunt, nag, hassle *(informal)*, aggravate *(informal)*, prod, gall, ruffle, spur, prick, nettle, goad, irk, rile, get under your skin *(informal)*, get on your nerves *(informal)*, nark *(Brit., Austral. & N.Z. slang)*, hack you off *(informal)*, get in your hair *(informal)*

needless ADJECTIVE **= unnecessary**, excessive, pointless, gratuitous, useless, unwanted, redundant, superfluous, groundless, expendable, uncalled-for, dispensable, nonessential, undesired **OPPOSITE:** essential

needlework NOUN **= embroidery**, tailoring, stitching, sewing, needlecraft

needy ADJECTIVE **= poor**, deprived, disadvantaged, impoverished, penniless, destitute, poverty-stricken, underprivileged, indigent, down at heel *(informal)*, impecunious, dirt-poor, on the breadline *(informal)* **OPPOSITE:** wealthy

negate VERB **1 = invalidate**, reverse, cancel, wipe out, void, repeal, revoke, retract, rescind, neutralize, annul, nullify, obviate, abrogate, countermand: *These environmental protection laws could be negated if the European Community decides they interfere with trade.* **2 = deny**, oppose, contradict, refute, disallow, disprove, rebut, gainsay *(archaic, literary)*: *I can neither negate nor affirm this claim.* **OPPOSITE:** confirm

negation NOUN **1 = opposite**, reverse, contrary, contradiction, converse, antithesis, inverse, antonym: *He repudiates liberty and equality as the negation of order and government.* **2 = denial**, refusal, rejection, contradiction, renunciation, repudiation, disavowal, veto: *She shook her head in a gesture of negation.*

negative ADJECTIVE **1 = neutralizing**, invalidating, annulling, nullifying, counteractive: *This will have a very serious negative effect on economic recovery.* **2 = pessimistic**, cynical, unwilling, gloomy, antagonistic, jaundiced, uncooperative, contrary: *There's no point in going along to an interview with a negative attitude.* **OPPOSITE:** optimistic **3 = dissenting**, contradictory, refusing, denying, rejecting, opposing, resisting, contrary: *Dr. Velayati gave a vague but negative response.* **OPPOSITE:** assenting

▷ NOUN **= denial**, no, refusal, rejection, contradiction: *We were fobbed off with a crisp negative.*

neglect VERB **1 = disregard**, ignore, leave alone, turn your back on, fail to look after: *The woman denied that she had neglected her child.* **OPPOSITE:** look after **2 = shirk**, forget, overlook, omit, evade, pass over, skimp, procrastinate over, let slide, be remiss in *or* about: *If you don't keep an eye on them, children tend to neglect their homework.* **3 = fail**, forget, omit: *She neglected to inform me of her change of plans.*

▷ NOUN **1 = negligence**, inattention, unconcern: *hundreds of orphans, old and handicapped people, some of whom have since died of neglect* **OPPOSITE:** care **2 = shirking**, failure, oversight, carelessness, dereliction, forgetfulness, slackness, laxity, laxness, slovenliness, remissness: *her deliberate neglect of her professional duty*

neglected ADJECTIVE **1 = uncared-for**, abandoned, underestimated, disregarded, undervalued, unappreciated: *The fact that he is not coming today makes his grandmother feel neglected.* **2 = run down**, derelict, overgrown, uncared-for: *a neglected house with an overgrown garden*

negligence NOUN **= carelessness**, failure, neglect, disregard, shortcoming, omission, oversight, dereliction, forgetfulness, slackness, inattention, laxity, thoughtlessness, laxness, inadvertence, inattentiveness, heedlessness, remissness

negligent ADJECTIVE **= careless**, slack, thoughtless, unthinking, forgetful, slapdash, neglectful, heedless, slipshod, inattentive, remiss, unmindful, disregardful **OPPOSITE:** careful

negligible ADJECTIVE **= insignificant**, small, minute, minor, petty, trivial, trifling, unimportant, inconsequential, imperceptible, nickel-and-dime *(U.S. slang)* **OPPOSITE:** significant

negotiable ADJECTIVE **1 = debatable**, flexible, unsettled, undecided, open to discussion, discussable *or* discussible: *The manor is for sale at a negotiable price.* **2 = valid**, transferable, transactional: *The bonds may no longer be negotiable.*

negotiate VERB **1 = bargain**, deal, contract, discuss, debate, consult, confer, mediate, hold talks, arbitrate, cut a deal, conciliate, parley, discuss terms: *The president may be willing to negotiate with the democrats.* **2 = arrange**, manage, settle, work out, bring about, transact: *The local government and the army have negotiated a truce.* **3 = get**

n

round, clear, pass, cross, pass through, get over, get past, surmount: *I negotiated the corner on my motorbike.*

negotiation NOUN **1 = bargaining**, debate, discussion, transaction, dialogue, mediation, arbitration, wheeling and dealing *(informal)*: *We have had meaningful negotiations and I believe we are close to a deal.* **2 = arrangement**, management, settlement, working out, transaction, bringing about: *They intend to take no part in the negotiation of a new treaty of union.*

negotiator NOUN **= mediator**, ambassador, diplomat, delegate, intermediary, arbitrator, moderator, honest broker

neighbourhood *or (U.S.)* **neighborhood** NOUN **1 = district**, community, quarter, region, surroundings, locality, locale: *It seemed like a good neighbourhood to raise my children.* **2 = vicinity**, confines, proximity, precincts, environs, purlieus: *the loss of woodlands in the neighbourhood of large towns*

> **QUOTATIONS**
> The Bible tells us to love our neighbours, and also to love our enemies; probably because they are generally the same people
> [G. K. Chesterton]

neighbouring *or (U.S.)* **neighboring** ADJECTIVE **= nearby**, next, near, bordering, surrounding, connecting, adjacent, adjoining, abutting, contiguous, nearest
OPPOSITE: remote

neighbourly *or (U.S.)* **neighborly** ADJECTIVE **= helpful**, kind, social, civil, friendly, obliging, harmonious, amiable, considerate, sociable, genial, hospitable, companionable, well-disposed

Nemesis *(sometimes not cap.)* NOUN **= retribution**, fate, destruction, destiny, vengeance

neophyte NOUN **= novice**, student, pupil, recruit, amateur, beginner, trainee, apprentice, disciple, learner, tyro, probationer, novitiate, proselyte, catechumen

nepotism NOUN **= favouritism**, bias, patronage, preferential treatment, partiality

nerd *or* **nurd** NOUN **1 = bore**, obsessive, anorak *(informal)*, geek *(informal)*, trainspotter *(informal)*, dork *(slang)*, wonk *(informal)*, statto *(Brit. informal)*: *the outdated notion that users of the Internet are all sad computer nerds* **2 = fool**, weed, drip *(informal)*, sap *(slang)*, wally *(slang)*, sucker *(slang)*, wimp *(informal)*, booby, prat *(slang)*, plonker *(slang)*, twit *(informal, chiefly Brit.)*, simpleton, dipstick *(Brit. slang)*, schmuck *(U.S. slang)*, divvy *(Brit. slang)*, putz *(U.S. slang)*, wuss *(slang)*, eejit *(Scot. & Irish)*, dumb-ass *(slang)*, doofus *(slang, chiefly U.S.)*, dorba or dorb *(Austral. slang)*, bogan *(Austral. slang)*: *No woman in her right mind would look twice at such a charmless little nerd.*

nerve NOUN **1 = bravery**, courage, spirit, bottle *(Brit. slang)*, resolution, daring, determination, guts *(informal)*, pluck, grit, fortitude, vigour, coolness, balls *(taboo, slang)*, mettle, firmness, spunk *(informal)*, fearlessness, steadfastness, intrepidity, hardihood, gameness: *I never got up enough nerve to ask her out; If we keep our nerve, we might be able to bluff it out.* **2 = impudence**, face *(informal)*, front, neck *(informal)*, sauce *(informal)*, cheek *(informal)*, brass *(informal)*, gall, audacity, boldness, temerity, chutzpah *(U.S. & Canad. informal)*, insolence, impertinence, effrontery, brass neck *(Brit. informal)*, brazenness, sassiness *(U.S. slang)*: *He had the nerve to ask me to prove who I was.*
▷ PLURAL NOUN **= tension**, stress, strain, anxiety, butterflies (in your stomach) *(informal)*, nervousness, cold feet *(informal)*, heebie-jeebies *(slang)*, worry: *I just played badly. It wasn't nerves.*
get on someone's nerves = annoy, provoke, bug *(informal)*, needle *(informal)*, plague, irritate, aggravate *(informal)*, madden, ruffle, exasperate, nettle, irk, rile, peeve, get under your skin *(informal)*, nark *(Brit., Austral. & N.Z. slang)*, get up your nose *(informal)*, make your blood boil, piss you off *(taboo, slang)*, rub (someone) up the wrong way *(informal)*, get your goat *(slang)*, get in your hair *(informal)*, get on your wick *(Brit. slang)*, put your back up, hack you off *(informal)*
nerve yourself = brace yourself, prepare yourself, steel yourself, fortify yourself, gear yourself up, gee yourself up: *I nerved myself to face the pain.*
▸ *technical name:* neuron, neurone
▸ *related adjective:* neural

nerve-racking *or* **nerve-wracking** ADJECTIVE **= tense**, trying, difficult, worrying, frightening, distressing, daunting, harassing, stressful, harrowing, gut-wrenching

nervous ADJECTIVE *(often with* **of***)* **= apprehensive**, anxious, uneasy, edgy, worried, wired *(slang)*, tense, fearful, shaky, hysterical, neurotic, agitated, ruffled, timid, hyper *(informal)*, jittery *(informal)*, uptight *(informal)*, flustered, on edge, excitable, nervy *(Brit. informal)*, jumpy, twitchy *(informal)*, fidgety, timorous, highly strung, antsy *(informal)*, toey *(Austral. slang)*, adrenalized
OPPOSITE: calm

nervous breakdown NOUN **= collapse**, breakdown, crack-up *(informal)*, neurasthenia *(obsolete)*, nervous disorder

nervousness NOUN **= anxiety**, stress, tension, strain, unease, disquiet, agitation, trepidation, timidity, excitability, perturbation, edginess, worry, jumpiness, antsiness *(informal)*

nervy ADJECTIVE **= anxious**, nervous, tense, agitated, wired *(slang)*, restless, jittery *(informal)*, on edge, excitable, jumpy, twitchy *(informal)*, fidgety, adrenalized

nest NOUN **1 = refuge**, resort, retreat, haunt, den, hideaway: *He moved into a £2,000-a-month love nest with his blonde mistress.* **2 = hotbed**, den, breeding-ground: *Biarritz was notorious in those days as a nest of spies.*

nest egg NOUN **= savings**, fund(s), store, reserve, deposit, fall-back, cache

nestle VERB *(often with* **up** *or* **down***)* **= snuggle**, cuddle, huddle, curl up, nuzzle

nestling NOUN **= chick**, fledgling, baby bird

net[1] NOUN **= mesh**, netting, network, web, lattice, lacework, openwork: *the use of a net in greenhouses to protect crops against insects*
▷ VERB **= catch**, bag, capture, trap, nab *(informal)*, entangle, ensnare, enmesh: *Poachers have been netting fish to sell on the black market.*

net[2] *or* **nett** ADJECTIVE **1 = after taxes**, final, clear, take-home: *At the year end, net assets were £18 million.* **2 = final**, closing, ultimate, eventual, conclusive: *The party made a net gain of 210 seats.*
▷ VERB **= earn**, make, clear, gain, realize, bring in, accumulate, reap: *The state government expects to net about 1.46 billion rupees.*

nether ADJECTIVE **= lower**, bottom, beneath, underground, inferior, basal

nettle VERB **= irritate**, provoke, annoy, gall, sting, aggravate *(informal)*, incense, ruffle, exasperate, vex, goad, pique, get on your nerves *(informal)*, nark *(Brit., Austral. & N.Z. slang)*, hack you off *(informal)*

network NOUN **1 = web**, system, arrangement, grid, mesh, lattice, circuitry, nexus, plexus, interconnection, net: *The uterus is supplied with a network of blood vessels and nerves.* **2 = maze**, warren, labyrinth: *Strasbourg, with its rambling network of medieval streets*

neurosis NOUN **= obsession**, instability, mental illness, abnormality, phobia, derangement, mental disturbance, psychological *or* emotional disorder

neurotic ADJECTIVE **= unstable**, nervous, disturbed, anxious, abnormal, obsessive, compulsive, manic, unhealthy, hyper *(informal)*, twitchy *(informal)*, overwrought, maladjusted **OPPOSITE:** rational

neuter VERB **= castrate**, doctor *(informal)*, emasculate, spay, dress, fix *(informal)*, geld

neutral ADJECTIVE **1 = unbiased**, impartial, disinterested, even-handed, dispassionate, sitting on the fence, uninvolved, noncommittal, nonpartisan, unprejudiced, nonaligned, unaligned, noncombatant, nonbelligerent: *Those who had decided to remain neutral now found themselves forced to take sides.* **OPPOSITE:** biased **2 = expressionless**, dull, blank, deadpan, toneless: *He told her about the death, describing the events in as neutral a manner as he could.* **3 = uncontroversial** *or* **noncontroversial**, safe, inoffensive: *Stick to talking about neutral subjects on your first meeting.* **4 = colourless**, achromatic: *I tend to wear neutral colours like grey and beige.*

neutrality NOUN **= impartiality**, detachment, noninterference, nonpartisanship, noninvolvement, nonalignment, noninterventionism

neutralize *or* **neutralise** VERB **= counteract**, cancel, offset, undo, compensate for, negate, invalidate, counterbalance, nullify

never ADVERB **1 = at no time**, not once, not ever: *She was never really well after that.* **OPPOSITE:** always **2 = under no circumstances**, no way, not at all, on no account, not on your life *(informal)*, not on your nelly *(Brit. slang)*, not for love nor money *(informal)*, not ever: *I would never do anything to hurt him.*

> **USAGE**
> *Never* is sometimes used in informal speech and writing as an emphatic form of *not*, with simple past tenses of certain verbs: *I never said that* – and in very informal speech as a denial in place of *did not*: *he says I hit him, but I never.* These uses of *never* should be avoided in careful writing.

never-never NOUN **= hire-purchase** *(Brit.)*, H.P. *(Brit.)*

nevertheless ADVERB **= even so**, still, however, yet, regardless, nonetheless, notwithstanding, in spite of that, (even) though, but

new ADJECTIVE **1 = modern**, recent, contemporary, up-to-date, latest, happening *(informal)*, different, current, advanced, original, fresh, novel, topical, state-of-the-art, ground-breaking, modish, newfangled, modernistic, ultramodern, all-singing, all-dancing: *a brilliant new invention that puts a world of information at your fingertips* **OPPOSITE:** old-fashioned **2 = brand new**, unused: *There are many boats, new and used, for sale.* **3 = extra**, more, added, new-found, supplementary: *Many are looking for a new source of income by taking on freelance work.* **4 = unfamiliar**, unaccustomed, strange, unknown: *I had been in my new job only a few days; She was still new to the art of bargaining.* **5 = renewed**, changed, improved, restored, altered, rejuvenated, revitalized: *The treatment made him feel like a new man.*

> **QUOTATIONS**
> There is no new thing under the sun
> [*Bible: Ecclesiastes*]

newcomer NOUN **1 = new arrival**, incomer, immigrant, stranger, foreigner, alien, settler: *He must be a newcomer to town.* **2 = beginner**, stranger, outsider, novice, new arrival, parvenu, Johnny-come-lately *(informal)*, noob *(derogatory, slang)*: *The candidates are all relative newcomers to politics.*

newly ADVERB **= recently**, just, lately, freshly, anew, latterly

newness NOUN **= novelty**, innovation, originality, freshness, strangeness, unfamiliarity
▸ *related prefix:* neo- ▸ *related phobia:* neophobia

news NOUN **= information**, latest *(informal)*, report, word, story, release, account, statement, advice, exposé, intelligence, scandal, rumour, leak, revelation, buzz, gossip, dirt *(U.S. slang)*, goss *(informal)*, disclosure, bulletin, dispatch, gen *(Brit. informal)*, communiqué, hearsay, tidings, news flash, scuttlebutt *(U.S. slang)*

> **QUOTATIONS**
> As cold waters to a thirsty soul, so is good news from another country
> [*Bible: Proverbs*]
>
> News may be true, but it is not truth, and reporters and officials seldom see it the same way
> [James Reston *The Artillery of the Press*]
>
> If people didn't give the news their news, and if everybody kept their news to themselves, the news wouldn't have any news
> [Andy Warhol *From A to B and Back Again*]
>
> When a dog bites a man, that is not news, because it happens so often. But if a man bites a dog, that is news
> [John B. Bogart]
>
> all the news that's fit to print
> [Adolph S. Ochs *motto of the New York Times*]

> **PROVERBS**
> *No news is good news*

newsworthy ADJECTIVE **= interesting**, important, arresting, significant, remarkable, notable, sensational, noteworthy

next ADJECTIVE **1 = following**, later, succeeding, subsequent: *I caught the next available flight.* **2 = adjacent**, closest, nearest, neighbouring, adjoining: *The man in the next chair was asleep.*
▷ ADVERB **= afterwards**, then, later, following, subsequently, thereafter: *I don't know what to do next.*

nexus NOUN **= connection**, link, tie, bond, junction, joining

nibble VERB *(often with* **at***)* **= bite**, eat, peck, pick at, nip, munch, gnaw: *He started to nibble his biscuit.*
▷ NOUN **= snack**, bite, taste, peck, crumb, morsel, titbit, soupçon *(French)*: *We each took a nibble of cheese.*

nice ADJECTIVE **1 = pleasant**, delightful, agreeable, good, attractive, charming, pleasurable, enjoyable: *We had a nice meal with a bottle of champagne.* **OPPOSITE:** unpleasant **2 = kind**, helpful, obliging, considerate: *It was nice of you to go to so much trouble.* **OPPOSITE:** unkind **3 = likable** *or* **likeable**, friendly, engaging, charming, pleasant, agreeable, amiable, prepossessing: *I've met your father and I think he's really nice.* **4 = polite**, cultured, refined, courteous, genteel, well-bred, well-mannered: *The kids are very well brought up and have nice manners.* **OPPOSITE:** vulgar **5 = precise**, fine, careful, strict, accurate, exact, exacting, subtle, delicate, discriminating, rigorous, meticulous, scrupulous, fastidious: *As a politician, he drew a nice distinction between his own opinions and the wishes of the majority.* **OPPOSITE:** vague

nicely ADVERB **1 = pleasantly**, well, delightfully, attractively, charmingly, agreeably, pleasingly, acceptably, pleasurably: *He's just written a book, nicely illustrated and not too technical.* **OPPOSITE:** unpleasantly **2 = kindly**, politely, thoughtfully, amiably, courteously: *He treated you very nicely and acted like a decent guy.* **3 = precisely**, exactly, accurately, finely, carefully, strictly, subtly, delicately, meticulously, rigorously, scrupulously: *I think this sums up the problem very nicely.* **OPPOSITE:** carelessly **4 = satisfactorily**, well, adequately, acceptably, passably: *She has a private income, so they manage very nicely.*

nicety NOUN **= fine point**, distinction, subtlety, nuance, refinement, minutiae

niche NOUN **1 = recess**, opening, corner, hollow, nook, alcove: *There was a niche in the rock where the path ended.* **2 = position**, calling, place, slot *(informal)*, vocation, pigeonhole *(informal)*: *Perhaps I will find my niche in a desk job.*

nick NOUN **= cut**, mark, scratch, score, chip, scar, notch, dent, snick: *The barbed wire had left only the tiniest nick below my right eye.*
▷ VERB **1 = steal**, pinch *(informal)*, swipe *(slang)*, pilfer, snitch *(slang)*: *We used to nick biscuits from the kitchen.* **2 = cut**, mark, score, damage, chip, scratch, scar, notch, dent, snick: *A sharp blade is likely to nick the skin and draw blood.*

nickname NOUN **= pet name**, label, diminutive, epithet, sobriquet, familiar name, moniker *or* monicker *(slang)*, handle *(slang)*

nifty ADJECTIVE **1 = slick**, excellent, sharp, smart, clever, neat, stylish, schmick *(Austral. informal)*: *This new adventure film features some nifty special effects.* **2 = agile**, quick, swift, skilful, deft: *Knight displayed all the nifty legwork of a champion bowler.*

Novelists part 1

Peter Abrahams *(South African)*
Chinua Achebe *(Nigerian)*
Douglas Adams *(English)*
Alain-Fournier *(French)*
James Aldridge *(Australian)*
Kingsley Amis *(English)*
Martin Amis *(English)*
Mulk Raj Anand *(Indian)*
Maya Angelou *(U.S.)*
Lucius Apuleius *(Roman)*
Jeffrey Archer *(English)*
Isaac Asimov *(U.S.)*
Margaret Atwood *(Canadian)*
Louis Auchincloss *(U.S.)*
Jane Austen *(English)*
Beryl Bainbridge *(English)*
R M Ballantyne *(Scottish)*
J G Ballard *(English)*
Honoré de Balzac *(French)*
Iain Banks *(Scottish)*
Lynne Reid Banks *(English)*
Pat Barker *(English)*
John Barth *(U.S.)*
H E Bates *(English)*
Nina Bawden *(English)*
Simone de Beauvoir *(French)*
Sybille Bedford *(British)*
Saul Bellow *(Canadian)*
Andrei Bely *(Russian)*
Thomas Berger *(U.S.)*
Maeve Binchy *(Irish)*
Alan Bleasdale *(English)*
Heinrich Böll *(German)*
Elizabeth Bowen *(Irish)*
Paul Bowles *(U.S.)*
William Boyd *(Scottish)*
Malcolm Bradbury *(English)*
Barbara Taylor Bradford *(English)*
André Brink *(South African)*
Louis Bromfield *(U.S.)*
Anne Brontë *(English)*
Charlotte Brontë *(English)*
Emily (Jane) Brontë *(English)*
Anita Brookner *(English)*
George Douglas Brown *(Scottish)*
George Mackay Brown *(Scottish)*
John Buchan *(Scottish)*
Pearl Buck *(U.S.)*
Mikhail Afanaseyev Bulgakov *(Russian)*
John Bunyan *(English)*
Anthony Burgess *(British)*
Fanny Burney *(English)*
Edgar Rice Burrows *(U.S.)*
William Burroughs *(U.S.)*
A S Byatt *(English)*
Italo Calvino *(Italian)*
Albert Camus *(French)*
Elias Canetti *(Bulgarian)*
Truman Capote *(U.S.)*
Peter Carey *(Australian)*
Angela Carter *(English)*
Barbara Cartland *(English)*
Willa Cather *(U.S.)*
Camilo José Cela *(Spanish)*
Miguel de Cervantes *(Spanish)*
Raymond Chandler *(U.S.)*
G K Chesterton *(English)*
Agatha (Mary Clarissa) Christie *(English)*
Arthur C Clarke *(English)*
James Clavell *(U.S.)*
Jon Cleary *(Australian)*
J M Coetzee *(South African)*
Colette *(French)*
(William) Wilkie Collins *(English)*
Richard Condon *(U.S.)*
Evan Connell *(U.S.)*
Joseph Conrad *(Polish-British)*
Catherine Cookson *(English)*
James Fenimore Cooper *(U.S.)*
Jilly Cooper *(English)*
Stephen Crane *(U.S.)*
(William) Robertson Davies *(Canadian)*
Daniel Defoe *(English)*
Len Deighton *(English)*
Don DeLillo *(U.S.)*
Anita Desai *(Indian)*
Peter De Vries *(U.S.)*
Charles (John Huffam) Dickens *(English)*
Joan Didion *(U.S.)*
Isak Dinesen *(Danish)*
Benjamin Disraeli *(English)*
J P Donleavy *(Irish)*
John Roderigo Dos Passos *(U.S.)*
Fyodor Mikhailovich Dostoevsky *(Russian)*
Arthur Conan Doyle *(Scottish)*
Roddy Doyle *(Irish)*
Margaret Drabble *(English)*
Alexandre Dumas *(French)*
Daphne Du Maurier *(English)*
Umberto Eco *(Italian)*
George Eliot *(English)*
Stanley Elkin *(U.S.)*
Alice Thomas Ellis *(English)*
Philip José Farmer *(U.S.)*
Howard Fast *(U.S.)*
William Faulkner *(U.S.)*
Henry Fielding *(English)*
F(rancis) Scott (Key) Fitzgerald *(U.S.)*
Penelope Fitzgerald *(English)*
Gustave Flaubert *(French)*
Richard Ford *(U.S.)*
E M Forster *(English)*
Frederick Forsyth *(English)*
John Fowles *(English)*
Janet Paterson Frame *(New Zealand)*
Dick Francis *(English)*
Michael Frayn *(English)*
Marilyn French *(U.S.)*
William Gaddis *(U.S.)*
Janice Galloway *(Scottish)*
Gabriel García Márquez *(Colombian)*
Helen Garner *(Australian)*
Elizabeth Gaskell *(English)*
Lewis Grassic Gibbon *(Scottish)*
André Gide *(French)*
Ellen Glasgow *(U.S.)*
Johann Wolfgang von Goethe *(German)*
Nikolai Vasilievich Gogol *(Russian)*
Herbert Gold *(U.S.)*
William (Gerald) Golding *(English)*
William Goldman *(U.S.)*
Oliver Goldsmith *(Anglo-Irish)*
Ivan Aleksandrovich Goncharov *(Russian)*
Nadine Gordimer *(South African)*
Maxim Gorky *(Russian)*
Günter (Wilhelm) Grass *(German)*
Alasdair Gray *(Scottish)*
Graham Greene *(English)*
John Grisham *(U.S.)*
David Guterson *(U.S.)*
Arthur Hailey *(Anglo-Canadian)*
Thomas Hardy *(English)*
L(eslie) P(oles) Hartley *(English)*
Nathaniel Hawthorne *(U.S.)*
Shirley Hazzard *(U.S.)*
Robert A Heinlein *(U.S.)*
Joseph Heller *(U.S.)*
Ernest Hemingway *(U.S.)*
Hermann Hesse *(German)*
Georgette Heyer *(English)*
Patricia Highsmith *(U.S.)*
Russell Hoban *(U.S.)*
James Hogg *(Scottish)*
Paul Horgan *(U.S.)*
Victor (Marie) Hugo *(French)*
Keri Hulme *(New Zealand)*
Evan Hunter *(U.S.)*
Zora Neale Hurston *(U.S.)*
Aldous Huxley *(English)*
John Irving *(U.S.)*
Kazuo Ishiguro *(British)*
Henry James *(U.S.-British)*
P D James *(English)*
Ruth Prawer Jhabvala *(Anglo-Polish)*
Erica Jong *(U.S.)*
James Joyce *(Irish)*
Franz Kafka *(Czech)*
Johanna Kaplan *(U.S.)*
Nikos Kazantazakis *(Greek)*
Molly Keane *(Anglo-Irish)*
James Kelman *(Scottish)*
Thomas Keneally *(Australian)*
Jack Kerouac *(U.S.)*
Ken Kesey *(U.S.)*
Stephen King *(U.S.)*
Charles Kingsley *(English)*
Rudyard Kipling *(English)*
Milan Kundera *(French-Czech)*
Pierre Choderlos de Laclos *(French)*
George Lamming *(Barbadian)*
Guiseppe Tomasi di Lampedusa *(Italian)*
D H Lawrence *(English)*
John Le Carré *(English)*
Harper Lee *(U.S.)*
Laurie Lee *(English)*
Sheridan Le Fanu *(Irish)*

niggle VERB **1 = bother**, concern, worry, trouble, disturb, rankle: *I realise now that the things which used to niggle me didn't really matter.* **2 = criticize**, provoke, annoy, plague, irritate, hassle *(informal)*, badger, find fault with, nag at, cavil, be on your back *(slang)*: *I don't react any more when opponents try to niggle me.*
▷ NOUN **= complaint**, moan, grievance, grumble, beef *(slang)*, bitch *(slang)*, lament, grouse, gripe *(informal)*, grouch *(informal)*: *The life we have built together is far more important than any minor niggle either of us might have.*

niggling ADJECTIVE **1 = irritating**, troubling, persistent, bothersome: *Both players have been suffering from niggling injuries.* **2 = petty**, minor, trifling, insignificant, unimportant, fussy, quibbling, picky *(informal)*, piddling *(informal)*, nit-picking *(informal)*, finicky, pettifogging: *They started having tiffs about the most niggling little things.*

nigh ADVERB **= almost**, about, nearly, close to, practically, approximately: *Accurate earthquake prediction is well nigh impossible.*
▷ ADJECTIVE **= near**, next, close, imminent, impending, at hand, upcoming: *The end of the world is nigh.*

night NOUN **= darkness**, dark, night-time, dead of night, night watches, hours of darkness
▶ *related adjective:* nocturnal

n

QUOTATIONS

Night hath a thousand eyes
[John Lyly *Maides Metamorphose*]

The night has a thousand eyes,
And the day but one
[F.W. Bourdillon *Light*]

Night is the half of life, and the better half
[Johann Wolfgang von Goethe *Wilhelm Meisters Lehrjahre*]

the huge and thoughtful night
[Walt Whitman *When Lilacs Last in the Dooryard Bloom'd*]

sable-vested night, eldest of things
[John Milton *Paradise Lost*]

nightfall NOUN **= evening**, sunset, twilight, dusk, sundown, eventide, gloaming *(Scot. poetic)*, eve *(archaic)*, evo *(Austral. slang)* **OPPOSITE:** daybreak

nightly ADJECTIVE **= nocturnal**, night-time: *One of the nurses came by on her nightly rounds.*
▷ ADVERB **= every night**, nights *(informal)*, each night, night after night: *She had prayed nightly for his safe return.*

nightmare NOUN **1 = bad dream**, hallucination, night terror: *Jane did not eat cheese because it gave her nightmares.* **2 = ordeal**, trial, hell, horror, torture, torment, tribulation, purgatory, hell on earth: *My years in prison were a nightmare.*

nightmarish ADJECTIVE **= terrifying**, frightening, disturbing, appalling, horrible, horrific, ghastly, hideous, harrowing, frightful

nihilism NOUN **= negativity**, rejection, denial, scepticism, cynicism, pessimism, renunciation, atheism, repudiation, agnosticism, unbelief, abnegation: *These disillusioned students embraced agnosticism, atheism, and nihilism.*

nil NOUN **1 = nothing**, love, zero, zip *(U.S. slang)*: *The score was 2-nil.* **2 = zero**, nothing, none, naught, zilch *(slang)*, zip *(U.S. slang)*: *The chances of success are virtually nil.*

nimble ADJECTIVE **1 = agile**, active, lively, deft, proficient, sprightly, nippy *(Brit. informal)*, spry, dexterous: *Lily, who was light and nimble on her feet, was learning to tap-dance.* **OPPOSITE:** clumsy **2 = alert**, ready, bright *(informal)*, sharp, keen, active, smart, quick-witted: *To keep your mind nimble, you must use it.*

nimbus NOUN **= halo**, atmosphere, glow, aura, ambience, corona, irradiation, aureole

nip[1] VERB **1** *(with* **along**, **up**, **out**, *Brit. informal)* **= pop**, go, run, rush, dash: *Could you nip down to the corner shop for some milk?* **2 = bite**, snap, nibble: *She was patting the dog when it nipped her finger.* **3 = pinch**, catch, grip, squeeze, clip, compress, tweak: *He gave Billy's cheek a nip between two rough fingers.*
nip something in the bud = thwart, check, frustrate: *It is important to recognize jealousy and to nip it in the bud before it gets out of hand.*

nip[2] NOUN **= dram**, shot *(informal)*, drop, taste, finger, swallow, portion, peg *(Brit.)*, sip, draught, sup, mouthful, snifter *(informal)*, soupçon *(French)*: *She had a habit of taking an occasional nip from a flask of cognac.*

nipper NOUN **1 = child**, girl, boy, baby, kid *(informal)*, infant, tot, little one, sprog *(slang)*, munchkin *(informal, chiefly U.S.)*, rug rat *(slang)*, littlie *(Austral. informal)*, ankle-biter *(Austral. slang)*, tacker *(Austral. slang)*: *I couldn't have been much more than a nipper when you last saw me.* **2 = pincer**, claw: *Just inside the ragworm's mouth is a sharp, powerful pair of nippers.*

nipple NOUN **= teat**, breast, udder, tit, pap, papilla, mamilla

nippy ADJECTIVE **1 = chilly**, biting, parky *(Brit. informal)*: *It can get quite nippy in the evenings.* **2 = fast** *(informal)*, quick, speedy: *This nippy new car has fold-down rear seats.* **3 = agile**, fast, quick, active, lively, nimble, sprightly, spry: *He's nippy, and well suited to badminton.*

nirvana NOUN **= paradise**, peace, joy, bliss, serenity, tranquillity

nitty-gritty NOUN **= basics**, facts, reality, essentials, core, fundamentals, substance, essence, bottom line, crux, gist, nuts and bolts, heart of the matter, ins and outs, brass tacks *(informal)*

no SENTENCE SUBSTITUTE **= not at all**, certainly not, of course not, absolutely not, never, no way, nay: *'Any problems?' – 'No, everything's fine.'* **OPPOSITE:** yes
▷ NOUN **1 = refusal**, rejection, denial, negation, veto: *My answer to that is an emphatic no.* **OPPOSITE:** consent **2 = objector**, protester, dissident, dissenter: *According to the latest poll, the noes have 50 per cent and the yeses 35 per cent.*

nob NOUN **= aristocrat**, fat cat *(slang, chiefly U.S.)*, toff *(Brit. slang)*, bigwig *(informal)*, celeb *(informal)*, big shot *(informal)*, big hitter *(informal)*, aristo *(informal)*, heavy hitter *(informal)*, nabob *(informal)*, V.I.P.

nobble VERB **1 = influence**, square, win over, pay off *(informal)*, corrupt, intimidate, bribe, get at, buy off, suborn, grease the palm *or* hand of *(slang)*: *The trial was stopped after allegations of attempts to nobble the jury.* **2 = disable**, handicap, weaken, incapacitate: *the drug used to nobble two horses at Doncaster last week* **3 = thwart**, check, defeat, frustrate, snooker, foil, baffle, balk, prevent: *Their plans were nobbled by jealous rivals.*

nobility NOUN **1 = aristocracy**, lords, elite, nobles, upper class, peerage, ruling class, patricians, high society: *They married into the nobility and entered the highest ranks of society.* **2 = dignity**, majesty, greatness, grandeur, magnificence, stateliness, nobleness: *I found Mr. Mandela supremely courteous, with a genuine nobility of bearing.* **3 = integrity**, honour, virtue, goodness, honesty, righteousness, probity, rectitude, worthiness, incorruptibility, uprightness: *There can be no doubt about the remarkable strength and nobility of her character.*

QUOTATIONS

New nobility is but the act of power, but ancient nobility is the act of time
[Francis Bacon *Essays*]

noble ADJECTIVE **1 = worthy**, generous, upright, honourable, virtuous, magnanimous: *He was an upright and noble man.* **OPPOSITE:** despicable **2 = dignified**, great, august, imposing, impressive, distinguished, magnificent, splendid, stately: *She was described by contemporaries as possessing a noble bearing and excellent manners.* **OPPOSITE:** lowly **3 = aristocratic**, lordly, titled, gentle *(archaic)*, patrician, blue-blooded, highborn: *Although he was of noble birth he lived as a poor man.* **OPPOSITE:** humble
▷ NOUN **= lord**, peer, aristocrat, nobleman, aristo *(informal)*: *In those days, many of the nobles and landowners were a law unto themselves.* **OPPOSITE:** commoner

nobody PRONOUN **= no-one**: *They were shut away in a little room where nobody could overhear.*
▷ NOUN **= nonentity**, nothing *(informal)*, lightweight *(informal)*, zero, no-mark *(Brit. slang)*, cipher: *A man in my position has nothing to fear from a nobody like you.* **OPPOSITE:** celebrity

nocturnal ADJECTIVE = **nightly**, night, of the night, night-time

nod VERB **1 = agree**, concur, assent, show agreement: *'Are you okay?' I asked. She nodded and smiled.* **2 = incline**, bob, bow, duck, dip: *She nodded her head in understanding.* **3 = signal**, indicate, motion, gesture: *He lifted his end of the canoe, nodding to me to take up mine.* **4 = salute**, acknowledge: *All the girls nodded and said 'Hi'.*
▷ NOUN **1 = signal**, sign, motion, gesture, indication: *Then, at a nod from their leader, they all sat.* **2 = salute**, greeting, acknowledgment: *I gave him a quick nod of greeting and slipped into the nearest chair.*

node NOUN = **nodule**, growth, swelling, knot, lump, bump, bud, knob, protuberance

noise NOUN = **sound**, talk, row, racket, outcry, clamour, din, clatter, uproar, babble, blare, fracas, commotion, pandemonium, rumpus, cry, tumult, hubbub **OPPOSITE:** silence

noisy ADJECTIVE **1 = rowdy**, chattering, strident, boisterous, vociferous, riotous, uproarious, obstreperous, clamorous: *a noisy group of drunken students* **OPPOSITE:** quiet **2 = loud**, piercing, deafening, tumultuous, ear-splitting, cacophonous, clamorous: *It may be necessary to ask a neighbour to turn down noisy music.* **OPPOSITE:** quiet

nomad NOUN = **wanderer**, migrant, rover, rambler, itinerant, drifter, vagabond

nomadic ADJECTIVE = **wandering**, travelling, roaming, migrant, roving, itinerant, migratory, vagrant, peripatetic

nomenclature NOUN = **terminology**, vocabulary, classification, taxonomy, phraseology, locution

nominal ADJECTIVE **1 = titular**, formal, purported, in name only, supposed, so-called, pretended, theoretical, professed, ostensible: *As he was still not allowed to run a company, his wife became its nominal head.* **2 = token**, small, symbolic, minimal, trivial, trifling, insignificant, inconsiderable: *The ferries carry bicycles for a nominal charge.*

nominate VERB **1 = propose**, suggest, recommend, submit, put forward: *The public will be able to nominate candidates for the awards.* **2 = appoint**, name, choose, commission, select, elect, assign, designate, empower: *It is legally possible for an elderly person to nominate someone to act for them.*

nomination NOUN **1 = proposal**, suggestion, recommendation: *a list of nominations for senior lectureships* **2 = appointment**, election, selection, designation, choice: *On Leo's death there were two main candidates for nomination as his replacement.*

nominee NOUN = **candidate**, applicant, entrant, contestant, aspirant, runner

QUOTATIONS
nominee: a modest gentleman shrinking from the distinction of private life and diligently seeking the honorable obscurity of public office
[Ambrose Bierce *The Devil's Dictionary*]

nonaligned ADJECTIVE = **neutral**, impartial, uninvolved, nonpartisan, noncombatant, nonbelligerent

nonchalance NOUN = **indifference**, insouciance, detachment, unconcern, cool *(slang)*, calm, apathy, composure, carelessness, equanimity, casualness, sang-froid, self-possession, dispassion, imperturbability

nonchalant ADJECTIVE = **indifferent**, cool, calm, casual, detached, careless, laid-back *(informal)*, airy, unconcerned, apathetic, dispassionate, unfazed *(informal)*, unperturbed, blasé, offhand, unemotional, insouciant, imperturbable **OPPOSITE:** concerned

noncommittal ADJECTIVE = **evasive**, politic, reserved, guarded, careful, cautious, neutral, vague, wary, discreet, tentative, ambiguous, indefinite, circumspect, tactful, equivocal, temporizing, unrevealing

nonconformist NOUN = **dissenter**, rebel, radical, protester, eccentric, maverick, heretic, individualist, iconoclast, dissentient **OPPOSITE:** traditionalist

nondescript ADJECTIVE = **undistinguished**, ordinary, dull, commonplace, unremarkable, run-of-the-mill, uninspiring, indeterminate, uninteresting, featureless, insipid, unexceptional, common or garden *(informal)*, mousy, characterless, unmemorable, vanilla *(informal)*, nothing to write home about **OPPOSITE:** distinctive

none PRONOUN **1 = not any**, nothing, zero, not one, nil, no part, not a bit, zilch *(slang, chiefly U.S. & Canad.)*, diddly *(U.S. slang)*: *I turned to bookshops and libraries seeking information and found none.* **2 = no-one**, nobody, not one: *None of us knew what to say to her.*

nonentity NOUN = **nobody**, lightweight *(informal)*, mediocrity, cipher, small fry, unimportant person

nonetheless SENTENCE CONNECTOR = **nevertheless**, however, yet, even so, despite that, in spite of that

nonevent NOUN = **flop** *(informal)*, failure, disappointment, fiasco, dud *(informal)*, washout, clunker *(informal)*

nonexistent ADJECTIVE = **imaginary**, imagined, fancied, fictional, mythical, unreal, hypothetical, illusory, insubstantial, hallucinatory **OPPOSITE:** real

nonplussed ADJECTIVE = **taken aback**, stunned, confused, embarrassed, puzzled, astonished, stumped, dismayed, baffled, bewildered, astounded, confounded, perplexed, disconcerted, mystified, fazed, dumbfounded, discomfited, flummoxed, discountenanced

nonsense NOUN **1 = rubbish**, hot air *(informal)*, waffle *(informal, chiefly Brit.)*, twaddle, pants *(slang)*, rot, crap *(slang)*, garbage *(informal)*, trash, bunk *(informal)*, tosh *(slang, chiefly Brit.)*, rhubarb, pap, foolishness, bilge *(informal)*, drivel, tripe *(informal)*, gibberish, guff *(slang)*, bombast, moonshine, claptrap *(informal)*, hogwash, hokum *(slang, chiefly U.S. & Canad.)*, blather, double Dutch *(Brit. informal)*, piffle *(informal)*, poppycock *(informal)*, balderdash, bosh *(informal)*, eyewash *(informal)*, stuff and nonsense, tommyrot, horsefeathers *(U.S. slang)*, bunkum *or* buncombe *(chiefly U.S.)*, bizzo *(Austral. slang)*, bull's wool *(Austral. & N.Z. slang)*: *Most orthodox doctors, however, dismiss this theory as complete nonsense.* **OPPOSITE:** sense **2 = idiocy**, folly, stupidity, absurdity, silliness, inanity, senselessness, ridiculousness, ludicrousness, fatuity: *Surely it is an economic nonsense to deplete the world of natural resources.*

nonsensical ADJECTIVE = **senseless**, crazy, silly, ridiculous, absurd, foolish, ludicrous, meaningless, irrational, incomprehensible, inane, asinine, cockamamie *(slang, chiefly U.S.)*

nonstarter NOUN = **dead loss**, dud *(informal)*, washout *(informal)*, no-hoper *(informal)*, turkey *(informal)*, lemon *(informal)*, loser, waste of space *or* time

nonstop ADJECTIVE = **continuous**, constant, relentless, uninterrupted, steady, endless, unbroken, interminable, incessant, unending, ceaseless, unremitting, unfaltering: *The training was non-stop and continued for three days.* **OPPOSITE:** occasional
▷ ADVERB = **continuously**, constantly, steadily, endlessly, relentlessly, perpetually, incessantly, without stopping, ceaselessly, interminably, unremittingly, uninterruptedly, unendingly, unfalteringly, unbrokenly: *The snow fell non-stop for 24 hours.*

nook NOUN = **niche**, corner, recess, cavity, crevice, alcove, cranny, inglenook *(Brit.)*, cubbyhole, opening

noon NOUN = **midday**, high noon, noonday, noontime, twelve noon, noontide: *The long day of meetings started at noon.*

norm NOUN = **standard**, rule, model, pattern, mean, type, measure, average, par, criterion, benchmark, yardstick: *Their actions departed from what she called the commonly accepted norms of behaviour.*

normal ADJECTIVE **1 = usual**, common, standard, average, natural, regular, ordinary, acknowledged, typical, conventional, routine, accustomed, habitual, run-of-the-mill: *The two* *countries have resumed normal diplomatic relations; The hospital claimed they were simply following their normal procedure.* **OPPOSITE:** unusual **2 = sane**, reasonable, rational, lucid, well-adjusted, compos mentis *(Latin)*, in your right mind, mentally sound, in possession of all your faculties: *Depressed patients are more likely to become ill than normal people.*

normality *or (U.S.)* **normalcy** NOUN **1 = regularity**, order, routine, ordinariness, naturalness, conventionality, usualness: *A semblance of normality has returned to the city after the attack.* **2 = sanity**, reason, balance, rationality, lucidity: *Behind the smiling facade of normality lurked a psychopathic serial killer.*

normally ADVERB **1 = usually**, generally, commonly, regularly, typically, ordinarily, as a rule, habitually: *Normally, the transportation system in Paris carries 950,000 passengers a day.* **2 = as usual**, naturally, properly, conventionally, in the usual way: *the failure of the blood to clot normally*

normative ADJECTIVE **= standardizing**, controlling, regulating, prescriptive, normalizing, regularizing

north ADJECTIVE **= northern**, polar, arctic, boreal, northerly: *On the north side of the mountain; a bitterly cold north wind*
▷ ADVERB **= northward(s)**, in a northerly direction: *The hurricane which had destroyed Honolulu was moving north.*

North Star NOUN **= Pole Star**, Polaris, lodestar

nose NOUN **1 = snout**, bill, beak, hooter *(slang)*, snitch *(slang)*, conk *(slang)*, neb *(archaic, dialect)*, proboscis, schnozzle *(slang, chiefly U.S.)*: *She's got funny eyes and a big nose.* **2 = instinct**, feeling, intuition, sixth sense
▷ VERB **= ease forward**, push, edge, shove, nudge: *The car nosed forward out of the drive; Ben drove past them, nosing his car into the garage.*
by a nose = only just, just, hardly, barely, scarcely, by the skin of your teeth
get up someone's nose = irritate, annoy, anger, madden, get *(informal)*, bug *(informal)*, aggravate *(informal)*, gall, exasperate, nettle, vex, irk, rile, peeve, get under someone's skin *(informal)*, get someone's back up, piss someone off *(taboo, slang)*, put someone's back up, nark *(Brit., Austral. & N.Z. slang)*, get someone's goat *(slang)*, make someone's blood boil, get someone's dander up *(informal)*, hack someone off *(informal)*
nose around *or* **about = search**, examine, investigate, explore, inspect, work over, fossick *(Austral. & N.Z.)*
nose something out = detect, smell, scent, sniff out
poke *or* **stick your nose into something = pry**, interfere, meddle, intrude, snoop *(informal)*, be inquisitive
▸ *related adjectives:* nasal, rhinal

> **QUOTATIONS**
> Give me a man with a good allowance of nose
> [Napoleon Bonaparte]

nose dive NOUN **1 = drop**, plunge, dive, plummet, sharp fall: *The catamaran sailed over the precipice and plunged into a nosedive.* **2 = sharp fall**, plunge, drop, dive, plummet: *My career has taken a nosedive in the past year or two.*
▷ VERB **1 = drop**, plunge, dive, plummet, fall sharply: *The cockpit was submerged as the plane nosedived into the water.* **2 = fall sharply**, drop, plunge, dive, plummet: *The value of the shares nosedived by £2.6 billion.*

nosey *or* **nosy** ADJECTIVE **= inquisitive**, curious, intrusive, prying, eavesdropping, snooping *(informal)*, busybody, interfering, meddlesome

nosh NOUN **1 = food**, eats *(slang)*, fare, grub *(slang)*, feed, tack *(informal)*, scoff *(slang)*, kai *(N.Z. informal)*, chow *(informal)*, sustenance, victuals, comestibles, nosebag *(slang)*, vittles *(obsolete, dialect)*, viands: *a restaurant which serves fine wines and posh nosh* **2 = meal**, repast: *We went for a nosh at our local Indian restaurant.*
▷ VERB **= eat**, consume, scoff *(slang)*, devour, feed on, munch, gobble, partake of, wolf down: *Guests mingled in the gardens, sipped wine, and noshed at cabaret tables; sipping enormous bowls of frothy cappuccino and noshing huge slabs of carrot cake*

nostalgia NOUN **= reminiscence**, longing, regret, pining, yearning, remembrance, homesickness, wistfulness

> **QUOTATIONS**
> Nostalgia isn't what it used to be
> [Anon.]

nostalgic ADJECTIVE **= sentimental**, longing, emotional, homesick, wistful, maudlin, regretful

notable ADJECTIVE **1 = remarkable**, marked, striking, unusual, extraordinary, outstanding, evident, pronounced, memorable, noticeable, uncommon, conspicuous, salient, noteworthy: *The most notable architectural feature of the town is its castle.* **OPPOSITE:** imperceptible
2 = prominent, famous, celebrated, distinguished, well-known, notorious, renowned, eminent, pre-eminent: *the notable occultist, Madame Blavatsky* **OPPOSITE:** unknown
▷ NOUN **= celebrity**, worthy, big name, dignitary, luminary, celeb *(informal)*, personage, megastar *(informal)*, notability, V.I.P.: *The notables attending included five Senators, two Supreme Court judges and three State Governors.*

notably ADVERB **= remarkably**, unusually, distinctly, extraordinarily, markedly, noticeably, strikingly, conspicuously, singularly, outstandingly, uncommonly, pre-eminently, signally: *a notably brave officer who had served under Wolfe at Quebec*

notation NOUN **1 = signs**, system, characters, code, symbols, script: *The dot in musical notation symbolizes an abrupt or staccato quality.* **2 = note**, record, noting, jotting: *He was checking the readings and making notations on a clipboard.*

notch NOUN **1 = level**, step, degree, grade, cut *(informal)*: *Average earnings in the economy moved up another notch in August.* **2 = cut**, nick, incision, indentation, mark, score, cleft: *The blade had a hole through the middle and a notch on one side.*
▷ VERB **= cut**, mark, score, nick, scratch, indent: *a bamboo walking stick with a notched handle*

note NOUN **1 = message**, letter, communication, memo, memorandum, epistle, e-mail, text: *Stevens wrote him a note asking him to come to his apartment.* **2 = record**, reminder, memo, memorandum, jotting, minute: *I made a note of his address.*
3 = annotation, comment, remark, gloss: *See note 16 on page 223.*
4 = document, form, record, certificate: *In the eyes of the law, signing a delivery note is seen as 'accepting' the goods.*
5 = symbol, mark, sign, indication, token: *He has never been able to read or transcribe musical notes.* **6 = tone**, touch, trace, hint, sound: *I detected a note of bitterness in his voice.*
▷ VERB **1 = notice**, see, observe, perceive: *Suddenly I noted that the rain had stopped.* **2 = bear in mind**, be aware, take into account: *Please note that there are a limited number of tickets.*
3 = mention, record, mark, indicate, register, remark: *The report noted a sharp drop in cases of sexually transmitted diseases.*
4 = write down, record, scribble, take down, set down, jot down, put in writing, put down in black and white: *A policeman was noting the number plates of passing cars.*
of note 1 = famous, prestigious, eminent, renowned, of standing, of character, of reputation, of consequence, celebrated: *Besides being an artist of great note, he can also be a fascinating conversationalist.*
2 = important, consequential, significant, of distinction: *She has published nothing of note in the last ten years.*
take note of something *or* **someone = notice**, note, regard, observe, heed, pay attention to: *Take note of the weather conditions.*

notebook NOUN **= notepad**, record book, exercise book, jotter, journal, diary, Filofax®, memorandum book

noted ADJECTIVE **= famous**, celebrated, recognized, distinguished, well-known, prominent, notorious, acclaimed, notable, renowned, eminent, conspicuous, illustrious **OPPOSITE:** unknown

noteworthy ADJECTIVE **= remarkable**, interesting, important, significant, extraordinary, outstanding, exceptional, notable **OPPOSITE:** ordinary

nothing PRONOUN **1 = nought**, zero, nil, naught, not a thing, zilch *(slang)*, sod all *(slang)*, damn all *(slang)*, zip *(U.S. slang)*: *I know nothing of these matters.* **2 = a trifle**, no big deal, a mere bagatelle: *'Thanks for all your help.' 'It was nothing.'* **3 = void**, emptiness, nothingness, nullity, nonexistence: *philosophical ideas of the void, the nothing and the 'un-thought'*
▷ NOUN **= nobody**, cipher, nonentity: *I went from being a complete nothing to all of a sudden having people calling me the new star of the Nineties.*

nothingness NOUN **1 = oblivion**, nullity, nonexistence, nonbeing: *There might be something beyond the grave, you know, and not just nothingness.* **2 = insignificance**, triviality, worthlessness, meaninglessness, unimportance: *the banal lyrics, clichéd song structures and light, fluffy nothingness of her latest album*

notice NOUN **1 = sign**, advertisement, poster, placard, warning, bill: *A few seaside guest houses had 'No Vacancies' notices in their windows.* **2 = notification**, warning, advice, intimation, news, communication, intelligence, announcement, instruction, advance warning, wake-up call, heads up *(U.S. & Canad.)*: *Unions are requested to give seven days' notice of industrial action.* **3 = review**, comment, criticism, evaluation, critique, critical assessment: *She got some good notices for her performance last night.* **4 = attention**, interest, note, regard, consideration, observation, scrutiny, heed, cognizance: *Nothing that went on in the hospital escaped her notice.* **OPPOSITE:** oversight **5 = the sack** *(informal)*, dismissal, discharge, the boot *(slang)*, the push *(slang)*, marching orders *(informal)*, the (old) heave-ho *(informal)*, your books or cards *(informal)*: *They predicted that many teachers would be given their notice by the end of next term.*
▷ VERB **= observe**, see, mind, note, spot, remark, distinguish, perceive, detect, heed, discern, behold *(archaic, literary)*, mark, eyeball *(slang)*: *People should not hesitate to contact the police if they notice anything suspicious.* **OPPOSITE:** overlook

noticeable ADJECTIVE **= obvious**, clear, striking, plain, bold, evident, distinct, manifest, conspicuous, unmistakable, salient, observable, perceptible, appreciable

notification NOUN **= announcement**, declaration, notice, statement, telling, information, warning, message, advice, intelligence, publication, notifying, heads up *(U.S. & Canad.)*

notify VERB **= inform**, tell, advise, alert to, announce, warn, acquaint with, make known to, apprise of

notion NOUN **1 = idea**, view, opinion, belief, concept, impression, judgment, sentiment, conception, apprehension, inkling, mental image or picture, picture: *I disagree with the notion that violence on TV causes acts of violence in society; He has a realistic notion of his capabilities.* **2 = whim**, wish, desire, fancy, impulse, inclination, caprice: *I had a whimsical notion to fly off to Rio that night.*

notional ADJECTIVE **= hypothetical**, ideal, abstract, theoretical, imaginary, speculative, conceptual, unreal, fanciful **OPPOSITE:** actual

notoriety NOUN **= infamy**, discredit, disrepute, dishonour, bad reputation, opprobrium, ill repute, obloquy

notorious ADJECTIVE **= infamous**, disreputable, opprobrious

notoriously ADVERB **= infamously**, disreputably

notwithstanding PREPOSITION **= despite**, in spite of, regardless of: *He despised Pitt, notwithstanding the similar views they both held.*
▷ SENTENCE CONNECTOR **= nevertheless**, however, though, nonetheless: *He doesn't want me there, but I'm going, notwithstanding.*

nought, naught, ought *or* **aught** NOUN **1 = zero**, nothing, nil: *Properties are graded from nought to ten for energy efficiency.* **2 = nothing**, zip *(U.S. slang)*, slang, nothingness, nada, zilch, sod all *(slang)*, damn all *(slang)*: *All our efforts came to nought.*

nourish VERB **1 = feed**, supply, sustain, nurture: *The food the mother eats nourishes both her and her baby.* **2 = encourage**, support, maintain, promote, sustain, foster, cultivate: *This attitude has been carefully nourished by a small group of journalists and scholars.*

nourishing ADJECTIVE **= nutritious**, beneficial, wholesome, healthful, health-giving, nutritive

nourishment NOUN **= food**, nutrition, sustenance, nutriment, tack *(informal)*, kai *(N.Z. informal)*, victuals, vittles *(obsolete, dialect)*

novel[1] NOUN **= story**, tale, fiction, romance, narrative: *He had all but finished writing a first novel.*

> QUOTATIONS
> Yes – oh dear yes – the novel tells a story
> [E.M. Forster *Aspects of the Novel*]
>
> There are three rules for writing the novel. Unfortunately, no one knows what they are
> [W. Somerset Maugham]
>
> novel: a short story padded
> [Ambrose Bierce *The Devil's Dictionary*]
>
> If you try to nail anything down in the novel, either it kills the novel, or the novel gets up and walks away with the nail
> [D.H. Lawrence *Phoenix*]

novel[2] ADJECTIVE **= new**, different, original, fresh, unusual, innovative, uncommon, singular, ground-breaking, left-field *(informal)*: *Staging your own murder mystery party is a novel way to entertain a group of friends.* **OPPOSITE:** ordinary

novelist NOUN **= author**, writer

novelty NOUN **1 = newness**, originality, freshness, innovation, surprise, uniqueness, strangeness, unfamiliarity: *The radical puritanism of Conceptual art and Minimalism had lost its novelty.* **2 = curiosity**, marvel, rarity, oddity, wonder: *In those days a motor car was still a novelty.* **3 = trinket**, souvenir, memento, bauble, bagatelle, gimcrack, trifle, gewgaw, knick-knack: *At Easter, we give them plastic eggs filled with small toys, novelties and coins.*

> QUOTATIONS
> A "new thinker", when studied closely, is merely a man who does not know what other people have thought
> [F.M. Colby]

novice NOUN **= beginner**, pupil, amateur, newcomer, trainee, apprentice, learner, neophyte, tyro, probationer, proselyte: *I'm a novice at these things. You're the professional.* **OPPOSITE:** expert

now ADVERB **1 = nowadays**, at the moment, these days: *Beef now costs over 30 roubles a pound.* **2 = immediately**, presently *(Scot. & U.S.)*, promptly, instantly, at once, straightaway: *Please tell him I need to talk to him now.*
now and then *or* **again = occasionally**, sometimes, at times, from time to time, on and off, on occasion, once in a while, intermittently, infrequently, sporadically: *Now and then he would pay us a brief visit.*

nowadays ADVERB **= now**, today, at the moment, these days, in this day and age

noxious ADJECTIVE **= harmful**, deadly, poisonous, unhealthy, hurtful, pernicious, injurious, unwholesome, noisome, pestilential, insalubrious, foul **OPPOSITE:** harmless

nuance NOUN **= subtlety**, degree, distinction, graduation, refinement, nicety, gradation

nub NOUN **= gist**, point, heart, core, essence, nucleus, kernel, crux, pith

nubile ADJECTIVE **= attractive**, sexy *(informal)*, desirable, ripe *(informal)*, marriageable

nucleus NOUN **= centre**, heart, focus, basis, core, pivot, kernel, nub

nude ADJECTIVE **= naked**, stripped, exposed, bare, uncovered, undressed, stark-naked, in the raw *(informal)*, disrobed, starkers *(informal)*, unclothed, in the buff *(informal)*, au naturel *(French)*, in the altogether *(informal)*, buck naked *(slang)*, unclad, undraped, in your birthday suit *(informal)*, scuddy *(slang)*, without a stitch on *(informal)*, in the bare scud *(slang)*, naked as the day you were born *(informal)* **OPPOSITE:** dressed

nudge VERB **1 = push**, touch, dig, jog, prod, elbow, shove, poke: *'Stop it,' he said, and nudged me in the ribs.* **2 = prompt**, influence, urge, persuade, spur, prod, coax, prevail upon: *Bit by bit Bob nudged Fritz into selling his controlling interest.*
▷ NOUN **1 = push**, touch, dig, elbow, bump, shove, poke, jog, prod: *She slipped her arm under his and gave him a nudge.* **2 = prompting**, push, encouragement, prod: *The challenge appealed to him. All he needed was a little nudge.*

nudity NOUN **= nakedness**, undress, nudism, bareness, deshabille

nugget NOUN **= lump**, piece, mass, chunk, clump, hunk

nuisance NOUN **= trouble**, problem, trial, bore, drag *(informal)*, bother, plague, pest, irritation, hassle *(informal)*, inconvenience, annoyance, pain *(informal)*, pain in the neck *(informal)*, pain in the backside *(informal)*, pain in the butt *(informal)* **OPPOSITE:** benefit

n

null ADJECTIVE
null and void = invalid, useless, void, worthless, ineffectual, valueless, inoperative

nullify VERB **1 = invalidate**, quash, revoke, render null and void, abolish, void, repeal, rescind, annul, abrogate **OPPOSITE:** validate **2 = cancel out**, counteract, negate, neutralize, obviate, countervail, bring to naught

numb ADJECTIVE **1 = unfeeling**, dead, frozen, paralysed, insensitive, deadened, immobilized, torpid, insensible: *His legs felt numb and his toes ached.* **OPPOSITE:** sensitive **2 = stupefied**, deadened, unfeeling, insensible: *The mother, numb with grief, had trouble speaking.*
▷ VERB **1 = stun**, knock out, paralyse, daze, stupefy: *For a while the shock of his letter numbed her.* **2 = deaden**, freeze, dull, paralyse, immobilize, benumb: *The cold numbed my fingers.*

number NOUN **1 = numeral**, figure, character, digit, integer: *None of the doors have numbers on them.* **2 = amount**, quantity, collection, total, count, sum, aggregate: *I have had an enormous number of letters from concerned parents.* **OPPOSITE:** shortage **3 = crowd**, horde, multitude, throng: *People turned out to vote in huge numbers.* **4 = group**, company, set, band, crowd, gang, coterie: *We had a stag night for one of our number who had decided to get married.* **5 = issue**, copy, edition, imprint, printing: *an article which appeared in the summer number of the magazine*
▷ VERB **1 = amount to**, come to, total, add up to: *They told me that their village numbered 100 or so.* **2 = calculate**, account, reckon, compute, enumerate: *One widely cited report numbered the dead at over 10,000.* **OPPOSITE:** guess **3 = include**, count: *He numbered several Americans among his friends.*

numbered ADJECTIVE **1 = reckoned**, totalled, counted: *The Liberian army is officially numbered at eight thousand strong.* **2 = limited**, restricted, limited in number: *Her days as leader are numbered.*

numbness NOUN **1 = deadness**, paralysis, insensitivity, dullness, torpor, insensibility: *I have recently been suffering from numbness in my fingers and toes.* **2 = torpor**, deadness, dullness, stupefaction: *She swung from emotional numbness to overwhelming fear and back again.*

numeral NOUN **= number**, figure, digit, character, symbol, cipher, integer

numerous ADJECTIVE **= many**, several, countless, lots, abundant, plentiful, innumerable, copious, manifold, umpteen *(informal)*, profuse, thick on the ground **OPPOSITE:** few

nuptial ADJECTIVE **= marital**, wedding, wedded, bridal, matrimonial, conjugal, connubial, hymeneal *(poetic)*

nuptials PLURAL NOUN *(sometimes singular)* **= wedding**, marriage, matrimony, espousal *(archaic)*

nurse VERB **1 = look after**, treat, tend, care for, take care of, minister to: *All the years he was sick my mother had nursed him.* **2 = harbour**, have, maintain, preserve, entertain, cherish, keep alive: *He nursed an ambition to lead his own orchestra.* **3 = breast-feed**, feed, nurture, nourish, suckle, wet-nurse: *She did not have enough milk to nurse the infant.*

nursery NOUN **= crèche**, kindergarten, playgroup, play-centre *(N.Z.)*

nurture NOUN **= upbringing**, training, education, instruction, rearing, development: *The human organism learns partly by nature, partly by nurture.*
▷ VERB **= bring up**, raise, look after, rear, care for, develop: *Parents want to know the best way to nurture and raise their children to adulthood.* **OPPOSITE:** neglect

nut NOUN **1 = kernel**, stone, seed, pip: *Nuts are a good source of vitamin E.* **2 = madman**, eccentric, flake *(slang, chiefly U.S.)*, psycho *(slang)*, crank *(informal)*, lunatic, maniac, loony *(slang)*, nutter *(Brit. slang)*, oddball *(informal)*, crackpot *(informal)*, wacko *(slang)*, nutcase *(slang)*, headcase *(informal)*, crazy *(informal)*: *Some nut with a gun walked in and just opened fire on the diners.* **3 = head**, skull, noggin: *He took a bottle and smashed me over the nut.*

nutrition NOUN **= food**, nourishment, sustenance, nutriment

nutritious ADJECTIVE **= nourishing**, beneficial, wholesome, healthful, health-giving, nutritive

nuts ADJECTIVE **= insane**, mad, crazy *(informal)*, bananas *(slang)*, barking *(slang)*, eccentric, batty *(slang)*, psycho *(slang)*, irrational, loony *(slang)*, demented, nutty *(slang)*, deranged, loopy *(informal)*, out to lunch *(informal)*, barking mad *(slang)*, gonzo *(slang)*, doolally *(slang)*, off your trolley *(slang)*, up the pole *(informal)*, as daft as a brush *(informal, chiefly Brit.)*, not the full shilling *(informal)*, wacko or whacko *(informal)*, off the air *(Austral. slang)*
nuts and bolts = essentials, basics, fundamentals, nitty-gritty *(informal)*, practicalities, ins and outs, details: *Social skills are the nuts and bolts of social interaction.*

nuzzle VERB **= snuggle**, cuddle, nudge, burrow, nestle

nymph NOUN **1 = sylph**, dryad, naiad, hamadryad, Oceanid *(Greek myth)*, oread: *In the depths of a river, the three water nymphs – the Rhinemaidens – play and sing.* **2 = girl**, lass, maiden, maid, damsel: *They had one daughter, an exquisite nymph named Jacqueline.*

Oo

oasis NOUN 1 = **watering hole**: *The province was largely a wasteland with an occasional oasis.* 2 = **haven**, retreat, refuge, sanctuary, island, resting place, sanctum: *an oasis of peace in a troubled world*

oath NOUN 1 = **promise**, bond, pledge, vow, word, compact, covenant, affirmation, sworn statement, avowal, word of honour: *a solemn oath by members to help each other* 2 = **swear word**, curse, obscenity, blasphemy, expletive, four-letter word, cuss *(informal)*, profanity, strong language, imprecation, malediction: *Weller let out a foul oath and hurled himself upon him.*

> QUOTATIONS
> He who cheats with an oath acknowledges that he is afraid of his enemy, but that he thinks little of God
> [Plutarch *Lives: Lysander*]
>
> Oaths are but words, and words but wind
> [Samuel Butler *Hudibras*]
>
> Let your yea be yea; and your nay, nay
> [*Bible: James*]

obedience NOUN = **compliance**, yielding, submission, respect, conformity, reverence, deference, observance, subservience, submissiveness, docility, complaisance, tractability, dutifulness, conformability **OPPOSITE:** disobedience

> QUOTATIONS
> They who know the least obey the best
> [George Farquhar]

obedient ADJECTIVE = **submissive**, yielding, compliant, under control, respectful, law-abiding, well-trained, amenable, docile, dutiful, subservient, deferential, tractable, acquiescent, biddable, accommodating, passive, meek, ingratiating, malleable, pliant, unresisting, bootlicking *(informal)*, obeisant, duteous **OPPOSITE:** disobedient

obese ADJECTIVE = **fat**, overweight, heavy, solid, gross, plump, stout, fleshy, beefy *(informal)*, tubby, portly, outsize, roly-poly, rotund, podgy, corpulent, elephantine, paunchy, well-upholstered *(informal)*, Falstaffian **OPPOSITE:** thin

obesity *or* **obeseness** NOUN = **fatness**, flab, heaviness, a weight problem, grossness, corpulence, beef *(informal)*, embonpoint *(French)*, rotundity, fleshiness, stoutness, portliness, bulkiness, podginess, tubbiness **OPPOSITE:** thinness

obey VERB 1 = **submit to**, surrender (to), give way to, succumb to, bow to, give in to, yield to, serve, cave in to *(informal)*, take orders from, do what you are told by: *Cissie obeyed her mother without question.* **OPPOSITE:** disobey 2 = **submit**, yield, surrender, give in, give way, succumb, cave in, toe the line, knuckle under *(informal)*, do what is expected, come to heel, get into line: *If you love me, you will obey.* 3 = **carry out**, follow, perform, respond to, implement, fulfil, execute, discharge, act upon, carry through: *The commander refused to obey an order.* **OPPOSITE:** disregard 4 = **abide by**, keep, follow, comply with, observe, mind, embrace, hold to, heed, conform to, keep to, adhere to, be ruled by: *Most people obey the law.*

object[1] NOUN 1 = **thing**, article, device, body, item, implement, entity, gadget, contrivance: *an object the shape of a coconut* 2 = **purpose**, aim, end, point, plan, idea, reason, goal, design, target, principle, function, intention, objective, intent, motive, end in view, end purpose, the why and wherefore: *The object of the exercise is to raise money for charity.* 3 = **target**, victim, focus, butt, recipient: *She was an object of pity among her friends.*

object[2] VERB 1 *(often with* **to***)* = **protest against**, oppose, say no to, kick against *(informal)*, argue against, draw the line at, take exception to, raise objections to, cry out against, complain against, take up the cudgels against, expostulate against: *A lot of people objected to the plan.* **OPPOSITE:** accept 2 = **disagree**, demur, remonstrate, expostulate, express disapproval: *We objected strongly.* **OPPOSITE:** agree

objection NOUN = **protest**, opposition, complaint, doubt, exception, dissent, outcry, censure, disapproval, niggle *(informal)*, protestation, scruple, demur, formal complaint, counter-argument, cavil, remonstrance, demurral **OPPOSITE:** agreement

> QUOTATIONS
> A technical objection is the first refuge of a scoundrel
> [Heywood Broun]

objectionable ADJECTIVE = **offensive**, annoying, irritating, unacceptable, unpleasant, rude, intolerable, undesirable, distasteful, obnoxious, deplorable, displeasing, unseemly, disagreeable, repugnant, abhorrent, beyond the pale, insufferable, detestable, discourteous, uncivil, unmannerly, exceptionable, dislikable *or* dislikeable **OPPOSITE:** pleasant

objective ADJECTIVE 1 = **factual**, real, circumstantial: *He has no objective evidence to support his claim.* 2 = **unbiased**, detached, just, fair, judicial, open-minded, equitable, impartial, impersonal, disinterested, even-handed, dispassionate, unemotional, uninvolved, unprejudiced, uncoloured: *I would like your objective opinion on this.* **OPPOSITE:** subjective
▷ NOUN = **purpose**, aim, goal, end, plan, hope, idea, design, target, wish, scheme, desire, object, intention, ambition, aspiration, Holy Grail *(informal)*, end in view, why and wherefore: *His objective was to play golf and win.*

objectively ADVERB = **impartially**, neutrally, fairly, justly, without prejudice, dispassionately, with an open mind, equitably, without fear or favour, even-handedly, without bias, disinterestedly, with objectivity *or* impartiality

objectivity NOUN = **impartiality**, detachment, neutrality, equity, fairness, disinterest, open-mindedness, even-handedness, impersonality, disinterestedness, dispassion, nonpartisanship, lack of bias, equitableness **OPPOSITE:** subjectivity

obligation NOUN 1 = **duty**, compulsion: *Students usually feel an obligation to attend lectures.* 2 = **task**, job, duty, work, calling, business, charge, role, function, mission, province, assignment, pigeon *(informal)*, chore: *I feel that's my obligation, to do whatever is possible.* 3 = **responsibility**, duty, liability, accountability, culpability, answerability, accountableness: *I have an ethical and moral obligation to my client.*

obligatory ADJECTIVE 1 = **compulsory**, required, necessary, essential, binding, enforced, mandatory, imperative, unavoidable, requisite, coercive, de rigueur *(French)*: *Third-party insurance is obligatory when driving in Italy.* **OPPOSITE:** optional 2 = **customary**, regular, usual, popular, normal, familiar, conventional, fashionable, bog-standard *(Brit. & Irish slang)*: *This hotel has every facility, including the obligatory swimming-pool.*

oblige VERB 1 = **compel**, make, force, require, bind, railroad *(informal)*,

O

constrain, necessitate, coerce, impel, dragoon, obligate: *This decree obliges unions to delay strikes.* **2 = help**, assist, serve, benefit, please, favour, humour, accommodate, indulge, gratify, do someone a service, put yourself out for, do (someone) a favour *or* a kindness, meet the wants *or* needs of: *He is always ready to oblige journalists with information.* **OPPOSITE:** bother

obliged ADJECTIVE **1 = forced**, required, bound, compelled, obligated, duty-bound, under an obligation, under compulsion, without any option: *I was obliged to answer their questions.* **2 = grateful**, in (someone's) debt, thankful, indebted, appreciative, beholden: *I am extremely obliged to you.*

obliging ADJECTIVE **= accommodating**, kind, helpful, willing, civil, friendly, polite, cooperative, agreeable, amiable, courteous, considerate, hospitable, unselfish, good-natured, eager to please, complaisant **OPPOSITE:** unhelpful

oblique ADJECTIVE **1 = indirect**, implied, roundabout, backhanded, evasive, elliptical, circuitous, circumlocutory, inexplicit, periphrastic: *It was an oblique reference to his time in prison.* **OPPOSITE:** direct **2 = slanting**, angled, sloped, sloping, inclined, tilted, tilting, slanted, diagonal, at an angle, asymmetrical, canted, aslant, slantwise, atilt, cater-cornered *(U.S. informal)*: *The mountain ridge runs at an oblique angle to the coastline.* **3 = sidelong**, sideways, covert, indirect, furtive, surreptitious: *She gave him an oblique glance.*

obliquely ADVERB **1 = indirectly**, evasively, not in so many words, circuitously, in a roundabout manner *or* way: *He referred obliquely to a sordid event in her past.* **2 = at an angle**, sideways, diagonally, sidelong, aslant, slantwise, aslope: *The muscle runs obliquely downwards inside the abdominal cavity.*

obliterate VERB **1 = destroy**, eliminate, devastate, waste, wreck, wipe out, demolish, ravage, eradicate, desolate, annihilate, put paid to, raze, blow to bits, extirpate, blow sky-high, destroy root and branch, kennet *(Austral. slang)*, jeff *(Austral. slang)*, wipe from *or* off the face of the earth: *Whole villages were obliterated by the fire.* **OPPOSITE:** create **2 = eradicate**, remove, eliminate, cancel, get rid of, wipe out, erase, excise, delete, extinguish, root out, efface, blot out, expunge, extirpate: *He drank to obliterate the memory of what had occurred.*

oblivion NOUN **= neglect**, anonymity, insignificance, obscurity, limbo, nothingness, unimportance: *Most of these performers will fail and sink into oblivion.*

oblivious ADJECTIVE *(usually with* **of** *or* **to***)* **= unaware**, unconscious, ignorant, regardless, careless, negligent, blind to, unaffected by, impervious to, forgetful, deaf to, unconcerned about, neglectful, heedless, inattentive, insensible, unmindful, unobservant, disregardful, incognizant **OPPOSITE:** aware

> **USAGE**
> It was formerly considered incorrect to use *oblivious* and *unaware* as synonyms, but this use is now acceptable. When employed with this meaning, *oblivious* should be followed either by *to* or *of*, *to* being much the commoner.

obnoxious ADJECTIVE **= loathsome**, offensive, nasty, foul, disgusting, unpleasant, revolting, obscene, sickening, vile, horrid, repellent, repulsive, objectionable, disagreeable, nauseating, odious, hateful, repugnant, reprehensible, abhorrent, abominable, insufferable, execrable, detestable, hateable, dislikable *or* dislikeable, yucky *or* yukky *(slang)*, yucko *(Austral. slang)* **OPPOSITE:** pleasant

obscene ADJECTIVE **1 = indecent**, dirty, offensive, gross, foul, coarse, filthy, vile, improper, immoral, pornographic, suggestive, blue, loose, shameless, lewd, depraved, X-rated *(informal)*, bawdy, salacious, prurient, impure, lascivious, smutty, ribald, unwholesome, scabrous, immodest, licentious, indelicate, unchaste: *I'm no prude, but I think these photos are obscene.* **OPPOSITE:** decent **2 = offensive**, shocking, evil, disgusting, outrageous, revolting, sickening, vile, wicked, repellent, atrocious, obnoxious, heinous, nauseating, odious, loathsome, abominable, detestable: *It was obscene to spend millions producing unwanted food.*

obscenity NOUN **1 = indecency**, pornography, impurity, impropriety, vulgarity, smut, prurience, coarseness, crudity, licentiousness, foulness, outrageousness, blueness, immodesty, suggestiveness, lewdness, dirtiness, grossness, vileness, filthiness, bawdiness, unseemliness, indelicacy, smuttiness, salacity: *He justified the use of obscenity on the grounds that it was art.* **OPPOSITE:** decency **2 = swear word**, curse, oath, expletive, four-letter word, cuss *(informal)*, profanity, vulgarism: *They shouted obscenities at us as we passed.*

obscure ADJECTIVE **1 = unknown**, minor, little-known, humble, unfamiliar, out-of-the-way, unseen, lowly, unimportant, unheard-of, unsung, nameless, undistinguished, inconspicuous, unnoted, unhonoured, unrenowned: *The hymn was written by an obscure Greek composer.* **OPPOSITE:** famous **2 = abstruse**, involved, complex, confusing, puzzling, subtle, mysterious, deep, vague, unclear, doubtful, mystical, intricate, ambiguous, enigmatic, esoteric, perplexing, occult, opaque, incomprehensible, arcane, cryptic, unfathomable, recondite, clear as mud *(informal)*: *The contract is written in obscure language.* **OPPOSITE:** straightforward **3 = unclear**, hidden, uncertain, confused, mysterious, concealed, doubtful, indefinite, indeterminate: *The word is of obscure origin.* **OPPOSITE:** well-known **4 = indistinct**, vague, blurred, dark, clouded, faint, dim, gloomy, veiled, murky, fuzzy, shadowy, cloudy, misty, hazy, indistinguishable, indeterminate, dusky, undefined, out of focus, ill-defined, obfuscated, indiscernible, tenebrous: *The hills were just an obscure shape in the mist.* **OPPOSITE:** clear
▷ VERB **1 = obstruct**, hinder, block out: *Trees obscured his vision.* **2 = hide**, cover (up), screen, mask, disguise, conceal, veil, cloak, shroud, camouflage, envelop, encase, enshroud: *The building is almost completely obscured by a huge banner.* **OPPOSITE:** expose

obscurity NOUN **1 = insignificance**, oblivion, unimportance, non-recognition, inconsequence, lowliness, inconspicuousness, namelessness, ingloriousness: *His later life was spent in obscurity and loneliness.* **2 = vagueness**, complexity, ambiguity, intricacy, incomprehensibility, inexactitude, woolliness, abstruseness, impreciseness, impenetrableness, reconditeness, lack of preciseness: *Hunt was irritated by the obscurity of his reply.* **OPPOSITE:** clarity **3 = darkness**, dark, shadows, shade, gloom, haze, blackness, murk, dimness, murkiness, haziness, duskiness, shadiness, shadowiness, indistinctness: *the vast branches vanished into deep indigo obscurity above my head*

observable ADJECTIVE **= noticeable**, clear, obvious, open, striking, apparent, visible, patent, evident, distinct, manifest, blatant, conspicuous, unmistakable, discernible, salient, recognizable, detectable, perceptible, appreciable, perceivable

observance NOUN **1** *(with* **of***)* **= carrying out of**, attention to, performance of, respect for, notice of, honouring of, observation of, compliance with, adherence to, fulfilment of, discharge of, obedience to, keeping of, heeding of, conformity to: *Councils should ensure strict observance of laws.* **OPPOSITE:** disregard for **2 = ceremony**, rite, procedure, service, form, act, practice, tradition, celebration, custom, ritual, formality, ceremonial, ordinance, liturgy:

Novelists part 2

Ursula Le Guin *(U.S.)*
Mikhail Yurievich Lermontov *(Russian)*
Doris Lessing *(Rhodesian)*
Primo Levi *(Italian)*
(Harry) Sinclair Lewis *(U.S.)*
Penelope Lively *(English)*
David Lodge *(English)*
Jack London *(U.S.)*
Alison Lurie *(U.S.)*
Carson McCullers *(U.S.)*
George MacDonald *(Scottish)*
Ian McEwan *(English)*
William McIlvanney *(Scottish)*
Henry MacKenzie *(Scottish)*
Bernard McLaverty *(Irish)*
Alistair MacLean *(Scottish)*
Naguib Mahfouz *(Egyptian)*
Norman Mailer *(U.S.)*
Bernard Malamud *(U.S.)*
David Malouf *(Australian)*
Thomas Mann *(German)*
Kamala Markandaya *(Indian)*
Ngaio Marsh *(New Zealand)*
Allan Massie *(Scottish)*
Somerset Maugham *(English)*
Guy de Maupassant *(French)*
Francois Mauriac *(French)*
Herman Melville *(U.S.)*
George Meredith *(English)*
James A Michener *(U.S.)*
Henry Miller *(U.S.)*
Yukio Mishima *(Japanese)*
Margaret Mitchell *(U.S.)*
Naomi Mitchison *(Scottish)*
Brian Moore *(Irish-Canadian)*
Toni Morrison *(U.S.)*
John Mortimer *(English)*
Penelope Mortimer *(Welsh)*
Iris Murdoch *(Irish)*
Vladimir Vladimirovich Nabokov *(Russian-U.S.)*
V S Naipaul *(Trinidadian)*
Ngugi wa Thiong'o *(Kenyan)*
Joyce Carol Oates *(U.S.)*
Edna O'Brien *(Irish)*
Flann O'Brien *(Irish)*
Kenzaburo Oë *(Japanese)*
Liam O'Flaherty *(Irish)*
John O'Hara *(U.S.)*
Ben Okri *(Nigerian)*
Margaret Oliphant *(Scottish)*
Michael Ondaatje *(Canadian)*
Baroness Emmuska Orczy *(Hungarian-British)*
George Orwell *(English)*
Cynthia Ozick *(U.S.)*
Boris Leonidovich Pasternak *(Russian)*
Allan Paton *(South African)*
Harold Porter *(Australian)*
Katherine Anne Porter *(U.S.)*
Terry Pratchett *(English)*
J B Priestley *(English)*
V S Pritchett *(English)*
E Annie Proulx *(U.S.)*
Marcel Proust *(French)*
Mario Puzo *(U.S.)*
Thomas Pynchon *(U.S.)*
Ellery Queen *(U.S.)*
Ann Radcliffe *(English)*
Raja Rao *(Indian)*
Frederic Raphael *(U.S.)*
Erich Maria Remarque *(German)*
Ruth Rendell *(English)*
Mordecai Richler *(Canadian)*
Harold Robbins *(U.S.)*
Henry Roth *(U.S.)*
(Ahmed) Salman Rushdie *(Indian-British)*
Vita Sackville-West *(English)*
Antoine de Saint-Exupéry *(French)*
J D Salinger *(U.S.)*
George Sand *(French)*
William Saroyan *(U.S.)*
Jean-Paul Sartre *(French)*
Dorothy L Sayers *(English)*
Olive Schreiner *(South African)*
Walter Scott *(Scottish)*
Hubert Selby Jr. *(U.S.)*
Mary Shelley *(English)*
Carol Shields *(Canadian-American)*
Mikhail Alexandrovich Sholokhov *(Russian)*
Nevil Shute *(Anglo-Austrian)*
Georges Simenon *(Belgian)*
Claude Simon *(French)*
Isaac Bashevis Singer *(U.S.)*
Iain Crichton Smith *(Scottish)*
Zadie Smith *(British)*
Tobias George Smollett *(Scottish)*
Alexander Isayevich Solzhenitsyn *(Russian)*
Muriel Spark *(Scottish)*
Howard Spring *(Welsh)*
C K Stead *(New Zealand)*
Gertrude Stein *(U.S.)*
John Steinbeck *(U.S.)*
Stendhal *(French)*
Laurence Sterne *(Irish-British)*
Robert Louis Stevenson *(Scottish)*
J I M Stewart *(Scottish)*
Mary Stewart *(English)*
Bram Stoker *(Irish)*
Robert Stone *(U.S.)*
Harriet Elizabeth Beecher Stowe *(U.S.)*
William Styron *(U.S.)*
Patrick Süskind *(German)*
Graham Swift *(English)*
Jonathan Swift *(Irish)*
William Makepeace Thackeray *(English)*
Paul Theroux *(U.S.)*
J(ohn) R(onald) R(euel) Tolkien *(English)*
Leo Tolstoy *(Russian)*
John Kennedy Toole *(U.S.)*
Nigel Tranter *(Scottish)*
Rose Tremain *(English)*
William Trevor *(Irish)*
Anthony Trollope *(English)*
Joanna Trollope *(English)*
Ivan Sergeyevich Turgenev *(Russian)*
Amos Tutuola *(Nigerian)*
Mark Twain *(U.S.)*
Anne Tyler *(U.S.)*
John Updike *(U.S.)*
Leon Uris *(U.S.)*
Laurens Van der Post *(South African)*
Mario Vargos Llosa *(Peruvian)*
Jules Verne *(French)*
Gore Vidal *(U.S.)*
Voltaire *(French)*
Kurt Vonnegut *(U.S.)*
Alice Walker *(U.S.)*
Robert Penn Warren *(U.S.)*
Keith Waterhouse *(English)*
Evelyn Waugh *(English)*
Fay Weldon *(English)*
H G Wells *(English)*
Irvine Welsh *(Scottish)*
Eudora Welty *(U.S.)*
Mary Wesley *(English)*
Morris West *(Australian)*
Rebecca West *(Irish)*
Edith Wharton *(U.S.)*
Oscar Wilde *(Irish)*
Thornton Wilder *(U.S.)*
Michael Wilding *(Australian)*
Jeanette Winterson *(English)*
P(elham) G(renville) Wodehouse *(English-U.S.)*
Thomas Clayton Wolfe *(U.S.)*
Tom Wolfe *(U.S.)*
Tobias Wolff *(U.S.)*
Virginia Woolf *(English)*
Herman Wouk *(U.S.)*
Richard Nathaniel Wright *(U.S.)*
Frank Yerby *(U.S.)*
Marguerite Yourcenar *(French)*
Evgeny Ivanovich Zamyatin *(Russian)*
Emile Zola *(French)*

Numerous religious observances set the rhythm of the day.

observant ADJECTIVE **1 = attentive**, quick, alert, perceptive, concentrating, careful, vigilant, mindful, watchful, wide-awake, sharp-eyed, eagle-eyed, keen-eyed, on your toes, heedful: *An observant doctor can detect depression from expression and posture.* **OPPOSITE:** unobservant **2 = devout**, godly, holy, orthodox, pious, obedient, reverent: *This is a profoundly observant Islamic country.*

observation NOUN **1 = watching**, study, survey, review, notice, investigation, monitoring, attention, consideration, examination, inspection, scrutiny, surveillance, contemplation, cognition, perusal: *careful observation of the movement of the planets* **2 = comment**, finding, thought, note, statement, opinion, remark, explanation, reflection, exposition, utterance, pronouncement, annotation, elucidation, obiter dictum *(Latin)*: *This book contains observations about the nature of addiction.* **3 = remark**, thought, comment, statement, opinion, reflection, assertion, utterance, animadversion: *Is that a criticism or just an observation?* **4** *(with* **of***)* **= observance of**, attention to, compliance with, notice of, honouring of, adherence to, fulfilment of, discharge of, heeding of, carrying out of: *strict observation of oil quotas*

observe VERB **1 = watch**, study, view, look at, note, check, regard, survey, monitor, contemplate, check out *(informal)*, look on, keep an eye on *(informal)*, gaze at, pay attention to, keep track of, scrutinize, keep tabs on *(informal)*, recce *(slang)*, keep under observation, watch like a hawk, take a dekko at *(Brit. slang)*: *He studies and observes the behaviour of babies.* **2 = notice**, see, note, mark, discover, spot, regard, witness, clock *(Brit. slang)*, distinguish, perceive, detect, discern, behold *(archaic, literary)*, eye, eyeball *(slang)*, peer at, espy, get a load of *(informal)*: *In 1664 Hooke observed a reddish spot on the surface of the planet.* **3 = remark**, say, comment, state, note, reflect, mention, declare, opine, pass comment, animadvert: *'I like your hair that way,' he observed.* **4 = comply with**, keep, follow, mind, respect, perform, carry out, honour, fulfil, discharge, obey, heed, conform to, adhere to, abide by: *Forcing motorists to observe speed restrictions is difficult.* **OPPOSITE:** disregard

observer NOUN **1 = witness**, viewer, spectator, looker-on, watcher, onlooker, eyewitness, bystander, spotter, fly on the wall, beholder: *A casual observer would have assumed they were lovers.* **2 = commentator**, commenter, reporter, special correspondent: *Political observers believe there may be a general election soon.* **3 = monitor**, inspector, watchdog, supervisor, overseer, scrutineer: *A UN observer should attend the conference.*

> **QUOTATIONS**
> I am a camera with its shutter open, quite passive, recording, not thinking
> [Christopher Isherwood *Goodbye to Berlin*]

obsess VERB *(often with* **with** *or* **by***)* **= preoccupy**, dominate, grip, absorb, possess, consume, rule, haunt, plague, hound, torment, bedevil, monopolize, be on your mind, engross, prey on your mind, be uppermost in your thoughts

obsessed ADJECTIVE **= absorbed**, dominated, gripped, caught up, haunted, distracted, hung up *(slang)*, preoccupied, immersed, beset, in the grip, infatuated, fixated, having a one-track mind **OPPOSITE:** indifferent

obsession NOUN **= preoccupation**, thing *(informal)*, complex, enthusiasm, addiction, hang-up *(informal)*, mania, phobia, fetish, fixation, infatuation, ruling passion, pet subject, hobbyhorse, idée fixe *(French)*, bee in your bonnet *(informal)*

obsessive ADJECTIVE **= compulsive**, fixed, gripping, consuming, haunting, tormenting, irresistible, neurotic, besetting, uncontrollable, obsessional

obsolete ADJECTIVE **= outdated**, old, passé, ancient, antique, old-fashioned, dated, discarded, extinct, past it, out of date, archaic, disused, out of fashion, out, antiquated, anachronistic, outmoded, musty, old hat, behind the times, superannuated, antediluvian, outworn, démodé *(French)*, out of the ark *(informal)*, vieux jeu *(French)* **OPPOSITE:** up-to-date

obstacle NOUN **1 = obstruction**, block, barrier, hurdle, hazard, snag, impediment, blockage, hindrance: *She had to navigate her way round trolleys and other obstacles.* **2 = hindrance**, check, bar, block, difficulty, barrier, handicap, hurdle, hitch, drawback, snag, deterrent, uphill *(S. African)*, obstruction, stumbling block, impediment: *Overcrowding remains a large obstacle to improving conditions.* **OPPOSITE:** help

obstinacy NOUN **= stubbornness**, persistence, tenacity, perseverance, resolution, intransigence, firmness, single-mindedness, inflexibility, obduracy, doggedness, relentlessness, wilfulness, resoluteness, pig-headedness, pertinacity, tenaciousness, mulishness **OPPOSITE:** flexibility

> **QUOTATIONS**
> Obstinacy in a bad cause, is but constancy in a good
> [Thomas Browne *Religio Medici*]

obstinate ADJECTIVE **= stubborn**, dogged, determined, persistent, firm, perverse, intractable, inflexible, wilful, tenacious, recalcitrant, steadfast, unyielding, opinionated, intransigent, immovable, headstrong, unmanageable, cussed, strong-minded, unbending, obdurate, stiff-necked, unshakable, self-willed, refractory, pig-headed, bull-headed, mulish, contumacious, pertinacious **OPPOSITE:** flexible

obstruct VERB **1 = block**, close, bar, cut off, plug, choke, clog, barricade, shut off, stop up, bung up *(informal)*: *Lorries obstructed the road completely.* **2 = hold up**, stop, check, bar, block, prevent, arrest, restrict, interrupt, slow down, hamstring, interfere with, hamper, inhibit, clog, hinder, retard, impede, get in the way of, bring to a standstill, cumber: *Drivers who park illegally obstruct the flow of traffic.* **3 = impede**, prevent, frustrate, hold up, slow down, hamstring, interfere with, hamper, hold back, thwart, hinder, retard, get in the way of, trammel, cumber: *The authorities are obstructing the investigation.* **OPPOSITE:** help **4 = obscure**, screen, cut off, cover, hide, mask, shield: *She positioned herself so as not to obstruct his view.*

obstruction NOUN **1 = obstacle**, bar, block, difficulty, barrier, hazard, barricade, snag, impediment, hindrance: *drivers parking near his house and causing an obstruction* **2 = blockage**, stoppage, occlusion: *The boy was suffering from a bowel obstruction.* **3 = hindrance**, stop, check, bar, block, difficulty, barrier, restriction, handicap, obstacle, restraint, deterrent, stumbling block, impediment, trammel: *Americans viewed the army as an obstruction to legitimate economic development.* **OPPOSITE:** help

obstructive ADJECTIVE **= unhelpful**, difficult, awkward, blocking, delaying, contrary, stalling, inhibiting, restrictive, hindering, uncooperative, disobliging, unaccommodating **OPPOSITE:** helpful

obtain VERB **1 = get**, gain, acquire, land, net, pick up, bag, secure, get hold of, come by, procure, get your hands on, score *(slang)*, come into possession of: *Evans was trying to obtain a false passport.* **OPPOSITE:** lose **2 = achieve**, get, gain, realize, accomplish, attain: *The perfect body has always been difficult to obtain.* **3 = prevail**, hold, stand, exist, be the case, abound, predominate, be in force, be current, be prevalent: *The longer this situation obtains, the bigger the problems will be.*

obtainable ADJECTIVE **1 = available**, to be had, procurable: *This herb is obtainable from health food shops.* **2 = attainable**, accessible, achievable, at your fingertips, at your disposal, reachable, realizable, gettable, accomplishable: *That's new information that isn't obtainable by other means.*

obtuse ADJECTIVE **= stupid**, simple, slow, thick, dull, dim, dense, dumb *(informal)*, sluggish, retarded, simple-minded, dozy *(Brit. informal)*, witless, stolid, dopey *(informal)*, moronic, brainless, uncomprehending, cretinous, unintelligent, half-witted, slow on the uptake *(informal)*, braindead *(informal)*, dumb-ass *(informal)*, doltish, dead from the neck up *(informal)*, boneheaded *(slang)*, thickheaded, dull-witted, imperceptive, slow-witted, muttonheaded *(slang)*, thick as mince *(Scot. informal)*, woodenheaded *(informal)* **OPPOSITE:** clever

obviate VERB **= avert**, avoid, remove, prevent, counter, do away with, preclude, counteract, ward off, stave off, forestall, render unnecessary

obvious ADJECTIVE **= clear**, open, plain, apparent, visible, bold, patent, evident, distinct, pronounced, straightforward, explicit, manifest, transparent, noticeable, blatant, conspicuous, overt, unmistakable, palpable, unequivocal, undeniable, salient, recognizable, unambiguous, self-evident, indisputable, perceptible, much in evidence, unquestionable, open-and-shut, cut-and-dried *(informal)*, undisguised, incontrovertible, self-explanatory, unsubtle, unconcealed, clear as a bell, staring you in the face *(informal)*, right under your nose *(informal)*, sticking out a mile *(informal)*, plain as the nose on your face *(informal)*
OPPOSITE: unclear

obviously ADVERB **1 = clearly**, of course, certainly, needless to say, without doubt, assuredly: *There are obviously exceptions to this.* **2 = plainly**, patently, undoubtedly, evidently, manifestly, markedly, without doubt, unquestionably, undeniably, beyond doubt, palpably, indubitably, incontrovertibly, irrefutably, incontestably: *She's obviously cleverer than I am.*

occasion NOUN **1 = time**, moment, point, stage, incident, instance, occurrence, juncture: *I often think fondly of an occasion some years ago.*
2 = function, event, affair, do *(informal)*, happening, experience, gathering, celebration, occurrence, social occasion: *It will be a unique family occasion.* **3 = opportunity**, chance, time, opening, window: *It is always an occasion for setting out government policy.*
4 = reason, cause, call, ground(s), basis, excuse, incentive, motive, warrant, justification, provocation, inducement: *You had no occasion to speak to him like that.*
▷ VERB **= cause**, begin, produce, create, effect, lead to, inspire, result in, generate, prompt, provoke, induce, bring about, originate, evoke, give rise to, precipitate, elicit, incite, engender: *The incident occasioned a full-scale parliamentary row.*

occasional ADJECTIVE **= infrequent**, odd, rare, casual, irregular, sporadic, intermittent, few and far between, desultory, periodic
OPPOSITE: constant

occasionally ADVERB **= sometimes**, at times, from time to time, on and off, now and then, irregularly, on occasion, now and again, periodically, once in a while, every so often, at intervals, off and on, (every) now and then **OPPOSITE:** constantly

occult ADJECTIVE **= supernatural**, dark, magical, mysterious, psychic, mystical, mystic, unearthly, unnatural, esoteric, uncanny, arcane, paranormal, abstruse, recondite, preternatural, cabbalistic, supranatural: *organizations which campaign against paganism and occult practices*
the occult = magic, witchcraft, sorcery, wizardry, enchantment, occultism, black art, necromancy, theurgy: *his unhealthy fascination with the occult*

occultism NOUN **= black magic**, magic, witchcraft, wizardry, sorcery, the black arts, necromancy, diabolism, theurgy, supernaturalism

occupancy NOUN **= occupation**, use, residence, holding, term, possession, tenure, tenancy, habitation, inhabitancy

occupant NOUN **= occupier**, resident, tenant, user, holder, inmate, inhabitant, incumbent, dweller, denizen, addressee, lessee, indweller

occupation NOUN **1 = job**, work, calling, business, line (of work), office, trade, position, post, career, situation, activity, employment, craft, profession, pursuit, vocation, livelihood, walk of life: *I was looking for an occupation which would allow me to travel.* **2 = hobby**, pastime, diversion, relaxation, sideline, leisure pursuit, (leisure) activity: *Hang-gliding is a dangerous occupation.* **3 = invasion**, seizure, conquest, incursion, subjugation, foreign rule: *the deportation of Jews from Paris during the German occupation* **4 = occupancy**, use, residence, holding, control, possession, tenure, tenancy, habitation, inhabitancy: *She is seeking an order for 'sole use and occupation' of the house.*

occupied ADJECTIVE **1 = in use**, taken, full, engaged, unavailable: *three beds, two of which were occupied* **2 = inhabited**, peopled, lived-in, settled, tenanted: *The house was occupied by successive generations of farmers.*
OPPOSITE: uninhabited **3 = busy**, engaged, employed, working, active, tied up *(informal)*, engrossed, hard at work, in harness, hard at it *(informal)*, rushed off your feet: *I forgot about it because I was so occupied with other things.*

occupy VERB **1 = inhabit**, own, live in, stay in *(Scot.)*, be established in, dwell in, be in residence in, establish yourself in, ensconce yourself in, tenant, reside in, lodge in, take up residence in, make your home, abide in: *the couple who occupy the flat above mine* **OPPOSITE:** vacate **2 = invade**, take over, capture, seize, conquer, keep, hold, garrison, overrun, annex, take possession of, colonize: *Alexandretta had been occupied by the French in 1918.* **OPPOSITE:** withdraw
3 = hold, control, dominate, possess: *Men still occupy more positions of power than women.* **4 = take up**, consume, tie up, use up, monopolize, keep busy *or* occupied: *Her parliamentary career has occupied all of her time.* **5** *(often passive)* **= engage**, interest, involve, employ, busy, entertain, absorb, amuse, divert, preoccupy, immerse, hold the attention of, engross, keep busy *or* occupied: *I had other matters to occupy me that day.* **6 = fill**, take up, cover, fill up, utilize, pervade, permeate, extend over: *The tombs occupy two thirds of the church.*

occur VERB **1 = happen**, take place, come about, follow, result, chance, arise, turn up *(informal)*, come off *(informal)*, ensue, crop up *(informal)*, transpire *(informal)*, befall, materialize, come to pass *(archaic)*, betide, eventuate: *The deaths occurred when troops tried to disperse the demonstrators.* **2 = exist**, appear, be found, develop, obtain, turn up, be present, be met with, manifest itself, present itself, show itself: *The disease occurs throughout Africa.*
occur to someone = come to mind, strike someone, dawn on someone, come to someone, spring to mind, cross someone's mind, present itself to someone, enter someone's head, offer itself to someone, suggest itself to someone: *It didn't occur to me to check my insurance policy.*

USAGE
It is usually regarded as incorrect to talk of pre-arranged events *occurring* or *happening*. For this meaning a synonym such as *take place* would be more appropriate: *the wedding took place* (not *occurred* or *happened*) *in the afternoon.*

occurrence NOUN **1 = incident**, happening, event, fact, matter, affair, proceeding, circumstance, episode, adventure, phenomenon, transaction: *Traffic jams are now a daily occurrence.* **2 = existence**, instance, appearance, manifestation, materialization: *the greatest occurrence of heart disease in the over-65s*

odd ADJECTIVE **1 = peculiar**, strange, unusual, different, funny, extraordinary, bizarre, weird, exceptional, eccentric, abnormal, queer, rum *(Brit. slang)*, deviant, unconventional, far-out *(slang)*, quaint, kinky *(informal)*, off-the-wall *(slang)*, outlandish, whimsical, oddball *(informal)*, out of the ordinary, offbeat, left-field *(informal)*, freakish, freaky *(slang)*, wacko *(slang)*, outré, daggy *(Austral. & N.Z. informal)*: *He'd* *always been odd, but not to this extent.* **2 = unusual**, different, strange, rare, funny *(slang)*, extraordinary, remarkable, bizarre, fantastic, curious, weird, exceptional, peculiar, abnormal, queer, irregular, uncommon, singular, uncanny, outlandish, out of the ordinary, freakish, atypical, freaky: *Something odd began to happen.* **OPPOSITE:** normal **3 = occasional**, various, varied, random, casual, seasonal, irregular, periodic, miscellaneous, sundry, incidental, intermittent, infrequent: *He did various odd jobs around the place.* **OPPOSITE:** regular **4 = spare**, remaining, extra, surplus, single, lone, solitary, uneven, leftover, unmatched, unpaired: *I found an odd sock in the washing machine.* **OPPOSITE:** matched

odd man *or* **odd one out = misfit**, exception, outsider, freak, eccentric, maverick, oddball *(informal)*, nonconformist, fish out of water *(informal)*, square peg in a round hole *(informal)*: *All my family smoke apart from me – I'm the odd man out.*

oddity NOUN **1 = misfit**, eccentric, crank *(informal)*, nut *(slang)*, maverick, flake *(slang, chiefly U.S.)*, oddball *(informal)*, loose cannon, nonconformist, odd man out, wacko *(slang)*, screwball *(slang, chiefly U.S. & Canad.)*, card *(informal)*, fish out of water, square peg (in a round hole) *(informal)*, odd fish *(Brit. informal)*, odd bird *(informal)*, rara avis *(Latin)*, weirdo or weirdie *(informal)*: *He's a bit of an oddity, but quite harmless.* **2 = strangeness**, abnormality, peculiarity, eccentricity, weirdness, singularity, incongruity, oddness, unconventionality, queerness, unnaturalness, bizarreness, freakishness, extraordinariness, outlandishness: *I was struck by the oddity of this question.* **3 = irregularity**, phenomenon, anomaly, freak, abnormality, rarity, quirk, eccentricity, kink, peculiarity, idiosyncrasy, singularity, unorthodoxy, unconventionality: *the oddities of the Welsh legal system*

odds PLURAL NOUN **= probability**, chances, likelihood: *What are the odds of that happening?*

at odds 1 = in conflict, arguing, quarrelling, in opposition to, at loggerheads, in disagreement, at daggers drawn, on bad terms: *He was at odds with his neighbour.* **2 = at variance**, conflicting, contrary to, at odds, out of line, out of step, at sixes and sevens *(informal)*, not in keeping, out of harmony: *Her inexperience is at odds with the tale she tells.*

odds and ends = scraps, bits, pieces, remains, rubbish, fragments, litter, debris, shreds, remnants, bits and pieces, bric-a-brac, bits and bobs, oddments, odds and sods, leavings, miscellanea, sundry *or* miscellaneous items: *She packed her clothes and a few other odds and ends.*

odious ADJECTIVE **= offensive**, nasty, foul, disgusting, horrible, unpleasant, revolting, obscene, sickening, vile, horrid, repellent, unsavoury, obnoxious, unpalatable, repulsive, disagreeable, nauseating, hateful, repugnant, loathsome, abhorrent, abominable, execrable, detestable, yucky *or* yukky *(slang)*, yucko *(Austral. slang)*
OPPOSITE: delightful

odour *or (U.S.)* **odor** NOUN **1 = smell**, scent, perfume, fragrance, stink, bouquet, aroma, whiff, stench, pong *(Brit. informal)*, niff *(Brit. slang)*, redolence, malodour, fetor: *the faint odour of whisky on his breath*
2 = atmosphere, feeling, air, quality, spirit, tone, climate, flavour, aura, vibe *(slang)*: *a tantalising odour of scandal*

Odyssey NOUN *(often not cap.)* **= journey**, tour, trip, passage, quest, trek, expedition, voyage, crusade, excursion, pilgrimage, jaunt, peregrination

of PREPOSITION **= about**, on, concerning, regarding, with respect to, as regards

> USAGE
> *Of* is sometimes used instead of *have* in phrases such as *should have*, *could have*, and *might have*. This is because, when people are speaking, they often drop the *h* at the beginning of *have*, making the word's pronunciation very similar to that of *of*. Using *of* in this way is, however, regarded as nonstandard, and in writing it should definitely be avoided.

off ADVERB **1 = away**, out, apart, elsewhere, aside, hence, from here: *He went off on his own.* **2 = absent**, gone, unavailable, not present, inoperative, nonattendant: *She was off sick 27 days last year.*
▷ ADJECTIVE **1 = cancelled**, abandoned, postponed, shelved: *Today's game is off.* **2 = bad**, rotten, rancid, mouldy, high, turned, spoiled, sour, decayed, decomposed, putrid: *Food starts to smell when it goes off.* **3 = unacceptable**, poor, unsatisfactory, disappointing, inadequate, second-rate, shoddy, displeasing, below par, mortifying, substandard, disheartening: *Coming home drunk like that – it's a bit off, isn't it?*

off and on = occasionally, sometimes, at times, from time to time, on and off, now and then, irregularly, on occasion, now and again, periodically, once in a while, every so often, intermittently, at intervals, sporadically, every once in a while, (every) now and again: *We lived together, off and on, for two years.*

offbeat ADJECTIVE **= unusual**, odd, strange, novel, extraordinary, bizarre, weird, way-out *(informal)*, eccentric, queer, rum *(Brit. slang)*, uncommon, Bohemian, unconventional, far-out *(slang)*, idiosyncratic, kinky *(informal)*, off-the-wall *(slang)*, unorthodox, oddball *(informal)*, out of the ordinary, left-field *(informal)*, freaky *(slang)*, wacko *(slang)*, outré, daggy *(Austral. & N.Z. informal)* **OPPOSITE:** conventional

offence *or (U.S.)* **offense** NOUN **1 = crime**, wrong, sin, lapse, fault, violation, wrongdoing, trespass, felony, misdemeanour, delinquency, misdeed, transgression, peccadillo, unlawful act, breach of conduct: *It is a criminal offence to sell goods which are unsafe.* **2 = outrage**, shock, anger, trouble, bother, grief *(informal)*, resentment, irritation, hassle *(informal)*, wrath, indignation, annoyance, ire *(literary)*, displeasure, pique, aggravation, hard feelings, umbrage, vexation, wounded feelings: *The book might be published without creating offence.* **3 = insult**, injury, slight, hurt, harm, outrage, put-down *(slang)*, injustice, snub, affront, indignity, displeasure, rudeness, slap in the face *(informal)*, insolence: *His behaviour was an offence to his hosts.*

take offence = be offended, resent, be upset, be outraged, be put out *(informal)*, be miffed *(informal)*, be displeased, take umbrage, be disgruntled, be affronted, be piqued, take the needle *(informal)*, get riled, take the huff, go into a huff, be huffy: *You're very quick to take offence today.*

offend VERB **1 = distress**, upset, outrage, pain, wound, slight, provoke, insult, annoy, irritate, put down, dismay, snub, aggravate *(informal)*, gall, agitate, ruffle, disconcert, vex, affront, displease, rile, pique, give offence, hurt (someone's) feelings, nark *(Brit., Austral. & N.Z. slang)*, cut to the quick, miff *(informal)*, tread on (someone's) toes *(informal)*, put (someone's) nose out of joint, put (someone's) back up, disgruntle, get (someone's) goat *(slang)*, hack someone off *(informal)*: *He had no intention of offending the community.* **OPPOSITE:** please **2 = disgust**, revolt, turn (someone) off *(informal)*, put off, sicken, repel, repulse, nauseate, gross out *(U.S. slang)*, make (someone) sick, turn someone's stomach, be disagreeable to, fill with loathing: *The smell of cigar smoke offends me.* **3 = break the law**, sin, err, do wrong, fall, fall from grace, go astray: *alleged criminals who offend while on bail*

offended ADJECTIVE **= upset**, pained, hurt, bothered, disturbed, distressed, outraged, stung, put out *(informal)*, grieved, disgruntled, agitated, ruffled, resentful, affronted, miffed *(informal)*, displeased, in a huff, piqued, huffy, tooshie *(Austral. slang)*

offender NOUN **= criminal**, convict, con *(slang)*, crook, lag *(slang)*, villain, culprit, sinner, delinquent, felon, jailbird, wrongdoer, miscreant, malefactor, evildoer, transgressor, lawbreaker, perp *(U.S. & Canad. informal)*

offensive ADJECTIVE **1 = insulting**, rude, abusive, embarrassing, slighting, annoying, irritating, degrading, affronting, contemptuous, disparaging, displeasing, objectionable, disrespectful, scurrilous, detestable, discourteous, uncivil, unmannerly: *offensive remarks about minority groups* **OPPOSITE:** respectful **2 = disgusting**, gross, nasty, foul, unpleasant, revolting, stinking, sickening, vile, repellent, unsavoury, obnoxious, unpalatable, objectionable, disagreeable, nauseating, odious, repugnant, loathsome, abominable, grotty *(slang)*, detestable, noisome, yucky or yukky *(slang)*, festy *(Austral. slang)*, yucko *(Austral. slang)*: *the offensive smell of manure* **OPPOSITE:** pleasant **3 = attacking**, threatening, aggressive, striking, hostile, invading, combative: *The troops were in an offensive position.* **OPPOSITE:** defensive
▷ NOUN **= attack**, charge, campaign, strike, push *(informal)*, rush, assault, raid, drive, invasion, onslaught, foray, incursion: *The armed forces have launched an offensive to recapture lost ground.*

offer VERB **1 = present with**, give, hand, hold out to: *Rhys offered him an apple.* **2 = provide**, present, furnish, make available, afford, place at (someone's) disposal: *Western governments have offered aid.* **OPPOSITE:** withhold **3 = volunteer**, come forward, offer your services, be at (someone's) service: *Peter offered to help us.* **4 = propose**, suggest, advance, extend, submit, put forward, put forth: *They offered no suggestion as to how it might be done.* **5 = give**, show, bring, provide, render, impart: *His mother and sister rallied round offering comfort.* **6 = put up for sale**, sell, put on the market, put under the hammer: *The house is being offered at 1.5 million pounds.* **7 = bid**, submit, propose, extend, tender, proffer: *He offered a fair price for the land.*
▷ NOUN **1 = proposal**, suggestion, proposition, submission, attempt, endeavour, overture: *He has refused all offers of help.* **2 = bid**, tender, bidding price: *We've made an offer for the house.*

offering NOUN **1 = contribution**, gift, donation, present, subscription, hand-out, stipend, widow's mite: *funds from local church offerings* **2 = sacrifice**, tribute, libation, burnt offering, oblation *(in religious contexts)*: *a Shinto ritual in which offerings are made to the great Sun*

offhand ADJECTIVE **= casual**, informal, indifferent, careless, abrupt, cavalier, aloof, unconcerned, curt, uninterested, glib, cursory, couldn't-care-less, apathetic, perfunctory, blasé, brusque, take-it-or-leave-it *(informal)*, nonchalant, lackadaisical, unceremonious, offhanded: *Consumers found the attitude of its staff offhand.* **OPPOSITE:** attentive
▷ ADVERB **= off the cuff** *(informal)*, spontaneously, impromptu, just like that *(informal)*, ad lib, extempore, off the top of your head *(informal)*, without preparation, extemporaneously: *I couldn't tell you offhand how long he's worked here.*

office NOUN **1 = place of work**, workplace, base, workroom, place of business: *He had an office just big enough for a desk and chair.* **2 = branch**, department, division, section, wing, subdivision, subsection: *Downing Street's press office* **3 = post**, place, role, work, business, service, charge, situation, commission, station, responsibility, duty, function, employment, capacity, appointment, occupation: *the honour and dignity of the office of President*
▷ PLURAL NOUN **= support**, help, backing, aid, favour, assistance, intervention, recommendation, patronage, mediation, advocacy, auspices, aegis, moral support, intercession, espousal: *Thanks to his good offices, a home has been found for the birds.*

officer NOUN **1 = official**, executive, agent, representative, bureaucrat, public servant, appointee, dignitary, functionary, office-holder, office bearer: *a local education authority officer* **2 = police officer**, detective, PC, police constable, police man, police woman: *an officer in the West Midlands police force*

official ADJECTIVE **1 = authorized**, approved, formal, sanctioned, licensed, proper, endorsed, warranted, legitimate, authentic, ratified, certified, authoritative, accredited, bona fide, signed and sealed, ex officio, ex cathedra, straight from the horse's mouth *(informal)*: *An official announcement is expected later today.* **OPPOSITE:** unofficial **2 = formal**, prescribed, bureaucratic, ceremonial, solemn, ritualistic: *his official duties*
▷ NOUN **= officer**, executive, agent, representative, bureaucrat, public servant, appointee, dignitary, functionary, office-holder, office bearer: *a senior UN official*

officiate VERB **1 = preside**, conduct, celebrate: *Bishop Silvester officiated at the funeral.* **2 = superintend**, supervise, be in charge, run, control, serve, manage, direct, handle, chair, look after, overlook, oversee, preside, take charge, adjudicate, emcee *(informal)*: *He has been chosen to officiate at the cup final.*

offing NOUN
in the offing = imminent, coming, close, near, coming up, gathering, on the way, in the air, forthcoming, looming, brewing, hovering, impending, at hand, upcoming, on the cards, on the horizon, in the wings, in the pipeline, nigh *(archaic)*, in prospect, close at hand, fast-approaching, in the immediate future, just round the corner: *A general amnesty for political prisoners may be in the offing.*

off-key ADJECTIVE **= cacophonous**, harsh, jarring, grating, shrill, jangling, discordant, dissonant, inharmonious, unmelodious

off-load VERB **= get rid of**, shift, dump, dispose of, unload, dispense with, jettison, foist, see the back of, palm off: *Prices have been cut by developers anxious to offload unsold apartments.*

off-putting ADJECTIVE **= discouraging**, upsetting, disturbing, frustrating, nasty, formidable, intimidating, dismaying, unsettling, daunting, dampening, unnerving, disconcerting, unfavourable, dispiriting, discomfiting

offset VERB **= cancel out**, balance, set off, make up for, compensate for, redeem, counteract, neutralize, counterbalance, nullify, obviate, balance out, counterpoise, countervail

offshoot NOUN **= by-product**, development, product, branch, supplement, complement, spin-off, auxiliary, adjunct, appendage, outgrowth, appurtenance

offspring NOUN **1 = child**, baby, kid *(informal)*, youngster, infant, successor, babe, toddler, heir, issue, tot, descendant, wean *(Scot.)*, little one, brat, bairn *(Scot.)*, nipper *(informal)*, chit, scion, babe in arms *(informal)*, sprog *(slang)*, munchkin *(informal, chiefly U.S.)*, rug rat *(slang)*, littlie *(Austral. informal)*, ankle-biter *(Austral. slang)*, tacker *(Austral. slang)*: *She was less anxious about her offspring than she had been.* **OPPOSITE:** parent **2 = children**, kids *(informal)*, young, family, issue, stock, seed *(chiefly biblical)*, fry, successors, heirs, spawn, descendants, brood, posterity, lineage, progeny, scions: *Characteristics are often passed from parents to offspring.*

often ADVERB **= frequently**, much, generally, commonly, repeatedly, again and again, very often, oft *(archaic, poetic)*, over and over again, time and again, habitually, time after time, customarily, oftentimes *(archaic)*, not infrequently, many a time, ofttimes *(archaic)* **OPPOSITE:** never

ogle VERB **= leer at**, stare at, eye up *(informal)*, gawp at *(Brit. slang)*, give the once-over *(informal)*, make sheep's eyes at *(informal)*, give the glad eye *(informal)*, lech or letch after *(informal)*

ogre NOUN **1 = fiend**, monster, beast, villain, brute, bogeyman: *Some people think of bank managers as ogres.* **2 = monster**, giant, devil, beast, demon, bogey, spectre, fiend, ghoul, bogeyman, bugbear: *an ogre and a princess in a fairy tale*

oil NOUN **1 = lubricant**, grease, lubrication, fuel oil: *Her car had run out of oil.* **2 = lotion**, cream, balm, salve, liniment, embrocation, solution: *sun-tan oil*
▷ VERB **= lubricate**, grease, make slippery: *A crew of assistants oiled the mechanism until it worked perfectly.*

oily ADJECTIVE **1 = greasy**, slick, slimy, fatty, slippery, oleaginous, smeary: *traces of an oily substance*
2 = sycophantic, smooth, flattering, slick, plausible, hypocritical, fawning, grovelling, glib, ingratiating, fulsome, deferential, servile, unctuous, obsequious, smarmy (*Brit. informal*), mealy-mouthed, toadying: *He asked in an oily voice what he could do for them today.*

ointment NOUN **= salve**, dressing, cream, lotion, balm, lubricant, emollient, liniment, embrocation, unguent, cerate

O.K. *or* **okay** SENTENCE SUBSTITUTE **= all right**, right, yes, agreed, very good, roger, very well, ya (*S. African*), righto (*Brit. informal*), okey-dokey (*informal*), chur (*N.Z. informal*), yebo (*S. African informal*): *'Shall I ring you later?' – 'OK.'*
▷ ADJECTIVE **1 = all right**, fine, fitting, fair, in order, correct, approved, permitted, suitable, acceptable, convenient, allowable: *Is it OK if I bring a friend with me?*
OPPOSITE: unacceptable **2 = fine**, good, average, middling, fair, all right, acceptable, adequate, satisfactory, not bad (*informal*), so-so (*informal*), tolerable, up to scratch (*informal*), passable, unobjectionable: *'Did you enjoy the film?' – 'It was okay.'*
OPPOSITE: unsatisfactory **3 = well**, all right, safe, sound, healthy, hale, unharmed, uninjured, unimpaired: *Would you go and check the baby's ok?*
▷ VERB **= approve**, allow, pass, agree to, permit, sanction, second, endorse, authorize, ratify, go along with, consent to, validate, countenance, give the go-ahead, rubber-stamp (*informal*), say yes to, give the green light, assent to, give the thumbs up (*informal*), concur in, give your consent to, give your blessing to: *His doctor wouldn't OK the trip.*
▷ NOUN **= authorization**, agreement, sanction, licence, approval, go-ahead (*informal*), blessing, permission, consent, say-so (*informal*), confirmation, mandate, endorsement, green light, ratification, assent, seal of approval, approbation: *He gave the okay to issue a new press release.*

old ADJECTIVE **1 = aged**, elderly, ancient, getting on, grey, mature, past it (*informal*), venerable, patriarchal, grey-haired, antiquated, over the hill (*informal*), senile, grizzled, decrepit, hoary, senescent, advanced in years, full of years, past your prime: *He was considered too old for the job.*
OPPOSITE: young **2 = tumbledown**, ruined, crumbling, decayed, shaky, disintegrating, worn-out, done, tottering, ramshackle, rickety, decrepit, falling to pieces: *a dilapidated old farmhouse* **3 = worn**, ragged, shabby, frayed, cast-off, tattered, tatty, threadbare: *Dress in old clothes for gardening.* **4 = out of date**, old-fashioned, dated, passé, antique, outdated, obsolete, archaic, unfashionable, antiquated, outmoded, behind the times, superannuated, out of style, antediluvian, out of the ark (*informal*), démodé (*French*): *They got rid of all their old, outdated office equipment.*
OPPOSITE: up-to-date **5 = former**, earlier, past, previous, prior, one-time, erstwhile, late, quondam, whilom (*archaic*), ex-: *Mark was heartbroken when Jane returned to her old boyfriend.* **6 = long-standing**, established, fixed, enduring, abiding, long-lasting, long-established, time-honoured: *He is an old enemy of mine.* **7 = early**, ancient, original, remote, of old, antique, aboriginal, primitive, archaic, gone by, bygone, undeveloped, primordial, primeval, immemorial, of yore, olden (*archaic*), pristine: *How did people manage in the old days before electricity?* **8 = stale**, common, commonplace, worn-out, banal, threadbare, trite, old hat, insipid, hackneyed, overused, repetitious, unoriginal, platitudinous, cliché-ridden, timeworn: *He trotted out all the same old excuses as before.* **9 = long-established**, seasoned, experienced, tried, tested, trained, professional, skilled, expert, master, qualified, familiar, capable, veteran, practised, accomplished, vintage, versed, hardened, competent, skilful, adept, knowledgeable, age-old, of long standing, well-versed: *She's an old campaigner at this game.*
10 = customary, established, traditional, conventional, historic, long-established, time-honoured, of long standing: *They dance, and sing the old songs they sang at home.*

> **QUOTATIONS**
> No man is ever so old but he thinks he can live another year
> [Cicero *De Senectute*]

> **PROVERBS**
> *There's many a good tune played on an old fiddle*
> *You can't teach an old dog new tricks*

old-fashioned ADJECTIVE **1 = out of date**, ancient, dated, outdated, unfashionable, antiquated, outmoded, passé, old hat, behind the times, fusty, out of style, démodé (*French*), out of the ark (*informal*), not with it (*informal*), (old-)fogeyish: *She always wears such boring, old-fashioned clothes.* **OPPOSITE:** up-to-date
2 = oldfangled, square (*informal*), outdated, old, past, dead, past it (*informal*), obsolete, old-time, archaic, unfashionable, superannuated, obsolescent, out of the ark (*informal*): *She has some old-fashioned values.*

old man NOUN **1 = senior citizen**, grandfather (*slang*), patriarch, old age pensioner, old person, old-timer (*U.S.*), elder, elder statesman, wrinkly (*informal*), old codger (*informal*), old stager, greybeard, coffin-dodger (*slang*), oldster (*informal*), O.A.P. (*Brit.*), koro (*N.Z.*): *a wizened, bent-over old man*
2 = father, pop (*informal*), dad (*informal*), daddy (*informal*), pa (*informal*), old boy (*informal*), papa (*old-fashioned, informal*), pater, paterfamilias: *My old man used to work down the mines.* **3 = manager**, boss (*informal*), supervisor, governor (*informal*), ganger, superintendent, gaffer (*informal*), foreman, overseer, baas (*S. African*): *Why's the old man got it in for you?*

old person NOUN **= senior citizen**, senior, retired person, old age pensioner, elder, pensioner (*slang*), coffin-dodger (*slang*), elderly person, O.A.P. (*Brit.*)

> **USAGE**
> While not as offensive as *coffin-dodger* and some of the other synonyms listed here, phrases such as *old man*, *old woman*, *old person*, and *elderly person* may still cause offence. It is better to use *senior citizen* or *senior*.

old-time ADJECTIVE **= old-fashioned**, traditional, vintage, ancient, antique, old-style, bygone

old-world ADJECTIVE **= traditional**, old-fashioned, picturesque, quaint, archaic, gentlemanly, courteous, gallant, courtly, chivalrous, ceremonious

Olympian ADJECTIVE **= majestic**, kingly, regal, royal, august, grand, princely, imperial, glorious, noble, splendid, elevated, awesome, dignified, regal, stately, sublime, lofty, pompous, grandiose, exalted, rarefied, godlike: *She affects an Olympian disdain for their opinions.*

omen NOUN **= portent**, sign, warning, threat, indication, foreshadowing, foreboding, harbinger, presage, forewarning, writing on the wall, prognostication, augury, prognostic, foretoken

> **QUOTATIONS**
> May the gods avert this omen
> [Cicero *Third Philippic*]
>
> omen: a sign that something will happen if nothing happens
> [Ambrose Bierce *The Devil's Dictionary*]

ominous ADJECTIVE **= threatening**, menacing, sinister, dark, forbidding, grim, fateful, foreboding, unpromising, portentous, baleful, inauspicious, premonitory, unpropitious, minatory, bodeful
OPPOSITE: promising

omission NOUN **1 = exclusion**, removal, leaving out, elimination, deletion, excision, noninclusion: *her*

O

The Language of EM Forster

Edward Morgan Forster (1879–1970) was a distinguished author and academic whose reputation rests on the six novels he produced between 1905 and 1924 (although one of these, *Maurice*, was published only posthumously). His fiction addresses issues of class, colonialism, Englishness, and sexuality and was loosely associated with the work of the Bloomsbury group of writers, which included Virginia Woolf.

Despite the philosophical and emotional complexity of Forster's novels, his writing contains a high proportion of short, grammatically simple sentences, often consisting of only one clause. These frequently begin with a conjunction, as in:

But now it was impossible.

And, so, and *for* are also used with unusual frequency by Forster at the start of a sentence. This tendency is part of a colloquial register that is characteristic of his writing, even in his celebrated critical work *Aspects of the Novel*. Indeed, in this text Forster even apologizes for his 'talkative' tone. A further ingredient of this informality is the occasional appearance of the authorial voice in the narrative. At the opening of a chapter in *The Longest Journey*, for example, Forster intersperses a development in the plot with a reflection on the act of writing that produces it:

Meanwhile he was a husband. Perhaps his union should have been emphasised before.

The strategy of making the reader aware of the constructedness of the text is more commonly associated with the 'postmodernism' of the second half of the 20th century than with the modernism that was in vogue at the time of Forster's literary productivity.

Another notable facet of Forster's language is his use of rhetorical questions. These often occur in free indirect speech when a character's thoughts are contained within the third person narration, as in these lines from *A Room with a View*:

'Now the old man attacked Miss Bartlett almost violently: Why should she not change? What possible objection had she?'

While this is a well-established literary device that dates back to Chaucer and beyond, it was also utilized extensively by Virginia Woolf in producing a 'stream of consciousness' that gives the reader access to the minds of the characters. Forster's enthusiasm for it might, then, be seen as an example of his coherence with a broader modernist emphasis on interior experience.

Three of Forster's novels are concerned to a large extent with travel and tourism and he also produced three works of travel writing, two on Egypt and one on India. Interestingly, there are more references to *Italy* in Forster's work than to *England*. Accordingly, in *A Room with a View* and *Where Angels Fear to Tread* there are numerous references to *Baedeker*, the most popular makers of guidebooks in Forster's time. Often *Baedeker* is used when the book itself is not present, as Forster's characters engage with what it would be like to be abroad without their guide, as in:

And no, you are not, not, NOT to look at your **Baedeker**.

Just as *Baedeker* is no longer a word in common usage, there are other examples of alterations in the language of travel since Forster was publishing. There are slightly more occurrences of the now slightly outmoded *motor* than the modern vernacular *car*. Motor is used as both a noun and a verb, as in:

My husband and our daughter are **motoring**.

Reflecting the status of the railway as the predominant form of transport in the early years of the 20th century, there are twice as many usages of *train* as either of these. The now largely obsolete mode of transport of a horse and *carriage* is also prominent, especially in the Italian novels.

omission from the guest list **OPPOSITE:** inclusion **2 = failure**, neglect, default, negligence, oversight, carelessness, dereliction, forgetfulness, slackness, laxity, laxness, slovenliness, neglectfulness, remissness: *an injury occasioned by any omission of the defendant* **3 = gap**, space, blank, exclusion, lacuna: *There is one noticeable omission in your article.*

omit VERB **1 = leave out**, miss (out), drop, exclude, eliminate, skip, give (something) a miss *(informal)*: *Our apologies for omitting your name from the article.* **OPPOSITE:** include **2 = forget**, fail, overlook, neglect, pass over, lose sight of, leave (something) undone, let (something) slide: *She had omitted to tell him she was married.*

omnipotence NOUN **= supremacy**, sovereignty, dominance, domination, mastery, primacy, ascendancy, pre-eminence, predominance, invincibility, supreme power, absolute rule, undisputed sway: *leaders who use violent discipline to assert their omnipotence* **OPPOSITE:** powerlessness

omnipotent ADJECTIVE **= almighty**, supreme, invincible, all-powerful **OPPOSITE:** powerless

once ADVERB **1 = on one occasion**, one time, one single time: *I only met her once, very briefly.* **2 = at one time**, in the past, previously, formerly, long ago, in the old days, once upon a time, in times past, in times gone by: *I lived there once, before I was married.*
▷ CONJUNCTION **= as soon as**, when, after, the moment, immediately, the instant: *Once she got inside the house, she slammed the door.*
at once 1 = immediately, now, right now, straight away, directly, promptly, instantly, right away, without delay, without hesitation, forthwith, this (very) minute, pronto *(informal)*, this instant, straightway *(archaic)*, posthaste, tout de suite *(French)*: *I must go at once.* **2 = simultaneously**, together, at the same time, all together, in concert, in unison, concurrently, in the same breath, in chorus, at *or* in one go *(informal)*: *They all started talking at once.*
once and for all = for the last time, finally, completely, for good, positively, permanently, for ever, decisively, inexorably, conclusively, irrevocably, for all time, inescapably, with finality, beyond the shadow of a doubt: *We have to resolve this matter once and for all.*
once in a while = occasionally, sometimes, at times, from time to time, on and off, irregularly, on occasion, now and again, periodically, every now and then, every so often, at intervals, off and on: *He phones me once in a while.*

oncoming ADJECTIVE **1 = approaching**, advancing, looming, onrushing: *He skidded into the path of an oncoming car.* **2 = forthcoming**, coming, approaching, expected, threatening, advancing, gathering, imminent, impending, upcoming, fast-approaching: *the oncoming storm*

one-horse ADJECTIVE **= small**, slow, quiet, minor, obscure, sleepy, unimportant, small-time *(informal)*, backwoods, tinpot *(Brit. informal)*

onerous ADJECTIVE **= trying**, hard, taxing, demanding, difficult, heavy, responsible, grave, crushing, exhausting, exacting, formidable, troublesome, oppressive, weighty, laborious, burdensome, irksome, backbreaking, exigent **OPPOSITE:** easy

one-sided ADJECTIVE **1 = unequal**, unfair, uneven, unjust, unbalanced, lopsided, inequitable, ill-matched: *It was a totally one-sided competition.* **OPPOSITE:** equal **2 = biased**, prejudiced, weighted, twisted, coloured, unfair, partial, distorted, partisan, warped, slanted, unjust, discriminatory, lopsided: *She gave a very one-sided account of the affair.* **OPPOSITE:** unbiased

one-time ADJECTIVE **= former**, previous, prior, sometime, late, erstwhile, quondam, ci-devant *(French)*, ex-

ongoing ADJECTIVE **= in progress**, current, growing, developing, advancing, progressing, evolving, unfolding, unfinished, extant

onlooker NOUN **= spectator**, witness, observer, viewer, looker-on, watcher, eyewitness, bystander

only ADJECTIVE **= sole**, one, single, individual, exclusive, unique, lone, solitary, one and only: *She was the only applicant for the job.*
▷ ADVERB **1 = just**, simply, purely, merely, no more than, nothing but, but, at most, at a push: *At the moment it's only a theory.* **2 = hardly**, just, barely, only just, scarcely, at most, at a push: *I only have enough money for one ticket.* **3 = exclusively**, entirely, purely, solely: *Computers are only for use by class members.*

onset NOUN **= beginning**, start, rise, birth, kick-off *(informal)*, outbreak, starting point, inception, commencement **OPPOSITE:** end

onslaught NOUN **= attack**, charge, campaign, strike, rush, assault, raid, invasion, offensive, blitz, onset, foray, incursion, onrush, inroad **OPPOSITE:** retreat

onus NOUN **= burden**, weight, responsibility, worry, task, stress, load, obligation, liability

onwards *or* **onward** ADVERB **= forward**, on, forwards, ahead, beyond, in front, forth

ooze[1] VERB **1 = seep**, well, drop, escape, strain, leak, drain, sweat, filter, bleed, weep, drip, trickle, leach, dribble, percolate: *Blood was still oozing from the wound.* **2 = emit**, release, leak, sweat, bleed, discharge, drip, leach, give out, dribble, exude, give off, excrete, overflow with, pour forth: *The cut was oozing a clear liquid.* **3 = exude**, emit, radiate, display, exhibit, manifest, emanate, overflow with: *Graham positively oozed confidence.*

ooze[2] NOUN **= mud**, clay, dirt, muck, silt, sludge, mire, slime, slob *(Irish)*, gloop *(informal)*, alluvium: *He thrust his hand into the ooze and brought out a large toad.*

opaque ADJECTIVE **1 = cloudy**, clouded, dull, dim, muddied, muddy, murky, hazy, filmy, turbid, lustreless: *The bathroom has an opaque glass window.* **OPPOSITE:** clear **2 = incomprehensible**, obscure, unclear, difficult, puzzling, baffling, enigmatic, perplexing, impenetrable, unintelligible, cryptic, unfathomable, abstruse, obfuscated, beyond comprehension: *the opaque language of the official report* **OPPOSITE:** lucid

open ADJECTIVE **1 = unclosed**, unlocked, ajar, unfastened, yawning, gaping, unlatched, unbolted, partly open, unbarred, off the latch: *an open door* **OPPOSITE:** closed **2 = unsealed**, unstoppered: *an open bottle of milk* **OPPOSITE:** unopened **3 = extended**, expanded, unfolded, stretched out, spread out, unfurled, straightened out, unrolled: *A newspaper lay open on the coffee table.* **OPPOSITE:** shut **4 = frank**, direct, natural, plain, innocent, straightforward, sincere, transparent, honest, candid, truthful, upfront *(informal)*, plain-spoken, above board, unreserved, artless, ingenuous, guileless, straight from the shoulder *(informal)*: *She has an open, trusting nature.* **OPPOSITE:** sly **5 = obvious**, clear, frank, plain, apparent, visible, patent, evident, distinct, pronounced, manifest, transparent, noticeable, blatant, conspicuous, downright, overt, unmistakable, palpable, recognizable, avowed, flagrant, perceptible, much in evidence, undisguised, unsubtle, barefaced, unconcealed: *their open dislike of each other* **OPPOSITE:** hidden **6 = receptive**, welcoming, sympathetic, responsive, amenable: *He seems open to suggestions.* **7 = susceptible**, subject, exposed, vulnerable, in danger, disposed, liable, wide open, unprotected, at the mercy of, left open, laid bare, an easy target for, undefended, laid open, defenceless against, unfortified: *They left themselves open to accusations of double standards.* **OPPOSITE:** defended **8 = unresolved**, unsettled, undecided, debatable, up in the air, moot, arguable, yet to be decided: *It is an open question how long his commitment will last.* **9 = clear**, free, passable, uncluttered, unhindered, unimpeded, navigable, unobstructed, unhampered: *The emergency services will do their best to keep the highway open.* **OPPOSITE:** obstructed **10 = unenclosed**, wide, rolling,

O

sweeping, exposed, extensive, bare, spacious, wide-open, undeveloped, uncrowded, unfenced, not built-up, unsheltered: *Police will continue their search of nearby open ground.* **OPPOSITE:** enclosed **11 = undone**, gaping, unbuttoned, unzipped, agape, unfastened: *Her blouse was open to the waist.* **OPPOSITE:** fastened **12 = available**, to hand, accessible, handy, vacant, on hand, obtainable, attainable, at your fingertips, at your disposal: *There are a wide range of career opportunities open to young people.* **13 = general**, public, free, catholic, broad, universal, blanket, unconditional, across-the-board, unqualified, all-inclusive, unrestricted, overarching, free to all, nondiscriminatory, one-size-fits-all: *an open invitation* **OPPOSITE:** restricted **14 = vacant**, free, available, empty, up for grabs *(informal)*, unoccupied, unfilled, unengaged: *The job is still open.* **15 = generous**, kind, liberal, charitable, benevolent, prodigal, bountiful, open-handed, unstinting, beneficent, bounteous, munificent, ungrudging: *the public's open and generous response to the appeal* **16 = gappy**, loose, lacy, porous, honeycombed, spongy, filigree, fretted, holey, openwork: *Ciabatta has a distinctive crisp crust and open texture.* ▷ VERB **1 = unfasten**, unlock, unclasp, throw wide, unbar, unclose: *He opened the window and looked out.* **OPPOSITE:** close **2 = unwrap**, uncover, undo, unravel, untie, unstrap, unseal, unlace: *The Inspector opened the parcel.* **OPPOSITE:** wrap **3 = uncork**, crack (open): *Let's open another bottle of wine.* **4 = unfold**, spread (out), expand, stretch out, unfurl, unroll: *When you open the map, you will find it is divided into squares.* **OPPOSITE:** fold **5 = clear**, unblock: *Police have opened the road again after the crash.* **OPPOSITE:** block **6 = undo**, loosen, unbutton, unfasten: *He opened his shirt to show me his scar.* **OPPOSITE:** fasten **7 = begin business**: *The new shopping complex opens tomorrow.* **8 = start**, begin, launch, trigger, kick off *(informal)*, initiate, commence, get going, instigate, kick-start, inaugurate, set in motion, get (something) off the ground *(informal)*, enter upon: *They are now ready to open negotiations.* **OPPOSITE:** end **9 = begin**, start, commence: *The service opened with a hymn.* **OPPOSITE:** end

open-air MODIFIER **= outdoor**, outside, out-of-door(s), alfresco

open-and-shut ADJECTIVE **= straightforward**, simple, obvious, routine, clear-cut, foregone, noncontroversial

opening ADJECTIVE **= first**, early, earliest, beginning, premier, primary, initial, maiden, inaugural, commencing, introductory, initiatory: *the season's opening game* ▷ NOUN **1 = beginning**, start, launch, launching, birth, dawn, outset, starting point, onset, overture, initiation, inauguration, inception, commencement, kickoff *(informal)*, opening move: *the opening of peace talks* **OPPOSITE:** ending **2 = hole**, break, space, tear, split, crack, gap, rent, breach, slot, outlet, vent, puncture, rupture, aperture, cleft, chink, fissure, orifice, perforation, interstice: *He squeezed through an opening in the fence.* **OPPOSITE:** blockage **3 = opportunity**, chance, break *(informal)*, time, place, moment, window, occasion, look-in *(informal)*: *All she needed was an opening to show her capabilities.* **4 = job**, position, post, situation, opportunity, vacancy: *We don't have any openings just now, but we'll call you.*

openly ADVERB **1 = frankly**, plainly, in public, honestly, face to face, overtly, candidly, unreservedly, unhesitatingly, forthrightly, straight from the shoulder *(informal)*: *We can now talk openly about AIDS.* **OPPOSITE:** privately **2 = blatantly**, publicly, brazenly, unashamedly, shamelessly, in full view, flagrantly, unabashedly, wantonly, undisguisedly, without pretence: *He was openly gay.* **OPPOSITE:** secretly

open-minded ADJECTIVE **= unprejudiced**, liberal, free, balanced, catholic, broad, objective, reasonable, enlightened, tolerant, impartial, receptive, unbiased, even-handed, dispassionate, fair-minded, broad-minded, undogmatic **OPPOSITE:** narrow-minded

openness NOUN **= frankness**, honesty, truthfulness, naturalness, bluntness, forthrightness, ingenuousness, artlessness, guilelessness, candidness, freeness, open-heartedness, absence of reserve, candour *or* (U.S.) candor, sincerity *or* sincereness, unreservedness

> **QUOTATIONS**
> I will wear my heart upon my sleeve
> [William Shakespeare *Othello*]

operate VERB **1 = manage**, run, direct, handle, govern, oversee, supervise, preside over, be in charge of, call the shots in, superintend, call the tune in: *Until his death he owned and operated a huge company.* **2 = function**, work, act, be in business, be in action: *allowing commercial businesses to operate in the country* **3 = run**, work, use, control, drive, manoeuvre: *The men were trapped as they operated a tunnelling machine.* **4 = work**, go, run, perform, function: *the number of fax machines operating around the world* **OPPOSITE:** break down **5 = perform surgery**, carry out surgery, put someone under the knife *(informal)*: *The surgeons had to decide quickly whether or not to operate.*

operation NOUN **1 = undertaking**, process, affair, organization, proceeding, procedure, coordination: *A major rescue operation is under way.* **2 = manoeuvre**, campaign, movement, exercise, assault, deployment: *a full-scale military operation* **3 = business**, concern, firm, organization, corporation, venture, enterprise: *The company has converted its mail-order operation into an e-business.* **4 = surgery**, surgical operation, surgical intervention: *an operation to reduce a bloodclot on the brain* **5 = performance**, working, running, action, movement, functioning, motion, manipulation: *Dials monitor every aspect of the operation of the aircraft.* **6 = effect**, force, activity, agency, influence, impact, effectiveness, instrumentality: *This change is due to the operation of several factors.* **in operation = in action**, current, effective, going, functioning, active, in effect, in business, operative, in force: *The night-time curfew remains in operation.*

operational ADJECTIVE **= working**, going, running, ready, functioning, operative, viable, functional, up and running, workable, usable, in working order **OPPOSITE:** inoperative

operative ADJECTIVE **1 = in force**, current, effective, standing, functioning, active, efficient, in effect, in business, operational, functional, in operation, workable, serviceable: *The scheme was operative by the end of 1983.* **OPPOSITE:** inoperative **2 = relevant**, important, key, fitting, significant, appropriate, crucial, influential, apt, applicable, indicative, pertinent, apposite, germane: *A small whisky may help you sleep – 'small' being the operative word.* ▷ NOUN **1 = worker**, hand, employee, mechanic, labourer, workman, artisan, machinist, working man *or* working woman: *In an automated car plant there is not a human operative to be seen.* **2 = spy**, secret agent, double agent, secret service agent, undercover agent, mole, foreign agent, fifth columnist, nark *(Brit., Austral. & N.Z. slang)*: *The CIA wants to protect its operatives.*

operator NOUN **1 = worker**, hand, driver, mechanic, operative, conductor, technician, handler, skilled employee: *He first of all worked as a machine operator.* **2 = contractor**, dealer, trader, administrator: *the country's largest cable TV operator* **3 = manipulator**, worker, mover, Machiavellian, mover and shaker, machinator, wheeler-dealer *(informal)*, wirepuller: *one of the shrewdest political operators in the Arab world*

opiate NOUN **= narcotic**, drug, downer *(slang)*, painkiller, sedative, tranquillizer, bromide, anodyne, analgesic, soporific, pacifier, nepenthe

opine VERB **= suggest**, say, think, believe, judge, suppose, declare, conclude, venture, volunteer, imply,

O

intimate, presume, conjecture, surmise, ween *(poetic)*, give as your opinion

opinion NOUN **1 = belief**, feeling, view, idea, theory, notion, conviction, point of view, sentiment, viewpoint, persuasion, conjecture: *Most who expressed an opinion spoke favourably of him.* **2 = estimation**, view, impression, assessment, judgment, evaluation, conception, appraisal, considered opinion: *That has improved my already favourable opinion of him.*
be of the opinion = believe, think, hold, consider, judge, suppose, maintain, imagine, guess *(informal, chiefly U.S. & Canad.)*, reckon, conclude, be convinced, speculate, presume, conjecture, postulate, surmise, be under the impression: *Frank is of the opinion that there has been a cover-up.*
matter of opinion = debatable point, debatable, open question, open to question, moot point, open for discussion, matter of judgment: *Whether or not it is a work of art is a matter of opinion.*

> **QUOTATIONS**
> We can never be sure that the opinion we are endeavouring to stifle is a false opinion; and if we were sure, stifling it would be an evil still
> [John Stuart Mill *On Liberty*]
>
> There are as many opinions as there are people; each has his own correct way
> [Terence *Phormio*]
>
> New opinions are always suspected, and usually opposed, without any other reason but because they are not already common
> [John Locke *Essay concerning Human Understanding*]
>
> A man can brave opinion, a woman must submit to it
> [Mme de Staël *Delphine*]
>
> Where an opinion is general, it is usually correct
> [Jane Austen *Mansfield Park*]
>
> A study of the history of opinion is a necessary preliminary to the emancipation of the mind
> [John Maynard Keynes *The End of Laissez-Faire*]
>
> When a man gives his opinion, he's a man. When a woman gives her opinion, she's a bitch
> [Bette Davis]
>
> They that approve a private opinion, call it opinion; but they that mislike it, heresy; and yet heresy signifies no more than private opinion
> [Thomas Hobbes *Leviathan*]
>
> Opinion in good men is but knowledge in the making
> [John Milton *Areopagitica*]

opinionated ADJECTIVE **= dogmatic**, prejudiced, biased, arrogant, adamant, stubborn, assertive, uncompromising, single-minded, inflexible, bigoted, dictatorial, imperious, overbearing, obstinate, doctrinaire, obdurate, cocksure, pig-headed, self-assertive, bull-headed **OPPOSITE:** open-minded

opponent NOUN **1 = adversary**, rival, enemy, the opposition, competitor, challenger, foe, contestant, antagonist: *Mr Kennedy's opponent in the leadership contest* **OPPOSITE:** ally **2 = opposer**, dissident, objector, dissentient, disputant: *He became an outspoken opponent of the old Soviet system.* **OPPOSITE:** supporter

opportune ADJECTIVE **= timely**, fitting, fit, welcome, lucky, appropriate, suitable, happy, proper, convenient, fortunate, favourable, apt, advantageous, auspicious, fortuitous, well-timed, propitious, heaven-sent, felicitous, providential, seasonable, falling into your lap **OPPOSITE:** inopportune

opportunism NOUN **= expediency**, convenience, exploitation, realism, manipulation, pragmatism, capitalization, realpolitik, utilitarianism, making hay while the sun shines *(informal)*, striking while the iron is hot *(informal)*, unscrupulousness, Machiavellianism

> **QUOTATIONS**
> There is a tide in the affairs of men,
> Which, taken at the flood, leads on to fortune
> [William Shakespeare *Julius Caesar*]

opportunity NOUN **= chance**, opening, time, turn, hour, break *(informal)*, moment, window, possibility, occasion, slot, scope, look-in *(informal)*

> **PROVERBS**
> *When the cat's away, the mice will play*
> *Never look a gift horse in the mouth*
> *When one door shuts, another door opens*
> *Strike while the iron is hot*
> *There is no time like the present*
> *He who hesitates is lost*

oppose VERB **= be against**, fight (against), check, bar, block, prevent, take on, counter, contest, resist, confront, face, combat, defy, thwart, contradict, withstand, stand up to, hinder, struggle against, obstruct, fly in the face of, take issue with, be hostile to, counterattack, speak (out) against, be in opposition to, be in defiance of, strive against, set your face against, take *or* make a stand against **OPPOSITE:** support

opposed ADJECTIVE **1** *(with* **to***)* **= against**, anti *(informal)*, hostile, adverse, contra *(informal)*, in opposition, averse, antagonistic, inimical, (dead) set against: *I am utterly opposed to any form of terrorism.* **2 = contrary**, opposite, conflicting, opposing, clashing, counter, adverse, contradictory, in opposition, incompatible, antithetical, antipathetic, dissentient: *people with views almost diametrically opposed to his own*

opposing ADJECTIVE **1 = conflicting**, different, opposed, contrasting, opposite, differing, contrary, contradictory, incompatible, irreconcilable: *I have a friend who holds the opposing view.* **2 = rival**, warring, conflicting, clashing, competing, enemy, opposite, hostile, combatant, antagonistic, antipathetic: *The leader said he still favoured a dialogue between the opposing sides.*

opposite ADJECTIVE **1 = facing**, other, opposing: *the opposite side of the room* **2 = different**, conflicting, opposed, contrasted, contrasting, unlike, differing, contrary, diverse, adverse, at odds, contradictory, inconsistent, dissimilar, divergent, irreconcilable, at variance, poles apart, diametrically opposed, antithetical, streets apart: *Everything he does is opposite to what is considered normal behaviour.* **OPPOSITE:** alike **3 = rival**, conflicting, opposed, opposing, competing, hostile, antagonistic, inimical: *They fought on opposite sides during the War of Independence.*
▷ PREPOSITION *(often with* **to***)* **= facing**, face to face with, across from, eyeball to eyeball with *(informal)*: *She sat opposite her at breakfast.*
▷ NOUN **= reverse**, contrary, converse, antithesis, the other extreme, contradiction, inverse, the other side of the coin *(informal)*, obverse: *She's very shy, but her sister is quite the opposite.*

> **PROVERBS**
> *Opposites attract*

opposition NOUN **1 = hostility**, resistance, resentment, disapproval, obstruction, animosity, aversion, antagonism, antipathy, obstructiveness, counteraction, contrariety: *Much of the opposition to this plan has come from the media.* **OPPOSITE:** support **2 = opponent(s)**, competition, rival(s), enemy, competitor(s), other side, challenger(s), foe, contestant(s), antagonist(s): *The team inflicted a crushing defeat on the opposition.*

oppress VERB **1 = subjugate**, abuse, suppress, wrong, master, overcome, crush, overwhelm, put down, subdue, overpower, persecute, rule over, enslave, maltreat, hold sway over, trample underfoot, bring someone to heel, tyrannize over, rule with an iron hand, bring someone under the yoke: *Men still oppress women both physically and socially.* **OPPOSITE:** liberate **2 = depress**, burden, discourage, torment, daunt, harass, afflict, sadden, vex, weigh down, dishearten, cast someone down, dispirit, take the heart out of, deject, lie *or* weigh heavy upon, make someone despondent: *The atmosphere in the room oppressed her.*

oppressed ADJECTIVE **= downtrodden**, abused, exploited, subject, burdened, distressed, slave, disadvantaged, helpless, misused, enslaved, prostrate, underprivileged, subservient, subjugated, browbeaten, maltreated, tyrannized, henpecked **OPPOSITE:** liberated

oppression NOUN = **persecution**, control, suffering, abuse, injury, injustice, cruelty, domination, repression, brutality, suppression, severity, tyranny, authoritarianism, harshness, despotism, ill-treatment, subjugation, subjection, maltreatment **OPPOSITE:** justice

> **QUOTATIONS**
> the most potent weapon in the hands of the oppressor is the mind of the oppressed
> [Steve Biko *'Black Consciousness and the Quest for a True Humanity'*]

oppressive ADJECTIVE **1 = tyrannical**, severe, harsh, heavy, overwhelming, cruel, brutal, authoritarian, unjust, repressive, Draconian, autocratic, inhuman, dictatorial, coercive, imperious, domineering, overbearing, burdensome, despotic, high-handed, peremptory, overweening, tyrannous: *The new laws will be as oppressive as those they replace.* **OPPOSITE:** merciful **2 = stifling**, close, heavy, sticky, overpowering, suffocating, stuffy, humid, torrid, sultry, airless, muggy: *The oppressive afternoon heat had quite tired him out.*

oppressor NOUN = **persecutor**, tyrant, bully, scourge, tormentor, despot, autocrat, taskmaster, iron hand, slave-driver, harrier, intimidator, subjugator

opt VERB = **choose**, decide, prefer, select, elect, see fit, make a selection: *Students can opt to stay in residence.* **OPPOSITE:** reject
opt for something *or* **someone** = **choose**, pick, select, take, adopt, go for, designate, decide on, single out, espouse, fix on, plump for, settle upon, exercise your discretion in favour of: *You may wish to opt for one method or the other.*

optimistic ADJECTIVE **1 = hopeful**, positive, confident, encouraged, can-do *(informal)*, bright, assured, cheerful, rosy, buoyant, idealistic, Utopian, sanguine, expectant, looking on the bright side, buoyed up, disposed to take a favourable view, seen through rose-coloured spectacles: *Michael was in a jovial and optimistic mood.* **OPPOSITE:** pessimistic **2 = encouraging**, promising, bright, good, cheering, reassuring, satisfactory, rosy, heartening, auspicious, propitious: *an optimistic forecast that the economy would pick up by the end of the year* **OPPOSITE:** discouraging

optimum ADJECTIVE = **ideal**, best, highest, finest, choicest, perfect, supreme, peak, outstanding, first-class, foremost, first-rate, flawless, superlative, pre-eminent, most excellent, A1 *or* A-one *(informal)*, most favourable *or* advantageous **OPPOSITE:** worst

option NOUN = **choice**, alternative, selection, preference, freedom of choice, power to choose, election

optional ADJECTIVE = **voluntary**, open, discretionary, possible, extra, elective, up to the individual, noncompulsory **OPPOSITE:** compulsory

opulence *or* **opulency** NOUN **1 = luxury**, riches, wealth, splendour, prosperity, richness, affluence, voluptuousness, lavishness, sumptuousness, luxuriance: *the opulence of the hotel's sumptuous interior* **2 = wealth**, means, riches *(informal)*, capital, resources, assets, fortune, substance, prosperity, affluence, easy circumstances, prosperousness: *He is surrounded by possessions which testify to his opulence.* **OPPOSITE:** poverty

opulent ADJECTIVE **1 = luxurious**, expensive, magnificent, costly, splendid, lavish, sumptuous, plush *(informal)*, ritzy *(slang)*, de luxe, well-appointed: *an opulent lifestyle* **2 = rich**, wealthy, prosperous, propertied, loaded *(slang)*, flush *(informal)*, affluent, well-off, well-heeled *(informal)*, well-to-do, moneyed, filthy rich, stinking rich *(informal)*, made of money *(informal)*, minted *(Brit. slang)*: *the spoilt child of an opulent father* **OPPOSITE:** poor

opus NOUN = **work**, piece, production, creation, composition, work of art, brainchild, oeuvre *(French)*

oracle NOUN **1 = prophet**, diviner, sage, seer, clairvoyant, augur, soothsayer, sibyl, prophesier: *Ancient peoples consulted the oracle and the shaman for advice.* **2 = prophecy**, vision, revelation, forecast, prediction, divination, prognostication, augury, divine utterance: *Aeneas had begged the Sibyl to speak her oracle in words.*

oral ADJECTIVE = **spoken**, vocal, verbal, unwritten, viva voce

orange

SHADES OF ORANGE

amber	gold	peach
burnt sienna	grenadine	tangerine
	ochre	terracotta

oration NOUN = **speech**, talk, address, lecture, discourse, harangue, homily, spiel *(informal)*, disquisition, declamation, whaikorero *(N.Z.)*

orator NOUN = **public speaker**, speaker, lecturer, spokesperson, declaimer, rhetorician, Cicero, spieler *(informal)*, word-spinner, spokesman *or* spokeswoman

oratory NOUN = **rhetoric**, eloquence, public speaking, speech-making, expressiveness, fluency, a way with words, declamation, speechifying, grandiloquence, spieling *(informal)*, whaikorero *(N.Z.)*

orb NOUN = **sphere**, ball, circle, globe, round

orbit NOUN **1 = path**, course, track, cycle, circle, revolution, passage, rotation, trajectory, sweep, ellipse, circumgyration: *the point at which the planet's orbit is closest to the sun* **2 = sphere of influence**, reach, range, influence, province, scope, sphere, domain, compass, ambit: *Eisenhower acknowledged that Hungary lay within the Soviet orbit.*
▷ VERB = **circle**, ring, go round, compass, revolve around, encircle, circumscribe, gird, circumnavigate: *the first satellite to orbit the Earth*

orchestrate VERB **1 = organize**, plan, run, set up, arrange, be responsible for, put together, see to *(informal)*, marshal, coordinate, concert, stage-manage: *The colonel orchestrated the rebellion from inside his army jail.* **2 = score**, set, arrange, adapt: *He was orchestrating the first act of his opera.*

ordain VERB **1 = appoint**, call, name, commission, select, elect, invest, install, nominate, anoint, consecrate, frock: *Her brother was ordained as a priest in 1982.* **2 = order**, will, rule, demand, require, direct, establish, command, dictate, prescribe, pronounce, lay down, decree, instruct, enact, legislate, enjoin: *He ordained that women should be veiled in public.* **3 = predestine**, fate, intend, mark out, predetermine, foreordain, destine, preordain: *His future seemed ordained right from the start.*

ordeal NOUN = **hardship**, trial, difficulty, test, labour, suffering, trouble(s), nightmare, burden, torture, misery, agony, torment, anguish, toil, affliction, tribulation(s), baptism of fire **OPPOSITE:** pleasure

order VERB **1 = command**, instruct, direct, charge, demand, require, bid, compel, enjoin, adjure: *Williams ordered him to leave.* **OPPOSITE:** forbid **2 = decree**, rule, demand, establish, prescribe, pronounce, ordain: *The President has ordered a full investigation.* **OPPOSITE:** ban **3 = request**, ask (for), book, demand, seek, call for, reserve, engage, apply for, contract for, solicit, requisition, put in for, send away for: *I often order goods over the Internet these days.* **4 = arrange**, group, sort, class, position, range, file, rank, line up, organize, set out, sequence, catalogue, sort out, classify, array, dispose, tidy, marshal, lay out, tabulate, systematize, neaten, put in order, set in order, put to rights: *Entries in the book are ordered alphabetically.* **OPPOSITE:** disarrange
▷ NOUN **1 = instruction**, ruling, demand, direction, command, say-so *(informal)*, dictate, decree, mandate, directive, injunction, behest, stipulation: *They were arrested and executed on the orders of Stalin.*

O

2 = request, booking, demand, commission, application, reservation, requisition: *The company say they can't supply our order.* **3 = sequence**, grouping, ordering, line, series, structure, chain, arrangement, line-up, succession, disposal, array, placement, classification, layout, progression, disposition, setup *(informal)*, categorization, codification: *List the key headings and sort them in a logical order.* **4 = organization**, system, method, plan, pattern, arrangement, harmony, symmetry, regularity, propriety, neatness, tidiness, orderliness: *The wish to impose order upon confusion is a kind of intellectual instinct.* **OPPOSITE:** chaos **5 = peace**, control, law, quiet, calm, discipline, law and order, tranquillity, peacefulness, lawfulness: *He has the power to use force to maintain public order.* **6 = society**, company, group, club, union, community, league, association, institute, organization, circle, corporation, lodge, guild, sect, fellowship, fraternity, brotherhood, sisterhood, sodality: *the Benedictine order of monks* **7 = class**, set, rank, degree, grade, sphere, caste: *He maintained that the higher orders of society must rule the lower.* **8 = kind**, group, class, family, form, sort, type, variety, cast, species, breed, strain, category, tribe, genre, classification, genus, ilk, subdivision, subclass, taxonomic group: *the order of insects Coleoptera, better known as beetles*

in order 1 = tidy, ordered, neat, arranged, trim, orderly, spruce, well-kept, well-ordered, shipshape, spick-and-span, trig *(archaic, dialect)*, in apple-pie order *(informal)*: *We tried to keep the room in order.* **2 = appropriate**, right, fitting, seemly, called for, correct, suitable, acceptable, proper, to the point, apt, applicable, pertinent, befitting, well-suited, well-timed, apposite, germane, to the purpose, meet *(archaic)*, O.K. *or* okay *(informal)*: *I think an apology would be in order.*

out of order 1 = not working, broken, broken-down, ruined, bust *(informal)*, defective, wonky *(Brit. slang)*, not functioning, out of commission, on the blink *(slang)*, on its last legs, inoperative, kaput *(informal)*, in disrepair, gone haywire *(informal)*, nonfunctional, on the fritz *(U.S. slang)*, gone phut *(informal)*, U.S. *(informal)*: *The phone is out of order.* **2 = improper**, wrong, unsuitable, not done, not on *(informal)*, unfitting, vulgar, out of place, unseemly, untoward, unbecoming, impolite, off-colour, out of turn, uncalled-for, not cricket *(informal)*, indelicate, indecorous: *Don't you think that remark was a bit out of order?*

PROVERBS

A place for everything, and everything in its place
There's a time and a place for everything

orderly ADJECTIVE **1 = well-behaved**, controlled, disciplined, quiet, restrained, law-abiding, nonviolent, peaceable, decorous: *The organizers guided them in orderly fashion out of the building.* **OPPOSITE:** disorderly **2 = well-organized**, ordered, regular, in order, organized, trim, precise, neat, tidy, systematic, businesslike, methodical, well-kept, shipshape, systematized, well-regulated, in apple-pie order *(informal)*: *The vehicles were parked in orderly rows.* **OPPOSITE:** disorganized

ordinance NOUN **= rule**, order, law, ruling, standard, guide, direction, principle, command, regulation, guideline, criterion, decree, canon, statute, fiat, edict, dictum, precept

ordinarily ADVERB **= usually**, generally, normally, commonly, regularly, routinely, in general, as a rule, habitually, customarily, in the usual way, as is usual, as is the custom, in the general run (of things) **OPPOSITE:** seldom

ordinary ADJECTIVE **1 = usual**, standard, normal, common, established, settled, regular, familiar, household, typical, conventional, routine, stock, everyday, prevailing, accustomed, customary, habitual, quotidian, wonted: *It was just an ordinary day for us.* **2 = commonplace**, plain, modest, humble, stereotyped, pedestrian, mundane, vanilla *(slang)*, stale, banal, unremarkable, prosaic, run-of-the-mill, humdrum, homespun, uninteresting, workaday, common or garden *(informal)*, unmemorable: *My life seems pretty ordinary compared to yours.* **3 = average**, middling, fair, indifferent, not bad, mediocre, so-so *(informal)*, unremarkable, tolerable, run-of-the-mill, passable, undistinguished, uninspired, unexceptional, bog-standard *(Brit. & Irish slang)*, no great shakes *(informal)*, dime-a-dozen *(informal)*: *The food here is cheap, but very ordinary.* **OPPOSITE:** extraordinary

out of the ordinary = unusual, different, odd, important, special, striking, surprising, significant, strange, exciting, rare, impressive, extraordinary, outstanding, remarkable, bizarre, distinguished, unexpected, curious, exceptional, notable, unfamiliar, abnormal, queer, uncommon, singular, unconventional, noteworthy, atypical: *Have you noticed anything out of the ordinary about him?*

ordnance NOUN **= weapons**, arms, guns, artillery, cannon, firearms, weaponry, big guns, armaments, munitions, materiel, instruments of war

organ NOUN **1 = body part**, part of the body, member, element, biological structure: *damage to the muscles and internal organs* **2 = newspaper**, paper, medium, voice, agency, channel, vehicle, journal, publication, rag *(informal)*, gazette, periodical, mouthpiece: *the People's Daily, the official organ of the Chinese Commmunist Party*

organic ADJECTIVE **1 = natural**, biological, living, live, vital, animate, biotic: *Oxygen is vital to all organic life on Earth.* **2 = systematic**, ordered, structured, organized, integrated, orderly, standardized, methodical, well-ordered, systematized: *City planning treats the city as an organic whole.* **3 = integral**, fundamental, constitutional, structural, inherent, innate, immanent: *The history of Russia is an organic part of European history.*

organism NOUN **= creature**, being, thing, body, animal, structure, beast, entity, living thing, critter *(U.S. dialect)*

organize *or* **organise** VERB **1 = arrange**, run, plan, form, prepare, establish, set up, shape, schedule, frame, look after, be responsible for, construct, constitute, devise, put together, take care of, see to *(informal)*, get together, marshal, contrive, get going, coordinate, fix up, straighten out, lay the foundations of, lick into shape, jack up *(N.Z. informal)*: *We need someone to help organize our campaign.* **OPPOSITE:** disrupt **2 = put in order**, arrange, group, list, file, index, catalogue, classify, codify, pigeonhole, tabulate, inventory, systematize, dispose: *He began to organize his papers.* **OPPOSITE:** muddle

orgasm NOUN **= climax**, coming *(taboo, slang)*, pleasure, the big O *(informal)*, (sexual) satisfaction

orgy NOUN **1 = party**, celebration, rave *(Brit. slang)*, revel, festivity, bender *(informal)*, debauch, revelry, carouse, Saturnalia, bacchanal, rave-up *(Brit. slang)*, bacchanalia, carousal, hooley *or* hoolie *(chiefly Irish & N.Z.)*: *a drunken orgy* **2 = spree**, fit, spell, run, session, excess, bout, indulgence, binge *(informal)*, splurge, surfeit, overindulgence: *He blew £43,000 in an 18-month orgy of spending.*

orient *or* **orientate** VERB **= adjust**, settle, adapt, tune, convert, alter, compose, accommodate, accustom, reconcile, align, harmonize, familiarize, acclimatize, find your feet *(informal)*: *It will take some time to orient yourself to this new way of thinking.*

orient yourself = get your bearings, get the lie of the land, establish your location: *She lay still for a few seconds, trying to orient herself.*

orientation NOUN **1 = inclination**, tendency, bias, leaning, bent, disposition, predisposition, predilection, proclivity, partiality, turn of mind: *The party is liberal and democratic in orientation.* **2 = induction**, introduction, breaking in, adjustment, settling in, adaptation, initiation, assimilation, familiarization, acclimatization: *the company's policy on recruiting and orientation* **3 = position**, situation,

O

The Language of RD Blackmore

Richard Dorridge Blackmore (1825–1900) was one of the most famous English novelists of the second half of the 19th century. Although many of his works have since fallen from popularity, *Lorna Doone*, a romance set in the late 17th century in south-west England, remains a popular classic.

Little is the one of the adjectives which Blackmore uses most frequently. *Little* most frequently modifies words for children, including *boy, girl, maid, maiden, child, fellow, ones,* and *things*. The adjectives that most often collocate with *little* are *poor* and *quiet*, as in:

The **poor little things** looked up at her in wonder ...

Great is another one of Blackmore's 100 most frequently used words, although, interestingly, neither *little* nor *great* are among the 100 most commonly used words in the *Bank of English*, Collins' corpus of present-day English. Blackmore most frequently uses *great* in the phrase *a great deal*:

I was **a great deal** too worn out to cry or sob.

However, in the sense 'of exceptional talents or achievements', *great* also frequently modifies *man* and *people*, although never *woman*.

Old and *young* are also common adjectives in Blackmore, both generally collocating with words for people. When talking about a female, Blackmore is more likely to talk about a *young lady* than a *young woman*; conversely, *old woman* occurs far more frequently than *old lady*. The other adjectives with which *young* tends to collocate are mostly of a positive nature, such as *fine, brave, lovely, nice, fair, bright, beautiful, gallant, stout,* and *handsome*. However, there is also a significant collocation between *young* and *poor*, and *poor* is in fact the adjective that most frequently collocates with *old*, as in 'the poor old man'. It should be noted, however, that there is also a significant collocation between *old* and *fine*, as in 'the fine old gentleman'.

Mother and *father* are also common nouns in the writings of RD Blackmore. Both are frequently modified by the adjective *dear* and also by the adjective *poor*. However, it is interesting that *father* and *mother* collocate with quite different verbs. *Mother* is the most common subject of the verb *tell*, as in:

... her **mother** always told him not to be in any hurry ...

Father, on the other hand, is the most common subject of the verbs *allow* and *refuse*, as in:

My **father** had never allowed me much acquaintance with other children ...

... his own **father** had refused to see him ...

These collocations reflect traditional parental roles, which have only in recent decades become less fixed in the Western world.

The adverb *scarcely* is another word which occurs frequently in the works of Blackmore. The most significant collocation with *scarcely* is the verb *know*, as in:

I **scarcely knew** whom to believe, or what.

Scarcely often also occurs with the adverb *ever*, as in, '... I scarcely ever spoke of him.' Again, it is interesting to compare Blackmore's use of *scarcely* with evidence from the *Bank of English*. In the *Bank of English*, *scarcely* does not appear among the 7,500 most commonly used words. *Scarcely* is, however, one of Blackmore's 300 most frequently used words.

One of Blackmore's signature traits is his vivid and beautiful descriptions of nature, and this is also reflected in his use of language, with words such as *water, light, land, sea, wind, air,* and even *nature* itself all occurring frequently in his writings.

location, site, bearings, direction, arrangement, whereabouts, disposition, coordination: *The orientation of the church is such that the front faces the square.*

orifice NOUN = **opening**, space, hole, split, mouth, gap, rent, breach, vent, pore, rupture, aperture, cleft, chink, fissure, perforation, interstice

origin NOUN **1 = beginning**, start, birth, source, launch, foundation, creation, dawning, early stages, emergence, outset, starting point, onset, genesis, initiation, inauguration, inception, font *(poetic)*, commencement, fountain, fount, origination, fountainhead, mainspring: *theories about the origin of life* **OPPOSITE:** end **2 = root**, source, basis, beginnings, base, cause, spring, roots, seed, foundation, nucleus, germ, provenance, derivation, wellspring, fons et origo *(Latin)*: *What is the origin of the word 'honeymoon'?* **3 = ancestry**, family, race, beginnings, stock, blood, birth, heritage, ancestors, descent, pedigree, extraction, lineage, forebears, antecedents, parentage, forefathers, genealogy, derivation, progenitors, stirps: *people of Asian origin*

original ADJECTIVE **1 = first**, earliest, early, initial, aboriginal, primitive, pristine, primordial, primeval, autochthonous: *The Dayaks were the original inhabitants of Borneo.* **2 = initial**, first, starting, opening, primary, inaugural, commencing, introductory: *Let's stick to the original plan.* **OPPOSITE:** final **3 = authentic**, real, actual, genuine, legitimate, first generation, bona fide, the real McCoy: *The company specializes in selling original movie posters.* **OPPOSITE:** copied **4 = new**, fresh, novel, different, unusual, unknown, unprecedented, innovative, unfamiliar, unconventional, seminal, ground-breaking, untried, innovatory, newfangled: *an original idea* **OPPOSITE:** unoriginal **5 = creative**, inspired, imaginative, artistic, fertile, ingenious, visionary, inventive, resourceful: *a chef with an original touch and a measure of inspiration*
▷ NOUN **1 = prototype**, master, pattern: *Photocopy the form and send the original to your employer.* **OPPOSITE:** copy **2 = character**, eccentric, case *(informal)*, card *(informal)*, nut *(slang)*, flake *(slang, chiefly U.S.)*, anomaly, oddity, oddball *(informal)*, nonconformist, wacko *(slang)*, odd bod *(informal)*, queer fish *(Brit. informal)*, weirdo or weirdie *(informal)*: *He's an original, this one, and a good storyteller.*

> **QUOTATIONS**
> Original thought is like original sin: both happened before you were born to people you could not have possibly met
> [Fran Lebowitz *Social Studies*]

originality NOUN = **novelty**, imagination, creativity, innovation, new ideas, individuality, ingenuity, freshness, uniqueness, boldness, inventiveness, cleverness, resourcefulness, break with tradition, newness, unfamiliarity, creative spirit, unorthodoxy, unconventionality, creativeness, innovativeness, imaginativeness **OPPOSITE:** conventionality

> **QUOTATIONS**
> He was dull in a new way, and that made many people think him great
> [Dr. Johnson]

originally ADVERB = **initially**, first, firstly, at first, primarily, at the start, in the first place, to begin with, at the outset, in the beginning, in the early stages

originate VERB **1 = begin**, start, emerge, come, issue, happen, rise, appear, spring, flow, be born, proceed, arise, dawn, stem, derive, commence, emanate, crop up *(informal)*, come into being, come into existence: *The disease originated in Africa.* **OPPOSITE:** end **2 = invent**, produce, create, form, develop, design, launch, set up, introduce, imagine, institute, generate, come up with *(informal)*, pioneer, evolve, devise, initiate, conceive, bring about, formulate, give birth to, contrive, improvise, dream up *(informal)*, inaugurate, think up, set in motion: *No-one knows who originated this story.*

originator NOUN = **creator**, father *or* mother, founder, author, maker, framer, designer, architect, pioneer, generator, inventor, innovator, prime mover, initiator, begetter

ornament NOUN **1 = decoration**, trimming, accessory, garnish, frill, festoon, trinket, bauble, flounce, gewgaw, knick-knack, furbelow, falderal: *Christmas tree ornaments* **2 = embellishment**, trimming, decoration, embroidery, elaboration, adornment, ornamentation: *Her dress was plain and without ornament.*
▷ VERB = **decorate**, trim, adorn, enhance, deck, array, dress up, enrich, brighten, garnish, gild, do up *(informal)*, embellish, emblazon, festoon, bedeck, beautify, prettify, bedizen *(archaic)*, engarland: *The Egyptians ornamented their mirrors with carved handles of ivory, gold, or wood.*

ornamental ADJECTIVE = **decorative**, pretty, attractive, fancy, enhancing, for show, embellishing, showy, beautifying, nonfunctional

ornamentation NOUN = **decoration**, trimming, frills, garnishing, embroidery, enrichment, elaboration, embellishment, adornment, beautification, ornateness

ornate ADJECTIVE = **elaborate**, fancy, decorated, detailed, beautiful, complex, busy, complicated, elegant, extravagant, baroque, ornamented, fussy, flowery, showy, ostentatious, rococo, florid, bedecked, overelaborate, high-wrought, aureate **OPPOSITE:** plain

orthodox ADJECTIVE **1 = established**, official, accepted, received, common, popular, traditional, normal, regular, usual, ordinary, approved, familiar, acknowledged, conventional, routine, customary, well-established, kosher *(informal)*: *These ideas are now being incorporated into orthodox medical treatment.* **OPPOSITE:** unorthodox **2 = conformist**, conservative, traditional, strict, devout, observant, doctrinal: *orthodox Jews* **OPPOSITE:** nonconformist

orthodoxy NOUN **1 = doctrine**, teaching, opinion, principle, belief, convention, canon, creed, dogma, tenet, precept, article of faith: *He departed from prevailing orthodoxies and broke new ground.* **2 = conformity**, received wisdom, traditionalism, inflexibility, conformism, conventionality: *a return to political orthodoxy* **OPPOSITE:** nonconformity

oscillate VERB **1 = fluctuate**, swing, vary, sway, waver, veer, rise and fall, vibrate, undulate, go up and down, seesaw: *The needle indicating volume was oscillating wildly.* **2 = waver**, change, swing, shift, vary, sway, alternate, veer, ebb and flow, vacillate, seesaw: *She oscillated between elation and despair.* **OPPOSITE:** settle

oscillation NOUN **1 = fluctuation**, swing, variation, instability, imbalance, wavering, volatility, variability, unpredictability, seesawing, disequilibrium, capriciousness, mutability, inconstancy, changeableness: *a slight oscillation in world temperature* **2 = wavering**, swing, shift, swaying, alteration, veering, seesawing, vacillation: *his oscillation between scepticism and credulity*

ostensible ADJECTIVE = **apparent**, seeming, supposed, alleged, so-called, pretended, exhibited, manifest, outward, superficial, professed, purported, avowed, specious

ostensibly ADVERB = **apparently**, seemingly, supposedly, outwardly, on the surface, on the face of it, superficially, to all intents and purposes, professedly, speciously, for the ostensible purpose of

ostentatious ADJECTIVE = **pretentious**, extravagant, flamboyant, flash *(informal)*, loud, dashing, inflated, conspicuous, vulgar, brash, high-flown, flashy, pompous, flaunted, flaunting, grandiose, crass, gaudy, showy, swanky *(informal)*, snobbish, puffed up, specious, boastful, obtrusive, highfalutin *(informal)*, arty-farty *(informal)*, magniloquent, bling *(slang)* **OPPOSITE:** modest

ostracism NOUN **= exclusion**, boycott, isolation, exile, rejection, expulsion, avoidance, cold-shouldering, renunciation, banishment **OPPOSITE:** acceptance

other DETERMINER **1 = additional**, more, further, new, added, extra, fresh, spare, supplementary, auxiliary: *No other details are available at the moment.* **2 = different**, alternative, contrasting, distinct, diverse, dissimilar, separate, alternative, substitute, alternate, unrelated, variant: *Try to find other words and phrases to give variety to your writing.* **3 = remaining**, left-over, residual, extant: *The other pupils were taken to an exhibition.*

otherwise SENTENCE CONNECTOR **= or else**, or, if not, or then: *Write it down, otherwise you'll forget it.* ▷ ADVERB **1 = apart from that**, in other ways, in (all) other respects: *a caravan slightly dented but otherwise in good condition* **2 = differently**, any other way, in another way, contrarily, contrastingly, in contrary fashion: *I believed he would be home soon – I had no reason to think otherwise.*

ounce NOUN **= shred**, bit, drop, trace, scrap, grain, particle, fragment, atom, crumb, snippet, speck, whit, iota

oust VERB **= expel**, turn out, dismiss, exclude, exile, discharge, throw out, relegate, displace, topple, banish, eject, depose, evict, dislodge, unseat, dispossess, send packing, turf out *(informal)*, disinherit, drum out, show someone the door, give the bum's rush *(slang)*, throw out on your ear *(informal)*

out ADJECTIVE **1 = not in**, away, elsewhere, outside, gone, abroad, from home, absent, not here, not there, not at home: *I tried to phone you last night, but you were out.* **2 = extinguished**, ended, finished, dead, cold, exhausted, expired, used up, doused, at an end: *There was an occasional spark but the fire was out.* **OPPOSITE:** alight **3 = in bloom**, opening, open, flowering, blooming, in flower, in full bloom: *The daffodils are out now.* **4 = available**, on sale, in the shops, at hand, to be had, purchasable, procurable: *Their new album is out next week.* **5 = not allowed**, banned, forbidden, ruled out, vetoed, not on *(informal)*, unacceptable, prohibited, taboo, verboten *(German)*: *Drinking is bad enough, but smoking is right out.* **OPPOSITE:** allowed **6 = out of date**, dead, square *(informal)*, old-fashioned, dated, outdated, unfashionable, antiquated, outmoded, passé, old hat, behind the times, out of style, démodé *(French)*, not with it *(informal)*: *Romance is making a comeback. Cynicism is out.* **OPPOSITE:** fashionable **7 = inaccurate**, wrong, incorrect, faulty, off the mark, erroneous, off target, wide of the mark: *Our calculations were only slightly out.* **OPPOSITE:** accurate **8 = revealed**, exposed, common knowledge, public knowledge, (out) in the open: *The secret about his drug addiction is out.* **OPPOSITE:** kept secret ▷ VERB **= expose**, uncover, unmask: *The New York gay action group recently outed an American Congressman.*

out-and-out ADJECTIVE **= absolute**, complete, total, perfect, sheer, utter, outright, thorough, downright, consummate, unqualified, unmitigated, dyed-in-the-wool, thoroughgoing, unalloyed, arrant, deep-dyed *(usually derogatory)*

outbreak NOUN **1 = eruption**, burst, explosion, epidemic, rash, outburst, flare-up, flash, spasm, upsurge: *an outbreak of violence involving hundreds of youths; This outbreak of flu is no worse than normal.* **2 = onset**, beginning, outset, opening, dawn, commencement: *On the outbreak of war he expected to be called up.*

outburst NOUN **1 = explosion**, surge, outbreak, eruption, flare-up **2 = fit**, storm, attack, gush, flare-up, eruption, spasm, outpouring, paroxysm

outcast NOUN **= pariah**, exile, outlaw, undesirable, untouchable, leper, vagabond, wretch, persona non grata *(Latin)*

outclass VERB **= surpass**, top, beat, cap *(informal)*, exceed, eclipse, overshadow, excel, transcend, outstrip, outdo, outshine, leave standing *(informal)*, tower above, go one better than *(informal)*, be a cut above *(informal)*, run rings around *(informal)*, outdistance, outrank, put in the shade, leave *or* put in the shade

outcome NOUN **= result**, end, consequence, conclusion, end result, payoff *(informal)*, upshot

outcry NOUN **= protest**, complaint, objection, cry, dissent, outburst, disapproval, clamour, uproar, commotion, protestation, exclamation, formal complaint, hue and cry, hullaballoo, demurral

outdated ADJECTIVE **= old-fashioned**, dated, obsolete, out of date, passé, antique, archaic, unfashionable, antiquated, outmoded, behind the times, out of style, obsolescent, démodé *(French)*, out of the ark *(informal)*, oldfangled **OPPOSITE:** modern

outdo VERB **= surpass**, best, top, beat, overcome, exceed, eclipse, overshadow, excel, transcend, outstrip, get the better of, outclass, outshine, tower above, outsmart *(informal)*, outmanoeuvre, go one better than *(informal)*, run rings around *(informal)*, outfox, outdistance, be one up on, score points off, put in the shade, outjockey

outdoor ADJECTIVE **= open-air**, outside, out-of-door(s), alfresco **OPPOSITE:** indoor

outer ADJECTIVE **1 = external**, outside, outward, exterior, exposed, outermost: *Peel away the outer skin of the onion.* **OPPOSITE:** inner **2 = surface**, external, outward, exterior, superficial: *Our preoccupation with appearance goes much deeper than the outer image.* **3 = outlying**, remote, distant, provincial, out-of-the-way, peripheral, far-flung: *the outer suburbs of the city* **OPPOSITE:** central

outfit NOUN **1 = costume**, dress, clothes, clothing, suit, gear *(informal)*, get-up *(informal)*, kit, ensemble, apparel, attire, garb, togs *(informal)*, threads *(slang)*, schmutter *(slang)*, rigout *(informal)*: *She was wearing an outfit we'd bought the previous day.* **2 = group**, company, team, set, party, firm, association, unit, crowd, squad, organization, crew, gang, corps, setup *(informal)*, galère *(French)*: *He works for a private security outfit.* ▷ VERB **1 = equip**, stock, supply, turn out, appoint, provision, furnish, fit out, deck out, kit out, fit up, accoutre: *Homes can be outfitted with security lights for a few hundred dollars.* **2 = dress**, clothe, attire, deck out, kit out, rig out: *The travel company outfitted their staff in coloured jerseys.*

outfitter NOUN **= clothier**, tailor, couturier, dressmaker, seamstress, haberdasher *(U.S.)*, costumier, garment maker, modiste

outflow NOUN **1 = stream**, issue, flow, rush, emergence, spate, deluge, outpouring, effusion, emanation, efflux: *an increasing outflow of refugees from the country* **2 = discharge**, flow, jet, cascade, ebb, gush, drainage, torrent, deluge, spurt, spout, outpouring, outfall, efflux, effluence, debouchment: *an outflow of fresh water from a river*

outgoing ADJECTIVE **1 = leaving**, last, former, past, previous, retiring, withdrawing, prior, departing, erstwhile, late, ex-: *the outgoing director of the Edinburgh International Festival* **OPPOSITE:** incoming **2 = sociable**, open, social, warm, friendly, accessible, expansive, cordial, genial, affable, extrovert, approachable, gregarious, communicative, convivial, demonstrative, unreserved, companionable: *She is very friendly and outgoing.* **OPPOSITE:** reserved

outgoings PLURAL NOUN **= expenses**, costs, payments, expenditure, overheads, outlay

outgrowth NOUN **1 = product**, result, development, fruit, consequence, outcome, legacy, emergence, derivative, spin-off, by-product, end result, offshoot, upshot: *Her first book is an outgrowth of an art project she began in 1988.* **2 = offshoot**, shoot, branch, limb, projection, sprout, node, outcrop, appendage, scion, protuberance, excrescence: *a new organism develops as an outgrowth or bud*

outing NOUN **= journey**, run, trip, tour, expedition, excursion, spin *(informal)*, ramble, jaunt, pleasure trip

outlandish ADJECTIVE **= strange**, odd, extraordinary, wonderful, funny, bizarre, fantastic, astonishing, eye-popping *(informal)*, curious, weird, foreign, alien, exotic, exceptional, peculiar, eccentric, abnormal, out-of-the-way, queer, irregular, singular, grotesque, far-out *(slang)*, unheard-of, preposterous, off-the-wall *(slang)*, left-field *(informal)*, freakish, barbarous, outré, daggy *(Austral. & N.Z. informal)* **OPPOSITE:** normal

outlast VERB **= outlive**, survive, live after, outstay, live on after, endure beyond, outwear, remain alive after

outlaw NOUN **= bandit**, criminal, thief, crook, robber, fugitive, outcast, delinquent, felon, highwayman, desperado, marauder, brigand, lawbreaker, footpad *(archaic)*: *a band of desperate outlaws*
▷ VERB **1 = ban**, bar, veto, forbid, condemn, exclude, embargo, suppress, prohibit, banish, disallow, proscribe, make illegal, interdict: *The German government has outlawed some fascist groups.* **OPPOSITE:** legalise
2 = banish, excommunicate, ostracize, put a price on (someone's) head: *He should be outlawed for his crimes against the state.*

outlay NOUN **= expenditure**, cost, spending, charge, investment, payment, expense(s), outgoings, disbursement

outlet NOUN **1 = shop**, store, supermarket, market, mart, boutique, emporium, hypermarket: *the largest retail outlet in the city*
2 = channel, release, medium, avenue, vent, conduit, safety valve, means of expression: *He found an outlet for his emotions in his music.* **3 = pipe**, opening, channel, passage, tube, exit, canal, way out, funnel, conduit, duct, orifice, egress: *The leak was caused by a fracture in the cooling water outlet.*

outline NOUN **1 = summary**, review, résumé, abstract, summing-up, digest, rundown, compendium, main features, synopsis, rough idea, précis, bare facts, thumbnail sketch, recapitulation, abridgment: *There follows an outline of the survey findings.*
2 = draft, plan, drawing, frame, tracing, rough, framework, sketch, skeleton, layout, delineation, preliminary form: *an outline of a plan to reduce the country's national debt* **3 = shape**, lines, form, figure, profile, silhouette, configuration, contour(s), delineation, lineament(s): *He could see only the hazy outline of the trees.*
▷ VERB **1 = summarize**, review, draft, plan, trace, sketch (in), sum up, encapsulate, delineate, rough out, adumbrate: *The methods outlined in this book are only suggestions.* **2 = silhouette**, etch, delineate: *The building was a beautiful sight, outlined against the starry sky.*

outlive VERB **= survive**, outlast, live on after, endure beyond, remain alive after

outlook NOUN **1 = attitude**, views, opinion, position, approach, mood, perspective, point of view, stance, viewpoint, disposition, standpoint, frame of mind: *The illness had a profound effect on his outlook.* **2 = prospect(s)**, future, expectations, forecast, prediction, projection, probability, prognosis: *The economic outlook is one of rising unemployment.* **3 = view**, prospect, scene, aspect, perspective, panorama, vista: *The house has an expansive southern outlook over the valley.*

outlying ADJECTIVE **= remote**, isolated, distant, outer, provincial, out-of-the-way, peripheral, far-off, secluded, far-flung, faraway, in the middle of nowhere, off the beaten track, backwoods, godforsaken

outmanoeuvre or *(U.S.)* **outmaneuver** VERB **= outwit**, outdo, get the better of, circumvent, outflank, outsmart *(informal)*, steal a march on *(informal)*, put one over on *(informal)*, outfox, run rings round *(informal)*, outthink, outgeneral, outjockey

outmoded ADJECTIVE **= old-fashioned**, passé, dated, out, dead, square *(informal)*, ancient, antique, outdated, obsolete, out-of-date, old-time, archaic, unfashionable, superseded, bygone, antiquated, anachronistic, olden *(archaic)*, behind the times, superannuated, fossilized, out of style, antediluvian, outworn, obsolescent, démodé *(French)*, out of the ark *(informal)*, not with it *(informal)*, oldfangled **OPPOSITE:** modern

out of date ADJECTIVE **1 = old-fashioned**, ancient, dated, discarded, extinct, outdated, stale, obsolete, démodé *(French)*, archaic, unfashionable, superseded, antiquated, outmoded, passé, old hat, behind the times, superannuated, out of style, outworn, obsolescent, out of the ark *(informal)*, oldfangled: *processes using out-of-date technology and very old equipment* **OPPOSITE:** modern
2 = invalid, expired, lapsed, void, superseded, elapsed, null and void: *These tax records are now out of date.*

out of the way ADJECTIVE
1 = remote, far, distant, isolated, lonely, obscure, far-off, secluded, inaccessible, far-flung, faraway, outlying, in the middle of nowhere, off the beaten track, backwoods, godforsaken, unfrequented: *I like travelling to out-of-the-way places.*
OPPOSITE: nearby **2 = unusual**, surprising, odd, strange, extraordinary, remarkable, bizarre, unexpected, curious, exceptional, notable, peculiar, abnormal, queer, uncommon, singular, unconventional, outlandish, out of the ordinary, left-field *(informal)*, atypical: *He did not seem to think her behaviour at all out of the way.*

outpouring NOUN **= outburst**, storm, stream, explosion, surge, outbreak, deluge, eruption, spasm, paroxysm, effusion, issue

output NOUN **= production**, manufacture, manufacturing, yield, productivity, outturn *(rare)*

outrage NOUN **1 = indignation**, shock, anger, rage, fury, hurt, resentment, scorn, wrath, ire *(literary)*, exasperation, umbrage, righteous anger: *The decision has provoked outrage from human rights groups.* **2 = atrocity**, crime, horror, evil, cruelty, brutality, enormity, barbarism, inhumanity, abomination, barbarity, villainy, act of cruelty: *The terrorists' latest outrage is a bomb attack on a busy station.*
▷ VERB **= offend**, shock, upset, pain, wound, provoke, insult, infuriate, incense, gall, madden, vex, affront, displease, rile, scandalize, give offence, nark *(Brit., Austral. & N.Z. slang)*, cut to the quick, make your blood boil, put (someone's) nose out of joint, put (someone's) back up, disgruntle: *Many people have been outraged by these comments.*

outrageous ADJECTIVE **1 = atrocious**, shocking, terrible, violent, offensive, appalling, cruel, savage, horrible, beastly, horrifying, vicious, ruthless, infamous, disgraceful, scandalous, wicked, barbaric, unspeakable, inhuman, diabolical, heinous, flagrant, egregious, abominable, infernal, fiendish, villainous, nefarious, iniquitous, execrable, godawful *(slang)*, hellacious *(U.S. slang)*: *I must apologize for my friend's outrageous behaviour.* **OPPOSITE:** mild
2 = unreasonable, unfair, excessive, steep *(informal)*, shocking, over the top *(slang)*, extravagant, too great, scandalous, preposterous, unwarranted, exorbitant, extortionate, immoderate, O.T.T. *(slang)*: *Charges for long-distance telephone calls are absolutely outrageous.*
OPPOSITE: reasonable

outright ADJECTIVE **1 = absolute**, complete, total, direct, perfect, pure, sheer, utter, thorough, wholesale, unconditional, downright, consummate, unqualified, undeniable, out-and-out, unadulterated, unmitigated, thoroughgoing, unalloyed, arrant, deep-dyed *(usually derogatory)*: *He told me an outright lie.*
2 = definite, clear, certain, straight, flat, absolute, black-and-white, decisive, straightforward, clear-cut, unmistakable, unequivocal, unqualified, unambiguous, cut-and-dried *(informal)*, incontrovertible, uncontestable: *She failed to win an outright victory.*
▷ ADVERB **1 = openly**, frankly, plainly, face to face, explicitly, overtly, candidly, unreservedly, unhesitatingly, forthrightly, straight from the shoulder *(informal)*: *Why are you being so mysterious? Why can't you just*

tell me outright? **2 = absolutely**, completely, totally, fully, entirely, thoroughly, wholly, utterly, to the full, without hesitation, to the hilt, one hundred per cent, straightforwardly, without restraint, unmitigatedly, lock, stock and barrel: *His plan was rejected outright.* **3 = instantly**, immediately, at once, straight away, cleanly, on the spot, right away, there and then, instantaneously: *The driver was killed outright in the crash.*

outset NOUN **= beginning**, start, opening, early days, starting point, onset, inauguration, inception, commencement, kickoff *(informal)* **OPPOSITE:** finish

outside ADJECTIVE **1 = external**, outer, exterior, surface, extreme, outdoor, outward, superficial, extraneous, outermost, extramural: *Cracks are beginning to appear on the outside wall.* **OPPOSITE:** inner **2 = remote**, small, unlikely, slight, slim, poor, distant, faint, marginal, doubtful, dubious, slender, meagre, negligible, inconsiderable: *I thought I had an outside chance of winning.*
▷ ADVERB **= outdoors**, out, out of the house, out-of-doors: *I went outside and sat on the steps.*
▷ NOUN **= exterior**, face, front, covering, skin, surface, shell, coating, finish, façade, topside: *the outside of the building; Grill until the outsides are browned.*

> **USAGE**
> The use of *outside of* and *inside of*, although fairly common, is generally thought to be incorrect or nonstandard: *She waits outside* (not *outside of*) *the school.*

outsider NOUN **= stranger**, incomer, visitor, foreigner, alien, newcomer, intruder, new arrival, unknown, interloper, odd one out, nonmember, outlander

outsize ADJECTIVE **1 = huge**, great, large, giant, massive, enormous, monster, immense, mega *(slang)*, jumbo *(informal)*, gigantic, monumental, mammoth, bulky, colossal, mountainous, oversized, stupendous, gargantuan, elephantine, ginormous *(informal)*, Brobdingnagian, humongous *or* humungous *(U.S. slang)*: *An outsize teddy bear sat on the bed.* **OPPOSITE:** tiny **2 = extra-large**, large, generous, ample, roomy: *Often outsize clothes are made from cheap fabric.*

outskirts PLURAL NOUN **= edge**, borders, boundary, suburbs, fringe, perimeter, vicinity, periphery, suburbia, environs, purlieus, faubourgs

outsmart VERB **= outwit**, trick, take in *(informal)*, cheat, deceive, defraud, dupe, gull *(archaic)*, get the better of, swindle, circumvent, outperform, make a fool of *(informal)*, outmanoeuvre, go one better than *(informal)*, put one over on *(informal)*, outfox, run rings round *(informal)*, pull a fast one on *(informal)*, outthink, outjockey

outspan VERB **= relax**, chill out *(slang, chiefly U.S.)*, take it easy, loosen up, laze, lighten up *(slang)*, put your feet up, hang loose *(slang)*, let yourself go *(informal)*, let your hair down *(informal)*, mellow out *(informal)*, make yourself at home

outspoken ADJECTIVE **= forthright**, open, free, direct, frank, straightforward, blunt, explicit, downright, candid, upfront *(informal)*, unequivocal, undisguised, plain-spoken, unreserved, unconcealed, unceremonious, free-spoken, straight from the shoulder *(informal)*, undissembling **OPPOSITE:** reserved

outstanding ADJECTIVE **1 = excellent**, good, great, important, special, fine, noted, champion, celebrated, brilliant, impressive, superb, distinguished, well-known, prominent, superior, first-class, exceptional, notable, world-class, exquisite, admirable, eminent, exemplary, first-rate, stellar *(informal)*, superlative, top-notch *(informal)*, mean *(slang)*, pre-eminent, meritorious, estimable, tiptop, A1 *or* A-one *(informal)*, booshit *(Austral. slang)*, exo *(Austral. slang)*, sik *(Austral. slang)*, rad *(informal)*, phat *(slang)*, schmick *(Austral. informal)*, beaut *(informal)*, barrie *(Scot. slang)*, belting *(Brit. slang)*, pearler *(Austral. slang)*: *an outstanding tennis player* **OPPOSITE:** mediocre **2 = conspicuous**, marked, striking, arresting, signal, remarkable, memorable, notable, eye-catching, salient, noteworthy: *an area of outstanding natural beauty* **3 = unpaid**, remaining, due, owing, ongoing, pending, payable, unsettled, unresolved, uncollected: *The total debt outstanding is $70 billion.* **4 = undone**, left, not done, omitted, unfinished, incomplete, passed over, unfulfilled, not completed, unperformed, unattended to: *Complete any work outstanding from yesterday.*

outstrip VERB **1 = exceed**, eclipse, overtake, top, cap *(informal)*, go beyond, surpass, outdo: *In 1989 and 1990 demand outstripped supply.* **2 = surpass** *(informal)*, beat, leave behind, eclipse, overtake, best, top, better, overshadow, outdo, outclass, outperform, outshine, leave standing *(informal)*, tower above, get ahead of, go one better than *(informal)*, run rings around, knock spots off *(informal)*, put in the shade: *In pursuing her ambition she outstripped everyone else.* **3 = outdistance**, shake off, outrun, outpace: *He soon outstripped the other runners.*

outward ADJECTIVE **= apparent**, seeming, outside, surface, external, outer, superficial, ostensible **OPPOSITE:** inward

outwardly ADVERB **= apparently**, externally, seemingly, it seems that, on the surface, it appears that, ostensibly, on the face of it, superficially, to the eye, to all intents and purposes, to all appearances, as far as you can see, professedly

outweigh VERB **= override**, cancel (out), eclipse, offset, make up for, compensate for, redeem, supersede, neutralize, counterbalance, nullify, take precedence over, prevail over, obviate, balance out, preponderate, outbalance

outwit VERB **= outsmart** *(informal)*, get the better of, circumvent, outperform, outmanoeuvre, go one better than *(informal)*, put one over on *(informal)*, outfox, run rings round *(informal)*, pull a fast one on *(informal)*, outthink, outjockey

oval ADJECTIVE **= elliptical**, egg-shaped, ovoid, ovate, ellipsoidal, oviform

ovation NOUN **= applause**, hand, cheering, cheers, praise, tribute, acclaim, clapping, accolade, plaudits, big hand, commendation, hand-clapping, acclamation, laudation **OPPOSITE:** derision

over PREPOSITION **1 = above**, on top of, atop: *He looked at himself in the mirror over the fireplace.* **2 = on top of**, on, across, upon: *His coat was thrown over a chair.* **3 = across**, past, (looking) onto: *a room with a wonderful view over the river* **4 = more than**, above, exceeding, in excess of, upwards of: *Smoking kills over 100,000 people in Britain a year.* **5 = about**, regarding, relating to, with respect to, re, concerning, apropos of, anent *(Scot.)*: *You're making a lot of fuss over nothing.*
▷ ADVERB **1 = above**, overhead, in the sky, on high, aloft, up above: *Planes flew over every 15 minutes or so.* **2 = extra**, more, other, further, beyond, additional, in addition, surplus, in excess, left over, unused, supplementary, auxiliary: *There were two for each of us, and one over.*
▷ ADJECTIVE **= finished**, by, done (with), through, ended, closed, past, completed, complete, gone, in the past, settled, concluded, accomplished, wrapped up *(informal)*, bygone, at an end, ancient history *(informal)*, over and done with: *I think the worst is over now.*
over and above = in addition to, added to, on top of, besides, plus, let alone, not to mention, as well as, over and beyond: *Costs have gone up 7% over and above inflation.*
over and over (again) = repeatedly, frequently, again and again, often, many times, time and (time) again, time after time, ad nauseam: *He plays the same song over and over again.*

> **QUOTATIONS**
> It ain't over till it's over
> [attributed to Yogi Berra]
> ▸ *related prefixes:* hyper-, super-, supra-, sur-

O

overall ADJECTIVE = **total**, full, whole, general, complete, long-term, entire, global, comprehensive, gross, blanket, umbrella, long-range, inclusive, all-embracing, overarching: *Cut down your overall intake of calories.*
▷ ADVERB = **in general**, generally, mostly, all things considered, on average, in (the) large, on the whole, predominantly, in the main, in the long term, by and large, all in all, on balance, generally speaking, taking everything into consideration: *Overall, I was disappointed with the result.*

overawed ADJECTIVE = **intimidated**, threatened, alarmed, frightened, scared, terrified, cowed, put off, daunted, unnerved

overbearing ADJECTIVE = **domineering**, lordly, superior, arrogant, authoritarian, oppressive, autocratic, masterful, dictatorial, coercive, bossy (*informal*), imperious, haughty, tyrannical, magisterial, despotic, high-handed, peremptory, supercilious, officious, overweening, iron-handed **OPPOSITE:** submissive

overblown ADJECTIVE **1** = **excessive**, exaggerated, over the top (*slang*), too much, inflated, extravagant, overdone, disproportionate, undue, fulsome, intemperate, immoderate, O.T.T. (*slang*): *The reporting of the story was fair, though a little overblown.* **2** = **inflated**, rhetorical, high-flown, pompous, pretentious, flowery, florid, turgid, bombastic, windy, grandiloquent, fustian, magniloquent, aureate, euphuistic: *The book contains a heavy dose of overblown lyrical description.*

overcast ADJECTIVE = **cloudy**, grey, dull, threatening, dark, clouded, dim, gloomy, dismal, murky, dreary, leaden, clouded over, sunless, louring *or* lowering **OPPOSITE:** bright

overcharge VERB = **cheat**, con (*informal*), do (*slang*), skin (*slang*), stiff (*slang*), sting (*informal*), rip off (*slang*), fleece, defraud, surcharge, swindle, stitch up (*slang*), rook (*slang*), short-change, diddle (*informal*), take for a ride (*informal*), cozen

overcome VERB **1** = **defeat**, beat, conquer, master, tank (*slang*), crush, overwhelm, overthrow, lick (*informal*), undo, subdue, rout, overpower, quell, triumph over, best, get the better of, trounce, worst, clobber (*slang*), stuff (*slang*), vanquish, surmount, subjugate, prevail over, wipe the floor with (*informal*), make mincemeat of (*informal*), blow (someone) out of the water (*slang*), come out on top of (*informal*), bring (someone) to their knees (*informal*), render incapable, render powerless, be victorious over, render helpless: *the satisfaction of overcoming a rival* **2** = **conquer**, beat, master, survive, weather, curb, suppress, subdue, rise above, quell, triumph over, get the better of, vanquish: *I have fought to overcome my fear of spiders.*

overdo VERB = **exaggerate**, overstate, overuse, overplay, do to death (*informal*), belabour, carry *or* take too far, make a production (out) of (*informal*), lay (something) on thick (*informal*): *He overdid his usually quite funny vitriol.* **OPPOSITE:** minimize
overdo it = **overwork**, go too far, go overboard, strain *or* overstrain yourself, burn the midnight oil, burn the candle at both ends (*informal*), wear yourself out, bite off more than you can chew, have too many irons in the fire, overtire yourself, drive yourself too far, overburden yourself, overload yourself, overtax your strength, work your fingers to the bone: *When you start your running programme, don't be tempted to overdo it.*

overdone ADJECTIVE **1** = **overcooked**, burnt, spoiled, dried up, charred, burnt to a crisp *or* cinder: *The meat was overdone and the vegetables disappointing.* **2** = **excessive**, too much, unfair, unnecessary, exaggerated, over the top (*slang*), needless, unreasonable, disproportionate, undue, hyped, preposterous, inordinate, fulsome, immoderate, overelaborate, beyond all bounds, O.T.T. (*slang*): *In fact, all the panic about the drought in Britain was overdone.* **OPPOSITE:** minimized

overdue ADJECTIVE **1** = **delayed**, belated, late, late in the day, long delayed, behind schedule, tardy, not before time (*informal*), behind time, unpunctual, behindhand: *I'll go and pay an overdue visit to my mother.* **OPPOSITE:** early **2** = **unpaid**, owing: *a strike aimed at forcing the government to pay overdue salaries*

overflow VERB **1** = **spill over**, discharge, well over, run over, pour over, pour out, bubble over, brim over, surge over, slop over, teem over: *the sickening stench of raw sewage overflowing from toilets* **2** = **flood**, swamp, submerge, cover, drown, soak, immerse, inundate, deluge, pour over: *The river has overflowed its banks in several places.*
▷ NOUN **1** = **flood**, flooding, spill, discharge, spilling over, inundation: *Carpeting is damaged from the overflow of water from a bathtub.* **2** = **surplus**, extra, excess, overspill, inundation, overabundance, additional people *or* things: *Tents have been set up next to hospitals to handle the overflow.*

overflowing ADJECTIVE = **full**, abounding, swarming, rife, plentiful, thronged, teeming, copious, bountiful, profuse, brimful, overfull, superabundant **OPPOSITE:** deficient

overhang VERB = **project (over)**, extend (over), loom (over), stand out (over), bulge (over), stick out (over), protrude (over), jut (over), impend (over)

overhaul VERB **1** = **check**, service, maintain, examine, restore, tune (up), repair, go over, inspect, fine tune, do up (*informal*), re-examine, recondition: *The plumbing was overhauled a year ago.* **2** = **overtake**, pass, leave behind, catch up with, get past, outstrip, get ahead of, draw level with, outdistance: *Beattie led for several laps before he was overhauled by Itoh.*
▷ NOUN = **check**, service, examination, going-over (*informal*), inspection, once-over (*informal*), checkup, reconditioning: *The study says there must be a complete overhaul of air traffic control systems.*

overhead ADJECTIVE = **raised**, suspended, elevated, aerial, overhanging: *people who live under or near overhead cables*
▷ ADVERB = **above**, in the sky, on high, aloft, up above: *planes passing overhead* **OPPOSITE:** underneath

overheads PLURAL NOUN = **running costs**, expenses, outgoings, operating costs, oncosts

overjoyed ADJECTIVE = **delighted**, happy, pleased, thrilled, ecstatic, jubilant, joyous, joyful, elated, over the moon (*informal*), euphoric, rapturous, rapt, only too happy, gladdened, on cloud nine (*informal*), transported, cock-a-hoop, blissed out, in raptures, tickled pink (*informal*), deliriously happy, in seventh heaven, floating on air, stoked (*Austral. & N.Z. informal*) **OPPOSITE:** heartbroken

overlay VERB = **cover**, coat, blanket, adorn, mantle, ornament, envelop, veneer, encase, inlay, superimpose, laminate, overspread: *The floor was overlaid with rugs of Oriental design; a very large dark wood table overlaid in glass*
▷ NOUN = **covering**, casing, wrapping, decoration, veneer, adornment, ornamentation, appliqué: *Silver overlay is bonded to the entire surface.*

overlook VERB **1** = **look over** *or* **out on**, have a view of, command a view of, front on to, give upon, afford a view of: *The rooms overlooked the garden.* **2** = **miss**, forget, neglect, omit, disregard, pass over, fail to notice, leave undone, slip up on, leave out of consideration: *We overlook all sorts of warning signals about our health.* **OPPOSITE:** notice **3** = **ignore**, excuse, forgive, pardon, disregard, condone, turn a blind eye to, wink at, blink at, make allowances for, let someone off with, let pass, let ride, discount, pass over, take no notice of, be oblivious to, pay no attention to, turn a deaf ear to, shut your eyes to: *satisfying relationships that enable them to overlook each other's faults*

overly ADVERB = **too**, very, extremely, exceedingly, unduly, excessively, unreasonably, inordinately, immoderately, over-

overpower VERB **1** = **overcome**, master, overwhelm, overthrow, subdue, quell, get the better of, subjugate, prevail over, immobilize, bring (someone) to their knees (*informal*), render incapable, render powerless, render helpless, get the

The Language of Ralph Waldo Emerson

Ralph Waldo Emerson (1803–82) was an American essayist, poet, and philosopher. He was greatly concerned with the creation of an American literary style distinct from – and as great as – that of Europe. Because of this, he is generally considered to be one of the key figures in the formation of an American national literature.

In Emerson's 1836 essay, *Nature*, he argues that more can be learned from personal experiences with nature than can be learned from history. This is an important point, given that America does not have the same cultural heritage as Europe. The noun *nature* is in fact one of Emerson's 50 most frequently used words. It is interesting to compare this with the data in the *Bank of English*, Collins' corpus of present-day English, where *nature* is not even among the 1000 most frequently occurring words.

In Emerson's writings, the word *nature* is frequently found in both of its main senses: that of physical life not controlled by man, and that of the fundamental qualities of a person or thing. The adjectives which most commonly modify *nature* in Emerson's writings are *human* and *spiritual*; *nature* is here being used in the latter sense, that of something's fundamental qualities. Another significant collocation with *nature* in Emerson's writings is *art*, as in:

> They are the kings of the world who give the color of their present thought to all **nature** and all **art**.

In this case, the collocation is with the former sense of *nature*, that of physical life not controlled by man. This collocation between art and nature is unsurprising, given Emerson's preoccupation with the development of an American artistic culture.

The only noun to occur more frequently than *nature* in Emerson's writings is *man*. Emerson makes extensive use of the *man of* construction, with frequent occurrences of phrases such as *man of talent, man of genius, man of science, man of thought, man of the world,* and *man of letters*. Emerson was, in his words, keen for there to be 'creative reading as well as creative writing' in America – this was an important part of the new tradition which he envisaged – and these collocations reflect Emerson's desire for a society of thoughtful and intelligent readers.

As might be expected, both *mind* and *thought* are also commonly used by Emerson, each noun placed among his 100 most commonly used words. *Mind* is modified on several occasions by the adjective *superior*, whereas the most notable adjectival modifier of *thought* is *new*, as in:

> There are new lands, new men, **new thoughts**.

Perhaps predictably, given the frequency of its occurrence in the above example, the adjective *new* is also among Emerson's 100 most frequently used words. As well as commonly modifiying *thought*, it frequently collocates with *era*. Again, from this, we can discern Emerson's concern with the creation of a *new* literary tradition for America, not just a poor imitation of European tradition.

Power is another one of Emerson's 100 most frequently used words, although its most significant collocates – *mental* and *intellectual* – reveal that he is talking about a personal power which all people can achieve, rather than a power over other people. The phrase *power of expression* is also found several times in Emerson's writings, reflecting his belief in the importance of language, the vehicle by which the new thoughts and ideas in which he was interested could be communicated to others. However, on this point, it should be noted that it was not in Emerson's nature to directly tell the reader his conclusions; in fact, Emerson's meaning is often elusive. Emerson's writing style leaves it to the reader to make connections between the thoughts and ideas which he introduces in his essays. Such a writing style encourages the 'creative reading' for which he hoped, encouraging the reader to participate in the search for truth.

upper hand over: *It took four policemen to overpower him.* **2 = beat**, defeat, tank *(slang)*, crush, lick *(informal)*, triumph over, best, clobber *(slang)*, stuff *(slang)*, vanquish, be victorious (over), wipe the floor with *(informal)*, make mincemeat of *(informal)*, worst: *Britain's tennis No.1 yesterday overpowered his American rival.* **3 = overwhelm**, overcome, bowl over *(informal)*, stagger: *I was so overpowered by shame that I was unable to speak.*

overpowering ADJECTIVE **1 = overwhelming**, powerful, extreme, compelling, irresistible, breathtaking, compulsive, invincible, uncontrollable: *The desire for revenge can be overpowering.* **2 = strong**, marked, powerful, distinct, sickening, unbearable, suffocating, unmistakable, nauseating: *There was an overpowering smell of garlic.* **3 = forceful**, powerful, overwhelming, dynamic, compelling, persuasive, overbearing: *his overpowering manner*

overrate VERB **= overestimate**, glorify, overvalue, oversell, make too much of, rate too highly, assess too highly, overpraise, exaggerate the worth of, overprize, think *or* expect too much of, think too highly of, attach too much importance to

override VERB **1 = outweigh**, overcome, eclipse, supersede, take precedence over, prevail over, outbalance: *His work frequently overrides all other considerations.* **2 = overrule**, reverse, cancel, overturn, set aside, repeal, quash, revoke, disallow, rescind, upset, rule against, invalidate, annul, nullify, ride roughshod over, outvote, countermand, trample underfoot, make null and void: *The senate failed by one vote to override the President's veto.* **3 = ignore**, reject, discount, overlook, set aside, disregard, pass over, take no notice of, take no account of, pay no attention to, turn a deaf ear to: *He overrode all opposition to his plans.*

overriding ADJECTIVE **= major**, chief, main, prime, predominant, leading, controlling, final, ruling, determining, primary, supreme, principal, ultimate, dominant, compelling, prevailing, cardinal, sovereign, paramount, prevalent, pivotal, top-priority, overruling, preponderant, number one **OPPOSITE:** minor

overrule VERB **= reverse**, alter, cancel, recall, discount, overturn, set aside, override, repeal, quash, revoke, disallow, rescind, rule against, invalidate, annul, nullify, outvote, countermand, make null and void **OPPOSITE:** approve

overrun VERB **1 = overwhelm**, attack, assault, occupy, raid, invade, penetrate, swamp, rout, assail, descend upon, run riot over: *A group of rebels overran the port; A military group overran them and took four of them off.* **2 = spread over**, overwhelm, choke, swamp, overflow, infest, inundate, permeate, spread like wildfire, swarm over, surge over, overgrow: *The flower beds were overrun with weeds.* **3 = exceed**, go beyond, surpass, overshoot, outrun, run over *or* on: *Costs overran the budget by about 30%.*

overseer NOUN **= supervisor**, manager, chief, boss *(informal)*, master, inspector, superior, administrator, steward, superintendent, gaffer *(informal, chiefly Brit.)*, foreman, super *(informal)*, baas *(S. African)*

overshadow VERB **1 = spoil**, ruin, mar, wreck, scar, blight, crool *or* cruel *(Austral. slang)*, mess up, take the edge off, put a damper on, cast a gloom upon, take the pleasure *or* enjoyment out of: *Her mother's illness overshadowed her childhood.* **2 = outshine**, eclipse, surpass, dwarf, rise above, take precedence over, tower above, steal the limelight from, leave *or* put in the shade, render insignificant by comparison, throw into the shade: *I'm sorry to say that she overshadowed her less attractive sister.* **3 = shade**, cloud, eclipse, darken, overcast, adumbrate: *one of the towers that overshadow the square*

oversight NOUN **1 = mistake**, error, slip, fault, misunderstanding, blunder, lapse, omission, boob *(Brit. slang)*, gaffe, slip-up *(informal)*, delinquency, inaccuracy, carelessness, howler *(informal)*, goof *(informal)*, bloomer *(Brit. informal)*, clanger *(informal)*, miscalculation, error of judgment, faux pas, inattention, laxity, boo-boo *(informal)*, erratum, barry *or* Barry Crocker *(Austral. slang)*: *By an unfortunate oversight, full instructions do not come with the product.* **2 = supervision**, keeping, control, charge, care, management, handling, administration, direction, custody, stewardship, superintendence: *I had the oversight of their collection of manuscripts.*

overt ADJECTIVE **= open**, obvious, plain, public, clear, apparent, visible, patent, evident, manifest, noticeable, blatant, downright, avowed, flagrant, observable, undisguised, barefaced, unconcealed **OPPOSITE:** hidden

overtake VERB **1 = pass**, leave behind, overhaul, catch up with, get past, draw level with, outdistance, go by *or* past: *He overtook the truck and pulled into the inside lane.* **2 = outdo**, top, exceed, eclipse, surpass, outstrip, get the better of, outclass, outshine, best, go one better than *(informal)*, outdistance, be one up on: *Japan has overtaken Britain as the Mini's biggest market.* **3 = befall**, hit, happen to, come upon, take by surprise, catch off guard, catch unawares, catch unprepared: *Tragedy was about to overtake him.* **4 = engulf**, overwhelm, hit, strike, consume, swamp, envelop, swallow up: *A sudden flood of panic overtook me.*

overthrow VERB **= defeat**, beat, master, overcome, crush, overwhelm, conquer, bring down, oust, lick *(informal)*, topple, subdue, rout, overpower, do away with, depose, trounce, unseat, vanquish, subjugate, dethrone: *The government was overthrown in a military coup three years ago.* **OPPOSITE:** uphold
▷ NOUN **= downfall**, end, fall, defeat, collapse, ruin, destruction, breakdown, ousting, undoing, rout, suppression, displacement, subversion, deposition, unseating, subjugation, dispossession, disestablishment, dethronement: *They were charged with plotting the overthrow of the state.* **OPPOSITE:** preservation

overtone NOUN *(often plural)* **= connotation**, association, suggestion, sense, hint, flavour, implication, significance, nuance, colouring, innuendo, undercurrent, intimation

overture NOUN **= prelude**, opening, introduction, introductory movement: *the William Tell Overture* **OPPOSITE:** finale

overtures PLURAL NOUN **= approach**, offer, advance, proposal, appeal, invitation, tender, proposition, opening move, conciliatory move: *He had begun to make clumsy yet endearing overtures of friendship.* **OPPOSITE:** rejection

overturn VERB **1 = tip over**, spill, topple, upturn, capsize, upend, keel over, overbalance: *The lorry went out of control, overturned and smashed into a wall; Two salmon fishermen died when their boat overturned.* **2 = knock over** *or* **down**, upset, upturn, tip over, upend: *Alex jumped up so violently that he overturned the table.* **3 = reverse**, change, alter, cancel, abolish, overthrow, set aside, repeal, quash, revoke, overrule, override, negate, rescind, invalidate, annul, nullify, obviate, countermand, declare null and void, overset: *The Russian parliament overturned his decision.* **4 = overthrow**, defeat, destroy, overcome, crush, bring down, oust, topple, do away with, depose, unseat, dethrone: *He accused his opponents of wanting to overturn the government.*

overweight ADJECTIVE **= fat**, heavy, stout, huge, massive, solid, gross, hefty, ample, plump, bulky, chunky, chubby, obese, fleshy, beefy *(informal)*, tubby *(informal)*, portly, outsize, buxom, roly-poly, rotund, podgy, corpulent, elephantine, well-padded *(informal)*, well-upholstered *(informal)*, broad in the beam *(informal)*, on the plump side **OPPOSITE:** underweight

overwhelm VERB **1 = overcome**, overpower, devastate, stagger, get the better of, bowl over *(informal)*, prostrate, knock (someone) for six *(informal)*, render speechless, render incapable, render powerless, render helpless, sweep (someone) off his *or*

her feet, take (someone's) breath away: *He was overwhelmed by a longing for times past.* **2 = destroy**, beat, defeat, overcome, smash, crush, massacre, conquer, wipe out, overthrow, knock out, lick *(informal)*, subdue, rout, eradicate, overpower, quell, annihilate, put paid to, vanquish, subjugate, immobilize, make mincemeat of *(informal)*, cut to pieces: *One massive Allied offensive would overwhelm the weakened enemy.*
3 = swamp, bury, flood, crush, engulf, submerge, beset, inundate, deluge, snow under: *The small Pacific island could be overwhelmed by rising sea levels.*

overwhelming ADJECTIVE
1 = overpowering, strong, powerful, towering, vast, stunning, extreme, crushing, devastating, shattering, compelling, irresistible, breathtaking, compulsive, forceful, unbearable, uncontrollable: *She felt an overwhelming desire to have another child.* **OPPOSITE:** negligible **2 = vast**, huge, massive, enormous, tremendous, immense, very large, astronomic, humongous *or* humungous *(U.S. slang)*: *An overwhelming majority of small businesses fail within the first two years.* **OPPOSITE:** insignificant

overwork VERB **1 = wear yourself out**, burn the midnight oil, burn the candle at both ends, bite off more than you can chew, strain yourself, overstrain yourself, work your fingers to the bone, overtire yourself, drive yourself too far, overburden yourself, overload yourself, overtax yourself: *You've been overworking – you need a holiday.* **2 = exploit**, exhaust, fatigue, weary, oppress, wear out, prostrate, overtax, drive into the ground, be a slave-driver *or* hard taskmaster to: *He overworks his staff.*

> **QUOTATIONS**
> overwork: a dangerous disorder affecting high public functionaries who want to go fishing
> [Ambrose Bierce *The Devil's Dictionary*]

overwrought ADJECTIVE
1 = distraught, upset, excited, desperate, wired *(slang)*, anxious, distressed, tense, distracted, frantic, in a state, hysterical, wound up *(informal)*, worked up *(informal)*, agitated, uptight *(informal)*, on edge, strung out *(informal)*, out of your mind, keyed up, overexcited, in a tizzy *(informal)*, at the end of your tether, wrought-up, beside yourself, in a twitter *(informal)*, tooshie *(Austral. slang)*, adrenalized: *When I'm feeling overwrought, I try to take some time out to relax.* **OPPOSITE:** calm
2 = overelaborate, contrived, overdone, flamboyant, baroque, high-flown, ornate, fussy, flowery, busy, rococo, florid, grandiloquent, euphuistic, overembellished, overornate: *He writes pretentious, overwrought poetry.*

owe VERB **= be in debt (to)**, be in arrears (to), be overdrawn (by), be beholden to, be under an obligation to, be obligated *or* indebted (to)

owing ADJECTIVE **= unpaid**, due, outstanding, owed, payable, unsettled, overdue
owing to = because of, thanks to, as a result of, on account of, by reason of

own DETERMINER **= personal**, special, private, individual, particular, exclusive: *She insisted on having her own room.*
▷ VERB **= possess**, have, keep, hold, enjoy, retain, be responsible for, be in possession of, have to your name: *His father owns a local pub.*
hold your own = keep going, compete, get on, get along, stand your ground, keep your head above water, keep your end up, maintain your position: *Placed in brilliant company at Eton, he more than held his own.*
on your own 1 = alone, by yourself, all alone, unaccompanied, on your tod *(Brit. slang)*: *I need some time on my own.* **2 = independently**, alone, singly, single-handedly, by yourself, unaided, without help, unassisted, left to your own devices, under your own steam, off your own bat, by your own efforts, (standing) on your own two feet: *I work best on my own.*

owner NOUN **= possessor**, holder, proprietor, freeholder, titleholder, proprietress, proprietrix, landlord *or* landlady, master *or* mistress, deed holder

ownership NOUN **= possession**, occupation, tenure, dominion, occupancy, proprietorship, proprietary rights, right of possession

Pp

pace NOUN **1 = speed**, rate, momentum, tempo, progress, motion, clip *(informal)*, lick *(informal)*, velocity: *driving at a steady pace* **2 = step**, walk, stride, tread, gait: *Their pace quickened as they approached their cars.* **3 = footstep**, step, stride: *I took a pace backwards.*
▷ VERB **= stride**, walk, pound, patrol, walk up and down, march up and down, walk back and forth: *He paced the room nervously.*

pacific ADJECTIVE **1 = nonaggressive**, pacifist, nonviolent, friendly, gentle, mild, peace-loving, peaceable, dovish, nonbelligerent, dovelike: *a country with a pacific policy*
OPPOSITE: aggressive
2 = peacemaking, diplomatic, appeasing, conciliatory, placatory, propitiatory, irenic, pacificatory: *He spoke in a pacific voice.*

pacifist NOUN **= peace lover**, dove, conscientious objector, peacenik *(informal)*, conchie *(informal)*, peacemonger, satyagrahi *(rare)*, passive resister

pacify VERB **= calm (down)**, appease, placate, still, content, quiet, moderate, compose, soften, soothe, allay, assuage, make peace with, mollify, ameliorate, conciliate, propitiate, tranquillize, smooth someone's ruffled feathers, clear the air with, restore harmony to: *Is this just something to pacify the critics?*

pack VERB **1 = package**, load, store, bundle, batch, stow: *They offered me a job packing goods in a warehouse.* **2 = cram**, charge, crowd, press, fill, stuff, jam, compact, mob, ram, wedge, compress, throng, tamp: *All her possessions were packed into the back of her car; Thousands of people packed into the mosque.*
▷ NOUN **1 = packet**, box, package, carton: *a pack of cigarettes* **2 = bundle**, kit, parcel, load, burden, bale, rucksack, truss, knapsack, back pack, kitbag, fardel *(archaic)*: *I hid the money in my pack.* **3 = group**, crowd, collection, company, set, lot, band, troop, crew, drove, gang, deck, bunch, mob, flock, herd, assemblage: *a pack of journalists who wanted to interview him*
pack someone off = send away, dismiss, send packing *(informal)*, bundle out, hustle out: *The children were packed off to bed.*
pack something in 1 = resign from, leave, give up, quit *(informal)*, chuck *(informal)*, jack in *(informal)*: *I've just packed in my job.* **2 = stop**, give up, kick *(informal)*, cease, chuck *(informal)*, leave off, jack in, desist from: *He's trying to pack in smoking.*
pack something up 1 = put away, store, tidy up: *He began packing up his things.* **2 = stop**, finish, give up, pack in *(Brit. informal)*, call it a day *(informal)*, call it a night *(informal)*: *He's packed up coaching and retired.*
pack up = break down, stop, fail, stall, give out, conk out *(informal)*: *Our car packed up.*
send someone packing = send away, dismiss, discharge, give someone the bird *(informal)*, give someone the brushoff *(slang)*, send someone about his *or* her business, send someone away with a flea in his *or* her ear *(informal)*: *He was sent packing in disgrace.*

package NOUN **1 = parcel**, box, container, packet, carton: *I tore open the package.* **2 = collection**, lot, unit, combination, compilation: *A complete package of teaching aids, course notes and case studies had been drawn up.*
▷ VERB **= pack**, box, wrap up, parcel (up), batch: *The coffee beans are ground and packaged for sale.*

packaging NOUN **= wrapping**, casing, covering, cover, box, packing, wrapper

packed ADJECTIVE **= filled**, full, crowded, jammed, crammed, swarming, overflowing, overloaded, seething, congested, jam-packed, chock-full, bursting at the seams, cram-full, brimful, chock-a-block, packed like sardines, hoatching *(Scot.)*, loaded *or* full to the gunwales
OPPOSITE: empty

packet NOUN **1 = container**, box, package, wrapping, poke *(dialect)*, carton, wrapper: *He wrote the number on the back of a cigarette packet.* **2 = package**, parcel: *the cost of sending letters and packets abroad* **3 = a fortune**, lot(s), pot(s) *(informal)*, a bomb *(Brit. slang)*, a pile *(informal)*, big money, a bundle *(slang)*, big bucks *(informal, chiefly U.S.)*, a small fortune, a mint, a wad *(U.S. & Canad. slang)*, megabucks *(U.S. & Canad. slang)*, an arm and a leg *(informal)*, a bob or two *(Brit. informal)*, a tidy sum *(informal)*, a king's ransom *(informal)*, a pretty penny *(informal)*, top whack *(informal)*: *You could save yourself a packet.*

pact NOUN **= agreement**, contract, alliance, treaty, deal, understanding, league, bond, arrangement, bargain, convention, compact, protocol, covenant, concord, concordat

pad[1] NOUN **1 = wad**, dressing, pack, padding, compress, wadding: *He placed a pad of cotton wool over the cut.* **2 = cushion**, filling, stuffing, pillow, bolster, upholstery: *seat-pad covers which tie to the backs of your chairs* **3 = notepad**, block, tablet, notebook, jotter, writing pad: *Have a pad and pencil ready.* **4 = home**, flat, apartment, place, room, quarters, hang-out *(informal)*, bachelor apartment *(Canad.)*: *He's bought himself a bachelor pad.* **5 = paw**, foot, sole: *My cat has an infection in the pad of its foot.*
▷ VERB **= pack**, line, fill, protect, shape, stuff, cushion: *Pad the seat with a pillow.*
pad something out = lengthen, stretch, elaborate, inflate, fill out, amplify, augment, spin out, flesh out, eke out, protract: *He padded out his article with a lot of quotations.*

pad[2] VERB **= sneak**, creep, steal, pussyfoot *(informal)*, go barefoot: *He padded around in his slippers.*

padding NOUN **1 = filling**, stuffing, packing, wadding: *the chair's foam rubber padding* **2 = waffle** *(informal, chiefly Brit.)*, hot air *(informal)*, verbiage, wordiness, verbosity, prolixity: *Politicians fill their speeches with a lot of padding.*

paddle[1] NOUN **= oar**, sweep, scull: *He used a piece of driftwood as a paddle.*
▷ VERB **= row**, pull, scull: *paddling around the South Pacific in a kayak*

paddle[2] VERB **= wade**, splash (about), slop, plash: *The children were paddling in the stream.*

paddy NOUN **= temper**, tantrum, bad mood, passion, rage, pet, fit of pique, fit of temper, foulie *(Austral. slang)*, hissy fit *(informal)*, strop *(informal)*

paean *or (sometimes U.S.)* **pean** NOUN **= eulogy**, tribute, panegyric, hymn of praise, encomium

pagan NOUN **= heathen**, infidel, unbeliever, polytheist, idolater: *He has been a practising pagan for years.*
▷ ADJECTIVE **= heathen**, infidel, irreligious, polytheistic, idolatrous, heathenish: *Britain's ancient pagan heritage*

page[1] NOUN **1 = folio**, side, leaf, sheet: *Turn to page four of your books.* **2 = period**, chapter, phase, era, episode, time, point, event, stage, incident, epoch: *a new page in the country's history*

page[2] NOUN **1 = attendant**, bellboy *(U.S.)*, pageboy, footboy: *He worked as a page in a hotel.* **2 = servant**, attendant, squire, pageboy, footboy: *He served as page to a noble lord.*
▷ VERB **= call**, seek, summon, call out for, send for: *He was paged repeatedly as the flight was boarding.*

pageant NOUN **= show**, display, parade, ritual, spectacle, procession, extravaganza, tableau: *a traditional Christmas pageant*

pageantry NOUN = **spectacle**, show, display, drama, parade, splash *(informal)*, state, glitter, glamour, grandeur, splendour, extravagance, pomp, magnificence, theatricality, showiness

pain NOUN **1** = **suffering**, discomfort, trouble, hurt, irritation, tenderness, soreness: *a disease that causes excruciating pain* **2** = **ache**, smarting, stinging, aching, cramp, throb, throbbing, spasm, pang, twinge, shooting pain: *I felt a sharp pain in my lower back.* **3** = **sorrow**, suffering, torture, distress, despair, grief, misery, agony, sadness, torment, hardship, bitterness, woe, anguish, heartache, affliction, tribulation, desolation, wretchedness: *Her eyes were filled with pain.*
▷ PLURAL NOUN = **trouble**, labour, effort, industry, care, bother, diligence, special attention, assiduousness: *He got little thanks for his pains.*
▷ VERB **1** = **distress**, worry, hurt, wound, torture, grieve, torment, afflict, sadden, disquiet, vex, agonize, cut to the quick, aggrieve: *It pains me to think of an animal being in distress.* **2** = **hurt**, chafe, cause pain to, cause discomfort to: *His ankle still pained him.*

pained ADJECTIVE = **distressed**, worried, hurt, injured, wounded, upset, unhappy, stung, offended, aggrieved, anguished, miffed *(informal)*, reproachful

painful ADJECTIVE **1** = **sore**, hurting, smarting, aching, raw, tender, throbbing, inflamed, excruciating: *Her glands were swollen and painful.* **OPPOSITE:** painless **2** = **distressing**, unpleasant, harrowing, saddening, grievous, distasteful, agonizing, disagreeable, afflictive: *His remark brought back painful memories.* **OPPOSITE:** pleasant **3** = **difficult**, arduous, trying, hard, severe, troublesome, laborious, vexatious: *the long and painful process of getting divorced* **OPPOSITE:** easy **4** = **terrible**, awful, dreadful, dire, excruciating, abysmal, gut-wrenching, eye-watering, godawful *(informal)*, extremely bad: *The interview was painful to watch.*

painfully ADVERB = **distressingly**, clearly, sadly, unfortunately, markedly, excessively, alarmingly, woefully, dreadfully, deplorably

painkiller NOUN = **analgesic**, drug, remedy, anaesthetic, sedative, palliative, anodyne

painless ADJECTIVE **1** = **pain-free**, without pain: *The operation is a brief, painless procedure.* **2** = **simple**, easy, fast, quick, no trouble, effortless, trouble-free: *There are no painless solutions to the problem.*

painstaking ADJECTIVE = **thorough**, careful, meticulous, earnest, exacting, strenuous, conscientious, persevering, diligent, scrupulous, industrious, assiduous, thoroughgoing, punctilious, sedulous **OPPOSITE:** careless

paint NOUN = **colouring**, colour, stain, dye, tint, pigment, emulsion: *a pot of red paint*
▷ VERB **1** = **colour**, cover, coat, decorate, stain, whitewash, daub, distemper, apply paint to: *They painted the walls yellow.* **2** = **depict**, draw, portray, figure, picture, represent, sketch, delineate, catch a likeness: *He was painting a portrait of his wife.* **3** = **describe**, capture, portray, depict, evoke, recount, bring to life, make you see, conjure up a vision, put graphically, tell vividly: *The report paints a grim picture of life in the city.*
paint the town red = **celebrate**, revel, carouse, live it up *(informal)*, make merry, make whoopee *(informal)*, go on a binge *(informal)*, go on a spree, go on the town: *Thousands of football fans painted the town red after the match.*

> **QUOTATIONS**
> And those who paint 'em truest praise 'em most
> [Joseph Addison *The Campaign*]
>
> Every time I paint a portrait I lose a friend
> [John Singer Sargent]

pair NOUN **1** = **set**, match, combination, doublet, matched set, two of a kind: *a pair of socks* **2** = **couple**, brace, duo, twosome: *A pair of teenage boys were arrested.*
▷ VERB *(often with* **off***)* = **team**, match (up), join, couple, marry, wed, twin, put together, bracket, yoke, pair off: *Each trainee is paired with an experienced worker.*

> **USAGE**
> Like other collective nouns, *pair* takes a singular or a plural verb according to whether it is seen as a unit or as a collection of two things: *the pair are said to dislike each other; a pair of good shoes is essential.*

pal NOUN = **friend**, companion, mate *(informal)*, buddy *(informal)*, comrade, chum *(informal)*, crony, cock *(Brit. informal)*, main man *(slang, chiefly U.S.)*, homeboy *(slang, chiefly U.S.)*, cobber *(Austral. & N.Z. old-fashioned, informal)*, boon companion, E hoa *(N.Z.)*

palatable ADJECTIVE **1** = **delicious**, tasty, luscious, savoury, delectable, mouthwatering, appetizing, toothsome, yummo *(Austral. slang)*: *flavourings designed to make the food more palatable* **OPPOSITE:** unpalatable **2** = **acceptable**, pleasant, agreeable, fair, attractive, satisfactory, enjoyable: *There is no palatable way of sacking someone.*

palate NOUN = **taste**, heart, stomach, appetite

palatial ADJECTIVE = **magnificent**, grand, imposing, splendid, gorgeous, luxurious, spacious, majestic, regal, stately, sumptuous, plush *(informal)*, illustrious, grandiose, opulent, de luxe, splendiferous *(facetious)*

pale[1] ADJECTIVE **1** = **light**, soft, faded, subtle, muted, bleached, pastel, light-coloured: *a pale blue dress* **2** = **dim**, weak, faint, feeble, thin, wan, watery: *A pale light seeped through the window.* **3** = **white**, pasty, bleached, washed-out, wan, bloodless, colourless, pallid, anaemic, ashen, sallow, whitish, ashy, like death warmed up *(informal)*: *She looked pale and tired.* **OPPOSITE:** rosy-cheeked **4** = **poor**, weak, inadequate, pathetic, feeble: *a pale imitation of the real thing*
▷ VERB **1** = **fade**, dull, diminish, decrease, dim, lessen, grow dull, lose lustre: *My problems paled in comparison with his.* **2** = **become pale**, blanch, whiten, go white, lose colour: *Her face paled at the news.*

pale[2] NOUN = **post**, stake, paling, upright, picket, slat, palisade: *the pales of the fence*
beyond the pale = **unacceptable**, not done, forbidden, irregular, indecent, unsuitable, improper, barbaric, unspeakable, out of line, unseemly, inadmissible: *His behaviour was beyond the pale.*

pall[1] NOUN **1** = **cloud**, shadow, veil, mantle, shroud: *A pall of black smoke drifted over the cliff-top.* **2** = **gloom**, damp, dismay, melancholy, damper, check: *His depression cast a pall on the proceedings.*

pall[2] VERB *(often with* **on***)* = **become boring**, become dull, become tedious, become tiresome, jade, cloy, become wearisome: *The glamour of her job soon palled.*

pallid ADJECTIVE = **pale**, wan, pasty, colourless, anaemic, ashen, sallow, whitish, cadaverous, waxen, ashy, like death warmed up *(informal)*, wheyfaced: *His thin, pallid face broke into a smile.*

pallor NOUN = **paleness**, whiteness, lack of colour, wanness, bloodlessness, ashen hue, pallidness

palm NOUN = **hand**, hook, paw *(informal)*, mitt *(slang)*, meathook *(slang)*: *He wiped his sweaty palm.*
in the palm of your hand = **in your power**, in your control, in your clutches, at your mercy: *He had the board of directors in the palm of his hand.*
palm someone off = **fob off**, dismiss, disregard, pooh-pooh *(informal)*: *Mark was palmed off with a series of excuses.*
palm something off on someone = **foist on**, force upon, impose upon, pass off, thrust upon, unload upon: *They palm a lot of junk off on the tourists.*

palpable ADJECTIVE = **obvious**, apparent, patent, clear, plain, visible, evident, manifest, open, blatant, conspicuous, unmistakable, salient

paltry ADJECTIVE **1** = **meagre**, petty, trivial, trifling, beggarly, derisory, measly, piddling *(informal)*, inconsiderable: *He was fined the paltry sum of $50.* **OPPOSITE:** considerable **2** = **insignificant**, trivial, worthless, unimportant, small, low, base, minor, slight, petty, trifling, Mickey Mouse *(slang)*, piddling *(informal)*, toytown *(slang)*, poxy *(slang)*, nickel-and-dime *(U.S. slang)*, picayune *(U.S.)*, twopenny-halfpenny *(Brit. informal)*: *She had no interest in such paltry concerns.* **OPPOSITE:** important

pamper VERB = **spoil**, indulge, gratify, baby, pet, humour, pander to, fondle, cosset, coddle, mollycoddle, wait on (someone) hand and foot, cater to your every whim

pamphlet NOUN = **booklet**, leaflet, brochure, circular, tract, folder

pan[1] NOUN = **pot**, vessel, container, saucepan: *Heat the butter in a large pan.* ▷ VERB **1 = criticize**, knock, blast, hammer *(Brit. informal)*, slam *(slang)*, rubbish *(informal)*, roast *(informal)*, put down, slate *(informal)*, censure, slag (off) *(slang)*, tear into *(informal)*, flay, lambast(e), throw brickbats at *(informal)*: *His first movie was panned by the critics.* **2 = sift out**, look for, wash, search for: *People came westward in the 1800s to pan for gold in Sierra Nevada.*
pan out = work out, happen, result, come out, turn out, culminate, come to pass *(archaic)*, eventuate: *None of his ideas panned out.*

pan[2] VERB = **move along** *or* **across**, follow, track, sweep, scan, traverse, swing across: *A television camera panned the crowd.*

panacea NOUN = **cure-all**, elixir, nostrum, heal-all, sovereign remedy, universal cure

panache NOUN = **style**, spirit, dash, flair, verve, swagger, flourish, élan, flamboyance, brio

pandemonium NOUN = **uproar**, confusion, chaos, turmoil, racket, clamour, din, commotion, rumpus, bedlam, babel, tumult, hubbub, ruction *(informal)*, hullabaloo, hue and cry, ruckus *(informal)* **OPPOSITE:** order

pander VERB
pander to something *or* **someone = indulge**, please, satisfy, gratify, cater to, play up to *(informal)*, fawn on

pang NOUN **1 = pain**, stab, sting, stitch, ache, wrench, prick, spasm, twinge, throe *(rare)*: *pangs of hunger* **2 = twinge**, stab, prick, spasm, qualm, gnawing: *She felt a pang of guilt about the way she was treating him.*

panic NOUN = **fear**, alarm, horror, terror, anxiety, dismay, hysteria, fright, agitation, consternation, trepidation, a flap *(informal)*: *The earthquake has caused panic among the population.* ▷ VERB **1 = go to pieces**, overreact, become hysterical, have kittens *(informal)*, lose your nerve, be terror-stricken, lose your bottle *(Brit. slang)*: *The guests panicked and screamed when the bomb went off.* **2 = alarm**, scare, terrify, startle, unnerve: *The dogs were panicked by the noise.*

panicky ADJECTIVE = **frightened**, worried, afraid, nervous, distressed, fearful, frantic, frenzied, hysterical, worked up, windy *(slang)*, agitated, jittery *(informal)*, in a flap *(informal)*, antsy *(informal)*, in a tizzy *(informal)* **OPPOSITE:** calm

panic-stricken *or* **panic-struck** ADJECTIVE = **frightened**, alarmed, scared, terrified, startled, horrified, fearful, frenzied, hysterical, agitated, unnerved, petrified, aghast, panicky, scared stiff, in a cold sweat *(informal)*, frightened to death, terror-stricken, horror-stricken, frightened out of your wits

panoply NOUN **1 = array**, range, display, collection: *The film features a vast panoply of special effects.* **2 = trappings**, show, dress, get-up *(informal)*, turnout, attire, garb, insignia, regalia, raiment *(archaic, poetic)*: *all the panoply of a royal wedding*

panorama NOUN **1 = view**, prospect, scenery, vista, bird's-eye view, scenic view: *He looked out over a panorama of hills and valleys.* **2 = survey**, perspective, overview, overall picture: *The play presents a panorama of the history of communism.*

panoramic ADJECTIVE **1 = wide**, overall, extensive, scenic, bird's-eye: *I had a panoramic view of the city.* **2 = comprehensive**, general, extensive, sweeping, inclusive, far-reaching, all-embracing: *the panoramic sweep of his work*

pant VERB = **puff**, blow, breathe, gasp, throb, wheeze, huff, heave, palpitate: *He was panting with the effort of the climb.* ▷ NOUN = **gasp**, puff, wheeze, huff: *His breath was coming in short pants.*
pant for something = long for, want, desire, crave for, covet, yearn for, thirst for, hunger for, pine for, hanker after, ache for, sigh for, set your heart on, eat your heart out over, suspire for *(archaic, poetic)*: *They left the audience panting for more.*

panting ADJECTIVE **1 = out of breath**, winded, gasping, puffed, puffing, breathless, puffed out, short of breath, out of puff, out of whack *(informal)*: *She collapsed, panting, at the top of the stairs.* **2 = eager**, raring, anxious, impatient, champing at the bit *(informal)*, all agog: *He came down here panting to be rescued from the whole ghastly mess.*

pants PLURAL NOUN **1 = underpants**, briefs, drawers, knickers, panties, boxer shorts, Y-fronts®, broekies *(S. African)*, underdaks *(Austral. slang)*: *a matching set of bra and pants* **2 = trousers**, slacks: *He was wearing brown corduroy pants and a white shirt.*

pap NOUN = **rubbish**, trash, trivia, drivel

paper NOUN **1 = newspaper**, news, daily, journal, organ, rag *(informal)*, tabloid, gazette, broadsheet: *The story is in all the papers.* **2 = essay**, study, article, analysis, script, composition, assignment, thesis, critique, treatise, dissertation, monograph: *He has just written a paper on the subject.* **3 = examination**, test, exam: *the applied mathematics paper* **4 = report**, study, survey, inquiry: *a new government paper on European policy* ▷ PLURAL NOUN **1 = letters**, records, documents, file, diaries, archive, paperwork, dossier: *After her death, her papers were collected and published.* **2 = documents**, records, certificates, identification, deeds, identity papers, I.D. *(informal)*: *people who were trying to leave the country with forged papers* ▷ VERB = **wallpaper**, line, hang, paste up, cover with paper: *We have papered this room in grey.*
on paper 1 = in writing, written down, on (the) record, in print, in black and white: *It is important to get something down on paper.* **2 = in theory**, ideally, theoretically, in the abstract: *On paper, he is the best man for the job.*

parable NOUN = **lesson**, story, fable, allegory, moral tale, exemplum

parade NOUN **1 = procession**, march, ceremony, pageant, train, review, column, spectacle, tattoo, motorcade, cavalcade, cortège: *A military parade marched slowly through the streets.* **2 = show**, display, exhibition, spectacle, array: *A glittering parade of celebrities attended the event.* ▷ VERB **1 = march**, process, file, promenade: *More than four thousand people paraded down the Champs Elysées.* **2 = flaunt**, show, display, exhibit, show off *(informal)*, air, draw attention to, brandish, vaunt, make a show of: *He was a modest man who never paraded his wealth.* **3 = strut**, show off *(informal)*, swagger, swank: *She loves to parade around in designer clothes.*

paradigm NOUN = **model**, example, original, pattern, ideal, norm, prototype, archetype, exemplar

paradise NOUN **1 = heaven**, Promised Land, Zion *(Christianity)*, Happy Valley *(Islam)*, City of God, Elysian fields, garden of delights, divine abode, heavenly kingdom: *They believe they will go to paradise when they die.* **2 = Garden of Eden**, Eden: *Adam and Eve's expulsion from Paradise* **3 = bliss**, delight, heaven, felicity, utopia, seventh heaven: *This job is paradise compared to my last one.*

> **QUOTATIONS**
> Two paradises 'twere in one
> To live in paradise alone
> [Andrew Marvell *The Garden*]

paradox NOUN = **contradiction**, mystery, puzzle, ambiguity, anomaly, inconsistency, enigma, oddity, absurdity

paradoxical ADJECTIVE = **contradictory**, inconsistent, impossible, puzzling, absurd, baffling, riddling, ambiguous, improbable, confounding, enigmatic, illogical, equivocal, oracular

paragon NOUN = **model**, standard, pattern, ideal, criterion, norm, jewel,

The Language of Anna Sewell

Famous for her only novel, the 1877 'autobiography of a horse' *Black Beauty*, Anna Sewell (1820–78) came from a devoutly religious family in the East of England. She suffered from poor health for much of her life and was introduced to writing by her mother who published a number of evangelical tales for children.

Written from the first-person perspective of a horse, *Black Beauty* is a notable example of anthropomorphism through which the animals that Sewell's narrative centres on are made to display completely human thought processes and to converse in grammatical, if simple, English. Sewell's aim in this was to bring public attention to welfare issues surrounding the treatment of horses in Victorian Britain. Accordingly, many of the adjectives that Sewell's equine hero, Beauty, applies to his fellow horses indicate either their physical or mental state. Often these are compound adjectives, some of which are in relatively common usage, such as *good-tempered*, *well-made*, and *broken-down*. Others are less familiar, as in *high-mettled*, *useful-looking*, and *dejected-looking*.

As might be expected in a work focused on cruelty, many of Sewell's verbs suggest suffering. After *ride*, *horse* is most commonly the object of *flog* and *spoil*, while others that occur in this vein include *ill-use*, *whip*, and *ruin*. In describing humans, Sewell presents Beauty frequently employing *master*, with *good* the most salient adjective associated with it. The most commonly occurring noun with *good*, however, is *deal* forming an expression of degree that is now used far less than it was in Sewell's time:

> Merrylegs was a **good deal** put out at being 'mauled about,' as he said, 'by a boy who knew nothing.'

In keeping with the theme of compassion in Sewell's writing, *gentle* and *kind* are other common adjectives and occur in the majority of cases to suggest the desirable human attitude to horses:

> I grew very fond of him, he was so **gentle** and **kind**; he seemed to know just how a horse feels, and when he cleaned me he knew the tender places and the ticklish places; when he brushed my head he went as carefully over my eyes.

Kind collocates most frequently with *words* followed by *master* while nouns that occur with *gentle* include *voice*, *hand*, and *friend*. Indeed, *hand* functions repeatedly for Sewell as a metonym for human conduct, occurring also with *hard* and *heavy* in the context of violence and with *light* and *good* in the context of more appropriate human actions. Horses' *feet*, meanwhile, appear as the cause of much discomfort to them throughout the text, generally in the context of horseshoes:

> Of course my shoeless **foot** suffered dreadfully; the hoof was broken and split down to the very quick, and the inside was terribly cut by the sharpness of the stones.

By contrast human tenderness is often expressed through a close attention to horses' feet.

Sewell's sensitive attitude has been seen as indicative of a markedly sentimental strain in her writing. A tendency towards an exaggeratedly emotional stance might be illustrated by her extensive use of the exclamation mark. At times this gives additional emphasis to the brutal situation Sewell describes:

> ...it was no accident! it was a cruel, shameful, cold-blooded act!

Chastisement also produces exclamation (as in *bad boy!*), as do sudden exhortations of shock or surprise: *oh!* and *what!* Sewell's frequent use of *very* is another of her strategies for intensifying the experiences she depicts, though this tends to be used to accentuate the positive rather than to draw further attention to the horses' misery. Occurrences of *very good* far outnumber those of *very bad* and *fond*, *glad*, *handsome*, and *fine* are next in salience.

masterpiece, prototype, paradigm, archetype, epitome, exemplar, apotheosis, quintessence, nonesuch *(archaic)*, nonpareil, best *or* greatest thing since sliced bread *(informal)*, cynosure

paragraph NOUN **= section**, part, notice, item, passage, clause, portion, subdivision

parallel NOUN **1 = equivalent**, counterpart, match, equal, twin, complement, duplicate, analogue, likeness, corollary: *It is an ecological disaster with no parallel in the modern era.* **OPPOSITE:** opposite **2 = similarity**, correspondence, correlation, comparison, analogy, resemblance, likeness, parallelism: *Detectives realised there were parallels between the two murders.* **OPPOSITE:** difference
▷ VERB **1 = correspond to**, compare with, agree with, complement, conform to, be alike, chime with, correlate to: *His remarks paralleled those of the president.* **OPPOSITE:** differ from **2 = match**, equal, duplicate, keep pace (with), measure up to: *His achievements have never been paralleled.*
▷ ADJECTIVE **1 = matching**, correspondent, corresponding, like, similar, uniform, resembling, complementary, akin, analogous: *He describes the rise in tuberculosis as an epidemic parallel to that of AIDS.* **OPPOSITE:** different **2 = equidistant**, alongside, aligned, side by side, coextensive: *seventy-two ships, drawn up in two parallel lines* **OPPOSITE:** divergent

paralyse VERB **1 = disable**, cripple, lame, debilitate, incapacitate: *Her sister had been paralysed in a road accident.* **2 = freeze**, stun, numb, petrify, transfix, stupefy, halt, stop dead, immobilize, anaesthetize, benumb: *He was paralysed with fear.* **3 = immobilize**, freeze, halt, disable, cripple, arrest, incapacitate, bring to a standstill: *The strike has virtually paralysed the country.*

paralysis NOUN **1 = immobility**, palsy, paresis *(Pathology)*: *paralysis of the legs* **2 = standstill**, breakdown, stoppage, shutdown, halt, stagnation, inactivity: *The unions have brought about a total paralysis of trade.*

parameter NOUN *(usually plural)* **= limit**, constant, restriction, guideline, criterion, framework, limitation, specification

paramount ADJECTIVE **= principal**, prime, first, chief, main, capital, primary, supreme, outstanding, superior, dominant, cardinal, foremost, eminent, predominant, pre-eminent **OPPOSITE:** secondary

paranoid ADJECTIVE **1 = suspicious**, worried, nervous, fearful, apprehensive, antsy *(informal)*: *We live in an increasingly paranoid and fearful society.* **2 = obsessive**, disturbed, unstable, manic, neurotic, mentally ill, psychotic, deluded, paranoiac: *his increasingly paranoid delusions*

paraphernalia NOUN **= equipment**, things, effects, material, stuff, tackle, gear, baggage, apparatus, belongings, clobber *(Brit. slang)*, accoutrements, impedimenta, appurtenances, equipage

paraphrase VERB **= reword**, interpret, render, restate, rehash, rephrase, express in other words *or* your own words: *Baxter paraphrased the contents of the press release.*
▷ NOUN **= rewording**, version, interpretation, rendering, translation, rendition, rehash, restatement, rephrasing: *The following is a paraphrase of his remarks.*

parasite NOUN **= sponger** *(informal)*, sponge *(informal)*, drone *(Brit.)*, leech, hanger-on, scrounger *(informal)*, bloodsucker *(informal)*, cadger, quandong *(Austral. slang)*

parasitic *or* **parasitical** ADJECTIVE **= scrounging** *(informal)*, sponging *(informal)*, cadging, bloodsucking *(informal)*, leechlike

parcel NOUN **1 = package**, case, box, pack, packet, bundle, carton: *They sent parcels of food and clothing.* **2 = plot**, area, property, section, patch, tract, allotment, piece of land: *These small parcels of land were sold to the local people.* **3 = group**, crowd, pack, company, lot, band, collection, crew, gang, bunch, batch: *He described them, quite rightly, as a parcel of rogues.*
▷ VERB *(often with* **up***)* **= wrap**, pack, package, tie up, do up, gift-wrap, box up, fasten together: *We parcelled up our unwanted clothes to take to the charity shop.*
parcel something out = distribute, divide, portion, allocate, split up, dispense, allot, carve up, mete out, dole out, share out, apportion, deal out: *The inheritance was parcelled out equally among the three brothers.*

parched ADJECTIVE **1 = dried out** *or* **up**, dry, withered, scorched, arid, torrid, shrivelled, dehydrated, waterless: *Showers poured down upon the parched earth.* **2 = thirsty**, dry, dehydrated, drouthy *(Scot.)*: *After all that exercise, I was parched.*

pardon VERB **= acquit**, free, release, liberate, reprieve, remit, amnesty, let off *(informal)*, exonerate, absolve, exculpate: *Hundreds of political prisoners were pardoned and released.*
OPPOSITE: punish
▷ NOUN **1 = forgiveness**, mercy, indulgence, absolution, grace: *He asked God's pardon for his sins.*
OPPOSITE: condemnation
2 = acquittal, release, discharge, amnesty, reprieve, remission, exoneration: *They lobbied the government on his behalf and he was granted a pardon.*
OPPOSITE: punishment
pardon me = forgive me, excuse me: *Pardon me for asking, but what business is it of yours?*

> **QUOTATIONS**
> God will pardon me. It is His trade
> [Heinrich Heine *on his deathbed*]

pare VERB **1 = peel**, cut, skin, trim, clip, shave: *Pare the rind thinly from the lemon.* **2 = cut back**, cut, reduce, crop, decrease, dock, prune, shear, lop, retrench: *Local authorities must pare down their budgets.*

parent NOUN **1 = father** *or* **mother**, sire, progenitor, begetter, procreator, old *(Austral. & N.Z. informal)*, oldie *(Austral. informal)*, patriarch: *Both her parents were killed in a car crash.*
2 = source, cause, author, root, origin, architect, creator, prototype, forerunner, originator, wellspring: *He is regarded as one of the parents of modern classical music.*

parentage NOUN **= family**, birth, origin, descent, line, race, stock, pedigree, extraction, ancestry, lineage, paternity, derivation

> **QUOTATIONS**
> Men are generally more careful of the breed of their horses and dogs than of their children
> [William Penn *Some Fruits of Solitude*]

parenthood NOUN **= fatherhood** *or* **motherhood**, parenting, rearing, bringing up, nurturing, upbringing, child rearing, baby *or* child care, fathering *or* mothering

> **QUOTATIONS**
> Before I got married I had six theories about bringing up children; now I have six children, and no theories
> [John Wilmot, Earl of Rochester]

pariah NOUN **= outcast**, exile, outlaw, undesirable, untouchable, leper, unperson

parings PLURAL NOUN **= peelings**, skins, slices, clippings, peel, fragments, shavings, shreds, flakes, rind, snippets, slivers

parish NOUN **1 = district**, community: *the vicar of a small parish in a West Country town* **2 = community**, fold, flock, church, congregation, parishioners, churchgoers: *The whole parish will object if he is appointed as priest.*
▸ *related adjective:* parochial

parity NOUN **= equality**, correspondence, consistency, equivalence, quits *(informal)*, par, unity, similarity, likeness, uniformity, equal terms, sameness, parallelism, congruity

park NOUN **1 = recreation ground**, garden, playground, pleasure garden, playpark, domain *(N.Z.)*, forest park *(N.Z.)*: *We went for a brisk walk round the park.* **2 = parkland**, grounds, estate, lawns, woodland, grassland: *a manor house in six acres of park and woodland* **3 = field**, pitch, playing field: *Chris was the best player on the park.*
▷ VERB **1 = leave**, stop, station, position: *He found a place to park the car.* **2 = put (down)**, leave, place, stick, deposit, dump, shove, plonk *(informal)*: *Just park your bag on the floor.*

parlance NOUN **= language**, talk, speech, tongue, jargon, idiom, lingo

p

(*informal*), phraseology, manner of speaking

parliament NOUN **1 = assembly**, council, congress, senate, convention, legislature, talking shop (*informal*), convocation: *The Bangladesh Parliament has approved the policy.* **2 = sitting**, diet: *The legislation will be passed in the next parliament.* **3** (*with cap.*) **= Houses of Parliament**, the House, Westminster, Mother of Parliaments, the House of Commons and the House of Lords, House of Representatives (N.Z.): *Questions have been raised in Parliament regarding this issue.*

> **QUOTATIONS**
> A parliament can do any thing but make a man a woman, and a woman a man
> [2nd Earl of Pembroke]
>
> A Parliament is nothing less than a big meeting of more or less idle people
> [Walter Bagehot *The English Constitution*]
>
> England is the mother of Parliaments
> [John Bright *speech at Birmingham*]

parliamentary ADJECTIVE **= governmental**, congressional, legislative, law-making, law-giving, deliberative

parlour *or (U.S.)* **parlor** NOUN **1 = sitting room**, lounge, living room, drawing room, front room, reception room, best room: *The guests were shown into the parlour.* **2 = establishment**, shop, store, salon: *a funeral parlour*

parlous ADJECTIVE **= dangerous**, difficult, desperate, risky, dire, hazardous, hairy (*slang*), perilous, chancy (*informal*)

parochial ADJECTIVE **= provincial**, narrow, insular, limited, restricted, petty, narrow-minded, inward-looking, small-minded, parish-pump **OPPOSITE:** cosmopolitan

parody NOUN **1 = takeoff** (*informal*), imitation, satire, caricature, send-up (*Brit. informal*), spoof (*informal*), lampoon, skit, burlesque, piss-take (*informal*): *a parody of a well-know soap opera* **2 = travesty**, farce, caricature, mockery, apology for: *His trial was a parody of justice.*
▷ VERB **= take off** (*informal*), mimic, caricature, send up (*Brit. informal*), spoof (*informal*), travesty, lampoon, poke fun at, burlesque, satirize, do a takeoff of (*informal*): *It was easy to parody his rather pompous manner of speaking.*

paroxysm NOUN **= outburst**, attack, fit, seizure, flare-up (*informal*), eruption, spasm, convulsion

parrot VERB **= repeat**, echo, imitate, copy, reiterate, mimic

parry VERB **1 = evade**, avoid, fence off, dodge, duck (*informal*), shun, sidestep, circumvent, fight shy of: *He parried questions about his involvement in the affair.* **2 = ward off**, block, deflect, repel, rebuff, fend off, stave off, repulse, hold at bay: *My opponent parried every blow I got close enough to attempt.*

parsimonious ADJECTIVE **= mean**, stingy, penny-pinching (*informal*), miserly, near (*informal*), saving, sparing, grasping, miserable, stinting, frugal, niggardly, penurious, tightfisted, close-fisted, mingy (*Brit. informal*), cheeseparing, skinflinty, snoep (*S. African informal*) **OPPOSITE:** extravagant

parson NOUN **= clergyman**, minister, priest, vicar, divine, incumbent, reverend (*informal*), preacher, pastor, cleric, rector, curate, churchman, man of God, man of the cloth, ecclesiastic

part NOUN **1 = piece**, share, proportion, percentage, lot, bit, section, sector, slice, scrap, particle, segment, portion, fragment, lump, fraction, chunk, wedge: *A large part of his earnings went on repaying the bank loan.* **OPPOSITE:** entirety **2** (*often plural*) **= region**, area, district, territory, neighbourhood, quarter, vicinity, neck of the woods (*informal*), airt (*Scot.*): *It's a beautiful part of the country; That kind of behaviour doesn't go down too well round these parts.* **3 = component**, bit, piece, unit, element, ingredient, constituent, module: *The engine only has three moving parts.* **4 = branch**, department, division, office, section, wing, subdivision, subsection: *He works in a different part of the company.* **5 = organ**, member, limb: *hands, feet, and other body parts* **6 = role**, representation, persona, portrayal, depiction, character part: *the actor who played the part of the doctor in the soap* **7 = lines**, words, script, dialogue: *She's having a lot of trouble learning her part.* **8 = duty**, say, place, work, role, hand, business, share, charge, responsibility, task, function, capacity, involvement, participation: *He felt a sense of relief now that his part in this business was over.* **9 = side**, behalf: *There's no hurry on my part.*
▷ VERB **1 = divide**, separate, break, tear, split, rend, detach, sever, disconnect, cleave, come apart, disunite, disjoin: *The clouds parted and a shaft of sunlight broke through; He parted the bushes with his stick.* **OPPOSITE:** join **2 = part company**, separate, break up, split up, say goodbye, go (their) separate ways: *We parted on bad terms.* **OPPOSITE:** meet
for the most part = mainly, largely, generally, chiefly, mostly, principally, on the whole, in the main: *For the most part, they try to keep out of local disputes.*
in good part = good-naturedly, well, cheerfully, cordially, without offence: *He took their jokes in good part.*
in part = partly, a little, somewhat, slightly, partially, to some degree, to a certain extent, in some measure: *His extreme reaction was due, in part, to his deep fear of rejection.*
on the part of = by, in, from, made by, carried out by: *There was a change of mood on the part of the government.*
part with something = give up, abandon, yield, sacrifice, surrender, discard, relinquish, renounce, let go of, forgo: *He was reluctant to part with his money, even in such a good cause.*
take part in = participate in, be involved in, join in, play a part in, be instrumental in, have a hand in, partake in, take a hand in, associate yourself with, put your twopence-worth in: *Thousands of students have taken part in the demonstrations.*

partake VERB
partake in something = participate in, share in, take part in, engage in, enter into: *Do you partake in dangerous sports?*
partake of something 1 = consume, take, share, receive, eat: *They were happy to partake of our food and drink.* **2 = display**, exhibit, evoke, hint at, be characterized by: *These groups generally partake of a common characteristic.*

> **USAGE**
> The phrase *partake of* is sometimes inappropriately used as if it were a synonym of *eat* or *drink*. In strict usage, you can only *partake of* food or drink which is available for several people to share.

partial ADJECTIVE **1 = incomplete**, limited, unfinished, imperfect, fragmentary, uncompleted: *Their policy only met with partial success.* **OPPOSITE:** complete **2 = biased**, prejudiced, discriminatory, partisan, influenced, unfair, one-sided, unjust, predisposed, tendentious: *Some of the umpiring in the tournament was partial.* **OPPOSITE:** unbiased

partially ADVERB **= partly**, somewhat, moderately, in part, halfway, piecemeal, not wholly, fractionally, incompletely, to a certain extent *or* degree

participant NOUN **= participator**, party, member, player, associate, shareholder, contributor, stakeholder, partaker

participate VERB **= take part**, be involved, engage, perform, join, enter, partake, have a hand, get in on the act, be a party to, be a participant, come to the party **OPPOSITE:** refrain from

participation NOUN **= taking part**, contribution, partnership, involvement, assistance, sharing in, joining in, partaking

particle NOUN **= bit**, piece, scrap, grain, molecule, atom, shred, crumb, mite, jot, speck, mote, whit, tittle, iota

particular ADJECTIVE **1 = specific**, special, express, exact, precise, distinct, peculiar: *What particular aspects of the job are you interested in?* **OPPOSITE:** general **2 = special**, exceptional, notable, uncommon,

marked, unusual, remarkable, singular, noteworthy, especial: *Stress is a particular problem for women; This is a question of particular importance for us.* **3 = fussy**, demanding, critical, exacting, discriminating, meticulous, fastidious, dainty, choosy *(informal)*, picky *(informal)*, finicky, pernickety *(informal)*, overnice, nit-picky *(informal)*: *Ted was very particular about the colours he used.* **OPPOSITE:** indiscriminate **4 = detailed**, minute, precise, thorough, selective, painstaking, circumstantial, itemized, blow-by-blow: *a very particular account of the history of sociology*
▷ NOUN *(usually plural)* **= detail**, fact, feature, item, circumstance, specification: *The nurses at the admission desk asked for her particulars.*
in particular = especially, particularly, expressly, specifically, exactly, distinctly: *Why should he have noticed me in particular?*

particularly ADVERB **1 = specifically**, expressly, explicitly, especially, in particular, distinctly: *I particularly asked for a seat by the window.* **2 = especially**, surprisingly, notably, unusually, exceptionally, decidedly, markedly, peculiarly, singularly, outstandingly, uncommonly: *The number of fatal road accidents has been particularly high.*

parting NOUN **1 = farewell**, departure, goodbye, leave-taking, adieu, valediction: *It was a dreadfully emotional parting.* **2 = division**, breaking, split, separation, rift, partition, detachment, rupture, divergence: *Through a parting in the mist, we saw a huddle of buildings.*
▷ MODIFIER **= farewell**, last, final, departing, valedictory: *Her parting words made him feel empty and alone.*

partisan ADJECTIVE **1 = prejudiced**, one-sided, biased, partial, sectarian, factional, tendentious: *He is too partisan to be a referee.* **OPPOSITE:** unbiased **2 = underground**, resistance, guerrilla, irregular: *the hide-out of a Bulgarian partisan leader*
▷ NOUN **1 = supporter**, champion, follower, backer, disciple, stalwart, devotee, adherent, upholder, votary: *At first the young poet was a partisan of the Revolution.* **OPPOSITE:** opponent **2 = underground fighter**, guerrilla, irregular, freedom fighter, resistance fighter: *He was rescued by some Italian partisans.*

partition NOUN **1 = screen**, wall, barrier, divider, room divider: *offices divided only by a glass partition* **2 = division**, splitting, dividing, separation, segregation, severance: *the fighting which followed the partition of India*
▷ VERB **1 = separate**, screen, divide, fence off, wall off: *Two rooms have been created by partitioning a single larger room.* **2 = divide**, separate, segment, split up, share, section, portion, cut up, apportion, subdivide, parcel out: *Korea was partitioned in 1945.*

partly ADVERB **= partially**, relatively, somewhat, slightly, in part, halfway, not fully, in some measure, incompletely, up to a certain point, to a certain degree *or* extent
OPPOSITE: completely

> **USAGE**
> *Partly* and *partially* are to some extent interchangeable, but *partly* should be used when referring to a part or parts of something: *the building is partly* (not *partially*) *made of stone*, while *partially* is preferred for the meaning *to some extent*: *his mother is partially* (not *partly*) *sighted.*

partner NOUN **1 = spouse**, consort, bedfellow, significant other *(U.S. informal)*, mate, better half *(Brit. informal)*, helpmate, husband *or* wife, Wag *(informal)*: *Wanting other friends doesn't mean you don't love your partner.* **2 = companion**, collaborator, accomplice, ally, colleague, associate, mate, team-mate, participant, comrade, confederate, bedfellow, copartner: *They were partners in crime.* **3 = associate**, colleague, collaborator, copartner: *He is a partner in a Chicago law firm.*

partnership NOUN **1 = cooperation**, association, alliance, sharing, union, connection, participation, copartnership: *the partnership between Germany's banks and its businesses* **2 = company**, firm, corporation, house, interest, society, conglomerate, cooperative: *As the partnership prospered, the employees shared in the benefits.*

party NOUN **1 = faction**, association, alliance, grouping, set, side, league, camp, combination, coalition, clique, coterie, schism, confederacy, cabal: *opposing political parties* **2 = get-together** *(informal)*, celebration, do *(informal)*, social, at-home, gathering, function, reception, bash *(informal)*, rave *(Brit. slang)*, festivity, knees-up *(Brit. informal)*, beano *(Brit. slang)*, social gathering, shindig *(informal)*, soirée, wrap party, rave-up *(Brit. slang)*, after party, hooley *or* hoolie *(chiefly Irish & N.Z.)*: *We threw a huge birthday party.* **3 = group**, team, band, company, body, unit, squad, gathering, crew, gang, bunch *(informal)*, detachment *(Military)*: *a party of explorers* **4 = litigant**, defendant, participant, contractor *(Law)*, plaintiff: *It has to be proved that he is the guilty party.*

pass VERB **1 = go by** *or* **past**, overtake, drive past, lap, leave behind, pull ahead of: *A car passed me going quite fast.* **OPPOSITE:** stop **2 = go**, move, travel, roll, progress, flow, proceed, move onwards: *He passed through the doorway to ward B.* **3 = run**, move, stroke: *He passed a hand through her hair.* **4 = give**, hand, send, throw, exchange, transfer, deliver, toss, transmit, convey, chuck *(informal)*, let someone have: *He passed the books to the librarian.* **5 = be left**, come, be bequeathed, be inherited by: *His mother's estate passed to him after her death.* **6 = kick**, hit, loft, head, lob: *Their team passed the ball better than ours did.* **7 = elapse**, progress, go by, lapse, wear on, go past, tick by: *As the years passed, he grew discontented with his marriage.* **8 = end**, go, die, disappear, fade, cease, vanish, dissolve, expire, terminate, dwindle, evaporate, wane, ebb, melt away, blow over: *This crisis will pass eventually; Her feelings lightened as the storm passed.* **9 = spend**, use (up), kill, fill, waste, employ, occupy, devote, beguile, while away: *The children passed the time playing in the streets.* **10 = exceed**, beat, overtake, go beyond, excel, surpass, transcend, outstrip, outdo, surmount: *They were the first company in their field to pass the £2 billion turnover mark.* **11 = be successful in**, qualify (in), succeed (in), graduate (in), get through, do, pass muster (in), come up to scratch (in) *(informal)*, gain a pass (in): *Kevin has just passed his driving test.* **OPPOSITE:** fail **12 = approve**, accept, establish, adopt, sanction, decree, enact, authorize, ratify, ordain, validate, legislate (for): *The Senate passed the bill by a vote of seventy-three to twenty-four.* **OPPOSITE:** ban **13 = pronounce**, deliver, issue, set forth: *Passing sentence, the judge described the crime as odious.* **14 = utter**, speak, voice, express, declare: *We passed a few remarks about the weather.* **15 = discharge**, release, expel, evacuate, emit, let out, eliminate *(rare)*: *The first symptom is extreme pain when passing urine.*
▷ NOUN **1 = licence**, ticket, permit, permission, passport, warrant, identification, identity card, authorization: *Can I see your boarding pass, please?* **2 = gap**, route, canyon, col, gorge, ravine, defile: *The monastery is in a remote mountain pass.* **3 = predicament**, condition, situation, state, stage, pinch, plight, straits, state of affairs, juncture: *Things have come to a pretty pass when people are afraid to go out after dark.*
make a pass at someone = make advances to, proposition, hit on *(U.S. & Canad. slang)*, come on to *(informal)*, make a play for *(informal)*, make an approach to, make sexual overtures to: *Was he just being friendly, or was he making a pass at her?*
pass as *or* **for something** *or* **someone = be mistaken for**, be taken for, impersonate, be accepted as, be regarded as: *He was trying to pass as one of the locals.*
pass away *or* **on = die**, pass on, depart (this life), buy it *(U.S. slang)*, expire, check out *(U.S. slang)*, pass over, kick it *(slang)*, croak *(slang)*, go belly-up *(slang)*, snuff it *(informal)*, peg out *(informal)*, kick the bucket *(slang)*, buy the farm *(U.S. slang)*, peg it *(informal)*, decease, shuffle off this mortal coil, cark it *(Austral. & N.Z. informal)*, pop your clogs *(informal)*: *He unfortunately*

passed away last year.
pass off 1 = take place, happen, occur, turn out, go down *(U.S. & Canad.)*, be completed, go off, fall out, be finished, pan out: *The event passed off without any major incidents.* **2 = come to an end**, disappear, vanish, die away, fade out *or* away: *The effects of the anaesthetic gradually passed off.*
pass out = faint, drop, black out *(informal)*, swoon *(literary)*, lose consciousness, keel over *(informal)*, flake out *(informal)*, become unconscious: *She got drunk and passed out.*
pass someone over = overlook, ignore, discount, pass by, disregard, not consider, take no notice of, not take into consideration, pay no attention to: *She claimed she was repeatedly passed over for promotion.*
pass something out = hand out, distribute, dole out, deal out: *They were passing out leaflets in the street.*
pass something over = disregard, forget, ignore, skip, omit, pass by, not dwell on: *Let's pass over that subject.*
pass something up = miss, ignore, let slip, refuse, decline, reject, neglect, forgo, abstain from, let (something) go by, give (something) a miss *(informal)*: *It's too good a chance to pass up.*
pass something *or* someone off as something *or* someone = misrepresent, palm something *or* someone off, falsely represent, disguise something *or* someone, dress something *or* someone up: *horse meat being passed off as ground beef*

> **USAGE**
> The past participle of *pass* is sometimes wrongly spelt *past*: *the time for recriminations has passed* (not *past*).

passable ADJECTIVE **1 = adequate**, middling, average, fair, all right, ordinary, acceptable, moderate, fair enough, mediocre, so-so *(informal)*, tolerable, not too bad, allowable, presentable, admissible, unexceptional, half-pie *(N.Z. informal)*: *The meal was passable, but nothing special.* **OPPOSITE:** unsatisfactory **2 = clear**, open, navigable, unobstructed, traversable, crossable: *muddy mountain roads that are barely passable* **OPPOSITE:** impassable

passage NOUN **1 = corridor**, hallway, passageway, hall, lobby, entrance, exit, doorway, aisle, entrance hall, vestibule: *The toilets are up the stairs and along the passage to your right.* **2 = alley**, way, opening, close *(Brit.)*, course, road, channel, route, path, lane, avenue, thoroughfare: *He spotted someone lurking in the passage between the two houses.* **3 = extract**, reading, piece, section, sentence, text, clause, excerpt, paragraph, verse, quotation: *He read a passage from the Bible.* **4 = movement**, passing, advance, progress, flow, motion, transit, progression: *the passage of troops through Spain* **5 = transition**, change, move, development, progress, shift, conversion, progression, metamorphosis: *the passage from school to college* **6 = establishment**, passing, legislation, sanction, approval, acceptance, adoption, ratification, enactment, authorization, validation, legalization: *It has been 200 years since the passage of the Bill of Rights.* **7 = journey**, crossing, tour, trip, trek, voyage: *We arrived after a 10-hour passage by ship.* **8 = safe-conduct**, right to travel, freedom to travel, permission to travel, authorization to travel: *They were granted safe passage to Baghdad.*

passageway NOUN **= corridor**, passage, hallway, hall, lane, lobby, entrance, exit, alley, aisle, wynd *(Scot.)*

passé ADJECTIVE **= out-of-date**, old-fashioned, dated, outdated, obsolete, unfashionable, antiquated, outmoded, old hat, outworn, démodé *(French)*

passenger NOUN **= traveller**, rider, fare, commuter, hitchhiker, pillion rider, fare payer

passer-by NOUN **= bystander**, witness, observer, viewer, spectator, looker-on, watcher, onlooker, eyewitness

passing ADJECTIVE **1 = momentary**, fleeting, short-lived, transient, ephemeral, short, brief, temporary, transitory, evanescent, fugacious *(rare)*: *people who dismissed mobile phones as a passing fad* **2 = superficial**, short, quick, slight, glancing, casual, summary, shallow, hasty, cursory, perfunctory, desultory: *He only gave us a passing glance.*
▷ NOUN **1 = end**, finish, loss, vanishing, disappearance, termination, dying out, expiry, expiration: *the passing of an era* **2 = death**, demise, decease, passing on *or* away: *His passing will be mourned by many people.*
in passing = incidentally, on the way, by the way, accidentally, en passant, by the bye: *She only mentioned you in passing.*

passion NOUN **1 = love**, desire, affection, lust, the hots *(slang)*, attachment, itch, fondness, adoration, infatuation, ardour, keenness, concupiscence: *Romeo's passion for Juliet* **2 = emotion**, feeling, fire, heat, spirit, transport, joy, excitement, intensity, warmth, animation, zeal, zest, fervour, eagerness, rapture, ardour: *Her eyes were blazing with passion.* **OPPOSITE:** indifference **3 = mania**, fancy, enthusiasm, obsession, bug *(informal)*, craving, fascination, craze, infatuation: *She has a passion for gardening; Television is his passion.* **4 = rage**, fit, storm, anger, fury, resentment, outburst, frenzy, wrath, indignation, flare-up *(informal)*, ire, vehemence, paroxysm: *Sam flew into a passion at the suggestion; He killed the woman in a fit of passion.*

> **QUOTATIONS**
> In passion, the body and the spirit seek expression outside of self
> [John Boorman *journal entry*]
>
> A man who has not passed through the inferno of his passions has never overcome them
> [Carl Gustav Jung *Memories, Dreams, Reflections*]

passionate ADJECTIVE **1 = emotional**, excited, eager, enthusiastic, animated, strong, warm, wild, intense, flaming, fierce, frenzied, ardent, fervent, heartfelt, impassioned, zealous, impulsive, vehement, impetuous, fervid: *He made a passionate speech about his commitment to peace.* **OPPOSITE:** unemotional **2 = loving**, erotic, hot, sexy *(informal)*, aroused, sensual, ardent, steamy *(informal)*, wanton, amorous, lustful, desirous: *a passionate embrace* **OPPOSITE:** cold

passionately ADVERB **1 = emotionally**, eagerly, enthusiastically, vehemently, excitedly, strongly, warmly, wildly, fiercely, intensely, fervently, impulsively, ardently, zealously, animatedly, with all your heart, frenziedly, impetuously, fervidly: *He spoke passionately about the country's moral crisis.* **OPPOSITE:** unemotionally **2 = lovingly**, with passion, erotically, ardently, sexily *(informal)*, sensually, lustfully, amorously, steamily *(informal)*, libidinously, desirously: *She kissed him passionately.* **OPPOSITE:** coldly

passive ADJECTIVE **1 = submissive**, resigned, compliant, receptive, lifeless, docile, nonviolent, quiescent, acquiescent, unassertive, unresisting: *their passive acceptance of the new regime* **OPPOSITE:** spirited **2 = inactive**, inert, uninvolved, non-participating: *He took a passive role in the interview.* **OPPOSITE:** active

password NOUN **= watchword**, key word, magic word *(informal)*, open sesame

past NOUN **1 = former times**, history, long ago, antiquity, the good old days, yesteryear *(literary)*, times past, the old times, days gone by, the olden days, days of yore: *In the past, things were very different.* **OPPOSITE:** future **2 = background**, life, experience, history, past life, life story, career to date: *shocking revelations about his past*
▷ ADJECTIVE **1 = former**, late, early, recent, previous, ancient, prior, long-ago, preceding, foregoing, erstwhile, bygone, olden: *a return to the turbulence of past centuries* **OPPOSITE:** future **2 = previous**, former, one-time, sometime, erstwhile, quondam, ex-: *I was still longing for my past lover* **3 = last**, recent, previous, preceding: *the events of the past few days* **4 = over**, done, ended, spent, finished, completed, gone, forgotten, accomplished, extinct,

elapsed, over and done with: *The great age of exploration is past.*
▷ PREPOSITION **1 = after**, beyond, later than, over, outside, farther than, in excess of, subsequent to: *It's well past your bedtime.* **2 = by**, across, in front of: *She dashed past me and ran out of the room.*
▷ ADVERB **= on**, by, along: *The ambulance drove past.*

USAGE
The past participle of *pass* is sometimes wrongly spelt *past*: *the time for recrimination has passed* (not *past*).

paste NOUN **1 = adhesive**, glue, cement, gum, mucilage: *wallpaper paste* **2 = purée**, pâté, spread: *tomato paste*
▷ VERB **= stick**, fix, glue, cement, gum, fasten: *pasting labels on bottles*

pastel ADJECTIVE **= pale**, light, soft, delicate, muted, soft-hued
OPPOSITE: bright

pastiche NOUN **1 = medley**, mixture, blend, motley, mélange *(French)*, miscellany, farrago, hotchpotch, gallimaufry: *The world menu may be a pastiche of dishes from many countries.* **2 = parody**, take-off, imitation: *a pastiche of Botticelli's Birth of Venus*

pastime NOUN **= activity**, game, sport, entertainment, leisure, hobby, relaxation, recreation, distraction, amusement, diversion

pastor NOUN **= clergyman**, minister, priest, vicar, divine, parson, rector, curate, churchman, ecclesiastic

pastoral ADJECTIVE **1 = ecclesiastical**, priestly, ministerial, clerical: *the pastoral duties of bishops* **2 = rustic**, country, simple, rural, idyllic, bucolic, Arcadian, georgic *(literary)*, agrestic: *a tranquil pastoral scene*

pasture NOUN **= grassland**, grass, meadow, grazing, lea *(poetic)*, grazing land, pasturage, shieling *(Scot.)*

pasty ADJECTIVE **= pale**, unhealthy, wan, sickly, pallid, anaemic, sallow, like death warmed up *(informal)*, wheyfaced

pat[1] VERB **= stroke**, touch, tap, pet, slap, dab, caress, fondle: *She patted me on the knee.*
▷ NOUN **1 = tap**, stroke, slap, clap, dab, light blow: *He gave her an encouraging pat on the shoulder.* **2 = lump**, cake, portion, dab, small piece: *a pat of butter*

pat[2] ADJECTIVE **= glib**, easy, ready, smooth, automatic, slick, simplistic, facile: *There's no pat answer to your question.*
off pat = perfectly, precisely, exactly, flawlessly, faultlessly: *He doesn't have the answer off pat.*

patch NOUN **1 = spot**, bit, stretch, scrap, shred, small piece: *a damp patch on the carpet* **2 = plot**, area, ground, land, tract: *the little vegetable patch in her backyard* **3 = reinforcement**, piece of fabric, piece of cloth, piece of material, piece sewn on: *jackets with patches on the elbows*
▷ VERB **1** *(often with* **up***)* **= sew (up)**, mend, repair, reinforce, stitch (up): *elaborately patched blue jeans* **2** *(often with* **up***)* **= mend**, cover, fix, reinforce: *They patched the barn roof.*
patch things up = settle, make friends, placate, bury the hatchet, conciliate, settle differences, smooth something over: *He's trying to patch things up with his wife.*

patchwork NOUN **= mixture**, confusion, jumble, medley, hash, pastiche, mishmash, hotchpotch

patchy ADJECTIVE **1 = uneven**, irregular, variegated, spotty, mottled, dappled: *Bottle tans can make your legs look a patchy orange colour.*
OPPOSITE: even **2 = irregular**, varying, variable, random, erratic, uneven, sketchy, fitful, bitty, inconstant, scattershot: *The response to the strike call has been patchy.* **OPPOSITE:** constant

patent NOUN **= copyright**, licence, franchise, registered trademark: *He had a number of patents for his inventions.*
▷ ADJECTIVE **= obvious**, apparent, evident, blatant, open, clear, glaring, manifest, transparent, conspicuous, downright, unmistakable, palpable, unequivocal, flagrant, indisputable, unconcealed: *This was a patent lie.*

paternal ADJECTIVE **1 = fatherly**, concerned, protective, benevolent, vigilant, solicitous, fatherlike: *He has always taken a paternal interest in her.* **2 = patrilineal**, patrimonial: *my paternal grandparents*

paternity NOUN **= fatherhood**, fathership *(rare)*

path NOUN **1 = way**, road, walk, track, trail, avenue, pathway, footpath, walkway *(chiefly U.S.)*, towpath, footway, berm *(N.Z.)*: *We followed the path along the clifftops.* **2 = route**, way, course, direction, passage: *A group of reporters blocked his path; The tornado wrecked everything in its path.* **3 = course**, way, road, track, route, procedure: *The country is on the path to economic recovery.*

pathetic ADJECTIVE **1 = sad**, moving, touching, affecting, distressing, tender, melting, poignant, harrowing, heartbreaking, plaintive, heart-rending, gut-wrenching, pitiable: *It was a pathetic sight, watching the people queue for food.*
OPPOSITE: funny **2 = inadequate**, useless, feeble, poor, sorry, wet *(Brit. informal)*, pants *(informal)*, miserable, petty, worthless, meagre, pitiful, woeful, deplorable, lamentable, trashy, measly, crummy *(slang)*, crappy *(slang)*, rubbishy, poxy *(slang)*: *That's the most pathetic excuse I've ever heard.*

pathfinder NOUN **= pioneer**, guide, scout, explorer, discoverer, trailblazer

pathos NOUN **= sadness**, poignancy, plaintiveness, pitifulness, pitiableness

patience NOUN **1 = forbearance**, tolerance, composure, serenity, cool *(slang)*, restraint, calmness, equanimity, toleration, sufferance, even temper, imperturbability: *She lost her patience and shrieked, 'Just shut up, will you?'* **OPPOSITE:** impatience
2 = endurance, resignation, submission, fortitude, persistence, long-suffering, perseverance, stoicism, constancy: *a burden which he has borne with great patience*

> **QUOTATIONS**
> Genius is only a greater aptitude for patience
> [Comte de Buffon]
>
> Patience is the virtue of an ass
> [Lord Lansdowne]
>
> They also serve who only stand and wait
> [John Milton *Sonnet on his Blindness*]
>
> **PROVERBS**
> *All things come to those who wait*
> *Rome was not built in a day*
> *Patience is a virtue*

patient NOUN **= sick person**, case, sufferer, invalid: *He specialized in the treatment of cancer patients.*
▷ ADJECTIVE **1 = forbearing**, understanding, forgiving, mild, accommodating, tolerant, indulgent, lenient, even-tempered: *He was endlessly kind and patient with children.*
OPPOSITE: impatient **2 = long-suffering**, resigned, calm, enduring, quiet, composed, persistent, philosophical, serene, persevering, stoical, submissive, self-possessed, uncomplaining, untiring: *years of patient devotion to her family*

> **QUOTATIONS**
> That patient is not like to recover who makes the doctor his heir
> [Thomas Fuller *Gnomologia*]

patois NOUN **1 = dialect**, vernacular: *In France patois was spoken in rural regions.* **2 = jargon**, slang, vernacular, patter, cant, lingo *(informal)*, argot: *people from the ghetto who speak street patois*

patriarch NOUN **= father**, old man, elder, grandfather, sire, paterfamilias, greybeard

patrician NOUN **= aristocrat**, peer, noble, nobleman, aristo *(informal)*: *He was a patrician, born to wealth.*
▷ ADJECTIVE **= aristocratic**, noble, lordly, high-class, blue-blooded, highborn: *a member of a patrician German family*

patriot NOUN **= nationalist**, loyalist, chauvinist, flag-waver *(informal)*, lover of your country

> **QUOTATIONS**
> No man can be a patriot on an empty stomach
> [W.C. Brann *Old Glory*]
>
> Patriot: The person who can holler the loudest without knowing what he is hollering about
> [Mark Twain]

patriotic ADJECTIVE **= nationalistic**, loyal, flag-waving *(informal)*, chauvinistic, jingoistic

Waffle-free Writing

Most of us have been guilty of waffling at some time or another, ie of 'speaking or writing in a vague or wordy manner'. Some people do this unconsciously, especially in public speaking or conversation, repeating the same points again and again, becoming distracted and bringing in irrelevant matters, or merely filling in regrettable pauses or gaps in one's discourse with words and expressions that add nothing to the gist of what is being said. Sometimes this is merely stalling for time, waiting for your thoughts to organize themselves or for the apposite phrasing to come to mind.

However, what may be acceptable in informal speaking is far from desirable in most forms of writing. Outside of formal examination essays, in which a student who has run out of things to say may be tempted to witter on pointlessly in order to meet a set word count, most writing works better when it is shorn of useless material. Repeating what you have already said will at best bore the reader. It could also cause confusion, leading the reader to suspect that they have missed some subtle point, some difference between what they have already been told and its latest reiteration.

If you are writing a descriptive passage of, say, travel journalism, or an artistic form of fiction, it may be that conciseness is not a priority and that extravagant language is perfectly in keeping with the subject matter. In factual writing, such as news journalism, business reports, or instruction manuals, as long as the meaning is clear then 'less is better'. It is vital to concentrate on the task and keep reading what you have written, making sure that you have put the point across without unnecessary verbiage, trimming back wherever necessary. If you fail to do this, a reader may be forgiven for concluding that you have not thought very deeply about what you wanted to say, that your ideas are woolly, or that you are careless and disorganized.

Try to keep your writing free from pompous-sounding and over-elaborate language. No-one with any sense is going to be impressed by this. Obviously, in scientific or technical writing there will be vocabulary that has precise meaning and which cannot be simplified without the risk of becoming vague. However, clarity in general writing often consists in not using lots of words where fewer will do, refraining from unnecessary jargon or currently fashionable expressions, and avoiding long or overly-technical terms when simple language is perfectly adequate. You may think that *at this moment in time* sounds important or official, but what you are essentially saying is *now*. Similarly, *on a daily basis* adds nothing that *daily* or *every day* don't cover. If you want to say *because*, why not do so? There's no point in reaching for the alternative circumlocutions beloved by poor writers that convey the same thing, such as *by virtue of the fact that* or *due to the fact that*. There's no need to trot out *to all intents and purposes* when *practically* or *essentially* will do the job. Perhaps you think *within the timescale of* has a nice ring to it? Maybe so, but *during* means exactly the same.

To illustrate, here is a passage characterized by waffle, followed immediately by a revised version that is much more concise and to the point, yet sacrifices none of the meaning. Which is more of a chore to read?

> *The current writer is strongly of the opinion that, during the course of the school year, in the majority of cases, students will, in all probability benefit in a very real sense from extending their involvement in homework by something in the neighbourhood of four hours on a weekly basis.*

> *I think most students will benefit from doing another four or so hours of homework each week.*

Of course, nobody really writes like the first passage (or do they?). This is akin to bludgeoning the reader over the head instead of clearly giving him or her the necessary information. However, this example may be taken as a warning to resist the temptation to dress up simple points to no purpose other than to sound clever or fill up space.

patriotism NOUN = **nationalism**, loyalty, flag-waving *(informal)*, jingoism, love of your country

QUOTATIONS

I only regret that I have but one life to lose for my country
[Nathan Hale *prior to his execution by the British in 1776*]

It is a sweet and honourable thing to die for your country (dulce et decorum est pro patria mori)
[Horace *Odes*]

Patriotism is the last refuge of a scoundrel
[Dr. Johnson]

And so, my fellow Americans; ask not what your country can do for you – ask what you can do for your country. My fellow citizens of the world; ask not what America will do for you, but what together we can do for the freedom of man
[John F. Kennedy *inaugural address*]

England expects that every man will do his duty
[Horatio Nelson *said at the Battle of Trafalgar*]

What do I mean by patriotism in the context of our times? ... a sense of national responsibility ... a patriotism which is not short, frenzied outbursts of emotion, but the tranquil and steady dedication of a lifetime
[Adlai Stevenson *speech to the American Legion Convention*]

Never was patriot yet, but was a fool
[John Dryden *Absalom and Achitophel*]

That kind of patriotism which consists in hating all other nations
[Elizabeth Gaskell *Sylvia's Lovers*]

You'll never have a quiet world until you knock the patriotism out of the human race
[George Bernard Shaw *O'Flaherty V.C.*]

Our country, right or wrong!
[Stephen Decatur *toast*]

If I should die, think only this of me,
That there's some corner of a foreign field
That is for ever England
[Rupert Brooke *The Soldier*]

Patriotism is a lively sense of collective responsibility. Nationalism is a silly cock crowing on its own dunghill
[Richard Aldington *The Colonel's Daughter*]

patriotism: combustible rubbish ready to the torch of any one ambitious to illuminate his name
[Ambrose Bierce *The Devil's Dictionary*]

patrol VERB = **police**, guard, keep watch (on), pound, range (over), cruise, inspect, safeguard, make the rounds (of), keep guard (on), walk *or* pound the beat (of): *Prison officers continued to patrol the grounds.*
▷ NOUN = **guard**, watch, garrison, watchman, sentinel, patrolman: *Gunmen opened fire after they were challenged by a patrol.*

patron NOUN **1** = **supporter**, friend, champion, defender, sponsor, guardian, angel *(informal)*, advocate, backer, helper, protagonist, protector, benefactor, philanthropist: *Catherine the Great was a patron of the arts and sciences.* **2** = **customer**, client, buyer, frequenter, shopper, habitué: *Like so many of its patrons, he could not resist the food at the Savoy.*

patronage NOUN = **support**, promotion, sponsorship, backing, help, aid, championship, assistance, encouragement, espousal, benefaction

patronize VERB **1** = **talk down to**, look down on, treat as inferior, treat like a child, be lofty with, treat condescendingly: *a doctor who does not patronize his patients* **2** = **support**, promote, sponsor, back, help, fund, maintain, foster, assist, subscribe to, befriend: *Some believe it is not the job of the government to patronize the arts.* **3** = **be a customer** *or* **client of**, deal with, frequent, buy from, trade with, shop at, do business with: *the record stores he patronized*

patronizing ADJECTIVE = **condescending**, superior, stooping, lofty, gracious, contemptuous, haughty, snobbish, disdainful, supercilious, toffee-nosed *(slang, chiefly Brit.)* OPPOSITE: respectful

patter[1] VERB = **tap**, beat, pat, pelt, spatter, rat-a-tat, pitter-patter, pitapat: *All night the sleet pattered on the tin roof.*
▷ NOUN = **tapping**, pattering, pitter-patter, pitapat: *the patter of the driving rain on the window*

patter[2] NOUN **1** = **spiel** *(informal)*, line, pitch, monologue: *Don't be taken in by the sales patter.* **2** = **chatter**, prattle, nattering, jabber, gabble, yak *(slang)*: *the cheery patter of DJs* **3** = **jargon**, slang, vernacular, cant, lingo *(informal)*, patois, argot: *the famous Glasgow patter*

pattern NOUN **1** = **order**, plan, system, method, arrangement, sequence, orderliness: *All three attacks followed the same pattern.* **2** = **design**, arrangement, motif, figure, device, decoration, ornament, decorative design: *curtains in a light floral pattern* **3** = **plan**, design, original, guide, instructions, diagram, stencil, template: *a sewing pattern* **4** = **model**, example, standard, original, guide, par, criterion, norm, prototype, paradigm, archetype, paragon, exemplar, cynosure: *the ideal pattern of a good society*

paucity NOUN = **scarcity**, lack, poverty, shortage, deficiency, rarity, dearth, smallness, insufficiency, slenderness, sparseness, slightness, sparsity, meagreness, paltriness, scantiness

paunch NOUN = **belly**, beer-belly *(informal)*, spread *(informal)*, corporation *(informal)*, pot, spare tyre *(Brit. slang)*, middle-age spread *(informal)*, potbelly, large abdomen, muffin top *(informal)*, puku *(N.Z.)*

pauper NOUN = **down-and-out**, have-not, bankrupt, beggar, insolvent, indigent, poor person, mendicant

pause VERB = **stop briefly**, delay, hesitate, break, wait, rest, halt, cease, interrupt, deliberate, waver, take a break, discontinue, desist, have a breather *(informal)*: *He paused briefly before answering.* OPPOSITE: continue
▷ NOUN = **stop**, break, delay, interval, hesitation, stay, wait, rest, gap, halt, interruption, respite, lull, stoppage, interlude, cessation, let-up *(informal)*, breathing space, breather *(informal)*, intermission, discontinuance, entr'acte, caesura: *There was a brief pause in the conversation.*
OPPOSITE: continuance

QUOTATIONS

The right word may be effective, but no word was ever as effective as a rightly timed pause
[Mark Twain]

pave VERB = **cover**, floor, surface, flag, concrete, tile, tar, asphalt, macadamize

paw VERB = **manhandle**, grab, maul, molest, handle roughly

pawn[1] VERB = **hock** *(informal, chiefly U.S.)*, pop *(Brit. informal)*, stake, mortgage, deposit, pledge, hazard, wager: *He pawned his wedding ring.*

pawn[2] NOUN = **tool**, instrument, toy, creature, puppet, dupe, stooge *(slang)*, plaything, cat's-paw: *He is being used as a political pawn by the President.*

pay VERB **1** = **reward**, compensate, reimburse, recompense, requite, remunerate, front up: *They are paid well for doing such a difficult job.* **2** = **spend**, offer, give, fork out *(informal)*, remit, cough up *(informal)*, shell out *(informal)*: *I was prepared to pay anything for that car.* **3** = **settle**, meet, clear, foot, honour, discharge, liquidate, square up: *If you cannot pay your debts, you can file for bankruptcy.* **4** = **bring in**, earn, return, net, yield: *This job pays $500 a week.* **5** = **be profitable**, make money, make a return, provide a living, be remunerative: *She took over her husband's restaurant and made it pay.* **6** = **benefit**, serve, repay, be worthwhile, be advantageous: *It pays to invest in protective clothing.* **7** = **give**, extend, present with, grant, render, hand out, bestow, proffer: *My husband never pays me compliments or says he loves me.*
▷ NOUN = **wages**, income, payment, earnings, fee, reward, hire, salary, compensation, allowance, remuneration, takings, reimbursement, hand-outs,

recompense, stipend, emolument, vacation pay (*Canad.*), meed (*archaic*): *the workers' complaints about pay and conditions*
pay off = **succeed**, work, be successful, be effective, be profitable: *Her persistence paid off in the end.*
pay someone back = **get even with** (*informal*), punish, repay, retaliate, hit back at, reciprocate, recompense, get revenge on, settle a score with, get your own back on, revenge yourself on, avenge yourself for: *It was her chance to pay him back for humiliating her.*
pay someone off 1 = **bribe**, corrupt, oil (*informal*), get at, buy off, suborn, grease the palm of (*slang*): *corrupt societies where officials have to be paid off* 2 = **dismiss**, fire, sack (*informal*), discharge, let go, lay off, kennet (*Austral. slang*), jeff (*Austral. slang*): *Most of the staff are being paid off at the end of the month.*
pay something back = **repay**, return, square, refund, reimburse, settle up: *I'll pay you back that money tomorrow.*
pay something off = **settle**, clear, square, discharge, liquidate, pay in full: *It would take him the rest of his life to pay off that loan.*
pay something out = **spend**, lay out (*informal*), expend, cough up (*informal*), shell out (*informal*), disburse, fork out or over or up (*slang*): *football clubs who pay out millions of pounds for players*
pay up = **pay**, fork out (*informal*), stump up (*Brit. informal*), make payment, pay in full, settle up, come up with the money: *We claimed a refund, but the company wouldn't pay up.*

> **PROVERBS**
> *He who pays the piper calls the tune*
> *You pays your money and you takes your choice*

payable ADJECTIVE = **due**, outstanding, owed, owing, mature, to be paid, obligatory, receivable

payment NOUN 1 = **remittance**, advance, deposit, premium, portion, instalment: *a deposit of £50, followed by three monthly payments of £15* 2 = **settlement**, paying, discharge, outlay, remittance, defrayal: *He sought payment of a sum which he claimed was owed to him.* 3 = **wages**, fee, reward, hire, remuneration: *It is reasonable to expect proper payment for this work.*

payoff NOUN 1 = **bribe**, incentive, cut (*informal*), payment, sweetener (*informal*), bung (*Brit. informal*), inducement, kick-back (*informal*), backhander (*informal*), hush money (*informal*): *payoffs from drugs exporters* 2 = **settlement**, payment, reward, payout, recompense: *a $1m divorce payoff* 3 = **outcome**, result, consequence, conclusion, climax, finale, culmination, the crunch (*informal*), upshot, moment of truth, clincher (*informal*), punch line: *The payoff of the novel is patently predictable.*

peace NOUN 1 = **truce**, ceasefire, treaty, armistice, pacification, conciliation, cessation of hostilities: *They hope the treaty will bring peace to Southeast Asia.* **OPPOSITE:** war 2 = **stillness**, rest, quiet, silence, calm, hush, tranquillity, seclusion, repose, calmness, peacefulness, quietude, restfulness: *All I want is a bit of peace and quiet.* 3 = **serenity**, calm, relaxation, composure, contentment, repose, equanimity, peacefulness, placidity, harmoniousness: *People always felt a sense of peace in her company.* 4 = **harmony**, accord, agreement, concord, amity: *a period of relative peace in the country's industrial relations*

> **QUOTATIONS**
> Peace hath her victories
> No less renowned than war
> [John Milton *Sonnet, To the Lord General Cromwell, May 1652*]
>
> Let him who desires peace, prepare for war
> [Vegetius *De Re Militari*]
>
> Peace is not the absence of war. Lasting peace is rooted in justice
> [David Trimble]
>
> You can't separate peace from freedom because no one can be at peace unless he has his freedom
> [Malcolm X *Prospects for Peace in 1965*]
>
> If peace cannot be maintained with honour, it is no longer peace
> [Lord John Russell *speech*]
>
> In the arts of peace Man is a bungler
> [George Bernard Shaw *Man and Superman*]
>
> the peace of God, which passeth all understanding
> [*Bible: Philippians*]
>
> They shall beat their swords into ploughshares, and their spears into pruning-hooks
> [*Bible: Isaiah*]
>
> War makes rattling good history; but Peace is poor reading
> [Thomas Hardy *The Dynasts*]
>
> He that makes a good war makes a good peace
> [George Herbert *Outlandish Proverbs*]
>
> peace: in international affairs, a period of cheating between two periods of fighting
> [Ambrose Bierce *The Devil's Dictionary*]

peaceable ADJECTIVE = **peace-loving**, friendly, gentle, peaceful, mild, conciliatory, amiable, pacific, amicable, placid, inoffensive, dovish, unwarlike, nonbelligerent

peaceful ADJECTIVE 1 = **at peace**, friendly, harmonious, amicable, cordial, nonviolent, without hostility, free from strife, on friendly or good terms: *Their relations with most of these people were peaceful.* **OPPOSITE:** hostile 2 = **peace-loving**, conciliatory, peaceable, placatory, irenic, pacific, unwarlike: *warriors who killed or enslaved the peaceful farmers* **OPPOSITE:** belligerent 3 = **calm**, still, quiet, gentle, pleasant, soothing, tranquil, placid, restful, chilled (*informal*): *a peaceful scene* **OPPOSITE:** agitated 4 = **serene**, placid, undisturbed, untroubled, unruffled: *I felt relaxed and peaceful.*

peacemaker NOUN = **mediator**, appeaser, arbitrator, conciliator, pacifier, peacemonger

> **QUOTATIONS**
> Blessed are the peacemakers; for they shall be called the children of God
> [*Bible: St. Matthew*]

peak NOUN 1 = **high point**, crown, climax, culmination, zenith, maximum point, apogee, acme, ne plus ultra (*Latin*): *His career was at its peak when he died.* 2 = **point**, top, tip, summit, brow, crest, pinnacle, apex, aiguille: *the snow-covered peaks of the Alps* ▷ VERB = **culminate**, climax, come to a head, be at its height, reach its highest point, reach the zenith: *Temperatures have peaked at over 30 degrees Celsius.*

peal VERB = **ring**, sound, toll, resound, chime, resonate, tintinnabulate: *The church bells pealed at the stroke of midnight.* ▷ NOUN 1 = **ring**, sound, ringing, clamour, chime, clang, carillon, tintinnabulation: *the great peals of the Abbey bells* 2 = **clap**, sound, crash, blast, roar, rumble, resounding, reverberation: *great peals of thunder* 3 = **roar**, fit, shout, scream, gale, howl, shriek, hoot: *She burst into peals of laughter.*

pearly ADJECTIVE 1 = **iridescent**, mother-of-pearl, opalescent, nacreous, margaric, margaritic: *a suit covered with pearly buttons* 2 = **ivory**, creamy, milky, silvery: *pearly white teeth*

peasant NOUN 1 = **rustic**, countryman, hind (*obsolete*), swain (*archaic*), son of the soil, churl (*archaic*): *land given to peasants for food production* 2 = **boor**, provincial, hick (*informal, chiefly U.S. & Canad.*), lout, yokel, country bumpkin, hayseed (*U.S. & Canad. informal*), churl: *Why should I let a lot of peasants traipse over my property?*

peck VERB 1 = **pick**, bite, hit, strike, tap, poke, jab, prick, nibble: *The crow pecked his hand.* 2 = **kiss**, plant a kiss, give someone a smacker, give someone a peck or kiss: *She walked up to him and pecked him on the cheek.* ▷ NOUN = **kiss**, smacker, osculation (*rare*): *He gave me a peck on the lips.*

peculiar ADJECTIVE 1 = **odd**, strange, unusual, bizarre, funny, extraordinary, curious, weird, exceptional, eccentric, abnormal, out-of-the-way, queer, uncommon, singular, unconventional, far-out (*slang*), quaint, off-the-wall (*slang*), outlandish, offbeat, freakish, wacko (*slang*), outré, daggy (*Austral. & N.Z. informal*): *He has a very peculiar sense of humour.* **OPPOSITE:** ordinary

2 = special, private, individual, personal, particular, unique, characteristic, distinguishing, distinct, idiosyncratic: *He has his own peculiar way of doing things.* **OPPOSITE:** common **3** (*with* **to**) **= specific to**, restricted to, appropriate to, endemic to: *surnames peculiar to this area*

peculiarity NOUN **1 = oddity**, abnormality, eccentricity, weirdness, queerness, bizarreness, freakishness: *the peculiarity of her behaviour* **2 = quirk**, caprice, mannerism, whimsy, foible, idiosyncrasy, odd trait: *He had many little peculiarities.* **3 = characteristic**, mark, feature, quality, property, attribute, trait, speciality, singularity, distinctiveness, particularity: *a strange peculiarity of the Soviet system*

pecuniary ADJECTIVE **= monetary**, economic, financial, capital, commercial, fiscal, budgetary

pedantic ADJECTIVE **1 = hairsplitting**, particular, formal, precise, fussy, picky (*informal*), nit-picking (*informal*), punctilious, priggish, pedagogic, overnice: *all his pedantic quibbles about grammar* **2 = academic**, pompous, schoolmasterly, stilted, erudite, scholastic, didactic, bookish, abstruse, donnish, sententious: *His lecture was pedantic and uninteresting.*

peddle VERB **= sell**, trade, push (*informal*), market, hawk, flog (*slang*), vend, huckster, sell door to door

peddler *or* **pedlar** NOUN **= seller**, vendor, hawker, duffer (*dialect*), huckster, door-to-door salesman, cheap-jack (*informal*), colporteur

P

pedestal NOUN **= support**, stand, base, foot, mounting, foundation, pier, plinth, dado (*Architecture*): *a bronze statue on a granite pedestal*
put someone on a pedestal = worship, dignify, glorify, exalt, idealize, ennoble, deify, apotheosize: *Since childhood, I put my parents on a pedestal.*

pedestrian NOUN **= walker**, foot-traveller, footslogger: *In Los Angeles, a pedestrian is a rare spectacle.* **OPPOSITE:** driver
▷ ADJECTIVE **= dull**, flat, ordinary, boring, commonplace, mundane, mediocre, plodding, banal, prosaic, run-of-the-mill, humdrum, unimaginative, uninteresting, uninspired, ho-hum (*informal*), no great shakes (*informal*), half-pie (*N.Z. informal*): *His style is so pedestrian that the book is really boring.* **OPPOSITE:** exciting

pedigree MODIFIER **= purebred**, thoroughbred, full-blooded: *A pedigree dog will never cost less than a three-figure sum.*
▷ NOUN **= lineage**, family, line, race, stock, blood, breed, heritage, descent, extraction, ancestry, family tree, genealogy, derivation: *a countess of impeccable pedigree*

pedlar *see* **peddler**

peek VERB **= glance**, look, peer, spy, take a look, peep, eyeball (*slang*), sneak a look, keek (*Scot.*), snatch a glimpse, take *or* have a gander (*informal*): *She peeked at him through a crack in the wall.*
▷ NOUN **= glance**, look, glimpse, blink, peep, butcher's (*Brit. slang*), gander (*informal*), look-see (*slang*), shufti (*Brit. slang*), keek (*Scot.*): *I had a quick peek into the bedroom.*

peel NOUN **= rind**, skin, peeling, epicarp, exocarp: *grated lemon peel*
▷ VERB **= skin**, scale, strip, pare, shuck, flake off, decorticate (*rare*), take the skin *or* rind off: *She sat down and began peeling potatoes.*

peep VERB **1 = peek**, look, peer, spy, eyeball (*slang*), sneak a look, steal a look, keek (*Scot.*), look surreptitiously, look from hiding: *Now and then she peeped to see if he was watching her.* **2 = appear briefly**, emerge, pop up, spring up, issue from, peer out, peek from, show partially: *Purple and yellow flowers peeped between the rocks.*
▷ NOUN **= look**, glimpse, peek, butcher's (*Brit. slang*), gander (*informal*), look-see (*slang*), shufti (*Brit. slang*), keek (*Scot.*): *He took a peep at his watch.*

peer[1] NOUN **1 = noble**, lord, count, duke, earl, baron, aristocrat, viscount, marquess, marquis, nobleman, aristo (*informal*): *He was made a life peer in 1981.* **2 = equal**, like, match, fellow, contemporary, coequal, compeer: *His personality made him popular with his peers.*

peer[2] VERB **= squint**, look, spy, gaze, scan, inspect, peep, peek, snoop, scrutinize, look closely: *She peered at him sleepily over the bedclothes.*

peerage NOUN **= aristocracy**, peers, nobility, lords and ladies, titled classes

> **QUOTATIONS**
> When I want a peerage, I shall buy it like an honest man
> [Lord Northcliffe]

peerless ADJECTIVE **= unequalled**, excellent, unique, outstanding, unparalleled, superlative, unrivalled, second to none, incomparable, unmatched, unsurpassed, matchless, beyond compare, nonpareil **OPPOSITE:** mediocre

peeved ADJECTIVE **= irritated**, upset, annoyed, put out, hacked off (*U.S. slang*), sore, galled, exasperated, nettled, vexed, irked, riled, piqued, tooshie (*Austral. slang*)

peg NOUN **= pin**, spike, rivet, skewer, dowel, spigot: *He builds furniture using wooden pegs instead of nails.*
▷ VERB **1 = fasten**, join, fix, secure, attach, make fast: *trying to peg a sheet on to the washing line* **2 = fix**, set, control, limit, freeze: *The bank wants to peg interest rates at 9%.*

pejorative ADJECTIVE **= derogatory**, negative, slighting, unpleasant, belittling, disparaging, debasing, deprecatory, uncomplimentary, depreciatory, detractive, detractory

pelt[1] VERB **1 = shower**, beat, strike, pepper, batter, thrash, bombard, wallop (*informal*), assail, pummel, hurl at, cast at, belabour, sling at: *Crowds started to pelt police cars with stones.* **2 = pour**, teem, rain hard, bucket down (*informal*), rain cats and dogs (*informal*): *It's pelting down with rain out there.* **3 = rush**, charge, shoot, career, speed, tear, belt (*slang*), dash, hurry, barrel (along) (*informal, chiefly U.S. & Canad.*), whizz (*informal*), stampede, run fast, burn rubber (*informal*): *She pelted down the stairs in her nightgown.*

pelt[2] NOUN **= coat**, fell, skin, hide: *mink which had been bred for their pelts*

pen[1] VERB **= write (down)**, draft, compose, pencil, draw up, scribble, take down, inscribe, scrawl, jot down, dash off, commit to paper: *She penned a short memo to his private secretary.*

> **QUOTATIONS**
> Beneath the rule of men entirely great
> The pen is mightier than the sword
> [Edward Bulwer-Lytton *Richelieu*]

pen[2] NOUN **= enclosure**, pound, fold, cage, coop, hutch, corral (*chiefly U.S. & Canad.*), sty: *a holding pen for sheep*
▷ VERB **= enclose**, confine, cage, pound, mew (up), fence in, impound, hem in, coop up, hedge in, shut up *or* in: *The cattle had been milked and penned for the night.*

penal ADJECTIVE **= disciplinary**, punitive, corrective, penalizing, retributive

penalize VERB **1 = punish**, discipline, correct, handicap, award a penalty against (*Sport*), impose a penalty on: *Players who break the rules will be penalized.* **2 = put at a disadvantage**, handicap, cause to suffer, unfairly disadvantage, inflict a handicap on: *Old people are being penalized for being pensioners.*

penalty NOUN **= punishment**, price, fine, handicap, forfeit, retribution, forfeiture

penance NOUN **= atonement**, punishment, penalty, reparation, expiation, sackcloth and ashes, self-punishment, self-mortification

penchant NOUN **= liking**, taste, tendency, turn, leaning, bent, bias, inclination, affinity, disposition, fondness, propensity, predisposition, predilection, proclivity, partiality, proneness

pending ADJECTIVE **1 = undecided**, unsettled, in the balance, up in the air, undetermined: *The cause of death was listed as pending.* **2 = forthcoming**, imminent, prospective, impending, in the wind, in the offing: *Customers have been inquiring about the pending price rises.*
▷ PREPOSITION **= awaiting**, until, waiting for, till: *The judge has suspended the ban, pending a full inquiry.*

penetrate VERB **1 = pierce**, enter, go through, bore, probe, stab, prick, perforate, impale: *The needle penetrated the skin.* **2 = pervade**, enter, permeate, filter through, suffuse, seep through, get in through, percolate through: *A cool breeze penetrated the mosquito netting.* **3 = infiltrate**, enter, get in to, make inroads into, sneak in to *(informal)*, work *or* worm your way into: *They had managed to penetrate Soviet defences.* **4 = grasp**, understand, work out, figure out *(informal)*, unravel, discern, comprehend, fathom, decipher, suss (out) *(slang)*, get to the bottom of: *long answers that were often difficult to penetrate*

penetrating ADJECTIVE **1 = sharp**, harsh, piercing, carrying, piping, loud, intrusive, strident, shrill, high-pitched, ear-splitting: *Her voice was nasal and penetrating.* **OPPOSITE:** sweet **2 = pungent**, biting, strong, powerful, sharp, heady, pervasive, aromatic: *a most wonderful penetrating smell and taste* **3 = piercing**, cutting, biting, sharp, freezing, fierce, stinging, frosty, bitterly cold, arctic: *A raw, penetrating wind was blowing in off the plain.* **4 = intelligent**, quick, sharp, keen, critical, acute, profound, discriminating, shrewd, discerning, astute, perceptive, incisive, sharp-witted, perspicacious, sagacious: *a penetrating mind* **OPPOSITE:** dull **5 = perceptive**, searching, sharp, keen, alert, probing, discerning: *a penetrating stare* **OPPOSITE:** unperceptive

penetration NOUN **1 = piercing**, entry, entrance, invasion, puncturing, incision, perforation: *the penetration of eggs by more than one sperm* **2 = entry**, entrance, inroad: *US penetration of Japanese markets*

pennant NOUN **= flag**, jack, banner, ensign, streamer, burgee *(Nautical)*, pennon, banderole

penniless ADJECTIVE **= poor**, broke *(informal)*, bankrupt, impoverished, short, ruined, strapped *(slang)*, needy, cleaned out *(slang)*, destitute, poverty-stricken, down and out, skint *(Brit. slang)*, indigent, down at heel, impecunious, dirt-poor *(informal)*, on the breadline, flat broke *(informal)*, penurious, on your uppers, stony-broke *(Brit. slang)*, necessitous, in queer street, moneyless, without two pennies to rub together *(informal)*, without a penny to your name **OPPOSITE:** rich

penny-pinching ADJECTIVE **= mean**, close, near *(informal)*, frugal, stingy, scrimping, miserly, niggardly, tightfisted, Scrooge-like, mingy *(Brit. informal)*, cheeseparing, snoep *(S. African informal)* **OPPOSITE:** generous

pension NOUN **= allowance**, benefit, welfare, annuity, superannuation

pensioner NOUN **= senior citizen**, retired person, retiree *(U.S.)*, old-age pensioner, O.A.P.

pensive ADJECTIVE **= thoughtful**, serious, sad, blue *(informal)*, grave, sober, musing, preoccupied, melancholy, solemn, reflective, dreamy, wistful, mournful, contemplative, meditative, sorrowful, ruminative, in a brown study *(informal)*, cogitative **OPPOSITE:** carefree

pent-up ADJECTIVE **= suppressed**, checked, curbed, inhibited, held back, stifled, repressed, smothered, constrained, bridled, bottled-up

penury NOUN **= poverty**, want, need, privation, destitution, straitened circumstances, beggary, indigence, pauperism

people PLURAL NOUN **1 = persons**, humans, individuals, folk *(informal)*, men and women, human beings, humanity, mankind, mortals, the human race, Homo sapiens: *People should treat the planet with respect.* **2 = the public**, the crowd, the masses, the general public, the mob, the herd, the grass roots, the rank and file, the multitude, the populace, the proletariat, the rabble, the plebs, the proles *(derogatory, slang, chiefly Brit.)*, the commonalty, (the) hoi polloi: *the will of the people* **3 = nation**, public, community, subjects, population, residents, citizens, folk, inhabitants, electors, populace, tax payers, citizenry, (general) public: *the people of Rome* **4 = race**, tribe, ethnic group: *the native peoples of Central and South America* **5 = family**, parents, relations, relatives, folk, folks *(informal)*, clan, kin, next of kin, kinsmen, nearest and dearest, kith and kin, your own flesh and blood, rellies *(Austral. slang)*: *My people still live in Ireland.*
▷ VERB **= inhabit**, occupy, settle, populate, colonize: *a small town peopled by workers and families*

> **QUOTATIONS**
> The voice of the people is the voice of God
> [Alcuin *Epistles*]

pep NOUN **= energy**, life, spirit, zip *(informal)*, vitality, animation, vigour, verve, high spirits, gusto, get-up-and-go *(informal)*, brio, vivacity, liveliness, vim *(slang)*: *They need something to put the pep back in their lives.*
pep something *or* **someone up = enliven**, inspire, stimulate, animate, exhilarate, quicken, invigorate, jazz up *(informal)*, vitalize, vivify: *an attempt to pep up your sex life*

pepper NOUN **= seasoning**, flavour, spice: *Season the mixture with salt and pepper.*
▷ VERB **1 = pelt**, hit, shower, scatter, blitz, riddle, rake, bombard, assail, strafe, rain down on: *He was peppered with shrapnel.* **2 = sprinkle**, spot, scatter, dot, stud, fleck, intersperse, speck, spatter, freckle, stipple, bespatter: *The road was peppered with glass.*

peppery ADJECTIVE **= hot**, fiery, spicy, pungent, highly seasoned, piquant **OPPOSITE:** mild

perceive VERB **1 = see**, notice, note, identify, discover, spot, observe, remark, recognize, distinguish, glimpse, make out, pick out, discern, behold, catch sight of, espy, descry: *I perceived a number of changes.* **2 = understand**, sense, gather, get *(informal)*, know, see, feel, learn, realize, conclude, appreciate, grasp, comprehend, get the message about, deduce, apprehend, suss (out) *(slang)*, get the picture about: *He was beginning to perceive the true nature of their relationship.* **3 = consider**, believe, judge, suppose, rate, deem, adjudge: *How real do you perceive this threat to be?*

perceptible ADJECTIVE **= noticeable**, clear, obvious, apparent, visible, evident, distinct, tangible, blatant, conspicuous, palpable, discernible, recognizable, detectable, observable, appreciable, perceivable **OPPOSITE:** imperceptible

perception NOUN **1 = awareness**, understanding, sense, impression, feeling, idea, taste, notion, recognition, observation, consciousness, grasp, sensation, conception, apprehension: *how our perception of death affects the way we live* **2 = understanding**, intelligence, observation, discrimination, insight, sharpness, cleverness, keenness, shrewdness, acuity, discernment, perspicacity, astuteness, incisiveness, perceptiveness, quick-wittedness, perspicuity: *It did not require a great deal of perception to realise what he meant.*

perceptive ADJECTIVE **= observant**, acute, intelligent, discerning, quick, aware, sharp, sensitive, alert, penetrating, discriminating, shrewd, responsive, astute, intuitive, insightful, percipient, perspicacious **OPPOSITE:** obtuse

perch VERB **1 = sit**, rest, balance, settle: *He perched on the corner of the desk.* **2 = place**, put, rest, balance: *His glasses were perched precariously on his head.* **3 = land**, alight, roost: *A blackbird perched on the parapet outside the window.*
▷ NOUN **= resting place**, post, branch, pole, roost: *The canary fell off its perch.*

percolate VERB **1 = penetrate**, filter, seep, pervade, permeate, transfuse: *These truths begin to percolate through our minds.* **2 = filter**, brew, perk *(informal)*: *the machine I use to percolate my coffee* **3 = seep**, strain, drain, filter, penetrate, drip, leach, ooze, pervade, permeate, filtrate: *Water cannot percolate through the clay.*

perennial ADJECTIVE **= continual**, lasting, continuing, permanent, constant, enduring, chronic, persistent, abiding, lifelong, perpetual, recurrent, never-ending, incessant, unchanging, inveterate

perfect ADJECTIVE **1 = faultless**, correct, pure, accurate, faithful, impeccable, exemplary, flawless, foolproof, blameless: *Nobody's perfect;*

He spoke perfect English. **OPPOSITE:** deficient **2 = excellent**, ideal, supreme, superb, splendid, sublime, superlative: *This is a perfect time to buy a house.* **3 = immaculate**, impeccable, flawless, spotless, unblemished, untarnished, unmarred: *The car is in perfect condition.* **OPPOSITE:** flawed **4 = complete**, absolute, sheer, utter, consummate, out-and-out, unadulterated, unmitigated, unalloyed: *She behaved like a perfect fool.* **OPPOSITE:** partial **5 = exact**, true, accurate, precise, right, close, correct, strict, faithful, spot-on *(Brit. informal)*, on the money *(U.S.)*, unerring: *She spoke in a perfect imitation of her father's voice.*
▷ VERB **= improve**, develop, polish, elaborate, refine, cultivate, hone: *He worked hard to perfect his drawing technique.* **OPPOSITE:** mar

perfection NOUN **1 = excellence**, integrity, superiority, purity, wholeness, sublimity, exquisiteness, faultlessness, flawlessness, perfectness, immaculateness: *the quest for physical perfection* **2 = the ideal**, the crown, the last word, one in a million *(informal)*, a paragon, the crème de la crème, the acme, a nonpareil, the beau idéal *(French)*: *She seems to be perfection itself.* **3 = accomplishment**, achieving, achievement, polishing, evolution, refining, completion, realization, fulfilment, consummation: *the woman credited with the perfection of this technique*

perfectionist NOUN **= stickler**, purist, formalist, precisionist, precisian

perfectly ADVERB **1 = completely**, totally, entirely, absolutely, quite, fully, altogether, thoroughly, wholly, utterly, consummately, every inch: *These mushrooms are perfectly safe to eat.* **OPPOSITE:** partially **2 = flawlessly**, ideally, wonderfully, superbly, admirably, supremely, to perfection, exquisitely, superlatively, impeccably, like a dream, faultlessly: *The system worked perfectly.* **OPPOSITE:** badly

perforate VERB **= pierce**, hole, bore, punch, drill, penetrate, puncture, honeycomb

perform VERB **1 = do**, achieve, carry out, effect, complete, satisfy, observe, fulfil, accomplish, execute, bring about, pull off, act out, transact: *people who have performed outstanding acts of bravery* **2 = fulfil**, carry out, execute, discharge: *Each part of the engine performs a different function.* **3 = present**, act (out), stage, play, produce, represent, put on, render, depict, enact, appear as: *students performing Shakespeare's Macbeth* **4 = appear on stage**, act: *He began performing in the early fifties.*

performance NOUN **1 = presentation**, playing, acting (out), staging, production, exhibition, interpretation, representation, rendering, portrayal, rendition: *They are giving a performance of Bizet's Carmen.* **2 = show**, appearance, concert, gig *(informal)*, recital: *The band did three performances at the Royal Albert Hall.* **3 = work**, acts, conduct, exploits, feats: *The study looked at the performance of 18 surgeons.* **4 = functioning**, running, operation, working, action, behaviour, capacity, efficiency, capabilities: *What is the car's performance like?* **5 = carrying out**, practice, achievement, discharge, execution, completion, accomplishment, fulfilment, consummation: *the performance of his duties* **6 = carry-on** *(informal, chiefly Brit.)*, business, to-do, act, scene, display, bother, fuss, pantomime *(informal, chiefly Brit.)*, song and dance *(informal)*, palaver, rigmarole, pother: *She made a big performance of cooking the dinner.*

> **QUOTATIONS**
> The only true performance is the one which attains madness
> [Mick Jagger]

performer NOUN **= artiste**, player, Thespian, trouper, play-actor, actor *or* actress

perfume NOUN **1 = fragrance**, scent, essence, incense, cologne, eau de toilette, eau de cologne, attar: *The room smelled of her mother's perfume.* **2 = scent**, smell, fragrance, bouquet, aroma, odour, sweetness, niff *(Brit. slang)*, redolence, balminess: *the perfume of roses*

perfunctory ADJECTIVE **= offhand**, routine, wooden, automatic, stereotyped, mechanical, indifferent, careless, superficial, negligent, sketchy, unconcerned, cursory, unthinking, slovenly, heedless, slipshod, inattentive **OPPOSITE:** thorough

perhaps ADVERB **= maybe**, possibly, it may be, it is possible (that), conceivably, as the case may be, perchance *(archaic)*, feasibly, for all you know, happen *(Northern English dialect)*

peril NOUN **1 = danger**, risk, threat, hazard, menace, jeopardy, perilousness: *sailors in peril on the sea* **2** *(often plural)* **= pitfall**, problem, risk, hazard: *the perils of starring in a TV commercial* **OPPOSITE:** safety

perilous ADJECTIVE **= dangerous**, threatening, exposed, vulnerable, risky, unsure, hazardous, hairy *(slang)*, unsafe, precarious, parlous *(archaic)*, fraught with danger, chancy *(informal)*

perimeter NOUN **= boundary**, edge, border, bounds, limit, margin, confines, periphery, borderline, circumference, ambit **OPPOSITE:** centre

period NOUN **1 = time**, term, season, space, run, stretch, spell, phase, patch *(Brit. informal)*, interval, span: *a period of a few months* **2 = age**, generation, years, time, days, term, stage, date, cycle, era, epoch, aeon: *the Victorian period*

periodic ADJECTIVE **= recurrent**, regular, repeated, occasional, periodical, seasonal, cyclical, sporadic, intermittent, every so often, infrequent, cyclic, every once in a while, spasmodic, at fixed intervals

periodical NOUN **= publication**, paper, review, magazine, journal, weekly, monthly, organ, serial, quarterly, zine *(informal)*: *The walls were lined with books and periodicals.*
▷ ADJECTIVE **= recurrent**, regular, repeated, occasional, seasonal, cyclical, sporadic, intermittent, every so often, infrequent, cyclic, every once in a while, spasmodic, at fixed intervals: *periodical fits of depression*

peripheral ADJECTIVE **1 = secondary**, beside the point, minor, marginal, irrelevant, superficial, unimportant, incidental, tangential, inessential: *That information is peripheral to the main story.* **2 = outermost**, outside, external, outer, exterior, borderline, perimetric: *development in the peripheral areas of large towns*

periphery NOUN **= boundary**, edge, border, skirt, fringe, verge, brink, outskirts, rim, hem, brim, perimeter, circumference, outer edge, ambit

perish VERB **1 = die**, be killed, be lost, expire, pass away, lose your life, decease, cark it *(Austral. & N.Z. slang)*: *the ferry disaster in which 193 passengers perished* **2 = be destroyed**, fall, decline, collapse, disappear, vanish, go under: *Civilizations do eventually decline and perish.* **3 = rot**, waste away, break down, decay, wither, disintegrate, decompose, moulder: *The rubber lining had perished.*

perishable ADJECTIVE **= short-lived**, biodegradable, easily spoilt, decomposable, liable to rot **OPPOSITE:** non-perishable

perjury NOUN **= lying under oath**, false statement, forswearing, bearing false witness, giving false testimony, false oath, oath breaking, false swearing, violation of an oath, wilful falsehood

perk NOUN **= bonus**, benefit, extra, plus, dividend, icing on the cake, fringe benefit, perquisite

perk up VERB **= cheer up**, recover, rally, revive, look up, brighten, take heart, recuperate, buck up *(informal)*: *She perked up and began to laugh.*
perk something *or* **someone up = liven someone up**, revive someone, cheer someone up, pep someone up: *A brisk stroll will perk you up.*

perky ADJECTIVE **= lively**, spirited, bright, sunny, cheerful, animated, upbeat *(informal)*, buoyant, bubbly, cheery, bouncy, genial, jaunty, chirpy *(informal)*, sprightly, vivacious, in fine fettle, full of beans *(informal)*, gay, bright-eyed and bushy-tailed *(informal)*

permanence NOUN **= continuity**, survival, stability, duration, endurance, immortality, durability,

The Language of HG Wells

Herbert George Wells (1866–1946) was an English novelist and social commentator most commonly associated with science fiction, though his output was multifaceted, comprising works of politics and comedy alongside his numerous imaginations of the future.

Unsurprisingly, *science* appears often in Wells' writings. The most salient adjectives with *science* are *physical, biological, modern,* and *medical,* while it is most frequently the subject of the verb *have*, as in:

> The development of **science has** lifted famine and pestilence from the shoulders of man, and it will yet lift war.

As the prominence of *biological* as a modifier of *science* indicates, Wells was frequently drawn to evolutionary questions of human development over time. Most famously, *The Time Machine* depicts the descent of the human species by the year 802,701 into the effete *Eloi* and the ape-like *Morlocks*. Such *strange* beings are a recurrent theme in Wells' scientific romances. Indeed, beyond the commonplace usage of *strange thing* ("the strange thing is', explained Lagune.'), the most salient nouns appearing with *strange* are *world, creature, orchid, experience, sense, beast, star, sound, moth,* and *planet*. Strangeness thus comprises most prominently for Wells distant places, mysterious zoological and botanical specimens, and unusual human experiences.

Space is also a familiar motif to readers of Wells. The frequency of the science fictional staple of *outer space*, however, is significantly lower than that of the more versatile *open space*. This occurs to evoke both Wells' terrestrial settings and his alien or future worlds:

> ...at last I emerged upon a small **open space**, and as I did so, a Morlock came blundering towards me.

Likewise, *great, wide, empty,* and *infinite* in conjunction with *space* provide other frequent indicators of exposed landscapes. In contrast to Wells' emphasis on the large and bare nature of his outdoors, his indoor spaces are notably compact with *little, private,* and *small* the most common adjectival modifiers of *room*.

World as well as featuring in combination with *strange* is often associated with verbs with a political resonance. *Rule, dominate, save,* and *govern* reveal the dramatic texture of Wells' novels, as, for example, in the invasion of the Earth in *The War of the Worlds*. They also testify, however, to Well's commitment to left-wing politics. A dedicated socialist and one-time member of the radical Fabian society, Wells' concern with political justice and social reform is expounded in his novels and in numerous works of non-fiction. *Social* often occurs with *order, organisation, system,* and *development* in Wells' political critiques. A less familiar usage today, is the term *social body* that Wells and many of his contemporaries also used to refer to society at large:

> It is integral in the New Republican idea that the process of Schooling, which is the common atrium to all public service, should be fairly uniform throughout the **social body**.

Wells at times extended this metaphor into specific anatomical areas, writing, for example, of the *brain and nervous system* of the *social body*. The *public body, general body* and *religious body* are similar versions of the same metaphorical register, though none of these appears as frequently in Wells' work as the more literal *dead body*.

Stylistically, a recurring feature of Wells' writing is the use of a framing narrative to introduce the novel's often improbable events. *The Island of Doctor Moreau* introduces a grotesque tale of vivisection on a remote Pacific island by describing the discovery by his nephew of the papers of the supposedly crazed Charles Edward Prendrick which then comprises the rest of the narrative. Accordingly, *incredible* and *remarkable* appear several times in Wells' writing as adjectives modifying *story*:

> 'It's a most **remarkable story**,' he said. He looked very wise and grave indeed. 'It's really,' said Mr. Bunting with judicial emphasis, 'a most **remarkable story**.'

finality, perpetuity, constancy, continuance, dependability, permanency, fixity, indestructibility, fixedness, lastingness, perdurability *(rare)*

permanent ADJECTIVE **1 = lasting**, fixed, constant, enduring, persistent, eternal, abiding, perennial, durable, perpetual, everlasting, unchanging, immutable, indestructible, immovable, invariable, imperishable, unfading: *Heavy drinking can cause permanent damage to the brain.* **OPPOSITE:** temporary **2 = long-term**, established, secure, stable, steady, long-lasting: *a permanent job* **OPPOSITE:** temporary

permanently ADVERB **= for ever**, constantly, continually, always, invariably, perennially, persistently, eternally, perpetually, steadfastly, indelibly, in perpetuity, enduringly, unwaveringly, immutably, lastingly, immovably, abidingly, unchangingly, unfadingly **OPPOSITE:** temporarily

permeable ADJECTIVE **= penetrable**, porous, absorbent, spongy, absorptive, pervious

permeate VERB **1 = infiltrate**, fill, pass through, pervade, filter through, spread through, diffuse throughout: *Bias against women permeates every level of the judicial system.* **2 = pervade**, saturate, charge, fill, pass through, penetrate, infiltrate, imbue, filter through, spread through, impregnate, seep through, percolate, soak through, diffuse throughout: *The water will eventually permeate through the surrounding concrete.*

permissible ADJECTIVE **= permitted**, acceptable, legitimate, legal, all right, sanctioned, proper, authorized, lawful, allowable, kosher *(informal)*, admissible, legit *(slang)*, licit, O.K. *or* okay *(informal)* **OPPOSITE:** forbidden

permission NOUN **= authorization**, sanction, licence, approval, leave, freedom, permit, go-ahead *(informal)*, liberty, consent, allowance, tolerance, green light, assent, dispensation, carte blanche, blank cheque, sufferance **OPPOSITE:** prohibition

permissive ADJECTIVE **= tolerant**, liberal, open-minded, indulgent, easy-going, free, lax, lenient, forbearing, acquiescent, latitudinarian, easy-oasy *(slang)* **OPPOSITE:** strict

permit VERB **1 = allow**, admit, grant, sanction, let, suffer, agree to, entitle, endure, license, endorse, warrant, tolerate, authorize, empower, consent to, give the green light to, give leave *or* permission: *I was permitted to bring my camera into the concert; The German constitution does not permit the sending of troops.* **OPPOSITE:** forbid **2 = enable**, let, allow, cause: *This method of cooking permits the heat to penetrate evenly.*
▷ NOUN **= licence**, pass, document, certificate, passport, visa, warrant, authorization: *He has to apply for a permit before looking for a job.* **OPPOSITE:** prohibition

permutation NOUN **= transformation**, change, shift, variation, modification, alteration, mutation, transmutation, transposition

pernicious ADJECTIVE **= wicked**, bad, damaging, dangerous, evil, offensive, fatal, deadly, destructive, harmful, poisonous, malicious, malign, malignant, detrimental, hurtful, malevolent, noxious, venomous, ruinous, baleful, deleterious, injurious, noisome, baneful *(archaic)*, pestilent, maleficent

perpendicular ADJECTIVE **1 = upright**, straight, vertical, plumb, on end: *the perpendicular wall of sandstone* **2 = at right angles**, at 90 degrees: *The left wing dipped until it was perpendicular to the ground.*

perpetrate VERB **= commit**, do, perform, carry out, effect, be responsible for, execute, inflict, bring about, enact, wreak

> **USAGE**
> *Perpetrate* and *perpetuate* are sometimes confused: *he must answer for the crimes he has perpetrated* (not *perpetuated*); *the book helped to perpetuate* (not *perpetrate*) *some of the myths surrounding his early life*.

perpetual ADJECTIVE **1 = everlasting**, permanent, endless, eternal, lasting, enduring, abiding, perennial, infinite, immortal, never-ending, unending, unchanging, undying, sempiternal *(literary)*: *the regions of perpetual night at the lunar poles* **OPPOSITE:** temporary **2 = continual**, repeated, constant, endless, continuous, persistent, perennial, recurrent, never-ending, uninterrupted, interminable, incessant, ceaseless, unremitting, unfailing, unceasing: *her perpetual complaints* **OPPOSITE:** brief

perpetuate VERB **= maintain**, preserve, sustain, keep up, keep going, continue, keep alive, immortalize, eternalize **OPPOSITE:** end

perplex VERB **= puzzle**, confuse, stump, baffle, bewilder, muddle, confound, beset, mystify, faze, befuddle, flummox, bemuse, dumbfound, nonplus, mix you up

perplexing ADJECTIVE **= puzzling**, complex, confusing, complicated, involved, hard, taxing, difficult, strange, weird, mysterious, baffling, bewildering, intricate, enigmatic, mystifying, inexplicable, thorny, paradoxical, unaccountable, knotty, labyrinthine

perplexity NOUN **1 = puzzlement**, confusion, bewilderment, incomprehension, bafflement, mystification, stupefaction: *There was utter perplexity in both their expressions.* **2** *(usually plural)* **= complexity**, difficulty, mystery, involvement, puzzle, paradox, obscurity, enigma, intricacy, inextricability: *the perplexities of quantum mechanics*

per se ADVERB **= in itself**, essentially, as such, in essence, by itself, of itself, by definition, intrinsically, by its very nature

persecute VERB **1 = victimize**, hunt, injure, pursue, torture, hound, torment, martyr, oppress, pick on, molest, ill-treat, maltreat: *They have been persecuted for their beliefs.* **OPPOSITE:** mollycoddle **2 = harass**, bother, annoy, bait, tease, worry, hassle *(informal)*, badger, pester, vex, be on your back *(slang)*: *He described his first wife as constantly persecuting him.* **OPPOSITE:** leave alone

perseverance NOUN **= persistence**, resolution, determination, dedication, stamina, endurance, tenacity, diligence, constancy, steadfastness, doggedness, purposefulness, pertinacity, indefatigability, sedulity

> **QUOTATIONS**
> If at first you don't succeed,
> Try, try, try again
> [William E. Hickson *Try and Try Again*]
>
> The best way out is always through
> [Robert Frost *A Servant to Servants*]

persevere VERB **= keep going**, continue, go on, carry on, endure, hold on *(informal)*, hang on, persist, stand firm, plug away *(informal)*, hold fast, remain firm, stay the course, keep your hand in, pursue your goal, be determined *or* resolved, keep on *or* at, stick at *or* to **OPPOSITE:** give up

persist VERB **1 = continue**, last, remain, carry on, endure, keep up, linger, abide: *Consult your doctor if the symptoms persist.* **2 = persevere**, continue, go on, carry on, hold on *(informal)*, keep on, keep going, press on, not give up, stand firm, soldier on *(informal)*, stay the course, plough on, be resolute, stick to your guns *(informal)*, show determination, crack on *(informal)*: *He urged them to persist with their efforts to bring about peace.*

persistence NOUN **= determination**, resolution, pluck, stamina, grit, endurance, tenacity, diligence, perseverance, constancy, steadfastness, doggedness, pertinacity, indefatigability, tirelessness

persistent ADJECTIVE **1 = continuous**, constant, relentless, lasting, repeated, endless, perpetual, continual, never-ending, interminable, unrelenting, incessant, unremitting: *flooding caused by persistent rain* **OPPOSITE:** occasional **2 = determined**, dogged, fixed, steady, enduring, stubborn, persevering, resolute, tireless, tenacious, steadfast, obstinate, indefatigable, immovable, assiduous, obdurate, stiff-necked, unflagging, pertinacious: *He phoned again this morning – he's very persistent.* **OPPOSITE:** irresolute

person NOUN **= individual**, being, body, human, soul, creature, human being, mortal, living soul, man *or* woman: *He's the only person who can do the job.*

in person 1 = personally, yourself: *She collected the award in person.* **2 = in the flesh**, actually, physically, bodily: *It was the first time she had seen him in person.*

> **QUOTATIONS**
> A person is a person because he recognizes others as persons [Desmond Tutu *speech at enthronement as Anglican archbishop of Cape Town*]

persona NOUN **= personality**, part, face, front, role, character, mask, façade, public face, assumed role

personable ADJECTIVE **= pleasant**, pleasing, nice, attractive, charming, handsome, good-looking, winning, agreeable, amiable, affable, presentable, likable *or* likeable **OPPOSITE:** unpleasant

personage NOUN **= personality**, celebrity, big name, somebody, worthy, notable, public figure, dignitary, luminary, celeb *(informal)*, big shot *(informal)*, megastar *(informal)*, big noise *(informal)*, well-known person, V.I.P.

personal ADJECTIVE **1 = own**, special, private, individual, particular, peculiar, privy: *That's my personal property!* **2 = individual**, special, particular, exclusive: *I'll give it my personal attention.* **3 = private**, intimate, confidential: *prying into his personal life* **4 = offensive**, critical, slighting, nasty, insulting, rude, belittling, disparaging, derogatory, disrespectful, pejorative: *a series of personal comments about my family* **5 = physical**, intimate, bodily, corporal, corporeal: *personal hygiene*

personality NOUN **1 = nature**, character, make-up, identity, temper, traits, temperament, psyche, disposition, individuality: *She has such a kind, friendly personality.* **2 = character**, charm, attraction, charisma, attractiveness, dynamism, magnetism, pleasantness, likableness *or* likeableness: *a woman of great personality and charm* **3 = celebrity**, star, big name, notable, household name, famous name, celeb *(informal)*, personage, megastar *(informal)*, well-known face, well-known person: *a radio and television personality*

personalized ADJECTIVE **= customized**, special, private, individual, distinctive, tailor-made, individualized, monogrammed

personally ADVERB **1 = in your opinion**, for yourself, in your book, for your part, from your own viewpoint, in your own view: *Personally, I think it's a waste of time.* **2 = by yourself**, alone, independently, solely, on your own, in person, in the flesh: *The minister will answer the allegations personally.* **3 = individually**, specially, subjectively, individualistically: *This topic interests me personally.* **4 = privately**, in private, off the record: *Personally he was quiet, modest and unobtrusive.*

personification NOUN **= embodiment**, image, representation, re-creation, portrayal, incarnation, likeness, semblance, epitome

personify VERB **= embody**, represent, express, mirror, exemplify, symbolize, typify, incarnate, image *(rare)*, epitomize, body forth

personnel NOUN **= employees**, people, members, staff, workers, men and women, workforce, human resources, helpers, liveware

perspective NOUN **1 = outlook**, attitude, context, angle, overview, way of looking, frame of reference, broad view: *The death of my mother gave me a new perspective on life.* **2 = objectivity**, proportion, relation, relativity, relative importance: *helping her to get her problems into perspective* **3 = view**, scene, prospect, outlook, panorama, vista: *stretching away along the perspective of a tree-lined, wide avenue*

perspiration NOUN **= sweat**, moisture, wetness, exudation

perspire VERB **= sweat**, glow, swelter, drip with sweat, break out in a sweat, pour with sweat, secrete sweat, be damp *or* wet *or* soaked with sweat, exude sweat

persuade VERB **1 = talk (someone) into**, urge, advise, prompt, influence, counsel, win (someone) over, induce, sway, entice, coax, incite, prevail upon, inveigle, bring (someone) round *(informal)*, twist (someone's) arm, argue (someone) into: *My husband persuaded me to come.* **OPPOSITE:** dissuade **2 = cause**, prompt, lead, move, influence, motivate, induce, incline, dispose, impel, actuate: *the event which persuaded the United States to enter the war* **3 = convince**, satisfy, assure, prove to, convert to, cause to believe: *Derek persuaded me of the feasibility of the idea.*

persuasion NOUN **1 = urging**, influencing, conversion, inducement, exhortation, wheedling, enticement, cajolery, blandishment, soft power, inveiglement: *It took all her powers of persuasion to induce them to stay.* **2 = belief**, views, opinion, party, school, side, camp, faith, conviction, faction, cult, sect, creed, denomination, tenet, school of thought, credo, firm belief, certitude, fixed opinion: *people who are of a different political persuasion*

persuasive ADJECTIVE **= convincing**, telling, effective, winning, moving, sound, touching, impressive, compelling, influential, valid, inducing, logical, credible, plausible, forceful, eloquent, weighty, impelling, cogent **OPPOSITE:** unconvincing

pertain to VERB **= relate to**, concern, refer to, regard, be part of, belong to, apply to, bear on, befit, be relevant to, be appropriate to, appertain to

pertinent ADJECTIVE **= relevant**, fitting, fit, material, appropriate, pat, suitable, proper, to the point, apt, applicable, apposite, apropos, admissible, germane, to the purpose, ad rem *(Latin)* **OPPOSITE:** irrelevant

perturb VERB **= disturb**, worry, trouble, upset, alarm, bother, unsettle, agitate, ruffle, unnerve, disconcert, disquiet, vex, fluster, faze, discountenance, discompose

perturbed ADJECTIVE **= disturbed**, worried, troubled, shaken, upset, alarmed, nervous, anxious, uncomfortable, uneasy, fearful, restless, flurried, agitated, disconcerted, disquieted, flustered, ill at ease, antsy *(informal)* **OPPOSITE:** relaxed

peruse VERB **= read**, study, scan, check, examine, inspect, browse, look through, eyeball *(slang)*, work over, scrutinize, run your eye over, surf *(Computing)*

pervade VERB **= spread through**, fill, affect, penetrate, infuse, permeate, imbue, suffuse, percolate, extend through, diffuse through, overspread

pervasive ADJECTIVE **= widespread**, general, common, extensive, universal, prevalent, ubiquitous, rife, pervading, permeating, inescapable, omnipresent

perverse ADJECTIVE **1 = stubborn**, contrary, unreasonable, dogged, contradictory, troublesome, rebellious, wayward, delinquent, intractable, wilful, unyielding, obstinate, intransigent, headstrong, unmanageable, cussed *(informal)*, obdurate, stiff-necked, disobedient, wrong-headed, refractory, pig-headed, miscreant, mulish, cross-grained, contumacious: *You're just being perverse.* **OPPOSITE:** cooperative **2 = ill-natured**, cross, surly, petulant, crabbed, fractious, spiteful, churlish, ill-tempered, stroppy *(Brit. slang)*, cantankerous, peevish, shrewish: *He seems to take a perverse pleasure in being disagreeable.* **OPPOSITE:** good-natured **3 = abnormal**, incorrect, unhealthy, improper, deviant, depraved: *perverse sexual practices*

perversion NOUN **1 = deviation**, vice, abnormality, aberration, kink *(Brit. informal)*, wickedness, depravity, immorality, debauchery, unnaturalness, kinkiness *(slang)*, vitiation: *The most frequent sexual perversion is fetishism.* **2 = distortion**, twisting, corruption, misuse, misrepresentation, misinterpretation, falsification: *a monstrous perversion of justice*

perversity NOUN = **contrariness**, intransigence, obduracy, waywardness, contradictoriness, wrong-headedness, refractoriness, contumacy, contradictiveness, frowardness *(archaic)*

pervert VERB **1 = distort**, abuse, twist, misuse, warp, misinterpret, misrepresent, falsify, misconstrue: *officers attempting to pervert the course of justice* **2 = corrupt**, degrade, subvert, deprave, debase, desecrate, debauch, lead astray: *He was accused of perverting the nation's youth.*
▷ NOUN = **deviant**, degenerate, sicko *(informal)*, sleazeball *(slang)*, debauchee, weirdo *or* weirdie *(informal)*: *You're nothing but a sick pervert.*

perverted ADJECTIVE = **unnatural**, sick, corrupt, distorted, abnormal, evil, twisted, impaired, warped, misguided, unhealthy, immoral, deviant, wicked, kinky *(slang)*, depraved, debased, debauched, aberrant, vitiated, pervy *(slang)*, sicko *(slang)*

pessimism NOUN = **gloominess**, depression, despair, gloom, cynicism, melancholy, hopelessness, despondency, dejection, glumness

pessimist NOUN = **defeatist**, cynic, melancholic, worrier, killjoy, prophet of doom, misanthrope, wet blanket *(informal)*, gloom merchant *(informal)*, doomster

pessimistic ADJECTIVE = **gloomy**, dark, despairing, bleak, resigned, sad, depressed, cynical, hopeless, melancholy, glum, dejected, foreboding, despondent, morose, fatalistic, distrustful, downhearted, misanthropic **OPPOSITE:** optimistic

pest NOUN **1 = infection**, bug, insect, plague, epidemic, blight, scourge, bane, pestilence, gogga *(S. African informal)*: *all kinds of pests like flies and mosquitoes; bacterial, fungal, and viral pests of the plants themselves* **2 = nuisance**, bore, trial, pain *(informal)*, drag *(informal)*, bother, irritation, gall, annoyance, bane, pain in the neck *(informal)*, vexation, thorn in your flesh: *My neighbour's a real pest.*

pester VERB = **annoy**, worry, bother, disturb, bug *(informal)*, plague, torment, get at, harass, nag, hassle *(informal)*, harry, aggravate *(informal)*, fret, badger, pick on, irk, bedevil, chivvy, get on your nerves *(informal)*, bend someone's ear *(informal)*, drive you up the wall *(slang)*, be on your back *(slang)*, get in your hair *(informal)*

pestilence NOUN = **plague**, epidemic, visitation, pandemic

pet ADJECTIVE **1 = favourite**, chosen, special, personal, particular, prized, preferred, favoured, dearest, cherished, fave *(informal)*, dear to your heart: *The proceeds will be split between her pet charities.* **2 = tame**, trained, domestic, house, domesticated, house-trained *(Brit.)*, house-broken: *One in four households owns a pet dog.*
▷ NOUN = **favourite**, treasure, darling, jewel, idol, fave *(informal)*, apple of your eye, blue-eyed boy *or* girl *(Brit. informal)*: *They taunted her about being the teacher's pet.*
▷ VERB **1 = fondle**, pat, stroke, caress: *A woman sat petting a cocker spaniel.* **2 = pamper**, spoil, indulge, cosset, baby, dote on, coddle, mollycoddle, wrap in cotton wool: *She had petted her son all his life.* **3 = cuddle**, kiss, snog *(Brit. slang)*, smooch *(informal)*, neck *(informal)*, canoodle *(slang)*: *They were kissing and petting on the couch.*

peter out VERB = **die out**, stop, fail, run out, fade, dwindle, evaporate, wane, give out, ebb, come to nothing, run dry, taper off

petite ADJECTIVE = **small**, little, slight, delicate, dainty, dinky *(Brit. informal)*, elfin

petition NOUN **1 = appeal**, round robin, list of signatures: *We presented the government with a petition signed by 4,500 people.* **2 = entreaty**, appeal, address, suit, application, request, prayer, plea, invocation, solicitation, supplication: *a humble petition to Saint Anthony*
▷ VERB = **appeal**, press, plead, call (upon), ask, urge, sue, pray, beg, crave, solicit, beseech, entreat, adjure, supplicate: *She is petitioning to regain custody of the child.*

petrified ADJECTIVE **1 = terrified**, horrified, shocked, frozen, stunned, appalled, numb, dazed, speechless, aghast, dumbfounded, stupefied, scared stiff, terror-stricken: *He was petrified at the thought of having to make a speech.* **2 = fossilized**, ossified, rocklike: *a block of petrified wood*

petrify VERB **1 = terrify**, horrify, amaze, astonish, stun, appal, paralyse, astound, confound, transfix, stupefy, immobilize, dumbfound: *His story petrified me.* **2 = fossilize**, set, harden, solidify, ossify, turn to stone, calcify: *Bird and bat guano petrifies into a mineral called taranakite.*

petty ADJECTIVE **1 = trivial**, inferior, insignificant, little, small, slight, trifling, negligible, unimportant, paltry, measly *(informal)*, contemptible, piddling *(informal)*, inconsiderable, inessential, nickel-and-dime *(U.S. slang)*: *Rows would start over petty things.* **OPPOSITE:** important **2 = small-minded**, mean, cheap, grudging, shabby, spiteful, stingy, ungenerous, mean-minded: *I think that attitude is a bit petty.* **OPPOSITE:** broad-minded **3 = minor**, lower, junior, secondary, lesser, subordinate, inferior: *Wilson was not a man who dealt with petty officials.*

petulance NOUN = **sulkiness**, bad temper, irritability, spleen, pique, sullenness, ill-humour, peevishness, querulousness, crabbiness, waspishness, pettishness

petulant ADJECTIVE = **sulky**, cross, moody, sour, crabbed, impatient, pouting, perverse, irritable, crusty, sullen, bad-tempered, ratty *(Brit. & N.Z. informal)*, fretful, waspish, querulous, peevish, ungracious, cavilling, huffy, fault-finding, snappish, ill-humoured, captious **OPPOSITE:** good-natured

phantom NOUN = **spectre**, ghost, spirit, shade *(literary)*, spook *(informal)*, apparition, wraith, revenant, phantasm

phase NOUN = **stage**, time, state, point, position, step, development, condition, period, chapter, aspect, juncture: *The crisis is entering a crucial phase.*
phase something in = **introduce**, incorporate, ease in, start: *Reforms will be phased in over the next three years.*
phase something out = **eliminate**, close, pull, remove, replace, withdraw, pull out, axe *(informal)*, wind up, run down, terminate, wind down, ease off, taper off, deactivate, dispose of gradually: *The present system of military conscription should be phased out.*

phenomenal ADJECTIVE = **extraordinary**, outstanding, remarkable, fantastic, unique, unusual, marvellous, exceptional, notable, sensational, uncommon, singular, miraculous, stellar *(informal)*, prodigious, unparalleled, wondrous *(archaic, literary)* **OPPOSITE:** unremarkable

phenomenon NOUN **1 = occurrence**, happening, fact, event, incident, circumstance, episode: *scientific explanations of this natural phenomenon* **2 = wonder**, sensation, spectacle, sight, exception, miracle, marvel, prodigy, rarity, nonpareil, black swan: *The Loch Ness monster is not the only bizarre phenomenon that bookmakers take bets on.*

> **USAGE**
> Although *phenomena* is often treated as a singular, this is not grammatically correct. *Phenomenon* is the singular form of this word, and *phenomena* the plural; so *several new phenomena were recorded in his notes* is correct, but *that is an interesting phenomena* is not.

philanthropic ADJECTIVE = **humanitarian**, generous, charitable, benevolent, kind, humane, gracious, altruistic, public-spirited, beneficent, kind-hearted, munificent, almsgiving, benignant **OPPOSITE:** selfish

philanthropist NOUN = **humanitarian**, patron, benefactor, giver, donor, contributor, altruist, almsgiver

philanthropy NOUN = **humanitarianism**, charity, generosity, patronage, bounty, altruism, benevolence, munificence, beneficence, liberality, public-

p

spiritedness, benignity, almsgiving, brotherly love, charitableness, kind-heartedness, generousness, open-handedness, largesse *or* largess

philistine NOUN **= boor**, barbarian, yahoo, lout, bourgeois, hoon *(Austral. & N.Z.)*, ignoramus, lowbrow, vulgarian, cougan *(Austral. slang)*, scozza *(Austral. slang)*, bogan *(Austral. slang)*: *The man's a total philistine when it comes to the arts.*
▷ ADJECTIVE *(sometimes not cap)* **= uncultured**, ignorant, crass, tasteless, bourgeois, uneducated, boorish, unrefined, uncultivated, anti-intellectual, lowbrow, inartistic: *the country's philistine, consumerist mentality*

philosopher NOUN **= thinker**, theorist, sage, wise man, logician, metaphysician, dialectician, seeker after truth

> **QUOTATIONS**
> It is one of the chief skills of the philosopher not to occupy himself with questions which do not concern him
> [Ludwig Wittgenstein *Tractatus Logico-Philosophicus*]
>
> There is no statement so absurd that no philosopher will make it
> [Cicero *De Divinatione*]
>
> There was never yet philosopher
> That could endure the toothache patiently
> [William Shakespeare *Much Ado About Nothing*]
>
> The philosophers have only interpreted the world in various ways; the point, however, is to change it
> [Karl Marx *Theses on Feuerbach*]
>
> I have tried too in my time to be a philosopher; but, I don't know how, cheerfulness was always breaking in
> [Oliver Edwards]
>
> what I understand by 'philosopher': a terrible explosive in the presence of which everything is in danger
> [Friedrich Nietzsche *Ecce Homo*]

philosophical *or* **philosophic** ADJECTIVE **1 = theoretical**, abstract, learned, wise, rational, logical, thoughtful, erudite, sagacious: *a philosophical discourse* **OPPOSITE:** practical **2 = stoical**, calm, composed, patient, cool, collected, resigned, serene, tranquil, sedate, impassive, unruffled, imperturbable: *He was remarkably philosophical about his failure.* **OPPOSITE:** emotional

> **QUOTATIONS**
> What, knocked a tooth out? Never mind, dear, laugh it off, laugh it off; it's all part of life's rich pageant
> [Arthur Marshall *The Games Mistress*]

philosophy NOUN **1 = thought**, reason, knowledge, thinking, reasoning, wisdom, logic, metaphysics: *He studied philosophy and psychology at Cambridge.* **2 = outlook**, values, principles, convictions, thinking, beliefs, doctrine, ideology, viewpoint, tenets, world view, basic idea, attitude to life, Weltanschauung *(German)*: *his philosophy of non-violence*

phlegm NOUN **= mucus**, catarrh, sputum, mucous secretion

phlegmatic ADJECTIVE **= unemotional**, indifferent, cold, heavy, dull, sluggish, matter-of-fact, placid, stoical, lethargic, bovine, apathetic, frigid, lymphatic, listless, impassive, stolid, unfeeling, undemonstrative
OPPOSITE: emotional

phobia NOUN **= fear**, horror, terror, thing about *(informal)*, obsession, dislike, dread, hatred, loathing, distaste, revulsion, aversion to, repulsion, irrational fear, detestation, overwhelming anxiety about
OPPOSITE: liking ▷ *See themed panel* **Phobias** *on page 506*

phone NOUN **1 = telephone**, blower *(informal)*, dog and bone *(slang)*: *I spoke to her on the phone only yesterday.* **2 = call**, ring *(informal, chiefly Brit.)*, bell *(Brit. slang)*, buzz *(informal)*, tinkle *(Brit. informal)*: *If you need anything, give me a phone.*
▷ VERB **= call**, telephone, ring (up) *(informal, chiefly Brit.)*, give someone a call, give someone a ring *(informal, chiefly Brit.)*, make a call, give someone a buzz *(informal)*, give someone a bell *(Brit. slang)*, give someone a tinkle *(Brit. informal)*, get on the blower *(informal)*: *I got more and more angry as I waited for her to phone.*

phoney ADJECTIVE **1 = fake**, affected, assumed, trick, put-on, false, forged, imitation, sham, pseudo *(informal)*, counterfeit, feigned, spurious: *He used a phoney accent.* **OPPOSITE:** genuine **2 = bogus**, false, fake, pseudo *(informal)*, ersatz: *phoney 'experts'*
▷ NOUN **1 = faker**, fraud, fake, pretender, humbug, impostor, pseud *(informal)*: *He was a liar, a cheat, and a phoney.* **2 = fake**, sham, forgery, counterfeit: *This passport is a phoney.*

photograph NOUN **= picture**, photo *(informal)*, shot, image, print, slide, snap *(informal)*, snapshot, transparency, likeness: *He wants to take some photographs of the house.*
▷ VERB **= take a picture of**, record, film, shoot, snap *(informal)*, take (someone's) picture, capture on film, get a shot of: *I hate being photographed.*

photographic ADJECTIVE **1 = pictorial**, visual, graphic, cinematic, filmic: *The bank is able to use photographic evidence of who used the machine.* **2 = accurate**, minute, detailed, exact, precise, faithful, retentive: *a photographic memory*

phrase NOUN **= expression**, saying, remark, motto, construction, tag, quotation, maxim, idiom, utterance, adage, dictum, way of speaking, group of words, locution: *the Latin phrase, 'mens sana in corpore sano'*
▷ VERB **= express**, say, word, put, term, present, voice, frame, communicate, convey, utter, couch, formulate, put into words: *The speech was carefully phrased.*

physical ADJECTIVE **1 = corporal**, fleshly, bodily, carnal, somatic, corporeal: *the physical problems caused by the illness* **2 = earthly**, fleshly, mortal, incarnate, unspiritual: *They were still aware of the physical world around them.* **3 = material**, real, substantial, natural, solid, visible, sensible, tangible, palpable: *There is no physical evidence to support the story.*

physician NOUN **= doctor**, specialist, doc *(informal)*, healer, medic *(informal)*, general practitioner, medical practitioner, medico *(informal)*, doctor of medicine, sawbones *(slang)*, G.P., M.D.

> **QUOTATIONS**
> Physician, heal thyself
> [*Bible: St. Luke*]
>
> Cured yesterday of my disease,
> I died last night of my physician
> [Matthew Prior *The Remedy Worse than the Disease*]

physique NOUN **= build**, form, body, figure, shape, structure, make-up, frame, constitution

pick VERB **1 = select**, choose, identify, elect, nominate, sort out, specify, opt for, single out, mark out, plump for, hand-pick, decide upon, cherry-pick, fix upon, settle on *or* upon, sift out, flag up: *He had picked ten people to interview for the jobs.* **OPPOSITE:** reject **2 = gather**, cut, pull, collect, take in, harvest, pluck, garner, cull: *He helped his mother pick fruit.* **3 = provoke**, start, cause, stir up, incite, instigate, foment: *He picked a fight with a waiter and landed in jail.* **4 = open**, force, crack *(informal)*, break into, break open, prise open, jemmy *(informal)*: *He picked the lock, and rifled through the papers in each drawer.*
▷ NOUN **1 = choice**, decision, choosing, option, selection, preference: *We had the pick of winter coats from the shop.* **2 = best**, prime, finest, tops *(slang)*, choicest, flower, prize, elect, pride, elite, cream, jewel in the crown, the crème de la crème: *These boys are the pick of the under-15 cricketers in the country.*
pick at something = nibble (at), peck at, have no appetite for, play *or* toy with, push round the plate, eat listlessly: *She picked at her breakfast.*
pick on someone 1 = torment, bully, bait, tease, get at *(informal)*, badger, persecute, hector, goad, victimize, have it in for *(informal)*, tyrannize, have a down on *(informal)*: *Bullies pick on smaller children.* **2 = choose**, select, prefer, elect, single out, fix on, settle upon: *He needed to confess to someone – he just happened to pick on me.*

PHOBIAS

Phobia	Meaning
acerophobia	sourness
achluophobia	darkness
acrophobia	heights
aerophobia	air
agoraphobia	open spaces
aichurophobia	points
ailurophobia	cats
akousticophobia	sound
algophobia	pain
amakaphobia	carriages
amathophobia	dust
androphobia	men
anemophobia	wind
anginophobia	narrowness
anthropophobia	man
antlophobia	flood
apeirophobia	infinity
aquaphobia	water
arachnophobia	spiders
asthenophobia	weakness
astraphobia	lightning
atephobia	ruin
aulophobia	flute
bacilliphobia	microbes
barophobia	gravity
basophobia	walking
batrachophobia	reptiles
belonephobia	needles
bibliophobia	books
brontophobia	thunder
cancerophobia	cancer
cheimaphobia	cold
chionophobia	snow
chrematophobia	money
chronophobia	duration
chrystallophobia	crystals
claustrophobia	closed spaces
cnidophobia	stings
cometophobia	comets
cromophobia	colour
cyberphobia	computers
cynophobia	dogs
demonophobia	demons
demophobia	crowds
dermatophobia	skin
dikephobia	justice
doraphobia	fur
eisoptrophobia	mirrors
electrophobia	electricity
enetephobia	pins
entomophobia	insects

Phobia	Meaning
eosophobia	dawn
eremophobia	solitude
ereuthophobia	blushing
ergasiophobia	work
genophobia	sex
geumaphobia	taste
graphophobia	writing
gymnophobia	nudity
gynophobia	women
hadephobia	hell
haematophobia	blood
hamartiophobia	sin
haptophobia	touch
harpaxophobia	robbers
hedonophobia	pleasure
helminthophobia	worms
hodophobia	travel
homichlophobia	fog
homophobia	homosexuals
hormephobia	shock
hydrophobia	water
hypegiaphobia	responsibility
hypnophobia	sleep
ideophobia	ideas
kakorraphiaphobia	failure
katagelophobia	ridicule
kenophobia	void
kinesophobia	motion
kleptophobia	stealing
kopophobia	fatigue
kristallophobia	ice
laliophobia	stuttering
linonophobia	string
logophobia	words
lyssophobia	insanity
maniaphobia	insanity
mastigophobia	flogging
mechanophobia	machinery
metallophobia	metals
meteorophobia	meteors
misophobia	contamination
monophobia	one thing
musicophobia	music
musophobia	mice
necrophobia	corpses
nelophobia	glass
neophobia	newness
nephophobia	clouds
nosophobia	disease
nyctophobia	night
ochlophobia	crowds

Phobia	Meaning
ochophobia	vehicles
odontophobia	teeth
oikophobia	home
olfactophobia	smell
ommatophobia	eyes
oneirophobia	dreams
ophidiophobia	snakes
ornithophobia	birds
ouranophobia	heaven
panphobia	everything
pantophobia	everything
parthenophobia	girls
pathophobia	disease
peniaphobia	poverty
phasmophobia	ghosts
phobophobia	fears
photophobia	light
pnigerophobia	smothering
poinephobia	punishment
polyphobia	many things
potophobia	drink
pteronophobia	feathers
pyrophobia	fire
Russophobia	Russia
rypophobia	soiling
Satanophobia	Satan
selaphobia	flesh
siderophobia	stars
sitophobia	food
spermaphobia	germs
spermatophobia	germs
stasiphobia	standing
stygiophobia	hell
taphephobia	being buried alive
technophobia	technology
teratophobia	giving birth to a monster
thaasophobia	sitting
thalassophobia	sea
thanatophobia	death
theophobia	God
thermophobia	heat
tonitrophobia	thunder
toxiphobia	poison
tremophobia	trembling
triskaidekaphobia	thirteen
xenophobia	strangers *or* foreigners
zelophobia	jealousy
zoophobia	animals

pick someone up = arrest, nick *(slang, chiefly Brit.)*, bust *(informal)*, do *(slang)*, lift *(slang)*, run in *(slang)*, nail *(informal)*, collar *(informal)*, pinch *(informal)*, pull in *(Brit. slang)*, nab *(informal)*, apprehend, take someone into custody, feel your collar *(slang)*: *The police picked him up within the hour.*

pick something *or* **someone out 1 = identify**, notice, recognize, distinguish, perceive, discriminate, make someone *or* something out, tell someone *or* something apart, single someone *or* something out: *He wasn't difficult to pick out when the bus drew in.* **2 = select**, choose, decide on, take, sort out, opt for, cull, plump for, hand-pick: *Pick out a painting you think she'd like.*

pick something up 1 = learn, master, acquire, get the hang of *(informal)*, become proficient in: *Where did you pick up your English?* **2 = obtain**, get, find, buy, score *(slang)*, discover, purchase, acquire, locate, come across, come by, unearth, garner, stumble across, chance upon, happen upon: *Auctions can be great places to pick up a bargain.*

pick something *or* **someone up 1 = lift**, raise, gather, take up, grasp, uplift, hoist: *He picked his cap up from the floor; They had to pick him up and carry on.* **2 = collect**, get, call for, go for, go to get, fetch, uplift *(Scot.)*, go and get, give someone a lift *or* a ride: *We drove to the airport to pick her up; He went to Miami where he had arranged to pick up the money.*

pick up 1 = improve, recover, rally, get better, bounce back, make progress, make a comeback *(informal)*, perk up, turn the corner, gain ground, take a turn for the better, be on the road to

The Language of Jerome K Jerome

Jerome Klapka Jerome (1859–1927) was a comic dramatist and novelist most remembered for his classic tale of a boating holiday *Three Men in a Boat* and its sequel *Three Men on the Bummel*. Born in Walsall in England's West Midlands, Jerome's early life was marked by relative poverty until his literary successes brought him financial security. A distinctive feature of his prose fiction is his use of a summary of events at the start of each chapter, a device most associated with such literary greats as Milton.

Among Jerome's now seldom-read works is his collection of essays *Idle Thoughts of an Idle Fellow* and he was also for a time editor of the monthly magazine *The Idler*. The language of *idleness*, consequently, is something to which Jerome returns. *Idle* is applied most to a *fellow* and is not only used as an adjective but also indicates a pastime, as in:

> I like **idling** when I ought not to be **idling**.

Most likely to be *lazy* in Jerome's work, meanwhile, are *people*, a *hussy*, or a *devil*.

The colloquial usage of *devil* in this uncapitalized form was common in the late 19th and early 20th centuries. By far the most frequent adjective occurring with *devil* is *poor*, constituting a commonplace expression of pity. *Little devil* also appears on several occasions in Jerome's writing, often with an additional adjective such as *funny* or *plucky*. *The Devil himself*, sometimes capitalized and sometimes not in Jerome's work, is another recurrent usage of the word that generally occurs at moments of heightened emotion. Other colloquial usages by Jerome include the use of *your* before a nationality to suggest a characteristic supposedly shared by all residents of that country. With *Three Men on a Bummel* set in part in Germany, *your German* is the most common example of this pattern, for example:

> ... **your German** would no more think of sitting on the grass than would an English bishop dream of rolling down One Tree Hill.

German, indeed, is by far the most frequent indicator of nationality in Jerome's work, appearing considerably in excess of *English* or *British*.

A verb that appears to be used with unusual frequency by Jerome is *creep*. This collocates with the adverbs *back*, *forward*, *stealthily*, and *upstairs*. With *back*, *creep* indicates not only a surreptitious movement but also at times a shift in emotional register, as in:

> The sternness faded from the beautiful face, the tenderness crept back.

Other things that *creep* are *shadows*, *smiles*, and *flesh* while the gerund *creeping* is associated with *fear*.

The focus on boating in Jerome's most cele-brated text reflects its rise in popularity among the middle and working classes during this era. The social class most often mentioned by Jerome is the *working class* followed by *middle class* and then by *high* or *superior*. The identification of a *certain class* of people also occurs along with the slightly different usage of *class* in the context of travel, as in *second class ticket*.

Somewhat is used as a modifier by Jerome with notable regularity. The adjectives it is attached to most often are *curious* and *difficult*, although there are also some more idiosyncratic usages, such as:

> George has a cousin, who is usually described in the charge-sheet as a medical student, so that he naturally has a somewhat family-physicianary way of putting things.

In this similarly comic vein, Jerome also describes characters as being *somewhat vulgar-noisy*, *somewhat vulture-like*, or *somewhat rabbit-like*. At times the use of *somewhat* involves a logical contradiction as in *somewhat unpronounceable*. The verb modified most by *somewhat* is *surprise*, while *puzzle* and *confuse* also feature.

recovery: *Industrial production is beginning to pick up.* **2 = recover**, improve, rally, get better, mend, perk up, turn the corner, be on the mend, take a turn for the better: *A good dose of tonic will help you to pick up.*

pick your way = tread carefully, work through, move cautiously, walk tentatively, find *or* make your way: *I picked my way among the rubble.*

picket VERB **= blockade**, boycott, demonstrate outside: *The miners went on strike and picketed the power station.*
▷ NOUN **1 = demonstration**, strike, blockade: *Demonstrators have set up a twenty-four-hour picket.* **2 = protester**, demonstrator, picketer, flying picket: *Ten hotels were damaged by pickets in the weekend strike.* **3 = lookout**, watch, guard, patrol, scout, spotter, sentry, sentinel, vedette *(Military)*: *Troops are still manning pickets and patrolling the area.* **4 = stake**, post, pale, paling, peg, upright, palisade, stanchion: *The area was fenced in with pickets to keep out the animals.*

pickings PLURAL NOUN **= profits**, returns, rewards, earnings, yield, proceeds, spoils, loot, plunder, gravy *(slang)*, booty, ill-gotten gains

pickle VERB **= preserve**, marinade, keep, cure, steep: *Herrings can be salted, smoked and pickled; Pickle your favourite vegetables while they're still fresh.*
▷ NOUN **1 = chutney**, relish, piccalilli: *jars of pickle* **2 = predicament**, spot *(informal)*, fix *(informal)*, difficulty, bind *(informal)*, jam *(informal)*, dilemma, scrape *(informal)*, hot water *(informal)*, uphill *(S. African)*, quandary, tight spot: *Connie had got herself into a real pickle this time.*

P

pick-me-up NOUN **= tonic**, drink, pick-up *(slang)*, bracer *(informal)*, refreshment, stimulant, shot in the arm *(informal)*, restorative

pick-up NOUN **= improvement**, recovery, rise, gain, rally, strengthening, revival, upturn, change for the better, upswing

picky ADJECTIVE **= fussy**, particular, critical, carping, fastidious, dainty, choosy, finicky, cavilling, pernickety *(informal)*, fault-finding, captious, nit-picky *(informal)*

picnic NOUN **1 = excursion**, fête champêtre *(French)*, barbecue, barbie *(informal)*, cookout *(U.S. & Canad.)*, alfresco meal, déjeuner sur l'herbe *(French)*, clambake *(U.S. & Canad.)*, outdoor meal, outing: *We're going on a picnic tomorrow.* **2** *(used in negative constructions)* **= walkover** *(informal)*, breeze *(U.S. & Canad. informal)*, pushover *(slang)*, snap *(informal)*, child's play *(informal)*, piece of cake *(Brit. informal)*, cinch *(slang)*, cakewalk *(informal)*, duck soup *(U.S. slang)*: *Emigrating is no picnic.*

pictorial ADJECTIVE **= graphic**, striking, illustrated, vivid, picturesque, expressive, scenic, representational

picture NOUN **1 = representation**, drawing, painting, portrait, image, print, illustration, sketch, portrayal, engraving, likeness, effigy, delineation, similitude: *drawing a small picture with coloured chalks* **2 = photograph**, photo, still, shot, image, print, frame, slide, snap, exposure, portrait, snapshot, transparency, enlargement: *I saw his picture in the paper.* **3 = film**, movie *(U.S. informal)*, flick *(slang)*, feature film, motion picture: *a director of epic pictures* **4 = idea**, vision, concept, impression, notion, visualization, mental picture, mental image: *I'm trying to get a picture of what kind of person you are.* **5 = description**, impression, explanation, report, account, image, sketch, depiction, re-creation: *I want to give you a clear picture of what we are trying to do.* **6 = personification**, model, embodiment, soul, essence, archetype, epitome, perfect example, exemplar, quintessence, living example: *Six years after the operation, he remains a picture of health.*
▷ VERB **1 = imagine**, see, envision, visualize, conceive of, fantasize about, conjure up an image of, see in the mind's eye: *She pictured herself working with animals.* **2 = represent**, show, describe, draw, paint, illustrate, portray, sketch, render, depict, delineate: *The goddess Demeter is pictured holding an ear of wheat.* **3 = show**, photograph, capture on film: *Betty is pictured here with her award.*
▸ *related adjective:* pictorial

QUOTATIONS
One picture is worth ten thousand words
[Frederick R. Barnard *Printers' Ink*]

PROVERBS
Every picture tells a story

picturesque ADJECTIVE **1 = interesting**, pretty, beautiful, attractive, charming, scenic, quaint: *the Algarve's most picturesque village* **OPPOSITE:** unattractive **2 = vivid**, striking, graphic, colourful, memorable: *Every inn had a quaint and picturesque name.* **OPPOSITE:** dull

piddling ADJECTIVE **= trivial**, little, petty, worthless, insignificant, pants *(informal)*, useless, fiddling, trifling, unimportant, paltry, Mickey Mouse *(slang)*, puny, derisory, measly *(informal)*, crappy *(slang)*, toytown *(slang)*, piffling, poxy *(slang)*, nickel-and-dime *(U.S. slang)* **OPPOSITE:** significant

piece NOUN **1 = bit**, section, slice, part, share, division, block, length, quantity, scrap, segment, portion, fragment, fraction, chunk, wedge, shred, slab, mouthful, morsel, wodge *(Brit. informal)*: *Another piece of cake?; a piece of wood* **2 = component**, part, section, bit, unit, segment, constituent, module: *The equipment was taken down the shaft in pieces.* **3 = instance**, case, example, sample, specimen, occurrence: *a highly complex piece of legislation* **4 = item**, report, story, bit *(informal)*, study, production, review, article: *There was a piece about him on television.* **5 = composition**, work, production, opus: *an orchestral piece* **6 = work of art**, work, creation: *The cabinets display a wide variety of porcelain pieces.* **7 = share**, cut *(informal)*, slice, percentage, quantity, portion, quota, fraction, allotment, subdivision: *They got a small piece of the net profits.*

go *or* **fall to pieces = break down**, fall apart, disintegrate, lose control, crumple, crack up *(informal)*, have a breakdown, lose your head: *She went to pieces when her husband died.*

of a piece (with) = like, the same (as), similar (to), consistent (with), identical (to), analogous (to), of the same kind (as): *These essays are of a piece with his earlier work; Thirties design and architecture was all of a piece.*

piecemeal ADJECTIVE **= unsystematic**, interrupted, partial, patchy, intermittent, spotty, fragmentary: *piecemeal changes to the constitution*
▷ ADVERB **= bit by bit**, slowly, gradually, partially, intermittently, at intervals, little by little, fitfully, by degrees, by fits and starts: *It was built piecemeal over some 130 years.*

pied ADJECTIVE **= variegated**, spotted, streaked, irregular, flecked, motley, mottled, dappled, multicoloured, piebald, parti-coloured, varicoloured

pier NOUN **1 = jetty**, wharf, quay, promenade, landing place: *The lifeboats were moored at the pier.* **2 = pillar**, support, post, column, pile, piling, upright, buttress: *the cross-beams bracing the piers of the jetty*

pierce VERB **1 = penetrate**, stab, spike, enter, bore, probe, drill, run through, lance, puncture, prick, transfix, stick into, perforate, impale: *Pierce the skin of the potato with a fork.* **2 = hurt**, cut, wound, strike, touch, affect, pain, move, excite, stir, thrill, sting, rouse, cut to the quick: *Her words pierced Lydia's heart like an arrow.*

piercing ADJECTIVE **1 = penetrating**, sharp, loud, shattering, shrill, high-pitched, ear-splitting: *a piercing whistle* **OPPOSITE:** low **2 = perceptive**, searching, aware, bright *(informal)*, sharp, keen, alert, probing, penetrating, shrewd, perspicacious, quick-witted: *He fixes you with a piercing stare.* **OPPOSITE:** unperceptive **3 = sharp**, shooting, powerful, acute, severe, intense, painful, stabbing, fierce, racking, exquisite, excruciating, agonizing: *I felt a piercing pain in my abdomen.* **4 = cold**, biting, keen, freezing, bitter, raw, arctic, nipping, numbing, frosty, wintry, nippy: *a piercing wind*

piety NOUN **= holiness**, duty, faith, religion, grace, devotion, reverence, sanctity, veneration, godliness, devoutness, dutifulness, piousness

pig NOUN **1 = hog**, sow, boar, piggy, swine, grunter, piglet, porker, shoat: *He keeps poultry, pigs and goats.* **2 = slob**, hog *(informal)*, guzzler *(slang)*, glutton, gannet *(informal)*, sloven, greedy guts *(slang)*: *He's just a greedy pig.* **3 = brute**, monster, scoundrel, animal, beast, rogue, swine, rotter, boor: *Her ex-husband was a real pig to her.*
▸ *related adjective:* porcine ▸ *name of male:* boar ▸ *name of female:* sow ▸ *name of young:* piglet ▸ *collective noun:* litter ▸ *name of home:* sty

pigeon NOUN **= squab**, bird, dove, culver *(archaic)*

pigment NOUN **= colour**, colouring, paint, stain, dye, tint, tincture, colouring matter, colorant, dyestuff

piker NOUN **= slacker**, shirker, skiver *(Brit. slang)*, loafer, layabout, idler, passenger, do-nothing, dodger, good-for-nothing, bludger *(Austral. & N.Z. informal)*, gold brick *(U.S. slang)*, scrimshanker *(Brit. Military slang)*

pile[1] NOUN **1 = heap**, collection, mountain, mass, stack, rick, mound, accumulation, stockpile, hoard, assortment, assemblage: *a pile of books* **2** *(often plural)* **= lot(s)**, mountain(s), load(s) *(informal)*, oceans, wealth, great deal, stack(s), abundance, large quantity, oodles *(informal)*, shedload *(Brit. informal)*: *I've got piles of questions for you.* **3 = mansion**, building, residence, manor, country house, seat, big house, stately home, manor house: *a stately pile in the country* **4 = fortune**, bomb *(Brit. slang)*, pot, packet *(slang)*, mint, big money, wad *(U.S. & Canad. slang)*, big bucks *(informal, chiefly U.S.)*, megabucks *(U.S. & Canad. slang)*, tidy sum *(informal)*, pretty penny *(informal)*, top whack *(informal)*: *He made a pile in various business ventures.*
▷ VERB **1 = load**, stuff, pack, stack, charge, heap, cram, lade: *He was piling clothes into the case.* **2 = crowd**, pack, charge, rush, climb, flood, stream, crush, squeeze, jam, flock, shove: *They all piled into the car.*
pile something up 1 = gather (up), collect, assemble, stack (up), mass, heap (up), load up: *Bulldozers piled up huge mounds of dirt.* **2 = collect**, accumulate, gather in, pull in, amass, hoard, stack up, store up, heap up: *Their aim is to pile up the points and aim for a qualifying place.*
pile up = accumulate, collect, gather (up), build up, amass: *Her mail had piled up inside the front door.*

pile[2] NOUN **= foundation**, support, post, column, piling, beam, upright, pier, pillar: *wooden houses set on piles along the shore*

pile[3] NOUN **= nap**, fibre, down, hair, surface, fur, plush, shag, filament: *the carpet's thick pile*

piles PLURAL NOUN **= haemorrhoids**: *More women than men suffer from piles.*

pile-up NOUN **= collision**, crash, accident, smash, smash-up *(informal)*, multiple collision

pilfer VERB **= steal**, take, rob, lift *(informal)*, nick *(slang, chiefly Brit.)*, appropriate, rifle, pinch *(informal)*, swipe *(slang)*, embezzle, blag *(slang)*, walk off with, snitch *(slang)*, purloin, filch, snaffle *(Brit. informal)*, thieve

pilgrim NOUN **= traveller**, crusader, wanderer, devotee, palmer, haji *(Islam)*, wayfarer

> QUOTATIONS
> pilgrim: a traveler that is taken seriously
> [Ambrose Bierce *The Devil's Dictionary*]

pilgrimage NOUN **= journey**, tour, trip, mission, expedition, crusade, excursion, hajj *(Islam)*

pill NOUN **= tablet**, capsule, pellet, bolus, pilule: *a sleeping pill*
a bitter pill (to swallow) = trial, pain *(informal)*, bore, drag *(informal)*, pest, nuisance, pain in the neck *(informal)*: *You're too old to be given a job. That's a bitter pill to swallow.*

pillage VERB **= plunder**, strip, sack, rob, raid, spoil *(archaic)*, rifle, loot, ravage, ransack, despoil, maraud, reive *(dialect)*, depredate *(rare)*, freeboot, spoliate: *Soldiers went on a rampage, pillaging stores and shooting.*
▷ NOUN **= plundering**, sacking, robbery, plunder, sack, devastation, marauding, depredation, rapine, spoliation: *There were no signs of violence or pillage.*

pillar NOUN **1 = support**, post, column, piling, prop, shaft, upright, pier, obelisk, stanchion, pilaster: *the pillars supporting the roof* **2 = supporter**, leader, rock, worthy, mainstay, leading light *(informal)*, tower of strength, upholder, torchbearer: *My father had been a pillar of the community.*

pillory VERB **= ridicule**, denounce, stigmatize, brand, lash, show someone up, expose someone to ridicule, cast a slur on, heap *or* pour scorn on, hold someone up to shame

pilot NOUN **1 = airman**, captain, flyer, aviator, aeronaut: *He spent seventeen years as an airline pilot.* **2 = helmsman**, guide, navigator, leader, director, conductor, coxswain, steersman: *The pilot steered the ship safely inside the main channel.*
▷ VERB **1 = fly**, control, operate, be at the controls of: *the first person to pilot an aircraft across the Pacific* **2 = navigate**, drive, manage, direct, guide, handle, conduct, steer: *Local fishermen piloted the boats.* **3 = direct**, lead, manage, conduct, steer: *We are piloting the strategy through Parliament.*
▷ MODIFIER **= trial**, test, model, sample, experimental: *a pilot show for a new TV series*

pimp NOUN **= procurer**, go-between, bawd *(archaic)*, mack daddy *(slang, chiefly U.S.)*, white-slaver, pander, panderer, whoremaster *(archaic)*: *Every hooker I ever met had a pimp.*
▷ VERB **= procure**, sell, tout, solicit, live off immoral earnings: *He sold drugs, and also did a bit of pimping on the side.*

pimple NOUN **= spot**, boil, swelling, pustule, zit *(slang)*, papule *(Pathology)*, plook *(Scot.)*

pin NOUN **1 = tack**, nail, needle, safety pin: *Use pins to keep the material in place as you work.* **2 = peg**, rod, brace, bolt: *the steel pin holding his left leg together*
▷ VERB **1 = fasten**, stick, attach, join, fix, secure, nail, clip, staple, tack, affix: *They pinned a notice to the door.* **2 = hold fast**, hold down, press, restrain, constrain, immobilize, pinion: *I pinned him against the wall.*
pin someone down = force, pressure, compel, put pressure on, pressurize, nail someone down, make someone commit themselves: *She couldn't pin him down to a decision.*
pin something down 1 = determine, identify, locate, name, specify, designate, pinpoint, home in on: *It has taken until now to pin down its exact location.* **2 = trap**, confine, constrain, bind, squash, tie down, nail down, immobilize: *The wreckage of the cockpit had pinned down my legs.*

pinch VERB **1 = nip**, press, squeeze, grasp, compress, tweak: *She pinched his arm as hard as she could.* **2 = hurt**, crush, squeeze, pain, confine, cramp, chafe: *shoes which pinch our toes* **3 = steal**, rob, snatch, lift *(informal)*, nick *(slang, chiefly Brit.)*, swipe *(slang)*, knock off *(slang)*, blag *(slang)*, pilfer, snitch *(slang)*, purloin, filch, snaffle *(Brit. informal)*: *pickpockets who pinched his wallet*
▷ NOUN **1 = nip**, squeeze, tweak: *She gave him a little pinch.* **2 = dash**, bit, taste, mite, jot, speck, small quantity, smidgen *(informal)*, soupçon *(French)*: *a pinch of salt* **3 = emergency**, crisis, difficulty, plight, scrape *(informal)*, strait, uphill *(S. African)*, predicament, extremity, hardship: *I'd trust her in a pinch.*

pinched ADJECTIVE **= thin**, starved, worn, drawn, gaunt, haggard, careworn, peaky **OPPOSITE:** plump

pine VERB **= waste**, decline, weaken, sicken, sink, flag, fade, decay, dwindle, wither, wilt, languish, droop: *While away from her children, she pined dreadfully.*
pine for something *or* **someone 1 = long**, ache, crave, yearn, sigh, carry a torch, eat your heart out over, suspire *(archaic, poetic)*: *She was pining for her lost husband.* **2 = hanker after**, crave, covet, wish for, yearn for, thirst for, hunger for, lust after: *pining for a mythical past*

pink ADJECTIVE **= rosy**, rose, salmon, flushed, reddish, flesh coloured, roseate: *his pink face*
▷ NOUN **= best**, summit, height, peak, perfection, acme: *the pink of perfection*
in the pink = in good health, strong, blooming, very healthy, in fine fettle, in perfect health, in excellent shape, hale and hearty, fit as a fiddle: *A glass of red wine a day will keep you in the pink.*

pinnacle NOUN **1 = summit**, top, height, peak, eminence: *He plunged 80 ft from a rocky pinnacle.* **2 = height**, top, crown, crest, meridian, zenith, apex, apogee, acme, vertex: *He had reached the pinnacle of his career.*

pinpoint VERB **1 = identify**, discover, spot, define, distinguish, put your finger on: *It was impossible to pinpoint the cause of death.* **2 = locate**, find, spot, identify, home in on, zero in on, get a fix on: *trying to pinpoint his precise location*

pint NOUN **= beer**, jar (*Brit. informal*), jug (*Brit. informal*), ale

pint-sized ADJECTIVE **= small**, little, tiny, wee, pocket-sized, miniature, diminutive, midget, teeny-weeny, teensy-weensy, pygmy *or* pigmy

pioneer NOUN **1 = founder**, leader, developer, innovator, founding father, trailblazer: *one of the pioneers in embryology work* **2 = settler**, explorer, colonist, colonizer, frontiersman: *abandoned settlements of early European pioneers*
▷ VERB **= develop**, create, launch, establish, start, prepare, discover, institute, invent, open up, initiate, originate, take the lead on, instigate, map out, show the way on, lay the groundwork on: *the scientist who invented and pioneered DNA tests*

pious ADJECTIVE **1 = religious**, godly, devoted, spiritual, holy, dedicated, righteous, devout, saintly, God-fearing, reverent: *He was brought up by pious female relatives.* **OPPOSITE:** irreligious **2 = self-righteous**, hypocritical, sanctimonious, goody-goody, unctuous, holier-than-thou, pietistic, religiose: *They were derided as pious, self-righteous bores.* **OPPOSITE:** humble

pipe NOUN **1 = tube**, drain, canal, pipeline, line, main, passage, cylinder, hose, conduit, duct, conveyor: *The liquid is conveyed along a pipe.* **2 = clay (pipe)**, briar, calabash (*rare*), meerschaum, hookah (*rare*): *He gave up cigarettes and started smoking a pipe.* **3 = whistle**, horn, recorder, fife, flute, wind instrument, penny whistle: *Pan is often pictured playing a reed pipe.*
▷ VERB **= convey**, channel, supply, conduct, bring in, transmit, siphon: *The gas is piped through a coil surrounded by water.*
pipe down = be quiet, shut up (*informal*), hush, stop talking, quieten down, shush, button it (*slang*), belt up (*slang*), shut your mouth, hold your tongue, put a sock in it (*Brit. slang*), button your lip (*slang*): *Just pipe down and I'll tell you what I want.*
pipe up = speak, volunteer, speak up, have your say, raise your voice, make yourself heard, put your oar in: *'That's right, mister,' another child piped up.*

pipe dream NOUN **= daydream**, dream, notion, fantasy, delusion, vagary, reverie, chimera, castle in the air

pipeline NOUN **= tube**, passage, pipe, line, conduit, duct, conveyor: *a natural-gas pipeline*
in the pipeline = on the way, expected, coming, close, near, being prepared, anticipated, forthcoming, under way, brewing, imminent, in preparation, in production, in process, in the offing: *A 2.9 per cent pay increase is already in the pipeline.*

piquant ADJECTIVE **1 = spicy**, biting, sharp, stinging, tart, savoury, pungent, tangy, highly-seasoned, peppery, zesty, with a kick (*informal*), acerb: *a mixed salad with a piquant dressing* **OPPOSITE:** mild **2 = interesting**, spirited, stimulating, lively, sparkling, provocative, salty, racy, scintillating: *There was a piquant novelty about her books.* **OPPOSITE:** dull

pique NOUN **= resentment**, offence, irritation, annoyance, huff, displeasure, umbrage, hurt feelings, vexation, wounded pride: *In a fit of pique, he threw down his bag.*
▷ VERB **1 = arouse**, excite, stir, spur, stimulate, provoke, rouse, goad, whet, kindle, galvanize: *This phenomenon piqued Dr. Morris's interest.* **2 = displease**, wound, provoke, annoy, get (*informal*), sting, offend, irritate, put out, incense, gall, nettle, vex, affront, mortify, irk, rile, peeve (*informal*), nark (*Brit., Austral. & N.Z. slang*), put someone's nose out of joint (*informal*), miff (*informal*), hack off (*informal*): *She was piqued by his lack of enthusiasm.*

piracy NOUN **1 = robbery**, stealing, theft, hijacking, infringement, buccaneering, rapine, freebooting: *Seven of the fishermen have been formally charged with piracy.* **2 = illegal copying**, bootlegging, plagiarism, copyright infringement, illegal reproduction: *Video piracy is a criminal offence.*

pirate NOUN **= buccaneer**, raider, rover, filibuster, marauder, corsair, sea wolf, freebooter, sea robber, sea rover: *In the nineteenth century, pirates roamed the seas.*
▷ VERB **= copy**, steal, reproduce, bootleg, lift (*informal*), appropriate, borrow, poach, crib (*informal*), plagiarize: *pirated copies of music tapes*

pirouette NOUN **= spin**, turn, whirl, pivot, twirl: *a ballerina famous for her pirouettes*
▷ VERB **= spin**, turn, whirl, pivot, twirl: *She pirouetted in front of the mirror.*

pit NOUN **1 = coal mine**, mine, shaft, colliery, mine shaft: *Up to ten pits and ten thousand jobs could be lost.* **2 = hole**, gulf, depression, hollow, trench, crater, trough, cavity, abyss, chasm, excavation, pothole: *He lost his footing and began to slide into the pit.*
▷ VERB **= scar**, mark, hole, nick, notch, dent, gouge, indent, dint, pockmark: *The plaster was pitted and the paint scuffed.*
pit something *or* **someone against something** *or* **someone = set against**, oppose, match against, measure against, put in competition with, put in opposition to: *You will be pitted against people as good as you are.*

pitch NOUN **1 = sports field**, ground, stadium, arena, park, field of play: *a cricket pitch* **2 = tone**, sound, key, frequency, timbre, modulation: *He raised his voice to a higher pitch.* **3 = level**, point, degree, summit, extent, height, intensity, high point: *Tensions have reached such a pitch in the area that the army have been called in.* **4 = talk**, line, patter, spiel (*informal*): *He was impressed with her hard sales pitch.*
▷ VERB **1 = throw**, launch, cast, toss, hurl, fling, chuck (*informal*), sling, lob (*informal*), bung (*Brit. slang*), heave: *Simon pitched the empty bottle into the lake.* **2 = fall**, drop, plunge, dive, stagger, tumble, topple, plummet, fall headlong, (take a) nosedive: *He pitched head-first over the low wall.* **3 = set up**, place, station, locate, raise, plant, settle, fix, put up, erect: *He had pitched his tent in the yard.* **4 = toss (about)**, roll, plunge, flounder, lurch, wallow, welter, make heavy weather: *The ship was pitching and rolling as if in mid-ocean.*
pitch in = help, contribute, participate, join in, cooperate, chip in (*informal*), get stuck in (*Brit. informal*), lend a hand, muck in (*Brit. informal*), do your bit, lend a helping hand: *Everyone pitched in to help.*

pitch-black *or* **pitch-dark** ADJECTIVE **= dark**, black, jet, raven, ebony, sable, unlit, jet-black, inky, Stygian, pitchy, unilluminated

pitfall NOUN **= danger**, difficulty, peril, catch, trap, hazard, drawback, snag, uphill (*S. African*), banana skin (*informal*)

pithy ADJECTIVE **= succinct**, pointed, short, brief, to the point, compact, meaningful, forceful, expressive, concise, terse, laconic, trenchant, cogent, epigrammatic, finely honed **OPPOSITE:** long-winded

pitiful ADJECTIVE **1 = pathetic**, distressing, miserable, harrowing, heartbreaking, grievous, sad, woeful, deplorable, lamentable, heart-rending, gut-wrenching, wretched, pitiable, piteous: *It was the most pitiful sight I had ever seen.* **OPPOSITE:** funny **2 = inadequate**, mean, low, miserable, dismal, beggarly, shabby, insignificant, paltry, despicable, measly, contemptible: *Many of them work as farm labourers for pitiful wages.* **OPPOSITE:** adequate **3 = worthless**, base, sorry, vile, abject, scurvy: *a pitiful performance* **OPPOSITE:** admirable

pitiless ADJECTIVE **= merciless**, ruthless, heartless, harsh, cruel, brutal, relentless, callous, inhuman, inexorable, implacable, unsympathetic, cold-blooded, uncaring, unfeeling, cold-hearted, unmerciful, hardhearted **OPPOSITE:** merciful

pittance NOUN **= peanuts** (*slang*), trifle, modicum, drop, mite, chicken feed *(slang)*, slave wages, small allowance

pitted ADJECTIVE = **scarred**, marked, rough, scratched, dented, riddled, blemished, potholed, indented, eaten away, holey, pockmarked, rutty

pity NOUN **1 = compassion**, understanding, charity, sympathy, distress, sadness, sorrow, kindness, tenderness, condolence, commiseration, fellow feeling: *He felt a sudden tender pity for her.*
OPPOSITE: mercilessness **2 = shame**, crime *(informal)*, sin *(informal)*, misfortune, bad luck, sad thing, bummer *(slang)*, crying shame, source of regret: *It's a pity you couldn't come.*
3 = mercy, kindness, clemency, leniency, forbearance, quarter: *a killer who had no pity for his victims*
▷ VERB = **feel sorry for**, feel for, sympathize with, grieve for, weep for, take pity on, empathize with, bleed for, commiserate with, have compassion for, condole with: *I don't know whether to hate him or pity him.*
take pity on something *or* **someone** = **have mercy on**, spare, forgive, pity, pardon, reprieve, show mercy to, feel compassion for, put out of your misery, relent against: *She took pity on him because he was homeless.*

pivot NOUN **1 = hub**, centre, heart, hinge, focal point, kingpin: *A large group of watercolours forms the pivot of the exhibition.* **2 = axis**, swivel, axle, spindle, fulcrum: *The pedal had sheared off at the pivot.*
▷ VERB = **turn**, spin, revolve, rotate, swivel, twirl: *The boat pivoted on its central axis.*

pivotal ADJECTIVE = **crucial**, central, determining, vital, critical, decisive, focal, climactic

pixie NOUN = **elf**, fairy, brownie, sprite, peri

placard NOUN = **notice**, bill, advertisement, poster, sticker, public notice, affiche *(French)*

placate VERB = **calm**, satisfy, humour, soothe, appease, assuage, pacify, mollify, win someone over, conciliate, propitiate

place NOUN **1 = spot**, point, position, site, area, situation, station, location, venue, whereabouts, locus: *the place where the temple actually stood* **2 = region**, city, town, quarter, village, district, neighbourhood, hamlet, vicinity, locality, locale, dorp *(S. African)*: *the opportunity to visit new places*
3 = position, point, spot, location: *He returned the album to its place on the shelf.*
4 = space, position, seat, chair: *There was a single empty place left at the table.*
5 = job, position, post, situation, office, employment, appointment, berth *(informal)*, billet *(informal)*: *All the candidates won places on the ruling council.*
6 = home, house, room, property, seat, flat, apartment, accommodation, pad *(slang)*, residence, mansion, dwelling, manor, abode, domicile, bachelor apartment *(Canad.)*: *Let's all go back to my place!* **7 = duty**, right, job, charge, concern, role, affair, responsibility, task, function, prerogative: *It is not my place to comment.*
▷ VERB **1 = lay (down)**, leave, put (down), set (down), stand, sit, position, rest, plant, station, establish, stick *(informal)*, settle, fix, arrange, lean, deposit, locate, set out, install, prop, dispose, situate, stow, bung *(Brit. slang)*, plonk *(informal)*, array: *Chairs were placed in rows for the parents.* **2 = put**, lay, set, invest, pin: *Children place their trust in us.* **3 = classify**, class, group, put, order, sort, rank, arrange, grade, assign, categorize: *The authorities have placed the drug in Class A.* **4 = entrust to**, give to, assign to, appoint to, allocate to, find a home for: *The twins were placed in a foster home.*
5 = identify, remember, recognize, pin someone down, put your finger on, put a name to, set someone in context: *I know we've met, but I can't place you.*
in place of = **instead of**, rather than, in exchange for, as an alternative to, taking the place of, in lieu of, as a substitute for, as a replacement for: *Cooked kidney beans can be used in place of French beans.*
in your/his/her/their place = **situation**, position, circumstances, shoes *(informal)*: *If I were in your place I'd see a lawyer as soon as possible.*
know one's place = **know one's rank**, know one's standing, know one's position, know one's footing, know one's station, know one's status, know one's grade, know one's niche: *a society where everyone knows their place*
put someone in their place = **humble**, humiliate, deflate, crush, mortify, take the wind out of someone's sails, cut someone down to size *(informal)*, take someone down a peg *(informal)*, make someone eat humble pie, bring someone down to size *(informal)*, make someone swallow their pride, settle someone's hash *(informal)*: *She put him in his place with just a few words.*
take place = **happen**, occur, go on, go down *(U.S. & Canad.)*, arise, come about, crop up, transpire *(informal)*, befall, materialize, come to pass *(archaic)*, betide: *Similar demonstrations also took place elsewhere.*

placement NOUN **1 = positioning**, stationing, arrangement, location, ordering, distribution, locating, installation, deployment, disposition, emplacement: *The treatment involves the placement of electrodes in the inner ear.*
2 = appointment, employment, engagement, assignment: *He had a six-month work placement with the Japanese government.*

placid ADJECTIVE **1 = calm**, cool, quiet, peaceful, even, collected, gentle, mild, composed, serene, tranquil, undisturbed, unmoved, untroubled, unfazed *(informal)*, unruffled, self-possessed, imperturbable, equable, even-tempered, unexcitable, chilled *(informal)*: *She was a placid child who rarely cried.*
OPPOSITE: excitable **2 = still**, quiet, calm, peaceful, serene, tranquil, undisturbed, halcyon, unruffled: *the placid waters of Lake Erie*
OPPOSITE: rough

plagiarism NOUN = **copying**, borrowing, theft, appropriation, infringement, piracy, lifting *(informal)*, cribbing *(informal)*

> QUOTATIONS
> If you steal from one author, it's plagiarism; if you steal from many, it's research
> [Wilson Mizner]

plague NOUN **1 = disease**, infection, epidemic, contagion, pandemic, pestilence, lurgy *(informal)*: *A cholera plague had killed many prisoners of war.*
2 = infestation, invasion, epidemic, influx, host, swarm, multitude: *The city is under threat from a plague of rats.*
3 = bane, trial, cancer, evil, curse, torment, blight, calamity, scourge, affliction: *the cynicism which is the plague of our generation* **4 = nuisance**, problem, pain *(informal)*, bother, pest, hassle *(informal)*, annoyance, irritant, aggravation *(informal)*, vexation, thorn in your flesh: *Those children can be a real plague at times.*
▷ VERB **1 = torment**, trouble, pain, torture, haunt, afflict: *She was plagued by weakness, fatigue, and dizziness.*
2 = pester, trouble, bother, disturb, annoy, tease, harry, harass, hassle, fret, badger, persecute, molest, vex, bedevil, get on your nerves *(informal)*, give someone grief *(Brit. & S. African)*, be on your back *(slang)*, get in your hair *(informal)*: *I'm not going to plague you with a lot of questions.*

plain ADJECTIVE **1 = unadorned**, simple, basic, severe, pure, bare, modest, stark, restrained, muted, discreet, austere, spartan, unfussy, unvarnished, unembellished, unornamented, unpatterned, bare-bones: *a plain grey stone house, distinguished by its unspoilt simplicity*; *Her dress was plain, but it hung well on her.*
OPPOSITE: ornate **2 = clear**, obvious, patent, evident, apparent, visible, distinct, understandable, manifest, transparent, overt, unmistakable, lucid, unambiguous, comprehensible, legible: *It was plain to me that he was having a nervous breakdown.*
OPPOSITE: hidden
3 = straightforward, open, direct, frank, bold, blunt, sincere, outspoken, honest, downright, candid, forthright, upfront *(informal)*, artless, ingenuous, guileless: *his reputation for plain speaking*
OPPOSITE: roundabout **4 = ugly**, ordinary, unattractive, homely *(U.S. &*

Canad.), not striking, unlovely, unprepossessing, not beautiful, no oil painting *(informal)*, ill-favoured, unalluring: *a shy, rather plain girl with a pale complexion* **OPPOSITE:** attractive **5 = ordinary**, homely, common, simple, modest, everyday, commonplace, lowly, unaffected, unpretentious, frugal, workaday: *We are just plain people.* **OPPOSITE:** sophisticated
▷ NOUN **= flatland**, plateau, prairie, grassland, mesa, lowland, steppe, open country, pampas, tableland, veld, llano: *Once there were 70 million buffalo on the plains.*

plain-spoken ADJECTIVE **= blunt**, direct, frank, straightforward, open, explicit, outright, outspoken, downright, candid, forthright, upfront *(informal)*, unequivocal **OPPOSITE:** tactful

plaintive ADJECTIVE **= sorrowful**, sad, pathetic, melancholy, grievous, pitiful, woeful, wistful, mournful, heart-rending, rueful, grief-stricken, disconsolate, doleful, woebegone, piteous

plan NOUN **1 = scheme**, system, design, idea, programme, project, proposal, strategy, method, suggestion, procedure, plot, device, scenario, proposition, contrivance: *She met her creditors to propose a plan for making repayments.* **2 = diagram**, map, drawing, chart, illustration, representation, sketch, blueprint, layout, delineation, scale drawing: *Draw a plan of the garden.*
▷ VERB **1 = devise**, arrange, prepare, scheme, frame, plot, draft, organize, outline, invent, formulate, contrive, think out, concoct: *I had been planning a trip to the West Coast.* **2 = intend**, aim, mean, propose, purpose, contemplate, envisage, foresee: *The rebel soldiers plan to strike again.* **3 = design**, outline, draw up a plan of, architect: *The company is planning a theme park on the site.*

plane NOUN **1 = aeroplane**, aircraft, jet, airliner, jumbo jet: *He had plenty of time to catch his plane.* **2 = flat surface**, the flat, horizontal, level surface: *a building with angled planes* **3 = level**, position, stage, footing, condition, standard, degree, rung, stratum, echelon: *life on a higher plane of existence*
▷ ADJECTIVE **= level**, even, flat, regular, plain, smooth, uniform, flush, horizontal: *a plane surface*
▷ VERB **= skim**, sail, skate, glide: *The boats planed across the lake with the greatest of ease.*

planet

PLANETS

Earth	Mercury	Uranus
Jupiter	Neptune	Venus
Mars	Saturn	

plant[1] NOUN **= flower**, bush, vegetable, herb, weed, shrub: *Water each plant as often as required.*
▷ VERB **1 = sow**, scatter, set out, transplant, implant, put in the ground: *He intends to plant fruit and vegetables.* **2 = seed**, sow, implant: *They are going to plant the area with grass and trees.* **3 = place**, put, set, settle, fix: *She planted her feet wide and bent her knees slightly.* **4 = hide**, put, place, conceal: *So far no-one has admitted to planting the bomb in the hotel.* **5 = place**, put, establish, found, fix, institute, root, lodge, insert, sow the seeds of, imbed: *Sir Eric had evidently planted the idea in her mind.*
▸ *related mania:* florimania

QUOTATIONS

What is a weed? A plant whose virtues have not been discovered
[Ralph Waldo Emerson *Fortune of the Republic*]

Just now the lilac is in bloom,
All before my little room
[Rupert Brooke *Grantchester*]

plant[2] NOUN **1 = factory**, works, shop, yard, mill, foundry: *The plant provides forty per cent of the country's electricity.* **2 = machinery**, equipment, gear, apparatus: *Firms may invest in plant and equipment abroad where costs are cheaper.*

plaque NOUN **= plate**, panel, medal, tablet, badge, slab, brooch, medallion, cartouch(e)

plaster NOUN **1 = mortar**, stucco, gypsum, plaster of Paris, gesso: *a sculpture in plaster by Rodin* **2 = bandage**, dressing, sticking plaster, Elastoplast®, adhesive plaster: *Put a piece of plaster on the graze.*
▷ VERB **= cover**, spread, coat, smear, overlay, daub, besmear, bedaub: *She gets sunburn even when she plasters herself in lotion.*

plastic ADJECTIVE **1 = false**, artificial, synthetic, superficial, sham, pseudo *(informal)*, spurious, specious, meretricious, phoney *or* phony *(informal)*: *When girls wear too much make-up, they look plastic.* **OPPOSITE:** natural **2 = pliant**, soft, flexible, supple, pliable, tensile, ductile, mouldable, fictile: *The mud is as soft and plastic as butter.* **OPPOSITE:** rigid

plate NOUN **1 = platter**, dish, dinner plate, salver, trencher *(archaic)*: *Scott piled his plate with food.* **2 = helping**, course, serving, dish, portion, platter, plateful: *a huge plate of bacon and eggs* **3 = layer**, panel, sheet, slab: *The beam is strengthened by a steel plate 6 millimetres thick.* **4 = illustration**, picture, photograph, print, engraving, lithograph: *The book has 55 colour plates.*
▷ VERB **= coat**, gild, laminate, face, cover, silver, nickel, overlay, electroplate, anodize, platinize: *small steel balls plated with chrome or gold*

plateau NOUN **1 = upland**, table, highland, mesa, tableland: *a high, flat plateau of cultivated land* **2 = levelling off**, level, stage, stability: *The economy is stuck on a plateau of slow growth.*

platform NOUN **1 = stage**, stand, podium, rostrum, dais, soapbox: *Nick finished his speech and jumped down from the platform.* **2 = policy**, programme, principle, objective(s), manifesto, tenet(s), party line: *The party has announced a platform of economic reforms; They won a landslide victory on a nationalist platform.*

platitude NOUN **= cliché**, stereotype, commonplace, banality, truism, bromide, verbiage, inanity, trite remark, hackneyed saying

Platonic ADJECTIVE *(often not cap)* **= nonphysical**, ideal, intellectual, spiritual, idealistic, transcendent

platoon NOUN **= squad**, company, group, team, outfit *(informal)*, patrol, squadron

platter NOUN **= plate**, dish, tray, charger, salver, trencher *(archaic)*

plaudits PLURAL NOUN **= approval**, acclaim, applause, praise, clapping, ovation, kudos, congratulation, round of applause, commendation, approbation, acclamation

plausible ADJECTIVE **1 = believable**, possible, likely, reasonable, credible, probable, persuasive, conceivable, tenable, colourable, verisimilar: *That explanation seems entirely plausible to me.* **OPPOSITE:** unbelievable **2 = glib**, smooth, specious, smooth-talking, smooth-tongued, fair-spoken: *He was so plausible he conned us all.*

play VERB **1 = amuse yourself**, have fun, frolic, sport, fool, romp, revel, trifle, caper, frisk, gambol, entertain yourself, engage in games: *The children played in the garden.* **2 = take part in**, be involved in, engage in, participate in, compete in, be in a team for: *I used to play basketball.* **3 = compete against**, challenge, take on, rival, oppose, vie with, contend against: *Northern Ireland will play Latvia tomorrow.* **4 = perform**, carry out, execute: *Someone had played a trick on her.* **5 = act**, portray, represent, perform, impersonate, act the part of, take the part of, personate *(rare)*: *His ambition is to play the part of Dracula.* **6 = perform on**, strum, make music on: *Do you play the guitar?* **7** *(often with* **about** *or* **around***)* **= fool around**, toy, fiddle, trifle, mess around, take something lightly: *He's not working, he's just playing around.*
▷ NOUN **1 = amusement**, pleasure, leisure, games, sport, fun, entertainment, relaxation, a good time, recreation, enjoyment, romping, larks, capering, frolicking, junketing, fun and games, revelry, skylarking, living it up *(informal)*, gambolling, horseplay, merrymaking, me-time: *Try to strike a balance between work and play; a few hours of play until you go to bed* **2 = drama**, show, performance, piece, comedy, entertainment, tragedy, farce, soap

The Language of Oscar Wilde

Oscar Wilde (1854–1900) was an Irish dramatist, novelist, poet, and essayist whose literary reputation is intertwined with his ostentatious public persona and tragic personal life. Renowned for the sharpness of his repartee, the adjective *Wildean* has come to designate a flamboyant wit most apparent in his published work in such society comedies as *A Woman of No Importance* and *Lady Windermere's Fan*.

A prominent feature of Wilde's language is his use of paradox, often based on remarks he reportedly made in real life. This consists of a self-contradictory statement that aims to unsettle an established truth. For example, in *The Picture of Dorian Gray* Lord Henry Wotton remarks:

> I can believe anything, provided that it is quite incredible.

Wilde frequently uses this pattern to make his characters and the social norm they represent seem a little ridiculous, and is representative of his playful approach to convention. Such concise pronouncements are also indicative of Wilde's mastery of an epigrammatic style in which short, punchy sentences provide a memorable, and in Wilde's case very quotable, statement. Wilde often concluded his epigrams with the parting comment *that is all*:

> ...one should never talk of a moral or an immoral poem – poems are either well written or badly written, **that is all**.

More broadly, wordplay is a favourite device of Wilde's as in the pun of the title of *The Importance of Being Earnest*. The connection of the man's name *Ernest* and the quality of being *earnest* provide the basis for the plot's elaborate twists and turns and the numerous confusions of its characters' identities.

As a writer connected with the aesthetic movement of the late 19th century, Wilde is often drawn in his work to *beauty* and the *beautiful*. By a considerable distance, the noun most commonly modified by *beautiful* is *thing*. For the most part this refers to an abstract principle or set of ideals rather than to a specific object:

> ...devotion to beauty and to the creation of **beautiful things** is the test of all great civilised nations.

Followed by *beautiful thing* in salience is *beautiful work* and this most frequently pertains to a *beautiful work of art*. *Beautiful surroundings* provides another recurrent usage that reveals the importance of decoration for Wilde in his life and work. Indeed, *decorative* is the most salient modifier of *art* in Wilde's writing. Commonly associated with *beauty* is *colour* and accordingly colours appear prominently among Wilde's choice of adjectives. Wilde's literary palette is topped by *white* (most frequently with *hand* then *foot*), followed by *red* (most commonly with *rose*), *black* (with *velvet* most salient), *blue* (*eye*), *green* (*corn*), *yellow* (*gold*), *purple* (*robe*), and *scarlet* (*thread*). These luxuriant colours and textures indicate *pleasure* as a strong theme in Wilde's work. Most frequently *pleasure* is the object of the verbs *give*, *take*, and *find*, and despite the famous difficulties of Wilde's later life its usage far exceeds that of *pain* or *suffering*.

Wilde's interest in art for its own sake is manifested in the adjectives he most commonly applies to an *artist*. The most common of these is *great* and the second most common is *true*, with *perfect*, *individual*, and *real* also featuring strongly. This demonstrates both Wilde's dedication to the aesthetic life and also his role as a theorist of art, on which he often pronounces with his characteristic terseness:

> A **true artist** takes no notice whatever of the public.

Among forms of art, Wilde's work makes most frequent reference to *poetry*, followed by *music*, the *novel*, *painting*, *drama*, and *sculpture*. Of these, *poetry* and *painting* appear together more frequently than the others.

opera, soapie *or* soapy *(Austral. slang)*, pantomime, stage show, television drama, radio play, masque, dramatic piece: *The company put on a play about the homeless.*
in play = in *or* **for fun**, for sport, for a joke, for a lark *(informal)*, as a prank, for a jest: *It was done only in play, but they got a ticking off from the police.*
play around = philander, have an affair, carry on *(informal)*, fool around, dally, sleep around *(informal)*, womanize, play away from home *(informal)*: *Up to 75 per cent of married men may be playing around.*
play at something = pretend to be, pose as, impersonate, make like *(U.S. & Canad. informal)*, profess to be, assume the role of, give the appearance of, masquerade as, pass yourself off as: *rich people just playing at being farmers*
play on *or* **upon something = take advantage of**, abuse, exploit, impose on, trade on, misuse, milk, make use of, utilize, profit by, capitalize on, turn to your account: *I felt as if I was playing on her generosity.*
play something down = minimize, make light of, gloss over, talk down, underrate, underplay, pooh-pooh *(informal)*, soft-pedal *(informal)*, make little of, set no store by: *Western diplomats have played down the significance of the reports.*
play something up = emphasize, highlight, underline, magnify, stress, accentuate, point up, call attention to, turn the spotlight on, bring to the fore: *This increase in crime is definitely being played up by the media.*
play up 1 = hurt, be painful, bother you, trouble you, be sore, pain you, give you trouble, give you gyp *(Brit. & N.Z. slang)*: *My bad back is playing up again.* **2 = malfunction**, not work properly, be on the blink *(slang)*, be wonky *(Brit. slang)*: *The engine has started playing up.* **3 = be awkward**, misbehave, give trouble, be disobedient, give someone grief *(Brit. & S. African)*, be stroppy *(Brit. slang)*, be bolshie *(Brit. informal)*: *The kids always play up in his class.*
play up to someone = butter up, flatter, pander to, crawl to, get in with, suck up to *(informal)*, curry favour with, toady, fawn over, keep someone sweet, bootlick *(informal)*, ingratiate yourself to *or* with: *She plays up to journalists in the media.*

playboy NOUN **= womanizer**, philanderer, rake, socialite, man about town, pleasure seeker, lady-killer *(informal)*, roué, lover boy *(slang)*, ladies' man

player NOUN **1 = sportsman** *or* **sportswoman**, competitor, participant, contestant, team member: *top chess players* **2 = musician**, artist, performer, virtuoso, instrumentalist, music maker: *a professional trumpet player* **3 = performer**, entertainer, Thespian, trouper, actor or actress: *Oscar nominations went to all five leading players.*

playful ADJECTIVE **1 = joking**, humorous, jokey, arch, teasing, coy, tongue-in-cheek, jesting, flirtatious, good-natured, roguish, waggish: *She gave her husband a playful slap.* **2 = lively**, spirited, cheerful, merry, mischievous, joyous, sprightly, vivacious, rollicking, impish, frisky, puckish, coltish, kittenish, frolicsome, ludic *(literary)*, sportive, gay, larkish *(informal)*: *They tumbled around like playful children.*
OPPOSITE: sedate

playmate NOUN **= friend**, companion, comrade, chum *(informal)*, pal *(informal)*, cobber *(Austral. & N.Z. old-fashioned, informal)*, playfellow

plaything NOUN **= toy**, amusement, game, pastime, trifle, trinket, bauble, gimcrack, gewgaw

playwright NOUN **= dramatist**, scriptwriter, tragedian, dramaturge, dramaturgist

plea NOUN **1 = appeal**, request, suit, prayer, begging, petition, overture, entreaty, intercession, supplication: *an impassioned plea to mankind to act to save the planet* **2 = suit**, cause, action, allegation: *We will enter a plea of not guilty.* **3 = excuse**, claim, defence, explanation, justification, pretext, vindication, extenuation: *He murdered his wife, but got off on a plea of insanity.*

plead VERB **1 = appeal**, ask, request, beg, petition, crave, solicit, implore, beseech, entreat, importune, supplicate: *He was kneeling on the floor pleading for mercy.* **2 = allege**, claim, argue, maintain, assert, put forward, adduce, use as an excuse: *The guards pleaded that they were only obeying orders.*

pleasant ADJECTIVE **1 = pleasing**, nice, welcome, satisfying, fine, lovely, acceptable, amusing, refreshing, delightful, enjoyable, gratifying, agreeable, pleasurable, delectable, lekker *(S. African slang)*: *a pleasant surprise* **OPPOSITE:** horrible **2 = friendly**, nice, agreeable, likable *or* likeable, engaging, charming, cheerful, cheery, good-humoured, amiable, genial, affable, congenial: *He was most anxious to seem agreeable and pleasant.*
OPPOSITE: disagreeable

pleasantry NOUN **= comment**, remark, casual remark, polite remark

please VERB **= delight**, entertain, humour, amuse, suit, content, satisfy, charm, cheer, indulge, tickle, gratify, gladden, give pleasure to, tickle someone pink *(informal)*: *This comment pleased her immensely.*
OPPOSITE: annoy

pleased ADJECTIVE **= happy**, delighted, contented, satisfied, thrilled, glad, tickled, gratified, over the moon *(informal)*, chuffed *(Brit. slang)*, euphoric, rapt, in high spirits, tickled pink *(informal)*, pleased as punch *(informal)*

pleasing ADJECTIVE **1 = enjoyable**, satisfying, attractive, charming, entertaining, delightful, gratifying, agreeable, pleasurable: *a pleasing view* **OPPOSITE:** unpleasant **2 = likable** *or* **likeable**, attractive, engaging, charming, winning, entertaining, amusing, delightful, polite, agreeable, amiable: *a pleasing personality* **OPPOSITE:** disagreeable

pleasurable ADJECTIVE **= enjoyable**, pleasant, diverting, good, nice, welcome, fun, lovely, entertaining, delightful, gratifying, agreeable, congenial

pleasure NOUN **1 = happiness**, delight, satisfaction, enjoyment, bliss, gratification, contentment, gladness, delectation: *We exclaimed with pleasure when we saw them.*
OPPOSITE: displeasure
2 = amusement, joy, recreation, diversion, solace, jollies *(slang)*, beer and skittles *(informal)*: *Watching TV is our only pleasure.* **OPPOSITE:** duty **3 = wish**, choice, desire, will, mind, option, preference, inclination: *Let me get you a drink. What's your pleasure?*

> **QUOTATIONS**
>
> Everyone is dragged on by their favourite pleasure
> [Virgil *Eclogue*]
>
> Pleasure's a sin, and sometimes sin's a pleasure
> [Lord Byron *Don Juan*]
>
> Sweet is pleasure after pain
> [John Dryden *Alexander's Feast*]
>
> The rapturous, wild, and ineffable pleasure
> Of drinking at somebody else's expense
> [Henry Sambrooke Leigh *Carols of Cockayne*]
>
> Pleasure is nothing else but the intermission of pain
> [John Selden *Table Talk*]
>
> One half of the world cannot understand the pleasures of the other
> [Jane Austen *Emma*]

pledge NOUN **1 = promise**, vow, assurance, word, undertaking, warrant, oath, covenant, word of honour: *a pledge to step up cooperation between the states* **2 = guarantee**, security, deposit, bail, bond, collateral, earnest, pawn, gage, surety: *items held in pledge for loans*
▷ VERB **1 = promise**, vow, vouch, swear, contract, engage, undertake, give your word, give your word of honour, give your oath: *I pledge that by next year we will have the problem solved.* **2 = bind**, guarantee, mortgage, engage, gage *(archaic)*: *He asked her to pledge the house as security for the loan.*

plenary ADJECTIVE **1 = full**, open, general, whole, complete, entire: *a plenary session of the Central Committee* **2 = complete**, full, sweeping,

p

absolute, thorough, unlimited, unconditional, unqualified, unrestricted: *The president has plenary power in some areas of foreign policy.*

plentiful ADJECTIVE **1 = abundant**, liberal, generous, lavish, complete, ample, infinite, overflowing, copious, inexhaustible, bountiful, profuse, thick on the ground, bounteous (*literary*), plenteous: *a plentiful supply* **OPPOSITE:** scarce **2 = productive**, bumper, fertile, prolific, fruitful, luxuriant, plenteous: *a celebration that gives thanks for a plentiful harvest*

plenty NOUN **1 = abundance**, wealth, luxury, prosperity, fertility, profusion, affluence, opulence, plenitude, fruitfulness, copiousness, plenteousness, plentifulness: *You are fortunate to be growing up in a time of peace and plenty.* **2** (*usually with* **of**) **= lots of** (*informal*), enough, a great deal of, masses of, quantities of, piles of (*informal*), mountains of, a good deal of, stacks of, heaps of (*informal*), a mass of, a volume of, an abundance of, a plethora of, a quantity of, a fund of, oodles of (*informal*), a store of, a mine of, a sufficiency of: *There was still plenty of time.*

> **QUOTATIONS**
> Plenty has made me poor
> [Ovid *Metamorphoses*]

plethora NOUN **= excess**, surplus, glut, profusion, surfeit, overabundance, superabundance, superfluity **OPPOSITE:** shortage

pliable ADJECTIVE **1 = flexible**, plastic, supple, lithe, limber, malleable, pliant, tensile, bendy, ductile, bendable: *The baskets are made with young, pliable spruce roots.* **OPPOSITE:** rigid **2 = compliant**, susceptible, responsive, manageable, receptive, yielding, adaptable, docile, impressionable, easily led, pliant, tractable, persuadable, influenceable, like putty in your hands: *His young queen was pliable and easily influenced.* **OPPOSITE:** stubborn

plight NOUN **= difficulty**, condition, state, situation, trouble, circumstances, dilemma, straits, predicament, extremity, perplexity

plod VERB **1 = trudge**, drag, tread, clump, lumber, tramp, stomp (*informal*), slog: *He plodded slowly up the hill.* **2 = slog away**, labour, grind away (*informal*), toil, grub, persevere, soldier on, plough through, plug away (*informal*), drudge, peg away: *He is still plodding away at the same job.*

plot[1] NOUN **1 = plan**, scheme, intrigue, conspiracy, cabal, stratagem, machination, covin (*Law*): *a plot to overthrow the government* **2 = story**, action, subject, theme, outline, scenario, narrative, thread, story line: *the plot of a cheap spy novel*
▷ VERB **1 = plan**, scheme, conspire, intrigue, manoeuvre, contrive, collude, cabal, hatch a plot, machinate: *They are awaiting trial for plotting against the state.* **2 = devise**, design, project, lay, imagine, frame, conceive, brew, hatch, contrive, concoct, cook up (*informal*): *a meeting to plot the survival strategy of the party* **3 = chart**, mark, draw, map, draft, locate, calculate, outline, compute: *We were trying to plot the course of the submarine.*

> **QUOTATIONS**
> Ay, now the plot thickens very much upon us
> [George Villiers Buckingham *The Rehearsal*]

plot[2] NOUN **= patch**, lot, area, ground, parcel, tract, allotment: *a small plot of land for growing vegetables*

plotter NOUN **= conspirator**, architect, intriguer, planner, conspirer, strategist, conniver, Machiavellian, schemer, cabalist

plough *or* **plow** (*U.S.*) VERB **= turn over**, dig, till, ridge, cultivate, furrow, break ground: *They ploughed 100,000 acres of virgin moorland.*
plough into something *or* **someone = plunge into**, crash into, smash into, career into, shove into, hurtle into, bulldoze into: *The car veered off the road and ploughed into a culvert.*
plough through something = forge, cut, drive, press, push, plunge, surge, stagger, wade, flounder, trudge, plod: *Mr Dambar watched her plough through the grass.*

ploy NOUN **= tactic**, move, trick, device, game, scheme, manoeuvre, dodge, ruse, gambit, subterfuge, stratagem, contrivance, wile

pluck VERB **1 = pull out** *or* **off**, pick, draw, collect, gather, harvest: *I plucked a lemon from the tree.* **2 = tug**, catch, snatch, clutch, jerk, yank, tweak, pull at: *He plucked the cigarette from his mouth.* **3 = strum**, pick, finger, twang, thrum, plunk: *Nell was plucking a harp.*
▷ NOUN **= courage**, nerve, heart, spirit, bottle (*Brit. slang*), resolution, determination, guts (*informal*), grit, bravery, backbone, mettle, boldness, spunk (*informal*), intrepidity, hardihood: *Cynics might sneer at him but you have to admire his pluck.*

plucky ADJECTIVE **= courageous**, spirited, brave, daring, bold, game, hardy, heroic, gritty, feisty (*informal, chiefly U.S. & Canad.*), gutsy (*slang*), intrepid, valiant, doughty, undaunted, unflinching, spunky (*informal*), ballsy (*taboo, slang*), mettlesome, (as) game as Ned Kelly (*Austral. slang*) **OPPOSITE:** cowardly

plug NOUN **1 = stopper**, cork, bung, spigot, stopple: *A plug had been inserted in the drill hole.* **2 = mention**, advertisement, advert (*Brit. informal*), push, promotion, publicity, puff, hype, good word: *The show was little more than a plug for her new film.*
▷ VERB **1 = seal**, close, stop, fill, cover, block, stuff, pack, cork, choke, stopper, bung, stop up, stopple: *Crews are working to plug a major oil leak.* **2 = mention**, push, promote, publicize, advertise, build up, puff, hype, write up: *If I hear another actor plugging his latest book I will scream.*
plug away = slog away, labour, toil away, grind away (*informal*), peg away, plod away, drudge away: *I just keep plugging away at this job, although I hate it.*

plum MODIFIER **= choice**, prize, first-class

plumb VERB **= delve into**, measure, explore, probe, sound out, search, go into, penetrate, gauge, unravel, fathom: *her attempts to plumb my innermost emotions*
▷ ADVERB **= exactly**, precisely, bang, slap, spot-on (*Brit. informal*): *The hotel is set plumb in the middle of the High Street.*

plume NOUN **= feather**, crest, quill, pinion, aigrette

plummet VERB **1 = drop**, fall, crash, nosedive, descend rapidly: *Share prices have plummeted.* **2 = plunge**, fall, drop, crash, tumble, swoop, stoop, nosedive, descend rapidly: *The car plummeted off a cliff.*

plummy ADJECTIVE **= deep**, posh (*informal, chiefly Brit.*), refined, upper-class, fruity, resonant

plump[1] ADJECTIVE **= chubby**, fat, stout, full, round, burly, obese, fleshy, beefy (*informal*), tubby, portly, buxom, dumpy, roly-poly, well-covered, rotund, podgy, corpulent, well-upholstered (*informal*): *Maria was small and plump with a mass of curly hair.* **OPPOSITE:** scrawny

plump[2] VERB **= flop**, fall, drop, sink, dump, slump: *Breathlessly, she plumped down next to Katrina.*
plump for something *or* **someone = choose**, favour, go for, back, support, opt for, side with, come down in favour of: *In the end, we plumped for an endowment mortgage.*

plunder VERB **1 = loot**, strip, sack, rob, raid, devastate, spoil, rifle, ravage, ransack, pillage, despoil: *They plundered and burned the town.* **2 = steal**, rob, take, nick (*informal*), pinch (*informal*), embezzle, pilfer, thieve: *a settlement to recover money plundered from government coffers*
▷ NOUN **1 = pillage**, sacking, robbery, marauding, rapine, spoliation: *a guerrilla group infamous for torture and plunder* **2 = loot**, spoils, prey, booty, swag (*slang*), ill-gotten gains: *Pirates swarmed the seas in search of easy plunder.*

plunge VERB **1 = descend**, fall, drop, crash, pitch, sink, go down, dive, tumble, plummet, nosedive: *50 people died when a bus plunged into a river.* **2 = hurtle**, charge, career, jump, tear, rush, dive, dash, swoop, lurch: *I plunged forward, calling her name.* **3 = submerge**, sink, duck, dip, immerse, douse, dunk: *She plunged her face into a bowl of cold water.* **4 = throw**, cast, pitch, propel: *conflicts which threaten to plunge the country into chaos*

5 = fall steeply, drop, crash *(informal)*, go down, slump, plummet, take a nosedive *(informal)*: *Net profits plunged 73% last year.*
▷ NOUN **1 = fall**, crash *(informal)*, slump, drop, tumble: *the stock market plunge* **2 = dive**, jump, duck, swoop, descent, immersion, submersion: *a refreshing plunge into cold water*

plurality NOUN **= multiplicity**, variety, diversity, profusion, numerousness

plus PREPOSITION **= and**, with, added to, coupled with, with the addition of: *Send a cheque for £18.99 plus £2 for postage and packing.*
▷ NOUN **= advantage**, benefit, asset, gain, extra, bonus, perk *(Brit. informal)*, good point, icing on the cake: *A big plus is that the data can be stored on a PC.*
▷ ADJECTIVE **= additional**, added, extra, positive, supplementary, add-on: *Accessibility is the other plus point of the borough.*

USAGE
When you have a sentence with more than one subject linked by *and*, this makes the subject plural and means it should take a plural verb: *the doctor and all the nurses were* (not *was*) *waiting for the patient.* However, where the subjects are linked by *plus*, *together with*, or *along with*, the number of the verb remains just as it would have been if the extra subjects had not been mentioned. Therefore you would say *the doctor, together with all the nurses, was* (not *were*) *waiting for the patient.*

p

plush ADJECTIVE **= luxurious**, luxury, costly, lavish, rich, sumptuous, opulent, palatial, ritzy *(slang)*, de luxe
OPPOSITE: cheap

ply[1] VERB **1 = provide**, supply, shower, lavish, regale: *Elsie plied her with food and drink.* **2 = bombard**, press, harass, besiege, beset, assail, importune: *Giovanni plied him with questions.* **3 = work at**, follow, exercise, pursue, carry on, practise: *streetmarkets with stallholders plying their trade* **4 = travel**, go, ferry, shuttle: *The brightly-coloured boats ply between the islands.* **5 = use**, handle, employ, swing, manipulate, wield, utilize: *With startling efficiency, the chef plied his knives.*

ply[2] NOUN **= thickness**, leaf, sheet, layer, fold, strand: *The plastic surfaces are covered with teak ply.*

poach VERB **1 = steal**, rob, plunder, hunt or fish illegally: *Many national parks are invaded by people poaching game.* **2 = take**, steal, appropriate, snatch *(informal)*, nab *(informal)*, purloin: *allegations that it had poached members from other unions*

pocket NOUN **= pouch**, bag, sack, hollow, compartment, receptacle: *a canvas container with customised pockets for each tool*
▷ MODIFIER **= small**, compact, miniature, portable, little, potted *(informal)*, concise, pint-size(d) *(informal)*, abridged: *a pocket dictionary*
▷ VERB **= steal**, take, lift *(informal)*, appropriate, pilfer, purloin, filch, help yourself to, snaffle *(Brit. informal)*: *He pocketed a wallet from the bedside of a dead man.*

pod NOUN **= shell**, case, hull, husk, shuck

podium NOUN **= platform**, stand, stage, rostrum, dais

poem NOUN **= verse**, song, lyric, rhyme, sonnet, ode, verse composition

QUOTATIONS
A poem should not mean
but be
[Archibald McLeish *Ars Poetica*]

poet NOUN **= bard**, rhymer, lyricist, lyric poet, versifier, maker *(archaic)*, elegist

QUOTATIONS
The poet is the priest of the invisible
[Wallace Stevens *Adagia*]

A poet's hope: to be,
like some valley cheese,
local, but prized elsewhere
[W.H. Auden *Shorts II*]

For that fine madness still he did retain
Which rightly should possess a poet's brain
[Michael Drayton *To Henry Reynolds, of Poets and Poesy*]

Immature poets imitate; mature poets steal
[T.S. Eliot *The Sacred Wood*]

The poet is always indebted to the universe, paying interest and fines on sorrow
[Vladimir Mayakovsky *Conversation with an Inspector of Taxes about Poetry*]

All a poet can do today is warn
[Wilfred Owen *Poems (preface)*]

Sir, I admit your general rule
That every poet is a fool;
But you yourself may serve to show it,
That every fool is not a poet
[Alexander Pope *Epigram from the French*]

poetic ADJECTIVE **1 = figurative**, creative, lyric, symbolic, lyrical, rhythmic, rhythmical, songlike: *Heidegger's interest in the poetic, evocative uses of language* **2 = lyrical**, lyric, rhythmic, elegiac, rhythmical, metrical: *There's a very rich poetic tradition in Gaelic.*

poetry NOUN **= verse**, poems, rhyme, rhyming, poesy *(archaic)*, verse composition, metrical composition

QUOTATIONS
Poetry is a kind of ingenious nonsense
[Isaac Barrow]

Poetry is what gets lost in translation
[Robert Frost]

Poetry is a search for ways of communication; it must be conducted with openness, flexibility, and a constant readiness to listen
[Fleur Adcock]

Poetry is the spontaneous overflow of powerful feelings; it takes its origin from emotion recollected in tranquillity
[William Wordsworth *Lyrical Ballads (preface)*]

Poetry is at bottom a criticism of life
[Matthew Arnold *Essays in Criticism*]

Poetry is a subject as precise as geometry
[Gustave Flaubert *letter*]

Poetry is a way of taking life by the throat
[Robert Frost]

As civilization advances, poetry almost necessarily declines
[Lord Macaulay *Essays*]

Poetry (is) a speaking picture, with this end; to teach and delight
[Sir Philip Sidney *The Defence of Poetry*]

Poetry is truth in its Sunday clothes
[Joseph Roux *Meditations of a Parish Priest*]

Prose = words in their best order; poetry = the best words in their best order
[Samuel Taylor Coleridge *Table Talk*]

Imaginary gardens with real toads in them
[Marianne Moore *Poetry*]

Poetry is something more philosophical and more worthy of serious attention than history
[Aristotle *Poetics*]

Prose is when all the lines except the last go on to the end. Poetry is when some of them fall short of it
[Jeremy Bentham]

I am two fools, I know,
For loving, and for saying so
In whining poetry
[John Donne *The Triple Fool*]

Poetry's a mere drug, Sir
[George Farquhar *Love and a Battle*]

I'd as soon write free verse as play tennis with the net down
[Robert Frost]

If poetry comes not as naturally as the leaves to a tree it had better not come at all
[John Keats *letter*]

Writing a book of poetry is like dropping a rose petal down the Grand Canyon and waiting for the echo
[Don Marquis]

rhyme being... but the invention of a barbarous age, to set off wretched matter and lame metre
[John Milton *Paradise Lost (preface)*]

> Most people ignore most poetry because
> most poetry ignores most people
> [Adrian Mitchell *Poems*]
>
> All that is not prose is verse; and all that is not verse is prose
> [Molière *Le Bourgeois Gentilhomme*]
>
> My subject is War, and the pity of War. The Poetry is in the pity
> [Wilfred Owen *Poems (preface)*]
>
> it is not poetry, but prose run mad
> [Alexander Pope *An Epistle to Dr. Arbuthnot*]

po-faced ADJECTIVE = **humourless**, disapproving, solemn, prim, puritanical, narrow-minded, stolid, prudish, strait-laced

pogey NOUN = **benefits**, the dole (*Brit. & Austral.*), welfare, social security, unemployment benefit, state benefit, allowance

poignancy NOUN = **sadness**, emotion, sentiment, intensity, feeling, tenderness, pathos, emotionalism, plaintiveness, evocativeness, piteousness

poignant ADJECTIVE = **moving**, touching, affecting, upsetting, sad, bitter, intense, painful, distressing, pathetic, harrowing, heartbreaking, agonizing, heart-rending, gut-wrenching

point NOUN **1** = **essence**, meaning, subject, question, matter, heart, theme, import, text, core, burden, drift, thrust, proposition, marrow, crux, gist, main idea, nub, pith: *You have missed the main point of my argument.* **2** = **purpose**, aim, object, use, end, reason, goal, design, intention, objective, utility, intent, motive, usefulness: *What's the point of all these questions?* **3** = **aspect**, detail, feature, side, quality, property, particular, respect, item, instance, characteristic, topic, attribute, trait, facet, peculiarity, nicety: *The most interesting point about the village is its religion.* **4** = **place**, area, position, station, site, spot, location, locality, locale: *The town square is a popular meeting point for tourists.* **5** = **moment**, time, stage, period, phase, instant, juncture, moment in time, very minute: *At this point, Diana arrived.* **6** = **stage**, level, position, condition, degree, pitch, circumstance, extent: *It got to the point where he had to leave.* **7** = **end**, tip, sharp end, top, spur, spike, apex, nib, tine, prong: *the point of a knife* **8** = **score**, tally, mark: *Sort the answers out and add up the points.* **9** = **headland**, head, bill, cape, ness (*archaic*), promontory, foreland: *a long point of land reaching southwards into the sea* **10** = **pinpoint**, mark, spot, dot, fleck, speck: *a point of light in an otherwise dark world*
▷ VERB **1** (*usually followed by* **at** *or* **to**) = **aim**, level, train, direct: *A man pointed a gun at them and pulled the trigger.* **2** = **face**, look, direct: *He controlled the car until it was pointing forwards again.*
beside the point = **irrelevant**, inappropriate, pointless, peripheral, unimportant, incidental, unconnected, immaterial, inconsequential, nothing to do with it, extraneous, neither here nor there, off the subject, inapplicable, not to the point, inapposite, without connection, inconsequent, not pertinent, not germane, not to the purpose: *Brian didn't like it, but that was beside the point.*
point at *or* **to something** *or* **someone** = **indicate**, show, signal, point to, point out, specify, designate, gesture towards: *I pointed at the boy sitting nearest me.*
point of view **1** = **opinion**, view, attitude, belief, feeling, thought, idea, approach, judgment, sentiment, viewpoint, way of thinking, way of looking at it: *His point of view is that money isn't everything.* **2** = **perspective**, side, position, stance, stand, angle, outlook, orientation, viewpoint, slant, standpoint, frame of reference: *Try to look at it from my point of view.*
point something *or* **someone out** **1** = **identify**, show, point to, indicate, finger (*informal, chiefly U.S.*), single out, call attention to, draw *or* call attention to, flag up: *She pointed him out to me as we drove past.* **2** = **allude to**, reveal, mention, identify, indicate, bring up, specify, draw *or* call attention to, flag up: *We all too easily point out other people's failings.*
point something up = **emphasize**, stress, highlight, underline, make clear, accent, spotlight, draw attention to, flag up, underscore, play up, accentuate, foreground, focus attention on, give prominence to, turn the spotlight on, bring to the fore, put emphasis on: *Politicians pointed up the differences between the two countries.*
point to something **1** = **denote**, reveal, indicate, show, suggest, evidence, signal, signify, be evidence of, bespeak (*literary*): *All the evidence pointed to his guilt.* **2** = **refer to**, mention, indicate, specify, single out, touch on, call attention to: *Gooch pointed to their bowling as the key to their success.*
to the point = **relevant**, appropriate, apt, pointed, short, fitting, material, related, brief, suitable, applicable, pertinent, terse, pithy, apposite, apropos, germane: *The description he gave was brief and to the point.*

point-blank ADJECTIVE = **direct**, plain, blunt, explicit, abrupt, express, downright, categorical, unreserved, straight-from-the-shoulder: *He gave a point-blank refusal.*
▷ ADVERB = **directly**, openly, straight, frankly, plainly, bluntly, explicitly, overtly, candidly, brusquely, straightforwardly, forthrightly: *Mr Patterson was asked point-blank if he would resign.*

pointed ADJECTIVE **1** = **sharp**, edged, acute, barbed: *the pointed end of the chisel* **2** = **cutting**, telling, biting, sharp, keen, acute, accurate, penetrating, pertinent, incisive, trenchant: *a pointed remark*

pointer NOUN **1** = **hint**, tip, suggestion, warning, recommendation, caution, piece of information, piece of advice: *Here are a few pointers to help you make a choice.* **2** = **indicator**, hand, guide, needle, arrow: *The pointer indicates the pressure on the dial.*

pointless ADJECTIVE = **senseless**, meaningless, futile, fruitless, unproductive, stupid, silly, useless, absurd, irrelevant, in vain, worthless, ineffectual, unprofitable, nonsensical, aimless, inane, unavailing, without rhyme or reason **OPPOSITE:** worthwhile

poise NOUN **1** = **composure**, cool (*slang*), presence, assurance, dignity, equilibrium, serenity, coolness, aplomb, calmness, equanimity, presence of mind, sang-froid, savoir-faire, self-possession: *It took a moment for Mark to recover his poise.* **2** = **grace**, balance, equilibrium, elegance: *Ballet classes are important for poise.*

poised ADJECTIVE **1** = **ready**, waiting, prepared, standing by, on the brink, in the wings, all set: *US forces are poised for a massive air, land and sea assault.* **2** = **composed**, calm, together (*informal*), collected, dignified, graceful, serene, suave, urbane, self-confident, unfazed (*informal*), debonair, unruffled, nonchalant, self-possessed: *Rachel appeared poised and calm.* **OPPOSITE:** agitated

poison NOUN **1** = **toxin**, venom, bane (*archaic*): *Poison from the weaver fish causes paralysis and swelling.* **2** = **contamination**, corruption, contagion, cancer, virus, blight, bane, malignancy, miasma, canker: *the poison of crime and violence spreading through the city*
▷ VERB **1** = **murder**, kill, give someone poison, administer poison to: *There were rumours that she had poisoned her husband.* **2** = **contaminate**, foul, infect, spoil, pollute, blight, taint, adulterate, envenom, befoul: *The land has been completely poisoned by chemicals.* **3** = **corrupt**, colour, undermine, bias, sour, pervert, warp, taint, subvert, embitter, deprave, defile, jaundice, vitiate, envenom: *ill-feeling that will poison further negotiations*

poisonous ADJECTIVE **1** = **toxic**, fatal, deadly, lethal, mortal, virulent, noxious, venomous, baneful (*archaic*), mephitic: *All parts of the yew tree are poisonous.* **2** = **evil**, vicious, malicious, corrupting, pernicious, baleful, baneful (*archaic*), pestiferous: *poisonous attacks on the Church*

p

poke VERB **1 = jab**, hit, push, stick, dig, punch, stab, thrust, butt, elbow, shove, nudge, prod: *Lindy poked him in the ribs.* **2 = protrude**, stick, thrust, jut: *His fingers poked through the worn tips of his gloves.*
▷ NOUN **= jab**, hit, dig, punch, thrust, butt, nudge, prod: *John smiled and gave Richard a playful poke.*

polar ADJECTIVE **= opposite**, opposed, contrary, contradictory, antagonistic, antithetical, diametric, antipodal: *economists at polar ends of the politico-economic spectrum*

polarity NOUN **= opposition**, contradiction, paradox, ambivalence, dichotomy, duality, contrariety

pole[1] NOUN **= rod**, post, support, staff, standard, bar, stick, stake, paling, shaft, upright, pillar, mast, picket, spar, stave: *The sign hung at the top of a large pole.*

pole[2] NOUN **= extremity**, limit, terminus, antipode: *The two mayoral candidates represent opposite poles of the political spectrum.*
poles apart = at opposite extremes, incompatible, irreconcilable, worlds apart, miles apart, like chalk and cheese *(Brit.)*, like night and day, widely separated, completely different, at opposite ends of the earth: *Her views on Europe are poles apart from those of her successor.*

polemic NOUN **= argument**, attack, debate, dispute, controversy, rant, tirade, diatribe, invective, philippic *(rare)*

polemics NOUN **= dispute**, debate, argument, discussion, controversy, contention, wrangling, disputation, argumentation

police NOUN **= the law** *(informal)*, police force, constabulary, the fuzz *(slang)*, law enforcement agency, boys in blue *(informal)*, the Old Bill *(slang)*, the rozzers *(slang)*: *The police have arrested twenty people following the disturbances.*
▷ VERB **1 = control**, patrol, guard, watch, protect, regulate, keep the peace, keep in order: *the UN force whose job it is to police the border* **2 = monitor**, check, observe, oversee, supervise: *the body which polices the investment management business*

police officer NOUN **= cop** *(slang)*, officer, pig *(offensive, slang)*, bobby *(informal)*, copper *(slang)*, constable, peeler *(Irish & Brit. obsolete, slang)*, gendarme *(slang)*, fuzz *(slang)*, woodentop *(slang)*, bizzy *(informal)*, flatfoot *(slang)*, rozzer *(slang)*, policeman *or* policewoman

> **QUOTATIONS**
> A policeman's lot is not a happy one
> [W.S. Gilbert *The Pirates of Penzance*]

policy NOUN **1 = procedure**, plan, action, programme, practice, scheme, theory, code, custom, stratagem: *plans which include changes in foreign policy* **2 = line**, rules, approach, guideline, protocol: *significant changes in Britain's policy on global warming*

polish NOUN **1 = varnish**, wax, glaze, lacquer, japan: *The air smelt of furniture polish.* **2 = sheen**, finish, sparkle, glaze, gloss, brilliance, brightness, veneer, lustre, smoothness: *I admired the high polish of his boots.* **3 = style**, class *(informal)*, finish, breeding, grace, elegance, refinement, finesse, urbanity, suavity, politesse: *She was enormously popular for her charm and polish.*
▷ VERB **1 = shine**, wax, clean, smooth, rub, buff, brighten, burnish, furbish: *Every morning he polished his shoes.* **2** *(often with up)* **= perfect**, improve, enhance, refine, finish, correct, cultivate, brush up, touch up, emend: *Polish up your writing skills on a one-week course.*
polish someone off = eliminate, take out *(slang)*, get rid of, dispose of, do away with, blow away *(slang, chiefly U.S.)*, beat someone once and for all: *a chance to polish off their bitter local rivals*
polish something off = finish, down, shift *(informal)*, wolf, consume, put away, eat up, swill: *He polished off the whole box of truffles on his own.*

polished ADJECTIVE **1 = elegant**, sophisticated, refined, polite, cultivated, civilized, genteel, suave, finished, urbane, courtly, well-bred: *He is polished, charming and articulate.* **OPPOSITE:** unsophisticated
2 = accomplished, professional, masterly, fine, expert, outstanding, skilful, adept, impeccable, flawless, superlative, faultless: *a polished performance* **OPPOSITE:** amateurish
3 = shining, bright, smooth, gleaming, glossy, slippery, burnished, glassy, furbished: *a highly polished surface* **OPPOSITE:** dull

polite ADJECTIVE **1 = mannerly**, civil, courteous, affable, obliging, gracious, respectful, well-behaved, deferential, complaisant, well-mannered: *He was a quiet and very polite young man.* **OPPOSITE:** rude **2 = refined**, cultured, civilized, polished, sophisticated, elegant, genteel, urbane, courtly, well-bred: *Certain words are not acceptable in polite society.* **OPPOSITE:** uncultured

politeness NOUN **= courtesy**, decency, correctness, etiquette, deference, grace, civility, graciousness, common courtesy, complaisance, courteousness, respectfulness, mannerliness, obligingness

> **QUOTATIONS**
> Politeness is organized indifference
> [Paul Valéry *Tel Quel*]

politic ADJECTIVE **= wise**, diplomatic, sensible, discreet, prudent, advisable, expedient, judicious, tactful, sagacious, in your best interests

political ADJECTIVE **1 = governmental**, government, state, parliamentary, constitutional, administrative, legislative, civic, ministerial, policy-making, party political: *a democratic political system* **2 = factional**, party, militant, partisan: *I'm not political, I take no interest in politics.*

> **QUOTATIONS**
> Man is by nature a political animal
> [Aristotle *Politics*]

politician NOUN **= statesman** *or* **stateswoman**, representative, senator *(U.S.)*, congressman *(U.S.)*, Member of Parliament, legislator, public servant, congresswoman *(U.S.)*, politico *(informal, chiefly U.S.)*, lawmaker, office bearer, M.P., elected offical

> **QUOTATIONS**
> An honest politician is one who when bought stays bought
> [Simon Cameron]
>
> A statesman is a politician who has been dead ten or fifteen years
> [Harry S. Truman]
>
> A politician is an animal that can sit on a fence and keep both ears to the ground
> [H.L. Mencken]
>
> Since a politician never believes what he says, he is always astonished when others do
> [Charles de Gaulle]
>
> Well, in politics, I'm a complete neutral; I think they're all scoundrels without exception
> [H.L. Mencken]
>
> a politician is an arse upon which everyone has sat except a man
> [e e cummings *1 X 1 (no. 10)*]
>
> There are no good and bad politicians, only bad ones and worse
> [*Spanish anarchist slogan*]
>
> 'Do you pray for the senators, Dr. Hale?'
> 'No, I look at the senators and I pray for the country.'
> [Edward Everett Hale]
>
> A statesman is a politician who places himself at the service of the nation. A politician is a statesman who places the nation at his service
> [Georges Pompidou]
>
> The politician who never made a mistake never made a decision
> [John Major]
>
> Ninety-eight percent of the adults in this country are decent, hard-working, honest Americans. It's the other lousy two percent that get all the publicity. But then – we elected them
> [Lily Tomlin]

politics NOUN **1 = affairs of state**, government, government policy, public affairs, civics: *He quickly involved himself in politics.* **2 = political beliefs**, party politics, political allegiances, political leanings, political sympathies: *My politics are well to the left of centre.* **3 = political science**, polity, statesmanship, civics, statecraft: *He studied politics and medieval history.*

The Language of Miles Franklin

Stella Maria Sarah Miles Franklin (1879–1954) was an Australian writer and feminist. Her first and most famous work, *My Brilliant Career*, is a semi-autobiographical novel about a young girl growing up in late-19th-century rural Australia. Franklin's other works include *Some Everyday Folk and Dawn*, a novel about provincial Australian life.

An important feature of Franklin's novels is family life, and this is reflected in her most frequent nouns, several of which refer to family members: *mother, grandma, child, father, aunt. Father* is particularly frequent in *My Brilliant Career*, where the narrator's inadequate father is captured in the collocates, such as *drunken father, lazy father, father's drinking*, and *father's fault*.

Woman is also one of Franklin's five most frequent nouns. It is often used in aphoristic statements to describe the narrators', or characters', perceptions of female identity:

> Provided a **woman** is beautiful allowance will be made for all her shortcomings.
>
> **Women**, he asserted, were the bane of society and the ruination of all men.

Over a tenth of the occurrences of *woman* in *Some Everyday Folk and Dawn* occur within five words of *vote*, for example:

> Old Hollis there says he won't **vote** this year because the women have one.
>
> I think the **women** ought to **vote** if they want to. There's nothing to stop 'em voting and doing their housework as well.

This novel was written not long after Australian women were given the vote, and Franklin captures the ensuing debate, portraying characters who oppose suffrage and those who support it (even those, as in the second quotation, whose reasons are somewhat questionable).

The most frequent adjective in Franklin's works is *good*, some of the most salient collocates of which are *girl* ('I was a good girl and honoured my parents') and *match* ('good matches are few'). *Beautiful* and *pretty* are also among Franklin's forty most frequent adjectives, reflecting the importance of physical appearance in her novels (the narrator of *My Beautiful Career* is plagued by her plainness). Both *beautiful* and *pretty* tend to be used to refer to girls and their features: *a soft pretty face; a pretty head with a wealth of bright hair*; *a beautiful and vivacious girl. Nice*, on the other hand, is more often used in reference to men ('she should marry some nice youngster with means to place her in a setting befitting her intelligence and beauty'), indicating the extent to which the appearance of women was regarded as much more important than that of men. *Handsome* is less frequent, and, as in modern English, refers both to men and to a particular kind of beautiful and stately woman.

At the beginning of *Some Everyday Folk and Dawn*, Franklin helpfully offers the reader a 'glossary of colloquialisms and slang terms', where Australian words are given with 'American Equivalents' and 'English Interpretation' alongside. For example, *to smoodge* is translated into American as 'to be a 'sucker'', and into English as 'To curry favour at the expense of independence'; *sollicker* is 'somewhat equivalent to 'corker'', 'something excessive'. These notes help the non-Australian reader with examples such as:

> 'Blow it all, don't **smoodge** so. It ain't long since you was all rared up on yer hind legs showin' how things would go to fury if wimmen had the vote.'
>
> '...if he was a bloke I felt fit to wallop, I'd give him a nice **sollicker** under the ear...'

However, it is interesting to note that Franklin sometimes assumes a slang term to be Australian when it is not. For example, she gives the 'Australian' term 'two 'bob'', translated into English as 'two shillings'; *bob* meaning 'shilling', however, was originally an English word.

The examples above also show the way that Franklin represents the dialect of her characters, with spellings such as *wimmen* and *yer*, non-standard grammar such as *you was*, and lively colloquialisms such as *wallop* and *blow it all*.

4 = power struggle, machinations, opportunism, realpolitik, Machiavellianism: *He doesn't know how to handle office politics.*

> **QUOTATIONS**
>
> Politics is the art of the possible
> [Prince Otto von Bismarck]
>
> A week is a long time in politics
> [Harold Wilson]
>
> Politics is not the art of the possible. It consists in choosing between the disastrous and the unpalatable
> [John Kenneth Galbraith *Ambassador's Journal*]
>
> Politics...has always been the systematic organisation of hatreds
> [Henry Brooks Adams *The Education of Henry Adams*]
>
> Practical politics consists in ignoring facts
> [Henry Brooks Adams *The Education of Henry Adams*]
>
> In politics the middle way is none at all
> [John Adams]
>
> In politics, what begins in fear usually ends in folly
> [Samuel Taylor Coleridge *Table Talk*]
>
> There is a holy mistaken zeal in politics as well as in religion. By persuading others, we convince ourselves
> [Junius *Public Advertiser*]
>
> Politics is war without bloodshed while war is politics with bloodshed
> [Mao Tse-tung]
>
> The argument of the broken window pane is the most valuable argument in modern politics
> [Emmeline Pankhurst]
>
> Politics is perhaps the only profession for which no preparation is thought necessary
> [Robert Louis Stevenson *Familiar Studies of Men and Books*]
>
> Most schemes of political improvement are very laughable things
> [Dr. Johnson]
>
> politics: a strife of interests masquerading as a contest of principles. The conduct of public affairs for private advantage
> [Ambrose Bierce *The Devil's Dictionary*]

> **PROVERBS**
>
> *Politics makes strange bedfellows*

poll NOUN **1 = survey**, figures, count, sampling, returns, ballot, tally, census, canvass, Gallup Poll, (public) opinion poll: *Polls show that the party is losing support.* **2 = election**, vote, voting, referendum, ballot, plebiscite: *In 1945, Churchill was defeated at the polls.*
▷ VERB **1 = question**, interview, survey, sample, ballot, canvass: *More than 18,000 people were polled.* **2 = gain**, return, record, register, tally: *He had polled enough votes to force a second ballot.*

pollute VERB **1 = contaminate**, dirty, mar, poison, soil, foul, infect, spoil, stain, taint, adulterate, make filthy, smirch, befoul: *beaches polluted by sewage pumped into the sea* **OPPOSITE:** decontaminate **2 = defile**, violate, corrupt, sully, deprave, debase, profane, desecrate, dishonour, debauch, besmirch: *a man accused of polluting the minds of children* **OPPOSITE:** honour

pollution NOUN **1 = contamination**, dirtying, corruption, taint, adulteration, foulness, defilement, uncleanness, vitiation, carbon footprint: *environmental pollution* **2 = waste**, poisons, dirt, impurities: *the level of pollution in the river*

pomp NOUN **1 = ceremony**, grandeur, splendour, state, show, display, parade, flourish, pageant, magnificence, solemnity, pageantry, ostentation, éclat: *the pomp and splendour of the English aristocracy* **2 = show**, pomposity, grandiosity, vainglory: *The band have trawled new depths of pomp and self-indulgence.*

pompous ADJECTIVE **1 = self-important**, affected, arrogant, pretentious, bloated, grandiose, imperious, showy, overbearing, ostentatious, puffed up, portentous, magisterial, supercilious, pontifical, vainglorious: *What a pompous little man he is.* **OPPOSITE:** unpretentious **2 = grandiloquent**, high-flown, inflated, windy, overblown, turgid, bombastic, boastful, flatulent, arty-farty *(informal)*, fustian, orotund, magniloquent: *She winced at his pompous phraseology.* **OPPOSITE:** simple

pond NOUN **= pool**, tarn, small lake, fish pond, duck pond, millpond, lochan *(Scot.)*, dew pond

ponder VERB **= think about**, consider, study, reflect on, examine, weigh up, contemplate, deliberate about, muse on, brood on, meditate on, mull over, puzzle over, ruminate on, give thought to, cogitate on, rack your brains about, excogitate

ponderous ADJECTIVE **1 = dull**, laboured, pedestrian, dreary, heavy, tedious, plodding, tiresome, lifeless, stilted, stodgy, pedantic, long-winded, verbose, prolix: *He had a dense, ponderous writing style.* **2 = clumsy**, awkward, lumbering, laborious, graceless, elephantine, heavy-footed, unco *(Austral. slang)*: *He strolled about with a ponderous, heavy gait.* **OPPOSITE:** graceful

pontificate VERB **= expound**, preach, sound off, pronounce, declaim, lay down the law, hold forth, dogmatize, pontify

pool[1] NOUN **1 = swimming pool**, lido, swimming bath(s) *(Brit.)*, bathing pool *(archaic)*: *a heated indoor pool* **2 = pond**, lake, mere, tarn: *Beautiful gardens filled with pools and fountains.* **3 = puddle**, drop, patch, splash: *There were pools of water on the gravel drive.*

pool[2] NOUN **1 = supply**, reserve, fall-back: *the available pool of manpower* **2 = kitty**, bank, fund, stock, store, pot, jackpot, stockpile, hoard, cache: *a reserve pool of cash*
▷ VERB **= combine**, share, merge, put together, amalgamate, lump together, join forces on: *We pooled our savings to start up a new business.*

poor ADJECTIVE **1 = impoverished**, broke *(informal)*, badly off, hard up *(informal)*, short, in need, needy, on the rocks, penniless, destitute, poverty-stricken, down and out, skint *(Brit. slang)*, in want, indigent, down at heel, impecunious, dirt-poor *(informal)*, on the breadline, flat broke *(informal)*, penurious, on your uppers, stony-broke *(Brit. slang)*, necessitous, in queer street, without two pennies to rub together *(informal)*, on your beam-ends: *He was one of thirteen children from a poor family.* **OPPOSITE:** rich **2 = unfortunate**, pathetic, miserable, unlucky, hapless, pitiful, luckless, wretched, ill-starred, pitiable, ill-fated: *I feel sorry for that poor child.* **OPPOSITE:** fortunate **3 = inferior**, unsatisfactory, mediocre, second-rate, sorry, weak, pants *(informal)*, rotten *(informal)*, faulty, feeble, worthless, shabby, shoddy, low-grade, below par, substandard, low-rent *(informal)*, crappy *(slang)*, valueless, no great shakes *(informal)*, rubbishy, poxy *(slang)*, not much cop *(Brit. slang)*, half-pie *(N.Z. informal)*, bodger or bodgie *(Austral. slang)*: *The wine is very poor; He was a poor actor.* **OPPOSITE:** excellent **4 = meagre**, inadequate, insufficient, reduced, lacking, slight, miserable, pathetic, incomplete, scant, sparse, deficient, skimpy, measly, scanty, pitiable, niggardly, straitened, exiguous: *poor wages and terrible working conditions; A poor crop has sent vegetable prices spiralling.* **OPPOSITE:** ample **5 = unproductive**, barren, fruitless, bad, bare, exhausted, depleted, impoverished, sterile, infertile, unfruitful: *Mix in some planting compost to improve poor soil when you dig.* **OPPOSITE:** productive

poorly ADVERB **= badly**, incompetently, inadequately, crudely, inferiorly, unsuccessfully, insufficiently, shabbily, unsatisfactorily, inexpertly: *poorly built houses* **OPPOSITE:** well
▷ ADJECTIVE **= ill**, sick, ailing, unwell, crook *(Austral. & N.Z. informal)*, seedy *(informal)*, below par, out of sorts, off colour, under the weather *(informal)*, indisposed, feeling rotten *(informal)*: *I've just phoned Julie and she's still poorly.* **OPPOSITE:** healthy

pop NOUN **1 = soft drink**, ginger *(Scot.)*, soda *(U.S. & Canad.)*, fizzy drink, cool drink *(S. African)*: *He still visits the village shop for buns and fizzy pop.* **2 = bang**, report, crack, noise, burst, explosion:

Each corn kernel will make a loud pop when cooked.
▷ VERB **1 = burst**, crack, snap, bang, explode, report, go off (with a bang): *The champagne cork popped and shot to the ceiling.* **2 = protrude**, bulge, stick out: *My eyes popped at the sight of so much food.* **3 = put**, insert, push, stick, slip, thrust, tuck, shove: *He plucked a grape from the bunch and popped it into his mouth.* **4** *(often with* **in, out,** *etc)* **= call**, visit, appear, drop in *(informal)*, leave quickly, come *or* go suddenly, nip in *or* out *(Brit. informal)*: *Wendy popped in for a quick visit on Monday night.*

pope NOUN **= Holy Father**, pontiff, His Holiness, Bishop of Rome, Vicar of Christ
▸ *related adjective:* papal

populace NOUN **= people**, crowd, masses, mob, inhabitants, general public, multitude, throng, rabble, hoi polloi, Joe Public *(slang)*, Joe Six-Pack *(U.S. slang)*, commonalty

popular ADJECTIVE **1 = well-liked**, liked, favoured, celebrated, in, accepted, favourite, famous, approved, in favour, fashionable, in demand, sought-after, fave *(informal)*: *This is the most popular game ever devised.* **OPPOSITE:** unpopular **2 = common**, general, standard, widespread, prevailing, stock, current, public, conventional, universal, prevalent, ubiquitous: *the popular misconception that dinosaurs were all lumbering giants* **OPPOSITE:** rare

popularity NOUN **1 = favour**, fame, esteem, acclaim, regard, reputation, approval, recognition, celebrity, vogue, adoration, renown, repute, idolization, lionization: *His authority and popularity have declined.* **2 = currency**, acceptance, circulation, vogue, prevalence: *This theory has enjoyed tremendous popularity among sociologists.*

popularize VERB **1 = make something popular**, spread the word about, disseminate, universalize, give mass appeal to: *the first person to popularize rock 'n' roll in China* **2 = simplify**, make available to all, give currency to, give mass appeal to: *a magazine devoted to popularizing science*

popularly ADVERB **= generally**, commonly, widely, usually, regularly, universally, traditionally, ordinarily, conventionally, customarily

populate VERB **1 = inhabit**, people, live in, occupy, reside in, dwell in *(formal)*: *the native people who populate areas around the city* **2 = settle**, people, occupy, pioneer, colonize: *North America was populated largely by Europeans.*

population NOUN **= inhabitants**, people, community, society, residents, natives, folk, occupants, populace, denizens, citizenry

> **QUOTATIONS**
> Population, when unchecked, increases in a geometrical ratio. Subsistence only increases in an arithmetical ratio
> [Thomas Malthus *The Principle of Population*]

populous ADJECTIVE **= populated**, crowded, packed, swarming, thronged, teeming, heavily populated, overpopulated

pore[1] NOUN **= opening**, hole, outlet, orifice, stoma: *microscopic pores in the plant's leaves*

pore[2] VERB **1** *(followed by* **over***)* **= study**, read, examine, go over, scrutinize, peruse: *We spent whole afternoons poring over travel brochures.* **2** *(followed by* **over, on,** *or* **upon***)* **= contemplate**, ponder, brood, dwell on, work over: *One day historians will pore over these strange months.*

pornographic ADJECTIVE **= obscene**, erotic, indecent, blue, dirty, offensive, rude, sexy, filthy, lewd, risqué, X-rated *(informal)*, salacious, prurient, smutty

pornography NOUN **= obscenity**, porn *(informal)*, erotica, dirt, filth, indecency, porno *(informal)*, smut

> **QUOTATIONS**
> Pornography is the attempt to insult sex, to do dirt on it
> [D.H. Lawrence *Phoenix*]

porous ADJECTIVE **= permeable**, absorbent, spongy, absorptive, penetrable, pervious
OPPOSITE: impermeable

port NOUN **= harbour**, haven, anchorage, seaport, roadstead

> **PROVERBS**
> *Any port in a storm*

portable ADJECTIVE **= light**, compact, convenient, handy, lightweight, manageable, movable, easily carried, portative

portal NOUN **= doorway**, door, entry, way in, entrance, gateway, entrance way

portent NOUN **= omen**, sign, warning, threat, indication, premonition, foreshadowing, foreboding, harbinger, presage, forewarning, prognostication, augury, presentiment, prognostic

portentous ADJECTIVE **1 = pompous**, solemn, ponderous, self-important, pontifical: *There was nothing portentous or solemn about him.* **2 = significant**, alarming, sinister, ominous, important, threatening, crucial, forbidding, menacing, momentous, fateful, minatory, bodeful: *portentous prophecies of doom*

porter[1] NOUN **= baggage attendant**, carrier, bearer, baggage-carrier: *A porter slammed the baggage compartment doors.*

porter[2] NOUN **= doorman**, caretaker, janitor, concierge, gatekeeper: *a porter at the block of flats*

portion NOUN **1 = part**, bit, piece, section, scrap, segment, fragment, fraction, chunk, wedge, hunk, morsel: *I have spent a large portion of my life here.* **2 = helping**, serving, piece, plateful: *fish and chips at about £2.70 a portion* **3 = share**, division, allowance, lot, measure, quantity, quota, ration, allocation, allotment: *his portion of the inheritance*

portly ADJECTIVE **= stout**, fat, overweight, plump, large, heavy, ample, bulky, burly, obese, fleshy, beefy *(informal)*, tubby *(informal)*, rotund, corpulent

portrait NOUN **1 = picture**, painting, image, photograph, representation, sketch, likeness, portraiture: *Lucian Freud has been asked to paint a portrait of the Queen.* **2 = description**, account, profile, biography, portrayal, depiction, vignette, characterization, thumbnail sketch: *a beautifully written and sensitive portrait of a great woman*

portray VERB **1 = play**, take the role of, act the part of, represent, personate *(rare)*: *He portrayed the king in a revival of 'Camelot'.* **2 = describe**, present, depict, evoke, delineate, put in words: *The novelist accurately portrays provincial domestic life.* **3 = represent**, draw, paint, illustrate, sketch, figure, picture, render, depict, delineate: *the landscape as portrayed by painters such as Poussin* **4 = characterize**, describe, represent, depict, paint a mental picture of: *complaints about the way women are portrayed in adverts*

portrayal NOUN **1 = performance**, interpretation, enacting, take *(informal, chiefly U.S.)*, acting, impersonation, performance as, characterization, personation *(rare)*: *He is well known for his portrayal of a prison guard in 'The Last Emperor'.* **2 = depiction**, picture, representation, sketch, rendering, delineation: *a near-monochrome portrayal of a wood infused with silvery light* **3 = description**, account, representation: *an often funny portrayal of a friendship between two boys* **4 = characterization**, representation, depiction: *The media persists in its portrayal of us as muggers and dope sellers.*

pose VERB **1 = present**, cause, produce, create, lead to, result in, constitute, give rise to: *His ill health poses serious problems.* **2 = ask**, state, advance, put, set, submit, put forward, posit, propound: *When I posed the question 'Why?', he merely shrugged.* **3 = position yourself**, sit, model, strike a pose, arrange yourself: *The six foreign ministers posed for photographs.* **4 = put on airs**, affect, posture, show off *(informal)*, strike an attitude, attitudinize: *He criticized them for posing pretentiously.*
▷ NOUN **1 = posture**, position, bearing, attitude, stance, mien *(literary)*: *We have had several sittings in various poses.* **2 = act**, role, façade, air, front, posturing, pretence, masquerade, mannerism, affectation, attitudinizing: *In many writers modesty is a pose, but in him it seems to be genuine.*
pose as something *or* **someone = impersonate**, pretend to be, sham,

P

feign, profess to be, masquerade as, pass yourself off as: *The team posed as drug dealers to trap the ringleaders.*

poser[1] NOUN **= puzzle**, problem, question, riddle, enigma, conundrum, teaser, tough one, vexed question, brain-teaser *(informal)*, knotty point

poser[2] NOUN **= show-off** *(informal)*, poseur, posturer, masquerader, hot dog *(chiefly U.S.)*, impostor, exhibitionist, self-publicist, mannerist, attitudinizer

posh ADJECTIVE **1 = smart**, grand, exclusive, luxury, elegant, fashionable, stylish, luxurious, classy *(slang)*, swish *(informal, chiefly Brit.)*, up-market, swanky *(informal)*, ritzy *(slang)*, schmick *(Austral. informal)*: *I took her to a posh hotel for a cocktail.* **2 = upper-class**, high-class, top-drawer, plummy, high-toned, la-di-da *(informal)*: *He sounded very posh on the phone.*

posit VERB **= put forward**, advance, submit, state, assume, assert, presume, predicate, postulate, propound

position NOUN **1 = location**, place, point, area, post, situation, station, site, spot, bearings, reference, orientation, whereabouts, locality, locale: *The ship's position was reported to the coastguard.* **2 = posture**, attitude, arrangement, pose, stance, disposition: *He had raised himself into a sitting position.* **3 = status**, place, standing, class, footing, station, rank, reputation, importance, consequence, prestige, caste, stature, eminence, repute: *their changing role and position in society* **4 = job**, place, post, opening, office, role, situation, duty, function, employment, capacity, occupation, berth *(informal)*, billet *(informal)*: *He took up a position with the Arts Council.* **5 = place**, standing, rank, status: *The players resumed their battle for the no. 1 position.* **6 = situation**, state, condition, set of circumstances, plight, strait(s), predicament: *He's going to be in a difficult position if things go badly.* **7 = attitude**, view, perspective, point of view, standing, opinion, belief, angle, stance, outlook, posture, viewpoint, slant, way of thinking, standpoint: *He usually takes a moderate position.*
▷ VERB **= place**, put, set, stand, stick *(informal)*, settle, fix, arrange, locate, sequence, array, dispose, lay out: *Position trailing plants near the edges of the basket.*

positive ADJECTIVE **1 = beneficial**, effective, useful, practical, helpful, progressive, productive, worthwhile, constructive, pragmatic, efficacious: *Working abroad should be a positive experience.* **OPPOSITE:** harmful **2 = certain**, sure, convinced, confident, satisfied, assured, free from doubt: *I'm positive she said she'd be here.* **OPPOSITE:** uncertain **3 = definite**, real, clear, firm, certain, direct, express, actual, absolute, concrete, decisive, explicit, affirmative, clear-cut, unmistakable, conclusive, unequivocal, indisputable, categorical, incontrovertible, nailed-on *(slang)*: *There was no positive evidence.* **OPPOSITE:** inconclusive **4 = absolute**, complete, perfect, right *(Brit. informal)*, real, total, rank, sheer, utter, thorough, downright, consummate, veritable, unqualified, out-and-out, unmitigated, thoroughgoing, unalloyed: *He was in a positive fury.*

positively ADVERB **1 = definitely**, surely, firmly, certainly, absolutely, emphatically, unquestionably, undeniably, categorically, unequivocally, unmistakably, with certainty, assuredly, without qualification: *This is positively the worst thing I can imagine.* **2 = really**, completely, simply, plain *(informal)*, absolutely, thoroughly, utterly, downright: *He was positively furious.*

possess VERB **1 = own**, have, hold, be in possession of, be the owner of, have in your possession, have to your name: *He is said to possess a huge fortune.* **2 = be endowed with**, have, enjoy, benefit from, be born with, be blessed with, be possessed of, be gifted with: *individuals who possess the qualities of sense and discretion* **3 = control**, influence, dominate, consume, obsess, bedevil, mesmerize, eat someone up, fixate, put under a spell: *Absolute terror possessed her.* **4 = seize**, hold, control, dominate, occupy, haunt, take someone over, bewitch, take possession of, have power over, have mastery over: *It was as if the spirit of his father possessed him.*

possessed ADJECTIVE **= crazed**, haunted, cursed, obsessed, raving, frenzied, consumed, enchanted, maddened, demented, frenetic, berserk, bewitched, bedevilled, under a spell, hag-ridden

possession NOUN **1 = ownership**, control, custody, hold, hands, tenure, occupancy, proprietorship: *These documents are now in the possession of the authorities.* **2 = province**, territory, colony, dominion, protectorate: *All of these countries were once French possessions.*
▷ PLURAL NOUN **= property**, things, effects, estate, assets, wealth, belongings, chattels, goods and chattels: *People had lost their homes and all their possessions.*

possessive ADJECTIVE **1 = jealous**, controlling, dominating, domineering, proprietorial, overprotective: *Danny could be very jealous and possessive of me.* **2 = selfish**, grasping, acquisitive: *He's very possessive about his toys.*

possibility NOUN **1 = feasibility**, likelihood, plausibility, potentiality, practicability, workableness: *a debate about the possibility of political reform* **2 = likelihood**, chance, risk, odds, prospect, liability, hazard, probability: *There is still a possibility of unrest in the country.* **3** *(often plural)* **= potential**, promise, prospects, talent, capabilities, potentiality: *This situation has great possibilities.*

> QUOTATIONS
> Probable impossibilities are to be preferred to improbable possibilities
> [Aristotle *Poetics*]

possible ADJECTIVE **1 = feasible**, viable, workable, achievable, within reach, on *(informal)*, practicable, attainable, doable, realizable: *Everything is possible if we want it enough.* **OPPOSITE:** unfeasible **2 = likely**, potential, anticipated, probable, odds-on, on the cards: *One possible solution is to take legal action.* **OPPOSITE:** improbable **3 = conceivable**, likely, credible, plausible, hypothetical, imaginable, believable, thinkable: *It's just possible that he was trying to put me off the trip.* **OPPOSITE:** inconceivable **4 = aspiring**, would-be, promising, hopeful, prospective, wannabe *(informal)*: *a possible presidential contender*

> QUOTATIONS
> Everything is possible, including the impossible
> [Benito Mussolini]
>
> With God all things are possible
> [*Bible: St. Matthew*]

> USAGE
> Although it is very common to talk about something's being *very possible* or *more possible*, many people object to such uses, claiming that *possible* describes an absolute state, and therefore something can only be either *possible* or *not possible*. If you want to refer to different degrees of probability, a word such as *likely* or *easy* may be more appropriate than *possible*, for example *it is very likely that he will resign* (not *very possible*).

possibly ADVERB **1 = perhaps**, maybe, God willing, perchance *(archaic)*, mayhap *(archaic)*, peradventure *(archaic)*, haply *(archaic)*: *Exercise may possibly protect against heart attacks.* **2 = at all**, in any way, conceivably, by any means, under any circumstances, by any chance: *I couldn't possibly answer that.*

post[1] NOUN **= support**, stake, pole, stock, standard, column, pale, shaft, upright, pillar, picket, palisade, newel: *Eight wooden posts were driven into the ground.*
▷ VERB **= put up**, announce, publish, display, advertise, proclaim, publicize, promulgate, affix, stick something up, make something known, pin something up: *Officials began posting warning notices.*

post[2] NOUN **1 = job**, place, office, position, situation, employment, appointment, assignment, berth

(informal), billet *(informal)*: *Sir Peter has held several senior military posts.* **2 = position**, place, base, beat, station: *Quick, men, back to your posts!*
▷ VERB **= station**, assign, put, place, position, establish, locate, situate, put on duty: *After training she was posted to Brixton.*

post[3] NOUN **1 = mail**, collection, delivery, postal service, snail mail *(informal)*: *You'll receive your book through the post; rushing to catch the post* **2 = correspondence**, letters, cards, mail: *He flipped through the post without opening any of it.*
▷ VERB **= send (off)**, forward, mail, get off, transmit, dispatch, consign: *I'm posting you a cheque tonight.* **keep someone posted = notify**, brief, advise, inform, report to, keep someone informed, keep someone up to date, apprise, fill someone in on *(informal)*: *Keep me posted on your progress.*

poster NOUN **= notice**, bill, announcement, advertisement, sticker, placard, public notice, affiche *(French)*

posterior NOUN **= bottom**, behind *(informal)*, bum *(Brit. slang)*, seat, rear, tail *(informal)*, butt *(U.S. & Canad. informal)*, buns *(U.S. slang)*, buttocks, backside, rump, rear end, derrière *(euphemistic)*, tush *(U.S. slang)*, fundament, jacksy *(Brit. slang)*: *her curvaceous posterior*
▷ ADJECTIVE **= rear**, back, hinder, hind: *the posterior lobe of the pituitary gland*

posterity NOUN **= the future**, future generations, succeeding generations

postpone VERB **= put off**, delay, suspend, adjourn, table, shelve, defer, put back, hold over, put on ice *(informal)*, put on the back burner *(informal)*, take a rain check on *(U.S. & Canad. informal)* **OPPOSITE:** go ahead with

postponement NOUN **= delay**, stay, suspension, moratorium, respite, adjournment, deferment, deferral

postscript NOUN **= P.S.**, addition, supplement, appendix, afterthought, afterword

postulate VERB **= presuppose**, suppose, advance, propose, assume, put forward, take for granted, predicate, theorize, posit, hypothesize

posture NOUN **1 = bearing**, set, position, attitude, pose, stance, carriage, disposition, mien *(literary)*: *She walked haltingly and her posture was stooped.* **2 = attitude**, feeling, mood, point of view, stance, outlook, inclination, disposition, standpoint, frame of mind: *None of the banks changed their posture on the deal as a result of the inquiry.*
▷ VERB **= show off** *(informal)*, pose, affect, hot-dog *(chiefly U.S.)*, make a show, put on airs, try to attract attention, attitudinize, do something for effect

posy NOUN **= bouquet**, spray, buttonhole, corsage, nosegay, boutonniere

pot NOUN **1 = container**, bowl, pan, vessel, basin, vase, jug, cauldron, urn, utensil, crock, skillet, potjie *(S. African)*: *metal cooking pots; Use a large terracotta pot or a wooden tub.* **2 = jackpot**, bank, prize, stakes, purse: *The pot for this Saturday's draw stands at over £18 million.* **3 = kitty**, funds, pool: *If there is more money in the pot, all the members will benefit proportionally.* **4 = paunch**, beer belly *or* gut *(informal)*, spread *(informal)*, corporation *(informal)*, gut, bulge, spare tyre *(Brit. slang)*, pot belly: *He's already developing a pot from all the beer he drinks.*

pot-bellied ADJECTIVE **= fat**, overweight, bloated, obese, distended, corpulent, paunchy

pot belly NOUN **= paunch**, beer belly *or* gut *(informal)*, spread *(informal)*, corporation *(informal)*, pot, gut, spare tyre *(Brit. slang)*, middle-age spread *(informal)*, puku *(N.Z.)*

potency NOUN **1 = influence**, might, force, control, authority, energy, potential, strength, capacity, mana *(N.Z.)*: *the extraordinary potency of his personality* **2 = persuasiveness**, force, strength, muscle, effectiveness, sway, forcefulness, cogency, impressiveness: *His remarks have added potency given the current situation.* **3 = power**, force, strength, effectiveness, efficacy: *The potency of the wine increases with time.* **4 = vigour**, puissance: *Alcohol abuse in men can reduce sexual potency.*

potent ADJECTIVE **1 = powerful**, commanding, dynamic, dominant, influential, authoritative: *a potent political force* **2 = persuasive**, telling, convincing, effective, impressive, compelling, forceful, cogent: *a potent electoral message* **OPPOSITE:** unconvincing **3 = strong**, powerful, mighty, vigorous, forceful, efficacious, puissant: *The drug is extremely potent, but can have unpleasant side-effects.* **OPPOSITE:** weak

potentate NOUN **= ruler**, king, prince, emperor, monarch, sovereign, mogul, overlord

potential ADJECTIVE **1 = possible**, future, likely, promising, budding, embryonic, undeveloped, unrealized, probable: *potential customers* **2 = hidden**, possible, inherent, dormant, latent: *We are aware of the potential dangers.*
▷ NOUN **= ability**, possibilities, capacity, capability, the makings, what it takes *(informal)*, aptitude, wherewithal, potentiality: *The boy has potential.*

potion NOUN **= concoction**, mixture, brew, tonic, cup, dose, draught, elixir, philtre

potter VERB *(usually with* **around** *or* **about**) **= mess about**, fiddle *(informal)*, tinker, dabble, fritter, footle *(informal)*, poke along, fribble

pottery NOUN **= ceramics**, terracotta, crockery, earthenware, stoneware

potty ADJECTIVE **= crazy**, eccentric, crackers *(Brit. slang)*, barmy *(slang)*, touched, soft *(informal)*, silly, foolish, daft *(informal)*, off-the-wall *(slang)*, oddball *(informal)*, off the rails, dotty *(slang, chiefly Brit.)*, loopy *(informal)*, crackpot *(informal)*, out to lunch *(informal)*, dippy *(slang)*, gonzo *(slang)*, doolally *(slang)*, off your trolley *(slang)*, up the pole *(informal)*, off your chump *(slang)*, wacko *or* whacko *(informal)*, off the air *(Austral. slang)*, porangi *(N.Z.)*, daggy *(Austral. & N.Z. informal)*

pouch NOUN **= bag**, pocket, sack, container, purse, poke *(dialect)*

pounce VERB **= attack**, strike, jump, leap, swoop: *Before I could get to the pigeon, the cat pounced.*

pound[1] NOUN **= enclosure**, yard, pen, compound, kennels, corral *(chiefly U.S. & Canad.)*: *The dog has been sent to the pound.*

pound[2] VERB **1** *(sometimes with* **on**) **= beat**, strike, hammer, batter, thrash, thump, pelt, clobber *(slang)*, pummel, belabour, beat *or* knock seven bells out of *(informal)*, beat the living daylights out of: *He pounded the table with his fist.* **2 = crush**, powder, bruise, bray *(dialect)*, pulverize: *She paused as she pounded the maize grains.* **3 = pulsate**, beat, pulse, throb, palpitate, pitapat: *I'm sweating and my heart is pounding.* **4** *(often with* **out**) **= thump**, beat, hammer, bang: *A group of tribal drummers pounded out an unrelenting beat.* **5 = stomp**, tramp, march, thunder *(informal)*, clomp: *I pounded up the stairs to my room and slammed the door.*

pour VERB **1 = let flow**, spill, splash, dribble, drizzle, slop *(informal)*, slosh *(informal)*, decant: *Francis poured a generous measure of whisky into the glass.* **2 = flow**, stream, run, course, rush, emit, cascade, gush, spout, spew: *Blood was pouring from his broken nose.* **3 = rain**, sheet, pelt (down), teem, bucket down *(informal)*, rain cats and dogs *(informal)*, come down in torrents, rain hard *or* heavily: *It has been pouring all week.* **4 = stream**, crowd, flood, swarm, gush, throng, teem: *The northern forces poured across the border.*

> **USAGE**
> The spelling of *pour* (as in *she poured cream on her strudel*) should be carefully distinguished from that of *pore over* or *through* (as in *she pored over the manuscript*).

pout VERB **= sulk**, glower, mope, look sullen, purse your lips, look petulant, pull a long face, lour *or* lower, make a moue, turn down the corners of your mouth: *He whined and pouted like a kid when he didn't get what he wanted.*
▷ NOUN **= sullen look**, glower, long face, moue *(French)*: *She jutted her lower lip out in a pout.*

poverty NOUN **1 = pennilessness**, want, need, distress, necessity, hardship, insolvency, privation, penury, destitution, hand-to-mouth existence, beggary, indigence, pauperism, necessitousness: *41 per cent of Brazilians live in absolute poverty.* **OPPOSITE:** wealth **2 = scarcity**, lack, absence, want, deficit, shortage, deficiency, inadequacy, dearth, paucity, insufficiency, sparsity: *a poverty of ideas* **OPPOSITE:** abundance **3 = barrenness**, deficiency, infertility, sterility, aridity, bareness, poorness, meagreness, unfruitfulness: *the poverty of the soil* **OPPOSITE:** fertility

QUOTATIONS

The greatest of evils and the worst of crimes is poverty
[George Bernard Shaw *Major Barbara*]

Anyone who has ever struggled with poverty knows how extremely expensive it is to be poor
[James Baldwin *Nobody Knows My Name*]

Give me not poverty lest I steal
[Daniel Defoe *Review (later incorporated into Moll Flanders)*]

The want of money is the root of all evil
[Samuel Butler *Erewhon*]

No man should commend poverty unless he is poor
[Saint Bernard]

People don't resent having nothing nearly as much as too little
[Ivy Compton-Burnett *A Family and a Fortune*]

PROVERBS

Poverty is not a crime

poverty-stricken ADJECTIVE **= penniless**, broke *(informal)*, bankrupt, impoverished, short, poor, distressed, beggared, needy, destitute, down and out, skint *(Brit. slang)*, indigent, down at heel, impecunious, dirt-poor *(informal)*, on the breadline, flat broke *(informal)*, penurious, on your uppers, stony-broke *(Brit. slang)*, in queer street, without two pennies to rub together *(informal)*, on your beam-ends

powder NOUN **= dust**, pounce *(rare)*, talc, fine grains, loose particles: *a fine white powder*
▷ VERB **1 = dust**, cover, scatter, sprinkle, strew, dredge: *Powder the puddings with icing sugar.* **2 = grind**, crush, pound, pestle, pulverize, granulate: *Mix all the powdered ingredients together.*

powdery ADJECTIVE **= fine**, dry, sandy, dusty, loose, crumbling, grainy, chalky, crumbly, granular, pulverized, friable

power NOUN **1 = control**, authority, influence, command, sovereignty, sway, dominance, domination, supremacy, mastery, dominion, ascendancy, mana *(N.Z.)*: *women who have reached positions of great power and influence* **2 = ability**, capacity, faculty, property, potential, capability, competence, competency: *He was so drunk that he had lost the power of speech.* **OPPOSITE:** inability **3 = authority**, right, licence, privilege, warrant, prerogative, authorization: *The Prime Minister has the power to dismiss senior ministers.* **4 = strength**, might, energy, weight, muscle, vigour, potency, brawn, hard power: *He had no power in his left arm.* **OPPOSITE:** weakness **5 = forcefulness**, force, strength, punch *(informal)*, intensity, potency, eloquence, persuasiveness, cogency, powerfulness: *the power of his rhetoric*

powerful ADJECTIVE **1 = influential**, dominant, controlling, commanding, supreme, prevailing, sovereign, authoritative, puissant, skookum *(Canad.)*: *You're a powerful woman – people will listen to you.* **OPPOSITE:** powerless **2 = strong**, strapping, mighty, robust, vigorous, potent, energetic, sturdy, stalwart: *a big, powerful man* **OPPOSITE:** weak **3 = persuasive**, convincing, effective, telling, moving, striking, storming, dramatic, impressive, compelling, authoritative, forceful, weighty, forcible, cogent, effectual: *a powerful drama about a corrupt city leader*

powerfully ADVERB **= strongly**, hard, vigorously, forcibly, forcefully, mightily, with might and main

powerless ADJECTIVE **1 = defenceless**, vulnerable, dependent, subject, tied, ineffective, unarmed, disenfranchised, over a barrel *(informal)*, disfranchised: *political systems that keep women poor and powerless* **2 = weak**, disabled, helpless, incapable, paralysed, frail, feeble, debilitated, impotent, ineffectual, incapacitated, prostrate, infirm, etiolated: *His leg muscles were powerless with lack of use.* **OPPOSITE:** strong

practicable ADJECTIVE **= feasible**, possible, viable, workable, achievable, attainable, doable, within the realm of possibility, performable **OPPOSITE:** unfeasible

practical ADJECTIVE **1 = functional**, efficient, realistic, pragmatic: *practical suggestions on how to improve your diet* **OPPOSITE:** impractical **2 = empirical**, real, applied, actual, hands-on, in the field, experimental, factual: *theories based on practical knowledge* **OPPOSITE:** theoretical **3 = sensible**, ordinary, realistic, down-to-earth, mundane, matter-of-fact, no-nonsense, businesslike, hard-headed, workaday, grounded: *She is always so practical and full of common sense.* **OPPOSITE:** impractical **4 = feasible**, possible, sound, viable, constructive, workable, practicable, doable: *We do not yet have any practical way to prevent cancer.* **OPPOSITE:** impractical **5 = useful**, ordinary, appropriate, sensible, everyday, functional, utilitarian, serviceable: *clothes which are practical as well as stylish* **6 = skilled**, working, seasoned, trained, experienced, qualified, veteran, efficient, accomplished, proficient: *people with practical experience of running businesses* **OPPOSITE:** inexperienced

USAGE

A distinction is usually made between *practical* and *practicable*. *Practical* refers to a person, idea, project, etc, as being more concerned with or relevant to practice than theory: *he is a very practical person; the idea had no practical application*. *Practicable* refers to a project or idea as being capable of being done or put into effect: *the plan was expensive, yet practicable*.

practically ADVERB **1 = almost**, nearly, close to, essentially, virtually, basically, fundamentally, all but, just about, in effect, very nearly, to all intents and purposes, well-nigh: *He'd known the old man practically all his life.* **2 = sensibly**, reasonably, matter-of-factly, realistically, rationally, pragmatically, with common sense, unsentimentally: *'Let me help you to bed,' Helen said, practically.*

practice NOUN **1 = custom**, use, way, system, rule, method, tradition, habit, routine, mode, usage, wont, praxis, usual procedure, tikanga *(N.Z.)*: *a public inquiry into bank practices* **2 = training**, study, exercise, work-out, discipline, preparation, drill, rehearsal, repetition: *netball practice* **3 = profession**, work, business, career, occupation, pursuit, vocation: *improving his skills in the practice of medicine* **4 = business**, company, office, firm, enterprise, partnership, outfit *(informal)*: *He worked in a small legal practice.* **5 = use**, experience, action, effect, operation, application, enactment: *attempts to encourage the practice of safe sex*

practise VERB **1 = rehearse**, study, prepare, perfect, repeat, go through, polish, go over, refine, run through: *Lauren practises the concerto every day.* **2 = do**, train, exercise, work out, drill, warm up, keep your hand in: *practising for a gym display* **3 = carry out**, follow, apply, perform, observe, engage in, live up to, put into practice: *Astronomy continued to be practised in Byzantium.* **4 = work at**, pursue, carry on, undertake, specialize in, ply your trade: *He practised as a lawyer for thirty years.*

practised ADJECTIVE **= skilled**, trained, experienced, seasoned, able, expert, qualified, accomplished, versed, proficient **OPPOSITE:** inexperienced

pragmatic ADJECTIVE **= practical**, efficient, sensible, realistic, down-to-earth, matter-of-fact, utilitarian, businesslike, hard-headed **OPPOSITE:** idealistic

praise VERB **1 = acclaim**, approve of, honour, cheer, admire, applaud, compliment, congratulate, pay tribute to, laud, extol, sing the praises

The Language of Thomas Hardy

Thomas Hardy (1840–1928) was a novelist and poet whose work is deeply grounded in the rural West of England where he was born and lived most of his life. Although he considered himself primarily a poet, Hardy's fiction is firmly established among the great achievements of English literature. Such classics as *Tess of the D'Urbervilles* and *Jude the Obscure* are substantial and tragic, and reveal what is often considered a pessimistic turn of mind.

In his novels Hardy transformed his native region into the fictional county of Wessex. With a consistent focus on the lives of the rural working class, his writing is notable for extensive use of the idioms of West Country speech. Specific features of the 'Wessex tongue', as it is described in *Jude the Obscure*, include the use of *en* usually as a substitute for *him*:

> O, sure. Now I know **en** as well as any man can be known. And you know **en** very well too, don't ye.

Past participles of strong verbs often appear in the dialect of Hardy's characters in a weak form. For example, *saw* becomes *seed* and *knew* becomes *knowed*. Abbreviations such as *wi'* for *with* and *ha'* for *have* are another common feature, along with contractions like *t'other* for *the other* or *'tis* for *it is*.

Another element of the specific texture of Hardy's writing is his use of proper nouns. The names he assigns to his characters are unusual, vivid, and expressive. *The Return of the Native*, for instance, boasts Clym Yeobright, Eustacia Vye, Damon Wildeve, Diggory Venn, and Susan Nunsuch. Hints of the organic and agricultural are frequently embedded in such names. The *yeo* of Yeobright, for example, subtly recalling the yeomen who populate Hardy's Wessex. Gabriel Oak and Fanny Robin from *Far From the Madding Crowd* provide a more explicit illustration of the natural world's significant role in Hardy's work. Place names reveal a comparably lyrical register, although they generally refer to existing towns and villages in the West of England. Sandbourne, Knollsea, and Kingsbere are examples of the poetic feel of Hardy's places.

Hardy's interest in the landscape and rural occupations of his Wessex is often conveyed in extended descriptive passages. A characteristic feature of Hardy's descriptions is the coinage of compound words that add detail and emotional texture to his prose, by, for example, combining a verb and a noun as in:

> ...there was nothing left for her to do but to continue upon that **starve-acre** farm till she could again summon courage to face the Vicarage.

Other similar manipulations of language are particularly common in Hardy's poetry, where he at times uses adjectives as verbs, such as:

> he **darked** my cottage door.

Sentences in Hardy's fiction can be very long and can run to several clauses. An aspect of this wordiness is the use of a chain of adjectives, rather than a single descriptor:

> The irresistible, universal, automatic tendency to find sweet pleasure somewhere...

Sound, music, and voice form an important motif in Hardy's work; indeed, 'The Voice' is the title of one of his most famous poems. Across his work by far the most common adjective with *voice* is *low*. Similarly, *faint*, *slight*, and *only* occur most commonly with *sound*. This emphasis on quietness is also expressed in Hardy's usage of the verb *hear*. The most salient modifiers of *hear* are *not*, followed by *never*, with *distinctly* much less common, indicating the prominence of silence in Hardy's work in addition to the lowness of *voice*. Conversely, *silence* figures most strongly as the object of the verb *break*, with *keep silence* being considerably less frequent.

of, pat someone on the back, cry someone up, big up *(slang)*, eulogize, take your hat off to, crack someone up *(informal)*: *Many praised him for taking a strong stand.* **OPPOSITE:** criticize **2 = give thanks to**, bless, worship, adore, magnify *(archaic)*, glorify, exalt, pay homage to: *She asked the congregation to praise God.*
▷ NOUN **1 = approval**, acclaim, applause, cheering, tribute, compliment, congratulations, ovation, accolade, good word, kudos, eulogy, commendation, approbation, acclamation, panegyric, encomium, plaudit, laudation: *I have nothing but praise for the police.* **OPPOSITE:** criticism **2 = thanks**, glory, worship, devotion, homage, adoration: *Hindus were singing hymns in praise of the god Rama.*

prance VERB **1 = dance**, bound, leap, trip, spring, jump, skip, romp, caper, cavort, frisk, gambol, cut a rug *(informal)*: *The cheerleaders pranced on the far side of the pitch.* **2 = strut**, parade, stalk, show off *(informal)*, swagger, swank *(informal)*: *models prancing around on the catwalk*

prank NOUN **= trick**, lark *(informal)*, caper, frolic, escapade, practical joke, skylarking *(informal)*, antic, jape

prattle VERB **= chatter**, babble, waffle *(informal, chiefly Brit.)*, run on, rabbit on *(Brit. informal)*, witter on *(informal)*, patter, drivel, clack, twitter, jabber, gabble, rattle on, blather, blether, run off at the mouth *(slang)*, earbash *(Austral. & N.Z. slang)*: *She prattled on until I wanted to scream.*
▷ NOUN **= chatter**, talk, babble, waffle *(informal)*, rambling, wittering *(informal)*, prating, drivel, jabber, gabble, blather, blether: *I had had enough of his mindless prattle.*

pray VERB **1 = say your prayers**, offer a prayer, recite the rosary: *He spent his time in prison praying and studying.* **2 = beg**, ask, plead, petition, urge, request, sue, crave, invoke, call upon, cry, solicit, implore, beseech, entreat, importune, adjure, supplicate: *They prayed for help.*

> **QUOTATIONS**
> pray: to ask that the laws of the universe be annulled in behalf of a single petitioner confessedly unworthy
> [Ambrose Bierce *The Devil's Dictionary*]

prayer NOUN **1 = supplication**, devotion, communion: *The night was spent in prayer and meditation.* **2 = orison**, litany, invocation, intercession: *prayers of thanksgiving* **3 = plea**, appeal, suit, request, petition, entreaty, supplication: *Say a quick prayer I don't get stopped for speeding.*

> **QUOTATIONS**
> More things are wrought by prayer
> Than this world dreams of
> [Alfred, Lord Tennyson *Morte d'Arthur*]
>
> When the gods wish to punish us
> they answer our prayers
> [Oscar Wilde *An Ideal Husband*]
>
> The wish for prayer is a prayer in itself
> [Georges Bernanos *Journal d'un cure de campagne*]
>
> In prayer the lips ne'er act the winning part,
> Without the sweet concurrence of the heart
> [Robert Herrick *The Heart*]
>
> One single grateful thought raised to heaven is the most perfect prayer
> [G.E. Lessing *Minna von Barnhelm*]

preach VERB **1** *(often with* **to***)* **= deliver a sermon**, address, exhort, evangelize, preach a sermon, orate: *The bishop preached to a huge crowd.* **2 = urge**, teach, champion, recommend, advise, counsel, advocate, exhort: *The movement preaches revolution.*

preacher NOUN **= clergyman**, minister, parson, missionary, evangelist, revivalist

preamble NOUN **= introduction**, prelude, preface, foreword, overture, opening move, proem, prolegomenon, exordium, opening statement *or* remarks

precarious ADJECTIVE **1 = insecure**, dangerous, uncertain, tricky, risky, doubtful, dubious, unsettled, dodgy *(Brit., Austral. & N.Z. informal)*, unstable, unsure, hazardous, shaky, hairy *(slang)*, perilous, touch and go, dicey *(informal, chiefly Brit.)*, chancy *(informal)*, built on sand, shonky *(Austral. & N.Z. informal)*: *Our financial situation had become precarious.* **OPPOSITE:** secure **2 = dangerous**, unstable, shaky, slippery, insecure, unsafe, unreliable, unsteady: *They crawled up a precarious rope ladder.* **OPPOSITE:** stable

precaution NOUN **= safeguard**, insurance, protection, provision, safety measure, preventative measure, belt and braces *(informal)*: *This is purely a safety precaution.*

precede VERB **1 = go before**, introduce, herald, pave the way for, usher in, antedate, antecede, forerun: *Intensive negotiations preceded the vote.* **2 = go ahead of**, lead, head, go before, take precedence: *Alice preceded them from the room.* **3 = preface**, introduce, go before, launch, prefix: *the information that precedes the paragraph in question*

precedence NOUN **= priority**, lead, rank, preference, superiority, supremacy, seniority, primacy, pre-eminence, antecedence

precedent NOUN **= instance**, example, authority, standard, model, pattern, criterion, prototype, paradigm, antecedent, exemplar, previous example

preceding ADJECTIVE **1 = previous**, earlier, former, above, foregoing, aforementioned, anterior, aforesaid: *Please refer back to the preceding chapter.* **2 = past**, earlier, former, prior, foregoing: *the student revolution of the preceding years*

precept NOUN **1 = rule**, order, law, direction, principle, command, regulation, instruction, decree, mandate, canon, statute, ordinance, commandment, behest, dictum: *the precepts of Buddhism* **2 = maxim**, saying, rule, principle, guideline, motto, dictum, axiom, byword: *the precept, 'If a job's worth doing, it's worth doing well'*

precinct NOUN **= area**, quarter, section, sector, district, zone: *a pedestrian precinct*
▷ PLURAL NOUN **= district**, limits, region, borders, bounds, boundaries, confines, neighbourhood, milieu, surrounding area, environs, purlieus: *No-one carrying arms is allowed within the precincts of the temple.*

precious ADJECTIVE **1 = valuable**, expensive, rare, fine, choice, prized, dear, costly, high-priced, exquisite, invaluable, priceless, recherché, inestimable: *jewellery and precious objects belonging to her mother* **OPPOSITE:** worthless **2 = loved**, valued, favourite, prized, dear, dearest, treasured, darling, beloved, adored, cherished, fave *(informal)*, idolized, worth your *or* its weight in gold: *her most precious possession* **3 = affected**, artificial, fastidious, twee *(Brit. informal)*, chichi, overrefined, overnice: *Actors, he decided, were all precious and neurotic.*

precipice NOUN **= cliff**, crag, rock face, cliff face, height, brink, bluff, sheer drop, steep cliff, scarp

precipitate VERB **1 = quicken**, trigger, accelerate, further, press, advance, hurry, dispatch, speed up, bring on, hasten, push forward, expedite: *The killings in the city have precipitated the worst crisis yet.* **2 = throw**, launch, cast, discharge, hurl, fling, let fly, send forth: *Dust was precipitated into the air.*
▷ ADJECTIVE **1 = hasty**, hurried, frantic, rash, reckless, impulsive, madcap, ill-advised, precipitous, impetuous, indiscreet, heedless, harum-scarum: *I don't think we should make any precipitate decisions.* **2 = sudden**, quick, brief, rushing, violent, plunging, rapid, unexpected, swift, abrupt, without warning, headlong, breakneck: *the precipitate collapse of European communism*

precipitous ADJECTIVE **1 = sheer**, high, steep, dizzy, abrupt, perpendicular, falling sharply: *a steep, precipitous cliff* **2 = hasty**, sudden, hurried, precipitate, abrupt, harum-scarum: *the stock market's precipitous drop*

> **USAGE**
> Some people think the use of *precipitous* to mean 'hasty' is incorrect, and that *precipitate* should be used instead.

precise ADJECTIVE **1 = exact**, specific, actual, particular, express, fixed, correct, absolute, accurate, explicit, definite, clear-cut, literal,

p

unequivocal, surgical: *We will never know the precise details of his death.* **OPPOSITE:** vague **2 = strict**, particular, exact, nice, formal, careful, stiff, rigid, meticulous, inflexible, scrupulous, fastidious, prim, puritanical, finicky, punctilious, ceremonious: *They speak very precise English.* **OPPOSITE:** inexact

precisely ADVERB **1 = exactly**, bang on, squarely, correctly, absolutely, strictly, accurately, plumb *(informal)*, slap on *(informal)*, square on, on the dot, smack on *(informal)*: *The meeting began at precisely 4.00 p.m.* **2 = just so**, yes, absolutely, exactly, quite so, you bet *(informal)*, without a doubt, on the button *(informal)*, indubitably: *'Is that what you meant?' – 'Precisely.'* **3 = just**, entirely, absolutely, altogether, exactly, in all respects: *That is precisely what I suggested.* **4 = word for word**, literally, exactly, to the letter, neither more nor less: *Please repeat precisely what she said.*

precision NOUN **= exactness**, care, accuracy, fidelity, correctness, rigour, nicety, particularity, exactitude, meticulousness, definiteness, dotting the i's and crossing the t's, preciseness

preclude VERB **1 = rule out**, put a stop to, obviate, make impossible, make impracticable: *At 84, John feels his age precludes much travelling.* **2 = prevent**, stop, check, exclude, restrain, prohibit, inhibit, hinder, forestall, debar: *Poor English precluded them from ever finding a job.*

precocious ADJECTIVE **= advanced**, developed, forward, quick, bright, smart **OPPOSITE:** backward

preconceived ADJECTIVE **= presumed**, premature, predetermined, presupposed, prejudged, forejudged

preconception NOUN **= preconceived idea** *or* **notion**, notion, prejudice, bias, presumption, predisposition, presupposition, prepossession

precondition NOUN **= necessity**, essential, requirement, prerequisite, must, sine qua non *(Latin)*, must-have

precursor NOUN **1 = forerunner**, pioneer, predecessor, forebear, antecedent, originator: *Real tennis, a precursor of the modern game, originated in the eleventh century.* **2 = herald**, usher, messenger, vanguard, forerunner, harbinger: *The deal should not be seen as a precursor to a merger.*

predatory ADJECTIVE **1 = hunting**, ravening, carnivorous, rapacious, raptorial, predacious: *predatory birds like the eagle* **2 = plundering**, ravaging, pillaging, marauding, thieving, despoiling: *predatory gangs* **3 = rapacious**, greedy, voracious, vulturous, vulturine: *predatory business practices*

predecessor NOUN **1 = previous job holder**, precursor, forerunner, antecedent, former job holder, prior job holder: *He learned everything he knew from his predecessor.* **2 = ancestor**, forebear, antecedent, forefather, tupuna *or* tipuna *(N.Z.)*: *opportunities our predecessors never had*

predetermined ADJECTIVE **1 = fated**, predestined, preordained, meant, doomed, foreordained, pre-elected, predestinated: *our predetermined fate* **2 = prearranged**, set, agreed, set up, settled, fixed, cut and dried *(informal)*, preplanned, decided beforehand, arranged in advance: *The capsules release the drug at a predetermined time.*

predicament NOUN **= fix** *(informal)*, state, situation, spot *(informal)*, corner, hole *(slang)*, emergency, mess, jam *(informal)*, dilemma, pinch, plight, scrape *(informal)*, hot water *(informal)*, pickle *(informal)*, how-do-you-do *(informal)*, quandary, tight spot

predict VERB **= foretell**, forecast, divine, foresee, prophesy, call, augur, presage, portend, prognosticate, forebode, soothsay, vaticinate *(rare)*

> **QUOTATIONS**
> You can only predict things after they happen
> [Eugène Ionesco]

predictable ADJECTIVE **= likely**, expected, sure, certain, anticipated, reliable, foreseen, on the cards, foreseeable, sure-fire *(informal)*, calculable **OPPOSITE:** unpredictable

prediction NOUN **= prophecy**, forecast, prognosis, divination, prognostication, augury, soothsaying, sortilege

predilection NOUN **= liking**, love, taste, weakness, fancy, leaning, tendency, preference, bias, inclination, penchant, fondness, propensity, predisposition, proclivity, partiality, proneness

predispose VERB **= incline**, influence, prepare, prompt, lead, prime, affect, prejudice, bias, induce, dispose, sway, make you of a mind to

predisposed ADJECTIVE **1 = inclined**, willing, given, minded, ready, agreeable, amenable: *Franklin was predisposed to believe him.* **2 = susceptible**, subject, prone, liable: *Some people are genetically predisposed to diabetes.*

predisposition NOUN **1 = inclination**, tendency, disposition, bent, bias, willingness, likelihood, penchant, propensity, predilection, proclivity, potentiality, proneness: *the predisposition to behave in a certain way* **2 = susceptibility**, tendency, proneness: *a hereditary predisposition to the disease*

predominance NOUN **1 = prevalence**, weight, preponderance, greater number: *An interesting note was the predominance of London club players.* **2 = dominance**, hold, control, edge, leadership, sway, supremacy, mastery, dominion, upper hand, ascendancy, paramountcy: *their economic predominance*

predominant ADJECTIVE **1 = main**, chief, prevailing, notable, paramount, prevalent, preponderant: *Amanda's predominant emotion was one of confusion.* **2 = principal**, leading, important, prime, controlling, ruling, chief, capital, primary, supreme, prominent, superior, dominant, sovereign, top-priority, ascendant: *He played a predominant role in shaping French economic policy* **OPPOSITE:** minor

predominantly ADVERB **= mainly**, largely, chiefly, mostly, generally, principally, primarily, on the whole, in the main, for the most part, to a great extent, preponderantly

predominate VERB **1 = be in the majority**, dominate, prevail, stand out, be predominant, be most noticeable, preponderate: *All nationalities were represented, but the English and American predominated.* **2 = prevail**, rule, reign, hold sway, get the upper hand, carry weight: *a society where Islamic principles predominate*

pre-eminence NOUN **= superiority**, distinction, excellence, supremacy, prestige, prominence, transcendence, renown, predominance, paramountcy

pre-eminent ADJECTIVE **= outstanding**, supreme, paramount, chief, excellent, distinguished, superior, renowned, foremost, consummate, predominant, transcendent, unrivalled, incomparable, peerless, unsurpassed, unequalled, matchless

preen VERB **1** *(often reflexive)* **= smarten**, admire, dress up, doll up *(slang)*, trim, array, deck out, spruce up, prettify, primp, trig *(archaic, dialect)*, titivate, prink: *He spent half an hour preening in front of the mirror; 20 minutes preening themselves every morning* **2 = clean**, smooth, groom, tidy, plume: *The linnet shook herself and preened a few feathers on her breast.*

preen yourself = pride yourself, congratulate yourself, give yourself a pat on the back, pique yourself, plume yourself: *His only negative feature is the desire to brag and preen himself over his abilities.*

preface NOUN **= introduction**, preliminary, prelude, preamble, foreword, prologue, proem, prolegomenon, exordium: *the preface to the English edition of the novel*
▷ VERB **= introduce**, precede, open, begin, launch, lead up to, prefix: *I will preface what I am going to say with a few lines from Shakespeare.*

prefer VERB **1 = like better**, favour, go for, pick, select, adopt, fancy, opt for, single out, plump for, incline towards, be partial to: *Do you prefer a particular sort of music?* **2 = choose**, elect, opt for, pick, wish, desire, would

P

rather, would sooner, incline towards: *I prefer to go on self-catering holidays.*

preferable ADJECTIVE **= better**, best, chosen, choice, preferred, recommended, favoured, superior, worthier, more suitable, more desirable, more eligible
OPPOSITE: undesirable

> **USAGE**
> Since *preferable* already means 'more desirable', it is better when writing not to say something is *more preferable* or *most preferable*.

preferably ADVERB **= ideally**, if possible, rather, sooner, much rather, by choice, much sooner, as a matter of choice, in *or* for preference

preference NOUN **1 = liking**, wish, taste, desire, bag *(slang)*, leaning, bent, bias, cup of tea *(informal)*, inclination, penchant, fondness, predisposition, predilection, proclivity, partiality: *Whatever your preference, we have a product to suit you.* **2 = first choice**, choice, favourite, election, pick, option, selection, top of the list, fave *(informal)*: *He enjoys all styles of music, but his preference is opera.* **3 = priority**, first place, precedence, advantage, favouritism, pride of place, favoured treatment: *Candidates with the right qualifications should be given preference.*

preferential ADJECTIVE **= privileged**, favoured, superior, better, special, partial, partisan, advantageous

prefigure VERB **= foreshadow**, suggest, indicate, intimate, presage, portend, shadow forth, adumbrate, foretoken

P

pregnancy NOUN **= gestation**, gravidity
▸ *related adjectives:* antenatal, postnatal, maternity

pregnant ADJECTIVE **1 = expectant**, expecting *(informal)*, with child, in the club *(Brit. slang)*, in the family way *(informal)*, gravid, preggers *(Brit. informal)*, enceinte, in the pudding club *(slang)*, big *or* heavy with child: *Tina was pregnant with their first child.* **2 = meaningful**, pointed, charged, significant, telling, loaded, expressive, eloquent, weighty, suggestive: *There was a long, pregnant silence.* **3** (with **with**) **= full of**, rich in, fraught with, teeming with, replete with, abounding in, abundant in, fecund with: *The songs are pregnant with irony and insight.*

prehistoric ADJECTIVE **= earliest**, early, primitive, primordial, primeval

prejudice NOUN **1 = discrimination**, racism, injustice, sexism, intolerance, bigotry, unfairness, chauvinism, narrow-mindedness, faith hate: *a victim of racial prejudice* **2 = bias**, preconception, partiality, preconceived notion, warp, jaundiced eye, prejudgment: *the male prejudices which Dr Greer identifies* **3 = harm**, damage, hurt, disadvantage, loss, mischief, detriment, impairment: *I feel sure it can be done without prejudice to anybody's principles.*
▷ VERB **1 = bias**, influence, colour, poison, distort, sway, warp, slant, predispose, jaundice, prepossess: *I think your upbringing has prejudiced you.* **2 = harm**, damage, hurt, injure, mar, undermine, spoil, impair, hinder, crool *or* cruel *(Austral. slang)*: *He claimed that the media coverage had prejudiced his chance of a fair trial.*

> **QUOTATIONS**
> Drive out prejudices through the door, and they will return through the window
> [Frederick the Great *letter to Voltaire*]
>
> prejudice: a vagrant opinion without visible means of support
> [Ambrose Bierce *The Devil's Dictionary*]
>
> Who's 'im, Bill?
> A stranger!
> 'Eave 'arf a brick at 'im
> [*Punch*]

prejudiced ADJECTIVE **= biased**, influenced, unfair, one-sided, conditioned, partial, partisan, discriminatory, bigoted, intolerant, opinionated, narrow-minded, jaundiced, prepossessed
OPPOSITE: unbiased

prejudicial ADJECTIVE **= harmful**, damaging, undermining, detrimental, hurtful, unfavourable, counterproductive, deleterious, injurious, inimical, disadvantageous

preliminary ADJECTIVE **1 = first**, opening, trial, initial, test, pilot, prior, introductory, preparatory, exploratory, initiatory, prefatory, precursory: *Preliminary talks began yesterday.* **2 = qualifying**, eliminating: *the last match of the preliminary rounds*
▷ NOUN **= introduction**, opening, beginning, foundation, start, preparation, first round, prelude, preface, overture, initiation, preamble, groundwork, prelims: *Today's survey is a preliminary to a more detailed one.*

prelude NOUN **1 = introduction**, beginning, preparation, preliminary, start, commencement, curtain-raiser: *The protests are now seen as the prelude to last year's uprising.* **2 = overture**, opening, introduction, introductory movement: *the third-act Prelude of Parsifal*

premature ADJECTIVE **1 = early**, untimely, before time, unseasonable: *a twenty-four-year-old man suffering from premature baldness* **2 = hasty**, rash, too soon, precipitate, impulsive, untimely, ill-considered, jumping the gun, ill-timed, inopportune, overhasty: *It now seems their optimism was premature.* **3 = preterm**, prem *(informal)*, preemie *(U.S. & Canad. informal)*: *a greater risk of having a premature baby*

prematurely ADVERB **1 = too early**, too soon, before your time, preterm: *Danny was born prematurely.* **2 = overhastily**, rashly, too soon, precipitately, too hastily, half-cocked, at half-cock: *He may have spoken just a little prematurely.*

premeditated ADJECTIVE **= planned**, calculated, deliberate, considered, studied, intended, conscious, contrived, intentional, wilful, aforethought, prepense
OPPOSITE: unplanned

premier NOUN **= head of government**, prime minister, chancellor, chief minister, P.M.: *Australia's premier Paul Keating*
▷ ADJECTIVE **= chief**, leading, top, first, highest, head, main, prime, primary, principal, arch, foremost: *the country's premier opera company*

premiere NOUN **= first night**, opening, debut, first showing, first performance

premise NOUN **= assumption**, proposition, thesis, ground, argument, hypothesis, assertion, postulate, supposition, presupposition, postulation: *the premise that men and women are on equal terms in this society*

premises PLURAL NOUN **= building(s)**, place, office, property, site, establishment

premium NOUN **1 = fee**, charge, payment, instalment: *an increase in insurance premiums* **2 = surcharge**, extra charge, additional fee *or* charge: *Customers are not willing to pay a premium.* **3 = bonus**, reward, prize, percentage *(informal)*, perk *(Brit. informal)*, boon, bounty, remuneration, recompense, perquisite: *Shareholders did not receive a premium on the price of their shares.*
at a premium = in great demand, valuable, expensive, rare, costly, scarce, in short supply, hard to come by, like gold dust, beyond your means, not to be had for love or money: *Tickets to the game are at a premium.*

premonition NOUN **= feeling**, idea, intuition, suspicion, hunch, apprehension, misgiving, foreboding, funny feeling *(informal)*, presentiment, feeling in your bones

preoccupation NOUN **1 = obsession**, concern, hang-up *(informal)*, fixation, pet subject, hobbyhorse, idée fixe *(French)*, bee in your bonnet: *Her main preoccupation from an early age was boys.* **2 = absorption**, musing, oblivion, abstraction, daydreaming, immersion, reverie, absent-mindedness, brown study, inattentiveness, absence of mind, pensiveness, engrossment, prepossession, woolgathering: *He kept sinking back into gloomy preoccupation.*

preoccupied ADJECTIVE **1 = absorbed**, taken up, caught up, lost, intent, wrapped up, immersed, engrossed, rapt: *They were preoccupied with their own* *concerns.* **2 = lost in thought**, abstracted, distracted, unaware, oblivious, faraway, absent-minded, heedless, distrait, in a brown study: *He was too preoccupied to notice what was going on.*

preparation NOUN **1 = groundwork**, development, preparing, arranging, devising, getting ready, thinking-up, putting in order: *Behind any successful event lies months of preparation.* **2 = readiness**, expectation, provision, safeguard, precaution, anticipation, foresight, preparedness, alertness: *a military build-up in preparation for war* **3** *(usually plural)* **= arrangement**, plan, measure, provision: *Final preparations are under way for the celebration.* **4 = mixture**, cream, medicine, compound, composition, lotion, concoction, amalgam, ointment, tincture: *a specially formulated natural skin preparation*

preparatory ADJECTIVE **= introductory**, preliminary, opening, basic, primary, elementary, prefatory, preparative: *At least a year's preparatory work will be needed.*
preparatory to = before, prior to, in preparation for, in advance of, in anticipation of: *Sloan cleared his throat preparatory to speaking.*

prepare VERB **1 = make** *or* **get ready**, arrange, draw up, form, fashion, get up *(informal)*, construct, assemble, contrive, put together, make provision, put in order, jack up *(N.Z. informal)*: *He said the government must prepare an emergency plan for evacuation.* **2 = equip**, fit, adapt, adjust, outfit, furnish, fit out, accoutre: *The crew has been preparing the ship for storage.* **3 = train**, guide, prime, direct, coach, brief, discipline, groom, put someone in the picture: *It is a school's job to prepare students for university studies.* **4 = make**, cook, put together, get, produce, assemble, muster, concoct, fix up, dish up, rustle up *(informal)*: *She found him in the kitchen, preparing dinner.* **5 = get ready**, plan, anticipate, make provision, lay the groundwork, make preparations, arrange things, get everything set: *They were not given enough time to prepare for the election battle.* **6 = practise**, get ready, train, exercise, warm up, get into shape: *giving the players a chance to prepare for the match*

prepared ADJECTIVE **1 = willing**, minded, able, ready, inclined, disposed, in the mood, predisposed, of a mind: *Are you prepared to take industrial action?* **2 = ready**, set, all set: *I was prepared for a long wait.* **3 = fit**, primed, in order, arranged, in readiness, all systems go *(informal)*: *The country is fully prepared for war.*

preparedness NOUN **= readiness**, order, preparation, fitness, alertness

preponderance NOUN **1 = predominance**, instance, dominance, prevalence: *the huge preponderance of males among homeless people* **2 = greater part**, mass, bulk, weight, lion's share, greater numbers, extensiveness: *The preponderance of the evidence strongly supports his guilt.* **3 = domination**, power, sway, superiority, supremacy, dominion, ascendancy: *In 1965, the preponderance of West Germany over East had become even greater.*

preposterous ADJECTIVE **= ridiculous**, bizarre, incredible, outrageous, shocking, impossible, extreme, crazy, excessive, absurd, foolish, ludicrous, extravagant, unthinkable, unreasonable, insane, irrational, monstrous, senseless, out of the question, laughable, exorbitant, nonsensical, risible, asinine, cockamamie *(slang, chiefly U.S.)*

prerequisite NOUN **= requirement**, must, essential, necessity, condition, qualification, imperative, precondition, requisite, sine qua non *(Latin)*, must-have: *Good self-esteem is a prerequisite for a happy life.*
▷ ADJECTIVE **= required**, necessary, essential, called for, vital, mandatory, imperative, indispensable, obligatory, requisite, of the essence, needful: *Young children can be taught the prerequisite skills necessary to learn to read.*

prerogative NOUN **= right**, choice, claim, authority, title, due, advantage, sanction, liberty, privilege, immunity, exemption, birthright, droit, perquisite

presage VERB **= portend**, point to, warn of, signify, omen, bode, foreshadow, augur, betoken, adumbrate, forebode, foretoken: *Diplomats fear the incidents presage a new chapter in the conflict.*
▷ NOUN **= omen**, sign, warning, forecast, prediction, prophecy, portent, harbinger, intimation, forewarning, prognostication, augury, prognostic, auspice: *Soldiers used to believe a raven was a presage of coming battle.*

prescient ADJECTIVE **= foresighted**, psychic, prophetic, divining, discerning, perceptive, clairvoyant, far-sighted, divinatory, mantic

prescribe VERB **1 = specify**, order, direct, stipulate, write a prescription for: *Our doctor prescribed antibiotics for her throat infection.* **2 = ordain**, set, order, establish, rule, require, fix, recommend, impose, appoint, command, define, dictate, assign, lay down, decree, stipulate, enjoin: *The judge said he was passing the sentence prescribed by law.*

prescription NOUN **1 = instruction**, direction, formula, script *(informal)*, recipe: *These drugs are freely available without a prescription.* **2 = medicine**, drug, treatment, preparation, cure, mixture, dose, remedy: *I'm not sleeping, even with that new prescription the doctor gave me at my last appointment.*

prescriptive ADJECTIVE **= dictatorial**, rigid, authoritarian, legislating, dogmatic, didactic, preceptive

presence NOUN **1 = being**, existence, company, residence, attendance, showing up, companionship, occupancy, habitation, inhabitance: *His presence in the village could only stir up trouble; the presence of a carcinogen in the water* **2 = proximity**, closeness, vicinity, nearness, neighbourhood, immediate circle, propinquity: *conscious of being in the presence of a great man* **3 = personality**, bearing, appearance, aspect, air, ease, carriage, aura, poise, demeanour, self-assurance, mien *(literary)*, comportment: *Hendrix's stage presence appealed to thousands of teenage rebels.* **4 = spirit**, ghost, manifestation, spectre, apparition, shade *(literary)*, wraith, supernatural being, revenant, eidolon, atua *(N.Z.)*, wairua *(N.Z.)*: *The house was haunted by shadows and unseen presences.*
presence of mind = level-headedness, assurance, composure, poise, cool *(slang)*, wits, countenance, coolness, aplomb, alertness, calmness, equanimity, self-assurance, phlegm, quickness, sang-froid, self-possession, unflappability *(informal)*, imperturbability, quick-wittedness, self-command, collectedness: *Someone had the presence of mind to call for an ambulance.*

present[1] ADJECTIVE **1 = current**, existing, immediate, contemporary, instant, present-day, existent, extant: *the government's present economic difficulties* **2 = here**, there, near, available, ready, nearby, accounted for, to hand, at hand, in attendance: *The whole family was present.* **OPPOSITE:** absent **3 = in existence**, existing, existent, extant: *This vitamin is naturally present in breast milk.*
at present = just now, now, presently, currently, at the moment, right now, nowadays, at this time, at the present time, in this day and age: *At present, children under 14 are not permitted in bars.*
for the present = for now, for a while, in the meantime, temporarily, for the moment, for the time being, provisionally, not for long, for the nonce: *The ministers agreed that sanctions should remain in place for the present.*
the present = now, today, the time being, here and now, this day and age, the present moment: *His struggle to reconcile the past with the present.*

present[2] NOUN **= gift**, offering, grant, favour, donation, hand-out, endowment, boon, bounty, gratuity, prezzie *(informal)*, benefaction, bonsela *(S. African)*, koha *(N.Z.)*, largesse *or* largess: *The vase was a wedding present.*
▷ VERB **1 = give**, award, hand over, offer, grant, donate, hand out,

P

furnish, confer, bestow, entrust, proffer, put at someone's disposal: *The queen presented the prizes to the winning captain.* **2 = put forward**, offer, suggest, raise, state, produce, introduce, advance, relate, declare, extend, pose, submit, tender, hold out, recount, expound, proffer, adduce: *We presented three options to the unions for discussion.* **3 = put on**, stage, perform, give, show, mount, render, put before the public: *The theatre is presenting a new production of 'Hamlet'.* **4 = launch**, display, demonstrate, parade, exhibit, unveil: *presenting a new product or service to the market-place* **5 = introduce**, make known, acquaint someone with: *Fox stepped forward and presented him to Jack.*

presentable ADJECTIVE **1 = tidy**, elegant, well groomed, becoming, trim, spruce, dapper, natty *(informal)*, smartly dressed, fit to be seen: *She managed to make herself presentable in time for work.* **OPPOSITE:** unpresentable **2 = satisfactory**, suitable, decent, acceptable, proper, good enough, respectable, not bad *(informal)*, tolerable, passable, O.K. *or* okay *(informal)*: *His score had reached a presentable total.* **OPPOSITE:** unsatisfactory

presentation NOUN **1 = giving**, award, offering, donation, investiture, bestowal, conferral: *at the presentation ceremony* **2 = appearance**, look, display, packaging, arrangement, layout: *Keep the presentation of the dish simple.* **3 = performance**, staging, production, show, arrangement, representation, portrayal, rendition: *Scottish Opera's presentation of Das Rheingold*

present-day ADJECTIVE **= current**, modern, present, recent, contemporary, up-to-date, latter-day, newfangled

presently ADVERB **1 = at present**, currently, now, today, these days, nowadays, at the present time, in this day and age, at the minute *(Brit. informal)*: *The island is presently uninhabited.* **2 = soon**, shortly, directly, before long, momentarily *(U.S. & Canad.)*, in a moment, in a minute, pretty soon *(informal)*, anon *(archaic)*, by and by, in a short while, in a jiffy *(informal)*, erelong *(archaic, poetic)*: *Just take it easy and you'll feel better presently.*

preservation NOUN **1 = upholding**, keeping, support, security, defence, maintenance, perpetuation: *the preservation of the status quo* **2 = protection**, safety, maintenance, conservation, salvation, safeguarding, safekeeping: *the preservation of buildings of historic interest* **3 = storage**, smoking, drying, bottling, freezing, curing, chilling, candying, pickling, conserving, tinning: *the preparation, cooking and preservation of food*

PROVERBS

Self-preservation is the first law of nature

preserve VERB **1 = maintain**, keep, continue, retain, sustain, keep up, prolong, uphold, conserve, perpetuate, keep alive: *We will do everything we can to preserve peace.* **OPPOSITE:** end **2 = protect**, keep, save, maintain, guard, defend, secure, shelter, shield, care for, safeguard, conserve: *We need to preserve the rainforests.* **OPPOSITE:** attack **3 = keep**, save, store, can, dry, bottle, salt, cure, candy, pickle, conserve: *ginger preserved in syrup*

▷ NOUN **1** *(often plural)* **= jam**, jelly, conserve, marmalade, confection, sweetmeat, confiture: *jars of pear and blackberry preserves* **2 = area**, department, field, territory, province, arena, orbit, sphere, realm, domain, specialism: *The conduct of foreign policy is largely the preserve of the president.* **3 = reserve**, reservation, sanctuary, game reserve: *one of the world's great wildlife preserves*

preside VERB **= officiate**, chair, moderate, be chairperson: *He presided at the closing ceremony.*

preside over something *or* **someone = run**, lead, head, control, manage, direct, conduct, govern, administer, supervise, be at the head of, be in authority: *The question of who should preside over the next full commission was being debated.*

press VERB **1 = push (down)**, depress, lean on, bear down, press down, force down: *her hands pressing down on the desk*; *He pressed a button and the door closed.* **2 = push**, squeeze, jam, thrust, ram, wedge, shove: *He pressed his back against the door.* **3 = hug**, squeeze, embrace, clasp, crush, encircle, enfold, hold close, fold in your arms: *I pressed my child closer to my heart and shut my eyes.* **4 = urge**, force, beg, petition, sue, enforce, insist on, compel, constrain, exhort, implore, enjoin, pressurize, entreat, importune, supplicate: *The trade unions are pressing him to stand firm.* **5 = plead**, present, lodge, submit, tender, advance insistently: *mass strikes and demonstrations to press their demands* **6 = steam**, finish, iron, smooth, flatten, put the creases in: *Vera pressed his shirt.* **7 = compress**, grind, reduce, mill, crush, pound, squeeze, tread, pulp, mash, trample, condense, pulverize, tamp, macerate: *The grapes are hand-picked and pressed.* **8 = crowd**, push, gather, rush, surge, mill, hurry, cluster, flock, herd, swarm, hasten, seethe, throng: *As the music stopped, the crowd pressed forward.*

the press 1 = newspapers, the papers, journalism, news media, Fleet Street, fourth estate: *Today the British press is full of articles on the subject.* **2 = journalists**, correspondents, reporters, photographers, columnists, pressmen, newsmen, journos *(slang)*, gentlemen of the press: *He looked relaxed and calm as he faced the press.*

QUOTATIONS

The job of the press is to encourage debate, not to supply the public with information
[Christopher Lasch *Journalism, Publicity, and the Lost Art of Political Argument*]

Thou god of our idolatry, the press...
Thou fountain, at which drink the good and wise;
Thou ever-bubbling spring of endless lies;
Like Eden's dread probationary tree,
Knowledge of good and evil is from thee
[William Cowper *The Progress of Error*]

pressing ADJECTIVE **= urgent**, serious, burning, vital, crucial, imperative, important, constraining, high-priority, now or never, importunate, exigent **OPPOSITE:** unimportant

pressure NOUN **1 = force**, crushing, squeezing, compressing, weight, compression, heaviness: *The pressure of his fingers had relaxed.* **2 = power**, influence, force, obligation, constraint, sway, compulsion, coercion: *He may be putting pressure on her to agree.* **3 = stress**, demands, difficulty, strain, press, heat, load, burden, distress, hurry, urgency, hassle *(informal)*, uphill *(S. African)*, adversity, affliction, exigency: *The pressures of modern life are great.*

pressurize VERB **= force**, drive, compel, intimidate, coerce, dragoon, breathe down someone's neck, browbeat, press-gang, twist someone's arm *(informal)*, turn on the heat *(informal)*, put the screws on *(slang)*

prestige NOUN **= status**, standing, authority, influence, credit, regard, weight, reputation, honour, importance, fame, celebrity, distinction, esteem, stature, eminence, kudos, cachet, renown, Brownie points, mana *(N.Z.)*

prestigious ADJECTIVE **= celebrated**, respected, prominent, great, important, imposing, impressive, influential, esteemed, notable, renowned, eminent, illustrious, reputable, exalted **OPPOSITE:** unknown

presumably ADVERB **= it would seem**, probably, likely, apparently, most likely, seemingly, doubtless, on the face of it, in all probability, in all likelihood, doubtlessly

presume VERB **1 = believe**, think, suppose, assume, guess *(informal, chiefly U.S. & Canad.)*, take it, take for granted, infer, conjecture, postulate, surmise, posit, presuppose: *I presume you're here on business.* **2 = dare**, venture, undertake, go so far as, have the audacity, take the liberty, make bold, make so bold as: *I wouldn't presume to question your judgement.*

presume on something *or* **someone = depend on**, rely on, exploit, take

Poetry

Poets

Dannie Abse *(Welsh)*
(Karen) Fleur Adcock *(New Zealander)*
Conrad (Potter) Aiken *(U.S.)*
Anna Akhamatova *(Russian)*
Maya Angelou *(U.S.)*
Guillaume Apollinaire *(French)*
Ludovico Ariosto *(Italian)*
Matthew Arnold *(English)*
W(ystan) H(ugh) Auden *(English-U.S.)*
Charles Pierre Baudelaire *(French)*
Patricia Beer *(English)*
Hilaire Belloc *(British)*
John Berryman *(U.S.)*
John Betjeman *(English)*
Elizabeth Bishop *(U.S.)*
William Blake *(English)*
Edmund Blunden *(English)*
Joseph Brodsky *(Russian-American)*
Rupert (Chawner) Brooke *(English)*
Gwendolyn Brooks *(U.S.)*
Elizabeth Barrett Browning *(English)*
Robert Browning *(English)*
Robert Burns *(Scottish)*
(George Gordon) Byron *(British)*
Callimachus *(Greek)*
Luis Vaz de Camoëns *(Portuguese)*
Thomas Campion *(English)*
Raymond Carver *(U.S.)*
Gaius Valerius Catullus *(Roman)*
Charles Causley *(English)*
Geoffrey Chaucer *(English)*
Amy Clampitt *(U.S.)*
John Clare *(English)*
Samuel Taylor Coleridge *(English)*
William Cowper *(English)*
George Crabbe *(English)*
e(dward) e(stlin) cummings *(U.S.)*
Dante (Alighieri) *(Italian)*
Cecil Day Lewis *(Irish)*
Walter de la Mare *(English)*
Emily Dickinson *(U.S.)*
John Donne *(English)*
H D (Hilda Doolittle) *(U.S.)*
John Dryden *(English)*
Carol Ann Duffy *(Scottish)*
William Dunbar *(Scottish)*
Douglas Dunn *(Scottish)*
Geoffrey Dutton *(Australian)*
T(homas) S(tearns) Eliot *(U.S.-British)*
Paul Éluard *(French)*
Ralph Waldo Emerson *(U.S.)*
William Empson *(English)*
Edward Fitzgerald *(English)*
Robert Fitzgerald *(Australian)*
Robert (Lee) Frost *(U.S.)*
Allen Ginsberg *(U.S.)*
Johann Wolfgang von Goethe *(German)*
Robert Graves *(English)*
Thomas Gray *(English)*
Thom Gunn *(English)*
Seamus Heaney *(Irish)*
Adrian Henri *(English)*
Robert Henryson *(Scottish)*
George Herbert *(English)*
Robert Herrick *(English)*
Hesiod *(Greek)*
Geoffrey Hill *(English)*
Ralph Hodgson *(English)*
Homer *(Greek)*
Thomas Hood *(English)*
Gerard Manley Hopkins *(English)*
Horace *(Roman)*
A(lfred) E(dward) Housman *(English)*
Ted Hughes *(English)*
Elizabeth Jennings *(English)*
Samuel Johnson *(English)*
Ben Jonson *(English)*
Juvenal *(Roman)*
Patrick Kavanagh *(Irish)*
John Keats *(English)*
Sidney Keyes *(English)*
(Joseph) Rudyard Kipling *(English)*
Jean de La Fontaine *(French)*
Alphonse Marie Louis de Prat de Lamartine *(French)*
Walter Savage Landor *(English)*
William Langland *(English)*
Philip Larkin *(English)*
Tom Leonard *(Scottish)*
Henry Wadsworth Longfellow *(U.S.)*
Amy Lowell *(U.S.)*
Robert Lowell *(U.S.)*
Richard Lovelace *(English)*
Lucretius *(Roman)*
Thomas Macauley *(English)*
Norman MacCaig *(Scottish)*
Hugh MacDiarmid *(Scottish)*
Roger McGough *(English)*
Sorley MacLean *(Scottish)*
Louis MacNeice *(Irish)*
Stéphane Mallarmé *(French)*
Martial *(Roman)*
Andrew Marvell *(English)*
John Masefield *(English)*
Edna St Vincent Millay *(U.S.)*
John Milton *(English)*
Marianne Moore *(U.S.)*
Edwin Morgan *(Scottish)*
Andrew Motion *(English)*
Edwin Muir *(Scottish)*
Ogden Nash *(U.S.)*
Pablo Neruda *(Chilean)*
Frank O'Hara *(U.S.)*
Omar Khayyam *(Persian)*
Ovid *(Roman)*
Wilfred Owen *(British)*
Brian Patten *(English)*
Octavio Paz *(Mexican)*
Petrarch *(Italian)*
Pindar *(Greek)*
Sylvia Plath *(U.S.)*
Alexander Pope *(English)*
Peter Porter *(Australian)*
Ezra (Loomis) Pound *(U.S.)*
Sextus Propertius *(Roman)*
Aleksander Sergeyevich Pushkin *(Russian)*
Kathleen Raine *(English)*
Adrienne Rich *(U.S.)*
Laura Riding *(U.S.)*
Rainer Maria Rilke *(Austro-German)*
Arthur Rimbaud *(French)*
(John Wilmot) Rochester *(English)*
Theodore Huebner Roethke *(U.S.)*
Isaac Rosenberg *(English)*
Christina Georgina Rossetti *(English)*
Dante Gabriel Rossetti *(English)*
Saint-John Perse *(French)*
Sappho *(Greek)*
Siegfried Sassoon *(English)*
Johann Christoph Friedrich von Schiller *(German)*
Delmore Schwarz *(U.S.)*
Sir Walter Scott *(Scottish)*
Jaroslav Seifert *(Czech)*
William Shakespeare *(English)*
Percy Bysshe Shelley *(English)*
Sir Philip Sidney *(English)*
Edith Sitwell *(English)*
John Skelton *(English)*
Christopher Smart *(English)*
Stevie Smith *(English)*
Robert Southey *(English)*
Stephen Spender *(English)*
Edmund Spenser *(English)*
Wallace Stevens *(U.S.)*
Algernon Charles Swinburne *(English)*
Wislawa Szymborska *(Polish)*
Torquato Tasso *(Italian)*
Alfred, Lord Tennyson *(English)*
Dylan (Marlais) Thomas *(Welsh)*
Edward Thomas *(English)*
R(onald) S(tuart) Thomas *(Welsh)*
James Thomson *(Scottish)*
Paul Verlaine *(French)*
Alfred Victor de Vigny *(French)*
François Villon *(French)*
Virgil *(Roman)*
Derek Walcott *(West Indian)*
Francis Charles Webb *(Australian)*
Walt Whitman *(U.S.)*
William Wordsworth *(English)*
Judith Wright *(Australian)*
Thomas Wyatt *(English)*
W(illiam) B(utler) Yeats *(Irish)*

advantage of, count on, bank on, take liberties with, trust in *or* to: *He's presuming on your good nature.*

> **QUOTATIONS**
> Dr. Livingstone, I presume?
> [Henry Morton Stanley *How I Found Livingstone*]

presumption NOUN **1 = assumption**, opinion, belief, guess, hypothesis, anticipation, conjecture, surmise, supposition, presupposition, premise: *the presumption that a defendant is innocent until proved guilty* **2 = cheek** (*informal*), front, neck (*informal*), nerve (*informal*), assurance, brass (*informal*), gall (*informal*), audacity, boldness, temerity, chutzpah (*U.S. & Canad. informal*), insolence, impudence, effrontery, brass neck (*Brit. informal*), sassiness (*U.S. informal*), presumptuousness, forwardness: *He had the presumption to answer me back.*

presumptuous ADJECTIVE **= pushy** (*informal*), forward, bold, arrogant, presuming, rash, audacious, conceited, foolhardy, insolent, overweening, overconfident, overfamiliar, bigheaded (*informal*), uppish (*Brit. informal*), too big for your boots **OPPOSITE:** shy

presuppose VERB **= presume**, consider, accept, suppose, assume, take it, imply, take for granted, postulate, posit, take as read

presupposition NOUN **= assumption**, theory, belief, premise, hypothesis, presumption, preconception, supposition, preconceived idea

pretence NOUN **1 = deception**, invention, sham, fabrication, acting, faking, simulation, deceit, feigning, charade, make-believe, trickery, falsehood, subterfuge, fakery: *struggling to keep up the pretence that all was well* **OPPOSITE:** candour **2 = show**, posturing, artifice, affectation, display, appearance, posing, façade, veneer, pretentiousness, hokum (*slang, chiefly U.S. & Canad.*): *She was completely without guile or pretence.* **OPPOSITE:** reality **3 = pretext**, claim, excuse, show, cover, mask, veil, cloak, guise, façade, masquerade, semblance, ruse, garb, wile: *He claimed the police beat him up under the pretence that he was resisting arrest.*

pretend VERB **1 = feign**, affect, assume, allege, put on, fake, make out, simulate, profess, sham, counterfeit, falsify, impersonate, dissemble, dissimulate, pass yourself off as: *He pretended to be asleep.* **2 = make believe**, suppose, imagine, play, act, make up, play the part of: *She can sunbathe and pretend she's in Spain; The children pretended to be animals.* **3 = lay claim**, claim, allege, aspire, profess, purport: *I cannot pretend to understand the problem.*

pretended ADJECTIVE **= feigned**, alleged, so-called, phoney *or* phony (*informal*), false, pretend (*informal*), fake, imaginary, bogus, professed, sham, purported, pseudo (*informal*), counterfeit, spurious, fictitious, avowed, ostensible

pretender NOUN **= claimant**, claimer, aspirant

pretension NOUN **1 = affectation**, hypocrisy, conceit, show, airs, vanity, snobbery, pomposity, self-importance, ostentation, pretentiousness, snobbishness, vainglory, showiness: *We liked him for his honesty and lack of pretension.* **2** (*usually plural*) **= aspiration**, claim, demand, profession, assumption, assertion, pretence: *one of the few fashion designers who does not have pretensions to be an artist*

pretentious ADJECTIVE **= affected**, mannered, exaggerated, pompous, assuming, hollow, inflated, extravagant, high-flown, flaunting, grandiose, conceited, showy, ostentatious, snobbish, puffed up, bombastic, specious, grandiloquent, vainglorious, high-sounding, highfalutin (*informal*), overambitious, arty-farty (*informal*), magniloquent **OPPOSITE:** unpretentious

pretext NOUN **= guise**, excuse, veil, show, cover, appearance, device, mask, ploy, cloak, simulation, pretence, semblance, ruse, red herring, alleged reason

pretty ADJECTIVE **1 = attractive**, appealing, beautiful, sweet, lovely, charming, fair, fetching, good-looking, cute, graceful, bonny, personable, comely, prepossessing, fit (*Brit. informal*): *She's a charming and pretty girl.* **OPPOSITE:** plain **2 = pleasant**, fine, pleasing, nice, elegant, trim, delicate, neat, tasteful, dainty, bijou: *comfortable sofas covered in a pretty floral print*
▷ ADVERB **= fairly**, rather, quite, kind of (*informal*), somewhat, moderately, reasonably: *I had a pretty good idea what she was going to do.*

prevail VERB **1 = win**, succeed, triumph, overcome, overrule, be victorious, carry the day, prove superior, gain mastery: *We hoped that common sense would prevail.* **2 = be widespread**, abound, predominate, be current, be prevalent, preponderate, exist generally: *A similar situation prevails in America.*
prevail on *or* **upon someone = persuade**, influence, convince, prompt, win over, induce, incline, dispose, sway, talk into, bring round: *Do you think she can be prevailed upon to do it?*

prevailing ADJECTIVE **1 = widespread**, general, established, popular, common, set, current, usual, ordinary, fashionable, in style, customary, prevalent, in vogue: *individuals who have gone against the prevailing opinion* **2 = predominating**, ruling, main, existing, principal: *the prevailing weather conditions in the area*

prevalence NOUN **= commonness**, frequency, regularity, currency, universality, ubiquity, common occurrence, pervasiveness, extensiveness, widespread presence, rampancy, rifeness

prevalent ADJECTIVE **= common**, accepted, established, popular, general, current, usual, widespread, extensive, universal, frequent, everyday, rampant, customary, commonplace, ubiquitous, rife, habitual **OPPOSITE:** rare

prevent VERB **= stop**, avoid, frustrate, restrain, check, bar, block, anticipate, hamper, foil, inhibit, head off, avert, thwart, intercept, hinder, obstruct, preclude, impede, counteract, ward off, balk, stave off, forestall, defend against, obviate, nip in the bud: *These methods prevent pregnancy; We took steps to prevent it happening.* **OPPOSITE:** help

prevention NOUN **= elimination**, safeguard, precaution, anticipation, thwarting, avoidance, deterrence, forestalling, prophylaxis, preclusion, obviation

> **QUOTATIONS**
> Prevention is better than cure
> [Desiderius Erasmus *Adagia*]

preventive *or* **preventative** ADJECTIVE **1 = precautionary**, protective, hampering, hindering, deterrent, impeding, pre-emptive, obstructive, inhibitory: *They accused the police of failing to take adequate preventive measures.* **2 = prophylactic**, protective, precautionary, counteractive: *preventive medicine*

preview NOUN **= sample**, sneak preview, trailer, sampler, taster, foretaste, advance showing: *He had gone to see a preview of the play.*
▷ VERB **= sample**, taste, give a foretaste of: *We preview this season's collections from Paris.*

previous ADJECTIVE **1 = earlier**, former, past, prior, one-time, preceding, sometime, erstwhile, antecedent, anterior, quondam, ex-: *He had a daughter from a previous marriage.* **OPPOSITE:** later **2 = preceding**, past, prior, foregoing: *He recalled what Bob had told him the previous night.*

previously ADVERB **= before**, earlier, once, in the past, formerly, back then, until now, at one time, hitherto, beforehand, a while ago, heretofore, in days *or* years gone by

prey NOUN **1 = quarry**, game, kill: *These animals were the prey of hyenas.* **2 = victim**, target, mark, mug (*Brit. slang*), dupe, fall guy (*informal*): *Old people are easy prey for con men.*
prey on something *or* **someone 1 = hunt**, live off, eat, seize, devour, feed upon: *The larvae prey on small aphids.* **2 = victimize**, bully, intimidate, exploit, take advantage of, bleed (*informal*), blackmail, terrorize: *unscrupulous men who preyed on young runaways* **3 = worry**, trouble, burden,

distress, haunt, hang over, oppress, weigh down, weigh heavily: *This was the question that preyed on his mind.*

price NOUN **1 = cost**, value, rate, charge, bill, figure, worth, damage *(informal)*, amount, estimate, fee, payment, expense, assessment, expenditure, valuation, face value, outlay, asking price: *a sharp increase in the price of petrol; What's the price on that one?* **2 = consequences**, penalty, cost, result, sacrifice, toll, forfeit: *He's paying the price for pushing his body so hard.* **3 = reward**, bounty, compensation, premium, recompense: *He is still at large despite the high price on his head.*
▷ VERB **= evaluate**, value, estimate, rate, cost, assess, put a price on: *The shares are priced at 330p.*
at any price = whatever the cost, regardless, no matter what the cost, anyhow, cost what it may, expense no object: *We want the hostages home at any price.*

priceless ADJECTIVE **= valuable**, expensive, precious, invaluable, rich, prized, dear, rare, treasured, costly, cherished, incomparable, irreplaceable, incalculable, inestimable, beyond price, worth a king's ransom, worth your *or* its weight in gold **OPPOSITE:** worthless

pricey *or* **pricy** ADJECTIVE **= expensive**, dear, steep *(informal)*, costly, high-priced, exorbitant, over the odds *(Brit. informal)*, extortionate

prick VERB **1 = pierce**, stab, puncture, bore, pink, punch, lance, jab, perforate, impale: *She pricked her finger with a needle.* **2 = move**, trouble, touch, pain, wound, distress, grieve: *Most were sympathetic once we had pricked their consciences.*
▷ NOUN **1 = pang**, smart, sting, spasm, gnawing, twinge, prickle: *She felt a prick on the back of her neck.* **2 = puncture**, cut, hole, wound, gash, perforation, pinhole: *a tiny hole no bigger than a pin prick*
prick up = raise, point, rise, stand erect: *The dog's ears pricked up at the sound.*

prickle VERB **1 = tingle**, smart, sting, twitch, itch: *His scalp prickled under his wig.* **2 = prick**, stick into, nick, jab: *The pine needles prickled her skin.*
▷ NOUN **1 = tingling**, smart, chill, tickle, tingle, pins and needles *(informal)*, goose bumps, goose flesh: *A prickle at the nape of my neck reminds me of my fears.* **2 = spike**, point, spur, needle, spine, thorn, barb: *an erect stem covered at the base with prickles*

prickly ADJECTIVE **1 = spiny**, barbed, thorny, bristly, brambly, briery: *The grass was prickly and damp.* **2 = itchy**, sharp, smarting, stinging, crawling, pricking, tingling, scratchy, prickling: *a hot prickly feeling at the back of her eyes* **3 = irritable**, edgy, grumpy, touchy, bad-tempered, fractious, petulant, stroppy *(Brit. slang)*, cantankerous, tetchy, ratty *(Brit. & N.Z. informal)*, chippy *(informal)*, waspish, shirty *(slang, chiefly Brit.)*, peevish, snappish, liverish, pettish: *You know how prickly she can be.* **4 = difficult**, complicated, tricky, trying, involved, intricate, troublesome, thorny, knotty, ticklish: *The issue is likely to prove a prickly one.*

pride NOUN **1 = satisfaction**, achievement, fulfilment, delight, content, pleasure, joy, gratification: *the sense of pride in a job well done* **2 = self-respect**, honour, ego, dignity, self-esteem, self-image, self-worth, amour-propre *(French)*: *Her rejection was a severe blow to his pride.* **3 = conceit**, vanity, arrogance, pretension, presumption, snobbery, morgue *(French)*, hubris, smugness, self-importance, egotism, self-love, hauteur, pretentiousness, haughtiness, loftiness, vainglory, superciliousness, bigheadedness *(informal)*: *His pride may still be his downfall.* **OPPOSITE:** humility **4 = elite**, pick, best, choice, flower, prize, cream, glory, boast, treasure, jewel, gem, pride and joy: *This glittering dress is the pride of her collection.*
pride yourself on something = be proud of, revel in, boast of, glory in, vaunt, take pride in, brag about, crow about, exult in, congratulate yourself on, flatter yourself, pique yourself, plume yourself: *He prides himself on being able to organize his own life.*

> **QUOTATIONS**
> Pride goeth before destruction, and a haughty spirit before a fall
> [*Bible: Proverbs*]
>
> And the Devil did grin, for his darling sin
> Is pride that apes humility
> [Samuel Taylor Coleridge *The Devil's Thoughts*]

priest NOUN **= clergyman**, minister, father, divine, vicar, pastor, cleric, curate, churchman, padre *(informal)*, holy man, man of God, man of the cloth, ecclesiastic, father confessor

> **QUOTATIONS**
> Once we had wooden chalices and golden priests, now we have golden chalices and wooden priests
> [Ralph Waldo Emerson *The Preacher*]
>
> In all the ages of the world, priests have been the enemy of liberty
> [David Hume *Essays Moral, Political, and Literary*]
>
> The clergyman is expected to be a kind of human Sunday
> [Samuel Butler *The Way of All Flesh*]
>
> A priest,
> A piece of mere church furniture at best
> [William Cowper *Tirocinium*]

priestly ADJECTIVE **= ecclesiastic**, pastoral, clerical, canonical, hieratic, sacerdotal, priestlike

prim ADJECTIVE **= prudish**, particular, formal, proper, precise, stiff, fussy, fastidious, puritanical, demure, starchy *(informal)*, prissy *(informal)*, strait-laced, priggish, schoolmarmish *(Brit. informal)*, old-maidish *(informal)*, niminy-piminy **OPPOSITE:** liberal

primacy NOUN **= supremacy**, leadership, command, dominance, superiority, dominion, ascendancy, pre-eminence

prima donna NOUN **= diva**, star, leading lady, female lead

primal ADJECTIVE **1 = basic**, prime, central, first, highest, greatest, major, chief, main, most important, principal, paramount: *the most primal of human fears* **2 = earliest**, prime, original, primary, first, initial, primitive, pristine, primordial: *Yeats's remarks about folklore and the primal religion*

primarily ADVERB **1 = chiefly**, largely, generally, mainly, especially, essentially, mostly, basically, principally, fundamentally, above all, on the whole, for the most part: *Public order is primarily an urban problem.* **2 = at first**, originally, initially, in the first place, in the beginning, first and foremost, at *or* from the start: *These machines were primarily intended for use in editing.*

primary ADJECTIVE **1 = chief**, leading, main, best, first, highest, greatest, top, prime, capital, principal, dominant, cardinal, paramount: *His primary aim in life is to be happy.* **OPPOSITE:** subordinate **2 = basic**, essential, radical, fundamental, ultimate, underlying, elemental, bog-standard *(informal)*: *our primary needs of air, food and water*

prime ADJECTIVE **1 = main**, leading, chief, central, major, ruling, key, senior, primary, supreme, principal, ultimate, cardinal, paramount, overriding, foremost, predominant, pre-eminent, number-one *(informal)*: *Political stability is a prime concern.* **2 = best**, top, select, highest, capital, quality, choice, selected, excellent, superior, first-class, first-rate, grade-A: *It was one of the City's prime locations.* **3 = fundamental**, original, basic, primary, underlying: *A prime cause of deforestation was the burning of charcoal to melt ore into iron.*
▷ NOUN **= peak**, flower, bloom, maturity, height, perfection, best days, heyday, zenith, full flowering: *She was in her intellectual prime.*
▷ VERB **1 = inform**, tell, train, coach, brief, fill in *(informal)*, groom *(informal)*, notify, clue in *(informal)*, gen up *(Brit. informal)*, give someone the lowdown, clue up *(informal)*: *The press corps has been primed to avoid this topic.* **2 = prepare**, set up, load, equip, get ready, make ready: *They had primed the bomb to go off in an hour's time.*

primeval *or* **primaeval** ADJECTIVE **1 = earliest**, old, original, ancient, primitive, first, early, pristine, primal, prehistoric, primordial: *a vast expanse of primeval swamp* **2 = primal**, primitive, natural, basic, inherited,

P

inherent, hereditary, instinctive, innate, congenital, primordial, inborn, inbred: *a primeval urge*

primitive ADJECTIVE **1 = uncivilized**, savage, barbarian, barbaric, undeveloped, uncultivated: *studies of primitive societies* **OPPOSITE:** civilized **2 = early**, first, earliest, original, primary, elementary, pristine, primordial, primeval: *primitive birds from the dinosaur era* **OPPOSITE:** modern **3 = simple**, naive, childlike, untrained, undeveloped, unsophisticated, untutored: *primitive art* **OPPOSITE:** sophisticated **4 = crude**, simple, rough, rude, rudimentary, unrefined: *primitive tools* **OPPOSITE:** elaborate

primordial ADJECTIVE **1 = primeval**, primitive, first, earliest, pristine, primal, prehistoric: *Twenty million years ago this was dense primordial forest.* **2 = fundamental**, original, basic, radical, elemental: *primordial particles generated by the Big Bang*

prince NOUN **= ruler**, lord, monarch, sovereign, crown prince, liege, potentate, prince regent, crowned head, dynast

princely ADJECTIVE **1 = substantial**, considerable, goodly, large, huge, massive, enormous, tidy *(informal)*, whopping (great) *(informal)*, sizable *or* sizeable: *It cost them the princely sum of seventy-five pounds.* **2 = regal**, royal, imposing, magnificent, august, grand, imperial, noble, sovereign, majestic, dignified, stately, lofty, high-born: *the embodiment of princely magnificence*

princess NOUN **= ruler**, lady, monarch, sovereign, liege, crowned head, crowned princess, dynast, princess regent

principal ADJECTIVE **= main**, leading, chief, prime, first, highest, controlling, strongest, capital, key, essential, primary, most important, dominant, arch, cardinal, paramount, foremost, pre-eminent: *Their principal concern is that of winning the next election.* **OPPOSITE:** minor
▷ NOUN **1 = headmaster** *or* **headmistress**, head *(informal)*, director, dean, head teacher, rector, master *or* mistress: *the principal of the local high school* **2 = boss**, head, leader, director, chief *(informal)*, master, ruler, superintendent, baas *(S. African)*, sherang *(Austral. & N.Z.)*: *the principal of the company* **3 = star**, lead, leader, prima ballerina, first violin, leading man *or* lady, coryphée: *soloists and principals of The Scottish Ballet orchestra* **4 = capital**, money, assets, working capital, capital funds: *Use the higher premiums to pay the interest and principal on the debt.*

principally ADVERB **= mainly**, largely, chiefly, especially, particularly, mostly, primarily, above all, predominantly, in the main, for the most part, first and foremost

principle NOUN **1 = morals**, standards, ideals, honour, virtue, ethics, integrity, conscience, morality, decency, scruples, probity, rectitude, moral standards, sense of duty, moral law, sense of honour, uprightness, kaupapa *(N.Z.)*: *He would never compromise his principles; They had great trust in him as a man of principle.* **2 = belief**, rule, standard, attitude, code, notion, criterion, ethic, doctrine, canon, creed, maxim, dogma, tenet, dictum, credo, axiom: *a violation of the basic principles of Marxism* **3 = rule**, idea, law, theory, basis, truth, concept, formula, fundamental, assumption, essence, proposition, verity, golden rule, precept: *the principles of quantum theory*
in principle 1 = in general, generally, all things considered, on the whole, in the main, by and large, in essence, all in all, on balance: *I agree with this plan in principle.* **2 = in theory**, ideally, on paper, theoretically, in an ideal world, en principe *(French)*: *In principle, it should be possible.*

> **QUOTATIONS**
> It is always easier to fight for one's principles than to live up to them
> [Alfred Adler]
>
> The most useful thing about a principle is that it can always be sacrificed to expediency
> [W. Somerset Maugham *The Circle*]

> **USAGE**
> *Principle* and *principal* are often confused: *the principal* (not *principle*) *reason for his departure; the plan was approved in principle* (not *principal*).

principled ADJECTIVE **= moral**, ethical, upright, honourable, just, correct, decent, righteous, conscientious, virtuous, scrupulous, right-minded, high-minded

print VERB **1 = run off**, publish, copy, reproduce, issue, engrave, go to press, put to bed *(informal)*: *It costs far less to press a CD than to print a book.* **2 = publish**, release, circulate, issue, disseminate: *a questionnaire printed in the magazine* **3 = mark**, impress, stamp, imprint: *printed with a paisley pattern*
▷ NOUN **1 = photograph**, photo, snap: *a black and white print of the children* **2 = picture**, plate, etching, engraving, lithograph, woodcut, linocut: *Hogarth's famous series of prints* **3 = copy**, photo *(informal)*, picture, reproduction, replica: *There was a huge print of 'Le Déjeuner Sur l'Herbe' on the wall.* **4 = type**, lettering, letters, characters, face, font, fount, typeface: *columns of tiny print*
in print 1 = published, printed, on the streets, on paper, in black and white, out: *the appearance of his poems in print* **2 = available**, current, on the market, in the shops, on the shelves, obtainable: *The book has been in print for over 40 years.*
out of print = unavailable, unobtainable, no longer published, o.p.: *The book is now out of print, but can be found in libraries.*

prior ADJECTIVE **= earlier**, previous, former, preceding, foregoing, antecedent, aforementioned, pre-existing, anterior, pre-existent: *He claimed he had no prior knowledge of the protest.*
prior to = before, preceding, earlier than, in advance of, previous to: *A man was seen in the area prior to the shooting.*

priority NOUN **1 = prime concern**, first concern, primary issue, most pressing matter: *The government's priority should be better health care.* **2 = precedence**, preference, greater importance, primacy, predominance: *The school gives priority to science and maths.* **3 = supremacy**, rank, the lead, superiority, precedence, prerogative, seniority, right of way, pre-eminence: *the premise that economic development has priority over the environment*

priory NOUN **= monastery**, abbey, convent, cloister, nunnery, religious house

prise *see* **prize**

prison NOUN **= jail**, confinement, can *(slang)*, pound, nick *(Brit. slang)*, stir *(slang)*, cooler *(slang)*, jug *(slang)*, dungeon, clink *(slang)*, glasshouse *(Military, informal)*, gaol, penitentiary *(U.S.)*, slammer *(slang)*, lockup, quod *(slang)*, penal institution, calaboose *(U.S. informal)*, choky *(slang)*, poky *or* pokey *(U.S. & Canad. slang)*, boob *(Austral. slang)*

> **QUOTATIONS**
> Prison is a second-by-second assault on the soul, a day-to-day degradation of the self
> [Mumia Abu-Jamal *Live From Death Row*]
>
> Stone walls do not a prison make,
> Nor iron bars a cage
> [Richard Lovelace *To Althea, from Prison*]
>
> Prisons are built with stones of Law, brothels with bricks of Religion
> [William Blake *The Marriage of Heaven and Hell*]

prisoner NOUN **1 = convict**, con *(slang)*, lag *(slang)*, jailbird: *the large number of prisoners sharing cells* **2 = captive**, hostage, detainee, internee: *wartime hostages and concentration-camp prisoners*

> **QUOTATIONS**
> Only free men can negotiate. Prisoners cannot enter into contracts
> [Nelson Mandela]

prissy ADJECTIVE **= prim**, precious, fussy, fastidious, squeamish, prudish, finicky, strait-laced, schoolmarmish *(Brit. informal)*, old-maidish *(informal)*, niminy-piminy, overnice, prim and proper

pristine ADJECTIVE **= new**, pure, virgin, immaculate, untouched, unspoiled, virginal, unsullied, uncorrupted, undefiled

privacy NOUN **= seclusion**, isolation, solitude, retirement, retreat, separateness, sequestration, privateness

private ADJECTIVE **1 = nonpublic**, independent, commercial, privatised, private-enterprise, denationalized: *a joint venture with private industry* **2 = exclusive**, individual, privately owned, own, special, particular, reserved: *He has had to sell his private plane.* **OPPOSITE:** public **3 = secret**, confidential, covert, inside, closet, unofficial, privy *(archaic)*, clandestine, off the record, hush-hush *(informal)*, in camera: *He held a private meeting with the country's political party leaders.* **OPPOSITE:** public **4 = personal**, individual, secret, intimate, undisclosed, unspoken, innermost, unvoiced: *I've always kept my private and professional life separate; He hardly ever betrayed his private thoughts.* **5 = secluded**, secret, separate, isolated, concealed, retired, sequestered, not overlooked: *It was the only reasonably private place they could find to talk.* **OPPOSITE:** busy **6 = solitary**, reserved, retiring, withdrawn, discreet, secretive, self-contained, reclusive, reticent, insular, introvert, uncommunicative: *Gould was an intensely private individual.* **OPPOSITE:** sociable
▷ NOUN **= enlisted man** *(U.S.)*, tommy *(Brit. informal)*, private soldier, Tommy Atkins *(Brit. informal)*, squaddie or squaddy *(Brit. slang)*: *The rest of the gunners in the battery were privates.*
in private = in secret, privately, personally, behind closed doors, in camera, between ourselves, confidentially: *I think we should discuss this in private.*

privation NOUN **= want**, poverty, need, suffering, loss, lack, distress, misery, necessity, hardship, penury, destitution, neediness, indigence

privilege NOUN **= right**, benefit, due, advantage, claim, freedom, sanction, liberty, concession, franchise, entitlement, prerogative, birthright

privileged ADJECTIVE **1 = special**, powerful, advantaged, favoured, ruling, honoured, entitled, elite, indulged: *They were a wealthy and privileged elite.* **2 = confidential**, special, inside, exceptional, privy, off the record, not for publication: *This data is privileged information.*

privy NOUN **= lavatory**, closet, bog *(slang)*, latrine, outside toilet, earth closet, pissoir *(French)*, bogger *(Austral. slang)*, brasco *(Austral. slang)*: *an outside privy*
▷ ADJECTIVE *(with* **to***)* **= informed of**, aware of, in on, wise to *(slang)*, hip to *(slang)*, in the loop, apprised of, cognizant of, in the know about *(informal)*: *Only three people were privy to the facts.*

prize[1] NOUN **1 = reward**, cup, award, honour, premium, medal, trophy, accolade: *He won a prize in the Leeds Piano Competition.* **2 = winnings**, haul, jackpot, stakes, purse, windfall: *A single winner is in line for a jackpot prize of £8 million.* **3 = goal**, hope, gain, aim, desire, ambition, conquest, Holy Grail *(informal)*: *A settlement of the dispute would be a great prize.*
▷ MODIFIER **= champion**, best, winning, top, outstanding, award-winning, first-rate, top-notch *(informal)*: *a prize bull*

prize[2] VERB **= value**, appreciate, treasure, esteem, cherish, hold dear, regard highly, set store by: *These items are greatly prized by collectors.*

prize[3] or **prise** VERB **1 = force**, pull, lever: *He tried to prize the dog's jaws open.* **2 = drag**, force, draw, wring, extort: *We had to prize the story out of him.*

probability NOUN **1 = likelihood**, prospect, chance, odds, expectation, liability, presumption, likeliness: *There is a high probability of success.* **2 = chance**, odds, possibility, likelihood: *the probability of life on other planets*

probable ADJECTIVE **= likely**, possible, apparent, reasonable to think, most likely, presumed, credible, plausible, feasible, odds-on, on the cards, presumable **OPPOSITE:** unlikely

probably ADVERB **= likely**, perhaps, maybe, possibly, presumably, most likely, doubtless, in all probability, in all likelihood, perchance *(archaic)*, as likely as not

probation NOUN **= trial period**, test, trial, examination, apprenticeship, initiation, novitiate

probe VERB **1** *(often with* **into***)* **= examine**, research, go into, investigate, explore, test, sound, search, look into, query, verify, sift, analyze, dissect, delve into, work over, scrutinize: *The more they probed into his background, the more suspicious they became.* **2 = explore**, examine, poke, prod, feel around: *A doctor probed deep in his shoulder wound for shrapnel.*
▷ NOUN **= investigation**, study, research, inquiry, analysis, examination, exploration, scrutiny, inquest, scrutinization: *a federal grand-jury probe into corruption within the FDA*

probity NOUN **= integrity**, worth, justice, honour, equity, virtue, goodness, morality, honesty, fairness, fidelity, sincerity, righteousness, rectitude, truthfulness, trustworthiness, uprightness

problem NOUN **1 = difficulty**, trouble, dispute, plight, obstacle, dilemma, headache *(informal)*, disagreement, complication, predicament, quandary: *the economic problems of the inner city* **2 = puzzle**, question, riddle, enigma, conundrum, teaser, poser, brain-teaser *(informal)*, bitch *(slang)*: *a mathematical problem*
▷ MODIFIER **= difficult**, disturbed, troublesome, unruly, delinquent, uncontrollable, intractable, recalcitrant, intransigent, unmanageable, disobedient, ungovernable, refractory, maladjusted: *Sometimes a problem child is placed in a special school.*

> **PROVERBS**
> *A problem shared is a problem halved*

problematic ADJECTIVE **= tricky**, puzzling, uncertain, doubtful, dubious, unsettled, questionable, enigmatic, debatable, moot, problematical, chancy *(informal)*, open to doubt **OPPOSITE:** clear

procedure NOUN **= method**, policy, process, course, system, form, action, step, performance, operation, practice, scheme, strategy, conduct, formula, custom, routine, transaction, plan of action, modus operandi *(Latin)*

proceed VERB **1 = begin**, go ahead, get going, make a start, get under way, set something in motion: *I had no idea how to proceed.* **2 = continue**, go on, progress, carry on, go ahead, get on, press on, crack on *(informal)*: *The defence is not yet ready to proceed with the trial.* **OPPOSITE:** discontinue **3 = go on**, continue, advance, progress, carry on, go ahead, move on, move forward, press on, push on, make your way, crack on *(informal)*: *She proceeded along the hallway.* **OPPOSITE:** stop **4 = arise**, come, follow, issue, result, spring, flow, stem, derive, originate, ensue, emanate: *Does Othello's downfall proceed from a flaw in his character?*

proceeding NOUN **= action**, process, procedure, move, act, step, measure, venture, undertaking, deed, occurrence, course of action

proceeds PLURAL NOUN **= income**, profit, revenue, returns, produce, products, gain, earnings, yield, receipts, takings

process NOUN **1 = procedure**, means, course, system, action, performance, operation, measure, proceeding, manner, transaction, mode, course of action: *The best way to find out is by a process of elimination.* **2 = development**, growth, progress, course, stage, step, movement, advance, formation, evolution, unfolding, progression: *the evolutionary process of Homo sapiens* **3 = method**, system, practice, technique, procedure: *the cost of the production process* **4 = action**, case, trial, suit: *steps in the impeachment process against the president*
▷ VERB **1 = prepare**, treat, convert, transform, alter, refine: *silicon chips process electrical signals; facilities to process the beans before export* **2 = handle**, manage, action, deal with, fulfil, take care of, dispose of: *A number of applications are being processed at the moment.*

procession NOUN **= parade**, train, march, file, column, motorcade, cavalcade, cortege: *a funeral procession*

proclaim VERB **1 = announce**, declare, advertise, show, publish, indicate, blaze (abroad), herald, circulate, trumpet, affirm, give out, profess, promulgate, make known, enunciate, blazon (abroad), shout from the housetops *(informal)*: *He continues to proclaim his innocence.* **OPPOSITE:** keep secret **2 = pronounce**, announce, declare: *He launched a coup and proclaimed himself president.*

proclamation NOUN **1 = declaration**, notice, announcement, decree, manifesto, edict, pronouncement, pronunciamento: *A formal proclamation of independence was issued eight days ago.* **2 = publishing**, broadcasting, announcement, publication, declaration, notification, pronouncement, promulgation: *his proclamation of the good news*

proclivity NOUN **= tendency**, liking, leaning, inclination, bent, weakness, bias, disposition, penchant, propensity, kink, predisposition, predilection, partiality, proneness, liableness

procrastinate VERB **= delay**, stall, postpone, prolong, put off, defer, adjourn, retard, dally, play for time, gain time, temporize, play a waiting game, protract, drag your feet *(informal)*, be dilatory **OPPOSITE:** hurry (up)

procrastination NOUN **= delay**, hesitation, slowness, slackness, dilatoriness, temporization

> **QUOTATIONS**
> Procrastination is the thief of time
> [Edward Young *The Complaint: Night Thoughts*]
>
> Never put off till tomorrow what you can do today
> [Lord Chesterfield *letter to his son*]
>
> procrastination is the
> art of keeping
> up with yesterday
> [Don Marquis *archy and mehitabel*]

p

procure VERB **= obtain**, get, find, buy, win, land, score *(slang)*, gain, earn, pick up, purchase, secure, appropriate, acquire, manage to get, get hold of, come by, lay hands on

prod VERB **1 = poke**, push, dig, shove, propel, nudge, jab, prick: *He prodded Murray with the shotgun.* **2 = prompt**, move, urge, motivate, spur, stimulate, rouse, stir up, incite, egg on, goad, impel, put a bomb under *(informal)*: *a tactic to prod the government into spending more on the Health Service*
▷ NOUN **1 = poke**, push, boost, dig, elbow, shove, nudge, jab: *He gave the donkey a prod in the backside.* **2 = prompt**, boost, signal, cue, reminder, stimulus: *She won't do it without a prod from you.* **3 = goad**, stick, spur, poker: *a cattle prod*

prodigal ADJECTIVE **1 = extravagant**, excessive, reckless, squandering, wasteful, wanton, profligate, spendthrift, intemperate, immoderate, improvident: *his prodigal habits* **OPPOSITE:** thrifty **2** *(often with* **of**) **= lavish**, bountiful, unstinting, unsparing, bounteous, profuse: *You are prodigal of both your toil and your talent.* **OPPOSITE:** generous

prodigious ADJECTIVE **1 = huge**, giant, massive, vast, enormous, tremendous, immense, gigantic, monumental, monstrous, mammoth, colossal, stellar *(informal)*, stupendous, inordinate, immeasurable: *This business generates cash in prodigious amounts.* **OPPOSITE:** tiny **2 = wonderful**, striking, amazing, unusual, dramatic, impressive, extraordinary, remarkable, fantastic *(informal)*, fabulous, staggering, marvellous, startling, exceptional, abnormal, phenomenal, astounding, miraculous, stupendous, flabbergasting *(informal)*: *He impressed everyone with his prodigious memory.* **OPPOSITE:** ordinary

prodigy NOUN **= genius**, talent, wizard, mastermind, whizz *(informal)*, whizz kid *(informal)*, wunderkind, brainbox, child genius, wonder child, up-and-comer *(informal)*

produce VERB **1 = cause**, lead to, result in, effect, occasion, generate, trigger, make for, provoke, set off, induce, bring about, give rise to, engender: *The drug is known to produce side-effects.* **2 = make**, build, create, develop, turn out, manufacture, construct, invent, assemble, put together, originate, fabricate, mass-produce: *The company produces circuitry for communications systems.* **3 = create**, develop, write, turn out, compose, originate, churn out *(informal)*: *So far he has produced only one composition he deems suitable for performance.* **4 = yield**, provide, grow, bear, give, supply, afford, render, furnish: *The plant produces sweet fruit with deep red flesh.* **5 = bring forth**, bear, deliver, breed, give birth to, beget, bring into the world: *Some species of snake produce live young.* **6 = show**, provide, present, advance, demonstrate, offer, come up with, exhibit, put forward, furnish, bring forward, set forth, bring to light: *They challenged him to produce evidence to support his allegations.* **7 = display**, show, present, proffer: *You must produce your passport upon re-entering the country.* **8 = present**, stage, direct, put on, do, show, mount, exhibit, put before the public: *He produced Broadway's longest show.*
▷ NOUN **= fruit and vegetables**, goods, food, products, crops, yield, harvest, greengrocery *(Brit.)*: *I buy organic produce whenever possible.*

producer NOUN **1 = director**, promoter, impresario, régisseur *(French)*: *a freelance film producer* **2 = maker**, manufacturer, builder, creator, fabricator: *producers of precision instruments and electrical equipment* **3 = grower**, farmer: *They are producers of high-quality wines.*

> **QUOTATIONS**
> There'd be a great improvement if they shot less film and more producers
> [Samuel Goldwyn]

product NOUN **1 = goods**, produce, production, creation, commodity, invention, merchandise, artefact, concoction: *Try to get the best products at the lowest price.* **2 = result**, fruit, consequence, yield, returns, issue, effect, outcome, legacy, spin-off, end result, offshoot, upshot: *The company is the product of a merger.*

production NOUN **1 = producing**, making, manufacture, manufacturing, construction, assembly, preparation, formation, fabrication, origination: *two companies involved in the production of the steel pipes* **2 = creation**, development, fashioning, composition, origination: *the apparent lack of skill in the production of much new modern art* **3 = management**, administration, direction: *the story behind the show's production* **4 = presentation**, staging, mounting: *a critically acclaimed production of Othello*

productive ADJECTIVE **1 = fertile**, rich, producing, prolific, plentiful, fruitful, teeming, generative, fecund: *fertile and productive soil* **OPPOSITE:** barren **2 = creative**, dynamic, vigorous, energetic, inventive: *a highly productive writer of fiction* **3 = useful**, rewarding, valuable, profitable, effective, worthwhile, beneficial, constructive, gratifying, fruitful, advantageous, gainful: *a productive relationship* **OPPOSITE:** useless

productivity NOUN **= output**, production, capacity, yield, efficiency, mass production, work rate, productive capacity, productiveness

profane ADJECTIVE **1 = sacrilegious**, wicked, irreverent, sinful, disrespectful, heathen, impure, godless, ungodly, irreligious, impious, idolatrous: *a hard-drinking, profane Irishman* **OPPOSITE:** religious **2 = crude**, foul, obscene, abusive, coarse, filthy, vulgar, blasphemous: *a campaign against suggestive and profane lyrics in country songs* **3 = secular**, lay, temporal, unholy, worldly, unconsecrated, unhallowed, unsanctified: *Churches should not be used for profane or secular purposes.*
▷ VERB **= desecrate**, violate, abuse, prostitute, contaminate, pollute, pervert, misuse, debase, defile, vitiate, commit sacrilege: *They have profaned the traditions of the Church.*

profess VERB **1 = claim**, allege, pretend, fake, make out, sham, purport, feign, act as if, let on, dissemble: *'I don't know,' he replied, professing innocence.* **2 = state**, admit,

The Language of Joseph Furphy

Joseph Furphy (1843–1912) was an Australian writer who wrote under the pseudonym 'Tom Collins', and is generally considered the father of the Australian novel. His most famous work is *Such Is Life: Being Certain Aspects from the Diary of Tom Collins*, a series of stories about late-19th-century rural Australia, woven together by the travelling narrator. *Such is Life* has been praised for its insight into Australian life and its realistic portrayal of rural characters such as bullock drivers, travellers, and squatters.

One of the most striking features of Furphy's prose is the juxtaposition of the high-flown language of the narrator (Furphy was a very literate man; apparently he was memorising passages of Shakespeare and the Bible by the age of seven) and the dialect spoken by the characters he meets. The following passage is typical:

> 'It's this way,' said Mosey imperatively, and deftly weaving into his address the thin red line of puissant adjective; 'You dunno what you're doin' when you're foolin' with this run.'

Puissant ('potent') adjectives are a recurrent feature in the dialogue in *Such is Life*: Furphy uses the symbol *adj.* in brackets to indicate a swear-word, rather like the ****s used nowadays. *Adv.* is also occasionally used if the omitted expletive is used as an adverb, which draws further attention to the distance between the literate narrator (who makes distinctions between parts of speech) and the speakers (who, we suspect, would not):

> An' here's them (adj.) sneaks gone; an' Martin he'll be on top o' me in about two (adj.) twos; an' me left by my own (adj.) self...

> Lord stan' by us now! for we'll git (adv.) near hung if we're caught.

The passages above also show other features which characterise Furphy's representation of rural speech: contractions such as *o'*, *dunno* and *doin'*; spellings showing pronunciations, as in *git* for *get*; and non-standard grammar, for example *them sneaks*.

Furphy's most frequent words indicate the concrete realism of his subject matter. *Man* is the noun which occurs most often, and it is regularly used with a modifier to indicate profession or role, for example *boundary man, circus man,* and *station man.* Other frequent nouns include *horse, bullock,* and *station* (in the specific Australian sense 'ranch'). *Mile* is also frequent as the characters talk about their travels: it is notable that the narrator tends to use the plural *miles* after a cardinal number, while the characters he meets tend to use the dialectal singular *mile*:

> ...a hundred **miles** back in that leafy solitude...

> I won't fetch the station much short o' fifty **mile**; an' there ain't a middlin' camp the whole road.

Australia occurs seven times in *Such is Life*, while *Australian* as a noun occurs six times, always in generic statements about the identity of 'the Australian' (or, once, 'you Australians'):

> 'It is not in our cities or townships, it is not in our agricultural or mining areas, that **the Australian** attains full consciousness of his own nationality...'

Australian as an adjective is slightly more frequent, with eighteen occurrences. It is used to describe people, places, and, in several cases, fiction and poetry (*Australian novelist, Australian pioneer of poetry, Australian authoresses*) as Furphy contemplates the development of Australian literature, in which he played such an important role.

Furphy's work is also replete with words specific to life in Australia, such as *narangy* (a particular rank of person who works on a ranch) and *nilla-nilla* (a kind of wooden tool). Other words refer to the flora and fauna of Australia, such as *salt-bush* (a plant which grows in arid regions) and *bilby-hole* (the burrow of a *bilby*, a kind of marsupial).

announce, maintain, own, confirm, declare, acknowledge, confess, assert, proclaim, affirm, certify, avow, vouch, aver, asseverate: *He professed that he was content with the arrangements.*

professed ADJECTIVE **1 = supposed**, would-be, alleged, so-called, apparent, pretended, purported, self-styled, ostensible, soi-disant (*French*): *their professed concern for justice* **2 = declared**, confirmed, confessed, proclaimed, certified, self-confessed, avowed, self-acknowledged: *He was a professed anarchist.*

profession NOUN **= occupation**, calling, business, career, employment, line, office, position, sphere, vocation, walk of life, line of work, métier

professional ADJECTIVE **1 = qualified**, trained, skilled, white-collar: *professional people like doctors and engineers* **2 = expert**, experienced, finished, skilled, masterly, efficient, crack (*slang*), polished, practised, ace (*informal*), accomplished, slick, competent, adept, proficient: *She told me we'd done a really professional job.* **OPPOSITE:** amateurish
▷ NOUN **= expert**, authority, master, pro (*informal*), specialist, guru, buff (*informal*), wizard, adept, whizz (*informal*), maestro, virtuoso, hotshot (*informal*), past master, dab hand (*Brit. informal*), wonk (*informal*), maven (*U.S.*), fundi (*S. African*): *a dedicated professional*

professor NOUN **= don** (*Brit.*), fellow (*Brit.*), prof (*informal*), head of faculty

> **QUOTATIONS**
> A professor is one who talks in someone else's sleep
> [W.H. Auden]

proffer VERB **1 = offer**, hand over, present, extend, hold out: *He proffered a box of cigarettes.* **2 = suggest**, propose, volunteer, submit, tender, propound: *They have not yet proffered an explanation of how the accident happened.*

proficiency NOUN **= skill**, ability, know-how (*informal*), talent, facility, craft, expertise, competence, accomplishment, mastery, knack, aptitude, dexterity, expertness, skilfulness

proficient ADJECTIVE **= skilled**, trained, experienced, qualified, able, expert, masterly, talented, gifted, capable, efficient, clever, accomplished, versed, competent, apt, skilful, adept, conversant **OPPOSITE:** unskilled

profile NOUN **1 = outline**, lines, form, figure, shape, silhouette, contour, side view: *His handsome profile was turned away from us.* **2 = biography**, sketch, vignette, characterization, thumbnail sketch, character sketch: *The newspaper published comparative profiles of the candidates.* **3 = analysis**, study, table, review, survey, chart, examination, diagram, graph: *a profile of the hospital's catchment area*

profit NOUN **1** (*often plural*) **= earnings**, winnings, return, revenue, gain, boot (*dialect*), yield, proceeds, percentage (*informal*), surplus, receipts, bottom line, takings, emoluments: *The bank made pre-tax profits of £3.5 million.* **OPPOSITE:** loss **2 = benefit**, good, use, interest, value, gain, advantage, advancement, mileage (*informal*), avail: *They saw little profit in risking their lives to capture the militants.* **OPPOSITE:** disadvantage
▷ VERB **1 = make money**, clear up, gain, earn, clean up (*informal*), rake in (*informal*), make a killing (*informal*), make a good thing of (*informal*): *The dealers profited shamelessly at my family's expense.* **2 = benefit**, help, serve, aid, gain, promote, contribute to, avail, be of advantage to: *So far the French alliance has profited the rebels very little.*

profitable ADJECTIVE **1 = money-making**, lucrative, paying, commercial, rewarding, worthwhile, cost-effective, fruitful, gainful, remunerative: *Drug manufacturing is the most profitable business in America.* **2 = beneficial**, useful, rewarding, valuable, productive, worthwhile, fruitful, advantageous, expedient, serviceable: *a profitable exchange of ideas* **OPPOSITE:** useless

profligacy NOUN **= extravagance**, excess, squandering, waste, recklessness, wastefulness, lavishness, prodigality, improvidence

profligate ADJECTIVE **= extravagant**, reckless, squandering, wasteful, prodigal, spendthrift, immoderate, improvident

profound ADJECTIVE **1 = sincere**, acute, intense, great, keen, extreme, hearty, heartfelt, abject, deeply felt, heartrending: *The overwhelming feeling is profound shock and anger.* **OPPOSITE:** insincere **2 = wise**, learned, serious, deep, skilled, subtle, penetrating, philosophical, thoughtful, sage, discerning, weighty, insightful, erudite, abstruse, recondite, sagacious: *a book full of profound and challenging insights* **OPPOSITE:** uninformed **3 = complete**, intense, absolute, serious (*informal*), total, extreme, pronounced, utter, consummate, unqualified, out-and-out: *A profound silence fell.* **OPPOSITE:** slight **4 = radical**, extensive, thorough, far-reaching, exhaustive, thoroughgoing: *the profound changes brought about by World War I*

profoundly ADVERB **= greatly**, very, deeply, seriously, keenly, extremely, thoroughly, sincerely, intensely, acutely, heartily, to the core, abjectly, to the nth degree, from the bottom of your heart

profundity NOUN **= insight**, intelligence, depth, wisdom, learning, penetration, acumen, erudition, acuity, perspicacity, sagacity, perceptiveness, perspicuity

profuse ADJECTIVE **1 = plentiful**, ample, prolific, abundant, overflowing, teeming, copious, bountiful, luxuriant: *This plant produces profuse bright-blue flowers.* **OPPOSITE:** sparse **2 = extravagant**, liberal, generous, excessive, lavish, exuberant, prodigal, fulsome, open-handed, unstinting, immoderate: *Helena's profuse thanks were met with only a nod.* **OPPOSITE:** moderate

profusion NOUN **= abundance**, wealth, excess, quantity, surplus, riot, multitude, bounty, plethora, exuberance, glut, extravagance, cornucopia, oversupply, plenitude, superabundance, superfluity, lavishness, luxuriance, prodigality, copiousness

progenitor NOUN **1 = ancestor**, parent, forebear, forefather, begetter, procreator, primogenitor: *the Arabian stallions which were the progenitors of all modern thoroughbreds* **2 = originator**, source, predecessor, precursor, forerunner, antecedent, instigator: *the man who is considered the progenitor of modern drama*

progeny NOUN **1 = children**, family, young, issue, offspring, descendants: *They set aside funds to ensure the welfare of their progeny.* **2 = race**, stock, breed, posterity (*archaic*), seed (*chiefly biblical*), lineage, scions: *They claimed to be the progeny of Genghis Khan.*

prognosis NOUN **= forecast**, prediction, diagnosis, expectation, speculation, projection, surmise, prognostication

programme NOUN **1 = plan**, scheme, strategy, procedure, project, plan of action: *the programme for reform outlined by the Soviet President* **2 = schedule**, plan, agenda, timetable, listing, list, line-up, calendar, order: *the programme of events for the forthcoming year* **3 = course**, curriculum, syllabus: *a detailed ten-step programme of study with attainment targets* **4 = show**, performance, production, broadcast, episode, presentation, transmission, telecast, podcast: *a series of TV programmes on global warming*
▷ VERB **1 = schedule**, plan, timetable, book, bill, list, design, arrange, work out, line up, organize, lay on, formulate, map out, itemize, prearrange: *His homework is more manageable now because it is programmed into his schedule.* **2 = set**, fix: *Most VCRs can be programmed using a remote control handset.*

progress NOUN **1 = development**, increase, growth, advance, gain, improvement, promotion, breakthrough, step forward, advancement, progression, headway, betterment, amelioration: *The two sides made little progress towards agreement; The doctors say they are pleased with her progress.* **OPPOSITE:** regression **2 = movement forward**, passage, advancement, progression, course,

advance, headway, onward movement: *The road was too rough for further progress in the car.* **OPPOSITE:** movement backward
▷ VERB **1 = move on**, continue, travel, advance, proceed, go forward, gain ground, forge ahead, make inroads (into), make headway, make your way, cover ground, make strides, gather way, crack on *(informal)*: *He progressed slowly along the coast in an easterly direction.* **OPPOSITE:** move back
2 = develop, improve, advance, better, increase, grow, gain, get on, come on, mature, blossom, ameliorate: *He came round to see how our work was progressing.* **OPPOSITE:** get behind
in progress = going on, happening, continuing, being done, occurring, taking place, proceeding, under way, ongoing, being performed, in operation: *The game was already in progress when we took our seats.*

QUOTATIONS

Printing, gunpowder, and the magnet... these three have changed the whole face and state of things throughout the world
[Francis Bacon *Essays*]

What we call progress is the exchange of one nuisance for another nuisance
[Havelock Ellis *Impressions and Comments*]

Perhaps the best definition of progress would be the continuing efforts of men and women to narrow the gap between the convenience of the powers that be and the unwritten charter
[Nadine Gordimer *Speak Out: The Necessity of Protest*]

Is it progress if a cannibal uses a knife and fork?
[Stanislaw Lec *Unkempt Thoughts*]

You can't say civilization don't advance, however, for in every war they kill you in a new way
[Will Rogers]

That's one small step for a man, one giant leap for mankind
[Neil Armstrong *on his first steps on the moon's surface*]

PROVERBS

One step at a time

progression NOUN **1 = progress**, advance, advancement, gain, headway, furtherance, movement forward: *Both drugs slow the progression of HIV.* **2 = sequence**, course, order, series, chain, cycle, string, succession: *the steady progression of events in my life*

progressive ADJECTIVE **1 = enlightened**, liberal, modern, advanced, radical, enterprising, go-ahead, revolutionary, dynamic, avant-garde, reformist, up-and-coming, forward-looking: *The children go to a progressive school.* **2 = growing**, continuing, increasing, developing, advancing, accelerating, ongoing, continuous, intensifying, escalating: *One symptom of the disease is a progressive loss of memory.*

prohibit VERB **1 = forbid**, ban, rule out, veto, outlaw, disallow, proscribe, debar, interdict: *the law which prohibits trading on Sunday* **OPPOSITE:** permit
2 = prevent, restrict, rule out, stop, hamper, hinder, constrain, obstruct, preclude, impede, make impossible: *The contraption prohibited any movement.* **OPPOSITE:** allow

prohibited ADJECTIVE **= forbidden**, barred, banned, illegal, not allowed, vetoed, taboo, off limits, proscribed, verboten *(German)*

prohibition NOUN **= ban**, boycott, embargo, bar, veto, prevention, exclusion, injunction, disqualification, interdiction, interdict, proscription, disallowance, forbiddance, restraining order *(U.S., Law)*

prohibitive ADJECTIVE **1 = exorbitant**, excessive, steep *(informal)*, high-priced, preposterous, sky-high, extortionate, beyond your means: *The cost of private treatment can be prohibitive.*
2 = prohibiting, forbidding, restraining, restrictive, repressive, suppressive, proscriptive: *prohibitive regulations*

project NOUN **1 = scheme**, plan, job, idea, design, programme, campaign, operation, activity, proposal, venture, enterprise, undertaking, occupation, proposition, plan of action: *a local development project* **2 = assignment**, task, homework, piece of research: *Students complete their projects at their own pace.*
▷ VERB **1 = forecast**, expect, estimate, predict, reckon, calculate, gauge, extrapolate, predetermine: *Africa's population is projected to double by 2025.*
2 = plan, propose, design, scheme, purpose, frame, draft, outline, devise, contemplate, contrive, map out: *His projected visit to Washington had to be postponed.* **3 = launch**, shoot, throw, cast, transmit, discharge, hurl, fling, propel: *The hardware can be used for projecting nuclear missiles.* **4 = stick out**, extend, stand out, bulge, beetle, protrude, overhang, jut: *A piece of metal projected out from the side.*

projectile NOUN **= missile**, shell, bullet, rocket

projection NOUN **= forecast**, estimate, reckoning, prediction, calculation, estimation, computation, extrapolation

proletarian ADJECTIVE **= working-class**, common, cloth-cap *(informal)*, plebeian, blue-singlet *(Austral. slang)*: *the issue of proletarian world solidarity*
▷ NOUN **= worker**, commoner, Joe Bloggs *(Brit. informal)*, pleb, plebeian, prole *(derogatory, slang, chiefly Brit.)*: *The proletarians have nothing to lose but their chains.*

proletariat NOUN **= working class**, the masses, lower classes, commoners, the herd, wage-earners, lower orders, the common people, hoi polloi, plebs, the rabble, the great unwashed *(derogatory)*, labouring classes, proles *(derogatory, slang, chiefly Brit.)*, commonalty **OPPOSITE:** ruling class

proliferate VERB **= increase**, expand, breed, mushroom, escalate, multiply, burgeon, snowball, run riot, grow rapidly

proliferation NOUN **= multiplication**, increase, spread, build-up, concentration, expansion, extension, step-up *(informal)*, escalation, intensification

prolific ADJECTIVE **1 = productive**, creative, fertile, inventive, copious: *a prolific writer of novels and short stories*
2 = fruitful, fertile, abundant, rich, rank, teeming, bountiful, luxuriant, generative, profuse, fecund: *Closer planting will give you a more prolific crop.*
OPPOSITE: unproductive

prologue NOUN **= introduction**, preliminary, prelude, preface, preamble, foreword, proem, exordium

prolong VERB **= lengthen**, continue, perpetuate, draw out, extend, delay, stretch out, carry on, spin out, drag out, make longer, protract
OPPOSITE: shorten

promenade NOUN **1 = walkway**, parade, boulevard, prom, esplanade, public walk: *a fine promenade running past the boathouses* **2 = stroll**, walk, turn, airing, constitutional, saunter: *Take a tranquil promenade along a stretch of picturesque coastline.*
▷ VERB **1 = stroll**, walk, saunter, take a walk, perambulate, stretch your legs: *People came out to promenade along the front.* **2 = parade**, strut, swagger, flaunt: *attracting attention as he promenaded up and down the street in his flashy clothes*

prominence NOUN **1 = fame**, name, standing, rank, reputation, importance, celebrity, distinction, prestige, greatness, eminence, pre-eminence, notability, outstandingness: *He came to prominence during the World Cup in Italy.*
2 = conspicuousness, weight, precedence, top billing, specialness, salience, markedness: *Many papers give prominence to reports of the latest violence.*
3 = protrusion, swelling, projection, bulge, jutting, protuberance: *Birds have a prominence on the breast bone called a keel.*

prominent ADJECTIVE **1 = famous**, leading, top, chief, important, main, noted, popular, respected, celebrated, outstanding, distinguished, well-known, notable, renowned, big-time *(informal)*, foremost, eminent, major league *(informal)*, pre-eminent, well-thought-of: *a prominent member of the Law Society*

OPPOSITE: unknown **2 = noticeable**, striking, obvious, outstanding, remarkable, pronounced, blatant, conspicuous, to the fore, unmistakable, eye-catching, salient, in the foreground, easily seen, obtrusive: *the lighthouses that are still a prominent feature of the Scottish coast* **OPPOSITE:** inconspicuous **3 = jutting**, projecting, standing out, bulging, hanging over, protruding, protuberant, protrusive: *a low forehead and prominent eyebrows* **OPPOSITE:** indented

promiscuity NOUN **= licentiousness**, profligacy, sleeping around *(informal)*, permissiveness, abandon, incontinence, depravity, immorality, debauchery, laxity, dissipation, looseness, amorality, lechery, laxness, wantonness, libertinism, promiscuousness

> **QUOTATIONS**
> She speaks eighteen languages. And she can't say no in any of them [Dorothy Parker]
>
> You were born with your legs apart. They'll send you to the grave in a Y-shaped coffin [Joe Orton *What the Butler Saw*]

promiscuous ADJECTIVE **= licentious**, wanton, profligate, debauched, fast, wild, abandoned, loose, immoral, lax, dissipated, unbridled, dissolute, libertine, of easy virtue, unchaste **OPPOSITE:** chaste

promise VERB **1 = guarantee**, pledge, vow, swear, contract, assure, undertake, warrant, plight, stipulate, vouch, take an oath, give an undertaking to, cross your heart, give your word: *They promised they would deliver it on Friday.* **2 = seem likely**, look like, hint at, show signs of, bespeak, augur, betoken, lead you to expect, hold out hopes of, give hope of, bid fair, hold a probability of: *The seminar promises to be most instructive.*
▷ NOUN **1 = guarantee**, word, bond, vow, commitment, pledge, undertaking, assurance, engagement, compact, oath, covenant, word of honour: *If you make a promise, you should keep it.* **2 = potential**, ability, talent, capacity, capability, flair, aptitude: *He first showed promise as an athlete in grade school.*

> **QUOTATIONS**
> Whom the gods wish to destroy they first call promising [Cyril Connolly *Enemies of Promise*]
>
> We promise according to our hopes, and perform according to our fears [La Rochefoucauld *Maxims*]
>
> Promises and pie-crust are made to be broken [Jonathan Swift *Polite Conversation*]

promising ADJECTIVE **1 = encouraging**, likely, bright, reassuring, hopeful, favourable, rosy, auspicious, propitious, full of promise: *a new and promising stage in the negotiations* **OPPOSITE:** unpromising **2 = talented**, able, gifted, rising, likely, up-and-coming: *one of the school's brightest and most promising pupils*

promontory NOUN **= point**, cape, head, spur, ness *(archaic)*, headland, foreland

promote VERB **1 = help**, back, support, further, develop, aid, forward, champion, encourage, advance, work for, urge, boost, recommend, sponsor, foster, contribute to, assist, advocate, stimulate, endorse, prescribe, speak for, nurture, push for, espouse, popularize, gee up: *His country will do everything possible to promote peace.* **OPPOSITE:** impede **2 = advertise**, sell, hype, publicize, push, plug *(informal)*, puff, call attention to, beat the drum for *(informal)*: *He has announced a full British tour to promote his new album.* **3 = raise**, upgrade, elevate, honour, dignify, exalt, kick upstairs *(informal)*, aggrandize: *I was promoted to editor and then editorial director.* **OPPOSITE:** demote

promoter NOUN **1 = organizer**, arranger, entrepreneur, impresario: *one of the top boxing promoters in Britain* **2 = supporter**, champion, advocate, campaigner, helper, proponent, stalwart, mainstay, upholder: *Aaron Copland was a most energetic promoter of American music.*

promotion NOUN **1 = rise**, upgrading, move up, advancement, elevation, exaltation, preferment, aggrandizement, ennoblement: *rewarding outstanding employees with promotion* **2 = publicity**, advertising, hype, pushing, plugging *(informal)*, propaganda, advertising campaign, hard sell, media hype, ballyhoo *(informal)*, puffery *(informal)*, boosterism: *The company spent a lot of money on advertising and promotion.* **3 = encouragement**, backing, support, development, progress, boosting, advancement, advocacy, cultivation, espousal, furtherance, boosterism: *dedicated to the promotion of new ideas and research*

prompt VERB **1 = cause**, move, inspire, stimulate, occasion, urge, spur, provoke, motivate, induce, evoke, give rise to, elicit, incite, instigate, impel, call forth: *The recession has prompted consumers to cut back on buying cars.* **OPPOSITE:** discourage **2 = remind**, assist, cue, help out, prod, jog the memory, refresh the memory: *'What was that you were saying about a guided tour?' he prompted her.*
▷ ADJECTIVE **1 = immediate**, quick, rapid, instant, timely, early, swift, on time, speedy, instantaneous, punctual, pdq *(slang)*, unhesitating: *an inflammation of the eyeball which needs prompt treatment* **OPPOSITE:** slow **2 = quick**, ready, efficient, eager, willing, smart, alert, brisk, responsive, expeditious: *I was impressed by the prompt service I received.* **OPPOSITE:** inefficient
▷ ADVERB **= exactly**, sharp, promptly, on the dot, punctually: *The invitation specifies eight o'clock prompt.*
▷ NOUN **= reminder**, hint, cue, help, spur, stimulus, jog, prod, jolt: *Her blushes were saved by a prompt from her host.*

promptly ADVERB **1 = immediately**, instantly, swiftly, directly, quickly, at once, speedily, by return, pronto *(informal)*, unhesitatingly, hotfoot, pdq *(slang)*, posthaste: *She lay down and promptly fell asleep.* **2 = punctually**, on time, spot on *(informal)*, bang on *(informal)*, on the dot, on the button *(U.S.)*, on the nail: *We left the hotel promptly at seven.*

promulgate VERB **1 = make known**, issue, announce, publish, spread, promote, advertise, broadcast, communicate, proclaim, circulate, notify, make public, disseminate: *Such behaviour promulgates a negative image of the British.* **2 = make official**, pass, declare, decree: *bills limiting the FDA's authority to promulgate such regulations*

prone ADJECTIVE **1 = liable**, given, subject, inclined, tending, bent, disposed, susceptible, apt, predisposed: *For all her experience, she was still prone to nerves.* **OPPOSITE:** disinclined **2 = face down**, flat, lying down, horizontal, prostrate, recumbent, procumbent: *Bob slid from his chair and lay prone on the floor.* **OPPOSITE:** face up

pronounce VERB **1 = say**, speak, voice, stress, sound, utter, articulate, enunciate, vocalize: *Have I pronounced your name correctly?* **2 = declare**, announce, judge, deliver, assert, proclaim, decree, affirm: *A specialist has pronounced him fully fit; They took time to pronounce their verdict.*

pronounced ADJECTIVE **= noticeable**, clear, decided, strong, marked, striking, obvious, broad, evident, distinct, definite, conspicuous, unmistakable, salient **OPPOSITE:** imperceptible

pronouncement NOUN **= announcement**, statement, declaration, judgment, decree, manifesto, proclamation, notification, edict, dictum, promulgation, pronunciamento

pronunciation NOUN **= intonation**, accent, speech, stress, articulation, inflection, diction, elocution, enunciation, accentuation

> **USAGE**
> The *-un-* in *pronunciation* should be written and pronounced in the same way as the *-un-* in *unkind*. It is incorrect to add an *o* after the *u* to make this word look and sound more like *pronounce*.

proof NOUN **1 = evidence**, demonstration, testimony, confirmation, verification, certification, corroboration, authentication, substantiation,

attestation: *You must have proof of residence in the state.* **2 = trial print**, pull, slip, galley, page proof, galley proof, trial impression: *I'm correcting the proofs of the Spanish edition right now.*
▷ ADJECTIVE **= impervious**, strong, tight, resistant, impenetrable, repellent: *The fortress was proof against attack.*

prop VERB **1 = lean**, place, set, stand, position, rest, lay, balance, steady: *He propped his bike against the fence.* **2** *(often with* **up***)* **= support**, maintain, sustain, shore, hold up, brace, uphold, bolster, truss, buttress: *Plaster ceilings are propped with scaffolding.*
▷ NOUN **1 = support**, stay, brace, mainstay, truss, buttress, stanchion: *The timber is reinforced with three steel props on a concrete foundation.* **2 = mainstay**, support, sustainer, anchor, backbone, cornerstone, upholder: *The army is one of the main props of the government.*

propaganda NOUN **= information**, advertising, promotion, publicity, hype, brainwashing, disinformation, ballyhoo *(informal)*, agitprop, newspeak, boosterism

propagandist NOUN **= publicist**, advocate, promoter, proponent, evangelist, proselytizer, pamphleteer, indoctrinator

propagate VERB **1 = spread**, publish, promote, broadcast, proclaim, transmit, circulate, diffuse, publicize, disseminate, promulgate, make known: *They propagated subversive political doctrines.* **OPPOSITE:** suppress
2 = produce, generate, engender, increase: *The easiest way to propagate a vine is to take cuttings.* **3 = reproduce**, breed, multiply, proliferate, beget, procreate: *Tomatoes rot in order to transmit their seed and propagate the species.*

propagation NOUN **1 = spreading**, spread, promotion, communication, distribution, circulation, transmission, diffusion, dissemination, promulgation: *working towards the propagation of true Buddhism*
2 = reproduction, generation, breeding, increase, proliferation, multiplication, procreation: *the successful propagation of a batch of new plants*

propel VERB **1 = drive**, launch, start, force, send, shoot, push, thrust, shove, set in motion: *The rocket is designed to propel the spacecraft.*
OPPOSITE: stop **2 = impel**, drive, push, prompt, spur, motivate: *He is propelled by the need to avenge his father.*
OPPOSITE: hold back

propensity NOUN **= tendency**, leaning, weakness, inclination, bent, liability, bias, disposition, penchant, susceptibility, predisposition, proclivity, proneness, aptness

proper ADJECTIVE **1 = real**, actual, genuine, true, bona fide, kosher *(informal)*, dinkum *(Austral. & N.Z. informal)*: *Two out of five people do not have a proper job.* **2 = correct**, accepted, established, appropriate, right, formal, conventional, accurate, exact, precise, legitimate, orthodox, apt: *Please ensure that the proper procedures are followed.* **OPPOSITE:** improper
3 = polite, right, becoming, seemly, fitting, fit, mannerly, suitable, decent, gentlemanly, refined, respectable, befitting, genteel, de rigueur *(French)*, ladylike, meet *(archaic)*, decorous, punctilious, comme il faut *(French)*: *In those days it was not thought proper for a woman to be on the stage.* **OPPOSITE:** unseemly
4 = characteristic, own, special, individual, personal, particular, specific, peculiar, respective: *Make sure everything is in its proper place.*

properly ADVERB **1 = correctly**, rightly, fittingly, appropriately, legitimately, accurately, suitably, aptly, deservedly, as intended, in the true sense, in the accepted *or* approved manner: *The debate needs to be conducted properly.* **OPPOSITE:** incorrectly
2 = politely, respectfully, ethically, decently, respectably, decorously, punctiliously: *It's about time that brat learned to behave properly.*
OPPOSITE: badly

property NOUN **1 = possessions**, goods, means, effects, holdings, capital, riches, resources, estate, assets, wealth, belongings, chattels: *Security forces confiscated weapons and stolen property.* **2 = land**, holding, title, estate, acres, real estate, freehold, realty, real property: *He inherited a family property near Stamford.* **3 = quality**, feature, characteristic, mark, ability, attribute, virtue, trait, hallmark, peculiarity, idiosyncrasy: *A radio signal has both electrical and magnetic properties.*

> **QUOTATIONS**
> Property is theft
> [Pierre-Joseph Proudhon *Qu'est-ce que la Propriété?*]

prophecy NOUN **1 = prediction**, forecast, revelation, prognosis, foretelling, prognostication, augury, sortilege, vaticination *(rare)*: *Nostradamus's prophecy of the end of the world* **2 = second sight**, divination, augury, telling the future, soothsaying: *a child born with the gift of prophecy*

prophesy VERB **= predict**, forecast, divine, foresee, augur, presage, foretell, forewarn, prognosticate, soothsay, vaticinate *(rare)*

prophet *or* **prophetess** NOUN **= soothsayer**, forecaster, diviner, oracle, seer, clairvoyant, augur, sibyl, prognosticator, prophesier

> **QUOTATIONS**
> A prophet is not without honour, but in his own country
> [*Bible: St. Mark*]

prophetic ADJECTIVE **= predictive**, foreshadowing, presaging, prescient, divinatory, oracular, sibylline, prognostic, mantic, vatic *(rare)*, augural, fatidic *(rare)*

propitious ADJECTIVE **= favourable**, timely, promising, encouraging, bright, lucky, fortunate, prosperous, rosy, advantageous, auspicious, opportune, full of promise

proponent NOUN **= supporter**, friend, champion, defender, advocate, patron, enthusiast, subscriber, backer, partisan, exponent, apologist, upholder, vindicator, spokesman *or* spokeswoman

proportion NOUN **1 = part**, share, cut *(informal)*, amount, measure, division, percentage, segment, quota, fraction: *A proportion of the rent is met by the city council.* **2 = relative amount**, relationship, distribution, ratio: *the proportion of women in the profession; the proportion of length to breadth*
3 = balance, agreement, harmony, correspondence, symmetry, concord, congruity: *an artist with a special feel for colour and proportion*
▷ PLURAL NOUN **= dimensions**, size, volume, capacity, extent, range, bulk, scope, measurements, magnitude, breadth, expanse, amplitude: *In the tropics, plants grow to huge proportions.*

proportional *or* **proportionate** ADJECTIVE **= correspondent**, equivalent, corresponding, even, balanced, consistent, comparable, compatible, equitable, in proportion, analogous, commensurate
OPPOSITE: disproportionate

proposal NOUN **= suggestion**, plan, programme, scheme, offer, terms, design, project, bid, motion, recommendation, tender, presentation, proposition, overture

propose VERB **1 = put forward**, present, suggest, advance, come up with, submit, tender, proffer, propound: *We are about to propose some changes to the system.* **2 = intend**, mean, plan, aim, design, scheme, purpose, have in mind, have every intention: *I propose to spend my entire life travelling.*
3 = nominate, name, present, introduce, invite, recommend, put up: *He was proposed for renomination as party chairman.* **4 = offer marriage**, pop the question *(informal)*, ask for someone's hand (in marriage), pay suit: *Merton proposed to her on bended knee.*

proposition NOUN **1 = task**, problem, activity, job, affair, venture, undertaking: *Designing his own flat was quite a different proposition to designing for clients.* **2 = theory**, idea, argument, concept, thesis, hypothesis, theorem, premise, postulation: *the proposition that monarchs derived their authority by divine right* **3 = proposal**, plan, suggestion, scheme, bid, motion, recommendation: *I want to make you a business proposition.* **4 = advance**, pass *(informal)*, proposal, overture, improper suggestion, come-on *(informal)*: *unwanted sexual propositions*

p

▷ VERB **= make a pass at**, solicit, accost, make an indecent proposal to, make an improper suggestion to: *He had allegedly tried to proposition Miss Hawes.*

> QUOTATIONS
> It is more important that a proposition be interesting than that it be true
> [A.N. Whitehead *Adventures of Ideas*]

propound VERB **= put forward**, present, advance, propose, advocate, submit, suggest, lay down, contend, postulate, set forth

proprietor *or* **proprietress** NOUN **= owner**, landowner, freeholder, possessor, titleholder, deed holder, landlord *or* landlady

propriety NOUN **1 = decorum**, manners, courtesy, protocol, good form, decency, breeding, delicacy, modesty, respectability, etiquette, refinement, politeness, good manners, rectitude, punctilio, seemliness: *Their sense of social propriety is eroded.* **OPPOSITE:** indecorum **2 = correctness**, fitness, appropriateness, rightness, aptness, seemliness, suitableness: *They questioned the propriety of the corporation's use of public money.*
the proprieties = etiquette, the niceties, the civilities, the amenities, the done thing, the social graces, the rules of conduct, the social conventions, social code, accepted conduct, kawa (N.Z.), tikanga (N.Z.): *respectable couples who observe the proprieties but loathe each other*

propulsion NOUN **= power**, pressure, push, thrust, momentum, impulse, impetus, motive power, impulsion, propelling force

prosaic ADJECTIVE **= dull**, ordinary, boring, routine, flat, dry, everyday, tame, pedestrian, commonplace, mundane, matter-of-fact, stale, banal, uninspiring, humdrum, trite, unimaginative, hackneyed, workaday, vapid **OPPOSITE:** exciting

proscribe VERB **1 = prohibit**, ban, forbid, boycott, embargo, interdict: *They are proscribed by federal law from owning guns.* **OPPOSITE:** permit **2 = condemn**, reject, damn, denounce, censure: *Slang is reviled and proscribed by pedants and purists.* **3 = outlaw**, exclude, exile, expel, banish, deport, expatriate, excommunicate, ostracize, blackball, attaint (*archaic*): *He was proscribed in America, where his estate was put up for sale.*

prosecute VERB **1 = take someone to court**, try, sue, summon, indict, do (*slang*), arraign, seek redress, put someone on trial, litigate, bring suit against, bring someone to trial, put someone in the dock, bring action against, prefer charges against: *The police have decided not to prosecute him.* **2 = conduct**, continue, manage, direct, pursue, work at, carry on, practise, engage in, discharge, persist, see through, follow through, persevere, carry through: *To prosecute this war is costing the country fifteen million pounds a day.*

prospect NOUN **1 = likelihood**, chance, possibility, plan, hope, promise, proposal, odds, expectation, probability, anticipation, presumption: *There is little prospect of having these questions answered.* **2 = idea**, thought, outlook, contemplation: *the pleasant prospect of a quiet night in* **3 = view**, perspective, landscape, scene, sight, vision, outlook, spectacle, panorama, vista: *The windows overlooked the superb prospect of the hills.*
▷ PLURAL NOUN **= possibilities**, openings, chances, future, potential, expectations, outlook, scope: *I chose to work abroad to improve my career prospects.*
▷ VERB **= look**, search, seek, survey, explore, drill, go after, dowse: *The companies are prospecting for oil not far from here.*

prospective ADJECTIVE **1 = potential**, possible, to come, about to be, upcoming, soon-to-be: *The story is a warning to other prospective buyers.* **2 = expected**, coming, future, approaching, likely, looked-for, intended, awaited, hoped-for, anticipated, forthcoming, imminent, destined, eventual, on the cards: *The terms of the prospective deal are spelled out clearly.*

prospectus NOUN **= catalogue**, plan, list, programme, announcement, outline, brochure, handbook, syllabus, synopsis, conspectus

prosper VERB **= succeed**, advance, progress, thrive, make it (*informal*), flower, get on, do well, flourish, bloom, make good, be fortunate, grow rich, fare well

prosperity NOUN **= success**, riches, plenty, ease, fortune, wealth, boom, luxury, well-being, good times, good fortune, the good life, affluence, life of luxury, life of Riley (*informal*), prosperousness **OPPOSITE:** poverty

prosperous ADJECTIVE **1 = wealthy**, rich, affluent, well-off, in the money (*informal*), blooming, opulent, well-heeled (*informal*), well-to-do, moneyed, in clover (*informal*), minted (*Brit. slang*): *the youngest son of a prosperous family* **OPPOSITE:** poor **2 = successful**, booming, thriving, flourishing, doing well, prospering, on a roll, on the up and up (*Brit.*), palmy: *He has developed a prosperous business.* **OPPOSITE:** unsuccessful

prostitute NOUN **= whore**, hooker (*U.S. slang*), pro (*slang*), brass (*slang*), tart (*informal*), hustler (*U.S. & Canad. slang*), moll (*slang*), call girl, courtesan, working girl (*facetious, slang*), harlot, streetwalker, camp follower, loose woman, fallen woman, scrubber (*Brit. & Austral. slang*), strumpet, trollop, white slave, bawd (*archaic*), cocotte, fille de joie (*French*): *He admitted that he had paid for sex with a prostitute.*
▷ VERB **= cheapen**, sell out, pervert, degrade, devalue, squander, demean, debase, profane, misapply: *His friends said that he had prostituted his talents.*

prostitution NOUN **= harlotry**, the game (*slang*), vice, the oldest profession, whoredom, streetwalking, harlot's trade, Mrs. Warren's profession

prostrate ADJECTIVE **1 = prone**, fallen, flat, horizontal, abject, bowed low, kowtowing, procumbent: *Percy was lying prostrate with his arms outstretched.* **2 = exhausted**, overcome, depressed, drained, spent, worn out, desolate, dejected, inconsolable, at a low ebb, fagged out (*informal*): *After my mother's death, I was prostrate with grief.* **3 = helpless**, overwhelmed, disarmed, paralysed, powerless, reduced, impotent, defenceless, brought to your knees: *Gaston was prostrate on his sickbed.*
▷ VERB **= exhaust**, tire, drain, fatigue, weary, sap, wear out, fag out (*informal*): *patients who have been prostrated by fatigue*
prostrate yourself = bow down, submit, kneel, cringe, grovel, fall at someone's feet, bow, kowtow, bend the knee, abase yourself, cast yourself, fall on your knees: *They prostrated themselves before the king in awe and fear.*

protagonist NOUN **1 = supporter**, leader, champion, advocate, exponent, mainstay, prime mover, standard-bearer, moving spirit, torchbearer: *an active protagonist of his country's membership of the EU* **2 = leading character**, lead, principal, central character, hero *or* heroine: *the protagonist of J.D. Salinger's novel*

protean ADJECTIVE **= changeable**, variable, volatile, versatile, temperamental, ever-changing, mercurial, many-sided, mutable, polymorphous, multiform

protect VERB **= keep someone safe**, defend, keep, support, save, guard, secure, preserve, look after, foster, shelter, shield, care for, harbour, safeguard, watch over, stick up for (*informal*), cover up for, chaperon, give someone sanctuary, take someone under your wing, mount *or* stand guard over **OPPOSITE:** endanger

protection NOUN **1 = safety**, charge, care, defence, protecting, security, guarding, custody, safeguard, preservation, aegis, guardianship, safekeeping: *The primary duty of parents is the protection of their children.* **2 = safeguard**, cover, guard, shelter, screen, barrier, shield, refuge, buffer, bulwark: *Innocence is no protection from the evils in our society.* **3 = armour**, cover, screen, barrier, shelter, shield, bulwark: *Riot shields acted as protection against the attack.*

protective ADJECTIVE **1 = protecting**, covering, sheltering, shielding,

P

Who and Whom in Classic Literature

One of the main ways that English has changed over the past thousand years or so is in its loss of word endings to mark case. In Old English (as in Latin, German, and many other languages) a noun had a different ending depending on whether it was the subject of a sentence (where it was in the 'nominative case') or the object (where it was in the 'accusative case'). In present-day English, however, we make no distinction. For example, *this tree* has the same form when it is the subject - '**this tree** is green' - and when it is the object - 'I like **this tree**'. The exception is pronouns: we *do* make a distinction between subject and object in sentences such as '**I** love Tom' and 'Tom loves **me**'; '**she** helps Jean' and 'Jean helps **her**'. These do not cause a problem for English speakers. However, another pair of pronouns does: *who* and *whom*. *Whom* is the accusative form, and is the traditionally correct option in a sentence such as '**Whom** did you see?'; this is evident if we answer with another pronoun, which would also be in the accusative case - 'I saw **him**' - and would sound completely wrong in the nominative case - 'I saw he'. *Who* is the subject or nominative form, and is used in sentences such as 'Who saw it?', the answer being something like '**He** saw it'. However, in recent years *whom* has become less frequent - particularly in everyday English, where it is felt to be too formal and stuffy - and *who* is coming to be used in both subject and object position. In the *Bank of English*, Collins' corpus of present-day English, *who* is nearly thirty times more frequent than *whom*; in the spoken part of the corpus, *who* is over forty times more frequent.

In classic literature of the 18th to 20th centuries, *whom* was much more frequent, occurring five times as often as it does in present-day English. Some of the authors who use *whom* most frequently are Sir Walter Scott, Henry Fielding, Samuel Johnson, and Abraham Lincoln. Examples include:

> Of all the fellows **whom** I ever saw haunted by terrors of this nature... (Sir Walter Scott)

However, it is notable that even those authors who write in a more informal style use *whom* in contexts where a modern writer would be more likely to choose *who*:

> And, gadzooks! The boy **whom** he had pursued last night had been just about Jackson's size and build! (PG Wodehouse)

Another difference between classic literature and modern literature is the contexts in which *whom* is used. In the *Bank of English*, over two-thirds of the occurrences of *whom* follow a preposition; in the spoken part of the *Bank of English*, nearly three-quarters are of this type, in examples such as:

> ...she had a cluster of admirers, **most of whom** were older than her. (Bank of English)

In this type of sentence, *whom* is the only option without rephrasing the sentence; *most of who* would be very non-standard. In classic literature, there is a more even split between *whom* following a preposition and *whom* in other constructions such as the ones quoted above.

Perhaps surprisingly, though, the related pair *whomever* and *whoever* are distributed differently. *Whomever* is very infrequent in both modern and classic writing, occurring less than once per million words, but it is actually *less* frequent in classic literature. Furthermore, there are several cases where *whoever* is used when *whomever* would be the grammatically correct form, for example:

> He having consented, she told him then, he should follow her, but told him, **whoever he saw**, he must speak to no body but her. (Daniel Defoe)

> All I cared for was that, wherever you came from, whatever you had done, **whoever you had loved**, you were mine at last. (Thomas Hardy)

This suggests that, even though grammatical case was followed with regard to *whom* and *who*, the distinction between *whomever* and *whoever* was already being lost in the 18th and 19th centuries.

safeguarding, insulating: *Protective gloves reduce the absorption of chemicals through the skin.* **2 = caring**, defensive, motherly, fatherly, warm, careful, maternal, vigilant, watchful, paternal, possessive: *He is very protective towards his sisters.*

protector NOUN **1 = defender**, champion, guard, guardian, counsel, advocate, patron, safeguard, bodyguard, benefactor, guardian angel, tower of strength, knight in shining armour: *Many mothers see their son as a protector and provider.* **2 = guard**, screen, protection, shield, pad, cushion, buffer: *Ear protectors must be worn when operating this equipment.*

protégé *or* **protégée** NOUN **= charge**, student, pupil, ward, discovery, dependant

protest VERB **1 = object**, demonstrate, oppose, complain, disagree, cry out, disapprove, say no to, demur, take exception, remonstrate, kick against *(informal)*, expostulate, take up the cudgels, express disapproval: *Women took to the streets to protest against the arrests.* **2 = assert**, argue, insist, maintain, declare, vow, testify, contend, affirm, profess, attest, avow, asseverate: *'I never said that,' he protested.* ▷ NOUN **1 = demonstration**, march, rally, sit-in, demo *(informal)*, hikoi *(N.Z.)*: *The opposition staged a protest against the government.* **2 = objection**, complaint, declaration, dissent, outcry, disapproval, protestation, demur, formal complaint, remonstrance, demurral: *a protest against people's growing economic hardship*

p

QUOTATIONS

The lady doth protest too much methinks
[William Shakespeare *Hamlet*]

protestation NOUN **= declaration**, pledge, vow, oath, profession, affirmation, avowal, asseveration

protester NOUN **1 = demonstrator**, rebel, dissident, dissenter, agitator, picketers, protest marcher: *anti-abortion protesters* **2 = objector**, opposer, complainer, opponent, dissident, dissenter: *Protesters say the government is corrupt.*

protocol NOUN **1 = code of behaviour**, manners, courtesies, conventions, customs, formalities, good form, etiquette, propriety, decorum, rules of conduct, politesse, p's and q's: *He is a stickler for royal protocol.* **2 = agreement**, contract, treaty, convention, pact, compact, covenant, concordat: *the Montreal Protocol to phase out use and production of CFCs*

prototype NOUN **= original**, model, precedent, first, example, standard, paradigm, archetype, mock-up

protracted ADJECTIVE **= extended**, long, prolonged, lengthy, time-consuming, never-ending, drawn-out, interminable, spun out, dragged out, long-drawn-out, overlong

protrude VERB **= stick out**, start (from), point, project, pop *(of an eye)*, extend, come through, stand out, bulge, shoot out, jut, stick out like a sore thumb, obtrude

proud ADJECTIVE **1 = satisfied**, pleased, content, contented, honoured, thrilled, glad, gratified, joyful, appreciative, well-pleased: *I am proud to be a Scot.* **OPPOSITE:** dissatisfied **2 = glorious**, rewarding, memorable, pleasing, satisfying, illustrious, gratifying, exalted, red-letter: *My daughter's graduation was a proud moment for me.* **3 = distinguished**, great, grand, imposing, magnificent, noble, august, splendid, eminent, majestic, stately, illustrious: *The American Indians were a proud and noble people.* **OPPOSITE:** lowly **4 = conceited**, vain, arrogant, stuck-up *(informal)*, lordly, imperious, narcissistic, overbearing, snooty *(informal)*, haughty, snobbish, egotistical, self-satisfied, disdainful, self-important, presumptuous, boastful, supercilious, high and mighty *(informal)*, toffee-nosed *(slang, chiefly Brit.)*, too big for your boots *or* breeches: *She has a reputation for being proud and arrogant.* **OPPOSITE:** humble

prove VERB **1 = turn out**, come out, end up, be found to be: *In the past this process has proved difficult.* **2 = verify**, establish, determine, show, evidence, confirm, demonstrate, justify, ascertain, bear out, attest, substantiate, corroborate, authenticate, evince, show clearly: *new evidence that could prove their innocence* **OPPOSITE:** disprove

proven ADJECTIVE **= established**, accepted, proved, confirmed, tried, tested, checked, reliable, valid, definite, authentic, certified, verified, attested, undoubted, dependable, trustworthy

provenance NOUN **= origin**, source, birthplace, derivation

proverb NOUN **= saying**, saw, maxim, gnome, adage, dictum, aphorism, byword, apophthegm

proverbial ADJECTIVE **= conventional**, accepted, traditional, famous, acknowledged, typical, well-known, legendary, notorious, customary, famed, archetypal, time-honoured, self-evident, unquestioned, axiomatic

provide VERB **1 = supply**, give, contribute, provision, distribute, outfit, equip, accommodate, donate, furnish, dispense, part with, fork out *(informal)*, stock up, cater to, purvey: *I will be happy to provide you with a copy of the report; They did not provide any food.* **OPPOSITE:** withhold **2 = give**, bring, add, produce, present, serve, afford, yield, lend, render, impart: *The summit will provide an opportunity for discussions on the crisis.* **3 = stipulate**, state, require, determine, specify, lay down: *The treaty provides that, by 2010, the U.S. must have removed its military bases.*
provide for someone = support, look after, care for, keep, maintain, sustain, take care of, fend for: *He can't even provide for his family.*
provide for *or* **against something = take precautions against**, plan for, prepare for, anticipate, arrange for, get ready for, make plans for, make arrangements for, plan ahead for, take measures against, forearm for: *James had provided for just such an emergency.*

providence NOUN **= fate**, fortune, destiny, God's will, divine intervention, predestination

provider NOUN **1 = supplier**, giver, source, donor, benefactor: *Japan is the largest provider of foreign aid in the world.* **2 = breadwinner**, supporter, earner, mainstay, wage earner: *A husband's job is to be a good provider.*

providing *or* **provided** CONJUNCTION *(often with* **that***)* **= on condition that**, if, subject to, given that, on the assumption that, in the event that, with the proviso that, contingent upon, with the understanding that, as long as, if and only if, upon these terms

province NOUN **1 = region**, section, county, district, territory, zone, patch, colony, domain, dependency, tract: *the Algarve, Portugal's southernmost province* **2 = area**, business, concern, responsibility, part, line, charge, role, post, department, field, duty, function, employment, capacity, orbit, sphere, turf *(U.S. slang)*, pigeon *(Brit. informal)*: *Industrial research is the province of the Department of Trade and Industry.*

provincial ADJECTIVE **1 = regional**, state, local, county, district, territorial, parochial: *The local and provincial elections take place in June.* **2 = rural**, country, local, home-grown, rustic, homespun, hick *(informal, chiefly U.S. & Canad.)*, backwoods: *My accent gave away my provincial roots.* **OPPOSITE:** urban **3 = parochial**, insular, narrow-minded, unsophisticated, limited, narrow, small-town *(chiefly U.S.)*, uninformed, inward-looking, small-minded, parish-pump, upcountry: *The audience was dull and very provincial.* **OPPOSITE:** cosmopolitan ▷ NOUN **= yokel**, hick *(informal, chiefly U.S. & Canad.)*, rustic, country cousin, hayseed *(U.S. & Canad. informal)*: *French provincials looking for work in Paris*

provision NOUN **1 = supplying**, giving, providing, supply, delivery, distribution, catering, presentation, equipping, furnishing, allocation, fitting out, purveying, accoutrement: *the provision of military supplies to the Khmer Rouge* **2 = arrangement**, plan, planning, preparation, precaution, contingency, prearrangement: *There is no provision for funding performance-related pay increases.* **3 = facilities**, services,

funds, resources, means, opportunities, arrangements, assistance, concession(s), allowance(s), amenities: *Special provision should be made for single mothers.* **4 = condition**, term, agreement, requirement, demand, rider, restriction, qualification, clause, reservation, specification, caveat, proviso, stipulation: *a provision that would allow existing regulations to be reviewed*
▷ PLURAL NOUN **= food**, supplies, stores, feed, fare, rations, eats *(slang)*, groceries, tack *(informal)*, grub *(slang)*, foodstuff, kai *(N.Z. informal)*, sustenance, victuals, edibles, comestibles, provender, nosebag *(slang)*, vittles *(obsolete, dialect)*, viands, eatables: *On board were enough provisions for two weeks.*

provisional ADJECTIVE **1 = temporary**, interim, transitional, stopgap, pro tem: *the possibility of setting up a provisional coalition government* **OPPOSITE:** permanent **2 = conditional**, limited, qualified, contingent, tentative, provisory: *The times stated are provisional and subject to confirmation.* **OPPOSITE:** definite

proviso NOUN **= condition**, requirement, provision, strings, rider, restriction, qualification, clause, reservation, limitation, stipulation

provocation NOUN **1 = cause**, reason, grounds, motivation, justification, stimulus, inducement, incitement, instigation, casus belli *(Latin)*: *The soldiers fired without provocation.* **2 = offence**, challenge, insult, taunt, injury, dare, grievance, annoyance, affront, indignity, red rag, vexation: *They kept their tempers in the face of severe provocation.*

provocative ADJECTIVE **1 = offensive**, provoking, insulting, challenging, disturbing, stimulating, annoying, outrageous, aggravating *(informal)*, incensing, galling, goading: *Their behaviour was called provocative and antisocial.* **2 = suggestive**, tempting, stimulating, exciting, inviting, sexy *(informal)*, arousing, erotic, seductive, alluring, tantalizing: *sexually provocative behaviour*

provoke VERB **1 = anger**, insult, annoy, offend, irritate, infuriate, hassle *(informal)*, aggravate *(informal)*, incense, enrage, gall, put someone out, madden, exasperate, vex, affront, chafe, irk, rile, pique, get on someone's nerves *(informal)*, get someone's back up, put someone's back up, try someone's patience, nark *(Brit., Austral. & N.Z. slang)*, make someone's blood boil, get in someone's hair *(informal)*, rub someone up the wrong way, hack someone off *(informal)*: *I didn't want to do anything to provoke him.* **OPPOSITE:** pacify **2 = rouse**, cause, produce, lead to, move, fire, promote, occasion, excite, inspire, generate, prompt, stir, stimulate, motivate, induce, bring about, evoke, give rise to, precipitate, elicit, inflame, incite, instigate, kindle, foment, call forth, draw forth, bring on *or* down: *His comments have provoked a shocked reaction.* **OPPOSITE:** curb

> **QUOTATIONS**
> No-one provokes me with impunity (Nemo me impune lacessit)
> *[Motto of the Crown of Scotland and of all Scottish regiments]*

prowess NOUN **1 = skill**, ability, talent, expertise, facility, command, genius, excellence, accomplishment, mastery, attainment, aptitude, dexterity, adroitness, adeptness, expertness: *He's always bragging about his prowess as a cricketer.* **OPPOSITE:** inability **2 = bravery**, daring, courage, heroism, mettle, boldness, gallantry, valour, fearlessness, intrepidity, hardihood, valiance, dauntlessness, doughtiness: *a race of people noted for their fighting prowess* **OPPOSITE:** cowardice

prowl VERB **= move stealthily**, hunt, patrol, range, steal, cruise, stalk, sneak, lurk, roam, rove, scavenge, slink, skulk, nose around

proximity NOUN **= nearness**, closeness, vicinity, neighbourhood, juxtaposition, contiguity, propinquity, adjacency

proxy NOUN **= representative**, agent, deputy, substitute, factor, attorney, delegate, surrogate

prudence NOUN **1 = caution**, care, discretion, vigilance, wariness, circumspection, canniness, heedfulness: *He urged prudence rather than haste on any new resolution.* **2 = wisdom**, common sense, good sense, good judgment, sagacity, judiciousness: *acting with prudence and judgment* **3 = thrift**, economy, planning, saving, precaution, foresight, providence, preparedness, good management, husbandry, frugality, forethought, economizing, far-sightedness, careful budgeting: *A lack of prudence may lead to financial problems.*

> **QUOTATIONS**
> I would rather worry without need than live without heed
> [Beaumarchais *The Barber of Seville*]
> Prudence is a rich, ugly, old maid courted by incapacity
> [William Blake *Proverbs of Hell*]

> **PROVERBS**
> *Take care of the pennies and the pounds will look after themselves*
> *A stitch in time saves nine*
> *Waste not, want not*

prudent ADJECTIVE **1 = cautious**, careful, wary, discreet, canny, vigilant, circumspect: *He is taking a prudent and cautious approach.* **OPPOSITE:** careless **2 = wise**, politic, sensible, sage, shrewd, discerning, judicious, sagacious: *We believed ours was the prudent and responsible course of action.* **OPPOSITE:** unwise **3 = thrifty**, economical, sparing, careful, canny, provident, frugal, far-sighted: *In private, she is prudent and even frugal.* **OPPOSITE:** extravagant

prudish ADJECTIVE **= prim**, formal, proper, stuffy, puritanical, demure, squeamish, narrow-minded, starchy *(informal)*, prissy *(informal)*, strait-laced, Victorian, priggish, schoolmarmish *(Brit. informal)*, old-maidish *(informal)*, niminy-piminy, overmodest, overnice **OPPOSITE:** broad-minded

prune VERB **1 = cut**, trim, clip, dock, shape, cut back, shorten, snip, lop, pare down: *You have to prune the bushes if you want fruit.* **2 = reduce**, cut, cut back, trim, cut down, pare down, make reductions in: *Economic hard times are forcing the company to prune their budget.*

prurient ADJECTIVE **1 = lecherous**, longing, lewd, salacious, lascivious, itching, hankering, voyeuristic, lustful, libidinous, desirous, concupiscent: *our prurient fascination with sexual scandals* **2 = indecent**, dirty, erotic, obscene, steamy *(informal)*, pornographic, X-rated *(informal)*, salacious, smutty: *the film's harshly prurient and cynical sex scenes*

pry VERB **= be inquisitive**, peer, interfere, poke, peep, meddle, intrude, snoop *(informal)*, nose into, be nosy *(informal)*, be a busybody, ferret about, poke your nose in *or* into *(informal)*

prying ADJECTIVE **= inquisitive**, spying, curious, interfering, meddling, intrusive, eavesdropping, snooping *(informal)*, snoopy *(informal)*, impertinent, nosy *(informal)*, meddlesome

psalm NOUN **= hymn**, carol, chant, paean, song of praise

pseudonym NOUN **= false name**, alias, incognito, stage name, pen name, assumed name, nom de guerre, nom de plume, professional name

psyche NOUN **= soul**, mind, self, spirit, personality, individuality, subconscious, true being, anima, essential nature, pneuma *(Philosophy)*, innermost self, inner man, wairua *(N.Z.)*

psychedelic ADJECTIVE **1 = hallucinogenic**, mind-blowing *(informal)*, psychoactive, hallucinatory, mind-bending *(informal)*, psychotropic, mind-expanding, consciousness-expanding, psychotomimetic: *experimenting with psychedelic drugs* **2 = multicoloured**, wild, crazy, freaky *(slang)*, kaleidoscopic: *psychedelic patterns*

psychiatrist NOUN **= psychotherapist**, analyst, therapist, psychologist, shrink *(slang)*, psychoanalyst, psychoanalyser, headshrinker *(slang)*

QUOTATIONS
We believe that civilization has been created under the pressure of the exigencies of life at the cost of satisfaction of the instincts [Sigmund Freud *Introductory Lectures on Psychoanalysis*]

Anyone who goes to see a psychiatrist needs his head examined [Samuel Goldwyn]

To us he is no more a person now but a whole climate of opinion [W.H. Auden (of Sigmund Freud) *In Memory of Sigmund Freud*]

psychic ADJECTIVE **1 = supernatural**, mystic, occult, clairvoyant, telepathic, extrasensory, preternatural, telekinetic: *Trevor helped police by using his psychic powers.* **2 = mystical**, spiritual, magical, other-worldly, paranormal, preternatural: *He declared his total disbelief in psychic phenomena.* **3 = psychological**, emotional, mental, spiritual, inner, psychiatric, cognitive, psychogenic: *Childhood mistreatment is the primary cause of every kind of psychic disorder.*
▷ NOUN **= clairvoyant**, fortune teller: *a natural psychic who used Tarot as a focus for his intuition*

psychological ADJECTIVE **1 = mental**, emotional, intellectual, inner, cognitive, cerebral: *the treatment of psychological disorders* **2 = imaginary**, psychosomatic, unconscious, subconscious, subjective, irrational, unreal, all in the mind: *My GP dismissed my back pains as purely psychological.*

P

psychology NOUN **1 = behaviourism**, study of personality, science of mind: *He is Professor of Psychology at Bedford Community College.* **2 = way of thinking**, attitude, behaviour, temperament, mentality, thought processes, mental processes, what makes you tick, mental make-up: *a fascination with the psychology of serial killers*

QUOTATIONS
There is no psychology; there is only biography and autobiography [Thomas Szasz *The Second Sin*]

The trouble with Freud is that he never had to play the old Glasgow Empire on a Saturday night after Rangers and Celtic had both lost [Ken Dodd]

psychopath NOUN **= madman**, lunatic, maniac, psychotic, nutter (*Brit. slang*), nutcase (*slang*), sociopath, headcase (*informal*), mental case (*slang*), headbanger (*informal*), insane person, crazy (*informal*)

psychotic ADJECTIVE **= mad**, mental (*slang*), insane, lunatic, demented, unbalanced, deranged, psychopathic, round the bend (*Brit. slang*), certifiable, off your head (*slang*), off your trolley (*slang*), not right in the head, non compos mentis (*Latin*), off your rocker (*slang*), off your chump: *He was diagnosed as psychotic and schizophrenic.*
▷ NOUN **= lunatic**, maniac, psychopath, nut (*slang*), psycho (*slang*), loony (*slang*), nutter (*Brit. slang*), nutcase (*slang*), headcase (*informal*), mental case (*slang*), headbanger (*informal*), crazy (*informal*)

pub *or* **public house** NOUN **= tavern**, bar, inn, local (*Brit. informal*), saloon, watering hole (*facetious, slang*), boozer (*Brit., Austral. & N.Z. informal*), beer parlour (*Canad.*), beverage room (*Canad.*), roadhouse, hostelry (*archaic, facetious*), alehouse (*archaic*), taproom

QUOTATIONS
There is nothing which has yet been contrived by man, by which so much happiness is produced, as by a good tavern or inn [Dr. Johnson]

puberty NOUN **= adolescence**, teenage, teens, young adulthood, pubescence, awkward age, juvenescence

public NOUN **= people**, society, country, population, masses, community, nation, everyone, citizens, voters, electorate, multitude, populace, hoi polloi, Joe Public (*slang*), Joe Six-Pack (*U.S. slang*), Main Street (*U.S. & Canad.*), commonalty: *The poll is a test of the public's confidence in the government.*
▷ ADJECTIVE **1 = civic**, government, state, national, local, official, community, social, federal, civil, constitutional, municipal: *a substantial part of public spending* **2 = general**, popular, national, shared, common, widespread, universal, collective: *Parliament's decision was in line with public opinion.* **3 = open**, community, accessible, communal, open to the public, unrestricted, free to all, not private: *a public library* **OPPOSITE:** private **4 = well-known**, leading, important, respected, famous, celebrated, recognized, distinguished, prominent, influential, notable, renowned, eminent, famed, noteworthy, in the public eye: *He hit out at public figures who commit adultery.* **5 = known**, published, exposed, open, obvious, acknowledged, recognized, plain, patent, notorious, overt, in circulation: *She was reluctant to make her views public.* **OPPOSITE:** secret

publication NOUN **1 = pamphlet**, book, newspaper, magazine, issue, title, leaflet, brochure, booklet, paperback, hardback, periodical, zine (*informal*), handbill, blog (*informal*): *a renewed campaign against pornographic publications* **2 = announcement**, publishing, broadcasting, reporting, airing, appearance, declaration, advertisement, disclosure, proclamation, notification, dissemination, promulgation: *We have no comment regarding the publication of these photographs.*

publicity NOUN **1 = advertising**, press, promotion, hype, boost, build-up, plug (*informal*), puff, ballyhoo (*informal*), puffery (*informal*), boosterism: *Much advance publicity was given to the talks.* **2 = attention**, exposure, fame, celebrity, fuss, public interest, limelight, notoriety, media attention, renown, public notice: *The case has generated enormous publicity.*

QUOTATIONS
All publicity is good, except an obituary notice [Brendan Behan]

publicize VERB **1 = advertise**, promote, plug (*informal*), hype, push, spotlight, puff, play up, write up, spread about, beat the drum for (*informal*), give publicity to, bring to public notice: *The author appeared on TV to publicize her latest book.* **2 = make known**, report, reveal, publish, broadcast, leak, disclose, proclaim, circulate, make public, divulge: *He never publicized his plans.* **OPPOSITE:** keep secret

public-spirited ADJECTIVE **= altruistic**, generous, humanitarian, charitable, philanthropic, unselfish, community-minded

publish VERB **1 = put out**, issue, produce, print, bring out: *His latest book will be published in May.* **2 = announce**, reveal, declare, spread, advertise, broadcast, leak, distribute, communicate, disclose, proclaim, circulate, impart, publicize, divulge, promulgate, shout from the rooftops (*informal*), blow wide open (*slang*): *The paper did not publish his name for legal reasons.*

QUOTATIONS
Publish and be damned [Duke of Wellington]

pucker VERB **= wrinkle**, tighten, purse, pout, contract, gather, knit, crease, compress, crumple, ruffle, furrow, screw up, crinkle, draw together, ruck up, ruckle: *She puckered her lips and kissed him on the nose.*
▷ NOUN **= wrinkle**, fold, crease, crumple, ruck, crinkle, ruckle: *small puckers in the material*

pudding NOUN **= dessert**, afters (*Brit. informal*), sweet, pud (*informal*), second course, last course

puerile ADJECTIVE **= childish**, juvenile, naive, weak, silly, ridiculous, foolish, petty, trivial, irresponsible, immature, infantile, inane, babyish, jejune **OPPOSITE:** mature

puff VERB **1 = smoke**, draw, drag (*slang*), suck, inhale, pull at *or* on: *He gave a wry smile as he puffed on his cigarette.* **2 = breathe heavily**, pant, exhale, blow, gasp, gulp, wheeze, fight for breath, puff and pant: *I could see he was unfit, because he was puffing.* **3 = promote**, push, plug (*informal*), hype, publicize, advertise, praise, crack up (*informal*), big up (*slang*), overpraise: *TV correspondents puffing the new digital channels*

▷ NOUN **1 = drag**, pull *(slang)*, smoke: *She was taking quick puffs at her cigarette.* **2 = blast**, breath, flurry, whiff, draught, gust, emanation: *an occasional puff of air stirring the brittle leaves* **3 = advertisement**, ad *(informal)*, promotion, plug *(informal)*, good word, commendation, sales talk, favourable mention, piece of publicity: *an elaborate puff for his magazine*
puff out *or* **up = swell**, expand, enlarge, inflate, stick out, dilate, distend, bloat: *His chest puffed out with pride.*

puffy ADJECTIVE **= swollen**, enlarged, inflated, inflamed, bloated, puffed up, distended

pugnacious ADJECTIVE **= aggressive**, contentious, irritable, belligerent, combative, petulant, antagonistic, argumentative, bellicose, irascible, quarrelsome, hot-tempered, choleric, disputatious, aggers *(Austral. slang)*, biffo *(Austral. slang)* **OPPOSITE:** peaceful

puke VERB **= vomit**, be sick, throw up *(informal)*, spew, heave, regurgitate, disgorge, retch, be nauseated, chuck *(Austral. & N.Z. informal)*, barf *(U.S. slang)*, chunder *(slang, chiefly Austral.)*, upchuck *(U.S. slang)*, do a technicolour yawn *(slang)*, toss your cookies *(U.S. slang)*

pull VERB **1 = draw**, haul, drag, trail, tow, tug, jerk, yank, prise, wrench, lug, wrest: *I helped pull him out of the water.* **OPPOSITE:** push **2 = extract**, pick, remove, gather, take out, weed, pluck, cull, uproot, draw out: *Wes was in the yard pulling weeds when we drove up.* **OPPOSITE:** insert **3 = attract**, draw, bring in, tempt, lure, interest, entice, pull in, magnetize: *The organizers have to employ performers to pull a crowd.* **OPPOSITE:** repel **4 = strain**, tear, stretch, rend, rip, wrench, dislocate, sprain: *Dave pulled a back muscle and could hardly move.*
▷ NOUN **1 = tug**, jerk, yank, twitch, heave: *The tooth must be removed with a firm, straight pull.* **OPPOSITE:** shove **2 = attraction**, appeal, lure, fascination, force, draw, influence, magnetism, enchantment, drawing power, enticement, allurement: *No matter how much you feel the pull of the past, try to look to the future.* **3 = force**, exertion, magnetism, forcefulness: *the pull of gravity* **4 = puff**, drag *(slang)*, inhalation: *He took a deep pull of his cigarette.* **5 = influence**, power, authority, say, standing, weight, advantage, muscle, sway, prestige, clout *(informal)*, leverage, kai *(N.Z. informal)*: *Using all his pull in parliament, he obtained the necessary papers.*
pull a fast one on someone = trick, cheat, con *(informal)*, take advantage of, deceive, defraud, swindle, bamboozle *(informal)*, hoodwink, take for a ride *(informal)*, put one over on *(informal)*: *Someone had pulled a fast one on her over a procedural matter.*
pull in = draw in, stop, park, arrive, come in, halt, draw up, pull over, come to a halt: *He pulled in at the side of the road and got out of the car.*
pull out (of) 1 = withdraw, retire from, abandon, quit, step down from, back out, bow out, stop participating in: *An injury forced him to pull out of the race.* **2 = leave**, abandon, get out, quit, retreat from, depart, evacuate: *The militia has agreed to pull out of Beirut.*
pull someone in = arrest, nail *(informal)*, bust *(informal)*, lift *(slang)*, run in *(slang)*, collar *(informal)*, pinch *(informal)*, nab *(informal)*, take someone into custody, feel someone's collar *(slang)*: *The police pulled him in for questioning.*
pull someone up = reprimand, lecture, rebuke, reproach, carpet *(informal)*, censure, scold, berate, castigate, admonish, chastise, tear into *(informal)*, read the riot act to, tell someone off *(informal)*, reprove, upbraid, take someone to task, tick someone off *(informal)*, read someone the riot act, bawl someone out *(informal)*, dress someone down *(informal)*, lambaste, give someone an earful, chew someone out *(U.S. & Canad. informal)*, tear someone off a strip *(Brit. informal)*, haul someone over the coals, give someone a dressing down, give someone a rocket *(Brit. & N.Z. informal)*, slap someone on the wrist, rap someone over the knuckles: *My boss pulled me up about my timekeeping.*
pull something apart *or* **to pieces 1 = dismantle**, strip down, disassemble, take something apart, break something up, take something to bits: *You'll have to pull it apart and start all over again.* **2 = criticize**, attack, blast, pan *(informal)*, slam *(slang)*, put down, run down, slate *(informal)*, tear into *(informal)*, lay into *(informal)*, flay, diss *(slang, chiefly U.S.)*, find fault with, lambast(e), pick holes in: *The critics pulled his new book to pieces.*
pull something down = demolish, level, destroy, dismantle, remove, flatten, knock down, take down, tear down, bulldoze, raze, lay waste, raze to the ground, kennet *(Austral. slang)*, jeff *(Austral. slang)*: *They'd pulled the school down.*
pull something in 1 = attract, draw, pull, bring in, lure: *his ability to pull in a near capacity crowd for a match* **2 = earn**, make, clear, gain, net, collect, be paid, pocket, bring in, gross, take home, rake in: *I only pull in £15,000 a year as a social worker.*
pull something off 1 = succeed in, manage, establish, effect, complete, achieve, engineer, carry out, crack *(informal)*, fulfil, accomplish, execute, discharge, clinch, bring about, carry off, perpetrate, bring off: *Labour might just pull off its third victory in a row.* **2 = remove**, detach, rip off, tear off, doff, wrench off: *He pulled off his shirt.*
pull something out = produce, draw, bring out, draw out: *He pulled out a gun and threatened us.*
pull something up = uproot, raise, lift, weed, dig up, dig out, rip up: *Pull up weeds by hand and put them on the compost heap.*
pull through = survive, improve, recover, rally, come through, get better, be all right, recuperate, turn the corner, pull round, get well again: *Everyone waited to see whether he would pull through or not.*
pull up = stop, park, halt, arrive, brake, draw up, come to a halt, reach a standstill: *The cab pulled up and the driver jumped out.*
pull yourself together = get a grip on yourself, recover, get over it, buck up *(informal)*, snap out of it *(informal)*, get your act together, regain your composure: *He pulled himself together and got back to work.*

pulp NOUN **1 = paste**, mash, pap, mush, semisolid, pomace, semiliquid: *The olives are crushed to a pulp by stone rollers.* **2 = flesh**, meat, marrow, soft part: *Use the whole fruit, including the pulp, which is high in fibre.*
▷ MODIFIER **= cheap**, sensational, lurid, mushy *(informal)*, trashy, rubbishy: *lurid '50s pulp fiction*
▷ VERB **= crush**, squash, mash, pulverize: *Onions can be boiled and pulped to a puree.*

pulsate VERB **= throb**, pound, beat, hammer, pulse, tick, thump, quiver, vibrate, thud, palpitate

pulse NOUN **= beat**, rhythm, vibration, beating, stroke, throb, throbbing, oscillation, pulsation: *the repetitive pulse of the music*
▷ VERB **= beat**, tick, throb, vibrate, pulsate: *Her feet pulsed with pain.*

pummel VERB **= beat**, punch, pound, strike, knock, belt *(informal)*, hammer, bang, batter, thump, clobber *(slang)*, lambast(e), beat the living daylights out of, rain blows upon, beat *or* knock seven bells out of *(informal)*

pump VERB **1 = drive out**, empty, drain, force out, bail out, siphon, draw off: *drill rigs that are busy pumping natural gas* **2 = supply**, send, pour, inject: *The government must pump more money into community care.* **3 = interrogate**, probe, quiz, cross-examine, grill *(informal)*, worm out of, give someone the third degree, question closely: *He ran in every five minutes to pump me for details.*
pump something up = inflate, blow up, fill up, dilate, puff up, aerate: *I was trying to pump up my back tyre.*

pun NOUN **= play on words**, quip, double entendre, witticism, paronomasia *(Rhetoric)*, equivoque

> **QUOTATIONS**
> A man who could make so vile a pun would not scruple to pick a pocket
> [John Dennis]

punch[1] VERB **= hit**, strike, box, smash, belt *(informal)*, slam, plug *(slang)*, bash *(informal)*, sock *(slang)*, clout *(informal)*, slug, swipe *(informal)*, biff *(slang)*, bop *(informal)*, wallop *(informal)*, pummel:

p

After punching him on the chin, she hit him over the head.
▷ NOUN **1 = blow**, hit, knock, bash *(informal)*, plug *(slang)*, sock *(slang)*, thump, clout *(informal)*, jab, swipe *(informal)*, biff *(slang)*, bop *(informal)*, wallop *(informal)*: *He's asking for a punch on the nose.* **2 = effectiveness**, force, bite, impact, point, drive, vigour, verve, forcefulness: *The film lacks punch and pace.*

punch² VERB **= pierce**, cut, bore, drill, pink, stamp, puncture, prick, perforate: *I took a pen and punched holes in the carton.*

punch-up NOUN **= fight**, row, argument, set-to *(informal)*, scrap *(informal)*, brawl, free-for-all *(informal)*, dust-up *(informal)*, shindig *(informal)*, battle royal, stand-up fight *(informal)*, dingdong, shindy *(informal)*, bagarre *(French)*, biffo *(Austral. slang)*

punchy ADJECTIVE **= effective**, spirited, dynamic, lively, storming *(informal)*, aggressive, vigorous, forceful, incisive, in-your-face *(slang)*

punctual ADJECTIVE **= on time**, timely, early, prompt, strict, exact, precise, in good time, on the dot, seasonable **OPPOSITE:** late

punctuality NOUN **= promptness**, readiness, regularity, promptitude

> **QUOTATIONS**
> Punctuality is the politeness of kings
> [Louis XVIII]
>
> Punctuality is the thief of time
> [Oscar Wilde]
>
> Punctuality is the virtue of the bored
> [Evelyn Waugh *diary*]

punctuate VERB **= interrupt**, break, pepper, sprinkle, intersperse, interject

puncture NOUN **1 = flat tyre**, flat, flattie *(N.Z.)*: *Someone helped me to mend the puncture.* **2 = hole**, opening, break, cut, nick, leak, slit, rupture, perforation: *an instrument used to make a puncture in the abdominal wall*
▷ VERB **1 = pierce**, cut, nick, penetrate, prick, rupture, perforate, impale, bore a hole (in): *The bullet punctured his stomach.* **2 = deflate**, go down, go flat: *The tyre is guaranteed never to puncture.* **3 = humble**, discourage, disillusion, flatten, deflate, take down a peg *(informal)*: *a witty column which punctures celebrity egos*

pundit NOUN **= expert**, guru, maestro, buff *(informal)*, wonk *(informal)*, fundi *(S. African)*, one of the cognoscenti, (self-appointed) expert *or* authority

pungent ADJECTIVE **1 = strong**, hot, spicy, seasoned, sharp, acid, bitter, stinging, sour, tart, aromatic, tangy, acrid, peppery, piquant, highly flavoured, acerb: *The more herbs you use, the more pungent the sauce will be.* **OPPOSITE:** mild **2 = cutting**, pointed, biting, acute, telling, sharp, keen, stinging, piercing, penetrating, poignant, stringent, scathing, acrimonious, barbed, incisive, sarcastic, caustic, vitriolic, trenchant, mordant, mordacious: *He enjoyed the play's shrewd and pungent social analysis.* **OPPOSITE:** dull

punish VERB **= discipline**, correct, castigate, chastise, beat, sentence, whip, lash, cane, flog, scourge, chasten, penalize, bring to book, slap someone's wrist, throw the book at, rap someone's knuckles, give someone the works *(slang)*, give a lesson to

punishable ADJECTIVE **= culpable**, criminal, chargeable, indictable, blameworthy, convictable

punishing ADJECTIVE **= hard**, taxing, demanding, grinding, wearing, tiring, exhausting, uphill, gruelling, strenuous, arduous, burdensome, backbreaking **OPPOSITE:** easy

punishment NOUN **1 = penalizing**, discipline, correction, retribution, what for *(informal)*, chastening, just deserts, chastisement, punitive measures: *The man is guilty and he deserves punishment.* **2 = penalty**, reward, sanction, penance, comeuppance *(slang)*: *The usual punishment is a fine.* **3 = beating**, abuse, torture, pain, victimization, manhandling, maltreatment, rough treatment: *He took a lot of punishment in the first few rounds of the fight.* **4 = rough treatment**, abuse, maltreatment: *This bike isn't designed to take that kind of punishment.*

> **QUOTATIONS**
> Let the punishment fit the crime
> [W.S. Gilbert *The Mikado*]
>
> Whoso sheddeth man's blood, by man shall his blood be shed
> [*Bible: Genesis*]
>
> They have sown the wind, and they shall reap the whirlwind
> [*Bible: Hosea*]
>
> Men are not hanged for stealing horses, but that horses may not be stolen
> [George Savile, Marquess of Halifax *Political, Moral, and Miscellaneous Thoughts*]

punitive ADJECTIVE **= retaliatory**, in retaliation, vindictive, in reprisal, revengeful, retaliative, punitory

punt VERB **= bet**, back, stake, gamble, lay, wager: *He punted the lot on Little Nell in the third race.*
▷ NOUN **= bet**, stake, gamble, wager: *I like to take the odd punt on the stock exchange.*

punter NOUN **1 = gambler**, better, backer, punt *(chiefly Brit.)*: *Punters are expected to gamble £70m on the Grand National.* **2 = customer**, guest, client, patron, member of the audience: *The show ended when an irate punter punched one of the performers.* **3 = person**, guy *(informal)*, fellow, bloke *(Brit. informal)*, man in the street: *Most of these artists are not known to the ordinary punter.*

puny ADJECTIVE **1 = feeble**, weak, frail, little, tiny, weakly, stunted, diminutive, sickly, undeveloped, pint-sized *(informal)*, undersized, underfed, dwarfish, pygmy *or* pigmy: *Our Kevin has always been a puny lad.* **OPPOSITE:** strong **2 = insignificant**, minor, petty, inferior, trivial, worthless, trifling, paltry, inconsequential, piddling *(informal)*: *the puny resources at our disposal*

pup *or* **puppy** NOUN **= whippersnapper**, braggart, whelp, jackanapes, popinjay

pupil NOUN **1 = student**, scholar, schoolboy *or* schoolgirl, schoolchild: *a school with over 1,000 pupils* **OPPOSITE:** teacher **2 = learner**, student, follower, trainee, novice, beginner, apprentice, disciple, protégé, neophyte, tyro, catechumen: *Goldschmidt became a pupil of the composer Franz Schreker.* **OPPOSITE:** instructor

puppet NOUN **1 = marionette**, doll, glove puppet, sock puppet, finger puppet: *The show features huge inflatable puppets.* **2 = pawn**, tool, instrument, creature, dupe, gull *(archaic)*, figurehead, mouthpiece, stooge, cat's-paw: *The ministers have denied that they are puppets of a foreign government.*

purchase VERB **= buy**, pay for, obtain, get, score *(slang)*, gain, pick up, secure, acquire, invest in, shop for, get hold of, come by, procure, make a purchase: *She purchased a tuna sandwich and a carton of orange juice; Most of the shares were purchased by brokers.* **OPPOSITE:** sell
▷ NOUN **1 = acquisition**, buy, investment, property, gain, asset, possession: *She opened the bag and looked at her purchases.* **2 = grip**, hold, support, footing, influence, edge, advantage, grasp, lever, leverage, foothold, toehold: *I got a purchase on the rope and pulled.*

purchaser NOUN **= buyer**, customer, consumer, vendee *(Law)* **OPPOSITE:** seller

pure ADJECTIVE **1 = unmixed**, real, clear, true, simple, natural, straight, perfect, genuine, neat, authentic, flawless, unalloyed: *The ancient alchemists tried to transmute base metals into pure gold.* **OPPOSITE:** adulterated **2 = clean**, immaculate, sterile, wholesome, sanitary, spotless, sterilized, squeaky-clean, unblemished, unadulterated, untainted, disinfected, uncontaminated, unpolluted, pasteurized, germ-free: *demands for pure and clean river water* **OPPOSITE:** contaminated **3 = theoretical**, abstract, philosophical, speculative, academic, conceptual, hypothetical, conjectural, non-practical: *Physics isn't just about pure science with no practical applications.* **OPPOSITE:** practical

The Language of Frances Hodgson Burnett

Frances Hodgson Burnett (1849–1924) was a novelist and playwright of British birth who emigrated to America in her teens. She is most remembered for her writing for children, in particular *The Secret Garden* and *Little Lord Fauntleroy* which present an idealistic vision of childhood innocence in the face of sometimes difficult social circumstances.

Burnett's writing is often structured around transformation, as in the young aristocrat Colin's growth from a bad-tempered invalid to a healthy, active boy in *The Secret Garden*. Consequently, synonyms for unhappiness are a prominent aspect of Burnett's language as she depicts the first stages of the journey to an improved situation. *Alone* is a frequent indicator of a forlorn state and often collocates with parts of a house or with items of furniture. The most common place to be *alone* is a *room*, though there are numerous more specific locations, such as a *closet*, *chamber*, *attic*, and *parlour* and yet more specific places within these, for example *bed* or *armchair*. The more general lament of being *alone in the world* is another recurrent descriptor of this predicament.

Similarly, the adjective *lonely* most frequently modifies *life*, *place*, and *child* though more unusually it is also used with *look*, as in:

> But though the **lonely** look passed away from Sara's face she never quite forgot the garret at Miss Minchin's.

This focus on the child's eyes as the site of her discontent represents a recurrent motif in Burnett's work. *Eyes* are frequently used by Burnett to indicate mood. As well as *lonely* they can be *hungry*, *wild*, *solemn*, *fierce*, *wistful*, *mournful*, *dreamy*, or *mad*. Alongside the most familiar adjectives applied to *eyes* (*blue* or *dark*, for example), Burnett consistently pays attention to their size. *Great* and *big* are two of the most salient adjectives with *eyes* and there are often more precise depictions of scale, such as:

> ... her soft, dull eyes looked twice their natural size, and seemed to stare piteously at people.

Accordingly, one of the most frequent nouns occurring with *grow* is *eyes*. This usage encompasses both emotion and dimensions and there is often a connection between the two as the increase in size reveals a particular state of mind, generally excitement or fear. Burnett is also drawn to the *face* in her writing. By far the most salient adjective in this context is *little*, although once again, there is a strong leaning towards words expressive of suffering, such as *pale*, *haggard*, *thin*, *sharp*, and *delicate*. *Queer* is among the other most common terms of distress employed by Burnett, and in contrast to today's most common usage, suggests sickness when applied to a person or, more broadly, strangeness when employed in other contexts.

Unsurprisingly, given the setting of her most famous work in a garden, horticulture supplies Burnett with another prominent semantic field. In describing *flowers*, *white* followed by *blue* are her adjectives of choice. For *trees*, *huge*, *bare*, and *green* are the most salient with a broad range of more evocative compound adjectives occurring too, such as *heavy-branched*, *close-growing* and *soot-blackened*. This area of interest provides Burnett with the source of numerous metaphors and similes. *Bloom* indicates not just the flourishing of plants but also the developing of childhood into adulthood, as in the phrase *blooming youth*. *Like a flower* conveys a similar sense of natural human wellbeing, as in:

> No one had ever looked at her in this way before, but being herself a thing which had grown **like a flower**, she felt no shyness, and was only glad.

Like a bird is another organic simile that recurs in Burnett's writing.

4 = complete, total, perfect, absolute, mere, sheer, patent, utter, outright, thorough, downright, palpable, unqualified, out-and-out, unmitigated: *The old man turned to give her a look of pure surprise.*
OPPOSITE: qualified **5 = innocent**, virgin, modest, good, true, moral, maidenly, upright, honest, immaculate, impeccable, righteous, virtuous, squeaky-clean, blameless, chaste, virginal, unsullied, guileless, uncorrupted, unstained, undefiled, unspotted: *a pure and chaste maiden*
OPPOSITE: corrupt

> **QUOTATIONS**
> My strength is as the strength of ten
> Because my heart is pure
> [Alfred, Lord Tennyson *Sir Galahad*]
>
> Unto the pure all things are pure
> [*Bible: II Timothy*]

purely ADVERB **= absolutely**, just, only, completely, simply, totally, entirely, exclusively, plainly, merely, solely, wholly

purgatory NOUN **= torment**, agony, murder *(informal)*, hell *(informal)*, torture, misery, hell on earth

purge VERB **1 = rid**, clear, cleanse, strip, empty, void: *They voted to purge the party of 'hostile and anti-party elements'.* **2 = get rid of**, kill, remove, dismiss, axe *(informal)*, expel, wipe out, oust, eradicate, eject, do away with, liquidate, exterminate, sweep out, rout out, wipe from the face of the earth, rid somewhere of: *They have purged thousands from the upper levels of the civil service; They purged any individuals suspected of loyalty to the king.*
3 = cleanse, clear, purify, wash, clean out, expiate: *He lay still, trying to purge his mind of anxiety.*
▷ NOUN **= removal**, elimination, crushing, expulsion, suppression, liquidation, cleanup, witch hunt, eradication, ejection: *a thorough purge of people associated with the late ruler*

purify VERB **1 = clean**, filter, cleanse, refine, clarify, disinfect, fumigate, decontaminate, sanitize, detoxify: *Plants can filter and purify the air in your office.* **OPPOSITE:** contaminate
2 = absolve, cleanse, redeem, exonerate, sanctify, exculpate, shrive, lustrate: *They believe that bathing in the Ganges at certain holy places purifies the soul.* **OPPOSITE:** sully

purist NOUN **= stickler**, traditionalist, perfectionist, classicist, pedant, formalist, literalist

puritan NOUN **= moralist**, fanatic, zealot, prude, pietist, rigorist: *He delighted in dealing with subjects that enraged puritans.*
▷ ADJECTIVE **= strict**, austere, puritanical, narrow, severe, intolerant, ascetic, narrow-minded, moralistic, prudish, hidebound, strait-laced: *Paul has always had a puritan streak.*

> **QUOTATIONS**
> The Puritan hated bear-baiting, not because it gave pain to the bear, but because it gave pleasure to the spectators
> [Lord Macaulay *History of England*]

puritanical ADJECTIVE **= strict**, forbidding, puritan, stuffy, narrow, severe, proper, stiff, rigid, disapproving, austere, fanatical, bigoted, prim, ascetic, narrow-minded, prudish, strait-laced
OPPOSITE: liberal

puritanism NOUN **= strictness**, austerity, severity, zeal, piety, rigidity, fanaticism, narrowness, asceticism, moralism, prudishness, rigorism, piousness

> **QUOTATIONS**
> Puritanism: The haunting fear that someone, somewhere may be happy
> [H.L. Mencken *Chrestomathy*]

purity NOUN **1 = cleanness**, clarity, cleanliness, brilliance, genuineness, wholesomeness, fineness, clearness, pureness, faultlessness, immaculateness, untaintedness: *the purity of the air in your working environment*
OPPOSITE: impurity **2 = innocence**, virtue, integrity, honesty, decency, sincerity, virginity, piety, chastity, rectitude, guilelessness, virtuousness, chasteness, blamelessness: *The American Female Reform Society promoted sexual purity.*
OPPOSITE: immorality

purple

SHADES OF PURPLE

amethyst	magenta
aubergine	mauve
burgundy	mulberry
carmine	pansy
claret	peach-blow
dubonnet	periwinkle
gentian	plum
gentian blue	puce
heather	royal purple
heliotrope	Tyrian purple
indigo	violet
lavender	wine
lilac	

purport VERB **= claim**, allege, proclaim, maintain, declare, pretend, assert, pose as, profess

purpose NOUN **1 = reason**, point, idea, goal, grounds, design, aim, basis, principle, function, object, intention, objective, motive, motivation, justification, impetus, the why and wherefore: *The purpose of the occasion was to raise money for charity.* **2 = aim**, end, plan, hope, view, goal, design, project, target, wish, scheme, desire, object, intention, objective, ambition, aspiration, Holy Grail *(informal)*: *They are prepared to go to any lengths to achieve their purpose.*
3 = determination, commitment, resolve, will, resolution, initiative, enterprise, ambition, conviction, motivation, persistence, tenacity, firmness, constancy, single-mindedness, steadfastness: *The teachers are enthusiastic and have a sense of purpose.* **4 = use**, good, return, result, effect, value, benefit, profit, worth, gain, advantage, outcome, utility, merit, mileage *(informal)*, avail, behoof *(archaic)*: *Talking about it will serve no purpose.*
on purpose = deliberately, purposely, consciously, intentionally, knowingly, wilfully, by design, wittingly, calculatedly, designedly: *Was it an accident, or did she do it on purpose?*

> **USAGE**
> The two concepts *purposeful* and *on purpose* should be carefully distinguished. *On purpose* and *purposely* have roughly the same meaning, and imply that a person's action is deliberate, rather than accidental. However, *purposeful* and its related adverb *purposefully* refer to the way that someone acts as being full of purpose or determination.

purposeful ADJECTIVE **= determined**, resolved, resolute, decided, firm, settled, positive, fixed, deliberate, single-minded, tenacious, strong-willed, steadfast, immovable, unfaltering **OPPOSITE:** undecided

purposely ADVERB **= deliberately**, expressly, consciously, intentionally, knowingly, with intent, on purpose, wilfully, by design, calculatedly, designedly **OPPOSITE:** accidentally

purse NOUN **1 = pouch**, wallet, money-bag: *I dug the money out of my purse.* **2 = handbag**, bag, shoulder bag, pocket book, clutch bag: *She reached into her purse for her cigarettes.* **3 = funds**, means, money, resources, treasury, wealth, exchequer, coffers, wherewithal: *The money will go into the public purse, helping to lower taxes.*
4 = prize, winnings, award, gift, reward: *She is tipped to win the biggest purse in women's pro volleyball history.*
▷ VERB **= pucker**, close, contract, tighten, knit, wrinkle, pout, press together: *She pursed her lips in disapproval.*

pursue VERB **1 = engage in**, follow, perform, conduct, wage, tackle, take up, work at, carry on, practise, participate in, prosecute, ply, go in for, apply yourself to: *Japan would continue to pursue the policies laid down at the summit.* **2 = try for**, seek, desire, search for, aim for, aspire to, work towards, strive for, have as a goal: *Mr Menendez has aggressively pursued success.*
3 = continue, maintain, carry on, keep on, hold to, see through, adhere to, persist in, proceed in, persevere in: *If your request is denied, don't be afraid to pursue the matter.* **4 = follow**, track, hunt, chase, dog, attend, shadow, accompany, harry, tail *(informal)*, haunt, plague, hound, stalk, harass,

go after, run after, hunt down, give chase to: *She pursued the man who had stolen her bag.* **OPPOSITE:** flee **5 = court**, woo, pay attention to, make up to (*informal*), chase after, pay court to, set your cap at: *He had pursued her, and within weeks they had become lovers.* **OPPOSITE:** fight shy of

pursuit NOUN **1 = quest**, seeking, search, aim, aspiration, striving towards: *individuals in pursuit of their dreams; the pursuit of happiness* **2 = pursuing**, seeking, tracking, search, hunt, hunting, chase, trail, trailing: *Police had obstructed justice by hindering the pursuit of terrorists.* **3 = occupation**, activity, interest, line, pleasure, hobby, pastime, vocation: *They both love outdoor pursuits.*

push VERB **1 = shove**, force, press, thrust, drive, knock, sweep, plunge, elbow, bump, ram, poke, propel, nudge, prod, jostle, hustle, bulldoze, impel, manhandle: *They pushed him into the car.* **OPPOSITE:** pull **2 = press**, operate, depress, squeeze, activate, hold down: *He got into the lift and pushed the button for the second floor.* **3 = make** or **force your way**, move, shoulder, inch, squeeze, thrust, elbow, shove, jostle, work your way, thread your way: *I pushed through the crowds and on to the escalator.* **4 = urge**, encourage, persuade, spur, drive, press, influence, prod, constrain, incite, coerce, egg on, impel, browbeat, exert influence on, inspan (*S. African*): *Her parents kept her in school and pushed her to study.* **OPPOSITE:** discourage **5 = promote**, advertise, hype, publicize, boost, plug (*informal*), puff, make known, propagandize, cry up: *Advertisers often use scientific doublespeak to push their products.*
▷ NOUN **1 = shove**, thrust, butt, elbow, poke, nudge, prod, jolt: *He gave me a sharp push.* **OPPOSITE:** pull **2 = effort**, charge, attack, campaign, advance, assault, raid, offensive, sally, thrust, blitz, onset: *All that was needed was one final push, and the enemy would be vanquished once and for all.* **3 = drive**, go (*informal*), energy, initiative, enterprise, ambition, determination, pep, vitality, vigour, dynamism, get-up-and-go (*informal*), gumption (*informal*): *He lacked the push to succeed in his chosen vocation.*
push off = go away, leave, get lost (*informal*), clear off (*informal*), take off (*informal*), depart, beat it (*slang*), light out (*informal*), hit the road (*slang*), hook it (*slang*), slope off, pack your bags (*informal*), make tracks, buzz off (*informal*), hop it (*informal*), shove off (*informal*), skedaddle (*informal*), naff off (*informal*), be off with you, sling your hook (*informal*), make yourself scarce (*informal*), voetsek (*S. African offensive*), rack off (*Austral. & N.Z. slang*): *Do me a favour and push off, will you?*
the push = dismissal, the sack (*informal*), discharge, the boot (*slang*), your cards (*informal*), your books (*informal*), your marching orders (*informal*), the kiss-off (*slang, chiefly U.S. & Canad.*), the (old) heave-ho (*informal*), the order of the boot (*slang*): *Two cabinet ministers also got the push.*

pushed ADJECTIVE (*often with* **for**) **= short of**, pressed, rushed, tight, hurried, under pressure, in difficulty, up against it (*informal*)

pushover NOUN **1 = sucker** (*slang*), mug (*Brit. slang*), stooge (*slang*), soft touch (*slang*), chump (*informal*), walkover (*informal*), easy game (*informal*), easy *or* soft mark (*informal*): *He's a tough negotiator – you won't find him a pushover.* **2 = piece of cake** (*Brit. informal*), breeze (*U.S. & Canad. informal*), picnic (*informal*), child's play (*informal*), plain sailing, doddle (*Brit. slang*), walkover (*informal*), cinch (*slang*), cakewalk (*informal*), duck soup (*U.S. slang*): *You might think Hungarian is a pushover to learn, but it isn't.* **OPPOSITE:** challenge

pushy ADJECTIVE **= forceful**, aggressive, assertive, brash, loud, offensive, ambitious, bold, obnoxious, presumptuous, obtrusive, officious, bumptious, self-assertive **OPPOSITE:** shy

put VERB **1 = place**, leave, set, position, rest, park (*informal*), plant, establish, lay, stick (*informal*), settle, fix, lean, deposit, dump (*informal*), prop, lay down, put down, situate, set down, stow, bung (*informal*), plonk (*informal*): *She put her bag on the floor.* **2 = consign to**, place, commit to, doom to, condemn to: *She was put in prison for her beliefs.* **3 = impose**, subject, levy, inflict: *The government has put a big tax on beer, wine and spirits.* **4 = express**, state, word, phrase, set, pose, utter: *To put it bluntly, he doesn't give a damn.* **5 = present**, suggest, advance, propose, offer, forward, submit, tender, bring forward, proffer, posit, set before, lay before: *He sat there listening as we put our suggestions to him.*
put-down = humiliation, slight, snub, knock (*informal*), dig, sneer, rebuff, barb, sarcasm, kick in the teeth (*slang*), gibe, disparagement, one in the eye (*informal*)
put someone away = commit, confine, cage (*informal*), imprison, certify, institutionalize, incarcerate, put in prison, put behind bars, lock up *or* away: *He's insane! He should be put away for life.*
put someone down = humiliate, shame, crush, show up, reject, dismiss, condemn, slight, criticize, snub, have a go at (*informal*), deflate, denigrate, belittle, disparage, deprecate, mortify, diss (*slang, chiefly U.S.*): *She's always putting her husband down in public.*
put someone off 1 = discourage, intimidate, deter, daunt, dissuade, demoralize, scare off, dishearten: *We tried to visit the abbey but were put off by the queues.* **2 = disconcert**, confuse, unsettle, throw (*informal*), distress, rattle (*informal*), dismay, perturb, faze, discomfit, take the wind out of someone's sails, nonplus, abash: *All this noise is putting me off.*
put someone out 1 = inconvenience, trouble, upset, bother, disturb, impose upon, discomfit, discommode, incommode: *Thanks for the offer, but I couldn't put you out like that.* **2 = annoy**, anger, provoke, irritate, disturb, harass, confound, exasperate, disconcert, nettle, vex, perturb, irk, put on the spot, take the wind out of someone's sails, discountenance, discompose: *They were quite put out to find me in charge.*
put someone up 1 = accommodate, house, board, lodge, quarter, entertain, take someone in, billet, give someone lodging: *She asked if I could put her up for a few days.* **2 = nominate**, put forward, offer, present, propose, recommend, float, submit: *The new party is putting up 15 candidates for 22 seats.*
put someone up to something = encourage, urge, persuade, prompt, incite, egg on, goad, put the idea into someone's head: *How do you know he asked me out? Did you put him up to it?*
put something across *or* **over = communicate**, explain, clarify, express, get through, convey, make clear, spell out, get across, make yourself understood: *The opposition parties were hampered from putting across their message.*
put something aside *or* **by 1 = save**, store, stockpile, deposit, hoard, cache, lay by, stow away, salt away, keep in reserve, squirrel away: *Encourage children to put some money aside each week.* **2 = disregard**, forget, ignore, bury, discount, set aside, pay no heed to: *We should put aside our differences and discuss this sensibly.*
put something away 1 = store away, replace, put back, tidy up, clear away, tidy away, return to its place: *She began putting away the dishes.* **2 = save**, set aside, put aside, keep, deposit, put by, stash away, store away: *He had been able to put away money, to insure against old age.* **3 = consume**, devour, eat up, demolish (*informal*), gobble, guzzle, polish off (*informal*), gulp down, wolf down, pig out on (*informal*): *The food was superb, and we put away a fair amount of it.*
put something down 1 = record, write down, list, enter, log, take down, inscribe, set down, transcribe, put in black and white: *Never put anything down on paper which might be used in evidence.* **2 = repress**, crush, suppress, check, silence, overthrow, squash, subdue, quash, quell, stamp out: *Soldiers went in to put down a rebellion.* **3 = put to sleep**, kill, destroy, do away with, put away, put out of its misery: *Magistrates ordered that the dog should be put down at once.*
put something down to something

p

= attribute, blame, ascribe, set down, impute, chalk up: *You may be a sceptic and put it down to coincidence.*
put something forward = recommend, present, suggest, introduce, advance, propose, press, submit, tender, nominate, prescribe, move for, proffer: *He has put forward new peace proposals.*
put something off = postpone, delay, defer, adjourn, put back, hold over, reschedule, put on ice, put on the back burner *(informal)*, take a rain check on *(U.S. & Canad. informal)*: *The Association has put the event off until December.*
put something on 1 = don, dress in, slip into, pull on, climb into, change into, throw on, get dressed in, fling on, pour yourself into, doll yourself up in: *She put on her coat and went out.* **2 = present**, stage, perform, do, show, produce, mount: *The band are putting on a UK show before the end of the year.* **3 = add**, gain, increase by: *I've put on a stone since I stopped training.* **4 = bet**, back, place, chance, risk, lay, stake, hazard, wager: *They put £20 on Matthew scoring the first goal.* **5 = fake**, affect, assume, simulate, feign, make believe, play-act: *Anything becomes funny if you put on an American accent.*
put something out 1 = issue, release, publish, broadcast, bring out, circulate, make public, make known: *The French news agency put out a statement from the Trade Minister.* **2 = extinguish**, smother, blow out, stamp out, douse, snuff out, quench: *Firemen tried to free the injured and put out the blaze.*
put something up 1 = build, raise, set up, construct, erect, fabricate: *He was putting up a new fence round the garden.* **2 = offer**, present, mount, put forward: *In the end they surrendered without putting up any resistance.* **3 = provide**, advance, invest, contribute, give, pay up, supply, come up with, pledge, donate, furnish, fork out *(informal)*, cough up *(informal)*, shell out *(informal)*: *The state agreed to put up the money to start his company.*
put up with something *or* **someone = stand**, suffer, bear, take, wear *(Brit. informal)*, stomach, endure, swallow, brook, stand for, lump *(informal)*, tolerate, hack *(slang)*, abide, countenance: *I won't put up with this kind of behaviour from you.*
put upon someone = take advantage of, trouble, abuse, harry, exploit, saddle, take for granted, put someone out, inconvenience, beset, overwork, impose upon, take for a fool: *Don't allow people to put upon you or take you for granted.*

putative ADJECTIVE **= supposed**, reported, assumed, alleged, presumed, reputed, imputed, presumptive, commonly believed

put-down = humiliation, slight, snub, knock *(informal)*, dig, sneer, rebuff, barb, sarcasm, kick in the teeth *(slang)*, gibe, disparagement, one in the eye *(informal)*

puzzle VERB **= perplex**, beat *(slang)*, confuse, baffle, stump, bewilder, confound, mystify, faze, flummox, bemuse, nonplus: *What puzzles me is why nobody has complained before now.*
▷ NOUN **1 = problem**, riddle, maze, labyrinth, question, conundrum, teaser, poser, brain-teaser *(informal)*: *a word puzzle* **2 = mystery**, problem, paradox, enigma, conundrum: *the puzzle of why there are no Stone Age cave paintings in Britain*
puzzle over something = think about, study, wonder about, mull over, muse on, think hard about, ponder on, brood over, ask yourself about, cudgel *or* rack your brains: *puzzling over the complexities of Shakespeare's verse*
puzzle something out = solve, work out, figure out, unravel, see, get, crack, resolve, sort out, clear up, decipher, think through, suss (out) *(slang)*, get the answer of, find the key to, crack the code of: *I stared at the symbols, trying to puzzle out their meaning.*

puzzled ADJECTIVE **= perplexed**, beaten, confused, baffled, lost, stuck, stumped, doubtful, at sea, bewildered, mixed up, at a loss, mystified, clueless, nonplussed, flummoxed, in a fog, without a clue

puzzlement NOUN **= perplexity**, questioning, surprise, doubt, wonder, confusion, uncertainty, bewilderment, disorientation, bafflement, mystification, doubtfulness

puzzling ADJECTIVE **= perplexing**, baffling, bewildering, hard, involved, misleading, unclear, ambiguous, enigmatic, incomprehensible, mystifying, inexplicable, unaccountable, knotty, unfathomable, labyrinthine, full of surprises, abstruse, beyond you, oracular **OPPOSITE:** simple

pygmy *or* **pigmy** MODIFIER **= small**, miniature, dwarf, tiny, wee, stunted, diminutive, minuscule, midget, elfin, undersized, teeny-weeny, Lilliputian, dwarfish, teensy-weensy, pygmean: *The pygmy hippopotamus is less than 6 ft long.*
▷ NOUN **1 = midget**, dwarf, shrimp *(informal)*, Lilliputian, Tom Thumb, munchkin *(informal, chiefly U.S.)*, homunculus, manikin: *an encounter with the Ituri Forest pygmies*
2 = nonentity, nobody, lightweight *(informal)*, mediocrity, cipher, small fry, pipsqueak *(informal)*: *He saw the politicians of his day as pygmies, not as giants.*

Qq

quack NOUN **= charlatan**, fraud, fake, pretender, humbug, impostor, mountebank, phoney *or* phony *(informal)*: *The man was a quack after all, just as Rosalinda had warned.*
▷ MODIFIER **= fake**, fraudulent, phoney *or* phony *(informal)*, pretended, sham, counterfeit: *Why do intelligent people find quack remedies so appealing?*

quaff VERB **= drink**, gulp, swig *(informal)*, have, down, swallow, slug, guzzle, imbibe, partake of

quagmire NOUN **1 = predicament**, difficulty, quandary, pass, fix *(informal)*, jam *(informal)*, dilemma, pinch, plight, scrape *(informal)*, muddle, pickle *(informal)*, impasse, entanglement, imbroglio: *a political quagmire* **2 = bog**, marsh, swamp, slough, fen, mire, morass, quicksand, muskeg *(Canad.)*: *Overnight rain had turned the grass airstrip into a quagmire.*

quail VERB **= shrink**, cringe, flinch, shake, faint, tremble, quake, shudder, falter, droop, blanch, recoil, cower, blench, have cold feet *(informal)*

quaint ADJECTIVE **1 = unusual**, odd, curious, original, strange, bizarre, fantastic, old-fashioned, peculiar, eccentric, queer, rum *(Brit. slang)*, singular, fanciful, whimsical, droll: *When visiting restaurants, be prepared for some quaint customs.* **OPPOSITE:** ordinary **2 = old-fashioned**, charming, picturesque, antique, gothic, old-world, antiquated: *Whisky-making is treated as a quaint cottage industry.* **OPPOSITE:** modern

quake VERB **= shake**, tremble, quiver, move, rock, shiver, throb, shudder, wobble, waver, vibrate, pulsate, quail, totter, convulse

qualification NOUN **1 = eligibility**, quality, ability, skill, capacity, fitness, attribute, capability, endowment(s), accomplishment, achievement, aptitude, suitability, suitableness: *That time with him is my qualification to write the book.* **2 = condition**, restriction, proviso, requirement, rider, exception, criterion, reservation, allowance, objection, limitation, modification, exemption, prerequisite, caveat, stipulation: *The empirical evidence is subject to many qualifications.*

qualified ADJECTIVE **1 = capable**, trained, experienced, seasoned, able, fit, expert, talented, chartered, efficient, practised, licensed, certificated, equipped, accomplished, eligible, competent, skilful, adept, knowledgeable, proficient: *Demand has far outstripped supply of qualified teachers.* **OPPOSITE:** untrained **2 = restricted**, limited, provisional, conditional, reserved, guarded, bounded, adjusted, moderated, adapted, confined, modified, tempered, cautious, refined, amended, contingent, tentative, hesitant, circumscribed, equivocal: *He answers both questions with a qualified yes.* **OPPOSITE:** unconditional

qualify VERB **1 = certify**, equip, empower, train, ground, condition, prepare, fit, commission, ready, permit, sanction, endow, capacitate: *The course does not qualify you to practise as a therapist.* **OPPOSITE:** disqualify **2 = be described**, count, be considered as, be named, be counted, be eligible, be characterized, be designated, be distinguished: *13 percent of households qualify as poor.* **3 = restrict**, limit, reduce, vary, ease, moderate, adapt, modify, regulate, diminish, temper, soften, restrain, lessen, mitigate, abate, tone down, assuage, modulate, circumscribe: *I would qualify that by putting it into context.*

quality NOUN **1 = standard**, standing, class, condition, value, rank, grade, merit, classification, calibre: *high quality paper and plywood* **2 = excellence**, status, merit, position, value, worth, distinction, virtue, superiority, calibre, eminence, pre-eminence: *a college of quality* **3 = characteristic**, feature, attribute, point, side, mark, property, aspect, streak, trait, facet, quirk, peculiarity, idiosyncrasy: *He wanted to introduce mature people with leadership qualities.* **4 = nature**, character, constitution, make, sort, kind, worth, description, essence: *The pretentious quality of the poetry.*

qualm NOUN **= misgiving**, doubt, uneasiness, regret, anxiety, uncertainty, reluctance, hesitation, remorse, apprehension, disquiet, scruple, compunction, twinge *or* pang of conscience

quandary NOUN **= difficulty**, dilemma, predicament, puzzle, uncertainty, embarrassment, plight, strait, impasse, bewilderment, perplexity, delicate situation, cleft stick

quantity NOUN **1 = amount**, lot, total, sum, part, portion, quota, aggregate, number, allotment: *a vast quantity of food* **2 = size**, measure, mass, volume, length, capacity, extent, bulk, magnitude, greatness, expanse: *the sheer quantity of data can cause problems.*

> **USAGE**
> The use of a plural noun after *quantity of*, as in *a large quantity of bananas*, used to be considered incorrect, the objection being that the word *quantity* should only be used to refer to an uncountable amount, which was grammatically regarded as a singular concept. Nowadays, however, most people consider the use of *quantity* with a plural noun to be acceptable.

quarrel NOUN **= disagreement**, fight, row, difference (of opinion), argument, dispute, controversy, breach, scrap *(informal)*, disturbance, misunderstanding, contention, feud, fray, brawl, spat, squabble, strife, wrangle, skirmish, vendetta, discord, fracas, commotion, tiff, altercation, broil, tumult, dissension, affray, shindig *(informal)*, disputation, dissidence, shindy *(informal)*, bagarre *(French)*, biffo *(Austral. slang)*: *I had a terrible quarrel with my other brothers.* **OPPOSITE:** accord
▷ VERB **= disagree**, fight, argue, row, clash, dispute, scrap *(informal)*, differ, fall out *(informal)*, brawl, squabble, spar, wrangle, bicker, be at odds, lock horns, cross swords, fight like cat and dog, go at it hammer and tongs, altercate: *My brother quarrelled with my father.* **OPPOSITE:** get on *or* along (with)

quarrelsome ADJECTIVE **= argumentative**, belligerent, pugnacious, cross, contentious, irritable, combative, fractious, petulant, ill-tempered, irascible, cantankerous, litigious, querulous, peevish, choleric, disputatious **OPPOSITE:** easy-going

quarry NOUN **= prey**, victim, game, goal, aim, prize, objective

quarter NOUN **1 = district**, region, neighbourhood, place, point, part, side, area, position, station, spot, territory, zone, location, province, colony, locality: *He wandered through the Chinese quarter.* **2 = mercy**, pity, compassion, favour, charity, sympathy, tolerance, kindness, forgiveness, indulgence, clemency, leniency, forbearance, lenity: *It is bloody brutal work, with no quarter given.*
▷ VERB **= accommodate**, house, lodge, place, board, post, station, install, put up, billet, give accommodation, provide with accommodation: *Our soldiers are quartered in Peredelkino.*

quarters PLURAL NOUN **= lodgings**, rooms, accommodation, post, station, chambers, digs (*Brit. informal*), shelter, lodging, residence, dwelling, barracks, abode, habitation, billet, domicile, cantonment (*Military*)

quash VERB **1 = annul**, overturn, reverse, cancel, overthrow, set aside, void, revoke, overrule, rescind, invalidate, nullify, declare null and void: *The Appeal Court has quashed the convictions.* **2 = suppress**, crush, put down, beat, destroy, overthrow, squash, subdue, repress, quell, extinguish, quench, extirpate: *an attempt to quash regional violence*

quaver VERB **= tremble**, shake, quiver, thrill, quake, shudder, flicker, flutter, waver, vibrate, pulsate, oscillate, trill, twitter

queasy ADJECTIVE **1 = sick**, ill, nauseous, squeamish, upset, uncomfortable, crook (*Austral. & N.Z. informal*), queer, unwell, giddy, nauseated, groggy (*informal*), off colour, bilious, indisposed, green about the gills (*informal*), sickish: *He was prone to sickness and already felt queasy.* **2 = uneasy**, concerned, worried, troubled, disturbed, anxious, uncertain, restless, ill at ease, fidgety: *Some people feel queasy about how their names and addresses have been obtained.*

queen NOUN **1 = sovereign**, ruler, monarch, leader, Crown, princess, majesty, head of state, Her Majesty, empress, crowned head: *the time she met the Queen* **2 = leading light**, star, favourite, celebrity, darling, mistress, idol, big name, doyenne: *the queen of crime writing*

queer ADJECTIVE **1 = strange**, odd, funny, unusual, extraordinary, remarkable, curious, weird, peculiar, abnormal, rum (*Brit. slang*), uncommon, erratic, singular, eerie, unnatural, unconventional, uncanny, disquieting, unorthodox, outlandish, left-field (*informal*), anomalous, droll, atypical, outré: *If you ask me, there's something queer going on.* **OPPOSITE:** normal **2 = faint**, dizzy, giddy, queasy, light-headed, reeling: *Wine before beer and you'll feel queer.*

quell VERB **1 = suppress**, crush, put down, defeat, overcome, conquer, subdue, stifle, overpower, quash, extinguish, stamp out, vanquish, squelch: *Troops eventually quelled the unrest.* **2 = calm**, quiet, silence, moderate, dull, soothe, alleviate, appease, allay, mitigate, assuage, pacify, mollify, deaden: *He is trying to quell fears of a looming crisis.*

quench VERB **1 = satisfy**, appease, allay, satiate, slake, sate: *He stopped to quench his thirst at a stream.* **2 = put out**, extinguish, douse, end, check, destroy, crush, suppress, stifle, smother, snuff out, squelch: *Fire crews struggled to quench the fire.*

query NOUN **1 = question**, inquiry, enquiry, problem, demand: *If you have any queries, please contact us.* **2 = doubt**, suspicion, reservation, objection, hesitation, scepticism: *I read the query in the guide's eyes.*
▷ VERB **1 = question**, challenge, doubt, suspect, dispute, object to, distrust, mistrust, call into question, disbelieve, feel uneasy about, throw doubt on, harbour reservations about: *No one queried my decision.* **2 = ask**, inquire *or* enquire, question: *'Is there something else?' he queried.*

quest NOUN **1 = search**, hunt, mission, enterprise, undertaking, exploration, crusade: *his quest to find true love* **2 = expedition**, journey, adventure, voyage, pilgrimage: *Sir Guy the Seeker came on his quest to Dunstanburgh Castle.*

question NOUN **1 = inquiry**, enquiry, query, investigation, examination, interrogation: *He refused to answer further questions on the subject.* **OPPOSITE:** answer **2 = difficulty**, problem, doubt, debate, argument, dispute, controversy, confusion, uncertainty, query, contention, misgiving, can of worms (*informal*), dubiety: *There's no question about their success.* **3 = issue**, point, matter, subject, problem, debate, proposal, theme, motion, topic, proposition, bone of contention, point at issue: *The whole question of aid is a tricky political one.*
▷ VERB **1 = interrogate**, cross-examine, interview, examine, investigate, pump (*informal*), probe, grill (*informal*), quiz, ask questions, sound out, catechize: *A man is being questioned by police.* **2 = dispute**, challenge, doubt, suspect, oppose, query, distrust, mistrust, call into question, disbelieve, impugn, cast aspersions on, cast doubt upon, controvert: *It never occurs to them to question the doctor's decisions.* **OPPOSITE:** accept
in question = under discussion, at issue, under consideration, in doubt, on the agenda, to be discussed, for debate, open to debate: *The film in question detailed allegations about party corruption.*
out of the question = impossible, unthinkable, inconceivable, not on (*informal*), hopeless, unimaginable, unworkable, unattainable, unobtainable, not feasible, impracticable, unachievable, unrealizable, not worth considering, not to be thought of: *Is a tax increase still out of the question?*

questionable ADJECTIVE **= dubious**, suspect, doubtful, controversial, uncertain, suspicious, dodgy (*Brit., Austral. & N.Z. informal*), unreliable, shady (*informal*), debatable, unproven, fishy (*informal*), moot, arguable, iffy (*informal*), equivocal, problematical, disputable, controvertible, dubitable, shonky (*Austral. & N.Z. informal*) **OPPOSITE:** indisputable

questionnaire NOUN **= set of questions**, form, survey form, question sheet

queue NOUN **= line**, row, file, train, series, chain, string, column, sequence, succession, procession, crocodile (*Brit. informal*), progression, cavalcade, concatenation

quibble VERB **= split hairs**, carp, cavil, prevaricate, beat about the bush, equivocate, nit-pick (*informal*): *Let's not quibble.*
▷ NOUN **= objection**, complaint, niggle, protest, criticism, nicety, equivocation, prevarication, cavil, quiddity, sophism: *These are minor quibbles.*

quick ADJECTIVE **1 = fast**, swift, speedy, express, active, cracking (*Brit. informal*), smart, rapid, fleet, brisk, hasty, headlong, nippy (*informal*), pdq (*slang*): *Europe has moved a long way at a quick pace.* **OPPOSITE:** slow **2 = brief**, passing, hurried, flying, fleeting, summary, lightning, short-lived, hasty, cursory, perfunctory: *I just popped in for a quick chat.* **OPPOSITE:** long **3 = immediate**, instant, prompt, sudden, abrupt, instantaneous, expeditious: *The President has admitted there is no quick end in sight.* **4 = excitable**, passionate, impatient, abrupt, hasty, irritable, touchy, curt, petulant, irascible, testy: *She had inherited her father's quick temper.* **OPPOSITE:** calm **5 = intelligent**, bright (*informal*), alert, sharp, acute, smart, clever, all there (*informal*), shrewd, discerning, astute, receptive, perceptive, quick-witted, quick on the uptake (*informal*), nimble-witted: *The older adults are not as quick in their thinking.* **OPPOSITE:** stupid

quicken VERB **1 = speed up**, hurry, accelerate, hasten, gee up (*informal*): *He quickened his pace a little.* **2 = stimulate**, inspire, arouse, excite, strengthen, revive, refresh, activate, animate, rouse, incite, resuscitate, energize, revitalize, kindle, galvanize, invigorate, reinvigorate, vitalize, vivify: *Thank you for quickening my spiritual understanding.*

quickly ADVERB **1 = swiftly**, rapidly, hurriedly, speedily, fast, quick, hastily, briskly, at high speed, apace, at full speed, hell for leather (*informal*), like lightning, at the speed of light, at full tilt, hotfoot, at a rate of knots (*informal*), like the clappers (*Brit. informal*), pdq (*slang*), like nobody's business (*informal*), with all speed, posthaste, lickety-split (*U.S. informal*), like greased lightning (*informal*), at *or* on the double, flatstick (*S. African slang*): *She turned and ran quickly up the stairs to the flat above.* **OPPOSITE:** slowly **2 = soon**, speedily, as soon as possible, momentarily (*U.S.*), instantaneously, pronto (*informal*), a.s.a.p. (*informal*): *You can become fitter quickly and easily.* **3 = immediately**, instantly, at once, directly, promptly, abruptly, without delay, expeditiously: *The meeting quickly adjourned.*

quick-witted ADJECTIVE **= clever**, bright (*informal*), sharp, keen, smart,

Mark Twain's Use of Nouns

Mark Twain was the no-nonsense pen name of the splendidly monickered Samuel Langhorne Clemens (1835–1910). The son of a Missouri lawyer, his lively youth was spent, among other occupations, as a printer's apprentice, silver prospector and, most famously, river-boat pilot, a period which he chronicled in *Life on the Mississippi* (1883). He is most often remembered as the author of *The Adventures of Tom Sawyer* (1876) and the darker and more sophisticated *The Adventures of Huckleberry Finn* (1885, often nominated in votes for the Great American Novel). However, his output as novelist, short story writer, and journalist was vast, and the often-applied label 'humorist' scarcely does justice to his fierce satires on intolerance, hypocrisy, and the growth of US imperialism.

His language was often complimented (and just as often condemned) for its reflection of everyday speech, and he prided himself on his use of dialect, above all in *Huckleberry Finn*, stating in its preface:

> In this book a number of dialects are used, to wit: the Missouri negro dialect; the extremest form of the backwoods Southwestern dialect; the ordinary 'Pike County' dialect; and four modified varieties of this last. ... I make this explanation for the reason that without it many readers would suppose that all these characters were trying to talk alike and not succeeding.

One colloquial noun frequently used in the novel is the most controversial in all of Twain's writings – the word *nigger*. Twain's characters (and especially Huck) often seem to use this in a purely descriptive way, with no particular intended slur – an indication in itself of how deeply ingrained are their racist assumptions. Nevertheless, the use of this particular noun has, unsurprisingly, caused much controversy in recent years, and has even led to bans by some American school libraries.

As an outspoken critic of public misdeeds, it is not surprising that the word *office* occurs widely in his writings. It is used in the sense of 'place of business', as in 'attorney's office' (the most frequent possessor) and 'telegraph', 'patent', or 'dead letter office'. It is also found in the sense of 'post or occupation', as in something to 'hold', 'accept', or 'vacate' – or, indeed, to seek by fair means or foul:

> Several times since your election persons wanting **office** have asked me 'to use my influence' with you in their behalf.

The now rather rare sense of 'service' also occurs quite often, as in 'to perform an office for someone', 'deferential little offices of courtesy' or:

> a hireling nurse to whom was delegated the mother's tenderest **office**

As a commentator-at-large on the follies of humanity, it is natural that *people* should have come frequently to Twain's pen. However, the phrase *the American people* occurs only a little over once per million words, much less often than in the works of his contemporary American authors. Fenimore Cooper used it twice as often, Hawthorne three times as frequently, and Harriet Beecher Stowe eight times (though all fade in comparison with Lincoln, who as President during the Civil War doubtless had good reason to use the phrase almost 70 times per million words!). Twain may well have instinctively shunned the potentially demagogic phrase – an irony this most American of authors would no doubt have savoured had it been pointed out to him.

One oddity thrown up by a word search of Twain's work is the use of the archaic pronoun *ye*, which occurs over 500 times. This is not, however, an indication of high-flown rhetorical appeals (the kind which Twain would invariably have found suspect), but an indication of the rather creaky language Twain manufactured for the dialogue in his historical fantasies such as *The Prince and the Pauper* (1882, set in 16th-century London), or the even further-flung *A Connecticut Yankee in King Arthur's Court* (1889).

alert, shrewd, astute, perceptive **OPPOSITE:** slow

quid pro quo NOUN = **exchange**, interchange, tit for tat, equivalent, compensation, retaliation, reprisal, substitution

quiet ADJECTIVE **1 = soft**, low, muted, lowered, whispered, faint, suppressed, stifled, hushed, muffled, inaudible, indistinct, low-pitched: *A quiet murmur passed through the classroom.* **OPPOSITE:** loud **2 = peaceful**, silent, hushed, soundless, noiseless: *She was received in a small, quiet office.* **OPPOSITE:** noisy **3 = calm**, peaceful, tranquil, contented, gentle, mild, serene, pacific, placid, restful, untroubled, chilled *(informal)*: *She wanted a quiet life.* **OPPOSITE:** exciting **4 = still**, motionless, calm, peaceful, tranquil, untroubled: *a look of quiet satisfaction* **OPPOSITE:** troubled **5 = undisturbed**, isolated, secluded, private, secret, retired, sequestered, unfrequented: *a quiet rural backwater* **OPPOSITE:** crowded **6 = silent**, dumb: *I told them to be quiet and go to sleep.* **7 = reserved**, retiring, shy, collected, gentle, mild, composed, serene, sedate, meek, placid, docile, unflappable *(informal)*, phlegmatic, peaceable, imperturbable, equable, even-tempered, unexcitable: *He's a nice quiet man.* **OPPOSITE:** excitable **8 = subdued**, conservative, plain, sober, simple, modest, restrained, unassuming, unpretentious, unobtrusive: *They dress in quiet colours.* **OPPOSITE:** bright
▷ NOUN = **peace**, rest, tranquillity, ease, silence, solitude, serenity, stillness, repose, calmness, quietness, peacefulness, restfulness: *He wants some peace and quiet.* **OPPOSITE:** noise

quieten VERB **1 = silence**, subdue, stifle, still, stop, quiet, mute, hush, quell, muffle, shush *(informal)*: *She tried to quieten her breathing.* **2 = soothe**, calm, allay, dull, blunt, alleviate, appease, lull, mitigate, assuage, mollify, deaden, tranquillize, palliate: *It took a long time to quieten the paranoia of the West.* **OPPOSITE:** provoke

quietly ADVERB **1 = noiselessly**, silently: *She closed the door quietly.* **2 = softly**, in hushed tones, in a low voice *or* whisper, inaudibly, in an undertone, under your breath: *'This is goodbye, isn't it?' she said quietly.* **3 = privately**, secretly, confidentially: *quietly planning their next move* **4 = calmly**, serenely, placidly, patiently, mildly, meekly, contentedly, dispassionately, undemonstratively: *She sat quietly watching all that was going on around her.* **5 = silently**, in silence, mutely, without talking, dumbly: *Amy stood quietly in the door watching him.* **6 = modestly**, humbly, unobtrusively, diffidently, unpretentiously, unassumingly, unostentatiously: *He is quietly confident about the magazine's chances.*

quilt NOUN = **bedspread**, duvet, comforter *(U.S.)*, downie *(informal)*, coverlet, eiderdown, counterpane, doona *(Austral.)*, continental quilt

quintessential ADJECTIVE = **ultimate**, essential, typical, fundamental, definitive, archetypal, prototypical

quip NOUN = **joke**, sally, jest, riposte, wisecrack *(informal)*, retort, counterattack, pleasantry, repartee, gibe, witticism, bon mot, badinage

quirk NOUN = **peculiarity**, eccentricity, mannerism, foible, idiosyncrasy, habit, fancy, characteristic, trait, whim, oddity, caprice, fetish, aberration, kink, vagary, singularity, idée fixe *(French)*

quirky ADJECTIVE = **odd**, unusual, eccentric, idiosyncratic, curious, peculiar, unpredictable, rum *(Brit. slang)*, singular, fanciful, whimsical, capricious, offbeat

quit VERB **1 = resign (from)**, leave, retire (from), pull out (of), surrender, chuck *(informal)*, step down (from) *(informal)*, relinquish, renounce, pack in *(informal)*, abdicate: *He figured he would quit his job before he was fired* **2 = stop**, give up, cease, end, drop, abandon, suspend, halt, discontinue, belay *(Nautical)*: *I was trying to quit smoking at the time.* **OPPOSITE:** continue **3 = leave**, depart from, go out of, abandon, desert, exit, withdraw from, forsake, go away from, pull out from, decamp from: *Police were called when he refused to quit the building.*

quite ADVERB **1 = somewhat**, rather, fairly, reasonably, kind of *(informal)*, pretty *(informal)*, relatively, moderately, to some extent, comparatively, to some degree, to a certain extent: *I was doing quite well, but I wasn't earning a lot of money.* **2 = absolutely**, perfectly, completely, totally, fully, entirely, precisely, considerably, wholly, in all respects, without reservation: *It is quite clear that we were firing in self defence.*

quiver VERB = **shake**, tremble, shiver, quake, shudder, agitate, vibrate, pulsate, quaver, convulse, palpitate: *Her bottom lip quivered and big tears rolled down her cheeks.*
▷ NOUN = **shake**, tremble, shiver, throb, shudder, tremor, spasm, vibration, tic, convulsion, palpitation, pulsation: *I felt a quiver of panic.*

quixotic ADJECTIVE = **unrealistic**, idealistic, romantic, absurd, imaginary, visionary, fanciful, impractical, dreamy, Utopian, impulsive, fantastical, impracticable, chivalrous, unworldly, chimerical

quiz NOUN = **examination**, questioning, interrogation, interview, investigation, grilling *(informal)*, cross-examination, cross-questioning, the third degree *(informal)*: *Man faces quiz over knife death.*
▷ VERB = **question**, ask, interrogate, examine, investigate, pump *(informal)*, grill *(informal)*, catechize: *Sybil quizzed her about life as a working girl.*

quizzical ADJECTIVE = **mocking**, questioning, inquiring, curious, arch, teasing, bantering, sardonic, derisive, supercilious

quota NOUN = **share**, allowance, ration, allocation, part, cut *(informal)*, limit, proportion, slice, quantity, portion, assignment, whack *(informal)*, dispensation

quotation NOUN **1 = passage**, quote *(informal)*, excerpt, cutting, selection, reference, extract, citation: *He illustrated his argument with quotations from Pasternak.* **2 = estimate**, price, tender, rate, cost, charge, figure, quote *(informal)*, bid price: *Get several written quotations and check exactly what's included in the cost.*

> **QUOTATIONS**
> Every quotation contributes something to the stability or enlargement of the language
> [Dr. Johnson *Dictionary of the English Language (preface)*]

quote VERB **1 = repeat**, recite, reproduce, recall, echo, extract, excerpt, proclaim, parrot, paraphrase, retell: *Then suddenly he quoted a line from the play.* **2 = refer to**, cite, give, name, detail, relate, mention, instance, specify, spell out, recount, recollect, make reference to, adduce: *Most newspapers quote the warning.*

Rr

rabble NOUN **1 = mob**, crowd, herd, swarm, horde, throng, canaille: *a rabble of gossip columnists* **2 = commoners**, proletariat, common people, riffraff, crowd, masses, trash (*chiefly U.S. & Canad.*), scum, lower classes, populace, peasantry, dregs, hoi polloi, the great unwashed (*derogatory*), canaille, lumpenproletariat, commonalty: *They are forced to socialise with the rabble.* **OPPOSITE:** upper classes

rabid ADJECTIVE **1 = fanatical**, extreme, irrational, fervent, zealous, bigoted, intolerant, narrow-minded, intemperate: *the rabid state media* **OPPOSITE:** moderate **2 = crazed**, wild, violent, mad, raging, furious, frantic, frenzied, infuriated, berserk, maniacal, berko (*Austral. slang*): *The tablets gave him the look of a rabid dog.*

race[1] NOUN **1 = competition**, contest, chase, dash, pursuit, contention: *a running race in a Cambridge quadrangle* **2 = contest**, competition, rivalry, contention: *the race for the White House*
▷ VERB **1 = compete against**, run against: *They may even have raced each other.* **2 = compete**, run, contend, take part in a race: *He, too, will be racing here again soon.* **3 = run**, fly, career, speed, tear, dash, hurry, barrel (along) (*informal, chiefly U.S. & Canad.*), dart, gallop, zoom, hare (*Brit. informal*), hasten, burn rubber (*informal*), go like a bomb (*Brit. & N.Z. informal*), run like mad (*informal*): *They raced away out of sight.*

race[2] NOUN **= people**, ethnic group, nation, blood, house, family, line, issue, stock, type, seed (*chiefly biblical*), breed, folk, tribe, offspring, clan, kin, lineage, progeny, kindred: *We welcome students of all races, faiths and nationalities.*

> **QUOTATIONS**
> Say it loud! I'm black and I'm proud!
> [James Brown]
>
> No race has the last word on culture and on civilization
> [Marcus Garvey *speech*]
>
> There are only two races on this planet – the intelligent and the stupid
> [John Fowles]

racial ADJECTIVE **= ethnic**, ethnological, national, folk, genetic, tribal, genealogical

rack NOUN **= frame**, stand, structure, framework: *a luggage rack*
▷ VERB **= torture**, distress, torment, harass, afflict, oppress, harrow, crucify, agonize, pain, excruciate: *a teenager racked with guilt*

racket NOUN **1 = noise**, row, shouting, fuss, disturbance, outcry, clamour, din, uproar, commotion, pandemonium, rumpus, babel, tumult, hubbub, hullabaloo, ballyhoo (*informal*): *The racket went on past midnight.* **2 = fraud**, scheme, criminal activity, illegal enterprise: *a drugs racket*

racy ADJECTIVE **1 = risqué**, naughty, indecent, bawdy, blue, broad, spicy (*informal*), suggestive, smutty, off colour, immodest, indelicate, near the knuckle (*informal*): *Her novels may be racy but they don't fight shy of larger issues.* **2 = lively**, spirited, exciting, dramatic, entertaining, stimulating, sexy (*informal*), sparkling, vigorous, energetic, animated, heady, buoyant, exhilarating, zestful: *very high-quality wines with quite a racy character*

radiance NOUN **1 = happiness**, delight, pleasure, joy, warmth, rapture, gaiety: *There was a new radiance about her.* **2 = brightness**, light, shine, glow, glitter, glare, gleam, brilliance, lustre, luminosity, incandescence, resplendence, effulgence: *The dim bulb cast a soft radiance over his face.*

radiant ADJECTIVE **1 = happy**, glowing, ecstatic, joyful, sent (*informal*), gay, delighted, beaming, joyous, blissful, rapturous, rapt, on cloud nine (*informal*), beatific, blissed out (*informal*), floating on air: *On her wedding day the bride looked truly radiant.* **OPPOSITE:** miserable **2 = bright**, brilliant, shining, glorious, beaming, glowing, sparkling, sunny, glittering, gleaming, luminous, resplendent, incandescent, lustrous, effulgent: *Out on the bay the morning is radiant.* **OPPOSITE:** dull

radiate VERB **1 = emit**, spread, send out, disseminate, pour, shed, scatter, glitter, gleam: *Thermal imagery will show up objects radiating heat.* **2 = shine**, emanate, be diffused: *From here contaminated air radiates out to the open countryside.* **3 = show**, display, demonstrate, exhibit, emanate, give off or out: *She radiates happiness and health.* **4 = spread out**, diverge, branch out: *the narrow streets which radiate from the Cathedral Square*

radiation NOUN **= emission**, rays, emanation

radical ADJECTIVE **1 = extreme**, complete, entire, sweeping, violent, severe, excessive, thorough, drastic: *periods of radical change* **2 = revolutionary**, extremist, fanatical: *political tension between radical and conservative politicians* **3 = fundamental**, natural, basic, essential, native, constitutional, organic, profound, innate, deep-seated, thoroughgoing: *the radical differences between them* **OPPOSITE:** superficial
▷ NOUN **= extremist**, revolutionary, militant, fanatic: *a former left-wing radical who was involved with the civil rights movement* **OPPOSITE:** conservative

> **QUOTATIONS**
> A radical is a man with both feet firmly planted in the air
> [Franklin D. Roosevelt *radio broadcast*]

raffle NOUN **= draw**, lottery, sweepstake, sweep

rage NOUN **1 = fury**, temper, frenzy, rampage, tantrum, foulie (*Austral. slang*), hissy fit (*informal*), strop (*Brit. informal*): *I flew into a rage.* **OPPOSITE:** calmness **2 = anger**, violence, passion, obsession, madness, raving, wrath, mania, agitation, ire, vehemence, high dudgeon: *The people are full of fear and rage.* **3 = craze**, fashion, enthusiasm, vogue, fad (*informal*), latest thing: *the latest technological rage*
▷ VERB **1 = be at its height**, surge, rampage, be uncontrollable, storm: *The war rages on and the time has come to take sides.* **2 = be furious**, rave, blow up (*informal*), fume, lose it (*informal*), fret, seethe, crack up (*informal*), see red (*informal*), chafe, lose the plot (*informal*), go ballistic (*slang, chiefly U.S.*), rant and rave, foam at the mouth, lose your temper, blow a fuse (*slang, chiefly U.S.*), fly off the handle (*informal*), be incandescent, go off the deep end (*informal*), throw a fit (*informal*), wig out (*slang*), go up the wall (*slang*), blow your top, lose your rag (*slang*), be beside yourself, flip your lid (*slang*): *He was annoyed, no doubt, but not raging.* **OPPOSITE:** stay calm

ragged ADJECTIVE **1 = tatty**, worn, poor, torn, rent, faded, neglected, rundown, frayed, shabby, worn-out, seedy, scruffy, in tatters, dilapidated, tattered, threadbare, unkempt, in rags, down at heel, the worse for wear, in holes, having seen better days, scraggy: *I am usually happiest in ragged jeans and a t-shirt.* **OPPOSITE:** smart **2 = rough**, fragmented, crude, rugged, notched, irregular, unfinished, uneven, jagged, serrated: *She tore her tights on the ragged edge of a desk*

raging ADJECTIVE **= furious**, mad, raving, fuming, frenzied, infuriated, incensed, enraged, seething, fizzing (*Scot.*), incandescent, foaming at the mouth, fit to be tied *(slang)*, boiling mad *(informal)*, beside yourself, doing your nut *(Brit. slang)*, off the air *(Austral. slang)*

raid VERB **1 = steal from**, break into, plunder, pillage, sack: *The guerrillas raided banks and destroyed a police barracks.* **2 = attack**, invade, assault, rifle, forage *(Military)*, fall upon, swoop down upon, reive *(dialect)*: *8th century Vikings set off to raid the coasts of Europe.* **3 = make a search of**, search, bust *(informal)*, descend on, make a raid on, make a swoop on: *Fraud squad officers raided the firm's offices.*
▷ NOUN **1 = attack**, invasion, seizure, onset, foray, sortie, incursion, surprise attack, hit-and-run attack, sally, inroad, irruption: *The rebels attempted a surprise raid on a military camp.* **2 = bust** *(informal)*, swoop, descent, surprise search: *a raid on a house by thirty armed police*

raider NOUN **= attacker**, thief, robber, plunderer, invader, forager *(Military)*, marauder, reiver *(dialect)*

rail VERB **= complain**, attack, abuse, blast, put down, criticize, censure, scold, castigate, revile, tear into *(informal)*, fulminate, inveigh, upbraid, lambast(e), vituperate, vociferate

railing NOUN **= fence**, rails, barrier, paling, balustrade

rain NOUN **1 = rainfall**, fall, showers, deluge, drizzle, downpour, precipitation, raindrops, cloudburst: *You'll get soaked standing out in the rain.* **2 = shower**, flood, stream, hail, volley, spate, torrent, deluge: *A rain of stones descended on the police.*
▷ VERB **1 = pour**, pelt (down), teem, bucket down *(informal)*, fall, shower, drizzle, rain cats and dogs *(informal)*, come down in buckets *(informal)*: *It rained the whole weekend.* **2 = fall**, shower, be dropped, sprinkle, be deposited: *Rockets, mortars and artillery rained on buildings.* **3 = bestow**, pour, shower, lavish: *Banks rained money on commercial real estate developers.*
▸ *related adjectives:* pluvial, pluvious

QUOTATIONS
The rain it raineth every day
[William Shakespeare *Twelfth Night*]

PROVERBS
It never rains but it pours

rainy ADJECTIVE **= wet**, damp, drizzly, showery OPPOSITE: dry

raise VERB **1 = lift**, move up, elevate, uplift, heave: *He raised his hand to wave.* **2 = set upright**, lift, elevate: *She raised herself on one elbow.* **3 = increase**, reinforce, intensify, heighten, advance, boost, strengthen, enhance, put up, exaggerate, hike (up) *(informal)*, enlarge, escalate, inflate, aggravate, magnify, amplify, augment, jack up: *Two incidents in recent days have raised the level of concern.* OPPOSITE: reduce **4 = make louder**, heighten, amplify, louden: *Don't you raise your voice to me!* **5 = collect**, get, gather, obtain: *events held to raise money* **6 = mobilize**, form, mass, rally, recruit, assemble, levy, muster: *Landed nobles provided courts of justice and raised troops.* **7 = cause**, start, produce, create, occasion, provoke, bring about, originate, give rise to, engender: *a joke that raised a smile* **8 = put forward**, suggest, introduce, advance, bring up, broach, moot: *He had been consulted and had raised no objections.* **9 = bring up**, develop, rear, nurture: *the house where she was raised* **10 = grow**, produce, rear, cultivate, propagate: *He raises 2,000 acres of wheat and hay.* **11 = breed**, keep: *She raised chickens and pigs.* **12 = build**, construct, put up, erect: *They raised a church in the shape of a boat.* OPPOSITE: demolish **13 = promote**, upgrade, elevate, advance, prefer, exalt, aggrandize: *He was to be raised to the rank of ambassador.* OPPOSITE: demote

rake[1] VERB **1 = scrape**, break up, scratch, scour, harrow, hoe: *The beach is raked and cleaned daily.* **2 = gather**, collect, scrape together, scrape up, remove: *I watched the men rake leaves into heaps.* **3 = strafe**, pepper, enfilade: *The caravan was raked with bullets.* **4 = graze**, scratch, scrape: *Ragged fingernails raked her skin.* **5** *(with* **through***)* **= search**, hunt, examine, scan, comb, scour, ransack, forage, scrutinize, fossick *(Austral. & N.Z.)*: *Many can only survive by raking through dustbins.*

rake[2] NOUN **= libertine**, playboy, swinger *(slang)*, profligate, lecher, roué, sensualist, voluptuary, debauchee, rakehell *(archaic)*, dissolute man, lech *or* letch *(informal)*: *As a young man I was a rake.* OPPOSITE: puritan

rakish ADJECTIVE **= dashing**, smart, sporty, flashy, breezy, jaunty, dapper, natty *(informal)*, debonair, snazzy *(informal)*, raffish, devil-may-care

rally NOUN **1 = gathering**, mass meeting, convention, convocation, meeting, conference, congress, assembly, congregation, muster, hui *(N.Z.)*: *They held a rally to mark international human rights day.* **2 = recovery**, improvement, comeback *(informal)*, revival, renewal, resurgence, recuperation, turn for the better: *After a brief rally, shares returned to 126p.* OPPOSITE: relapse
▷ VERB **1 = gather together**, unite, bring together, regroup, reorganize, reassemble, re-form: *He rallied his own supporters for a fight.* **2 = recover**, improve, pick up, revive, get better, come round, perk up, recuperate, turn the corner, pull through, take a turn for the better, regain your strength, get your second wind: *He rallied enough to thank his doctor.* OPPOSITE: get worse

ram VERB **1 = hit**, force, drive into, strike, crash, impact, smash, slam, dash, run into, butt, collide with: *They used a lorry to ram the main gate.* **2 = cram**, pound, force, stuff, pack, hammer, jam, thrust, tamp: *He rammed the key into the lock and kicked the front door open.*

ramble NOUN **= walk**, tour, trip, stroll, hike, roaming, excursion, roving, saunter, traipse *(informal)*, peregrination, perambulation: *an hour's ramble through the woods*
▷ VERB **1 = walk**, range, drift, wander, stroll, stray, roam, rove, amble, saunter, straggle, traipse *(informal)*, go walkabout *(Austral.)*, perambulate, stravaig *(Scot. & Northern English dialect)*, peregrinate: *freedom to ramble across the moors* **2** *(often with* **on***)* **= babble**, wander, rabbit (on) *(Brit. informal)*, chatter, waffle *(informal, chiefly Brit.)*, digress, rattle on, maunder, witter on *(informal)*, expatiate, run off at the mouth *(slang)*: *Sometimes she tended to ramble.*

rambler NOUN **= walker**, roamer, wanderer, rover, hiker, drifter, stroller, wayfarer

rambling ADJECTIVE **1 = sprawling**, spreading, trailing, irregular, straggling: *that rambling house with its bizarre contents* **2 = long-winded**, incoherent, disjointed, prolix, irregular, diffuse, disconnected, desultory, wordy, circuitous, discursive, digressive, periphrastic: *He wrote a rambling letter to his wife.* OPPOSITE: concise

ramification NOUN **= consequences**, results, developments, complications, sequel, upshot

ramp NOUN **= slope**, grade, incline, gradient, inclined plane, rise

rampage VERB **= go berserk**, tear, storm, rage, run riot, run amok, run wild, go ballistic *(slang)*, go ape *(slang)*: *He used a sword to defend his shop from a rampaging mob.*
on the rampage = berserk, wild, violent, raging, destructive, out of control, rampant, amok, riotous, berko *(Austral. slang)*: *a bull that went on the rampage*

rampant ADJECTIVE **1 = widespread**, rank, epidemic, prevalent, rife, exuberant, uncontrolled, unchecked, unrestrained, luxuriant, profuse, spreading like wildfire: *the rampant corruption of the administration* **2 = unrestrained**, wild, violent, raging, aggressive, dominant, excessive, outrageous, out of control, rampaging, out of hand, uncontrollable, flagrant, unbridled, vehement, wanton, riotous, on the rampage, ungovernable: *rampant civil and military police atrocities* **3 = upright**, standing, rearing, erect: *a shield with a lion rampant*

rampart NOUN **= defence**, wall, parapet, fortification, security, guard, fence, fort, barricade, stronghold, bastion, embankment, bulwark, earthwork, breastwork

ramshackle ADJECTIVE **= rickety**, broken-down, crumbling, shaky, unsafe, derelict, flimsy, tottering, dilapidated, decrepit, unsteady, tumbledown, jerry-built **OPPOSITE:** stable

rancid ADJECTIVE **= rotten**, sour, foul, bad, off, rank, tainted, stale, musty, fetid, putrid, fusty, strong-smelling, frowsty **OPPOSITE:** fresh

rancour NOUN **= hatred**, hate, spite, hostility, resentment, bitterness, grudge, malice, animosity, venom, antipathy, spleen, enmity, ill feeling, bad blood, ill will, animus, malevolence, malignity, chip on your shoulder *(informal)*, resentfulness

random ADJECTIVE **1 = chance**, spot, casual, stray, accidental, arbitrary, incidental, indiscriminate, haphazard, unplanned, fortuitous, aimless, desultory, hit or miss, purposeless, unpremeditated, adventitious: *The competitors will be subject to random drug testing.* **OPPOSITE:** planned **2 = casual**, arbitrary, indiscriminate, unplanned, aimless, purposeless, unpremeditated: *random violence against innocent children*
at random = haphazardly, randomly, arbitrarily, casually, accidentally, irregularly, by chance, indiscriminately, aimlessly, willy-nilly, unsystematically, purposelessly, adventitiously: *We received several answers and we picked one at random.*

randy ADJECTIVE **= lustful**, hot, sexy *(informal)*, turned-on *(slang)*, aroused, raunchy *(slang)*, horny *(slang)*, amorous, lascivious, lecherous, sexually excited, concupiscent, satyric

range NOUN **1 = series**, variety, selection, assortment, lot, collection, gamut: *The two men discussed a range of issues.* **2 = limits**, reach, distance, sweep, extent, pale, confines, parameters *(informal)*, ambit: *The average age range is between 35 and 55.* **3 = scope**, area, field, bounds, province, orbit, span, domain, compass, latitude, radius, amplitude, purview, sphere: *The trees on the mountain within my range of vision had all been felled.* **4 = row**, series, line, file, rank, chain, string, sequence, tier: *the massive mountain ranges to the north*
▷ VERB **1 = vary**, run, reach, extend, go, stretch, fluctuate: *offering merchandise ranging from the everyday to the esoteric* **2 = arrange**, order, line up, sequence, array, dispose, draw up, align: *More than 1,500 police are ranged against them.* **3 = roam**, explore, wander, rove, sweep, cruise, stroll, ramble, traverse: *They range widely in search of carrion.* **4 = group**, class, file, rank, arrange, grade, catalogue, classify, bracket, categorize, pigeonhole: *The pots are all ranged in neat rows.*

rank[1] NOUN **1 = status**, level, position, grade, order, standing, sort, quality, type, station, division, degree, classification, echelon: *He eventually rose to the rank of captain.* **2 = class**, dignity, caste, nobility, stratum: *Each rank of the peerage was respected.* **3 = row**, line, file, column, group, range, series, formation, tier: *Ranks of police in riot gear stood nervously by.*
▷ VERB **1 = order**, class, grade, classify, dispose: *Universities were ranked according to marks scored in seven areas.* **2 = arrange**, sort, position, range, line up, locate, sequence, array, marshal, align: *Daffodils were ranked along a crazy paving path.*
rank and file 1 = general public, body, majority, mass, masses, Joe (and Eileen) Public *(slang)*, Joe Six-Pack *(U.S. slang)*: *There was widespread support for him among the rank and file.* **2 = lower ranks**, men, troops, soldiers, other ranks, private soldiers: *the rank and file of the Red Army*

rank[2] ADJECTIVE **1 = absolute**, complete, total, gross, sheer, excessive, utter, glaring, thorough, extravagant, rampant, blatant, downright, flagrant, egregious, unmitigated, undisguised, arrant: *He accused his rival of rank hypocrisy.* **2 = foul**, off, bad, offensive, disgusting, revolting, stinking, stale, pungent, noxious, disagreeable, musty, rancid, fetid, putrid, fusty, strong-smelling, gamey, noisome, mephitic, olid, yucky or yukky *(slang)*, festy *(Austral. slang)*: *the rank smell of unwashed clothes* **3 = abundant**, flourishing, lush, luxuriant, productive, vigorous, dense, exuberant, profuse, strong-growing: *brambles and rank grass*

rankle VERB **= annoy**, anger, irritate, gall, fester, embitter, chafe, irk, rile, get on your nerves *(informal)*, get your goat *(slang)*, hack you off *(informal)*

ransack VERB **1 = search**, go through, rummage through, rake through, explore, comb, scour, forage, turn inside out, fossick *(Austral. & N.Z.)*: *Why should they be allowed to ransack your bag?* **2 = plunder**, raid, loot, pillage, strip, sack, gut, rifle, ravage, despoil: *Demonstrators ransacked and burned the house where he was staying.*

ransom NOUN **1 = payment**, money, price, payoff: *The demand for the ransom was made by telephone.* **2 = release**, rescue, liberation, redemption, deliverance: *the eventual ransom of the victim*
▷ VERB **= buy the freedom of**, release, deliver, rescue, liberate, buy (someone) out *(informal)*, redeem, set free, obtain or pay for the release of: *The same system was used for ransoming or exchanging captives.*

rant VERB **= shout**, roar, yell, rave, bellow, cry, spout *(informal)*, bluster, declaim, vociferate: *I don't rant and rave or throw tea cups.*
▷ NOUN **= tirade**, rhetoric, bluster, diatribe, harangue, bombast, philippic, vociferation, fanfaronade *(rare)*: *As the boss began his rant, I stood up and went out.*

rap VERB **1 = hit**, strike, knock, crack, tap: *A guard raps his stick on a metal hand rail.* **2 = reprimand**, knock *(informal)*, blast, pan *(informal)*, carpet *(informal)*, criticize, censure, scold, tick off *(informal)*, castigate, diss *(slang, chiefly U.S.)*, read the riot act, lambast(e), chew out *(U.S. & Canad. informal)*, give a rocket *(Brit. & N.Z. informal)*: *The minister rapped the banks over their treatment of small businesses.* **3 = talk**, chat, discourse, converse, shoot the breeze *(slang, chiefly U.S.)*, confabulate: *Today we're going to rap about relationships.*
▷ NOUN **1 = blow**, knock, crack, tap, clout *(informal)*: *There was a light rap on the door.* **2 = rebuke**, sentence, blame, responsibility, punishment, censure, chiding: *You'll be facing a federal rap for aiding and abetting an escaped convict.*

rapacious ADJECTIVE **= greedy**, grasping, insatiable, ravenous, preying, plundering, predatory, voracious, marauding, extortionate, avaricious, wolfish, usurious

rape VERB **= sexually assault**, violate, abuse, ravish, force, outrage: *A young woman was brutally raped in her own home.*
▷ NOUN **1 = sexual assault**, violation, ravishment, outrage: *Ninety per cent of all rapes and violent assaults went unreported.* **2 = plundering**, pillage, depredation, despoliation, rapine, spoliation, despoilment, sack: *the rape of the environment*

rapid ADJECTIVE **1 = sudden**, prompt, speedy, precipitate, express, fleet, swift, quickie *(informal)*, expeditious: *the country's rapid economic growth* **OPPOSITE:** gradual **2 = quick**, fast, hurried, swift, brisk, hasty, flying, pdq *(slang)*: *He walked at a rapid pace along Charles Street.* **OPPOSITE:** slow

rapidity NOUN **= speed**, swiftness, promptness, speediness, rush, hurry, expedition, dispatch, velocity, haste, alacrity, quickness, briskness, fleetness, celerity, promptitude, precipitateness

rapidly ADVERB **= quickly**, fast, swiftly, briskly, promptly, hastily, precipitately, in a hurry, at speed, hurriedly, speedily, apace, in a rush, in haste, like a shot, pronto *(informal)*, hell for leather, like lightning, expeditiously, hotfoot, like the clappers *(Brit. informal)*, pdq *(slang)*, like nobody's business *(informal)*, posthaste, with dispatch, like greased lightning *(informal)*

rapport NOUN **= bond**, understanding, relationship, link, tie, sympathy, harmony, affinity, empathy, interrelationship

rapprochement NOUN **= reconciliation**, softening, reunion, détente, reconcilement, restoration of harmony **OPPOSITE:** dissension

rapt ADJECTIVE **1 = spellbound**, entranced, enthralled, engrossed, held, gripped, fascinated, absorbed, intent, preoccupied, carried away: *I noticed that everyone was watching me with rapt attention.* **OPPOSITE:** uninterested

2 = rapturous, enchanted, captivated, bewitched, sent, transported, delighted, charmed, ecstatic, blissful, ravished, enraptured, blissed out: *He played to a rapt audience.*

rapture NOUN **= ecstasy**, delight, enthusiasm, joy, transport, spell, happiness, bliss, euphoria, felicity, rhapsody, exaltation, cloud nine *(informal)*, seventh heaven, delectation, beatitude, ravishment

rapturous ADJECTIVE **= ecstatic**, delighted, enthusiastic, rapt, sent *(informal)*, happy, transported, joyous, exalted, joyful, over the moon *(informal)*, overjoyed, blissful, ravished, euphoric, on cloud nine *(informal)*, blissed out *(informal)*, rhapsodic, in seventh heaven, floating on air

rare[1] ADJECTIVE **1 = priceless**, rich, precious, invaluable: *She collects rare plants.* **2 = uncommon**, unusual, exceptional, out of the ordinary, few, strange, scarce, singular, sporadic, sparse, infrequent, thin on the ground, recherché: *I think big families are extremely rare nowadays.*
OPPOSITE: common **3 = superb**, great, fine, excellent, extreme, exquisite, admirable, superlative, choice, incomparable, peerless: *She has a rare ability to record her observations on paper.*

rare[2] ADJECTIVE **= underdone**, bloody, undercooked, half-cooked, half-raw: *Waiter, I specifically asked for this steak rare.*

rarefied ADJECTIVE **= exclusive**, select, esoteric, cliquish, private, occult, clannish

rarely ADVERB **= seldom**, hardly, almost never, hardly ever, little, once in a while, infrequently, on rare occasions, once in a blue moon *(informal)*, only now and then, scarcely ever: *I rarely wear a raincoat because I spend most of my time in a car.* **OPPOSITE:** often

raring ADJECTIVE
raring to = eager to, impatient to, longing to, yearning to, willing to, ready to, keen to, desperate to, enthusiastic to, avid to, champing at the bit to *(informal)*, keen as mustard to, athirst to

rarity NOUN **1 = curio**, find, treasure, pearl, one-off, curiosity, gem, collector's item: *Other rarities include an interview with Presley.*
2 = uncommonness, scarcity, infrequency, unusualness, shortage, strangeness, singularity, sparseness: *This indicates the rarity of such attacks.*

rascal NOUN **= rogue**, devil, villain, scoundrel, disgrace, rake, pickle *(Brit. informal)*, imp, scally *(Northwest English dialect)*, wretch, knave *(archaic)*, ne'er-do-well, reprobate, scallywag *(informal)*, good-for-nothing, miscreant, scamp, wastrel, bad egg *(old-fashioned, informal)*, blackguard, varmint *(informal)*, rapscallion, caitiff *(archaic)*, wrong 'un *(Austral. slang)*, nointer *(Austral. slang)*

r

rash[1] ADJECTIVE **= reckless**, hasty, impulsive, imprudent, premature, adventurous, careless, precipitate, brash, audacious, headlong, madcap, ill-advised, foolhardy, unwary, thoughtless, unguarded, headstrong, impetuous, indiscreet, unthinking, helter-skelter, ill-considered, hot-headed, heedless, injudicious, incautious, venturesome, harebrained, harum-scarum: *Don't do anything rash until the feelings subside.*
OPPOSITE: cautious

rash[2] NOUN **1 = outbreak of spots**, (skin) eruption: *I noticed a rash on my leg.*
2 = spate, series, wave, flood, succession, plague, outbreak, epidemic: *a rash of internet-related companies*

rasp VERB **= scrape**, grind, rub, scour, excoriate, abrade: *The blade rasped over his skin.*
▷ NOUN **= grating**, grinding, scratch, scrape: *the rasp of something being drawn across the sand*

rasping *or* **raspy** ADJECTIVE **= harsh**, rough, hoarse, gravelly, jarring, grating, creaking, husky, croaking, gruff, croaky

rat NOUN **1 = traitor**, grass *(Brit. informal)*, betrayer, deceiver, informer, defector, deserter, double-crosser, quisling, stool pigeon, nark *(Brit., Austral. & N.Z. slang)*, snake in the grass, two-timer *(informal)*, fizgig *(Austral. slang)*: *He was known as 'The Rat', even before the bribes had come to light.* **2 = rogue**, scoundrel, heel *(slang)*, cad *(old-fashioned, informal, Brit.)*, bounder *(old-fashioned, slang, Brit.)*, rotter *(slang, chiefly Brit.)*, bad lot, shyster *(informal, chiefly U.S.)*, ratfink *(slang, chiefly U.S. & Canad.)*, wrong 'un *(Austral. slang)*: *What did you do with the gun you took from that little rat?*
rat on someone = betray, denounce, tell on, shop *(slang, chiefly Brit.)*, grass *(Brit. slang)*, peach *(slang)*, squeal *(slang)*, incriminate *(informal)*, blow the whistle on *(informal)*, spill the beans *(informal)*, snitch *(slang)*, blab, let the cat out of the bag, blow the gaff *(Brit. slang)*, nark *(Brit., Austral. & N.Z. slang)*, put the finger on *(informal)*, spill your guts *(slang)*, inculpate, clype *(Scot.)*, dob in *(Austral. slang)*: *They were accused of encouraging children to rat on their parents.*

rate NOUN **1 = speed**, pace, tempo, velocity, time, measure, gait, frequency: *The rate at which hair grows can be agonisingly slow.* **2 = degree**, standard, scale, proportion, percentage, ratio: *bank accounts paying above the average rate of interest*
3 = charge, price, cost, fee, tax, figure, dues, duty, hire, toll, tariff: *specially reduced rates*
▷ VERB **1 = evaluate**, consider, rank, reckon, class, value, measure, regard, estimate, count, grade, assess, weigh, esteem, classify, appraise, adjudge: *The film was rated excellent by 90 per cent of children.* **2 = deserve**, merit, be entitled to, be worthy of: *Her attire did not rate a second glance.*
at any rate = in any case, anyway, nevertheless, anyhow, at all events: *Well, at any rate, let me thank you for all you did.*

rather ADVERB **1 = preferably**, sooner, instead, more readily, more willingly: *I'd rather stay at home than fight against the holiday crowds.* **2 = to some extent**, quite, sort of *(informal)*, kind of *(informal)*, a little, a bit, pretty *(informal)*, fairly, relatively, somewhat, slightly, moderately, to some degree: *I'm afraid it's rather a long story.*

ratify VERB **= approve**, sign, establish, confirm, bind, sanction, endorse, uphold, authorize, affirm, certify, consent to, validate, bear out, corroborate, authenticate
OPPOSITE: annul

rating NOUN **= position**, evaluation, classification, placing, rate, order, standing, class, degree, estimate, rank, status, grade, designation

ratio NOUN **= proportion**, rate, relationship, relation, arrangement, percentage, equation, fraction, correspondence, correlation

ration NOUN **= allowance**, quota, allotment, provision, helping, part, share, measure, dole, portion: *The meat ration was down to one pound per person per week.*
▷ VERB **1 = limit**, control, restrict, save, budget, conserve: *Staples such as bread, rice and tea are already being rationed.*
2 = distribute, issue, deal, dole, allocate, give out, allot, mete, apportion, measure out, parcel out: *I had a flask so I rationed out cups of tea.*

rational ADJECTIVE **1 = sensible**, sound, wise, reasonable, intelligent, realistic, logical, enlightened, sane, lucid, judicious, sagacious, grounded: *a rational decision* **2 = reasoning**, thinking, cognitive, cerebral, ratiocinative: *Man, as a rational being, may act against his impulses.* **3 = sane**, balanced, normal, all there *(informal)*, lucid, of sound mind, compos mentis *(Latin)*, in your right mind: *Rachel looked calmer and more rational now.*
OPPOSITE: insane

rationale NOUN **= reason**, grounds, theory, principle, philosophy, logic, motivation, exposition, raison d'être *(French)*

rationalize VERB **1 = justify**, excuse, account for, vindicate, explain away, make allowances for, make excuses for, extenuate: *It's easy to rationalize gambling.* **2 = reason out**, resolve, think through, elucidate, apply logic to: *an attempt to rationalize my feelings*
3 = streamline, trim, make more efficient, make cuts in: *They have been unable or unwilling to modernize and rationalize the business.*

rattle VERB **1 = clatter**, bang, jangle: *She slams the kitchen door so hard I hear dishes rattle.* **2 = shake**, jiggle, jolt, vibrate, bounce, jar, jounce: *He gently*

Mark Twain's Use of Adjectives

Twain is noted for the vigour of his prose, rooted as it is in American popular speech – indeed the later US writer HL Mencken said of him that he was 'the true father of our national literature, the first genuinely American artist of the blood royal'. In his writing Twain was mindful of the law of diminishing returns as far as elaboration is concerned, and observed in a letter of 1878:

> God only exhibits his thunder and lightning at intervals, and so they always command attention. These are God's adjectives. You thunder and lightning too much; the reader ceases to get under the bed, by and by.

Twain famously and characteristically summarized this view in the pithy advice given in his novel *Pudd'nhead Wilson* (1894), 'As to the Adjective: when in doubt, strike it out.' An examination of his adjective use indicates that by far the commonest in his writing is the plain and simple *good*, and that the most frequent context for this is the colloquial phrase 'a good deal', as in 'a young printer wanders around a good deal, seeking and finding work.' Other common adjectives are similarly down to earth and to the point, such as *right*, *true*, *fine*, *noble*, and *strong*. Negative words are rarer, but we do find a small stock of words of disapprobation, including *odious* and *repulsive*, though the latter is mostly used of ugliness. *Awful* is an interesting case, as it is frequently used in the older sense of 'filled with awe' – the adjective pairing 'solemn and awful' is found across a wide range of his writings – but at the same time the word is used colloquially in the more modern sense (usually with adverbial effect), as when Tom Sawyer says of his teeth that 'one of them's loose, and it aches perfectly awful'.

Twain's parsimonious way with descriptive words makes it all the more startlingly effective when he does break free with a run of adjectives, for example in his description of Joan of Arc as:

> one who was wholly noble, pure, truthful, brave, compassionate, generous, pious, unselfish, modest, blameless as the very flowers in the fields ...

(though here again we note the simplicity of most of the words chosen – all the more apt to describe a peasant girl ranged against throngs of duplicitous clerics and princes).

One less common adjective he uses is *pathetic*, but not, of course, in the modern pejorative sense. He describes the hazy reminiscing of some ageing pioneers as:

> amazingly funny , and at the same time deeply **pathetic**; for they had seen so much, these time-worn veterans, and had suffered so much

A search for other possible negative uses of common adjectives mostly comes up short. *Low* is almost always used in a physical sense, and only very rarely as in 'a low, mean swindle', though *cheap* can be used other than of price, as in the phrase 'cheap and trivial', or in the mouth of one of Twain's characters:

> We had some sharp words, and I felt pretty **cheap**, to come banging into a grave old person like that.

One case where Twain did go against his natural bent for adjectival simplicity was in his attacks on the German language, and what he called its 'forsaken wind-galled nine-jointed words'. However, in general it was not by a judicious use of precise but abstruse epithets that Twain achieved his most telling effects, but rather by effective deployment of relatively workaday adjectives. Thus he describes (and deflates) Goethe as 'that meek idolater of provincial three carat royalty and nobility', or castigates US foreign policy in the Philippines, presented by President McKinley as 'Benevolent Assimilation', but which Twain devastatingly glossed as 'the pious new name of the musket'.

rattled the cage and whispered to the canary. **3 = fluster**, shake, upset, frighten, scare, disturb, disconcert, perturb, faze, discomfit, discountenance, put (someone) off his stride, discompose, put (someone) out of countenance: *She refused to be rattled by his lawyer.*
rattle on = prattle, rabbit (on) (*Brit. informal*), chatter, witter (*informal*), cackle, yak (away) (*slang*), gibber, jabber, gabble, blether, prate, run on, earbash (*Austral. & N.Z. slang*): *He listened in silence as she rattled on.*
rattle something off = recite, list, run through, rehearse, reel off, spiel off (*informal*): *He could rattle off yards of poetry.*

ratty ADJECTIVE **= irritable**, cross, angry, annoyed, crabbed, impatient, snappy, touchy, tetchy, testy, short-tempered, tooshie (*Austral. slang*)

raucous ADJECTIVE **= harsh**, rough, loud, noisy, grating, strident, rasping, husky, hoarse **OPPOSITE:** quiet

raunchy ADJECTIVE **= sexy**, sexual, steamy (*informal*), earthy, suggestive, lewd, lusty, bawdy, salacious, smutty, lustful, lecherous, ribald, coarse

ravage VERB **= destroy**, ruin, devastate, wreck, shatter, gut, spoil, loot, demolish, plunder, desolate, sack, ransack, pillage, raze, lay waste, wreak havoc on, despoil, leave in ruins: *The soldiers had ravaged the village.*
▷ NOUN (*often plural*) **= damage**, destruction, devastation, desolation, waste, ruin, havoc, demolition, plunder, pillage, depredation, ruination, rapine, spoliation: *the ravages of a cold, wet climate*

rave VERB **1 = rant**, rage, roar, thunder, fume, go mad (*informal*), babble, splutter, storm, be delirious, talk wildly: *She cried and raved for weeks.* **2 = enthuse**, praise, gush, be delighted by, be mad about (*informal*), big up (*slang*), rhapsodize, be wild about (*informal*), cry up: *She raved about the new foods she ate while she was there.*
▷ NOUN **= party**, rave-up (*Brit. slang*), do (*informal*), affair, celebration, bash (*informal*), blow-out (*slang*), beano (*Brit. slang*), hooley or hoolie (*chiefly Irish & N.Z.*): *an all-night rave*
▷ MODIFIER **= enthusiastic**, excellent, favourable, ecstatic, laudatory: *The show has drawn rave reviews from the critics.*

ravenous ADJECTIVE **1 = starving**, starved, very hungry, famished, esurient: *a pack of ravenous animals* **OPPOSITE:** sated **2 = greedy**, insatiable, avaricious, covetous, grasping, insatiate: *He had moderated his ravenous appetite.*

ravine NOUN **= canyon**, pass, gap (*U.S.*), gorge, clough (*dialect*), gully, defile, linn (*Scot.*), gulch (*U.S. & Canad.*), flume

raving ADJECTIVE **= mad**, wild, raging, crazy, furious, frantic, frenzied, hysterical, insane, irrational, crazed, berserk, delirious, rabid, out of your mind, gonzo (*slang*), berko (*Austral. slang*), off the air (*Austral. slang*)

ravish VERB **1 = rape**, sexually assault, violate, abuse, force, outrage: *Her ravished body was found a week later.* **2 = enchant**, transport, delight, charm, fascinate, entrance, captivate, enrapture, spellbind, overjoy: *an eerie power to ravish the eye and seduce the soul*

> QUOTATIONS
> He in a few minutes ravished this fair creature, or at least would have ravished her, if she had not, by a timely compliance, prevented him [Henry Fielding *Jonathan Wild*]

ravishing ADJECTIVE **= enchanting**, beautiful, lovely, stunning (*informal*), charming, entrancing, gorgeous, dazzling, delightful, radiant, drop-dead (*slang*), bewitching

raw ADJECTIVE **1 = unrefined**, natural, crude, unprocessed, basic, rough, organic, coarse, unfinished, untreated, unripe: *two ships carrying raw sugar* **OPPOSITE:** refined **2 = uncooked**, natural, fresh, bloody (*of meat*), undressed, unprepared: *a popular dish made of raw fish* **OPPOSITE:** cooked **3 = sore**, open, skinned, sensitive, tender, scratched, grazed, chafed, abraded: *the drag of the rope against the raw flesh of my shoulder* **4 = frank**, plain, bare, naked, realistic, brutal, blunt, candid, unvarnished, unembellished: *the raw passions of nationalism* **OPPOSITE:** embellished **5 = inexperienced**, new, green, ignorant, immature, unskilled, callow, untrained, untried, undisciplined, unseasoned, unpractised: *He is still raw but his potential shows.* **OPPOSITE:** experienced **6 = chilly**, biting, cold, freezing, bitter, wet, chill, harsh, piercing, damp, unpleasant, bleak, parky (*Brit. informal*): *a raw December morning*

ray NOUN **1 = beam**, bar, flash, shaft, gleam: *The first rays of light spread over the horizon.* **2 = trace**, spark, flicker, glimmer, hint, indication, scintilla: *I can offer you a slender ray of hope.*

raze VERB **= destroy**, level, remove, ruin, demolish, flatten, knock down, pull down, tear down, throw down, bulldoze, kennet (*Austral. slang*), jeff (*Austral. slang*)

re PREPOSITION **= concerning**, about, regarding, respecting, with regard to, on the subject of, in respect of, with reference to, apropos, anent (*Scot.*)

> USAGE
> In contexts such as *re your letter, your remarks have been noted* or *he spoke to me re your complaint*, *re* is common in business or official correspondence. In spoken and in general written English *with reference to* is preferable in the former case and *about* or *concerning* in the latter. Even in business correspondence, the use of *re* is often restricted to the letter heading.

reach VERB **1 = arrive at**, get to, get as far as, make, attain, land at: *He did not stop until he reached the door.* **2 = attain**, get to, amount to: *We're told the figure could reach 100,000 next year.* **3 = touch**, grasp, extend to, get (a) hold of, stretch to, go as far as, contact: *Can you reach your toes with your fingertips?* **4 = contact**, get in touch with, get through to, make contact with, get, find, communicate with, get hold of, establish contact with: *I'll tell her you've been trying to reach her.* **5 = come to**, move to, rise to, fall to, drop to, sink to: *a nightshirt that reached to his knees* **6 = achieve**, come to, arrive at: *They are meeting in Lusaka in an attempt to reach a compromise.*
▷ NOUN **1 = grasp**, range, distance, stretch, sweep, capacity, extent, extension, scope: *The clothes they model are in easy reach of every woman.* **2 = jurisdiction**, power, influence, command, compass, mastery, ambit: *The elite are no longer beyond the reach of the law.*

react VERB **= respond**, act, proceed, behave, conduct yourself

reaction NOUN **1 = response**, acknowledgment, feedback, answer, reply: *He showed no reaction when the judge pronounced his sentence.* **2 = counteraction**, compensation, backlash, recoil, counterbalance, counterpoise: *All new fashion starts out as a reaction against existing convention.* **3 = conservatism**, the right, counter-revolution, obscurantism: *their victory against the forces of reaction and conservatism*

reactionary ADJECTIVE **= conservative**, right-wing, counter-revolutionary, obscurantist, blimpish: *narrow and reactionary ideas about family life* **OPPOSITE:** radical
▷ NOUN **= conservative**, die-hard, right-winger, rightist, counter-revolutionary, obscurantist, Colonel Blimp: *Critics viewed him as a reactionary, even a monarchist.* **OPPOSITE:** radical

read VERB **1 = scan**, study, look at, refer to, glance at, pore over, peruse, run your eye over: *He read through the pages slowly and carefully.* **2 = recite**, deliver, utter, declaim, speak, announce: *Jay reads poetry so beautifully.* **3 = understand**, interpret, comprehend, construe, decipher, perceive the meaning of, see, discover: *He could read words at 18 months.* **4 = register**, show, record, display, indicate: *The sign on the bus read 'Private: Not in Service'.*

readable ADJECTIVE **1 = enjoyable**, interesting, gripping, entertaining, pleasant, enthralling, easy to read, worth reading: *This is an impeccably researched and very readable book.* **OPPOSITE:** dull **2 = legible**, clear, plain, understandable, comprehensible, intelligible, decipherable: *a typewritten and readable script* **OPPOSITE:** illegible

readily ADVERB **1 = willingly**, freely, quickly, gladly, eagerly, voluntarily, cheerfully, with pleasure, with good

grace, lief *(rare)*: *When I was invited to the party, I readily accepted.*
OPPOSITE: reluctantly **2 = promptly**, quickly, easily, smoothly, at once, straight away, right away, effortlessly, in no time, speedily, without delay, without hesitation, without difficulty, unhesitatingly, hotfoot, without demur, pdq *(slang)*: *I don't readily make friends.*
OPPOSITE: with difficulty

readiness NOUN **1 = willingness**, inclination, eagerness, keenness, aptness, gameness *(informal)*: *their readiness to co-operate with the new US envoy* **2 = preparedness**, preparation, fitness, maturity, ripeness: *a constant state of readiness for war* **3 = promptness**, facility, ease, skill, dexterity, rapidity, quickness, adroitness, handiness, promptitude: *the warmth of his personality and the readiness of his wit*
in readiness = prepared, set, waiting, primed, ready, all set, waiting in the wings, at the ready, at *or* on hand, fit: *Everything was in readiness for the President's arrival.*

reading NOUN **1 = perusal**, study, review, examination, inspection, scrutiny: *This knowledge makes the second reading as enjoyable as the first.*
2 = learning, education, knowledge, scholarship, erudition, edification, book-learning: *a man of great imagination, of wide reading and deep learning* **3 = recital**, performance, rendering, rendition, lesson, lecture, sermon, homily: *a poetry reading*
4 = interpretation, take *(informal, chiefly U.S.)*, understanding, treatment, version, construction, impression, grasp, conception: *There is a reading of this situation which upsets people.*

ready ADJECTIVE **1 = prepared**, set, primed, organized, all set, in readiness: *It took her a long time to get ready for church.*
OPPOSITE: unprepared **2 = completed**, arranged: *Everything's ready for the family to move in.* **3 = mature**, ripe, mellow, ripened, fully developed, fully grown, seasoned: *In a few days' time the sprouts will be ready to eat.* **4 = willing**, happy, glad, disposed, game *(informal)*, minded, keen, eager, inclined, prone, have-a-go *(informal)*, apt, agreeable, predisposed: *She was always ready to give interviews.* **OPPOSITE:** reluctant
5 = prompt, smart, quick, bright, sharp, keen, acute, rapid, alert, clever, intelligent, handy, apt, skilful, astute, perceptive, expert, deft, resourceful, adroit, quick-witted, dexterous: *I didn't have a ready answer for this dilemma.* **OPPOSITE:** slow
6 = available, handy, at the ready, at your fingertips, present, near, accessible, convenient, on call, on tap *(informal)*, close to hand, at *or* on hand: *I'm afraid I don't have much ready cash.*
OPPOSITE: unavailable **7** *(with* **to***)* **= on the point of**, close to, about to, on the verge of, likely to, in danger of, liable to, on the brink of: *She looked ready to cry.*
▷ VERB **= prepare**, get set, organize, get ready, order, arrange, equip, fit out, make ready, jack up *(N.Z. informal)*: *John's soldiers were readying themselves for the final assault.*

real ADJECTIVE **1 = true**, genuine, sincere, honest, factual, existent, dinkum *(Austral. & N.Z. informal)*, unfeigned: *No, it wasn't a dream. It was real.* **2 = genuine**, authentic, bona fide, dinkum *(Austral. & N.Z. informal)*: *the smell of real leather* **OPPOSITE:** fake
3 = proper, true, valid, legitimate: *His first real girlfriend.* **4 = true**, actual: *This was the real reason for her call.* **5 = typical**, true, genuine, sincere, unaffected, dinkum *(Austral. & N.Z. informal)*, unfeigned: *Their expressions of regret did not smack of real sorrow.* **6 = complete**, right, total, perfect, positive, absolute, utter, thorough, veritable, out-and-out: *You must think I'm a real idiot.*

realistic ADJECTIVE **1 = practical**, real, sensible, rational, common-sense, sober, pragmatic, down-to-earth, matter-of-fact, businesslike, level-headed, hard-headed, unsentimental, unromantic, grounded: *a realistic view of what we can afford* **OPPOSITE:** impractical
2 = attainable, reasonable, sensible: *Establish deadlines that are more realistic.*
3 = lifelike, true to life, authentic, naturalistic, true, natural, genuine, graphic, faithful, truthful, representational, vérité: *The language is foul and the violence horribly realistic.*

reality NOUN **1 = fact**, truth, certainty, realism, validity, authenticity, verity, actuality, materiality, genuineness, verisimilitude, corporeality: *Fiction and reality were increasingly blurred.*
2 = truth, fact, actuality: *the harsh reality of top international competition*
in reality = in fact, really, actually, in truth, as a matter of fact, in actuality, in point of fact: *He came across as streetwise, but in reality he was not.*

> **QUOTATIONS**
> Reality is that which, when you stop believing in it, doesn't go away
> [Philip K. Dick *I Hope I Shall Arrive Soon*]
>
> Human kind
> Cannot bear very much reality
> [T.S. Eliot *East Coker*]

realization NOUN **1 = awareness**, understanding, recognition, perception, imagination, consciousness, grasp, appreciation, conception, comprehension, apprehension, cognizance, aha moment *(informal)*, light bulb moment *(informal)*: *There is a growing realization that things cannot go on like this for much longer.* **2 = achievement**, carrying-out, completion, accomplishment, fulfilment, consummation, effectuation: *the realization of his worst fears*

realize VERB **1 = become aware of**, understand, recognize, appreciate, take in, grasp, conceive, catch on *(informal)*, comprehend, twig *(Brit. informal)*, get the message, apprehend, become conscious of, be cognizant of: *As soon as we realized what was going on, we moved the children away.* **2 = fulfil**, achieve, accomplish, make real: *Realize your dreams! Pursue your passions!*
3 = achieve, do, effect, complete, perform, fulfil, accomplish, bring about, consummate, incarnate, bring off, make concrete, bring to fruition, actualize, make happen, effectuate, reify, carry out *or* through: *The kaleidoscopic quality of the book is brilliantly realized on stage.* **4 = sell for**, go for, bring *or* take in, make, get, clear, produce, gain, net, earn, obtain, acquire: *A selection of correspondence from P.G. Wodehouse realized £1,232.*

really ADVERB **1 = certainly**, absolutely, undoubtedly, genuinely, positively, categorically, without a doubt, assuredly, verily, surely: *I really do feel that some people are being unfair.*
2 = truly, actually, in fact, indeed, in reality, in actuality: *My father didn't really love her.*

realm NOUN **1 = field**, world, area, province, sphere, department, region, branch, territory, zone, patch, orbit, turf *(U.S. slang)*: *the realm of politics*
2 = kingdom, state, country, empire, monarchy, land, province, domain, dominion, principality: *Defence of the realm is crucial.*

reap VERB **1 = get**, win, gain, obtain, acquire, derive: *We are not in this to reap immense financial rewards.* **2 = collect**, gather, bring in, harvest, garner, cut: *a group of peasants reaping a harvest of fruit and vegetables*

rear[1] NOUN **1 = back part**, back: *He settled back in the rear of the taxi.*
OPPOSITE: front **2 = back**, end, tail, rearguard, tail end, back end: *Musicians played at the front and rear of the procession.*
▷ MODIFIER **= back**, aft, hind, hindmost, after *(Nautical)*, last, following, trailing: *the rear end of a tractor* **OPPOSITE:** front

rear[2] VERB **1 = bring up**, raise, educate, care for, train, nurse, foster, nurture: *I was reared in east Texas.* **2 = breed**, keep: *She spends a lot of time rearing animals.*
3 *(often with* **up** *or* **over***)* **= rise**, tower, soar, loom: *The exhibition hall reared above me behind a high fence.*

reason NOUN **1 = cause**, grounds, purpose, motive, end, goal, design, target, aim, basis, occasion, object, intention, incentive, warrant, impetus, inducement, why and wherefore *(informal)*: *There is a reason for every important thing that happens.*
2 = justification, case, grounds, defence, argument, explanation, excuse, apology, rationale, exposition, vindication, apologia: *I hope you have a good reason for your behaviour.* **3 = sense**, mind, reasoning, understanding, brains, judgment, logic, mentality,

r

intellect, comprehension, apprehension, sanity, rationality, soundness, sound mind, ratiocination: *a conflict between emotion and reason* **OPPOSITE:** emotion
▷ VERB **= deduce**, conclude, work out, solve, resolve, make out, infer, draw conclusions, think, ratiocinate, syllogize: *I reasoned that changing my diet would lower my cholesterol level.*
in *or* **within reason = within limits**, within reasonable limits, within bounds: *I will take any job that comes along, within reason.*
reason with someone = persuade, debate with, remonstrate with, bring round, urge, win over, argue with, dispute with, dissuade, prevail upon (*informal*), expostulate with, show (someone) the error of his ways, talk into *or* out of: *All he wanted was to reason with one of them.*

USAGE
Many people object to the expression *the reason is because*, on the grounds that it is repetitive. It is therefore advisable to use either *this is because* or *the reason is that*.

reasonable ADJECTIVE **1 = sensible**, reasoned, sound, practical, wise, intelligent, rational, logical, sober, credible, plausible, sane, judicious, grounded: *He's a reasonable sort of chap.* **OPPOSITE:** irrational **2 = fair**, just, right, acceptable, moderate, equitable, justifiable, well-advised, well-thought-out, tenable: *a perfectly reasonable decision* **OPPOSITE:** unfair **3 = within reason**, fit, proper: *It seems reasonable to expect rapid urban growth.* **OPPOSITE:** impossible **4 = low**, cheap, competitive, moderate, modest, inexpensive, tolerable: *His fees were quite reasonable.* **5 = average**, fair, moderate, modest, tolerable, O.K. *or* okay (*informal*): *The boy answered him in reasonable French.*

r

reasoned ADJECTIVE **= sensible**, clear, logical, systematic, judicious, well-thought-out, well-presented, well-expressed

reasoning NOUN **1 = thinking**, thought, reason, analysis, logic, deduction, cogitation, ratiocination: *the reasoning behind the decision* **2 = case**, argument, proof, interpretation, hypothesis, exposition, train of thought: *She was not really convinced by their line of reasoning.*

reassure VERB **= encourage**, comfort, bolster, hearten, cheer up, buoy up, gee up, restore confidence to, inspirit, relieve (someone) of anxiety, put *or* set your mind at rest

rebate NOUN **= refund**, discount, reduction, bonus, allowance, deduction

rebel NOUN **1 = revolutionary**, resistance fighter, insurgent, secessionist, mutineer, insurrectionary, revolutionist: *fighting between rebels and government forces* **2 = nonconformist**, dissenter, heretic, apostate, schismatic: *She had been a rebel at school.*
▷ VERB **1 = revolt**, resist, rise up, mutiny, take to the streets, take up arms, man the barricades: *Poverty-stricken citizens could rise up and rebel.* **2 = defy**, dissent, disobey, come out against, refuse to obey, dig your heels in (*informal*): *The child who rebels against his parents is unlikely to be overlooked.* **3 = recoil**, shrink, shy away, flinch, show repugnance: *His free spirit rebelled at this demand.*
▷ MODIFIER **= rebellious**, revolutionary, insurgent, mutinous, insubordinate, insurrectionary: *Many soldiers in this rebel platoon joined as teenagers.*

QUOTATIONS
What is a rebel? A man who says no
[Albert Camus *The Rebel*]

To be a rebel is not to be a revolutionary. It is more often but a way of spinning one's wheels deeper in the sand
[Kate Millett *Sexual Politics*]

No one can go on being a rebel too long without turning into an autocrat
[Lawrence Durrell *Balthazar*]

rebellion NOUN **1 = resistance**, rising, revolution, revolt, uprising, mutiny, insurrection, insurgency, insurgence: *They soon put down the rebellion.* **2 = nonconformity**, dissent, defiance, heresy, disobedience, schism, insubordination, apostasy: *He engaged in a small act of rebellion against his heritage.*

QUOTATIONS
A little rebellion now and then is a good thing
[Thomas Jefferson *letter to James Madison*]

Rebellion to tyrants is obedience to God
[John Bradshaw]

rebellious ADJECTIVE **1 = defiant**, difficult, resistant, intractable, recalcitrant, obstinate, unmanageable, incorrigible, refractory, contumacious: *a rebellious teenager* **OPPOSITE:** obedient **2 = revolutionary**, rebel, disorderly, unruly, turbulent, disaffected, insurgent, recalcitrant, disloyal, seditious, mutinous, disobedient, ungovernable, insubordinate, insurrectionary: *a rebellious and dissident territory* **OPPOSITE:** obedient

rebirth NOUN **= revival**, restoration, renaissance, renewal, resurrection, reincarnation, regeneration, resurgence, new beginning, revitalization, renascence

rebound VERB **1 = bounce**, ricochet, spring back, return, resound, recoil: *His shot rebounded from a post.* **2 = misfire**, backfire, recoil, boomerang: *Mia realised her trick had rebounded on her.*

rebuff VERB **= reject**, decline, refuse, turn down, cut, check, deny, resist, slight, discourage, put off, snub, spurn, knock back (*slang*), brush off (*slang*), repulse, cold-shoulder: *He wanted to go out with with Julie but she rebuffed him.* **OPPOSITE:** encourage
▷ NOUN **= rejection**, defeat, snub, knock-back, check, opposition, slight, refusal, denial, brush-off (*slang*), repulse, thumbs down, cold shoulder, slap in the face (*informal*), kick in the teeth (*slang*), discouragement: *The results of the poll dealt a humiliating rebuff to Mr Jones.* **OPPOSITE:** encouragement

rebuke VERB **= scold**, censure, reprimand, reproach, blame, lecture, carpet (*informal*), berate, tick off (*informal*), castigate, chide, dress down (*informal*), admonish, tear into (*informal*), tell off (*informal*), take to task, read the riot act, reprove, upbraid, bawl out (*informal*), haul (someone) over the coals (*informal*), chew out (*U.S. & Canad. informal*), tear (someone) off a strip (*informal*), give a rocket (*Brit. & N.Z. informal*), reprehend: *He has been seriously rebuked.* **OPPOSITE:** praise
▷ NOUN **= scolding**, censure, reprimand, reproach, blame, row, lecture, wigging (*Brit. slang*), ticking-off (*informal*), dressing-down (*informal*), telling-off (*informal*), admonition, tongue-lashing, reproof, castigation, reproval: *'Silly little boy' was his favourite expression of rebuke.* **OPPOSITE:** praise

rebut VERB **= disprove**, defeat, overturn, quash, refute, negate, invalidate, prove wrong, confute

rebuttal NOUN **= disproof**, negation, refutation, invalidation, confutation, defeat

recalcitrant ADJECTIVE **= disobedient**, contrary, unwilling, defiant, stubborn, wayward, unruly, uncontrollable, intractable, wilful, obstinate, unmanageable, ungovernable, refractory, insubordinate, contumacious **OPPOSITE:** obedient

recall VERB **1 = recollect**, remember, call up, evoke, reminisce about, call to mind, look *or* think back to, mind (*dialect*): *I recalled the way they had been dancing together.* **2 = call back**: *Parliament was recalled from its summer recess.* **3 = annul**, withdraw, call in, take back, cancel, repeal, call back, revoke, retract, rescind, nullify, countermand, abjure: *The order was recalled.*
▷ NOUN **1 = recollection**, memory, remembrance: *He had a total recall of her spoken words.* **2 = annulment**, withdrawal, repeal, cancellation, retraction, revocation, nullification, rescission, rescindment: *The appellant sought a recall of the order.*

recant VERB **= withdraw**, take back, retract, disclaim, deny, recall, renounce, revoke, repudiate, renege, disown, disavow, forswear, abjure, unsay, apostatize **OPPOSITE:** maintain

recede VERB **1 = fall back**, withdraw, retreat, draw back, return, go back, retire, back off, regress, retrogress, retrocede: *As she receded into the distance he waved goodbye.* **2 = lessen**, decline, subside, abate, sink, fade, shrink, diminish, dwindle, wane, ebb: *The illness began to recede.*

receipt NOUN **1 = sales slip**, proof of purchase, voucher, stub, acknowledgment, counterfoil: *I wrote her a receipt for the money.* **2 = receiving**, delivery, reception, acceptance, recipience: *the receipt of your order*
▷ PLURAL NOUN **= takings**, return, profits, gains, income, gate, proceeds: *He was tallying the day's receipts.*

receive VERB **1 = get**, accept, be given, pick up, collect, obtain, acquire, take, derive, be in receipt of, accept delivery of: *I received your letter.* **2 = experience**, suffer, bear, go through, encounter, meet with, sustain, undergo, be subjected to: *He received a blow to the head.* **3 = greet**, meet, admit, welcome, entertain, take in, accommodate, be at home to: *The following evening the duchess was again receiving guests.*

recent ADJECTIVE **= new**, modern, contemporary, up-to-date, late, young, happening *(informal)*, current, fresh, novel, latter, present-day, latter-day **OPPOSITE:** old

recently ADVERB **= not long ago**, newly, lately, currently, freshly, of late, latterly

receptacle NOUN **= container**, holder, repository

reception NOUN **1 = party**, gathering, get-together, social gathering, do *(informal)*, social, function, entertainment, celebration, bash *(informal)*, festivity, knees-up *(Brit. informal)*, shindig *(informal)*, soirée, levee, rave-up *(Brit. slang)*: *a glittering wedding reception* **2 = response**, reaction, acknowledgment, recognition, treatment, welcome, greeting: *He received a cool reception to his speech.* **3 = receiving**, admission, acceptance, receipt, recipience: *the production, distribution and reception of medical knowledge*

receptive ADJECTIVE **= open**, sympathetic, favourable, amenable, interested, welcoming, friendly, accessible, susceptible, open-minded, hospitable, approachable, open to suggestions: *The voters had seemed receptive to his ideas.* **OPPOSITE:** narrow-minded

recess NOUN **1 = break**, rest, holiday, closure, interval, vacation, respite, intermission, cessation of business, schoolie *(Austral.)*: *Parliament returns to work today after its summer recess.* **2 = alcove**, corner, bay, depression, hollow, niche, cavity, nook, oriel, indentation: *a discreet recess next to a fireplace* **3** *(often plural)* **= depths**, reaches, heart, retreats, bowels, innards *(informal)*, secret places, innermost parts, penetralia: *He emerged from the dark recesses of the garage.*

recession NOUN **= depression**, drop, decline, credit crunch, slump, downturn **OPPOSITE:** boom

> **QUOTATIONS**
> It's a recession when your neighbour loses his job; it's a depression when you lose yours
> [Harry S. Truman]

recherché ADJECTIVE **= refined**, rare, exotic, esoteric, arcane, far-fetched, choice

recipe NOUN **= directions**, instructions, ingredients, receipt *(obsolete)*: *I can give you the recipe for these biscuits*
a recipe for something = method, formula, prescription, process, programme, technique, procedure, modus operandi: *Large-scale inflation is a recipe for disaster.*

> **QUOTATIONS**
> All recipes are built on the belief that somewhere at the beginning of the chain there is a cook who does not use them
> [John Thorne *'Cuisine Mécanique'*]

reciprocal ADJECTIVE **= mutual**, corresponding, reciprocative, reciprocatory, exchanged, equivalent, alternate, complementary, interchangeable, give-and-take, interdependent, correlative **OPPOSITE:** unilateral

reciprocate VERB **= return**, requite, feel in return, match, respond, equal, return the compliment

recital NOUN **1 = performance**, rendering, rehearsal, reading: *a solo recital* **2 = account**, telling, story, detailing, statement, relation, tale, description, narrative, narration, enumeration, recapitulation: *It was a depressing recital of childhood abuse.* **3 = recitation**, repetition: *The album features a recital of 13th century Latin prayers.*

recitation NOUN **= recital**, reading, performance, piece, passage, lecture, rendering, narration, telling

recite VERB **= perform**, relate, deliver, repeat, rehearse, declaim, recapitulate, do your party piece *(informal)*

reckless ADJECTIVE **= careless**, wild, rash, irresponsible, precipitate, hasty, mindless, negligent, headlong, madcap, ill-advised, regardless, foolhardy, daredevil, thoughtless, indiscreet, imprudent, heedless, devil-may-care, inattentive, incautious, harebrained, harum-scarum, overventuresome **OPPOSITE:** cautious

reckon VERB **1 = think**, believe, suppose, imagine, assume, guess *(informal, chiefly U.S. & Canad.)*, fancy, conjecture, surmise, be of the opinion: *He reckoned he was still fond of her.* **2 = consider**, hold, rate, account, judge, think of, regard, estimate, count, evaluate, esteem, deem, gauge, look upon, appraise: *The sale has been held up because the price is reckoned to be too high.* **3 = count**, figure, total, calculate, compute, add up, tally, number, enumerate: *The 'normal' by-election swing against a government is reckoned at about 5 per cent.*
reckon on *or* **upon something = rely on**, count on, bank on, depend on, hope for, calculate, trust in, take for granted: *He reckons on being world heavyweight champion.*
reckon with something *or* **someone** *(used in negative constructions)* **= take into account**, expect, plan for, anticipate, be prepared for, bear in mind, foresee, bargain for, take cognizance of: *He had not reckoned with the strength of her feelings for him.*
to be reckoned with = powerful, important, strong, significant, considerable, influential, weighty, consequential, skookum *(Canad.)*: *This act was a signal that he was someone to be reckoned with.*

reckoning NOUN **1 = count**, working, estimate, calculation, adding, counting, addition, computation, summation: *By my reckoning we were seven or eight kilometres away.* **2 = day of retribution**, doom, judgment day, last judgment: *the day of reckoning*

reclaim VERB **1 = retrieve**, get *or* take back, rescue, regain, reinstate: *I've come to reclaim my property.* **2 = regain**, restore, salvage, recapture, regenerate: *The Netherlands has been reclaiming farmland from water.* **3 = rescue**, reform, redeem: *He set out to fight the drug infestation by reclaiming a youth from the local gangs.*

recline VERB **= lean**, lie (down), stretch out, rest, lounge, sprawl, loll, repose, be recumbent **OPPOSITE:** stand up

recluse NOUN **= hermit**, solitary, ascetic, anchoress, monk, anchorite, eremite

reclusive ADJECTIVE **= solitary**, retiring, withdrawn, isolated, secluded, cloistered, monastic, recluse, ascetic, sequestered, hermit-like, hermitic, eremitic **OPPOSITE:** sociable

recognition NOUN **1 = identification**, recall, recollection, discovery, detection, remembrance: *He searched for a sign of recognition on her face.* **2 = acceptance**, acknowledgment, understanding, admission, perception, awareness, concession, allowance, confession, realization, avowal: *They welcomed his recognition of the recession.* **3 = acknowledgment**, approval: *His government did not receive full recognition until July.* **4 = approval**, honour, appreciation, salute, gratitude, acknowledgment: *At last, her father's work has received popular recognition.*

recognize VERB **1 = identify**, know, place, remember, spot, notice, recall, make out, recollect, know again, put your finger on: *The receptionist recognized him at once.* **2 = acknowledge**, see, allow, understand, accept, admit, grant, realize, concede, perceive, confess, be aware of, take on board, avow: *I recognize my own shortcomings.* **OPPOSITE:** ignore **3 = approve**, acknowledge, appreciate, greet, honour: *Most doctors appear to recognize homeopathy as a legitimate form of medicine.* **4 = appreciate**, respect, notice, salute: *He had the insight to recognize their talents.*

recoil VERB **1 = jerk back**, kick, react, rebound, spring back, resile: *I recoiled in horror.* **2 = draw back**, shrink, falter, shy away, flinch, quail, balk at: *People used to recoil from the idea of getting into debt.* ▷ NOUN **1 = jerking back**, reaction, springing back: *His reaction was as much a rebuff as a physical recoil.* **2 = kickback**, kick: *The policeman fires again, tensed against the recoil.*

recollect VERB **= remember**, mind *(dialect)*, recall, reminisce, summon up, call to mind, place

recollection NOUN **= memory**, recall, impression, remembrance, reminiscence, mental image

recommend VERB **1 = advocate**, suggest, propose, approve, endorse, commend: *Ask your doctor to recommend a suitable treatment.* **OPPOSITE:** disapprove of **2 = put forward**, approve, endorse, commend, vouch for, praise, big up *(slang)*, speak well of, put in a good word for: *He recommended me for a promotion.* **3 = advise**, suggest, advance, propose, urge, counsel, advocate, prescribe, put forward, exhort, enjoin: *I recommend that you consult your doctor.* **4 = make attractive**, make interesting, make appealing, make acceptable: *These qualities recommended him to Olivier.*

recommendation NOUN **1 = advice**, proposal, suggestion, counsel, urging: *The committee's recommendations are unlikely to be made public.* **2 = commendation**, reference, praise, sanction, approval, blessing, plug *(informal)*, endorsement, advocacy, testimonial, good word, approbation, favourable mention: *The best way of finding a solicitor is by personal recommendation.*

recompense NOUN **= compensation**, pay, payment, satisfaction, amends, repayment, remuneration, reparation, indemnity, restitution, damages, emolument, indemnification, requital: *He demands no financial recompense for his troubles.* ▷ VERB **= compensate**, reimburse, redress, repay, pay for, satisfy, make good, make up for, make amends for, indemnify, requite, make restitution for: *If they succeed in court, they will be fully recompensed for their loss.*

reconcile VERB **1 = resolve**, settle, square, adjust, compose, rectify, patch up, harmonize, put to rights: *It is possible to reconcile these apparently opposing perspectives.* **2 = reunite**, bring back together, make peace between, pacify, conciliate: *He never believed he and Susan would be reconciled.* **3 = make peace between**, reunite, propitiate, bring to terms, restore harmony between, re-establish friendly relations between: *my attempt to reconcile him and Toby*

reconcile yourself to something *(often passive)* **= accept**, resign yourself to, get used to, put up with *(informal)*, submit to, yield to, make the best of, accommodate yourself to: *She reconciled herself to never seeing him again.*

reconciliation NOUN **1 = reunion**, conciliation, rapprochement *(French)*, appeasement, détente, pacification, propitiation, understanding, reconcilement: *The couple have separated but he wants a reconciliation.* **OPPOSITE:** separation **2 = accommodation**, settlement, compromise: *the reconciliation of our differences*

reconnaissance NOUN **= inspection**, survey, investigation, observation, patrol, scan, exploration, scouting, scrutiny, recce *(slang)*, reconnoitring

reconsider VERB **= rethink**, review, revise, think again, think twice, reassess, re-examine, have second thoughts, change your mind, re-evaluate, think over, think better of, take another look at

> **QUOTATIONS**
> Second thoughts are the wisest
> [Euripides *Hippolytus*]

reconstruct VERB **1 = rebuild**, reform, restore, recreate, remake, renovate, remodel, re-establish, regenerate, reorganize, reassemble: *The government must reconstruct the shattered economy.* **2 = build up a picture of**, build up, piece together, deduce: *Elaborate efforts were made to reconstruct what had happened.*

record NOUN **1 = document**, file, register, log, report, minute, account, entry, journal, diary, memorial, archives, memoir, chronicle, memorandum, annals, blog *(informal)*: *Keep a record of all the payments.* **2 = evidence**, trace, documentation, testimony, witness, memorial, remembrance: *There's no record of any marriage or children.* **3 = disc**, recording, single, release, album, waxing *(informal)*, LP, vinyl, EP, forty-five, platter *(U.S. slang)*, seventy-eight, gramophone record, black disc: *This is one of my favourite records.* **4 = background**, history, performance, career, track record *(informal)*, curriculum vitae: *His record reveals a tough streak.* ▷ VERB **1 = set down**, report, minute, note, enter, document, register, preserve, log, put down, chronicle, write down, enrol, take down, inscribe, transcribe, chalk up *(informal)*, put on record, put on file: *In her letters she records the domestic and social details of life in China.* **2 = make a recording of**, cut, video, tape, lay down *(slang)*, wax *(informal)*, videotape, tape-record, put on wax *(informal)*: *She recorded a new album in Nashville.* **3 = register**, show, read, contain, indicate, give evidence of: *The test records the electrical activity of the brain.*

off the record 1 = confidentially, in private, in confidence, unofficially, sub rosa, under the rose: *May I speak off the record?* **2 = confidential**, private, unofficial, not for publication: *Those remarks were supposed to be off the record.*

recorder NOUN **= chronicler**, archivist, historian, scorer, clerk, registrar, scribe, diarist, scorekeeper, annalist

recording NOUN **= record**, video, tape, disc, gramophone record, cut *(informal)*

recount VERB **= tell**, report, detail, describe, relate, repeat, portray, depict, rehearse, recite, tell the story of, narrate, delineate, enumerate, give an account of

recoup VERB **= regain**, recover, make good, retrieve, redeem, win back

recourse NOUN **= option**, choice, alternative, resort, appeal, resource, remedy, way out, refuge, expedient

recover VERB **1 = get better**, improve, get well, recuperate, pick up, heal, revive, come round, bounce back, mend, turn the corner, pull through, convalesce, be on the mend, take a turn for the better, get back on your feet, feel yourself again, regain your health *or* strength: *He is recovering after sustaining a knee injury.* **OPPOSITE:** relapse **2 = rally**: *The stock market index fell by 80% before it began to recover.* **3 = save**, rescue, retrieve, salvage, reclaim: *Rescue teams recovered a few more survivors from the rubble.* **OPPOSITE:** abandon **4 = recoup**, restore, repair, get back, regain, make good, retrieve, reclaim, redeem, recapture, win back, take back, repossess, retake, find again: *Legal action is being taken to try and recover the money.* **OPPOSITE:** lose

recovery NOUN **1 = improvement**, return to health, rally, healing, revival, mending, recuperation, convalescence, turn for the better: *He made a remarkable recovery from a shin injury.* **2 = revival**, improvement, rally, restoration, rehabilitation, upturn, betterment, amelioration: *In many sectors of the economy the recovery has started.* **3 = retrieval**, repossession, reclamation, restoration, repair, redemption, recapture: *the recovery of a painting by Turner*

recreation NOUN **= leisure**, play, sport, exercise, fun, relief, pleasure, entertainment, relaxation, enjoyment, distraction, amusement, diversion, refreshment, beer and skittles *(informal)*, me-time

r

Mark Twain's Use of Verbs

Mark Twain was not equivocal in his disdain for adverbs and adjectives – his view of the former can be found in an essay elsewhere in this volume, and his dictum about adjectives was this: 'when in doubt, strike it out.' He left a scanter direct record of his opinion about verbs, but from his own writing, and his writing on other languages, we can infer that he held the verb in high esteem and see that he used it to great effect.

In two of Twain's most mirthful essays –'Italian With Grammar' and 'The Awful German Language' – he devotes considerable discussion to the difficulty (for him) of dealing with the verbs in these two languages. The intention is clearly comic, but modern readers of the essays will recognize, behind the hilarity, Twain's frustration at not being able to negotiate foreign verbs. He casts a number of good-natured aspersions on the irregularities in foreign verbs and there is a certain irony in this – because in his own writing, he uses the verb (often with introduced irregularities) as a primary marker of the colloquialism that is one of his hallmarks. Here are a few examples from his novels in which the verbs have the primary responsibility for conveying local colour and rustic character to the reader:

> Then I slid out quiet and throwed the snakes clear away amongst the bushes; for I warn't going to let Jim find out it was all my fault, not if I could help it.
>
> he hears a horse a-coming behind him, and sees old Baldy Shepherdson a-linkin' after him with his gun in his hand and his white hair a-flying in the wind
>
> in my opinion he never could've raised the men, and if he did, as like as not he would've got licked
>
> I've ciphered over it a good deal, and it's my opinion that some of it is knowledge but the main bulk of it is instink.

Twain has Huckleberry Finn make a regular verb out of *throw* in one sentence, and further irregularize *be* with the dialect spelling *warn't* (for *weren't*) in the following sentence. In the second passage, he uses the circumfix *a-________ing* around three verbs (*come, link, fly*) as a way of conveying rural colloquialism, in a passage that is otherwise in fairly standard English. This circumfix (as in *a-coming*) was in fact common in 17th-century English, and lives on today in some Southern US dialects.

The third passage above ends *he would've got licked*, a construction that will have a somewhat natural sound to British readers – but in fact most Americans would render this as *he would've gotten licked*, this being one of the uses of *get* for which Americans prefer the older participle. So again, Twain tweaks the form of a verb just slightly to suggest the folksiness of his speaker. All of the passages use slangish verbs which also move the text out of a standard register toward the colloquial.

The foregoing artifice, however, tells only half the story. Twain is equally adept with verbs in a standard register, as here in this longer passage from *Roughing It*. Here he is at his best, always ready with the right verb in the right place.

> I remembered how helpless I was that day, and how humiliated; how ashamed I was of having intimated to the girl that I had always owned the horse and was accustomed to grandeur; how hard I tried to appear easy, and even vivacious, under suffering that was consuming my vitals; how placidly and maliciously the girl smiled, and kept on smiling, while my hot blushes baked themselves into a permanent blood-pudding in my faces; how the horse ambled from one side of the street to the other and waited complacently before every third house two minutes and a quarter while I belabored his back and reviled him in my heart.

recrimination NOUN **= bickering**, retaliation, counterattack, mutual accusation, retort, quarrel, squabbling, name-calling, countercharge

recruit VERB **1 = gather**, take on, obtain, engage, round up, enrol, procure, proselytize: *He helped to recruit volunteers to go to Pakistan.* **2 = assemble**, raise, levy, muster, mobilize: *He's managed to recruit an army of crooks.* **3 = enlist**, draft, impress, enrol: *He had the forlorn job of trying to recruit soldiers.* **OPPOSITE:** dismiss
▷ NOUN **= beginner**, trainee, apprentice, novice, convert, initiate, rookie *(informal)*, helper, learner, neophyte, tyro, greenhorn *(informal)*, proselyte: *A new recruit could well arrive later this week.*

rectify VERB **= correct**, right, improve, reform, square, fix, repair, adjust, remedy, amend, make good, mend, redress, put right, set the record straight, emend

rectitude NOUN **1 = morality**, principle, honour, virtue, decency, justice, equity, integrity, goodness, honesty, correctness, righteousness, probity, incorruptibility, scrupulousness, uprightness: *people of the utmost rectitude* **OPPOSITE:** immorality **2 = correctness**, justice, accuracy, precision, verity, rightness, soundness, exactness: *Has the rectitude of this principle ever been formally contested?*

recuperate VERB **= recover**, improve, pick up, get better, mend, turn the corner, convalesce, be on the mend, get back on your feet, regain your health

recur VERB **= happen again**, return, come back, repeat, persist, revert, reappear, come and go, come again

recurrent ADJECTIVE **= periodic**, continued, regular, repeated, frequent, recurring, repetitive, cyclical, habitual **OPPOSITE:** one-off

recycle VERB **= reprocess**, reuse, salvage, reclaim, save, freecycle

red NOUN **1 = crimson**, scarlet, ruby, vermilion, rose, wine, pink, cherry, cardinal, coral, maroon, claret, carmine: *a deep shade of red* **2 = communist**, socialist, revolutionary, militant, Marxist, leftist, left-winger, lefty *(informal)*, Trotskyite
▷ ADJECTIVE **1 = crimson**, scarlet, ruby, vermilion, rose, wine, pink, cherry, cardinal, coral, maroon, claret, carmine: *a red coat* **2 = flushed**, embarrassed, blushing, suffused, florid, shamefaced, rubicund: *She was red with shame.* **3 = chestnut**, flaming, reddish, flame-coloured, bay, sandy, foxy, Titian, carroty, ginger: *Her red hair flowed out in the wind.* **4 = bloodshot**, inflamed, red-rimmed: *He rubbed his red eyes.* **5 = rosy**, healthy, glowing, blooming, ruddy, roseate: *rosy red cheeks*
in the red = in debt, bankrupt, on the rocks, insolvent, in arrears, overdrawn, owing money, in deficit, showing a loss, in debit: *The theatre is in the red.*
see red = lose your temper, boil, lose it *(informal)*, seethe, go mad *(informal)*, crack up *(informal)*, lose the plot *(informal)*, go ballistic *(slang, chiefly U.S.)*, blow a fuse *(slang, chiefly U.S.)*, fly off the handle *(informal)*, become enraged, go off the deep end *(informal)*, wig out *(slang)*, go up the wall *(slang)*, blow your top, lose your rag *(slang)*, be beside yourself with rage *(informal)*, be *or* get very angry, go off your head *(slang)*: *I didn't mean to break his nose. I just saw red.*
▸ *related adjectives:* rubicund, ruddy

red-blooded ADJECTIVE **= vigorous**, manly, lusty, virile, strong, vital, robust, hearty

redden VERB **= flush**, colour (up), blush, crimson, suffuse, go red, go beetroot *(informal)*

redeem VERB **1 = reinstate**, absolve, restore to favour, rehabilitate: *He had realized the mistake he had made and wanted to redeem himself.* **2 = make up for**, offset, make good, compensate for, outweigh, redress, atone for, make amends for, defray: *Work is the way people seek to redeem their sins.* **3 = trade in**, cash (in), exchange, change: *The voucher will be redeemed for one toy.* **4 = buy back**, recover, regain, retrieve, reclaim, win back, repossess, repurchase, recover possession of: *the date upon which you plan to redeem the item* **5 = save**, free, deliver, rescue, liberate, ransom, set free, extricate, emancipate, buy the freedom of, pay the ransom of: *a new female spiritual force to redeem the world* **6 = fulfil**, meet, keep, carry out, satisfy, discharge, make good, hold to, acquit, adhere to, abide by, keep faith with, be faithful to, perform: *They must redeem that pledge.*

redemption NOUN **1 = compensation**, amends, reparation, atonement, expiation: *trying to make some redemption for his actions* **2 = salvation**, release, rescue, liberation, ransom, emancipation, deliverance: *offering redemption from our sins* **3 = paying-off**, paying back: *redemption of the loan* **4 = trade-in**, recovery, retrieval, repurchase, repossession, reclamation, quid pro quo: *cash redemptions and quota payments*

red-handed ADJECTIVE **= in the act**, with your pants down *(U.S. slang)*, (in) flagrante delicto, with your fingers *or* hand in the till *(informal)*, bang to rights *(slang)*

red-hot ADJECTIVE **1 = very hot**, burning, heated, steaming, searing, scorching, scalding, piping hot **2 = exciting**, inspiring, sensational *(informal)*, electrifying **3 = passionate**, thrilling, sexy, arousing, titillating

redolent ADJECTIVE **1 = reminiscent**, evocative, suggestive, remindful: *a sad tale, redolent with regret* **2 = scented**, perfumed, fragrant, aromatic, sweet-smelling, odorous: *The air was redolent of cinnamon and apple.*

redoubtable ADJECTIVE **= formidable**, strong, powerful, terrible, awful, mighty, dreadful, fearful, fearsome, resolute, valiant, doughty

redress VERB **1 = make amends for**, pay for, make up for, compensate for, put right, recompense for, make reparation for, make restitution for: *Victims are turning to litigation to redress wrongs done to them.* **2 = put right**, reform, balance, square, correct, ease, repair, relieve, adjust, regulate, remedy, amend, mend, rectify, even up, restore the balance: *to redress the economic imbalance*
▷ NOUN **= amends**, payment, compensation, reparation, restitution, atonement, recompense, requital, quittance: *a legal battle to seek some redress from the government*

reduce VERB **1 = lessen**, cut, contract, lower, depress, moderate, dial down, weaken, diminish, turn down, decrease, slow down, cut down, shorten, dilute, impair, curtail, wind down, abate, tone down, debase, truncate, abridge, downsize,

SHADES OF RED

auburn	carroty	crimson	ginger	mulberry	poppy	rust	Titian
baby pink	cerise	cyclamen	grenadine	old rose	puce	salmon pink	Turkey red
bay	cherry	damask	gules	oxblood	raspberry	sandy	vermeil
burgundy	chestnut	dubonnet	*(Heraldry)*	oyster pink	rose	scarlet	vermilion
burnt sienna	cinnabar	flame	henna	peach	roseate	shell pink	wine
cardinal red	claret	flesh	liver	peach-blow	rosy	strawberry	
carmine	copper	foxy	magenta	pink	ruby	tea rose	
carnation	coral	fuchsia	maroon	plum	russet	terracotta	

downscale, kennet *(Austral. slang)*, jeff *(Austral. slang)*: *Consumption is being reduced by 25 per cent.* **OPPOSITE:** increase **2 = degrade**, downgrade, demote, lower in rank, break, humble, humiliate, bring low, take down a peg *(informal)*, lower the status of: *They wanted the army reduced to a police force.* **OPPOSITE:** promote **3 = drive**, force, bring, bring to the point of: *He was reduced to begging for a living.* **4 = cheapen**, cut, lower, discount, slash, mark down, bring down the price of: *Companies should reduce prices today.*

redundancy NOUN **1 = layoff**, sacking, dismissal: *They hope to avoid future redundancies.* **2 = unemployment**, the sack *(informal)*, the axe *(informal)*, joblessness: *Thousands of employees are facing redundancy.* **3 = superfluity**, surplus, surfeit, superabundance: *the redundancy of its two main exhibits*

redundant ADJECTIVE **1 = superfluous**, extra, surplus, excessive, unnecessary, unwanted, inordinate, inessential, supernumerary, de trop *(French)*, supererogatory: *the conversion of redundant buildings to residential use* **OPPOSITE:** essential **2 = tautological**, wordy, repetitious, verbose, padded, diffuse, prolix, iterative, periphrastic, pleonastic: *The last couplet collapses into redundant adjectives.*

reek VERB **1 = stink**, smell, pong *(Brit. informal)*, smell to high heaven, hum *(slang)*: *Your breath reeks.* **2** (with **of**) **= be redolent of**, suggest, smack of, testify to, be characterized by, bear the stamp of, be permeated by, be suggestive *or* indicative of: *The whole thing reeks of hypocrisy.*
▷ NOUN **= stink**, smell, odour, stench, pong *(Brit. informal)*, effluvium, niff *(Brit. slang)*, malodour, mephitis, fetor: *He smelt the reek of whisky.*

reel VERB **1 = stagger**, rock, roll, pitch, stumble, sway, falter, lurch, wobble, waver, totter: *He lost his balance and reeled back.* **2 = whirl**, swim, spin, revolve, swirl, twirl, go round and round: *The room reeled and he jammed his head down.*

refer VERB **1 = pass on**, transfer, deliver, commit, hand over, submit, turn over, consign: *He could refer the matter to the high court.* **2 = direct**, point, send, guide, recommend: *He referred me to a book on the subject.*
refer to something *or* **someone** **1 = allude to**, mention, cite, speak of, bring up, invoke, hint at, touch on, make reference to, make mention of: *He referred to a recent trip to Canada.* **2 = relate to**, concern, apply to, pertain to, be relevant to: *The term 'electronics' refers to electrically-induced action.* **3 = consult**, go, apply, turn to, look up, have recourse to, seek information from: *He referred briefly to his notebook.*

> **USAGE**
> It is usually unnecessary to add *back* to the verb *refer*, since the sense of *back* is already contained in the *re-* part of this word. For example, you might say *This refers to* (not *refers back to*) *what has already been said. Refer back* is only considered acceptable when used to mean 'return a document or question to the person it came from for further consideration', as in *he referred the matter back to me.*

referee NOUN **= umpire**, umpie *(Austral. slang)*, judge, ref *(informal)*, arbiter, arbitrator, adjudicator: *The referee stopped the fight.*
▷ VERB **= umpire**, judge, mediate, adjudicate, arbitrate: *He has refereed in two World Cups.*

reference NOUN **1 = allusion**, note, mention, remark, quotation: *He summed up his philosophy, with reference to Calvin.* **2 = citation**: *I would have found a brief list of references useful.* **3 = testimonial**, recommendation, credentials, endorsement, certification, good word, character reference: *The firm offered to give her a reference.*

referendum NOUN **= public vote**, popular vote, plebiscite

refine VERB **1 = purify**, process, filter, cleanse, clarify, distil, rarefy: *Oil is refined so as to remove naturally occurring impurities.* **2 = improve**, perfect, polish, temper, elevate, hone: *Surgical techniques are constantly being refined.*

refined ADJECTIVE **1 = purified**, processed, pure, filtered, clean, clarified, distilled: *refined sugar* **OPPOSITE:** unrefined **2 = cultured**, civil, polished, sophisticated, gentlemanly, elegant, polite, cultivated, gracious, civilized, genteel, urbane, courtly, well-bred, ladylike, well-mannered: *His speech and manner are refined.* **OPPOSITE:** coarse **3 = discerning**, fine, nice, sensitive, exact, subtle, delicate, precise, discriminating, sublime, fastidious, punctilious: *refined tastes*

refinement NOUN **1 = subtlety**, nuance, nicety, fine point: *the refinements of the game* **2 = sophistication**, finish, style, culture, taste, breeding, polish, grace, discrimination, courtesy, civilization, precision, elegance, delicacy, cultivation, finesse, politeness, good manners, civility, gentility, good breeding, graciousness, urbanity, fastidiousness, fineness, courtliness, politesse: *a girl who possessed both dignity and refinement* **3 = purification**, processing, filtering, cleansing, clarification, distillation, rectification, rarefaction: *the refinement of crude oil*

reflect VERB **1 = show**, reveal, express, display, indicate, demonstrate, exhibit, communicate, manifest, bear out, bespeak, evince: *Concern was reflected in the government's budget.* **2 = throw back**, return, mirror, echo, reproduce, imitate, give back: *The glass appears to reflect light naturally.* **3** (usually followed by **on**) **= consider**, think, contemplate, deliberate, muse, ponder, meditate, mull over, ruminate, cogitate, wonder: *I reflected on the child's future.*

reflection NOUN **1 = image**, echo, counterpart, mirror image: *Meg stared at her reflection in the mirror.* **2 = criticism**, censure, slur, reproach, imputation, derogation, aspersion: *Infection with head lice is no reflection on personal hygiene.* **3 = consideration**, thinking, pondering, deliberation, thought, idea, view, study, opinion, impression, observation, musing, meditation, contemplation, rumination, perusal, cogitation, cerebration: *After days of reflection she decided to write back.*

reflective ADJECTIVE **= thoughtful**, contemplative, meditative, pensive, reasoning, pondering, deliberative, ruminative, cogitating

reform NOUN **= improvement**, amendment, correction, rehabilitation, renovation, betterment, rectification, amelioration: *a programme of economic reform*
▷ VERB **1 = improve**, better, correct, restore, repair, rebuild, amend, reclaim, mend, renovate, reconstruct, remodel, rectify, rehabilitate, regenerate, reorganize, reconstitute, revolutionize, ameliorate, emend: *his plans to reform the country's economy* **2 = mend your ways**, go straight *(informal)*, shape up *(informal)*, get it together *(informal)*, turn over a new leaf, get your act together *(informal)*, clean up your act *(informal)*, pull your socks up *(Brit. informal)*, get back on the straight and narrow *(informal)*: *Under such a system where is the incentive to reform?*

refrain[1] VERB **= stop**, avoid, give up, cease, do without, renounce, abstain, eschew, leave off, desist, forbear, kick *(informal)*: *She refrained from making any comment.*

refrain[2] NOUN **= chorus**, song, tune, melody: *a refrain from an old song*

refresh VERB **1 = revive**, cool, freshen, revitalize, cheer, stimulate, brace, rejuvenate, kick-start *(informal)*, enliven, breathe new life into, invigorate, revivify, reanimate, inspirit: *The lotion cools and refreshes the skin.* **2 = replenish**, restore, repair, renew, top up, renovate: *She appeared, her make-up refreshed.* **3 = stimulate**, prompt, renew, jog, prod, brush up *(informal)*: *Allow me to refresh your memory.*

refreshing ADJECTIVE **1 = new**, different, original, novel: *refreshing new ideas* **2 = stimulating**, fresh, cooling, bracing, invigorating, revivifying, thirst-quenching, inspiriting: *Herbs have been used for centuries to make refreshing drinks.* **OPPOSITE:** tiring

refreshment NOUN **1 = revival**, restoration, renewal, stimulation, renovation, freshening, reanimation, enlivenment, repair: *a place where city dwellers come to find spiritual refreshment* **2** *(plural)* **= food and drink**, drinks, snacks, titbits, kai *(N.Z. informal)*: *Some refreshments would be nice.*

refrigerate VERB **= cool**, freeze, chill, keep cold

refrigerator NOUN **= fridge**, chiller, cooler, ice-box *(U.S. & Canad.)*

refuge NOUN **1 = protection**, security, shelter, harbour, asylum: *They took refuge in a bomb shelter.* **2 = haven**, resort, retreat, sanctuary, hide-out, bolt hole: *We climbed up a winding track towards a mountain refuge.*

refugee NOUN **= exile**, émigré, displaced person, runaway, fugitive, escapee

refund NOUN **= repayment**, reimbursement, return: *They plan to demand a refund.*
▷ VERB **= repay**, return, restore, make good, pay back, reimburse, give back: *She will refund you the purchase price.*

refurbish VERB **= renovate**, restore, repair, clean up, overhaul, revamp, mend, remodel, do up *(informal)*, refit, fix up *(informal, chiefly U.S. & Canad.)*, spruce up, pimp up, pimp out, re-equip, set to rights

refusal NOUN **= rejection**, denial, defiance, rebuff, knock-back *(slang)*, thumbs down, repudiation, kick in the teeth *(slang)*, negation, no: *a refusal of planning permission*
first refusal = option, choice, opportunity, consideration: *A tenant may have a right of first refusal if a property is offered for sale.*

refuse[1] VERB **1 = decline**, reject, turn down, say no to, repudiate: *I could hardly refuse his invitation.* **2 = deny**, decline, withhold: *She was refused access to her children.* **OPPOSITE:** allow

refuse[2] NOUN **= rubbish**, waste, sweepings, junk *(informal)*, litter, garbage *(chiefly U.S.)*, trash, sediment, scum, dross, dregs, leavings, dreck *(slang, chiefly U.S.)*, offscourings, lees: *a weekly collection of refuse*

refute VERB **= disprove**, counter, discredit, prove false, silence, overthrow, negate, rebut, give the lie to, blow out of the water *(slang)*, confute **OPPOSITE:** prove

> **USAGE**
> The use of *refute* to mean *deny* as in *I'm not refuting the fact that* is thought by some people to be incorrect. In careful writing it may be advisable to use *refute* only where there is an element of disproving something through argument and evidence, as in *we haven't got evidence to refute their hypothesis*.

regain VERB **1 = recover**, get back, retrieve, redeem, recapture, win back, take back, recoup, repossess, retake: *Troops have regained control of the city.* **2 = get back to**, return to, reach again, reattain: *Davis went to regain his carriage.*

regal ADJECTIVE **= royal**, majestic, kingly *or* queenly, noble, princely, proud, magnificent, sovereign, fit for a king *or* queen

regale VERB **1 = entertain**, delight, amuse, divert, gratify: *He was constantly regaled with amusing stories.* **2 = serve**, refresh, ply: *On Sunday evenings we were usually regaled with a roast dinner.*

regalia PLURAL NOUN **= trappings**, gear, decorations, finery, apparatus, emblems, paraphernalia, garb, accoutrements, rigout *(informal)*, bling *(slang)*

regard VERB **1 = consider**, see, hold, rate, view, value, account, judge, treat, think of, esteem, deem, look upon, adjudge: *I regard creativity as both a gift and a skill.* **2 = look at**, view, eye, watch, observe, check, notice, clock *(Brit. slang)*, remark, check out *(informal)*, gaze at, behold, eyeball *(U.S. slang)*, scrutinize, get a load of *(informal)*, take a dekko at *(Brit. slang)*: *She regarded him curiously for a moment.*
▷ NOUN **1 = respect**, esteem, deference, store, thought, love, concern, care, account, note, reputation, honour, consideration, sympathy, affection, attachment, repute: *I have a very high regard for him and what he has achieved.* **2 = look**, gaze, scrutiny, stare, glance: *This gave a look of calculated menace to his regard.* **3** *(plural)* **= good wishes**, respects, greetings, compliments, best wishes, salutations, devoirs: *Give my regards to your family.*
as regards = concerning, regarding, relating to, pertaining to: *As regards the war, he believed in victory at any price.*
in this regard = on this point, on this matter, on this detail, in this respect: *In this regard nothing has changed.*
with regard to = concerning, regarding, relating to, with respect to, as regards: *The UN has urged sanctions with regard to trade in arms.*

> **USAGE**
> The word *regard* in the expression *with regard to* is singular, and has no *s* at the end. People often make the mistake of saying *with regards to*, perhaps being influenced by the phrase *as regards*.

regarding PREPOSITION **= concerning**, about, as to, on the subject of, re, respecting, in respect of, as regards, with reference to, in re, in the matter of, apropos, in *or* with regard to

regardless ADVERB **= in spite of everything**, anyway, nevertheless, nonetheless, in any case, no matter what, for all that, rain or shine, despite everything, come what may: *Despite her recent surgery she has been carrying on regardless.*
▷ ADJECTIVE *(with* **of***)* **= irrespective of**, disregarding, unconcerned about, heedless of, unmindful of: *It takes in anybody regardless of religion, colour or creed.*

regenerate VERB **= renew**, restore, revive, renovate, change, reproduce, uplift, reconstruct, re-establish, rejuvenate, kick-start *(informal)*, breathe new life into, invigorate, reinvigorate, reawaken, revivify, give a shot in the arm, inspirit
OPPOSITE: degenerate

regime NOUN **1 = government**, rule, management, administration, leadership, establishment, reign: *the collapse of the fascist regime* **2 = plan**, course, system, policy, programme, scheme, regimen: *a drastic regime of economic reform*

region NOUN **= area**, country, place, part, land, quarter, division, section, sector, district, territory, zone, province, patch, turf *(U.S. slang)*, tract, expanse, locality: *a remote mountain region*

regional ADJECTIVE **= local**, district, provincial, parochial, sectional, zonal

register NOUN **= list**, record, roll, file, schedule, diary, catalogue, log, archives, chronicle, memorandum, roster, ledger, annals: *registers of births, deaths and marriages*
▷ VERB **1 = enrol**, sign on *or* up, enlist, list, note, enter, check in, inscribe, set down: *Have you come to register at the school?* **2 = record**, catalogue, chronicle, take down: *We registered his birth.* **3 = indicate**, show, record, read: *The meter registered loads of 9 and 10 kg.* **4 = show**, mark, record, reflect, indicate, betray, manifest, bespeak: *Many people registered no symptoms when they became infected.* **5 = express**, say, show, reveal, display, exhibit: *Workers stopped work to register their protest.* **6 = have an effect**, get through, sink in, make an impression, tell, impress, come home, dawn on: *What I said sometimes didn't register in her brain.*

regress VERB **= revert**, deteriorate, return, go back, retreat, lapse, fall back, wane, recede, ebb, degenerate, relapse, lose ground, turn the clock back, backslide, retrogress, retrocede, fall away *or* off **OPPOSITE:** progress

regret VERB **1 = be** *or* **feel sorry about**, feel remorse about, be upset about, rue, deplore, bemoan, repent (of), weep over, bewail, cry over spilt milk: *She regrets having given up her home.* **OPPOSITE:** be satisfied with **2 = mourn**, miss, grieve for *or* over: *I regret the passing of the old era.*
▷ NOUN **1 = remorse**, compunction, self-reproach, pang of conscience, bitterness, repentance, contrition, penitence, ruefulness: *He has no regrets about retiring.* **2 = sorrow**, disappointment, grief, lamentation: *He expressed great regret.* **OPPOSITE:** satisfaction

regretful ADJECTIVE **= sorry**, disappointed, sad, ashamed, apologetic, mournful, rueful, contrite, sorrowful, repentant, remorseful, penitent

USAGE
Regretful and *regretfully* are sometimes wrongly used where *regrettable* and *regrettably* are meant. A simple way of making the distinction is that when you regret something YOU have done, you are *regretful*: *he gave a regretful smile; he smiled regretfully*. In contrast, when you are sorry about an occurrence you did not yourself cause, you view the occurrence as *regrettable*: *this is a regrettable* (not *regretful*) *mistake; regrettably* (not *regretfully*, i.e. because of circumstances beyond my control) *I shall be unable to attend*.

regrettable ADJECTIVE **= unfortunate**, wrong, disappointing, sad, distressing, unhappy, shameful, woeful, deplorable, ill-advised, lamentable, pitiable

regular ADJECTIVE **1 = frequent**, daily: *Take regular exercise.* **2 = normal**, common, established, usual, ordinary, typical, routine, everyday, customary, commonplace, habitual, unvarying: *Children are encouraged to make reading a regular routine.* **OPPOSITE:** infrequent **3 = steady**, consistent: *a very regular beat* **4 = even**, level, balanced, straight, flat, fixed, smooth, uniform, symmetrical: *regular rows of wooden huts* **OPPOSITE:** uneven **5 = methodical**, set, ordered, formal, steady, efficient, systematic, orderly, standardized, dependable, consistent: *an unfailingly regular procedure* **OPPOSITE:** inconsistent **6 = official**, standard, established, traditional, classic, correct, approved, formal, sanctioned, proper, prevailing, orthodox, time-honoured, bona fide: *The regular method is to take your cutting, and insert it into the compost.*

regulate VERB **1 = control**, run, order, rule, manage, direct, guide, handle, conduct, arrange, monitor, organize, govern, administer, oversee, supervise, systematize, superintend: *a powerful body to regulate the stock market* **2 = moderate**, control, modulate, settle, fit, balance, tune, adjust: *He breathed deeply, trying to regulate the pound of his heartbeat.*

regulation NOUN **1 = rule**, order, law, direction, procedure, requirement, dictate, decree, canon, statute, ordinance, commandment, edict, precept, standing order: *new safety regulations* **2 = control**, government, management, administration, direction, arrangement, supervision, governance, rule: *They also have responsibility for the regulation of nurseries.*
▷ MODIFIER **= conventional**, official, standard, required, normal, usual, prescribed, mandatory, customary: *He wears the regulation dark suit of corporate America.*

regurgitate VERB **= disgorge**, throw up *(informal)*, chuck up *(slang, chiefly U.S.)*, puke up *(slang)*, sick up *(informal)*, spew out *or* up

rehabilitate VERB **1 = reintegrate**: *Considerable efforts have been made to rehabilitate patients.* **2 = restore**, convert, renew, adjust, rebuild, make good, mend, renovate, reconstruct, reinstate, re-establish, fix up *(informal, chiefly U.S. & Canad.)*, reconstitute, recondition, reinvigorate: *a programme for rehabilitating low-income housing*

rehash NOUN **= reworking**, rewrite, new version, rearrangement: *It was a rehash of an old script.*
▷ VERB **= rework**, rewrite, rearrange, change, alter, reshuffle, make over, reuse, rejig *(informal)*, refashion: *The tour seems to rely heavily on rehashed old favourites.*

rehearsal NOUN **= practice**, rehearsing, practice session, run-through, reading, preparation, drill, going-over *(informal)*

rehearse VERB **1 = practise**, prepare, run through, go over, train, act, study, ready, repeat, drill, try out, recite: *A group of actors are rehearsing a play about Joan of Arc.* **2 = recite**, practise, go over, run through, tell, list, detail, describe, review, relate, depict, spell out, recount, narrate, trot out *(informal)*, delineate, enumerate: *Anticipate any tough questions and rehearse your answers.*

reign VERB **1 = be supreme**, prevail, predominate, hold sway, be rife, be rampant: *A relative calm reigned over the city.* **2 = rule**, govern, be in power, occupy *or* sit on the throne, influence, command, administer, hold sway, wear the crown, wield the sceptre: *Henry II, who reigned from 1154 to 1189*
▷ NOUN **= rule**, sovereignty, supremacy, power, control, influence, command, empire, monarchy, sway, dominion, hegemony, ascendancy: *Queen Victoria's reign*

USAGE
The words *rein* and *reign* should not be confused; note the correct spellings in *he gave full rein to his feelings* (not *reign*); and *it will be necessary to rein in public spending* (not *reign in*).

reimburse VERB **= pay back**, refund, repay, recompense, return, restore, compensate, indemnify, remunerate

rein NOUN **= control**, harness, bridle, hold, check, restriction, brake, curb, restraint: *He wrapped his horse's reins round his left wrist.*
give (a) free rein to something *or* **someone = give a free hand (to)**, give carte blanche (to), give a blank cheque (to), remove restraints (from), indulge, let go, give way (to), give (someone) his *or* her head: *They gave him a free rein with time to mould a decent side.*
rein something in *or* **back = check**, control, limit, contain, master, curb, restrain, hold back, constrain, bridle, keep in check: *He promised the government would rein back inflation.*

reincarnation NOUN **= rebirth**, metempsychosis, transmigration of souls

reinforce VERB **1 = support**, strengthen, fortify, toughen, stress, prop, supplement, emphasize, underline, harden, bolster, stiffen, shore up, buttress: *They had to reinforce the walls with exterior beams.* **2 = increase**, extend, add to, strengthen, supplement, augment: *Troops and police have been reinforced.*

reinforcement NOUN **1 = strengthening**, increase, supplement, enlargement, fortification, amplification, augmentation: *the reinforcement of peace and security around the world* **2 = support**, stay, shore, prop, brace, buttress: *There are reinforcements on all doors.* **3** *(plural)* **= reserves**, support, auxiliaries, additional *or* fresh troops: *troop reinforcements*

reinstate VERB **= restore**, recall, bring back, re-establish, return, rehabilitate

reiterate VERB **= repeat**, restate, say again, retell, do again, recapitulate, iterate

reject VERB **1 = rebuff**, drop, jilt, desert, turn down, ditch *(slang)*, break with, spurn, refuse, say no to, repulse, throw over: *people who have been rejected by their lovers* **OPPOSITE:** accept **2 = deny**, decline, abandon, exclude, veto, discard, relinquish, renounce, spurn, eschew, leave off, throw off, disallow, forsake, retract, repudiate, cast off, disown, forgo, disclaim, forswear, swear off, wash your hands of: *They are rejecting the values on which Thatcherism was built.* **OPPOSITE:** approve **3 = discard**, decline, eliminate, scrap, bin, jettison, cast aside, throw away *or* out: *Seventeen publishers rejected the manuscript.* **OPPOSITE:** accept
▷ NOUN **1 = castoff**, second, discard, flotsam, clunker *(informal)*: *a hat that looks like a reject from an army patrol* **OPPOSITE:** treasure **2 = failure**, loser, flop: *I'm an outsider, a reject, a social failure; a reject of Real Madrid*

rejection NOUN **1 = denial**, veto, dismissal, exclusion, abandonment, spurning, casting off, disowning, thumbs down, renunciation, repudiation, eschewal: *his rejection of our values* **OPPOSITE:** approval **2 = rebuff**, refusal, knock-back *(slang)*, kick in the teeth *(slang)*, bum's rush *(slang)*, the (old) heave-ho *(informal)*, brushoff *(slang)*: *These feelings of rejection and hurt remain.* **OPPOSITE:** acceptance

rejoice VERB **= be glad**, celebrate, delight, be happy, joy, triumph, glory, revel, be overjoyed, exult, jump for joy, make merry **OPPOSITE:** lament

rejoicing NOUN **= happiness**, delight, joy, triumph, celebration, cheer, festivity, elation, gaiety, jubilation, revelry, exultation, gladness, merrymaking

rejoin VERB **= reply**, answer, respond, retort, come back with, riposte, return

rejuvenate VERB **= revitalize**, restore, renew, refresh, regenerate, breathe new life into, reinvigorate, revivify, give new life to, reanimate, make young again, restore vitality to

relapse VERB **1 = lapse**, revert, degenerate, slip back, fail, weaken, fall back, regress, backslide, retrogress: *He was relapsing into his usual gloom.* **2 = worsen**, deteriorate, sicken, weaken, fail, sink, fade: *In 90 per cent of cases the patient will relapse within six months.* **OPPOSITE:** recover
▷ NOUN **1 = lapse**, regression, fall from grace, reversion, backsliding, recidivism, retrogression: *a relapse into the nationalism of the nineteenth century* **2 = worsening**, setback, deterioration, recurrence, turn for the worse, weakening: *The sufferer can experience frequent relapses.* **OPPOSITE:** recovery

relate VERB **= tell**, recount, report, present, detail, describe, chronicle, rehearse, recite, impart, narrate, set forth, give an account of: *He was relating a story he had once heard.*
relate to something *or* **someone** **1 = concern**, refer to, apply to, have to do with, pertain to, be relevant to, bear upon, appertain to, have reference to: *papers relating to the children* **2 = connect with**, associate with, link with, couple with, join with, ally with, correlate to, coordinate with: *how language relates to particular cultural codes*

related ADJECTIVE **1 = associated**, linked, allied, joint, accompanying, connected, affiliated, akin, correlated, interconnected, concomitant, cognate, agnate: *equipment and accessories for diving and related activities* **OPPOSITE:** unconnected **2 = akin**, kin, kindred, cognate, consanguineous, agnate: *He is related by marriage to some of the complainants.* **OPPOSITE:** unrelated

relation NOUN **1 = similarity**, link, bearing, bond, application, comparison, tie-in, correlation, interdependence, pertinence, connection: *This theory bears no relation to reality.* **2 = relative**, kin, kinsman *or* kinswoman, rellie *(Austral. slang)*: *I call him Uncle though he's no relation.*
▷ PLURAL NOUN **1 = dealings**, relationship, rapport, communications, meetings, terms, associations, affairs, contact, connections, interaction, intercourse, liaison: *The company has a track record of good employee relations.* **2 = family**, relatives, tribe, clan, kin, kindred, kinsmen, kinsfolk, ainga (N.Z.), rellies *(Austral. slang)*: *All my relations come from the place.*

relationship NOUN **1 = association**, bond, communications, connection, conjunction, affinity, rapport, kinship: *Money problems place great stress on close family ps.* **2 = affair**, romance, liaison, amour, intrigue: *She likes to have a relationship with her leading men.* **3 = connection**, link, proportion, parallel, ratio, similarity, tie-up, correlation, read-across: *the relationship between culture and power*

> **QUOTATIONS**
> A relationship, I think, is like a shark, you know? It has to constantly move forward or it dies. And I think what we got on our hands is a dead shark
> [Woody Allen *Annie Hall*]

relative NOUN **= relation**, connection, kinsman *or* kinswoman, member of your *or* the family, cuzzie *or* cuzzie-bro *(N. Z.)*, rellie *(Austral. slang)*: *Do relatives of yours still live in Siberia?*
▷ ADJECTIVE **1 = comparative**: *a period of relative calm* **2 = corresponding**, respective, reciprocal: *the relative importance of education in 50 countries* **3** (with **to**) **= in proportion to**, corresponding to, proportionate to, proportional to: *The satellite remains in one spot relative to the earth's surface.*

relatively ADVERB **= comparatively**, rather, somewhat, to some extent, in *or* by comparison

relax VERB **1 = be** *or* **feel at ease**, chill out *(slang, chiefly U.S.)*, take it easy, loosen up, laze, lighten up *(slang)*, put your feet up, hang loose *(slang)*, let yourself go *(informal)*, let your hair down *(informal)*, mellow out *(informal)*, make yourself at home, outspan *(S. African)*, take your ease: *I ought to relax and stop worrying about it.* **OPPOSITE:** be alarmed **2 = calm down**, calm, unwind, loosen up, tranquillize: *Do something that you know relaxes you.* **3 = make less tense**, soften, loosen up, unbend, rest: *Massage is used to relax muscles.* **4 = lessen**, reduce, ease, relieve, weaken, loosen, let up, slacken: *He gradually relaxed his grip on the arms of the chair.* **OPPOSITE:** tighten **5 = moderate**, ease, relieve, weaken, diminish, mitigate, slacken: *Rules governing student conduct have been relaxed in recent years.* **OPPOSITE:** tighten up

relaxation NOUN **1 = leisure**, rest, fun, pleasure, entertainment, recreation, enjoyment, amusement, refreshment, beer and skittles *(informal)*, me-time: *You should be able to find the odd moment for relaxation.* **2 = lessening**, easing, reduction, weakening, moderation, let-up *(informal)*, slackening, diminution, abatement: *There will be no relaxation of army pressure.*

relaxed ADJECTIVE **1 = easy-going**, easy, casual, informal, laid-back *(informal)*, mellow, leisurely, downbeat *(informal)*, unhurried, nonchalant, free and easy, mild, insouciant, untaxing, chilled *(informal)*: *Try to adopt a more relaxed manner.* **2 = comfortable**, easy-going, casual, laid-back *(informal)*, informal, chilled *(informal)*: *The atmosphere at lunch was relaxed.*

relay VERB **= broadcast**, carry, spread, communicate, transmit, send out

release VERB **1 = set free**, free, discharge, liberate, drop, deliver, loose, let go, undo, let out, extricate, untie, disengage, emancipate, unchain, unfasten, turn loose, unshackle, unloose, unfetter, unbridle, manumit: *He was released from custody the next day.* **OPPOSITE:** imprison **2 = acquit**, excuse, exempt, let go, dispense, let off, exonerate, absolve: *He wants to be released from any promise between us.* **3 = issue**, publish, make public, make known, break, present, launch, distribute, unveil, put out, circulate, disseminate: *They're not releasing any more details yet.* **OPPOSITE:** withhold
▷ NOUN **1 = liberation**, freedom, delivery, liberty, discharge, emancipation, deliverance, manumission, relief: *the secret negotiations necessary to secure the release of the hostages* **OPPOSITE:** imprisonment **2 = acquittal**, exemption, let-off *(informal)*, dispensation, absolution, exoneration, acquittance: *a blessed release from the obligation to work* **3 = issue**, announcement, publication, proclamation, offering: *a meeting held after the release of the report*

relegate VERB **1 = demote**, degrade, downgrade, declass: *Other newspapers relegated the item to the middle pages.* **2 = banish**, exile, expel, throw out, oust, deport, eject, expatriate: *a team about to be relegated to the second division*

relent VERB **1 = be merciful**, yield, give in, soften, give way, come round, capitulate, acquiesce, change your mind, unbend, forbear, show mercy, have pity, melt, give quarter: *Finally his mother relented.* **OPPOSITE:** show no mercy **2 = ease**, die down, let up, fall, drop, slow, relax, weaken, slacken: *If the bad weather relents the game will be finished today.* **OPPOSITE:** intensify

relentless ADJECTIVE **1 = merciless**, hard, fierce, harsh, cruel, grim, ruthless, uncompromising, unstoppable, inflexible, unrelenting, unforgiving, inexorable, implacable, unyielding, remorseless, pitiless, undeviating: *He was the most relentless enemy I have ever known.* **OPPOSITE:** merciful **2 = unremitting**, sustained, punishing, persistent, unstoppable, unbroken, unrelenting, incessant, unabated, nonstop, unrelieved, unflagging, unfaltering: *The pressure now was relentless.*

relevant ADJECTIVE **= significant**, appropriate, proper, related, fitting, material, suited, relative, to the point, apt, applicable, pertinent, apposite, admissible, germane, to the purpose, appurtenant, ad rem *(Latin)* **OPPOSITE:** irrelevant

reliable ADJECTIVE **1 = dependable**, trustworthy, honest, responsible, sure, sound, true, certain, regular, stable, faithful, predictable, upright,

R

Mark Twain's Use of Adverbs

I am dead to adverbs; they cannot excite me. To misplace an adverb is a thing which I am able to do with frozen indifference; it can never give me a pang.

– 'Reply to a Boston Girl,' *Atlantic Monthly*, June 1880

From this famous pronouncement by Mark Twain a reader might conclude that Twain was indifferent at best, and possibly even hostile, to adverbs. What he says and what he does, however, are in this case not the same thing, and before drawing conclusions about his use of adverbs it would do well to consider another of Twain's aphorisms: 'Often, how louder and clearer than any tongue, does dumb circumstantial evidence speak.'

Twain was no stranger to adverbs. They appear in all of his writing, and the more frequent of English's adverbs – *really, nearly, merely, hardly,* for example – occur with roughly the same frequency as they do in other writers. Collocations including adverbs that are tantamount to cliché (even in Twain's day) are not less frequent in his writing than in the writing of his contemporaries: you will find a fairly typical sprinkling of *perfectly aware, finally decide,* and *simply because* in all of Twain. He was particularly fond of *presently* and used it to move the action forward in many his works, such as here in *The Adventures of Tom Sawyer:*

> **Presently** the confusion took form, and through the fog of battle Tom appeared, seated astride the new boy, and pounding him with his fists.

For adverbs with more semantic content, however, a different pattern emerges: they tend to occur quite a lot more in his nonfiction than in his fiction. The adverb *picturesquely*, for example, is used less than 20 times in his oeuvre, with two-thirds of its occurrences in nonfiction. Fewer than a quarter of the occurrences of *commonly* are in his fiction. Is there a reason for this pattern?

The prevalence of dialect and colloquialism in his best-known novels may come to mind, and this does in fact appear to explain a relative dearth of adverbs in Twain's fiction. Take, for example, this passage from *Huckleberry Finn*, when the legendary raft ride down the Mississippi is well underway:

> Next day, towards night, we laid up under a little willow towhead out in the middle, where there was a village on each side of the river, and the duke and the king begun to lay out a plan for working them towns. Jim he spoke to the duke, and said he hoped it wouldn't take but a few hours, because it got mighty heavy and tiresome to him when he had to lay all day in the wigwam tied with the rope. You see, when we left him all alone we had to tie him, because if anybody happened on to him all by himself and not tied it wouldn't look much like he was a runaway nigger, you know.

Twain lays out the entire scene with hardly a single adverb that provides any semantic content – and perhaps displays to some degree his stated indifference towards that part of speech. Twain is particularly good, however, at letting a well-placed adverb convey his trademark wit and irony. Note here, for example, the adverbs *apparently* and *naturally*, one at the beginning of a sentence and one at the end, that edge his language definitively in the humorous direction he favours:

> He said he believed that if you were to strip the nation naked and send a stranger through the crowd, he couldn't tell the king from a quack doctor, nor a duke from a hotel clerk. **Apparently** here was a man whose brains had not been reduced to an ineffectual mush by idiotic training.

> The body was dragged over to let the king and the swells look down upon it. They were stupefied with astonishment **naturally**.

The evidence suggests that Twain was in fact not as doctrinaire about the use of adverbs as he professed to be. Like many other great writers, he put them to work when he had a job for them to do.

staunch, reputable, trusty, unfailing, tried and true: *She was efficient and reliable.* **OPPOSITE:** unreliable **2 = safe**, dependable: *Japanese cars are so reliable.* **3 = definitive**, sound, dependable, trustworthy: *There is no reliable evidence.*

reliance NOUN **1 = dependency**, dependence: *the country's increasing reliance on foreign aid* **2 = trust**, confidence, belief, faith, assurance, credence, credit: *If you respond immediately, you will guarantee people's reliance on you.*

relic NOUN **= remnant**, vestige, memento, trace, survival, scrap, token, fragment, souvenir, remembrance, keepsake

relief NOUN **1 = ease**, release, comfort, cure, remedy, solace, balm, deliverance, mitigation, abatement, alleviation, easement, palliation, assuagement: *The news will come as a great relief.* **2 = rest**, respite, let-up, relaxation, break, diversion, refreshment *(informal)*, remission, breather *(informal)*: *a self-help programme which can give lasting relief* **3 = aid**, help, support, assistance, sustenance, succour: *famine relief*

relieve VERB **1 = ease**, soothe, alleviate, allay, relax, comfort, calm, cure, dull, diminish, soften, console, appease, solace, mitigate, abate, assuage, mollify, salve, palliate: *Drugs can relieve much of the pain.* **OPPOSITE:** intensify **2 = free**, release, deliver, discharge, exempt, unburden, disembarrass, disencumber: *He felt relieved of a burden.* **3 = take over from**, substitute for, stand in for, take the place of, give (someone) a break *or* rest: *At seven o'clock the night nurse came in to relieve her.* **4 = help**, support, aid, sustain, assist, succour, bring aid to: *a programme to relieve poor countries*

religion NOUN **= belief**, faith, theology, creed ▷ *See themed panel* **Religion** *on facing page*

QUOTATIONS

Religion is by no means a proper subject of conversation in a mixed company
[Earl of Chesterfield]

There is only one religion, though there are a hundred versions of it
[George Bernard Shaw *Plays Unpleasant (preface)*]

Religion enables us to ignore nothingness and get on with the jobs of life
[John Updike *Self-Consciousness*]

I count religion but a childish toy,
And hold there is no sin but ignorance
[Christopher Marlowe *The Jew of Malta*]

Religion...is the opium of the people
[Karl Marx *Critique of Hegel's Philosophy of Right*]

Things have come to a pretty pass when religion is allowed to invade the sphere of private life
[Lord Melbourne]

The true meaning of religion is thus not morality, but morality touched by emotion
[Matthew Arnold *Literature and Dogma*]

Science without religion is lame, religion without science is blind
[Albert Einstein *Out of My Later Years*]

Any system of religion that has any thing in it that shocks the mind of a child cannot be a true system
[Thomas Paine *The Age of Reason*]

I am a Millionaire. That is my religion
[George Bernard Shaw *Major Barbara*]

I can't talk religion to a man with bodily hunger in his eyes
[George Bernard Shaw *Major Barbara*]

The one certain way for a woman to hold a man is to leave him for religion
[Muriel Spark *The Comforters*]

We have just enough religion to make us hate, but not enough to make us love one another
[Jonathan Swift *Thoughts on Various Subjects*]

I am for religion against religions
[Victor Hugo *Les Misérables*]

Time consecrates;
And what is grey with age becomes religion
[Friedrich von Schiller *Die Piccolomini*]

If you talk to God you are praying; if God talks to you, you have schizophrenia
[Thomas Szasz *The Second Sin*]

One religion is as true as another
[Robert Burton *Anatomy of Melancholy*]

Christians have burnt each other, quite persuaded
That all the apostles would have done as they did
[Lord Byron *Don Juan*]

The nearer the Church the further from God
[Bishop Lancelot Andrews *Of the Nativity*]

To become a popular religion, it is only necessary for a superstition to enslave a philosophy
[Dean Inge *Idea of Progress*]

Religion's in the heart, not in the knees
[Douglas Jerrold *The Devil's Ducat*]

Religion is the frozen thought of men out of which they build temples
[Jiddu Krishnamurti]

religious ADJECTIVE **1 = spiritual**, holy, sacred, divine, theological, righteous, sectarian, doctrinal, devotional, scriptural: *different religious beliefs* **2 = conscientious**, exact, faithful, rigid, rigorous, meticulous, scrupulous, fastidious, unerring, unswerving, punctilious: *The clientele turned up, with religious regularity, every night.*

relinquish VERB **= give up**, leave, release, drop, abandon, resign, desert, quit, yield, hand over, surrender, withdraw from, let go, retire from, renounce, waive, vacate, say goodbye to, forsake, cede, repudiate, cast off, forgo, abdicate, kiss (something) goodbye, lay aside

relish VERB **1 = enjoy**, like, prefer, taste, appreciate, savour, revel in, luxuriate in: *He ate quietly, relishing his meal.* **OPPOSITE:** dislike **2 = look forward to**, fancy, delight in, lick your lips over: *She is not relishing the prospect of another spell in prison.*
▷ NOUN **1 = enjoyment**, liking, love, taste, fancy, stomach, appetite, appreciation, penchant, zest, fondness, gusto, predilection, zing *(informal)*, partiality: *The three men ate with relish.* **OPPOSITE:** distaste **2 = condiment**, seasoning, sauce, appetizer: *pots of spicy relish*

reluctance NOUN **= unwillingness**, dislike, loathing, distaste, aversion, backwardness, hesitancy, disinclination, repugnance, indisposition, disrelish

reluctant ADJECTIVE **= unwilling**, slow, backward, grudging, hesitant, averse, recalcitrant, loath, disinclined, unenthusiastic, indisposed **OPPOSITE:** willing

USAGE
Reticent is quite commonly used nowadays as a synonym of *reluctant* and followed by *to* and a verb. In careful writing it is advisable to avoid this use, since many people would regard it as mistaken.

rely on VERB **1 = depend on**, lean on: *They relied heavily on the advice of their advisors.* **2 = be confident of**, bank on, trust, count on, bet on, reckon on, lean on, be sure of, have confidence in, swear by, repose trust in: *I know I can rely on you to sort it out.*

remain VERB **1 = stay**, continue, go on, stand, dwell, bide: *The three men remained silent.* **2 = stay behind**, wait, delay, stay put, tarry: *He remained at home with his family.* **OPPOSITE:** go **3 = continue**, be left, endure, persist, linger, hang in the air, stay: *There remains deep mistrust of his government.*

remainder NOUN **= rest**, remains, balance, trace, excess, surplus, butt, remnant, relic, residue, stub, vestige(s), tail end, dregs, oddment, leavings, residuum

remaining ADJECTIVE **1 = left-over**, surviving, outstanding, lingering, unfinished, residual: *Stir in the remaining ingredients.* **2 = surviving**, lasting, persisting, abiding, extant: *They purged remaining memories of his reign.*

R

RELIGION

Religions

- animism
- Babi *or* Babism
- Baha'ism
- Buddhism
- Christianity
- Confucianism
- druidism
- heliolatry
- Hinduism
- Islam
- Jainism
- Judaism
- Macumba
- Manichaeism
- Mithraism
- Orphism
- paganism
- Rastafarianism
- Ryobu Shinto
- Santeria
- Satanism
- Scientology *(trademark)*
- shamanism
- Shango
- Shembe
- Shinto
- Sikhism
- Taoism
- voodoo
- Yezidis
- Zoroastrianism

Religious books

- Adi Granth
- Apocrypha
- Atharveda
- Ayurveda
- Bhagavad-Gita
- Bible
- Book of Mormon
- Granth *or* Guru Granth Sahib
- I Ching
- Koran
- Li Chi
- Lu
- Mahabharata
- New Testament
- Old Testament
- Ramayana
- Rigveda
- Samaveda
- Shi Ching
- Siddhanta
- Su Ching
- Talmud
- Tipitaka
- Torah
- Tripitaka
- Veda
- Yajurveda

Religious buildings

- abbey
- bethel
- cathedral
- chapel
- church
- convent
- gurdwara
- Kaaba
- marae
- monastery
- mosque
- synagogue
- tabernacle
- temple

Religious clothing

- alb
- almuce
- amice
- biretta
- calotte
- canonicals
- capuche
- cassock
- chasuble
- chimere
- clerical collar
- clericals
- coif
- cope
- cornet
- cotta
- cowl
- dalmatic
- dog collar
- gremial
- guimpe
- habit
- infulae
- maniple
- mantelletta
- mitre
- mozzetta
- pallium
- peplos
- pontificals
- rochet
- scapular
- shovel hat
- soutane
- superhumeral
- surcingle
- surplice
- tippet
- wimple
- zucchetto

Religious festivals

- Advent
- Al Hijrah
- Ascension Day
- Ash Wednesday
- Baisakhi
- Bodhi Day
- Candlemas
- Ching Ming
- Christmas
- Corpus Christi
- Day of Atonement
- Dhammacakka
- Diwali
- Dragon Boat Festival
- Dussehra
- Easter
- Eid ul-Adha
- Eid ul-Fitr
- Epiphany
- Feast of Tabernacles
- Good Friday
- Guru Nanak's Birthday
- Hanukah
- Hirja
- Hola Mohalla
- Holi
- Janamashtami
- Lailat ul-Barah
- Lailat ul-Isra Wal Mi'raj
- Lailat ul-Qadr
- Lent
- Mahashivaratri
- Maundy Thursday
- Michaelmas
- Moon Festival
- Palm Sunday
- Passion Sunday
- Passover
- Pentecost
- Pesach
- Purim
- Quadragesima
- Quinquagesima
- Raksha Bandhan
- Ramadan
- Rama Naumi
- Rogation
- Rosh Hashanah
- Septuagesima
- Sexagesima
- Shavuot
- Shrove Tuesday
- Sukkoth
- Trinity
- Wesak
- Whitsun
- Winter Festival
- Yom Kippur
- Yuan Tan

Buddhism, Schools of

- Foism
- Geluk
- Hinayana
- Jodo
- Kagyü
- Lamaism
- Mahayana
- Nichiren
- Nyingma
- Pure Land Buddhism
- Rinjai
- Sakya
- Soka Gakkai
- Soto
- Tendai
- Theravada
- Vajrayana
- Zen

Christian denominations and sects

- Adventism
- Amish
- Anabaptism
- Anglicanism
- Baptist Church
- Byzantine Church
- Calvinism
- Catholicism
- Christadelphianism
- Christian Science
- Congregationalism
- Coptic Church
- Dutch Reformed Church
- Eastern Orthodox Church
- Episcopal Church
- Evangelicalism
- Greek Orthodox Church
- Jehovah's Witnesses
- Lutheranism
- Maronite Church
- Methodism
- Moravian Church
- Mormons *or* Latter-day Saints
- New Jerusalem Church
- Orthodox Church
- Pentecostalism
- Plymouth Brethren
- Presbyterianism
- Protestantism
- Quakerism
- Roman Catholicism
- Russian Orthodox Church
- Salvation Army
- Seventh-Day Adventism
- Shakerism
- Society of Friends
- Unification Church
- Unitarianism

Hindu denominations and sects

- Hare Krishna
- Saivaism
- Saktas
- Vaishnavism

Jewish denominations and sects

- Chassidism, Chasidism, Hassidism, *or* Hasidism
- Conservative Judaism
- Liberal Judaism
- Orthodox Judaism
- Reform Judaism
- Zionism

Muslim denominations and sects

- Alaouites *or* Alawites
- Druse *or* Druze
- Imami
- Ismaili *or* Isma'ili
- Nizari
- Shiah, Shia *or* Shiite
- Sufism
- Sunni
- Wahhabism *or* Wahabism
- Zaidi

remains PLURAL NOUN **1 = remnants**, leftovers, remainder, scraps, rest, pieces, balance, traces, fragments, debris, residue, crumbs, vestiges, detritus, dregs, odds and ends, oddments, leavings: *the remains of their picnic* **2 = relics**: *There are Roman remains all around us.* **3 = corpse**, body, carcass, cadaver: *The remains of a man had been found.*

remark VERB **1 = comment**, say, state, reflect, mention, declare, observe, pass comment, animadvert: *I remarked that I would go shopping that afternoon.* **2 = notice**, note, observe, perceive, see, mark, regard, make out, heed, espy, take note *or* notice of: *Everyone has remarked what a lovely lady she is.*
▷ NOUN **1 = comment**, observation, reflection, statement, thought, word, opinion, declaration, assertion, utterance: *She has made outspoken remarks on the issue.* **2 = notice**, thought, comment, attention, regard, mention, recognition, consideration, observation, heed, acknowledgment: *He had never found the situation worthy of remark.*

remarkable ADJECTIVE **= extraordinary**, striking, outstanding, famous, odd, strange, wonderful, signal, rare, unusual, impressive, surprising, distinguished, prominent, notable, phenomenal, uncommon, conspicuous, singular, miraculous, noteworthy, pre-eminent **OPPOSITE:** ordinary

remedy NOUN **1 = solution**, relief, redress, antidote, corrective, panacea, countermeasure: *a remedy for economic ills* **2 = cure**, treatment, specific, medicine, therapy, antidote, panacea, restorative, relief, nostrum, physic *(rare)*, medicament, counteractive: *natural remedies to overcome winter infections*
▷ VERB **1 = put right**, redress, rectify, reform, fix, correct, solve, repair, relieve, ameliorate, set to rights: *A great deal has been done to remedy the situation.* **2 = cure**, treat, heal, help, control, ease, restore, relieve, soothe, alleviate, mitigate, assuage, palliate: *He's been remedying a hamstring injury.*

remember VERB **1 = recall**, think back to, recollect, reminisce about, retain, recognize, call up, summon up, call to mind: *He was remembering the old days.* **OPPOSITE:** forget **2 = bear in mind**, keep in mind: *Remember that each person reacts differently.* **3 = look back (on)**, commemorate: *He is remembered for being bad at games.*

remembrance NOUN **1 = commemoration**, memorial, testimonial: *They wore black in remembrance of those who had died.* **2 = souvenir**, token, reminder, monument, relic, remembrancer *(archaic)*, memento, keepsake: *As a remembrance, he left a photo album.* **3 = memory**, recollection, thought, recall, recognition, retrospect, reminiscence, anamnesis: *He had clung to the remembrance of things past.*

> **QUOTATIONS**
> There's rosemary, that's for remembrance
> [William Shakespeare *Hamlet*]

remind VERB **= jog your memory**, prompt, refresh your memory, make you remember: *Can you remind me to buy a bottle of milk?*
remind someone of something *or* **someone = bring to mind**, call to mind, put in mind, awaken memories of, call up, bring back to: *She reminds me of the wife of the pilot.*

reminisce VERB **= recall**, remember, look back, hark back, review, think back, recollect, live in the past, go over in the memory

reminiscences PLURAL NOUN **= recollections**, memories, reflections, retrospections, reviews, recalls, memoirs, anecdotes, remembrances

reminiscent ADJECTIVE **= suggestive**, evocative, redolent, remindful, similar

remission NOUN **1 = lessening**, abatement, abeyance, lull, relaxation, ebb, respite, moderation, let-up *(informal)*, alleviation, amelioration: *The disease is in remission.* **2 = reduction**, lessening, suspension, decrease, diminution: *It had been raining hard all day, without remission.* **3 = pardon**, release, discharge, amnesty, forgiveness, indulgence, exemption, reprieve, acquittal, absolution, exoneration, excuse: *I've got 10 years and there's no remission for drug offenders.*

remit NOUN **= instructions**, brief, guidelines, authorization, terms of reference, orders: *That issue is not within the remit of the group.*
▷ VERB **1 = send**, post, forward, mail, transmit, dispatch: *Many immigrants regularly remit money to their families.* **2 = cancel**, stop, halt, repeal, rescind, desist, forbear: *Every creditor shall remit the claim that is held against a neighbour.* **3 = lessen**, diminish, abate, ease up, reduce, relax, moderate, weaken, decrease, soften, dwindle, alleviate, wane, fall away, mitigate, slacken: *an episode of 'baby blues' which eventually remitted*

remittance NOUN **= payment**, fee, consideration, allowance

remnant NOUN **= remainder**, remains, trace, fragment, end, bit, rest, piece, balance, survival, scrap, butt, shred, hangover, residue, rump, leftovers, stub, vestige, tail end, oddment, residuum

remonstrate VERB **= protest**, challenge, argue, take issue, object, complain, dispute, dissent, take exception, expostulate

remorse NOUN **= regret**, shame, guilt, pity, grief, compassion, sorrow, anguish, repentance, contrition, compunction, penitence, self-reproach, pangs of conscience, ruefulness, bad *or* guilty conscience

> **QUOTATIONS**
> remorse, the fatal egg by pleasure laid
> [William Cowper *The Progress of Error*]

remorseless ADJECTIVE **= pitiless**, hard, harsh, cruel, savage, ruthless, callous, merciless, unforgiving, implacable, inhumane, unmerciful, hardhearted, uncompassionate: *the capacity for quick, remorseless violence*

remote ADJECTIVE **1 = distant**, far, isolated, lonely, out-of-the-way, far-off, secluded, inaccessible, faraway, outlying, in the middle of nowhere, off the beaten track, backwoods, godforsaken: *a remote farm in the hills* **OPPOSITE:** nearby **2 = far**, distant, obscure, far-off: *particular events in the remote past* **3 = slight**, small, outside, poor, unlikely, slim, faint, doubtful, dubious, slender, meagre, negligible, implausible, inconsiderable: *The chances of his surviving are pretty remote.* **OPPOSITE:** strong **4 = aloof**, cold, removed, reserved, withdrawn, distant, abstracted, detached, indifferent, faraway, introspective, uninterested, introverted, uninvolved, unapproachable, uncommunicative, standoffish: *She looked so remote.* **OPPOSITE:** outgoing

removal NOUN **1 = extraction**, stripping, withdrawal, purging, abstraction, uprooting, displacement, eradication, erasure, subtraction, dislodgment, expunction, taking away *or* off *or* out: *the removal of a small lump* **2 = dismissal**, expulsion, elimination, ejection, dispossession: *His removal from power was illegal.* **3 = move**, transfer, departure, relocation, flitting *(Scot. & Northern English dialect)*: *Home removals are best done in cool weather.*

remove VERB **1 = take out**, withdraw, extract, abstract: *Remove the cake from the oven.* **OPPOSITE:** insert **2 = take off**, doff: *He removed his jacket.* **OPPOSITE:** put on **3 = erase**, eliminate, take out: *This treatment removes the most stubborn stains.* **4 = dismiss**, eliminate, get rid of, discharge, abolish, expel, throw out, oust, relegate, purge, eject, do away with, depose, unseat, see the back of, dethrone, show someone the door, give the bum's rush *(slang)*, throw out on your ear *(informal)*: *The senate voted to remove him.* **OPPOSITE:** appoint **5 = get rid of**, wipe out, erase, eradicate, blow away *(slang, chiefly U.S.)*, blot out, expunge: *Most of her fears have been removed.* **6 = take away**, move, pull, transfer, detach, displace, do away with, dislodge, cart off *(slang)*, carry off *or* away: *They tried to remove the barricades which had been erected.* **OPPOSITE:** put back **7 = delete**, shed, get rid of, erase, excise, strike out, efface, expunge: *They intend to remove up to 100 offensive words.* **8 = move**, transfer, transport, shift, quit, depart, move away, relocate, vacate, flit *(Scot. & Northern English dialect)*: *They removed to America.* **9 = kill**, murder, do in *(slang)*, eliminate, take out *(slang)*, get rid of, execute, wipe out, dispose of, assassinate, do away with, liquidate, bump off *(slang)*, wipe from the face of the earth: *If someone irritates you, remove him, destroy him.*

remuneration NOUN **= payment**, income, earnings, salary, pay, return, profit, fee, wages, reward, compensation, repayment, reparation, indemnity, retainer, reimbursement, recompense, stipend, emolument, meed *(archaic)*

renaissance *or* **renascence** NOUN **= rebirth**, revival, restoration, renewal, awakening, resurrection, regeneration, resurgence, reappearance, new dawn, re-emergence, reawakening, new birth

rend VERB **= tear**, break, split, rip, pull, separate, divide, crack, burst, smash, disturb, shatter, pierce, fracture, sever, wrench, splinter, rupture, cleave, lacerate, rive, tear to pieces, sunder *(literary)*, dissever

render VERB **1 = make**, cause to become, leave: *It has so many errors as to render it useless.* **2 = provide**, give, show, pay, present, supply, deliver, contribute, yield, submit, tender, hand out, furnish, turn over, make available: *Any assistance you can render him will be helpful.* **3 = deliver**, give, return, announce, pronounce: *The Board was slow to render its verdict.* **4 = translate**, put, explain, interpret, reproduce, transcribe, construe, restate: *150 Psalms rendered into English* **5** *(sometimes followed by* **up***)* **= give up**, give, deliver, yield, hand over, surrender, turn over, relinquish, cede: *I render up my soul to God.* **6 = represent**, interpret, portray, depict, do, give, play, act, present, perform: *a powerful, bizarre, and beautifully rendered story*

rendezvous NOUN **1 = appointment**, meeting, date, engagement, tryst *(archaic)*, assignation: *I had decided to keep my rendezvous with him.* **2 = meeting place**, venue, gathering point, place of assignation, trysting-place *(archaic)*: *Their rendezvous would be the hotel at the airport.*
▷ VERB **= meet**, assemble, get together, come together, collect, gather, rally, muster, converge, join up, be reunited: *The plan was to rendezvous on Sunday afternoon.*

rendition NOUN **1 = performance**, arrangement, interpretation, rendering, take *(informal, chiefly U.S.)*, reading, version, delivery, presentation, execution, portrayal, depiction: *The musicians broke into a rousing rendition of the song.* **2 = translation**, reading, version, construction, explanation, interpretation, transcription: *a rendition of the works of Conrad*

renegade NOUN **= deserter**, rebel, betrayer, dissident, outlaw, runaway, traitor, defector, mutineer, turncoat, apostate, backslider, recreant *(archaic)*: *He was a renegade – a traitor.*
▷ MODIFIER **= traitorous**, rebel, dissident, outlaw, runaway, rebellious, unfaithful, disloyal, backsliding, mutinous, apostate, recreant *(archaic)*: *The renegade policeman supplied details of the murder.*

renege VERB **= break your word**, go back, welsh *(slang)*, default, back out, repudiate, break a promise

renew VERB **1 = recommence**, continue, extend, repeat, resume, prolong, reopen, recreate, reaffirm, re-establish, rejuvenate, regenerate, restate, begin again, revitalize, bring up to date: *He renewed his attack on government policy.* **2 = reaffirm**, resume, breathe new life into, recommence: *They renewed their friendship.* **3 = replace**, refresh, replenish, restock: *Cells are constantly renewed.* **4 = restore**, repair, transform, overhaul, mend, refurbish, renovate, refit, fix up *(informal, chiefly U.S. & Canad.)*, modernize: *the cost of renewing the buildings*

renounce VERB **1 = disown**, reject, abandon, quit, discard, spurn, eschew, leave off, throw off, forsake, retract, repudiate, cast off, abstain from, recant, forswear, abjure, swear off, wash your hands of: *She renounced terrorism.* **2 = disclaim**, deny, decline, give up, resign, relinquish, waive, renege, forgo, abdicate, abjure, abnegate: *He renounced his claim to the throne.* **OPPOSITE:** assert

renovate VERB **= restore**, repair, refurbish, do up *(informal)*, reform, renew, overhaul, revamp, recreate, remodel, rehabilitate, refit, fix up *(informal, chiefly U.S. & Canad.)*, modernize, reconstitute, recondition

renown NOUN **= fame**, note, distinction, repute, mark, reputation, honour, glory, celebrity, acclaim, stardom, eminence, lustre, illustriousness

renowned ADJECTIVE **= famous**, noted, celebrated, well-known, distinguished, esteemed, acclaimed, notable, eminent, famed, illustrious **OPPOSITE:** unknown

rent[1] VERB **1 = hire**, lease: *He rented a car.* **2 = let**, lease: *She rented rooms to university students.*
▷ NOUN **= hire**, rental, lease, tariff, fee, payment: *She worked to pay the rent.*

rent[2] NOUN **1 = tear**, split, rip, slash, slit, gash, perforation, hole: *a small rent in the silk* **2 = opening**, break, hole, crack, breach, flaw, chink: *welling up from a rent in the ground*

renunciation NOUN **1 = rejection**, giving up, denial, abandonment, spurning, abstention, repudiation, forswearing, disavowal, abnegation, eschewal, abjuration: *a renunciation of terrorism* **2 = giving up**, resignation, surrender, waiver, disclaimer, abdication, relinquishment, abjuration: *the renunciation of territory*

repair[1] VERB **1 = mend**, fix, recover, restore, heal, renew, patch, make good, renovate, patch up, put back together, restore to working order: *He has repaired the roof.* **OPPOSITE:** damage **2 = put right**, make up for, compensate for, rectify, square, retrieve, redress: *They needed to repair the damage done by the interview.*
▷ NOUN **1 = mend**, restoration, overhaul, adjustment: *Many of the buildings are in need of repair.* **2 = darn**, mend, patch: *She spotted a couple of obvious repairs in the dress.* **3 = condition**, state, form, shape *(informal)*, nick *(informal)*, fettle: *The road was in bad repair.*

repair[2] VERB **= go**, retire, withdraw, head for, move, remove, leave for, set off for, betake yourself: *We repaired to the pavilion for lunch.*

reparation NOUN **= compensation**, damages, repair, satisfaction, amends, renewal, redress, indemnity, restitution, atonement, recompense, propitiation, requital

repay VERB **1 = pay back**, refund, settle up, return, square, restore, compensate, reimburse, recompense, requite, remunerate: *It will take 30 years to repay the loan.* **2 = reward**, make restitution: *How can I ever repay such kindness?*

repeal VERB **= abolish**, reverse, revoke, annul, recall, withdraw, cancel, set aside, rescind, invalidate, nullify, obviate, abrogate, countermand, declare null and void: *The government has just repealed that law.* **OPPOSITE:** pass
▷ NOUN **= abolition**, withdrawal, cancellation, rescinding, annulment, revocation, nullification, abrogation, rescission, invalidation, rescindment: *a repeal of the age of consent law* **OPPOSITE:** passing

repeat VERB **1 = reiterate**, restate, recapitulate, iterate: *He repeated that he had been misquoted.* **2 = retell**, relate, quote, renew, echo, replay, reproduce, rehearse, recite, duplicate, redo, rerun, reshow: *I repeated the story to a delighted audience.*
▷ NOUN **1 = repetition**, echo, duplicate, reiteration, recapitulation: *a repeat of Wednesday's massive protests* **2 = rerun**, replay, reproduction, reshowing: *There's nothing except repeats on TV.*

USAGE
Since the sense of *again* is already contained within the *re-* part of the word *repeat*, it is unnecessary to say that something is *repeated again*.

repeatedly ADVERB **= over and over**, often, frequently, many times, again and again, time and (time) again, time after time, many a time and oft *(archaic, poetic)*

repel VERB **1 = drive off**, fight, refuse, check, decline, reject, oppose, resist,

I

confront, parry, hold off, rebuff, ward off, beat off, repulse, keep at arm's length, put to flight: *troops ready to repel an attack* **OPPOSITE:** submit to **2 = disgust**, offend, revolt, sicken, nauseate, put you off, make you sick, gross you out *(U.S. slang)*, turn you off *(informal)*, make you shudder, turn your stomach, give you the creeps *(informal)*: *excitement which frightened and repelled her* **OPPOSITE:** delight

repellent ADJECTIVE **1 = disgusting**, offensive, revolting, obscene, sickening, distasteful, horrid, obnoxious, repulsive, noxious, nauseating, odious, hateful, repugnant, off-putting *(Brit. informal)*, loathsome, abhorrent, abominable, cringe-making *(Brit. informal)*, yucky *or* yukky *(slang)*, yucko *(Austral. slang)*, discouraging: *She still found the place repellent.* **2 = proof**, resistant, repelling, impermeable: *a shower repellent jacket*

repent VERB **= regret**, lament, rue, sorrow, be sorry about, deplore, be ashamed of, relent, atone for, be contrite about, feel remorse about, reproach yourself for, see the error of your ways, show penitence

> **QUOTATIONS**
> When I consider how my life is spent,
> I hardly ever repent
> [Ogden Nash *Reminiscent Reflection*]

repentance NOUN **= regret**, guilt, grief, sorrow, remorse, contrition, compunction, penitence, self-reproach, sackcloth and ashes, sorriness

> **QUOTATIONS**
> Repentance is the virtue of weak minds
> [John Dryden *The Indian Emperor*]
>
> Amendment is repentance
> [Thomas Fuller *Gnomologia*]
>
> Joy shall be in heaven over one sinner that repenteth, more than over ninety and nine just persons, which need no repentance
> [*Bible: St. Luke*]
>
> Repentance is but want of power to sin
> [John Dryden *Palamon and Arcite*]

repercussion NOUN **= consequences**, result, side effects, backlash, sequel

repertoire NOUN **= range**, list, stock, supply, store, collection, repertory, repository

repertory NOUN **= repertoire**, list, range, stock, supply, store, collection, repository

repetition NOUN **1 = recurrence**, repeating, reappearance, duplication, echo: *He wants to avoid repetition of the confusion.* **2 = repeating**, redundancy, replication, duplication, restatement, iteration, reiteration, tautology, recapitulation, repetitiousness: *He could have cut much of the repetition and saved pages.*

repetitive ADJECTIVE **= monotonous**, boring, dull, mechanical, tedious, recurrent, unchanging, samey *(informal)*, unvaried

replace VERB **1 = take the place of**, follow, succeed, oust, take over from, supersede, supplant, stand in lieu of, fill (someone's) shoes *or* boots, step into (someone's) shoes *or* boots: *the man who deposed and replaced him* **2 = substitute**, change, exchange, switch, swap, commute: *Replace that liquid with salt, sugar and water.* **3 = put back**, restore: *Replace the caps on the bottles.*

replacement NOUN **1 = replacing**: *the replacement of damaged or lost books* **2 = successor**, double, substitute, stand-in, fill-in, proxy, surrogate, understudy: *a replacement for the injured player*

replenish VERB **1 = fill**, top up, refill, replace, renew, furnish: *He went to replenish her glass.* **OPPOSITE:** empty **2 = refill**, provide, stock, supply, fill, make up, restore, top up, reload, restock: *stock to replenish the shelves*

replete ADJECTIVE **1 = filled**, stuffed, jammed, crammed, abounding, brimming, teeming, glutted, well-stocked, jam-packed, well-provided, chock-full, brimful, full to bursting, charged: *The harbour was replete with boats.* **OPPOSITE:** empty **2 = sated**, full, gorged, full up, satiated: *replete after a heavy lunch* **OPPOSITE:** hungry

replica NOUN **1 = reproduction**, model, copy, imitation, facsimile, carbon copy: *It was a replica, for display only.* **OPPOSITE:** original **2 = duplicate**, copy, carbon copy: *The child was a replica of her mother.*

replicate VERB **= copy**, follow, repeat, reproduce, recreate, ape, mimic, duplicate, reduplicate

reply VERB **= answer**, respond, retort, return, come back, counter, acknowledge, react, echo, rejoin, retaliate, write back, reciprocate, riposte, make an answer: *He replied that this was absolutely impossible.*
▷ NOUN **= answer**, response, reaction, counter, echo, comeback *(informal)*, retort, retaliation, acknowledgment, riposte, counterattack, return, rejoinder, reciprocation: *They went ahead without waiting for a reply.*

report VERB **1 = inform of**, communicate, announce, mention, declare, recount, give an account of, bring word on: *I reported the theft to the police.* **2** *(often with* **on***)* **= communicate**, publish, record, announce, tell, state, air, detail, describe, note, cover, document, give an account of, relate, broadcast, pass on, proclaim, circulate, relay, recite, narrate, write up: *Several newspapers reported the decision.* **3 = present yourself**, come, appear, arrive, turn up, be present, show up *(informal)*, clock in *or* on: *None of them had reported for duty.*
▷ NOUN **1 = article**, story, dispatch, piece, message, communiqué, write-up: *Press reports vary dramatically.* **2 = account**, record, detail, note, statement, relation, version, communication, tale, description, declaration, narrative, summary, recital: *a full report of what happened here tonight* **3** *(often plural)* **= news**, word, information, announcement, tidings: *There were no reports of casualties.* **4 = bang**, sound, crash, crack, noise, blast, boom, explosion, discharge, detonation, reverberation: *There was a loud report as the fuel tanks exploded.* **5 = rumour**, talk, buzz, gossip, goss *(informal)*, hearsay, scuttlebutt *(U.S. slang)*: *According to report, she made an impact at the party.* **6 = repute**, character, regard, reputation, fame, esteem, eminence: *He is true, manly, and of good report.*

reporter NOUN **= journalist**, writer, correspondent, newscaster, hack *(derogatory)*, announcer, pressman, journo *(slang)*, newshound *(informal)*, newspaperman *or* newspaperwoman

repose[1] NOUN **1 = rest**, relaxation, inactivity, restfulness: *He had a still, almost blank, face in repose.* **2 = peace**, rest, quiet, ease, relaxation, respite, tranquillity, stillness, inactivity, quietness, quietude, restfulness: *The atmosphere is one of repose.* **3 = composure**, dignity, peace of mind, poise, serenity, tranquillity, aplomb, calmness, equanimity, self-possession: *She has a great deal of natural repose.*
▷ VERB **= lie**, rest, sleep, relax, lie down, recline, take it easy, slumber, rest upon, lie upon, drowse, outspan *(S. African)*, take your ease: *They repose on couches.*

repose[2] VERB **= place**, put, store, invest, deposit, lodge, confide, entrust: *Little trust can be reposed in such promises.*

repository NOUN **= store**, archive, storehouse, depository, magazine, treasury, warehouse, vault, depot, emporium, receptacle: *The church became a repository for police files.*

reprehensible ADJECTIVE **= blameworthy**, bad, disgraceful, shameful, delinquent, errant, unworthy, objectionable, culpable, ignoble, discreditable, remiss, erring, opprobrious, condemnable, censurable **OPPOSITE:** praiseworthy

represent VERB **1 = act for**, speak for: *the lawyers representing the victims* **2 = stand for**, substitute for, play the part of, assume the role of, serve as: *He will represent the president at ceremonies.* **3 = express**, equal, correspond to, symbolize, equate with, mean, betoken: *Circle the letter that represents the sound.* **4 = exemplify**, embody, symbolize, typify, personify, epitomize: *You represent everything British racing needs.* **5 = depict**, show, describe, picture, express, illustrate, outline,

The Language of Sir Arthur Conan Doyle

Sir Arthur Conan Doyle (1859–1930) was born in Edinburgh and first pursued a career in medicine, eventually establishing himself as a general practitioner in an English coastal town near Portsmouth. He began writing short stories to supplement his income and it was in one of these, *A Study in Scarlet* (1887), that he introduced to the world the character that would make both of them famous: Sherlock Holmes.

As a trained physician, Doyle was steeped in the methods and analytical approach of science, and the great detective Holmes was a master of logic and deduction. This mode of inquiry is reflected in Doyle's use of language, where his most commonly used verbs are *ask, show, answer,* and *understand.*

> 'If I take it up I must **understand** every detail,' said he. 'Take time to consider. The smallest point may be the most essential.'

Holmes is often called in by clients to get to the bottom of some mystery or other, some occurrence that seems to defy rational explanation. His less intellectually gifted friend Dr Watson comes in handy as the pupil to whom the master makes his insightful expositions. It is hardly surprising that among Doyle's most frequently used adjectives are *strange* and *singular*. The latter, of course, carries its now largely outdated sense of 'odd' or 'unusual'.

> 'A **singular** set of people, Watson – the man himself the most **singular** of them all.'

It should be borne in mind that the exploits of Holmes and Watson do not represent Doyle's only ventures in fiction. Not only did he explore science fiction in his novels about Professor Challenger (such as *The Lost World*), he was also greatly interested in history, particularly 'the age of chivalry'. His historical novels such as *The White Company* (1891) and *Sir Nigel* (1906) may not be much read nowadays but they were highly popular in their time. It is this vein of writing that introduces an element of period language, of deliberately chosen archaisms, into Doyle's writing. It would no doubt surprise many readers to discover that the word *sire* is used by Doyle, the great pioneer of crime fiction, just as often as the word *police*.

> 'Bethink you, **sire**, that this de Chargny and his comrades know nothing of their plans having gone awry.'

Similarly, the word *knight* occurs more often than *crime*, and in terms of proper names, Doyle's fiction shows a greater use of *Saxon* than *Sherlock*.

It is interesting to digress a little from the language that Doyle actually uses to an expression that he certainly does *not*. The phrase 'Elementary, my dear Watson' is the cliché that is inevitably linked to Sherlock Holmes and most people believe that this is a characteristic utterance. However, Doyle's incarnation of the great detective never came out with precisely this formula, which was the product of a much later film script. The closest that Doyle comes to putting these words into Holmes' mouth is in the following exchange from *The Crooked Man:*

> 'Excellent!' I cried. '**Elementary**,' said he.
> 'It is one of those instances where the reasoner can produce an effect which seems remarkable to his neighbour, because the latter has missed the one little point which is the basis of the deduction.'

portray, sketch, render, designate, reproduce, evoke, denote, delineate: *God is represented as male.*
represent someone as something *or* **someone = make out to be**, describe as: *They tend to represent him as a guru.*

representation NOUN **1 = body of representatives**, committee, embassy, delegates, delegation: *They have no representation in congress.* **2 = picture**, model, image, portrait, illustration, sketch, resemblance, likeness: *a life-like representation of Christ* **3 = portrayal**, depiction, account, relation, description, narrative, narration, delineation: *the representation of women in film and literature* **4** *(often plural)* **= statement**, argument, explanation, exposition, remonstrance, expostulation, account: *We have made representations to ministers.*

representative NOUN **1 = delegate**, member, agent, deputy, commissioner, councillor, proxy, depute *(Scot.)*, spokesman *or* spokeswoman: *trade union representatives* **2 = member**, congressman *or* congresswoman *(U.S.)*, member of parliament, Member of Congress *(U.S.)*, M.P.: *the representative for Eastleigh* **3 = agent**, salesman, rep, traveller, commercial traveller: *She was a sales representative.*
▷ ADJECTIVE **1 = chosen**, elected, delegated, elective: *a representative government* **2 = typical**, characteristic, archetypal, exemplary, illustrative: *fairly representative groups of adults* **OPPOSITE:** uncharacteristic **3 = symbolic**, evocative, emblematic, typical: *images chosen as representative of English life*

repress VERB **1 = control**, suppress, hold back, bottle up, check, master, hold in, overcome, curb, restrain, inhibit, overpower, keep in check: *People who repress their emotions risk having nightmares.* **OPPOSITE:** release **2 = hold back**, suppress, stifle, smother, silence, swallow, muffle: *I couldn't repress a sigh of admiration.* **3 = subdue**, abuse, crush, quash, wrong, persecute, quell, subjugate, maltreat, trample underfoot, tyrannize over, rule with an iron hand: *They have been repressed for decades.* **OPPOSITE:** liberate

repression NOUN **1 = subjugation**, control, constraint, domination, censorship, tyranny, coercion, authoritarianism, despotism: *a society conditioned by violence and repression* **2 = suppression**, crushing, prohibition, quashing, dissolution: *extremely violent repression of opposition* **3 = inhibition**, control, holding in, restraint, suppression, bottling up: *the repression of intense feelings*

repressive ADJECTIVE **= oppressive**, tough, severe, absolute, harsh, authoritarian, dictatorial, coercive, tyrannical, despotic **OPPOSITE:** democratic

reprieve VERB **= grant a stay of execution to**, pardon, let off the hook *(slang)*, postpone *or* remit the punishment of: *Fourteen people, waiting to be hanged, have been reprieved.*
▷ NOUN **= stay of execution**, suspension, amnesty, pardon, remission, abeyance, deferment, postponement of punishment: *a reprieve for eight people waiting to be hanged*

reprimand VERB **= blame**, censure, rebuke, reproach, check, lecture, carpet *(informal)*, scold, tick off *(informal)*, castigate, chide, dress down *(informal)*, admonish, tear into *(informal)*, tell off *(informal)*, take to task, read the riot act, tongue-lash, reprove, upbraid, slap on the wrist *(informal)*, bawl out *(informal)*, rap over the knuckles, haul over the coals *(informal)*, chew out *(U.S. & Canad. informal)*, tear (someone) off a strip *(Brit. informal)*, give (someone) a rocket *(Brit. & N.Z. informal)*, reprehend, give (someone) a row *(informal)*, send (someone) away with a flea in his *or* her ear *(informal)*: *He was reprimanded by a teacher.* **OPPOSITE:** praise
▷ NOUN **= blame**, talking-to *(informal)*, row, lecture, wigging *(Brit. slang)*, censure, rebuke, reproach, ticking-off *(informal)*, dressing-down *(informal)*, telling-off *(informal)*, admonition, tongue-lashing, reproof, castigation, reprehension, flea in your ear *(informal)*: *He has been given a severe reprimand.* **OPPOSITE:** praise

reprisal NOUN **= retaliation**, revenge, vengeance, retribution, an eye for an eye, counterstroke, requital

reproach VERB **= blame**, criticize, rebuke, reprimand, abuse, blast, condemn, carpet *(informal)*, discredit, censure, have a go at *(informal)*, scold, disparage, chide, tear into *(informal)*, diss *(slang, chiefly U.S.)*, defame, find fault with, take to task, read the riot act to, reprove, upbraid, lambast(e), bawl out *(informal)*, chew out *(U.S. & Canad. informal)*, tear (someone) off a strip *(Brit. informal)*, give a rocket *(Brit. & N.Z. informal)*, reprehend: *She is quick to reproach anyone.*
▷ NOUN **1 = rebuke**, lecture, wigging *(Brit. slang)*, censure, reprimand, scolding, ticking-off *(informal)*, dressing-down *(informal)*, telling-off *(informal)*, admonition, tongue-lashing, reproof, castigation, reproval: *Her reproach was automatic.* **2 = censure**, blame, abuse, contempt, condemnation, scorn, disapproval, opprobrium, odium, obloquy: *He looked at her with reproach.* **3 = disgrace**, shame, slight, stain, discredit, stigma, slur, disrepute, blemish, indignity, ignominy, dishonour: *The shootings were a reproach to all of us.*

reproduce VERB **1 = copy**, recreate, replicate, duplicate, match, represent, mirror, echo, parallel, imitate, emulate: *The effect has proved hard to reproduce.* **2 = print**, copy, transcribe: *permission to reproduce this article* **3 = breed**, produce young, procreate, generate, multiply, spawn, propagate, proliferate: *Women are defined by their ability to reproduce.*

reproduction NOUN **1 = copy**, picture, print, replica, imitation, duplicate, facsimile: *a reproduction of a religious painting* **OPPOSITE:** original **2 = breeding**, procreation, propagation, increase, generation, proliferation, multiplication: *what doctors call 'assisted human reproduction'*

Republican ADJECTIVE **= right-wing**, Conservative, red *(U.S.)*: *Senator John McCain, Mr Bush's rival for the Republican nomination*
▷ NOUN **= right-winger**, Conservative: *President Clinton is under pressure from Republicans in Congress.*

repudiate VERB **1 = reject**, renounce, retract, disown, abandon, desert, reverse, cut off, discard, revoke, forsake, cast off, rescind, disavow, turn your back on, abjure, wash your hands of: *He repudiated any form of nationalism.* **OPPOSITE:** assert **2 = deny**, oppose, disagree with, rebuff, refute, disprove, rebut, disclaim, gainsay *(archaic, literary)*: *He repudiated the charges.*

repugnant ADJECTIVE **1 = distasteful**, offensive, foul, disgusting, revolting, sickening, vile, horrid, repellent, obnoxious, objectionable, nauseating, odious, hateful, loathsome, abhorrent, abominable, yucky *or* yukky *(slang)*, yucko *(Austral. slang)*: *His actions were improper and repugnant.* **OPPOSITE:** pleasant **2 = incompatible**, opposed, hostile, adverse, contradictory, inconsistent, averse, antagonistic, inimical, antipathetic: *It is repugnant to the values of our society.* **OPPOSITE:** compatible

repulse VERB **1 = drive back**, check, defeat, fight off, repel, rebuff, ward off, beat off, throw back: *The army were prepared to repulse any attack.* **2 = reject**, refuse, turn down, snub, disregard, disdain, spurn, rebuff, give the cold shoulder to: *She repulsed him with undisguised venom.*
▷ NOUN **1 = defeat**, check: *the repulse of invaders in 1785* **2 = rejection**, refusal, snub, spurning, rebuff, knock-back *(slang)*, cold shoulder, kick in the teeth *(slang)*, the (old) heave-ho *(informal)*: *If he meets with a repulse he will not be cast down.*

> **USAGE**
> Some people think that the use of *repulse* in sentences such as *he was repulsed by what he saw* is incorrect and that the correct word is *repel*.

repulsive ADJECTIVE **= disgusting**, offensive, foul, ugly, forbidding, unpleasant, revolting, obscene, sickening, hideous, vile, distasteful, horrid, repellent, obnoxious, objectionable, disagreeable, nauseating, odious, hateful, loathsome, abhorrent, abominable, yucky *or* yukky *(slang)*, yucko *(Austral. slang)* **OPPOSITE:** delightful

reputable ADJECTIVE **= respectable**, good, excellent, reliable, worthy, legitimate, upright, honourable, honoured, trustworthy, creditable, estimable, well-thought-of, of good repute **OPPOSITE:** disreputable

reputation NOUN **= name**, standing, credit, character, honour, fame, distinction, esteem, stature, eminence, renown, repute

repute NOUN **1 = reputation**, standing, fame, celebrity, distinction, esteem, stature, eminence, estimation, renown: *The UN's repute has risen immeasurably.* **2 = name**, character, reputation: *a house of ill-repute*

reputed ADJECTIVE **1 = supposed**, said, seeming, held, believed, thought, considered, accounted, regarded, estimated, alleged, reckoned, rumoured, deemed: *a man reputed to be in his nineties* **2 = apparent**, supposed, putative, ostensible: *They booked the ballroom for a reputed $15,000 last year.*

reputedly ADVERB **= supposedly**, apparently, allegedly, seemingly, ostensibly

request VERB **1 = ask for**, apply for, appeal for, put in for, demand, desire, pray for, beg for, requisition, beseech: *I requested a copy of the form.* **2 = invite**, call for, beg, petition, beseech, entreat, supplicate: *They requested him to leave.* **3 = seek**, ask (for), sue for, solicit: *the right to request a divorce*
▷ NOUN **1 = appeal**, call, demand, plea, desire, application, prayer, petition, requisition, solicitation, entreaty, supplication, suit: *They agreed to his request for help.* **2 = asking**, plea, begging: *At his request, they attended some of the meetings.*

require VERB **1 = need**, crave, depend upon, have need of, want, miss, lack, wish, desire, stand in need of: *A baby requires warmth and physical security.* **2 = demand**, take, involve, call for, entail, necessitate: *This requires thought, effort, and a certain ruthlessness.* **3 = order**, demand, direct, command, compel, exact, oblige, instruct, call upon, constrain, insist upon: *The rules require employers to provide safety training.* **4 = ask**, enjoin: *She was required to take to the stage.*

> **USAGE**
> The use of *require to* as in *I require to see the manager* or *you require to complete a special form* is thought by many people to be incorrect. Useful alternatives are: *I need to see the manager* and *you are required to complete a special form.*

required ADJECTIVE **= obligatory**, prescribed, compulsory, mandatory, needed, set, demanded, necessary, called for, essential, recommended, vital, unavoidable, requisite, de rigueur *(French)* **OPPOSITE:** optional

requirement NOUN **= necessity**, demand, specification, stipulation, want, need, must, essential, qualification, precondition, requisite, prerequisite, sine qua non *(Latin)*, desideratum, must-have

requisite ADJECTIVE **= necessary**, needed, required, called for, essential, vital, mandatory, indispensable, obligatory, prerequisite, needful: *She filled in the requisite paperwork.*
▷ NOUN **= necessity**, condition, requirement, precondition, need, must, essential, prerequisite, sine qua non *(Latin)*, desideratum, must-have: *a major requisite for the work of the analysts*

requisition VERB **1 = take over**, appropriate, occupy, seize, commandeer, take possession of: *The vessel was requisitioned by the British Navy.* **2 = demand**, call for, request, apply for, put in for: *the task of requisitioning men and supplies*
▷ NOUN **1 = demand**, request, call, application, summons: *a requisition for a replacement typewriter* **2 = takeover**, occupation, seizure, appropriation, commandeering: *They are against the requisition of common land.*

rescind VERB **= annul**, recall, reverse, cancel, overturn, set aside, void, repeal, quash, revoke, retract, invalidate, obviate, abrogate, countermand, declare null and void **OPPOSITE:** confirm

rescue VERB **1 = save**, get out, save the life of, extricate, free, release, deliver, recover, liberate, set free, save (someone's) bacon *(Brit. informal)*: *Helicopters rescued nearly 20 people.* **OPPOSITE:** desert **2 = salvage**, deliver, redeem, come to the rescue of: *He rescued a 14th century barn from demolition.*
▷ NOUN **= saving**, salvage, deliverance, extrication, release, relief, recovery, liberation, salvation, redemption: *the rescue of the crew of a ship*

research NOUN **= investigation**, study, inquiry, analysis, examination, probe, exploration, scrutiny, experimentation, delving, groundwork, fact-finding: *His groundbreaking research will be vital in future developments.*
▷ VERB **= investigate**, study, examine, experiment, explore, probe, analyse, look into, work over, scrutinize, make inquiries, do tests, consult the archives: *They research the needs of both employers and staff.*

resemblance NOUN **= similarity**, correspondence, conformity, semblance, image, comparison, parallel, counterpart, analogy, affinity, closeness, parity, likeness, kinship, facsimile, sameness, comparability, similitude **OPPOSITE:** dissimilarity

resemble VERB **= be like**, look like, favour *(informal)*, mirror, echo, parallel, be similar to, duplicate, take after, remind you of, bear a resemblance to, put you in mind of

resent VERB **= be bitter about**, dislike, object to, grudge, begrudge, take exception to, be offended by, be angry about, take offence at, take umbrage at, harbour a grudge against, take as an insult, bear a grudge about, be in a huff about, take amiss to, have hard feelings about **OPPOSITE:** be content with

resentful ADJECTIVE **= bitter**, hurt, wounded, angry, offended, put out, jealous, choked, incensed, grudging, exasperated, aggrieved, indignant, irate, miffed *(informal)*, embittered, unforgiving, peeved *(informal)*, in a huff, piqued, huffy, in high dudgeon, revengeful, huffish, tooshie *(Austral. slang)* **OPPOSITE:** content

resentment NOUN **= bitterness**, indignation, ill feeling, ill will, hurt, anger, rage, fury, irritation, grudge, wrath, malice, animosity, huff, ire, displeasure, pique, rancour, bad blood, umbrage, vexation, chip on your shoulder *(informal)*

> **QUOTATIONS**
> It is very difficult to get up resentment towards persons whom one has never seen
> [Cardinal Newman *Apologia pro Vita Sua*]

reservation NOUN **1** *(often plural)* **= doubt**, scepticism, scruples, demur, hesitancy: *Their demands were met with some reservations.* **2 = reserve**, territory, preserve, homeland, sanctuary, tract, enclave, rez *(U.S. & Canad. slang)*: *a Navaho Indian from a North American reservation*

reserve VERB **1 = book**, prearrange, pre-engage, engage, bespeak: *I'll reserve a table for five.* **2 = put by**, secure, retain: *Ask your newsagent to reserve your copy today.* **3 = keep**, hold, save, husband, store, retain, preserve, set aside, withhold, hang on to, conserve, stockpile, hoard, lay up, put by, keep back: *Strain and reserve the cooking liquor.* **4 = delay**, postpone, withhold, put off, defer, keep back: *The Court has reserved its judgement.*
▷ NOUN **1 = store**, fund, savings, stock, capital, supply, reservoir, fall-back, stockpile, hoard, backlog, cache: *The country's reserves of petrol are running very low.* **2 = park**, reservation, preserve, sanctuary, tract, forest park *(N.Z.)*: *monkeys at the wildlife reserve* **3 = shyness**, silence, restraint, constraint, reluctance, formality, modesty, reticence, coolness, aloofness, secretiveness, taciturnity: *I hope you'll overcome your reserve.* **4 = reservation**, doubt, delay, uncertainty, indecision, hesitancy, vacillation, irresolution, dubiety: *I committed myself without reserve* **5 = substitute**, extra, spare, alternative, fall-back, auxiliary: *In this sport, you always have to have reserves.*

reserved ADJECTIVE **1 = uncommunicative**, cold, cool,

retiring, formal, silent, modest, shy, cautious, restrained, secretive, aloof, reticent, prim, demure, taciturn, unresponsive, unapproachable, unsociable, undemonstrative, standoffish, close-mouthed, unforthcoming: *He was unemotional and reserved.* **OPPOSITE:** uninhibited **2 = set aside**, taken, kept, held, booked, retained, engaged, restricted, spoken for: *Three coaches were reserved for us boys.*

reservoir NOUN **1 = lake**, pond, basin: *Torrents of water gushed into the reservoir.* **2 = repository**, store, tank, holder, container, receptacle: *It was on his desk next to the ink reservoir.* **3 = store**, stock, source, supply, reserves, fund, pool, accumulation, stockpile: *the body's short-term reservoir of energy*

reside VERB **1 = live**, lodge, dwell, have your home, remain, stay, settle, abide, hang out *(informal)*, sojourn: *She resides with her invalid mother.* **OPPOSITE:** visit **2 = be present**, lie, exist, consist, dwell, abide, rest with, be intrinsic to, inhere, be vested: *Happiness does not reside in money.*

residence NOUN **1 = home**, house, household, dwelling, place, quarters, flat, lodging, pad *(slang)*, abode, habitation, domicile: *There was a stabbing at a residence next door.* **2 = mansion**, seat, hall, palace, villa, manor: *She's staying at her country residence.* **3 = stay**, tenancy, occupancy, occupation, sojourn: *He returned to his place of residence.*

resident NOUN **1 = inhabitant**, citizen, denizen, indweller, local: *Ten per cent of residents live below the poverty line.* **OPPOSITE:** nonresident **2 = tenant**, occupant, lodger: *Council house residents purchasing their own homes* **3 = guest**, lodger: *Bar closed on Sunday except to hotel residents.*
▷ ADJECTIVE **1 = inhabiting**, living, settled, dwelling: *He had been resident in Brussels since 1967.* **OPPOSITE:** nonresident **2 = local**, neighbourhood: *The resident population of the inner city has risen.*

residual ADJECTIVE **= remaining**, net, unused, leftover, vestigial, nett, unconsumed

residue NOUN **= remainder**, remains, remnant, leftovers, rest, extra, balance, excess, surplus, dregs, residuum

resign VERB **1 = quit**, leave, step down *(informal)*, vacate, abdicate, call it a day or night, give or hand in your notice: *He has resigned after only ten weeks in office.* **2 = give up**, abandon, yield, hand over, surrender, turn over, relinquish, renounce, forsake, cede, forgo: *He has resigned his seat in parliament.*
resign yourself to something = accept, reconcile yourself to, succumb to, submit to, bow to, give in to, yield to, acquiesce to: *I simply resigned myself to staying indoors.*

resignation NOUN **1 = leaving**, notice, retirement, departure, surrender, abandonment, abdication, renunciation, relinquishment: *He has withdrawn his letter of resignation.* **2 = acceptance**, patience, submission, compliance, endurance, fortitude, passivity, acquiescence, forbearing, sufferance, nonresistance: *He sighed with profound resignation.* **OPPOSITE:** resistance

resigned ADJECTIVE **= stoical**, patient, subdued, long-suffering, compliant, submissive, acquiescent, unresisting, unprotesting

resilient ADJECTIVE **1 = flexible**, plastic, elastic, supple, bouncy, rubbery, pliable, springy, whippy: *some resilient plastic material* **OPPOSITE:** rigid **2 = tough**, strong, hardy, buoyant, feisty *(informal, chiefly U.S. & Canad.)*, bouncy, irrepressible, quick to recover: *I'm a resilient kind of person.* **OPPOSITE:** weak

resist VERB **1 = oppose**, fight, battle against, refuse, check, weather, dispute, confront, combat, defy, curb, thwart, stand up to, hinder, contend with, counteract, hold out against, put up a fight (against), countervail: *They resisted our attempts to modernize distribution.* **OPPOSITE:** accept **2 = fight against**, fight, struggle against, put up a fight (against): *He tried to resist arrest.* **3 = refrain from**, refuse, avoid, turn down, leave alone, keep from, forgo, abstain from, forbear, prevent yourself from: *Try to resist giving him advice.* **OPPOSITE:** indulge in **4 = withstand**, repel, be proof against: *bodies trained to resist the cold*

Resistance NOUN **= freedom fighters**, underground, guerrillas, partisans, irregulars, maquis

resistance NOUN **1 = opposition**, hostility, aversion: *In remote villages there is a resistance to change.* **2 = fighting**, fight, battle, struggle, combat, contention, defiance, obstruction, impediment, intransigence, hindrance, counteraction: *The protesters offered no resistance.*

resistant ADJECTIVE **1 = opposed**, hostile, dissident, unwilling, defiant, intractable, combative, recalcitrant, antagonistic, intransigent: *Some people are resistant to the idea of exercise.* **2 = impervious**, hard, strong, tough, unaffected, unyielding, insusceptible: *The body may be less resistant if it is cold.*

resolute ADJECTIVE **= determined**, set, firm, dogged, fixed, constant, bold, relentless, stubborn, stalwart, staunch, persevering, inflexible, purposeful, tenacious, undaunted, strong-willed, steadfast, obstinate, unwavering, immovable, unflinching, unbending, unshakable, unshaken **OPPOSITE:** irresolute

resolution NOUN **1 = declaration**, motion, verdict, judgment: *The UN had passed two major resolutions.* **2 = decision**, resolve, intention, aim, purpose, determination, intent: *It had been her resolution to lose weight.* **3 = determination**, energy, purpose, resolve, courage, dedication, fortitude, sincerity, tenacity, perseverance, willpower, boldness, firmness, staying power, stubbornness, constancy, earnestness, obstinacy, steadfastness, doggedness, relentlessness, resoluteness, staunchness: *He implemented policy with resolution and single-mindedness.* **4 = solution**, end, settlement, outcome, finding, answer, working out, solving, sorting out, unravelling, upshot: *a peaceful resolution to the crisis*

resolve VERB **1 = work out**, answer, solve, find the solution to, clear up, crack, fathom, suss (out) *(slang)*, elucidate: *We must find a way to resolve these problems.* **2 = decide**, determine, undertake, make up your mind, agree, design, settle, purpose, intend, fix, conclude: *She resolved to report the matter.* **3 = change**, convert, transform, alter, metamorphose, transmute: *The spirals of light resolved into points.* **4 = dispel**, explain, remove, clear up, banish: *Many years of doubt were finally resolved.*
▷ NOUN **1 = determination**, resolution, courage, willpower, boldness, firmness, earnestness, steadfastness, resoluteness: *He doesn't weaken in his resolve.* **OPPOSITE:** indecision **2 = decision**, resolution, undertaking, objective, design, project, purpose, conclusion, intention: *the resolve to enforce a settlement using troops*

resonant ADJECTIVE **1 = sonorous**, full, rich, ringing, booming, vibrant: *He responded with a resonant laugh.* **2 = echoing**, resounding, reverberating, reverberant: *a hall, resonant with the sound of violins*

resort NOUN **1 = holiday centre**, spot, retreat, haunt, refuge, tourist centre, watering place *(Brit.)*: *a genteel resort on the south coast* **2 = recourse to**, reference to: *without resort to illegal methods*
resort to something = have recourse to, turn to, fall back on, bring into play, use, exercise, employ, look to, make use of, utilize, avail yourself of: *We were forced to resort to violence.*

resound VERB **1 = echo**, resonate, reverberate, fill the air, re-echo: *The soldiers' boots resounded in the street.* **2 = ring**: *The whole place resounded with music.*

resounding ADJECTIVE **= echoing**, full, sounding, rich, ringing, powerful, booming, vibrant, reverberating, resonant, sonorous

resource NOUN **1 = supply**, source, reserve, stockpile, hoard: *a great resource of teaching materials* **2 = facility**: *The directory is a valuable resource.* **3 = means**, course, resort, device, expedient: *The only resource left to allay*

her husband's pain was opium.
▷ PLURAL NOUN **1 = funds**, means, holdings, money, capital, wherewithal, riches, materials, assets, wealth, property: *They do not have the resources to feed themselves properly.* **2 = reserves**, supplies, stocks: *We are overpopulated, straining the earth's resources.*

resourceful ADJECTIVE **= ingenious**, able, bright, talented, sharp, capable, creative, clever, imaginative, inventive, quick-witted
OPPOSITE: unimaginative

respect VERB **1 = think highly of**, value, regard, honour, recognize, appreciate, admire, esteem, adore, revere, reverence, look up to, defer to, venerate, set store by, have a good *or* high opinion of: *I want him to respect me as a career woman.* **2 = show consideration for**, regard, notice, honour, observe, heed, attend to, pay attention to: *Trying to respect her wishes, I said I'd leave.* **3 = abide by**, follow, observe, comply with, obey, heed, keep to, adhere to: *It's about time they respected the law.* **OPPOSITE:** disregard
▷ NOUN **1 = regard**, honour, recognition, esteem, appreciation, admiration, reverence, estimation, veneration, approbation, props (*U.S. slang*): *I have tremendous respect for him.*
OPPOSITE: contempt
2 = consideration, kindness, deference, friendliness, tact, thoughtfulness, solicitude, kindliness, considerateness: *They should be treated with respect.*
3 = particular, way, point, matter, sense, detail, feature, aspect, characteristic, facet: *He's simply wonderful in every respect.*
▷ PLURAL NOUN **= greetings**, regards, compliments, good wishes, salutations, devoirs: *He visited the hospital to pay his respects to her.*
in respect of *or* **with respect to = concerning**, in relation to, in connection with, with regard to, with reference to, apropos of: *The system is not working in respect of training.*

respectable ADJECTIVE
1 = honourable, good, respected, decent, proper, worthy, upright, admirable, honest, dignified, venerable, reputable, decorous, estimable: *He came from a respectable middle-class family.*
OPPOSITE: disreputable **2 = decent**, neat, tidy (*informal*), spruce: *At last I have something respectable to wear.*
3 = reasonable, considerable, substantial, fair, tidy (*informal*), ample, tolerable, presentable, appreciable, fairly good, sizable *or* sizeable, goodly: *respectable and highly attractive rates of return* **OPPOSITE:** small

respectful ADJECTIVE **= polite**, civil, mannerly, humble, gracious, courteous, obedient, submissive, self-effacing, dutiful, courtly, deferential, reverential, solicitous, reverent, regardful, well-mannered

respective ADJECTIVE **= specific**, own, several, individual, personal, particular, various, separate, relevant, corresponding

respite NOUN **1 = pause**, break, rest, relief, halt, interval, relaxation, recess, interruption, lull, cessation, let-up (*informal*), breathing space, breather (*informal*), hiatus, intermission: *I rang home during a brief respite at work.* **2 = reprieve**, stay, delay, suspension, moratorium, postponement, adjournment: *Devaluation would only give the economy brief respite.*

resplendent ADJECTIVE **= brilliant**, radiant, splendid, glorious, bright, shining, beaming, glittering, dazzling, gleaming, luminous, lustrous, refulgent (*literary*), effulgent, irradiant

respond VERB **1 = answer**, return, reply, come back, counter, acknowledge, retort, rejoin: *'Of course,' she responded scornfully.*
OPPOSITE: remain silent **2** (*often with* **to**) **= reply to**, answer: *He was quick to respond to questions.* **3 = react**, retaliate, reciprocate, take the bait, rise to the bait, act in response: *He responded to the attacks by exacting suitable retribution.*

response NOUN **= answer**, return, reply, reaction, comeback (*informal*), feedback, retort, acknowledgment, riposte, counterattack, rejoinder, counterblast

responsibility NOUN **1 = duty**, business, job, role, task, accountability, answerability: *The 600 properties were his responsibility.* **2 = fault**, blame, liability, guilt, culpability, burden: *They have admitted responsibility for the accident.* **3 = obligation**, duty, liability, charge, care: *This helps employees balance work and family responsibilities.* **4 = authority**, power, importance, mana (*N.Z.*): *a better-paying job with more responsibility* **5 = job**, task, function, role, pigeon (*informal*): *I'm glad it's not my responsibility to be their guardian.* **6 = level-headedness**, stability, maturity, reliability, rationality, dependability, trustworthiness, conscientiousness, soberness, sensibleness: *I think she's shown responsibility.*

> **QUOTATIONS**
> Uneasy lies the head that wears a crown
> [William Shakespeare *Henry IV, part II*]
> The buck stops here
> [Harry S. Truman *motto on his desk at the White House*]

responsible ADJECTIVE **1 = to blame**, guilty, at fault, culpable: *He felt responsible for her death.* **2 = in charge**, in control, at the helm, in authority, carrying the can (*informal*): *the minister responsible for the environment*
3 = accountable, subject, bound, liable, amenable, answerable, duty-bound, chargeable, under obligation: *I'm responsible to my board of directors.* **OPPOSITE:** unaccountable
4 = sensible, sound, adult, stable, mature, reliable, rational, sober, conscientious, dependable, trustworthy, level-headed: *He's a very responsible sort of person.*
OPPOSITE: unreliable
5 = authoritative, high, important, executive, decision-making: *demoted to less responsible jobs*

responsive ADJECTIVE **= sensitive**, open, aware, sharp, alive, forthcoming, sympathetic, awake, susceptible, receptive, reactive, perceptive, impressionable, quick to react **OPPOSITE:** unresponsive

rest[1] VERB **1 = relax**, sleep, take it easy, lie down, idle, nap, be calm, doze, sit down, slumber, kip (*Brit. slang*), snooze (*informal*), laze, lie still, be at ease, put your feet up, take a nap, drowse, mellow out (*informal*), have a snooze (*informal*), refresh yourself, outspan (*S. African*), zizz (*Brit. informal*), have forty winks (*informal*), take your ease: *He has been advised to rest for two weeks.*
OPPOSITE: work **2 = stop**, have a break, break off, take a breather (*informal*), stay, halt, cease, discontinue, knock off (*informal*), desist, come to a standstill: *They rested only once that morning.* **OPPOSITE:** keep going **3 = depend**, turn, lie, be founded, hang, be based, rely, hinge, reside: *Such a view rests on incorrect assumptions.* **4 = place**, lay, repose, stretch out, stand, sit, lean, prop: *He rested his arms on the back of the chair.*
5 = be placed, sit, lie, be supported, recline: *Matt's elbow rested on the table.*
▷ NOUN **1 = sleep**, snooze (*informal*), lie-down, nap, doze, slumber, kip (*Brit. slang*), siesta, forty winks (*informal*), zizz (*Brit. informal*): *Go home and have a rest.* **2 = relaxation**, repose, leisure, idleness, me-time: *I feel in need of some rest.* **OPPOSITE:** work **3 = pause**, break, breather, time off, stop, holiday, halt, interval, vacation, respite, lull, interlude, cessation, breathing space (*informal*), intermission: *He took a rest from teaching.* **4 = refreshment**, release, relief, ease, comfort, cure, remedy, solace, balm, deliverance, mitigation, abatement, alleviation, easement, palliation, assuagement: *some rest from the intense concentration* **5 = inactivity**, a halt, a stop, a standstill, motionlessness: *The plane came to rest in a field.* **6 = support**, stand, base, holder, shelf, prop, trestle: *Keep your elbow on the arm rest.* **7 = calm**, tranquillity, stillness, somnolence: *a remote part of the valley for those seeking rest and relaxation*
at rest 1 = motionless, still, stopped, at a standstill, unmoving: *When you are at rest you breathe with your tummy muscles.*
2 = calm, still, cool, quiet, pacific, peaceful, composed, serene, tranquil, at peace, sedate, placid, undisturbed,

restful, untroubled, unperturbed, unruffled, unexcited: *with your mind at rest* **3 = asleep**, resting, sleeping, napping, dormant, crashed out *(slang)*, dozing, slumbering, snoozing *(informal)*, fast asleep, sound asleep, out for the count, dead to the world *(informal)*: *She is at rest; don't disturb her.*

rest² NOUN **= remainder**, remains, excess, remnants, others, balance, surplus, residue, rump, leftovers, residuum: *The rest is thrown away.*
▷ VERB **= continue being**, keep being, remain, stay, be left, go on being: *Of one thing we may rest assured.*

restaurant NOUN **= café**, diner *(chiefly U.S. & Canad.)*, bistro, cafeteria, trattoria, tearoom, eatery *or* eaterie

restful ADJECTIVE **= relaxing**, quiet, relaxed, comfortable, pacific, calm, calming, peaceful, soothing, sleepy, serene, tranquil, placid, undisturbed, languid, unhurried, tranquillizing, chilled *(informal)* **OPPOSITE:** busy

restitution NOUN **1 = compensation**, satisfaction, amends, refund, repayment, redress, remuneration, reparation, indemnity, reimbursement, recompense, indemnification, requital: *The victims are demanding full restitution.* **2 = return**, return, replacement, restoration, reinstatement, re-establishment, reinstallation: *the restitution of their equal rights as citizens*

restive ADJECTIVE **= restless**, nervous, uneasy, impatient, agitated, unruly, edgy, jittery *(informal)*, recalcitrant, on edge, fractious, ill at ease, jumpy, fretful, fidgety, refractory, unquiet, antsy *(informal)* **OPPOSITE:** calm

restless ADJECTIVE **1 = unsettled**, worried, troubled, nervous, disturbed, anxious, uneasy, agitated, unruly, edgy, fidgeting, on edge, ill at ease, restive, jumpy, fitful, fretful, fidgety, unquiet, antsy *(informal)*: *My father seemed very restless and excited.* **OPPOSITE:** relaxed **2 = sleepless**, disturbed, wakeful, unsleeping, insomniac, tossing and turning: *He had spent a restless few hours on the plane.* **3 = moving**, active, wandering, unsettled, unstable, bustling, turbulent, hurried, roving, transient, nomadic, unsteady, changeable, footloose, irresolute, inconstant, having itchy feet: *He led a restless life.* **OPPOSITE:** settled

restlessness NOUN **1 = movement**, activity, turmoil, unrest, instability, bustle, turbulence, hurry, transience, inconstancy, hurry-scurry, unsettledness: *increasing sounds of restlessness* **2 = restiveness**, anxiety, disturbance, nervousness, disquiet, agitation, insomnia, jitters *(informal)*, uneasiness, edginess, heebie-jeebies *(slang)*, jumpiness, fretfulness, ants in your pants *(slang)*, fitfulness, inquietude, worriedness: *She complained of hyperactivity and restlessness.*

restoration NOUN **1 = reinstatement**, return, revival, restitution, re-establishment, reinstallation, replacement: *the restoration of diplomatic relations* **OPPOSITE:** abolition **2 = repair**, recovery, reconstruction, renewal, rehabilitation, refurbishing, refreshment, renovation, rejuvenation, revitalization: *I specialized in the restoration of old houses.* **OPPOSITE:** demolition

restore VERB **1 = reinstate**, re-establish, reintroduce, reimpose, re-enforce, reconstitute: *The army has been brought in to restore order.* **OPPOSITE:** abolish **2 = revive**, build up, strengthen, bring back, refresh, rejuvenate, revitalize, revivify, reanimate: *We will restore her to health.* **OPPOSITE:** make worse **3 = re-establish**, replace, reinstate, give back, reinstall, retrocede: *Civil rights were restored in a matter of days.* **4 = repair**, refurbish, renovate, reconstruct, fix (up), recover, renew, rebuild, mend, rehabilitate, touch up, recondition, retouch, set to rights: *They partly restored a local castle.* **OPPOSITE:** demolish **5 = return**, replace, recover, bring back, send back, hand back: *Their horses and goods were restored.*

restrain VERB **1 = hold back**, hold, control, check, contain, prevent, restrict, handicap, confine, curb, hamper, rein, harness, subdue, hinder, constrain, curtail, bridle, debar, keep under control, have on a tight leash, straiten: *He grabbed my arm, partly to restrain me.* **OPPOSITE:** encourage **2 = control**, keep in, limit, govern, suppress, inhibit, repress, muzzle, keep under control: *She was unable to restrain her desperate anger.* **3 = imprison**, hold, arrest, jail, bind, chain, confine, detain, tie up, lock up, fetter, manacle, pinion: *Police restrained her on July 28.* **OPPOSITE:** release

restrained ADJECTIVE **1 = controlled**, reasonable, moderate, self-controlled, soft, calm, steady, mild, muted, reticent, temperate, undemonstrative: *He felt he'd been very restrained.* **OPPOSITE:** hot-headed **2 = unobtrusive**, discreet, subdued, tasteful, quiet: *Her black suit was restrained and expensive.* **OPPOSITE:** garish

restraint NOUN **1 = limitation**, limit, check, ban, boycott, embargo, curb, rein, taboo, bridle, disqualification, interdict, restraining order *(U.S., Law)*: *Criminals could cross into the country without restraint.* **OPPOSITE:** freedom **2 = self-control**, self-discipline, self-restraint, self-possession, pulling your punches: *They behaved with more restraint than I'd expected.* **OPPOSITE:** self-indulgence **3 = constraint**, limitation, inhibition, moderation, hold, control, restriction, prevention, suppression, hindrance, curtailment: *A Bill of Rights would act as a restraint on judicial power.*

restrict VERB **1 = limit**, fix, regulate, specify, curb, ration, keep within bounds or limits: *a move to restrict the number of students on campus at any one time* **OPPOSITE:** widen **2 = hamper**, impede, handicap, restrain, cramp, inhibit, straiten: *The shoulder straps restrict movement.*

restriction NOUN **1 = control**, rule, condition, check, regulation, curb, restraint, constraint, confinement, containment, demarcation, stipulation: *the relaxation of travel restrictions* **2 = limitation**, handicap, inhibition: *the restrictions of urban living*

result NOUN **1 = consequence**, effect, outcome, end result, issue, event, development, product, reaction, fruit, sequel, upshot: *This is the result of eating too much fatty food.* **OPPOSITE:** cause **2 = outcome**, conclusion, end, decision, termination: *They were surprised by the result of their trials.*
▷ VERB *(often followed by* **from***)* **= arise**, follow, issue, happen, appear, develop, spring, flow, turn out, stem, derive, ensue, emanate, eventuate: *Many hair problems result from what you eat.*
result in something = end in, bring about, cause, lead to, wind up, finish with, culminate in, terminate in: *Fifty per cent of road accidents result in head injuries.*

resume VERB **1 = begin again**, continue, go on with, proceed with, carry on, reopen, restart, recommence, reinstitute, take up *or* pick up where you left off: *They are expected to resume the search early today.* **OPPOSITE:** discontinue **2 = take up again**, assume again: *After the war he resumed his duties at the college.* **3 = occupy again**, take back, reoccupy: *She resumed her seat.*

résumé NOUN **1 = summary**, synopsis, abstract, précis, review, digest, epitome, rundown, recapitulation: *I will leave you a résumé of his speech.* **2 = curriculum vitae**, CV, career history, details, biography: *I mailed him my résumé this week.*

resumption NOUN **= continuation**, carrying on, reopening, renewal, restart, resurgence, new beginning, re-establishment, fresh outbreak

resurgence NOUN **= revival**, return, renaissance, resurrection, resumption, rebirth, re-emergence, recrudescence, renascence

resurrect VERB **1 = revive**, renew, bring back, kick-start *(informal)*, reintroduce, breathe new life into: *Attempts to resurrect the ceasefire have failed.* **2 = restore to life**, raise from the dead: *Only the True Cross was able to resurrect a dead youth.*

resurrection NOUN **1 = revival**, restoration, renewal, resurgence, return, comeback *(informal)*, renaissance, rebirth, reappearance,

R

The Language of Marcus Clarke

Marcus Andrew Hislop Clarke (1846–81) was an Australian novelist and poet. He is remembered for his classic novel *For the Term of his Natural Life* (originally published as a serial, which tells the story of a young man, Rufus Dawes, who was transported to Australia for a murder he did not commit. Clarke visited a penal settlement in Tasmania as part of his research, and the novel has been praised for its realistic portrayal of the brutalities of the penal system.

Not surprisingly, words relating to life as a prisoner are among the most frequent nouns in the novel: *prisoner, prison*, and *convict*. *Convict* is often used as a noun – *the unhappy convict, the tameless convict, the convict's death* – and as a noun modifier in phrases such as *convict settlement, convict disciplinarian*, and *convict servant*. It is rarely used as a verb except in the participle form, as in *convicted felon*.

Another frequent noun is *sea*, which has a prominent role in the novel and is often personified as *hungry, ravenous, remorseless, angry, relentless*, and *all-devouring*. The sun is also portrayed as an *enemy*, and is often described as beating down relentlessly. These personifications prefigure the tragic ending, where Dawes and his loved one, Sylvia, are swept to sea. (At least, that is the ending of the novel; the original serialization ended in Dawes' survival.) In the final passage, Dawes' and Sylvia's deaths, and their accompanying understanding of life, are described as a tempest:

> The mists which shroud our self-knowledge become transparent, and we are smitten with sudden lightning-like comprehension of our own misused power over our fate. This much we feel and know, but who can coldly describe the hurricane which thus o'erwhelms him?

The aftermath of the couple's death is also portrayed through the pathetic fallacy of the calm after the storm: 'The tempest was over. As the sun rose higher the air grew balmy, the ocean placid; and, golden in the rays of the new risen morning, the wreck and its burden drifted out to sea.'

Clarke's most frequent adjectives represent the despair and brutality in the novel: notable are *terrible, desperate*, and *horrible*. We read of *desperate hopes, desperate schemes*, and *desperate courage*; *terrible experiences* and *terrible journeys*; *horrible madness* and *horrible dreams*. *Unhappy* is almost twice as frequent as *happy*, and, whereas the former usually describes people (*unhappy man, unhappy convict*), the latter tends to describe times in the past (*those happy days*) or is used in the sense of 'felicitious' (*happy suggestion, happy medium*). People are not happy except in the abstract:

> I think of **happier men**, with fair wives and clinging children ... – and a hideous wild beast seems to stir within me ...

Another frequent adjective is *strange*, which occurs more than twelve times as often in Clarke's work as it does in the *Bank of English*, Collins' corpus of present-day English. It is used in the sense 'unfamiliar' in, for example, *strange noise, strange behaviour*; there are also many uses of the sense 'unaccountable', in *strange concurrence, strange accident*, and *strange fate*, where characters are 'drawn together by that **strange fate** of circumstances which creates events'. This is interesting in light of a frequent criticism of the novel – that the plot relied heavily on unrealistic coincidences.

One feature of the novel is Clarke's representation and glossing of prison slang. For example, after using the word **ovalled** Clarke explains in a footnote that "To oval' is a term in use among convicts, and means so to bend the round ring of the ankle fetter that the heel can be drawn up through it.' Elsewhere the explanation is part of the text:

> '... How could the poor man compose such an ingenious piece of cryptography?' 'If you mean, **fake up** that paper,' returned Frere, unconsciously dropping into **prison slang**, 'I'll tell you.'

As with so many slang terms, *fake up* has widened in use over the years: whereas it was slang in the nineteenth century, it has now entered general colloquial English. Other 'slang' terms which Clarke highlights are *row* meaning 'argument' and *kid* meaning 'child', both of which are also in everyday usage.

resuscitation, renascence: *This is a resurrection of an old story.* **OPPOSITE:** killing off **2 = raising** *or* **rising from the dead**, return from the dead: *the Resurrection of Jesus Christ* **OPPOSITE:** demise

> **QUOTATIONS**
> I am the resurrection, and the life
> [*Bible: St. John*]

resuscitate VERB **1 = give artificial respiration to**, save, quicken, bring to life, bring round, give the kiss of life to: *A paramedic tried to resuscitate her.* **2 = revive**, rescue, restore, renew, resurrect, revitalize, breathe new life into, revivify, reanimate: *his promise to resuscitate the failing economy*

retain VERB **1 = maintain**, keep, reserve, preserve, keep up, uphold, nurture, continue to have, hang *or* hold onto: *He retains a deep respect for the profession.* **2 = keep**, keep possession of, hang *or* hold onto, save: *They want to retain a strip 33ft wide on the eastern shore.* **OPPOSITE:** let go **3 = remember**, recall, bear in mind, keep in mind, memorize, recollect, impress on the memory: *She needs tips on how to retain facts.* **OPPOSITE:** forget

retainer NOUN **1 = fee**, advance, deposit: *I'll need a five-hundred-dollar retainer.* **2 = servant**, domestic, attendant, valet, supporter, dependant, henchman, footman, lackey, vassal, flunky: *the ever-faithful family retainer*

retaliate VERB **= pay someone back**, hit back, strike back, reciprocate, take revenge, get back at someone, get even with *(informal)*, even the score, get your own back *(informal)*, wreak vengeance, exact retribution, give as good as you get *(informal)*, take an eye for an eye, make reprisal, give (someone) a taste of his *or* her own medicine, give tit for tat, return like for like **OPPOSITE:** turn the other cheek

retaliation NOUN **= revenge**, repayment, vengeance, reprisal, retribution, tit for tat, an eye for an eye, reciprocation, counterstroke, requital, counterblow, a taste of your own medicine

> **QUOTATIONS**
> The smallest worm will turn, being trodden on
> [William Shakespeare *Henry VI, part III*]

retard VERB **= slow down**, check, arrest, delay, handicap, stall, brake, detain, defer, clog, hinder, obstruct, impede, set back, encumber, decelerate, hold back *or* up **OPPOSITE:** speed up

retch VERB **= gag**, be sick, vomit, regurgitate, chuck *(Austral. & N.Z. informal)*, throw up *(informal)*, spew, heave, puke *(slang)*, disgorge, barf *(U.S. slang)*, chunder *(slang, chiefly Austral.)*, upchuck *(U.S. slang)*, do a technicolour yawn *(slang)*, toss your cookies *(U.S. slang)*

reticence NOUN **= silence**, reserve, restraint, quietness, secretiveness, taciturnity, uncommunicativeness, unforthcomingness

reticent ADJECTIVE **= uncommunicative**, reserved, secretive, unforthcoming, quiet, silent, restrained, taciturn, tight-lipped, unspeaking, close-lipped, mum **OPPOSITE:** communicative

retinue NOUN **= attendants**, entourage, escort, servants, following, train, suite, aides, followers, cortege

retire VERB **1 = stop working**, give up work, be pensioned off, be put out to grass *(informal)*: *In 1974 he retired.* **2 = withdraw**, leave, remove, exit, go away, depart, absent yourself, betake yourself: *He retired from the room with his colleagues.* **3 = go to bed**, turn in *(informal)*, go to sleep, hit the sack *(slang)*, go to your room, kip down *(Brit. slang)*, hit the hay *(slang)*: *She retires early most nights.* **4 = retreat**, withdraw, pull out, give way, recede, pull back, back off, decamp, give ground: *He was wounded, but did not retire from the field.*

retirement NOUN **= withdrawal**, retreat, privacy, loneliness, obscurity, solitude, seclusion

retiring ADJECTIVE **= shy**, reserved, quiet, modest, shrinking, humble, timid, coy, meek, reclusive, reticent, unassuming, self-effacing, demure, diffident, bashful, aw-shucks, timorous, unassertive **OPPOSITE:** outgoing

retort VERB **= reply**, return, answer, respond, counter, rejoin, retaliate, come back with, riposte, answer back: *'Who do you think you're talking to?' she retorted.*
▷ NOUN **= reply**, answer, response, comeback, riposte, rejoinder: *His sharp retort made an impact.*

retract VERB **1 = withdraw**, take back, revoke, disown, deny, recall, reverse, cancel, repeal, renounce, go back on, repudiate, rescind, renege on, back out of, disavow, recant, disclaim, abjure, eat your words, unsay: *He hurriedly sought to retract the statement.* **2 = draw in**, pull in, pull back, reel in, sheathe: *A cat in ecstasy will extend and retract his claws.*

retreat VERB **= withdraw**, retire, back off, draw back, leave, go back, shrink, depart, fall back, recede, pull back, back away, recoil, give ground, turn tail: *They were forced to retreat.* **OPPOSITE:** advance
▷ NOUN **1 = flight**, retirement, departure, withdrawal, evacuation: *The army was in full retreat.* **OPPOSITE:** advance **2 = refuge**, haven, resort, retirement, shelter, haunt, asylum, privacy, den, sanctuary, hideaway, seclusion: *He spent yesterday in his country retreat.*

retrenchment NOUN **= cutback**, cuts, economy, reduction, pruning, contraction, cost-cutting, rundown, curtailment, tightening your belt **OPPOSITE:** expansion

retribution NOUN **= punishment**, retaliation, reprisal, redress, justice, reward, reckoning, compensation, satisfaction, revenge, repayment, vengeance, Nemesis, recompense, an eye for an eye, requital

> **QUOTATIONS**
> Though the mills of God grind slowly, yet they grind exceeding small;
> Though with patience He stands waiting, with exactness grinds He all
> [Henry Wadsworth Longfellow *Retribution*]

retrieve VERB **1 = get back**, regain, repossess, fetch back, recall, recover, restore, recapture: *He retrieved his jacket from the seat.* **2 = redeem**, save, rescue, repair, salvage, win back, recoup: *He could retrieve the situation.*

retro ADJECTIVE **= old-time**, old, former, past, period, antique, old-fashioned, nostalgic, old-world, bygone, of yesteryear

retrograde ADJECTIVE **= deteriorating**, backward, regressive, retrogressive, declining, negative, reverse, retreating, worsening, downward, waning, relapsing, inverse, degenerative

retrospect NOUN **= hindsight**, review, afterthought, re-examination, survey, recollection, remembrance, reminiscence **OPPOSITE:** foresight

return VERB **1 = come back**, go back, repair, retreat, turn back, revert, reappear: *More than 350,000 people have returned home.* **OPPOSITE:** depart **2 = put back**, replace, restore, render, transmit, convey, send back, reinstate, take back, give back, carry back, retrocede: *The car was not returned on time.* **OPPOSITE:** keep **3 = give back**, repay, refund, pay back, remit, reimburse, recompense: *They promised to return the money.* **OPPOSITE:** keep **4 = reciprocate**, requite, feel in return, respond to: *Her feelings are not returned.* **5 = recur**, come back, repeat, persist, revert, happen again, reappear, come and go, come again: *The pain returned in waves.* **6 = announce**, report, come to, deliver, arrive at, bring in, submit, render: *They returned a verdict of not guilty.* **7 = earn**, make, net, yield, bring in, repay: *The business returned a handsome profit.* **OPPOSITE:** lose **8 = elect**, choose, pick, vote in: *He has been returned as leader of the party.*
▷ NOUN **1 = reappearance**: *his sudden return to London* **OPPOSITE:** departure **2 = restoration**, replacement, reinstatement, re-establishment: *Their demand was for the return of acres of forest.* **OPPOSITE:** removal **3 = recurrence**, repetition, reappearance, reversion, persistence: *It was like the return of his youth.* **4 = profit**, interest, benefit, gain, income, advantage, revenue, yield,

proceeds, takings, boot *(dialect)*: *They have seen no return on their investment.*
5 = repayment, reward, compensation, reparation, reimbursement, recompense, reciprocation, requital, retaliation, meed *(archaic)*: *What do I get in return for taking part in your experiment?*
6 = statement, report, form, list, account, summary: *a new analysis of the census returns*

revamp VERB **= renovate**, restore, overhaul, refurbish, rehabilitate, do up *(informal)*, patch up, refit, repair, fix up *(informal, chiefly U.S. & Canad.)*, recondition, give a face-lift to

reveal VERB **1 = make known**, disclose, give away, make public, tell, announce, publish, broadcast, leak, communicate, proclaim, betray, give out, let out, impart, divulge, let slip, let on, take the wraps off *(informal)*, blow wide open *(slang)*, get off your chest *(informal)*: *She has refused to reveal her daughter's whereabouts.*
OPPOSITE: keep secret **2 = show**, display, bare, exhibit, unveil, uncover, manifest, unearth, unmask, lay bare, bring to light, expose to view: *A grey carpet was removed to reveal the pine floor.*
OPPOSITE: hide

revel VERB **= celebrate**, rave *(Brit. slang)*, carouse, live it up *(informal)*, push the boat out *(Brit. informal)*, whoop it up *(informal)*, make merry, paint the town red *(informal)*, go on a spree, roister: *I'm afraid I revelled the night away.*
▷ NOUN *(often plural)* **= merrymaking**, party, celebration, rave *(Brit. slang)*, gala, spree, festivity, beano *(Brit. slang)*, debauch, saturnalia, bacchanal, rave-up *(Brit. slang)*, jollification, carousal, hooley *or* hoolie *(chiefly Irish & N.Z.)*, carouse: *The revels often last until dawn.*
revel in something = enjoy, relish, indulge in, delight in, savour, thrive on, bask in, wallow in, lap up, take pleasure in, drool over, luxuriate in, crow about, rejoice over, gloat about, rub your hands: *She revelled in her freedom.*

revelation NOUN **1 = disclosure**, discovery, news, broadcast, exposé, announcement, publication, exposure, leak, uncovering, confession, divulgence: *revelations about his private life* **2 = exhibition**, telling, communication, broadcasting, discovery, publication, exposure, leaking, unveiling, uncovering, manifestation, unearthing, giveaway, proclamation, exposition: *the revelation of his private life*

reveller NOUN **= merrymaker**, carouser, pleasure-seeker, partygoer, roisterer, celebrator

revelry NOUN **= merrymaking**, partying, fun, celebration, rave *(Brit. slang)*, spree, festivity, beano *(Brit. slang)*, debauch, debauchery, carouse, jollity, saturnalia, roistering, rave-up *(Brit. slang)*, jollification, carousal, hooley *or* hoolie *(chiefly Irish & N.Z.)*

revenge NOUN **= retaliation**, satisfaction, vengeance, reprisal, retribution, vindictiveness, an eye for an eye, requital: *in revenge for the murder of her lover*
▷ VERB **= avenge**, repay, vindicate, pay (someone) back, take revenge for, requite, even the score for, get your own back for *(informal)*, make reprisal for, take an eye for an eye for: *The relatives wanted to revenge the dead man's murder.*

QUOTATIONS
An eye for an eye, a tooth for a tooth
[*Bible: Exodus*]

Revenge is a kind of wild justice, which the more man's nature runs to, the more ought law to weed it out
[Francis Bacon *Essays*]

Sweet is revenge – especially to women
[Lord Byron *Don Juan*]

PROVERBS
Revenge is a dish best served cold
Don't get mad, get even
Revenge is sweet

revenue NOUN **= income**, interest, returns, profits, gain, rewards, yield, proceeds, receipts, takings
OPPOSITE: expenditure

reverberate VERB **= echo**, ring, resound, vibrate, re-echo

reverberation NOUN **= echo**, ringing, resonance, resounding, vibration, re-echoing

revere VERB **= be in awe of**, respect, honour, worship, adore, reverence, exalt, look up to, defer to, venerate, have a high opinion of, put on a pedestal, think highly of
OPPOSITE: despise

reverence NOUN **= respect**, honour, worship, admiration, awe, devotion, homage, deference, adoration, veneration, high esteem: *in mutual support and reverence for the dead*
OPPOSITE: contempt
▷ VERB **= revere**, respect, honour, admire, worship, adore, pay homage to, venerate, be in awe of, hold in awe: *Some men even seem to reverence them.*

reverent ADJECTIVE **= respectful**, awed, solemn, deferential, loving, humble, adoring, devout, pious, meek, submissive, reverential
OPPOSITE: disrespectful

reverie NOUN **= daydream**, musing, preoccupation, trance, abstraction, daydreaming, inattention, absent-mindedness, brown study, woolgathering, castles in the air *or* Spain

reverse VERB **1 = change**, alter, cancel, overturn, overthrow, set aside, undo, repeal, quash, revoke, overrule, retract, negate, rescind, invalidate, annul, obviate, countermand, declare null and void, overset, upset: *They have made it clear they will not reverse the decision.* **OPPOSITE:** implement
2 = turn round, turn over, turn upside down, upend: *The curve of the spine may be reversed under such circumstances.*
3 = transpose, change, move, exchange, transfer, switch, shift, alter, swap, relocate, rearrange, invert, interchange, reorder: *He reversed the position of the two stamps.*
4 = go backwards, retreat, back up, turn back, backtrack, move backwards, back: *He reversed and drove away.* **OPPOSITE:** go forward
▷ NOUN **1 = opposite**, contrary, converse, antithesis, inverse, contradiction: *There is absolutely no evidence. Quite the reverse.*
2 = misfortune, check, defeat, blow, failure, disappointment, setback, hardship, reversal, adversity, mishap, affliction, repulse, trial, misadventure, vicissitude: *They have suffered a major reverse.* **3 = back**, rear, other side, wrong side, underside, flip side, verso: *on the reverse of the coin*
OPPOSITE: front
▷ ADJECTIVE **1 = opposite**, contrary, converse, inverse: *The wrong attitude will have the reverse effect.* **2 = backward**, inverted, back to front: *We will take them in reverse order.*

revert VERB **1 = go back**, return, come back, resume, lapse, recur, relapse, regress, backslide, take up where you left off: *He reverted to smoking heavily.*
2 = return: *The property reverts to the freeholder.*

USAGE
Since the concept *back* is already contained in the *re-* part of the word *revert*, it is unnecessary to say that someone *reverts back* to a particular type of behaviour.

review NOUN **1 = re-examination**, revision, rethink, retrospect, another look, reassessment, fresh look, second look, reconsideration, re-evaluation, recapitulation: *She has announced a review of adoption laws.*
2 = survey, report, study, analysis, examination, scrutiny, perusal: *a review on the training and education of over-16s* **3 = critique**, commentary, evaluation, critical assessment, study, notice, criticism, judgment: *We've never had a good review in the press.*
4 = inspection, display, parade, procession, march past: *an early morning review of the troops*
5 = magazine, journal, periodical, zine *(informal)*: *He was recruited to write for the Edinburgh Review.*
▷ VERB **1 = reconsider**, revise, rethink, run over, reassess, re-examine, re-evaluate, think over, take another look at, recapitulate, look at again, go over again: *The next day we reviewed the previous day's work.* **2 = assess**, write a critique of, study, judge, discuss, weigh, evaluate, criticize, read through, give your opinion of: *I see that no papers have reviewed my book.*

3 = inspect, check, survey, examine, vet, check out *(informal)*, scrutinize, give (something *or* someone) the once-over *(informal)*: *He reviewed the troops.* **4 = look back on**, remember, recall, reflect on, summon up, recollect, call to mind: *Review all the information you need.*

reviewer NOUN **= critic**, judge, commentator, connoisseur, arbiter, essayist

revile VERB **= malign**, abuse, knock *(informal)*, rubbish *(informal)*, run down, smear, libel, scorn, slag (off) *(slang)*, reproach, denigrate, vilify, slander, defame, bad-mouth *(slang, chiefly U.S. & Canad.)*, traduce, calumniate, vituperate, asperse

revise VERB **1 = change**, review, modify, reconsider, re-examine: *He soon came to revise his opinion.* **2 = edit**, correct, alter, update, amend, rewrite, revamp, rework, redo, emend: *Three editors handled revising the articles.* **3 = study**, go over, run through, cram *(informal)*, memorize, reread, swot up on *(Brit. informal)*: *I have to revise maths tonight.*

revision NOUN **1 = emendation**, editing, updating, correction, rewriting: *The phase of writing that is important is revision.* **2 = change**, review, amendment, modification, alteration, re-examination: *The government will make a number of revisions.* **3 = studying**, cramming *(informal)*, memorizing, swotting *(Brit. informal)*, rereading, homework: *They prefer to do their revision at home.*

revitalize VERB **= reanimate**, restore, renew, refresh, resurrect, rejuvenate, breathe new life into, bring back to life, revivify

revival NOUN **1 = resurgence**: *There is no chance of a revival in car sales.* OPPOSITE: decline **2 = reawakening**, restoration, renaissance, renewal, awakening, resurrection, refreshment, quickening, rebirth, resuscitation, revitalization, recrudescence, reanimation, renascence, revivification: *a revival of nationalism and the rudiments of democracy*

revive VERB **1 = revitalize**, restore, rally, renew, renovate, rekindle, kick-start *(informal)*, breathe new life into, invigorate, reanimate: *an attempt to revive the economy* **2 = bring round**, awaken, animate, rouse, resuscitate, bring back to life: *They tried in vain to revive him.* **3 = come round**, recover, quicken, spring up again: *After three days in a coma, he revived.* **4 = refresh**, restore, comfort, cheer, renew, resurrect, rejuvenate, revivify: *Superb food and drink revived our little band.* OPPOSITE: exhaust

revoke VERB **= cancel**, recall, withdraw, reverse, abolish, set aside, repeal, renounce, quash, take back, call back, retract, repudiate, negate, renege, rescind, invalidate, annul, nullify, recant, obviate, disclaim, abrogate, countermand, declare null and void OPPOSITE: endorse

revolt NOUN **= uprising**, rising, revolution, rebellion, mutiny, defection, insurrection, insurgency, putsch, sedition: *a revolt by ordinary people against the leaders*
▷ VERB **1 = rebel**, rise up, resist, defect, mutiny, take to the streets, take up arms (against): *The townspeople revolted.* **2 = disgust**, offend, turn off *(informal)*, sicken, repel, repulse, nauseate, gross out *(U.S. slang)*, shock, turn your stomach, make your flesh creep, give you the creeps *(informal)*: *He entirely revolts me.*

revolting ADJECTIVE **= disgusting**, shocking, offensive, appalling, nasty, foul, horrible, obscene, sickening, distasteful, horrid, repellent, obnoxious, repulsive, nauseating, repugnant, loathsome, abhorrent, abominable, nauseous, cringe-making *(Brit. informal)*, noisome, yucky *or* yukky *(slang)*, yucko *(Austral. slang)* OPPOSITE: delightful

revolution NOUN **1 = revolt**, rising, coup, rebellion, uprising, mutiny, insurgency, coup d'état, putsch: *after the French Revolution* **2 = transformation**, shift, innovation, upheaval, reformation, metamorphosis, sea change, drastic *or* radical change: *a revolution in ship design and propulsion* **3 = rotation**, turn, cycle, circle, wheel, spin, lap, circuit, orbit, whirl, gyration, round: *The gear drives a wheel 1/10th revolution per cycle.*

revolutionary ADJECTIVE **1 = rebel**, radical, extremist, subversive, insurgent, seditious, mutinous, insurrectionary: *Do you know anything about the revolutionary movement?* OPPOSITE: reactionary **2 = innovative**, new, different, novel, radical, fundamental, progressive, experimental, drastic, avant-garde, ground-breaking, thoroughgoing: *His trumpet-playing was quite revolutionary.* OPPOSITE: conventional
▷ NOUN **= rebel**, insurgent, mutineer, insurrectionary, revolutionist, insurrectionist: *The revolutionaries laid down their arms.* OPPOSITE: reactionary

> QUOTATIONS
> The most radical revolutionary will become a conservative on the day after the revolution
> [Hannah Arendt]

revolutionize VERB **= transform**, reform, revamp, modernize, metamorphose, break with the past

revolve VERB **1 = go round**, circle, orbit, gyrate: *The satellite revolves around the earth.* **2 = rotate**, turn, wheel, spin, twist, whirl: *The entire circle revolved slowly.* **3 = consider**, study, reflect, think about, deliberate, ponder, turn over (in your mind), meditate, mull over, think over, ruminate: *He revolved the new notion dizzily in his mind.*

revulsion NOUN **= disgust**, loathing, distaste, aversion, recoil, abomination, repulsion, abhorrence, repugnance, odium, detestation OPPOSITE: liking

reward NOUN **1 = prize**: *He earned his reward for contributions to the struggle.* **2 = punishment**, desert, retribution, comeuppance *(slang)*, just deserts, requital: *He'll get his reward before long.* **3 = payment**, return, benefit, profit, gain, prize, wages, honour, compensation, bonus, premium, merit, repayment, bounty, remuneration, recompense, meed *(archaic)*, requital: *They last night offered a £10,000 reward.* OPPOSITE: penalty
▷ VERB **= compensate**, pay, honour, repay, recompense, requite, remunerate, make it worth your while: *Their generosity will be rewarded.* OPPOSITE: penalize

rewarding ADJECTIVE **= satisfying**, fulfilling, gratifying, edifying, economic, pleasing, valuable, profitable, productive, worthwhile, beneficial, enriching, fruitful, advantageous, gainful, remunerative OPPOSITE: unrewarding

rewrite VERB **= revise**, correct, edit, recast, touch up, redraft, emend

rhetoric NOUN **1 = hyperbole**, rant, hot air *(informal)*, pomposity, bombast, wordiness, verbosity, fustian, grandiloquence, magniloquence: *He has continued his warlike rhetoric.* **2 = oratory**, eloquence, public speaking, speech-making, elocution, declamation, speechifying, grandiloquence, spieling *(informal)*, whaikorero *(N.Z.)*: *the noble institutions, such as political rhetoric*

rhetorical ADJECTIVE **1 = oratorical**, verbal, linguistic, stylistic: *a rhetorical device used to emphasize moments in the text* **2 = high-flown**, flamboyant, windy, flashy, pompous, pretentious, flowery, showy, florid, bombastic, hyperbolic, verbose, oratorical, grandiloquent, high-sounding, declamatory, arty-farty *(informal)*, silver-tongued, magniloquent: *He disgorges a stream of rhetorical flourishes.*

rhyme NOUN **= poem**, song, verse, ode: *He has taught her a little rhyme.*
rhyme or reason *(used in negative constructions)* **= sense**, meaning, plan, planning, system, method, pattern, logic: *He picked people without rhyme or reason.*

rhythm NOUN **1 = beat**, swing, accent, pulse, tempo, cadence, lilt: *His music fused the rhythms of jazz and classical music.* **2 = metre**, time, measure *(Prosody)*: *the rhythm and rhyme inherent in nursery rhymes* **3 = pattern**, movement, flow, periodicity: *This is the rhythm of the universe.*

> QUOTATIONS
> It Don't Mean a Thing if it Ain't Got that Swing
> [Duke Ellington *song title*]

rhythmic *or* **rhythmical** ADJECTIVE **= cadenced**, throbbing, periodic, pulsating, flowing, musical, harmonious, lilting, melodious, metrical

rich ADJECTIVE **1 = wealthy**, affluent, well-off, opulent, propertied, rolling *(slang)*, loaded *(slang)*, flush *(informal)*, prosperous, well-heeled *(informal)*, well-to-do, moneyed, filthy rich, stinking rich *(informal)*, made of money *(informal)*, minted *(Brit. slang)*: *You're going to be a very rich man.* **OPPOSITE:** poor **2 = well-stocked**, full, productive, ample, abundant, plentiful, copious, well-provided, well-supplied, plenteous: *a rich supply of fresh, clean water* **OPPOSITE:** scarce **3 = full-bodied**, heavy, sweet, delicious, fatty, tasty, creamy, spicy, juicy, luscious, savoury, succulent, flavoursome, highly-flavoured: *the hearty rich foods of Gascony* **OPPOSITE:** bland **4 = fruitful**, productive, fertile, prolific, fecund: *Farmers grow rice in the rich soil.* **OPPOSITE:** barren **5 = abounding**, full, luxurious, lush, abundant, exuberant, well-endowed: *The bees buzzed around a garden rich with flowers.* **6 = resonant**, full, deep, mellow, mellifluous, dulcet: *He spoke in that deep rich voice which made them all swoon.* **OPPOSITE:** high-pitched **7 = vivid**, strong, deep, warm, bright, intense, vibrant, gay: *an attractive, glossy rich red colour* **OPPOSITE:** dull **8 = costly**, fine, expensive, valuable, superb, elegant, precious, elaborate, splendid, gorgeous, lavish, exquisite, sumptuous, priceless, palatial, beyond price: *This is a Baroque church with a rich interior.* **OPPOSITE:** cheap **9 = funny**, amusing, ridiculous, hilarious, ludicrous, humorous, laughable, comical, risible, side-splitting: *That's rich, coming from him.*

> **QUOTATIONS**
>
> Let me tell you about the very rich. They are different from you and me
> [F. Scott Fitzgerald *The Rich Boy*]
>
> I am rich beyond the dreams of avarice
> [Edward Moore *The Gamester*]
>
> It is easier for a camel to go through the eye of a needle, than for a rich man to enter into the kingdom of God
> [*Bible: St. Matthew*]

riches PLURAL NOUN **1 = wealth**, money, property, gold, assets, plenty, fortune, substance, treasure, abundance, richness, affluence, opulence, top whack *(informal)*: *Some people want fame or riches.* **OPPOSITE:** poverty **2 = resources**, treasures: *Russia's vast natural riches*

> **QUOTATIONS**
>
> The chief enjoyment of riches consists in the parade of riches
> [Adam Smith *Wealth of Nations*]
>
> Riches are a good handmaid, but the worst mistress
> [Francis Bacon *De Dignitate et Augmentis Scientiarum*]

richly ADVERB **1 = elaborately**, lavishly, elegantly, splendidly, exquisitely, expensively, luxuriously, gorgeously, sumptuously, opulently, palatially: *The rooms are richly decorated.* **2 = fully**, well, thoroughly, amply, appropriately, properly, suitably, in full measure: *He achieved the success he so richly deserved.*

rickety ADJECTIVE **= shaky**, broken, weak, broken-down, frail, insecure, feeble, precarious, derelict, flimsy, wobbly, imperfect, tottering, ramshackle, dilapidated, decrepit, unsteady, unsound, infirm, jerry-built

rid VERB **= free**, clear, deliver, relieve, purge, lighten, unburden, disabuse, make free, disembarrass, disencumber, disburden: *an attempt to rid the country of corruption*
get rid of something *or* **someone = dispose of**, throw away *or* out, dispense with, dump, remove, eliminate, expel, unload, shake off, eject, do away with, jettison, weed out, see the back of, wipe from the face of the earth, give the bum's rush to *(slang)*: *The owner needs to get rid of the car.*

riddle[1] NOUN **1 = puzzle**, problem, conundrum, teaser, poser, rebus, brain-teaser *(informal)*, Chinese puzzle: *Tell me a riddle.* **2 = enigma**, question, secret, mystery, puzzle, conundrum, teaser, problem: *a riddle of modern architecture*

riddle[2] VERB **1 = pierce**, pepper, puncture, perforate, honeycomb: *Attackers riddled two homes with gunfire.* **2 = pervade**, fill, spread through, mar, spoil, corrupt, impair, pervade, infest, permeate: *She was found to be riddled with cancer; The report was riddled with errors.*

ride VERB **1 = control**, handle, sit on, manage: *I saw a girl riding a horse.* **2 = travel**, be carried, be supported, be borne, go, move, sit, progress, journey: *I was riding on the back of a friend's bicycle.*
▷ NOUN **= journey**, drive, trip, lift, spin *(informal)*, outing, whirl *(informal)*, jaunt: *Would you like to go for a ride?*

ridicule VERB **= laugh at**, mock, make fun of, make a fool of, humiliate, taunt, sneer at, parody, caricature, jeer at, scoff at, deride, send up *(Brit. informal)*, lampoon, poke fun at, chaff, take the mickey out of *(informal)*, satirize, pooh-pooh, laugh out of court, make a monkey out of, make someone a laughing stock, laugh to scorn: *I admire her for allowing them to ridicule her.*
▷ NOUN **= mockery**, scorn, derision, laughter, irony, rib, taunting, sneer, satire, jeer, banter, sarcasm, chaff, gibe, raillery: *He was subjected to public ridicule.*

ridiculous ADJECTIVE **= laughable**, stupid, incredible, silly, outrageous, absurd, foolish, unbelievable, hilarious, ludicrous, preposterous, farcical, comical, zany, nonsensical, derisory, inane, risible, contemptible, cockamamie *(slang, chiefly U.S.)* **OPPOSITE:** sensible

> **QUOTATIONS**
>
> It is only one step from the sublime to the ridiculous
> [Napoleon Bonaparte]
>
> The sublime and the ridiculous are often so nearly related, that it is difficult to class them separately. One step above the sublime, makes the ridiculous; and one step above the ridiculous, makes the sublime again
> [Thomas Paine *The Age of Reason*]

rife ADJECTIVE **1 = widespread**, abundant, plentiful, rampant, general, common, current, raging, universal, frequent, prevailing, epidemic, prevalent, ubiquitous: *Speculation is rife that he'll be sacked.* **2** *(usually with* **with**) **= abounding**, seething, teeming: *Hollywood soon became rife with rumours.*

rifle VERB **1 = rummage**, go, rake, fossick *(Austral. & N.Z.)*: *The men rifled through his clothing.* **2 = ransack**, rob, burgle, loot, strip, sack, gut, plunder, pillage, despoil: *The child rifled the till while her mother distracted the postmistress.*

rift NOUN **1 = breach**, difference, division, split, separation, falling out *(informal)*, disagreement, quarrel, alienation, schism, estrangement: *They hope to heal the rift with their father.* **2 = split**, opening, space, crack, gap, break, fault, breach, fracture, flaw, cleavage, cleft, chink, crevice, fissure, cranny: *In the open bog are many rifts and potholes.*

rig VERB **1 = fix**, doctor, engineer *(informal)*, arrange, fake, manipulate, juggle, tamper with, fiddle with *(informal)*, falsify, trump up, gerrymander: *She accused her opponents of rigging the vote.* **2 = equip**, fit out, kit out, outfit, supply, turn out, provision, furnish, accoutre: *He had rigged the dinghy for a sail.*
rig something up = set up, build, construct, put up, arrange, assemble, put together, erect, improvise, fix up, throw together, cobble together: *I rigged up a shelter with a tarpaulin.*

right ADJECTIVE **1 = correct**, true, genuine, accurate, exact, precise, valid, authentic, satisfactory, spot-on *(Brit. informal)*, factual, on the money *(U.S.)*, unerring, admissible, dinkum *(Austral. & N.Z. informal)*, veracious, sound: *That's absolutely right!* **OPPOSITE:** wrong **2 = proper**, done, becoming, seemly, fitting, fit, appropriate, suitable, desirable, comme il faut *(French)*: *Make sure you approach it in the right way.* **OPPOSITE:** inappropriate

3 = favourable, due, ideal, convenient, rightful, advantageous, opportune, propitious: *at the right time in the right place* **OPPOSITE:** disadvantageous **4 = just**, good, fair, moral, proper, ethical, upright, honourable, honest, equitable, righteous, virtuous, lawful: *It's not right, leaving her like this.* **OPPOSITE:** unfair **5 = sane**, sound, balanced, normal, reasonable, rational, all there *(informal)*, lucid, unimpaired, compos mentis *(Latin)*: *I think he's not right in the head actually.* **6 = healthy**, well, fine, fit, in good health, in the pink, up to par: *He just didn't look right.* **OPPOSITE:** unwell
▷ ADVERB **1 = correctly**, truly, precisely, exactly, genuinely, accurately, factually, aright: *He guessed right about some things.* **OPPOSITE:** wrongly **2 = suitably**, fittingly, appropriately, properly, aptly, satisfactorily, befittingly: *They made sure I did everything right.* **OPPOSITE:** improperly **3 = exactly**, squarely, precisely, bang, slap-bang *(informal)*: *It caught me right in the middle of the forehead.* **4 = directly**, straight, precisely, exactly, unswervingly, without deviation, by the shortest route, in a beeline: *It was taken right there on a conveyor belt* **5 = all the way**, completely, totally, perfectly, entirely, absolutely, altogether, thoroughly, wholly, utterly, quite: *The candle had burned right down.* **6 = straight**, directly, immediately, quickly, promptly, instantly, straightaway, without delay: *She'll be right down.* **OPPOSITE:** indirectly **7 = properly**, fittingly, fairly, morally, honestly, justly, ethically, honourably, righteously, virtuously: *If you're not treated right, let us know.* **8 = favourably**, well, fortunately, for the better, to advantage, beneficially, advantageously: *I hope things will turn out right.* **OPPOSITE:** badly
▷ NOUN **1 = prerogative**, interest, business, power, claim, authority, title, due, freedom, licence, permission, liberty, privilege: *a woman's right to choose* **2 = justice**, good, reason, truth, honour, equity, virtue, integrity, goodness, morality, fairness, legality, righteousness, propriety, rectitude, lawfulness, uprightness: *a fight between right and wrong* **OPPOSITE:** injustice
▷ VERB **= rectify**, settle, fix, correct, repair, sort out, compensate for, straighten, redress, vindicate, put right: *We've made progress in righting the wrongs of the past.*
by rights = in fairness, properly, justly, equitably: *Negotiations should, by rights, have been conducted by him.*
put something to rights = order, arrange, straighten out: *He decided to put matters to rights.*

QUOTATIONS

We hold these truths to be self-evident: that all men are created equal; that they are endowed by their Creator with inalienable rights; that among these are life, liberty, and the pursuit of happiness [Thomas Jefferson *The Declaration of Independence*]

How forcible are right words [*Bible: Job*]

Natural rights is simple nonsense; natural and imprescriptible rights, rhetorical nonsense – nonsense upon stilts [Jeremy Bentham *Anarchical Fallacies*]

right away ADVERB **= immediately**, now, directly, promptly, instantly, at once, right off, straightaway, without delay, without hesitation, straight off *(informal)*, forthwith, pronto *(informal)*, this instant, posthaste

righteous ADJECTIVE **= virtuous**, good, just, fair, moral, pure, ethical, upright, honourable, honest, equitable, law-abiding, squeaky-clean, blameless **OPPOSITE:** wicked

righteousness NOUN **= virtue**, justice, honour, equity, integrity, goodness, morality, honesty, purity, probity, rectitude, faithfulness, uprightness, blamelessness, ethicalness

rightful ADJECTIVE **= lawful**, just, real, true, due, legal, suitable, proper, valid, legitimate, authorized, bona fide, de jure

right-wing ADJECTIVE **= conservative**, Tory, reactionary **OPPOSITE:** left-wing

rigid ADJECTIVE **1 = strict**, set, fixed, exact, rigorous, stringent, austere, severe: *Hospital routines for nurses are very rigid.* **OPPOSITE:** flexible **2 = inflexible**, harsh, stern, adamant, uncompromising, unrelenting, unyielding, intransigent, unbending, invariable, unalterable, undeviating: *My father is very rigid in his thinking.* **3 = stiff**, inflexible, inelastic: *rigid plastic containers* **OPPOSITE:** pliable

rigorous ADJECTIVE **1 = strict**, hard, firm, demanding, challenging, tough, severe, exacting, harsh, stern, rigid, stringent, austere, inflexible: *rigorous military training* **OPPOSITE:** soft **2 = thorough**, meticulous, painstaking, scrupulous, nice, accurate, exact, precise, conscientious, punctilious: *He is rigorous in his control of expenditure.* **OPPOSITE:** careless

rigour NOUN **1** *(often plural)* **= ordeal**, suffering, trial, hardship, privation: *the rigours of childbirth* **2 = strictness**, austerity, rigidity, firmness, hardness, harshness, inflexibility, stringency, asperity, sternness: *We need to address such challenging issues with rigour.* **3 = thoroughness**, accuracy, precision, exactitude, exactness, conscientiousness, meticulousness, punctiliousness, preciseness: *His work is built round academic rigour and years of insight.*

rile VERB **= anger**, upset, provoke, bug *(informal)*, annoy, irritate, aggravate *(informal)*, gall, nettle, vex, irk, pique, peeve *(informal)*, get under your skin *(informal)*, get on your nerves *(informal)*, nark *(Brit., Austral. & N.Z. slang)*, get your goat *(slang)*, try your patience, rub you up the wrong way, get *or* put your back up, hack you off *(informal)*

rim NOUN **1 = edge**, lip, brim, flange: *She looked at him over the rim of her glass.* **2 = border**, edge, trim, circumference: *a round mirror with white metal rim* **3 = margin**, border, verge, brink: *round the eastern rim of the Mediterranean*

rind NOUN **1 = skin**, peel, outer layer, epicarp: *grated lemon rind* **2 = crust**, husk, integument: *Cut off the rind of the cheese*

ring[1] VERB **1 = phone**, call, telephone, buzz *(informal, chiefly Brit.)*: *He rang me at my mother's.* **2 = chime**, sound, toll, resound, resonate, reverberate, clang, peal: *He heard the school bell ring.* **3 = reverberate**, resound, resonate: *The whole place was ringing with music.*
▷ NOUN **1 = call**, phone call, buzz *(informal, chiefly Brit.)*: *We'll give him a ring as soon as we get back.* **2 = chime**, knell, peal: *There was a ring of the bell.*

USAGE

Rang is the past tense of the verb *ring*, as in *he rang the bell*. *Rung* is the past participle, as in *he has already rung the bell*, and care should be taken not to use it as if it were a variant form of the past tense.

ring[2] NOUN **1 = circle**, round, band, circuit, loop, hoop, halo: *a ring of blue smoke* **2 = arena**, enclosure, circus, rink: *The fight continued in the ring.* **3 = gang**, group, association, band, cell, combine, organization, circle, crew *(informal)*, knot, mob, syndicate, cartel, junta, clique, coterie, cabal: *investigation of an international crime ring*
▷ VERB **= encircle**, surround, enclose, encompass, seal off, girdle, circumscribe, hem in, gird: *The area is ringed by troops.*

rinse VERB **= wash**, clean, wet, dip, splash, cleanse, bathe, wash out: *After washing always rinse the hair in clear water.*
▷ NOUN **= wash**, wetting, dip, splash, bath: *plenty of lather followed by a rinse with cold water*

riot NOUN **1 = disturbance**, row, disorder, confusion, turmoil, quarrel, upheaval, fray, strife, uproar, turbulence, commotion, lawlessness, street fighting, tumult, donnybrook, mob violence: *Twelve inmates have been killed during a riot.* **2 = display**, show, splash, flourish, extravaganza, profusion: *The garden was a riot of colour.* **3 = laugh**, joke, scream *(informal)*, blast *(U.S. slang)*, hoot *(informal)*, lark: *It was a riot when I introduced my two cousins!*
▷ VERB **= rampage**, take to the streets, run riot, go on the rampage, fight in the streets, raise an uproar: *They rioted in protest against the government.*

r

Henry James's Use of Nouns

The action of Henry James's novels generally takes place indoors – in places such as drawing rooms, hotels, and theatres. Nouns relating to the natural world are relatively infrequent in his writing. His focus is on his characters' internal life, and on their perceptions of, and relations with, other people. Among the nouns he uses most frequently are ones relating to these concerns, such as *sense, word, idea, mind, manner, effect,* and *impression. Sense* is a particularly Jamesian word; it almost always means 'feeling' as in *a sense of honour*; *a sense of deeper dangers*, rather than 'meaning', or the moral quality described by 'good sense'. James's very frequent use of 'sense' also has to do with his preference for noun constructions rather than the verbal ones that are more normal in English: this is a preference which is characteristic of written French. Thus, instead of *feel that*, followed by a clause, he much more often chooses *have a sense of* followed by a noun or gerund:

> Even while Selina spoke Laura **had** a cold, horrible **sense of** not believing her, and at the same time a desire, colder still, to extract a reiteration of the pledge.

The meaning of this sentence could roughly be expressed by verbs – Laura felt that she did not believe Selina, but she wanted to make her repeat her promise. This version contains one common noun, whereas James uses four, and thereby depicts Laura's feelings in a much more complex and subtle way. In James's sentence both *sense* and *desire* are objects of the verb *have:* the grammar matches the simultaneity of Laura's two feelings, and because *sense* is a noun, it can be modified by two powerful adjectives, *cold* and *horrible*. A further link between Laura's two feelings is made by the repetition of one of the adjectives (*colder still*). The very formal noun *reiteration* is in keeping with Laura's cold determination.

Another Jamesian noun is *air*, used in relation to appearance, as in *an air of animated sympathy*; *her air of momentary submission and self-control*. Rather than such a verb as 'seem' with an adjective, James very often chooses the locution *have an air of*, followed by a noun, or indeed several nouns, modified by several adjectives:

> Pickering **had the air of** an ingenuous young philosopher sitting at the feet of an austere muse, and not of a sentimental spendthrift dangling about some supreme incarnation of levity.

James's characters form *impressions* from what people say, and from non-verbal signals, including *manner*, another frequently-occurring noun:

> Her **manner** hasn't changed and I have no reason to suppose that she likes me any the less; but she makes a strange impression on me – she makes me uneasy.

Impressions also depend on *tone*, this being the word used to describe the way people present themselves when they talk. James's characters are acutely sensitive to *tone*, and may react to it angrily:

> When the elder man took that **tone**, the **tone** of vast experience and a fastidiousness justified by ineffable recollections, our friend was more provoked than he could say...

Conversation is very important in Henry James, and he has so great a partiality for nouns that it is not surprising that he felt the need for a noun to describe a person one is engaged in conversation with. Thus, instead of more natural phrases, such as 'the man I was talking to', or 'the woman I was talking to', he uses *my interlocutor*, or *my interlocutress*. While their equivalents are not uncommon in French, these words have not been used much by other English writers. James, however, uses them quite often, even in the context of quite informal dialogue:

> 'You know you're wrong, my dear,' said her **interlocutress**, with angry little eyes.

run riot 1 = rampage, go wild, be out of control, raise hell, let yourself go, break *or* cut loose, throw off all restraint: *Rampaging prisoners ran riot through the jail.* **2 = grow profusely**, luxuriate, spread like wildfire, grow like weeds: *Virginia creeper ran riot up the walls.*

> **QUOTATIONS**
> A riot is at bottom the language of the unheard
> [Martin Luther King Jr. *Where Do We Go From Here?*]
>
> riot: a popular entertainment given to the military by innocent bystanders
> [Ambrose Bierce *The Devil's Dictionary*]

riotous ADJECTIVE **1 = reckless**, wild, outrageous, lavish, rash, luxurious, extravagant, wanton, unrestrained, intemperate, heedless, immoderate: *They wasted their lives in riotous living.* **2 = unrestrained**, wild, loud, noisy, boisterous, rollicking, uproarious, orgiastic, side-splitting, rambunctious *(informal)*, saturnalian, roisterous: *Dinner was often a riotous affair.* **3 = unruly**, violent, disorderly, rebellious, rowdy, anarchic, tumultuous, lawless, mutinous, ungovernable, uproarious, refractory, insubordinate, rampageous: *a riotous mob of hooligans* **OPPOSITE:** orderly

rip VERB **1 = tear**, cut, score, split, burst, rend, slash, hack, claw, slit, gash, lacerate: *I tried not to rip the paper.* **2 = be torn**, tear, split, burst, be rent: *I felt the banner rip as we were pushed in opposite directions.*
▷ NOUN **= tear**, cut, hole, split, rent, slash, slit, cleavage, gash, laceration: *She looked at the rip in her new dress.*
rip someone off = cheat, trick, rob, con *(informal)*, skin *(slang)*, stiff *(slang)*, steal from, fleece, defraud, dupe, swindle, diddle *(informal)*, do the dirty on *(Brit. informal)*, gyp *(slang)*, cozen, scam *(slang)*: *Ticket touts ripped them off.*

ripe ADJECTIVE **1 = ripened**, seasoned, ready, mature, mellow, fully developed, fully grown: *Always choose firm but ripe fruit.* **OPPOSITE:** unripe **2 = right**, suitable: *Conditions are ripe for an outbreak of cholera.* **3 = mature**: *He lived to the ripe old age of 65.* **4 = suitable**, timely, ideal, favourable, auspicious, opportune: *The time is ripe for high-level dialogue.* **OPPOSITE:** unsuitable **5** *(with* **for**) **= ready for**, prepared for, eager for, in readiness for: *Do you think she's ripe for romance again?*

ripen VERB **= mature**, season, develop, get ready, burgeon, come of age, come to fruition, grow ripe, make ripe

rip-off *or* **ripoff** NOUN **= cheat**, con *(informal)*, scam *(slang)*, con trick *(informal)*, fraud, theft, sting *(informal)*, robbery, exploitation, swindle, daylight robbery *(informal)*

riposte NOUN **= retort**, return, answer, response, reply, sally, comeback *(informal)*, counterattack, repartee, rejoinder: *He glanced at her, expecting a cheeky riposte.*
▷ VERB **= retort**, return, answer, reply, respond, come back, rejoin, reciprocate: *'You look kind of funny,' she riposted blithely.*

ripple NOUN **1 = wave**, tremor, oscillation, undulation: *the ripples on the sea's calm surface* **2 = flutter**, thrill, tremor, tingle, vibration, frisson: *The news sent a ripple of excitement through the Security Council.*

rise VERB **1 = get up**, stand up, get to your feet: *He rose slowly from his chair.* **2 = arise**, surface, get out of bed, rise and shine: *He had risen early and gone to work.* **3 = go up**, climb, move up, ascend: *The sun had risen high in the sky.* **OPPOSITE:** descend **4 = loom**, tower: *The building rose before him.* **5 = get steeper**, mount, climb, ascend, go uphill, slope upwards: *the slope of land that rose from the house* **OPPOSITE:** drop **6 = increase**, mount, soar: *We need to increase our charges in order to meet rising costs.* **OPPOSITE:** decrease **7 = grow**, go up, intensify: *His voice rose almost to a scream.* **8 = rebel**, resist, revolt, mutiny, take up arms, mount the barricades: *The people wanted to rise against the oppression.* **9 = advance**, progress, get on, be promoted, prosper, go places *(informal)*, climb the ladder, work your way up: *She has risen to the top of her organization.*
▷ NOUN **1 = upward slope**, incline, elevation, ascent, hillock, rising ground, acclivity, kopje *or* koppie *(S. African)*: *I climbed to the top of the rise.* **2 = increase**, climb, upturn, upswing, advance, improvement, ascent, upsurge, bounce, upward turn: *the prospect of another rise in interest rates* **OPPOSITE:** decrease **3 = pay increase**, raise *(U.S.)*, increment: *He will get a rise of nearly £4,000.* **4 = advancement**, progress, climb, promotion, aggrandizement: *They celebrated the regime's rise to power.*
give rise to something = cause, produce, effect, result in, provoke, bring about, bring on: *The picture gave rise to speculation.*

risible ADJECTIVE **= ridiculous**, ludicrous, laughable, farcical, funny, amusing, absurd, hilarious, humorous, comical, droll, side-splitting, rib-tickling *(informal)*

risk NOUN **1 = danger**, chance, possibility, speculation, uncertainty, hazard: *There is a small risk of brain damage.* **2 = gamble**, chance, venture, speculation, leap in the dark: *This was one risk that paid off.* **3 = peril**, jeopardy: *He would not put their lives at risk.*
▷ VERB **1 = stand a chance of**: *Those who fail to register risk severe penalties.* **2 = dare**, endanger, jeopardize, imperil, venture, gamble, hazard, take a chance on, put in jeopardy, expose to danger: *She risked her life to help a woman.*

risky ADJECTIVE **= dangerous**, hazardous, unsafe, perilous, uncertain, tricky, dodgy *(Brit., Austral. & N.Z. informal)*, precarious, touch-and-go, dicey *(informal, chiefly Brit.)*, fraught with danger, chancy *(informal)*, shonky *(Austral. & N.Z. informal)* **OPPOSITE:** safe

risqué ADJECTIVE **= suggestive**, blue, daring, naughty, improper, racy, bawdy, off colour, ribald, immodest, indelicate, near the knuckle *(informal)*, Rabelaisian

rite NOUN **= ceremony**, custom, ritual, act, service, form, practice, procedure, mystery, usage, formality, ceremonial, communion, ordinance, observance, sacrament, liturgy, solemnity

ritual NOUN **1 = ceremony**, rite, ceremonial, sacrament, service, mystery, communion, observance, liturgy, solemnity: *This is the most ancient and holiest of the rituals.* **2 = custom**, tradition, routine, convention, form, practice, procedure, habit, usage, protocol, formality, ordinance, tikanga *(N.Z.)*, lockstep *(U.S. & Canad.)*: *Italian culture revolves around the ritual of eating.*
▷ ADJECTIVE **= ceremonial**, formal, conventional, routine, prescribed, stereotyped, customary, procedural, habitual, ceremonious: *Here, the conventions required me to make the ritual noises.*

ritzy ADJECTIVE **= luxurious**, grand, luxury, elegant, glittering, glamorous, stylish, posh *(informal, chiefly Brit.)*, sumptuous, plush *(informal)*, high-class, opulent, swanky *(informal)*, de luxe, schmick *(Austral. informal)*

rival NOUN **1 = opponent**, competitor, contender, challenger, contestant, adversary, antagonist, emulator: *He finished two seconds ahead of his rival.* **OPPOSITE:** supporter **2 = equal**, match, fellow, equivalent, peer, compeer: *He is a pastry chef without rival.*
▷ VERB **= compete with**, match, equal, oppose, compare with, contend, come up to, emulate, vie with, measure up to, be a match for, bear comparison with, seek to displace: *Cassettes cannot rival the sound quality of CDs.*
▷ MODIFIER **= competing**, conflicting, opposed, opposing, competitive, emulating: *It would be no use having two rival companies.*

rivalry NOUN **= competition**, competitiveness, vying, opposition, struggle, conflict, contest, contention, duel, antagonism, emulation

river NOUN **1 = stream**, brook, creek, beck, waterway, tributary, rivulet, watercourse, burn *(Scot.)*: *boating on the river* **2 = flow**, rush, flood, spate, torrent: *A river of lava was flowing down the mountainside towards the village.*
▸ *related adjective:* fluvial

riveting ADJECTIVE **= enthralling**, arresting, gripping, fascinating, absorbing, captivating, hypnotic, engrossing, spellbinding

road NOUN **1 = roadway**, street, highway, motorway, track, direction, route, path, lane, avenue, pathway, thoroughfare, course, ice road *(Canad.)*: *There was very little traffic on the roads.* **2 = way**, path: *on the road to recovery*

roam VERB **= wander**, walk, range, travel, drift, stroll, stray, ramble, prowl, meander, rove, stravaig *(Scot. & Northern English dialect)*, peregrinate

roar VERB **1 = thunder**, crash, rumble: *the roaring waters of Niagara Falls* **2 = guffaw**, laugh heartily, hoot, crack up *(informal)*, bust a gut *(informal)*, split your sides *(informal)*: *He threw back his head and roared.* **3 = cry**, shout, yell, howl, bellow, clamour, bawl, bay, vociferate: *'I'll kill you for that,' he roared.* ▷ NOUN **1 = rumble**, thunder: *the roar of traffic* **2 = guffaw**, hoot, belly laugh *(informal)*: *There were roars of laughter as he stood up.* **3 = cry**, crash, shout, yell, howl, outcry, bellow, clamour: *the roar of lions in the distance*

rob VERB **1 = steal from**, hold up, rifle, mug *(informal)*, stiff *(slang)*: *Police said he had robbed a man hours earlier.* **2 = raid**, hold up, sack, loot, plunder, burgle, ransack, pillage: *A man who tried to rob a bank was sentenced yesterday.* **3 = dispossess**, con *(informal)*, rip off *(slang)*, skin *(slang)*, cheat, defraud, swindle, despoil, gyp *(slang)*: *I was robbed by a used-car dealer.* **4 = deprive**, strip, do out of *(informal)*: *I can't forgive him for robbing me of an Olympic gold.*

robber NOUN **= thief**, raider, burglar, looter, stealer, fraud, cheat, pirate, bandit, plunderer, mugger *(informal)*, highwayman, con man *(informal)*, fraudster, swindler, brigand, grifter *(slang, chiefly U.S. & Canad.)*, footpad *(archaic)*, rogue trader

robbery NOUN **1 = burglary**, raid, hold-up, rip-off *(slang)*, stick-up *(slang, chiefly U.S.)*, home invasion *(Austral. & N.Z.)*: *He committed dozens of armed robberies.* **2 = theft**, stealing, fraud, steaming *(informal)*, mugging *(informal)*, plunder, swindle, pillage, embezzlement, larceny, depredation, filching, thievery, rapine, spoliation: *He was serving a sentence for robbery.*

robe NOUN **1 = gown**, costume, vestment, habit: *a fur-lined robe of green silk* **2 = dressing gown**, wrapper, bathrobe, negligée, housecoat, peignoir: *She put on a robe and went down to the kitchen.*

robot NOUN **= machine**, automaton, android, mechanical man

> **QUOTATIONS**
> The three fundamental Rules of Robotics... One, a robot may not injure a human being, or, through inaction, allow a human being to come to harm... Two... a robot must obey the orders given it by human beings except where such orders would conflict with the First law... Three, a robot must protect its own existence as long as such protection does not conflict with the First or Second Laws
> [Isaac Asimov I, *Robot*]

robust ADJECTIVE **1 = strong**, tough, powerful, athletic, well, sound, fit, healthy, strapping, hardy, rude, vigorous, rugged, muscular, sturdy, hale, stout, staunch, hearty, husky *(informal)*, in good health, lusty, alive and kicking, fighting fit, sinewy, brawny, in fine fettle, thickset, fit as a fiddle *(informal)*, able-bodied: *His robust physique counts for much in the modern game.* **OPPOSITE:** weak **2 = rough**, raw, rude, coarse, raunchy *(slang)*, earthy, boisterous, rollicking, unsubtle, indecorous, roisterous: *a robust sense of humour* **OPPOSITE:** refined **3 = straightforward**, practical, sensible, realistic, pragmatic, down-to-earth, hard-headed, common-sensical: *She has a robust attitude to children, and knows how to deal with them.*

rock[1] NOUN **1 = stone**, boulder: *She sat cross-legged on the rock.* **2 = tower of strength**, foundation, cornerstone, mainstay, support, protection, anchor, bulwark: *She was the rock of the family.*

rock[2] VERB **1 = sway**, pitch, swing, reel, toss, lurch, wobble, roll: *His body rocked from side to side.* **2 = shock**, surprise, shake, stun, astonish, stagger, jar, astound, daze, dumbfound, set you back on your heels *(informal)*: *His death rocked the fashion business.*

rocky[1] ADJECTIVE **= rough**, rugged, stony, craggy, pebbly, boulder-strewn: *The paths are often very rocky.*

rocky[2] ADJECTIVE **= unstable**, weak, uncertain, doubtful, shaky, unreliable, wobbly, rickety, unsteady, undependable: *Their relationship had gotten off to a rocky start.*

rod NOUN **1 = stick**, bar, pole, shaft, switch, crook, cane, birch, dowel: *reinforced with steel rods* **2 = staff**, baton, mace, wand, sceptre: *It was a witch-doctor's rod.*

rogue NOUN **1 = scoundrel**, crook *(informal)*, villain, fraudster, sharper, fraud, cheat, devil, deceiver, charlatan, con man *(informal)*, swindler, knave *(archaic)*, ne'er-do-well, reprobate, scumbag *(slang)*, blackguard, mountebank, grifter *(slang, chiefly U.S. & Canad.)*, skelm *(S. African)*, rorter *(Austral. slang)*, wrong 'un *(slang)*: *He wasn't a rogue at all.* **2 = scamp**, rascal, scally *(Northwest English dialect)*, rapscallion, nointer *(Austral. slang)*: *a loveable rogue*

role NOUN **1 = job**, part, position, post, task, duty, function, capacity: *His role in the events has been pivotal.* **2 = part**, character, representation, portrayal, impersonation: *Shakespearean women's roles*

roll VERB **1 = turn**, wheel, spin, reel, go round, revolve, rotate, whirl, swivel, pivot, twirl, gyrate: *The car went off the road and rolled over into a ditch.* **2 = trundle**, go, move: *The lorry slowly rolled forward.* **3 = flow**, run, course, slide, glide, purl: *Tears rolled down her cheeks.* **4** *(often with* **up***)* **= wind**, bind, wrap, twist, curl, coil, swathe, envelop, entwine, furl, enfold: *He took off his sweater and rolled it into a pillow.* **5** *(often with* **out***)* **= level**, even, press, spread, smooth, flatten: *Rub in and roll out the pastry.* **6 = toss**, rock, lurch, reel, tumble, sway, wallow, billow, swing, welter: *The ship was still rolling in the troughs.* **7 = rumble**, boom, echo, drum, roar, thunder, grumble, resound, reverberate: *guns firing, drums rolling, cymbals clashing* **8 = sway**, reel, stagger, lurch, lumber, waddle, swagger: *They rolled about in hysterics.* **9 = pass**, go past, elapse: *The years roll by and look at us now.* ▷ NOUN **1 = reel**, ball, bobbin, cylinder: *a roll of blue insulated wire* **2 = rumble**, boom, drumming, roar, thunder, grumble, resonance, growl, reverberation: *They heard the roll of drums.* **3 = register**, record, list, table, schedule, index, catalogue, directory, inventory, census, chronicle, scroll, roster, annals: *A new electoral roll should be drawn up.* **4 = tossing**, rocking, rolling, pitching, swell, lurching, wallowing: *despite the roll of the boat* **5 = turn**, run, spin, rotation, cycle, wheel, revolution, reel, whirl, twirl, undulation, gyration: *Control the roll of the ball.*

rollicking[1] ADJECTIVE **= boisterous**, spirited, lively, romping, merry, hearty, playful, exuberant, joyous, carefree, jaunty, cavorting, sprightly, jovial, swashbuckling, frisky, rip-roaring *(informal)*, devil-may-care, full of beans *(informal)*, frolicsome, sportive: *outrageous, and a rollicking good read* **OPPOSITE:** sedate

rollicking[2] NOUN **= scolding**, lecture, reprimand, telling-off, roasting *(informal)*, wigging *(Brit. slang)*, ticking off *(informal)*, dressing-down *(informal)*, tongue-lashing *(informal)*: *Whoever was responsible got a rollicking.*

romance NOUN **1 = love affair**, relationship, affair, intrigue, attachment, liaison, amour, affair of the heart, affaire (du coeur) *(French)*: *a holiday romance* **2 = love**: *He still finds time for romance.* **3 = excitement**, colour, charm, mystery, adventure, sentiment, glamour, fascination, nostalgia, exoticness: *We want to recreate the romance of old train journeys.* **4 = story**, novel, tale, fantasy, legend, fiction, fairy tale, love story, melodrama, idyll, tear-jerker *(informal)*: *Her taste in fiction was for historical romances.*

romantic ADJECTIVE **1 = loving**, tender, passionate, fond, sentimental, sloppy *(informal)*, amorous, mushy *(informal)*, soppy *(Brit.*

informal), lovey-dovey, icky (*informal*): *They enjoyed a romantic dinner for two.* **OPPOSITE:** unromantic **2 = idealistic**, unrealistic, visionary, high-flown, impractical, dreamy, utopian, whimsical, quixotic, starry-eyed: *He has a romantic view of rural society.* **OPPOSITE:** realistic **3 = exciting**, charming, fascinating, exotic, mysterious, colourful, glamorous, picturesque, nostalgic: *romantic images from travel brochures* **OPPOSITE:** unexciting **4 = fictitious**, made-up, fantastic, fabulous, legendary, exaggerated, imaginative, imaginary, extravagant, unrealistic, improbable, fairy-tale, idyllic, fanciful, wild, chimerical: *Both figures have become the stuff of romantic legends.* **OPPOSITE:** realistic

▷ NOUN **= idealist**, romancer, visionary, dreamer, utopian, Don Quixote, sentimentalist: *You're a hopeless romantic*

QUOTATIONS

Is not this the true romantic feeling – not to desire to escape life, but to prevent life from escaping you? [Thomas Wolfe]

romp VERB **= frolic**, sport, skip, have fun, revel, caper, cavort, frisk, gambol, make merry, rollick, roister, cut capers: *Dogs romped happily in the garden.*

▷ NOUN **= frolic**, lark (*informal*), caper: *a romp in the snow and slush*

romp home *or* **in = win easily**, walk it (*informal*), win hands down, run away with it, win by a mile (*informal*): *He romped home with 141 votes.*

room NOUN **1 = chamber**, office, apartment: *He excused himself and left the room.* **2 = space**, area, territory, volume, capacity, extent, expanse, elbowroom: *There wasn't enough room for all the gear.* **3 = opportunity**, scope, leeway, play, chance, range, occasion, margin, allowance, compass, latitude: *There's a lot of room for you to express yourself.*

roomy ADJECTIVE **= spacious**, large, wide, broad, extensive, generous, ample, capacious, commodious, sizable *or* sizeable **OPPOSITE:** cramped

root[1] NOUN **1 = stem**, tuber, rhizome, radix, radicle: *the twisted roots of an apple tree* **2 = source**, cause, heart, bottom, beginnings, base, seat, occasion, seed, foundation, origin, core, fundamental, essence, nucleus, starting point, germ, crux, nub, derivation, fountainhead, mainspring: *We got to the root of the problem.*

▷ PLURAL NOUN **= sense of belonging**, origins, heritage, birthplace, home, family, cradle: *I am proud of my Brazilian roots.*

root and branch 1 = complete, total, entire, radical, thorough: *in need of root and branch reform* **2 = completely**, finally, totally, entirely, radically, thoroughly, wholly, utterly, without exception, to the last man: *They want to deal with the problem root and branch.*

root something *or* **someone out 1 = get rid of**, remove, destroy, eliminate, abolish, cut out, erase, eradicate, do away with, uproot, weed out, efface, exterminate, extirpate, wipe from the face of the earth: *The generals have to root out traitors.* **2 = discover**, find, expose, turn up, uncover, unearth, bring to light, ferret out: *It shouldn't take long to root out the cause of the problem.*

▸ *related adjective:* radical

root[2] VERB **= dig**, hunt, nose, poke, burrow, delve, ferret, pry, rummage, forage, rootle: *She rooted through the bag.*

rooted ADJECTIVE **= deep-seated**, firm, deep, established, confirmed, fixed, radical, rigid, entrenched, ingrained, deeply felt

rootless ADJECTIVE **= footloose**, homeless, roving, transient, itinerant, vagabond

rope NOUN **= cord**, line, cable, strand, hawser: *He tied the rope around his waist.*

▷ VERB **= tie**, bind, moor, lash, hitch, fasten, tether, pinion, lasso: *I roped myself to the chimney.*

know the ropes = be experienced, know the score (*informal*), be knowledgeable, know what's what, be an old hand, know your way around, know where it's at (*slang*), know all the ins and outs: *She got to know the ropes.*

rope someone in *or* **into something = persuade**, involve, engage, enlist, talk into, drag in, inveigle: *I got roped into helping.*

roster NOUN **= rota**, listing, list, table, roll, schedule, register, agenda, catalogue, inventory, scroll

rostrum NOUN **= stage**, stand, platform, podium, dais

rosy ADJECTIVE **1 = glowing**, fresh, blooming, flushed, blushing, radiant, reddish, ruddy, healthy-looking, roseate, rubicund: *She had bright, rosy cheeks.* **OPPOSITE:** pale **2 = promising**, encouraging, bright, reassuring, optimistic, hopeful, sunny, cheerful, favourable, auspicious, rose-coloured, roseate: *Is the future really so rosy?* **OPPOSITE:** gloomy **3 = pink**, red, rose-coloured, roseate: *the rosy brick buildings*

rot VERB **1 = decay**, break down, spoil, corrupt, deteriorate, taint, perish, degenerate, fester, decompose, corrode, moulder, go bad, putrefy: *The grain will start rotting in the silos.* **2 = crumble**, disintegrate, become rotten: *It is not true to say that this wood never rots.* **3 = deteriorate**, decline, languish, degenerate, wither away, waste away: *I was left to rot nine years for a crime I didn't commit.*

▷ NOUN **1 = decay**, disintegration, corrosion, decomposition, corruption, mould, blight, deterioration, canker, putrefaction, putrescence: *Investigations revealed rot in the beams.* **2 = nonsense**, rubbish, drivel, twaddle, malarkey, pants (*slang*), crap (*slang*), garbage (*chiefly U.S.*), trash, bunk (*informal*), hot air (*informal*), tosh (*slang, chiefly Brit.*), pap, bilge (*informal*), tripe (*informal*), guff (*slang*), moonshine, claptrap (*informal*), hogwash, hokum (*slang, chiefly U.S. & Canad.*), codswallop (*Brit. slang*), piffle (*informal*), poppycock (*informal*), balderdash, bosh (*informal*), eyewash (*informal*), stuff and nonsense, flapdoodle (*slang*), tommyrot, horsefeathers (*U.S. slang*), bunkum *or* buncombe (*chiefly U.S.*), bizzo (*Austral. slang*), bull's wool (*Austral. & N.Z. slang*): *You do talk rot!*

▸ *related adjective:* putrid

rotary ADJECTIVE **= revolving**, turning, spinning, rotating, rotational, gyratory, rotatory

rotate VERB **1 = revolve**, turn, wheel, spin, reel, go round, swivel, pivot, gyrate, pirouette: *The earth rotates round the sun.* **2 = follow in sequence**, switch, alternate, interchange, take turns: *The members of the club can rotate.*

rotation NOUN **1 = revolution**, turning, turn, wheel, spin, spinning, reel, orbit, pirouette, gyration: *the daily rotation of the earth upon its axis* **2 = sequence**, switching, cycle, succession, interchanging, alternation: *crop rotation and integration of livestock*

rotten ADJECTIVE **1 = decaying**, bad, rank, foul, corrupt, sour, stinking, tainted, perished, festering, decomposed, decomposing, mouldy, mouldering, fetid, putrid, putrescent, festy (*Austral. slang*): *The smell is like rotten eggs.* **OPPOSITE:** fresh **2 = crumbling**, decayed, disintegrating, perished, corroded, unsound: *The bay window is rotten.* **3 = bad**, disappointing, unfortunate, unlucky, regrettable, deplorable: *What rotten luck!* **4 = despicable**, mean, base, dirty, nasty, unpleasant, filthy, vile, wicked, disagreeable, contemptible, scurrilous: *You rotten swine!* **5 = unwell**, poorly (*informal*), ill, sick, rough (*informal*), bad, crook (*Austral. & N.Z. informal*), below par, off colour, under the weather (*informal*), ropey *or* ropy (*Brit. informal*): *I felt rotten with the flu.* **6 = inferior**, poor, sorry, inadequate, unacceptable, punk, duff (*Brit. informal*), unsatisfactory, lousy (*slang*), low-grade, substandard, ill-considered, crummy (*slang*), ill-thought-out, poxy (*slang*), of a sort *or* of sorts, ropey *or* ropy (*Brit. informal*), bodger *or* bodgie (*Austral. slang*): *I thought it was a rotten idea.* **7 = corrupt**, immoral, deceitful, untrustworthy, bent (*slang*), crooked (*informal*), vicious, degenerate, mercenary, treacherous, dishonest, disloyal, faithless, venal, dishonourable, perfidious: *There was something rotten in our legal system.* **OPPOSITE:** honourable

rotund ADJECTIVE **1 = plump**, rounded, heavy, fat, stout, chubby, obese, fleshy, tubby, portly, roly-poly, podgy, corpulent: *A rotund gentleman appeared.* **OPPOSITE:** skinny **2 = pompous**, orotund, magniloquent, full: *writing rotund passages of purple prose* **3 = round**, rounded, spherical, bulbous, globular, orbicular: *rotund towers, moats and drawbridges* **4 = sonorous**, round, rich, resonant, orotund: *the wonderfully rotund tones of the presenter*

rough ADJECTIVE **1 = uneven**, broken, rocky, rugged, irregular, jagged, bumpy, stony, craggy: *She made her way across the rough ground.* **OPPOSITE:** even **2 = coarse**, disordered, tangled, hairy, fuzzy, bushy, shaggy, dishevelled, uncut, unshaven, tousled, bristly, unshorn: *people who looked rough and stubbly* **OPPOSITE:** smooth **3 = boisterous**, hard, tough, rugged, arduous: *Rugby's a rough game.* **4 = ungracious**, blunt, rude, coarse, bluff, curt, churlish, bearish, brusque, uncouth, unrefined, inconsiderate, impolite, loutish, untutored, discourteous, unpolished, indelicate, uncivil, uncultured, unceremonious, ill-bred, unmannerly, ill-mannered: *He was rough and common.* **OPPOSITE:** refined **5 = unpleasant**, hard, difficult, tough, uncomfortable, drastic, unjust: *Women have a rough time in our society.* **OPPOSITE:** easy **6 = unwell**, poorly (*informal*), ill, upset, sick, crook (*Austral. & N.Z. informal*), rotten (*informal*), below par, off colour, under the weather (*informal*), not a hundred per cent (*informal*), ropey or ropy (*Brit. informal*): *The lad is still feeling a bit rough.* **7 = approximate**, estimated: *We were only able to make a rough estimate.* **OPPOSITE:** exact **8 = vague**, general, sketchy, imprecise, hazy, foggy, amorphous, inexact: *I've got a rough idea of what he looks like.* **9 = basic**, quick, raw, crude, unfinished, incomplete, hasty, imperfect, rudimentary, sketchy, cursory, shapeless, rough-and-ready, unrefined, formless, rough-hewn, untutored, unpolished: *Make a rough plan of the space.* **OPPOSITE:** complete **10 = rough-hewn**, crude, uncut, unpolished, raw, undressed, unprocessed, unhewn, unwrought: *a rough wooden table* **11 = stormy**, wild, turbulent, agitated, choppy, tempestuous, inclement, squally: *The ships collided in rough seas.* **OPPOSITE:** calm **12 = grating**, harsh, jarring, raucous, rasping, husky, discordant, gruff, cacophonous, unmusical, inharmonious: *'Wait!' a rough voice commanded.* **OPPOSITE:** soft **13 = harsh**, tough, sharp, severe, nasty, cruel, rowdy, curt, unfeeling: *I was a bit rough with you this morning.* **OPPOSITE:** gentle
▷ NOUN **1 = outline**, draft, mock-up, preliminary sketch, suggestion: *Editors are always saying that the roughs are better.* **2 = thug**, tough, casual, rowdy, hoon (*Austral. & N.Z.*), bully boy, bruiser, ruffian, lager lout, roughneck (*slang*), ned (*Scot. slang*), cougan (*Austral. slang*), scozza (*Austral. slang*), bogan (*Austral. slang*): *The roughs of the town are out.*
rough and ready 1 = makeshift, adequate, crude, provisional, improvised, sketchy, thrown together, cobbled together, stopgap: *Here is a rough and ready measurement.* **2 = unrefined**, shabby, untidy, unkempt, unpolished, ungroomed, ill-groomed, daggy (*Austral. & N.Z. informal*): *The soldiers were a bit rough and ready.*
rough and tumble 1 = fight, struggle, scrap (*informal*), brawl, scuffle, punch-up (*Brit. informal*), fracas, affray (*Law*), dust-up (*informal*), shindig (*informal*), donnybrook, scrimmage, roughhouse (*slang*), shindy (*informal*), melee or mêlée, biffo (*Austral. slang*): *the rough and tumble of political combat* **2 = disorderly**, rough, scrambled, scrambling, irregular, rowdy, boisterous, haphazard, indisciplined: *He enjoys rough and tumble play.*
rough someone up = beat up, batter, thrash, do over (*Brit., Austral. & N.Z. slang*), work over (*slang*), mistreat, manhandle, maltreat, bash up (*informal*), beat the living daylights out of (*informal*), knock about or around, beat or knock seven bells out of (*informal*): *They roughed him up a bit*
rough something out = outline, plan, draft, sketch, suggest, block out, delineate, adumbrate: *He roughed out a framework for their story.*

round NOUN **1 = series**, session, cycle, sequence, succession, bout: *This is the latest round of job cuts.* **2 = stage**, turn, level, period, division, session, lap: *in the third round of the cup* **3 = sphere**, ball, band, ring, circle, disc, globe, orb: *small fresh rounds of goat's cheese* **4 = course**, turn, tour, circuit, beat, series, schedule, routine, compass, ambit: *The consultant did his morning round.* **5 = bullet**, shot, shell, discharge, cartridge: *live rounds of ammunition*
▷ ADJECTIVE **1 = spherical**, rounded, bowed, curved, circular, cylindrical, bulbous, rotund, globular, curvilinear, ball-shaped, ring-shaped, disc-shaped, annular, discoid, orbicular: *the round church known as* The New Temple **2 = complete**, full, whole, entire, solid, unbroken, undivided: *a round dozen* **3 = plump**, full, rounded, ample, fleshy, roly-poly, rotund, full-fleshed: *She was a small, round person in her early sixties.*
▷ VERB **= go round**, circle, skirt, flank, bypass, encircle, turn, circumnavigate: *The boats rounded the Cape.*
round on someone = attack, abuse, turn on, retaliate against, have a go at (*Brit. slang*), snap at, wade into, lose your temper with, bite (someone's) head off (*informal*): *He has rounded on his critics.*
round something off = complete, close, settle, crown, cap, conclude, finish off, put the finishing touch to, bring to a close: *A fireworks display rounded off the day.*
round something *or* **someone up = gather**, assemble, bring together, muster, group, drive, collect, rally, herd, marshal: *The police rounded up a number of suspects.*

roundabout ADJECTIVE **1 = indirect**, meandering, devious, tortuous, circuitous, evasive, discursive, circumlocutory: *a roundabout route* **OPPOSITE:** direct **2 = oblique**, implied, indirect, evasive, circuitous, circumlocutory, periphrastic: *indirect or roundabout language*

roundly ADVERB **= thoroughly**, sharply, severely, bitterly, fiercely, bluntly, intensely, violently, vehemently, rigorously, outspokenly, frankly

roundup NOUN **1 = summary**, survey, collation: *a roundup of the day's news* **2 = muster**, collection, rally, assembly, herding: *What keeps a cowboy ready for another roundup?*

rouse VERB **1 = wake up**, call, wake, awaken: *She roused him at 8.30.* **2 = excite**, move, arouse, stir, disturb, provoke, anger, startle, animate, prod, exhilarate, get going, agitate, inflame, incite, whip up, galvanize, bestir: *He did more to rouse the crowd than anybody else.* **3 = stimulate**, provoke, arouse, incite, instigate: *It roused a feeling of rebellion in him.*

rousing ADJECTIVE **= lively**, moving, spirited, exciting, inspiring, stirring, stimulating, vigorous, brisk, exhilarating, inflammatory, electrifying **OPPOSITE:** dull

rout VERB **= defeat**, beat, overthrow, thrash, stuff (*slang*), worst, destroy, chase, tank (*slang*), crush, scatter, conquer, lick (*informal*), dispel, drive off, overpower, clobber (*slang*), wipe the floor with (*informal*), cut to pieces, put to flight, drub, put to rout, throw back in confusion: *The Norman army routed the English opposition.*
▷ NOUN **= defeat**, beating, hiding (*informal*), ruin, overthrow, thrashing, licking (*informal*), pasting (*slang*), shambles, debacle, drubbing, overwhelming defeat, headlong flight, disorderly retreat: *The retreat turned into a rout.*

route NOUN **1 = way**, course, road, direction, path, journey, passage, avenue, itinerary: *the most direct route to the town centre* **2 = beat**, run, round, circuit: *They would go out on his route and check him.*
▷ VERB **1 = direct**, lead, guide, steer, convey: *Approaching cars will be routed into two lanes.* **2 = send**, forward, dispatch: *plans to route every emergency call through three exchanges*

USAGE
When adding *-ing* to the verb *route* to form the present participle, it is more conventional, and clearer, to keep the final *e* from the end of the

verb stem: *routeing*. The spelling *routing* in this sense is also possible, but keeping the *e* distinguishes it from *routing*, which is the participle formed from the verb *rout* meaning 'to defeat'.

routine NOUN **1 = procedure**, programme, way, order, practice, method, pattern, formula, custom, usage, wont, lockstep (*U.S. & Canad.*): *The players had to change their daily routine.* **2 = grind** (*informal*), monotony, banality, groove, boredom, chore, the doldrums, dullness, sameness, ennui, drabness, deadness, dreariness, tediousness, lifelessness: *the mundane routine of her life*
▷ ADJECTIVE **1 = usual**, standard, normal, customary, ordinary, familiar, typical, conventional, everyday, habitual, workaday, wonted: *a series of routine medical tests* **OPPOSITE:** unusual **2 = boring**, dull, predictable, tedious, tiresome, run-of-the-mill, humdrum, unimaginative, clichéd, uninspired, mind-numbing, hackneyed, unoriginal: *So many days are routine and uninteresting.*

rove VERB **= wander**, range, cruise, drift, stroll, stray, roam, ramble, meander, traipse (*informal*), gallivant, gad about, stravaig (*Scot. & Northern English dialect*)

rover NOUN **= wanderer**, traveller, gypsy, rolling stone, rambler, transient, nomad, itinerant, ranger, drifter, vagrant, stroller, bird of passage, gadabout (*informal*)

row[1] NOUN **= line**, bank, range, series, file, rank, string, column, sequence, queue, tier: *a row of pretty little cottages*
in a row = consecutively, running, in turn, one after the other, successively, in sequence: *They have won five championships in a row.*

row[2] NOUN **1 = quarrel**, dispute, argument, squabble, tiff, trouble, controversy, scrap (*informal*), fuss, falling-out (*informal*), fray, brawl, fracas, altercation, slanging match (*Brit.*), shouting match (*informal*), shindig (*informal*), ruction (*informal*), ruckus (*informal*), shindy (*informal*), bagarre (*French*): *A man was stabbed to death in a family row.* **2 = disturbance**, noise, racket, uproar, commotion, rumpus, tumult: *'Whatever is that row?' she demanded.* **3 = telling-off**, talking-to (*informal*), lecture, reprimand, ticking-off (*informal*), dressing-down (*informal*), rollicking (*Brit. informal*), tongue-lashing, reproof, castigation, flea in your ear (*informal*): *I can't give you a row for scarpering off.*
▷ VERB **= quarrel**, fight, argue, dispute, scrap (*informal*), brawl, squabble, spar, wrangle, go at it hammer and tongs: *They rowed all the time.*

rowdy ADJECTIVE **= disorderly**, rough, loud, noisy, unruly, boisterous, loutish, wild, uproarious, obstreperous: *He has complained about rowdy neighbours.* **OPPOSITE:** orderly
▷ NOUN **= hooligan**, tough, rough (*informal*), casual, ned (*Scot. slang*), brawler, yahoo, lout, troublemaker, tearaway (*Brit.*), ruffian, lager lout, yob *or* yobbo (*Brit. slang*), cougan (*Austral. slang*), scozza (*Austral. slang*), bogan (*Austral. slang*): *The owner kept a baseball bat to deal with rowdies.*

royal ADJECTIVE **1 = regal**, kingly *or* queenly, princely, imperial, sovereign, monarchical, kinglike *or* queenlike: *an invitation to a royal garden party* **2 = splendid**, august, grand, impressive, superb, magnificent, superior, majestic, stately: *She was given a royal welcome on her first visit to Britain.*

rub VERB **1 = stroke**, smooth, massage, caress, knead: *He rubbed his arms and stiff legs.* **2 = polish**, clean, shine, wipe, scour: *She took off her glasses and rubbed them.* **3 = spread**, put, apply, smear: *He rubbed oil into my aching back.* **4 = chafe**, scrape, grate, abrade: *Smear cream on to prevent it from rubbing.*
▷ NOUN **1 = massage**, caress, kneading: *She sometimes asks if I want a back rub.* **2 = polish**, stroke, shine, wipe: *Give them a rub with a clean, dry cloth.*
rub something out = erase, remove, cancel, wipe out, excise, delete, obliterate, efface, expunge: *She began rubbing out the pencilled marks.*
the rub = difficulty, problem, catch, trouble, obstacle, hazard, hitch, drawback, snag, uphill (*S. African*), impediment, hindrance: *And therein lies the rub.*

rubbish NOUN **1 = waste**, refuse, scrap, junk (*informal*), litter, debris, crap (*slang*), garbage (*chiefly U.S.*), trash, lumber, offal, dross, dregs, flotsam and jetsam, grot (*slang*), dreck (*slang, chiefly U.S.*), offscourings: *unwanted household rubbish*
2 = nonsense, garbage (*chiefly U.S.*), drivel, malarkey, twaddle, pants (*slang*), rot, crap (*slang*), trash, hot air (*informal*), tosh (*slang, chiefly Brit.*), pap, bilge (*informal*), tripe (*informal*), gibberish, guff (*slang*), havers (*Scot.*), moonshine, claptrap (*informal*), hogwash, hokum (*slang, chiefly U.S. & Canad.*), codswallop (*Brit. slang*), piffle (*informal*), poppycock (*informal*), balderdash, bosh (*informal*), wack (*U.S. slang*), eyewash (*informal*), stuff and nonsense, flapdoodle (*slang*), tommyrot, horsefeathers (*U.S. slang*), bunkum *or* buncombe (*chiefly U.S.*), bizzo (*Austral. slang*), bull's wool (*Austral. & N.Z. slang*): *He's talking rubbish.*

ruddy ADJECTIVE **1 = rosy**, red, fresh, healthy, glowing, blooming, flushed, blushing, radiant, reddish, sanguine, florid, sunburnt, rosy-cheeked, rubicund: *He had a naturally ruddy complexion.* **OPPOSITE:** pale **2 = red**, pink, scarlet, ruby, crimson, reddish, roseate: *barges, with their sails ruddy brown*

rude ADJECTIVE **1 = impolite**, insulting, cheeky, abrupt, short, blunt, abusive, curt, churlish, disrespectful, brusque, offhand, impertinent, insolent, inconsiderate, peremptory, impudent, discourteous, uncivil, unmannerly, ill-mannered: *He's rude to her friends.* **OPPOSITE:** polite
2 = uncivilized, low, rough, savage, ignorant, coarse, illiterate, uneducated, brutish, barbarous, scurrilous, boorish, uncouth, unrefined, loutish, untutored, graceless, ungracious, unpolished, oafish, uncultured: *a rude barbarian*
3 = vulgar, gross, crude: *He made a rude gesture with his finger.* **OPPOSITE:** refined
4 = unpleasant, sharp, violent, sudden, harsh, startling, abrupt: *It came as a rude shock.* **5 = roughly-made**, simple, rough, raw, crude, primitive, makeshift, rough-hewn, artless, inelegant, inartistic: *He had already constructed a rude cabin.*
OPPOSITE: well-made

rudiment NOUN (*often plural*) **= basics**, elements, essentials, fundamentals, beginnings, foundation, nuts and bolts, first principles

rudimentary ADJECTIVE
1 = primitive, undeveloped: *It had been extended into a kind of rudimentary kitchen.* **2 = basic**, fundamental, elementary, early, primary, initial, introductory: *He had only a rudimentary knowledge of French.* **3 = undeveloped**, embryonic, vestigial: *a rudimentary backbone called a notochord* **OPPOSITE:** complete

rue VERB **= regret**, mourn, grieve, lament, deplore, bemoan, repent, be sorry for, weep over, sorrow for, bewail, kick yourself for, reproach yourself for

rueful ADJECTIVE **= regretful**, sad, dismal, melancholy, grievous, pitiful, woeful, sorry, mournful, plaintive, lugubrious, contrite, sorrowful, repentant, doleful, remorseful, penitent, pitiable, woebegone, conscience-stricken, self-reproachful
OPPOSITE: unrepentant

ruffle VERB **1 = disarrange**, disorder, wrinkle, mess up, rumple, tousle, derange, discompose, dishevel, muss (*U.S. & Canad.*): *She let the wind ruffle her hair.* **2 = annoy**, worry, trouble, upset, confuse, stir, disturb, rattle (*informal*), irritate, put out, unsettle, shake up (*informal*), harass, hassle (*informal*), agitate, unnerve, disconcert, disquiet, nettle, vex, fluster, perturb, faze, peeve (*informal*), hack off (*informal*): *My refusal to let him ruffle me infuriated him.*
OPPOSITE: calm

rugged ADJECTIVE **1 = rocky**, broken, rough, craggy, difficult, ragged, stark, irregular, uneven, jagged, bumpy: *a rugged mountainous terrain*
OPPOSITE: even **2 = strong-featured**, lined, worn, weathered, wrinkled, furrowed, leathery, rough-hewn, weather-beaten: *A look of disbelief crossed his rugged face.* **OPPOSITE:** delicate

r

Henry James's Use of Adjectives

Henry James uses adjectives profusely: in the following passage from *What Maisie Knew*, every noun, except one, is qualified by an adjective - and sometimes by two. Maisie's fear is strongly conveyed by the repetition of *frightening* - a word a child would use - while the more literary adjectives *unenlivened* and *invidious* convey the detached narrator's ironic, adult view of the situation. The final adjective - *very* - contributes little to the sense, but is important to the rhythm of the sentence, as James's adjectives often are:

> ... there was only a frightening silence, unenlivened even by the invidious enquiries of former years, which culminated, according to its stern nature, in a still more frightening old woman, a figure awaiting her on the very doorstep.

In this novel authorial detachment is also to be seen in James's references to Maisie as *our young lady*. Instances of this literary use of the possessive, such as *our narrative*; *our hero*, are found throughout James's writing. The effect is slightly jocular; we are distanced from the action by this reminder that we are reading a book;

> a lady ... paused there and looked very hard at **our heroine**.

Many of the adjectives that occur most frequently in James's novels and stories are ones that express feelings, very often feelings about people - words such as *charming, beautiful, extraordinary, wonderful, pretty, handsome, pleasant*. James uses *charming* somewhat more than *beautiful*, and very much more than Anglo-Saxon words such as *pretty* and *lovely*. He uses it much more frequently than any adjective of colour, and the word occurs much more often in his writing than it does in that of other English writers. This may well be because of 'the inveterate habit of French' in James's writing that was noted by the editor of *The Atlantic Monthly*, which published his first stories. When James wrote *charming*, he might have been thinking *charmant*. The French element in his English is very much more noticeable than any influence of his American origins.

Two other adjectives that show his tendency to gallicism are *large* and *immense*. James uses *large* in its common English sense of 'big', with nouns such as *house, room, size, amount*. He also, however, often uses it in its French sense of 'wide', with nouns such as *road, experience, opportunities, freedom*. A person covers another *with his large look*; another shakes his head *with large loose bitterness*. Similarly, James uses *immense* in its normal meaning of 'huge' with nouns such as *theatre, hotel, array, charm*. In French the word can also be applied to people who are outstanding, and James sometimes adopts that usage:

> 'She's the sweetest little thing I've ever seen.'
> 'She's certainly **immense**. I mean she's the real thing.'

James's characters are acutely self-aware, and keenly observant of others: *conscious* and *aware* are adjectives that occur frequently. James uses the phrases *become aware*, and *become conscious* much oftener when tracing the growth of understanding than he does the verb *'realize'*, which in the 19th century was generally used with objects such as *profit* or *project* - George Eliot, for example, never uses the word to mean 'understand'. Used to modify nouns, *conscious* has several meanings in James's writing: 'deliberate', as in *conscious purpose*; 'self-conscious', as in *conscious blush*; 'self-aware', as in *her charming, conscious, coquettish little face*. At times the word is strongly positive; it describes the possession of a fine sensitivity to the feelings of others that is so important in James's novels:

> Her eyes met his, in which it seemed to her that as well as in his voice there was **conscious** sympathy, entreaty, vindication, tenderness.

3 = well-built, strong, tough, robust, sturdy: *this rugged all-steel design* **4 = tough**, strong, hardy, robust, vigorous, muscular, sturdy, hale, burly, husky *(informal)*, beefy *(informal)*, brawny: *He's rugged and durable, but not the best technical boxer.* **OPPOSITE:** delicate **5 = stern**, hard, severe, rough, harsh, sour, rude, crabbed, austere, dour, surly, gruff: *a fairly rugged customer*

ruin VERB **1 = destroy**, devastate, wreck, trash *(slang)*, break, total *(slang)*, defeat, smash, crush, overwhelm, shatter, overturn, overthrow, bring down, demolish, raze, lay waste, lay in ruins, wreak havoc upon, bring to ruin, bring to nothing, kennet *(Austral. slang)*, jeff *(Austral. slang)*: *Roads have been destroyed and crops ruined.* **OPPOSITE:** create **2 = bankrupt**, break, impoverish, beggar, pauperize: *She accused him of ruining her financially.* **3 = spoil**, damage, mar, mess up, blow *(slang)*, injure, undo, screw up *(informal)*, botch, mangle, cock up *(Brit. slang)*, disfigure, make a mess of, bodge *(informal)*, crool or cruel *(Austral. slang)*: *The original decor was all ruined during renovation.* **OPPOSITE:** improve
▷ NOUN **1 = bankruptcy**, insolvency, destitution: *Recent inflation has driven them to the brink of ruin.* **2 = disrepair**, decay, disintegration, ruination, wreckage: *The vineyards were falling into ruin.* **3 = destruction**, fall, the end, breakdown, damage, defeat, failure, crash, collapse, wreck, overthrow, undoing, havoc, Waterloo, downfall, devastation, dissolution, subversion, nemesis, crackup *(informal)*: *It is the ruin of society.* **OPPOSITE:** preservation

r

ruinous ADJECTIVE **1 = destructive**, devastating, shattering, fatal, deadly, disastrous, dire, withering, catastrophic, murderous, pernicious, noxious, calamitous, baleful, deleterious, injurious, baneful *(archaic)*: *the ruinous effects of the conflict* **2 = ruined**, broken-down, derelict, ramshackle, dilapidated, in ruins, decrepit: *They passed by the ruinous building.*

rule NOUN **1 = regulation**, order, law, ruling, guide, direction, guideline, decree, ordinance, dictum: *the rule against retrospective prosecution* **2 = precept**, principle, criterion, canon, maxim, tenet, axiom: *An important rule is to drink plenty of water.* **3 = procedure**, policy, standard, method, way, course, formula: *according to the rules of quantum theory* **4 = custom**, procedure, practice, routine, form, condition, tradition, habit, convention, wont, order or way of things: *The usual rule is to start as one group.* **5 = government**, power, control, authority, influence, administration, direction, leadership, command, regime, empire, reign, sway, domination, jurisdiction, supremacy, mastery, dominion, ascendancy, mana *(N.Z.)*: *the winding-up of British rule over the territory*
▷ VERB **1 = govern**, lead, control, manage, direct, guide, regulate, administer, oversee, preside over, have power over, reign over, command over, have charge of: *the feudal lord who ruled this land* **2 = reign**, govern, be in power, hold sway, wear the crown, be in authority, be number one *(informal)*: *He ruled for eight years.* **3 = control**, dominate, monopolize, tyrannize, be pre-eminent, have the upper hand over: *Fear can rule our lives.* **4 = decree**, find, decide, judge, establish, determine, settle, resolve, pronounce, lay down, adjudge: *The court ruled that laws passed by the assembly remained valid.* **5 = be prevalent**, prevail, predominate, hold sway, be customary, preponderate, obtain: *A ferocious form of anarchy ruled here.*
as a rule = usually, generally, mainly, normally, on the whole, for the most part, ordinarily, customarily: *As a rule, these tourists take far too many souvenirs with them.*
rule someone out = exclude, eliminate, disqualify, ban, prevent, reject, dismiss, forbid, prohibit, leave out, preclude, proscribe, obviate, debar: *a suspension which ruled him out of the grand final*
rule something out = reject, exclude, eliminate: *Local detectives have ruled out foul play.*

> **QUOTATIONS**
> He shall rule them with a rod of iron
> [*Bible: Revelation*]
>
> My people and I have come to an agreement which satisfies us both. They are to say what they please, and I am to do what I please
> [Frederick the Great]
>
> The hand that rocks the cradle
> Is the hand that rules the world
> [William Ross Wallace *John O'London's Treasure Trove*]
>
> Rules and models destroy genius and art
> [William Hazlitt *Sketches and Essays*]

ruler NOUN **1 = governor**, leader, lord, commander, controller, monarch, sovereign, head of state, potentate, crowned head, emperor or empress, king or queen, prince or princess: *He was an indecisive ruler.* **2 = measure**, rule, yardstick, straight edge: *taking measurements with a ruler*

ruling ADJECTIVE **1 = governing**, upper, reigning, controlling, leading, commanding, dominant, regnant: *the domination of the ruling class* **2 = predominant**, dominant, prevailing, preponderant, chief, main, current, supreme, principal, prevalent, pre-eminent, regnant: *a ruling passion for liberty and equality* **OPPOSITE:** minor
▷ NOUN **= decision**, finding, resolution, verdict, judgment, decree, adjudication, pronouncement: *He tried to have the court ruling overturned.*

rum ADJECTIVE **= strange**, odd, suspect, funny, unusual, curious, weird, suspicious, peculiar, dodgy *(Brit., Austral. & N.Z. informal)*, queer, singular, shonky *(Austral. & N.Z. informal)*

ruminate VERB **= ponder**, think, consider, reflect, contemplate, deliberate, muse, brood, meditate, mull over things, chew over things, cogitate, rack your brains, turn over in your mind

rummage VERB **= search**, hunt, root, explore, delve, examine, ransack, forage, fossick *(Austral. & N.Z.)*, rootle

rumour NOUN **= story**, news, report, talk, word, whisper, buzz, gossip, dirt *(U.S. slang)*, goss *(informal)*, hearsay, canard, tidings, scuttlebutt *(U.S. slang)*, bush telegraph, bruit *(archaic)*: *There's a strange rumour going around.*
be rumoured = be said, be told, be reported, be published, be circulated, be whispered, be passed around, be put about, be noised abroad: *It was rumoured that he'd been interned in an asylum.*

rump NOUN **= buttocks**, bottom, rear, backside *(informal)*, tail *(informal)*, seat, butt *(U.S. & Canad. informal)*, bum *(Brit. slang)*, buns *(U.S. slang)*, rear end, posterior, haunch, hindquarters, derrière *(euphemistic)*, croup, jacksy *(Brit. slang)*

rumple VERB **= ruffle**, crush, disorder, dishevel, wrinkle, crease, crumple, screw up, mess up, pucker, crinkle, scrunch, tousle, derange, muss *(U.S. & Canad.)*

rumpus NOUN **= commotion**, row, noise, confusion, fuss, disturbance, disruption, furore, uproar, tumult, brouhaha, shindig *(informal)*, hue and cry, kerfuffle *(informal)*, shindy *(informal)*

run VERB **1 = race**, speed, rush, dash, hurry, career, barrel (along) *(informal, chiefly U.S. & Canad.)*, sprint, scramble, bolt, dart, gallop, hare *(Brit. informal)*, jog, scud, hasten, scurry, stampede, scamper, leg it *(informal)*, lope, hie, hotfoot: *I excused myself and ran back to the telephone.* **OPPOSITE:** dawdle **2 = flee**, escape, take off *(informal)*, depart, bolt, clear out, beat it *(slang)*, leg it *(informal)*, make off, abscond, decamp, take flight, do a runner *(slang)*, scarper *(Brit. slang)*, slope off, cut and run *(informal)*, make a run for it, fly the coop *(U.S. & Canad. informal)*, beat a retreat, show a clean pair of heels, skedaddle *(informal)*, take a powder *(U.S. & Canad. slang)*, take it on the lam *(U.S. & Canad. slang)*, take to your heels: *As they closed in on him, he turned and ran.* **OPPOSITE:** stay **3 = take part**, compete: *I was running in the marathon.* **4 = continue**, go, stretch, last, reach, lie, range, extend, proceed: *the trail which ran through the*

beech woods **OPPOSITE:** stop
5 = compete, stand, contend, be a candidate, put yourself up for, take part, challenge, re-offer (*Canad. politics*): *He announced he would run for president.* **6 = manage**, lead, direct, be in charge of, own, head, control, boss (*informal*), operate, handle, conduct, look after, carry on, regulate, take care of, administer, oversee, supervise, mastermind, coordinate, superintend: *His father ran a prosperous business.* **7 = go**, work, operate, perform, function, be in business, be in action, tick over: *the staff who have kept the bank running* **8 = perform**, carry out: *He ran a lot of tests.* **9 = work**, go, operate, function: *The tape recorder was still running.* **10 = drive**: *I ran a 1960 Rover 100.* **11 = operate**, go: *A shuttle bus runs frequently.* **12 = give a lift to**, drive, carry, transport, convey, bear, manoeuvre, propel: *Can you run me to work?* **13 = pass**, go, move, roll, slide, glide, skim: *He winced as he ran his hand over his ribs.* **14 = flow**, pour, stream, cascade, go, move, issue, proceed, leak, spill, discharge, gush, spout, course: *cisterns to catch rainwater as it ran off the walls* **15 = spread**, mix, bleed, be diffused, lose colour: *The ink had run on the wet paper.* **16 = circulate**, spread, creep, go round: *A buzz of excitement ran through the crowd.* **17 = publish**, feature, display, print: *The paper ran a series of scathing editorials.* **18 = melt**, dissolve, liquefy, go soft, turn to liquid: *The pitch between the planks of the deck melted and ran.* **19 = unravel**, tear, ladder, come apart, come undone: *ladders in your tights gradually running all the way up your leg* **20 = smuggle**, deal in, traffic in, bootleg, ship, sneak: *I started running guns again.*
▷ NOUN **1 = race**, rush, dash, sprint, gallop, jog, spurt: *a six mile run* **2 = ride**, drive, trip, lift, journey, spin (*informal*), outing, excursion, jaunt, joy ride (*informal*): *Take them for a run in the car.* **3 = sequence**, period, stretch, spell, course, season, round, series, chain, cycle, string, passage, streak: *Their run of luck is holding.* **4 = type**, sort, kind, class, variety, category, order: *outside the common run of professional athletes* **5 = tear**, rip, ladder, snag: *She had a huge run in her tights.* **6 = enclosure**, pen, coop: *My mother had a little chicken run.* **7 = direction**, way, course, current, movement, progress, flow, path, trend, motion, passage, stream, tendency, drift, tide, tenor: *The only try came against the run of play.* **8** (with **on**) **= sudden demand for**, pressure for, rush for: *A run on sterling has killed hopes of a rate cut.*
in the long run = in the end, eventually, in time, ultimately, at the end of the day, in the final analysis, when all is said and done, in the fullness of time: *Things could get worse in the long run.*
on the run 1 = escaping, fugitive, in flight, at liberty, on the loose, on the lam (*U.S. & Canad. slang*): *The four men still on the run are Rule 43 prisoners.* **2 = in retreat**, defeated, fleeing, retreating, running away, falling back, in flight: *I knew I had him on the run.* **3 = hurrying**, hastily, in a hurry, at speed, hurriedly, in a rush, in haste: *We ate lunch on the run.*
run across something *or* **someone = meet**, encounter, meet with, come across, run into, bump into, come upon, chance upon: *We ran across some old friends.*
run away = flee, escape, take off, bolt, run off, clear out, beat it (*slang*), abscond, decamp, take flight, hook it (*slang*), do a runner (*slang*), scarper (*Brit. slang*), cut and run (*informal*), make a run for it, turn tail, do a bunk (*Brit. slang*), scram (*informal*), fly the coop (*U.S. & Canad. informal*), show a clean pair of heels, skedaddle (*informal*), take a powder (*U.S. & Canad. slang*), take it on the lam (*U.S. & Canad. slang*), take to your heels, do a Skase (*Austral. informal*): *I ran away from home when I was sixteen.*
run away with something *or* **someone 1 = abscond with**, run off with, elope with: *She ran away with a man called Allen.* **2 = win easily**, walk it (*informal*), romp home, win hands down, win by a mile (*informal*): *She ran away with the gold medal.*
run into someone = meet, encounter, bump into, run across, chance upon, come across *or* upon: *He ran into him in the corridor.*
run into something 1 = be beset by, encounter, meet with, come across *or* upon, face, experience, be confronted by, happen on *or* upon: *They ran into financial problems.* **2 = collide with**, hit, strike, ram, bump into, crash into, dash against: *The driver ran into a tree.*
run off = flee, escape, bolt, run away, clear out, make off, decamp, take flight, hook it (*slang*), do a runner (*slang*), scarper (*Brit. slang*), cut and run (*informal*), turn tail, fly the coop (*U.S. & Canad. informal*), show a clean pair of heels, skedaddle (*informal*), take a powder (*U.S. & Canad. slang*), take it on the lam (*U.S. & Canad. slang*), take to your heels: *He then ran off towards a nearby underground railway station.*
run off with someone = run away with, elope with, abscond with: *He ran off with a younger woman.*
run off with something = steal, take, lift (*informal*), nick (*slang, chiefly Brit.*), pinch (*informal*), swipe (*slang*), run away with, make off with, embezzle, misappropriate, purloin, filch, walk *or* make off with: *Who ran off with the money?*
run out 1 = be used up, dry up, give out, peter out, fail, finish, cease, be exhausted: *Supplies are running out.* **2 = expire**, end, terminate: *the day my visa ran out*
run out of something = exhaust your supply of, be out of, be cleaned out, have no more, have none left, have no remaining: *The plane ran out of fuel.*
run out on someone = desert, abandon, strand, run away from, forsake, rat on (*informal*), leave high and dry, leave holding the baby, leave in the lurch: *You can't run out on your wife and children like that.*
run over = overflow, spill over, brim over: *Water ran over the sides and trickled down on to the floor.*
run over something 1 = exceed, overstep, go over the top of, go beyond the bounds of, go over the limit of: *Phase one has run over budget.* **2 = review**, check, survey, examine, go through, go over, run through, rehearse, reiterate: *Let's run over the instructions again.*
run over something *or* **someone = knock down**, hit, strike, run down, knock over: *He ran over a six-year-old child.*
run someone in = arrest, apprehend, pull in (*Brit. slang*), take into custody, lift (*slang*), pick up, jail, nail (*informal*), bust (*informal*), collar (*informal*), pinch (*informal*), nab (*informal*), throw in jail, take to jail, feel your collar (*slang*): *They had run him in on a petty charge.*
run something in = break in gently, run gently: *He hardly had the time to run the car in.*
run something off = produce, print, duplicate, churn out (*informal*): *They ran off some copies for me.*
run something *or* **someone down 1 = criticize**, denigrate, belittle, revile, knock (*informal*), rubbish (*informal*), put down, slag (off) (*slang*), disparage, decry, vilify, diss (*slang, chiefly U.S.*), defame, bad-mouth (*slang, chiefly U.S. & Canad.*), speak ill of, asperse: *He was running down state schools.* **2 = downsize**, cut, drop, reduce, trim, decrease, cut back, curtail, pare down, kennet (*Austral. slang*), jeff (*Austral. slang*): *The property business could be sold or run down.* **3 = knock down**, hit, strike, run into, run over, knock over: *He was in the roadway and I nearly ran him down.*
run through something 1 = review, check, survey, examine, go through, look over, run over: *I ran through the options with him.* **2 = rehearse**, read, practise, go over, run over: *I ran through the handover procedure.* **3 = squander**, waste, exhaust, throw away, dissipate, fritter away, spend like water, blow (*slang*): *The country had run through its public food stocks.*

runaway ADJECTIVE **1 = easily won**, easy, effortless: *a runaway success* **2 = out of control**, uncontrolled: *The runaway car careered into a bench.* **3 = escaped**, wild, fleeing, loose, fugitive: *a runaway horse*
▷ NOUN **= fugitive**, escaper, refugee, deserter, truant, escapee, absconder: *a teenage runaway*

rundown *or* **run-down** ADJECTIVE **1 = exhausted**, weak, tired, drained, fatigued, weary, unhealthy, worn-out, debilitated, below par, under the weather (*informal*), enervated, out of condition, peaky: *She started to feel rundown last December.* **OPPOSITE:** fit

2 = dilapidated, broken-down, shabby, worn-out, seedy, ramshackle, dingy, decrepit, tumbledown: *a rundown block of flats*
▷ NOUN **= summary**, review, briefing, résumé, outline, sketch, run-through, synopsis, recap *(informal)*, précis: *Here's a rundown of the options*

run-in **= fight**, row, argument, dispute, set-to *(informal)*, encounter, brush, confrontation, quarrel, skirmish, tussle, altercation, face-off *(slang)*, dust-up *(informal)*, contretemps, biffo *(Austral. slang)*

runner NOUN **1 = athlete**, miler, sprinter, harrier, jogger: *a marathon runner* **2 = messenger**, courier, errand boy, dispatch bearer: *a bookie's runner* **3 = stem**, shoot, sprout, sprig, offshoot, tendril, stolon *(Botany)*: *strawberry runners*

running NOUN **1 = management**, control, administration, direction, conduct, charge, leadership, organization, regulation, supervision, coordination, superintendency: *in charge of the day-to-day running of the party* **2 = working**, performance, operation, functioning, maintenance: *the smooth running of the machine*
▷ ADJECTIVE **1 = continuous**, constant, perpetual, uninterrupted, incessant, unceasing: *The song turned into a running joke between them.* **2 = in succession**, together, unbroken, on the trot *(informal)*: *She never seems the same woman two days running.* **3 = flowing**, moving, streaming, coursing: *Wash the lentils under cold, running water.*

runny ADJECTIVE **= flowing**, liquid, melted, fluid, diluted, watery, streaming, liquefied

run-of-the-mill ADJECTIVE **= ordinary**, middling, average, fair, modest, commonplace, common, vanilla *(informal)*, mediocre, banal, tolerable, passable, undistinguished, unimpressive, unexciting, unexceptional, bog-standard *(Brit. & Irish slang)*, no great shakes *(informal)*, dime-a-dozen *(informal)*
OPPOSITE: exceptional

run-up NOUN **= time leading up to**, approach, build-up, preliminaries

rupture NOUN **1 = hernia** *(Medical)*: *a rupture of the abdominal aorta* **2 = breach**, split, hostility, falling-out *(informal)*, disagreement, contention, feud, disruption, quarrel, rift, break, bust-up *(informal)*, dissolution, altercation, schism, estrangement: *a major rupture between the two countries* **3 = break**, tear, split, crack, rent, burst, breach, fracture, cleavage, cleft, fissure: *ruptures in a 60-mile pipeline on the island*
▷ VERB **1 = break**, separate, tear, split, crack, burst, rend, fracture, sever, puncture, cleave: *Tanks can rupture and burn in a collision.* **2 = cause a breach**, split, divide, disrupt, break off, come between, dissever: *an accident which ruptured the bond between them*

rural ADJECTIVE **1 = agricultural**, country, agrarian, upcountry, agrestic: *These plants grow in the more rural areas.* **2 = rustic**, country, hick *(informal, chiefly U.S. & Canad.)*, pastoral, bucolic, sylvan, Arcadian, countrified: *the old rural way of life*
OPPOSITE: urban

ruse NOUN **= trick**, deception, ploy, hoax, device, manoeuvre, dodge, sham, artifice, blind, subterfuge, stratagem, wile, imposture

rush VERB **1 = hurry**, run, race, shoot, fly, career, speed, tear, dash, sprint, scramble, bolt, dart, hasten, scurry, stampede, lose no time, make short work of, burn rubber *(informal)*, make haste, hotfoot: *Someone inside the building rushed out.* **OPPOSITE:** dawdle **2 = push**, hurry, accelerate, dispatch, speed up, quicken, press, hustle, expedite: *The Act was rushed through after a legal loophole was discovered.* **3 = attack**, storm, capture, overcome, charge at, take by storm: *They rushed the entrance.*
▷ NOUN **1 = dash**, charge, race, scramble, stampede, expedition, speed, dispatch: *The explosion caused panic and a mad rush for the doors.* **2 = hurry**, urgency, bustle, haste, hustle, helter-skelter, hastiness: *the rush not to be late for school* **3 = surge**, flow, gush: *A rush of affection swept over him.* **4 = attack**, charge, push, storm, assault, surge, onslaught: *Throw something noisy and feign a rush at him.*
▷ ADJECTIVE **= hasty**, fast, quick, hurried, emergency, prompt, rapid, urgent, swift, brisk, cursory, expeditious: *I guess you could call it a rush job.* **OPPOSITE:** leisurely

rust NOUN **1 = corrosion**, oxidation: *a decaying tractor, red with rust* **2 = mildew**, must, mould, rot, blight: *canker, rust, mildew or insect attack*
▷ VERB **1 = corrode**, tarnish, oxidize: *The bolt on the door had rusted* **2 = deteriorate**, decline, decay, stagnate, atrophy, go stale: *If you rest, you rust.*

rustic ADJECTIVE **1 = rural**, country, pastoral, bucolic, sylvan, Arcadian, countrified, upcountry, agrestic: *the rustic charms of a country lifestyle*
OPPOSITE: urban **2 = simple**, homely, plain, homespun, unsophisticated, unrefined, artless, unpolished: *wonderfully rustic old log cabins*
OPPOSITE: grand
▷ NOUN **= yokel**, peasant, hick *(informal, chiefly U.S. & Canad.)*, bumpkin, swain *(archaic)*, hillbilly, country boy, clod, boor, country cousin, hayseed *(U.S. & Canad. informal)*, clodhopper *(informal)*, son of the soil, clown, countryman *or* countrywoman: *rustics in from the country* **OPPOSITE:** sophisticate

rustle VERB **= crackle**, whisper, swish, whoosh, crinkle, whish, crepitate, susurrate *(literary)*: *The leaves rustled in the wind.*
▷ NOUN **= crackle**, whisper, rustling, crinkling, crepitation, susurration *or* susurrus *(literary)*: *with a rustle of her frilled petticoats*

rusty ADJECTIVE **1 = corroded**, rusted, oxidized, rust-covered: *travelling around in a rusty old van* **2 = out of practice**, weak, impaired, sluggish, stale, deficient, not what it was, unpractised: *Your French is a bit rusty.* **3 = reddish-brown**, chestnut, reddish, russet, coppery, rust-coloured: *Her hair was rusty brown.* **4 = croaking**, cracked, creaking, hoarse, croaky: *his mild, rusty voice*

rut NOUN **1 = habit**, routine, dead end, humdrum existence, system, pattern, groove: *I don't like being in a rut.* **2 = groove**, score, track, trough, furrow, gouge, pothole, indentation, wheel mark: *deep ruts left by the truck's heavy wheels*

ruthless ADJECTIVE **= merciless**, hard, severe, fierce, harsh, cruel, savage, brutal, stern, relentless, adamant, ferocious, callous, heartless, unrelenting, inhuman, inexorable, remorseless, barbarous, pitiless, unfeeling, hard-hearted, without pity, unmerciful, unpitying
OPPOSITE: merciful

rutted ADJECTIVE **= grooved**, cut, marked, scored, holed, furrowed, gouged, indented

Ss

sable ADJECTIVE **1 = black**, jet, raven, jetty, ebony, ebon *(poetic)*: *thick sable lashes* **2 = dark**, black, dim, gloomy, dismal, dreary, sombre, shadowy: *Night enveloped me in its sable mantle.*

sabotage VERB **1 = damage**, destroy, wreck, undermine, disable, disrupt, cripple, subvert, incapacitate, vandalize, throw a spanner in the works *(Brit. informal)*: *The main pipeline was sabotaged by rebels.* **2 = disrupt**, ruin, wreck, spoil, interrupt, interfere with, obstruct, intrude, crool *or* cruel *(Austral. slang)*: *My ex-wife deliberately sabotages my access to the children.*
▷ NOUN **1 = damage**, destruction, wrecking, vandalism, deliberate damage: *The bombing was a spectacular act of sabotage.* **2 = disruption**, ruining, wrecking, spoiling, interference, intrusion, interruption, obstruction: *political sabotage of government policy*

saboteur NOUN **= demonstrator**, rebel, dissident, hooligan, vandal, delinquent, dissenter, agitator, protest marcher

sac NOUN **= pouch**, bag, pocket, bladder, pod, cyst, vesicle

saccharine ADJECTIVE **= sickly**, honeyed, sentimental, sugary, nauseating, soppy *(Brit. informal)*, cloying, maudlin, syrupy *(informal)*, mawkish, icky *(informal)*, treacly, oversweet

sack[1] NOUN **= bag**, pocket, poke *(Scot.)*, sac, pouch, receptacle: *a sack of potatoes*
▷ VERB **= dismiss**, fire *(informal)*, axe *(informal)*, discharge, kick out *(informal)*, give (someone) the boot *(slang)*, give (someone) his marching orders, kiss off *(slang, chiefly U.S. & Canad.)*, give (someone) the push *(informal)*, give (someone) the bullet *(Brit. slang)*, give (someone) his books *(informal)*, give (someone) the elbow, give (someone) his cards, kennet *(Austral. slang)*, jeff *(Austral. slang)*: *He was sacked for slapping a schoolboy.*
hit the sack = go to bed, retire, turn in *(informal)*, bed down, hit the hay *(slang)*: *I hit the sack early.*
the sack = dismissal, discharge, the boot *(slang)*, the axe *(informal)*, the chop *(Brit. slang)*, the push *(slang)*, the (old) heave-ho *(informal)*, termination of employment, the order of the boot *(slang)*: *People who make mistakes can be given the sack the same day.*

sack[2] VERB **= plunder**, loot, pillage, destroy, strip, rob, raid, ruin, devastate, spoil, rifle, demolish, ravage, lay waste, despoil, maraud, depredate *(rare)*: *Imperial troops sacked the French ambassador's residence in Rome.*
▷ NOUN **= plundering**, looting, pillage, waste, rape, ruin, destruction, ravage, plunder, devastation, depredation, despoliation, rapine: *the sack of Troy*

sacred ADJECTIVE **1 = holy**, hallowed, consecrated, blessed, divine, revered, venerable, sanctified: *shrines and sacred places* **OPPOSITE:** secular **2 = religious**, holy, ecclesiastical, hallowed, venerated: *the awe-inspiring sacred art of the Renaissance masters*
OPPOSITE: unconsecrated
3 = inviolable, protected, sacrosanct, secure, hallowed, inalienable, invulnerable, inviolate, unalterable: *My memories are sacred.*

sacrifice VERB **1 = offer**, offer up, immolate: *The priest sacrificed a chicken.* **2 = give up**, abandon, relinquish, lose, surrender, let go, do without, renounce, forfeit, forego, say goodbye to: *She sacrificed family life when her career took off.*
▷ NOUN **1 = offering**, immolation, oblation, hecatomb: *animal sacrifices to the gods* **2 = surrender**, loss, giving up, resignation, rejection, waiver, abdication, renunciation, repudiation, forswearing, relinquishment, eschewal, self-denial: *They have not suffered any sacrifice of identity.*

> **QUOTATIONS**
> Never in the field of human conflict was so much owed by so many to so few
> [Winston Churchill *speech to the House of Commons*]
>
> Too long a sacrifice
> Can make a stone of the heart
> [W.B. Yeats *Easter 1916*]
>
> Greater love hath no man than this, that a man lay down his life for his friends
> [*Bible: St. John*]
>
> **PROVERBS**
> *You cannot make an omelette without breaking eggs*

sacrificial ADJECTIVE **= propitiatory**, atoning, reparative, expiatory, oblatory

sacrilege NOUN **= desecration**, violation, blasphemy, mockery, heresy, irreverence, profanity, impiety, profanation, profaneness
OPPOSITE: reverence

sacrosanct ADJECTIVE **= inviolable**, sacred, inviolate, untouchable, hallowed, sanctified, set apart

sad ADJECTIVE **1 = unhappy**, down, low, blue, depressed, gloomy, grieved, dismal, melancholy, sombre, glum, wistful, mournful, dejected, downcast, grief-stricken, tearful, lugubrious, pensive, disconsolate, doleful, heavy-hearted, down in the dumps *(informal)*, cheerless, lachrymose, woebegone, down in the mouth *(informal)*, low-spirited, triste *(archaic)*, sick at heart: *The loss left me feeling sad and empty.* **OPPOSITE:** happy **2 = tragic**, moving, upsetting, dark, sorry, depressing, disastrous, dismal, pathetic, poignant, harrowing, grievous, pitiful, calamitous, heart-rending, pitiable: *the sad news that he had been killed in a motor-cycle accident* **3 = deplorable**, bad, sorry, terrible, distressing, unfortunate, miserable, dismal, shabby, heartbreaking, regrettable, lamentable, wretched, to be deplored: *It's a sad truth that children are the biggest victims of passive smoking.*
OPPOSITE: good **4 = regrettable**, disappointing, distressing, unhappy, unfortunate, unsatisfactory, woeful, deplorable, lamentable: *a sad state of affairs* **OPPOSITE:** fortunate

sadden VERB **= upset**, depress, distress, grieve, desolate, cast down, bring tears to your eyes, make sad, dispirit, make your heart bleed, aggrieve, deject, cast a gloom upon

saddle VERB **= burden**, load, lumber *(Brit. informal)*, charge, tax, task, encumber

sadism NOUN **= cruelty**, savagery, brutality, severity, ferocity, spite, ruthlessness, depravity, harshness, inhumanity, barbarity, callousness, viciousness, bestiality, heartlessness, brutishness, spitefulness, bloodthirstiness, murderousness, mercilessness, fiendishness, hard-heartedness

sadistic ADJECTIVE **= cruel**, savage, brutal, beastly, vicious, ruthless, perverted, perverse, inhuman, barbarous, fiendish

sadness NOUN **= unhappiness**, sorrow, grief, tragedy, depression, the blues, misery, melancholy, poignancy, despondency, bleakness, heavy heart, dejection, wretchedness, gloominess, mournfulness, dolour *(poetic)*, dolefulness, cheerlessness, sorrowfulness **OPPOSITE:** happiness

safe ADJECTIVE **1 = protected**, secure, in safety, impregnable, out of danger, safe and sound, in safe hands, out of harm's way, free from harm: *Keep your camera safe from sand.*
OPPOSITE: endangered **2 = all right**, fine, intact, unscathed, unhurt,

unharmed, undamaged, out of the woods, O.K. *or* okay *(informal)*: *Where is Sophie? Is she safe?* **3 = cautious**, prudent, sure, conservative, reliable, realistic, discreet, dependable, trustworthy, circumspect, on the safe side, unadventurous, tried and true: *I shall conceal myself at a safe distance from the battlefield.* **OPPOSITE:** risky **4 = risk-free**, sound, secure, certain, impregnable, riskless: *We are assured by our engineers that the building is safe.* **5 = harmless**, wholesome, innocuous, pure, tame, unpolluted, nontoxic, nonpoisonous: *a clean, inexpensive and safe fuel* **OPPOSITE:** dangerous ▷ NOUN **= strongbox**, vault, coffer, repository, deposit box, safe-deposit box: *The files are now in a safe.*

safeguard VERB **= protect**, guard, defend, save, screen, secure, preserve, look after, shield, watch over, keep safe: *international action to safeguard the ozone layer* ▷ NOUN **= protection**, security, defence, guard, shield, armour, aegis, bulwark, surety: *A system like ours lacks adequate safeguards for civil liberties.*

safely ADVERB **= in safety**, securely, with impunity, without risk, with safety, safe and sound

safety NOUN **1 = security**, protection, safeguards, assurance, precautions, immunity, safety measures, impregnability: *The report makes recommendations to improve safety on aircraft.* **OPPOSITE:** risk **2 = shelter**, haven, protection, cover, retreat, asylum, refuge, sanctuary: *the safety of your own home*

sag VERB **1 = sink**, bag, droop, fall, drop, seat *(of a skirt, etc)*, settle, slump, dip, give way, bulge, swag, hang loosely, fall unevenly: *The shirt's cuffs won't sag and lose their shape after washing.* **2 = drop**, sink, slump, flop, droop, loll: *He shrugged and sagged into a chair.* **3 = decline**, fall, slip, tire, slide, flag, slump, weaken, wilt, wane, cave in, droop: *Some of the tension he builds up begins to sag.*

S

saga NOUN **1 = carry-on** *(informal)*, to-do, performance *(informal)*, rigmarole, soap opera, pantomime *(informal)*: *the whole saga of Hoddle's dismissal* **2 = epic**, story, tale, legend, adventure, romance, narrative, chronicle, yarn, fairy tale, folk tale, roman-fleuve *(French)*: *a Nordic saga of giants and trolls*

sage NOUN **= wise man**, philosopher, guru, authority, expert, master, elder, pundit, Solomon, mahatma, Nestor, savant, Solon, man of learning, tohunga *(N.Z.)*: *ancient Chinese sages* ▷ ADJECTIVE **= wise**, learned, intelligent, sensible, politic, acute, discerning, prudent, canny, judicious, perspicacious, sagacious, sapient: *He was famous for his sage advice to young painters.*

sail NOUN **= sheet**, canvas: *The white sails billow with the breezes they catch.* ▷ VERB **1 = go by water**, cruise, voyage, ride the waves, go by sea: *We sailed upstream.* **2 = set sail**, embark, get under way, put to sea, put off, leave port, hoist sail, cast *or* weigh anchor: *The boat is due to sail tonight.* **3 = pilot**, steer, navigate, captain, skipper: *I shall get myself a little boat and sail her around the world.* **4 = glide**, sweep, float, shoot, fly, wing, soar, drift, skim, scud, skirr: *We got into the lift and sailed to the top floor.*
sail through something = cruise through, walk through, romp through, pass easily, succeed easily at: *She sailed through her maths exams.*
set sail = put to sea, embark, get under way, put off, leave port, hoist sail, cast *or* weigh anchor: *He loaded his vessel with another cargo and set sail.*

sailor NOUN **= mariner**, marine, seaman, salt, tar *(informal)*, hearty *(informal)*, navigator, sea dog, seafarer, matelot *(slang, chiefly Brit.)*, Jack Tar, seafaring man, lascar, leatherneck *(slang)*

saintly ADJECTIVE **= virtuous**, godly, holy, religious, sainted, blessed, worthy, righteous, devout, pious, angelic, blameless, god-fearing, beatific, sinless, saintlike, full of good works
▷ *See themed panel* **Saints** *on page 604*

> **QUOTATIONS**
> Saintliness is also a temptation
> [Jean Anouilh *Beckett*]

sake NOUN **= purpose**, interest, cause, reason, end, aim, principle, objective, motive: *For the sake of historical accuracy, permit us to state the true facts.*
for someone's sake = in someone's interests, to someone's advantage, on someone's account, for the benefit of, for the good of, for the welfare of, out of respect for, out of consideration for, out of regard for: *I trust you to do a good job for Stan's sake.*

salacious ADJECTIVE **= obscene**, indecent, pornographic, blue, erotic, steamy *(informal)*, lewd, X-rated *(informal)*, bawdy, smutty, lustful, ribald, ruttish

salary NOUN **= pay**, income, wage, fee, payment, wages, earnings, allowance, remuneration, recompense, stipend, emolument

sale NOUN **1 = selling**, marketing, dealing, trading, transaction, disposal, vending: *Efforts were made to limit the sale of alcohol.* **2 = auction**, fair, mart, bazaar: *The Old Master was bought at the Christie's sale.*

salient ADJECTIVE **= prominent**, outstanding, important, marked, striking, arresting, signal, remarkable, pronounced, noticeable, conspicuous

saliva NOUN **= spit**, dribble, drool, slaver, spittle, sputum

sallow ADJECTIVE **= wan**, pale, sickly, pasty, pallid, unhealthy, yellowish, anaemic, bilious, jaundiced-looking, peely-wally *(Scot.)* **OPPOSITE:** rosy

sally NOUN **= witticism**, joke, quip, crack *(informal)*, retort, jest, riposte, wisecrack *(informal)*, bon mot, smart remark: *He had thus far succeeded in fending off my conversational sallies.* ▷ VERB **= go forth**, set out, rush, issue, surge, erupt: *She would sally out on a bitter night to keep her appointments.*

salon NOUN **1 = shop**, store, establishment, parlour, boutique: *a beauty salon* **2 = sitting room**, lounge, living room, parlour, drawing room, front room, reception room, morning room: *His apartment was the most famous literary salon in Russia.*

salt NOUN **1 = seasoning**, sodium chloride, table salt, rock salt: *a pinch of salt* **2 = sailor**, marine, seaman, mariner, tar *(informal)*, hearty *(informal)*, navigator, sea dog, seafarer, matelot *(slang, chiefly Brit.)*, Jack Tar, seafaring man, lascar, leatherneck *(slang)*: *'Did he look like an old sea salt?' I asked, laughing.* ▷ ADJECTIVE **= salty**, salted, saline, brackish, briny: *Put a pan of salt water on to boil.*
rub salt into the wound = make something worse, add insult to injury, fan the flames, aggravate matters, magnify a problem: *I had no intention of rubbing salt into his wounds.*
with a grain *or* **pinch of salt = sceptically**, suspiciously, cynically, doubtfully, with reservations, disbelievingly, mistrustfully: *You have to take these findings with a pinch of salt.*

salty ADJECTIVE **= salt**, salted, saline, brackish, briny, over-salted, brak *(S. African)*

salubrious ADJECTIVE **= healthy**, beneficial, good for you, wholesome, invigorating, salutary, healthful, health-giving: *your salubrious lochside hotel*

salutary ADJECTIVE **= beneficial**, useful, valuable, helpful, profitable, good, practical, good for you, advantageous

salute VERB **1 = greet**, welcome, acknowledge, address, kiss, hail, salaam, accost, pay your respects to, doff your cap to, mihi *(N.Z.)*: *He stepped out and saluted the general.* **2 = honour**, acknowledge, recognize, take your hat off to *(informal)*, pay tribute *or* homage to: *The statement salutes the changes of the past year.* ▷ NOUN **= greeting**, recognition, salutation, address, kiss, salaam, obeisance: *He raised his hand in salute.*

salvage VERB **= save**, recover, rescue, restore, repair, get back, retrieve, redeem, glean, repossess, fetch back: *They studied flight recorders salvaged from the wreckage.* ▷ NOUN **1 = rescue**, saving, recovery, release, relief, liberation, salvation, deliverance, extrication: *The salvage of the ship went on.* **2 = scrap**, remains, waste, junk, offcuts: *They climbed up on the rock with their salvage.*

salvation NOUN **1 = saving**, rescue, recovery, restoration, salvage, redemption, deliverance: *those whose marriages are beyond salvation* **OPPOSITE:** ruin **2 = lifeline**, escape,

Henry James's Use of Verbs

Henry James (1843–1916) was born into an intellectual and wealthy New York family. In his youth he travelled often to Europe; later he lived in Paris, and eventually he settled in London. He took British citizenship in 1915. He was a prolific writer of novels, short stories, essays, and plays. His novels include *Washington Square* (1880), *The Portrait of a Lady* (1881), *The Bostonians* (1888), *The Wings of the Dove* (1902), and *The Ambassadors* (1903). His plays were less successful than his novels and stories, but his great interest in the theatre, and experience of writing dramatic dialogue, contributed to the style of his novels, and the central importance of dialogue in them.

James's novels are full of talk, and verbs of speaking are extremely frequent. In addition to neutral, common verbs such as *say, tell, ask speak, reply*, James uses many more literary synonyms: *remark, observe, utter, rejoin*, and a great number of verbs that indicate the particular way in which people speak: *cry, exclaim, murmur, ejaculate, break off, break out uncontrollably, appeal, demand*. Speakers in James's novels and stories are hesitant, and self-conscious; they are wary of what they may reveal about themselves, or uncertain of the reaction of they will elicit. This caution is indicated by the frequent use of *venture* with verbs of speaking:

> 'That's what your mother said to me',
> I **ventured to observe**. She was not offended, but she rose from her seat and stood looking at me a moment.

In James's writing, even spontaneity can be calculated: speakers venture to *exclaim, break out, ejaculate*:

> 'How much you've all been through!'
> I **ventured to ejaculate**.

Listeners are attentive and probing, luring their interlocutors into self-revelation:

> 'You draw a fellow out and put him off guard, and then you laugh at him.'

Very often people and their situations and behaviour are regarded as puzzles to be worked out: *What Maisie Knew*, for example, is about a little girl's very partial understanding of her own situation, and of her warring parents. Elsewhere *understand* as used by James often implies an acquisition of knowledge that is dramatic and full of emotional significance:

> She has felt and suffered, and now she **understands**!

When the object of the verb is a person, the act of understanding is seen as conferring a kind of power over them. This is true also of *see*, which James often uses in the sense of *understand*:

> Eugenio had, in an interview of five minutes, **understood** her.

> I had immediately **seen** them. I had seized their type.

Much of James's diction is Latinate, and at times very formal, particularly in narrative sections, but he also uses idiomatic language, such as Anglo-Saxon phrasal verbs, eg *draw out, pull off, give up, make out, take up, let down, get up*. He quite often prefers phrasal verbs that are actually less common, but more vivid, than their Latinate equivalents – such as *break out, break in, get off*, rather than *exclaim, interrupt, escape*. He uses *throw out* not only with objects such as *hint, question, idea*, but followed by a clause, as in *...her mother threw out that they had often talked about me...* This sounds somewhat odd, and perhaps makes one wonder what exactly the mother meant by her commonplace remark. Phrasal verbs are thus both colloquial, and imprecise, and James exploits both these qualities: in *What Maisie Knew*, the little girl employs the parlance of her humble governess, Mrs Wix, when concealing things from her doll: *... there were matters one couldn't "go into" with a pupil*. She also, when thinking of her mother, so often absent and so difficult to understand, sees her as *shading off into the unknowable*.

SAINTS

Saint	Feast day	Saint	Feast day	Saint	Feast day
Agatha	5 February	Francis of Assisi	4 October	Martin de Porres	3 November
Agnes	31 January	Francis of Sales	24 January	Martin of Tours (France)	11 November
Aidan	31 August	Francis Xavier	3 December	Mary	15 August
Alban	22 June	Geneviève (Paris)	3 January	Mary Magdalene	22 July
Albertus Magnus	15 November	George (England)	23 April	Matthew *or* Levi	21 September
Aloysius (patron saint of youth)	21 June	Gertrude	16 November	Matthias	14 May
Ambrose	7 December	Gilbert of Sempringham	4 February	Methodius	14 February
Andrew (Scotland)	30 November	Giles (cripples, beggars, and lepers)	1 September	Michael	29 September
Anne	26 July	Gregory I (the Great)	3 September	Neot	31 July
Anselm	21 April	Gregory VII *or* Hildebrand	25 May	Nicholas (Russia, children, sailors, merchants, and pawnbrokers)	6 December
Anthony	17 January	Gregory of Nazianzus	2 January	Nicholas I (the Great)	13 November
Anthony of Padua	13 June	Gregory of Nyssa	9 March	Ninian	16 September
Athanasius	2 May	Gregory of Tours	17 November	Olaf	29 July
Augustine of Hippo	28 August	Hilary of Poitiers	13 January	Oliver Plunket	1 July
Barnabas	11 June	Hildegard of Bingen	17 September	Oswald	28 February
Bartholomew	24 August	Helen *or* Helena	18 August	Pachomius	14 May
Basil	2 January	Helier	16 July	Patrick (Ireland)	17 March
Bede	25 May	Ignatius	17 October	Paul	29 June
Benedict	11 July	Ignatius of Loyola	31 July	Paulinus	10 October
Bernadette of Lourdes	16 April	Isidore of Seville	4 April	Paulinus of Nola	22 June
Bernard of Clairvaux	20 August	James	23 October	Peter *or* Simon Peter	29 June
Bernard of Menthon	28 May	James the Less	3 May	Philip	3 May
Bonaventura	15 July	Jane Frances de Chantal	12 December	Philip Neri	26 May
Boniface	5 June	Jerome	30 September	Pius V	30 April
Brendan	16 May	Joachim	26 July	Pius X	21 August
Bridget, Bride *or* Brigid (Ireland)	1 February	Joan of Arc	30 May	Polycarp	26 January *or* 23 February
Bridget *or* Birgitta (Sweden)	23 July	John	27 December	Rose of Lima	23 August
Catherine of Alexandria	25 November	John Bosco	31 January	Sebastian	20 January
Catherine of Siena (the Dominican Order)	29 April	John Chrysostom	13 September	Silas	13 July
Cecilia (music)	22 November	John Ogilvie	10 March	Simon Zelotes	28 October
Charles Borromeo	4 November	John of Damascus	4 December	Stanislaw *or* Stanislaus (Poland)	11 April
Christopher (travellers)	25 July	John of the Cross	14 December	Stanislaus Kostka	13 November
Clare of Assisi	11 August	John the Baptist	24 June	Stephen	26 *or* 27 December
Clement I	23 November	Joseph	19 March	Stephen of Hungary	16 *or* 20 August
Clement of Alexandria	5 December	Joseph of Arimathaea	17 March	Swithin	15 July
Columba *or* Colmcille	9 June	Joseph of Copertino	18 September	Teresa *or* Theresa of Avila	15 October
Crispin (shoemakers)	25 October	Jude	28 October	Thérèse de Lisieux	1 October
Crispinian (shoemakers)	25 October	Justin	1 June	Thomas	3 July
Cuthbert	20 March	Kentigern *or* Mungo	14 January	Thomas à Becket	29 December
Cyprian	16 September	Kevin	3 June	Thomas Aquinas	28 January
Cyril	14 February	Lawrence	10 August	Thomas More	22 June
Cyril of Alexandria	27 June	Lawrence O'Toole	14 November	Timothy	26 January
David (Wales)	1 March	Leger	2 October	Titus	26 January
Denis *or* Denys (France)	9 October	Leo I (the Great)	10 November	Ursula	21 October
Dominic	7 August	Leo II	3 July	Valentine	14 February
Dorothy	6 February	Leo III	12 June	Veronica	12 July
Dunstan	19 May	Leo IV	17 July	Vincent de Paul	27 September
Edmund	20 November	Leonard	6 November	Vitus	15 June
Edward the Confessor	13 October	Lucy	13 December	Vladimir	15 July
Edward the Martyr	18 March	Luke	18 October	Wenceslaus	28 September
Elizabeth	5 November	Malachy	3 November	Wilfrid	12 October
Elizabeth of Hungary	17 November	Margaret	20 July		
Elmo	2 June	Margaret of Scotland (in Scotland)	10 June, 16 November		
Ethelbert	25 February	Maria Goretti	6 July		
		Mark	25 April		
		Martha	29 July		

relief, preservation: *I consider books my salvation.*

QUOTATIONS

> Work out your own salvation with fear and trembling
> [*Bible: Philippians*]

salve VERB = **ease**, soothe, appease, still, allay, pacify, mollify, tranquillize, palliate: *I give myself treats and justify them to salve my conscience.*

▷ NOUN = **balm**, cream, medication, lotion, lubricant, ointment, emollient, liniment, dressing, unguent: *a soothing salve for sore, dry lips*

salvo NOUN = **barrage**, storm, bombardment, strafe, cannonade

same ADJECTIVE **1** = **identical**, similar, alike, equal, twin, equivalent,

corresponding, comparable, duplicate, indistinguishable, interchangeable: *The houses were all the same.* **OPPOSITE:** different **2 = the very same**, very, one and the same, selfsame: *Bernard works at the same institution as Arlette.* **3 = aforementioned**, aforesaid, selfsame: *Wristwatches: £5. Inscription of same: £25.* **4 = unchanged**, consistent, constant, uniform, unaltered, unfailing, invariable, unvarying, changeless: *Always taking the ingredients from here means the beers stay the same.* **OPPOSITE:** altered
all the same 1 = nevertheless, still, regardless, nonetheless, after all, in any case, for all that, notwithstanding, in any event, anyhow, just the same, be that as it may: *She didn't understand the joke but laughed all the same.* **2 = unimportant**, insignificant, immaterial, inconsequential, of no consequence, of little account, not worth mentioning: *It's all the same to me whether he goes or not.*

USAGE
The use of *same* as in *If you send us your order for the materials, we will deliver same tomorrow* is common in business and official English. In general English, however, this use of the word is best avoided, as it may sound rather stilted: *May I borrow your book? I will return it* (not *same*) *tomorrow.*

sameness NOUN **= similarity**, resemblance, uniformity, likeness, oneness, standardization, indistinguishability, identicalness

sample NOUN **1 = specimen**, example, model, pattern, instance, representative, indication, illustration, exemplification: *We're giving away 2000 free samples.* **2 = cross section**, test, sampling: *We based our analysis on a random sample of more than 200 males.*
▷ VERB **= test**, try, check out *(informal)*, experience, taste, examine, evaluate, inspect, experiment with, appraise, partake of: *We sampled a selection of different bottled waters.*

sanctify VERB **1 = consecrate**, bless, anoint, set apart, hallow, make sacred: *Their marriage has not been sanctified in a Christian church.* **2 = cleanse**, redeem, purify, absolve: *May the God of peace sanctify you entirely.*

sanctimonious ADJECTIVE **= pious**, smug, hypocritical, pi *(Brit. slang)*, too good to be true, self-righteous, self-satisfied, goody-goody *(informal)*, unctuous, holier-than-thou, priggish, pietistic, canting, pharisaical

sanction VERB **= permit**, back, support, allow, approve, entitle, endorse, authorize, countenance, vouch for, lend your name to: *He may seem ready to sanction the use of force.* **OPPOSITE:** forbid
▷ NOUN **1** *(often plural)* **= ban**, restriction, boycott, embargo, exclusion, penalty, deterrent, prohibition, coercive measures: *He expressed his opposition to lifting the sanctions.* **OPPOSITE:** permission **2 = permission**, backing, support, authority, approval, allowance, confirmation, endorsement, countenance, ratification, authorization, approbation, O.K. *or* okay *(informal)*, stamp *or* seal of approval: *The king could not enact laws without the sanction of parliament.* **OPPOSITE:** ban

sanctity NOUN **= sacredness**, inviolability, inalienability, hallowedness, sacrosanctness

sanctuary NOUN **1 = protection**, shelter, refuge, haven, retreat, asylum: *Some of them have sought sanctuary in the church.* **2 = reserve**, park, preserve, reservation, national park, tract, nature reserve, conservation area: *a bird sanctuary*

sanctum NOUN **1 = refuge**, retreat, den, private room: *His bedroom is his inner sanctum.* **2 = sanctuary**, shrine, altar, holy place, Holy of Holies: *the inner sanctum of the mosque*

sand NOUN **= beach**, shore, strand *(literary)*, dunes: *miles of golden sands*

sane ADJECTIVE **1 = rational**, normal, all there *(informal)*, lucid, of sound mind, compos mentis *(Latin)*, in your right mind, mentally sound, in possession of all your faculties: *He seemed perfectly sane.* **OPPOSITE:** insane **2 = sensible**, sound, reasonable, balanced, moderate, sober, judicious, level-headed, grounded: *a sane and safe energy policy* **OPPOSITE:** foolish

sanguine ADJECTIVE **= cheerful**, confident, optimistic, assured, hopeful, buoyant, in good heart **OPPOSITE:** gloomy

sanitary ADJECTIVE **= hygienic**, clean, healthy, wholesome, salubrious, unpolluted, germ-free

sanitation NOUN **= hygiene**, cleanliness, sewerage

sanity NOUN **1 = mental health**, reason, rationality, stability, normality, right mind *(informal)*, saneness: *He and his wife finally had to move, just to preserve their sanity.* **OPPOSITE:** insanity **2 = common sense**, sense, good sense, rationality, level-headedness, judiciousness, soundness of judgment: *He's been looking at ways of introducing some sanity into the market.* **OPPOSITE:** stupidity

sap[1] NOUN **1 = juice**, essence, vital fluid, secretion, lifeblood, plant fluid: *The leaves, bark and sap are common ingredients of herbal remedies.* **2 = fool**, jerk *(slang, chiefly U.S. & Canad.)*, idiot, noodle, wally *(slang)*, wet *(Brit. informal)*, charlie *(Brit. informal)*, drip *(informal)*, gull *(archaic)*, prat *(slang)*, plonker *(slang)*, noddy, twit *(informal)*, chump *(informal)*, oaf, simpleton, nitwit *(informal)*, ninny, nincompoop, dweeb *(U.S. slang)*, wuss *(slang)*, Simple Simon, weenie *(U.S. informal)*, muggins *(Brit. slang)*, eejit *(Scot. & Irish)*, dumb-ass *(slang)*, numpty *(Scot. informal)*, doofus *(slang, chiefly U.S.)*, nerd *or* nurd *(slang)*, numskull *or* numbskull, dorba *or* dorb *(Austral. slang)*, bogan *(Austral. slang)*: *her poor sap of a husband*

sap[2] VERB **= weaken**, drain, undermine, rob, exhaust, bleed, erode, deplete, wear down, enervate, devitalize: *I was afraid the sickness had sapped my strength.*

sarcasm NOUN **= irony**, satire, cynicism, contempt, ridicule, bitterness, scorn, sneering, mockery, venom, derision, vitriol, mordancy, causticness

sarcastic ADJECTIVE **= ironical**, cynical, satirical, cutting, biting, sharp, acid, mocking, taunting, sneering, acrimonious, backhanded, contemptuous, disparaging, sardonic, caustic, bitchy *(informal)*, vitriolic, acerbic, derisive, ironic, mordant, sarky *(Brit. informal)*, mordacious, acerb

sardonic ADJECTIVE **= mocking**, cynical, dry, bitter, sneering, jeering, malicious, wry, sarcastic, derisive, ironical, mordant, mordacious

sash NOUN **= belt**, girdle, waistband, cummerbund

Satan NOUN **= The Devil**, Lucifer, Prince of Darkness, Lord of the Flies, Mephistopheles, Beelzebub, Old Nick *(informal)*, The Evil One, Apollyon, Old Scratch *(informal)*

satanic ADJECTIVE **= evil**, demonic, hellish, black, malignant, wicked, inhuman, malevolent, devilish, infernal, fiendish, accursed, iniquitous, diabolic, demoniac, demoniacal **OPPOSITE:** godly

sate VERB **= satisfy**, satiate, slake, indulge to the full

satellite NOUN **1 = spacecraft**, communications satellite, sputnik, space capsule: *The rocket launched two satellites.* **2 = moon**, secondary planet: *the satellites of Jupiter*

satire NOUN **1 = mockery**, wit, irony, ridicule, sarcasm: *It's an easy target for satire.* **2 = parody**, mockery, caricature, send-up *(Brit. informal)*, spoof *(informal)*, travesty, takeoff *(informal)*, lampoon, skit, burlesque: *A sharp satire on the American political process.*

QUOTATIONS
It's hard not to write satire
[Juvenal *Satires*]

Satire is a sort of glass, wherein beholders do generally discover everybody's face but their own
[Jonathan Swift *The Battle of the Books*]

satirical *or* **satiric** ADJECTIVE **= mocking**, ironical, cynical, cutting, biting, bitter, taunting, pungent,

S

incisive, sarcastic, sardonic, caustic, vitriolic, burlesque, mordant, Rabelaisian, mordacious

satisfaction NOUN **1 = fulfilment**, pleasure, achievement, joy, relish, glee, gratification, pride, complacency: *She felt a small glow of satisfaction.* **OPPOSITE:** dissatisfaction **2 = compensation**, damages, justice, amends, settlement, redress, remuneration, reparation, vindication, restitution, reimbursement, atonement, recompense, indemnification, requital: *Buyers have the right to go to court and demand satisfaction.* **OPPOSITE:** injury **3 = contentment**, content, comfort, ease, pleasure, well-being, happiness, enjoyment, peace of mind, gratification, satiety, repletion, contentedness: *a state of satisfaction* **OPPOSITE:** discontent

satisfactory ADJECTIVE **= adequate**, acceptable, good enough, average, fair, all right, suitable, sufficient, competent, up to scratch, passable, up to standard, up to the mark **OPPOSITE:** unsatisfactory

satisfied ADJECTIVE **1 = contented**, happy, content, pacified, pleased: *our satisfied customers* **OPPOSITE:** dissatisfied **2 = sure**, smug, convinced, positive, easy in your mind: *People must be satisfied that the treatment is safe.*

satisfy VERB **1 = content**, please, indulge, fill, feed, appease, gratify, pander to, assuage, pacify, quench, mollify, surfeit, satiate, slake, sate: *The pace of change has not been quick enough to satisfy everyone.* **OPPOSITE:** dissatisfy **2 = convince**, persuade, assure, reassure, dispel (someone's) doubts, put (someone's) mind at rest: *He has to satisfy us that real progress will be made.* **OPPOSITE:** dissuade **3 = comply with**, meet, fulfil, answer, serve, fill, observe, obey, conform to: *The procedures should satisfy certain basic requirements.* **OPPOSITE:** fail to meet

satisfying ADJECTIVE **= satisfactory**, pleasing, gratifying, pleasurable, cheering

saturate VERB **1 = flood**, overwhelm, swamp, overrun, deluge, glut: *Both sides are saturating the airwaves.* **2 = soak**, steep, drench, seep, imbue, douse, impregnate, suffuse, ret *(flax, etc)*, wet through, waterlog, souse, drouk *(Scot.)*: *If the filter has been saturated with motor oil, discard it.*

saturated ADJECTIVE **= soaked**, soaking (wet), drenched, sodden, dripping, waterlogged, sopping (wet), wet through, soaked to the skin, wringing wet, droukit *or* drookit *(Scot.)*

sauce NOUN **= dressing**, dip, relish, condiment

saucy ADJECTIVE **= impudent**, cheeky *(informal)*, impertinent, forward, fresh *(informal)*, flip *(informal)*, rude, sassy *(U.S. informal)*, pert, disrespectful, flippant, presumptuous, insolent, lippy *(U.S. & Canad. slang)*, smart-alecky *(informal)*

saunter VERB **= stroll**, wander, amble, roam, ramble, meander, rove, take a stroll, mosey *(informal)*, stravaig *(Scot. & Northern English dialect)*: *We watched our fellow students saunter into the building.*
▷ NOUN **= stroll**, walk, amble, turn, airing, constitutional, ramble, promenade, breather, perambulation: *She began a slow saunter towards the bonfire.*

sausage NOUN **= banger**

savage ADJECTIVE **1 = cruel**, brutal, vicious, bloody, fierce, harsh, beastly, ruthless, ferocious, murderous, ravening, sadistic, inhuman, merciless, diabolical, brutish, devilish, bloodthirsty, barbarous, pitiless, bestial: *This was a savage attack on a defenceless young girl.* **OPPOSITE:** gentle **2 = wild**, fierce, ferocious, unbroken, feral, untamed, undomesticated: *a strange and savage animal encountered at the zoo* **OPPOSITE:** tame **3 = primitive**, undeveloped, uncultivated, uncivilized, in a state of nature, nonliterate: *a savage people* **4 = uncultivated**, rugged, unspoilt, uninhabited, waste, rough, uncivilized, unfrequented: *stunning images of a wild and savage land* **OPPOSITE:** cultivated
▷ NOUN **1 = native**, barbarian, heathen, indigene, primitive person, autochthon: *a frozen desert peopled by uncouth savages* **2 = lout**, yob *(Brit. slang)*, brute, bear, monster, beast, barbarian, fiend, yahoo, hoon *(Austral. & N.Z.)*, yobbo *(Brit. slang)*, roughneck *(slang)*, boor, cougan *(Austral. slang)*, scozza *(Austral. slang)*, bogan *(Austral. slang)*: *Our orchestra is a bunch of savages.*
▷ VERB **1 = maul**, tear, claw, attack, mangle, lacerate, mangulate *(Austral. slang)*: *The animal turned on him and he was savaged to death.* **2 = criticize**, attack, knock *(informal)*, blast, pan *(informal)*, slam *(slang)*, put down, slate *(informal)*, have a go (at) *(informal)*, disparage, tear into *(informal)*, find fault with, lambast(e), pick holes in, pick to pieces, give (someone *or* something) a bad press: *The show had already been savaged by the critics.* **OPPOSITE:** praise

> **QUOTATIONS**
> as savage as a bear with a sore head
> [Captain Marryat *The King's Own*]

savagery NOUN **= cruelty**, brutality, ferocity, ruthlessness, sadism, inhumanity, barbarity, viciousness, bestiality, fierceness, bloodthirstiness

save VERB **1 = rescue**, free, release, deliver, recover, get out, liberate, salvage, redeem, bail out, come to someone's rescue, set free, save the life of, extricate, save someone's bacon *(Brit. informal)*: *She could have saved him from this final disaster.* **OPPOSITE:** endanger **2 = keep**, reserve, set aside, store, collect, gather, hold, hoard, hide away, lay by, put by, salt away, treasure up, keep up your sleeve *(informal)*, put aside for a rainy day: *I thought we were saving money for a holiday.* **OPPOSITE:** spend **3 = protect**, keep, guard, preserve, look after, take care of, safeguard, salvage, conserve, keep safe: *a final attempt to save 40,000 jobs* **4 = budget**, be economical, economize, scrimp and save, retrench, be frugal, make economies, be thrifty, tighten your belt *(informal)*: *The majority of people intend to save.* **5 = put aside**, keep, reserve, collect, retain, set aside, amass, put by: *Scraps of material were saved, cut up and pieced together for quilts.* **6 = prevent**, avoid, spare, rule out, avert, obviate: *This will save the expense and trouble of buying two pairs.*

saving NOUN **= economy**, discount, reduction, bargain, cut: *Use these vouchers for some great savings on holidays.*
▷ PLURAL NOUN **= nest egg**, fund, store, reserves, resources, fall-back, provision for a rainy day: *Many people lost all their savings when the bank collapsed.*

Saviour NOUN **= Christ**, Jesus, the Messiah, the Redeemer

saviour NOUN **= rescuer**, deliverer, defender, guardian, salvation, protector, liberator, Good Samaritan, redeemer, preserver, knight in shining armour, friend in need

savour VERB **1 = relish**, like, delight in, revel in, luxuriate in, gloat over: *We won't pretend we savour the prospect of a month in prison.* **2 = enjoy**, appreciate, relish, delight in, revel in, partake of, drool over, luxuriate in, enjoy to the full, smack your lips over: *Savour the flavour of each mouthful.*
▷ NOUN **1 = flavour**, taste, smell, relish, smack, zest, tang, zing *(informal)*, piquancy: *The rich savour of the beans give this dish its character.* **2 = zest**, interest, spice, excitement, salt, flavour: *Life without Anna had no savour.*

savoury ADJECTIVE **1 = spicy**, rich, delicious, tasty, luscious, palatable, tangy, dainty, delectable, mouthwatering, piquant, full-flavoured, scrumptious *(informal)*, appetizing, toothsome, yummo *(Austral. slang)*: *Italian cooking is best known for its savoury dishes.* **OPPOSITE:** tasteless **2 = wholesome**, decent, respectable, honest, reputable, apple-pie *(informal)*: *He does not have a particularly savoury reputation.* **OPPOSITE:** disreputable
▷ PLURAL NOUN **= appetizers**, nibbles, apéritifs, canapés, titbits, hors d'oeuvres: *I'll make some cheese straws or savouries.*

savvy NOUN **= understanding**, perception, grasp, ken, comprehension, apprehension: *He is known for his political savvy.*
▷ ADJECTIVE **= shrewd**, sharp, astute, knowing, fly *(slang)*, keen, smart, clever, intelligent, discriminating, discerning, canny, perceptive, artful, far-sighted, far-seeing, long-headed,

S

perspicacious, sagacious: *She was a pretty savvy woman.*

say VERB **1 = state**, declare, remark, add, announce, maintain, mention, assert, affirm, asseverate: *She said she was very impressed.* **2 = speak**, utter, voice, express, pronounce, come out with (*informal*), put into words, give voice or utterance to: *I hope you didn't say anything about me.* **3 = make known**, reveal, disclose, divulge, answer, reply, respond, give as your opinion: *I must say that that rather shocked me, too.* **4 = suggest**, express, imply, communicate, disclose, give away, convey, divulge: *That says a lot about the power of their marketing people.* **5 = suppose**, supposing, imagine, assume, presume: *Say you lived in Boston, Massachusetts.* **6 = estimate**, suppose, guess, conjecture, surmise, dare say, hazard a guess: *I'd say she must be at least a size 20.* **7 = recite**, perform, deliver, do, read, repeat, render, rehearse, orate: *How am I going to go on and say those lines tonight?* **8 = allege**, report, claim, hold, suggest, insist, maintain, rumour, assert, uphold, profess, put about that: *He says he did it after the police pressured him.*
▷ NOUN **1 = influence**, power, control, authority, weight, sway, clout (*informal*), predominance, mana (*N.Z.*): *The students wanted more say in the running of the university.* **2 = chance to speak**, vote, voice, crack (*informal*), opportunity to speak, turn to speak: *Let him have his say.*
to say the least = at the very least, without any exaggeration, to put it mildly: *The result was, to say the least, fascinating.*

saying NOUN **= proverb**, maxim, adage, saw, slogan, gnome, dictum, axiom, aphorism, byword, apophthegm: *that old saying: 'Charity begins at home'*
go without saying = be obvious, be understood, be taken for granted, be accepted, be self-evident, be taken as read, be a matter of course: *It should go without saying that you shouldn't smoke.*

say-so NOUN **= assertion**, authority, agreement, word, guarantee, sanction, permission, consent, assurance, assent, authorization, dictum, asseveration, O.K. *or* okay (*informal*)

scalding ADJECTIVE **= burning**, boiling, searing, blistering, piping hot

scale[1] NOUN **= flake**, plate, layer, lamina: *a thing with scales all over its body*

scale[2] NOUN **1 = degree**, size, range, spread, extent, dimensions, scope, magnitude, breadth: *He underestimates the scale of the problem.* **2 = system of measurement**, register, measuring system, graduated system, calibration, calibrated system: *an earthquake measuring five-point-five on the Richter scale* **3 = ranking**, ladder, spectrum, hierarchy, series, sequence, progression, pecking order (*informal*): *This has become a reality for increasing numbers across the social scale.* **4 = ratio**, proportion, relative size: *The map, on a scale of 1:10,000, shows over 5,000 individual paths.*
▷ VERB **= climb up**, mount, go up, ascend, surmount, scramble up, clamber up, escalade: *The men scaled a wall and climbed down scaffolding on the other side.*
scale something down = reduce, cut, moderate, slow down, cut down, wind down, tone down, downsize, kennet (*Austral. slang*), jeff (*Austral. slang*): *The air rescue operation has now been scaled down.*
scale something up = expand, extend, blow up, enlarge, lengthen, magnify, amplify, augment: *Simply scaling up a size 10 garment often leads to disaster.*

scaly ADJECTIVE **1 = squamous**, squamate, lamellose, lamelliform: *The brown rat has prominent ears and a long scaly tail.* **2 = flaky**, scabrous, scurfy, furfuraceous (*Medical*), squamous *or* squamose (*Biology*), squamulose: *If your skin becomes red, sore or very scaly, consult your doctor.*

scamper VERB **= run**, dash, dart, fly, hurry, sprint, romp, beetle, hasten, scuttle, scurry, scoot

scan VERB **1 = glance over**, skim, look over, eye, check, clock (*Brit. slang*), examine, check out (*informal*), run over, eyeball (*slang*), size up (*informal*), get a load of (*informal*), look someone up and down, run your eye over, take a dekko at (*Brit. slang*), surf (*Computing*): *She scanned the advertisement pages of the newspaper.* **2 = survey**, search, investigate, sweep, con (*archaic*), scour, scrutinize, take stock of, recce (*slang*): *The officer scanned the room.*
▷ NOUN **1 = look**, glance, skim, browse, flick, squint, butcher's (*Brit. slang*), brief look, dekko (*Brit. slang*), shufti (*Brit. slang*): *I've had a quick scan through your book again.* **2 = examination**, scanning, ultrasound: *He was rushed to hospital for a brain scan.*

scandal NOUN **1 = disgrace**, crime, offence, sin, embarrassment, wrongdoing, skeleton in the cupboard, dishonourable behaviour, discreditable behaviour: *a financial scandal* **2 = gossip**, goss (*informal*), talk, rumours, dirt, slander, tattle, dirty linen (*informal*), calumny, backbiting, aspersion: *He loved gossip and scandal.* **3 = shame**, offence, disgrace, stigma, infamy, opprobrium, obloquy: *She braved the scandal of her husband's love child.* **4 = outrage**, shame, insult, disgrace, injustice, crying shame: *It is a scandal that a person can be stopped for no reason by the police.*

> QUOTATIONS
> It is public scandal that constitutes offence, and to sin in secret is not to sin at all
> [Molière *Le Tartuffe*]

scandalous ADJECTIVE **1 = shocking**, disgraceful, outrageous, offensive, appalling, foul, dreadful, horrifying, obscene, monstrous, unspeakable, atrocious, frightful, abominable: *They would be sacked for criminal or scandalous behaviour.* OPPOSITE: decent **2 = slanderous**, gossiping, scurrilous, untrue, defamatory, libellous: *Newspaper columns were full of scandalous tales.* OPPOSITE: laudatory **3 = outrageous**, shocking, infamous, disgraceful, monstrous, shameful, atrocious, unseemly, odious, disreputable, opprobrious, highly improper: *a scandalous waste of money* OPPOSITE: proper

scant ADJECTIVE **1 = inadequate**, insufficient, meagre, sparse, little, limited, bare, minimal, deficient, barely sufficient: *There is scant evidence of strong economic growth to come.* OPPOSITE: adequate **2 = small**, limited, inadequate, insufficient, meagre, measly, scanty, inconsiderable: *The hole was a scant 0.23 inches in diameter.*

scanty ADJECTIVE **1 = meagre**, sparse, poor, thin, narrow, sparing, restricted, bare, inadequate, pathetic, insufficient, slender, scant, deficient, exiguous: *So far, what scanty evidence we have points to two subjects.* **2 = skimpy**, short, brief, tight, thin: *a model in scanty clothing*

scapegoat NOUN **= fall guy**, whipping boy

scar NOUN **1 = mark**, injury, wound, trauma (*Pathology*), blemish, cicatrix: *He had a scar on his forehead.* **2 = trauma**, suffering, pain, strain, torture, disturbance, anguish: *emotional scars that come from having been abused*
▷ VERB **= mark**, disfigure, damage, brand, mar, mutilate, maim, blemish, deface, traumatize, disfeature: *He was scarred for life during a pub fight.*

scarce ADJECTIVE **1 = in short supply**, wanting, insufficient, deficient, at a premium, thin on the ground: *Food was scarce and expensive.* OPPOSITE: plentiful **2 = rare**, few, unusual, uncommon, few and far between, infrequent, thin on the ground: *I'm unemployed, so luxuries are scarce.* OPPOSITE: common

scarcely ADVERB **1 = hardly**, barely, only just, scarce (*archaic*): *He could scarcely breathe.* **2 = by no means**, hardly, not at all, definitely not, under no circumstances, on no account: *It can scarcely be coincidence.*

scarcity NOUN **= shortage**, lack, deficiency, poverty, want, dearth, paucity, insufficiency, infrequency, undersupply, rareness OPPOSITE: abundance

scare VERB **= frighten**, alarm, terrify, panic, shock, startle, intimidate, dismay, daunt, terrorize, put the wind up (someone) (*informal*), give (someone) a fright, give (someone) a turn (*informal*), affright (*archaic*): *She's just trying to scare me.*
▷ NOUN **1 = fright**, shock, start: *We got*

S

a bit of a scare. **2 = panic**, hysteria: *the doctor at the centre of an Aids scare* **3 = alert**, warning, alarm: *a security scare over a suspect package*

scared ADJECTIVE **= afraid**, alarmed, frightened, terrified, shaken, cowed, startled, fearful, unnerved, petrified, panicky, terrorized, panic-stricken, scared stiff, terror-stricken

scarf NOUN **= muffler**, stole, headscarf, comforter, cravat, neckerchief, headsquare

scary ADJECTIVE **= frightening**, alarming, terrifying, shocking, chilling, horrifying, intimidating, horrendous, hairy *(slang)*, unnerving, spooky *(informal)*, creepy *(informal)*, hair-raising, spine-chilling, bloodcurdling

scathing ADJECTIVE **= critical**, cutting, biting, harsh, savage, brutal, searing, withering, belittling, sarcastic, caustic, scornful, vitriolic, trenchant, mordant, mordacious

scatter VERB **1 = throw about**, spread, sprinkle, strew, broadcast, shower, fling, litter, sow, diffuse, disseminate: *He began by scattering seed and putting in plants.* **OPPOSITE:** gather **2 = disperse**, separate, break up, dispel, disband, dissipate, disunite, put to flight: *After dinner, everyone scattered.* **OPPOSITE:** assemble

scattering NOUN **= sprinkling**, few, handful, scatter, smattering, smatter

scavenge VERB **= search**, hunt, forage, rummage, root about, fossick *(Austral. & N.Z.)*, scratch about

scenario NOUN **1 = situation**, sequence of events, chain of events, course of events, series of developments: *That apocalyptic scenario cannot be ruled out.* **2 = story line**, résumé, outline, sketch, summary, rundown, synopsis: *I will write an outline of the scenario.*

scene NOUN **1 = act**, part, division, episode: *the opening scene* **2 = setting**, set, background, location, backdrop, mise en scène *(French)*: *The lights go up, revealing a scene of chaos.* **3 = incident**, happening, event, episode: *There were emotional scenes as the refugees enjoyed their first breath of freedom.* **4 = site**, place, setting, area, position, stage, situation, spot, whereabouts, locality: *Riot vans were on the scene in minutes.* **5 = world**, business, environment, preserve, arena, realm, domain, milieu, thing, field of interest: *the local music scene; Sport just isn't my scene.* **6 = view**, prospect, panorama, vista, landscape, tableau, outlook: *James Lynch's country scenes* **7 = fuss**, to-do, row, performance, upset, drama, exhibition, carry-on *(informal, chiefly Brit.)*, confrontation, tantrum, commotion, hue and cry, display of emotion, hissy fit *(informal)*: *I'm sorry I made such a scene.* **8 = section**, part, sequence, segment, clip: *She was told to cut some scenes from her new series.*

scenery NOUN **1 = landscape**, view, surroundings, terrain, vista: *Sometimes they just drive slowly down the lane enjoying the scenery.* **2 = set**, setting, backdrop, flats, décor, stage set: *There was a break while the scenery was changed.*

scenic ADJECTIVE **= picturesque**, beautiful, spectacular, striking, grand, impressive, breathtaking, panoramic

scent NOUN **1 = fragrance**, smell, perfume, bouquet, aroma, odour, niff *(Brit. slang)*, redolence: *She could smell the scent of her mother's lacquer.* **2 = trail**, track, spoor: *A police dog picked up the murderer's scent.* **3 = perfume**, fragrance, cologne, eau de toilette *(French)*, eau de cologne *(French)*, toilet water: *a bottle of scent*
▷ VERB **= smell**, sense, recognize, detect, sniff, discern, sniff out, nose out, get wind of *(informal)*, be on the track *or* trail of: *dogs which scent the hidden birds*

scented ADJECTIVE **= fragrant**, perfumed, aromatic, sweet-smelling, redolent, ambrosial, odoriferous

sceptic NOUN **1 = doubter**, cynic, scoffer, disbeliever, Pyrrhonist: *He was a born sceptic.* **2 = agnostic**, doubter, unbeliever, doubting Thomas: *a lifelong religious sceptic*

> **QUOTATIONS**
> I am too much of a sceptic to deny the possibility of anything
> [T.H. Huxley]

sceptical ADJECTIVE **= doubtful**, cynical, dubious, questioning, doubting, hesitating, scoffing, unconvinced, disbelieving, incredulous, quizzical, mistrustful, unbelieving **OPPOSITE:** convinced

scepticism NOUN **= doubt**, suspicion, disbelief, cynicism, incredulity

schedule NOUN **1 = plan**, programme, agenda, calendar, timetable, itinerary, list of appointments: *He has been forced to adjust his schedule.* **2 = list**, catalogue, inventory, syllabus: *a detailed written schedule*
▷ VERB **= plan**, set up, book, programme, arrange, organize, timetable: *No new talks are scheduled.*

schematic ADJECTIVE **= graphic**, representational, illustrative, diagrammatic, diagrammatical

scheme NOUN **1 = plan**, programme, strategy, system, design, project, theory, proposal, device, tactics, course of action, contrivance: *a private pension scheme* **2 = plot**, dodge, ploy, ruse, game *(informal)*, shift, intrigue, conspiracy, manoeuvre, machinations, subterfuge, stratagem: *a quick money-making scheme*
▷ VERB **= plot**, plan, intrigue, manoeuvre, conspire, contrive, collude, wheel and deal, machinate: *Everyone's always scheming and plotting.*

scheming ADJECTIVE **= calculating**, cunning, sly, designing, tricky, slippery, wily, artful, conniving, Machiavellian, foxy, deceitful, underhand, duplicitous **OPPOSITE:** straightforward

schism NOUN **= division**, break, split, breach, separation, rift, splintering, rupture, discord, disunion

schmick ADJECTIVE **1 = excellent**, outstanding, good, great, fine, prime, capital, noted, choice, champion, cool *(informal)*, select, brilliant, very good, cracking *(Brit. informal)*, crucial *(slang)*, mean *(slang)*, superb, distinguished, fantastic, magnificent, superior, sterling, worthy, first-class, marvellous, exceptional, terrific, splendid, notable, mega *(slang)*, topping *(Brit. slang)*, sovereign, dope *(slang)*, world-class, exquisite, admirable, exemplary, wicked *(slang)*, first-rate, def *(slang)*, superlative, top-notch *(informal)*, brill *(informal)*, pre-eminent, meritorious, estimable, tiptop, bodacious *(slang, chiefly U.S.)*, boffo *(slang)*, jim-dandy *(slang)*, A1 *or* A-one *(informal)*, bitchin' *(U.S. slang)*, chillin' *(U.S. slang)*, booshit *(Austral. slang)*, exo *(Austral. slang)*, sik *(Austral. slang)*, rad *(informal)*, phat *(slang)*, beaut *(informal)*, barrie *(Scot. slang)*, belting *(Brit. slang)*, pearler *(Austral. slang)* **OPPOSITE:** terrible **2 = stylish**, smart, chic, polished, fashionable, trendy *(Brit. informal)*, classy *(slang)*, in fashion, snappy, in vogue, dapper, natty *(informal)*, snazzy *(informal)*, modish, well turned-out, dressy *(informal)*, à la mode, voguish, funky **OPPOSITE:** scruffy

scholar NOUN **1 = intellectual**, academic, man of letters, bookworm, egghead *(informal)*, savant, bluestocking *(usually derogatory)*, acca *(Austral. slang)*: *The library attracts thousands of scholars and researchers.* **2 = student**, pupil, learner, schoolboy *or* schoolgirl: *She could be a good scholar if she didn't let her mind wander so much.*

> **QUOTATIONS**
> The ink of the scholar is more sacred than the blood of the martyr
> [Mohammed]

scholarly ADJECTIVE **= learned**, academic, intellectual, lettered, erudite, scholastic, well-read, studious, bookish, swotty *(Brit. informal)* **OPPOSITE:** uneducated

scholarship NOUN **1 = grant**, award, payment, exhibition, endowment, fellowship, bursary: *scholarships for women over 30* **2 = learning**, education, culture, knowledge, wisdom, accomplishments, attainments, lore, erudition, academic study, book-learning: *I want to take advantage of your lifetime of scholarship.*

scholastic ADJECTIVE **= learned**, academic, scholarly, lettered, literary, bookish

school NOUN **1 = academy**, college, institution, institute, discipline, seminary, educational institution, centre of learning, alma mater: *a boy*

Henry James's Use of Adverbs

In the writing of Henry James, the frequency of *so*, (adverb and conjunction), is twice that found for the word in the Collins *Bank of English* fiction wordlist. This can be explained by the fact that *so* is used much more in spoken English than in written English – and a large part of James's novels and stories consists of dialogue. Another factor is his characters' propensity for superlatives and exclamations: *so frightful; so dreadful; so ugly; so kind, so very kind; so very, very sorry*. Another very frequently used adverb that has a superlative meaning is *quite*. Whereas in modern usage the commonest meaning of this word is 'moderately', in the 19th century it generally meant 'utterly', as in *quite alone*; *I quite despair*; *of quite another type*, and this is the sense in which James most often uses it. Occasionally his meaning could be misconstrued: in the following description from *A Little Tour of France*, the censorious young monk travelling with the nice old priest thinks him utterly frivolous, not just somewhat frivolous:

> Indeed, he was a very childish and delightful old priest, and his companion evidently thought him quite frivolous.

A similar change of meaning has happened with *fairly* – which in previous centuries was used with verbs with the now uncommon sense of 'absolutely', as in 'the days fairly flew by'. James often uses the word in this way:

> ... there was something in this lady's large assured attack that fairly intimidated him.

James uses descriptive adverbs lavishly and idiosyncratically, particularly in his famously labyrinthine late novels. The adverbial counterparts of many of his favourite adjectives, such as *charmingly, beautifully, wonderfully, immensely* occur frequently, as in *say/smile charmingly; charmingly pretty/grateful*; *wonderfully kind/graceful*. These uses are unsurprising, but *immensely* sounds odd with verbs such as *want* and *wish*, and downright bizarre with *thresh out* – and yet it conveys the enjoyment and energy of a discussion:

> ... at the first rehearsals, ... they threshed things out **immensely** in a corner of the stage.

Beautifully, too, modifies unexpected verbs, such as *understand, believe, plead, indulge, hope*. One does not normally think of these as actions that can be done *beautifully* – but the oddness serves to emphasize the emotional response of an observer:

> ... there was never a word he had said to her that she hadn't **beautifully** understood.

The following extract from a sentence in the late novel, *The Wings of the Dove*, contains twelve adverbs:

> ... a friend who would **moreover** be, **wonderfully**, the **most** appointed, the **most thoroughly** adjusted of the whole collection, inasmuch as he would **somehow** wear the character **scientifically**, **ponderably**, **proveably** – not **just loosely** and **sociably**.

The meaning of this stream of language is far from clear, but the adverbs create a strong rhythm, and a kind of coherence. The impression of a person following a train of thought is conveyed by *moreover*, and her excitement is conveyed by *wonderfully*. The repetition of *most* seems to give coherence, as does the group of three adverbs ending in -ly. The fact that there are three of them is probably more important than the meaning of the last two – in the Collins *Bank of English* fiction wordlist only Henry James uses *ponderably* and *proveably* (the latter has come to be used in scientific contexts). The final adverb too is questionable as regards its meaning – here it seems to mean 'in a social way': 'socially', in fact. Elsewhere James uses *sociably* in the usual way – with verbs such as *say, reply, ask*. Here he uses it for stylistic reasons – because its final *-ably* balances the final two syllables of *ponderably* and *proveably*.

who was in my class at school **2 = group**, set, circle, following, class, faction, followers, disciples, sect, devotees, denomination, clique, adherents, schism: *the Chicago school of economists* **3 = way of life**, creed, faith, outlook, persuasion, school of thought: *He was never a member of any school.*
▷ VERB **= train**, prime, coach, prepare, discipline, educate, drill, tutor, instruct, verse, indoctrinate: *He is schooled to spot trouble.*

> **QUOTATIONS**
> School is where you go between when your parents can't take you and industry can't take you
> [John Updike]
>
> A school is not a factory. Its raison d'être is to provide opportunity for experience
> [J.L. Carr *The Harpole Report*]

schooling NOUN **1 = teaching**, education, tuition, formal education, book-learning: *Normal schooling has been severely disrupted.* **2 = training**, coaching, instruction, grounding, preparation, drill, guidance: *the schooling of horses*

schoolteacher NOUN **= schoolmaster** *or* **schoolmistress**, instructor, pedagogue, schoolmarm *(informal)*, dominie *(Scot.)*

science NOUN **= discipline**, body of knowledge, branch of knowledge

scientific ADJECTIVE
1 = technological, technical, chemical, biological, empirical, factual: *scientific research*
2 = systematic, accurate, exact, precise, controlled, mathematical: *the scientific study of capitalist development*

scientist NOUN **= researcher**, inventor, boffin *(informal)*, technophile

> **QUOTATIONS**
> When a distinguished but elderly scientist states that something is possible, he is almost certainly right. When he states that something is impossible, he is very probably wrong. (Clarke's First Law)
> [Arthur C. Clarke *Profile of the Future*]
>
> It is a good morning exercise for a research scientist to discard a pet hypothesis every day before breakfast. It keeps him young
> [Konrad Lorenz *On Aggression*]
>
> When I find myself in the company of scientists, I feel like a shabby curate who has strayed by mistake into a drawing room full of dukes
> [W.H. Auden *The Dyer's Hand*]
>
> I don't know what I may seem to the world, but as to myself, I seem to have been only like a boy playing on the sea-shore and diverting myself in now and then finding a smoother pebble or a prettier shell than ordinary, whilst the great ocean of truth lay all undiscovered before me
> [Isaac Newton]
>
> The physicists have known sin; and this is a knowledge which they cannot lose
> [J. Robert Oppenheimer *Open Mind*]
>
> Nature, and Nature's laws lay hid in night
> God said, Let Newton be! and all was light
> [Alexander Pope *Epitaph: Intended for Sir Isaac Newton*]

scintillating ADJECTIVE **= brilliant**, exciting, stimulating, lively, sparkling, bright, glittering, dazzling, witty, animated

scion NOUN **= descendant**, child, offspring, successor, heir

scoff[1] VERB **= scorn**, mock, laugh at, ridicule, knock *(informal)*, taunt, despise, sneer, jeer, deride, slag (off) *(slang)*, flout, belittle, revile, make light of, poke fun at, twit, gibe, pooh-pooh, make sport of: *At first I scoffed at the notion.*

scoff[2] VERB **= gobble (up)**, wolf, devour, bolt, cram, put away, guzzle, gulp down, gorge yourself on, gollop, stuff yourself with, cram yourself on, make a pig of yourself on *(informal)*: *I scoffed the lot!*

scold VERB **= reprimand**, censure, rebuke, rate, blame, lecture, carpet *(informal)*, slate *(informal, chiefly Brit.)*, nag, go on at, reproach, berate, tick off *(informal)*, castigate, chide, tear into *(informal)*, tell off *(informal)*, find fault with, remonstrate with, bring (someone) to book, take (someone) to task, read the riot act, reprove, upbraid, bawl out *(informal)*, give (someone) a talking-to *(informal)*, haul (someone) over the coals *(informal)*, chew out *(U.S. & Canad. informal)*, give (someone) a dressing-down *(informal)*, tear (someone) off a strip *(Brit. informal)*, give a rocket *(Brit. & N.Z. informal)*, vituperate, give (someone) a row, have (someone) on the carpet *(informal)* **OPPOSITE:** praise

scolding NOUN **= ticking-off**, row, lecture, wigging *(Brit. slang)*, rebuke *(informal)*, dressing-down *(informal)*, telling-off *(informal)*, tongue-lashing, piece of your mind, (good) talking-to *(informal)*

scoop VERB **= win**, get, receive, land, gain, achieve, net, earn, pick up, bag *(informal)*, secure, collect, obtain, procure, come away with: *films which scooped awards around the world*
▷ NOUN **1 = ladle**, spoon, dipper: *a small ice-cream scoop* **2 = spoonful**, lump, dollop *(informal)*, ball, ladleful: *She gave him an extra scoop of clotted cream.*
3 = exclusive, exposé, coup, revelation, sensation, inside story: *one of the biggest scoops in the history of newspapers*
scoop something out 1 = take out, empty, dig out, scrape out, spoon out, bail *or* bale out: *Cut a marrow in half and scoop out the seeds.* **2 = dig**, shovel, excavate, gouge, hollow out: *A hole had been scooped out next to the house.*
scoop something *or* **someone up = gather up**, lift, pick up, take up, sweep up *or* away: *He began to scoop his things up frantically; I wanted to scoop him up in my arms and give him a hug.*

scoot VERB **= dash**, run, dart, sprint, bolt, zip, scuttle, scurry, scamper, skitter, skedaddle *(informal)*, skirr

scope NOUN **1 = opportunity**, room, freedom, space, liberty, latitude, elbowroom, leeway: *He believed in giving his staff scope for initiative.* **2 = range**, capacity, reach, area, extent, outlook, orbit, span, sphere, ambit, purview, field of reference: *the scope of a novel*

scorch VERB **= burn**, sear, char, roast, blister, wither, blacken, shrivel, parch, singe

scorching ADJECTIVE **= burning**, boiling, baking, flaming, tropical, roasting, searing, fiery, sizzling, red-hot, torrid, sweltering, broiling, unbearably hot

score VERB **1 = gain**, win, achieve, make, get, net, bag, obtain, bring in, attain, amass, notch up *(informal)*, chalk up *(informal)*: *They scored 282 points in their first innings.* **2 = go down well with (someone)**, impress, triumph, make a hit *(informal)*, make a point, gain an advantage, put yourself across, make an impact *or* impression: *He told them he had scored with the girl.* **3 = arrange**, set, orchestrate, adapt: *He scored a piece for a chamber music ensemble.* **4 = cut**, scratch, nick, mark, mar, slash, scrape, notch, graze, gouge, deface, indent, crosshatch: *Lightly score the surface of the steaks with a sharp cook's knife.*
▷ NOUN **1 = rating**, mark, grade, percentage: *low maths scores* **2 = points**, result, total, outcome: *The final score was 4-1.* **3 = composition**, soundtrack, arrangement, orchestration: *the composer of classic film scores*
4 = grievance, wrong, injury, injustice, grudge, bone of contention, bone to pick: *They had a score to settle with each other.* **5 = charge**, bill, account, total, debt, reckoning, tab *(U.S. informal)*, tally, amount due: *So what is the score anyway?*
▷ PLURAL NOUN **= lots**, loads, many, millions, gazillions *(informal)*, hundreds, hosts, crowds, masses, droves, an army, legions, swarms, multitudes, myriads, very many, a flock, a throng, a great number: *Campaigners lit scores of bonfires.*
score something out *or* **through = cross out**, delete, strike out, cancel, obliterate, put a line through: *Words and sentences had been scored out and underlined.*

scorn NOUN **= contempt**, disdain, mockery, derision, despite, slight, sneer, sarcasm, disparagement, contumely, contemptuousness, scornfulness: *They greeted the proposal with scorn.* **OPPOSITE:** respect
▷ VERB **= despise**, reject, disdain,

slight, snub, shun, be above, spurn, rebuff, deride, flout, look down on, scoff at, make fun of, sneer at, hold in contempt, turn up your nose at *(informal)*, contemn, curl your lip at, consider beneath you: *People scorn me as a single parent; people who scorned traditional methods* **OPPOSITE:** respect

> **QUOTATIONS**
> Heav'n has no rage, like love to hatred turn'd,
> Nor Hell a fury, like a woman scorn'd
> [William Congreve *The Mourning Bride*]

scornful ADJECTIVE = **contemptuous**, insulting, mocking, defiant, withering, sneering, slighting, jeering, scoffing, scathing, sarcastic, sardonic, haughty, disdainful, insolent, derisive, supercilious, contumelious

scornfully ADVERB = **contemptuously**, with contempt, dismissively, disdainfully, with disdain, scathingly, witheringly, with a sneer, slightingly, with lip curled

scotch VERB = **put an end to**, destroy, smash, devastate, wreck, thwart, scupper, extinguish, put paid to, nip in the bud, bring to an end, put the lid on, put the kibosh on

Scots ADJECTIVE = **Scottish**, Caledonian

> **QUOTATIONS**
> There are few more impressive sights in the world than a Scotsman on the make
> [J.M. Barrie *What Every Woman Knows*]

scoundrel NOUN = **rogue**, villain, heel *(slang)*, cheat, swine, rascal, son-of-a-bitch *(slang, chiefly U.S. & Canad.)*, scally *(Northwest English dialect)*, wretch, incorrigible, knave *(archaic)*, rotter *(slang, chiefly Brit.)*, ne'er-do-well, reprobate, scumbag *(slang)*, good-for-nothing, miscreant, scamp, bad egg *(old-fashioned, informal)*, blackguard, scapegrace, caitiff *(archaic)*, dastard *(archaic)*, skelm *(S. African)*, wrong 'un *(Austral. slang)*

scour[1] VERB = **scrub**, clean, polish, rub, cleanse, buff, burnish, whiten, furbish, abrade: *He decided to scour the sink.*

scour[2] VERB = **search**, hunt, comb, ransack, forage, look high and low, go over with a fine-tooth comb: *We scoured the telephone directory for clues.*

scourge NOUN **1** = **affliction**, plague, curse, terror, pest, torment, misfortune, visitation, bane, infliction: *Drugs are a scourge that is devastating our society.* **OPPOSITE:** benefit **2** = **whip**, lash, thong, switch, strap, cat-o'-nine-tails: *a heavy scourge with a piece of iron lashed into its knot*
▷ VERB **1** = **afflict**, plague, curse, torment, harass, terrorize, excoriate: *Economic anarchy scourged the post-war world.* **2** = **whip**, beat, lash, thrash, discipline, belt *(informal)*, leather, punish, whale, cane, flog, trounce, castigate, wallop *(informal)*, chastise, lather *(informal)*, horsewhip, tan (someone's) hide *(slang)*, take a strap to: *They were scourging him severely.*

scout NOUN = **vanguard**, lookout, precursor, outrider, reconnoitrer, advance guard: *They set off, two men out in front as scouts.*
▷ VERB = **reconnoitre**, investigate, check out, case *(slang)*, watch, survey, observe, spy, probe, recce *(slang)*, spy out, make a reconnaissance, see how the land lies: *I have people scouting the hills already.*
scout around *or* **round** = **search**, look for, hunt for, fossick *(Austral. & N.Z.)*, cast about *or* around, ferret about *or* around: *They scouted around for more fuel.*

scowl VERB = **glower**, frown, look daggers, grimace, lour *or* lower: *She scowled at the two men as they entered the room.*
▷ NOUN = **glower**, frown, dirty look, black look, grimace: *He met the remark with a scowl.*

scrabble VERB = **scrape**, scratch, scramble, dig, claw, paw, grope, clamber

scramble VERB **1** = **struggle**, climb, clamber, push, crawl, swarm, scrabble, move with difficulty: *He scrambled up a steep bank.* **2** = **strive**, rush, contend, vie, run, push, hasten, jostle, jockey for position, make haste: *More than a million fans are expected to scramble for tickets.* **3** = **jumble**, mix up, muddle, shuffle, entangle, disarrange: *The latest machines scramble the messages.*
▷ NOUN **1** = **clamber**, ascent: *the scramble to the top of the cliffs* **2** = **race**, competition, struggle, rush, confusion, hustle, free-for-all *(informal)*, commotion, melee *or* mêlée: *the scramble for jobs*

scrap[1] NOUN **1** = **piece**, fragment, bit, trace, grain, particle, portion, snatch, part, atom, remnant, crumb, mite, bite, mouthful, snippet, sliver, morsel, modicum, iota: *a fire fuelled by scraps of wood* **2** = **waste**, junk, off cuts: *cut up for scrap*
▷ PLURAL NOUN = **leftovers**, remains, bits, scrapings, leavings: *children foraging for scraps of food*
▷ VERB = **get rid of**, drop, abandon, shed, break up, ditch *(slang)*, junk *(informal)*, chuck *(informal)*, discard, write off, demolish, trash *(slang)*, dispense with, jettison, toss out, throw on the scrapheap, throw away *or* out: *We should scrap nuclear and chemical weapons.* **OPPOSITE:** bring back

scrap[2] NOUN = **fight**, battle, row, argument, dispute, set-to *(informal)*, disagreement, quarrel, brawl, squabble, wrangle, scuffle, tiff, dust-up *(informal)*, shindig *(informal)*, scrimmage, shindy *(informal)*, bagarre *(French)*, biffo *(Austral. slang)*: *He has never been one to avoid a scrap.*
▷ VERB = **fight**, argue, row, fall out *(informal)*, barney *(informal)*, squabble, spar, wrangle, bicker, have words, come to blows, have a shouting match *(informal)*: *They are always scrapping.*

scrape VERB **1** = **rake**, sweep, drag, brush: *She went round the car scraping the frost off the windows.* **2** = **grate**, grind, scratch, screech, squeak, rasp: *The only sound is that of knives and forks scraping against china.* **3** = **graze**, skin, scratch, bark, scuff, rub, abrade: *She stumbled and fell, scraping her palms and knees.* **4** = **clean**, remove, scour: *She scraped food off the plates into the bin.*
▷ NOUN = **predicament**, trouble, difficulty, spot *(informal)*, fix *(informal)*, mess, distress, dilemma, plight, tight spot, awkward situation, pretty pickle *(informal)*: *We got into terrible scrapes.*
scrape something together = **collect**, save, muster, get hold of, amass, hoard, glean, dredge up, rake up *or* together: *They only just managed to scrape the money together.*

scrapheap NOUN
on the scrapheap = **discarded**, ditched *(slang)*, redundant, written off, jettisoned, put out to grass *(informal)*

scrappy ADJECTIVE = **incomplete**, sketchy, piecemeal, disjointed, perfunctory, thrown together, fragmentary, bitty

scratch VERB **1** = **rub**, scrape, claw at: *The old man lifted his cardigan to scratch his side.* **2** = **mark**, cut, score, damage, grate, graze, etch, lacerate, incise, make a mark on: *Knives will scratch the worktop.*
▷ NOUN = **mark**, scrape, graze, blemish, gash, laceration, claw mark: *I pointed to a number of scratches on the tile floor.*
scratch something out = **erase**, eliminate, delete, cancel, strike off, annul, cross out: *She scratched out the word 'frightful'.*
not up to scratch = **inadequate**, unacceptable, unsatisfactory, incapable, insufficient, incompetent, not up to standard, not up to snuff *(informal)*: *This work just isn't up to scratch.*

scrawl VERB = **scribble**, doodle, squiggle: *graffiti scrawled on school walls*
▷ NOUN = **scribble**, doodle, squiggle: *a hasty, barely decipherable scrawl*

scrawny ADJECTIVE = **thin**, lean, skinny, angular, gaunt, skeletal, bony, lanky, undernourished, skin-and-bones *(informal)*, scraggy, rawboned, macilent *(rare)*

scream VERB = **cry**, yell, shriek, screech, squeal, shrill, bawl, howl, holler *(informal)*, sing out: *If I hear one more joke about my hair, I shall scream.*
▷ NOUN **1** = **cry**, yell, howl, wail, outcry, shriek, screech, yelp: *Hilda let out a scream.* **2** = **laugh**, card *(informal)*, riot *(slang)*, comic, character *(informal)*, caution *(informal)*, sensation, wit, comedian, entertainer, wag, joker, hoot *(informal)*: *He's a scream, isn't he?*

S

screech VERB **= shriek**, scream, yell, howl, wail, squeal, holler: *She was screeching at them.*
▷ NOUN **= cry**, scream, shriek, squeal, squawk, yelp: *The figure gave a screech.*

screen NOUN **= cover**, guard, shade, shelter, shield, hedge, partition, cloak, mantle, shroud, canopy, awning, concealment, room divider: *They put a screen in front of me.*
▷ VERB **1 = broadcast**, show, put on, present, air, cable, beam, transmit, relay, televise, put on the air: *The series is likely to be screened in January.* **2 = cover**, hide, conceal, shade, mask, veil, cloak, shroud, shut out: *The road is screened by a block of flats.* **3 = investigate**, test, check, examine, scan: *They need to screen everyone at risk of contracting the illness.* **4 = process**, sort, examine, grade, filter, scan, evaluate, gauge, sift: *It was their job to screen information for their bosses.* **5 = protect**, guard, shield, defend, shelter, safeguard: *They deliberately screened him from knowledge of their operations.*

screw NOUN **= nail**, pin, tack, rivet, fastener, spike: *Each bracket is fixed to the wall with just three screws.*
▷ VERB **1 = fasten**, fix, attach, bolt, clamp, rivet: *I like the sort of shelving that you screw on the wall.* **2 = turn**, twist, tighten, work in: *Screw down the lid fairly tightly.* **3 = contort**, twist, distort, contract, wrinkle, warp, crumple, deform, pucker: *He screwed his face into an expression of mock pain.* **4 = cheat**, do *(slang)*, rip (someone) off *(slang)*, skin *(slang)*, trick, con, stiff *(slang)*, sting *(informal)*, deceive, fleece, dupe, overcharge, rook *(slang)*, bamboozle *(informal)*, diddle *(informal)*, take (someone) for a ride *(informal)*, put one over on (someone) *(informal)*, pull a fast one (on someone) *(informal)*, take to the cleaners *(informal)*, sell a pup (to) *(slang)*, hornswoggle *(slang)*: *We've been screwed.* **5** *(often with* **out of***)* **= squeeze**, wring, extract, wrest, bleed someone of something: *rich nations screwing money out of poor nations*
put the screws on someone = coerce, force, compel, drive, squeeze, intimidate, constrain, oppress, pressurize, browbeat, press-gang, bring pressure to bear on, hold a knife to someone's throat: *They had to put the screws on Harper to get the information they needed.*
screw something up 1 = contort, contract, wrinkle, knot, knit, distort, crumple, pucker: *She screwed up her eyes.* **2 = bungle**, botch, mess up, spoil, bitch (up) *(slang)*, queer *(informal)*, cock up *(Brit. slang)*, mishandle, make a mess of *(slang)*, mismanage, make a hash of *(informal)*, make a nonsense of, bodge *(informal)*, flub *(U.S. slang)*, louse up *(slang)*, crool or cruel *(Austral. slang)*: *Get out. Haven't you screwed things up enough already?*

scribble VERB **= scrawl**, write, jot, pen, scratch, doodle, dash off

scribe NOUN **= secretary**, clerk, scrivener *(archaic)*, notary *(archaic)*, amanuensis, copyist

script NOUN **1 = text**, lines, words, book, copy, dialogue, manuscript, libretto: *Jenny's writing a film script.* **2 = handwriting**, writing, hand, letters, calligraphy, longhand, penmanship: *She wrote the letter in an elegant script.*
▷ VERB **= write**, draft, compose, author: *I scripted and directed both films.*

scripture NOUN **= The Bible**, The Word, The Gospels, The Scriptures, The Word of God, The Good Book, Holy Scripture, Holy Writ, Holy Bible, The Book of Books

> **QUOTATIONS**
> The devil can cite Scripture for his purpose
> [William Shakespeare *The Merchant of Venice*]

Scrooge NOUN **= miser**, penny-pincher *(informal)*, skinflint, cheapskate *(informal)*, tightwad *(U.S. & Canad. slang)*, niggard, money-grubber *(informal)*, meanie *or* meany *(informal, chiefly Brit.)*

scrounge VERB **= cadge**, beg, sponge *(informal)*, bum *(informal)*, touch (someone) for *(slang)*, blag *(slang)*, wheedle, mooch *(slang)*, forage for, hunt around (for), sorn *(Scot.)*, freeload *(slang)*, bludge *(Austral. & N.Z. informal)*

scrounger NOUN **= parasite**, freeloader *(slang)*, sponger *(informal)*, bum *(informal)*, cadger, bludger *(Austral. & N.Z. informal)*, sorner *(Scot.)*, quandong *(Austral. slang)*

scrub VERB **1 = scour**, clean, polish, rub, wash, cleanse, buff, exfoliate: *The corridors are scrubbed clean.* **2 = cancel**, drop, give up, abandon, abolish, forget about, call off, delete, do away with, discontinue: *The whole thing had to be scrubbed.*

scruff NOUN **= nape**, scrag *(informal)*

scruffy ADJECTIVE **= shabby**, untidy, ragged, rundown, messy, sloppy *(informal)*, seedy, squalid, tattered, tatty, unkempt, disreputable, scrubby *(Brit. informal)*, grungy, slovenly, mangy, sluttish, slatternly, ungroomed, frowzy, ill-groomed, draggletailed *(archaic)*, daggy *(Austral. & N.Z. informal)* **OPPOSITE:** neat

scrumptious ADJECTIVE **= delicious**, delectable, inviting, magnificent, exquisite, luscious, succulent, mouthwatering, yummy *(slang)*, appetizing, moreish *(informal)*, yummo *(Austral. slang)*

scrunch VERB **= crumple**, crush, squash, crunch, mash, ruck up

scruple NOUN **= misgiving**, hesitation, qualm, doubt, difficulty, caution, reluctance, second thoughts, uneasiness, perplexity, compunction, squeamishness, twinge of conscience

scrupulous ADJECTIVE **1 = moral**, principled, upright, honourable, conscientious: *I have been scrupulous about telling them the truth.* **OPPOSITE:** unscrupulous **2 = careful**, strict, precise, minute, nice, exact, rigorous, meticulous, painstaking, fastidious, punctilious: *scrupulous attention to detail* **OPPOSITE:** careless

scrutinize VERB **= examine**, study, inspect, research, search, investigate, explore, probe, analyse, scan, sift, dissect, work over, pore over, peruse, inquire into, go over with a fine-tooth comb

scrutiny NOUN **= examination**, study, investigation, search, inquiry, analysis, inspection, exploration, sifting, once-over *(informal)*, perusal, close study

scud VERB **= fly**, race, speed, shoot, blow, sail, skim

scuffle NOUN **= fight**, set-to *(informal)*, scrap *(informal)*, disturbance, fray, brawl, barney *(informal)*, ruck *(slang)*, skirmish, tussle, commotion, rumpus, affray *(Law)*, shindig *(informal)*, ruction *(informal)*, ruckus *(informal)*, scrimmage, shindy *(informal)*, bagarre *(French)*, biffo *(Austral. slang)*: *Violent scuffles broke out.*
▷ VERB **= fight**, struggle, clash, contend, grapple, jostle, tussle, come to blows, exchange blows: *Police scuffled with some of the protesters.*

sculpture NOUN **= statue**, figure, model, bust, effigy, figurine, statuette: *a collection of 20th-century sculptures*
▷ VERB **= carve**, form, cut, model, fashion, shape, mould, sculpt, chisel, hew, sculp: *He sculptured the figure in marble.*

scum NOUN **1 = rabble**, trash *(chiefly U.S. & Canad.)*, riffraff, rubbish, dross, lowest of the low, dregs of society, canaille *(French)*, ragtag and bobtail: *They're cultureless scum drifted from elsewhere.* **2 = impurities**, film, crust, froth, scruff, dross, offscourings: *scum around the bath*

scungy ADJECTIVE **= sordid**, seedy, sleazy, squalid, mean, dirty, foul, filthy, unclean, wretched, seamy, slovenly, skanky *(slang)*, slummy, festy *(Austral. slang)*: *He was living in some scungy flat on the outskirts of town.*

scupper VERB **= destroy**, ruin, wreck, defeat, overwhelm, disable, overthrow, demolish, undo, torpedo, put paid to, discomfit

scurrilous ADJECTIVE **= slanderous**, scandalous, defamatory, low, offensive, gross, foul, insulting, infamous, obscene, abusive, coarse, indecent, vulgar, foul-mouthed, salacious, ribald, vituperative, scabrous, Rabelaisian

scurry VERB **= hurry**, race, dash, fly, sprint, dart, whisk, skim, beetle, scud, scuttle, scoot, scamper: *The attack began, sending residents scurrying for cover.* **OPPOSITE:** amble

S

▷ NOUN = **flurry**, race, bustle, whirl, scampering: *a mad scurry for a suitable venue*

scuttle VERB = **run**, scurry, scamper, rush, hurry, scramble, hare (*Brit. informal*), bustle, beetle, scud, hasten, scoot, scutter (*Brit. informal*)

sea NOUN **1** = **ocean**, the deep, the waves, the drink (*informal*), the briny (*informal*), main: *Most of the kids have never seen the sea.* **2** = **mass**, lot, lots (*informal*), army, host, crowd, collection, sheet, assembly, mob, congregation, legion, abundance, swarm, horde, multitude, myriad, throng, expanse, plethora, profusion, concourse, assemblage, vast number, great number: *Down below them was the sea of upturned faces.*
▷ MODIFIER = **marine**, ocean, maritime, aquatic, oceanic, saltwater, ocean-going, seagoing, pelagic, briny, salt: *a sea vessel*
at sea = **bewildered**, lost, confused, puzzled, uncertain, baffled, adrift, perplexed, disconcerted, at a loss, mystified, disoriented, bamboozled (*informal*), flummoxed, at sixes and sevens: *I'm totally at sea with popular culture.*
▸ *related adjectives*: marine, maritime

QUOTATIONS
the wine-dark sea
[Homer *Iliad*]

ocean: a body of water occupying about two-thirds of a world made for man – who has no gills
[Ambrose Bierce *The Devil's Dictionary*]

seafaring ADJECTIVE = **nautical**, marine, naval, maritime, oceanic

seal VERB = **settle**, clinch, conclude, consummate, finalize, shake hands on (*informal*): *McLaren are close to sealing a deal with Renault.*
▷ NOUN **1** = **sealant**, sealer, adhesive: *Wet the edges where the two crusts join, to form a seal.* **2** = **authentication**, stamp, confirmation, assurance, ratification, notification, insignia, imprimatur, attestation: *the President's seal of approval*
set the seal on something = **confirm**, establish, assure, stamp, ratify, validate, attest, authenticate: *Many are hoping that this visit may set the seal on a new relationship between them.*

seam NOUN **1** = **joint**, closure, suture (*Surgery*): *The seam of her tunic was split from armpit to hem.* **2** = **layer**, vein, stratum, lode: *The average UK coal seam is one metre thick.*

sear VERB = **wither**, burn, blight, brand, scorch, sizzle, shrivel, cauterize, desiccate, dry up *or* out

search VERB = **examine**, check, investigate, explore, probe, inspect, comb, inquire, sift, scour, ferret, pry, ransack, forage, scrutinize, turn upside down, rummage through, frisk (*informal*), cast around, rifle through, leave no stone unturned, turn inside out, fossick (*Austral. & N.Z.*), go over with a fine-tooth comb: *Armed troops searched the hospital yesterday.*
▷ NOUN = **hunt**, look, inquiry, investigation, examination, pursuit, quest, going-over (*informal*), inspection, exploration, scrutiny, rummage: *There was no chance of him being found alive and the search was abandoned.*
search for something *or* **someone** = **look for**, seek, hunt for, pursue, go in search of, cast around for, go in pursuit of, go in quest of, ferret around for, look high and low for: *The Turkish security forces have started searching for the missing men.*

searching ADJECTIVE = **keen**, sharp, probing, close, severe, intent, piercing, penetrating, thorough, quizzical OPPOSITE: superficial

searing ADJECTIVE **1** = **acute**, sharp, intense, shooting, violent, severe, painful, distressing, stabbing, fierce, stinging, piercing, sore, excruciating, gut-wrenching: *She woke to a searing pain in her feet.* **2** = **cutting**, biting, severe, bitter, harsh, scathing, acrimonious, barbed, hurtful, sarcastic, sardonic, caustic, vitriolic, trenchant, mordant, mordacious, acerb: *They have long been subject to searing criticism.*

season NOUN = **period**, time, term, spell, time of year: *birds arriving for the breeding season*
▷ VERB **1** = **flavour**, salt, spice, lace, salt and pepper, enliven, pep up, leaven: *Season the meat with salt and pepper.* **2** = **mature**, age, condition, prime, prepare, temper, mellow, ripen, acclimatize: *Ensure that the new wood has been seasoned.* **3** = **make experienced**, train, mature, prepare, discipline, harden, accustom, toughen, inure, habituate, acclimatize, anneal: *Both actors seem to have been seasoned by experience.*

SEASONS

Season	Related adjective
spring	vernal
summer	aestival *or* estival
autumn	autumnal
winter	hibernal *or* hiemal

seasoned ADJECTIVE = **experienced**, veteran, mature, practised, old, weathered, hardened, long-serving, battle-scarred, time-served, well-versed OPPOSITE: inexperienced

seasoning NOUN = **flavouring**, spice, salt and pepper, condiment

seat NOUN **1** = **chair**, bench, stall, throne, stool, pew, settle: *Stephen returned to his seat.* **2** = **membership**, place, constituency, chair, incumbency: *He lost his seat to the Tories.* **3** = **centre**, place, site, heart, capital, situation, source, station, location, headquarters, axis, cradle, hub: *Gunfire broke out around the seat of government.* **4** = **mansion**, house, residence, abode, ancestral hall: *her family's ancestral seat in Scotland*
▷ VERB **1** = **sit**, place, settle, set, fix, deposit, locate, install: *He waved towards a chair, and seated himself at the desk.* **2** = **hold**, take, accommodate, sit, contain, cater for, have room *or* capacity for: *The theatre seats 570.*

seating NOUN = **accommodation**, room, places, seats, chairs

secede VERB = **withdraw**, leave, resign, separate, retire, quit, pull out, break with, split from, disaffiliate, apostatize

secession NOUN = **withdrawal**, break, split, defection, seceding, apostasy, disaffiliation

SEAS AND OCEANS

Seas

Adriatic	Banda	Celebes	Inland	Marmara *or* Marmora	Ross	Weddell
Aegean	Barents	Ceram	Ionian	Mediterranean	Sargasso	White
Amundsen	Beaufort	China	Irish	Nordenskjöld	Scotia	Yellow *or* Hwang Hai
Andaman	Bellingshausen	Chukchi	Japan	North	Solomon	
Arabian	Bering	Coral	Java	Norwegian	South China	
Arafura	Bismarck	East China	Kara	Okhotsk	Sulu	
Aral	Black *or* Euxine	East Siberian	Laptev	Philippine	Tasman	
Azov	Caribbean	Flores	Ligurian	Red	Timor	
Baltic	Caspian	Icarian	Lincoln		Tyrrhenian	

Oceans

Antarctic *or* Southern, Arctic, Atlantic, Indian, Pacific

secluded ADJECTIVE **= private**, sheltered, isolated, remote, lonely, cut off, solitary, out-of-the-way, tucked away, cloistered, sequestered, off the beaten track, unfrequented **OPPOSITE:** public

seclusion NOUN **= privacy**, isolation, solitude, hiding, retirement, shelter, retreat, remoteness, ivory tower, concealment, purdah

second[1] ADJECTIVE **1 = next**, following, succeeding, subsequent, sophomore (*U.S. & Canad.*): *the second day of his visit to Delhi* **2 = additional**, other, further, extra, alternative, repeated: *Her second attempt proved disastrous.* **3 = spare**, duplicate, alternative, additional, back-up: *The suitcase contained clean shirts and a second pair of shoes.* **4 = inferior**, secondary, subordinate, supporting, lower, lesser: *They have to rely on their second string strikers.*
▷ NOUN **= supporter**, assistant, aide, partner, colleague, associate, backer, helper, collaborator, henchman, right-hand man, cooperator: *He shouted to his seconds, 'I did it!'*
▷ VERB **= support**, back, endorse, forward, promote, approve, go along with, commend, give moral support to: *He seconded the motion against fox hunting.*

second[2] NOUN **= moment**, minute, instant, flash, tick (*Brit. informal*), sec (*informal*), twinkling, split second, jiffy (*informal*), trice, twinkling of an eye, two shakes of a lamb's tail (*informal*), bat of an eye (*informal*)

secondary ADJECTIVE
1 = subordinate, minor, lesser, lower, inferior, unimportant, second-rate: *Refugee problems remained of secondary importance.* **OPPOSITE:** main
2 = resultant, resulting, contingent, derived, derivative, indirect, second-hand, consequential: *There was evidence of secondary tumours.* **OPPOSITE:** original

second-class ADJECTIVE **1 = inferior**, lesser, second-best, unimportant, second-rate, low-class: *Too many airlines treat our children as second-class citizens.* **2 = mediocre**, second-rate, mean, middling, ordinary, inferior, indifferent, commonplace, insignificant, so-so (*informal*), outclassed, uninspiring, undistinguished, uninspired, bog-standard (*Brit. & Irish slang*), no great shakes (*informal*), déclassé, half-pie (*N.Z. informal*), fair to middling (*informal*): *a second-class education*

second-hand ADJECTIVE **= used**, old, handed down, hand-me-down (*informal*), nearly new, reach-me-down (*informal*), preloved (*Austral. slang*)

secondly ADVERB **= next**, second, moreover, furthermore, also, in the second place

second-rate ADJECTIVE **= inferior**, mediocre, poor, cheap, pants (*slang*), commonplace, tacky (*informal*), shoddy, low-grade, tawdry, low-quality, substandard, low-rent (*informal, chiefly U.S.*), (strictly) for the birds (*informal*), two-bit (*U.S. & Canad. slang*), end-of-the-pier (*Brit. informal*), no great shakes (*informal*), cheap and nasty (*informal*), rubbishy, dime-a-dozen (*informal*), bush-league (*Austral. & N.Z. informal*), not much cop (*Brit. slang*), tinhorn (*U.S. slang*), bodger *or* bodgie (*Austral. slang*) **OPPOSITE:** first-rate

secrecy NOUN **1 = mystery**, stealth, concealment, furtiveness, cloak and dagger, secretiveness, huggermugger (*archaic*), clandestineness, covertness: *He shrouded his business dealings in secrecy.* **2 = confidentiality**, privacy: *The secrecy of the confessional.* **3 = privacy**, silence, retirement, solitude, seclusion: *These problems had to be dealt with in the secrecy of your own cell.*

> **QUOTATIONS**
> If you would wish another to keep your secret, first keep it yourself
> [Seneca *Hippolytus*]

secret ADJECTIVE **1 = undisclosed**, unknown, confidential, underground, undercover, unpublished, under wraps, unrevealed: *Soldiers have been training at a secret location.* **2 = concealed**, hidden, disguised, covered, camouflaged, unseen: *It has a secret compartment hidden behind the magical mirror.* **OPPOSITE:** unconcealed **3 = undercover**, covert, furtive, shrouded, behind someone's back, conspiratorial, hush-hush (*informal*), surreptitious, cloak-and-dagger, backstairs: *I was heading on a secret mission that made my flesh crawl.* **OPPOSITE:** open **4 = secretive**, reserved, withdrawn, close, deep, discreet, enigmatic, reticent, cagey (*informal*), unforthcoming: *the secret man behind the masks* **OPPOSITE:** frank **5 = mysterious**, cryptic, abstruse, classified, esoteric, occult, clandestine, arcane, recondite, cabbalistic: *a secret code* **OPPOSITE:** straightforward
▷ NOUN **1 = private affair**, confidence, skeleton in the cupboard: *I can't tell you; it's a secret.* **2 = key**, answer, formula, recipe: *The secret of success is honesty and fair dealing.*
in secret = secretly, surreptitiously, slyly, behind closed doors, incognito, by stealth, in camera, huggermugger (*archaic*): *Dan found out that I'd been meeting my ex-boyfriend in secret.*
▸ *related adjective:* cryptic

> **QUOTATIONS**
> They have a skeleton in their closet
> [William Makepeace Thackeray *The Newcomes*]
>
> I know that's a secret, for it's whispered every where
> [William Congreve *Love for Love*]
>
> For secrets are edged tools,
> And must be kept from children and from fools
> [John Dryden *Sir Martin Mar-All*]

secret agent NOUN **= spy**, undercover agent, spook (*U.S. & Canad. informal*), nark (*Brit., Austral. & N.Z. slang*), cloak-and-dagger man

secrete[1] VERB **= give off**, emit, emanate, exude, extrude: *The sweat glands secrete water.*

secrete[2] VERB **= hide**, conceal, stash (*informal*), cover, screen, secure, bury, harbour, disguise, veil, shroud, stow, cache, stash away (*informal*): *She secreted the gun in the kitchen cabinet.* **OPPOSITE:** display

secretion NOUN **= discharge**, emission, excretion, exudation, extravasation (*Medical*)

secretive ADJECTIVE **= reticent**, reserved, withdrawn, close, deep, enigmatic, cryptic, cagey (*informal*), uncommunicative, unforthcoming, tight-lipped, playing your cards close to your chest, clamlike **OPPOSITE:** open

secretly ADVERB **= in secret**, privately, surreptitiously, quietly, covertly, behind closed doors, in confidence, in your heart, furtively, in camera, confidentially, on the fly (*slang, chiefly Brit.*), stealthily, under the counter, clandestinely, unobserved, on the sly, in your heart of hearts, behind (someone's) back, in your innermost thoughts, on the q.t. (*informal*)

sect NOUN **= group**, division, faction, party, school, camp, wing, denomination, school of thought, schism, splinter group

sectarian ADJECTIVE **= narrow-minded**, partisan, fanatic, fanatical, limited, exclusive, rigid, parochial, factional, bigoted, dogmatic, insular, doctrinaire, hidebound, clannish, cliquish: *sectarian religious groups* **OPPOSITE:** tolerant
▷ NOUN **= bigot**, extremist, partisan, disciple, fanatic, adherent, zealot, true believer, dogmatist: *He remains a sectarian.*

section NOUN **1 = part**, piece, portion, division, sample, slice, passage, component, segment, fragment, fraction, instalment, cross section, subdivision: *a geological section of a rock* **2 = district**, area, region, sector, zone: *Kolonarai is a lovely residential section of Athens.*

sectional ADJECTIVE **= regional**, local, separate, divided, exclusive, partial, separatist, factional, localized

sector NOUN **1 = part**, division, category, stratum, subdivision: *the nation's manufacturing sector* **2 = area**, part, region, district, zone, quarter: *Officers were going to retake sectors of the city.*

secular ADJECTIVE **= worldly**, state, lay, earthly, civil, temporal, profane, laic, nonspiritual, laical **OPPOSITE:** religious

secure VERB **1 = obtain**, get, acquire, land (*informal*), score (*slang*), gain, pick up, get hold of, come by, procure,

S

The Language of Beatrix Potter

Helen Beatrix Potter (1866–1943) is best known as the author and illustrator of 23 popular children's books, including *The Tale of Peter Rabbit, The Tale of Squirrel Nutkin* and *The Tailor of Gloucester,* all celebrated for their endearing animal characters and charming illustrations.

Many of these anthropomorphic tales relate the adventures of a young animal as it narrowly avoids being turned into someone else's dinner before escaping and returning to the safety of home, and the nouns Potter uses most are simple everyday ones designating the places (*house, kitchen, hole, home, wood, garden*), characters (*rabbit, mouse, pig, rat*), objects, and events (*sack, fire, coat, pie, dinner*) involved. The verbs and adjectives employed most are of a similarly undemanding nature (*say, go, come, get, look, sit, run, good, old, big*). However, while the words she uses most often are the relatively short and simple ones that one might expect, Potter is not afraid to pepper her work with plenty of more formal vocabulary that children would find challenging (*indolent, impertinent, improvident, superfluous, doleful, lamentable, throstle, wainscot, gimlet*).

Not only do Potter's animals have shoes and clothes, they are also depicted in very human terms: they *wring* their paws, *recover* their *manners,* are *anxious parents* and are *driven distracted*; Mrs. Tittlemouse is described as *a resourceful person,* while a particular fox is a *bushy long-tailed gentleman.* Adult animals are given anthropomorphic titles (***Mrs.*** *Tittlemouse,* ***Mr.*** *Jackson, Old* ***Mr.*** *Bouncer*), and family members are sometimes addressed or referred to using a relationship word (***Cousin*** *Peter,* ***Uncle*** *Bouncer*). It may be worth noting that *Uncle Bouncer*'s name follows the archaic title-plus-surname pattern shared with *Uncle Pumblechook* in Dickens' *Great Expectations;* in current usage *Uncle* and *Aunt* are usually followed by a first name.

Potter's language is at times quite formal; she avoids contracted forms, except sometimes in speech, forms the negative of non-auxiliary *have* with *not* alone, and has her characters talk to one another with politeness and formality, often using high-register Latinate words and now rare constructions:

> 'Will not the string be very indigestible,
> Anna Maria?'

The polite formality of the animals' speech contrasts humorously with the less lofty aims and motives that the reader, if not the protagonist, knows them to harbour:

> 'Madam, have you lost your way?'

Today's writers use *upon* far less frequently than *on* except in certain set expressions. While Potter employs it only half as much as *on,* she does so in contexts where it sounds unnaturally formal or odd to a modern reader (for example, *outside* ***upon*** *the landing* and *get* ***upon*** *my nerves).*

When Potter was writing, the use of *may* for requesting or granting permission was more common than nowadays, so usage that strikes us as very formal would not have seemed so then:

> 'You **may** sleep on the rug,' said Mr. Peter
> Thomas Piperson.

In the above example, the name *Peter Thomas Piperson* is an allusion to the nursery rhyme, *Tom, Tom the Piper's son,* parts of which are quoted elsewhere in the same story. Beatrix Potter often uses excerpts or adaptations of nursery rhymes in her tales, something which, along with her frequent *'Once upon a time'* openings, serves to root her stories firmly in tradition:

> 'Your house is on fire, Mother Ladybird! Fly
> away home to your children!'

Beatrix Potter uses many more exclamation marks in her texts than is common in present-day writing and she is also far fonder of the semi-colon than are most modern writers, sometimes using it in unexpected places, such as before *but*:

> This looks like the end of the story; but it isn't.

make sure of, win possession of: *His achievements helped him to secure the job.* **OPPOSITE:** lose **2 = attach**, stick, fix, bind, pin, lash, glue, fasten, rivet: *The frames are secured by horizontal rails to the back wall.* **OPPOSITE:** detach **3 = guarantee**, insure, ensure, assure: *The loan is secured against your home.* **OPPOSITE:** endanger
▷ ADJECTIVE **1 = safe**, protected, shielded, sheltered, immune, unassailable, impregnable: *We shall make sure our home is as secure as possible.* **OPPOSITE:** unprotected **2 = fast**, firm, fixed, tight, stable, steady, fortified, fastened, dependable, immovable: *Shelves are only as secure as their fixings.* **OPPOSITE:** insecure **3 = reliable**, definite, solid, absolute, conclusive, in the bag *(informal)*: *demands for secure wages and employment* **4 = confident**, sure, easy, certain, assured, reassured: *She felt secure and protected when she was with him.* **OPPOSITE:** uneasy

security NOUN **1 = precautions**, defence, safeguards, guards, protection, surveillance, safety measures: *under pressure to tighten airport security* **2 = assurance**, confidence, conviction, certainty, reliance, sureness, positiveness, ease of mind, freedom from doubt: *He loves the security of a happy home life.* **OPPOSITE:** insecurity **3 = pledge**, insurance, guarantee, hostage, collateral, pawn, gage, surety: *The banks will pledge the land as security.* **4 = protection**, cover, safety, retreat, asylum, custody, refuge, sanctuary, immunity, preservation, safekeeping: *He could not remain long in a place of security.* **OPPOSITE:** vulnerability

sedate ADJECTIVE **1 = calm**, collected, quiet, seemly, serious, earnest, cool, grave, proper, middle-aged, composed, sober, dignified, solemn, serene, tranquil, placid, staid, demure, unflappable *(informal)*, unruffled, decorous, imperturbable: *She took them to visit her sedate, elderly cousins.* **OPPOSITE:** wild **2 = unhurried**, easy, relaxed, comfortable, steady, gentle, deliberate, leisurely, slow-moving, chilled *(informal)*: *We set off again at a more sedate pace.*

sedative ADJECTIVE **= calming**, relaxing, soothing, allaying, anodyne, soporific, sleep-inducing, tranquillizing, calmative, lenitive: *Amber bath oil has a sedative effect.*
▷ NOUN **= tranquillizer**, narcotic, sleeping pill, opiate, anodyne, calmative, downer *or* down *(slang)*: *They use opium as a sedative.*

sedentary ADJECTIVE **= inactive**, sitting, seated, desk, motionless, torpid, desk-bound **OPPOSITE:** active

sediment NOUN **= dregs**, grounds, residue, lees, deposit, precipitate, settlings

sedition NOUN **= rabble-rousing**, treason, subversion, agitation, disloyalty, incitement to riot

seduce VERB **1 = tempt**, attract, lure, entice, mislead, deceive, beguile, allure, decoy, ensnare, lead astray, inveigle: *The view of the lake and plunging cliffs seduces visitors.* **2 = corrupt**, ruin *(archaic)*, betray, deprave, dishonour, debauch, deflower: *a fifteen-year-old seduced by a man twice her age*

seduction NOUN **1 = temptation**, lure, snare, allure, enticement: *The seduction of the show is the fact that the kids are in it.* **2 = corruption**, ruin *(archaic)*, defloration: *his seduction of a minor*

seductive ADJECTIVE **= tempting**, inviting, attractive, sexy *(informal)*, irresistible, siren, enticing, provocative, captivating, beguiling, alluring, bewitching, ravishing, flirtatious, come-to-bed *(informal)*, come-hither *(informal)*, hot *(informal)*

see VERB **1 = perceive**, note, spot, notice, mark, view, eye, check, regard, identify, sight, witness, clock *(Brit. slang)*, observe, recognize, distinguish, glimpse, check out *(informal)*, make out, heed, discern, behold, eyeball *(slang)*, catch a glimpse of, catch sight of, espy, get a load of *(slang)*, descry, take a dekko at *(Brit. slang)*, lay *or* clap eyes on *(informal)*: *I saw a man making his way towards me.* **2 = understand**, get, follow, realize, know, appreciate, take in, grasp, make out, catch on *(informal)*, comprehend, fathom, get the hang of *(informal)*, get the drift of: *Oh, I see what you're saying.* **3 = foresee**, picture, imagine, anticipate, divine, envisage, visualize, foretell: *We can see a day when all people live side by side.* **4 = find out**, learn, discover, determine, investigate, verify, ascertain, make inquiries: *I'd better go and see if she's all right.* **5 = consider**, decide, judge, reflect, deliberate, mull over, think over, make up your mind, give some thought to: *We'll see what we can do, Miss.* **6 = make sure**, mind, ensure, guarantee, take care, make certain, see to it: *See that you take care of him.* **7 = accompany**, show, escort, lead, walk, attend, usher: *He didn't offer to see her to her car.* **8 = speak to**, receive, interview, consult, confer with: *The doctor can see you now.* **9 = meet**, encounter, come across, run into, happen on, bump into, run across, chance on: *I saw her last night at Monica's.* **10 = go out with**, court, date *(informal, chiefly U.S.)*, walk out with *(obsolete)*, keep company with, go steady with *(informal)*, consort *or* associate with, step out with *(informal)*: *My husband was still seeing her.*
see about something = take care of, deal with, look after, see to, attend to: *I must see about selling the house.*
see something through = persevere (with), keep at, persist, stick out *(informal)*, see out, stay to the bitter end: *He will not be credited with seeing the project through.*
see through something *or* **someone = be undeceived by**, penetrate, be wise to *(informal)*, fathom, get to the bottom of, not fall for, have (someone's) number *(informal)*, read (someone) like a book: *I saw through your little ruse from the start.*
see to something *or* **someone = take care of**, manage, arrange, look after, organize, be responsible for, sort out, attend to, take charge of, do: *Franklin saw to the luggage.*
seeing as = since, as, in view of the fact that, inasmuch as: *Seeing as he is a doctor, I would assume he has a modicum of intelligence.*

> **PROVERBS**
> *What the eye doesn't see, the heart doesn't grieve over*
> *What you see is what you get*
> *Seeing is believing*

> **USAGE**
> It is common to hear *seeing as how*, as in *Seeing as how the bus is always late, I don't need to hurry*. However, the use of *how* here is considered incorrect or nonstandard, and should be avoided.

seed NOUN **1 = grain**, pip, germ, kernel, egg, embryo, spore, ovum, egg cell, ovule: *a packet of cabbage seed* **2 = beginning**, start, suspicion, germ, inkling: *His questions were meant to plant seeds of doubt in our minds.* **3 = origin**, source, nucleus: *the seed of an idea* **4 = offspring**, children, descendants, issue, race, successors, heirs, spawn, progeny, scions: *a curse on my seed*
go *or* **run to seed = decline**, deteriorate, degenerate, decay, go downhill *(informal)*, go to waste, go to pieces, let yourself go, go to pot, go to rack and ruin, retrogress: *If unused, winter radishes run to seed in spring.*

seedy ADJECTIVE **1 = shabby**, rundown, scruffy, old, worn, faded, decaying, grubby, dilapidated, tatty, unkempt, grotty *(slang)*, crummy *(slang)*, down at heel, slovenly, mangy, manky *(Scot. dialect)*, scungy *(Austral. & N.Z.)*: *a seedy hotel close to the red light district* **OPPOSITE:** smart **2 = unwell**, ill, poorly *(informal)*, crook *(Austral. & N.Z. informal)*, ailing, sickly, out of sorts, off colour, under the weather *(informal)*, peely-wally *(Scot.)*: *All right, are you? Not feeling seedy?*

seek VERB **1 = look for**, pursue, search for, be after, hunt, go in search of, go in pursuit of, go gunning for, go in quest of: *They have had to seek work as labourers.* **2 = request**, invite, ask for, petition, plead for, solicit, beg for, petition for: *The couple have sought help from marriage guidance counsellors.* **3 = try**, attempt, aim, strive, endeavour, essay, aspire to, have a go at *(informal)*: *He also denied that he would seek to annex the country.*

> **QUOTATIONS**
> Seek, and ye shall find
> [*Bible: St. Matthew*]

seem VERB **= appear**, give the impression of being, look, look to be, sound as if you are, look as if you are, look like you are, strike you as being, have the *or* every appearance of being

seeming ADJECTIVE **= apparent**, appearing, outward, surface, illusory, ostensible, specious, quasi-

seemingly ADVERB **= apparently**, outwardly, on the surface, ostensibly, on the face of it, to all intents and purposes, to all appearances, as far as anyone could tell

seep VERB **= ooze**, well, leak, soak, bleed, weep, trickle, leach, exude, permeate, percolate

seer NOUN **= prophet**, augur, predictor, soothsayer, sibyl

seesaw VERB **= alternate**, swing, fluctuate, teeter, oscillate, go from one extreme to the other

seethe VERB **1 = be furious**, storm, rage, fume, simmer, be in a state *(informal)*, see red *(informal)*, be incensed, be livid, go ballistic *(slang, chiefly U.S.)*, foam at the mouth, be incandescent, get hot under the collar *(informal)*, wig out *(slang)*, breathe fire and slaughter: *Under the surface she was seething.* **2 = boil**, bubble, foam, churn, fizz, ferment, froth: *a seething cauldron of broth*

segment NOUN **= section**, part, piece, division, slice, portion, wedge, compartment

segregate VERB **= set apart**, divide, separate, isolate, single out, discriminate against, dissociate
OPPOSITE: unite

segregation NOUN **= separation**, discrimination, apartheid, isolation

seize VERB **1 = grab**, grip, grasp, take, snatch, clutch, snap up, pluck, fasten, latch on to, lay hands on, catch *or* take hold of: *an otter seizing a fish*
OPPOSITE: let go **2 = take by storm**, take over, acquire, occupy, conquer, annex, usurp: *Troops have seized the airport and radio stations.* **3 = confiscate**, appropriate, commandeer, impound, take possession of, requisition, sequester, expropriate, sequestrate: *Police were reported to have seized all copies of the newspaper.* **OPPOSITE:** hand back **4 = capture**, catch, arrest, get, nail *(informal)*, grasp, collar *(informal)*, hijack, abduct, nab *(informal)*, apprehend, take captive: *Men carrying sub-machine guns seized the five soldiers.*
OPPOSITE: release

seizure NOUN **1 = attack**, fit, spasm, convulsion, paroxysm: *I was prescribed drugs to control seizures.* **2 = taking**, grabbing, annexation, confiscation, commandeering: *the seizure of territory through force* **3 = capture**, arrest, apprehension, abduction: *a mass seizure of hostages*

seldom ADVERB **= rarely**, occasionally, not often, infrequently, once in a blue moon *(informal)*, hardly ever, scarcely ever **OPPOSITE:** often

select VERB **= choose**, take, pick, prefer, opt for, decide on, single out, adopt, fix on, cherry-pick, settle upon: *They selected only bright pupils.*
OPPOSITE: reject
▷ ADJECTIVE **1 = choice**, special, prime, picked, selected, excellent, rare, superior, first-class, posh *(informal, chiefly Brit.)*, first-rate, hand-picked, top-notch *(informal)*, recherché: *a select group of French cheeses*
OPPOSITE: ordinary **2 = exclusive**, elite, privileged, limited, cliquish: *a meeting of a very select club*
OPPOSITE: indiscriminate

selection NOUN **1 = choice**, choosing, pick, option, preference: *Make your selection from the list.* **2 = anthology**, collection, medley, choice, line-up, mixed bag *(informal)*, potpourri, miscellany: *this selection of popular songs*

selective ADJECTIVE **= particular**, discriminating, critical, careful, discerning, astute, discriminatory, tasteful, fastidious
OPPOSITE: indiscriminate

self-assurance NOUN **= confidence**, self-confidence, poise, nerve, assertiveness, self-possession, positiveness

self-centred ADJECTIVE **= selfish**, narcissistic, self-absorbed, inward looking, self-seeking, egotistic, wrapped up in yourself

self-confidence NOUN **= self-assurance**, confidence, poise, nerve, self-respect, aplomb, self-reliance, high morale

self-confident ADJECTIVE **= self-assured**, confident, assured, secure, poised, fearless, self-reliant, sure of yourself

self-conscious ADJECTIVE **= embarrassed**, nervous, uncomfortable, awkward, insecure, diffident, ill at ease, sheepish, bashful, aw-shucks, shamefaced, like a fish out of water, out of countenance

self-control NOUN **= willpower**, restraint, self-discipline, cool, coolness, calmness, self-restraint, self-mastery, strength of mind *or* will

> **QUOTATIONS**
> He that would govern others, first should be
> The master of himself
> [Philip Massinger *The Bondman*]

self-denial NOUN **= self-sacrifice**, renunciation, asceticism, abstemiousness, selflessness, unselfishness, self-abnegation

> **QUOTATIONS**
> Deny yourself! You must deny yourself! That is the song that never ends
> [Johann Wolfgang von Goethe *Faust*]

self-esteem NOUN **= self-respect**, confidence, courage, vanity, boldness, self-reliance, self-assurance, self-regard, self-possession, amour-propre *(French)*, faith in yourself, pride in yourself

self-evident ADJECTIVE **= obvious**, clear, undeniable, inescapable, written all over (something), cut-and-dried *(informal)*, incontrovertible, axiomatic, manifestly *or* patently true

self-government NOUN **= independence**, democracy, sovereignty, autonomy, devolution, self-determination, self-rule, home rule

self-important ADJECTIVE **= conceited**, arrogant, pompous, strutting, swaggering, cocky, pushy *(informal)*, overbearing, presumptuous, bumptious, swollen-headed, bigheaded, full of yourself

self-indulgence NOUN **= extravagance**, excess, incontinence, dissipation, self-gratification, intemperance, sensualism

selfish ADJECTIVE **= self-centred**, self-interested, greedy, mercenary, self-seeking, ungenerous, egoistic *or* egoistical, egotistic *or* egotistical, looking out for number one *(informal)*
OPPOSITE: unselfish

selfless ADJECTIVE **= unselfish**, generous, altruistic, self-sacrificing, magnanimous, self-denying, ungrudging

self-reliant ADJECTIVE **= independent**, capable, self-sufficient, self-supporting, able to stand on your own two feet *(informal)*
OPPOSITE: dependent

self-respect NOUN **= pride**, dignity, self-esteem, morale, amour-propre *(French)*, faith in yourself

self-restraint NOUN **= self-control**, self-discipline, willpower, patience, forbearance, abstemiousness, self-command

self-righteous ADJECTIVE **= sanctimonious**, smug, pious, superior, complacent, hypocritical, pi *(Brit. slang)*, too good to be true, self-satisfied, goody-goody *(informal)*, holier-than-thou, priggish, pietistic, pharisaic

self-sacrifice NOUN **= selflessness**, altruism, self-denial, generosity, self-abnegation

self-satisfied ADJECTIVE **= smug**, complacent, proud of yourself, well-pleased, puffed up, self-congratulatory, flushed with success, pleased with yourself, like a cat that has swallowed the canary, too big for your boots *or* breeches

self-styled ADJECTIVE **= so-called**, would-be, professed, self-appointed, soi-disant *(French)*, quasi-

sell VERB **1 = trade**, dispose of, exchange, barter, put up for sale: *I sold everything I owned except for my car and books.* **OPPOSITE:** buy **2 = deal in**, market, trade in, stock, handle, retail, hawk, merchandise, peddle, traffic in, vend, be in the business of: *It sells everything from hair ribbons to oriental rugs.*

OPPOSITE: buy **3 = promote**, put across, gain acceptance for: *She is hoping she can sell the idea to clients.*
sell out of something = run out of, be out of stock of: *Hardware stores have sold out of water pumps and tarpaulins.*

seller NOUN **= dealer**, merchant, vendor, agent, representative, rep, retailer, traveller, supplier, shopkeeper, purveyor, tradesman, salesman *or* saleswoman

semblance NOUN **= appearance**, show, form, air, figure, front, image, bearing, aspect, mask, similarity, resemblance, guise, façade, pretence, veneer, likeness, mien

semen NOUN **= sperm**, seed *(archaic, dialect)*, scum *(U.S. slang)*, seminal fluid, spermatic fluid

seminal ADJECTIVE **= influential**, important, ground-breaking, original, creative, productive, innovative, imaginative, formative

send VERB **1 = dispatch**, forward, direct, convey, consign, remit: *He sent a basket of exotic fruit and a card.* **2 = transmit**, broadcast, communicate: *The space probe Voyager sent back pictures of Triton.* **3 = propel**, hurl, fling, shoot, fire, deliver, cast, let fly: *He let me go with a thrust of his wrist that sent me flying.*
send something *or* **someone up = mock**, mimic, parody, spoof *(informal)*, imitate, take off *(informal)*, make fun of, lampoon, burlesque, take the mickey out of *(informal)*, satirize: *a spoof that sends up the macho world of fighter pilots*

sendoff NOUN **= farewell**, departure, leave-taking, valediction, going-away party

send-up NOUN **= parody**, take-off *(informal)*, satire, mockery, spoof *(informal)*, imitation, skit, mickey-take *(informal)*

senile ADJECTIVE **= doddering**, doting, decrepit, failing, imbecile, gaga *(informal)*, in your dotage, in your second childhood

> **USAGE**
> Words such as *senile* and *geriatric* are only properly used as medical terms. They are very insulting when used loosely to describe a person of advanced years. Care should be taken when using *old* and its synonyms, as they can all potentially cause offence.

senility NOUN **= dotage**, Alzheimer's disease, infirmity, senile dementia, decrepitude, senescence, second childhood, caducity, loss of your faculties

senior ADJECTIVE **1 = higher ranking**, superior: *Television and radio needed many more women in senior jobs.*
OPPOSITE: subordinate **2 = the elder**, major *(Brit.)*: *George Bush Senior*
OPPOSITE: junior

senior citizen NOUN **= pensioner**, retired person, old age pensioner, O.A.P., elder, old *or* elderly person

seniority NOUN **= superiority**, rank, priority, precedence, longer service

sensation NOUN **1 = feeling**, sense, impression, perception, awareness, consciousness: *A sensation of burning or tingling may be felt in the hands.*
2 = excitement, surprise, thrill, stir, scandal, furore, agitation, commotion: *She caused a sensation at the Montreal Olympics.* **3 = hit**, wow *(slang, chiefly U.S.)*, crowd puller *(informal)*: *the film that turned her into an overnight sensation*

sensational ADJECTIVE **1 = amazing**, dramatic, thrilling, revealing, spectacular, eye-popping *(informal)*, staggering, startling, horrifying, breathtaking, astounding, lurid, electrifying, hair-raising: *The world champions suffered a sensational defeat.*
OPPOSITE: dull **2 = shocking**, scandalous, exciting, yellow *(of the press)*, melodramatic, shock-horror *(facetious)*, sensationalistic: *sensational tabloid newspaper reports*
OPPOSITE: unexciting **3 = excellent**, brilliant, superb, mean *(slang)*, topping *(Brit. slang)*, cracking *(Brit. informal)*, crucial *(slang)*, impressive, smashing *(informal)*, fabulous *(informal)*, first class, marvellous, exceptional, mega *(slang)*, sovereign, awesome *(slang)*, def *(slang)*, brill *(informal)*, out of this world *(informal)*, mind-blowing *(informal)*, bodacious *(slang, chiefly U.S.)*, boffo *(slang)*, jim-dandy *(slang)*, chillin' *(U.S. slang)*, booshit *(Austral. slang)*, exo *(Austral. slang)*, sik *(Austral. slang)*, rad *(informal)*, phat *(slang)*, schmick *(Austral. informal)*, beaut *(informal)*, barrie *(Scot. slang)*, belting *(Brit. slang)*, pearler *(Austral. slang)*, funky: *Her voice is sensational.*
OPPOSITE: ordinary

sense NOUN **1 = faculty**, sensibility: *a keen sense of smell* **2 = feeling**, impression, perception, awareness, consciousness, atmosphere, aura, intuition, premonition, presentiment: *There is no sense of urgency on either side.* **3 = understanding**, awareness, appreciation: *He has an impeccable sense of timing.* **4** *(sometimes plural)* **= intelligence**, reason, understanding, brains *(informal)*, smarts *(slang, chiefly U.S.)*, judgment, discrimination, wisdom, wit(s), common sense, sanity, sharpness, tact, nous *(Brit. slang)*, cleverness, quickness, discernment, gumption *(Brit. informal)*, sagacity, clear-headedness, mother wit: *When he was younger he had a bit more sense.*
OPPOSITE: foolishness **5 = point**, good, use, reason, value, worth, advantage, purpose, logic: *There's no sense in pretending this doesn't happen.*
6 = meaning, definition, interpretation, significance, message, import, substance, implication, drift, purport, nuance, gist, signification, denotation: *a noun which has two senses*
▷ VERB **= perceive**, feel, understand, notice, pick up, suspect, realize, observe, appreciate, grasp, be aware of, divine, discern, just know, have a (funny) feeling *(informal)*, get the impression, apprehend, have a hunch: *He had sensed what might happen.*
OPPOSITE: be unaware of

senseless ADJECTIVE **1 = pointless**, mad, crazy, stupid, silly, ridiculous, absurd, foolish, daft *(informal)*, ludicrous, meaningless, unreasonable, irrational, inconsistent, unwise, mindless, illogical, incongruous, idiotic, nonsensical, inane, fatuous, moronic, unintelligent, asinine, imbecilic, dumb-ass *(slang)*, without rhyme or reason, halfwitted: *acts of senseless violence* **OPPOSITE:** sensible
2 = unconscious, stunned, insensible, out, cold, numb, numbed, deadened, unfeeling, out cold, anaesthetized, insensate: *Then I saw my boy lying senseless on the floor.*
OPPOSITE: conscious

sensibility NOUN **1 = awareness**, insight, intuition, taste, appreciation, delicacy, discernment, perceptiveness: *Everything he writes demonstrates the depths of his sensibility.*
OPPOSITE: lack of awareness **2** *(often plural)* **= feelings**, emotions, sentiments, susceptibilities, moral sense: *The challenge offended their sensibilities.*

sensible ADJECTIVE **1 = wise**, practical, prudent, shrewd, well-informed, judicious, well-advised: *It might be sensible to get a solicitor.*
OPPOSITE: foolish **2 = intelligent**, practical, reasonable, rational, sound, realistic, sober, discriminating, discreet, sage, shrewd, down-to-earth, matter-of-fact, prudent, sane, canny, judicious, far-sighted, sagacious, grounded: *She was a sensible girl and did not panic.*
OPPOSITE: senseless

sensitive ADJECTIVE **1 = thoughtful**, kind, kindly, concerned, patient, attentive, tactful, unselfish: *He was always so sensitive and caring.*
2 = delicate, tender: *gentle cosmetics for sensitive skin* **3 = susceptible**, responsive, reactive, easily affected: *My eyes are overly sensitive to bright light.*
4 = touchy, oversensitive, easily upset, easily offended, easily hurt, umbrageous *(rare)*: *Young people are very sensitive about their appearance.*
OPPOSITE: insensitive **5 = precise**, fine, acute, keen, responsive, perceptive: *an extremely sensitive microscope* **OPPOSITE:** imprecise

sensitivity NOUN **1 = susceptibility**, responsiveness, reactivity, receptiveness, sensitiveness, reactiveness: *the sensitivity of cells to chemotherapy* **2 = consideration**, patience, thoughtfulness: *concern and sensitivity for each other's feelings*
3 = touchiness, oversensitivity: *an*

atmosphere of extreme sensitivity over the situation **4 = responsiveness**, precision, keenness, acuteness: *the sensitivity of the detector*

sensual ADJECTIVE **1 = sexual**, sexy *(informal)*, erotic, randy *(informal, chiefly Brit.)*, steamy *(informal)*, raunchy *(slang)*, lewd, lascivious, lustful, lecherous, libidinous, licentious, unchaste: *He was a very sensual person.* **2 = physical**, bodily, voluptuous, animal, luxurious, fleshly, carnal, epicurean, unspiritual: *sensual pleasure*

sensuality NOUN **= eroticism**, sexiness *(informal)*, voluptuousness, prurience, licentiousness, carnality, lewdness, salaciousness, lasciviousness, animalism, libidinousness, lecherousness

sensuous ADJECTIVE **= pleasurable**, pleasing, sensory, gratifying

sentence NOUN **1 = punishment**, prison term, condemnation: *He was given a four-year sentence.* **2 = verdict**, order, ruling, decision, judgment, decree, pronouncement: *When she heard of the sentence, she said: 'Is that all?'* ▷ VERB **1 = condemn**, doom: *A military court sentenced him to death in his absence.* **2 = convict**, condemn, penalize, pass judgment on, mete out justice to: *They sentenced him for punching a policewoman.*

sentient ADJECTIVE **= feeling**, living, conscious, live, sensitive, reactive

sentiment NOUN **1 = feeling**, thought, idea, view, opinion, attitude, belief, judgment, persuasion, way of thinking: *The Foreign Secretary echoed this sentiment.* **2 = sentimentality**, emotion, tenderness, romanticism, sensibility, slush *(informal)*, emotionalism, tender feeling, mawkishness, soft-heartedness, overemotionalism: *Laura kept that letter out of sentiment.*

sentimental ADJECTIVE **= romantic**, touching, emotional, tender, pathetic, nostalgic, sloppy *(informal)*, tearful, corny *(slang)*, impressionable, mushy *(informal)*, maudlin, simpering, weepy *(informal)*, slushy *(informal)*, mawkish, tear-jerking *(informal)*, drippy *(informal)*, schmaltzy *(slang)*, icky *(informal)*, gushy *(informal)*, soft-hearted, overemotional, dewy-eyed, three-hankie *(informal)* **OPPOSITE:** unsentimental

sentimentality NOUN **= romanticism**, nostalgia, tenderness, gush *(informal)*, pathos, slush *(informal)*, mush *(informal)*, schmaltz *(slang)*, sloppiness *(informal)*, emotionalism, bathos, mawkishness, corniness *(slang)*, play on the emotions, sob stuff *(informal)*

sentinel NOUN **= guard**, watch, lookout, sentry, picket, watchman

separate ADJECTIVE **1 = unconnected**, individual, particular, divided, divorced, isolated, detached, disconnected, discrete, unattached, disjointed: *The two things are separate and mutually irrelevant.* **OPPOSITE:** connected **2 = individual**, independent, apart, distinct, autonomous: *We both live our separate lives.* **OPPOSITE:** joined ▷ VERB **1 = divide**, detach, disconnect, come between, disentangle, keep apart, disjoin: *Police moved in to separate the two groups.* **OPPOSITE:** combine **2 = come apart**, split, break off, come away: *The nose section separates from the fuselage.* **OPPOSITE:** connect **3 = sever**, disconnect, break apart, split in two, divide in two, uncouple, bifurcate: *Separate the garlic into cloves.* **OPPOSITE:** join **4 = split up**, part, divorce, break up, part company, get divorced, be estranged, go different ways: *Her parents separated when she was very young.* **5 = distinguish**, mark, single out, set apart, make distinctive, set at variance *or* at odds: *What separates terrorism from other acts of violence?* **OPPOSITE:** link

separated ADJECTIVE **1 = estranged**, parted, split up, separate, apart, broken up, disunited, living apart *or* separately: *Most single parents are either separated or divorced.* **2 = disconnected**, parted, divided, separate, disassociated, disunited, sundered, put asunder: *They're trying their best to bring together separated families.*

separately ADVERB **1 = alone**, independently, apart, personally, not together, severally: *Chris had insisted that we went separately to the club.* **OPPOSITE:** together **2 = individually**, singly, one by one, one at a time: *Cook the stuffing separately.*

separation NOUN **1 = division**, break, segregation, detachment, severance, disengagement, dissociation, disconnection, disjunction, disunion, disconnect: *a permanent separation from his son* **2 = split-up**, parting, split, divorce, break-up, farewell, rift, estrangement, leave-taking: *They agreed to a trial separation.*

septic ADJECTIVE **= infected**, poisoned, toxic, festering, pussy, putrid, putrefying, suppurating, putrefactive

sequel NOUN **1 = follow-up**, continuation, development: *She is currently writing a sequel.* **2 = consequence**, result, outcome, conclusion, end, issue, payoff *(informal)*, upshot: *The arrests were a direct sequel to the investigations.*

sequence NOUN **1 = succession**, course, series, order, chain, cycle, arrangement, procession, progression: *the sequence of events that led to the murder* **2 = order**, structure, arrangement, ordering, placement, layout, progression: *The chronological sequence gives the book an element of structure.*

serene ADJECTIVE **= calm**, peaceful, tranquil, composed, sedate, placid, undisturbed, untroubled, unruffled, imperturbable, chilled *(informal)* **OPPOSITE:** troubled

serenity NOUN **= calm**, peace, tranquillity, composure, peace of mind, stillness, calmness, quietness, peacefulness, quietude, placidity

serf NOUN **= vassal**, servant, slave, thrall, bondsman, varlet *(archaic)*, helot, villein, liegeman

series NOUN **1 = sequence**, course, chain, succession, run, set, line, order, train, arrangement, string, progression: *a series of explosions* **2 = drama**, serial, soap *(informal)*, sitcom *(informal)*, soap opera, soapie *or* soapy *(Austral. slang)*, situation comedy: *Channel 4's 'GBH' won best drama series.*

serious ADJECTIVE **1 = grave**, bad, critical, worrying, dangerous, acute, alarming, severe, extreme, grievous: *His condition was serious but stable.* **2 = important**, crucial, urgent, pressing, difficult, worrying, deep, significant, grim, far-reaching, momentous, fateful, weighty, no laughing matter, of moment *or* consequence: *I regard this as a serious matter.* **OPPOSITE:** unimportant **3 = thoughtful**, detailed, careful, deep, profound, in-depth: *It was a question which deserved serious consideration.* **4 = deep**, sophisticated, highbrowed: *a serious novel* **5 = solemn**, earnest, grave, stern, sober, thoughtful, sedate, glum, staid, humourless, long-faced, pensive, unsmiling: *He's quite a serious person.* **OPPOSITE:** light-hearted **6 = sincere**, determined, earnest, resolved, genuine, deliberate, honest, resolute, in earnest: *You really are serious about this, aren't you?* **OPPOSITE:** insincere

seriously ADVERB **1 = truly**, no joking *(informal)*, in earnest, all joking aside: *Seriously, though, something must be done about it.* **2 = badly**, severely, gravely, critically, acutely, sorely, dangerously, distressingly, grievously: *Three people were seriously injured in the blast.*

seriousness NOUN **1 = importance**, gravity, urgency, moment, weight, danger, significance: *the seriousness of the crisis* **2 = solemnity**, gravity, earnestness, sobriety, gravitas, sternness, humourlessness, staidness, sedateness: *They had shown a commitment and a seriousness of purpose.*

sermon NOUN **= homily**, address, exhortation

serpentine ADJECTIVE **= twisting**, winding, snaking, crooked, coiling, meandering, tortuous, sinuous, twisty, snaky

serrated ADJECTIVE **= notched**, toothed, sawtoothed, serrate, serrulate, sawlike, serriform *(Biology)*

servant NOUN **= attendant**, domestic, slave, maid, help, helper, retainer, menial, drudge, lackey, vassal, skivvy *(chiefly Brit.)*, servitor *(archaic)*, varlet *(archaic)*, liegeman

serve VERB **1 = work for**, help, aid, assist, be in the service of: *soldiers who have served their country well* **2 = perform**,

do, complete, go through, fulfil, pass, discharge: *He had served an apprenticeship as a bricklayer.* **3 = be adequate**, do, suffice, answer, suit, content, satisfy, be good enough, be acceptable, fill the bill *(informal)*, answer the purpose: *This little book should serve.* **4 = present**, provide, supply, deliver, arrange, set out, distribute, dish up, purvey: *Serve it with French bread.*
serve as something *or* **someone = act as**, function as, do the work of, do duty as: *She ushered me into the front room, which served as her office.*

QUOTATIONS
They also serve who only stand and wait
[John Milton *Sonnet 16*]

PROVERBS
If you would be well served, serve yourself

service NOUN **1 = facility**, system, resource, utility, amenity: *a campaign for better social services* **2 = ceremony**, worship, rite, function, observance: *The President was attending the morning service.* **3 = work**, labour, employment, business, office, duty, employ: *If a young woman did not have a dowry, she went into domestic service.* **4 = check**, servicing, maintenance check: *The car needs a service.*
▷ VERB **= overhaul**, check, maintain, tune (up), repair, go over, fine tune, recondition: *Make sure that all gas fires are serviced annually.*

serviceable ADJECTIVE **= useful**, practical, efficient, helpful, profitable, convenient, operative, beneficial, functional, durable, usable, dependable, advantageous, utilitarian, hard-wearing
OPPOSITE: useless

servile ADJECTIVE **= subservient**, cringing, grovelling, mean, low, base, humble, craven, fawning, abject, submissive, menial, sycophantic, slavish, unctuous, obsequious, toadying, bootlicking *(informal)*, toadyish

serving NOUN **= portion**, helping, plateful

servitude NOUN **= slavery**, bondage, enslavement, bonds, chains, obedience, thrall, subjugation, serfdom, vassalage, thraldom

session NOUN **= meeting**, hearing, sitting, term, period, conference, congress, discussion, assembly, seminar, get-together *(informal)*

set[1] VERB **1 = put**, place, lay, park *(informal)*, position, rest, plant, station, stick, deposit, locate, lodge, situate, plump, plonk: *He took the case out of her hand and set it on the floor.* **2 = switch on**, turn on, activate, programme: *I forgot to set my alarm and I overslept.* **3 = adjust**, regulate, coordinate, rectify, synchronize: *He set his watch, then waited for five minutes.* **4 = embed**, fix, mount, install, fasten: *a gate set in a high wall* **5 = arrange**, decide (upon), settle, name, establish, determine, fix, schedule, appoint, specify, allocate, designate, ordain, fix up, agree upon: *A date will be set for a future meeting.* **6 = assign**, give, allot, prescribe: *We will train you first before we set you a task.* **7 = harden**, stiffen, condense, solidify, cake, thicken, crystallize, congeal, jell, gelatinize: *Lower the heat and allow the omelette to set on the bottom.* **8 = go down**, sink, dip, decline, disappear, vanish, subside: *The sun sets at about 4pm in winter.* **9 = prepare**, lay, spread, arrange, make ready: *She had set the table and was drinking coffee at the hearth.*
▷ ADJECTIVE **1 = established**, planned, decided, agreed, usual, arranged, rigid, definite, inflexible, hard and fast, immovable: *A set period of fasting is supposed to bring us closer to godliness.* **2 = strict**, firm, rigid, hardened, stubborn, entrenched, inflexible, hidebound: *They have very set ideas about how to get the message across.*
OPPOSITE: flexible **3 = conventional**, stock, standard, traditional, formal, routine, artificial, stereotyped, rehearsed, hackneyed, unspontaneous: *Use the subjunctive in some set phrases and idioms.*
▷ NOUN **1 = scenery**, setting, scene, stage setting, stage set, mise-en-scène *(French)*: *a movie set* **2 = position**, bearing, attitude, carriage, turn, fit, hang, posture: *the set of his shoulders*
set on *or* **upon something = determined to**, intent on, bent on, resolute about: *She was set on going to an all-girls school.*
set about someone = assault, attack, mug *(informal)*, assail, sail into *(informal)*, lambast(e), belabour: *Several thugs set about him with clubs.*
set about something = begin, start, get down to, attack, tackle, set to, get to work, sail into *(informal)*, take the first step, wade into, get cracking *(informal)*, make a start on, roll up your sleeves, get weaving *(informal)*, address yourself to, put your shoulder to the wheel *(informal)*: *He set about proving she was completely wrong.*
set off = leave, set out, depart, embark, start out, sally forth: *I set off, full of optimism.*
set on *or* **upon someone = attack**, beat up, assault, turn on, mug *(informal)*, set about, ambush, go for, sic, pounce on, fly at, work over *(slang)*, assail, sail into *(informal)*, fall upon, lay into *(informal)*, put the boot in *(slang)*, pitch into *(informal)*, let fly at, beat *or* knock seven bells out of *(informal)*: *We were set upon by three youths.*
set out = embark, set off, start out, begin, get under way, hit the road *(slang)*, take to the road, sally forth: *When setting out on a long walk, always wear suitable boots.*
set someone against someone = alienate, oppose, divide, drive a wedge between, disunite, estrange, set at odds, make bad blood between, make mischief between, set at cross purposes, set by the ears *(informal)*, sow dissension amongst: *The case has set neighbour against neighbour in the village.*
set someone up 1 = finance, back, fund, establish, promote, build up, subsidize: *Grandfather set them up in a liquor business.* **2 = prepare**, prime, warm up, dispose, make ready, put in order, put in a good position: *The win set us up perfectly for the match in Belgium.*
set something against something = balance, compare, contrast, weigh, juxtapose: *a considerable sum when set against the maximum wage*
set something aside 1 = reserve, keep, save, separate, select, single out, earmark, keep back, set apart, put on one side: *£130 million would be set aside for repairs to schools.* **2 = reject**, dismiss, reverse, cancel, overturn, discard, quash, overrule, repudiate, annul, nullify, abrogate, render null and void: *The decision was set aside because one of the judges had links with the defendant.*
set something back = hold up, slow, delay, hold back, hinder, obstruct, retard, impede, slow up: *a risk of public protest that could set back reforms*
set off 1 = detonate, trigger (off), explode, ignite, light, set in motion, touch off: *Who set off the bomb?* **2 = cause**, start, produce, generate, prompt, trigger (off), provoke, bring about, give rise to, spark off, set in motion: *It set off a storm of speculation.* **3 = enhance**, show off, throw into relief, bring out the highlights in: *Blue suits you – it sets off the colour of your hair.*
set something out 1 = arrange, present, display, lay out, exhibit, array, dispose, set forth, expose to view: *Set out the cakes attractively.* **2 = explain**, list, describe, detail, elaborate, recount, enumerate, elucidate, itemize, particularize: *He has written a letter setting out his views.*
set something up 1 = arrange, organize, prepare, make provision for, prearrange: *an organization that sets up meetings* **2 = establish**, begin, found, institute, install, initiate: *He set up the company four years ago.* **3 = build**, raise, construct, put up, assemble, put together, erect, elevate: *The activists set up a peace camp at the border.* **4 = assemble**, put up: *I set up the computer so that they could work from home.*

set[2] NOUN **1 = series**, collection, assortment, kit, outfit, batch, compendium, assemblage, coordinated group, ensemble: *Only she and Mr Cohen had complete sets of keys to the shop.* **2 = group**, company, crowd, circle, class, band, crew *(informal)*, gang, outfit, faction, sect, posse *(informal)*, clique, coterie, schism: *the popular watering hole for the literary set*

setback NOUN **= hold-up**, check, defeat, blow, upset, reverse, disappointment, hitch, misfortune, rebuff, whammy *(informal, chiefly U.S.)*, bummer *(slang)*, bit of trouble

S

The Language of Daniel Defoe

Daniel Defoe (1660–1731) was a prolific journalist, novelist, and writer of pamphlets. His style of writing is plain and utilitarian, eschewing Latinate or literary terms and tending not to aspire to the more allusive and polished prose of contemporary stylists, such as Swift, or the Augustan poets, such as Pope.

His best-remembered works include the novels *Robinson Crusoe* (1719), *Colonel Jack* (1722), and *Moll Flanders* (1722), and his blend of journalism and fiction *A Journal of the Plague Year* (1722). Much of his prodigious output has been largely forgotten but with *Robinson Crusoe*, his tale of a shipwrecked mariner struggling to survive on a desert island, he contributed two new terms to the English language which endure to this day. The title, of course, became a label for anyone enduring a harsh and lonely existence, and his hero's servant, Man Friday, became a byword for any loyal male servant or assistant. By extension of the latter he may be said to be responsible for the much later coining of *girl Friday*, meaning a versatile female employee.

Defoe was also an entrepreneur, taking a not always successful part in such ventures as the wine trade, hosiery and the manufacture of tiles, and the world of business bulks large in his writings. This can be seen in his language in which many of the most common nouns spring from this sphere of activity, such as *money, business, work, trade, tradesman,* and *merchant*. The word *tradesman*, for example, occurs far more frequently than *gentleman*.

> By the easiness of **terms** on which the **merchant** may have **money**, he is encouraged to **venture** further in **trade** than otherwise he would do.

This pattern is also shown in his use of verbs, in which such terms as *pay, lose,* and *receive* are amongst the most common. His characters are often described as paying *debts, rent, excise, premiums, quotas. customs, rates,* and *quarterage*.

Defoe's language is also very much of its time, and many of his most prevalent usages would strike a 21st-century reader as archaic. Such terms include *'tis, nay,* and *thou*. Among the words he uses that are still current, it is often an older, outdated meaning that he has in mind. Examples of this include his use of *observe* to mean both 'see' and 'remark', *distemper* to mean a human illness, *discover* to mean 'uncover' or 'bring to light' rather than 'find', and *discourse* to mean 'discussion'.

> Either the **distemper** did not come immediately by contagion from body to body, or, if it did, then a body may be capable to continue infected without the disease **discovering** itself many days, nay, weeks together.

Defoe as a journalist and pamphleteer was very much caught up in the political, religious and economic issues of his age and his language abounds with such terms as *king, army, power, prince, nation, Parliament, liberty,* and *public*; as well as *God, Devil, spirit, Christian, church, religion, Quaker* and *Heaven*.

> Banks, being established by **public authority**, ought also, as all **public things** are, to be under limitations and restrictions from that **authority**.

In 1702 one of his pamphlets, *The Shortest Way with the Dissenters*, satirized the religious intolerance of the contemporary establishment, recommending that all religious Dissenters (a minority of which he himself was one) should be put to death. This earned him a term of imprisonment, as a preamble to which he spent three days in the public pillory. Typical of his resilience and resourcefulness was the mock ode he composed while in prison, *Hymn to the Pillory*.

setting NOUN = **surroundings**, site, location, set, scene, surround, background, frame, context, perspective, backdrop, scenery, locale, mise en scène *(French)*

settle VERB **1** = **resolve**, work out, put an end to, straighten out, set to rights: *They agreed to try and settle their dispute by negotiation.* **2** = **pay**, clear, square (up), discharge: *I settled the bill for my coffee and his two glasses of wine.* **3** = **move to**, take up residence in, live in, dwell in, inhabit, reside in, set up home in, put down roots in, make your home in: *He visited Paris and eventually settled there.* **4** = **colonize**, populate, people, pioneer: *This was one of the first areas to be settled by Europeans.* **5** = **make comfortable**, bed down: *Albert settled himself on the sofa.* **6** = **subside**, fall, sink, decline: *Once its impurities had settled, the oil could be graded.* **7** = **land**, alight, descend, light, come to rest: *The birds settled less than two hundred paces away.* **8** = **calm**, quiet, relax, relieve, reassure, compose, soothe, lull, quell, allay, sedate, pacify, quieten, tranquillize: *They needed a win to settle their nerves.* **OPPOSITE:** disturb
settle on *or* **upon something** *or* **someone** = **decide on**, choose, pick, select, adopt, agree on, opt for, fix on, elect for: *We finally settled on a Mercedes estate.*

settlement NOUN **1** = **agreement**, arrangement, resolution, working out, conclusion, establishment, adjustment, confirmation, completion, disposition, termination: *Our objective must be to secure a peace settlement.* **2** = **payment**, clearing, discharge, clearance, defrayal: *ways to delay the settlement of debts* **3** = **colony**, community, outpost, peopling, hamlet, encampment, colonization, kainga *or* kaika (N.Z.): *a Muslim settlement*

settler NOUN = **colonist**, immigrant, pioneer, colonizer, frontiersman

setup NOUN = **arrangement**, system, structure, organization, conditions, circumstances, regime

sever VERB **1** = **cut**, separate, split, part, divide, rend, detach, disconnect, cleave, bisect, disunite, cut in two, sunder, disjoin: *Oil was still gushing from the severed fuel line.* **OPPOSITE:** join **2** = **discontinue**, terminate, break off, abandon, dissolve, put an end to, dissociate: *He was able to sever all emotional bonds to his family.* **OPPOSITE:** continue

several ADJECTIVE = **various**, different, diverse, divers *(archaic)*, assorted, disparate, indefinite, sundry: *one of several failed attempts*

severe ADJECTIVE **1** = **serious**, critical, terrible, desperate, alarming, extreme, awful, distressing, appalling, drastic, catastrophic, woeful, ruinous: *a business with severe cash flow problems* **2** = **acute**, extreme, intense, burning, violent, piercing, racking, searing, tormenting, exquisite, harrowing, unbearable, agonizing, insufferable, torturous, unendurable: *He woke up blinded and in severe pain.* **3** = **tough**, hard, difficult, taxing, demanding, fierce, punishing, exacting, rigorous, stringent, arduous, unrelenting: *He had faced an appallingly severe task in the jungle.* **OPPOSITE:** easy **4** = **strict**, hard, harsh, cruel, rigid, relentless, drastic, oppressive, austere, Draconian, unrelenting, inexorable, pitiless, unbending, iron-handed: *This was a dreadful crime and a severe sentence is necessary.* **OPPOSITE:** lenient **5** = **grim**, serious, grave, cold, forbidding, stern, sober, disapproving, dour, unsmiling, flinty, strait-laced, tight-lipped: *He had a severe look that disappeared when he smiled.* **OPPOSITE:** genial **6** = **plain**, simple, austere, classic, restrained, functional, Spartan, ascetic, unadorned, unfussy, unembellished, bare-bones: *wearing her felt hats and severe grey suits* **OPPOSITE:** fancy **7** = **harsh**, cutting, biting, scathing, satirical, caustic, astringent, vitriolic, mordant, unsparing, mordacious: *The team has suffered severe criticism from influential figures.* **OPPOSITE:** kind

severely ADVERB **1** = **seriously**, badly, extremely, gravely, hard, sorely, dangerously, critically, acutely: *the severely depressed construction industry* **2** = **strictly**, harshly, sternly, rigorously, sharply, like a ton of bricks *(informal)*, with an iron hand, with a rod of iron: *They should punish these drivers more severely.*

severity NOUN = **strictness**, seriousness, harshness, austerity, rigour, toughness, hardness, stringency, sternness, severeness

sew VERB = **stitch**, tack, seam, hem

sex NOUN **1** = **gender**: *differences between the sexes* **2** = **facts of life**, sexuality, reproduction, the birds and the bees *(informal)*: *a campaign to help parents talk about sex with their children* **3** = **lovemaking**, sexual relations, copulation, the other *(informal)*, screwing *(taboo, slang)*, intimacy, going to bed (with someone), shagging *(Brit. taboo, slang)*, nookie *(slang)*, fornication, coitus, rumpy-pumpy *(slang)*, legover *(slang)*, coition, rumpo *(slang)*: *The entire film revolves around sex and drugs.*

QUOTATIONS

The pleasure is momentary, the position ridiculous, and the expense damnable
[attributed to Lord Chesterfield]

When I hear his steps outside my door I lie down on my bed, close my eyes, open my legs, and think of England
[Lady Hillingdon]

Sex is what you can get. For some people, most people, it's the most important thing they can get without being born rich or smart or stealing
[Don DeLillo *Underworld*]

Sexual intercourse began
In nineteen sixty-three
(Which was rather late for me) -
Between the end of the 'Chatterley' ban
And the Beatles' first LP
[Philip Larkin *Annus Mirabilis*]

Continental people have sex lives; the English have hot-water bottles
[George Mikes *How to be an Alien*]

Is sex dirty? Only if it's done right
[Woody Allen *Everything You Always Wanted to Know About Sex*]

That [sex] was the most fun I ever had without laughing
[Woody Allen *Annie Hall*]

My mother used to say, Delia, if S-E-X ever rears its ugly head, close your eyes before you see the rest of it
[Alan Ayckbourn *Bedroom Farce*]

It doesn't matter what you do in the bedroom as long as you don't do it in the street and frighten the horses
[Mrs. Patrick Campbell]

While we have sex in the mind, we truly have none in the body
[D.H. Lawrence *Leave Sex Alone*]

There is more difference within the sexes than between them
[Ivy Compton-Burnett]

sex appeal NOUN = **desirability**, attractiveness, allure, glamour, sensuality, magnetism, sexiness *(informal)*, oomph *(informal)*, it *(informal)*, voluptuousness, seductiveness

sexual ADJECTIVE **1** = **carnal**, erotic, intimate, of the flesh, coital: *Men's sexual fantasies often have little to do with their sexual desire.* **2** = **sexy**, erotic, sensual, inviting, bedroom, provoking, arousing, naughty, provocative, seductive, sensuous, suggestive, voluptuous, slinky, titillating, flirtatious, come-hither *(informal)*, kissable, beddable: *exchanging sexual glances*

sexual intercourse NOUN = **copulation**, sex *(informal)*, the other *(informal)*, union, coupling, congress, mating, commerce *(archaic)*, screwing *(taboo, slang)*, intimacy, penetration, shagging *(Brit. taboo, slang)*, nookie *(slang)*, consummation, bonking *(informal)*, coitus, carnal knowledge, rumpy-pumpy *(slang)*, legover *(slang)*, coition

sexuality NOUN = **desire**, lust, eroticism, sensuality, virility, sexiness *(informal)*, voluptuousness, carnality, bodily appetites

sexy ADJECTIVE = **erotic**, sensual, seductive, inviting, bedroom,

S

provoking, arousing, naughty, provocative, sensuous, suggestive, voluptuous, slinky, titillating, flirtatious, come-hither *(informal)*, kissable, beddable, hot *(informal)*

shabby ADJECTIVE **1 = tatty**, worn, ragged, scruffy, faded, frayed, worn-out, tattered, threadbare, down at heel, the worse for wear, having seen better days: *His clothes were old and shabby.* **OPPOSITE:** smart **2 = rundown**, seedy, mean, neglected, dilapidated: *a rather shabby Naples hotel* **3 = mean**, low, rotten *(informal)*, cheap, dirty, shameful, low-down *(informal)*, shoddy, unworthy, despicable, contemptible, scurvy, dishonourable, ignoble, ungentlemanly: *It was hard to know why the man deserved such shabby treatment.* **OPPOSITE:** fair

shack NOUN **= hut**, cabin, shanty, lean-to, dump *(informal)*, hovel, shiel *(Scot.)*, shieling *(Scot.)*, whare *(N.Z.)*

shackle VERB **1 = hamper**, limit, restrict, restrain, hamstring, inhibit, constrain, obstruct, impede, encumber, tie (someone's) hands: *The trade unions are shackled by the law.* **2 = fetter**, chain, handcuff, secure, bind, hobble, manacle, trammel, put in irons: *She was shackled to a wall.*
▷ NOUN *(often plural)* **= fetter**, chain, iron, bond, handcuff, hobble, manacle, leg-iron, gyve *(archaic)*: *He unbolted the shackles on Billy's hands.*

shade NOUN **1 = hue**, tone, colour, tint: *The walls were painted in two shades of green.* **2 = shadow**, screen, shadows, coolness, shadiness: *Exotic trees provide welcome shade.* **3 = dash**, trace, hint, suggestion, suspicion, small amount, semblance: *There was a shade of irony in her voice.* **4 = nuance**, difference, degree, graduation, subtlety: *the capacity to convey subtle shades of meaning* **5 = screen**, covering, cover, blind, curtain, shield, veil, canopy: *She left the shades down and the lights off.* **6 = ghost**, spirit, shadow, phantom, spectre, manes, apparition, eidolon, kehua *(N.Z.)*: *His writing benefits from the shade of Lincoln hovering over his shoulder.*
▷ VERB **1 = darken**, shadow, cloud, dim, cast a shadow over, shut out the light: *a health resort whose beaches are shaded by palm trees* **2 = cover**, protect, screen, hide, shield, conceal, obscure, veil, mute: *You've got to shade your eyes or close them altogether.*

shadow NOUN **1 = silhouette**, shape, outline, profile: *All he could see was his shadow.* **2 = shade**, dimness, darkness, gloom, cover, protection, shelter, dusk, obscurity, gloaming *(Scot. poetic)*, gathering darkness: *Most of the lake was in shadow.*
▷ VERB **1 = shade**, screen, shield, darken, overhang, cast a shadow over: *The hood shadowed her face.* **2 = follow**, dog, tail *(informal)*, trail, stalk, spy on: *shadowed by a large and highly visible body of police*

shadowy ADJECTIVE **1 = dark**, shaded, dim, gloomy, shady, obscure, murky, dusky, funereal, crepuscular, tenebrous, tenebrious: *I watched him from a shadowy corner.* **2 = vague**, indistinct, faint, ghostly, obscure, dim, phantom, imaginary, unreal, intangible, illusory, spectral, undefined, nebulous, dreamlike, impalpable, unsubstantial, wraithlike: *the shadowy shape of a big barge loaded with logs*

shady ADJECTIVE **1 = shaded**, cool, shadowy, dim, leafy, bowery, bosky *(literary)*, umbrageous: *After flowering, place the pot in a shady spot.* **OPPOSITE:** sunny **2 = crooked**, dodgy *(Brit., Austral. & N.Z. informal)*, unethical, suspect, suspicious, dubious, slippery, questionable, unscrupulous, fishy *(informal)*, shifty, disreputable, untrustworthy, shonky *(Austral. & N.Z. informal)*: *Be wary of people who try to talk you into shady deals.* **OPPOSITE:** honest

shaft NOUN **1 = tunnel**, hole, passage, burrow, passageway, channel: *old mine shafts* **2 = handle**, staff, pole, rod, stem, upright, baton, shank: *a drive shaft* **3 = ray**, beam, gleam, streak: *A brilliant shaft of sunlight burst through the doorway.*

shaggy ADJECTIVE **= unkempt**, rough, tousled, hairy, long-haired, hirsute, unshorn **OPPOSITE:** smooth

shake VERB **1 = jiggle**, agitate, joggle: *Shake the rugs well and hang them out.* **2 = tremble**, shiver, quake, shudder, quiver: *I stood there, crying and shaking with fear.* **3 = rock**, sway, shudder, wobble, waver, totter, oscillate: *The plane shook frighteningly as it hit the high, drenching waves.* **4 = wave**, wield, flourish, brandish: *They shook clenched fists.* **5 = upset**, shock, frighten, disturb, distress, move, rattle *(informal)*, intimidate, unnerve, discompose, traumatize: *The news of his escape had shaken them all.* **6 = undermine**, threaten, disable, weaken, impair, sap, debilitate, subvert, pull the rug out from under *(informal)*: *It won't shake the football world if we beat them.*
▷ NOUN **= vibration**, trembling, quaking, shock, jar, disturbance, jerk, shiver, shudder, jolt, tremor, agitation, convulsion, pulsation, jounce: *blurring of photos caused by camera shake*
shake someone off = leave behind, lose, get rid of, get away from, elude, get rid of, throw off, get shot of *(slang)*, rid yourself of, give the slip: *He had shaken off his pursuers.*
shake someone up = upset, shock, frighten, disturb, distress, rattle *(informal)*, unsettle, unnerve, discompose: *He was shaken up when he was thrown from his horse.*
shake something off = get rid of, lose, recuperate from: *He just couldn't shake off that cough.*
shake something up = restructure, reorganize, mix, overturn, churn (up), turn upside down: *Directors and shareholders are preparing to shake things up.*

shaky ADJECTIVE **1 = unstable**, weak, precarious, tottering, rickety: *Our house will remain on shaky foundations unless the architect sorts out the basement.* **OPPOSITE:** stable **2 = unsteady**, faint, trembling, faltering, wobbly, tremulous, quivery, all of a quiver *(informal)*: *Even small operations can leave you feeling a bit shaky.* **3 = uncertain**, suspect, dubious, questionable, unreliable, unsound, iffy *(informal)*, unsupported, undependable: *We knew we may have to charge them on shaky evidence.* **OPPOSITE:** reliable

shallow ADJECTIVE **= superficial**, surface, empty, slight, foolish, idle, trivial, meaningless, flimsy, frivolous, skin-deep **OPPOSITE:** deep

sham NOUN **= fraud**, imitation, hoax, pretence, forgery, counterfeit, pretender, humbug, impostor, feint, pseud *(informal)*, wolf in sheep's clothing, imposture, phoney *or* phony *(informal)*: *Their promises were exposed as a hollow sham.* **OPPOSITE:** the real thing
▷ ADJECTIVE **= false**, artificial, bogus, pretended, mock, synthetic, imitation, simulated, pseudo *(informal)*, counterfeit, feigned, spurious, ersatz, pseud *(informal)*, phoney *or* phony *(informal)*: *a sham marriage* **OPPOSITE:** real

shambles NOUN **1 = chaos**, mess, disorder, confusion, muddle, havoc, anarchy, disarray, madhouse, disorganization: *The economy is a shambles.* **2 = mess**, state, jumble, untidiness: *The boat's interior was an utter shambles.*

shambling ADJECTIVE **= clumsy**, awkward, shuffling, lurching, lumbering, unsteady, ungainly, unco *(Austral. slang)*

shambolic ADJECTIVE **= disorganized**, disordered, chaotic, confused, muddled, inefficient, anarchic, topsy-turvy, at sixes and sevens, in total disarray, unsystematic

shame NOUN **1 = embarrassment**, humiliation, chagrin, ignominy, compunction, mortification, loss of face, abashment: *I was, to my shame, a coward.* **OPPOSITE:** shamelessness **2 = disgrace**, scandal, discredit, contempt, smear, degradation, disrepute, reproach, derision, dishonour, infamy, opprobrium, odium, ill repute, obloquy: *I don't want to bring shame on the family name.* **OPPOSITE:** honour
▷ VERB **1 = embarrass**, disgrace, humiliate, humble, disconcert, mortify, take (someone) down a peg *(informal)*, abash: *Her son's affair had humiliated and shamed her.* **OPPOSITE:** make proud **2 = dishonour**, discredit, degrade, stain, smear, blot, debase, defile: *I wouldn't shame my family by trying that.* **OPPOSITE:** honour
put something *or* **someone to shame = show up**, disgrace, eclipse, surpass,

S

outstrip, outclass: *His playing really puts me to shame.*

QUOTATIONS
It is a most miserable thing to feel ashamed of home
[Charles Dickens *Great Expectations*]

shameful ADJECTIVE **= disgraceful**, outrageous, scandalous, mean, low, base, infamous, indecent, degrading, vile, wicked, atrocious, unworthy, reprehensible, ignominious, dastardly, unbecoming, dishonourable **OPPOSITE:** admirable

shameless ADJECTIVE **= brazen**, audacious, flagrant, abandoned, corrupt, hardened, indecent, brash, improper, depraved, wanton, unabashed, profligate, unashamed, incorrigible, insolent, unprincipled, impudent, dissolute, reprobate, immodest, barefaced, unblushing

shanty NOUN **= shack**, shed, cabin, hut, lean-to, hovel, shiel *(Scot.)*, bothy *(Scot.)*, shieling *(Scot.)*

shape NOUN **1 = appearance**, form, aspect, guise, likeness, semblance: *The glass bottle is the shape of a woman's torso.* **2 = form**, profile, outline, lines, build, cut, figure, silhouette, configuration, contours: *the shapes of the trees against the sky* **3 = pattern**, model, frame, mould: *Carefully cut round the shape of the design you wish to use.* **4 = condition**, state, health, trim, kilter, fettle: *He was still in better shape than many young men.*
▷ VERB **1 = form**, make, produce, create, model, fashion, mould: *Like it or not, our families shape our lives.* **2 = mould**, form, make, fashion, model, frame: *Cut the dough in half and shape each half into a loaf.*

shapeless ADJECTIVE **= formless**, irregular, amorphous, unstructured, misshapen, asymmetrical **OPPOSITE:** well-formed

shapely ADJECTIVE **= well-formed**, elegant, trim, neat, graceful, well-turned, curvaceous, sightly, comely, well-proportioned

share NOUN **= part**, portion, quota, ration, lot, cut *(informal)*, due, division, contribution, proportion, allowance, whack *(informal)*, allotment: *I have had more than my share of adventures.*
▷ VERB **1 = divide**, split, distribute, assign, apportion, parcel out, divvy up *(informal)*: *the small income he has shared with his brother* **2 = go halves on**, go fifty-fifty on *(informal)*, go Dutch on *(informal)*: *Share the cost of the flowers.*

sharp ADJECTIVE **1 = keen**, cutting, sharpened, honed, jagged, knife-edged, razor-sharp, serrated, knifelike: *Using a sharp knife, cut away the pith and peel from both fruits.* **OPPOSITE:** blunt **2 = quick-witted**, clever, astute, knowing, ready, quick, bright, alert, subtle, penetrating, apt, discerning, on the ball *(informal)*, perceptive, observant, long-headed: *He is very sharp and swift with repartee.* **OPPOSITE:** dim **3 = cutting**, biting, severe, bitter, harsh, scathing, acrimonious, barbed, hurtful, sarcastic, sardonic, caustic, vitriolic, trenchant, mordant, mordacious, acerb: *'Don't criticize your mother,' was his sharp reprimand.* **OPPOSITE:** gentle **4 = sudden**, marked, abrupt, extreme, distinct: *There's been a sharp rise in the rate of inflation.* **OPPOSITE:** gradual **5 = clear**, distinct, clear-cut, well-defined, crisp: *All the footmarks are quite sharp and clear.* **OPPOSITE:** indistinct **6 = sour**, tart, pungent, hot, burning, acid, acerbic, acrid, piquant, acetic, vinegary, acerb: *a colourless, almost odourless liquid with a sharp, sweetish taste* **OPPOSITE:** bland **7 = stylish**, smart, fashionable, trendy *(informal)*, chic, classy *(slang)*, snappy, natty *(informal)*, dressy, schmick *(Austral. informal)*: *Now politics is all about the right haircut and a sharp suit.* **8 = acute**, violent, severe, intense, painful, shooting, distressing, stabbing, fierce, stinging, piercing, sore, excruciating, gut-wrenching: *I felt a sharp pain in my lower back.*
▷ ADVERB **= promptly**, precisely, exactly, on time, on the dot, punctually: *She planned to unlock the store at 8.00 sharp.* **OPPOSITE:** approximately

sharpen VERB **= make sharp**, hone, whet, grind, edge, strop, put an edge on

shatter VERB **1 = smash**, break, burst, split, crack, crush, explode, demolish, shiver, implode, pulverize, crush to smithereens: *Safety glass won't shatter if it's broken.* **2 = destroy**, ruin, wreck, blast, disable, overturn, demolish, impair, blight, torpedo, bring to nought: *Something like that really shatters your confidence.* **3 = devastate**, shock, stun, crush, overwhelm, upset, break (someone's) heart, knock the stuffing out of (someone) *(informal)*, traumatize: *the tragedy which had shattered him*

shattered ADJECTIVE **1 = devastated**, crushed, upset, gutted *(slang)*: *I am absolutely shattered to hear the news.* **2 = exhausted**, drained, worn out, spent, done in *(informal)*, all in *(slang)*, wiped out *(informal)*, weary, knackered *(slang)*, clapped out *(Brit., Austral. & N.Z. informal)*, tired out, ready to drop, dog-tired *(informal)*, zonked *(slang)*, dead tired *(informal)*, dead beat *(informal)*, shagged out *(Brit. slang)*, jiggered *(informal)*: *He was shattered and too tired to concentrate.*

shattering ADJECTIVE **= devastating**, stunning, severe, crushing, overwhelming, paralysing

shave VERB **1 = trim**, crop: *It's a pity you shaved your moustache off.* **2 = scrape**, plane, trim, shear, pare: *I set the log on the ground and shaved off the bark.* **3 = brush past**, touch, graze: *The ball shaved the goalpost.*

shed[1] NOUN **= hut**, shack, lean-to, outhouse, lockup, bothy *(chiefly Scot.)*, whare *(N.Z.)*: *a garden shed*

shed[2] VERB **1 = drop**, spill, scatter: *Some of the trees were already beginning to shed their leaves.* **2 = cast off**, discard, moult, slough off, exuviate: *a snake who has shed its skin* **3 = give out**, cast, emit, give, throw, afford, radiate, diffuse, pour forth: *as dawn sheds its first light*

sheen NOUN **= shine**, gleam, gloss, polish, brightness, lustre, burnish, patina, shininess

sheepish ADJECTIVE **= embarrassed**, uncomfortable, ashamed, silly, foolish, self-conscious, chagrined, mortified, abashed, shamefaced **OPPOSITE:** unembarrassed

sheer ADJECTIVE **1 = total**, complete, absolute, utter, rank, pure, downright, unqualified, out-and-out, unadulterated, unmitigated, thoroughgoing, unalloyed, arrant: *acts of sheer desperation* **OPPOSITE:** moderate **2 = steep**, abrupt, perpendicular, precipitous: *There was a sheer drop just outside my window.* **OPPOSITE:** gradual **3 = fine**, thin, transparent, see-through, gossamer, diaphanous, gauzy: *sheer black tights* **OPPOSITE:** thick

sheet NOUN **1 = page**, leaf, folio, piece of paper: *I was able to fit it all on one sheet.* **2 = plate**, piece, panel, slab, pane: *a cracked sheet of glass* **3 = coat**, film, layer, membrane, surface, stratum, veneer, overlay, lamina: *a sheet of ice* **4 = expanse**, area, stretch, sweep, covering, blanket: *Sheets of rain slanted across the road.*

shell NOUN **1 = husk**, case, pod, shuck: *They cracked the nuts and removed their shells.* **2 = carapace**, armour: *The baby tortoise tucked his head in his shell.* **3 = frame**, structure, hull, framework, skeleton, chassis: *The solid feel of the car's shell is impressive.*
▷ VERB **1 = remove the shells from**, husk, shuck *(U.S.)*: *She shelled and ate a few nuts.* **2 = bomb**, barrage, bombard, attack, strike, blitz, strafe: *The rebels shelled the densely-populated suburbs near the port.*
shell something out = pay out, fork out *(slang)*, expend, give, hand over, lay out *(informal)*, disburse, ante up *(informal, chiefly U.S.)*: *You won't have to shell out a fortune for it.*

shelter NOUN **1 = cover**, screen, awning, shiel *(Scot.)*: *a bus shelter* **2 = protection**, safety, refuge, cover, security, defence, sanctuary: *the hut where they were given food and shelter* **3 = refuge**, haven, sanctuary, retreat, asylum: *a shelter for homeless women*
▷ VERB **1 = take shelter**, hide, seek refuge, take cover: *a man sheltering in a doorway* **2 = protect**, shield, harbour, safeguard, cover, hide, guard, defend, take in: *A neighbour sheltered the boy for seven days.* **OPPOSITE:** endanger

sheltered ADJECTIVE **1 = screened**, covered, protected, shielded, secluded: *a shallow-sloping beach next to a sheltered bay* **OPPOSITE:** exposed

S

2 = protected, screened, shielded, quiet, withdrawn, isolated, secluded, cloistered, reclusive, ensconced, hermitic, conventual: *She had a sheltered upbringing.*

shelve VERB **= postpone**, put off, defer, table *(U.S.)*, dismiss, freeze, suspend, put aside, hold over, mothball, pigeonhole, lay aside, put on ice, put on the back burner *(informal)*, hold in abeyance, take a rain check on *(U.S. & Canad. informal)*

shepherd NOUN **= drover**, stockman, herdsman, grazier: *The shepherd was filled with terror.*
▷ VERB **= guide**, conduct, steer, convoy, herd, marshal, usher: *She was shepherded by her guards up the rear ramp of the aircraft.*
▸ *related adjective:* pastoral

QUOTATIONS
The Lord is my shepherd; I shall not want
[*Bible: Psalm 23*]

sherang NOUN **= boss**, manager, head, leader, director, chief, executive, owner, master, governor *(informal)*, employer, administrator, supervisor, superintendent, gaffer *(informal, chiefly Brit.)*, foreman, overseer, kingpin, big cheese *(old-fashioned, slang)*, baas *(S. African)*, numero uno *(informal)*, Mister Big *(slang, chiefly U.S.)*

shield NOUN **1 = protection**, cover, defence, screen, guard, ward *(archaic)*, shelter, safeguard, aegis, rampart, bulwark: *innocents used as a human shield against attack* **2 = buckler**, escutcheon *(Heraldry)*, targe *(archaic)*: *a warrior with sword and shield*
▷ VERB **= protect**, cover, screen, guard, defend, shelter, safeguard: *He shielded his head from the sun with an old sack.*

shift VERB **1 = move**, drift, move around, veer, budge, swerve, change position: *The entire pile shifted and slid, thumping onto the floor.* **2 = remove**, move, transfer, displace, relocate, rearrange, transpose, reposition: *We shifted the vans and used the area for skateboarding.*
▷ NOUN **1 = change**, switch, shifting, modification, alteration, displacement, about-turn, permutation, fluctuation: *a shift in policy* **2 = move**, transfer, removal, veering, rearrangement: *There has been a shift of the elderly to this state.*

shifty ADJECTIVE **= untrustworthy**, sly, devious, scheming, tricky, slippery, contriving, wily, crafty, evasive, furtive, deceitful, underhand, unprincipled, duplicitous, fly-by-night *(informal)* **OPPOSITE:** honest

shimmer VERB **= gleam**, twinkle, glimmer, dance, glisten, scintillate: *The lights shimmered on the water.*
▷ NOUN **= gleam**, glimmer, iridescence, unsteady light: *a shimmer of starlight*

shine VERB **1 = gleam**, flash, beam, glow, sparkle, glitter, glare, shimmer, radiate, twinkle, glimmer, glisten, emit light, give off light, scintillate: *It is a mild morning and the sun is shining.* **2 = polish**, buff, burnish, brush, rub up: *Let him dust and shine the furniture.* **3 = be outstanding**, stand out, excel, star, be distinguished, steal the show, be conspicuous, be pre-eminent, stand out in a crowd: *He conspicuously failed to shine academically.*
▷ NOUN **1 = polish**, gloss, sheen, glaze, lustre, patina: *The wood has been recently polished to bring back the shine.* **2 = brightness**, light, sparkle, radiance: *There was a sparkle about her, a shine of anticipation.*

shining ADJECTIVE **1 = outstanding**, glorious, splendid, leading, celebrated, brilliant, distinguished, eminent, conspicuous, illustrious: *She is a shining example to us all.* **2 = bright**, brilliant, gleaming, beaming, sparkling, glittering, shimmering, radiant, luminous, glistening, resplendent, aglow, effulgent, incandescent: *shining brass buttons*

shiny ADJECTIVE **= bright**, gleaming, glossy, glistening, polished, burnished, lustrous, satiny, sheeny, agleam

ship NOUN **= vessel**, boat, craft

shirk VERB **1 = dodge**, avoid, evade, get out of, duck (out of) *(informal)*, shun, sidestep, body-swerve *(Scot.)*, bob off *(Brit. slang)*, scrimshank *(Brit. Military slang)*: *We will not shirk the task of considering the need for further action.* **2 = skive** *(Brit. slang)*, slack, idle, malinger, swing the lead, gold-brick *(U.S. slang)*, bob off *(Brit. slang)*, bludge *(Austral. & N.Z. informal)*, scrimshank *(Brit. Military slang)*: *He was sacked for shirking.*

shiver VERB **= shudder**, shake, tremble, quake, quiver, palpitate: *He shivered in the cold.*
▷ NOUN **= tremble**, shudder, quiver, thrill, trembling, flutter, tremor, frisson: *Alice gave a shiver of delight.*
the shivers = the shakes, a chill *(informal)*, goose pimples, goose flesh, chattering teeth: *My boss gives me the shivers.*

shock NOUN **1 = upset**, blow, trauma, bombshell, turn *(informal)*, distress, disturbance, consternation, whammy *(informal, chiefly U.S.)*, state of shock, rude awakening, bolt from the blue, prostration: *The extent of the violence came as a shock.* **2 = impact**, blow, jolt, clash, encounter, jarring, collision: *Steel barriers can bend and absorb the shock.* **3 = start**, scare, fright, turn, jolt: *It gave me quite a shock to see his face on the screen.*
▷ VERB **1 = shake**, stun, stagger, jar, shake up *(informal)*, paralyse, numb, jolt, stupefy, shake out of your complacency: *Relief workers were shocked by what they saw.* **2 = horrify**, appal, disgust, outrage, offend, revolt, unsettle, sicken, agitate, disquiet, nauseate, raise someone's eyebrows, scandalize, gross out *(U.S. slang)*, traumatize, give (someone) a turn *(informal)*: *They were easily shocked in those days.*

shocking ADJECTIVE **1 = terrible**, appalling, dreadful, bad, fearful, dire, horrendous, ghastly, from hell *(informal)*, deplorable, abysmal, frightful, godawful *(slang)*: *I must have been in a shocking state last night.* **2 = appalling**, outrageous, disgraceful, offensive, distressing, disgusting, horrible, dreadful, horrifying, revolting, obscene, sickening, ghastly, hideous, monstrous, scandalous, disquieting, unspeakable, atrocious, repulsive, nauseating, odious, loathsome, abominable, stupefying, hellacious *(U.S. slang)*: *This was a shocking invasion of privacy.* **OPPOSITE:** wonderful

shoddy ADJECTIVE **= inferior**, poor, second-rate, cheap, tacky *(informal)*, tawdry, tatty, trashy, low-rent *(informal, chiefly U.S.)*, slipshod, cheapo *(informal)*, rubbishy, junky *(informal)*, cheap-jack *(informal)*, bodger *or* bodgie *(Austral. slang)* **OPPOSITE:** excellent

shoemaker NOUN **= cobbler**, bootmaker, souter *(Scot.)*

shoot VERB **1 = open fire on**, blast *(slang)*, hit, kill, bag, plug *(slang)*, bring down, blow away *(slang, chiefly U.S.)*, zap *(slang)*, pick off, pump full of lead *(slang)*: *The police had orders to shoot anyone who attacked them.* **2 = fire**, launch, discharge, project, hurl, fling, propel, emit, let fly: *He shot an arrow into the air.* **3 = speed**, race, rush, charge, fly, spring, tear, flash, dash, barrel (along) *(informal, chiefly U.S. & Canad.)*, bolt, streak, dart, whisk, whizz *(informal)*, hurtle, scoot, burn rubber *(informal)*: *They had almost reached the boat when a figure shot past them.*
▷ NOUN **= sprout**, branch, bud, twig, sprig, offshoot, scion, slip: *This week saw the first pink shoots of the new season's crop.*

shop NOUN **= store**, market, supermarket, mart, boutique, emporium, hypermarket, dairy *(N.Z.)*

shore NOUN **= beach**, coast, sands, strand *(poetic)*, lakeside, waterside, seaboard *(chiefly U.S.)*, foreshore, seashore

shore up VERB **= support**, strengthen, reinforce, prop, brace, underpin, augment, buttress

short ADJECTIVE **1 = brief**, fleeting, short-term, short-lived, momentary: *We had a short meeting.* **OPPOSITE:** long **2 = concise**, brief, succinct, clipped, summary, compressed, curtailed, terse, laconic, pithy, abridged, compendious, sententious: *This is a short note to say thank you.* **OPPOSITE:** lengthy **3 = small**, little, wee, squat, diminutive, petite, dumpy, knee high to a grasshopper,

S

fubsy (*archaic, dialect*), knee high to a gnat: *I'm tall and thin and he's short and fat.* **OPPOSITE:** tall **4 = abrupt**, sharp, terse, curt, blunt, crusty, gruff, brusque, offhand, testy, impolite, discourteous, uncivil: *She was definitely short with me.* **OPPOSITE:** polite **5 = crumbly**, crisp, brittle, friable: *a crisp short pastry* **6 = scarce**, wanting, low, missing, limited, lacking, tight, slim, inadequate, insufficient, slender, scant, meagre, sparse, deficient, scanty: *Money was short in those days.* **OPPOSITE:** plentiful
▷ ADVERB **= abruptly**, suddenly, unaware, by surprise, without warning: *He had no insurance and was caught short when his house was burgled.* **OPPOSITE:** gradually

shortage NOUN **= deficiency**, want, lack, failure, deficit, poverty, shortfall, inadequacy, scarcity, dearth, paucity, insufficiency **OPPOSITE:** abundance

shortcoming NOUN **= failing**, fault, weakness, defect, flaw, drawback, imperfection, frailty, foible, weak point

shorten VERB **1 = cut**, reduce, decrease, cut down, trim, diminish, dock, cut back, prune, lessen, curtail, abbreviate, truncate, abridge, downsize: *The day surgery will help to shorten waiting lists.* **OPPOSITE:** increase **2 = turn up**, trim: *It's a simple matter to shorten trouser legs.*

short-lived ADJECTIVE **= brief**, short, temporary, fleeting, passing, transient, ephemeral, transitory, impermanent

shortly ADVERB **1 = soon**, presently, before long, anon (*archaic*), in a little while, any minute now, erelong (*archaic, poetic*): *Their trial will begin shortly.* **2 = curtly**, sharply, abruptly, tartly, tersely, succinctly, briefly, concisely, in a few words: *'I don't know you,' he said shortly, 'and I'm in a hurry.'*

S

short-sighted ADJECTIVE **1 = near-sighted**, myopic, blind as a bat: *Testing showed her to be very short-sighted.* **2 = imprudent**, injudicious, ill-advised, unthinking, careless, impractical, ill-considered, improvident, impolitic, seeing no further than (the end of) your nose: *I think we're being very short-sighted.*

shot NOUN **1 = discharge**, report, gunfire, crack, blast, explosion, bang: *Guards at the training base heard the shots.* **2 = ammunition**, bullet, slug, pellet, projectile, lead, ball: *These guns are lighter and take more shot for their size.* **3 = marksman**, shooter, markswoman: *He was not a particularly good shot because of his eyesight.* **4 = strike**, throw, lob: *He had only one shot at goal.* **5 = attempt**, go (*informal*), try, turn, chance, effort, opportunity, crack (*informal*), essay, stab (*informal*), endeavour: *He will be given a shot at the world title.*
a shot in the arm = boost, lift, encouragement, stimulus, impetus, fillip, geeing-up: *A win would provide a much-needed shot in the arm for the team.*
have a shot = make an attempt, have a go, try, have a crack (*informal*), try your luck, have a stab (*informal*), have a bash (*informal*), tackle: *Why don't you have a shot at it?*
like a shot = at once, immediately, in a flash, quickly, eagerly, unhesitatingly, like a bat out of hell (*slang*): *I heard the key in the front door and I was out of bed like a shot.*

shoulder VERB **1 = bear**, carry, take on, accept, assume, be responsible for, take upon yourself: *He has to shoulder the consequences of his father's mistakes.* **2 = push**, thrust, elbow, shove, jostle, press: *He shouldered past her and opened the door.*
give someone the cold shoulder = snub, ignore, blank (*slang*), put down, shun, rebuff, kick in the teeth (*slang*), ostracize, send someone to Coventry, cut (*informal*): *He was given the cold shoulder by his former friends.*
rub shoulders with someone = mix with, associate with, consort with, hobnob with, socialize with, fraternize with: *I was destined to rub shoulders with the most unexpected people.*
shoulder to shoulder 1 = side by side, abreast, next to each other: *walking shoulder to shoulder with their heads bent against the rain* **2 = together**, united, jointly, as one, in partnership, in cooperation, in unity: *My party will stand shoulder to shoulder with the Prime Minister and his Government.*

shout VERB **= cry (out)**, call (out), yell, scream, roar, shriek, bellow, bawl, holler (*informal*), raise your voice: *We began to shout for help.*
▷ NOUN **= cry**, call, yell, scream, roar, shriek, bellow: *I heard a distant shout.*
shout someone down = drown out, overwhelm, drown, silence: *The hecklers began to shout down the speakers.*

shove VERB **= push**, shoulder, thrust, elbow, drive, press, crowd, propel, jostle, impel: *He shoved her out of the way.*
▷ NOUN **= push**, knock, thrust, elbow, bump, nudge, jostle: *She gave Gracie a shove in the back.*
shove off = go away, leave, clear off (*informal*), depart, go to hell (*informal*), push off (*informal*), slope off, pack your bags (*informal*), scram (*informal*), get on your bike (*Brit. slang*), take yourself off, vamoose (*slang, chiefly U.S.*), sling your hook (*Brit. slang*), rack off (*Austral. & N.Z. slang*): *Why don't you just shove off and leave me alone?*

shovel NOUN **= spade**, scoop: *She dug the foundation with a pick and shovel.*
▷ VERB **1 = move**, scoop, dredge, shift, load, heap: *He had to get out and shovel snow.* **2 = stuff**, spoon, ladle: *shovelling food into his mouth*

show VERB **1 = indicate**, demonstrate, prove, reveal, display, evidence, point out, manifest, testify to, evince, flag up: *These figures show an increase in unemployment.* **OPPOSITE:** disprove **2 = display**, exhibit, put on display, present, put on show, put before the public: *What made you decide to show your paintings?* **3 = guide**, lead, conduct, accompany, direct, steer, escort: *Let me show you to my study.* **4 = demonstrate**, describe, explain, teach, illustrate, instruct: *Claire showed us how to make a chocolate roulade.* **5 = be visible**, be seen: *I'd driven both ways down this road, but the tracks didn't show.* **OPPOSITE:** be invisible **6 = express**, display, reveal, indicate, register, demonstrate, disclose, manifest, divulge, make known, evince: *She had enough time to show her gratitude.* **OPPOSITE:** hide **7 = turn up**, come, appear, arrive, attend, show up (*informal*), put in *or* make an appearance: *There was always a chance he wouldn't show.* **8 = broadcast**, transmit, air, beam, relay, televise, put on the air, podcast: *The drama will be shown on American TV.*
▷ NOUN **1 = display**, view, sight, spectacle, array: *Spring brings a lovely show of green and yellow striped leaves.* **2 = exhibition**, fair, display, parade, expo (*informal*), exposition, pageant, pageantry: *the Chelsea flower show* **3 = appearance**, display, pose, profession, parade, ostentation: *The change in government is more for show than for real.* **4 = pretence**, appearance, semblance, illusion, pretext, likeness, affectation: *We need to make a show of acknowledging their expertise.* **5 = programme**, broadcast, presentation, production: *I had my own TV show.* **6 = entertainment**, performance, play, production, drama, musical, presentation, theatrical performance: *How about going to see a show in London?*
show off = boast, brag, blow your own trumpet, swagger, hot-dog (*chiefly U.S.*), strut your stuff (*chiefly U.S.*), make a spectacle of yourself: *He had been showing off at the poker table.*
show someone up = embarrass, shame, let down, mortify, put to shame, show in a bad light: *He wanted to teach her a lesson for showing him up.*
show something off = exhibit, display, parade, advertise, demonstrate, spread out, flaunt: *She was showing off her engagement ring.*
show something up = reveal, expose, highlight, pinpoint, unmask, lay bare, put the spotlight on: *The awards showed up the fact that TV has been a washout this year.*

showdown NOUN **= confrontation**, crisis, clash, moment of truth, face-off (*slang*)

shower NOUN **1 = deluge**, downpour: *a shower of rain* **2 = profusion**, plethora: *They were reunited in a shower of kisses and tears.*
▷ VERB **1 = cover**, dust, spray, sprinkle: *They were showered with rice in the traditional manner.* **2 = inundate**, load, heap, lavish, pour, deluge: *He showered her with emeralds and furs; She showered gifts on us.*

The Language of Jonathan Swift

Jonathan Swift (1667–1745) was an Irish prose writer, poet, and clergyman renowned as the foremost satirist of his day. While he was a prolific author of tracts, sermons, and pamphlets, often with a strident political agenda, his most famous work is the fictional *Gulliver's Travels* which parodies the exploration narratives that were increasingly popular in the early 18th century.

The aim of satire is to expose what the author sees as corruption, injustice, or pomposity, generally by means of comic exaggeration. It operates by producing the understanding among readers that the narrator's words are not to be taken at face value. An example of this is the infamous suggestion by the narrator of Swift's *A Modest Proposal* that babies should be eaten as a solution for poverty in Ireland. As part of his satirical method, Swift's narrators often address the *reader* directly. The most salient adjectives with *reader* indicate that flattery is a common component of this mode, as the narrator ostensibly tries to win the reader over to his point of view. *Courteous, gentle, curious, candid,* and *judicious* all feature recurrently and promote a superficial intimacy between reader and narrator that the content of the narrative undercuts. The lack of credibility that this aims towards is expressed in the adverbs that collocate with the verb *believe*. *Hardly*, in particular, contributes to the aura of improbability, as in:

> ... perhaps I should be **hardly believed**; at least a severe critic would be apt to think I enlarged a little, as travellers are often suspected to do.

Other adverbs, by contrast, suggest naïve self-confidence in the narration: *verily, generally, firmly,* and *easily* indicate the narrator's claim to truthfulness from which the reader is expected to dissent.

A prominent aspect of Swift's satirical register is his concern with the human body and especially with sickness and the body's baser functions. His scatological interest leads him at times to expletives (in the poem 'The Lady's Dressing Room', for example), and frequently to a grotesque attention to the details of decay. Consequently, Swift is often drawn to language that evokes smell, *odious* being one such term, used most commonly in combination with *animal* as in the moment when Gulliver is reunited with his wife after a lengthy period of travel:

> ... having not been used to the touch of that **odious animal** for so many years, I fell into a swoon for almost an hour.

Such disgusted evocations of a woman demonstrate what has often been identified as a misogynist strain to Swift's writing (or at least an interest in writing about misogyny). The most salient adjectives with woman, however, are the relatively neutral and commonplace *young* and *old*, while *lady*, similarly, is most frequently used with *young* and *great*.

Some notable differences in language from Swift's era to the present day include the use of *farther* for further, as in:

> Our journey was somewhat **farther** than from London to St. Alban's.

Among the numerous other usages common in Swift's work but now largely obsolete are *hath* for *has*, *frighted* for what would now be *frightened* and *whereof* in place of our modern *of which* or *of what*. In accordance with the convention of his age, capital letters are used much more liberally in Swift's texts than in today's writing. Although some recent editions of Swift adjust this to modern tastes, in early editions nouns are routinely capitalized:

> I am not in the least provoked at the sight of a Lawyer, a Pick-pocket, a Colonel, a Fool, a Lord, a Gamester, a Politician, a Whoremonger, a Physician, an Evidence, a Suborner, an Attorney, a Traitor, or the like.

showing NOUN **1 = display**, staging, presentation, exhibition, demonstration: *a private showing of the hit film* **2 = performance**, demonstration, track record, show, appearance, impression, account of yourself: *On this showing he has a big job ahead of him.*

showman NOUN **= performer**, entertainer, artiste, player, Thespian, trouper, play-actor, actor *or* actress

show-off NOUN **= exhibitionist**, boaster, swaggerer, hot dog *(chiefly U.S.)*, poseur, egotist, braggart, braggadocio, peacock, figjam *(Austral. slang)*

showy ADJECTIVE **= ostentatious**, flamboyant, flashy, flash *(informal)*, loud, over the top *(informal)*, brash, pompous, pretentious, gaudy, garish, tawdry, splashy *(informal)*, tinselly **OPPOSITE:** tasteful

shred NOUN **1 = strip**, bit, piece, scrap, fragment, rag, ribbon, snippet, sliver, tatter: *Cut the cabbage into fine long shreds.* **2 = particle**, trace, scrap, grain, atom, jot, whit, iota: *There is not a shred of truth in this story.*

shrew NOUN **= nag**, fury, dragon *(informal)*, spitfire, virago, vixen, harpy, harridan, termagant *(rare)*, scold, Xanthippe: *After the first visit he announced that his stepmother was a shrew.*

> **QUOTATIONS**
> It is better to dwell in a corner of the housetop, than with a brawling woman in a wide house
> [*Bible: Proverbs*]
>
> A continual dropping in a very rainy day and a contentious woman are alike
> [*Bible: Proverbs*]

shrewd ADJECTIVE **= astute**, clever, sharp, knowing, fly *(slang)*, keen, acute, smart, calculated, calculating, intelligent, discriminating, cunning, discerning, sly, canny, perceptive, wily, crafty, artful, far-sighted, far-seeing, long-headed, perspicacious, sagacious **OPPOSITE:** naive

shrewdly ADVERB **= astutely**, perceptively, cleverly, knowingly, artfully, cannily, with consummate skill, sagaciously, far-sightedly, perspicaciously, with all your wits about you

shriek VERB **= scream**, cry, yell, howl, wail, whoop, screech, squeal, holler: *She shrieked and leapt from the bed.*
▷ NOUN **= scream**, cry, yell, howl, wail, whoop, screech, squeal, holler: *a shriek of joy*

shrill ADJECTIVE **= piercing**, high, sharp, acute, piping, penetrating, screeching, high-pitched, ear-splitting, ear-piercing **OPPOSITE:** deep

shrink VERB **= decrease**, dwindle, lessen, grow *or* get smaller, contract, narrow, diminish, fall off, shorten, wrinkle, wither, drop off, deflate, shrivel, downsize **OPPOSITE:** grow

shrivel VERB **= wither**, dry (up), wilt, shrink, wrinkle, dwindle, dehydrate, desiccate, wizen

shrivelled ADJECTIVE **= withered**, dry, dried up, wrinkled, shrunken, wizened, desiccated, sere *(archaic)*

shroud NOUN **1 = winding sheet**, grave clothes, cerecloth, cerement: *a burial shroud* **2 = covering**, veil, mantle, screen, cloud, pall: *a parked car huddled under a shroud of grey snow*
▷ VERB **= conceal**, cover, screen, hide, blanket, veil, cloak, swathe, envelop: *Mist shrouded the outline of the palace.*

shudder VERB **= shiver**, shake, tremble, quake, quiver, convulse: *She shuddered with cold.*
▷ NOUN **= shiver**, trembling, tremor, quiver, spasm, convulsion: *She recoiled with a shudder.*

shuffle VERB **1 = shamble**, stagger, stumble, dodder: *She shuffled across the kitchen.* **2 = scuffle**, drag, scrape, scuff: *He shuffled his feet along the gravel path.* **3 = rearrange**, jumble, mix, shift, disorder, disarrange, intermix: *The silence lengthened as he unnecessarily shuffled some papers.*

shun VERB **= avoid**, steer clear of, keep away from, evade, eschew, shy away from, cold-shoulder, have no part in, fight shy of, give (someone *or* something) a wide berth, body-swerve *(Scot.)*

shut VERB **= close**, secure, fasten, bar, seal, slam, push to, draw to: *Just make sure you shut the gate after you.* **OPPOSITE:** open
▷ ADJECTIVE **= closed**, fastened, sealed, locked: *A smell of burning came from behind the shut door.* **OPPOSITE:** open

shut down = stop work, halt work, cease operating, close down, cease trading, discontinue: *Smaller constructors had been forced to shut down.*

shut someone out = exclude, bar, keep out, black, lock out, ostracize, debar, blackball: *I was set to shut out anyone else who came knocking.*

shut someone up 1 = silence, gag, hush, muzzle, fall silent, button it *(slang)*, pipe down *(slang)*, hold your tongue, put a sock in it *(Brit. slang)*, keep your trap shut *(slang)*, cut the cackle *(informal)*, button your lip *(slang)*: *A sharp put-down was the only way he knew of shutting her up.* **2 = confine**, cage, imprison, keep in, box in, intern, incarcerate, coop up, immure: *They shut him up in a windowless tower.*

shut something in = confine, cage, enclose, imprison, impound, pound, wall off *or* up: *The door enables us to shut the birds in in bad weather.*

shut something out = block out, screen, hide, cover, mask, veil: *I shut out the memory that was too painful to dwell on.*

shuttle VERB **= go back and forth**, commute, go to and fro, alternate, ply, shunt, seesaw

shy ADJECTIVE **1 = timid**, self-conscious, bashful, reserved, retiring, nervous, modest, aw-shucks, shrinking, backward, coy, reticent, self-effacing, diffident, mousy: *He is painfully shy when it comes to talking to women.* **OPPOSITE:** confident **2 = cautious**, wary, hesitant, suspicious, reticent, distrustful, chary: *You should not be shy of having your say.* **OPPOSITE:** reckless
▷ VERB *(sometimes with* **off** *or* **away***)* **= recoil**, flinch, draw back, start, rear, buck, wince, swerve, balk, quail, take fright: *The horse shied as the wind sent sparks flying.*

shyness NOUN **= timidity**, self-consciousness, bashfulness, modesty, nervousness, lack of confidence, reticence, diffidence, timorousness, mousiness, timidness

sick ADJECTIVE **1 = unwell**, ill, poorly *(informal)*, diseased, weak, crook *(Austral. & N.Z. informal)*, under par *(informal)*, ailing, feeble, laid up *(informal)*, under the weather *(informal)*, indisposed, on the sick list *(informal)*: *He's very sick.* **OPPOSITE:** well **2 = nauseous**, ill, queasy, nauseated, green about the gills *(informal)*, qualmish: *The very thought of food made him feel sick.* **3 = tired**, bored, fed up, weary, jaded, blasé, satiated: *I am sick of hearing all these people moaning.* **4 = morbid**, cruel, sadistic, black, macabre, ghoulish: *a sick joke about a cat*

sicken VERB **1 = disgust**, revolt, nauseate, repel, gross out *(U.S. slang)*, turn your stomach, make your gorge rise: *What he saw there sickened him, despite years of police work.* **2 = fall ill**, take sick, ail, go down with something, contract something, be stricken by something: *Many of them sickened and died.*

sickening ADJECTIVE **= disgusting**, revolting, vile, offensive, foul, distasteful, repulsive, nauseating, loathsome, nauseous, gut-wrenching, putrid, stomach-turning *(informal)*, cringe-making *(Brit. informal)*, noisome, yucky *or* yukky *(slang)*, yucko *(Austral. slang)* **OPPOSITE:** delightful

sickly ADJECTIVE **1 = unhealthy**, weak, delicate, ailing, feeble, infirm, in poor health, indisposed: *He had been a sickly child.* **2 = pale**, wan, pasty, bloodless, pallid, sallow, ashen-faced, waxen, peaky: *his pale, sickly face and woebegone expression* **3 = nauseating**, revolting *(informal)*, cloying, icky *(informal)*: *the sickly smell of rum* **4 = sentimental**, romantic, sloppy *(informal)*, corny *(slang)*, mushy *(informal)*, weepy *(informal)*, slushy *(informal)*, mawkish, tear-jerking *(informal)*, schmaltzy *(slang)*, gushy *(informal)*: *a sickly sequel to the flimsy series*

sickness NOUN **1 = illness**, disorder, ailment, disease, complaint, bug *(informal)*, affliction, malady, infirmity, indisposition, lurgy *(informal)*: *a sickness that affects children* **2 = nausea**, queasiness: *He felt a great rush of sickness.* **3 = vomiting**, nausea, upset stomach, throwing up *(informal)*, puking *(slang)*, retching, barfing *(U.S. slang)*: *Symptoms include sickness and diarrhoea.*

side NOUN **1 = border**, margin, boundary, verge, flank, rim, perimeter, periphery, edge: *Park at the side of the road.* **OPPOSITE:** middle **2 = face**, surface, facet: *The copier only copies onto one side of the paper.* **3 = half**, part: *the right side of your face* **4 = district**, area, region, quarter, sector, neighbourhood, vicinity, locality, locale, neck of the woods *(informal)*: *He lives on the south side of Edinburgh.* **5 = party**, camp, faction, cause: *Both sides appealed for a new ceasefire.* **6 = point of view**, viewpoint, position, opinion, angle, slant, standpoint: *those with the ability to see all sides of a question* **7 = team**, squad, crew, line-up: *Italy were the better side.* **8 = aspect**, feature, angle, facet: *He is in charge of the civilian side of the UN mission.*
▹ ADJECTIVE **= subordinate**, minor, secondary, subsidiary, lesser, marginal, indirect, incidental, ancillary: *The refugees were treated as a side issue.* **OPPOSITE:** main
side with someone = support, back, champion, agree with, stand up for, second, favour, defend, team up with *(informal)*, go along with, befriend, join with, sympathize with, be loyal to, take the part of, associate yourself with, ally yourself with: *They side with the forces of evil.*
▸ *related adjective:* lateral

PROVERBS
There are two sides to every question

sidestep VERB **= avoid**, dodge, evade, duck *(informal)*, skirt, skip, bypass, elude, circumvent, find a way round, body-swerve *(Scot.)*

sidetrack VERB **= distract**, divert, lead off the subject, deflect

sidewalk NOUN **= pavement**, footpath *(Austral. & N.Z.)*

sideways ADVERB **1 = indirectly**, obliquely: *He glanced sideways at her.* **2 = to the side**, laterally, crabwise: *They moved sideways, their arms still locked together.*
▹ ADJECTIVE **= sidelong**, side, slanted, oblique: *Alfred shot him a sideways glance.*

sidle VERB **= edge**, steal, slink, inch, creep, sneak

siege NOUN **= blockade**, encirclement, besiegement

siesta NOUN **= nap**, rest, sleep, doze, kip *(Brit. slang)*, snooze *(informal)*, catnap, forty winks *(informal)*, zizz *(Brit. informal)*

sieve NOUN **= strainer**, sifter, colander, screen, riddle, tammy cloth: *Press the raspberries through a fine sieve to form a puree.*
▹ VERB **= sift**, filter, strain, separate, pan, bolt, riddle: *Sieve the icing sugar into the bowl.*

sift VERB **1 = part**, filter, strain, separate, pan, bolt, riddle, sieve: *Sift the flour and baking powder into a medium-sized mixing bowl.* **2 = examine**, investigate, go through, research, screen, probe, analyse, work over, pore over, scrutinize: *He has sifted the evidence and summarized it clearly.*

sigh VERB **1 = breathe out**, exhale, moan, suspire *(archaic)*: *Dad sighed and stood up.* **2 = moan**, complain, groan, grieve, lament, sorrow: *'Everyone forgets,' she sighed.*
sigh for something *or* **someone = long for**, yearn for, pine for, mourn for, languish over, eat your heart out over: *sighing for the good old days*

sight NOUN **1 = vision**, eyes, eyesight, seeing, eye: *My sight is failing and I can't see to read any more.* **2 = spectacle**, show, scene, display, exhibition, vista, pageant: *Among the most spectacular sights are the great sea-bird colonies.* **3 = view**, field of vision, range of vision, eyeshot, viewing, ken, visibility: *The Queen's carriage came into sight.* **4 = eyesore**, mess, spectacle, fright *(informal)*, monstrosity, blot on the landscape *(informal)*: *She looked a sight in the street-lamps.*
▹ VERB **= spot**, see, observe, distinguish, perceive, make out, discern, behold: *A fleet of ships was sighted in the North Sea.*
▸ *related adjectives:* optical, visual

PROVERBS
Out of sight, out of mind

sign NOUN **1 = symbol**, mark, character, figure, device, representation, logo, badge, emblem, ensign, cipher: *Equations are generally written with a two-bar equals sign.* **2 = figure**, form, shape, outline: *The priest made the sign of the cross over him.* **3 = gesture**, signal, motion, indication, cue, gesticulation: *They gave him the thumbs-up sign.* **4 = notice**, board, warning, signpost, placard: *a sign saying that the highway was closed* **5 = indication**, evidence, trace, mark, note, signal, suggestion, symptom, hint, proof, gesture, clue, token, manifestation, giveaway, vestige, spoor: *His face and movements rarely betrayed any sign of nerves.* **6 = omen**, warning, portent, foreboding, presage, forewarning, writing on the wall, augury, auspice, wake-up call: *It is a sign of things to come.*
▹ VERB **1 = gesture**, indicate, signal, wave, beckon, gesticulate, use sign language: *She signed to me to go out.* **2 = autograph**, initial, inscribe, subscribe, set your hand to: *I got him to sign my copy of his book.*
sign someone up = engage, recruit, employ, take on, hire, contract, take on board *(informal)*, put on the payroll, take into service: *Spalding wants to sign you up.*
sign something away = give up, relinquish, renounce, lose, transfer, abandon, surrender, dispose of, waive, forgo: *The Duke signed away his inheritance.*
sign up = enlist, join, volunteer, register, enrol, join up: *He signed up as a steward.*

signal NOUN **1 = flare**, rocket, beam, beacon, smoke signal, signal fire: *They fired three distress signals.* **2 = cue**, sign, nod, prompting, go-ahead *(informal)*, reminder, green light: *You mustn't fire without my signal.* **3 = sign**, gesture, indication, mark, note, evidence, expression, proof, token, indicator, manifestation: *The event was seen as a signal of support.*
▹ VERB **= gesture**, sign, wave, indicate, nod, motion, beckon, gesticulate, give a sign to: *She signalled a passing taxi.*

significance NOUN **= importance**, import, consequence, matter, moment, weight, consideration, gravity, relevance, magnitude, impressiveness

significant ADJECTIVE **1 = important**, notable, serious, material, vital, critical, considerable, momentous, weighty, noteworthy: *It is the first drug that seems to have a significant effect on this disease.* **OPPOSITE:** insignificant **2 = meaningful**, expressive, eloquent, knowing, meaning, expressing, pregnant, indicative, suggestive: *The old woman gave her a significant glance.* **OPPOSITE:** meaningless

signify VERB **= indicate**, show, mean, matter, suggest, announce, evidence, represent, express, imply, exhibit, communicate, intimate, stand for, proclaim, convey, be a sign of, symbolize, denote, connote, portend, betoken, flag up

silence NOUN **1 = quiet**, peace, calm, hush, lull, stillness, quiescence, noiselessness: *They stood in silence.* **OPPOSITE:** noise **2 = reticence**, dumbness, taciturnity, speechlessness, muteness, uncommunicativeness: *The court ruled that his silence should be entered as a plea of not guilty.* **OPPOSITE:** speech
▹ VERB **= quieten**, still, quiet, cut off, subdue, stifle, cut short, quell, muffle, deaden, strike dumb: *The shock silenced him completely.* **OPPOSITE:** make louder

silent ADJECTIVE **1 = mute**, dumb, speechless, wordless, mum, struck dumb, voiceless, unspeaking: *They both fell silent.* **OPPOSITE:** noisy **2 = uncommunicative**, quiet, taciturn, tongue-tied, unspeaking, nonvocal, not talkative: *He was a serious, silent man.* **3 = quiet**, still, hushed, soundless, noiseless, muted, stilly *(poetic)*: *The heavy guns have again fallen silent.* **OPPOSITE:** loud **4 = unspoken**, implied, implicit, tacit, understood, unexpressed: *He watched with silent contempt.*

silently ADVERB **1 = quietly**, in silence, soundlessly, noiselessly, inaudibly, without a sound: *as silently as a mouse*

S

2 = mutely, dumbly, in silence, wordlessly, speechlessly: *He could no longer stand by silently while these rumours persisted.*

silhouette NOUN **= outline**, form, shape, profile, delineation: *The dark silhouette of the castle ruins.*
▷ VERB **= outline**, delineate, etch: *firefighters silhouetted against the burning wreckage*

silky ADJECTIVE **= smooth**, soft, sleek, velvety, silken

silly ADJECTIVE **1 = stupid**, ridiculous, absurd, daft, inane, childish, immature, senseless, frivolous, preposterous, giddy, goofy *(informal)*, idiotic, dozy *(Brit. informal)*, fatuous, witless, puerile, brainless, asinine, dumb-ass *(slang)*, dopy *(slang)*: *That's a silly thing to say.* **OPPOSITE:** clever
2 = foolish, stupid, unwise, inappropriate, rash, irresponsible, reckless, foolhardy, idiotic, thoughtless, imprudent, inadvisable: *Don't go doing anything silly now, will you?*
OPPOSITE: sensible
▷ NOUN **= fool**, twit *(informal)*, goose *(informal)*, clot *(Brit. informal)*, wally *(slang)*, prat *(slang)*, plonker *(slang)*, duffer *(informal)*, simpleton, ignoramus, nitwit *(informal)*, ninny, silly-billy *(informal)*, dweeb *(U.S. slang)*, putz *(U.S. slang)*, eejit *(Scot. & Irish)*, doofus *(slang, chiefly U.S.)*, nerd *or* nurd *(slang)*, dorba *or* dorb *(Austral. slang)*, bogan *(Austral. slang)*: *Come on, silly, we'll miss all the fun.*

silt NOUN **= sediment**, deposit, residue, ooze, sludge, alluvium: *The lake was almost solid with silt and vegetation.*
silt something up = clog up, block up, choke up, obstruct, stop up, jam up, dam up, bung up, occlude, congest: *The soil washed from the hills is silting up the dams.*

silver NOUN **= silverware**, silver plate: *He beat the rugs and polished the silver.*
▷ ADJECTIVE **= snowy**, white, grey, silvery, greyish-white, whitish-grey: *He had thick silver hair which needed cutting.*

similar ADJECTIVE **1 = alike**, uniform, resembling, corresponding, comparable, much the same, homogeneous, of a piece, homogenous, cut from the same cloth, congruous: *The sisters looked very similar.* **OPPOSITE:** different **2** *(with* **to***)* **= like**, much the same as, comparable to, analogous to, close to, cut from the same cloth as: *The accident was similar to one that happened in 1973.*

> **USAGE**
> *As* should not be used after *similar* – so *Wilson held a similar position to Jones* is correct, but not *Wilson held a similar position as Jones*; and *The system is similar to the one in France* is correct, but not *The system is similar as in France.*

similarity NOUN **= resemblance**, likeness, sameness, agreement, relation, correspondence, analogy, affinity, closeness, concordance, congruence, comparability, point of comparison, similitude
OPPOSITE: difference

> **PROVERBS**
> *Birds of a feather flock together*

similarly ADVERB **1 = in the same way**, the same, identically, in a similar fashion, uniformly, homogeneously, undistinguishably: *Most of the men who now gathered round him were similarly dressed.* **2 = likewise**, in the same way, by the same token, correspondingly, in like manner: *Similarly a baby's cry is instantly identified by the mother.*

simmer VERB **1 = bubble**, stew, boil gently, seethe, cook gently: *Turn the heat down so the sauce simmers gently.*
2 = fume, seethe, smoulder, burn, smart, rage, boil, be angry, see red *(informal)*, be tense, be agitated, be uptight *(informal)*: *He simmered with rage.*
simmer down = calm down, grow quieter, control yourself, unwind *(informal)*, contain yourself, collect yourself, cool off *or* down, get down off your high horse *(informal)*: *After an hour or so, she finally managed to simmer down.*

simper VERB **= smile coyly**, smirk, smile self-consciously, smile affectedly

simpering ADJECTIVE **= coy**, affected, flirtatious, coquettish, kittenish

simple ADJECTIVE **1 = uncomplicated**, clear, plain, understandable, coherent, lucid, recognizable, unambiguous, comprehensible, intelligible, uninvolved: *simple pictures and diagrams* **OPPOSITE:** complicated
2 = easy, straightforward, not difficult, light, elementary, manageable, effortless, painless, uncomplicated, undemanding, easy-peasy *(slang)*: *The job itself had been simple enough.* **3 = plain**, natural, basic, classic, severe, Spartan, uncluttered, unadorned, unfussy, unembellished, bare-bones: *She's shunned Armani for a simple blouse and jeans.*
OPPOSITE: elaborate **4 = pure**, mere, sheer, unalloyed: *His refusal to talk was simple stubbornness.* **5 = artless**, innocent, naive, natural, frank, green, sincere, simplistic, unaffected, childlike, unpretentious, unsophisticated, ingenuous, guileless: *He was as simple as a child.*
OPPOSITE: sophisticated
6 = unpretentious, modest, humble, homely, lowly, rustic, uncluttered, unfussy, unembellished: *It was a simple home.* **OPPOSITE:** fancy

simple-minded ADJECTIVE **= stupid**, simple, foolish, backward, idiot, retarded, idiotic, moronic, brainless, feeble-minded, addle-brained, dead from the neck up *(informal)*, a bit lacking *(informal)*, dim-witted

simplicity NOUN
1 = straightforwardness, ease, clarity, obviousness, easiness, clearness, absence of complications, elementariness: *The apparent simplicity of his plot is deceptive.*
OPPOSITE: complexity **2 = plainness**, restraint, purity, clean lines, naturalness, lack of adornment: *fussy details that ruin the simplicity of the design*
OPPOSITE: elaborateness

simplify VERB **= make simpler**, facilitate, streamline, disentangle, dumb down, make intelligible, reduce to essentials, declutter

simplistic ADJECTIVE
= oversimplified, shallow, facile, naive, oversimple

> **USAGE**
> Since *simplistic* already has 'too' as part of its meaning, some people object to something being referred to as *too simplistic* or *oversimplistic*, and it is best to avoid such uses in serious writing.

simply ADVERB **1 = just**, only, merely, purely, solely: *The table is simply a chipboard circle on a base.* **2 = totally**, really, completely, absolutely, altogether, wholly, utterly, unreservedly: *He's simply wonderful in every respect.* **3 = clearly**, straightforwardly, directly, plainly, intelligibly, unaffectedly: *The book is clearly and simply written.* **4 = plainly**, naturally, modestly, with restraint, unpretentiously, without any elaboration: *He dressed simply and led a quiet family life.* **5 = without doubt**, surely, certainly, definitely, unquestionably, undeniably, unmistakably, beyond question, beyond a shadow of (a) doubt: *It was simply the greatest night any of us ever had.*

simulate VERB **= pretend**, act, feign, affect, assume, put on, reproduce, imitate, sham, fabricate, counterfeit, make believe

simulated ADJECTIVE **1 = pretended**, put-on, feigned, assumed, artificial, make-believe, insincere, phoney *or* phony *(informal)*: *He performed a simulated striptease.* **2 = synthetic**, artificial, fake, substitute, mock, imitation, man-made, sham, pseudo *(informal)*: *a necklace of simulated pearls*

simultaneous ADJECTIVE
= coinciding, concurrent, contemporaneous, coincident, synchronous, happening at the same time

simultaneously ADVERB **= at the same time**, together, all together, in concert, in unison, concurrently, in the same breath, in chorus

sin NOUN **1 = wickedness**, wrong, evil, crime, error, trespass, immorality, transgression, iniquity, sinfulness, unrighteousness, ungodliness: *Sin can be forgiven, but never condoned.* **2 = crime**, offence, misdemeanour, error, wrongdoing, misdeed, transgression, act of evil, guilt: *Was it a sin to have believed too much in themselves?*

▷ VERB **= transgress**, offend, lapse, err, trespass *(archaic)*, fall from grace, go astray, commit a sin, do wrong: *They charged him with sinning against God and man.*

SEVEN DEADLY SINS

anger	gluttony
covetousness *or* avarice	lust
	pride
envy	sloth

QUOTATIONS

I count religion but a childish toy
And hold there is no sin but ignorance
[Christopher Marlowe *The Jew of Malta*]

Be sure your sin will find you out
[*Bible: Numbers*]

I used to be Snow White – but I drifted
[Mae West]

The wages of sin is death
[*Bible: Romans*]

more sinn'd against than sinning
[William Shakespeare *King Lear*]

All good biography, as all good fiction, comes down to the study of original sin, of our inherent disposition to choose death when we ought to choose life
[Rebecca West *Time and Tide*]

There's no such thing as an original sin
[Elvis Costello *I'm not Angry*]

Though your sins be as scarlet, they shall be as white as snow
[*Bible: Isaiah*]

He that toucheth pitch shall be defiled therewith
[*Bible: Ecclesiasticus*]

If we say that we have no sin, we deceive ourselves, and the truth is not in us
[*Bible: I John*]

It is public scandal that constitutes offence, and to sin in secret is not to sin at all
[Molière *Le Tartuffe*]

PROVERBS

Old sins cast long shadows

sincere ADJECTIVE **= honest**, genuine, real, true, serious, natural, earnest, frank, open, straightforward, candid, unaffected, no-nonsense, heartfelt, upfront *(informal)*, bona fide, wholehearted, dinkum *(Austral. & N.Z. informal)*, artless, guileless, unfeigned **OPPOSITE:** false

sincerely ADVERB **= honestly**, really, truly, genuinely, seriously, earnestly, wholeheartedly, in good faith, in earnest, in all sincerity, from the bottom of your heart

sincerity NOUN **= honesty**, truth, candour, frankness, seriousness, good faith, probity, bona fides *(Law)*, genuineness, straightforwardness, artlessness, guilelessness, wholeheartedness

sinewy ADJECTIVE **= muscular**, strong, powerful, athletic, robust, wiry, brawny

sinful ADJECTIVE **= wicked**, bad, criminal, guilty, corrupt, immoral, erring, unholy, depraved, iniquitous, ungodly, irreligious, unrighteous, morally wrong **OPPOSITE:** virtuous

sing VERB **1 = croon**, carol, chant, warble, yodel, pipe, vocalize: *Go on, then, sing us a song!* **2 = trill**, chirp, warble, make melody: *Birds were already singing in the garden.*

sing out = call (out), cry (out), shout, yell, holler *(informal)*, halloo: *'See you,' Jeff sang out.*

USAGE

Sang is the past tense of the verb *sing*, as in *She sang sweetly*. *Sung* is the past participle, as in *We have sung our song*, and care should be taken not to use it as if it were a variant form of the past tense.

singe VERB **= burn**, sear, scorch, char

singer NOUN **= vocalist**, divo *or* diva *(fem.)*, crooner, minstrel, soloist, cantor, troubadour, chorister, chanteuse *(fem.)*, balladeer, songster *or* songstress

single ADJECTIVE **1 = one**, sole, lone, solitary, only, only one, unique, singular: *A single shot rang out.* **2 = individual**, particular, separate, distinct: *Every single house had been damaged.* **3 = unmarried**, free, unattached, a bachelor *or* bachelorette, unwed: *The last I heard she was still single, still out there.* **4 = separate**, individual, exclusive, undivided, unshared: *A single room at the hotel costs £36 a night.* **5 = simple**, unmixed, unblended, uncompounded: *single malt whisky*

single something *or* **someone out = pick**, choose, select, separate, distinguish, fix on, set apart, winnow, put on one side, pick on *or* out, flag up: *He singled me out for special attention.*

single-handed ADVERB **= unaided**, on your own, by yourself, alone, independently, solo, without help, unassisted, under your own steam

single-minded ADJECTIVE **= determined**, dogged, fixed, dedicated, stubborn, tireless, steadfast, unwavering, unswerving, hellbent *(informal)*, undeviating, monomaniacal

singly ADVERB **= one by one**, individually, one at a time, separately, one after the other

singular ADJECTIVE **1 = single**, individual: *The pronoun 'you' can be singular or plural.* **2 = remarkable**, unique, extraordinary, outstanding, exceptional, rare, notable, eminent, uncommon, conspicuous, prodigious, unparalleled, noteworthy: *a smile of singular sweetness* **OPPOSITE:** ordinary **3 = unusual**, odd, strange, extraordinary, puzzling, curious, peculiar, eccentric, out-of-the-way, queer, oddball *(informal)*, atypical, wacko *(slang)*, outré, daggy *(Austral. & N.Z. informal)*: *He was without doubt a singular character.* **OPPOSITE:** conventional

singularity NOUN **= oddity**, abnormality, eccentricity, peculiarity, strangeness, idiosyncrasy, irregularity, particularity, oddness, queerness, extraordinariness, curiousness

singularly ADVERB **= remarkably**, particularly, exceptionally, especially, seriously *(informal)*, surprisingly, notably, unusually, extraordinarily, conspicuously, outstandingly, uncommonly, prodigiously

sinister ADJECTIVE **= threatening**, evil, menacing, forbidding, dire, ominous, malign, disquieting, malignant, malevolent, baleful, injurious, bodeful **OPPOSITE:** reassuring

sink NOUN **= basin**, washbasin, hand basin, wash-hand basin: *The sink was full of dirty dishes.*

▷ VERB **1 = scupper**, scuttle: *In a naval battle your aim is to sink the enemy's ship.* **2 = go down**, founder, go under, submerge, capsize: *The boat was beginning to sink fast.* **3 = slump**, drop, flop, collapse, droop: *Kate laughed, and sank down again to her seat.* **4 = fall**, drop, decline, slip, plunge, plummet, subside, relapse, abate, retrogress: *Pay increases have sunk to around seven per cent.* **5 = drop**, fall: *Her voice had sunk to a whisper.* **6 = stoop**, descend, be reduced to, succumb, lower yourself, debase yourself, demean yourself: *You know who you are, be proud of it and don't sink to his level.* **7 = decline**, die, fade, fail, flag, weaken, diminish, decrease, deteriorate, decay, worsen, dwindle, lessen, degenerate, depreciate, go downhill *(informal)*: *He's still alive, but sinking fast.* **OPPOSITE:** improve **8 = dig**, bore, drill, drive, lay, put down, excavate: *the site where Stephenson sank his first mineshaft*

sinner NOUN **= wrongdoer**, offender, evildoer, trespasser *(archaic)*, reprobate, miscreant, malefactor, transgressor

sinuous ADJECTIVE **= curving**, winding, meandering, crooked, coiling, tortuous, undulating, serpentine, curvy, lithe, twisty, mazy

sip VERB **= drink**, taste, sample, sup: *Jessica sipped her drink thoughtfully.*

▷ NOUN **= swallow**, mouthful, swig, drop, taste, thimbleful: *Harry took a sip of bourbon.*

siren NOUN **1 = alert**, warning, signal, alarm: *It sounds like an air raid siren.* **2 = seductress**, vamp *(informal)*, femme fatale *(French)*, witch, charmer, temptress, Lorelei, Circe: *She's a voluptuous siren with a husky voice.*

sissy or **cissy** NOUN **= wimp**, softie *(informal)*, weakling, baby, wet *(Brit. informal)*, coward *(informal)*, jessie *(Scot. slang)*, pansy, pussy *(slang, chiefly U.S.)*, mummy's boy, mollycoddle, namby-pamby, wuss *(slang)*, milksop, milquetoast *(U.S.)*, sisspot *(informal)*: *They were rough kids and thought we were sissies.*
▷ ADJECTIVE **= wimpish** or **wimpy** *(informal)*, soft *(informal)*, weak, wet *(Brit. informal)*, cowardly, feeble, unmanly, effeminate, namby-pamby, wussy *(slang)*, sissified *(informal)*: *Far from being sissy, it takes a real man to admit he's not perfect.*

sit VERB **1 = take a seat**, perch, settle down, be seated, take the weight off your feet: *Eva pulled up a chair and sat beside her husband.* **2 = place**, set, put, position, rest, lay, settle, deposit, situate: *She found her chair and sat it in the usual spot.* **3 = be a member of**, serve on, have a seat on, preside on: *He was asked to sit on numerous committees.* **4 = convene**, meet, assemble, officiate, be in session: *Parliament sits for only 28 weeks out of 52.*

site NOUN **1 = area**, ground, plot, patch, tract: *He became a hod carrier on a building site.* **2 = location**, place, setting, point, position, situation, spot, whereabouts, locus: *the site of Moses' tomb*
▷ VERB **= locate**, put, place, set, position, establish, install, situate: *He said chemical weapons had never been sited in Germany.*

sitting NOUN **1 = session**, period: *Dinner was in two sittings.* **2 = meeting**, hearing, session, congress, consultation, get-together *(informal)*: *the recent emergency sittings*

situation NOUN **1 = position**, state, case, condition, circumstances, equation, plight, status quo, state of affairs, ball game *(informal)*, kettle of fish *(informal)*: *We are in a difficult financial situation.* **2 = scenario**, the picture *(informal)*, the score *(informal)*, state of affairs, lie of the land: *They looked at each other and weighed up the situation.* **3 = location**, place, setting, position, seat, site, spot, locality, locale: *The garden is in a beautiful situation.*

sixth sense NOUN **= intuition**, second sight, clairvoyance

size NOUN **= dimensions**, extent, measurement(s), range, amount, mass, length, volume, capacity, proportions, bulk, width, magnitude, greatness, vastness, immensity, bigness, largeness, hugeness: *books of various sizes*
size something or **someone up = assess**, evaluate, appraise, take stock of, eye up, get the measure of, get (something) taped *(Brit. informal)*: *He spent the entire evening sizing me up intellectually.*

sizeable or **sizable** ADJECTIVE **= large**, considerable, substantial, goodly, decent, respectable, tidy *(informal)*, decent-sized, largish

sizzle VERB **= hiss**, spit, crackle, sputter, fry, frizzle

skeletal ADJECTIVE **= emaciated**, wasted, gaunt, skin-and-bone *(informal)*, cadaverous, hollow-cheeked, lantern-jawed, fleshless, worn to a shadow

skeleton NOUN **1 = bones**, bare bones: *a human skeleton* **2 = frame**, shell, framework, basic structure: *Only skeletons of buildings remained in the area.* **3 = plan**, structure, frame, draft, outline, framework, sketch, abstract, blueprint, main points: *a skeleton of policy guidelines*
▷ MODIFIER **= minimum**, reduced, minimal, essential: *Only a skeleton staff remains to see anyone interested around the site.*

sketch NOUN **1 = drawing**, design, draft, delineation: *a sketch of a soldier* **2 = draft**, outline, framework, plan, frame, rough, skeleton, layout, lineament(s): *I had a basic sketch of a plan.* **3 = skit**, piece, scene, turn, act, performance, item, routine, number: *a five-minute humorous sketch*
▷ VERB **= draw**, paint, outline, represent, draft, portray, depict, delineate, rough out: *I sketched the scene with my pen and paper.*

sketchy ADJECTIVE **= incomplete**, rough, vague, slight, outline, inadequate, crude, superficial, unfinished, skimpy, scrappy, cursory, perfunctory, cobbled together, bitty **OPPOSITE:** complete

skid VERB **= slide**, slip, slither, coast, glide, skim, veer, toboggan

skilful ADJECTIVE **= expert**, skilled, masterly, trained, experienced, able, professional, quick, clever, practised, accomplished, handy, competent, apt, adept, proficient, adroit, dexterous **OPPOSITE:** clumsy

skill NOUN **= expertise**, ability, proficiency, experience, art, technique, facility, talent, intelligence, craft, competence, readiness, accomplishment, knack, ingenuity, finesse, aptitude, dexterity, cleverness, quickness, adroitness, expertness, handiness, skilfulness **OPPOSITE:** clumsiness

skilled ADJECTIVE **= expert**, professional, accomplished, trained, experienced, able, masterly, practised, skilful, proficient, a dab hand at *(Brit. informal)* **OPPOSITE:** unskilled

skim VERB **1 = remove**, separate, cream, take off: *Skim off the fat.* **2 = glide**, fly, coast, sail, float, brush, dart: *seagulls skimming over the waves* **3** *(usually with* **over** *or* **through***)* **= scan**, glance, run your eye over, thumb or leaf through: *I only had time to skim over the script before I came here.*

skimp VERB **= stint**, scrimp, be sparing with, pinch, withhold, scant, cut corners, scamp, be mean with, be niggardly, tighten your belt **OPPOSITE:** be extravagant

skimpy ADJECTIVE **= inadequate**, insufficient, scant, meagre, short, tight, thin, sparse, scanty, miserly, niggardly, exiguous

skin NOUN **1 = complexion**, colouring, skin tone: *His skin is clear and smooth.* **2 = hide**, fleece, pelt, fell, integument, tegument: *That was real crocodile skin.* **3 = peel**, rind, husk, casing, outside, crust: *banana skins* **4 = film**, coating, coat, membrane: *Stir the custard occasionally to prevent a skin forming.*
▷ VERB **1 = peel**, pare, hull: *two tomatoes, skinned, peeled and chopped* **2 = scrape**, graze, bark, flay, excoriate, abrade: *He fell down and skinned his knee.*
by the skin of one's teeth = narrowly, only just, by a whisker *(informal)*, by a narrow margin, by a hair's-breadth: *He won, but only by the skin of his teeth.*
get under your skin = annoy, irritate, aggravate *(informal)*, needle *(informal)*, nettle, irk, grate on, get on your nerves *(informal)*, get in your hair *(informal)*, rub you up the wrong way, hack you off *(informal)*: *Her mannerisms can just get under your skin and needle you.*

skin-deep ADJECTIVE **= superficial**, surface, external, artificial, shallow, on the surface, meaningless

skinny ADJECTIVE **= thin**, lean, scrawny, skeletal, emaciated, twiggy, undernourished, skin-and-bone *(informal)*, scraggy **OPPOSITE:** fat

skip VERB **1 = hop**, dance, bob, trip, bounce, caper, prance, cavort, frisk, gambol: *She was skipping along the pavement.* **2 = miss out**, omit, leave out, overlook, pass over, eschew, forgo, skim over, give (something) a miss: *It is important not to skip meals.* **3 = miss**, cut *(informal)*, bunk off *(slang)*, play truant from, wag *(dialect)*, dog it or dog off *(dialect)*: *Her daughter started skipping school.*

skirmish NOUN **= fight**, battle, conflict, incident, clash, contest, set-to *(informal)*, encounter, brush, combat, scrap *(informal)*, engagement, spat *(U.S.)*, tussle, fracas, affray *(Law)*, dust-up *(informal)*, scrimmage, biffo *(Austral. slang)*, boilover *(Austral.)*: *Border skirmishes are common.*
▷ VERB **= fight**, clash, come to blows, scrap *(informal)*, collide, grapple, wrangle, tussle, lock horns, cross swords: *Police skirmished with youths on a council estate last Friday.*

skirt VERB **1 = border**, edge, lie alongside, line, fringe, flank: *We raced across a large field that skirted the slope of the hill.* **2** *(often with* **around** *or* **round***)* **= go round**, bypass, walk round, circumvent: *She skirted around the edge of the room to the door.* **3** *(often with* **around** *or* **round***)* **= avoid**, evade, steer clear of,

S

The Language of James Joyce

The Irish writer James Augustine Aloysius Joyce (1882–1941) was one of the most celebrated authors of the 20th century. His major early works were *Dubliners,* a collection of vignettes about life in late-19th-century Dublin, and *A Portrait of the Artist as a Young Man,* the story of the internal coming of age of Stephen Dedalus, Joyce's alter ego. *Ulysses* was perhaps Joyce's masterpiece, and is often considered the first and greatest modernist novel. It tells the story of Leopold Bloom as he spends a day winding his way through the streets of Dublin. The narrative parallels that of Homer's *Odyssey,* but the action is internal, and the most important aspect of the book is the workings of the characters' minds. *Ulysses* was followed by *Finnegan's Wake,* a dreamscape prose-poem which, with its heavy use of neologisms, puns, and allusions, has often eluded comprehension.

Appropriately enough, one of Joyce's twenty most frequent nouns is *word,* which is often used as a character ruminates on the nature of a word, as in this example from *Dubliners*:

> Every night as I gazed up at the window I said softly to myself the **word** paralysis. It had always sounded strangely in my ears, like the **word** gnomon in the Euclid and the **word** simony in the Catechism.

Similarly, Stephen Dedalus ponders on the nature of the word *God* (another of Joyce's top twenty nouns), reflecting that 'there were different names for God in all the different languages in the world' but 'still God remained always the same God and God's real name was God.' Words and names are never casual for Joyce: they are heavy with meaning.

Joyce's words don't tend to enter into repeated or predictable phrases. *Word* itself is modified by a wide variety of adjectives such as *frolicsome, pregnant, scurvy,* and *wedded* ('Wavewhite wedded words shimmering on the dim tide'). Another frequent noun is *soul,* meaning both 'spirit' and 'person': souls in Joyce can be *bat-like, Godpossibled,* and *obscure. Soft* is a frequent adjective, and it is often used in novel ways, as in *soft grey silence* and *soft liquid joy.* Physical descriptions are also inventive. *Face* is Joyce's tenth most frequent noun, and faces are not only bearded but *beardframed*; not round but *harvestmoon.*

One of the most striking features of Joyce's prose is his sentence structure, which he uses to express the workings of his characters' minds. In *A Portrait of the Artist as a Young Man,* Joyce captures the child Stephen's disjointed images and associations through the use of short simple one-clause sentences with no conjunctions:

> His mother put on the oilsheet. That had the queer smell. His mother had a nicer smell than his father.

In *Ulysses,* we find an example of a different but just as effective kind of sentence structure, or lack of it, as we get inside the mind of Molly Bloom:

> Yes because he never did a thing like that before as ask to get his breakfast in bed with a couple of eggs since the City arms hotel when he used to be pretending to be laid up with a sick voice doing his highness to make himself interesting to that old faggot Mrs Riordan that he thought he had a great leg of and she never left us a farthing...

This stream-of-consciousness style, a style also used by other modernist writers such as Virginia Woolf, aimed to represent the flow of people's thoughts, which work by association and move from impression to impression without logical coherence. In this passage, which is the first part of an entire chapter in this mode, we enter Molly's mind as she leaps from one image to another. The lack of punctuation contributes to the authentic impression of unstructured flow, and this chapter has been praised as one of the most successful examples of stream-of-consciousness style in literature.

sidestep, circumvent, detour, body-swerve (*Scot.*): *They have, until now, skirted around the issue.*
▷ NOUN (*often plural*) = **border**, edge, margin, fringe, outskirts, rim, hem, periphery, purlieus: *the skirts of the hill*

skit NOUN = **parody**, spoof (*informal*), travesty, takeoff (*informal*), burlesque, turn, sketch

skittish ADJECTIVE = **nervous**, lively, excitable, jumpy, restive, fidgety, highly strung, antsy (*informal*)
OPPOSITE: calm

skookum ADJECTIVE = **powerful**, influential, big, dominant, controlling, commanding, supreme, prevailing, sovereign, authoritative, puissant

skulduggery NOUN = **trickery**, swindling, machinations, duplicity, double-dealing, fraudulence, shenanigan(s) (*informal*), unscrupulousness, underhandedness

skulk VERB **1** = **creep**, sneak, slink, pad, prowl: *He skulked off.* **2** = **lurk**, hide, lie in wait, loiter: *skulking in the safety of the car*

sky NOUN = **heavens**, firmament, upper atmosphere, azure (*poetic*), welkin (*archaic*), vault of heaven, rangi (*N.Z.*)
▸ *related adjective:* celestial

slab NOUN = **piece**, slice, lump, chunk, wedge, hunk, portion, nugget, wodge (*Brit. informal*)

slack ADJECTIVE **1** = **limp**, relaxed, loose, lax, flaccid, not taut: *The electronic pads work slack muscles to astounding effect.* **2** = **loose**, hanging, flapping, baggy: *The wind had gone, leaving the sails slack.* **OPPOSITE:** taut
3 = **slow**, quiet, inactive, dull, sluggish, slow-moving: *busy times and slack periods* **OPPOSITE:** busy
4 = **negligent**, lazy, lax, idle, easy-going, inactive, tardy, slapdash, neglectful, slipshod, inattentive, remiss, asleep on the job (*informal*): *Many publishers have simply become far too slack.* **OPPOSITE:** strict
▷ NOUN **1** = **surplus**, excess, overflow, leftover, glut, surfeit, overabundance, superabundance, superfluity: *Buying-to-let could stimulate the housing market by reducing the slack.* **2** = **room**, excess, leeway, give (*informal*), play, looseness: *He cranked in the slack, and the ship was moored.*
▷ VERB = **shirk**, idle, relax, flag, neglect, dodge, skive (*Brit. slang*), bob off (*Brit. slang*), bludge (*Austral. & N.Z. informal*): *He had never let a foreman see him slacking.*

slacken VERB = **lessen**, reduce, decrease, ease (off), moderate, diminish, slow down, drop off, abate, let up, slack off

slacker NOUN = **layabout**, shirker, loafer, skiver (*Brit. slang*), idler, passenger, do-nothing, piker (*Austral. & N.Z. slang*), dodger, good-for-nothing, bludger (*Austral. & N.Z. informal*), gold brick (*U.S. slang*), scrimshanker (*Brit. Military slang*)

slag NOUN = **tart** (*informal*), scrubber (*Brit. & Austral. slang*), whore, pro (*slang*), brass (*slang*), prostitute, hooker (*U.S. slang*), hustler (*U.S. & Canad. slang*), moll (*slang*), call girl, courtesan, working girl (*facetious, slang*), harlot, slapper (*Brit. slang*), streetwalker, camp follower, loose woman, fallen woman, strumpet, trollop, white slave, bawd (*archaic*), cocotte, fille de joie (*French*): *She became a slag, a tart, a hustler, a lost girl.*
slag something *or* **someone off** = **criticize**, abuse, malign, slam, insult, mock, slate, slang, deride, berate, slander, diss (*slang, chiefly U.S.*), lambast(e), flame (*informal*): *People keep slagging me off.*

slam VERB **1** = **bang**, crash, smash, thump, shut with a bang, shut noisily: *She slammed the door and locked it behind her.* **2** = **throw**, dash, hurl, fling: *They slammed him up against a wall.*
3 = **criticize**, attack, blast, pan (*informal*), damn, slate (*informal*), shoot down (*informal*), castigate, vilify, pillory, tear into (*informal*), diss (*slang, chiefly U.S.*), lambast(e), excoriate: *The director slammed the claims as an outrageous lie.*

slander NOUN = **defamation**, smear, libel, scandal, misrepresentation, calumny, backbiting, muckraking, obloquy, aspersion, detraction: *He is now suing the company for slander.*
OPPOSITE: praise
▷ VERB = **defame**, smear, libel, slur, malign, detract, disparage, decry, vilify, traduce, backbite, blacken (someone's) name, calumniate, muckrake: *He has been questioned on suspicion of slandering the politician.*
OPPOSITE: praise

PROVERBS
Throw enough dirt and some will stick
Give a dog a bad name and hang him

slang NOUN = **colloquialisms**, jargon, idioms, argot, informal language

slant VERB **1** = **slope**, incline, tilt, list, bend, lean, heel, shelve, skew, cant, bevel, angle off: *The morning sun slanted through the glass roof.* **2** = **bias**, colour, weight, twist, angle, distort: *The coverage was deliberately slanted to make the home team look good.*
▷ NOUN **1** = **slope**, incline, tilt, gradient, pitch, ramp, diagonal, camber, declination: *The house is on a slant.* **2** = **bias**, emphasis, prejudice, angle, leaning, point of view, viewpoint, one-sidedness: *They give a slant to every single news item that's put on the air.*

slanting ADJECTIVE = **sloping**, angled, inclined, tilted, tilting, sideways, slanted, bent, diagonal, oblique, at an angle, canted, on the bias, aslant, slantwise, atilt, cater-cornered (*U.S. informal*)

slap VERB **1** = **smack**, hit, strike, beat, bang, clap, clout (*informal*), cuff, whack, swipe, spank, clobber (*slang*), wallop (*informal*), lay one on (*slang*): *He would push and slap her once in a while.*
2 = **plaster**, apply, spread, daub: *We now routinely slap sunscreen on ourselves before venturing out.*
▷ NOUN = **smack**, blow, whack, wallop (*informal*), bang, clout (*informal*), cuff, swipe, spank: *He reached forward and gave her a slap.*
a slap in the face = **insult**, humiliation, snub, affront, blow, rejection, put-down, rebuke, rebuff, repulse: *They treated any pay rise of less than 5% as a slap in the face.*

slapstick NOUN = **farce**, horseplay, buffoonery, knockabout comedy

slap-up ADJECTIVE = **luxurious**, lavish, sumptuous, princely, excellent, superb, magnificent, elaborate, splendid, first-rate, no-expense-spared, fit for a king

slash VERB **1** = **cut**, slit, gash, lacerate, score, rend, rip, hack: *He nearly bled to death after slashing his wrists.* **2** = **reduce**, cut, decrease, drop, lower, moderate, diminish, cut down, lessen, curtail: *Everyone agrees that subsidies have to be slashed.*
▷ NOUN = **cut**, slit, gash, rent, rip, incision, laceration: *deep slashes in the meat*

slate VERB = **criticize**, blast, pan (*informal*), slam (*slang*), blame, roast (*informal*), censure, rebuke, slang, scold, berate, castigate, rail against, tear into (*informal*), lay into (*informal*), pitch into (*informal*), take to task, lambast(e), flame (*informal*), excoriate, haul over the coals (*informal*), tear (someone) off a strip (*informal*), rap (someone's) knuckles

slaughter VERB **1** = **kill**, murder, massacre, destroy, do in (*slang*), execute, dispatch, assassinate, blow away (*slang, chiefly U.S.*), annihilate, bump off (*slang*): *Thirty-four people were slaughtered while queueing up to cast their votes.* **2** = **butcher**, kill, slay, destroy, massacre, exterminate: *Whales and dolphins are still being slaughtered for commercial gain.* **3** = **defeat**, thrash, vanquish, stuff (*slang*), tank (*slang*), hammer (*informal*), crush, overwhelm, lick (*informal*), undo, rout, trounce, wipe the floor with (*informal*), blow out of the water (*slang*): *He slaughtered his opponent in three sets.*
▷ NOUN = **slaying**, killing, murder, massacre, holocaust, bloodshed, carnage, liquidation, extermination, butchery, blood bath: *The annual slaughter of wildlife is horrific.*

slaughterhouse NOUN = **abattoir**, butchery, shambles

slave NOUN **1** = **servant**, serf, vassal, bondsman, slavey (*Brit. informal*), varlet (*archaic*), villein, bondservant: *still living as slaves in the desert*
2 = **drudge**, skivvy (*chiefly Brit.*), scullion (*archaic*), bitch (*slang*): *Mum says to Dad, 'I'm not your slave, you know!'*
▷ VERB = **toil**, labour, grind (*informal*),

drudge, sweat, graft, slog, skivvy (*Brit.*), work your fingers to the bone: *slaving over a hot stove*

slaver VERB = **dribble**, drool, salivate, slobber

slavery NOUN = **enslavement**, servitude, subjugation, captivity, bondage, thrall, serfdom, vassalage, thraldom **OPPOSITE:** freedom

> QUOTATIONS
> There're two people in the world that are not likeable: a master and a slave
> [Nikki Giovanni *A Dialogue [with James Baldwin]*]
> Slavery they can have anywhere. It is a weed that grows on every soil
> [Edmund Burke *On Conciliation with America*]
> That state is a state of slavery in which a man does what he likes to do in his spare time and in his working time that which is required of him
> [Eric Gill *Art-nonsense and Other Essays*]

slavish ADJECTIVE **1 = imitative**, unimaginative, unoriginal, conventional, second-hand, uninspired: *a slavish follower of fashion* **OPPOSITE:** original **2 = servile**, cringing, abject, submissive, grovelling, mean, low, base, fawning, despicable, menial, sycophantic, obsequious: *slavish devotion* **OPPOSITE:** rebellious

slay VERB **1 = kill**, destroy, slaughter, eliminate, massacre, butcher, dispatch, annihilate, exterminate: *the hill where he slew the dragon* **2 = murder**, kill, assassinate, do in (*slang*), eliminate, massacre, slaughter, do away with, exterminate, mow down, rub out (*U.S. slang*): *Two Australian tourists were slain.*

sleaze NOUN = **corruption**, fraud, dishonesty, fiddling (*informal*), bribery, extortion, venality, shady dealings (*informal*), crookedness (*informal*), unscrupulousness

sleazy ADJECTIVE = **squalid**, seedy, sordid, low, rundown, tacky (*informal*), disreputable, crummy (*slang*), scungy (*Austral. & N.Z.*)

sleek ADJECTIVE = **glossy**, shiny, lustrous, smooth, silky, velvety, well-groomed **OPPOSITE:** shaggy

sleep NOUN = **slumber(s)**, rest, nap, doze, kip (*Brit. slang*), snooze (*informal*), repose, hibernation, siesta, dormancy, beauty sleep (*informal*), forty winks (*informal*), shuteye (*slang*), zizz (*Brit. informal*): *Try and get some sleep.*
▷ VERB = **slumber**, drop off (*informal*), doze, kip (*Brit. slang*), snooze (*informal*), snore, hibernate, nod off (*informal*), take a nap, catnap, drowse, go out like a light, take forty winks (*informal*), zizz (*Brit. informal*), be in the land of Nod, rest in the arms of Morpheus: *I've not been able to sleep for the last few nights.*

sleepless ADJECTIVE **1 = wakeful**, disturbed, restless, insomniac, unsleeping: *I have sleepless nights worrying about her.* **2 = alert**, vigilant, watchful, wide awake, unsleeping: *his sleepless vigilance*

sleepwalking NOUN = **somnambulism**, noctambulation, noctambulism, somnambulation

sleepy ADJECTIVE **1 = drowsy**, sluggish, lethargic, heavy, dull, inactive, somnolent, torpid: *I was beginning to feel amazingly sleepy.* **OPPOSITE:** wide-awake **2 = soporific**, hypnotic, somnolent, sleep-inducing, slumberous: *How long we spent there in that sleepy heat, I don't know.* **3 = quiet**, peaceful, dull, tranquil, inactive: *a sleepy little town* **OPPOSITE:** busy

slender ADJECTIVE **1 = slim**, narrow, slight, lean, svelte, willowy, sylphlike: *He gazed at her slender neck.* **OPPOSITE:** chubby **2 = faint**, slight, remote, slim, thin, weak, fragile, feeble, flimsy, tenuous: *the first slender hope of peace* **OPPOSITE:** strong **3 = meagre**, little, small, inadequate, insufficient, scant, scanty, inconsiderable: *the Government's slender 21-seat majority* **OPPOSITE:** large

sleuth NOUN = **detective**, private eye (*informal*), (private) investigator, tail (*informal*), dick (*slang, chiefly U.S.*), gumshoe (*U.S. slang*), sleuthhound (*informal*)

slice NOUN = **piece**, segment, portion, wedge, sliver, helping, share, cut: *water flavoured with a slice of lemon*
▷ VERB = **cut**, divide, carve, segment, sever, dissect, cleave, bisect: *She sliced the cake.*

slick ADJECTIVE **1 = efficient**, professional, smart, smooth, streamlined, masterly, sharp, deft, well-organized, adroit: *His style is slick and visually exciting.* **2 = skilful**, deft, adroit, dextrous, dexterous, professional, polished: *a slick gear change* **OPPOSITE:** clumsy **3 = glib**, smooth, sophisticated, plausible, polished, specious, meretricious: *a slick, suit-wearing detective*
▷ VERB = **smooth**, oil, grease, sleek, plaster down, make glossy, smarm down (*Brit. informal*): *She had slicked her hair.*

slide VERB = **slip**, slither, glide, skim, coast, toboggan, glissade: *She slipped and slid downhill on her backside.*
let something slide = **neglect**, forget, ignore, pass over, turn a blind eye to, gloss over, push to the back of your mind, let ride: *The company had let environmental standards slide.*

slight ADJECTIVE **1 = small**, minor, insignificant, negligible, weak, modest, trivial, superficial, feeble, trifling, meagre, unimportant, paltry, measly, insubstantial, scanty, inconsiderable: *It's only made a slight difference.* **OPPOSITE:** large **2 = slim**, small, delicate, spare, fragile, lightly-built: *a man of slight build* **OPPOSITE:** sturdy
▷ VERB = **snub**, insult, ignore, rebuff, affront, neglect, put down, despise, scorn, disdain, disparage, cold-shoulder, treat with contempt, show disrespect for, give offence *or* umbrage to: *They felt slighted by not being adequately consulted.* **OPPOSITE:** compliment
▷ NOUN = **insult**, snub, affront, contempt, disregard, indifference, disdain, rebuff, disrespect, slap in the face (*informal*), inattention, discourtesy, (the) cold shoulder: *a child weeping over an imagined slight* **OPPOSITE:** compliment

slightly ADVERB = **a little**, a bit, somewhat, moderately, marginally, a shade, to some degree, on a small scale, to some extent *or* degree

slim ADJECTIVE **1 = slender**, slight, trim, thin, narrow, lean, svelte, willowy, sylphlike: *She is pretty, of slim build, with blue eyes.* **OPPOSITE:** chubby **2 = slight**, remote, faint, distant, slender: *a slim chance* **OPPOSITE:** strong
▷ VERB = **lose weight**, diet, get thinner, get into shape, slenderize (*chiefly U.S.*): *Some people will gain weight no matter how hard they try to slim.* **OPPOSITE:** put on weight

slimy ADJECTIVE **1 = viscous**, clammy, glutinous, muddy, mucous, gloopy (*informal*), oozy, miry: *Her hand touched something cold and slimy.* **2 = obsequious**, creepy, unctuous, smarmy (*Brit. informal*), oily, grovelling, soapy (*slang*), sycophantic, servile, toadying: *his slimy business partner*

sling VERB **1 = throw**, cast, toss, hurl, fling, chuck (*informal*), lob (*informal*), heave, shy: *She slung her coat over the desk chair.* **2 = hang**, swing, suspend, string, drape, dangle: *We slept in hammocks slung beneath the roof.*
▷ NOUN = **harness**, support, bandage, strap: *She was back at work with her arm in a sling.*

slink VERB = **creep**, steal, sneak, slip, prowl, skulk, pussyfoot (*informal*)

slinky ADJECTIVE = **figure-hugging**, clinging, sleek, close-fitting, skintight

slip[1] VERB **1 = fall**, trip (over), slide, skid, lose your balance, miss *or* lose your footing: *Be careful not to slip.* **2 = slide**, fall, drop, slither: *The hammer slipped out of her grasp.* **3 = sneak**, creep, steal, insinuate yourself: *She slipped downstairs and out of the house.*
▷ NOUN = **mistake**, failure, error, blunder, lapse, omission, boob (*Brit. slang*), oversight, slip-up (*informal*), indiscretion, bloomer (*Brit. informal*), faux pas, slip of the tongue, imprudence, barry *or* Barry Crocker (*Austral. slang*): *There must be no slips.*
give someone the slip = **escape from**, get away from, evade, shake (someone) off, elude, lose (someone), flee, dodge, outwit, slip through someone's fingers: *He gave reporters the*

S

slip by leaving by the back door at midnight. **let something slip = give away**, reveal, disclose, divulge, leak, come out with *(informal)*, let out *(informal)*, blurt out, let the cat out of the bag: *I bet he'd let slip that I'd gone to America.* **slip away = get away**, escape, disappear, break away, break free, get clear of, take French leave: *He slipped away in the early hours to exile in France.* **slip up = make a mistake**, go wrong, blunder, mistake, boob *(Brit. slang)*, err, misjudge, miscalculate, drop a brick *or* clanger *(informal)*: *You will see exactly where you are slipping up.*

slip² NOUN **= strip**, piece, sliver: *little slips of paper*

slippery ADJECTIVE **1 = smooth**, icy, greasy, glassy, slippy *(informal, dialect)*, unsafe, lubricious *(rare)*, skiddy *(informal)*: *The floor was wet and slippery.* **2 = untrustworthy**, tricky, cunning, false, treacherous, dishonest, devious, crafty, evasive, sneaky, two-faced, shifty, foxy, duplicitous: *a slippery customer*

slit VERB **= cut (open)**, rip, slash, knife, pierce, lance, gash, split open: *They say somebody slit her throat.*
▷ NOUN **1 = cut**, gash, incision, tear, rent, fissure: *Make a slit in the stem.* **2 = opening**, split, crack, aperture, chink, space: *She watched them through a slit in the curtain.*

slither VERB **= slide**, slip, glide, snake, undulate, slink, skitter

sliver NOUN **= shred**, fragment, splinter, slip, shaving, flake, paring

slob NOUN **= layabout**, lounger, loafer, couch potato *(slang)*, idler, good-for-nothing

slog VERB **1 = work**, labour, toil, slave, plod, persevere, plough through, sweat blood *(informal)*, apply yourself to, work your fingers to the bone, peg away at, keep your nose to the grindstone: *While slogging at your work, have you neglected your marriage?* **2 = trudge**, tramp, plod, trek, hike, traipse *(informal)*, yomp, walk heavily, footslog: *The men had to slog up a muddy incline.*
▷ NOUN **1 = work**, labour, toil, industry, grind *(informal)*, effort, struggle, pains, sweat *(informal)*, painstaking, exertion, donkey-work, blood, sweat, and tears *(informal)*: *There is little to show for two years of hard slog.* **2 = trudge**, tramp, trek, hike, traipse *(informal)*, yomp, footslog: *a slog through heather and bracken*

slogan NOUN **= catch phrase**, motto, jingle, rallying cry, tag-line, catchword, catchcry *(Austral.)*

slop VERB **= spill**, splash, overflow, splatter, spatter, slosh *(informal)*

slope NOUN **= inclination**, rise, incline, tilt, descent, downgrade *(chiefly U.S.)*, slant, ramp, gradient, brae *(Scot.)*, scarp, declination, declivity: *a mountain slope*
▷ VERB **= slant**, incline, drop away, fall, rise, pitch, lean, tilt: *The garden sloped quite steeply.* **slope off = slink away**, slip away, steal away, skulk, creep away, make yourself scarce: *She sloped off quietly on Saturday afternoon.*

sloping ADJECTIVE **= slanting**, leaning, inclined, inclining, oblique, atilt

sloppy ADJECTIVE **1 = careless**, slovenly, slipshod, messy, clumsy, untidy, amateurish, hit-or-miss *(informal)*, inattentive: *I won't accept sloppy work from my students.* **2 = sentimental**, mushy *(informal)*, soppy *(Brit. informal)*, slushy *(informal)*, wet *(Brit. informal)*, gushing, banal, trite, mawkish, icky *(informal)*, overemotional, three-hankie *(informal)*: *some sloppy love-story* **3 = wet**, watery, slushy, splashy, sludgy: *sloppy foods*

slosh VERB **1 = splash**, wash, slop, break, plash: *The water sloshed around the bridge.* **2 = wade**, splash, flounder, paddle, dabble, wallow, swash: *We sloshed through the mud together.*

slot NOUN **1 = opening**, hole, groove, vent, slit, aperture, channel: *He dropped a coin in the slot and dialled.* **2 = place**, time, space, spot, opening, position, window, vacancy, niche: *Visitors can book a time slot a week or more in advance.*
▷ VERB **= fit**, slide, insert, put, place: *She slotted a fresh filter into the machine.*

sloth NOUN **= laziness**, inactivity, idleness, inertia, torpor, sluggishness, slackness, indolence

slouch VERB **= lounge**, slump, flop, sprawl, stoop, droop, loll, lean

slouching ADJECTIVE **= shambling**, lumbering, ungainly, awkward, uncouth, loutish

slow ADJECTIVE **1 = unhurried**, sluggish, leisurely, easy, measured, creeping, deliberate, lagging, lazy, plodding, slow-moving, loitering, ponderous, leaden, dawdling, laggard, lackadaisical, tortoise-like, sluggardly: *He moved in a slow, unhurried way.* **OPPOSITE:** quick **2 = prolonged**, time-consuming, protracted, long-drawn-out, lingering, gradual: *The distribution of passports has been a slow process.* **3 = unwilling**, reluctant, loath, averse, hesitant, disinclined, indisposed: *He was not slow to take up the offer.* **4 = late**, unpunctual, behindhand, behind, tardy: *My watch is slow.* **5 = stupid**, dim, dense, thick, dull, dumb *(informal)*, retarded, bovine, dozy *(Brit. informal)*, unresponsive, obtuse, slow on the uptake *(informal)*, braindead *(informal)*, dull-witted, blockish, slow-witted, intellectually handicapped *(Austral.)*: *He got hit in the head and he's been a bit slow since.* **OPPOSITE:** bright **6 = dull**, quiet, boring, dead, tame, slack, sleepy, sluggish, tedious, stagnant, unproductive, inactive, one-horse *(informal)*, uneventful, uninteresting, wearisome, dead-and-alive *(Brit.)*, unprogressive: *Island life is too slow for her liking.* **OPPOSITE:** exciting
▷ VERB **1** *(often with* **down***)* **= decelerate**, brake, lag: *The car slowed down as they passed customs.* **2** *(often with* **down***)* **= delay**, hold up, hinder, check, restrict, handicap, detain, curb, retard, rein in: *Damage to the turbine slowed the work down.*
OPPOSITE: speed up

> **USAGE**
> While not as unkind as *thick* and *stupid*, words like *slow* and *backward*, when used to talk about a person's mental abilities, are both unhelpful and likely to cause offence. It is preferable to say that a person has *special educational needs* or *learning difficulties*.

slowly ADVERB **= gradually**, steadily, by degrees, unhurriedly, taking your time, at your leisure, at a snail's pace, in your own (good) time, ploddingly, inchmeal **OPPOSITE:** quickly

sludge NOUN **= sediment**, ooze, silt, mud, muck, residue, slop, mire, slime, slush, slob *(Irish)*, dregs, gloop *(informal)*

sluggish ADJECTIVE **= inactive**, slow, lethargic, listless, heavy, dull, lifeless, inert, slow-moving, unresponsive, phlegmatic, indolent, torpid, slothful: *feeling sluggish after a big meal* **OPPOSITE:** energetic

sluice VERB **= drain**, cleanse, flush, drench, wash out, wash down

slum NOUN **= hovel**, ghetto, shanty

slumber NOUN **= sleep**, nap, doze, rest, kip *(Brit. informal)*, snooze *(informal)*, siesta, catnap, forty winks *(informal)*: *He had fallen into exhausted slumber.*
▷ VERB **= sleep**, nap, doze, kip *(Brit. slang)*, snooze *(informal)*, lie dormant, drowse, zizz *(Brit. informal)*: *The older three girls are still slumbering peacefully.*

slump VERB **1 = fall**, decline, sink, plunge, crash, collapse, slip, deteriorate, fall off, plummet, go downhill *(informal)*: *Net profits slumped.* **OPPOSITE:** increase **2 = sag**, bend, hunch, droop, slouch, loll: *I closed the door and slumped into a chair.*
▷ NOUN **1 = fall**, drop, decline, crash, collapse, reverse, lapse, falling-off, downturn, depreciation, trough, meltdown *(informal)*: *a slump in property prices* **OPPOSITE:** increase **2 = recession**, depression, stagnation, inactivity, hard *or* bad times: *the slump of the early 1980s*

slur NOUN **= insult**, stain, smear, stigma, disgrace, discredit, blot, affront, innuendo, calumny, insinuation, aspersion: *yet another slur on the integrity of the police*
▷ VERB **= mumble**, stammer, stutter, stumble over, falter, mispronounce, garble, speak unclearly: *He repeated himself and slurred his words a lot.*

S

slut NOUN **= tart** *(informal)*, slag *(Brit. slang)*, slapper *(Brit. slang)*, sket *(Brit. derogatory slang)*, scrubber *(Brit. & Austral. slang)*, trollop, drab *(archaic)*, sloven, slattern, hornbag *(Austral. slang)*

sly ADJECTIVE **1 = roguish**, knowing, arch, mischievous, impish: *His lips were spread in a sly smile.* **2 = cunning**, scheming, devious, secret, clever, subtle, tricky, covert, astute, wily, insidious, crafty, artful, furtive, conniving, Machiavellian, shifty, foxy, underhand, stealthy, guileful: *She is devious, sly and manipulative.* **OPPOSITE:** open **3 = secret**, furtive, surreptitious, stealthy, sneaking, covert, clandestine: *They were giving each other sly looks across the room.*
on the sly = secretly, privately, covertly, surreptitiously, under the counter *(informal)*, on the quiet, behind (someone's) back, like a thief in the night, underhandedly, on the q.t. *(informal)*: *Was she meeting some guy on the sly?*

smack VERB **1 = slap**, hit, strike, pat, tap, sock *(slang)*, clap, cuff, swipe, box, spank: *She smacked me on the side of the head.* **2 = drive**, hit, strike, thrust, impel: *He smacked the ball against the post.*
▷ NOUN **= slap**, blow, whack, clout *(informal)*, cuff, crack, swipe, spank, wallop *(informal)*: *I end up shouting at him or giving him a smack.*
▷ ADVERB **= directly**, right, straight, squarely, precisely, exactly, slap *(informal)*, plumb, point-blank: *smack in the middle of the city*
smack of something = be suggestive *or* **indicative of**, suggest, smell of, testify to, reek of, have all the hallmarks of, betoken, be redolent of, bear the stamp of: *His comments smacked of racism.*

small ADJECTIVE **1 = little**, minute, tiny, slight, mini, miniature, minuscule, diminutive, petite, teeny, puny, pint-sized *(informal)*, pocket-sized, undersized, teeny-weeny, Lilliputian, teensy-weensy, pygmy *or* pigmy: *She is small for her age.* **OPPOSITE:** big **2 = intimate**, close, private: *a small select group of friends* **3 = young**, little, growing up, junior, wee, juvenile, youthful, immature, unfledged, in the springtime of life: *What were you like when you were small?* **4 = unimportant**, minor, trivial, insignificant, little, lesser, petty, trifling, negligible, paltry, piddling *(informal)*: *No detail was too small to escape her attention.* **OPPOSITE:** important **5 = modest**, small-scale, humble, unpretentious: *shops, restaurants and other small businesses* **OPPOSITE:** grand **6 = soft**, low, inaudible, low-pitched, noiseless: *a very small voice* **7 = meagre**, inadequate, insufficient, scant, measly, scanty, limited, inconsiderable: *a diet of one small meal a day* **OPPOSITE:** ample

small-minded ADJECTIVE **= petty**, mean, rigid, grudging, envious, bigoted, intolerant, narrow-minded, hidebound, ungenerous **OPPOSITE:** broad-minded

small-time ADJECTIVE **= minor**, insignificant, unimportant, petty, no-account *(U.S. informal)*, piddling *(informal)*, of no consequence, of no account

smart ADJECTIVE **1 = chic**, trim, neat, fashionable, stylish, fine, elegant, trendy *(Brit. informal)*, spruce, snappy, natty *(informal)*, modish, well turned-out, schmick *(Austral. informal)*: *I was dressed in a smart navy-blue suit.* **OPPOSITE:** scruffy **2 = clever**, bright, intelligent, quick, sharp, keen, acute, shrewd, apt, ingenious, astute, canny, quick-witted: *He thinks he's much smarter than Sarah.* **OPPOSITE:** stupid **3 = fashionable**, stylish, chic, genteel, in vogue, voguish *(informal)*: *smart dinner parties* **4 = brisk**, quick, lively, vigorous, spirited, cracking *(informal)*, spanking, jaunty: *We set off at a smart pace.*
▷ VERB **= sting**, burn, tingle, pain, hurt, throb: *My eyes smarted from the smoke.*

smarten VERB *(often with* **up***)* **= tidy**, spruce up, groom, beautify, put in order, put to rights, gussy up *(slang, chiefly U.S.)*

smash VERB **1 = break**, crush, shatter, crack, demolish, shiver, disintegrate, pulverize, crush to smithereens: *A crowd of youths started smashing windows.* **2 = shatter**, break, disintegrate, split, crack, explode, splinter: *The bottle smashed against a wall.* **3 = collide**, crash, meet head-on, clash, come into collision: *The train smashed into the car at 40 mph.* **4 = destroy**, ruin, wreck, total *(slang)*, defeat, overthrow, trash *(slang)*, lay waste: *Police staged a raid to smash one of Britain's biggest crack factories.*
▷ NOUN **1 = success**, hit, winner, triumph *(informal)*, belter *(slang)*, sensation, smash hit, sellout: *It is the public who decide if a film is a smash or a flop.* **2 = collision**, crash, accident, pile-up *(informal)*, smash-up *(informal)*: *He was near to death after a car smash.* **3 = crash**, smashing, clatter, clash, bang, thunder, racket, din, clattering, clang: *the smash of falling crockery*

smashing ADJECTIVE **= excellent**, mean *(slang)*, great *(informal)*, wonderful, topping *(Brit. slang)*, brilliant *(informal)*, cracking *(Brit. informal)*, crucial *(slang)*, superb, fantastic *(informal)*, magnificent, fabulous *(informal)*, first-class, marvellous, terrific *(informal)*, sensational *(informal)*, mega *(slang)*, sovereign, awesome *(slang)*, world-class, exhilarating, fab *(informal, chiefly Brit.)*, super *(informal)*, first-rate, def *(slang)*, superlative, brill *(informal)*, stupendous, out of this world *(informal)*, bodacious *(slang, chiefly U.S.)*, boffo *(slang)*, jim-dandy *(slang)*, chillin' *(U.S. slang)*, booshit *(Austral. slang)*, exo *(Austral. slang)*, sik *(Austral. slang)*, rad *(informal)*, phat *(slang)*, schmick *(Austral. informal)* **OPPOSITE:** awful

smattering NOUN **= modicum**, dash, rudiments, bit, elements, sprinkling, passing acquaintance, nodding acquaintance, smatter

smear VERB **1 = spread over**, daub, rub on, cover, coat, plaster, bedaub: *Smear a little olive oil over the inside of the salad bowl.* **2 = slander**, tarnish, malign, vilify, blacken, sully, besmirch, traduce, calumniate, asperse, drag (someone's) name through the mud: *a crude attempt to smear her* **3 = smudge**, soil, dirty, stain, sully, besmirch, smirch: *a face covered by a heavy beard, smeared with dirt*
▷ NOUN **1 = smudge**, daub, streak, blot, blotch, splotch, smirch: *a smear of gravy* **2 = slander**, libel, defamation, vilification, whispering campaign, calumny, mudslinging: *a smear by his rivals*

smell NOUN **1 = odour**, scent, fragrance, perfume, bouquet, aroma, whiff, niff *(Brit. slang)*, redolence: *the smell of freshly baked bread* **2 = stink**, stench, reek, pong *(Brit. informal)*, niff *(Brit. slang)*, malodour, fetor: *horrible smells*
▷ VERB **1 = stink**, reek, pong *(Brit. informal)*, hum *(slang)*, whiff *(Brit. slang)*, stink to high heaven *(informal)*, niff *(Brit. slang)*, be malodorous: *Do my feet smell?* **2 = sniff**, scent, get a whiff of, nose: *We could smell the gas.*
▸ *related adjective:* olfactory

smelly ADJECTIVE **= stinking**, reeking, fetid, foul-smelling, high, strong, foul, putrid, strong-smelling, stinky *(informal)*, malodorous, evil-smelling, noisome, whiffy *(Brit. slang)*, pongy *(Brit. informal)*, mephitic, niffy *(Brit. slang)*, olid, festy *(Austral. slang)* **OPPOSITE:** fragrant

smile VERB **= grin**, beam, smirk, twinkle, grin from ear to ear: *He smiled and waved.*
▷ NOUN **= grin**, beam, smirk: *She gave a wry smile.*

smirk NOUN **= smug smile**, grin, simper: *Wipe that smirk off your face!*
▷ VERB **= give a smug look**, grin, simper

smitten ADJECTIVE **1 = infatuated**, charmed, captivated, beguiled, bewitched, bowled over *(informal)*, enamoured, swept off your feet: *They were totally smitten with each other.* **2 = afflicted**, struck, beset, laid low, plagued: *smitten with yellow fever*

smoky ADJECTIVE **= thick**, murky, hazy

smooth ADJECTIVE **1 = even**, level, flat, plane, plain, flush, horizontal, unwrinkled: *a smooth surface* **OPPOSITE:** uneven **2 = sleek**, polished, shiny, glossy, silky, velvety, glassy, mirror-like: *The flagstones were worn smooth by centuries of use.*

OPPOSITE: rough **3 = mellow**, pleasant, mild, soothing, bland, agreeable: *This makes the flavour much smoother.* **4 = flowing**, steady, fluent, regular, uniform, rhythmic: *This exercise is done in one smooth motion.* **5 = calm**, peaceful, serene, tranquil, undisturbed, unruffled, equable: *This was only a brief upset in their smooth lives.* **OPPOSITE:** troubled **6 = easy**, effortless, untroubled, well-ordered: *A number of problems marred the smooth running of this event.* **7 = suave**, slick, persuasive, urbane, silky, glib, facile, ingratiating, debonair, unctuous, smarmy (*Brit. informal*): *Twelve extremely good-looking, smooth young men have been picked as finalists.*
▷ VERB **1 = flatten**, level, press, plane, iron: *She stood up and smoothed down her frock.* **2 = ease**, aid, assist, facilitate, pave the way, make easier, help along, iron out the difficulties of: *smoothing the path towards a treaty* **OPPOSITE:** hinder

smoothness NOUN **1 = evenness**, regularity, levelness, flushness, unbrokenness: *The lawn was rich, weed-free, and trimmed to smoothness.* **2 = fluency**, finish, flow, ease, polish, rhythm, efficiency, felicity, smooth running, slickness, effortlessness: *the strength and smoothness of his movements* **3 = sleekness**, softness, smooth texture, silkiness, velvetiness: *the smoothness of her skin* **4 = suavity**, urbanity, oiliness, glibness, smarminess (*Brit. informal*): *His cleverness, smoothness even, made his relationships uneasy.*

smother VERB **1 = extinguish**, put out, stifle, snuff: *They tried to smother the flames.* **2 = suffocate**, choke, strangle, stifle: *He had attempted to smother his sixteen-week-old son.* **3 = suppress**, stifle, repress, hide, conceal, muffle, keep back: *She tried to smother her feelings of panic.* **4 = overwhelm**, cover, shower, surround, heap, shroud, inundate, envelop, cocoon: *He smothered her with kisses.* **5 = stifle**, suppress, hold in, restrain, hold back, repress, muffle, bottle up, keep in check: *trying to smother our giggles* **6 = smear**, cover, spread: *Luckily, it wasn't smothered in creamy sauce.*

smoulder VERB **1 = smoke**, burn slowly: *Whole blocks had been turned into smouldering rubble.* **2 = seethe**, rage, fume, burn, boil, simmer, fester, be resentful, smart: *He smouldered as he drove home for lunch.*

smudge NOUN **= smear**, blot, smut, smutch: *smudges of blood*
▷ VERB **1 = smear**, blur, blot: *Smudge the outline using a cotton-wool bud.* **2 = mark**, soil, dirty, daub, smirch: *She kissed me, careful not to smudge me with her fresh lipstick.*

smug ADJECTIVE **= self-satisfied**, superior, complacent, conceited, self-righteous, holier-than-thou, priggish, self-opinionated

smuggler NOUN **= trafficker**, runner, bootlegger, moonshiner (*U.S.*), rum-runner, contrabandist

snack NOUN **= light meal**, bite, refreshment(s), nibble, titbit, bite to eat, elevenses (*Brit. informal*)

snag NOUN **= difficulty**, hitch, problem, obstacle, catch, hazard, disadvantage, complication, drawback, inconvenience, downside, stumbling block, the rub: *A police crackdown hit a snag when villains stole one of their cars.*
▷ VERB **= catch**, tear, rip, hole: *He snagged his suit.*

snake NOUN **= serpent**: *He was caught with his pet snake in his pocket.*
▷ VERB **= wind**, twist, curve, turn, bend, ramble, meander, deviate, zigzag: *The road snaked through the forested mountains.*
▶ *related adjective:* serpentine

snap VERB **1 = break**, split, crack, separate, fracture, give way, come apart: *The brake pedal had just snapped.* **2 = pop**, click, crackle: *He snapped the cap on his ballpoint.* **3 = speak sharply**, bark, lash out at, flash, retort, snarl, growl, fly off the handle at (*informal*), jump down (someone's) throat (*informal*): *I'm sorry, I didn't mean to snap at you.* **4 = bite at**, bite, nip: *The poodle yapped and snapped at our legs.*
▷ NOUN **1 = crack**, pop, crash, report, burst, explosion, clap: *Every minute or so I could hear a snap, a crack and a crash as another tree went down.* **2 = pop**, crack, smack, whack: *He shut the book with a snap and stood up.*
▷ MODIFIER **= instant**, immediate, sudden, abrupt, spur-of-the-moment, unpremeditated: *I think this is too important for a snap decision.*
snap out of it = get over it, recover, cheer up, perk up, liven up, pull yourself together (*informal*), get a grip on yourself: *Come on, snap out of it!*
snap something up = grab, seize, take advantage of, swoop down on, pounce upon, avail yourself of: *a queue of people waiting to snap up the bargains*

snappy ADJECTIVE **1 = smart**, fashionable, stylish, trendy (*Brit. informal*), chic, dapper, up-to-the-minute, natty (*informal*), modish, voguish, schmick (*Austral. informal*): *snappy sports jackets* **2 = irritable**, cross, bad-tempered, tart, impatient, edgy, touchy, tetchy, ratty (*Brit. & N.Z. informal*), testy, waspish, quick-tempered, snappish, like a bear with a sore head (*informal*), apt to fly off the handle (*informal*): *He wasn't irritable or snappy.*
make it snappy = hurry (up), be quick, get a move on (*informal*), buck up (*informal*), make haste, look lively, get your skates on: *Look at the pamphlets, and make it snappy.*

snare NOUN **= trap**, net, wire, gin, pitfall, noose, springe: *an animal caught in a snare*
▷ VERB **= trap**, catch, net, wire, seize, entrap, springe: *He'd snared a rabbit earlier in the day.*

snarl[1] VERB **1 = growl**, show its teeth (*of an animal*): *The dogs snarled at the intruders.* **2 = snap**, bark, lash out, speak angrily, jump down someone's throat, speak roughly: *'Call that a good performance?' he snarled.*

snarl[2]
snarl something up = tangle, complicate, muddle, embroil, entangle, entwine, ravel, enmesh: *The group had succeeded in snarling up rush-hour traffic throughout the country.*

snatch VERB **1 = grab**, seize, wrench, wrest, take, grip, grasp, clutch, take hold of: *He snatched the telephone from me.* **2 = steal**, take, nick (*slang, chiefly Brit.*), pinch (*informal*), swipe (*slang*), lift (*informal*), pilfer, filch, shoplift, thieve, walk *or* make off with: *He snatched her bag and threw her to the ground.* **3 = win**, take, score, gain, secure, obtain: *They snatched a third goal.* **4 = save**, free, rescue, pull, recover, get out, salvage, extricate: *He was snatched from the jaws of death at the last minute.*
▷ NOUN **= bit**, part, fragment, piece, spell, snippet, smattering: *I heard snatches of the conversation.*

snazzy ADJECTIVE **= stylish**, smart, dashing, with it (*informal*), attractive, sophisticated, flamboyant, sporty, flashy, jazzy (*informal*), showy, ritzy (*slang*), raffish, schmick (*Austral. informal*)

sneak VERB **1 = slink**, slip, steal, pad, sidle, skulk: *Don't sneak away and hide.* **2 = slip**, smuggle, spirit: *He snuck me a cigarette.*
▷ NOUN **= informer**, grass (*Brit. slang*), betrayer, telltale, squealer (*slang*), Judas, accuser, stool pigeon, snake in the grass, nark (*Brit., Austral. & N.Z. slang*), fizgig (*Austral. slang*): *He is disloyal, distrustful and a sneak.*
▷ MODIFIER **= secret**, quick, clandestine, furtive, stealthy: *We can give you this exclusive sneak preview.*

sneaking ADJECTIVE **1 = nagging**, worrying, persistent, niggling, uncomfortable: *a sneaking suspicion* **2 = secret**, private, hidden, suppressed, unexpressed, unvoiced, unavowed, unconfessed, undivulged: *a sneaking admiration*

sneaky ADJECTIVE **= sly**, dishonest, devious, mean, low, base, nasty, cowardly, slippery, unreliable, malicious, unscrupulous, furtive, disingenuous, shifty, snide, deceitful, contemptible, untrustworthy, double-dealing

sneer VERB **1 = scorn**, mock, ridicule, laugh, jeer, disdain, scoff, deride, look down on, snigger, sniff at, gibe, hold in contempt, hold up to ridicule, turn up your nose (*informal*): *There is too great a readiness to sneer at anything they do.* **2 = say contemptuously**, snigger: *'I wonder what you people do with your lives,' he sneered.*
▷ NOUN **1 = scorn**, ridicule, mockery,

The Language of Thomas Chandler Haliburton

Thomas Chandler Haliburton (1796–1865) was a Canadian politician and author who is best remembered for his series of satirical books about 'Sam Slick', including *The Clockmaker; or, the sayings and doings of Samuel Slick, of Slickville* (originally serialised in the *Novascotian*); *The Attaché; or, Sam Slick in England*; and *Nature and Human Nature*. These books are collections of anecdotes about the character Sam Slick, a Yankee clockmaker, as he travels in Nova Scotia and England. Haliburton used these anecdotes to satirize Nova Scotians, Americans, and Britons alike, and the books were very successful on both sides of the Atlantic.

Some of Haliburton's most frequent nouns refer to the people that he comments on: *folk, people,* and *critters. Folk* is the most frequent of the three, particularly in *The Clockmaker,* and is almost always used in the plural form, as in 'No wonder the folks are poor.' *People* is more frequent in *Nature and Human Nature. Critter,* a dialectal variant of *creature,* usually means 'animal' or 'insect' in modern American English; Haliburton's characters usually use it to refer to people, as in 'Sam, you are the most conceited critter I ever knew.' There are also several instances of the tautological *created critter*. That *critter* and *folk* should occur more frequently than *people* is evidence of Haliburton's use of colloquial and informal speech as a tool for satire.

Other frequent words, both nouns and adjectives, refer to countries and nationalities. *Country* itself is among the ten most frequent nouns, often used as characters reflect on the state of the nation. Verbs of which *country* is the object include *ruin,* the now archaic *ruinate, derange,* and *ransack*:

> ... them aristocrats, they'll **ruinate the country** [Canada], they spend the whole revenu on themselves ...

There are more occurrences of *Nova Scotia* than there are of *Canada,* but *Nova Scotian* is quite rare, and *Novascotian* as one word is even rarer. *Nova Scotia* is sometimes used as an adjective, as in *a Nova Scotia doctor, the Nova Scotia coast,* and *Nova Scotia politics. Yankee* is also frequent, both as a noun ('I have the honour to be a Yankee') and an adjective (*Yankee galls, that Yankee way*). There are also a couple of instances of *Yankeedoodledum* meaning 'place where Yankees are from'. Sam comments on the use of the word *Yankee* as referring to 'Eastern folk' (showing that it had widened from its original reference to New Englanders only; it has, of course, since widened further in British English to refer to all Americans):

> The southerners, who are both as proud and as sarcy as the British, call us Eastern folk **Yankees** as a term of reproach, because having no slaves, we are obliged to be our own niggers and do our own work, which isn't considered very genteel ...

Other points of interest in this passage are the word *sarcy* meaning 'impudent, sarcastic', which has revived in modern slang; the use of the word *nigger,* which did not have the same taboo as it does now; and the curious apostrophe placement in *is'nt* (rather than the expected *isn't*), which appears a few times in Haliburton's representation of speech.

Yankee is also used to refer to the language of Yankees – 'I don't understand Yankee yet, says he' – which is appropriate given the nature of Sam's language. His speech captures many features of colloquial American English, such as the frequent use of *ain't*; novel word-forms such as *splendiferous*; and *guess* meaning 'think, suppose', sometimes without a pronoun:

> **Guess** I'll go, and pack up my fixing and have 'em ready to land.

Another characteristic of speech in these books is the use of adjectives as adverbs, as in *dreadful lonely* and *a terrible powerful man.* The colloquial *plaguy* meaning 'extremely' is also frequent, and there are even some examples of *plague* as an adverb, as in 'Oh, I was plague scared.'

It was only in the early 19th century that the first dictionaries of American English were written, and indeed that 'American English' was recognized as a distinct variety. In the language of Sam Slick we find a fascinating representation of colloquial American English in these early stages.

derision, jeer, disdain, snigger, gibe, snidery: *Best-selling authors may have to face the sneers of the literati.* **2 = contemptuous smile**, snigger, curl of the lip: *His mouth twisted in a contemptuous sneer.*

> **QUOTATIONS**
> Who can refute a sneer?
> [Revd. William Paley *Principles of Moral and Political Philosophy*]
>
> Damn with faint praise, assent with civil leer,
> And, without sneering, teach the rest to sneer
> [Alexander Pope *Epistle to Dr. Arbuthnot*]

snide *or* **snidey** ADJECTIVE **= nasty**, sneering, malicious, mean, cynical, unkind, hurtful, sarcastic, disparaging, spiteful, insinuating, scornful, shrewish, ill-natured, snarky *(informal)*

sniff VERB **1 = breathe in**, inhale, snuffle, snuff: *She wiped her face and sniffed loudly.* **2 = smell**, nose, breathe in, scent, get a whiff of: *Suddenly, he stopped and sniffed the air.* **3 = inhale**, breathe in, suck in, draw in: *He'd been sniffing glue.*

sniffy ADJECTIVE **= contemptuous**, superior, condescending, haughty, scornful, disdainful, supercilious

snigger VERB **= laugh**, giggle, sneer, snicker, titter: *The tourists snigger at the locals' outdated ways and dress.*
▷ NOUN **= laugh**, giggle, sneer, snicker, titter: *trying to suppress a snigger*

snip VERB **= cut**, nick, clip, crop, trim, dock, notch, nip off: *Snip the corners off the card.*
▷ NOUN **= bargain**, steal *(informal)*, good buy, giveaway: *a snip at £74.25*

snipe VERB **= criticize**, knock *(informal)*, put down, carp, bitch, have a go (at) *(informal)*, jeer, denigrate, disparage

snippet NOUN **= piece**, scrap, fragment, part, particle, snatch, shred

snob NOUN **= elitist**, highbrow, social climber

snobbery NOUN **= arrogance**, airs, pride, pretension, condescension, snobbishness, snootiness *(informal)*, side *(Brit. slang)*, uppishness *(Brit. informal)*

snobbish ADJECTIVE **= superior**, arrogant, stuck-up *(informal)*, patronizing, condescending, snooty *(informal)*, pretentious, uppity *(informal)*, high and mighty *(informal)*, toffee-nosed *(slang, chiefly Brit.)*, hoity-toity *(informal)*, high-hat *(informal, chiefly U.S.)*, uppish *(Brit. informal)* **OPPOSITE:** humble

snoop VERB **1 = investigate**, explore, have a good look at, prowl around, nose around, peer into: *He's been snooping around her hotel.* **2 = spy**, poke your nose in, nose, interfere, pry *(informal)*: *Governments have been known to snoop into innocent citizens' lives.*
▷ NOUN **= look**, search, nose, prowl, investigation: *He had a snoop around.*

snooty ADJECTIVE **= snobbish**, superior, aloof, pretentious, stuck-up *(informal)*, condescending, proud, haughty, disdainful, snotty, uppity *(informal)*, supercilious, high and mighty *(informal)*, toffee-nosed *(slang, chiefly Brit.)*, hoity-toity *(informal)*, high-hat *(informal, chiefly U.S.)*, uppish *(Brit. informal)*, toplofty *(informal)* **OPPOSITE:** humble

snooze NOUN **= doze**, nap, kip *(Brit. slang)*, siesta, catnap, forty winks *(informal)*: *The bird is enjoying a snooze.*
▷ VERB **= doze**, drop off *(informal)*, nap, kip *(Brit. slang)*, nod off *(informal)*, catnap, drowse, take forty winks *(informal)*: *He snoozed in front of the television.*

snub VERB **= insult**, slight, put down, humiliate, cut *(informal)*, shame, humble, rebuff, mortify, cold-shoulder, kick in the teeth *(slang)*, give (someone) the cold shoulder, give (someone) the brush-off *(slang)*, cut dead *(informal)*: *He snubbed her in public and made her feel an idiot.*
▷ NOUN **= insult**, put-down, humiliation, affront, slap in the face *(informal)*, brush-off *(slang)*: *He took it as a snub.*

snug ADJECTIVE **1 = cosy**, warm, comfortable, homely, sheltered, intimate, comfy *(informal)*: *a snug log cabin* **2 = tight**, close, trim, neat: *a snug black T-shirt and skin-tight black jeans*

snuggle VERB **= nestle**, cuddle up

so SENTENCE CONNECTOR **= therefore**, thus, hence, consequently, then, as a result, accordingly, for that reason, whence, thence, ergo

soak VERB **1 = steep**, immerse, submerge, infuse, marinate *(Cookery)*, dunk, submerse: *Soak the beans for two hours.* **2 = wet**, damp, saturate, drench, douse, moisten, suffuse, wet through, waterlog, souse, drouk *(Scot.)*: *Soak the soil around each bush with at least 4 gallons of water.* **3 = penetrate**, pervade, permeate, enter, get in, infiltrate, diffuse, seep, suffuse, make inroads (into): *Rain had soaked into the sand.*
soak something up = absorb, suck up, take in *or* up, drink in, assimilate: *Wrap in absorbent paper after frying to soak up excess oil.*

soaking ADJECTIVE **= soaked**, dripping, saturated, drenched, sodden, waterlogged, streaming, sopping, wet through, soaked to the skin, wringing wet, like a drowned rat, droukit *or* drookit *(Scot.)*

soar VERB **1 = rise**, increase, grow, mount, climb, go up, rocket, swell, escalate, shoot up: *soaring unemployment* **2 = fly**, rise, wing, climb, ascend, fly up: *Buzzards soar overhead at a great height.* **OPPOSITE:** plunge **3 = tower**, rise, climb, go up: *The steeple soars skyward.*

sob VERB **= cry**, weep, blubber, greet *(Scot.)*, howl, bawl, snivel, shed tears, boohoo: *She began to sob again, burying her face in the pillow.*
▷ NOUN **= cry**, whimper, howl: *Her body was racked by violent sobs.*

sober ADJECTIVE **1 = abstinent**, temperate, abstemious, moderate, on the wagon *(informal)*: *He was dour and uncommunicative when stone sober.* **OPPOSITE:** drunk **2 = serious**, practical, realistic, sound, cool, calm, grave, reasonable, steady, composed, rational, solemn, lucid, sedate, staid, level-headed, dispassionate, unruffled, clear-headed, unexcited, grounded: *We are now far more sober and realistic.* **OPPOSITE:** frivolous **3 = plain**, dark, sombre, quiet, severe, subdued, drab: *He dresses in sober grey suits.* **OPPOSITE:** bright
▷ VERB **1** *(usually with* **up***)* **= come to your senses**: *He was left to sober up in a police cell.* **OPPOSITE:** get drunk **2** *(usually with* **up***)* **= clear your head**: *These events sobered him up considerably*

sobriety NOUN **1 = abstinence**, temperance, abstemiousness, moderation, self-restraint, soberness, nonindulgence: *the boredom of a lifetime of sobriety* **2 = seriousness**, gravity, steadiness, restraint, composure, coolness, calmness, solemnity, reasonableness, level-headedness, staidness, sedateness: *the values society depends upon, such as honesty, sobriety and trust*

so-called ADJECTIVE **= alleged**, supposed, professed, pretended, self-styled, ostensible, soi-disant *(French)*

sociability NOUN **= friendliness**, conviviality, cordiality, congeniality, neighbourliness, affability, gregariousness, companionability, social intelligence

sociable ADJECTIVE **= friendly**, social, outgoing, warm, neighbourly, accessible, cordial, genial, affable, approachable, gregarious, convivial, companionable, conversable **OPPOSITE:** unsociable

social ADJECTIVE **1 = communal**, community, collective, group, public, general, common, societal: *the tightly woven social fabric of small towns* **2 = sociable**, friendly, companionable, neighbourly: *We ought to organize more social events.* **3 = organized**, gregarious: *social insects like bees and ants*
▷ NOUN **= get-together** *(informal)*, party, gathering, function, do *(informal)*, reception, bash *(informal)*, social gathering: *church socials*
▷ *See themed panel* **Social Networking** *on facing page*

socialize VERB **= mix**, interact, mingle, be sociable, meet, go out, entertain, get together, fraternize, be a good mixer, get about *or* around

society NOUN **1 = the community**, social order, people, the public, the population, humanity, civilization, mankind, the general public, the world at large: *This reflects attitudes and values prevailing in society.* **2 = culture**, community, population: *those*

SOCIAL NETWORKING

Social Networking and Social Bookmarking Sites

Bebo
Blogger
Blogster *(trademark)*
Classmates *(trademark)*
Delicious
Digg
Facebook
Fark *(trademark)*
Flickr *(trademark)*
Freecycle *(trademark)*
Friends Reunited
Friendster
Google Buzz
Hi5
Last.fm
LinkedIn *(trademark)*
LiveMocha *(trademark)*
Mixi
Mixx
Mumsnet
MySpace *(trademark)*
Newsvine
NowPublic
Orkut
Reddit
Renren Network
StumbleUpon
Tweetmeme
Twitter *(trademark)*
VampireFreaks
VoxSwap
Windows Live Spaces *(trademark)*
Yahoo Buzz *(trademark)*
ZombieFriends

Social Networking Terms

add
app
avatar
Beboer
block
blog
chat
comment
defriend
group
hashtag
follow
friend
friend request
inbox
instant message *or* IM
like
microblog
news feed
panic button
phishing
plugin
poke
profile
retweet
status
tag
unfriend
update
tweet
wall

responsible for destroying our African heritage and the fabric of our society **3 = organization**, group, club, union, league, association, institute, circle, corporation, guild, fellowship, fraternity, brotherhood *or* sisterhood: *the historical society* **4 = upper classes**, gentry, upper crust *(informal)*, elite, the swells *(informal)*, high society, the top drawer, polite society, the toffs *(Brit. slang)*, the smart set, beau monde, the nobs *(slang)*, the country set, haut monde *(French)*: *The couple tried to secure themselves a position in society.* **5 = companionship**, company, fellowship, friendship, camaraderie: *I largely withdrew from the society of others.*

QUOTATIONS

Human life in common is only made possible when a majority comes together which is stronger than any separate individual and which remains united against all separate individuals
[Sigmund Freud *Civilization and its Discontents*]

Man did not enter into society to become worse than he was before, nor to have fewer rights than he had before, but to have those rights better secured
[Thomas Paine *The Rights of Man*]

There is no such thing as society
[Margaret Thatcher]

He who is unable to live in society, or who has no need because he is sufficient for himself, must be either a beast or a god
[Aristotle *Politics*]

sodden ADJECTIVE **= soaked**, saturated, sopping, drenched, soggy, waterlogged, marshy, boggy, miry, droukit *or* drookit *(Scot.)*

sodomy NOUN **= anal intercourse**, anal sex, buggery

sofa NOUN **= couch**, settee, divan, chaise longue, chesterfield, ottoman

soft ADJECTIVE **1 = velvety**, smooth, silky, furry, feathery, downy, fleecy, like a baby's bottom *(informal)*: *Regular use of a body lotion will keep the skin soft and supple.* OPPOSITE: rough **2 = yielding**, flexible, pliable, cushioned, elastic, malleable, spongy, springy, cushiony: *She lay down on the soft, comfortable bed.* OPPOSITE: hard **3 = soggy**, swampy, marshy, boggy, squelchy, quaggy: *The horse didn't handle the soft ground very well.* **4 = squashy**, sloppy, mushy, spongy, squidgy *(Brit. informal)*, squishy, gelatinous, squelchy, pulpy, doughy: *a simple bread made with a soft dough* **5 = pliable**, flexible, supple, malleable, plastic, elastic, tensile, ductile *(of a metal)*, bendable, mouldable, impressible: *Aluminium is a soft metal.* **6 = quiet**, low, gentle, sweet, whispered, soothing, murmured, muted, subdued, mellow, understated, melodious, mellifluous, dulcet, soft-toned: *When he woke again he could hear soft music; She spoke in a soft whisper.* OPPOSITE: loud **7 = lenient**, easy-going, lax, liberal, weak, indulgent, permissive, spineless, boneless, overindulgent: *He says the measure is soft and weak on criminals.* OPPOSITE: harsh **8 = kind**, tender, sentimental, compassionate, sensitive, gentle, pitying, sympathetic, tenderhearted, touchy-feely *(informal)*: *a very soft and sensitive heart* **9 = easy**, comfortable, undemanding, cushy *(informal)*, easy-peasy *(slang)*: *a soft option* **10 = pale**, light, subdued, pastel, pleasing, bland, mellow: *The room was tempered by the soft colours.* OPPOSITE: bright **11 = dim**, faint, dimmed: *His skin looked golden in the soft light.* OPPOSITE: bright **12 = mild**, delicate, caressing, temperate, balmy: *a soft breeze* **13 = feeble-minded**, simple, silly, foolish, daft *(informal)*, soft in the head *(informal)*, a bit lacking *(informal)*: *They were wary of him, thinking he was soft in the head.*

soften VERB **1 = melt**, tenderize: *Soften the butter mixture in a small saucepan.* **2 = lessen**, moderate, diminish, temper, lower, relax, ease, calm, modify, cushion, soothe, subdue, alleviate, lighten, quell, muffle, allay, mitigate, abate, tone down, assuage: *He could not think how to soften the blow of what he had to tell her.*

soggy ADJECTIVE **= sodden**, saturated, moist, heavy, soaked, dripping, waterlogged, sopping, mushy, spongy, pulpy

soil[1] NOUN **1 = earth**, ground, clay, dust, dirt, loam: *regions with sandy soils* **2 = territory**, country, land, region, turf *(U.S. slang)*, terrain: *The issue of foreign troops on Turkish soil is a sensitive one.*

soil[2] VERB **= dirty**, foul, stain, smear, muddy, pollute, tarnish, spatter, sully, defile, besmirch, smirch, bedraggle, befoul, begrime: *Young people don't want to do things that soil their hands.* OPPOSITE: clean

sojourn NOUN **= stay**, visit, stop, rest, stopover

solace NOUN **= comfort**, consolation, help, support, relief, succour, alleviation, assuagement: *I found solace in writing when my father died.*
▷ VERB **= comfort**, console, soothe: *They solaced themselves with their fan mail.*

soldier NOUN **= fighter**, serviceman, trooper, warrior, Tommy *(Brit. informal)*, GI *(U.S. informal)*, military man, redcoat, enlisted man *(U.S.)*, man-at-arms, squaddie *or* squaddy *(Brit. slang)*

sole ADJECTIVE **= only**, one, single, individual, alone, exclusive, solitary, singular, one and only

solely ADVERB **= only**, completely, entirely, exclusively, alone, singly, merely, single-handedly

solemn ADJECTIVE **1 = serious**, earnest, grave, sober, thoughtful, sedate, glum, staid, portentous: *His solemn little face broke into smiles.*

S

OPPOSITE: cheerful **2 = formal**, august, grand, imposing, impressive, grave, majestic, dignified, ceremonial, stately, momentous, awe-inspiring, ceremonious: *This is a solemn occasion.* **OPPOSITE:** informal **3 = sacred**, religious, holy, ritual, venerable, hallowed, sanctified, devotional, reverential: *a solemn religious ceremony* **OPPOSITE:** irreligious

solemnity NOUN **1 = seriousness**, gravity, formality, grandeur, gravitas, earnestness, portentousness, momentousness, impressiveness: *the solemnity of the occasion* **2** *(often plural)* **= ritual**, proceedings, ceremony, rite, formalities, ceremonial, observance, celebration: *the constitutional solemnities*

solicit VERB **1 = request**, seek, ask for, petition, crave, pray for, plead for, canvass, beg for: *He's already solicited their support on health care reform.* **2 = appeal to**, ask, call on, lobby, press, beg, petition, plead with, implore, beseech, entreat, importune, supplicate: *They were soliciting Nader's supporters to re-register as Republicans.*

solicitous ADJECTIVE **= concerned**, caring, attentive, careful

solid ADJECTIVE **1 = firm**, hard, compact, dense, massed, concrete: *a tunnel carved through 50ft of solid rock* **OPPOSITE:** unsubstantial **2 = strong**, stable, sturdy, sound, substantial, unshakable: *I stared up at the square, solid house.* **OPPOSITE:** unstable **3 = pure**, unalloyed, unmixed, complete: *The taps appeared to be made of solid gold.* **4 = continuous**, unbroken, uninterrupted: *a solid line* **5 = reliable**, decent, dependable, upstanding, serious, constant, sensible, worthy, upright, sober, law-abiding, trusty, level-headed, estimable: *a good, solid member of the community* **OPPOSITE:** unreliable **6 = sound**, real, reliable, good, genuine, dinkum *(Austral. & N.Z. informal)*: *Some solid evidence was what was required.* **OPPOSITE:** unsound

S

solidarity NOUN **= unity**, harmony, unification, accord, stability, cohesion, team spirit, camaraderie, unanimity, soundness, concordance, esprit de corps, community of interest, singleness of purpose, like-mindedness, kotahitanga *(N.Z.)*

solidify VERB **= harden**, set, congeal, cake, jell, coagulate, cohere

soliloquy NOUN **= monologue**, address, speech, aside, oration, dramatic monologue

> **USAGE**
> Although *soliloquy* and *monologue* are close in meaning, you should take care when using one as a synonym of the other. Both words refer to a long speech by one person, but a *monologue* can be addressed to other people, whereas in a *soliloquy* the speaker is always talking to himself or herself.

solitary ADJECTIVE **1 = unsociable**, retiring, reclusive, unsocial, isolated, lonely, cloistered, lonesome, friendless, companionless: *Paul was a shy, pleasant, solitary man.* **OPPOSITE:** sociable **2 = lone**, alone: *His evenings were spent in solitary drinking.* **3 = isolated**, remote, out-of-the-way, desolate, hidden, sequestered, unvisited, unfrequented: *a boy of eighteen in a solitary house in the Ohio countryside* **OPPOSITE:** busy

solitude NOUN **1 = isolation**, privacy, seclusion, retirement, loneliness, ivory tower, reclusiveness: *Imagine long golden beaches where you can wander in solitude.* **2 = wilderness**, waste, desert, emptiness, wasteland: *travelling by yourself in these vast solitudes*

> **QUOTATIONS**
> far from the madding crowd's
> ignoble strife
> [Thomas Gray *Elegy Written in a Country Churchyard*]
>
> Solitude should teach us how to die
> [Lord Byron *Childe Harold*]
>
> That inward eye
> Which is the bliss of solitude
> [William Wordsworth *I Wandered Lonely as a Cloud*]
>
> Two paradises 'twere in one
> To live in paradise alone
> [Andrew Marvell *The Garden*]

solution NOUN **1 = answer**, resolution, key, result, solving, explanation, unfolding, unravelling, clarification, explication, elucidation: *the ability to sort out effective solutions to practical problems* **2 = mixture**, mix, compound, blend, suspension, solvent, emulsion: *a warm solution of liquid detergent*

solve VERB **= answer**, work out, resolve, explain, crack, interpret, unfold, clarify, clear up, unravel, decipher, expound, suss (out) *(slang)*, get to the bottom of, disentangle, elucidate

solvent ADJECTIVE **= financially sound**, secure, in the black, solid, profit-making, in credit, debt-free, unindebted

sombre ADJECTIVE **1 = gloomy**, sad, sober, grave, dismal, melancholy, mournful, lugubrious, joyless, funereal, doleful, sepulchral: *The pair were in sombre mood.* **OPPOSITE:** cheerful **2 = dark**, dull, gloomy, sober, drab: *a worried official in sombre black* **OPPOSITE:** bright

somebody NOUN **= celebrity**, big name, public figure, name, star, heavyweight *(informal)*, notable, superstar, household name, dignitary, luminary, bigwig *(informal)*, celeb *(informal)*, big shot *(informal)*, personage, megastar *(informal)*, big wheel *(slang)*, big noise *(informal)*, big hitter *(informal)*, heavy hitter *(informal)*, person of note, V.I.P., someone, muckymuck*(Canad. informal)* **OPPOSITE:** nobody

someday ADVERB **= one day**, eventually, ultimately, sooner or later, one of these (fine) days, in the fullness of time

somehow ADVERB **= one way or another**, come what may, come hell or high water *(informal)*, by fair means or foul, by hook or (by) crook, by some means or other

sometime ADVERB **= some day**, one day, at some point in the future, sooner or later, one of these days, by and by: *Why don't you come and see me sometime?*
▷ ADJECTIVE **= former**, one-time, erstwhile, ex-, late, past, previous: *She was in her early thirties, a sometime actress, dancer and singer.*

> **USAGE**
> *Sometime* as a single word should only be used to refer to an unspecified point in time. When referring to a considerable length of time, you should use *some time*. Compare: *It was some time after, that the rose garden was planted*, i.e. after a considerable period of time, with *It was sometime after the move that the rose garden was planted*, i.e. at some unspecified point after the move, but not necessarily a long time after.

sometimes ADVERB **= occasionally**, at times, now and then, from time to time, on occasion, now and again, once in a while, every now and then, every so often, off and on **OPPOSITE:** always

son NOUN **= male child**, boy, lad *(informal)*, descendant, son and heir
▸ *related adjective:* filial

> **QUOTATIONS**
> A wise son maketh a glad father; but a foolish son is the heaviness of his mother
> [*Bible: Proverbs*]

> **PROVERBS**
> *Like father like son*

song NOUN **= ballad**, air, tune, lay, strain, carol, lyric, chant, chorus, melody, anthem, number, hymn, psalm, shanty, pop song, ditty, canticle, canzonet, choon *(slang)*, waiata *(N.Z.)*

song and dance NOUN **= fuss**, to-do, flap *(informal)*, performance *(informal)*, stir, pantomime *(informal)*, commotion, ado, shindig *(informal)*, kerfuffle *(informal)*, hoo-ha, pother, shindy *(informal)*

soon ADVERB **= before long**, shortly, in the near future, in a minute, anon *(archaic)*, in a short time, in a little while, any minute now, betimes *(archaic)*, in two shakes of a lamb's tail, erelong *(archaic, poetic)*, in a couple of shakes

sooner ADVERB **1 = earlier**, before, already, beforehand, ahead of time: *I thought she would have recovered sooner.* **2 = rather**, more readily, by preference, more willingly: *They would sooner die than stay in London.*

> USAGE
> *When* is sometimes used instead of *than* after *no sooner*, but this use is generally regarded as incorrect: *no sooner had he arrived than* (not *when*) *the telephone rang.*

soothe VERB **1 = calm**, still, quiet, hush, settle, calm down, appease, lull, mitigate, pacify, mollify, smooth down, tranquillize: *He would take her in his arms and soothe her.* **OPPOSITE:** upset **2 = relieve**, ease, alleviate, dull, diminish, assuage: *Lemon tisanes with honey can soothe sore throats.* **OPPOSITE:** irritate

soothing ADJECTIVE **1 = calming**, relaxing, peaceful, quiet, calm, restful: *Put on some nice soothing music.* **2 = emollient**, palliative, balsamic, demulcent, easeful, lenitive: *Cold tea is very soothing for burns.*

sophisticated ADJECTIVE **1 = complex**, advanced, complicated, subtle, delicate, elaborate, refined, intricate, multifaceted, highly-developed: *a large and sophisticated new telescope* **OPPOSITE:** simple **2 = cultured**, refined, cultivated, worldly, cosmopolitan, urbane, jet-set, world-weary, citified, worldly-wise: *Recently her tastes have become more sophisticated.* **OPPOSITE:** unsophisticated

sophistication NOUN **= poise**, worldliness, savoir-faire, urbanity, finesse, savoir-vivre (*French*), worldly wisdom

soporific ADJECTIVE **= sleep-inducing**, hypnotic, sedative, sleepy, somnolent, tranquillizing, somniferous (*rare*)

soppy ADJECTIVE **= sentimental**, corny (*slang*), slushy (*informal*), soft (*informal*), silly, daft (*informal*), weepy (*informal*), mawkish, drippy (*informal*), lovey-dovey, schmaltzy (*slang*), icky (*informal*), gushy (*informal*), overemotional, three-hankie (*informal*)

sorcerer *or* **sorceress** NOUN **= magician**, witch, wizard, magus, warlock, mage (*archaic*), enchanter, necromancer

sorcery NOUN **= black magic**, witchcraft, black art, necromancy, spell, magic, charm, wizardry, enchantment, divination, incantation, witchery

sordid ADJECTIVE **1 = base**, degraded, shameful, low, vicious, shabby, vile, degenerate, despicable, disreputable, debauched: *He put his head in his hands as his sordid life was exposed.* **OPPOSITE:** honourable **2 = dirty**, seedy, sleazy, squalid, mean, foul, filthy, unclean, wretched, seamy, slovenly, slummy, scungy (*Austral. & N.Z.*), festy (*Austral. slang*): *the attic windows of their sordid little rooms* **OPPOSITE:** clean

sore ADJECTIVE **1 = painful**, smarting, raw, tender, burning, angry, sensitive, irritated, inflamed, chafed, reddened: *My chest is still sore from the surgery.* **2 = annoyed**, cross, angry, pained, hurt, upset, stung, irritated, grieved, resentful, aggrieved, vexed, irked, peeved (*informal*), tooshie (*Austral. slang*), hoha (*N.Z.*): *The result of it is that they are all feeling very sore at you.* **3 = annoying**, distressing, troublesome, harrowing, grievous: *Timing is frequently a sore point.* **4 = urgent**, desperate, extreme, dire, pressing, critical, acute: *The prime minister is in sore need of friends.*
▷ NOUN **= abscess**, boil, ulcer, inflammation, gathering: *All of us had long sores on our backs.*

sorrow NOUN **1 = grief**, sadness, woe, regret, distress, misery, mourning, anguish, unhappiness, heartache, heartbreak, affliction: *It was a time of great sorrow.* **OPPOSITE:** joy **2 = hardship**, trial, tribulation, affliction, worry, trouble, blow, woe, misfortune, bummer (*slang*): *the joys and sorrows of family life* **OPPOSITE:** good fortune
▷ VERB **= grieve**, mourn, lament, weep, moan, be sad, bemoan, agonize, eat your heart out, bewail: *She was lamented by a large circle of sorrowing friends and acquaintances.* **OPPOSITE:** rejoice

> QUOTATIONS
> There is no greater sorrow than to recall a time of happiness in misery
> [Dante *Divine Comedy*]
>
> Into each life some rain must fall
> [Henry Wadsworth Longfellow]
>
> Sorrow makes us wise
> [Alfred Tennyson *In Memoriam*]
>
> Sorrow is tranquillity remembered in emotion
> [Dorothy Parker *Here Lies*]

sorrowful ADJECTIVE **= sad**, unhappy, miserable, sorry, depressed, painful, distressed, grieving, dismal, afflicted, melancholy, tearful, heartbroken, woeful, mournful, dejected, rueful, lugubrious, wretched, disconsolate, doleful, heavy-hearted, down in the dumps (*informal*), woebegone, piteous, sick at heart

sorry ADJECTIVE **1 = regretful**, apologetic, contrite, repentant, guilt-ridden, remorseful, penitent, shamefaced, conscience-stricken, in sackcloth and ashes, self-reproachful: *She was very sorry about all the trouble she'd caused.* **OPPOSITE:** unapologetic **2 = sympathetic**, moved, full of pity, pitying, compassionate, commiserative: *I am very sorry for the family.* **OPPOSITE:** unsympathetic **3 = sad**, distressed, unhappy, grieved, melancholy, mournful, sorrowful, disconsolate: *What he must not do is sit around at home feeling sorry for himself.* **OPPOSITE:** happy **4 = wretched**, miserable, pathetic, mean, base, poor, sad, distressing, dismal, shabby, vile, paltry, pitiful, abject, deplorable, pitiable, piteous: *She is in a sorry state.*

sort NOUN **= kind**, type, class, make, group, family, order, race, style, quality, character, nature, variety, brand, species, breed, category, stamp, description, denomination, genus, ilk: *What sort of person is he?*
▷ VERB **= arrange**, group, order, class, separate, file, rank, divide, grade, distribute, catalogue, classify, categorize, tabulate, systematize, put in order: *He sorted the materials into their folders.*
out of sorts 1 = irritable, cross, edgy, tense, crabbed, snarling, prickly, snappy, touchy, bad-tempered, petulant, ill-tempered, irascible, cantankerous, tetchy, ratty (*Brit. & N.Z. informal*), testy, fretful, grouchy (*informal*), peevish, crabby, dyspeptic, choleric, crotchety, oversensitive, snappish, ill-humoured, narky (*Brit. slang*), out of humour: *Lack of sleep can leave us feeling jaded and out of sorts.* **2 = depressed**, miserable, in low spirits, down, low, blue, sad, unhappy, gloomy, melancholy, mournful, dejected, despondent, dispirited, downcast, long-faced, sorrowful, disconsolate, crestfallen, down in the dumps (*informal*), down in the mouth (*informal*), mopy: *You are feeling out of sorts and unable to see the wood for the trees.* **3 = unwell**, ill, sick, poorly (*informal*), funny (*informal*), crook (*Austral. & N.Z. informal*), ailing, queer, unhealthy, seedy (*informal*), laid up (*informal*), queasy, infirm, dicky (*Brit. informal*), off colour, under the weather (*informal*), at death's door, indisposed, on the sick list (*informal*), not up to par, valetudinarian, green about the gills (*informal*), not up to snuff (*informal*): *At times, he has seemed lifeless and out of sorts.*
sort of = rather, somewhat, as it were, slightly, moderately, in part, reasonably: *I sort of made my own happiness.*

> USAGE
> It is common in informal speech to combine singular and plural in sentences like *These sort of distinctions are becoming blurred*. This is not acceptable in careful writing, where the plural must be used consistently: *These sorts of distinctions are becoming blurred.*

so-so ADJECTIVE **= average**, middling, fair, ordinary, moderate, adequate, respectable, indifferent, not bad (*informal*), tolerable, run-of-the-mill, passable, undistinguished, fair to middling (*informal*), O.K. *or* okay (*informal*)

soul NOUN **1 = spirit**, essence, psyche, life, mind, reason, intellect, vital force, animating principle, wairua (*N.Z.*): *Such memories stirred in his soul.* **2 = embodiment**, essence, incarnation, epitome, personification, quintessence, type: *With such celebrated clients, she necessarily remains the soul of discretion.* **3 = person**, being, human, individual, body, creature, mortal, man *or* woman: *a tiny village of only 100 souls* **4 = feeling**, force, energy, vitality, animation, fervour, ardour, vivacity: *an ice goddess without soul*

soulful ADJECTIVE **= expressive**, sensitive, eloquent, moving, profound, meaningful, heartfelt, mournful

soulless ADJECTIVE **1 = characterless**, dull, bland, mundane, ordinary, grey, commonplace, dreary, mediocre, drab, uninspiring, colourless, featureless, unexceptional: *a clean but soulless hotel* **2 = unfeeling**, dead, cold, lifeless, inhuman, harsh, cruel, callous, unkind, unsympathetic, spiritless: *He was big and brawny with soulless eyes.*

sound[1] NOUN **1 = noise**, racket, din, report, tone, resonance, hubbub, reverberation: *Peter heard the sound of gunfire.* **2 = idea**, impression, implication(s), drift: *Here's a new idea we like the sound of.* **3 = cry**, noise, peep, squeak: *She didn't make a sound.* **4 = tone**, music, note, chord: *the soulful sound of the violin* **5 = earshot**, hearing, hearing distance: *I was born and bred within the sound of the cathedral bells.*
▷ VERB **1 = toll**, set off: *A young man sounds the bell to start the Sunday service.* **2 = resound**, echo, go off, toll, set off, chime, resonate, reverberate, clang, peal: *A silvery bell sounded somewhere.* **3 = seem**, seem to be, appear to be, give the impression of being, strike you as being: *She sounded a bit worried.*
▸ *related adjectives:* sonic, acoustic

sound[2] ADJECTIVE **1 = fit**, healthy, robust, firm, perfect, intact, vigorous, hale, unhurt, undamaged, uninjured, unimpaired, hale and hearty: *His body was still sound.* **OPPOSITE:** frail **2 = sturdy**, strong, solid, stable, substantial, durable, stout, well-constructed: *a perfectly sound building* **3 = safe**, secure, reliable, proven, established, recognized, solid, stable, solvent, reputable, tried and true: *a sound financial proposition* **OPPOSITE:** unreliable **4 = sensible**, wise, reasonable, right, true, responsible, correct, proper, reliable, valid, orthodox, rational, logical, prudent, trustworthy, well-founded, level-headed, right-thinking, well-grounded, grounded: *They are trained nutritionists who can give sound advice on diets.* **OPPOSITE:** irresponsible **5 = deep**, peaceful, unbroken, undisturbed, untroubled: *She has woken me out of a sound sleep.* **OPPOSITE:** troubled

sound[3]
sound someone out = question, interview, survey, poll, examine, investigate, pump *(informal)*, inspect, canvass, test the opinion of: *Sound him out gradually.*
sound something out = investigate, research, examine, probe, look into, test the water, put out feelers, see how the land lies, carry out an investigation of: *They are discreetly sounding out blue-chip American banks.*

sound[4] NOUN **= channel**, passage, strait, inlet, fjord, voe, arm of the sea: *a blizzard blasting great drifts of snow across the sound*

sour ADJECTIVE **1 = sharp**, acid, tart, bitter, unpleasant, pungent, acetic, acidulated, acerb: *The stewed apple was sour even with honey.* **OPPOSITE:** sweet **2 = rancid**, turned, gone off, fermented, unsavoury, curdled, unwholesome, gone bad, off: *tiny fridges full of sour milk* **OPPOSITE:** fresh **3 = bitter**, cynical, crabbed, tart, discontented, grudging, acrimonious, embittered, disagreeable, churlish, ill-tempered, jaundiced, waspish, grouchy *(informal)*, ungenerous, peevish, ill-natured: *He became a sour, lonely old man.* **OPPOSITE:** good-natured
▷ VERB **= embitter**, disenchant, alienate, envenom: *The experience, she says, has soured her.*

source NOUN **1 = cause**, origin, derivation, beginning, author: *This gave me a clue as to the source of the problem.* **2 = informant**, authority, documentation: *a major source of information about the arts* **3 = origin**, spring, fount, fountainhead, wellspring, rise: *the source of the Tiber*

souvenir NOUN **= keepsake**, token, reminder, relic, remembrancer *(archaic)*, memento

sovereign ADJECTIVE **1 = supreme**, ruling, absolute, chief, royal, principal, dominant, imperial, unlimited, paramount, regal, predominant, monarchal, kingly *or* queenly: *No contract can absolutely restrain a sovereign power.* **2 = excellent**, efficient, efficacious, effectual: *wild garlic, a sovereign remedy in any healer's chest*
▷ NOUN **= monarch**, ruler, king *or* queen, chief, shah, potentate, supreme ruler, emperor *or* empress, prince *or* princess, tsar *or* tsarina: *the first British sovereign to set foot on Spanish soil*

sovereignty NOUN **= supreme power**, domination, supremacy, primacy, sway, ascendancy, kingship, suzerainty, rangatiratanga *(N.Z.)*

sow VERB **= scatter**, plant, seed, lodge, implant, disseminate, broadcast, inseminate

space NOUN **1 = room**, volume, capacity, extent, margin, extension, scope, play, expanse, leeway, amplitude, spaciousness, elbowroom: *The furniture proved impractical because it took up too much space.* **2 = gap**, opening, interval, gulf, cavity, aperture: *The space underneath could be used as a storage area.* **3 = period**, interval, time, while, span, duration, time frame, timeline: *They've come a long way in a short space of time.* **4 = outer space**, the universe, the galaxy, the solar system, the cosmos: *launching satellites into space* **5 = blank**, gap, interval: *Affix your stamps on the space provided.*

spaceman *or* **spacewoman** NOUN **= astronaut**, cosmonaut, space cadet, space traveller

spacious ADJECTIVE **= roomy**, large, huge, broad, vast, extensive, ample, expansive, capacious, uncrowded, commodious, comfortable, sizable *or* sizeable **OPPOSITE:** cramped

span NOUN **1 = period**, term, duration, spell: *The batteries had a life span of six hours.* **2 = extent**, reach, spread, length, distance, stretch: *With a span of 6ft, her wings dominated the stage.*
▷ VERB **= extend across**, cross, bridge, cover, link, vault, traverse, range over, arch across: *the humped iron bridge spanning the railway*

spank VERB **= smack**, slap, whack, belt *(informal)*, tan *(slang)*, slipper *(informal)*, cuff, wallop *(informal)*, give (someone) a hiding *(informal)*, put (someone) over your knee

spanking[1] ADJECTIVE **1 = smart**, brand-new, fine, gleaming: *a spanking new car* **2 = fast**, quick, brisk, lively, smart, vigorous, energetic, snappy: *The film moves along at a spanking pace.*

spanking[2] NOUN **= smacking**, hiding *(informal)*, whacking, slapping, walloping *(informal)*: *Andrea gave her son a sound spanking.*

spar VERB **= argue**, row, squabble, dispute, scrap *(informal)*, fall out *(informal)*, spat *(U.S.)*, wrangle, skirmish, bicker, have a tiff

spare ADJECTIVE **1 = back-up**, reserve, second, extra, relief, emergency, additional, substitute, fall-back, auxiliary, in reserve: *He could have taken a spare key.* **2 = extra**, surplus, leftover, over, free, odd, unwanted, in excess, unused, superfluous, supernumerary: *They don't have a lot of spare cash.* **OPPOSITE:** necessary **3 = free**, leisure, unoccupied: *In her spare time she raises funds for charity.* **4 = thin**, lean, slim, slender, slight, meagre, gaunt, wiry, lank: *She was thin and spare, with a shapely intelligent face.* **OPPOSITE:** plump **5 = meagre**, sparing, modest, economical, frugal, scanty: *The two rooms were spare and neat, stripped bare of ornaments.*
▷ VERB **1 = afford**, give, grant, do without, relinquish, part with, allow, bestow, dispense with, manage without, let someone have: *He suggested that his country could not spare the troops.* **2 = have mercy on**, pardon, have pity on, leave, release, excuse, let off *(informal)*, go easy on *(informal)*, be merciful to, grant pardon to, deal leniently with, refrain from hurting, save (from harm): *Not a man was spared.* **OPPOSITE:** show no mercy to

S

Shakespeare

Characters in Shakespeare	Play
Sir Andrew Aguecheek	Twelfth Night
Antonio	The Merchant of Venice
Ariel	The Tempest
Autolycus	The Winter's Tale
Banquo	Macbeth
Bassanio	The Merchant of Venice
Beatrice	Much Ado About Nothing
Sir Toby Belch	Twelfth Night
Benedick	Much Ado About Nothing
Bolingbroke	Richard II
Bottom	A Midsummer Night's Dream
Brutus	Julius Caesar
Caliban	The Tempest
Casca	Julius Caesar
Cassio	Othello
Cassius	Julius Caesar
Claudio	Much Ado About Nothing, Measure for Measure
Claudius	Hamlet
Cordelia	King Lear
Demetrius	A Midsummer Night's Dream
Desdemona	Othello
Dogberry	Much Ado About Nothing
Edmund	King Lear
Enobarbus	Antony and Cleopatra
Falstaff	Henry IV Parts I and II, The Merry Wives of Windsor
Ferdinand	The Tempest
Feste	Twelfth Night
Fluellen	Henry V
Gertrude	Hamlet
Gloucester	King Lear
Goneril	King Lear
Guildenstern	Hamlet
Hamlet	Hamlet
Helena	All's Well that Ends Well, A Midsummer Night's Dream
Hermia	A Midsummer Night's Dream
Hotspur	Henry IV Part I
Iago	Othello
John of Gaunt	Richard II
Juliet	Romeo and Juliet
Julius Caesar	Julius Caesar
Katharina or Kate	The Taming of the Shrew
Kent	King Lear
Laertes	Hamlet
Lear	King Lear
Lysander	A Midsummer Night's Dream
Macbeth	Macbeth
Lady Macbeth	Macbeth
Macduff	Macbeth
Malcolm	Macbeth
Malvolio	Twelfth Night
Mercutio	Romeo and Juliet
Miranda	The Tempest
Oberon	A Midsummer Night's Dream
Octavius	Antony and Cleopatra
Olivia	Twelfth Night
Ophelia	Hamlet
Orlando	As You Like It
Orsino	Twelfth Night
Othello	Othello
Perdita	The Winter's Tale
Petruchio	The Taming of the Shrew
Pistol	Henry IV Part II, Henry V, The Merry Wives of Windsor
Polonius	Hamlet
Portia	The Merchant of Venice
Prospero	The Tempest
Puck	A Midsummer Night's Dream
Mistress Quickly	The Merry Wives of Windsor
Regan	King Lear
Romeo	Romeo and Juliet
Rosalind	As You Like It
Rosencrantz	Hamlet
Sebastian	The Tempest, Twelfth Night
Shylock	The Merchant of Venice
Titania	A Midsummer Night's Dream
Touchstone	As You Like It
Tybalt	Romeo and Juliet
Viola	Twelfth Night

Plays of Shakespeare

All's Well that Ends Well
Antony and Cleopatra
As You Like It
The Comedy of Errors
Coriolanus
Cymbeline
Hamlet
Henry IV Part I
Henry IV Part II
Henry V
Henry VI Part I
Henry VI Part II
Henry VI Part III
Henry VIII
Julius Caesar
King John
King Lear
Love's Labour's Lost
Macbeth
Measure for Measure
The Merchant of Venice
The Merry Wives of Windsor
A Midsummer Night's Dream
Much Ado About Nothing
Othello
Pericles, Prince of Tyre
Richard II
Richard III
Romeo and Juliet
The Taming of the Shrew
The Tempest
Timon of Athens
Titus Andronicus
Troilus and Cressida
Twelfth Night
The Two Gentlemen of Verona
The Winter's Tale

sparing ADJECTIVE **= economical**, frugal, thrifty, saving, careful, prudent, cost-conscious, chary, money-conscious **OPPOSITE:** lavish

spark NOUN **1 = flicker**, flash, gleam, glint, spit, flare, scintillation: *Sparks flew in all directions.* **2 = trace**, hint, scrap, atom, jot, vestige, scintilla: *Even Oliver felt a tiny spark of excitement.*
▷ VERB *(often with* **off**) **= start**, stimulate, provoke, excite, inspire, stir, trigger (off), set off, animate, rouse, prod, precipitate, kick-start, set in motion, kindle, touch off: *What was it that sparked your interest in motoring?*

sparkle VERB **= glitter**, flash, spark, shine, beam, glow, gleam, wink, shimmer, twinkle, dance, glint, glisten, glister *(archaic)*, scintillate: *His bright eyes sparkled.*
▷ NOUN **1 = glitter**, flash, gleam, spark, dazzle, flicker, brilliance, twinkle, glint, radiance: *There was a sparkle in her eye that could not be hidden.* **2 = vivacity**, life, spirit, dash, zip *(informal)*, vitality, animation, panache, gaiety, élan, brio, liveliness, vim *(slang)*: *There was little sparkle in their performance.*

sparse ADJECTIVE **= scattered**, scarce, meagre, sporadic, few and far between, scanty **OPPOSITE:** thick

Spartan ADJECTIVE **= austere**, severe, frugal, ascetic, plain, disciplined, extreme, strict, stern, bleak, rigorous, stringent, abstemious, self-denying, bare-bones

spasm NOUN **1 = convulsion**, contraction, paroxysm, twitch, throe *(rare)*: *A lack of magnesium causes muscles to go into spasm.* **2 = burst**, fit, outburst, seizure, frenzy, eruption, access: *He felt a spasm of fear.*

spasmodic ADJECTIVE **= sporadic**, irregular, erratic, intermittent, jerky, fitful, convulsive

S

spat NOUN **= quarrel**, dispute, squabble, controversy, contention, bickering, tiff, altercation

spate NOUN **1 = flood**, flow, torrent, rush, deluge, outpouring **2 = series**, sequence, course, chain, succession, run, train, string

spatter VERB **= splash**, spray, sprinkle, soil, dirty, scatter, daub, speckle, splodge, bespatter, bestrew

spawn VERB **= generate**, produce, give rise to, start, prompt, provoke, set off, bring about, spark off, set in motion: *His novels spawned both movies and television shows.*

speak VERB **1 = talk**, say something: *The President spoke of the need for territorial compromise.* **2 = articulate**, say, voice, pronounce, utter, tell, state, talk, express, communicate, make known, enunciate: *The very act of speaking the words gave him comfort.* **3 = converse**, talk, chat, discourse, confer, commune, exchange views, shoot the breeze *(slang, chiefly U.S. & Canad.)*, korero (N.Z.): *It was very emotional when we spoke again.* **4 = lecture**, talk, discourse, spout *(informal)*, make a speech, pontificate, give a speech, declaim, hold forth, spiel *(informal)*, address an audience, deliver an address, speechify: *Last month I spoke in front of two thousand people in Birmingham.*
speak for something *or* **someone 1 = represent**, act for *or* on behalf of, appear for, hold a brief for, hold a mandate for: *It was the job of the church to speak for the underprivileged.* **2 = support**, back, champion, defend, promote, advocate, fight for, uphold, commend, espouse, stick up for *(informal)*: *a role in which he would be seen as speaking for the Government*

speaker NOUN **= orator**, public speaker, lecturer, spokesperson, mouthpiece, spieler *(informal)*, word-spinner, spokesman *or* spokeswoman

spearhead VERB **= lead**, head, pioneer, launch, set off, initiate, lead the way, set in motion, blaze the trail, be in the van, lay the first stone

special ADJECTIVE **1 = exceptional**, important, significant, particular, unique, unusual, extraordinary, distinguished, memorable, gala, festive, uncommon, momentous, out of the ordinary, one in a million, red-letter, especial: *I usually reserve these outfits for special occasions.* **OPPOSITE:** ordinary **2 = major**, chief, main, primary: *He is a special correspondent for Newsweek magazine.* **3 = specific**, particular, distinctive, certain, individual, appropriate, characteristic, precise, peculiar, specialized, especial: *It requires a very special brand of courage to fight dictators.* **OPPOSITE:** general

specialist NOUN **= expert**, authority, professional, master, consultant, guru, buff *(informal)*, whizz *(informal)*, connoisseur, boffin *(Brit. informal)*, hotshot *(informal)*, wonk *(informal)*, maven *(U.S.)*, fundi *(S. African)*

speciality NOUN **1 = forte**, strength, special talent, métier, specialty, bag *(slang)*, claim to fame, pièce de résistance *(French)*, distinctive *or* distinguishing feature: *His speciality was creating rich, creamy sauces.* **2 = special subject**, specialty *(chiefly U.S. & Canad.)*, field of study, branch of knowledge, area of specialization: *His speciality was the history of Germany.*

species NOUN **= kind**, sort, type, group, class, variety, breed, category, description, genus

specific ADJECTIVE **1 = particular**, special, characteristic, distinguishing, peculiar, definite, especial: *the specific needs of the individual* **OPPOSITE:** general **2 = precise**, exact, explicit, definite, limited, express, clear-cut, unequivocal, unambiguous: *I asked him to be more specific.* **OPPOSITE:** vague **3 = peculiar**, appropriate, individual, particular, personal, unique, restricted, idiosyncratic, endemic: *Send your résumé with a covering letter that is specific to that particular job.*

specification NOUN **= requirement**, detail, particular, stipulation, condition, qualification

specify VERB **= state**, designate, spell out, stipulate, name, detail, mention, indicate, define, cite, individualize, enumerate, itemize, be specific about, particularize

specimen NOUN **1 = sample**, example, individual, model, type, pattern, instance, representative, exemplar, exemplification: *a perfect specimen of a dinosaur fossil* **2 = example**, model, exhibit, embodiment, type: *a fine specimen of manhood*

specious ADJECTIVE **= fallacious**, misleading, deceptive, plausible, unsound, sophistic, sophistical, casuistic

speck NOUN **1 = mark**, spot, dot, stain, blot, fleck, speckle, mote: *There is a speck of blood by his ear.* **2 = particle**, bit, grain, dot, atom, shred, mite, jot, modicum, whit, tittle, iota: *He leaned forward and brushed a speck of dust off his shoes.*

speckled ADJECTIVE **= flecked**, spotted, dotted, sprinkled, spotty, freckled, mottled, dappled, stippled, brindled, speckledy

spectacle NOUN **1 = show**, display, exhibition, event, performance, sight, parade, extravaganza, pageant: *a director passionate about music and spectacle* **2 = sight**, wonder, scene, phenomenon, curiosity, marvel, laughing stock: *the bizarre spectacle of an actor desperately demanding an encore*

spectacles PLURAL NOUN **= glasses**, specs *(informal)*, eyeglasses *(U.S.)*, eyewear

spectacular ADJECTIVE **= impressive**, striking, dramatic, stunning *(informal)*, marked, grand, remarkable, fantastic *(informal)*, magnificent, staggering, splendid, dazzling, sensational, breathtaking, eye-catching: *The results have been spectacular.* **OPPOSITE:** unimpressive
▷ NOUN **= show**, display, spectacle, extravaganza: *a television spectacular*

spectator NOUN **= onlooker**, observer, viewer, witness, looker-on, watcher, eyewitness, bystander, beholder **OPPOSITE:** participant

spectral ADJECTIVE **= ghostly**, unearthly, eerie, supernatural, weird, phantom, shadowy, uncanny, spooky *(informal)*, insubstantial, incorporeal, wraithlike

spectre NOUN **= ghost**, spirit, phantom, presence, vision, shadow, shade *(literary)*, apparition, wraith, kehua *(N.Z.)*

speculate VERB **1 = conjecture**, consider, wonder, guess, contemplate, deliberate, muse, meditate, surmise, theorize, hypothesize, cogitate: *The reader can* *speculate about what will happen next.* **2 = gamble**, risk, venture, hazard, have a flutter *(informal)*, take a chance with, play the market: *They speculated in property whose value has now dropped.*

speculation NOUN **1 = theory**, opinion, hypothesis, conjecture, guess, consideration, deliberation, contemplation, surmise, guesswork, supposition: *I had published my speculations about the future of the universe.* **2 = gamble**, risk, gambling, hazard: *speculation on the Stock Exchange*

speculative ADJECTIVE **1 = hypothetical**, academic, theoretical, abstract, tentative, notional, conjectural, suppositional: *He has written a speculative biography of Christopher Marlowe.* **2 = risky**, uncertain, hazardous, unpredictable, dicey *(informal, chiefly Brit.)*, chancy *(informal)*: *a speculative venture*

speech NOUN **1 = communication**, talk, conversation, articulation, discussion, dialogue, intercourse: *the development of speech in children* **2 = diction**, pronunciation, articulation, delivery, fluency, inflection, intonation, elocution, enunciation: *His speech became increasingly thick and nasal.* **3 = language**, tongue, utterance, jargon, dialect, idiom, parlance, articulation, diction, lingo *(informal)*, enunciation: *the way common letter clusters are pronounced in speech* **4 = talk**, address, lecture, discourse, harangue, homily, oration, spiel *(informal)*, disquisition, whaikorero *(N.Z.)*: *He delivered his speech in French.*

> QUOTATIONS
>
> A speech is poetry: cadence, rhythm, imagery, sweep! A speech reminds us that words, like children, have the power to make dance the dullest beanbag of a heart
> [Peggy Noonan *What I Saw at the Revolution*]
>
> A speech is like a love-affair. Any fool can start it, but to end it requires considerable skill
> [Lord Mancroft]
>
> Speech is the small-change of silence
> [George Meredith *The Ordeal of Richard Feverel*]
>
> Human speech is like a cracked kettle on which we tap crude rhythms for bears to dance to, while we long to make music that will melt the stars
> [Gustave Flaubert *Madame Bovary*]

speechless ADJECTIVE **= dumb**, dumbfounded, lost for words, dumbstruck, astounded, shocked, mum, amazed, silent, mute, dazed, aghast, inarticulate, tongue-tied, wordless, thunderstruck, unable to get a word out *(informal)*

speed NOUN **1 = rate**, pace, momentum, tempo, velocity: *He drove off at high speed.* **2 = velocity**, swiftness, acceleration, precipitation, rapidity, quickness, fastness, briskness, speediness, precipitateness: *Speed is the essential ingredient of all athletics.* **3 = swiftness**, rush, hurry, expedition, haste, rapidity, quickness, fleetness, celerity: *I was amazed at his speed of working.* **OPPOSITE:** slowness
▷ VERB **1 = race**, rush, hurry, zoom, career, bomb (along), tear, flash, belt (along) *(slang)*, barrel (along) *(informal, chiefly U.S. & Canad.)*, sprint, gallop, hasten, press on, quicken, lose no time, get a move on *(informal)*, burn rubber *(informal)*, bowl along, put your foot down *(informal)*, step on it *(informal)*, make haste, go hell for leather *(informal)*, exceed the speed limit, go like a bomb *(Brit. & N.Z. informal)*, go like the wind, go like a bat out of hell: *The engine noise rises only slightly as I speed along.* **OPPOSITE:** crawl **2 = help**, further, advance, aid, promote, boost, assist, facilitate, impel, expedite: *Invest in low-cost language courses to speed your progress.* **OPPOSITE:** hinder
speed something up = accelerate, promote, hasten, help along, further, forward, advance: *Excessive drinking will speed up the ageing process.*

> USAGE
>
> The past tense of *speed up* is *speeded up* (not *sped up*), for example *I speeded up to overtake the lorry*. The past participle is also *speeded up*, for example *I had already speeded up when I spotted the police car*.

speedy ADJECTIVE **= quick**, fast, rapid, swift, express, winged, immediate, prompt, fleet, hurried, summary, precipitate, hasty, headlong, quickie *(informal)*, expeditious, fleet of foot, pdq *(slang)* **OPPOSITE:** slow

spell[1] VERB **= indicate**, mean, signify, suggest, promise, point to, imply, amount to, herald, augur, presage, portend: *The report spells more trouble.*
spell something out = make clear *or* **plain**, specify, make explicit, clarify, elucidate, explicate: *How many times do I have to spell it out?*

spell[2] NOUN **1 = incantation**, charm, sorcery, exorcism, abracadabra, witchery, conjuration, makutu *(N.Z.)*: *Vile witch! She cast a spell on me!* **2 = enchantment**, magic, fascination, glamour, allure, bewitchment, mojo *(U.S. slang)*: *The King also falls under her spell.*

spell[3] NOUN **= period**, time, term, stretch, turn, course, season, patch, interval, bout, stint: *There has been a spell of dry weather.*

spellbound ADJECTIVE **= entranced**, gripped, fascinated, transported, charmed, hooked, possessed, bemused, captivated, enthralled, bewitched, transfixed, rapt, mesmerized, under a spell

spelling NOUN **= orthography**

> QUOTATIONS
>
> My spelling is Wobbly. It's good spelling but it Wobbles, and the letters get in the wrong place
> [A.A. Milne *Winnie-the-Pooh*]
>
> 'Do you spell it with a "V" or a "W"?' 'That depends upon the taste and fancy of the speller, my Lord.'
> [Charles Dickens *Pickwick Papers*]
>
> orthography: the science of spelling by the eye instead of the ear
> [Ambrose Bierce *The Devil's Dictionary*]

spend VERB **1 = pay out**, fork out *(slang)*, expend, lay out, splash out *(Brit. informal)*, shell out *(informal)*, disburse: *They have spent £23m on new players.* **OPPOSITE:** save **2 = apply**, use, employ, concentrate, invest, put in, devote, lavish, exert, bestow: *This energy could be much better spent taking some positive action.* **3 = pass**, fill, occupy, while away: *We spent the night in a hotel.* **4 = use up**, waste, squander, blow *(slang)*, empty, drain, exhaust, consume, run through, deplete, dissipate, fritter away: *My stepson was spending money like it grew on trees.* **OPPOSITE:** save

spendthrift NOUN **= squanderer**, spender, profligate, prodigal, big spender, waster, wastrel: *I was a natural spendthrift when I was single.* **OPPOSITE:** miser
▷ ADJECTIVE **= wasteful**, extravagant, prodigal, profligate, improvident: *his father's spendthrift ways* **OPPOSITE:** economical

spent ADJECTIVE **1 = used up**, finished, gone, consumed, expended: *The money was spent.* **2 = exhausted**, drained, worn out, bushed *(informal)*, all in *(slang)*, shattered *(informal)*, weakened, wiped out *(informal)*, wearied, weary, played out *(informal)*, burnt out, fagged (out) *(informal)*, whacked *(Brit. informal)*, debilitated, knackered *(slang)*, prostrate, clapped out *(Brit., Austral. & N.Z. informal)*, tired out, ready to drop *(informal)*, dog-tired *(informal)*, zonked *(informal)*, dead beat *(informal)*, shagged out *(Brit. slang)*, done in *or* up *(informal)*: *After all that exertion, we were completely spent.*

sperm NOUN **1 = spermatozoon**, reproductive cell, male gamete: *Conception occurs when a single sperm fuses with an egg.* **2 = semen**, seed *(archaic, dialect)*, spermatozoa, scum *(U.S. slang)*, come *or* cum *(taboo)*, jism *or* jissom *(taboo)*: *the ejaculation of sperm*

spew VERB **1 = shed**, discharge, send out, issue, throw out, eject, diffuse, emanate, exude, cast out: *An oil tanker spewed its cargo into the sea.* **2 = vomit**, throw up *(informal)*, puke *(slang)*, chuck *(Austral. & N.Z. informal)*, spit out, regurgitate, disgorge, barf *(U.S. slang)*, chunder *(slang, chiefly Austral.)*, belch forth, upchuck *(U.S. slang)*, do a technicolour yawn *(slang)*, toss your cookies *(U.S. slang)*: *Let's get out of his way before he starts spewing.*

sphere NOUN **1 = ball**, globe, orb, globule, circle: *The cactus will form a large sphere crested with golden thorns.* **2 = field**, range, area, department, function, territory, capacity, province, patch, scope, turf (*U.S. slang*), realm, domain, compass, walk of life: *the sphere of international politics* **3 = rank**, class, station, status, stratum: *life outside academic spheres of society*

spherical ADJECTIVE **= round**, globular, globe-shaped, rotund, orbicular

spice NOUN **1 = seasoning**, condiment: *herbs and spices* **2 = excitement**, kick (*informal*), zest, colour, pep, zip (*informal*), tang, zap (*slang*), gusto, zing (*informal*), piquancy: *The spice of danger will add to the lure.*

spicy ADJECTIVE **1 = hot**, seasoned, pungent, aromatic, savoury, tangy, piquant, flavoursome: *Thai food is hot and spicy.* **2 = risqué**, racy, off-colour, ribald, hot (*informal*), broad, improper, suggestive, unseemly, titillating, indelicate, indecorous: *spicy anecdotes about his sexual adventures*

spider NOUN
▸ *related phobia:* arachnophobia

spiel NOUN **= patter**, speech, pitch, recital, harangue, sales talk, sales patter

spike NOUN **= point**, stake, spur, pin, nail, spine, barb, tine, prong: *a 15-foot wall topped with iron spikes*
▷ VERB **1 = drug**, lace, dope, cut, contaminate, adulterate: *drinks spiked with tranquillizers* **2 = impale**, spit, spear, stick: *She was spiked on a railing after a 20ft plunge.*

spill VERB **1 = tip over**, upset, overturn, capsize, knock over, topple over: *He always spilled the drinks.* **2 = shed**, scatter, discharge, throw off, disgorge, spill *or* run over: *A number of bags had split and were spilling their contents.* **3 = slop**, flow, pour, run, overflow, slosh, splosh: *It doesn't matter if red wine spills on this floor.* **4 = emerge**, flood, pour, mill, stream, surge, swarm, crowd, teem: *When the bell rings, more than 1,000 children spill from the classrooms.*
▷ NOUN **= spillage**, flood, leak, leakage, overspill: *An oil spill could be devastating for wildlife.*

spin VERB **1 = revolve**, turn, rotate, wheel, twist, reel, whirl, twirl, gyrate, pirouette, birl (*Scot.*): *The Earth spins on its own axis.* **2 = reel**, swim, whirl, be giddy, be in a whirl, grow dizzy: *My head was spinning from the wine.* **3 = tell**, relate, recount, develop, invent, unfold, concoct, narrate: *She had spun a story that was too good to be true.*
▷ NOUN **1 = drive**, ride, turn, hurl (*Scot.*), whirl, joy ride (*informal*): *Think twice about going for a spin by the light of the silvery moon.* **2 = revolution**, roll, whirl, twist, gyration: *a spin of the roulette wheel*
spin something out = prolong, extend, lengthen, draw out, drag out, delay, amplify, pad out, protract, prolongate: *They will try to spin out the conference into next autumn.*

spindly ADJECTIVE **= lanky**, gangly, spidery, leggy, twiggy, attenuated, gangling, spindle-shanked

spine NOUN **1 = backbone**, vertebrae, spinal column, vertebral column: *fractures of the hip and spine* **2 = barb**, spur, needle, spike, ray, quill: *Carry a pair of thick gloves to protect you from hedgehog spines.* **3 = determination**, resolution, backbone, resolve, drive, conviction, fortitude, persistence, tenacity, perseverance, willpower, firmness, constancy, single-mindedness, steadfastness, doggedness, resoluteness, indomitability: *If you had any spine, you wouldn't let her walk all over you like that.*

spine-chilling ADJECTIVE **= frightening**, terrifying, horrifying, scary (*informal*), eerie, spooky (*informal*), hair-raising, bloodcurdling

spineless ADJECTIVE **= weak**, soft, cowardly, ineffective, feeble, yellow (*informal*), inadequate, pathetic, submissive, squeamish, vacillating, boneless, gutless (*informal*), weak-willed, weak-kneed (*informal*), faint-hearted, irresolute, spiritless, lily-livered, without a will of your own **OPPOSITE:** brave

spiral ADJECTIVE **= coiled**, winding, corkscrew, circular, scrolled, whorled, helical, cochlear, voluted, cochleate (*Biology*): *a spiral staircase*
▷ NOUN **= coil**, helix, corkscrew, whorl, screw, curlicue: *Larks were rising in spirals from the ridge.*

spirit[1] NOUN **1 = soul**, life, psyche, essential being: *The human spirit is virtually indestructible.* **2 = life force**, vital spark, breath, mauri (*N.Z.*): *His spirit left him during the night.* **3 = ghost**, phantom, spectre, vision, shadow, shade (*literary*), spook (*informal*), apparition, sprite, atua (*N.Z.*), kehua (*N.Z.*): *Do you believe in the existence of evil spirits?* **4 = courage**, guts (*informal*), grit, balls (*taboo, slang*), backbone, spunk (*informal*), gameness, ballsiness (*taboo, slang*), dauntlessness, stoutheartedness: *She was a very brave girl and everyone admired her spirit.* **5 = liveliness**, energy, vigour, life, force, fire, resolution, enterprise, enthusiasm, sparkle, warmth, animation, zest, mettle, ardour, earnestness, brio: *They played with spirit.* **6 = attitude**, character, quality, humour, temper, outlook, temperament, complexion, disposition: *They approached the talks in a conciliatory spirit.* **7 = heart**, sense, nature, soul, core, substance, essence, lifeblood, quintessence, fundamental nature: *the real spirit of the Labour movement* **8 = intention**, meaning, purpose, substance, intent, essence, purport, gist: *the spirit of the treaty* **9 = feeling**, atmosphere, character, feel, quality, tone, mood, flavour, tenor, ambience, vibes (*slang*): *I appreciate the sounds, smells and the spirit of the place.* **10 = resolve**, will, drive, resolution, conviction, motivation, dedication, backbone, fortitude, persistence, tenacity, perseverance, willpower, firmness, constancy, single-mindedness, steadfastness, doggedness, resoluteness, indomitability: *It takes a lot of spirit to win with 10 men.* **11** (*plural*) **= mood**, feelings, morale, humour, temper, tenor, disposition, state of mind, frame of mind: *A bit of exercise will help lift his spirits.*

spirit[2] NOUN (*often plural*) **= strong alcohol**, liquor, the hard stuff (*informal*), firewater, strong liquor

spirited ADJECTIVE **= lively**, vigorous, energetic, animated, game, active, bold, sparkling, have-a-go (*informal*), courageous, ardent, feisty (*informal, chiefly U.S. & Canad.*), plucky, high-spirited, sprightly, vivacious, spunky (*informal*), mettlesome, (as) game as Ned Kelly (*Austral. slang*)
OPPOSITE: lifeless

spiritual ADJECTIVE **1 = nonmaterial**, immaterial, incorporeal: *She lived entirely by spiritual values.*
OPPOSITE: material **2 = sacred**, religious, holy, divine, ethereal, devotional, otherworldly: *A man in priestly clothes offered spiritual guidance.*

spit VERB **1 = expectorate**, sputter, flob (*Brit. informal*): *They spat at me and taunted me.* **2 = eject**, discharge, throw out: *I spat it on to my plate.*
▷ NOUN **= saliva**, dribble, spittle, drool, slaver, sputum: *When he took a corner kick he was showered with spit.*

spite NOUN **= malice**, malevolence, ill will, hate, hatred, gall, animosity, venom, spleen, pique, rancour, bitchiness (*slang*), malignity, spitefulness: *Never had she met such spite and pettiness.* **OPPOSITE:** kindness
▷ VERB **= annoy**, hurt, injure, harm, provoke, offend, needle (*informal*), put out, gall, nettle, vex, pique, discomfit, put someone's nose out of joint (*informal*), hack someone off (*informal*): *He was giving his art collection away for nothing, to spite them.* **OPPOSITE:** benefit
in spite of = despite, regardless of, notwithstanding, in defiance of, (even) though: *Their love of life comes in spite of considerable hardship.*

> **PROVERBS**
> *Don't cut off your nose to spite your face*

spiteful ADJECTIVE **= malicious**, nasty, vindictive, cruel, malignant, barbed, malevolent, venomous, bitchy (*informal*), snide, rancorous, catty (*informal*), splenetic, shrewish, ill-disposed, ill-natured

spitting image NOUN **= double**, lookalike, (dead) ringer (*slang*), picture, spit (*informal, chiefly Brit.*), clone, replica, likeness, living image, spit and image (*informal*)

S

splash VERB **1 = paddle**, plunge, bathe, dabble, wade, wallow: *A lot of people were in the water, splashing about.* **2 = scatter**, shower, spray, sprinkle, spread, wet, strew, squirt, spatter, slop, slosh *(informal)*: *He closed his eyes tight, and splashed the water on his face.* **3 = spatter**, mark, stain, smear, speck, speckle, blotch, splodge, bespatter: *The carpet was splashed with beer stains.* **4 = dash**, break, strike, wash, batter, surge, smack, buffet, plop, plash: *waves splashing against the side of the boat* ▷ NOUN **1 = splashing**, dashing, plash, beating, battering, swashing: *I would sit alone and listen to the splash of water on the rocks.* **2 = dash**, touch, spattering, splodge: *Add a splash of lemon juice to flavour the butter.* **3 = spot**, burst, patch, stretch, spurt: *splashes of colour* **4 = blob**, spot, smudge, stain, smear, fleck, speck: *splashes of ink over a glowing white surface*
make a splash = cause a stir, make an impact, cause a sensation, cut a dash, be ostentatious: *He knows how to make a splash in the House of Lords.*

spleen NOUN **= spite**, anger, bitterness, hostility, hatred, resentment, wrath, gall, malice, animosity, venom, bile, bad temper, acrimony, pique, rancour, ill will, animus, malevolence, vindictiveness, malignity, spitefulness, ill humour, peevishness

splendid ADJECTIVE **1 = excellent**, wonderful, marvellous, mean *(slang)*, great *(informal)*, topping *(Brit. slang)*, fine, cracking *(Brit. informal)*, crucial *(slang)*, fantastic *(informal)*, first-class, glorious, mega *(slang)*, sovereign, awesome *(slang)*, def *(slang)*, brill *(informal)*, bodacious *(slang, chiefly U.S.)*, boffo *(slang)*, chillin' *(U.S. slang)*, booshit *(Austral. slang)*, exo *(Austral. slang)*, sik *(Austral. slang)*, rad *(informal)*, phat *(slang)*, schmick *(Austral. informal)*, beaut *(informal)*, barrie *(Scot. slang)*, belting *(Brit. slang)*, pearler *(Austral. slang)*: *The book includes a wealth of splendid photographs.* **OPPOSITE:** poor **2 = magnificent**, grand, imposing, impressive, rich, superb, costly, gorgeous, dazzling, lavish, luxurious, sumptuous, ornate, resplendent, splendiferous *(facetious)*: *a splendid Victorian mansion* **OPPOSITE:** squalid **3 = glorious**, superb, magnificent, grand, brilliant, rare, supreme, outstanding, remarkable, sterling, exceptional, renowned, admirable, sublime, illustrious: *a splendid career in publishing* **OPPOSITE:** ignoble

splendour NOUN **= magnificence**, glory, grandeur, show, display, ceremony, luxury, spectacle, majesty, richness, nobility, pomp, opulence, solemnity, éclat, gorgeousness, sumptuousness, stateliness, resplendence, luxuriousness: *They met in the splendour of the hotel.* **OPPOSITE:** squalor

splice VERB **= join**, unite, graft, marry, wed, knit, mesh, braid, intertwine, interweave, yoke, plait, entwine, interlace, intertwist

splinter NOUN **= sliver**, fragment, chip, needle, shaving, flake, paring: *a splinter in the finger* ▷ VERB **= shatter**, split, fracture, shiver, disintegrate, break into fragments: *The ruler cracked and splintered into pieces.*

split VERB **1 = break**, crack, burst, snap, break up, open, give way, splinter, gape, come apart, come undone: *In a severe gale the ship split in two.* **2 = cut**, break, crack, snap, chop, cleave, hew: *He started on the main course while she split the avocados.* **3 = divide**, separate, disunite, disrupt, disband, cleave, pull apart, set at odds, set at variance: *It is feared they could split the government.* **4 = diverge**, separate, branch, fork, part, go separate ways: *that place where the road split in two* **5 = tear**, rend, rip, slash, slit: *The seat of his short grey trousers split.* **6 = share out**, divide, distribute, halve, allocate, partition, allot, carve up, dole out, apportion, slice up, parcel out, divvy up *(informal)*: *Split the wages between you.* ▷ NOUN **1 = division**, break, breach, rift, difference, disruption, rupture, discord, divergence, schism, estrangement, dissension, disunion: *a split in the party* **2 = separation**, break, divorce, break-up, split-up, disunion: *The split from her husband was acrimonious.* **3 = crack**, tear, rip, damage, gap, rent, breach, slash, slit, fissure: *The seat had a few small splits around the corners.* ▷ ADJECTIVE **1 = divided**, ambivalent, bisected: *The Kremlin is deeply split in its approach to foreign policy.* **2 = broken**, cracked, snapped, fractured, splintered, ruptured, cleft: *a split finger nail*
split on someone = betray, tell on, shop *(slang, chiefly Brit.)*, sing *(slang, chiefly U.S.)*, grass *(Brit. slang)*, give away, squeal *(slang)*, inform on, spill your guts *(slang)*, dob in *(Austral. slang)*: *If I wanted to tell, I'd have split on you before now.*
split up = break up, part, separate, divorce, disband, part company, go separate ways: *I was beginning to think that we would never split up.*

spoil VERB **1 = ruin**, destroy, wreck, damage, total *(slang)*, blow *(slang)*, injure, upset, harm, mar, scar, undo, trash *(slang)*, impair, mess up, blemish, disfigure, debase, deface, put a damper on, crool *or* cruel *(Austral. slang)*: *It is important not to let mistakes spoil your life.* **OPPOSITE:** improve **2 = overindulge**, indulge, pamper, baby, cosset, coddle, spoon-feed, mollycoddle, kill with kindness: *Grandparents are often tempted to spoil their grandchildren.* **OPPOSITE:** deprive **3 = indulge**, treat, pamper, satisfy, gratify, pander to, regale: *Spoil yourself with a new perfume this summer.* **4 = go bad**, turn, go off *(Brit. informal)*, rot, decay, decompose, curdle, mildew, addle, putrefy, become tainted: *Fats spoil by becoming tainted.*

spoils PLURAL NOUN **= booty**, loot, plunder, gain, prizes, prey, pickings, pillage, swag *(slang)*, boodle *(slang, chiefly U.S.)*, rapine: *Competing warlords and foreign powers scrambled for political spoils.*

spoken ADJECTIVE **= verbal**, voiced, expressed, uttered, oral, said, told, unwritten, phonetic, by word of mouth, put into words, viva voce: *written and spoken communication skills*
spoken for 1 = reserved, booked, claimed, chosen, selected, set aside: *The top jobs in the party are already spoken for.* **2 = engaged**, taken, going out with someone, betrothed *(archaic)*, going steady: *Both girls, I remind him, are spoken for.*

spokesperson NOUN **= speaker**, official, spokesman *or* spokeswoman, voice, spin doctor *(informal)*, mouthpiece

spongy ADJECTIVE **= porous**, light, absorbent, springy, cushioned, elastic, cushiony

sponsor VERB **= back**, fund, finance, promote, subsidize, patronize, put up the money for, lend your name to: *They are sponsoring a major pop art exhibition.* ▷ NOUN **= backer**, patron, promoter, angel *(informal)*, guarantor: *the new sponsors of the League Cup*

spontaneous ADJECTIVE **= unplanned**, impromptu, unprompted, willing, free, natural, voluntary, instinctive, impulsive, unforced, unbidden, unconstrained, unpremeditated, extempore, uncompelled **OPPOSITE:** planned

spontaneously ADVERB **= voluntarily**, freely, instinctively, impromptu, off the cuff *(informal)*, on impulse, impulsively, in the heat of the moment, extempore, off your own bat, of your own accord, quite unprompted

spoof NOUN **= parody**, takeoff *(informal)*, satire, caricature, mockery, send-up *(Brit. informal)*, travesty, lampoon, burlesque

spook NOUN **= ghost**, spirit, phantom, spectre, soul, shade *(literary)*, manes, apparition, wraith, revenant, phantasm, eidolon, kehua *(N.Z.)*: *She woke up to see a spook hovering over her bed.* ▷ VERB **= frighten**, alarm, scare, terrify, startle, intimidate, daunt, unnerve, petrify, scare (someone) stiff, put the wind up (someone) *(informal)*, scare the living daylights out of (someone) *(informal)*, make your hair stand on end *(informal)*, get the wind up, make your blood run cold, throw into a panic, scare the bejesus out of *(informal)*, affright *(archaic)*, freeze your blood, make (someone) jump out of his skin *(informal)*, throw into a fright: *But was it the wind that spooked her?*

spooky ADJECTIVE *(informal)* = **eerie**, frightening, chilling, ghostly, weird, mysterious, scary *(informal)*, unearthly, supernatural, uncanny, creepy *(informal)*, spine-chilling

sporadic ADJECTIVE = **intermittent**, occasional, scattered, isolated, random, on and off, irregular, infrequent, spasmodic, scattershot **OPPOSITE:** steady

sport NOUN **1** = **game**, exercise, recreation, play, entertainment, amusement, diversion, pastime, physical activity: *I'd say football is my favourite sport.* **2** = **fun**, kidding *(informal)*, joking, teasing, ridicule, joshing *(slang, chiefly U.S. & Canad.)*, banter, frolic, jest, mirth, merriment, badinage, raillery: *Had themselves a bit of sport first, didn't they?*
▷ VERB = **wear**, display, flaunt, boast, exhibit, flourish, show off, vaunt: *He was fat-faced, heavily-built and sported a red moustache.*

sporting ADJECTIVE = **fair**, sportsmanlike, game *(informal)*, gentlemanly **OPPOSITE:** unfair

sporty ADJECTIVE **1** = **athletic**, outdoor, energetic, hearty: *He would go to the ballgames with his sporty friends.* **2** = **casual**, stylish, jazzy *(informal)*, loud, informal, trendy *(Brit. informal)*, flashy, jaunty, showy, snazzy *(informal)*, raffish, rakish, gay, schmick *(Austral. informal)*: *The moustache gave him a certain sporty air.*

spot NOUN **1** = **mark**, stain, speck, scar, flaw, taint, blot, smudge, blemish, daub, speckle, blotch, discoloration: *The floorboards were covered with white spots.* **2** = **pimple**, blackhead, pustule, zit *(slang)*, plook *(Scot.)*, acne: *Never squeeze blackheads, spots or pimples.* **3** = **bit**, little, drop, bite, splash, small amount, tad, morsel: *We've given all the club members tea, coffee and a spot of lunch.* **4** = **place**, situation, site, point, position, scene, location, locality: *They returned to the remote spot where they had left him.* **5** = **predicament**, trouble, difficulty, mess, plight, hot water *(informal)*, quandary, tight spot: *In a tight spot there is no one I would sooner see than Frank.*
▷ VERB **1** = **see**, observe, catch sight of, identify, sight, recognize, detect, make out, pick out, discern, behold *(archaic, literary)*, espy, descry: *He left the party seconds before smoke was spotted coming up the stairs.* **2** = **mark**, stain, dot, soil, dirty, scar, taint, tarnish, blot, fleck, spatter, sully, speckle, besmirch, splodge, splotch, mottle, smirch: *a brown shoe spotted with paint*

spotless ADJECTIVE **1** = **clean**, immaculate, impeccable, white, pure, virgin, shining, gleaming, snowy, flawless, faultless, unblemished, virginal, unsullied, untarnished, unstained: *Every morning cleaners make sure everything is spotless.* **OPPOSITE:** dirty **2** = **blameless**, squeaky-clean, unimpeachable, innocent, chaste, irreproachable, above reproach: *He was determined to leave a spotless record behind him.* **OPPOSITE:** reprehensible

spotlight NOUN **1** = **search light**, headlight, floodlight, headlamp, foglamp: *the light of a powerful spotlight from a police helicopter* **2** = **attention**, limelight, public eye, interest, fame, notoriety, public attention: *Webb is back in the spotlight.*
▷ VERB = **highlight**, feature, draw attention to, focus attention on, accentuate, point up, give prominence to, throw into relief: *a new book spotlighting female entrepreneurs*

spot-on ADJECTIVE = **accurate**, exact, precise, right, correct, on the money *(U.S.)*, unerring, punctual (to the minute), hitting the nail on the head *(informal)*, on the bull's-eye *(informal)*

spotted ADJECTIVE = **speckled**, dotted, flecked, pied, specked, mottled, dappled, polka-dot

spotty ADJECTIVE **1** = **pimply**, pimpled, blotchy, poor-complexioned, plooky-faced *(Scot.)*: *She was rather fat, and her complexion was muddy and spotty.* **2** = **inconsistent**, irregular, erratic, uneven, fluctuating, patchy, sporadic: *His attendance record was spotty.*

spouse NOUN = **partner**, mate, husband *or* wife, companion, consort, significant other *(U.S. informal)*, better half *(humorous)*, her indoors *(Brit. slang)*, helpmate

spout VERB **1** = **stream**, shoot, gush, spurt, jet, spray, surge, discharge, erupt, emit, squirt: *In a storm, water spouts out of the blowhole just like a whale.* **2** = **hold forth**, talk, rant, go on *(informal)*, rabbit (on) *(Brit. informal)*, ramble (on), pontificate, declaim, spiel *(informal)*, expatiate, orate, speechify: *She would go red in the face and start to spout.*

sprawl VERB = **loll**, slump, lounge, flop, slouch

spray[1] NOUN **1** = **droplets**, moisture, fine mist, drizzle, spindrift, spoondrift: *The moon was casting a rainbow through the spray of the waterfall.* **2** = **aerosol**, sprinkler, atomizer: *an insect-repellent spray*
▷ VERB = **scatter**, shower, sprinkle, diffuse: *A shower of seeds sprayed into the air and fell on the grass; We sprayed the area with weedkiller.*

spray[2] NOUN = **sprig**, floral arrangement, branch, bough, shoot, corsage: *a small spray of freesias*

spread VERB **1** = **open (out)**, extend, stretch, unfold, sprawl, unfurl, fan out, unroll: *He spread his coat over the bed.* **2** = **extend**, open, stretch: *He stepped back and spread his hands wide.* **3** = **coat**, cover, smear, smother: *Spread the bread with the cream cheese.* **4** = **smear**, apply, rub, put, smooth, plaster, daub: *Spread the cream over the skin and allow it to remain for 12 hours.* **5** = **grow**, increase, develop, expand, widen, mushroom, escalate, proliferate, multiply, broaden: *The sense of fear is spreading in residential neighbourhoods.* **6** = **space out**, stagger: *The course is spread over a five-week period.* **7** = **circulate**, publish, broadcast, advertise, distribute, scatter, proclaim, transmit, make public, publicize, propagate, disseminate, promulgate, make known, blazon, bruit: *Someone has been spreading rumours about us.* **OPPOSITE:** suppress **8** = **diffuse**, cast, shed, radiate: *The overall flaring tends to spread light.*
▷ NOUN **1** = **increase**, development, advance, spreading, expansion, transmission, proliferation, advancement, escalation, diffusion, dissemination, dispersal, suffusion: *The greatest hope for reform is the gradual spread of information.* **2** = **extent**, reach, span, stretch, sweep, compass: *The rhododendron grows to 18 inches with a spread of 24 inches.* **3** = **feast**, banquet, blowout *(slang)*, repast, array: *They put on a spread of sandwiches for us.*

spree NOUN **1** = **fling**, binge *(informal)*, orgy, splurge: *They went on a spending spree.* **2** = **binge**, bender *(informal)*, orgy, revel *(informal)*, jag *(slang)*, junketing, beano *(Brit. slang)*, debauch, carouse, bacchanalia, carousal: *They attacked two London shops after a drinking spree.*

sprightly ADJECTIVE = **lively**, spirited, active, energetic, animated, brisk, nimble, agile, jaunty, gay, perky, vivacious, spry, bright-eyed and bushy-tailed **OPPOSITE:** inactive

spring NOUN **1** = **springtime**, springtide *(literary)*: *We met again in the spring of 1977.* **2** = **source**, root, origin, well, beginning, cause, fount, fountainhead, wellspring: *the hidden springs of consciousness* **3** = **flexibility**, give *(informal)*, bounce, resilience, elasticity, recoil, buoyancy, springiness, bounciness: *Put some spring back into your old sofa.*
▷ VERB **1** = **jump**, bound, leap, bounce, hop, rebound, vault, recoil: *The lion roared once and sprang.* **2** *(usually followed by* **from***)* = **originate**, come, derive, start, issue, grow, emerge, proceed, arise, stem, descend, be derived, emanate, be descended: *The art springs from the country's Muslim heritage.*
▷ MODIFIER = **vernal**, springlike: *Walking carefree through the fresh spring rain.*

springy ADJECTIVE = **flexible**, elastic, resilient, bouncy, rubbery, spongy

sprinkle VERB = **scatter**, dust, strew, pepper, shower, spray, powder, dredge

sprinkling NOUN = **scattering**, dusting, scatter, few, dash, handful, sprinkle, smattering, admixture

sprint VERB = **run**, race, shoot, tear, dash, barrel (along) *(informal, chiefly U.S. & Canad.)*, dart, hare *(Brit. informal)*, whizz *(informal)*, scamper, hotfoot, go like a bomb *(Brit. & N.Z. informal)*, put on a burst of speed, go at top speed

sprite NOUN = **spirit**, fairy, elf, nymph, brownie, pixie, apparition, imp,

S

The Language of Mary Shelley

Mary Shelley (1797–1851) was an English writer, most famous for her Gothic novel *Frankenstein; or, The Modern Prometheus.* She was the wife of the Romantic poet Percy Bysshe Shelley, and the daughter of the political philosopher William Godwin and the feminist philosopher Mary Wollstonecraft. *Frankenstein* is the story of a scientist, Victor Frankenstein, who creates a human-like being that eventually destroys him. The novel explores the relationship between creator and created, the loneliness of the outcast monster, and the danger of excessive knowledge. Shelley's other works include the novella *Mathilda,* which tells the story of a young girl's depression and death after her father's confession of incestuous love for her, and the futuristic novel *The Last Man,* about the survivors of a world devastated by plague.

Given the themes of Shelley's novels, it is not surprising that her most frequent noun is *life.* In *Frankenstein,* the doctor's creation is *given life* and *infused with life*; life is *renewed* and *received*; it is frequently *miserable.* The phrase *life and death* recurs in all of Shelley's novels; *life and love*, however, is found in *The Last Man* and *Mathilda* but not in *Frankenstein. Death* is also among Shelley's ten most frequent nouns, but it is much more frequent in *The Last Man* than in *Frankenstein.* In all her novels, death is often personified:

> **Death** snatches away many blooming children.
>
> **Death** had hunted us through the course of many months.

Another of Shelley's most frequent nouns is *heart,* sometimes as a physical entity which *beats* and *palpitates,* but more often as the seat of emotion: hearts *sicken*; they are *wounded, heavy, aching,* and *sorrowing.* Also among Shelley's twenty most frequent nouns are *hope* and *friend,* which act as beacons in the bleakness of the novels. *Friends* are frequently *beloved,* but they are not numerous; the phrase *only friend* is recurrent. Similarly, *hope* is *cherished* and *dear,* but it is also *extinguished,* and there are several instances of the phrases *last hope, small hope,* and *only hope.*

Shelley's most frequent adjective is *own,* often collocating with *heart, mind,* and *hand,* and used to emphasize the moral responsibility of her characters:

> You would not call it murder if you could precipitate me into one of those ice-rifts and destroy my frame, the work of your **own hands**.

Another frequent adjective is *human,* often in phrases such as *human being* and *human form,* but also used to underline the very inhumanity of Dr Frankenstein's actions:

> ... often did my **human** nature turn with loathing from my occupation.

Other frequent adjectives are *miserable* (often in *miserable wretch*) and *dark,* which is used in descriptions of the physical settings of the novels (*dark mass, dark ravine, dark mountain*) but also to describe the underside of the human soul (*dark melancholy, dark passions*).

The continued influence of *Frankenstein* in modern culture is evident in the fact that the word *Frankenstein* has come to be used generically to describe monstrous creations, for example in the phrase *Frankenstein food,* a facetious phrase for genetically modified food. Furthermore, *Frankenstein* is sometimes used incorrectly to refer to a monster itself (rather than its creator). In the novel, however, the monster has no name, indicating his lack of identity: he is a *monster, fiend,* or *being*; or, more often, a *daemon* or a *devil,* emphasising the metaphor of Victor Frankenstein as God and the monster as Satan (although a very sympathetic Satan). The monster calls himself a *creature,* using the word with a focus on the original sense 'one who is created', and reminding Victor of the responsibility which that word entails:

> I am **thy creature**, and I will be even mild and docile to my natural lord and king.

goblin, leprechaun, peri, dryad, naiad, sylph, Oceanid *(Greek myth)*, atua *(N.Z.)*

sprout VERB **1 = germinate**, bud, shoot, push, spring, vegetate: *It only takes a few days for beans to sprout.* **2 = grow**, develop, blossom, ripen: *Leaf-shoots were beginning to sprout on the hawthorn.*

spruce ADJECTIVE **= smart**, trim, neat, elegant, dainty, dapper, natty *(informal)*, well-groomed, well turned out, trig *(archaic, dialect)*, as if you had just stepped out of a bandbox, soigné *or* soignée **OPPOSITE:** untidy

spry ADJECTIVE **= active**, sprightly, quick, brisk, supple, nimble, agile, nippy *(Brit. informal)* **OPPOSITE:** inactive

spur VERB **= incite**, drive, prompt, press, urge, stimulate, animate, prod, prick, goad, impel: *His friend's plight had spurred him into taking part.*
▷ NOUN **= stimulus**, incentive, impetus, motive, impulse, inducement, incitement, kick up the backside *(informal)*: *Redundancy is the spur for many to embark on new careers.*
on the spur of the moment = on impulse, without thinking, impulsively, on the spot, impromptu, unthinkingly, without planning, impetuously, unpremeditatedly: *They admitted they had taken a vehicle on the spur of the moment.*

spurious ADJECTIVE **= false**, bogus, sham, pretended, artificial, forged, fake, mock, imitation, simulated, contrived, pseudo *(informal)*, counterfeit, feigned, ersatz, specious, unauthentic, phoney *or* phony *(informal)* **OPPOSITE:** genuine

spurn VERB **= reject**, slight, scorn, rebuff, put down, snub, disregard, despise, disdain, repulse, cold-shoulder, kick in the teeth *(slang)*, turn your nose up at *(informal)*, contemn *(formal)* **OPPOSITE:** accept

spurt VERB **= gush**, shoot, burst, jet, surge, erupt, spew, squirt: *I saw flames spurt from the roof.*
▷ NOUN **1 = gush**, jet, burst, spray, surge, eruption, squirt: *A spurt of diesel came from one valve and none from the other.* **2 = burst**, rush, surge, fit, access, spate: *I flushed bright red as a spurt of anger flashed through me.*

spy NOUN **= undercover agent**, secret agent, double agent, secret service agent, foreign agent, mole, fifth columnist, nark *(Brit., Austral. & N.Z. slang)*: *He was jailed for five years as an alleged British spy.*
▷ VERB **1 = be a spy**, snoop *(informal)*, gather intelligence: *I never agreed to spy for the United States.* **2** *(usually followed by* **on***)* **= watch**, follow, shadow, tail *(informal)*, trail, keep watch on, keep under surveillance: *He had his wife spied on for evidence in a divorce case.* **3 = catch sight of**, see, spot, notice, sight, observe, glimpse, behold *(archaic, literary)*, set eyes on, espy, descry: *He was walking down the street when he spied an old friend.*

spying NOUN **= espionage**, reconnaissance, infiltration, undercover work

squabble VERB **= quarrel**, fight, argue, row, clash, dispute, scrap *(informal)*, fall out *(informal)*, brawl, spar, wrangle, bicker, have words, fight like cat and dog, go at it hammer and tongs: *Mother is devoted to Dad although they squabble all the time.*
▷ NOUN **= quarrel**, fight, row, argument, dispute, set-to *(informal)*, scrap *(informal)*, disagreement, barney *(informal)*, spat *(U.S.)*, difference of opinion, tiff, bagarre *(French)*: *There have been minor squabbles about phone bills.*

squad NOUN **= team**, group, band, company, force, troop, crew, gang

squalid ADJECTIVE **1 = dirty**, filthy, seedy, sleazy, sordid, low, nasty, foul, disgusting, rundown, decayed, repulsive, poverty-stricken, unclean, fetid, slovenly, skanky *(slang)*, slummy, yucky *or* yukky *(slang)*, yucko *(Austral. slang)*, festy *(Austral. slang)*: *The migrants have been living in squalid conditions.* **OPPOSITE:** hygienic **2 = unseemly**, sordid, inappropriate, unsuitable, out of place, improper, undignified, disreputable, unbecoming, unrefined, out of keeping, discreditable, indelicate, in poor taste, indecorous, unbefitting: *the squalid pursuit of profit*

squalor NOUN **= filth**, wretchedness, sleaziness, decay, foulness, slumminess, squalidness, meanness **OPPOSITE:** luxury

squander VERB **= waste**, spend, fritter away, blow *(slang)*, consume, scatter, run through, lavish, throw away, misuse, dissipate, expend, misspend, be prodigal with, frivol away, spend like water **OPPOSITE:** save

square NOUN **1 = town square**, close, quad, market square, quadrangle, village square: *The house is located in one of Pimlico's prettiest squares.* **2 = conservative**, dinosaur, traditionalist, die-hard, stick-in-the-mud *(informal)*, fuddy-duddy *(informal)*, old buffer *(Brit. informal)*, antediluvian, back number *(informal)*, (old) fogey: *I'm a square, man. I adore Steely Dan.*
▷ ADJECTIVE **1 = fair**, just, straight, genuine, decent, ethical, straightforward, upright, honest, equitable, upfront *(informal)*, on the level *(informal)*, kosher *(informal)*, dinkum *(Austral. & N.Z. informal)*, above board, fair and square, on the up and up: *We are asking for a square deal.* **2 = old-fashioned**, straight *(slang)*, conservative, conventional, dated, bourgeois, out of date, stuffy, behind the times, strait-laced, out of the ark *(informal)*, Pooterish: *I felt so square in my three-piece suit.* **OPPOSITE:** fashionable
▷ VERB *(often followed by* **with***)* **= agree**, match, fit, accord, correspond, tally, conform, reconcile, harmonize: *His dreams did not square with reality.*

squash VERB **1 = crush**, press, flatten, mash, pound, smash, distort, pulp, compress, stamp on, trample down: *She made clay models and squashed them flat again.* **2 = suppress**, put down *(slang)*, quell, silence, sit on *(informal)*, crush, quash, annihilate: *The troops would stay in position to squash the first murmur of trouble.* **3 = embarrass**, put down, humiliate, shame, disgrace, degrade, mortify, debase, discomfit, take the wind out of someone's sails, put (someone) in his *(or* her) place, take down a peg *(informal)*: *Worried managers would be sacked or simply squashed.*

squawk VERB **1 = cry**, crow, screech, hoot, yelp, cackle: *I threw pebbles at the hens, and that made them jump and squawk.* **2 = complain**, protest, squeal *(informal, chiefly Brit.)*, kick up a fuss *(informal)*, raise Cain *(slang)*: *He squawked that the deal was a double cross.*
▷ NOUN **1 = cry**, crow, screech, hoot, yelp, cackle: *rising steeply into the air with an angry squawk* **2 = scream**, cry, yell, wail, shriek, screech, squeal, yelp, yowl: *She gave a loud squawk when the water was poured on her.*

squeak VERB **= squeal**, pipe, peep, shrill, whine, yelp

squeal VERB **1 = scream**, yell, shriek, screech, yelp, wail, yowl: *Jennifer squealed with delight and hugged me.* **2 = complain**, protest, moan, squawk *(informal)*, kick up a fuss *(informal)*: *They went squealing to the European Commission.* **3 = inform on**, grass *(Brit. slang)*, betray, shop *(slang, chiefly Brit.)*, sing *(slang, chiefly U.S.)*, peach *(slang)*, tell all, spill the beans *(informal)*, snitch *(slang)*, blab, rat on *(informal)*, sell (someone) down the river *(informal)*, blow the gaff *(Brit. slang)*, spill your guts *(slang)*, dob in *(Austral. slang)*: *There was no question of squealing to the police.*
▷ NOUN **= scream**, shriek, screech, yell, scream, wail, yelp, yowl: *At that moment there was a squeal of brakes; the squeal of piglets*

squeamish ADJECTIVE **1 = queasy**, sick, nauseous, queer, sickish, qualmish: *I feel squeamish at the sight of blood.* **OPPOSITE:** strong-stomached **2 = fastidious**, particular, delicate, nice *(rare)*, scrupulous, prudish, prissy *(informal)*, finicky, strait-laced, punctilious: *A meeting with this man is not for the socially squeamish.* **OPPOSITE:** coarse

squeeze VERB **1 = press**, crush, squash, pinch: *Dip the bread in the water and squeeze it dry.* **2 = clutch**, press, grip, crush, pinch, squash, nip, compress, wring: *He squeezed her arm reassuringly.* **3 = extract**, force, press, express: *Joe squeezed some juice from the oranges.* **4 = cram**, press, crowd, force, stuff, pack, jam, thrust, ram, wedge, jostle: *Somehow they managed to squeeze into the tight space.* **5 = pressurize**, lean on *(informal)*, bring pressure to bear on,

S

milk, bleed *(informal)*, oppress, wrest, extort, put the squeeze on *(informal)*, put the screws on *(informal)*: *The investigators are accused of squeezing the residents for information.* **6 = hug**, embrace, cuddle, clasp, enfold, hold tight: *He longed to just scoop her up and squeeze her.*
▷ NOUN **1 = press**, grip, clasp, crush, pinch, squash, nip, wring **2 = crush**, jam, squash, press, crowd, congestion: *The lift holds six people, but it's a bit of a squeeze.* **3 = hug**, embrace, cuddle, hold, clasp, handclasp: *She gave her teddy bear a squeeze.*

squint VERB **= peer**, screw up your eyes, narrow your eyes, look through narrowed eyes: *The girl squinted at the photograph.*
▷ NOUN **= cross eyes**, strabismus: *she had a bad squint in her right eye*

squirm VERB **= wriggle**, twist, writhe, shift, flounder, wiggle, fidget

squirt VERB **= spurt**, shoot, gush, burst, jet, surge, erupt, spew: *The water squirted from its throat.*
▷ NOUN **= spurt**, jet, burst, gush, surge, eruption: *a squirt of air freshener*

stab VERB **= pierce**, cut, gore, run through, stick, injure, wound, knife, thrust, spear, jab, puncture, bayonet, transfix, impale, spill blood: *Somebody stabbed him in the stomach.*
▷ NOUN **1 = attempt**, go *(informal)*, try, shot *(informal)*, crack *(informal)*, essay, endeavour: *Several times tennis stars have had a stab at acting.* **2 = twinge**, prick, pang, ache: *a stab of pain just above his eye*
stab someone in the back = betray, double-cross *(informal)*, sell out *(informal)*, sell, let down, inform on, do the dirty on *(Brit. slang)*, break faith with, play false, give the Judas kiss to, dob in *(Austral. slang)*: *She has been stabbed in the back by her supposed 'friends'.*

stability NOUN **= firmness**, strength, soundness, durability, permanence, solidity, constancy, steadiness, steadfastness **OPPOSITE:** instability

stable ADJECTIVE **1 = secure**, lasting, strong, sound, fast, sure, established, permanent, constant, steady, enduring, reliable, abiding, durable, deep-rooted, well-founded, steadfast, immutable, unwavering, invariable, unalterable, unchangeable: *a stable marriage* **OPPOSITE:** insecure **2 = well-balanced**, balanced, sensible, reasonable, rational, mentally sound: *Their characters are fully formed and they are both very stable children.* **3 = solid**, firm, secure, fixed, substantial, sturdy, durable, well-made, well-built, immovable, built to last: *This structure must be stable.* **OPPOSITE:** unstable

stack NOUN **1 = pile**, heap, mountain, mass, load, cock, rick, clamp *(Brit. Agriculture)*, mound: *There were stacks of books on the bedside table and floor.* **2 = lot**, mass, load *(informal)*, ton *(informal)*, heap *(informal)*, large quantity, great amount: *If the job's that good, you'll have stacks of money.*
▷ VERB **= pile**, heap up, load, assemble, accumulate, amass, stockpile, bank up: *They are stacked neatly in piles of three.*

staff NOUN **1 = workers**, employees, personnel, workforce, team, organization: *The staff were very good.* **2 = stick**, pole, rod, prop, crook, cane, stave, wand, sceptre: *We carried a staff that was notched at various lengths.*

stage NOUN **= step**, leg, phase, point, level, period, division, length, lap, juncture: *the final stage of the tour*
▷ VERB **1 = present**, produce, perform, put on, do, give, play: *She staged her first play in the late 1970s.* **2 = organize**, mount, arrange, lay on, orchestrate, engineer: *In the middle of this year the government staged a huge military parade.*

stagger VERB **1 = totter**, reel, sway, falter, lurch, wobble, waver, teeter: *He was staggering and had to lean on the bar.* **2 = astound**, amaze, stun, surprise, shock, shake, overwhelm, astonish, confound, take (someone) aback, bowl over *(informal)*, stupefy, strike (someone) dumb, throw off balance, give (someone) a shock, dumbfound, nonplus, flabbergast *(informal)*, take (someone's) breath away: *The whole thing staggers me.*

stagnant ADJECTIVE **1 = stale**, still, standing, quiet, sluggish, motionless, brackish: *Mosquitoes have been thriving in stagnant water on building sites.* **OPPOSITE:** flowing **2 = inactive**, declining, stagnating, slow, depressed, sluggish, slow-moving: *Mass movements are often a factor in the awakening of stagnant societies.*

stagnate VERB **= vegetate**, decline, deteriorate, rot, decay, idle, rust, languish, stand still, fester, go to seed, lie fallow: *His career had stagnated.*

staid ADJECTIVE **= sedate**, serious, sober, quiet, calm, grave, steady, composed, solemn, demure, decorous, self-restrained, set in your ways **OPPOSITE:** wild

stain NOUN **1 = mark**, spot, blot, blemish, discoloration, smirch: *a black stain* **2 = stigma**, shame, disgrace, slur, reproach, blemish, dishonour, infamy, blot on the escutcheon: *a stain on the honour of its war dead* **3 = dye**, colour, tint: *Give each surface two coats of stain.*
▷ VERB **1 = mark**, soil, discolour, dirty, tarnish, tinge, spot, blot, blemish, smirch: *Some foods can stain teeth, as of course can smoking.* **2 = dye**, colour, tint: *a technique biologists use to stain proteins* **3 = disgrace**, taint, blacken, sully, corrupt, contaminate, deprave, defile, besmirch, drag through the mud: *It was too late. Their reputation had been stained.*

stake[1] NOUN **= pole**, post, spike, stick, pale, paling, picket, stave, palisade: *Drive in a stake before planting the tree.*
▷ VERB **= support**, secure, prop, brace, tie up, tether: *The plants are susceptible to wind, and should be well staked.*
stake something out = lay claim to, define, outline, mark out, demarcate, delimit: *The time has come for Hindus to stake out their claim to their own homeland.*

stake[2] NOUN **1 = bet**, ante, wager, chance, risk, venture, hazard: *The game was usually played for high stakes between two large groups.* **2 = interest**, share, involvement, claim, concern, investment: *a stake in the plot*
▷ VERB **= bet**, gamble, wager, chance, risk, venture, hazard, jeopardize, imperil, put on the line: *He has staked his reputation on the outcome.*
at stake = to lose, at risk, being risked: *The tension was naturally high for a game with so much at stake.*

stale ADJECTIVE **1 = old**, hard, dry, decayed, fetid: *a lump of stale bread* **OPPOSITE:** fresh **2 = musty**, stagnant, fusty: *the smell of stale sweat* **3 = tasteless**, flat, sour, insipid: *The place smelled of stale beer and dusty carpets.* **4 = unoriginal**, banal, trite, common, flat, stereotyped, commonplace, worn-out, antiquated, threadbare, old hat, insipid, hackneyed, overused, repetitious, platitudinous, cliché-ridden: *repeating stale jokes to kill the time* **OPPOSITE:** original

stalemate NOUN **= deadlock**, draw, tie, impasse, standstill

stalk VERB **1 = pursue**, follow, track, hunt, shadow, tail *(informal)*, haunt, creep up on: *He stalks his victims like a hunter after a deer.* **2 = march**, pace, stride, strut, flounce: *If his patience is tried at meetings he has been known to stalk out.*

stall[1] VERB **1 = hinder**, obstruct, impede, block, check, arrest, halt, slow down, hamper, thwart, sabotage: *an attempt to stall the negotiations* **2 = play for time**, delay, hedge, procrastinate, stonewall, beat about the bush *(informal)*, temporize, drag your feet: *Thomas had spent all week stalling over a decision..* **3 = hold up**, delay, detain, divert, distract: *Shop manager Brian Steel stalled the man until the police arrived.*

stall[2] VERB **= stop dead**, jam, seize up, catch, stick, stop short: *The engine stalled.*
▷ NOUN **1 = stand**, table, counter, booth, kiosk: *market stalls selling local fruits* **2 = enclosure**, pen, coop, corral, sty: *mucking out the animal stalls*

stalwart ADJECTIVE **1 = loyal**, faithful, strong, firm, true, constant, resolute, dependable, steadfast, true-blue, tried and true: *a stalwart supporter of the colonial government* **2 = strong**, strapping, robust, athletic, vigorous, rugged, manly, hefty *(informal)*, muscular, sturdy, stout, husky *(informal)*, beefy *(informal)*, lusty, sinewy, brawny: *I was never in any danger with my stalwart bodyguard around me.* **OPPOSITE:** puny

stamina NOUN **= staying power**, endurance, resilience, force, power,

S

energy, strength, resistance, grit, vigour, tenacity, power of endurance, indefatigability, lustiness

stammer VERB **= stutter**, falter, splutter, pause, hesitate, hem and haw, stumble over your words: *She stammered her way through an introduction.*
▷ NOUN **= speech impediment**, stutter, speech defect: *A speech-therapist cured his stammer.*

stamp NOUN **1 = imprint**, mark, brand, cast, mould, signature, earmark, hallmark: *You may live only where the stamp in your passport says you may.* **2 = stomp** *(informal)*, stump, clump, tramp, clomp: *the stamp of feet on the stairs* **3 = type**, sort, kind, form, cut, character, fashion, cast, breed, description: *Montgomerie's style is of a different stamp.*
▷ VERB **1 = print**, mark, fix, impress, mould, imprint, engrave, inscribe: *'Eat before July 14' was stamped on the label.* **2 = stomp** *(informal)*, stump, clump, tramp, clomp: *She stamped her feet on the pavement to keep out the cold.* **3 = trample**, step, tread, crush: *He received a ban last week after stamping on the referee's foot.* **4 = identify**, mark, brand, label, reveal, exhibit, betray, pronounce, show to be, categorize, typecast: *They had stamped me as a bad woman.*
stamp something out = eliminate, destroy, eradicate, crush, suppress, put down, put out, scotch, quell, extinguish, quench, extirpate: *on-the-spot fines to stamp the problems out*

stampede NOUN **= rush**, charge, flight, scattering, rout: *There was a stampede for the exit.*
▷ VERB **= bolt**, run, charge, race, career, rush, dash: *The crowd stampeded and many were crushed or trampled underfoot.*

stance NOUN **1 = attitude**, stand, position, viewpoint, standpoint: *They have maintained a consistently neutral stance.* **2 = posture**, carriage, bearing, deportment: *The woman detective shifted her stance from one foot to the other.*

stand VERB **1 = be upright**, be erect, be vertical: *She was standing beside my bed staring down at me.* **2 = get to your feet**, rise, stand up, straighten up: *Becker stood and shook hands with Ben.* **3 = be located**, be, sit, perch, nestle, be positioned, be sited, be perched, be situated *or* located: *The house stands alone on top of a small hill.* **4 = be valid**, be in force, continue, stay, exist, prevail, remain valid: *The supreme court says the convictions still stand.* **5 = put**, place, position, set, mount: *Stand the plant in the open in a sunny, sheltered place.* **6 = sit**, rest, mellow, maturate: *The salad improves if made in the open and left to stand.* **7 = resist**, endure, withstand, wear *(Brit. slang)*, weather, undergo, defy, tolerate, stand up to, hold out against, stand firm against: *Ancient wisdom has stood the test of time.* **8 = tolerate**, bear, abide, suffer, stomach, endure, brook, hack *(slang)*, submit to, thole *(dialect)*: *He hates vegetables and can't stand curry.* **9 = take**, bear, handle, cope with, experience, sustain, endure, undergo, put up with *(informal)*, withstand, countenance: *I can't stand any more. I'm going to run away.*
▷ NOUN **1 = position**, attitude, stance, opinion, determination, standpoint, firm stand: *His tough stand won some grudging admiration.* **2 = stall**, booth, kiosk, table: *She bought a hot dog from a stand on a street corner.* **3 = grandstand**: *The people in the stands are cheering with all their might.* **4 = support**, base, platform, place, stage, frame, rack, bracket, tripod, dais, trivet: *The teapot came with a stand to catch the drips.*
stand by 1 = be prepared, wait, stand ready, prepare yourself, wait in the wings: *Stand by for details.* **2 = look on**, watch, not lift a finger, wait, turn a blind eye: *The police just stood by and watched as the missiles rained down on us.*
stand by someone = support, back, champion, defend, take (someone's) part, uphold, befriend, be loyal to, stick up for *(informal)*: *I wouldn't break the law for a friend, but I would stand by her if she did.*
stand by something = support, maintain, defend, champion, justify, sustain, endorse, assert, uphold, vindicate, stand up for, espouse, speak up for, stick up for *(informal)*: *The decision has been made and I have got to stand by it.*
stand for something 1 = represent, mean, signify, denote, indicate, exemplify, symbolize, betoken: *What does EEC stand for?* **2 = tolerate**, suffer, bear, endure, put up with, wear *(Brit. informal)*, brook, lie down under *(informal)*: *It's outrageous, and we won't stand for it any more.*
stand in for someone = be a substitute for, represent, cover for, take the place of, replace, understudy, hold the fort for, do duty for, deputize for: *I had to stand in for her on Tuesday when she didn't show up.*
stand out 1 = be conspicuous, be striking, be prominent, be obvious, be highlighted, attract attention, catch the eye, be distinct, stick out like a sore thumb *(informal)*, stare you in the face *(informal)*, be thrown into relief, bulk large, stick out a mile *(informal)*, leap to the eye: *Every tree, wall and fence stood out against dazzling white fields.* **2 = project**, protrude, bristle: *Her hair stood out in spikes.*
stand up for something *or* **someone = support**, champion, defend, uphold, side with, stick up for *(informal)*, come to the defence of: *They stood up for what they believed to be right.*
stand up to something *or* **someone 1 = withstand**, take, bear, weather, cope with, resist, endure, tolerate, hold out against, stand firm against: *Is this building going to stand up to the strongest gales?* **2 = resist**, oppose, confront, tackle, brave, defy: *Women are now aware of their rights and are prepared to stand up to their employers.*

standard NOUN **1 = level**, grade: *There will be new standards of hospital cleanliness.* **2 = criterion**, measure, guideline, example, model, average, guide, pattern, sample, par, norm, gauge, benchmark, yardstick, touchstone: *systems that were by later standards absurdly primitive* **3** *(often plural)* **= principles**, ideals, morals, rule, ethics, canon, moral principles, code of honour: *My father has always had high moral standards.* **4 = flag**, banner, pennant, colours, ensign, pennon: *a gleaming limousine bearing the royal standard*
▷ ADJECTIVE **1 = usual**, normal, customary, set, stock, average, popular, basic, regular, typical, prevailing, orthodox, staple, one-size-fits-all: *It was standard practice for them to advise in cases of murder.* **OPPOSITE:** unusual **2 = accepted**, official, established, classic, approved, recognized, definitive, authoritative: *a standard text in several languages* **OPPOSITE:** unofficial

QUOTATIONS
Standards are always out of date. That's what makes them standards
[Alan Bennett *Forty Years On*]

standardize VERB **= bring into line**, stereotype, regiment, assimilate, mass-produce, institutionalize

stand-in NOUN **= substitute**, deputy, replacement, reserve, surrogate, understudy, locum, stopgap

standing NOUN **1 = status**, position, station, footing, condition, credit, rank, reputation, eminence, estimation, repute: *He has improved his country's standing abroad.* **2 = duration**, existence, experience, continuance: *My girlfriend of long standing left me.*
▷ ADJECTIVE **1 = permanent**, lasting, fixed, regular, repeated, perpetual: *a standing offer* **2 = upright**, erect, vertical, rampant *(Heraldry)*, perpendicular, upended: *standing stones*

standpoint NOUN **= point of view**, position, angle, viewpoint, stance, vantage point

staple ADJECTIVE **= principal**, chief, main, key, basic, essential, primary, fundamental, predominant

star NOUN **1 = heavenly body**, sun, celestial body: *The nights were pure with cold air and lit with stars.* **2 = celebrity**, big name, celeb *(informal)*, megastar *(informal)*, name, draw, idol, luminary, leading man *or* lady, lead, hero *or* heroine, principal, main attraction: *Not all football stars are ill-behaved louts.*
▷ PLURAL NOUN **= horoscope**, forecast, astrological chart: *There was nothing in my stars to say I'd have problems.*
▷ VERB **= play the lead**, appear, feature, perform: *He's starred in dozens of films.* ▷ *See themed panel* **Stars and Constellations** *on facing page*

starchy ADJECTIVE **= formal**, stiff, stuffy, conventional, precise, prim, punctilious, ceremonious

S

STARS AND CONSTELLATIONS

Stars

Aldebaran
Betelgeuse
Polaris, the Pole Star, *or* the North Star
Sirius, the Dog Star, Canicula, *or* Sothis
the Sun
Vega

Constellations

Latin name	English name	Latin name	English name
Andromeda	Andromeda	Leo	Lion
Antila	Air Pump	Leo Minor	Little Lion
Apus	Bird of Paradise	Lepus	Hare
Aquarius	Water Bearer	Libra	Scales
Aquila	Eagle	Lupus	Wolf
Ara	Altar	Lynx	Lynx
Aries	Ram	Lyra	Harp
Auriga	Charioteer	Mensa	Table
Boötes	Herdsman	Microscopium	Microscope
Caelum	Chisel	Monoceros	Unicorn
Camelopardalis	Giraffe	Musca	Fly
Cancer	Crab	Norma	Level
Canes Venatici	Hunting Dogs	Octans	Octant
Canis Major	Great Dog	Ophiuchus	Serpent Bearer
Canis Minor	Little Dog	Orion	Orion
Capricornus	Sea Goat	Pavo	Peacock
Carina	Keel	Pegasus	Winged Horse
Cassiopeia	Cassiopeia	Perseus	Perseus
Centaurus	Centaur	Phoenix	Phoenix
Cepheus	Cepheus	Pictor	Easel
Cetus	Whale	Pisces	Fishes
Chamaeleon	Chameleon	Piscis Austrinus	Southern Fish
Circinus	Compasses	Puppis	Ship's Stern
Columba	Dove	Pyxis	Mariner's Compass
Coma Bernices	Bernice's Hair	Reticulum	Net
Corona Australis	Southern Crown	Sagitta	Arrow
Corona Borealis	Northern Crown	Sagittarius	Archer
Corvus	Crow	Scorpius	Scorpion
Crater	Cup	Sculptor	Sculptor
Crux	Southern Cross	Scutum	Shield
Cygnus	Swan	Serpens	Serpent
Delphinus	Dolphin	Sextans	Sextant
Dorado	Swordfish	Taurus	Bull
Draco	Dragon	Telescopium	Telescope
Equuleus	Little Horse	Triangulum	Triangle
Eridanus	River Eridanus	Triangulum Australe	Southern Triangle
Fornax	Furnace	Tucana	Toucan
Gemini	Twins	Ursa Major	Great Bear (contains the Plough *or* (*U.S.*) Big Dipper)
Grus	Crane		
Hercules	Hercules	Ursa Minor	Little Bear *or* (*U.S.*) Little Dipper
Horologium	Clock	Vela	Sails
Hydra	Sea Serpent	Virgo	Virgin
Hydrus	Water Snake	Volans	Flying Fish
Indus	Indian	Vulpecula	Fox
Lacerta	Lizard		

stare VERB **= gaze**, look, goggle, watch, gape, eyeball (*slang*), ogle, gawp (*Brit. slang*), gawk, rubberneck (*slang*)

stark ADJECTIVE **1 = plain**, simple, harsh, basic, bare, grim, straightforward, blunt, bald: *The stark truth is that we are paying more now than we ever were.* **2 = sharp**, clear, striking, distinct, clear-cut: *in stark contrast* **3 = austere**, severe, plain, bare, harsh, unadorned, bare-bones: *the stark, white, characterless fireplace in the drawing room* **4 = bleak**, grim, barren, hard, cold, depressing, dreary, desolate, forsaken, godforsaken, drear (*literary*): *a stark landscape of concrete, wire and utility equipment* **5 = absolute**, pure, sheer, utter, downright, patent, consummate, palpable, out-and-out, flagrant, unmitigated, unalloyed, arrant: *They are motivated, he said, by stark fear.*
▷ ADVERB **= absolutely**, quite, completely, clean, entirely, altogether, wholly, utterly: *I gasped again. He must have gone stark staring mad.*

start VERB **1 = set about**, begin, proceed, embark upon, take the plunge (*informal*), take the first step, make a beginning, put your hand to the plough (*informal*): *She started cleaning the kitchen.* **OPPOSITE:** stop **2 = begin**, arise, originate, issue, appear, commence, get under way, come into being, come into existence, first see the light of day: *The fire is thought to have started in an upstairs room.* **OPPOSITE:** end **3 = set in motion**, initiate, instigate, open, trigger, kick off (*informal*), originate, get going, engender, kick-start, get (something) off the ground (*informal*), enter upon, get *or* set *or* start the ball rolling: *Who started the fight?* **OPPOSITE:** stop **4 = establish**, begin, found, father,

create, launch, set up, introduce, institute, pioneer, initiate, inaugurate, lay the foundations of: *Now is probably as good a time as any to start a business.* **OPPOSITE:** terminate **5 = start up**, activate, get something going: *He started the car, which hummed smoothly.* **OPPOSITE:** turn off **6 = jump**, shy, jerk, twitch, flinch, recoil: *Rachel started at his touch.*
▷ NOUN **1 = beginning**, outset, opening, birth, foundation, dawn, first step(s), onset, initiation, inauguration, inception, commencement, kickoff *(informal)*, opening move: *She demanded to know why she had not been told from the start.* **OPPOSITE:** end **2 = jump**, jerk, twitch, spasm, convulsion: *He gave a start of surprise and astonishment.*

startle VERB **= surprise**, shock, alarm, frighten, scare, agitate, take (someone) aback, make (someone) jump, give (someone) a turn *(informal)*

startling ADJECTIVE **= surprising**, shocking, alarming, extraordinary, sudden, unexpected, staggering, unforeseen, jaw-dropping

starving ADJECTIVE **= hungry**, starved, ravenous, famished, hungering, sharp-set, esurient, faint from lack of food, ready to eat a horse *(informal)*

stash VERB **= store**, stockpile, save up, hoard, hide, secrete, stow, cache, lay up, salt away, put aside for a rainy day: *He had stashed money away in secret offshore bank accounts.*
▷ NOUN **= hoard**, supply, store, stockpile, cache, collection: *A large stash of drugs had been found aboard the yacht.*

state NOUN **1 = country**, nation, land, republic, territory, federation, commonwealth, kingdom, body politic: *Mexico is a secular state.* **2 = province**, region, district, area, territory, federal state: *Leaders of the Southern States are meeting in Louisville.* **3 = government**, ministry, administration, executive, regime, powers-that-be: *The state does not collect enough revenue to cover its expenditure.* **4 = condition**, shape, state of affairs: *When we moved here the walls and ceiling were in an awful state.* **5 = frame of mind**, condition, spirits, attitude, mood, humour: *When you left our place, you weren't in a fit state to drive.* **6 = ceremony**, glory, grandeur, splendour, dignity, majesty, pomp: *Nelson's body lay in state in the Painted Hall after the battle of Trafalgar.* **7 = circumstances**, situation, position, case, pass, mode, plight, predicament: *You shouldn't be lifting heavy things in your state.*
▷ VERB **= say**, report, declare, specify, put, present, explain, voice, express, assert, utter, articulate, affirm, expound, enumerate, propound, aver, asseverate: *Clearly state your address and telephone number.*
in a state 1 = distressed, upset, agitated, disturbed, anxious, ruffled, uptight *(informal)*, flustered, panic-stricken, het up, all steamed up *(slang)*: *I was in a terrible state because nobody could understand why I had this illness.* **2 = untidy**, disordered, messy, muddled, cluttered, jumbled, in disarray, topsy-turvy, higgledy-piggledy *(informal)*: *The living room was in a dreadful state.*

stately ADJECTIVE **= grand**, majestic, dignified, royal, august, imposing, impressive, elegant, imperial, noble, regal, solemn, lofty, pompous, ceremonious **OPPOSITE:** lowly

statement NOUN **1 = announcement**, declaration, communication, explanation, communiqué, proclamation, utterance: *He now disowns that statement, saying he was depressed when he made it.* **2 = account**, report, testimony, evidence: *statements from witnesses to the event*

state-of-the-art ADJECTIVE **= latest**, newest, up-to-date, up-to-the-minute **OPPOSITE:** old-fashioned

static ADJECTIVE **= stationary**, still, motionless, fixed, constant, stagnant, inert, immobile, unmoving, stock-still, unvarying, changeless **OPPOSITE:** moving

station NOUN **1 = railway station**, stop, stage, halt, terminal, train station, terminus: *She went with him to the station to see him off.* **2 = headquarters**, base, depot: *He was taken to the police station for questioning.* **3 = channel**, wavelength, broadcasting company: *Which radio station do you usually listen to?* **4 = position**, rank, status, standing, post, situation, grade, sphere: *The vast majority knew their station in life and kept to it.* **5 = post**, place, location, position, situation, seat: *Police said the bomb was buried in the sand near a lifeguard station.*
▷ VERB **= assign**, post, locate, set, establish, fix, install, garrison: *I was stationed there just after the war.*

stationary ADJECTIVE **= motionless**, standing, at a standstill, parked, fixed, moored, static, inert, unmoving, stock-still **OPPOSITE:** moving

> **USAGE**
> This word, which is always an adjective, is occasionally wrongly used where 'paper products' are meant: *in the stationery* (not *stationary*) *cupboard.*

statuesque ADJECTIVE **= well-proportioned**, stately, Junoesque, imposing, majestic, dignified, regal

stature NOUN **1 = height**, build, size: *She was a little short in stature.* **2 = importance**, standing, prestige, size, rank, consequence, prominence, eminence, high station: *This club has grown in stature over the last 20 years.*

status NOUN **1 = position**, rank, grade, degree: *promoted to the status of foreman* **2 = prestige**, standing, authority, influence, weight, reputation, honour, importance, consequence, fame, distinction, eminence, renown, mana (N.Z.): *She cheated banks to satisfy her desire for money and status.* **3 = state of play**, development, progress, condition, evolution, progression: *Please keep us informed of the status of this project.*

statute NOUN **= law**, act, rule, regulation, decree, ordinance, enactment, edict

staunch ADJECTIVE **= loyal**, faithful, stalwart, sure, strong, firm, sound, true, constant, reliable, stout, resolute, dependable, trustworthy, trusty, steadfast, true-blue, immovable, tried and true

stay VERB **1 = remain**, continue to be, linger, stand, stop, wait, settle, delay, halt, pause, hover, abide, hang around *(informal)*, reside, stay put, bide, loiter, hang in the air, tarry, put down roots, establish yourself: *Hundreds of people defied army orders to stay at home.* **OPPOSITE:** go **2** *(often with* **at***)* **= lodge**, visit, sojourn *(literary)*, put up at, be accommodated at: *He tried to stay at the hotel a few days every year.* **3 = continue**, remain, go on, survive, endure: *Nothing stays the same for long.* **4 = suspend**, put off, defer, adjourn, hold over, hold in abeyance, prorogue: *The finance ministry stayed the execution to avoid upsetting a nervous market.*
▷ NOUN **1 = visit**, stop, holiday, stopover, sojourn *(literary)*: *An experienced Italian guide is provided during your stay.* **2 = postponement**, delay, suspension, stopping, halt, pause, reprieve, remission, deferment: *The court dismissed defence appeals for a permanent stay of execution.*

staying power NOUN **= endurance**, strength, stamina, toughness

steadfast ADJECTIVE **1 = loyal**, faithful, stalwart, staunch, constant, steady, dedicated, reliable, persevering, dependable: *a steadfast friend* **OPPOSITE:** undependable **2 = resolute**, firm, fast, fixed, stable, intent, single-minded, unwavering, immovable, unflinching, unswerving, unfaltering: *He remained steadfast in his belief that he had done the right thing.* **OPPOSITE:** irresolute

steady ADJECTIVE **1 = continuous**, even, regular, constant, consistent, persistent, rhythmic, unbroken, habitual, uninterrupted, incessant, ceaseless, unremitting, unwavering, nonstop, unvarying, unfaltering, unfluctuating: *the steady beat of the drums* **OPPOSITE:** irregular **2 = stable**, fixed, secure, firm, safe, immovable, on an even keel: *Make sure the camera is steady.* **OPPOSITE:** unstable **3 = regular**, established: *a steady boyfriend* **4 = dependable**, sensible, reliable, balanced, settled, secure, calm, supportive, sober, staunch, serene, sedate, staid, steadfast, level-headed,

S

Foreign Plurals in Classic Literature

With the exception of a few irregular cases such as *child/children* and *mouse/mice*, forming the plural of a noun is usually straightforward in English: we simply add an '-s' so that *shoe* becomes *shoes* and *thought* becomes *thoughts*. The problems arise when we try to form plurals of foreign nouns. Do we say *indices* or *indexes*; *formulae* or *formulas*? All of these are correct: the first in each pair is the Latinate plural; the second the English one; both *index* and *formula* have become naturalized English words to the extent that native plurals are seen as acceptable. What about *octopuses* or .... – it is tempting to offer *octopi* as an alternative, but since *octopus* derives from Greek rather than Latin, *octopi* would be incorrect and *octopuses* is the accepted plural. (Only pedants use the Greek *octopodes*.) Other foreign plurals cause difficulties because they are no longer felt to be plural. We know that *datum* is singular and *data* is plural, but *data* is in the process of being reinterpreted as an uncountable noun (rather like *information*) and is often used with a singular verb, as in '**this data is** all wrong'. A similar situation can be seen with *media*, the plural of *medium*. In current usage *media* usually refers to mass media, ie television, radio, and newspapers, and is often treated as an uncountable noun ('the **media has** sensationalized the events'), even though this usage is often frowned upon.

In classic literature of the eighteenth to early twentieth century, Latinate plurals seem to have caused fewer problems than they do today. *Data* is almost always treated as a plural noun, for example:

> Meanwhile, we shall put the case aside until more accurate **data are** available. (Conan Doyle)

Indeed, in the entire corpus of classic authors which was examined, only one example of *data* as a singular was found, in one of Jack London's essays:

> From all **this data** I concluded that if I began immediately and worked and saved until I was fifty years of age, I could then stop working. (Jack London)

Other frequent Latinate plurals in classic literature are *memoranda, strata,* and *phenomena*. Again, these are almost always treated as plurals, although there are occasional examples of *strata* treated as a singular (one of these again from the works of Jack London):

> For, as a general rule, the more ancient **the strata is** in which the limestone is found, the harder the limestone is. (Charles Kingsley)

> And if they fire it, it means the entire Ebano oil field. The **strata's** too broken. (Jack London)

One consequence of the modern tendency to treat Latinate plurals as singulars is that the singular forms have become increasingly rare. In the *Bank of English*, Collins' corpus of present-day English, *strata* is three times as common as *stratum*, *criteria* is seven times as common as *criteria* and, remarkably, *data* is almost 700 times more frequent than *datum*. In classic literature, on the other hand, the singular form *stratum* is about as frequent as the plural *strata*, while *criterion* is actually more common than *criteria*. However, *datum* was already quite infrequent, occurring twenty times less frequently than *data*.

For those who worry over *indexes* and *indices* or *formula* and *formulae*, it is perhaps comforting that they occur with approximately equal frequency in classic literature. HG Wells had a preference for *formulae*, but other writers including Edith Wharton, George Eliot, and Henry James were more likely to choose *formulas*.

serious-minded, imperturbable, equable, unchangeable, having both feet on the ground: *He was firm and steady, unlike other men she knew.* **OPPOSITE:** undependable

steal VERB **1 = take**, nick *(slang, chiefly Brit.)*, pinch *(informal)*, lift *(informal)*, cabbage *(Brit. slang)*, swipe *(slang)*, half-inch *(old-fashioned, slang)*, heist *(U.S. slang)*, embezzle, blag *(slang)*, pilfer, misappropriate, snitch *(slang)*, purloin, filch, prig *(Brit. slang)*, shoplift, thieve, be light-fingered, peculate, walk *or* make off with: *People who are drug addicts come in and steal stuff.* **2 = copy**, take, plagiarize, appropriate, pinch *(informal)*, pirate, poach: *They solved the problem by stealing an idea from nature.* **3 = sneak**, slip, creep, flit, tiptoe, slink, insinuate yourself: *They can steal away at night and join us.*

stealth NOUN **= secrecy**, furtiveness, slyness, sneakiness, unobtrusiveness, stealthiness, surreptitiousness: *Both sides advanced by stealth*

stealthy ADJECTIVE **= secret**, secretive, furtive, sneaking, covert, sly, clandestine, sneaky, skulking, underhand, surreptitious

steamy ADJECTIVE **1 = erotic**, hot *(slang)*, sexy *(informal)*, sensual, raunchy *(slang)*, lewd, carnal, titillating, prurient, lascivious, lustful, lubricious *(formal, literary)*: *He'd had a steamy affair with an office colleague.* **2 = muggy**, damp, humid, sweaty, like a sauna: *a steamy café*

steep[1] ADJECTIVE **1 = sheer**, precipitous, perpendicular, abrupt, headlong, vertical: *a narrow, steep-sided valley* **OPPOSITE:** gradual **2 = sharp**, sudden, abrupt, marked, extreme, distinct: *Unemployment has shown a steep rise.* **3 = high**, excessive, exorbitant, extreme, stiff, unreasonable, overpriced, extortionate, uncalled-for: *The annual premium can be a little steep.* **OPPOSITE:** reasonable

steep[2] VERB **= soak**, immerse, marinate *(Cookery)*, damp, submerge, drench, moisten, macerate, souse, imbrue *(rare)*: *green beans steeped in olive oil*

steeped ADJECTIVE **= saturated**, pervaded, permeated, filled, infused, imbued, suffused

steer VERB **1 = drive**, control, direct, handle, conduct, pilot, govern, be in the driver's seat: *What is it like to steer a ship of this size?* **2 = direct**, lead, guide, conduct, escort, show in *or* out: *Nick steered them into the nearest seats.*
steer clear of something *or* **someone = avoid**, evade, fight shy of, shun, eschew, circumvent, body-swerve *(Scot.)*, give a wide berth to, sheer off: *A lot of people steer clear of these sensitive issues.*

stem[1] NOUN **= stalk**, branch, trunk, shoot, stock, axis, peduncle: *He cut the stem for her and handed her the flower.*
stem from something = originate from, be caused by, derive from, arise from, flow from, emanate from, develop from, be generated by, be brought about by, be bred by, issue forth from: *Much of the instability stems from the economic effects of the war.*

stem[2] VERB **= stop**, hold back, staunch, stay *(archaic)*, check, contain, dam, curb, restrain, bring to a standstill, stanch: *He was still conscious, trying to stem the bleeding with his right hand.*

stench NOUN **= stink**, whiff *(Brit. slang)*, reek, pong *(Brit. informal)*, foul smell, niff *(Brit. slang)*, malodour, mephitis, noisomeness

step NOUN **1 = pace**, stride, footstep: *I took a step towards him.* **2 = footfall**: *He heard steps in the corridor.* **3 = stair**, tread, rung: *He slowly climbed the steps.* **4 = move**, measure, action, means, act, proceeding, procedure, manoeuvre, deed, expedient: *He greeted the agreement as the first step towards peace.* **5 = stage**, point, phase: *Aristotle took the scientific approach a step further.* **6 = gait**, walk: *He quickened his step.* **7 = level**, rank, remove, degree: *This is the final step in the career ladder.*
▷ VERB **= walk**, pace, tread, move: *the first man to step on the moon*
in step = in agreement, in harmony, in unison, in line, coinciding, conforming, in conformity: *Now they are more in step and more in love with each other.*
mind *or* **watch your step = be careful**, take care, look out, be cautious, be discreet, take heed, tread carefully, be canny, be on your guard, mind how you go, have your wits about you, mind your p's and q's: *Hey! she thought. Watch your step, girl!*
out of step = in disagreement, out of line, out of phase, out of harmony, incongruous, pulling different ways: *They jogged in silence a while, faces lowered, out of step.*
step down *or* **aside = resign**, retire, quit, leave, give up, pull out, bow out, abdicate: *Many would prefer to see him step aside in favour of a younger man.*
step in = intervene, take action, become involved, chip in *(informal)*, intercede, take a hand: *If no agreement was reached, the army would step in.*
step something up = increase, boost, intensify, up, raise, accelerate, speed up, escalate, augment: *Security is being stepped up to deal with the increase in violence.*
take steps = take action, act, intervene, move in, take the initiative, take measures: *They agreed to take steps to avoid confrontation.*

PROVERBS
one step at a time

stereotype NOUN **= formula**, cliché, pattern, mould, received idea: *Accents can reinforce a stereotype.*
▷ VERB **= categorize**, typecast, pigeonhole, dub, standardize, take to be, ghettoize, conventionalize: *He was stereotyped by some as a renegade.*

stereotyped ADJECTIVE **= unoriginal**, stock, standard, tired, conventional, played out, stale, banal, standardized, mass-produced, corny *(slang)*, threadbare, trite, hackneyed, overused, platitudinous, cliché-ridden

sterile ADJECTIVE **1 = germ-free**, antiseptic, sterilized, disinfected, aseptic: *He always made sure that any cuts were protected by sterile dressings.* **OPPOSITE:** unhygienic **2 = barren**, infertile, unproductive, childless, infecund: *a sterile male* **OPPOSITE:** fertile

sterilize VERB **= disinfect**, purify, fumigate, decontaminate, autoclave, sanitize: *Sulphur is also used to sterilize equipment.*

sterling ADJECTIVE **= excellent**, sound, fine, first-class, superlative

stern ADJECTIVE **1 = strict**, harsh, rigorous, hard, cruel, grim, rigid, relentless, drastic, authoritarian, austere, inflexible, unrelenting, unyielding, unsparing: *He said stern measures would be taken against the killers.* **OPPOSITE:** lenient **2 = severe**, serious, forbidding, steely, boot-faced *(informal)*, flinty: *Her father was stern and hard to please.* **OPPOSITE:** friendly

stew NOUN **= hash**, goulash, ragout, olla, olio, olla podrida: *She served him a bowl of beef stew.*
▷ VERB **= braise**, boil, simmer, casserole: *Stew the apple and blackberries to make a thick pulp.*
in a stew = troubled, concerned, anxious, worried, fretting, in a panic, in a lather *(informal)*: *Highly charged emotions have you in a stew.*

stick[1] NOUN **1 = twig**, branch, birch, offshoot: *people carrying bundles of dry sticks to sell for firewood* **2 = cane**, staff, pole, rod, stake, switch, crook, baton, wand, sceptre: *Crowds armed with sticks and stones took to the streets.* **3 = abuse**, criticism, flak *(informal)*, blame, knocking *(informal)*, hostility, slagging *(slang)*, denigration, critical remarks, fault-finding: *It's not motorists who give you the most stick, it's the general public.*

stick[2] VERB **1 = put**, place, set, position, drop, plant, store, lay, stuff, fix, deposit, install, plonk: *He folded the papers and stuck them in a drawer.* **2 = poke**, dig, stab, insert, thrust, pierce, penetrate, spear, prod, jab, transfix: *They stuck a needle in my back; The knife stuck in his chest.* **3 = fasten**, fix, bind, hold, bond, attach, hold on, glue, fuse, paste, adhere, affix: *Stick down any loose bits of flooring.* **4 = adhere**, cling, cleave, become joined, become cemented, become welded: *The soil sticks to the blade and blocks the plough.* **5 = stay**, remain, linger, persist: *That song has stuck in my head for years.* **6 = catch**, lodge, jam, stop, clog, snag, be embedded, be bogged down, come

S

to a standstill, become immobilized: *The dagger stuck tightly in the silver scabbard.* **7 = tolerate**, take, stand, stomach, endure, hack *(slang)*, abide, bear up under: *How long did you stick that abuse for?*
stick out = protrude, stand out, jut out, show, project, bulge, obtrude: *Your label's sticking out.*
stick something out 1 = offer, present, extend, hold out, advance, reach out, stretch out, proffer: *He stuck his hand out in welcome.* **2 = endure**, bear, put up with *(informal)*, weather, take it *(informal)*, see through, soldier on, last out, grin and bear it *(informal)*: *I know the job's tough, but try to stick it out a bit longer.*
stick to something 1 = keep to, persevere in, cleave to: *Stick to well-lit roads.* **2 = adhere to**, honour, hold to, keep to, abide by, stand by: *We must stick to the rules.*
stick up for someone = defend, support, champion, uphold, stand up for, take the part *or* side of: *Thanks for sticking up for me.*

stickler NOUN **= fanatic**, nut *(slang)*, maniac *(informal)*, purist, perfectionist, pedant, martinet, hard taskmaster, fusspot *(Brit. informal)*

sticky ADJECTIVE **1 = adhesive**, gummed, adherent, grippy: *Peel away the sticky paper.* **2 = gooey**, tacky *(informal)*, syrupy, viscous, glutinous, gummy, icky *(informal)*, gluey, clinging, claggy *(dialect)*, viscid: *a weakness for rich meat dishes and sticky puddings* **3 = difficult**, awkward, tricky, embarrassing, painful, nasty, delicate, unpleasant, discomforting, hairy *(slang)*, thorny, barro *(Austral. slang)*: *He found himself in a not inconsiderably sticky situation.* **4 = humid**, close, sultry, oppressive, sweltering, clammy, muggy: *sticky days in the middle of August*

stiff ADJECTIVE **1 = inflexible**, rigid, unyielding, hard, firm, tight, solid, tense, hardened, brittle, taut, solidified, unbending, inelastic: *The film is crammed with corsets, bustles and stiff collars.* **OPPOSITE:** flexible **2 = unsupple**, arthritic, creaky *(informal)*, rheumaticky: *I'm stiff all over right now.* **OPPOSITE:** supple **3 = formal**, constrained, forced, laboured, cold, mannered, wooden, artificial, uneasy, chilly, unnatural, austere, pompous, prim, stilted, starchy *(informal)*, punctilious, priggish, standoffish, ceremonious, unrelaxed: *They always seemed a little awkward with each other, a bit stiff and formal.* **OPPOSITE:** informal **4 = vigorous**, great, strong: *The film faces stiff competition for the nomination.* **5 = severe**, strict, harsh, hard, heavy, sharp, extreme, cruel, drastic, rigorous, stringent, oppressive, austere, inexorable, pitiless: *stiff anti-drugs laws* **6 = strong**, fresh, powerful, vigorous, brisk: *a stiff breeze rustling the trees* **7 = difficult**, hard, tough, exacting, formidable, trying, fatiguing, uphill, arduous, laborious: *the stiff climb to the finish*

stifle VERB **1 = suppress**, repress, prevent, stop, check, silence, curb, restrain, cover up, gag, hush, smother, extinguish, muffle, choke back: *Critics have accused them of trying to stifle debate.* **2 = restrain**, suppress, repress, smother: *She makes no attempt to stifle a yawn.*

stigma NOUN **= disgrace**, shame, dishonour, mark, spot, brand, stain, slur, blot, reproach, imputation, smirch

stigmatize VERB **= brand**, label, denounce, mark, discredit, pillory, defame, cast a slur upon

still ADJECTIVE **1 = motionless**, stationary, at rest, calm, smooth, peaceful, serene, tranquil, lifeless, placid, undisturbed, inert, restful, unruffled, unstirring: *He sat very still for several minutes.* **OPPOSITE:** moving **2 = silent**, quiet, hushed, noiseless, stilly *(poetic)*: *The night air was very still.* **OPPOSITE:** noisy
▷ VERB **= quieten**, calm, subdue, settle, quiet, silence, soothe, hush, alleviate, lull, tranquillize: *Her crying slowly stilled; The people's voice has been stilled.* **OPPOSITE:** get louder
▷ NOUN **= stillness**, peace, quiet, silence, hush, tranquillity: *It was the only noise in the still of the night.* **OPPOSITE:** noise
▷ ADVERB **= yet**, even now, up until now, up to this time: *I still dream of home.*
▷ SENTENCE CONNECTOR **= however**, but, yet, nevertheless, for all that, notwithstanding: *Despite the ruling, he was still found guilty; It won't be easy. Still, I'll do my best.*

stilted ADJECTIVE **= stiff**, forced, wooden, laboured, artificial, inflated, constrained, unnatural, high-flown, pompous, pretentious, pedantic, bombastic, grandiloquent, high-sounding, arty-farty *(informal)*, fustian **OPPOSITE:** natural

stimulant NOUN **= pick-me-up**, tonic, restorative, upper *(slang)*, reviver, bracer *(informal)*, energizer, pep pill *(informal)*, excitant, analeptic **OPPOSITE:** sedative

stimulate VERB **= encourage**, inspire, prompt, fire, fan, urge, spur, provoke, turn on *(slang)*, arouse, animate, rouse, prod, quicken, inflame, incite, instigate, goad, whet, impel, foment, gee up

stimulating ADJECTIVE **= exciting**, inspiring, stirring, provoking, intriguing, rousing, provocative, exhilarating, thought-provoking, galvanic **OPPOSITE:** boring

stimulus NOUN **= incentive**, spur, encouragement, impetus, provocation, inducement, goad, incitement, fillip, shot in the arm *(informal)*, clarion call, geeing-up

sting VERB **1 = hurt**, burn, wound: *The nettles stung their legs.* **2 = smart**, burn, pain, hurt, tingle: *His cheeks were stinging from the icy wind.* **3 = anger**, provoke, infuriate, incense, gall, inflame, nettle, rile, pique: *Some of the criticism has really stung him.*
▷ NOUN **= smarting**, pain, stinging, pricking, soreness, prickling: *This won't hurt – you will just feel a little sting.*

stingy ADJECTIVE **1 = mean**, penny-pinching *(informal)*, miserly, near, parsimonious, scrimping, illiberal, avaricious, niggardly, ungenerous, penurious, tightfisted, close-fisted, mingy *(Brit. informal)*, cheeseparing, snoep *(S. African informal)*: *The West is stingy with aid.* **2 = insufficient**, inadequate, meagre, small, pathetic, scant, skimpy, measly *(informal)*, scanty, on the small side: *Many people may consider this a rather stingy amount.*

stink VERB **1 = reek**, pong *(Brit. informal)*, whiff *(Brit. slang)*, stink to high heaven *(informal)*, offend the nostrils: *We all stank and nobody minded.* **2 = be bad**, be no good, be rotten, be offensive, be abhorrent, have a bad name, be detestable, be held in disrepute: *I think their methods stink.*
▷ NOUN **1 = stench**, pong *(Brit. informal)*, foul smell, foulness, malodour, fetor, noisomeness: *The stink was overpowering.* **2 = fuss**, to-do, row, upset, scandal, stir, disturbance, uproar, commotion, rumpus, hubbub, brouhaha, deal of trouble *(informal)*: *The family's making a hell of a stink.*

stinker NOUN **= scoundrel**, heel, sod *(slang)*, cad *(Brit. informal)*, swine, bounder *(Brit. old-fashioned, slang)*, cur, rotter *(slang, chiefly Brit.)*, nasty piece of work *(informal)*, dastard *(archaic)*, wrong 'un *(slang)*

stinking ADJECTIVE **1 = rotten**, disgusting, unpleasant, vile, contemptible, wretched: *I had a stinking cold.* **2 = foul-smelling**, smelly, reeking, fetid, malodorous, noisome, whiffy *(Brit. slang)*, pongy *(Brit. informal)*, mephitic, ill-smelling, niffy *(Brit. slang)*, olid, festy *(Austral. slang)*, yucko *(Austral. slang)*: *They were locked up in a stinking cell.*

stint NOUN **= term**, time, turn, bit, period, share, tour, shift, stretch, spell, quota, assignment: *a five-year stint in Hong Kong*
▷ VERB **= be mean**, hold back, be sparing, scrimp, skimp on, save, withhold, begrudge, economize, be frugal, be parsimonious, be mingy *(Brit. informal)*, spoil the ship for a ha'porth of tar: *He didn't stint on the special effects.*

stipulate VERB **= specify**, agree, require, promise, contract, settle, guarantee, engage, pledge, lay down, covenant, postulate, insist upon, lay down *or* impose conditions

stipulation NOUN **= condition**, requirement, provision, term, contract, agreement, settlement, rider, restriction, qualification, clause, engagement, specification, precondition, prerequisite, proviso, sine qua non *(Latin)*

stir VERB **1 = mix**, beat, agitate: *Stir the soup for a few seconds.* **2 = move**, change position: *The two women lay on their backs, not stirring.* **3 = get moving**, move, get a move on *(informal)*, hasten, budge, make an effort, be up and about *(informal)*, look lively *(informal)*, shake a leg *(informal)*, exert yourself, bestir yourself: *Stir yourself! We've got a visitor.* **4 = stimulate**, move, excite, fire, raise, touch, affect, urge, inspire, prompt, spur, thrill, provoke, arouse, awaken, animate, rouse, prod, quicken, inflame, incite, instigate, electrify, kindle: *I was intrigued by him, stirred by his intellect.* **OPPOSITE:** inhibit **5 = spur**, drive, prompt, stimulate, prod, press, urge, animate, prick, incite, goad, impel: *The sight of them stirred him into action.*
▷ NOUN **= commotion**, to-do, excitement, activity, movement, disorder, fuss, disturbance, bustle, flurry, uproar, ferment, agitation, ado, tumult: *His film has caused a stir in America.*

stirring ADJECTIVE **= exciting**, dramatic, thrilling, moving, spirited, inspiring, stimulating, lively, animating, rousing, heady, exhilarating, impassioned, emotive, intoxicating

stock NOUN **1 = shares**, holdings, securities, investments, bonds, equities: *Stock prices have dropped.* **2 = property**, capital, assets, funds: *The Fisher family holds 40% of the stock.* **3 = goods**, merchandise, wares, range, choice, variety, selection, commodities, array, assortment: *We took a decision to withdraw a quantity of stock from sale.* **4 = supply**, store, reserve, fund, reservoir, stockpile, hoard, cache: *a stock of ammunition* **5 = lineage**, descent, extraction, ancestry, house, family, line, race, type, variety, background, breed, strain, pedigree, forebears, parentage, line of descent: *We are both from working-class stock.* **6 = livestock**, cattle, beasts, domestic animals: *I am carefully selecting the breeding stock.*
▷ VERB **1 = sell**, supply, handle, keep, trade in, deal in: *The shop stocks everything from cigarettes to recycled loo paper.* **2 = fill**, supply, provide with, provision, equip, furnish, fit out, kit out: *I worked stocking shelves in a grocery store.*
▷ ADJECTIVE **1 = hackneyed**, standard, usual, set, routine, stereotyped, staple, commonplace, worn-out, banal, run-of-the-mill, trite, overused: *National security is the stock excuse for keeping things confidential.* **2 = regular**, traditional, usual, basic, ordinary, conventional, staple, customary: *They supply stock sizes outside the middle range.*
stock up with something = store (up), lay in, hoard, save, gather, accumulate, amass, buy up, put away, replenish supplies of: *New Yorkers have been stocking up with bottled water.*
take stock = review the situation, weigh up, appraise, estimate, size up *(informal)*, see how the land lies: *It was time to take stock of my life.*

stocky ADJECTIVE **= thickset**, solid, sturdy, chunky, stubby, dumpy, stumpy, mesomorphic

stodgy ADJECTIVE **1 = heavy**, filling, substantial, leaden, starchy: *He was disgusted by the stodgy pizzas on sale in London.* **OPPOSITE:** light **2 = dull**, boring, stuffy, formal, tedious, tiresome, staid, unimaginative, turgid, uninspired, unexciting, ho-hum, heavy going, fuddy-duddy *(informal)*, dull as ditchwater: *stodgy old fogies* **OPPOSITE:** exciting

stoical ADJECTIVE **= resigned**, long-suffering, phlegmatic, philosophic, cool, calm, indifferent, stoic, dispassionate, impassive, stolid, imperturbable

stoicism NOUN **= resignation**, acceptance, patience, indifference, fortitude, long-suffering, calmness, fatalism, forbearance, stolidity, dispassion, impassivity, imperturbability

stolen ADJECTIVE **= hot** *(slang)*, bent *(slang)*, hooky *(slang)*

stolid ADJECTIVE **= apathetic**, unemotional, dull, heavy, slow, wooden, stupid, bovine, dozy *(Brit. informal)*, obtuse, lumpish, doltish **OPPOSITE:** lively

stomach NOUN **1 = belly**, inside(s) *(informal)*, gut *(informal)*, abdomen, tummy *(informal)*, puku *(N.Z.)*: *My stomach is completely full.* **2 = tummy**, pot, spare tyre *(informal)*, paunch, breadbasket *(slang)*, potbelly: *This exercise strengthens the stomach, buttocks and thighs.* **3 = inclination**, taste, desire, appetite, relish, mind: *They have no stomach for a fight.*
▷ VERB **= bear**, take, tolerate, suffer, endure, swallow, hack *(slang)*, abide, put up with *(informal)*, submit to, reconcile *or* resign yourself to: *I could never stomach the cruelty involved in the wounding of animals.*

stone NOUN **1 = masonry**, rock: *He could not tell if the floor was wood or stone.* **2 = rock**, pebble: *The crowd began throwing stones.* **3 = pip**, seed, pit, kernel: *Old men sat beneath the plane trees and spat cherry stones at my feet.*

stony ADJECTIVE **1 = rocky**, rough, gritty, gravelly, rock-strewn, pebble: *a stony track* **2 = cold**, icy, hostile, hard, harsh, blank, adamant, indifferent, chilly, callous, heartless, merciless, unforgiving, inexorable, frigid, expressionless, unresponsive, pitiless, unfeeling, obdurate: *The stony look he was giving her made it hard to think.*

stooge NOUN **= pawn**, puppet, fall guy *(informal)*, butt, foil, patsy *(slang, chiefly U.S. & Canad.)*, dupe, henchman, lackey

stoop VERB **1 = hunch**, be bowed *or* round-shouldered: *She was taller than he was and stooped slightly.* **2 = bend**, lean, bow, duck, descend, incline, kneel, crouch, squat: *He stooped to pick up the carrier bag of groceries.*
▷ NOUN **= slouch**, slump, droop, sag, bad posture, round-shoulderedness: *He was a tall, thin fellow with a slight stoop.*
stoop to something = resort to, sink to, descend to, deign to, condescend to, demean yourself by, lower yourself by: *How could anyone stoop to doing such a thing?*

stop VERB **1 = quit**, cease, refrain, break off, put an end to, pack in *(Brit. informal)*, discontinue, leave off, call it a day *(informal)*, desist, belay *(Nautical)*, bring *or* come to a halt *or* standstill: *I've been told to lose weight and stop smoking.* **OPPOSITE:** start **2 = prevent**, suspend, cut short, close, break, check, bar, arrest, silence, frustrate, axe *(informal)*, interrupt, restrain, hold back, intercept, hinder, repress, impede, rein in, forestall, nip (something) in the bud: *I think she really would have liked to stop everything right there.* **OPPOSITE:** facilitate **3 = end**, conclude, finish, be over, cut out *(informal)*, terminate, come to an end, peter out: *The music stopped and the lights were turned up.* **OPPOSITE:** continue **4 = cease**, shut down, discontinue, desist: *His heart stopped three times.* **OPPOSITE:** continue **5 = halt**, pause, stall, draw up, pull up: *The car failed to stop at an army checkpoint.* **OPPOSITE:** keep going **6 = pause**, wait, rest, hesitate, deliberate, take a break, have a breather *(informal)*, stop briefly: *She doesn't stop to think about what she's saying.* **7 = stay**, rest, put up, lodge, sojourn *(literary)*, tarry, break your journey: *He insisted we stop at a small restaurant just outside Atlanta.*
▷ NOUN **1 = halt**, standstill: *He slowed the car almost to a stop.* **2 = station**, stage, halt, destination, depot, termination, terminus: *They waited at a bus stop.* **3 = stay**, break, visit, rest, stopover, sojourn *(literary)*: *The last stop in his lengthy tour was Paris.*

stopgap NOUN **= makeshift**, improvisation, temporary expedient, shift, resort, substitute: *It is not an acceptable long term solution, just a stopgap.*
▷ MODIFIER **= makeshift**, emergency, temporary, provisional, improvised, impromptu, rough-and-ready: *It was only ever intended as a stopgap solution.*

stoppage NOUN **1 = stopping**, halt, standstill, close, arrest, lay-off, shutdown, cutoff, abeyance, discontinuance: *a seven-hour stoppage by air-traffic controllers* **2 = blockage**, obstruction, stopping up, occlusion: *The small traffic disturbance will soon grow into a complete stoppage.*

store NOUN **1 = shop**, outlet, department store, market,

S

supermarket, mart, emporium, chain store, hypermarket: *Bombs were planted in stores in Manchester and Blackpool.* **2 = supply**, stock, reserve, lot, fund, mine, plenty, provision, wealth, quantity, reservoir, abundance, accumulation, stockpile, hoard, plethora, cache: *I handed over my store of chocolate biscuits.* **3 = repository**, warehouse, depot, storehouse, depository, storeroom: *a grain store*
▷ VERB **1** *(often with* **away** *or* **up***)* **= put by**, save, hoard, keep, stock, husband, reserve, deposit, accumulate, garner, stockpile, put aside, stash *(informal)*, salt away, keep in reserve, put aside for a rainy day, lay by *or* in: *storing away cash that will come in useful later on* **2 = put away**, put in storage, put in store, lock away: *Some types of garden furniture must be stored inside in the winter.* **3 = keep**, hold, preserve, maintain, retain, conserve: *chips for storing data*
set great store by something = value, prize, esteem, appreciate, hold in high regard, think highly of: *a retail group that sets great store by traditional values*

storm NOUN **1 = tempest**, blast, hurricane, gale, tornado, cyclone, blizzard, whirlwind, gust, squall: *the violent storms which whipped America's East Coast* **2 = outburst**, row, stir, outcry, furore, violence, anger, passion, outbreak, turmoil, disturbance, strife, clamour, agitation, commotion, rumpus, tumult, hubbub: *The photos caused a storm when they were first published.* **3 = roar**, thunder, clamour, din: *His speech was greeted with a storm of applause.* **4 = barrage**, volley, salvo, rain, shower, spray, discharge, fusillade: *a storm of missiles*
▷ VERB **1 = rush**, stamp, flounce, fly, stalk, stomp *(informal)*: *After a bit of an argument, he stormed out.* **2 = rage**, fume, rant, complain, thunder, rave, scold, bluster, go ballistic *(slang, chiefly U.S.)*, fly off the handle *(informal)*, wig out *(slang)*: *'It's a fiasco,' he stormed.* **3 = attack**, charge, rush, assault, beset, assail, take by storm: *The refugees decided to storm the embassy.*

stormy ADJECTIVE **1 = wild**, rough, tempestuous, raging, dirty, foul, turbulent, windy, blustering, blustery, gusty, inclement, squally: *the long stormy winter of 1942* **2 = rough**, wild, turbulent, tempestuous, raging: *the stormy waters that surround the British Isles* **3 = angry**, heated, fierce, passionate, fiery, impassioned, tumultuous: *The letter was read at a stormy meeting.*

story NOUN **1 = tale**, romance, narrative, record, history, version, novel, legend, chronicle, yarn, recital, narration, urban myth, urban legend, fictional account: *a popular love story with a happy ending* **2 = anecdote**, account, tale, report, detail, relation: *The parents all shared interesting stories about their children.* **3 = lie**, falsehood, fib, fiction, untruth, porky *(Brit. slang)*, pork pie *(Brit. slang)*, white lie: *He invented some story about a cousin.* **4 = report**, news, article, feature, scoop, news item: *Those are some of the top stories in the news.*

storyteller NOUN **= raconteur**, author, narrator, romancer, novelist, chronicler, bard, fabulist, spinner of yarns, anecdotist

stout ADJECTIVE **1 = fat**, big, heavy, overweight, plump, bulky, substantial, burly, obese, fleshy, tubby, portly, rotund, corpulent, on the large *or* heavy side: *exercises ideal for stout women of maturer years*
OPPOSITE: slim **2 = strong**, strapping, muscular, tough, substantial, athletic, hardy, robust, vigorous, sturdy, stalwart, husky *(informal)*, hulking, beefy *(informal)*, lusty, brawny, thickset, able-bodied: *a great stout fellow, big in brawn and bone*
OPPOSITE: puny **3 = brave**, bold, courageous, fearless, resolute, gallant, intrepid, valiant, plucky, doughty, indomitable, dauntless, lion-hearted, valorous: *The invasion was held up by unexpectedly stout resistance.*
OPPOSITE: timid

stow VERB **= pack**, load, put away, store, stuff, deposit, jam, tuck, bundle, cram, stash *(informal)*, secrete

straggle VERB **= trail**, drift, wander, range, lag, stray, roam, ramble, rove, loiter, string out

straggly ADJECTIVE **= spread out**, spreading, rambling, untidy, loose, drifting, random, straying, irregular, aimless, disorganized, straggling

straight ADJECTIVE **1 = direct**, unswerving, undeviating: *Keep the boat in a straight line.* **OPPOSITE:** indirect **2 = level**, even, right, square, true, smooth, in line, aligned, horizontal: *There wasn't a single straight wall in the building.* **OPPOSITE:** crooked **3 = frank**, plain, straightforward, blunt, outright, honest, downright, candid, forthright, bold, point-blank, upfront *(informal)*, unqualified: *a straight answer to a straight question* **OPPOSITE:** evasive **4 = successive**, consecutive, continuous, through, running, solid, sustained, uninterrupted, nonstop, unrelieved: *They'd won twelve straight games before they lost.*
OPPOSITE: discontinuous
5 = conventional, conservative, orthodox, traditional, square *(informal)*, bourgeois, Pooterish: *Dorothy was described as a very straight woman.* **OPPOSITE:** fashionable
6 = honest, just, fair, decent, reliable, respectable, upright, honourable, equitable, law-abiding, trustworthy, above board, fair and square: *You need to be straight with them to gain their respect.*
OPPOSITE: dishonest **7 = undiluted**, pure, neat, unadulterated, unmixed: *a large straight whisky, with ice* **8 = in order**, organized, arranged, sorted out, neat, tidy, orderly, shipshape, put to rights: *We need to get the house straight again before they come home.*
OPPOSITE: untidy
▷ ADVERB **1 = directly**, precisely, exactly, as the crow flies, unswervingly, by the shortest route, in a beeline: *Straight ahead were the low cabins of the motel.* **2 = immediately**, directly, promptly, instantly, at once, straightaway, without delay, without hesitation, forthwith, unhesitatingly, before you could say Jack Robinson *(informal)*: *As always, we went straight to the experts for advice.*
3 = frankly, honestly, point-blank, candidly, pulling no punches *(informal)*, in plain English, with no holds barred: *I told him straight that I had been looking for another job.*

straightaway ADVERB **= immediately**, now, at once, directly, instantly, on the spot, right away, there and then, this minute, straightway *(archaic)*, without more ado, without any delay

straighten VERB **= neaten**, arrange, tidy (up), order, spruce up, smarten up, put in order, set *or* put to rights: *She looked in the mirror and straightened her hair.*
straighten something out = sort out, resolve, put right, settle, correct, work out, clear up, rectify, disentangle, unsnarl: *My sister had come in with her common sense and straightened things out.*

straightforward ADJECTIVE **1 = simple**, easy, uncomplicated, routine, elementary, clear-cut, undemanding, easy-peasy *(slang)*: *The question seemed straightforward enough.*
OPPOSITE: complicated **2 = honest**, open, direct, genuine, sincere, candid, truthful, forthright, upfront *(informal)*, dinkum *(Austral. & N.Z. informal)*, above board, guileless: *I was impressed by his straightforward intelligent manner.* **OPPOSITE:** devious

strain[1] NOUN **1 = pressure**, stress, difficulty, demands, burden, adversity: *The prison service is already under considerable strain.* **2 = stress**, pressure, anxiety, difficulty, distress, nervous tension: *She was tired and under great strain.* **3 = worry**, effort, struggle, tension, hassle: *the strain of being responsible for the mortgage*
OPPOSITE: ease **4 = burden**, tension: *Place your hands under your buttocks to take some of the strain off your back.* **5 = injury**, wrench, sprain, pull, tension, tautness, tensity *(rare)*: *a groin strain*
6 = tune, air, melody, measure *(poetic)*, lay, song, theme: *She could hear the tinny strains of a chamber orchestra.*
▷ VERB **1 = stretch**, test, tax, overtax, push to the limit: *Resources will be further strained by new demands for housing.*
2 = injure, wrench, sprain, damage, pull, tear, hurt, twist, rick: *He strained his back during a practice session.*
3 = strive, struggle, endeavour,

S

labour, go for it *(informal)*, bend over backwards *(informal)*, go for broke *(slang)*, go all out for *(informal)*, bust a gut *(informal)*, give it your best shot *(informal)*, make an all-out effort *(informal)*, knock yourself out *(informal)*, do your damnedest *(informal)*, give it your all *(informal)*, break your back *or* neck *(informal)*, rupture yourself *(informal)*: *Several thousand supporters strained to catch a glimpse of the new president.* **OPPOSITE:** relax **4 = sieve**, filter, sift, screen, separate, riddle, purify: *Strain the stock and put it back in the pan.*

strain² NOUN **1 = trace**, suggestion, suspicion, tendency, streak, trait: *There was a strain of bitterness in his voice.* **2 = breed**, type, stock, family, race, blood, descent, pedigree, extraction, ancestry, lineage: *a particularly beautiful strain of Swiss pansies*

strained ADJECTIVE **1 = tense**, difficult, uncomfortable, awkward, embarrassed, stiff, uneasy, constrained, self-conscious, unrelaxed: *a period of strained relations* **OPPOSITE:** relaxed **2 = forced**, put on, false, artificial, unnatural, laboured: *His laughter seemed a little strained.* **OPPOSITE:** natural

strait NOUN *(often plural)* **= channel**, sound, narrows, stretch of water, sea passage: *Thousands of vessels pass through the straits annually.*
▷ PLURAL NOUN **= difficulty**, crisis, mess, pass, hole *(slang)*, emergency, distress, dilemma, embarrassment, plight, hardship, uphill *(S. African)*, predicament, extremity, perplexity, panic stations *(informal)*, pretty *or* fine kettle of fish *(informal)*: *If we had a child, we'd be in really dire straits.*

strand NOUN **= filament**, fibre, thread, length, lock, string, twist, rope, wisp, tress

stranded ADJECTIVE **1 = beached**, grounded, marooned, ashore, shipwrecked, aground, cast away: *He returned to his stranded vessel yesterday afternoon.* **2 = helpless**, abandoned, high and dry, left in the lurch: *He left me stranded by the side of the road.*

strange ADJECTIVE **1 = odd**, unusual, curious, weird, wonderful, rare, funny, extraordinary, remarkable, bizarre, fantastic, astonishing, marvellous, exceptional, peculiar, eccentric, abnormal, out-of-the-way, queer, irregular, rum *(Brit. slang)*, uncommon, singular, perplexing, uncanny, mystifying, unheard-of, off-the-wall *(slang)*, oddball *(informal)*, unaccountable, left-field *(informal)*, outré, curiouser and curiouser, daggy *(Austral. & N.Z. informal)*: *There was something strange about the flickering blue light.* **OPPOSITE:** ordinary **2 = out of place**, lost, uncomfortable, awkward, bewildered, disoriented, ill at ease, like a fish out of water: *I felt strange in his office, realizing how absurd it was.* **OPPOSITE:** comfortable **3 = unfamiliar**, new, unknown, foreign, novel, alien, exotic, untried, unexplored, outside your experience: *I ended up alone in a strange city.* **OPPOSITE:** familiar

stranger NOUN **1 = unknown person**: *Sometimes I feel like I'm living with a stranger.* **2 = newcomer**, incomer, foreigner, guest, visitor, unknown, alien, new arrival, outlander: *Being a stranger in town can be a painful experience.*
a stranger to something = unaccustomed to, new to, unused to, ignorant of, inexperienced in, unversed in, unpractised in, unseasoned in: *He is no stranger to controversy.*
▸ *related phobia:* xenophobia

QUOTATIONS
a stranger in a strange land
[*Bible: Exodus*]

strangle VERB **1 = throttle**, choke, asphyxiate, garrotte, strangulate, smother, suffocate: *He was almost strangled by his parachute harness straps.* **2 = suppress**, inhibit, subdue, stifle, gag, repress, overpower, quash, quell, quench: *His creative drive has been strangled by his sense of guilt.*

strap NOUN **= tie**, thong, leash, belt: *Nancy gripped the strap of her beach bag.*
▷ VERB **= fasten**, tie, secure, bind, lash, buckle, truss: *She strapped the gun belt around her waist.*

strapping ADJECTIVE **= well-built**, big, powerful, robust, hefty *(informal)*, sturdy, stalwart, burly, husky *(informal)*, hulking, beefy *(informal)*, brawny, well set-up

stratagem NOUN **= trick**, scheme, manoeuvre, plan, plot, device, intrigue, dodge, ploy, ruse, artifice, subterfuge, feint, wile

strategic ADJECTIVE **1 = tactical**, calculated, deliberate, planned, politic, diplomatic: *a strategic plan for reducing the rate of infant mortality* **2 = crucial**, important, key, vital, critical, decisive, cardinal: *an operation to take the strategic island*

strategy NOUN **1 = policy**, procedure, planning, programme, approach, scheme, manoeuvring, grand design: *Community involvement is now integral to company strategy.* **2 = plan**, approach, scheme, manoeuvring, grand design: *the basic principles of my strategy*

stratum NOUN **1 = class**, group, level, station, estate, rank, grade, category, bracket, caste: *It was an enormous task that affected every stratum of society.* **2 = layer**, level, seam, table, bed, vein, tier, stratification, lode: *The rock strata show that the region was intensely dry 15,000 years ago.*

USAGE
The word *strata* is the plural form of *stratum*, and should not be used as if it is a singular form: so you would say *This stratum of society is often disregarded*, or *These strata of society are often disregarded*, but not *This strata of society is often disregarded*.

stray VERB **1 = wander**, roam, go astray, range, drift, meander, rove, straggle, lose your way, be abandoned or lost: *A railway line crosses the park so children must not be allowed to stray.* **2 = drift**, wander, roam, meander, rove: *She could not keep her eyes from straying towards him.* **3 = digress**, diverge, deviate, ramble, get sidetracked, go off at a tangent, get off the point: *Anyway, as usual, we seem to have strayed from the point.*
▷ MODIFIER **= lost**, abandoned, homeless, roaming, vagrant: *A stray dog came up to him.*
▷ ADJECTIVE **= random**, chance, freak, accidental, odd, scattered, erratic, scattershot: *An 8-year-old boy was killed by a stray bullet.*

streak NOUN **1 = band**, line, strip, stroke, layer, slash, vein, stripe, smear: *There are these dark streaks on the surface of the moon.* **2 = trace**, touch, element, strain, dash, vein: *He's still got a mean streak.*
▷ VERB **1 = fleck**, smear, daub, band, slash, stripe, striate: *Rain had begun to streak the window pains.* **2 = speed**, fly, tear, sweep, flash, barrel (along) *(informal, chiefly U.S. & Canad.)*, whistle, sprint, dart, zoom, whizz *(informal)*, hurtle, burn rubber *(informal)*, move like greased lightning *(informal)*: *A meteorite streaked across the sky.*

stream NOUN **1 = river**, brook, creek *(U.S.)*, burn *(Scot.)*, beck, tributary, bayou, rivulet, rill, freshet: *a mountain stream* **2 = flow**, current, rush, run, course, drift, surge, tide, torrent, outpouring, tideway: *a continuous stream of lava* **3 = succession**, series, flood, chain, battery, volley, avalanche, barrage, torrent: *a never-ending stream of jokes*
▷ VERB **1 = flow**, run, pour, course, issue, flood, shed, spill, emit, glide, cascade, gush, spout: *Tears streamed down their faces.* **2 = rush**, fly, speed, tear, flood, pour: *The traffic streamed past him.*

streamer NOUN **= banner**, flag, pennant, standard, colours, ribbon, ensign, pennon

streamlined ADJECTIVE **= efficient**, organized, modernized, rationalized, smooth, slick, sleek, well-run, time-saving, smooth-running

street NOUN **= road**, lane, avenue, terrace, row, boulevard, roadway, thoroughfare
up one's street = to one's liking, to one's taste, one's cup of tea *(informal)*, pleasing, familiar, suitable, acceptable, compatible, congenial: *She loved it, this was right up her street.*

strength NOUN **1 = might**, muscle, brawn, sinew, brawniness: *He threw it forward with all his strength.* **OPPOSITE:** weakness **2 = will**, spirit, resolution, resolve, courage, character, nerve, determination, pluck, stamina, grit, backbone, fortitude, toughness, tenacity,

The Language of Edgar Allan Poe

Edgar Allan Poe (1809–49) was an American poet, writer, and literary critic. He is best known for his short stories, and is often considered to be the father of this mode. He was also one of the earliest writers of detective fiction in English. Poe's stories are dark and gothic, dealing with themes of death, madness, and guilt. For example, in one of his most famous stories, 'The Tell-Tale Heart', the narrator murders an old man, chops his body up and hides the parts under the floor. He eventually gives away his guilt by losing his mind over what he believes to be the noise of the old man's heart continuing to beat under the floorboards.

The noun most frequently used in Poe's works is *time*, which is often modified by *long*. Indeed, time is an oppressive concept in Poe's stories: another frequent noun is *hour*, and as well as being *long*, *hours* are *evil*, *corrosive*, and *leaden-footed*. We read of the *many hours* in which horror is endured:

> **Long – long – long** – many minutes, many hours, many days, have I heard it – yet I dared not – oh, pity me, miserable wretch that I am! – I dared not – *I dared not speak!*

Furthermore, time is often presented as negative in phrases such as *no longer* and *no more*. *Nevermore* occurs only in Poe's famous poem 'The Raven' (in which the bird of the title – the 'prophet' and 'thing of evil' – ominously repeats the word *nevermore*) but *no more* is frequent in Poe's other works, occurring more than five times as often as it does in modern English, in sentences such as 'He was stone dead. His eye would trouble me **no more**.' *Nothing more* is also frequent, and *nothing* on its own occurs nearly three times as often in Poe's works as in general modern English, in sentences such as:

> I felt **nothing**; yet dreaded to move a step, lest I should be impeded by the walls of a tomb.

The repeated use of negatives such as these contributes to the overall sense of emptiness and despair in Poe's works.

Day and *night* are also among Poe's fifteen most frequent nouns, and their collocates evoke the gothic nature of his work. *Day* tends to be used neutrally as a simple reference to time, in phrases such as *the next day* and *a few days*. *Night*, on the other hand, has much stronger connotations: nights are *eternal*, *sleepless*, *wakeful*, *dreary*, and *fearful*

Poe's most frequent adjective is *great*, and its most frequent collocate is *difficulty*; we read of characters finding *great difficulty* breathing, for example. Another of Poe's top ten adjectives is *long*, and all its most frequent collocates relate to time: *long intervals*, *long hours*, *long periods*, and a *long time*. *Human* is also recurrent, often with reference to evidence in the detective stories, in collocations such as *human hair* and *human bones*. It is also used to distance and depersonalize characters, for example in *a shrouded human figure*.

The most striking feature of Poe's use of adverbs is his tendency to repeat them in order to build tension and suspense:

> ...but **gradually – very gradually** – I came to look upon it with unutterable loathing.

> I undid the lantern **cautiously – oh, so cautiously – cautiously** (for the hinges creaked)...

Poe also uses emphatic adverbs frequently: characters are *utterly* speechless; the sun is *entirely* blotted from the sky; a head is *absolutely* severed from its body; limbs are *exceedingly* emaciated.

Another distinctive feature of Poe's prose is his use of punctuation. He makes heavy use of dashes and exclamation marks to portray the often disjointed and violent emotions of his narrators and characters, as in the final lines of 'The Tell-Tale Heart':

> 'Villains!' I shrieked, 'dissemble no more! I admit the deed! – tear up the planks! – here, here! – it is the beating of his hideous heart!'

willpower, mettle, firmness, strength of character, steadfastness, moral fibre: *Something gave me the strength to overcome the difficulty.* **3 = health**, fitness, vigour, lustiness: *It'll take a while before you regain full strength.* **4 = mainstay**, anchor, tower of strength, security, succour: *He was my strength during that terrible time.* **5 = toughness**, soundness, robustness, sturdiness, stoutness: *He checked the strength of the cables.* **6 = force**, power, intensity, energy, vehemence, intenseness: *He was surprised at the strength of his own feeling.* **OPPOSITE:** weakness **7 = potency**, effectiveness, concentration, efficacy: *maximum-strength migraine tablets* **8 = strong point**, skill, asset, advantage, talent, forte, speciality, aptitude: *Take into account your own strengths and weaknesses.* **OPPOSITE:** failing

strengthen VERB **1 = fortify**, encourage, harden, toughen, consolidate, stiffen, hearten, gee up, brace up, give new energy to: *Such antagonism, he has asserted, strengthened his resolve.* **OPPOSITE:** weaken **2 = reinforce**, support, confirm, establish, justify, enhance, intensify, bolster, substantiate, buttress, corroborate, give a boost to: *Research would strengthen the case for socialist reform.* **3 = bolster**, harden, reinforce, give a boost to: *Any experience can teach and strengthen you.* **4 = heighten**, intensify: *Every day of sunshine strengthens the feeling of optimism.* **5 = make stronger**, build up, invigorate, restore, nourish, rejuvenate, give strength to: *Yoga can be used to strengthen the immune system.* **6 = support**, brace, steel, reinforce, consolidate, harden, bolster, augment, buttress: *The builders will have to strengthen the existing joists with additional timber.* **7 = become stronger**, intensify, heighten, gain strength: *As it strengthened, the wind was veering southerly.*

strenuous ADJECTIVE **1 = demanding**, hard, tough, exhausting, taxing, uphill, arduous, laborious, Herculean, tough going, toilsome, unrelaxing: *Avoid strenuous exercise in the evening.* **OPPOSITE:** easy **2 = tireless**, determined, zealous, strong, earnest, spirited, active, eager, bold, persistent, vigorous, energetic, resolute: *Strenuous efforts have been made to improve conditions in the jail.*

stress VERB **1 = emphasize**, highlight, underline, repeat, draw attention to, dwell on, underscore, accentuate, point up, rub in, flag up, harp on, belabour: *He stressed the need for new measures.* **2 = place the emphasis on**, emphasize, give emphasis to, place the accent on, lay emphasis upon: *She stresses the syllables as though teaching a child.*
▷ NOUN **1 = emphasis**, importance, significance, force, weight, urgency: *Japanese car makers are laying ever more stress on European sales.* **2 = strain**, pressure, worry, tension, burden, anxiety, trauma, oppression, hassle (*informal*), nervous tension: *Katy could not think clearly when under stress.* **3 = accent**, beat, emphasis, accentuation, ictus: *the misplaced stress on the first syllable*

> **QUOTATIONS**
> I don't have ulcers, I give them
> [Harry Cohn]

stressful ADJECTIVE **= worrying**, anxious, tense, taxing, demanding, tough, draining, exhausting, exacting, traumatic, agitating, nerve-racking

stretch VERB **1 = extend**, cover, spread, reach, unfold, put forth, unroll: *an artificial reef stretching the length of the coast* **2 = last**, continue, go on, extend, carry on, reach: *Protests stretched into their second week.* **3 = expand**, lengthen, be elastic, be stretchy: *The cables are designed not to stretch.* **4 = pull**, distend, pull out of shape, strain, swell, tighten, rack, inflate, lengthen, draw out, elongate: *Make sure you don't stretch the pastry as you ease it into the corners.* **5 = hold out**, offer, present, extend, proffer: *She stretched out her hand and slowly led him upstairs.*
▷ NOUN **1 = expanse**, area, tract, spread, distance, sweep, extent: *It's a very dangerous stretch of road.* **2 = period**, time, spell, stint, run, term, bit, space: *He would study for eight- to ten-hour stretches.*

strew VERB **= scatter**, spread, litter, toss, sprinkle, disperse, bestrew

stricken ADJECTIVE **= affected**, hit, afflicted, struck, injured, struck down, smitten, laid low

strict ADJECTIVE **1 = severe**, harsh, stern, firm, rigid, rigorous, stringent, austere: *French privacy laws are very strict.* **OPPOSITE:** easy-going **2 = stern**, firm, severe, harsh, authoritarian, austere, no-nonsense: *My parents were very strict.* **3 = exact**, accurate, precise, close, true, particular, religious, faithful, meticulous, scrupulous: *the strictest sense of the word* **4 = devout**, religious, orthodox, pious, pure, reverent, prayerful: *a strict Catholic* **5 = absolute**, complete, total, perfect, utter: *Your enquiry will be handled in strict confidence.*

stricture NOUN **= criticism**, censure, stick (*slang*), blame, rebuke, flak (*informal*), bad press, animadversion

strident ADJECTIVE **= harsh**, jarring, grating, clashing, screeching, raucous, shrill, rasping, jangling, discordant, clamorous, unmusical, stridulant, stridulous **OPPOSITE:** soft

strife NOUN **= conflict**, battle, struggle, row, clash, clashes, contest, controversy, combat, warfare, rivalry, contention, quarrel, friction, squabbling, wrangling, bickering, animosity, discord, dissension

strike NOUN **= walkout**, industrial action, mutiny, revolt, stop-work *or* stop-work meeting (*Austral.*): *a call for a strike*
▷ VERB **1 = walk out**, take industrial action, down tools, revolt, mutiny: *their recognition of the worker's right to strike* **2 = hit**, smack, thump, pound, beat, box, knock, punch, hammer, deck (*slang*), slap, sock (*slang*), chin (*slang*), buffet, clout (*informal*), cuff, clump (*slang*), swipe, clobber (*slang*), smite, wallop (*informal*), lambast(e), lay a finger on (*informal*), lay one on (*slang*), beat *or* knock seven bells out of (*informal*): *She took two steps forward and struck him across the mouth.* **3 = drive**, propel, force, hit, smack, wallop (*informal*): *He struck the ball straight into the hospitality tents.* **4 = collide with**, hit, run into, bump into, touch, smash into, come into contact with, knock into, be in collision with: *He was killed when a car struck him.* **5 = knock**, bang, smack, thump, beat, smite: *He fell and struck his head on the stone floor.* **6 = affect**, move, hit, touch, devastate, overwhelm, leave a mark on, make an impact *or* impression on: *He was suddenly struck with a sense of loss.* **7 = attack**, assault someone, fall upon someone, set upon someone, lay into someone (*informal*): *The killer says he will strike again.* **8 = occur to**, hit, come to, register (*informal*), come to the mind of, dawn on *or* upon: *At this point, it suddenly struck me that I was wasting my time.* **9 = seem to**, appear to, look to, give the impression to: *He struck me as a very serious but friendly person.* **10 = move**, touch, impress, hit, affect, overcome, stir, disturb, perturb, make an impact on: *She was struck by his simple, spellbinding eloquence.* **11 = achieve**, arrive at, attain, reach, effect, arrange: *You have to strike a balance between sleep and homework.* **12** (*sometimes with* **upon**) **= discover**, find, come upon *or* across, reach, encounter, turn up, uncover, unearth, hit upon, light upon, happen *or* chance upon, stumble upon *or* across: *He realized he had just struck oil.*
strike out = set out, set off, start out, sally forth: *They left the car and struck out along the muddy track.*
strike someone down = kill, destroy, slay, ruin, afflict, smite, bring low, deal a deathblow to: *a great sporting hero, struck down at 49*
strike something out *or* **off** *or* **through = score out**, delete, cross out, remove, cancel, erase, excise, efface, expunge: *The censor struck out the next two lines.*

striking ADJECTIVE **1 = distinct**, noticeable, conspicuous, clear, obvious, evident, manifest, unmistakable, observable, perceptible, appreciable: *He bears a striking resemblance to Lenin.* **2 = impressive**, dramatic, stunning (*informal*), wonderful, extraordinary, outstanding, astonishing,

S

memorable, dazzling, noticeable, conspicuous, drop-dead *(slang)*, out of the ordinary, forcible, jaw-dropping, eye-popping *(informal)*: *She was a striking woman with long blonde hair.* **OPPOSITE:** unimpressive

string NOUN **1 = cord**, yarn, twine, strand, fibre, thread: *He held out a small bag tied with string.* **2 = series**, line, row, file, sequence, queue, succession, procession: *The landscape is broken only by a string of villages.* **3 = sequence**, run, series, chain, succession, streak: *The incident was the latest in a string of attacks.* ▷ PLURAL NOUN **1 = stringed instruments**: *The strings provided a melodic background.* **2 = conditions**, catches *(informal)*, provisos, stipulations, requirements, riders, obligations, qualifications, complications, prerequisites: *an offer made in good faith, with no strings attached* ▷ VERB **= hang**, stretch, suspend, sling, thread, loop, festoon: *He had strung a banner across the wall.* **string along with someone = accompany**, go with, go along with, chaperon: *Can I string along with you for a while?* **string someone along = deceive**, fool, take (someone) for a ride *(informal)*, kid *(informal)*, bluff, hoax, dupe, put one over on (someone) *(informal)*, play fast and loose with (someone) *(informal)*, play (someone) false: *She was stringing him along even after they were divorced.*

stringent ADJECTIVE **= strict**, tough, rigorous, demanding, binding, tight, severe, exacting, rigid, inflexible **OPPOSITE:** lax

stringy ADJECTIVE **= fibrous**, tough, chewy, sinewy, gristly, wiry

strip[1] VERB **1 = undress**, disrobe, unclothe, uncover yourself: *Women residents stripped naked in protest.* **2 = plunder**, rob, loot, empty, sack, deprive, ransack, pillage, divest, denude: *The soldiers have stripped the civilians of their passports.*

strip[2] NOUN **1 = piece**, shred, bit, band, slip, belt, tongue, ribbon, fillet, swathe: *Serve with strips of fresh raw vegetables.* **2 = stretch**, area, tract, expanse, extent: *a short boat ride across a narrow strip of water*

striped ADJECTIVE **= banded**, stripy, barred, striated

stripy *or* **stripey** ADJECTIVE **= banded**, striped, streaky

strive VERB **= try**, labour, struggle, fight, attempt, compete, strain, contend, endeavour, go for it *(informal)*, try hard, toil, make every effort, go all out *(informal)*, bend over backwards *(informal)*, do your best, go for broke *(slang)*, leave no stone unturned, bust a gut *(informal)*, do all you can, give it your best shot *(informal)*, jump through hoops *(informal)*, break your neck *(informal)*, exert yourself, make an all-out effort *(informal)*, knock yourself out *(informal)*, do your utmost, do your damnedest *(informal)*, give it your all *(informal)*, rupture yourself *(informal)*

stroke VERB **= caress**, rub, fondle, pat, pet: *She was smoking a cigarette and stroking her cat.* ▷ NOUN **1 = apoplexy**, fit, seizure, attack, shock, collapse: *He had a minor stroke in 1987, which left him partly paralysed.* **2 = mark**, line, slash: *Fill in gaps by using short, upward strokes of the pencil.* **3 = movement**, action, motion: *I turned and swam a few strokes further out to sea.* **4 = blow**, hit, knock, pat, rap, thump, swipe: *He was sending the ball into the net with each stroke.* **5 = feat**, move, achievement, accomplishment, movement: *At the time, his appointment seemed a stroke of genius.*

stroll VERB **= walk**, ramble, amble, wander, promenade, saunter, stooge *(slang)*, take a turn, toddle, make your way, mooch *(slang)*, mosey *(informal)*, stretch your legs: *We strolled back, put the kettle on and settled down.* ▷ NOUN **= walk**, promenade, turn, airing, constitutional, excursion, ramble, breath of air: *After dinner, I took a stroll around the city.*

strong ADJECTIVE **1 = powerful**, muscular, tough, capable, athletic, strapping, hardy, sturdy, stout, stalwart, burly, beefy *(informal)*, virile, Herculean, sinewy, brawny: *I'm not strong enough to carry him.* **OPPOSITE:** weak **2 = fit**, sound, healthy, robust, hale, in good shape, in good condition, lusty, fighting fit, fit as a fiddle: *It took me a long while to feel well and strong again.* **3 = self-confident**, determined, tough, brave, aggressive, courageous, high-powered, forceful, resilient, feisty *(informal, chiefly U.S. & Canad.)*, resolute, resourceful, tenacious, plucky, hard-nosed *(informal)*, steadfast, unyielding, hard as nails, self-assertive, stout-hearted, two-fisted, firm in spirit: *Eventually I felt strong enough to look at him.* **OPPOSITE:** timid **4 = durable**, substantial, sturdy, reinforced, heavy-duty, well-built, well-armed, hard-wearing, well-protected, on a firm foundation: *Around its summit, a strong wall had been built.* **OPPOSITE:** flimsy **5 = forceful**, powerful, intense, vigorous: *A strong current seemed to be moving the whole boat.* **6 = extreme**, radical, drastic, strict, harsh, rigid, forceful, uncompromising, Draconian, unbending: *She is known to hold strong views on Cuba.* **7 = decisive**, firm, forceful, decided, determined, severe, resolute, incisive: *The government will take strong action against any further strikes.* **8 = persuasive**, convincing, compelling, telling, great, clear, sound, effective, urgent, formidable, potent, well-established, clear-cut, overpowering, weighty, well-founded, redoubtable, trenchant, cogent: *The evidence that such investment promotes growth is strong.* **9 = pungent**, powerful, concentrated, pure, undiluted: *strong aftershave* **OPPOSITE:** bland **10 = highly-flavoured**, hot, spicy, piquant, biting, sharp, heady, overpowering, intoxicating, highly-seasoned: *It's a good strong flavour, without being overpowering.* **11 = keen**, deep, acute, eager, fervent, zealous, vehement: *He has a strong interest in paintings and owns a fine collection.* **12 = intense**, deep, passionate, ardent, fierce, profound, forceful, fervent, deep-rooted, vehement, fervid: *Having strong unrequited feelings for someone is hard.* **13 = staunch**, firm, keen, dedicated, fierce, ardent, eager, enthusiastic, passionate, fervent: *The Deputy Prime Minister is a strong supporter of the plan.* **14 = distinct**, marked, clear, unmistakable: *'Good, Mr Royle,' he said in English with a strong French accent.* **OPPOSITE:** slight **15 = bright**, brilliant, dazzling, loud, bold, stark, glaring: *strong colours* **OPPOSITE:** dull

strong-arm MODIFIER **= bullying**, threatening, aggressive, violent, terror, forceful, high-pressure, coercive, terrorizing, thuggish

stronghold NOUN **1 = bastion**, fortress, bulwark, fastness: *The seat was a stronghold of the Labour Party.* **2 = refuge**, haven, retreat, sanctuary, hide-out, bolt hole: *Shetland is the last stronghold of otters in the British Isles.*

strong-minded ADJECTIVE **= determined**, resolute, strong-willed, firm, independent, uncompromising, iron-willed, unbending

strong point NOUN **= forte**, strength, speciality, advantage, asset, strong suit, métier, long suit *(informal)*

stroppy ADJECTIVE **= awkward**, difficult, obstreperous, destructive, perverse, unhelpful, cantankerous, bloody-minded *(Brit. informal)*, quarrelsome, litigious, uncooperative

structure NOUN **1 = arrangement**, form, make-up, make, design, organization, construction, fabric, formation, configuration, conformation, interrelation of parts: *The chemical structure of this particular molecule is very unusual.* **2 = building**, construction, erection, edifice, pile: *The house was a handsome four-storey brick structure.* ▷ VERB **= arrange**, organize, design, shape, build up, assemble, put together: *You have begun to structure your time.*

struggle VERB **1 = strive**, labour, toil, work, strain, go for it *(informal)*, make every effort, go all out *(informal)*, bend over backwards *(informal)*, go for broke *(slang)*, bust a gut *(informal)*, give it your best shot *(informal)*, break your neck *(informal)*, exert yourself, make an all-out effort *(informal)*, work like a Trojan, knock yourself out *(informal)*,

do your damnedest *(informal)*, give it your all *(informal)*, rupture yourself *(informal)*: *They had to struggle against all kinds of adversity.* **2 = fight**, battle, wrestle, grapple, compete, contend, scuffle, lock horns: *We were struggling for the gun when it went off.* **3 = have trouble**, have problems, have difficulties, fight, come unstuck: *The company is struggling to find customers.*
▷ NOUN **1 = problem**, battle, effort, trial, strain: *Life became a struggle.* **2 = effort**, labour, toil, work, grind *(informal)*, pains, scramble, long haul, exertion: *a young lad's struggle to support his poverty-stricken family* **3 = fight**, battle, conflict, clash, contest, encounter, brush, combat, hostilities, strife, skirmish, tussle, biffo *(Austral. slang)*: *He died in a struggle with prison officers.*

strut VERB **= swagger**, parade, stalk, peacock, prance

stub NOUN **1 = butt**, end, stump, tail, remnant, tail end, fag end *(informal)*, dog-end *(informal)*: *an ashtray of cigarette stubs* **2 = counterfoil**: *Those who still have their ticket stubs, please contact the arena.*

stubborn ADJECTIVE **= obstinate**, dogged, inflexible, fixed, persistent, intractable, wilful, tenacious, recalcitrant, unyielding, headstrong, unmanageable, unbending, obdurate, stiff-necked, unshakeable, self-willed, refractory, pig-headed, bull-headed, mulish, cross-grained, contumacious **OPPOSITE:** compliant

stubby ADJECTIVE **= stumpy**, short, squat, stocky, chunky, dumpy, thickset, fubsy *(archaic, dialect)*

stuck ADJECTIVE **1 = fastened**, fast, fixed, joined, glued, cemented: *She had got something stuck between her teeth.* **2 = trapped**, caught, ensnared: *I don't want to get stuck in another job like that.* **3 = burdened**, saddled, lumbered, landed, loaded, encumbered: *Many people are now stuck with fixed-rate mortgages.* **4 = baffled**, stumped, at a loss, beaten, nonplussed, at a standstill, bereft of ideas, up against a brick wall *(informal)*, at your wits' end: *They will be there to help if you're stuck.*
be stuck on something *or* **someone = infatuated with**, obsessed with, keen on, enthusiastic about, mad about, wild about *(informal)*, hung up on *(slang)*, crazy about, for, *or* over *(informal)*: *She's stuck on him because he was her first lover.*
get stuck into something = set about, tackle, get down to, make a start on, take the bit between your teeth: *The sooner we get stuck into this, the sooner we'll finish.*

stuck-up ADJECTIVE **= snobbish**, arrogant, conceited, proud, patronizing, condescending, snooty *(informal)*, haughty, uppity *(informal)*, high and mighty *(informal)*, toffee-nosed *(slang, chiefly Brit.)*, hoity-toity *(informal)*, swollen-headed, bigheaded *(informal)*, uppish *(Brit. informal)*

student NOUN **1 = undergraduate**, scholar: *a 23-year-old medical student* **2 = pupil**, scholar, schoolchild, schoolboy or schoolgirl: *She's a former student of the school.* **3 = learner**, observer, trainee, apprentice, disciple: *a passionate student of history*

studied ADJECTIVE **= planned**, calculated, deliberate, conscious, intentional, wilful, purposeful, premeditated, well-considered **OPPOSITE:** unplanned

studio NOUN **= workshop**, shop, workroom, atelier

studious ADJECTIVE **1 = scholarly**, academic, intellectual, serious, earnest, hard-working, thoughtful, reflective, diligent, meditative, bookish, assiduous, sedulous: *I was a very quiet, studious little girl.* **OPPOSITE:** unacademic **2 = intent**, attentive, watchful, listening, concentrating, careful, regardful: *He had a look of studious concentration on his face.* **OPPOSITE:** careless **3 = deliberate**, planned, conscious, calculated, considered, studied, designed, thoughtful, intentional, wilful, purposeful, premeditated, prearranged: *the studious refusal of most of these firms to get involved in politics*

study VERB **1 = learn**, cram *(informal)*, swot (up) *(Brit. informal)*, read up, hammer away at, bone up on *(informal)*, burn the midnight oil, mug up *(Brit. slang)*: *The rehearsals make it difficult for her to study for her law exams.* **2 = examine**, survey, look at, scrutinize, peruse: *Debbie studied her friend's face for a moment.* **3 = contemplate**, read, examine, consider, go into, con *(archaic)*, pore over, apply yourself (to): *I invite every citizen to carefully study the document.*
▷ NOUN **1 = examination**, investigation, analysis, consideration, inspection, scrutiny, contemplation, perusal, cogitation: *the use of maps and visual evidence in the study of local history* **2 = piece of research**, survey, report, paper, review, article, inquiry, investigation: *the first study of English children's attitudes* **3 = learning**, lessons, school work, academic work, reading, research, cramming *(informal)*, swotting *(Brit. informal)*, book work: *She gave up her studies to have a family.* **4 = office**, room, studio, workplace, den, place of work, workroom: *I went through the papers in his study.*

> **QUOTATIONS**
> Of making many books there is no end; and much study is a weariness of the flesh
> [*Bible: Ecclesiastes*]

stuff NOUN **1 = things**, gear, possessions, effects, materials, equipment, objects, tackle, kit, junk, luggage, belongings, trappings, bits and pieces, paraphernalia, clobber *(Brit. slang)*, impedimenta, goods and chattels: *He pointed to a duffle bag. 'That's my stuff.'* **2 = nonsense**, rubbish, rot, trash, bunk *(informal)*, foolishness, humbug, twaddle, tripe *(informal)*, baloney *(informal)*, verbiage, claptrap, malarkey *(informal)*, bunkum, poppycock *(informal)*, balderdash, pants *(slang)*, bosh *(informal)*, stuff and nonsense, tommyrot, bizzo *(Austral. slang)*, bull's wool *(Austral. & N.Z. slang)*: *Don't tell me you believe in all that stuff.* **3 = substance**, material, essence, matter, staple, pith, quintessence: *The idea that we can be what we want has become the stuff of TV commercials.*
▷ VERB **1 = shove**, force, push, squeeze, jam, ram, wedge, compress, stow: *His trousers were stuffed inside the tops of his boots.* **2 = cram**, fill, pack, load, crowd: *wallets stuffed with dollars*

stuffing NOUN **1 = filling**, forcemeat: *a stuffing for turkey, guinea fowl or chicken* **2 = wadding**, filling, packing, quilting, kapok: *She made a wig from pillow stuffing.*

stuffy ADJECTIVE **1 = staid**, conventional, dull, old-fashioned, deadly, dreary, pompous, formal, prim, stilted, musty, stodgy, uninteresting, humourless, fusty, strait-laced, priggish, as dry as dust, old-fogeyish, niminy-piminy, prim and proper: *stuffy attitudes* **2 = airless**, stifling, oppressive, close, heavy, stale, suffocating, sultry, fetid, muggy, unventilated, fuggy, frowsty: *It was hot and stuffy in the classroom.* **OPPOSITE:** airy

stumble VERB **1 = trip**, fall, slip, reel, stagger, falter, flounder, lurch, come a cropper *(informal)*, lose your balance, blunder about: *The smoke was so thick that I stumbled on the first step.* **2 = totter**, reel, stagger, blunder, falter, lurch, wobble, teeter: *I stumbled into the telephone box and dialled 999.* **3 = falter**, hesitate, stammer, stutter, fluff *(informal)*: *His voiced wavered and he stumbled over his words.*
stumble across *or* **on** *or* **upon something** *or* **someone = discover**, find, come across, encounter, run across, chance upon, happen upon, light upon, blunder upon: *History relates that they stumbled on a magnificent waterfall.*

stumbling block NOUN **= obstacle**, difficulty, bar, barrier, hurdle, hazard, snag, uphill *(S. African)*, obstruction, impediment, hindrance

stump NOUN **= tail end**, end, remnant, remainder: *The tramp produced a stump of candle from his pocket.*
▷ VERB **1 = baffle**, confuse, puzzle, snooker, foil, bewilder, confound, perplex, mystify, outwit, stymie, flummox, bring (someone) up short, dumbfound, nonplus: *Well, maybe I stumped you on that one.* **2 = stamp**, clump, stomp *(informal)*, trudge, plod, clomp: *The marshal stumped out of the room.*
stump something up = pay, fork out *(slang)*, shell out *(informal)*, contribute,

hand over, donate, chip in *(informal)*, cough up *(informal)*, come across with *(informal)*: *Customers do not have to stump up cash for at least four weeks.*

stumped ADJECTIVE **= baffled**, perplexed, at a loss, floored *(informal)*, at sea, stymied, nonplussed, flummoxed, brought to a standstill, uncertain which way to turn, at your wits' end

stun VERB **1 = overcome**, shock, amaze, confuse, astonish, stagger, bewilder, astound, overpower, confound, stupefy, strike (someone) dumb, knock (someone) for six *(informal)*, dumbfound, flabbergast *(informal)*, hit (someone) like a ton of bricks *(informal)*, take (someone's) breath away: *Many cinema-goers were stunned by the film's violent and tragic end.* **2 = daze**, knock out, stupefy, numb, benumb: *He stood his ground and took a heavy blow that stunned him.*

stung ADJECTIVE **= hurt**, wounded, angered, roused, incensed, exasperated, resentful, nettled, goaded, piqued

stunned ADJECTIVE **= staggered**, shocked, devastated, numb, astounded, bowled over *(informal)*, gobsmacked *(Brit. slang)*, dumbfounded, flabbergasted *(informal)*, struck dumb, at a loss for words

stunner NOUN **= beauty**, looker *(informal, chiefly U.S.)*, lovely *(slang)*, dish *(informal)*, sensation, honey *(informal)*, good-looker, dazzler, peach *(informal)*, wow *(slang, chiefly U.S.)*, dolly *(slang)*, knockout *(informal)*, heart-throb, charmer, eyeful *(informal)*, smasher *(informal)*, humdinger *(slang)*, glamour puss, beaut *(Austral. & N.Z. slang)*

stunning ADJECTIVE **= wonderful**, beautiful, impressive, great *(informal)*, striking, brilliant, dramatic, lovely, remarkable, smashing *(informal)*, heavenly, devastating *(informal)*, spectacular, marvellous, splendid, gorgeous, dazzling, sensational *(informal)*, drop-dead *(slang)*, ravishing, out of this world *(informal)*, jaw-dropping, eye-popping *(informal)* **OPPOSITE:** unimpressive

stunt NOUN **= feat**, act, trick, exploit, deed, tour de force *(French)*

stunted ADJECTIVE **= undersized**, dwarfed, little, small, tiny, diminutive, dwarfish

stupefy VERB **= astound**, shock, amaze, stun, stagger, bewilder, numb, daze, confound, knock senseless, dumbfound

stupendous ADJECTIVE **1 = wonderful**, brilliant, amazing, stunning *(informal)*, superb, overwhelming, fantastic *(informal)*, tremendous *(informal)*, fabulous *(informal)*, surprising, staggering, marvellous, sensational *(informal)*, breathtaking, phenomenal, astounding, prodigious, wondrous *(archaic, literary)*, mind-boggling *(informal)*, out of this world *(informal)*, mind-blowing *(informal)*, jaw-dropping, surpassing belief: *This stupendous novel keeps you gripped to the end.* **OPPOSITE:** unremarkable **2 = huge**, vast, enormous, mega *(slang)*, gigantic, colossal: *a stupendous amount of money* **OPPOSITE:** tiny

stupid ADJECTIVE **1 = unintelligent**, thick, dumb *(informal)*, simple, slow, dull, dim, dense, sluggish, deficient, crass, gullible, simple-minded, dozy *(Brit. informal)*, witless, stolid, dopey *(informal)*, moronic, obtuse, brainless, cretinous, half-witted, slow on the uptake *(informal)*, braindead *(informal)*, dumb-ass *(slang)*, doltish, dead from the neck up, thickheaded, slow-witted, Boeotian, thick as mince *(Scot. informal)*, woodenheaded *(informal)*: *I'm not stupid, you know.* **OPPOSITE:** intelligent **2 = silly**, foolish, daft *(informal)*, rash, trivial, ludicrous, meaningless, irresponsible, pointless, futile, senseless, mindless, laughable, short-sighted, ill-advised, idiotic, fatuous, nonsensical, half-baked *(informal)*, inane, crackpot *(informal)*, unthinking, puerile, unintelligent, asinine, imbecilic, crackbrained: *I wouldn't call it art. It's just stupid and tasteless; You won't go and do anything stupid, will you?* **OPPOSITE:** sensible **3 = senseless**, dazed, groggy, punch-drunk, insensate, semiconscious, into a daze: *She would drink herself stupid.*

> **QUOTATIONS**
>
> He that reads and grows no wiser seldom suspects his own deficiency, but complains of hard words and obscure sentences, and asks why books are written which cannot be understood
> [Dr. Johnson *The Idler*]
>
> Nothing sways the stupid more than arguments they can't understand
> [Cardinal De Retz *Mémoires*]
>
> He's so dumb he can't fart and chew gum at the same time (often euphemistically 'walk and chew gum')
> [Lyndon B Johnson (of Gerald Ford)]

stupidity NOUN **1 = lack of intelligence**, imbecility, obtuseness, simplicity, thickness, slowness, dullness, dimness, dumbness *(informal)*, feeble-mindedness, lack of brain, denseness, brainlessness, doziness *(Brit. informal)*, asininity, dopiness *(slang)*, thickheadedness: *I stared at him, astonished by his stupidity.* **2 = silliness**, folly, foolishness, idiocy, madness, absurdity, futility, lunacy, irresponsibility, pointlessness, inanity, rashness, impracticality, foolhardiness, senselessness, bêtise *(rare)*, ludicrousness, puerility, fatuousness, fatuity: *I can't get over the stupidity of their decision.*

stupor NOUN **= daze**, numbness, unconsciousness, trance, coma, inertia, lethargy, torpor, stupefaction, insensibility

sturdy ADJECTIVE **1 = robust**, hardy, vigorous, powerful, athletic, muscular, stalwart, staunch, hearty, lusty, brawny, thickset: *She was a short, sturdy woman in her early sixties.* **OPPOSITE:** puny **2 = substantial**, secure, solid, durable, well-made, well-built, built to last: *The camera was mounted on a sturdy tripod.* **OPPOSITE:** flimsy

stutter NOUN **= stammer**, falter, speech impediment, speech defect, hesitance: *He spoke with a pronounced stutter.*
▷ VERB **= stammer**, stumble, falter, hesitate, splutter, speak haltingly: *I was trembling so hard, I thought I would stutter when I spoke.*

style NOUN **1 = manner**, way, method, approach, technique, custom, mode: *Our children's different learning styles created many problems.* **2 = elegance**, taste, chic, flair, polish, grace, dash, sophistication, refinement, panache, élan, cosmopolitanism, savoir-faire, smartness, urbanity, stylishness, bon ton *(French)*, fashionableness, dressiness *(informal)*: *She has not lost her grace and style.* **3 = design**, form, cut: *Several styles of hat were available.* **4 = type**, sort, kind, spirit, pattern, variety, appearance, tone, strain, category, characteristic, genre, tenor: *six scenes in the style of a classical Greek tragedy* **5 = fashion**, trend, mode, vogue, rage: *The longer length of skirt is the style at the moment.* **6 = luxury**, ease, comfort, elegance, grandeur, affluence, gracious living: *The £17 million settlement allowed her to live in style to the end.* **7 = mode of expression**, phrasing, turn of phrase, wording, treatment, expression, vein, diction, phraseology: *The author's style is wonderfully anecdotal.*
▷ VERB **1 = design**, cut, tailor, fashion, shape, arrange, adapt: *classically styled clothes* **2 = call**, name, term, address, label, entitle, dub, designate, christen, denominate: *people who would like to style themselves as arms dealers*

stylish ADJECTIVE **= smart**, chic, polished, fashionable, trendy *(Brit. informal)*, classy *(slang)*, in fashion, snappy, in vogue, dapper, natty *(informal)*, snazzy *(informal)*, modish, well turned-out, dressy *(informal)*, à la mode, voguish, schmick *(Austral. informal)*, bling *(slang)*, funky **OPPOSITE:** scruffy

stymie VERB **= frustrate**, defeat, foil, thwart, puzzle, stump, snooker, hinder, confound, mystify, balk, flummox, throw a spanner in the works *(Brit. informal)*, nonplus, spike (someone's) guns

suave ADJECTIVE **= smooth**, charming, urbane, debonair, worldly, cool *(informal)*, sophisticated, polite, gracious, agreeable, courteous, affable, smooth-tongued

subconscious NOUN = **mind**, psyche: *the hidden power of the subconscious* ▷ ADJECTIVE = **hidden**, inner, suppressed, repressed, intuitive, latent, innermost, subliminal: *a subconscious cry for affection* **OPPOSITE:** conscious

subdue VERB **1** = **overcome**, defeat, master, break, control, discipline, crush, humble, put down, conquer, tame, overpower, overrun, trample, quell, triumph over, get the better of, vanquish, beat down, get under control, get the upper hand over, gain ascendancy over: *They admit they have not been able to subdue the rebels.* **2** = **moderate**, control, check, suppress, soften, repress, mellow, tone down, quieten down: *He forced himself to subdue and overcome his fears.* **OPPOSITE:** arouse

subdued ADJECTIVE **1** = **quiet**, serious, sober, sad, grave, restrained, repressed, solemn, chastened, dejected, downcast, crestfallen, repentant, down in the mouth, sadder and wiser, out of spirits: *He faced the press, initially, in a somewhat subdued mood.* **OPPOSITE:** lively **2** = **hushed**, soft, quiet, whispered, murmured, muted: *The conversation around them was resumed, but in subdued tones.* **OPPOSITE:** loud **3** = **dim**, soft, subtle, muted, shaded, low-key, understated, toned down, unobtrusive: *The lighting was subdued.* **OPPOSITE:** bright

subject NOUN **1** = **topic**, question, issue, matter, point, business, affair, object, theme, substance, subject matter, field of inquiry *or* reference: *It was I who first raised the subject of plastic surgery.* **2** = **branch of study**, area, field, discipline, speciality, branch of knowledge: *a tutor in maths and science subjects* **3** = **participant**, case, patient, victim, client, guinea pig *(informal)*: *Subjects in the study were forced to follow a modified diet.* **4** = **citizen**, resident, native, inhabitant, national: *Roughly half of them are British subjects.* **5** = **dependant**, subordinate, vassal, liegeman: *His subjects regard him as a great and wise monarch.* ▷ ADJECTIVE = **subordinate**, dependent, satellite, inferior, captive, obedient, enslaved, submissive, subservient, subjugated: *colonies and other subject territories* ▷ VERB = **put through**, expose, submit, lay open, make liable: *He had subjected her to four years of beatings and abuse.* **subject to 1** = **liable to**, open to, exposed to, vulnerable to, prone to, susceptible to, disposed to: *Prices may be subject to alteration.* **2** = **bound by**, under the control of, constrained by: *It could not be subject to another country's laws.* **3** = **dependent on**, contingent on, controlled by, conditional on: *The merger is subject to certain conditions.*

subjective ADJECTIVE = **personal**, emotional, prejudiced, biased, instinctive, intuitive, idiosyncratic, nonobjective **OPPOSITE:** objective

subjugate VERB = **conquer**, master, overcome, defeat, crush, suppress, put down, overthrow, tame, lick *(informal)*, subdue, overpower, quell, rule over, enslave, vanquish, hold sway over, bring to heel, bring (someone) to his knees, bring under the yoke

sublimate VERB = **channel**, transfer, divert, redirect, turn

sublime ADJECTIVE = **noble**, magnificent, glorious, high, great, grand, imposing, elevated, eminent, majestic, lofty, exalted, transcendent **OPPOSITE:** lowly

subliminal ADJECTIVE = **subconscious**, unconscious

submerge VERB **1** = **flood**, swamp, engulf, drown, overflow, inundate, deluge: *The river burst its banks, submerging an entire village.* **2** = **immerse**, plunge, dip, duck, dunk: *Submerge the pieces of fish in the poaching liquid and simmer.* **3** = **sink**, plunge, go under water: *Just as I shot at it, the crocodile submerged again.* **4** = **overwhelm**, swamp, engulf, overload, inundate, deluge, snow under, overburden: *He was suddenly submerged in an avalanche of scripts and offers.*

submerged ADJECTIVE = **immersed**, sunk, underwater, drowned, submarine, sunken, undersea, subaqueous, submersed, subaquatic

submission NOUN **1** = **surrender**, yielding, giving in, cave-in *(informal)*, capitulation, acquiescence: *The army intends to take the city or force it into submission.* **2** = **presentation**, submitting, handing in, entry, tendering: *the submission of a dissertation* **3** = **proposal**, argument, contention: *A written submission has to be prepared.* **4** = **compliance**, obedience, submissiveness, meekness, resignation, deference, passivity, docility, tractability, unassertiveness: *She nodded her head in submission.*

submissive ADJECTIVE = **meek**, passive, obedient, compliant, patient, resigned, yielding, accommodating, humble, subdued, lowly, abject, amenable, docile, dutiful, ingratiating, malleable, deferential, pliant, obsequious, uncomplaining, tractable, acquiescent, biddable, unresisting, bootlicking *(informal)*, obeisant **OPPOSITE:** obstinate

submit VERB **1** = **surrender**, yield, give in, agree, bend, bow, endure, tolerate, comply, put up with *(informal)*, succumb, defer, stoop, cave in *(informal)*, capitulate, accede, acquiesce, toe the line, knuckle under, resign yourself, lay down arms, hoist the white flag, throw in the sponge: *If I submitted to their demands, they would not press the allegations.* **2** = **present**, hand in, tender, put forward, table, commit, refer, proffer: *They submitted their reports to the Chancellor yesterday.* **3** = **suggest**, claim, argue, propose, state, put, move, advance, volunteer, assert, contend, propound: *I submit that you knew exactly what you were doing.*

subordinate NOUN = **inferior**, junior, assistant, aide, second, attendant, dependant, underling, subaltern, bitch *(slang)*: *Nearly all her subordinates adored her.* **OPPOSITE:** superior ▷ ADJECTIVE **1** = **inferior**, lesser, lower, junior, subject, minor, secondary, dependent, subservient: *Sixty of his subordinate officers followed his example.* **OPPOSITE:** superior **2** = **subsidiary**, supplementary, auxiliary, ancillary: *It was an art in which words were subordinate to images.*

subordination NOUN = **inferiority**, servitude, subjection, inferior *or* secondary status

subscribe to VERB **1** = **support**, agree with, advocate, consent to, endorse, countenance, acquiesce with: *I've personally never subscribed to the view.* **2** = **contribute to**, give to, donate to, chip in to *(informal)*: *I subscribe to a few favourable charities.*

subscription NOUN = **membership fee**, charge, dues, annual payment

subsequent ADJECTIVE = **following**, later, succeeding, after, successive, ensuing, consequent **OPPOSITE:** previous

subsequently ADVERB = **later**, afterwards, in the end, consequently, in the aftermath (of), at a later date

subservient ADJECTIVE **1** = **servile**, submissive, deferential, subject, inferior, abject, sycophantic, slavish, obsequious, truckling, bootlicking *(informal)*: *Her willingness to be subservient to her children isolated her.* **OPPOSITE:** domineering **2** = **subordinate**, subsidiary, accessory, auxiliary, conducive, ancillary: *The individual's needs are seen as subservient to the group's.*

subside VERB **1** = **decrease**, diminish, lessen, ease, moderate, dwindle, wane, recede, ebb, abate, let up, peter out, slacken, melt away, quieten, level off, de-escalate: *The pain had subsided during the night.* **OPPOSITE:** increase **2** = **collapse**, sink, cave in, drop, lower, settle: *Does that mean that the whole house is subsiding?* **3** = **drop**, fall, decline, ebb, descend: *Local officials say the flood waters have subsided.*

subsidence NOUN = **sinking**, settling, collapse, settlement

subsidiary NOUN = **branch**, division, section, office, department, wing, subdivision, subsection, local office: *a subsidiary of the American multinational* ▷ ADJECTIVE = **secondary**, lesser, subordinate, minor, supplementary, auxiliary, supplemental, contributory, ancillary, subservient: *a subsidiary position* **OPPOSITE:** main

S

The Language of W Somerset Maugham

William Somerset Maugham (1874–1965) was a successful dramatist, novelist, and author of short stories. Born at the British embassy in Paris, Maugham travelled widely throughout his life and his time overseas provided him with the inspiration for much of his most successful material. Two of his most celebrated works are the largely autobiographical *Of Human Bondage* and his fictional reconstruction of the lives of the British authors Thomas Hardy and Hugh Walpole, *Cakes and Ale*. Both these texts take their titles from quotations (the first from Spinoza, the second from Shakespeare), a strategy that Maugham employed on several occasions.

An interesting feature of Maugham's writing is the frequency with which he is drawn to an oral frame of reference. *Lip* is unusually common although it is modified by fairly typical adjectives, *red* being the most salient, followed by *thin* and *upper*. The *lips* of Maugham's characters *tremble* far more often than they *smile*, and they also *tighten*, *twitch*, and *quiver*. *Mouths* meanwhile are most frequently *large*, *red*, or *sensual*. Oral verbs are led in frequency by *eat*, followed closely by *kiss* and then *drink*. *Tongue* appears less in an anatomical sense and more often to describe the qualities or characteristics of speech, either its mood (as in *sharp* or *bitter tongue*) or the particular language, for example:

> ... friendly gossip with persons of a different **tongue** and country.

Another adjective that occurs with *tongue* in this sense is *native*, which evidently testifies to Maugham's engagement with questions of empire at a period in which it was beginning to decline.

Used as both an adjective and a noun, *native* is a familiar part of the outdated rhetoric of British colonial rule. As an adjective it occurs most frequently in Maugham's work with *village*. As a noun, it appears with a wide range of adjectives, the most common of which is *half-caste*, indicating a typically imperialist interest in race. But despite the continuing presence of the language of empire in Maugham's work, his own approach to these themes is characterized by a distinct lack of enthusiasm, even at times cynicism.

Maugham's sceptical literary temperament also translates to a preference for age over youth. *Old* occurs over twice as many times as *young* throughout his work. Within this pattern *old man* is nearly three times as common as *old woman*, while *old* also appears in a number of colloquial usages that are now seldom heard. *Old fellow*, *old chap*, and *old boy* are the most common of these in Maugham's writing and generally function as terms of endearment, as in:

> My dear **old boy**, you know I wouldn't do anything to hurt you.

Another colloquial usage of *old* that has nothing specifically to do with age is the phrase *funny old*, a general expression of strangeness as in *funny old thing*.

Sickness in Maugham's work is most likely to carry emotional rather than medical connotations. Most commonly his characters would be *sick* with *apprehension*, *fear*, or *love*, or they might also appear *sick at heart*. In a similar vein, *heart* often appears with *sink* as an indication of a sudden deterioration in circumstances, as in:

> Presently when her letters came his **heart sank**.

In accordance with common usage, more prevalent with *heart* than *sink* is *beat*. This familiar collocation is notable in Maugham's work for the consistent use of adverbs indicative of distress as once again he uses descriptions of the body to depict states of mind. The relatively neutral *quickly* is the most salient of these, though others suggest more pronounced agitation, such as *violently*, *horribly*, or *furiously*.

subsidize VERB **= fund**, finance, support, promote, sponsor, underwrite, put up the money for

subsidy NOUN **= aid**, help, support, grant, contribution, assistance, allowance, financial aid, stipend, subvention

subsist VERB **= stay alive**, survive, keep going, make ends meet, last, live, continue, exist, endure, eke out an existence, keep your head above water, sustain yourself

subsistence NOUN **= living**, maintenance, upkeep, keep, support, existence, survival, livelihood

substance NOUN **1 = material**, body, stuff, element, fabric, texture: *The substance that causes the problem comes from the barley.* **2 = importance**, significance, concreteness: *It is questionable whether anything of substance has been achieved.* **3 = meaning**, main point, gist, matter, subject, theme, import, significance, essence, pith, burden, sum and substance: *The substance of his discussions doesn't really matter.* **4 = truth**, fact, reality, certainty, validity, authenticity, verity, verisimilitude: *There is no substance in any of these allegations.* **5 = wealth**, means, property, assets, resources, estate, affluence: *mature men of substance*

substandard ADJECTIVE **= inferior**, inadequate, unacceptable, damaged, imperfect, second-rate, shoddy

substantial ADJECTIVE **1 = big**, significant, considerable, goodly, large, important, generous, worthwhile, tidy *(informal)*, ample, sizable *or* sizeable: *That is a very substantial improvement in the current situation.* **OPPOSITE:** small **2 = solid**, sound, sturdy, strong, firm, massive, hefty, durable, bulky, well-built: *those fortunate enough to have a fairly substantial property to sell* **OPPOSITE:** insubstantial

substantially ADVERB **1 = considerably**, significantly, very much, greatly, seriously *(informal)*, remarkably, markedly, noticeably, appreciably: *The price was substantially higher than had been expected.* **2 = essentially**, largely, mainly, materially, in the main, in essence, to a large extent, in substance, in essentials: *He checked the details given and found them substantially correct.*

substantiate VERB **= support**, prove, confirm, establish, affirm, verify, validate, bear out, corroborate, attest to, authenticate **OPPOSITE:** disprove

substitute VERB **1 = replace**, exchange, swap, change, switch, commute, interchange: *They were substituting violence for dialogue.* **2** *(with* **for***)* **= stand in for**, cover for, take over from, relieve, act for, double for, fill in for, hold the fort for, be in place of, deputize for: *Her parents are trying to be supportive but they can't substitute for Jackie as a mother.*
▷ NOUN **= replacement**, reserve, equivalent, surrogate, deputy, relief, representative, sub, temporary, stand-by, makeshift, proxy, temp *(informal)*, expedient, locum, depute *(Scot.)*, stopgap, locum tenens: *She is seeking a substitute for the man who broke her heart.*

substitution NOUN **= replacement**, exchange, switch, swap, change, interchange

subterfuge NOUN **= trick**, dodge, ploy, shift, manoeuvre, deception, evasion, pretence, pretext, ruse, artifice, duplicity, stratagem, deviousness, machination

subtle ADJECTIVE **1 = faint**, slight, implied, delicate, indirect, understated, insinuated: *a subtle hint* **OPPOSITE:** obvious **2 = crafty**, cunning, sly, designing, scheming, intriguing, shrewd, ingenious, astute, devious, wily, artful, Machiavellian: *He is a subtle character, you know.* **OPPOSITE:** straightforward **3 = muted**, soft, subdued, low-key, toned down: *subtle shades of brown* **4 = fine**, minute, narrow, tenuous, hair-splitting: *There was, however, a subtle distinction between the two lawsuits.*

subtlety NOUN **1 = fine point**, refinement, nicety, sophistication, delicacy, intricacy, discernment: *All those linguistic subtleties get lost when a book goes into translation.* **2 = skill**, acumen, astuteness, ingenuity, guile, cleverness, deviousness, sagacity, acuteness, craftiness, artfulness, slyness, wiliness: *She analyses herself with great subtlety.* **3 = sensitivity**, diplomacy, discretion, delicacy, understanding, skill, consideration, judgment, perception, finesse, thoughtfulness, discernment, savoir-faire, adroitness: *They had obviously been hoping to approach the topic with more subtlety.*

subtract VERB **= take away**, take off, deduct, remove, withdraw, diminish, take from, detract **OPPOSITE:** add

suburb NOUN **= residential area**, neighbourhood, outskirts, precincts, suburbia, environs, purlieus, dormitory area *(Brit.)*, faubourgs

subversive ADJECTIVE **= seditious**, inflammatory, incendiary, underground, undermining, destructive, overthrowing, riotous, insurrectionary, treasonous, perversive: *The play was promptly banned as subversive and possibly treasonous.*
▷ NOUN **= dissident**, terrorist, saboteur, insurrectionary, quisling, fifth columnist, deviationist, seditionary, seditionist: *Agents regularly rounded up suspected subversives.*

subvert VERB **1 = overturn**, destroy, undermine, upset, ruin, wreck, demolish, sabotage: *an alleged plot to subvert the state* **2 = corrupt**, pervert, deprave, poison, contaminate, confound, debase, demoralize, vitiate: *an attempt to subvert culture from within*

succeed VERB **1 = triumph**, win, prevail: *Some people will succeed in their efforts to stop smoking.* **2 = work out**, work, be successful, come off *(informal)*, do the trick *(informal)*, turn out well, go like a bomb *(Brit. & N.Z. informal)*, go down a bomb *(informal, chiefly Brit.)*, do the business *(informal)*: *a move which would make any future talks even more unlikely to succeed* **3 = make it** *(informal)*, do well, be successful, arrive *(informal)*, triumph, thrive, flourish, make good, prosper, cut it *(informal)*, make the grade *(informal)*, get to the top, crack it *(informal)*, hit the jackpot *(informal)*, bring home the bacon *(informal)*, make your mark *(informal)*, gain your end, carry all before you, do all right for yourself: *the skills and qualities needed to succeed* **OPPOSITE:** fail **4 = take over from**, replace, assume the office of, fill (someone's) boots, step into (someone's) boots: *He is almost certain to succeed him as chairman.* **5** *(with* **to***)* **= take over**, assume, attain, acquire, come into, inherit, accede to, come into possession of: *He eventually succeeded to the post in 1998.* **6 = follow**, come after, follow after, replace, be subsequent to, supervene: *He succeeded Trajan as emperor in AD 117.* **OPPOSITE:** precede

success NOUN **1 = victory**, triumph, positive result, favourable outcome: *the success of European business in building a stronger partnership* **OPPOSITE:** failure **2 = prosperity**, fortune, luck, fame, eminence, ascendancy: *Nearly all of them believed work was the key to success.* **3 = hit** *(informal)*, winner, smash *(informal)*, triumph, sensation, wow *(slang)*, best seller, market leader, smash hit *(informal)*: *We hope it will be a commercial success.* **OPPOSITE:** flop *(informal)* **4 = big name**, star, hit *(informal)*, somebody, celebrity, sensation, megastar *(informal)*, V.I.P.: *Everyone who knows her says she will be a great success.* **OPPOSITE:** nobody

QUOTATIONS

Eighty percent of success is showing up
[Woody Allen]

It is not enough to succeed. Others must fail
[Gore Vidal]

Failure is inevitable. Success is elusive
[Steven Spielberg]

Getting on is the opium of the middle classes
[Walter James]

To succeed in the world we must look foolish but be wise
[C.L. de Montesquieu *Pensées*]

Success has ruin'd many a man
[Benjamin Franklin *Poor Richard's Almanack*]

The road to success is full of women pushing their husbands along
[Lord Thomas Dewar]

The moral flabbiness born of the exclusive worship of the bitch-goddess success
[William James *Letter to H G Wells*]

The secret of business success is honesty and sincerity. If you can fake those, you've got it made
[attributed to Groucho Marx]

If A is success in life, then A equals x plus y plus z. Work is x; y is play; and z is keeping your mouth shut
[Albert Einstein]

Success is relative;
It is what we can make of the mess we have made of things
[T.S. Eliot *The Family Reunion*]

success: the one unpardonable sin against one's fellows
[Ambrose Bierce *The Devil's Dictionary*]

Be nice to people on your way up because you'll meet 'em on your way down
[Wilson Mizner]

PROVERBS
Nothing succeeds like success
There is always room at the top

successful ADJECTIVE **1 = triumphant**, victorious, lucky, fortunate: *The successful candidate will be announced in June.* **2 = thriving**, profitable, productive, paying, effective, rewarding, booming, efficient, flourishing, unbeaten, lucrative, favourable, fruitful, efficacious, moneymaking: *One of the keys to successful business is careful planning.* **OPPOSITE:** unprofitable **3 = top**, prosperous, acknowledged, wealthy, out in front *(informal)*, going places, at the top of the tree: *She is a successful lawyer.*

QUOTATIONS
A successful man is one who makes more money than his wife can spend
[Lana Turner]

successfully ADVERB **= well**, favourably, in triumph, with flying colours, famously *(informal)*, swimmingly, victoriously

succession NOUN **1 = series**, run, sequence, course, order, train, flow, chain, cycle, procession, continuation, progression: *He took a succession of jobs which have stood him in good stead.* **2 = taking over**, assumption, inheritance, elevation, accession, entering upon: *She is now seventh in line of succession to the throne.*
in succession = one after the other, running, successively, consecutively, on the trot *(informal)*, one behind the other: *They needed to reach the World Cup final for the third time in succession.*

successive ADJECTIVE **= consecutive**, following, succeeding, in a row, in succession, sequent

succinct ADJECTIVE **= brief**, to the point, concise, compact, summary, condensed, terse, laconic, pithy, gnomic, compendious, in a few well-chosen words
OPPOSITE: rambling

succour NOUN **= help**, support, aid, relief, comfort, assistance: *Have you offered comfort and succour to your friend?*
▷ VERB **= help**, support, aid, encourage, nurse, comfort, foster, assist, relieve, minister to, befriend, render assistance to, give aid and encouragement to: *They had left nothing to succour a dung beetle, let alone a human.*

succulent ADJECTIVE **= juicy**, moist, luscious, rich, lush, mellow, mouthwatering

succumb VERB **1** *(often with* **to***)* **= surrender (to)**, yield (to), submit (to), give in (to), give way (to), go under (to), cave in (to) *(informal)*, capitulate (to), knuckle under (to): *Don't succumb to the temptation to have just one cigarette.* **OPPOSITE:** beat **2** *(with* **to**, *an illness)* **= catch**, fall victim to, fall ill with: *I was determined not to succumb to the virus.*

suck VERB **1 = drink**, sip, draw: *They waited in silence and sucked their drinks through straws.* **2 = take**, draw, pull, extract: *The air is sucked out by a high-powered fan.*
suck up to someone = ingratiate yourself with, play up to *(informal)*, curry favour with, flatter, pander to, toady, butter up, keep in with *(informal)*, fawn on, truckle, lick someone's boots, dance attendance on, get on the right side of, worm yourself into (someone's) favour: *She kept sucking up to the teachers.*

sucker NOUN **= fool**, mug *(Brit. slang)*, dupe, victim, butt, sap *(slang)*, pushover *(slang)*, sitting duck *(informal)*, sitting target, putz *(U.S. slang)*, cat's paw, easy game *or* mark *(informal)*, nerd *or* nurd *(slang)*, dorba *or* dorb *(Austral. slang)*, bogan *(Austral. slang)*

sudden ADJECTIVE **= quick**, rapid, unexpected, swift, hurried, abrupt, hasty, impulsive, unforeseen
OPPOSITE: gradual

suddenly ADVERB **= abruptly**, all of a sudden, all at once, unexpectedly, out of the blue *(informal)*, without warning, on the spur of the moment

sue VERB **1 = take (someone) to court**, prosecute, bring an action against (someone), charge, summon, indict, have the law on (someone) *(informal)*, prefer charges against (someone), institute legal proceedings against (someone): *The company could be sued for damages.* **2 = appeal for**, plead, beg, petition, solicit, beseech, entreat, supplicate: *He realized that suing for peace was the only option.*

suffer VERB **1 = be in pain**, hurt, ache, be racked, have a bad time, go through a lot *(informal)*, go through the mill *(informal)*, feel wretched: *Can you assure me that my father is not suffering?* **2 = be affected**, have trouble with, be afflicted, be troubled with: *I realized he was suffering from shock.* **3 = undergo**, experience, sustain, feel, bear, go through, endure: *The peace process has suffered a serious blow now.* **4 = deteriorate**, decline, get worse, fall off, be impaired: *I'm not surprised that your studies are suffering.* **5 = tolerate**, stand, put up with *(informal)*, support, bear, endure, hack *(Brit. informal)*, abide: *She doesn't suffer fools gladly and, in her view, most people are fools.*

suffering NOUN **= pain**, torture, distress, agony, misery, ordeal, discomfort, torment, hardship, anguish, affliction, martyrdom

suffice VERB **= be enough**, do, be sufficient, be adequate, answer, serve, content, satisfy, fill the bill *(informal)*, meet requirements, tick all the boxes

sufficient ADJECTIVE **= adequate**, enough, ample, satisfactory, enow *(archaic)* **OPPOSITE:** insufficient

suffocate VERB **1 = choke**, stifle, smother, asphyxiate: *They were suffocated as they slept.* **2 = be choked**, be stifled, be smothered, be asphyxiated: *He either suffocated, or froze to death.*

suffuse VERB **= spread through** *or* **over**, flood, infuse, cover, steep, bathe, mantle, pervade, permeate, imbue, overspread, transfuse

suggest VERB **1 = recommend**, propose, advise, move, advocate, prescribe, put forward, offer a suggestion: *I suggest you ask him some specific questions about his past.* **2 = indicate**, lead you to believe: *The figures suggest that their success is conditional on this restriction.* **3 = hint at**, imply, insinuate, intimate, get at, drive at *(informal)*: *What exactly are you suggesting?* **4 = bring to mind**, evoke, remind you of, connote, make you think of, put you in mind of: *Its hairy body suggests a mammal.*

suggestion NOUN
1 = recommendation, proposal, proposition, plan, motion: *I have lots of suggestions for the park's future.* **2 = hint**, implication, insinuation, intimation: *There is absolutely no suggestion of any mainstream political party involvement.* **3 = trace**, touch, hint, breath, indication, whisper, suspicion, intimation: *that fashionably faint suggestion of a tan*

suggestive ADJECTIVE **= smutty**, rude, indecent, improper, blue, provocative, spicy *(informal)*, racy, unseemly, titillating, risqué, bawdy, prurient, off colour, ribald, immodest, indelicate: *A female employee claimed he made suggestive remarks to her.*
suggestive of = reminiscent of, indicative of, redolent of, evocative of: *These headaches were most suggestive of raised blood pressure.*

suit NOUN **1 = outfit**, costume, ensemble, dress, clothing, habit: *a smart suit and tie* **2 = lawsuit**, case, trial, proceeding, cause, action, prosecution, industrial tribunal: *The judge dismissed the suit.*
▷ VERB **1 = be acceptable to**, please, satisfy, do, answer, gratify: *They will only release information if it suits them.* **2 = agree with**, become, match, go with, correspond with, conform to, befit, harmonize with: *I don't think a sedentary life would altogether suit me.*
follow suit = copy someone, emulate someone, accord with someone, take your cue from someone, run with the herd: *The Dutch seem set to follow suit.*

suitability NOUN **= appropriateness**, fitness, rightness, aptness

suitable ADJECTIVE **1 = appropriate**, right, fitting, fit, suited, acceptable, becoming, satisfactory, apt, befitting: *She had no other dress suitable for the occasion.* **OPPOSITE:** inappropriate **2 = seemly**, fitting, becoming, due, proper, correct: *Was it really suitable behaviour for someone who wants to be taken seriously?* **OPPOSITE:** unseemly **3 = suited**, appropriate, in keeping with, in character, cut out for: *a resort where the slopes are more suitable for young children* **OPPOSITE:** out of keeping **4 = pertinent**, relevant, applicable, fitting, appropriate, to the point, apt, apposite, germane: *Give a few people an idea of suitable questions to ask.* **OPPOSITE:** irrelevant **5 = convenient**, timely, appropriate, well-timed, opportune, commodious: *He could think of no less suitable moment to mention the idea.* **OPPOSITE:** inopportune

suite NOUN **1 = rooms**, apartment, set of rooms, living quarters: *a suite at the Paris Hilton* **2 = set**, series, collection: *We will run a suite of checks.* **3 = attendants**, escorts, entourage, train, followers, retainers, retinue: *Fox and his suite sat there, looking uncertain.*

suitor NOUN **= admirer**, young man, beau, follower (*obsolete*), swain (*archaic*), wooer

sulk VERB **= be sullen**, brood, be in a huff, pout, be put out, have the hump (*Brit. informal*)

sulky ADJECTIVE **= huffy**, sullen, petulant, cross, put out, moody, perverse, disgruntled, aloof, resentful, vexed, churlish, morose, querulous, ill-humoured, in the sulks

sullen ADJECTIVE **= morose**, cross, moody, sour, gloomy, brooding, dour, surly, glowering, sulky, unsociable, out of humour **OPPOSITE:** cheerful

sully VERB **1 = dishonour**, ruin, disgrace, besmirch, smirch: *Reputations are easily sullied and business lost.* **2 = defile**, dirty, stain, spot, spoil, contaminate, pollute, taint, tarnish, blemish, befoul: *I felt loath to sully the gleaming brass knocker by handling it.*

sultry ADJECTIVE **1 = humid**, close, hot, sticky, stifling, oppressive, stuffy, sweltering, muggy: *The climax came one sultry August evening.* **OPPOSITE:** cool **2 = seductive**, sexy (*informal*), sensual, voluptuous, passionate, erotic, provocative, amorous, come-hither (*informal*): *a dark-haired sultry woman*

sum NOUN **1 = amount**, quantity, volume: *Large sums of money were lost.* **2 = calculation**, figures, arithmetic, problem, numbers, reckonings, mathematics, maths (*Brit. informal*), tally, math (*U.S. informal*), arithmetical problem: *I can't do my sums.* **3 = total**, aggregate, entirety, sum total: *The sum of all the angles of a triangle is 180 degrees.* **4 = totality**, whole: *The sum of evidence points to the crime resting on them.*
sum something *or* **someone up = size up**, estimate (*informal*), get the measure of, form an opinion of: *My mother probably summed her up better than I ever could.*

summarily ADVERB **= immediately**, promptly, swiftly, on the spot, speedily, without delay, arbitrarily, at short notice, forthwith, expeditiously, peremptorily, without wasting words

summarize VERB **= sum up**, recap, review, outline, condense, encapsulate, epitomize, abridge, précis, recapitulate, give a rundown of, put in a nutshell, give the main points of

summary NOUN **= synopsis**, résumé, précis, recapitulation, review, outline, extract, essence, abstract, summing-up, digest, epitome, rundown, compendium, abridgment: *Here's a summary of the day's news.*
▷ ADJECTIVE **1 = hasty**, cursory, perfunctory, arbitrary: *The four men were killed after a summary trial.* **2 = concise**, brief, compact, condensed, laconic, succinct, pithy, compendious: *a summary profit and loss statement*

summit NOUN **1 = meeting**, talks, conference, discussion, negotiation, dialogue: *a NATO summit held in Rome* **2 = peak**, top, tip, pinnacle, apex, head, crown, crest: *the first man to reach the summit of Mount Everest* **OPPOSITE:** base **3 = height**, pinnacle, culmination, peak, high point, zenith, acme, crowning point: *This is just a molehill on the way to the summit of her ambitions.* **OPPOSITE:** depths

summon VERB **1 = send for**, call, bid, invite, rally, assemble, convene, call together, convoke: *Howe summoned a doctor and hurried over.* **2** (*often with* **up**) **= gather**, muster, draw on, invoke, mobilize, call into action: *We couldn't even summon up the energy to open the envelope.*

sumptuous ADJECTIVE **= luxurious**, rich, grand, expensive, superb, magnificent, costly, splendid, posh (*informal, chiefly Brit.*), gorgeous, lavish, extravagant, plush (*informal*), opulent, palatial, ritzy (*slang*), de luxe, splendiferous (*facetious*) **OPPOSITE:** plain

sun NOUN **= Sol** (*Roman myth*), Helios (*Greek myth*), Phoebus (*Greek myth*), daystar (*poetic*), eye of heaven, Phoebus Apollo (*Greek myth*): *The sun was now high in the southern sky.*
sun yourself = sunbathe, tan, bask: *She was last seen sunning herself in a riverside park.*
▸ *related adjective:* solar

sundry DETERMINER **= various**, several, varied, assorted, some, different, divers (*archaic*), miscellaneous

sunk ADJECTIVE **= ruined**, lost, finished, done for (*informal*), on the rocks, all washed up (*informal*), up the creek without a paddle (*informal*)

sunken ADJECTIVE **1 = submerged**, immersed, submersed: *Try diving for sunken treasure.* **2 = lowered**, buried, depressed, recessed, below ground, at a lower level: *Steps led down to the sunken bath.* **3 = hollow**, drawn, haggard, hollowed, concave: *an elderly man with sunken cheeks*

sunny ADJECTIVE **1 = bright**, clear, fine, brilliant, radiant, luminous, sunlit, summery, unclouded, sunshiny, without a cloud in the sky: *The weather was surprisingly warm and sunny.* **OPPOSITE:** dull **2 = cheerful**, happy, cheery, smiling, beaming, pleasant, optimistic, buoyant, joyful, genial, chirpy (*informal*), blithe, light-hearted: *The staff wear big sunny smiles.* **OPPOSITE:** gloomy

sunrise NOUN **= dawn**, daybreak, break of day, daylight, aurora (*poetic*), sunup, cockcrow, dayspring (*poetic*)

sunset NOUN **= nightfall**, dusk, sundown, eventide, gloaming (*Scot. poetic*), close of (the) day

super ADJECTIVE **= excellent**, wonderful, marvellous, mean (*slang*), topping (*Brit. slang*), cracking (*Brit. informal*), crucial (*slang*), outstanding, smashing (*informal*), superb, magnificent, glorious, terrific (*informal*), sensational (*informal*), mega (*slang*), sovereign, awesome (*slang*), def (*slang*), top-notch (*informal*), brill (*informal*), incomparable, out of this world (*informal*), peerless, matchless, boffo (*slang*), jim-dandy (*slang*), chillin' (*U.S. slang*), booshit (*Austral. slang*), exo (*Austral. slang*), sik (*Austral. slang*), rad (*informal*), phat (*slang*), schmick (*Austral. informal*)

superb ADJECTIVE **1 = splendid**, excellent, magnificent, topping (*Brit. slang*), fine, choice, grand, superior, divine, marvellous, gorgeous, mega (*slang*), awesome (*slang*), world-class, exquisite, breathtaking, first-rate, superlative, unrivalled, brill (*informal*), bodacious (*slang, chiefly U.S.*), boffo (*slang*), splendiferous (*facetious*), of the first water, chillin' (*U.S. slang*), booshit (*Austral. slang*), exo (*Austral. slang*), sik (*Austral. slang*), rad (*informal*), phat (*slang*), schmick (*Austral. informal*): *a superb 18-hole golf course* **OPPOSITE:** inferior **2 = magnificent**, superior, marvellous, exquisite, breathtaking, admirable, superlative,

S

unrivalled, splendiferous *(facetious)*: *With superb skill he managed to make a perfect landing.* **OPPOSITE:** terrible

superficial ADJECTIVE **1 = shallow**, frivolous, empty-headed, empty, silly, lightweight, trivial: *a superficial yuppie with no intellect whatsoever* **OPPOSITE:** serious **2 = hasty**, cursory, perfunctory, passing, nodding, hurried, casual, sketchy, facile, desultory, slapdash, inattentive: *He only gave it a superficial glance through.* **OPPOSITE:** thorough **3 = slight**, surface, external, cosmetic, on the surface, exterior, peripheral, skin-deep: *It may well look different but the changes are only superficial.* **OPPOSITE:** profound

superficially ADVERB **= at first glance**, apparently, on the surface, ostensibly, externally, at face value, to the casual eye

superfluous ADJECTIVE **= excess**, surplus, redundant, remaining, extra, spare, excessive, unnecessary, in excess, needless, left over, on your hands, surplus to requirements, uncalled-for, unneeded, residuary, supernumerary, superabundant, pleonastic *(Rhetoric)*, unrequired, supererogatory **OPPOSITE:** necessary

superhuman ADJECTIVE **= heroic**, phenomenal, prodigious, stupendous, herculean

superintend VERB **= supervise**, run, oversee, control, manage, direct, handle, look after, overlook, administer, inspect

superintendent NOUN **1 = supervisor**, director, manager, chief, governor, inspector, administrator, conductor, controller, overseer: *He became superintendent of the bank's East African branches.* **2 = warden**, caretaker, curator, keeper, porter, custodian, watchman, janitor, concierge: *He lost his job as a building superintendent.*

superior ADJECTIVE **1 = better**, higher, greater, grander, preferred, prevailing, paramount, surpassing, more advanced, predominant, unrivalled, more extensive, more skilful, more expert, a cut above *(informal)*, streets ahead *(informal)*, running rings around *(informal)*: *a woman greatly superior to her husband in education* **OPPOSITE:** inferior **2 = first-class**, excellent, first-rate, good, fine, choice, exclusive, distinguished, exceptional, world-class, good quality, admirable, high-class, high-calibre, de luxe, of the first order, booshit *(Austral. slang)*, exo *(Austral. slang)*, sik *(Austral. slang)*, rad *(informal)*, phat *(slang)*, schmick *(Austral. informal)*: *He's got a superior car, and it's easy to win races that way.* **OPPOSITE:** average **3 = higher-ranking**, senior, higher-level, upper-level: *negotiations between mutineers and their superior officers* **4 = supercilious**, patronizing, condescending, haughty, disdainful, lordly, lofty, airy, pretentious, stuck-up *(informal)*, snobbish, on your high horse *(informal)*: *Finch gave a superior smile.* ▷ NOUN **= boss**, senior, director, manager, chief *(informal)*, principal, supervisor, baas *(S. African)*, sherang *(Austral. & N.Z.)*: *my immediate superior* **OPPOSITE:** subordinate

> **USAGE**
> *Superior* should not be used with *than*: *He is a better* (not *a superior*) *poet than his brother; His poetry is superior to* (not *than*) *his brother's.*

superiority NOUN **= supremacy**, lead, advantage, excellence, prevalence, ascendancy, pre-eminence, preponderance, predominance

> **QUOTATIONS**
> Superiority is always detested [Baltasar Gracián *The Art of Worldly Wisdom*]

superlative ADJECTIVE **= supreme**, excellent, outstanding, highest, greatest, crack *(slang)*, magnificent, surpassing, consummate, stellar *(informal)*, unparalleled, transcendent, unrivalled, peerless, unsurpassed, matchless, of the highest order, of the first water **OPPOSITE:** average

supernatural ADJECTIVE **= paranormal**, mysterious, unearthly, uncanny, dark, hidden, ghostly, psychic, phantom, abnormal, mystic,

THE SUPERNATURAL

PEOPLE WITH SUPERNATURAL POWERS

archimage, channeller, clairaudient, clairvoyant, conjurer, diviner, dowser, enchanter, enchantress, exorcist, fortune-teller, hag, hex, mage, magician, magus, medium, necromancer, rainmaker, seer, shaman, siren, sorcerer, sorceress, spaewife *(Scot.)*, superhero, thaumaturge, warlock, water diviner, water witch, white witch, witch, witch doctor, witch master, wizard

SUPERNATURAL CREATURES

angel, banshee, brownie, demon, devil, dwarf, dybbuk, elf, fairy, fairy godmother, familiar, fay, genie, ghost, ghoul, giant, gnome, goblin, god *or* goddess, golem, gremlin, guardian angel, hobgoblin, imp, incubus, jinni, kachina, kelpie, lamia, leprechaun, little people *or* folk, monster, ogre, peri, phantom, pixie, poltergeist, sandman, selkie *(Scot.)*, spectre, sprite, succubus, sylph, troll, vampire, werewolf *or* lycanthrope, wraith, zombie

SUPERNATURAL TERMS

abracadabra, amulet, apport, aura, black magic *or* the Black Art, charm, clairaudience, clairvoyance, cryptaesthesia, curse, divination, ectoplasm, evil eye, exorcism, extrasensory perception *or* ESP, fate, fetish, grigri, grimoire, hex, hoodoo, incantation, invultuation, Indian sign, jinx, juju, kismet, levitation, magic circle, magic spell, magic wand, mojo, necromancy, obi *or* obeah, Ouija *(trademark)*, parapsychology, pentagram, philtre, portent, possession, premonition, reincarnation, rune, seance, second sight, sigil, sixth sense, spell, talisman, talking in tongues, xenoglossia, *or* xenoglossy, telaesthesia, telegnosis, telekinesis *or* psychokinesis, telepathy, voodoo, wand, white magic, witching hour miraculous, unnatural, occult, spectral, preternatural, supranatural

> QUOTATIONS
> There are more things in Heaven
> and earth, Horatio,
> Than are dreamt of in your
> philosophy
> [William Shakespeare *Hamlet*]

supersede VERB **= replace**, displace, usurp, supplant, remove, take over, oust, take the place of, fill *or* step into (someone's) boots

supervise VERB **1 = observe**, guide, monitor, oversee, keep an eye on: *He supervised and trained more than 400 volunteers.* **2 = oversee**, run, manage, control, direct, handle, conduct, look after, be responsible for, administer, inspect, preside over, keep an eye on, be on duty, superintend, have *or* be in charge of: *One of his jobs was supervising the dining room.*

supervision NOUN **= superintendence**, direction, instruction, control, charge, care, management, administration, guidance, surveillance, oversight, auspices, stewardship

supervisor NOUN **= boss** *(informal)*, manager, superintendent, chief, inspector, administrator, steward, gaffer *(informal, chiefly Brit.)*, foreman, overseer, baas *(S. African)*

supervisory ADJECTIVE **= managerial**, administrative, overseeing, superintendent, executive

supine ADJECTIVE **1 = flat on your back**, flat, horizontal, recumbent: *a statue of a supine dog* **OPPOSITE:** prone **2 = lethargic**, passive, lazy, idle, indifferent, careless, sluggish, negligent, inert, languid, uninterested, apathetic, lymphatic, listless, indolent, heedless, torpid, slothful, spiritless: *a willing and supine executive*

supplant VERB **= replace**, oust, displace, supersede, remove, take over, undermine, overthrow, unseat, take the place of

supple ADJECTIVE **1 = pliant**, flexible, pliable, plastic, bending, elastic: *The leather is supple and sturdy enough to last for years.* **OPPOSITE:** rigid **2 = flexible**, lithe, limber, lissom(e), loose-limbed: *Paul was incredibly supple and strong.* **OPPOSITE:** stiff

supplement VERB **= add to**, reinforce, complement, augment, extend, top up, fill out: *I suggest supplementing your diet with vitamins E and A.*
▷ NOUN **1 = pull-out**, insert, magazine section, added feature, sidebar: *a special supplement to a monthly financial magazine* **2 = appendix**, sequel, add-on, complement, postscript, addendum, codicil, sidebar: *the supplement to the Encyclopedia Britannica* **3 = addition**, extra, surcharge: *The single room supplement is £11 a night.*

supplementary ADJECTIVE **= additional**, extra, complementary, accompanying, secondary, auxiliary, add-on, supplemental, ancillary

supply VERB **1 = provide**, give, furnish, produce, stock, store, grant, afford, contribute, yield, come up with, outfit, endow, purvey, victual: *an agreement not to supply chemical weapons to these countries* **2 = furnish**, provide, equip, endow: *a pipeline which will supply the city with natural gas* **3 = meet**, provide for, fill, satisfy, fulfil, be adequate for, cater to *or* for: *a society that looks to the government to supply their needs*
▷ NOUN **= store**, fund, stock, source, reserve, quantity, reservoir, stockpile, hoard, cache: *The brain requires a constant supply of oxygen.*
▷ PLURAL NOUN **= provisions**, necessities, stores, food, materials, items, equipment, rations, foodstuff, provender: *The country's only supplies are those it can import by lorry.*

support VERB **1 = help**, back, champion, second, aid, forward, encourage, defend, promote, take (someone's) part, strengthen, assist, advocate, uphold, side with, go along with, stand up for, espouse, stand behind, hold (someone's) hand, stick up for *(informal)*, succour, buoy up, boost (someone's) morale, take up the cudgels for, be a source of strength to: *He supported the hardworking people.* **OPPOSITE:** oppose **2 = provide for**, maintain, look after, keep, fund, finance, sustain, foster, take care of, subsidize: *I have children to support, and a home to be maintained.* **OPPOSITE:** live off **3 = bear out**, confirm, verify, substantiate, corroborate, document, endorse, attest to, authenticate, lend credence to: *The evidence does not support the argument.* **OPPOSITE:** refute **4 = bear**, hold up, carry, sustain, prop (up), reinforce, hold, brace, uphold, bolster, underpin, shore up, buttress: *the thick wooden posts that supported the ceiling*
▷ NOUN **1 = furtherance**, backing, promotion, championship, approval, assistance, encouragement, espousal: *They are prepared to resort to violence in support of their views.* **2 = help**, protection, comfort, friendship, assistance, blessing, loyalty, patronage, moral support, succour: *We hope to continue to have her close support and friendship.* **OPPOSITE:** opposition **3 = aid**, help, benefits, relief, assistance: *the EC's proposal to cut agricultural support* **4 = prop**, post, foundation, back, lining, stay, shore, brace, pillar, underpinning, stanchion, stiffener, abutment: *Rats had been gnawing at the supports of the house.* **5 = supporter**, prop, mainstay, tower of strength, second, stay, backer, backbone, comforter: *Andrew is terrific. He's been such a support to me.* **OPPOSITE:** antagonist **6 = upkeep**, maintenance, keep, livelihood, subsistence, sustenance: *He failed to send child support.*

supporter NOUN **= follower**, fan, advocate, friend, champion, ally, defender, sponsor, patron, helper, protagonist, adherent, henchman, apologist, upholder, well-wisher **OPPOSITE:** opponent

supportive ADJECTIVE **= helpful**, caring, encouraging, understanding, reassuring, sympathetic
▸ *related prefix:* pro-

suppose VERB **1 = imagine**, believe, consider, conclude, fancy, conceive, conjecture, postulate, hypothesize: *Where do you suppose he's got to?* **2 = think**, imagine, expect, judge, assume, guess *(informal, chiefly U.S. & Canad.)*, calculate *(U.S. dialect)*, presume, take for granted, infer, conjecture, surmise, dare say, opine, presuppose, take as read: *The problem was more complex than he supposed.*

supposed ADJECTIVE **1** *(usually with* **to***)* **= meant**, expected, required, obliged: *He produced a handwritten list of nine men he was supposed to kill.* **2 = presumed**, alleged, professed, reputed, accepted, assumed, rumoured, hypothetical, putative, presupposed: *What is it his son is supposed to have said?*

supposedly ADVERB **= presumably**, allegedly, ostensibly, theoretically, by all accounts, purportedly, avowedly, hypothetically, at a guess, professedly **OPPOSITE:** actually

supposition NOUN **= belief**, idea, notion, view, theory, speculation, assumption, hypothesis, presumption, conjecture, surmise, guesswork

suppress VERB **1 = stamp out**, stop, check, crush, conquer, overthrow, subdue, put an end to, overpower, quash, crack down on, quell, extinguish, clamp down on, snuff out, quench, beat down, trample on, drive underground: *drug traffickers who flourish despite attempts to suppress them* **OPPOSITE:** encourage **2 = check**, inhibit, subdue, stop, quell, quench: *strong evidence that ultraviolet light can suppress immune responses* **3 = restrain**, cover up, withhold, stifle, contain, silence, conceal, curb, repress, smother, keep secret, muffle, muzzle, hold in check, hold in *or* back: *Liz thought of Barry and suppressed a smile.* **4 = conceal**, hide, keep secret, hush up, stonewall, sweep under the carpet, draw a veil over, keep silent about, keep dark, keep under your hat *(informal)*: *At no time did they try to persuade me to suppress the information.*

suppression NOUN **1 = elimination**, crushing, crackdown, check, extinction, prohibition, quashing, dissolution, termination, clampdown: *They were imprisoned after the suppression of pro-democracy protests.* **2 = inhibition**, blocking, restriction,

S

The Language of DH Lawrence

David Herbert Richards Lawrence was born in Nottinghamshire in 1885 and died in France in 1930. He was an author, poet, dramatist, essayist, and literary critic. His most famous novels include *The Rainbow*, *Women in Love*, *Sons and Lovers*, and *Lady Chatterley's Lover*. His treatment of sexuality in his works led to accusations of obscenity and to censorship.

The word *soul* is the twentieth most commonly used noun in Lawrence's work, but doesn't appear until position 987 in the most frequently used words in fiction in Collins' *Bank of English*. Souls *leap* and *groan*, are *inflamed* and *wretched* and we are urged to *possess our own souls*. A distinction is made between the physicality of the body and the spirituality of the soul:

> She was a young, powerful, passionate woman,
> and she was unsatisfied **body and soul**.

Soul, in fact, appears more than 270 times more than *body* in Lawrence's writing.

Unsurprisingly, *love* is another common noun in Lawrence's work. Lawrence's characters *make* love, are *in love* and love is frequently *passionate*, *spiritual*, and *pure*. However, more significant are the frequencies of the words *passion* and *desire*, which don't appear at all in the top thousand most frequently occurring words in fiction in the *Bank of English*:

> She could see the sombre **passion and desire**
> and dissatisfaction in them, and she wanted not
> to see it any more.

Flower is also used frequently in Lawrence's writings, but again doesn't appear in the top thousand fiction words in the *Bank of English*. Flowers bring a burst of colour to Lawrence's often *black, industrial countryside* and are used as sensual imagery:

> Rhythmically, Miriam was swaying and stroking
> the **flower** with her mouth.

The strength, fragility, and the beauty of flowers are compared to people, unusually to men as well as women. In *Women in Love*, Ursula is described as 'frail like a flower just unfolded', in *Sons and Lovers*, Arthur Morel is 'the flower of the family' and in *England, My England*, Winifrid is 'like a ruddy hard flower of the field'.

The word *dark* is a frequently occurring adjective. Further investigation reveals that this word is often repeated with particular stylistic effect and is, in fact, a typical example of the use of repetition in Lawrence's writing:

> They saw a man come from the dark building,
> with a lighted lantern which swung golden, and
> made that his dark feet walked in a halo of snow.
> He was a small, dark figure in the darkened
> snow. He unlatched the door of an outhouse.
> A smell of cows, hot, animal, almost like beef,
> came out on the heavily cold air. There was a
> glimpse of two cattle in their dark stall, then the
> door was shut again, and not a chink of light
> showed.

In this short passage from *Women in Love*, the words *dark* and *darkened* appear 5 times. These words contrast with the repetition of *light*, which is also echoed in the words *golden* and *halo*. *Snow* also occurs twice, again contrasting with *dark* and emphasizing *light*. The word *door* is another repeated word which continues repetition in the language by means of alliteration with *dark* and *darkened*. Alliteration also occurs in *saw*, *swung*, *snow*, *small*, and *smell*, in *come*, *cows*, *cold*, and *cattle*, in *light* and *lantern*, in *golden* and *glimpse* and in *shut* and *showed*. The polyphonic nature of Lawrence's language is further demonstrated by repetition of vowel sounds in *man*, *lantern*, *unlatched*, and *animal*, and also in *golden*, *halo*, *snow*, and *cold*.

restraint, smothering: *suppression of the immune system* **3 = concealment**, covering, hiding, disguising, camouflage: *A mother's suppression of her own feelings can cause problems.* **4 = hiding**, hushing up, stonewalling: *suppression of official documents*

> **QUOTATIONS**
> Everybody knows there is no fineness or accuracy of suppression: if you hold down one thing, you hold down the adjoining
> [Saul Bellow *The Adventures of Augie March*]

supremacy NOUN **= domination**, dominance, ascendancy, sovereignty, sway, lordship, mastery, dominion, primacy, pre-eminence, predominance, supreme power, absolute rule, paramountcy

supreme ADJECTIVE **1 = paramount**, surpassing, superlative, prevailing, sovereign, predominant, incomparable, mother of all *(informal)*, unsurpassed, matchless: *The lady conspired to seize supreme power.* **OPPOSITE:** least **2 = chief**, leading, principal, first, highest, head, top, prime, cardinal, foremost, pre-eminent, peerless: *He proposes to make himself the supreme overlord.* **OPPOSITE:** lowest **3 = ultimate**, highest, greatest, utmost, final, crowning, extreme, culminating: *My eldest son made the supreme sacrifice in Vietnam.*

supremo NOUN **= head**, leader, boss *(informal)*, director, master, governor, commander, principal, ruler, baas *(S. African)*

sure ADJECTIVE **1 = certain**, positive, clear, decided, convinced, persuaded, confident, satisfied, assured, definite, free from doubt: *She was no longer sure how she felt about him.* **OPPOSITE:** uncertain **2 = inevitable**, guaranteed, bound, assured, in the bag *(slang)*, inescapable, irrevocable, ineluctable, nailed-on *(slang)*: *Another victory is now sure.* **OPPOSITE:** unsure **3 = reliable**, accurate, dependable, effective, precise, honest, unmistakable, undoubted, undeniable, trustworthy, never-failing, trusty, foolproof, infallible, indisputable, sure-fire *(informal)*, unerring, well-proven, unfailing, tried and true: *a sure sign of rain* **OPPOSITE:** unreliable **4 = secure**, firm, steady, fast, safe, solid, stable: *A doctor's sure hands may perform surgery.*

surely ADVERB **1 = it must be the case that**, assuredly: *If I can accept this situation, surely you can?* **2 = undoubtedly**, certainly, definitely, inevitably, doubtless, for certain, without doubt, unquestionably, inexorably, come what may, without fail, indubitably, doubtlessly, beyond the shadow of a doubt: *He knew that under the surgeon's knife he would surely die.*

surety NOUN **1 = security**, guarantee, deposit, insurance, bond, safety, pledge, bail, warranty, indemnity: *a surety of £2,500* **2 = guarantor**, sponsor, hostage, bondsman, mortgagor: *I agreed to stand surety for Arthur to be bailed out.*

surface NOUN **1 = covering**, face, exterior, side, top, skin, plane, facet, veneer: *The road surface had started breaking up.* **2 = façade**, outward appearance: *A much wider controversy was bubbling under the surface.*
▷ MODIFIER **= superficial**, external, outward, exterior: *Doctors believed it was just a surface wound.*
▷ VERB **1 = emerge**, come up, come to the surface: *He surfaced, gasping for air.* **2 = appear**, emerge, arise, come to light, crop up *(informal)*, transpire, materialize: *The emotions will surface at some point in life.*
on the surface = at first glance, apparently, outwardly, seemingly, ostensibly, superficially, to all appearances, to the casual eye: *On the surface the elections appear to be democratic.*

surfeit NOUN **= excess**, plethora, glut, satiety, overindulgence, superabundance, superfluity **OPPOSITE:** shortage

surge NOUN **1 = rush**, flood, upsurge, sudden increase, uprush: *a new surge of interest in Dylan's work* **2 = flow**, wave, rush, roller, breaker, gush, upsurge, outpouring, uprush: *The bridge was destroyed in a tidal surge during a storm.* **3 = tide**, roll, rolling, swell, swirling, billowing: *the beating and surge of the sea* **4 = rush**, wave, storm, outburst, torrent, eruption: *He was overcome by a sudden surge of jealousy.*
▷ VERB **1 = rush**, pour, stream, rise, swell, spill, swarm, seethe, gush, well forth: *The crowd surged out from the church.* **2 = roll**, rush, billow, heave, swirl, eddy, undulate: *Fish and seaweed rose, caught motionless in the surging water.* **3 = sweep**, rush, storm: *Panic surged through her.*

surly ADJECTIVE **= ill-tempered**, cross, churlish, crabbed, perverse, crusty, sullen, gruff, bearish, sulky, morose, brusque, testy, grouchy *(informal)*, curmudgeonly, ungracious, uncivil, shrewish **OPPOSITE:** cheerful

surmise VERB **= guess**, suppose, imagine, presume, consider, suspect, conclude, fancy, speculate, infer, deduce, come to the conclusion, conjecture, opine, hazard a guess: *He surmised that he had discovered one of the illegal streets.*
▷ NOUN **= guess**, speculation, assumption, thought, idea, conclusion, notion, suspicion, hypothesis, deduction, inference, presumption, conjecture, supposition: *His surmise proved correct.*

surmount VERB **= overcome**, master, conquer, pass, exceed, surpass, overpower, triumph over, vanquish, prevail over

surpass VERB **= outdo**, top, beat, best, cap *(informal)*, exceed, eclipse, overshadow, excel, transcend, outstrip, outshine, tower above, go one better than *(informal)*, put in the shade

surpassing ADJECTIVE **= supreme**, extraordinary, outstanding, exceptional, rare, phenomenal, stellar *(informal)*, transcendent, unrivalled, incomparable, matchless

surplus NOUN **= excess**, surfeit, superabundance, superfluity: *Germany suffers from a surplus of teachers.* **OPPOSITE:** shortage
▷ ADJECTIVE **= extra**, spare, excess, remaining, odd, in excess, left over, unused, superfluous: *Few people have large sums of surplus cash.* **OPPOSITE:** insufficient

surprise NOUN **1 = shock**, start, revelation, jolt, bombshell, eye-opener *(informal)*, bolt from the blue, turn-up for the books *(informal)*: *It is perhaps no surprise to see her attempting a comeback.* **2 = amazement**, astonishment, wonder, incredulity, stupefaction: *To my surprise I am in a room where I see one of my mother's sisters.*
▷ VERB **1 = amaze**, astonish, astound, stun, startle, stagger, disconcert, take aback, bowl over *(informal)*, leave open-mouthed, nonplus, flabbergast *(informal)*, take (someone's) breath away: *We'll solve the case ourselves and surprise everyone.* **2 = catch unawares** *or* **off-guard**, catch napping, catch on the hop *(informal)*, burst in on, spring upon, catch in the act *or* red-handed, come down on like a bolt from the blue: *The army surprised their enemy near the village of Blenheim.*

> **QUOTATIONS**
> Surprises are foolish things. The pleasure is not enhanced, and the inconvenience is often considerable
> [Jane Austen *Emma*]

surprised ADJECTIVE **= amazed**, astonished, startled, disconcerted, at a loss, taken aback, speechless, incredulous, open-mouthed, nonplussed, thunderstruck, unable to believe your eyes

surprising ADJECTIVE **= amazing**, remarkable, incredible, astonishing, wonderful, unusual, extraordinary, unexpected, staggering, marvellous, startling, astounding, jaw-dropping, eye-popping *(informal)*, unlooked-for

surrender VERB **1 = give in**, yield, submit, give way, quit, succumb, cave in *(informal)*, capitulate, throw in the towel, lay down arms, give yourself up, show the white flag: *We'll never surrender to the terrorists.* **OPPOSITE:** resist **2 = give up**, abandon, relinquish, resign, yield, concede, part with, renounce, waive, forgo, cede, deliver up: *She had to surrender all rights to her property.*
▷ NOUN **= submission**, yielding, cave-in *(informal)*, capitulation, resignation, renunciation, relinquishment: *the unconditional surrender of the rebels*

S

surreptitious ADJECTIVE **= secret**, clandestine, furtive, sneaking, veiled, covert, sly, fraudulent, unauthorized, underhand, stealthy **OPPOSITE:** open

surrogate NOUN **= substitute**, deputy, representative, stand-in, proxy

surround VERB **1 = enclose**, ring, encircle, encompass, envelop, close in on, fence in, girdle, hem in, environ, enwreath: *The church was surrounded by a rusted wrought-iron fence.* **2 = besiege**, beset, lay siege to, invest *(rare)*: *When the car stopped it was surrounded by police and militiamen.*

surrounding ADJECTIVE **= nearby**, neighbouring: *Aerial bombing of the surrounding area is continuing.*

surroundings PLURAL NOUN **= environment**, setting, background, location, neighbourhood, milieu, environs: *a peaceful holiday home in beautiful surroundings*

surveillance NOUN **= observation**, watch, scrutiny, supervision, control, care, direction, inspection, vigilance, superintendence, dataveillance

> **QUOTATIONS**
> Big Brother is watching you
> [George Orwell *1984*]

survey NOUN **1 = poll**, study, research, review, inquiry, investigation, opinion poll, questionnaire, census: *According to the survey, overall world trade has also slackened.* **2 = examination**, inspection, scrutiny, overview, once-over *(informal)*, perusal: *He sniffed the perfume she wore, then gave her a quick survey.* **3 = valuation**, estimate, assessment, appraisal: *a structural survey undertaken by a qualified surveyor*
▷ VERB **1 = interview**, question, poll, study, research, investigate, sample, canvass: *Only 18 percent of those surveyed opposed the idea.* **2 = look over**, view, scan, examine, observe, contemplate, supervise, inspect, eyeball *(slang)*, scrutinize, size up, take stock of, eye up, recce *(slang)*, reconnoitre: *He pushed himself to his feet and surveyed the room.* **3 = measure**, estimate, prospect, assess, appraise, triangulate: *Geological experts were commissioned to survey the land.*

survive VERB **1 = remain alive**, live, pull through, last, exist, live on, endure, hold out, subsist, keep body and soul together *(informal)*, be extant, fight for your life, keep your head above water: *Drugs that dissolve blood clots can help heart-attack victims survive.* **2 = continue**, last, live on, pull through: *Rejected by the people, can the organization survive at all?* **3 = live longer than**, outlive, outlast: *Most women will survive their spouses.*

susceptibility NOUN **= vulnerability**, weakness, liability, propensity, predisposition, proneness

susceptible ADJECTIVE **1 = responsive**, sensitive, receptive, alive to, impressionable, easily moved, suggestible: *He was unusually susceptible to flattery.* **OPPOSITE:** unresponsive **2** *(usually with* **to***)* **= liable**, inclined, prone, given, open, subject, vulnerable, disposed, predisposed: *Walking with weights makes the shoulders susceptible to injury.* **OPPOSITE:** resistant

suspect VERB **1 = believe**, feel, guess, consider, suppose, conclude, fancy, speculate, conjecture, surmise, hazard a guess, have a sneaking suspicion, think probable: *I suspect they were right.* **OPPOSITE:** know **2 = distrust**, doubt, mistrust, smell a rat *(informal)*, harbour suspicions about, have your doubts about: *You don't really think he suspects you, do you?* **OPPOSITE:** trust
▷ ADJECTIVE **= dubious**, doubtful, dodgy *(Brit., Austral. & N.Z. informal)*, questionable, fishy *(informal)*, iffy *(informal)*, open to suspicion, shonky *(Austral. & N.Z. informal)*: *Delegates evacuated the building when a suspect package was found.* **OPPOSITE:** innocent

suspend VERB **1 = postpone**, delay, put off, arrest, cease, interrupt, shelve, withhold, defer, adjourn, hold off, cut short, discontinue, lay aside, put in cold storage: *The union suspended strike action this week.* **OPPOSITE:** continue **2 = remove**, expel, eject, debar: *Julie was suspended from her job shortly after the incident.* **OPPOSITE:** reinstate **3 = hang**, attach, dangle, swing, append: *chandeliers suspended on heavy chains from the ceiling*

suspense NOUN **= uncertainty**, doubt, tension, anticipation, expectation, anxiety, insecurity, expectancy, apprehension: *a writer who holds the suspense throughout her tale*

suspension NOUN **= postponement**, delay, break, stay, breaking off, interruption, moratorium, respite, remission, adjournment, abeyance, deferment, discontinuation, disbarment

suspicion NOUN **1 = feeling**, theory, impression, intuition, conjecture, surmise, funny feeling *(informal)*, presentiment: *Police had suspicions that it was not a natural death.* **2 = distrust**, scepticism, mistrust, doubt, misgiving, qualm, lack of confidence, wariness, bad vibes *(slang)*, dubiety, chariness: *Our culture harbours deep suspicions of big-time industry.* **3 = idea**, notion, hunch, guess, impression, conjecture, surmise, gut feeling *(informal)*, supposition: *I have a sneaking suspicion that they are going to succeed.* **4 = trace**, touch, hint, shadow, suggestion, strain, shade, streak, tinge, glimmer, soupçon *(French)*: *large blooms of white with a suspicion of pale pink*
above suspicion = blameless, unimpeachable, above reproach, pure, honourable, virtuous, sinless, like Caesar's wife: *He was a respected academic and above suspicion*

> **QUOTATIONS**
> Caesar's wife should be above suspicion
> [Julius Caesar]
>
> There is no smoke without fire
> [Plautus *Curculio*]

suspicious ADJECTIVE **1 = distrustful**, suspecting, sceptical, doubtful, apprehensive, leery *(slang)*, mistrustful, unbelieving, wary: *He has his father's suspicious nature.* **OPPOSITE:** trusting **2 = suspect**, dubious, questionable, funny, doubtful, dodgy *(Brit., Austral. & N.Z. informal)*, queer, irregular, shady *(informal)*, fishy *(informal)*, of doubtful honesty, open to doubt *or* misconstruction, shonky *(Austral. & N.Z. informal)*: *two suspicious-looking characters* **OPPOSITE:** beyond suspicion **3 = odd**, strange, mysterious, dark, dubious, irregular, questionable, murky *(informal)*, shady *(informal)*, fishy: *Four people have died in suspicious circumstances.*

sustain VERB **1 = maintain**, continue, keep up, prolong, keep going, keep alive, protract: *He has sustained his fierce social conscience.* **2 = suffer**, experience, undergo, feel, bear, endure, withstand, bear up under: *Every aircraft in there has sustained some damage.* **3 = help**, aid, comfort, foster, assist, relieve, nurture: *I am sustained by letters of support.* **4 = keep alive**, nourish, provide for: *not enough food to sustain a mouse* **5 = support**, carry, bear, keep up, uphold, keep from falling: *The magnets have lost the capacity to sustain the weight.* **6 = uphold**, confirm, endorse, approve, ratify, verify, validate: *The court sustained his objection.*

sustained ADJECTIVE **= continuous**, constant, steady, prolonged, perpetual, unremitting, nonstop **OPPOSITE:** periodic

sustenance NOUN **1 = nourishment**, food, provisions, rations, refreshments, kai *(N.Z. informal)*, daily bread, victuals, edibles, comestibles, provender, aliment, eatables, refection: *The state provided a basic quantity of food for daily sustenance.* **2 = support**, maintenance, livelihood, subsistence: *everything that is necessary for the sustenance of the offspring*

svelte ADJECTIVE **= slender**, lithe, willowy, graceful, slinky, lissom(e), sylphlike

swagger VERB **1 = stride**, parade, strut, prance: *The burly brute swaggered forward, towering over me, and shouted.* **2 = show off**, boast, brag, hot-dog *(chiefly U.S.)*, bluster, swank *(informal)*, gasconade *(rare)*: *It's bad manners to swagger about how rich you are.*
▷ NOUN **1 = strut**: *He walked with something of a swagger.* **2 = ostentation**, show, display, showing off *(informal)*, bluster, swashbuckling, swank *(informal)*, braggadocio, gasconade *(rare)*: *What he needed was confidence and a bit of swagger.*

S

swallow VERB **1 = eat**, down *(informal)*, consume, devour, absorb, swig *(informal)*, swill, wash down, ingest: *Polly took a bite of the apple, chewed and swallowed it.* **2 = gulp**, drink: *He took a glass of Scotch and swallowed it down.* **3 = believe**, accept, buy *(slang)*, fall for, take (something) as gospel: *I too found this story a little hard to swallow.* **4 = suppress**, hold in, restrain, contain, hold back, stifle, repress, bottle up, bite back, choke back: *Gordon swallowed the anger he felt.*
swallow something *or* **someone up 1 = engulf**, overwhelm, overrun, consume: *Weeds had swallowed up the garden.* **2 = absorb**, assimilate, envelop: *Wage costs swallow up two-thirds of the turnover.*

swamp NOUN **= bog**, marsh, quagmire, moss *(Scot. & Northern English dialect)*, slough, fen, mire, morass, everglade(s) (U.S.), pakihi (N.Z.), muskeg *(Canad.)*: *Much of the land is desert or swamp.*
▷ VERB **1 = flood**, engulf, submerge, inundate, deluge: *The Ventura river burst its banks, swamping a mobile home park.* **2 = overload**, overwhelm, inundate, besiege, beset, snow under: *We swamp them with praise, make them think that they are important.*

swampy ADJECTIVE **= boggy**, waterlogged, marshy, wet, fenny, miry, quaggy, marish *(obsolete)*

swank VERB **= show off**, swagger, give yourself airs, posture *(informal)*, hot-dog *(chiefly U.S.)*, put on side *(Brit. slang)*: *I never swank about the things I have been lucky enough to win.*
▷ NOUN **= boastfulness**, show, ostentation, display, swagger, vainglory: *There was no swank in Martin.*

swanky ADJECTIVE **= ostentatious**, grand, posh *(informal, chiefly Brit.)*, rich, expensive, exclusive, smart, fancy, flash, fashionable, glamorous, stylish, gorgeous, lavish, luxurious, sumptuous, plush *(informal)*, flashy, swish *(informal, chiefly Brit.)*, glitzy *(slang)*, showy, ritzy *(slang)*, de luxe, swank *(informal)*, plushy *(informal)*, schmick *(Austral. informal)*
OPPOSITE: modest

swap *or* **swop** VERB **= exchange**, trade, switch, traffic, interchange, barter

swarm NOUN **= multitude**, crowd, mass, army, host, drove, flock, herd, horde, myriad, throng, shoal, concourse, bevy: *A swarm of people encircled the hotel.*
▷ VERB **1 = crowd**, flock, throng, mass, stream, congregate: *People swarmed to the shops, buying up everything in sight.* **2 = teem**, crawl, be alive, abound, bristle, be overrun, be infested: *Within minutes the area was swarming with officers.*

swarthy ADJECTIVE **= dark-skinned**, black, brown, dark, tawny, dusky, swart *(archaic)*, dark-complexioned

swashbuckling ADJECTIVE **= dashing**, spirited, bold, flamboyant, swaggering, gallant, daredevil, mettlesome, roisterous

swastika NOUN **= crooked cross**, fylfot

swath *or* **swathe** NOUN **= area**, section, stretch, patch, tract: *On May 1st the army took over another swathe of territory.*

swathe VERB **= wrap**, drape, envelop, bind, lap, fold, bandage, cloak, shroud, swaddle, furl, sheathe, enfold, bundle up, muffle up, enwrap: *She swathed her enormous body in thin black fabrics.*

sway VERB **1 = move from side to side**, rock, wave, roll, swing, bend, lean, incline, lurch, oscillate, move to and fro: *The people swayed back and forth with arms linked.* **2 = influence**, control, direct, affect, guide, dominate, persuade, govern, win over, induce, prevail on: *Don't ever be swayed by fashion.*
▷ NOUN **= power**, control, influence, government, rule, authority, command, sovereignty, jurisdiction, clout *(informal)*, dominion, predominance, ascendancy: *How can mothers keep daughters under their sway?*
hold sway = prevail, rule, predominate, reign: *Here, a completely different approach seems to hold sway.*

swear VERB **1 = curse**, cuss *(informal)*, blaspheme, turn the air blue *(informal)*, be foul-mouthed, take the Lord's name in vain, utter profanities, imprecate: *It is wrong to swear and shout.* **2 = vow**, promise, take an oath, warrant, testify, depose, attest, avow, give your word, state under oath, pledge yourself: *Alan swore that he would do everything in his power to help us.* **3 = declare**, assert, affirm, swear blind, asseverate: *I swear I've told you all I know.*
swear by something = believe in, trust, depend on, rely on, have confidence in: *Many people swear by vitamin C's ability to ward off colds.*

swearing NOUN **= bad language**, cursing, profanity, blasphemy, cussing *(informal)*, foul language, imprecations, malediction

> QUOTATIONS
> Expletive deleted
> [editor of Nixon's Watergate tapes]

swearword NOUN **= oath**, curse, obscenity, expletive, four-letter word, cuss *(informal)*, profanity

sweat NOUN **1 = perspiration**, moisture, dampness: *He wiped the sweat off his face and looked around.* **2 = panic**, anxiety, state *(informal)*, worry, distress, flap *(informal)*, agitation, fluster, lather *(informal)*, tizzy *(informal)*, state of anxiety: *She was in a sweat about the exam.*
▷ VERB **1 = perspire**, swelter, break out in a sweat, exude moisture, glow: *Already they were sweating as the sun beat down upon them.* **2 = worry**, fret, agonize, lose sleep over, be on tenterhooks, torture yourself, be on pins and needles *(informal)*: *It gives sales chiefs something to sweat about.*
sweat something out = endure, see (something) through, stick it out *(informal)*, stay the course: *I just had to sweat it out and hope.*

sweaty ADJECTIVE **= perspiring**, sweating, sticky, clammy, bathed *or* drenched *or* soaked in perspiration, glowing

sweep VERB **1 = brush**, clean: *She was in the kitchen sweeping the floor.* **2 = clear**, remove, brush, clean: *I swept rainwater off the flat top of a gravestone.* **3 = sail**, pass, fly, tear, zoom, glide, skim, scud, hurtle: *The car swept past the gate house.* **4 = swagger**, sail, breeze, stride, stroll, glide, flounce: *She swept into the conference room.*
▷ NOUN **1 = movement**, move, swing, stroke, gesture: *She indicated the garden with a sweep of her hand.* **2 = arc**, bend, curve: *the great sweep of the bay* **3 = extent**, range, span, stretch, scope, compass: *the whole sweep of German social and political history*

sweeping ADJECTIVE **1 = indiscriminate**, blanket, across-the-board, wholesale, exaggerated, overstated, unqualified, overdrawn: *sweeping generalizations about ability based on gender* **2 = wide-ranging**, global, comprehensive, wide, broad, radical, extensive, all-inclusive, all-embracing, overarching, thoroughgoing: *sweeping economic reforms* **OPPOSITE:** limited

sweet ADJECTIVE **1 = sugary**, sweetened, cloying, honeyed, saccharine, syrupy, icky *(informal)*, treacly: *a mug of sweet tea* **OPPOSITE:** sour **2 = fragrant**, perfumed, aromatic, redolent, sweet-smelling: *the sweet smell of a summer garden* **OPPOSITE:** stinking **3 = fresh**, clean, pure, wholesome: *I gulped a breath of sweet air.* **4 = melodious**, musical, harmonious, soft, mellow, silvery, tuneful, dulcet, sweet-sounding, euphonious, silver-toned, euphonic: *the sweet sounds of Mozart* **OPPOSITE:** harsh **5 = charming**, kind, gentle, tender, affectionate, agreeable, amiable, sweet-tempered: *He was a sweet man but when he drank he tended to quarrel.* **OPPOSITE:** nasty **6 = delightful**, appealing, cute, taking, winning, fair, beautiful, attractive, engaging, lovable, winsome, cutesy *(informal, chiefly U.S.)*, likable *or* likeable: *a sweet little baby girl* **OPPOSITE:** unpleasant **7 = beloved**, dear, darling, dearest, pet, treasured, precious, cherished: *my dear, sweet mother*
▷ NOUN **1** *(usually plural)* **= confectionery**, candy (U.S.), sweetie, lolly *(Austral. & N.Z.)*, sweetmeat, bonbon: *They've always enjoyed fish and chips – and sweets and cakes.* **2 = dessert**, pudding, afters *(Brit. informal)*, sweet course: *The sweet was a mousse flavoured with whisky and topped with cream.*

S

sweet on = in love with, keen on, infatuated with, gone on *(slang)*, fond of, taken with, enamoured of, head over heels in love with, obsessed *or* bewitched by, wild *or* mad about *(informal)*: *It was rumoured that she was sweet on him.*

sweeten VERB **1 = sugar**: *He liberally sweetened his coffee.* **2 = soften**, ease, alleviate, relieve, temper, cushion, mellow, make less painful: *They sweetened the deal with a rather generous cash payment.* **3 = mollify**, appease, soothe, pacify, soften up, sugar the pill: *He is likely to try to sweeten them with pledges of fresh aid.*

sweetheart NOUN **1 = dearest**, beloved, sweet, angel, treasure, honey, dear, sweetie *(informal)*: *Happy birthday, sweetheart!* **2 = love**, boyfriend *or* girlfriend, beloved, lover, steady *(informal)*, flame *(informal)*, darling, follower *(obsolete)*, valentine, admirer, suitor, beau, swain *(archaic)*, truelove, leman *(archaic)*, inamorata *or* inamorato: *I married my childhood sweetheart, in Liverpool.*

swell VERB **1 = increase**, rise, grow, mount, expand, accelerate, escalate, multiply, grow larger: *The human population swelled as migrants moved south.* **OPPOSITE:** decrease **2 = expand**, increase, grow, rise, extend, balloon, belly, enlarge, bulge, protrude, well up, billow, fatten, dilate, puff up, round out, be inflated, become larger, distend, bloat, tumefy, become bloated *or* distended: *The limbs swell to an enormous size.* **OPPOSITE:** shrink
▷ NOUN **= wave**, rise, surge, billow: *the swell of the incoming tide*

swelling NOUN **= enlargement**, lump, puffiness, bump, blister, bulge, inflammation, dilation, protuberance, distension, tumescence
▸ *related adjective:* tumescent

sweltering ADJECTIVE **= hot**, burning, boiling, steaming, baking, roasting, stifling, scorching, oppressive, humid, torrid, sultry, airless

swerve VERB **= veer**, turn, swing, shift, bend, incline, deflect, depart from, skew, diverge, deviate, turn aside, sheer off

swift ADJECTIVE **1 = quick**, immediate, prompt, rapid, instant, abrupt, ready, expeditious: *We need to make a swift decision.* **2 = fast**, quick, rapid, flying, express, winged, sudden, fleet, hurried, speedy, spanking, nimble, quickie *(informal)*, nippy *(Brit. informal)*, fleet-footed: *a swift runner*
OPPOSITE: slow

swiftly ADVERB **1 = quickly**, rapidly, speedily, without losing time: *They have acted swiftly and decisively.* **2 = fast**, promptly, hurriedly, apace, pronto *(informal)*, double-quick, hell for leather, like lightning, hotfoot, like the clappers *(Brit. informal)*, posthaste, like greased lightning *(informal)*, nippily *(Brit. informal)*, in less than no time, as fast as your legs can carry you, (at) full tilt, pdq *(slang)*: *Lenny moved swiftly and silently across the front lawn.*

swill VERB **1 = drink**, gulp, swig *(informal)*, guzzle, drain, consume, swallow, imbibe, quaff, bevvy *(dialect)*, toss off, bend the elbow *(informal)*, pour down your gullet: *A crowd of men were standing around swilling beer.* **2** *(often with* **out***)* **= rinse**, wash out, sluice, flush, drench, wash down: *He swilled out the mug and left it on the draining board.*
▷ NOUN **= waste**, slops, mash, mush, hogwash, pigswill, scourings: *The porker ate swill from a trough.*

swindle VERB **= cheat**, do *(slang)*, con, skin *(slang)*, trick, stiff *(slang)*, sting *(informal)*, rip (someone) off *(slang)*, deceive, fleece, defraud, dupe, overcharge, rook *(slang)*, bamboozle *(informal)*, diddle *(informal)*, take (someone) for a ride *(informal)*, put one over on (someone) *(informal)*, pull a fast one (on someone) *(informal)*, bilk (of), take to the cleaners *(informal)*, sell a pup (to) *(slang)*, cozen, hornswoggle *(slang)*, scam *(slang)*: *He swindled investors out of millions of pounds.*
▷ NOUN **= fraud**, fiddle *(Brit. informal)*, rip-off *(slang)*, racket, scam *(slang)*, sting *(informal)*, deception, imposition, deceit, trickery, double-dealing, con trick *(informal)*, sharp practice, swizzle *(Brit. informal)*, knavery, swizz *(Brit. informal)*, roguery, fastie *(Austral. slang)*: *He fled to Switzerland rather than face trial for a tax swindle.*

swing VERB **1 = brandish**, wave, shake, flourish, wield, dangle: *She was swinging a bottle of wine by its neck.*
2 = sway, rock, wave, veer, vibrate, oscillate, move back and forth, move to and fro: *The sail of the little boat swung from one side to the other.* **3** *(usually with* **round***)* **= turn**, veer, swivel, twist, curve, rotate, pivot, turn on your heel: *The canoe found the current and swung around.* **4 = hit out**, strike, swipe, lash out at, slap: *I picked up his baseball bat and swung at the man's head.* **5 = hang**, dangle, be suspended, suspend, move back and forth: *He looks cute swinging from a branch.*
▷ NOUN **1 = swaying**, sway: *a woman walking with a slight swing to her hips*
2 = fluctuation, change, shift, switch, variation: *Dieters can suffer from violent mood swings.*
in full swing = at its height, under way, on the go *(informal)*: *The international rugby season was in full swing.*

swingeing ADJECTIVE **= severe**, heavy, drastic, huge, punishing, harsh, excessive, daunting, stringent, oppressive, Draconian, exorbitant

swipe VERB **1 = hit out**, strike, slap, lash out at: *She swiped at him as though he were a fly.* **2 = steal**, nick *(slang, chiefly Brit.)*, pinch *(informal)*, lift *(informal)*, appropriate, cabbage *(Brit. slang)*, make off with, pilfer, purloin, filch, snaffle *(Brit. informal)*: *People kept trying to swipe my copy of the New York Times.*
▷ NOUN **= blow**, slap, smack, clip *(informal)*, thump, clout *(informal)*, cuff, clump *(slang)*, wallop *(informal)*: *He gave Andrew a swipe on the ear.*

swirl VERB **= whirl**, churn, spin, twist, boil, surge, agitate, eddy, twirl

swish ADJECTIVE **= smart**, grand, posh *(informal, chiefly Brit.)*, exclusive, elegant, swell *(informal)*, fashionable, sumptuous, ritzy *(slang)*, de luxe, plush *or* plushy *(informal)*

switch NOUN **1 = control**, button, lever, on/off device: *a light switch*
2 = change, shift, transition, conversion, reversal, alteration, about-turn, change of direction: *New technology made the switch to oil possible.*
▷ VERB **1 = change**, shift, convert, divert, deviate, change course: *I'm switching to a new gas supplier.*
2 = exchange, trade, swap, replace, substitute, rearrange, interchange: *The ballot boxes have been switched.*
switch something off = turn off, shut off, deactivate, cut: *She switched off the coffee-machine.*
switch something on = turn on, put on, set off, activate, set in motion: *He pointed the torch at his feet and tried to switch it on.*

swivel VERB **= turn**, spin, revolve, rotate, pivot, pirouette, swing round

swollen ADJECTIVE **= enlarged**, bloated, puffy, inflamed, puffed up, distended, tumescent, oedematous, dropsical, tumid, edematous

swoop VERB **1 = pounce**, attack, charge, rush, descend: *The terror ended when armed police swooped on the car.*
2 = drop, plunge, dive, sweep, descend, plummet, pounce, stoop: *The hawk swooped and soared away carrying something.*
▷ NOUN **= raid**, attack, assault, surprise search: *a swoop on a German lorry*

swop *see* swap

sword NOUN **= blade**, brand *(archaic)*, trusty steel: *the stubby sword used by ancient Roman gladiators*

swot VERB **= study**, revise, cram *(informal)*, work, get up *(informal)*, pore over, bone up on *(informal)*, burn the midnight oil, mug up *(Brit. slang)*, toil over, apply yourself to, lucubrate *(rare)*

sycophant NOUN **= crawler**, yes man, toady, slave, parasite, cringer, fawner, hanger-on, sponger, flatterer, truckler, lickspittle, apple polisher *(U.S. slang)*, bootlicker *(informal)*, toadeater *(rare)*, suckhole *(Austral. slang)*

sycophantic ADJECTIVE **= obsequious**, grovelling, ingratiating, servile, crawling, flattering, cringing, fawning, slimy, slavish, unctuous, smarmy *(Brit. informal)*, toadying, parasitical, bootlicking *(informal)*, timeserving

syllabus NOUN **= course of study**, curriculum

symbol NOUN **1 = metaphor**, image, sign, representation, token: *To them the monarchy is a special symbol of nationhood.* **2 = representation**, sign, figure, mark, type, image, token, logo, badge, emblem, glyph: *I frequently use sunflowers as symbols of strength.*

symbolic ADJECTIVE **1 = representative**, token, emblematic, allegorical: *The move today was largely symbolic.* **2 = figurative**, representative: *symbolic representations of landscape*

symbolize VERB **= represent**, signify, stand for, mean, exemplify, denote, typify, personify, connote, betoken, body forth

symmetrical ADJECTIVE **= balanced**, regular, proportional, in proportion, well-proportioned **OPPOSITE:** unbalanced

symmetry NOUN **= balance**, proportion, regularity, form, order, harmony, correspondence, evenness

sympathetic ADJECTIVE **1 = caring**, kind, understanding, concerned, feeling, interested, kindly, warm, tender, pitying, supportive, responsive, affectionate, compassionate, commiserating, warm-hearted, condoling: *It may be that he sees you only as a sympathetic friend.* **OPPOSITE:** uncaring **2 = supportive**, encouraging, pro, approving of, friendly to, in sympathy with, well-disposed towards, favourably disposed towards: *They were sympathetic to our cause.* **3 = like-minded**, compatible, agreeable, friendly, responsive, appreciative, congenial, companionable, well-intentioned: *She sounds a most sympathetic character.* **OPPOSITE:** uncongenial

sympathetically ADVERB **= feelingly**, kindly, understandingly, warmly, with interest, with feeling, sensitively, with compassion, appreciatively, perceptively, responsively, warm-heartedly

sympathizer NOUN **= supporter**, partisan, protagonist, fellow traveller, well-wisher

sympathize with VERB **1 = feel for**, pity, empathize with, commiserate with, bleed for, have compassion for, grieve with, offer consolation for, condole with, share another's sorrow, feel your heart go out to: *I must tell you how much I sympathize with you for your loss.* **OPPOSITE:** have no feelings for **2 = agree with**, support, side with, understand, identify with, go along with, be in accord with, be in sympathy with: *Some Europeans sympathize with the Americans over the issue.* **OPPOSITE:** disagree with

sympathy NOUN **1 = compassion**, understanding, pity, empathy, tenderness, condolence(s), thoughtfulness, commiseration, aroha *(N.Z.)*: *We expressed our sympathy for her loss.* **OPPOSITE:** indifference **2 = affinity**, agreement, rapport, union, harmony, warmth, correspondence, fellow feeling, congeniality: *I still have sympathy with this point of view.* **OPPOSITE:** opposition

symptom NOUN **1 = sign**, mark, indication, warning: *patients with flu symptoms* **2 = manifestation**, sign, indication, mark, evidence, expression, proof, token: *Your problem with sleep is just a symptom of a larger problem.*

symptomatic ADJECTIVE **= indicative**, characteristic, suggestive

synonymous with ADJECTIVE **= equivalent to**, the same as, identical to, similar to, identified with, equal to, tantamount to, interchangeable with, one and the same as

synopsis NOUN **= summary**, review, résumé, outline, abstract, digest, epitome, rundown, condensation, compendium, précis, aperçu *(French)*, abridgment, conspectus, outline sketch

synthesis NOUN **= combining**, integration, amalgamation, unification, welding, coalescence

synthetic ADJECTIVE **= artificial**, manufactured, fake, man-made, mock, simulated, sham, pseudo *(informal)*, ersatz **OPPOSITE:** real

system NOUN **1 = arrangement**, structure, organization, scheme, combination, classification, coordination, setup *(informal)*: *a multi-party system of government* **2 = network**, organization, web, grid, set of channels: *a news channel on a local cable system* **3 = method**, practice, technique, procedure, routine, theory, usage, methodology, frame of reference, modus operandi, fixed order: *the decimal system of metric weights and measures*

systematic ADJECTIVE **= methodical**, organized, efficient, precise, orderly, standardized, businesslike, well-ordered, systematized **OPPOSITE:** unmethodical

The Language of Joseph Conrad

Joseph Conrad (1857–1924) was born as Jozef Teodor Konrad Korzeniowski to Polish parents in the Ukraine. He made a career first in the French, then in the British merchant marine before becoming a naturalized British subject in 1886. He published his first novel, *Almayer's Folly*, in 1895 and there followed a succession of novels and short stories featuring his favourite themes of the sea, adventure, and espionage, such as *Lord Jim* (1900), *The Secret Agent* (1907), and *Under Western Eyes* (1911). English was, of course, not his first language but his third (after Polish and French) but his writing demonstrates that he became an acknowledged master of it.

He chose to write in English as he had long admired Great Britain both as a great sea power, especially contrasted with his Polish homeland that was under the heel of Russia, and as the source of the literature he most enjoyed. On a more practical level, he was perfectly aware that attempting to publish in Polish would severely restrict his readership, and after quitting the sea he soon had a young family to support. Despite his naturalization and marriage to an English wife, he retained a marked Polish accent for the rest of his life, which often made him reluctant to give public talks from fear of not being understood, but he himself claimed that if he had not written in English he would not have written at all.

Typical Conrad prose is spare and direct, rather than fancy or long-winded. He mainly deals with practical people, men who get things done despite their moral uncertainties or spiritual fears, and Conrad's language reflects this. As may be expected from the nautical setting of many of his works, nouns of the sea (such as *sea, water, ship, boat*) are recurrent, even in the metaphors he uses:

> ....the big office desk, with one of its legs broken, careened over like the hull of a stranded **ship**...

In keeping with Conrad's characteristic terseness, two of the adjectives he uses most are those eternal opposites *white* and *black*. In his novels and stories that have a tropical setting Conrad makes frequent mention of the white uniforms of sailors, the white clouds in blue skies, the white dresses of the European women contrasted with the more colourful clothing (or lack of it) among the indigenous peoples. However, there is no getting away from the fact that the majority of his uses of *white* are in terms of skin colour, of race. His most frequent collocations are *man, men* and *woman*.

> Almayer in his quality of **white** man – as Lingard before him – had somewhat better relations with the up-river tribes.

It has to be remembered that Conrad was writing at the time of great imperial expansion by European powers and America, a time in which white people unthinkingly saw themselves as bringing 'civilization' to inferior cultures, and he is merely reflecting the accepted belief of his contemporaries that race was important in defining character. This is not to say that Conrad was a white supremacist; indeed he often shows white people at a disadvantage when seen from a non-white point of view:

> They fought without arms, like wild beasts, after the manner of **white men**.

On the other hand, as could be predicted from the author of *Heart of Darkness*, Conrad's use of *black* is less about race than about suggesting mystery, things not understood, the impenetrability of jungle and of the night.

> 'How dark it is,' he muttered to himself – 'one would think the world had been painted black.'

Tt

tab NOUN **= flap**, tag, label, ticket, flag, marker, sticker

table NOUN **1 = counter**, bench, stand, board, surface, slab, work surface: *I placed his drink on the small table.* **2 = list**, chart, tabulation, record, roll, index, register, digest, diagram, inventory, graph, synopsis, itemization: *Consult the table on page 104.* **3 = food**, spread (*informal*), board, diet, fare, kai (*N.Z. informal*), victuals: *She always sets a marvellous table.*
▹ VERB **= submit**, propose, put forward, move, suggest, enter, file, lodge, moot: *They've tabled a motion criticizing the government for inaction.*

tableau NOUN **= picture**, scene, representation, arrangement, spectacle

taboo *or* **tabu** ADJECTIVE **= forbidden**, banned, prohibited, ruled out, not allowed, unacceptable, outlawed, unthinkable, not permitted, disapproved of, anathema, off limits, frowned on, proscribed, beyond the pale, unmentionable: *Cancer is a taboo subject.* **OPPOSITE:** permitted
▹ NOUN **= prohibition**, ban, restriction, disapproval, anathema, interdict, proscription, tapu (*N.Z.*): *Not all men respect the taboo against bedding a friend's woman.*

tacit ADJECTIVE **= implied**, understood, implicit, silent, taken for granted, unspoken, inferred, undeclared, wordless, unstated, unexpressed **OPPOSITE:** stated

taciturn ADJECTIVE **= uncommunicative**, reserved, reticent, unforthcoming, quiet, withdrawn, silent, distant, dumb, mute, aloof, antisocial, tight-lipped, close-lipped **OPPOSITE:** communicative

tack NOUN **= nail**, pin, stud, staple, rivet, drawing pin, thumbtack (*U.S.*), tintack: *Use a staple gun or upholstery tacks.*
▹ VERB **1 = fasten**, fix, attach, pin, nail, staple, affix: *He had tacked this note to the door.* **2 = stitch**, sew, hem, bind, baste: *Tack the cord around the cushion.*
tack something on to something = append, add, attach, tag, annex: *The childcare bill is to be tacked on to the budget plan.*

tackle NOUN **1 = block**, stop, challenge: *a tackle by a full-back* **2 = rig**, rigging, apparatus: *I finally hoisted him up with a block and tackle.*
▹ VERB **1 = deal with**, take on, set about, wade into, get stuck into (*informal*), sink your teeth into, apply yourself to, come *or* get to grips with, step up to the plate (*informal*): *We need to tackle these problems and save people's lives.* **2 = undertake**, deal with, attempt, try, begin, essay, engage in, embark upon, get stuck into (*informal*), turn your hand to, have a go *or* stab at (*informal*): *My husband is quite good at DIY and wants to tackle the job himself.*
3 = intercept, block, bring down, stop, challenge: *He tackled the quarter-back.*

tacky[1] ADJECTIVE **= sticky**, wet, adhesive, gummy, icky (*informal*), gluey: *If the finish is still tacky, leave to harden.*

tacky[2] ADJECTIVE (*informal*) **1 = vulgar**, cheap, tasteless, nasty, sleazy, naff (*Brit. slang*): *tacky red sunglasses*
2 = seedy, shabby, shoddy: *The whole thing is dreadfully tacky.*

tact NOUN **= diplomacy**, understanding, consideration, sensitivity, delicacy, skill, judgment, perception, discretion, finesse, thoughtfulness, savoir-faire, adroitness **OPPOSITE:** tactlessness

> **PROVERBS**
> *Least said, soonest mended*

tactful ADJECTIVE **= diplomatic**, politic, discreet, prudent, understanding, sensitive, polished, careful, subtle, delicate, polite, thoughtful, perceptive, considerate, judicious **OPPOSITE:** tactless

tactic NOUN **= policy**, approach, course, way, means, move, line, scheme, plans, method, trick, device, manoeuvre, tack, ploy, stratagem: *His tactic to press on paid off.*

tactical ADJECTIVE **= strategic**, politic, shrewd, smart, diplomatic, clever, cunning, skilful, artful, foxy, adroit **OPPOSITE:** impolitic

tactician NOUN **= strategist**, campaigner, planner, mastermind, general, director, brain (*informal*), coordinator, schemer

tactics PLURAL NOUN **= strategy**, campaigning, manoeuvres, generalship: *guerrilla tactics*

tag NOUN **= label**, tab, sticker, note, ticket, slip, flag, identification, marker, flap, docket: *Staff wore name tags and called inmates by their first names.*
▹ VERB **1 = label**, mark, flag, ticket, identify, earmark: *Important trees were tagged to protect them from machinery.*
2 = name, call, label, term, style, dub, nickname, christen: *The critics still tagged him with his old name.*

tail NOUN **1 = extremity**, appendage, brush, rear end, hindquarters, hind part, empennage: *The cattle were swinging their tails to disperse the flies.*
2 = train, end, trail, tailpiece: *a comet tail* **3 = buttocks**, behind (*informal*), bottom, butt (*U.S. & Canad. informal*), bum (*Brit. slang*), rear (*informal*), buns (*U.S. slang*), backside (*informal*), rump, rear end, posterior, derrière (*euphemistic*), jacksy (*Brit. slang*): *He desperately needs a kick in the tail.*
4 = ponytail, braid, plait, tress, pigtail: *She wore bleached denims with her golden tail of hair swinging.*
▹ VERB **= follow**, track, shadow, trail, stalk, keep an eye on, dog the footsteps of: *Officers had tailed the gang in an undercover inquiry.*
turn tail = run away, flee, run off, escape, take off (*informal*), retreat, make off, hook it (*slang*), run for it (*informal*), scarper (*Brit. slang*), cut and run, show a clean pair of heels, skedaddle (*informal*), take to your heels: *I turned tail and fled in the direction of the house.*
▸ *related adjective:* caudal

tailor NOUN **= outfitter**, couturier, dressmaker, seamstress, clothier, costumier, garment maker: *He's the grandson of an East End tailor.*
▹ VERB **= adapt**, adjust, modify, cut, style, fit, fashion, shape, suit, convert, alter, accommodate, mould, customize: *scripts tailored to American comedy audiences*
▸ *related adjective:* sartorial

tailor-made ADJECTIVE **1 = perfect**, right, ideal, suitable, just right, right up your street (*informal*), up your alley: *This job was tailor-made for me.* **2 = made-to-measure**, fitted, cut to fit, made to order: *his expensive tailor-made shirt*

taint VERB **1 = disgrace**, shame, dishonour, brand, ruin, blacken, stigmatize: *They said that the elections had been tainted by corruption.* **2 = spoil**, ruin, contaminate, damage, soil, dirty, poison, foul, infect, stain, corrupt, smear, muddy, pollute, blight, tarnish, blot, blemish, sully, defile, adulterate, besmirch, vitiate, smirch: *Rancid oil will taint the flavour.* **OPPOSITE:** purify

take VERB **1 = grip**, grab, seize, catch, grasp, clutch, get hold of, clasp, take hold of, lay hold of: *He took her by the shoulders and shook her.* **2 = carry**, bring, bear, transport, ferry, haul, convey, fetch, cart, tote (*informal*): *I'll take these papers home and read them.*
OPPOSITE: send **3 = accompany**, lead, bring, guide, conduct, escort, convoy, usher: *She was taken to hospital.*
4 = remove, draw, pull, fish, withdraw, extract, abstract: *He took a handkerchief from his pocket.* **5 = steal**,

nick (*slang, chiefly Brit.*), appropriate, pocket, pinch (*informal*), carry off, swipe (*slang*), run off with, blag (*slang*), walk off with, misappropriate, cart off (*slang*), purloin, filch, help yourself to, gain possession of: *The burglars took just about anything they could carry.* **OPPOSITE:** return **6 = capture**, arrest, seize, abduct, take into custody, ensnare, entrap, lay hold of: *Marines went in and took 15 prisoners.* **OPPOSITE:** release **7 = tolerate**, stand, bear, suffer, weather, go through, brave, stomach, endure, undergo, swallow, brook, hack (*slang*), abide, put up with (*informal*), withstand, submit to, countenance, pocket, thole (*Scot.*): *His rudeness was becoming hard to take.* **OPPOSITE:** avoid **8 = require**, need, involve, demand, call for, entail, necessitate: *Walking across the room took all her strength.* **9 = accept**, assume, take on, undertake, adopt, take up, enter upon: *When I took the job, I thought I could change the system.* **OPPOSITE:** reject **10 = understand**, follow, comprehend, get, see, grasp, apprehend: *They've turned sensible, if you take my meaning.* **11 = hire**, book, rent, lease, reserve, pay for, engage, make a reservation for: *My wife and I have taken the cottage for a month.* **12 = perform**, have, do, make, effect, accomplish, execute: *She took her driving test last week.* **13 = ingest**, consume, swallow, inhale: *She's been taking sleeping pills.* **14 = consume**, have, drink, eat, imbibe: *She took tea with Nanny every day.* **15 = have room for**, hold, contain, accommodate, accept: *The place could just about take 2000 people.* **16 = work**, succeed, do the trick (*informal*), have effect, be efficacious: *If the cortisone doesn't take, I may have to have surgery.* **OPPOSITE:** fail

▷ NOUN **= takings**, profits, revenue, return, gate, yield, proceeds, haul, receipts: *It added another $11.8 million to the take.*

take it = assume, suppose, presume, expect, imagine, guess (*informal, chiefly U.S. & Canad.*): *I take it you're a friend of theirs.*

take off 1 = lift off, leave the ground, take to the air, become airborne: *We eventually took off at 11am and arrived in Venice at 1.30pm.* **2 = depart**, go, leave, split (*slang*), disappear, set out, strike out, beat it (*slang*), hit the road (*slang*), abscond, decamp, hook it (*slang*), slope off, pack your bags (*informal*): *He took off at once and headed home.*

take on = get upset, get excited, make a fuss, break down, give way: *Please don't take on so. I'll help you.*

take someone for something = regard as, see as, believe to be, consider to be, think of as, deem to be, perceive to be, hold to be, judge to be, reckon to be, presume to be, look on as: *Do you take me for an idiot?*

take someone in 1 = let in, receive, admit, board, welcome, harbour, accommodate, take care of, put up, billet: *The monastery has taken in 26 refugees.* **2 = deceive**, fool, con (*informal*), do (*slang*), trick, cheat, mislead, dupe, gull (*archaic*), swindle, hoodwink, pull the wool over someone's eyes (*informal*), bilk, cozen, scam (*slang*): *He was a real charmer who totally took me in.*

take someone off = parody, imitate, mimic, mock, ridicule, ape, caricature, send up (*Brit. informal*), spoof (*informal*), travesty, impersonate, lampoon, burlesque, satirize: *He can take off his father to perfection.*

take someone on 1 = compete against, face, contend with, fight, oppose, vie with, pit yourself against, enter the lists against, match yourself against: *I knew I couldn't take him on if it came to a fight.* **2 = engage**, employ, hire, retain, enlist, enrol: *A publishing firm agreed to take him on.*

take something back 1 = return, bring back, send back, hand back: *I'm going to take it back and ask for a refund.* **2 = retract**, withdraw, renounce, renege on, disavow, recant, disclaim, unsay: *Take back what you said about Jeremy!* **3 = regain**, get back, reclaim, recapture, repossess, retake, reconquer: *The government took back control of the city.*

take something down 1 = remove, take off, extract: *He went to the bookcase and took down a volume.* **2 = dismantle**, demolish, take apart, disassemble, level, tear down, raze, take to pieces: *They took down the barricades that had been erected.* **3 = make a note of**, record, write down, minute, note, set down, transcribe, put on record: *I took down his comments in shorthand.*

take something in 1 = understand, absorb, grasp, digest, comprehend, assimilate, get the hang of (*informal*): *She seemed to take in all he said.* **2 = include**, contain, comprise, cover, embrace, encompass: *The constituency takes in a population of more than 4 million people.*

take something off = remove, discard, strip off, drop, peel off, doff, divest yourself of: *She took off her spectacles.*

take something on 1 = accept, tackle, undertake, shoulder, have a go at (*informal*), agree to do, address yourself to, step up to the plate (*informal*): *No one was able or willing to take on the job.* **2 = acquire**, assume, come to have: *His writing took on a feverish intensity.*

take something over = gain control of, take command of, assume control of, come to power in, become leader of: *They took over Rwanda under a League of Nations mandate.*

take something up 1 = start, begin, engage in, assume, adopt, become involved in: *He didn't want to take up a competitive sport.* **2 = occupy**, absorb, consume, use up, cover, fill, waste, squander, extend over: *I don't want to take up too much of your time.* **3 = resume**, continue, go on with, pick up, proceed with, restart, carry on with, recommence, follow on with, begin something again: *His wife takes up the story.*

take to someone = like, get on with, warm to, be taken with, be pleased by, become friendly with, conceive an affection for: *Did the children take to him?*

take to something 1 = start, resort to, make a habit of, have recourse to: *They had taken to aimlessly wandering through the streets.* **2 = head for**, make for, run for, flee to: *He took to the roof of his home when police officers came round.*

takeoff NOUN **1 = departure**, launch, liftoff: *The aircraft crashed soon after takeoff.* **2 = parody**, imitation, send-up (*Brit. informal*), mocking, satire, caricature, spoof (*informal*), travesty, lampoon, piss-take (*informal*): *an inspired takeoff of the two sisters*

takeover NOUN **= merger**, coup, change of leadership, incorporation

tale NOUN **1 = story**, narrative, anecdote, account, relation, novel, legend, fiction, romance, saga, short story, yarn (*informal*), fable, narration, conte (*French*), spiel (*informal*), urban myth, urban legend: *a collection of poems and folk tales* **2 = lie**, fabrication, falsehood, fib, untruth, spiel (*informal*), tall story (*informal*), rigmarole, cock-and-bull story (*informal*): *He's always ready to spin a tall tale about the one that got away.*

> **QUOTATIONS**
> And so from hour to hour we ripe and ripe,
> And then from hour to hour we rot and rot;
> And thereby hangs a tale
> [William Shakespeare *As You Like It*]

> **PROVERBS**
> *A tale never loses in the telling*

talent NOUN **= ability**, gift, aptitude, power, skill, facility, capacity, bent, genius, expertise, faculty, endowment, forte, flair, knack

> **QUOTATIONS**
> Talent is like electricity. We don't understand electricity. We use it
> [Maya Angelou]
>
> Genius does what it must, and talent does what it can
> [E.G. Bulwer-Lytton]
>
> Mediocrity knows nothing higher than itself, but talent instantly recognizes genius
> [Sir Arthur Conan Doyle *The Valley of Fear*]

talented ADJECTIVE **= gifted**, able, expert, master, masterly, brilliant, ace (*informal*), artistic, consummate, first-rate, top-notch (*informal*), adroit

talisman NOUN **= charm**, mascot, amulet, lucky charm, fetish, juju

talk VERB **1 = speak**, chat, chatter, converse, communicate, rap (*slang*), articulate, witter (*informal*), gab (*informal*), express yourself, prattle, natter, shoot the breeze (*U.S. slang*),

prate, run off at the mouth *(slang)*, earbash *(Austral. & N.Z. slang)*: *The boys all began to talk at once.* **2 = discuss**, confer, hold discussions, negotiate, palaver, parley, confabulate, have a confab *(informal)*, chew the rag *or* fat *(slang)*, korero *(N.Z.)*: *Let's talk about these new ideas of yours.* **3 = inform**, shop *(slang, chiefly Brit.)*, grass *(Brit. slang)*, sing *(slang, chiefly U.S.)*, squeal *(slang)*, squeak *(informal)*, tell all, spill the beans *(informal)*, give the game away, blab, let the cat out of the bag, reveal information, spill your guts *(slang)*: *They'll talk; they'll implicate me.*
▷ NOUN **1 = speech**, lecture, presentation, report, address, seminar, discourse, sermon, symposium, dissertation, harangue, oration, disquisition, whaikorero *(N.Z.)*: *The guide gave us a brief talk on the history of the site.* **2 = discussion**, tête-à-tête, conference, dialogue, consultation, heart-to-heart, confabulation, confab *(informal)*, powwow, korero *(N.Z.)*: *I think it's time we had a talk.* **3 = conversation**, chat, natter, crack *(Scot. & Irish)*, rap *(slang)*, jaw *(slang)*, chatter, gab *(informal)*, chitchat, blether, blather: *We had a long talk about her father.* **4 = gossip**, rumour, hearsay, tittle-tattle, goss *(informal)*: *There has been a lot of talk about me getting married.* **5 = language**, words, speech, jargon, slang, dialect, lingo *(informal)*, patois, argot: *children babbling on in baby talk* **6** *(often plural)* **= meeting**, conference, discussions, negotiations, congress, summit, mediation, arbitration, conciliation, conclave, palaver, parley, hui *(N.Z.)*: *Talks between strikers and government have broken down.*
talk big = boast, exaggerate, brag, crow, vaunt, bluster, blow your own trumpet: *men who talk big and drive fast cars*
talk someone into something = persuade, convince, win someone over, sway, bring round *(informal)*, sweet-talk someone into, prevail on *or* upon: *He talked me into marrying him.*

talkative ADJECTIVE **= loquacious**, chatty, garrulous, long-winded, big-mouthed *(slang)*, wordy, effusive, gabby *(informal)*, voluble, gossipy, verbose, mouthy, prolix
OPPOSITE: reserved

talker NOUN **= speaker**, lecturer, orator, conversationalist, chatterbox, speechmaker

talking-to NOUN **= reprimand**, lecture, rebuke, scolding, row, criticism, wigging *(Brit. slang)*, slating *(informal)*, reproach, ticking-off *(informal)*, dressing-down *(informal)*, telling-off *(informal)*, reproof, rap on the knuckles **OPPOSITE:** praise

tall ADJECTIVE **1 = lofty**, big, giant, long-legged, lanky, leggy: *Being tall can make you incredibly self-confident.* **2 = high**, towering, soaring, steep, elevated, lofty: *a lawn of tall, waving grass* **OPPOSITE:** short

tally VERB **1 = agree**, match, accord, fit, suit, square, parallel, coincide, correspond, conform, concur, harmonize: *The figures didn't seem to tally.* **OPPOSITE:** disagree **2 = count up**, total, compute, keep score: *When the final numbers are tallied, sales will probably have fallen.*
▷ NOUN **= record**, score, total, count, reckoning, running total: *They do not keep a tally of visitors to the palace.*

tame ADJECTIVE **1 = domesticated**, unafraid, docile, broken, gentle, fearless, obedient, amenable, tractable, used to human contact: *tame animals at a children's zoo or farm* **OPPOSITE:** wild **2 = submissive**, meek, compliant, subdued, manageable, obedient, docile, spiritless, unresisting: *a tame and gullible newspaper journalist* **OPPOSITE:** stubborn **3 = unexciting**, boring, dull, bland, tedious, flat, tiresome, lifeless, prosaic, uninspiring, humdrum, uninteresting, insipid, vapid, wearisome: *The report was pretty tame stuff.* **OPPOSITE:** exciting
▷ VERB **1 = domesticate**, train, break in, gentle, pacify, house-train, make tame: *They were the first to tame horses.* **OPPOSITE:** make fiercer **2 = subdue**, suppress, master, discipline, curb, humble, conquer, repress, bridle, enslave, subjugate, bring to heel, break the spirit of: *Two regiments were called out to tame the crowds.*
OPPOSITE: arouse

tamper *(usually with* **with***)* VERB **1 = interfere with**, tinker with, meddle with, alter, fiddle with *(informal)*, mess about with, muck about with *(Brit. slang)*, monkey around with, fool about with *(informal)*: *He found his computer had been tampered with.* **2 = influence**, fix *(informal)*, rig, corrupt, manipulate: *I don't want to be accused of tampering with the evidence.*

tang NOUN **1 = scent**, smell, odour, perfume, fragrance, aroma, reek, redolence: *She could smell the salty tang of the sea.* **2 = taste**, bite, flavour, edge, relish, smack, savour, zest, sharpness, piquancy, spiciness, zestiness: *Some liked its strong, fruity tang.* **3 = trace**, touch, tinge, suggestion, hint, whiff, smattering: *His criticism seemed to have acquired a tang of friendliness.*

tangible ADJECTIVE **= definite**, real, positive, solid, material, physical, actual, substantial, objective, concrete, evident, manifest, palpable, discernible, tactile, perceptible, corporeal, touchable
OPPOSITE: intangible

tangle NOUN **1 = knot**, mass, twist, web, jungle, mat, coil, snarl, mesh, ravel, entanglement: *a tangle of wires* **2 = mess**, jam, fix *(informal)*, confusion, complication, maze, mix-up, shambles, labyrinth, entanglement, imbroglio: *I was thinking what a tangle we had got ourselves into.*
▷ VERB **1 = twist**, knot, mat, coil, snarl, mesh, entangle, interlock, kink, interweave, ravel, interlace, enmesh, intertwist: *a huge mass of hair, all tangled together*
OPPOSITE: disentangle **2** *(sometimes with* **up***)* **= entangle**, catch, ensnare, entrap: *Animals get tangled in fishing nets and drown.* **3 = confuse**, mix up, muddle, jumble, scramble: *Themes get tangled in his elliptical storytelling.*
tangle with someone = come into conflict with, come up against, cross swords with, dispute with, contend with, contest with, lock horns with: *They are not the first bank to tangle with the taxman recently.*

tangled ADJECTIVE **1 = knotted**, twisted, matted, messy, snarled, jumbled, entangled, knotty, tousled: *tugging a comb through her tangled hair* **2 = complicated**, involved, complex, confused, messy, mixed-up, convoluted, knotty: *His personal life has become more tangled than ever.*

tangy ADJECTIVE **= sharp**, tart, piquant, biting, fresh, spicy, pungent, briny, acerb

tantalize *or* **tantalise** VERB **= torment**, tease, taunt, torture, provoke, entice, lead on, titillate, make someone's mouth water, keep someone hanging on

tantamount ADJECTIVE
tantamount to = equivalent to, equal to, as good as, synonymous with, the same as, commensurate with

tantrum NOUN **= outburst**, temper, hysterics, fit, storm, paddy *(Brit. informal)*, wax *(informal, chiefly Brit.)*, flare-up, paroxysm, bate *(Brit. slang)*, ill humour, foulie *(Austral. slang)*, hissy fit *(informal)*, strop *(Brit. informal)*

tap[1] VERB **= knock**, strike, pat, rap, beat, touch, drum: *Tap the egg lightly with a teaspoon.*
▷ NOUN **= knock**, pat, rap, beat, touch, drumming, light blow: *A tap on the door interrupted him.*

tap[2] NOUN **1 = valve**, spout, faucet *(U.S. & Canad.)*, spigot, stopcock: *She turned on the taps.* **2 = bug** *(informal)*, listening device, wiretap, bugging device, hidden microphone: *Ministers are not subject to phone taps.*
▷ VERB **= listen in on**, monitor, bug *(informal)*, spy on, eavesdrop on, wiretap: *laws allowing the police to tap telephones*
on tap 1 = available, ready, standing by, to hand, on hand, at hand, in reserve: *He's already got surveyors on tap to measure for the road.* **2 = on draught**, cask-conditioned, from barrels, not bottled *or* canned: *They only have one beer on tap.*

tape NOUN **= binding**, strip, band, string, ribbon: *The books were all tied up with tape.*
▷ VERB **1 = record**, video, tape-record, make a recording of: *She has just taped an interview.* **2** *(sometimes with* **up***)* **= bind**, secure, stick, seal, wrap: *I taped the base of the feather onto the velvet.*

t

taper VERB **= narrow**, thin, attenuate, come to a point, become thinner, become narrow: *The trunk doesn't taper very much.*
taper off = decrease, dwindle, lessen, reduce, fade, weaken, wane, subside, wind down, die out, die away, thin out: *Immigration is beginning to taper off.*

tardy ADJECTIVE **1 = late**, overdue, unpunctual, belated, dilatory, behindhand: *He was as tardy as ever for our appointment.* **2 = slow**, belated, delayed: *the agency's tardy response to the hurricane*

target NOUN **1 = mark**, goal, bull's-eye: *We threw knives at targets.* **2 = goal**, aim, objective, end, mark, object, intention, ambition, Holy Grail *(informal)*: *school leavers who fail to reach their targets* **3 = victim**, butt, prey, quarry, scapegoat: *In the past they have been the targets of racist abuse.*

tariff NOUN **1 = tax**, rate, duty, toll, levy, excise, impost, assessment: *America wants to eliminate tariffs on items such as electronics.* **2 = price list**, charges, schedule: *electricity tariffs and telephone charges*

tarnish VERB **1 = stain**, dull, discolour, spot, soil, dim, rust, darken, blot, blemish, befoul, lose lustre *or* shine: *It never rusts or tarnishes.*
OPPOSITE: brighten **2 = damage**, taint, blacken, sully, drag through the mud, smirch: *His image was tarnished by the savings and loans scandal.*
OPPOSITE: enhance
▷ NOUN **= stain**, taint, discoloration, spot, rust, blot, blemish: *The tarnish lay thick on the inside of the ring.*

tarry VERB **= linger**, remain, loiter, wait, delay, pause, hang around *(informal)*, lose time, bide, dally, take your time, dawdle, drag your feet *or* heels **OPPOSITE:** hurry

tart[1] NOUN **= pie**, pastry, pasty, tartlet, patty: *a slice of home-made tart*

tart[2] ADJECTIVE **1 = sharp**, acid, sour, bitter, pungent, tangy, astringent, piquant, vinegary, acidulous, acerb: *a slightly tart wine* **OPPOSITE:** sweet
2 = cutting, biting, sharp, short, wounding, nasty, harsh, scathing, acrimonious, barbed, hurtful, caustic, astringent, vitriolic, trenchant, testy, mordant, snappish, mordacious: *The words were more tart than she had intended.* **OPPOSITE:** kind

tart[3] NOUN **= slut**, prostitute, hooker *(U.S. slang)*, whore, slag *(Brit. slang)*, call girl, working girl *(facetious, slang)*, harlot, streetwalker, loose woman, fallen woman, scrubber *(Brit. & Austral. slang)*, strumpet, trollop, floozy *(slang)*, woman of easy virtue, fille de joie *(French)*, hornbag *(Austral. slang)*: *He said I looked like a tart.*

task NOUN **= job**, duty, assignment, work, business, charge, labour, exercise, mission, employment, enterprise, undertaking, occupation, chore, toil: *He had the unenviable task of breaking the bad news.*
▷ VERB **= charge**, assign to, entrust: *The minister was tasked with checking that aid was spent wisely.*
take someone to task = criticize, blame, blast, lecture, carpet *(informal)*, censure, rebuke, reprimand, reproach, scold, tear into *(informal)*, tell off *(informal)*, diss *(slang, chiefly U.S.)*, read the riot act to, reprove, upbraid, lambast(e), bawl out *(informal)*, chew out *(U.S. & Canad. informal)*, tear (someone) off a strip *(Brit. informal)*, give a rocket to *(Brit. & N.Z. informal)*: *The country's intellectuals are being taken to task.*

taste NOUN **1 = flavour**, savour, relish, smack, tang: *Nettles have a surprisingly sweet taste.* **OPPOSITE:** blandness
2 = bit, bite, drop, swallow, sip, mouthful, touch, sample, dash, nip, spoonful, morsel, titbit, soupçon *(French)*: *He took another small taste.*
3 = liking, preference, penchant, fondness, partiality, desire, fancy, leaning, bent, appetite, relish, inclination, palate, predilection: *She developed a taste for journeys to hazardous regions.* **OPPOSITE:** dislike
4 = refinement, style, judgment, culture, polish, grace, discrimination, perception, appreciation, elegance, sophistication, cultivation, discernment: *She has very good taste in clothes.* **OPPOSITE:** lack of judgment
5 = propriety, discretion, correctness, delicacy, tact, politeness, nicety, decorum, tactfulness: *I do not feel your actions were in good taste.*
OPPOSITE: impropriety
▷ VERB **1** *(often with* **of**) **= have a flavour of**, smack of, savour of: *The drink tastes like chocolate.* **2 = sample**, try, test, relish, sip, savour, nibble: *Cut off a small piece of meat and taste it.*
3 = distinguish, perceive, discern, differentiate: *You can taste the chilli in the dish.* **4 = experience**, know, undergo, partake of, feel, encounter, meet with, come up against, have knowledge of: *He had tasted outdoor life, and didn't want to come home.* **OPPOSITE:** miss
▸ *related noun:* gustation

> **QUOTATIONS**
> Taste is the feminine of genius
> [Edward Fitzgerald *Letters*]
>
> No one ever went broke underestimating the taste of the American public
> [H.L. Mencken]
>
> Taste is the only morality. Tell me what you like, and I'll tell you who you are
> [John Ruskin]
>
> Taste is the enemy of creativeness
> [Pablo Picasso]

> **PROVERBS**
> *There's no accounting for tastes*
> *Beauty is in the eye of the beholder*
> *One man's meat is another man's poison*

tasteful ADJECTIVE **= refined**, stylish, elegant, cultured, beautiful, smart, charming, polished, delicate, artistic, handsome, cultivated, discriminating, exquisite, graceful, harmonious, urbane, fastidious, aesthetically pleasing, in good taste
OPPOSITE: tasteless

tasteless ADJECTIVE **1 = gaudy**, cheap, vulgar, tacky *(informal)*, flashy, naff *(Brit. slang)*, garish, inelegant, tawdry: *spectacularly tasteless objets d'art*
OPPOSITE: tasteful **2 = vulgar**, crude, improper, low, gross, rude, coarse, crass, unseemly, indiscreet, tactless, uncouth, impolite, graceless, indelicate, indecorous: *a tasteless remark* **3 = insipid**, bland, flat, boring, thin, weak, dull, mild, tame, watered-down, uninteresting, uninspired, vapid, flavourless: *The fish was mushy and tasteless.* **OPPOSITE:** tasty

tasty ADJECTIVE **= delicious**, luscious, palatable, delectable, good-tasting, savoury, full-flavoured, yummy *(slang)*, flavoursome, scrumptious *(informal)*, appetizing, toothsome, flavourful, sapid, lekker *(S. African slang)*, yummo *(Austral. slang)*
OPPOSITE: bland

tattletale NOUN **= gossip**, busybody, babbler, prattler, chatterbox *(informal)*, blether, chatterer, bigmouth *(slang)*, scandalmonger, gossipmonger

tatty ADJECTIVE **= shabby**, seedy, scruffy, worn, poor, neglected, ragged, run-down, frayed, worn out, dilapidated, tattered, tawdry, threadbare, rumpled, bedraggled, unkempt, down at heel, the worse for wear, having seen better days
OPPOSITE: smart

taunt VERB **= jeer**, mock, tease, ridicule, provoke, insult, torment, sneer, deride, revile, twit, guy *(informal)*, gibe: *Other youths taunted him about his clothes.*
▷ NOUN **= jeer**, dig, insult, ridicule, cut, teasing, provocation, barb, derision, sarcasm, gibe: *For years they suffered racist taunts.*

taut ADJECTIVE **1 = tense**, rigid, tight, stressed, stretched, strained, flexed: *When muscles are taut or cold, there is more chance of injury.* **OPPOSITE:** relaxed
2 = tight, stretched, rigid, tightly stretched: *The clothes line is pulled taut and secured.* **OPPOSITE:** slack

tavern NOUN **= inn**, bar, pub *(informal, chiefly Brit.)*, public house, watering hole *(facetious, slang)*, boozer *(Brit., Austral. & N.Z. informal)*, beer parlour *(Canad.)*, beverage room *(Canad.)*, hostelry, alehouse *(archaic)*, taproom

> **QUOTATIONS**
> There is nothing which has yet been contrived by man, by which so much happiness is produced as by a good tavern or inn
> [Dr. Johnson]

tawdry ADJECTIVE **= vulgar**, cheap, tacky *(informal)*, flashy, tasteless, plastic *(slang)*, glittering, naff *(Brit. slang)*, gaudy, tatty, showy, tinsel,

raffish, gimcrack, meretricious, tinselly, cheap-jack *(informal)*
OPPOSITE: stylish

tax NOUN **1 = charge**, rate, duty, toll, levy, tariff, excise, contribution, assessment, customs, tribute, imposition, tithe, impost: *a cut in tax on new cars* **2 = strain**, demand, burden, pressure, weight, load, drain: *less of a tax on her bodily resources*
▷ VERB **1 = charge**, impose a tax on, levy a tax on, rate, demand, assess, extract, exact, tithe: *The government taxes profits of corporations at a high rate.* **2 = strain**, push, stretch, try, test, task, load, burden, drain, exhaust, weaken, weary, put pressure on, sap, wear out, weigh heavily on, overburden, make heavy demands on, enervate: *Overcrowding has taxed the city's ability to deal with waste.* **3 = accuse**, charge, blame, confront, impeach, incriminate, arraign, impugn, lay at your door: *Writers to the letters column taxed me with shallowness.*
OPPOSITE: acquit

QUOTATIONS

In this world nothing can be said to be certain, except death and taxes
[Benjamin Franklin *letter to Jean Baptiste Le Roy*]

The Chancellor of the Exchequer is a man whose duties make him more or less of a taxing machine. He is entrusted with a certain amount of misery which it is his duty to distribute as fairly as he can
[Robert Lowe, Viscount Sherbrooke *speech*]

To tax and to please, no more than to love and to be wise, is not given to men
[Edmund Burke *On American Taxation*]

If you tax too high, the revenue will yield nothing
[Ralph Waldo Emerson]

Only the little people pay taxes
[Leona Helmsley]

Death and taxes and childbirth! There's never any convenient time for any of them
[Margaret Mitchell *Gone with the Wind*]

Read my lips: no new taxes
[George Bush *speech during election campaign – later, he raised taxes*]

Taxation without representation is tyranny
[James Otis]

What is the difference between a taxidermist and a tax collector? The taxidermist takes only your skin
[Mark Twain]

Income Tax has made more Liars out of the American people than Golf
[Will Rogers *The Illiterate Digest*]

taxing ADJECTIVE **= demanding**, trying, wearing, heavy, tough, tiring, punishing, exacting, stressful, sapping, onerous, burdensome, wearisome, enervating
OPPOSITE: easy

teach VERB **1 = instruct**, train, coach, school, direct, advise, inform, discipline, educate, drill, tutor, enlighten, impart, instil, inculcate, edify, give lessons in: *a programme to teach educational skills; She taught me to read.* **2** *(often with* **how**) **= show**, train, demonstrate: *George had taught him how to ride a horse.*

teacher NOUN **= instructor**, coach, tutor, don, guide, professor, trainer, lecturer, guru, mentor, educator, handler, schoolteacher, pedagogue, dominie *(Scot.)*, master *or* mistress, schoolmaster *or* schoolmistress

QUOTATIONS

We teachers can only help the work going on, as servants wait upon a master
[Maria Montessori *The Absorbent Mind*]

A teacher affects eternity; he can never tell where his influence stops
[Henry Brooks Adams *The Education of Henry Adams*]

The true teacher defends his pupils against his own personal influence
[A. Bronson Alcot]

He who can, does. He who cannot, teaches
[George Bernard Shaw *Maxims for Revolutionists*]

I owe a lot to my teachers and mean to pay them back some day
[Stephen Leacock]

It is when the gods hate a man with uncommon abhorrence that they drive him into the profession of a schoolmaster
[Seneca]

team NOUN **1 = side**, squad, troupe: *The team failed to qualify for the final.* **2 = group**, company, set, body, band, crew, gang, line-up, bunch, posse *(informal)*: *Mr Hunter and his management team* **3 = pair**, span, yoke: *Ploughing is no longer done with a team of oxen.*
team up = join, unite, work together, cooperate, couple, link up, get together, yoke, band together, collaborate, join forces: *He suggested that we team up for a working holiday in France.*

teamwork NOUN **= cooperation**, collaboration, unity, concert, harmony, fellowship, coordination, joint action, esprit de corps

tear VERB **1 = rip**, split, rend, shred, rupture, sunder: *She very nearly tore my overcoat.* **2 = run**, rip, ladder, snag: *Too fine a material may tear.* **3 = scratch**, cut (open), gash, lacerate, injure, mangle, cut to pieces, cut to ribbons, mangulate *(Austral. slang)*: *He'd torn his skin trying to do it barehanded.* **4 = pull apart**, claw, lacerate, sever, mutilate, mangle, mangulate *(Austral. slang)*: *Canine teeth are for tearing flesh.* **5 = rush**, run, charge, race, shoot, fly, career, speed, belt *(slang)*, dash, hurry, barrel (along) *(informal, chiefly U.S. & Canad.)*, sprint, bolt, dart, gallop, zoom, burn rubber *(informal)*: *The door flew open and she tore into the room.* **6** *(often with* **away** *or* **from**) **= pull**, seize, rip, grab, snatch, pluck, yank, wrench, wrest: *She tore the windscreen wipers from his car.*
▷ NOUN **= hole**, split, rip, run, rent, snag, rupture: *I peered through a tear in the van's curtains.*

tearaway NOUN **= hooligan**, delinquent, tough, rough *(informal)*, rowdy, ruffian, roughneck *(slang)*, good-for-nothing

tearful ADJECTIVE **1 = weeping**, crying, sobbing, in tears, whimpering, blubbering, weepy *(informal)*, lachrymose: *She was tearful when asked to talk about it.* **2 = sad**, pathetic, poignant, upsetting, distressing, harrowing, pitiful, woeful, mournful, lamentable, sorrowful, pitiable, dolorous: *a tearful farewell*

tears PLURAL NOUN **= crying**, weeping, sobbing, wailing, whimpering, blubbering, lamentation: *She was very near to tears.*
in tears = weeping, crying, sobbing, whimpering, blubbering, visibly moved: *He was in tears at the funeral.*
▸ *related adjectives:* lacrimal, lachrymal, lacrymal

tease VERB **1 = mock**, bait, wind up *(Brit. slang)*, worry, bother, provoke, annoy, needle *(informal)*, plague *(informal)*, rag, rib *(informal)*, torment, ridicule, taunt, aggravate *(informal)*, badger, pester, vex, goad, bedevil, take the mickey out of *(informal)*, twit, chaff, guy *(informal)*, gibe, pull someone's leg *(informal)*, make fun of: *He teased me mercilessly about going there.* **2 = tantalize**, lead on, flirt with, titillate: *When did you last flirt with him or tease him?*

technical ADJECTIVE **= scientific**, technological, skilled, specialist, specialized, hi-tech *or* high-tech

technique NOUN **1 = method**, way, system, approach, means, course, style, fashion, manner, procedure, mode, MO, modus operandi: *tests performed using a new technique* **2 = skill**, art, performance, craft, touch, know-how *(informal)*, facility, delivery, execution, knack, artistry, craftsmanship, proficiency, adroitness: *He went abroad to improve his tennis technique.*

tedious ADJECTIVE **= boring**, dull, dreary, monotonous, tiring, annoying, fatiguing, drab, banal, tiresome, lifeless, prosaic, laborious, humdrum, uninteresting, long-drawn-out, mind-numbing, irksome, unexciting, soporific, ho-hum *(informal)*, vapid, wearisome, deadly dull, prosy, dreich *(Scot.)*
OPPOSITE: exciting

t

The Language of William Makepeace Thackeray

William Makepeace Thackeray (1811–1863) was born in Calcutta – his father was a senior official of the East India Company – and was sent to England at the age of four. In later years he disliked his public school, left Cambridge without graduating, travelled in Europe, abandoned legal studies, gambled away his inheritance, and eventually supported himself by writing. He wrote for magazines, including *Punch*, and in 1848 achieved tremendous success with his lively and entertaining novel *Vanity Fair*, part of which takes place at Waterloo. He was hailed as a rival to Dickens though, in fact, in style and outlook he has more in common with Henry Fielding. Among his other novels are *Pendennis* (1850), *Henry Esmond* (1852), and *The Newcomes* (1855).

In one of his many asides in *Vanity Fair*, Thackeray promises that there some 'terrific chapters' coming presently, but begs 'the good-natured reader' to remember

> ...that we are only discoursing at present about a stockbroker's family..., who are taking walks, or luncheon, or dinner, or talking and making love* as people do in common life...
>
> (**to make love* in the 19th century did not have its modern sense)

He goes on to say that he had three options for his treatment of his subject matter – the genteel, the romantic, or the facetious – and he chose the third.

Thackeray takes a humorous view of his characters, often jocularly applying to them commendatory or affectionate adjectives such as *good, honest, gallant*, or *poor*, as in *the good old lady; honest German folks; the gallant stout gentleman; poor fat Jos.* When he refers to people as *worthy*, he is usually being ironic:

> It is very likely that this **worthy** couple never absolutely conspired and agreed together in so many words: the one to cajole the young gentleman, whilst the other won his money at cards ...

Thackeray's writing abounds in descriptions, and he uses adjectives of colour profusely in them: *red* occurs more frequently in his work than *true, late, early*, or *rich*. Faces, hair, cheeks, waistcoats, and eyes are *red*, and embarrassed people *turn red*. Often colour contributes to a comic effect, but it can be startlingly grotesque:

> The scar cut by the diamond on his white, bald, shining forehead made a burning red mark; his red whiskers were dyed of a purple hue, which made his pale face look still paler.

Thackeray's focus is on people, and a large proportion of his most-used nouns relate to people and family relationships, such as *man, lady, gentleman, friend, boy, mother, father.* More frequent than *home, son*, or *love*, however, is the word *money.* The phrase *no money* occurs often, as does *more money*, and *ready money*. There are a good many citations for *bailiff*, and for *dun*, used both as a noun meaning 'debt collector', and as a verb meaning 'to pursue debtors'. Thackeray himself had financial problems and so do his characters.

Thackeray is particularly adept at presenting reported speech. Unlike other 19th-century authors, he does not constantly strive to find synonyms for *say*, and his repetition of *say* in the following passage in no way reduces the violence of the man's words:

> 'Send the children out of the room. Go!' **said** he.... The urchins, always frightened before him, retired: their mother would have followed too. 'Not you,' he **said**. 'You stop.'

He also uses short, simple sentences to telling effect in descriptions – as when poor Dobbin looks after the carriage that is taking away the girl he loves, and the man she has just married:

> William Dobbin stood in the church-porch, looking at it, a queer figure. The small crew of spectators jeered him. He was not thinking about them or their laughter.

tedium NOUN = **boredom**, monotony, dullness, routine, the doldrums, banality, sameness, ennui, drabness, deadness, dreariness, tediousness, lifelessness **OPPOSITE:** excitement

teem[1] VERB = **be full of**, abound, swarm, bristle, brim, overflow, be abundant, burst at the seams, be prolific, be crawling, pullulate: *The forest below him seethed and teemed with life.*

teem[2] VERB (*often with* **down** *or* **with rain**) = **pour**, lash, pelt (down), sheet, stream, belt (*slang*), bucket down (*informal*), rain cats and dogs (*informal*): *The wedding was supposed to be outside but it teemed with rain.*

teeming[1] ADJECTIVE = **full**, packed, crowded, alive, thick, bursting, numerous, crawling, swarming, abundant, bristling, brimming, overflowing, fruitful, replete, chock-full, brimful, chock-a-block: *The area is usually teeming with tourists.* **OPPOSITE:** lacking

teeming[2] ADJECTIVE = **pouring**, lashing, pelting, sheeting, streaming, belting (*slang*), bucketing down (*informal*): *I arrived early to find it teeming with rain.*

teenage ADJECTIVE = **youthful**, adolescent, juvenile, immature

teenager NOUN = **youth**, minor, adolescent, juvenile, girl, boy

teeny ADJECTIVE = **tiny**, minute, wee, miniature, microscopic, diminutive, minuscule, teeny-weeny, teensy-weensy

teeter VERB = **wobble**, rock, totter, balance, stagger, sway, tremble, waver, pivot, seesaw

telegram NOUN = **cable**, wire (*informal*), telegraph, telex, radiogram

telegraph VERB = **cable**, wire (*informal*), transmit, telex, send

telepathy NOUN = **mind-reading**, ESP, sixth sense, clairvoyance, extrasensory perception, psychometry, thought transference

telephone NOUN = **phone**, blower (*informal*), mobile, mobile phone *or* (*informal*) moby, cellphone *or* cellular phone (*U.S.*), handset, dog and bone (*slang*), iPhone (*trademark*): *They usually exchanged messages by telephone.*
▷ VERB = **call**, phone, ring (*chiefly Brit.*), buzz (*informal*), dial, call up, give someone a call, give someone a ring (*informal, chiefly Brit.*), give someone a buzz (*informal*), give someone a bell (*Brit. slang*), put a call through to, give someone a tinkle (*Brit. informal*), get on the blower to (*informal*): *I had to telephone him to say I was sorry.*

QUOTATIONS

The telephone gives us the happiness of being together yet safely apart
[Mason Cooley *City Aphorisms*]

The telephone, which interrupts the most serious conversations and cuts short the most weighty observations, has a romance of its own
[Virginia Woolf *The Common Reader*]

telephone: an invention of the devil which abrogates some of the advantages of making a disagreeable person keep his distance
[Ambrose Bierce *The Devil's Dictionary*]

telescope NOUN = **glass**, scope (*informal*), spyglass: *The telescope enables us to see deeper into the universe than ever.*
▷ VERB = **shorten**, contract, compress, cut, trim, shrink, tighten, condense, abbreviate, abridge, capsulize: *Film naturally tends to telescope time.* **OPPOSITE:** lengthen

television NOUN = **TV**, telly (*Brit. informal*), small screen (*informal*), the box (*Brit. informal*), receiver, the tube (*slang*), TV set, gogglebox (*Brit. slang*), idiot box (*slang*)

QUOTATIONS

Television tells a story in a way that requires no imagination
[Witold Rybczynski]

I find television very educational. Every time someone switches it on I go into another room and read a good book
[Groucho Marx]

Television has brought back murder into the home – where it belongs
[Alfred Hitchcock]

tell VERB **1** = **inform**, notify, make aware, say to, state to, warn, reveal to, express to, brief, advise, disclose to, proclaim to, fill in, speak about to, confess to, impart, alert to, divulge, announce to, acquaint with, communicate to, mention to, make known to, apprise, utter to, get off your chest (*informal*), let know, flag up: *I called her to tell her how spectacular it looked.* **2** = **describe**, relate, recount, report, portray, depict, chronicle, rehearse, narrate, give an account of: *He told his story to the Sunday Times.* **3** = **instruct**, order, command, direct, bid, enjoin: *She told me to come and help clean the house.* **4** = **see**, make out, discern, understand, discover, be certain, comprehend: *It was impossible to tell where the bullet had entered.* **5** = **distinguish**, discriminate, discern, differentiate, identify: *I can't really tell the difference between their policies and ours.* **6** = **have** *or* **take effect**, register, weigh, have force, count, take its toll, carry weight, make its presence felt: *The pressure began to tell as rain closed in after 20 laps.*

tell someone off = **reprimand**, rebuke, scold, lecture, carpet (*informal*), censure, reproach, berate, chide, tear into (*informal*), read the riot act to, reprove, upbraid, take to task, tick off (*informal*), bawl out (*informal*), chew out (*U.S. & Canad. informal*), tear off a strip (*Brit. informal*), give a piece of your mind to, haul over the coals (*informal*), give a rocket to (*Brit. & N.Z. informal*): *He never listened to us when we told him off.*

telling ADJECTIVE = **effective**, significant, considerable, marked, striking, powerful, solid, impressive, influential, decisive, potent, forceful, weighty, forcible, trenchant, effectual **OPPOSITE:** unimportant

temerity NOUN = **audacity**, nerve (*informal*), cheek, gall (*informal*), front, assurance, pluck, boldness, recklessness, chutzpah (*U.S. & Canad. informal*), impudence, effrontery, impulsiveness, rashness, brass neck (*Brit. informal*), foolhardiness, sassiness (*U.S. informal*), forwardness, heedlessness

temper NOUN **1** = **irritability**, anger, irascibility, passion, resentment, irritation, annoyance, petulance, surliness, ill humour, peevishness, hot-headedness: *I hope he can control his temper.* **OPPOSITE:** good humour **2** = **frame of mind**, character, nature, attitude, mind, mood, constitution, humour, vein, temperament, tenor, disposition: *He's known for his placid temper.* **3** = **rage**, fury, bad mood, passion, paddy (*Brit. informal*), wax (*informal, chiefly Brit.*), tantrum, bate (*Brit. slang*), fit of pique, foulie (*Austral. slang*), hissy fit (*informal*), strop (*Brit. informal*): *She was still in a temper when I arrived.* **4** = **self-control**, composure, cool (*slang*), calm, good humour, tranquillity, coolness, calmness, equanimity: *I've never seen him lose his temper.* **OPPOSITE:** anger
▷ VERB **1** = **moderate**, restrain, tone down, calm, soften, soothe, lessen, allay, mitigate, abate, assuage, mollify, soft-pedal (*informal*), palliate, admix: *He had to learn to temper his enthusiasm.* **OPPOSITE:** intensify **2** = **strengthen**, harden, toughen, anneal: *a new way of tempering glass* **OPPOSITE:** soften

temperament NOUN = **nature**, character, personality, quality, spirit, make-up, soul, constitution, bent, stamp, humour, tendencies, tendency, temper, outlook, complexion, disposition, frame of mind, mettle, cast of mind: *His impulsive temperament regularly got him into difficulties.*

temperamental ADJECTIVE **1** = **moody**, emotional, touchy, sensitive, explosive, passionate, volatile, fiery, impatient, erratic, neurotic, irritable, mercurial, excitable, capricious, petulant, hot-headed, hypersensitive, highly strung, easily upset, unstable: *a man given to temperamental outbursts and paranoia* **OPPOSITE:** even-tempered **2** = **unreliable**, unpredictable, undependable, inconsistent, erratic, inconstant, unstable: *The machine guns could be temperamental.* **OPPOSITE:** reliable **3** = **natural**, inherent, innate, constitutional, ingrained, congenital, inborn: *Some temperamental qualities are not easily detected by parents.*

t

temperance NOUN **1 = teetotalism**, abstinence, sobriety, abstemiousness: *a reformed alcoholic extolling the joys of temperance* **2 = moderation**, restraint, self-control, self-discipline, continence, self-restraint, forbearance: *The age of hedonism was replaced by a new era of temperance.* **OPPOSITE:** excess

> QUOTATIONS
> Temperance is the greatest of all the virtues
> [Plutarch *Moralia*]

temperate ADJECTIVE **1 = mild**, moderate, balmy, fair, cool, soft, calm, gentle, pleasant, clement, agreeable: *The valley keeps a temperate climate throughout the year.* **OPPOSITE:** extreme **2 = moderate**, dispassionate, self-controlled, calm, stable, reasonable, sensible, mild, composed, equable, even-tempered, self-restrained: *His final report was more temperate than earlier ones.* **OPPOSITE:** unrestrained

tempest NOUN **1 = storm**, hurricane, gale, tornado, cyclone, typhoon, squall: *torrential rain and howling tempest* **2 = uproar**, storm, furore, disturbance, upheaval, ferment, commotion, tumult: *I hadn't foreseen the tempest my request would cause.* **OPPOSITE:** calm

tempestuous ADJECTIVE **1 = passionate**, intense, turbulent, heated, wild, excited, emotional, violent, flaming, hysterical, stormy, impassioned, uncontrolled, boisterous, feverish: *the couple's tempestuous relationship* **OPPOSITE:** peaceful **2 = stormy**, turbulent, inclement, raging, windy, boisterous, blustery, gusty, squally: *adverse winds and tempestuous weather*

temple NOUN **= shrine**, church, sanctuary, holy place, place of worship, house of God

tempo NOUN **= pace**, time, rate, beat, measure *(Prosody)*, speed, metre, rhythm, cadence, pulse

temporal ADJECTIVE **1 = secular**, worldly, lay, earthly, mundane, material, civil, fleshly, mortal, terrestrial, carnal, profane, sublunary: *Clergy should not be preoccupied with temporal matters.* **2 = temporary**, passing, transitory, fleeting, short-lived, fugitive, transient, momentary, evanescent, impermanent, fugacious: *The temporal gifts that Fortune grants in this world are finally worthless.*

temporarily ADVERB **= briefly**, for the moment, for the time being, momentarily, for a moment, for a short time, for a little while, fleetingly, for a short while, pro tem, for the nonce

temporary ADJECTIVE **1 = impermanent**, passing, transitory, brief, fleeting, interim, short-lived, fugitive, transient, momentary, ephemeral, evanescent, pro tem, here today and gone tomorrow, pro tempore *(Latin)*, fugacious: *a temporary loss of memory* **OPPOSITE:** permanent **2 = short-term**, acting, interim, supply, stand-in, fill-in, caretaker, provisional, stopgap, pop-up: *She was working as a temporary teacher at a Belfast school.*

tempt VERB **1 = attract**, draw, appeal to, allure, whet the appetite of, make your mouth water: *Can I tempt you with a little puff pastry?* **2 = entice**, lure, lead on, invite, woo, seduce, coax, decoy, inveigle: *Don't let credit tempt you to buy something you can't afford.* **OPPOSITE:** discourage **3 = provoke**, try, test, risk, dare, bait, fly in the face of: *As soon as you talk about never losing, it's tempting fate.*

temptation NOUN **1 = enticement**, lure, inducement, pull, come-on *(informal)*, invitation, bait, coaxing, snare, seduction, decoy, allurement, tantalization: *the many temptations to which they will be exposed* **2 = appeal**, draw, attraction, attractiveness: *The thrill and the temptation of crime is very strong.*

> QUOTATIONS
> The best way to get the better of temptation is to yield to it
> [Clementina Stirling Graham *Mystifications*]
>
> Music and women I cannot but give way to, whatever my business is
> [Samuel Pepys *Diary*]
>
> I can resist everything except temptation
> [Oscar Wilde *Lady Windermere's Fan*]
>
> No temptation can ever be measured by the value of its object
> [Colette]
>
> The serpent beguiled me, and I did eat
> [*Bible: Genesis*]
>
> Get thee behind me, Satan
> [*Bible: St. Matthew*]
>
> Watch and pray, that ye enter not into temptation; the spirit indeed is willing but the flesh is weak
> [*Bible: St. Matthew*]
>
> The last temptation is the greatest treason: To do the right deed for the wrong reason
> [T.S. Eliot *Murder in the Cathedral*]

tempting ADJECTIVE **= inviting**, enticing, seductive, alluring, attractive, mouthwatering, appetizing **OPPOSITE:** uninviting

tenacious ADJECTIVE **1 = stubborn**, dogged, determined, persistent, sure, firm, adamant, staunch, resolute, inflexible, strong-willed, steadfast, unyielding, obstinate, intransigent, immovable, unswerving, obdurate, stiff-necked, pertinacious: *He is regarded as a persistent and tenacious interviewer.* **OPPOSITE:** irresolute **2 = firm**, dogged, persistent, unyielding, unswerving: *a tenacious belief* **3 = strong**, firm, fast, iron, tight, clinging, forceful, immovable, unshakeable: *He has a particularly tenacious grip on life.* **4 = retentive**, good, photographic, unforgetful: *her analytical mind and tenacious memory* **5 = adhesive**, clinging, sticky, glutinous, gluey, mucilaginous: *tenacious catarrh in the nasal passages and lungs*

tenacity NOUN **= perseverance**, resolution, determination, application, resolve, persistence, diligence, intransigence, firmness, stubbornness, inflexibility, obstinacy, steadfastness, obduracy, doggedness, strength of will, strength of purpose, resoluteness, pertinacity, staunchness

tenancy NOUN **1 = lease**, residence, occupancy, holding, renting, possession, occupation: *Check the terms of your tenancy closely.* **2 = period of office**, tenure, incumbency, time in office: *Baroness Thatcher's nine-year tenancy*

tenant NOUN **= leaseholder**, resident, renter, occupant, holder, inhabitant, occupier, lodger, boarder, lessee

tend[1] VERB **= be inclined**, be likely, be liable, have a tendency, be apt, be prone, trend, lean, incline, be biased, be disposed, gravitate, have a leaning, have an inclination: *Lighter cars tend to be noisy.*

tend[2] VERB **1 = take care of**, look after, care for, keep, watch, serve, protect, feed, handle, attend, guard, nurse, see to, nurture, minister to, cater for, keep an eye on, wait on, watch over: *For years he tended her in her illness.* **OPPOSITE:** neglect **2 = maintain**, take care of, nurture, cultivate, manage: *The grey-haired lady dug and tended her garden.* **OPPOSITE:** neglect

tendency NOUN **1 = trend**, drift, movement, turning, heading, course, drive, bearing, direction, bias: *the government's tendency towards secrecy in recent years* **2 = inclination**, leaning, bent, liability, readiness, disposition, penchant, propensity, susceptibility, predisposition, predilection, proclivity, partiality, proneness: *He has a tendency towards snobbery.*

tender[1] ADJECTIVE **1 = gentle**, loving, kind, caring, warm, sympathetic, fond, sentimental, humane, affectionate, compassionate, benevolent, considerate, merciful, amorous, warm-hearted, tenderhearted, softhearted, touchy-feely *(informal)*: *tender, loving care* **OPPOSITE:** harsh **2 = romantic**, moving, touching, emotional, sentimental, poignant, evocative, soppy *(Brit. informal)*: *a tragic, tender love story* **3 = vulnerable**, young, sensitive, new, green, raw, youthful, inexperienced, immature, callow, impressionable, unripe, wet behind the ears *(informal)*: *He had become attracted to the game at the tender age of* *seven.* **OPPOSITE:** experienced **4 = sensitive**, painful, sore, smarting, raw, bruised, irritated, aching, inflamed: *My tummy felt very tender.* **5 = fragile**, delicate, frail, soft, weak, feeble, breakable: *The newborn looked so fragile and tender.* **6 = difficult**, sensitive, tricky, dangerous, complicated, risky, touchy, ticklish: *Even his continuing presence remains a tender issue.*

tender[2] VERB **= offer**, present, submit, give, suggest, propose, extend, volunteer, hand in, put forward, proffer: *She quickly tendered her resignation.*
▷ NOUN **= offer**, bid, estimate, proposal, suggestion, submission, proffer: *Builders will be asked to submit a tender for the work.*

tenderness NOUN **1 = gentleness**, love, affection, liking, care, consideration, sympathy, pity, humanity, warmth, mercy, attachment, compassion, devotion, kindness, fondness, sentimentality, benevolence, humaneness, amorousness, warm-heartedness, softheartedness, tenderheartedness: *She smiled, politely, rather than with tenderness.* **OPPOSITE:** harshness **2 = soreness**, pain, sensitivity, smart, bruising, ache, aching, irritation, inflammation, rawness, sensitiveness, painfulness: *There is still some tenderness on her tummy.* **3 = fragility**, vulnerability, weakness, sensitivity, softness, feebleness, sensitiveness, frailness, delicateness: *the vulnerability and tenderness he brings to the role*

tenet NOUN **= principle**, rule, doctrine, creed, view, teaching, opinion, belief, conviction, canon, thesis, maxim, dogma, precept, article of faith, kaupapa *(N.Z.)*

tenor NOUN **= meaning**, trend, drift, way, course, sense, aim, purpose, direction, path, theme, substance, burden, tendency, intent, purport

tense ADJECTIVE **1 = strained**, uneasy, stressful, fraught, charged, difficult, worrying, exciting, uncomfortable, knife-edge, nail-biting, nerve-racking: *the tense atmosphere of the talks* **2 = nervous**, wound up *(informal)*, edgy, strained, wired *(slang)*, anxious, under pressure, restless, apprehensive, jittery *(informal)*, uptight *(informal)*, on edge, jumpy, twitchy *(informal)*, overwrought, strung up *(informal)*, on tenterhooks, fidgety, keyed up, antsy *(informal)*, wrought up, adrenalized: *He had been very tense, but he finally relaxed.* **OPPOSITE:** calm **3 = rigid**, strained, taut, stretched, tight: *She lay, eyes shut, body tense.* **OPPOSITE:** relaxed
▷ VERB **= tighten**, strain, brace, tauten, stretch, flex, stiffen: *His stomach muscles tensed.* **OPPOSITE:** relax

tension NOUN **1 = strain**, stress, nervousness, pressure, anxiety, unease, apprehension, suspense, restlessness, the jitters *(informal)*, edginess: *Smiling relieves tension and stress.* **OPPOSITE:** calmness **2 = friction**, hostility, unease, antagonism, antipathy, enmity, ill feeling: *The tension between the two countries is likely to remain.* **3 = rigidity**, tightness, stiffness, pressure, stress, stretching, straining, tautness: *Slowly, the tension in his face dispersed.*

tentative ADJECTIVE **1 = unconfirmed**, provisional, indefinite, test, trial, pilot, preliminary, experimental, unsettled, speculative, pencilled in, exploratory, to be confirmed, TBC, conjectural: *They have reached a tentative agreement to hold talks next month.* **OPPOSITE:** confirmed **2 = hesitant**, cautious, uncertain, doubtful, backward, faltering, unsure, timid, undecided, diffident, iffy *(informal)*: *My first attempts at complaining were very tentative.* **OPPOSITE:** confident

tenuous ADJECTIVE **1 = slight**, weak, dubious, shaky, doubtful, questionable, insignificant, flimsy, sketchy, insubstantial, nebulous: *Links between the provinces were seen to be tenuous.* **OPPOSITE:** strong **2 = fine**, slim, delicate, attenuated, gossamer: *She was holding onto life by a tenuous thread.*

tenure NOUN **1 = occupancy**, holding, occupation, residence, tenancy, possession, proprietorship: *Lack of security of tenure meant that many became homeless.* **2 = term of office**, term, incumbency, period in office, time: *his short tenure of the Labour leadership*

tepid ADJECTIVE **1 = lukewarm**, warmish, slightly warm: *She bent to the tap and drank the tepid water.* **2 = unenthusiastic**, half-hearted, indifferent, cool, lukewarm, apathetic: *His nomination has received tepid support in the Senate.* **OPPOSITE:** enthusiastic

term NOUN **1 = word**, name, expression, title, label, phrase, denomination, designation, appellation, locution: *What's the medical term for a heart attack?* **2 = session**, course, quarter *(U.S.)*, semester, trimester *(U.S.)*: *the summer term* **3 = period**, time, spell, while, season, space, interval, span, duration, incumbency: *a 12-month term of service* **4 = conclusion**, end, close, finish, culmination, fruition: *Older women are just as capable of carrying a baby to term.*
▷ VERB **= call**, name, label, style, entitle, tag, dub, designate, describe as, denominate: *He had been termed a temporary employee.*

terminal ADJECTIVE **1 = fatal**, deadly, lethal, killing, mortal, incurable, inoperable, untreatable: *terminal cancer* **2 = final**, last, closing, finishing, concluding, ultimate, terminating: *Endowments pay a terminal bonus at maturity.* **OPPOSITE:** initial
▷ NOUN **= terminus**, station, depot, end of the line: *Only the original ochre facade of the nearby railway terminal remains.*

terminate VERB **1 = end**, stop, conclude, finish, complete, axe *(informal)*, cut off, wind up, put an end to, discontinue, pull the plug on *(informal)*, belay *(Nautical)*, bring or come to an end: *Her next remark abruptly terminated the conversation.* **OPPOSITE:** begin **2 = cease**, end, close, finish, run out, expire, lapse: *His contract terminates at the end of the season.* **3 = abort**, end: *She finally decided to terminate the pregnancy.*

termination NOUN **1 = ending**, end, close, finish, conclusion, wind-up, completion, cessation, expiry, cut-off point, finis, discontinuation: *a dispute which led to the abrupt termination of trade* **OPPOSITE:** beginning **2 = abortion**, ending, discontinuation: *You should have a medical after the termination of a pregnancy.*

terminology NOUN **= language**, terms, vocabulary, jargon, cant, lingo *(informal)*, nomenclature, patois, phraseology, argot

terminus NOUN **= end of the line**, terminal, station, depot, last stop, garage

terms PLURAL NOUN **1 = language**, terminology, phraseology, manner of speaking: *The video explains in simple terms how the tax works.* **2 = conditions**, particulars, provisions, provisos, stipulations, qualifications, premises *(Law)*, specifications: *the terms of the Helsinki agreement* **3 = relationship**, standing, footing, relations, position, status: *We shook hands and parted on good terms.* **4 = price**, rates, charges, fee, payment: *They provide favourable terms to shops that invest in their services.*
come to terms = come to an agreement, reach agreement, come to an understanding, conclude agreement: *Even if they came to terms, investors would object to the merger.*
come to terms with something = learn to live with, come to accept, be reconciled to, reach acceptance of: *She had come to terms with the fact that she would always be ill.*

> **USAGE**
> Many people object to the use of *in terms of* as an all-purpose preposition replacing phrases such as 'as regards', 'about', and so forth in a context such as the following: *In terms of trends in smoking habits, there is good news.* They would maintain that in strict usage it should be used to specify a relationship, as in: *Obesity is defined in terms of body mass index, which involves a bit of cumbersome maths.* Nevertheless, despite objections, it is very commonly used as a link word, particularly in speech.

terrain NOUN **= ground**, country, land, landscape, topography, going

terrestrial ADJECTIVE **= earthly**, worldly, global, mundane, sublunary, tellurian, terrene

terrible ADJECTIVE **1 = awful**, shocking, appalling, terrifying, horrible, dreadful, horrifying, dread, dreaded, fearful, horrendous, monstrous, harrowing, gruesome, horrid, unspeakable, frightful, hellacious *(U.S. slang)*: *Thousands suffered terrible injuries in the disaster.* **2 = bad**, awful, dreadful, beastly *(informal)*, dire, abysmal, abhorrent, poor, offensive, foul, unpleasant, revolting, rotten *(informal)*, obscene, hideous, vile, from hell *(informal)*, obnoxious, repulsive, frightful, odious, hateful, loathsome, godawful *(slang)*: *I have the most terrible nightmares.* **OPPOSITE:** wonderful **3 = serious**, desperate, severe, extreme, bad, dangerous, insufferable: *He claimed that he had a terrible pain in his head; We are in terrible trouble.* **OPPOSITE:** mild

terribly ADVERB **1 = very much**, greatly, very, much, dreadfully, seriously, extremely, gravely, desperately, thoroughly, decidedly, awfully *(informal)*, exceedingly: *He has suffered terribly in losing his best friend.* **2 = extremely**, very, much, greatly, dreadfully, seriously, desperately, thoroughly, decidedly, awfully *(informal)*, exceedingly: *I'm terribly sorry to bother you at this hour.*

terrific ADJECTIVE **1 = excellent**, great *(informal)*, wonderful, mean *(slang)*, topping *(Brit. slang)*, fine, brilliant, very good, cracking *(Brit. informal)*, amazing, outstanding, smashing *(informal)*, superb, fantastic *(informal)*, ace *(informal)*, magnificent, fabulous *(informal)*, marvellous, sensational *(informal)*, sovereign, awesome *(slang)*, breathtaking, super *(informal)*, brill *(informal)*, stupendous, bodacious *(slang, chiefly U.S.)*, boffo *(slang)*, jim-dandy *(slang)*, chillin' *(U.S. slang)*, booshit *(Austral. slang)*, exo *(Austral. slang)*, sik *(Austral. slang)*, ka pai *(N.Z.)*, rad *(informal)*, phat *(slang)*, schmick *(Austral. informal)*, beaut *(informal)*, barrie *(Scot. slang)*, belting *(Brit. slang)*, pearler *(Austral. slang)*: *What a terrific idea!* **OPPOSITE:** awful **2 = intense**, great, huge, terrible, enormous, severe, extreme, awful, tremendous, fierce, harsh, excessive, dreadful, horrific, fearful, awesome, gigantic, monstrous: *There was a terrific bang and a great cloud of smoke.*

terrified ADJECTIVE **= frightened**, scared, petrified, alarmed, intimidated, awed, panic-stricken, scared to death, scared stiff, terror-stricken, horror-struck, frightened out of your wits

terrify VERB **= frighten**, scare, petrify, alarm, intimidate, terrorize, scare to death, put the fear of God into, make your hair stand on end, fill with terror, make your flesh creep, make your blood run cold, frighten out of your wits

territory NOUN **= district**, area, land, region, state, country, sector, zone, province, patch, turf *(U.S. slang)*, domain, terrain, tract, bailiwick

terror NOUN **1 = fear**, alarm, dread, fright, panic, anxiety, intimidation, fear and trembling: *I shook with terror whenever I flew in an aeroplane.* **2 = nightmare**, monster, bogeyman, devil, fiend, bugbear, scourge: *the many obscure terrors that haunted the children of that period*

terrorize *or* **terrorise** VERB **1 = bully**, menace, intimidate, threaten, oppress, coerce, strong-arm *(informal)*, browbeat: *In his childhood he liked to terrorize his young siblings.* **2 = terrify**, alarm, frighten, scare, intimidate, petrify, scare to death, strike terror into, put the fear of God into, fill with terror, frighten out of your wits, inspire panic in: *The government had the helicopter gunships to terrorize the population.*

terse ADJECTIVE **1 = curt**, abrupt, brusque, short, rude, tart, snappy, gruff: *His tone was terse as he asked the question.* **OPPOSITE:** polite **2 = concise**, short, brief, clipped, neat, to the point, crisp, compact, summary, condensed, incisive, elliptical, laconic, succinct, pithy, monosyllabic, gnomic, epigrammatic, aphoristic, sententious: *He issued a terse statement, saying the decision will be made on Monday.* **OPPOSITE:** lengthy

test VERB **1 = check**, try, investigate, assess, research, prove, analyse, experiment with, try out, verify, assay, put something to the proof, put something to the test, run something up the flagpole: *Test the temperature of the water with your wrist.* **2 = examine**, put someone to the test, put someone through their paces: *He tested him on verbs and gave him a forfeit for each one he got wrong.*
▷ NOUN **1 = trial**, research, check, investigation, attempt, analysis, assessment, proof, examination, evaluation, acid test: *High levels of dioxin were confirmed by scientific tests.* **2 = examination**, paper, assessment, evaluation: *Only 922 pupils passed the test.*

testament NOUN **1 = proof**, evidence, testimony, witness, demonstration, tribute, attestation, exemplification: *His house is a testament to his Gothic tastes.* **2 = will**, last wishes: *a codicil to my will and testament*

testify VERB **= bear witness**, state, swear, certify, declare, witness, assert, affirm, depose *(Law)*, attest, corroborate, vouch, evince, give testimony, asseverate **OPPOSITE:** disprove

testimonial NOUN **= reference**, recommendation, credential, character, tribute, certificate, endorsement, commendation

> **USAGE**
> *Testimonial* is sometimes wrongly used where *testimony* is meant: *His re-election is a testimony (not a testimonial) to his popularity with his constituents.*

testimony NOUN **1 = evidence**, information, statement, witness, profession, declaration, confirmation, submission, affirmation, affidavit, deposition, corroboration, avowal, attestation: *His testimony was an important element of the case.* **2 = proof**, evidence, demonstration, indication, support, manifestation, verification, corroboration: *Her living room piled with documents is a testimony to her dedication to her work.*

testing ADJECTIVE **= difficult**, trying, demanding, taxing, challenging, searching, tough, exacting, formidable, rigorous, strenuous, arduous **OPPOSITE:** undemanding

testy ADJECTIVE **= irritable**, cross, grumpy, crabbed, impatient, snappy, sullen, touchy, bad-tempered, petulant, irascible, cantankerous, peppery, tetchy, ratty *(Brit. & N.Z. informal)*, quarrelsome, fretful, short-tempered, waspish, peevish, quick-tempered, splenetic, snappish, liverish, captious

tetchy ADJECTIVE **= irritable**, cross, grumpy, crabbed, impatient, snappy, sullen, touchy, bad-tempered, petulant, irascible, cantankerous, peppery, ratty *(Brit. & N.Z. informal)*, testy, quarrelsome, fretful, short-tempered, waspish, peevish, quick-tempered, splenetic, snappish, liverish, captious

tether NOUN **= leash**, rope, lead, bond, chain, restraint, fastening, shackle, fetter, halter: *The eagle sat on a tether, looking fierce.*
▷ VERB **= tie**, secure, bind, chain, rope, restrain, fasten, shackle, leash, fetter, manacle: *He dismounted, tethering his horse to a tree.*
at the end of your tether = exasperated, exhausted, at your wits' end, finished, out of patience, at the limit of your endurance: *She was emotionally at the end of her tether.*

text NOUN **1 = contents**, words, content, wording, body, matter, subject matter, main body: *The photographs enhance the clarity of the text.* **2 = words**, wording: *A CD-ROM can store up to 250,000 pages of text.* **3 = transcript**, script: *the text of Dr. Runcie's speech* **4 = reference book**, textbook, source, reader: *reluctant readers of GCSE set texts* **5 = passage**, extract, line, sentence, paragraph, verse: *I'll read the text aloud first.* **6 = subject**, matter, topic, argument, theme, thesis, motif: *His work served as the text of secret debates.*

texture NOUN **= feel**, quality, character, consistency, structure, surface, constitution, fabric, tissue, grain, weave, composition

thank VERB **= say thank you to**, express gratitude to, show gratitude to, show your appreciation to

thankful ADJECTIVE **= grateful**, pleased, relieved, obliged, in (someone's) debt, indebted, appreciative, beholden **OPPOSITE:** ungrateful

thankless ADJECTIVE **= unrewarding**, unappreciated **OPPOSITE:** rewarding

thanks PLURAL NOUN **= gratitude**, appreciation, thanksgiving, credit, recognition, acknowledgment, gratefulness: *They accepted their certificates with words of thanks.*
thanks to = because of, through, due to, as a result of, owing to, by reason of: *Thanks to recent research, effective treatment is available.*

thaw VERB **= melt**, dissolve, soften, defrost, warm, liquefy, unfreeze **OPPOSITE:** freeze

theatre

THEATRE TERMS

act	off-Broadway
backstage	off-off-Broadway
catastrophe	offstage
chorus	opera house
circle	orchestra *or* orchestra pit
Comédie Française	overact
coup de théâtre	prompt
crush bar	prompter
cue	prop
curtain	proscenium arch
curtain call	resting
curtain-raiser	role
curtain speech	scene
downstage	scene dock *or* bay
dramatis personae	scenery
entr'acte	script
entrance	soliloquy
exit	soubrette
first night	speech
first-night nerves	stage
flat	stage direction
flies	stage door
fluff	stage fright
front of house	stagehand
gallery	stage left
gods	stage manager
greasepaint	stage right
greenroom	stage-struck
ham	stage whisper
house	stalls
juvenile	theatre-in-the-round
leading lady	Thespian
leading man	understudy
lines	unities
monologue	upstage
noises off	wings

theatrical ADJECTIVE **1 = dramatic**, stage, Thespian, dramaturgical: *major theatrical productions* **2 = exaggerated**, dramatic, melodramatic, histrionic, affected, camp (*informal*), mannered, artificial, overdone, unreal, pompous, stilted, showy, ostentatious, hammy (*informal*), ceremonious, stagy, actorly or actressy: *In a theatrical gesture he clamped his hand over his eyes.*
OPPOSITE: natural

theft NOUN **= stealing**, robbery, thieving, fraud, rip-off (*slang*), swindling, embezzlement, pilfering, larceny, purloining, thievery

theme NOUN **1 = motif**, leitmotif, recurrent image, unifying idea: *The need to strengthen the family has become a recurrent theme.* **2 = subject**, idea, topic, matter, argument, text, burden, essence, thesis, subject matter, keynote, gist, through-line (*Austral., U.S., & Canad.*): *The novel's central theme is the conflict between men and women.*

theological ADJECTIVE **= religious**, ecclesiastical, doctrinal, divine

theorem NOUN **= proposition**, statement, formula, rule, principle, thesis, hypothesis, deduction, dictum

theoretical *or* **theoretic** ADJECTIVE **1 = abstract**, pure, speculative, ideal, impractical: *theoretical physics*
OPPOSITE: practical **2 = hypothetical**, academic, notional, unproven, conjectural, postulatory: *There is a theoretical risk, but there is seldom a problem.*

theorize *or* **theorise** VERB **= speculate**, conjecture, hypothesize, project, suppose, guess, formulate, propound, blue-sky

theory NOUN **1 = hypothesis**, philosophy, system of ideas, plan, system, science, scheme, proposal, principles, ideology, thesis: *He produced a theory about historical change.*
OPPOSITE: fact **2 = belief**, feeling, speculation, assumption, guess, hunch, presumption, conjecture, surmise, supposition: *There was a theory that he wanted to marry her.*

therapeutic ADJECTIVE **= beneficial**, healing, restorative, good, corrective, remedial, salutary, curative, salubrious, ameliorative, analeptic, sanative **OPPOSITE:** harmful

therapist NOUN **= psychologist**, analyst, psychiatrist, shrink (*informal*), counsellor, healer, psychotherapist, psychoanalyst, trick cyclist (*informal*)

therapy NOUN **= remedy**, treatment, cure, healing, method of healing, remedial treatment

therefore ADVERB **= consequently**, so, thus, as a result, hence, accordingly, for that reason, whence, thence, ergo

thesaurus NOUN **= wordbook**, wordfinder

thesis NOUN **1 = proposition**, theory, hypothesis, idea, view, opinion, proposal, contention, line of argument: *This thesis does not stand up to close inspection.* **2 = dissertation**, paper, treatise, essay, composition, monograph, disquisition: *He was awarded his PhD for a thesis on industrial robots.* **3 = premise**, subject, statement, proposition, theme, topic, assumption, postulate, surmise, supposition: *His central thesis is that crime is up because children do not learn self-control.*

thick ADJECTIVE **1 = bulky**, broad, big, large, fat, solid, substantial, hefty, plump, sturdy, stout, chunky, stocky, meaty, beefy, thickset: *He folded his thick arms across his chest.* **OPPOSITE:** thin **2 = wide**, across, deep, broad, in extent *or* diameter: *The folder was two inches thick.* **3 = dense**, close, heavy, deep, compact, impenetrable, lush: *He led the rescuers through the thick undergrowth.* **4 = heavy**, heavyweight, dense, chunky, bulky, woolly: *She wore a thick tartan skirt.* **5 = opaque**, heavy, dense, impenetrable: *The smoke was blueish-black and thick.* **6 = viscous**, concentrated, stiff, condensed, clotted, coagulated, gelatinous, semi-solid, viscid: *The sauce is thick and rich.* **OPPOSITE:** runny **7 = crowded**, full, packed, covered, filled, bursting, jammed, crawling, choked, crammed, swarming, abundant, bristling, brimming, overflowing, seething, thronged, teeming, congested, replete, chock-full, bursting at the seams, chock-a-block: *The area is so thick with people that the police close the streets.* **OPPOSITE:** empty **8 = husky**, rough, hoarse, distorted, muffled, croaking, inarticulate, throaty, indistinct, gravelly, guttural, raspy, croaky: *His voice was thick with bitterness.* **OPPOSITE:** clear **9 = strong**, marked, broad, decided, rich, distinct, pronounced: *He answered questions in a thick accent.*
OPPOSITE: slight **10 = stupid**, slow, dull, dense, insensitive, dozy (*Brit. informal*), dopey (*informal*), moronic, obtuse, brainless, blockheaded, braindead (*informal*), dumb-ass (*informal*), thickheaded, dim-witted (*informal*), slow-witted: *How could she have been so thick?* **OPPOSITE:** clever **11 = friendly**, close, intimate, familiar, pally (*informal*), devoted, well in (*informal*), confidential, inseparable, on good terms, chummy (*informal*), hand in glove, buddy-buddy (*slang, chiefly U.S. & Canad.*), palsy-walsy (*informal*), matey *or* maty (*Brit. informal*): *You're thick with the girl, aren't you?*
OPPOSITE: unfriendly
▷ NOUN **= middle**, centre, heart, focus, core, midst, hub: *I enjoy being in the thick of things.*

thicken VERB **= set**, condense, congeal, cake, gel, clot, jell, coagulate, inspissate (*archaic*) **OPPOSITE:** thin

thicket NOUN **= wood**, grove, woodland, brake, clump, covert, hurst (*archaic*), copse, coppice, spinney (*Brit.*)

thick-skinned ADJECTIVE **= insensitive**, tough, callous, hardened, hard-boiled (*informal*), impervious, stolid, unfeeling, case-hardened, unsusceptible **OPPOSITE:** sensitive

Jane Austen's Use of Nouns

The most frequently used nouns in Jane Austen's novels are *Mr., Mrs.* and *Miss.* Modern day instances of these terms are limited to occurrences of formal usage and would not be used by family members or friends when addressing each other. However, the frequent use of these terms in Jane Austen's writing is an indicator of a more formal society. In *Pride and Prejudice,* Mrs. Bennet even addresses her husband as *Mr Bennet.* In *Emma,* when Emma persuades Harriet that Harriet is the object of Mr Elton's affections, even in her emotional state, Harriet still refers to her friend as *dear Miss Woodhouse.* This is also indicative of the social order of Austen's society: Emma is Harriet's friend but she is socially superior to her and Harriet knows her place.

Tellingly, the most salient modifiers of *marriage* in Jane Austen's work are *imprudent* and *unprosperous. Happy* appears rather further down the list. The most salient verbs used with marriage are *expedite* and *prevent.* In the late 18th and early 19th centuries, the only way for a woman to improve her position in society and achieve financial security was through marriage and a high value was placed on a socially and financially beneficial union. Marriages in Jane Austen's world are treated rather like contracts and are *secured, planned,* and *concluded.* In *Pride and Prejudice,* Charlotte believes that happiness in marriage is *entirely a matter of chance* and:

> Without thinking highly either of men or matrimony, marriage had always been her object; it was the only provision for well-educated young women of small fortune, and however uncertain of giving happiness, must be their pleasantest preservative from want.

Nothing is the fifth most frequently used word in Jane Austen's writings, whereas *anything* is used three times less. Jane Austen's characters frequently *know, see, say,* and *hear nothing,* though occasionally *don't say* or *do anything.* In *Northanger Abbey,* Catherine *knew nothing of drawing – nothing of taste.* Here *nothing* is used in preference to negation of the verb *know* and use of the noun *anything.*

Jane Austen uses many polysyllabic nouns derived from French and Latin: *acquaintance, consequence, disposition, agitation, and solicitude,* to name a few. Such nouns are used not only by the narrator, but also by the characters themselves. Occasionally, the writer humorously exploits the use of non-native words by characters in order to expose their pretentiousness and vulgarity. In *Emma,* Mrs. Elton refers to her husband as her *caro sposo* and she speaks boastfully of her brother and sister's mode of transport:

> They will have their **barouche-landau**, of course, which holds four perfectly; and therefore, without saying any thing of our carriage, we should be able to explore the different beauties extremely well. They would hardly come in their **chaise**, I think, at that season of the year. Indeed, when the time draws on, I shall decidedly recommend their bringing the **barouche-landau**; it will be so very much preferable.

In the above passage, Mrs Elton is the only character to use the expression *barouche-landau* and her vulgarity is further emphasised by the fact that she uses it four times in the same conversation.

The word *sense* is another significant noun in Jane Austen's writings. She uses the word to parody the literary genre of romanticism and sensibility that was in vogue at the end of the 18th century. In *Sense and Sensibility,* Elinor is portrayed as sensible and composed but is concerned by *the excess of her sister's sensibility,* by Marianne's exaggerated idealism and romantic notions, but believes that:

> A few years however will settle her opinions on the reasonable basis of common sense and observation.

thief NOUN = **robber**, crook *(informal)*, burglar, stealer, bandit, plunderer, mugger *(informal)*, shoplifter, embezzler, pickpocket, pilferer, swindler, purloiner, housebreaker, footpad *(archaic)*, cracksman *(slang)*, larcenist

> **QUOTATIONS**
> Thieves respect property. They merely wish the property to become their property that they may more perfectly respect it
> [G.K. Chesterton *The Man who was Thursday*]

> **PROVERBS**
> *Set a thief to catch a thief*

thin ADJECTIVE **1 = narrow**, fine, attenuate, attenuated, threadlike: *A thin cable carries the signal to a computer.* **OPPOSITE:** thick **2 = slim**, spare, lean, slight, slender, skinny, light, meagre, skeletal, bony, lanky, emaciated, spindly, underweight, scrawny, lank, undernourished, skin and bone, scraggy, thin as a rake: *a tall, thin man with grey hair* **OPPOSITE:** fat **3 = watery**, weak, diluted, dilute, runny, rarefied, wishy-washy *(informal)*: *The soup was thin and clear.* **OPPOSITE:** viscous **4 = meagre**, sparse, scanty, poor, scattered, inadequate, insufficient, deficient, paltry: *The crowd had been thin for the first half of the match.* **OPPOSITE:** plentiful **5 = fine**, delicate, flimsy, sheer, transparent, see-through, translucent, skimpy, gossamer, diaphanous, filmy, unsubstantial: *Her gown was thin and she shivered from the cold.* **OPPOSITE:** thick **6 = unconvincing**, inadequate, feeble, poor, weak, slight, shallow, insufficient, superficial, lame, scant, flimsy, scanty, unsubstantial: *The evidence is thin, and to some extent, ambiguous.* **OPPOSITE:** convincing **7 = wispy**, thinning, sparse, scarce, scanty: *She had pale thin yellow hair.*
▷ VERB **1 = prune**, trim, cut back, weed out: *It would have been better to thin the trees over several winters.* **2 = dilute**, water down, weaken, attenuate: *Aspirin thins the blood, letting it flow more easily.*

thing NOUN **1 = object**, article, implement, machine, device, tool, instrument, mechanism, apparatus, gadget, gizmo *(informal)*, contrivance, whatsit *(informal)*, doo-dah *(informal)*, thingummy *(informal)*, thingummyjig *(informal)*: *What's that thing in the middle of the fountain?* **2 = substance**, stuff, element, being, body, material, fabric, texture, entity: *The Earth is mainly made of iron and silicon and things like that.* **3 = concept**, idea, notion, conception: *Literacy isn't the same thing as intelligence.* **4 = matter**, issue, subject, thought, concern, worry, topic, preoccupation: *There were far more serious things on my mind.* **5 = affair**, situation, state of affairs, state, circumstance, scenario: *This war thing is upsetting me.* **6 = fact**, detail, particular, point, factor, piece of information: *The first thing parents want to know is what sex the baby is.* **7 = feature**, point, detail, something, particular, factor, item, aspect, facet: *If you could change one thing about yourself, what would it be?* **8 = happening**, event, incident, proceeding, phenomenon, occurrence, eventuality: *A strange thing happened.* **9 = phobia**, fear, complex, horror, terror, hang-up *(informal)*, aversion, neurosis, bee in your bonnet *(informal)*: *She had a thing about spiders.* **10 = obsession**, liking, preoccupation, mania, quirk, fetish, fixation, soft spot, predilection, idée fixe *(French)*: *He's got a thing about red hair.* **11 = remark**, comment, statement, observation, declaration, utterance, pronouncement: *No, some things are better left unsaid.* **12** *(often plural)* **= possessions**, stuff, gear, belongings, goods, effects, clothes, luggage, baggage, bits and pieces, paraphernalia, clobber *(Brit. slang)*, odds and ends, chattels, impedimenta: *She told him to take his things and not come back.* **13 = equipment**, gear, tool, stuff, tackle, implement, kit, apparatus, utensil, accoutrement: *He forgot his shaving things.* **14 = circumstances**, the situation, the state of affairs, matters, life, affairs: *Everyone agrees things are getting better.*

think VERB **1 = believe**, hold that, be of the opinion, conclude, esteem, conceive, be of the view: *I think there should be a ban on tobacco advertising.* **2 = anticipate**, expect, figure *(U.S. informal)*, suppose, imagine, guess *(informal, chiefly U.S. & Canad.)*, reckon *(informal)*, presume, envisage, foresee, surmise: *I think he'll do a great job for us.* **3 = judge**, consider, estimate, reckon, deem, regard as: *She thought he was about seventeen years old.* **4 = ponder**, reflect, contemplate, deliberate, brood, meditate, ruminate, cogitate, rack your brains, be lost in thought, cerebrate: *She closed her eyes for a moment, trying to think.* **5 = remember**, recall, recollect, review, think back to, bring to mind, call to mind: *I was trying to think what else we had to do.*
▷ NOUN **= ponder**, consideration, muse, assessment, reflection, deliberation, contemplation: *I'll have a think about that.*
think something over = consider, contemplate, ponder, reflect upon, give thought to, consider the pros and cons of, weigh up, rack your brains about, chew over *(informal)*, mull over, turn over in your mind: *She says she needs time to think it over.*
think something up = devise, create, imagine, manufacture, come up with, invent, contrive, improvise, visualize, concoct, dream up, trump up: *'Where did you get that idea?' – 'I just thought it up.'*

> **QUOTATIONS**
> I think, therefore I am
> [René Descartes *Le Discours de la Méthode*]

thinker NOUN **= philosopher**, intellect *(informal)*, wise man, sage, brain *(informal)*, theorist, mastermind, mahatma

thinking NOUN **= reasoning**, thoughts, philosophy, idea, view, position, theory, opinion, conclusions, assessment, judgment, outlook, conjecture: *There was a strong theoretical dimension to his thinking.*
▷ ADJECTIVE **= thoughtful**, intelligent, cultured, reasoning, sophisticated, rational, philosophical, reflective, contemplative, meditative, ratiocinative: *Thinking people on both sides will applaud this book.*

third-rate ADJECTIVE **= mediocre**, bad, inferior, indifferent, poor, duff *(Brit. informal)*, shoddy, poor-quality, low-grade, no great shakes *(informal)*, not much cop *(informal)*, cheap-jack, half-pie *(N.Z. informal)*, of a sort *or* of sorts, ropey *or* ropy *(Brit. informal)*, bodger *or* bodgie *(Austral. slang)*

thirst NOUN **1 = dryness**, thirstiness, drought, craving to drink: *Instead of tea or coffee, drink water to quench your thirst.* **2 = craving**, hunger, appetite, longing, desire, passion, yen *(informal)*, ache, lust, yearning, eagerness, hankering, keenness: *their ever-growing thirst for cash* **OPPOSITE:** aversion

thirsty ADJECTIVE **1 = parched**, dry, dehydrated: *If a baby is thirsty, it feeds more often.* **2** (with **for**) **= eager for**, longing for, hungry for, dying for, yearning for, lusting for, craving for, thirsting for, burning for, hankering for, itching for, greedy for, desirous of, avid for, athirst for: *People should understand how thirsty for revenge they are.*

thorn NOUN **= prickle**, spike, spine, barb: *Roses will always have thorns, but with care they can be avoided.*
thorn in your side = irritation, nuisance, annoyance, trouble, bother, torture, plague, curse, pest, torment, hassle *(informal)*, scourge, affliction, irritant, bane: *She's a real thorn in his side.*

thorny ADJECTIVE **1 = prickly**, spiky, spiny, pointed, sharp, barbed, bristly, spinous, bristling with thorns: *thorny hawthorn trees* **2 = troublesome**, difficult, problematic(al), trying, hard, worrying, tough, upsetting, awkward, unpleasant, sticky *(informal)*, harassing, irksome, ticklish, vexatious: *the thorny issue of immigration policy*

thorough ADJECTIVE
1 = comprehensive, full, complete, sweeping, intensive, in-depth, exhaustive, all-inclusive, all-embracing, leaving no stone unturned: *We are making a thorough investigation.* **OPPOSITE:** cursory **2 = careful**, conscientious, painstaking, efficient, meticulous, exhaustive, scrupulous, assiduous: *The men were expert, thorough and careful.* **OPPOSITE:** careless **3 = complete**,

total, absolute, utter, perfect, entire, pure, sheer, outright, downright, unqualified, out-and-out, unmitigated, arrant, deep-dyed *(usually derogatory)*: *I was a thorough little academic snob.* **OPPOSITE:** partial

thoroughbred ADJECTIVE **= purebred**, pedigree, pure-blooded, blood, full-blooded, of unmixed stock **OPPOSITE:** mongrel

thoroughfare NOUN **1 = road**, way, street, highway, roadway, passageway, avenue **2 = access**, way, passage

thoroughly ADVERB **1 = carefully**, completely, fully, comprehensively, sweepingly, efficiently, inside out, meticulously, painstakingly, scrupulously, assiduously, intensively, from top to bottom, conscientiously, exhaustively, leaving no stone unturned: *a thoroughly researched and illuminating biography* **OPPOSITE:** carelessly **2 = fully**, completely, throughout, inside out, through and through: *Food must be reheated thoroughly.* **3 = completely**, quite, totally, perfectly, entirely, absolutely, utterly, to the full, downright, to the hilt, without reservation: *We returned home thoroughly contented.* **OPPOSITE:** partly

though CONJUNCTION **= although**, while, even if, despite the fact that, allowing, granted, even though, albeit, notwithstanding, even supposing, tho' *(U.S. poetic)*: *He's very attractive, though he certainly isn't a ladykiller.*
▷ ADVERB **= nevertheless**, still, however, yet, nonetheless, all the same, for all that, notwithstanding: *I like him. He makes me angry sometimes, though.*

thought NOUN **1 = thinking**, consideration, reflection, deliberation, regard, musing, meditation, contemplation, introspection, rumination, navel-gazing *(slang)*, cogitation, brainwork, cerebration: *After much thought I decided to end my marriage.* **2 = opinion**, view, belief, idea, thinking, concept, conclusion, assessment, notion, conviction, judgment, conception, conjecture, estimation: *It is my thought that the situation will be resolved.*
3 = consideration, study, attention, care, regard, scrutiny, heed: *He had given some thought to what she had told him.*
4 = intention, plan, idea, design, aim, purpose, object, notion: *They had no thought of surrendering.* **5 = hope**, expectation, dream, prospect, aspiration, anticipation: *He had now banished all thought of retirement.*
6 = concern, care, regard, anxiety, sympathy, compassion, thoughtfulness, solicitude, attentiveness: *They had no thought for others who might get hurt.*

thoughtful ADJECTIVE **1 = reflective**, pensive, contemplative, meditative, thinking, serious, musing, wistful, introspective, rapt, studious, lost in thought, deliberative, ruminative, in a brown study: *He was looking very thoughtful.* **OPPOSITE:** shallow
2 = considerate, kind, caring, kindly, helpful, attentive, unselfish, solicitous: *a thoughtful and caring man* **OPPOSITE:** inconsiderate

thoughtless ADJECTIVE
1 = inconsiderate, rude, selfish, insensitive, unkind, uncaring, indiscreet, tactless, impolite, undiplomatic: *a minority of thoughtless and inconsiderate people*
OPPOSITE: considerate **2 = unthinking**, stupid, silly, careless, regardless, foolish, rash, reckless, mindless, negligent, inadvertent, ill-considered, tactless, absent-minded, imprudent, slapdash, neglectful, heedless, slipshod, inattentive, injudicious, remiss, unmindful, unobservant, ditsy *or* ditzy *(slang)*: *It was thoughtless of her to mention it.*
OPPOSITE: wise

thrall NOUN **= slavery**, bondage, servitude, enslavement, subjugation, serfdom, subjection, vassalage, thraldom

thrash VERB **1 = defeat**, beat, hammer *(informal)*, stuff *(slang)*, tank *(slang)*, crush, overwhelm, slaughter *(informal)*, lick *(informal)*, paste *(slang)*, rout, maul, trounce, clobber *(slang)*, run rings around *(informal)*, wipe the floor with *(informal)*, make mincemeat of *(informal)*, blow someone out of the water *(slang)*, drub, beat someone hollow *(Brit. informal)*: *They thrashed their opponents 5-0.* **2 = beat**, wallop, whip, hide *(informal)*, belt *(informal)*, leather, tan *(slang)*, cane, lick *(informal)*, paste *(slang)*, birch, flog, scourge, spank, clobber *(slang)*, lambast(e), flagellate, horsewhip, give someone a (good) hiding *(informal)*, drub, take a stick to, beat *or* knock seven bells out of *(informal)*: *'Liar!' she screamed, as she thrashed the child.* **3 = thresh**, flail, jerk, plunge, toss, squirm, writhe, heave, toss and turn: *He collapsed on the floor, thrashing his legs about.*
thrash something out = settle, resolve, discuss, debate, solve, argue out, have out, talk over: *an effort to thrash out differences about which they have strong feelings*

thrashing NOUN **1 = defeat**, beating, hammering *(informal)*, hiding *(informal)*, pasting *(slang)*, rout, mauling, trouncing, drubbing: *She dropped only eight points in her thrashing of the former champion.* **2 = beating**, hiding *(informal)*, belting *(informal)*, whipping, tanning *(slang)*, lashing, caning, pasting *(slang)*, flogging, drubbing, chastisement: *She knew if she was caught she would get a thrashing.*

thread NOUN **1 = strand**, fibre, yarn, filament, line, string, cotton, twine: *a hat embroidered with golden threads*
2 = theme, motif, train of thought, course, direction, strain, plot, drift, tenor, story line: *the thread running through the book*
▷ VERB **= move**, pass, inch, ease, thrust, meander, squeeze through, pick your way: *She threaded her way back through the crowd.*

threadbare ADJECTIVE **1 = shabby**, worn, frayed, old, ragged, worn-out, scruffy, tattered, tatty, down at heel: *She sat cross-legged on a square of threadbare carpet.* **OPPOSITE:** new **2 = hackneyed**, common, tired, stale, corny *(slang)*, stock, familiar, conventional, stereotyped, commonplace, well-worn, trite, clichéd, overused, cliché-ridden: *the government's threadbare domestic policies*
OPPOSITE: original

threat NOUN **1 = danger**, risk, hazard, menace, peril: *the threat of tropical storms* **2 = threatening remark**, menace, commination, intimidatory remark: *He may be forced to carry out his threat to resign.* **3 = warning**, foreshadowing, foreboding: *The people who lived there felt a permanent sense of threat.*

threaten VERB **1 = intimidate**, bully, menace, terrorize, warn, cow, lean on *(slang)*, pressurize, browbeat, make threats to: *He tied her up and threatened her with a knife.* **OPPOSITE:** defend
2 = endanger, jeopardize, put at risk, imperil, put in jeopardy, put on the line: *The newcomers directly threaten the livelihood of current workers.*
OPPOSITE: protect **3 = be imminent**, hang over, be in the air, loom, be in the offing, hang over someone's head, impend: *Plants must be covered with a leaf mould if frost threatens.*

threatening ADJECTIVE **1 = menacing**, bullying, intimidatory, terrorizing, minatory, comminatory: *The police should have charged them with threatening behaviour.* **2 = ominous**, sinister, forbidding, grim, baleful, inauspicious, bodeful: *a threatening atmosphere of rising tension and stress*
OPPOSITE: promising

threesome NOUN **= trio**, trinity, trilogy, triplet, triad, triumvirate, troika, triptych, triplex, trine, triune

threshold NOUN **1 = entrance**, doorway, door, doorstep, sill, doorsill: *He stopped at the threshold of the bedroom.*
2 = start, beginning, opening, dawn, verge, brink, outset, starting point, inception: *We are on the threshold of a new era in astronomy.* **OPPOSITE:** end
3 = limit, margin, starting point, minimum: *She has a low threshold of boredom, and needs constant stimulation.*

thrift NOUN **= economy**, prudence, frugality, saving, parsimony, carefulness, good husbandry, thriftiness **OPPOSITE:** extravagance

thrifty ADJECTIVE **= economical**, prudent, provident, frugal, saving, sparing, careful, parsimonious
OPPOSITE: extravagant

thrill NOUN **1 = pleasure**, charge *(slang)*, kick *(informal)*, glow, sensation, buzz *(slang)*, high, stimulation, tingle, titillation, flush of excitement: *I remember the thrill of opening presents on Christmas morning.* **OPPOSITE:** tedium **2 = trembling**, throb, shudder, flutter, fluttering, tremor, quiver, vibration: *He felt a thrill of fear, of adrenaline.*
▷ VERB **= excite**, stimulate, arouse, move, send *(slang)*, stir, flush, tingle, electrify, titillate, give someone a kick: *The electric atmosphere both thrilled and terrified him.*

thrilling ADJECTIVE **= exciting**, gripping, stimulating, stirring, sensational, rousing, riveting, electrifying, hair-raising, rip-roaring *(informal)* **OPPOSITE:** boring

thrive VERB **= prosper**, do well, flourish, increase, grow, develop, advance, succeed, get on, boom, bloom, wax, burgeon, grow rich **OPPOSITE:** decline

thriving ADJECTIVE **= successful**, doing well, flourishing, growing, developing, healthy, booming, wealthy, blooming, prosperous, burgeoning, going strong **OPPOSITE:** unsuccessful

throaty ADJECTIVE **= hoarse**, husky, gruff, low, deep, thick, guttural

throb VERB **1 = pulsate**, pound, beat, pulse, thump, palpitate: *His head throbbed.* **2 = vibrate**, pulse, resonate, pulsate, reverberate, shake, judder *(informal)*: *The engines throbbed.*
▷ NOUN **1 = pulse**, pounding, beat, thump, thumping, pulsating, palpitation: *The bruise on his stomach ached with a steady throb.* **2 = vibration**, pulse, throbbing, resonance, reverberation, judder *(informal)*, pulsation: *His head jerked up at the throb of the engine.*

throes PLURAL NOUN **= pains**, spasms, pangs, fit, stabs, convulsions, paroxysm: *The animal twitched in its final death throes.*
in the throes of something = in the midst of, in the process of, suffering from, struggling with, wrestling with, toiling with, anguished by, agonized by, in the pangs of: *The country is in the throes of a general election.*

throng NOUN **= crowd**, mob, horde, press, host, pack, mass, crush, jam, congregation, swarm, multitude, concourse, assemblage: *An official pushed through the throng.*
▷ VERB **1 = crowd**, flock, congregate, troop, bunch, herd, cram, converge, hem in, mill around, swarm around: *the multitudes that throng around the Pope* **OPPOSITE:** disperse **2 = pack**, fill, crowd, press, jam: *They throng the beaches in July and August.*

throttle VERB **1 = strangle**, choke, garrotte, strangulate: *He tried to throttle her with wire.* **2 = suppress**, inhibit, stifle, control, silence, gag: *The over-valuation of sterling is throttling industry.*

through PREPOSITION **1 = via**, by way of, by, between, past, in and out of, from end to end of, from one side to the other of: *The path continues through a tunnel of trees.* **2 = because of**, by way of, by means of, by virtue of, with the assistance of, as a consequence or result of: *the thought of someone suffering through a mistake of mine* **3 = using**, via, by way of, by means of, by virtue of, with the assistance of: *I got it cheap through a friend in the trade.* **4 = during**, throughout, in the middle of, for the duration of, in: *trips at home and abroad all through the year*
▷ ADJECTIVE **1** *(with* **with***)* **= finished with**, done with, having had enough of: *I'm through with women.*
2 = completed, done, finished, ended, terminated: *It would guarantee employment once her schooling was through.*
through and through = completely, totally, fully, thoroughly, entirely, altogether, wholly, utterly, to the core, unreservedly: *People assume they know me through and through as soon as we meet.*

throughout PREPOSITION **1 = right through**, all through, everywhere in, for the duration of, during the whole of, through the whole of, from end to end of: *The same themes are repeated throughout the film.* **2 = all over**, all through, everywhere in, through the whole of, over the length and breadth of: *He now runs projects throughout Africa.*
▷ ADVERB **1 = from start to finish**, right through, the whole time, all the time, from the start, all through, from beginning to end: *The concert wasn't bad, but people talked throughout.*
2 = all through, right through, in every nook and cranny: *Throughout, the walls are white.*

throw VERB **1 = hurl**, toss, fling, send, project, launch, cast, pitch, shy, chuck *(informal)*, propel, sling, lob *(informal)*, heave, put: *He spent hours throwing a tennis ball against a wall.*
2 = toss, fling, chuck *(informal)*, cast, hurl, sling, heave, put: *He threw his jacket onto the back seat.* **3 = dislodge**, unseat, upset, overturn, hurl to the ground: *The horse reared, throwing its rider.*
4 = confuse, baffle, faze, astonish, confound, unnerve, disconcert, perturb, throw you out, throw you off, dumbfound, discompose, put you off your stroke, throw you off your stride, unsettle: *He threw me by asking if I went in for martial arts.*
▷ NOUN **= toss**, pitch, fling, put, cast, shy, sling, lob *(informal)*, heave: *One of the judges thought it was a foul throw.*
throw someone off 1 = disconcert, unsettle, faze, throw *(informal)*, upset, confuse, disturb, put you off your stroke, throw you off your stride: *I lost my first serve in the first set; it threw me off a bit.* **2 = escape from**, lose, leave behind, get away from, evade, shake off, elude, outrun, outdistance, give someone the slip, show a clean pair of heels to: *He threw off his pursuers by pedalling across the state line.*
throw someone out = expel, eject, evict, dismiss, get rid of, oust, kick out *(informal)*, show the door to, turf out *(Brit. informal)*, give the bum's rush to *(slang)*, kiss off *(slang, chiefly U.S. & Canad.)*: *I wanted to kill him, but instead I just threw him out.*
throw something away 1 = discard, dump *(informal)*, get rid of, reject, scrap, axe *(informal)*, bin *(informal)*, ditch *(slang)*, junk *(informal)*, chuck *(informal)*, throw out, dispose of, dispense with, jettison, cast off: *I never throw anything away.* **2 = waste**, lose, blow *(slang)*, squander, fritter away, fail to make use of, make poor use of: *Failing to tackle the problem would be throwing away an opportunity.*
throw something off = cast off, shake off, rid yourself of, free yourself of, drop, abandon, discard: *a country ready to throw off the shackles of its colonial past*
throw something out 1 = discard, dump *(informal)*, get rid of, reject, scrap, bin *(informal)*, ditch *(slang)*, junk *(informal)*, chuck *(informal)*, throw away, dispose of, dispense with, jettison, cast off: *Never throw out milk that is about to go off.* **2 = emit**, radiate, give off, diffuse, disseminate, put forth: *a workshop throwing out a pool of light*
throw something up 1 = throw together, jerry-build, run up, slap together: *Scrap metal dwellings are thrown up in any available space.* **2 = produce**, reveal, bring to light, bring forward, bring to the surface, bring to notice: *These studies have thrown up some interesting results.* **3 = give up**, leave, abandon, quit, chuck *(informal)*, resign from, relinquish, renounce, step down from *(informal)*, jack in: *He threw up his job as party chairman.*
throw up = vomit, be sick, spew, puke *(slang)*, chuck *(Austral. & N.Z. informal)*, heave, regurgitate, disgorge, retch, barf *(U.S. slang)*, chunder *(slang, chiefly Austral.)*, upchuck *(U.S. slang)*, do a technicolour yawn *(slang)*, toss your cookies *(U.S. slang)*: *He threw up over a seat next to me.*

throwaway ADJECTIVE **= casual**, passing, offhand, careless, understated, unthinking, ill-considered

thrust VERB **1 = push**, force, shove, drive, press, plunge, jam, butt, ram, poke, propel, prod, impel: *They thrust him into the back of a jeep.* **2 = shove**, push, shoulder, lunge, jostle, elbow or shoulder your way: *She thrust her way into the crowd.* **3** *(often with* **through** *or* **into***)* **= stab**, stick, jab, pierce: *How can I thrust a knife into my son's heart?*
▷ NOUN **1 = stab**, pierce, lunge: *Two of the knife thrusts were fatal.* **2 = push**, shove, poke, prod: *a thrust of his hand that sent the lad reeling* **3 = momentum**, impetus, drive, motive power, motive force, propulsive force: *It provides the thrust that makes the craft move forward.*

thud NOUN **= thump**, crash, knock, smack, clump, wallop *(informal)*, clunk, clonk: *She tripped and fell with a sickening thud.*
▷ VERB **= thump**, crash, knock, smack, clump, wallop *(informal)*, clunk, clonk: *She ran upstairs, her bare feet thudding on the wood.*

thug NOUN **= ruffian**, hooligan, tough, heavy *(slang)*, killer, murderer, robber, gangster, assassin, bandit, mugger *(informal)*, cut-throat, bully boy, bruiser *(informal)*, tsotsi *(S. African)*

thumb NOUN **= digit**: *She bit her thumb, not looking at me.*
▷ VERB **1 = handle**, finger, mark, soil, maul, mess up, dog-ear: *a well-thumbed copy of Who's Who* **2 = hitch**, request *(informal)*, signal for, hitchhike: *Thumbing a lift once had a carefree image.*
all thumbs = clumsy, inept, cack-handed *(informal)*, maladroit, butterfingered *(informal)*, ham-fisted *(informal)*, unco *(Austral. slang)*: *Can you open this? I'm all thumbs.*
thumbs down = disapproval, refusal, rejection, no, rebuff, negation: *Brokers have given the firm the thumbs down.*
thumbs up = approval, go-ahead *(informal)*, acceptance, yes, encouragement, green light, affirmation, O.K. *or* okay *(informal)*: *The film got a general thumbs up from the critics.*
thumb through something = flick through, browse through, leaf through, glance at, turn over, flip through, skim through, riffle through, scan the pages of, run your eye over: *He had the drawer open and was thumbing through files.*

thumbnail ADJECTIVE **= brief**, short, concise, quick, compact, succinct, pithy

thump NOUN **1 = blow**, knock, punch, rap, smack, clout *(informal)*, whack, swipe, wallop *(informal)*: *He felt a thump on his shoulder.* **2 = thud**, crash, bang, clunk, thwack: *There was a loud thump as the horse crashed into the van.*
▷ VERB **1 = strike**, hit, punch, pound, beat, knock, deck *(slang)*, batter, rap, chin *(slang)*, smack, thrash, clout *(informal)*, whack, swipe, clobber *(slang)*, wallop *(informal)*, lambast(e), belabour, lay one on *(slang)*, beat *or* knock seven bells out of *(informal)*: *He thumped me, nearly knocking me over.*
2 = thud, crash, bang, thwack: *She thumped her hand on the witness box.*
3 = throb, pound, beat, pulse, pulsate, palpitate: *My heart was thumping wildly.*

thumping ADJECTIVE **= huge**, massive, enormous, great, impressive, tremendous, excessive, terrific, thundering *(slang)*, titanic, gigantic, monumental, mammoth, colossal, whopping *(informal)*, stellar *(informal)*, exorbitant, gargantuan, elephantine, humongous *or* humungous *(U.S. slang)*
OPPOSITE: insignificant

thunder NOUN **= rumble**, crash, crashing, boom, booming, explosion, rumbling, pealing, detonation, cracking: *the thunder of the sea on the rocks*
▷ VERB **1 = rumble**, crash, blast, boom, explode, roar, clap, resound, detonate, reverberate, crack, peal: *the sound of the guns thundering in the fog* **2 = shout**, roar, yell, bark, bellow, declaim: *'It's your money. Ask for it!' she thundered.* **3 = rail**, curse, fulminate: *He started thundering about feminists and liberals.*

thunderous ADJECTIVE **= loud**, noisy, deafening, booming, roaring, resounding, tumultuous, ear-splitting

thus ADVERB **1 = in this way**, so, like this, as follows, like so, in this manner, in this fashion, to such a degree: *She explained her mistake thus.*
2 = therefore, so, hence, consequently, accordingly, for this reason, ergo, on that account: *women's access to the basic means of production, and thus to political power*

thwart VERB **= frustrate**, stop, foil, check, defeat, prevent, oppose, snooker, baffle, hinder, obstruct, impede, balk, outwit, stymie, cook someone's goose *(informal)*, put a spoke in someone's wheel *(informal)*
OPPOSITE: assist

tic NOUN **= twitch**, jerk, spasm

tick NOUN **1 = check mark**, mark, line, stroke, dash: *Place a tick in the appropriate box.* **2 = click**, tap, tapping, clicking, clack, ticktock: *He sat listening to the tick of the grandfather clock.* **3 = moment**, second, minute, shake *(informal)*, flash, instant, sec *(informal)*, twinkling, split second, jiffy *(informal)*, trice, half a mo *(Brit. informal)*, two shakes of a lamb's tail *(informal)*, bat of an eye *(informal)*: *I'll be back in a tick.*
▷ VERB **1 = mark**, indicate, mark off, check off, choose, select: *Please tick here if you do not want to receive such mailings.*
2 = click, tap, clack, ticktock: *A clock ticked busily from the kitchen counter.*
tick someone off = scold, rebuke, tell off *(informal)*, lecture, carpet *(informal)*, censure, reprimand, reproach, berate, chide, tear into *(informal)*, reprove, upbraid, take to task, read the riot act to, bawl out *(informal)*, chew out *(U.S. & Canad. informal)*, tear off a strip *(Brit. informal)*, haul over the coals *(informal)*, give a rocket to *(Brit. & N.Z. informal)*: *His mum ticked him off when they got home.*
tick something off = mark off, check off, put a tick at: *He ticked off my name on a piece of paper.*

ticket NOUN **1 = voucher**, pass, coupon, card, slip, certificate, token, chit: *They were queueing to get tickets for the football match.* **2 = label**, tag, marker, sticker, card, slip, tab, docket: *a price ticket*

tickle VERB **= amuse**, delight, entertain, please, divert, gratify, titillate **OPPOSITE:** bore

tide NOUN **1 = current**, flow, stream, course, ebb, undertow, tideway: *They used to sail with the tide.* **2 = course**, direction, trend, current, movement, tendency, drift: *They talked of reversing the tide of events.*
tide someone over = keep you going, see you through, keep the wolf from the door, keep your head above water, bridge the gap for: *He wanted to borrow some money to tide him over.*

tidings PLURAL NOUN **= news**, report, word, message, latest *(informal)*, information, communication, intelligence, bulletin, gen *(Brit. informal)*

tidy ADJECTIVE **1 = neat**, orderly, ordered, clean, trim, systematic, spruce, businesslike, well-kept, well-ordered, shipshape, spick-and-span, trig *(archaic, dialect)*, in apple-pie order *(informal)*: *Having a tidy desk can sometimes seem impossible.*
OPPOSITE: untidy **2 = organized**, neat, fastidious, methodical, smart, efficient, spruce, businesslike, well-groomed, well turned out: *She wasn't a tidy person.* **3 = considerable**, large, substantial, good, goodly, fair, healthy, generous, handsome, respectable, ample, largish, sizable *or* sizeable: *The opportunities are there to make a tidy profit.* **OPPOSITE:** small
▷ VERB **= neaten**, straighten, put in order, order, clean, groom, spruce up, put to rights, put in trim: *She made her bed and tidied her room.*
OPPOSITE: disorder

tie VERB **1 = fasten**, bind, join, unite, link, connect, attach, knot, truss, interlace: *He tied the ends of the plastic bag together.* **OPPOSITE:** unfasten
2 = tether, secure, rope, moor, lash, make fast: *She tied her horse to a fence post.* **3 = restrict**, limit, confine, hold, bind, restrain, hamper, hinder: *I wouldn't like to be tied to catching the last train home.* **OPPOSITE:** free **4 = draw**, be even, be level, be neck and neck, match, equal: *Both teams had tied on points and goal difference.*
▷ NOUN **1 = fastening**, binding, link, band, bond, joint, connection, string, rope, knot, cord, fetter, ligature: *little empire-line coats with ribbon ties* **2 = bond**, relationship, connection, duty, commitment, obligation, liaison, allegiance, affinity, affiliation, kinship: *She had family ties in France.*
3 = draw, dead heat, deadlock, stalemate: *The first game ended in a tie.*
4 = match, game, contest, fixture, meeting, event, trial, bout: *They'll meet the winners of the first-round tie.*
5 = encumbrance, restriction, limitation, check, handicap, restraint, hindrance, bind *(informal)*: *It's a bit of a tie, going there every Sunday.*
tie in with something 1 = link, relate to, connect, be relevant to, come in to, have a bearing on: *subjects which tie in with whatever you enjoy about painting*
2 = fit in with, coincide with, coordinate with, harmonize with, occur simultaneously with: *Our wedding date had to tie in with Dave's leaving the army.*

tie something up **1 = secure**, lash, tether, make fast, moor, attach, rope: *I had tied the boat up in the marina and furled my sail.* **2 = conclude**, settle, wrap up *(informal)*, end, wind up, terminate, finish off, bring to a close: *They hope to tie up a deal within the next few weeks.*
tie something *or* **someone up** **= bind**, restrain, pinion, truss up: *Don't you think we should tie him up and put a guard over him?*

tie in *or* **tie-in** NOUN **= link**, connection, relation, relationship, association, tie-up, liaison, coordination, hook-up

tier NOUN **= row**, bank, layer, line, order, level, series, file, rank, storey, stratum, echelon

tie-up NOUN **= link**, association, connection, relationship, relation, liaison, tie-in, coordination, hook-up, linkup

tiff NOUN **= quarrel**, row, disagreement, words, difference, dispute, scrap *(informal)*, falling-out *(informal)*, squabble, petty quarrel

tight ADJECTIVE **1 = close-fitting**, narrow, cramped, snug, constricted, close: *His jeans were too tight.* **OPPOSITE:** loose **2 = secure**, firm, fast, fixed: *Keep a tight grip on my hand.* **3 = taut**, stretched, tense, rigid, stiff: *Pull the elastic tight and knot the ends.* **OPPOSITE:** slack **4 = strict**, stringent, severe, tough, harsh, stern, rigid, rigorous, uncompromising, inflexible, unyielding: *tight control of media coverage* **OPPOSITE:** easy-going **5 = sealed**, watertight, impervious, sound, proof, hermetic: *Cover with foil and the lid to ensure a tight seal.* **OPPOSITE:** open **6 = close**, even, well-matched, near, hard-fought, evenly-balanced: *It was a very tight match.* **OPPOSITE:** uneven **7 = miserly**, mean, stingy, close, sparing, grasping, parsimonious, niggardly, penurious, tightfisted: *Are you so tight you won't even spend a few quid?* **OPPOSITE:** generous **8 = difficult**, tough, dangerous, tricky, sticky *(informal)*, hazardous, troublesome, problematic, precarious, perilous, worrisome, ticklish: *They teach you to use your head and get out of a tight spot.* **9 = drunk**, intoxicated, flying *(slang)*, bombed *(slang)*, stoned *(slang)*, wasted *(slang)*, smashed *(slang)*, steaming *(slang)*, wrecked *(slang)*, out of it *(slang)*, plastered *(slang)*, blitzed *(slang)*, lit up *(slang)*, stewed *(slang)*, pickled *(informal)*, bladdered *(slang)*, under the influence *(informal)*, tipsy, legless *(informal)*, paralytic *(informal)*, sozzled *(informal)*, steamboats *(Scot. slang)*, tiddly *(slang, chiefly Brit.)*, half cut *(Brit. slang)*, zonked *(slang)*, blotto *(slang)*, inebriated, out to it *(Austral. & N.Z. slang)*, three sheets to the wind *(slang)*, in your cups, half seas over *(Brit. informal)*, bevvied *(dialect)*, pie-eyed *(slang)*: *He laughed loudly. There was no doubt he was tight.* **OPPOSITE:** sober

tighten VERB **1 = close**, narrow, strengthen, squeeze, harden, constrict: *He answered by tightening his grip on her shoulder.* **OPPOSITE:** slacken **2 = stretch**, strain, tense, tauten, stiffen, rigidify: *He flung his whole weight back, tightening the rope.* **OPPOSITE:** slacken **3 = fasten**, secure, screw, fix: *I used my thumbnail to tighten the screw.* **OPPOSITE:** unfasten

tight-lipped ADJECTIVE **= secretive**, reticent, uncommunicative, reserved, quiet, silent, mute, taciturn, close-mouthed, unforthcoming, close-lipped

till[1] VERB **= cultivate**, dig, plough, work, turn over: *freshly tilled fields*

till[2] NOUN **= cash register**, cash box, cash drawer: *He checked the register. There was money in the till.*

tilt VERB **= slant**, tip, slope, list, lean, heel, incline, cant: *The boat instantly tilted, filled and sank.*
▷ NOUN **1 = slope**, angle, inclination, list, pitch, incline, slant, cant, camber, gradient: *the tilt of the earth's axis* **2 = joust**, fight, tournament, lists, clash, set-to *(informal)*, encounter, combat, duel, tourney: *The crowd cheered and the tilt began.*

timber NOUN **1 = beams**, boards, planks: *a bird nesting in the timbers of the roof* **2 = wood**, logs: *These forests have been exploited for timber since Saxon times.*

timbre NOUN **= tone**, sound, ring, resonance, colour, tonality, tone colour, quality of sound

time NOUN **1 = period**, while, term, season, space, stretch, spell, phase, interval, span, period of time, stint, duration, length of time, time frame, timeline: *For a long time I didn't tell anyone.* **2 = occasion**, point, moment, stage, instance, point in time, juncture: *It seemed like a good time to tell her.* **3 = age**, days, era, year, date, generation, duration, epoch, chronology, aeon: *The design has remained unchanged since the time of the pharaohs.* **4 = tempo**, beat, rhythm, measure, metre: *A reel is in four-four time.* **5 = lifetime**, day, life, season, duration, life span, allotted span: *I wouldn't change anything if I had my time again.* **6 = heyday**, prime, peak, hour, springtime, salad days, best years or days: *He was a very good jockey in his time.*
▷ VERB **1 = measure**, judge, clock, count: *He timed each performance with a stopwatch.* **2 = schedule**, set, plan, book, programme, set up, fix, arrange, line up, organize, timetable, slate *(U.S.)*, fix up, prearrange: *We had timed our visit for March 7.* **3 = regulate**, control, calculate: *an alarm timed to go off every hour on the hour*
at one time **= once**, previously, formerly, for a while, hitherto, once upon a time: *At one time, 400 people lived in the village.*
at times **= sometimes**, occasionally, from time to time, now and then, on occasion, once in a while, every now and then, every so often: *The debate was highly emotional at times.*
for the time being **= for now**, meanwhile, meantime, in the meantime, temporarily, for the moment, for the present, pro tem, for the nonce: *The situation is calm for the time being.*
from time to time **= occasionally**, sometimes, now and then, at times, on occasion, once in a while, every now and then, every so often: *Her daughters visited her from time to time.*
in good time **1 = on time**, early, ahead of schedule, ahead of time, with time to spare: *We always make sure we're home in good time for the programme.* **2 = promptly**, quickly, rapidly, swiftly, speedily, with dispatch: *Ninety-three per cent of the students received their loans in good time.*
in no time **= quickly**, rapidly, swiftly, in a moment, in a flash, speedily, in an instant, apace, before you know it, in a trice, in a jiffy *(informal)*, in two shakes of a lamb's tail *(informal)*, before you can say Jack Robinson: *At his age he'll heal in no time.*
in time **1 = on time**, on schedule, in good time, at the appointed time, early, with time to spare: *I arrived in time for my flight to London.* **2 = eventually**, one day, ultimately, sooner or later, someday, in the fullness of time, by and by: *He would sort out his own problems in time.*
on time **= punctual(ly)**, prompt(ly), on schedule, in good time, on the dot: *Don't worry, she'll be on time; The train arrived on time and she stepped out.*
time and again **= over and over again**, repeatedly, time after time: *Time and again political parties have failed to tackle this issue.*
▸ *related adjective:* temporal

QUOTATIONS

But meanwhile it is flying,
irretrievable time is flying
[Virgil *Georgics*]

Time is the best medicine
[Ovid *Remedia Amoris*]

Every instant of time is a pinprick
of eternity
[Marcus Aurelius *Meditations*]

Wait for that wisest of Counsellors,
Time
[Pericles]

To every thing there is a season, and
a time
to every purpose under heaven:
A time to be born, and a time to die
...
A time to love, and a time to hate;
A time of war, and a time of peace
[*Bible: Ecclesiastes*]

Come what may,
Time and the hour runs through
the roughest day
[William Shakespeare *Macbeth*]

t

Jane Austen's Use of Adjectives

From a linguistic point of view, the works of Jane Austen are extremely interesting. As she wrote around the beginning of the nineteenth century, many of the terms that she used have changed in meaning or become obsolete.

For example, the *saucy looks* given by Emma Woodhouse in *Emma* have none of today's suggestive overtones, and the word *safe* is used in *Northanger Abbey* in the phrase *with a safe conscience* meaning 'with a clear conscience'.

The adjective *handsome* is now commonly used of men, women, and buildings in the sense 'attractive' and of sums of money meaning 'large', but is also used by Jane Austen in *Emma* to describe an elegantly written letter:

> I suppose you have heard of the **handsome** letter Mr. Frank Churchill has written to Mrs. Weston?

Merry is now used of people in the senses 'happy' or 'tipsy', of sights or sounds in the sense 'cheerful' and in specific phrases such as *Merry Christmas* and to *make merry*. Jane Austen also used this word of a pastime in the sense 'pleasing':

> Harriet was very ready to speak of the share he had had in their moonlight walks and **merry** evening games.

In modern day usage, the adjective *nice* has become overused to the point that it is almost meaningless. It is used in the vague general sense 'agreeable'. However, this adjective originally had quite specific senses:

> Mrs. Norris accepted the compliment, and admired the **nice** discernment of character which could so well distinguish merit.

The above extract from *Mansfield Park* shows the adjective being used in the sense 'subtle'. Even by the beginning of the nineteenth century, though, this adjective had lost much of its power and distinct uses. In *Northanger Abbey*, Catherine describes her book as *nice* and is mocked by Henry:

> 'Very true,' said Henry 'and this is a very **nice** day, and we are taking a very **nice** walk, and you are two very **nice** young ladies. Oh! It is a very **nice** word indeed! It does for everything. Originally perhaps it was applied only to express neatness, propriety, delicacy, or refinement – people were nice in their dress, in their sentiments, or their choice. But now every commendation on every subject is comprised in that one word.'

The most common modern-day sense of *happy* is 'pleased' or 'joyful' and is used of people. However, in the following extract from *Pride and Prejudice*, the author also uses the adjective in the sense 'fortunate':

> 'For we must attribute this **happy** conclusion,' she added, 'in a great measure to his kindness.'

In modern usage it is common to talk of *fine clothes* ('smart clothes'), but in Jane Austen's day *fine* was also used of a person, meaning 'pretty'. In *Northanger Abbey*, her mother describes Isabella as the handsomest of her children, *a fine young woman*. In this novel she also uses the word in a predicative position meaning 'well-dressed'. We learn that Mrs Allen's passion is clothing and she has *a most harmless delight in being fine*.

Some words and expressions have become very rare or even obsolete. For example, in *Mansfield Park* Fanny says that Henry *was really not unagreeable*. The word *unagreeable* is now rarely used and the more common word is *disagreeable*.

Time, the subtle thief of youth
[John Milton *Sonnet 7*]

Remember that time is money
[Benjamin Franklin *Advice to a Young Tradesman*]

Men talk of killing time, while time quietly kills them
[Dion Boucicault *London Assurance*]

The innocent and the beautiful have no enemy but time
[W.B. Yeats *in memory of Eva Gore-Booth and Con Markiewicz*]

Time goes, you say? Ah, no!
Alas, Time stays, we go
[Henry Austin Dobson *The Paradox of Time*]

Time rushes by and yet time is frozen. Funny how we get so exact about time at the end of life and at its beginning
[Sister Helen Prejean]

PROVERBS
Time and tide wait for no man
Time flies (tempus fugit)
Time is a great healer
Time will tell

time-honoured ADJECTIVE = **long-established**, traditional, customary, old, established, fixed, usual, ancient, conventional, venerable, age-old

timeless ADJECTIVE = **eternal**, lasting, permanent, enduring, abiding, immortal, everlasting, ceaseless, immutable, indestructible, undying, ageless, imperishable, deathless, changeless: *His work has a timeless quality.* **OPPOSITE:** temporary

timely ADJECTIVE = **opportune**, appropriate, well-timed, prompt, suitable, convenient, at the right time, judicious, punctual, propitious, seasonable **OPPOSITE:** untimely

timetable NOUN **1** = **schedule**, programme, agenda, list, diary, calendar, order of the day: *The timetable was hopelessly optimistic.* **2** = **syllabus**, course, curriculum, programme, teaching programme: *Latin was not included on the timetable.*

timid ADJECTIVE = **nervous**, shy, retiring, modest, shrinking, fearful, cowardly, apprehensive, coy, diffident, bashful, mousy, timorous, pusillanimous, faint-hearted, irresolute **OPPOSITE:** bold

tincture NOUN = **tinge**, trace, hint, colour, touch, suggestion, shade, flavour, dash, stain, smack, aroma, tint, hue, soupçon *(French)*

tinge NOUN **1** = **tint**, colour, shade, cast, wash, stain, dye, tincture: *His skin had an unhealthy greyish tinge.* **2** = **trace**, bit, drop, touch, suggestion, dash, pinch, smack, sprinkling, smattering, soupçon *(French)*: *Could there have been a slight tinge of envy in her voice?*
▷ VERB = **tint**, colour, shade, stain, dye: *The living room was tinged yellow by the sunlight.*

tingle VERB = **prickle**, sting, itch, tickle, have goose pimples: *The backs of her thighs tingled.*
▷ NOUN = **prickling**, stinging, itch, itching, tickle, tickling, pins and needles *(informal)*: *I felt a sudden tingle in my fingers.*

tinker VERB = **meddle**, play, toy, monkey, potter, fiddle *(informal)*, dabble, mess about, muck about *(Brit. slang)*

tinsel ADJECTIVE = **showy**, flashy, gaudy, cheap, plastic *(slang)*, superficial, sham, tawdry, ostentatious, trashy, specious, gimcrack, meretricious, pinchbeck

tint NOUN **1** = **shade**, colour, tone, hue, cast: *Its leaves show a purple tint.* **2** = **dye**, wash, stain, rinse, tinge, tincture: *a tint on your hair.* **3** = **hint**, touch, trace, suggestion, shade, tinge: *His words had more than a tint of truth to them.*
▷ VERB = **dye**, colour, stain, rinse, tinge, tincture: *Eyebrows can be tinted with the same dye.*

tiny ADJECTIVE = **small**, little, minute, slight, mini, wee, miniature, trifling, insignificant, negligible, microscopic, diminutive, petite, puny, pint-sized *(informal)*, infinitesimal, teeny-weeny, Lilliputian, dwarfish, teensy-weensy, pygmy *or* pigmy **OPPOSITE:** huge

tip[1] NOUN **1** = **end**, point, head, extremity, sharp end, nib, prong: *She poked and shifted things with the tip of her walking stick.* **2** = **peak**, top, summit, pinnacle, crown, cap, zenith, apex, spire, acme, vertex: *After dusk, the tip of the cone will light up.*
▷ VERB = **cap**, top, crown, surmount, finish: *a missile tipped with three warheads*

tip[2] NOUN **1** = **gratuity**, gift, reward, present, sweetener *(informal)*, perquisite, baksheesh, pourboire *(French)*: *I gave the barber a tip.* **2** = **hint**, suggestion, piece of information, piece of advice, gen *(Brit. informal)*, pointer, piece of inside information, heads up *(U.S. & Canad.)*: *A good tip is to buy the most expensive lens you can afford.*
▷ VERB **1** = **reward**, remunerate, give a tip to, sweeten *(informal)*: *Do you think it's customary to tip the waiters?* **2** = **predict**, back, recommend, think of: *He was widely tipped for success.*

tip[3] VERB **1** = **pour**, drop, empty, dump, drain, spill, discharge, unload, jettison, offload, slop *(informal)*, slosh *(informal)*, decant: *She took the plate and tipped the contents into the bin.* **2** = **dump**, empty, ditch *(slang)*, unload, pour out: *the costs of tipping rubbish in landfills*
▷ NOUN = **dump**, midden, rubbish heap, refuse heap: *I took a load of rubbish and grass cuttings to the tip.*
tip off = **advise**, warn, caution, forewarn, give a clue to, give a hint to, tip someone the wink *(Brit. informal)*: *He tipped police off on his carphone.*

tip-off NOUN = **hint**, word, information, warning, suggestion, clue, pointer, inside information, word of advice, heads up *(U.S. & Canad.)*

tipple VERB = **drink**, imbibe, tope, indulge *(informal)*, swig, quaff, take a drink, bevvy *(dialect)*, bend the elbow *(informal)*: *You may be tempted to tipple unobserved.*
▷ NOUN = **alcohol**, drink, booze *(informal)*, poison *(informal)*, liquor, John Barleycorn: *My favourite tipple is a glass of port.*

tipsy ADJECTIVE = **tiddly** *(slang, chiefly Brit.)*, fuddled, slightly drunk, happy *(informal)*, merry *(Brit. informal)*, mellow, woozy *(slang, chiefly Brit.)*

tirade NOUN = **outburst**, diatribe, harangue, abuse, lecture, denunciation, invective, fulmination, philippic

tire VERB **1** = **exhaust**, drain, fatigue, weary, fag *(informal)*, whack *(Brit. informal)*, wear out, wear down, take it out of *(informal)*, knacker *(slang)*, enervate: *If driving tires you, take the train.* **OPPOSITE:** refresh **2** = **flag**, become tired, fail, droop: *He tired easily, and was unable to sleep well at night.*

tired ADJECTIVE **1** = **exhausted**, fatigued, weary, spent, done in *(informal)*, flagging, all in *(slang)*, drained, sleepy, fagged *(informal)*, whacked *(Brit. informal)*, worn out, drooping, knackered *(slang)*, drowsy, clapped out *(Brit., Austral. & N.Z. informal)*, enervated, ready to drop, dog-tired *(informal)*, zonked *(slang)*, dead beat *(informal)*, tuckered out *(Austral. & N.Z. informal)*, asleep *or* dead on your feet *(informal)*, leggy: *He is tired and he has to rest after his long trip.* **OPPOSITE:** energetic **2** = **bored**, fed up, weary, sick, annoyed, irritated, exasperated, irked, hoha *(N.Z.)*: *I was tired of being a bookkeeper.* **OPPOSITE:** enthusiastic about **3** = **hackneyed**, stale, well-worn, old, stock, familiar, conventional, corny *(slang)*, threadbare, trite, clichéd, outworn: *I didn't want to hear one of his tired excuses.* **OPPOSITE:** original

tireless ADJECTIVE = **energetic**, vigorous, industrious, determined, resolute, indefatigable, unflagging, untiring, unwearied **OPPOSITE:** exhausted

tiresome ADJECTIVE = **boring**, annoying, irritating, trying, wearing, dull, tedious, exasperating, monotonous, laborious, uninteresting, irksome, wearisome, vexatious **OPPOSITE:** interesting

tiring ADJECTIVE = **exhausting**, demanding, wearing, tough, exacting, fatiguing, wearying, strenuous, arduous, laborious, enervative

tissue NOUN **1** = **matter**, material, substance, stuff, structure: *As we age we lose muscle tissue.* **2** = **paper**, wipe, paper handkerchief, wrapping paper: *a box of tissues* **3** = **series**, pack, collection, mass, network, chain, combination, web, accumulation, fabrication, conglomeration, concatenation: *It was all a tissue of lies which ended in his resignation.*

titan NOUN **= giant**, superman, colossus, leviathan

titanic ADJECTIVE **= gigantic**, huge, giant, massive, towering, vast, enormous, mighty, immense, jumbo *(informal)*, monstrous, mammoth, colossal, mountainous, stellar *(informal)*, prodigious, stupendous, herculean, elephantine, humongous *or* humungous *(U.S. slang)*

titbit *or (esp. U.S.)* **tidbit** NOUN **= delicacy**, goody, dainty, morsel, treat, snack, choice item, juicy bit, bonne bouche *(French)*

tit for tat NOUN **= retaliation**, like for like, measure for measure, an eye for an eye, a tooth for a tooth, blow for blow, as good as you get: *a dangerous game of tit for tat*

tithe NOUN **= tax**, levy, duty, assessment, tribute, toll, tariff, tenth, impost

titillate VERB **= excite**, stimulate, arouse, interest, thrill, provoke, turn on *(slang)*, tease, tickle, tantalize

titillating ADJECTIVE **= exciting**, stimulating, interesting, thrilling, arousing, sensational, teasing, provocative, lurid, suggestive, lewd

title NOUN **1 = heading**, name, caption, label, legend, inscription: *The book was first published under the title 'A Place for Us'.* **2 = name**, designation, epithet, term, handle *(slang)*, nickname, denomination, pseudonym, appellation, sobriquet, nom de plume, moniker *or* monicker *(slang)*: *Her husband was honoured with the title 'Sir Denis'.* **3 = championship**, trophy, laurels, bays, crown, honour: *He has retained his title as world chess champion.* **4 = ownership**, right, claim, privilege, entitlement, tenure, prerogative, freehold: *He never had title to the property.*
▷ VERB **= name**, call, term, style, label, tag, designate: *a new book titled 'The Golden Thirteen'*

titter VERB **= snigger**, laugh, giggle, chuckle, chortle *(informal)*, tee-hee, te-hee

toad NOUN
▸ *related adjective:* batrachian ▸ *name of young:* tadpole

toast[1] VERB **1 = brown**, grill, crisp, roast: *Toast the bread lightly on both sides.* **2 = warm (up)**, heat (up), thaw, bring back to life: *a bar with an open fire for toasting feet after a day skiing*

toast[2] NOUN **1 = tribute**, drink, compliment, salute, health, pledge, salutation: *We drank a toast to Miss Jacobs.* **2 = favourite**, celebrity, darling, talk, pet, focus of attention, hero *or* heroine, blue-eyed boy *or* girl *(Brit. informal)*: *She was the toast of Paris.*
▷ VERB **= drink to**, honour, pledge to, salute, drink (to) the health of: *They toasted her with champagne.*

QUOTATIONS

If I am obliged to bring religion into after-dinner toasts (which indeed does not seem quite the thing)
I shall drink... to Conscience first, and to the Pope afterwards
[Cardinal Newman *Letter Addressed to the Duke of Norfolk*]

Here's tae us; wha's like us?
Gey few, and they're a' deid
[Scottish toast]

to-do NOUN **= fuss**, performance *(informal)*, disturbance, bother, stir, turmoil, unrest, flap *(informal)*, quarrel, upheaval, bustle, furore, uproar, agitation, commotion, rumpus, tumult, brouhaha, ruction *(informal)*, hue and cry, hoo-ha

together ADVERB **1 = collectively**, jointly, closely, as one, with each other, in conjunction, side by side, mutually, hand in hand, as a group, in partnership, in concert, in unison, shoulder to shoulder, cheek by jowl, in cooperation, in a body, hand in glove: *Together they swam to the ship.* **OPPOSITE:** separately **2 = at the same time**, simultaneously, in unison, as one, (all) at once, en masse, concurrently, contemporaneously, with one accord, at one fell swoop: *'Yes,' they said together.*
▷ ADJECTIVE **= self-possessed**, calm, composed, well-balanced, cool, stable, well-organized, well-adjusted, grounded: *She was very headstrong, and very together.*

toil NOUN **= hard work**, industry, labour, effort, pains, application, sweat, graft *(informal)*, slog, exertion, drudgery, travail, donkey-work, elbow grease *(informal)*, blood, sweat and tears *(informal)*: *It is only toil which gives meaning to things.*
OPPOSITE: idleness
▷ VERB **1 = labour**, work, struggle, strive, grind *(informal)*, sweat *(informal)*, slave, graft *(informal)*, go for it *(informal)*, slog, grub, bend over backwards *(informal)*, drudge, go for broke *(slang)*, push yourself, bust a gut *(informal)*, give it your best shot *(informal)*, break your neck *(informal)*, work like a dog, make an all-out effort *(informal)*, work like a Trojan, knock yourself out *(informal)*, do your damnedest *(informal)*, give it your all *(informal)*, work your fingers to the bone, rupture yourself *(informal)*: *Boys toiled in the hot sun to finish the wall.* **2 = struggle**, trek, slog, trudge, push yourself, fight your way, drag yourself, footslog: *He had his head down as he toiled up the hill.*

toilet NOUN **1 = lavatory**, bathroom, loo *(Brit. informal)*, bog *(slang)*, gents *or* ladies, can *(U.S. & Canad. slang)*, john *(slang, chiefly U.S. & Canad.)*, head(s) *(Nautical slang)*, throne *(informal)*, closet, privy, cloakroom *(Brit.)*, urinal, latrine, washroom, powder room, ablutions *(Military, informal)*, dunny *(Austral. & N.Z. old-fashioned, informal)*, water closet, khazi *(slang)*, pissoir *(French)*, little boy's room *or* little girl's room *(informal)*, (public) convenience, W.C., bogger *(Austral. slang)*, brasco *(Austral. slang)*: *She made him flush the pills down the toilet.* **2 = bathroom**, washroom, gents *or* ladies *(Brit. informal)*, privy, outhouse, latrine, powder room, water closet, pissoir *(French)*, ladies' room, little boy's *or* little girl's room, W.C.: *I ran to the toilet, vomiting.*

token NOUN **= symbol**, mark, sign, note, evidence, earnest, index, expression, demonstration, proof, indication, clue, representation, badge, manifestation: *He sent her a gift as a token of his appreciation.*
▷ ADJECTIVE **= nominal**, symbolic, minimal, hollow, superficial, perfunctory: *weak token gestures with no real consequences*

tolerable ADJECTIVE **1 = bearable**, acceptable, allowable, supportable, endurable, sufferable: *He described their living conditions as tolerable.*
OPPOSITE: intolerable **2 = fair**, O.K. *or* okay *(informal)*, middling, average, all right, ordinary, acceptable, reasonable, good enough, adequate, indifferent, not bad *(informal)*, mediocre, so-so *(informal)*, run-of-the-mill, passable, unexceptional, fairly good, fair to middling: *Is there anywhere tolerable to eat in town?*
OPPOSITE: dreadful

tolerance NOUN **1 = broad-mindedness**, charity, sympathy, patience, indulgence, forbearance, permissiveness, magnanimity, open-mindedness, sufferance, lenity: *his tolerance and understanding of diverse human nature* **OPPOSITE:** intolerance **2 = endurance**, resistance, stamina, fortitude, resilience, toughness, staying power, hardness, hardiness: *She has a high tolerance for pain.* **3 = resistance**, immunity, resilience, non-susceptibility: *Your body will build up a tolerance to most drugs.*

tolerant ADJECTIVE **= broad-minded**, understanding, sympathetic, open-minded, patient, fair, soft, catholic, charitable, indulgent, easy-going, long-suffering, lax, lenient, permissive, magnanimous, free and easy, forbearing, kind-hearted, unprejudiced, complaisant, latitudinarian, unbigoted, easy-oasy *(slang)* **OPPOSITE:** intolerant

tolerate VERB **1 = endure**, stand, suffer, bear, take, stomach, undergo, swallow, hack *(slang)*, abide, put up with *(informal)*, submit to, thole *(Scot.)*: *She can no longer tolerate the position that she's in.* **2 = allow**, accept, permit, sanction, take, receive, admit, brook, indulge, put up with *(informal)*, condone, countenance, turn a blind eye to, wink at: *I will not tolerate breaches of the code of conduct.* **OPPOSITE:** forbid

toleration NOUN **1 = acceptance**, endurance, indulgence, sanction, allowance, permissiveness, sufferance, condonation: *They urged toleration of mixed marriages.* **2 = religious freedom**, freedom of conscience, freedom of worship: *his views on religious toleration, education and politics*

toll[1] VERB **1 = ring**, sound, strike, chime, knell, clang, peal: *Church bells tolled and black flags fluttered.* **2 = announce**, call, signal, warn of: *Big Ben tolled the midnight hour.* ▷ NOUN **= ringing**, ring, tolling, chime, knell, clang, peal: *the insistent toll of the bell in the church tower*

toll[2] NOUN **1 = charge**, tax, fee, duty, rate, demand, payment, assessment, customs, tribute, levy, tariff, impost: *Opponents of motorway tolls say they would force cars onto smaller roads.* **2 = damage**, cost, loss, roll, penalty, sum, number, roster, inroad: *There are fears that the death toll may be higher.* **3 = adverse effects**, price, cost, suffering, damage, penalty, harm: *Winter takes its toll on your health.*

tomb NOUN **= grave**, vault, crypt, mausoleum, sarcophagus, catacomb, sepulchre, burial chamber

tombstone NOUN **= gravestone**, memorial, monument, marker, headstone

tome NOUN **= book**, work, title, volume, opus, publication

tomorrow NOUN

> **QUOTATIONS**
> Take therefore no thought for the morrow; for the morrow shall take thought for the things of itself [*Bible: St. Matthew*]
>
> After all, tomorrow is another day [Margaret Mitchell *Gone with the Wind*]

> **PROVERBS**
> *Tomorrow never comes*

tone NOUN **1 = pitch**, stress, volume, accent, force, strength, emphasis, inflection, intonation, timbre, modulation, tonality: *He spoke in a low tone to her.* **2 = volume**, timbre, tonality: *the clear tone of the bell* **3 = character**, style, approach, feel, air, effect, note, quality, spirit, attitude, aspect, frame, manner, mood, drift, grain, temper, vein, tenor: *The tone of the letter was very friendly.* **4 = colour**, cast, shade, tint, tinge, hue: *Each brick also varies slightly in tone.* ▷ VERB **= harmonize**, match, blend, suit, go well with: *Her sister toned with her in a turquoise print dress.*

tone something down 1 = moderate, temper, soften, restrain, subdue, play down, dampen, mitigate, modulate, soft-pedal *(informal)*: *He toned down his militant statement after the meeting.* **2 = reduce**, moderate, soften, lessen: *He was asked to tone down the spices and garlic in his recipes.*

tone something up = get into condition, trim, shape up, freshen, tune up, sharpen up, limber up, invigorate, get in shape: *Regular exercise will tone up your stomach muscles.*

tongue NOUN **1 = language**, speech, vernacular, talk, dialect, idiom, parlance, lingo *(informal)*, patois, argot: *They feel passionately about their native tongue.* **2 = utterance**, voice, speech, articulation, verbal expression: *her sharp wit and quick tongue* ▸ *related adjective:* lingual

tongue-tied ADJECTIVE **= speechless**, dumb, mute, inarticulate, dumbstruck, struck dumb, at a loss for words **OPPOSITE:** talkative

tonic NOUN **= stimulant**, boost, bracer *(informal)*, refresher, cordial, pick-me-up *(informal)*, fillip, shot in the arm *(informal)*, restorative, livener, analeptic, roborant

too ADVERB **1 = also**, as well, further, in addition, moreover, besides, likewise, to boot, into the bargain: *Depression may be expressed physically too.* **2 = excessively**, very, extremely, overly, unduly, unreasonably, inordinately, exorbitantly, immoderately, over-: *I'm afraid you're too late; she's gone.*

tool NOUN **1 = implement**, device, appliance, apparatus, machine, instrument, gadget, utensil, contraption, contrivance: *The best tool for the purpose is a pair of shears.* **2 = means**, agency, vehicle, medium, agent, intermediary, wherewithal: *The video has become an invaluable teaching tool.* **3 = puppet**, creature, pawn, dupe, stooge *(slang)*, jackal, minion, lackey, flunkey, hireling, cat's-paw: *He became the tool of the security services.* ▷ VERB **= make**, work, cut, shape, chase, decorate, ornament: *We have a beautifully tooled glass replica of it.*

top NOUN **1 = peak**, summit, head, crown, height, ridge, brow, crest, high point, pinnacle, culmination, meridian, zenith, apex, apogee, acme, vertex: *I came down alone from the top of the mountain.* **OPPOSITE:** bottom **2 = lid**, cover, cap, cork, plug, stopper, bung: *the plastic tops from aerosol containers* **3 = first place**, head, peak, lead, highest rank, high point: *The US will be at the top of the medals table.* ▷ ADJECTIVE **1 = highest**, upper, loftiest, furthest up, uppermost, topmost: *Our new flat was on the top floor.* **2 = leading**, best, first, highest, greatest, lead, head, prime, finest, crowning, crack *(informal)*, elite, superior, dominant, foremost, pre-eminent: *He was the top student in physics.* **OPPOSITE:** lowest **3 = chief**, most important, principal, most powerful, highest, lead, head, ruling, leading, main, commanding, prominent, notable, sovereign, eminent, high-ranking, illustrious: *I need to have the top people in this company work together.* **4 = prime**, best, select, first-class, capital, quality, choice, excellent, premier, superb, elite, superior, top-class, A1 *(informal)*, top-quality, first-rate, top-notch *(informal)*, grade A, top-grade: *a candlelit dinner at a top restaurant* ▷ VERB **1 = lead**, head, command, be at the top of, be first in: *What happens if the socialists top the poll?* **2 = cover**, coat, garnish, finish, crown, cap, overspread: *To serve, top the fish with cooked leeks.* **3 = surpass**, better, beat, improve on, cap, exceed, best, eclipse, go beyond, excel, transcend, outstrip, outdo, outshine: *How are you ever going to top that?* **OPPOSITE:** not be as good as **4 = reach the top of**, scale, mount, climb, conquer, crest, ascend, surmount: *As they topped the hill he saw the town in the distance.*

over the top = excessive, too much, going too far, inordinate, over the limit, a bit much *(informal)*, uncalled-for, immoderate: *The special effects are a bit over the top, but I enjoyed it.*

top something up 1 = fill (up), refresh, recharge, refill, replenish, freshen: *He topped her glass up, complaining that she was a slow drinker.* **2 = supplement**, boost, add to, enhance, augment: *The bank topped up their loan to £5000.*

topic NOUN **= subject**, point, question, issue, matter, theme, text, thesis, subject matter

topical ADJECTIVE **= current**, popular, contemporary, up-to-date, up-to-the-minute, newsworthy

topple VERB **1 = fall over**, fall, collapse, tumble, overturn, capsize, totter, tip over, keel over, overbalance, fall headlong: *He released his hold and toppled slowly backwards.* **2 = knock over**, upset, knock down, tip over: *Wind and rain toppled trees and electricity lines.* **3 = overthrow**, overturn, bring down, oust, unseat, bring low: *the revolution which toppled the regime*

topsy-turvy ADJECTIVE **= confused**, upside-down, disorderly, chaotic, messy, mixed-up, jumbled, inside-out, untidy, disorganized, disarranged **OPPOSITE:** orderly

torment VERB **1 = torture**, pain, distress, afflict, rack, harrow, crucify, agonize, excruciate: *At times, memories returned to torment her.* **OPPOSITE:** comfort **2 = tease**, annoy, worry, trouble, bother, provoke, devil *(informal)*, harry, plague, irritate, hound, harass, hassle *(informal)*, aggravate *(informal)*, persecute, pester, vex, bedevil, chivvy, give someone grief *(Brit. & S. African)*, lead someone a merry dance *(Brit. informal)*: *My older brother used to torment me by singing it to me.* ▷ NOUN **1 = suffering**, distress, misery, pain, hell, torture, agony, anguish: *He spent days in torment while they searched for her.* **OPPOSITE:** bliss **2 = trouble**, worry, bother, plague, irritation, hassle *(informal)*, nuisance, annoyance, bane, pain in the neck *(informal)*: *the torments of being a writer*

torn ADJECTIVE **1 = cut**, split, rent, ripped, ragged, slit, lacerated: *a torn photograph* **2 = undecided**, divided,

t

uncertain, split, unsure, wavering, vacillating, in two minds (*informal*), irresolute: *I know the administration was very torn on this subject.*

tornado NOUN = **whirlwind**, storm, hurricane, gale, cyclone, typhoon, tempest, squall, twister (*U.S. informal*), windstorm

torpor NOUN = **inactivity**, apathy, inertia, lethargy, passivity, laziness, numbness, sloth, stupor, drowsiness, dullness, sluggishness, indolence, languor, listlessness, somnolence, inertness, stagnancy, accidie (*Theology*), inanition, torpidity
OPPOSITE: vigour

torrent NOUN **1 = stream**, flow, rush, flood, tide, spate, cascade, gush, effusion, inundation: *A torrent of water rushed into the reservoir.* **2 = downpour**, flood, shower, deluge, rainstorm: *The rain came down in torrents.* **3 = outburst**, stream, barrage, hail, spate, outpouring, effusion: *He directed a torrent of abuse at me.*

torrid ADJECTIVE **1 = hot**, tropical, burning, dry, boiling, flaming, blistering, stifling, fiery, scorched, scorching, sizzling, arid, sultry, sweltering, parched, parching, broiling: *the torrid heat of a Spanish summer* **2 = passionate**, intense, sexy (*informal*), hot, flaming, erotic, ardent, steamy (*informal*), fervent: *He is locked in a torrid affair with a mystery older woman.*

tortuous ADJECTIVE **1 = winding**, twisting, meandering, bent, twisted, curved, crooked, indirect, convoluted, serpentine, zigzag, sinuous, circuitous, twisty, mazy: *a tortuous mountain route* **2 = complicated**, involved, misleading, tricky, indirect, ambiguous, roundabout, deceptive, devious, convoluted, mazy: *long and tortuous negotiations*
OPPOSITE: straightforward

> **USAGE**
> The adjective *tortuous* is sometimes confused with *torturous*. A *tortuous* road is one that winds or twists, while a *torturous* experience is one that involves pain, suffering, or discomfort.

torture VERB **1 = torment**, abuse, persecute, afflict, martyr, scourge, molest, crucify, mistreat, ill-treat, maltreat, put on the rack: *Police are convinced she was tortured and killed.*
OPPOSITE: comfort **2 = distress**, torment, worry, trouble, pain, rack, afflict, harrow, agonize, give someone grief (*Brit. & S. African*), inflict anguish on: *He would not torture her further by arguing.*
▷ NOUN **1 = ill-treatment**, abuse, torment, persecution, martyrdom, maltreatment, harsh treatment: *alleged cases of torture and murder by security forces* **2 = agony**, suffering, misery, anguish, hell, distress, torment, heartbreak: *Waiting for the result was torture.* **OPPOSITE:** bliss

toss VERB **1 = throw**, pitch, hurl, fling, project, launch, cast, shy, chuck (*informal*), flip, propel, sling, lob (*informal*): *He screwed the paper up and tossed it into the fire.* **2 = shake**, turn, mix, stir, tumble, agitate, jiggle: *Toss the apple slices in the mixture.* **3 = heave**, labour, rock, roll, pitch, lurch, jolt, wallow: *The small boat tossed about in the high seas like a cork.* **4 = thrash (about)**, twitch, wriggle, squirm, writhe: *I felt as though I'd been tossing and turning all night.*
▷ NOUN **= throw**, cast, pitch, shy, fling, lob (*informal*): *Decisions are almost made with the toss of a die.*

tot NOUN **1 = infant**, child, baby, toddler, mite, wean (*Scot.*), little one, sprog (*slang*), munchkin (*informal, chiefly U.S.*), rug rat (*slang*), littlie (*Austral. informal*), ankle-biter (*Austral. slang*), tacker (*Austral. slang*): *They may hold a clue to the missing tot.* **2 = measure**, shot (*informal*), finger, nip, slug, dram, snifter (*informal*), toothful: *a tot of dark rum*
tot something up = add up, calculate, sum (up), total, reckon, compute, tally, enumerate, count up: *Now tot up the points you've scored.*

total NOUN **= sum**, mass, entirety, grand total, whole, amount, aggregate, totality, full amount, sum total: *The companies have a total of 1,776 employees.* **OPPOSITE:** part
▷ ADJECTIVE **= complete**, absolute, utter, whole, perfect, entire, sheer, outright, all-out, thorough, unconditional, downright, undisputed, consummate, unqualified, out-and-out, undivided, overarching, unmitigated, thoroughgoing, arrant, deep-dyed (*usually derogatory*): *The car was in a total mess; I mean I'm not a total idiot.*
OPPOSITE: partial
▷ VERB **1 = amount to**, make, come to, reach, equal, run to, number, add up to, correspond to, work out as, mount up to, tot up to: *Their exports will total £85 million this year.* **2 = add up**, work out, sum up, compute, reckon, tot up: *They haven't totalled the exact figures.*
OPPOSITE: subtract

totalitarian ADJECTIVE **= dictatorial**, authoritarian, one-party, oppressive, undemocratic, monolithic, despotic, tyrannous **OPPOSITE:** democratic

totality NOUN **1 = entirety**, unity, fullness, wholeness, completeness, entireness: *He did not want to reform the system in its totality.* **2 = aggregate**, whole, entirety, all, total, sum, sum total: *We must take into consideration the totality of the evidence.*

totally ADVERB **= completely**, entirely, absolutely, quite, perfectly, fully, comprehensively, thoroughly, wholly, utterly, consummately, wholeheartedly, unconditionally, to the hilt, one hundred per cent, unmitigatedly **OPPOSITE:** partly

totter VERB **1 = stagger**, stumble, reel, sway, falter, lurch, wobble, walk unsteadily: *He tottered to the fridge to get another beer.* **2 = shake**, sway, rock, tremble, quake, shudder, lurch, waver, quiver, vibrate, teeter, judder: *The balconies begin to tremble and totter in the smoke and fumes.*

touch VERB **1 = feel**, handle, finger, stroke, brush, make contact with, graze, caress, fondle, lay a finger on, palpate: *Her tiny hand gently touched my face.* **2 = come into contact**, meet, contact, border, brush, come together, graze, adjoin, converge, be in contact, abut, impinge upon: *Their knees were touching.* **3 = tap**, hit, strike, push, pat: *As the aeroplane came down, the wing touched a pile of rubble.* **4 = affect**, mark, involve, strike, get to (*informal*), influence, inspire, impress, get through to, have an effect on, make an impression on: *a guilt that in some way touches everyone* **5 = consume**, take, drink, eat, partake of: *He doesn't drink much, and he never touches drugs.*
6 = move, upset, stir, disturb, melt, soften, tug at someone's heartstrings (*often facetious*), leave an impression on: *It has touched me deeply to see how these people live.* **7 = match**, rival, equal, compare with, parallel, come up to, come near, be on a par with, be a match for, hold a candle to (*informal*), be in the same league as: *No one can touch these girls for professionalism.* **8 = get involved in**, use, deal with, handle, have to do with, utilize, be a party to, concern yourself with: *These days no sports will touch tobacco advertising.*
9 = reach, hit (*informal*), come to, rise to, arrive at, attain, get up to: *The winds had touched storm-force the day before.*
▷ NOUN **1 = contact**, push, stroke, brush, press, tap, poke, nudge, prod, caress, fondling: *Even a light touch on the face can trigger this pain.* **2 = feeling**, feel, handling, physical contact, palpation, tactility: *Our sense of touch is programmed to diminish with age.* **3 = bit**, spot, trace, drop, taste, suggestion, hint, dash, suspicion, pinch, smack, small amount, tinge, whiff, jot, speck, smattering, intimation, tincture: *She thought she might have a touch of flu.* **4 = style**, approach, method, technique, way, manner, characteristic, trademark, handiwork: *The striker was unable to find his scoring touch.* **5 = awareness**, understanding, acquaintance, familiarity: *They've lost touch with what is happening in the country.*
6 = communication, contact, association, connection, correspondence: *In my job one tends to lose touch with friends.* **7 = skill**, ability, flair, art, facility, command, craft, mastery, knack, artistry, virtuosity, deftness, adroitness: *You don't want to lose your touch. You should get some practice.*
8 = influence, hand, effect, management, direction: *This place is crying out for a woman's touch.*
touch and go = risky, close, near,

dangerous, critical, tricky, sticky *(informal)*, hazardous, hairy *(slang)*, precarious, perilous, nerve-racking, parlous: *It was touch and go whether we'd go bankrupt.*
touch on *or* **upon something = refer to**, cover, raise, deal with, mention, bring in, speak of, hint at, allude to, broach, make allusions to: *The film touches on these issues, but only superficially.*
touch something off 1 = trigger (off), start, begin, cause, provoke, set off, initiate, arouse, give rise to, ignite, stir up, instigate, spark off, set in motion, foment: *The massacre touched off a new round of violence.* **2 = ignite**, light, fire, set off, detonate, put a match to: *set enormous fuel fires raging, or touch off explosions*
touch something up 1 = enhance, revamp, renovate, patch up, brush up, gloss over, polish up, retouch, titivate, give a face-lift to: *He got up regularly to touch up the painting.* **2 = improve**, perfect, round off, enhance, dress up, finish off, embellish, put the finishing touches to: *Use these tips to touch up your image.*
▸ *related adjectives:* haptic, tactile, tactual

touched ADJECTIVE **1 = moved**, affected, upset, impressed, stirred, disturbed, melted, softened, swayed: *I was touched to hear that he finds me engaging.* **2 = mad**, crazy, nuts *(slang)*, daft *(informal)*, batty *(slang)*, cuckoo *(informal)*, barmy *(slang)*, nutty *(slang)*, bonkers *(slang, chiefly Brit.)*, loopy *(informal)*, crackpot *(informal)*, out to lunch *(informal)*, gonzo *(slang)*, not all there, doolally *(slang)*, off your trolley *(slang)*, up the pole *(informal)*, soft in the head *(informal)*, not right in the head, off your rocker *(slang)*, nutty as a fruitcake *(slang)*, wacko *or* whacko *(informal)*, off the air *(Austral. slang)*: *They thought I was a bit touched.*

touching ADJECTIVE **= moving**, affecting, sad, stirring, tender, melting, pathetic, poignant, heartbreaking, emotive, pitiful, pitiable, piteous

touchstone NOUN **= standard**, measure, par, criterion, norm, gauge, yardstick

touchy ADJECTIVE **1 = oversensitive**, irritable, bad-tempered, cross, crabbed, grumpy, surly, petulant, irascible, tetchy, ratty *(Brit. & N.Z. informal)*, testy, thin-skinned, grouchy *(informal)*, querulous, peevish, quick-tempered, splenetic, easily offended, captious, pettish, toey *(N.Z. slang)*: *She is very touchy about her past.* **OPPOSITE:** thick-skinned **2 = delicate**, sensitive, tricky, risky, sticky *(informal)*, thorny, knotty, ticklish: *a touchy subject*

tough ADJECTIVE **1 = strong**, determined, aggressive, high-powered, feisty *(informal, chiefly U.S. & Canad.)*, hard-nosed *(informal)*, self-confident, unyielding, hard as nails, two-fisted, self-assertive, badass *(slang, chiefly U.S.)*: *She is tough and ambitious.* **OPPOSITE:** weak **2 = hardy**, strong, seasoned, fit, strapping, hardened, vigorous, sturdy, stout, stalwart, resilient, brawny, hard as nails: *He's small, but he's tough, and I expect him to do well in the match.* **3 = violent**, rough, vicious, ruthless, pugnacious, hard-bitten, ruffianly, two-fisted: *He shot three people, earning his reputation as a tough guy.* **4 = strict**, severe, stern, hard, firm, exacting, adamant, resolute, draconian, intractable, inflexible, merciless, unforgiving, unyielding, unbending: *He announced tough measures to limit the money supply.* **OPPOSITE:** lenient **5 = hard**, difficult, exhausting, troublesome, uphill, strenuous, arduous, thorny, laborious, irksome: *Whoever wins the election is going to have a tough job.* **6 = resilient**, hard, resistant, durable, strong, firm, solid, stiff, rigid, rugged, sturdy, inflexible, cohesive, tenacious, leathery, hard-wearing, robust: *tough leather boots and trousers* **OPPOSITE:** fragile
▹ NOUN **= ruffian**, heavy *(slang)*, rough *(informal)*, bully, thug, hooligan, brute, rowdy, bravo, bully boy, bruiser *(informal)*, roughneck *(slang)*, tsotsi *(S. African)*: *Three burly toughs elbowed their way to the front.*

tour NOUN **1 = circuit**, course, round: *the first official cricket tour of South Africa for 22 years* **2 = journey**, expedition, excursion, trip, progress, outing, jaunt, junket, peregrination: *week five of my tour of European cities*
▹ VERB **1 = travel round**, holiday in, travel through, journey round, trek round, go on a trip through: *A few years ago they toured the country in a roadshow.* **2 = visit**, explore, go round, inspect, walk round, drive round, sightsee: *You can tour the site in modern coaches fitted with videos.*

tourist NOUN **= traveller**, journeyer, voyager, tripper, globetrotter, holiday-maker, sightseer, excursionist

> **QUOTATIONS**
> You perceive I generalize with intrepidity from single instances. It is the tourist's custom
> [Mark Twain]

tournament NOUN **1 = competition**, meeting, match, event, series, contest: *Here is a player capable of winning a world tournament.* **2 = joust**, the lists, tourney: *a medieval tournament with displays of archery, armour and combat*

tousled ADJECTIVE **= dishevelled**, disordered, tangled, ruffled, messed up, rumpled, disarranged, disarrayed

tout VERB **1 = recommend**, promote, endorse, support, tip, urge, approve, praise, commend, speak well of: *the advertising practice of using performers to tout products* **2 = solicit**, canvass, drum up, bark *(U.S. informal)*, spiel: *He visited several foreign countries to tout for business.*
▹ NOUN **= seller**, solicitor, barker, canvasser, spieler: *a ticket tout*

tow VERB **= drag**, draw, pull, trail, haul, tug, yank, hale, trawl, lug

towards PREPOSITION **1 = in the direction of**, to, for, on the way to, on the road to, en route for: *She walked down the corridor towards the foyer.* **2 = regarding**, about, concerning, respecting, in relation to, with regard to, with respect to, apropos: *You must develop your own attitude towards religion.* **3 = just before**, nearing, close to, coming up to, almost at, getting on for, shortly before: *There's a forecast of cooler weather towards the end of the week.*

tower NOUN **1 = column**, pillar, turret, belfry, steeple, obelisk: *an eleventh-century house with 120-foot high towers* **2 = stronghold**, castle, fort, refuge, keep, fortress, citadel, fortification: *troops occupied the first two floors of the tower*
▹ VERB *(often with* **over***)* **= rise**, dominate, loom, top, mount, rear, soar, overlook, surpass, transcend, ascend, be head and shoulders above, overtop: *He stood up and towered over her.*

towering ADJECTIVE **1 = tall**, high, great, soaring, elevated, gigantic, lofty, colossal: *towering cliffs of black granite* **2 = impressive**, imposing, supreme, striking, extraordinary, outstanding, magnificent, superior, paramount, surpassing, sublime, stellar *(informal)*, prodigious, transcendent: *a towering figure in British politics* **3 = intense**, violent, extreme, excessive, burning, passionate, mighty, fiery, vehement, inordinate, intemperate, immoderate: *I saw her in a towering rage only once.*

toxic ADJECTIVE **= poisonous**, deadly, lethal, harmful, pernicious, noxious, septic, pestilential, baneful *(archaic)* **OPPOSITE:** harmless

toy NOUN **= plaything**, game, doll: *He was really too old for children's toys.*
toy with something = play with, consider, trifle with, flirt with, dally with, entertain the possibility of, amuse yourself with, think idly of: *He toyed with the idea of going to China.*

trace NOUN **1 = bit**, drop, touch, shadow, suggestion, hint, dash, suspicion, tinge, trifle, whiff, jot, tincture, iota: *Wash them in cold water to remove all traces of sand.* **2 = remnant**, remains, sign, record, mark, evidence, indication, token, relic, vestige: *The church has traces of fifteenth-century frescoes.* **3 = track**, trail, footstep, path, slot, footprint, spoor, footmark: *He disappeared mysteriously without a trace.*
▹ VERB **1 = search for**, follow, seek out, track, determine, pursue, unearth, ascertain, hunt down: *I first went there to trace my roots.* **2 = find**, track (down), discover, trail, detect, unearth, hunt down, ferret out, locate: *Police are anxious to trace a man seen leaving the*

t

Jane Austen's Use of Verbs

It should come as no surprise to those moderately well acquainted with the world of Jane Austen's novels that the verb *marry* occurs in her novels over 60% more often than does the verb *love*. A dreamy romantic she was not, and she had a proper regard for the life-defining drama of the marriage race – what might happen afterwards was, it seems, of much less concern.

In a similar way, free-flowing emotion is not the norm in her writing, and it is revealing that the verb *cry* is almost always used in the sense 'exclaim', while *weep* seldom occurs, and even when it does may be the product of something other than love-sickness or sorrow:

> Kitty was the only one who shed tears; but she did **weep** from vexation and envy.

There are certainly many examples of *feel*, but this verb may have as its object intellectual matters ('doubt', 'conviction', or 'scruple', for example) as well as emotions such as 'alarm', 'pang', or 'dislike'.

We might assume that a verb like *entertain* would be used chiefly to refer to the parties, balls, and other social events around which the social lives of her characters revolve. In fact, the objects of this verb are almost invariably mental, such as a 'suspicion', 'design' (in the sense 'plan'), 'partiality', or, most often of all, 'hope' (of what need hardly be spelled out):

> Let no one presume to give the feelings of a young woman on receiving the assurance of that affection of which she has scarcely allowed herself to **entertain** a hope.

An investigation of this kind into the use of verbs in the novels confirms what most attentive readers will have long intuited. The real arena of action is as much, if not more, the interior life of the characters as their relatively narrow social circles. Verbs suggesting dramatic action such as *kill* or *rob* occur rarely (the former usually referring to the fate of poultry rather than humans). *Grieve* occurs rather more frequently, but it is used not for death, but the slights and traumas of social intercourse, as when a character says of prospective in-laws that she would be 'exceedingly grieved at their disapprobation'. In this sense *grieve* is matched by the equally frequent *mortify*, as we follow the author's careful depiction of the psychological mechanisms by which the iron laws of social propriety rule the world of the novels.

Her quaintly archaic spellings *shew* for 'show', and *chuse* for 'choose' are often modernized by contemporary editors, but there are less superficial verbal differences which remind us that she was writing some 200 years ago. For example, though her characters may *suffer*, as we do, from pain, depression or the heat, this verb is also used in the sense 'allow or permit':

> ... he **suffered** the girls at last to seize the advantage of an outer door.

... that is to say, he let them escape from him into the garden! Another now archaic usage is the employment of *occasion* as a verb, in the sense 'cause', as when Elizabeth Bennet tells Mr Darcy she is 'sorry to have occasioned pain to anyone.'

It is only in her first novel, *Sense and Sensibility* (1811), that we find the, to us, jarring use of *was* in the second person:

> I felt sure that you was angry with me.

This had been on its way to becoming standard usage in the second half of the 18th century, but a successful rearguard action by prescriptive grammarians such as Lowth saw it consigned to non-standard usage, where it remains today. As it is mainly the relatively poorly educated Lucy Steele who uses the form, this presumably indicates the author's feeling for it as a questionable usage.

house. **3 = outline**, chart, sketch, draw, map out, depict, mark out, delineate: *I traced the course of the river on the map.* **4 = copy**, map, draft, outline, sketch, reproduce, draw over: *She learnt to draw by tracing pictures from story books.*

track NOUN **1 = path**, way, road, route, trail, pathway, footpath: *We set off once more, over a rough mountain track.* **2 = course**, line, path, orbit, trajectory, flight path: *following the track of a hurricane* **3 = line**, rail, tramline: *A woman fell onto the railway track.*
▷ VERB **= follow**, pursue, chase, trace, tail *(informal)*, dog, shadow, trail, stalk, hunt down, follow the trail of: *He thought he had better track this creature and kill it.*
keep track of something *or* **someone = keep up with**, follow, monitor, watch, keep an eye on, keep in touch with, keep up to date with: *It's hard to keep track of time here.*
lose track of something *or* **someone = lose**, lose sight of, misplace: *It's so easy to lose track of who's playing who and when.*
track something *or* **someone down = find**, catch, capture, apprehend, discover, expose, trace, unearth, dig up, hunt down, sniff out, bring to light, ferret out, run to earth *or* ground: *They are doing all they can to track down terrorists.*

tracks PLURAL NOUN **= trail**, marks, impressions, traces, imprints, prints: *He suddenly noticed tyre tracks on the bank ahead; The killer returned to the scene to cover his tracks.*

tract[1] NOUN **= area**, lot, region, estate, district, stretch, quarter, territory, extent, zone, plot, expanse: *A vast tract of land is ready for development.*

tract[2] NOUN **= treatise**, essay, leaflet, brochure, booklet, pamphlet, dissertation, monograph, homily, disquisition, tractate: *She produced a feminist tract, 'Comments on Birth Control'.*

t

traction NOUN **= grip**, resistance, friction, adhesion, purchase

trade NOUN **1 = commerce**, business, transactions, buying and selling, dealing, exchange, traffic, truck, barter: *The ministry has control over every aspect of foreign trade.* **2 = job**, employment, calling, business, line, skill, craft, profession, occupation, pursuit, line of work, métier, avocation: *He was a jeweller by trade.* **3 = exchange**, deal, swap, interchange: *It wouldn't exactly have been a fair trade.*
▷ VERB **1 = deal**, do business, buy and sell, exchange, traffic, truck, bargain, peddle, barter, transact, cut a deal, have dealings: *They had years of experience trading with the west.* **2 = exchange**, switch, swap, barter: *They traded land for goods and money.* **3 = operate**, run, deal, do business: *The company is thought to be trading at a loss.*
▸ *related adjective:* mercantile

trader NOUN **= dealer**, marketer, buyer, broker, supplier, merchant, seller, purveyor, merchandiser

tradesman NOUN **= craftsman**, workman, artisan, journeyman, skilled worker

tradition NOUN **1 = customs**, institution, ritual, folklore, lore, praxis, tikanga *(N.Z.)*: *a country steeped in tradition* **2 = established practice**, custom, convention, habit, ritual, unwritten law: *She has carried on the family tradition of giving away plants.*

traditional ADJECTIVE **1 = old-fashioned**, old, established, conventional, fixed, usual, transmitted, accustomed, customary, ancestral, long-established, unwritten, time-honoured: *Traditional teaching methods can put students off learning.* **OPPOSITE:** revolutionary **2 = folk**, old, historical: *traditional Indian music*

traffic NOUN **1 = transport**, movement, vehicles, transportation, freight, coming and going: *There was heavy traffic on the roads.* **2 = trade**, dealing, commerce, buying and selling, business, exchange, truck, dealings, peddling, barter, doings: *traffic in illicit drugs*
▷ VERB *(often with* **in***)* **= trade**, market, deal, exchange, truck, bargain, do business, buy and sell, peddle, barter, cut a deal, have dealings, have transactions: *Anyone who trafficked in illegal drugs was brought to justice.*

tragedy NOUN **= disaster**, catastrophe, misfortune, adversity, calamity, affliction, whammy *(informal, chiefly U.S.)*, bummer *(slang)*, grievous blow **OPPOSITE:** fortune

tragic *or* **tragical** ADJECTIVE **1 = distressing**, shocking, sad, awful, appalling, fatal, deadly, unfortunate, disastrous, dreadful, dire, catastrophic, grievous, woeful, lamentable, ruinous, calamitous, wretched, ill-starred, ill-fated: *the tragic loss of so many lives* **OPPOSITE:** fortunate **2 = sad**, miserable, dismal, pathetic, heartbreaking, anguished, mournful, heart-rending, sorrowful, doleful, pitiable: *She is a tragic figure.* **OPPOSITE:** happy

trail NOUN **1 = path**, track, route, way, course, road, pathway, footpath, beaten track, single track: *He was following a broad trail through the trees.* **2 = tracks**, path, mark, marks, wake, trace, scent, footsteps, footprints, spoor: *They would take no action except that of following her trail.* **3 = wake**, stream, tail, slipstream: *the high vapour trail of an aircraft*
▷ VERB **1 = follow**, track, chase, pursue, dog, hunt, shadow, trace, tail *(informal)*, hound, stalk, keep an eye on, keep tabs on *(informal)*, run to ground: *Two detectives were trailing him.* **2 = drag**, draw, pull, sweep, stream, haul, tow, dangle, droop: *She came down the stairs, trailing the coat behind her.* **3 = lag**, follow, drift, wander, linger, trudge, fall behind, plod, meander, amble, loiter, straggle, traipse *(informal)*, dawdle, hang back, tag along *(informal)*, bring up the rear, drag yourself: *I spent a long afternoon trailing behind him.*
trail away *or* **off = fade away** *or* **out**, sink, weaken, diminish, decrease, dwindle, shrink, lessen, subside, fall away, peter out, die away, tail off, taper off, grow weak, grow faint: *'But he of all men...' her voice trailed away.*

train VERB **1 = instruct**, school, prepare, improve, coach, teach, guide, discipline, rear, educate, drill, tutor, rehearse: *We train them in bricklaying and other building techniques.* **2 = exercise**, prepare, work out, practise, do exercise, get into shape: *They have spent a year training for the race.* **3 = aim**, point, level, position, direct, focus, sight, line up, turn on, fix on, zero in, bring to bear: *She trained her binoculars on the horizon.*
▷ NOUN **1 = convoy**, file, rank, string, column, queue, succession, caravan, procession, progression, cavalcade: *a long train of oil tankers* **2 = sequence**, series, chain, string, set, course, order, cycle, trail, succession, progression, concatenation: *a train of events which would culminate in tragedy* **3 = tail**, trail, appendage: *a velvet dress, bias cut with a train* **4 = retinue**, following, entourage, court, staff, household, suite, cortège: *Toby arrived with his train of medical students*

trainer NOUN **= coach**, manager, guide, adviser, tutor, instructor, counsellor, guru, handler

training NOUN **= instruction**, practice, schooling, grounding, education, preparation, exercise, working out, body building, tutelage: *He had no formal training as a decorator; He will soon be back in training for next year.*

traipse *or* **trapse** *(informal)* VERB **= trudge**, trail, tramp, slouch, drag yourself, footslog: *He traipsed from one doctor to another.*
▷ NOUN **= trudge**, trek, tramp, slog, long walk: *It's rather a long traipse from here. Let's take a bus.*

trait NOUN **= characteristic**, feature, quality, attribute, quirk, peculiarity, mannerism, idiosyncrasy, lineament

traitor NOUN **= betrayer**, deserter, turncoat, deceiver, informer, renegade, defector, Judas, double-crosser *(informal)*, quisling, apostate, miscreant, fifth columnist, snake in the grass *(informal)*, back-stabber, fizgig *(Austral. slang)* **OPPOSITE:** loyalist

trajectory NOUN **= path**, line, course, track, flight, route, flight path

tramp VERB **1 = trudge**, march, stamp, stump, toil, plod, traipse *(informal)*, walk heavily: *They put on their coats and tramped through the fallen snow.* **2 = hike**, walk, trek, roam, march, range,

ramble, slog, rove, yomp, footslog: *He spent a month tramping in the hills around Balmoral.*
▷ NOUN **1 = vagrant**, bum (*informal*), derelict, drifter, down-and-out, hobo (*chiefly U.S.*), vagabond, bag lady (*chiefly U.S.*), dosser (*Brit. slang*), derro (*Austral. slang*): *an old tramp who slept rough in our neighbourhood* **2 = tread**, stamp, footstep, footfall: *the slow, heavy tramp of feet on the staircase* **3 = hike**, march, trek, ramble, slog: *He had just come from a day-long tramp on some wild moor.*

trample VERB **= stamp**, crush, squash, tread, flatten, run over, walk over

trance NOUN **= daze**, dream, spell, ecstasy, muse, abstraction, rapture, reverie, stupor, unconsciousness, hypnotic state

tranquil ADJECTIVE **1 = peaceful**, quiet, calm, serene, still, cool, pacific, composed, at peace, sedate, placid, undisturbed, restful, untroubled, unperturbed, unruffled, unexcited, chilled (*informal*): *The place was tranquil and appealing.* **2 = calm**, quiet, peaceful, serene, still, cool, pacific, composed, sedate, placid, undisturbed, restful, untroubled, unperturbed, unruffled, unexcited, chilled (*informal*): *She settled into a life of tranquil celibacy.*
OPPOSITE: troubled

tranquillity or (*sometimes U.S.*) **tranquility** NOUN **1 = peace**, calm, quiet, hush, composure, serenity, stillness, coolness, repose, rest, calmness, equanimity, quietness, peacefulness, quietude, placidity, restfulness, sedateness: *The hotel is a haven of peace and tranquillity.* **2 = calm**, peace, composure, serenity, stillness, coolness, repose, calmness, equanimity, quietness, peacefulness, quietude, placidity, imperturbability, restfulness, sedateness: *He has a tranquillity and maturity that I desperately need.* **OPPOSITE:** agitation

tranquillizer, tranquilliser or (*U.S.*) **tranquilizer** NOUN **= sedative**, opiate, barbiturate, downer (*slang*), red (*slang*), bromide

transact VERB **= carry out**, handle, conduct, do, manage, perform, settle, conclude, negotiate, carry on, accomplish, execute, take care of, discharge, see to, prosecute, enact

transaction NOUN **1 = deal**, matter, affair, negotiation, business, action, event, proceeding, enterprise, bargain, coup, undertaking, deed, occurrence: *plans to disclose a business transaction with British Telecommunications* **2** (*plural*) **= records**, minutes, affairs, proceedings, goings-on (*informal*), annals, doings: *the transactions of the Metallurgical Society of Great Britain*

transcend VERB **= surpass**, exceed, go beyond, rise above, leave behind, eclipse, excel, outstrip, outdo, outshine, overstep, go above, leave in the shade (*informal*), outrival, outvie

transcendence or **transcendency** NOUN **= greatness**, excellence, superiority, supremacy, ascendancy, pre-eminence, sublimity, paramountcy, incomparability, matchlessness

transcendent ADJECTIVE **= unparalleled**, unique, extraordinary, superior, exceeding, sublime, consummate, unrivalled, second to none, pre-eminent, transcendental, incomparable, peerless, unequalled, matchless

transcribe VERB **1 = write out**, reproduce, take down, copy out, note, transfer, set out, rewrite: *Every telephone call will be recorded and transcribed.* **2 = translate**, interpret, render, transliterate: *He decided to transcribe the work for piano.*

transcript NOUN **= copy**, record, note, summary, notes, version, carbon, log, translation, manuscript, reproduction, duplicate, transcription, carbon copy, transliteration, written version

transfer VERB **= move**, carry, remove, transport, shift, transplant, displace, relocate, transpose, change: *The person can be transferred from wheelchair to seat with relative ease.*
▷ NOUN **= transference**, move, removal, handover, change, shift, transmission, translation, displacement, relocation, transposition: *Arrange for the transfer of medical records to your new doctor.*

transfix VERB **= stun**, hold, fascinate, paralyse, petrify, mesmerize, hypnotize, stop dead, root to the spot, engross, rivet the attention of, spellbind, halt or stop in your tracks
OPPOSITE: bore

transform VERB **1 = change**, convert, alter, translate, reconstruct, metamorphose, transmute, renew, transmogrify (*humorous*): *the speed at which your body transforms food into energy* **2 = make over**, overhaul, revamp, remake, renovate, remodel, revolutionize, redo, transfigure, restyle: *A cheap table can be transformed by an attractive cover.*

transformation NOUN **1 = change**, conversion, alteration, metamorphosis, transmutation, renewal, transmogrification (*humorous*): *the transformation of an attic room into a study* **2 = revolution**, radical change, sea change, revolutionary change, transfiguration: *He has undergone a personal transformation.*

transgress VERB **1 = misbehave**, sin, offend, break the law, err, lapse, fall from grace, go astray, be out of order, do or go wrong: *If a politician transgresses, it is his own fault.* **2 = go beyond**, exceed, infringe, overstep, break, defy, violate, trespass, contravene, disobey, encroach upon: *He had transgressed the boundaries of good taste.*

transgression NOUN **= crime**, wrong, fault, error, offence, breach, sin, lapse, violation, wrongdoing, infringement, trespass, misdemeanour, misdeed, encroachment, misbehaviour, contravention, iniquity, peccadillo, infraction

transient ADJECTIVE **= brief**, passing, short-term, temporary, short, flying, fleeting, short-lived, fugitive, momentary, ephemeral, transitory, evanescent, impermanent, here today and gone tomorrow, fugacious
OPPOSITE: lasting

transit NOUN **= movement**, transfer, transport, passage, travel, crossing, motion, transportation, carriage, shipment, traverse, conveyance, portage: *They halted transit of EU livestock.*
▷ VERB **= pass**, travel, cross, journey, traverse, move: *They have been allowed back into Kuwait by transitting through Baghdad.*
in transit = en route, on the way, on the road, on the move, in motion, on the go (*informal*), on the journey, while travelling, during transport, during passage: *We cannot be held responsible for goods lost in transit.*

transition NOUN **= change**, passing, development, shift, passage, conversion, evolution, transit, upheaval, alteration, progression, flux, metamorphosis, changeover, transmutation, metastasis

transitional ADJECTIVE **1 = changing**, passing, fluid, intermediate, unsettled, developmental, transitionary: *a transitional period following a decade of civil war*
2 = temporary, working, acting, short-term, interim, fill-in, caretaker, provisional, makeshift, make-do, stopgap, pro tem: *a meeting to set up a transitional government*

transitory ADJECTIVE **= short-lived**, short, passing, brief, short-term, temporary, fleeting, transient, flying, momentary, ephemeral, evanescent, impermanent, here today and gone tomorrow, fugacious
OPPOSITE: lasting

translate VERB **1 = render**, put, change, convert, interpret, decode, transcribe, construe, paraphrase, decipher, transliterate: *Only a small number of his books have been translated into English.* **2 = put in plain English**, explain, make clear, clarify, spell out, simplify, gloss, unravel, decode, paraphrase, decipher, elucidate, rephrase, reword, state in layman's language: *Translating IT jargon is the key to the IT director's role.* **3 = convert**, change, turn, transform, alter, render, metamorphose, transmute, transfigure: *Your decision must be translated into specific actions.*
4 = transfer, move, send, relocate, carry, remove, transport, shift, convey, transplant, transpose:

t

The local-government minister was translated to Wales.

translation NOUN **1 = interpretation**, version, rendering, gloss, rendition, decoding, transcription, paraphrase, transliteration: *his excellent English translation of 'Faust'* **2 = conversion**, change, rendering, transformation, alteration, metamorphosis, transfiguration, transmutation: *the translation of these goals into classroom activities*

translator NOUN **= interpreter**, transcriber, paraphraser, decipherer, linguist, metaphrast, paraphrast, transliterator

translucent ADJECTIVE **= semitransparent**, clear, limpid, lucent, diaphanous, pellucid

transmission NOUN **1 = transfer**, spread, spreading, communication, passing on, circulation, dispatch, relaying, mediation, imparting, diffusion, transference, dissemination, conveyance, channelling: *the transmission of knowledge and skills* **2 = broadcasting**, showing, putting out, relaying, sending: *The transmission of the programme was brought forward.* **3 = programme**, broadcast, show, production, telecast, podcast: *A webcast is a transmission using the internet.*

transmit VERB **1 = broadcast**, put on the air, televise, relay, send, air, radio, send out, disseminate, beam out, podcast: *letters begging them to transmit the programme daily* **2 = pass on**, carry, spread, communicate, take, send, forward, bear, transfer, transport, hand on, convey, dispatch, hand down, diffuse, remit, impart, disseminate: *mosquitoes that transmit disease to humans*

transmute VERB **= transform**, change, convert, alter, metamorphose, transfigure, alchemize

transparency NOUN **1 = photograph**, slide, exposure, photo, picture, image, print, plate, still: *The first colour photo was a transparency of a tartan ribbon.* **2 = clarity**, translucency, translucence, clearness, limpidity, transparence, diaphaneity, filminess, diaphanousness, gauziness, limpidness, pellucidity, pellucidness, sheerness: *It is a condition that affects the transparency of the lenses.* **OPPOSITE:** opacity **3 = frankness**, openness, candour, directness, forthrightness, straightforwardness: *openness and transparency in the government's decision-making* **OPPOSITE:** ambiguity

transparent ADJECTIVE **1 = clear**, sheer, see-through, lucid, translucent, crystal clear, crystalline, limpid, lucent, diaphanous, gauzy, filmy, pellucid: *a sheet of transparent coloured plastic* **OPPOSITE:** opaque **2 = frank**, open, direct, straight, straightforward, candid, forthright, unequivocal, unambiguous, plain-spoken: *striving to establish a transparent parliamentary democracy* **OPPOSITE:** unclear **3 = obvious**, plain, apparent, visible, bold, patent, evident, distinct, explicit, easy, understandable, manifest, recognizable, unambiguous, undisguised, as plain as the nose on your face (*informal*), perspicuous: *The meaning of their actions is transparent.* **OPPOSITE:** uncertain

transpire VERB **1 = become known**, emerge, come out, be discovered, come to light, be disclosed, be made public: *It transpired that he had left his driving licence at home.* **2 = happen**, occur, take place, arise, turn up, come about, come to pass (*archaic*): *Nothing is known about what transpired at the meeting.*

> **USAGE**
> It is sometimes maintained that *transpire* should not be used to mean 'happen' or 'occur', as in *the event transpired late in the evening*, and that the word is properly used to mean 'become known', as in *it transpired later that the thief had been caught*. The word is, however, widely used in the first sense, especially in spoken English.

transplant VERB **1 = implant**, transfer, graft: *The operation to transplant a kidney is now fairly routine.* **2 = transfer**, take, bring, carry, remove, transport, shift, convey, fetch, displace, relocate, uproot: *Marriage had transplanted her from London to Manchester.*

transport VERB **1 = convey**, take, run, move, bring, send, carry, bear, remove, ship, transfer, deliver, conduct, shift, ferry, haul, fetch: *There's no petrol so it's difficult to transport goods.* **2 = enrapture**, move, delight, entrance, enchant, carry away, captivate, electrify, ravish, spellbind: *I have never seen any man so completely transported by excitement.* **3 = exile**, banish, deport, sentence to transportation: *He was transported to Italy and interned.*
▷ NOUN **1 = vehicle**, wheels (*informal*), transportation, conveyance: *Have you got your own transport?* **2 = transference**, carrying, shipping, delivery, distribution, removal, transportation, carriage, shipment, freight, haulage, conveyance, freightage: *Safety rules had been breached during transport of radioactive fuel.* **3** (*often plural*) **= ecstasy**, delight, heaven, happiness, bliss, euphoria, rapture, enchantment, cloud nine (*informal*), seventh heaven, ravishment: *transports of joy* **OPPOSITE:** despondency

transpose VERB **1 = transplant**, move, transfer, shift, displace, relocate, reposition: *Genetic engineers transpose bits of material from one organism to another.* **2 = interchange**, switch, swap, reorder, change, move, exchange, substitute, alter, rearrange: *Many people inadvertently transpose the digits of the code.*

transverse ADJECTIVE **= crossways**, diagonal, oblique, crosswise, athwart

trap NOUN **1 = snare**, net, booby trap, gin, toils (*old-fashioned*), pitfall, noose, springe: *He came across a bird caught in a trap.* **2 = ambush**, set-up (*informal*), device, lure, bait, honey trap, ambuscade (*old-fashioned*): *He failed to keep the appointment after sensing a police trap.* **3 = trick**, set-up (*informal*), deception, ploy, ruse, artifice, trickery, subterfuge, stratagem, wile, device: *He was trying to decide whether the question was a trap.*
▷ VERB **1 = catch**, snare, ensnare, entrap, take, corner, bag, lay hold of, enmesh, lay a trap for, run to earth *or* ground: *The locals were trying to trap and kill the birds.* **2 = trick**, fool, cheat, lure, seduce, deceive, dupe, beguile, gull, cajole, ensnare, hoodwink, wheedle, inveigle: *Were you trying to trap her into making an admission?* **3 = capture**, catch, arrest, seize, take, lift (*slang*), secure, nail (*informal*), collar (*informal*), nab (*informal*), apprehend, take prisoner, take into custody: *To trap the killer they had to play him at his own game.*

trapped ADJECTIVE **= caught**, cornered, snared, ensnared, stuck (*informal*), netted, surrounded, cut off, at bay, in a tight corner, in a tight spot, with your back to the wall

trappings PLURAL NOUN **= accessories**, trimmings, paraphernalia, finery, things, fittings, dress, equipment, gear, fixtures, decorations, furnishings, ornaments, livery, adornments, panoply, accoutrements, fripperies, bells and whistles, raiment (*archaic, poetic*), bling (*slang*)

trash NOUN **1 = nonsense**, rubbish, garbage (*informal*), rot, pants (*slang*), crap (*slang*), hot air (*informal*), tosh (*slang, chiefly Brit.*), pap, bilge (*informal*), drivel, twaddle, tripe (*informal*), guff (*slang*), moonshine, hogwash, malarkey, hokum (*slang, chiefly U.S. & Canad.*), piffle (*informal*), poppycock (*informal*), inanity, balderdash, bosh (*informal*), eyewash (*informal*), kak (*S. African taboo, slang*), trumpery, tommyrot, foolish talk, horsefeathers (*U.S. slang*), bunkum *or* buncombe (*chiefly U.S.*), bizzo (*Austral. slang*), bull's wool (*Austral. & N.Z. slang*): *Don't read that awful trash.* **OPPOSITE:** sense **2 = litter**, refuse, waste, rubbish, sweepings, junk (*informal*), garbage, dross, dregs, dreck (*slang, chiefly U.S.*), offscourings: *The yards are overgrown and cluttered with trash.*

trashy ADJECTIVE **= worthless**, cheap, inferior, shabby, flimsy, shoddy, tawdry, tinsel, thrown together, crappy (*slang*), meretricious, rubbishy, poxy (*slang*), catchpenny, cheap-jack (*informal*), of a sort *or* of sorts **OPPOSITE:** excellent

trauma NOUN **1 = shock**, suffering, worry, pain, stress, upset, strain, torture, distress, misery, disturbance, ordeal, anguish, upheaval, jolt: *I'd been through the trauma of losing a house.* **2 = injury**, damage, hurt, wound, agony: *spinal trauma*

traumatic ADJECTIVE **= shocking**, upsetting, alarming, awful, disturbing, devastating, painful, distressing, terrifying, scarring, harrowing **OPPOSITE:** calming

travel VERB **1 = go**, journey, proceed, make a journey, move, walk, cross, tour, progress, wander, trek, voyage, roam, ramble, traverse, rove, take a trip, make your way, wend your way: *You can travel to Helsinki tomorrow.* **2 = be transmitted**, move, advance, proceed, get through: *Light travels at around 300 million metres per second.*
▷ NOUN *(usually plural)* **= journey**, wandering, expedition, globetrotting, walk, tour, touring, movement, trip, passage, voyage, excursion, ramble, peregrination: *He collects things for the house on his travels.*
▸ *related adjective:* itinerant

QUOTATIONS

I'll put a girdle round the earth
In forty minutes
[William Shakespeare *A Midsummer Night's Dream*]

I have recently been all round the world and have formed a very poor opinion of it
[Sir Thomas Beecham]

Travel, at its best, is a process of continually conquering disbelief
[Michael Palin *Pole to Pole*]

Travel is glamorous only in retrospect
[Paul Theroux]

In America there are two classes of travel – first class and with children
[Robert Benchley]

They change their clime, but not their minds, who rush across the sea
[Horace *Epistles*]

Whenever I prepare for a journey
I prepare as though for death
[Katherine Mansfield *Journal*]

A man who has not seen Italy, is always conscious of an inferiority, from his not having seen what it is expected a man should see. The grand object of travelling is to see the shores of the Mediterranean
[Dr. Johnson]

For my part, I travel not to go anywhere, but to go. I travel for travel's sake. The great affair is to move
[Robert Louis Stevenson *Travels with a Donkey*]

Airplane travel is nature's way of making you look like your passport photo
[Al Gore]

PROVERBS

Travel broadens the mind

traveller NOUN **1 = voyager**, tourist, passenger, journeyer, explorer, hiker, tripper, globetrotter, holiday-maker, wayfarer, excursionist: *Many air travellers suffer puffy ankles during long flights.* **2 = travelling salesman**, representative, rep, salesman, sales rep, commercial traveller, agent: *My father was a commercial traveller who migrated from Scotland.*

travelling ADJECTIVE **= itinerant**, moving, touring, mobile, wandering, unsettled, roaming, migrant, restless, roving, nomadic, migratory, peripatetic, wayfaring

traverse VERB **1 = cross**, go across, travel over, make your way across, cover, range, bridge, negotiate, wander, go over, span, roam, ply: *I traversed the narrow pedestrian bridge.* **2 = cut across**, pass over, stretch across, extend across, lie across: *a steep-sided valley traversed by streams*

travesty NOUN **= mockery**, distortion, parody, caricature, sham, send-up *(Brit. informal)*, spoof *(informal)*, perversion, takeoff *(informal)*, lampoon, burlesque

treacherous ADJECTIVE **1 = disloyal**, deceitful, untrustworthy, duplicitous, false, untrue, unreliable, unfaithful, faithless, double-crossing *(informal)*, double-dealing, perfidious, traitorous, treasonable, recreant *(archaic)*: *The President spoke of the treacherous intentions of the enemy.* **OPPOSITE:** loyal **2 = dangerous**, tricky, risky, unstable, hazardous, icy, slippery, unsafe, unreliable, precarious, deceptive, perilous, slippy *(informal, dialect)*: *The current of the river is fast-flowing and treacherous.* **OPPOSITE:** safe

treachery NOUN **= betrayal**, infidelity, treason, duplicity, disloyalty, double-cross *(informal)*, double-dealing, stab in the back, perfidy, faithlessness, perfidiousness **OPPOSITE:** loyalty

tread VERB **= step**, walk, march, pace, stamp, stride, hike, tramp, trudge, plod: *She trod casually, enjoying the sensation of bare feet on grass.*
▷ NOUN **= step**, walk, pace, stride, footstep, gait, footfall: *We could hear their heavy tread and an occasional coarse laugh.*
tread on something 1 = crush underfoot, step on, stamp on, trample (on), stomp on, squash, flatten: *Oh sorry, I didn't mean to tread on your foot.* **2 = repress**, crush, suppress, subdue, oppress, quell, bear down on, subjugate, ride roughshod over: *Paid lawyers would tread on the farmers' interests.*

treason NOUN **= disloyalty**, mutiny, treachery, subversion, disaffection, duplicity, sedition, perfidy, lese-majesty, traitorousness **OPPOSITE:** loyalty

QUOTATIONS

Treason doth never prosper, what's the reason
For if it prosper, none dare call it treason
[Sir John Harington *Epigrams*]

treasure NOUN **1 = riches**, money, gold, fortune, wealth, valuables, jewels, funds, cash: *It was here, the buried treasure, she knew it was.* **2 = angel**, darling, find, star *(informal)*, prize, pearl, something else *(informal)*, jewel, gem, paragon, one in a million *(informal)*, one of a kind *(informal)*, nonpareil: *Charlie? Oh he's a treasure, loves children.*
▷ VERB **= prize**, value, worship, esteem, adore, cherish, revere, venerate, hold dear, love, idolize, set great store by, dote upon, place great value on: *She treasures her memories of those joyous days.*

treasury NOUN **1 = funds**, money, capital, finances, resources, assets, revenues, exchequer, coffers: *reconciling accounts with the central bank and its treasury* **2 = storehouse**, bank, store, vault, hoard, cache, repository: *He had been compiling a treasury of jokes.*

treat VERB **1 = behave towards**, deal with, handle, act towards, use, consider, serve, manage, regard, look upon: *He treated most women with indifference.* **2 = take care of**, minister to, attend to, give medical treatment to, doctor *(informal)*, nurse, care for, medicate, prescribe medicine for, apply treatment to: *An experienced nurse treats all minor injuries.* **3** *(often with* **to***)* **= provide**, give, buy, stand *(informal)*, pay for, entertain, feast, lay on, regale, wine and dine, take out for, foot *or* pay the bill: *She was always treating him to ice cream.* **4 = negotiate**, bargain, consult, have talks, confer, come to terms, parley, make a bargain, make terms: *They assumed we were treating with the rebels.*
▷ NOUN **1 = entertainment**, party, surprise, gift, celebration, feast, outing, excursion, banquet, refreshment: *a birthday treat* **2 = pleasure**, delight, joy, thrill, satisfaction, enjoyment, gratification, source of pleasure, fun: *It's a real treat to see someone doing justice to the film.*
treat of something = deal with, discuss, go into, be concerned with, touch upon, discourse upon: *part of Christian theology that treats of the afterlife*

treatise NOUN **= paper**, work, writing, study, essay, thesis, tract, pamphlet, exposition, dissertation, monograph, disquisition

treatment NOUN **1 = care**, medical care, nursing, medicine, surgery, therapy, healing, medication, therapeutics, ministrations: *Many patients are not getting the treatment they need.* **2 = cure**, remedy, medication, medicine: *a new treatment for eczema* **3** *(often with* **of***)* **= handling**, dealings

t

with, behaviour towards, conduct towards, management, reception, usage, manipulation, action towards: *She was shocked at his treatment of her.*

treaty NOUN = **agreement**, pact, contract, bond, alliance, bargain, convention, compact, covenant, entente, concordat

trek NOUN **1 = slog**, tramp, long haul, footslog: *It's a bit of a trek, but it's worth it.* **2 = journey**, hike, expedition, safari, march, odyssey: *He is on a trek through the South Gobi desert.*
▷ VERB **1 = journey**, march, range, hike, roam, tramp, rove, go walkabout (*Austral.*): *trekking through the jungles* **2 = trudge**, plod, traipse (*informal*), footslog, slog: *They trekked from shop to shop looking for knee-length socks.*

tremble VERB **1 = shake**, shiver, quake, shudder, quiver, teeter, totter, quake in your boots, shake in your boots *or* shoes: *He began to tremble all over.* **2 = vibrate**, rock, shake, quake, wobble, oscillate: *He felt the earth tremble under him.*
▷ NOUN = **shake**, shiver, quake, shudder, wobble, tremor, quiver, vibration, oscillation: *I'll never forget the tremble in his hand.*

tremendous ADJECTIVE **1 = huge**, great, towering, vast, enormous, terrific, formidable, immense, awesome, titanic, gigantic, monstrous, mammoth, colossal, whopping (*informal*), stellar (*informal*), prodigious, stupendous, gargantuan: *I felt a tremendous pressure on my chest.* **OPPOSITE:** tiny **2 = excellent**, great, wonderful, brilliant, mean (*slang*), topping (*Brit. slang*), cracking (*Brit. informal*), amazing, extraordinary, fantastic (*informal*), ace (*informal*), incredible, fabulous (*informal*), marvellous, exceptional, terrific (*informal*), sensational (*informal*), sovereign, awesome (*slang*), super (*informal*), brill (*informal*), bodacious (*slang, chiefly U.S.*), boffo (*slang*), jim-dandy (*slang*), chillin' (*U.S. slang*), booshit (*Austral. slang*), exo (*Austral. slang*), sik (*Austral. slang*), rad (*informal*), phat (*slang*), schmick (*Austral. informal*), beaut (*informal*), barrie (*Scot. slang*), belting (*Brit. slang*), pearler (*Austral. slang*): *I thought it was absolutely tremendous.* **OPPOSITE:** terrible

tremor NOUN **1 = shake**, shaking, tremble, trembling, shiver, quaking, wobble, quiver, quivering, agitation, vibration, quaver: *He felt a tremor in his arm.* **2 = earthquake**, shock, quake (*informal*), tremblor (*U.S. informal*): *The minute-long tremor measured 6.8 on the Richter Scale.*

trench NOUN = **ditch**, cut, channel, drain, pit, waterway, gutter, trough, furrow, excavation, earthwork, fosse, entrenchment

trenchant ADJECTIVE **1 = scathing**, pointed, cutting, biting, sharp, keen, acute, severe, acid, penetrating, tart, pungent, incisive, hurtful, sarcastic, caustic, astringent, vitriolic, acerbic, piquant, mordant, acidulous, mordacious: *He was shattered by the trenchant criticism.* **OPPOSITE:** kind **2 = clear**, driving, strong, powerful, effective, distinct, crisp, explicit, vigorous, potent, energetic, clear-cut, forceful, emphatic, unequivocal, salient, well-defined, effectual, distinctly defined: *His comment was trenchant and perceptive.*
OPPOSITE: vague

trend NOUN **1 = tendency**, swing, drift, inclination, current, direction, flow, leaning, bias: *a trend towards part-time employment* **2 = fashion**, craze, fad (*informal*), mode, look, thing, style, rage, vogue, mania: *The record may well start a trend.*
▷ VERB = **tend**, turn, head, swing, flow, bend, lean, incline, veer, run: *Unemployment is still trending down.*

trendy ADJECTIVE = **fashionable**, in (*slang*), now (*informal*), latest, with it (*informal*), flash (*informal*), stylish, in fashion, in vogue, up to the minute, modish, voguish, schmick (*Austral. informal*), funky: *a trendy London nightclub*
▷ NOUN = **poser** (*informal*), pseud (*informal*): *an example of what happens when you get a few trendies in power*

trepidation NOUN = **anxiety**, fear, worry, alarm, emotion, excitement, dread, butterflies (*informal*), shaking, disturbance, dismay, trembling, fright, apprehension, tremor, quivering, nervousness, disquiet, agitation, consternation, jitters (*informal*), cold feet (*informal*), uneasiness, palpitation, cold sweat (*informal*), perturbation, the heebie-jeebies (*slang*) **OPPOSITE:** composure

trespass VERB **1 = intrude**, infringe, encroach, enter without permission, invade, poach, obtrude: *They were trespassing on private property.* **2** (*often with* **against**, *archaic*) = **sin**, offend, transgress, commit a sin: *Forgive those who trespass against us.*
▷ NOUN **1 = intrusion**, infringement, encroachment, unlawful entry, invasion, poaching, wrongful entry: *You could be prosecuted for trespass.* **2 = sin**, crime, fault, error, offence, breach, misconduct, wrongdoing, misdemeanour, delinquency, misdeed, transgression, misbehaviour, iniquity, infraction, evildoing, injury: *Forgive us our trespasses.*

tress NOUN (*often plural*) = **hair**, lock, curl, braid, plait, pigtail, ringlet

triad NOUN = **threesome**, triple, trio, trinity, trilogy, triplet, triumvirate, triptych, trine, triune

trial NOUN **1 = hearing**, case, court case, inquiry, contest, tribunal, lawsuit, appeal, litigation, industrial tribunal, court martial, legal proceedings, judicial proceedings, judicial examination: *New evidence showed that he lied at the trial* **2 = test**, testing, experiment, evaluation, check, examination, audition, assay, dry run (*informal*), assessment, proof, probation, appraisal, try-out, test-run, pilot study, dummy run: *They have been treated with drugs in clinical trials.* **3 = hardship**, suffering, trouble, pain, load, burden, distress, grief, misery, ordeal, hard times, woe, unhappiness, adversity, affliction, tribulation, wretchedness, vexation, cross to bear: *the trials of adolescence* **4 = nuisance**, drag (*informal*), bother, plague (*informal*), pest, irritation, hassle (*informal*), bane, pain in the neck (*informal*), vexation, thorn in your flesh *or* side: *The whole affair has been a terrible trial for us all.*
▷ ADJECTIVE = **experimental**, probationary, testing, pilot, provisional, exploratory: *a trial period*

tribe NOUN = **race**, ethnic group, people, family, class, stock, house, division, blood, seed (*chiefly biblical*), sept, gens, clan, caste, dynasty, hapu (*N.Z.*), iwi (*N.Z.*)

tribulation NOUN = **trouble**, care, suffering, worry, trial, blow, pain, burden, distress, grief, misery, curse, ordeal, hardship, sorrow, woe, hassle (*informal*), misfortune, bad luck, unhappiness, heartache, adversity, affliction, bummer (*slang*), wretchedness, vexation, ill fortune, cross to bear **OPPOSITE:** joy

tribunal NOUN = **hearing**, court, trial, bar, bench, industrial tribunal, judgment seat, judicial examination

tribute NOUN = **accolade**, testimonial, eulogy, recognition, respect, gift, honour, praise, esteem, applause, compliment, gratitude, acknowledgment, commendation, panegyric, encomium, laudation
OPPOSITE: criticism

trick NOUN **1 = joke**, put-on (*slang*), gag (*informal*), stunt, spoof (*informal*), caper, prank, frolic, practical joke, antic, jape, leg-pull (*Brit. informal*), cantrip (*Scot.*): *We are playing a trick on a man who keeps bothering me.* **2 = deception**, trap, fraud, con (*slang*), sting (*informal*), manoeuvre, dodge, ploy, scam (*slang*), imposition, gimmick, device, hoax, deceit, swindle, ruse, artifice, subterfuge, canard, feint, stratagem, wile, imposture, fastie (*Austral. slang*): *That was a really mean trick.* **3 = sleight of hand**, device, feat, stunt, juggle, legerdemain: *He shows me card tricks.* **4 = secret**, skill, device, knack, art, hang (*informal*), technique, know-how (*informal*), gift, command, craft, expertise: *She showed me all the tricks of the trade.* **5 = mannerism**, habit, characteristic, trait, quirk, peculiarity, foible, idiosyncrasy, practice, crotchet: *all her little tricks and funny voices*
▷ VERB = **deceive**, trap, have someone on, take someone in (*informal*), fool, cheat, con (*informal*), kid (*informal*), stiff (*slang*), sting (*informal*), mislead, hoax, defraud, dupe, gull (*archaic*), delude,

Jane Austen's Use of Adverbs

Jane Austen (1775–1817) was the youngest of the seven children of a clergyman. She never married and her life was lived, as far as we can tell, largely uneventfully within the domestic sphere. Her first (anonymously) published novel was *Sense and Sensibility* (1811), which was followed by *Pride and Prejudice* (1813), *Mansfield Park* (1814) and *Emma* (1816). *Persuasion* and *Northanger Abbey*, her satire on the Gothic novel, were published the year after her death. Her sharply observed comedies of domestic manners and the marriage market have brought her a posthumous fame and esteem which contrast markedly with her secluded life.

Jane Austen begins her most popular novel, *Pride and Prejudice*, with what is arguably the most easily recognizable use of an adverb in English literature:

> It is a truth **universally** acknowledged, that a single man in possession of a good fortune must be in want of a wife.

The adverb *universally* occurs comparatively rarely in her work as a whole, but this would not prevent most of her devotees from instantly completing this sentence, given the opening clause.

Among the more frequent adverbs are those which might judiciously modify a judgement, such as *quite* and *rather*, but another equally recurrent item is *indeed*, often used by characters to effusively assure others of their sincerity:

> I always take the part of my own sex. I do **indeed**. I give you notice – You will find me a formidable antagonist on that point.

Turning to adverbs of manner, these are relatively rarer (as might be expected), but it is perhaps a surprise to find the robust *heartily* among the more common. While this does occur with 'ashamed' and 'sorry', it also appears with 'glad', and by far the commonest verb it accompanies is 'laugh'. Again, characters – and especially leading characters – speak *warmly* (whether to insist, protest, thank, or agree) much more often than *coolly*. Hardly anyone, on the other hand, is said to speak *coldly*, and when they do the effect is all the more shocking, most memorably when Darcy utters thus his dismissive initial judgement of Elizabeth Bennet, that she is 'tolerable, but not handsome enough to tempt *me*.'

The adverb *nicely* is most often used with 'dressed', but not in the blandly approving contemporary sense, as is indicated when the same word is used with 'talk', implying discrimination and good judgement. Curiously, the word is also used in a culinary context, by Emma Woodhouse's valetudinarian father, as he frets over the threat to digestion from pork:

> ... unless one could be sure of their making it into steaks, **nicely** fried, as ours are fried, without the smallest grease, and not roast it, for no stomach can bear roast pork.

One notable grammatical aspect of Jane Austen's adverb usage is the postverbal positioning of *not* with certain verbs:

> Emma dared not attempt any immediate reply.

The onward historical march of 'do/did' seems to have temporarily halted here, as also with 'doubt not' and 'know/knew not'. This also occurs with 'need not', which in subsequent English has developed into the twin forms 'needn't' and 'don't need to'. The contracted negative *n't* is never used except in direct speech, and on occasion seems to be particularly associated with less educated speech – which may not necessarily be confined to the less socially advantaged characters, as is indicated by the vigorously non-standard (perhaps old-fashioned) remark of the well-connected gossip Mrs Jennings in *Sense and Sensibility*:

> Well, it **don't** signify talking.

swindle, impose upon, bamboozle (*informal*), hoodwink, put one over on (*informal*), pull the wool over someone's eyes, pull a fast one on (*informal*), scam (*slang*): *He'll be upset when he finds out how you tricked him.*

do the trick = **work**, fit the bill, have effect, achieve the desired result, produce the desired result, take care of the problem, be effective *or* effectual, do the business (*informal*): *Sometimes a few choice words will do the trick.*

trickery NOUN = **deception**, fraud, cheating, con (*informal*), hoax, pretence, deceit, dishonesty, swindling, guile, double-dealing, skulduggery (*informal*), chicanery, hanky-panky (*informal*), hokum (*slang, chiefly U.S. & Canad.*), monkey business (*informal*), funny business, jiggery-pokery (*informal, chiefly Brit.*), imposture **OPPOSITE:** honesty

trickle VERB = **dribble**, run, drop, stream, creep, crawl, drip, ooze, seep, exude, percolate: *A tear trickled down his cheek.*

▷ NOUN = **dribble**, drip, seepage, thin stream: *There was not so much as a trickle of water.*

trickster NOUN = **deceiver**, fraud, cheat, joker, hoaxer, pretender, hustler (*U.S. informal*), con man (*informal*), impostor, fraudster, swindler, practical joker, grifter (*slang, chiefly U.S. & Canad.*), chiseller (*informal*), rorter (*Austral. slang*), rogue trader

tricky ADJECTIVE **1** = **difficult**, sensitive, complicated, delicate, risky, sticky (*informal*), hairy (*informal*), problematic, thorny, touch-and-go, knotty, dicey (*informal*), ticklish: *This could be a very tricky problem.*
OPPOSITE: simple **2** = **crafty**, scheming, subtle, cunning, slippery, sly, deceptive, devious, wily, artful, foxy, deceitful: *They could encounter some tricky political manoeuvring.*
OPPOSITE: open

trifle NOUN = **knick-knack**, nothing, toy, plaything, bauble, triviality, bagatelle, gewgaw: *He had no money to spare on trifles.*

a trifle = **slightly**, a little, a bit, somewhat, rather, moderately, marginally, a shade, to some degree, on a small scale, to some extent *or* degree: *He found both locations just a trifle disappointing.*

> **QUOTATIONS**
> a snapper-up of unconsidered trifles
> [William Shakespeare *The Winter's Tale*]

trifling ADJECTIVE = **insignificant**, small, tiny, empty, slight, silly, shallow, petty, idle, trivial, worthless, negligible, unimportant, frivolous, paltry, minuscule, puny, measly, piddling (*informal*), inconsiderable, valueless, nickel-and-dime (*U.S. slang*), footling (*informal*)
OPPOSITE: significant

trigger VERB = **bring about**, start, cause, produce, generate, prompt, provoke, set off, activate, give rise to, elicit, spark off, set in motion
OPPOSITE: prevent

trim ADJECTIVE **1** = **neat**, nice, smart, compact, tidy, orderly, spruce, dapper, natty (*informal*), well-groomed, well-ordered, well turned-out, shipshape, spick-and-span, trig (*archaic, dialect*), soigné *or* soignée: *The neighbour's gardens were trim and neat.*
OPPOSITE: untidy **2** = **slender**, fit, slim, sleek, streamlined, shapely, svelte, willowy, lissom: *The driver was a trim young woman of about thirty.*

▷ VERB **1** = **cut**, crop, clip, dock, shave, barber, tidy, prune, shear, pare, lop, even up, neaten: *My friend trims my hair every eight weeks.* **2** = **decorate**, dress, array, adorn, embroider, garnish, ornament, embellish, deck out, bedeck, beautify, trick out: *jackets trimmed with crocheted flowers*

▷ NOUN **1** = **decoration**, edging, border, piping, trimming, fringe, garnish, frill, embellishment, adornment, ornamentation: *a white satin scarf with black trim* **2** = **condition**, form, health, shape (*informal*), repair, fitness, wellness, order, fettle: *He is already getting in trim for the big day.*
3 = **cut**, crop, trimming, clipping, shave, pruning, shearing, tidying up: *His hair needed a trim.*

trimming NOUN = **decoration**, edging, border, piping, fringe, garnish, braid, frill, festoon, embellishment, adornment, ornamentation: *the lace trimming on her satin nightgown*

▷ PLURAL NOUN **1** = **extras**, accessories, garnish, ornaments, accompaniments, frills, trappings, paraphernalia, appurtenances: *a Thanksgiving dinner of turkey and all the trimmings* **2** = **clippings**, ends, cuttings, shavings, brash, parings: *Use any pastry trimmings to decorate the apples.*

trinity NOUN = **threesome**, triple, trio, trilogy, triplet, triad, triumvirate, triptych, trine, triune

trinket NOUN = **ornament**, bauble, knick-knack, piece of bric-a-brac, nothing, toy, trifle, bagatelle, gimcrack, gewgaw, bibelot, kickshaw

trio NOUN = **threesome**, triple, trinity, trilogy, triplet, triad, triumvirate, triptych, trine, triune

trip NOUN **1** = **journey**, outing, excursion, day out, run, drive, travel, tour, spin (*informal*), expedition, voyage, ramble, foray, jaunt, errand, junket (*informal*): *On the Thursday we went out on a day trip.* **2** = **stumble**, fall, slip, blunder, false move, misstep, false step: *Slips, trips and falls were monitored using a daily calendar.*

▷ VERB **1** (*often with* **up**) = **stumble**, fall, fall over, slip, tumble, topple, stagger, misstep, lose your balance, make a false move, lose your footing, take a spill: *She tripped and broke her hip.* **2** = **skip**, dance, spring, hop, caper, flit, frisk, gambol, tread lightly: *They tripped along without a care in the world.*
3 = **take drugs**, get high (*informal*), get stoned (*slang*), turn on (*slang*): *One night I was tripping on acid.* **4** = **activate**, turn on, flip, release, pull, throw, engage, set off, switch on: *He set the timer, then tripped the switch.*

trip someone up = **catch out**, trap, confuse, unsettle, disconcert, throw you off, wrongfoot, put you off your stride: *Your own lies will trip you up.*

tripe NOUN = **nonsense**, rot, trash, twaddle, rubbish, pants (*slang*), crap (*slang*), garbage (*informal*), hot air (*informal*), tosh (*slang, chiefly Brit.*), pap, bilge (*informal*), drivel, guff (*slang*), moonshine, claptrap (*informal*), hogwash, hokum (*slang, chiefly U.S. & Canad.*), piffle (*informal*), poppycock (*informal*), inanity, balderdash, bosh (*informal*), eyewash (*informal*), trumpery, tommyrot, foolish talk, horsefeathers (*U.S. slang*), bunkum *or* buncombe (*chiefly U.S.*), bizzo (*Austral. slang*), bull's wool (*Austral. & N.Z. slang*)

triple ADJECTIVE **1** = **treble**, three times, three times as much as: *The kitchen is triple the size it used to be.*
2 = **three-way**, threefold, tripartite: *Germany, Austria and Italy formed the Triple Alliance.*

▷ VERB = **treble**, triplicate, increase threefold: *I got a great new job and my salary tripled.*

triplet NOUN = **threesome**, triple, trio, trinity, trilogy, triad, triumvirate, trine, triune

tripper NOUN = **tourist**, holiday-maker, sightseer, excursionist, journeyer, voyager

trite ADJECTIVE = **unoriginal**, worn, common, stock, ordinary, tired, routine, dull, stereotyped, hack, pedestrian, commonplace, stale, banal, corny (*slang*), run-of-the-mill, threadbare, clichéd, uninspired, hackneyed, bromidic
OPPOSITE: original

triumph NOUN **1** = **success**, victory, accomplishment, mastery, hit (*informal*), achievement, smash (*informal*), coup, sensation, feat, conquest, attainment, smash hit (*informal*), tour de force (*French*), walkover (*informal*), feather in your cap, smasheroo (*slang*): *Cataract operations are a triumph of modern surgery.*
OPPOSITE: failure **2** = **joy**, pride, happiness, rejoicing, elation, jubilation, exultation: *Her sense of triumph was short-lived.*

▷ VERB **1** (*often with* **over**) = **succeed**, win, overcome, prevail, best, dominate, overwhelm, thrive, flourish, subdue, prosper, get the better of, vanquish, come out on top (*informal*), carry the day, take the honours: *a symbol of good triumphing over evil* **OPPOSITE:** fail **2** = **rejoice**, celebrate, glory, revel, swagger, drool, gloat, exult, jubilate, crow: *the* *euphoria, the sense of triumphing together as a nation*

triumphant ADJECTIVE **1 = victorious**, winning, successful, dominant, conquering, undefeated: *the triumphant team* **OPPOSITE:** defeated **2 = celebratory**, rejoicing, jubilant, triumphal, proud, glorious, swaggering, elated, exultant, boastful, cock-a-hoop: *his triumphant return home*

trivia NOUN **= minutiae**, details, trifles, trivialities, petty details **OPPOSITE:** essentials

trivial ADJECTIVE **= unimportant**, little, small, minor, slight, everyday, petty, meaningless, commonplace, worthless, trifling, insignificant, negligible, frivolous, paltry, incidental, puny, inconsequential, trite, inconsiderable, valueless, nickel-and-dime *(U.S. slang)* **OPPOSITE:** important

> **QUOTATIONS**
> What mighty contests rise from trivial things
> [Alexander Pope *The Rape of the Lock*]

triviality NOUN **1 = insignificance**, frivolity, smallness, pettiness, worthlessness, meaninglessness, unimportance, littleness, slightness, triteness, paltriness, inconsequentiality, valuelessness, negligibility, much ado about nothing: *news items of quite astonishing triviality* **OPPOSITE:** importance **2 = trifle**, nothing, detail, technicality, petty detail, no big thing, no great matter: *He accused me of making a great fuss about trivialities.* **OPPOSITE:** essential

> **PROVERBS**
> *Little things please little minds*

troop NOUN **1 = group**, company, team, body, unit, band, crowd, pack, squad, gathering, crew *(informal)*, drove, gang, bunch *(informal)*, flock, herd, contingent, swarm, horde, multitude, throng, posse *(informal)*, bevy, assemblage: *She was aware of a little troop of travellers watching them.* **2** *(plural)* **= soldiers**, men, armed forces, servicemen, fighting men, military, army, soldiery: *the deployment of more than 35,000 troops from a dozen countries*
▷ VERB **= flock**, march, crowd, stream, parade, swarm, throng, traipse *(informal)*: *The VIPs trooped into the hall and sat down.*

trophy NOUN **1 = prize**, cup, award, bays, laurels: *They could win a trophy this year.* **2 = souvenir**, spoils, relic, memento, booty, keepsake: *lines of stuffed animal heads, trophies of his hunting hobby*

tropical ADJECTIVE **= hot**, stifling, lush, steamy, humid, torrid, sultry, sweltering **OPPOSITE:** cold

trot VERB **= run**, jog, scamper, lope, go briskly, canter: *I trotted down the steps and out to the shed.*
▷ NOUN **= run**, jog, lope, brisk pace, canter: *He walked briskly, but without breaking into a trot.*
on the trot = one after the other, in a row, in succession, without break, without interruption, consecutively: *She lost five games on the trot.*
trot something out = repeat, relate, exhibit, bring up, reiterate, recite, come out with, bring forward, drag up: *Was it really necessary to trot out the same old stereotypes?*

troubadour NOUN **= minstrel**, singer, poet, balladeer, lyric poet, jongleur

trouble NOUN **1 = bother**, problems, concern, worry, stress, difficulty *(informal)*, anxiety, distress, grief *(Brit. & S. African)*, irritation, hassle *(informal)*, strife, inconvenience, unease, disquiet, annoyance, agitation, commotion, unpleasantness, vexation: *You've caused a lot of trouble.* **2** *(often plural)* **= distress**, problem, suffering, worry, pain, anxiety, grief, torment, hardship, sorrow, woe, irritation, hassle *(informal)*, misfortune, heartache, disquiet, annoyance, agitation, tribulation, bummer *(slang)*, vexation: *She tells me her troubles. I tell her mine.* **OPPOSITE:** pleasure **3 = ailment**, disease, failure, complaint, upset, illness, disorder, disability, defect, malfunction: *He had never before had any heart trouble.* **4 = disorder**, fighting, row, conflict, bother, grief *(Brit. & S. African)*, unrest, disturbance, to-do *(informal)*, discontent, dissatisfaction, furore, uproar, scuffling, discord, fracas, commotion, rumpus, breach of the peace, tumult, affray *(Law)*, brouhaha, ructions, hullabaloo *(informal)*, kerfuffle *(Brit. informal)*, hoo-ha *(informal)*, biffo *(Austral. slang)*, boilover *(Austral.)*: *Riot police are being deployed to prevent any trouble.* **OPPOSITE:** peace **5 = problem**, bother, concern, pest, irritation, hassle *(informal)*, nuisance, inconvenience, irritant, cause of annoyance: *He's no trouble at all, but his brother is rude and selfish.* **6 = effort**, work, thought, care, labour, struggle, pains, bother, grief *(Brit. & S. African)*, hassle *(informal)*, inconvenience, exertion: *You've saved us a lot of trouble by helping.* **OPPOSITE:** convenience **7 = difficulty**, hot water *(informal)*, predicament, deep water *(informal)*, spot *(informal)*, danger, mess, dilemma, scrape *(informal)*, pickle *(informal)*, dire straits, tight spot: *a charity that helps women in trouble with the law*
▷ VERB **1 = bother**, worry, upset, disturb, distress, annoy, plague, grieve, torment, harass, hassle *(informal)*, afflict, pain, fret, agitate, sadden, perplex, disconcert, disquiet, pester, vex, perturb, faze, give someone grief *(Brit. & S. African)*, discompose, put *or* get someone's back up, hack you off *(informal)*: *Is anything troubling you?* **OPPOSITE:** please **2 = afflict**, hurt, bother, cause discomfort to, pain, grieve: *The ulcer had been troubling her for several years.* **3 = inconvenience**, disturb, burden, put out, impose upon, discommode, incommode: *'Good morning. I'm sorry to trouble you.'* **OPPOSITE:** relieve **4 = take pains**, take the time, make an effort, go to the effort of, exert yourself: *He yawns, not troubling to cover his mouth.* **OPPOSITE:** avoid

> **QUOTATIONS**
> Man is born unto trouble
> [*Bible: Job*]
>
> Double, double, toil and trouble
> [William Shakespeare *Macbeth*]

> **PROVERBS**
> *Never trouble trouble till trouble troubles you*

troublemaker NOUN **= mischief-maker**, firebrand, instigator, agitator, bad apple *(U.S. informal)*, rabble-rouser, agent provocateur *(French)*, stirrer *(informal)*, incendiary, rotten apple *(Brit. informal)*, meddler, stormy petrel **OPPOSITE:** peace-maker

> **QUOTATIONS**
> Better to have him inside the tent pissing out, than outside pissing in
> [Lyndon B Johnson (of J Edgar Hoover)]

troublesome ADJECTIVE **1 = bothersome**, trying, taxing, demanding, difficult, worrying, upsetting, annoying, irritating, tricky, harassing, oppressive, arduous, tiresome, inconvenient, laborious, burdensome, hard, worrisome, irksome, wearisome, vexatious, importunate, pestilential, plaguy *(informal)*: *The economy has become a troublesome problem for the party.* **OPPOSITE:** simple **2 = disorderly**, violent, turbulent, rebellious, unruly, rowdy, recalcitrant, undisciplined, uncooperative, refractory, insubordinate: *Parents may find that a troublesome teenager becomes unmanageable.* **OPPOSITE:** well-behaved

trough NOUN **= manger**, crib, water trough

trounce VERB **= defeat someone heavily** *or* **utterly**, beat, thrash, slaughter *(informal)*, stuff *(slang)*, tank *(slang)*, hammer *(informal)*, crush, overwhelm, lick *(informal)*, paste *(slang)*, rout, walk over *(informal)*, clobber *(slang)*, run rings around *(informal)*, wipe the floor with *(informal)*, make mincemeat of, blow someone out of the water *(slang)*, give someone a hiding *(informal)*, drub, beat someone hollow *(Brit. informal)*, give someone a pasting *(slang)*

troupe NOUN **= company**, group, band, cast, ensemble

truancy NOUN **= absence**, shirking, skiving *(Brit. slang)*, malingering, absence without leave

truant NOUN **= absentee**, skiver *(Brit. slang)*, shirker, dodger, runaway, delinquent, deserter, straggler,

malingerer: *She became a truant at the age of ten.*
▷ ADJECTIVE = **absent**, missing, skiving (*Brit. slang*), absent without leave, A.W.O.L.: *Neither the parents nor the truant students showed up at court.*
▷ VERB = **absent yourself**, play truant, skive (*Brit. slang*), bunk off (*slang*), desert, run away, dodge, wag (*dialect*), go missing, shirk, malinger, bob off (*Brit. slang*): *In his fourth year he was truanting regularly.*

truce NOUN = **ceasefire**, break, stay, rest, peace, treaty, interval, moratorium, respite, lull, cessation, let-up (*informal*), armistice, intermission, cessation of hostilities

truculent ADJECTIVE = **hostile**, defiant, belligerent, bad-tempered, cross, violent, aggressive, fierce, contentious, combative, sullen, scrappy (*informal*), antagonistic, pugnacious, ill-tempered, bellicose, obstreperous, itching *or* spoiling for a fight (*informal*), aggers (*Austral. slang*) **OPPOSITE:** amiable

trudge VERB = **plod**, trek, tramp, traipse (*informal*), march, stump, hike, clump, lumber, slog, drag yourself, yomp, walk heavily, footslog: *We had to trudge up the track back to the station.*
▷ NOUN = **tramp**, march, haul, trek, hike, slog, traipse (*informal*), yomp, footslog: *We were reluctant to start the long trudge home.*

true ADJECTIVE **1** = **correct**, right, accurate, exact, precise, valid, legitimate, factual, truthful, veritable, bona fide, veracious: *Everything I had heard about him was true.* **OPPOSITE:** false **2** = **actual**, real, natural, pure, genuine, proper, authentic, dinkum *or* dinky-di (*Austral. & N.Z. informal*): *I allowed myself to acknowledge my true feelings.*
3 = **faithful**, loyal, devoted, dedicated, firm, fast, constant, pure, steady, reliable, upright, sincere, honourable, honest, staunch, trustworthy, trusty, dutiful, true-blue, unswerving: *He was always true to his wife.* **OPPOSITE:** unfaithful
4 = **exact**, perfect, correct, accurate, proper, precise, spot-on (*Brit. informal*), on target, unerring: *The score is usually a true reflection of events on the pitch.* **OPPOSITE:** inaccurate
▷ ADVERB **1** = **truthfully**, honestly, veritably, veraciously, rightly: *Does the lad speak true?* **2** = **precisely**, accurately, on target, perfectly, correctly, properly, unerringly: *Most of the bullets hit true.*

true-blue ADJECTIVE = **staunch**, confirmed, constant, devoted, dedicated, loyal, faithful, orthodox, uncompromising, trusty, unwavering, dyed-in-the-wool

truism NOUN = **cliché**, commonplace, platitude, axiom, stock phrase, trite saying

truly ADVERB **1** = **genuinely**, really, correctly, truthfully, rightly, in fact, precisely, exactly, legitimately, accurately, in reality, in truth, beyond doubt, without a doubt, authentically, beyond question, factually, in actuality, veritably, veraciously: *a truly democratic system* **OPPOSITE:** falsely **2** = **really**, very, greatly, indeed, seriously (*informal*), extremely, to be sure, exceptionally, verily: *a truly splendid man* **3** = **faithfully**, firmly, constantly, steadily, honestly, sincerely, staunchly, dutifully, loyally, honourably, devotedly, with all your heart, with dedication, with devotion, confirmedly: *He truly loved his children.*

trump VERB = **outdo**, top, cap, surpass, score points off, excel: *The Socialists tried to trump this with their slogan.*
trump something up = **invent**, create, make up, manufacture, fake, contrive, fabricate, concoct, cook up (*informal*): *He insists that charges against him have been trumped up.*

trumped up ADJECTIVE = **invented**, made-up, manufactured, false, fake, contrived, untrue, fabricated, concocted, falsified, cooked-up (*informal*), phoney *or* phony (*informal*) **OPPOSITE:** genuine

trumpet NOUN **1** = **horn**, clarion, bugle: *Picking up his trumpet, he gave it a quick blow.* **2** = **roar**, call, cry, bay, bellow: *The elephant gave a loud trumpet.*
▷ VERB = **proclaim**, advertise, extol, tout (*informal*), announce, publish, broadcast, crack up (*informal*), sound loudly, shout from the rooftops, noise abroad: *He is trumpeted as the greatest talent of his generation.* **OPPOSITE:** keep secret
blow your own trumpet = **boast**, crow, brag, vaunt, sing your own praises, big yourself up (*slang, chiefly Caribbean*): *The cameramen have good reason to blow their own trumpets.*

truncate VERB = **shorten**, cut, crop, trim, clip, dock, prune, curtail, cut short, pare, lop, abbreviate: *I'm going to truncate the time I spend at work.* **OPPOSITE:** lengthen

truncheon NOUN = **club**, staff, stick, baton, cudgel, mere (*N.Z.*), patu (*N.Z.*)

trunk NOUN **1** = **stem**, stock, stalk, bole: *toadstools growing on fallen tree trunks* **2** = **chest**, case, box, crate, bin, suitcase, locker, coffer, casket, portmanteau, kist (*Scot. & Northern English dialect*): *He had left most of his records in a trunk in the attic.* **3** = **body**, torso: *Simultaneously, raise your trunk six inches above the ground.* **4** = **snout**, nose, proboscis: *It could exert the suction power of an elephant's trunk.*

truss VERB (*often with* **up**) = **tie**, secure, bind, strap, fasten, tether, pinion, make fast: *She trussed him with the bandage and gagged his mouth.*
▷ NOUN **1** = **support**, pad, bandage: *For a hernia he introduced the simple solution of a truss.* **2** = **joist**, support, stay, shore, beam, prop, brace, strut, buttress, stanchion: *the bridge's arched, steel truss*

trust NOUN **1** = **confidence**, credit, belief, faith, expectation, conviction, assurance, certainty, reliance, credence, certitude: *There's a feeling of warmth and trust here.* **OPPOSITE:** distrust **2** = **responsibility**, duty, obligation: *She held a position of trust, which was generously paid.*
3 = **custody**, care, guard, protection, guardianship, safekeeping, trusteeship: *The British Library holds its collection in trust for the nation.*
▸ *related adjective:* fiducial
▷ VERB **1** = **believe in**, have faith in, depend on, count on, bank on, lean on, rely upon, swear by, take at face value, take as gospel, place reliance on, place your trust in, pin your faith on, place *or* have confidence in: *'I trust you completely,' he said.* **OPPOSITE:** distrust **2** = **entrust**, commit, assign, confide, consign, put into the hands of, allow to look after, hand over, turn over, sign over, delegate: *I'd been willing to trust my life to him.* **3** = **expect**, believe, hope, suppose, assume, guess (*informal*), take it, presume, surmise, think likely: *We trust that they are considering our suggestion.*

trustful *or* **trusting** ADJECTIVE = **unsuspecting**, simple, innocent, optimistic, naive, confiding, gullible, unwary, unguarded, credulous, unsuspicious **OPPOSITE:** suspicious

trustworthy ADJECTIVE = **dependable**, responsible, principled, mature, sensible, reliable, ethical, upright, true, honourable, honest, staunch, righteous, reputable, truthful, trusty, steadfast, level-headed, to be trusted **OPPOSITE:** untrustworthy

trusty ADJECTIVE = **reliable**, dependable, trustworthy, responsible, solid, strong, firm, true, steady, faithful, straightforward, upright, honest, staunch **OPPOSITE:** unreliable

truth NOUN **1** = **reality**, fact(s), real life, actuality: *Is it possible to separate truth from fiction?* **OPPOSITE:** unreality **2** = **truthfulness**, fact, accuracy, honesty, precision, validity, legitimacy, authenticity, correctness, sincerity, verity, candour, veracity, rightness, genuineness, exactness, factuality, factualness: *There is no truth in this story.* **OPPOSITE:** inaccuracy **3** = **fact**, law, reality, certainty, maxim, verity, axiom, truism, proven principle: *It's a universal truth that we all die eventually.* **4** = **honesty**, principle, honour, virtue, integrity, goodness, righteousness, candour, frankness, probity, rectitude, incorruptibility, uprightness: *His mission is to uphold truth, justice and the American way.* **OPPOSITE:** dishonesty

truthful ADJECTIVE **1** = **honest**, frank, candid, upfront (*informal*), true, straight, reliable, faithful, straightforward, sincere, forthright, trustworthy, plain-spoken, veracious:

t

We are all fairly truthful about our personal lives. **OPPOSITE:** dishonest **2 = true**, correct, accurate, exact, realistic, precise, literal, veritable, naturalistic: *They had not given a truthful account of what actually happened.*
OPPOSITE: untrue

try VERB **1 = attempt**, seek, aim, undertake, essay, strive, struggle, endeavour, have a go, go for it (*informal*), make an effort, have a shot (*informal*), have a crack (*informal*), bend over backwards (*informal*), do your best, go for broke (*slang*), make an attempt, move heaven and earth, bust a gut (*informal*), give it your best shot (*informal*), have a stab (*informal*), break your neck (*informal*), exert yourself, make an all-out effort (*informal*), knock yourself out (*informal*), have a whack (*informal*), do your damnedest (*informal*), give it your all (*informal*), front up, rupture yourself (*informal*): *He secretly tried to block her advancement in the Party.* **2 = experiment with**, try out, put to the test, test, taste, examine, investigate, sample, evaluate, check out, inspect, appraise: *It's best not to try a new recipe on such an important occasion.* **3 = judge**, hear, consider, examine, adjudicate, adjudge, pass judgement on: *The case was tried in Tampa, a changed venue with an all-white jury.* **4 = tax**, test, trouble, pain, stress, upset, tire, strain, drain, exhaust, annoy, plague, irritate, weary, afflict, sap, inconvenience, wear out, vex, irk, make demands on, give someone grief (*Brit. & S. African*): *She really tried my patience.*
▷ NOUN **= attempt**, go (*informal*), shot (*informal*), effort, crack (*informal*), essay, stab (*informal*), bash (*informal*), endeavour, whack (*informal*): *I didn't really expect anything, but it was worth a try.*
try something out = test, experiment with, appraise, put to the test, taste, sample, evaluate, check out, inspect, put into practice: *She knew I wanted to try the boat out at the weekend.*

trying ADJECTIVE **= annoying**, hard, taxing, difficult, tough, upsetting, irritating, fatiguing, stressful, aggravating (*informal*), troublesome, exasperating, arduous, tiresome, vexing, irksome, wearisome, bothersome
OPPOSITE: straightforward

tsar or **czar** NOUN **= head**, chief, boss, big cheese (*informal*), baas (*S. African*), head honcho (*informal*), sherang (*Austral. & N.Z.*): *He was appointed 'drugs tsar' by Bill Clinton.*

tubby ADJECTIVE **= fat**, overweight, plump, stout, chubby, obese, portly, roly-poly, podgy, corpulent, paunchy

tuck VERB **= push**, stick, stuff, slip, ease, insert, pop (*informal*): *He tried to tuck his shirt inside his trousers.*
▷ NOUN **1 = food**, eats (*slang*), tack (*informal*), scoff (*slang*), grub (*slang*), kai (*N.Z. informal*), nosh (*slang*), victuals, comestibles, nosebag (*slang*), vittles (*obsolete, dialect*): *The wags from the rival house were ready to snaffle his tuck.* **2 = fold**, gather, pleat, pinch: *a tapered tuck used to take in fullness and control shape in a garment*
tuck in = eat up, get stuck in (*informal*), eat heartily, fall to, chow down (*slang*): *Tuck in, it's the last hot food you'll get for a while.*
tuck someone in = make snug, wrap up, put to bed, bed down, swaddle: *I read her a story and tucked her in.*

tuft NOUN **= clump**, bunch, shock, collection, knot, cluster, tussock, topknot

tug VERB **1 = pull**, drag, pluck, jerk, yank, wrench, lug: *A little boy tugged at her sleeve excitedly.* **2 = drag**, pull, haul, tow, lug, heave, draw: *She tugged him along by his arm.*
▷ NOUN **= pull**, jerk, yank, wrench, drag, haul, tow, traction, heave: *My head was snapped backwards by a tug on my air hose.*

tuition NOUN **= training**, schooling, education, teaching, lessons, instruction, tutoring, tutelage

tumble VERB **= fall**, drop, topple, plummet, roll, pitch, toss, stumble, flop, trip up, fall head over heels, fall headlong, fall end over end: *The dog had tumbled down the cliff.*
▷ NOUN **= fall**, drop, roll, trip, collapse, plunge, spill, toss, stumble, flop, headlong fall: *He injured his knee in a tumble from his horse.*

tummy NOUN **= stomach**, belly, abdomen, corporation (*informal*), pot, gut (*informal*), paunch, tum (*informal*), spare tyre (*informal*), breadbasket (*slang*), potbelly

tumour or (*U.S.*) **tumor** NOUN **= growth**, cancer, swelling, lump, carcinoma (*Pathology*), sarcoma (*Medical*), neoplasm (*Medical*)

tumult NOUN **1 = disturbance**, trouble, chaos, turmoil, storms, upset, stir, disorder, excitement, unrest, upheaval, havoc, mayhem, strife, disarray, turbulence, ferment, agitation, convulsions, bedlam: *the recent tumult in global financial markets* **2 = clamour**, row, outbreak, racket, din, uproar, fracas, commotion, pandemonium, babel, hubbub, hullabaloo: *Round one ended to a tumult of whistles, screams and shouts.*
OPPOSITE: silence

tumultuous ADJECTIVE **1 = turbulent**, exciting, confused, disturbed, hectic, stormy, agitated: *the tumultuous changes in Eastern Europe* **OPPOSITE:** quiet **2 = wild**, excited, riotous, unrestrained, violent, raging, disorderly, fierce, passionate, noisy, restless, unruly, rowdy, boisterous, full-on (*informal*), lawless, vociferous, rumbustious, uproarious, obstreperous, clamorous: *Delegates greeted the news with tumultuous applause.*

tune NOUN **1 = melody**, air, song, theme, strain(s), motif, jingle, ditty, choon (*slang*), melody line: *She was humming a merry little tune.* **2 = harmony**, pitch, euphony: *It was an ordinary voice, but he sang in tune.*
▷ VERB **1 = tune up**, adjust, bring into harmony: *They were quietly tuning their instruments.* **2 = regulate**, adapt, modulate, harmonize, attune, pitch: *He will rapidly be tuned to the keynote of his new associates.*

tuneful ADJECTIVE **= melodious**, musical, pleasant, harmonious, melodic, catchy, consonant (*Music*), symphonic, mellifluous, easy on the ear (*informal*), euphonious, euphonic
OPPOSITE: discordant

tunnel NOUN **= passage**, underpass, passageway, subway, channel, hole, shaft: *two new railway tunnels through the Alps*
▷ VERB **= dig**, dig your way, burrow, mine, bore, drill, excavate: *The rebels tunnelled out of a maximum security jail.*

turbulence NOUN **= confusion**, turmoil, unrest, instability, storm, boiling, disorder, upheaval, agitation, commotion, pandemonium, tumult, roughness **OPPOSITE:** peace

turbulent ADJECTIVE **1 = wild**, violent, disorderly, agitated, rebellious, unruly, rowdy, boisterous, anarchic, tumultuous, lawless, unbridled, riotous, undisciplined, seditious, mutinous, ungovernable, uproarious, refractory, obstreperous, insubordinate: *six turbulent years of rows and reconciliations* **2 = stormy**, rough, raging, tempestuous, boiling, disordered, furious, unsettled, foaming, unstable, agitated, tumultuous, choppy, blustery: *I had to have a boat that could handle turbulent seas.*
OPPOSITE: calm

turf NOUN **1 = grass**, green, sward: *They shuffled slowly down the turf towards the cliff's edge.* **2 = sod**, divot, clod: *Lift the turfs carefully – they can be reused elsewhere.*
the turf = horse-racing, the flat, racecourse, racetrack, racing: *He has sent out only three winners on the turf this year.*
turf someone out = throw out, evict, cast out, kick out (*informal*), fire (*informal*), dismiss, sack (*informal*), bounce (*slang*), discharge, expel, oust, relegate, banish, eject, dispossess, chuck out (*informal*), fling out, kiss off (*slang, chiefly U.S. & Canad.*), show someone the door, give someone the sack (*informal*), give someone the bum's rush (*slang*), kennet (*Austral. slang*), jeff (*Austral. slang*): *stories of people being turfed out and ending up on the streets*

turgid ADJECTIVE **= pompous**, inflated, windy, high-flown, pretentious, grandiose, flowery, overblown, stilted, ostentatious, fulsome, bombastic, grandiloquent, arty-farty (*informal*), fustian, orotund, magniloquent, sesquipedalian, tumid

turmoil NOUN **= confusion**, trouble, violence, row, noise, stir, disorder,

chaos, disturbance, upheaval, bustle, flurry, strife, disarray, uproar, turbulence, ferment, agitation, commotion, pandemonium, bedlam, tumult, hubbub, brouhaha
OPPOSITE: peace

turn VERB **1** *(sometimes with* **round***)* = **change course**, swing round, wheel round, veer, move, return, go back, switch, shift, reverse, swerve, change position: *He turned abruptly and walked away.* **2** = **rotate**, spin, go round (and round), revolve, roll, circle, wheel, twist, spiral, whirl, swivel, pivot, twirl, gyrate, go round in circles, move in a circle: *As the wheel turned, the potter shaped the clay.* **3** = **go round**, come round, negotiate, pass, corner, pass around, take a bend: *The taxi turned the corner of the lane and stopped.* **4** *(with* **into***)* = **change**, transform, fashion, shape, convert, alter, adapt, mould, remodel, form, mutate, refit, metamorphose, transmute, transfigure: *She turned the house into a beautiful home.* **5** = **shape**, form, fashion, cast, frame, construct, execute, mould, make: *finely-turned metal* **6** = **sicken**, upset, nauseate: *The true facts will turn your stomach.* **7** = **go bad**, go off *(Brit. informal)*, curdle, go sour, become rancid: *milk starting to turn in the refrigerator* **8** = **make rancid**, spoil, sour, taint: *They are stupid and ugly enough to turn milk.*
▷ NOUN **1** = **rotation**, turning, cycle, circle, revolution, spin, twist, reversal, whirl, swivel, pivot, gyration: *The rear sprocket will turn only twice for one turn of the pedals.* **2** = **change of direction**, bend, curve, change of course, shift, departure, deviation: *You can't do a right-hand turn here.* **3** = **direction**, course, tack, swing, tendency, drift, bias: *The scandal took a new turn today.* **4** = **opportunity**, go, spell, shot *(informal)*, time, try, round, chance, period, shift, crack *(informal)*, succession, fling, stint, whack *(informal)*: *Let each child have a turn at fishing.* **5** = **stroll**, airing, walk, drive, ride, spin *(informal)*, circuit, constitutional, outing, excursion, promenade, jaunt, saunter: *I think I'll just go up and take a turn round the deck.* **6** = **deed**, service, act, action, favour, gesture: *He did you a good turn by resigning.* **7** = **shock**, start, surprise, scare, jolt, fright: *It gave me quite a turn.* **8** = **inclination**, talent, gift, leaning, bent, bias, flair, affinity, knack, propensity, aptitude: *She has a turn for gymnastic exercises.*
by turns = **alternately**, in succession, turn and turn about, reciprocally: *His tone was by turns angry and aggrieved.*
to a turn = **perfectly**, correctly, precisely, exactly, just right: *sweet tomatoes roasted to a turn*
turn off = **branch off**, leave, quit, depart from, deviate, change direction, take a side road, take another road: *He turned off only to find that he was trapped in the main square; The truck turned off the main road along the gravelly track.*
turn on someone = **attack**, assault, fall on, round on, lash out at, assail, lay into *(informal)*, let fly at, lose your temper with: *The demonstrators turned on the police.*
turn on something = **depend on**, hang on, rest on, hinge on, be decided by, balance on, be contingent on, pivot on: *It all turns on what his real motives are.*
turn out 1 = **prove to be**, transpire, become apparent, happen, emerge, become known, develop, come to light, crop up *(informal)*: *It turned out that I knew the person who got shot.* **2** = **end up**, happen, result, work out, evolve, come to be, come about, transpire, pan out *(informal)*, eventuate: *Things don't always turn out the way we expect.* **3** = **come**, be present, turn up, show up *(informal)*, go, appear, attend, gather, assemble, put in an appearance: *Thousands of people turned out for the funeral.*
turn over = **overturn**, tip over, flip over, upend, be upset, reverse, capsize, keel over: *The buggy turned over and she was thrown out.*
turn someone off = **repel**, bore, put someone off, disgust, offend, irritate, alienate, sicken, displease, nauseate, gross someone out *(U.S. slang)*, disenchant, lose your interest: *Aggressive men turn me off completely.*
turn someone on = **arouse**, attract, excite, thrill, stimulate, please, press someone's buttons *(slang)*, work someone up, titillate, ring someone's bell *(U.S. slang)*, arouse someone's desire: *The body that turns men on doesn't have to be perfect.*
turn someone out = **expel**, drive out, evict, throw out, fire *(informal)*, dismiss, sack *(informal)*, axe *(informal)*, discharge, oust, relegate, banish, deport, put out, cashier, unseat, dispossess, kick out *(informal)*, cast out, drum out, show the door, turf out *(Brit. informal)*, give someone the sack *(informal)*, give someone the bum's rush *(slang)*, kiss off *(slang, chiefly U.S. & Canad.)*, kennet *(Austral. slang)*, jeff *(Austral. slang)*: *It was a monastery but the authorities turned all the monks out.*
turn something down 1 = **refuse**, decline, reject, spurn, rebuff, say no to, repudiate, abstain from, throw something out: *I thanked him for the offer but turned it down.* **2** = **lower**, soften, reduce the volume of, mute, lessen, muffle, quieten, diminish: *The police told the DJs to turn down the music.*
turn something in = **hand in**, return, deliver, give back, give up, hand over, submit, surrender, tender: *He told her to turn in her library books.*
turn something off = **switch off**, turn out, put out, stop, kill, cut out, shut down, unplug, flick off: *She had turned off the light to go to sleep.*
turn something on = **switch on**, put on, activate, start, start up, ignite, kick-start, set in motion, energize: *Why haven't you turned the lights on?*
turn something out 1 = **turn off**, put out, switch off, extinguish, disconnect, unplug, flick off: *I'll read till they come round to turn the lights out.* **2** = **produce**, make, process, finish, manufacture, assemble, put together, put out, bring out, fabricate, churn out: *They have been turning out great furniture for 400 years.*
turn something over 1 = **flip over**, flick through, leaf through: *She was turning over the pages of the directory.* **2** = **consider**, think about, contemplate, ponder, reflect on, wonder about, mull over, think over, deliberate on, give thought to, ruminate about, revolve: *You could see her turning things over in her mind.* **3** = **hand over**, transfer, deliver, commit, give up, yield, surrender, pass on, render, assign, commend, give over: *The lawyer turned over the release papers.* **4** = **start up**, warm up, activate, switch on, crank, set something in motion, set something going, switch on the ignition of: *I squeezed into the seat and turned the engine over.*
turn something up 1 = **find**, reveal, discover, expose, come up with, disclose, unearth, dig up, bring to light: *Investigations have never turned up any evidence.* **2** = **increase**, raise, boost, enhance, intensify, amplify, increase the volume of, make louder: *I turned the volume up.*
turn up 1 = **arrive**, come, appear, show up *(informal)*, show *(informal)*, attend, put in an appearance, show your face: *He turned up on Christmas Day with a friend.* **2** = **come to light**, be found, show up, pop up, materialize, appear: *The rare spoon turned up in an old house in Devon.*

PROVERBS
One good turn deserves another
A bad penny always turns up

turning NOUN **1** = **turn-off**, turn, junction, crossroads, side road, exit: *Take the next turning on the right.* **2** = **bend**, turn, curve

turning point NOUN = **crossroads**, critical moment, decisive moment, change, crisis, crux, moment of truth, point of no return, moment of decision, climacteric, tipping point

turn-off NOUN = **turning**, turn, branch, exit, side road

turnout NOUN = **attendance**, crowd, audience, gate, assembly, congregation, number, throng, assemblage

turnover NOUN **1** = **output**, business, production, flow, volume, yield, productivity, outturn *(rare)*: *The company had a turnover of £3.8 million.* **2** = **movement**, replacement, coming and going, change: *Short-term contracts increase staff turnover.*

tussle VERB = **fight**, battle, struggle, scrap *(informal)*, contend, wrestle, vie,

Introduction to the Corpus

The essays in this thesaurus aim to take a new approach to style, vocabulary, and usage, by analysing the language of some of the best-loved classics of the past three centuries, and, in addition, the language of two of the most widely-read contemporary British newspapers, *The Times* and *The Sun*. There are over eighty essays on classic prose-writers from Britain, Ireland, the United States, Canada, Australia, New Zealand, and South Africa. Included are novelists such as Jane Austen, Mark Twain, and James Joyce; short-story writers such as Edgar Allan Poe and Katherine Mansfield; and children's authors such as Lewis Carroll and LM Montgomery. Some eminent non-fiction writers are also covered, such as Abraham Lincoln, whose language is recorded in his speeches and letters. As well as essays on individuals, there are several discussions of linguistic features of classic literature in general; attention has been paid to areas which are considered problematic or controversial today, such as the split infinitive and the use of *who* and *whom*. In addition, there are six essays comparing the language used in *The Times* with that of *The Sun*.

The essays are all based on the analysis of a *corpus*, an electronic searchable collection of texts. Both *The Times* and *The Sun* are included in Collins' corpus of present-day English, the *Bank of English*. (References to *The Times* include *The Sunday Times*, while references to *The Sun* also cover its Sunday sister, *The News of the World*.) For the classic authors, a new corpus was built for the purpose: out-of-copyright texts by each author were collected, tagged for linguistic analysis, and put together as a single corpus.

These corpora allow for highly sophisticated linguistic analysis. For each author, a list of their most frequent words, or *lemmas*, was created. (A lemma is a word with all its inflections; so, for example, if one of Charles Dickens' most frequent lemmas is *man*, this includes the plural form *men* as well as singular *man*.) Lists of parts of speech were also generated to show, for instance, what Jane Austen's most frequent adjectives were. Using these lists as guides, words were then viewed using a concordance programme. For example, a search for the adjective *sensible* in Austen's works yields a list of examples including:

a <sensible> man about seven or eight-and-thirty
became gradually <sensible> that he was inviting her
more <sensible> of the disadvantages she has been under

From these few examples it is evident that Austen uses *sensible* to mean both 'intelligent, having good sense' (as in *a sensible man*) and 'aware' (in *sensible that* and *sensible of*). In addition, *word sketches* were created for particular words. The word sketch (developed by Lexical Computing, Ltd) is a tool which presents a profile of a word and its *collocates* – other words which it tends to be associated with. For example, a word sketch of *sensible* in Austen's works shows that it most frequently collocates with *man* (in the 'intelligent' sense) and that characters are *sensible of* ('aware of') a range of feelings and qualities such as *pleasure*, *impropriety*, and *change*.

Comparisons were also made between different parts of corpora, for example between *The Times* and *The Sun*, or between an eighteenth-century writer's use of a word and the use of that word in modern English. All comparisons of frequency were based on the relative size of the corpora, and calculated per million words of text.

In addition, searches were made of particular grammatical patterns. For example, one can search for the word *to* and the bare infinitive of a verb, with one or more intervening words. This yields examples of split infinitives such as *to reasonably hope* and *to totally omit*. Or one can find out how often the traditionally plural noun *data* is used as a singular, by searching for *data* followed by a singular verb and finding examples such as *the data is available*. Such examples have to be manually checked (for example to exclude sentences such as *the collection of data is laborious*, where the verb relates to *collection* rather than *data*). As in all corpus linguistic studies, the corpus is only the starting-point, and requires human analysis. The essays in this thesaurus aim to combine computational analysis with human interpretation in order to offer glimpses of the way that the English language has been used by some of its greatest writers.

brawl, grapple, scuffle: *They ended up tussling with the security staff.*
▷ NOUN **= fight**, scrap (*informal*), brawl, scuffle, battle, competition, struggle, conflict, contest, set-to (*informal*), bout, contention, fray, punch-up (*Brit. informal*), fracas, shindig (*informal*), scrimmage, shindy (*informal*), bagarre (*French*), biffo (*Austral. slang*): *The referee booked him for a tussle with the goalie.*

tutelage NOUN **= guidance**, education, instruction, preparation, schooling, charge, care, teaching, protection, custody, tuition, dependence, patronage, guardianship, wardship

tutor NOUN **= teacher**, coach, instructor, educator, guide, governor, guardian, lecturer, guru, mentor, preceptor, master *or* mistress, schoolmaster *or* schoolmistress: *He surprised his tutors by failing the exam.*
▷ VERB **= teach**, educate, school, train, coach, guide, discipline, lecture, drill, instruct, edify, direct: *She was at home, being tutored with her brothers.*

tutorial NOUN **= seminar**, lesson, individual instruction: *Methods of study include lectures, tutorials and practical work.*
▷ ADJECTIVE **= teaching**, coaching, guiding, instructional: *Students may seek tutorial guidance.*

TV NOUN **= television**, telly (*Brit. informal*), the box (*Brit. informal*), receiver, the tube (*slang*), television set, TV set, small screen (*informal*), gogglebox (*Brit. slang*), idiot box (*slang*)

twaddle NOUN **= nonsense**, rubbish, rot, garbage (*informal*), pants (*slang*), gossip, crap (*slang*), trash, hot air (*informal*), tosh (*slang, chiefly Brit.*), waffle (*informal, chiefly Brit.*), pap, bilge (*informal*), drivel, tripe (*informal*), guff (*slang*), tattle, moonshine, verbiage, gabble, claptrap (*informal*), gobbledegook (*informal*), hogwash, hokum (*slang, chiefly U.S. & Canad.*), rigmarole, blather, piffle (*informal*), poppycock (*informal*), inanity, balderdash, bosh (*informal*), eyewash (*informal*), trumpery, tommyrot, foolish talk, horsefeathers (*U.S. slang*), bunkum *or* buncombe (*chiefly U.S.*), bizzo (*Austral. slang*), bull's wool (*Austral. & N.Z. slang*)

tweak VERB **= twist**, pull, pinch, jerk, squeeze, nip, twitch: *He tweaked my ear roughly.*
▷ NOUN **= twist**, pull, squeeze, pinch, jerk, nip, twitch: *a tweak on the ear*

twee ADJECTIVE **1 = sweet**, pretty, cute, sentimental, quaint, dainty, cutesy (*informal, chiefly U.S.*), bijou, precious: *twee musical boxes shaped like cottages* **2 = sentimental**, over-sentimental, soppy (*Brit. informal*), mawkish, affected, precious: *Although twee at times, the script is well-constructed.*

twiddle VERB **= fiddle with**, adjust, finger, play with, juggle, wiggle (*informal*), twirl, jiggle, monkey with (*informal*)

twig¹ NOUN **= branch**, stick, sprig, offshoot, shoot, spray, withe: *There was a slight sound of a twig breaking underfoot.*

twig² VERB **= understand**, get, see, find out, grasp, make out, rumble (*Brit. informal*), catch on (*informal*), comprehend, fathom, tumble to (*informal*): *By the time she'd twigged what it was all about, it was too late.*

twilight NOUN **1 = dusk**, evening, sunset, early evening, nightfall, sundown, gloaming (*Scot. poetic*), close of day, evo (*Austral. slang*): *They returned at twilight and set off for the bar.* **OPPOSITE:** dawn **2 = half-light**, gloom, dimness, semi-darkness: *the deepening autumn twilight* **3 = decline**, last years, final years, closing years, autumn, downturn, ebb, last phase: *Now they are both in the twilight of their careers.* **OPPOSITE:** height
▷ ADJECTIVE **1 = evening**, dim, darkening, evo (*Austral. slang*): *the summer twilight sky* **2 = declining**, last, final, dying, ebbing: *the twilight years of the Hapsburg Empire*

twin NOUN **= double**, counterpart, mate, match, fellow, clone, duplicate, lookalike, likeness, ringer (*slang*), corollary: *the twin of the chair she had at the cottage*
▷ VERB **= pair**, match, join, couple, link, yoke: *The borough is twinned with Kasel in Germany.*
▷ ADJECTIVE **= identical**, matched, matching, double, paired, parallel, corresponding, dual, duplicate, twofold, geminate: *the twin spires of the cathedral*

twine NOUN **= string**, cord, yarn, strong thread: *a ball of twine*
▷ VERB **1 = twist together**, weave, knit, braid, splice, interweave, plait, entwine, interlace, twist: *He twined his fingers into hers.* **2 = coil**, wind, surround, bend, wrap, twist, curl, loop, spiral, meander, encircle, wreathe: *These strands of molecules twine around each other.*

twinge NOUN **1 = pang**, twitch, tweak, throe (*rare*), twist: *I would have twinges of guilt occasionally.* **2 = pain**, sharp pain, gripe, stab, bite, twist, stitch, pinch, throb, twitch, prick, spasm, tweak, tic: *the occasional twinge of indigestion*

twinkle VERB **= sparkle**, flash, shine, glitter, gleam, blink, flicker, wink, shimmer, glint, glisten, scintillate, coruscate: *At night, lights twinkle in distant villages across the valleys.*
▷ NOUN **1 = sparkle**, light, flash, spark, shine, glittering, gleam, blink, flicker, wink, shimmer, glimmer, glistening, scintillation, coruscation: *A kindly twinkle came into his eyes.* **2 = moment**, second, shake (*informal*), flash, instant, tick (*Brit. informal*), twinkling, split second, jiffy (*informal*), trice, two shakes of a lamb's tail (*informal*): *Hours can pass in a twinkle.*

twinkling *or* **twink** NOUN **= moment**, second, flash, instant, tick (*Brit. informal*), twinkle, split second, jiffy (*informal*), trice, two shakes of a lamb's tail (*informal*), shake (*informal*), bat of an eye (*informal*)

twirl VERB **1 = twiddle**, turn, rotate, wind, spin, twist, revolve, whirl: *She twirled an empty glass in her fingers.* **2 = turn**, whirl, wheel, spin, twist, pivot, gyrate, pirouette, turn on your heel: *Several hundred people twirl around the dance floor.*
▷ NOUN **= turn**, spin, rotation, whirl, wheel, revolution, twist, pirouette, gyration: *with a twirl of his silver-handled cane*

twist VERB **1 = coil**, curl, wind, plait, wrap, screw, twirl: *She twisted her hair into a bun.* **2 = intertwine**, wind, weave, braid, interweave, plait, entwine, twine, wreathe, interlace: *The fibres are twisted together during spinning.* **3 = distort**, screw up, contort, mangle, mangulate (*Austral. slang*): *The car was left a mess of twisted metal.* **OPPOSITE:** straighten **4 = sprain**, turn, rick, wrench: *He fell and twisted his ankle.* **5 = misrepresent**, distort, misquote, alter, change, pervert, warp, falsify, garble: *It's a shame the way the media can twist your words.* **6 = squirm**, wriggle, writhe: *He tried to twist out of my grasp.*
▷ NOUN **1 = surprise**, change, turn, development, revelation: *This little story has a twist in its tail.* **2 = development**, emphasis, variation, slant: *The battle of the sexes took on a new twist.* **3 = wind**, turn, spin, swivel, twirl: *The bag is resealed with a simple twist of the valve.* **4 = coil**, roll, curl, hank, twine: *the bare bulb hanging from a twist of flex* **5 = curve**, turn, bend, loop, arc, kink, zigzag, convolution, dog-leg, undulation: *the twists and turns of the existing track* **6 = trait**, fault, defect, peculiarity, bent, characteristic, flaw, deviation, quirk, eccentricity, oddity, aberration, imperfection, kink, foible, idiosyncrasy, proclivity, crotchet: *If only she could alter this personality twist.* **7 = sprain**, turn, pull, jerk, wrench: *A twist of the ankle denied him a place on the substitutes' bench.*

twit NOUN **= fool**, idiot, jerk (*slang, chiefly U.S. & Canad.*), charlie (*Brit. informal*), dope (*informal*), clown, ass, plank (*Brit. slang*), berk (*Brit. slang*), wally (*slang*), prat (*slang*), plonker (*slang*), geek (*slang*), chump (*informal*), oaf, simpleton, airhead (*slang*), dipstick (*Brit. slang*), gonzo (*slang*), schmuck (*U.S. slang*), dork (*slang*), nitwit (*informal*), blockhead, ninny, divvy (*Brit. slang*), pillock (*Brit. slang*), halfwit, silly-billy (*informal*), nincompoop, dweeb (*U.S. slang*), putz (*U.S. slang*), weenie (*U.S. informal*), eejit (*Scot. & Irish*), dumb-ass (*slang*), numpty (*Scot. informal*), doofus (*slang, chiefly U.S.*), juggins (*Brit. informal*), dickwit (*slang*), nerd *or* nurd (*slang*), numbskull *or* numskull, twerp *or* twirp *(informal)*, dorba *or* dorb *(Austral. slang)*, bogan *(Austral. slang)*

twitch VERB **1 = jerk**, blink, flutter, jump, squirm: *His left eyelid twitched involuntarily.* **2 = pull (at)**, snatch (at), tug (at), pluck (at), yank (at): *He twitched his curtains to check on callers.*
▷ NOUN **= jerk**, tic, spasm, twinge, jump, blink, flutter, tremor: *He developed a nervous twitch.*

twitter VERB **1 = chirrup**, whistle, chatter, trill, chirp, warble, cheep, tweet: *There were birds twittering in the trees.* **2 = chatter**, chat, rabbit (on) *(Brit. informal)*, gossip, babble, gab *(informal)*, prattle, natter, jabber, blather, prate: *They were twittering excitedly about their new dresses.*
▷ NOUN **= chirrup**, call, song, cry, whistle, chatter, trill, chirp, warble, cheep, tweet: *She would waken to the twitter of birds.*

two-faced ADJECTIVE **= hypocritical**, false, deceiving, treacherous, deceitful, untrustworthy, insincere, double-dealing, duplicitous, dissembling, perfidious, Janus-faced **OPPOSITE:** honest

tycoon NOUN **= magnate**, capitalist, baron, industrialist, financier, fat cat *(slang, chiefly U.S.)*, mogul, captain of industry, potentate, wealthy businessman, big cheese *(slang, old-fashioned)*, plutocrat, big noise *(informal)*, merchant prince

type NOUN **1 = kind**, sort, class, variety, group, form, order, style, species, breed, strain, category, stamp, kidney, genre, classification, ilk, subdivision: *There are various types of the disease.* **2 = print**, printing, face, case, characters, font, fount: *The correction has already been set in type.*

typhoon NOUN **= storm**, tornado, cyclone, tempest, squall, tropical storm

typical ADJECTIVE **1 = archetypal**, standard, model, normal, classic, stock, essential, representative, usual, conventional, regular, characteristic, orthodox, indicative, illustrative, archetypical, stereotypical: *such typical schoolgirl pastimes as horse-riding and reading* **OPPOSITE:** unusual **2 = characteristic**, in keeping, in character, true to type: *That's just typical of you, isn't it?* **3 = average**, normal, usual, conventional, routine, regular, orthodox, predictable, run-of-the-mill, bog-standard *(Brit. & Irish slang)*: *not exactly your typical Sunday afternoon stroll*

typify VERB **= represent**, illustrate, sum up, characterize, embody, exemplify, personify, incarnate, epitomize

tyrannical *or* **tyrannic** ADJECTIVE **= oppressive**, cruel, authoritarian, dictatorial, severe, absolute, unreasonable, arbitrary, unjust, autocratic, inhuman, coercive, imperious, domineering, overbearing, magisterial, despotic, high-handed, peremptory, overweening, tyrannous **OPPOSITE:** liberal

tyranny NOUN **= oppression**, cruelty, dictatorship, authoritarianism, reign of terror, despotism, autocracy, absolutism, coercion, high-handedness, harsh discipline, unreasonableness, imperiousness, peremptoriness **OPPOSITE:** liberality

> **QUOTATIONS**
> Tyranny is always better organised than freedom
> [Charles Péguy *Basic Verities*]

tyrant NOUN **= dictator**, bully, authoritarian, oppressor, despot, autocrat, absolutist, martinet, slave-driver, Hitler

> **QUOTATIONS**
> The hand of vengeance found the bed
> To which the purple tyrant fled;
> The iron hand crushed the tyrant's head,
> And became a tyrant in his stead
> [William Blake *The Grey Monk*]
>
> Tyrants seldom want pretexts
> [Edmund Burke *letter to a Member of the National Assembly*]
>
> Nature has left this tincture in the blood,
> That all men would be tyrants if they could
> [Daniel Defoe *The History of the Kentish Petition*]
>
> When he laughed, respectable senators burst with laughter,
> And when he cried the little children died in the streets
> [W.H. Auden *Epitaph on a Tyrant*]

tyro *or* **tiro** NOUN **= beginner**, novice, apprentice, learner, neophyte, rookie *(informal)*, greenhorn *(informal)*, catechumen

Uu

ubiquitous ADJECTIVE **= ever-present**, pervasive, omnipresent, all-over, everywhere, universal

ugly ADJECTIVE **1 = unattractive**, homely *(chiefly U.S.)*, plain, unsightly, unlovely, unprepossessing, not much to look at, no oil painting *(informal)*, ill-favoured, hard-featured, hard-favoured: *She makes me feel dowdy and ugly.* **OPPOSITE:** beautiful **2 = unpleasant**, shocking, terrible, offensive, nasty, disgusting, revolting, obscene, hideous, monstrous, vile, distasteful, horrid, repulsive, frightful, objectionable, disagreeable, repugnant: *an ugly scene* **OPPOSITE:** pleasant **3 = bad-tempered**, nasty, sullen, surly, threatening, dangerous, angry, forbidding, menacing, sinister, ominous, malevolent, spiteful, baleful, bodeful: *He's in an ugly mood today.* **OPPOSITE:** good-natured

ulcer NOUN **= sore**, abscess, gathering, peptic ulcer, gumboil

ulterior ADJECTIVE **= hidden**, secret, concealed, personal, secondary, selfish, covert, undisclosed, unexpressed **OPPOSITE:** obvious

ultimate ADJECTIVE **1 = final**, eventual, conclusive, last, end, furthest, extreme, terminal, decisive: *He said it is still not possible to predict the ultimate outcome.* **2 = fundamental**, basic, primary, radical, elemental: *the ultimate cause of what's happened* **3 = supreme**, highest, greatest, maximum, paramount, most significant, superlative, topmost: *Of course the ultimate authority remained the presidency.* **4 = worst**, greatest, utmost, extreme: *Treachery was the ultimate sin.* **5 = best**, greatest, supreme, optimum, quintessential: *the ultimate luxury foods*
▷ NOUN **= epitome**, height, greatest, summit, peak, extreme, perfection, the last word: *This hotel is the ultimate in luxury.*

ultimately ADVERB **1 = finally**, eventually, in the end, after all, at last, at the end of the day, sooner or later, in the fullness of time, in due time: *a tough but ultimately worthwhile struggle* **2 = fundamentally**, essentially, basically, primarily, at heart, deep down: *Ultimately, Bismarck's revisionism scarcely affected British interests.*

ultra-modern ADJECTIVE **= advanced**, progressive, avant-garde, futuristic, ahead of its time, modernistic, neoteric *(rare)*

umbrella NOUN **1 = brolly** *(Brit. informal)*, parasol, sunshade, gamp: *Harry held an umbrella over Dawn.* **2 = cover**, protection, guardianship, backing, support, charge, care, agency, responsibility, guidance, patronage, auspices, aegis, safe keeping, protectorship: *under the moral umbrella of the United Nations*

umpire NOUN **= referee**, judge, ref *(informal)*, arbiter, arbitrator, moderator, adjudicator, umpie *(Austral. slang)*: *The umpire's decision is final.*
▷ VERB **= referee**, judge, adjudicate, arbitrate, call *(Sport)*, moderate, mediate: *He umpired for school football matches.*

umpteen ADJECTIVE **= very many**, numerous, countless, millions, gazillions *(informal)*, considerable, a good many, a thousand and one, ever so many

unable ADJECTIVE *(with* **to***)* **= incapable**, inadequate, powerless, unfit, unfitted, not able, impotent, not up to, unqualified, ineffectual, not equal to **OPPOSITE:** able

unaccountable ADJECTIVE **1 = inexplicable**, mysterious, baffling, odd, strange, puzzling, peculiar, incomprehensible, inscrutable, unfathomable, unexplainable: *He had an unaccountable change of mind.* **OPPOSITE:** understandable **2 = not answerable**, exempt, not responsible, free, unliable: *Economic policy should not be run by an unaccountable committee.*

unaccustomed ADJECTIVE **1 = unfamiliar**, unusual, unexpected, new, special, surprising, strange, remarkable, unprecedented, uncommon, out of the ordinary, unwonted: *He comforted me with unaccustomed gentleness.* **OPPOSITE:** familiar **2** *(with* **to***)* **= not used to**, unfamiliar with, unused to, not given to, a newcomer to, a novice at, inexperienced at, unversed in, unpractised in: *They were unaccustomed to such military setbacks.* **OPPOSITE:** used to

unaffected[1] ADJECTIVE **= natural**, genuine, unpretentious, simple, plain, straightforward, naive, sincere, honest, unassuming, unspoilt, unsophisticated, dinkum *(Austral. & N.Z. informal)*, artless, ingenuous, without airs, unstudied: *this unaffected, charming couple* **OPPOSITE:** pretentious

unaffected[2] ADJECTIVE *(often with* **by***)* **= impervious to**, unchanged, untouched, unimpressed, unmoved, unaltered, not influenced, unresponsive to, unstirred: *She seemed totally unaffected by what she'd drunk.* **OPPOSITE:** affected

unanimity NOUN **= agreement**, accord, consensus, concert, unity, harmony, chorus, unison, assent, concord, one mind, concurrence, like-mindedness **OPPOSITE:** disagreement

unanimous ADJECTIVE **1 = agreed**, united, in agreement, agreeing, at one, harmonious, like-minded, concordant, of one mind, of the same mind, in complete accord: *Editors were unanimous in their condemnation of the proposals.* **OPPOSITE:** divided **2 = united**, common, concerted, solid, consistent, harmonious, undivided, congruent, concordant, unopposed: *the unanimous vote for Hungarian membership* **OPPOSITE:** split

unanimously ADVERB **= without exception**, by common consent, without opposition, with one accord, unitedly, nem. con.

unarmed ADJECTIVE **= defenceless**, helpless, unprotected, without arms, unarmoured, weaponless **OPPOSITE:** armed

unassailable ADJECTIVE **= undeniable**, indisputable, irrefutable, sound, proven, positive, absolute, conclusive, incontrovertible, incontestable: *His legal position is unassailable.* **OPPOSITE:** doubtful

unassuming ADJECTIVE **= modest**, quiet, humble, meek, simple, reserved, retiring, unpretentious, unobtrusive, self-effacing, diffident, unassertive, unostentatious **OPPOSITE:** conceited

unattached ADJECTIVE **1 = single**, available, unmarried, on your own, by yourself, a free agent, not spoken for, left on the shelf, footloose and fancy-free, unengaged: *Those who are unattached may find that a potential mate is very close.* **2** *(often with* **to***)* **= independent (from)**, unaffiliated (to), nonaligned (to), free (from), autonomous (from), uncommitted (to): *There's one nursery which is unattached to any school.* **OPPOSITE:** attached (to)

unavoidable ADJECTIVE **= inevitable**, inescapable, inexorable, sure, certain, necessary, fated, compulsory, obligatory, bound to happen, ineluctable

unaware ADJECTIVE **= ignorant**, unconscious, oblivious, in the dark *(informal)*, unsuspecting, uninformed, unknowing, heedless,

u

unenlightened, unmindful, not in the loop *(informal)*, incognizant **OPPOSITE:** aware

unawares ADVERB **1 = by surprise**, unprepared, off guard, suddenly, unexpectedly, abruptly, aback, without warning, on the hop *(Brit. informal)*, caught napping: *The suspect was taken unawares.* **OPPOSITE:** prepared **2 = unknowingly**, unwittingly, unconsciously: *They were entertaining an angel unawares.* **OPPOSITE:** knowingly

unbalanced ADJECTIVE **1 = deranged**, disturbed, unstable, touched, mad, crazy, barking *(slang)*, eccentric, insane, irrational, erratic, lunatic, demented, unsound, unhinged, loopy *(informal)*, out to lunch *(informal)*, barking mad *(slang)*, gonzo *(slang)*, not all there, doolally *(slang)*, off your trolley *(slang)*, up the pole *(informal)*, non compos mentis *(Latin)*, not the full shilling *(informal)*, wacko *or* whacko *(informal)*, off the air *(Austral. slang)*, daggy *(Austral. & N.Z. informal)*: *He was shown to be mentally unbalanced.* **2 = biased**, one-sided, prejudiced, unfair, partial, partisan, unjust, inequitable: *unbalanced and unfair reporting* **3 = irregular**, not balanced, lacking: *unbalanced and uncontrolled diets* **4 = shaky**, unstable, wobbly: *The Loganair BAe 46 was noticeably unbalanced.* **OPPOSITE:** stable

unbearable ADJECTIVE **= intolerable**, insufferable, unendurable, too much *(informal)*, unacceptable, oppressive, insupportable **OPPOSITE:** tolerable

unbeatable ADJECTIVE **1 = unsurpassed**, matchless, unsurpassable: *These resorts remain unbeatable in terms of price.* **2 = invincible**, unstoppable, indomitable, unconquerable: *The opposition was unbeatable.*

unbeaten ADJECTIVE **= undefeated**, winning, triumphant, victorious, unsurpassed, unbowed, unvanquished, unsubdued

unbelievable ADJECTIVE **1 = wonderful**, excellent, superb, fantastic *(informal)*, mean *(slang)*, great *(informal)*, topping *(Brit. slang)*, bad *(slang)*, cracking *(Brit. informal)*, crucial *(slang)*, smashing *(informal)*, magnificent, fabulous *(informal)*, divine *(informal)*, glorious, terrific *(informal)*, splendid, sensational *(informal)*, mega *(slang)*, sovereign, awesome *(slang)*, colossal, super *(informal)*, wicked *(informal)*, def *(slang)*, brill *(informal)*, stupendous, bodacious *(slang, chiefly U.S.)*, boffo *(slang)*, jim-dandy *(slang)*, chillin' *(U.S. slang)*, booshit *(Austral. slang)*, exo *(Austral. slang)*, sik *(Austral. slang)*, rad *(informal)*, phat *(slang)*, schmick *(Austral. informal)*, beaut *(informal)*, barrie *(Scot. slang)*, belting *(Brit. slang)*, pearler *(Austral. slang)*: *His guitar solos are just unbelievable.* **OPPOSITE:** terrible **2 = incredible**, impossible, unthinkable, astonishing, staggering, questionable, improbable, inconceivable, preposterous, unconvincing, unimaginable, outlandish, far-fetched, implausible, beyond belief, jaw-dropping, eye-popping *(informal)*, cock-and-bull *(informal)*: *I find it unbelievable that people can accept this sort of behaviour.* **OPPOSITE:** believable

unbeliever NOUN **= atheist**, sceptic, disbeliever, agnostic, infidel, doubting Thomas

unborn ADJECTIVE **= expected**, awaited, embryonic, in utero *(Latin)*

unbridled ADJECTIVE **= unrestrained**, uncontrolled, unchecked, violent, excessive, rampant, unruly, full-on *(informal)*, wanton, riotous, intemperate, ungovernable, unconstrained, licentious, ungoverned, uncurbed

unbroken ADJECTIVE **1 = intact**, whole, undamaged, complete, total, entire, solid, untouched, unscathed, unspoiled, unimpaired: *Against all odds her glasses remained unbroken after the explosion.* **OPPOSITE:** broken **2 = continuous**, uninterrupted, constant, successive, endless, progressive, incessant, ceaseless, unremitting: *The ruling party has governed the country for an unbroken thirty years.* **OPPOSITE:** interrupted **3 = undisturbed**, uninterrupted, sound, fast, deep, profound, untroubled, unruffled: *We maintained an almost unbroken silence.* **4 = untamed**, wild, undomesticated: *The car plunged like an unbroken horse.*

unburden VERB **1 = reveal**, confide, disclose, lay bare, unbosom: *He had to unburden his soul to somebody.* **2 = unload**, relieve, discharge, lighten, disencumber, disburden, ease the load of: *The human touch is one of the surest ways of unburdening stresses.* **unburden yourself = confess**, come clean about *(informal)*, get something off your chest *(informal)*, tell all about, empty yourself, spill your guts about *(slang)*, make a clean breast of something: *Many came to unburden themselves of emotional problems.*

uncanny ADJECTIVE **1 = weird**, strange, mysterious, queer, unearthly, eerie, supernatural, unnatural, spooky *(informal)*, creepy *(informal)*, eldritch *(poetic)*, preternatural: *I had this uncanny feeling that Alice was warning me.* **2 = extraordinary**, remarkable, incredible, unusual, fantastic, astonishing, exceptional, astounding, singular, miraculous, unheard-of, prodigious: *The hero bears an uncanny resemblance to Kirk Douglas.*

uncertain ADJECTIVE **1 = unsure**, undecided, at a loss, vague, unclear, doubtful, dubious, ambivalent, hazy, hesitant, vacillating, in two minds, undetermined, irresolute: *He stopped, uncertain how to put the question tactfully.* **OPPOSITE:** sure **2 = doubtful**, undetermined, unpredictable, insecure, questionable, ambiguous, unreliable, precarious, indefinite, indeterminate, incalculable, iffy *(informal)*, changeable, indistinct, chancy, unforeseeable, unsettled, unresolved, in the balance, unconfirmed, up in the air, unfixed, conjectural, sketchy *(informal)*: *Students all over the country are facing an uncertain future.* **OPPOSITE:** decided

uncertainty NOUN **1 = unpredictability**, precariousness, state of suspense, ambiguity, unreliability, fickleness, inconclusiveness, chanciness, changeableness: *a period of political uncertainty* **OPPOSITE:** predictability **2 = doubt**, confusion, dilemma, misgiving, qualm, bewilderment, quandary, puzzlement, perplexity, mystification: *The magazine ignores all the uncertainties males currently face.* **OPPOSITE:** confidence **3 = hesitancy**, hesitation, indecision, lack of confidence, vagueness, irresolution: *There was a hint of uncertainty in his voice.*

uncharted ADJECTIVE **= unexplored**, unknown, undiscovered, strange, virgin, unfamiliar, unplumbed, not mapped

> **USAGE**
> *Unchartered* is sometimes mistakenly used where *uncharted* is meant: *We did not want to pioneer in completely uncharted* (not *unchartered*) *territory.*

unclean ADJECTIVE **1 = dirty**, soiled, foul, contaminated, polluted, nasty, filthy, defiled, impure, scuzzy *(slang, chiefly U.S.)*: *By bathing in unclean water, they expose themselves to contamination.* **OPPOSITE:** clean **2 = immoral**, corrupt, impure, evil, dirty, nasty, foul, polluted, filthy, scuzzy *(slang, chiefly U.S.)*: *unclean thoughts*

uncomfortable ADJECTIVE **1 = uneasy**, troubled, disturbed, embarrassed, distressed, awkward, out of place, self-conscious, disquieted, ill at ease, discomfited, like a fish out of water: *The request for money made them feel uncomfortable.* **OPPOSITE:** comfortable **2 = painful**, awkward, irritating, hard, rough, troublesome, disagreeable, causing discomfort: *Wigs are hot and uncomfortable to wear constantly.*

uncommitted ADJECTIVE **= undecided**, uninvolved, nonpartisan, nonaligned, free, floating, neutral, not involved, unattached, free-floating, (sitting) on the fence

uncommon ADJECTIVE **1 = rare**, unusual, odd, novel, strange, bizarre, curious, peculiar, unfamiliar, scarce, queer, singular, few and far between, out of the ordinary, infrequent, thin on the ground: *Cancer of the breast in young women is uncommon.* **OPPOSITE:** common

2 = extraordinary, rare, remarkable, special, outstanding, superior, distinctive, exceptional, unprecedented, notable, singular, unparalleled, noteworthy, inimitable, incomparable: *Both are blessed with an uncommon ability to fix things.*
OPPOSITE: ordinary

uncommonly ADVERB
1 = exceptionally, very, extremely, remarkably, particularly, strangely, seriously *(informal)*, unusually, peculiarly, to the nth degree: *Mary was uncommonly good at tennis.* **2** *(used in negative constructions)* **= rarely**, occasionally, seldom, not often, infrequently, hardly ever, only now and then, scarcely ever: *Not uncommonly, family strains may remain hidden behind complaints.*

uncompromising ADJECTIVE
= inflexible, strict, rigid, decided, firm, tough, stubborn, hardline, die-hard, inexorable, steadfast, unyielding, obstinate, intransigent, unbending, obdurate, stiff-necked

unconcerned ADJECTIVE
= untroubled, relaxed, unperturbed, nonchalant, easy, careless, not bothered, serene, callous, carefree, unruffled, blithe, insouciant, unworried, not giving a toss *(informal)*
OPPOSITE: concerned

unconditional ADJECTIVE **= absolute**, full, complete, total, positive, entire, utter, explicit, outright, unlimited, downright, unqualified, unrestricted, out-and-out, plenary, categorical, unreserved **OPPOSITE:** qualified

unconscious ADJECTIVE **1 = senseless**, knocked out, out cold *(informal)*, out, stunned, numb, dazed, blacked out *(informal)*, in a coma, comatose, stupefied, asleep, out for the count *(informal)*, insensible, dead to the world *(informal)*: *By the time ambulancemen arrived he was unconscious.*
OPPOSITE: awake **2 = unaware**, ignorant, oblivious, unsuspecting, lost to, blind to, in ignorance, unknowing: *Mr Battersby was apparently quite unconscious of their presence.*
OPPOSITE: aware **3 = unintentional**, unwitting, unintended, inadvertent, accidental, unpremeditated: *'You're well out of it,' he said with unconscious brutality.* **OPPOSITE:** intentional
4 = subconscious, automatic, suppressed, repressed, inherent, reflex, instinctive, innate, involuntary, latent, subliminal, unrealized, gut *(informal)*: *an unconscious desire expressed solely during sleep*

unconventional ADJECTIVE
1 = unusual, unorthodox, odd, eccentric, different, individual, original, bizarre, way-out *(informal)*, informal, irregular, bohemian, far-out *(slang)*, idiosyncratic, off-the-wall *(slang)*, oddball *(informal)*, individualistic, out of the ordinary, offbeat, left-field *(informal)*, freakish, atypical, nonconformist, wacko *(slang)*, outré, uncustomary, daggy *(Austral. & N.Z. informal)*: *He was known for his unconventional behaviour.*
OPPOSITE: conventional
2 = unorthodox, original, unusual, irregular, atypical, different, uncustomary: *The vaccine had been produced by an unconventional technique.*
OPPOSITE: normal

uncover VERB **1 = reveal**, find, discover, expose, encounter, turn up, detect, disclose, unveil, come across, unearth, dig up, divulge, chance on, root out, unmask, lay bare, make known, blow the whistle on *(informal)*, bring to light, smoke out, take the wraps off, blow wide open *(slang)*, stumble on *or* across: *Auditors said they had uncovered evidence of fraud.*
OPPOSITE: conceal **2 = open**, unveil, unwrap, show, strip, expose, bare, lay bare, lift the lid, lay open: *When the seedlings sprout, uncover the tray.*

undaunted ADJECTIVE **= undeterred**, unflinching, not discouraged, not put off, brave, bold, courageous, gritty, fearless, resolute, gallant, intrepid, steadfast, indomitable, dauntless, undismayed, unfaltering, nothing daunted, undiscouraged, unshrinking

undecided ADJECTIVE **1 = unsure**, uncertain, uncommitted, torn, doubtful, dubious, wavering, hesitant, ambivalent, dithering *(chiefly Brit.)*, in two minds, irresolute, swithering *(Scot.)*: *She was still undecided as to what career she wanted to pursue.*
OPPOSITE: sure **2 = unsettled**, open, undetermined, vague, pending, tentative, in the balance, indefinite, debatable, up in the air, moot, iffy *(informal)*, unconcluded: *The release date for his record is still undecided.*
OPPOSITE: settled

undeniable ADJECTIVE **= certain**, evident, undoubted, incontrovertible, clear, sure, sound, proven, obvious, patent, manifest, beyond (a) doubt, unassailable, indisputable, irrefutable, unquestionable, beyond question, incontestable, indubitable
OPPOSITE: doubtful

under PREPOSITION **1 = below**, beneath, underneath, on the bottom of: *A path runs under the trees.*
OPPOSITE: over **2 = subordinate to**, subject to, reporting to, directed by, governed by, inferior to, secondary to, subservient to, junior to: *I am the new manager and you will be working under me.*
3 = included in, belonging to, subsumed under, comprised in: *under section 4 of the Family Law Reform Act*
▷ ADVERB **= below**, down, beneath, downward, to the bottom: *A hand came from behind and pushed his head under.*
OPPOSITE: up
▸ *related prefix:* sub-

undercover ADJECTIVE **= secret**, covert, clandestine, private, hidden, intelligence, underground, spy, concealed, confidential, hush-hush *(informal)*, surreptitious
OPPOSITE: open

undercurrent NOUN **1 = undertone**, feeling, atmosphere, sense, suggestion, trend, hint, flavour, tendency, drift, murmur, tenor, aura, tinge, vibes *(slang)*, vibrations, overtone, hidden feeling: *a deep undercurrent of racism in British society*
2 = undertow, tideway, riptide, rip, rip current, crosscurrent, underflow: *He tried to swim after him but the strong undercurrent swept them apart.*

undercut VERB **= underprice**, sell cheaply, sell at a loss, undersell, sacrifice, undercharge

underdog NOUN **= weaker party**, victim, loser, little fellow *(informal)*, outsider, fall guy *(informal)*

underestimate VERB
1 = undervalue, understate, underrate, diminish, play down, minimize, downgrade, miscalculate, trivialize, rate too low, underemphasize, hold cheap, misprize: *Never underestimate what you can learn from a group of like-minded people.*
OPPOSITE: overestimate
2 = underrate, undervalue, belittle, sell short *(informal)*, not do justice to, rate too low, set no store by, hold cheap, think too little of: *The first lesson I learnt was never to underestimate the enemy.* **OPPOSITE:** overrate

> **USAGE**
> *Underestimate* is sometimes wrongly used where *overestimate* is meant: *The importance of his work cannot be overestimated* (not *cannot be underestimated*).

undergo VERB **= experience**, go through, be subjected to, stand, suffer, bear, weather, sustain, endure, withstand, submit to

underground ADJECTIVE
1 = subterranean, basement, lower-level, sunken, covered, buried, below the surface, below ground, subterrestrial: *a rundown shopping area with an underground car park* **2 = secret**, undercover, covert, hidden, guerrilla, revolutionary, concealed, confidential, dissident, closet, subversive, clandestine, renegade, insurgent, hush-hush *(informal)*, surreptitious, cloak-and-dagger, hugger-mugger, insurrectionist, hole-and-corner, radical: *accused of organizing and financing an underground youth movement*
the underground 1 = the tube *(Brit.)*, the subway, the metro: *The underground is ideal for getting to work in Milan.* **2 = the Resistance**, partisans, freedom fighters, the Maquis: *US dollars were smuggled into the country to aid the underground.*

undergrowth NOUN **= scrub**, brush, underwood, bracken, brambles, briars, underbrush, brushwood, underbush

u

The Language of Olive Schreiner

Olive Schreiner (1855–1920) was a South African author who published her most famous work *The Story of an African Farm* under the pseudonym Ralph Iron. Her writing has a strong political agenda, marked particularly by a sharp critique of British imperialism and a commitment to female enfranchisement.

A striking feature of her fiction is the inclusion of a number of Afrikaans words. *Boer*, the Dutch for farmer, came to denote a South African settler of Dutch origin. It was in relatively common usage in English the late 19th and early 20th centuries, largely as a result of the successive *Boer* wars of this period. Occasionally, Schreiner uses the term to denote an individual farmer rather than a group of people, as in:

> At one desolate farm the **Boer** had a good deal to tell.

In Schreiner's work the most common Afrikaans word is *kopje*. Literally meaning 'little head', this signifies a small hill on the South African grasslands (or *veld*) and is often used by Schreiner to describe the exact location of her characters in a geographical setting otherwise devoid of prominent landmarks. People are variously *at the foot of, on the side of, on the other side of, behind, or halfway up* Schreiner's kopjes, which are often more specifically identified as *little*. Indeed, the only other adjectives she applies to them in her work are *broken, solitary, dark,* and *ironstone*. *Kraal*, in English a cattle enclosure, is the second most salient Afrikaans word in Schreiner's writing, while *mealies*, a kind of South African corn, also occurs on numerous occasions.

One of Schreiner's notable stylistic characteristics is the use of repetition. This occurs with remarkable frequency in her use of dialogue, often to signal a crisis, as in:

> 'Oh, I can't, I can't! I shall die! I shall die!' said Bonaparte, putting his hands to his side.

At other moments repetition in dialogue highlights perseverance and often consists of a reiteration of a gerund, such as *painting, painting, painting*. Beyond her rendering of her characters' speech, repetition adds both emphasis and a poetic ambience to Schreiner's descriptions. Often this evokes the passing of time, as in *again and yet again, month by month,* or the *long, long night*. Accordingly, in writing of *time*, the most common adjective is *long*. *Long*, indeed, applies most commonly in Schreiner's work to measurements of *time*, occurring most frequently with *year*, but also prominently with *night, age, month,* and *day*, although *grass* is also recurrent.

Schreiner's writing style is also notable for its simplicity. *Said* is nearly always the verb that indicates speech. In adjectives Schreiner has a leaning towards colour, but she is also drawn towards language that creates an other-worldly atmosphere. One of her lesser-known works is titled *Dreams* and this constitutes a prominent semantic field in her writing. *Dream* occurs most frequently with *beautiful*, while the verb it is most commonly the object of is *dream*, illustrating both Schreiner's preference for uncomplicated lexical choices and inclination to repetition, as in:

> And in the dark I **dreamt** a **dream**.

In a historical period in which spiritualism was of increasing popularity, *spirit* and *spiritual* also recur significantly. *Soul* is another salient word and *angels* are frequent visitors to Schreiner's prose.

A point of typographical interest is Schreiner's use of italics. This occurs notably with adverbs. In the first few pages of *The Story of an African Farm*, for example, *slightly, distinctly, systematically,* and *always* are all italicised, as are several pronouns, as in:

> ***I*** think he is a liar.

Occasional longer passages in italics indicate quotation or deliver an interior monologue.

underhand ADJECTIVE = **sly**, secret, crooked *(informal)*, devious, sneaky, secretive, fraudulent, treacherous, dishonest, deceptive, clandestine, unscrupulous, crafty, unethical, furtive, deceitful, surreptitious, stealthy, dishonourable, below the belt *(informal)*, underhanded **OPPOSITE:** honest

underline VERB **1 = emphasize**, stress, highlight, bring home, accentuate, point up, give emphasis to, call *or* draw attention to: *The report underlined his concern that standards were at risk.* **OPPOSITE:** minimize **2 = underscore**, mark, italicize, rule a line under: *Take two pens and underline the positive and negative words.*

underling NOUN = **subordinate**, inferior, minion, servant, slave, cohort *(chiefly U.S.)*, retainer, menial, nonentity, lackey, hireling, flunky, understrapper

underlying ADJECTIVE **1 = fundamental**, basic, essential, root, prime, primary, radical, elementary, intrinsic, basal: *To stop a problem you have to understand its underlying causes.* **2 = hidden**, concealed, lurking, veiled, latent: *hills with the hard underlying rock poking through the turf*

undermine VERB = **weaken**, sabotage, subvert, compromise, disable, debilitate **OPPOSITE:** reinforce

underpinning NOUN = **support**, base, foundation, footing, groundwork, substructure

underprivileged ADJECTIVE = **disadvantaged**, poor, deprived, in need, impoverished, needy, badly off, destitute, in want, on the breadline

underrate VERB = **underestimate**, discount, undervalue, belittle, disparage, fail to appreciate, not do justice to, set (too) little store by, misprize **OPPOSITE:** overestimate

understand VERB **1 = comprehend**, get, take in, perceive, grasp, know, see, follow, realize, recognize, appreciate, be aware of, penetrate, make out, discern, twig *(Brit. informal)*, fathom, savvy *(slang)*, apprehend, conceive of, suss *(Brit. informal)*, get to the bottom of, get the hang of *(informal)*, tumble to *(informal)*, catch on to *(informal)*, cotton on to *(informal)*, make head or tail of *(informal)*, get your head round: *I think you understand my meaning.* **2 = sympathize with**, appreciate, be aware of, be able to see, take on board *(informal)*, empathize with, commiserate with, show compassion for: *Trish had not exactly understood his feelings.* **3 = believe**, hear, learn, gather, think, see, suppose, notice, assume, take it, conclude, fancy, presume, be informed, infer, surmise, hear tell, draw the inference: *I understand you've heard about David and Lorna.*

QUOTATIONS
In the long course of history, having people who understand your thought is much greater security than another submarine
[J. William Fulbright *speaking of the Fulbright scholarship programme*]

understandable ADJECTIVE = **reasonable**, natural, normal, justified, expected, inevitable, legitimate, logical, predictable, accountable, on the cards *(informal)*, foreseeable, to be expected, justifiable, unsurprising, excusable, pardonable

understanding NOUN **1 = perception**, knowledge, grasp, sense, know-how *(informal)*, intelligence, judgment, awareness, appreciation, insight, skill, penetration, mastery, comprehension, familiarity with, discernment, proficiency: *They have to have a basic understanding of computers.* **OPPOSITE:** ignorance **2 = agreement**, deal, promise, arrangement, accord, contract, bond, pledge, bargain, pact, compact, concord, gentlemen's agreement: *We had not set a date but there was an understanding between us.* **OPPOSITE:** disagreement **3 = belief**, view, opinion, impression, interpretation, feeling, idea, conclusion, notion, conviction, judgment, assumption, point of view, perception, suspicion, viewpoint, hunch, way of thinking, estimation, supposition, sneaking suspicion, funny feeling: *It is my understanding that this has been going on for many years.* ▷ ADJECTIVE = **sympathetic**, kind, compassionate, considerate, kindly, accepting, patient, sensitive, forgiving, discerning, tolerant, responsive, perceptive, forbearing: *Her boss, who was very understanding, gave her time off.* **OPPOSITE:** unsympathetic

QUOTATIONS
Shallow understanding from people of good will is more frustrating than absolute misunderstanding from people of ill will
[Martin Luther King Jr. *Letter from Birmingham Jail*]

The ill and unfit choice of words wonderfully obstructs the understanding
[Francis Bacon *Novum Organum*]

I shall light a candle of understanding in thine heart, which shall not be put out
[*Bible: II Esdras*]

understood ADJECTIVE **1 = assumed**, presumed, accepted, taken for granted: *The management is understood to be very unwilling to agree.* **2 = implied**, implicit, unspoken, inferred, tacit, unstated: *The technical equality of all officers was understood.*

understudy NOUN = **stand-in**, reserve, substitute, double, sub, replacement, fill-in

undertake VERB **1 = take on**, embark on, set about, commence, try, begin, attempt, tackle, enter upon, endeavour to do: *She undertook the arduous task of monitoring the elections.* **2 = agree**, promise, contract, guarantee, engage, pledge, covenant, commit yourself, take upon yourself: *He undertook to edit the text himself.*

undertaker NOUN = **funeral director**, mortician *(U.S.)*

undertaking NOUN **1 = task**, business, operation, project, game, attempt, effort, affair, venture, enterprise, endeavour: *Organizing the show has been a massive undertaking.* **2 = promise**, commitment, pledge, word, vow, assurance, word of honour, solemn word: *British Coal gave an undertaking that it was maintaining the pits.*

undertone NOUN **1 = murmur**, whisper, low tone, subdued voice: *Well-dressed clients were talking in polite undertones as they ate.* **2 = undercurrent**, suggestion, trace, hint, feeling, touch, atmosphere, flavour, tinge, vibes *(slang)*: *The sobbing voice had an undertone of anger.*

undervalue VERB = **underrate**, underestimate, minimize, look down on, misjudge, depreciate, make light of, set no store by, hold cheap, misprize **OPPOSITE:** overrate

underwater ADJECTIVE = **submerged**, submarine, immersed, sunken, undersea, subaqueous, subaquatic

under way ADJECTIVE = **in progress**, going on, started, begun, in business, in motion, in operation, afoot

underwear NOUN = **underclothes**, lingerie, undies *(informal)*, smalls *(informal)*, undergarments, unmentionables *(humorous)*, underclothing, underthings, underlinen, broekies *(S. African informal)*, underdaks *(Austral. slang)*

underweight ADJECTIVE = **skinny**, puny, emaciated, undernourished, skin and bone *(informal)*, undersized, half-starved, underfed

underworld NOUN **1 = criminals**, gangsters, organized crime, gangland *(informal)*, criminal element: *a wealthy businessman with underworld connections* **2 = nether world**, hell, Hades, the inferno, nether regions, infernal region, abode of the dead: *Persephone, goddess of the underworld*

underwrite VERB = **finance**, back, fund, guarantee, sponsor, insure, ratify, subsidize, bankroll *(U.S. informal)*, provide security, provide capital for

undesirable ADJECTIVE = **unwanted**, unwelcome, disagreeable, objectionable, offensive, disliked, unacceptable, dreaded, unpopular, unsuitable, out of place, unattractive, distasteful, unsavoury, obnoxious, repugnant, unpleasing, unwished-for **OPPOSITE:** desirable

undo VERB **1 = open**, unfasten, loose, loosen, unlock, unwrap, untie, disengage, unbutton, disentangle, unstrap, unclasp: *I managed to undo a corner of the parcel.* **2 = reverse**, cancel, offset, wipe out, neutralize, invalidate, annul, nullify: *It would be difficult to undo the damage that had been done.* **3 = ruin**, defeat, destroy, wreck, shatter, upset, mar, undermine, overturn, quash, subvert, bring to naught: *Their hopes of a victory were undone by a goal from John Barnes.*

undoing NOUN **= downfall**, weakness, curse, trouble, trial, misfortune, blight, affliction, the last straw, fatal flaw

undone[1] ADJECTIVE **= unfinished**, left, outstanding, not done, neglected, omitted, incomplete, passed over, unfulfilled, not completed, unperformed, unattended to: *She left nothing undone that needed attention.* **OPPOSITE:** finished

undone[2] ADJECTIVE **= ruined**, destroyed, overcome, hapless, forlorn, prostrate, wretched: *He is undone by his lack of inner substance.*

undoubted ADJECTIVE **= certain**, sure, definite, confirmed, positive, obvious, acknowledged, patent, evident, manifest, transparent, clear-cut, undisputed, indisputable, unquestioned, unquestionable, incontrovertible, indubitable, nailed-on *(slang)*

undoubtedly ADVERB **= certainly**, definitely, undeniably, surely, of course, doubtless, without doubt, unquestionably, unmistakably, assuredly, beyond question, beyond a shadow of (a) doubt

undress VERB **= strip**, strip naked, disrobe, take off your clothes, peel off, doff your clothes: *She went out, leaving Rachel to undress and have her shower.* ▷ NOUN **= nakedness**, nudity, disarray, deshabille: *Every cover showed a woman in a state of undress.*

undue ADJECTIVE **= excessive**, too much, inappropriate, extreme, unnecessary, extravagant, needless, unsuitable, improper, too great, disproportionate, unjustified, unwarranted, unseemly, inordinate, undeserved, intemperate, uncalled-for, overmuch, immoderate **OPPOSITE:** appropriate

undulate VERB **= wave**, roll, surge, swell, ripple, rise and fall, billow, heave

unduly ADVERB **= excessively**, overly, too much, unnecessarily, disproportionately, improperly, unreasonably, extravagantly, out of all proportion, inordinately, unjustifiably, overmuch, immoderately **OPPOSITE:** reasonably

undying ADJECTIVE **= eternal**, everlasting, perpetual, continuing, permanent, constant, perennial, infinite, unending, indestructible, undiminished, imperishable, deathless, inextinguishable, unfading, sempiternal *(literary)* **OPPOSITE:** short-lived

unearth VERB **1 = discover**, find, reveal, expose, turn up, uncover, bring to light, ferret out, root up: *No evidence has yet been unearthed.* **2 = dig up**, excavate, exhume, dredge up, disinter: *Fossil hunters have unearthed the bones of an elephant.*

unearthly ADJECTIVE **1 = eerie**, strange, supernatural, ghostly, weird, phantom, uncanny, spooky *(informal)*, nightmarish, spectral, eldritch *(poetic)*, preternatural: *The sound was so serene that it seemed unearthly.* **2 = unreasonable**, ridiculous, absurd, strange, extraordinary, abnormal, unholy *(informal)*, ungodly *(informal)*: *They arranged to meet at the unearthly hour of seven in the morning.*

uneasiness NOUN **= anxiety**, apprehension, misgiving, worry, doubt, alarm, suspicion, nervousness, disquiet, agitation, qualms, trepidation, perturbation, apprehensiveness, dubiety **OPPOSITE:** ease

uneasy ADJECTIVE **1 = anxious**, worried, troubled, upset, wired *(slang)*, nervous, disturbed, uncomfortable, unsettled, impatient, restless, agitated, apprehensive, edgy, jittery *(informal)*, perturbed, on edge, ill at ease, restive, twitchy *(informal)*, like a fish out of water, antsy *(informal)*, discomposed: *He looked uneasy and refused to answer questions.* **OPPOSITE:** relaxed **2 = precarious**, strained, uncomfortable, tense, awkward, unstable, shaky, insecure, constrained: *An uneasy calm has settled over Los Angeles.* **3 = disturbing**, upsetting, disquieting, worrying, troubling, bothering, dismaying: *This is an uneasy book.*

uneconomic ADJECTIVE **= unprofitable**, loss-making, non-profit-making, nonpaying, nonviable **OPPOSITE:** profitable

unemployed ADJECTIVE **= out of work**, redundant, laid off, jobless, idle, on the dole *(Brit. informal)*, out of a job, workless, resting *(of an actor)* **OPPOSITE:** working

unequal ADJECTIVE **1 = disproportionate**, uneven, unbalanced, unfair, irregular, unjust, inequitable, ill-matched: *the unequal power relationships between men and women* **2 = different**, differing, dissimilar, unlike, varying, variable, disparate, unmatched, not uniform: *These pipes appear to me to be all of unequal length.* **OPPOSITE:** identical **3** *(with* **to***)* **= not up to**, not qualified for, inadequate for, insufficient for, found wanting in, not cut out for *(informal)*, incompetent at: *Her critics say that she has proved unequal to the task she was set.*

unequalled or *(U.S.)* **unequaled** ADJECTIVE **= incomparable**, supreme, unparalleled, paramount, transcendent, unrivalled, second to none, pre-eminent, inimitable, unmatched, peerless, unsurpassed, matchless, beyond compare, without equal, nonpareil

unequivocal ADJECTIVE **= clear**, absolute, definite, certain, direct, straight, positive, plain, evident, black-and-white, decisive, explicit, manifest, clear-cut, unmistakable, unambiguous, cut-and-dried *(informal)*, incontrovertible, indubitable, uncontestable, nailed-on *(slang)* **OPPOSITE:** vague

unerring ADJECTIVE **= accurate**, sure, certain, perfect, exact, impeccable, faultless, infallible, unfailing

uneven ADJECTIVE **1 = rough**, bumpy, not flat, not level, not smooth: *He staggered on the uneven surface of the car park.* **OPPOSITE:** level **2 = irregular**, unsteady, fitful, variable, broken, fluctuating, patchy, intermittent, jerky, changeable, spasmodic, inconsistent: *He could hear that her breathing was uneven.* **3 = unequal**, unfair, one-sided, ill-matched: *It was an uneven contest.* **4 = lopsided**, unbalanced, asymmetrical, odd, out of true, not parallel: *a flat head accentuated by a short, uneven crew-cut*

uneventful ADJECTIVE **= humdrum**, ordinary, routine, quiet, boring, dull, commonplace, tedious, monotonous, unremarkable, uninteresting, unexciting, unexceptional, ho-hum *(informal)*, unmemorable, unvaried **OPPOSITE:** exciting

unexpected ADJECTIVE **= unforeseen**, surprising, unanticipated, chance, sudden, astonishing, startling, unpredictable, accidental, abrupt, out of the blue, unannounced, fortuitous, unheralded, unlooked-for, not bargained for **OPPOSITE:** expected

> **PROVERBS**
> *Expect the unexpected*

unfailing ADJECTIVE **1 = continuous**, endless, persistent, unlimited, continual, never-failing, boundless, bottomless, ceaseless, inexhaustible, unflagging: *He continued to appear in the office with unfailing regularity.* **2 = reliable**, constant, dependable, sure, true, certain, loyal, faithful, staunch, infallible, steadfast, tried and true: *He had the unfailing care and support of Erica, his wife.* **OPPOSITE:** unreliable

unfair ADJECTIVE **1 = biased**, prejudiced, unjust, one-sided, partial, partisan, arbitrary, discriminatory, bigoted, inequitable: *Some have been sentenced to long prison terms after unfair trials.* **2 = unscrupulous**, crooked *(informal)*, dishonest, unethical, wrongful, unprincipled, dishonourable, unsporting: *nations*

involved in unfair trade practices
OPPOSITE: ethical

unfaithful ADJECTIVE **1 = faithless**, untrue, two-timing *(informal)*, adulterous, fickle, inconstant, unchaste: *She was frequently left alone by her unfaithful husband.* **OPPOSITE:** faithful **2 = disloyal**, false, treacherous, deceitful, faithless, perfidious, traitorous, treasonable, false-hearted, recreant *(archaic)*: *They denounced him as unfaithful to the traditions of the Society.* **OPPOSITE:** loyal

unfamiliar ADJECTIVE **1 = strange**, new, unknown, different, novel, unusual, curious, alien, out-of-the-way, uncommon, little known, unaccustomed, beyond your ken: *She grew many plants that were unfamiliar to me.* **OPPOSITE:** familiar **2** *(with* **with***)* **= unacquainted with**, a stranger to, unaccustomed to, inexperienced in, uninformed about, unversed in, uninitiated in, unskilled at, unpractised in, unconversant with: *She speaks no Japanese and is unfamiliar with Japanese culture.* **OPPOSITE:** acquainted with

unfathomable ADJECTIVE **1 = baffling**, incomprehensible, inexplicable, deep, profound, esoteric, impenetrable, unknowable, abstruse, indecipherable: *How unfathomable and odd is life!* **2 = immeasurable**, bottomless, unmeasured, unplumbed, unsounded: *Her eyes were black, unfathomable pools.*

unfavourable *or (U.S.)* **unfavorable** ADJECTIVE **= adverse**, bad, unfortunate, disadvantageous, threatening, contrary, unlucky, ominous, untimely, untoward, unpromising, unsuited, inauspicious, ill-suited, inopportune, unseasonable, unpropitious, infelicitous: *Unfavourable economic conditions were blocking a recovery.*

unfinished ADJECTIVE **1 = incomplete**, uncompleted, half-done, lacking, undone, in the making, imperfect, unfulfilled, unaccomplished: *Jane Austen's unfinished novel* **2 = natural**, rough, raw, bare, crude, unrefined, unvarnished, unpolished: *unfinished wood ready for you to varnish or paint* **OPPOSITE:** polished

unfit ADJECTIVE **1 = out of shape**, feeble, unhealthy, debilitated, flabby, decrepit, in poor condition, out of trim, out of kilter: *Many children are so unfit they are unable to do basic exercises.* **OPPOSITE:** healthy **2 = incapable**, inadequate, incompetent, no good, useless, not up to, unprepared, ineligible, unqualified, untrained, ill-equipped, not equal, not cut out: *They were utterly unfit to govern America.* **OPPOSITE:** capable **3 = unsuitable**, inadequate, inappropriate, useless, not fit, not designed, unsuited, ill-adapted: *I can show them plenty of houses unfit for human habitation.* **OPPOSITE:** suitable

unflappable ADJECTIVE **= imperturbable**, cool, collected, calm, composed, level-headed, unfazed *(informal)*, impassive, unruffled, self-possessed, not given to worry **OPPOSITE:** excitable

unflinching ADJECTIVE **= determined**, firm, steady, constant, bold, stalwart, staunch, resolute, steadfast, unwavering, immovable, unswerving, unshaken, unfaltering, unshrinking **OPPOSITE:** wavering

unfold VERB **1 = develop**, happen, progress, grow, emerge, occur, take place, expand, work out, mature, evolve, blossom, transpire, bear fruit: *The outcome depends on conditions as well as how events unfold.* **2 = reveal**, tell, present, show, describe, explain, illustrate, disclose, uncover, clarify, divulge, narrate, make known: *Mr Wills unfolds his story with evident enjoyment.* **3 = open**, spread out, undo, expand, flatten, straighten, stretch out, unfurl, unwrap, unroll: *He quickly unfolded the blankets and spread them on the mattress.*

unfortunate ADJECTIVE **1 = disastrous**, calamitous, inopportune, adverse, untimely, unfavourable, untoward, ruinous, ill-starred, infelicitous, ill-fated: *Through some unfortunate accident, the information reached me a day late.* **OPPOSITE:** opportune **2 = regrettable**, deplorable, lamentable, inappropriate, unsuitable, ill-advised, unbecoming: *the unfortunate incident of the upside-down Canadian flag* **OPPOSITE:** becoming **3 = unlucky**, poor, unhappy, doomed, cursed, hopeless, unsuccessful, hapless, luckless, out of luck, wretched, star-crossed, unprosperous: *charity days to raise money for unfortunate people* **OPPOSITE:** fortunate

unfounded ADJECTIVE **= groundless**, false, unjustified, unproven, unsubstantiated, idle, fabricated, spurious, trumped up, baseless, without foundation, without basis **OPPOSITE:** justified

unfriendly ADJECTIVE **1 = hostile**, cold, distant, sour, chilly, aloof, surly, antagonistic, disagreeable, quarrelsome, unsociable, ill-disposed, unneighbourly: *She spoke in a loud, rather unfriendly voice.* **OPPOSITE:** friendly **2 = unfavourable**, hostile, inhospitable, alien, inauspicious, inimical, uncongenial, unpropitious, unkind: *We got an unfriendly reception from the hotel-owner.* **OPPOSITE:** congenial

ungainly ADJECTIVE **= awkward**, clumsy, inelegant, lumbering, slouching, gawky, uncouth, gangling, loutish, uncoordinated, ungraceful, lubberly, unco *(Austral. slang)* **OPPOSITE:** graceful

unguarded ADJECTIVE **1 = unprotected**, vulnerable, defenceless, undefended, open to attack, unpatrolled: *The U-boat entered in through a narrow unguarded eastern entrance.* **2 = careless**, rash, unwary, foolhardy, thoughtless, indiscreet, unthinking, ill-considered, imprudent, heedless, incautious, undiplomatic, impolitic, uncircumspect: *He was tricked by a reporter into an unguarded comment.* **OPPOSITE:** cautious

unhappiness NOUN **= sadness**, depression, misery, gloom, sorrow, melancholy, heartache, despondency, blues, dejection, wretchedness, low spirits: *There was a lot of unhappiness in my adolescence.*

unhappy ADJECTIVE **1 = sad**, depressed, miserable, down, low, blue, gloomy, melancholy, mournful, dejected, despondent, dispirited, downcast, long-faced, sorrowful, disconsolate, crestfallen, down in the dumps *(informal)*: *Her marriage is in trouble and she is desperately unhappy.* **OPPOSITE:** happy **2 = unlucky**, unfortunate, hapless, luckless, cursed, wretched, ill-omened, ill-fated: *I have already informed your unhappy father of your expulsion.* **OPPOSITE:** fortunate **3 = inappropriate**, awkward, clumsy, unsuitable, inept, ill-advised, tactless, ill-timed, injudicious, infelicitous, malapropos, untactful: *The legislation represents in itself an unhappy compromise.* **OPPOSITE:** apt

> **QUOTATIONS**
> Those who are unhappy have no need for anything in this world but people capable of giving them their attention
> [Simone Weil *Waiting on God*]

unhealthy ADJECTIVE **1 = harmful**, detrimental, unwholesome, noxious, deleterious, insanitary, noisome, insalubrious: *the unhealthy environment of a coal mine* **OPPOSITE:** beneficial **2 = sick**, sickly, unwell, poorly *(informal)*, weak, delicate, crook *(Austral. & N.Z. informal)*, ailing, frail, feeble, invalid, unsound, infirm, in poor health: *a poorly dressed, unhealthy looking fellow with a poor complexion* **OPPOSITE:** well **3 = weak**, unsound, ailing: *a clear sign of an unhealthy economy* **OPPOSITE:** strong **4 = unwholesome**, morbid, bad, negative, corrupt, corrupting, degrading, undesirable, demoralizing, baneful *(archaic)*: *an unhealthy obsession with secrecy* **OPPOSITE:** wholesome

unheard-of ADJECTIVE **1 = unprecedented**, inconceivable, undreamed of, new, novel, unique, unusual, unbelievable, singular, ground-breaking, never before encountered, unexampled: *In those days, it was unheard-of for a woman to work after marriage.* **2 = shocking**, extreme, outrageous, offensive, unacceptable, unthinkable, disgraceful, preposterous, outlandish: *the unheard-of rate of a bottle of rum for $30* **3 = obscure**, unknown,

u

undiscovered, unfamiliar, little known, unsung, unremarked, unregarded: *an unheard-of comic waiting for his big break to come along*

unhinge VERB = **unbalance**, confuse, derange, disorder, unsettle, madden, craze, confound, distemper *(archaic)*, dement, drive you out of your mind

unholy ADJECTIVE **1 = shocking**, awful, appalling, dreadful, outrageous, horrendous, unearthly, ungodly *(informal)*: *The economy is still in an unholy mess.* **2 = evil**, vile, wicked, base, corrupt, immoral, dishonest, sinful, heinous, depraved, profane, iniquitous, ungodly, irreligious: *He screamed unholy things at me.*
OPPOSITE: holy

unification NOUN = **union**, uniting, alliance, combination, coalition, merger, federation, confederation, fusion, amalgamation, coalescence

uniform NOUN **1 = regalia**, suit, livery, colours, habit, regimentals: *He was dressed in his uniform for parade.* **2 = outfit**, dress, costume, attire, gear *(informal)*, get-up *(informal)*, ensemble, garb: *Mark's is the uniform of the young male traveller.*
▷ ADJECTIVE **1 = consistent**, unvarying, similar, even, same, matching, regular, constant, equivalent, identical, homogeneous, unchanging, equable, undeviating: *Chips should be cut into uniform size and thickness.* **OPPOSITE:** varying **2 = alike**, similar, identical, like, same, equal, selfsame: *Along each wall stretched uniform green metal filing cabinets.*

uniformity NOUN **1 = regularity**, similarity, sameness, constancy, homogeneity, evenness, invariability: *Caramel was used to maintain uniformity of colour in the brandy.* **2 = monotony**, sameness, tedium, dullness, flatness, drabness, lack of diversity: *the dull uniformity of the houses*

unify VERB = **unite**, join, combine, merge, consolidate, bring together, fuse, confederate, amalgamate, federate **OPPOSITE:** divide

uninterested ADJECTIVE = **indifferent**, unconcerned, apathetic, bored, distant, listless, impassive, blasé, unresponsive, uninvolved, incurious
OPPOSITE: concerned

union NOUN **1 = joining**, uniting, unification, combination, coalition, merger, mixture, blend, merging, integration, conjunction, fusion, synthesis, amalgamating, amalgam, amalgamation: *The Romanian majority in the province voted for union with Romania.* **2 = alliance**, league, association, coalition, federation, confederation, confederacy, Bund: *the question of which countries should join the currency union* **3 = marriage**, match, wedlock, matrimony: *Even Louis began to think their union was not blessed.* **4 = intercourse**, coupling, copulation, the other *(informal)*, nookie *(slang)*, coitus, rumpy-pumpy *(slang)*, coition: *the joys of sexual union*

unique ADJECTIVE **1 = distinct**, special, exclusive, peculiar, only, single, lone, solitary, one and only, sui generis: *The area has its own unique language, Catalan.* **2 = unparalleled**, unrivalled, incomparable, inimitable, unmatched, peerless, unequalled, matchless, without equal, nonpareil, unexampled: *She was a woman of unique talent and determination.*

unit NOUN **1 = entity**, whole, item, feature, piece, portion, module: *Agriculture was based in the past on the family as a unit.* **2 = section**, company, group, force, detail, division, cell, squad, crew, outfit, faction, corps, brigade, regiment, battalion, legion, contingent, squadron, garrison, detachment, platoon: *a secret military unit* **3 = measure**, quantity, measurement: *The liver can only burn up one unit of alcohol in an hour.* **4 = part**, section, segment, class, element, component, constituent, tutorial: *designed for teachers to plan a study unit on marine mammals*

unite VERB **1 = join**, link, combine, couple, marry, wed, blend, incorporate, merge, consolidate, unify, fuse, amalgamate, coalesce, meld: *They have agreed to unite their efforts to bring peace.* **OPPOSITE:** separate **2 = cooperate**, ally, join forces, league, band, associate, pool, collaborate, confederate, pull together, join together, close ranks, club together: *The two parties have been trying to unite since the New Year.*
OPPOSITE: split

united ADJECTIVE **1 = in agreement**, agreed, unanimous, one, like-minded, in accord, of like mind, of one mind, of the same opinion: *Every party is united on the need for parliamentary democracy.* **2 = combined**, leagued, allied, unified, pooled, concerted, collective, affiliated, in partnership, banded together: *the first elections in a united Germany for fifty-eight years*

unity NOUN **1 = union**, unification, coalition, federation, integration, confederation, amalgamation: *the future of European economic unity* **2 = wholeness**, integrity, oneness, union, unification, entity, singleness, undividedness: *The deer represents the unity of the universe.* **OPPOSITE:** disunity **3 = agreement**, accord, consensus, peace, harmony, solidarity, unison, assent, unanimity, concord, concurrence: *Speakers at the rally mouthed sentiments of unity.*
OPPOSITE: disagreement

> **QUOTATIONS**
> We must indeed all hang together, or, most assuredly, we shall all hang separately
> [Benjamin Franklin *on his signing of the Declaration of Independence*]
>
> All for one; one for all
> [Alexandre Dumas *The Three Musketeers*]
>
> By uniting we stand, by dividing we fall
> [John Dickinson *The Patriot's Appeal*]

universal ADJECTIVE **1 = widespread**, general, common, whole, total, entire, catholic, unlimited, ecumenical, omnipresent, all-embracing, overarching, one-size-fits-all: *proposals for universal health care* **2 = global**, worldwide, international, pandemic: *universal diseases*

> **USAGE**
> The use of *more universal* as in *his writings have long been admired by fellow scientists, but his latest book should have more universal appeal* is acceptable in modern English usage.

universality NOUN = **comprehensiveness**, generalization, generality, totality, completeness, ubiquity, all-inclusiveness

universally ADVERB = **without exception**, uniformly, everywhere, always, invariably, across the board, in all cases, in every instance

universe NOUN = **cosmos**, space, creation, everything, nature, heavens, the natural world, macrocosm, all existence

> **QUOTATIONS**
> The more the universe seems comprehensible, the more it also seems pointless
> [Steven Weinberg *The First Three Minutes*]
>
> The universe is not hostile, nor yet is it friendly. It is simply indifferent
> [Revd. John H. Holmes *A Sensible Man's View of Religion*]
>
> Had I been present at the Creation, I would have given some useful hints for the better ordering of the universe
> [attributed to Alfonso 'the Wise', King of Castile]
>
> Now, my own suspicion is that the Universe is not only queerer than we suppose, but queerer than we *can* suppose
> [J.B.S. Haldane *Possible Worlds*]

unjust ADJECTIVE = **unfair**, prejudiced, biased, wrong, one-sided, partial, partisan, unjustified, wrongful, undeserved, inequitable, unmerited
OPPOSITE: fair

unkempt ADJECTIVE **1 = uncombed**, tousled, shaggy, ungroomed: *His hair was unkempt and filthy.* **2 = untidy**, scruffy, dishevelled, disordered, messy, sloppy *(informal)*, shabby, rumpled, bedraggled, slovenly, blowsy, sluttish, slatternly, disarranged, ungroomed, disarrayed, frowzy, daggy *(Austral. & N.Z. informal)*: *an unkempt old man*
OPPOSITE: tidy

unkind ADJECTIVE **= cruel**, mean, nasty, spiteful, harsh, malicious, insensitive, unfriendly, inhuman, unsympathetic, uncaring, thoughtless, unfeeling, inconsiderate, uncharitable, unchristian, hardhearted **OPPOSITE:** kind

unknown ADJECTIVE **1 = strange**, new, undiscovered, uncharted, unexplored, virgin, remote, alien, exotic, outlandish, unmapped, untravelled, beyond your ken: *a perilous expedition, through unknown terrain* **2 = unidentified**, mysterious, anonymous, unnamed, nameless, incognito: *Unknown thieves had forced their way into the apartment.* **3 = obscure**, little known, minor, humble, unfamiliar, insignificant, lowly, unimportant, unheard-of, unsung, inconsequential, undistinguished, unrenowned: *He was an unknown writer.* **OPPOSITE:** famous

unleash VERB **= release**, let go, let loose, free, untie, unloose, unbridle

unlike PREPOSITION **1 = different from**, dissimilar to, not resembling, far from, not like, distinct from, incompatible with, unrelated to, distant from, unequal to, far apart from, divergent from, not similar to, as different as chalk and cheese from *(informal)*: *She was unlike him in every way except her eyes.* **OPPOSITE:** similar to **2 = contrasted with**, not like, in contradiction to, in contrast with *or* to, as opposed to, differently from, opposite to: *Unlike aerobics, walking entails no expensive fees.*

unlikely ADJECTIVE **1 = improbable**, doubtful, remote, slight, faint, not likely, unimaginable: *A military coup seems unlikely.* **OPPOSITE:** probable **2 = unbelievable**, incredible, unconvincing, implausible, questionable, cock-and-bull *(informal)*: *I smiled sincerely, to encourage him to buy this unlikely story.* **OPPOSITE:** believable

unlimited ADJECTIVE **1 = infinite**, endless, countless, great, vast, extensive, immense, stellar *(informal)*, limitless, boundless, incalculable, immeasurable, unbounded, illimitable: *An unlimited number of copies can be made from the original.* **OPPOSITE:** finite **2 = total**, full, complete, absolute, unconditional, unqualified, unfettered, unrestricted, all-encompassing, unconstrained: *You'll also have unlimited access to the swimming pool.* **OPPOSITE:** restricted

unload VERB **1 = empty**, clear, unpack, dump, discharge, off-load, disburden, unlade: *Unload everything from the boot and clean it thoroughly.* **2 = unburden**, relieve, lighten, disburden: *He unloaded the horse where the track dead-ended.*

unlock VERB **= open**, undo, unfasten, release, unbolt, unlatch, unbar

unlucky ADJECTIVE **1 = unfortunate**, unhappy, disastrous: *Argentina's unlucky defeat by Ireland* **OPPOSITE:** fortunate **2 = ill-fated**, doomed, inauspicious, ominous, untimely, unfavourable, cursed, ill-starred, ill-omened: *13 was to prove an unlucky number.*

> **QUOTATIONS**
> now and then
> there is a person born
> who is so unlucky
> that he runs into accidents
> which started to happen
> to someone else
> [Don Marquis *archys life of mehitabel*]

unmask VERB **= reveal**, expose, uncover, discover, disclose, unveil, show up, lay bare, bring to light, uncloak

unmistakable ADJECTIVE **= clear**, certain, positive, decided, sure, obvious, plain, patent, evident, distinct, pronounced, glaring, manifest, blatant, conspicuous, palpable, unequivocal, unambiguous, indisputable **OPPOSITE:** doubtful

unmitigated ADJECTIVE **1 = unrelieved**, relentless, unalleviated, intense, harsh, grim, persistent, oppressive, unbroken, unqualified, unabated, undiminished, unmodified, unredeemed: *She leads a life of unmitigated misery.* **2 = complete**, absolute, utter, perfect, rank, sheer, total, outright, thorough, downright, consummate, out-and-out, thoroughgoing, arrant, deep-dyed *(usually derogatory)*: *A senior policeman had called him an unmitigated liar.*

unnatural ADJECTIVE **1 = abnormal**, odd, strange, unusual, extraordinary, bizarre, perverted, queer, irregular, perverse, supernatural, uncanny, outlandish, unaccountable, anomalous, freakish, aberrant: *The altered landscape looks unnatural and weird.* **OPPOSITE:** normal **2 = false**, forced, artificial, studied, laboured, affected, assumed, mannered, strained, stiff, theatrical, contrived, self-conscious, feigned, stilted, insincere, factitious, stagy, phoney *or* phony *(informal)*: *She gave him a bright, determined smile which seemed unnatural.* **OPPOSITE:** genuine **3 = inhuman**, evil, monstrous, wicked, savage, brutal, ruthless, callous, heartless, cold-blooded, fiendish, unfeeling: *Murder is an unnatural act.* **OPPOSITE:** humane

unnecessary ADJECTIVE **= needless**, excessive, unwarranted, useless, pointless, not needed, redundant, wasteful, gratuitous, superfluous, wanton, expendable, surplus to requirements, uncalled-for, dispensable, unneeded, nonessential, inessential, unmerited, to no purpose, unrequired, supererogatory **OPPOSITE:** essential

unnerve VERB **= shake**, upset, disconcert, disturb, intimidate, frighten, rattle *(informal)*, discourage, dismay, daunt, disarm, confound, fluster, faze, unman, demoralize, unhinge, psych out *(informal)*, throw off balance, dishearten, dispirit **OPPOSITE:** strengthen

unoccupied ADJECTIVE **1 = empty**, vacant, uninhabited, untenanted, tenantless: *The house was unoccupied at the time of the explosion.* **2 = idle**, unemployed, inactive, disengaged, at leisure, at a loose end: *Portraits of unoccupied youths and solitary females predominate.*

unofficial ADJECTIVE **1 = unconfirmed**, off the record, unsubstantiated, private, personal, unauthorized, undocumented, uncorroborated: *Unofficial estimates speak of at least two hundred dead.* **2 = unauthorized**, informal, unsanctioned, casual, wildcat: *Rail workers have voted to continue their unofficial strike.*

unparalleled ADJECTIVE **= unequalled**, exceptional, unprecedented, rare, unique, singular, consummate, superlative, unrivalled, incomparable, unmatched, peerless, unsurpassed, matchless, beyond compare, without equal

unpleasant ADJECTIVE **1 = nasty**, bad, horrid, distressing, annoying, irritating, miserable, troublesome, distasteful, obnoxious, unpalatable, displeasing, repulsive, objectionable, disagreeable, abhorrent, irksome, unlovely, execrable, eye-watering: *They tolerated what they felt was an unpleasant situation.* **OPPOSITE:** nice **2 = obnoxious**, disagreeable, vicious, malicious, rude, mean, cruel, poisonous, unattractive, unfriendly, vindictive, venomous, mean-spirited, inconsiderate, impolite, unloveable, ill-natured, unlikable *or* unlikeable: *He was very unpleasant indeed.* **OPPOSITE:** likable *or* likeable

unpleasantness NOUN **1 = hostility**, animosity, antagonism, bad feeling, malice, rudeness, offensiveness, abrasiveness, argumentativeness, unfriendliness, quarrelsomeness, ill humour *or* will: *Most offices are riddled with sniping and general unpleasantness.* **OPPOSITE:** friendliness **2 = nastiness**, awfulness, grimness, trouble, misery, woe, ugliness, unacceptability, dreadfulness, disagreeableness, horridness: *the unpleasantness of surgery and chemotherapy* **OPPOSITE:** pleasantness

unpopular ADJECTIVE **= disliked**, rejected, unwanted, avoided, shunned, unwelcome, undesirable, unattractive, detested, out of favour, unloved, out in the cold, cold-shouldered, not sought out, sent to Coventry *(Brit.)* **OPPOSITE:** popular

unprecedented ADJECTIVE **1 = unparalleled**, unheard-of, exceptional, new, original, novel, unusual, abnormal, singular, ground-breaking, unrivalled, freakish, unexampled: *Such a move is unprecedented.* **2 = extraordinary**,

The Language of Herman Melville

The American novelist, short story writer, and poet Herman Melville (1819–91) was born in New York City. He took to a merchant navy career at the age of nineteen and made several voyages to such exotic locations as the Marquesas Islands of Polynesia. One voyage in particular, on board a whaling ship, furnished him with the experiences that would later inform his best-known novel *Moby-Dick* (1851).

While not all of Melville's writings have a nautical theme or setting (for example the novel *Pierre, or The Ambiguities* is wholly land-locked, being set in New York State) a look at his characteristic language shows that things of the sea play a predominant part. Among his most common nouns (in descending order of frequency) are: *ship, sea, whale, sailor, boat, water, deck, crew, vessel, seaman,* and *voyage:*

> At length, as the **ship**, gliding on past three or
> four **vessels** at **anchor** in the **roadstead**-one,
> a **man-of-war** just furling her **sails**-came nigh
> Falmouth town, Israel, from his perch, saw
> crowds in violent commotion on the **shore**.

There can be no doubt that Melville's seagoing world is very much a masculine one. At this period few women would have been aboard the kind of ships that Melville writes about, from men-of-war to merchant vessels to whalers. This is shown in the relative paucity of female nouns (although a ship, of course, is always female) in his writings. Words like *lady, wife,* or *woman* are much less frequent than, for example, *death, book,* or *fish*.

It can be argued that Melville's view of the world is dark and pessimistic, particularly in *Moby-Dick* and *Billy Budd*. His heroes are often doomed, both to fail in their endeavours and, often, to lose their lives in unredeeming ways. This is borne out in his language by the fact that the noun *death* is more often to be met with than, say, *love* or *hope*. Similarly, occurrences of the more hopeful adverb *always* are greatly outnumbered by instances of the doom-laden finality of *never*.

One of Melville's most commonly used adjectives is *white*. This is hardly surprising, given that the eponymous Moby-Dick is a great white sperm whale. Captain Ahab, who pursues this whale around the globe, stumps about the deck on an artificial leg made of white whalebone; *white sails* and *white birds* abound. This colour, or absence of colour, is at once suggestive of purity and of mystery. It is blank, ambiguous, and unknowable.

> In the distance, a great **white** mass lazily rose,
> and rising higher and higher, and disentangling
> itself from the azure, at last gleamed before our
> prow like a **snow**-slide, new slid from the hills.

Another commonly used adjective is *strange*. Melville is nothing if not a metaphysical writer, and he is greatly concerned with the mysterious and the ineffable.

> ...that deep, blue, bottomless soul, pervading
> mankind and nature; and every **strange**,
> half-seen, gliding, beautiful thing that eludes him.

Archaic vocabulary is relatively common in Melville's writings, with great use of *ye* (which, of course, might be expected in sailors' talk anyway), *thy,* and *thee*. In part this is because many of his characters, especially among the Nantucket whalers in *Moby-Dick,* are Quakers, and these even-then old-fashioned terms of address were considered characteristic of their discourse. However, another reason for this is that Melville's language often echoes that of the King James Bible. He uses biblical-sounding language to convey portentousness, a sense of great natural forces at work, and overtones of the inevitability of fate and retribution.

> 'Roll on, **thou** deep and dark blue ocean, roll!
> Ten thousand blubber-hunters sweep over **thee**
> in vain.'

amazing, remarkable, outstanding, fantastic, marvellous, exceptional, phenomenal, uncommon: *The scheme has been hailed as an unprecedented success.*

unprofessional ADJECTIVE **1 = unethical**, unfitting, improper, lax, negligent, unworthy, unseemly, unprincipled: *He was also fined $150 for unprofessional conduct.* **2 = amateurish**, amateur, incompetent, inefficient, cowboy *(informal)*, inexperienced, untrained, slapdash, slipshod, inexpert: *He rubbished his team for another unprofessional performance.* **OPPOSITE:** skilful

unqualified ADJECTIVE **1 = unfit**, incapable, incompetent, not up to, unprepared, ineligible, ill-equipped, not equal to: *She was unqualified for the job.* **2 = unconditional**, complete, total, absolute, utter, outright, thorough, downright, consummate, unrestricted, out-and-out, categorical, unmitigated, unreserved, thoroughgoing, without reservation, arrant, deep-dyed *(usually derogatory)*: *The event was an unqualified success.*

unquestionable ADJECTIVE **= certain**, undeniable, indisputable, clear, sure, perfect, absolute, patent, definite, manifest, unmistakable, conclusive, flawless, unequivocal, faultless, self-evident, irrefutable, incontrovertible, incontestable, indubitable, beyond a shadow of doubt, nailed-on *(slang)* **OPPOSITE:** doubtful

unravel VERB **1 = solve**, explain, work out, resolve, interpret, figure out *(informal)*, make out, clear up, suss (out) *(slang)*, get to the bottom of, get straight, puzzle out: *She wanted to unravel the mystery of her husband's disappearance.* **2 = undo**, separate, disentangle, free, unwind, extricate, straighten out, untangle, unknot: *He could unravel knots that others could not even attempt.*

unreadable ADJECTIVE **1 = turgid**, heavy going, badly written, dry as dust: *Most computer ads used to be unreadable.* **2 = illegible**, undecipherable, crabbed: *She scribbled an unreadable address on the receipt.*

unreal ADJECTIVE **= imaginary**, make-believe, illusory, fabulous, visionary, mythical, fanciful, fictitious, intangible, immaterial, storybook, insubstantial, nebulous, dreamlike, impalpable, chimerical, phantasmagoric

unreasonable ADJECTIVE **1 = biased**, arbitrary, irrational, illogical, blinkered, opinionated, headstrong: *The strikers were being unreasonable in their demands.* **OPPOSITE:** open-minded **2 = excessive**, steep *(informal)*, exorbitant, unfair, absurd, extravagant, unjust, too great, undue, preposterous, unwarranted, far-fetched, extortionate, uncalled-for, immoderate: *unreasonable increases in the price of petrol* **OPPOSITE:** moderate

unrelenting ADJECTIVE **1 = merciless**, tough, ruthless, relentless, cruel, stern, inexorable, implacable, intransigent, remorseless, pitiless, unsparing: *in the face of severe opposition and unrelenting criticism* **2 = steady**, constant, continuous, endless, perpetual, continual, unbroken, incessant, unabated, ceaseless, unremitting, unwavering: *an unrelenting downpour of rain*

unremitting ADJECTIVE **= constant**, continuous, relentless, perpetual, continual, unbroken, incessant, diligent, unabated, unwavering, indefatigable, remorseless, assiduous, unceasing, sedulous, unwearied

unrest NOUN **= discontent**, rebellion, dissatisfaction, protest, turmoil, upheaval, strife, agitation, discord, disaffection, sedition, tumult, dissension **OPPOSITE:** peace

unrivalled ADJECTIVE **= unparalleled**, incomparable, unsurpassed, supreme, unmatched, peerless, unequalled, matchless, beyond compare, without equal, nonpareil, unexcelled

unruffled ADJECTIVE **1 = calm**, cool, collected, peaceful, composed, serene, tranquil, sedate, placid, undisturbed, unmoved, unfazed *(informal)*, unperturbed, unflustered: *Anne had remained unruffled, very cool and controlled.* **2 = smooth**, even, level, flat, unbroken: *the unruffled surface of the pool*

unruly ADJECTIVE **= uncontrollable**, wild, unmanageable, disorderly, turbulent, rebellious, wayward, rowdy, intractable, wilful, lawless, fractious, riotous, headstrong, mutinous, disobedient, ungovernable, refractory, obstreperous, insubordinate **OPPOSITE:** manageable

unsafe ADJECTIVE **= dangerous**, risky, hazardous, threatening, uncertain, unstable, insecure, unreliable, precarious, treacherous, perilous, unsound **OPPOSITE:** safe

unsavoury ADJECTIVE **1 = unpleasant**, nasty, obnoxious, offensive, revolting, distasteful, repellent, repulsive, objectionable, repugnant: *The sport has long been associated with unsavoury characters.* **2 = unappetizing**, unpalatable, distasteful, sickening, disagreeable, nauseating: *unsavoury school meals* **OPPOSITE:** appetizing

unscathed ADJECTIVE **= unharmed**, unhurt, uninjured, whole, sound, safe, untouched, unmarked, in one piece, unscarred, unscratched

unscrupulous ADJECTIVE **= unprincipled**, corrupt, crooked *(informal)*, ruthless, improper, immoral, dishonest, unethical, exploitative, dishonourable, roguish, unconscionable, knavish, conscienceless, unconscientious **OPPOSITE:** honourable

unseat VERB **1 = depose**, overthrow, oust, remove, dismiss, discharge, displace, dethrone: *It is not clear who was behind the attempt to unseat the President.* **2 = throw**, unsaddle, unhorse: *She was unseated on her first ride.*

unseemly ADJECTIVE **= improper**, inappropriate, unsuitable, out of place, undignified, disreputable, unbecoming, unrefined, out of keeping, discreditable, indelicate, in poor taste, indecorous, unbefitting **OPPOSITE:** proper

unseen ADJECTIVE **1 = unobserved**, undetected, unperceived, lurking, unnoticed, unobtrusive: *I can now accept that there are unseen forces at work.* **2 = hidden**, concealed, invisible, veiled, obscure: *playing computer games against unseen opponents*

unselfish ADJECTIVE **= generous**, selfless, noble, kind, liberal, devoted, humanitarian, charitable, disinterested, altruistic, self-sacrificing, magnanimous, self-denying

unsettle VERB **= disturb**, trouble, upset, throw *(informal)*, bother, confuse, disorder, rattle *(informal)*, agitate, ruffle, unnerve, disconcert, unbalance, fluster, perturb, faze, throw into confusion, throw off balance, discompose, throw into disorder, throw into uproar

unsettled ADJECTIVE **1 = unstable**, shaky, insecure, disorderly, unsteady: *Britain's unsettled political scene also worries some investors.* **2 = restless**, tense, uneasy, troubled, shaken, confused, wired *(slang)*, disturbed, anxious, agitated, unnerved, flustered, perturbed, on edge, restive, adrenalized: *To tell the truth, I'm a bit unsettled tonight.* **3 = unresolved**, undecided, undetermined, open, doubtful, debatable, up in the air, moot: *They were in the process of resolving all the unsettled issues.* **4 = inconstant**, changing, unpredictable, variable, uncertain, changeable: *Despite the unsettled weather, we had a marvellous weekend.* **5 = owing**, due, outstanding, pending, payable, in arrears: *Liabilities related to unsettled transactions are recorded.*

unsightly ADJECTIVE **= ugly**, unattractive, repulsive, unpleasant, revolting *(informal)*, hideous, horrid, disagreeable, unprepossessing **OPPOSITE:** attractive

unskilled ADJECTIVE **= unprofessional**, inexperienced, unqualified, untrained, uneducated, amateurish, cowboy *(informal)*, untalented **OPPOSITE:** skilled

unsophisticated ADJECTIVE **1 = simple**, plain, uncomplicated, straightforward, unrefined, uninvolved, unspecialized, uncomplex: *music of a crude kind which unsophisticated audiences enjoyed* **OPPOSITE:** advanced **2 = naive**, innocent, inexperienced, unworldly,

u

unaffected, childlike, natural, artless, ingenuous, guileless: *She was quite unsophisticated in the ways of the world.*

unsound ADJECTIVE **1 = flawed**, faulty, weak, false, shaky, unreliable, invalid, defective, illogical, erroneous, specious, fallacious, ill-founded: *The thinking is muddled and fundamentally unsound.* **2 = unstable**, shaky, insecure, unsafe, unreliable, flimsy, wobbly, tottering, rickety, unsteady, not solid: *The church was structurally unsound.* **OPPOSITE:** stable **3 = unhealthy**, unstable, unbalanced, diseased, ill, weak, delicate, ailing, frail, defective, unwell, deranged, unhinged: *He was rejected as an army conscript as being of unsound mind.*

unspeakable ADJECTIVE **= dreadful**, shocking, appalling, evil, awful, overwhelming, horrible, unbelievable, monstrous, from hell *(informal)*, inconceivable, unimaginable, repellent, abysmal, frightful, heinous, odious, indescribable, loathsome, abominable, ineffable, beyond words, execrable, unutterable, inexpressible, beyond description, hellacious *(U.S. slang)*, too horrible for words

unstable ADJECTIVE **1 = changeable**, volatile, unpredictable, variable, fluctuating, unsteady, fitful, inconstant: *The situation is unstable and potentially dangerous.* **OPPOSITE:** constant **2 = insecure**, shaky, precarious, unsettled, wobbly, tottering, rickety, unsteady, not fixed: *a house built on unstable foundations* **3 = unpredictable**, irrational, erratic, inconsistent, unreliable, temperamental, capricious, changeable, untrustworthy, vacillating: *He was emotionally unstable.* **OPPOSITE:** level-headed

unsteady ADJECTIVE **1 = unstable**, shaky, insecure, unsafe, precarious, treacherous, rickety, infirm: *a slightly unsteady item of furniture* **2 = reeling**, wobbly, tottering: *The boy was unsteady, staggering around the room.* **3 = erratic**, unpredictable, volatile, unsettled, wavering, unreliable, temperamental, changeable, vacillating, flighty, inconstant: *She knew the impact an unsteady parent could have on a young girl.*

unsung ADJECTIVE **= unacknowledged**, unrecognized, unappreciated, unknown, neglected, anonymous, disregarded, unnamed, uncelebrated, unhonoured, unacclaimed, unhailed

unswerving ADJECTIVE **= firm**, staunch, steadfast, constant, true, direct, devoted, steady, dedicated, resolute, single-minded, unwavering, unflagging, untiring, unfaltering, undeviating

untangle VERB **1 = disentangle**, unravel, sort out, extricate, straighten out, untwist, unsnarl: *trying to untangle several reels of film* **OPPOSITE:** entangle **2 = solve**, clear up, straighten out, understand, explain, figure out *(informal)*, clarify, unravel, fathom, get to the bottom of, elucidate, suss out *(informal)*, puzzle out: *Lawyers began trying to untangle the complex affairs of the bank.* **OPPOSITE:** complicate

untenable ADJECTIVE **= unsustainable**, indefensible, unsound, groundless, weak, flawed, shaky, unreasonable, illogical, fallacious, insupportable **OPPOSITE:** justified

unthinkable ADJECTIVE **1 = impossible**, out of the question, inconceivable, unlikely, not on *(informal)*, absurd, unreasonable, improbable, preposterous, illogical: *Her strong Catholic beliefs made abortion unthinkable.* **2 = inconceivable**, incredible, unbelievable, unimaginable, beyond belief, beyond the bounds of possibility: *Monday's unthinkable tragedy*

unthinking ADJECTIVE **1 = thoughtless**, insensitive, tactless, rude, blundering, inconsiderate, undiplomatic: *He doesn't say those silly things that unthinking people say.* **2 = impulsive**, senseless, unconscious, mechanical, rash, careless, instinctive, oblivious, negligent, unwitting, witless, inadvertent, heedless, unmindful: *Bruce was no unthinking vandal.* **OPPOSITE:** deliberate

untidy ADJECTIVE **1 = messy**, disordered, chaotic, littered, muddled, cluttered, jumbled, rumpled, shambolic, bedraggled, unkempt, topsy-turvy, higgledy-piggledy *(informal)*, mussy *(U.S. informal)*, muddly, disarrayed: *Clothes were thrown in the luggage in an untidy heap.* **OPPOSITE:** neat **2 = unkempt**, dishevelled, tousled, disordered, messy, ruffled, scruffy, rumpled, bedraggled, ratty *(informal)*, straggly, windblown, disarranged, mussed up *(informal)*, daggy *(Austral. & N.Z. informal)*: *a thin man with untidy hair* **3 = sloppy**, messy *(informal)*, slovenly, slipshod, slatternly: *I'm untidy in most ways.* **OPPOSITE:** methodical

untie VERB **= undo**, free, release, loosen, unfasten, unbind, unstrap, unclasp, unlace, unknot, unmoor, unbridle

until PREPOSITION **1 = till**, up to, up till, up to the time, as late as **2 = before**, up to, prior to, in advance of, previous to, pre-

▷ CONJUNCTION **1 = till**, up to, up till, up to the time, as late as **2 = before**, up to, prior to, in advance of, previous to

USAGE
The use of *until such time as* (as in *Industrial action will continue until such time as our demands are met*) is unnecessary and should be avoided: *Industrial action will continue until our demands are met.* The use of *up* before *until* is also redundant and should be avoided: *the talks will continue until* (not *up until*) *23rd March.*

untimely ADJECTIVE **1 = early**, premature, before time, unseasonable: *His mother's untimely death had a catastrophic effect on him.* **OPPOSITE:** timely **2 = ill-timed**, inappropriate, badly timed, inopportune, unfortunate, awkward, unsuitable, inconvenient, mistimed, inauspicious: *Your readers would have seen the article as at best untimely.* **OPPOSITE:** well-timed

untold ADJECTIVE **1 = indescribable**, unthinkable, unimaginable, unspeakable, undreamed of, unutterable, inexpressible: *This might do untold damage to her health.* **2 = countless**, incalculable, innumerable, myriad, numberless, uncounted, uncountable, unnumbered, measureless: *the glittering prospect of untold riches* **3 = undisclosed**, unknown, unrevealed, private, secret, hidden, unrelated, unpublished, unrecounted: *the untold story of children's suffering*

untoward ADJECTIVE **= unfavourable**, unfortunate, disastrous, adverse, contrary, annoying, awkward, irritating, unlucky, inconvenient, untimely, inauspicious, inimical, ill-timed, vexatious, inopportune

untrue ADJECTIVE **1 = false**, lying, wrong, mistaken, misleading, incorrect, inaccurate, sham, dishonest, deceptive, spurious, erroneous, fallacious, untruthful: *The allegations were completely untrue.* **OPPOSITE:** true **2 = unfaithful**, disloyal, deceitful, treacherous, two-faced, faithless, false, untrustworthy, perfidious, forsworn, traitorous, inconstant: *untrue to the basic tenets of socialism* **OPPOSITE:** faithful

untruth NOUN **= lie**, fabrication, falsehood, fib, story, tale, fiction, deceit, whopper *(informal)*, porky *(Brit. slang)*, pork pie *(Brit. slang)*, falsification, prevarication: *The Authority accused estate agents of using blatant untruths.*

unused ADJECTIVE **1 = new**, untouched, remaining, fresh, intact, immaculate, pristine: *unused containers of food and drink* **2 = remaining**, leftover, unconsumed, left, available, extra, unutilized: *Throw away any unused cream when it has reached the expiry date.* **3** (with **to**) **= unaccustomed to**, new to, unfamiliar with, not up to, not ready for, a stranger to, inexperienced in, unhabituated to: *Mother was entirely unused to such hard work.*

unusual ADJECTIVE **1 = rare**, odd, strange, extraordinary, different, surprising, novel, bizarre, unexpected, curious, weird *(informal)*, unfamiliar, abnormal, queer, phenomenal, uncommon, out of the ordinary, left-field *(informal)*, unwonted: *rare and unusual plants* **OPPOSITE:** common **2 = extraordinary**, unique, remarkable, exceptional, notable, phenomenal, uncommon, singular, unconventional, out of the ordinary, atypical: *He was an unusual man with great business talents.* **OPPOSITE:** average

unveil VERB **= reveal**, publish, launch, introduce, release, display, broadcast, demonstrate, expose, bare, parade, exhibit, disclose, uncover, bring out, make public, flaunt, divulge, lay bare, make known, bring to light, put on display, lay open, put on show, put on view **OPPOSITE:** conceal

unwarranted ADJECTIVE **= unnecessary**, unjustified, indefensible, wrong, unreasonable, unjust, gratuitous, unprovoked, inexcusable, groundless, uncalled-for

unwary ADJECTIVE **= careless**, rash, reckless, hasty, thoughtless, unguarded, indiscreet, imprudent, heedless, incautious, uncircumspect, unwatchful **OPPOSITE:** cautious

unwell ADJECTIVE **= ill**, poorly *(informal)*, sick, crook *(Austral. & N.Z. informal)*, ailing, unhealthy, sickly, out of sorts, off colour, under the weather *(informal)*, in poor health, at death's door, indisposed, green about the gills **OPPOSITE:** well

unwieldy ADJECTIVE **1 = bulky**, massive, hefty, clumsy, weighty, ponderous, ungainly, clunky *(informal)*: *They came panting up to his door with their unwieldy baggage.* **2 = awkward**, cumbersome, inconvenient, burdensome, unmanageable, unhandy: *His firm must contend with the unwieldy Russian bureaucracy.*

unwilling ADJECTIVE **1 = disinclined**, reluctant, averse, loath, slow, opposed, resistant, not about, not in the mood, indisposed: *Initially the government was unwilling to accept the defeat.* **OPPOSITE:** willing **2 = reluctant**, grudging, unenthusiastic, resistant, involuntary, averse, demurring, laggard *(rare)*: *He finds himself an unwilling participant in school politics.* **OPPOSITE:** eager

unwind VERB **1 = relax**, wind down, take it easy, slow down, sit back, calm down, take a break, loosen up, quieten down, let yourself go, mellow out *(informal)*, make yourself at home, outspan *(S. African)*: *It helps them to unwind after a busy day at work.* **2 = unravel**, undo, uncoil, slacken, disentangle, unroll, unreel, untwist, untwine: *One of them unwound a length of rope from around his waist.*

unwise ADJECTIVE **= foolish**, stupid, silly, rash, irresponsible, reckless, senseless, short-sighted, ill-advised, foolhardy, inane, indiscreet, ill-judged, ill-considered, imprudent, inadvisable, asinine, injudicious, improvident, impolitic **OPPOSITE:** wise

unwitting ADJECTIVE **1 = unintentional**, involuntary, inadvertent, chance, accidental, unintended, unplanned, undesigned, unmeant: *It had been an unwitting blunder on his part.* **OPPOSITE:** deliberate **2 = unknowing**, innocent, unsuspecting, unconscious, unaware, ignorant: *We're unwitting victims of the system.* **OPPOSITE:** knowing

unworthy ADJECTIVE **1 = undeserving**, not good enough, not fit, not worth, ineligible, not deserving: *You may feel unworthy of the attention and help people offer you.* **OPPOSITE:** deserving **2 = dishonourable**, base, contemptible, degrading, disgraceful, shameful, disreputable, ignoble, discreditable: *Aren't you amazed by how loving the father is to his unworthy son?* **OPPOSITE:** commendable **3** *(with* **of***)* **= unbefitting**, beneath, unfitting to, unsuitable for, inappropriate to, improper to, out of character with, out of place with, unbecoming to: *His accusations are unworthy of a prime minister.*

unwritten ADJECTIVE **1 = oral**, word-of-mouth, unrecorded, vocal: *the unwritten stories of his infancy and childhood* **2 = understood**, accepted, tacit, traditional, conventional, silent, customary, implicit, unformulated: *They obey the one unwritten rule that binds them all – no talking.*

up NOUN
ups and downs = fluctuations, changes, vicissitudes, moods, ebb and flow

up-and-coming ADJECTIVE **= promising**, ambitious, go-getting *(informal)*, pushing, eager

upbeat ADJECTIVE **= cheerful**, positive, optimistic, promising, encouraging, looking up, hopeful, favourable, rosy, buoyant, heartening, cheery, forward-looking

upbringing NOUN **= education**, training, breeding, rearing, care, raising, tending, bringing-up, nurture, cultivation

update VERB **= bring up to date**, improve, correct, renew, revise, upgrade, amend, overhaul, streamline, modernize, rebrand

upgrade VERB **1 = improve**, better, update, reform, add to, enhance, refurbish, renovate, remodel, make better, modernize, spruce up, ameliorate: *Medical facilities are being reorganized and upgraded.* **2 = promote**, raise, advance, boost, move up, elevate, kick upstairs *(informal)*, give promotion to: *He was upgraded to security guard.* **OPPOSITE:** demote

upheaval NOUN **= disturbance**, revolution, disorder, turmoil, overthrow, disruption, eruption, cataclysm, violent change

uphill ADJECTIVE **1 = ascending**, rising, upward, mounting, climbing: *a long, uphill journey* **OPPOSITE:** descending **2 = arduous**, hard, taxing, difficult, tough, exhausting, punishing, gruelling, strenuous, laborious, wearisome, Sisyphean: *It had been an uphill struggle to achieve what she wanted.*

uphold VERB **1 = support**, back, defend, aid, champion, encourage, maintain, promote, sustain, advocate, stand by, stick up for *(informal)*: *upholding the artist's right to creative freedom* **2 = confirm**, support, sustain, endorse, approve, justify, hold to, ratify, vindicate, validate: *The crown court upheld the magistrate's decision.*

upkeep NOUN **1 = maintenance**, running, keep, subsistence, support, repair, conservation, preservation, sustenance: *The money will be used for the estate's upkeep.* **2 = running costs**, expenses, overheads, expenditure, outlay, operating costs, oncosts *(Brit.)*: *subsidies for the upkeep of kindergartens and orphanages*

uplift VERB **= improve**, better, raise, advance, inspire, upgrade, refine, cultivate, civilize, ameliorate, edify: *Art was created to uplift the mind and the spirit.*
▷ NOUN **= improvement**, enlightenment, advancement, cultivation, refinement, enhancement, enrichment, betterment, edification: *literature intended for the uplift of the soul*

upper ADJECTIVE **1 = topmost**, top: *There is a smart restaurant on the upper floor.* **OPPOSITE:** bottom **2 = higher**, high: *the muscles of the upper back and chest* **OPPOSITE:** lower **3 = superior**, senior, higher-level, greater, top, important, chief, most important, elevated, eminent, higher-ranking: *the upper echelons of the Army* **OPPOSITE:** inferior

upper class ADJECTIVE **= aristocratic**, upper-class, noble, high-class, patrician, top-drawer, blue-blooded, highborn

uppermost ADJECTIVE **1 = top**, highest, topmost, upmost, loftiest, most elevated: *John was on the uppermost floor of the three-storey gatehouse.* **OPPOSITE:** bottom **2 = supreme**, greatest, chief, leading, main, primary, principal, dominant, paramount, foremost, predominant, pre-eminent: *Protection of sites is of uppermost priority.* **OPPOSITE:** least

upright ADJECTIVE **1 = vertical**, straight, standing up, erect, on end, perpendicular, bolt upright: *He moved into an upright position.* **OPPOSITE:** horizontal **2 = honest**, good, principled, just, true, faithful, ethical, straightforward, honourable, righteous, conscientious, virtuous, trustworthy, high-minded, above board, incorruptible, unimpeachable:

a very upright, trustworthy man **OPPOSITE:** dishonourable

uprising NOUN **= rebellion**, rising, revolution, outbreak, revolt, disturbance, upheaval, mutiny, insurrection, putsch, insurgence

uproar NOUN **1 = commotion**, noise, racket, riot, confusion, turmoil, brawl, mayhem, clamour, din, turbulence, pandemonium, rumpus, hubbub, hurly-burly, brouhaha, ruction *(informal)*, hullabaloo, ruckus *(informal)*, bagarre *(French)*: *The announcement caused uproar in the crowd.* **2 = protest**, outrage, complaint, objection, fuss, stink *(informal)*, outcry, furore, hue and cry: *The announcement could cause an uproar in the United States.*

uproot VERB **1 = displace**, remove, exile, disorient, deracinate: *the trauma of uprooting them from their homes* **2 = pull up**, dig up, root out, weed out, rip up, grub up, extirpate, deracinate, pull out by the roots: *fallen trees which have been uprooted by the storm*

upset ADJECTIVE **1 = distressed**, shaken, disturbed, worried, troubled, hurt, bothered, confused, unhappy, gutted *(Brit. informal)*, put out, dismayed, choked *(informal)*, grieved, frantic, hassled *(informal)*, agitated, ruffled, cut up *(informal)*, disconcerted, disquieted, overwrought, discomposed: *They are terribly upset by the breakup of their parents' marriage.* **2 = sick**, queasy, bad, poorly *(informal)*, ill, gippy *(slang)*: *Larry is suffering from an upset stomach.*
▷ VERB **1 = distress**, trouble, disturb, worry, alarm, bother, dismay, grieve, hassle *(informal)*, agitate, ruffle, unnerve, disconcert, disquiet, fluster, perturb, faze, throw someone off balance, give someone grief *(Brit. & S. African)*, discompose: *She warned me not to say anything to upset him.* **2 = tip over**, overturn, capsize, knock over, spill, topple over: *bumping into him, and almost upsetting the ginger ale* **3 = mess up**, spoil, disturb, change, confuse, disorder, unsettle, mix up, disorganize, turn topsy-turvy, put out of order, throw into disorder: *I was wondering whether that might upset my level of concentration.*
▷ NOUN **1 = distress**, worry, trouble, shock, bother, disturbance, hassle *(informal)*, disquiet, agitation, discomposure: *a source of continuity in times of worry and upset* **2 = reversal**, surprise, shake-up *(informal)*, defeat, sudden change: *She caused a major upset when she beat last year's finalist.* **3 = illness**, complaint, disorder, bug *(informal)*, disturbance, sickness, malady, queasiness, indisposition: *Paul was unwell last night with a stomach upset.*

upshot NOUN **= result**, consequence, outcome, end, issue, event, conclusion, sequel, finale, culmination, end result, payoff *(informal)*

upside down *or* **upside-down** ADVERB **= wrong side up**, bottom up, on its head: *The painting was hung upside down.*
▷ ADJECTIVE **1 = inverted**, overturned, upturned, on its head, bottom up, wrong side up: *Tony had an upside-down map of Britain on his wall.* **2 = confused**, disordered, chaotic, muddled, jumbled, in disarray, in chaos, topsy-turvy, in confusion, higgledy-piggledy *(informal)*, in disorder: *the upside-down sort of life that we've had*

upstanding ADJECTIVE **= honest**, principled, upright, honourable, good, moral, ethical, trustworthy, incorruptible, true **OPPOSITE:** immoral

upstart NOUN **= social climber**, nobody, nouveau riche *(French)*, parvenu, arriviste, status seeker

uptight ADJECTIVE **= tense**, wired *(slang)*, anxious, neurotic, uneasy, prickly, edgy, on the defensive, on edge, nervy *(Brit. informal)*, adrenalized

up-to-date ADJECTIVE **= modern**, fashionable, trendy *(Brit. informal)*, in, newest, now *(informal)*, happening *(informal)*, current, with it *(informal)*, stylish, in vogue, all the rage, up-to-the-minute, having your finger on the pulse **OPPOSITE:** out-of-date

upturn NOUN **= rise**, increase, boost, improvement, recovery, revival, advancement, upsurge, upswing

urban ADJECTIVE **= civic**, city, town, metropolitan, municipal, dorp *(S. African)*, inner-city

urbane ADJECTIVE **= sophisticated**, cultured, polished, civil, mannerly, smooth, elegant, refined, cultivated, cosmopolitan, civilized, courteous, suave, well-bred, debonair, well-mannered **OPPOSITE:** boorish

urchin NOUN **= ragamuffin**, waif, guttersnipe, brat, mudlark *(slang)*, gamin, street Arab *(offensive)*, young rogue

urge VERB **1 = beg**, appeal to, exhort, press, prompt, plead, put pressure on, lean on, solicit, goad, implore, enjoin, beseech, pressurize, entreat, twist someone's arm *(informal)*, put the heat on *(informal)*, put the screws on *(informal)*: *They urged parliament to approve plans for their reform programme.* **2 = advocate**, suggest, recommend, advise, back, support, champion, counsel, insist on, endorse, push for: *He urged restraint on the security forces.* **OPPOSITE:** discourage
▷ NOUN **= impulse**, longing, wish, desire, fancy, drive, yen *(informal)*, hunger, appetite, craving, yearning, itch *(informal)*, thirst, compulsion, hankering: *He had an urge to open a shop of his own.* **OPPOSITE:** reluctance

urge someone on = drive on, push, encourage, force, press, prompt, stimulate, compel, induce, propel, hasten, constrain, incite, egg on, goad, spur on, impel, gee up: *She had a strong and supportive sister who urged her on.*

urgency NOUN **= importance**, need, necessity, gravity, pressure, hurry, seriousness, extremity, exigency, imperativeness

urgent ADJECTIVE **1 = crucial**, desperate, pressing, great, important, crying, critical, immediate, acute, grave, instant, compelling, imperative, top-priority, now or never, exigent, not to be delayed: *There is an urgent need for food and water.* **OPPOSITE:** unimportant **2 = insistent**, earnest, determined, intense, persistent, persuasive, resolute, clamorous, importunate: *His mother leaned forward and spoke to him in urgent undertones.* **OPPOSITE:** casual

urinate VERB **= pee**, wee *(informal)*, leak *(slang)*, tinkle *(Brit. informal)*, piddle *(informal)*, spend a penny *(Brit. informal)*, make water, pass water, wee-wee *(informal)*, micturate, take a whizz *(slang, chiefly U.S.)*

usable ADJECTIVE **= serviceable**, working, functional, available, current, practical, valid, at your disposal, ready for use, in running order, fit for use, utilizable

usage NOUN **1 = use**, operation, employment, running, control, management, treatment, handling: *Parts of the motor wore out because of constant usage.* **2 = practice**, method, procedure, form, rule, tradition, habit, regime, custom, routine, convention, mode, matter of course, wont: *a fruitful convergence with past usage and custom*

use VERB **1 = employ**, utilize, make use of, work, apply, operate, exercise, practise, resort to, exert, wield, ply, put to use, bring into play, find a use for, avail yourself of, turn to account, call into play: *Officials used loud-hailers to call for calm.* **2** *(sometimes with* **up***)* **= consume**, go through, exhaust, spend, waste, get through, run through, deplete, dissipate, expend, fritter away: *You used all the ice cubes and didn't put the ice trays back.* **3 = take advantage of**, exploit, manipulate, abuse, milk, profit from, impose on, misuse, make use of, cash in on *(informal)*, walk all over *(informal)*, take liberties with: *Be careful she's not just using you.*
▷ NOUN **1 = usage**, employment, utilization, operation, application: *research related to microcomputers and their use in classrooms* **2 = service**, handling, wear and tear, treatment, practice, exercise: *Holes had developed, the result of many years of use.* **3 = purpose**, call, need, end, point, cause, reason, occasion, object, necessity: *You will no longer have a use for the car.* **4 = good**, point, help, service, value, benefit, profit, worth, advantage, utility, mileage *(informal)*, avail, usefulness: *There's no use you asking me any more questions about that.*

use something up = **consume**, drain, exhaust, finish, waste, absorb, run through, deplete, squander, devour, swallow up, burn up, fritter away: *They aren't the ones who use up the world's resources.*

used ADJECTIVE = **second-hand**, worn, not new, cast-off, hand-me-down (*informal*), nearly new, shopsoiled, reach-me-down (*informal*), preloved (*Austral. slang*) **OPPOSITE:** new

used to ADJECTIVE = **accustomed to**, familiar with, in the habit of, given to, at home in, attuned to, tolerant of, wont to, inured to, hardened to, habituated to

useful ADJECTIVE = **helpful**, effective, valuable, practical, of use, profitable, of service, worthwhile, beneficial, of help, fruitful, advantageous, all-purpose, salutary, general-purpose, serviceable **OPPOSITE:** useless

usefulness NOUN = **helpfulness**, value, worth, use, help, service, benefit, profit, utility, effectiveness, convenience, practicality, efficacy

useless ADJECTIVE **1** = **worthless**, of no use, valueless, pants (*slang*), ineffective, impractical, fruitless, unproductive, ineffectual, unworkable, disadvantageous, unavailing, bootless, unsuitable: *He realised that their money was useless in this country.* **OPPOSITE:** useful **2** = **pointless**, hopeless, futile, vain, idle, profitless: *She knew it was useless to protest.* **OPPOSITE:** worthwhile **3** = **inept**, no good, hopeless, weak, stupid, pants (*slang*), incompetent, ineffectual: *He was useless at any game with a ball.*

usher VERB = **escort**, lead, direct, guide, conduct, pilot, steer, show: *They were quickly ushered away.*
▷ NOUN = **attendant**, guide, doorman, usherette, escort, doorkeeper: *He did part-time work as an usher in a theatre.*
usher something in = **introduce**, launch, bring in, precede, initiate, herald, pave the way for, ring in, open the door to, inaugurate: *a unique opportunity to usher in a new era of stability in Europe*

usual ADJECTIVE = **normal**, customary, regular, expected, general, common, stock, standard, fixed, ordinary, familiar, typical, constant, routine, everyday, accustomed, habitual, bog-standard (*Brit. & Irish slang*), wonted **OPPOSITE:** unusual

usually ADVERB = **normally**, generally, mainly, commonly, regularly, mostly, routinely, on the whole, in the main, for the most part, by and large, most often, ordinarily, as a rule, habitually, as is usual, as is the custom

usurp VERB = **seize**, take over, assume, take, appropriate, wrest, commandeer, arrogate, infringe upon, lay hold of

utility NOUN = **usefulness**, use, point, benefit, service, profit, fitness, convenience, mileage (*informal*), avail, practicality, efficacy, advantageousness, serviceableness

utilize VERB = **use**, employ, deploy, take advantage of, resort to, make the most of, make use of, put to use, bring into play, have recourse to, avail yourself of, turn to account

utmost ADJECTIVE **1** = **greatest**, highest, maximum, supreme, extreme, paramount, pre-eminent: *Security matters are treated with the utmost seriousness.* **2** = **farthest**, extreme, last, final, outermost, uttermost, farthermost: *The break-up tested our resolve to its utmost limits.*
▷ NOUN = **best**, greatest, maximum, most, highest, hardest: *I'm going to do my utmost to climb as fast and as far as I can.*

utopia NOUN = **paradise**, heaven, Eden, bliss, perfect place, Garden of Eden, Shangri-la, Happy Valley, seventh heaven, ideal life, Erewhon

utopian ADJECTIVE = **perfect**, ideal, romantic, dream, fantasy, imaginary, visionary, airy, idealistic, fanciful, impractical, illusory, chimerical: *He was pursuing a utopian dream of world prosperity.*
▷ NOUN = **dreamer**, visionary, idealist, Don Quixote, romanticist: *Kennedy had no patience with dreamers or liberal utopians.*

utter[1] VERB = **say**, state, speak, voice, express, deliver, declare, mouth, breathe, pronounce, articulate, enunciate, put into words, verbalize, vocalize: *They departed without uttering a word.*

utter[2] ADJECTIVE = **absolute**, complete, total, perfect, positive, pure, sheer, stark, outright, all-out, thorough, downright, real, consummate, veritable, unqualified, out-and-out, unadulterated, unmitigated, thoroughgoing, arrant, deep-dyed (*usually derogatory*): *A look of utter confusion swept across his handsome face.*

utterance NOUN **1** = **speech**, words, statement, comment, opinion, remark, expression, announcement, observation, declaration, reflection, pronouncement: *the Queen's public utterances* **2** = **speaking**, voicing, expression, breathing, delivery, ejaculation, articulation, enunciation, vocalization, verbalization, vociferation: *the simple utterance of a few platitudes*

utterly ADVERB = **totally**, completely, absolutely, just, really, quite, perfectly, fully, entirely, extremely, altogether, thoroughly, wholly, downright, categorically, to the core, one hundred per cent, in all respects, to the nth degree, unqualifiedly

The Language of Lewis Carroll

Lewis Carroll was the pen-name of the Reverend Charles Lutwidge Dodgson (1832–98) an Oxford mathematics don most famous for his two Alice stories, *Alice's Adventures in Wonderland* and *Through the Looking-Glass and What Alice Found There*. He also published poetry and a number of academic works, most notably on algebra.

A distinctive feature of Carroll's writing is his use of nonsense, most prominently perhaps in his poems 'Jabberwocky' and 'The Hunting of the Snark.' Such writing works by reproducing the conventional rhythms of poetry and the usual syntax of English so that the words sound like they ought to make sense. The insertion of made-up nonsense words into these patterns, however, produces instead a playful avoidance of a clear semantic outcome, as in the famous opening of 'Jaberwocky:'

'Twas brilig, and the slithy toves
Did gyre and gimble in the wabe.

The different parts of speech are still clearly recognisable here. *Brilig*, *toves*, and *wabe* are evidently nouns, *gyre* and *gimble* are verbs, while *slithy* undoubtedly has the feel of an adjective. Some of these words are produced by compressing two different terms into one sound: as Humpty-Dumpty explains to Alice, '*slithy* means lithe and slimy.' Another strategy of Carroll's nonsense writing is the construction of sentences that make semantic sense but which are undercut by a failure of logic or by the bizarre flights of fantasy that occur throughout his literary works.

Riddles comprise an important aspect of this tendency towards the irrational. While usually operating as word puzzles with a complicated solution, in Carroll's work the idea of a solution is challenged. Accordingly, *mean* and *meaning* are important words in Carroll, often deployed in a negative sense of things slipping away from stable and familiar connotations.

'When I use a word,' Humpty Dumpty said, in rather a scornful tone, 'it means just what I choose it to mean – neither more nor less.'

The adjective used most commonly by Carroll is *little*, which most often modifies *fellow*, a generic term for a man or boy in popular usage in the late 19th and early 20th century but now rarely heard. *Little* is also frequently used with *lady*, *creature*, *boy*, and *brook*. The other adjective that features most with *little* is *poor*, not as an indication of poverty, but in the more general sense of misfortunate or distressed, as in:

... the **poor little** thing coughed violently for some time.

Large and *big*, by contrast appear relatively rarely. *Large* occurs most saliently with *eyes* though conversely the large size of the eyes at times only gives emphasis to the Alice's smallness, as in

The Frog looked at the door with his **large** dull **eyes** for a minute.

Smallness, then, is a central aspect of Alice's adventures with a shrinking potion famously providing her with the means to disappear down the rabbit hole and enter the fabulous world beneath.

Indeed, words suggesting beneath are recurrent in Carroll's writing, particularly *down* and *under*. While these words appear in a number of commonplace usages, such as 'under the circumstances', there are also numerous instances at which they refer to a specific place or object, often concealed below something else or to the possibility of hiding. *Under* is used in these contexts with *hedge*, *table*, *door*, *window*, *tree*, and *leaves*, as in:

You keep your head under the leaves, and snore away there, till you know no more what's going on in the world, than if you were a bud!

Carroll's use of underworlds was a significant part of his writing's intention to disappear from Victorian literary and social conventions into an alternative world of the grotesque and unlikely.

Vv

vacancy NOUN **1 = opening**, job, post, place, position, role, situation, opportunity, slot, berth *(informal)*, niche, job opportunity, vacant position, situation vacant: *They had a vacancy for a temporary secretary.* **2 = room**, space, available accommodation, unoccupied room: *The hotel only has a few vacancies left.*

vacant ADJECTIVE **1 = empty**, free, available, abandoned, deserted, to let, for sale, on the market, void, up for grabs, disengaged, uninhabited, unoccupied, not in use, unfilled, untenanted: *They came upon a vacant house.* **OPPOSITE:** occupied **2 = unfilled**, unoccupied: *The post has been vacant for some time.* **OPPOSITE:** taken **3 = blank**, vague, dreamy, dreaming, empty, abstracted, idle, thoughtless, vacuous, inane, expressionless, unthinking, absent-minded, incurious, ditzy *or* ditsy *(slang)*: *She had a dreamy, vacant look on her face.* **OPPOSITE:** thoughtful

vacate VERB **1 = leave**, quit, move out of, give up, withdraw from, evacuate, depart from, go away from, leave empty, relinquish possession of: *He vacated the flat and went back to stay with his parents.* **2 = quit**, leave, resign from, give up, withdraw from, chuck *(informal)*, retire from, relinquish, renounce, walk out on, pack in *(informal)*, abdicate, step down from *(informal)*, stand down from: *He recently vacated his post as Personnel Director.*

vacuous ADJECTIVE **= vapid**, stupid, inane, blank, vacant, unintelligent

vacuum NOUN **1 = gap**, lack, absence, space, deficiency, void: *The collapse of the army left a vacuum in the area.* **2 = emptiness**, space, void, gap, empty space, nothingness, vacuity: *The spinning turbine creates a vacuum.*

vagabond NOUN **= tramp**, bum *(informal)*, drifter, vagrant, migrant, rolling stone, wanderer, beggar, outcast, rover, nomad, itinerant, down-and-out, hobo *(U.S.)*, bag lady *(chiefly U.S.)*, wayfarer, dosser *(Brit. slang)*, knight of the road, person of no fixed address, derro *(Austral. slang)*: *He had lived as a vagabond, begging for food.*
▷ MODIFIER **= vagrant**, drifting, wandering, homeless, journeying, unsettled, roaming, idle, roving, nomadic, destitute, itinerant, down and out, rootless, footloose, fly-by-night *(informal)*, shiftless: *his impoverished, vagabond existence*

vagary NOUN *(usually plural)* **= whim**, caprice, unpredictability, sport, urge, fancy, notion, humour, impulse, quirk, conceit, whimsy, crotchet, sudden notion

vagrant NOUN **= tramp**, bum *(informal)*, drifter, vagabond, rolling stone, wanderer, beggar, derelict, itinerant, down-and-out, hobo *(U.S.)*, bag lady *(chiefly U.S.)*, dosser *(Brit. slang)*, pikey *(Brit. slang)*, person of no fixed address, derro *(Austral. slang)*: *He lived on the street as a vagrant.*
▷ ADJECTIVE **= vagabond**, drifting, wandering, homeless, journeying, unsettled, roaming, idle, roving, nomadic, destitute, itinerant, down and out, rootless, footloose, fly-by-night *(informal)*, shiftless: *the terrifying subculture of vagrant alcoholics* **OPPOSITE:** settled

vague ADJECTIVE **1 = unclear**, indefinite, hazy, confused, loose, uncertain, doubtful, unsure, superficial, incomplete, woolly, imperfect, sketchy, cursory: *Her description of her attacker was very vague.* **OPPOSITE:** clear **2 = imprecise**, unspecified, generalized, rough, loose, ambiguous, hazy, equivocal, ill-defined, non-specific, inexact, obfuscatory, inexplicit: *His answer was deliberately vague.* **3 = absent-minded**, absorbed, abstracted, distracted, unaware, musing, vacant, preoccupied, bemused, oblivious, dreamy, daydreaming, faraway, unthinking, heedless, inattentive, unheeding: *She had married a charming but rather vague Englishman.* **4 = indistinct**, blurred, unclear, dim, fuzzy, unknown, obscure, faint, shadowy, indefinite, misty, hazy, indistinguishable, amorphous, indeterminate, bleary, nebulous, out of focus, ill-defined, indiscernible: *He could just make out a vague shape in the distance.* **OPPOSITE:** distinct

vaguely ADVERB **1 = slightly**, rather, sort of *(informal)*, kind of *(informal)*, a little, a bit, somewhat, moderately, faintly, dimly, to some extent, kinda *(informal)*: *The voice was vaguely familiar.* **2 = absent-mindedly**, evasively, abstractedly, obscurely, vacantly, inattentively: *'What did you talk about?' 'Oh, this and that,' she replied vaguely.* **3 = roughly**, loosely, indefinitely, carelessly, in a general way, imprecisely: *'She's back there,' he said, waving vaguely behind him.*

vagueness NOUN **1 = impreciseness**, ambiguity, obscurity, looseness, inexactitude, woolliness, undecidedness, lack of preciseness: *the vagueness of the language used in the text* **OPPOSITE:** preciseness **2 = absent-mindedness**, abstraction, forgetfulness, confusion, inattention, disorganization, giddiness, dreaminess, befuddlement, empty-headedness: *her deliberately affected vagueness*

vain ADJECTIVE **1 = futile**, useless, pointless, unsuccessful, empty, hollow, idle, trivial, worthless, trifling, senseless, unimportant, fruitless, unproductive, abortive, unprofitable, time-wasting, unavailing, nugatory: *They worked all night in a vain attempt to finish on schedule.* **OPPOSITE:** successful **2 = conceited**, narcissistic, proud, arrogant, inflated, swaggering, stuck-up *(informal)*, cocky, swanky *(informal)*, ostentatious, egotistical, self-important, overweening, vainglorious, swollen-headed *(informal)*, pleased with yourself, bigheaded *(informal)*, peacockish: *She's a shallow, vain and self-centred woman.* **OPPOSITE:** modest
in vain 1 = useless, to no avail, unsuccessful, fruitless, wasted, vain, ineffectual, without success, to no purpose, bootless: *All her complaints were in vain.* **2 = uselessly**, to no avail, unsuccessfully, fruitlessly, vainly, ineffectually, without success, to no purpose, bootlessly: *He hammered the door, trying in vain to attract her attention.*

valiant ADJECTIVE **= brave**, heroic, courageous, bold, worthy, fearless, gallant, intrepid, plucky, doughty, indomitable, redoubtable, dauntless, lion-hearted, valorous, stouthearted **OPPOSITE:** cowardly

valid ADJECTIVE **1 = sound**, good, reasonable, just, telling, powerful, convincing, substantial, acceptable, sensible, rational, logical, viable, credible, sustainable, plausible, conclusive, weighty, well-founded, cogent, well-grounded: *Both sides have made valid points.* **OPPOSITE:** unfounded **2 = legal**, official, legitimate, correct, genuine, proper, in effect, authentic, in force, lawful, bona fide, legally binding, signed and sealed: *For foreign holidays you will need a valid passport.* **OPPOSITE:** invalid

validate VERB **1 = confirm**, prove, certify, substantiate, corroborate: *The evidence has been validated by historians.* **2 = authorize**, endorse, ratify, legalize, authenticate, make legally binding, set your seal on *or* to: *Give the retailer your winning ticket to validate.*

validity NOUN **1 = soundness**, force, power, grounds, weight, strength, foundation, substance, point, cogency: *Some people deny the validity of* *this claim.* **2 = legality**, authority, legitimacy, right, lawfulness: *They now want to challenge the validity of the vote.*

valley NOUN **= hollow**, dale, glen, vale, depression, dell, dingle, strath *(Scot.)*, cwm *(Welsh)*, coomb

valour *or (U.S.)* **valor** NOUN **= bravery**, courage, heroism, spirit, boldness, gallantry, derring-do *(archaic)*, fearlessness, intrepidity, doughtiness, lion-heartedness **OPPOSITE:** cowardice

valuable ADJECTIVE **1 = useful**, important, profitable, worthwhile, beneficial, valued, helpful, worthy, of use, of help, invaluable, serviceable, worth its weight in gold: *The experience was very valuable.* **OPPOSITE:** useless **2 = treasured**, esteemed, cherished, prized, precious, held dear, estimable, worth your weight in gold: *She was a valuable friend and an excellent teacher.* **3 = precious**, expensive, costly, dear, high-priced, priceless, irreplaceable: *valuable old books* **OPPOSITE:** worthless ▷ PLURAL NOUN **= treasures**, prized possessions, precious items, heirlooms, personal effects, costly articles: *Leave your valuables in the hotel safe.*

value NOUN **1 = importance**, use, benefit, worth, merit, point, help, service, sense, profit, advantage, utility, significance, effectiveness, mileage *(informal)*, practicality, usefulness, efficacy, desirability, serviceableness: *Studies are needed to see if these therapies have any value.* **OPPOSITE:** worthlessness **2 = cost**, price, worth, rate, equivalent, market price, face value, asking price, selling price, monetary worth: *The value of his investment has risen by more than 100%.* ▷ PLURAL NOUN **= principles**, morals, ethics, mores, standards of behaviour, code of behaviour, (moral) standards: *a return to traditional family values* ▷ VERB **1 = appreciate**, rate, prize, regard highly, respect, admire, treasure, esteem, cherish, think much of, hold dear, have a high opinion of, set store by, hold in high regard *or* esteem: *Do you value your best friend enough?* **OPPOSITE:** undervalue **2** *(with* **at***)* **= evaluate**, price, estimate, rate, cost, survey, assess, set at, appraise, put a price on: *I have had my jewellery valued for insurance purposes; cocaine valued at $53 million*

valued ADJECTIVE **= appreciated**, prized, esteemed, highly regarded, loved, dear, treasured, cherished

vandal NOUN **= hooligan**, ned *(Scot. slang)*, delinquent, rowdy, lager lout, graffiti artist, yob *or* yobbo *(Brit. slang)*, cougan *(Austral. slang)*, scozza *(Austral. slang)*, bogan *(Austral. slang)*

vanguard NOUN **= forefront**, front line, cutting edge, leaders, front, van, spearhead, forerunners, front rank, trailblazers, advance guard, trendsetters **OPPOSITE:** rearguard

vanish VERB **1 = disappear**, become invisible, be lost to sight, dissolve, evaporate, fade away, melt away, disappear from sight, exit, evanesce: *The aircraft vanished without trace.* **OPPOSITE:** appear **2 = die out**, disappear, pass away, end, fade, dwindle, cease to exist, become extinct, disappear from the face of the earth: *Dinosaurs vanished from the earth millions of years ago.*

vanity NOUN **1 = pride**, arrogance, conceit, airs, showing off *(informal)*, pretension, narcissism, egotism, self-love, ostentation, vainglory, self-admiration, affected ways, bigheadedness *(informal)*, conceitedness, swollen-headedness *(informal)*: *Men who use steroids are motivated by sheer vanity.* **OPPOSITE:** modesty **2 = futility**, uselessness, worthlessness, emptiness, frivolity, unreality, triviality, hollowness, pointlessness, inanity, unproductiveness, fruitlessness, unsubstantiality, profitlessness: *the futility of human existence and the vanity of wealth* **OPPOSITE:** value

QUOTATIONS

I've only been in love with a beer bottle and a mirror
[Sid Vicious]

Vanity is a vital aid to nature: completely and absolutely necessary to life. It is one of nature's ways to bind you to the earth
[Elizabeth Smart *Necessary Secrets*]

Vanity, like murder, will out
[Hannah Cowley *The Belle's Stratagem*]

Possibly, more people kill themselves and others out of hurt vanity than out of envy, jealousy, malice or desire for revenge
[Iris Murdoch *The Philosopher's Pupil*]

Vanity of vanities, all is vanity
[*Bible: Ecclesiastes*]

We are so vain that we even care for the opinion of those we don't care for
[Marie von Ebner-Eschenbach]

vanquish VERB **= defeat**, beat, conquer, reduce, stuff *(slang)*, master, tank *(slang)*, overcome, crush, overwhelm, put down, lick *(informal)*, undo, subdue, rout, repress, overpower, quell, triumph over, clobber *(slang)*, subjugate, run rings around *(informal)*, wipe the floor with *(informal)*, blow out of the water *(slang)*, put to flight, get the upper hand over, put to rout

vapour *or (U.S.)* **vapor** NOUN **= mist**, fog, haze, smoke, breath, steam, fumes, dampness, miasma, exhalation

variable ADJECTIVE **= changeable**, unstable, fluctuating, shifting, flexible, wavering, uneven, fickle, temperamental, mercurial, capricious, unsteady, protean, vacillating, fitful, mutable, inconstant, chameleonic **OPPOSITE:** constant

variance NOUN **OPPOSITE:** agreement **at variance = in disagreement**, conflicting, at odds, in opposition, out of line, at loggerheads, at sixes and sevens *(informal)*, out of harmony: *Many of his statements are at variance with the facts.*

variant ADJECTIVE **= different**, alternative, modified, derived, exceptional, divergent: *There are so many variant spellings of this name.* ▷ NOUN **= variation**, form, version, development, alternative, adaptation, revision, modification, permutation, transfiguration, aberration, derived form: *Bulimia was once seen as a variant of anorexia.*

variation NOUN **1 = alternative**, variety, modification, departure, innovation, variant: *This delicious variation on an omelette is easy to prepare.* **2 = variety**, change, deviation, difference, diversity, diversion, novelty, alteration, discrepancy, diversification, departure from the norm, break in routine: *Every day without variation my grandfather ate a plate of ham.* **OPPOSITE:** uniformity

varied ADJECTIVE **= different**, mixed, various, diverse, assorted, miscellaneous, sundry, motley, manifold, heterogeneous **OPPOSITE:** unvarying

variegated ADJECTIVE **= mottled**, pied, streaked, motley, many-coloured, parti-coloured, varicoloured

variety NOUN **1 = diversity**, change, variation, difference, diversification, heterogeneity, many-sidedness, multifariousness: *people who like variety in their lives and enjoy trying new things* **OPPOSITE:** uniformity **2 = range**, selection, assortment, mix, collection, line-up, mixture, array, cross section, medley, multiplicity, mixed bag *(informal)*, miscellany, motley collection, intermixture: *a store selling a wide variety of goods* **3 = type**, sort, kind, make, order, class, brand, species, breed, strain, category: *She grows 12 varieties of old-fashioned roses.*

QUOTATIONS

Variety's the very spice of life,
That gives all its flavour
[William Cowper *The Task*]

You should make a point of trying everything once, excepting incest and folk-dancing
[Sir Arnold Bax *Farewell My Youth*]

PROVERBS

Different strokes for different folks

various DETERMINER **= different**, assorted, miscellaneous, varied, differing, distinct, diverse, divers *(archaic)*, diversified, disparate, sundry, heterogeneous: *He plans to spread his capital between various bank accounts.* **OPPOSITE:** similar

▷ ADJECTIVE = **many**, numerous, countless, several, abundant, innumerable, sundry, manifold, profuse: *The methods employed are many and various.*

> **USAGE**
> The use of *different* after *various*, which seems to be most common in speech, is unnecessary and should be avoided in serious writing: *The disease exists in various forms* (not *in various different forms*).

varnish NOUN = **lacquer**, polish, glaze, japan, gloss, shellac: *The varnish comes in six natural shades.*
▷ VERB **1** = **lacquer**, polish, glaze, japan, gloss, shellac: *The painting still has to be varnished* **2** = **polish**, decorate, glaze, adorn, gild, lacquer, embellish: *The floors have all been varnished.*

vary VERB **1** = **differ**, be different, be dissimilar, disagree, diverge, be unlike: *As the rugs are all handmade, each one varies slightly.* **2** = **change**, shift, swing, transform, alter, fluctuate, oscillate, see-saw: *women whose moods vary according to their menstrual cycle* **3** = **alternate**, mix, diversify, reorder, intermix, bring variety to, permutate, variegate: *Try to vary your daily diet to include all the major food groups.* **4** = **modify**, change, alter, adjust: *The colour can be varied by adding filters.*

varying ADJECTIVE **1** = **different**, contrasting, inconsistent, varied, distinct, diverse, assorted, disparate, dissimilar, distinguishable, discrepant, streets apart: *Reporters gave varying figures on the number of casualties.* **2** = **changing**, variable, irregular, inconsistent, fluctuating: *The green table lamp flickered with varying intensity.* **OPPOSITE:** unchanging

vassal NOUN = **serf**, slave, bondsman, subject, retainer, thrall, varlet *(archaic)*, bondservant, liegeman

vast ADJECTIVE = **huge**, massive, enormous, great, wide, sweeping, extensive, tremendous, immense, mega *(slang)*, unlimited, gigantic, astronomical, monumental, monstrous, mammoth, colossal, never-ending, prodigious, limitless, boundless, voluminous, immeasurable, unbounded, elephantine, ginormous *(informal)*, vasty *(archaic)*, measureless, illimitable, humongous *or* humungous *(U.S. slang)* **OPPOSITE:** tiny

vault[1] NOUN **1** = **strongroom**, repository, depository: *The money was in storage in bank vaults.* **2** = **crypt**, tomb, catacomb, cellar, mausoleum, charnel house, undercroft: *He ordered that Matilda's body should be buried in the family vault.* **3** = **arch**, roof, ceiling, span: *the vault of a magnificent cathedral*

vault[2] VERB = **jump**, spring, leap, clear, bound, hurdle: *Ned vaulted over the low wall.*

vaunted ADJECTIVE = **boasted about**, flaunted, paraded, shown off, made much of, bragged about, crowed about, exulted in, made a display of, prated about

veer VERB = **change direction**, turn, swerve, shift, sheer, tack, be deflected, change course

vehemence NOUN = **forcefulness**, force, violence, fire, energy, heat, passion, emphasis, enthusiasm, intensity, warmth, vigour, zeal, verve, fervour, eagerness, ardour, earnestness, keenness, fervency **OPPOSITE:** indifference

vehement ADJECTIVE = **strong**, fierce, forceful, earnest, powerful, violent, intense, flaming, eager, enthusiastic, passionate, ardent, emphatic, fervent, impassioned, zealous, forcible, fervid **OPPOSITE:** half-hearted

vehicle NOUN **1** = **conveyance**, machine, motor vehicle, means of transport: *a vehicle which was somewhere between a tractor and a truck* **2** = **medium**, means, channel, mechanism, organ, apparatus, means of expression: *Her art became a vehicle for her political beliefs.*

veil NOUN **1** = **mask**, cover, shroud, film, shade, curtain, cloak: *She swathed her face in a veil of decorative muslin.* **2** = **screen**, mask, disguise, blind: *the chilling facts behind this veil of secrecy* **3** = **film**, cover, curtain, cloak, shroud: *He recognized the coast of England through the veil of mist.*
▷ VERB = **cover**, screen, hide, mask, shield, disguise, conceal, obscure, dim, cloak, mantle: *Her hair swept across her face, as if to veil it.* **OPPOSITE:** reveal

veiled ADJECTIVE = **disguised**, implied, hinted at, covert, masked, concealed, suppressed

vein NOUN **1** = **blood vessel**: *Many veins are found just under the skin.* **2** = **mood**, style, spirit, way, turn, note, key, character, attitude, atmosphere, tone, manner, bent, stamp, humour, tendency, mode, temper, temperament, tenor, inclination, disposition, frame of mind: *He also wrote several works in a lighter vein.* **3** = **streak**, element, thread, suggestion, strain, trace, hint, dash, trait, sprinkling, nuance, smattering: *The song has a vein of black humour running through it.* **4** = **seam**, layer, stratum, course, current, bed, deposit, streak, stripe, lode: *a rich deep vein of copper in the rock*
▸ *related adjective:* venous

velocity NOUN = **speed**, pace, rapidity, quickness, swiftness, fleetness, celerity

velvety ADJECTIVE = **soft**, smooth, downy, delicate, mossy, velvet-like

venal ADJECTIVE = **corrupt**, bent *(slang)*, crooked *(informal)*, prostituted, grafting *(informal)*, mercenary, sordid, rapacious, unprincipled, dishonourable, corruptible, purchasable **OPPOSITE:** honest

vendetta NOUN = **feud**, dispute, quarrel, enmity, bad blood, blood feud

veneer NOUN **1** = **mask**, show, façade, front, appearance, guise, pretence, semblance, false front: *He was able to fool people with his veneer of intellectuality.* **2** = **layer**, covering, finish, facing, film, gloss, patina, laminate, cladding, lamination: *bath panels fitted with a mahogany veneer*

venerable ADJECTIVE = **respected**, august, sage, revered, honoured, wise, esteemed, reverenced

venerate VERB = **respect**, honour, esteem, revere, worship, adore, reverence, look up to, hold in awe **OPPOSITE:** scorn

veneration NOUN = **respect**, esteem, reverence, worship, awe, deference, adoration

vengeance NOUN = **revenge**, retaliation, reprisal, retribution, avenging, an eye for an eye, settling of scores, requital, lex talionis: *She wanted vengeance for the loss of her daughter.* **OPPOSITE:** forgiveness
with a vengeance = **to the utmost**, greatly, extremely, to the full, and no mistake, to the nth degree, with no holds barred: *The problem has returned with a vengeance.*

> **QUOTATIONS**
> Vengeance is mine; I will repay, saith the Lord
> [*Bible: Romans*]

vengeful ADJECTIVE = **unforgiving**, relentless, avenging, vindictive, punitive, implacable, spiteful, retaliatory, rancorous, thirsting for revenge, revengeful

venom NOUN **1** = **malice**, hate, spite, bitterness, grudge, gall, acidity, spleen, acrimony, rancour, ill will, malevolence, virulence, pungency, malignity, spitefulness, maliciousness: *There was no mistaking the venom in his voice.* **OPPOSITE:** benevolence **2** = **poison**, toxin, bane: *snake handlers who grow immune to snake venom*

venomous ADJECTIVE **1** = **malicious**, vindictive, spiteful, hostile, savage, vicious, malignant, virulent, baleful, rancorous: *He made a venomous personal attack on his opponent.* **OPPOSITE:** benevolent **2** = **poisonous**, poison, toxic, virulent, noxious, baneful *(archaic)*, envenomed, mephitic: *The adder is Britain's only venomous snake.* **OPPOSITE:** harmless

vent NOUN = **outlet**, opening, hole, split, aperture, duct, orifice: *There was a small air vent in the ceiling.*
▷ VERB = **express**, release, voice, air, empty, discharge, utter, emit, come out with, pour out, give vent to, give expression to: *She telephoned her best friend to vent her frustration.* **OPPOSITE:** hold back

ventilate VERB **1** = **aerate**, fan, cool, refresh, air-condition, freshen, oxygenate: *The pit is ventilated by a steel fan.* **2** = **discuss**, air, bring out into the open, talk about, debate, examine,

V

broadcast, sift, scrutinize, make known: *Following a bereavement, people need a safe place to ventilate their feelings.*

venture VERB **1 = go**, travel, journey, set out, wander, stray, plunge into, rove, set forth: *Few Europeans had ventured beyond the Himalayas.* **2 = dare**, presume, have the courage to, be brave enough, hazard, go out on a limb *(informal)*, take the liberty, stick your neck out *(informal)*, go so far as, make so bold as, have the temerity *or* effrontery *or* nerve: *Each time I ventured to speak, I was ignored.* **3 = put forward**, offer, suggest, present, air, table, advance, propose, volunteer, submit, bring up, postulate, proffer, broach, posit, moot, propound, dare to say: *We were warned not to make fools of ourselves by venturing an opinion.*
▷ NOUN **= undertaking**, project, enterprise, chance, campaign, risk, operation, activity, scheme, task, mission, speculation, gamble, adventure, exploit, pursuit, fling, hazard, crusade, endeavour: *a Russian-American joint venture*

PROVERBS
Nothing ventured, nothing gained

veracity NOUN **1 = accuracy**, truth, credibility, precision, exactitude: *We have total confidence in the veracity of our research.* **2 = truthfulness**, integrity, honesty, candour, frankness, probity, rectitude, trustworthiness, uprightness: *He was shocked to find his veracity being questioned.*

verbal ADJECTIVE **1 = spoken**, oral, word-of-mouth, unwritten **2 = verbatim**, literal

verbally ADVERB **= orally**, vocally, in words, in speech, by word of mouth

verbatim ADVERB **= exactly**, to the letter, word for word, closely, precisely, literally, faithfully, rigorously, in every detail, letter for letter: *The president's speeches are reproduced verbatim in the state-run newspapers.*
▷ ADJECTIVE **= word for word**, exact, literal, close, precise, faithful, line by line, unabridged, unvarnished, undeviating, unembellished: *He gave me a verbatim report of the entire conversation.*

verdant ADJECTIVE **= green**, lush, leafy, grassy, fresh, flourishing

verdict NOUN **= decision**, finding, judgment, opinion, sentence, conclusion, conviction, adjudication, pronouncement

verge NOUN **1 = brink**, point, edge, threshold: *Carole was on the verge of tears.* **2 = border**, edge, margin, limit, extreme, lip, boundary, threshold, roadside, brim: *The car pulled over on to the verge off the road.*
verge on something = come near to, approach, border on, resemble, incline to, be similar to, touch on, be more or less, be tantamount to, tend towards, be not far from, incline towards: *a fury that verges on madness*

verification NOUN **= proof**, confirmation, validation, corroboration, authentication, substantiation

verify VERB **1 = check**, confirm, make sure, examine, monitor, check out *(informal)*, inspect: *A clerk simply verifies that the payment and invoice amount match.* **2 = confirm**, prove, substantiate, support, validate, bear out, attest, corroborate, attest to, authenticate: *The government has not verified any of these reports.* **OPPOSITE:** disprove

vernacular NOUN *(with* **the***)* **= speech**, jargon, idiom, parlance, cant, native language, dialect, patois, argot, vulgar tongue: *To use the vernacular of the day, Peter was square.*
▷ ADJECTIVE **= colloquial**, popular, informal, local, common, native, indigenous, vulgar: *dialects such as black vernacular English*

versatile ADJECTIVE **1 = adaptable**, flexible, all-round, resourceful, protean, multifaceted, many-sided, all-singing, all-dancing: *He stood out as one of the game's most versatile athletes.* **OPPOSITE:** unadaptable **2 = all-purpose**, handy, functional, variable, adjustable, all-singing, all-dancing: *a versatile piece of equipment* **OPPOSITE:** limited

versed ADJECTIVE *(with* **in***)* **= knowledgeable**, experienced, skilled, seasoned, qualified, familiar, practised, accomplished, competent, acquainted, well-informed, proficient, well up *(informal)*, conversant **OPPOSITE:** ignorant

version NOUN **1 = form**, variety, variant, sort, kind, class, design, style, model, type, brand, genre: *Ludo is a version of an ancient Indian racing game.* **2 = adaptation**, edition, interpretation, form, reading, copy, rendering, translation, reproduction, portrayal: *The English version is far inferior to the original French text.* **3 = account**, report, side, description, record, reading, story, view, understanding, history, statement, analysis, take *(informal, chiefly U.S.)*, construction, tale, impression, explanation, interpretation, rendering, narrative, chronicle, rendition, narration, construal: *She went public with her version of events.*

vertical ADJECTIVE **= upright**, sheer, perpendicular, straight (up and down), erect, plumb, on end, precipitous, vertiginous, bolt upright **OPPOSITE:** horizontal

vertigo NOUN **= dizziness**, giddiness, light-headedness, fear of heights, loss of balance, acrophobia, loss of equilibrium, swimming of the head

verve NOUN **= enthusiasm**, energy, spirit, life, force, punch *(informal)*, dash, pep, sparkle, zip *(informal)*, vitality, animation, vigour, zeal, gusto, get-up-and-go *(informal)*, élan, brio, vivacity, liveliness, vim *(slang)* **OPPOSITE:** indifference

very ADVERB **= extremely**, highly, greatly, really, deeply, particularly, seriously *(informal)*, truly, absolutely, terribly, remarkably, unusually, jolly *(Brit.)*, wonderfully, profoundly, decidedly, awfully *(informal)*, acutely, exceedingly, excessively, noticeably, eminently, superlatively, uncommonly, surpassingly: *I am very grateful to you for all your help.*
▷ ADJECTIVE **1 = exact**, actual, precise, same, real, express, identical, unqualified, selfsame: *Those were his very words to me.* **2 = ideal**, perfect, right, fitting, appropriate, suitable, spot on *(Brit. informal)*, apt, just the job *(Brit. informal)*: *the very person we need for the job*

vessel NOUN **1 = ship**, boat, craft, barque *(poetic)*: *a Moroccan fishing vessel* **2 = container**, receptacle, can, bowl, tank, pot, drum, barrel, butt, vat, bin, jar, basin, tub, jug, pitcher, urn, canister, repository, cask: *plastic storage vessels*

vest VERB
vest in something *or* **someone** *(usually passive)* **= place**, invest, entrust, settle, lodge, confer, endow, bestow, consign, put in the hands of, be devolved upon: *All the authority was vested in one man.*
vest with something *(usually passive)* **= endow with**, furnish with, entrust with, empower with, authorize with: *The mass media has been vested with considerable power.*

vestibule NOUN **= hall**, lobby, foyer, porch, entrance hall, portico, anteroom

vestige NOUN **= trace**, sign, hint, scrap, evidence, indication, suspicion, glimmer: *She had lost every vestige of her puppy fat.*

vet NOUN **= veterinary surgeon**, veterinarian *(U.S.)*, animal doctor
▷ VERB **= check**, examine, investigate, check out, review, scan, look over, appraise, scrutinize, size up *(informal)*, give the once-over *(informal)*, pass under review

veteran NOUN **= old hand**, master, pro *(informal)*, old-timer, past master, trouper, warhorse *(informal)*, old stager: *Graf was already a tennis veteran at the age of 21.* **OPPOSITE:** novice
▷ MODIFIER **= long-serving**, seasoned, experienced, old, established, expert, qualified, mature, practised, hardened, adept, proficient, well trained, battle-scarred, worldly-wise: *Tony Benn, the veteran Labour MP and former Cabinet Minister*

veto NOUN **= ban**, dismissal, rejection, vetoing, boycott, embargo, prohibiting, prohibition, suppression, knock-back *(informal)*, interdict, declination, preclusion, nonconsent: *congressmen who tried to override the president's veto of the bill* **OPPOSITE:** ratification
▷ VERB **= ban**, block, reject, rule out,

kill *(informal)*, negative, turn down, forbid, boycott, prohibit, disallow, put a stop to, refuse permission to, interdict, give the thumbs down to, put the kibosh on *(slang)*: *De Gaulle vetoed Britain's application to join the EEC.* **OPPOSITE:** pass

vex VERB **= annoy**, bother, irritate, worry, trouble, upset, disturb, distress, provoke, bug *(informal)*, offend, needle *(informal)*, plague, put out, tease, torment, harass, hassle *(informal)*, aggravate *(informal)*, afflict, fret, gall, agitate, exasperate, nettle, pester, displease, rile, pique, peeve *(informal)*, grate on, get on your nerves *(informal)*, nark *(Brit., Austral. & N.Z. slang)*, give someone grief *(Brit. & S. African)*, get your back up, put your back up, hack you off *(informal)* **OPPOSITE:** soothe

vexed ADJECTIVE **1 = annoyed**, upset, irritated, worried, troubled, bothered, confused, disturbed, distressed, provoked, put out, fed up, tormented, harassed, aggravated *(informal)*, afflicted, agitated, ruffled, exasperated, perplexed, nettled, miffed *(informal)*, displeased, riled, peeved *(informal)*, hacked off *(U.S. slang)*, out of countenance, tooshie *(Austral. slang)*, hoha *(N.Z.)*: *He was vexed by the art establishment's rejection of his work.* **2 = controversial**, disputed, contested, moot, much debated: *Later the minister raised the vexed question of refugees.*

viable ADJECTIVE **= workable**, practical, feasible, suitable, realistic, operational, applicable, usable, practicable, serviceable, operable, within the bounds of possibility **OPPOSITE:** unworkable

vibes *(sometimes singular)* PLURAL NOUN **1 = feelings**, emotions, response, reaction: *I don't like the guy – I have bad vibes about him.* **2 = atmosphere**, aura, vibrations, feeling, emanation: *a club with really good vibes*

vibrant ADJECTIVE **1 = energetic**, dynamic, sparkling, vivid, spirited, storming, alive, sensitive, colourful, vigorous, animated, responsive, electrifying, vivacious, full of pep *(informal)*: *Tom was drawn to her by her vibrant personality.* **2 = vivid**, bright, brilliant, intense, clear, rich, glowing, colourful, highly-coloured: *His shirt was a vibrant shade of green.*

vibrate VERB **1 = shake**, tremble, shiver, fluctuate, quiver, oscillate, judder *(informal)*: *Her whole body seemed to vibrate with terror.* **2 = throb**, pulse, resonate, pulsate, reverberate: *The noise vibrated through the whole house.*

vibration NOUN **1 = shaking**, shake, trembling, quake, quaking, shudder, shuddering, quiver, oscillation, judder *(informal)*: *The vibration dislodged the pins from the plane's rudder.* **2 = throbbing**, pulse, thumping, hum, humming, throb, resonance, tremor, drone, droning, reverberation, pulsation: *They heard a distant low vibration in the distance.*

vicarious ADJECTIVE **= indirect**, substitute, surrogate, by proxy, empathetic, at one remove

vice NOUN **1 = fault**, failing, weakness, limitation, defect, deficiency, flaw, shortcoming, blemish, imperfection, frailty, foible, weak point, infirmity: *Having the odd flutter on the horses is his only vice.* **OPPOSITE:** good point **2 = wickedness**, evil, corruption, sin, depravity, immorality, iniquity, profligacy, degeneracy, venality, turpitude, evildoing: *offences connected with vice, gaming and drugs* **OPPOSITE:** virtue

vice versa ADVERB **= the other way round**, conversely, in reverse, contrariwise

vicinity NOUN **= neighbourhood**, area, district, precincts, locality, environs, neck of the woods *(informal)*, purlieus

vicious ADJECTIVE **1 = savage**, brutal, violent, bad, dangerous, foul, cruel, ferocious, monstrous, vile, atrocious, diabolical, heinous, abhorrent, barbarous, fiendish: *He suffered a vicious attack by a gang of youths.* **OPPOSITE:** gentle **2 = depraved**, corrupt, wicked, infamous, degraded, worthless, degenerate, immoral, sinful, debased, profligate, unprincipled: *a vicious criminal incapable of remorse* **OPPOSITE:** virtuous **3 = malicious**, vindictive, spiteful, mean, cruel, venomous, bitchy *(informal)*, defamatory, rancorous, backbiting, slanderous: *a vicious attack on an innocent woman's character* **OPPOSITE:** complimentary

> **QUOTATIONS**
> You can't expect a boy to be vicious till he's been to a good school
> [Saki *Reginald in Russia*]

vicissitude NOUN *(often plural)* **= variation**, change, shift, change of fortune, life's ups and downs *(informal)*

victim NOUN **1 = casualty**, sufferer, injured party, fatality: *an organization representing victims of the accident* **OPPOSITE:** survivor **2 = prey**, patsy *(slang, chiefly U.S. & Canad.)*, sucker *(slang)*, dupe, gull *(archaic)*, stooge, sitting duck *(informal)*, sitting target, innocent: *the victim of a particularly cruel hoax* **OPPOSITE:** culprit **3 = scapegoat**, sacrifice, martyr, fall guy *(informal)*, whipping boy: *A sacrificial victim was thrown to the judicial authorities.*

victimize *or* **victimise** VERB **= persecute**, bully, pick on, abuse, harass, discriminate against, lean on, have it in for *(informal)*, push around, give a hard time, demonize, have a down on *(informal)*, have your knife into

victor NOUN **= winner**, champion, conqueror, first, champ *(informal)*, vanquisher, top dog *(informal)*, prizewinner, conquering hero **OPPOSITE:** loser

victorious ADJECTIVE **= winning**, successful, triumphant, first, champion, conquering, vanquishing, prizewinning **OPPOSITE:** losing

victory NOUN **= win**, success, triumph, the prize, superiority, conquest, laurels, mastery, walkover *(informal)* **OPPOSITE:** defeat

vie VERB *(with* **with** *or* **for***)* **= compete**, struggle, contend, contest, strive, be rivals, match yourself against

view NOUN **1** *(sometimes plural)* **= opinion**, thought, idea, belief, thinking, feeling, attitude, reckoning, impression, notion, conviction, judgment, point of view, sentiment, viewpoint, persuasion, way of thinking, standpoint: *You should make your views known to your local MP.* **2 = scene**, picture, sight, prospect, aspect, perspective, landscape, outlook, spectacle, panorama, vista: *The view from our window was one of beautiful countryside.* **3 = vision**, sight, visibility, perspective, eyeshot, range *or* field of vision: *A group of riders came into view.* **4 = study**, review, survey, assessment, examination, scan, inspection, look, scrutiny, contemplation: *a concise but comprehensive view of basic economics* ▷ VERB **1 = regard**, see, consider, judge, perceive, treat, estimate, reckon, deem, look on, adjudge, think about *or* of: *America was viewed as a land of golden opportunity.* **2 = look at**, see, inspect, gaze at, eye, watch, check, regard, survey, witness, clock *(Brit. slang)*, examine, observe, explore, stare at, scan, contemplate, check out *(informal)*, behold, eyeball *(slang)*, gawp at, recce *(slang)*, get a load of *(informal)*, spectate, take a dekko at *(Brit. slang)*: *The mourners filed past to view the body.* **with a view to = with the aim** *or* **intention of**, in order to, so as to, in the hope of: *She joined a dating agency with a view to finding a husband.*

viewer NOUN **= watcher**, observer, spectator, onlooker, couch potato *(informal)*, TV watcher, one of an audience

viewpoint NOUN **= point of view**, perspective, angle, position, attitude, stance, slant, belief, conviction, feeling, opinion, way of thinking, standpoint, vantage point, frame of reference

vigilance NOUN **= watchfulness**, alertness, caution, observance, circumspection, attentiveness, carefulness

vigilant ADJECTIVE **= watchful**, alert, on the lookout, careful, cautious, attentive, circumspect, wide awake, on the alert, on your toes, wakeful, on your guard, on the watch, on the qui vive, keeping your eyes peeled *or* skinned *(informal)* **OPPOSITE:** inattentive

vigorous ADJECTIVE **1 = strenuous**, energetic, arduous, hard, taxing,

Choosing Suitable Names for Fictional Characters

Selecting a name for a character in a work of fiction is a small but important part of the creative process. A character can occasionally become so memorable that his or her name becomes synonymous with a particular type of personality and the name eventually becomes a word in its own right and an established part of the language: *Svengali*, *Scrooge*, and *Walter Mitty* being three notable examples.

A name should certainly be in keeping with a character's age, ethnicity, religion, and class, otherwise it will not ring true. A good source of inspiration is the phone book, although newspapers and film credits can be just as helpful. Specialist dictionaries of given names and surnames are also widely available, and these often have word origins that might help with selecting a name. One other useful if morbid source, especially for finding names for characters from previous generations, is a cemetery. Indeed, it has been claimed, perhaps rather fancifully, that Charles Dickens gained inspiration for one of his most famous characters, the miserly *Ebenezer Scrooge*, by looking at the grave of one Ebenezer Lennox Scroggie whose headstone identified him as a 'meal man' (a grain merchant) which Dickens supposedly misread as 'mean man'.

Real people's names are often an inspiration. Thriller writer Ian Fleming wanted his secret service agent to be 'an anonymous blunt instrument' and so chose the 'plainest-sounding' name he could find, which happened to be the author of a bird-spotting book: *James Bond*. It has also been suggested that Bond's nemesis, the evil *Blofeld*, was inspired by a classmate of Fleming's at Eton, Thomas Blofeld (father of cricket commentator, Henry).

Some authors want there to be no doubt as to the nature of their characters and choose names - sometimes known as 'aptronyms' - that clearly reveal their owner's personality. Charles Dickens was especially noted for this and *Hard Times* provides three good examples: the hypocritical *Josiah Bounderby*, the grimly utilitarian educationalist *Thomas Gradgrind*, and his dull protégé the teacher *Mr M'Choakumchild*. Some contemporary writers use this technique, and the egocentric and hedonistic *John Self* from Martin Amis's novel *Money* is a modern example of this tradition.

An 'everyman' type of character often crops up in fiction and their ordinariness and decentness can be expressed through their name: George Orwell's *Winston Smith*, Douglas Adams' *Arthur Dent*, and JK Rowling's *Harry Potter* being three well-known examples.

Harry Potter, as fans of the series will know, is one of the few names created by JK Rowling that is not meaningful, although the author often draws inspiration from languages other than English. For example, the bullying *Draco Malfoy*'s first name is that of the harsh ancient Athenian lawgiver from whose name is derived 'draconian', and his surname seems to be derived from French 'mal foi' (bad faith). *Voldemort* similarly appears to be derived from French, with 'flight (or theft) from death' being a possible translation. French is not the only language that has inspired fictional names, of course, and from Latin comes Jules Verne's *Captain Nemo* (meaning 'no-one'), while the name of *Alex*, the thuggish protagonist of Anthony Burgess's *A Clockwork Orange*, could well be derived from Latin 'a-lex' (without the law). Inspired by ancient northern European languages, JRR Tolkien derived the name of the Hobbit *Frodo* from the Old English word *fród* meaning 'wise by experience', while the Ring-obsessed *Gollum* may well get his name from Germanic words meaning 'gold', 'treasure', or 'precious'.

Finally, a source even closer to home is one's own name and if a writer wishes to pen a character either strongly or vaguely resembling him- or herself then an anagram might be suitable. Vladimir Nabokov certainly found this strategy useful during the writing of *Lolita* where he turned his own name into the character *Vivian Darkbloom*.

active, intense, exhausting, rigorous, brisk: *Avoid vigorous exercise for a few weeks.* **2 = spirited**, lively, energetic, active, intense, dynamic, sparkling, animated, forceful, feisty *(informal)*, spanking, high-spirited, sprightly, vivacious, forcible, effervescent, full of energy, zippy *(informal)*, spunky *(informal)*: *The choir and orchestra gave a vigorous performance of Haydn's oratorio.* **OPPOSITE:** lethargic **3 = strong**, powerful, robust, sound, healthy, vital, lively, flourishing, hardy, hale, hearty, lusty, virile, alive and kicking, red-blooded, fighting fit, full of energy, full of beans *(informal)*, hale and hearty, fit as a fiddle *(informal)*: *He was a vigorous, handsome young man.* **OPPOSITE:** weak

vigorously ADVERB **1 = energetically**, hard, forcefully, strongly, all out, eagerly, with a vengeance, strenuously, like mad *(slang)*, lustily, hammer and tongs, with might and main: *She shivered and rubbed her arms vigorously.* **2 = forcefully**, strongly, vehemently, strenuously: *The police vigorously denied that excessive force had been used.*

vigour or *(U.S.)* **vigor** NOUN **= energy**, might, force, vitality, power, activity, spirit, strength, snap *(informal)*, punch *(informal)*, dash, pep, zip *(informal)*, animation, verve, gusto, dynamism, oomph *(informal)*, brio, robustness, liveliness, vim *(slang)*, forcefulness **OPPOSITE:** weakness

vile ADJECTIVE **1 = wicked**, base, evil, mean, bad, low, shocking, appalling, ugly, corrupt, miserable, vicious, humiliating, perverted, coarse, degrading, worthless, disgraceful, vulgar, degenerate, abject, sinful, despicable, depraved, debased, loathsome, contemptible, impure, wretched, nefarious, ignoble: *a vile and despicable crime* **OPPOSITE:** honourable **2 = disgusting**, foul, revolting, offensive, nasty, obscene, sickening, horrid, repellent, repulsive, noxious, nauseating, repugnant, loathsome, yucky or yukky *(slang)*, yucko *(Austral. slang)*: *the vile smell of his cigar smoke* **OPPOSITE:** pleasant

vilification NOUN **= denigration**, abuse, defamation, invective, calumny, mudslinging, disparagement, vituperation, contumely, aspersion, scurrility, calumniation

vilify VERB **= malign**, abuse, denigrate, knock *(informal)*, rubbish *(informal)*, run down, smear, slag (off) *(slang)*, berate, disparage, decry, revile, slander, dump on *(slang, chiefly U.S.)*, debase, defame, bad-mouth *(slang, chiefly U.S. & Canad.)*, traduce, speak ill of, pull to pieces *(informal)*, calumniate, vituperate, asperse **OPPOSITE:** praise

villain NOUN **1 = evildoer**, criminal, rogue, profligate, scoundrel, wretch, libertine, knave *(archaic)*, reprobate, miscreant, malefactor, blackguard, rapscallion, caitiff *(archaic)*, wrong 'un *(Austral. slang)*: *As a copper, I've spent my life putting villains like him away.* **2 = baddy** *(informal)*, antihero: *Darth Vader, the villain of the Star Wars trilogy* **OPPOSITE:** hero

villainous ADJECTIVE **= wicked**, evil, depraved, mean, bad, base, criminal, terrible, cruel, vicious, outrageous, infamous, vile, degenerate, atrocious, inhuman, sinful, diabolical, heinous, debased, hateful, scoundrelly, fiendish, ruffianly, nefarious, ignoble, detestable, blackguardly, thievish **OPPOSITE:** virtuous

vindicate VERB **1 = clear**, acquit, exonerate, absolve, let off the hook, exculpate, free from blame: *The director said he had been vindicated by the expert's report.* **OPPOSITE:** condemn **2 = support**, uphold, ratify, defend, excuse, justify, substantiate: *Subsequent events vindicated his policy.*

vindication NOUN **1 = exoneration**, pardon, acquittal, dismissal, discharge, amnesty, absolution, exculpating, exculpation: *He insisted on a complete vindication from the libel jury.* **2 = support**, defence, ratification, excuse, apology, justification, assertion, substantiation: *He called the success a vindication of his party's economic policy.*

vindictive ADJECTIVE **= vengeful**, malicious, spiteful, relentless, resentful, malignant, unrelenting, unforgiving, implacable, venomous, rancorous, revengeful, full of spleen **OPPOSITE:** merciful

vintage NOUN **1 = harvest**, year, crop, yield: *This wine is from one of the best vintages of the decade.* **2 = era**, period, origin, sort, type, generation, stamp, epoch, ilk, time of origin: *a Jeep of World War Two vintage*
▷ ADJECTIVE **1 = high-quality**, best, prime, quality, choice, select, rare, superior: *Gourmet food and vintage wines are also part of the service.* **2 = classic**, old, veteran, historic, heritage, enduring, antique, timeless, old-world, age-old, ageless: *This is vintage comedy at its best; vintage, classic and racing cars*

violate VERB **1 = break**, infringe, disobey, transgress, ignore, defy, disregard, flout, rebel against, contravene, fly in the face of, overstep, not comply with, take no notice of, encroach upon, pay no heed to, infract: *They violated the ceasefire agreement.* **OPPOSITE:** obey **2 = invade**, infringe on, disturb, upset, shatter, disrupt, impinge on, encroach on, intrude on, trespass on, obtrude on: *These journalists were violating her family's privacy.* **3 = desecrate**, profane, defile, abuse, outrage, pollute, deface, dishonour, vandalize, treat with disrespect, befoul: *Police are still searching for the people who violated the graves.* **OPPOSITE:** honour **4 = rape**, molest, sexually assault, ravish, abuse, assault, interfere with, sexually abuse, indecently assault, force yourself on: *He broke into a woman's home and attempted to violate her.*

violation NOUN **1 = breach**, abuse, infringement, contravention, trespass, transgression, infraction: *This is a flagrant violation of state law.* **2 = invasion**, intrusion, trespass, breach, disturbance, disruption, interruption, encroachment: *Legal action will be initiated for defamation and violation of privacy.* **3 = desecration**, sacrilege, defilement, profanation, spoliation: *This violation of the church is not the first such incident.* **4 = rape**, sexual assault, molesting, ravishing *(old-fashioned)*, abuse, sexual abuse, indecent assault, molestation: *the violation of women in war*

violence NOUN **1 = brutality**, bloodshed, savagery, fighting, terrorism, frenzy, thuggery, destructiveness, bestiality, strong-arm tactics *(informal)*, rough handling, bloodthirstiness, murderousness: *Twenty people were killed in the violence.* **2 = force**, power, strength, might, ferocity, brute force, fierceness, forcefulness, powerfulness: *The violence of the blow forced the hammer through his skull.* **3 = intensity**, passion, fury, force, cruelty, severity, fervour, sharpness, harshness, vehemence: *'There's no need,' she snapped with sudden violence.* **4 = power**, turbulence, wildness, raging, tumult, roughness, boisterousness, storminess: *The house was destroyed in the violence of the storm.*

> **QUOTATIONS**
> I say violence is necessary. It is as American as cherry pie
> [H. Rap Brown]
>
> All they that take the sword shall perish with the sword
> [*Bible: St. Matthew*]
>
> Violence is one of the most fun things to watch
> [Quentin Tarantino *at the screening of Pulp Fiction in Cannes*]
>
> Keep violence in the mind
> Where it belongs
> [Brian Aldiss *Barefoot in the Head*]

violent ADJECTIVE **1 = brutal**, aggressive, savage, wild, rough, fierce, bullying, cruel, vicious, destructive, ruthless, murderous, maddened, berserk, merciless, bloodthirsty, homicidal, pitiless, hot-headed, thuggish, maniacal, hot-tempered: *He was a violent man with a drink and drugs problem.* **OPPOSITE:** gentle **2 = sharp**, hard, powerful, forceful, strong, fierce, fatal, savage, deadly, brutal, vicious, lethal, hefty, ferocious, death-dealing: *She had died from a violent blow to the head.* **3 = intense**, acute, severe, biting, sharp, extreme, painful, harsh, excruciating, agonizing, inordinate: *He had violent stomach pains.* **4 = passionate**, intense, extreme, strong, wild, consuming, uncontrollable, vehement,

V

unrestrained, tempestuous, ungovernable: *his violent, almost pathological jealousy* **5 = fiery**, raging, fierce, flaming, furious, passionate, peppery, ungovernable: *I had a violent temper and was always in fights.* **6 = powerful**, wild, devastating, strong, storming, raging, turbulent, tumultuous, tempestuous, gale force, blustery, ruinous, full of force: *That night a violent storm arose and wrecked most of the ships.* **OPPOSITE:** mild

VIP NOUN **= celebrity**, big name, public figure, star, somebody, lion, notable, luminary, bigwig (*informal*), leading light (*informal*), big shot (*informal*), personage, big noise (*informal*), big hitter (*informal*), heavy hitter (*informal*), man *or* woman of the hour

virago NOUN **= harridan**, fury, shrew, vixen, scold, battle-axe (*informal*), termagant (*rare*)

virgin NOUN **= maiden**, maid (*archaic*), damsel (*archaic*), girl (*archaic*), celibate, vestal, virgo intacta: *I was a virgin until I was twenty-four years old.*
▷ ADJECTIVE **1 = untouched**, immaculate, fresh, new, pure, unused, pristine, flawless, unblemished, unadulterated, unsullied: *Within 40 years there will be no virgin forest left.* **OPPOSITE:** spoiled **2 = pure**, maidenly, chaste, immaculate, virginal, unsullied, vestal, uncorrupted, undefiled: *a society in which men still prize virgin brides* **OPPOSITE:** corrupted

virginal ADJECTIVE **1 = chaste**, pure, maidenly, virgin, immaculate, celibate, uncorrupted, undefiled: *She had always been a child in his mind, pure and virginal.* **2 = immaculate**, fresh, pristine, white, pure, untouched, snowy, undisturbed, spotless: *linen tablecloths of virginal white*

virginity NOUN **= chastity**, maidenhead, maidenhood

virile ADJECTIVE **= manly**, masculine, macho, strong, male, robust, vigorous, potent, forceful, lusty, red-blooded, manlike **OPPOSITE:** effeminate

virility NOUN **= masculinity**, manhood, potency, vigour, machismo **OPPOSITE:** effeminacy

virtual ADJECTIVE **= practical**, near, essential, implied, indirect, implicit, tacit, near enough, unacknowledged, in all but name

virtually ADVERB **= practically**, almost, nearly, in effect, in essence, as good as, to all intents and purposes, in all but name, for all practical purposes, effectually

virtue NOUN **1 = goodness**, honour, integrity, worth, dignity, excellence, morality, honesty, decency, respectability, nobility, righteousness, propriety, probity, rectitude, worthiness, high-mindedness, incorruptibility, uprightness, virtuousness, ethicalness: *His mother was held up to the family as a paragon of virtue.* **OPPOSITE:** vice **2 = merit**, strength, asset, plus (*informal*), attribute, good quality, good point, strong point: *His chief virtue is patience.* **OPPOSITE:** failing **3 = advantage**, benefit, merit, credit, usefulness, efficacy: *There is no virtue in overexercising.* **4 = chastity**, honour, virginity, innocence, purity, maidenhood, chasteness: *His many attempts on her virtue were all unavailing.* **OPPOSITE:** unchastity
by virtue of = because of, in view of, on account of, based on, thanks to, as a result of, owing to, by reason of, by dint of: *Mr Olaechea has British residency by virtue of his marriage.*

QUOTATIONS

Virtue is the fount whence honour springs
[Christopher Marlowe *Tamburlaine the Great*]

Virtue is its own reward
[Cicero *De Finibus*]

Virtue is like a rich stone, best plain set
[Francis Bacon *Essays*]

Who can find a virtuous woman?
For her price is far above rubies
[*Bible: Proverbs*]

For 'tis some virtue, virtue to commend
[William Congreve]

Virtue could see to do what Virtue would
By her own radiant light, though sun and moon
Were in the flat sea sunk
[John Milton *Comus*]

Against the threats
Of malice or of sorcery, or that power
Which erring men call chance, this I hold firm,
Virtue may be assailed, but never hurt,
Surprised by unjust force, but not enthralled
[John Milton *Comus*]

It is queer how it is always one's virtues and not one's vices that precipitate one into disaster
[Rebecca West *There Is No Conversation*]

The weakest of all weak things is a virtue which has not been tested in the fire
[Mark Twain *The Man That Corrupted Hadleyburg*]

I cannot praise a fugitive and cloistered virtue, unexercised and unbreathed, that never sallies out and sees her adversary, but slinks out of the race, where that immortal garland is to be run for, not without dust and heat... that which purifies us is trial, and trial is by what is contrary
[John Milton *Areopagitica*]

virtuosity NOUN **= mastery**, skill, brilliance, polish, craft, expertise, flair, panache, éclat

virtuoso NOUN **= master**, artist, genius, maestro, magician, grandmaster, maven (*U.S.*), master hand: *Canada's foremost piano virtuoso, Glenn Gould*
▷ MODIFIER **= masterly**, brilliant, dazzling, bravura (*Music*): *a virtuoso performance by a widely respected musician*

virtuous ADJECTIVE **1 = good**, moral, ethical, upright, honourable, excellent, pure, worthy, honest, righteous, exemplary, squeaky-clean, blameless, praiseworthy, incorruptible, high-principled: *The president is portrayed as a virtuous family man.* **OPPOSITE:** corrupt **2 = chaste**, pure, innocent, celibate, spotless, virginal, clean-living: *a prince who falls in love with a beautiful and virtuous maiden* **OPPOSITE:** promiscuous

virulent ADJECTIVE **1 = vicious**, vindictive, bitter, hostile, malicious, resentful, acrimonious, malevolent, spiteful, venomous, rancorous, splenetic, envenomed: *A virulent personal campaign is being waged against him.* **OPPOSITE:** benign **2 = deadly**, lethal, toxic, poisonous, malignant, pernicious, venomous, septic, infective, injurious, baneful (*archaic*): *A virulent form of the disease has appeared in Belgium.* **OPPOSITE:** harmless

viscous ADJECTIVE **= thick**, sticky, gooey (*informal*), adhesive, tenacious, clammy, syrupy, glutinous, gummy, gelatinous, icky (*informal*), gluey, treacly, mucilaginous, viscid

visible ADJECTIVE **= perceptible**, noticeable, observable, clear, obvious, plain, apparent, bold, patent, to be seen, evident, manifest, in sight, in view, conspicuous, unmistakable, palpable, discernible, salient, detectable, not hidden, distinguishable, unconcealed, perceivable, discoverable, anywhere to be seen **OPPOSITE:** invisible

vision NOUN **1 = image**, idea, dream, plans, hopes, prospect, ideal, concept, fancy, fantasy, conception, delusion, daydream, reverie, flight of fancy, mental picture, pipe dream, imago (*Psychoanalysis*), castle in the air, fanciful notion: *I have a vision of a society free of exploitation and injustice.* **2 = hallucination**, illusion, apparition, revelation, ghost, phantom, delusion, spectre, mirage, wraith, chimera, phantasm, eidolon: *She heard voices and saw visions of her ancestors.* **3 = sight**, seeing, eyesight, view, eyes, perception: *The disease causes blindness or serious loss of vision.* **4 = foresight**, imagination, perception, insight, awareness, inspiration, innovation, creativity, intuition, penetration, inventiveness, shrewdness, discernment, prescience, perceptiveness, farsightedness, breadth of view:

The government's lack of vision could have profound economic consequences.
5 = picture, dream, sight, delight, beauty, joy, sensation, spectacle, knockout (*informal*), beautiful sight, perfect picture, feast for the eyes, sight for sore eyes, pearler (*Austral. slang*), beaut (*Austral. & N.Z. slang*): *The girl was a vision in crimson organza.*

> **QUOTATIONS**
> Your old men shall dream dreams, your young men shall see visions
> [*Bible: Joel*]
>
> Where there is no vision, the people perish
> [*Bible: Proverbs*]

visionary ADJECTIVE **1 = idealistic**, romantic, unrealistic, utopian, dreaming, speculative, impractical, dreamy, unworkable, quixotic, starry-eyed, with your head in the clouds: *His ideas were dismissed as mere visionary speculation.* **OPPOSITE:** realistic
2 = prophetic, mystical, divinatory, predictive, oracular, sibylline, mantic, vatic (*rare*), fatidic (*rare*): *visionary experiences and contact with spirit beings*
3 = imaginary, fantastic, unreal, fanciful, ideal, idealized, illusory, imaginal (*Psychoanalysis*), chimerical, delusory: *the visionary worlds created by fantasy writers* **OPPOSITE:** real
▷ NOUN **1 = idealist**, romantic, dreamer, daydreamer, utopian, enthusiast (*archaic*), theorist, zealot, Don Quixote: *Visionaries see the world not as it is but as it could be.* **OPPOSITE:** realist
2 = prophet, diviner, mystic, seer, soothsayer, sibyl, scryer, spaewife (*Scot.*): *shamans, mystics and religious visionaries*

visit VERB **1 = call on**, go to see, drop in on (*informal*), stop by, look up, call in on, pop in on (*informal*), pay a call on, go see (*U.S.*), swing by (*informal*)
2 = stay at, stay with, spend time with, pay a visit to, be the guest of: *I want to visit my relatives in Scotland.*
3 = stay in, see, tour, explore, take in (*informal*), holiday in, go to see, stop by, spend time in, vacation in (*U.S.*), stop over in: *He'll be visiting four cities, including Cagliari in Sardinia.*
▷ NOUN **1 = call**, social call: *Helen recently paid me a visit.* **2 = trip**, stop, stay, break, tour, holiday, vacation (*informal*), stopover, sojourn: *the Pope's visit to Canada*

visitation NOUN **1 = apparition**, vision, manifestation, appearance, materialization: *He claims to have had a visitation from the Virgin Mary.*
2 = inspection, survey, examination, visit, review, scrutiny: *House-to-house visitation has been authorized by the Board of Health.*

visitor NOUN **= guest**, caller, company, visitant, manu(w)hiri (*N.Z.*)

vista NOUN **= view**, scene, prospect, landscape, panorama, perspective

visual ADJECTIVE **1 = optical**, optic, ocular: *the way our brain processes visual information* **2 = observable**, visible, perceptible, discernible: *There was no visual evidence to support his claim.*
OPPOSITE: imperceptible

visualize *or* **visualise** VERB **= picture**, imagine, think about, envisage, contemplate, conceive of, see in the mind's eye, conjure up a mental picture of

vital ADJECTIVE **1 = essential**, important, necessary, key, basic, significant, critical, radical, crucial, fundamental, urgent, decisive, cardinal, imperative, indispensable, requisite, life-or-death, must-have: *a blockade which could cut off vital oil and gas supplies* **OPPOSITE:** unnecessary
2 = lively, vigorous, energetic, spirited, dynamic, animated, vibrant, forceful, sparky, vivacious, full of beans (*informal*), zestful, full of the joy of living: *It is tragic to see how the disease has diminished a once vital person.*
OPPOSITE: lethargic

vitality NOUN **= energy**, vivacity, sparkle, go (*informal*), life, strength, pep, stamina, animation, vigour, exuberance, brio, robustness, liveliness, vim (*slang*), lustiness, vivaciousness **OPPOSITE:** lethargy

vitriolic ADJECTIVE **= venomous**, scathing, malicious, acid, bitter, destructive, withering, virulent, sardonic, caustic, bitchy (*informal*), acerbic, envenomed, dripping with malice

vivacious ADJECTIVE **= lively**, spirited, vital, gay, bubbling, sparkling, cheerful, jolly, animated, merry, upbeat (*informal*), high-spirited, ebullient, chirpy (*informal*), sparky, scintillating, sprightly, effervescent, full of life, full of beans (*informal*), frolicsome, sportive, light-hearted
OPPOSITE: dull

vivid ADJECTIVE **1 = clear**, detailed, realistic, telling, moving, strong, affecting, arresting, powerful, sharp, dramatic, stirring, stimulating, haunting, graphic, distinct, lively, memorable, unforgettable, evocative, lucid, lifelike, true to life, sharply-etched: *Last night I had a vivid dream which really upset me.* **OPPOSITE:** vague
2 = bright, brilliant, intense, clear, rich, glowing, colourful, highly-coloured: *a vivid blue sky* **OPPOSITE:** dull
3 = lively, strong, dynamic, striking, spirited, powerful, quick, storming, active, vigorous, energetic, animated, vibrant, fiery, flamboyant, expressive, vivacious, zestful: *one of the most vivid personalities in tennis* **OPPOSITE:** quiet

vixen NOUN **= shrew**, fury, spitfire, virago, harpy, scold, harridan, termagant (*rare*), hellcat

viz ADVERB **= namely**, that is to say, to wit, videlicet

vocabulary NOUN **1 = language**, words, lexicon, word stock, word hoard: *Children need to read to improve their vocabularies.* **2 = wordbook**, dictionary, glossary, lexicon: *I could not find this word in my small Italian-English vocabulary.*

vocal ADJECTIVE **1 = outspoken**, frank, blunt, forthright, strident, vociferous, noisy, articulate, expressive, eloquent, plain-spoken, clamorous, free-spoken: *He has been very vocal in his displeasure over the decision.*
OPPOSITE: quiet **2 = spoken**, voiced, uttered, oral, said, articulated, put into words: *a child's ability to imitate rhythms and vocal sounds*

vocation NOUN **= profession**, calling, job, business, office, trade, role, post, career, mission, employment, pursuit, life work, métier

> **QUOTATIONS**
> Many are called, but few are chosen
> [*Bible: St. Matthew*]

vociferous ADJECTIVE **= outspoken**, vocal, strident, noisy, shouting, loud, ranting, vehement, loudmouthed (*informal*), uproarious, obstreperous, clamorous **OPPOSITE:** quiet

vogue NOUN **= fashion**, trend, craze, style, the latest, the thing (*informal*), mode, last word, the rage, passing fancy, dernier cri (*French*): *the new vogue for herbal medicines*
▷ ADJECTIVE **= fashionable**, trendy (*Brit. informal*), in, now (*informal*), popular, with it (*informal*), prevalent, up-to-the-minute, modish, voguish: *The word 'talisman' has become a vogue word in sports writing.*
in vogue = popular, big, fashionable, all the rage, happening, accepted, current, cool, in favour, stylish, up to date, in use, prevalent, up to the minute, modish, trendsetting, schmick (*Austral. informal*): *Pale colours are in vogue this season.*

voice NOUN **1 = tone**, sound, language, articulation, power of speech: *Miriam's voice was strangely calm.* **2 = utterance**, expression, words, airing, vocalization, verbalization: *The crowd gave voice to their anger.* **3 = opinion**, will, feeling, wish, desire: *the voice of the opposition* **4 = say**, part, view, decision, vote, comment, input: *Our employees have no voice in how our company is run.*
5 = instrument, medium, spokesman *or* spokeswoman, agency, channel, vehicle, organ, spokesperson, intermediary, mouthpiece: *He claims to be the voice of the people.*
▷ VERB **= express**, say, declare, air, raise, table, reveal, mention, mouth, assert, pronounce, utter, articulate, come out with (*informal*), divulge, ventilate, enunciate, put into words, vocalize, give expression *or* utterance to: *Scientists have voiced concern that the disease could be passed to humans.*
▸ *related adjective:* vocal

void ADJECTIVE **1 = invalid**, null and void, inoperative, useless, ineffective, worthless, ineffectual, unenforceable, nonviable: *The elections were declared void by the former military ruler.* **2** (with **of**) **= devoid of**, without,

lacking, free from, wanting, bereft of, empty of, bare of, destitute of, vacant of: *His face was void of emotion as he left the room.*
▷ NOUN **1 = gap**, space, lack, want, hole, blank, emptiness: *His death has created a void which will never be filled.* **2 = emptiness**, space, vacuum, oblivion, blankness, nullity, vacuity: *the limitless void of outer space*
▷ VERB **= invalidate**, nullify, cancel, withdraw, reverse, undo, repeal, quash, revoke, disallow, retract, repudiate, negate, rescind, annul, abrogate, countermand, render invalid, abnegate: *The Supreme Court voided his conviction for murder.*

volatile ADJECTIVE **1 = changeable**, shifting, variable, unsettled, unstable, explosive, unreliable, unsteady, inconstant: *There have been riots before and the situation is volatile.* **OPPOSITE:** stable **2 = temperamental**, erratic, mercurial, up and down (*informal*), fickle, whimsical, giddy, flighty, over-emotional, inconstant: *She has a volatile temperament.* **OPPOSITE:** calm

volcano

VOLCANOES

Antisana
Apo
Askja
Cameroon
Chimborazo
Citlaltépetl
Corcovado
Cotopaxi
Egmont
Elgon
El Misti
Erciyas Dagi
Erebus
Etna
Fuji
Haleakala
Hekla
Helgafell
Huascarán
Iliamna
Ixtaccihuatl
Katmai
Kazbek
Kenya
Kilauea
Krakatoa
Lassen Peak
Llaima
Mauna Kea
Mauna Loa
Mayon
Mount St. Helens
Nevado de Colima
Nevado de Toluca
Paricutín
Pelée
Popocatépetl
Santa Maria
Semeru
Soufrière
Stromboli
Suribachi
Taal
Tambora
Teide
Tolima
Tristan da Cunha
Tungurahua
Vesuvius

volition NOUN **= free will**, will, choice, election, choosing, option, purpose, resolution, determination, preference, discretion

volley NOUN **= barrage**, blast, burst, explosion, shower, hail, discharge, bombardment, salvo, fusillade, cannonade

voluble ADJECTIVE **= talkative**, garrulous, loquacious, forthcoming, articulate, fluent, glib, blessed with the gift of the gab **OPPOSITE:** reticent

volume NOUN **1 = amount**, quantity, level, body, total, measure, degree, mass, proportion, bulk, aggregate: *the sheer volume of traffic on our motorways* **2 = capacity**, size, mass, extent, proportions, dimensions, bulk, measurements, magnitude, compass, largeness, cubic content: *When water is frozen it increases in volume.* **3 = book**, work, title, opus, publication, manual, tome, treatise, almanac, compendium: *a slim volume of English poetry* **4 = loudness**, sound, amplification: *He came round to complain about the volume of the music.*
▸ *related adjective:* cubical

voluminous ADJECTIVE **1 = large**, big, full, massive, vast, ample, bulky, billowing, roomy, cavernous, capacious: *She was swathed in a voluminous cloak.* **OPPOSITE:** small **2 = copious**, extensive, prolific, abundant, plentiful, profuse: *this author's voluminous writings and correspondence* **OPPOSITE:** scanty

voluntarily ADVERB **= willingly**, freely, by choice, without being asked, without prompting, lief (*rare*), on your own initiative, of your own free will, off your own bat, of your own accord, of your own volition

voluntary ADJECTIVE **1 = intentional**, intended, deliberate, planned, studied, purposed, calculated, wilful, done on purpose: *a voluntary act undertaken in full knowledge of the consequences* **OPPOSITE:** unintentional **2 = optional**, discretionary, up to the individual, open, unforced, unconstrained, unenforced, at your discretion, discretional, open to choice, uncompelled: *The extra course in Commercial French is voluntary.* **OPPOSITE:** obligatory **3 = unpaid**, volunteer, free, willing, honorary, gratuitous, pro bono (*Law*): *In her spare time she does voluntary work for the homeless.*

volunteer VERB **1 = offer**, step forward, offer your services, propose, let yourself in for (*informal*), need no invitation, present your services, proffer your services, put yourself at someone's disposal: *Aunt Mary volunteered to clean up the kitchen.* **OPPOSITE:** refuse **2 = suggest**, advance, put forward, venture, tender: *His wife volunteered an ingenious suggestion.*

voluptuous ADJECTIVE **1 = buxom**, shapely, curvaceous, erotic, ample, enticing, provocative, seductive (*informal*), well-stacked (*Brit. slang*), full-bosomed: *a voluptuous, well-rounded lady with glossy red hair* **2 = sensual**, luxurious, self-indulgent, hedonistic, sybaritic, epicurean, licentious, bacchanalian, pleasure-loving: *a life of voluptuous decadence*
OPPOSITE: abstemious

vomit VERB **1 = be sick**, throw up (*informal*), spew, chuck (*Austral. & N.Z. informal*), heave (*slang*), puke (*slang*), retch, barf (*U.S. slang*), chunder (*slang, chiefly Austral.*), belch forth, upchuck (*U.S. slang*), do a technicolour yawn, toss your cookies (*U.S. slang*): *Any dairy product made him vomit.* **2** (*often with* **up**) **= bring up**, throw up, regurgitate, chuck (up) (*slang, chiefly U.S.*), emit (*informal*), eject, puke (*slang*), disgorge, sick up (*informal*), spew out *or* up: *She vomited up all she had just eaten.*

voracious ADJECTIVE **1 = gluttonous**, insatiable, ravenous, hungry, greedy, ravening, devouring: *For their size, stoats are voracious predators.* **2 = avid**, prodigious, insatiable, uncontrolled, rapacious, unquenchable: *He was a voracious reader.* **OPPOSITE:** moderate

vortex NOUN **= whirlpool**, eddy, maelstrom, gyre, countercurrent

vote NOUN **1 = poll**, election, ballot, referendum, popular vote, plebiscite, straw poll, show of hands: *They took a vote and decided not to do it.* **2 = right to vote**, franchise, voting rights, suffrage, say, voice, enfranchisement: *Before that, women did not even have the vote.*
▷ VERB **1 = cast your vote**, go to the polls, mark your ballot paper: *Over half of the electorate did not vote in the last general election.* **2 = judge**, declare, pronounce, decree, adjudge: *They voted him Player of the Year.*
vote someone in = elect, choose, select, appoint, return, pick, opt for, designate, decide on, settle on, fix on, plump for, put in power: *The Prime Minister was voted in by a huge majority.*

voucher NOUN **= ticket**, token, coupon, pass, slip, chit, chitty (*Brit. informal*), docket

vouch for VERB **1 = guarantee**, back, certify, answer for, swear to, stick up for (*informal*), stand witness, give assurance of, asseverate, go bail for: *Kim's mother agreed to vouch for Maria and get her a job.* **2 = confirm**, support, affirm, attest to, assert, uphold: *I cannot vouch for the accuracy of the story.*

vow NOUN **= promise**, commitment, pledge, oath, profession, troth (*archaic*), avowal: *Most people still take their marriage vows seriously.*
▷ VERB **= promise**, pledge, swear, commit, engage, affirm, avow, bind yourself, undertake solemnly: *She vowed that some day she would return to live in France.*

voyage NOUN **= journey**, travels, trip, passage, expedition, crossing, sail, cruise, excursion: *He aims to follow Columbus's voyage to the West Indies.*
▷ VERB **= travel**, journey, tour, cruise, steam, take a trip, go on an expedition: *The boat is currently voyaging through the Barents Sea.*

vulgar ADJECTIVE **1 = tasteless**, common, flashy, low, gross, nasty, gaudy, tawdry, cheap and nasty, common as muck: *The decor is ugly, tasteless and vulgar.* **OPPOSITE:** tasteful **2 = crude**, dirty, rude, low, blue, nasty, naughty, coarse, indecent, improper, suggestive, tasteless, risqué, off colour, ribald, indelicate, indecorous:

an oaf with a taste for racist and vulgar jokes **3 = uncouth**, boorish, unrefined, impolite, ill-bred, unmannerly: *He was a vulgar old man, but he never swore in front of women.* **OPPOSITE:** refined **4 = vernacular**, native, common, general, ordinary: *translated from Latin into the vulgar tongue*

QUOTATIONS
It's worse than wicked, my dear, it's vulgar
[*Punch*]

vulgarity NOUN **1 = tastelessness**, bad taste, grossness, tawdriness, gaudiness, lack of refinement: *I hate the vulgarity of this room.* **OPPOSITE:** tastefulness **2 = crudeness**, rudeness, coarseness, crudity, ribaldry, suggestiveness, indelicacy, indecorum: *a comedian famous for his vulgarity and irreverence* **OPPOSITE:** decorum **3 = coarseness**, roughness, boorishness, rudeness, loutishness, oafishness, uncouthness: *For all his apparent vulgarity, Todd had a certain raw charm.* **OPPOSITE:** refinement

vulnerable ADJECTIVE **1 = susceptible**, helpless, unprotected, defenceless, exposed, weak, sensitive, tender, unguarded, thin-skinned: *criminals who prey on the more vulnerable members of our society* **OPPOSITE:** immune **2 = exposed**, open, unprotected, defenceless, accessible, wide open, open to attack, assailable: *Their tanks would be vulnerable to attack from the air.* **OPPOSITE:** well-protected

V

The Language of PG Wodehouse

The novelist and short-story writer Sir P(elham) G(renville) Wodehouse (1881–1975) was born in Guildford, Surrey. As well as writing over 100 books, he also wrote lyrics for several Broadway musical comedies, putting words to the music of George Gershwin, Irving Berlin, and Cole Porter. He was living in France when World War II broke out, and after being interned by the Nazis, he made some ill-considered, though innocent radio broadcasts from Berlin, which led to accusations of treachery in England. Consequently, he spent the rest of his life largely in the United States, becoming a naturalized American citizen in 1955, and receiving a long-overdue knighthood only shortly before his death.

The setting for his most popular books, such as the *Blandings* novels or the series featuring the feckless but amiable toff Bertie Wooster and his ever-capable manservant Jeeves, is the upper-class society of Britain between the World Wars. His prose was a light and comic version of literary English, leavened with contemporary slang and allusions to jazz, but it is deceptively finely honed. Not a comma is out of place, nor is any word or phrase used that is unnecessary. Wodehouse is a master of creating the most outlandishly vivid similes for his characters to utter:

> ...one of those robust, dynamic girls with the muscles of a welter-weight and a laugh like a squadron of cavalry charging on a tin bridge.

The young men who populate the Wodehousian world are often sufficiently well off to have nothing better to do than to fall in love (or convince themselves that they have) and *love* is one of the nouns he most frequently uses, as in:

> I'm most frightfully in **love** with somebody else.

However, it is a sign both of the morality of the period and the essential goodness of Wodehouse that whenever love rears its head, marriage is never far behind, and *marry* is one of the most ubiquitous verbs.

Another commonly used noun in the Wodehouse *oeuvre* is *chap*, which will hardly be surprising, given the everyday speech of the time. Examples of 'old chap' and 'my dear chap' abound, but it is just as common as a substitute for 'person' as it is as a form of address:

> ...he looked the sort of **chap** who might have a brother.

> They ought to sack a **chap** for doing that sort of thing.

Wodehouse characters are prone to enthusiasm and exaggeration; they tend to inflate what they say in order to ensure that their point is clearly put across and thus it is no surprise to find extensive use of the adverb *really*

> It was disarming to discover that he was **really** capital company.

Absolutely also occurs with great frequency, often, of course, when used as a single-word sentence of agreement or confirmation:

> 'Maud is a charming girl' – 'Oh, **absolutely**! One of the best.'

Simply is another example of this adverbial tendency:

> 'I think it's **simply** sickening the way girls want to do everything we do,' said Norris disgustedly.

Bertie Wooster is particularly fond of another Wodehouse language trait, the conversational abbreviation. Bertie often breakfasts on 'eggs and b.' Position becomes *posish*, as in:

> 'But with Gussie, the posish was entirely different',

and circumstances become *circs*, as in

> 'It seemed to me in the circs that there was but one thing to do.'

Ww

wacky ADJECTIVE = **unusual**, odd, wild, strange, crazy, silly, weird, way-out *(informal)*, eccentric, unpredictable, daft *(informal)*, irrational, erratic, Bohemian, unconventional, far-out *(slang)*, loony *(slang)*, kinky *(informal)*, off-the-wall *(slang)*, unorthodox, nutty *(slang)*, oddball, zany, goofy *(informal)*, offbeat *(informal)*, freaky *(slang)*, outré, gonzo *(slang)*, screwy *(informal)*, wacko *or* whacko *(informal)*, off the air *(Austral. slang)*

wad NOUN **1** = **bundle**, roll, bankroll *(U.S. & Canad.)*, pocketful: *a wad of banknotes* **2** = **mass**, ball, lump, hunk, piece, block, plug, chunk: *a wad of cotton wool*

waddle VERB = **shuffle**, shamble, totter, toddle, rock, stagger, sway, wobble

wade VERB **1** = **paddle**, splash, splash about, slop: *The boys were wading in the cold pool nearby.* **2** = **walk through**, cross, ford, pass through, go across, travel across, make your way across: *We had to wade the river and then climb out of the valley.*

wade in = **move in**, pitch in, dive in *(informal)*, set to work, advance, set to, get stuck in *(informal)*, buckle down: *I waded in to help, but I got pushed aside.*

wade into someone = **launch yourself at**, charge at, attack, rush, storm, tackle, go for, set about, strike at, assail, tear into *(informal)*, fall upon, set upon, lay into *(informal)*, light into *(informal)*: *The troops waded into the protesters with batons.*

wade into something = **get involved in**, tackle, pitch in, interfere in, dive in, plunge in, get stuck into: *The Stock Exchange yesterday waded into the debate on stamp duty.*

wade through something = **plough through**, trawl through, labour at, work your way through, toil at, drudge at, peg away at: *scientists who have to wade through tons of data*

W

waffle VERB *(often followed by* **on***)* = **chatter**, rabbit (on) *(Brit. informal)*, babble, drivel, prattle, jabber, gabble, rattle on, verbalize, blather, witter on *(informal)*, blether, run off at the mouth *(slang)*, prate, earbash *(Austral. & N.Z. slang)*: *some guy on TV waffling about political correctness*

▷ NOUN = **prattle**, nonsense, hot air *(informal)*, twaddle, padding, prating, gibberish, jabber, verbiage, blather, wordiness, verbosity, prolixity, bunkum *or* buncombe *(chiefly U.S.)*, bizzo *(Austral. slang)*, bull's wool *(Austral. & N.Z. slang)*: *I'm tired of his smug, sanctimonious waffle.*

waft VERB **1** = **drift**, float, be carried, be transported, coast, flow, stray, glide, be borne, be conveyed: *The scent of roses wafted through the open window.* **2** = **transport**, bring, carry, bear, guide, conduct, transmit, convey: *A slight breeze wafted the heavy scent of flowers past her.*

▷ NOUN = **current**, breath, puff, whiff, draught, breeze: *A waft of perfume reached Ingrid's nostrils.*

wag[1] VERB **1** = **wave**, shake, swing, waggle, stir, sway, flutter, waver, quiver, vibrate, wiggle, oscillate: *The dog was barking and wagging its tail wildly.* **2** = **waggle**, wave, shake, flourish, brandish, wobble, wiggle: *He wagged a disapproving finger at me.* **3** = **shake**, bob, nod: *She wagged her head in agreement.*

▷ NOUN **1** = **wave**, shake, swing, toss, sway, flutter, waver, quiver, vibration, wiggle, oscillation, waggle: *The dog gave a responsive wag of his tail.* **2** = **nod**, bob, shake: *a wag of the head*

wag[2] NOUN = **joker**, comic, wit, comedian, clown, card *(informal)*, kidder *(informal)*, jester, dag *(N.Z. informal)*, prankster, buffoon, trickster, humorist, joculator *or (fem.)* joculatrix: *My dad's always been a bit of a wag.*

wage NOUN *(often plural)* = **payment**, pay, earnings, remuneration, fee, reward, compensation, income, allowance, recompense, stipend, emolument: *efforts to set a minimum wage well above the poverty line*

▷ VERB = **engage in**, conduct, pursue, carry on, undertake, practise, prosecute, proceed with: *the three factions that had been waging a civil war*

> **QUOTATIONS**
> For the labourer is worthy of his hire
> *[Bible: St. Luke]*

wager VERB = **bet**, chance, risk, stake, lay, venture, put on, pledge, gamble, hazard, speculate, punt *(chiefly Brit.)*: *People had wagered a good deal of money on his winning the championship.*

▷ NOUN = **bet**, stake, pledge, gamble, risk, flutter *(Brit. informal)*, ante, punt *(chiefly Brit.)*, long shot: *punters placing wagers on the day's racing*

waggle VERB = **wag**, wiggle, wave, shake, flutter, wobble, oscillate

waif NOUN = **stray**, orphan, outcast, urchin, foundling

wail VERB = **cry**, weep, grieve, lament, keen, greet *(Scot. archaic)*, howl, whine, deplore, bemoan, bawl, bewail, yowl, ululate: *The woman began to wail for her lost child.*

▷ NOUN = **cry**, moan, sob, howl, keening, lament, bawl, lamentation, yowl, ululation: *Wails of grief were heard as visitors filed past the site of the disaster.*

wait VERB **1** = **stay**, remain, stop, pause, rest, delay, linger, hover, hang around *(informal)*, dally, loiter, tarry: *I waited at the corner for the lights to go green.* **OPPOSITE:** go **2** = **stand by**, delay, hold on *(informal)*, hold back, wait in the wings, mark time, hang fire, bide your time, kick your heels, cool your heels: *Let's wait and see what happens.* **3** = **be postponed**, be suspended, be delayed, be put off, be put back, be deferred, be put on hold *(informal)*, be shelved, be tabled, be held over, be put on ice *(informal)*, be put on the back burner *(informal)*: *I want to talk to you but it can wait.*

▷ NOUN = **delay**, gap, pause, interval, stay, rest, halt, hold-up, lull, stoppage, hindrance, hiatus, entr'acte: *After a long wait, someone finally picked up the phone.*

wait for *or* **on something** *or* **someone** = **await**, expect, look forward to, hope for, anticipate, look for: *I'm still waiting for a reply from him.*

wait on *or* **upon someone** = **serve**, tend to, look after, take care of, minister to, attend to, cater to: *The owner of the restaurant himself waited on us.*

wait up = **stay awake**, stay up, keep vigil: *I waited up for you till three in the morning.*

> **PROVERBS**
> *Don't count your chickens before they are hatched*
> *Don't cross the bridge till you come to it*

waiter NOUN = **attendant**, server, flunkey, steward, servant

waitress NOUN = **attendant**, server, stewardess, servant

waive VERB **1** = **give up**, relinquish, renounce, forsake, drop, abandon, resign, yield, surrender, set aside, dispense with, cede, forgo: *He pled guilty to the charges and waived his right to appeal.* **OPPOSITE:** claim **2** = **disregard**, ignore, discount, overlook, set aside, pass over, dispense with, brush aside, turn a blind eye to, forgo: *The council has agreed to waive certain statutory planning regulations.*

waiver NOUN = **renunciation**, surrender, remission, abdication, giving up, resignation, denial, setting aside, abandonment, disclaimer, disavowal, relinquishment, eschewal, abjuration

wake[1] VERB **1** = **awake**, stir, awaken, come to, arise, get up, rouse, get out

of bed, waken, bestir, rouse from sleep, bestir yourself: *It was still dark when I woke.* **OPPOSITE:** fall asleep
2 = awaken, arouse, rouse, waken, rouse someone from sleep: *She went upstairs at once to wake the children.*
3 = evoke, recall, excite, renew, stimulate, revive, induce, arouse, call up, awaken, rouse, give rise to, conjure up, stir up, rekindle, summon up, reignite: *Seeing him again upset her, because it woke painful memories.*
▷ NOUN **= vigil**, watch, funeral, deathwatch, tangi (N.Z.): *A funeral wake was in progress.*
wake someone up = activate, stimulate, enliven, galvanize, fire, excite, provoke, motivate, arouse, awaken, animate, rouse, mobilize, energize, kindle, switch someone on, stir someone up: *He needs a shock to wake him up a bit.*

USAGE
Both *wake* and its synonym *waken* can be used either with or without an object: *I woke/wakened my sister*, and also *I woke/wakened (up) at noon*. *Wake*, *wake up*, and occasionally *waken*, can also be used in a figurative sense, for example *Seeing him again woke painful memories*; and *It's time he woke up to his responsibilities*. The verbs *awake* and *awaken* are more commonly used in the figurative than the literal sense, for example *He awoke to the danger he was in.*

wake² NOUN **= slipstream**, wash, trail, backwash, train, track, waves, path: *Dolphins sometimes play in the wake of the boats.*
in the wake of = in the aftermath of, following, because of, as a result of, on account of, as a consequence of: *The move comes in the wake of new measures brought in by the government.*

waken VERB **1 = awaken**, wake, stir, wake up, stimulate, revive, awake, arouse, activate, animate, rouse, enliven, galvanize: *Have a cup of coffee to waken you.* **2 = wake up**, come to, get up, awake, awaken, be roused, come awake: *I dozed off and I only wakened when she came in.* **OPPOSITE:** fall asleep

Wales NOUN **= Cymru** (*Welsh*), Cambria (*Latin*)

walk VERB **1 = stride**, wander, stroll, trudge, go, move, step, march, advance, pace, trek, hike, tread, ramble, tramp, promenade, amble, saunter, take a turn, traipse (*informal*), toddle, make your way, mosey (*informal*), plod on, perambulate, footslog: *They walked in silence for a while.* **2 = travel on foot**, go on foot, hoof it (*slang*), foot it, go by shanks's pony (*informal*): *When I was your age I walked five miles to school.* **3 = escort**, take, see, show, partner, guide, conduct, accompany, shepherd, convoy, usher, chaperon: *He offered to walk me home.*
▷ NOUN **1 = stroll**, hike, ramble, tramp, turn, march, constitutional, trek, outing, trudge, promenade, amble, saunter, traipse (*informal*), breath of air, perambulation: *He often took long walks in the hills.* **2 = gait**, manner of walking, step, bearing, pace, stride, carriage, tread: *Despite his gangling walk, George was a good dancer.*
3 = path, pathway, footpath, track, way, road, lane, trail, avenue, pavement, alley, aisle, sidewalk (*chiefly U.S.*), walkway (*chiefly U.S.*), promenade, towpath, esplanade, footway, berm (*N.Z.*): *a covered walk consisting of a roof supported by columns*
walk of life = area, calling, business, line, course, trade, class, field, career, rank, employment, province, profession, occupation, arena, sphere, realm, domain, caste, vocation, line of work, métier: *In this job you meet people from all walks of life.*
walk out 1 = leave suddenly, storm out, get up and go, flounce out, vote with your feet, make a sudden departure, take off (*informal*): *Mr Mason walked out during the performance.* **2 = go on strike**, strike, revolt, mutiny, stop work, take industrial action, down tools, withdraw your labour: *Industrial action began this week, when most of the staff walked out.*
walk out on someone = abandon, leave, desert, strand, betray, chuck (*informal*), run away from, forsake, jilt, run out on (*informal*), throw over, leave high and dry, leave in the lurch: *Her husband walked out on her*

PROVERBS
We must learn to walk before we can run

walker NOUN **= hiker**, rambler, backpacker, wayfarer, footslogger, pedestrian

walkout NOUN **= strike**, protest, revolt, stoppage, industrial action

wall NOUN **1 = partition**, divider, room divider, screen, panel, barrier, enclosure: *We're going to knock down the dividing wall to give us one big room.*
2 = barricade, rampart, fortification, bulwark, blockade, embankment, parapet, palisade, stockade, breastwork: *The Romans breached the city walls and captured the city.* **3 = barrier**, obstacle, barricade, obstruction, check, bar, block, fence, impediment, hindrance: *I appealed for help but met the usual wall of silence.*
drive someone up the wall = infuriate, madden, exasperate, get on your nerves (*informal*), anger, provoke, annoy, irritate, aggravate (*informal*), incense, enrage, gall, rile, drive you crazy (*informal*), nark (*Brit., Austral. & N.Z. slang*), be like a red rag to a bull, make your blood boil, get your goat (*slang*), drive you insane, make your hackles rise, raise your hackles, send off your head (*slang*), get your back up, make you see red (*informal*), put your back up, hack you off (*informal*): *That tuneless humming of his drives me up the wall.*
go to the wall = fail, close down, go under, go out of business, fall, crash, collapse, fold (*informal*), be ruined, go bust (*informal*), go bankrupt, go broke (*informal*), go into receivership, become insolvent: *Even big companies are going to the wall these days.*
▸ *related adjective:* mural

wallet NOUN **= purse**, pocketbook, notecase, pouch, case, holder, moneybag

wallop VERB **1 = hit**, beat, strike, knock, belt (*informal*), deck (*slang*), bang, batter, bash (*informal*), pound, chin (*slang*), smack, thrash, thump, paste (*slang*), buffet, clout (*informal*), slug, whack, swipe, clobber (*slang*), pummel, tonk (*slang*), lambast(e), lay one on (*slang*), beat *or* knock seven bells out of (*informal*): *Once she walloped me over the head with a frying pan.*
2 = beat, defeat, slaughter, thrash, best, stuff (*slang*), worst, tank (*slang*), hammer (*informal*), crush, overwhelm, lick (*informal*), paste (*slang*), rout, walk over (*informal*), trounce, clobber (*slang*), vanquish, run rings around (*informal*), wipe the floor with (*informal*), make mincemeat of, blow out of the water (*slang*), drub, beat hollow (*Brit. informal*), defeat heavily *or* utterly: *England were walloped by Brazil in the finals.*
▷ NOUN **= blow**, strike, punch, thump, belt (*informal*), bash, sock (*slang*), smack, clout (*informal*), slug, whack, swipe, thwack, haymaker (*slang*): *With one brutal wallop, Clarke sent him flying.*

wallow VERB **1 = revel**, indulge, relish, savour, delight, glory, thrive, bask, take pleasure, luxuriate, indulge yourself: *All he wants to do is wallow in self-pity.* **OPPOSITE:** refrain from
2 = roll about, lie, tumble, wade, slosh, welter, splash around: *Hippos love to wallow in mud.*

wan ADJECTIVE **1 = pale**, white, washed out, pasty, faded, bleached, ghastly, sickly, bloodless, colourless, pallid, anaemic, discoloured, ashen, sallow, whitish, cadaverous, waxen, like death warmed up (*informal*), wheyfaced: *He looked wan and tired.* **OPPOSITE:** glowing **2 = dim**, weak, pale, faint, feeble: *The lamp cast a wan light through the swirls of fog.*

wand NOUN **= stick**, rod, cane, baton, stake, switch, birch, twig, sprig, withe, withy

wander VERB **= roam**, walk, drift, stroll, range, cruise, stray, ramble, prowl, meander, rove, straggle, traipse (*informal*), mooch around (*slang*), stravaig (*Scot. & Northern English dialect*), knock about *or* around, peregrinate: *He wandered aimlessly around the garden.*
▷ NOUN **= excursion**, turn, walk, stroll, cruise, ramble, meander, promenade, traipse (*informal*), mosey (*informal*), peregrination: *Let's go for a wander round the shops.*
wander off = stray, roam, go astray, lose your way, drift, depart, rove, straggle: *The child wandered off and got lost.*
wander off something = deviate,

diverge, veer, swerve, digress, go off at a tangent, go off course, lapse: *He has a tendency to wander off the point when he's talking.*

wanderer NOUN **= traveller**, rover, nomad, drifter, ranger, journeyer, gypsy, explorer, migrant, rolling stone, rambler, voyager, tripper, itinerant, globetrotter, vagrant, stroller, vagabond, wayfarer, bird of passage

wandering ADJECTIVE **= itinerant**, travelling, journeying, roving, drifting, homeless, strolling, voyaging, unsettled, roaming, rambling, nomadic, migratory, vagrant, peripatetic, vagabond, rootless, wayfaring

wane VERB **1 = decline**, flag, weaken, diminish, fall, fail, drop, sink, fade, decrease, dim, dwindle, wither, lessen, subside, ebb, wind down, die out, fade away, abate, draw to a close, atrophy, taper off: *His interest in her began to wane.* **OPPOSITE:** grow **2 = diminish**, decrease, dwindle: *The sliver of a waning moon was high in the sky.* **OPPOSITE:** wax

on the wane = declining, dropping, fading, weakening, dwindling, withering, lessening, subsiding, ebbing, dying out, on the way out, on the decline, tapering off, obsolescent, on its last legs, at its lowest ebb: *His career prospects were clearly on the wane.*

want VERB **1 = wish for**, desire, fancy, long for, crave, covet, hope for, yearn for, thirst for, hunger for, pine for, hanker after, set your heart on, feel a need for, have a yen for *(informal)*, have a fancy for, eat your heart out over, would give your eyeteeth for: *My husband really wants a new car.* **OPPOSITE:** have **2 = need**, demand, require, call for, have need of, stand in need of: *The grass wants cutting.* **3 = should**, need, must, ought: *You want to look where you're going, mate.* **4 = desire**, fancy, long for, crave, wish for, yearn for, thirst for, hanker after, burn for: *Come on, darling. I want you.* **5 = lack**, need, require, be short of, miss, be deficient in, be without, fall short in: *Our team still wants one more player.*
▷ NOUN **1 = lack**, need, absence, shortage, deficiency, famine, default, shortfall, inadequacy, scarcity, dearth, paucity, shortness, insufficiency, non-existence, scantiness: *The men were daily becoming weaker for want of rest.* **OPPOSITE:** abundance **2 = poverty**, need, hardship, privation, penury, destitution, neediness, hand-to-mouth existence, indigence, pauperism, pennilessness, distress: *He said they were fighting for freedom from want.* **OPPOSITE:** wealth **3 = wish**, will, need, demand, desire, requirement, fancy, yen *(informal)*, longing, hunger, necessity, appetite, craving, yearning, thirst, whim, hankering: *The company needs to respond to the wants of our customers.*

W

wanting ADJECTIVE **1 = deficient**, poor, disappointing, inadequate, pathetic, inferior, insufficient, faulty, not good enough, defective, patchy, imperfect, sketchy, unsound, substandard, leaving much to be desired, not much cop *(Brit. slang)*, not up to par, not up to expectations, bodger *or* bodgie *(Austral. slang)*: *He examined her work and found it wanting.* **OPPOSITE:** adequate **2 = lacking**, missing, absent, incomplete, needing, short, shy: *I feel as if something important is wanting in my life.* **OPPOSITE:** complete

wanton ADJECTIVE **1 = wilful**, needless, senseless, unjustified, willed, evil, cruel, vicious, deliberate, arbitrary, malicious, wicked, purposeful, gratuitous, malevolent, spiteful, unprovoked, groundless, unjustifiable, uncalled-for, motiveless: *the unnecessary and wanton destruction of our environment* **OPPOSITE:** justified **2 = promiscuous**, immoral, shameless, licentious, fast, wild, abandoned, loose, dissipated, lewd, profligate, debauched, lustful, lecherous, dissolute, libertine, libidinous, of easy virtue, unchaste: *Women behaving with the same sexual freedom as men are considered wanton.* **OPPOSITE:** puritanical

war NOUN **1 = conflict**, drive, attack, fighting, fight, operation, battle, movement, push, struggle, clash, combat, offensive, hostilities, hostility, warfare, expedition, crusade, strife, bloodshed, jihad, enmity, armed conflict: *matters of war and peace* **OPPOSITE:** peace **2 = campaign**, drive, attack, operation, movement, push, mission, offensive, crusade: *the war against organized crime*
▷ VERB **= fight**, battle, clash, wage war, campaign, struggle, combat, contend, go to war, do battle, make war, take up arms, bear arms, cross swords, conduct a war, engage in hostilities, carry on hostilities: *The two tribes warred to gain new territory.* **OPPOSITE:** make peace
▸ *related adjectives:* belligerent, martial

QUOTATIONS

War is nothing but the continuation of politics by other means
[Karl von Clausewitz *On War*]

Politics is war without bloodshed while war is politics with bloodshed
[Mao Zedong *On Protracted War*]

There was never a good war, or a bad peace
[Benjamin Franklin]

War makes rattling good history; but Peace is poor reading
[Thomas Hardy *The Dynasts*]

He that makes a good war makes a good peace
[George Herbert *Outlandish Proverbs*]

O I know they make war because they want peace; they hate so that they may live; and they destroy the present to make the world safe for the future. When have they not done and said they did it for that?
[Elizabeth Smart *Necessary Secrets*]

For what can war but endless war still breed?
[John Milton *Sonnet, On the Lord General Fairfax*]

Above all, this book is not concerned with Poetry,
The subject of it is War, and the Pity of War.
The Poetry is in the Pity
[Wilfred Owen *Poems (preface)*]

As long as war is regarded as wicked, it will always have its fascination. When it is looked upon as vulgar, it will cease to be popular
[Oscar Wilde *The Critic as Artist*]

In war, whichever side may call itself the victor, there are no winners, but all are losers
[Neville Chamberlain]

War is too serious a matter to entrust to military men
[Georges Clemenceau]

War is like love, it always finds a way
[Bertolt Brecht *Mother Courage and Her Children*]

It is easier to make war than to make peace
[Georges Clemenceau]

During the time men live without a common power to keep them all in awe, they are in that condition which is called war; and such a war as is of every man against every man
[Thomas Hobbes *Leviathan*]

History is littered with the wars which everybody knew would never happen
[Enoch Powell *speech to the Conservative Party Conference*]

Let slip the dogs of war
[William Shakespeare *Julius Caesar*]

War is the trade of kings
[John Dryden *King Arthur*]

The quickest way of ending a war is to lose it
[George Orwell *Shooting an Elephant*]

Sometime they'll give a war and nobody will come
[Carl Sandburg *'The People, Yes'*]

Since war begins in the minds of men, it is in the minds of men that the defences of peace must be constructed
[*Constitution of UNESCO*]

The next war will be fought with atom bombs and the one after that with spears
[Harold Urey]

A bayonet is a weapon with a worker at each end
[*pacifist slogan*]

Fighting for peace is like fucking for virginity
[*anti-war graffiti*]

War will cease when men refuse to fight
[*pacifist slogan*]

After each war there is a little less democracy to save
[Brooks Atkinson *Once Around the Sun*]

What if someone gave a war and
Nobody came?
Life would ring the bells of Ecstasy
and Forever be Itself again
[Allen Ginsberg *The Fall of America*]

In the fall the war was always there but we did not go to it any more
[Ernest Hemingway *Men Without Women*]

The Falklands thing was a fight between two bald men over a comb
[Jorge Luis Borges]

PROVERBS
All is fair in love and war

warble VERB **= sing**, trill, chirp, twitter, chirrup, make melody, pipe, quaver: *A flock of birds was warbling in the trees.*
▷ NOUN **= song**, trill, quaver, twitter, call, cry, chirp, chirrup: *the soft warble of her speaking voice*

ward NOUN **1 = room**, department, unit, quarter, division, section, apartment, cubicle: *A toddler was admitted to the emergency ward.* **2 = district**, constituency, area, division, zone, parish, precinct: *Canvassers are focusing on marginal wards in this election.* **3 = dependant**, charge, pupil, minor, protégé: *Richard became Burton's legal ward and took his name by deed poll.*
ward someone off = drive off, resist, confront, fight off, block, oppose, thwart, hold off, repel, fend off, beat off, keep someone at bay, keep someone at arm's length: *She may have tried to ward off her assailant.*
ward something off 1 = avert, turn away, fend off, stave off, avoid, block, frustrate, deflect, repel, forestall: *A rowan cross was hung over the door to ward off evil.* **2 = parry**, avert, deflect, fend off, avoid, block, repel, turn aside: *He lifted his hands as if to ward off a blow.*

warden NOUN **1 = steward**, guardian, administrator, superintendent, caretaker, curator, warder, custodian, watchman, janitor: *He was a warden at the local parish church.* **2 = jailer**, prison officer, guard, screw *(slang)*, keeper, captor, turnkey *(archaic)*, gaoler: *The prisoners seized three wardens.* **3 = governor**, head, leader, director, manager, chief, executive, boss *(informal)*, commander, ruler, controller, overseer, baas *(S. African)*: *A new warden took over the prison.* **4 = ranger**, keeper, guardian, protector, custodian, official: *a safari park warden*

warder or **wardress** *(chiefly Brit.)* NOUN **= jailer**, guard, screw *(slang)*, warden, prison officer, keeper, captor, custodian, turnkey *(archaic)*, gaoler

wardrobe NOUN **1 = clothes cupboard**, cupboard, closet *(U.S.)*, clothes-press, cabinet: *Hang your dress up in the wardrobe.* **2 = clothes**, outfit, apparel, clobber *(Brit. slang)*, attire, collection of clothes: *splurging on an expensive new wardrobe of clothes*

warehouse NOUN **= store**, depot, storehouse, repository, depository, stockroom

wares PLURAL NOUN **= goods**, produce, stock, products, stuff, commodities, merchandise, lines

warfare NOUN **= war**, fighting, campaigning, battle, struggle, conflict, combat, hostilities, strife, bloodshed, jihad, armed struggle, discord, enmity, armed conflict, clash of arms, passage of arms **OPPOSITE:** peace

warily ADVERB **1 = cautiously**, carefully, discreetly, with care, tentatively, gingerly, guardedly, circumspectly, watchfully, vigilantly, cagily *(informal)*, heedfully: *He backed warily away from the animal.* **OPPOSITE:** carelessly **2 = suspiciously**, uneasily, guardedly, sceptically, cagily *(informal)*, distrustfully, mistrustfully, charily: *The two men eyed each other warily.*

wariness NOUN **1 = caution**, care, attention, prudence, discretion, deliberation, foresight, vigilance, alertness, forethought, circumspection, mindfulness, watchfulness, carefulness, caginess *(informal)*, heedfulness: *Extreme wariness is the safest policy when dealing with these substances.* **OPPOSITE:** carelessness **2 = suspicion**, scepticism, distrust, mistrust: *the country's obsessive wariness of foreigners*

QUOTATIONS
Call no man foe, but never love a stranger
[Stella Benson *This is the End*]

warlike ADJECTIVE **= belligerent**, military, aggressive, hostile, martial, combative, unfriendly, antagonistic, pugnacious, argumentative, bloodthirsty, hawkish, bellicose, quarrelsome, militaristic, inimical, sabre-rattling, jingoistic, warmongering, aggers *(Austral. slang)*, biffo *(Austral. slang)* **OPPOSITE:** peaceful

warm ADJECTIVE **1 = balmy**, mild, temperate, pleasant, fine, bright, sunny, agreeable, sultry, summery, moderately hot: *The weather was so warm I had to take off my jacket.* **OPPOSITE:** cool **2 = cosy**, snug, toasty *(informal)*, comfortable, homely, comfy *(informal)*: *Nothing beats coming home to a warm house.* **3 = moderately hot**, heated: *A warm bath will help to relax you.* **OPPOSITE:** cool **4 = thermal**, winter, thick, chunky, woolly: *Some people can't afford warm clothes.* **OPPOSITE:** cool **5 = mellow**, relaxing, pleasant, agreeable, restful: *The basement hallway is painted a warm yellow.* **6 = affable**, kindly, friendly, affectionate, loving, happy, tender, pleasant, cheerful, hearty, good-humoured, amiable, amicable, cordial, sociable, genial, congenial, hospitable, approachable, amorous, good-natured, likable *or* likeable: *We were instantly attracted by his warm personality.* **OPPOSITE:** unfriendly **7 = near**, close, hot, near to the truth: *Am I getting warm? Am I right?*
▷ VERB **= warm up**, heat, thaw (out), heat up: *She went to warm her hands by the fire.* **OPPOSITE:** cool down
warm something or **someone up 1 = heat**, thaw, heat up: *He blew on his hands to warm them up.* **2 = rouse**, stimulate, stir up, animate, interest, excite, provoke, turn on *(slang)*, arouse, awaken, exhilarate, incite, whip up, galvanize, put some life into, get something *or* someone going, make something *or* someone enthusiastic: *They went on before us to warm up the audience.*

warm-hearted ADJECTIVE **= kindly**, loving, kind, warm, gentle, generous, tender, pleasant, mild, sympathetic, affectionate, compassionate, hearty, cordial, genial, affable, good-natured, kind-hearted, tender-hearted **OPPOSITE:** cold-hearted

warmth NOUN **1 = heat**, snugness, warmness, comfort, homeliness, hotness: *She went in, drawn by the warmth of the fire.* **OPPOSITE:** coolness **2 = affection**, feeling, love, goodwill, kindness, tenderness, friendliness, cheerfulness, amity, cordiality, affability, kindliness, heartiness, amorousness, hospitableness, fondness: *He greeted us both with warmth.* **OPPOSITE:** hostility

warn VERB **1 = notify**, tell, remind, inform, alert, tip off, give notice, make someone aware, forewarn, apprise, give fair warning: *They warned him of the dangers of sailing alone.* **2 = advise**, urge, recommend, counsel, caution, commend, exhort, admonish, put someone on his *or* her guard: *My mother warned me not to interfere.*

warning NOUN **1 = caution**, information, advice, injunction, notification, caveat, word to the wise: *health warnings on cigarette packets* **2 = notice**, notification, word, sign, threat, tip, signal, alarm, announcement, hint, alert, tip-off *(informal)*, heads up *(U.S. & Canad.)*: *The soldiers opened fire without warning.* **3 = omen**, sign, forecast, indication, token, prediction, prophecy, premonition, foreboding, portent, presage, augury, foretoken, rahui *(N.Z.)*: *a warning of impending doom* **4 = reprimand**, talking-to *(informal)*, caution, censure, counsel, carpeting *(Brit. informal)*, rebuke, reproach, scolding, berating, ticking-off *(informal)*, chiding, dressing down *(informal)*, telling-off *(informal)*,

admonition, upbraiding, reproof, remonstrance: *He was given a severe warning from the referee.*
▷ ADJECTIVE = **cautionary**, threatening, ominous, premonitory, admonitory, monitory, bodeful: *Pain can act as a warning signal that something is wrong.*

warp VERB **1 = distort**, bend, twist, buckle, deform, disfigure, contort, misshape, malform: *Rainwater had warped the door's timber.* **2 = become distorted**, bend, twist, contort, become deformed, become misshapen: *Plastic can warp in the sun.* **3 = pervert**, twist, corrupt, degrade, deprave, debase, desecrate, debauch, lead astray: *Their minds have been warped by their experiences.*
▷ NOUN = **twist**, turn, bend, defect, flaw, distortion, deviation, quirk, imperfection, kink, contortion, deformation: *small warps in the planking*

warrant VERB = **call for**, demand, require, merit, rate, commission, earn, deserve, permit, sanction, excuse, justify, license, authorize, entail, necessitate, be worthy of, give ground for: *The allegations are serious enough to warrant an investigation.*
▷ NOUN = **authorization**, permit, licence, permission, security, authority, commission, sanction, pledge, warranty, carte blanche: *Police have issued a warrant for his arrest.*

warranty NOUN = **guarantee**, promise, contract, bond, pledge, certificate, assurance, covenant

warring ADJECTIVE = **hostile**, fighting, conflicting, opposed, contending, at war, embattled, belligerent, combatant, antagonistic, warlike, bellicose, ill-disposed

warrior NOUN = **soldier**, combatant, fighter, gladiator, champion, brave, trooper, military man, fighting man, man-at-arms

wary ADJECTIVE **1 = suspicious**, sceptical, mistrustful, suspecting, guarded, apprehensive, cagey *(informal)*, leery *(slang)*, distrustful, on your guard, chary, heedful: *My mother always told me to be wary of strangers.* **2 = watchful**, careful, alert, cautious, prudent, attentive, vigilant, circumspect, heedful: *Keep a wary eye on children when they are playing near water.* **OPPOSITE:** careless

wash VERB **1 = clean**, scrub, sponge, rinse, scour, cleanse: *He got a job washing dishes in a pizza parlour.* **2 = launder**, clean, wet, rinse, dry-clean, moisten: *The colours will fade a little each time you wash the shirt.* **3 = rinse**, clean, scrub, lather: *It took a long time to wash the mud out of his hair.* **4 = bathe**, bath, shower, take a bath *or* shower, clean yourself, soak, sponge, douse, freshen up, lave *(archaic)*, soap, scrub yourself down: *There was a sour smell about him, as if he had not washed for days.* **5 = lap**, break, dash, roll, flow, surge, splash, slap, ripple, swish, splosh: *The sea washed against the shore.* **6 = move**, overcome, touch, upset, stir, disturb, perturb, surge through, tug at someone's heartstrings *(often facetious)*: *A wave of despair washed over him.* **7** *(used in negative constructions)* **= be plausible**, stand up, hold up, pass muster, hold water, stick, carry weight, be convincing, bear scrutiny: *All those excuses simply won't wash with me.*
▷ NOUN **1 = laundering**, cleaning, clean, cleansing: *That coat could do with a good wash.* **2 = bathe**, bath, shower, dip, soak, scrub, shampoo, rinse, ablution: *She had a wash and changed her clothes.* **3 = backwash**, slipstream, path, trail, train, track, waves, aftermath: *The wash from a passing ship overturned their dinghy.* **4 = splash**, roll, flow, sweep, surge, swell, rise and fall, ebb and flow, undulation: *The steady wash of waves on the shore calmed me.* **5 = coat**, film, covering, layer, screen, coating, stain, overlay, suffusion: *He painted a wash of colour over the entire surface.*
wash something away = **erode**, corrode, eat into, wear something away, eat something away: *The topsoil is washed away by flood rains.*
wash something *or* **someone away** = **sweep away**, carry off, bear away: *Flood waters washed him away.*

washed out ADJECTIVE **1 = pale**, light, flat, mat, muted, drab, lacklustre, watery, lustreless: *The room was now dull and flat with washed-out colours.* **2 = wan**, drawn, pale, pinched, blanched, haggard, bloodless, colourless, pallid, anaemic, ashen, chalky, peaky, deathly pale: *She tried to hide her washed-out face behind large, dark glasses.* **3 = faded**, bleached, blanched, colourless, stonewashed: *a washed-out blue denim jacket* **4 = exhausted**, drained, worn-out, tired-out, spent, drawn, done in *(informal)*, all in *(slang)*, fatigued, wiped out *(informal)*, weary, knackered *(slang)*, clapped out *(Austral. & N.Z. informal)*, dog-tired *(informal)*, zonked *(slang)*, dead on your feet *(informal)*: *She looked washed-out and listless.* **OPPOSITE:** lively

washout NOUN **1 = failure**, disaster, disappointment, flop *(informal)*, mess, fiasco, dud *(informal)*, clunker *(informal)*: *The concert was a total washout.* **OPPOSITE:** success **2 = loser**, failure, incompetent, no-hoper: *As a husband, he's a complete washout.*

waste VERB **1 = squander**, throw away, blow *(slang)*, run through, lavish, misuse, dissipate, fritter away, frivol away *(informal)*: *We can't afford to waste money on another holiday.* **OPPOSITE:** save **2** *(followed by* **away***)* **= wear out**, wither, deplete, debilitate, drain, undermine, exhaust, disable, consume, gnaw, eat away, corrode, enfeeble, sap the strength of, emaciate: *a cruel disease which wastes the muscles*
▷ NOUN **1 = squandering**, misuse, loss, expenditure, extravagance, frittering away, lost opportunity, dissipation, wastefulness, misapplication, prodigality, unthriftiness: *The whole project is a complete waste of time and resources.* **OPPOSITE:** saving **2 = rubbish**, refuse, debris, sweepings, scrap, litter, garbage, trash, leftovers, offal, dross, dregs, leavings, offscourings: *This country produces 10 million tonnes of toxic waste every year.* **3** *(usually plural)* **= desert**, wilds, wilderness, void, solitude, wasteland: *the barren wastes of the Sahara*
▷ ADJECTIVE **1 = unwanted**, useless, worthless, unused, leftover, superfluous, unusable, supernumerary: *suitable locations for the disposal of waste products* **OPPOSITE:** necessary **2 = uncultivated**, wild, bare, barren, empty, devastated, dismal, dreary, desolate, unproductive, uninhabited: *Yarrow can be found growing wild on waste ground.* **OPPOSITE:** cultivated
lay something waste = **devastate**, destroy, ruin, spoil, total *(slang)*, sack, undo, trash *(slang)*, ravage, raze, kennet *(Austral. slang)*, jeff *(Austral. slang)*, despoil, wreak havoc upon, depredate *(rare)*: *The war has laid waste large regions of the country.*
waste away = **decline**, dwindle, wither, perish, sink, fade, crumble, decay, wane, ebb, wear out, atrophy: *People dying from cancer grow thin and visibly waste away.*

PROVERBS
It's no use making shoes for geese

USAGE
Waste and *wastage* are to some extent interchangeable, but many people think that *wastage* should not be used to refer to loss resulting from human carelessness, inefficiency, etc: *a waste* (not *a wastage*) *of time, money, effort, etc.*

wasteful ADJECTIVE = **extravagant**, lavish, prodigal, profligate, ruinous, spendthrift, uneconomical, improvident, unthrifty, thriftless **OPPOSITE:** thrifty

wasteland NOUN = **wilderness**, waste, wild, desert, void

waster NOUN = **layabout**, loser, good-for-nothing, shirker, piker *(Austral. & N.Z. slang)*, drone, loafer, skiver *(Brit. slang)*, idler, ne'er-do-well, wastrel, malingerer, bludger *(Austral. & N.Z. informal)*

watch VERB **1 = look at**, observe, regard, eye, see, mark, view, note, check, clock *(Brit. slang)*, stare at, contemplate, check out *(informal)*, look on, gaze at, pay attention to, eyeball *(slang)*, peer at, leer at, get a load of *(informal)*, feast your eyes on, take a butcher's at *(Brit. informal)*, take a dekko at *(Brit. slang)*: *The man was standing in the doorway watching him.* **2 = spy on**, follow, track, monitor,

Writers and Dramatists

Children's writers

Louisa May Alcott *(U.S.)*
Hans Christian Andersen *(Danish)*
Lynn Reid Banks *(English)*
J(ames) M(atthew) Barrie *(Scottish)*
Judy Blume *(U.S.)*
Enid (Mary) Blyton *(English)*
Elinor M(ary) Brent-Dyer *(English)*
Lewis Carroll *(English)*
Babette Cole *(British)*
Eoin Colfer *(Irish)*
Susan Coolidge *(U.S.)*
Karen Cushman *(U.S.)*
Roald Dahl *(British)*
Anne Digby *(English)*
Dr Seuss *(U.S.)*
Anne Fine *(English)*
Kenneth Grahame *(Scottish)*
Laura Ingalls Wilder *(U.S.)*
Mick Inkpen *(English)*
Robin Jarvis *(English)*
Diana Wynne Jones *(Welsh)*
Dick King-Smith *(English)*
C(live) S(taples) Lewis *(English)*
A(lan) A(lexander) Milne *(English)*
Michael Morpurgo *(English)*
Jill Murphy *(English)*
E(dith) Nesbit *(English)*
Terry Pratchett *(English)*
Philip Pullman *(English)*
Chris Riddell *(English)*
J K Rowling *(British)*
Louis Sachar *(U.S.)*
Paul Stewart *(English)*
Noel Streatfield *(English)*
Jacqueline Wilson *(English)*

Short story writers

Giovanni Boccaccio *(Italian)*
Jorge Luis Borges *(Argentinian)*
Stephen Crane *(U.S.)*
Arthur Conan Doyle *(British)*
Joel Chandler Harris *(U.S.)*
Nathaniel Hawthorne *(U.S.)*
Washington Irving *(U.S.)*
Carson McCullers *(U.S.)*
Katherine Mansfield *(N.Z.-British)*
W(illiam) Somerset Maugham *(English)*
(Henri René Albert) Guy de Maupassant *(French)*
Herman Melville *(U.S.)*
H(ector) H(ugh) Munro *(Scottish)*
O. Henry *(U.S.)*
Dorothy Parker *(U.S.)*
Edgar Allan Poe *(U.S.)*

Non-fiction writers

Joseph Addison *(English)*
Aesop *(Greek)*
Roger Ascham *(English)*
James Boswell *(Scottish)*
John Bunyan *(English)*
Edmund Burke *(British)*
Jane Welsh Carlyle *(Scottish)*
Thomas Carlyle *(Scottish)*
William Godwin *(English)*
Marcus Tullius Cicero *(Roman)*
William Cobbett *(English)*
Desiderius Erasmus *(Dutch)*
Edward Gibbon *(English)*
William Hazlitt *(English)*
R.H. Hutton *(English)*
Thomas Jefferson *(U.S.)*
Jerome K(lapka) Jerome *(English)*
Samuel Johnson *(English)*
Margery Kempe *(English)*
Lord Chesterfield *(English)*
John Lyly *(English)*
Thomas Malory *(English)*
Michel Eyquem de Montaigne *(French)*
Tom Paine *(English-U.S.)*
Samuel Pepys *(English)*
François Rabelais *(French)*
John Ruskin *(English)*
Richard Steele *(English)*
Leslie Stephen *(English)*
Thomas Traherne *(English)*
Izaak Walton *(English)*
Mary Wollstonecraft *(English)*

Dramatists

Aeschylus *(Greek)*
Edward Albee *(U.S.)*
Robert Amos *(Australian)*
Jean Anouilh *(French)*
Aristophanes *(Greek)*
Alan Ayckbourn *(English)*
Pierre Augustin Caron de Beaumarchais *(French)*
Francis Beaumont *(English)*
Samuel Beckett *(Irish)*
Brendan Behan *(Irish)*
Alan Bleasdale *(English)*
Edward Bond *(English)*
Bertolt Brecht *(German)*
Pedro Calderón de la Barca *(Spanish)*
George Chapman *(English)*
Anton Pavlovich Chekhov *(Russian)*
William Congreve *(English)*
Pierre Corneille *(French)*
Noël (Pierce) Coward *(English)*
Thomas Dekker *(English)*
John Dryden *(English)*
T(homas) S(tearns) Eliot *(U.S.-British)*
Euripides *(Greek)*
John Fletcher *(English)*
Dario Fo *(Italian)*
John Ford *(English)*
Brian Friel *(Irish)*
John Galsworthy *(English)*
Jean Genet *(French)*
(Hippolyte) Jean Giraudoux *(French)*
Johann Wolfgang von Goethe *(German)*
Nikolai Gogol *(Russian)*
Oliver Goldsmith *(Irish)*
Robert Greene *(English)*
David Hare *(English)*
Gerhart Johann Robert Hauptmann *(German)*
Václav Havel *(Czech)*
Eugène Ionesco *(Romanian-French)*
Ben Jonson *(English)*
George Kaiser *(German)*
Tony Kushner *(U.S.)*
Thomas Kyd *(English)*
Ray Lawler *(Australian)*
Liz Lochhead *(Scottish)*
Lope de Vega *(Spanish)*
Federico Garcia Lorca *(Spanish)*
Maurice Maeterlinck *(Belgian)*
David Mamet *(U.S.)*
Christopher Marlowe *(English)*
John Marston *(English)*
Menander *(Greek)*
Arthur Miller *(U.S.)*
Molière *(French)*
Barry Oakley *(Australian)*
Sean O'Casey *(Irish)*
Eugene (Gladstone) O'Neill *(U.S.)*
Joe Orton *(English)*
John Osborne *(English)*
Thomas Otway *(English)*
John Patrick *(U.S.)*
Arthur Wing Pinero *(English)*
Harold Pinter *(English)*
Luigi Pirandello *(Italian)*
Titus Maccius Plautus *(Roman)*
Hal Porter *(Australian)*
Aleksander Sergeyevich Pushkin *(Russian)*
Jean Baptiste Racine *(French)*
Terence Mervyn Rattigan *(English)*
John Romeril *(Australian)*
Willy Russell *(English)*
Thomas Sackville *(English)*
Jean-Paul Sartre *(French)*
Johann Christoph Friedrich von Schiller *(German)*
Lucius Annaeus Seneca *(Roman)*
Alan Seymour *(Australian)*
Peter Shaffer *(English)*
William Shakespeare *(English)*
George Bernard Shaw *(Irish)*
Sam Shepard *(U.S.)*
Richard Brinsley Sheridan *(Irish)*
Robert Sherwood *(U.S.)*
Sophocles *(Greek)*
Wole Soyinka *(Nigerian)*
Tom Stoppard *(Czech-English)*
August Strindberg *(Swedish)*
John Millington Synge *(Irish)*
Terence *(Roman)*
John Webster *(English)*
Oscar Wilde *(Irish)*
Thornton Wilder *(U.S.)*
Tennessee Williams *(U.S.)*
David Keith Williamson *(Australian)*
William Wycherly *(English)*

keep an eye on, stake out, keep tabs on *(informal)*, keep watch on, keep under observation, keep under surveillance: *I had the feeling we were being watched.* **3 = guard**, keep, mind, protect, tend, look after, shelter, take care of, safeguard, superintend: *Parents can't be expected to watch their children 24 hours a day.*
▷ NOUN **1 = wristwatch**, timepiece, pocket watch, clock, chronometer: *He looked at his watch and checked the time.* **2 = guard**, eye, attention, supervision, surveillance, notice, observation, inspection, vigil, lookout, vigilance: *Keep a close watch on him while I'm gone.*
watch out *or* **watch it** *or* **watch yourself = be careful**, look out, be wary, be alert, be on the lookout, be vigilant, take heed, have a care, be on the alert, watch yourself, keep your eyes open, be watchful, be on your guard, mind out, be on (the) watch, keep a sharp lookout, keep a weather eye open, keep your eyes peeled *or* skinned *(informal)*, pay attention: *Watch out if you're walking home after dark.*
watch out for something *or* **someone = keep a sharp lookout for**, look out for, be alert for, be on the alert for, keep your eyes open for, be on your guard for, be on (the) watch for, be vigilant for, keep a weather eye open for, be watchful for, keep your eyes peeled *or* skinned for *(informal)*: *We had to watch out for unexploded mines.*

watchdog NOUN **1 = guardian**, monitor, inspector, protector, custodian, scrutineer: *the government's consumer watchdog, the Office of Fair Trading* **2 = guard dog**: *A good watchdog can be a faithful friend as well as a deterrent to intruders.*

watchful ADJECTIVE **= alert**, attentive, vigilant, observant, guarded, suspicious, wary, on the lookout, circumspect, wide awake, on your toes, on your guard, on the watch, on the qui vive, heedful
OPPOSITE: careless

watchman NOUN **= guard**, security guard, security man, custodian, caretaker

watchword NOUN **= motto**, slogan, maxim, byword, rallying cry, battle cry, catch phrase, tag-line, catchword, catchcry *(Austral.)*

water NOUN **1 = liquid**, aqua, Adam's ale *or* wine, H_2O, wai *(N.Z.)*: *Could I have a glass of water, please?* **2** *(often plural)* **= sea**, main, waves, ocean, depths, briny: *the open waters of the Arctic Ocean*
▷ VERB **1 = sprinkle**, spray, soak, irrigate, damp, hose, dampen, drench, douse, moisten, souse, fertigate *(Austral.)*: *Water the plants once a week.* **2 = get wet**, cry, weep, become wet, exude water: *His eyes were watering from the smoke.*
hold water = be sound, work, stand up, be convincing, hold up, make sense, be logical, ring true, be credible, pass the test, be plausible, be tenable, bear examination *or* scrutiny: *This argument simply doesn't hold water.*
water something down 1 = dilute, add water to, put water in, weaken, water, doctor, thin, adulterate: *He always waters his whisky down before drinking it.* **2 = moderate**, weaken, temper, curb, soften, qualify, tame, mute, play down, mitigate, tone down, downplay, adulterate, soft-pedal: *The government has no intention of watering down its social security reforms.*
▸ *related adjectives:* aquatic, aqueous
▸ *related prefix:* hydro- ▸ *related phobia:* hydrophobia

> **QUOTATIONS**
> Water, water, every where,
> And all the boards did shrink;
> Water, water, every where.
> Nor any drop to drink.
> [Samuel Taylor Coleridge *The Ancient Mariner*]
>
> Water taken in moderation cannot hurt anybody
> [Mark Twain *Notebook*]

waterfall NOUN **= cascade**, fall, cataract, chute, linn *(Scot.)*, force *(Northern English dialect)*

waterlogged ADJECTIVE **= soaked**, saturated, drenched, sodden, streaming, dripping, sopping, wet through, wringing wet, droukit *or* drookit *(Scot.)*

watertight ADJECTIVE
1 = waterproof, hermetically sealed, sealed, water-resistant, sound, coated, impermeable, weatherproof, water-repellent, damp-proof, rubberized: *The batteries are enclosed in a watertight compartment.* **OPPOSITE:** leaky
2 = foolproof, firm, sound, perfect, conclusive, flawless, undeniable, unassailable, airtight, indisputable, impregnable, irrefutable, unquestionable, incontrovertible: *The police had a watertight case against their suspect.* **OPPOSITE:** weak

watery ADJECTIVE **1 = pale**, thin, weak, faint, feeble, washed-out, wan, colourless, anaemic, insipid, wishy-washy *(informal)*: *A watery light began to show through the branches.* **2 = diluted**, thin, weak, dilute, watered-down, tasteless, runny, insipid, washy, adulterated, wishy-washy *(informal)*, flavourless, waterish: *a plateful of watery cabbage soup* **OPPOSITE:** concentrated **3 = wet**, damp, moist, soggy, humid, marshy, squelchy: *a wide watery sweep of marshland* **4 = liquid**, fluid, aqueous, hydrous: *There was a watery discharge from her ear.* **5 = tearful**, moist, weepy, lachrymose *(formal)*, tear-filled, rheumy: *Emma's eyes were red and watery.*

wave VERB **1 = signal**, sign, gesture, gesticulate: *He waved to us from across the street.* **2 = guide**, point, direct, indicate, signal, motion, gesture, nod, beckon, point in the direction: *The policeman waved to us to go on.* **3 = brandish**, swing, flourish, wield, wag, move something to and fro, shake: *The protesters were waving banners and shouting.* **4 = flutter**, flap, stir, waver, shake, swing, sway, ripple, wag, quiver, undulate, oscillate, move to and fro: *Flags were waving gently in the breeze.*
▷ NOUN **1 = gesture**, sign, signal, indication, gesticulation: *Paddy spotted Mary Anne and gave her a cheery wave.* **2 = ripple**, breaker, sea surf, swell, ridge, roller, comber, billow: *the sound of waves breaking on the shore* **3 = outbreak**, trend, rash, upsurge, sweep, flood, tendency, surge, groundswell: *the current wave of violence in schools* **4 = stream**, flood, surge, spate, current, movement, flow, rush, tide, torrent, deluge, upsurge: *the wave of immigrants flooding into the country*

waver VERB **1 = hesitate**, dither *(chiefly Brit.)*, vacillate, be irresolute, falter, fluctuate, seesaw, blow hot and cold *(informal)*, be indecisive, hum and haw, be unable to decide, shillyshally *(informal)*, be unable to make up your mind, swither *(Scot.)*: *Some military commanders wavered over whether to support the coup.* **OPPOSITE:** be decisive
2 = flicker, wave, shake, vary, reel, weave, sway, tremble, wobble, fluctuate, quiver, undulate, totter: *The shadows of the dancers wavered on the wall.*

wax VERB **1 = increase**, rise, grow, develop, mount, expand, swell, enlarge, fill out, magnify, get bigger, dilate, become larger: *Portugal and Spain had vast empires which waxed and waned.* **OPPOSITE:** wane **2 = become fuller**, become larger, enlarge, get bigger: *One should plant seeds and cuttings when the moon is waxing.*

way NOUN **1 = method**, means, system, process, approach, practice, scheme, technique, manner, plan, procedure, mode, course of action: *Freezing is a great way to preserve most foods.* **2 = manner**, style, fashion, mode: *He had a strange way of talking.* **3 = aspect**, point, sense, detail, feature, particular, regard, respect, characteristic, facet: *In some ways, we are better off than we were before.* **4** *(often plural)* **= custom**,

WATERFALLS

Angel Falls	Itatinga	Ribbon	Victoria Falls
Churchill Falls	Kaieteur Falls	Roraima	Yellowstone Falls
Cleve-Garth	Niagara Falls	Sutherland Falls	Yosemite Falls
Cuquenan	Ormeli	Tysse	
Iguaçú Falls	Pilao	Vestre Mardola	

manner, habit, idiosyncrasy, style, practice, nature, conduct, personality, characteristic, trait, usage, wont, tikanga (N.Z.): *You'll have to get used to my mother's odd little ways.* **5 = route**, direction, course, road, path: *Can you tell me the way to the station?* **6 = access**, street, road, track, channel, route, path, lane, trail, avenue, highway, pathway, thoroughfare: *He came round the back way.* **7 = journey**, approach, advance, progress, passage: *She said she'd pick me up on her way to work.* **8 = room**, opening, space, elbowroom: *The ranks of soldiers parted and made way for her.* **9 = distance**, length, stretch, journey, trail: *We've a long way to go yet.* **10 = condition**, state, shape *(informal)*, situation, status, circumstances, plight, predicament, fettle: *He's in a bad way, but he'll live.* **11 = will**, demand, wish, desire, choice, aim, pleasure, ambition: *It's bad for a child to get its own way all the time.*

by the way = incidentally, in passing, in parenthesis, en passant, by the bye: *By the way, how did your seminar go?*

give way 1 = collapse, give, fall, crack, break down, subside, cave in, crumple, fall to pieces, go to pieces: *The whole ceiling gave way and fell in on us.* **2 = concede**, yield, back down, make concessions, accede, acquiesce, acknowledge defeat: *I knew he'd give way if I nagged enough.*

give way to something = be replaced by, be succeeded by, be supplanted by: *The numbness gave way to anger*

under way = in progress, going, started, moving, begun, on the move, in motion, afoot, on the go *(informal)*: *A full-scale security operation is now under way.*

ways and means = capability, methods, procedure, way, course, ability, resources, capacity, tools, wherewithal: *discussing ways and means of improving productivity*

PROVERBS

The longest way round is the shortest way home

way-out ADJECTIVE **= outlandish**, eccentric, unconventional, unorthodox, advanced, wild, crazy, bizarre, weird, progressive, experimental, avant-garde, far-out *(slang)*, off-the-wall *(slang)*, oddball *(informal)*, offbeat, freaky *(slang)*, outré, wacko or whacko *(informal)*, off the air *(Austral. slang)*

wayward ADJECTIVE **= erratic**, unruly, wilful, unmanageable, disobedient, contrary, unpredictable, stubborn, perverse, rebellious, fickle, intractable, capricious, obstinate, headstrong, changeable, flighty, incorrigible, obdurate, ungovernable, self-willed, refractory, insubordinate, undependable, inconstant, mulish, cross-grained, contumacious, froward *(archaic)* **OPPOSITE:** obedient

weak ADJECTIVE **1 = feeble**, exhausted, frail, debilitated, spent, wasted, weakly, tender, delicate, faint, fragile, shaky, sickly, languid, puny, decrepit, unsteady, infirm, anaemic, effete, enervated: *I was too weak to move my arms and legs.* **OPPOSITE:** strong **2 = deficient**, wanting, poor, lacking, inadequate, pathetic, faulty, substandard, under-strength: *His eyesight had always been weak.* **OPPOSITE:** effective **3 = ineffectual**, pathetic, cowardly, powerless, soft, impotent, indecisive, infirm, spineless, boneless, timorous, weak-kneed *(informal)*, namby-pamby, irresolute: *a weak man who let his wife walk all over him* **OPPOSITE:** firm **4 = slight**, faint, feeble, pathetic, shallow, hollow: *He managed a weak smile and said, 'Don't worry about me.'* **5 = faint**, soft, quiet, slight, small, low, poor, distant, dull, muffled, imperceptible: *Her voice was so weak we could hardly hear her.* **OPPOSITE:** loud **6 = fragile**, brittle, flimsy, unsound, fine, delicate, frail, dainty, breakable: *The animals escaped through a weak spot in the fence.* **7 = unsafe**, exposed, vulnerable, helpless, wide open, unprotected, untenable, defenceless, unguarded: *The trade unions are in a very weak position.* **OPPOSITE:** secure **8 = unconvincing**, unsatisfactory, lame, invalid, flimsy, inconclusive, pathetic: *The evidence against him was too weak to hold up in court.* **OPPOSITE:** convincing **9 = tasteless**, thin, diluted, watery, runny, insipid, wishy-washy *(informal)*, under-strength, milk-and-water, waterish: *a weak cup of tea* **OPPOSITE:** strong

weaken VERB **1 = reduce**, undermine, moderate, diminish, temper, impair, lessen, sap, mitigate, invalidate, soften up, take the edge off: *Her opponents believe that her authority has been fatally weakened.* **OPPOSITE:** boost **2 = wane**, fail, diminish, dwindle, lower, flag, fade, give way, lessen, abate, droop, ease up: *Family structures are weakening and breaking up; The storm was finally beginning to weaken* **OPPOSITE:** grow **3 = sap the strength of**, tire, exhaust, debilitate, depress, disable, cripple, incapacitate, enfeeble, enervate: *Malnutrition weakens the patient.* **OPPOSITE:** strengthen

weakness NOUN **1 = frailty**, fatigue, exhaustion, fragility, infirmity, debility, feebleness, faintness, decrepitude, enervation: *Symptoms of anaemia include weakness and fatigue.* **OPPOSITE:** strength **2 = liking**, appetite, penchant, soft spot, passion, inclination, fondness, predilection, proclivity, partiality, proneness: *Carol has a great weakness for ice cream.* **OPPOSITE:** aversion **3 = powerlessness**, vulnerability, impotence, meekness, irresolution, spinelessness, ineffectuality, timorousness, cravenness, cowardliness: *People are always taking advantage of his weakness.* **4 = inadequacy**, deficiency, transparency, lameness, hollowness, implausibility, flimsiness, unsoundness, tenuousness: *She was quick to spot the weakness in his argument.* **5 = failing**, fault, defect, deficiency, flaw, shortcoming, blemish, imperfection, Achilles' heel, chink in your armour, lack: *His main weakness was his violent temper.* **OPPOSITE:** strong point

QUOTATIONS

Frailty, thy name is woman!
[William Shakespeare *Hamlet*]

PROVERBS

A chain is no stronger than its weakest link

wealth NOUN **1 = riches**, fortune, prosperity, affluence, goods, means, money, funds, property, cash, resources, substance, possessions, big money, big bucks *(informal, chiefly U.S.)*, opulence, megabucks *(U.S. & Canad. slang)*, lucre, pelf: *The discovery of oil brought untold wealth to the island.* **OPPOSITE:** poverty **2 = property**, funds, capital, estate, assets, fortune, possessions: *His personal wealth is estimated at over 50 million dollars.* **3 = abundance**, store, plenty, richness, bounty, profusion, fullness, cornucopia, plenitude, copiousness: *The city boasts a wealth of beautiful churches and museums.* **OPPOSITE:** lack

▸ *related mania:* plutomania

QUOTATIONS

In every well-governed state, wealth is a sacred thing; in democracies it is the only sacred thing
[Anatole France *L'Île des pingouins*]

It is easier for a camel to go through the eye of a needle, than for a rich man to enter the kingdom of God
[*Bible: St. Mark*]

I am rich beyond the dreams of avarice
[Edward Moore *The Gamester*]

wealthy ADJECTIVE **= rich**, prosperous, affluent, well-off, loaded *(slang)*, comfortable, flush *(informal)*, in the money *(informal)*, opulent, well-heeled *(informal)*, well-to-do, moneyed, quids in *(slang)*, filthy rich, rolling in it *(slang)*, on Easy Street *(informal)*, stinking rich *(slang)*, made of money *(informal)*, minted *(Brit. slang)*: *a wealthy international businessman* **OPPOSITE:** poor

wear VERB **1 = be dressed in**, have on, dress in, be clothed in, carry, sport *(informal)*, bear, put on, clothe yourself in: *He was wearing a dark green uniform.* **2 = show**, present, bear, display, assume, put on, exhibit: *Millson's face wore a smug expression.* **3 = deteriorate**, fray, wear thin, become threadbare: *The living room carpet is beginning to wear.* **4 = accept** *(Brit. informal)*, take, allow, permit, stomach, swallow *(informal)*, brook, stand for, fall for, put up with *(informal)*, countenance: *I asked if I could work part-time, but the company wouldn't wear it.*

▷ NOUN **1 = clothes**, things, dress, gear (*informal*), attire, habit, outfit, costume, threads (*slang*), garments, apparel, garb, raiments: *The shops stock an extensive range of beach wear.* **2 = usefulness**, use, service, employment, utility, mileage (*informal*): *You'll get more wear out of a car if you look after it properly.* **3 = damage**, wear and tear, use, erosion, friction, deterioration, depreciation, attrition, corrosion, abrasion: *a large, well-upholstered armchair which showed signs of wear* **OPPOSITE:** repair
wear down = be eroded, erode, be consumed, wear away: *Eventually the parts start to wear down.*
wear off 1 = subside, disappear, fade, weaken, diminish, decrease, dwindle, wane, ebb, abate, peter out, lose strength, lose effect: *Her initial excitement soon began to wear off.* **2 = rub away**, disappear, fade, abrade: *The paint is discoloured and little bits have worn off.*
wear out = deteriorate, become worn, become useless, wear through, fray: *Eventually the artificial joint wears out and has to be replaced.*
wear someone down = undermine, reduce, chip away at (*informal*), fight a war of attrition against, overcome gradually: *his sheer persistence in wearing down the opposition*
wear someone out = exhaust, tire, fatigue, weary, impair, sap, prostrate, knacker (*slang*), frazzle (*informal*), fag someone out (*informal*), enervate: *The past few days had really worn him out.*
wear something down = erode, grind down, consume, impair, corrode, grind down, rub away, abrade: *Rabbits wear down their teeth with constant gnawing.*
wear something out = erode, go through, consume, use up, wear holes in, make worn: *He wore his shoes out wandering around the streets.*

weariness NOUN **= tiredness**, fatigue, exhaustion, lethargy, drowsiness, lassitude, languor, listlessness, prostration, enervation **OPPOSITE:** energy

wearing ADJECTIVE **= tiresome**, trying, taxing, tiring, exhausting, fatiguing, oppressive, exasperating, irksome, wearisome **OPPOSITE:** refreshing

weary ADJECTIVE **1 = tired**, exhausted, drained, worn out, spent, done in (*informal*), flagging, all in (*slang*), fatigued, wearied, sleepy, fagged (*informal*), whacked (*Brit. informal*), jaded, drooping, knackered (*slang*), drowsy, clapped out (*Austral. & N.Z. informal*), enervated, ready to drop, dog-tired (*informal*), zonked (*slang*), dead beat (*informal*), asleep *or* dead on your feet (*informal*): *She sank to the ground, too weary to walk another step.* **OPPOSITE:** energetic **2 = fed up**, bored, sick (*informal*), discontented, impatient, indifferent, jaded, sick and tired (*informal*), browned-off (*informal*): *He was growing weary of his wife's constant complaints.* **OPPOSITE:** excited **3 = tiring**, taxing, wearing, arduous, tiresome, laborious, irksome, wearisome, enervative: *a long, weary journey in search of food and water* **OPPOSITE:** refreshing
▷ VERB **1 = grow tired**, tire, sicken, have had enough, become bored: *He had wearied of teaching in state universities.* **2 = bore**, annoy, plague, sicken, jade, exasperate, vex, irk, try the patience of, make discontented: *Her nagging and criticism wearied him so much that he left her.* **OPPOSITE:** excite **3 = tire**, tax, burden, drain, fatigue, fag (*informal*), sap, wear out, debilitate, take it out of (*informal*), tire out, enervate: *Her pregnancy wearied her to the point of exhaustion.* **OPPOSITE:** invigorate

weather NOUN **= climate**, conditions, temperature, forecast, outlook, meteorological conditions, elements: *I don't like hot weather much.*
▷ VERB **1 = toughen**, season, wear, expose, harden: *The stones have been weathered by centuries of wind and rain.* **2 = withstand**, stand, suffer, survive, overcome, resist, brave, endure, come through, get through, rise above, live through, ride out, make it through (*informal*), surmount, pull through, stick it out (*informal*), bear up against: *The company has weathered the recession.* **OPPOSITE:** surrender to
under the weather = ill, unwell, poorly (*informal*), sick, rough (*informal*), crook (*Austral. & N.Z. informal*), ailing, not well, seedy (*informal*), below par, queasy, out of sorts, nauseous, off-colour (*Brit.*), indisposed, peaky, ropy (*Brit. informal*), wabbit (*Scot. informal*): *I'm feeling a bit under the weather today.*

> **QUOTATIONS**
> Summer has set in with its usual severity
> [Samuel Taylor Coleridge]
>
> 'Tis the hard grey weather
> Breeds hard English men
> [Charles Kingsley *The Three Fishers*]
>
> weather: the climate of an hour
> [Ambrose Bierce *The Devil's Dictionary*]

> **PROVERBS**
> *Red sky at night, shepherd's delight; red sky in the morning, shepherd's warning*

weave VERB **1 = knit**, twist, intertwine, plait, unite, introduce, blend, incorporate, merge, mat, fuse, braid, entwine, intermingle, interlace: *She then weaves the fibres together to make the traditional Awatum basket.* **2 = zigzag**, wind, move in and out, crisscross, weave your way: *The cyclists wove in and out of the traffic.* **3 = create**, tell, recount, narrate, make, build, relate, make up, spin, construct, invent, put together, unfold, contrive, fabricate: *The author weaves a compelling tale of life in London during the war.*

web NOUN **1 = cobweb**, spider's web: *He was caught like a fly in a web.* **2 = mesh**, net, netting, screen, webbing, weave, lattice, latticework, interlacing, lacework: *a delicate web of fine lace* **3 = tangle**, series, network, mass, chain, knot, maze, toils, nexus: *a complex web of financial dealings*

wed VERB **1 = get married to**, espouse, get hitched to (*slang*), be united to, plight your troth to (*old-fashioned*), get spliced to (*informal*), take as your husband *or* wife: *In 1952 he wed his childhood sweetheart.* **OPPOSITE:** divorce **2 = get married**, marry, be united, tie the knot (*informal*), take the plunge (*informal*), get hitched (*slang*), get spliced (*informal*), become man and wife, plight your troth (*old-fashioned*): *The pair wed in a secret ceremony in front of just nine guests.* **OPPOSITE:** divorce **3 = unite**, combine, bring together, amalgamate, join, link, marry, ally, connect, blend, integrate, merge, unify, make one, fuse, weld, interweave, yoke, coalesce, commingle: *a film which weds stunning visuals and a first-class score* **OPPOSITE:** divide

wedding NOUN **= marriage**, nuptials, wedding ceremony, marriage ceremony, marriage service, wedding service, nuptial rite, espousals

wedge VERB **= squeeze**, force, lodge, jam, crowd, block, stuff, pack, thrust, ram, cram, stow: *He wedged himself between the door and the radiator.*
▷ NOUN **= block**, segment, l ump, chunk, triangle, slab, hunk, chock, wodge (*Brit. informal*): *a wedge of cheese*

wedlock NOUN **= marriage**, matrimony, holy matrimony, married state, conjugal bond

wee ADJECTIVE **= little**, small, minute, tiny, miniature, insignificant, negligible, microscopic, diminutive, minuscule, teeny, itsy-bitsy (*informal*), teeny-weeny, titchy (*Brit. informal*), teensy-weensy, pygmy *or* pigmy

weedy ADJECTIVE **= weak**, thin, frail, skinny, feeble, ineffectual, puny, undersized, weak-kneed (*informal*), namby-pamby, nerdy *or* nurdy (*slang*)

weekly ADJECTIVE **= once a week**, hebdomadal, hebdomadary: *her weekly visit to her parents' house*
▷ ADVERB **= every week**, once a week, by the week, hebdomadally: *The group meets weekly.*

weep VERB **= cry**, shed tears, sob, whimper, complain, keen, greet (*Scot.*), moan, mourn, grieve, lament, whinge (*informal*), blubber, snivel, ululate, blub (*slang*), boohoo **OPPOSITE:** rejoice

weepy ADJECTIVE **= tearful**, crying, weeping, sobbing, whimpering, close to tears, blubbering, lachrymose, on the verge of tears: *After her mother's death she was depressed and weepy for months.*
▷ NOUN **= tear-jerker** (*informal*): *The film is an old-fashioned weepy with fine performances by both stars.*

weigh VERB **1 = have a weight of**, tip the scales at *(informal)*: *His wife weighs over 22 stone.* **2 = measure the weight of**, put someone *or* something on the scales, measure how heavy someone *or* something is: *They counted and weighed the fruits.* **3 = consider**, study, examine, contemplate, evaluate, ponder, mull over, think over, eye up, reflect upon, give thought to, meditate upon, deliberate upon: *He is weighing the possibility of filing charges against the doctor.* **4 = compare**, balance, contrast, juxtapose, place side by side: *We must weigh the pros and cons of each method.* **5 = matter**, carry weight, cut any ice *(informal)*, impress, tell, count, have influence, be influential: *His opinion doesn't weigh much with me, I'm afraid.*
weigh on someone = oppress, burden, depress, distress, plague, prey, torment, hang over, bear down, gnaw at, cast down, take over: *The separation weighed on both of them.*
weigh someone down 1 = burden, overload, encumber, overburden, tax, weight, strain, handicap, saddle, hamper: *The soldiers were weighed down by their heavy packs.* **2 = oppress**, worry, trouble, burden, depress, haunt, plague, get down, torment, take control of, hang over, beset, prey on, bear down, gnaw at, cast down, press down on, overburden, weigh upon, lie heavy on: *He could not shake off the guilt that weighed him down.*
weigh someone up = assess, judge, gauge, appraise, eye someone up, size someone up *(informal)*: *As soon as I walked into his office I could see him weighing me up.*
weigh something out = measure, dole out, apportion, deal out: *I weighed out portions of tea and sugar.*

weight NOUN **1 = heaviness**, mass, burden, poundage, pressure, load, gravity, tonnage, heft *(informal)*, avoirdupois: *Try to reduce the weight of the load.* **2 = load**, mass, ballast, heavy object: *Straining to lift heavy weights can cause back injury.* **3 = importance**, force, power, moment, value, authority, influence, bottom, impact, import, muscle, consequence, substance, consideration, emphasis, significance, sway, clout *(informal)*, leverage, efficacy, mana *(N.Z.)*, persuasiveness: *That argument no longer carries much weight.* **4 = burden**, pressure, load, strain, oppression, albatross, millstone, encumbrance: *He heaved a sigh of relief. 'That's a great weight off my mind.'* **5 = preponderance**, mass, bulk, main body, most, majority, onus, lion's share, greatest force, main force, best *or* better part: *The weight of evidence suggests that he is guilty.*
▷ VERB **1** *(often with* **down***)* **= load**, ballast, make heavier: *The body was weighted down with bricks.* **2 = bias**, load, slant, unbalance: *The electoral law is still heavily weighted in favour of the ruling party.* **3 = burden**, handicap, oppress, impede, weigh down, encumber, overburden: *His life was a struggle, weighted with failures and disappointments.*

weighty ADJECTIVE **1 = important**, serious, significant, critical, crucial, considerable, substantial, grave, solemn, momentous, forcible, consequential, portentous: *Surely such weighty matters merit a higher level of debate?* **OPPOSITE:** unimportant **2 = heavy**, massive, dense, hefty *(informal)*, cumbersome, ponderous, burdensome: *Simon lifted a weighty volume from the shelf.* **3 = onerous**, taxing, demanding, difficult, worrying, crushing, exacting, oppressive, burdensome, worrisome, backbreaking: *the weighty responsibility of organizing the entire event*

weird ADJECTIVE **1 = strange**, odd, unusual, bizarre, ghostly, mysterious, queer, unearthly, eerie, grotesque, supernatural, unnatural, far-out *(slang)*, uncanny, spooky *(informal)*, creepy *(informal)*, eldritch *(poetic)*: *I had such a weird dream last night.* **OPPOSITE:** normal **2 = bizarre**, odd, strange, unusual, queer, grotesque, unnatural, creepy *(informal)*, outlandish, freakish: *I don't like that guy – he's really weird.* **OPPOSITE:** ordinary

weirdo *or* **weirdie** NOUN **= eccentric**, nut *(slang)*, freak *(informal)*, crank *(informal)*, loony *(slang)*, nutter *(Brit. slang)*, oddball *(informal)*, crackpot *(informal)*, nutcase *(slang)*, headcase *(informal)*, headbanger *(informal)*, queer fish *(Brit. informal)*

welcome VERB **1 = greet**, meet, receive, embrace, hail, usher in, say hello to, roll out the red carpet for, offer hospitality to, receive with open arms, bid welcome, karanga *(N.Z.)*, mihi *(N.Z.)*, haeremai *(N.Z.)*: *Several people came out to welcome me.* **OPPOSITE:** reject **2 = accept gladly**, appreciate, embrace, approve of, be pleased by, give the thumbs up to *(informal)*, be glad about, express pleasure *or* satisfaction at: *They welcomed the move but felt it did not go far enough.*
▷ NOUN **= greeting**, welcoming, entertainment, reception, acceptance, hail, hospitality, salutation, haeremai *(N.Z.)*: *There was a wonderful welcome waiting for him when he arrived.* **OPPOSITE:** rejection
▷ ADJECTIVE **1 = pleasing**, wanted, accepted, appreciated, acceptable, pleasant, desirable, refreshing, delightful, gratifying, agreeable, pleasurable, gladly received: *a welcome change from the usual routine* **OPPOSITE:** unpleasant **2 = wanted**, at home, invited: *I was really made to feel welcome.* **OPPOSITE:** unwanted **3 = free**, invited: *Non-residents are welcome to use our facilities.*

weld VERB **1 = join**, link, bond, bind, connect, cement, fuse, solder, braze: *It's possible to weld stainless steel to ordinary steel.* **2 = unite**, combine, blend, consolidate, unify, fuse, meld: *The miracle was that Rose had welded them into a team.*
▷ NOUN **= joint**, bond, seam, juncture: *The weld on the outlet pipe was visibly fractured.*

welfare NOUN **1 = wellbeing**, good, interest, health, security, benefit, success, profit, safety, protection, fortune, comfort, happiness, prosperity, prosperousness: *Above all we must consider the welfare of the children.* **2 = state benefit**, support, benefits, pensions, dole *(slang)*, social security, unemployment benefit, state benefits, pogey *(Canad.)*: *proposed cuts in welfare*

well[1] ADVERB **1 = skilfully**, expertly, adeptly, with skill, professionally, correctly, properly, effectively, efficiently, adequately, admirably, ably, conscientiously, proficiently: *All the team members played well.* **OPPOSITE:** badly **2 = satisfactorily**, nicely, smoothly, successfully, capitally, pleasantly, happily, famously *(informal)*, splendidly, agreeably, like nobody's business *(informal)*, in a satisfactory manner: *I thought the interview went very well.* **OPPOSITE:** badly **3 = thoroughly**, completely, fully, carefully, effectively, efficiently, rigorously: *Mix all the ingredients well.* **4 = intimately**, closely, completely, deeply, fully, personally, profoundly: *How well do you know him?* **OPPOSITE:** slightly **5 = carefully**, closely, minutely, fully, comprehensively, accurately, in detail, in depth, extensively, meticulously, painstakingly, rigorously, scrupulously, assiduously, intensively, from top to bottom, methodically, attentively, conscientiously, exhaustively: *This is obviously a man who's studied his subject well.* **6 = favourably**, highly, kindly, warmly, enthusiastically, graciously, approvingly, admiringly, with admiration, appreciatively, with praise, glowingly, with approbation: *He speaks very well of you.* **OPPOSITE:** unfavourably **7 = considerably**, easily, very much, significantly, substantially, markedly: *Franklin did not turn up until well after midnight.* **8 = fully**, highly, greatly, completely, amply, very much, thoroughly, considerably, sufficiently, substantially, heartily, abundantly: *I am well aware of how much she has suffered.* **9 = possibly**, probably, certainly, reasonably, conceivably, justifiably: *The murderer may well be someone who was close to the victim.* **10 = decently**, right, kindly, fittingly, fairly, easily, correctly, properly, readily, politely, suitably, generously, justly, in all fairness, genially, civilly, hospitably: *My parents always treated me well.* **OPPOSITE:** unfairly **11 = prosperously**, comfortably, splendidly, in comfort, in (the lap of) luxury, flourishingly, without

hardship: *We manage to live very well on our combined salaries.*
▷ ADJECTIVE **1 = healthy**, strong, sound, fit, blooming, robust, hale, hearty, in good health, alive and kicking, fighting fit *(informal)*, in fine fettle, up to par, fit as a fiddle, able-bodied, in good condition: *I hope you're well.* **OPPOSITE:** ill
2 = satisfactory, good, right, fine, happy, fitting, pleasing, bright, useful, lucky, proper, thriving, flourishing, profitable, fortunate: *He was satisfied that all was well.*
OPPOSITE: unsatisfactory
3 = advisable, useful, proper, prudent, agreeable: *It would be well to check the facts before you speak out.*
OPPOSITE: inadvisable
as well = also, too, in addition, moreover, besides, to boot, into the bargain: *I like the job, and the people I work with are very nice as well.*
as well as = including, along with, in addition to, not to mention, at the same time as, over and above: *food and other goods, as well as energy supplies such as gas and oil*

well² NOUN **1 = hole**, bore, pit, shaft: *the cost of drilling an oil well*
2 = waterhole, source, spring, pool, fountain, fount: *I had to fetch water from the well.* **3 = source**, fund, mine, treasury, reservoir, storehouse, repository, fount, wellspring: *a man with a well of experience and insight*
▷ VERB **1 = flow**, trickle, seep, run, issue, spring, pour, jet, burst, stream, surge, discharge, trickle, gush, ooze, seep, exude, spurt, spout: *Blood welled from a gash in his thigh.* **2 = rise**, increase, grow, mount, surge, swell, intensify: *He could feel the anger welling inside him.*

well-balanced ADJECTIVE
1 = sensible, rational, level-headed, well-adjusted, together *(slang)*, sound, reasonable, sober, sane, judicious, grounded: *a sensible, well-balanced individual* **OPPOSITE:** unbalanced
2 = well-proportioned, proportional, graceful, harmonious, symmetrical: *Intervals of depth are essential to a well-balanced composition.*

well-bred ADJECTIVE **1 = polite**, ladylike, well-brought-up, well-mannered, cultured, civil, mannerly, polished, sophisticated, gentlemanly, refined, cultivated, courteous, gallant, genteel, urbane, courtly: *She was too well-bred to make personal remarks.*
OPPOSITE: ill-bred **2 = aristocratic**, gentle, noble, patrician, blue-blooded, well-born, highborn: *He was clearly of well-bred stock.*

well-groomed ADJECTIVE **= smart**, trim, neat, tidy, spruce, well-dressed, dapper, well turned out, soigné *or* soignée

well-heeled ADJECTIVE **= prosperous**, rich, wealthy, affluent, loaded *(slang)*, comfortable, flush *(informal)*, well-off, in the money *(informal)*, opulent, well-to-do, moneyed, well-situated, in clover *(informal)*, minted *(Brit. slang)*

well-informed ADJECTIVE
= educated, aware, informed, acquainted, knowledgeable *or* knowledgable, understanding, well-educated, in the know *(informal)*, well-read, conversant, au fait *(French)*, in the loop *(informal)*, well-grounded, au courant *(French)*, clued-up *(informal)*, cognizant *or* cognisant, well-versed

well-known ADJECTIVE **1 = famous**, important, celebrated, prominent, great, leading, noted, august, popular, familiar, distinguished, esteemed, acclaimed, notable, renowned, eminent, famed, illustrious, on the map, widely known: *He liked to surround himself with attractive or well-known people.*
2 = familiar, common, established, popular, everyday, widely known: *It is a well-known fact that smoking can cause lung cancer.*

well-mannered ADJECTIVE **= polite**, civil, mannerly, gentlemanly, gracious, respectful, courteous, genteel, well-bred, ladylike

well-nigh ADVERB **= almost**, nearly, virtually, practically, next to, all but, just about, more or less

well-off ADJECTIVE **1 = rich**, wealthy, comfortable, affluent, loaded *(slang)*, flush *(informal)*, prosperous, well-heeled *(informal)*, well-to-do, moneyed, minted *(Brit. slang)*: *My family was quite well-off.* **OPPOSITE:** poor
2 = fortunate, lucky, comfortable, thriving, flourishing, successful: *Compared to some of the people in my ward, I feel quite well off.*

well-to-do ADJECTIVE **= rich**, wealthy, affluent, well-off, loaded *(slang)*, comfortable, flush *(informal)*, prosperous, well-heeled *(informal)*, moneyed, minted *(Brit. slang)*
OPPOSITE: poor

well-worn ADJECTIVE **1 = stale**, tired, stereotyped, commonplace, banal, trite, hackneyed, overused, timeworn: *To use a well-worn cliché, she does not suffer fools gladly.* **2 = shabby**, worn, faded, ragged, frayed, worn-out, scruffy, tattered, tatty, threadbare: *He was dressed casually in a sweater and well-worn jeans.*

welter NOUN **= jumble**, confusion, muddle, hotchpotch, web, mess, tangle

wend VERB
wend your way = go, move, travel, progress, proceed, make for, direct your course

wet ADJECTIVE **1 = damp**, soaked, soaking, dripping, saturated, moist, drenched, watery, soggy, sodden, waterlogged, moistened, dank, sopping, aqueous, wringing wet: *He rubbed his wet hair with a towel.*
OPPOSITE: dry **2 = rainy**, damp, drizzly, showery, raining, pouring, drizzling, misty, teeming, humid, dank, clammy: *It was a miserable wet day.*
OPPOSITE: sunny **3 = feeble**, soft, weak, silly, foolish, ineffectual, weedy *(informal)*, spineless, effete, boneless, timorous, namby-pamby, irresolute, wussy *(slang)*, nerdy *or* nurdy *(slang)*: *I despised him for being so wet and spineless.*
▷ VERB **= moisten**, spray, damp, dampen, water, dip, splash, soak, steep, sprinkle, saturate, drench, douse, irrigate, humidify, fertigate *(Austral.)*: *Wet the fabric with a damp sponge before ironing.* **OPPOSITE:** dry
▷ NOUN **1 = rain**, rains, damp, drizzle, wet weather, rainy season, rainy weather, damp weather: *They had come in from the cold and the wet.*
OPPOSITE: fine weather **2 = moisture**, water, liquid, damp, humidity, condensation, dampness, wetness, clamminess: *splashing around in the wet of the puddles* **OPPOSITE:** dryness

whack VERB **= strike**, hit, beat, box, belt *(informal)*, deck *(slang)*, bang, rap, slap, bash *(informal)*, sock *(slang)*, chin *(slang)*, smack, thrash, thump, buffet, clout *(informal)*, slug, cuff, swipe, clobber *(slang)*, wallop *(informal)*, thwack, lambast(e), lay one on *(slang)*, beat *or* knock seven bells out of *(informal)*: *Someone whacked him on the head with a baseball bat.*
▷ NOUN **1 = blow**, hit, box, stroke, belt *(informal)*, bang, rap, slap, bash *(informal)*, sock *(slang)*, smack, thump, buffet, clout *(informal)*, slug, cuff, swipe, wallop *(informal)*, wham, thwack: *He gave the donkey a whack across the back with a stick.* **2 = share**, part, cut *(informal)*, bit, portion, quota, allotment: *I pay a sizeable whack of capital gains tax.* **3 = attempt**, go *(informal)*, try, turn, shot *(informal)*, crack *(informal)*, stab *(informal)*, bash *(informal)*: *Let me have a whack at trying to fix the car.*

whacking ADJECTIVE **= huge**, big, large, giant, enormous, extraordinary, tremendous, gigantic, great, monstrous, mammoth, whopping *(informal)*, prodigious, elephantine, humongous *or* humungous *(U.S. slang)*

whale NOUN
▸ *related adjective:* cetacean ▸ *name of male:* bull ▸ *name of female:* cow ▸ *name of young:* calf ▸ *collective nouns:* school, gam, run

wharf NOUN **= dock**, pier, berth, quay, jetty, landing stage

wheedle VERB **= coax**, talk, court, draw, persuade, charm, worm, flatter, entice, cajole, inveigle

wheel NOUN **= disc**, ring, hoop: *a bicycle wheel*
▷ VERB **1 = push**, trundle, roll: *He wheeled his bike into the alley beside the house.* **2 = turn**, swing, spin, revolve, rotate, whirl, swivel: *He wheeled around to face her.* **3 = circle**, orbit, go round, twirl, gyrate: *A flock of crows wheeled overhead.*
at *or* **behind the wheel = driving**,

Sir Walter Scott's Use of Nouns

Sir Walter Scott (1771–1832) was a Scottish writer who is renowned for his historical novels, including *Ivanhoe*, *Rob Roy*, *Waverley*, and *The Heart of Midlothian*. In his own day, he was popular both in Britain and abroad, and became known as 'The Wizard of the North'. His works have been criticized for glorifying war, and his reputation suffered in the early 20th century because of this, but they have renewed appeal today.

Honour and *duty* are central themes in Scott's novels, and are both among his hundred most frequent nouns. *Honour* is often described as *great*, *knightly*, and *distinguished*, and there is even a particular quality of *Scottish honour*. *Duty* is often *military*, but also *religious* and even *sacred*; and again, the Scots are portrayed as having particular excellence in this regard:

> ...he contrived... to send considerable assistance to his sole remaining parent, a **sacred duty**, of which the Scotch are seldom negligent.

Character is also frequent, both in the concrete sense 'person' and the abstract sense 'qualities, nature'. In the latter sense it is sometimes modified by *national* and *Scottish*, where Scott again considers the intrinsic nature of Scottishness:

> It is well known, that much, both of what is good and bad in the Scottish national **character**, arises out of the intimacy of their family connections.

War is central to Scott's novels, and *sword, blood, soldier, enemy, battle*, and *war* itself all appear in his two hundred most frequently used nouns. *War* is often found in the compound *civil war*, particularly in phrases such as *the evils/miseries/plague of civil war*:

> ...for I think you have already seen enough of the evils of **civil war**, to be wary of again awakening its terrors in a peaceful and happy country.

Neighbour war - referring to war with a neighbouring country - is also used twice in *The Black Dwarf*, set in the borders of Scotland. One interesting shift in usage is that *make war* is about twice as frequent in Scott's novels as *wage war*, whereas the latter has become much more frequent in modern English.

As with *war*, the collocates of *battle* do not suggest its glorification: battles are described as *bloody, fatal, desperate*, and *unhappy*. Rather, it is the people who fight in battles who are romanticized: *soldiers* are *gallant, brave, valiant*, and *distinguished*. Even *enemies* are occasionally *honorouble* and *generous*, and are otherwise admirably strong, described as *powerful* and *deadly*. Enemies are also classified by type and history as *mortal, feudal*, and *hereditary*. *Knight* is frequent, particularly in the medieval novel *Ivanhoe*, and we often read of knights who are *brave, noble*, and *gallant*. The epitome of medieval chivalry was the *knight-errant* who travelled the land in search of noble quests; Scott's works feature several uses of this phrase in various forms: *knight errant*, the hyphenated *knight-errant*, and *errant knight*.

One of the most famous poems of the First World War was Wilfred Owen's 'Dulce et Decorum est', which laid bare the absurdity of the Roman poet Horace's ode *Dulce et decorum est pro patria mori* ('How sweet and fitting it is to die for one's country'). In light of this, it is not surprising that Scott's books fell out of favour in the early 20th century; *death*, one of the hundred most frequent nouns, is sometimes described as *glorious* and *honourable*. However, Scott does not portray the concept of noble death in war as black-and-white: *death* is also *bloody* and *cruel;* and in one line from *Waverley*, the supposed honour of death is balanced by the honest human admission that it is a *pis-aller*, a last resort:

> The next best thing to victory is honourable death; but it is a **pis-aller**, and one would rather a foe had it than one's self.

steering, in the driving seat, in the driver's seat: *He persuaded his wife to say she was at the wheel when the car crashed.*

wheeze VERB **= gasp**, whistle, cough, hiss, rasp, catch your breath, breathe roughly: *His chest problems made him wheeze constantly.*
▷ NOUN **1 = gasp**, whistle, cough, hiss, rasp: *He puffed up the stairs, emitting a wheeze at every breath.* **2 = trick**, plan, idea, scheme, stunt, ploy, expedient, ruse: *He came up with a clever wheeze to get round the problem.*

whereabouts PLURAL NOUN **= position**, situation, site, location

wherewithal NOUN **= resources**, means, money, funds, capital, supplies, ready *(informal)*, essentials, ready money

whet VERB **= stimulate**, increase, excite, stir, enhance, provoke, arouse, awaken, animate, rouse, quicken, incite, kindle, pique
OPPOSITE: suppress

whiff NOUN **1 = smell**, hint, scent, sniff, aroma, odour, draught, niff *(Brit. slang)*: *He caught a whiff of her perfume.* **2 = stink**, stench, reek, pong *(Brit. informal)*, niff *(Brit. slang)*, malodour, hum *(slang)*: *the nauseating whiff of rotting flesh* **3 = trace**, suggestion, hint, suspicion, bit, drop, note, breath, whisper, shred, crumb, tinge, jot, smidgen *(informal)*, soupçon *(French)*: *Not a whiff of scandal has ever tainted his private life.* **4 = puff**, breath, flurry, waft, rush, blast, draught, gust: *At the first whiff of smoke, the alarm will go off.*
▷ VERB **= stink**, stench, reek, pong *(Brit. informal)*, niff *(Brit. slang)*, hum *(slang)*: *These socks whiff a bit, don't they?*

whim NOUN **= impulse**, sudden notion, caprice, fancy, sport, urge, notion, humour, freak, craze, fad *(informal)*, quirk, conceit, vagary, whimsy, passing thought, crotchet

whimper VERB **= cry**, moan, sob, weep, whine, whinge *(informal)*, grizzle *(informal, chiefly Brit.)*, blubber, snivel, blub *(slang)*, mewl: *She lay at the bottom of the stairs, whimpering in pain.*
▷ NOUN **= sob**, moan, whine, snivel: *David's crying subsided to a whimper.*

W

whimsical ADJECTIVE **= fanciful**, odd, funny, unusual, fantastic, curious, weird, peculiar, eccentric, queer, flaky *(slang, chiefly U.S.)*, singular, quaint, playful, mischievous, capricious, droll, freakish, fantastical, crotchety, chimerical, waggish: *He had an offbeat, whimsical sense of humour.*

whine VERB **1 = cry**, sob, wail, whimper, sniffle, snivel, moan: *He could hear a child whining in the background.* **2 = complain**, grumble, gripe *(informal)*, whinge *(informal)*, moan, cry, beef *(slang)*, carp, sob, wail, grouse, whimper, bleat, grizzle *(informal, chiefly Brit.)*, grouch *(informal)*, bellyache *(slang)*, kvetch *(U.S. slang)*: *She's always calls to whine about her problems.*
▷ NOUN **1 = cry**, moan, sob, wail, whimper, plaintive cry: *His voice became a pleading whine.* **2 = drone**, note, hum: *the whine of air-raid sirens* **3 = complaint**, moan, grumble, grouse, gripe *(informal)*, whinge *(informal)*, grouch *(informal)*, beef *(slang)*: *Her conversation is one long whine about her husband.*

whinge VERB **= complain**, moan, grumble, grouse, gripe *(informal)*, beef *(slang)*, carp, bleat, grizzle *(informal, chiefly Brit.)*, grouch *(informal)*, bellyache *(slang)*, kvetch *(U.S. slang)*: *people who whinge about their alleged misfortunes*
▷ NOUN **= complaint**, moan, grumble, whine, grouse, gripe *(informal)*, grouch, beef *(slang)*: *It must be depressing having to listen to everyone's whinges.*

whip NOUN **= lash**, cane, birch, switch, crop, scourge, thong, rawhide, riding crop, horsewhip, bullwhip, knout, cat-o'-nine-tails: *Prisoners were regularly beaten with a whip.*
▷ VERB **1 = lash**, cane, flog, beat, switch, leather, punish, strap, tan *(slang)*, thrash, lick *(informal)*, birch, scourge, spank, castigate, lambast(e), flagellate, give a hiding *(informal)*: *He was whipped with a studded belt.* **2 = dash**, shoot, fly, tear, rush, dive, dart, whisk, flit: *I whipped into a parking space.* **3 = whisk**, beat, mix vigorously, stir vigorously: *Whip the cream until it is thick.* **4 = incite**, drive, push, urge, stir, spur, provoke, compel, hound, prod, work up, get going, agitate, prick, inflame, instigate, goad, foment: *an accomplished orator who could whip a crowd into hysteria* **5 = beat**, thrash, trounce, wipe the floor with *(informal)*, best, defeat, stuff *(slang)*, worst, overcome, hammer *(informal)*, overwhelm, conquer, lick *(informal)*, rout, overpower, outdo, clobber *(slang)*, take apart *(slang)*, run rings around *(informal)*, blow out of the water *(slang)*, make mincemeat out of *(informal)*, drub: *Our school can whip theirs at football and rugby.*
whip someone up = rouse, excite, provoke, arouse, stir up, work up, agitate, inflame: *McCarthy whipped up Americans into a frenzy of anti-Communist activity.*
whip something out = pull out, produce, remove, jerk out, show, flash, seize, whisk out, snatch out: *Bob whipped out his notebook.*

whipping NOUN **= beating**, lashing, thrashing, caning, hiding *(informal)*, punishment, tanning *(slang)*, birching, flogging, spanking, the strap, flagellation, castigation, leathering

whirl VERB **1 = spin**, turn, circle, wheel, twist, reel, rotate, pivot, twirl: *Hearing a sound behind her, she whirled round.* **2 = rotate**, roll, twist, revolve, swirl, twirl, gyrate, pirouette: *The smoke whirled and grew into a monstrous column.* **3 = feel dizzy**, swim, spin, reel, go round: *My head whirled in a giddiness like that of intoxication.*
▷ NOUN **1 = revolution**, turn, roll, circle, wheel, spin, twist, reel, swirl, rotation, twirl, pirouette, gyration, birl *(Scot.)*: *the whirl of snowflakes in the wind* **2 = bustle**, round, series, succession, flurry, merry-go-round: *Her life is one long whirl of parties.* **3 = confusion**, daze, dither *(chiefly Brit.)*, giddiness: *My thoughts are in a complete whirl.* **4 = tumult**, spin, stir, agitation, commotion, hurly-burly: *I was caught up in a terrible whirl of emotion.*
give something a whirl = attempt, try, have a go at *(informal)*, have a crack at *(informal)*, have a shot at *(informal)*, have a stab at *(informal)*, have a bash at, have a whack at *(informal)*: *Why not give acupuncture a whirl?*

whirlwind NOUN **1 = tornado**, hurricane, cyclone, typhoon, twister *(U.S.)*, dust devil, waterspout: *They scattered like leaves in a whirlwind.* **2 = turmoil**, chaos, swirl, mayhem, uproar, maelstrom, welter, bedlam, tumult, hurly-burly, madhouse: *a whirlwind of frenzied activity*
▷ MODIFIER **= rapid**, short, quick, swift, lightning, rash, speedy, hasty, impulsive, headlong, impetuous: *He got married after a whirlwind romance.*
OPPOSITE: unhurried

whisk VERB **1 = rush**, sweep, hurry: *I was whisked away in a police car.* **2 = pull**, whip *(informal)*, snatch, take: *The waiter whisked our plates away.* **3 = speed**, race, shoot, fly, career, tear, rush, sweep, dash, hurry, barrel (along) *(informal, chiefly U.S. & Canad.)*, sprint, dart, hasten, burn rubber *(informal)*, go like the clappers *(Brit. informal)*, hightail it *(U.S. informal)*, wheech *(Scot. informal)*: *She whisked out of the room.* **4 = flick**, whip, sweep, brush, wipe, twitch: *The dog whisked its tail around in excitement.* **5 = beat**, mix vigorously, stir vigorously, whip, fluff up: *Whisk together the sugar and the egg yolks.*
▷ NOUN **1 = flick**, sweep, brush, whip, wipe: *With one whisk of its tail, the horse brushed the flies off.* **2 = beater**, mixer, blender: *Using a whisk, beat the mixture until it thickens.*

whisky NOUN **= Scotch**, malt, rye, bourbon, firewater, John Barleycorn, usquebaugh *(Gaelic)*, barley-bree *(Scot.)*

> **QUOTATIONS**
> Freedom and Whisky gang thegither!
> [Robert Burns *The Author's Earnest Cry and Prayer*]
>
> a torchlight procession marching down your throat
> [John L. O'Sullivan (of whisky)]

whisper VERB **1 = murmur**, breathe, mutter, mumble, purr, speak in hushed tones, say softly, say sotto voce, utter under the breath: *'Keep your voice down,' I whispered.* **OPPOSITE:** shout **2 = gossip**, hint, intimate, murmur,

insinuate, spread rumours: *People started whispering that the pair were having an affair.* **3 = rustle**, sigh, moan, murmur, hiss, swish, sough, susurrate *(literary)*: *The leaves whispered and rustled in the breeze.*
▷ NOUN **1 = murmur**, mutter, mumble, undertone, low voice, soft voice, hushed tone: *Men were talking in whispers in the corridor.* **2 = rumour**, report, word, story, hint, buzz, gossip, dirt *(U.S. slang)*, goss *(informal)*, innuendo, insinuation, scuttlebutt *(U.S. slang)*: *I've heard a whisper that he is planning to resign.* **3 = rustle**, sigh, sighing, murmur, hiss, swish, soughing, susurration *or* susurrus *(literary)*: *the slight whisper of the wind in the grass* **4 = hint**, shadow, suggestion, trace, breath, suspicion, fraction, tinge, whiff: *There is a whisper of conspiracy about the whole affair.*

whit NOUN **= bit**, drop, piece, trace, scrap, dash, grain, particle, fragment, atom, pinch, shred, crumb, mite, jot, speck, modicum, least bit, iota

white ADJECTIVE **1 = pale**, grey, ghastly, wan, pasty, bloodless, pallid, ashen, waxen, like death warmed up *(informal)*, wheyfaced: *He turned white and began to stammer.* **2 = silver**, grey, snowy, grizzled, hoary: *an old man with white hair*
whiter than white = immaculate, innocent, virtuous, saintly, clean, pure, worthy, noble, stainless, impeccable, exemplary, spotless, squeaky-clean, unblemished, untainted, unsullied, irreproachable, uncorrupted

white-collar ADJECTIVE **= clerical**, office, executive, professional, salaried, nonmanual

whiten VERB **1 = pale**, blanch, go white, turn pale, blench, fade, etiolate: *His face whitened as he heard the news.* **OPPOSITE:** darken **2 = bleach**, lighten: *toothpastes that whiten the teeth* **OPPOSITE:** darken

whitewash VERB **= cover up**, conceal, suppress, camouflage, make light of, gloss over, extenuate: *The administration is whitewashing the regime's actions.* **OPPOSITE:** expose
▷ NOUN **= cover-up**, deception, camouflage, concealment, extenuation: *The report's findings were condemned as total whitewash.*

whittle VERB **= carve**, cut, hew, shape, trim, shave, pare: *Chitty sat in his rocking chair whittling a piece of wood.*
whittle something away = undermine, reduce, destroy, consume, erode, eat away, wear away, cut down, cut, decrease, prune, scale down: *I believe the Government's aim is to whittle away the Welfare State.*

whole NOUN **1 = total**, all, lot, everything, aggregate, sum total, the entire amount: *Taken as a percentage of the whole, it has to be a fairly minor part.* **2 = unit**, body, piece, object, combination, unity, entity, ensemble, entirety, fullness, totality: *The different components combine to form a complete whole.* **OPPOSITE:** part
▷ ADJECTIVE **1 = complete**, full, total, entire, integral, uncut, undivided, unabridged, unexpurgated, uncondensed: *I have now read the whole book.* **OPPOSITE:** partial **2 = undamaged**, intact, unscathed, unbroken, good, sound, perfect, mint, untouched, flawless, unhurt, faultless, unharmed, in one piece, uninjured, inviolate, unimpaired, unmutilated: *I struck the glass with all my might, but it remained whole.* **OPPOSITE:** damaged
▷ ADVERB **= in one piece**, in one: *Snakes swallow their prey whole.*
on the whole 1 = all in all, altogether, all things considered, by and large, taking everything into consideration: *On the whole, I think it's better if I don't come with you.* **2 = generally**, in general, for the most part, as a rule, chiefly, mainly, mostly, principally, on average, predominantly, in the main, to a large extent, as a general rule, generally speaking: *On the whole, women are having children much later these days.*

wholehearted ADJECTIVE **= sincere**, complete, committed, genuine, real, true, determined, earnest, warm, devoted, dedicated, enthusiastic, emphatic, hearty, heartfelt, zealous, unqualified, unstinting, unreserved, unfeigned **OPPOSITE:** half-hearted

wholesale ADJECTIVE **= extensive**, total, mass, sweeping, broad, comprehensive, wide-ranging, blanket, outright, far-reaching, indiscriminate, all-inclusive: *the wholesale destruction of life on this planet* **OPPOSITE:** limited
▷ ADVERB **= extensively**, comprehensively, across the board, all at once, indiscriminately, without exception, on a large scale: *The army was burning down houses and killing villagers wholesale.*

wholesome ADJECTIVE **1 = moral**, nice, clean, pure, decent, innocent, worthy, ethical, respectable, honourable, uplifting, righteous, exemplary, virtuous, apple-pie *(informal)*, squeaky-clean, edifying: *It was all good, wholesome fun.* **OPPOSITE:** corrupt **2 = healthy**, good, strengthening, beneficial, nourishing, nutritious, sanitary, invigorating, salutary, hygienic, healthful, health-giving: *The food was filling and wholesome.* **OPPOSITE:** unhealthy

wholly ADVERB **1 = completely**, totally, perfectly, fully, entirely, comprehensively, altogether, thoroughly, utterly, heart and soul, one hundred per cent *(informal)*, in every respect: *The accusation is wholly without foundation.* **OPPOSITE:** partly **2 = solely**, only, exclusively, without exception, to the exclusion of everything else: *societies which rely wholly on farming to survive*

whoop VERB **= cry**, shout, scream, cheer, yell, shriek, hoot, holler *(informal)*: *The audience whooped and cheered with delight.*
▷ NOUN **= cry**, shout, scream, cheer, yell, shriek, hoot, holler *(informal)*, hurrah, halloo: *A wild frenzy of whoops and yells arose outside.*

whopper NOUN **1 = big lie**, fabrication, falsehood, untruth, tall story *(informal)*, fable: *He's always telling whoppers about his sex life.* **2 = giant**, monster, jumbo *(informal)*, mammoth, colossus, leviathan, crackerjack *(informal)*: *As comets go, it is a whopper.*

whopping ADJECTIVE **= gigantic**, great, big, large, huge, giant, massive, enormous, extraordinary, tremendous, monstrous, whacking *(informal)*, mammoth, prodigious, elephantine, humongous *or* humungous *(U.S. slang)*

whore NOUN **= prostitute**, hooker *(U.S. slang)*, tart *(informal)*, streetwalker, tom *(Brit. slang)*, brass *(slang)*, slag *(Brit. slang)*, hustler *(U.S. & Canad. slang)*, call girl, courtesan, working girl *(facetious, slang)*, harlot, loose woman, fallen woman, scrubber *(Brit. & Austral. slang)*, strumpet, trollop, lady of the night, cocotte, woman of easy virtue, demimondaine, woman of ill repute, fille de joie *(French)*, demirep *(rare)*: *There were pimps and whores standing on every street corner.*
▷ VERB **= sleep around**, womanize, wanton *(informal)*, wench *(archaic)*, fornicate, lech *or* letch *(informal)*: *His eldest son gambled, whored and drank.*

whorl NOUN **= swirl**, spiral, coil, twist, vortex, helix, corkscrew

wicked ADJECTIVE **1 = bad**, evil, corrupt, vile, guilty, abandoned, foul, vicious, worthless, shameful, immoral, scandalous, atrocious, sinful, heinous, depraved, debased, devilish, amoral, egregious, abominable, fiendish, villainous, unprincipled, nefarious, dissolute, iniquitous, irreligious, black-hearted, impious, unrighteous, maleficent, flagitious: *She flew at me, shouting how evil and wicked I was.* **OPPOSITE:** virtuous **2 = mischievous**, playful, impish, devilish, arch, teasing, naughty, cheeky, rascally, incorrigible, raffish, roguish, rakish, tricksy, puckish, waggish: *She has a delightfully wicked sense of humour.* **OPPOSITE:** well-behaved **3 = agonizing**, terrible, acute, severe, intense, awful, painful, fierce, mighty, dreadful, fearful, gut-wrenching: *A wicked pain shot through his injured elbow.* **4 = harmful**, terrible, intense, mighty, crashing, dreadful, destructive, injurious: *The wind gets so wicked you want to stay indoors while the sea rages.* **OPPOSITE:** harmless **5 = expert**, great *(informal)*, strong, powerful, masterly, wonderful, outstanding, remarkable, ace *(informal)*, first-class, marvellous, mighty, dazzling, skilful, A1 *(informal)*, adept, deft, adroit: *John's a wicked tennis player. He always wins.*

wide ADJECTIVE **1 = spacious**, broad, extensive, ample, roomy, commodious: *The doorway should be wide enough to allow wheelchair access.* **OPPOSITE:** confined **2 = baggy**, full, loose, ample, billowing, roomy, voluminous, capacious, oversize, generously cut: *Wear the shirt loose over wide trousers.* **3 = expanded**, dilated, fully open, distended: *His eyes were wide with disbelief.* **OPPOSITE:** shut **4 = broad**, comprehensive, extensive, wide-ranging, large, catholic, expanded, sweeping, vast, immense, ample, inclusive, expansive, exhaustive, encyclopedic, far-ranging, compendious: *The brochure offers a wide choice of hotels and holiday homes.* **OPPOSITE:** restricted **5 = extensive**, general, far-reaching, overarching: *The case has attracted wide publicity.* **6 = large**, broad, vast, immense: *the wide variation in the ages and backgrounds of the candidates* **7 = distant**, off, away, remote, off course, off target: *The shot was several feet wide.*
▷ ADVERB **1 = fully**, completely, right out, as far as possible, to the furthest extent: *He opened his mouth wide.* **OPPOSITE:** partly **2 = off target**, nowhere near, astray, off course, off the mark: *The big striker fired wide and missed an easy goal.*

wide-eyed ADJECTIVE **1 = naive**, green, trusting, credulous, simple, innocent, impressionable, unsophisticated, ingenuous, wet behind the ears *(informal)*, unsuspicious, as green as grass: *He told tall stories to a wide-eyed group of tourists.* **2 = staring**, spellbound, gobsmacked *(Brit. slang)*, dumbfounded, agog, agape, thunderstruck, goggle-eyed, awe-stricken: *She was wide-eyed in astonishment.*

widen VERB **1 = broaden**, expand, enlarge, dilate, spread, extend, stretch, open wide, open out *or* up: *He had an operation to widen an artery in his heart.* **OPPOSITE:** narrow **2 = get wider**, spread, extend, expand, broaden, open wide, open out *or* up: *The river widens considerably as it begins to turn east.* **OPPOSITE:** narrow

wide-open ADJECTIVE **1 = outspread**, spread, outstretched, splayed, fully open, fully extended, gaping: *He came towards her with his arms wide open in welcome.* **2 = unprotected**, open, exposed, vulnerable, at risk, in danger, susceptible, defenceless, in peril: *The virus leaves the body wide open to infection.* **3 = uncertain**, unsettled, unpredictable, up for grabs *(informal)*, indeterminate, anybody's guess *(informal)*: *The match was still wide open when it reached half-time.*

widespread ADJECTIVE **= common**, general, popular, sweeping, broad, extensive, universal, epidemic, wholesale, far-reaching, prevalent, rife, pervasive, far-flung
OPPOSITE: limited

width NOUN **= breadth**, extent, span, wideness, reach, range, measure, scope, diameter, compass, thickness, girth

wield VERB **1 = brandish**, flourish, manipulate, swing, use, manage, handle, employ, ply: *He was attacked by an assailant wielding a kitchen knife.* **2 = exert**, hold, maintain, exercise, have, control, manage, apply, command, possess, make use of, utilize, put to use, be possessed of, have at your disposal: *He remains chairman, but wields little power in the company.*

wife NOUN **= spouse**, woman *(informal)*, partner, mate, bride, old woman *(informal)*, old lady *(informal)*, little woman *(informal)*, significant other *(U.S. informal)*, better half *(humorous)*, her indoors *(Brit. slang)*, helpmate, helpmeet, (the) missis *or* missus *(informal)*, femme, vrou *(S. African)*, wahine *(N.Z.)*, wifey *(informal)*, Wag *(informal)* ▸ *related adjective*: uxorial

> **QUOTATIONS**
>
> If you get a good wife you'll become happy; if you get a bad one, you'll become a philosopher
> [Socrates]
>
> Wives are young men's mistresses, companions for middle age, and old men's nurses
> [Francis Bacon]
>
> An ideal wife is any woman who has an ideal husband
> [Booth Tarkington]
>
> I... chose my wife, as she did her wedding gown, not for a fine glossy surface, but such qualities as would wear well
> [Oliver Goldsmith *The Vicar of Wakefield*]
>
> My fairest, my espoused, my latest found,
> Heaven's last best gift, my ever new delight
> [John Milton *Paradise Lost*]
>
> best image of myself and dearer half
> [John Milton *Paradise Lost*]
>
> A good husband should be deaf and a good wife blind
> [*French proverb*]

wiggle VERB **1 = jerk**, shake, twitch, wag, jiggle, waggle: *She wiggled her fingers to attract his attention.* **2 = squirm**, twitch, writhe, shimmy: *A little worm was wiggling on the pavement.*
▷ NOUN **= jerk**, shake, twitch, wag, squirm, writhe, jiggle, waggle, shimmy: *With a wiggle of her hips, she slid out of her skirt.*

wild ADJECTIVE **1 = untamed**, fierce, savage, ferocious, unbroken, feral, undomesticated, free, warrigal *(Austral. literary)*: *The organization is calling for a total ban on the trade of wild animals.* **OPPOSITE:** tame **2 = uncultivated**, natural, native, indigenous: *The lane was lined with wild flowers.* **OPPOSITE:** cultivated **3 = desolate**, empty, desert, deserted, virgin, lonely, uninhabited, godforsaken, uncultivated, uncivilized, trackless, unpopulated: *one of the few wild areas remaining in the South East* **OPPOSITE:** inhabited **4 = stormy**, violent, rough, intense, raging, furious, howling, choppy, tempestuous, blustery: *The recent wild weather has caused millions of pounds' worth of damage.* **5 = excited**, mad *(informal)*, crazy *(informal)*, eager, nuts *(slang)*, enthusiastic, raving, frantic, daft *(informal)*, frenzied, hysterical, avid, potty *(Brit. informal)*, delirious, agog: *The children were wild with excitement.* **OPPOSITE:** unenthusiastic **6 = uncontrolled**, violent, rough, disorderly, noisy, chaotic, turbulent, wayward, unruly, rowdy, boisterous, lawless, unfettered, unbridled, riotous, unrestrained, unmanageable, impetuous, undisciplined, ungovernable, self-willed, uproarious: *When drunk, he became wild and violent.* **OPPOSITE:** calm **7 = mad** *(informal)*, furious, fuming, infuriated, incensed, enraged, very angry, irate, livid *(informal)*, in a rage, on the warpath *(informal)*, hot under the collar *(informal)*, beside yourself, tooshie *(Austral. slang)*, off the air *(Austral. slang)*: *When I told him what I had done, he was wild.* **8 = outrageous**, fantastic, foolish, rash, extravagant, reckless, preposterous, giddy, madcap, foolhardy, flighty, ill-considered, imprudent, impracticable: *I was just a kid and full of wild ideas.* **OPPOSITE:** practical **9 = dishevelled**, disordered, untidy, unkempt, tousled, straggly, windblown, daggy *(Austral. & N.Z. informal)*: *They were alarmed by his wild hair and staring eyes.* **10 = passionate**, mad *(informal)*, ardent, fervent, zealous, fervid: *She's just wild about him.* **11 = uncivilized**, fierce, savage, primitive, rude, ferocious, barbaric, brutish, barbarous: *the wild tribes which still roam the northern plains with their horse herds* **OPPOSITE:** civilized
the wilds = wilderness, desert, wasteland, middle of nowhere *(informal)*, backwoods, back of beyond *(informal)*, uninhabited area: *They went canoeing in the wilds of Canada.*
run wild 1 = grow unchecked, spread, ramble, straggle: *The front garden is running wild.* **2 = go on the rampage**, stray, rampage, run riot, cut loose, run free, kick over the traces, be undisciplined, abandon all restraint: *She lets her children run wild.*

wilderness NOUN **1 = wilds**, waste, desert, wasteland, uncultivated region: *He looked out over a wilderness of mountain, lake and forest.* **2 = tangle**,

W

confusion, maze, muddle, clutter, jumble, welter, congeries, confused mass: *The neglected cemetery was a wilderness of crumbling gravestones and parched grass.*

wildlife NOUN = **flora and fauna**, animals, fauna

wile NOUN = **cunning**, craft, fraud, cheating, guile, artifice, trickery, chicanery, craftiness, artfulness, slyness: *His wit and wile has made him one of the sharpest politicians in the Cabinet.*
▷ PLURAL NOUN = **ploys**, tricks, devices, lures, manoeuvres, dodges, ruses, artifices, subterfuges, stratagems, contrivances, impositions: *She never hesitated to use her feminine wiles to get her own way.*

wilful *or* **willful** ADJECTIVE
1 = intentional, willed, intended, conscious, voluntary, deliberate, purposeful, volitional: *Wilful neglect of the environment has caused this problem.*
OPPOSITE: unintentional
2 = obstinate, dogged, determined, persistent, adamant, stubborn, perverse, uncompromising, intractable, inflexible, unyielding, intransigent, headstrong, obdurate, stiff-necked, self-willed, refractory, pig-headed, bull-headed, mulish, froward *(archaic)*: *a spoilt and wilful teenager* **OPPOSITE:** obedient

will NOUN **1 = determination**, drive, aim, purpose, commitment, resolution, resolve, intention, spine, backbone, tenacity, willpower, single-mindedness, doggedness, firmness of purpose: *He lacked the will to confront her.*
2 = wish, mind, desire, pleasure, intention, fancy, preference, inclination: *He was forced to leave the country against his will.* **3 = choice**, decision, option, prerogative, volition: *the concept of free will*
4 = decree, wish, desire, command, dictate, ordinance: *He has submitted himself to the will of God.* **5 = testament**, declaration, bequest(s), last wishes, last will and testament: *Attached to his will was a letter he had written just before his death.*
▷ VERB **1 = decree**, order, cause, effect, direct, determine, bid, intend, command, resolve, bring about, ordain: *They believed they would win because God had willed it.* **2 = wish**, want, choose, prefer, desire, elect, opt, see fit: *Say what you will about him, but he's always been a good provider.* **3 = bequeath**, give, leave, transfer, gift, hand on, pass on, confer, hand down, settle on: *She had willed all her money to her brother, Frank.*
at will = as you please, at your discretion, as you think fit, at your pleasure, at your desire, at your whim, at your inclination, at your wish: *Some yoga practitioners can slow their heart rates down at will.*
▸ *related adjectives:* voluntary, volitive

PROVERBS
Where there's a will there's a way

willing ADJECTIVE **1 = inclined**, prepared, happy, pleased, content, in favour, consenting, disposed, favourable, agreeable, in the mood, compliant, amenable, desirous, so-minded, nothing loath: *There are some questions which they will not be willing to answer.* **OPPOSITE:** unwilling
2 = ready, game *(informal)*, eager, enthusiastic: *He had plenty of willing volunteers to help him clear up.*
OPPOSITE: reluctant

willingly ADVERB = **readily**, freely, gladly, happily, eagerly, voluntarily, cheerfully, with pleasure, without hesitation, by choice, with all your heart, lief *(rare)*, of your own free will, of your own accord
OPPOSITE: unwillingly

willingness NOUN = **inclination**, will, agreement, wish, favour, desire, enthusiasm, consent, goodwill, disposition, volition, agreeableness
OPPOSITE: reluctance

willowy ADJECTIVE = **slender**, slim, graceful, supple, lithe, limber, svelte, lissom(e), sylphlike

willpower NOUN = **self-control**, drive, resolution, resolve, determination, grit, self-discipline, single-mindedness, fixity of purpose, firmness of purpose *or* will, force *or* strength of will **OPPOSITE:** weakness

willy-nilly ADVERB **1 = whether you like it or not**, necessarily, of necessity, perforce, whether or no, whether desired or not, nolens volens *(Latin)*: *We were dragged willy-nilly into the argument.* **2 = haphazardly**, at random, randomly, without order, without method, without planning, any old how *(informal)*: *The papers were just bundled into the drawers willy-nilly.*

wilt VERB **1 = droop**, wither, sag, shrivel, become limp *or* flaccid: *The roses wilted the day after she bought them.*
2 = weaken, sag, languish, droop: *She began to wilt in the morning heat.*
3 = wane, fail, sink, flag, fade, diminish, dwindle, wither, ebb, melt away, lose courage: *Their resolution wilted in the face of such powerful opposition.*

wily ADJECTIVE = **cunning**, designing, scheming, sharp, intriguing, arch, tricky, crooked, shrewd, sly, astute, deceptive, crafty, artful, shifty, foxy, cagey *(informal)*, deceitful, underhand, guileful, fly *(slang)*
OPPOSITE: straightforward

wimp NOUN = **weakling**, wet *(Brit. slang)*, mouse, drip *(informal)*, coward, jessie *(Scot. slang)*, pussy *(slang, chiefly U.S.)*, jellyfish *(informal)*, sissy, doormat *(slang)*, wuss *(slang)*, milksop, softy *or* softie

win VERB **1 = be victorious in**, succeed in, prevail in, come first in, finish first in, be the victor in, gain victory in, achieve first place in: *He does not have any reasonable chance of winning the election.* **OPPOSITE:** lose **2 = be victorious**, succeed, triumph, overcome, prevail, conquer, come first, finish first, carry the day, sweep the board, take the prize, gain victory, achieve mastery, achieve first place, carry all before you, topscore *(informal)*: *Our team is confident of winning again this year.* **OPPOSITE:** lose **3 = gain**, get, receive, land, catch, achieve, net, earn, pick up, bag *(informal)*, secure, collect, obtain, acquire, accomplish, attain, procure, come away with: *The first correct entry will win the prize.*
OPPOSITE: forfeit
▷ NOUN = **victory**, success, triumph, conquest: *Arsenal's run of eight games without a win* **OPPOSITE:** defeat
win someone over *or* **round = convince**, influence, attract, persuade, convert, charm, sway, disarm, allure, prevail upon, bring *or* talk round: *He had won over a significant number of his opponents.*

wince VERB = **flinch**, start, shrink, cringe, quail, recoil, cower, draw back, blench: *He tightened his grip on her arm until she winced in pain.*
▷ NOUN = **flinch**, start, cringe: *She gave a wince at the memory of their first date.*

wind[1] NOUN **1 = air**, blast, breath, hurricane, breeze, draught, gust, zephyr, air-current, current of air: *During the night the wind had blown down the fence.* **2 = flatulence**, gas, flatus: *tablets to treat trapped wind* **3 = breath**, puff, respiration: *A punch in the stomach knocked the wind out of me.* **4 = nonsense**, talk, boasting, hot air, babble, bluster, humbug, twaddle *(informal)*, gab *(informal)*, verbalizing, blather, codswallop *(informal)*, eyewash *(informal)*, idle talk, empty talk, bizzo *(Austral. slang)*, bull's wool *(Austral. & N.Z. slang)*: *You're just talking a lot of wind.*
get wind of something = hear about, learn of, find out about, become aware of, be told about, be informed of, be made aware of, hear tell of, have brought to your notice, hear on the grape vine *(informal)*: *I don't want the press to get wind of our plans at this stage.*
in the wind = imminent, coming, near, approaching, on the way, looming, brewing, impending, on the cards *(informal)*, in the offing, about to happen, close at hand: *By the mid-1980s, economic change was in the wind again.*
put the wind up someone = scare, alarm, frighten, panic, discourage, unnerve, scare off, frighten off: *I had an anonymous letter that really put the wind up me.*

PROVERBS
It's an ill wind that blows nobody any good

wind[2] VERB **1 = meander**, turn, bend, twist, curve, snake, ramble, twist and turn, deviate, zigzag: *The Moselle winds through some 160 miles of tranquil countryside.* **2 = wrap**, twist, reel, curl, loop, coil, twine, furl, wreathe: *She wound the sash round her waist.* **3 = coil**, curl, spiral, encircle, twine: *The snake wound around my leg.*
wind down 1 = calm down, unwind,

take it easy, unbutton *(informal)*, put your feet up, de-stress *(informal)*, outspan *(S. African)*, cool down *or* off: *I need a drink to help me wind down.* **2 = subside**, decline, diminish, come to an end, dwindle, tail off, taper off, slacken off: *The relationship was winding down by more or less mutual agreement.*

wind someone up 1 = irritate, excite, anger, annoy, exasperate, nettle, work someone up, pique, make someone nervous, put someone on edge, make someone tense, hack you off *(informal)*: *This woman kept winding me up by talking over me.* **2 = tease**, kid *(informal)*, have someone on *(informal)*, annoy, rag *(informal)*, rib *(informal)*, josh *(informal)*, vex, make fun of, take the mickey out of *(informal)*, send someone up *(informal)*, pull someone's leg *(informal)*, jerk *or* yank someone's chain *(informal)*: *You're joking. Come on, you're just winding me up.*

wind something up 1 = end, finish, settle, conclude, tie up, wrap up, finalize, bring to a close, tie up the loose ends of *(informal)*: *The President is about to wind up his visit to Somalia.* **2 = close down**, close, dissolve, terminate, liquidate, put something into liquidation: *The bank seems determined to wind up the company.*

wind up = end up, be left, find yourself, finish up, fetch up *(informal)*, land up, end your days: *You're going to wind up a bitter and lonely old man.*

winded ADJECTIVE **= out of breath**, panting, puffed, breathless, gasping for breath, puffed out, out of puff, out of whack *(informal)*

windfall NOUN **= godsend**, find, jackpot, bonanza, stroke of luck, manna from heaven, pot of gold at the end of the rainbow **OPPOSITE:** misfortune

winding ADJECTIVE **= twisting**, turning, bending, curving, crooked, spiral, indirect, roundabout, meandering, tortuous, convoluted, serpentine, sinuous, circuitous, twisty, anfractuous, flexuous **OPPOSITE:** straight

windy ADJECTIVE **= breezy**, wild, stormy, boisterous, blustering, windswept, tempestuous, blustery, gusty, inclement, squally, blowy **OPPOSITE:** calm

wing NOUN **1 = organ of flight**, pinion *(poetic)*, pennon *(poetic)*: *The bird flapped its wings furiously.* **2 = annexe**, part, side, section, extension, adjunct, ell *(U.S.)*: *We were given an office in the empty west wing of the building.* **3 = faction**, grouping, group, set, side, arm, section, camp, branch, circle, lobby, segment, caucus, clique, coterie, schism, cabal: *the liberal wing of the Democratic party*

▷ VERB **1 = fly**, soar, glide, take wing: *Several birds broke cover and went winging over the lake.* **2 = hurry**, fly, race, speed, streak, zoom, hasten, hurtle: *He was soon winging his way home to rejoin his family.* **3 = wound**, hit, nick, clip, graze: *He shot at the bird but only managed to wing it.*

wink VERB **1 = blink**, bat, flutter, nictate, nictitate: *Brian winked an eye at me, giving me his seal of approval.* **2 = twinkle**, flash, shine, sparkle, gleam, shimmer, glimmer: *From the hotel window, they could see lights winking on the bay.*

▷ NOUN **1 = blink**, flutter, nictation, nictitation: *Diana gave me a reassuring wink.* **2 = twinkle**, flash, sparkle, gleam, blink, glimmering, glimmer: *In the distance, he noticed the wink of a red light.*

wink at something = condone, allow, ignore, overlook, tolerate, put up with *(informal)*, disregard, turn a blind eye to, blink at, connive at, pretend not to notice, shut your eyes to: *Corrupt police have been known to wink at crimes in return for bribes.*

winner NOUN **= victor**, first, champion, master, champ *(informal)*, conqueror, vanquisher, prizewinner, conquering hero **OPPOSITE:** loser

winning ADJECTIVE **1 = victorious**, first, top, successful, unbeaten, conquering, triumphant, undefeated, vanquishing, top-scoring, unvanquished: *The winning team returned home to a heroes' welcome.* **2 = charming**, taking, pleasing, sweet, attractive, engaging, lovely, fascinating, fetching, delightful, cute, disarming, enchanting, endearing, captivating, amiable, alluring, bewitching, delectable, winsome, prepossessing, likable *or* likeable: *She had great charm and a winning personality.* **OPPOSITE:** unpleasant

▷ PLURAL NOUN **= spoils**, profits, gains, prize, proceeds, takings, booty: *The poker player collected his winnings and left.*

winsome ADJECTIVE **= charming**, taking, winning, pleasing, pretty, fair, sweet, attractive, engaging, fascinating, pleasant, fetching, cute, disarming, enchanting, endearing, captivating, agreeable, amiable, alluring, bewitching, delectable, comely, likable *or* likeable, fit *(Brit. informal)*

wintry ADJECTIVE **1 = cold**, freezing, frozen, harsh, icy, chilly, snowy, frosty, hibernal: *The wintry weather continues to sweep across the country.* **OPPOSITE:** warm **2 = unfriendly**, cold, cool, remote, distant, bleak, chilly, frigid, cheerless: *Melissa gave him a wintry smile and walked on without a word.*

wipe VERB **1 = clean**, dry, polish, brush, dust, rub, sponge, mop, swab: *She wiped her hands on the towel.* **2 = erase**, remove, take off, get rid of, take away, rub off, efface, clean off, sponge off: *Gleb wiped the sweat from his face.*

▷ NOUN **= rub**, clean, polish, brush, lick, sponge, mop, swab: *I'll give the surfaces a wipe with some disinfectant.*

wipe something *or* **someone out = destroy**, eliminate, take out *(slang)*, massacre, slaughter, erase, eradicate, blow away *(slang, chiefly U.S.)*, obliterate, liquidate *(informal)*, annihilate, efface, exterminate, expunge, extirpate, wipe from the face of the earth *(informal)*, kill to the last man, kennet *(Austral. slang)*, jeff *(Austral. slang)*: *a fanatic who is determined to wipe out anyone who opposes him*

wiry ADJECTIVE **1 = lean**, strong, tough, thin, spare, skinny, stringy, sinewy: *a wiry and athletic young man* **OPPOSITE:** flabby **2 = stiff**, rough, coarse, curly, kinky, bristly: *wiry black hair*

wisdom NOUN **1 = understanding**, learning, knowledge, intelligence, smarts *(slang, chiefly U.S.)*, judgment, insight, enlightenment, penetration, comprehension, foresight, erudition, discernment, sagacity, sound judgment, sapience: *a man respected for his wisdom and insight* **OPPOSITE:** foolishness **2 = prudence**, reason, circumspection, judiciousness: *Many have expressed doubts about the wisdom of the decision.* **OPPOSITE:** folly

▸ *related adjective:* sagacious

QUOTATIONS

Knowledge comes, but wisdom lingers
[Alfred, Lord Tennyson *Locksley Hall*]

Wisdom denotes the pursuing of the best ends by the best means
[Francis Hutcheson *Inquiry into the Original of our Ideas of Beauty and Virtue*]

The art of being wise is the art of knowing what to overlook
[William James *Principles of Psychology*]

Be wiser than other people if you can, but do not tell them so
[Lord Chesterfield]

wise enough to play the fool
[William Shakespeare *Twelfth Night*]

The price of wisdom is above rubies
[*Bible: Job*]

Some folks are wise, and some are otherwise
[Tobias Smollett *Roderick Random*]

But where shall wisdom be found? And where is the place of understanding?
[*Bible: Job*]

Wisdom is the principal thing; therefore get wisdom; and with all thy getting get understanding
[*Bible: Proverbs*]

It is the province of knowledge to speak and it is the privilege of wisdom to listen
[Oliver Wendell Holmes *The Poet at the Breakfast-Table*]

PROVERBS

Don't teach your grandmother to suck eggs

Sir Walter Scott's Use of Adjectives

Many of Scott's most frequent adjectives describe features of personality or character, such as *kind, wise, worthy, honest, gallant,* and *brave. Knights, armies,* and *soldiers* are *gallant* or *brave,* whereas *worthy* is often used to refer to people who are representatives of the church, for example *clergyman, deacon,* and *monk. Honest* is used alongside *man, gentleman, fellow,* and *lad,* and is often used in conjunction with the adjective *douce,* a Scots term meaning 'sedate' or 'peaceable':

> 'And how's that **douce honest** man, your father?' Jeanie was saved the pain of answering this hypocritical question by the appearance of the Laird himself.

Another frequent adjective is *gentle,* sometimes in the sense 'mild, kind', for example in *gentle spirit* and *gentle voice,* but sometimes in the older sense 'of honourable birth', in phrases such as *in right of his gentle blood.*

One interesting feature of Scott's adjectival usage is his use of *old* contrasting with the Scots term *auld. Old* appears over seven times as often as *auld,* although both are among his hundred most frequent adjectives. *Old* is used most with nouns referring to people, such as *friend, woman,* and *man.* This too is the case with *auld,* but the nouns that *auld* combines with are usually Scots terms and are often negative, for example *deevil* ('devil'), *fule* ('fool'), and *besom* (a derogatory term meaning 'woman'):

> 'G--d, I have gude cause to remember her,' said Peter, 'for she turned a dyvour on my hands, the **auld besom**!'

This suggests that the adjective *auld* is often used to provide emphasis. Adjectives used in conjunction with *auld* include *gude* ('good'), *daft,* and *doited* ('foolish'). As with *old, auld* tends to be the adjective that appears second when used in conjunction with another adjective, for example in 'my gude auld house' and 'daft auld songs'. However, we occasionally find it in first position, as in 'auld doited fule' and 'auld rusty lass', an unusual construction to modern ears.

Scott used – and popularized – many other adjectives which are still found in modern Scots, including *canny* ('prudent, cautious'), *dour* ('sullen'), *thrawn* ('crooked'), and *wee* ('small'), as well as some which have become less common, such as *skeely* ('skilful') and *fendy* ('thrifty'):

> 'Alice is both **canny** and **fendy**,' said the bold Evan Dhu, with a cock of his bonnet, 'and I ken nocht to hinder me to marry her myself'

Scott's novels were popular all over the world, not only in Scotland, and part of their international success was a result of his ability to capture Scots dialogue without making it inaccessible to readers. In the passage just quoted, most of the words are understandable to a reader of English, with only a few common Scots expressions sprinkled throughout (*canny, fendy, ken,* and *nocht*). Furthermore, Scott sometimes draws the reader's attention to a 'Scottish phrase':

> His countenance was wild, haggard, and highly excited, or, as the **Scottish phrase** expresses it, much 'raised.'

As well as modifying *phrase,* the adjective *Scottish* is often used to refer to people (*Scottish knight* and *Scottish nobility*), qualities (*Scottish honour*), and features of culture (*Scottish history* and *Scottish superstition*). *Scots* is also sometimes used as an adjective, for example in *Scots song.* Less frequently, the adjective *Scotch* is used, as in *Scotch lassies, Scotch manners,* and *Scotch laws.* This usage has since become obsolete, and in modern English, *Scotch* is only found in set phrases such as *Scotch mist* and *Scotch egg,* and, of course, as a noun referring to whisky.

In addition to Scots terms, Scott peppers his novels with archaic words. Although much of his language is firmly that of the 19th century, the use of adjectives such as *scatheless* 'unharmed' and *soothfast* 'true' conjure up a sense of the historical settings of his novels.

wise ADJECTIVE **1 = sage**, knowing, understanding, aware, informed, clever, intelligent, sensible, enlightened, shrewd, discerning, perceptive, well-informed, erudite, sagacious, sapient, clued-up (*informal*), grounded: *She has the air of a wise woman.* **OPPOSITE:** foolish **2 = sensible**, sound, politic, informed, reasonable, clever, intelligent, rational, logical, shrewd, prudent, judicious, well-advised: *She had made a very wise decision.* **OPPOSITE:** unwise

wisecrack NOUN **= joke**, sally, gag (*informal*), quip, jibe, barb, jest, witticism, smart remark, pithy remark, sardonic remark

wish NOUN **1 = desire**, liking, want, longing, hope, urge, intention, fancy (*informal*), ambition, yen (*informal*), hunger, aspiration, craving, lust, yearning, inclination, itch (*informal*), thirst, whim, hankering: *Clearly she had no wish for his company.* **OPPOSITE:** aversion **2 = request**, will, want, order, demand, desire, command, bidding, behest (*literary*): *The decision was made against the wishes of the party leader.*
▷ VERB **1 = want**, feel, choose, please, desire, think fit: *We can dress as we wish nowadays.* **2 = require**, ask, order, direct, bid, desire, command, instruct: *I will do as you wish.* **3 = bid**, greet with: *He wished me a good morning.*
wish for = desire, want, need, hope for, long for, crave, covet, aspire to, yearn for, thirst for, hunger for, hanker for, sigh for, set your heart on, desiderate: *They both wished for a son to carry on the family business.*

> **PROVERBS**
> *The wish is father to the thought*
> *If wishes were horses, beggars would ride*

wisp NOUN **= piece**, twist, strand, thread, shred, snippet

wispy ADJECTIVE **1 = straggly**, fine, thin, frail, wisplike: *Grey wispy hair straggled down to her shoulders.* **2 = thin**, light, fine, delicate, fragile, flimsy, ethereal, insubstantial, gossamer, diaphanous, wisplike: *a wispy chiffon dress*

wistful ADJECTIVE **= melancholy**, longing, dreaming, sad, musing, yearning, thoughtful, reflective, dreamy, forlorn, mournful, contemplative, meditative, pensive, disconsolate

wit NOUN **1 = humour**, fun, quips, banter, puns, pleasantry, repartee, wordplay, levity, witticisms, badinage, jocularity, facetiousness, drollery, raillery, waggishness, wittiness: *Bill was known for his biting wit.* **OPPOSITE:** seriousness **2 = humorist**, card (*informal*), comedian, wag, joker, dag (*N.Z. informal*), punster, epigrammatist: *a man who fancied himself as a great wit* **3 = cleverness**, mind, reason, understanding, sense, brains, smarts (*slang, chiefly U.S.*), judgment, perception, wisdom, insight, common sense, intellect, comprehension, ingenuity, acumen, nous (*Brit. slang*), discernment, practical intelligence: *The information is there for anyone with the wit to use it.* **OPPOSITE:** stupidity

witch NOUN **= enchantress**, magician, hag, crone, occultist, sorceress, Wiccan, necromancer

> **QUOTATIONS**
> witch: (1) An ugly and repulsive old woman, in a wicked league with the devil. (2) A beautiful and attractive young woman, in wickedness a league beyond the devil
> [Ambrose Bierce *The Devil's Dictionary*]

witchcraft NOUN **= magic**, spell, witching, voodoo, the occult, wizardry, black magic, enchantment, occultism, sorcery, incantation, Wicca, the black art, witchery, necromancy, sortilege, makutu (*N.Z.*)

withdraw VERB **1 = remove**, pull, take off, pull out, extract, take away, pull back, draw out, draw back: *Cassandra withdrew her hand from Roger's; He reached into his pocket and withdrew a piece of paper.* **2 = take out**, extract, draw out: *They withdrew 100 dollars from their bank account.* **3 = retreat**, go, leave (*informal*), retire, depart, pull out, fall back, pull back, back out, back off, cop out (*slang*), disengage from: *Troops withdrew from the country last March.* **OPPOSITE:** advance **4 = go**, leave, retire, retreat, depart, make yourself scarce, absent yourself: *The waiter poured the wine and then withdrew.* **5 = pull out**, leave, drop out, secede, disengage, detach yourself, absent yourself: *The African National Congress threatened to withdraw from the talks.* **6 = retract**, recall, take back, revoke, rescind, disavow, recant, disclaim, abjure, unsay: *He withdrew his remarks and said he had not intended to cause offence.*

withdrawal NOUN **1 = removal**, ending, stopping, taking away, abolition, elimination, cancellation, termination, extraction, discontinuation: *the withdrawal of foreign aid* **2 = exit**, retirement, departure, pull-out, retreat, exodus, evacuation, disengagement: *the withdrawal of troops from Eastern Europe* **3 = departure**, retirement, exit, secession: *his withdrawal from government in 1946* **4 = retraction**, recall, disclaimer, repudiation, revocation, disavowal, recantation, rescission, abjuration: *The charity insists on a withdrawal of the accusations.*

withdrawn ADJECTIVE **= uncommunicative**, reserved, retiring, quiet, silent, distant, shy, shrinking, detached, aloof, taciturn, introverted, timorous, unforthcoming **OPPOSITE:** outgoing

wither VERB **1 = wilt**, dry, decline, shrink, decay, disintegrate, perish, languish, droop, shrivel, desiccate: *Farmers have watched their crops wither because of the drought.* **OPPOSITE:** flourish **2 = waste**, decline, shrink, shrivel, atrophy: *His leg muscles had withered from lack of use.* **3 = fade**, decline, wane, perish: *His dream of being a famous footballer withered and died.* **OPPOSITE:** increase **4 = humiliate**, blast, shame, put down, snub, mortify, abash: *Mary withered me with a glance.*

withering ADJECTIVE **= scornful**, blasting, devastating, humiliating, snubbing, blighting, hurtful, mortifying

withhold VERB **1 = keep secret**, keep, refuse, hide, reserve, retain, sit on (*informal*), conceal, suppress, hold back, keep back: *Police withheld the victim's name until her relatives had been informed.* **OPPOSITE:** reveal **2 = hold back**, check, resist, suppress, restrain, repress, keep back: *She could not withhold a scornful comment as he passed.* **OPPOSITE:** release

withstand VERB **= resist**, take, face, suffer, bear, weather, oppose, take on, cope with, brave, confront, combat, endure, defy, tolerate, put up with (*informal*), thwart, stand up to, hold off, grapple with, hold out against, stand firm against **OPPOSITE:** give in to

witless ADJECTIVE **= foolish**, crazy, stupid, silly, dull, daft (*informal*), senseless, goofy (*informal*), idiotic, dozy (*Brit. informal*), inane, loopy (*informal*), crackpot (*informal*), moronic, obtuse, unintelligent, empty-headed, asinine, imbecilic, braindead (*informal*), dumb-ass (*slang*), halfwitted, rattlebrained (*slang*)

witness NOUN **1 = observer**, viewer, spectator, looker-on, watcher, onlooker, eyewitness, bystander, beholder: *No witnesses of the crash have come forward.* **2 = testifier**, deponent, attestant: *Eleven witnesses were called to testify.*
▷ VERB **1 = see**, mark, view, watch, note, notice, attend, observe, perceive, look on, be present at, behold (*archaic, literary*): *Anyone who witnessed the attack is urged to contact the police.* **2 = countersign**, sign, endorse, validate: *Ask a friend to witness your signature on the application.*
bear witness 1 = confirm, show, prove, demonstrate, bear out, testify to, be evidence of, corroborate, attest to, be proof of, vouch for, evince, betoken, be a monument to, constitute proof of: *Many of his poems bear witness to the years he spent in India.* **2 = give evidence**, testify, depose, give testimony, depone: *His mother bore witness in court that he had been at home that night.*
▶ *related adjective:* testimonial

witter VERB **= chatter**, chat, rabbit (on) (*Brit. informal*), babble, waffle (*informal, chiefly Brit.*), cackle, twaddle, clack, burble, gab (*informal*), prattle, tattle, jabber, blab, gabble, blather, blether, prate, earbash *(Austral. & N.Z. slang)*

witty ADJECTIVE **= humorous**, gay, original, brilliant, funny, clever, amusing, lively, sparkling, ingenious, fanciful, whimsical, droll, piquant, facetious, jocular, epigrammatic, waggish **OPPOSITE:** dull

QUOTATIONS

A witty woman is a treasure; a witty beauty is a power
[George Meredith *Diana of the Crossways*]

wizard NOUN **1 = magician**, witch, shaman, sorcerer, occultist, magus, conjuror, warlock, mage *(archaic)*, enchanter, necromancer, thaumaturge *(rare)*, tohunga *(N.Z.)*: *Merlin, the legendary wizard who worked magic for King Arthur* **2 = genius**, star, expert, master, ace *(informal)*, guru, buff *(informal)*, adept, whizz *(informal)*, prodigy, maestro, virtuoso, hotshot *(informal)*, rocket scientist *(informal, chiefly U.S.)*, wiz *(informal)*, whizz kid *(informal)*, wonk *(informal)*, maven *(U.S.)*, fundi *(S. African)*, up-and-comer *(informal)*: *a mathematical wizard at Harvard University*

wizardry NOUN **1 = expertise**, skill, know-how *(informal)*, craft, mastery, cleverness, expertness: *a piece of technical wizardry* **2 = magic**, witching, witchcraft, voodoo, enchantment, occultism, sorcery, the black art, witchery, necromancy, conjuration, sortilege: *Hogwarts School of Witchcraft and Wizardry*

wizened ADJECTIVE **= wrinkled**, lined, worn, withered, dried up, shrivelled, gnarled, shrunken, sere *(archaic)* **OPPOSITE:** rounded

wobble VERB **1 = shake**, rock, sway, tremble, quake, waver, teeter, totter, seesaw: *The ladder wobbled on the uneven ground.* **2 = tremble**, shake, vibrate: *My voice wobbled with nerves.* **3 = hesitate**, waver, fluctuate, dither *(chiefly Brit.)*, be undecided, vacillate, shillyshally *(informal)*, be unable to make up your mind, swither *(Scot.)*: *He dithered and wobbled when questioned on his policies.*
▷ NOUN **1 = unsteadiness**, shake, tremble, quaking: *He rode off on his bicycle with only a slight wobble.*
2 = unsteadiness, shake, tremor, vibration: *There was a distinct wobble in her voice when she replied.*

wobbly ADJECTIVE **1 = unstable**, shaky, unsafe, uneven, teetering, unbalanced, tottering, rickety, unsteady, wonky *(Brit. slang)*: *I was sitting on a wobbly plastic chair.*
2 = unsteady, weak, unstable, shaky, quivery, all of a quiver *(informal)*: *His legs felt wobbly after the long flight.*
3 = shaky, unsteady, tremulous: *'I want to go home,' she said in a wobbly voice.*

woe NOUN **1 = misery**, suffering, trouble, pain, disaster, depression, distress, grief, agony, gloom, sadness, hardship, sorrow, anguish, misfortune, unhappiness, heartache, heartbreak, adversity, dejection, wretchedness: *He listened to my tale of woe.* **OPPOSITE:** happiness
2 = problem, trouble, trial, burden, grief, misery, curse, hardship, sorrow, misfortune, heartache, heartbreak, affliction, tribulation: *He did not tell his friends about all his woes.*

woeful ADJECTIVE **1 = wretched**, sad, unhappy, tragic, miserable, gloomy, grieving, dismal, pathetic, afflicted, pitiful, anguished, agonized, disconsolate, doleful, pitiable: *those woeful people to whom life had dealt a bad hand* **OPPOSITE:** happy **2 = sad**, distressing, tragic, miserable, gloomy, dismal, pathetic, harrowing, heartbreaking, grievous, mournful, plaintive, heart-rending, sorrowful, doleful, piteous: *a woeful ballad about lost love* **OPPOSITE:** happy **3 = pitiful**, mean, bad, poor, shocking, sorry, disappointing, terrible, awful, appalling, disastrous, inadequate, dreadful, miserable, hopeless, rotten *(informal)*, pathetic, catastrophic, duff *(Brit. informal)*, feeble, disgraceful, lousy *(slang)*, grievous, paltry, deplorable, abysmal, lamentable, calamitous, wretched, pitiable, godawful *(slang)*, not much cop *(Brit. slang)*: *the team's recent woeful performance*

wolf VERB *(often with* **down***)* **= devour**, stuff, bolt, cram, scoff *(slang)*, gulp, gobble, pack away *(informal)*, gorge on, gollop: *I was in the changing room wolfing down tea and sandwiches.*
OPPOSITE: nibble
▷ NOUN **= womanizer**, seducer, Don Juan, Casanova, philanderer, Lothario, lecher, ladykiller, lech *or* letch *(informal)*: *My grandfather is still an old wolf.*
▸ *related adjective:* lupine ▸ *name of female:* bitch ▸ *name of young:* cub, whelp ▸ *collective nouns:* pack, rout, herd

woman NOUN **1 = lady**, girl, miss, female, bird *(slang)*, dame *(slang)*, ho *(U.S. derogatory, slang)*, sheila *(Austral. & N.Z. informal)*, vrou *(S. African)*, maiden *(archaic)*, chick *(slang)*, maid *(archaic)*, gal *(slang)*, lass, lassie *(informal)*, wench *(facetious)*, adult female, she, charlie *(Austral. slang)*, chook *(Austral. slang)*, femme, wahine *(N.Z.)*: *No woman in her right mind would ever want to go out with you.* **OPPOSITE:** man
2 = girlfriend, girl, wife, partner, mate, lover, bride, mistress, spouse, old lady *(informal)*, sweetheart, significant other *(U.S. informal)*, ladylove, wifey *(informal)*: *I know my woman will never leave me, whatever I do.*
3 = maid, domestic, char *(informal)*, housekeeper, lady-in-waiting, chambermaid, handmaiden, charwoman, maidservant, female servant: *Catriona had been nagging him to get a woman in to clean once a week.*
▸ *related prefixes:* gyn-, gyno-, gynaeco-

QUOTATIONS

She floats, she hesitates; in a word, she's a woman
[Jean Racine *Athalie*]

The meaning of what it is to be a woman has never been more open-ended and therefore more filled with anxiety
[Nancy Friday *What is a Real Woman?*]

Women have served all these centuries as looking-glasses possessing the magic and delicious power of reflecting the figure of man at twice its natural size
[Virginia Woolf *A Room of One's Own*]

The individual woman is required ... a thousand times a day to choose either to accept her appointed role and thereby rescue her good disposition out of the wreckage of her self-respect, or else follow an independent line of behavior and rescue her self-respect out of the wreckage of her good disposition
[Jeannette Rankin]

When a woman behaves like a man why doesn't she behave like a nice man?
[Edith Evans]

The great question that has never been answered, and which I have not yet been able to answer, despite my thirty years of research into the feminine soul, is 'What does a woman want?'
[Sigmund Freud]

A woman can look both moral and exciting – if she also looks as if it was quite a struggle
[Edna Ferber]

I think being a woman is like being Irish ... Everyone says you're important and nice, but you take second place all the same
[Iris Murdoch *The Red and the Green*]

Fickle and changeable always is woman
[Virgil *Aeneid*]

A man is as old as he's feeling,
A woman as old as she looks
[Mortimer Collins *The Unknown Quantity*]

Men play the game, women know the score
[Roger Woddis]

A complete woman is probably not a very admirable creature. She is manipulative, uses other people to get her own way, and works within whatever system she is in
[Anita Brookner]

The prime truth of woman, the universal mother...that if a thing is worth doing, it is worth doing badly
[G.K. Chesterton *What's Wrong with the World*]

One is not born a woman; one becomes one
[Simone de Beauvoir *The Second Sex*]

Woman was God's second blunder
[Friedrich Nietzsche *Der Antichrist*]

Being a woman is of special interest only to aspiring male transsexuals. To actual women it is merely a good excuse not to play football
[Fran Lebowitz *Metropolitan Life*]

The greatest glory of a woman is to be least talked about by men
[Pericles]

A woman seldom writes her mind but in her postscript
[Sir Richard Steele *The Spectator*]

A woman without a man is like a fish without a bicycle
[attributed to Gloria Steinem]

Frailty, thy name is woman!
[William Shakespeare *Hamlet*]

Men, at most, differ as Heaven and earth,
But women, worst and best, as Heaven and Hell
[Alfred, Lord Tennyson *Merlin and Vivien*]

A woman, especially, if she have the misfortune of knowing anything, should conceal it as well as she can
[Jane Austen *Northanger Abbey*]

A woman's place is in the wrong
[James Thurber]

I expect that woman will be the last thing civilized by man
[George Meredith]

A woman who thinks she is intelligent demands equal rights with men. A woman who is intelligent does not
[Colette]

Whatever women do they must do twice as well as men to be thought half as good. Luckily this is not difficult
[Charlotte Whitton]

I hate women because they always know where things are
[James Thurber]

Most women are not as young as they are painted
[Sir Max Beerbohm]

She's the sort of woman who lives for others – you can tell the others by their hunted expression
[C.S. Lewis *The Screwtape Letters*]

A woman knows enough if she knows enough to mend our shirts and cook us a steak
[Pierre-Joseph Proudhon]

Man has his will; but woman has her way
[O.W. Holmes]

All women become like their mothers. That is their tragedy. No man does. That's his
[Oscar Wilde *The Importance of Being Earnest*]

When women go wrong, men go right after them
[Mae West]

Women – one half of the human race at least – care fifty times more for a marriage than a ministry
[Walter Bagehot *The English Constitution*]

Women can't forgive failure
[Anton Chekhov *The Seagull*]

Women, then, are only children of a larger growth
[Lord Chesterfield *Letters to his Son*]

Can anything be more absurd than keeping women in a state of ignorance, and yet so vehemently to insist on their resisting temptation?
[Vicesimus Knox]

Women are really much nicer than men: no wonder we like them
[Kingsley Amis *A Bookshop Idyll*]

Any woman who chooses to behave like a full human being should be warned that the armies of the status quo will treat her as something of a dirty joke
[Gloria Steinem *Outrageous Acts and Everyday Rebellions*]

There are only three things to be done with a woman. You can love her, suffer for her, or turn her into literature
[Lawrence Durrell *Justine*]

If all men are born free, how is it that all women are born slaves?
[Mary Astell *Some Reflections upon Marriage*]

Good women always think it is their fault when someone else is being offensive. Bad women never take the blame for anything
[Anita Brookner *Hotel du Lac*]

O fairest of creation, last and best
Of all God's works
[John Milton *Paradise Lost*]

Music and women I cannot but give way to, whatever my business is
[Samuel Pepys *Diary*]

PROVERBS

A woman's place is in the home
Hell hath no fury like a woman scorned
A woman's work is never done

womanly ADJECTIVE **1 = feminine**, motherly, female, warm, tender, matronly, ladylike: *the accepted womanly qualities of compassion and unselfishness* **2 = curvaceous**, ample, voluptuous, shapely, curvy *(informal)*, busty *(informal)*, buxom, full-figured, Rubenesque, Junoesque: *a womanly figure*

wonder VERB **1 = think**, question, doubt, puzzle, speculate, query, ponder, inquire, ask yourself, meditate, be curious, conjecture, be inquisitive: *I wonder what he's up to; We were wondering where you were.* **2 = be amazed**, stare, marvel, be astonished, gape, boggle, be awed, be flabbergasted *(informal)*, gawk, be dumbstruck, stand amazed: *I wondered at the arrogance of the man.*
▷ NOUN **1 = amazement**, surprise, curiosity, admiration, awe, fascination, astonishment, bewilderment, wonderment, stupefaction: *'How did you know that?' Bobby exclaimed in wonder.* **2 = phenomenon**, sight, miracle, spectacle, curiosity, marvel, prodigy, rarity, portent, wonderment, nonpareil: *a fascinating lecture on the wonders of nature*

THE SEVEN WONDERS OF THE ANCIENT WORLD

Colossus of Rhodes
Hanging Gardens of Babylon
Mausoleum of Halicarnassus
Pharos of Alexandria
Phidias' statue of Zeus at Olympia
Pyramids of Egypt
Temple of Artemis at Ephesus

wonderful ADJECTIVE **1 = excellent**, mean *(slang)*, great *(informal)*, topping *(Brit. slang)*, brilliant, cracking *(Brit. informal)*, outstanding, smashing *(informal)*, superb, fantastic *(informal)*, tremendous, ace *(informal)*, magnificent, fabulous *(informal)*, marvellous, terrific, sensational *(informal)*, sovereign, awesome *(slang)*, admirable, super *(informal)*, brill *(informal)*, stupendous, out of this world *(informal)*, tiptop, bodacious *(slang, chiefly U.S.)*, boffo *(slang)*, jim-dandy *(slang)*, chillin' *(U.S. slang)*, booshit *(Austral. slang)*, exo *(Austral. slang)*, sik *(Austral. slang)*, rad *(informal)*, phat *(slang)*, schmick *(Austral. informal)*: *I've always thought he was a wonderful actor.* **OPPOSITE:** terrible **2 = remarkable**, surprising, odd, strange, amazing, extraordinary, fantastic, incredible, astonishing, staggering, eye-popping *(informal)*, marvellous, startling, peculiar, awesome, phenomenal, astounding, miraculous, unheard-of, wondrous *(archaic, literary)*, awe-inspiring, jaw-dropping: *This is a wonderful achievement for one so young.* **OPPOSITE:** ordinary

wonky ADJECTIVE **1 = askew**, squint *(informal)*, awry, out of alignment, skewwhiff *(Brit. informal)*: *The wheels of the trolley kept going wonky.* **2 = shaky**, weak, wobbly, unsteady, infirm: *He's got a wonky knee.*

wont ADJECTIVE **= accustomed**, used, given, in the habit of: *Both have made mistakes, as human beings are wont to do.*

▷ NOUN **= habit**, use, way, rule, practice, custom: *Keith woke early, as was his wont.*

woo VERB **1 = seek**, cultivate, try to attract, curry favour with, seek to win, solicit the goodwill of: *The bank wooed customers by offering low interest rates.* **2 = court**, chase, pursue, spark (*rare*), importune, seek to win, pay court to, seek the hand of, set your cap at (*old-fashioned*), pay your addresses to, pay suit to, press your suit with: *The penniless author successfully wooed and married Roxanne.*

wood NOUN **1 = timber**, planks, planking, lumber (*U.S.*): *The floor is made of polished wood.* **2 = woodland**, trees, forest, grove, hurst (*archaic*), thicket, copse, coppice, bushland: *After dinner they went for a walk through the wood.* **3 = firewood**, fuel, logs, kindling: *We gathered wood for the fire.*
out of the wood(s) (*used in negative constructions*) **= safe**, clear, secure, in the clear, out of danger, home and dry (*Brit. slang*), safe and sound: *The nation's economy is not out of the woods yet.*
▸ *related adjectives:* ligneous, sylvan

wooded ADJECTIVE **= tree-covered**, forested, timbered, woody, sylvan (*poetic*), tree-clad

wooden ADJECTIVE **1 = made of wood**, timber, woody, of wood, ligneous: *the shop's bare brick walls and wooden floorboards* **2 = awkward**, stiff, rigid, clumsy, lifeless, stilted, ungainly, gauche, gawky, inelegant, graceless, maladroit: *The film is marred by the wooden acting of the star.*
OPPOSITE: graceful
3 = expressionless, empty, dull, blank, vacant, lifeless, deadpan, colourless, glassy, unresponsive, unemotional, emotionless, spiritless: *It's hard to tell from his wooden expression whether he's happy or sad.*

wool NOUN **1 = fleece**, hair, coat: *These shawls are made from the wool of mountain goats.* **2 = yarn**: *a ball of wool*
pull the wool over someone's eyes = deceive, kid (*informal*), trick, fool, take in (*informal*), con (*slang*), dupe, delude, bamboozle (*informal*), hoodwink, put one over on (*slang*), pull a fast one on someone (*informal*), lead someone up the garden path (*informal*): *a phony psychic who pulled the wool over everyone's eyes*

woolly or (*sometimes U.S.*) **wooly** ADJECTIVE **1 = woollen**, fleecy, made of wool: *She wore a woolly hat with pompoms.* **2 = vague**, confused, clouded, blurred, unclear, muddled, fuzzy, indefinite, hazy, foggy, nebulous, ill-defined, indistinct: *It is no good setting vague, woolly goals – we need a specific aim.*
OPPOSITE: precise **3 = downy**, hairy, shaggy, flocculent: *The plant has silvery, woolly leaves.*
▷ NOUN **= sweater**, jersey, jumper, pullover: *Bring a woolly – it can get cold here at night.*

word NOUN **1 = term**, name, expression, designation, appellation (*formal*), locution, vocable: *The word 'ginseng' comes from the Chinese word 'Shen-seng'.* **2 = chat**, tête-à-tête, talk, discussion, consultation, chitchat, brief conversation, colloquy, confabulation, confab (*informal*), heart-to-heart, powwow (*informal*): *James, could I have a quick word with you?* **3 = comment**, remark, expression, declaration, utterance, brief statement: *I'd like to say a word of thanks to everyone who helped me.* **4 = message**, news, latest (*informal*), report, information, account, notice, advice, communication, intelligence, bulletin, dispatch, gen (*Brit. informal*), communiqué, intimation, tidings, heads up (*U.S. & Canad.*): *There is no word from the authorities on the reported attack.* **5 = promise**, guarantee, pledge, undertaking, vow, assurance, oath, parole, word of honour, solemn oath, solemn word: *He simply cannot be trusted to keep his word.* **6 = command**, will, order, go-ahead (*informal*), decree, bidding, mandate, commandment, edict, ukase (*rare*): *I want nothing said about this until I give the word.*
▷ VERB **= express**, say, state, put, phrase, utter, couch, formulate: *If I had written the letter, I might have worded it differently.*
in a word = briefly, in short, in a nutshell, to sum up, succinctly, concisely, not to put too fine a point on it, to put it briefly: *'Don't you like her?' 'In a word – no.'*
the last word 1 = final say, ultimatum: *Our manager has the last word on all major decisions.* **2 = summation**, finis: *We'll let this gentleman have the last word.*
the last word in something = epitome, newest, best, latest, crown, cream, rage, ultimate, vogue, perfection, mother of all (*informal*), quintessence, the crème de la crème, ne plus ultra (*French*), dernier cri (*French*): *The spa is the last word in luxury.*
▸ *related adjectives:* lexical, verbal

QUOTATIONS

In the beginning was the Word
[*Bible: St. John*]

Words are, of course, the most powerful drug used by mankind
[Rudyard Kipling]

For words, like Nature, half reveal
And half conceal the Soul within
[Alfred, Lord Tennyson]

I am a bear of Very Little Brain, and long words Bother me
[A.A. Milne *Winnie-the-Pooh*]

'When I use a word,' Humpty Dumpty said in a rather scornful tone, 'it means just what I choose it to mean – neither more nor less.'
[Lewis Carroll *Through the Looking-Glass*]

Words just say what you want them to say; they don't know any better
[A.L. Kennedy *The Role of Notable Silences in Scottish History*]

and once sent out, a word takes wing beyond recall
[Horace *Epistles*]

Words are the physicians of a mind diseased
[Aeschylus *Prometheus Bound*]

Thought flies and words go on foot
[Julien Green *Journal*]

How often misused words generate misleading thoughts
[Herbert Spencer *Principles of Ethics*]

Words are the tokens current and accepted for conceits, as moneys are for values
[Francis Bacon *The Advancement of Learning*]

Words are wise men's counters, they do but reckon by them
[Thomas Hobbes *Leviathan*]

Oaths are but words, and words but wind
[Samuel Butler *Hudibras*]

wording NOUN **= phraseology**, words, language, phrasing, terminology, choice of words, mode of expression

wordy ADJECTIVE **= long-winded**, rambling, windy, diffuse, garrulous, discursive, loquacious, verbose, prolix, pleonastic (*rare*)
OPPOSITE: brief

work VERB **1 = be employed**, do business, have a job, earn a living, be in work, hold down a job: *I want to work, I don't want to be on welfare.*
2 = labour, sweat, slave, toil, slog (away), drudge, peg away, exert yourself, break your back: *My father worked hard all his life.* **OPPOSITE:** relax
3 = function, go, run, operate, perform, be in working order: *The pump doesn't work and we have no running water.* **OPPOSITE:** be out of order
4 = succeed, work out, pay off (*informal*), be successful, be effective, do the trick (*informal*), do the business (*informal*), get results, turn out well, have the desired result, go as planned, do the business (*informal*): *Most of these diets don't work.*
5 = accomplish, cause, create, effect, achieve, carry out, implement, execute, bring about, encompass, contrive: *Modern medicine can work miracles.* **6 = handle**, move, excite, manipulate, rouse, stir up, agitate, incite, whip up, galvanize: *a performer with the ability to work an audience*
7 = cultivate, farm, dig, till, plough: *Farmers worked the fertile valleys.*
8 = operate, use, move, control, drive, manage, direct, handle, manipulate, wield, ply: *I learnt how to work the forklift.*
9 = manipulate, make, form, process, fashion, shape, handle, mould, knead: *Work the dough with your hands until it is very smooth.* **10 = progress**, move, force, manoeuvre, make your way: *Rescuers were still working their way towards the trapped men.* **11 = move**, twitch, writhe, convulse, be agitated:

His face was working in his sleep. **12 = contrive**, handle, fix *(informal)*, swing *(informal)*, arrange, exploit, manipulate, pull off, fiddle *(informal)*, bring off: *Some clever people work it so that they never have to pay taxes.*
▷ NOUN **1 = employment**, calling, business, job, line, office, trade, duty, craft, profession, occupation, pursuit, livelihood, métier: *What kind of work do you do?* **OPPOSITE:** play **2 = effort**, industry, labour, grind *(informal)*, sweat, toil, slog, exertion, drudgery, travail *(literary)*, elbow grease *(facetious)*: *This needs time and a lot of hard work.* **OPPOSITE:** leisure **3 = task**, jobs, projects, commissions, duties, assignments, chores, yakka *(Austral. & N.Z. informal)*: *I used to take work home, but I don't do it any more.* **4 = handiwork**, doing, act, feat, deed: *Police say the bombing was the work of extremists.* **5 = creation**, performance, piece, production, opus, achievement, composition, oeuvre *(French)*, handiwork: *In my opinion, this is Rembrandt's greatest work.*

work out 1 = happen, go, result, develop, come out, turn out, evolve, pan out *(informal)*: *Things didn't work out as planned.* **2 = succeed**, flourish, go well, be effective, prosper, go as planned, prove satisfactory, do the business *(informal)*: *I hope everything works out for you in your new job.* **3 = exercise**, train, practise, drill, warm up, do exercises: *I work out at a gym twice a week.*

work out at something = amount to, come to, reach, add up to, reach a total of: *The price per pound works out at £3.20.*

work someone up = excite, move, spur, wind up *(informal)*, arouse, animate, rouse, stir up, agitate, inflame, incite, instigate, get someone all steamed up *(slang)*: *By now she had worked herself up so much that she couldn't sleep.*

work something out 1 = solve, find out, resolve, calculate, figure out, clear up, suss (out) *(slang)*, puzzle out: *It took me some time to work out what was going on.* **2 = plan**, form, develop, arrange, construct, evolve, devise, elaborate, put together, formulate, contrive: *Negotiators are due to meet today to work out a compromise.*

work something up = generate, rouse, instigate, foment, enkindle: *Malcolm worked up the courage to ask his grandfather for help.*

QUOTATIONS

I just don't happen to think [work]'s an appropriate subject for an ethic
[Barbara Ehrenreich *Goodbye to the Work Ethic*]

Work expands so as to fill the time available for its completion
[N. Northcote Parkinson *Parkinson's Law*]

I mean, really: *Why work?* Simply to buy more *stuff?*
[Douglas Coupland *Generation X*]

Work is the curse of the drinking classes
[Oscar Wilde]

Work is the great cure of all maladies and miseries that ever beset mankind
[Thomas Carlyle]

If any would not work, neither should he eat
[Bible: II Thessalonians]

All that matters is love and work
[attributed to Sigmund Freud]

Anyone can do any amount of work, provided it isn't the work he is supposed to be doing
[Robert Benchley]

PROVERBS

All work and no play makes Jack a dull boy

workable ADJECTIVE **= viable**, possible, practical, feasible, practicable, doable
OPPOSITE: unworkable

workaday ADJECTIVE **= ordinary**, common, familiar, practical, routine, everyday, commonplace, mundane, prosaic, run-of-the-mill, humdrum, bog-standard *(Brit. & Irish slang)*
OPPOSITE: extraordinary

worker NOUN **= employee**, hand, labourer, workman, craftsman, artisan, tradesman, wage earner, proletarian, working man *or* working woman

QUOTATIONS

The proletarians have nothing to lose but their chains. They have a world to win. Workers of all countries unite!
[Marx & Engels *The Communist Manifesto*]

working ADJECTIVE **1 = employed**, labouring, in work, in a job: *Like most working women, I use a lot of convenience foods.* **2 = functioning**, going, running, operating, active, operative, operational, functional, usable, serviceable, in working order: *the oldest working steam engine in the world* **3 = effective**, useful, practical, sufficient, adequate: *I used to have a good working knowledge of French.*
▷ NOUN **= operation**, running, action, method, functioning, manner, mode of operation: *computer systems which mimic the workings of the human brain*
▷ PLURAL NOUN **= mine**, pit, shaft, quarry, excavations, diggings: *housing which was built over old mine workings*

workman NOUN **= labourer**, hand, worker, employee, mechanic, operative, craftsman, artisan, tradesman, journeyman, artificer *(rare)*

PROVERBS

A bad workman always blames his tools

workmanlike ADJECTIVE **= efficient**, professional, skilled, expert, masterly, careful, satisfactory, thorough, skilful, adept, painstaking, proficient **OPPOSITE:** amateurish

workmanship NOUN **= skill**, work, art, technique, manufacture, craft, expertise, execution, artistry, craftsmanship, handiwork, handicraft

workout NOUN **= exercise**, training, drill, warm-up, training session, practice session, exercise session

works PLURAL NOUN **1 = factory**, shop, plant, mill, workshop: *the belching chimneys of the steelworks at Corby* **2 = writings**, productions, output, canon, oeuvre *(French)*: *the complete works of Milton* **3 = deeds**, acts, actions, doings: *a religious order who dedicated their lives to prayer and good works* **4 = mechanism**, workings, parts, action, insides *(informal)*, movement, guts *(informal)*, machinery, moving parts, innards *(informal)*: *The box held what looked like the works of a large clock.*

workshop NOUN **1 = seminar**, class, discussion group, study group, masterclass: *She runs a writing workshop for women.* **2 = factory**, works, shop, plant, mill: *a small workshop for repairing secondhand motorcycles* **3 = workroom**, studio, atelier: *He got a job in the workshop of a local tailor.*

world NOUN **1 = earth**, planet, globe, earthly sphere: *It's a beautiful part of the world.* **2 = mankind**, man, men, everyone, the public, everybody, humanity, human race, humankind, the race of man: *The world was shocked by this heinous crime.* **3 = sphere**, system, area, field, environment, province, kingdom, realm, domain: *The publishing world had never seen an event quite like this.* **4 = life**, nature, existence, creation, universe, cosmos: *Be happy, in this world and the next!* **5 = planet**, star, orb, heavenly body: *conditions which would support life on other worlds* **6 = period**, times, days, age, era, epoch: *What was life like for the ordinary man in the medieval world?*

a world of = a huge amount of, a mountain of, a wealth of, a great deal of, a good deal of, an abundance of, an enormous amount of, a vast amount of: *They may look alike but there's a world of difference between them.*

for all the world = exactly, just like, precisely, in every way, to all intents and purposes, just as if, in every respect: *He looked for all the world as if he was dead.*

on top of the world = overjoyed, happy, ecstatic, elated, over the moon *(informal)*, exultant, on cloud nine *(informal)*, cock-a-hoop, in raptures, beside yourself with joy, stoked *(Austral. & N.Z. informal)*: *After his win, he was on top of the world.*

out of this world = wonderful, great *(informal)*, excellent, superb, fantastic *(informal)*, incredible, fabulous *(informal)*, marvellous, unbelievable, awesome *(slang)*, indescribable, bodacious *(slang, chiefly U.S.)*, booshit *(Austral. slang)*, exo *(Austral. slang)*, sik *(Austral. slang)*, rad *(informal)*, phat

W

Sir Walter Scott's Use of Verbs

A large part of the appeal of Walter Scott's novels is their historical settings, and, like all historical novelists, Scott uses language to evoke a sense of bygone years. This is particularly evident in his verbs, where he often uses the older *-eth* endings of third person singulars, as in *he loveth* and *she hath*. This form ultimately derives from Old English, and was the norm up until around the 17th century, when it began to be replaced with the *-s* form that we know today: *he loves, she has*. Scott makes frequent use of the function words *hath* and *doth*, particularly in *Ivanhoe* (set in the Middle Ages) and *Kenilworth* (set in the 16th century):

> 'The monk **hath** some fair penitent to shrive to-night, that he is in such a hurry to depart,' said De Bracy.

Has is more frequent in *Waverley* and *Rob Roy*, set in the 18th century, although there are smatterings of *hath* in these as well. Scott also uses *-eth* forms of other verbs, even those borrowed from Latin: the resulting polysyllabic nature of these verbs makes them rather cumbersome and even more noticeable as archaisms:

> If ingratitude **comprehendeth** every vice...

> We shall learn whether this Hakim **hath** really the art of curing which he **professeth**...

> ...we islanders love not blows, save those of holy Church, who **chasteneth** whom she **loveth**.

In addition, Scott makes frequent use of the old *thou-you* distinction which modern English has lost: *thou* is used, like French *tu* and German *Du*, to address individuals, close friends, and subordinates; *you* is used, like *vous* and *Sie*, to address groups, people one does not know, and people in authority. *Thou* is used throughout Scott's novels to create a sense of pastness, and with it verbs ending in *-st*: *thou hast, thou didst, thou lovest*, and so on. However, there are occasional uses of the modern form:

> **Thou** shall not want one faithful friend To share the cruel fates' decree.

> 'And how much money,' continued Isaac, 'has **thou** brought with thee?

The use of *shall* and *has* here (rather than *shalt* and *hast*) remind us that this is not the language that came naturally to Scott: rather, it is a created language intended to strike the reader as old.

Other archaic features of Scott's prose include the use of the impersonal verb *methinks*, which was already fossilized by Shakespeare's time and is only used jocularly in modern English. His novels are also peppered with verbs such as *forespeak* ('prophesy, predict') and *aroint* ('begone!'):

> For I would sooner face fifty deevils as my master's ghaist, or even his wraith; wherefore, **aroint** ye, if ye were ten times my master, unless ye come in bodily shape, lith and limb.

The centrality of fighting and war is evident in Scott's verbs. *Die* is unsurprisingly frequent; people *die a death, die bitterly* or *bravely, die by the sword*, and *die in exile/poverty/peace/misery*. There are many descriptions of *fighting*, and people *fight bravely, valiantly*, and *well*. Archaism is again evident in Scott's use of the past participle form *foughten* alongside the more modern *fought*: it is used both as an adjective (*a foughten field*) and as a verb (*the field must be foughten*). The archaic *slay* is almost as frequent as its synonym *kill*, but Scott almost always uses it in the participle form *slain*, as in *they were both slain in battle* and *a new slain knight*. Other verbs are not immediately obvious as associated with war, but upon investigation it is evident that they are often used in a war-related sense in Scott's novels. The most salient collocates with *draw*, for example, are *sword* and *weapon*, and there are also examples of *drawing blood*. *Fall* is often used in phrases associated with fighting: armies *fall back* and soldiers *fall down* or *fall in battle*; they also occasionally *fall with honour*.

(slang), schmick *(Austral. informal)*: *The food in this place is simply out of this world.*

worldly ADJECTIVE **1 = earthly**, lay, physical, fleshly, secular, mundane, terrestrial, temporal, carnal, profane, sublunary: *It is time you woke up and focused your thoughts on more worldly matters.* **OPPOSITE:** spiritual **2 = materialistic**, grasping, selfish, greedy, avaricious, covetous, worldly-minded: *He has repeatedly criticized Western churches as being too worldly.* **OPPOSITE:** nonmaterialistic **3 = worldly-wise**, knowing, experienced, politic, sophisticated, cosmopolitan, urbane, blasé, well versed in the ways of the world: *He was worldly and sophisticated, quite unlike me.* **OPPOSITE:** naive

> **QUOTATIONS**
> Be wisely worldly, be not worldly wise
> [Francis Quarles *Emblems*]

worldwide ADJECTIVE **= global**, general, international, universal, ubiquitous, omnipresent, pandemic **OPPOSITE:** limited

worn ADJECTIVE **1 = ragged**, shiny, frayed, shabby, tattered, tatty, threadbare, the worse for wear: *an elderly man in well-cut but worn clothes* **2 = haggard**, lined, drawn, pinched, wizened, careworn: *A sudden smile lit up his worn face.* **3 = exhausted**, spent, tired, fatigued, wearied, weary, played-out *(informal)*, worn-out, jaded, tired out: *She looked tired and worn.*

worn out ADJECTIVE **1 = worn**, done, used, broken-down, ragged, useless, rundown, frayed, used-up, shabby, tattered, tatty, threadbare, decrepit, clapped out *(Brit., Austral. & N.Z. informal)*, moth-eaten: *Always replace worn out tyres with the same brand.* **2 = exhausted**, spent, done in *(informal)*, tired, all in *(slang)*, fatigued, wiped out *(informal)*, weary, played-out, knackered *(slang)*, prostrate, clapped out *(Austral. & N.Z. informal)*, tired out, dog-tired *(informal)*, zonked *(slang)*, shagged out *(Brit. slang)*, fit to drop, jiggered *(dialect)*, dead or out on your feet *(informal)*: *I was exhausted – worn out by the strain I'd been under.* **OPPOSITE:** refreshed

W

worried ADJECTIVE **= anxious**, concerned, troubled, upset, afraid, bothered, frightened, wired *(slang)*, nervous, disturbed, distressed, tense, distracted, uneasy, fearful, tormented, distraught, apprehensive, perturbed, on edge, ill at ease, overwrought, fretful, hot and bothered, unquiet, antsy *(informal)* **OPPOSITE:** unworried

worrisome ADJECTIVE **= disturbing**, worrying, upsetting, distressing, troublesome, disquieting, vexing, perturbing, irksome, bothersome

worry VERB **1 = be anxious**, be concerned, be worried, obsess, brood, fret, agonize, feel uneasy, get in a lather *(informal)*, get in a sweat *(informal)*, get in a tizzy *(informal)*, get overwrought: *I worry about my daughter constantly.* **OPPOSITE:** be unconcerned **2 = trouble**, upset, harry, bother, disturb, distress, annoy, plague, irritate, tease, unsettle, torment, harass, hassle *(informal)*, badger, hector, disquiet, pester, vex, perturb, tantalize, importune, make anxious: *'Why didn't you tell us?' 'I didn't want to worry you.'* **OPPOSITE:** soothe
▷ NOUN **1 = anxiety**, concern, care, fear, trouble, misery, disturbance, torment, woe, irritation, unease, apprehension, misgiving, annoyance, trepidation, perplexity, vexation: *His last years were overshadowed by financial worry.* **OPPOSITE:** peace of mind **2 = problem**, care, trouble, trial, bother, plague, pest, torment, irritation, hassle *(informal)*, annoyance, vexation: *Robert's health had always been a worry to his wife.*

worsen VERB **1 = deteriorate**, decline, sink, decay, get worse, degenerate, go downhill *(informal)*, go from bad to worse, take a turn for the worse, retrogress: *The security forces had to intervene to prevent the situation from worsening.* **OPPOSITE:** improve **2 = aggravate**, damage, exacerbate, make worse: *These options would actually worsen the economy and add to the deficit.* **OPPOSITE:** improve

worship VERB **1 = revere**, praise, respect, honour, adore, glorify, reverence, exalt, laud, pray to, venerate, deify, adulate: *people who still worship the pagan gods* **OPPOSITE:** dishonour **2 = love**, adore, idolize, put on a pedestal: *The children worship their father.* **OPPOSITE:** despise
▷ NOUN **= reverence**, praise, love, regard, respect, honour, glory, prayer(s), devotion, homage, adulation, adoration, admiration, exaltation, glorification, deification, laudation: *The temple had been a centre of worship of the goddess Hathor.*

worth NOUN **1 = value**, price, rate, cost, estimate, valuation: *The total worth of the Australian sharemarket is now close to $520 billion.* **OPPOSITE:** worthlessness **2 = merit**, value, quality, importance, desert(s), virtue, excellence, goodness, estimation, worthiness: *She did not appreciate her husband's true worth until he was gone.* **OPPOSITE:** unworthiness **3 = usefulness**, value, benefit, quality, importance, utility, excellence, goodness: *The client has little means of judging the worth of the advice he is given.* **OPPOSITE:** uselessness

worthless ADJECTIVE **1 = valueless**, poor, miserable, trivial, trifling, paltry, trashy, measly, wretched, two a penny *(informal)*, rubbishy, poxy *(slang)*, nickel-and-dime *(U.S. slang)*, wanky *(taboo, slang)*, a dime a dozen, nugatory, negligible: *This piece of old junk is totally worthless.* **OPPOSITE:** valuable **2 = useless**, meaningless, pointless, futile, no use, insignificant, unimportant, ineffectual, unusable, unavailing, not much cop *(Brit. slang)*, inutile, not worth a hill of beans *(chiefly U.S.)*, negligible, pants *(slang)*: *Training is worthless unless there is proof that it works.* **OPPOSITE:** useful **3 = good-for-nothing**, base, abandoned, useless, vile, abject, despicable, depraved, contemptible, ignoble: *Murphy was an evil, worthless man.* **OPPOSITE:** honourable

worthwhile ADJECTIVE **= useful**, good, valuable, helpful, worthy, profitable, productive, beneficial, meaningful, constructive, justifiable, expedient, gainful **OPPOSITE:** useless

worthy ADJECTIVE **= praiseworthy**, good, excellent, deserving, valuable, decent, reliable, worthwhile, respectable, upright, admirable, honourable, honest, righteous, reputable, virtuous, dependable, commendable, creditable, laudable, meritorious, estimable: *worthy members of the community* **OPPOSITE:** disreputable
▷ NOUN **= dignitary**, notable, luminary, bigwig *(informal)*, big shot *(informal)*, personage, big hitter *(informal)*, heavy hitter *(informal)*: *The event brought together worthies from many fields.* **OPPOSITE:** nobody

would-be ADJECTIVE **= budding**, potential, so-called, professed, dormant, self-styled, latent, wannabe *(informal)*, unfulfilled, undeveloped, self-appointed, unrealized, manqué, soi-disant *(French)*, quasi-

wound NOUN **1 = injury**, cut, damage, hurt, harm, slash, trauma *(Pathology)*, gash, lesion, laceration: *Six soldiers are reported to have died of their wounds.* **2** *(often plural)* **= trauma**, injury, shock, pain, offence, slight, torture, distress, insult, grief, torment, anguish, heartbreak, pang, sense of loss: *Her experiences have left deep psychological wounds.*
▷ VERB **1 = injure**, cut, hit, damage, wing, hurt, harm, slash, pierce, irritate, gash, lacerate: *The driver of the bus was wounded by shrapnel.* **2 = offend**, shock, pain, hurt, distress, annoy, sting, grieve, mortify, cut to the quick, hurt the feelings of, traumatize: *He was deeply wounded by the treachery of his closest friends.*

> **QUOTATIONS**
> what wound did ever heal but by degrees?
> [William Shakespeare *Othello*]

wounding ADJECTIVE **= hurtful**, pointed, cutting, damaging, acid, bitter, slighting, offensive, distressing, insulting, cruel, savage, stinging, destructive, harmful, malicious, scathing, grievous, barbed, unkind, pernicious, caustic, spiteful, vitriolic, trenchant, injurious, maleficent

wrangle VERB **= argue**, fight, row, dispute, scrap, disagree, fall out *(informal)*, contend, quarrel, brawl, squabble, spar, bicker, have words, altercate: *The two parties are still wrangling over the timing of the election.*
▷ NOUN **= argument**, row, clash, dispute, contest, set-to *(informal)*, controversy, falling-out *(informal)*, quarrel, brawl, barney *(informal)*, squabble, bickering, tiff, altercation, slanging match *(Brit.)*, angry exchange, argy-bargy *(Brit. informal)*, bagarre *(French)*: *He was involved in a legal wrangle with the Health Secretary.*

wrap VERB **1 = cover**, surround, fold, enclose, roll up, cloak, shroud, swathe, muffle, envelop, encase, sheathe, enfold, bundle up: *She wrapped the baby in a blanket.* **OPPOSITE:** uncover **2 = pack**, package, parcel (up), tie up, gift-wrap: *Harry had wrapped some presents for the children.* **OPPOSITE:** unpack **3 = bind**, wind, fold, swathe: *She wrapped a handkerchief round her bleeding hand.* **OPPOSITE:** unwind
▷ NOUN **= cloak**, cape, stole, mantle, shawl: *a model wearing a leopard-print wrap*
wrap something up 1 = giftwrap, pack, package, enclose, bundle up, enwrap: *We spent the evening wrapping up Christmas presents.* **2 = end**, conclude, wind up, terminate, finish off, round off, tidy up, polish off, bring to a close: *NATO defence ministers wrap up their meeting in Brussels today.*
wrap up = dress warmly, muffle up, wear something warm, put warm clothes on: *Make sure you wrap up warmly before you go out.*

wrapper NOUN **= cover**, case, paper, packaging, wrapping, jacket, envelope, sleeve, sheath

wrath NOUN **= anger**, passion, rage, temper, fury, resentment, irritation, indignation, ire, displeasure, exasperation, choler **OPPOSITE:** satisfaction

> **QUOTATIONS**
> The tigers of wrath are wiser than the horses of instruction
> [William Blake *Proverbs of Hell*]
>
> I was angry with my friend,
> I told my wrath, my wrath did end.
> I was angry with my foe,
> I told it not, my wrath did grow
> [William Blake *A Poison Tree*]
>
> nursing her wrath to keep it warm
> [Robert Burns *Tam o' Shanter*]
>
> wrath: anger of a superior quality and degree, appropriate to exalted characters and momentous occasions
> [Ambrose Bierce *The Devil's Dictionary*]

wreak VERB **1 = create**, work, cause, visit, effect, exercise, carry out, execute, inflict, bring about: *Violent storms wreaked havoc on the coast.* **2 = unleash**, express, indulge, vent, gratify, give vent to, give free rein to: *He wreaked vengeance on the men who had betrayed him.*

wreath NOUN **= garland**, band, ring, crown, loop, festoon, coronet, chaplet

wreathe VERB **1 = surround**, envelop, encircle, enfold, coil around, writhe around, enwrap: *Cigarette smoke wreathed her face.* **2 = festoon**, wind, crown, wrap, twist, coil, adorn, intertwine, interweave, entwine, twine, engarland: *The temple's huge columns were wreathed in laurels.*

wreck VERB **1 = destroy**, break, total *(slang)*, smash, ruin, devastate, mar, shatter, spoil, demolish, sabotage, trash *(slang)*, ravage, dash to pieces, kennet *(Austral. slang)*, jeff *(Austral. slang)*: *Vandals wrecked the garden.* **OPPOSITE:** build **2 = spoil**, blow *(slang)*, ruin, devastate, shatter, undo, screw up *(informal)*, cock up *(Brit. slang)*, play havoc with, crool or cruel *(Austral. slang)*: *His life has been wrecked by the tragedy.* **OPPOSITE:** save **3 = run aground**, strand, shipwreck, run onto the rocks: *His ship was wrecked off the coast of Ireland.*
▷ NOUN **1 = shipwreck**, derelict, hulk, sunken vessel: *the wreck of a sailing ship* **2 = ruin**, mess, destruction, overthrow, undoing, disruption, devastation, desolation: *a broken man contemplating the wreck of his life* **OPPOSITE:** preservation **3 = remains**, pieces, ruin, fragments, debris, rubble, hulk, wrack **4 = accident**, smash, pile-up: *He was killed in a car wreck.*

wrench VERB **1 = twist**, force, pull, tear, rip, tug, jerk, yank, wring, wrest: *They wrenched open the passenger door and got into the car.* **2 = sprain**, strain, rick, distort: *He had wrenched his ankle badly in the fall.*
▷ NOUN **1 = twist**, pull, rip, tug, jerk, yank: *The rope stopped his fall with a wrench that broke his neck.* **2 = sprain**, strain, twist: *We are hoping the injury is just a wrench.* **3 = blow**, shock, pain, ache, upheaval, uprooting, pang: *I knew it would be a wrench to leave home.* **4 = spanner**, adjustable spanner, shifting spanner: *He took a wrench from his toolbox.*

wrest VERB **1 = seize**, take, win, extract: *He has been trying to wrest control from the central government.* **2 = pull**, force, strain, seize, twist, extract, wrench, wring: *She wrested the suitcase from the chauffeur's grasp.*

wrestle VERB **= fight**, battle, struggle, combat, contend, strive, grapple, tussle, scuffle

wretch NOUN **1 = poor thing**, unfortunate, poor soul, poor devil *(informal)*, miserable creature: *Before the wretch had time to reply, he was shot.* **2 = scoundrel**, rat *(informal)*, worm, villain, rogue, outcast, swine, rascal, son-of-a-bitch *(slang, chiefly U.S. & Canad.)*, profligate, vagabond, ruffian, cur, rotter *(slang, chiefly Brit.)*, scumbag *(slang)*, good-for-nothing, miscreant, bad egg *(old-fashioned, informal)*, blackguard, wrong 'un *(Austral. slang)*: *I think he's a mean-minded, vindictive old wretch.*

wretched ADJECTIVE **1 = unfortunate**, poor, sorry, hapless, pitiful, luckless, star-crossed, pitiable: *wretched people living in abject poverty* **2 = worthless**, poor, sorry, miserable, pathetic, inferior, paltry, deplorable: *What a wretched excuse!* **OPPOSITE:** excellent **3 = shameful**, mean, low, base, shabby, vile, low-down *(informal)*, paltry, despicable, contemptible, scurvy, crappy *(slang)*, poxy *(slang)*: *Politicians – I hate the whole wretched lot of them.* **OPPOSITE:** admirable **4 = ill**, poorly, sick, crook *(Austral. & N.Z. informal)*, sickly, unwell, off colour *(Brit. informal)*, under the weather *(informal)*: *The flu was making him feel absolutely wretched.*

wriggle VERB **1 = jiggle**, turn, twist, jerk, squirm, writhe: *The audience were fidgeting and wriggling in their seats.* **2 = wiggle**, jerk, wag, jiggle, waggle: *She pulled off her shoes and stockings and wriggled her toes.* **3 = crawl**, snake, worm, twist and turn, zigzag, slink: *Bauman wriggled along the passage on his stomach.*
▷ NOUN **= twist**, turn, jerk, wag, squirm, wiggle, jiggle, waggle: *With a wriggle, he freed himself from her grasp and ran off.*
wriggle out of something = twist, avoid, duck, dodge, extricate yourself from, talk your way out of, worm your way out of: *The government is trying to wriggle out of its responsibilities.*

wring VERB **= twist**, force, squeeze, extract, screw, wrench, coerce, wrest, extort

wrinkle NOUN **1 = line**, fold, crease, furrow, pucker, crow's-foot, corrugation: *His face was covered with wrinkles.* **2 = crease**, gather, fold, crumple, furrow, rumple, pucker, crinkle, corrugation: *He noticed a wrinkle in the material.*
▷ VERB **= crease**, line, gather, fold, crumple, ruck, furrow, rumple, pucker, crinkle, corrugate: *I wrinkled the velvet; The skin around her eyes had begun to wrinkle.* **OPPOSITE:** smooth

writ NOUN **= summons**, document, decree, indictment, court order, subpoena, arraignment

write VERB **1 = record**, copy, scribble, take down, inscribe, set down, transcribe, jot down, put in writing, commit to paper, indite, put down in black and white: *Write your name and address at the top of the page.* **2 = compose**, create, author, draft, pen, draw up: *She wrote articles for magazines in Paris.* **3 = correspond**, get in touch, keep in touch, write a letter, drop a line, drop a note, e-mail: *Why didn't you write and let me know you were coming?*
write something off 1 = wreck, total

(slang), crash, destroy, trash *(slang)*, smash up, damage beyond repair: *John's written off four cars. Now he sticks to public transport.* **2 = cancel**, shelve, forget about, cross out, score out, give up for lost: *The President persuaded the West to write off Polish debts.*

write something or someone off = disregard, ignore, dismiss, regard something *or* someone as finished, consider something *or* someone as unimportant: *He is fed up with people writing him off because of his age.*

QUOTATIONS

No man but a blockhead ever wrote, except for money
[Dr. Johnson]

writer NOUN **= author**, novelist, hack, columnist, scribbler, scribe, essayist, penman, wordsmith, man of letters, penpusher, littérateur, penny-a-liner *(rare)*

QUOTATIONS

The wise writer ... writes for the youth of his own generation, the critics of the next, and the schoolmasters of ever afterward
[F. Scott Fitzgerald *Some Sort of Epic Grandeur*]

Some editors are failed writers – but so are most writers
[T.S. Eliot]

Writers, like teeth, are divided into incisors and grinders
[Walter Bagehot *Estimates of some Englishmen and Scotchmen*]

writhe VERB **= squirm**, struggle, twist, toss, distort, thrash, jerk, wriggle, wiggle, contort, convulse, thresh

writing NOUN **1 = script**, hand, print, printing, fist *(informal)*, scribble, handwriting, scrawl, calligraphy, longhand, penmanship, chirography: *It's a little difficult to read your writing.* **2 = document**, work, book, letter, title, opus, publication, literature, composition, belle-lettre: *Althusser's writings are focused mainly on France.*

TEXT MESSAGING ABBREVIATIONS AND SYMBOLS

Abbreviation or symbol	Meaning
A3	anytime, anywhere, anyplace
AAM	as a matter of fact
AFAIK	as far as I know
AFK	away from keyboard
al2gethr	altogether
ALrlt	all right
ATB	all the best
ATK	at the keyboard
ATM	at the moment
ATTN	attention
B	be
B4	before
BAK	back at keyboard
BBL	be back later
BCNU	be seeing you
BFN *or* B4N	bye for now
BK *or* COZ	because
BF	boyfriend
BR	bathroom
BRB	be right back
BRT	be right there
BS	bullshit
BWD	backward
BY	busy
C	see
CIAO	goodbye
CMIIW	correct me if I'm wrong
CU	see you
CUL8R	see you later
CYA	see you
EVR	ever
EZ	easy
FC	fingers crossed
FONE	phone
4	for *or* four
4EVA	for ever
F2T	free to talk
FWD	forward
FWIW	for what it's worth
FYI	for your information
GAL	get a life
G9	genius
GF	girlfriend
GG	good game
GGG *or* GGL	giggle
GMTA	great minds think alike
GR8	great
HAND	have a nice day
H8	hate
HD	hold
IC	I see
IDD	indeed
ILU	I love you
IMHO	in my humble *or* honest opinion
IMNSHO	in my not so humble opinion
IMO	in my opinion
IOW	in other words
IRL	in real life
IRW	in the real world
IFYWIMAITYD	if you know what I mean and I think you do
K	okay
KISS	keep it simple, stupid
KIT	keep in touch
L8	late
L8R	later
LDR	long-distance relationship
LO	hello
LOL	laughing out loud
LTNS	long time no see
LUV	love
LZ	loser
M8	mate
MSG	message
MT	empty
MTG	meeting
NE	any
NE1	anyone
Njoy	enjoy
NO1	no-one
NRN	no reply necessary
OFN	often
OIC	oh I see
PCM	please call me
PLS	please
PLU	people like us
PPL	people
PRT	party
PRW	parents are watching
Q	queue
QL	cool
QT	quiet
R	are
RGDS	regards
ROFL	rolling on floor laughing
ROFLOL	rolling on floor laughing out loud
ROTFL	rolling on the floor laughing
ROTFLOL	rolling on the floor laughing out loud
RUOK	are you OK?
SIT	stay in touch
SK8	skate
SOHF	sense of humour failure
SOM1	someone
THX *or* TX	thanks
Ti2GO	time to go
2	to, too, *or* two
2DAY	today
2MORO	tomorrow
2NITE	tonight
TTYL	talk to you later
TXT	text
U	you
U2	you too
U4E	yours for ever
UR	you are *or* your
W8	wait
WADYA	what do you
WAN2	want to
WAN2TLK	want to talk?
WB	welcome back
WK	week
WKND	weekend
WIV	with
W/O	without
WOT	what
WTG	way to go!
X	kiss
XLNT	excellent
XOXO	hugs and kisses

W

WRITING

Types of Writing

acrostics, apologia, article, autobiography, belles-lettres, biography, blogging, calligraphy, causerie, citizen journalism, comedy, cryptograph, dialectic, diary, dissertation, drama, elegy, encomium, epitaph, epithalamium *or* epithalamion, erotica, essay, eulogy, fan fiction *or* fanfic, fansub, fantasy, farce, fiction, fisking, glossary, gonzo journalism, hagiography, history, historiography, homily, journalism, lexicography, libretto, lyric, memoirs, microblogging, miscellany, nanopublishing, nonfiction, novel, novella, parody, play, podcasting, poetry, pornography, prose, radio play, review, rhapsody, romance, saga, satire, screenplay, script, sermon, short fiction, short story, story, teleplay, tragedy, tweet, vlogging, vodcasting

Types of Writer

agony aunt *or* uncle, amorist, annotator, aphorist, apologist, belletrist, belligerati, biographer, blogger, bloggerati, calligrapher, columnist, comedian, commentator, copywriter, cryptographer, dialogist, diarist, dramatist, editor, elegist, encomiast, epitaphist, essayist, eulogist, fantasist, farceur, freelancer, gazetteer, ghostwriter, glossator, glossarist, glossist, *or* glossographer, gonzo journalist, gossip columnist, hagiographer, historian, historiographer, homilist, huckster (*U.S.*), humourist *or* humorist (*U.S.*), journalist, lexicographer, librettist, lyricist, microblogger, miscellanist, moralist, novelist, parodist, playwright, poet, pornographer, reporter, rhapsodist, satirist, screenwriter, scribe, scriptwriter, sermonist, telewriter, tragedian, troubadour, tweeter

QUOTATIONS

Writing, at its best, is a lonely life
[Ernest Hemingway *speech, accepting the Nobel Prize for Literature*]

I think writing does come out of a deep well of loneliness and a desire to fill some kind of gap
[Jay McInerney]

Would you not like to try all sorts of lives – one is so very small – but that is the satisfaction of writing – one can impersonate so many people
[Katherine Mansfield *letter*]

What is written without effort is in general read without pleasure
[Dr. Johnson *Johnsonian Miscellanies*]

Many suffer from the incurable disease of writing, and it becomes chronic in their sick minds
[Juvenal *Satires*]

All writing is garbage
[Antonin Artaud *Selected Writings*]

wrong ADJECTIVE **1 = amiss**, faulty, unsatisfactory, not right, defective, awry: *Pain is the body's way of telling us that something is wrong.* **2 = incorrect**, mistaken, false, faulty, inaccurate, untrue, erroneous, off target, unsound, in error, wide of the mark, fallacious, off base (*U.S. & Canad. informal*), off beam (*informal*), way off beam (*informal*): *That was the wrong answer – try again.* **3 = inappropriate**, incorrect, unfitting, unsuitable, unhappy, not done, unacceptable, undesirable, improper, unconventional, incongruous, unseemly, unbecoming, indecorous, inapt, infelicitous, malapropos: *I'm always embarrassing myself by saying the wrong thing.* **OPPOSITE:** correct **4 = bad**, criminal, illegal, evil, unfair, crooked, unlawful, illicit, immoral, unjust, dishonest, wicked, sinful, unethical, wrongful, under-the-table, reprehensible, dishonourable, iniquitous, not cricket (*informal*), felonious, blameworthy: *It was wrong of you to leave her alone in the house.* **OPPOSITE:** moral **5 = defective**, not working, faulty, out of order, awry, askew, out of commission: *We think there's something wrong with the computer.* **6 = opposite**, inside, reverse, inverse: *Iron the t-shirt on the wrong side to prevent damage to the design.*
▷ ADVERB **1 = incorrectly**, badly, wrongly, mistakenly, erroneously, inaccurately: *You've spelled my name wrong.* **OPPOSITE:** correctly **2 = amiss**, astray, awry, askew: *Where did we go wrong with our children?*
▷ NOUN **1 = wickedness**, injustice, unfairness, inequity, immorality, iniquity, sinfulness: *He doesn't seem to know the difference between right and wrong.* **OPPOSITE:** morality **2 = offence**, injury, crime, abuse, error, sin, injustice, grievance, infringement, trespass, misdeed, transgression, infraction, bad *or* evil deed: *I intend to right the wrong done to you.* **OPPOSITE:** good deed
▷ VERB **= mistreat**, abuse, hurt, injure, harm, cheat, take advantage of, discredit, oppress, malign, misrepresent, dump on (*slang, chiefly U.S.*), impose upon, dishonour, ill-treat, maltreat, ill-use: *She felt she had been wronged.* **OPPOSITE:** treat well
go wrong 1 = fail, flop (*informal*), fall through, come to nothing, miscarry, misfire, come to grief (*informal*), go pear-shaped (*informal*): *Nearly everything that could go wrong has gone wrong.* **2 = make a mistake**, boob (*Brit. slang*), err, slip up (*informal*), go astray: *I think I've gone wrong somewhere in my calculations.* **3 = break down**, fail, malfunction, misfire, cease to function, conk out (*informal*), go on the blink (*slang*), go kaput (*informal*), go phut (*informal*): *If your video recorder goes wrong, you can have it repaired.* **4 = lapse**, sin, err, fall from grace, go astray, go to the bad, go off the straight and narrow (*informal*): *We condemn teenagers who go wrong and punish those who step out of line.*

wrongful ADJECTIVE **= improper**, illegal, unfair, inappropriate, unlawful, illicit, immoral, unjust, illegitimate, unethical, groundless **OPPOSITE:** rightful

wry ADJECTIVE **1 = ironic**, dry, mocking, sarcastic, sardonic, droll, pawky (*Scot.*), mordacious: *a wry sense of humour* **2 = contorted**, twisted, crooked, distorted, warped, uneven, deformed, awry, askew, aslant, skewwhiff (*Brit. informal*): *She cast a wry grin in his direction.* **OPPOSITE:** straight

W

Xmas NOUN **= Christmas**, Noel, festive season, Yule *(archaic)*, Yuletide *(archaic)*, Christmastime, Christmastide, Crimbo *(Brit. informal)*

QUOTATIONS
'Twas the night before Christmas, when all through the house
Not a creature was stirring, not even a mouse
[Clement C. Moore *A Visit from St. Nicholas*]

X-ray NOUN **= radiograph**, x-ray image

X

Sir Walter Scott's Use of Adverbs

Among Scott's preferred adverbs are archaic terms such as *forth, yonder,* and *hither.* Armies and horses *sally forth* and are *poured forth* in war; blood *pours forth*; fires *break forth*; people *set forth* on journeys and *pour forth* words, prayers and thanks. In most of these expressions, *out* is now used, for example in *set out, pour out* and *break out. Forth* was already becoming archaic in Scott's day, and he uses it to imbue his historical novels with a sense of the past. *Hither* is also frequent, and most often combines with *come, return,* and *summon,* as well as *venture, gallop,* and *hasten.* Other adverbs which would have struck his readers as old forms are *fain* ('gladly'), *withal* ('as well'), and *certes* ('certainly'), and poetic contractions such as *o'er* and *e'en* are used liberally. Scott also uses many *wh-* adverbs which were already archaic in his own time, such as *wherefore, whence, whilom* ('at one time'), *wherethrough* ('because of which'), *whereuntil* ('on to which'), *whither,* and *whitherward* ('in which direction'):

> We see not **whence** the eddy comes,
> nor **whitherward** it is tending.

> an effigy... burned on the spot **whilom**
> occupied by a stately Maypole...

Some of his adverbs are specifically Scots, for example *yestreen* meaning 'yesterday evening' and *whiles* meaning 'sometimes':

> I was at the place where he had
> rested **yestreen**...

> ...but she was **whiles** well, and **whiles** ill,
> sometimes with them, and other times away
> frae them...

In the second example, the alternation between *whiles, sometimes,* and *other times* shows Scott's ability to balance Scots and English to make his novels accessible to his wide international readership. *Ay* and *aye* are also frequent, *ay* meaning 'yes' and *aye* meaning 'always', although the spellings are sometimes interchanged.

Scott also makes extensive use of manner and emphatic adverbs; for example, *truly* is over twice as frequent in his novels as it is in the *Bank of English,* Collins' corpus of present-day English. Scott sometimes uses it in its original sense 'correctly, truthfully', referring to those who *speak, say, guess, prophesy, augur,* and *judge truly.* However, we also find examples of its extended emphatic sense 'completely':

> and when he attempted to smile, in polite
> acquiescence to the truth of what the King told
> him, the grimace which he made
> was **truly** diabolical.

Other intensive adverbs that Scott favours are *deeply* (people *colour, blush, sigh, groan,* and *muse deeply,* and are *deeply impressed, engaged,* and *affected*) and *fully* (especially in *fully understand* and *fully equipped*). Another example is *utterly,* which occurs nearly three times as often in Scott's works as in the *Bank of English.* Its connotations have also shifted slightly over time: while in modern English it can be used to modify a positive adjective - one can be *utterly charming, utterly relaxed* or *utterly content* - it is only used in a negative way in Scott's works, collocating with words such as *ruined, confounded,* and *incapable.* Furthermore, *utterly* is almost always used in modern English before a participle (eg *utterly contented* or *utterly astounded*), whereas in Scott there are several examples of *utterly,* following a verb, for example *resign utterly, fail utterly,* and *slay utterly*:

> ... The voice that cried, Slay, slay - smite - slay
> **utterly** - let not your eye have pity! slay **utterly**,
> old and young, the maiden, the child, and the
> woman whose head is grey - Defile the house
> and fill the courts with the slain!

Yy

yahoo NOUN **= philistine**, savage, lout, beast, barbarian, brute, rowdy, hoon *(Austral. & N.Z.)*, roughneck *(slang)*, boor, churl, yob *or* yobbo *(Brit. slang)*, cougan *(Austral. slang)*, scozza *(Austral. slang)*, bogan *(Austral. slang)*

yak VERB **= gossip**, go on, gab *(informal)*, rabbit (on) *(Brit. informal)*, run on, jaw *(slang)*, chatter, spout, waffle *(informal, chiefly Brit.)*, yap *(informal)*, tattle, jabber, blather, chew the fat *(slang)*, witter on *(informal)*, run off at the mouth

yank VERB **= pull**, tug, jerk, seize, snatch, pluck, hitch, wrench: *She yanked the child back into the house.*
▷ NOUN **= pull**, tug, jerk, snatch, hitch, wrench, tweak: *Grabbing his ponytail, Shirley gave it a yank.*

yap VERB **1 = yelp**, bark, woof, yip *(chiefly U.S.)*: *The little dog yapped frantically.* **2 = talk**, go on, rabbit (on) *(Brit. informal)*, gossip, jaw *(slang)*, chatter, spout, babble, waffle *(informal, chiefly Brit.)*, prattle, jabber, blather, run off at the mouth *(slang)*, earbash *(Austral. & N.Z. slang)*: *She keeps yapping at me about Joe.*

yardstick NOUN **= standard**, measure, criterion, gauge, benchmark, touchstone, par

yarn NOUN **1 = thread**, fibre, cotton, wool: *vegetable-dyed yarn* **2 = story**, tale, anecdote, account, narrative, fable, reminiscence, urban myth, tall story, urban legend, cock-and-bull story *(informal)*: *Doug has a yarn or two to tell me about his trips into the bush.*

yawning ADJECTIVE **= gaping**, wide, huge, vast, wide-open, cavernous

yearly ADJECTIVE **= annual**, each year, every year, once a year: *a yearly meeting*
▷ ADVERB **= annually**, every year, by the year, once a year, per annum: *Interest is paid yearly.*

yearn VERB *(often with* **for***)* **= long**, desire, pine, pant, hunger, ache, lust, crave, covet, itch, languish, hanker after, have a yen for *(informal)*, eat your heart out over, set your heart upon, suspire *(archaic, poetic)*, would give your eyeteeth for

yell VERB **= scream**, shout, cry out, howl, call out, wail, shriek, screech, squeal, bawl, holler *(informal)*, yelp, call at the top of your voice: *He was out there shouting and yelling.*
OPPOSITE: whisper
▷ NOUN **= scream**, cry, shout, roar, howl, shriek, whoop, screech, squeal, holler *(informal)*, yelp, yowl: *He let out a yell.* **OPPOSITE:** whisper

yellow NOUN **= lemon**, gold, amber
▷ ADJECTIVE **= cowardly**, spineless, gutless, chicken *(informal)*, craven *(informal)*, faint-hearted, yellow-bellied *(informal)*, lily-livered

yelp VERB **= bark**, howl, yap, yip *(chiefly U.S.)*, yowl: *Her dog yelped and came to heel.*
▷ NOUN **= cry**, squeal: *She gave a yelp of pain.*

yen NOUN **= longing**, desire, craving, yearning, passion, hunger, ache, itch, thirst, hankering

yet ADVERB **1 = so far**, until now, up to now, still, as yet, even now, thus far, up till now, up to the present time: *They haven't finished yet.* **2 = now**, right now, just now, so soon, already: *Don't get up yet.* **3 = still**, further, in addition, as well, moreover, besides, to boot, additionally, over and above, into the bargain: *This weekend yet more uniformed soldiers were posted at official buildings.*
▷ CONJUNCTION **= nevertheless**, still, however, for all that, notwithstanding, just the same, be that as it may: *I don't eat much, yet I am a size 16.*

yield VERB **1 = bow**, submit, give in, surrender, give way, succumb, cave in *(informal)*, capitulate, knuckle under, resign yourself: *She yielded to general pressure.* **2 = relinquish**, resign, hand over, surrender, turn over, part with, make over, cede, give over, bequeath, abdicate, deliver up: *He may yield control.* **OPPOSITE:** retain
3 = surrender, give up, give in, concede defeat, cave in *(informal)*, throw in the towel, admit defeat, accept defeat, give up the struggle, knuckle under, raise the white flag, lay down your arms, cry quits: *Their leader refused to yield.* **4 = produce**, give, provide, pay, return, supply, bear, net, earn, afford, generate, bring in, furnish, bring forth: *400,000 acres of land yielded a crop worth $1.75 billion.*
OPPOSITE: use up
▷ NOUN **1 = produce**, crop, harvest, output: *improving the yield of the crop*
2 = profit, return, income, revenue, earnings, takings: *the yield on a bank's investment* **OPPOSITE:** loss
yield to something = comply with, agree to, concede, allow, grant, permit, go along with, bow to, consent to, accede to: *Television officials had yielded to demands.*

yielding ADJECTIVE **1 = soft**, pliable, springy, elastic, resilient, supple, spongy, unresisting, quaggy: *the soft yielding cushions* **2 = submissive**, obedient, compliant, docile, easy, flexible, accommodating, pliant, tractable, acquiescent, biddable: *women's yielding nature*
OPPOSITE: obstinate

yob *or* **yobbo** NOUN **= thug**, hooligan, lout, heavy *(slang)*, tough, rough *(informal)*, rowdy, yahoo, hoon *(Austral. & N.Z. slang)*, hoodlum, ruffian, roughneck *(slang)*, tsotsi *(S. African)*, cougan *(Austral. slang)*, scozza *(Austral. slang)*, bogan *(Austral. slang)*

yoke NOUN **1 = oppression**, slavery, bondage, servitude, service, burden, enslavement, serfdom, servility, vassalage, thraldom: *People are suffering under the yoke of capitalism.* **2 = harness**, coupling, tackle, chain, collar, tack: *He put a yoke around his body and pulled along the cart.*
▷ VERB **1 = unite**, join, link, tie, bond, bind, connect: *They are yoked by money and votes.* **2 = harness**, join, couple, link, tie, connect, bracket, hitch, inspan *(S. African)*: *a plough team of eight oxen yoked in pairs*

young ADJECTIVE **1 = immature**, juvenile, youthful, little, growing, green, junior, infant, adolescent, callow, unfledged, in the springtime of life: *I was still too young to understand what was going on.* **OPPOSITE:** old
2 = early, new, undeveloped, fledgling, newish, not far advanced: *the larvae, the young stages of the worm*
OPPOSITE: advanced
▷ NOUN **= offspring**, baby, litter,

SHADES OF YELLOW

almond	bistre	champagne	eau de nil	gold *or* golden	maize	ochre	straw
amber	buff	cinnamon	ecru	jasmine	mustard	old gold	tea rose
beige	butternut	citron	eggshell	lemon	nankeen	primrose	topaz
bisque	canary yellow	daffodil	gamboge	magnolia	oatmeal	saffron	tortoiseshell

family, issue, brood, little ones, progeny: *The hen may not be able to feed its young.* **OPPOSITE:** parent

youngster NOUN **= youth**, girl, boy, kid *(informal)*, lad, teenager, juvenile, cub, young person, lass, young adult, pup *(informal, chiefly Brit.)*, urchin, teenybopper *(slang)*, young shaver *(informal)*, young 'un *(informal)*

youth NOUN **1 = immaturity**, adolescence, early life, young days, boyhood *or* girlhood, salad days, juvenescence: *the comic books of my youth* **OPPOSITE:** old age **2 = boy**, lad, youngster, kid *(informal)*, teenager, young man, adolescent, teen *(informal)*, stripling, young shaver *(informal)*: *gangs of youths who broke windows and looted shops* **OPPOSITE:** adult **3 = young people**, the young, the younger generation, teenagers, the rising generation: *He represents the opinions of the youth of today.* **OPPOSITE:** old people

QUOTATIONS

Youth's a stuff will not endure
[William Shakespeare *Twelfth Night*]

Young men have more virtue than old men; they have more generous sentiments in every respect
[Dr. Johnson]

Youth, which is forgiven everything, forgives itself nothing: age, which forgives itself anything, is forgiven nothing
[George Bernard Shaw *Maxims for Revolutionists*]

Whom the gods love di.es young
[Menander *Mouostichoi*]

The whining schoolboy, with his satchel
And shining morning face, creeping like snail
Unwillingly to school
[William Shakespeare *As You Like It*]

Bliss was it in that dawn to be alive,
But to be young was very heaven
[William Wordsworth *The Prelude*]

Youth is a disease that must be borne with patiently! Time, indeed, will cure it
[R.H. Benson]

I've never understood why people consider youth a time of freedom and joy. It's probably because they have forgotten their own
[Margaret Atwood *Hair Jewelry*]

Hope I die before I get old
[Pete Townshend *My Generation*]

The atrocious crime of being a young man... I shall neither attempt to palliate nor deny
[William Pitt, Earl of Chatham]

PROVERBS

Youth must be served

youthful ADJECTIVE **1 = young**, juvenile, childish, immature, boyish, pubescent, girlish, puerile: *youthful enthusiasm and high spirits* **OPPOSITE:** elderly **2 = vigorous**, fresh, active, young looking, young at heart, spry: *I'm a very youthful 50.* **OPPOSITE:** tired

Zz

zany ADJECTIVE = **comical**, crazy, nutty *(slang)*, funny, eccentric, wacky *(slang)*, loony *(slang)*, oddball *(informal)*, madcap, goofy *(informal)*, kooky *(U.S. informal)*, clownish, wacko *or* whacko *(informal)*, off the air *(Austral. slang)*

zeal NOUN = **enthusiasm**, passion, zest, fire, spirit, warmth, devotion, verve, fervour, eagerness, gusto, militancy, fanaticism, ardour, earnestness, keenness, fervency **OPPOSITE:** apathy

zealot NOUN = **fanatic**, enthusiast, extremist, militant, maniac, fiend *(informal)*, bigot

zealous ADJECTIVE = **enthusiastic**, passionate, earnest, burning, spirited, keen, devoted, eager, militant, ardent, fanatical, fervent, impassioned, rabid, fervid **OPPOSITE:** apathetic

zenith NOUN = **height**, summit, peak, top, climax, crest, high point, pinnacle, meridian, apex, high noon, apogee, acme, vertex **OPPOSITE:** lowest point

zero NOUN **1** = **nought**, nothing, nil, naught, cipher: *a scale ranging from zero to seven* **2** = **rock bottom**, the bottom, an all-time low, a nadir, as low as you can get, the lowest point *or* ebb: *My spirits were at zero.*
zero in on something **1** = **zoom in on**, focus on, aim at, train on, home in on: *He raised the binoculars again and zeroed in on an eleventh-floor room.* **2** = **focus on**, concentrate on, home in on, pinpoint, converge on: *Critics have zeroed in on his weakness.*

zest NOUN **1** = **enjoyment**, love, appetite, relish, interest, joy, excitement, zeal, gusto, keenness, zing *(informal)*, delectation: *He has a zest for life and a quick intellect.* **OPPOSITE:** aversion **2** = **flavour**, taste, savour, kick *(informal)*, spice, relish, smack, tang, piquancy, pungency: *Lemon oil adds zest to your cuppa.* **3** = **rind**, skin, peel, outer layer: *the zest and juice of the lemon*

zip VERB = **speed**, shoot, fly, tear, rush, flash, dash, hurry, barrel (along) *(informal, chiefly U.S. & Canad.)*, buzz, streak, hare *(Brit. informal)*, zoom, whizz *(informal)*, hurtle, pelt, burn rubber *(informal)*: *My craft zipped along the bay.*
▷ NOUN = **energy**, go *(informal)*, life, drive, spirit, punch *(informal)*, pep, sparkle, vitality, vigour, verve, zest, gusto, get-up-and-go *(informal)*, oomph *(informal)*, brio, zing *(informal)*, liveliness, vim *(slang)*, pizzazz *or* pizazz *(informal)*: *He gave the choreography his usual class and zip.* **OPPOSITE:** lethargy

zodiac

SIGNS OF THE ZODIAC

Aquarius (the Water Carrier)
Aries (the Ram)
Cancer (the Crab)
Capricorn (the Goat)
Gemini (the Twins)
Leo (the Lion)
Libra (the Scales)
Pisces (the Fishes)
Sagittarius (the Archer)
Scorpio (the Scorpion)
Taurus (the Bull)
Virgo (the Virgin)

zone NOUN = **area**, region, section, sector, district, territory, belt, sphere, tract

zoom VERB = **speed**, shoot, fly, tear, rush, flash, dash, barrel (along) *(informal, chiefly U.S. & Canad.)*, buzz, streak, hare *(Brit. informal)*, zip *(informal)*, whizz *(informal)*, hurtle, pelt, burn rubber *(informal)*